The Broadview Anthology of
Social and Political Thought

VOLUME I
From Plato to Nietzsche

The Broadview Anthology of
Social and Political Thought

VOLUME I
From Plato to Nietzsche

GENERAL EDITORS

Andrew Bailey
Samantha Brennan
Will Kymlicka
Jacob Levy
Alex Sager
Clark Wolf

broadview press

Library and Archives Canada Cataloguing in Publication

The Broadview anthology of social and political thought / general editors, Andrew Bailey ... [et al.].

Includes bibliographical references and index.
Contents: v. 1. From Plato to Nietzsche.
ISBN 978-1-55111-742-3 (v. 1)

1. Social sciences—Philosophy—Textbooks. 2. Political science—Philosophy—Textbooks. I. Bailey, Andrew, 1969- II. Title: Anthology of social and political thought.

B72.B76 2008   300.1   C2008-900804-9

Broadview Press is an independent, international publishing house, incorporated in 1985. Broadview believes in shared ownership, both with its employees and with the general public; since the year 2000 Broadview shares have traded publicly on the Toronto Venture Exchange under the symbol BDP.

We welcome comments and suggestions regarding any aspect of our publications—please feel free to contact us at the addresses below or at broadview@broadviewpress.com.

North America
PO Box 1243, Peterborough, Ontario, Canada K9J 7H5
2215 Kenmore Ave., Buffalo, New York, USA 14207
Tel: (705) 743-8990; Fax: (705) 743-8353
email: customerservice@broadviewpress.com

UK, Ireland, and continental Europe
NBN International, Estover Road, Plymouth, UK PL6 7PY
Tel: 44 (0) 1752 202300; Fax: 44 (0) 1752 202330
email: enquiries@nbninternational.com

Australia and New Zealand
UNIREPS, University of New South Wales
Sydney, NSW, 2052 Australia
Tel: 61 2 9664 0999; Fax: 61 2 9664 5420
email: info.press@unsw.edu.au

www.broadviewpress.com

Broadview Press acknowledges the financial support of the Government of Canada through the Book Publishing Industry Development Program (BPIDP) for our publishing activities.

PRINTED IN CANADA

Contributing Editors and Writers

Editorial Coordinators
Alex Sager
Don LePan

Developmental Editor
Robert M. Martin

Textual Editor
John Burbidge

Design Coordinator
Eileen Eckert

Production Editors
Judith Earnshaw
Tara Lowes

Permissions Coordinator
Chris Griffin

Contributing Editors

Elizabeth Brake	Ann Levey
John Burbidge	Robert M. Martin
Ryoa Chung	A.P. Martinich
Ryan Chynces	Alex Sager
Mark Hulliung	Janet Sisson
Ian Johnston	Patricia Springborg
Victoria Kamsler	Lisa H. Schwartzman
Don LePan	

Contributing Writers

Elizabeth Brake	Ann Levey
John Burbige	Robert M. Martin
Ryoa Chung	Lisa H. Schwartzman
Mark Hulliung	Patricia Springborg
Victoria Kamsler	Dave White

Editorial Advisors

Scott Anderson	Cressida Heyes
David Archard	Ann Levey
Thom Brooks	Karen Houle
Elizabeth Brake	Martin Tweedale
Deen Chatterjee	Leif Wenar

Contents

PART I The Classical Period

PART II The Medieval Period

PART III The Early Modern Period

PART IV The Nineteenth Century

Preface

In recent decades anthologies of social and political thought have generally taken one of two directions. One approach has been to deal with the major figures, stopping more or less at the beginning of the twentieth century—"Plato to Nietzsche" has been a common configuration. The other has been to focus on the period starting around 1970—the era of Rawls and rights-based liberalism, and the reaction to this work, of course, but also the era of powerful new waves in feminist thought. The two approaches have existed largely in isolation from each other, and to a large extent that has reflected pedagogical practice, with separate courses or groups of courses at many universities covering classical and contemporary political thought.

This anthology bridges that divide in one obvious respect, through the inclusion of material from the period 1900 to 1970. It also breaks new ground in a variety of ways. Readers will notice, for example, that the range of figures included in every era is broader than is customary. Along with Plato and Aristotle one may find Thucydides, Seneca and Cicero; along with Augustine and Aquinas one may find Al-Farabi, Marsilius of Padua, and de Pisan; along with Locke, Rousseau and Wollstonecraft one may find de Gouges and Constant. Noteworthy throughout is the extent to which women are included; this anthology recognizes as few other general collections have done the degree to which thinkers ranging from de Pisan, Wollstonecraft and Astell to de Beauvoir, Okin, and Nussbaum have made vitally important contributions.

In giving appropriate space to figures such as these, the general editors have had no wish to displace figures traditionally acknowledged as central. Indeed, we have endeavoured with these central figures not only to include complete (when possible) or substantial selections from core readings, but also to provide some material rarely or never previously included in this type of anthology. Along with selections from the *Republic*, the complete *Apology*, and the complete *Crito*, for example, we include selections from Plato's *Laws* (in a new translation); along with selections from Rawls's *Theory of Justice* we include his important essay "The Idea of an Overlapping Consensus"; and so on.

To have attempted all this within the compass of a single volume would have resulted in a book that was very unwieldy; with this in mind, we have from its early stages conceived of the project as a two-volume work. Our hope is that publishing in this way will allow for a high degree of pedagogical flexibility. Courses focusing either on "Plato to Nietzsche" or on the twentieth and twenty-first centuries will obviously require only one of the two volumes. For courses covering the full range of political thought the volumes are available packaged together at a special price. And for special situations it is also possible to make special arrangements; if, for example, a course focuses on several figures included in volume 1, together with a limited amount from volume 2, the publisher can prepare a course pack of the needed material from the second volume, and ship that together with the bound-book volume 1 at a special price for the student.

If *The Broadview Anthology* fills in many gaps in covering the full range of political thought, it also recognizes that there may often be good reasons for approaching twentieth- and twenty-first-century political thought rather differently than is the norm for earlier periods. Notably, a thematic organization is often felt to be suitable for the later period, a chronological organization for earlier periods. With that in mind, we present the figures in volume 1 in this anthology in chronological order, but group the selections in volume 2 under three broad thematic headings, each with its own substantial introduction. In these sections, we have included many early- and mid-twentieth-century writings to reflect the importance of sometimes neglected themes such as power, the state, gender, race, and post-colonialism. Inevitably, there is overlap between these sections, and certainly some selections could equally well have been included in a section other than the one in which they appear. It should be emphasized that the sectional divisions are intended to provide a loose framework, not to impose a prescriptive view as to how the material should be taught; the present arrangement in no way precludes instructors from discussing a particular selection in conjunction with those in other sections. But we hope it will provide for the second volume a pedagogically more useful structure than would a strictly chronological arrangement.

All too often with anthologies it is assumed that what is important is *only* the selections themselves, and how they are arranged. Our working principle with *The Broadview Anthology* has been very different. We believe issues of translation are of real importance, and we have made substantial efforts to include in these pages translations that are both accurate and accessible to the reader. We also believe that thorough annotation and extensive introductory material are vital to the success of an anthology with twenty-first-century readers. Whereas most anthologies of political thought include only minimal annotations, we make it a practice to gloss any reference not likely to be familiar to undergraduate readers. Rather than brief headnotes, we provide substantial introductions even to figures not generally acknowledged as occupying a central place in political thought. For the figures who have been generally acknowledged to be of central importance,[1] we go further, providing extended introductions designed to help students place the figure in a broad context of history and intellectual history as well as of political thought, and to steer them clear of common misconceptions. And, for virtually all figures included within the anthology, we provide something that one might not imagine in this age

of the visual would be as unusual as it is in anthologies of political thought—illustration.

All in all, *The Broadview Anthology* is a project as ambitious as it is wide-ranging. With a view to the great challenges involved, we have conceived of the project from the outset as a broadly collaborative effort. The general editors have taken the lead in setting out the general shape of the anthology and in choosing the individual selections; the general editors have also reviewed and had a hand in shaping the introductory materials. But a large number of others have played vitally important roles—offering their advice as to what should and should not be included, commenting on texts and translations, and in many cases drafting annotations and superb introductory material. Their very substantial contributions are acknowledged following the title page; without their help it would surely have been impossible to produce this anthology in a timely fashion, and to them both the general editors and the publishers extend profound thanks.

---

1   There is of course substantial room for disagreement as to which figures *are* of central importance, particularly in the context of an anthology designed for undergraduate teaching. Though no choice of selections will be entirely free from controversy, we have consulted with many professors in the philosophy and political science departments to construct a complete as possible table of contents that gives each figure her or his appropriate weight.

Acknowledgments

To a much greater extent than most anthologies, *The Broadview Anthology of Social and Political Thought* is a collaborative effort. The many who contributed by drafting introductory material, preparing annotations, or editing texts are listed immediately following the listing of the general editors on the title page. Special mention should here be made of the contributions of Prof. Robert M. Martin of Dalhousie University, who not only led the way in the drafting of introductions and notes but also assisted significantly in the preliminary editing of material drafted by others; of Victoria Kamsler of Princeton University, who has made very significant contributions both to the medieval and to the twentieth-century sections; and of Dr. Janet Sisson of Mount Royal College, whose contributions to the anthology's first section have been extensive and invaluable. Several others in-house at Broadview—notably, former Broadview Philosophy editors Tania Therien and Ryan Chynces—made significant contributions that should also be acknowledged.

Invaluable too has been the assistance of the dozens of academics who have been kind enough to offer their advice at one time or another during the preparation of the anthology on the specifics as to what should or should not be included, on various issues relating to translation, on the nuances of titling the anthology, and on a number of other matters. Following is a partial list; we apologize to any we have inadvertently omitted.

◆　◆　◆　◆　◆

Barbara Arniel, University of British Columbia

Farid Abdel-Nour, San Diego State University

Terence Ball, Arizona State University

Nandita Biswas Mellamphy, University of Western Ontario

William Buschert, University of Saskatchewan

Don Carmichael, University of Alberta

William Chaloupka, Colorado State University (Fort Collins)

B. Cooper, University of Calgary

Jack Crittenden, Arizona State University

Richard Dagger, Arizona State University

Shadia Drury, University of Regina

Allison Dube, University of Calgary

Avigail Eisenberg, University of Victoria

Cecil L Eubanks, Louisiana State University

Catherine Frost, McMaster University

Joshua D. Goldstein, University of Calgary

Thomas Heilke, University of Kansas

Peter Ives, University of Winnipeg

Catherine Kellogg, University of Alberta

Ed King, Concordia University

Jennet Kirkpatrick, University of Michigan

Mika LaVaque-Manty, University of Michigan

Douglas G Long, University of Western Ontario

Allan MacLeod, University of Saskatchewan

Anne Manuel, University of Michigan

Kirstie McClure, University of California, Los Angeles

Dennis McKerlie, University of Calgary

Margaret Ogrodnick, University of Manitoba

Anthony Parel, University of Calgary

John Seaman, McMaster University

Richard Sigurdson, University of Manitoba

Travis Smith, Concordia University

Christina Tarnopolsky, McGill University

Richard Vernon, University of Western Ontario

Ann Ward, University of Regina

PART I

The Classical Period

THUCYDIDES
(c. 400 BCE)

T HUCYDIDES AND HIS PREDECESSOR HERODOTUS COM-
pete for the title "Father of History." Herodotus was
arguably the first to write history in anything like the form
that we recognize. But Herodotus did little to separate fact
from myth within the rambling succession of stories he
recounted. In contrast, Thucydides' groundbreaking work,
History of the Peloponnesian War was chronological and
factual. It was also philosophical, building on theoretical
postulates about human nature and historical development,
and presenting concrete historical events as case studies
illustrating more general phenomena.

Not much is known about Thucydides' life. He was born
of a prominent aristocratic family, probably around 460
BCE. Serving as a general in 424, he commanded Athenian
forces in Thrace, but failed to prevent an important Spartan victory, and, as punishment, was exiled from Athens.
He spent much of the next 20 years in Sparta, collecting
information from the other side of the great Peloponnesian
War (430–404 BCE), and writing his account of it. At the
conclusion of the war he returned to Athens; he died a few
years later, around the turn of the century.

Thucydides was clearly influenced by the Sophists,
a group of professional instructors who were a dominant
educational force in fifth-century Athens. Sophist education put rhetoric and argument to the fore, an emphasis
powerfully reflected in Thucydides' *History*, a quarter
of which is made up of imagined debates and orations.
Thucydides' cynical view of human nature—as he depicts
them, people are chiefly motivated by fear, ambition, and
greed—also connects with elements of the Sophists' teaching, as do strands of naturalism, determinism, empiricism and materialism in his writing. In all these respects
his work foreshadows that of Thomas Hobbes, who was
greatly impressed by Thucydides and published a translation of his *History* in 1628. The two of them share the
view that democracy is unstable and untrustworthy, and
inherently prone to collapse into lawlessness. Thucydides is
often taken to be the first important figure in the tradition
of political realism—"realpolitik"—which extends through
Hobbes, Machiavelli, and Weber, and which holds that
what drives history most powerfully is self-interest and the
struggle to acquire power.

♦ ♦ ♦ ♦ ♦

History of the Peloponnesian War, 2.40

Pericles' Funeral Oration

In the same winter the Athenians gave a funeral at the public cost to those who had first fallen in this war. It was a
custom of their ancestors, and the manner of it is as follows.
Three days before the ceremony, the bones of the dead are
laid out in a tent which has been erected; and their friends
bring to their relatives such offerings as they please. In the
funeral procession cypress coffins are borne in carts, one for
each tribe; the bones of the deceased being placed in the
coffin of their tribe. Among these is carried one empty bier
decked for the missing, that is, for those whose bodies could
not be recovered. Any citizen or foreigner who pleases, joins
in the procession: and the female relatives are there to wail
at the burial. The dead are laid in the public burial vault in
the Beautiful suburb of the city, in which those who fall in
war are always buried; with the exception of those slain at
Marathon,[1] who for their singular and extraordinary valor
were interred on the spot where they fell. After the bodies
have been laid in the earth, a man chosen by the state, of approved wisdom and eminent reputation, pronounces over
them an appropriate panegyric;[2] after which all leave. Such
is the manner of the burying; and throughout the whole
of the war, whenever the occasion arose, the established
custom was observed. These, however, were the first that
had fallen, and Pericles,[3] son of Xanthippus, was chosen to
pronounce their eulogy. When the proper time arrived, he
advanced from the burial vault to an elevated platform in

---

1   *Marathon*   Town in Greece, site of a famous Athenian victory
    over the Persians in 490 BCE. (A legendary run of 46 kilometers
    to Athens by a messenger reporting this victory gives the race its
    name.)
2   *panegyric*   Formal public oration in praise of a person.
3   *Pericles*   (495–429 BCE)   Prominent Athenian statesman, gen-
    eral, and orator.

order to be heard by as many of the crowd as possible, and spoke as follows:

"Most of my predecessors in this place have commended the lawgiver who added this speech to our other funeral customs, telling us that it is well that it should be delivered at the burial of those who fall in battle. For myself, I should have thought that the worth which had displayed itself in deeds would be sufficiently rewarded by honors also shown by deeds; such as you now see in this funeral prepared at the people's cost. And I could have wished that the reputations of many brave men were not to be imperiled in the mouth of a single individual, to stand or fall according as he spoke well or ill. For it is hard to speak properly upon a subject where it is even difficult to convince your hearers that you are speaking the truth. On the one hand, the friend who is familiar with every fact of the story may think that some point has not been set forth with that fullness which he wishes and knows it to deserve; on the other, he who is a stranger to the matter may be led by envy to suspect exaggeration if he hears anything above his own nature. For men can endure to hear others praised only so long as they can each persuade themselves of their own ability to equal the actions recounted: when this point is passed, envy comes in and with it incredulity. However, since our ancestors have stamped this custom with their approval, it becomes my duty to obey the law and to try to satisfy your individual wishes and opinions as best I may.

"I shall begin with our ancestors: it is both just and proper that they should have the honor of the first mention on an occasion like the present. They dwelt in the country without break in the succession from generation to generation, and handed it down free to the present time by their valor. And if our more remote ancestors deserve praise, much more do our own fathers, who added to their inheritance the empire which we now possess, and spared no pains to be able to leave their acquisitions to us of the present generation. Lastly, there are few parts of our dominions that have not been augmented by those of us here, who are still more or less in the vigor of life; while the mother country has been furnished by us with everything that can enable her to depend on her own resources whether for war or for peace. That part of our history which tells of the military achievements which gave us our several possessions, or of the ready valor with which either we or our fathers stemmed the tide of Greek or foreign aggression, is a theme too familiar to my hearers for me to dilate on, and I shall therefore pass it by.

But what was the road by which we reached our position, what the form of government under which our greatness grew, what the national habits out of which it sprang; these are questions which I may try to solve before I proceed to my panegyric; since I think this to be a subject upon which on the present occasion a speaker may properly dwell, and to which the whole assemblage, whether citizens or foreigners, may listen with advantage.

"Our constitution does not copy the laws of neighboring states; we are rather a pattern to others than imitators ourselves. Its administration favors the many instead of the few; this is why it is called a democracy. If we look to the laws, they afford equal justice to all in their private differences; if to social standing, advancement in public life falls to reputation for capacity, class considerations not being allowed to interfere with merit; nor again does poverty bar the way, for if a man is able to serve the state, he is not hindered by the obscurity of his condition. The freedom which we enjoy in our government extends also to our ordinary life. There, far from exercising a jealous surveillance over each other, we do not feel called upon to be angry with our neighbor for doing what he likes, or even to indulge in those injurious looks which cannot fail to be offensive, although they inflict no positive penalty. But all this ease in our private relations does not make us lawless as citizens. Against this fear is our chief safeguard, teaching us to obey the magistrates and the laws, particularly such as regard the protection of the injured, whether they are actually on the statute book, or belong to that code which, although unwritten, yet cannot be broken without acknowledged disgrace.

"Further, we provide plenty of means for the mind to refresh itself from business. We celebrate games and sacrifices all the year round, and the elegance of our private establishments forms a daily source of pleasure and helps to banish bad temper; while the magnitude of our city draws the produce of the world into our harbor, so that to the Athenian the fruits of other countries are as familiar a luxury as those of his own.

"If we turn to our military policy, there also we differ from our antagonists. We throw open our city to the world, and have no laws excluding foreigners from any opportunity of learning or observing, although the eyes of an enemy may occasionally profit by our liberality; trusting less in system and policy than to the native spirit of our citizens; while in education, where our rivals from their very cradles by a painful discipline seek after manliness, at Athens we live exactly as we please, and yet are just as ready to encounter every legitimate danger. In proof of this it may be noticed that the Spartans do not invade our country alone, but bring with them all their confederates; while we Athenians advance unsupported into the territory of a neighbor, and fighting upon a foreign soil usually vanquish with ease men who are defending their homes. Our united force was never yet encountered by any enemy, because we have at once to attend to our navy and to dispatch our citizens by land upon a hundred different services; so that, wherever they engage with some such fraction of our strength, a success against a detachment is magnified into a victory over the nation, and a defeat into a reverse suffered at the hands of our entire people. And yet if with habits not of labor but of ease, and courage not of art but of nature, we are still willing to encounter danger, we have the double advantage of escaping the experience of hardships in anticipation and of facing them in the hour of need as fearlessly as those who are never free from them.

"Nor are these the only points in which our city is worthy of admiration. We cultivate refinement without extravagance and knowledge without effeminacy; wealth we employ more for use than for show, and place the real disgrace of poverty not in owning to the fact but in declining the struggle against it. Our public men have, besides politics, their private affairs to attend to, and our ordinary citizens, though occupied with the pursuits of industry, are still fair judges of public matters; for, unlike any other nation, regarding him who takes no part in these duties not as unambitious but as useless, we Athenians are able to deliberate if we cannot act, and, instead of looking on discussion as a stumbling-block in the way of action, we think it an indispensable preliminary to any wise action at all. Again, in our enterprises we present the singular spectacle of daring and deliberation, each carried to its highest point, and both united in the same persons; although usually decision is the fruit of ignorance, hesitation of reflection. But the palm[1] of courage will surely be awarded most justly to those who best know the difference between hardship and pleasure and yet are never tempted to shrink from danger. In generosity we are equally singular, acquiring our friends by conferring, not by receiving, favors. Yet, of course, the doer of the favor is the firmer friend of the two, in order by continued kindness to keep the recipient in his debt; while the debtor feels less keenly from the very consciousness that

the return he makes will be a payment, not a free gift. And it is only the Athenians, who, fearless of consequences, confer their benefits not from calculations of expediency, but in the confidence of liberality.

"In short, I say that as a city we are the school of Greece, while I doubt if the world can produce a man who, where he has only himself to depend upon, is equal to so many emergencies, and graced by so happy a versatility, as the Athenian. And that this is no mere boast thrown out for the occasion, but plain matter of fact, proven by the power of the state acquired by these habits. For Athens alone of her contemporaries is found when tested to be greater than her reputation, and alone gives no occasion to her assailants to blush at the antagonist by whom they have been worsted, or to her subjects to question her title by merit to rule. Rather, the admiration of the present and succeeding ages will be ours, since we have not left our power without witness, but have shown it by mighty proofs; and far from needing a Homer for our panegyrist, or other of his craft whose verses might charm for the moment only for the impression which they gave, only to melt at the touch of fact, we have forced every sea and land to be the highway of our daring, and everywhere, whether for evil or for good, have left imperishable monuments behind us. Such is the Athens for which these men, in the assertion of their resolve not to lose her, nobly fought and died; and well may every one of their survivors be ready to suffer in her cause.

"Indeed if I have dwelt at some length upon the character of our country, it has been to show that our stake in the struggle is not the same as theirs who have no such blessings to lose, and also that the praise of the men over whom I am now speaking might be by definite proofs established. That panegyric is now in a great measure complete; for the Athens that I have celebrated is only what the heroism of these and their like have made her, men whose fame, unlike that of most Greeks, will be found to be in proportion to what is deserved. And if a test of worth be needed, it is to be found in their closing scene, and this not only in cases in which it set the final seal upon their merit, but also in those in which it gave the first intimation of their having any. For there is justice in the claim that steadfastness in his country's battles should be as a cloak to cover a man's other imperfections; since the good action has blotted out the bad, and his merit as a citizen more than outweighed his demerits as an individual. But none of these allowed either wealth with its prospect of future enjoyment to unnerve his spirit, or poverty with its hope of a day of freedom and

---

1   *palm* A palm leaf was awarded and carried as the symbol of victory or success.

riches to tempt him to shrink from danger. No, holding that vengeance upon their enemies was more to be desired than any personal blessings, and reckoning this to be the most glorious of hazards, they joyfully determined to accept the risk, to make sure of their vengeance, and to let their wishes wait; and while committing to hope the uncertainty of final success, in the business before them they thought fit to act boldly and trust in themselves. Thus choosing to die resisting, rather than to live submitting, they fled only from dishonor, but met danger face to face, and after one brief moment, while at the summit of their fortune, escaped, not from their fear, but from their glory.

"So died these men as was suitable for Athenians. You, their survivors, must determine to have as unfaltering a resolution in the field, though you may pray that it may have a happier issue. And not contented with ideas derived only from words of the advantages which are bound up with the defense of your country, though these would furnish a valuable text to a speaker even before an audience so alive to them as the present, you must yourselves realize the power of Athens, and feed your eyes upon her from day to day, till love of her fills your hearts; and then, when you recognize all her greatness, you must reflect that it was by courage, sense of duty, and a keen feeling of honor in action that men were enabled to win all this, and that no personal failure in an enterprise could make them consent to deprive their country of their valor, but they laid it at her feet as the most glorious contribution that they could offer. For this offering of their lives made in common by them all they each of them individually received that renown which never grows old, and for a burial vault, not so much that in which their bones have been deposited, but that noblest of shrines wherein their glory is laid up to be eternally remembered upon every occasion on which deed or story shall call for its commemoration. For heroes have the whole earth for their tomb; and in lands far from their own, where the column with its epitaph declares it, there is enshrined in every breast a record unwritten with no carved stone to preserve it, except that of the heart. These take as your model and, judging happiness to be the fruit of freedom and freedom of valor, never decline the dangers of war. For it is not the miserable that would most justly be unsparing of their lives; these have nothing to hope for: it is rather they to whom continued life may bring reverses as yet unknown, and to whom a fall, if it came, would be most tremendous in its consequences. And surely, to a man of spirit, the degradation of cowardice must be immeasurably more grievous than the unfelt death which strikes him in the midst of his strength and patriotism!

"Comfort, therefore, not condolence, is what I have to offer to the parents of the dead who may be here. Numberless are the chances to which, as they know, the life of man is subject; but fortunate indeed are they who draw for their lot a death so glorious as that which has caused your mourning, and to whom life has been so exactly measured as to terminate in the happiness in which it has been passed. Still I know that this is a hard saying, especially when those are in question of whom you will constantly be reminded by seeing in the homes of others blessings of which once you also boasted: for grief is felt not so much for the lack of what we have never known, as for the loss of that to which we have been long accustomed. Yet you who are still of an age to beget children must bear up in the hope of having others in their place; not only will they help you to forget those whom you have lost, but will be to the state at once a reinforcement and a security; for never can a fair or just policy be expected of the citizen who does not, like his fellows, bring to the decision the interests and apprehensions of a father. While those of you who have passed your prime must congratulate yourselves with the thought that the best part of your life was fortunate, and that the brief span that remains will be cheered by the fame of the departed. For it is only the love of honor that never grows old; and honor it is, not gain, as some would have it, that rejoices the heart of age and helplessness.

"Turning to the sons or brothers of the dead, I see an arduous struggle before you. When a man is gone, all are inclined to praise him, and should your merit be ever so transcendent, you will still find it difficult not merely to overtake, but even to approach their renown. The living have envy to contend with, while those who are no longer in our path are honored with a goodwill into which rivalry does not enter. On the other hand, if I must say anything on the subject of female excellence to those of you who will now be in widowhood, it will be all comprised in this brief exhortation. Great will be your glory in not falling short of your natural character; and greatest will be hers who is least talked of among the men, whether for good or for bad.

"My task is now finished. I have performed it to the best of my ability, and in word, at least, the requirements of the law are now satisfied. If deeds be in question, those who are here interred have received part of their honors already, and for the rest, their children will be brought up till manhood at the public expense: the state thus offers a valuable prize, as the garland of victory in this race of valor, for the reward both of those who have fallen and their survivors. And where the rewards for merit are greatest, there are found the best citizens.

"And now that you have brought to a close your lamentations for your relatives, you may depart."

◆ ◆ ◆ ◆ ◆

History of the Peloponnesian War, 5.84-116

Melian Dialogue

... The next summer Alcibiades[1] sailed with twenty ships to Argos and seized three hundred suspected Spartan sympathizers, whom the Athenians forthwith lodged in the neighboring islands of their empire. The Athenians also made an expedition against the isle of Melos with thirty ships of their own, six Chian, and two Lesbian vessels, sixteen hundred foot-soldiers, three hundred archers, and twenty mounted archers from Athens, and about fifteen hundred hoplites[2] from the allies and the islanders. The Melians are a colony of Sparta that would not submit to the Athenians like the other islanders, and at first remained neutral and took no part in the struggle, but afterwards, when the Athenians used violence against them and plundered their territory, they assumed an attitude of open hostility. Cleomedes son of Lycomedes, and Tisias son of Tisimachus, the generals, encamping in Melian territory with the Athenian forces, before doing any harm to their land, sent envoys to negotiate. The Melians did not bring these envoys before the people, but bade them state the object of their mission to the magistrates and the few; then the Athenian envoys spoke as follows:

Athenians: Since the negotiations are not to go on before the people, in order that we may not be able to speak straight on without interruption, and deceive the ears of the multitude by seductive arguments which would pass without refutation (for we know that this is the meaning of our being

brought before the few), what if you who sit there were to pursue a method more cautious still! Make no set speech yourselves, but interrupt us at whatever you do not like, and settle that before going any farther. And first tell us if this proposition of ours suits you.

The Melian commissioners answered:

Melians: To the fairness of calmly instructing each other as you propose there is nothing to object; but your military preparations are too far advanced to be consistent with what you say, as we see you are come to be judges in your own cause. All we can reasonably expect from this negotiation is war, if we prove to have right on our side and refuse to submit, or in the contrary case, slavery.

Athenians: If you have met us to reason about your suspicions about the future, or for anything else than to consult, for the sake of the safety of your state, about the facts that you see before you, we will cease talking; otherwise we will go on.

Melians: It is natural and excusable for men in our position to think and argue in more ways than one. However, the question in this conference is, as you say, the safety of our country; and the discussion, if you please, can proceed in the way which you propose.

Athenians: For ourselves, we shall not trouble you with specious pretenses—either of how we have a right to our empire because we overthrew the Mede, or are now attacking you because of wrong that you have done us—and make a long speech which would not be believed; and in return we hope that you, instead of thinking to influence us by saying that you did not join the Spartans, although their colonists, or that you have done us no wrong, will aim at what is feasible, holding in view what we both really do think; since you know as well as we do that the way the world works is that justice is only in question between equals in power, while the strong do what they can and the weak accept what they must.

Melians: As we think, at any rate, it is expedient—we speak as we are obliged, since you enjoin us to let right alone and talk only of interest—that you should not destroy a principle that is our common protection, namely, that one in danger is allowed to invoke what is fair and right, and even to profit by arguments not strictly valid if they can be persuasive. And you have as much interest in this as anyone, as your fall would be a signal for the heaviest vengeance and an example for the world to meditate upon.

---

1   *Alcibiades*   Athenian statesman and general who played a major role in the Peloponnesian War.
2   *hoplites*   Heavy infantrymen.

Athenians: The end of our empire, if end it should, does not frighten us: a rival empire like Sparta, even if Sparta was our real antagonist, is not so terrible to the vanquished as an attack by our own subjects overpowering their rulers. This, however, is a risk that we are content to take. We will now proceed to show you that we have come here in the interest of our empire, and that we shall say what we are now going to say, for the preservation of your country; as we would desire to exercise that empire over you without trouble, and see you preserved for the good of us both.

Melians: And how, pray, could it turn out as good for us to serve as for you to rule?

Athenians: Because you would have the advantage of submitting before suffering the worst, and we should gain by not destroying you.

Melians: So you would not consent to our being neutral, friends instead of enemies, but allies of neither side?

Athenians: No; for your hostility cannot hurt us that much; your friendship will be an sign to our subjects of our weakness, and your enmity of our power.

Melians: Is that your subjects' idea of equity—that you would put those who have nothing to do with you in the same category with people who are most of them your own colonists, or conquered rebels?

Athenians: As far as right goes they think there is no difference between them, and that if any maintain their independence it is because they are strong, and that if we do not molest them it is because we are afraid; so that besides extending our empire we should gain in security by your subjection; the fact that you are islanders and weaker than others rendering it all the more important that you should not succeed in thwarting the masters of the sea.

Melians: But do you consider that there is no security in the policy which we indicate? For here again if you debar us from talking about justice and invite us to obey your interest, we also must explain ours, and try to persuade you, if the two happen to coincide. How can you avoid making enemies of all existing neutrals who shall look at our case and conclude from it that one day or another you will attack them? And what does this do but make greater the enemies that you have already, and force others to become enemies who would otherwise have never thought of it?

Athenians: Why, the fact is that mainlanders generally give us but little alarm; the liberty which they enjoy will long prevent their taking precautions against us; it is rather islanders like yourselves, outside our empire, and subjects smarting under the yoke, who would be the most likely to take a rash step and lead themselves and us into obvious danger.

Melians: Well then, if you risk so much to retain your empire, and your subjects risk so much to get rid of it, it would surely be great weakness and cowardice in us who are still free not to try everything that can be tried, before submitting to your yoke.

Athenians: Not if you are well advised; for the contest is not an equal one, with honor as the prize and shame as the penalty; rather, it is a question of self-preservation and of not resisting those who are far stronger than you are.

Melians: But we know that the fortune of war is sometimes more impartial than the disproportion of numbers might lead one to suppose; to submit is to give ourselves over to despair, while action still preserves for us a hope that we may stand erect.

Athenians: Hope, danger's comforter, may be indulged in by those who have abundant resources, if not without loss, at all events without ruin; but its nature is to be extravagant, and those who go so far as to stake everything on a venture see it in its true colors only when they are ruined; but when that discovery would have enabled them to guard against it, they never lack hope. Let not this be the case with you, who are weak and whose fate hangs on a single turn of the scale; nor be like the vulgar, who, abandoning such security as human means may still afford, when visible hopes fail them in extremity, turn to the invisible, to prophecies and oracles, and other such inventions that delude men with hopes and lead them to their destruction.

Melians: You may be sure that we are as well aware as you of the difficulty of contending against your power and fortune, unless the terms be equal. But we trust that the gods may grant us fortune as good as yours, since we are just men fighting against injustice, and what we lack in power will be made up by the alliance of the Spartans, who are bound, if only to avoid shame, to come to the aid of their kindred. Our confidence, therefore, after all is not so utterly irrational.

Athenians: When you speak of the favor of the gods, we may as fairly hope for that as yourselves; neither our pretensions nor our conduct being in any way contrary to what men believe of the gods, or practice among themselves. Of the gods we believe, and of men we know, that by a necessary law of their nature they rule wherever they can. And it is not as if we were the first to make this law, or to act upon it when made: we found it existing before us, and shall leave it to exist forever after us; all we do is to make use of it, knowing that you and everybody else, having the same power as we have, would do the same as we do. Thus, as far as the gods are concerned, we have no fear and no reason to fear that we shall be at a disadvantage. But when we come to your notion about the Spartans, which leads you to believe that shame will make them help you, here we bless your simplicity but do not envy your folly. The Spartans, when their own interests or their country's laws are in question, are the worthiest men alive; of their conduct toward others much might be said, but no clearer idea of it could be given than by briefly stating that of all the men we know they are most conspicuous in considering that what they find agreeable is honorable, and that what they find expedient is just. Such a way of thinking does not promise much for the safety which you now unreasonably count upon.

Melians: But it is for this very reason that we now trust to their respect for expediency to prevent them from betraying the Melians, their colonists, and thereby losing the confidence of their friends in Greece and helping their enemies.

Athenians: Then you do not adopt the view that expediency goes with security, while justice and honor cannot be followed without danger; and that the Spartans generally court danger as little as possible.

Melians: But we believe that they would be more likely to face even danger for our sake, and with more confidence than for others, as our nearness to the Peloponnesus makes it easier for them to act; and our common blood insures our fidelity.

Athenians: Yes, but what a prospective ally trusts is not the good will of those who ask his aid, but a decided superiority of power for action; and the Spartans look to this even more than others. At least, such is their distrust of their home resources that it is only with the aid of numerous allies that they attack a neighbor; now is it likely that while we are masters of the sea they will cross over to an island?

Melians: But they would have others to send. The Cretan sea is a wide one, and it is more difficult for those who command it to intercept others, than for those who wish to elude them to do so safely. And should the Spartans miscarry in this, they would turn against your land, and upon those left of your allies whom Brasidas did not reach; and instead of places which are not yours, you will have to fight for your own country and your own confederacy.

Athenians: Some diversion of the kind you speak of you may one day experience, only to learn, as others have done, that the Athenians never once withdrew from a siege for fear of others. But we are struck by the fact, that after saying you would consult for the safety of your country, in all this discussion you have mentioned nothing which a man might trust in and think he might be saved by. Your strongest arguments depend upon hope and the future, and your actual resources are too scanty, as compared with those arrayed against you, for you to come out victorious. You will therefore show great blindness of judgment, if, after allowing us to retire from this meeting, you have not found some counsel more prudent than this. You will surely not be influenced by the idea of disgrace which proves so fatal to mankind when they face dangers that are disgraceful, and at the same time too plain to be mistaken; in too many cases the very men that have their eyes perfectly open to what they are rushing into, let the thing called disgrace, by the mere influence of a seductive name, lead them on to a point at which they become so enslaved by the phrase as in fact to fall willfully into hopeless disaster, and incur disgrace which is more disgraceful when accompanied by error, than when it comes as the result of misfortune. This, if you are well advised, you will guard against; and you will not think it dishonorable to submit to the greatest city in Greece, when it makes you the reasonable offer of becoming a tribute-paying ally, without ceasing to enjoy the country that belongs to you; nor when you have the choice given you between war and security, will you be so blinded as to choose the worse. And it is certain that those who do not yield to their equals, who keep terms with their superiors, and are reasonable toward their inferiors, on the whole succeed best. Think over the matter, therefore, after our withdrawal, and reflect once and again that it is for your country that you are consulting, that you have only one country, and that upon this one deliberation depends its prosperity or ruin.

The Athenians now withdrew from the conference; and the Melians, left to themselves, came to a decision much the same as what they had maintained in the discussion, and answered, "Our resolution, Athenians, is the same as it was at first. We will not in a moment deprive of freedom a city that has been inhabited these seven hundred years; but we put our trust in the fortune by which the gods have preserved it until now, and in the help of men, that is, of the Spartans; and so we will try and save ourselves. Meanwhile we invite you to allow us to be friends to you and foes to neither party, and to retire from our country after making such a treaty as shall seem fit to us both."

Such was the answer of the Melians. The Athenians now departing from the conference said, "Well, you alone, as it seems to us, judging from these resolutions, regard what is future as more certain than what is before your eyes, and what is out of sight, in your eagerness, as already coming to pass; and as you have staked your fortune and your hopes most on the Spartans, and trusted most in them, so will you be most completely deceived."

The Athenian envoys now returned to the army; and as the Melians showed no signs of yielding, the generals at once commenced hostilities, and built a wall around the city of Melos, dividing the work among the different states. Subsequently the Athenians returned home with most of their army, leaving behind them a certain number of their own citizens and of the allies to keep guard by land and sea. The force thus left stayed on and besieged the place.

About the same time the Argives invaded the territory of Phliasia and lost eighty men cut off in an ambush by the Phliasians and Argive exiles. Meanwhile the Athenians at Pylos took so much plunder from the Spartans that the latter, although they still refrained from breaking off the treaty and going to war with Athens, yet proclaimed that any of their people that chose to might plunder the Athenians. The Corinthians also commenced hostilities with the

Athenians for private quarrels of their own; but the rest of the Peloponnesians stayed quiet.

Meanwhile the Melians attacked by night and captured part of the Athenian lines near the market, and killed some of the men, and brought in corn and all else that they could find useful to them, and so returned and kept quiet, while the Athenians took measures to keep better guard in future. Summer was now over.

The next winter the Spartans intended to invade the Argive territory, but arriving at the frontier found the sacrifices for crossing unfavorable, and went back again. This attempt of theirs made the Argives suspicious of certain of their fellow citizens, some of whom they arrested; others, however, escaped them. About the same time the Melians again took another part of the Athenian lines which were only a few of the garrison. Reinforcements afterwards arriving from Athens in consequence, under the command of Philocrates son of Demeas, and the siege was now pressed vigorously; and as there was some treachery taking place inside, the Melians surrendered unconditionally to the Athenians, who put to death all the grown men whom they took, and sold the women and children for slaves, and subsequently sent out five hundred colonists and settled the place themselves.

PLATO
(c. 427 – c. 347 BCE)

Who Was Plato?

Tʜᴇ ʜɪsᴛᴏʀɪᴄᴀʟ ᴅᴇᴛᴀɪʟs ᴏғ Pʟᴀᴛᴏ's ʟɪғᴇ ᴀʀᴇ sᴏᴍᴇ-what obscure, though we know more about his life than about the lives of most ancient philosophers and he is the first whose entire philosophical corpus survives. He is traditionally thought to have been born in about 427 BCE and to have died in 347 BCE. His family, who lived in the Greek city-state of Athens, was aristocratic and probably wealthy. Legend has it that Plato's father, Ariston, was descended from Codrus, the last king of Athens. His mother, Perictione, was related to the great Solon, who around 570 BCE had reformed the earlier Draconic Athenian constitution. Solon cancelled all debts secured on the person and made the practice of securing debt in this way illegal. He replaced the hereditary aristocracy with a citizenship whose ranks were based on wealth. Solon's reforms were considered to have removed conditions that might otherwise have led to civil war and tyranny; although he himself could have become a tyrant, he chose instead what he thought was the best for everyone. All parties complained they were disadvantaged, but the threat of tyranny was postponed for over 30 years. When democracy was finally introduced, Solon's constitution provided the basis from which the new constitution grew.

While Plato was still a boy his father died, and his mother married Pyrilampes, a friend of the revered Athenian statesman Pericles who in the 450s had transformed Athens into one of the greatest cities in the Greek world. As a young man Plato probably fought with the Athenian army against Sparta during the Peloponnesian war (431–404 BCE)—which Athens lost—and he may have served again around 395 when Athens was involved in the Corinthian war (395–386 BCE).

Given his family connections, Plato looked set to play a prominent role in Athenian political life and as it

happened, when he was about 23, a political revolution occurred in Athens that could have catapulted Plato into public affairs. The coup swept the previous democratic rulers—who had just lost the war against Sparta—out of power and into exile, and replaced them with the so-called Thirty Tyrants, several of whom were friends and relatives of Plato: two of these, Critias and Charmides, appear in his dialogues. It seems that Plato, an idealistic young man, expected that this revolution would usher in a new era of justice and good government, but he was soon disillusioned; the new regime proved to be even more violent and corrupt than the old. He withdrew from public life in disgust.

The rule of the Thirty lasted only about 90 days before the exiled democrats were restored to power, and Plato—impressed by their relative lenience towards the coup leaders—apparently thought again about entering politics. But then, in 399 BCE, three citizens brought trumped-up charges against Plato's old friend and mentor Socrates, accusing him of impiety towards the city's gods and of corrupting the youth of Athens. It is not clear how far this prosecution was inspired by political opposition to Socrates, who had associated with members of the Thirty tyrants, among others. Socrates was convicted by the majority of a jury of 501 citizens and—since he declared that he would rather die than give up philosophy (even though he would probably not have been executed had he chosen exile as a penalty)—he was executed by being given a poison, hemlock, to drink. Plato records the trial and death of Socrates in a series of three speeches attributed to Socrates in his own defense, the *Apology*, and in the dialogues *Crito*, and *Phaedo*. In the so-called *Seventh Letter* (which Plato may have written when he was seventy years old; if it was not by him, it was probably written by one of his disciples shortly after his death), Plato recounts:

The result was that I, who had at first been full of eagerness for public affairs, when I considered all this and saw how things were shifting about every which way, at last became dizzy. I didn't cease to consider ways of improving this particular situation, however, and, indeed, of reforming the whole constitution. But as far as action was concerned, I kept waiting for favorable moments and finally saw clearly that the constitutions of all actual cities are bad and that their laws are almost beyond redemption without extraordinary resources and luck as well. Hence I was compelled to say in praise of the true philosophy that it enables us to discern what is just for a city or an individual in every case and that the human race will have no respite from evils until those who are really and truly philosophers acquire political power or until, through some divine dispensation, those who rule and have political authority in cities become real philosophers.

After the death of Socrates, it appears that Plato, along with some other philosophical followers of Socrates, fled Athens and went west to the city of Megara to stay with the philosopher Eucleides (a follower of the great Greek philosopher Parmenides of Elea). He may also have visited Egypt, though his travels at this time are shrouded in myth. It appears that Plato started writing in earnest at about this time; certainly, the earliest writings that have come down to us date from this point.

Almost all of Plato's writings are in the form of dialogues between two or more characters, and in most of them the character that takes the leading role in the discussion is that of Socrates. Writing in the dialogue form was not unique to Plato; for example, a friend of Socrates', the general Xenophon, wrote a number of dialogues that provide another major source of Socrates' life. Plato, though, was by far the greatest practitioner of the dialogue form. Since Plato never wrote himself into any of his dialogues, it is often—though not uncontroversially—assumed that the views expressed by the character of Socrates more or less correspond with those that Plato is trying to put forward (though Plato, in the 7th letter, claims that he never expressed his own views in his writings).

Later, when Plato was about 40, he made another trip away from Athens, visiting Italy to talk with the Pythagorean philosophers who lived there, and Syracuse on the island of Sicily. There, during a long stay, he became close friends with Dion, the brother-in-law of the ruling tyrant Dionysius I.[1] Dion became Plato's pupil, and (according to legend) came to prefer a philosophical life of moral goodness to the pleasure, luxury, and power of his surroundings. Exactly what happened next is historically unclear, but there is some reason to believe that Plato was captured by a displeased Dionysius and sold into slavery, and that he was rescued from the slave market only by having his freedom purchased by Anniceris the Cyrenaic (or possibly by Dion).

On Plato's return to Athens he bought some land in the precinct named for an Athenian hero called Academus, and there, in about 385 BCE, he founded the first European research centre (or at least, the first of which there is any real historical knowledge). Because of its location this school was called the Academy; it was to remain in existence for more than 900 years, until 529 CE. For most of the rest of his life, Plato stayed at the Academy, directing its studies, and he probably wrote the *Republic* there in about 380 BCE. Very quickly, the school became a vital centre for research in all kinds of subjects, both theoretical and practical: it was probably one of the first cradles for the subjects of metaphysics, epistemology, psychology, ethics, politics, aesthetics and mathematical science, and members were invited by various Greek city-states to help draft new political constitutions. All known mathematicians of the fourth century had links to the Academy. Theaetetus of Athens and Eudoxus of Cnidus, together with Plato's Italian friend Archytas of Tarentum, helped to develop the mathematics that form the latter part of Euclid's *Elements*.

In 368 Dionysius I of Sicily died and Dion persuaded his successor, Dionysius II, to send for Plato to advise him on how the state should be run. Plato, who was now about sixty, agreed to go, albeit with some misgivings; possibly he hoped to make the younger Dionysius an example of a philosopher-king and to put the doctrines of the *Republic* into practice. If so, the experiment was a disastrous failure. Plato was held as a prisoner on Sicily for nearly two years until, in 360, he was finally able to escape and return to Athens for good. He died thirteen years later, at the ripe age of 80.

---

1   Indeed, Plato later wrote an epitaph for Dion in which he spoke of his deep love for Dion.

What Was Plato's Overall Philosophical Project?

Plato is often regarded as the inventor of Western philosophy—and with some justification. His thought encompassed nearly all of the areas that are central to philosophy today—including metaphysics, epistemology, ethics, political theory, aesthetics, and the philosophy of science and mathematics—and for the first time in European history dealt with them in a unified way.[1] Plato thought of philosophy as a special discipline with its own intellectual method, and he was convinced that it had an absolutely foundational importance in human life. Only philosophy, Plato thought, could provide genuine understanding, since only philosophy scrutinized the assumptions that other disciplines left unquestioned. Furthermore, according to Plato, philosophy reveals a realm of comprehensive and unitary hidden truths—indeed, a whole level of reality which is undetectable by the senses—which goes far beyond everyday common sense and which, when properly understood, has the power to revolutionize the way we live our lives and organize our societies. Philosophy, and only philosophy, holds the key to genuine human happiness and well-being.

This realm of objects that Plato claimed to have discovered is generally known as that of the Platonic Forms. The Forms—according to Plato—are changeless, eternal objects, which lie outside of both the physical world and the minds of individuals, and which can only be encountered through pure thought (rather than sensation). One of Plato's favorite examples of a Form is the mathematical property of Equality. In a dialogue called the *Phaedo* he argues that Equality itself cannot be identical with two equal sticks, or with any other group of physical objects of equal length, since we could always be mistaken about whether any two observed objects are really equal with one another, but we could not possibly be mistaken about Equality itself and somehow take *it* to be unequal. When two sticks are equal in length, therefore, they "participate in" Equality—it is their relation to Equality which makes them equal rather than unequal—but Equality itself is an abstract object which exists over and above all the instances of equal things. The Form of Equality is what one succeeds in understanding when one has a proper conception of what equality really is

in itself: real knowledge, therefore, comes not from observation but from acquaintance with the Forms. Other central examples of Forms, for Plato, are Sameness, Number, Motion, Beauty, Justice, Piety and (the most important Form of all) Goodness.

What is the Structure of These Readings?

The *Apology*, the *Crito*, and *The Death of Socrates* (taken from the concluding section of the *Phaedo*) provide the most vivid and comprehensive account of the trial and execution of Socrates. (The historian Xenophon [c. 321–355 BCE] provides the only other surviving contemporary account.) Plato was present at the trial and in his *Apology*—the title comes from the Greek *apologia* which means "defense"—he depicts Socrates, before a jury of 501 Athenian citizens, addressing the charges of Meletus, Anytus, and Lycon that he has been corrupting the youth and worshipping false gods. In his last speech, Socrates recounts how his "*daimon*"—an inner voice that Socrates interprets as having a supernatural source—led him in search for truth, justice, knowledge and the good. It also caused him to question his fellow citizens, particularly those who pretended to possess knowledge; as Plato portrays him, Socrates prodding his fellow citizens is like a gadfly "upon a great and noble horse which was somewhat sluggish because of its size and needed to be stirred up" (30e). Socrates' habit of humiliating prominent figures by revealing their ignorance was widely resented, and that resentment may well have been shared by members of the jury; Socrates succeeds in making Meletus contradict himself, but the jury nonetheless convicts Socrates. The *Apology* has played an important role in the traditions of political thought that are critical of democratic government—and, more broadly, clearly figures in the shaping of Plato's own anti-democratic political views.

The *Crito* is a dialogue between Socrates and his old friend Crito on the nature of justice. Crito attempts to persuade Socrates to try to avoid execution, arguing that Socrates has a responsibility to his sons. Socrates replies that it is impossible to determine whether he is acting rightly or wrongly without inquiring into the nature of justice, and he proceeds to initiate an inquiry into this question. The discussion provides support for a form of social contract theory, from the standpoint of which Socrates argues that it would be unjust to violate the laws. A community requires laws, which depend on the support of the citizens. Since Socrates was educated in Athens and chose to remain and

---

1   In fact the mathematician and philosopher Alfred North Whitehead (1861–1947) was famously moved to say that: "The safest general characterization of the European philosophical tradition is that it consists of a series of footnotes to Plato."

raise his children there, he has expressed his support for the laws; thus, disobeying them would be to commit an injustice.

The bulk of the *Phaedo*, written some time after the *Apology* and *Crito*, consists of a discussion of arguments for the immortality of the soul. In the conclusion of the *Phaedo*, Socrates explains to his friends why he should not fear death, before drinking the hemlock poison.

Plato's most important social and political work, the *Republic*, is written in the form of a dramatic dialogue. The narrator Socrates, speaking directly to the reader, is describing a conversation he took part in which is supposed to have happened yesterday at the Athenian port city of Piraeus. The dialogue is traditionally divided into ten parts or "Books." The aim of the *Republic* is to discover what justice (*dikaiosunē*) is and to establish that it is preferable to injustice. Book 1 (which, some interpreters believe, may have been originally written as a separate dialogue) is a preliminary discussion of these issues, and Books 2 to 4 contain a discussion of the nature of justice. Books 5 to 7 are—according to Socrates—a digression, but the discussion they contain serves to connect Plato's account of justice to human motivation and the Good. In Books 8 and 9 Plato argues that justice is more beneficial than injustice. Book 10 is often considered an epilogue to the argument; it deals with a few final objections, such as the suggestion that Plato's conclusions contradict the teachings of contemporary poets.

At the start of Book 2 it is made clear that the discussion of Book 1 has been unsatisfactory, and that the issues need to be explored in more depth. The main argument begins with an important distinction between three kinds of good thing, of varying value. The question which the discussants then agree to pursue (and which occupies the rest of the *Republic*) is: how important is it to actually *be* just. Does the just man with a bad reputation have a happier life than the unjust man who has the reputation of being just? Glaucon and Adeimantus make the case as forcefully as they are able that justice is, in itself, far less beneficial than injustice, and challenge Socrates to respond.

Although the topic, so far, has been justice in the individual—the difference between a just and an unjust person—Socrates turns to considering justice in the city (*polis*) where it is displayed "in a larger size and on a larger surface." He discusses the origin of the city, or of human society, and connects this to what he considers to be natural differences between types of people; people, according to Socrates, are

not self-sufficient but are naturally suited to play particular specialized roles (such as shoemaker, farmer, or builder) in a cooperative social system. Socrates describes the historical growth of this first, ideal society and suggests that, after a time, it will need to develop a warrior class who evolve into the "guardians" and rulers of the city. The end of Book 2 and the start of Book 3 contain an extensive discussion of the proper forms of education for the city's guardians, and Socrates then explains how these rulers should be selected. He suggests at this point that the guardian class should be split into two—the warriors and the rulers—and that the rest of the city's citizens should be told a "noble falsehood" to legitimize and enforce the distinction between the classes of rulers and ruled.

Book 4 begins with an examination of the place of happiness and individual wealth in the ideal society, and the role of the guardians in preserving social order. Socrates is then, he says, ready to examine the ideal city he has conjured to see how it manifests the virtue of justice. He explains that the city has three parts (rulers, soldiers, and the productive class) and four virtues (wisdom, courage, moderation, and justice), and that the city—itself, not merely its individual citizens—has these virtues in virtue of its structure. Socrates then develops an account of the virtuous and just individual that parallels that he has just given of the city: the soul (*psychē*), he says, has a tripartite structure (reason, spirit, and desire) and virtue consists in the proper ordering of these parts.

At the start of Book 5, Socrates claims that he has now shown that justice is worth having for its own sake; he prepares to move on to show that it is valuable also for its consequences. However he is interrupted by some of the parties to the conversation, who demand that he amplify his account of the relationship between women and men in the ideal state. Socrates does so, and also talks more about the role and nature of the guardians, calling the best among them "philosopher kings." He defends the idea that philosophers are best suited to rule by arguing that they alone know the true nature of the Good; the allegory of the cave at the start of Book 7 is part of his attempt to explain what he means by this.

Book 8 returns us to the main thread of the argument of the *Republic*, and here Socrates begins to make his case that being just benefits the individual—that the just person has a more pleasant life than an unjust one. Once again Socrates begins by considering justice and injustice at the level of society, in order to shed light on individuals. He does so by describing a sequence of four types of increasingly unjust state: timocracy (in which the rulers are motivated by selfish love of honor), oligarchy (in which the rulers are motivated by desire for wealth), democracy (in which there is no unifying principle for society at all), and tyranny (in which the state is run by a dictator, with no concern for its welfare). These, Socrates argues, parallel four types of unjust person. The discussion culminates, in Book 9, in an account of how unpleasant life is for a tyrant, as compared to the life of a philosopher-king.

The *Laws* is one of Plato's later dialogues and Socrates does not appear here as a protagonist. Set on the island of Crete, it is a dialogue between an Athenian Stranger, a Spartan citizen (Megillus) and a Cretan politician Clinias. As in the *Republic*, the topic of discussion is the laws for a city, but unlike the *Republic*, these laws are not for an ideal city; rather, they are meant to be applied to an actual city. (Here it should be noted that Plato almost certainly revised some of the views he expressed in the *Republic*: to observe that the claim that the respective works treat ideal and actual cities does not fully capture the differences between the two works.) The first two books of the *Laws* (the first section of the first book is included here) ask about the proper end (*telos*) of legislation. As in the *Republic*, Plato's answer is that the lawgiver must aim at virtue and the legislation should foster the virtues (courage, justice, moderation, and wisdom) in the city's citizens. Books 4 to 12 discuss in detail the constitution and the social and political institutions for a new Cretan city *Magnesia*. Plato sets outs rules about the population (with a maximum of 5,040 households), property (with a maximum amount permitted depending on class), common meals (funded jointly by the households), and military training. Unusually for the time, the *Laws* treats women as citizens (though ones with no independent right to property), making them eligible to vote and hold office, as well as liable for military training. Among the most important requirements in the *Laws* is that lawgivers must attempt to persuade the citizens that the laws are just, rather than relying on mere force.

Some Useful Background Information

i) All the characters that take part in the discussions of the *Republic* were historical figures. Glaucon and Adeimantus, for example, were actually Plato's brothers, and Thrasymachus was a well-known contemporary teacher of rhetoric,

oratory and "sophist" philosophy. The main character of the *Republic*, however, is of course its narrator Socrates.

Socrates was Plato's primary intellectual influence: though he left no writings, Socrates' personality and ideas were so powerful that he appears to have had a tremendous impact upon everyone he encountered, inspiring either intense devotion or intense irritation. Socrates' main philosophical concern was the ethical question of how one's life should best be lived, and his method was to engage in systematic cross-examination (*elenchus*) of those he encountered, challenging them to state and then justify their own beliefs about justice and virtue. Socrates frequently demonstrated to his conversants that their uncritically considered beliefs about moral virtue were self-contradictory and hence that those beliefs *had* no justification. The state of bewildered awareness of their own ignorance in which Socrates left his unfortunate victims is called *aporia*, and Socrates' technique of remorseless questioning is sometimes known as the "aporetic method."

Though Socrates was famous for insisting that he was wiser than his fellow Athenians only because he alone realized that he knew nothing, he did subscribe to a handful of substantive philosophical positions, two of which in particular he passed on to Plato. First, for Socrates, virtue (*aretē*) is a kind of knowledge: that is, to be a virtuous person is, fundamentally, to *understand* what the good—the right thing to do—is, in much the same way as being an expert shoemaker consists in knowing everything there is to know about shoes. Socrates (and Plato after him) therefore held that it was vitally important to find correct definitions—or to understand the essence (*eidos*)—of ethical concepts; otherwise, we will not know how to live. In this way, ethical research would parallel mathematical research, in which the researcher tries to establish definitions for fundamental objects and then to prove results about those objects.

The second crucial Socratic doctrine is that the real essence of a person is not his or her body but her soul, and that this soul is immortal: the health of one's own soul is thus of paramount importance, and is far more significant than the mere slings and arrows of physical life. Indeed Socrates was convinced that, even while we are living in the physical world, the quality of our souls is a far more important determinant of our happiness than external circumstances like health, wealth, popularity, or power.

ii) The topic of the *Republic* is *dikaiosunē*, a Greek word that is usually translated into English as "justice." Although, strangely enough, it is a matter of some controversy just what exactly Plato means by *dikaiosunē* (and thus just what exactly the *Republic* is about!), it is clear that the notion covers more than we might normally understand by the word "justice," though probably somewhat less than we would today understand by "morality." That is, Plato is not merely interested in the virtue of treating other people fairly and impartially (in the *Republic*, he is hardly interested at all in the formulation and administration of civil and criminal law: in the *Laws*, on the other hand, he develops a system of laws). Rather, Plato is discussing something like *the right way to live*, where it is understood (as was generally assumed by the ancient Greeks) that human beings are *social* animals, for whom the good life can only exist in a particular sort of political context; and understood as well that all the virtues—such as courage, moderation, generosity and even piety—have to do, in one way or another, with our relationships with other people. By "justice," then, Plato probably means all the areas of morality that regulate our relationships with other people.

On the other hand, it is important to notice that Plato does *not* think of justice as primarily a way of behaving, or as a set of rules for correct action, or as a kind of relationship between people. Justice, for Plato, is an *internal property of individual souls*, and only secondarily of their actions. You have the virtue of justice if your soul has a certain kind of configuration, and then it is this virtue of yours which regulates your treatment of other people; but your treatment of other people is not *itself* justice; it is just the manifestation of your justice. To put it another way, you are not a just person because your actions are just—on the contrary, your actions are just because you are.

iii) The description of the "popular view" of justice by Glaucon and Adeimantus is philosophically slightly more complicated than it might at first seem. In this context it is useful one to bear in mind the distinction between what are often called the "artificial" and the "natural" consequences of justice. The artificial consequences of justice are those "rewards and reputations" which society provides for those who give the appearance of being just. They are artificial rewards because they would not exist if it were not for human social conventions and practices. Even more importantly, they are connected only to the *appearance* of justice rather than to justice itself. Thus, someone who appeared just but was not would still get all the artificial rewards of justice. On the other hand, the natural rewards of being just are supposed to follow simply from justice itself, in the way that health, sight and

knowledge have, in themselves, beneficial consequences for their possessors.

iv) Plato devotes an important section of the *Republic* to discussing justice in the city. In ancient Greece, the city was the primary political unit—approximately equivalent to states or societies today. Although the Greeks at the time did think of themselves as members of a common people, their main allegiance was to their home *polis*, and cities differed widely in their culture and forms of government.

One final point: it is important to Plato to establish that the arrangement of his ideal city is *natural*—that is, roughly, a consequence of human nature; a social structure that is uniquely suited to the human species—rather than merely being the best of several possible conventional ways of organizing society.

Some Common Misconceptions

i) The main protagonists of the *Republic*—Glaucon, Adeimantus, and Socrates—*agree* that justice is good in itself. In Book 2, Glaucon and Adeimantus present certain arguments as strongly as they can in order to force Socrates to give a proper response to them, but they do not themselves endorse the conclusion of those arguments (and they hope that Socrates will be able to give them a legitimate means to escape that conclusion).

ii) The discussion in the *Republic* is ultimately about the benefits of justice *for just people themselves*, not for those they interact with or for society in general. That is, the topic is whether *acting justly* is intrinsically worthwhile (rather than whether it is nice to be treated justly by others).

iii) Socrates would agree that the division of labor in society contributes to economic efficiency, but this is not his main reason for holding that people must specialize in particular tasks (Book 3). His view is that people are born with particular aptitudes, and that this fits them naturally to cooperate with others by playing a particular role, complementary to the roles played by others in that society. It is not only for the greater good of the whole that everyone should fulfill the roles to which they are naturally suited; it is also the case that doing so is the only way for the individuals to fulfill their innate potential.

iv) There is a tendency for modern readers to see Plato's vision of the ideal state as disconcertingly totalitarian and classist. This response is something one should take seriously. However, it is also important to bear in mind that the state Socrates conjures is ideal also in the sense that it is not supposed to describe any actual state. He is arguing that *if* a city were ruled by perfectly wise and incorruptible leaders *then* it would be prudent and right for citizens who lacked the innate ability and careful education of their leaders to defer to them. It need not follow from this, for example, that *we* ought implicitly to trust and obey our own governments.

How Important and Influential Are These Writings?

It is difficult to overestimate the influence of Plato's thought on many philosophers, beginning with Aristotle, who responds to him in the *Nicomachean Ethics* and the *Politics*. The *Apology* has continued to play an important role in discussions of democracy and its pitfalls, while the *Crito's* early version of the social contract theory—along with its posing of the question of whether or not unjust laws should be obeyed—has retained a central place in political philosophy and in discussions of civil disobedience.

The *Republic* is generally acknowledged to be one of the greatest works in all philosophy. Though it presents only a partial picture of Plato's developing philosophical views, it is the dialogue in which most of his central ideas—about metaphysics, epistemology, politics, psychology, and aesthetics, as well as about ethics and politics—come together into a single unified theory.

One of Plato's key contributions to political thought was to introduce the idea that there could be a body of expert knowledge whose content, when applied, would make it possible to resolve political problems, reverse social decline, and generate social harmony. Such harmony was under Plato's theory a more achievable goal than it has seemed to many other philosophers and theorists, simply because Plato understood there to be an underlying harmony of real interests for human beings; the proper role of the state, in his view, is to help establish and maintain this harmony. For Plato, justice is not what serves the interests of the strongest but what preserves the happiness of the state as a whole.

Although most of the particular constitutional recommendations of the *Republic*—abolition of the family, female equality, the outlawing of personal wealth, and so on—were rejected or ignored for much of the subsequent history of political thought, many of the book's other ideals have resonated in many eras: the political importance of education; the idea that there is a relation between class structure, social order, and individual psychology; the idea that freedom is valuable only if it is under the control of reason; the notion that intellectual and moral superiority makes it appropriate for a certain group of people to rule; and the concept of an intrinsically social nature for human beings.

◆ ◆ ◆ ◆ ◆

Apology[1]

I do not know, men of Athens,[2] how my accusers affected you; as for me, I was almost carried away in spite of myself, so persuasively did they speak. And yet, hardly anything of what they said is true. Of the many lies they told, one in particular surprised me, namely that you should be careful not to be deceived by an accomplished speaker like me. That they were not ashamed to be immediately proved wrong by the facts, when I show myself not to be an accomplished speaker at all, that I thought was most shameless on their part—unless indeed they call an accomplished speaker the man who speaks the truth. If they mean that, I would agree that I am an orator, but not after their manner, for indeed, as I say, practically nothing they said was true. From me you will hear the whole truth, though not, by Zeus, gentlemen, expressed in embroidered and stylized phrases like theirs, but things spoken at random and expressed in the first words that come to mind, for I put my trust in the justice of what I say, and let none of you expect anything else. It would not be fitting at my age, as it might be for a young man, to toy with words when I appear before you.

One thing I do ask and beg of you, gentlemen: if you hear me making my defense in the same kind of language as I am accustomed to use in the marketplace by the bankers'

1   *Apology* The word *apology* is a transliteration, not a translation, of the Greek *apologia*, which means *defense*.

2   *men of Athens* Jurors were selected by lot from all the male citizens 30 years of age or older who offered themselves on the given day for service. They thus functioned as representatives of the Athenian people and the Athenian democracy. In cases such as that of Socrates, they judged on behalf of the whole citizen body whether or not their interests had been undermined by the accused's behavior. Hence Socrates can address them as if he were addressing the people of Athens at large, and in particular the partisans of the democracy against its oligarchic opponents (see, for example, 21a, 32d). Socrates addresses the jury as "men of Athens" rather than employing the usual mode of address "gentlemen of the jury" (as Meletus does at 26d). At 40a he explains that only those who voted to acquit him deserve that honor.

tables,[1] where many of you have heard me, and elsewhere,
d do not be surprised or create a disturbance on that account.
The position is this: this is my first appearance in a lawcourt,
at the age of seventy; I am therefore simply a stranger to the
manner of speaking here. Just as if I were really a stranger,
you would certainly excuse me if I spoke in that dialect and
18 manner in which I had been brought up, so too my present
request seems a just one, for you to pay no attention to my
manner of speech—be it better or worse but to concentrate
your attention on whether what I say is just or not, for the
excellence of a judge lies in this, as that of a speaker lies in
telling the truth.

It is right for me, gentlemen, to defend myself first
against the first lying accusations made against me and my
first accusers, and then against the later accusations and the
b later accusers. There have been many who have accused me
to you for many years now, and none of their accusations
are true. These I fear much more than I fear Anytus and his
friends,[2] though they too are formidable. These earlier ones,
however, are more so, gentlemen; they got hold of most of
you from childhood, persuaded you and accused me quite
falsely, saying that there is a man called Socrates, a wise
man, a student of all things in the sky and below the earth,
c who makes the worse argument the stronger. Those who
spread that rumor, gentlemen, are my dangerous accusers,
for their hearers believe that those who study these things
do not even believe in the gods. Moreover, these accusers
are numerous, and have been at it a long time; also, they
spoke to you at an age when you would most readily believe
them, some of you being children and adolescents, and they
won their case by default, as there was no defense.

What is most absurd in all this is that one cannot even
d know or mention their names unless one of them is a writer
of comedies.[3] Those who maliciously and slanderously per-

suaded you—who also, when persuaded themselves then
persuaded others—all those are most difficult to deal with:
one cannot bring one of them into court or refute him; one
must simply fight with shadows, as it were, in making one's
defense, and cross-examine when no one answers. I want
you to realize too that my accusers are of two kinds: those
who have accused me recently, and the old ones I mention;
and to think that I must first defend myself against the lat- e
ter, for you have also heard their accusations first, and to a
much greater extent than the more recent.

Very well then, men of Athens. I must surely defend 19
myself and attempt to uproot from your minds in so short
a time the slander that has resided there so long. I wish this
may happen, if it is in any way better for you and me, and
that my defense may be successful, but I think this is very
difficult and I am fully aware of how difficult it is. Even so,
let the matter proceed as the god may wish, but I must obey
the law and make my defense.

Let us then take up the case from its beginning. What
is the accusation from which arose the slander in which b
Meletus trusted when he wrote out the charge against me?
What did they say when they slandered me? I must, as if
they were my actual prosecutors, read the affidavit they
would have sworn. It goes something like this: Socrates is
guilty of wrongdoing in that he busies himself studying
things in the sky and below the earth; he makes the worse
into the stronger argument, and he teaches these same c
things to others. You have seen this yourself in the comedy
of Aristophanes, a Socrates swinging about there,[4] saying
he was walking on air and talking a lot of other nonsense
about things of which I know nothing at all. I do not speak
in contempt of such knowledge, if someone is wise in these
things—lest Meletus bring more cases against me—but,
gentlemen, I have no part in it, and on this point I call
upon the majority of you as witnesses. I think it right that
all those of you who have heard me conversing, and many d
of you have, should tell each other if anyone of you has ever
heard me discussing such subjects to any extent at all. From
this you will learn that the other things said about me by
the majority are of the same kind.

Not one of them is true. And if you have heard from
anyone that I undertake to teach people and charge a fee for

---

1 *the bankers' tables* The bankers or money-changers had their
counters in the marketplace. It seems that this was a favorite place
for gossip.

2 *Anytus and his friends* His friends were Meletus and Lycon; the
three of them were prosecuting. The leader of the prosecution
was Meletus, a young man who probably held a grudge against
Socrates; Anytus hated the sophists and probably regarded Socrates
as one of them; Lycon was a rhetorician. Anytus is mentioned
specially, because he was the most politically influential of these,
having played an important part in the restoration of Athenian
democracy.

3 *writer of comedies* This is Aristophanes, Greek comic dramatist
(c. 446 BCE–c. 388 BCE). Socrates refers below (19c) to the character Socrates in his *Clouds*, first produced in 423 BCE; in that

play Socrates is presented as a dubious scientific practitioner and
amoral atheist rhetorician.

4 *a Socrates swinging about there* In the play, the satire of Socrates'
to desire to inquire into higher things is given physical form
through the depiction of Socrates in a hanging basket.

e it, that is not true either. Yet I think it a fine thing to be able to teach people as Gorgias of Leontini does, and Prodicus of Ceos, and Hippias of Elis.[1] Each of these men can go to any city and persuade the young, who can keep company with anyone of their own fellow citizens they want without pay-
20 ing, to leave the company of these, to join with themselves, pay them a fee, and be grateful to them besides. Indeed, I learned that there is another wise man from Paros who is visiting us, for I met a man who has spent more money on Sophists than everybody else put together, Callias, the son of Hipponicus. So I asked him—he has two sons—"Cal-lias," I said, "if your sons were colts or calves, we could find and engage a supervisor for them who would make them
b excel in their proper qualities, some horse breeder or farmer. Now since they are men, whom do you have in mind to supervise them? Who is an expert in this kind of excellence, the human and social kind? I think you must have given thought to this since you have sons. Is there such a person," I asked, "or is there not?" "Certainly there is," he said. "Who is he?" I asked, "What is his name, where is he from? And what is his fee?" "His name, Socrates, is Evenus, he comes from Paros, and his fee is five minas."[2] I thought Evenus a
c happy man, if he really possesses this art, and teaches for so moderate a fee. Certainly I would pride and preen myself if I had this knowledge, but I do not have it, gentlemen.

One of you might perhaps interrupt me and say: "But Socrates, what is your occupation? From where have these slanders come? For surely if you did not busy yourself with something out of the common, all these rumors and talk would not have arisen unless you did something other than most people. Tell us what it is, that we may not speak
d inadvisedly about you." Anyone who says that seems to be right, and I will try to show you what has caused this reputation and slander. Listen then. Perhaps some of you will think I am jesting, but be sure that all that I shall say is true. What has caused my reputation is none other than

a certain kind of wisdom. What kind of wisdom? Human wisdom, perhaps. It may be that I really possess this, while those whom I mentioned just now are wise with a wisdom
e more than human; else I cannot explain it, for I certainly do not possess it, and whoever says I do is lying and speaks to slander me. Do not create a disturbance, gentlemen, even if you think I am boasting, for the story I shall tell does not originate with me, but I will refer you to a trustworthy source. I shall call upon the god at Delphi[3] as witness to the existence and nature of my wisdom, if it be such. You know Chaerephon. He was my friend from youth, and the friend
21 of most of you, as he shared your exile and your return.[4] You surely know the kind of man he was, how impulsive in any course of action. He went to Delphi at one time and ventured to ask the oracle—as I say, gentlemen, do not create a disturbance—he asked if any man was wiser than I, and the Pythian replied that no one was wiser. Chaerephon is dead, but his brother will testify to you about this.

b Consider that I tell you this because I would inform you about the origin of the slander. When I heard of this reply I asked myself: "Whatever does the god mean? What is his riddle? I am very conscious that I am not wise at all; what then does he mean by saying that I am the wisest? For surely he does not lie; it is not legitimate for him to do so." For a long time I was at a loss as to his meaning; then I very reluc-tantly turned to some such investigation as this; I went to
c one of those reputed wise, thinking that there, if anywhere, I could refute the oracle and say to it: "This man is wiser than I, but you said I was." Then, when I examined this man—there is no need for me to tell you his name, he was one of our public men—my experience was something like this: I thought that he appeared wise to many people and especially to himself, but he was not. I then tried to show
d him that he thought himself wise, but that he was not. As a result he came to dislike me, and so did many of the by-standers. So I withdrew and thought to myself: "I am wiser than this man; it is likely that neither of us knows anything worthwhile, but he thinks he knows something when he does not, whereas when I do not know, neither do I think I know; so I am likely to be wiser than he to this small extent, that I do not think I know what I do not know." After this I

---

1 *Gorgias ... Hippias* These were all well-known Sophists (profes-sional teachers, criticized by Plato for their amorality and cyni-cism). Gorgias, after whom Plato named one of his dialogues, was a celebrated rhetorician and teacher of rhetoric. Two dialogues, the authenticity of which has been doubted, are named after Hip-pias, whose knowledge was encyclopedic. Prodicus was known for his insistence on the precise meaning of words. Both he and Hippias are characters in *Protagoras* (named after another famous Sophist).

2 *five minas* A mina equaled 100 drachmas. In Socrates' time one drachma was the daily wage of a day-laborer. So Evenus' fee was a considerable sum.

3 *the god at Delphi* The god Apollo had a very famous shrine at Delphi, where his oracles were delivered through the mouth of a priestess, the "Pythian."

4 *your exile and your return* In 404 BCE, a coup seized the govern-ment and sent opponents into exile for a year, till the democracy was restored.

approached another man, one of those thought to be wiser
e   than he, and I thought the same thing, and so I came to be
disliked both by him and by many others.

After that I proceeded systematically. I realized, to
my sorrow and alarm, that I was getting unpopular, but I
thought that I must attach the greatest importance to the
god's oracle, so I must go to all those who had any reputation
for knowledge to examine its meaning. And by the dog,[1]
22 men of Athens—for I must tell you the truth—I experienced something like this: in my investigation in the service
of the god I found that those who had the highest reputation were nearly the most deficient, while those who were
thought to be inferior were more knowledgeable. I must
give you an account of my journeyings as if they were labors
I had undertaken to prove the oracle irrefutable. After the
politicians, I went to the poets, the writers of tragedies and
b   dithyrambs and the others, intending in their case to catch
myself being more ignorant than they. So I took up those
poems with which they seemed to have taken most trouble
and asked them what they meant, in order that I might at
the same time learn something from them. I am ashamed to
tell you the truth, gentlemen, but I must. Almost all the by-
standers might have explained the poems better than their
authors could. I soon realized that poets do not compose
c   their poems with knowledge, but by some inborn talent and
by inspiration, like seers and prophets who also say many
fine things without any understanding of what they say. The
poets seemed to me to have had a similar experience. At the
same time I saw that, because of their poetry, they thought
themselves very wise men in other respects, which they were
not. So there again I withdrew, thinking that I had the same
advantage over them as I had over the politicians.

Finally I went to the craftsmen, for I was conscious of
d   knowing practically nothing, and I knew that I would find
that they had knowledge of many fine things. In this I was
not mistaken; they knew things I did not know, and to that
extent they were wiser than I. But, men of Athens, the good
craftsmen seemed to me to have the same fault as the poets:
each of them, because of his success at his craft, thought
himself very wise in other most important pursuits, and this
error of theirs overshadowed the wisdom they had, so that
e   I asked myself, on behalf of the oracle, whether I should
prefer to be as I am, with neither their wisdom nor their

---

1   *by the dog* A curious oath, occasionally used by Socrates as well
    as other Greeks as a somewhat humorous oath replacing the name
    of a real deity; it appears in a longer form in *Gorgias* (482b) as "by
    the dog, the god of the Egyptians."

ignorance, or to have both. The answer I gave myself and
the oracle was that it was to my advantage to be as I am.

As a result of this investigation, men of Athens, I acquired much unpopularity, of a kind that is hard to deal   23
with and is a heavy burden; many slanders came from these
people and a reputation for wisdom, for in each case the
bystanders thought that I myself possessed the wisdom that
I proved that my interlocutor did not have. What is probable, gentlemen, is that in fact the god is wise and that his
oracular response meant that human wisdom is worth little
or nothing, and that when he says this man, Socrates, he is
using my name as an example, as if he said: "This man among   b
you, mortals, is wisest who, like Socrates, understands that
his wisdom is worthless." So even now I continue this investigation as the god bade me—and I go around seeking
out anyone, citizen or stranger, whom I think wise. Then if
I do not think he is, I come to the assistance of the god and
show him that he is not wise. Because of this occupation,
I do not have the leisure to engage in public affairs to any
extent, nor indeed to look after my own, but I live in great
poverty because of my service to the god.   c

Furthermore, the young men who follow me around of
their own free will, those who have most leisure, the sons
of the very rich, take pleasure in hearing people questioned;
they themselves often imitate me and try to question others.
I think they find an abundance of men who believe they
have some knowledge but know little or nothing. The result
is that those whom they question are angry, not with themselves but with me. They say: "That man Socrates is a pesti-   d
lential fellow who corrupts the young." If one asks them
what he does and what he teaches to corrupt them, they are
silent, as they do not know, but, so as not to appear at a loss,
they mention those accusations that are available against all
philosophers, about "things in the sky and things below the
earth," about "not believing in the gods" and "making the
worse the stronger argument"; they would not want to tell
the truth, I'm sure, that they have been proved to lay claim
to knowledge when they know nothing. These people are   e
ambitious, violent, and numerous; they are continually and
convincingly talking about me; they have been filling your
ears for a long time with vehement slanders against me.
From them Meletus attacked me, and Anytus and Lycon,
Meletus being vexed on behalf of the poets, Anytus on behalf of the craftsmen and the politicians, Lycon on behalf of   24
the orators, so that, as I started out by saying, I should be
surprised if I could rid you of so much slander in so short a
time. That, men of Athens, is the truth for you. I have hid-

den or disguised nothing. I know well enough that this very conduct makes me unpopular, and this is proof that what I say is true, that such is the slander against me, and that such are its causes. If you look into this either now or later, this is what you will find.

Let this suffice as a defense against the charges of my earlier accusers. After this I shall try to defend myself against Meletus, that good and patriotic man, as he says he is, and my later accusers. As these are a different lot of accusers, let us again take up their sworn deposition. It goes something like this: Socrates is guilty of corrupting the young and of not believing in the gods in whom the city believes, but in other new spiritual things? Such is their charge. Let us examine it point by point.

He says that I am guilty of corrupting the young, but I say that Meletus is guilty of dealing frivolously with serious matters, of irresponsibly bringing people into court, and of professing to be seriously concerned with things about none of which he has ever cared, and I shall try to prove that this is so. Come here and tell me, Meletus. Surely you consider it of the greatest importance that our young men be as good as possible?[1]

Indeed I do.

Come then, tell these men who improves them. You obviously know, in view of your concern.[2] You say you have discovered the one who corrupts them, namely me, and you bring me here and accuse me to these men. Come, inform these men and tell them who it is who improves them. You see, Meletus, that you are silent and know not what to say. Does this not seem shameful to you and a sufficient proof of what I say, that you have not been concerned with any of this? Tell me, my good sir, who improves our young men?

The laws.

That is not what I am asking, but what person who has knowledge of the laws to begin with?

These jurymen, Socrates.

How do you mean, Meletus? Are these able to educate the young and improve them?

Certainly.

All of them, or some but not others?

All of them.

Very good, by Hera. You mention a great abundance of benefactors. But what about the audience? Do they improve the young or not?

They do, too.

What about the members of Council?

The Councilors, also.

But, Meletus, what about the assembly?[3] Do members of the assembly corrupt the young, or do they all improve them?

They improve them.

All the Athenians, it seems, make the young into fine good men, except me, and I alone corrupt them. Is that what you mean?

That is most definitely what I mean.

You condemn me to a great misfortune. Tell me: does this also apply to horses, do you think? That all men improve them and one individual corrupts them? Or is quite the contrary true, one individual is able to improve them, or very few, namely, the horse breeders, whereas the majority, if they have horses and use them, corrupt them? Is that not the case, Meletus, both with horses and all other animals? Of course it is, whether you and Anytus say so or not. It would be a very happy state of affairs if only one person corrupted our youth, while the others improved them.

You have made it sufficiently obvious, Meletus, that you have never had any concern for our youth; you show your indifference clearly; that you have given no thought to the subjects about which you bring me to trial.

And by Zeus, Meletus, tell us also whether it is better for a man to live among good or wicked fellow citizens. Answer, my good man, for I am not asking a difficult question. Do not the wicked do some harm to those who are ever closest to them, whereas good people benefit them?—Certainly.

And does the man exist who would rather be harmed than benefited by his associates? Answer, my good sir, for the law orders you to answer. Is there any man who wants to be harmed?—Of course not.

Come now, do you accuse me here of corrupting the young and making them worse deliberately or unwillingly?

Deliberately.

What follows, Meletus? Are you so much wiser at your age than I am at mine that you understand that wicked people always do some harm to their closest neighbors

---

1 *Surely you ... as possible?* Socrates here drops into his usual method of discussion by question and answer. This, no doubt, is what Plato had in mind, at least in part, when he made him ask the indulgence of the jury if he spoke "in his usual manner."

2 *in view of your concern* A play on words: "Meletus" means "caring person."

3 *members of Council ... the assembly* The Council was a body of 500 men, elected annually by lot, that prepared the agenda for meetings of the assembly and (together with the magistrates) conducted the public business of Athens. The assembly was open to all male citizens.

e while good people do them good, but I have reached such a pitch of ignorance that I do not realize this, namely that if I make one of my associates wicked I run the risk of being harmed by him so that I do such a great evil deliberately, as you say? I do not believe you, Meletus, and I do not think anyone else will. Either I do not corrupt the young or, if I

26 do, it is unwillingly, and you are lying in either case. Now if I corrupt them unwillingly, the law does not require you to bring people to court for such unwilling wrongdoings, but to get hold of them privately, to instruct them and exhort them; for clearly, if I learn better, I shall cease to do what I am doing unwillingly. You, however, have avoided my company and were unwilling to instruct me, but you bring me here, where the law requires one to bring those who are in need of punishment, not of instruction.

And so, men of Athens, what I said is clearly true: Me-
b letus has never been at all concerned with these matters. Nonetheless tell us, Meletus, how you say that I corrupt the young; or is it obvious from your deposition that it is by teaching them not to believe in the gods in whom the city believes but in other new spiritual things? Is this not what you say I teach and so corrupt them?—That is most certainly what I do say.

Then by those very gods about whom we are talking, Meletus, make this clearer to me and to these men: I cannot
c be sure whether you mean that I teach the belief that there are some gods—and therefore I myself believe that there are gods and am not altogether an atheist, nor am I guilty of that—not, however, the gods in whom the city believes, but others, and that this is the charge against me, that they are others. Or whether you mean that I do not believe in gods at all, and that this is what I teach to others.

This is what I mean, that you do not believe in gods at all.
d You are a strange fellow, Meletus. Why do you say this? Do I not believe, as other men do, that the sun and the moon are gods?[1]

No, by Zeus, gentlemen of the jury, for he says that the sun is stone, and the moon earth.

My dear Meletus, do you think you are prosecuting Anaxagoras?[2] Are you so contemptuous of these men and

think them so ignorant of letters as not to know that the books of Anaxagoras of Clazomenae are full of those theories, and further, that the young men learn from me what they can buy from time to time for a drachma, at most, in the bookshops, and ridicule Socrates if he pretends that e these theories are his own, especially as they are so absurd? Is that, by Zeus, what you think of me, Meletus, that I do not believe that there are any gods? That is what I say, that you do not believe in the gods at all.

You cannot be believed, Meletus, even, I think, by yourself. The man appears to me, men of Athens, highly insolent and uncontrolled. He seems to have made this deposition out of insolence, violence, and youthful zeal. He is like one who composed a riddle and is trying it out: "Will the wise 27 Socrates realize that I am jesting and contradicting myself, or shall I deceive him and others?" I think he contradicts himself in the affidavit, as if he said: "Socrates is guilty of not believing in gods but believing in gods," and surely that is the part of a jester!

Examine with me, gentlemen, how he appears to contradict himself, and you, Meletus, answer us. Remember, gentlemen, what I asked you when I began, not to create a b disturbance if I proceed in my usual manner.

Does any man, Meletus, believe in human activities who does not believe in humans? Make him answer, and not again and again create a disturbance. Does any man who does not believe in horses believe in horsemen's activities? Or in flute-playing activities but not in fluteplayers? No, my good sir, no man could. If you are not willing to answer, I will tell you and these men. Answer the next question, however. Does any man believe in spiritual activities c who does not believe in spirits?—No one.

Thank you for answering, if reluctantly, when these gentlemen made you. Now you say that I believe in spiritual things and teach about them, whether new or old, but at any rate spiritual things according to what you say, and to this you have sworn in your deposition. But if I believe in spiritual things I must quite inevitably believe in spirits. Is that not so? It is indeed. I shall assume that you agree, as you do not answer. Do we not believe spirits to be either d gods or the children of gods? Yes or no?

Of course.

Then since I do believe in spirits, as you admit, if spirits are gods, this is what I mean when I say you speak in

---

1 *Do I not believe ... are gods?* Sun and moon worship were common in Greece.
2 *Anaxagoras* Anaxagorus of Clazomenae, born about the beginning of the fifth century BCE, came to Athens as a young man and spent his time in the pursuit of natural philosophy. He taught that the sun and moon are fragments of the earth that glow from

heat caused by their movement. Socrates leads the discussion to him as a parallel to his own case; he left Athens after being prosecuted for impiety.

riddles and in jest, as you state that I do not believe in gods and then again that I do, since I do believe in spirits. If on the other hand the spirits are children of the gods, bastard children of the gods by nymphs or some other mothers, as they are said to be, what man would believe children of the gods to exist, but not gods? That would be just as absurd as

e to believe the young of horses and asses, namely mules, to exist, but not to believe in the existence of horses and asses. You must have made this deposition, Meletus, either to test us or because you were at a loss to find any true wrongdoing of which to accuse me. There is no way in which you could persuade anyone of even small intelligence that it is possible for one and the same man to believe in spiritual but not

28 also in divine things, and then again for that same man to believe neither in spirits nor in gods nor in heroes.

I do not think, men of Athens, that it requires a prolonged defense to prove that I am not guilty of the charges in Meletus' deposition, but this is sufficient. On the other hand, you know that what I said earlier is true, that I am very unpopular with many people. This will be my undoing, if I am undone, not Meletus or Anytus but the slanders and envy of many people. This has destroyed many other good

b men and will, I think, continue to do so. There is no danger that it will stop at me.

Someone might say: "Are you not ashamed, Socrates, to have followed the kind of occupation that has led to your being now in danger of death?" However, I should be right to reply to him: "You are wrong, sir, if you think that a man who is any good at all should take into account the risk of life or death; he should look to this only in his actions, whether what he does is right or wrong, whether he is acting like a good or a bad man." According to your view,

c all the heroes who died at Troy were inferior people, especially the son of Thetis who was so contemptuous of danger compared with disgrace. When he was eager to kill Hector, his goddess mother warned him, as I believe, in some such words as these: "My child, if you avenge the death of your comrade, Patroclus, and you kill Hector, you will die yourself, for your death is to follow immediately after Hector's." Hearing this, he despised death and danger and was much

d more afraid to live a coward who did not avenge his friends. "Let me die at once," he said, "when once I have given the wrongdoer his deserts, rather than remain here, a laughing-stock by the curved ships, a burden upon the earth." Do you think he gave thought to death and danger?[1]

---

1   *the son of Thetis ... danger*   The scene between Thetis and Achilles
     is from Book 18 of the *Iliad*.

This is the truth of the matter, men of Athens: wherever a man has taken a position that he believes to be best, or has been placed by his commander, there he must I think remain and face danger, without a thought for death or anything

e else, rather than disgrace. It would have been a dreadful way to behave, men of Athens, if, at Potidaea, Amphipolis, and Delium, I had, at the risk of death, like anyone else, remained at my post where those you had elected to command had ordered me, and then, when the god ordered me, as I thought and believed, to live the life of a philosopher, to examine myself and others, I had abandoned my post for fear of death or anything else. That would have been

29 a dreadful thing, and then I might truly have justly been brought here for not believing that there are gods, disobeying the oracle, fearing death, and thinking I was wise when I was not. To fear death, gentlemen, is no other than to think oneself wise when one is not, to think one knows what one does not know. No one knows whether death may not be the greatest of all blessings for a man, yet men fear it as if they know that it is the greatest of evils. And surely it is the most

b blameworthy ignorance to believe that one knows what one does not know. It is perhaps on this point and in this respect, gentlemen, that I differ from the majority of men, and if I were to claim that I am wiser than anyone in anything, it would be in this, that, as I have no adequate knowledge of things in the underworld, so I do not think I have. I do know, however, that it is wicked and shameful to do wrong, to disobey one's superior, be he god or man. I shall never fear or avoid things of which I do not know, whether they may not be good rather than things that I know to be bad. Even if you acquitted me now and did not believe Anytus, who

c said to you that either I should not have been brought here in the first place, or that now I am here, you cannot avoid executing me, for if I should be acquitted, your sons would practice the teachings of Socrates and all be thoroughly corrupted; if you said to me in this regard: "Socrates, we do not believe Anytus now; we acquit you, but only on condition that you spend no more time on this investigation and do not practice philosophy, and if you are caught doing so you

d will die"; if, as I say, you were to acquit me on those terms, I would say to you: "Men of Athens, I am grateful and I am your friend, but I will obey the god rather than you, and as long as I draw breath and am able, I shall not cease to practice philosophy, to exhort you and in my usual way to point out to anyone of you whom I happen to meet: Good Sir, you are an Athenian, a citizen of the greatest city with the greatest reputation for both wisdom and power; are you e not ashamed of your eagerness to possess as much wealth, reputation, and honors as possible, while you do not care for nor give thought to wisdom or truth, or the best possible state of your soul?" Then, if one of you disputes this and says he does care, I shall not let him go at once or leave him, but I shall question him, examine him, and test him, and if I do not think he has attained the goodness that he says he

30 has, I shall reproach him because he attaches little importance to the most important things and greater importance to inferior things. I shall treat in this way anyone I happen to meet, young and old, citizen and stranger, and more so the citizens because you are more kindred to me. Be sure that this is what the god orders me to do, and I think there is no greater blessing for the city than my service to the god. For I go around doing nothing but persuading both young

b and old among you not to care for your body or your wealth in preference to or as strongly as for the best possible state of your soul, as I say to you: "Wealth does not bring about excellence, but excellence makes wealth and everything else good for men, both individually and collectively."[1]

Now if by saying this I corrupt the young, this advice must be harmful, but if anyone says that I give different advice, he is talking nonsense. On this point I would say to you, men of Athens: "Whether you believe Anytus or not,

c whether you acquit me or not, do so on the understanding that this is my course of action, even if I am to face death many times." Do not create a disturbance, gentlemen, but abide by my request not to cry out at what I say but to listen, for I think it will be to your advantage to listen, and I am about to say other things at which you will perhaps cry out. By no means do this. Be sure that if you kill the sort of man I say I am, you will not harm me more than yourselves. Neither Meletus nor Anytus can harm me in any way; he could not harm me, for I do not think it is permitted that

d a better man be harmed by a worse; certainly he might kill me, or perhaps banish or disfranchise me, which he and maybe others think to be great harm, but I do not think so. I think he is doing himself much greater harm doing what he is doing now, attempting to have a man executed unjustly. Indeed, men of Athens, I am far from making a defense now on my own behalf, as might be thought, but on yours, to prevent you from wrongdoing by mistreating

e the god's gift to you by condemning me; for if you kill me you will not easily find another like me. I was attached to

this city by the god—though it seems a ridiculous thing to say—as upon a great and noble horse which was somewhat sluggish because of its size and needed to be stirred up by a kind of gadfly. It is to fulfill some such function that I believe the god has placed me in the city. I never cease to rouse each and every one of you, to persuade and reproach you all day long and everywhere I find myself in your company. 31

Another such man will not easily come to be among you, gentlemen, and if you believe me you will spare me. You might easily be annoyed with me as people are when they are aroused from a doze, and strike out at me; if convinced by Anytus you could easily kill me, and then you could sleep on for the rest of your days, unless the god, in his care for you, sent you someone else. That I am the kind of person to be a gift of the god to the city you might realize from the fact that it does not seem like human nature for me to have b neglected all my own affairs and to have tolerated this neglect now for many years while I was always concerned with you, approaching each one of you like a father or an elder brother to persuade you to care for virtue. Now if I profited from this by charging a fee for my advice, there would be some sense to it, but you can see for yourselves that, for all their shameless accusations, my accusers have not been able in c their impudence to bring forward a witness to say that I have ever received a fee or ever asked for one. I, on the other hand, have a convincing witness that I speak the truth, my poverty.

It may seem strange that while I go around and give this advice privately and interfere in private affairs, I do not venture to go to the assembly and there advise the city. You have heard me give the reason for this in many places. I have d a divine or spiritual sign which Meletus has ridiculed in his deposition. This began when I was a child. It is a voice, and whenever it speaks it turns me away from something I am about to do, but it never encourages me to do anything. This is what has prevented me from taking part in public affairs, and I think it was quite right to prevent me. Be sure, men of Athens, that if I had long ago attempted to take part e in politics, I should have died long ago, and benefited neither you nor myself. Do not be angry with me for speaking the truth; no man will survive who genuinely opposes you or any other crowd and prevents the occurrence of many unjust and illegal happenings in the city. A man who really fights for justice must lead a private, not a public, life if he 32 is to survive for even a short time.

I shall give you great proofs of this, not words but what you esteem, deeds. Listen to what happened to me, that you may know that I will not yield to any man contrary to what is right, for fear of death, even if I should die at once for not

---

1 *"Wealth does not ... individually and collectively"* Alternatively, this sentence could be translated: "Wealth does not bring about excellence, but excellence brings about wealth and all other public and private blessings for men."

• - Socrates never collected fees for his advice → proof his poverty

[handwritten margin note: O— Case where Socrates opposed assembly on principles of law, despite the risks.]

yielding. The things I shall tell you are commonplace and smack of the lawcourts, but they are true. I have never held
b any other office in the city, but I served as a member of the Council, and our tribe Antiochis was presiding at the time when you wanted to try as a body the ten generals who had failed to pick up the survivors of the naval battle.[1] This was illegal, as you all recognized later. I was the only member of the presiding committee to oppose your doing something contrary to the laws, and I voted against it. The orators were ready to prosecute me and take me away, and your shouts
c were egging them on, but I thought I should run any risk on the side of law and justice rather than join you, for fear of prison or death, when you were engaged in an unjust course.

This happened when the city was still a democracy. When the oligarchy was established, the Thirty[2] summoned me to the Hall, along with four others, and ordered us to bring Leon from Salamis, that he might be executed. They gave many such orders to many people, in order to implicate as many as possible in their guilt. Then I showed again,
d not in words but in action, that, if it were not rather vulgar to say so, death is something I couldn't care less about, but that my whole concern is not to do anything unjust or impious. That government, powerful as it was, did not frighten me into any wrongdoing. When we left the Hall, the other four went to Salamis and brought in Leon, but I went home. I might have been put to death for this, had not the government fallen shortly afterwards. There are many
e who will witness to these events.

Do you think I would have survived all these years if I were engaged in public affairs and, acting as a good man must, came to the help of justice and considered this the most important thing? Far from it, men of Athens, nor
33 would any other man. Throughout my life, in any public activity I may have engaged in, I am the same man as I

am in private life. I have never come to an agreement with anyone to act unjustly, neither with anyone else nor with anyone of those who they slanderously say are my pupils. I have never been anyone's teacher. If anyone, young or old, desires to listen to me when I am talking and dealing with my own concerns, I have never begrudged this to anyone,
b but I do not converse when I receive a fee and not when I do not. I am equally ready to question the rich and the poor if anyone is willing to answer my questions and listen to what I say. And I cannot justly be held responsible for the good or bad conduct of these people, as I never promised to teach them anything and have not done so. If anyone says that he has learned anything from me, or that he heard anything privately that the others did not hear, be assured that he is not telling the truth.

Why then do some people enjoy spending considerable time in my company? You have heard why, men of Athens,
c I have told you the whole truth. They enjoy hearing those being questioned who think they are wise, but are not. And this is not unpleasant. To do this has, as I say, been enjoined upon me by the god, by means of oracles and dreams, and in every other way that a divine manifestation has ever ordered a man to do anything. This is true, gentlemen, and can easily be established.

If I corrupt some young men and have corrupted
d others, then surely some of them who have grown older and realized that I gave them bad advice when they were young should now themselves come up here to accuse me and avenge themselves. If they were unwilling to do so themselves, then some of their kindred, their fathers or brothers or other relations should recall it now if their family had been harmed by me. I see many of these present here, first Crito, my contemporary and fellow demesman, the father
e of Critobulus here; next Lysanias of Sphettus, the father of Aeschines here; also Antiphon the Cephisian, the father of Epigenes; and others whose brothers spent their time in this way; Nicostratus, the son of Theozotides, brother of Theodotus, and Theodotus has died so he could not influence him; Paralius here, son of Demodocus, whose brother was Theages; there is Adeimantus, son of Ariston, brother of
34 Plato here; Aeantidorus, brother of Apollodorus here.

I could mention many others, some one of whom surely Meletus should have brought in as witness in his own speech. If he forgot to do so, then let him do it now; I will yield time if he has anything of the kind to say. You will find quite the contrary, gentlemen. These men are all ready to come to the help of the corruptor, the man who has harmed

---

1   *ten generals … naval battle* This was the battle of Arginusae (south of Lesbos) in 406 BCE, the last Athenian victory of the war. A violent storm prevented the Athenian generals from rescuing their survivors. For this they were tried in Athens and sentenced to death by the assembly. They were tried in a body, and it is this to which Socrates objected in the Council's presiding committee which prepared the business of the assembly. He obstinately persisted in his opposition, in which he stood alone, and was overruled by the majority. Six generals who were in Athens were executed.

2   *the Thirty* This was the harsh oligarchy that was set up after the final defeat of Athens by Sparta in the Peloponnesian War in 404 BCE, and that ruled Athens for nine months in 404–403 before the democracy was restored.

[handwritten margin note: • —refused to get Leon of Salamis for execution, instead went home]

b their kindred, as Meletus and Anytus say. Now those who were corrupted might well have reason to help me, but the uncorrupted, their kindred who are older men, have no reason to help me except the right and proper one, that they know that Meletus is lying and that I am telling the truth.

Very well, gentlemen. This, and maybe other similar things, is what I have to say in my defense. Perhaps one of
c you might be angry as he recalls that when he himself stood trial on a less dangerous charge, he begged and implored the jurymen with many tears, that he brought his children and many of his friends and family into court to arouse as much pity as he could, but that I do none of these things, even though I may seem to be running the ultimate risk. Thinking of this, he might feel resentful towards me and,
d angry about this, cast his vote in anger. If there is such a one among you—I do not deem there is, but if there is—I think it would be right to say in reply: My good sir, I too have a household and, in Homer's phrase, I am not born "from oak or rock"[1] but from men, so that I have a family, indeed three sons, men of Athens, of whom one is an adolescent while two are children. Nevertheless, I will not beg you to acquit me by bringing them here. Why do I do none of these things? Not through arrogance, gentlemen,
e nor through lack of respect for you. Whether I am brave in the face of death is another matter, but with regard to my reputation and yours and that of the whole city, it does not seem right to me to do these things, especially at my age and with my reputation. For it is generally believed, whether it be true or false, that in certain respects Socrates is superior
35 to the majority of men. Now if those of you who are considered superior, be it in wisdom or courage or whatever other virtue makes them so, are seen behaving like that, it would be a disgrace. Yet I have often seen them do this sort of thing when standing trial, men who are thought to be somebody, doing amazing things as if they thought it a terrible thing to die, and as if they were to be immortal if you did not execute
b them. I think these men bring shame upon the city so that a stranger, too, would assume that those who are outstanding in virtue among the Athenians, whom they themselves select from themselves to fill offices of state and receive other honors, are in no way better than women. You should not act like that, men of Athens, those of you who have any reputation at all, and if we do, you should not allow it. You should make it very clear that you will more readily convict a man who performs these pitiful dramatics in court and so makes the city a laughingstock, than a man who keeps quiet.

Quite apart from the question of reputation, gentlemen, I do not think it right to supplicate the jury and to be
c acquitted because of this, but to teach and persuade them. It is not the purpose of a juryman's office to give justice as a favor to whoever seems good to him, but to judge according to law, and this he has sworn to do. We should not accustom you to perjure yourselves, nor should you make a habit of it. This is irreverent conduct for either of us.

Do not deem it right for me, men of Athens, that I should act towards you in a way that I do not consider to be good or just or pious, especially, by Zeus, as I am being pros-
d ecuted by Meletus here for impiety; clearly, if I convinced you by my supplication to do violence to your oath of office, I would be teaching you not to believe that there are gods, and my defense would convict me of not believing in them. This is far from being the case, gentlemen, for I do believe in them as none of my accusers do. I leave it to you and the god to judge me in the way that will be best for me and for you.

[The jury now gives its verdict of guilty, and Meletus asks for the penalty of death.]

There are many other reasons for my not being angry e
with you for convicting me, men of Athens, and what happened was not unexpected. I am much more surprised at the number of votes cast on each side, for I did not think the decision would be by so few votes but by a great many. As it is, a switch of only thirty votes would have acquitted me. I think myself that I have been cleared on Meletus' charges, and not only this, but it is clear to all that, if Anytus and Lycon had not joined him in accusing me, he would have been fined a thousand drachmas for not receiving a fifth of b the votes.

He assesses the penalty at death. So be it. What counter-assessment should I propose[2] to you, men of Athens? Clearly it should be a penalty I deserve, and what do I deserve to suffer or to pay because I have deliberately not led a quiet life but have neglected what occupies most people: wealth, household affairs, the position of general or public orator or the other offices, the political clubs and factions that exist in the city? I thought myself too honest to survive if I occupied c myself with those things. I did not follow that path that would have made me of no use either to you or to myself, but I went to each of you privately and conferred upon him

---

1 *"from oak or rock"* Homer, *Odyssey*, 19, 163.

2 *What counter-assessment should I propose* No penalty was provided for this (and some other crimes) by law. Instead, the prosecution and defendant both proposed a penalty and the jurors had to decide which of the two recommended penalties to impose.

○ – outlines how even men w/ reputation have brought their families to trial to get pity and sympathy, trying to undermine justice

O — if Socrates left, would he be quiet? — NO
— he wants to obey the God
— it's the greatest good to discuss virtue

PLATO – Apology   27

what I say is the greatest benefit, by trying to <u>persuade him</u> <u>not to care for any of his belongings before caring that he</u> <u>himself should be as good and as wise as possible, not to</u>
d <u>care for the city's possessions more than for the city itself,</u> <u>and to care for other things in the same way.</u> What do I deserve for being such a man? Some good, men of Athens, if I must truly make an assessment according to my deserts, and something suitable. What is suitable for a poor benefactor who needs leisure to exhort you? Nothing is more suitable, gentlemen, than for such a man to be fed in the Prytaneum[1] much more suitable for him than for anyone of you who has won a victory at Olympia with a pair or a team of horses.
e The Olympian victor makes you think yourself happy; I make you be happy. Besides, he does not need food, but I
37 do. So if I must make a just assessment of what I deserve, I assess it as this: free meals in the Prytaneum.

When I say this you may think, as when I spoke of appeals to pity and entreaties, that I speak arrogantly, but that is not the case, men of Athens; rather it is like this: I am convinced that I never willingly wrong anyone, but I am not convincing you of this, for we have talked together but a short time. If it were the law with us, as it is elsewhere, that
b a trial for life should not last one but many days, you would be convinced, but now it is not easy to dispel great slanders in a short time. Since I am convinced that I wrong no one, I am not likely to wrong myself, to say that I deserve some evil and to make some such assessment against myself. What should I fear? That I should suffer the penalty Meletus has assessed against me, of which I say I do not know whether it is good or bad? Am I then to choose in preference to this something that I know very well to be an evil and assess the
c penalty at that? Imprisonment? Why should I live in prison, always subjected to the ruling magistrates, the Eleven? A fine, and imprisonment until I pay it? That would be the same thing for me, as I have no money. Exile? For perhaps you might accept that assessment.

I should have to be inordinately fond of life, men of Athens, to be so unreasonable as to suppose that other men will easily tolerate my company and conversation when
d you, my fellow citizens, have been unable to endure them, but found them a burden and resented them so that you are now seeking to get rid of them. Far from it, gentlemen. It would be a fine life at my age to be driven out of one

city after another, for I know very well that wherever I go the young men will listen to my talk as they do here. If I drive them away, they will themselves persuade their elders to drive me out; if I do not drive them away, their fathers e and relations will drive me out on their behalf.

Perhaps someone might say, "But Socrates, if you leave us will you not be able to live quietly, without talking?" Now this is the most difficult point on which to convince some of you. If I say that it is impossible for me to keep quiet because that means disobeying the god, you will not 38 believe me and will think I am being ironical. On the other hand, if I say that it is the greatest good for a man to discuss virtue every day and those other things about which you hear me conversing and testing myself and others, for <u>the unexamined life is not worth living</u> for men, you will believe me even less.

What I say is true, gentlemen, but it is not easy to convince you. At the same time, I am not accustomed to think that I deserve any penalty. If I had money, I would assess b the penalty at the amount I could pay, for that would not hurt me, but I have none, unless you are willing to set the penalty at the amount I can pay, and perhaps I could pay you one mina of silver. So that is my assessment.

Plato here, men of Athens, and Crito and Critobulus and Apollodorus bid me put the penalty at thirty minas, and they will stand surety for the money. Well then, that is my assessment, and they will be sufficient guarantee of payment.

[The jury now votes again and sentences Socrates to death.]

It is for the sake of a short time, men of Athens, that you c will acquire the reputation and the guilt, in the eyes of those who want to denigrate the city, of having killed Socrates, a wise man, for they who want to revile you will say that I am wise even if I am not. If you had waited but a little while, this would have happened of its own accord. You see my age, that I am already advanced in years and close to death. I am d saying this not to all of you but to those who condemned me to death, and to these same ones I say: Perhaps you think that I was convicted for lack of such words as might have convinced you, if I thought I should say or do all I could to avoid my sentence. Far from it. <u>I was convicted because</u> <u>I lacked not words but boldness and shamelessness and the</u> <u>willingness to say to you what you would most</u> gladly have <u>heard from me, lamentations and tears and my saying and</u> e <u>doing many things that I say are unworthy of me but that</u> <u>you are accustomed to hear from others.</u> I did not think

---

1   *The Prytaneum*   Magistrates' hall or town hall of Athens in which public entertainments were given, particularly to Olympian victors on their return home. Free accommodation was provided there for distinguished citizens.

then that the danger I ran should make me do anything mean, nor do I now regret the nature of my defense. I would much rather die after this kind of defense than live after
39 making the other kind. Neither I nor any other man should, on trial or in war, contrive to avoid death at any cost. Indeed it is often obvious in battle that one could escape death by throwing away one's weapons and by turning to supplicate one's pursuers, and there are many ways to avoid death in every kind of danger if one will venture to do or say anything to avoid it. It is not difficult to avoid death, gentlemen; it is
b much more difficult to avoid wickedness, for it runs faster than death. Slow and elderly as I am, I have been caught by the slower pursuer, whereas my accusers, being clever and sharp, have been caught by the quicker, wickedness. I leave you now, condemned to death by you, but they are condemned by truth to wickedness and injustice. So I maintain my assessment, and they maintain theirs. This perhaps had to happen, and I think it is as it should be.

c   Now I want to prophesy to those who convicted me, for I am at the point when men prophesy most, when they are about to die. I say, gentlemen, to those who voted to kill me, that vengeance will come upon you immediately after my death, a vengeance much harder to bear than that which you took in killing me. You did this in the belief that you would avoid giving an account of your life, but I maintain that quite the opposite will happen to you. There will be
d more people to test you, whom I now held back, but you did not notice it. They will be more difficult to deal with as they will be younger and you will resent them more. You are wrong if you believe that by killing people you will prevent anyone from reproaching you for not living in the right way. To escape such tests is neither possible nor good, but it is best and easiest not to discredit others but to prepare oneself to be as good as possible. With this prophecy to you who convicted me, I part from you.

e   I should be glad to discuss what has happened with those who voted for my acquittal during the time that the officers of the court are busy and I do not yet have to depart to my death. So, gentlemen, stay with me awhile, for nothing prevents us from talking to each other while
40 it is allowed. To you, as being my friends, I want to show the meaning of what has occurred. A surprising thing has happened to me, jurymen—you I would rightly call jurymen.[1] At all previous times my familiar prophetic power,

my spiritual manifestation, frequently opposed me, even in small matters, when I was about to do something wrong, but now that, as you can see for yourselves, I was faced with what one might think, and what is generally thought to be, the worst of evils, my divine sign has not opposed me, b either when I left home at dawn, or when I came into court, or at any time that I was about to say something during my speech. Yet in other talks it often held me back in the middle of my speaking, but now it has opposed no word or deed of mine. What do I think is the reason for this? I will tell you. What has happened to me may well be a good thing, and those of us who believe death to be an evil are certainly mistaken. I have convincing proof of this, for it is c impossible that my familiar sign did not oppose me if I was not about to do what was right.

     Let us reflect in this way, too, that there is good hope that death is a blessing, for it is one of two things: either the dead are nothing and have no perception of anything, or it is, as we are told, a change and a relocating for the soul from here to another place. If it is complete lack of perception, like a dreamless sleep, then death would be a d great advantage. For I think that if one had to pick out that night during which a man slept soundly and did not dream, put beside it the other nights and days of his life, and then see how many days and nights had been better and more pleasant than that night, not only a private person but the great king would find them easy to count com- e pared with the other days and nights. If death is like this I say it is an advantage, for all eternity would then seem to be no more than a single night. If, on the other hand, death is a change from here to another place, and what we are told is true and all who have died are there, what great- er blessing could there be, gentlemen of the jury? If anyone arriving in Hades will have escaped from those who call 41 themselves jurymen here, and will find those true jurymen who are said to sit in judgment there, Minos and Rhada- manthus and Aeacus and Triptolemus and the other demi- gods who have been upright in their own life, would that be a poor kind of change? Again, what would one of you give to keep company with Orpheus and Musaeus, Hesiod and Homer? I am willing to die many times if that is true. It would be a wonderful way for me to spend my time b whenever I met Palamedes and Ajax, the son of Telamon, and any other of the men of old who died through an un- just conviction, to compare my experience with theirs. I think it would be pleasant. Most important, I could spend my time testing and examining people there, as I do here,

---

1   *you I would rightly call jurymen*   Previously he had called them "men of Athens" or "my friends."

as to who among them is wise, and who thinks he is, but is not.

What would one not give, gentlemen of the jury, for the opportunity to examine the man who led the great expedition against Troy, or Odysseus, or Sisyphus,[1] and innumerable other men and women one could mention. It would be an extraordinary happiness to talk with them, to keep company with them and examine them. In any case, they would certainly not put one to death for doing so. They are happier there than we are here in other respects, and for the rest of time they are deathless, if indeed what we are told is true.

c

You too must be of good hope as regards death, gentlemen of the jury, and keep this one truth in mind, that a good man cannot be harmed either in life or in death, and that his affairs are not neglected by the gods. What has happened to me now has not happened of itself, but it is clear to me that it was better for me to die now and to escape from trouble. That is why my divine sign did not oppose me at any point. So I am certainly not angry with those who convicted me, or with my accusers. Of course that was not their purpose when they accused and convicted me, but they thought they were hurting me, and for this they deserve blame. This much I ask from them: when my sons grow up, avenge yourselves by causing them the same kind of grief that I caused you, if you think they care for money or anything else more than they care for virtue, or if they think they are somebody when they are nobody. Reproach them as I reproach you, that they do not care for the right things and think they are worthy when they are not worthy of anything. If you do this, I shall have been justly treated by you, and my sons also.

d

e

42

Now the hour to part has come. I go to die, you go to live. Which of us goes to the better lot is known to no one, except the god.

◆ ◆ ◆ ◆ ◆

Crito

About the time of Socrates' trial, a state galley had set out on an annual religious mission to the small Aegean island of Delos, sacred to Apollo, and while it was away no execution was allowed to take place. So it was that Socrates was kept in prison for a month after the trial. The ship has now arrived at Cape Sunium in Attica and is thus expected at the Piraeus, Athens' port, momentarily. So Socrates' old and faithful friend, Crito, makes one last effort to persuade him to escape into exile, and all arrangements for this plan have been made. It is this conversation between the two old friends that Plato professes to report in this dialogue. It is, as Crito plainly tells him, his last chance, but Socrates will not take it, and he gives his reasons for his refusal.

[...]

Socrates: Why have you come so early, Crito? Or is it not still early?   43

Crito: It certainly is.

Socrates: How early?

Crito: Early dawn.

Socrates: I am surprised that the warder was willing to listen to you.

Crito: He is quite friendly to me by now, Socrates. I have been here often and I have given him something.

Socrates: Have you just come, or have you been here for some time?

Crito: A fair time.

Socrates: Then why did you not wake me right away but   b sit there in silence?

Crito: By Zeus no, Socrates. I would not myself want to be in distress and awake so long. I have been surprised to see you so peacefully asleep. It was on purpose that I did not wake you, so that you should spend your time most agreeably. Often in the past throughout my life, I have considered the way you live happy, and especially so now that you bear your present misfortune so easily and lightly.

Socrates: It would not be fitting at my age to resent the fact that I must die now.

---

1   *Minos ... Sisyphus*   Most of these are mythological: Minos, Rhadamanthys and Aeacus were mortal sons of Zeus, rewarded with the position of judges of the dead because they had established the first just laws on earth; Triptolemus was a demigod who brought agriculture to earth; Orpheus was a singer and a poet, and founder of the Orphic religious cult; Musaeus was a producer of sacred poetry and oracles; Palamedes was a clever inventor; Ajax was a king and Greek hero in the Trojan War; Odysseus was a cunning and eloquent Greek hero of the Trojan War, and protagonist of the *Odyssey*; Sisyphus, a king punished in the underworld by having perpetually to push a rock uphill. Possibly real figures were two revered Greek poets: Homer, author of the *Iliad* and the *Odyssey*, and Hesiod, whose only surviving works are *Works and Days* and the *Theogony*.

43c *Crito:* Other men of your age are caught in such misfortunes, but their age does not prevent them resenting their fate.

Socrates: That is so. Why have you come so early?

Crito: I bring bad news, Socrates, not for you, apparently, but for me and all your friends the news is bad and hard to bear. Indeed, I would count it among the hardest.

Socrates: What is it? Or has the ship arrived from Delos,

d at the arrival of which I must die?[1]

Crito: It has not arrived yet, but it will, I believe, arrive today, according to a message some men brought from Sunium,[2] where they left it. This makes it obvious that it will come today, and that your life must end tomorrow.

Socrates: May it be for the best. If it so please the gods, so be it. However, I do not think it will arrive today.

44 *Crito:* What indication have you of this?

Socrates: I will tell you. I must die the day after the ship arrives.

Crito: That is what those in authority say.

Socrates: Then I do not think it will arrive on this coming day, but on the next. I take to witness of this a dream I had a little earlier during this night. It looks as if it was the right time for you not to wake me.

Crito: What was your dream?

Socrates: I thought that a beautiful and comely woman

b dressed in white approached me. She called me and said: "Socrates, may you arrive at fertile Phythia[3] on the third day."

Crito: A strange dream, Socrates.

Socrates: But it seems clear enough to me, Crito.

Crito: Too clear it seems, my dear Socrates, but listen to me even now and be saved. If you die, it will not be a single misfortune for me. Not only will I be deprived of a friend, the like of whom I shall never find again, but many people who do not know you or me very well will think that

c I could have saved you if I were willing to spend money but

---

1   *at the arrival of which I must die*   Criminals could not be put to death while the sacred ship was at sea.

2   *Sunium*   A cape headland about sixty-five kilometers south-east of the city where ships headed for Athens could be sighted early.

3   *fertile Phythia*   A quotation from the ninth book of the *Iliad* (363). Achilles has rejected all the presents of Agamemnon for him to return to the battle, and threatens to go home. He says his ships will sail in the morning, and with good weather he might arrive on the third day "in fertile Phythia" (which is his home). Socrates takes the dream to mean that he will die, and his soul will find its home, on the third day. As always, counting the first member of a series, the third day is the day after tomorrow.

that I did not care to do so. Surely there can be no worse reputation than to be thought to value money more highly than one's friends, for the majority will not believe that you yourself were not willing to leave prison while we were eager for you to do so.

Socrates: My good Crito, why should we care so much for what the majority think? The most reasonable people, to whom one should pay more attention, will believe that things were done as they were done.

Crito: You see, Socrates: that one must also pay attention d to the opinion of the majority. Your present situation makes clear that the majority can inflict not the least but pretty well the greatest evils if one is slandered among them.

Socrates: Would that the majority could inflict the greatest evils, for they would then be capable of the greatest good, and that would be fine, but now they cannot do either. They cannot make a man either wise or foolish, but they inflict things haphazardly.

Crito: That may be so. But tell me this, Socrates, are e you anticipating that I and your other friends would have trouble with the informers if you escape from here, as having stolen you away, and that we should be compelled to lose all our property or pay heavy fines and suffer other punishment besides? If you have any such fear, forget it. We would be justified in running this risk to save you, and 45 worse, if necessary. Do follow my advice, and do not act differently.

Socrates: I do have these things in mind, Crito, and also many others.

Crito: Have no such fear. It is not much money that some people require to save you and get you out of here. Further, do you not see that those informers are cheap, and that not much money would be needed to deal with them? My money is available and is, I think, sufficient. If, because b of your affection for me, you feel you should not spend any of mine, there are those strangers here ready to spend money. One of them, Simmias the Theban, has brought enough for this very purpose. Gebes, too, and a good many others. So, as I say, do not let this fear make you hesitate to save yourself, nor let what you said in court trouble you, that you would not know what to do with yourself if you left Athens, for you would be welcomed in many places to c which you might go. If you want to go to Thessaly, I have friends there who will greatly appreciate you and keep you safe, so that no one in Thessaly will harm you.

Besides, Socrates, I do not think that what you are doing is just, to give up your life when you can save it, and to hasten your fate as your enemies would hasten it, and indeed have hastened it in their wish to destroy you. Moreover, I think you are betraying your sons by going away and leaving them, when you could bring them up and educate them. You thus show no concern for what their fate may be. They will probably have the usual fate of orphans. Either one should not have children, or one should share with them to the end the toil of upbringing and education. You seem to me to choose the easiest path, whereas one should choose the path a good and courageous man would choose, particularly when one claims throughout one's life to care for virtue.

I feel ashamed on your behalf and on behalf of us, your friends, lest all that has happened to you be thought due to cowardice on our part: the fact that your trial came to court when it need not have done so,[1] the handling of the trial itself, and now this absurd ending which will be thought to have got beyond our control through some cowardice and unmanliness on our part, since we did not save you, or you save yourself, when it was possible and could be done if we had been of the slightest use. Consider, Socrates, whether this is not only evil, but shameful, both for you and for us. Take counsel with yourself, or rather the time for counsel is past and the decision should have been taken, and there is no further opportunity, for this whole business must be ended tonight. If we delay now, then it will no longer be possible, it will be too late. Let me persuade you on every count, Socrates, and do not act otherwise.

Socrates: My dear Crito, your eagerness is worth much if it should have some right aim; if not, then the greater your keenness the more difficult it is to deal with. We must therefore examine whether we should act in this way or not, as not only now but at all times I am the kind of man who listens to nothing within me but the argument that on reflection seems best to me. I cannot, now that this fate has come upon me, discard the arguments I used; they seem to me much the same. I value and respect the same principles as before, and if we have no better arguments to bring up at this moment, be sure that I shall not agree with you, not even if the power of the majority were to frighten us with more bogeys, as if we were children, with threats of incarcerations and executions and confiscation of property. How should we examine this matter most reasonably? Would it be by taking up first your argument about the opinions of

men, whether it is sound in every case that one should pay attention to some opinions, but not to others? Or was that well-spoken before the necessity to die came upon me, but now it is clear that this was said in vain for the sake of argument, that it was in truth play and nonsense? I am eager to examine together with you, Crito, whether this argument will appear in any way different to me in my present circumstances, or whether it remains the same, whether we are to abandon it or believe it. It was said on every occasion by those who thought they were speaking sensibly, as I have just now been speaking, that one should greatly value some people's opinions, but not others. Does that seem to you a sound statement?

You, as far as a human being can tell, are exempt from the likelihood of dying tomorrow, so the present misfortune is not likely to lead you astray. Consider then, do you not think it a sound statement that one must not value all the opinions of men, but some and not others, nor the opinions of all men, but those of some and not of others? What do you say? Is this not well said?

Crito: It is.

Socrates: One should value the good opinions, and not the bad ones?

Crito: Yes.

Socrates: The good opinions are those of wise men, the bad ones those of foolish men?

Crito: Of course.

Socrates: Come then, what of statements such as this: Should a man professionally engaged in physical training pay attention to the praise and blame and opinion of any man, or to those of one man only, namely a doctor or trainer?

Crito: To those of one only.

Socrates: He should therefore fear the blame and welcome the praise of that one man, and not those of the many?

Crito: Obviously.

Socrates: He must then act and exercise, eat and drink in the way the one, the trainer and the one who knows, thinks right, not all the others?

Crito: That is so.

Socrates: Very well. And if he disobeys the one, disregards his opinion and his praises while valuing those of the many who have no knowledge, will he not suffer harm?

Crito: Of course.

Socrates: What is that harm, where does it tend, and what part of the man who disobeys does it affect?

---

1 *when it need not have done so* Socrates could have left the country and avoided trial.

• – Majority Opinion vs. Expert Opinion

Crito: Obviously the harm is to his body, which it ruins.

Socrates: Well said. So with other matters, not to enumerate them all, and certainly with actions just and unjust, shameful and beautiful, good and bad, about which we are now deliberating, should we follow the opinion of the many and fear it, or that of the one, if there is one who has knowledge of these things and before whom we feel fear and shame more than before all the others? If we do not follow his directions, we shall harm and corrupt that part of ourselves that is improved by just actions and destroyed by unjust actions. Or is there nothing in this?

Crito: I think there certainly is, Socrates.

Socrates: Come now, if we ruin that which is improved by health and corrupted by disease by not following the opinions of those who know, is life worth living for us when that is ruined? And that is the body, is it not?

Crito: Yes.

Socrates: And is life worth living with a body that is corrupted and in bad condition?

Crito: In no way.

Socrates: And is life worth living for us with that part of us corrupted that unjust action harms and just action benefits? Or do we think that part of us, whatever it is, that is concerned with justice and injustice, is inferior to the body?

Crito: Not at all.

Socrates: It is more valuable?

Crito: Much more.

Socrates: We should not then think so much of what the majority will say about us, but what he will say who understands justice and injustice, the one, that is, and the truth itself. So that, in the first place, you were wrong to believe that we should care for the opinion of the many about what is just, beautiful, good, and their opposites. "But," someone might say, "the many are able to put us to death."

Crito: That too is obvious, Socrates, and someone might well say so.

Socrates: And, my admirable friend, that argument that we have gone through remains, I think, as before. Examine the following statement in turn as to whether it stays the same or not, that the most important thing is not life, but the good life.

Crito: It stays the same.

Socrates: And that the good life, the beautiful life, and the just life are the same; does that still hold, or not?

Crito: It does hold.

Socrates: As we have agreed so far, we must examine next whether it is just for me to try to get out of here when the Athenians have not acquitted me. If it is seen to be just, we will try to do so; if it is not, we will abandon the idea. As for those questions you raise about money, reputation, the upbringing of children, Crito, those considerations in truth belong to those people who easily put men to death and would bring them to life again if they could, without thinking; I mean the majority of men. For us, however, since our argument leads to this, the only valid consideration, as we were saying just now, is whether we should be acting rightly in giving money and gratitude to those who will lead me out of here, and ourselves helping with the escape, or whether in truth we shall do wrong in doing all this. If it appears that we shall be acting unjustly, then we have no need at all to take into account whether we shall have to die if we stay here and keep quiet, or suffer in another way, rather than do wrong.

Crito: I think you put that beautifully, Socrates, but see what we should do.

Socrates: Let us examine the question together, my dear friend, and if you can make any objection while I am speaking, make it and I will listen to you, but if you have no objection to make, my dear Crito, then stop now from saying the same thing so often, that I must leave here against the will the Athenians. I think it important to persuade you before I act, and not to act against your wishes. See whether the start of our inquiry is adequately stated, and try to answer what I ask you in the way you think best.

Crito: I shall try.

Socrates: Do we say that one must never in any way do wrong willingly, or must one do wrong in one way and not in another? Is to do wrong never good or admirable, as we have agreed in the past, or have all these former agreements been washed out during the last few days? Have we at our age failed to notice for some time that in our serious discussions we were no different from children? Above all, is the truth such as we used to say it was, whether the majority agree or not, and whether we must still suffer worse things than we do now, or will be treated more gently, that nonetheless, wrongdoing or injustice is in every way harmful and shameful to the wrongdoer? Do we say so or not?

Crito: We do.

Socrates: So one must never do wrong.

Crito: Certainly not.

Socrates: Nor must one, when wronged, inflict wrong in return, as the majority believe, since one must never do wrong.

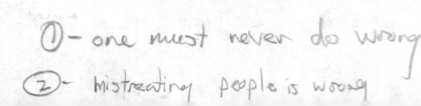

⑤ -breaking the laws is mistreatment, and will
lead to their distruction, as no one is
above the law. (Rule/Supremacy of Laws)   PLATO – Crito   33

c   *Crito:* That seems to be the case.

Socrates: Come now, should one mistreat anyone or not, Crito?

Crito: One must never do so.

Socrates: Well then, if one is oneself mistreated, is it right, as the majority say, to mistreat in return, or is it not?

Crito: It is never right.

② *Socrates:* Mistreating people is no different from wrongdoing.

Crito: That is true.

③ *Socrates:* One should never do wrong in return, nor mistreat any man, no matter how one has been mistreated
d   by him. And Crito, see that you do not agree to this, contrary to your belief. For I know that only a few people hold this view or will hold it, and there is no common ground between those who hold this view and those who do not, but they inevitably despise each other's views. So then consider very carefully whether we have this view in common, and whether you agree, and let this be the basis of our deliberation, that neither to do wrong nor to return a wrong is ever right, nor is bad treatment in return for bad treatment. Or do you disagree and do not share this view
e   as a basis for discussion? I have held it for a long time and still hold it now, but if you think otherwise, tell me now. If, however, you stick to our former opinion, then listen to the next point.

Crito: I stick to it and agree with you. So say on.

Socrates: Then I state the next point, or rather I ask you: when one has come to an agreement that is just with someone, should one fulfill it or cheat on it?

④ *Crito:* One should fulfill it.

Socrates: See what follows from this: if we leave here
50   without the city's permission, are we mistreating people whom we should least mistreat? And are we sticking to a just agreement, or not?

Crito: I cannot answer your question, Socrates. I do not know.

⑤ *Socrates:* Look at it this way. If, as we were planning to run away from here, or whatever one should call it, the laws and the state came and confronted us and asked: "Tell me, Socrates, what are you intending to do? Do you not
b   by this action you are attempting intend to destroy us, the laws, and indeed the whole city, as far as you are concerned? Or do you think it possible for a city not to be destroyed if the verdicts of its courts have no force but are nullified and set at naught by private individuals?" What shall we answer to this and other such arguments? For many things

could be said, especially by an orator on behalf of this law we are destroying, which orders that the judgments of the courts shall be carried out. Shall we say in answer, "The city   c wronged me, and its decision was not right." Shall we say that, or what?

Crito: Yes, by Zeus, Socrates, that is our answer.

Socrates: Then what if the laws said: "Was that the agreement between us, Socrates, or was it to respect the judgments that the city came to?" And if we wondered at their words, they would perhaps add: "Socrates, do not wonder at what we say but answer, since you are accustomed to proceed by question and answer. Come now, what accusation do you bring against us and the city, that you should try to   d destroy us? Did we not, first, bring you to birth, and was it not through us that your father married your mother and begat you? Tell us, do you find anything to criticize in those of us who are concerned with marriage?" And I would say that I do not criticize them. "Or in those of us concerned with the nurture of babies and the education that you too received? Were those assigned to that subject not right to instruct your father to educate you in the arts and in physical culture?" And I would say that they were right. "Very   e well," they would continue, "and after you were born and nurtured and educated, could you, in the first place, deny that you are our offspring and servant, both you and your forefathers? If that is so, do you think that we are on an equal footing as regards the right, and that whatever we do to you it is right for you to do to us? You were not on an   ⑥ equal footing with your father as regards the right, nor with   *Socrates is* your master if you had one, so as to retaliate for anything   *a subject* they did to you, to revile them if they reviled you, to beat   *51 to the* them if they beat you, and so with many other things. Do   *city, as* you think you have this right to retaliation against your   *a son to* country and its laws? That if we undertake to destroy you   *a father,* and think it right to do so, you can undertake to destroy us,   *can't break* as far as you can, in return? And will you say that you are   *the* right to do so, you who truly care for virtue? Is your wisdom   *Natural law* such as not to realize that your country is to be honored   *of their* more than your mother, your father and all your ancestors,   b *agreement* that it is more to be revered and more sacred, and that it counts for more among the gods and sensible men, that you must worship it, yield to it and placate its anger more than your father's? You must either persuade it or obey its orders, and endure in silence whatever it instructs you to endure, whether blows or bonds, and if it leads you into war to be wounded or killed, you must obey. To do so is right, and one must not give way or retreat or leave one's post, but

③ -responding to mistreatment, w/ mistreatment is wrong   and also to mistreat the 'govt' that has mistreated
                                                                                                                            socrates
④ - always fullfill 'just' agreements you've made   → leaving city is to break agreement :
         (it's wrong not to)

both in war and in courts and everywhere else, one must
c   obey the commands of one's city and country, or persuade
it as to the nature of justice. It is impious to bring violence
to bear against your mother or father, it is much more so
to use it against your country." What shall we say in reply,
Crito, that the laws speak the truth, or not?

Crito: I think they do.

(7) Socrates: "Reflect now, Socrates," the laws might say
"that if what we say is true, you are not treating us rightly
by planning to do what you are planning. We have given
you birth, nurtured you, educated you, we have given you
d   and all other citizens a share of all the good things we could.
Even so, by giving every Athenian the opportunity, once
arrived at voting age and having observed the affairs of the
city and us the laws, we proclaim that if we do not please
him, he can take his possessions and go wherever he pleases.
Not one of our laws raises any obstacle or forbids him, if he
is not satisfied with us or the city, if one of you wants to go
e   and live in a colony or wants to go anywhere else, and keep
his property. We say, however, that whoever of you remains,
when he sees how we conduct our trials and manage the
city in other ways, has in fact come to an agreement with us
to obey our instructions. We say that the one who disobeys
does wrong in three ways, first because in us he disobeys
his parents, also those who brought him up, and because,
in spite of his agreement, he neither obeys us nor, if we do
something wrong, does he try to persuade us to do better.
52   Yet we only propose things, we do not issue savage commands to do whatever we order; we give two alternatives,
either to persuade us or to do what we say. He does neither.
We do say that you too, Socrates, are open to those charges
if you do what you have in mind; you would be among,
not the least, but the most guilty of the Athenians." And if
I should say "Why so?" they might well be right to upbraid
(8) me and say that I am among the Athenians who most definitely came to that agreement with them. They might well
b   say: "Socrates, we have convincing proofs that we and the
city were congenial to you. You would not have dwelt here
most consistently of all the Athenians if the city had not
been exceedingly pleasing to you. You have never left the
city, even to see a festival, nor for any other reason except
military service; you have never gone to stay in any other
c   city, as people do; you have had no desire to know another
city or other laws; we and our city satisfied you.

"So decisively did you choose us and agree to be a
citizen under us. Also, you have had children in this city,
thus showing that it was congenial to you. Then at your

trial you could have assessed your penalty at exile if you
wished, and you are now attempting to do against the city's
wishes what you could then have done with her consent.
Then you prided yourself that you did not resent death,
but you chose, as you said, death in preference to exile.
Now, however, those words do not make you ashamed, and
you pay no heed to us, the laws, as you plan to destroy us,
and you act like the meanest type of slave by trying to run   d
away, contrary to your commitments and your agreement
to live as a citizen under us. First then, answer us on this
very point, whether we speak the truth when we say that
you agreed, not only in words but by your deeds, to live
in accordance with us." What are we to say to that, Crito?
Must we not agree?

Crito: We must, Socrates.

Socrates: "Surely," they might say, "you are breaking
the commitments and agreements that you made with us   e
without compulsion or deceit, and under no pressure of
time for deliberation. You have had seventy years during
which you could have gone away if you did not like us, and
if you thought our agreements unjust. You did not choose
to go to Sparta or to Crete, which you are always saying
are well governed, nor to any other city, Greek or foreign.   53
You have been away from Athens less than the lame or the
blind or other handicapped people. It is clear that the city
has been outstandingly more congenial to you than to other
Athenians, and so have we, the laws, for what city can please
without laws? Will you then not now stick to our agreements? You will, Socrates, if we can persuade you, and not
make yourself a laughingstock by leaving the city.

"For consider what good you will do yourself or your
friends by breaking our agreements and committing such a
wrong. It is pretty obvious that your friends will themselves   b
be in danger of exile, disfranchisement and loss of property.
As for yourself, if you go to one of the nearby cities—Thebes
or Megara, both are well governed—you will arrive as an
enemy to their government; all who care for their city will
look on you with suspicion, as a destroyer of the laws.[1] You
will also strengthen the conviction of the jury that they
passed the right sentence on you, for anyone who destroys   c
the laws could easily be thought to corrupt the youth and
the ignorant. Or will you avoid cities that are well governed
and men who are civilized? If you do this, will your life be

---

1   *Thebes or Megara ... destroyer of the laws*   These were neighboring
oligarchical states of Athens. Socrates would be seen an enemy
because he was a law-breaker (not a democrat).

(8) Socrates def. enjoyed citizen rights, he even stayed
his whole life in Athens, not leaving once, had a fam. here
* Decisively he chose to agree to be a citizen under Athens

worth living? Will you have social intercourse with them and not be ashamed to talk to them? And what will you say? The same as you did here, that virtue and justice are man's most precious possession, along with lawful behavior
d and the laws? Do you not think that Socrates would appear to be an unseemly kind of person? One must think so. Or will you leave those places and go to Crito's friends in Thessaly?[1] There you will find the greatest license and disorder, and they may enjoy hearing from you how absurdly you escaped from prison in some disguise, in a leather jerkin or some other things in which escapees wrap themselves, thus altering your appearance. Will there be no one to say that you, likely to live but a short time more, were so greedy for
e life that you transgressed the most important laws? Possibly, Socrates, if you do not annoy anyone, but if you do, many disgraceful things will be said about you.

"You will spend your time ingratiating yourself with all men, and be at their beck and call. What will you do in Thessaly but feast, as if you had gone to a banquet in Thes-
54 saly? As for those conversations of yours about justice and the rest of virtue, where will they be? You say you want to live for the sake of your children, that you may bring them up and educate them. How so? Will you bring them up and educate them by taking them to Thessaly and making strangers of them, that they may enjoy that too? Or not so, but they will be better brought up and educated here, while you are alive, though absent? Yes, your friends will look after them. Will they look after them if you go and live in Thessaly, but not if you go away to the underworld?
b If those who profess themselves your friends are any good at all, one must assume that they will.

"Be persuaded by us who have brought you up, Socrates. Do not value either your children or your life or anything else more than goodness, in order that when you arrive in Hades you may have all this as your defense before the rulers there. If you do this deed, you will not think it better or more just or more pious here, nor will anyone of your friends, nor will it be better for you when you arrive yonder. As it is, you depart, if you depart, after being
c wronged not by us, the laws, but by men; but if you depart after shamefully returning wrong for wrong and mistreatment for mistreatment, after breaking your agreements and commitments with us, after mistreating those you should mistreat least-yourself, your friends, your country, and us

we shall be angry with you while you are still alive, and our brothers, the laws of the underworld, will not receive you kindly, knowing that you tried to destroy us as far as you could. Do not let Crito persuade you, rather than us, to do d what he says."

Crito, my dear friend, be assured that these are the words I seem to hear, as the Corybants[2] seem to hear the music of their flutes, and the echo of these words resounds in me, and makes it impossible for me to hear anything else. As far as my present beliefs go, if you speak in opposition to them, you will speak in vain. However, if you think you can accomplish anything, speak.

Crito: I have nothing to say, Socrates.

Socrates: Let it be then, Crito, and let us act in this way, e since this is the way the god is leading us.

◆ ◆ ◆ ◆ ◆

Death Scene from the *Phaedo*

In Phaedo, *a number of Socrates' friends have come to visit him in prison on the last day of his life, as he will drink the hemlock at sundown. The main topic of their conversation is the nature of the soul and the arguments for its immortality. This takes up most of the dialogue. Then Socrates tells a rather elaborate myth on the shape of the earth in a hollow of which we live, and of which we know nothing of the splendors of its surface, the purer air and brighter heavens. The myth then deals with the dwelling places of various kinds of souls after death. The following passage immediately follows the conclusion of the myth, and concludes the dialogue.*

...

No sensible man would insist that these things are as I 114d have described them, but I think it is fitting for a man to risk the belief—for the risk is a noble one—that this, or something like this, is true about our souls and their dwelling places, since the soul is evidently immortal, and a man should repeat this to himself as if it were an incantation, which is why I have been prolonging my tale. That is the reason why a man should be of good cheer about his own e soul, if during life he has ignored the pleasures of the body and its ornamentation as of no concern to him and doing

1 *Thessaly* The Athenians associated this place with gluttony and dissipation.

2 *Corybants* Priests of the Asiatic goddess Cybele. The rites of the Corybants were accompanied by wild music, dancing, etc.

him more harm than good, but has seriously concerned himself with the pleasures of learning, and adorned his soul not with alien but with its own ornaments, namely, moderation, righteousness, courage, freedom, and truth, and in that state awaits his journey to the underworld.

Now you, Simmias, Cebes, and the rest of you, Socrates continued, will each take that journey at some other time but my fated day calls me now, as a tragic character might say, and it is about time for me to have my bath, for I think it better to have it before I drink the poison and save the women the trouble of washing the corpse.

When Socrates had said this Crito spoke. Very well, Socrates, what are your instructions to me and the others about your children or anything else? What can we do that would please you most?—Nothing new, Crito, said Socrates, but what I am always saying, that you will please me and mine and yourselves by taking good care of your own selves in whatever you do, even if you do not agree with me now, but if you neglect your own selves, and are unwilling to live following the tracks, as it were, of what we have said now and on previous occasions, you will achieve nothing even if you strongly agree with me at this moment.

We shall be eager to follow your advice, said Crito, but how shall we bury you?

In any way you like, said Socrates, if you can catch me and I do not escape you. And laughing quietly, looking at us, he said: I do not convince Crito that I am this Socrates talking to you here and ordering all I say, but he thinks that I am the thing which he will soon be looking at as a corpse, and so he asks how he shall bury me. I have been saying for some time and at some length that after I have drunk the poison I shall no longer be with you but will leave you to go and enjoy some good fortunes of the blessed, but it seems that I have said all this to him in vain in an attempt to reassure you and myself too. Give a pledge to Crito on my behalf, he said, the opposite pledge to that he gave the jury. He pledged that I would stay, you must pledge that I will not stay after I die, but that I shall go away, so that Crito will bear it more easily when he sees my body being burned or buried and will not be angry on my behalf, as if I were suffering terribly, and so that he should not say at the funeral that he is laying out, or carrying out, or burying Socrates. For know you well, my dear Crito, that to express oneself badly is not only faulty as far as the language goes, but does some harm to the soul. You must be of good cheer, and say you are burying my body, and bury it in any way you like and think most customary.

After saying this he got up and went to another room to take his bath, and Crito followed him and he told us to wait for him. So we stayed, talking among ourselves, questioning what had been said, and then again talking of the great misfortune that had befallen us. We all felt as if we had lost a father and would be orphaned for the rest of our lives. When he had washed, his children were brought to him—two of his sons were small and one was older—and the women of his household came to him. He spoke to them before Crito and gave them what instructions he wanted. Then he sent the women and children away, and he himself joined us. It was now close to sunset, for he had stayed inside for some time. He came and sat down after his bath and conversed for a short while, when the officer of the Eleven[1] came and stood by him and said: "I shall not reproach you as I do the others, Socrates. They are angry with me and curse me when obeying the orders of my superiors, I tell them to drink the poison. During the time you have been here I have come to know you in other ways as the noblest, the gentlest and the best man who has ever come here. So now too I know that you will not make trouble for me; you know who is responsible and you will direct your anger against them. You know what message I bring. Fare you well, and try to endure what you must as easily as possible." The officer was weeping as he turned away and went out. Socrates looked up at him and said: "Fare you well also, we shall do as you bid us." And turning to us he said: "How pleasant the man is! During the whole time I have been here he has come in and conversed with me from time to time, a most agreeable man. And how genuinely he now weeps for me. Come, Crito, let us obey him. Let someone bring the poison if it is ready; if not, let the man prepare it."

But Socrates, said Crito, I think the sun still shines upon the hills and has not yet set. I know that others drink the poison quite a long time after they have received the order, eating and drinking quite a bit, and some of them enjoy intimacy with their loved ones. Do not hurry; there is still some time.

It is natural, Crito, for them to do so, said Socrates, for they think they derive some benefit from doing this, but it is not fitting for me. I do not expect any benefit from drinking the poison a little later, except to become ridiculous in my own eyes for clinging to life, and be sparing of it when there is none left. So do as I ask and do not refuse me.

---

1 *the Eleven* Commissioners in charge of the prison.

Hearing this, Crito nodded to the slave who was standing near him; the slave went out and after a time came back with the man who was to administer the poison, carrying it made ready in a cup. When Socrates saw him he said: "Well, my good man, you are an expert in this, what must one do?"—"Just drink it and walk around until your legs feel heavy, and then lie down and it will act of itself." And he offered the cup to Socrates who took it quite cheerfully, Echecrates,[1] without a tremor or any change of feature or color, but looking at the man from under his eyebrows as was his wont, asked: "What do you say about pouring a libation from this drink? It is allowed?"—"We only mix as much as we believe will suffice," said the man.

I understand, Socrates said, but one is allowed, indeed one must, utter a prayer to the gods that the journey from here to yonder may be fortunate. This is my prayer and may it be so.

And while he was saying this, he was holding the cup, and then drained it calmly and easily. Most of us had been able to hold back our tears reasonably well up until then, but when we saw him drinking it and after he drank it, we could hold them back no longer; my own tears came in floods against my will. So I covered my face. I was weeping for myself, not for him—for my misfortune in being deprived of such a comrade. Even before me, Crito was unable to restrain his tears and got up. Apollodorus had not ceased from weeping before, and at this moment his noisy tears and anger made everybody present break down, except Socrates. "What is this," he said, "you strange fellows. It is mainly for this reason that I sent the women away, to avoid such unseemliness, for I am told one should die in good—omened silence. So keep quiet and control yourselves."

His words made us ashamed, and we checked our tears. He walked around, and when he said his legs were heavy he lay on his back as he had been told to do, and the man who had given him the poison touched his body, and after a while tested his feet and legs, pressed hard upon his foot and asked him if he felt this, and Socrates said no. Then he pressed his calves, and made his way up his body and showed us that it was cold and stiff. He felt it himself and said that when the cold reached his heart he would be gone. As his belly was getting cold Socrates uncovered his head—he had covered it—and said—these were his last words—"Crito, we owe a cock to Asclepius;[2] make this offering to him and do not forget."—"It shall be done," said Crito, "tell us if there is anything else." But there was no answer. Shortly afterwards Socrates made a movement; the man uncovered him and his eyes were fixed. Seeing this Crito closed his mouth and his eyes.

Such was the end of our comrade, Echecrates, a man who, we would say, was of all those we have known the best, and also the wisest and the most upright.

♦ ♦ ♦ ♦ ♦

The Republic

Book 1

I[3] went down to the Piraeus yesterday with Glaucon, the son of Ariston. I intended to say a prayer to the goddess,[4] and I also wanted to see how they would manage the festival, since this was its first celebration. I thought our own procession was a fine one and that which the Thracians had sent was no less outstanding. After we had said our prayer and witnessed the procession we started back toward the city. Polemarchus saw us from a distance as we were setting off for home and he told his slave to run and bid us wait for him. So the slave caught hold of my cloak from behind: "Polemarchus, he said, bids you wait for him." I turned round and asked where Polemarchus was. "There he is, coming up behind you, he said, please wait for him." And Glaucon said: "All right, we'll wait."

---

1   *Echecrates* Pythagorean philosopher. Most of what we know about him comes from the *Phaedo*.

2   *we owe a cock to Asclepius* A cock was sacrificed to Asclepius, God of healing, by the sick people who slept in his temples, hoping for a cure. Socrates apparently means that death is a cure for the ills of life.

3   *I* The narrator is Socrates.

4   *a prayer to the goddess* The expression "the goddess" in the work of an Athenian writer, especially when the scene is laid in Athens, usually refers to Athena, and it may do so here. However, we know from 354a, and the mention of the Thracians here, that the festival was that of Bendis, a Thracian goddess whose worship had recently been introduced in the Piraeus, and the reference may be to her.

c   Just then Polemarchus caught up with us. Adeimantus, the brother of Glaucon,[1] was with him, and so were Niceratus, the son of Nicias, and some others, presumably on their way from the procession.

Then Polemarchus said: Socrates, it looks to me as if you had started on your way back to the city.

Quite right, said I.

Do you see how many we are? he said.

Of course I do.

Well, he said, you must either be stronger than we are, or you must stay here.

Is there not another alternative, said I, namely that we may persuade you to let us go?

Could you, said he, persuade men who do not listen?

Not possibly, said Glaucon.

Well, you can take it that we are certainly not going to listen.

328   Adeimantus intervened: Do you really not know that there is to be a torch race on horseback this evening in honor of the goddess?

On horseback? said I, that is a novelty. Are they going to race on horseback and hand the torches on in relays, or how do you mean?

That's it, said Polemarchus, and there will be an all night festival besides, which will be worth seeing, and which we intend to watch after dinner. We shall be joined by many of
b our young men here and talk with them. So please do stay.

And Glaucon said: It seems that we'll have to stay.

If you think so, said I, then we must.

So we went to the home of Polemarchus, and there we found Lysias[2] and Euthydemus, the brothers of Polemarchus, also Thrasymachus of Chalcedon,[3] Charmantides of Paiania,[4] and Cleitophon the son of Aristonymus. Polemarchus' father Cephalus was also in the house. I thought he
c looked quite old, as I had not seen him for some time. He was sitting on a seat with a cushion, a wreath on his head, for he had been offering a sacrifice in the courtyard. There was a circle of seats there, and we sat down by him.

As soon as he saw me Cephalus welcomed me and said: Socrates, you don't often come down to the Piraeus to see us. You should. If it were still easy for me to walk to the city you would not need to come here, we would come to you, d but now you should come more often. You should realize that, to the extent that my physical pleasures get feebler, my desire for conversation, and the pleasure I take in it, increase. So be sure to come more often and talk to these youngsters, as you would to good friends and relations.

I replied: Indeed, Cephalus, I do enjoy conversing with men of advanced years. As from those who have traveled e along a road which we too will probably have to follow, we should enquire from them what kind of a road it is, whether rough and difficult or smooth and easy, and I should gladly learn from you what you think about this, as you have reached the point in life which the poets call "the threshold of old age," whether it is a difficult part of life, or how your experience would describe it to us.

Yes by Zeus, Socrates, he said, I will tell you what I 329 think of old age. A number of us who are more or less the same age often get together in accordance with the old adage.[5] When we meet, the majority of us bemoan their age: they miss the pleasures which were theirs in youth; they recall the pleasures of sex, drink, and feasts, and some other things that go with them, and they are angry as if they were deprived of important things, as if they then lived the good life and now were not living at all. Some others deplore the b humiliations which old age suffers in the household, and because of this they repeat again and again that old age is the cause of many evils. However, Socrates, I do not think that they blame the real cause. For if old age were the cause, then I should have suffered in the same way, and so would all others who have reached my age. As it is, I have met other old men who do not feel like that, and indeed I was present at one time when someone asked the poet Sophocles:[6] "How are you in regard to sex, Sophocles? Can you still make love c to a woman?" "Hush man," the poet replied, "I am very glad to have escaped from this, like a slave who has escaped from a mad and cruel master." I thought then that he was right, and I still think so, for a great peace and freedom from these things come with old age: after the tension of one's desires relaxes and ceases, then Sophocles' words certainly apply, it is an escape from many mad masters. As regards both sex d

---

1   *Adeimantus, the brother of Glaucon* Glaucon and Adeimantus are the brothers of Plato, who is not present. They carry the main burden of the conversation with Socrates from the beginning of the second book to the end of the work.

2   *Lysias* A famous writer of speeches for use in legal trials.

3   *Thrasymachus of Chalcedon* Sophist (c. 459–400 BCE) known for his critique of justice. His name translates as "fierce fighter" and reflects his character.

4   *Charmantides of Paiania* We have no information other than what is mentioned here.

5   *old adage* The old saying that like consorts with like.

6   *Sophocles* One of the three greatest Greek tragedians (495–406 BCE), the other two being Aeschylus (c. 525–456 BCE) and Euripides (c. 480–406 BCE).

and relations in the household there is one cause, Socrates, not old age but the manner of one's life: if it is moderate and contented, then old age too is but moderately burdensome; if it is not, then both old age and youth are hard to bear.

I wondered at his saying this and I wanted him to say
e   more, so I urged him on by saying: Cephalus, when you say this, I don't think most people would agree with you; they think you endure old age easily not because of your manner of life but because you are wealthy, for the wealthy, they say, have many things to encourage them.

What you say is true, he said. They would not agree. And there is something in what they say, but not as much as they think. What Themistocles[1] said is quite right: when
330   a man from Seriphus[2] was insulting him by saying that his high reputation was due to his city and not to himself, he replied that, had he been a Seriphian, he would not be famous, but neither would the other had he been an Athenian. The same can be applied to those who are not rich and find old age hard to bear—namely that a good man would not very easily bear old age in poverty, nor would a bad man, even if wealthy, be at peace with himself.

Did you inherit most of your wealth, Cephalus, I asked, or did you acquire it?

b   How much did I acquire, Socrates? As a moneymaker I stand between my grandfather and my father. My grandfather and namesake inherited about the same amount of wealth which I possess but multiplied it many times. My father, Lysanias, however, diminished that amount to even less than I have now. As for me, I am satisfied to leave to my sons here no less but a little more than I inherited.

The reason I asked, said I, is that you did not seem to
c   me to be overfond of money, and this is generally the case with those who have not made it themselves. Those who have acquired it by their own efforts are twice as fond of it as other men. Just as poets love their own poems and fathers love their children, so those who have made their money are attached to it as something they have made themselves, besides using it as other men do. This makes them poor company, for they are unwilling to give their approval to anything but money.

What you say is true, he said.

d   It surely is, said I. Now tell me this much more: What is the greatest benefit you have received from the enjoyment of wealth?

I would probably not convince many people in saying this, Socrates, he said, but you must realize that when a man approaches the time when he thinks he will die, he becomes fearful and concerned about things which he did not fear before. It is then that the stories we are told about the underworld, which he ridiculed before—that the man
e   who has sinned here will pay the penalty there—torture his mind lest they be true. Whether because of the weakness of old age, or because he is now closer to what happens there and has a clearer view, the man himself is filled with suspicion and fear, and he now takes account and examines whether he has wronged anyone. If he finds many sins in his
331   own life, he awakes from sleep in terror, as children do, and he lives with the expectation of evil. However, the man who knows he has not sinned has a sweet and good hope as his constant companion, a nurse to his old age, as Pindar[3] too puts it. The poet has expressed this charmingly, Socrates, that whoever lives a just and pious life

> Sweet is the hope that nurtures his heart,
> companion and nurse to his old age,
> a hope which governs the rapidly changing
> thoughts of mortals.

This is wonderfully well said. It is in this connection that I would say that wealth has its greatest value, not for everyone but for a good and well-balanced man. Not to
b   have lied to or deceived anyone even unwillingly, not to depart yonder in fear, owing either sacrifices to a god or money to a man: to this wealth makes a great contribution. It has many other uses, but benefit for benefit I would say that its greatest usefulness lies in this for an intelligent man, Socrates.

Beautifully spoken, Cephalus, said I, but are we to say
c   that justice or right[4] is simply to speak the truth and to pay back any debt one may have contracted? Or are these same actions sometimes right and sometimes wrong? I mean this sort of thing, for example: everyone would surely agree that if a friend has deposited weapons with you when he was sane, and he asks for them when he is out of his mind, you should not return them. The man who returns them is not

---

1   *Themistocles*   A fifth-century BCE Athenian statesman.
2   *Seriphus*   A small island of little importance.

3   *Pindar*   Greek lyric poet (c. 518–438 BCE).
4   *justice or right*   Throughout the *Republic* the Greek words *dikaios* and *dikaiosyne* are often used, as here, in a much wider sense than our words "just" and "justice" by which we must usually translate them. They may refer to "right" or "righteous" conduct in relation to others; their opposite *adikia* then has the general sense of wrongdoing.

doing right, nor is one who is willing to tell the whole truth to a man in such a state.

d What you say is correct, he answered.

This then is not a definition of right or justice, namely to tell the truth and pay one's debts.

It certainly is, said Polemarchus interrupting, if we are to put any trust in Simonides.[1]

And now, said Cephalus, I leave the argument to you, for I must go back and look after the sacrifice.

Do I then inherit your role? asked Polemarchus.

You certainly do, said Cephalus laughing, and as he said it he went off to sacrifice.

e Then do tell us, Polemarchus, said I, as the heir to the argument, what it is that Simonides stated about justice which you consider to be correct.

He stated, said he, that it is just to give to each what is owed to him, and I think he was right to say so.

Well now, I said, it is hard not to believe Simonides, for he is a wise and inspired man, but what does he mean? Perhaps you understand him, but I do not. Clearly he does not mean what we were saying just now, that anything he has deposited must be returned to a man who is not in his *332* right mind; yet anything he has deposited is owing to him. Is that not so?

Yes.

But it is not to be returned to him at all if he is out of his mind when he asks for it?

That's true.

Certainly Simonides meant something different from this when he says that to return what is owed is just.

He did indeed mean something different by Zeus, said he. He believes that one owes it to one's friends to do good to them, and not harm.

I understand, said I, that one does not give what is *b* owed or due if one gives back gold to a depositor, when giving back and receiving are harmful, and the two are friends. Is that not what you say Simonides meant?

Quite.

Well then, should one give what is due to one's enemies?

By all means, said he, what is in fact due to them, and I believe that is what is properly due from an enemy to an enemy, namely something harmful.

It seems, I said, that Simonides was suggesting the nature of the just poetically and in riddles. For he thought this *c* to be just, to give to each man what is proper to him, and he called this what is due.

Surely.

Then by Zeus, I said, if someone asked him: "Simonides, what does the craft[2] which we call medicine give that is due, and to whom?" What do you think his answer would be?

Clearly, it is the craft which prescribes medicines and food and drink for our bodies.

And what does the craft which we call cooking give that is due and fitting, and to whom?

It adds flavor to food.

Very well. What, and to whom, does that craft give *d* which we would call justice?

It must follow from what was said before, Socrates, that it is that which benefits one's friends and harms one's enemies.

He means then that to benefit one's friends and harm one's enemies is justice?

I think so.

And who is most capable of benefiting his friends and harming his enemies in matters of health and disease?

A physician.

And who can do so best when they are sailing and head-*e* ing into a storm?

A pilot.

What about the just man? In what activity and what task is he most able to benefit his friends and harm his enemies?

In waging war and in alliances, I think.

Very well. Now when people are not ill, my dear Polemarchus, the physician is no use to them?

True.

Nor is the pilot when they are not sailing?

That is so.

So to people who are not fighting a war the just man is useless?

I do not think so at all.

---

1 *Simonides* Simonides was a well-known lyric and elegiac poet and author of many epigrams. He died about 468 BCE around the time of Socrates' birth.

2 *craft* By *technê*, here translated "craft," Socrates refers to any art or craft which requires special knowledge. The word "art" has been avoided in the translation because it implies for us other factors than knowledge, and it is knowledge alone which Socrates has in mind. He then proceeds to equate "justice" with such a *technê*, as implying the knowledge of how to behave, on the well-known Socratic belief that virtue is knowledge.

Justice then is useful also in peace time?

333   It is.

And so is farming, is it not?

Yes.

For the producing of a harvest?

Yes.

And the cobbler's craft too?

Yes.

I think you would say for getting shoes?

Certainly.

Well then, what is it which justice helps one to use or acquire in peace time?

Contracts, Socrates.

By contracts you mean dealings between people, or something else?

That is what I mean.

b   Is the just man a good and useful associate in a game of checkers, or is the checkers player?

The checkers player.

And for putting together bricks and stones, is the just man a better and more useful associate than the builder?

Not at all.

In what kind of dealings then is the just man a better associate than the builder or the musician, as the musician is better than the just man in matters of music?

In money matters, I think.

Except perhaps, Polemarchus, when money is to be used, for whenever one needs to buy or sell a horse together,

c   I think the horse breeder is a more useful associate. Is that not so?

Apparently.

And when one needs to buy a boat, the shipbuilder or the captain of a ship?

So it seems.

In what joint use of silver and gold is the just man a more useful associate than the others?

Whenever one needs to deposit it and keep it safe.

You mean whenever there is no need to use it, but to keep it?

Quite so.

d   So it is whenever money is not being used that justice is useful?

I'm afraid so.

And whenever one needs to keep a pruning knife safe, but not to use it, justice is useful both in associations and in private. When you need to use it, however, it is the craft of vine dressing that is useful.

So it seems.

You will agree then that when one needs to keep a shield or a lyre safe and not use them, justice is a useful thing, but when you need to use them, it is the hoplite's[1] or the musician's craft which is useful.

That necessarily follows.

So with all other things, justice is useless in their use, but useful when they are not in use.

I fear so.

In that case, my friend, justice is not a very important   e thing if it is only useful for things not in use. Let us, however, investigate the following point: is not the man most capable of landing a blow in a fight, be it boxing or any other kind, also the most capable of guarding against blows?

Certainly.

And the man most able to guard against disease is also the man most able to inflict it unnoticed?

So it seems.

Further, the same man is a good guardian of a camp   334 who is also able to steal the plans of the enemy and be aware of their actions?

Quite so.

Whenever a man is a good guardian of anything, he is also a good thief of it.

Apparently.

If then the just man is good at guarding money, he is also good at stealing it.

So our argument shows.

The just man then has turned out to be a kind of thief. You may well have learned this from Homer;[2] for he likes Odysseus' maternal grandfather Autolycus, and at the same   b time he says that he excelled all men in thieving and perjury. It follows that justice, according to you and Homer and Simonides, appears to be a craft of thieving, of course to the advantage of one's friends and to the harm of one's enemies. Is this not what you meant?

No, by Zeus, he said, I don't any longer know what I meant, but this I still believe to be true, that justice is to benefit one's friends and harm one's enemies.

When you say friends, do you mean those whom a man   c believes to be helpful to him, or those who are helpful even if they do not appear to be so, and so with enemies?

---

1   *hoplite*   Heavily armed foot-soldier.
2   *Homer*   Author (eighth or seventh century BCE) of the *Iliad* and the *Odyssey* (to which this refers: 19, 392–98).

Probably, he said, one is fond of those whom one thinks to be good and helpful to one, and one hates those whom one considers bad and harmful.

Surely people make mistakes about this, and consider many to be helpful when they are not, and often make the opposite mistake about enemies?

They do.

Then good men are their enemies, and bad people their friends?

Quite so.

d   And so it is just and right for these mistaken people to benefit the bad and harm the good?

It seems so.

But the good are just and able to do no wrong?

True.

But according to your argument it is just to harm those who do no wrong.

Never, Socrates, he said. It is the argument that is wrong.

It is just to harm the wrongdoers and to benefit the just?

That statement, Socrates, seems much more attractive than the other.

Then, Polemarchus, for many who are mistaken in their
e   judgment it follows that it is just to harm their friends, for these are bad, and to benefit their enemies, who are good, and so we come to a conclusion which is the opposite of what we said was the meaning of Simonides.

That certainly follows, he said, but let us change our assumption; we have probably not defined the friend and the enemy correctly.

Where were we mistaken, Polemarchus?

When we said that a friend was one who was thought to be helpful.

How shall we change this now? I asked.

Let us state, he said, that a friend is one who is both thought to be helpful and also is; one who is thought to be,
335   but is not, helpful is thought to be a friend but is not. And so also with the enemy.

According to this argument then, the good man will be a friend, and the bad man an enemy.

Yes.

You want us to add to what we said before about the just, namely that it is just to benefit one's friend and harm one's enemy; to this you want us to make an addition and say that it is just to benefit the friend who is good and to harm the enemy who is bad?

Quite so, he said. This seems to me to be well said.   b

But, I said, is it the part of the just man to harm anyone at all?

Why certainly, he said, those who are bad and one's enemies.

Do horses become better or worse when they are harmed?

Worse.

Do they deteriorate in their excellence as dogs or as horses?

As horses.

And when dogs are harmed, they deteriorate in their excellence as dogs, not in that of horses?

Necessarily.

Shall we not say so about men too, that when they are   c harmed they deteriorate in their human excellence?

Quite so.

And is not justice a human excellence?

Of course.

Then men who are harmed, my friend, necessarily become more unjust.

So it appears.

Can musicians, by practicing music, make men unmusical?

Not possibly.

Or can teachers of horsemanship, by the practice of their craft, make them into non-horsemen?

Impossible.

Well then, can the just, by the practice of justice, make men unjust? Or, in a word, can good men, by the practice   d of their virtue,[1] make men bad?

They cannot.

---

1   *virtue*   The Greek word which this translation sometimes renders as "excellence" (for example, a few lines above) and sometimes as "virtue" is *arête*. The former translation is more generally suitable: for Plato, the *arête* of something—anything—is being all it can be—achieving its potential, fulfilling its purpose or function. Thus plants, animals, and even inanimate beings have an "excellence" particular to their own sort of thing. We ordinarily think of "virtue" as applying only to humans insofar as they have a quality that is morally good or admirable: hardly something applicable to plants or inanimate objects. For Plato, "virtue" in this sense is closely tied up with the "excellence" particular to humans: we are morally good insofar as we live up to our potential. This translation renders *arête* as "excellence" when it is being used primarily in the wider sense and "virtue" when it is being used in the second, narrower sense.

It is not the function of heat to cool things, but the opposite?

Yes.

Nor of dryness to make things wet but the opposite?

Quite so.

And it is not the function of the good to harm people, but the opposite?

It seems so.

And the just man is good?

Certainly.

It is not then the function of the just man, Polemarchus, to do harm to a friend or anyone else, but it is that of his opposite, the unjust man?

I think that you are entirely right, Socrates.

e   If, then, anyone tells us that it is just to give everyone his due, and he means by this that from the just man harm is due to his enemies and benefit due to his friends—the man who says that is not wise, for it is not true. We have shown that it is never just to harm anyone.

I agree.

You and I, I said, will therefore together fight anyone who tells us that Simonides said this, or Bias or Pittacus[1] or any other of our wise and blessed men.

Yes, and I am quite willing to join that fight.

336   Do you know, I said, to whom I think this saying belongs, that it is just to benefit one's friends and harm one's enemies?

To whom?

I think Periander said that, or Perdiccas, or Xerxes, or Ismenias of Corinth,[2] or some other wealthy man who believed himself to have great power.

What you say is very true.

Very well, said I. Since neither justice nor the just appears to be that either, what else might one say it is?

b   While we were speaking Thrasymachus often started to interrupt, but he was restrained by those who were sitting by him, for they wanted to hear the argument to the end. But when we paused after these last words of mine he could

no longer keep quiet. He gathered himself together like a wild beast about to spring, and he came at us as if to tear us to pieces.

Polemarchus and I were afraid and flustered as he roared into the middle of our company: What nonsense have you two been talking, Socrates? Why do you play the fool in   c thus giving way to each other? If you really want to know what justice is, don't only ask questions and then score off anyone who answers, and refute him. You know very well that it is much easier to ask questions than to answer them. Give an answer yourself and tell us what you say justice is. And don't tell me that it is the needful, or the advantageous,   d or the beneficial, or the gainful, or the useful, but tell me clearly and precisely what you mean, for I will not accept it if you utter such rubbish.

His words startled me, and glancing at him I was afraid. I think if I had not looked at him before he looked at me, I should have been speechless. As it was I had glanced at him first when our discussion began to exasperate him, so I was able to answer him and I said, trembling: do not be   e hard on us, Thrasymachus, if we have erred in our investigation, he and I; be sure that we err unwillingly. You surely do not believe that if we were searching for gold we would be unwilling to give way to each other and thus destroy our chance of finding it, but that when searching for justice, a thing more precious than much gold, we mindlessly give way to one another, and that we are not thoroughly in earnest about finding it. You must believe that, my friend, for I think we could not do it. So it is much more seemly that   337 you clever people should pity us than that you should be angry with us.

When he heard that he gave a loud and bitter laugh and said: By Heracles, that is just Socrates' usual irony.[3] I knew this, and I warned these men here before that you would not be willing to answer any questions but would pretend ignorance, and that you would do anything rather than give an answer, if anyone questioned you.

You are clever, Thrasymachus, I said, for you knew very well that if you asked anyone how much is twelve, and as you asked him you warned him: "Do not, my man, say that   b twelve is twice six, or three times four, or six times two, or four times three, for I will not accept such nonsense," it would be quite clear to you that no one can answer a

---

1   *Bias of Pittacus*   Bias of Priene in Ionia and Pittacus of Mytilene (both early sixth century BCE) were counted among the seven wise men of Greece.

2   *Periander ... Ismenias of Corinth*   Periander was a tyrant of Corinth (650–570 BCE); Perdiccas probably refers to the first king of Macedonia (eighth century BCE); Xerxes was the king of Persia who invaded Greece in the second Persian war; *Ismenias of Corinth* was a Theban politician of the fourth century BCE. All four are mentioned here as typical despots.

3   *irony*   Unlike this English word, the Greek word it translates, *eirōneia*, is applied only when someone intends to deceive. Thus Socrates is being accused of intentional deception, not of saying the opposite of what he obviously meant with humorous intent.

handwritten: → Thrasymachus' thesis about justice

question asked in those terms. And if he said to you: "What do you mean, Thrasymachus? Am I not to give any of the answers you mention, not even, you strange man, if it happens to be one of those things, but am I to say something which is not the truth, or what do you mean?" What answer c would you give him?

Well, he said, do you maintain that the two cases are alike?

They may well be, said I. Even if they are not, but the person you ask thinks they are, do you think him less likely to answer what he believes to be true, whether we forbid him or not?

And you will surely do the same, he said. Will you give one of the forbidden answers?

I shouldn't wonder, said I, if after investigation that was my opinion.

d What, he said, if I show you a different answer about justice from all these and a better one? What penalty do you think you should pay then?

What else, said I, but what is proper for an ignorant man to pay? It is fitting for him to learn from one who knows. And that is what I believe I would deserve.

You amuse me, he said. You must not only learn but pay the fee.

Yes, when I have the money, I said.

We have the money, said Glaucon. If it is a matter of money, speak, Thrasymachus, for we shall all contribute for Socrates.

e Quite so, said he, so that Socrates can carry on as usual: he gives no answer himself, and then, when someone else does give one, he takes up the argument and refutes it.

My dear man, I said, how could one answer, when in the first place he does not know and does not profess to know, and then, if he has an opinion, an eminent man forbids him to say what he believes? It is much more seemly for 338 you to answer, since you say you know and have something to say. Please do so. Do me that favor, and do not begrudge your teaching to Glaucon and the others.

While I was saying this, Glaucon and the others begged him to speak. It was obvious that Thrasymachus was eager to do so and earn their admiration, and that he thought he had a beautiful answer, but he pretended that he wanted b to win his point that I should be the one to answer. However, he agreed in the end, and then said: "There you have Socrates' wisdom; he himself is not willing to teach but he goes around learning from others, and then he is not even grateful."

When you say that I learn from others you are right, Thrasymachus, said I, but when you say that I am not grateful, that is not true. I show what gratitude I can, but I can only give praise. I have no money, but how enthusiastically I praise when someone seems to me to speak well is something you will realize quite soon after you have given your answer, for I think you will speak well.

→ Listen then, said he. I say that the just is nothing else c than the advantage of the stronger. Well, why don't you praise me? But you will not want to.

I must first understand your meaning, said I, for I do not know it yet. You say that the advantage of the stronger is just. What do you mean, Thrasymachus? Surely you do not mean such a thing as this: Poulydamas, the pancratist[1] athlete, is stronger than we are; it is to his advantage to eat beef to build up his physical strength. Do you mean that this food is also advantageous and just for us who are d weaker than he is?

You disgust me, Socrates, he said. Your trick is always to take up the argument at the point where you can damage it most.

Not at all, my dear sir, I said, but tell us more clearly what you mean.

Do you not know, he said, that some cities are ruled by a despot, others by the people, and others again by the aristocracy?

Of course.

And this element has the power and rules in every city?

Certainly.

Yes, and each government makes laws to its own ad- e vantage: democracy makes democratic laws, a despotism makes despotic laws, and so with the others, and when they have made these laws they declare this to be just for their subjects, that is, their own advantage, and they punish him who transgresses the laws as lawless and unjust. This then, my good man, is what I say justice is, the same in all cities, 339 the advantage of the established government, and correct reasoning will conclude that the just is the same everywhere, the advantage of the stronger.

Now I see what you mean, I said. Whether it is true or not I will try to find out. But you too, Thrasymachus, have given as an answer that the just is the advantageous whereas

---

1 *pancratist* The *pancratium* was a Greek athletic prize-fight in which boxing, wrestling, kicking, strangling, and even the breaking of limbs were all allowed.

you forbade that answer to me. True, you have added the words "of the stronger."

b   Perhaps, he said, you consider that an insignificant addition!

It is not clear yet whether or not it is significant. Obviously, we must investigate whether what you say is true. I agree that the just is some kind of advantage, but you add that it is the advantage of the stronger. I do not know. We must look into this.

Go on looking, he said.

We will do so, said I. Tell me, do you also say that obedience to the rulers is just?

I do.

c   And are the rulers in all cities infallible, or are they liable to error?

No doubt they are liable to error.

When they undertake to make laws, therefore, they make some correctly and make others incorrectly?

I think so.

✳ "Correctly" means that they make laws to their own advantage, and "incorrectly" not to their own advantage. Or how would you put it?

As you do.

And whatever laws they make must be obeyed by their subjects, and this is just?

Of course.

d □ Then, according to your argument, it is just to do not only what is to the advantage of the stronger, but also the opposite, what is not to their advantage.

What is that you are saying? he asked.

The same as you, I think, but let us examine it more fully. Have we not agreed that, in giving orders to their subjects, the rulers are sometimes in error as to what is best for themselves, yet it is just for their subjects to do whatever their rulers order. Is that much agreed?

I think so.

e □ Think then also, said I, that you have agreed that it is just to do what is to the disadvantage of the rulers and the stronger whenever they unintentionally give orders which are bad for themselves, and you say it is just for the others to obey their given orders. Does it not of necessity follow, my wise Thrasymachus, that it is just to do the opposite of what you said? The weaker are then ordered to do what is to the disadvantage of the stronger.

340   Yes by Zeus, Socrates, said Polemarchus, that is quite clear.

Yes, if you bear witness for him, interrupted Cleitophon.

What need of a witness? said Polemarchus. Thrasymachus himself agrees that the rulers sometimes give orders that are bad for themselves, and that it is just to obey them.

Thrasymachus maintained that it is just to obey the orders of the rulers, Polemarchus.

He also said that the just was the advantage of the stronger, Cleitophon. Having established those two points b he went on to agree that the stronger sometimes ordered the weaker, their subjects, to do what was disadvantageous to themselves. From these agreed premises it follows that what is of advantage to the stronger is no more just than what is not.

But, Cleitophon replied, he said that the advantage of the stronger is what the stronger believes to be of advantage to him. This the weaker must do, and that is what he defined the just to be.

That is not how he stated it, said Polemarchus.

It makes no difference, Polemarchus, I said. If Thrasyma- c chus now wants to put it that way, let us accept it. Tell me, Thrasymachus, was this what you intended to say justice is, namely that which appears to the stronger to be to his advantage, whether it is so or not? Shall we say that this is what you mean?

Not in the least, said he. Do you think that I would call stronger a man who is in error at the time he errs?

I did think you meant that, said I, when you said that the rulers were not infallible but were liable to error.

You are being captious, Socrates, he said. Do you call d a man a physician when he is in error in the treatment of patients, at the moment of, and in regard to this very error? Or would you call a man an accountant when he makes a miscalculation at the moment of, and with regard to this miscalculation? I think that we express ourselves in words which, taken literally, do say that the physician is in error, or the accountant, or the grammarian. But each of these, in so far as he is what we call him, never errs, so that, if you use e language with precision—and you want to be precise—no practitioner of a craft ever errs. It is when the knowledge of his craft leaves him that he errs, and at that time he is not a practitioner of it. No craftsman, wise man, or ruler is in error at the time that he is a ruler in the precise sense. 341 However, everyone will say that the physician or the ruler is in error. Take it then that this is now my answer to you. To speak with precision, the ruler, in so far as he is a ruler, unerringly decrees what is best for himself and this the subject must do. The just then is, as I said from the first, to do what is advantageous to the stronger.

Very well, Thrasymachus, said I. You think I am captious?

You certainly are, he said.

And you think that it was deliberate trickery on my part to ask you the questions I did ask?

I know it very well, he said, but it will not do you any
b good, for I would be well aware of your trickery; nor would you have the ability to force my agreement in open debate.

I would not even try, my good sir, I said, but in order to avoid a repetition of this, do define clearly whether it is the ruler in the ordinary or the precise sense whose advantage is to be pursued as that of the stronger.

I mean, he said, the ruler in the most exact sense. Now practice your trickery and your captiousness on this if you can, for I will not let any statement of yours pass, and you certainly won't be able to.

c Do you think, I said, that I am crazy enough to try to shave a lion or trick Thrasymachus?

You certainly tried just now, he said, though you are no good at it.

Enough of this sort of thing, I said. But tell me: is the physician in the strict sense, whom you mentioned just now, a moneymaker or one who treats the sick? Tell me about the real physician.

He is one who treats the sick, said he.

What about the ship's captain? Is he, to speak correctly, a ruler of sailors or a sailor?

A ruler of sailors.

d We should not, I think, take into account the fact that he sails in a ship, and we should not call him a sailor, for it is not on account of his sailing that he is called a ship's captain, but because of his craft and his authority over sailors.

True.

And there is something which is advantageous to each of these, that is: patients and sailors?

Certainly.

And is not the purpose of a craft's existence to seek and secure the advantageous in each case?

That's right.

Now is there any other advantage to each craft, except that it be as perfect as possible?

e What is the meaning of that question?

It is this, said I. If you asked me whether our body is sufficient unto itself, or has a further need I should answer: "It certainly has needs, and for this purpose the craft of medicine exists and has now been discovered, because the body is defective, not self-sufficient. So to provide it with

things advantageous to it the craft of medicine has been developed." Do you think I am correct in saying this or not?

Correct.

Well then, is the craft of medicine itself defective, or   342
is there any other craft which needs some further excellence—as the eyes are in need of sight, the ears of hearing, and, because of this need, they require some other craft to investigate and provide for this?—is there in the craft itself some defect, so that each craft requires another craft which will investigate what is beneficial to it, and then the investigating craft needs another such still, and so ad infinitum? b
Or does a craft investigate what is beneficial to it, or does it need neither itself nor any other to investigate what is required because of imperfections? There is in fact no defect or error of any kind in any craft, nor is it proper to any craft to seek what is to the advantage of anything but the object of its concern; it is itself pure and without fault, being itself correct, as long as it is wholly itself in the precise sense. Consider this with that preciseness of language which you mentioned. Is it so or otherwise?

It appears to be so.

The craft of medicine, I said, does not seek its own ad-   c
vantage but that of the body.

Yes.

Nor does horse-breeding seek its own advantage but that of horses. Nor does any other craft seek its own advantage—it has no further need—but that of its object.

That seems to be the case.

And surely, Thrasymachus, the crafts govern and have power over their object.

He agreed, but with great reluctance at this point.

No science of any kind seeks or orders its own advantage, but that of the weaker which is subject to it and governed by it.   d

He tried to fight this conclusion, but he agreed to this too in the end. And after he had, I said: Surely no physician either, in so far as he is a physician, seeks or orders what is advantageous to himself, but to his patient? For we agreed that the physician in the strict sense of the word is a ruler over bodies and not a moneymaker. Was this not agreed?

He said yes.

So the ship's captain in the strict sense is a ruler over   e
sailors, and not a sailor?

That has been agreed.

Does it not follow that the ship's captain and ruler will not seek and order what is advantageous to himself, but to the sailor, his subject.

O – Thrasymachus' third attack
↳ the unjust man wins out

He agreed, but barely.

So then, Thrasymachus, I said, no other ruler in any kind of government, in so far as he is a ruler, seeks what is to his own advantage or orders it, but that which is to the advantage of his subject who is the concern of his craft; it is this he keeps in view; all his words and actions are directed to this end.

343   When we reached this point in our argument and it was clear to all that the definition of justice had turned into its opposite, Thrasymachus, instead of answering, said: Tell me, Socrates, do you have a nanny?

What's this? said I. Had you not better answer than ask such questions? Because, he said, she is letting you go around with a snotty nose and does not wipe it when she needs to, if she leaves you without any knowledge of sheep or shepherds.

What is the particular point of that remark? I asked.

b   You think, he said, that shepherds and cowherds seek the good of their sheep or cattle, whereas their sole purpose in fattening them and looking after them is their own good and that of their master. Moreover, you believe that rulers in the cities, true rulers that is, have a different attitude towards their subjects than one has towards sheep, and that they think of anything else, night and day, than their own c advantage. You are so far from understanding the nature of justice and the just, of injustice and the unjust, that you do not realize that the just is really another's good, the advantage of the stronger and the ruler, but for the inferior who obeys it is a personal injury. Injustice on the other hand exercises its power over those who are truly naive and just, and those over whom it rules do what is of advantage to the other, the stronger, and, by obeying him, they make him happy, but themselves not in the least.

d   You must look at it in this way, my naive Socrates: the just is everywhere at a disadvantage compared with the unjust. First, in their contracts with one another: wherever two such men are associated you will never find, when the partnership ends, the just man to have more than the unjust, but less. Then, in their relation to the city: when taxes are to be paid, from the same income the just man pays more, the other less; but, when benefits are to be received, the e one gets nothing while the other profits much; whenever each of them holds a public office, the just man, even if he is not penalized in other ways, finds that his private affairs deteriorate through neglect while he gets nothing from the public purse because he is just; moreover, he is disliked by his household and his acquaintances whenever he refuses

them an unjust favor. The opposite is true of the unjust man in every respect. I repeat what I said before: the man of 344 great power gets the better deal. Consider him if you want to decide how much more it benefits him privately to be unjust rather than just. You will see this most easily if you turn your thoughts to the most complete form of injustice which brings the greatest happiness to the wrongdoer, while it makes those whom he wronged, and who are not willing to do wrong, most wretched. This most complete form is despotism; it does not appropriate other people's property little by little, whether secretly or by force, whether public or private, whether sacred objects or temple property, but appropriates it all at once.   b

When a wrongdoer is discovered in petty cases, he is punished and faces great opprobrium, for the perpetrators of these petty crimes are called temple robbers, kidnappers, housebreakers, robbers, and thieves, but when a man, besides appropriating the possessions of the citizens, manages to enslave the owners as well, then, instead of those ugly names he is called happy and blessed, not only by his fellow- c citizens but by all others who learn that he has run through the whole gamut of injustice. Those who give injustice a bad name do so because they are afraid, not of practicing but of suffering injustice.

And so, Socrates, injustice, if it is on a large enough scale, is a stronger, freer, and more powerful thing than justice and, as I said from the first, the just is what is advantageous to the stronger, while the unjust is to one's own advantage and benefit.

Having said this and poured this mass of close-packed d words into our ears as a bathman might a flood of water, Thrasymachus intended to leave, but those present did not let him, and made him stay for a discussion of his views. I too begged him to stay and I said: My dear Thrasymachus, after throwing such a speech at us, you want to leave before adequately instructing us or finding out whether you are right or not? Or do you think it a small thing to decide on a e whole way of living, which, if each of us adopted it, would make him live the most profitable life?

Do I think differently? said Thrasymachus.

You seem to, said I, or else you care nothing for us nor worry whether we'll live better or worse, in ignorance of what you say you know. Do, my good sir, show some keen- 345 ness to teach us. It will not be without value to you to be the benefactor of so many of us. For my own part, I tell you that I do not believe that injustice is more profitable than justice, not even if one gives it full scope and does not

put obstacles in its way. No, my friend. Let us assume the existence of an unjust man with every opportunity to do wrong, either because his misdeeds remain secret or because he has the power to battle things through; nevertheless he does not persuade me that injustice is more profitable than
b justice. Perhaps some other of us feels the same, and not only I. Come now, my good sir, really persuade us that we are wrong to esteem justice more highly than injustice in planning our life.

And how, said he, shall I persuade you, if you are not convinced by what I said just now? What more can I do? Am I to take my argument and pour it into your mind?

Zeus forbid! Don't you do that, but first stick to what you have said and, if you change your position, do so openly
c and do not deceive us. You see now, Thrasymachus—let us examine again what went before—that, while you first defined the true physician, you did not think it necessary later to observe the precise definition of the true shepherd, but you think that he fattens sheep, in so far as he is a shepherd, not with what is best for the sheep in mind, but like a guest about to be entertained at a feast, with a banquet in view,
d or again a sale, like a moneymaker, not a shepherd. The shepherd's craft is concerned only to provide what is best for the object of its care; as for the craft itself, it is sufficiently provided with all it needs to be at its best, as long as it does not fall short of being the craft of the shepherd. That is why I thought it necessary for us to agree just now that every kind of rule, as far as it truly rules, does not seek what is best for
e anything else than the subject of its rule and care, and this is true both of public and private kinds of rule. Do you think that those who rule over cities, the true rulers, rule willingly?

I don't think it, by Zeus, I know it, he said.

Well but, Thrasymachus, said I, do you not realize that in other kinds of rule no one is willing to rule, but they ask for pay, thinking that their rule will benefit not themselves
346 but their subjects. Tell me, does not every craft differ from every other in that it has a different function? Please do not give an answer contrary to what you believe, so that we can come to some conclusion.

Yes, that is what makes it different, he said.

And each craft benefits us in its own particular way, different from the others. For example, medicine gives us health, navigation safety while sailing, and so with the others.

Quite so.
b And the craft of earning pay gives us wages, for that is its function. Or would you call medicine the same craft

as navigation? Or, if you wish to define with precision as you proposed, if the ship's captain becomes healthy because sailing benefits his health, would you for that reason call his craft medicine?

Not at all, he said.

Nor would you call wage-earning medicine if someone is healthy while earning wages?

Certainly not.

Nor would you call medicine wage-earning if someone earns pay while healing?

No.
c So we agree that each craft brings its own benefit?

Be it so.

Whatever benefit all craftsmen receive in common must then result clearly from some craft which they pursue in common, and so are benefited by it.

It seems so.

We say then that if the practitioners of these crafts are benefited by earning a wage, this results from their practicing the wage earning craft.

He reluctantly agreed.

So this benefit to each, the receiving of pay, does not
d result from the practice of their own craft, but if we are to examine this precisely, medicine provides health while the craft of earning provides pay; house building provides a house, and the craft of earning which accompanies it provides a wage, and so with the other crafts; each fulfills its own function and benefits that with which it is concerned. If pay is not added, is there any benefit which the practitioner gets from his craft?

Apparently not.

Does he even provide a benefit when he works for
e nothing?

Yes, I think he does.

Is this not clear now, Thrasymachus, that no craft or rule provides its own advantage, but, as we have been saying for some time, it procures and orders what is of advantage to its subject; it aims at his advantage, that of the weaker, not of the stronger. That is why, my dear Thrasymachus, I said just now that no one willingly wants to rule, to handle and straighten out the affairs of others. They ask for pay 347 because the man who intends to practice his craft well never does what is best for himself, nor, when he gives such orders, does he give them in accordance with his craft, but he pursues the advantage of his subject. For that reason, then, it seems one must provide remuneration if they are to be willing to rule, whether money or honor, or a penalty if he does not rule.

What do you mean, Socrates? said Glaucon. I understand the two kinds of remuneration, but I do not understand what kind of penalty you mean, which you mention under the heading of remuneration.

b Then you do not understand the remuneration of the best men, I said, which makes them willing to rule. Do you not know that the love of honor and money are made a reproach, and rightly so?

I know that.

Therefore good men will not be willing to rule for the sake of either money or honor. They do not want to be called hirelings if they openly receive payment for ruling, nor, if they provide themselves with it secretly, to be called thieves. Nor will they do it for honor's sake, for they have no c love for it. So, if they are to be willing to rule, some compulsion or punishment must be brought to bear on them. That is perhaps why to seek office willingly, before one must, is thought shameful. Now the greatest punishment is to be ruled by a worse man than oneself if one is not willing to rule. I think it is the fear of this which makes men of good character rule whenever they do. They approach office not d as something good or something to be enjoyed, but as something necessary because they cannot entrust it to men better than, or even equal to, themselves. In a city of good men, if there were such, they would probably vie with each other in order not to rule, not, as now, in order to be rulers. There it would be quite clear that the nature of the true ruler is not to seek his own advantage but that of his subjects, and everyone, knowing this, would prefer to receive benefits rather than take the trouble to benefit others. In this matter I do not at all agree with Thrasymachus that the just is the advantage of the stronger, but we will look into this matter e another time. What seems to me of greater importance is what Thrasymachus is saying now, namely that the life of the unjust man is to be preferred to that of the just. Which will you choose, Glaucon, and which of our views do you consider the more truly spoken?

I certainly think that the life of the just is more profitable.

348 You have heard, said I, all the blessings of the unjust life which Thrasymachus enumerated just now?

I heard, said he, but I am not convinced.

Do you want us to persuade him, if we could find the means to do so, that what he says is not true?

Of course I want it, he said.

If we were to oppose him, I said, with a parallel set speech on the blessings of the just life, then another speech from him in turn, then another from us, we should have to count and measure the blessings mentioned on each side, b and we should need some judges to decide the case. If, on the other hand, we investigate the question, as we were doing, by seeking agreement with each other, then we can ourselves be both the judges and the advocates.

Quite so.

Which method do you prefer? I asked.

The second.

Come then, Thrasymachus, I said, answer us from the beginning. You say that complete injustice is more profitable than complete justice?

I certainly do say that, he said, and I have told you c why.

Well then, what about this: you call one of the two a virtue and the other a vice?

Of course.

That is, you call justice a virtue, and injustice a vice?

Is that likely, my good man, said he, since I say that injustice is profitable, and justice is not?

What then?

The opposite.

Do you call being just a vice?

No, but certainly high-minded foolishness.

And you call being unjust low-minded? d

No, I call it good judgment.

You consider the unjust then, Thrasymachus, to be good and knowledgeable?

Yes, he said, those who are able to carry injustice through to the end, who can bring cities and communities of men under their power. Perhaps you think I mean purse-snatchers? Not that those actions too are not profitable, if they are not found out, but they are not worth mentioning in comparison with what I am talking about.

I am not unaware of what you mean, I said, but this e point astonishes me: do you include injustice under virtue and wisdom, and justice among their opposites?

I certainly do.

That makes it harder, my friend, and it is not easy now to know what to say. If you had declared that injustice was more profitable, but agreed that it was a vice or shameful as some others do, we could have discussed it along the lines of general opinion. Now, obviously, you will say that it is fine and strong, and apply to it all the attributes which we used 349 to apply to justice, since you have been so bold as to include it under virtue and wisdom.

Your guess, he said, is quite right.

We must not, however, shrink from pursuing our argument and looking into this, so long as I am sure that you mean what you say. For I do not think you are joking now, Thrasymachus, but are saying what you believe to be true.

What difference, said he, does it make to you whether I believe it or not? Is it not my argument you are refuting?.

b No difference, said I, but try to answer this further question: do you think that the just man wants to get the better of the just?

Never, said he, for he would not, then be well mannered and simple, as he is now.

Does he want to overreach a just action?[1]

Not a just action either, he said.

Would he want to get the better of an unjust man, and would he deem that just or not?

He would want to, he said, and he would deem it right, but he would not be able to.

That was not my question, said I, but whether the just
c man wants and deems it right to outdo not a just man, but an unjust one?

That is so.

What about the unjust man? Would he deem it right to outdo the just man and the just action?

Of course he does, he said, since he deems it right to get the better of everybody.

So the unjust man will get the better of another unjust man or an unjust action and he will strive to get all he can from everyone?

That is so.

Let us put it this way, I said. The just man does not try to get the better of one like him but of one unlike
d him, whereas the unjust man overreaches the like and the unlike?

Very well put.

The unjust man, I said, is knowledgeable and good, and the just man is neither?

That is well said too.

It follows, I said, that the unjust man is like the knowledgeable and the good, while the just man is unlike them?

Of course that will be so, he said, being such a man he will be like such men, while the other is not like them.

Good. Each of them has the qualities of those he is like?

Why not?

Very well, Thrasymachus. Now you speak of one man
as musical, of another as unmusical? e

I do indeed.

Which is knowledgeable and which is not?

Of course the musical man is knowledgeable, the unmusical is not.

What he has knowledge of he is good at,[2] and he who has no knowledge is bad?

Yes.

Is not the same true of the physician?

The same.

Do you think, my dear sir, that any musician, when tuning his lyre, desires, in the tightening and relaxing of the strings, to do better than another musician or deems it right to get the better of him?

I don't think so.

But he wants to do better than a non-musician?

Necessarily.

What of a physician? When prescribing food or drink, 350
does he want to do better than another medical man or action?

Certainly not.

But better than the non-medical?

Yes.

In matters involving any kind of knowledge or ignorance, do you think that any expert would wish to achieve more than any other expert would do or say, rather than, in respect to the same action, achieve the same as anyone like himself?

Well perhaps, it must be as you say.

What about the non-expert? Does he not want to outdo b
the expert and the non-expert equally?

Perhaps.

---

1   *overreach a just action*   *Pleon echein* or *pleonexia*, literally "to have more," comes to mean "to outdo, to overreach, to do better than." Now there is one right note to strike in music and the musician has the necessary knowledge to do so. He will want to do this, but he will not want to do better than another musician with the same knowledge, which would be absurd. So the just man, if justice is a *technê*, a matter of knowledge (see 332c) will have the knowledge to do the right thing, and cannot want to do better than that, so he will not desire to outdo another just man with the same knowledge.

2   *What he has ... good at*   As before, the craftsman with sufficient knowledge is good at his craft, and his virtue or excellence as a craftsman depends on, in a sense is, that knowledge. Socrates assumes throughout that *dikaiosune* or justice in the sense it is here used (see 331c) is also a matter of knowledge, a *technê*. So the notion of "being good at one's craft" being a matter of knowledge is broadened to "being good is a matter of knowledge," i.e., the famous Socratic paradox that "virtue" (*aretê*) is knowledge.

The man with knowledge is wise?

I agree.

And the wise is good?

I agree.

So the good and wise does not wish to get the better of one like himself, but of the unlike and opposite?

Apparently.

But the bad and ignorant would want to get the better of his like and his opposite?

So it appears.

Now Thrasymachus, I said, we found that the unjust man tries to get the better of both those like and those unlike him. Did you not say so?

I did.

c   Yes, and the just man will not get the better of his like, but of one unlike him?

Yes.

The just man then, I said, resembles the wise and good, while the unjust resembles the bad and ignorant?

It may be so.

Further, we agreed that each will be such as the man he resembles?

We did so agree.

So we find that the just man has turned out to be good and wise, and the unjust man ignorant and bad.

Thrasymachus agreed to all this, not easily as I am tell-
d   ing it, but reluctantly and after being pushed. It was summer and he was perspiring profusely. And then I saw something I had never seen before: Thrasymachus blushing. After we had agreed that justice was virtue and wisdom, and injustice vice and ignorance, I said: Very well, let us consider this as established, but we also said that injustice was powerful, or don't you remember, Thrasymachus?

I remember, he said, but then I am not satisfied with what you are now saying. I could make a speech about it,
e   but if I should speak I know that you would say I am delivering a public oration. So either allow me to speak or, if you want to ask questions, ask them, and I will say "very well," and nod yes and no, as one does to old wives' tales.

Don't ever do that, I said, against your own opinion.

Just to please you, he said, since you won't let me speak. What else do you want?

Nothing at all, said I. If you will do this, do it. I will ask my questions.

Ask them then.

I am asking what I asked before, so that we may pro-
351 ceed with our argument about the relation of justice and injustice in an orderly way. It was said that injustice is more powerful and stronger than justice. But now, I said, since justice is wisdom and virtue, it will easily be shown to be also stronger than injustice which is ignorance; nobody could still not know that. However, I do not want to state this thus simply, Thrasymachus, but to look into it in some such way as this: would you say that it is unjust for a city to b undertake to enslave other cities unjustly and hold them in subjection, having enslaved many cities to its power?

Of course, he said, this is what the best city will do, the most completely unjust.

I understand that this was your argument, I said, but let me examine this point: will the city which has become stronger than another achieve this power without justice, or must it do so with the help of justice?

If what you said just now stands—that justice is wis- c dom—with the help of justice, but if things are as I stated them, with injustice.

I am delighted, Thrasymachus, that you do not merely nod yes or no, but that you answer in a very fine manner.

I am doing it to please you, he said.

You are doing well. Now please me also by answering this question: do you think that a city, an army, a band of robbers or thieves, or any other body of men which engages unjustly upon a common course, could achieve anything if they wrong one another?

No indeed. d

What if they do not wrong one another? Would they not achieve more?

Certainly.

Yes, for injustice, Thrasymachus, causes factions and hatreds and fights with one another, while justice brings a sense of common purpose and friendship. Is that not so?

Be it so, to agree with you.

You are doing well my good friend. Tell me this: if it is the result of injustice to bring hatred wherever it occurs, then its presence, whether among free men or slaves, will make them hate each other and quarrel, and be unable to achieve any common purpose?

Quite so. e

What if it occurs between two men? Will they not be at odds, hate each other, and be hostile to each other as well as to the just?

They will be.

Does injustice, my good sir, lose this capacity for dissension when it occurs within one individual, or will it preserve it intact?

Let it be preserved intact, he said.

It seems to follow that injustice, wherever it occurs, be it in a city, a family, an army, or anything else results in making it incapable of achieving anything as a unit because of the dissensions and differences it creates, and, further, it makes that unit hostile to itself, to its every enemy, and to the just. Is that not so?

Quite.

Even in one individual it has the same effect, which follows from its nature. First, it makes that individual incapable of achievement because he is at odds with himself and not of one mind. It makes him his own enemy, as well as the enemy of the just, does it not?

It does.

The gods too, my friend, are just.

Be it so.

So the unjust man is also an enemy of the gods, while the just man is their friend.

Bravely enjoy your feast of words, he said. I will not oppose you, to avoid unpopularity in this company.

Come then, said I, complete the feast for me by answering as you are now doing. The just are shown to be wiser and more able in action, while the unjust are not even able to act together, for surely, when we speak of a powerful achievement by unjust men acting in common, we are altogether far from the truth. They could not have kept their hands off each other if they had been completely bad, but clearly they had some justice which forbade them to wrong each other and their enemies at the same time. It was this which enabled them to do what they did. They started on their unjust course being half evil with injustice, for those who are completely evil and completely unjust are also completely incapable of achievement. I can see that this is so, and not as you at first assumed.

We must now examine whether the just also live a better life than the unjust and are happier, a point which we deferred for later investigation.[1] I think it is clear even now that they are, yet we must look into this further, for the argument concerns no casual topic, but one's whole manner of living.

Look into it, then.

I am looking, said I. Do you think there is such a thing as the function of a horse?

I do.

And would you define the function of a horse, or of anything else, as to do that which can be done only, or be done best, by means of it?

I do not understand your question, he said.

Put it like this: is it possible to see by any other means than the eyes?

Certainly not.

Further, could you hear by any other means than the ears?

Not possibly.

Then we are right to say that these are the functions of eyes and ears?

Quite so.

Further, would you use a dagger or a carving knife to trim the branches of a vine, or many other instruments?

Of course.

But you would not do it as well with any other instrument as with a pruning knife which was made for the purpose?

That is true.

Then shall we put it that this is the function of a pruning knife?

We shall.

Now I think you will understand my recent question better, when I inquired whether the function of each thing is to do that which it alone can perform, or perform better than anything else could.

I understand, he said, and I think that is the function of each.

Very well, said I. Does each thing to which a particular task is assigned also have its excellence? Let us go over the same ground again. We say that the eyes have a particular task?

Yes.

They also have their own excellence?

They have.

The ears too have a function?

Yes.

So they have their excellence?

That too.

Is that not the case with all other things?

It is.

Moreover, could the eyes perform their function well if they did not possess their own excellence or virtue, but their own vice instead?

How could they? he said. You mean blindness instead of sight?

---

1   *later investigation*   See 347e.

Whatever their virtue is, for I am not now asking that, but whether any agent performs its function well by means of its own excellence or virtue, or badly through its own badness or vice.

What you say is true.

So the ears, too, deprived of their own virtue, would perform their function badly.

Quite so.

d   And we could say the same about all other things?

I think so.

Come now, consider this point next: There is a function of the soul which you could not fulfill by means of any other thing, as for example: to take care of things, to rule, to deliberate, and other things of the kind; could we entrust these things to any other agent than the soul and say that they belong to it?

To no other.

What of living? Is that not a function of the soul?

It most certainly is.

So there is also an excellence of the soul?

We say so.

e   And, Thrasymachus, will the soul ever fulfill its function well if it is deprived of its own particular excellence, or is this impossible?

Impossible.

It is therefore inevitable that the bad soul rules and looks after things badly and that the good soul does all these things well.

Inevitable.

Now we have agreed that justice is excellence of the soul, and that injustice is vice of soul?

We have so agreed.

The just soul and the just man, then, will live well, and the unjust man will live badly.

So it seems, according to your argument.

354   Surely the one who lives well is blessed and happy, and the one who does not is the opposite.

Of course.

So the just man is happy, and the unjust one is wretched.

So be it.

It profits no one to be wretched, but to be happy.

Of course.

And so, my good Thrasymachus, injustice is never more profitable than justice.

Let that be your banquet of words, he said, at the feast of Bendis, Socrates.

Given by you, Thrasymachus, I said, after you became gentle and ceased to be angry with me. Yet I have not had   b
a good banquet, but that was my fault, not yours. I seem to have behaved as gluttons do, snatching at every dish that passes them and tasting it before they have reasonably enjoyed the one before. So I, before finding the answer to our first enquiry into the nature of justice, let that go and turned to investigate whether it was vice and ignorance or wisdom and virtue. Another argument came up after, that injustice was more profitable than justice, and I could not refrain from following, this up and abandoning the previous one so that the result of our discussion for me is that I know nothing; for, when I do not know what justice is, I   c
shall hardly know whether it is a kind of virtue or not, or whether the just man is unhappy or happy.

Book 2

When I had said this I thought I had done with the dis-   357
cussion, but evidently this was only a prelude. Glaucon on this occasion too showed boldness which is characteristic of him, and refused to accept Thrasymachus' abandoning the argument. He said: Do you, Socrates, want to appear to have persuaded us, or do you want truly to convince us that   b
it is better in every way to be just than unjust?

I would certainly wish to convince you truly, I said, if I could.

Well, he said, you are certainly not attaining your wish. Tell me, do you think there is a kind of good which we welcome not because we desire its consequences but for its own sake: joy, for example, and all the harmless pleasures which have no further consequences beyond the joy which one finds in them?

Certainly, said I, I think there is such a good.

Further, there is the good which we welcome for its own   c
sake and also for its consequences, knowledge for example and sight and health. Such things we somehow welcome on both counts.

Yes, said I.

Are you also aware of a third kind, he asked, such as physical training, being treated when ill, the practice of medicine, and other ways of making money? We should say that these are wearisome but beneficial to us; we should not want them for their own sake, but because of the rewards   d
and other benefits which result from them.

There is certainly such a third kind, I said, but why do you ask?

Under which of these headings do you put justice? he asked.

358   I would myself put it in the finest class, I said, that which is to be welcomed both for itself and for its consequences by any man who is to be blessed with happiness.

That is not the opinion of the many, he said; they would put it in the wearisome class, to be pursued for the rewards and popularity which come from a good reputation, but to be avoided in itself as being difficult.

I know that is the general opinion, I said. Justice has now for some time been objected to by Thrasymachus on this score while injustice was extolled, but it seems I am a slow learner.

b   Come then, he said, listen to me also to see whether you are still of the same opinion, for I think that Thrasymachus gave up before he had to, charmed by you as by a snake charmer. I am not yet satisfied by the demonstration on either side. I am eager to hear the nature of each, of justice and injustice, and what effect its presence has upon the soul. I want to leave out of account the rewards and consequences of each. So, if you agree, I will do the follow-

c ing: I will renew the argument of Thrasymachus; I will first state what people consider the nature and origin of justice; secondly, that all who practice it do so unwillingly as being something necessary but not good; thirdly, that they have good reason to do so, for, according to what people say, the life of the unjust man is much better than that of the just.

It is not that I think so, Socrates, but I am perplexed and my ears are deafened listening to Thrasymachus and in-

d numerable other speakers; I have never heard from anyone the sort of defense of justice that I want to hear, proving that it is better than injustice. I want to hear it praised for itself, and I think I am most likely to hear this from you. Therefore I am going to speak at length in praise of the unjust life and in doing so I will show you the way I want to hear you denouncing injustice and praising justice. See whether you want to hear what I suggest.

I want it more than anything else, I said. Indeed, what subject would a man of sense talk and hear about more often with enjoyment?

e   Splendid, he said, then listen while I deal with the first subject I mentioned: the nature and origin of justice.

They say that to do wrong is naturally good, to be wronged is bad, but the suffering of injury so far exceeds in badness the good of inflicting it that when men have done wrong to each other and suffered it, and have had a taste of both, those who are unable to avoid the latter and

practice the former decide that it is profitable to come to an 359 agreement with each other neither to inflict injury nor to suffer it. As a result they begin to make laws and covenants, and the law's command they call lawful and just. This, they say, is the origin and essence of justice; it stands between the best and the worst, the best being to do wrong without paying the penalty and the worst to be wronged without the power of revenge. The just then is a mean between two extremes; it is welcomed and honored because of men's lack b of the power to do wrong. The man who has that power, the real man, would not make a compact with anyone not to inflict injury or suffer it. For him that would be madness. This then, Socrates, is, according to their argument, the nature and origin of justice.

Even those who practice justice do so against their will because they lack the power to do wrong. This we could realize very clearly if we imagined ourselves granting to c both the just and the unjust the freedom to do whatever they liked. We could then follow both of them and observe where their desires led them, and we would catch the just man redhanded traveling the same road as the unjust. The reason is the desire for undue gain which every organism by nature pursues as a good, but the law forcibly sidetracks him to honor equality. The freedom I just mentioned would most easily occur if these men had the power which they say the ancestor of the Lydian Gyges[1] possessed. The story d is that he was a shepherd in the service of the ruler of Lydia. There was a violent rainstorm and an earthquake which broke open the ground and created a chasm at the place where he was tending sheep. Seeing this and marveling, he went down into it. He saw, besides many other wonders of which we are told, a hollow bronze horse. There were window-like openings in it; he climbed through them and caught sight of a corpse which seemed of more than human stature, wearing nothing but a ring of gold on its finger. e This ring the shepherd put on and came out. He arrived at the usual monthly meeting which reported to the king on the state of the flocks, wearing the ring. As he was sitting among the others he happened to twist the hoop of the ring towards himself, to the inside of his hand, and as he did this he became invisible to those sitting near him and they 360 went on talking as if he had gone. He marveled at this and, fingering the ring, he turned the hoop outward again and

---

1   *Gyges* There may be a connection between the Lydian Gyges mentioned in this allegory and Gyges the historical king of Lydia around 700 BCE.

became visible. Perceiving this he tested whether the ring had this power and so it happened: if he turned the hoop inwards he became invisible, but was visible when he turned it outwards. When he realized this, he at once arranged to become one of the messengers to the king. He went, committed adultery with the king's wife, attacked the king with her help, killed him, and took over the kingdom.

Now if there were two such rings, one worn by the just man, the other by the unjust, no one, as these people think, would be so incorruptible that he would stay on the path of justice or bring himself to keep away from other people's property and not touch it, when he could with impunity take whatever he wanted from the market, go into houses and have sexual relations with anyone he wanted, kill anyone, free all those he wished from prison, and do the other things which would make him like a god among men. His actions would be in no way different from those of the other and they would both follow the same path. This, some would say, is a great proof that no one is just willingly but under compulsion, so that justice is not one's private good, since wherever either thought he could do wrong with impunity he would do so. Every man believes that injustice is much more profitable to himself than justice, and any exponent of this argument will say that he is right. The man who did not wish to do wrong with that opportunity, and did not touch other people's property, would be thought by those who knew it to be very foolish and miserable. They would praise him in public, thus deceiving one another, for fear of being wronged. So much for my second topic.

As for the choice between the lives we are discussing, we shall be able to make a correct judgment about it only if we put the most just man and the most unjust man face to face; otherwise we cannot do so. By face to face I mean this: let us grant to the unjust the fullest degree of injustice and to the just the fullest justice, each being perfect in his own pursuit. First, the unjust man will act as clever craftsmen do—a top navigator for example or physician distinguishes what his craft can do and what it cannot; the former he will undertake, the latter he will pass by, and when he slips he can put things right. So the unjust man's correct attempts at wrongdoing must remain secret; the one who is caught must be considered a poor performer, for the extreme of injustice is to have a reputation for justice, and our perfectly unjust man must be granted perfection in injustice. We must not take this from him, but we must allow that, while committing the greatest crimes, he has provided himself with the greatest reputation for justice; if he makes a slip he must be able to put it right; he must be a sufficiently persuasive speaker if some wrongdoing of his is made public; he must be able to use force, where force is needed, with the help of his courage, his strength, and the friends and wealth with which he has provided himself.

Having described such a man, let us now in our argument put beside him the just man, simple as he is and noble, who, as Aeschylus put it,[1] does not wish to appear just but to be so. We must take away his reputation, for a reputation for justice would bring him honor and rewards, and it would then not be clear whether he is what he is for justice's sake or for the sake of rewards and honor. We must strip him of everything except justice and make him the complete opposite of the other. Though he does no wrong, he must have the greatest reputation for wrongdoing so that he may be tested for justice by not weakening under ill repute and its consequences. Let him go his incorruptible way until death with a reputation for injustice throughout his life, just though he is, so that our two men may reach the extremes, one of justice, the other of injustice, and let them be judged as to which of the two is the happier.

Whew! My dear Glaucon, I said, what a mighty scouring you have given those two characters, as if they were statues in a competition.[2]

I do the best I can, he replied. The two being such as I have described, there should be no difficulty in following the argument through as to what kind of life awaits each of them, but it must be said. And if what I say sounds rather boorish, Socrates, realize that it is not I who speak, but those who praise injustice as preferable to justice. They will say that the just man in these circumstances will be whipped, stretched on the rack, imprisoned, have his eyes burnt out, and, after suffering every kind of evil, he will be impaled and realize that one should not want to be just but to appear so. Indeed, Aeschylus' words are far more correctly applied to the unjust than to the just, for we shall be told that the unjust man pursues a course which is based on truth and not on appearances; he does not want to appear but to be unjust:

---

1   *as Aeschylus put it*   Aeschylus (525–456 BCE) was the first of the three great Greek tragedians. This and the quotation a few lines down are from *Seven Against Thebes*, 592–94, where it is said of Amphiaraus that "he did not wish to appear but to be the best," and continues, "he harbors in his heart a deep furrow, from which good counsels grow."

2   *a mighty scouring ... statues in a competition*   Officials called "burnishers" had the duty of cleaning cult statues.

He harvests in his heart a deep furrow
b   from which good counsels grow.

He rules his city because of his reputation for justice, he
marries into any family he wants to, he gives his children in
marriage to anyone he wishes, he has contractual and other
associations with anyone he may desire, and, beside all these
advantages, he benefits in the pursuit of gain because he
does not scruple to practice injustice. In any contest, public
or private, he is the winner, getting the better of his enemies
c   and accumulating wealth; he benefits his friends and does
harm to his enemies. To the gods he offers grand sacrifices
and gifts which will satisfy them, he can serve the gods much
better than the just man, and also such men as he wants to,
with the result that he is likely to be dearer to the gods. This
is what they say, Socrates, that both from gods and men the
unjust man secures a better life than the just.

d   After Glaucon had thus spoken I again had it in mind
to say something in reply, but his brother Adeimantus intervened: You surely do not think that enough has been said
from this point of view, Socrates?

Why not? said I.

The most important thing, that should have been said,
has not been said, he replied.

Well then, I said, let brother stand by brother. If Glaucon has omitted something, you come to his help. Yet what
he has said is sufficient to throw me and to make me incapable of coming to the help of justice.

e   Nonsense, he said. Hear what more I have to say, for we
should also go fully into the arguments opposite to those
he mentioned, those which praise justice and censure injustice, so that what I take to be Glaucon's intention may
be clearer. When fathers speak to their sons, they say one
363 must be just—and so do all who care for them, but they do
not praise justice itself, only the high reputations it leads
to, in order that the son, thought to be just, shall enjoy
those public offices, marriages, and the rest which Glaucon
mentioned, as they belong to the just man because of his
high repute; they lay even greater emphasis on the results of
reputation. They add popularity granted by the gods, and
mention abundant blessings which, they say, the gods grant
to the pious. So too the noble Hesiod[1] and Homer declare,
b   the one that for the just the gods make "the oak trees bear
acorns at the top and bees in the middle and their fleecy

sheep are heavy with their burden of wool"[2] and many other
blessings of like nature. The other says similar things:

(like the fame) of a goodly king who, in his piety,
upholds justice; for him the black earth bears
    wheat
and barley and the trees are heavy with fruit; his
sheep bear lambs continually and the sea
    provides its fish.[3]

Musaeus[4] and his son grant from the gods more robust pleasures to the just. Their words lead the just to the underworld,
and, seating them at table, provide them with a banquet
of the saints, crown them with wreaths, and make them
spend all their time drinking, as if they thought that the
finest reward of virtue was perpetual drunkenness. Others d
stretch the rewards of virtue from the gods even further,
for they say that the children and the children's children
and the posterity of the pious man who keeps his oaths will
survive into the future. Thus, and in other such ways, do
they praise justice. The impious and unjust they bury in
mud in the underworld, they force them to carry water in a
sieve, they bring them into disrepute while still living, and
they attribute to them all the punishments which Glaucon e
enumerated in the case of the just with a reputation for
injustice, but they have nothing else to say. This then is the
way people praise and blame justice and injustice.

Besides this, Socrates, look at another kind of argument
which is spoken in private, and also by the poets, concerning justice and injustice. All go on repeating with one voice 364
that justice and moderation are beautiful, but certainly difficult and burdensome, while incontinence and injustice are
sweet and easy, and shameful only by repute and by law.
They add that unjust deeds are for the most part more profitable than just ones. They freely declare, both in private
and in public, that the wicked who have wealth and other
forms of power are happy. They honor them but pay neither
honor nor attention to the weak and the poor, though they b
agree that these are better men than the others.

What men say about the gods and virtue is the most
amazing of all, namely that the gods too inflict misfortunes
and a miserable life upon many good men, and the opposite fate to their opposites. Begging priests and prophets
frequent the doors of the rich and persuade them that they

---

1   *Hesiod*   Like Homer, Hesiod was a revered very early Greek poet
and author of *Works and Days*—living perhaps in the seventh century BCE.

2   *the oak trees ... wool*   From Hesiod's *Works and Days*, 232–3.
3   *(like the fame) ... fish*   Homer, *Odyssey*, 19, 109.
4   *Musaeus*   Legendary poet closely connected with the mystery
religion of Orphism.

possess a god-given power to remedy by sacrifices and incantations at pleasant festivals any crime that the rich man
c or one of his ancestors may have committed. Moreover, if
one wishes to harass some enemy, then at little expense he
will be able to harm the just and the unjust alike, for by
means of spells and enchantments they can persuade the
gods to serve them. They bring the poets as witnesses to all
this, some harping on the easiness of vice, that

> Vice is easy to choose in abundance, the path is
d >   smooth and it dwells very near, but sweat is
>   placed by
>   the gods on the way to virtue,[1]

and a path which is long, rough, and steep; others quote
Homer as a witness that the gods can be influenced by men,
for he too said:[2]

> the gods themselves can be swayed by prayer, for
>   suppliant men can turn them from their purpose
>   by
e >   sacrifices and gentle prayers, by libations and
>   burnt offerings
>   whenever anyone has transgressed and sinned.

They offer in proof a mass of writings by Musaeus and Orpheus,[3] offspring, as they say, of Selene[4] and the Muses.[5]
In accordance with these they perform their ritual and
365 persuade not only individuals but whole cities that, both
for the living and for the dead, there are absolutions and
purifications for sin by means of sacrifices and pleasurable, playful rituals. These they call initiations which free
from punishment yonder, where a dreadful fate awaits the
uninitiated.

When all such sayings about the attitudes of men and
gods toward virtue and vice are so often repeated, what
effect, my dear Socrates, do we think they have upon the
minds of our youth? One who is naturally talented and able,
like a bee flitting from flower to flower gathering honey, to
flit over these sayings and to gather from them an impression of what kind of man he should be and of how best to
b travel along the road of life, would surely repeat to himself

the saying of Pindar: should I by justice or by crooked deceit scale this high wall and thus live my life fenced off from
other men? The advantages said to be mine if I am just are of
no use, I am told, unless I also appear so; while the troubles
and penalties are obvious. The unjust man, on the other
hand, who has secured for himself a reputation for justice,
lives, they tell me, the life of a god. Therefore, since appear- c
ance, as the wise men tell me, forcibly overwhelms truth
and controls happiness, this is altogether the way I should
live. I should build around me a façade that gives the illusion of justice to those who approach me and keep behind
this the greedy and crafty fox of the wise Archilochus.[6]

"But surely" someone objects, "it is not easy for vice to
remain hidden always." We shall reply that nothing is easy
which is of great import. Nevertheless, this is the way we d
must go if we are to be happy, and follow along the lines of
all we have been told. To protect our secret we shall form
sworn conspiratorial societies and political clubs. Besides,
there are teachers of persuasion who make one clever in
dealing with assemblies and with the courts. This will enable us to use persuasion here and force there, so that we
can secure our own advantage without penalty.

"But one cannot force the gods nor have secrets from
them." Well, if either they do not exist or do not concern
themselves with human affairs, why should we worry about
secrecy? If they do exist and do concern themselves, we have e
heard about them and know them from no other source
than our laws and our genealogizing poets, and these are
the very men who tell us that the gods can be persuaded and
influenced by gentle prayers and by offerings. We should
believe both or neither. If we believe them, we should do
wrong and then offer sacrifices from the proceeds. If we 366
are just, we shall not be punished by the gods but we shall
lose the profits of injustice. If we are unjust we shall get the
benefit of sins and transgressions, and afterwards persuade
the gods by prayer and escape without punishment. "But
in Hades we will pay the penalty for the crimes committed here, either ourselves or our children's children." "My
friend," the young man will reply as he does his reckoning,
"mystery rites have great potency, and so have the gods of
absolution, as the greatest cities tell us, and the children of b
the gods who have become poets and prophets tell us that
this is so."

---

1   *Vice is easy ... to virtue*   Hesiod, *Works and Days*, 287–89.
2   *he too said*   Homer, *Iliad*, 9, 497–501.
3   *Orpheus*   Like Museus, Orpheus was a (possibly wholly) mythological poet-musician associated with Orphism (thus its name).
4   *Selene*   The moon-goddess.
5   *the Muses*   Goddesses or lesser spirits personifying artistic
inspiration.

6   *the greedy ... Archilochus*   The fable in question is not extant, but
we do have a fragment attributed to Archilochus: "The fox has
many tricks; the hedgehog only one great trick."

For what reason then should we still choose justice rather than the greatest injustice? If we practice the latter with specious decorum we shall do well at the hands of gods and of men; we shall live and die as we intend, for so both the many and the eminent tell us. From all that
c has been said, Socrates, what possibility is there that any man of power, be it the power of mind or of wealth, of body or of birth, will be willing to honor justice and not laugh aloud when he hears it praised? And surely any man who can show that what we have said is untrue and has full knowledge that justice is best, will be full of forgiveness, and not of anger, for the unjust. He knows that only a man of godlike character whom injustice disgusts, or one who
d has superior knowledge, avoids injustice, and that no other man is willingly just, but through cowardice or old age or some other weakness objects to injustice, because he cannot practice it. That this is so is obvious, for the first of these men to acquire power is the first to do wrong as much as he is able.

The only reason for all this talk, Socrates, which led to Glaucon's speech and mine, is to say to you: Socrates, you
e strange man, not one of all of you who profess to praise justice, beginning with the heroes of old, whose words are left to us, to the present day—not one has ever blamed injustice or praised justice in any other way than by mentioning the reputations, honors, and rewards which follow justice. No one has ever adequately described, either in poetry or in private conversation, what the very presence of justice or injustice in his soul does to a man even if it remains hidden from gods and men; one is the greatest evil the soul can
367 contain, while the other, justice, is the greatest good. If you had treated the subject in this way and had persuaded us from youth, we should then not be watching one another to see we do no wrong, but every man would be his own best guardian and he would be afraid lest, by doing wrong, he live with the greatest evil.

Thrasymachus or anyone else might say what we have said, and perhaps more in discussing justice and injustice. I believe they would be vulgarly distorting the effect of each.
b To be quite frank with you, it is because I am eager to hear the opposite from you that I speak with all the emphasis I can muster. So do not merely give us a theoretical proof that justice is better than injustice, but tell us how each, in and by itself, affects a man, the one for good, the other for evil. Follow Glaucon's advice and do not take reputations into account, for if you do not deprive them of true reputation and attach false reputations to them, we shall say that you

are not praising justice but the reputation for it, or blaming injustice but the appearance of it, that you are encour-
c aging one to be unjust in secret, and that you agree with Thrasymachus that the just is another's good, the advantage of the stronger, while the unjust is one's own advantage and profit, though not the advantage of the weaker.

Since you have agreed that justice is one of the greatest goods, those which are worthy of attainment for their consequences, but much more for their own sake—sight,
d hearing, knowledge, health, and all other goods which are creative by what they are and not by what they seem—do praise justice in this regard: in what way does its very possession benefit a man and injustice harm him? Leave rewards and reputations for others to praise.

For others would satisfy me if they praised justice and blamed injustice in this way, extolling the rewards of the one and denigrating those of the other, but from you, unless you tell me to, I will not accept it, because you have spent
e your whole life investigating this and nothing else. Do not, therefore, give us a merely theoretical proof that justice is better than injustice, but tell us what effect each has in and by itself, the one for good, the other for evil, whether or not it be hidden from gods and men.

I had always admired the character of Glaucon and Adeimantus, and on this occasion I was quite delighted 368 with them as I listened and I said: You are the sons of a great man, and Glaucon's lover began his elegy well when he wrote, celebrating the repute you gained at the battle of Megara:

> Sons of Ariston, godlike offspring of a famous
> man.

That seems well deserved, my friends; you must be divinely inspired if you are not convinced that injustice is better than justice, and yet can speak on its behalf as you have done. And I do believe that you are really unconvinced by
b your own words. I base this belief on my knowledge of the way you live, for, if I had only your words to go by, I would not trust you. The more I trust you, however, the more I am at a loss what to do. I do not see how I can be of help; I feel myself incapable. I see a proof of this in the fact that I thought what I said to Thrasymachus showed that justice is better than injustice, but you refuse to accept this as adequate. On the other hand I do not see how I can refuse my help, for I fear it is even impious to be present when justice is being charged and to fail to come to her
c help as long as there is breath in one's body and one is still

able to speak. So the best course is to give her any assistance I can.

Glaucon and the others begged me to give any help I could, not to abandon the argument but to track down the nature of justice and injustice, and where the truth lay as regards the benefits of both. So I said what I had in mind: This investigation we are undertaking is not easy, I think, but requires keen eyesight. As we are not very clever, I said, I think we should adopt a method like this: if men who did not have keen eyesight were told to read small letters from a distance, and then someone noticed that these same letters were to be found somewhere else on a larger scale and on a larger object, it would, I think, be considered a piece of luck that they could read these first and then examine the smaller letters to see if they were the same.

That is certainly true, said Adeimantus, but what relevance do you see in it to our present search for justice?

I will tell you, I said. There is, we say, the justice of one man, and also the justice of a whole city?

Certainly.

And a city is larger than one man?

It is.

Perhaps there is more justice in the larger unit, and it may be easier to grasp. So, if you are willing, let us first investigate what justice is in the cities, and afterwards let us look for it in the individual, observing the similarities to the larger in the smaller.

Your proposal seems sound.

Well then, I said, if we observed the birth of a city in theory, we would also see its justice and injustice beginning to exist.

Probably.

And as the process went on, we may hope that the object of our search would be easier to discover.

Much easier.

Do you think we should attempt to carry this through? It is no small task, I think. Think it over.

We have, said Adeimantus. Carry on.

I think a city comes to be, I said, because not one of us is self-sufficient, but needs many things. Do you think a city is founded on any other principle?

On no other.

As they need many things, people make use of one another for various purposes. They gather many associates and helpers to live in one place, and to this settlement we give the name of city. Is that not so?

It is.

And they share with one another, both giving and taking, in so far as they do, because they think this better for themselves?

Quite so.

Come then, I said, let us create a city from the beginning in our discussion. And it is our needs, it seems, that will create it.

Of course.

Surely our first and greatest need is to provide food to sustain life.

It certainly is.

Our second need is for shelter, our third for clothes and such things.

Quite so.

Consider then, said I, how the city will adequately provide for all this. One man obviously must be a farmer, another a builder, and another a weaver. Or should we add a cobbler and some other craftsman to look after our physical needs?

All right.

So the essential minimum for the city is four or five men.

Apparently.

A further point: must each of them perform his own work as common for them all, for example the one farmer provide food for them all, and spend four times as much time and labor to provide food which is shared by the others, or will he not care for this but provide for himself a quarter of such food in a quarter of the time and spend the other three quarters, one in building a house, one in the production of clothes, and one to make shoes, and not trouble to associate with the others but for and by himself mind his own business?

Perhaps, Socrates, Adeimantus replied, the way you suggested first would be easier than the other.

By Zeus, said I, there is nothing surprising in this, for even as you were speaking I was thinking that, in the first place, each one of us is born somewhat different from the others, one more apt for one task, one for another. Don't you think so?

I do.

Further, does a man do better if he practices many crafts, or if, being one man, he restricts himself to one craft.

When he restricts himself to one.

This at any rate is clear, I think, that if one misses the proper time to do something, the opportunity to do it has gone.

Clear enough.

For I do not think that the thing to be done awaits the leisure of the doer, but the doer must of necessity adjust himself to the requirements of his task, and not consider this of secondary importance.

He must.

Both production and quality are improved in each case, and easier, if each man does one thing which is congenial to him, does it at the right time, and is free of other pursuits.

Most certainly.

We shall then need more than four citizens, Adeimantus, to provide the things we have mentioned. It is likely that the farmer will not make his own plough if it is to be a good one, nor his mattock, nor other agricultural implements. Neither will the builder, for he too needs many things; and the same is true of the weaver and the cobbler, is it not?

True.

Carpenters, metal workers, and many such craftsmen will share our little city and make it bigger.

Quite so.

Yet it will not be a very big settlement if we add cowherds, shepherds, and other herdsmen in order that our farmers have oxen to do their plowing, and the builders will join the farmers in the use of them as beasts of burden to transport their materials, while the weavers and cobblers will use their wool and hides.

Neither will it be a small city, said he, if it has to hold all these things.

And further, it is almost impossible to establish the city in the kind of place that will need no imports.

Impossible.

So we shall still need other people to bring what is needed from other cities.

We shall.

Now if one who serves in this way goes to the other city without a cargo of the things needed by those from whom he is to bring what his own people need, he will come away empty-handed, will he not?

I think so.

Therefore our citizens must not only produce enough for themselves at home, but also the things these others require, of the right quality and in the right quantity.

They must.

So we need more farmers and other craftsmen in our city.

We do.

Then again we need more people to service imports and exports. These are merchants, are they not?

Yes.

So we shall need merchants too.

Quite so.

And if the trade is by sea, we shall need a number of others who know how to sail the seas.

A good many, certainly.

A further point: how are they going to share the things that each group produces within the city itself? This association with each other was the very purpose for which we established the city.

Clearly, he said, they must do this by buying and selling.

It follows that we must have a market place and a currency for this exchange.

Certainly.

If the farmer brings some of his produce to market, or any other craftsman, and he does not arrive at the same time as those who want to exchange things with him, will he be sitting idly in the market place, away from his own work?

Not at all, he said. There will be people who realize this and engage in this service. In well-organized cities this will be pretty well those of feeble physique who are not fit for other work. They must stay around the market, buying for money from those who have something to sell, and then again selling at a price to those who want to buy.

To fill this need there will be retailers in our city. Do we not call retailers those who establish themselves in the market place for this service of buying and selling, while those who travel between cities are called merchants?

Quite so.

There are some others to serve, as I think, who are not worth admitting into our society for their intelligence, but they have sufficient physical strength for heavy labor. These sell the use of their strength; their reward for this is a wage and they are, I think, called wage-earners. Is that not so?

Certainly.

So the wage-earners complete our city.

I think so.

Well, Adeimantus, has our city now grown to its full size?

Perhaps.

Where then would justice and injustice be in it? With which of the parts we have examined has it come to be?

I do not notice them, Socrates, he said, unless it is in the relations of these very people to one another.

You may be right, I said, but we must look into it and not grow weary. First then let us see what kind of life our citizens will lead when they have thus been provided for. Obviously they will produce grain and wine and clothes and shoes. They will build their houses. In the summer they will strip for their work and go without shoes, though they will be adequately clothed and shod in the winter. For food they will make flour from wheat and meal from barley; they will bake the former and knead the latter; they will put their excellent cakes and loaves upon reeds or clean leaves; then, reclining upon a bed of strewn bryony and myrtle leaves, they will feast together with their children, drinking of their wine. Crowned with wreaths they will hymn the gods and enjoy each other, bearing no more children than their means allow, cautious to avoid poverty and war.

Glaucon interrupted and said: You make your people feast, it seems, without cooked dishes or seasoning.

True enough, I said, I was forgetting that they will need these, salt obviously and olives and cheese; they will boil roots and vegetables such as are found in the fields. We shall put sweetmeats before them consisting of figs and chickpeas and beans, and they will bake myrtles and acorns[1] before the fire, drinking moderately. So they will live at peace and in good health, and when they die at a ripe age they will bequeath a similar life to their offspring.

And he said: If you were founding a city of pigs, Socrates, what else would you fatten them on?

And how should I feed them, Glaucon? said I.

In the conventional way, he said. If they are not to be miserable they should recline on proper couches and dine at a table, with the cooked foods and delicacies which people have nowadays.

Very well, I said, I understand. We should examine not only the birth of a city, but of a luxurious city. This may not be a bad idea, for in examining such a one we might very well see how justice and injustice grow in the cities. Yet to me the true city is that which we described, like a healthy individual. However, if you wish, let us also observe the feverish city. There is nothing to prevent us. The things I mentioned would not, it seems, satisfy some people, nor would that kind of life. There will be couches, then, and tables and the other kinds of furniture. They must have cooked dishes and unguents and perfumes, and cour-tesans and pastries—various kinds of all these. We must no longer provide them only with the necessities we mentioned at first, houses and clothes and shoes, but we must call in painting and embroidery; we must acquire gold and ivory and all such things. Is that not so?

Yes.

We must then again enlarge our city. That healthy community is no longer adequate, but it must be swollen in bulk and filled with a multitude of things which are no longer necessities, as, for example, all kinds of hunters and artists,[2] many of them concerned with shapes and colors, many with music; poets and their auxiliaries, actors, choral dancers, and contractors; and makers of all kinds of instruments, including those needed for the beautification of women. And further we shall require more services in the city, or do you not think we shall need tutors, wet nurses, dry nurses, beauty parlors, barbers, and again chefs and cooks, also swineherds? These were not needed in our earlier city, but in this one there is need of them, as there will be for many other fatted beasts, once one eats them. Is that not so?

Of course.

And if we live like this we shall have far greater need of physicians than before.

Much greater.

The land which was adequate to feed the earlier population will become small and inadequate instead, shall we say?

That is so.

We must therefore annex a portion of our neighbors' land if we are to have sufficient pasture and plowland, and they will want to annex part of ours if they too have surrendered themselves to the limitless acquisition of wealth and overstepped the boundaries of the necessary.

Inevitably, Socrates.

So our next step is war, Glaucon, or what will be the situation?

As you describe it.

Let us say nothing as yet whether the effects of war are good or evil, I said, but only this, that we have now found the origin of war. It originates from the same source from which many evils both public and private come in their own time upon the state.

---

1 *myrtles and acorns* This is suspected to be a sexual pun: the Greek words for "myrtle" and "acorn" were employed as slang to denote female and male genitals.

2 *hunters and artists* Hunters are needed because the people are no longer vegetarians. The Greek word translated as artists is *mimētai*, literally "imitators."

Quite so.

Again, my friend, we shall need a city larger by not a
374 little, in fact larger by a whole army, which will go out and
fight on behalf of all this property and of the people we have
mentioned, against the invaders.

Why? he said, are the citizens themselves not able to
do so?[1]

Not, I said, if you and all of us were right to agree
when we fashioned our city: we agreed, if you remember,
that it was impossible for one man to practice many crafts
successfully.

That is true.

b   Well then, I said, do you not think that the contest of
war is a craft?

Definitely.

And does the cobbler's craft require more care than that
of the soldier?

Not at all.

We prevented the cobbler trying to be at the same time
a farmer or a weaver or a builder, and we said that he must
remain a cobbler so that the product of his craft be good;
c so with the others, each was to have one trade for which he
had a natural aptitude, stick to it for life, and keep away
from other crafts so as not to miss the opportunities to practice his own craft well. Is it not of the greatest importance
that matters of war be well performed? Or is fighting a war
so easy that a farmer can at the same time be a soldier and
so with the cobbler and any other craftsman? Yet no one
can become an adequate draughts or dice player if he does
not practice at it from childhood and only considers it a
d sideline. Can a man then pick up a shield or any other arm
or instrument of war and on the same day be an adequate
performer in a hoplite battle or any other kind? No other
instrument makes any man a craftsman or champion by
just being picked up, nor will it be of any use except to
one who has acquired the necessary knowledge and had sufficient practice.

If instruments could do this, they would be valuable
indeed, he said.

Therefore, I said, as the task of the guardian is most
e important, so he should have the most freedom from all
other pursuits, for he requires technical knowledge and the
greatest diligence.

I think so.

He also needs a nature which is suited to his pursuit,
does he not?

Of course.

It is then our task, to select, if we can, the man whose
nature is most suited to guard the city.

So it is.

By Zeus, I said, this is no small matter we have
raised. However, we must not weaken, so far as our ability
permits.

We must not.   375

Do you think, said I, that the nature of a pedigree
puppy[2] differs from that of a well-born youth as regards his
capacity to guard things?

What do you mean?

In so far as each of them must be quick to see things
and swift in the pursuit of what he has seen and also strong
if it is necessary to catch up with the enemy and fight to
the end.

They need all these qualities.

And he must be brave, if he is to fight well.

Of course.

And will a horse, a dog, or any other animal be brave,
if he is not high-spirited? Or have you noticed that a high
spirit is invincible and unbeatable? Its presence makes the b
whole soul fearless and unconquerable.

I have noticed it.

The physical qualities of the guardian are clear.

Yes.

And as far as the soul is concerned, he must be
high-spirited.

That too.

How then, Glaucon, said I, being of such a nature, will
they not be savage in their behavior to each other and to the
rest of the citizens?

That, by Zeus, will not be easy, he said.

Yet certainly they must be gentle to their own people, c
but hard for the enemy to deal with. Else they will not wait
for others to destroy the city but destroy it themselves first.

True.

What shall we do then? said I. Where shall we find a
character which is both gentle and high-spirited at the same
time? For a gentle nature is the opposite of a spirited one.

So it seems.

---

1   *are the citizens ... do so?* Citizen armies were the rule in earlier
     Greek history, but professional and mercenary armies came into
     their own in the fourth century BCE.

2   *puppy* Plato contrasts "puppy" (*skylax*) with "guardian"
     (*phylax*).

And surely if either of these qualities is missing, he cannot be a good guardian. The combination seems impossible, so it follows that a good guardian cannot exist.

I am afraid so.

So I was at a loss, but on reexamining what we had said: My friend, I said, we deserve to be in difficulties, for we have neglected the image we put forward.

How do you mean?

We have failed to notice that there exist some natures as we thought did not exist, combining these opposite qualities.

Where?

One might see this in other animals too, but not least in the one we compared to the guardian. You know that this type of character exists by nature in the pedigree dog. He is as gentle as one can be to those he is used to and knows, but the opposite to those he does not know.

Yes, I know that.

So the thing is possible, and our search for the good guardian is not against nature.

Apparently not.

Do you think that our future guardian, besides being high-spirited, must also naturally love wisdom?

How so? I do not understand.

You will see this also in dogs, which makes one marvel at the animal.

See what?

That whenever he sees a stranger he is angry, even though no harm has been done to him, but whomsoever he knows he welcomes even if he has never received anything good from him. Have you not wondered at this?

I have never, he said, paid any attention to the matter, but obviously this is how a dog behaves.

This is a smart way for a dog to behave, and his nature seems truly wisdom-loving.[1]

In what way?

In that he judges anything he sees as being friendly or hostile by no other criterion than that he knows the former

and does not know the latter. Surely anyone who distinguishes what he feels to be akin to him and its opposite by this criterion of knowledge and ignorance must be a lover of knowledge?

That must follow.

Surely loving knowledge and loving wisdom are the same thing? I said.

They are the same.

We are therefore encouraged to assume in the case of a man also, that if he is to be gentle toward his familiars and his acquaintances, he must be a lover of wisdom and a lover of knowledge.

Let us assume it.

So he who is to be a fine and good guardian of our city must be a lover of wisdom, high-spirited, swift and strong by nature.

That is altogether so.

This type of man would be available, as we saw, but how is he to be brought up and educated? The question is highly relevant to our investigation, since our primary purpose is to see how justice and injustice come to be in our city. We do not want to omit a necessary argument, nor speak at too great length.

At this point Glaucon's brother said: Certainly I expect that this inquiry will be very relevant to our purpose.

Then, by Zeus, Adeimantus, I said, we must not leave it out, even if its discussion may be somewhat long.

No indeed.

Come then, let us in theory educate our guardians as if we were telling a story and had the leisure to do so.

We must.

What will this education be? Or is it hard to find a better one than that which has been developed over a long period of time? It is in part physical training for the body and training in the arts[2] for the soul.

That is so.

---

1 *wisdom-loving* The Greek word is *philosophos*. Both it and the corresponding verb occur but rarely in texts before Plato; their meaning is quite general: intellectual curiosity, wanting to know things, without ulterior motive. The word is here introduced in its general sense, and the jest is less startling in Greek than in English. As the discussion proceeds the meaning deepens, and Plato uses the word in the central books of the *Republic* to describe his philosopher. Then "philosopher" is the only possible translation, but even so a Greek reader would have remained conscious of the etymological meaning.

2 *physical training ... training in the arts* The reference is to the conventional Greek education in *gymnastikê* and *mousikê*. The meaning of the first, physical training, is quite clear; *mousikê* is more difficult: sometimes the fine arts seem to be included, but the word refers mostly to poetry and music. Moreover, music, in Plato's time, was only beginning to be thought of as a separate art, and it was the combination of music and poetry which made up the song and was inspired by the Muses. "Music" is therefore a misleading translation. This translation uses the more general phrase "education in the arts" which includes all literature and, in Plato, even the "reasoned speech" of philosophy.

Do we not start education in the arts before physical training?

Of course.

Under the arts you include literature, or not?

I do.

There are two kinds of discourse, the true and the untrue

Yes.

377 They must be educated in both, but first in the untrue?

I do not understand your meaning, he said.

Do you not understand, I said, that we first tell stories to children. These are, in general, untrue, though there is some truth in them. And we tell stories to small children before we give them physical training.

That is so.

That is what I meant, that we must deal with the arts before physical training.

Correct.

b You know that the beginning of any process is most important, especially for anything young and tender. For it is at that time that it takes shape, and any mould one may want can be impressed upon it.

Very true.

Shall we then carelessly allow the children to hear any kind of stories composed by anybody, and to take into their souls beliefs which are for the most part contrary to those we think they should hold in maturity?

We shall certainly not allow that.

c Then we must first of all, it seems, control the story tellers. Whatever noble story they compose we shall select, but a bad one we must reject. Then we shall persuade nurses and mothers to tell their children those we have selected and by those stories to fashion their minds far more than they can shape their bodies by handling them. The majority of the stories they now tell must be thrown out.

Which do you mean?

We shall be able to examine the lesser by observing the larger. For they must all have much the same mold and the d same effect, whether they be large or small. Do you not think so?

I do, he said, but I do not know which you call large.

Those told, I said, by Hesiod and Homer and the other poets, for they put together fictitious stories and told them to men, and still do.

Which stories do you mean? said he, and why do you object to them?

Because of what one should object to first and most, especially if the fictitious is not well told.

As for instance?

Whenever any story gives a bad image of the nature e of gods[1] and heroes, like a painter drawing a bad picture, unlike the model he is wanting to portray.

You are right to object to that, he said, but how shall we proceed and what shall we say?

First, I said, the greatest lie[2] about the most important matters was that of the man who told bad fiction when he said that Ouranos did what Hesiod tells us he did, and how Cronos punished him for it.[3] Then again, even if the deeds 378 of Cronos and what he suffered from his son were true,[4] I do not think this should be told to foolish and young people; it should be passed over in silence. If there were some necessity to tell it, only a very few people should hear it, and in secret, after sacrificing not a pig but some great and scarce victim, so that as few people as possible should hear it.

Yes, he said, these stories are hard to deal with.

And they should not be told, Adeimantus, I said, in our b city. Nor should a young man hear it said that in committing the worst crimes he is not doing anything out of the way, or that, if he inflicts every kind of punishment upon an erring father, he is only doing the same as the first and greatest of the gods.

---

1   *gods*   It should be noted that throughout the *Republic*, as indeed elsewhere, Plato uses the singular *theos* and the plural *theoi* quite indifferently to denote a god, gods, or the gods. He even uses the singular with the article, the god. This, however, is the generic use of the article and does not refer to any particular god unless the context makes this obvious. It certainly does not imply any kind of monotheism, as a modern reader might think. All these expressions are equivalent, and refer to the gods or the divine nature generally.

2   *lie*   The Greek word *pseudos* means untruth, and need not imply a deliberate lie, though it frequently does. Hence "the lie in the soul" or "the true lie" is ignorance, i.e., untruth in the soul, as Plato goes on to argue, taking advantage of the ambiguity, though the expression is only slightly less paradoxical in Greek than in English.

3   *Ouranos did ... him for it*   Ouranos represented the sky or heaven. He was both the son and husband of Gaia, the earth. Gaia, in revenge for his having imprisoned their children, incited their leader Cronos to castrate him. The story of Ouranos and his castration by his son Cronos is told by Hesiod in *Theogony*, 154–210.

4   *if the deeds of Cronos ... were true*   Cronos, having castrated his father, became ruler of the universe, but was murdered by his son Zeus, who took over his rule. For the birth of Zeus and his revenge on his father Cronos see *Theogony*, 453–506.

No by Zeus, he said, I myself do not think these things are fit to be told.

Nor indeed, said I, any tales of gods warring and plot-
c ting and fighting against each other—these things are not true—if those who are to guard our city are to think it shameful to be easily driven to hate each other. Certainly stories of battles of giants must not be told nor embroidered, nor all the various stories of gods hating their kindred or friends. If we are to persuade our people that no citizen has ever hated another and that this is impious, then that is the kind of tale we should tell right away to small children, and to
d old men and women also, and to the middle-aged, and we must compel our poets to follow those guidelines. We shall not admit into our city stories about Hera being chained by her son, or of Hephaestus being hurled from heaven by his father when he intended to help his mother who was being beaten,[1] nor the battle of the gods in Homer, whether these stories are told allegorically or without allegory. The young cannot distinguish what is allegorical from what is not, and
e the beliefs they acquire at that age are hard to expunge and usually remain unchanged. That may be the reason why it is most important that the first stories they hear should be well told and dispose them to virtue.

That is reasonable, he said, but if someone were to ask us what these stories are, what should we say?

379 I answered: You and I, Adeimantus, are not poets now, but we are founding a city, and it is proper that founders should know the general lines which the poets must follow in telling their stories. These lines they will not be allowed to cross. We are not to compose their poems for them.

Correct, he said, but on this very point, what would be the general lines about the gods?

Something like this, I said: the god must always be represented as he is, whether in epic, lyric, or tragedy.

That must be.
b Now the god is good in truth and must be so presented.

What then?

Surely nothing good is harmful, or is it?

I don't think so.

And what is not harmful does no harm?

Not ever.

Does what does no harm work any evil?

No.

And what works no evil could not be the cause of evil.

How could it?

Further, the good is beneficial.

Yes.

It is the cause of well-being.

Yes.

The good then is not the cause of all things, but of good only; it is guiltless of evils.

I agree entirely.
c Neither is the god, since he is good, the cause of all things, as the many say, but of only a few things for men, of many he is guiltless. For good things are fewer than bad things in our life. For the good things no one else is responsible, but for evil things we must find some other cause, not the god.

I think what you say is very true.
d Therefore we shall not accept from Homer or any other this foolish mistake about the gods when he says:

There are two urns by the threshold of Zeus
one filled with good, the other with evil fates....

and the man to whom Zeus grants a mixture of these two

at one time meets with evil, at another with good

but the one who is given purely from the second urn,

evil famine drives him over the goodly earth,[2]
e nor shall we grant that Zeus is for us

of evil and good the distributor.

And if anyone tells us that the breaking of oaths and truce as Pandarus broke them, was brought about by Athena and Zeus we shall not approve, nor that the quarrel and judgment came about through Themis[3] and Zeus. Again, we
380 must not allow our youth to hear the words of Aeschylus:

a god makes mortals guilty
when he wants utterly to destroy a house.

---

1 *Hera being chained ... being beaten* Hera, wife of Zeus, rejected her son Hephaestus; in revenge, Hephaestus made a throne for her which bound her with invisible chains. Zeus threw him down to earth from Mount Olympus after he sided with Hera in an argument.

2 *There are two urns ... goodly earth* All three quotations are from *Iliad* 24, 527–32, but for the following the reference is unknown, as it is for the quotation from Aeschylus. The story of Athena urging Pandarus to break the truce is told in *Iliad* 4, 73–126.

3 *Themis* Daughter of Gaia and Ouranus in Greek mythology and embodiment of divine order, law and custom.

And if anyone composes a poem in which these lines occur, or the sufferings of Niobe,[1] or the fate of the house of Pelops,[2] or the Trojan tale,[3] or anything else of that kind, we must allow him to say either that these are not the work of a god or, if they are, then the poets must find the kind of explanation we are seeking, and say that the actions of the god are good and just, and that those who receive punishment are benefited thereby. We shall not allow the poet to say that those who pay the penalty are wretched and that it was a god who did this. If, on the other hand, they say that the wicked are wretched because they stand in need of punishment, and that in paying the penalty they are benefited by the gods, that we must allow. But to say that the god, himself good, is the cause of evil for anyone, that we shall fight in every way, and we shall not allow anyone to say it in his own city, if it is to be well governed, nor must anyone hear it said, neither young nor old, neither in verse or prose. It is impious to say these things; they do us no good, and they are inconsistent with themselves.

I like your law, he said, and I will vote for it.

This then is one of the rules and guidelines about the gods within which speakers must speak and poets compose, that the god is not the cause of all things but only of the good.

That is very satisfactory.

What about this second rule? Do you think that the god is a sorcerer, able to appear in different forms at different times, at times as himself yet changing his appearance into different shapes, sometimes deceiving us and making us think him different, or that he has one single form and is least likely to step out of it?

I cannot say offhand, he said.

What about this? Must he not, if he step out of his own form, be changed either of his own volition, or by another's?

Necessarily.

Now the best things are least liable to change or alteration. For example, the body by food or drink or labor, or any plant by sunshine and wind and the like; does not the healthiest and strongest change least?

Of course.

The strongest and most knowledgeable soul would be least disturbed and changed by any outside experience.

Yes.

So with all artifacts, furniture, and houses and clothes, those which are well made and good are least changed by time or anything else that happens to them.

That is so.

Anything then which is in good condition, either by nature or as the product of a craft, or both, is least changed by anything else.

That is likely.

Surely the god, and all that is his, are in every way best?

Of course.

Then the god would be the least likely to have many shapes.

Least of all.

Would he change and alter himself?

Clearly he does, if he changes at all.

Would he change himself into something better and more beautiful, or into something worse and uglier than himself?

The change must be for the worse, he said, if there is change, for we shall not say that the god is deficient in beauty or virtue.

Quite correct, I said, and do you think, Adeimantus, that anyone who was in such a perfect state, be he man or god, would deliberately make himself in any way worse?

Impossible.

It is then impossible, said I, for a god to want to change himself, but being, as is fitting, each of them as far as is possible best and most beautiful, he remains always simply in his own form.

That seems to me quite inevitable.

Then, my dear sir, I said, let no poet tell us that

> like unto strangers from every land
> the gods in various shapes frequent our towns[4]

nor tell us lies abut Proteus and Thetis; neither in their tragedies nor other poems bring on Hera in altered form, as a priestess begging for

---

1 *the sufferings of Niobe* After she boasted about her superiority to the goddess Leto (because she had more children than Leto did) the gods killed all fourteen of her children. Her mourning made her a conventional symbol for suffering.

2 *fate of the house of Pelops* Pelops, a mortal, was killed by his father Tantalus as a sacrifice to the gods, who detected the plot and brought him back to life. Various horrible disasters attended his own life and extended through his family down to his great-grandchildren (who included Agamemnon and Orestes).

3 *Trojan tale* The story of the Trojan War (told in Homer's *Iliad*.)

4 *Then, my dear ... our towns* The quotation is from Homer, *Odyssey* 17, 485–86.

the life-giving sons of the river, Argive Inachus,[1]

e   and many other such lies they must not tell. Nor must our mothers, believing them, terrify their children by telling bad stories, saying that some gods wander at night in the shape of strangers from many lands. These stories slander the gods, and at the same time make children more cowardly.

They must not be told.

Or do the gods themselves, though unable to change, make us believe that they appear in many forms, thus deceiving and beguiling us?

Perhaps.

382   How so? said I. Would a god be willing to lie, either in word or deed, by projecting a false appearance?

I do not know.

Do you not know, I said, that the true lie, if one may call it so, is hated by all gods and men?

What do you mean?

I mean this, I said: no one is willing to speak untruth with the most important part of himself about the most important subjects, but of all things he is most afraid to have untruth in that part.

I still do not understand, he said.

b   You think, I said, that I am saying something mysterious. I mean to lie and to be in a state of untruth about reality in one's soul, to be ignorant, and there to have and to hold untruth. This is what men most want to avoid, and they hate this state of soul most.

Quite so.

Surely, as I said just now, this would most correctly be called the true lie, the ignorance in the soul of the man who has been deceived. The verbal lie is a mere reflection of that which exists in the soul, a reflection of it which comes later,

c   and is not completely untrue. Is that not so?

Certainly.

And the real lie is hated not only by the gods, but also by men.

I think so.

What about the verbal lie? When and to whom is it useful and not deserving hatred? Is it not useful against one's enemies and those of one's so-called friends who, through madness or ignorance, are attempting to do some wrong, in order to turn them away from it? The lie then becomes

d   useful, like a drug. It is also useful in the case of those stories we mentioned just now, because of our ignorance of what

truly happened of old. We then make the fiction as like the truth as we can, and so make the lie or untruth useful.

That certainly is the case.

In which of these ways can the lie be useful to the god? Is it because of his ignorance of the past, making fiction as like truth as possible?

That would be ridiculous.

There is nothing of the fictional poet in the god?

I do not think so.

Would he lie for fear of his enemies?

Far from it.

e   Because of the ignorance or madness of his kindred?

None of the foolish or mad are friends of the gods, he said.

There is then no reason for the god to lie.

None.

Therefore the divine and the godlike do not lie at all.

Not at all.

The god then is simple and true in word and deed; he does not change himself nor deceive others, either by images or by words or by sending signs, either in visions or in dreams.

That is what I thought, he said, even as you spoke.   383

You agree then that this is our second rule according to which one should speak or compose poetry about the gods, that neither are they sorcerers who change, nor do they mislead us by lies in word or deed?

I agree.

We praise many things in Homer, but we will not approve of the dream which Zeus sent to Agamemnon,[2] nor of Aeschylus when he makes Thetis say that Apollo prophesied in song at her wedding the good fortune of her offspring: b

their long lives of disease quite free,
and my good fortunes pleasing to the gods,
he sang a paean and encouraged me.
I hoped the lips of Phoebus[3] would be truthful
those divine lips, with prophecy endowed.
Himself he sang, was present at the feast,
himself he said this, yet himself it is,
this same god, who killed my child.[4]

---

1   *Inachus*   Father of Io, who was persecuted by Hera, but the part of the story here referred to is unknown.

2   *dream ... Agamemnon*   In the second book of the *Iliad* Zeus sends a dream to Agamemnon to promise him success if he attacks Troy now. The promise is a lie.

3   *Phoebus*   Synonym for Apollo (Phoebus Apollo).

4   *their long ... child*   From an unknown play of Aeschylus. The point of the quotation is that Achilles, the son of Thetis, died very young, and Apollo's promise was false.

c Whenever anyone says such things about a god, we shall be angry and refuse him a chorus,[1] nor allow his poetry to be used in the education of the young, if our guardians are to be god-fearing and godlike, as far as man can be.

I altogether agree with these rules, he said, and I would make them into laws.

from Book 3

...

Shall we choose as our next topic of discussion which [...] men shall rule,[2] and which be ruled?

412c   Why not?

Now it is obvious that the rulers must be older men and that the younger must be ruled.

Obviously.

And that the rulers must be the best of them?

That too.

The best farmers are those who have to the highest degree the qualities required for farming?

Yes.

Now as the rulers must be the best among the guardians, they must have to the highest degree the qualities required to guard the city?

Yes.

And for this they must be intelligent, able, and also care for the city?

d   That is so.

Now one cares most for that which one loves.

Necessarily.

And one loves something most when one believes that what is good for it is good for oneself, and that when it is doing well the same is true of oneself, and so with the opposite.

Quite so, he said.

We must therefore select from among our guardians those who, as we test them, hold throughout their lives to
e the belief that it is right to pursue eagerly what they believe

---

1   *refuse him a chorus*   Deny him the funding to put on his play.
2   *which ... men shall rule*   This is the first appearance of the rulers who are to be chosen from the guardians and further tested and educated (414a and Books 6 and 7). There was an earlier mention of rulers at 389c, but there they were not said to be a special group of guardians which they now become—in fact the most important group in the state. The rest of the guardians are now to be considered their helpers or auxiliaries and are to carry out their orders.

---

to be to the advantage of the city, and who are in no way willing to do what is not.

Yes, for they are good men.

I think we must observe them at all ages to see whether they are guardians of this principle, and make sure that they cannot be tempted or forced to discard or forget the belief that they must do what is best for the city.

What, he said, do you mean by discarding?

I will tell you, I said. I think the discarding of a belief is either voluntary or involuntary; voluntary when the belief is false, and as a result of learning one changes one's mind,   413 involuntary when the belief is true.

I understand the voluntary discarding, but not the involuntary.

Really? Do you not think that men are unwilling to be deprived of good things, but willingly deprived of bad things? Is not untruth and missing the truth a bad thing, while to be truthful is good? And is not to have a true opinion to be truthful?

You are right, he said, and people are unwilling to be deprived of a true opinion.

But they can be so deprived by theft, or compulsion,   b or under a spell?

I do not understand even now.

I fear I must be talking like a tragic poet! I apply the word "theft" to those who change their mind or those who forget, not realizing that time or argument has robbed them of their belief. Do you understand now?

Yes.

By compulsion I mean those whom pain or suffering causes to change their mind.

That too I understand and you are right.

Those under a spell I think you would agree are those   c who change their mind because they are bewitched by pleasure or fear.

It seems to me, he said, that anything which deceives bewitches.

As I said just now, we must find out who are the best guardians of their belief that they must always do whatever they think to be in the best interest of the city. We must keep them under observation from childhood and set them tasks which would most easily lead one to forget this belief, or to be deceived. We must select the one who keeps on remembering and is not easily deceived, the other we will   d reject. Do you agree?

Yes.

We must also subject them to labors, sufferings, and contests in which to observe this.

Right.

Then, I said, for the third kind we must observe how they face bewitchment. Like those who lead colts into noise and tumult to see if they are fearful, so we must expose our young to fears and pleasures to test them, much more thoroughly than one tests gold in fire, and see whether a guardian is hard to bewitch and behaves well in all circumstances as a good guardian of himself and of the cultural education he has received, always showing himself a gracious and harmonious personality, the best man for himself and for the city. The one who is thus tested as a child, as a youth, and as an adult, and comes out of it untainted, is to be made a ruler as well as a guardian. He is to be honored both in life and after death and receive the most esteemed rewards in the form of tombs and memorials. The one who does not prove himself in this way is to be rejected. It seems to me, Glaucon, I said, that rulers and guardians must be selected and established in some such way as this, to speak in a general way and not in exact detail.

I also think it must be done in some such way.

These are the men whom it is most correct to call proper guardians, so that the enemies without shall not have the power, and their friends within shall not have the desire, to harm the city. Those young men whom we have called guardians hitherto we shall call auxiliaries to help the rulers in their decisions.

I agree.

What device could we find to make our rulers, or at any rate the rest of the city, believe us if we told them a noble fiction, one of those necessary untruths of which we have spoken?

What kind of fiction?

Nothing new, I said, but a Phoenician story which the poets say has happened in many places and made people believe them; it has not happened among us, though it might, and it will take a great deal of persuasion to have it believed.

You seem hesitant to tell your story, he said.

When you hear it you will realize that I have every reason to hesitate.

Speak without fear.

This is the story—yet I don't know that I am bold enough to tell it or what words I shall use. I shall first try to persuade the rulers and the soldiers, and then the rest of the city, that the upbringing and the education we gave them, and the experience that went with them, were a dream as it were, that in fact they were then being fashioned and

nurtured inside the earth, themselves and their weapons and their apparel. Then, when they were quite finished, the earth, being their mother, brought them out into the world. So even now they must take counsel for, and defend, the land in which they live as their mother and nurse, if someone attacks it, and they must think of their fellow-citizens as their earth-born brothers.

It is not for nothing that you were shy, he said, of telling your story.

Yes, I said, I had very good reason. Nevertheless, hear the rest of the tale. "All of you in the city are brothers" we shall tell them as we tell our story, "but the god who fashioned you mixed some gold in the nature of those capable of ruling because they are to be honored most. In those who are auxiliaries he has put silver, and iron and bronze in those who are farmers and other workers. You will for the most part produce children like yourselves but, as you are all related, a silver child will occasionally be born from a golden parent, and vice versa, and all the others from each other. So the first and most important command of the god to the rulers is that there is nothing they must guard better or watch more carefully than the mixture in the souls of the next generation. If their own offspring should be found to have iron or bronze in his nature, they must not pity him in any way, but give him the esteem appropriate to his nature; they must drive him out to join the workers and farmers. Then again, if an offspring of these is found to have gold or silver in his nature they will honor him and bring him up to join the rulers or guardians, for there is an oracle that the city will be ruined if ever it has an iron or bronze guardian. Can you suggest any device which will make our citizens believe this story?

I cannot see any way, he said, to make them believe it themselves, but the sons and later generations might, both theirs and those of other men.

Even that, I said, would help to make them care more for their city and each other, for I do understand what you mean. But let us leave this matter to later tradition. Let us now arm our earthborn and lead them forth with their rulers in charge. And as they march let them look for the best place in the city to have their camp, a site from which they could most easily control those within, if anyone is unwilling to obey the laws, and ward off any outside enemy who came like a wolf upon the flock. When they had established their camp and made the right sacrifices, let them see to their sleeping quarters, or what do you suggest?

I agree.

These must protect them adequately both in winter and summer.

Of course, he said, you mean their dwellings.

Yes, I said, dwellings for soldiers, not for money-makers.

416 What would you say is the difference? he asked.

I will try to tell you, I said. The most terrible and shameful thing for a shepherd is to train his dogs, who should help the flocks, in such a way that, through lack of discipline or hunger or bad habit, those very dogs maltreat the animals and behave like wolves rather than dogs.

Quite true.

b We must therefore take every precaution to see that our auxiliaries, since they are the stronger, do not behave like that toward the citizens, and become cruel masters instead of kindly allies.

We must watch this.

And a really good education would endow them with the greatest caution in this regard?

But surely they have had that.

And I said: Perhaps we should not assert this dogmatically, my dear Glaucon. What we can assert is what we were c saying just now, that they must have the correct education, whatever that is, in order to attain the greatest degree of gentleness toward each other and toward those whom they are protecting.

Right.

Besides this education, an intelligent man might say that they must have the amount of housing and of other property which would not prevent them from being the d best guardians and would not encourage them to maltreat the other citizens.

That would be true.

Consider then, said I, whether they should live in some such way as this if they are to be the kind of men we described: First, not one of them must possess any private property beyond what is essential. Further, none of them should have a house or a storeroom which anyone who wishes is not permitted to enter. Whatever moderate and e courageous warrior-athletes require will be provided by taxation upon the other citizens as a salary for their guardianship, no more and no less than they need over the year. They will have common messes and live together as soldiers in a camp. We shall tell them that the gold and silver they always have in their nature as a gift from the gods makes the possession of human gold unnecessary, indeed that it is impious for them to defile this divine possession by any admixture of the human kind of gold, because many an impious deed is committed in connection with the currency 417 of the majority, and their own must remain pure. For them alone among the city's population it is unlawful to touch or handle gold or silver; they must not be under the same roof with it, or wear any, or drink from gold or silver goblets; in this way they may preserve themselves and the city. If they themselves acquire private land and houses and currency, they will be household managers and farmers instead of guardians, hostile masters of the other citizens instead of b their allies; they will spend their whole life hating and being hated, plotting and being plotted against; they will be much more afraid of internal than of external enemies, and they will rush themselves and their city very close to ruin. For all these reasons, I said, let us say that the guardians must be provided with housing and other matters in this way, and these are the laws we shall establish.

Certainly, said Glaucon.

from Book 4

Adeimantus took up the argument and said: What defense, 419 Socrates, would you offer against the charge that you are not making your guardians very happy, and that through their own fault? The city is really in their power, yet they derive no good from this. Others own land, build grand and beautiful houses, acquire furnishings appropriate to them, make their own private sacrifices to the gods, entertain, also, as you mentioned just now, have gold and silver and all the possessions which are thought to belong to people who will be happy. One might well say that your guardians are simply settled in the city like paid mercenaries, with nothing to do but to watch over it. 420

Yes, said I. Moreover, they work for their keep and get no extra wages as the others do, so that if they want to leave the city privately they cannot do so; they have nothing to give their mistresses, nothing to spend in whatever other way they wish, as men do who are considered happy. You have omitted these and other such things from the charge.

Let these accusations be added, he said.

Now you ask what defense we shall offer? b

Yes.

I think we shall discover what to say if we follow the same path as before, I said. We shall say that it would not be at all surprising if these men too were very happy. In any case, in establishing our city, we are not aiming to make any one group outstandingly happy, but to make the whole city so, as far as possible. We thought that in such a city we would most easily find justice, find injustice in a badly governed one, and then decide what we have been looking for all the time. Now we think we are fashioning the happy city not by separating a few people in it and making them happy, but by making the whole city so. We shall look at the opposite kind of city presently. If someone came to us while we were painting a statue and objected because we did not apply the finest colors to the finest parts of the body, for the eyes are the most beautiful part, and they are not made purple but black, we should appear to offer a reasonable defense if we said: "My good sir, do not think that we must make the eyes so beautiful that they no longer appear to be eyes at all, and so with the other parts, but look to see whether by dealing with each part appropriately we are making the whole statue beautiful." And so now, do not force us to give our guardians the kind of happiness which would make them anything but guardians.

We know how to clothe our farmers too in purple robes, surround them with gold and tell them to work the land at their pleasure, and how to settle our potters on couches by the fire, feasting and passing the wine, put their wheel by them and tell them to make pots as much as they want; we know how to make all the others also happy in the same way, so that the whole city is happy. Do not exhort us to do this, however. If we do, the farmer will not be a farmer, nor the potter a potter; nor would anyone else fulfill any of the functions which make up the state. For the others this is less important: if shoemakers become inferior and corrupt, and claim to be what they are not, the state is not in peril, but, if the guardians of our laws and city only appear to be guardians and are not, you surely see that they destroy the city utterly, as they alone have the opportunity to govern it well and to make it happy.

If then we are making true guardians who are least likely to work wickedness upon the city, whereas our accuser makes some farmers into banqueters, happy as at some festival but not in a city, he would be talking about something else than a city. We should examine then, with this in mind, whether our aim in establishing our guardians should be to give them the greatest happiness, or whether we should in this matter look to the whole city and see how its greatest happiness can be secured. We must compel and persuade the auxiliaries and the guardians to be excellent performers of their own task, and so with all the others. As the whole city grows and is well governed, we must leave it to nature to provide each group with its share of happiness.

I think, he said, that you put that very well.

Will you also, said I, think that I speak reasonably when I make the next point which is closely akin to this?

What is that?

Consider whether these factors corrupt the other workers also, so that they become bad at their job?

What factors?

Wealth, I said, and poverty.

How do you mean?

Like this. Do you think that a potter who has become wealthy will still be willing to pay attention to his craft?

Not in any way.

He will become more idle and careless than he was?

Much.

And therefore become a worse potter?

Far worse.

And surely if poverty prevents him having the tools or anything else his craft needs, he will produce poorer work, and his sons or any others he may teach will not be as good workers.

Of course.

So both poverty and wealth make the products of the crafts worse, and the craftsmen too.

Apparently.

We have, it seems, found other dangers against which our guardians must guard most carefully, lest these should penetrate the city unnoticed.

What are these?

Both wealth and poverty, I said. The former makes for luxury, idleness, and political change, the latter for meanness, bad work, and change as well.

That is certainly true, he said, but please consider this point, Socrates: how will our city be able to fight a war, since it has not acquired wealth, especially if it has to fight against a mighty and wealthy opponent?

Obviously, I said, it will be harder to fight one such city than two.

How do you mean? said he.

First of all, said I, if they must fight, will they not be fighting as warrior-athletes against rich men?

As far as that goes, yes.

Well then, Adeimantus, I said, do you not think that one boxer who has had the best possible training could easily fight two rich and fat non-boxers?

Perhaps not at the same time.

Not even, said I, if he could run off and then turn round and hit the one close to him, and did this again and again in the stifling heat of the sun? Would he not be able, in his condition, to tackle even more than two?

That would certainly not be surprising.

And do you not think that the rich have more knowledge and experience of boxing than of fighting in war?

I do.

Our athletes would then most likely be able to fight with ease twice or three times their own numbers.

I will agree with you, for I think you are talking sense.

d What if they sent envoys to the other city and said, which is the truth: "We have no use for gold or silver and it is not lawful for us to possess them, but you can. So join us in this war and make the other side's possessions your own." Do you think that any people on hearing this would choose to fight against hardened and spare dogs rather than, with the dogs on their side, fight against sleek and soft sheep?

e No, I do not think so, he said, but if the wealth of the others came to be gathered together in one city, take care that this does not imperil your non-wealthy city.

You are fortunate, I said, if you think that any other city than the kind we are founding deserves the name.

What do you mean?

We must find a grander name for the others, as each of them is a cluster of cities, not one city, as they say in the 423 game.[1] Each of them, in any case, consists of two hostile cities, that of the poor and that of the rich, and each of these contains many. It would be a grave mistake to approach them as one, but if you approach them as many and give the possessions of one to the other, their wealth, their power, and even their persons, you will always have many allies and few enemies. As long as your city is governed with moderation as we have just established it, it will itself have greatness. I do not mean great repute but true greatness, even if it have only one thousand men to fight for it. You will not easily find one great city in this sense either among Greeks b or barbarians, though you will find a very large number that are thought to be great. Do you think differently?

By Zeus no.

This then would be the best limitation which our guardians should put upon the size of the city; they should then mark off the amount of land required for its size, and let the rest go.

What is this limitation?

I think, I said, that it is this: to let the city grow as long as it is willing to retain its unity, but not beyond that point.

Quite right.

c This then is another order we shall give our guardians: to watch most carefully that the city should not appear either small or big, but sufficient, and remain one.

This, he said, is indeed an easy order we shall give them!

Even easier than that, I said, is the one we mentioned before when we said that, if an offspring of the guardians is inferior, he must be sent off to join the other citizens, d and if the others have an able offspring, he must be taken into the guardian group. This was meant to make clear that the other citizens must each be directed to the one task for which each is naturally fitted, so that he should pursue that one task which is his own and be himself one person and not many, and the city itself be a unity and not a plurality.

That is an even easier order than the other!

These orders we give them, my good Adeimantus, I said, are not, as one might think, either numerous or important; they are all secondary, provided that they guard the e one great thing, as people say, though rather than great I would call it sufficient.

What is that?

Their education and their upbringing, I said. If they become cultured, moderate men, they will easily see these things for themselves, and other things too which we are now omitting, the acquiring of wives and children which must all accord with the old proverb, that the possessions of 424 friends must be held in common.[2]

That would be the best way.

Surely, I said, once our city gets a good start, it would go on growing in a circle. Good education and upbringing, if preserved, will lead to men of a better nature, and these in turn, if they cling to their education, will improve with each generation both in other respects and also in their children, just like other animals.

b Quite likely.

---

1   *as they say in the game*   The reference is obscure; it may be to an unknown saying or proverb, or to a game like checkers, where the pieces on each side, or perhaps any cluster of pieces, was called a *polis* or city, while the separate pieces were called dogs.

2   *the acquiring ... the best way*   The subject of marriage and children, here so lightly passed over, is fully dealt with in the fifth book.

Well, son of Ariston, I said, your city might now be said
427d to be established. The next step is for you to look inside it
with what light you can procure, to call upon your brother
and Polemarchus and the others, if we can somehow see
where justice resides in it, and where injustice, what the
difference is between them, and which of the two the man
who intends to be happy should possess, whether gods and
men recognize it or not.

Nonsense, said Glaucon. You promised to look for
them yourself because, you said it was impious for you not
e to come to the rescue of justice in every way you could.

True, I said, as you remind me; I must do so, but you
must help.

We will, he said.

I hope to find it, I said, in this way. I think our city, if it
is rightly founded, is completely good.

Necessarily so, he said.

Clearly then it is wise, brave, moderate, and just?[1]

Clearly.

Therefore whichever of these we find in the city, the rest
will be what we have not found?

428   You mean?

As with any four things, if we were looking for any one
of them in anything, if we first recognize it, that would be
enough, but if we recognize the other three first, then by
that very fact we recognize what we are looking for. For
clearly it can be no other than what is left.

Correct, he said.

So with these, since there are four, we must look for
them in the same way.

Obviously.

Now the first of them which I believe to be clear is wis-
b dom; and there seems to be something strange about it.

What is that? he said.

I think that the city which we have described is wise in
fact because it has sound judgment, is it not so?

Yes.

Now this very thing, sound judgment, is clearly some
kind of knowledge, for it is through knowledge, not ignorance, that people judge soundly.

Clearly.

There are many kinds of knowledge in the city.

Of course.

Would we call the city wise and sound in judgment
because of the knowledge of its carpenters?

Never through that, he said; we would then call it c
sound in carpentry.

Nor through the knowledge by which it judges which
wooden furniture is best would we call the city wise.

No indeed.

Nor because of its knowledge of brazen[2] things or of
any similar things?

Not through any of them.

Nor through the knowledge of how to raise a harvest
from the earth, but then we should call it agricultural.

I think so.

Well then, I said, is there some knowledge in the city we
have just founded and among some of the citizens, which
does not deliberate about any particular matter but about d
the city as a whole, how best to maintain good relations
both internally and with other cities?

There is.

What is this knowledge, I asked, and in whom does it
reside?

It is the knowledge of guardianship, he said, and it resides in those rulers whom just now we named the complete
guardians.

Then what does this knowledge entitle us to call the
city?

Really wise, he said, and of good judgment.

Do you think, I asked, that the metal-workers or these
true guardians are the more numerous in our city?

The metal-workers, he said, by far.

Of all those who are called by a certain name because
they have some knowledge, the guardians would be the least
numerous?

They are by far the fewest.

Then a whole city which is established according to nature would be wise because of the smallest group or part of
itself, the commanding or ruling group. This group seems
to be the smallest by nature and to it belongs a share in 429
that knowledge which, alone of them all, must be called
wisdom.

What you say is very true, he said.

We have now found, I don't know how, this to be itself
one of the four, and also where in the city it resides.

Our way of finding it, he said, seems good enough to
me.

---

1   *wise, brave, moderate, and just* The doctrine of the four cardinal
virtues is often met with in Plato. It seems to be referred to here as
well known. *Hosiotês* or piety is often added to the list.

2   *brazen* Made of brass.

It is surely not very difficult to see courage itself, through which the city is to be called brave, and where in the city it is to be found.

How?

b Who, I said, when calling the city cowardly or brave, would look anywhere else but to that part of it which makes war and campaigns on its behalf?

No one, he said, would look anywhere else.

I do not think, I said, that whether the other citizens were cowardly or brave would cause the city to be called one or the other.

It would not.

The city then is brave because of a part of itself which has the capacity always to preserve its belief about things c to be feared, that they are those things and those kinds of things which the lawgiver declared to be such in the course of their education. Or don't you call that courage?

I do not, he said, quite understand what you mean. Please repeat it.

I mean, said I, that courage is a kind of preservation.

What kind?

The preservation of the belief which has been inculcated by the law through one's education as to what things and what kinds of things are to be feared, and by always I meant to preserve this belief and not to lose it when one is in pain, d beset by pleasures and desires, and by fears. I will, if you like, make clear what I think this resembles by a simile.

I should like you to do so.

You know, I said, that dyers who want to dye wool purple, first of all pick out from many colors the natural white, and then prepare this in a number of ways so that it will absorb the color as well as possible, and only then dye e it. In what is dyed in this way the color is fast; no washing with or without soap can take it away. You also know what becomes of material which has not been dyed in this way, whether someone dyes it other colors or does not prepare the wool beforehand.

I know, he said, that it looks washed out and ridiculous.

Understand then, I said, that, as far as we could, we were doing something similar when we were selecting our 430 soldiers and were educating them in the arts and physical culture. What we were in fact contriving was that, in obeying us, they should absorb the laws most beautifully like a dye, so that, as they had the right nature and the proper education, their belief as to what they should fear and so on should become fast and that the detergents which are

extremely effective should not wash it out: pleasure, which is much more potent than any powder or soda or soap, and b pain, and fear and appetite. Now this capacity to preserve through everything the right and lawful belief as to what is to be feared and what is not, this is what I call and define as courage, unless you say otherwise.

I have, he said, nothing to say, for I assume that the right opinion about these same things which is not the result of education, such as you find in animals and slaves, you do not consider to be inculcated by law, and you do not call it courage but something else.

Very true, I said.

Then I accept your description of courage.

Accept also, I said, that it is civic courage,[1] and your acceptance will be sound. We shall discuss this subject more fully some other time, if you want to, but it is not the object of our investigation; justice is, and for that purpose I think this is sufficient.

You are quite right, he said.

There are now two qualities left for us to find in the city: moderation and that at which our whole investigation d is aimed, justice.

Quite so.

How could we find justice, so that we need not bother with moderation[2] any further?

I do not know, he said, and I should not want it to appear first, if that means that we do not investigate moderation. If you want to please me, look for moderation before the other.

I am certainly willing, I said; it would be wrong not e to be.

Look then.

We must do so, I said. Looked at from here, it is more like a consonance or harmony than the others we have considered hitherto.

How?

Moderation is a certain orderliness, I said, and mastery over certain pleasures and appetites, as people somehow

---

1   *civic courage*   In restricting courage here to civic or political courage, Plato seems to have in mind that the courage of the guardians, or at least of the auxiliaries, is based on habit and opinion only, not on knowledge, as is that of the philosopher; the mention of further discussion indicates that this should be clarified. We find such a distinction and clarification in the *Phaedo* 82b ff.

2   *moderation*   The Greek word translated as moderation is *sôphrosunê*. It has a very wide meaning: self-control, temperance, reasonableness, in some contexts chastity. Etymologically it seems to mean a man who remains equable under strain.

indicate by using the phrase self-control and other expressions which give a clue to its nature. Is that not so?

Most certainly.

Yet the expression self-control is laughable, for the controller of self and the self that is weaker and controlled is the
431 same person, and so with all those expressions. It is the same person that is referred to.

Of course.

But, I said, the expression seems to want to indicate that in the soul of the man himself there is a better and a worse part; whenever what is by nature the better part is in control of the worse, this is expressed by saying that the man is self-controlled or master of himself, and this is a term of praise. When, on the other hand, the smaller and better part, because of poor upbringing or bad company, is overpowered by the larger and worse, this is made a re-
b proach and called being defeated by oneself, and a man in that situation is called uncontrolled.

Properly so.

Look now, I said, at our new city and you will find one of those alternatives in it. You will say that it is rightly called self-controlled, since that in which the better rules the worse should be called moderate and self-controlled.

I am looking at it, and what you say is true.

Further, one would mostly find many and various ap-
c petites and pleasures of all kinds as well as pains in children and women and household slaves, and in the many and the inferior among those called free men.

Quite so.

But those that are simple and measured and directed by reasoning with intelligence and right belief you will meet with in but few people who are the best by nature and the best educated.

True.

You will see this also in your city; there the desires of the
d inferior many are controlled by the desires and the knowledge of the fewer and better?

I do indeed.

If any city is to be called in control of its pleasures and desires and of itself, this city is.

Most certainly.

And will it not be called moderate in all these respects?

Definitely.

Further, if the same opinion exists in any city among
e the rulers and also the ruled as to who should rule, it will be found in this city, do you not think?

Definitely.

And when that is the case, in which of the two kinds of citizens will you say that moderation exists, among the rulers or the ruled?

Among both, I suppose.

You see now how right we were to foresee that moderation resembles a kind of harmony?

How so?

Because, unlike courage and wisdom, each of which resided in one part of the city and made it, the one brave,   432
the other wise, moderation spreads throughout the whole, among the weakest and the strongest and those who are in between, be it in regard to knowledge or, if you wish, in physical strength or in numbers or in wealth or in anything else, and it makes them all sing the same tune. This unanimity would rightly be called moderation, agreement, that is, between the naturally worse and the naturally better as to which of the two must rule, both in the city and in each individual.

I quite agree.   b

Very well, I said. We have now found three of the four in the city, as far as our present discussion takes us. What would the remaining kind be which still makes the city share in virtue? Or is it clear that this is justice?

Quite clear.

So now we must concentrate our attention like hunters surrounding a copse, lest justice escape us and vanish without our seeing it, for obviously it is somewhere around   c
here. Look eagerly, now, in case you see it before I do, and tell me.

I wish I could, he said, but you will make a more sensible use of me if you take me to be a follower who can see things when you point them out.

Follow then, I said, and join me in a prayer.

I will do that, but you lead.

Indeed, I said, the place seems impenetrable and full of shadows; it is certainly dark and hard to hunt in. However, go on we must.

We must indeed.   d

As I looked I exclaimed: Aha! Glaucon, it looks as if there was a track, and I don't think our prey will altogether escape us.

Good news.

Surely, I said, we are being stupid.

In what way?

My good friend, it seems to have been rolling about right in front of our feet for some time, in fact from the beginning, and we did not see it. This was quite ridiculous

of us. As people sometimes look for the very thing they are
e holding in their hands, so we paid no attention to it, but
were looking away in the distance, which accounts for our
not seeing it.

What do you mean?

I mean, I said, that we have been mentioning it, and
hearing it mentioned, for a long time without understanding ourselves that we were, in a way, speaking of it.

This is a long prelude for someone who is impatient
to hear.

Well, I said, listen whether I am talking sense. I think
433 that justice is the very thing, or some form of the thing
which, when we were beginning to found our city, we said
had to be established throughout. We stated, and often repeated, if you remember, that everyone must pursue one
occupation of those in the city, that for which his nature
best fitted him.

Yes, we kept saying that.

Further, we have heard many people say, and have often
said ourselves, that justice is to perform one's own task and
b not to meddle with that of others.

We have said that.

This then, my friend, I said, when it happens, is in some
way justice, to do one's own job. And do you know what I
take to be a proof of this?

No, tell me.

I think what is left over of those things we have been
investigating, after moderation and courage and wisdom
have been found, was that which made it possible for those
three qualities to appear in the city and to continue as long
c as it was present. We also said that what remained after we
found the other three was justice.

It had to be.

And surely, I said, if we had to decide which of the four
will make the city good by its presence, it would be hard to
judge whether it is a common belief among the rulers and
the ruled, or the preservation among the soldiers of a law-
inspired belief as to the nature of what is, and what is not,
d to be feared, or the knowledge and guardianship of the rulers, or whether it is, above all, the presence of this fourth in
child and woman, slave and free, artisan, ruler and subject,
namely that each man, a unity in himself, performed his
own task and was not meddling with that of others.

How could this not be hard to judge?

It seems then that the capacity for each in the city to
perform his own task rivals wisdom, moderation, and cour-
e age as a source of excellence for the city.

It certainly does.

You would then describe justice as a rival to them for
excellence in the city?

Most certainly.

Look at it this way and see whether you agree: you will
order your rulers to act as judges in the courts of the city?

Surely.

And will their exclusive aim in delivering judgment not
be that no citizen should have what belongs to another or
be deprived of what is his own?

That would be their aim.

That being just?

Yes.

In some way then possession of one's own and the performance of one's own task could be agreed to be justice.[1] 434

That is so.

Consider then whether you agree with me in this: if a
carpenter attempts to do the work of a cobbler, or a cobbler
that of a carpenter, and they exchange their tools and the
esteem that goes with the job, or the same man tries to do
both, and all the other exchanges are made, do you think
that this does any great harm to the city?

No.

But I think that when one who is by nature a worker
or some other kind of moneymaker is puffed up by wealth, b
or by the mob, or by his own strength, or some other such
thing, and attempts to enter the warrior class, or one of the
soldiers tries to enter the group of counselors and guardians,
though he is unworthy of it, and these exchange their tools
and the public esteem, or when the same man tries to perform all these jobs together, then I think you will agree that
these exchanges and this meddling bring the city to ruin.

They certainly do.

The meddling and exchange between the three established orders does very great harm to the city and would c
most correctly be called wickedness.

Very definitely.

And you would call the greatest wickedness worked
against one's own city injustice?

Of course.

---

1 *possession of ... be justice* The difference between moderation
and justice seems clear in the Greek. The city is moderate if each
group is satisfied with its position in the state, and they all agree
as to who should rule. Justice is more positive, it implies that each
group actually performs its function in the state. Moreover, those
who are dissatisfied with their own are likely to interfere with the
work which properly belongs to others.

That then is injustice. And let us repeat that the doing of one's own job by the moneymaking, auxiliary, and guardian groups, when each group is performing its own task in the city, is the opposite, it is justice and makes the city just.

d   I agree with you that this is so.

Do not let us, I said, take this as quite final yet. If we find that this quality, when existing in each individual man, is agreed there too to be justice, then we can assent to this—for what can we say?—but if not, we must look for something else. For the present, let us complete that examination which we thought we should make, that if we tried to observe justice in something larger which contains it, this would make it easier to observe it in the individual.

e We thought that this larger thing was a city, and so we established the best city we could, knowing well that justice would be present in the good city. It has now appeared to us there, so let us now transfer it to the individual and, if it corresponds, all will be well. But if it is seen to be something different in the individual, then we must go back to the city
435 and examine this new notion of justice. By thus comparing and testing the two, we might make justice light up like fire from the rubbing of firesticks, and when it has become clear, we shall fix it firmly in our own minds.

You are following the path we set, and we must do so.

Well now, when you apply the same name to a thing whether it is big or small, are these two instances of it like or unlike with regard to that to which the same name applies?

They are alike in that, he said.

b   So the just man and the just city will be no different but alike as regards the very form of justice.

Yes, they will be.

Now the city was thought to be just when the three kinds of men within it each performed their own task, and it was moderate and brave and wise because of some other qualities and attitudes of the same groups.

True.

And we shall therefore deem it right, my friend, that
c the individual have the same parts in his own soul, and through the same qualities in those parts will correctly be given the same names.

That must be so.

Once again, my good man, I said, we have come upon an easy inquiry whether the soul has these three parts or not!

It does not look easy to us, he said. Perhaps the old saying is true, that all fine things are difficult.

So it seems, said I. I want you to know, Glaucon, that in my opinion we shall certainly not attain any precise answer d by following our present methods. There is another longer and fuller way which leads to such an answer. However, this way is perhaps good enough to accord with our previous statements and inquiries.

Is it not satisfactory? he asked. It is enough for me at the present time.

And indeed, I said, it will quite satisfy me.

Do not weary, he said, but continue.

Well then, I said, we are surely compelled to agree that e each of us has within himself the same parts and characteristics as the city? Where else would they come from? It would be ridiculous for anyone to think that spiritedness has not come to be in the city from individuals who are held to possess it, like the inhabitants of Thrace and Scythia and others who live to the north of us, or that the same is not true of the love of learning which one would attribute most 436 to our part of the world, or the love of money which one might say is conspicuously displayed by the Phoenicians and the Egyptians.

Certainly, he said.

This then is the case, I said, and it is not hard to understand.

No indeed.

But this is: whether we do everything with the same part of our soul, or one thing with one of the three parts, and another with another. Do we learn with one part of ourselves, get angry with another, and with some third part desire the pleasures of food and procreation and other things closely akin to them, or, when we set out after something, b do we act with the whole of our soul in each case? This will be hard to determine satisfactorily.

I think so too.

Let us try to determine in this way whether these parts are the same or different.

How?

It is clear that one thing cannot act in opposite ways or be in opposite states at the same time and in the same part of itself in relation to the same other thing; so if we find this happening we shall know that we are not dealing with one thing but with several.

Be it so.

Examine then what I am about to say.

Say on.

Is it possible for the same thing to stand still and to move at the same time in the same part of itself?

In no way.

Let us go into this more precisely to avoid disagreements later on. If someone were to say that a man is standing still but moving his hands and his head, and that therefore he is moving and standing still at the same time, I think we would not deem that the proper way to put it, but that one part of him is standing still and another part is moving. Is not that the way to express it?

It is.

Then if our interlocutor carried the objection further, and was smart enough to say that whole spinning tops stand still and move at the same time for, while remaining in the same spot, they turn round their axis, and so with anything else moving in a circular motion while staying in the same place, we would not agree because the parts of them in respect to which they stand still and move are not the same. We should say that these objects have an axis and a circumference; in their axis they stand still, for they do not wobble in any way, and their circumference moves in a circle; then, when the axis inclines left or right, frontward or backward, while the top goes round, it is not still at all.

And we would be right.

No such statements shall disturb us or make us believe that anything, while remaining itself, can ever be affected, or be, or act, in opposite ways at the same time, in the same part of itself in relation to the same other object.

They will not make me believe it at any rate.

Nevertheless, I said, in order to avoid having to go through all these objections one by one and taking a long time proving them untrue, let us assume that it is so and carry on. We agree that if the matter should ever be shown to be otherwise, all the consequences we have drawn from it will also be invalidated.

We must do so.

Would you not, I said, consider all the following as pairs of opposites: assent and dissent, to want to have something and to deny oneself, to take something to oneself and to cast it off? Whether they are actions or passive states makes no difference in this respect.

They are opposites.

Further, I said, thirst and hunger and the appetites as a whole, then again inclination and willingness, would you not include all these among the class of things we were mentioning? Would you not say that the soul of one who desires something longs for the object of his desire, or wants to take to itself what he wants to have, or again, in so far as he wants to be provided with something, the soul nods assent to itself as if someone were questioning it, because it yearns for it to be?

Yes.

Then we would include among what is altogether the opposite of these: being unwilling, lacking desire, since these lead to driving away or casting off from the soul.

Of course.

That being so, we will say that there is a class of things named appetites and that the most obvious of these are hunger and thirst?

We agree.

One of these is for drink, the other for food?

Yes.

Now in so far as it is mere thirst, is it a desire in the soul for something more than what we mentioned? For example, is thirst a thirst for a hot drink or a cold drink, a long or a short one, or, in a word, is it for a drink of a certain kind? Or is it that if you feel hot as well as thirsty, this adds a desire for cold or, if you feel cold, for hot. If the desire is great because of the presence of quantity it will make it a desire for much, and if it is little, for a little one, but thirst itself is never for anything different from its natural object, drink unqualified, and so too with hunger, for food.

That's it, he said, each desire itself is only for its natural object in each case, and additional circumstances add the qualifications, that is, for such and such an object.

Do not let us be disturbed, I said, because we are unprepared for it, by someone saying that no one just wants a drink but a good drink, or any food but good food. All men want good things. So that if thirst is a desire, it will be a desire for good, be it a drink or anything else for which it is a desire, and so with the other desires.

Perhaps the man who says this has a point, he said.

But surely, I said, in the case of all things that are related to another, when the first is qualified by a predicate, the second is too, but each in itself is unqualified and directed to an unqualified object.

I do not understand.

You do not understand that the greater is such as to be greater than something?

Quite so.

It is greater than the smaller?

Yes.

And that which is much greater is related to something much smaller?

Yes.

And that which is sometimes greater is related to that which is sometimes smaller.

Certainly.

c   So is the more numerous to the less numerous, the double to the half, and so with all things of the kind, the heavier to the lighter, the swifter to the slower, also the hot to the cold, and all similar things. Is that not so?

Quite.

Then what about knowledge? Does the same apply? Knowledge itself is directed to the thing itself which is learned, or whatever one should say that knowledge is relat-

d   ed to, and, when knowledge is qualified, it is of a qualified object. I mean this: when knowledge is of building a house it is called building-knowledge?

Yes indeed.

And is this not qualified as no other knowledge is?

Yes.

So when it becomes knowledge of a certain object, it becomes a certain kind of knowledge, and this is true of all crafts and sciences?

That is so.

This is what I was wanting to say, I said, if you understand now. In a relation between two things, when the first is unqualified by a predicate, so is the second, and when the first is qualified by a predicate, the second is too. I do

e   not mean that the predicate need be the same for them both—for example, knowledge of health or disease is not healthy or diseased, or the knowledge of good and evil does not itself become good or evil—but that when knowledge is no longer of its simple object but a qualification is added to the object, it follows that the knowledge itself is qualified. It is then no longer simply called knowledge but is qualified, as in this case it becomes medical knowledge.

I understand and I think that it is so.

439   As for thirst, I said, would you not include it as something which in itself is related to something else? Thirst is related to ...

I know, to drink.

Therefore when a predicate is added to the drink, one is also added to the thirst, but in itself thirst is not for a long drink or a short one, a good drink or a bad one, in a word not for a qualified drink, but thirst in itself is by nature for a drink without any qualification.

Quite true.

The soul of the thirsty, in so far as he is thirsty, does not

b   want anything else, only to drink; this is what it longs for and sets out to get.

Obviously.

Therefore if anything pulls it back when it is thirsty, there must be a different part in the soul from the part that is thirsty and, like an animal, leads him to drink: for we say that the same thing cannot act in contrary ways with the same part of itself toward the same object at the same time.

It cannot.

Just as I think it wrong to say that a man's hands at the same time push the bow away and draw it toward him. One ought to say that one hand pushes it away and the other draws it toward him.

Most certainly one should.   c

Shall we say that there are times when thirsty people are not willing to drink?

Certainly it happens often and to many people.

What then, I said, should one say about this? Is there not in their soul that which bids them drink, and also that which prevents them, that the latter is different and over-rules the other part?

I think so, he said.

And the preventing part comes into play as a result of reasoning, whereas the impulses that lead and drag him are   d due to emotive states and diseases?

Apparently.

It is therefore not unreasonable for us to say that these are two distinct parts, to call that with which it reasons the rational part of the soul, and that with which it lusts and feels hungry and thirsty and gets excited with other desires the irrational and appetitive part, the companion of repletions and pleasures.

That is a natural way for us to think.   e

Let these two then be described as two parts existing in the soul. Now is the spirited part by which we get angry a third part, or is it of the same nature as either of the other two?

Perhaps it is like the appetitive part.

I have, I said, heard a story which I believe, that Leontius, the son of Aglaion, as he came up from the Piraeus on the outside of the northern wall, saw the executioner with some corpses lying near him. Leontius felt a strong desire to look at them,[1] but at the same time he was disgusted and turned away. For a time he struggled with himself and

---

1   *Leontius felt ... to look at them*   Another source suggests that Leontius was known for his sexual attraction to boys as pale as corpses.

440 covered his face, but then, overcome by his desire, pushing his eyes wide open and rushing toward the corpses: "Look for yourselves," he said, "you evil things, get your fill of the beautiful sight!"

I've heard that story myself.

It certainly proves, I said, that anger sometimes wars against the appetites as one thing against another.

It does.

Besides, I said, we often see this elsewhere, when his

b appetites are forcing a man to act contrary to reason, and he rails at himself and is angry with that within himself which is compelling him to do so; of the two civic factions at odds, as it were, the spirited part becomes the ally of reason. I do not think that you can say that when reason has decided that it must not be opposed, you have ever perceived the spirited part associating itself with the appetites, either in yourself or in anyone else.

No by Zeus I have not.

c What happens, I said, when anyone thinks he is doing wrong? Is it not true that the nobler a man is, the less he can resent it if he suffers hunger or cold or anything of that kind at the hands of one whom he believes to be inflicting this on him justly, and as I say, does not his spirited part refuse to be aroused?

True.

What if a man believes himself wronged? I asked. Is the spirit within him not boiling and angry, fighting for what he believes to be just? Will he not endure hunger and cold

d and such things and carry on till he wins out? and not cease from noble actions until he either wins out or dies, or, like a dog by his shepherd, is called to heel by the reason within himself and quieted down?

The spirit certainly behaves as you say, he said. Moreover, in our city, we made the auxiliaries, like dogs, obey the rulers, the shepherds of the city.

You understand very well, I said, what I want to convey. In addition, reflect on this further point.

e What point?

The position of the spirited part seems the opposite of what we thought a short time ago. Then we thought of it as something appetitive, but now we say it is far from being that; in the civil war of the soul it aligns itself far more with the reasonable part.

Very much so.

Is it different from that also, or is it some part of reason, so that there are two parts of the soul instead of three, the reasonable and the appetitive? Or, as we had three separ-

ate parts holding our city together, the money-making, the 441 auxiliary and the deliberative, so in the soul the spirited is a third part, by nature the helper of reason, if it has not been corrupted by a bad upbringing?

It must be a third part.

Yes, I said, if it now appears to be different from the reasonable part, as earlier from the appetitive part.

It is not difficult, he said, to show that it is different. One can see this in children; they are full of spirit from birth, whereas a few of them seem to me never to acquire a share of reason, while the majority do not do so until late. b

By Zeus, I said, that is very well put. One can see this also in animals. Besides, our earlier quotation from Homer bears witness to it, where he says:

Striking his chest, he addressed his heart,[1]

for clearly Homer represents the part which reasons about c the better and the worse course, and which strikes his chest, as different from that which is angry without reasoning.

You are definitely right.

We have now made our difficult way through a sea of argument to reach this point, and we have fairly agreed that the same kinds of parts, and the same number of parts, exist in the soul of each individual as in our city.

That is so.

It necessarily follows that the individual is wise in the same way, and in the same part of himself, as the city.

Quite so.

And the part which makes the individual brave is the d same as that which makes the city brave, and in the same manner, and everything which makes for virtue is the same in both?

That necessarily follows.

Moreover, Glaucon, I think we shall say that a man is just in the same way as the city is just.

That too is inevitable.

We have surely not forgotten that the city was just because each of the three classes in it was fulfilling its own task.

I do not think, he said, that we have forgotten that.

We must remember then that each one of us within whom each part is fulfilling its own task will himself be just e and do his own work.

We must certainly remember this.

---

1   *Striking … heart*   Homer, *Odyssey* 20, 17.

Therefore it is fitting that the reasonable part should rule, it being wise and exercising foresight on behalf of the whole soul, and for the spirited part to obey it and be its ally.

Quite so.

Is it not then, as we were saying,[1] a mixture of artistic and physical culture which makes the two parts harmoni-442 ous, stretching and nurturing the reasonable part with fine speech and learning, relaxing and soothing the spirited part, and making it gentle by means of harmony and rhythm.

Very definitely, he said.

These two parts, then, thus nurtured and having truly learned their own role and being educated in it, will exercise authority over the appetitive part which is the largest part in any man's soul and is insatiable for possessions. They will watch over it to see that it is not filled with the so-called pleasures of the body, and by becoming enlarged and strong b thereby no longer does its own job but attempts to enslave and to rule over those over whom it is not fitted to rule, and so upsets everybody's whole life.

Quite so, he said.

These two parts will also most effectively stand on guard on behalf of the whole soul and the body, the one by planning, the other by fighting, following its leader, and by its courage fulfilling his decisions.

That is so.

It is this part which causes us to call an individual brave, c when his spirit preserves in the midst of pain and pleasure his belief in the declarations of reason as to what he should fear and what he should not.

Right.

And we shall call him wise because of that small part of himself which ruled in him and made those declarations, which possesses the knowledge of what is beneficial to each part, and of what is to the common advantage of all three.

Quite so.

Further, shall we not call him moderate because of the friendly and harmonious relations between these same parts, when the rulers and the ruled hold a common belief d that reason should rule, and, they do not rebel against it?

Moderation, he said, is surely just that, both in the individual and the city.

And he will be just in the way we have often described.

Necessarily.

Now, I said, has our notion of justice become at all indistinct? Does it appear to be something different from what it was seen to be in the city?

I do not think so.

If any part of our soul still disputes this, we could alto-gether confirm it by bringing up common arguments.   e

What are they?

For example, concerning the city and the man similar to it by nature and training, if we had to come to an agreement whether we think that this man has embezzled a deposit of gold and silver, who, do you think, would consider him to have done this rather than men of a different type?   443

No one would.

And he would have nothing to do with temple robber-ies, thefts, or betrayals, either of friends in his private life, or, in public life, of cities?

Nothing.

Further, he would be in no way untrustworthy in keep-ing an oath or any other agreement.

How could he be?

Adultery too, disrespect for parents, neglect of the gods would suit his character less than any other man's.

Much less.

And the reason for all this is that every part within him b fulfills its own function, be that ruling or being ruled?

Certainly that, and nothing else.

Are you still looking for justice to be anything else than this power which produces such men and such cities as we have described?

By Zeus, he said, not I.

We have then completely realized the dream we had when we suspected[2] that, by the grace of god, we came c upon a principle and mould of justice right at the beginning of the founding of our city.

Very definitely.

Indeed, Glaucon—and this is why it is useful—it was a sort of image of justice, namely that it was right for one who is by nature a cobbler to cobble and to do nothing else, and for the carpenter to carpenter, and so with the others.

Apparently.

And justice was in truth, it appears, something like this. It does not lie in a man's external actions, but in the way he acts within himself, really concerned with himself and d his inner parts. He does not allow each part of himself to

---

1   *as we were saying*   The reference is to the discussion of the effects of education in the arts and physical culture at 410–11. There both are said to have a good effect, but here Plato refers only to the effect of the arts upon both reason and spirit.

2   *when we suspected*   See 432d–443a.

perform the work of another, or the sections of his soul to meddle with one another. He orders what are in the true sense of the word his own affairs well; he is master of himself, puts things in order, is his own friend, harmonizes the three parts like the limiting notes of a musical scale, the high, the low, and the middle, and any others there may be between. He binds them all together, and himself from a plurality becomes a unity. Being thus moderate and harmonious, he now performs any action, be it about the acquisition of wealth, the care of his body, some public actions, or private contract.[1] In all these fields he thinks the just and beautiful action, which he names as such, to be that which preserves this inner harmony and indeed helps to achieve it, wisdom to be the knowledge which oversees this action, an unjust action to be that which always destroys it, and ignorance the belief which oversees that.

Socrates you are altogether right.

Very well, I said, we would then not be thought to be lying if we claim that we have found the just man, the just city, and the justice that is in them.

No by Zeus, we would not.

Shall we say so then?

Yes, let us.

Let that stand then, I said. After this we must, I think, look for injustice.

Obviously.

Surely it must be a kind of civil war between the three parts, a meddling and a doing of other people's task, a rebellion of one part against the whole soul in order to rule it, though this is not fitting, as the rebelling part is by nature fitted to serve, while the other part is by nature not fit to serve, for it is of the ruling kind. We shall say, I think, that such things, the turmoil and the straying, are injustice and license and cowardice and ignorance and, in a word, every kind of wickedness.

That is what they are.

If justice and injustice are now sufficiently clear to us, then so are unjust actions and wrongdoing on the one hand, just actions on the other, and all such things.

---

1 *he now ... private contract* Plato here (442e–443e) links his present more psychologically profound definition of justice and injustice as inner states of soul with the more external description of them in the first book. Clearly the unjust man who, in the argument with Thrasymachus, wanted to get the better of everybody (e.g., 349c) is here the man whose appetitive part is out of control and rebels against the ruling reason (442a). His antisocial conduct now follows from this.

How so?

Because they are no different from healthy and diseased actions; what those are in the body, these are in the soul.

In what way?

Healthy actions produce health, diseased ones, disease.

Yes.

Therefore just actions produce justice in a man, and unjust actions, injustice?

Inevitably.

To produce health in the body is to establish the parts of the body as ruler and ruled according to nature, while disease is that they rule and are ruled contrary to nature.

That is so.

Therefore to produce justice is to establish the parts of the soul as ruler and ruled according to nature, while injustice means they rule and are ruled contrary to nature.

Most certainly.

Excellence then seems to be a kind of health and beauty and well-being of the soul, while vice is disease and ugliness and weakness.

That is so.

Then do not fine pursuits lead one to acquire virtue, ugly ones to acquire vice?

Of necessity.

It is left for us to enquire, it seems, if it is more profitable to act justly, to engage in fine pursuits and be just, whether one is known to be so or not, or to do wrong and be unjust, provided one does not pay the penalty and is not improved by punishment.

But Socrates, he said, this enquiry strikes me as becoming ridiculous now that justice and injustice have been shown to be such as we described. It is generally thought that life is not worth living when the body's nature is ruined, even if every kind of food and drink, every kind of wealth and power are available; yet we are to enquire whether life will be worth living when our soul, the very thing by which we live, is confused and ruined, if only one can do whatever one wishes, except that one cannot do what will free one from vice and injustice and make one acquire justice and virtue.

Ridiculous indeed, I said, but as we have reached the point from which we can see the state of these things most clearly, we must not give up.

No by Zeus, he said, least of all must we give up.

Join me at this point, I said, that you may see how many forms of vice there are, as I think, that are worth looking at.

I follow you, only proceed.

Well now, I said, as it appears to me from this vantage point which we have reached in our discussion, there is one form of excellence and an infinite number of forms of vice, four of them worth calling to mind.

How do you mean?

It is likely, I said, that there are as many types of soul as there are specific forms of government.

How many then?

d   Five forms of government, I said, and five of soul.

Tell us which they are.

I mean, I said, that one is the form of government we have been describing; and it could have two names: if there is one outstanding man among the rulers it is called kingship; if there are more, aristocracy.[1]

True.

That then, I said I call one form; whether the rulers be e one or more, they would not disturb the worthwhile laws of the city, and to ensure this they would make use of the upbringing and education we have described.

It is not likely that they would change them, he said.

from Book 5

[...]

451c We must now, said I, go back to what should have been said earlier in sequence. However, this may well be the right way: after we have completed the parts that men must play, we turn to those of women, especially as you call on me to do so.

For men of such a nature and education as we have described there is, in my opinion, no other right way to deal with wives and children than following the road upon which we started them. We attempted, in our argument, to establish the men as guardians of the flock.

Yes.

d   Let us then give them for the birth and upbringing of children a system appropriate to that function and see whether it suits us or not.

How?

Like this: do we think that the wives of our guardian watchdogs should join in whatever guardian duties the men fulfill, join them in the hunt, and do everything else in common, or should we keep the women at home as unable

to do so because they must bear and rear their young, and leave to the men the labor and the whole care of the flock?

All things, he said, should be done in common, ex- e cept that the women are physically weaker and the men stronger.

And is it possible, I asked, to make use of living creatures for the same purposes unless you give them the same upbringing and education?

It is not possible.

So if we use the women for the same tasks as the men, they must be taught the same things.

Yes.   452

Now we gave the men artistic and physical culture.

Yes.

So we must give both also to the women, as well as training in war, and use them for the same tasks.

That seems to follow from what you say.

Perhaps, I said, many of the things we are saying, being contrary to custom, would stir up ridicule, if carried out in practice in the way we are telling them.

They certainly would, he said.

What, I asked, is the most ridiculous feature you see in this? Or is it obviously that women should exercise naked in the palaetra[2] along with the men, not only the young b women but the older women too, as the old men do in the gymnasia when their bodies are wrinkled and not pleasant to look at and yet they are fond of physical exercise?

Yes, by Zeus, he said, it would appear ridiculous as things stand now.

Surely, I said, now that we have started on this argument, we must not be afraid of all the jokes of the kind that the wits will make about such a change in physical and artistic culture, and not least about the women carrying c arms and riding horses.

You are right, he said.

As we have begun this discussion we must go on to the tougher part of the law and beg these people not to practice their own trade of comedy at our expense but to be serious and to remember that it is not very long since the Greeks thought it ugly and ridiculous, as the majority of barbarians still do, for men to be seen naked. When first the Cretans and then the Lacedaemonians started their physical training, the wits of those days could have ridiculed it all, or do d you not think so?

I do.

---

1   *aristocracy* Rule of the best.

2   *palaetra* (or palaestra) Wrestling school.

But I think that after it was found in practice to be better to strip than to cover up all those parts, then the spectacle ceased to be looked on as ridiculous because reasonable argument had shown that it was best. This showed that it is foolish to think anything ridiculous except what is bad, or to try to raise a laugh at any other spectacle than that of ignorance and evil as being ridiculous, as it is foolish to be in earnest about any other standard of beauty than that of the good.

Most certainly.

Must we not first agree whether our proposals are possible or not? And we must grant an opportunity for discussion to anyone who, in jest or seriously, wishes to argue the point whether female human nature can share all the tasks of the male sex, or none at all, or some but not others, and to which of the two waging war belongs. Would this not be the best beginning and likely to lead to the best conclusion?

Certainly.

Do you then want us to dispute among ourselves on behalf of those others, lest the other side of the argument fall by default?

There is nothing to stop us.

Let us then speak on their behalf: "Socrates and Glaucon, there is no need for others to argue with you. You yourselves, when you began to found your city, agreed that each person must pursue the one task for which he is fitted by nature." I think we did agree to this, of course. "Can you deny that a woman is by nature very different from a man?" Of course not. "And is it not proper to assign a different task to each according to their nature?" Certainly. "How then are you not wrong and contradicting yourselves when you say that men and women must do the same things, when they have quite separate natures?" Do you have any defense against that argument, my good friend?

That is not very easy offhand, he said, but I ask and beg you to explain the argument on our side, whatever it is.

It is these and many other difficulties that I foresaw, Glaucon, I said, when I was afraid and hesitated to tackle the law concerning the acquiring of wives and the upbringing of children.

By Zeus, he said, it does not seem at all easy.

It is not, said I, but the fact is that whether a man falls into a small swimming pool or in the middle of the ocean, he must swim all the same.

Certainly.

So then we must swim too and try to save ourselves from the sea of our argument, hoping that a dolphin will pick us up[1] or we may find some other miraculous deliverance.

It seems so.

Come now, said I, let us see if we can find a way out. We have agreed that a different nature must follow a different occupation and that the nature of man and woman is different, and we now say that different natures must follow the same pursuits. This is the accusation brought against us.

Surely.

How grand is the power of disputation, Glaucon.

Why?

Because, I said, many people fall into it unwittingly and think they are not disputing but conversing because they cannot analyze their subject into its parts, but they pursue mere verbal contradictions of what has been said, thus engaging in a dispute rather than in a conversation.

Many people, he said, have that experience, but does this also apply to us at the present moment?

It most certainly does, I said. I am afraid we have indeed unwittingly fallen into disputation.

How?

We are bravely, but in a disputatious and verbal fashion, pursuing the principle that a nature which is not the same must not engage in the same pursuits, but when we assigned different tasks to a different nature and the same to the same nature, we did not examine at all what kind of difference and sameness of nature we had in mind and in what regard we were distinguishing them.

No, we did not look into that.

We might therefore just as well, it seems, ask ourselves whether the nature of bald men and long-haired men is the same and not opposite, and then, agreeing that they are opposite, if we allow bald men to be cobblers, not allow long-haired men to be, or again if long-haired men are cobblers, not allow the others to be.

That would indeed be ridiculous.

Is it ridiculous for any other reason than because we did not fully consider their same or different natures in every respect but we were only watching the kind of difference and sameness which applied to those particular pursuits? For example, a male and a female physician, we said, have the same nature of soul, or do you not think so?

I do.

---

1   *a dolphin will pick us up* Herodotus, *Histories* 1.23–24 contains the story of the rescue of a drowning man by dolphins.

But a physician and a carpenter have a different nature?

Surely.

Therefore, I said, if the male and the female are seen to be different as regards a particular craft or other pursuit we shall say this must be assigned to one or the other. But if they seem to differ in this particular only, that the female e bears children while the male begets them, we shall say that there has been no kind of proof that a woman is different from a man as regards the duties we are talking about, and we shall still believe that our guardians and their wives should follow the same pursuits.

And rightly so.

Next we shall bid anyone who holds the contrary view 455 to instruct us in this: with regard to what craft or pursuit concerned with the establishment of the city is the nature of man and woman not the same but different?

That is right.

Someone else might very well say what you said a short time ago, that it is not easy to give an immediate reply, but that it would not be at all difficult after considering the question.

He might say that.

Do you then want us to beg the one who raises these b objections to follow us to see whether we can show him that no pursuit connected with the management of the city belongs in particular to a woman?

Certainly.

Come now, we shall say to him, give us an answer: did you mean that one person had a natural ability for a certain pursuit, while another had not, when the first learned it easily, the latter with difficulty? The one, after a brief period of instruction, was able to find things out for himself from what he had learned, while the other, after much instruction, could not even remember what he had learned; the former's body adequately served his mind, while the other's c physical reactions opposed his. Are there any other ways in which you distinguished the naturally gifted in each case from those who were not?

No one will say anything else.

Do you know of any occupation practiced by mankind in which the male sex is not superior to the female in all these respects? Or shall we pursue the argument at length by mentioning weaving, baking cakes, cooking vegetables, tasks in which the female sex certainly seems to distinguish itself, and in which it is most laughable of all for women to d be inferior to men?

What you say is true, he said, namely that one sex is much superior to the other in almost everything, yet many women are better than many men in many things, but on the whole it is as you say.

There is therefore no pursuit connected with city management which belongs to woman because she is a woman, or to a man because he is a man, but various natures are scattered in the same way among both kinds of persons. Woman by nature shares all pursuits, and so does man, but in all of e them woman is a physically weaker creature than man.

Certainly.

Shall we then assign them all to men, and none to a woman?

How can we?

One woman, we shall say, is a physician, another is not, one is by nature artistic, another is not.

Quite so.

One may be athletic or warlike, while another is not 456 warlike and has no love of athletics.

I think so.

Further, may not one woman love wisdom, another hate it, or one may be high-spirited, another be without spirit?

That too.

So one woman may have a guardian nature, the other not. Was it not a nature with these qualities which we selected among men for our male guardians too?

We did.

Therefore the nature of man and woman is the same as regards guarding the city, except in so far as she is physically weaker, and the man's nature stronger.

So it seems.

Such women must then be chosen along with such men b to live with them and share their guardianship, since they are qualified and akin to them by nature.

Certainly.

Must we not assign the same pursuits to the same natures?

The same.

We have come round then to what we said before, and we agree that it is not against nature to give to the wives of the guardians an education in the arts and physical culture.

Definitely not.

We are not legislating against nature or indulging in mere wishful thinking since the law we established is in ac- c cord with nature. It is rather the contrary present practice which is against nature as it seems.

It appears so.

Now we were to examine whether our proposals were possible and the best.

We were.

That they are possible is now agreed?

Yes.

After this we must seek agreement whether they are the best.

Clearly.

With a view to having women guardians, we should not have one kind of education to fashion the men, and another d for the women, especially as they have the same nature to begin with.

No, not another.

What is your opinion of this kind of thing?

Of what?

About thinking to yourself that one man is better and another worse, or do you think that they are all alike?

Certainly not.

In the city we were establishing, do you think the guardians are made better men by the education they have received, or the cobblers who were educated for their craft?

Your question is ridiculous.

I know, said I. Well, are these guardians not the best of e all the citizens?

By far.

Will then these women guardians not be the best of women?

That too by far.

Is there anything better for a city than to have the best possible men and women?

Nothing.

And it is the arts and physical culture, as we have de-457 scribed them, which will achieve this?

Of course.

So the institution we have established is not only possible but also the best.

That is so.

The women then must strip for their physical training, since they will be clothed in excellence. They must share in war and the other duties of the guardians about the city, and have no other occupation; the lighter duties will be assigned to them because of the weakness of their sex. The man who b laughs at the sight of naked women exercising for the best of reasons is "plucking the unripe fruit of laughter,"[1] he

understands nothing of what he is laughing at, it seems, nor what he is doing. For it is and always will be a fine saying that what is beneficial is beautiful, what is harmful is ugly.

Very definitely.

Let us say then that we have escaped from one wave of criticism in our discussion of the law about women, and we have not been altogether swamped when we laid it down that male and female guardians must share all their duties c in common, and our argument is consistent when it states that this is both possible and beneficial.

It is, he said, certainly no small wave from which you are escaping.

You will not say this was a big one when you see the one that follows, I said.

Speak up, then, he said, and let me see it.

I think, I said, that the law follows from the last and those that have gone before.

What law?

All these women shall be wives in common to all the d men, and not one of them shall live privately with any man; the children too should be held in common so that no parent shall know which is his own offspring, and no child shall know his parent.

This proposal raises far more doubts than the last, both as to its possibility and its usefulness, he said.

I do not think its usefulness will be disputed, I said, namely that it is not a great blessing to hold wives in common, and children too, provided it is possible. I think that most controversy will arise on the question of its possibility.

Both points, he said, will certainly be disputed.   e

You mean that I will have to fight a combination of arguments. I thought I could escape by running away from one of them, if you thought the proposal beneficial, and that it would only remain for me to argue its possibility.

I saw you running away, he said, but you must explain both.

Well, I said, I must take my punishment. Allow me, however, to indulge myself as if on holiday, as lazy-minded 458

---

1   *plucking ... laughter*   Plato is here adapting a phrase of Pindar, which survives as a fragment. The text is uncertain. As it stands

it means "They pluck from wisdom the unripe fruit of laughter," which does not seem to make much sense. The Pindaric phrase was "they pluck the unripe fruit of wisdom," i.e., their wisdom is not wisdom; it seems likely that Plato simply replaced *sophias* (of wisdom) by *geloiou* "they pluck the unripe fruit of laughter." As the original meant that their wisdom was no wisdom, the adaptation then means that their laughter is no true laughter, because what they laugh at is not laughable.

people feast on their own thoughts whenever they take a walk alone. Instead of finding out how something they desire may become a reality, such people pass over that question to avoid wearying themselves by deliberating on what is possible and what is not; they assume that what they desire is available; they arrange the details and enjoy themselves thinking about all they will do when it has come to pass, thus making a lazy mind even lazier. I am myself at this moment getting soft, and I want to delay consideration of the feasibility of our proposal until later. I will assume that it is feasible and examine, if you will allow me, how the rulers will arrange these things when they happen and I will argue that this will be most beneficial to the city and to the guardians. This I will try to examine along with you, and deal with the other question later, if you permit.

I permit it, he said, carry on with your examination.

I think that surely our rulers, if indeed they are worthy of the name, and their auxiliaries as well, will be willing, the latter to do what they are told, the former to give the orders, in part by obeying the laws themselves, and in part, in such matters as we have entrusted to them, by imitating these laws.

That is likely.

You then, as their lawgiver, just as you chose the men, will in the same manner choose the women and provide as far as possible those of the same nature. Since they have their dwellings and meals together and none of them possess anything of the kind as private property, they will be together and mix together both in the gymnasia and in the rest of their education and they will, I think, be driven by inborn necessity to have intercourse with one another. Or do you not think that what I say will of necessity happen?

The necessity is not of a mathematical but of an erotic kind, he said, and this is probably stronger in persuading and compelling the mass of the people.

Yes indeed, I said. The next point is, Glaucon, that promiscuity is impious in a city of fortunate people, nor will the rulers allow it.

It is not right.

After this we must obviously make marriage as sacred as possible, and sacred marriages will be those which are the most beneficial.

Most certainly.

How then will they be most beneficial? Tell me, Glaucon: I see that at home you have hunting dogs and quite a number of pedigree birds. Did you then, by Zeus, pay any attention to their unions and breeding?

In what way? he asked.

In the first place, though they are all of good stock, are there not some who are and prove themselves to be best?

There are.

Do you breed equally from them all, or are you anxious to breed most from the best?

From the best.

Further, do you breed from the youngest, or from the oldest, or from those in their prime?

From those in their prime.

And do you think that if they were not bred in this way, your stock of birds and dogs would deteriorate considerably?

I do.

Do you think things are any different in the case of horses and the other animals?

That would indeed be absurd.

Good gracious, my friend, I said, how great is our need for extremely able rulers if the same is true for the human race.

It is, but what about it?

Because they will need to use a good many drugs. For people who do not need drugs but are willing to follow a diet even an inferior physician will be sufficient, but when drugs are needed, we know that a bolder physician is required.

True, but what do you have in mind?

This, I said: our rulers will probably have to make considerable use of lies and deceit for the good of their subjects. We said that all such things are useful as a kind of drug.

And rightly so.

This "rightly" will occur frequently in matters of marriage and the bearing of children.

How so?

It follows from our previous agreement that the best men must have intercourse with the best women as frequently as possible, and the opposite is true of the very inferior men and women; the offspring of the former must be reared, but not the offspring of the latter, if our herd is to be of the highest possible quality. Only the rulers should know of these arrangements, if our herd of guardians is to avoid all dissension as far as possible.

Quite right.

Therefore certain festivals will be established by law at which we shall bring the brides and grooms together; there will also be sacrifices, and our poets must compose hymns to celebrate the marriages. The number of marriages we shall leave to the rulers to decide, in such a way as to keep the number of males as stable as possible, taking into account war, disease, and similar factors so that our city shall, as far as possible, become neither too big nor too small.

Right.

There will have to be some clever lots introduced, so that at each marriage celebration the inferior man we mentioned will blame chance but not the rulers.

Quite so.

b The young men who have distinguished themselves in war or in other ways must be given awards consisting of other prizes and also more abundant permission to sleep with women, so that we may have a good excuse to have as many children as possible begotten by them.

Right.

As the children are born, officials appointed for the purpose—be they men or women or both, since our offices are open to both women and men—will take them.

Yes.

c The children of good parents they will take to a rearing pen in the care of nurses living apart in a certain section of the city; the children of inferior parents, or any child of the others born defective, they will hide, as is fitting, in a secret and unknown place.[1]

Yes, he said, if the breed of the guardians is to remain pure.

The nurses will also see to it that the mothers are brought to the rearing pen when their breasts have milk, d but take every precaution that no mother shall know her own child; they will provide wet nurses if the number of mothers is insufficient; they will take care that the mothers suckle the children for only a reasonable time; the care of sleepless children and all other troublesome duties will belong to the wet nurses and other attendants.

You are making it very easy, he said, for the wives of the guardians to have children.

And that is fitting, I said. Let us take up the next point of our proposal: We said that the children's parents should be in their prime.

True.

---

1   *hide, as is fitting … unknown place*   Plato here recommends infanticide by exposure for these babies, a practice which was quite common in classical times (*cp.* 459d–e and 461b–c). Presumably the point of exposure rather than direct infanticide was that the responsibility was felt to be thrown upon the gods, for the child might be saved, as Oedipus was.

Do you agree that a reasonable interpretation of this is e twenty years for a woman and thirty years for a man?

Which years?

A woman, I said, is to bear children for the state from the age of twenty to the age of forty, a man after he has passed "his peak as a racer" begets children for the state till he reaches fifty.

This, he said, is the physical and mental peak for both. 461

If a man either younger or older than this meddles with procreation for the state, we shall declare his offence to be neither pious nor right as he begets for the city a child which, if it remains secret, will be born without benefit of the sacrifices and prayers which priests and priestesses and the whole city utter at every marriage festival, that the children of good and useful parents may always prove themselves better and more useful; but this child is born in darkness, the result of dangerous incontinence. b

Right.

The same law will apply, I said, if a man still of begetting years unites with a woman of child-bearing age without the sanction of the rulers; we shall say that he brings to the city an unauthorized and unhallowed bastard.

Quite right.

However, I think that when women and men have passed the age of having children, we shall leave them free to have intercourse with anyone they wish, with these c exceptions: for a man, his daughter or mother, or the daughter's daughters, or his mother's female progenitors; for a woman, a son or father, their male issue or progenitors. Having received these instructions they should be very careful not to bring a single child into the light, but if one should be conceived, and, forces its way to the light, they must deal with it knowing that no nurture is available for it.

This too, he said, is sensibly spoken, but how shall they know their fathers and daughters and those other relation- d ships you mentioned?

They have no means of knowing, I said, but all the children who are born in the tenth and seventh month after a man became a bridegroom he will call sons if they are male, daughters if they are female, and they will call him father, and so too he will call their offspring his grandchildren who in turn will call the first group their grandfathers and grandmothers. Those born during the time when their fathers and mothers were having children they will call their brothers and sisters, so that, as I said, these groups will have e no sexual relations with each other. But the law will allow brothers and sisters[1] to live together if the lot so falls and the Pythian[2] approves.

Quite right.

This then is the holding in common of wives and children for the guardians of your city. We must now confirm in our argument that it conforms with the rest of our constitution and is by far the best. Or how are we to proceed?

462   In that way, by Zeus.

Is not the first step towards agreement to ask ourselves what we say is the greatest good in the management of the city? At this the lawgiver must aim in making his laws. Also what is the greatest evil. Then we should examine whether the system we have just described follows the tracks of the good and not those of evil.

By all means.

Is there any greater evil we can mention for a city than

b whatever tears it apart into many communities instead of one?

There is not.

Do not common feelings of pleasure and pain bind the city together, when as nearly as possible all the citizens equally rejoice or feel pain at the same successes and failures?

Most certainly.

For such feelings to be isolated and private dissolves the

c city's unity, when some suffer greatly while others greatly rejoice at the same public or private events.

Of course.

And that sort of thing happens whenever such words as "mine" and "not mine"—and so with "another's"—are not used in unison.

Most certainly.

And the city which most closely resembles the individual? When one of us hurts his finger, the whole organism which binds body and soul together into the unitary system

d managed by the ruling part of it shares the pain at once throughout when one part suffers. This is why we say that the man has a pain in his finger, and the same can be said of any part of the man, both about the pain which any part suffers, and its pleasure when it finds relief.

Certainly, he said. As for your question, the best managed city certainly closely resembles such an organism.

And whenever anything good or bad happens to a single one of its citizens, such a city will certainly say that e this citizen is a part of itself, and the whole city will rejoice or suffer with him.

That must be so, if it has good laws.

It is time now, I said, for us to return to our own city and to look there for the features we have agreed on, whether it, or any other city, possesses them to the greatest degree.

We must do so.

Well then. There are rulers and people in the other cit- 463 ies as well as in this one?

There are.

And they all call each other fellow-citizens.

Of course.

Besides the word fellow-citizens, what do the people call the rulers in the other cities?

In many they call them masters, but in democracies they call them by this very name, rulers.[3]

What do the people call them in our city? Besides fellow citizens, what do they call the rulers?

Saviors and helpers.   b

And what do the rulers call the people?

Providers of food and wages.

What do the rulers call the people in the other cities?

Slaves.

And what do the rulers call each other?

Fellow rulers.

And ours?

Fellow guardians.

Can you tell me whether a ruler in the other cities might address one of his fellow rulers as his kinsman and another as an outsider?

Certainly, many could.

He then considers his kinsman, and addresses him, as his own, but not the outsider?   c

That is so.

What about your guardians? Can any of them consider any other of his fellow guardians an outsider and address him as such?

Not in any way, he said, for when he meets any one of them he will think he is meeting a brother or a sister, a father or a mother, a son or a daughter, their offspring or progenitors.

---

1   *brothers and sisters* Presumably natural brothers and sisters, since they will belong to different age groups and they have no means of discovering their relationship.

2   *the Pythian* The oracle at the temple of Apollo at Delphi.

---

3   *rulers* The Greek word is *archôn*, a general term for ruler. In Athens the board of archons served as the chief magistrates.

You put that very well, I said, but, further, tell me this: will you legislate these family relationships as names only, or must they act accordingly in all they do? Must a man show to his fathers the respect, solicitude, and obedience to parents required by law? Otherwise, if he acts differently, he will fare worse at the hands of gods and men as one whose actions are neither pious nor just. Will these be the sayings that ring in his ears on the part of all citizens from childhood both about their fathers, those pointed out to them as such, and about their other kindred—or will there be other voices?

It will be those, he said; it would be absurd if their lips spoke these names of kindred without appropriate action following.

So in our city more than any other, when any individual fares well or badly, they would all speak in unison the words we mentioned just now, namely that "mine" is doing well, or "mine" is doing badly.

That also is very true.

And we said that such a belief and its expression are followed by common feelings of pleasure and pain.

And we were right.

So our citizens will to the greatest extent share the same thing which they call "mine," with the result that they in the highest degree share common feelings of pleasure and pain.

Surely.

And besides other arrangements, the reason for this is the holding of wives and children in common among the guardians.

More than anything else.

This we agreed was the greatest blessing for a city, and we compared a well run city to the body's reactions to pain or pleasure in any part of it.

And we were right to agree on that.

So then the cause of the greatest good for our city has been shown to be the common ownership of wives and children among the auxiliaries.

Certainly.

And in this we are consistent with what went before, for we said somewhere that they must have no private houses or land or any private possessions, that they receive their upkeep from the other citizens as a wage for their guardianship, and that they must all spend it in common, if they are to be real guardians.

Right.

Does not what we said before and what we are saying now make them even more real guardians, and prevent them from tearing the city apart by not calling the same thing "mine," one man applying the word to one thing and another to another? One man would then drag into his own house whatever he could get hold of away from the others; another drag things into his different house to another wife and other children. This would make for private pleasures and pains at private events. Our people, on the other hand, will think of the same thing as their own, aim at the same goal, and, as far as possible, feel pleasure and pain in unison.

Most certainly.

What follows? Will not lawsuits and mutual accusations disappear from among them, one might say, since they own nothing but their body, everything else being held in common? Hence they will be spared all the dissension which is due to the possession of wealth, children, and families?

They will inevitably be spared them.

Nor could cases of violence or assault rightly occur among them, for we shall declare that it is a fine and just thing to defend oneself against those of the same age, thus compelling them to keep in good physical condition.

Right.

The law is right in this also, that if an angry man satisfied his anger in a personal encounter of this kind, he is less likely to turn to more important quarrels.

Certainly.

An older man will have authority over all the young, and be allowed to chastise them.

Obviously.

It is surely also obvious that a younger man, except by order of the rulers, shall not apply violence of any kind to, nor strike, an older man, nor fail to respect him in other ways. There are two adequate guardians to prevent this, namely shame and fear; shame will prevent him laying hands on his parents, fear because the others will come to the rescue of the victim, some as his sons, some as his brothers, and some as his fathers.

That follows, he said.

So the laws will induce people to live at peace with each other.

Very much so.

And if there is no discord among the guardians there is no danger that the rest of the city will start factions against them or among themselves.

No danger.

I hesitate to mention the petty evils they will escape: the poor man's flattery of the rich, the perplexities and sufferings involved in bringing up children and in making the necessary money to feed the household, sometimes borrowing, sometimes denying the debt, in one way or another providing enough money to hand over to their wives and household slaves to dispense; all the various troubles which men endure in these matters are quite obvious and sordid and not worth discussing.

d   They are clear even to the blind.

They will be free of all these, and they will live a life more blessed than that at of Olympian victors.

How?

Olympian victors are considered happy on account of only a small part of the blessings available to our guardians, whose victory is even finer and their upkeep from public funds more complete. The victory they gain is the safety of the whole city and the victor's crown they and their children receive is their nurture and all the necessities of life; they
e   receive rewards from their own city while they live, and at their death they are given a worthy funeral.

Certainly fine rewards.

Remember, said I, that earlier in our discussion someone—I forget who[1]—shocked us by saying that we did not
466   make our guardians happy, that while it was in their power to own all the possessions of our citizens, yet they possessed nothing. We said at the time that we would investigate later whether this would happen, but that our concern at the time was to make our guardians true guardians and the city as happy as we could, and that we would not concentrate our attention upon one group and make them happy in our city.

I remember.

Well now, if the life of the auxiliaries is indeed much finer and better than that of Olympian victors, it is not to
b   be compared to that of the cobblers or other craftsmen, or with that of the farmers?

I do not think so.

It is surely right to repeat here what I said then, that, if a guardian seeks happiness in such a way as not even to be a guardian nor to be satisfied with a life so stable and moderate and, as we maintain, so much the best; if a silly and youthful idea of happiness should come into his mind and
c   set him off to use his power to appropriate everything in the city as his own, he will realize the true wisdom of Hesiod's saying that somehow "the half is more than the whole."[2]

---

1   *someone—I forget who* The objection was made by Adeimantus at the beginning of the fourth book (419a).
2   *the half ... whole* Hesiod, *Works and Days* 40.

If he takes my advice, he said, he will stay with this kind of life.

You agree then, I said, that the women should be associated with the men in the way we have described in matters of education and child bearing, and in the guarding of the other citizens. Both when they remain in the city and when they go to war they must share the guardians'   d duties, hunt with them like hounds, share as far as possible in everything in every way. In doing so they will be acting for the best, and in no way contrary to woman's nature as compared with man's, as they were born to associate with one another.

I agree.

It now remains, I said, for us to determine whether this association can be brought about among human beings as it can among animals, and how it can be brought about.

You took the words out of my mouth.

As far as war is concerned, I said, the way they will wage   e it is clear, I think.

How so?

Men and women will campaign together; moreover they will take the sturdy among their children with them, in order that, like the children of other craftsmen, they may observe the actions which they will perform when they grow up. Moreover, in addition to observing these, they can assist   467 and help in all the duties of war and attend upon their fathers and mothers. Have you not noticed in the other crafts how the children of potters for example assist and observe for a long time before they engage in making pots?

Yes indeed.

Should those craftsmen take more care than the guardians in training their children by suitable experience and observation?

That would be quite ridiculous.

Besides, every living creature will fight better in the presence of its young.   b

That is true, but, Socrates, there is a considerable danger that, if they are defeated, as happens frequently in war, they will lose their children's lives as well as their own, thus making it impossible for the rest of the city to recover.

What you say is true, I said, but do you think that the first thing we should aim at is to take measures to avoid danger?

Certainly not.

Well then, if risks must be run, should one not run them where success will improve people?

Obviously.

c   And do you think that it makes little difference, and is not worth the risk, that the children, who are the future warriors, should observe matters of war?

No. It does make a difference with regard to what you are mentioning.

We must then make opportunities for the children to observe war while contriving to keep them safe, and all will be well, will it not?

Yes.

Well, said I, in the first place their fathers will know, as
d   far as men can, which expeditions are dangerous and which are not.

That is likely.

So they will take them on some expeditions, but be cautious about others.

Rightly.

And they will put in charge of them officers whose age and experience qualifies them to be leaders and tutors.

That is fitting.

However, many things have happened unexpectedly to many people.

Yes indeed.

With this in view, my friend, we must provide the children with wings while they are small, so that they can fly away and escape.
e   How do you mean?

They must as early as possible be mounted on horses and learn to ride before they are taken to observe warfare on horseback. Their horses should not be high-spirited or fond of fighting, but very swift and easy to manage. In this way they will observe their own future task best as well as most safely and, if the need arises, they will find safety in following their older commanders.

I think what you say is right.

468   What about the waging of war? What should be the attitude of the soldiers to each other and to the enemy? Are my ideas right or not?

What ideas?

Should not any solider who, through cowardice, deserts his post, throws away his arms, or behaves in any such manner be reduced to be a craftsman or a farmer?

Quite so.

And should not one who is captured alive be left to his captors as a gift to do with as they please?
b   Most certainly.

Do you not think that one who has distinguished himself and earned high esteem should first of all, while still on the campaign, be crowned with wreaths in turn by every youth and child who accompany the expedition?

I do.

Further, shaken by the hand?

That too.

But this, said I, I think you will not longer agree to?

What?

That he should kiss and be kissed by each of them.

That most of all, he said, and I would add this to the law: that as long as the campaign lasts, no one whom he c wants to kiss shall be allowed to refuse, the purpose being that if any one should be in love with another, whether male or female, he would be all the keener to carry off the prize for valour.

Excellent, I said, and we have already stated that, as a good man, more marriages will be available to him and that such men will be chosen as bridegrooms more often than the others, in order that a man of that kind may beget as many children as possible.

We have said so.

Indeed, according to Homer too it is right to honor by such means the brave among the young. He said that Ajax, d who was distinguished in war, "was rewarded with the long cut of the chine."[1] This is a proper way to honor a young and brave man as, beside the honor, it will also increase his strength.

Quite right.

Let us then, I said, follow Homer in these matters. We too shall, at our sacrifices and on all such occasions, honor good men according to their bravery, with hymns and in the other ways we were just mentioning, also with "seats e of honor, meats and well-filled wine cups,"[2] so that along with the honor we may continue to train our good men and women.

What you say is excellent.

As for those who died on the campaign, first we shall declare anyone who distinguished himself to belong to the golden race, shall we not?

That above all.

And shall we not believe Hesiod, whenever any of the golden race die, that they are

---

1   *was rewarded ... chine*   *Iliad*, 7, 321. The chine is a large cut of meat from the back of the animal. The king presented it to Ajax at a banquet—a sign of honor.

2   *seats of honor ... wine cups*   Homer, *Iliad*, 8, 162.

469   Sacred spirits living upon the earth
Noble, warding off evil, guardians of mortal men.[1]

We shall believe him.

We shall therefore enquire from the god what kind of distinguished burial we should give to those inspired and godlike men, and we shall follow his instructions.

Of course we shall.

b   Then, for the rest of time, we shall care for, and worship at, their graves as at those of divine spirits. We shall follow the same rites for anyone of those who have been judged to have lived an outstandingly good life, whether they die of old age or in any other way.

That is right.

Again, how will our soldiers act towards the enemy?

What do you have in mind?

First about enslavement. Do you think it right for Greeks to enslave Greek cities, or should they, as far as they can, not even allow any other city to do so, and make a c   habit of sparing the Greek race as a precaution against being enslaved by the barbarians?

It is altogether and in every way best, he said, to spare one another.

And they should not themselves acquire a Greek as a slave, and advise the other Greeks not to do so?

Definitely, he said, for in this way they would be better able to turn against the barbarian and keep from fighting each other.

Further, I said, should they despoil the dead of anything but their armor after a victory, or is stripping the dead d   a good thing? Do not cowards make this an excuse for not facing the enemy as if they were doing something essential when they keep skulking about a corpse, and has not many an army been lost through such greed?

Yes indeed.

Do you not think it mean and greedy to strip a corpse? Is it not womanish and small-minded to regard the body as your enemy, when the enemy himself has flitted away and left behind only the instrument with which he fought? Do e   you think such behavior any different from that of dogs who are angry with the stone that hits them and leave the thrower alone?

Not different at all.

They must therefore not strip corpses, nor refuse the enemy permission to pick up their dead.

By Zeus, he said, they certainly must not.

---

1   *Sacred spirits ... mortal men* Hesiod, *Works and Days* 122.

Nor shall we take the arms of the enemy to the temples to dedicate them, especially not the arms of other Greeks, if we care at all for goodwill among the Greeks. We should 470   rather be afraid of polluting the temples if we bring them such things from our own people, unless the god tells us to do so.

Quite right.

What about ravaging Greek land and burning the houses? How are your soldiers to behave to the enemy?

I would be glad to hear your opinion on this subject, he said.

I think they should do neither of those things, but destroy the year's harvest only. Do you want me to tell you b   why?

Surely I do.

It seems to me that as we have two terms, war and civil strife, so there are two things, and the terms apply to differences in two fields, one of one's own kindred, the other of outside strangers. Enmity with one's own is called civil strife, whereas enmity to strangers is called war.

What you say is to the point.

See then whether this too is to the point: I say that c   the Greek race is related and akin, while the barbarians are outsiders and strangers.

You are right.

We shall say then that Greeks fighting barbarians or barbarians fighting Greeks are at war, that they are natural enemies, and this enmity is to be called war; but when Greeks fight Greeks, they are by nature friends, and in those circumstances Greece is sick and in a state of civil strife, and this enmity is to be called civil strife.   d

Yes, I agree to think of it that way.

Note that in civil strife, as the term is generally used, wherever something of the kind occurs, and a city is divided against itself, if either party ravages the land of the others and burns their houses, this is considered an outrage and both parties unpatriotic, for if they loved their land they would never ravage it, their nurse and mother, though it is considered reasonable for the victors to carry off the harvest of the defeated. They should, however, keep in mind that e   they will not always be at war, and that peace will return.

This attitude is much more civilized than the other, he said.

Now, I said, the city you are founding is Greek, is it not?

It must be.

So your citizens will be good and civilized?

Yes indeed.

And will they not love Greece? Will they not consider Greece to be their own? Will they not share the religion of the other Greeks?

Very much so.

471 They will therefore consider their differences with Greeks, their kindred, as civil strife and will not call it war?

They will not.

They will then quarrel as people who one day will be reconciled?

Certainly.

They will therefore chasten their foes in a friendly spirit; they will not punish them with enslavement and destruction. They are chastisers, not enemies at war.

Quite so.

Being Greeks, they will not ravage Greece, they will not burn the houses, nor will they maintain that all the inhabitants of each city are their foes, men, women and children,
b but only a few, those who caused the quarrel. For all these reasons, as the majority are their friends, they will not ravage the country or destroy the houses. They will carry their quarrel to the point of compelling those who caused it to be punished by those who were guiltless and the victims of it.

I agree, he said, that this is how our citizens must behave toward their enemies, and toward barbarians they must behave as the Greeks now do toward each other.

Let us then make this a law for our guardians, neither to
c ravage the country nor to burn the houses.

Let us, he said, and let us also say that these things are well, as is what went before. But I think, Socrates, that if one lets you talk on these subjects, you will never remember the subject you postponed before you said all this, namely, that it is possible for this city to exist and how it can be brought about. I agree that, if it existed, all the things we have mentioned would be good for the city in which they occurred, including things you are leaving out: they would be excel-
d lent fighters against an enemy because they would be least likely to desert each other, since they know each other as, and call each other by the name of, brothers, fathers, sons. Moreover, if their women joined their campaigns, whether in the same ranks or drawn up behind as reserves, either to frighten the enemy or as reinforcements, should they ever be needed, I know that this would make them quite unbeatable. I also see that a number of good things would ensue for them at home which have not been mentioned. Take it
e that I agree that all these things would happen as well as innumerable others, if this kind of government were to exist.

Say no more on this subject but let us now try to convince ourselves of this, namely that it is possible and how it is possible. Let the rest go.

This is a sudden attack you have made upon my argu- 472 ment, I said, and you show no leniency towards my loitering. You may not realize that I have barely escaped from the first two waves of objections as you bring the third upon me, the biggest and most difficult to deal with. When you hear and see it you will surely be more lenient towards my natural hesitation and my fear to state, and attempt thoroughly to examine, such a paradox.

The more you speak like this, he said, the less we shall let you off from telling us how this city is possible. So speak b and do not waste time.

Well then, I said, we must first remember that we have come to this point while we were searching for the natures of justice and injustice.

We must, but what of it?

Nothing, but if we find out what justice is, shall we require that the just man be in no way different from that justice itself, and be like justice in every respect, or shall we c be satisfied if he comes as close to it as possible, and share in it far more than others?

That will satisfy us.

It was then to have a model, I said, that we were seeking the nature of justice itself, and of the completely just man, if he should exist, and what kind of man he would be if he did, and so with injustice and the most unjust man. Our purpose was, with these models before us, to see how they turned out as regards happiness and its opposite. Thus we would be forced to come to an agreement about ourselves, that he who was as like them as possible would also have a d life most like theirs. It was not our purpose to prove that these could exist.

What you say is true.

Do you think a man is any less a good painter if, having painted a model of what the most beautiful man would be, and having rendered all the details satisfactorily in his picture, he could not prove that such a man can come into being?

By Zeus, I do not.

Well then, do we not also say that we were making a model of a good city in our argument?

Certainly. e

Do you think our discussion less worthwhile if we cannot prove that it is possible to found a city such as we described?

Not at all.

And indeed, I said, that is the truth. But if we must, to please you, exert ourselves to pursue this topic, namely to show how and in what respect this might best be possible, then you in turn should agree that the same thing applies to this demonstration.

What thing?

Is it possible to realize anything in practice as it can be formulated in words or is it natural for practice to have a lesser grip on truth than theory,[1] even if some people do not think so? Will you first agree to this or not?

I agree.

Then do not compel me to show that the things we have described in theory can exist precisely in practice. If we are able to discover how the administration of a city can come closest to our theories, shall we say that we have found that those things are possible which you told us to prove so? Or will you not be satisfied with that measure of success? For I would be satisfied.

So would I.

Next, it seems, we should try to find out and to show what is now badly done in the cities which prevents them from being governed in this way, and what is the smallest change which would enable a city to reach our type of government—one change if possible, or, if not one, then two, or at any rate as few changes and as insignificant in their effects as possible.

By all means.

There is one change to which I think we could point which would accomplish this. It is certainly neither small nor easy, but it is possible.

What is it?

I have now come, I said, to what we likened to the greatest wave. However, it shall be said even if, like a wave of laughter, it will simply drown me in ridicule and contempt.

Say on.

And I said: Cities will have no respite from evil, my dear Glaucon, nor will the human race, I think, unless philosophers[2] rule as kings in the cities, or those whom we now call kings and rulers genuinely and adequately study philosophy, until, that is, political power and philosophy coalesce, and the various natures of those who now pursue the one to the exclusion of the other are forcibly debarred from doing so. Otherwise the city we have been describing will never grow into a possibility or see the light of day. It is because I saw how very paradoxical this statement would be that I have for some time hesitated to make it. It is hard to realize that there can be no happiness, public or private, in any other city.

Socrates, he said, you have uttered such a speech and statement that after speaking it you must expect a great many not undistinguished people to cast off their cloak at once and, thus stripped for action, to snatch any available weapon, make a determined rush at you and do astonishing things to you. Unless you can hold them off by argument and escape, you will really pay the penalty of general derision.

Well, I said, it is you who brought this on me.

And I was quite right, he said. However, I will not betray you but defend you by any means I can, by good will, by urging you on, and perhaps I could give you more appropriate answers than another. Try, with this assistance, to show the unbelievers that things are as you state them.

I must try, I said, with the considerable support that you offer. If we are to escape from the people you mention, I think we need to define for them whom we mean by philosophers when we venture to say that they must rule. Once this is clear, one should be able to defend oneself by showing that some people have a natural aptitude for philosophy and for leading the state, while others have not that aptitude and must follow the leader.

This would be the time for that definition.

Come then, follow me in this, if we can somehow explain it.

Lead on.

Will it be necessary to remind you, or do you remember, that when we say that a man loves something, it must

---

1   *Is it ... than theory* This sounds strange to us because we regard the practical and material world as more "true" and more real than theory; but to Plato, the unchanging Platonic Forms and such things as mathematical realities were not only more exact, but also more real and true than the world of phenomena. As these are always changing no real knowledge of them is possible, but only opinion or belief.

2   *philosophers* It is important to remember in this context that the word *philosophos*, which was not in common use before this time, retained its etymological meaning as "a lover of truth and wisdom." Plato is maintaining that a statesman needs to be a thinker, a lover of truth, beauty, and the Good, with a highly developed sense of values. The rest of this book and the next two are largely devoted to explaining the character and necessary training of the Platonic *philosophos*, and this includes practical experience.

be shown, if the word is properly applied to him, that he loves not one part of it and the other not, but that he is fond of all of it?

d   It seems, he said, that I need to be reminded, for I do not remember very well.

Your reply suited another man rather than you. An amorous man should not forget that all those in the bloom of youth stir and excite a boy lover and amorous man in some way, as all of them appear to deserve his care and attentions. Is that not how you people behave to beautiful youths? You will praise the snub-nosed as being charming,

e the hook-nosed you say is regal, the one in between is well proportioned, dark ones are manly in appearance, and the pale are children of the gods. As for the "honey-hued," do you think this very term is anything but the euphemistic invention of a lover who found it easy to tolerate sallowness as long as the boy was young? In a word, you will find

475 all kinds of terms and excuses not to reject anyone in the flower of his youth.

If, he said, you must take me as your example of how lovers behave, I will agree for the sake of the argument.

Further, I said, do you not see wine-lovers behave in the same way? They love every kind of wine and find every excuse to welcome it.

Certainly.

And I think you see lovers of honor, if they cannot be generals, be captains; if they cannot be honored by men of

b importance and dignity, they are content to be honored by insignificant and inferior men, for they have a passion for honor at any price.

Definitely so.

Do you agree, or not, that when we say that a man has a passion for something, we shall say that he desires that whole kind of thing, not just one part of it and not the other?

Yes, the whole of it.

The lover of wisdom, we shall say, has a passion for wisdom, not for this kind of wisdom and not that, but for every kind of wisdom?

True.

c As for one who is choosy about what he learns, especially if he is young and cannot yet give a reasoned account of what is useful and what is not, we shall not call him a lover of learning or a philosopher, just as we shall not say that a man who is difficult about his food is hungry or has an appetite for food. We shall not call him a lover of food but a bad feeder.

And we should be right.

But we shall rightly call a philosopher the man who is easily willing to learn every kind of knowledge, gladly turns to learning things, and is unsatiable in this respect. Is that not so?

And Glaucon said: That will include many strange d people: the lovers of spectacles seem to be included because of the pleasure they take in learning things, and the lovers of sounds seem to be the strangest folk to include among philosophers; they would never willingly attend a serious discussion or spend their time that way, but they run around to all the Dionysiac festivals[1] omitting none, either in the city or the villages, as if their ears were under contract to listen to every chorus. Are we to say that all these people, and those who learn similar things, and those who learn petty crafts, are philosophers?

No, I said, but they do resemble philosophers. e

Whom then, he asked, do you call the true philosophers?

Those who love the spectacle of truth, I said.

That is correct, he said, but what do you mean by it?

It would not be easy to explain to anyone else, but I think you will agree to this.

What?

Since the beautiful is the opposite of the ugly, they are two things.

Of course.

And since they are two, each is one? 476

I grant that too.

The same is true of the just and the unjust, the good and the bad, and all the Forms[2] each is itself one, but because they appear everywhere in association with actions, and bodies, and each other, each appears to be many.

You are right.

So, I said, I make this distinction: on one side are those whom you just now called lovers of spectacles and lovers of crafts and practical men, on the other side are those

---

1   *Dionysiac festivals* Festivals involving musical, poetical, and dramatic performances, banqueting, animal sacrifice, processions, etc.

2   *Forms* Abstract entities representing the ideal form of each type of thing. For Plato, these are the metaphysical basis of reality, and knowledge of these (not of their impure earthly counterparts) is true knowledge. The word *eidos* is here used for the first time in the *Republic* in this technical sense. The translation capitalizes words like Beauty, the Good, and the like when they refer specifically to a Platonic Form.

b whom we are discussing, and whom alone one would call philosophers.

How do you mean?

The lovers of sights and sounds, I said, like beautiful sounds and colors and shapes, and all the objects fashioned from them,[1] but their thought is unable to see and welcome the nature of Beauty itself.

That is surely the case, he said.

Those who can reach Beauty itself and see it in itself would be only a few, would they not?

c Certainly.

As for the man who believes in beautiful things but not in the existence of Beauty itself, nor is able to follow one who leads him to the knowledge of it, do you not think that his life is a dream rather than a reality? Consider: is this not dreaming, namely, whether asleep or awake, to think that a likeness is not a likeness but the reality which it resembles?

I certainly think that the man who does this is dreaming.

The man who, on the contrary, believes that there is d such a thing as Beauty itself, who can see both it and the things which share in it, and does not confuse the two, does he seem to you to live in a dream or in reality?

In reality certainly, he said.

His thought, since he knows, we could correctly call knowledge; that of the other we would call opinion, since he merely opines.

Quite so.

What if the man who has opinion but not knowledge is angry with us and disputes the truth of what we are saying? Shall we have some way to appease him and gently e persuade him, while hiding from him that he is not in his right mind?

We must have.

Come now, consider what we shall say to him. Or do you want us to enquire from him as follows—first telling him that nobody would grudge him any knowledge he may have, but that we should be glad to see that he knows something—"Tell us this: does the man who has knowledge know something or nothing?" You answer for him.

I will answer, he said, that he knows something.

Something that is, or is not?[2]

Something that is, for how could that which is not be 477 known?

In however many ways we examine the question, we can hold this to be certain: what fully is, is fully knowable, and what in no way is, is altogether unknowable.

That is quite certain.

Very well, now if anything is in such a state as to be and also not to be, will it not be intermediate between that which purely is and that which in no way is?

Yes, it will be between them.

Then, as knowledge is directed to what is, while ignorance is of necessity directed to what is not, we must find something intermediate between ignorance and knowledge b for that which lies between them, if there is such a thing.

Certainly.

Do we say that opinion is something?

Of course.

Is it a different capacity from knowledge or the same?

A different one.

Opinion then is directed to one object, and knowledge to another, according to the capacity of each?

That is so.

Knowledge then is by its nature directed to what is, to know it as it is—but I think it necessary first to make this distinction.

What distinction?

We shall say that capacities are a certain class of realities c which enable us to do what we are capable of doing, and so with anything else which is capable of doing anything. I mean sight for example, or hearing, are among the capacities, if you understand the class of things to which I want to refer.

---

1 *all the objects fashioned from them* Poetry fashioned from sounds; paintings from colors and shapes.

2 *Something that is, or is not?* The meaning of the passage which follows 476e–480 is disputed and possibly confused. According to one interpretation, when Plato speaks of "what is" he means the Platonic Forms. These, eternal and unchanging, are the object of the philosopher's knowledge, the only things which can be said to be real, indeed to *be*. Plato believed that the knowledge of these Forms of Beauty, Justice, and the rest would give his philosopher in the fields of ethics, aesthetics, and politics a knowledge as exact and as permanent as that of the mathematician in his field. So we have "that which is"—the Forms—at one extreme, total non-being or the nonexistent, of which of course no knowledge or perception is possible, at the other. The world of phenomena (the Greek word *phainomena* means appearances) lies somewhere between the two; it is in a perpetual state of flux or change; it offers no permanent objects of knowledge in the sense mentioned above, and therefore only opinion or belief of the phenomena is possible to Plato. So knowledge is of the Forms only, ignorance is of what is not in any sense, and opinion is of the physical world which shares both in being and non-being.

I understand.

Listen to what I think about them. I cannot see any color or shape of a capacity, or any such attribute as I see in many other things, looking to a few of which I distinguish some things from others for myself. In the case of a capacity d I can look only to this: to what it is directed and what it achieves, and in this way I called it a capacity; if it is related to the same object and achieves the same result I call it the same, while that which is related to a different object and achieves a different result I call a different capacity. How do you proceed?

In the same way.

Let us now go back, my good friend, I said. Would you say that knowledge is a capacity, or how do you classify it?

Among the capacities, he said, and the most powerful of all.

e   Further, do you count opinion as a capacity, or in what class do you put it?

In no other class, he said, for opinion is that by which we opine.

A short time ago you agreed that knowledge and opinion are not the same.

How, he answered, can any intelligent man say that a fallible thing is the same as an infallible one?

...

from Book 7

514   Next, I said, compare the effect of education and the lack of it upon our human nature to a situation like this: imagine men to be living in an underground cave-like dwelling place, which has a way up to the light along its whole width, but the entrance is a long way up. The men have been there from childhood, with their neck and legs in fet- b ters, so that they remain in the same place and can only see ahead of them, as their bonds prevent them turning their heads. Light is provided by a fire burning some way behind and above them. Between the fire and the prisoners, some way behind them and on a higher ground, there is a path across the cave and along this a low wall has been built, like the screen at a puppet show in front of the performers who show their puppets above it.

I see it.

See then also men carrying along that wall, so that they c overtop it, all kinds of artifacts, statues of men, reproduc- 515 tions of other animals in stone or wood fashioned in all

sorts of ways, and, as is likely, some of the carriers are talking while others are silent.

This is a strange picture, and strange prisoners.

They are like us, I said. Do you think, in the first place, that such men could see anything of themselves and each other[1] except the shadows which the fire casts upon the wall of the cave in front of them?

How could they, if they have to keep their heads still b throughout life?

And is not the same true of the objects carried along the wall?

Quite.

If they could converse with one another, do you not think that they would consider these shadows to be the real things?

Necessarily.

What if their prison had an echo which reached them from in front of them? Whenever one of the carriers passing behind the wall spoke, would they not think that it was the shadow passing in front of them which was talking? Do you agree?

By Zeus I do.

Altogether then, I said, such men would believe the c truth to be nothing else than the shadows of the artifacts?

They must believe that.

Consider then what deliverance from their bonds and the curing of their ignorance would be if something like this naturally happened to them. Whenever one of them was freed, had to stand up suddenly, turn his head, walk, and look up toward the light, doing all that would give him pain, the flash of the fire would make it impossible for him to see the objects of which he had earlier seen the shadows. d What do you think he would say if he was told that what he saw then was foolishness, that he was now somewhat closer to reality and turned to things that existed more fully, that he saw more correctly? If one then pointed to each of the objects passing by, asked him what each was, and forced him to answer, do you not think he would be at a loss and believe that the things which he saw earlier were truer than the things now pointed out to him?

Much truer.

---

1   *imagine men to be living ... themselves and each other* These shadows of themselves and each other are never mentioned again. A Platonic myth or parable, like a Homeric simile, is often elaborated in considerable detail. These contribute to the vividness of the picture but often have no other function, and it is a mistake to look for any symbolic meaning in them. It is the general picture that matters.

e   If one then compelled him to look at the fire itself, his eyes would hurt, he would turn round and flee toward those things which he could see, and think that they were in fact clearer than those now shown to him.

Quite so.

And if one were to drag him thence by force up the rough and steep path, and did not let him go before he was
516 dragged into the sunlight, would he not be in physical pain and angry as he was dragged along? When he came into the light, with the sunlight filling his eyes, he would not be able to see a single one of the things which are now said to be true.

Not at once, certainly.

I think he would need time to get adjusted before he could see things in the world above; at first he would see shadows most easily, then reflections of men and other things in water, then the things themselves. After this he would see objects in the sky and the sky itself more easily at
b night, the light of the stars and the moon more easily than the sun and the light of the sun during the day.

Of course.

Then, at last, he would be able to see the sun, not images of it in water or in some alien place, but the sun itself in its own place, and be able to contemplate it.

That must be so.

After this he would reflect that it is the sun which pro-
c vides the seasons and the years, which governs everything in the visible world, and is also in some way the cause of those other things which he used to see.

Clearly that would be the next stage.

What then? As he reminds himself of his first dwelling place, of the wisdom there and of his fellow prisoners, would he not reckon himself happy for the change, and pity them?

Surely.

And if the men below had praise and honors from each other, and prizes for the man who saw most clearly the shadows that passed before them, and who could best remember which usually came earlier and which later, and
d which came together and thus could most ably prophesy the future, do you think our man would desire those rewards and envy those who were honored and held power among the prisoners, or would he feel, as Homer put it, that he certainly wished to be "serf to another man without possessions upon the earth"[1] and go through any suffering, rather than share their opinions and live as they do?

Quite so, he said, I think he would rather suffer e
anything.

Reflect on this too, I said. If this man went down into the cave again and sat down in the same seat, would his eyes not be filled with darkness, coming suddenly out of the sunlight?

They certainly would.

And if he had to contend again with those who had remained prisoners in recognizing those shadows while his sight was affected and his eyes had not settled down—and 517
the time for this adjustment would not be short—would he not be ridiculed? Would it not be said that he had returned from his upward journey with his eyesight spoiled, and that it was not worthwhile even to attempt to travel upward? As for the man who tried to free them and lead them upward, if they could somehow lay their hands on him and kill him, they would do so.

They certainly would.

This whole image, my dear Glaucon, I said, must be related to what we said before. The realm of the visible b
should be compared to the prison dwelling, and the fire inside it to the power of the sun. If you interpret the upward journey and the contemplation of things above as the upward journey of the soul to the intelligible realm, you will grasp what I surmise since you were keen to hear it. Whether it is true or not only the god knows, but this is how I see it, namely that in the intelligible world the Form c
of the Good is the last to be seen, and with difficulty; when seen it must be reckoned to be for all the cause of all that is right and beautiful, to have produced in the visible world both light and the fount of light, while in the intelligible world it is itself that which produces and controls truth and intelligence, and he who is to act intelligently in public or in private must see it.

I share your thought as far as I am able.

Come then, share with me this thought also: do not be surprised that those who have reached this point are unwilling to occupy themselves with human affairs, and that their souls are always pressing upward to spend their time there, d
for this is natural if things are as our parable indicates.

That is very likely.

Further, I said, do you think it at all surprising that anyone coming to the evils of human life from the contemplation of the divine behaves awkwardly and appears

---

1   *serf to ... the earth*   Homer, *Odyssey* 11, 489–90, where Achilles says to Odysseus, on the latter's visit to the underworld, that he

would rather be a servant to a poor man on earth than king among the dead.

very ridiculous while his eyes are still dazzled and before he is sufficiently adjusted to the darkness around him, if he is compelled to contend in court or some other place about the shadows of justice or the objects of which they are shadows, and to carry through the contest about these in the way these things are understood by those who have never seen Justice itself?

That is not surprising at all.

Anyone with intelligence, I said, would remember that the eyes may be confused in two ways and from two causes, coming from light into darkness as well as from darkness into light. Realizing that the same applies to the soul, whenever he sees a soul disturbed and unable to see something, he will not laugh mindlessly but will consider whether it has come from a brighter life and is dimmed because unadjusted, or has come from greater ignorance into greater light and is filled with a brighter dazzlement. The former he would declare happy in its life and experience, the latter he would pity, and if he should wish to laugh at it, his laughter would be less ridiculous than if he laughed at a soul that has come from the light above.

What you say is very reasonable.

We must then, I said, if these things are true, think something like this about them, namely that education is not what some declare it to be; they say that knowledge is not present in the soul and that they put it in, like putting sight into blind eyes.

They surely say that.

Our present argument shows, I said, that the capacity to learn and the organ with which to do so are present in every person's soul. It is as if it were not possible to turn the eye from darkness to light without turning the whole body; so one must turn one's whole soul from the world of becoming until it can endure to contemplate reality, and the brightest of realities, which we say is the Good.

Yes.

Education then is the art of doing this very thing, this turning around, the knowledge of how the soul can most easily and most effectively be turned around; it is not the art of putting the capacity of sight into the soul; the soul possesses that already but it is not turned the right way or looking where it should. This is what education has to deal with.

That seems likely.

Now the other so-called virtues of the soul seem to be very close to those of the body—they really do not exist before and are added later by habit and practice—but the virtue of intelligence belongs above all to something more divine, it seems, which never loses its capacity but, according to which way it is turned, becomes useful and beneficial or useless and harmful. Have you never noticed in men who are said to be wicked but clever, how sharply their little soul looks into things to which it turns its attention? Its capacity for sight is not inferior, but it is compelled to serve evil ends, so that the more sharply it looks the more evils it works.

Quite so.

Yet if a soul of this kind had been hammered at from childhood and those excrescences had been knocked off it which belong to the world of becoming and have been fastened upon it by feasting, gluttony, and similar pleasures, and which like leaden weights draw the soul to look downward—if, being rid of these, it turned to look at things that are true, then the same soul of the same man would see these just as sharply as it now sees the things towards which it is directed.

That seems likely.

Further, is it not likely, I said, indeed it follows inevitably from what was said before, that the uneducated who have no experience of truth would never govern a city satisfactorily, nor would those who are allowed to spend their whole life in the process of educating themselves; the former would fail because they do not have a single goal at which all their actions, public and private, must aim; the latter because they would refuse to act, thinking that they have settled, while still alive, in the faraway islands of the blessed.[1]

True.

It is then our task as founders, I said, to compel the best natures to reach the study which we have previously said to be the most important, to see the Good and to follow that upward journey. When they have accomplished their journey and seen it sufficiently, we must not allow them to do what they are allowed to do today.

What is that?

To stay there, I said, and to refuse, to go down again to the prisoners in the cave, there to share both their labors and their honors, whether these be of little or of greater worth.

Are we then, he said, to do them an injustice by making them live a worse life when they could live a better one?

You are again forgetting, my friend, I said, that it is not the law's concern to make some one group in the city

---

1 *islands of the blessed* A place of eternal happy life after death.

outstandingly happy but to contrive to spread happiness throughout the city, by bringing the citizens into harmony with each other by persuasion or compulsion, and to make
520 them share with each other the benefits which each group can confer upon the community. The law has not made men of this kind in the city in order to allow each to turn in any direction they wish but to make use of them to bind the city together.

You are right, I had forgotten.

Consider then, Glaucon, I said, that we shall not be doing an injustice to those who have become philosophers in our city, and that what we shall say to them, when we compel them to care for and to guard the others, is just.
b For we shall say: "Those who become philosophers in other cities are justified in not sharing the city's labors, for they have grown into philosophy of their own accord, against the will of the government in each of those cities, and it is right that what grows of its own accord, as it owes no debt to anyone for its upbringing, should not be keen to pay it to anyone. But we have made you in our city kings and leaders of the swarm, as it were, both to your own advantage and to that of the rest of the city; you are better and more completely educated than those others, and you are better able to share in both kinds of life.[1] Therefore you
c must each in turn go down to live with other men and grow accustomed to seeing in the dark. When you are used to it you will see infinitely better than the dwellers below; you will know what each kind of image is and of what it is an image, because you have seen the truth of things beautiful and just and good, and so, for you as for us, the city will be governed as a waking reality and not as in a dream, as the majority of cities are now governed by men who are fighting shadows and striving against each other in order to rule as if
d this were a great good." For this is the truth: a city in which the prospective rulers are least keen to rule must of necessity be governed best and be most free from civil strife, whereas a city with the opposite kind of rulers is governed in the opposite way.

Quite so.

Do you think that those we nurtured will disobey us and refuse to share the labors of the city, each group in turn, though they may spend the greater part of their time dwelling with each other in a pure atmosphere?

They cannot, he said, for we shall be giving just orders e to just men, but each of them will certainly go to rule as to something that must be done, the opposite attitude from that of the present rulers in every city.

That is how it is, my friend, I said. If you can find a way of life which is better than governing for the prospective 521 governors, then a well-governed city can exist for you. Only in that city will the truly rich rule, not rich in gold but in the wealth which the happy man must have, a life with goodness and intelligence. If beggars hungry for private goods go into public life, thinking that they must snatch their good from it, the well-governed city cannot exist, for then office is fought for, and such a war at home inside the city destroys them and the city as well.

Very true.

Can you name, I said, any other life than that of true b philosophy which disdains political office?

No, by Zeus.

And surely it is those who are no lovers of governing who must govern. Otherwise, rival lovers of it will fight them.

Of course.

What other men will you compel to become guardians of the city rather than those who have the best knowledge of the principles that make for the best government of a city and who also know honors of a different kind, and a better life than the political?

No one else.

[...]

Book 8

Very well. These things then, Glaucon, are agreed. If a city 543 is to be well governed, wives, children, and all education must be in common, and so too their occupations in peace and war must be common to both sexes; their kings[2] must be those who are best in the practice of philosophy and the waging of war.

That is agreed.

---

1 *both kinds of life* Political leadership and philosophical contemplation.

2 *kings* Plato uses the terms "kings" and "kingship" of his ideal state or "aristocracy" in contrast with the other cities, both here and elsewhere (see 4, 445d). It implies rule by law, persuasion, and consent, not by force. For the lives of the guardians and their lack of private property see the end of Book 3 (415d on). The position of women and the family are discussed in Book 5 (from the beginning to 462).

b   We have further agreed that as soon as the rulers are established they will lead the soldiers and settle them in such dwellings as we have mentioned, in which there is no private property but which are common to all. Besides the houses, we have also agreed, if you remember, what kind of possessions they will have.

I remember, he said, that we thought that no one should acquire any of the things that other people now do, but c that, as athletes of war and guardians, they should receive their yearly keep from the other citizens as wages of their guardianship, their duty being to look after themselves and the rest of the city.

That is correct, I said. But come, since we have completed this discussion, let us recall the point at which we digressed to reach our present position, so that we may continue along the same path.

That offers no difficulty, he said, for then, much the same as now, you were talking as if you had completed the discussion of the city; you said that you would class as good d the city which you had described, and that the good man was he who resembled it, although it seems that you still 544 had a finer city and man about which to tell us. You then mentioned the other cities which were of the wrong kind, if this one was right. You said, as I remember, that there were four kinds of other cities which would be worth discussing, observing their errors, as well as the men corresponding to them. Our aim was to observe them all, to agree which was the best man and which the worst, and then to examine whether the best man was the happiest and the worst most wretched, or whether matters stood otherwise. I was asking b you to say which were these four kinds of cities when Polemarchus and Adeimantus interrupted,[1] and so you took up the argument again and have now arrived at this point.

Your recollection, I said, is quite correct.

Well then, like a wrestler, give me the same hold again and, as I ask the same question, do you try to give the answer which you were about to give then.

If indeed I can, said I.

Indeed, he said, I am myself eager to hear what four cities you meant.

c   You will hear these without difficulty, for they are those which have names. There is that which is praised by most people, the Cretan or Laconian.[2] The second kind, which is

also second in the praise it receives, is called oligarchy and it is full of many evils. Then there is a different one which comes into existence next, namely democracy. Then the noble dictatorship[3] which stands out from all these is the fourth and last diseased city. Or can you name another kind which is in a clearly different class? For hereditary dynasties d and bought kingships and some such other forms of rule are somewhere between these named kinds and one can find as many of them among the barbarians as among the Greeks.

One hears of many strange kinds, he said.

You realize, I said, that there are of necessity as many ways of life for men as there are types of cities? Or do you think that governments are born "from oak or rock"[4] and e not from the characters of the men who live in the cities, which characters tip the scales and drag other things after them?

I do not believe, he said, that they have any other origin.

Then if the cities are of five kinds, the dispositions of the individuals' souls must be five also.

Quite so.

We have already described the man who is like aristocracy, whom we correctly state to be the good and just man.

We have.   545

After this we must describe the worse types: the lover of victory and honor who corresponds to the Laconian city, then the oligarchic man, the democratic, and the dictatorial, in order to observe the most unjust man and contrast him with the most just. Thus we will complete our investigation of the relation between pure justice and pure injustice with regard to the happiness and wretchedness of the men who

---

3   *noble dictatorship*   The Greek words *tyrannis* and *tyrannos* do not mean tyranny or tyrant in our sense, though they are often rendered that way in translations. The *tyrannos* is one who seizes power for himself without legal justification, by some sort of coup, and the most exact modern equivalent seems to be dictator, and so it is translated here. A Greek *tyrannos* was sometimes a very good ruler. As Plato's main argument is that a *tyrannos* is bound by his absolute power to become a tyrant, that translation fits the later part of his argument very well, though it is probably better to keep the same term throughout. Plato is of course well aware that the "tyrannies" often preceded full democracy in Greek history. He is using a time sequence to illustrate what is really a psychological analysis of different kinds of states and different types of characters corresponding to them.

4   *from oak or rock*   A Homeric expression, as for example *Odyssey* 19, 163, where Penelope asks the supposed stranger (who is Odysseus) who he is and his ancestry "for you were not born from an oak or a rock."

---

1   *when Polemarchus ... interrupted*   At the beginning of the fifth book.

2   *Laconian*   Spartan.

possess these qualities. We shall then be persuaded either by
b Thrasymachus to practice injustice, or, in the light of our
present argument, to pursue justice.

This we must certainly do.

Shall we then, just as we began by seeking moral qualities in the cities, as being clearer, before we did so in individuals, also now examine the city which loves honor—I
have no other name for it, or should we call it a timocracy
c or timarchy[1]—and then examine that kind of individual,
then oligarchy and the oligarchic man, then again after
examining democracy we shall observe the democratic man;
then fourthly we shall come to the city under a dictator
and observe it, and then look into the dictatorial soul? Thus
we shall try to become well-qualified judges of the problem
which we set ourselves.

It would be reasonable for our investigation and decision to proceed in this way, he said.

Come now, I said, let us try to explain how timocracy
emerges from aristocracy. Or is it a simple principle that
d the cause of change in any government is to be found in
the ruling group itself, whenever discord breaks out in this
very group. While it remains of one mind, even if it be quite
small, it cannot be removed.

That is so.

How then, Glaucon, I asked, will our city be changed?
How will discord arise among the auxiliaries and the guardians, both between the two and among themselves? Do you
e want us to do like Homer and to pray to the Muses that
they may tell us "how discord first broke out,"[2] and shall we
say that they express themselves to us, as to children, in tragic language, playfully and in banter, though their language
is lofty, as if in earnest.

How so?

546 In some such way as this: "It is hard for a city composed in this way to change. But everything that is born
must perish. Not even a constitution such as this will last
forever but it must face dissolution, and its dissolution
will be as follows. Not only all plants which grow in the
earth but all animals which grow upon it have periods of
birth and barrenness of both soul and body whenever the
cycles of their existence complete the circumference of their

circles. These are short for the short-lived, and the opposite
for their opposites. Those whom you have educated to be
leaders in your city, though they are wise, still will not, as b
their reasoning is involved with sense perception, achieve
the right production and nonproduction of your race. This
will escape them, and they will at some time bring children
to birth when they should not.

"For a divine creature which is born there is a cycle contained in a perfect number; for man it is the first number
in which are found root—and square—increases, taking
three dimensions and four limits, of the numbers that make
things like and unlike, cause them to increase and decrease
and which make all things correspond and rational in relation to one another. Of these the lowest numbers in the c
ratio of four to three, married to five, give two harmonies
when multiplied three times, the one a square, so many
times a hundred, the other of equal length one way, but
oblong, the one side a hundred numbers obtained from the
rational diameters of five, each reduced by one, or from the
irrational diameters reduced by two, the other side being a
hundred cubes of three.[3]

---

3   *For a divine creature ... cubes of three*   The mock heroic invocation to the Muses and their talking in tragic language should
warn us not to take the mathematical myth which follows too
seriously or too literally. It is perhaps the most obscure and controversial passage in the whole of Plato's works. Scholars are not
even agreed as to whether there is one Platonic number or two.
The latter seems to be the case since he speaks of a number for
the "divinely created thing" (which it is admitted must be the
universe) and one for the human creature. The actual world-
number is again pretty well agreed on. It is three multiplied by
four multiplied by five (i.e., 60), multiplied three times by itself,
which is 12,960,000. This represented geometrically can be
thought of as a square of which the side is 3,600 or as a rectangle
of which the longer side is 4,800 and the shorter 2,700. That
much is clear. The human number seems to be the addition of
the cubes of 3, 4, and 5, which is 216 (James Adam, in his edition of *Republic*, 1902, points out that this is the shortest period
of human gestation in days: seven months each reckoned as 30
days plus the Pythagorean marriage number 6).
    The numbers 3, 4, and 5 were the sides of the first right-angled
triangle of which the sides are whole numbers. This is the triangle
of which the Pythagoreans made much mystical use. They are
obviously basic to both the Platonic numbers and are here the
numbers which make things "like and unlike." The sides of the
rectangle are 2,700 and 4,800, the latter being "obtained from"
the diameter of 5, i.e., the diameter of a square whose side is 5,
which is the root of 50, which is irrational, and the nearest rational number is 7 and the number "obtained from" this is 49,
from which we are told to subtract 1 (i.e., 48) while the number
obtained from the irrational diameter is of course 50, and from

---

1   *timocracy or timarchy*   These words can refer to rule either by the
propertied class or by rulers guided by principles of honor. Here
Plato means the second.

2   *how discord first broke out*   This is not a Homeric quotation but
an imitation of his epic style. Compare his invocation of the
Muses at *Iliad* 16, 112.

"This whole geometric number controls this kind of thing, namely better and worse births. Whenever your rulers, in ignorance of this, join brides and grooms at the wrong time, the children will be neither talented nor fortunate. The older generation will make the best of these rulers, they are nevertheless unworthy, and when they acquire their fathers' powers they will as guardians neglect us, the Muses, first of all, thinking the arts less important then they ought. Then, in the second place, they will neglect physical training, and so your young people will become less cultured. As a result you will have rulers who do not have the proper guardians' character to test the races of Hesiod[1] and your own—the golden, silver, copper,[2] and iron races. Iron will then be mixed with silver and copper with gold, and a lack of homogeneity will arise in the city, and discordant differences, and whenever these things happen they breed war and hostility. From such parentage,[3] we must declare, civil discord is born wherever it occurs."

We shall, he said, declare the Muses' answer to be correct.

And so it must be, said I, since they are Muses.

And what, he asked, do the Muses go on to say?

As civil discord arises, I said, two kinds, the copper and the iron, draw men along to money-making and the acquisition of land, a house, gold, and silver, while the other two kinds, the gold and the silver, not being poor but rich by nature, draw men's souls to virtue and the old order. Violently opposed to each other, they agree to a compromise: they distribute the land and houses as private property, and those whom they previously guarded and considered as free men, friends, and providers, they now enslave and hold as serfs and servants, while they themselves still take care of their protection and defense in war.

I think, he said, that this is how the change started.

---

this we are told to subtract 2 (i.e., 48) and a hundred times this is 4,800. Plato is obviously playing with numbers and the details are probably not of great importance.

Behind it all, however, is the serious conviction that the laws of the universe can be expressed mathematically; the totality of those laws, had we sufficient knowledge, would be the mathematical aspect of the supreme reality, one aspect of the Form of Good.

1 *the races of Hesiod* The reference is to Hesiod's myth of the five races of men which succeed each other (*Works and Days* 109–202).

2 *copper* In many translations (and elsewhere in this one): *bronze*. (Bronze is an alloy of copper and tin.) In some other translations: *brass* (which is an alloy of copper and zinc).

3 *From such parentage* A Homeric expression. See *Iliad* 6, 211.

This government then, I said, stands between aristocracy and oligarchy?

Certainly.

This is how it will change. And, having changed, how will it be managed? Clearly, it will be like the earlier government in some respects, and like oligarchy in others, being between the two, and it will also have some features of its own.

That is so.

It will honor the rulers; the fighting section of the state will take no part in agriculture, manual labor, or other ways of making money; it will eat communally and devote itself to physical exercise and training for war; in all these ways it will be like the earlier city?

Yes.

On the other hand it will be afraid to appoint wise men to office, because such men are no longer simple and earnest, but of mixed nature; it then turns to spirited and simpler-minded men who are born for war rather than for peace; the tricks and devices of war are now held in high esteem, and the city spends all its time in making war. Most of these features will be all its own.

Yes.

Such men, I said, will be greedy for money, as men are in oligarchies; they will prize gold and silver without restraint but in secret; they will have private treasuries and storing places where they can keep it hidden; their houses will enclose them, like private nests where they can spend a great deal of money on women and anyone else they may wish.

Very true.

They will also be mean with money, since they prize it and do not acquire it openly, but they will be ready to spend other people's money because of their passion for it. They will enjoy their pleasures in secret, escaping from the law as sons from their father. They have not been educated by persuasion but by force, because they have neglected the true Muse, that of discussion and philosophy, and have honored physical training more highly than the arts.

The city you mention, he said, is altogether a mixture of good and bad.

Yes, I said, it is indeed a mixture. There is only one thing which appears in it most clearly under the rule of the spirited part, namely the love of victory and of honors.

Very definitely.

This then, I said, is the kind of government it would be and how it would arise, to sketch the shape of it without working it out in detail, for even from a sketch we shall discern the most just and the most unjust man, and it would be an intolerably long task to describe every kind of city and every kind of character without omitting any detail.

Correct.

Who is now the man who corresponds to this city? How does he come to be and what kind of a man is he?

I think, said Adeimantus, that he would be very like Glaucon here as far as the love of victory goes.

e   Perhaps in that respect, I said, but in the following respects he would be very different.

In what respects? he said.

He must be rather obstinate and somewhat uncultured, though he likes the arts; he must like to hear things, but is
549 in no way a speaker; he would be harsh to his slaves, but not because he looks down on them as a man of good education does; toward free men, however, he would be gentle and quite obedient to those in power, being himself a lover of power and honors. He does not believe that the capacity to express oneself, or anything of that kind, should lead to power, but rather deeds in war and concerning war, as he is a lover of physical training and the hunt.

Yes, he said, that is the character of that city.

Such a man, I said, would despise money while young,
b but welcome it more and more as he grows older, for he has his share of the money-loving nature. He is not pure in his attitude to virtue because he lacks the best of guardians.

What is that?

Reasonable discourse, I said, with an admixture of the arts, for this dwells in a man as the sole preserver of his virtue throughout his life.

Well said.

This then is the timocratic youth, and he resembles this kind of city.

c   Quite so.

And he comes to be, I said, in some such manner as this. He is the son of a good father who lives in a city which is not well governed. The father avoids honors and office and lawsuits and all that kind of business; he is even willing to be put at a disadvantage in order to avoid trouble.

How, he said, does the timocrat come to be?

He becomes such in the first instance, I said, when he
d hears his mother being angry because her husband is not one of the rulers and she is less esteemed among other women on that account. Then she sees that he is not very concerned about money, that he does not fight back when he is insulted in private or in the courts or in public, and

that he bears all this with indifference. She also sees him always concentrating his mind upon his own thoughts, neither greatly honoring nor slighting her. Angered by all this, she tells her son that his father is unmanly and too easygoing, and all the things which women repeat over and over again about such men.

Yes, said Adeimantus, they do say many things which are characteristic of them.

You know too, I said, that these men's servants sometimes say similar things to the sons covertly, those servants who are thought to be well disposed. When they see the father failing to prosecute someone who owes him money or wrongs him in some other way, they advise the son that when he grows up he must take vengeance on all those people and be more of a man than his father. The boy hears
550 and sees the same kind of thing when he goes out, that those who restrict themselves to their own affairs are called foolish in the city and held in low esteem, while those who meddle with the affairs of others are honored and praised. The young man hears and sees all this, but on the other hand he also listens to what his father says, observes what he does from close at hand, and compares his actions with those of the others. So he is pulled both ways; his father
b nourishes the reasonable part of his soul and makes it grow, the others foster the spirited and the appetitive parts. As he is not a bad man by nature but keeps bad company, pulled both ways he has settled in the middle and has surrendered the rule over himself to the middle part, the victory-loving and spirited part, and becomes a proud and ambitious man.

I certainly think, he said, that you have given a full account of the birth of this type.

We have then, I said, the second type of city and the c
second type of man.

We have.

After this then, to quote Aeschylus, let us talk of "another man placed over against another city,"[1] or rather, according to our plan, talk of the city first.

Quite so.

The one to come after this city is, as I think, oligarchy.[2]

_____

1   *another man ... another city*   The line does not occur in the extant plays, but it may be an adaptation of *Seven Against Thebes* 451, where Etocles is assigning a defender to each gate.

2   *oligarchy*   Both Plato and Aristotle use the term "oligarchy" (which now means government by a small group) for what we

And what kind of constitution would you call oligarchy? he asked.

The constitution based on income, I said, in which the
d rich rule, while the poor have no share of power.

I understand.

So now we must first tell how the timarchy changes into an oligarchy?

Yes.

Surely, I said, the manner of this change is clear even to the blind.

How?

That private treasury, I said, which each man has, becomes filled with gold and destroys the constitution. First they find ways of spending it on themselves, they twist the laws for this purpose, and they themselves disobey it along with their wives.

Likely enough.

e Then as one man sees another doing this and envies him, they make the masses like themselves in this.

That is probable.

Then as they proceed further into money-making, the more they honor this the less they honor virtue. Or does not virtue stand in such opposition to wealth that if each were in the scale of a balance, they would ever incline in opposite directions?

Certainly.

551 When wealth and the wealthy are honored in a city, virtue and the virtuous are prized less.

Clearly.

What is honored is always practiced, and what is slighted is neglected.

That is so.

In the end the lovers of victory and honors become money-lovers and money-makers; they praise and admire the wealthy man and appoint him to office while they disregard the poor man.

Quite so.

Then they pass a law which is the characteristic of oli-
b garchy by establishing a wealth qualification, higher where the government is more oligarchic, of a lesser amount where it is less so, having previously declared that those whose possessions do not reach the stated amount are not qualified for office. They either enforce this by force of arms, or else they

have terrorized people before they established this kind of government. Is that not so?

It is.

This, in general terms, is how this kind of government is established.

Yes, he said, but how does it work? And what are the flaws which we said it had?   c

First of all, I said, is the very nature of the characteristic we mentioned. For look, would anyone appoint the pilots of a ship this way, by their wealth, and not entrust the ship to a poor man even if he was a better pilot?

People who did that, he said, would make a poor voyage.

Is that not also true of the rule of anything else?

I think so.

Except a city? I said, or does it also apply to a city?

More than to anything else, he said, in so far as this is the most difficult and the most important kind of rule.

This then is one considerable flaw of oligarchy?   d

So it appears.

Further, is the following flaw less than this?

What?

The fact that it is of necessity not one city but two, one of the poor and the other of the rich, living in the same place and always plotting against each other.

This, by Zeus, is just as big a flaw.

And this is not a fine feature either, that they are probably unable to fight a war, because they would be compelled either to arm the people and use them, and be more afraid   e
of them than of the enemy, or, if they did not do so, they would indeed be oligarchs, being so few, in the actual fighting. At the same time they would be unwilling to pay taxes, being lovers of money.

Not a fine feature.

Moreover, there is also what we strongly disapproved of before, that the same men in such a state would fulfill many functions, being farmers and money-makers and warriors   552
all at the same time. Or do you think this right?

Not right at all.

But look whether of all the evils this is not the greatest, which is first found in this city.

What evil?

That a man may sell all his possessions and another may buy them,[1] and, having sold them, he lives in the city

---

call "plutocracy" (government by the wealthy). But as the rich are always few, the usage combines the two ideas.

1   *That a man ... buy them*   In a number of Greek states it was illegal to sell the family land, which was the core of the family fortune in

without being any part of the community, neither a money-maker nor a craftsman, neither cavalry man nor hoplite, but one they call a pauper without means.

b   Yes, and this is the first city to allow this.

Yet this is not forbidden in an oligarchy. If it were, some would not be excessively rich and others utter paupers.

Correct.

However, consider this: when this man was rich and spending his money, was he of any greater use to the city in the ways we have just mentioned? He appeared to be one of the rulers, but in fact was neither ruler nor subject in the city, but merely someone who was spending money that was ready to hand.

c   That is so, he said. He appeared to be part of the community, but he was nothing but a spender.

Should we say then, I said, that, as a drone exists in a cell and is an affliction to the hive, so this man is a drone in the house and an affliction to the city?

Quite so, Socrates.

The god, Adeimantus, has fashioned all the winged drones without stings, but of these two-footed drones some are stingless, while others have dangerous stings. The sting-less ones continue as beggars into old age, but it is from
d   among those endowed with stings that all those we call criminals come.

Very true.

Clearly then, in any city where you see beggars there are thieves hidden in the place, and footpads[1] and temple robbers, and the doers of all such evil deeds.

Clearly.

And do you not notice the presence of beggars in oligarchies?

Almost everyone, he said, except the rulers.

e   Shall we not believe then that there are many criminals with stings in these cities, whom those in office deliberately keep in check by force?

We think so.

And shall we not say that it is the lack of education and a poor upbringing, as well as the condition of the city, that are the cause of the drones' presence?

We shall.

This then, or something like this, is the oligarchic city; it contains these many evils, and perhaps even more.

I think so.

That completes our picture of this city which they call 553 oligarchy, where the rulers are chosen for their wealth. Let us now examine the man who is like it, how he comes to be and the sort of man he is.

By all means.

Does he change from the timocrat we described to an oligarchic man mostly in this way?

Which way?

The timocrat's son at first emulates his father and fol-lows in his footsteps; then he suddenly sees him crashing against the city like a ship against a reef and spilling all b his possessions and even his life. He had been a general or held some other high office, then he is brought to court by informers and put to death or exiled or disfranchised and loses all his property.

That is likely to happen.

The son sees all this, suffers from it, and loses all his property. Then, fearing for his life, right away he drives from the throne in his own soul the love of honors and c the spirited part which ruled there. Humbled by poverty he turns greedily to making money; little by little he saves, works, and gathers property. Do you not think that this man would establish his appetitive and money-making part on that inner throne and make this a great king within himself, adorning him with golden tiaras and collars and girding him with Persian swords?[2]

I do think so.

The reasonable and spirited parts he makes sit upon d the ground beneath the king, one on either side, reducing them to slaves, the first he will not allow to reason about or examine anything else than how little money can be made into much; while he does not allow the other part to honor or admire anything but wealth and wealthy men, or to have any other ambition than the acquisition of wealth or of anything which may contribute to this.

No other change, he said, will as quickly or as certainly turn a young lover of honors into a lover of money.

And he then, I said, is the oligarchic man? e

---

a society where investment was obviously less developed and less reliable than in modern societies.

1   *footpads* Those who rob people on foot.

2   *this man ... Persian swords?* We should note that while the reason-able or philosophic part of the soul dominates in the "aristocrat," and the spirited part in the timocrat, it is the appetitive part which dominates in the last three cities and men, the difference being that in the oligarch the dominant desire is for money, which still requires some control, the democrat treats all desires as equal, and the dictator is ruled by his worst, his "unnecessary" appetites.

The change in the man is surely the same as that which made for an oligarchy in the city.

Let us look then whether he is similar to the city.

554 Let us.

He is like the city in the first place in that he attaches the greatest importance to money.

Of course.

Further, in that he is thrifty and a worker, satisfying only his necessary appetites, and makes no other expenditures, but he enslaves his other desires as vain.

Quite so.

He is somewhat squalid, I said, making a profit from everything; the sort of man the crowd approves of. Is this b not the man who resembles such a city?

I certainly think so, he said. Possessions are certainly held in honor by both the city and the man.

I do not think, I said, that such a man pays any attention to education.

I think not, he said. If he did he would not have chosen a blind leader[1] of his dance and honored him most.

Good, said I, but consider this: shall we not say that dronish appetites exist in him because of his lack of educa-c tion: some are beggarly, others are evil, but they are forcibly held in check by his other preoccupation?

Definitely.

Do you know where you should look to see their malpractices?

Where?

If he happens to be the guardian of orphans, or something of the kind, where he would have great opportunities to do wrong.

True.

Does this not make it clear that in his other associations where he has a good reputation and is thought to be just, d he forcibly holds his other evil appetites in check by means of some good part of himself? He does not persuade himself that it is better not to indulge them, nor does he tame them by reasoning, but he acts under the compulsion of fear, trembling for his other possessions.

Quite so.

And by Zeus, my friend, I said, you will find that when other people's money has to be spent, they have appetites which are akin to those of the drone.

That is most certainly true.

---

1   *blind leader* Plutus, the god of wealth, who is represented as blind, e.g., in the *Plutus* of Aristophanes.

Such a man would not, then, be without discord within himself, he is not one man but two, though generally his better appetites are in control of his worse.   e

That is so.

For this reason the man would be more respectable than many, but the true excellence of a harmonious soul, of one mind within itself, escapes him by far.

I think so.

Further, this thrifty man is a poor antagonist in any private contest for victory or some other fine rivalry, as he 555 is not willing to spend money for the sake of renown or for any contest of that kind. He is afraid to arouse his spending appetites or to call on them as allies to obtain victory, so he fights with only a small part of himself in the oligarchic manner, and so he is mostly defeated—and remains rich.

Quite so.

Have we any further doubt that the thrifty money-maker corresponds to the oligarchic city and is like it?   b

No doubt at all.

After this we must consider democracy, how it originated and how it functions once it has come into existence, in order that we should know the manner of life of the democratic man and put him beside the city for judgment.

We would be proceeding consistently in doing so.

Well, I said, the city changes from an oligarchy to a democracy in some such way as this, because of its insatiable desire to attain what it has set before itself as the good, namely the need to become as rich as possible.

How so?

I think that, in as much as those who rule in the city c do so because they have accumulated great possessions, they are not willing to prevent by law the intemperate among the young from spending and wasting their substance. Their intention is to buy them up and lend them money so that they themselves will become even richer and more honored.

Now this is quite clear: it is impossible to honor wealth in a city and at the same time for the citizens to acquire sufficient moderation; one or the other is inevitably neglected.   d

Quite clear.

Because of this neglect, and because they do not restrain the intemperate, men of good birth are often reduced to poverty in oligarchies.

Quite so.

So there they are in the city, with their stings and their weapons; some of them are in debt; some are disfranchised, some are both; they hate those who have acquired their

property and plot against them as well as against others,
e and they long for revolution.

That is so.

The money-makers on the other hand keep their eyes on the ground and do not appear to see them, but they injure anyone of the others who yields to them by providing him with money and exacting as interest many times the
556 principal sum, and so they create a considerable number of drones and beggars in the city.

Certainly a good many.

And as this evil flares up in the city they do not wish to quench it either in the way we mentioned, by preventing people doing whatever they please with their own, or by another law which might solve the problem.

What law?

One which is a second best but which compels people to pay attention to virtue, if it prescribes that the majority
b of private contracts be entered into at one's own risk; they would then be less shameless in their pursuit of money in the city and fewer of those evils we were mentioning just now would develop.

Far fewer.

But as it is now, I said, for all these reasons this is the condition to which the rulers reduce their subjects in the city. As for themselves and their children, do they not make the young fond of luxury, incapable of effort either physical
c or mental, soft in the face of pleasure and pain, and lazy besides?

Surely.

They neglect everything except making money, and care no more for virtue than the poor do.

Indeed they do not.

When rulers and subjects in this condition meet each other on a journey or on some other common pursuit, at festivals or on an embassy or on a campaign, on shipboard
d or in the army, and observe each other facing danger, on those occasions the poor are not despised by the rich. Often a poor man, spare and suntanned, stands in battle next to a rich man who is pale for lack of sun with much superfluous flesh, and sees him panting and at a loss. Do you not think that he would consider that it is through the cowardice of the poor that people like that are rich, and one poor man would say to the other as they met privately: "These men are
e at our mercy; they are no good."

I know very well that they do this.

Then, as a sick body needs only a slight shock from outside to fall into illness and sometimes even without this

it is in a state of civil strife, so a city which is in the same plight needs but a small excuse and, as one side brings in allies from an oligarchic city or the other from a democracy, the city is ill and fights itself, and sometimes a revolution occurs even without outside help.

Most certainly.

I think democracy comes when the poor are victorious,
557 kill some of the other side, expel others, and to the rest they give an equal share of political power and offices, and generally the offices are filled by lot in this city.

Yes, he said, that is how democracy is established, be it by force of arms or because those on the other side are frightened into exile.

How do they live then? I asked. Of what kind is this city? For clearly a man of this kind will turn out to be a
b democratic man.

Clearly.

First of all they are free, and the city becomes full of liberty and freedom of speech, and in it one can do anything one pleases.

So they say.

Where this opportunity exists, everyone will arrange his own life in any manner that pleases him.

Obviously.

And in this city above all others there would, I think,
c be all sorts of people.

Of course.

This is probably the most beautiful of all constitutions. Like a cloak embroidered with every kind of ornament, so this city, embroidered with every kind of character, would seem the most beautiful, and perhaps many would judge it to be so, like children and women gazing at embroideries of many colors.

They certainly would.

It is also, my good friend, I said, a convenient place to
d look for a constitution.

How do you mean?

It contains all kinds of constitutions because of its permissiveness, and the man who wants to establish a city, as we were doing, should probably go to a democracy as if it were an emporium of constitutions, pick out whatever type pleases him and establish that.

Perhaps he would not be at a loss for models.
e

In this city, I said, there is no compulsion to rule, even if you are capable of it, or again to be ruled if you do not want to be, or to be at war when the others are, or at peace unless you desire peace. If some law forbids you to hold

office or to go to law, you nevertheless do both if it occurs
558 to you to do so. Is that not a divine and pleasant life for the
time being?

Perhaps, he said, for the time being.

And is the placidity of some of their condemned criminals not civilized? Or have you not seen in this city men who
have been condemned to death or exile stay in the city in
spite of this? The criminal strolls around like a hero's ghost,
without anyone seeing him or giving him a thought.

Yes, I have seen many such.

b   The tolerance in such a city! It certainly does not show
any petty concern for trifles. Indeed it despises those things
we solemnly spoke of when we were founding our city, as
that, unless a man had an exceedingly fine nature, he would
never become a good man unless from early childhood he
played fine games and followed fine pursuits. How magnificently this city tramples all this underfoot and does not give a
thought to what a man was doing before he enters public life.
c   It honors him if only he says that he wishes the crowd well.

An altogether noble city!

These are the qualities of democracy, and others like
these, and it would seem to be a pleasant constitution without any rulers and with much variety, distributing a kind of
equality to the equal and the unequal alike.

We certainly know what you mean.

Look now, I said, what is a man like that in his private
life? Or should we first enquire, as we did with the city, how
he comes to be?

Yes.

Well, does it not happen like this? The son of that
d thrifty oligarch would be brought up by his father in his
way of life.

Of course.

So he too controls his pleasures by force, repressing the
spendthrift ones that do not make money. These he calls
unnecessary.

Clearly.

Should we first define the necessary and the unnecessary desires to avoid discussing in the dark?

We should.

Those we are unable to deny we would be right to call
e necessary or those of which the satisfaction benefits us, for
we are by nature compelled to satisfy them. Is that not so?

Certainly.

559   So we would be right to apply the term necessary to
them.

Yes.

As for those which one could avoid if one trained
oneself to avoid them from youth, which lead to no good
or indeed to the opposite, would we not rightly call these
unnecessary?

We certainly would.

Let us pick an example of each, so that we may grasp
them as a type.

We must do so.

Is not the desire to eat to the point of health and well-
being, the desire for bread and cooked food, necessary?   b

I think so.

The desire for bread is necessary on both counts; it is
useful and it keeps one alive.

Yes.

That for cooked food is necessary too, if it contributes
in any way to well-being.

Certainly.

What of the desire which goes beyond this, for strange
foods and the like. This can be restrained from youth, and
schooled to leave most people; it is harmful to the body, and
to the soul also as regards thought and moderation. Would
it not be correct to call this unnecessary?   c

Very correct.

Shall we say that these are also the spendthrift pleasures,
while the others are profitable because they are good for
doing work?

Surely.

And so with the pleasures of sex and the others.

Quite so.

When we called a man a drone, we meant one who is
full of such pleasures and desires and ruled by those which d
are unnecessary, while we called one who is ruled by necessary desires thrifty and oligarchic.

Quite so.

Let us then repeat that the democratic man evolves
from the oligarchic, and it seems to happen for the most
part as follows.

How?

Whenever a youth who was brought up in the miserly
manner we described, and without real education, has a
taste of the honey of the drones and frequents wild and
dangerous creatures who can provide all kinds of varied
pleasures from all sources, think that there is the beginning e
of the change of the oligarchy within him to democracy.

Quite inevitably.

Just as the city changed when one faction received help
from like-minded people outside, so the young man chan-

ges when help comes from the same type of desires outside to one of the factions within himself.

Definitely.

And, I think, if any contrary help comes to the oligarchic faction in him, either from his father or the rest of the household who exhort and reproach him, then there is faction and counterfaction within him and he battles against himself.

Quite so.

Sometimes the democratic element yields to the oligarchic, and some of his appetites are overcome, some are expelled, a kind of shame arises in the young man's soul, and order is restored.

That does sometimes happen.

But then again as desires are cast out, other desires akin to them are nurtured unawares, and because of the father's ignorance of proper upbringing, they grow numerous and strong.

Yes, that often happens.

They draw him into the same bad company, and while they are with him they breed another crowd of desires unnoticed.

Surely.

In the end they occupy the citadel of the young man's soul, as they see it empty of knowledge, fine pursuits, and true reasoning, which are the best guards and guardians in the minds of men whom the gods love.

Very much so.

Instead of these, false and boastful reasonings and beliefs rush up and occupy this same part of such a youth.

Definitely.

Will he then not return to these lotus-eaters[1] and live with them openly? And if some help comes from his household for the thrifty part of his soul, these boastful discourses close the gates of the royal wall within him and will not allow those allies to enter, nor will they admit as envoys the wiser discourses which are emissaries of older persons, while they themselves fight and conquer; reverence they call foolishness, and cast it out beyond the frontiers as a disfranchised exile; moderation they call cowardice; they abuse it and throw it out; they persuade him that measured and orderly expenditure is boorish and mean; and with the help of many useless desires they expel it over the border.

They do indeed.

___
1   *lotus-eaters* Lazy, self-indulgent people. (In Greek mythology, this condition was caused by eating lotus fruit.)

Having thus emptied and cleansed the soul of their victim, which is being initiated with splendid rites, they now introduce into it insolence and anarchy and extravagance and shamelessness wreathed and radiant among many followers, eulogizing them and calling them by fair names; insolence they call good breeding, anarchy freedom, extravagance munificence, shamelessness courage. Is it not in some such way, I said, that, being young, he changes from one brought up among necessary desires to one who lets loose and indulges in unnecessary and useless pleasures?

Yes indeed, that is clearly the case.

After this, I think, such a man spends his money, effort, and time no less upon unnecessary than upon necessary pleasures. If he is lucky and does not overstep the boundary of frenzy, then, as he grows older and the great tumult has spent itself, he welcomes back some of the exiles and does not surrender himself completely to the newcomers, he puts pleasures on an equal footing and so spends his life, always surrendering the government of himself to one, as if chosen by lot, until he is satisfied and then to another, not disdaining any but fulfilling them all equally.

Quite so.

He does not welcome true reasoning or allow it into the guardhouse; if someone tells him that some pleasures belong to good and beautiful desires, but others belong to evil ones, that one should prize and pursue the former while the latter must be restrained and mastered, he denies all this and declares that all pleasures are equal and must be equally prized.

A man in that condition would certainly do so.

And he lives on, yielding day by day to the desire at hand. At one time he drinks heavily to the accompaniment of the flute, at another he drinks only water and is wasting away; at one time he goes in for physical exercise, then again he does nothing and cares for nothing; at times he pretends to spend his time on philosophy; often he takes part in public affairs; he then leaps up from his seat and says and does whatever comes into his mind; if he happens to admire military men, he is carried in that direction, if moneyed men, he turns to making money; there is no plan or discipline in his life but he calls it pleasant, free, and blessed, and he follows it throughout his time.

You have certainly described the life of a man who believes in legal equality.

I also think, I said, that he is a fine man of great variety full of all sorts of characters, just like that city. Many men

562 and many women might envy his life, for it contains the greatest number of governments and ways of living. Shall we then place this man beside democracy as being correctly called the democratic man?

Let him so be placed.

The finest government and the finest kind of man remain for us to discuss, dictatorship and the dictatorial man.

They certainly do remain.

Come, my dear friend, what is dictatorship like? That it evolves from democracy is pretty clear.

Obviously.

Does it not evolve from democracy in much the same way as democracy does from oligarchy?

b How?

What they put before them as the good, which was the basis of oligarchy, was wealth, was it not?

Yes.

Then their insatiable desire for wealth, and their neglect of other things for money-making was what destroyed it, was it not?

True.

Now insatiability for what democracy defines as the good also destroys it.

And what do you say it defines as such?

Liberty, I said. This is what you would hear in a dem-
c ocracy is its finest possession, and that this is the reason why it is the only city worth living in for a man who is by nature free.

That too is very often said.

Well, this is just what I was going to say, that insatiability regarding this, and neglect of other things because of it, is the thing which changes this government too, and puts it in a condition in which it needs dictatorship.

How so?

I think that whenever a democracy athirst for liberty has
d bad cup-bearers to preside over it and drinks too deeply of the pure wine of liberty, then the rulers, unless they are very accommodating and give plenty of liberty, are punished by the city and accused of being foul oligarchs.

Yes, that is so.

It abuses those who obey the rulers as willing slaves and of no account, but it praises and honors, both in public and in private, rulers who behave like subjects and subjects who behave like rulers. Must not such a city reach the extreme
e of liberty?

Of course.

Liberty makes its way into private households and in the end it breeds anarchy even among the animals.

What do you mean?

I mean, for example, that a father will accustom himself to behave like a child and to fear his sons, while the son behaves like a father, and feels neither shame nor fear before his parents, in order to be free. A resident alien is the equal of a citizen and a citizen the equal of a resident alien, and so too a foreign visitor.

563 That is what happens.

Yes it does, I said, and so do other such small matters. A teacher in such a community is afraid of his pupils and flatters them, while the pupils think little of their teachers or their tutors. Altogether the young are thought to be the equals of the old and compete with them in word and deed, while the old accommodate themselves to the young, and are full of playfulness and pleasantries, thus aping the young b for fear of appearing disagreeable and authoritarian.

The uttermost liberty for the crowd is reached, my friend, I said, in such a city when bought slaves, both male and female, are no less free than those who bought them. And I almost forgot to mention what great equality exists between women and men.

Well then, to quote Aeschylus,[1] shall we speak what c now comes to our lips?

Certainly, I said, and I put it this way: No one who has not experienced it would believe how much freer the animals who serve man are here than anywhere else. As the proverb says, dogs are literally the equals of their mistresses, and indeed so are horses and donkeys, accustomed as they are to making their way freely and proudly along the streets, bumping into anyone they meet if he does not get out of their way, and everything else too is full of liberty. d

You are telling me what I know, he said, for I often experience this when I walk in the country.

To sum up, I said. All these things together, you notice, make the soul of the citizens so sensitive that if anyone brings up a word about slavery, they become angry and cannot endure it. And you know that in the end they take no notice of the laws, written or unwritten, in order that there should in no sense be a master over them. e

Quite so.

That then, my friend, I said, is that so fine and vigorous government from which dictatorship seems to me to evolve.

---

1 *to quote Aeschylus* The source of this quotation is not known.

Vigorous certainly, he said, but what follows?

The same disease, I said, which developed in oligarchy develops here also, more widespread and virulent because of the permissiveness, and it enslaves democracy. In fact, excessive action in one direction usually sets up a reaction in 564 the opposite direction. This happens in weather, in plants, in bodies, and not least in politics. So excessive liberty, whether in the individual or the state, is likely to change to excessive servitude and nothing else.

Likely enough.

So, I said, dictatorship is likely to evolve from democracy, the most severe and cruel servitude from pure liberty.

That is reasonable.

I do not think that was your question, however, but you b asked what was the disease which developed in oligarchy and also in democracy and enslaved it.

That is true.

I mentioned that class of idle and extravagant men, some of whom were very brave leaders while others were their more cowardly followers. This class we compared to drones, the former endowed with stings, the latter stingless.

Quite correct.

Now these two groups cause disturbances in any city they inhabit, as phlegm and bile do in the body. The good c physician therefore, and the lawgiver of a city, must, no less than the good beekeeper, take precautions ahead of time, in the first instance to prevent their presence, and if they should be present, to cut them out of the hive as quickly as possible, cells and all.

Yes, by Zeus, he must certainly do that.

Shall we take up the question in this way, so that we may see our way more clearly to decide what we want?

Which way?

Let us divide a democracy into three parts in our d argument as it is in reality. One part is this class of idlers, and it grows here no less than in oligarchy because of the permissiveness.

That is so.

And it is much more bitter here than there.

How so?

There it is bitter because it is disdained but, as it is kept out of office, it is lacking in experience and does not become strong. In a democracy, however, this class is the presiding element, with few exceptions. The most bitter speak and act, while the rest of them settle, buzzing around the speakers' platform, and will not tolerate the opposition e of another speaker so that everything is managed by them in this city, with a few exceptions.

That is certainly so.

Then there is also the following group which can be distinguished in the crowd.

Which is that?

When everybody is trying to make money, those who are the most steady by nature generally become the wealthiest.

Probably so.

They would provide the most and the most easily available honey for the drones.

Yes, for how can one take honey from those who have very little?

So I think that these rich are called the drones' pasture.

Pretty well.

The people would be a third part, those who work with 565 their own hands. They take no part in politics and have but few possessions. This is the most numerous and the most powerful element in a democracy whenever they are assembled.

It is, he said, but they are not willing to gather often, unless they get a share of the honey.

They always do take a share, I said, as much as their leaders can give them as they take it from the prosperous and distribute it to the people, though they keep the greater share of it to themselves.

Yes, he said, that is how the people get their share. b

And those from whom it is taken are compelled to defend themselves by speaking and acting before the people in so far as they can.

Of course.

They are accused by the other side of plotting against the people and of being oligarchs, even when they have no desire for revolution.

Quite so.

So in the end, when they see the people trying to harm them, not of its own free will but through ignorance and being deceived by their accusers, then indeed they truly do c become oligarchs, not willingly but that drone stings them with this evil too.

Definitely.

Then there are impeachments and judgments and trials on both sides.

Quite.

Now the people are always in the habit of elevating one man as their champion above all others, and they nurture him and make him great.

That is the custom.

d   It is clear that this championship of the people is the one and only root from which dictatorship and the dictator can grow.

Quite clear.

What is the beginning of the change from people's champion to dictator? Or does it clearly come when the champion begins to behave like the man in the story which is told about the temple of Lycaean Zeus[1] in Arcadia?

What story?

That the man who has tasted human flesh, a single piece of it cut up among the pieces from other sacrificial
e victims, must inevitably become a wolf. Have you not heard that story?

I have heard it.

So too the man who has become the people's champion and dominates the mob that obeys him, does not abstain from spilling kindred blood. He brings his enemy to trial on false charges, as they often do, and blots out a human life. His impious tongue and lips taste the murder of kindred. He drives his enemy into exile, kills him, while he throws
566 out hints to the people of the cancellation of debts and the redistribution of land. Is not such a man inevitably fated either to be killed by his enemies or to become a dictator and from being a man become a wolf?

Quite inevitably.

He is the one who stirs up factions against the owners of property.

He is.

If he is exiled and returns despite his enemies, he comes back as a full-fledged dictator.

Obviously.

b   If they are unable to expel him or to kill him by denouncing him to the city, then they plot secretly to kill him.

Yes, that usually happens.

All who have reached this point on the road to dictatorship discover the often quoted request of the dictator, namely to ask the people for a bodyguard, so that the safety of their helper may be assured.

c   Quite so.

They give it to him because, I believe, they are afraid for his safety but quite confident about themselves.

Yes indeed.

Then, when a man of property sees this and, with his property, is accused of being an enemy of the people, he, as

the oracle to Croesus put it, "flees to the banks of the many-pebbled Hermus; he does not stay, and is not ashamed of being a coward."[2]

He would not, he said, have another chance of being ashamed.

True, I said, for if he was caught he would be executed.

He most certainly would.

As for the champion, mighty he is but he does not mightily lie in the dust:[3] having brought down many others, d
he takes his stand as driver on the chariot of state, having now become from a champion a complete dictator.

What is to stop him?

Shall we now, I said, describe the happiness of the man, and of the city in which such a mortal arises?

Certainly, let us describe it.

Will he not, during the first days, and indeed for some time, smile in welcome at anyone he meets. He says he is no dictator and makes many promises both in private and e
in public. He has freed people from debt and redistributed the land to the people and to his own entourage, and he pretends to be gracious and gentle to all.

He must do that.

But I think that when he has dealt with his outside enemies by making peace with some and destroying others, and all is quiet on the external fronts, the first thing he always does is to stir up a war, so that the people shall feel the need of a leader.

That is likely.

Also in order that by paying war taxes they become 567
poor and are compelled to concern themselves with their daily needs and thus are less likely to plot against him.

Obviously.

Besides, if he suspects some of having thoughts of freedom and of not favoring his rule, he would have an excuse to destroy them by giving them up to the enemy. For all these reasons a dictator must always stir up war.

He must.

And because he does this, he is the more readily hated b
by the citizens?

Of course.

Then some of those who have helped to establish the dictatorship and hold positions of power speak freely to

---

1   Lycaean Zeus   Greek: Zeus the wolf-god—he was seen as having wolf-like features and characteristics in some regions.

2   the oracle to Croesus ... coward   The story of Croesus' oracle is found in Herodotus 1, 55.

3   mighty he is ... in the dust   See Homer, Iliad 16, 776, the fight around the body of Cebriones who "in his might mightily lay in the whirling dust, his horsemanship forgotten."

him and to each other; that is, the bravest of them reproach him for what is happening.

That is likely.

The dictator must eliminate them all if he is intending to rule, until he leaves no one who is of any account among his friends or his enemies.

Clearly.

He must therefore keep a sharp lookout for anyone who c is brave, proud, wise, or rich; so happy is he that he must be the enemy of them all, whether he wants to be or not, and plot against them until he has purged the city.

A fine purge!

Yes, I said, the opposite of that which the physicians apply to the body. They eliminate the worst and leave the best, he does the opposite.

He is compelled to do this, it seems, if he is to rule.

d A happy kind of necessity! said I, which binds him and orders him to live with a crowd of inferior people and to be hated by them, or not live at all.

That is how he must live.

And the more his actions make the citizens hate him, the more numerous and loyal a bodyguard he needs.

Of course.

Who will these loyal people be; and where will he get them from?

They will come flocking of their own accord, he said, if he pays them.

Drones by the dog! I think you mean foreign drones, I e said, from all kinds of places.

You are right.

But whom will he get from the city? For he would not want to ...

Do what?

Deprive citizens of their slaves by freeing them and enlisting them in his bodyguard.

He certainly will, he said, since they will also be the most loyal to him.

What a blessed sort of person you make the dictator 568 out to be, I said, if those are the kind of friends and loyal followers he has, after doing away with his earlier ones.

Anyway, that is the kind he has.

These friends admire him, I said, and the new citizens associate with him while the good citizens hate him and avoid him.

How could they not do so?

It is not for nothing that tragedy as a whole is thought to be wise, and Euripides is outstanding in it.

How so?

Because he said, and this shows a subtle mind, that "dictators are wise who keep company with the wise"; and b he clearly meant that the wise are the company they keep.[1] Also, he said, he eulogizes dictatorship as something god-like, and both he and the other poets say many things like that.

Surely, I said, being wise, the tragic poets will forgive us and those whose government is close to ours, if we do not admit them into our city because they praise dictatorship.

I think, he said, that the more subtle among them will. c

I believe, I said, that they go round the other cities, collect crowds, hire men with beautiful, resounding, and persuasive voices, and draw the cities to dictatorship and democracy.

They do indeed.

Besides this they receive pay and honors, especially from the dictators, as is natural, then from the democracies, but the higher they go on the ascending scale of governments, d the more their honors fail, as if unable to keep up with them for lack of breath.

That is certainly true.

But, I said, we have digressed here. Let us say again from what source the dictator's army, that beautiful, numerous, and varied body which never remains the same, draws its sustenance.

Clearly, he said, if there are sacred treasures in the city, he will spend them, as well as the property of his victims, for as long as these last, thus necessitating smaller taxes from the people.

What when these give out?

Obviously, he said, he and his fellow revelers and com- e panions and mistresses will have to be fed from his father's estate.

I understand, I said. You mean that the people, who fathered the dictatorship, will have to feed him and his companions.

They will certainly be compelled to do so.

How do you mean? said I. If the people get angry and say that it is not right for a young son to be kept by his

---

1   *dictators are wise ... the company they keep* An otherwise un-known fragment, but Euripides obviously meant that it is wise for dictators to keep company with the wise—and he probably meant rulers in general, for the word *tyrannos* is often used in tragedy in this more general sense. Plato would be well aware of this, but he is being ironic, as he so often is when dealing with tragedy, and indeed poetry generally.

father, but on the contrary for the father to be kept by the son, and that they did not father the dictatorship and put him in power, in order that, when he had grown great, they should be enslaved to their own slaves and feed him and his slaves and the other rabble; but they hoped that his championship would free them from the rich, the so-called best people in the city. They now order him and his companions to leave the city, like a father driving a son with his mob of fellow revelers from the house.

Then by Zeus, he said, the people will learn what kind of creature they fathered, welcomed, and caused to grow, and that they are the weaker trying to drive out the stronger.

How do you mean? I said. Will he dare to use violence against his father, and to strike him if he does not obey?

Yes, he said, after he has taken away his arms.

You are saying that the dictator is a parricide, I said, and a cruel nurse to old age. This is now an acknowledged tyranny and, as the saying goes, the people, in trying to avoid the smoke of servitude to free men, have fallen into the fire of having slaves as their masters, and, in the place of that vast and pure liberty, they have put upon themselves the harshest and most bitter slavery to slaves.

That indeed is what happened.

Well then, I said, shall we not be justified in saying that we have adequately described how dictatorship evolves from democracy, and what its nature is when it has so evolved?

Quite adequately.

from Book 9

[...]

Can you wonder then if those who have no experience of truth have many unsound opinions about many other things as well as about pleasure and pain and what is between them? When they descend to pain they believe what is true, namely that they are in pain, but when, after pain, they ascend to the middle they firmly believe that they have reached fulfillment and pleasure.

By Zeus, I would wonder much more if it were not so.

Think of it this way, I said: are not hunger and thirst and the like a sort of emptiness in the body?

Quite so.

And ignorance and lack of sense are an emptiness in the soul.

Of course.

So the man who takes his share of food and the man who acquires wisdom would be filled?

Very much so.

Which kinds of filling do you think have a greater share of reality, those which fill with bread, drink, meat, and every other kind of food, or the kind which fills with true opinion and knowledge and intelligence and, in a word, with every kind of virtue. Judge it this way: do you think that what is concerned with the unchanging and immortal and with truth, being itself of the same kind and existing in a receptacle of the same nature, is more real than what is concerned with the mortal and ever changing, being itself of that kind and existing in a receptacle of the same nature?

That which is concerned with the unchanging is by far the more real.

And does the reality of the unchanging partake to any greater extent of reality than of knowledge?

Not at all.

Or partake more of truth?

Not that either.

If it partook less of truth, it would partake less of reality?

Necessarily.

Therefore the kinds of filling concerned with the care of the body have less share in truth and reality than those concerned with the care of the soul?

Much less.

Do you not think that the same difference applies to the body itself and the soul?

Certainly.

It follows that what is filled with things more real, and is itself more real, is more truly filled than that which is filled with things less real and is itself less real?

Of course.

If to be filled with things appropriate to our nature is pleasurable, that which is in fact more filled with real things will make one rejoice more really and more truly in true pleasure, while that which partakes of things less real will be less truly and lastingly filled and partake of a less reliable and less true pleasure.

Quite inevitable.

Now those who have no experience of wisdom and virtue but are always occupied with feasts and the like are carried down and then back up to the middle, and so they wander throughout their life but they never reach beyond to what is the true above. They never look up to it nor are carried thither; they have never been truly filled with what truly exists, nor tasted any stable and pure pleasure. They look down always with their heads bent to the ground like b cattle; at the banquet tables they feed, fatten, and fornicate. To get their fill of such things they kick and butt each other with iron horns and hoofs and kill each other. They are insatiable as they do not fill the real and continent part of themselves with true realities.

Socrates, said Glaucon, you describe the life of the majority like an oracle.

Must they not live with pleasures that are mixed with pain, illusory images of true pleasures, which take their c color from the juxtaposition, so that both appear intense? They implant in the foolish mad passions for themselves and they are fought for as Stesichorus tells us that the wraith of Helen was fought for at Troy by men who did not know the truth.[1]

It must certainly be something like that.

Must not similar things happen to the man who satisfies his spirited part at all cost? His love of honors makes him envious, his love of victory makes him violent, his irritability d makes him angry, and he pursues the satisfaction of honors, victory, and anger without reasoning or intelligence.

Such things must happen to him also.

But then, I said, let us confidently assert that those desires of even the profit-loving and honor-loving parts, which follow knowledge and reason and pursue with their help those pleasures which intelligence prescribes, will attain the e truest pleasures possible for them, since they are following the truth. These pleasures are their own, if that which is best for each thing may be said to be fully its own.

Indeed it is.

If the whole soul follows the wisdom-loving part and there is no internal dissension, then each part will be able to fulfill its own task and be just in other respects, and also each will reap its own pleasures, the best and the truest as 587 far as possible.

Very definitely.

But when one of the other parts rules in the soul to any extent, it cannot find its own pleasure and it compels the other parts to pursue a pleasure that is alien to them and false.

That is so.

And those parts which are most remote from philosophy and reason are most likely to do this sort of thing.

Very much so.

Is not that which is most remote from reason also remote from law and order?

Clearly.

The most remote have been shown to be the lustful and b dictatorial appetites.

By far.

The least remote are the kingly and well ordered?

Yes.

So I think the dictator will be furthest away from enjoying true pleasure, and his own, while the king will be nearest to this.

It must be so.

So the dictator will lead the least pleasant life, and the king the most pleasant.

Definitely.

Do you know, I said, by how much the dictator's life is less pleasant than the king's?

If you tell me.

There are, it seems, one genuine and two bastard pleasures, and the dictator is at the extreme end of the latter. c He avoids both law and reason, and lives with certain slave pleasures as his bodyguard. It is not easy to say by how much he is inferior except perhaps in the following manner.

How?

The dictator was third distant from the oligarch, for the democratic man was between them.

Yes.

So he lives with an image of pleasure which is thrice[2] removed from the oligarch as to its truth, if what we said before is true?

Quite so.

Now the oligarch in turn was third from the king, if we identify the king and aristocrat.

Third he is. d

So the dictator is three times three times removed from true pleasure.

So it appears.

The image of dictatorial pleasure, according to the number of its dimensions, is a plane.[3] By squaring and

---

1   *the wraith ... the truth*   The story, referred to by Plato in the *Phaedrus* (243a), was that Stesichorus had written a poem defaming Helen and was struck with blindness. He then wrote a palinode (a poem retracting what was said in a previously written poem) and recovered his sight. The palinode was that Helen herself was never at Troy, but only a wraith or shadow of her. The *Helen* of Euripides is based on this story.

2   *thrice*   Three times because the Greeks always counted the first as well as the last number of a series, e.g., the day after tomorrow was the third day.

3   *a plane*   9 can be said to be a plane because it is the square of 3, but Plato does not say why he then cubes 9. Is it because we are

cubing this number it will become clear how large is the distance between the dictator and the king.

Clear at any rate to a mathematician.

e Turning this around, if one wants to know how far the king is superior to the dictator in the truth of his pleasure, he will find, if he completes his multiplication, that the king lives seven hundred and twenty-nine times more pleasantly than the dictator, and that the dictator is the same number of times more miserable.[1]

588 You have brought up an extraordinary calculation, he said, of the difference between the two men, the just and the unjust, as regards pleasure and pain.

Yet it is a true one, I said, and a number appropriate to human life, if days and nights and months and years are appropriate to them.

They surely are.

Then if the good and just man wins out over the bad and unjust to such an extent in pleasure, by how much more will he surpass him in the graciousness of his life, its beauty and excellence.

By Zeus yes, he certainly will.

b Very well, I said. As we have come to this point in our discussion, let us take up again what was said at first, which has led us to this. It was said at some point that injustice was to the benefit of the completely unjust man who had a reputation for justice, was it not?[2]

It certainly was.

Since we have fully agreed, I said, upon the effect of each, that is, of just and unjust behavior, let us now talk to the man who maintains this point of view.

How?

Let us in our argument fashion an image of the soul, so that he may understand the kind of thing he was saying.

c What kind of image?

One of the kind that are told in ancient legends about creatures like the Chimera,[3] Scylla,[4] Cerberus,[5] and many others in whose natures many different kinds had grown into one.

We are told of such creatures.

Fashion me then one kind of multiform beast with many heads, a ring of heads of both tame and wild animals, who is able to change these and grow them all out of himself.

d A work for a clever modeler, he said. However, as words are more malleable than wax and such things, take it as fashioned.

Then one other form, that of a lion, and another of a man, but the first form of all is much the largest, and the second second.

That is easy and it is done.

Gather the three into one, so that they somehow grow together.

All right.

Model around them on the outside the appearance of being one, a man, so that anyone who cannot see what is inside but only the outside cover will think it is one crea- e ture, a man.

Done.

Let us now tell the one who maintains that injustice benefits this man, and that justice brings him no advantage, that his words simply mean that it benefits the man to feed the multiform beast well and make it strong, as well as the lion and all that pertains to him, but to starve and weaken 589 the man within so that he is dragged along whithersoever one of the other two leads. He does not accustom one part to the other or make them friendly, but he leaves them alone to bite and fight and kill each other.

This is most certainly what one who praises injustice means.

On the other hand, one who maintains that justice is to our advantage would say that all our words and deeds would tend to make the man within the man the strong- b est. He would look after the many-headed beast as a farmer looks after his animals, fostering and domesticating the gentle heads and preventing the wild ones from growing.

---

concerned with a three dimensional world? In any case he wants the dictator to be as far removed from the king as possible.

1   *the king lives ... more miserable*   If Plato is following Philolaus who counted 364½ days in the year, there are 729 days *and* nights in the year, and the dictator is more miserable every day and every night. Plato may mean no more than that, though it seems that Philolaus also had a great year of 729 months.

2   *It was said ... was it not?*   The point was made at some length by Glaucon in Book 2, 361a ff.

3   *Chimera*   Fire-breathing female monster composed of lion, goat, and serpent.

4   *Scylla*   Also female, with six long necks, twelve dog-legs, and a fish's tail.

5   *Cerberus*   Three-headed dog with a snake for a tail who guarded the gate to Hades.

With the lion's nature as his ally, he will care for all of them and rear them by making them all friendly with each other and with himself.

This is most definitely the meaning of him who praises justice.

c What is said of justice is true in every way, and what is said on the other side is false, whether one examines it from the point of view of pleasure, of good repute, or of advantage; whereas he who condemns justice has nothing sound to say, and he does not know what he is condemning.

I don't think he does at all.

Let us then gently persuade him—he is not willingly wrong—by asking him: "My good sir, should we not say that beautiful and ugly traditions have originated as follows: d the beautiful are those which subordinate the beastlike parts of our nature to the human, or perhaps we should say to the divine, while the ugly enslave the gentler side to the wilder?" Will he agree or what?

He will agree if he takes my advice.

Can it benefit anyone, I said, to acquire gold unjustly if when he takes the gold he enslaves the best part of himself e to the most vicious part? Or, if by taking the gold he should make a slave of his son or daughter in the house of wild and evil men, it would certainly not benefit him to acquire even a great deal of gold on those terms.

If then he enslaves the most divine part of himself to the most ungodly and disgusting part and feels no pity for it, is he not wretched and is he not accepting a bribe of gold 590 for a more terrible death than Eriphyle when she accepted the necklace for her husband's life?[1]

Much more, said Glaucon. I will answer for him.

Then do you think that licentiousness has long been condemned because in a licentious man that terrible, that big, that multiform beast is let loose more than it should be?

Clearly.

Obstinacy and irritability are condemned whenever b the lion and snakelike[2] part is increased and stretched disproportionately?

Surely.

Are luxury and softness condemned because the slackening and looseness of this same part produce cowardice?

Of course.

And do not flattery and meanness come when this same spirited part is subordinated to the turbulent beast which accustoms it from youth to being abused for the sake of money and the beast's insatiability, and to become an ape instead of a lion?

Certainly.

c Why do you think the mechanical work of one's own hands is subject to reproach? Shall we say that it is so only when the best part of one's soul is naturally weak and cannot rule the animals within but pampers them and can learn nothing except ways to flatter them.

That is likely.

Therefore, in order that such a man be ruled by a principle similar to that which rules the best man, we say he must be enslaved to the best man, who has a divine ruler d within himself. It is not to harm the slave that we believe he must be ruled, as Thrasymachus thought subjects should be,[3] but because it is better for everyone to be ruled by divine intelligence. It is best that he should have this within himself, but if he has not, then it must be imposed from outside, so that, as far as possible, we should all be alike and friendly and governed by the same principle.

Quite right.

This, I said, is clearly the aim of the law which is the e ally of everyone in the city, and of our rule over children. We should not allow them to be free until we establish a government within them, as we did in the city, fostering the best in them with what is best in ourselves and securing 591 within the child a similar guardian and ruler, and then let him go free.

The law does make that clear.

How then and by what argument can we maintain, Glaucon, that injustice, licentiousness, and shameful actions are profitable, since they make a man more wicked, though he may acquire more riches or some other form of power?

We cannot.

Or that to do wrong without being discovered and not to pay the penalty is profitable? Does not one who remains b undiscovered become even more vicious, whereas within

---

1   *Eriphyle ... husband's life?*   She was bribed to persuade her husband to take part in a battle; he was killed, and her son murdered her in retaliation.

2   *snakelike*   The snake to represent the spirited part is a new image and presumably refers to the bad qualities developed by excessive development of that part as mentioned in 586c–d, or again when it has become an ape instead of a lion (590c).

3   *as Thrasymachus thought subjects should be*   Thrasymachus in the first book took the position that the subject must obey the ruler to the advantage of the ruler, not his own (See 339a and elsewhere).

the man who is discovered and punished the beast is calmed down and tamed; his whole soul, settling into its best nature, as it acquires moderation and justice together with wisdom, attains a more honored condition than a strong, beautiful, and healthy body, in so far as the soul is to be honored more than the body.

Most certainly.

c   The man of sense then will direct all his efforts to this end; firstly, he will prize such studies as make his soul like this, and he will disregard the others.

Obviously.

Then, I said, he will see to his bodily condition and nurture it in such a way that he does not entrust it to the irrational pleasure of the beast, turn himself that way, and live on that level. It is not even health he aims at, nor does he consider it most important that he should be strong, d healthy, or beautiful, unless he acquires moderation as a result, but he will cultivate harmony in his body for the sake of consonance in his soul.

That is altogether true, if he is truly to be a cultured man.

To the same end, there will be order and measure in his acquisition of wealth. He will not be panicked by the numbers of the crowd into accepting their idea of blessedness and increase his wealth without limit, and so have unlimited ills.

I do not think he will do so.

e   Looking to the government within, I said, he will guard against disturbances being caused there by too much wealth or too little, and he will direct, as far as he can, both the acquiring and spending of his possessions.

Very definitely.

592   He will have the same end in view as regards honors. He will share in, and willingly taste, those which he believes will make him a better man, but he will avoid both public and private honors which he believes will destroy the existing condition of his soul.

He will not then, he said, if that is his concern, be willing to go into politics.

Yes, by the dog, he will, I said, at least in his own kind of city, but not in his fatherland perhaps, unless divine good luck should be his.

I understand, he said, you mean in the city which we were founding and described, our city of words, for I do not b believe it exists anywhere on earth.

Perhaps, I said, it is a model laid up in heaven, for him who wishes to look upon, and as he looks, set up the gov-

ernment of his soul. It makes no difference whether it exists anywhere or will exist. He would take part in the public affairs of that city only, not of any other.

That is probable, he said.

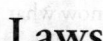

Laws

Book 1

The Scene: a summer day in Crete in the fourth century BCE.

Athenian visitor,[1] Kleinias the Cretan, Megillos the Spartan[2]

Athenian: Was it a god or a human, my foreign friends, who 624 is reputed to have laid down your laws for you?

Kleinias: A god, my friend, a god, to be absolutely right: among us it was Zeus, while among the Spartans, the home of Megillus here, I think they say it was Apollo.

Megillos: Yes.

Athenian: So do you say, with Homer,[3] that Minos[4] used to go for a conference with his father every ninth b year and he set up laws for your cities based on the god's pronouncements?

---

1   *visitor* "Visitor" translates "*xenos*" which is translated immediately below as "foreign friend" and thereafter mostly as "friend." The term denotes people from different cities who stand in a guest-host relation. We can assume that Kleinias is the host in Crete but all three men stand in a relation bound by rules of polite deference. The word is often translated "stranger," but that does not have the hospitable overtones of "*xenos*." (Non-Greek speakers were called "barbarians" [*barbaroi*] because they could only say "bar bar bar" and so were unintelligible to Greeks!)

2   *Kleinias the Cretan, Megillos the Spartan* Sparta and Crete had old constitutions. Aristotle discusses and compares them in *Politics* 2.9–10. Athens had a long and complex constitutional history, and the reformers were respected citizens.

3   *Homer* Reference to this passage can be found in Homer's *Odyssey* 19, 178–79.

4   *Minos* Mythical king of Crete, a son of Zeus and Europa. In Greek myth he and Rhadamanthus became two of the three judges of the dead when they died, because of their reputation for justice.

Kleinias: That's what we say: and also that Minos' brother Rhadamanthus—a name you will know—was the most just of men. We Cretans would say that he rightly won this reputation because of the way he handled judicial cases in those days.

Athenian: That praise is indeed noble, and especially fitting for a son of Zeus. Since you and this fellow were brought up under lawful habits of that kind, I expect you would not find it unpleasant to spend time now in discussion of a constitution and laws; we can talk and listen together throughout our journey. The road from Knossos to the cave and shrine of Zeus is quite long, I'm told, and in this heat we are sure to find resting-places along the way, shady ones among tall trees; at our age it would be appropriate for us to stop frequently at these and, by refreshing ourselves with conversation, make our way through the journey at our ease.

Kleinias: As one goes along, my friend, there are amazingly beautiful cypress trees in the groves and also meadows in which we can take leisurely rests.

Athenian: Well said!

Kleinias: Exactly: and when we have seen them, we'll have more to say. So let's be off, and may we have good luck on our journey.

Athenian: So be it. Now tell me, for what end has the law set up for you your communal meals, your gymnastic exercises and the kind of arms that you carry?

Kleinias: My friend, I think that our practices are easy for anyone to understand. You see, the nature of the whole Cretan landscape is not level like that in Thessaly—which is why they tend to use horses, while we go in for running. Our land is hilly and more suited to the practice of foot-racing. People have to use light arms in such terrain and be able to run without being weighed down; bows and arrows are suitably light weapons. These practices are thus all set up for warfare; and the lawgiver, I think, arranged them all with an eye to this end. It was probably through seeing that whenever they go on campaign, all the soldiers must eat together throughout, for their mutual protection, that he also set up the communal meals.

It seems to me that he judged the common people[1] foolish because they fail to understand that for all the people of a city, throughout their lives, there is always a continual war against all other cities. If in wartime it is necessary to eat together for the sake of protection, with some of both rulers and ruled appointed as guards, then the same should be done in peacetime. The legislator would say that's because what most people call "peace" is just a name; in reality, all cities are by nature in an undeclared state of war with all other cities. In this light, you will likely discover that our Cretan lawgiver organized all our institutions, both public and private ones, with an eye to war, and it is in virtue of this principle that he entrusted us with guardianship over the laws, supposing that unless one wins in war, no possession or practice is of any benefit, since all the goods of the conquered belong to the conquerors.

Athenian: You seem to me to have been very well trained, my friend, in analyzing Cretan institutions. But do explain this to me more clearly: you seem to me to be saying that the criterion for a well-governed city is that it should be organized so as to win in war against other cities. Isn't that so?

Kleinias: Of course: and I think our companion will think so too.

Me: How could a Spartan say anything else, honorable sir?

Athenian: Then if this is the right criterion for the relations among cities, is it any different between villages?

Kleinias: In no way.

Athenian: But the same?

Kleinias: Yes.

Athenian: Well then, for judging households in villages and men in those households, is the same criterion still applicable?

Kleinias: The same.

Athenian: In relation to himself too, should each person think of himself as one enemy against another? Or how else should we proceed?

Kleinias: Well, my Athenian friend—I would not want to call you "Attic"[2] as you seem to me to deserve to take your name from Athena. That's because you followed the argument by a very clear path to its starting point, so you will more easily understand why just now we were right to say that all are enemies of all, both in public life and privately within, being themselves pitted against themselves.

Athenian: What do you mean, you strange fellow?

---

1   *common people* Here "common people" translates *hoi polloi* (the many), a term used, often derogatively, to describe the lower classes in contrast to a smaller ruling group.

2   *Attic* The city of Athens is the centre of Attica, and an Athenian might be described as Attic or Athenian. Kleinias is complimenting the Athenian by noting his city's relation to Athena, the goddess of wisdom.

Kleinias: Right here, my foreign friend, in the victory of oneself over oneself, is the first and best of all victories; while being overcome by oneself is the worst and most shameful defeat of all. This way of talking clearly shows a war in each of us against ourselves.

Athenian: Now let's run the argument back the opposite way. Since each one of us is either superior to himself or inferior to himself, should we say or deny that a household and a village and a city have this same thing in themselves?

Kleinias: You mean that one is superior to itself and one is inferior?

Athenian: Yes.

Kleinias: That's another good question; everything *is* very much like this, especially in cities. In all those where the better people overcome the worse majority, the city would rightly be described as superior to itself and would most justly be praised for a victory of this kind; while the opposite would be true where things went the opposite way.

Athenian: We should pass over the question of whether the worse is ever superior to the better—that is a matter for a longer treatment—but now I understand you are talking about citizens who are related and born in the same city; when many unjust citizens come together, they will violently attack the smaller number of just citizens, trying to enslave them; when the unjust win, the city will rightly be described as inferior and bad, but wherever they are defeated, the city will be superior and good.

Kleinias: What you said sounds very strange: but one must agree that is how things are.

Athenian: Well then, let's reconsider this: many brothers may all be the sons of one man and one woman, and it will be no surprise if more of them are unjust and fewer just.

Kleinias: Of course not.

Athenian: It would not be fitting for you and me to pursue the point that when the wicked win, the household and the family would be *described* as "worse than itself," but as "better than itself" when the wicked are defeated. That's because its not for the way terms are used—well or not—that we are considering the language of the many,[1] but to find out what is by nature right or wrong in the case of laws.

Kleinias: Quite true, my foreign friend.

Megillos: I'd agree, that was a fine thing you said just now.

Athenian: Then let's consider this point: I suppose those brothers we just mentioned might come to have a judge?

Kleinias: Of course.

Athenian: Which is the better judge, the one who condemns all the bad ones to death and appoints the good to rule them, or the one who makes the good rule, but allows the worse to live if they are willing to be ruled? But suppose there were a judge who could take on a single divided family and reconcile them, without killing anybody; suppose too that by setting up laws, he could protect them against one another so that they remained friends throughout the future. Wouldn't we rank this third kind of judge as pre-eminent in virtue?

Kleinias: A judge and lawgiver of that sort would be far better.

Athenian: Yet he would set up the laws for them looking to quite the opposite of war.[2]

Kleinias: That's true.

Athenian: So what about the one who brings harmony to the city? Will he make rules for life by looking to external war or will he look rather to avoid the war that arises within the city, which we call "civil war"? Everybody passionately hopes this will never arise in his city and if it does, that it should be over as soon as possible.

Kleinias: He'd obviously look to avoiding civil war.

Athenian: If peace replaces war when one side is destroyed and the other victorious, is this to be preferred? Or if necessity required the citizens to devote their attention to outside enemies would it be better if peace and friendship arose through reconciliation?

Kleinias: All would prefer the second option for their cities.

Athenian: And wouldn't a legislator make the same choice?

Kleinias: Of course.

Athenian: So wouldn't every lawgiver set up all the laws for the sake of what is best?

Kleinias: Undoubtedly.

Athenian: The best is neither war nor civil war—one should reject the necessity of that—but rather it is peace and friendship towards one another. For a city to win a victory over itself is not one of the greatest goods, but among the necessities: that would otherwise be just like thinking that when a doctor has purified a sick body it

---

1 *the many* This is another use of *hoi polloi.*

2 *Yet he would set up ... opposite of war* His laws would be made to preserve peace within the city, not to prepare the city for war.

is in the best condition, ignoring the body which had never needed treatment. Similarly if one considered the happiness of a city or an individual in regard to war, he would not be a true statesman if he looked first and only towards external war, nor would he be a proper lawgiver if he did not make laws for war with the end of peace,

rather than setting up the laws for peace with an eye to warfare.

Kleinias: The argument does seem to have been rightly stated, my foreign friend, yet I'd be amazed if our laws and even more those of the Spartans were not all aimed wholly at success in external wars.

ARISTOTLE
(384 BCE – 322 BCE)

Who Was Aristotle?

ARISTOTLE WAS BORN IN 384 BCE IN STAGIRA, A SMALL town in the north-east corner of the Chalcidice peninsula in the kingdom of Macedon, many days journey north of the intellectual centers of Greece. Both his parents were descended from medical families. His father—Nicomachus, a physician at the Macedonian court—died when Aristotle was young, and he was first educated by his guardian Proxenus of Atarneus. At the age of seventeen Aristotle traveled to Athens to study at Plato's Academy. For most of his life thereafter he lived in foreign cities as a resident alien, and thus could take no active political role in those cities.

After Plato's death in about 347 BCE, Aristotle left Athens (possibly pushed out by a surge of anti-Macedonian feeling in the city—though another story suggests that he left in a fit of pique after failing to be granted the leadership of the Academy after Plato, and yet another account has it that Aristotle was unhappy with the Academy's turn towards pure mathematics under Plato's successor, Speusippus). He traveled to Atarneus on the coast of Asia Minor (present-day Turkey) where his mother's family had connections and where the pro-Macedonian tyrant, Hermias, was a patron of philosophical studies. There, with three of his colleagues from the Academy, Aristotle continued his researches at the town of Assos. Aristotle married Hermias' niece and adopted daughter, a woman called Pythias, and they had a daughter, also called Pythias.

This happy familial situation did not last long, however; in about 345 BCE Hermias was betrayed and executed (in a particularly grisly fashion) by the Persians. Aristotle and his family fled Assos and moved to the city of Mytilene on the nearby island of Lesbos, in the eastern Aegean Sea. There, with his friend Theophrastus, he engaged in a hugely impressive series of studies in botany, zoology and marine biology, collecting observations which were still of unrivalled scientific interest some two thousand years later. (Indeed, as late as the nineteenth century Charles Darwin was able to praise Aristotle's biological research as a work of genius which every professional biologist should read.)

Aristotle's stay on Lesbos also turned out to be of short duration: in 343 BCE he was invited by Philip II, the ruler of Macedonia, to return home to tutor the thirteen-year-old prince Alexander. Little is reliably known about Aristotle's life during this period—though many fanciful stories have been written about it. Three years later, on the death of Philip, Alexander became king and started the military career which, in fairly short order, made him the conqueror of much of the known world and earned him the epithet Alexander the Great. (One charming historical story claims that when Alexander embarked on his conquest of the East—his armies advanced as far as the Indian sub-continent—he took scientists with him whose sole job it was to report their discoveries back to Aristotle.)

In 335 BCE, after Alexander's troops had completed their conquest of the Greek city-states, Aristotle moved back to Athens where, once again, he started his own research institute. This was located in a building known as the Lyceum (after the grove, dedicated to Apollo Lyceus, where it stood), and it continued to flourish for 500 years after Aristotle's death.[1] There he spent the next twelve years teaching and writing—and building up the first known great library of the Greek world—and most of his philosophical writings we have probably date from this time. After his wife Pythias died, Aristotle lived with a woman called Herpyllis and they had a son, Nicomachus (named, as was the Greek custom, after his grandfather).

This peaceful existence was shattered when news of Alexander's death in Babylon (at the age of 33) reached Athens in 323 BCE. Almost instantly an open revolt against the Macedonian conquerors broke out, and Aristotle—because of his connection with Alexander—was suddenly no longer welcome in Athens. One of the citizens brought an indict-

---

1   Because philosophical discussions at the Lyceum were, after Aristotle's time, often conducted in a colonnaded walk called a *peripatos*, the members became known as "the Peripatetics."

ment of impiety towards him—the same "crime" for which Socrates had been executed by the Athenians three-quarters of a century earlier—and in order, as one tradition has it, to prevent the Athenians from sinning against philosophy a second time, Aristotle and his family beat a hasty retreat to Chalcis on the island of Euboea, where his mother's family had estates. There Aristotle soon died, in November 322 BCE, at the age of 62. In his humane and sensible will, preserved by Diogenes Laertius, Aristotle directed that Pythias' bones should be placed in his grave, in accordance with her wishes. He also freed several of his slaves and made generous and flexible financial provisions for Herpyllis and Nicomachus.

What Was Aristotle's Overall Philosophical Project?

Aristotle's life-work was nothing less than the attempt to collect together and systematically arrange all of human knowledge. His consuming ambition was to get as close as possible to *knowing everything*—about the natural world, the human social world, and even the unchanging and eternal world of the heavens and the gods. However, unlike many other philosophers with similar ambitions before and since, Aristotle probably did not believe that there is some single, unified set of truths—some single *theory*—which would provide the key to unlocking all of reality: he was not looking for a deeper and more authentic realm which lies behind and explains the world we live in, but instead was simply trying to find out as much as he could about *our* world, as we experience it. Thus, it is sometimes said that Aristotle's basic theoretical commitment was to *common sense*: he wanted to develop a system which would provide a place for both scientific and moral-political truths, but which did not depend on mysteriously invisible and inaccessible objects such as Plato's Forms (see the introduction to Plato).[1] For Aristotle, the ultimate reality is just the concrete world with which we are already acquainted made up of people, animals, plants, minerals, etc.—which Aristotle thought of as *substances* and their properties.

Often, Aristotle worked in the following way. After choosing a domain of study (such as rhetoric or metaphysics), he would begin by summarizing and laying out all the serious claims which had already been made about it—"what seems to be the case," including all the "reputable opinions" which have been recorded on the matter. He would also pay attention to the way in which the matters in question are ordinarily spoken of—the assumptions about them which are built into everyday language. Then, Aristotle would survey the puzzles or problems generated by this material, and would set out to try to solve those puzzles, preferably without disturbing too many of the received opinions. He typically would not stop there: new puzzles or objections would be raised by those solutions, and he would proceed to try and clear up those matters, and then the puzzles generated by those clarifications, and so on—each time, he hoped, getting closer to the final truth.

Since Aristotle did not believe in a single "theory of everything," he divided the different branches of knowledge, or "sciences," into three main groups: the theoretical sciences (whose aim is to discover truths), the practical sciences (which govern the performance of actions), and the productive sciences (whose goal is the making of objects). The major theoretical sciences, according to Aristotle, are theology—(which he thought of as the study of "changeless items")—mathematics, and the natural sciences; while the chief practical sciences are ethics and politics. Examples of productive sciences are poetics, rhetoric, medicine, and agriculture. According to Aristotle, these various sciences are quite different: although together they may help us to form a composite picture of reality, they share no single set of theoretical concepts or assumptions, no single methodology, and no single set of standards for scientific rigor. The proper methods of mathematics are different from those of zoology, which are different again from those of ethics.

On the other hand Aristotle believed that each science, or at least all the theoretical sciences, would share the same *structure*: Aristotle was the first philosopher to conceive of science as a body of knowledge arranged according to a particular logical structure; to him, geometry provided the model structure. As in geometry, there are two kinds of scientific truth, according to Aristotle: truths which are simply "evident" and need no explanation, and a much larger body of further truths which are justified or explained by being logically derived from the self-evident truths. (Aristotle more or less single-handedly *invented* the study of logic—which he called the science of "syllogisms"—partly in order to be able to describe the proper structure of scientific know-

---

1   Another contemporary theory to which Aristotle was opposed, also on the grounds of mystery-mongering, was a theory called "atomism," put forward by philosophers such as Leucippus (who flourished between 450 and 420 BCE) and Democritus (c. 460–371 BCE). This theory postulated the existence of huge numbers of invisibly tiny, eternal, unchangeable particles—*atoma*, Greek for "uncuttables"—whose hidden behaviors and interactions were supposed to explain all the observable properties of the visible spatio-temporal world.

ledge.) Unlike the case with geometry, however, Aristotle insisted that the "axioms" of any theoretical science—the self-evident truths upon which it is based—should ideally capture the *essences* of the things being described by that science. In this way, according to Aristotle, the logical structure of science would exactly reflect the structure of the world itself: just as the properties of things (say, plants) are caused by their essential natures, so will the claims of the relevant science (e.g., botany) be logically derived from its basic assumptions about the essences of the things in its domain.

Where, according to Aristotle, do we get these first principles of the different sciences *from*? The answer, Aristotle believed, was on the whole not from the exercise of pure reason but from careful *observation* of the world around us: by looking very hard and carefully at a particular domain (such as botany or ethics) we might be able to discern some fundamental truths about the things in that domain, from which everything else about it will follow. Because of this practical emphasis on observation rather than on thought in isolation, Aristotle is often thought of as "the father of modern empiricism." On the other hand, Aristotle never developed anything like an experimental method: his method for testing theories—verifying and falsifying them—consisted more in reasoned analysis than in empirical testing.

What Is the Structure of These Readings?

According to lists compiled of Aristotle's writings by later ancient biographers, Aristotle wrote some 150 works in his lifetime—ranging in length from essays to books—covering a huge variety of topics: logic, physics, biology, meteorology, philosophy of science, the history of science, metaphysics, psychology (including works on love, friendship, and the emotions), ethics and political theory, political science, rhetoric, poetics (and some original poetry), and political and legal history. Only a fraction of these writings—perhaps less than a fifth—still survive: many of Aristotle's works, including all of the dialogues he wrote for popular consumption, are now lost,[1] and much of what remains of his writings reads like notes either for his own

writings or for lectures he delivered at various times during his career. These were bequeathed with the rest of Aristotle's own library to Theophrastus, his successor at the Lyceum. Some of these notes may have been edited and re-edited, both by Aristotle and his successors; the *Nicomachean Ethics*, for example, is so-called because it is thought to have been edited by Aristotle's son Nicomachus after his father's death.[2] These "esoteric" writings we now have suffered a curious history, however, recorded by the Greek geographer Strabo (c. 64 BCE–21 CE) (Strabo *Geography* 13.1.4). They were left by Theophrastus to Neleus of Scepsis and he took them to Scepsis where they remained locked away in disorder, even buried for a time, until they were re-discovered, and finally brought by Sulla to Rome in about 86 BCE and edited in the form we have today by Andronicus of Rhodes, the then-head of the Peripatetic school.

The *Nicomachean Ethics* and the *Politics* are closely linked; Aristotle's political thought cannot be properly understood apart from his ethics. The *Nicomachean Ethics* is an inquiry into the nature of what is the highest good for human beings, and into how this good can be achieved. Aristotle's ethics is grounded in his views about biology, where every living being has its proper function. Unlike plants, which have nutritive capacities and aim at growth, and other animals, whose capacities are locomotive and perceptive, human beings are rational. The good for human beings, then, will require the use of reason.

Aristotle points out that some things are desired as a means to an end, whereas others are desired as ends in themselves. Money, for example, is only valuable since it allows the purchase of goods and services. His question is not merely what *things* are good for human beings—there is widespread agreement that many things are good, such as health, friendship, pleasure, etc.—but rather what is good *in itself*. The answer is *eudemonia* (variously translated as *happiness*, *flourishing*, and *living well*), since we seek it for its own sake.

Much of the *Nicomachean Ethics* is an examination of competing accounts of the nature of *eudamonia* and of its components, the virtues. Virtue (*aretê*), for Aristotle, can also be translated as "excellence" and includes intellectual virtues (e.g., theoretical wisdom, practical wisdom [*phronêsis*], etc.) as well as moral virtues (bravery, temperance, justice, etc.). Human happiness or living well, for

---

1   That so many works have been lost is a particular tragedy because Aristotle's prose style was particularly admired by the ancients. Yet perhaps (not unnaturally, considering their purpose) the lecture notes that are all that has survived are generally agreed to be rather dryly written: terse and elliptical, full of abrupt transitions, inadequate explanations, and technical jargon.

---

2   Aristotle's other main ethical work is called the *Eudemian Ethics*, possibly after its ancient editor Eudemus of Rhodes. There is a scholarly dispute over its relation to the *Nicomachean Ethics*.

Aristotle, consists in a life of virtuous activity in accordance with reason; thus much of the *Nicomachean Ethics* is an investigation of specific virtues. More generally, Aristotle proposes three candidates for the best life: a life devoted to the pursuit of physical pleasure, a life dedicated to politics, or a life engaged in intellectual contemplation. Pleasure is quickly dismissed and Aristotle proceeds to present arguments for the superiority of the life of intellectual contemplation. Though scholars generally agree that Aristotle considers the intellectual life to be superior, the political life is a clear second-best. In fact, unless some are willing to devote at least part of their lives to the art of politics, the intellectual life will be impossible.

The *Nicomachean Ethics* is traditionally divided into ten books (though the divisions into sections were probably not Aristotle's own). Book 1 examines the nature of the good for human beings and divides it into two categories: intellectual excellence and moral excellence. Books 2 to 4 deal with moral excellence, beginning with a general account of it and going on to discuss several of the moral virtues in detail. Book 5 looks at the virtue of justice. Aristotle distinguishes between two forms of justice, distributive and rectificatory. Distributive justice aims at fairness and distributes goods among community members according to their merit. Rectifactory justice remedies past injustices, restoring equality. Book 6 describes some of the forms of intellectual excellence. Book 7 deals with moral self-control and the nature of pleasure, and Books 8 and 9 are about friendship. Finally, Book 10 concludes with a discussion of *eudaimonia*, and of the role that education and society play in bringing about individual happiness. The final section of Book 10 introduces the subject of politics, namely the question of how to acquire legislative science, setting out the agenda for his *Politics*.

Though Aristotle's word for "politics" is *politikê* (short for *politikê epistêmê* or "political science"), he understands politics as a normative discipline, continuous with ethics. Political science, for Aristotle, is a practical science (distinct from contemplative sciences like physics and metaphysics, which are concerned with truth and knowledge; and productive sciences, which aim at creating useful or beautiful objects[1]) and aims at establishing the happiness and virtuous action of the city-state's inhabitants, not merely describing how political institutions function. The fundamental question in the *Politics* is what constitution or form of government *should* the lawgiver establish in order to foster the virtue of the citizens. Aristotle thus provides an account of the ideal (utopian) constitution, as well as conducting a detailed empirical study in order to determine which constitution is best given actual circumstances.

The *Politics* is composed of eight books. Book 1 discusses the purpose or end of the city, its origin, and also defends slavery and the subordination of women. Book 2 examines what citizens share, and includes an extended criticism of Socrates' proposal in the *Republic* that women and property be held in common. It also investigates cities of Sparta, Crete and Carthage and their constitutions. Book 3 deals with citizenship and the question of who should rule. This involves a detailed discussion of the different political regimes (see below). Books 4 to 6 discuss a variety of actual constitutions, their preservation and destruction, and the comparative merits of democracy and oligarchy. Book 7 sets out an account of the best constitution, whereas Book 8 (not included here) is primarily concerned with the education of children.

Aristotle famously argued that human beings are political animals (*Politics* 1, 2) and that human beings "naturally" form a city-state (*polis*). This is importantly different from the later social contract tradition, which locates the origins of the political society in an (artificial) agreement between individuals, usually to promote their mutual self-interest. Aristotle argues against this approach in *Politics* 3, 9. There is some controversy about what Aristotle means in his claim that the city-state is "natural," but the idea seems to be this: individuals naturally combine with members of the opposite sex for reproduction, while natural "masters" and "slaves"[2] join forces to profit from the master's intellect and the slave's labor; households arise naturally from these relationships; the city-state develops from these households, since only in a complex society can human beings perform their (rational) functions (e.g., the contemplative life is impossible in smaller communities when all members need to struggle to meet the necessities of life). Thus, the city-state is naturally prior to individuals, since only within the city-state can people exercise their natural functions.

The relationship between Aristotle's views on human nature, on the human good and on the political commun-

---

1   It may be noted that Aristotle frequently compares politics with the crafts; political science is also a productive science in the sense that it aims at the creation, preservation and reformation of political systems.

2   Aristotle notoriously argues in Book 1, 16 of the *Politics* that some individuals are natural slaves and lack a deliberative faculty, thus requiring that someone else rule over them.

ity is illuminated by his account of complete friendship in Book 8 of the *Nicomachean Ethics*. Aristotle suggests that friendship and justice are closely connected, since true friendship requires justice and city-states require friendship for their unity. Complete friendship is friendship of individuals with virtuous characters and requires living together, and achieving self-realization by jointly engaging in deliberations about the good of the city-state.

The goal of the politician is to provide a constitution—not merely a written document, but an organizing principle that structures the way of life of the citizens—for the city-state. Every community aims at some good and the best constitution is that which aims at the common advantage, rather than the advantage of the few. Aristotle and his colleagues collected 158 constitutions as part of his research, providing ample background for his discussion of how they fall short of the ideal constitutions. Aristotle groups the forms of government into three categories, each of which has a proper and a deviant form. Justice, as discussed above, involves the distribution of goods according to merit, so the best government is one in which each receives what is his or her due. Good governments rule in the interest of all citizens; bad governments rule according to their own interests. (It is important to emphasize that government rules in the interest of *citizens*, those who have the right to take part in politics; women, slaves, and, in most cases, foreigners and workers were excluded from citizenship and, in Aristotle's view, should not necessarily be taken into account.)

There are three basic forms of government, each of which can take a good or a bad form. The first form of government has one ruler. In a monarchy, the king rules for the good of the city; in a tyranny, the tyrant rules only for his own benefit. Aristotle considers monarchy the best form of government and tyranny the worst; he likens the relation of the tyrant over citizens to one of master over slaves. Monarchy, however, is difficult to achieve in practice, since men of such virtue are extremely rare. Second, in aristocracies (rule by the best persons) and oligarchies (rule by the wealthy), a few people rule. Aristocrats correctly realize that the best life is one of just actions. Oligarchs mistakenly believe that happiness consists in material wealth, and that equal political rights should be granted to those of equal wealth. The third case is that of rule by the many, Aristotle considers democracy to be a corrupt form of rule, though the least harmful of the three. He notes that the true distinction between oligarchy and democracy is between the rule of the wealthy and the rule of the poor, but adds that the rule of the poor

and the rule of the many will coincide, since the wealthy are always few. In a democracy, the many pursue their private pleasure, demanding liberty and equality among citizens, rather than the good of the city. The best practical (i.e., not ideal) form of government is a polity, which combines the institutions of democracy and oligarchy. In a polity, the many rule in the interests of the political community, but they adhere to the rule of law, which prevents them from taking advantage of the wealthy by expropriating their wealth or denying them political voice. Aristotle's discussion of polity is a landmark discussion of mixed government which has inspired political theorists from Polybius to Montesquieu to Madison and beyond.

Some Useful Background Information

i) Aristotle categorized ethics as a practical, rather than a theoretical, science. That is, the *Nicomachean Ethics* is written "not in order to know what virtue is, but in order to become good." In other words, for Aristotle, the point of ethics is not merely to know what good people are like, but to learn to act as good people do: the *Nicomachean Ethics* is intended to foster what he calls "practical wisdom" (*phronêsis*) in those who study it. The science of ethics is continuous, for Aristotle, with two other sciences: biology and politics. It is continuous with biology since ethics is the study of the good life for humankind *as a biological species*: a good life for the member of *any* species (such as a horse or a rubber plant) is a life of continuous flourishing, but what *counts* as flourishing will depend upon the biological nature of that species. And ethics is continuous with politics—the study of human society—since the arena in which human beings live their lives, developing as moral agents and exercising their moral capacities, is necessarily a social one. It is also the business of the political scientist to study human happiness in order to be able to judge among constitutions; in this sense, ethics is subordinate to politics.

ii) According to Aristotle, the goal of human lives is to achieve *eudaimonia*. *Eudaimonia* is usually translated as "happiness," but this can be misleading. The Greek word does not refer to a psychological state or feeling, such as that of pleasure, but instead denotes a certain kind of desirable *activity* or *way of life*—it is the activity of living well. The happy person is, for Aristotle, someone who has lived a genuinely *successful* or fulfilling life.

iii) Aristotle's understanding of nature, and in particular of biology, was what is called *teleological*: something's telos is its end, the final result that explains why it has been constructed the way it is. It is now commonplace to speak of this as a "goal," although in a functional, not an intentional sense; for Aristotle, all of nature is goal-directed in this sense. For example, the nature of natural processes (such as digestion) or biological organs (such as the eye) is plausibly determined by their *function*—their goal or *telos*—and not by their physical composition at some particular time. Eyes are things—any things—which have the function of seeing. Aristotle extended this model to the entire natural world, so that in his view, for example, the essence of fire consists in its goal (of, roughly, rising upwards), the essence of an acorn is its purpose to grow into an oak tree, and the essence of the species *horse* is to flourish and procreate as horses are supposed to do. Since human beings are as much a part of the biological world as anything else, for Aristotle, it follows that a proper understanding of human nature—and thus of the good life for human beings—must involve an investigation into the function of the human species.

Some Common Misconceptions

i) When Aristotle refers to the *telos*—the function or goal—of living creatures such as plants, animals and human beings, he is not thinking of these creatures as having a purpose for *something else*: he is not, for example, assuming that there is some great plan for the universe (perhaps God's plan) and that living creatures have a role to play in fulfilling this plan. Instead, for Aristotle, the *telos* of living creatures is *internal* to them: it is, so to speak, built in to their biological natures.

ii) It is sometimes easy to forget that Aristotle's Doctrine of the Mean urges us to avoid *both* excess and deficiency: for example, Aristotle's account not only instructs us to moderate our anger or curb our drinking, it also warns us against feeling too *little* anger or not drinking *enough* wine.

iii) When Aristotle refers to "the mean" of a certain spectrum of behavior, he does not intend to speak of something like an arithmetical average, and thus he is not suggesting that we should literally choose the *mid-point* of that range of behavior. The mean or mid-point of two numbers (as 6 is the mean of 2 and 10) is an example of what Aristotle calls a mean "in terms of the object," but Aristotle contrasts this mathematical use with his own usage of "mean," which is a mean "relative to us." For example, we should eat neither too many cookies nor too few cookies, but exactly how many cookies we should eat depends on our personal

circumstances (if we are overweight, how active our lifestyle is, how many other people also want some of the cookies, whether or not we are allergic to the nuts in the cookies, and so on). Certainly, Aristotle does not want to say that we should eat *exactly half* of all the available cookies. As Jonathan Barnes puts it, "it is as though I were to hand a man a pack of cards and urge him to pick the middle one—adding that by 'middle' I meant 'middle relative to the chooser,' and that any card in the pack may be middle in this sense."

iv) Aristotle does not think of his ethical theory as a sort of moral rulebook: Aristotle is not trying to find a theory that will, by itself, generate moral principles which will tell us how to act. Instead, he is trying to develop an account of moral *character*—a theory of the good person. It is salutary to recall that, although the topic of Aristotle's book is indeed *ēthika*, which is almost always translated into English as "ethics," the Greek word actually has a meaning closer to "matters to do with character." Similarly, when Aristotle writes of *ēthikē aretē*—which is almost invariably translated as "moral virtue"—the literal meaning of this phrase is "excellence of character," whereby "excellence" is meant simply what we would mean if we spoke of an excellent horse or an excellent axe. The sense of ethics in philosophy as involving *obedience to some sort of moral law* is substantially more recent than Aristotle, and has its roots (more or less) in the great monotheistic religions of Judaism, Christianity and Islam.

v) The Doctrine of the Mean does not apply to particular *actions*, but to *virtues*—to states of character. Thus, the idea is not that one always *acts* in a way which is intermediate between two extremes, but that one's actions are guided by a *character trait* which is neither excessive nor insufficient. For example, it might be the case that, in certain situations, someone possessing the virtue of generosity might nevertheless refuse to give anything at all away to a particular person in a particular circumstance (or, conversely, might give them everything they own); or a person with the virtue of being even-tempered might nevertheless find it appropriate, sometimes, to become very angry indeed (or, in another situation, to meekly suppress any feelings of anger whatsoever).

How Important and Influential Are These Writings?

Aristotle is considered by many professional philosophers to be the greatest philosopher who ever lived; throughout the Middle Ages he was referred to as simply "the Philosopher." The system of ethics developed by Aristotle in the *Nicomachean Ethics* has had a profound effect on all subsequent moral philosophy: in every age of philosophy it has been either fervently embraced or fiercely rejected, but it has never been ignored. So influential has it been, that several of its central tenets—such the idea as that morality consists in finding a "golden mean," or the notion that the rational aim of human life is happiness (though not necessarily pleasure)—have become part of our everyday moral consciousness. On the other hand, for much of the post-medieval period Aristotle's emphasis on the *virtues*, rather than on *types of action*, as the ground of morality was paid relatively little attention; more recently there has been a surge of interest in what is now called "virtue ethics," and Aristotle is generally considered the original source for this "new" theory. (Modern virtue theories, however, diverge from Aristotle's ethical philosophy in important ways: in particular, they tend to reject or ignore Aristotle's emphasis on *eudaimonia* as the ultimate moral good.)

Aristotle's political thought is similarly ubiquitous. Along with Plato, he dominates political philosophy from ancient times until the Renaissance, and his influence is particularly evident in the works of Al-Fārābi, Aquinas, Marsilius of Padua, and Machiavelli, as well as in those of modern philosophers such as Hobbes, Locke, Rousseau, Hegel and Nietzsche. Contemporary political scientists can trace their discipline to Aristotle's empirical examinations of Greek city-state constitutions. And in very different ways, Aristotle has continued to play a central role in twentieth- and twenty-first-century thought, particularly in the work of liberal philosophers Martha Nussbaum and John Rawls.

◆ ◆ ◆ ◆ ◆

Nicomachean Ethics

Book 1 [Happiness]

1094a 1 [Ends and goods]: Every craft and every line of inquiry, and likewise every action and decision, seems to seek some good; that is why some people were right to describe the good as what everything seeks. But the ends [that are sought] appear to differ; some are activities, and others are 5 products apart from the activities. Wherever there are ends apart from the actions, the products are by nature better than the activities.

Since there are many actions, crafts, and sciences, the ends turn out to be many as well; for health is the end of medicine, a boat of boat building, victory of generalship, and wealth of household management. But some of these 10 pursuits are subordinate to some one capacity; for instance, bridle making and every other science producing equipment for horses are subordinate to horsemanship, while this and every action in warfare are, in turn, subordinate to generalship, and in the same way other pursuits are subordinate to further ones. In all such cases, then, the ends of the ruling 15 sciences are more choiceworthy than all the ends subordinate to them, since the lower ends are also pursued for the sake of the higher. Here it does not matter whether the ends of the actions are the activities themselves, or something apart from them, as in the sciences we have mentioned.

2 [The highest good and political science[1]]: Suppose, then, that the things achievable by action have some end that we wish for because of itself, and because of which we wish for the other things, and that we do not choose everything 20 because of something else—for if we do, it will go on without limit, so that desire will prove to be empty and futile. Clearly, this end will be the good, that is to say, the best good.

Then surely knowledge of this good also carries great weight for [determining the best] way of life; if we know it, we are more likely, like archers who have a target to aim 25 at, to hit the right mark. If so, we should try to grasp, in outline at any rate, what the good is, and which is its proper science or capacity.

It seems proper to the most controlling science—the highest ruling science. And this appears characteristic of political science. For it is the one that prescribes which of   1094b the sciences ought to be studied in cities,[2] and which ones

---

1   *political science*   The art and science of ruling and managing a state.

2   *cities*   The most important large-scale political division in Aristotle's time was the "city-state"—a sovereign area controlled by the chief city within it. Examples were Athens, Sparta, and Corinth; these were independent states included within Greece (also known as Hellas), which was a geographical and cultural entity but not a political one. When Aristotle speaks of a "city" then, he is speaking of what we would think of as an independent sovereign nation.

each class in the city should learn, and how far; indeed we see that even the most honored capacities—generalship, household management,[1] and rhetoric, for instance—are subordinate to it. And since it uses the other sciences concerned with action, and moreover legislates what must be done and what avoided, its end will include the ends of the other sciences, and so this will be the human good. For even if the good is the same for a city as for an individual, still the good of the city is apparently a greater and more complete good to acquire and preserve. For while it is satisfactory to acquire and preserve the good even for an individual, it is finer and more divine to acquire and preserve it for a people and for cities. And so, since our line of inquiry seeks these [goods, for an individual and for a community], it is a sort of political science.

3 [The method of political science]: Our discussion will be adequate if we make things perspicuous enough to accord with the subject matter; for we would not seek the same degree of exactness in all sorts of arguments alike, any more than in the products of different crafts. Now, fine[2] and just things, which political science examines, differ and vary so much as to seem to rest on convention only, not on nature. But [this is not a good reason, since] goods also vary in the same way, because they result in harm to many people—for some have been destroyed because of their wealth, others because of their bravery. And so, since this is our subject and these are our premises, we shall be satisfied to indicate the truth roughly and in outline; since our subject and our premises are things that hold good usually [but not universally], we shall be satisfied to draw conclusions of the same sort.

Each of our claims, then, ought to be accepted in the same way [as claiming to hold good usually]. For the educated person seeks exactness in each area to the extent that the nature of the subject allows; for apparently it is just as mistaken to demand demonstrations[3] from a rhetorician as to accept [merely] persuasive arguments from a mathematician. Further, each person judges rightly what he knows, and is a good judge about that; hence the good judge in a given area is the person educated in that area, and the unqualifiedly good judge is the person educated in every area.

1095a

This is why a youth is not a suitable student of political science; for he lacks experience of the actions in life, which are the subject and premises of our arguments. Moreover, since he tends to follow his feelings, his study will be futile and useless; for the end [of political science] is action, not knowledge. It does not matter whether he is young in years or immature in character, since the deficiency does not depend on age, but results from following his feelings in his life and in a given pursuit; for an immature person, like an incontinent person, gets no benefit from his knowledge. But for those who accord with reason in forming their desires and in their actions, knowledge of political science will be of great benefit.

These are the preliminary points about the student, about the way our claims are to be accepted, and about what we propose to do.

4 [Common beliefs]: Let us, then, begin again. Since every sort of knowledge and decision pursues some good, what is the good that we say political science seeks? What, [in other words,] is the highest of all the goods achievable in action?

As far as its name goes, most people virtually agree; for both the many and the cultivated call it happiness,[4] and they suppose that living well and doing well are the same as being happy. But they disagree about what happiness is, and the many do not give the same answer as the wise.

For the many[5] think it is something obvious and evident—for instance, pleasure, wealth, or honor. Some take it to be one thing, others another. Indeed, the same person often changes his mind; for when he has fallen ill, he thinks happiness is health, and when he has fallen into poverty, he thinks it is wealth. And when they are conscious of their own ignorance, they admire anyone who speaks of something grand and above their heads. [Among the wise,] however, some used to think that besides these many goods

---

1   *household management*   For Aristotle, the "household" in question included all members of an extended family, together with its slaves.

2   *fine*   What Aristotle means here is sometimes rendered into English as "beautiful" or "noble"; there is an implied analogy to the beauty of a well-crafted artifact or literary production.

3   *demonstrations*   Strictly logical proofs, showing the necessity of a conclusion, of a sort that is possible in mathematics but is not possible in the empirical sciences or in less systematic everyday matters, which permit what Aristotle calls "merely persuasive" arguments.

4   *happiness*   The Greek *eudaimonia*. Casually translated as "happiness" but corresponds only roughly to the English term; it can also be translated as "human flourishing." It does not denote a subjective sense of well-being, but rather virtuous action over a complete life.

5   *the many*   Most people (the "vulgar"), in contrast here with the wise few.

there is some other good that exists in its own right and that causes all these goods to be goods.

Presumably, then, it is rather futile to examine all these beliefs, and it is enough to examine those that are most current or seem to have some argument for them.

We must notice, however, the difference between arguments from principles and arguments toward principles. For indeed Plato was right to be puzzled about this, when he used to ask if [the argument] set out from the principles or led toward them—just as on a race course the path may go from the starting line to the far end, or back again. For we should certainly begin from things known, but things are known in two ways; for some are known to us, some known without qualification. Presumably, then, *we* ought to begin from things known to *us*.

That is why we need to have been brought up in fine habits if we are to be adequate students of fine and just things, and of political questions generally. For we begin from the [belief] that [something is true]; if this is apparent enough to us, we can begin without also [knowing] why [it is true]. Someone who is well brought up has the beginnings, or can easily acquire them. Someone who neither has them nor can acquire them should listen to Hesiod:[1] "He who grasps everything himself is best of all; he is noble also who listens to one who has spoken well; but he who neither grasps it himself nor takes to heart what he hears from another is a useless man."

5 [The three lives]: But let us begin again from the point from which we digressed. For, it would seem, people quite reasonably reach their conception of the good, i.e., of happiness, from the lives [they lead]; for there are roughly three most favored lives: the lives of gratification, of political activity, and, third, of study.

The many, the most vulgar, would seem to conceive the good and happiness as pleasure, and hence they also like the life of gratification. In this they appear completely slavish, since the life they decide on is a life for grazing animals. Still, they have some argument in their defense, since many in positions of power feel as Sardanapallus[2] felt, [and also choose this life].

The cultivated people, those active [in politics], conceive the good as honor, since this is more or less the end [normally pursued] in the political life. This, however, appears to be too superficial to be what we are seeking; for it seems to depend more on those who honor than on the one honored, whereas we intuitively believe that the good is something of our own and hard to take from us. Further, it would seem, they pursue honor to convince themselves that they are good; at any rate, they seek to be honored by prudent people, among people who know them, and for virtue.[3] It is clear, then, that—in their view at any rate—virtue is superior [to honor].

Perhaps, indeed, one might conceive virtue more than honor to be the end of the political life. However, this also is apparently too incomplete [to be the good]. For it seems possible for someone to possess virtue but be asleep or inactive throughout his life, and, moreover, to suffer the worst evils and misfortunes. If this is the sort of life he leads, no one would count him happy, except to defend a philosopher's paradox. Enough about this, since it has been adequately discussed in the popular works as well.

The third life is the life of study, which we shall examine in what follows.

The moneymaker's life is in a way forced on him [not chosen for itself]; and clearly wealth is not the good we are seeking, since it is [merely] useful, [choiceworthy only] for some other end. Hence one would be more inclined to suppose that [any of] the goods mentioned earlier is the end, since they are liked for themselves. But apparently they are not [the end] either; and many arguments have been presented against them. Let us, then, dismiss them.

6 [The Platonic Form of the good]: Presumably, though, we had better examine the universal good, and puzzle out what is meant in speaking of it. This sort of inquiry is, to be sure, unwelcome to us, because those who introduced the Forms[4] were friends of ours; still, it presumably seems better, indeed only right, to destroy even what is close to us if that is the way to preserve truth. We must especially do this as philosophers, [lovers of wisdom]; for though we

---

1   *Hesiod* Prehistoric Greek poet (c. 700 BCE); he or Homer—nobody is sure who came first—was the first major Greek poet.
2   *Sardanapallus* A legendary Assyrian monarch, supposed to have lived in great luxury. Historians have been unable reliably to connect the legend with real historical events.
3   *virtue* This English word is used in this translation as well as in many others to translate the Greek word *aretê*. "Virtue" tends to suggest moral excellence only, however, whereas what Aristotle had in mind is excellence in general—the ability to perform well the appropriate function for which something is designed.
4   *those who introduced the Forms* Plato and Socrates.

love both the truth and our friends, reverence is due to the truth first.

Those who introduced this view did not mean to produce an Idea[1] for any [series] in which they spoke of prior and posterior [members]; that was why they did not mean to establish an Idea [of number] for [the series of] numbers. But the good is spoken of both in what-it-is [that is, substance], and in quality and relative; and what exists in its own right, that is, substance, is by nature prior to the relative, since a relative would seem to be an appendage and coincident of being. And so there is no common Idea over these.

Further, good is spoken of in as many ways as being [is spoken of]: in what-it-is, as god and mind; in quality, as the virtues; in quantity, as the measured amount; in relative, as the useful; in time, as the opportune moment; in place, as the [right] situation; and so on. Hence it is clear that the good cannot be some common and single universal; for if it were, it would be spoken of in only one [of the types of] predication, not in them all.

Further, if a number of things have a single Idea, there is also a single science of them; hence [if there were an Idea of good] there would also be some single science of all goods. But, in fact, there are many sciences even of the goods under one [type of] predication; for the science of the opportune moment, for instance, in war is generalship, in disease medicine. And similarly the science of the measured amount in food is medicine, in exertion gymnastics. [Hence there is no single science of the good, and so no Idea.]

One might be puzzled about what [the believers in Ideas] really mean in speaking of the So-and-So Itself, since Man Itself and man have one and the same account of man; for insofar as each is man, they will not differ at all. If that is so, then [Good Itself and good have the same account of good]; hence they also will not differ at all insofar as each is good, [hence there is no point in appealing to Good Itself].

Moreover, Good Itself will be no more of a good by being eternal; for a white thing is no whiter if it lasts a long time than if it lasts a day.

The Pythagoreans[2] would seem to have a more plausible view about the good, since they place the One[3] in the column of goods. Indeed, Speusippus[4] seems to have followed them. But let us leave this for another discussion.

A dispute emerges, however, about what we have said, because the arguments [in favor of the Idea] are not concerned with every sort of good. Goods pursued and liked in their own right are spoken of as one species of goods, whereas those that in some way tend to produce or preserve these goods, or to prevent their contraries, are spoken of as goods because of these and in a different way. Clearly, then, goods are spoken of in two ways, and some are goods in their own right, and others goods because of these. Let us, then, separate the goods in their own right from the [merely] useful goods, and consider whether goods in their own right correspond to a single Idea.

But what sorts of goods may we take to be goods in their own right? Are they the goods that are pursued even on their own—for instance, prudence, seeing, some types of pleasures, and honors? For even if we also pursue these because of something else, we may nonetheless take them to be goods in their own right. Alternatively, is nothing except the Idea good in its own right, so that the Form will be futile? But if these other things are also goods in their own right, then, [if there is an Idea of good,] the same account of good will have to turn up in all of them, just as the same account of whiteness turns up in snow and in chalk. In fact, however, honor, prudence, and pleasure have different and dissimilar accounts, precisely insofar as they are goods. Hence the good is not something common corresponding to a single Idea.

But how, then, is good spoken of? For it is not like homonyms resulting from chance. Is it spoken of from the fact that goods derive from one thing or all contribute to one thing? Or is it spoken of more by analogy? For as sight is to body, so understanding is to soul, and so on for other cases.

Presumably, though, we should leave these questions for now, since their exact treatment is more appropriate for another [branch of] philosophy. And the same is true about the Idea. For even if there is some one good predi-

1   *Idea* For Plato, the "Forms" or "Ideas" are, roughly speaking, archetypes—idealized abstractions—representing the pure nature of earthly imperfect objects. These have real existence—they are not just "ideas" in the sense of existing merely in our thoughts. Aristotle is quarrelling with the Platonic view that there is a "Form of the Good"—a single unified idealized picture of what good is.

2   *Pythagoreans* Followers of Pythagoras (c. 582–c. 507 BCE), the Greek philosopher, mystic, and mathematician.

3   *the One* For the Pythagoreans, the unity of all being (and non-being).

4   *Speusippus* Greek philosopher (407–339 BCE). Plato's nephew, he took over the Academy at Plato's death.

cated in common, or some separable good, itself in its own right, clearly that is not the sort of good a human being can achieve in action or possess; but that is the sort we are looking for now.

Perhaps, however, someone might think it is better to get to know the Idea with a view to the goods that we can possess and achieve in action; for [one might suppose that] if we have this as a sort of pattern, we shall also know better about the goods that are goods for us, and if we know about them, we shall hit on them. This argument certainly has some plausibility, but it would seem to clash with the sciences. For each of these, though it aims at some good and seeks to supply what is lacking, leaves out knowledge of the Idea; but if the Idea were such an important aid, surely it would not be reasonable for all craftsmen to know nothing about it and not even to look for it.

Moreover, it is a puzzle to know what the weaver or carpenter will gain for his own craft from knowing this Good Itself, or how anyone will be better at medicine or generalship from having gazed on the Idea Itself. For what the doctor appears to consider is not even health [universally, let alone good universally], but human health, and presumably the health of this human being even more, since he treats one particular patient at a time.

So much, then, for these questions.

7 [An account of the human good]: But let us return once again to the good we are looking for, and consider just what it could be. For it is apparently one thing in one action or craft, and another thing in another; for it is one thing in medicine, another in generalship, and so on for the rest. What, then, is the good of each action or craft? Surely it is that for the sake of which the other things are done; in medicine this is health, in generalship victory, in housebuilding a house, in another case something else, but in every action and decision it is the end, since it is for the sake of the end that everyone does the other actions. And so, if there is some end of everything achievable in action, the good achievable in action will be this end; if there are more ends than one, [the good achievable in action] will be these ends.

Our argument, then, has followed a different route to reach the same conclusion. But we must try to make this still more perspicuous. Since there are apparently many ends, and we choose some of them (for instance, wealth, flutes, and, in general, instruments) because of something else, it is clear that not all ends are complete. But the best good is apparently something complete. And so, if only one end is complete, the good we are looking for will be this end; if more ends than one are complete, it will be the most complete end of these.

We say that an end pursued in its own right is more complete than an end pursued because of something else, and that an end that is never choiceworthy because of something else is more complete than ends that are choiceworthy both in their own right and because of this end. Hence an end that is always choiceworthy in its own right, never because of something else, is complete without qualification.

Now happiness, more than anything else, seems complete without qualification. For we always choose it because of itself, never because of something else. Honor, pleasure, understanding, and every virtue we certainly choose because of themselves, since we would choose each of them even if it had no further result; but we also choose them for the sake of happiness, supposing that through them we shall be happy. Happiness, by contrast, no one ever chooses for their sake, or for the sake of anything else at all.

The same conclusion [that happiness is complete] also appears to follow from self-sufficiency. For the complete good seems to be self-sufficient. What we count as self-sufficient is not what suffices for a solitary person by himself, living an isolated life, but what suffices also for parents, children, wife, and, in general, for friends and fellow citizens, since a human being is a naturally political [animal]. Here, however, we must impose some limit; for if we extend the good to parents' parents and children's children and to friends of friends, we shall go on without limit; but we must examine this another time. Anyhow, we regard something as self-sufficient when all by itself it makes a life choiceworthy and lacking nothing; and that is what we think happiness does.

Moreover, we think happiness is most choiceworthy of all goods, [since] it is not counted as one good among many. [If it were] counted as one among many, then, clearly, we think it would be more choiceworthy if the smallest of goods were added; for the good that is added becomes an extra quantity of goods, and the larger of two goods is always more choiceworthy. Happiness, then, is apparently something complete and self-sufficient, since it is the end of the things achievable in action.

But presumably the remark that the best good is happiness is apparently something [generally] agreed, and we still need a clearer statement of what the best good is. Perhaps, then, we shall find this if we first grasp the function of a

25 human being. For just as the good, i.e., [doing] well, for a flautist, a sculptor, and every craftsman, and, in general, for whatever has a function and [characteristic] action, seems to depend on its function, the same seems to be true for a human being, if a human being has some function.

30 Then do the carpenter and the leather worker have their functions and actions, but has a human being no function? Is he by nature idle, without any function? Or, just as eye, hand, foot, and, in general, every [bodily] part apparently has its function, may we likewise ascribe to a human being some function apart from all of these?

What, then, could this be? For living is apparently shared with plants, but what we are looking for is the special 1098a function of a human being; hence we should set aside the life of nutrition and growth. The life next in order is some sort of life of sense perception; but this too is apparently shared with horse, ox, and every animal.

The remaining possibility, then, is some sort of life of action of the [part of the soul] that has reason. One [part] 5 of it has reason as obeying reason; the other has it as itself having reason and thinking. Moreover, life is also spoken of in two ways [as capacity and as activity], and we must take [a human being's special function to be] life as activity, since this seems to be called life more fully. We have found, then, that the human function is activity of the soul in accord with reason or requiring reason.

Now we say that the function of a [kind of thing]—of a harpist, for instance—is the same in kind as the function of an excellent individual of the kind—of an excellent harpist, 10 for instance. And the same is true without qualification in every case, if we add to the function the superior achievement in accord with the virtue; for the function of a harpist is to play the harp, and the function of a good harpist is to play it well. Moreover, we take the human function to be a certain kind of life, and take this life to be activity and actions of the soul that involve reason; hence the function 15 of the excellent man is to do this well and finely.

Now each function is completed well by being completed in accord with the virtue proper [to that kind of thing]. And so the human good proves to be activity of the soul in accord with virtue, and indeed with the best and most complete virtue, if there are more virtues than one. Moreover, it must be in a complete life. For one swallow 20 does not make a spring, nor does one day; nor, similarly, does one day or a short time make us blessed and happy.

This, then, is a sketch of the good; for, presumably, we must draw the outline first, and fill it in later. If the sketch is good, anyone, it seems, can advance and articulate it, and in such cases time discovers more, or is a good partner in discovery. That is also how the crafts have improved, since 25 anyone can add what is lacking [in the outline].

We must also remember our previous remarks, so that we do not look for the same degree of exactness in all areas, but the degree that accords with a given subject matter and is proper to a given line of inquiry. For the carpenter's and the geometer's inquiries about the right angle are different 30 also; the carpenter restricts himself to what helps his work, but the geometer inquires into what, or what sort of thing, the right angle is, since he studies the truth. We must do the same, then, in other areas too, [seeking the proper degree of exactness], so that digressions do not overwhelm our main task.

Nor should we make the same demand for an ex- 1098b planation in all cases. On the contrary, in some cases it is enough to prove rightly that [something is true, without also explaining why it is true]. This is so, for instance, with principles, where the fact that [something is true] is the first thing, that is to say, the principle.

Some principles are studied by means of induction,[1] some by means of perception, some by means of some sort of habituation, and others by other means. In each case we 5 should try to find them out by means suited to their nature, and work hard to define them rightly. For they carry great weight for what follows; for the principle seems to be more than half the whole, and makes evident the answer to many of our questions.

8 [Defense of the account of the good]: We should examine the principle, however, not only from the conclusion and 10 premises [of a deduction], but also from what is said about it; for all the facts harmonize with a true account, whereas the truth soon clashes with a false one.

Goods are divided, then, into three types, some called external, some goods of the soul, others goods of the body. We say that the goods of the soul are goods most fully, and 15 more than the others, and we take actions and activities of the soul to be [goods] of the soul. And so our account [of the good] is right, to judge by this belief anyhow—and it is an ancient belief, and accepted by philosophers.

---

1   *induction*   The sort of reasoning that moves from knowledge of particulars to knowledge of general truths.

Our account is also correct in saying that some sort of actions and activities are the end; for in that way the end turns out to be a good of the soul, not an external good.

The belief that the happy person lives well and does well also agrees with our account, since we have virtually said that the end is a sort of living well and doing well.

Further, all the features that people look for in happiness appear to be true of the end described in our account. For to some people happiness seems to be virtue; to others prudence; to others some sort of wisdom, to others again it seems to be these, or one of these, involving pleasure or requiring it to be added; others add in external prosperity as well. Some of these views are traditional, held by many, while others are held by a few men who are widely esteemed. It is reasonable for each group not to be completely wrong, but to be correct on one point at least, or even on most points.

First, our account agrees with those who say happiness is virtue [in general] or some [particular] virtue; for activity in accord with virtue is proper to virtue. Presumably, though, it matters quite a bit whether we suppose that the best good consists in possessing or in using—that is to say, in a state or in an activity [that actualizes the state]. For someone may be in a state that achieves no good—if, for instance, he is asleep or inactive in some other way—but this cannot be true of the activity; for it will necessarily act and act well. And just as Olympic prizes are not for the finest and strongest, but for the contestants—since it is only these who win—the same is true in life; among the fine and good people, only those who act correctly win the prize.

Moreover, the life of these active people is also pleasant in itself. For being pleased is a condition of the soul, [and hence is included in the activity of the soul]. Further, each type of person finds pleasure in whatever he is called a lover of; a horse, for instance, pleases the horse-lover, a spectacle the lover of spectacles. Similarly, what is just pleases the lover of justice, and in general what accords with virtue pleases the lover of virtue.

Now the things that please most people conflict, because they are not pleasant by nature, whereas the things that please lovers of the fine are things pleasant by nature. Actions in accord with virtue are pleasant by nature, so that they both please lovers of the fine and are pleasant in their own right.

Hence these people's life does not need pleasure to be added [to virtuous activity] as some sort of extra decoration; rather, it has its pleasure within itself. For besides the reasons already given, someone who does not enjoy fine actions is not good; for no one would call a person just, for instance, if he did not enjoy doing just actions, or generous if he did not enjoy generous actions, and similarly for the other virtues.

If this is so, actions in accord with the virtues are pleasant in their own right. Moreover, these actions are good and fine as well as pleasant; indeed, they are good, fine, and pleasant more than anything else is, since on this question the excellent person judges rightly, and his judgment agrees with what we have said.

Happiness, then, is best, finest, and most pleasant, and the Delian inscription[1] is wrong to distinguish these things: "What is most just is finest; being healthy is most beneficial; but it is most pleasant to win our heart's desire." For all three features are found in the best activities, and we say happiness is these activities, or [rather] one of them, the best one.

Nonetheless, happiness evidently also needs external goods to be added, as we said, since we cannot, or cannot easily, do fine actions if we lack the resources. For, first of all, in many actions we use friends, wealth, and political power just as we use instruments. Further, deprivation of certain [externals]—for instance, good birth, good children, beauty—mars our blessedness. For we do not altogether have the character of happiness if we look utterly repulsive or are ill-born, solitary, or childless; and we have it even less, presumably, if our children or friends are totally bad, or were good but have died.

And so, as we have said, happiness would seem to need this sort of prosperity added also. That is why some people identify happiness with good fortune, and others identify it with virtue.

9 [How is happiness achieved?]: This also leads to a puzzle: Is happiness acquired by learning, or habituation, or by some other form of cultivation? Or is it the result of some divine fate, or even of fortune?

First, then, if the gods give any gift at all to human beings, it is reasonable for them to give us happiness more than any other human good, insofar as it is the best of human goods. Presumably, however, this question is more suitable for a different inquiry.

---

1   *Delian inscription* Inscription for a temple composed by a man from Delos.

15   But even if it is not sent by the gods, but instead results from virtue and some sort of learning or cultivation, happiness appears to be one of the most divine things, since the prize and goal of virtue appears to be the best good, something divine and blessed. Moreover [if happiness comes in this way] it will be widely shared; for anyone who is not deformed [in his capacity] for virtue will be able to achieve
20   happiness through some sort of learning and attention.

And since it is better to be happy in this way than because of fortune, it is reasonable for this to be the way [we become] happy. For whatever is natural is naturally in the finest state possible. The same is true of the products of crafts and of every other cause, especially the best cause; and it would be seriously inappropriate to entrust what is greatest and finest to fortune.

25   The answer to our question is also evident from our account. For we have said that happiness is a certain sort of activity of the soul in accord with virtue, [and hence not a result of fortune]. Of the other goods, some are necessary conditions of happiness, while others are naturally useful and cooperative as instruments [but are not parts of it].

Further, this conclusion agrees with our opening re-
30   marks. For we took the goal of political science to be the best good; and most of its attention is devoted to the character of the citizens, to make them good people who do fine actions.

It is not surprising, then, that we regard neither ox, nor
1100a horse, nor any other kind of animal as happy; for none of them can share in this sort of activity. For the same reason a child is not happy either, since his age prevents him from doing these sorts of actions. If he is called happy, he is being congratulated [simply] because of anticipated blessedness;
5   for, as we have said, happiness requires both complete virtue and a complete life.

It needs a complete life because life includes many reversals of fortune, good and bad, and the most prosperous person may fall into a terrible disaster in old age, as the Trojan stories tell us about Priam.[1] If someone has suffered these sorts of misfortunes and comes to a miserable end, no one counts him happy.

10   [Can we be happy during our lifetime?]: Then should   10
we count no human being happy during his lifetime, but follow Solon's advice[2] to wait to see the end? But if we agree with Solon, can someone really be happy during the time after he has died? Surely that is completely absurd, especially when we say happiness is an activity.

We do not say, then, that someone is happy during the   15
time he is dead, and Solon's point is not this [absurd one], but rather that when a human being has died, we can safely pronounce [that he was] blessed [before he died], on the assumption that he is now finally beyond evils and misfortunes. But this claim is also disputable. For if a living person has good or evil of which he is not aware, a dead person also, it seems, has good or evil, if, for instance, he receives   20
honors or dishonors, and his children, and descendants in general, do well or suffer misfortune.

However, this conclusion also raises a puzzle. For even if someone has lived in blessedness until old age, and has died appropriately, many fluctuations of his descendants' fortunes may still happen to him; for some may be good   25
people and get the life they deserve, while the contrary may be true of others, and clearly they may be as distantly related to their ancestor as you please. Surely, then, it would be an absurd result if the dead person's condition changed along with the fortunes of his descendants, so that at one time he would turn out to have been happy [in his lifetime] and at another time he would turn out to have been miserable. But it would also be absurd if the condition of descendants did   30
not affect their ancestors at all or for any length of time.

But we must return to the previous puzzle, since that will perhaps also show us the answer to our present question. Let us grant that we must wait to see the end, and must then count someone blessed, not as now being blessed [during the time he is dead] but because he previously was blessed. Would it not be absurd, then, if, at the very time when he is happy, we refused to ascribe truly to him the   35
happiness he has? Such refusal results from reluctance to   1100b
call him happy during his lifetime, because of its ups and downs; for we suppose happiness is enduring and definitely not prone to fluctuate, but the same person's fortunes often turn to and fro. For clearly, if we take our cue from his fortunes, we shall often call him happy and then miserable   5

---

1   *Priam*   In Greek mythology, the ruler of Troy when it was defeated and destroyed during the Trojan War. In Homer's *Iliad*, he enters the Greek camp to plead movingly for the return of his son's dead body for burial; and finally he is killed by the son of Achilles.

2   *Solon's advice*   Sometimes rendered as: "Count no man happy until he be dead." Solon (c. 638–558 BCE) was an Athenian statesman, lawmaker, and poet.

again, thereby representing the happy person as a kind of chameleon, insecurely based.

But surely it is quite wrong to take our cue from someone's fortunes. For his doing well or badly does not rest on them. A human life, as we said, needs these added, but activities in accord with virtue control happiness, and the contrary activities control its contrary. Indeed, the present puzzle is further evidence for our account [of happiness]. For no human achievement has the stability of activities in accord with virtue, since these seem to be more enduring even than our knowledge of the sciences. Indeed, the most honorable among the virtues themselves are more enduring than the other virtues, because blessed people devote their lives to them more fully and more continually than to anything else—for this continual activity would seem to be the reason we do not forget them.

It follows, then, that the happy person has the [stability] we are looking for and keeps the character he has throughout his life. For always, or more than anything else, he will do and study the actions in accord with virtue, and will bear fortunes most finely, in every way and in all conditions appropriately, since he is truly "good, foursquare, and blameless."

Many events, however, are subject to fortune; some are minor, some major. Hence, minor strokes of good or ill fortune clearly will not carry any weight for his life. But many major strokes of good fortune will make it more blessed; for in themselves they naturally add adornment to it, and his use of them proves to be fine and excellent. Conversely, if he suffers many major misfortunes, they oppress and spoil his blessedness, since they involve pain and impede many activities. And yet, even here what is fine shines through, whenever someone bears many severe misfortunes with good temper, not because he feels no distress, but because he is noble and magnanimous.

And since it is activities that control life, as we said, no blessed person could ever become miserable, since he will never do hateful and base actions. For a truly good and prudent person, we suppose, will bear strokes of fortune suitably, and from his resources at any time will do the finest actions, just as a good general will make the best use of his forces in war, and a good shoemaker will make the finest shoe from the hides given to him, and similarly for all other craftsmen.

If this is so, the happy person could never become miserable, but neither will he be blessed if he falls into misfortunes as bad as Priam's. Nor, however, will he be inconstant

and prone to fluctuate, since he will neither be easily shaken from his happiness nor shaken by just any misfortunes. He will be shaken from it, though, by many serious misfortunes, and from these a return to happiness will take no short time. At best, it will take a long and complete length of time that includes great and fine successes.

Then why not say that the happy person is the one whose activities accord with complete virtue, with an adequate supply of external goods, not for just any time but for a complete life? Or should we add that he will also go on living this way and will come to an appropriate end, since the future is not apparent to us, and we take happiness to be the end, and altogether complete in every way? Given these facts [about the future and about happiness], we shall say that a living person who has, and will keep, the goods we mentioned is blessed, but blessed as a human being is. So much for a determination of this question.

11 [How happiness can be affected after one's death]: Still, it is apparently rather unfriendly and contrary to the [common] beliefs to claim that the fortunes of our descendants and all our friends contribute nothing. But since they can find themselves in many and various circumstances, some of which affect us more, some less, it is apparently a long—indeed endless—task to differentiate all the particular cases. Perhaps a general outline will be enough of an answer.

Misfortunes, then, even to the person himself, differ, and some have a certain gravity and weight for his life, whereas others would seem to be lighter. The same is true for the misfortunes of his friends; and it matters whether they happen to living or to dead people—much more than it matters whether lawless and terrible crimes are committed before a tragic drama begins or in the course of it.

In our reasoning, then, we should also take account of this difference, but even more account, presumably, of the puzzle about whether the dead share in any good or evil. For if we consider this, anything good or evil penetrating to the dead would seem to be weak and unimportant, either without qualification or for them. Even if the good or evil is not so weak and unimportant, still its importance and character are not enough to make people happy who are not already happy, or to take away the blessedness of those who are happy. And so, when friends do well, and likewise when they do badly, it appears to contribute something to the dead, but of a character and size that neither makes happy people not happy nor anything of this sort.

10 12 [Praise and honor]: Now that we have determined these points, let us consider whether happiness is something praiseworthy, or instead something honorable; for clearly it is not a capacity [which is neither praiseworthy nor honorable].

Whatever is praiseworthy appears to be praised for its character and its state in relation to something. We praise 15 the just and the brave person, for instance, and in general the good person and virtue, because of their actions and achievements; and we praise the strong person, the good runner, and each of the others because he naturally has a certain character and is in a certain state in relation to something good and excellent. This is clear also from praises of 20 the gods; for these praises appear ridiculous because they are referred to us, but they are referred to us because, as we said, praise depends on such a reference.

If praise is for these sorts of things, then clearly for the best things there is no praise, but something greater and better. And indeed this is how it appears. For the gods and the most godlike of men are [not praised, but] congratu-25 lated for their blessedness and happiness. The same is true of goods; for we never praise happiness, as we praise justice, but we count it blessed, as something better and more god-like [than anything that is praised].

Indeed, Eudoxus[1] seems to have used the right sort of argument in defending the supremacy of pleasure. By not praising pleasure, though it is a good, we indicate—so he 30 thought—that it is superior to everything praiseworthy; [only] the god and the good have this superiority since the other goods are [praised] by reference to them.

[Here he seems to have argued correctly.] For praise is given to virtue, since it makes us do fine actions; but cele-brations are for achievements, either of body or of soul. But an exact treatment of this is presumably more proper for 35 specialists in celebrations. For us, anyhow, it is clear from 1102a what has been said that happiness is something honorable and complete.

A further reason why this would seem to be correct is that happiness is a principle; for [the principle] is what we all aim at in all our other actions; and we take the principle and cause of goods to be something honorable and divine.

13 [Introduction to the virtues]: Since happiness is a certain 5 sort of activity of the soul in accord with complete virtue, we must examine virtue; for that will perhaps also be a way to study happiness better. Moreover, the true politician seems to have put more effort into virtue than into any-thing else, since he wants to make the citizens good and law-abiding. We find an example of this in the Spartan 10 and Cretan legislators and in any others who share their concerns. Since, then, the examination of virtue is proper for political science, the inquiry clearly suits our decision at the beginning.

It is clear that the virtue we must examine is human vir-tue,[2] since we are also seeking the human good and human 15 happiness. By human virtue we mean virtue of the soul, not of the body, since we also say that happiness is an activity of the soul. If this is so, it is clear that the politician must in some way know about the soul, just as someone setting out to heal the eyes must know about the whole body as well. 20 This is all the more true to the extent that political science is better and more honorable than medicine; even among doctors, the cultivated ones devote a lot of effort to find-ing out about the body. Hence the politician as well [as the student of nature] must study the soul. But he must study it for his specific purpose, far enough for his inquiry [into virtue]; for a more exact treatment would presumably take 25 more effort than his purpose requires.

[We] have discussed the soul sufficiently [for our pur-poses] in [our] popular works as well [as our less popular], and we should use this discussion. We have said, for in-stance, that one [part] of the soul is nonrational, while one has reason. Are these distinguished as parts of a body and everything divisible into parts are? Or are they two [only] 30 in definition, and inseparable by nature, as the convex and the concave are in a surface? It does not matter for present purposes.

Consider the nonrational [part]. One [part] of it, i.e., the cause of nutrition and growth, would seem to be plant-like and shared [with all living things]; for we can ascribe this capacity of the soul to everything that is nourished, 1102b including embryos, and the same capacity to full-grown living things, since this is more reasonable than to ascribe another capacity to them.

---

1 *Eudoxus* Eudoxus of Cnidus (c. 410–c. 355 BCE). Greek astronomer, mathematician, physician, scholar, and student of Plato. None of his writings survive.

2 *the virtue ... human virtue* For Aristotle, every kind of thing has its own sort of "virtue" (that is, excellence). That is why he speci-fies that it is *human* virtue that is of relevance here.

Hence the virtue of this capacity is apparently shared, not [specifically] human. For this part and this capacity more than others seem to be active in sleep, and here the good and the bad person are least distinct; hence happy people are said to be no better off than miserable people for half their lives. This lack of distinction is not surprising, since sleep is inactivity of the soul insofar as it is called excellent or base, unless to some small extent some movements penetrate [to our awareness], and in this way the decent person comes to have better images [in dreams] than just any random person has. Enough about this, however, and let us leave aside the nutritive part, since by nature it has no share in human virtue.

Another nature in the soul would also seem to be nonrational, though in a way it shares in reason. For in the continent and the incontinent person we praise their reason, that is to say, the [part] of the soul that has reason, because it exhorts them correctly and toward what is best; but they evidently also have in them some other [part] that is by nature something apart from reason, clashing and struggling with reason. For just as paralyzed parts of a body, when we decide to move them to the right, do the contrary and move off to the left, the same is true of the soul; for incontinent people have impulses in contrary directions. In bodies, admittedly, we see the part go astray, whereas we do not see it in the soul; nonetheless, presumably, we should suppose that the soul also has something apart from reason, countering and opposing reason. The [precise] way it is different does not matter.

However, this [part] as well [as the rational part] appears, as we said, to share in reason. At any rate, in the continent person it obeys reason; and in the temperate and the brave person it presumably listens still better to reason, since there it agrees with reason in everything.

The nonrational [part], then, as well [as the whole soul] apparently has two parts. For while the plantlike [part] shares in reason not at all, the [part] with appetites and in general desires shares in reason in a way, insofar as it both listens to reason and obeys it. This is the way in which we are said to "listen to reason" from father or friends, as opposed to the way in which [we "give the reason"] in mathematics. The nonrational part also [obeys and] is persuaded in some way by reason, as is shown by correction, and by every sort of reproof and exhortation.

1103a   If, then, we ought to say that this [part] also has reason, then the [part] that has reason, as well [as the nonrational part], will have two parts. One will have reason fully, by having it within itself; the other will have reason by listening to reason as to a father.

The division between virtues accords with this difference. For some virtues are called virtues of thought, others virtues of character; wisdom, comprehension, and prudence are called virtues of thought, generosity and temperance virtues of character. For when we speak of someone's character we do not say that he is wise or has good comprehension, but that he is gentle or temperate. And yet, we also praise the wise person for his state, and the states that are praiseworthy are the ones we call virtues.

Book 2 [Virtue of Character]

1 [How a virtue of character is acquired]: Virtue, then, is of two sorts, virtue of thought and virtue of character. Virtue of thought arises and grows mostly from teaching; that is why it needs experience and time. Virtue of character [i.e., of ēthos] results from habit [ethos]; hence its name "ethical," slightly varied from "ethos."[1]

Hence it is also clear that none of the virtues of character arises in us naturally. For if something is by nature in one condition, habituation cannot bring it into another condition. A stone, for instance, by nature moves downwards, and habituation could not make it move upwards, not even if you threw it up ten thousand times to habituate it; nor could habituation make fire move downwards, or bring anything that is by nature in one condition into another condition. And so the virtues arise in us neither by nature nor against nature. Rather, we are by nature able to acquire them, and we are completed through habit.

Further, if something arises in us by nature, we first have the capacity for it, and later perform the activity. This is clear in the case of the senses; for we did not acquire them by frequent seeing or hearing, but we already had them when we exercised them, and did not get them by exercising them. Virtues, by contrast, we acquire, just as we acquire crafts, by having first activated them. For we learn a craft by producing the same product that we must produce when we have learned it; we become builders, for

---

1   *Virtue of character ... "ethos"*   From the Greek word *ēthos* ("character") is derived the word *ethikos* ("theory of living") from which the English word "ethics" is derived. In pointing out the link between character and habit, Aristotle plays with the resemblance between that word and the word *ethos* ("habit"). These are related; a sense of the latter is "custom" or "usage."

1103b instance, by building, and we become harpists by playing the harp. Similarly, then, we become just by doing just actions, temperate by doing temperate actions, brave by doing brave actions.

What goes on in cities is also evidence for this. For the legislator makes the citizens good by habituating them, and this is the wish of every legislator; if he fails to do it well he misses his goal. Correct habituation distinguishes a good political system from a bad one.

Further, the sources and means that develop each virtue also ruin it, just as they do in a craft. For playing the harp makes both good and bad harpists, and it is analogous in the case of builders and all the rest; for building well makes good builders, and building badly makes bad ones. Otherwise no teacher would be needed, but everyone would be born a good or a bad craftsman.

It is the same, then, with the virtues. For what we do in our dealings with other people makes some of us just, some unjust; what we do in terrifying situations, and the habits of fear or confidence that we acquire, make some of us brave and others cowardly. The same is true of situations involving appetites and anger; for one or another sort of conduct in these situations makes some temperate and mild, others intemperate and irascible. To sum it up in a single account: a state [of character] results from [the repetition of] similar activities.

That is why we must perform the right activities, since differences in these imply corresponding differences in the states. It is not unimportant, then, to acquire one sort of habit or another, right from our youth. On the contrary, it is very important, indeed all-important.

2 [Habituation]: Our present discussion does not aim, as our others do, at study; for the purpose of our examination is not to know what virtue is, but to become good, since otherwise the inquiry would be of no benefit to us. And so we must examine the right ways of acting; for, as we have said, the actions also control the sorts of states we acquire.

First, then, actions should accord with the correct reason. That is a common [belief], and let us assume it. We shall discuss it later, and say what the correct reason is and how it is related to the other virtues.

1104a But let us take it as agreed in advance that every account of the actions we must do has to be stated in outline, not exactly. As we also said at the beginning, the type of accounts we demand should accord with the subject matter;

and questions about actions and expediency, like questions about health, have no fixed answers.

While this is the character of our general account, the account of particular cases is still more inexact. For these fall under no craft or profession; the agents themselves must consider in each case what the opportune action is, as doctors and navigators do. The account we offer, then, in our present inquiry is of this inexact sort; still, we must try to offer help.

First, then, we should observe that these sorts of states naturally tend to be ruined by excess and deficiency. We see this happen with strength and health—for we must use evident cases [such as these] as witnesses to things that are not evident. For both excessive and deficient exercise ruin bodily strength, and, similarly, too much or too little eating or drinking ruins health, whereas the proportionate amount produces, increases, and preserves it.

The same is true, then, of temperance, bravery, and the other virtues. For if, for instance, someone avoids and is afraid of everything, standing firm against nothing, he becomes cowardly; if he is afraid of nothing at all and goes to face everything, he becomes rash. Similarly, if he gratifies himself with every pleasure and abstains from none, he becomes intemperate; if he avoids them all, as boors do, he becomes some sort of insensible person. Temperance and bravery, then, are ruined by excess and deficiency, but preserved by the mean.

But these actions are not only the sources and causes both of the emergence and growth of virtues and of their ruin; the activities of the virtues [once we have acquired them] also consist in these same actions. For this is also true of more evident cases; strength, for instance, arises from eating a lot and from withstanding much hard labor, and it is the strong person who is most capable of these very actions. It is the same with the virtues. For abstaining from pleasures makes us become temperate, and once we have become temperate we are most capable of abstaining from pleasures. It is similar with bravery; habituation in disdain for frightening situations and in standing firm against them makes us become brave, and once we have become brave we shall be most capable of standing firm.

3 [The importance of pleasure and pain]: But we must take someone's pleasure or pain following on his actions to be a sign of his state. For if someone who abstains from bodily pleasures enjoys the abstinence itself, he is temperate; if he is grieved by it, he is intemperate. Again, if he stands firm

against terrifying situations and enjoys it, or at least does not find it painful, he is brave; if he finds it painful, he is cowardly. For virtue of character is about pleasures and pains.

10   For pleasure causes us to do base actions, and pain causes us to abstain from fine ones. That is why we need to have had the appropriate upbringing—right from early youth, as Plato says —to make us find enjoyment or pain in the right things; for this is the correct education.

Further, virtues are concerned with actions and feel-
15 ings; but every feeling and every action implies pleasure or pain; hence, for this reason too, virtue is about pleasures and pains. Corrective treatments also indicate this, since they use pleasures and pains; for correction is a form of medical treatment, and medical treatment naturally oper-ates through contraries.

Further, as we said earlier, every state of soul is naturally
20 related to and about whatever naturally makes it better or worse; and pleasures and pains make people base, from pur-suing and avoiding the wrong ones, at the wrong time, in the wrong ways, or whatever other distinctions of that sort are needed in an account. These [bad effects of pleasure and pain] are the reason why people actually define the virtues
25 as ways of being unaffected and undisturbed [by pleasures and pains]. They are wrong, however, because they speak of being unaffected without qualification, not of being un-affected in the right or wrong way, at the right or wrong time, and the added qualifications.

We assume, then, that virtue is the sort of state that does the best actions concerning pleasures and pains, and that vice is the contrary state.

The following will also make it evident that virtue and
30 vice are about the same things. For there are three objects of choice—fine, expedient, and pleasant—and three objects of avoidance—their contraries, shameful, harmful, and pain-ful. About all these, then, the good person is correct and the bad person is in error, and especially about pleasure. For
35 pleasure is shared with animals, and implied by every object
1105a of choice, since what is fine and what is expedient appear pleasant as well.

Further, pleasure grows up with all of us from infancy on. That is why it is hard to rub out this feeling that is dyed into our lives. We also estimate actions [as well as feel-ings]—some of us more, some less—by pleasure and pain.
5 For this reason, our whole discussion must be about these; for good or bad enjoyment or pain is very important for our actions.

Further, it is more difficult to fight pleasure than to fight spirit—and Heracleitus[1] tells us [how difficult it is to fight spirit]. Now both craft and virtue are in every case about what is more difficult, since a good result is even bet-ter when it is more difficult. Hence, for this reason also, the   10 whole discussion, for virtue and political science alike, must consider pleasures and pains; for if we use these well, we shall be good, and if badly, bad.

To sum up: Virtue is about pleasures and pains; the ac-tions that are its sources also increase it or, if they are done   15 badly, ruin it; and its activity is about the same actions as those that are its sources.

4 [Virtuous actions versus virtuous character]: Someone might be puzzled, however, about what we mean by say-ing that we become just by doing just actions and become temperate by doing temperate actions. For [one might sup-pose that] if we do grammatical or musical actions, we are   20 grammarians or musicians, and, similarly, if we do just or temperate actions, we are thereby just or temperate.

But surely actions are not enough, even in the case of crafts; for it is possible to produce a grammatical result by chance, or by following someone else's instructions. To be grammarians, then, we must both produce a grammatical result and produce it grammatically—that is to say, produce   25 it in accord with the grammatical knowledge in us.

Moreover, in any case, what is true of crafts is not true of virtues. For the products of a craft determine by their own qualities whether they have been produced well; and so it suffices that they have the right qualities when they have been produced. But for actions in accord with the virtues to be done temperately or justly it does not suffice that they themselves have the right qualities. Rather, the agent must   30 also be in the right state when he does them. First, he must know [that he is doing virtuous, actions]; second, he must decide on them, and decide on them for themselves; and, third, he must also do them from a firm and unchanging state.

As conditions for having a craft, these three do not   1105b count, except for the bare knowing. As a condition for hav-ing a virtue, however, the knowing counts for nothing, or [rather] for only a little, whereas the other two conditions

---

1   *Heracleitus* Heracleitus (also spelled *Heraclitus*) of Ephesus (c. 540–c. 475 BCE), a pre-Socratic Greek philosopher, was a very early theorist of science. He emphasized the universality of change ("flux") and the necessity of looking behind the illusory veil of appearances.

are very important, indeed all-important. And we achieve these other two conditions by the frequent doing of just and temperate actions.

Hence actions are called just or temperate when they are the sort that a just or temperate person would do. But the just and temperate person is not the one who [merely] does these actions, but the one who also does them in the way in which just or temperate people do them.

It is right, then, to say that a person comes to be just from doing just actions and temperate from doing temperate actions; for no one has the least prospect of becoming good from failing to do them.

The many, however, do not do these actions. They take refuge in arguments, thinking that they are doing philosophy, and that this is the way to become excellent people. They are like a sick person who listens attentively to the doctor, but acts on none of his instructions. Such a course of treatment will not improve the state of the sick person's body; nor will the many improve the state of their souls by this attitude to philosophy.

5 [Virtue of character: its genus]: Next we must examine what virtue is. Since there are three conditions arising in the soul—feelings, capacities, and states—virtue must be one of these.

By feelings I mean appetite, anger, fear, confidence, envy, joy, love, hate, longing, jealousy, pity, and in general whatever implies pleasure or pain. By capacities I mean what we have when we are said to be capable of these feelings—capable of being angry, for instance, or of being afraid or of feeling pity. By states I mean what we have when we are well or badly off in relation to feelings. If, for instance, our feeling is too intense or slack, we are badly off in relation to anger, but if it is intermediate, we are well off; the same is true in the other cases.

First, then, neither virtues nor vices are feelings. For we are called excellent or base insofar as we have virtues or vices, not insofar as we have feelings. Further, we are neither praised nor blamed insofar as we have feelings; for we do not praise the angry or the frightened person, and do not blame the person who is simply angry, but only the person who is angry in a particular way. We are praised or blamed, however, insofar as we have virtues or vices. Further, we are angry and afraid without decision; but the virtues are decisions of some kind, or [rather] require decision. Besides, insofar as we have feelings, we are said to be moved; but

insofar as we have virtues or vices, we are said to be in some condition rather than moved.

For these reasons the virtues are not capacities either; for we are neither called good nor called bad, nor are we praised or blamed, insofar as we are simply capable of feelings. Further, while we have capacities by nature, we do not become good or bad by nature; we have discussed this before.

If, then, the virtues are neither feelings nor capacities, the remaining possibility is that they are states. And so we have said what the genus of virtue is.

6 [Virtue of character: Its differentia]: But we must say not only, as we already have, that it is a state, but also what sort of state it is.

It should be said, then, that every virtue causes its possessors to be in a good state and to perform their functions well. The virtue of eyes, for instance, makes the eyes and their functioning excellent, because it makes us see well; and similarly, the virtue of a horse makes the horse excellent, and thereby good at galloping, at carrying its rider, and at standing steady in the face of the enemy. If this is true in every case, the virtue of a human being will likewise be the state that makes a human being good and makes him perform his function well.

We have already said how this will be true, and it will also be evident from our next remarks, if we consider the sort of nature that virtue has.

In everything continuous and divisible we can take more, less, and equal, and each of them either in the object itself or relative to us; and the equal is some intermediate between excess and deficiency. By the intermediate in the object I mean what is equidistant from each extremity; this is one and the same for all. But relative to us the intermediate is what is neither superfluous nor deficient; this is not one, and is not the same for all.

If, for instance, ten are many and two are few, we take six as intermediate in the object, since it exceeds [two] and is exceeded [by ten] by an equal amount, [four]. This is what is intermediate by numerical proportion. But that is not how we must take the intermediate that is relative to us. For if ten pounds [of food], for instance, are a lot for someone to eat, and two pounds a little, it does not follow that the trainer will prescribe six, since this might also be either a little or a lot for the person who is to take it—for Milo [the athlete] a little, but for the beginner in gymnastics a lot; and the same is true for running and wrestling. In this way every scientific expert avoids excess and deficiency and seeks and chooses what is intermediate—but intermediate relative to us, not in the object.

This, then, is how each science produces its product well, by focusing on what is intermediate and making the product conform to that. This, indeed, is why people regularly comment on well-made products that nothing could be added or subtracted; they assume that excess or deficiency ruins a good [result], whereas the mean preserves it. Good craftsmen also, we say, focus on what is intermediate when they produce their product. And since virtue, like nature, is better and more exact than any craft, it will also aim at what is intermediate.

By virtue I mean virtue of character; for this is about feelings and actions, and these admit of excess, deficiency, and an intermediate condition. We can be afraid, for instance, or be confident, or have appetites, or get angry, or feel pity, and in general have pleasure or pain, both too much and too little, and in both ways not well. But having these feelings at the right times, about the right things, toward the right people, for the right end, and in the right way, is the intermediate and best condition, and this is proper to virtue. Similarly, actions also admit of excess, deficiency, and an intermediate condition.

Now virtue is about feelings and actions, in which excess and deficiency are in error and incur blame, whereas the intermediate condition is correct and wins praise, which are both proper to virtue. Virtue, then, is a mean, insofar as it aims at what is intermediate.

Moreover, there are many ways to be in error—for badness is proper to the indeterminate, as the Pythagoreans pictured it, and good to the determinate.[1] But there is only one way to be correct. That is why error is easy and correctness is difficult, since it is easy to miss the target and difficult to hit it. And so for this reason also excess and deficiency are proper to vice, the mean to virtue; "for we are noble in only one way, but bad in all sorts of ways."

Virtue, then, is a state that decides, consisting in a mean, the mean relative to us, which is defined by reference to reason, that is to say, to the reason by reference to which the prudent person would define it. It is a mean between two vices, one of excess and one of deficiency.

It is a mean for this reason also: Some vices miss what is right because they are deficient, others because they are excessive, in feelings or in actions, whereas virtue finds and chooses what is intermediate.

That is why virtue, as far as its essence and the account stating what it is are concerned, is a mean, but, as far as the best [condition] and the good [result] are concerned, it is an extremity.

Now not every action or feeling admits of the mean. For the names of some automatically include baseness—for instance, spite, shamelessness, envy [among feelings], and adultery, theft, murder, among actions. For all of these and similar things are called by these names because they themselves, not their excesses or deficiencies, are base. Hence in doing these things we can never be correct, but must invariably be in error. We cannot do them well or not well—by committing adultery, for instance, with the right woman at the right time in the right way. On the contrary, it is true without qualification that to do any of them is to be in error.

[To think these admit of a mean], therefore, is like thinking that unjust or cowardly or intemperate action also admits of a mean, an excess and a deficiency. If it did, there would be a mean of excess, a mean of deficiency, an excess of excess and a deficiency of deficiency. On the contrary, just as there is no excess or deficiency of temperance or of bravery (since the intermediate is a sort of extreme), so also there is no mean of these vicious actions either, but whatever way anyone does them, he is in error. For in general there is no mean of excess or of deficiency, and no excess or deficiency of a mean.

7 [The particular virtues of character]: However, we must not only state this general account but also apply it to the particular cases. For among accounts concerning actions, though the general ones are common to more cases, the specific ones are truer, since actions are about particular cases, and our account must accord with these. Let us, then, find these from the chart.[2]

First, then, in feelings of fear and confidence the mean is bravery. The excessively fearless person is nameless (indeed many cases are nameless), and the one who is excessively confident is rash. The one who is excessive in fear and deficient in confidence is cowardly.

---

1 *indeterminate ... determinate* The "determinate" is the limited, orderly, specific; the "indeterminate" is the chaotic, open-ended, various.

2 *from the chart* That is, figuratively from a "table" organizing and classifying the phenomena.

5 In pleasures and pains—though not in all types, and in pains less than in pleasures —the mean is temperance and the excess intemperance. People deficient in pleasure are not often found, which is why they also lack even a name; let us call them insensible.

In giving and taking money the mean is generosity, the
10 excess wastefulness and the deficiency ungenerosity. Here the vicious people have contrary excesses and defects; for the wasteful person is excessive in spending and deficient in taking, whereas the ungenerous person is excessive in taking and deficient in spending. At the moment we are speaking
15 in outline and summary, and that is enough; later we shall define these things more exactly.

In questions of money there are also other conditions. Another mean is magnificence; for the magnificent person differs from the generous by being concerned with large matters, while the generous person is concerned with small. The excess is ostentation and vulgarity, and the deficiency is
20 stinginess. These differ from the vices related to generosity in ways we shall describe later.

In honor and dishonor the mean is magnanimity, the excess something called a sort of vanity, and the deficiency pusillanimity. And just as we said that generosity differs
25 from magnificence in its concern with small matters, similarly there is a virtue concerned with small honors, differing in the same way from magnanimity, which is concerned with great honors. For honor can be desired either in the right way or more or less than is right. If someone desires it to excess, he is called an honor-lover, and if his desire is deficient he is called indifferent to honor, but if he is intermedi-
30 ate he has no name. The corresponding conditions have no name either, except the condition of the honor-lover, which is called honor-loving.

This is why people at the extremes lay claim to the intermediate area. Moreover, we also sometimes call the intermediate person an honor-lover, and sometimes call him indifferent to honor; and sometimes we praise the
1108a honor-lover, sometimes the person indifferent to honor. We will mention later the reason we do this; for the moment, let us speak of the other cases in the way we have laid down.

5 Anger also admits of an excess, deficiency, and mean. These are all practically nameless; but since we call the intermediate person mild, let us call the mean mildness. Among the extreme people, let the excessive person be irascible, and his vice irascibility, and let the deficient person be a sort of inirascible person, and his deficiency inirascibility.

There are also three other means, somewhat similar to 10 one another, but different. For they are all concerned with common dealings in conversations and actions, but differ insofar as one is concerned with truth telling in these areas, the other two with sources of pleasure, some of which are found in amusement, and the others in daily life in general. Hence we should also discuss these states, so that we can better observe that in every case the mean is praiseworthy, 15 whereas the extremes are neither praiseworthy nor correct, but blameworthy. Most of these cases are also nameless, and we must try, as in the other cases also, to supply names ourselves, to make things clear and easy to follow.

In truth-telling, then, let us call the intermediate person 20 truthful, and the mean truthfulness; pretense that overstates will be boastfulness, and the person who has it boastful; pretense that understates will be self-deprecation, and the person who has it self-deprecating.

In sources of pleasure in amusements let us call the intermediate person witty, and the condition wit; the excess buffoonery and the person who has it a buffoon; and the 25 deficient person a sort of boor and the state boorishness.

In the other sources of pleasure, those in daily life, let us call the person who is pleasant in the right way friendly, and the mean state friendliness. If someone goes to excess with no [ulterior] aim, he will be ingratiating; if he does it for his own advantage, a flatterer. The deficient person, unpleasant in everything, will be a sort of quarrelsome and 30 ill-tempered person.

There are also means in feelings and about feelings. Shame, for instance, is not a virtue, but the person prone to shame as well as [the virtuous people we have described] receives praise. For here also one person is called intermediate, and another—the person excessively prone to shame, who is ashamed about everything—is called excessive; the person who is deficient in shame or never feels shame at all 35 is said to have no sense of disgrace; and the intermediate one is called prone to shame.

Proper indignation is the mean between envy and spite; 1108b these conditions are concerned with pleasure and pain at what happens to our neighbors. For the properly indignant person feels pain when someone does well undeservedly; the envious person exceeds him by feeling pain when anyone 5 does well, while the spiteful person is so deficient in feeling pain that he actually enjoys [other people's misfortunes].

There will also be an opportunity elsewhere to speak of these. We must consider justice after these. Since it is spoken of in more than one way, we shall distinguish its

two types and say how each of them is a mean. Similarly, we
10 must also consider the virtues that belong to reason.

8 [Relations between mean and extreme states]: Among
these three conditions, then, two are vices—one of excess,
one of deficiency—and one, the mean, is virtue. In a way,
each of them is opposed to each of the others, since each
15 extreme is contrary both to the intermediate condition and
to the other extreme, while the intermediate is contrary to
the extremes.

For, just as the equal is greater in comparison to the
smaller, and smaller in comparison to the greater, so also the
intermediate states are excessive in comparison to the deficiencies and deficient in comparison to the excesses—both
in feelings and in actions. For the brave person, for instance,
appears rash in comparison to the coward, and cowardly in
20 comparison to the rash person; the temperate person appears intemperate in comparison to the insensible person,
and insensible in comparison with the intemperate person;
and the generous person appears wasteful in comparison
to the ungenerous, and ungenerous in comparison to the
wasteful person. That is why each of the extreme people
tries to push the intermediate person to the other extreme,
25 so that the coward, for instance, calls the brave person rash,
and the rash person calls him a coward, and similarly in the
other cases.

Since these conditions of soul are opposed to each other
in these ways, the extremes are more contrary to each other
than to the intermediate. For they are further from each
other than from the intermediate, just as the large is further
30 from the small, and the small from the large, than either is
from the equal.

Further, sometimes one extreme—rashness or wastefulness, for instance—appears somewhat like the intermediate
state, bravery or generosity. But the extremes are most unlike one another; and the things that are furthest apart from
each other are defined as contraries. And so the things that
35 are further apart are more contrary.

In some cases the deficiency, in others the excess,
1109a is more opposed to the intermediate condition. For instance, cowardice, the deficiency, not rashness, the excess,
is more opposed to bravery, whereas intemperance, the
excess, not insensibility, the deficiency, is more opposed to
5 temperance.

This happens for two reasons: One reason is derived
from the object itself. Since sometimes one extreme is closer
and more similar to the intermediate condition, we oppose

the contrary extreme, more than this closer one, to the
intermediate condition. Since rashness, for instance, seems
to be closer and more similar to bravery, and cowardice 10
less similar, we oppose cowardice, more than rashness, to
bravery; for what is further from the intermediate condition
seems to be more contrary to it. This, then, is one reason,
derived from the object itself.

The other reason is derived from ourselves. For when
we ourselves have some natural tendency to one extreme
more than to the other, this extreme appears more opposed
to the intermediate condition. Since, for instance, we have 15
more of a natural tendency to pleasure, we drift more easily
toward intemperance than toward orderliness. Hence we
say that an extreme is more contrary if we naturally develop
more in that direction; and this is why intemperance is more
contrary to temperance, since it is the excess [of pleasure].

9 [How can we reach the mean?]: We have said enough, 20
then, to show that virtue of character is a mean and what
sort of mean it is; that it is a mean between two vices, one of
excess and one of deficiency; and that it is a mean because it
aims at the intermediate condition in feelings and actions.

That is why it is also hard work to be excellent. For
in each case it is hard work to find the intermediate; for 25
instance, not everyone, but only one who knows, finds the
midpoint in a circle. So also getting angry, or giving and
spending money, is easy and everyone can do it; but doing
it to the right person, in the right amount, at the right time,
for the right end, and in the right way is no longer easy, nor
can everyone do it. Hence doing these things well is rare, 30
praiseworthy, and fine.

That is why anyone who aims at the intermediate condition must first of all steer clear of the more contrary extreme, following the advice that Calypso[1] also gives: "Hold
the ship outside the spray and surge." For one extreme is
more in error, the other less. Since, therefore, it is hard to
hit the intermediate extremely accurately, the second-best
tack, as they say, is to take the lesser of the evils. We shall 35
succeed best in this by the method we describe.

We must also examine what we ourselves drift into eas- 1109b
ily. For different people have different natural tendencies
toward different goals, and we shall come to know our own
tendencies from the pleasure or pain that arises in us. We
must drag ourselves off in the contrary direction; for if we 5

---

1 *Calypso* In Homer's *Odyssey*, she is a sea nymph who is in love
with Odysseus and keeps him on her island for seven years.

pull far away from error, as they do in straightening bent wood, we shall reach the intermediate condition.

And in everything we must beware above all of pleasure and its sources; for we are already biased in its favor when we come to judge it. Hence we must react to it as the elders reacted to Helen,[1] and on each occasion repeat what they said; for if we do this, and send it off, we shall be less in error.

In summary, then, if we do these things we shall best be able to reach the intermediate condition. But presumably this is difficult, especially in particular cases, since it is not easy to define the way we should be angry, with whom, about what, for how long. For sometimes, indeed, we ourselves praise deficient people and call them mild, and sometimes praise quarrelsome people and call them manly.

Still, we are not blamed if we deviate a little in excess or deficiency from doing well, but only if we deviate a long way, since then we are easily noticed. But how great and how serious a deviation receives blame is not easy to define in an account; for nothing else perceptible is easily defined either. Such things are among particulars, and the judgment depends on perception.

This is enough, then, to make it clear that in every case the intermediate state is praised, but we must sometimes incline toward the excess, sometimes toward the deficiency; for that is the easiest way to hit the intermediate and good condition.

from Book 3 [The Individual Virtues of Character]

...

1115a 6 [Bravery: Its scope]: First let us discuss bravery. We have already made it apparent that there is a mean about feelings of fear and confidence. What we fear, clearly, is what is frightening, and such things are, speaking without qualifi-

cation, bad things; hence people define fear as expectation of something bad.

Certainly we fear all bad things—for instance, bad reputation, poverty, sickness, friendlessness, death—but they do not all seem to concern the brave person. For fear of some bad things, such as bad reputation, is actually right and fine, and lack of fear is shameful; for if someone fears bad reputation, he is decent and properly prone to shame, and if he has no fear of it, he has no feeling of disgrace. Some, however, call this fearless person brave, by a transference of the name; for he has some similarity to the brave person, since the brave person is also a type of fearless person.

Presumably it is wrong to fear poverty or sickness or, in general, [bad things] that are not the results of vice or caused by ourselves; still, someone who is fearless about these is not thereby brave. He is also called brave by similarity; for some people who are cowardly in the dangers of war are nonetheless generous, and face with confidence the [danger of] losing money.

Again, if someone is afraid of committing wanton aggression on children or women, or of being envious or anything of that sort, that does not make him cowardly. And if someone is confident when he is going to be whipped for his crimes, that does not make him brave.

Then what sorts of frightening conditions concern the brave person? Surely the most frightening; for no one stands firmer against terrifying conditions. Now death is most frightening of all, since it is a boundary, and when someone is dead nothing beyond it seems either good or bad for him any more. Still, not even death in all conditions—on the sea, for instance, or in sickness—seems to be the brave person's concern.

In what conditions, then, is death his concern? Surely in the finest conditions. Now such deaths are those in war, since they occur in the greatest and finest danger. This judgment is endorsed by the honors given in cities and by monarchs. Hence someone is called fully brave if he is intrepid in facing a fine death and the immediate dangers that bring death. And this is above all true of the dangers of war.

Certainly the brave person is also intrepid on the sea and in sickness, but not in the same way as seafarers are. For he has given up hope of safety, and objects to this sort of death [with nothing fine in it], but seafarers' experience makes them hopeful. Moreover, we act like brave men on occasions when we can use our strength, or when it is fine to be killed; and neither of these is true when we perish on the sea.

---

1   *as the elders reacted to Helen*   In Homer's *Iliad*, Helen of Sparta falls in love with Paris of Troy, and goes off with him, provoking the Trojan war. In *Iliad* 3,155, the Elders of Troy, revered as voices of wisdom and moderation, remark that they understand that her great beauty could provoke so horrible a war ("Who on earth could blame the Trojan and Achaean men-at-arms for suffering so long for such a woman's sake? Indeed, she is the very image of an immortal goddess"), but recommend that she be sent back ("All the same, and lovely as she is, let her sail home and not stay here to vex us and our children after us").

7 [Bravery: Its characteristic outlook]: Now what is frightening is not the same for everyone. We say, however, that some things are too frightening for a human being to resist; these, then, are frightening for everyone, at least for everyone with any sense. What is frightening, but not irresistible

10 for a human being, varies in its seriousness and degree; and the same is true of what inspires confidence.

The brave person is unperturbed, as far as a human being can be. Hence, though he will fear even the sorts of things that are not irresistible, he will stand firm against them, in the right way, as reason prescribes, for the sake of the fine, since this is the end aimed at by virtue.

It is possible to be more or less afraid of these frightening things, and also possible to be afraid of what is not

15 frightening as though it were frightening. The cause of error may be fear of the wrong thing, or in the wrong way, or at the wrong time, or something of that sort; and the same is true for things that inspire confidence.

Hence whoever stands firm against the right things and fears the right things, for the right end, in the right way, at the right time, and is correspondingly confident, is the brave person; for the brave person's actions and feelings accord with

20 what something is worth, and follow what reason prescribes.

Every activity aims at actions in accord with the state of character. Now to the brave person bravery is fine; hence the end it aims at is also fine, since each thing is defined by its end. The brave person, then, aims at the fine when he stands firm and acts in accord with bravery.

Among those who go to excess the excessively fearless

25 person has no name—we said earlier that many cases have no names. He would be some sort of madman, or incapable of feeling distress, if he feared nothing, neither earthquake nor waves, as they say about the Celts.

The person who is excessively confident about frightening things is rash. The rash person also seems to be a

30 boaster, and a pretender to bravery. At any rate, the attitude to frightening things that the brave person really has is the attitude that the rash person wants to appear to have; hence he imitates the brave person where he can. That is why most of them are rash cowards; for, rash though they are on these [occasions for imitation], they do not stand firm against anything frightening. Moreover, rash people are impetuous, wishing for dangers before they arrive, but they shrink from them when they come. Brave people, on the contrary, are eager when in action, but keep quiet until then.

The person who is excessively afraid is the coward, since

35 he fears the wrong things, and in the wrong way, and so on.

Certainly, he is also deficient in confidence, but his excessive pain distinguishes him more clearly. Hence, since he is afraid of everything, he is a despairing sort. The brave person, on the contrary, is hopeful, since [he is confident and] confidence is proper to a hopeful person.

1116a

Hence the coward, the rash person, and the brave person 5 are all concerned with the same things, but have different states related to them; the others are excessive or defective, but the brave person has the intermediate and right state.

As we have said, then, bravery is a mean about what 10 inspires confidence and about what is frightening in the conditions we have described; it chooses and stands firm because that is fine or because anything else is shameful. Dying to avoid poverty or erotic passion or something painful is proper to a coward, not to a brave person. For shirking burdens is softness, and such a person stands firm [in the face of death] to avoid an evil, not because standing firm 15 is fine.

8 [Conditions that resemble bravery]: Bravery, then, is something of this sort. But five other sorts of things are also called bravery.

The bravery of citizens comes first, since it looks most like bravery. For citizens seem to stand firm against dangers with the aim of avoiding reproaches and legal penalties and of winning honors; that is why the bravest seem to be those 20 who hold cowards in dishonor and do honor to brave people. That is how Homer also describes them when he speaks of Diomedes[1] and Hector: "Polydamas will be the first to heap disgrace on me"[2] and Diomedes say "For some time Hec- 25 tor speaking among the Trojans will say, 'The son of Tydeus fled from me.'"[3] This is most like the [genuine] bravery described above, because it results from a virtue; for it is caused

---

1 *Diomedes* In the *Iliad*, Diomedes and Ajax are the greatest warriors on the Greek side of the Trojan war. Diomedes was known for his wisdom and courage.

2 *Polydamas will be ... disgrace on me* In *Iliad* 22, Hector (son of the king, and Troy's mightiest warrior) is beseeched by his parents to come inside the walls of Troy, instead of standing outside to face Achilles in battle. In the quoted sentence, Hector is expressing concern about the reproach that he would receive if he did what they asked. Polydamas is a young Trojan commander who often urges prudence against Hector's rashness. The quoted sentence is *Iliad*, 22.10.

3 *For some time Hector ... fled from me* Diomedes replies here to Old Nestor, who urges him to withdraw from the fight where it seems the gods do not will victory for him. The passage is from *Iliad*, 22.148–49.

by shame and by desire for something fine, namely honor, and by aversion from reproach, which is shameful.

30   In this class we might also place those who are compelled by their superiors. However, they are worse to the extent that they act because of fear, not because of shame, and to avoid pain, not disgrace. For their commanders compel them, as Hector does; "If I notice anyone shrink-
35 ing back from the battle, nothing will save him from being eaten by the dogs."[1] Commanders who strike any troops
1116b who give ground, or who post them in front of ditches and suchlike, do the same thing, since they all compel them. The brave person, however, must be moved by the fine, not by compulsion.

Experience about a given situation also seems to be bravery; that is why Socrates actually thought that brav-
5   ery is scientific knowledge. Different people have this sort [of apparent courage] in different conditions. In wartime professional soldiers have it; for there seem to be many groundless alarms in war, and the professionals are the most familiar with these. Hence they appear brave, since others do not know that the alarms are groundless. Moreover, their
10 experience makes them most capable in attack and defense, since they are skilled in the use of their weapons, and have the best weapons for attack and defense. The result is that in fighting nonprofessionals they are like armed troops against unarmed, or trained athletes against ordinary people; for in these contests also the best fighters are the strongest and
15 physically fittest, not the bravest.

Professional soldiers, however, turn out to be cowards whenever the danger overstrains them and they are inferior in numbers and equipment. For they are the first to run, whereas the citizen troops stand firm and get killed; this was what happened at the temple of Hermes.[2] For the citizens
20 find it shameful to run, and find death more choiceworthy than safety at this cost. But the professionals from the start were facing the danger on the assumption of their superiority; once they learn their mistake, they run, since they are more afraid of being killed than of doing something shameful. That is not the brave person's character.

1   *If I notice ... eaten by the dogs* "Hector then cried out to the Trojans, 'Forward to the ships, and let the spoils be. If I see any man keeping back on the side of the wall away from the ships I will have him killed: his kinsmen and kinswomen shall not give him his dues of fire, but dogs shall tear him in pieces in front of our city'" (*Iliad*, 22).
2   *what happened ... temple of Hermes* Reference to a battle at Coronea c. 353 BCE between the Phonicians and Coroneans.

Spirit is also counted as bravery; for those who act on spirit also seem to be brave—as beasts seem to be when
25 they attack those who have wounded them—because brave people are also full of spirit. For spirit is most eager to run and face dangers; hence Homer's words, "put strength in his spirit," "aroused strength and spirit," and "his blood boiled." All these would seem to signify the arousal and the
30 impulse of spirit.

Now brave people act because of the fine, and their spirit cooperates with them. But beasts act because of pain; for they attack only because they have been wounded or frightened, (since they keep away from us in a forest). They are not brave, then, since distress and spirit drives them in an impulsive rush to meet danger, foreseeing none of the
35 terrifying prospects. For if they were brave, hungry asses would also be brave, since they keep on feeding even if they
1117a are beaten; and adulterers also do many daring actions because of lust.
5
Human beings as well as beasts find it painful to be angered, and pleasant to exact a penalty. But those who fight for these reasons are not brave, though they are good fighters; for they fight because of their feelings, not because of the fine nor as reason prescribes. Still, they have something similar [to bravery]. The [bravery] caused by spirit would seem to be the most natural sort, and to be [genuine] bravery once it has also acquired decision and the goal.

Hopeful people are not brave either; for their many vic-
10 tories over many opponents make them confident in dangers. They are somewhat, similar to brave people, since both are confident. But whereas brave people are confident for the reason given earlier, the hopeful are confident because they think they are stronger and nothing could happen to them; drunks do the same sort of thing, since they become hopeful. When things turn out differently from how they
15 expected, they run away. The brave person, on the contrary, stands firm against what is and appears frightening to a human being; he does this because it is fine to stand firm and shameful to fail.

Indeed, that is why someone who is unafraid and unperturbed in emergencies seems braver than [someone who is unafraid only] when he is warned in advance; for his action proceeds more from his state of character, because
20 it proceeds less from preparation. For if we are warned in advance, we might decide what to do [not only because of our state of character, but] also by reason and rational calculation; but in emergencies [we must decide] in accord with our state of character.

Those who act in ignorance also appear brave, and indeed they are close to hopeful people, though inferior to them insofar as they lack the self-esteem of hopeful people. That is why the hopeful stand firm for some time, whereas if ignorant people have been deceived and then realize or suspect that things are different, they run. That was what happened to the Argives when they stumbled on the Spartans and took them for Sicyonians.[1]

We have described, then, the character of brave people and of those who seem to be brave.

9 [Feelings proper to bravery]: Bravery is about feelings of confidence and fear—not, however, about both in the same way, but more about frightening things. For someone is brave if he is undisturbed and in the right state about these, more than if he is in this state about things inspiring confidence.

As we said, then, standing firm against what is painful makes us call people brave; that is why bravery is both painful and justly praised, since it is harder to stand firm against something painful than to refrain from something pleasant. Nonetheless, the end that bravery aims at deems to be pleasant, though obscured by its surroundings. This is what happens in athletic contests. For boxers find that the end they aim at, the crown and the honors, is pleasant, but, being made of flesh and blood, they find it distressing and painful to take the punches and to bear all the hard work; and because there are so many of these painful things, the end, being small, appears to have nothing pleasant in it.

And so, if the same is true for bravery, the brave person will find death and wounds painful, and suffer them unwillingly, but he will endure them because that is fine or because failure is shameful. Indeed, the truer it is that he has every virtue and the happier he is, the more pain he will feel at the prospect of death. For this sort of person, more than anyone, finds it worthwhile to be alive, and knows he is being deprived of the greatest goods, and this is painful. But he is no less brave for all that; presumably, indeed, he is all the braver, because he chooses what is fine in war at the cost of all these goods. It is not true, then, in the case of every virtue that its active exercise is pleasant; it is pleasant only insofar as we attain the end.

But presumably it is quite possible for brave people, given the character we have described, not to be the best soldiers. Perhaps the best will be those who are less brave, but possess no other good; for they are ready to face dangers, and they sell their lives for small gains.

So much for bravery. It is easy to grasp what it is, in outline at least, from what we have said.

...

Book 5 [Justice]

1 [Varieties of justice]: The questions we must examine about justice and injustice are these: What sorts of actions are they concerned with? What sort of mean is justice? What are the extremes between which justice is intermediate? Let us investigate them by the same line of inquiry as we used in the topics discussed before.

We see that the state everyone means in speaking of justice is the state that makes us just agents—[that is to say], the state that makes us do justice and wish what is just. In the same way they mean by injustice the state that makes us do injustice and wish what is unjust. That is why we also should first assume these things as an outline.

For what is true of sciences and capacities is not true of states. For while one and the same capacity or science seems to have contrary activities, a state that is a contrary has no contrary activities. Health, for instance, only makes us do healthy actions, not their contraries; for we say we are walking in a healthy way if [and only if] we are walking in the way a healthy person would.

Often one of a pair of contrary states is recognized from the other contrary; and often the states are recognized from their subjects. For if, for instance, the good state is evident, the bad state becomes evident too; and moreover the good state becomes evident from the things that have it, and the things from the state. For if, for instance, the good state is thickness of flesh, the bad state must be thinness of flesh, and the thing that produces the good state must be what produces thickness of flesh.

If one of a pair of contraries is spoken of in more ways than one, it follows, usually, that the other is too. If, for instance, the just is spoken of in more ways than one, so is the unjust.

Now it would seem that justice and injustice are both spoken of in more ways than one, but since their homonymy is close, the difference is unnoticed, and is less clear than it is with distant homonyms where the distance in appearance is wide (for instance, the bone below an

---

1   *what happened ... for Sicyonians*   Reference to events at the Long Walls of Corinth, 392 BCE.

30 animal's neck and what we lock doors with are called keys[1] homonymously).

Let us, then, find the number of ways an unjust person is spoken of. Both the lawless person and the overreaching and unfair person seem to be unjust; and so, clearly, both the lawful and the fair person will be just. Hence the just will be both the lawful and what is fair, and the unjust will 1129b be both the lawless and the unfair.

Since the unjust person is an overreacher, he will be concerned with goods—not with all goods, but only with those involved in good and bad fortune, goods which are, [considered] without qualification, always good, but for this or that person not always good. Though human beings pray 5 for these and pursue them, they are wrong; the right thing is to pray that what is good without qualification will also be good for us, but to choose [only] what is good for us.

Now the unjust person [who chooses these goods] does not choose more in every case; in the case of what is bad without qualification he actually chooses less. But since what is less bad also seems to be good in a way, and over-reaching aims at more of what is good, he seems to be an 10 overreacher. In fact he is unfair; for unfairness includes [all these actions], and is a common feature [of his choice of the greater good and of the lesser evil].

Since, as we saw, the lawless person is unjust and the lawful person is just, it clearly follows that whatever is lawful is in some way just; for the provisions of legislative science are lawful, and we say that each of them is just. In 15 every matter that they deal with, the laws aim either at the common benefit of all, or at the benefit of those in control, whose control rests on virtue or on some other such basis. And so in one way what we call just is whatever produces and maintains happiness and its parts for a political community.

20 Now the law instructs us to do the actions of a brave person—for instance, not to leave the battle-line, or to flee, or to throw away our weapons; of a temperate person—not to commit adultery or wanton aggression; of a mild person—not to strike or revile another; and similarly requires actions in accord with the other virtues, and prohibits ac-25 tions in accord with the vices. The correctly established law does this correctly, and the less carefully framed one does this worse.

This type of justice, then, is complete virtue, not com-plete virtue without qualification, but complete virtue in

relation to another. And that is why justice often seems to be supreme among the virtues, and "neither the evening star nor the morning star is so marvelous," and the proverb says, "And in justice all virtue is summed up." 30

Moreover, justice is complete virtue to the highest de-gree because it is the complete exercise of complete virtue. And it is the complete exercise because the person who has justice is able to exercise virtue in relation to another, not only in what concerns himself; for many are able to exercise virtue in their own concerns, but unable in what relates to another.

That is why Bias seems to have been correct in saying 1130a that ruling will reveal the man; for a ruler is automatically related to another, and in a community. That is also why justice is the only virtue that seems to be another person's good; because it is related to another; for it does what bene-5 fits another, either the ruler or the fellow member of the community.

The worst person, therefore, is the one who exercises his vice toward himself and his friends as well [as toward others]. And the best person is not the one who exercises virtue [only] toward himself, but the one who [also] exer-cises it in relation to another, since this is a difficult task.

This type of justice, then, is the whole, not a part, of virtue, and the injustice contrary to it is the whole, not a part, of vice. 10

Our discussion makes clear the difference between vir-tue and this type of justice. For virtue is the same as justice, but what it is to be virtue is not the same as what it is to be justice. Rather, insofar as virtue is related to another, it is justice, and insofar as it is a certain sort of state without qualification, it is virtue.

2 [Special justice contrasted with general]: But we are look-ing for the type of justice, since we say there is one, that 15 consists in a part of virtue, and correspondingly for the type of injustice that is a part of vice.

A sign that there is this type of justice and injustice is this: If someone's activities accord with the other vices—if, for instance, cowardice made him throw away his shield, or irritability made him revile someone, or ungenerosity made him fail to help someone with money—what he does is unjust, but not overreaching. But when someone acts from overreaching, in many cases his action accords with none 20 of these vices—certainly not all of them; but it still accords with some type of wickedness, since we blame him, and [in particular] it accords with injustice. Hence there is another

---

1   keys   In Greek, *kleis*.

type of injustice that is a part of the whole, and a way of being unjust that is a part of the whole that is contrary to law.

25   Further, if A commits adultery for profit and makes a profit, but B commits adultery because of his appetite, and spends money on it to his own loss, B seems intemperate rather than overreaching, but A seems unjust, not intemperate. Clearly, then, this is because A acts to make a profit.

Further, we can refer every other unjust action to some 30 vice—to intemperance if someone committed adultery, to cowardice if he deserted his comrade in the battle-line, to anger if he struck someone. But if he made an [unjust] profit, we can refer it to no other vice except injustice.

It is evident, then, that there is another type of injustice, special injustice, apart from injustice as a whole, and that it is synonymous with injustice as a whole, since the definition 1130b is in the same genus. For both have their area of competence in relation to another, but special injustice is concerned with honor or wealth or safety (or whatever single name will include all these), and aims at the pleasure that results from making a profit, whereas the concern of injustice as a whole 5 is whatever concerns the excellent person.

Clearly, then, there is more than one type of justice, and there is another type besides [the type that is] the whole of virtue; but we must still grasp what it is, and what sort of thing it is.

The unjust is divided into the lawless and the unfair, 10 and the just into the lawful and the fair. The injustice previously described, then, is concerned with the lawless. But the unfair is not the same as the lawless; it is related to it as part to whole, since whatever is unfair is lawless, but not everything lawless is unfair. Hence also the unfair type of injustice and the unfair way of being unjust are not the same as 15 the lawless type, but differ as parts from wholes. For unfair injustice is a part of the whole of injustice, and, similarly, fair justice is a part of the whole of justice. Hence we must describe special as well as general justice and injustice, and equally this way of being just or unjust.

20   Let us, then, set aside the type of justice and injustice that accords with the whole of virtue, justice being the exercise of the whole of virtue, and injustice of the whole of vice, in relation to another. And it is evident how we must distinguish the way of being just or unjust that accords with this type of justice and injustice. For most lawful actions, we might say, are those produced by virtue as a whole; for the law prescribes living in accord with each virtue, and for- 25 bids living in accord with each vice. Moreover, the actions

producing the whole of virtue are the lawful actions that the laws prescribe for education promoting the common good. We must wait till later, however, to determine whether the education that makes an individual an unqualified good man is a task for political science or for another science; for, presumably, being a good man is not the same as being every sort of good citizen.

Special justice, however, and the corresponding way of 30 being just have one species that is found in the distribution of honors or wealth or anything else that can be divided among members of a community who share in a political system; for here it is possible for one member to have a share equal or unequal to another's. A second species con- 1131a cerns rectification in transactions.

This second species has two parts, since one sort of transaction is voluntary, and one involuntary. Voluntary transactions (for instance, selling, buying, lending, pledging, renting, depositing, hiring out) are so called because 5 their principle is voluntary. Among involuntary transactions some are secret (for instance, theft, adultery, poisoning, pimping, slave-deception, murder by treachery, false witness), whereas others involve force (for instance, imprisonment, murder, plunder, mutilation, slander, insult).

3 [Justice in distribution]: Since the unjust person is unfair, 10 and what is unjust is unfair, there is clearly an intermediate between the unfair [extremes]. This is the fair; for in any action where too much and too little are possible, the fair [amount] is also possible. And so, if the unjust is unfair, the just is fair (ison), as seems true to everyone even without argument. And since the equal (ison) [and fair] is intermediate, the just is some sort of intermediate.

Since the equal involves at least two things [equal to 15 each other], it follows that the just must be intermediate and equal, and related to something, and for some people. Insofar as it is intermediate, it must be between too much and too little; insofar as it is equal, it involves two things; and insofar as it is just, it is just for some people. Hence the just requires four things at least; the people for whom it is just are two, and the [equal] things involved are two. 20

Equality for the people involved will be the same as for the things involved, since [in a just arrangement] the relation between the people will be the same as the relation between the things involved. For if the people involved are not equal, they will not [justly] receive equal shares; indeed, whenever equals receive unequal shares, or unequals equal shares, in a distribution, that is the source of quarrels and accusations.

25 This is also clear from considering what accords with worth. For all agree that the just in distributions must accord with some sort of worth, but what they call worth is not the same; supporters of democracy say it is free citizenship, some supporters of oligarchy say it is wealth, others good birth, while supporters of aristocracy say it is virtue.

30 Hence the just [since it requires equal shares for equal people] is in some way proportionate. For proportion is special to number as a whole, not only to numbers consisting of [abstract] units, since it is equality of ratios and requires at least four terms. Now divided proportion[1] clearly requires four terms. But so does continuous proportion,[2] since here we use one term as two, and mention it twice. If,
1131b for instance, line A is to line B as B is to C, B is mentioned twice; and so if B is introduced twice, the terms in the proportion will be four.

5 The just also requires at least four terms, with the same ratio [between the pairs], since the people [A and B] and the items [C and D] involved are divided in the same way. Term C, then, is to term D as A is to B, and, taking them alternately, B is to D as A is to C.[3] Hence there will also be the same relation of whole [A and C] to whole [B and D]; this is the relation in which the distribution pairs them, and it pairs them justly if this is how they are combined.

10 Hence the combination of term A with C and of B with D is the just in distribution, and this way of being just is intermediate, whereas the unjust is contrary to the proportionate. For the proportionate is intermediate, and the just is proportionate.

This is the sort of proportion that mathematicians call geometrical, since in geometrical proportion the relation of whole to whole is the same as the relation of each [part] to
15 each [part]. But this proportion [involved in justice] is not continuous, since there is no single term for both the person and the item. The just, then, is the proportionate, and the unjust is the counterproportionate. Hence [in an unjust action] one term becomes more and the other less; and this is indeed how it turns out in practice, since the one doing
20 injustice has more of the good, and the victim has less.

With an evil the ratio is reversed, since the lesser evil, compared to the greater, counts as a good; for the lesser evil is more choiceworthy than the greater, what is choiceworthy is good, and what is more choiceworthy is a greater good. This, then, is the first species of the just.

4 [Justice in rectification]: The other species is rectificatory,[4] 25 found in transactions both voluntary and involuntary. This way of being just belongs to a different species from the first.

For the just in distribution of common assets will always accord with the proportion mentioned above; for [just] 30 distribution from common funds will also accord with the ratio to one another of different people's deposits. Similarly, the way of being unjust that is opposed to this way of being just is what is counterproportionate.

The just in transactions, by contrast, though it is a sort of equality (and the unjust a sort of inequality), accords 1132a with numerical proportion, not with the [geometrical] proportion of the other species. For here it does not matter if a decent person has taken from a base person, or a base person from a decent person, or if a decent or a base person has committed adultery. Rather, the law looks only at differences in the harm [inflicted], and treats the people involved 5 as equals, if one does injustice while the other suffers it, and one has done the harm while the other has suffered it.

And so the judge tries to restore this unjust situation to equality, since it is unequal. For [not only when one steals from another but] also when one is wounded and the other wounds him, or one kills and the other is killed, the action and the suffering are unequally divided [with profit for the offender and loss for the victim]; and the judge tries to restore the [profit and] loss to a position of equality, by 10 subtraction from [the offender's] profit.

For in such cases, stating it without qualification, we speak of profit for the attacker who wounded his victim, for instance, even if that is not the proper word for some cases; and we speak of loss for the victim who suffers the wound. At any rate, when what was suffered has been measured, one part is called the [victim's] loss, and the other the [offender's] profit. Hence the equal is intermediate between more and 15 less. Profit and loss are more and less in contrary ways, since

---

1 *divided proportion* A divided proportion uses four different terms, saying, for example, that A is to B as C is to D.

2 *continuous proportion* A continuous proportion uses three: e.g., A is to B as B is to C.

3 *the people ... A is to C* Aristotle's idea here is that the ratio of distribution (of honor or reward) to two people, A and B, should be proportionate to their respective merit, C and D.

4 *rectificatory* Corrective. Aristotle is not interested in this section in what is usually considered punishment, but rather in correcting a wrong that has been done by awarding damages: removing the benefit from the wrongdoer and restoring it to the victim from whom it had been taken.

more good and less evil is profit, and the contrary is loss. The intermediate area between [profit and loss], we have found, is the equal, which we say is just. Hence the just in rectification is the intermediate between loss and profit.

20   That is why parties to a dispute resort to a judge, and an appeal to a judge is an appeal to the just; for the judge is intended to be a sort of living embodiment of the just. Moreover, they seek the judge as an intermediary, and in some cities they actually call a judge a "mediator," assuming that if they are awarded an intermediate amount, the award will be just. If, then, the judge is an intermediary, the just is in some way intermediate.

25   The judge restores equality, as though a line [AB] had been cut into unequal parts [AC and CB], and he removed from the larger part [AC] the amount [DC] by which it exceeds the half [AD] of the line [AB], and added this amount [DC] to the smaller part [CB]. And when the whole [AB] has been halved [into AD and DB], then they say that each person has what is properly his own, when he has got an equal share.

30   The equal [in this case] is intermediate, by numerical proportion, between the larger [AC] and the smaller line [CB]. This is also why it is called just (*dikaion*), because it is a bisection (*dicha*), as though we said bisected (*dichaion*), and the judge (*dikastes*) is a bisector (*dichastes*). For when [the same amount] is subtracted from one of two equal things and added to the other, then the one part exceeds the other by the two parts; for if a part had been subtracted 1132b from the one, but not added to the other, the larger part would have exceeded the smaller by just one part. Hence the larger part exceeds the intermediate by one part, and the intermediate from which [a part] was subtracted [exceeds the smaller] by one part.

In this way, then, we will recognize what we must subtract from the one who has more and add to the one who has less [to restore equality]; for to the one who has 5 less we must add the amount by which the intermediate exceeds what he has, and from the greatest amount [held by the one who has more] we must subtract the amount by which it exceeds the intermediate. Let lines AA' BB', and CC' be equal; let AE be subtracted from AA' and CD be added to CC', so that the whole line DCC' will exceed the line EA' by the parts CD and CF [where CF equals AE]; it follows that DCC' exceeds BB' by CD.[1]

These names "loss" and "profit" are derived from vol- 11 untary exchange. For having more than one's own share is called making a profit, and having less than what one had at the beginning is called suffering a loss, in buying and 15 selling, for instance, and in other transactions permitted by law. And when people get neither more nor less, but precisely what belongs to them, they say they have their own share and make neither a loss nor a profit. Hence the just is intermediate between a certain kind of loss and profit, since it is having the equal amount both before and after 20 [the transaction].

5 [Justice in exchange]: Some people, however, think reciprocity is also just without qualification. This was the Pythagoreans' view, since their definition stated without qualification that what is just is reciprocity with another.

The truth is that reciprocity suits neither distributive nor rectificatory justice, though people take even Rhada- 25 manthys'[2] [primitive] conception of justice to describe rectificatory justice: "If he suffered what he did, upright justice would be done." For in many cases reciprocity conflicts [with rectificatory justice]. If, for instance, a ruling official [exercising his office] wounded someone else, he must not be wounded in retaliation, but if someone wounded a rul- 30 ing official, he must not only be wounded but also receive corrective treatment. Moreover, the voluntary or involuntary character of the action makes a great difference.

In communities for exchange, however, this way of being just, reciprocity that is proportionate rather than equal, holds people together; for a city is maintained by proportionate reciprocity. For people seek to return either evil for evil, since otherwise [their condition] seems to be slavery, 1133a or good for good, since otherwise there is no exchange; and they are maintained [in a community] by exchange. Indeed, that is why they make a temple of the Graces prominent, so that there will be a return of benefits received. For this

---

2   *Rhadamanthys* Mythological king and one of the judges of the dead, renowned for his wisdom and justice. Aristotle associates him with justice as reciprocity—that is, that the evildoer should suffer in an equal amount to the suffering caused.

is what is special to grace; when someone has been gracious to us, we must do a service for him in return, and also ourselves take the lead in being gracious again.

It is diagonal combination that produces proportionate exchange. Let A be a builder, B a shoemaker, C a house, D a shoe. The builder must receive the shoemaker's product from him, and give him the builder's own product in return. If, then, first of all, proportionate equality is found, and, next, reciprocity is also achieved, the proportionate return will be reached. Otherwise it is not equal, and the exchange will not be maintained, since the product of one may well be superior to the product of the other. These products, then, must be equalized.

This is true of the other crafts also; for they would have been destroyed unless the producer produced the same thing, of the same quantity and quality as the thing affected underwent. For no community [for exchange] is formed from two doctors. It is formed from a doctor and a farmer, and, in general, from people who are different and unequal and who must be equalized.

This is why all items for exchange must be comparable in some way. Currency came along to do exactly this, and in a way it becomes an intermediate, since it measures everything, and so measures excess and deficiency—[for instance,] how many shoes are equal to a house. Hence, as builder is to shoemaker, so must the number of shoes be to a house; for if this does not happen, there will be no exchange and no community. But proportionate equality will not be reached unless they are equal in some way. Everything, then, must be measured by some one measure, as we said before.

In reality, this measure is need, which holds everything together; for if people needed nothing, or needed things to different extents, there would be either no exchange or not the same exchange. And currency has become a sort of pledge of need, by convention; in fact it has its name (*nomisma*) because it is not by nature, but by the current law (*nomos*), and it is within our power to alter it and to make it useless.

Reciprocity will be secured, then, when things are equalized, so that the shoemaker's product is to the farmer's as the farmer is to the shoemaker. However, they must be introduced into the figure of proportion not when they have already exchanged and one extreme has both excesses, but when they still have their own; in that way they will be equals and members of a community, because this sort of equality can be produced in them. Let A be a farmer, C food, B a shoemaker, and D his product that has been equalized; if this sort of reciprocity were not possible, there would be no community.

Now clearly need holds [a community] together as a single unit, since people with no need of each other, both of them or either one, do not exchange, as they exchange whenever another requires what one has oneself, such as wine, when they allow the export of corn. This, then, must be equalized.

If an item is not required at the moment, currency serves to guarantee us a future exchange, guaranteeing that the item will be there for us if we need it; for it must be there for us to take if we pay. Now the same thing happens to currency [as other goods], and it does not always count for the same; still, it tends to be more stable. Hence everything must have a price; for in that way there will always be exchange, and then there will be community.

Currency, then, by making things commensurate as a measure does, equalizes them; for there would be no community without exchange, no exchange without equality, no equality without commensuration. And so, though things so different cannot become commensurate in reality, they can become commensurate enough in relation to our needs.

Hence there must be some single unit fixed [as current] by a stipulation. This is why it is called currency; for this makes everything commensurate, since everything is measured by currency. Let A, for instance, be a house, B ten minae, C a bed. A is half of B if a house is worth five minae or equal to them; and C, the bed, is a tenth of B. It is clear, then, how many beds are equal to one house—five. This is clearly how exchange was before there was currency; for it does not matter whether a house is exchanged for five beds or for the currency for which five beds are exchanged.

We have now said what it is that is unjust and just. And now that we have defined them, it is clear that doing justice is intermediate between doing injustice and suffering injustice, since doing injustice is having too much and suffering injustice is having too little.

Justice is a mean, not as the other virtues are, but because it is about an intermediate condition, whereas injustice is about the extremes. Justice is the virtue in accord with which the just person is said to do what is just in accord with his decision, distributing good things and bad, both between himself and others and between others. He does not award too much of what is choiceworthy to

5 himself and too little to his neighbor (and the reverse with what is harmful), but awards what is proportionately equal; and he does the same in distributing between others.

Injustice, on the other hand, is related [in the same way] to the unjust. What is unjust is disproportionate excess and deficiency in what is beneficial or harmful; hence injustice is excess and deficiency because it concerns excess and
10 deficiency. The unjust person awards himself an excess of what is beneficial, [considered] without qualification, and a deficiency of what is harmful, and, speaking as a whole, he acts similarly [in distributions between] others, but deviates from proportion in either direction. In an unjust action getting too little good is suffering injustice, and getting too much is doing injustice.

15 So much, then, for the nature of justice and the nature of injustice, and similarly for just and unjust in general.

6 [Political justice]: Since it is possible to do injustice without thereby being unjust, what sort of injustice must someone do to be unjust by having one of the different types of injustice, by being a thief or adulterer or brigand, for instance?

Perhaps it is not the type of action that makes the difference [between merely doing injustice and being unjust].
20 For someone might lie with a woman and know who she is, but the principle might be feelings rather than decision. In that case he is not unjust, though he does injustice—not a thief, for instance, though he stole, not an adulterer though he committed adultery, and so on in the other cases.

Now we have previously described the relation of
25 reciprocity to the just. But we must recognize that we are inquiring not only into the just without qualification, but also into the politically just. This belongs to those who share in common a life aiming at self-sufficiency, who are free and either proportionately or numerically equal. Hence those who lack these features have nothing politically just in their relations, though they have something just insofar as it is similar to the politically just.

30 For the just belongs to those who have law in their relations. Law belongs to those among whom injustice is [possible]; for the judicial process is judgment that distinguishes the just from the unjust. Where there is injustice there is also doing injustice, though where there is doing injustice there need not also be injustice. And doing injustice is awarding to oneself too many of the things that, [considered] without qualification, are good, and too few of the things that, [considered] without qualification, are bad.

That is why we allow only reason, not a human being, 35 to be ruler. For a human being awards himself too many 1134b goods and becomes a tyrant; a ruler, however, is a guardian of the just, and hence of the equal [and so must not award himself too many goods].

If a ruler is just, he seems to profit nothing by it. For since he does not award himself more of what, [considered] without qualification, is good if it is not proportionate to him, he seems to labor for another's benefit. That is why 5 justice is said, as we also remarked before, to be another person's good. Hence some payment [for ruling] should be given; this is honor and privilege. The people who are not satisfied with these rewards are the ones who become tyrants.

The just for a master and a father is similar to this, not the same. For there is no unqualified injustice in relation to 10 what is one's own; one's own possession, or one's child until it is old enough and separated, is as though it were a part of oneself. Now no one decides to harm himself. Hence there is no injustice in relation to them, and so nothing politically unjust or just either. For we found that the politically just must accord with law, and belong to those who are naturally suited for law, and hence to those who have equality 15 in ruling and being ruled. [Approximation to this equality] explains why relations with a wife more than with children or possessions allow something to count as just; for that is the just in households. Still, this too is different from the politically just.

7 [Justice by nature and by law]: One part of the politically just is natural, and the other part legal. The natural has the 20 same validity everywhere alike, independent of its seeming so or not. The legal originally makes no difference [whether it is done] one way or another, but makes a difference whenever people have laid down the rule—that a mina is the price of a ransom, for instance, or that a goat rather than two sheep should be sacrificed. The legal also includes laws passed for particular cases (for instance, that sacrifices should be offered to Brasidas[1]) and enactments by decree.

Now some people think everything just is merely legal. 25 For the natural is unchangeable and equally valid everywhere—fire, for instance, burns both here and in Persia— whereas they see that the just changes [from city to city].

---

1   *to Brasidas*   That is, presumably, *in honor of* Brasidas, the courageous Spartan officer involved in the Peloponnesian War.

This is not so, though in a way it is so. With us, though presumably not at all with the gods, there is such a thing as the natural, but still all is changeable; despite the change
30 there is such a thing as what is natural and what is not.

Then what sort of thing, among those that [are changeable and hence] admit of being otherwise, is natural, and what sort is not natural, but legal and conventional, if both natural and legal are changeable? It is clear in other cases also, and the same distinction [between the natural and the unchangeable] will apply; for the right hand, for instance, is naturally superior, even though it is possible for everyone to
35 become ambidextrous.

1135a The sorts of things that are just by convention and expediency are like measures. For measures for wine and for corn are not of equal size everywhere, but in wholesale markets they are bigger, and in retail smaller. Similarly, the things that are just by human [enactment] and not by nature differ from place to place, since political systems also differ.
5 Still, only one system is by nature the best everywhere.

Each [type of] just and lawful [action] is related as a universal to the corresponding particulars; for the [particular] actions that are done are many, but each [type] is one, since it is universal.

An act of injustice is different from the unjust, and an
10 act of justice from the just. For the unjust is unjust by nature or enactment; when this has been done, it is an act of injustice, but before it is done it is only unjust. The same applies to an act of justice [in contrast to the just]. Here, however, the general [type of action contrary to an act of injustice] is more usually called a just act, and what is called an act of justice is the [specific type of just act] that rectifies an act of injustice.

15 Later we must examine each of these actions, to see what sorts of species, and how many, they have, and what they are concerned with.

8 [Justice, injustice, and the voluntary]: Given this account of just and unjust actions, one does injustice or does justice whenever one does them willingly. Whenever one does them unwillingly, one neither does justice nor does injustice, except coincidentally, since the actions one does
20 are coincidentally just or unjust.

An act of injustice and a just act are defined by the voluntary and the involuntary. For when the action is voluntary, the agent is blamed, and thereby also it is an act of injustice. And so something will be unjust without thereby being an act of injustice, if it is not also voluntary.

As I said before, I say that an action is voluntary just in case it is up to the agent, who does it in knowledge, and
25 [hence] not in ignorance of the person, instrument, and goal (for instance, whom he is striking, with what, and for what goal), and [does] each of these neither coincidentally nor by force (if, for instance, someone seized your hand and struck another [with it], you would not have done it willingly, since it was not up to you). But [a further distinction must be drawn about knowledge. For] it is possible that the victim is your father, and you know he is a human being or a bystander, but do not know he is your father. The same
30 distinction must be made for the goal and for the action as a whole.

Actions are involuntary, then, if they are done in ignorance; or they are not done in ignorance, but they are not up to the agent; or they are done by force. For we also do or undergo many of our natural [actions and processes], such 1135b as growing old and dying, in knowledge, but none of them is either voluntary or involuntary.

Both unjust and just actions may also be coincidental in the same way. For if someone returned a deposit unwillingly and because of fear, we ought to say that he neither 5 does anything just nor does justice, except coincidentally. Similarly, if someone is under compulsion and unwilling when he fails to return the deposit, we should say that he coincidentally does injustice and does something unjust.

In some of our voluntary actions we act on a previous decision, and in some we act without previous decision. We 10 act on a previous decision when we act on previous deliberation, and we act without previous decision when we act without previous deliberation.

Among the three ways of inflicting harms in a community, actions done with ignorance are errors if someone does neither the action he supposed, nor to the person, nor with the instrument, nor for the result he supposed. For he thought, for instance, that he was not hitting, or not hitting this person, or not for this result; but coincidentally 15 the result that was achieved was not what he thought (for instance, [he hit him] to graze, not to wound), or the victim or the instrument was not the one he thought.

If, then, the infliction of harm violates reasonable expectation, the action is a misfortune. If it does not violate reasonable expectation, but is done without vice, it is an error. For someone is in error if the principle of the cause is in him, and unfortunate when it is outside.

If he does it in knowledge, but without previous delib- 20 eration, it is an act of injustice; this is true, for instance, of actions caused by spirit and other feelings that are natural or necessary for human beings. For when someone inflicts these harms and commits these errors, he does injustice and these are acts of injustice; but he is not thereby unjust or wicked, since it is not vice that causes him to inflict the harm. But whenever his decision is the cause, he is unjust and vicious.

That is why it is right to judge that actions caused by spirit do not result from forethought [and hence do not result from decision], since the principle is not the agent who acted on spirit, but the person who provoked him to anger. Moreover the dispute is not about whether [the action caused by anger] happened or not, but about whether it was just, since anger is a response to apparent injustice. For they do not dispute about whether it happened or not, as they do in commercial transactions, where one party or the other must be vicious,[1] unless forgetfulness is the cause of the dispute. Rather [in cases of anger] they agree about the fact and dispute about which action was just; but [in commercial transactions] the [cheater] who has plotted against his victim knows very well [that what he is doing is unjust]. Hence [in cases of anger the agent] thinks he is suffering injustice, while [in transactions the cheater] does not think so.

1136a   If [the cheater's] decision causes him to inflict the harm, he does injustice, and this is the sort of act of injustice that makes an agent unjust, if it violates proportion or equality In the same way, a person is just if his decision causes him to do justice; one [merely] does justice if one merely does it voluntarily.

Some involuntary actions are to be pardoned, and some are not. For if someone's error is not only committed in ignorance, but also caused by ignorance, it is to be pardoned. But if, though committed in ignorance, it is caused not by ignorance but by some feeling that is neither natural nor human, it is not to be pardoned.

9 [Puzzles about justice and injustice]: If we have adequately defined suffering injustice and doing injustice, some puzzles might be raised.

First of all, are those bizarre words of Euripides[2] correct, where he says: "'I killed my mother—a short tale to tell.' 'Were both of you willing or both unwilling?'"? Is it really possible to suffer injustice willingly, or is it always involuntary, as doing injustice is always voluntary? And is it always one way or the other, or is it sometimes voluntary and sometimes involuntary?

The same question arises about receiving justice. Since doing justice is always voluntary [as doing injustice is], it is reasonable for the same opposition to apply in both cases, so that both receiving justice and suffering injustice will be either alike voluntary or alike involuntary. But it seems absurd in the case of receiving justice as well [as in the case of suffering injustice] for it to be always voluntary, since some people receive justice, but not willingly.

We might also raise the following puzzle: Does everyone who has received something unjust suffer injustice, or is it the same with receiving as it is with doing? For certainly it is possible, in the case both of doing and of receiving, to have a share in just things coincidentally; and clearly the same is true of unjust things, since doing something unjust is not the same as doing injustice, and suffering something unjust is not the same as suffering injustice. The same is true of doing justice and receiving it; for it is impossible to suffer injustice if no one does injustice and impossible to receive justice if no one does justice.

Now if doing injustice is simply harming someone willingly (and doing something willingly is doing it with knowledge of the victim, the instrument, and the way), and the incontinent person harms himself willingly, he suffers injustice willingly. Hence someone can do injustice to himself; and one of our puzzles was just this, whether someone can do injustice to himself. Further, someone's incontinence might cause him to be willingly harmed by another who is willing, so that it would be possible to suffer injustice willingly.

Perhaps, however, our definition [of doing injustice] was incorrect, and we should add to "harming with knowledge of the victim, the instrument, and the way," the further condition "against the wish of the victim." If so, someone is harmed and suffers something unjust willingly, but no one suffers injustice willingly. For no one wishes it, not even the incontinent, but he acts against his wish; for no one wishes for what he does not think is excellent, and what the incontinent does is not what he thinks it is right [and hence excellent] to do.

---

1   *where one ... be vicious* Where there is a disagreement about points of fact between the plaintiff and the defendant, one must be speaking falsely.

2   *Euripides* Great Greek tragedian (c. 480–406 BCE). The origin of this quotation is obscure, though in his play *Electra*, Orestes

---

and his sister Electra kill their mother.

And if someone gives away what is his own, as Homer says[1] Glaucus gave to Diomede "gold for bronze, a hundred cows' worth for nine cows worth," he does not suffer injustice. For it is up to him to give them, whereas suffering injustice is not up to him, but requires someone to do him injustice.

Clearly, then, suffering injustice is not voluntary.

Two further questions that we decided to discuss still remain: If A distributes to B more than B deserves, is it A, the distributor, or B, who has more, who does injustice? And is it possible to do injustice to oneself?

For if the first alternative is possible, and A rather than B does injustice, it follows that if A knowingly and willingly distributes more to B than to himself, A does injustice to himself. And indeed this is what a moderate person seems to do; for the decent person tends to take less than his share.

Perhaps, however, it is not true without qualification that he takes less. For perhaps he overreaches for some other good, such as reputation or the unqualifiedly fine. Moreover, our definition of doing injustice allows us to solve the puzzle. For since he suffers nothing against his own wish, he does not suffer injustice, at least not from his distribution, but, at most, is merely harmed.

But it is evidently the distributor who does injustice, and the one who has more does not always do it. For the one who does injustice is not the one who has an unjust share, but the one who willingly does what is unjust, that is to say, the one who has the principle of the action; this is the distributor, not the recipient. Besides, doing is spoken of in many ways, and there is a way in which inanimate things, or hands, or servants at someone else's order, kill; the recipient, then, does not do injustice, but does something that is unjust.

Further, if the distributor judged in ignorance, he does not do injustice in violation of what is legally just, and his judgment is not unjust; in a way, though, it is unjust, since what is legally just is different from what is primarily just. If, however, he judged unjustly, and did it knowingly, he himself as well [as the recipient] is overreaching—for gratitude or to exact a penalty.

And so someone who has judged unjustly for these reasons has also got more, exactly as though he got a share of the [profits of] the act of injustice. For he gave judgment about some land, for instance, on this condition [that he would share the profits], and what he got was not land, but money.

People think doing injustice is up to them; that is why they think that being just is also easy. But it is not. For lying with a neighbor's wife, wounding a neighbor, bribing, are all easy and up to us, but being in a certain state when we do them is not easy, and not up to us.

Similarly, people think it takes no wisdom to know the things that are just and unjust, because it is not difficult to comprehend what the laws speak of. But these are not the things that are just, except coincidentally. Knowing how actions must be done, and how distributions must be made, if they are to be just, takes more work than it takes to know about healthy things. And even in the case of healthy things, knowing about honey, wine, hellebore, burning, and cutting is easy, but knowing how these must be distributed to produce health, and to whom and when, takes all the work that it takes to be a doctor.

For the same reason they think doing injustice is no less proper to the just than to the unjust person, because the just person is no less, and even more, able to do each of the actions. For he is able to lie with a woman, and to wound someone; and the brave person, similarly, is able to throw away his shield, and to turn and run this way or that. But doing acts of cowardice or injustice is not doing these actions, except coincidentally; it is being in a certain state when we do them. Similarly, practicing medicine or healing is not cutting or not cutting, giving drugs or not giving them, but doing all these things in a certain way.

Just things belong to those who have a share in things that, [considered] without qualification, are good, who can have an excess or a deficiency of them. Some (as, presumably, the gods) can have no excess of them; others, the incurably evil, benefit from none of them, but are harmed by them all; others again benefit from these goods up to a point; and this is why the just is something human.

10 [Decency]: The next task is to discuss how decency is related to justice and how the decent[2] is related to the just.

---

1   *as Homer says*   Homer, *Iliad*, Book 6, 234–36.

2   *decent*   The Greek word *epieikes*, here translated as "decent," is, commentators agree, difficult to translate. Elsewhere it is translated variously as "equitable," "mild," "gentle," "forbearing," "yielding," "lenient," "unassertive," "fair," "fitting," "appropriate," "suitable," "proper," "magnanimous," "moderate." Aristotle's idea appears to be that a "decent" man, rather than merely obeying rules, can be counted on to be reasonable and nice even where rules leave off.

For on examination they appear as neither the same without qualification nor as states of different kinds. Sometimes we praise what is decent and the decent person, so that even when we praise someone for other things we transfer the term "decent" and use it instead of "good," making it clear that what is more decent is better. But sometimes, when we reason about the matter, it appears absurd for what is decent to be something apart from what is just, and still praiseworthy. For [apparently] either what is just is not excellent or what is decent is not excellent, if it is something other than what is just; or else, if they are both excellent, they are the same.

These, then, are roughly the claims that raise the puzzle about the decent; but they are all correct in a way, and none is contrary to any other. For the decent is better than one way of being just, but it is still just, and not better than the just by being a different kind of thing. Hence the same thing is just and decent; while both are excellent, what is decent is superior.

The puzzle arises because the decent is just, but is not the legally just, but a rectification of it. This is because all law is universal, but in some areas no universal rule can be correct; and so where a universal rule has to be made, but cannot be correct, the law chooses the [universal rule] that is usually [correct], well aware of the error being made. And the law is no less correct on this account; for the source of the error is not the law or the legislator, but the nature of the object itself, since that is what the subject matter of actions is bound to be like.

And so, whenever the law makes a universal rule, but in this particular case what happens violates the [intended scope of] the universal rule, on this point the legislator falls short, and has made an error by making an unqualified rule. Then it is correct to rectify the deficiency; this is what the legislator would have said himself if he had been present there, and what he would have prescribed, had he known, in his legislation.

That is why the decent is just, and better than a certain way of being just—not better than the unqualifiedly just, but better than the error that results from the omission of any qualification [in the rule]. And this is the nature of the decent—rectification of law insofar as the universality of law makes it deficient.

This is also the reason why not everything is guided by law. For on some matters legislation is impossible, and so a decree is needed. For the standard applied to the indefinite is itself indefinite, as the lead standard is in Lesbian building, where it is not fixed, but adapts itself to the shape of the stone; similarly, a decree is adapted to fit its objects.

It is clear from this what is decent, and clear that it is just, and better than a certain way of being just. It is also evident from this who the decent person is; for he is the one who decides on and does such actions, not an exact stickler for justice in the bad way, but taking less than he might even though he has the law on his side. This is the decent person, and his state is decency; it is a sort of justice, and not some state different from it.

11 [Injustice to oneself]: Is it possible to do injustice to oneself or not? The answer is evident from what has been said.

First of all, some just actions are the legal prescriptions in accord with each virtue; we are legally forbidden, for instance, to kill ourselves. Moreover, if someone illegally and willingly inflicts harm on another, not returning harm for harm, he does injustice (a person acting willingly is one who knows the victim and the instrument). Now if someone murders himself because of anger, he does this willingly, in violation of correct reason, when the law forbids it; hence he does injustice. But injustice to whom? Surely to the city,[1] not to himself, since he suffers it willingly, and no one willingly suffers injustice. That is why the city both penalizes him and inflicts further dishonor on him for destroying himself, on the ground that he does injustice to the city.

Now consider the type of injustice that belongs to an agent who is only unjust, not base generally. Clearly the corresponding type of unjust action is different from the first type. For this second type of unjust person is wicked in the same [special] way as the coward is, not by having total wickedness; hence his acts of injustice do not accord with total wickedness either. In this case also one cannot do injustice to oneself. For if one could, the same person could lose and get the same thing at the same time. But this is impossible; on the contrary, what is just or unjust must always involve more than one person.

Moreover, doing injustice is voluntary, and results from a decision, and strikes first; for a victim who retaliates does not seem to do injustice. But if someone does injustice to himself, he does and suffers the same thing at the same

---

1 *city* The word *polis*, often translated "city" in English editions of Aristotle, refers more exactly to a "city-state"—the most important large-scale political division in ancient Greece; city-states were in general politically independent, and in many ways similar to today's nation-states.

time. Further, on this view, it would be possible to suffer injustice willingly.

Besides, no one does injustice without doing one of the particular acts of injustice. But no one commits adultery with his own wife, or burgles his own house, or steals his own possessions.

And in general the puzzle about doing injustice to oneself is also solved by the distinction about voluntarily suffering injustice.

It is also evident that both doing and suffering injustice are bad, since one is having more, one having less, than the intermediate amount, just as in the case of health in medicine and fitness in gymnastics [both more and less than the intermediate amount are bad]. But doing injustice is worse; for it is blameworthy, involving vice that is either complete and unqualified or close to it (since not all voluntary doing of injustice is combined with [the state of] injustice). Suffering injustice, however, involves no vice or injustice.

In its own right, then, suffering injustice is less bad; and though it might still be coincidentally a greater evil, that is no concern of a craft. Rather, the craft says that pleurisy is a worse illness than a stumble, even though a stumble might sometimes coincidentally turn out worse—if, for instance, someone stumbled and by coincidence was captured by the enemy or killed because he fell.

It is possible for there to be a sort of justice, by similarity and transference, not of a person to himself, but of certain parts of a person—not every kind of justice, but the kind that belongs to masters or households. For in these discussions the part of the soul that has reason is distinguished from the nonrational part. People look at these and it seems to them that there is injustice to oneself, because in these parts it is possible to suffer something against one's own desires. Hence it is possible for those parts to be just to each other, as it is for ruler and ruled.

So much, then, for our definitions of justice and the other virtues of character.

...

Book 8 [Friendship]

1155a   1 [Common beliefs and questions]: After that, the next topic is friendship;[1] for it is a virtue, or involves virtue.

Further, it is most necessary for our life. For no one would choose to live without friends even if he had all the other goods. Indeed rich people and holders of powerful positions, even more than other people, seem to need friends. For how would one benefit from such prosperity if one had no opportunity for beneficence, which is most often displayed, and most highly praised, in relation to friends? And how would one guard and protect prosperity without friends, when it is all the more precarious the greater it is?

But in poverty also, and in the other misfortunes, people think friends are the only refuge. Moreover, the young need friends to keep them from error. The old need friends to care for them and support the actions that fail because of weakness. And those in their prime need friends to do fine actions; for "when two go together" they are more capable of understanding and acting.

Further, a parent would seem to have a natural friendship for a child, and a child for a parent, not only among human beings but also among birds and most kinds of animals. Members of the same species, and human beings most of all, have a natural friendship for each other; that is why we praise friends of humanity. And in our travels we can see how every human being is akin and beloved to a human being.

Moreover, friendship would seem to hold cities together, and legislators would seem to be more concerned about it than about justice. For concord would seem to be similar to friendship, and they aim at concord among all, while they try above all to expel civil conflict, which is enmity. Further, if people are friends, they have no need of justice, but if they are just they need friendship in addition; and the justice that is most just seems to belong to friendship.

But friendship is not only necessary, but also fine. For we praise lovers of friends, and having many friends seems to be a fine thing. Moreover, people think that the same people are good and also friends.

Still, there are quite a few disputed points about friendship.

For some hold it is a sort of similarity and that similar people are friends. Hence the sayings, "similar to similar," and "birds of a feather," and so on. On the other side, it is said that similar people are all like the proverbial potters, quarreling with each other.

---

1   *friendship* Aristotle's word here (*philia*) refers to something rather broader than what we would call "friendship": it includes also relationships characterized by affectionate regard and amiability, and even just those characterized simply by amiability.

1155b   On these questions some people inquire at a higher level, more proper to natural science. Euripides says that when earth gets dry it longs passionately for rain, and the holy heaven when filled with rain longs passionately to fall into the earth; and Heracleitus says that the opponent cooperates, the finest harmony arises from discordant elements, and all things come to be in struggle. Others, such as Empedocles,[1] oppose this view, and say that similar aims for similar.

Let us, then, leave aside the puzzles proper to natural science, since they are not proper to the present examination, and let us examine the puzzles that concern human [nature], and bear on characters and feelings. For instance, does friendship arise among all sorts of people, or can people not be friends if they are vicious? And is there one species of friendship, or are there more? Some people think there is only one species because friendship allows more and less. But here their confidence rests on an inadequate sign; for things of different species also allow more and less. We have spoken about these earlier.

2 [The object of friendship]: Perhaps these questions will become clear once we find out what it is that is lovable. For, it seems, not everything is loved, but [only] the lovable, and this is either good or pleasant or useful. However, it seems that the useful is the source of some good or some pleasure; hence the good and the pleasant are lovable as ends.

Now do people love the good, or the good for themselves? For sometimes these conflict; and the same is true of the pleasant. Each one, it seems, loves the good for himself; and while the good is lovable without qualification, the lovable for each one is the good for himself. In fact, each one loves not what *is* good for him, but what *appears* good for him; but this will not matter, since [what appears good for him] will be what appears lovable.

There are these three causes, then, of love. Now love for an inanimate thing is not called friendship, since there is no mutual loving, and no wishing of good to it. For it would presumably be ridiculous to wish good things to wine; the most you wish is its preservation so that you can have it. To a friend, however, it is said, you must wish goods for his own sake. If you wish good things in this way, but the same wish is not returned by the other, you would be said to have

[only] goodwill for the other. For friendship is said to be *reciprocated* goodwill.

But perhaps we should add that friends are aware of the reciprocated goodwill. For many a one has goodwill to people whom he has not seen but supposes to be decent or useful, and one of these might have the same goodwill toward him. These people, then, apparently have goodwill to each other, but how could we call them friends, given that they are unaware of their attitude to each other? [If they are to be friends], then, they must have goodwill to each other, wish goods and be aware of it, from one of the causes mentioned above.

3 [The three types of friendship]: Since these causes differ in species, so do the types of loving and types of friendship. Hence friendship has three species, corresponding to the three objects of love. For each object of love has a corresponding type of mutual loving, combined with awareness of it.

But those who love each other wish goods to each other [only] insofar as they love each other. Those who love each other for utility love the other not in his own right, but insofar as they gain some good for themselves from him. The same is true of those who love for pleasure; for they like a witty person not because of his character, but because he is pleasant to them.

Those who love for utility or pleasure, then, are fond of a friend because of what is good or pleasant for themselves, not insofar as the beloved is who he is, but insofar as he is useful or pleasant. Hence these friendships as well [as the friends] are coincidental, since the beloved is loved not insofar as he is who he is, but insofar as he provides some good or pleasure.

And so these sorts of friendships are easily dissolved, when the friends do not remain similar [to what they were]; for if someone is no longer pleasant or useful, the other stops loving him.

What is useful does not remain the same, but is different at different times. Hence, when the cause of their being friends is removed, the friendship is dissolved too, on the assumption that the friendship aims at these [useful results]. This sort of friendship seems to arise especially among older people, since at that age they pursue the advantageous, not the pleasant, and also among those in their prime or youth who pursue the expedient.

Nor do such people live together very much. For sometimes they do not even find each other pleasant. Hence they

---

1   *Empedocles*   Greek pre-Socratic philosopher (c. 490–430 BCE) who maintained that matter was composed of the four elements of water, air, earth, and fire, and that these were attracted or separated by the principles of love and strife respectively.

have no further need to meet in this way if they are not advantageous [to each other]; for each finds the other pleas-
30 ant [only] to the extent that he expects some good from him. The friendship of hosts and guests is taken to be of this type too.

The cause of friendship between young people seems to be pleasure. For their lives are guided by their feelings, and they pursue above all what is pleasant for themselves and what is at hand. But as they grow up [what they find] pleas-
35 ant changes too. Hence they are quick to become friends, and quick to stop; for their friendship shifts with [what they find] pleasant, and the change in such pleasure is quick.
1156b Young people are prone to erotic passion, since this mostly accords with feelings, and is caused by pleasure; that is why they love and quickly stop, often changing in a single day.

These people wish to spend their days together and to
5 live together; for this is how they gain [the good things] corresponding to their friendship.

But complete friendship is the friendship of good people similar in virtue; for they wish goods in the same way to each other insofar as they are good, and they are good in their own right. [Hence they wish goods to each other for each other's sake.] Now those who wish goods to
10 their friend for the friend's own sake are friends most of all; for they have this attitude because of the friend himself, not coincidentally. Hence these people's friendship lasts as long as they are good; and virtue is enduring.

Each of them is both good without qualification and good for his friend, since good people are both good with-out qualification and advantageous for each other. They are
15 pleasant in the same ways too, since good people are pleas-ant both without qualification and for each other. [They are pleasant for each other] because each person finds his own actions and actions of that kind pleasant, and the actions of good people are the same or similar.

It is reasonable that this sort of friendship is enduring, since it embraces in itself all the features that friends must
20 have. For the cause of every friendship is good or pleasure, either unqualified or for the lover; and every friendship accords with some similarity. And all the features we have mentioned are found in this friendship because of [the na-ture of] the friends themselves. For they are similar in this way [i.e., in being good]. Moreover, their friendship also has the other things—what is good without qualification and what is pleasant without qualification; and these are lovable most of all. Hence loving and friendship are found most of all and at their best in these friends.

These kinds of friendships are likely to be rare, since 25 such people are few. Further, they need time as well, to grow accustomed to each other; for, as the proverb says, they can-not know each other before they have shared their salt as often as it says, and they cannot accept each other or be friends until each appears lovable to the other and gains the other's confidence. Those who are quick to treat each other 30 in friendly ways wish to be friends, but are not friends, un-less they are also lovable, and know this. For though the wish for friendship comes quickly, friendship does not.

4 [Comparison between the types of friendship]: This sort of friendship, then, is complete both in time and in the other ways. In every way each friend gets the same things and similar things from each, and this is what must be true 35 of friends. Friendship for pleasure bears some resemblance 1157a to this complete sort, since good people are also pleasant to each other. And friendship for utility also resembles it, since good people are also useful to each other.

With these [incomplete friends] also, the friendships are most enduring whenever they get the same thing—pleasure, for instance—from each other, and, moreover, get it from 5 the same source, as witty people do, in contrast to the erotic lover and the boy he loves.

For the erotic lover and his beloved do not take pleasure in the same things; the lover takes pleasure in seeing his beloved, but the beloved takes pleasure in being courted by his lover. When the beloved's bloom is fading, some-times the friendship fades too; for the lover no longer finds pleasure in seeing his beloved, and the beloved is no longer 10 courted by the lover. Many, however, remain friends if they have similar characters and come to be fond of each other's characters from being accustomed to them. Those who ex-change utility rather than pleasure in their erotic relations are friends to a lesser extent and less enduring friends.

Those who are friends for utility dissolve the friendship 15 as soon as the advantage is removed; for they were never friends of each other, but of what was expedient for them.

Now it is possible for bad people as well [as good] to be friends to each other for pleasure or utility, for decent people to be friends to base people, and for someone with neither character to be a friend to someone with any character. Clearly, however, only good people can be friends to each other because of the other person himself; for bad people find no enjoyment in one another if they get no benefit. 20

Moreover, the friendship of good people is the only one that is immune to slander. For it is not easy to trust anyone

speaking against someone whom we ourselves have found reliable for a long time; and among good people there is trust, the belief that he would never do injustice, and all the other things expected in a true friendship. But in the other
25 types of friendship [distrust] may easily arise.

[These must be counted as types of friendship.] For people include among friends [not only the best type, but] also those who are friends for utility, as cities are—since alliances between cities seem to aim at expediency—and those who are fond of each other, as children are, for pleasure. Hence we must presumably also say that such people are
30 friends, but say that there are more species of friendship than one.

On this view, the friendship of good people insofar as they are good is friendship primarily and fully, but the other friendships are friendships by similarity. For insofar as there is something good, and [hence] something similar to [what one finds in the best kind], people [in the incomplete friendships] are friends; for what is pleasant is good to lovers of pleasure. But these [incomplete] types of friendship are not very regularly combined, and the same people
35 do not become friends for both utility and pleasure. For things that [merely] coincide with each other are not very regularly combined.

1157b Friendship has been assigned, then, to these species. Base people will be friends for pleasure or utility, since they are similar in that way. But good people will be friends because of themselves, since they are friends insofar as they are good. These, then, are friends without qualification;
5 the others are friends coincidentally and by being similar to these.

5 [State and activity in friendship]: Just as, in the case of the virtues, some people are called good in their state of character, others good in their activity, the same is true of friendship. For some people find enjoyment in each other by living together, and provide each other with good things. Others, however, are asleep or separated by distance, and so are not active in these ways, but are in the state that
10 would result in the friendly activities; for distance does not dissolve the friendship without qualification, but only its activity. But if the absence is long, it also seems to cause the friendship to be forgotten; hence the saying, "Lack of conversation has dissolved many a friendship."

Older people and sour people do not appear to be
15 prone to friendship. For there is little pleasure to be found in them, and no one can spend his days with what is painful or not pleasant, since nature appears to avoid above all what is painful and to aim at what is pleasant.

Those who welcome each other but do not live together would seem to have goodwill rather than friendship. For nothing is as proper to friends as living together; for while those who are in want desire benefit, blessedly happy people 20 [who want for nothing], no less than the others, desire to spend their days together, since a solitary life fits them least of all. But people cannot spend their time with each other if they are not pleasant and do not enjoy the same things, as they seem to in the friendship of companions.

Now the friendship of good people is friendship 25 most of all, as we have often said. For what is lovable and choiceworthy seems to be what is good or pleasant without qualification, and what is lovable and choiceworthy to each person seems to be what is good or pleasant to himself; and both of these make one good person lovable and choiceworthy to another good person.

Loving would seem to be a feeling, but friendship a state. For loving is directed no less toward inanimate things, 30 but reciprocal loving requires decision, and decision comes from a state; and [good people] wish good to the beloved for his own sake in accord with their state, not their feeling.

Moreover, in loving their friend they love what is good for themselves; for when a good person becomes a friend he becomes a good for his friend. Each of them loves what 35 is good for himself, and repays in equal measure the wish and the pleasantness of his friend; for friendship is said to be equality. And this is true above all in the friendship of 1158a good people.

6 [Activities characteristic of the different types of friendship]: Among sour people and older people, friendship is found less often, since they are worse-tempered and find less enjoyment in meeting people, so that they lack the features that seem most typical and most productive of friendship. That is why young people become friends quickly, 5 but older people do not, since they do not become friends with people in whom they find no enjoyment—nor do sour people. These people have goodwill to each other, since they wish goods and give help in time of need; but they scarcely count as friends, since they do not spend their days together or find enjoyment in each other, and these things seem to be 10 above all typical of friendship.

No one can have complete friendship for many people, just as no one can have an erotic passion for many at the same time; for [complete friendship, like erotic passion,] is like an excess, and an excess is naturally directed at a single individual. And just as it is difficult for many people to please the same person intensely at the same time, it is also difficult, presumably, for many to be good. [To find 15 out whether someone is really good], one must both have experience of him and be on familiar terms with him, which is extremely difficult. If, however, the friendship is for utility or pleasure, it is possible for many people to please; for there are many people of the right sort, and the services take little time.

Of these other two types of friendship, the friendship for pleasure is more like [real] friendship; for they get the same thing from each other, and they find enjoyment in 20 each other, or [rather] in the same things. This is what friendships are like among young people; for a generous [attitude] is found here more [than among older people], whereas it is mercenary people who form friendships for utility.

Moreover, blessedly happy people have no need of anything useful; but do need sources of pleasure. For they want to spend their lives with companions, and though what is painful is borne for a short time, no one could continuously 25 endure even the Good Itself if it were painful to him. That is why they seek friends who are pleasant. But, presumably, they must also seek friends who are good as well [as pleasant], and good for them too; for then they will have everything that friends must have.

Someone in a position of power appears to have separate groups of friends; for some are useful to him, others 30 pleasant, but the same ones are not often both. For he does not seek friends who are both pleasant and virtuous, or useful for fine actions, but seeks one group to be witty, when he pursues pleasure, and the other group to be clever in carrying out instructions; and the same person rarely has both features.

Though admittedly, as we have said, an excellent person is both pleasant and useful, he does not become a friend to a superior [in power and position] unless the 35 superior is also superior in virtue; otherwise he does not reach [proportionate] equality by having a proportionate superior. And this superiority both in power and in virtue is not often found.

1158b   The friendships we have mentioned involve equality, since both friends get the same and wish the same to each other, or exchange one thing for another—for instance, pleasure for benefit. But, as we have said, they are friend- 5 ships to a lesser extent, and less enduring.

They seem both to be and not to be friendships, because of their similarity and dissimilarity to the same thing. For, on the one hand, insofar as they are similar to the friendship of virtue, they are apparently friendships; for that type of friendship includes both utility and pleasure, and one of these types includes utility, the other pleasure. On the other hand, the friendship of virtue is enduring and immune to slander, whereas these change quickly, and differ from it in many 10 other ways as well; to that extent they are apparently not friendships, because of their dissimilarity to that best type.

7 [Friendship between unequals]: A different species of friendship is the one that rests on superiority—of a father toward his son, for instance, and in general of an older person toward a younger, of a man toward a woman, and of any sort of ruler toward the one he rules. These friendships also differ from each other. For friendship of parents 15 to children is not the same as that of rulers to ruled; nor is friendship of father to son the same as that of son to father, or of man to woman as that of woman to man. For each of these friends has a different virtue and a different function, and there are different causes of love. Hence the ways of loving are different, and so are the friendships.

Now each does not get the same thing from the other, 20 and must not seek it; but whenever children accord to their parents what they must accord to those who gave them birth, and parents accord what they must do to their children, their friendship is enduring and decent.

In all the friendships that rest on superiority, the loving must also be proportional; for instance, the better person, 25 and the more beneficial, and each of the others likewise, must be loved more than he loves; for when the loving accords with the comparative worth of the friends, equality is achieved in a way, and this seems to be proper to friendship.

Equality, however, does not appear to be the same in 30 friendship as in justice. For in justice equality is equality primarily in worth and secondarily in quantity; but in friendship it is equality primarily in quantity and secondarily in worth.

This is clear if friends come to be separated by some wide gap in virtue, vice, wealth, or something else; for then they are friends no more, and do not even expect to be. 35 This is most evident with gods, since they have the greatest superiority in all goods. But it is also clear with kings, since 1159a far inferior people do not expect to be their friends; nor do worthless people expect to be friends to the best or wisest.

Now in these cases there is no exact definition of how long people are friends. For even if one of them loses a lot, the friendship still endures; but if one is widely separated [from the other], as a god is [from a human being], it no longer endures.

This raises a puzzle: Do friends really wish their friend to have the greatest good, to be a god, for instance? For [if he becomes a god], *he* will no longer have friends, and hence no longer have goods, since friends are goods. If, then, we have been right to say that one friend wishes good things to the other for the sake of the other *himself*, the other must remain whatever sort of being he is. Hence it is to the other as a human being that a friend will wish the greatest goods—though presumably not all of them, since each person wishes goods most of all to himself.

8 [Giving and receiving in friendship]: Because the many love honor they seem to prefer being loved to loving. That is why they love flatterers. For the flatterer is a friend in an inferior position, or [rather] pretends to be one, and pretends to love more than he is loved; and being loved seems close to being honored, which the many certainly pursue.

It would seem, however, that they choose honor coincidentally, not in its own right. For the many enjoy being honored by powerful people because they expect to get whatever they need from them, and so enjoy the honor as a sign of this good treatment. Those who want honor from decent people with knowledge are seeking to confirm their own view of themselves, and so they are pleased because the judgment of those who say they are good makes them confident that they are good. Being loved, on the contrary, they enjoy in its own right. That is why it seems to be better than being honored, and friendship seems choiceworthy in its own right.

But friendship seems to consist more in loving than in being loved. A sign of this is the enjoyment a mother finds in loving. For sometimes she gives her child away to be brought up, and loves him as long as she knows about him; but she does not seek the child's love, if she cannot both [love and be loved]. She would seem to be satisfied if she sees the child doing well, and she loves the child even if ignorance prevents him from returning to her what is due to a mother.

Friendship, then, consists more in loving; and people who love their friends are praised; hence, it would seem, loving is the virtue of friends. And so friends whose love accords with the worth of their friends are enduring friends

and have an enduring friendship. This above all is how unequals as well as equals can be friends, since this is how they can be equalized.

Equality and similarity, and above all the similarity of those who are similar in being virtuous, is friendship. For virtuous people are enduringly [virtuous] in their own right, and enduring [friends] to each other. They neither request nor provide assistance that requires base actions, but, you might even say prevent this. For it is proper to good people to avoid error themselves and not to permit it in their friends.

Vicious people, by contrast, have no firmness, since they do not even remain similar to what they were. They become friends for a short time, enjoying each other's vice. Useful or pleasant friends, however, last longer, for as long as they supply each other with pleasures or benefits.

The friendship that seems to arise most from contraries is friendship for utility, of poor to rich, for instance, or ignorant to knowledgeable; for we aim at whatever we find we lack, and give something else in return. Here we might also include the erotic lover and his beloved, and the beautiful and the ugly. That is why an erotic lover also sometimes appears ridiculous, when he expects to be loved in the same way as he loves; that would presumably be a proper expectation if he were lovable in the same way, but it is ridiculous when he is not.

Presumably, however, contrary seeks contrary coincidentally, not in its own right, and desire is for the intermediate. For what is good for the dry, for instance, is to reach the intermediate, not to become wet, and the same is true for the hot, and so on. Let us, then, dismiss these questions, since they are rather extraneous to our concern.

9 [Friendship in communities]: As we said at the beginning, friendship and justice would seem to be about the same things and to be found in the same people. For in every community there seems to be some sort of justice, and some type of friendship also. At any rate, fellow voyagers and fellow soldiers are called friends, and so are members of other communities. And the extent of their community is the extent of their friendship, since it is also the extent of the justice found there. The proverb "What friends have is common" is correct, since friendship involves community.

But, whereas brothers and companions have everything in common, what people have in common in other types of community is limited, more in some communities and less in others, since some friendships are also closer than others, some less close.

35

1160a   What is just is also different, since it is not the same for parents toward children as for one brother toward another, and not the same for companions as for fellow citizens, and similarly with the other types of friendship. Similarly, what is unjust toward each of these is also different, and becomes more unjust as it is practiced on closer friends. It is more shocking, for instance, to rob a companion of money than to rob a fellow citizen, to fail to help a brother than a stranger, and to strike one's father than anyone else. Justice also naturally increases with friendship, since it involves the same people and extends over an equal area.

5

All the communities [mentioned], however, would seem to be parts of the political community. For people keep company for some advantage and to supply something contributing to their life. And the political community as well [as the others] seems both to have been originally formed and to endure for advantage; for legislators also aim at advantage, and the common advantage is said to be just.

10

Now the other types of community aim at partial advantage. Sea travelers, for instance, seek the advantage proper to a journey, in making money or something like that, while fellow soldiers seek the advantage proper to war, desiring either money or victory or a city; and the same is true of fellow members of a tribe or deme.[1] Some communities—religious societies and dining clubs—seem to arise for pleasure, since these are, respectively, for religious sacrifices and for companionship.

15

20

But all these communities would seem to be subordinate to the political community, since it aims not at some advantage close at hand, but at advantage for the whole of life. ... [We can see this in the arrangements that cities make for religious festivals. For] in performing sacrifices and arranging gatherings for these, people both accord honors to the gods and provide themselves with pleasant relaxations. For the long-established sacrifices and gatherings appear to take place after the harvesting of the crops, as a sort of first-fruits, since this was the time when people used to be most at leisure [and the time when relaxation would be most advantageous for the whole of life].

25

All the types of community, then, appear to be parts of the political community, and these sorts of communities imply the appropriate sorts of friendships.

30

---

1   *deme* Subdivision of the region that included Athens—a township.

10 [Political systems]: There are three species of political system (*politeia*), and an equal number of deviations, which are a sort of corruption of them. The first political system is kingship; the second aristocracy; and since the third rests on property (*timēma*), it appears proper to call it a timocratic system, thought most people usually call it a polity. The best of these is kingship and the worst timocracy.

35

The deviation from kingship is tyranny. For, though both are monarchies, they show the widest difference, since the tyrant considers his own advantage, but the king considers the advantage of his subjects. For someone is a king only if he is self-sufficient and superior in all goods; and since such a person needs nothing more, he will consider the subjects' benefit, not his own. For a king who is not like this would be only some sort of titular king. Tyranny is contrary to this; for the tyrant pursues his own good. It is more evident that [tyranny] is the worst [deviation than that timocracy is the worst political system]; but the worst is contrary to the best; [hence kingship is the best].

1160b

5

The transition from kingship is to tyranny. For tyranny is the degenerate condition of monarchy, and the vicious king becomes a tyrant.

10

The transition from aristocracy [rule of the best people] is to oligarchy [rule of the few], resulting from the badness of the rulers. They distribute the city's goods contrary to people's worth, so that they distribute all or most of the goods to themselves, and always assign ruling offices to the same people, counting wealth for most. Hence the rulers are few, and they are vicious people instead of the most decent.

15

The transition from timocracy is to democracy [rule by the people], since these border on each other. For timocracy is also meant to be rule by the majority, and all those with the property-qualification are equal; [and majority rule and equality are the marks of democracy]. Democracy is the least vicious [of the deviations]; for it deviates only slightly from the form of a [genuine] political system.

20

These, then, are the most frequent transitions from one political system to another, since they are the smallest and easiest.

Resemblances to these—indeed, a sort of pattern of them—can also be found in households. For the community of a father and his sons has the structure of kingship, since the father is concerned for his children. Indeed that is why Homer also calls Zeus father, since kingship is meant to be paternal rule.

25

Among the Persians, however, the father's rule is tyrannical, since he treats his sons as slaves. The rule of a master

30

over his slaves is also tyrannical, since it is the master's advantage that is achieved in it. This, then, appears a correct form of rule, whereas the Persian form appears erroneous, since the different types of rule suit different subjects.

The community of man and woman appears aristocratic. For the man's rule in the area where it is right accords with the worth [of each], and he commits to the woman what 35 is fitting for her. If, however, the man controls everything, he changes it into an oligarchy; for then his action does 1161a not accord with the worth [of each], or with the respect in which [each] is better. Sometimes, indeed, women rule because they are heiresses; these cases of rule do not accord with virtue, but result from wealth and power, as is true in oligarchies.

The community of brothers is like a timocratic [system], 5 since they are equal except insofar as they differ in age. That is why, if they differ very much in age, the friendship is no longer brotherly.

Democracy is found most of all in dwellings without a master, since everyone there is on equal terms; and also in those where the ruler is weak and everyone is free [to do what he likes].

10 11 [Friendships in political systems]: Friendship appears in each of the political systems, to the extent that justice appears also. A king's friendship to his subjects involves superior beneficence. For he benefits his subjects, since he is good and attends to them to ensure that they do well, as a shepherd attends to his sheep; hence Homer also called 15 Agamemnon[1] shepherd of the peoples.

A father's friendship resembles this, but differs in conferring a greater benefit, since the father is the cause of his children's being, which seems to be the greatest benefit, and of their nurture and education. These benefits are also ascribed to ancestors; and by nature a father is ruler over sons, ancestors over descendants, and a king over subjects.

20 All these are friendships of superiority. That is why parents are also honored. And what is just is not the same in each of these friendships, but it accords with worth; for so does the friendship.

The friendship of man to woman is the same as in an aristocracy. For it accords with virtue, in assigning more 25 good to the better, and assigning what is fitting to each. The same is true of what is just here.

---

1   *Agamemnon*   Chief commander of the Greeks during the Trojan War.

The friendship of brothers is similar to that of companions, since they are equal and of an age, and such people usually have the same feelings and characters. Friendship in a timocracy is similar to this. For there the citizens are meant to be equal and decent, and so rule in turn and on equal terms. The same is true, then, of their friendship.   30

In the deviations, however, justice is found only to a slight degree; and hence the same is true of friendship. There is least of it in the worst deviation; for in a tyranny there is little or no friendship.

For where ruler and ruled have nothing in common, they have no friendship, since they have no justice either. This is true for a craftsman in relation to his tool, and for   35 the soul in relation to the body. For in all these cases the   1161b user benefits what he uses, but there is neither friendship nor justice toward inanimate things. Nor is there any toward a horse or cow, or toward a slave, insofar as he is a slave. For master and slave have nothing in common, since a slave is a tool with a soul, while a tool is a slave without a soul.

Insofar as he is a slave, then, there is no friendship with   5 him. But there is friendship with him insofar as he is a human being. For every human being seems to have some relation of justice with everyone who is capable of community in law and agreement; hence [every human being seems] also [to have] friendship [with every human being], to the extent that [every human being] is a human being.

Hence there are friendships and justice to only a slight degree in tyrannies also, but to a much larger degree in   10 democracies; for there people are equal, and so have much in common.

12 [Friendships in families]: As we have said, then, every friendship is found in a community. But we should set apart the friendship of families and that of companions. The friendship of citizens, tribesmen, voyagers, and suchlike are more like friendships in a community, since they appear to   15 reflect some sort of agreement; and among these we may include the friendship of host and guest.

Friendship in families also seems to have many species, but they all seem to depend on paternal friendship. For a parent is fond of his children because he regards them as something of himself; and children are fond of a parent because they regard themselves as coming from him.

A parent knows better what has come from him than   20 the children know that they are from the parent; and the parent regards his children as his own more than the product regards the maker as its own. For a person regards what comes from him as his own, as the owner regards his tooth or hair or anything; but what has come from him regards its owner as its own not at all, or to a lesser degree. The length of time also matters. For a parent becomes fond of his children as soon as they are born, but children become fond of the parent when time has passed and they have acquired some comprehension or [at least] perception. And this also makes it clear why mothers love their children more [than fathers do].

A parent, then, loves his children as [he loves] himself. For what has come from him is a sort of other himself; [it is other because] it is separate. Children love a parent because they regard themselves as having come from him. Brothers love each other because they have come from the same [parents]. For the same relation to the parents makes the same thing for both of them; hence we speak of the same blood, the same stock, and so on. Hence they are the same thing in a way, in different [subjects].

Being brought up together and being of an age contributes largely to friendship; for "two of an age" [get on well], and those with the same character are companions. That is why the friendship of brothers and that of companions are similar. Cousins and other relatives are akin by being related to brothers, since that makes them descendants of the same parents [i.e., the parents of these brothers]. Some are more akin, others less, by the ancestor's being near to or far from them.

The friendship of children to a parent, like the friendship of human beings to a god, is friendship toward what is good and superior. For the parent conferred the greatest benefits on his children, since he is the cause of their being and nurture and of their education once they have been born. This sort of friendship also includes pleasure and utility, more than the friendship of unrelated people does, to the extent that [parents and children] have more of a life in common.

Friendship between brothers has the features of friendship between companions, especially when [the companions] are decent, or in general similar. For brothers are that much more akin to each other [than ordinary companions], and are fond of each other from birth; they are that much more similar in character when they are from the same parents, nurtured together and educated similarly; and the proof of their reliability over time is fullest and firmest. Among other relatives too the features of friendship are proportional [to the relation].

The friendship of man and woman also seems to be natural. For human beings form couples more naturally than they form cities, to the extent that the household is prior to the city, and more necessary, and childbearing is shared more widely among the animals. For the other animals, the community goes only as far as childbearing. Human beings, however, share a household not only for childbearing, but also for the benefits in their life. For the difference between them implies that their functions are divided, with different ones for the man and the woman; hence each supplies the other's needs by contributing a special function to the common good. For this reason their friendship seems to include both utility and pleasure.

And it may also be friendship for virtue, if they are decent. For each has a proper virtue, and this will be a source of enjoyment for them. Children seem to be another bond, and that is why childless unions are more quickly dissolved; for children are a common good for both, and what is common holds them together.

How should a man conduct his life toward his wife, or, in general, toward a friend? That appears to be the same as asking how they are to conduct their lives justly. For what is just is not the same for a friend toward a friend as toward a stranger, or the same toward a companion as toward a classmate.

13 [Disputes in friendships between equals]: There are three types of friendship, as we said at the beginning, and, within each type some friendships rest on equality, while others are in accord with superiority. For equally good people can be friends, but also. a better and a worse person; and the same is true of friends for pleasure or utility, since they may be either equal or unequal in their benefits. Hence equals must equalize in loving and in the other things, because of their equality; and unequals must make the return that is proportionate to the types of superiority.

Accusations and reproaches arise only or most often in friendship for utility. And this is reasonable. For friends for virtue are eager to benefit each other, since this is proper to virtue and to friendship; and if this is what they strain to achieve, there are no accusations or fights. For no one objects if the other loves and benefits him; if he is gracious, he retaliates by benefiting the other. And if the superior gets what he aims at, he will not accuse his friend of anything, since each of them desires what is good.

Nor are there many accusations among friends for pleasure. For both of them get what they want at the same time

15 if they enjoy spending their time together; and someone who accused his friend of not pleasing him would appear ridiculous, since he is free to spend his days without the friend's company.

Friendship for utility, however, is liable to accusations. For these friends deal with each other in the expectation of gaining benefits. Hence they always require more, thinking they have got less than is fitting; and they reproach the other because they get less than they require and deserve.
20 And those who confer benefits cannot supply as much as the recipients require.

There are two ways of being just, one unwritten, and one governed by rules of law. And similarly one type of friendship of utility would seem to depend on character,
25 and the other on rules. Accusations arise most readily if it is not the same sort of friendship when they dissolve it as it was when they formed it.

Friendship dependent on rules is the type that is on explicit conditions. One type of this is entirely mercenary and requires immediate payment. The other is more generous and postpones the time [of repayment], but in accordance with an agreement [requiring] one thing in return for another. In this sort of friendship it is clear and unambiguous what is owed, but the postponement is a friendly aspect of
30 it. That is why some cities do not allow legal actions in these cases, but think that people who have formed an arrangement on the basis of trust must put up with the outcome.

Friendship [for utility] that depends on character is not on explicit conditions. Someone makes a present or whatever it is, as to a friend, but expects to get back as much or more, since he assumes that it is not a free gift, but a loan.

If one party does not dissolve the friendship on the terms on which he formed it, he will accuse the other. This
35 happens because all or most people wish for what is fine, but decide to do what is beneficial; and while it is fine to
1163a do someone a good turn without aiming to receive one in return, it is beneficial to receive a good turn.

We should, if we can, make a return worthy of what we have received, [if the other has undertaken the friendship] willingly. For we should never make a friend of someone who is unwilling, but must suppose that we were in error at the beginning, and received a benefit from the wrong
5 person; for since it was not from a friend, and this was not why he was doing it, we must dissolve the arrangement as though we had received a good turn on explicit conditions. And we will agree to repay if we can. If we cannot repay, the giver would not even expect it. Hence we should repay if we can. We should consider at the beginning who is doing us a good turn, and on what conditions, so that we can put up with it on these conditions, or else decline it.

It is disputable whether we must measure [the return] 10 by the benefit accruing to the recipient, and make the return proportional to that, or instead by the good turn done by the benefactor. For a recipient says that what he got was a small matter for the benefactor, and that he could have gotten it from someone else instead, and so he belittles it. But the benefactor says it was the biggest thing he had, that 15 it could not be gotten from anyone else, and that he gave it when he was in danger or similar need.

Since the friendship is for utility, surely the benefit to the recipient must be the measure [of the return]. For he was the one who required it, and the benefactor supplies him on the assumption that he will get an equal return. Hence the aid has been as great as the benefit received, and 20 the recipient should return as much as he gained, or still more, since that is finer.

But in friendships in accord with virtue, there are no accusations. Rather, the decision of the benefactor would seem to be the measure, since the controlling element in virtue and character lies in decision.

14 [Disputes in friendships between unequals]: There are also disputes in friendships in accord with superiority, since 25 each friend expects to have more than the other, but whenever this happens the friendship is dissolved.

For the better person thinks it is fitting for him to have more, on the ground that more is fittingly allotted to the good person. And the more beneficial person thinks the same. For it is wrong, they say, for someone to have an equal share if he is useless; the result is a public service, not a friendship, if the benefits from the friendship do not accord 30 with the worth of the actions. [The superior party says this] because he notices that in a financial community the larger contributors gain more, and he thinks the same thing is right in a friendship.

But the needy person, the inferior party in the friendship, takes the opposite view, saying it is proper to a virtuous friend to supply his needy [friends]. For what use is it, as they say, to be an excellent or powerful person's friend if 35 you are not going to gain anything by it?

Well, each of them would seem to be correct in what he expects, and it is right for each of them to get more from 1163b the friendship—but not more of the same thing. Rather, the superior person should get more honor, and the needy person more profit, since honor is the reward of virtue and beneficence, while profit is what supplies need.

5 This also appears to be true in political systems. For someone who provides nothing for the community receives no honor, since what is common is given to someone who benefits the community, and honor is something common. For it is impossible both to make money off the community 10 and to receive honor from it at the same time; for no one endures the smaller share of everything. Hence someone who suffers a monetary loss [by holding office] receives honor in return, while someone who accepts gifts [in office] receives money [but not honor]; for distribution that accords with worth equalizes and preserves the friendship, as we have said.

This, then, is how we should treat unequals. If we benefit from them in money or virtue, we should return honor, 15 and thereby make what return we can. For friendship seeks what is possible, not what accords with worth, since that is impossible in some cases, as it is with honor to gods and parents. For no one could ever make a return in accord with their worth, but someone who attends to them as far as he is able seems to be a decent person.

That is why it might seem that a son is not free to disown his father, but a father is free to disown his son. For a 20 debtor should return what he owes, and since, no matter what a son has done, he has not made a worthy return for what his father has done for him, he is always the debtor. But the creditor is free to remit the debt, and hence the father is free to remit.

At the same time, however, it presumably seems that no one would ever withdraw from a son, except from one who was far gone in vice. For, quite apart from their natural 25 friendship, it is human not to repel aid. The son, however, if he is vicious, will want to avoid helping his father, or will not be keen on it. For the many wish to receive benefits, but they avoid doing them because they suppose it is unprofitable. So much, then, for these things.

...

from Book 10 [Happiness: Further Discussion]

...

6 [Conditions for happiness]: We have now finished our dis- 1176a cussion of the types of virtue; of friendship; and of pleasure. 30 It remains for us to discuss happiness in outline, since we take this to be the end of human [aims]. Our discussion will be shorter if we first take up again what we said before.

We said, then, that happiness is not a state. For if it were, someone might have it and yet be asleep for his whole 35 life, living the life of a plant, or suffer the greatest misfor- 1176b tunes. If we do not approve of this, we count happiness as an activity rather than a state, as we said before.

Some activities are necessary, i.e., choiceworthy for some other end, while others are choiceworthy in their own right. Clearly, then, we should count happiness as one of those activities that are choiceworthy in their own right, 5 not as one of those choiceworthy for some other end. For happiness lacks nothing, but is self-sufficient.

An activity is choiceworthy in its own right if nothing further apart from it is sought from it. This seems to be the character of actions in accord with virtue; for doing fine and excellent actions is choiceworthy for itself. But pleasant amusements also [seem to be choiceworthy in their own right]; for they are not chosen for other ends, since they ac- 10 tually cause more harm than benefit, by causing neglect of our bodies and possessions. Moreover, most of those people congratulated for their happiness resort to these sorts of pastimes. That is why people who are witty participants in them have a good reputation with tyrants, since they offer themselves as pleasant [partners] in the tyrant's aims, and 15 these are the sort of people the tyrant requires. And so these amusements seem to have the character of happiness because people in supreme power spend their leisure in them.

These sorts of people, however, are presumably no evidence. For virtue and understanding, the sources of excellent activities, do not depend on holding supreme power. Further, these powerful people have had no taste 20 of pure and civilized pleasure, and so they resort to bodily pleasures. But that is no reason to think these pleasures are most choiceworthy, since boys also think that the things they honor are best. Hence, just as different things appear honorable to boys and to men, it is reasonable that in the same way different things appear honorable to base and to decent people.

25 As we have often said, then, what is honorable and pleasant is what is so to the excellent person. To each type of person the activity that accords with his own proper state is most choiceworthy; hence the activity in accord with virtue is most choiceworthy to the excellent person [and hence is most honorable and pleasant].

Happiness, then, is not found in amusement; for it would be absurd if the end were amusement, and our life-
30 long efforts and sufferings aimed at amusing ourselves. For we choose practically everything for some other end—except for happiness, since it is [the] end; but serious work and toil aimed [only] at amusement appears stupid and excessively childish. Rather, it seems correct to amuse ourselves so that we can do something serious, as Anacharsis says; for amusement would seem to be relaxation, and it is
35 because we cannot toil continuously that we require relaxa-
1177a tion. Relaxation, then, is not [the] end; for we pursue it [to prepare] for activity. But the happy life seems to be a life in accord with virtue, which is a life involving serious actions, and not consisting in amusement.

Besides, we say that things to be taken seriously are better than funny things that provide amusement, and that in
5 each case the activity of the better part and the better person is more serious and excellent; and the activity of what is better is superior, and thereby has more the character of happiness.

Besides, anyone at all, even a slave, no less than the best person, might enjoy bodily pleasures; but no one would allow that a slave shares in happiness, if one does not [also allow that the slave shares in the sort of] life [needed for happiness]. Happiness, then, is found not in these pastimes,
10 but in the activities in accord with virtue, as we also said previously.

7 [Happiness and theoretical study]: If happiness is activity in accord with virtue, it is reasonable for it to accord with the supreme virtue, which will be the virtue of the best thing. The best is understanding, or whatever else seems to
15 be the natural ruler and leader, and to understand what is fine and divine, by being itself either divine or the most divine element in us. Hence complete happiness will be its activity in accord with its proper virtue; and we have said that this activity is the activity of study.

This seems to agree with what has been said before,
20 and also with the truth. For this activity is supreme, since understanding is the supreme element in us, and the objects of understanding are the supreme objects of knowledge.

Further, it is the most continuous activity, since we are more capable of continuous study than any continuous action.

Besides, we think pleasure must be mixed into happiness; and it is agreed that the activity in accord with wisdom is the most pleasant of the activities in accord with virtue. 25 Certainly, philosophy seems to have remarkably pure and firm pleasures, and it is reasonable for those who have knowledge to spend their lives more pleasantly than those who seek it.

Moreover, the self-sufficiency we spoke of will be found in study more than in anything else. For admittedly the wise person, the just person, and the other virtuous people all need the good things necessary for life. Still, when these are adequately supplied, the just person needs other people 30 as partners and recipients of his just actions; and the same is true of the temperate person, the brave person, and each of the others. But the wise person is able, and more able the wiser he is, to study even by himself; and though he presumably does it better with colleagues, even so he is more 1177b self-sufficient than any other [virtuous person].

Besides, study seems to be liked because of itself alone, since it has no result beyond having studied. But from the virtues concerned with action we try to a greater or lesser extent to gain something beyond the action itself.

Besides, happiness seems to be found in leisure; for we 5 deny ourselves leisure so that we can be at leisure, and fight wars so that we can be at peace. Now the virtues concerned with action have their activities in politics or war, and actions here seem to require trouble. This seems completely true for actions in war, since no one chooses to fight a war, and no one continues it, for the sake of fighting a war; for someone would have to be a complete murderer if he made 10 his friends his enemies so that there could be battles and killings. But the actions of the politician also deny us leisure; apart from political activities themselves, those actions seek positions of power and honors, or at least they seek happiness for the politician himself and for his fellow citizens, which is something different from political science itself, 15 and clearly is sought on the assumption that it is different.

Hence among actions in accord with the virtues those in politics and war are preeminently fine and great; but they require trouble, aim at some [further] end, and are choiceworthy for something other than themselves. But the activity of understanding, it seems, is superior in excellence 20 because it is the activity of study, aims at no end apart from itself, and has its own proper pleasure, which increases the

activity. Further, self-sufficiency, leisure, unwearied activity (as far as is possible for a human being), and any other features ascribed to the blessed person, are evidently features
25 of this activity. Hence a human being's complete happiness will be this activity, if it receives a complete span of life, since nothing incomplete is proper to happiness.

Such a life would be superior to the human level. For someone will live it not insofar as he is a human being, but insofar as he has some divine element in him. And the activity of this divine element is as much superior to the activity
30 in accord with the rest of virtue as this element is superior to the compound. Hence if understanding is something divine in comparison with a human being, so also will the life in accord with understanding be divine in comparison with human life. We ought not to follow the makers of proverbs and "Think human, since you are human," or "Think mortal, since you are mortal." Rather, as far as we can, we ought to be pro-immortal, and go to all lengths to live a
1178a life in accord with our supreme element; for however much this element may lack in bulk, by much more it surpasses everything in power and value.

Moreover, each person seems to be his understanding, if he is his controlling and better element. It would be absurd, then, if he were to choose not his own life, but something
5 else's. And what we have said previously will also apply now. For what is proper to each thing's nature is supremely best and most pleasant for it; and hence for a human being the life in accord with understanding will be supremely best and most pleasant, if understanding, more than anything else, is the human being. This life, then, will also be happiest.

8 [Theoretical study and the other virtues]: The life in accord with the other kind of virtue [i.e., the kind concerned
10 with action] is [happiest] in a secondary way because the activities in accord with this virtue are human. For we do just and brave actions, and the other actions in accord with the virtues, in relation to other people, by abiding by what fits each person in contracts, services, all types of actions, and also in feelings; and all these appear to be human conditions.
15 Indeed, some feelings actually seem to arise from the body; and in many ways virtue of character seems to be proper to feelings.

Besides, prudence is inseparable from virtue of character, and virtue of character from prudence. For the principles of prudence accord with the virtues of character; and correctness in virtues of character accords with prudence.
20 And since these virtues are also connected to feelings, they

are concerned with the compound. Since the virtues of the compound are human virtues, the life and the happiness in accord with these virtues is also human. The virtue of understanding, however, is separated [from the compound]. Let us say no more about it, since an exact account would be too large a task for our present project.

Moreover, it seems to need external supplies very little, or [at any rate] less than virtue of character needs them. For 25 let us grant that they both need necessary goods, and to the same extent; for there will be only a very small difference, even though the politician labors more about the body and suchlike. Still, there will be a large difference in [what is needed] for the [proper] activities [of each type of virtue]. For the generous person will need money for generous actions; and the just person will need it for paying debts, since 30 wishes are not clear, and people who are not just pretend to wish to do justice. Similarly, the brave person will need enough power, and the temperate person will need freedom [to do intemperate actions], if they are to achieve anything that the virtue requires. For how else will they, or any other virtuous people, make their virtue clear?

Moreover, it is disputed whether decision or action is 35 more in control of virtue, on the assumption that virtue depends on both. Well, certainly it is clear that the complete 1178b [good] depends on both; but for actions many external goods are needed, and the greater and finer the actions the more numerous are the external goods needed.

But someone who is studying needs none of these goods, for that activity at least; indeed, for study at least, we might say they are even hindrances. Insofar as he is a human 5 being, however, and [hence] lives together with a number of other human beings, he chooses to do the actions that accord with virtue. Hence he will need the sorts of external goods [that are needed for the virtues], for living a human life.

In another way also it appears that complete happiness is some activity of study. For we traditionally suppose that the gods more than anyone are blessed and happy; but what 10 sorts of actions ought we to ascribe to them? Just actions? Surely they will appear ridiculous making contracts, returning deposits, and so on. Brave actions? Do they endure what [they find] frightening and endure dangers because it is fine? Generous actions? Whom will they give to? And surely it would be absurd for them to have currency or 15 anything like that. What would their temperate actions be? Surely it is vulgar praise to say that they do not have base appetites. When we go through them all, anything that

concerns actions appears trivial and unworthy of the gods.
20 Nonetheless, we all traditionally suppose that they are alive
and active, since surely they are not asleep like Endymion.[1]
Then if someone is alive, and action is excluded, and production even more, what is left but study? Hence the gods'
activity that is superior in blessedness will be an activity of
study. And so the human activity that is most akin to the
gods' activity will, more than any others, have the character
of happiness.

A sign of this is the fact that other animals have no
25 share in happiness, being completely deprived of this activity of study. For the whole life of the gods is blessed, and
human life is blessed to the extent that it has something resembling this sort of activity; but none of the other animals
is happy, because none of them shares in study at all. Hence
happiness extends just as far as study extends, and the more
30 someone studies, the happier he is, not coincidentally but
insofar as he studies, since study is valuable in itself. And so
[on this argument] happiness will be some kind of study.

But happiness will need external prosperity also, since
we are human beings; for our nature is not self-sufficient for
35 study, but we need a healthy body, and need to have food
1179a and the other services provided. Still, even though no one
can be blessedly happy without external goods, we must not
think that to be happy we will need many large goods. For
self-sufficiency and action do not depend on excess.

Moreover, we can do fine actions even if we do not rule
earth and sea; for even from moderate resources we can do
5 the actions that accord with virtue. This is evident to see,
since many private citizens seem to do decent actions no less
than people in power do—even more, in fact. It is enough
if moderate resources are provided; for the life of someone
whose activity accords with virtue will be happy.

10 Solon surely described happy people well, when he said
they had been moderately supplied with external goods, had
done what he regarded as the finest actions, and had lived
their lives temperately. For it is possible to have moderate
possessions and still to do the right actions. And Anaxagoras[2] would seem to have supposed that the happy person
was neither rich nor powerful, since he said he would not
15 be surprised if the happy person appeared an absurd sort
of person to the many. For the many judge by externals,

since these are all they perceive. Hence the beliefs of the
wise would seem to accord with our arguments.

These considerations, then, produce some confidence.
But the truth in questions about action is judged from what
we do and how we live, since these are what control [the an-   20
swers to such questions]. Hence we ought to examine what
has been said by applying it to what we do and how we live;
and if it harmonizes with what we do, we should accept it,
but if it conflicts we should count it [mere] words.

The person whose activity accords with understanding
and who takes care of understanding would seem to be in
the best condition, and most loved by the gods. For if the
gods pay some attention to human beings, as they seem to,   25
it would be reasonable for them to take pleasure in what is
best and most akin to them, namely understanding; and
reasonable for them to benefit in return those who most of
all like and honor understanding, on the assumption that
these people attend to what is beloved by the gods, and act
correctly and finely. Clearly, all this is true of the wise per-   30
son more than anyone else; hence he is most loved by the
gods. And it is likely that this same person will be happiest;
hence, by this argument also, the wise person, more than
anyone else, will be happy.

[From Ethics to Politics]

9 [Moral education]: We have now said enough in outlines
about happiness and the virtues, and about friendship and
pleasures also. Should we, then, think that our decision [to   35
study these] has achieved its end? On the contrary, the aim   1179b
of studies about action, as we say, is surely not to study
and know about a given thing, but rather to act on our
knowledge. Hence knowing about virtue is not enough, but
we must also try to possess and exercise virtue, or become
good in any other way.

Now if arguments were sufficient by themselves to   5
make people decent, the rewards they would command
would justifiably have been many and large, as Theognis[3]
says, and rightly bestowed. In fact, however, arguments
seem to have enough influence to stimulate and encourage
the civilized ones among the young people, and perhaps to
make virtue take possession of a well-born character that
truly loves what is fine; but they seem unable to turn the   10
many toward being fine and good.

---

1   *Endymion* Aeolian shepherd in Greek mythology. In the version of his tale cited by Aristotle, Selene, the Titan goddess of the
moon, was so taken by how he looked while asleep that she asked
Zeus to grant him eternal sleep.
2   *Anaxagoras* Pre-Socratic Greek philosopher (c. 500–428 BCE).

---

3   *Theognis* Greek poet (c. 540–c. 480 BCE).

For the many naturally obey fear, not shame; they avoid what is base because of the penalties, not because it is disgraceful. For since they live by their feelings, they pursue their proper pleasures and the sources of them, and avoid the opposed pains, and have not even a notion of what is fine and [hence] truly pleasant, since they have had no taste of it.

What argument, then, could reform people like these? For it is impossible, or not easy, to alter by argument what has long been absorbed as a result of one's habits. But, presumably, we should be satisfied to achieve some share in virtue if we already have what we seem to need to become decent.

Now some think it is nature that makes people good; some think it is habit; some that it is teaching. The [contribution] of nature clearly is not up to us, but results from some divine cause in those who have it, who are the truly fortunate ones. Arguments and teaching surely do not prevail on everyone, but the soul of the student needs to have been prepared by habits for enjoying and hating finely, like ground that is to nourish seed. For someone who lives in accord with his feelings would not even listen to an argument turning him away, or comprehend it [if he did listen]; and in that state how could he be persuaded to change? And in general feelings seem to yield to force, not to argument. Hence we must already in some way have a character suitable for virtue, fond of what is fine and objecting to what is shameful.

It is difficult, however, for someone to be trained correctly for virtue from his youth if he has not been brought up under correct laws; for the many, especially the young, do not find it pleasant to live in a temperate and resistant way. That is why laws must prescribe their upbringing and practices; for they will not find these things painful when they get used to them.

1180a Presumably, however, it is not enough if they get the correct upbringing and attention when they are young; rather, they must continue the same practices and be habituated to them when they become men. Hence we need laws concerned with these things also, and in general with all of life. For the many yield to compulsion more than to argument, and to sanctions more than to the fine.

That is why legislators must, in some people's view, urge people toward virtue and exhort them to aim at the fine—on the assumption that anyone whose good habits have prepared him decently will listen to them—but must impose corrective treatments and penalties on anyone who

disobeys or lacks the right nature, and must completely expel an incurable. For the decent person, it is assumed, will attend to reason because his life aims at the fine, whereas the base person, since he desires pleasure, has to receive corrective treatment by pain, like a beast of burden. That is why it is said that the pains imposed must be those most contrary to the pleasures he likes.

As we have said, then, someone who is to be good must be finely brought up and habituated, and then must live in decent practices, doing base actions neither willingly nor unwillingly. And this will be true if his life follows some sort of understanding and correct order that prevails on him.

Now a father's instructions lack this power to prevail and compel; and so in general do the instructions of an individual man, unless he is a king or someone like that. Law, however, has the power that compels; and law is reason that proceeds from a sort of prudence and understanding. Besides, people become hostile to an individual human being who opposes their impulses, even if he is correct in opposing them, whereas a law's prescription of what is decent is not burdensome.

And yet, it is only in Sparta, or in a few other cities as well, that the legislator seems to have attended to upbringing and practices. In most other cities they are neglected, and an individual lives as he wishes, "laying down the rules for his children and wife," like a Cyclops.[1]

It is best, then, if the community attends to upbringing, and attends correctly. But if the community neglects it, it seems fitting for each individual to promote the virtue of his children and his friends—to be able to do it, or at least to decide to do it. From what we have said, however, it seems he will be better able to do it if he acquires legislative science. For, clearly, attention by the community works through laws, and decent attention works through excellent laws; and whether the laws are written or unwritten, for the education of one or of many, seems unimportant, as it is in music, gymnastics, and other practices. For just as in a city the provisions of law and the types of character [found in that city] have influence, similarly a father's words and habits have influence, and all the more because of kinship and because of the benefits he does; for his children are already fond of him and naturally ready to obey.

---

1   *Cyclops*   Mythological race of giants with a single central eye. Homer pictured them as lawless and barbaric in Book 9 of the *Odyssey*.

Further, education adapted to an individual is actually better than a common education for everyone, just as individualized medical treatment is better. For though generally a feverish patient benefits from rest and starvation, presumably some patient does not; nor does the boxing instructor impose the same way of fighting on everyone. Hence it seems that treatment in particular cases is more exactly right when each person gets special attention, since he then more often gets the suitable treatment.

Nonetheless a doctor, a gymnastics trainer, and everyone else will give the best individual attention if they also know universally what is good for all, or for these sorts. For sciences are said to be, and are, of what is common [to many particular cases]. Admittedly someone without scientific knowledge may well attend properly to a single person, if his experience has allowed him to take exact note of what happens in a given case, just as some people seem to be their own best doctors, though unable to help anyone else at all. Nonetheless, presumably, it seems that someone who wants to be an expert in a craft and a branch of study should progress to the universal, and come to know that, as far as possible; for that, as we have said, is what the sciences are about.

Then perhaps also someone who wishes to make people better by his attention, many people or few, should try to acquire legislative science, if laws are a means to make us good. For not just anyone can improve the condition of just anyone, or the person presented to him; but if someone can, it is the person with knowledge, just as in medical science and the others that require attention and prudence.

Next, then, should we examine whence and how someone might acquire legislative science? Just as in other cases [we go to the practitioner], should we go to the politicians, since, as we saw, legislative science seems to be a part of political science? Or does the case of political science appear different from the other sciences and capacities? For evidently, in the other cases, the same people, such as doctors or painters, who transmit the capacity to others actively practice it themselves. By contrast, it is the sophists[1] who advertise that they teach politics but none of them practices

it. Instead, those who practice it are the political activists, and they seem to act on some sort of capacity and experience rather than thought.

For evidently they neither write nor speak on such questions, though presumably it would be finer to do this than to compose speeches for the law courts or the Assembly; nor have they made politicians out of their own sons or any other friends of theirs. But it would be reasonable for them to do this if they were able; for there is nothing better than the political capacity that they could leave to their cities, and nothing better that they could decide to produce in themselves, or, therefore, in their closest friends.

Nonetheless, experience would seem to contribute quite a lot; otherwise people would not have become better politicians by familiarity with politics. That is why those who aim to know about political science would seem to need experience as well.

By contrast, those of the sophists who advertise [that they teach political science] appear to be a long way from teaching; for they are altogether ignorant about the sort of thing political science is, and the sorts of things it is about. For if they had known what it is, they would not have taken it to be the same as rhetoric, or something inferior to it, or thought it an easy task to assemble the laws with good reputations and then legislate. For they think they can select the best laws, as though the selection itself did not require comprehension, and as though correct judgment were not the most important thing, as it is in music.

[They are wrong;] for those with experience in each area judge the products correctly and comprehend the ways and means of completing them, and what fits with what; for if we lack experience, we must be satisfied with noticing that the product is well or badly made, as with painting. Now laws would seem to be the products of political science; how, then, could someone acquire legislative science, or judge which laws are best, from laws alone? For neither do we appear to become experts in medicine by reading textbooks.

And yet doctors not only try to describe the [recognized] treatments, but also distinguish different [bodily] states, and try to say how each type of patient might be cured and must be treated. And what they say seems to be useful to the experienced, though useless to the ignorant. Similarly, then, collections of laws and political systems might also, presumably, be most useful if we are capable of studying them and of judging what is done finely or in the contrary way, and what sorts of [elements] fit with what. Those who

---

1   *sophists* Group of professional teachers—of all subjects, but the biggest demand was for rhetoric, a skill which gave political advantage. Known for moral relativism and for political and philosophical cynicism, Sophists sometimes boasted that they could train one to argue for any position—to "make the worse appear the better," as Socrates says, citing the charges of his accusers who identified him with the Sophists in the *Apology*.

10 lack the [proper] state [of experience] when they go through these collections will not manage to judge finely, unless they can do it all by themselves [without training], though they might come to comprehend them better by going through them.

Since, then, our predecessors have left the area of legislation uncharted, it is presumably better to examine it ourselves instead, and indeed to examine political systems 15 in general, and so to complete the philosophy of human affairs, as far as we are able.

First, then, let us try to review any sound remarks our predecessors have made on particular topics. Then let us study the collected political systems, to see from them what sorts of things preserve and destroy cities, and political 20 systems of different types; and what causes some cities to conduct politics well, and some badly. For when we have studied these questions, we will perhaps grasp better what sort of political system is best; how each political system should be organized so as to be best; and what habits and laws it should follow.

Let us discuss this, then, starting from the beginning.[1]

◆ ◆ ◆ ◆ ◆

Politics

Book I

I

1252a Observation shows that every state[2] is a social organization of some kind, and that every social organization is directed at some good purpose; for mankind always act in order to obtain that which they think good. But, if all social organizations aim at some good, the state or political community, 5 which is the highest of all, and which embraces all the rest, aims at good in a greater degree than any other, and at the highest good.

---

1 *Let us ... the beginning* This sentence concludes Aristotle's *Nicomachean Ethics* and introduces his *Politics*.
2 *state* Aristotle's word *polis* here is sometimes translated "city." He was referring to the "city-states," the most politically significant large-scale divisions of Greece in those days; they correspond more closely to nations than to cities in today's world.

Some people mistakenly think that the qualifications of a statesman, king, householder, and slave-master are the same, and that they differ, not in kind, but only in the number of people they govern—the only difference being that the ruler over a few is called a master; over more, the 10 manager of a household; over a still larger number, a statesman or king. This view assumes that there would be no difference between a very large household and a very small state, and that the only distinction between the king and the statesman is that a ruler with sole authority is a king, but when people take turns ruling, according to the rules of 15 statesmanship, then the ruler is called a statesman.

But all this is a mistake; for governments differ in kind, as will be evident to any one who considers the matter according to the method which has hitherto guided us: as in other departments of science, so in politics, compound objects of study should always be analyzed into their simple 20 elements—their smallest parts. We must therefore look at the elements of which the state is composed, in order that we may see in what the different kinds of rule differ from one another, and whether any scientific result can be attained about each one of them.

2

He who thus considers things—a state or anything else—in 25 their origin and first growth will obtain the clearest view of them. In the first place there must be a union of those who cannot exist without each other. An example of this is the union of male and female, for the continuance of the race (a union which is not formed for a deliberate purpose, but because mankind has, in common with other animals and with plants, a natural desire to leave behind them an image of themselves); a second example is the union between nat- 30 ural ruler and subject, for the preservation of both. For a being capable of foresight is intended by nature to be lord and master, and that which can physically carry out the actions resulting from this foresight is intended to be ruled by the master—a natural slave; hence the master/slave relationship is advantageous to both.

Now nature has distinguished between the female and 1252b the slave. For nature is not like the blacksmith who made the all-purpose Delphian knife;[3] she makes each thing for a single use, and every instrument is best made when intend-

---

3 *Delphian knife* Tool that served as a knife, a file and a hammer.

ed for one and not for many uses. But among barbarians[1] no distinction is made between women and slaves, because there is no natural ruler among them: they are a community of slaves, male and female. For this reason the poets say "It is proper that Greeks should rule over barbarians";[2] as if they thought that the barbarian and the slave were by nature one.

Out of these two relationships between man and woman, master and slave, the first thing to arise is the family, and Hesiod is right when he says, "First house and wife and an ox for the plough,"[3] for the ox is the poor man's slave. The family is the association established by nature for the supply of men's everyday wants, and the members of it are called by Charondas[4] "companions of the cupboard," and by Epimenides the Cretan,[5] "companions of the manger." But when several families are united, and the association aims at something more than the supply of daily needs, the first society to be formed is the village. And the most natural form of the village appears to be that of the descendents of a single family, composed of the children and grandchildren, who are said to be "suckled with the same milk." And this is the reason why Greek states were originally governed by kings; because the Greeks were under royal rule before they came together, as the barbarians still are. Every family is monarchically ruled by the eldest, and therefore in the colonies of the family the monarchical form of government prevailed because they were of the same blood. As Homer says, "Each one gives law to his children and to his wives."[6] For they lived in scattered groups, as was the manner in ancient times. This is why people say that the gods have a king, because they themselves either are or were in ancient times under the rule of a king. For they imagine that not only the forms of the gods, but also their ways of life, are like their own.

When several villages are united in a single community, large enough to be self-sufficient or nearly, the state comes into existence; this originates to provide the bare needs of life, and continues in existence for the sake of a *good* life. And therefore, if the earlier forms of society are natural, so is the state, for the state is the end[7] of these earlier forms, and the nature of a thing is its end. For what each thing is when fully developed, we call its nature, whether we are speaking of a man, a horse, or a family. Besides, the final cause[8] and end of a thing is the best, and to be self-sufficing is the end and the best.

Hence it is evident that the state is a creation of nature, and that man is by nature a political animal. And he who by nature and not by mere accident is without a state, is either a bad man or above humanity; he is like the "Tribeless, lawless, heartless one,"[9] whom Homer denounces; a natural outcast, he is a lover of war; he is in the position of a solitary advanced piece in a board game.

Clearly man is more of a political animal than bees or any other gregarious animals. Nature, as we say, makes nothing in vain, and man is the only animal whom she has endowed with the gift of speech. And whereas mere voice is but an indication of pleasure or pain, and is therefore found in other animals (for their nature allows them to perceive pleasure and pain and to communicate them to one another, but nothing more), the power of speech is intended to express what is advantageous and inexpedient, and therefore likewise the just and the unjust. And it is a characteristic of man that he alone has any sense of good and evil, of just and unjust, and the like, and the association of living beings who have this sense makes a household and a state.

Further, the state is by nature clearly prior[10] to the household and to the individual, since the whole is necessarily prior to the part. For example, if a whole body were destroyed, there will be no foot or hand, except in an equivocal sense, as we might speak of a stone hand; for when destroyed in function the hand will be no better than that. Things are defined by their working and power; and we ought not to say that they are the same when they no longer have their proper function, but only that they have the same name. The proof that the state is a creation of na-

---

1   *barbarians*   Non-Greeks.
2   *It is proper ... barbarians*   Euripides, *Iphigenia in Aulis*, 1400.
3   *"First house ... the plough"*   Hesiod was a Greek poet, living around 700 BCE. This quote is from his long poem *Works and Days*.
4   *Charondas*   Sicilian lawgiver, c. 500 BCE.
5   *Epimenides the Cretan*   Semi-mythical poet-philosopher of the sixth century BCE. His works are now all lost.
6   *"Each one gives laws ... wives"*   *Odyssey* 9, 114. Homer here describes the society of the Cyclopes, which Aristotle took to be a representation of the structure of primitive society in general.

7   *end*   The Greek *telos* (end) refers to the full development or the aim of something.
8   *final cause*   One of the "four causes" Aristotle identifies as the four sorts of explanation one might give of something. The "final cause" of something is its *telos*, that for the sake of which a thing is done. (See *Physics* 2,8.)
9   *Tribeless, lawless, heartless one*   Homer, *Iliad* 9, 63.
10   *prior*   Preceding in an explanatory and conceptual sense: one must understand the state in order fully to understand the individual or the household.

ture and prior to the individual is that the individual, when isolated, is not self-suffing; and therefore he is like a part in relation to the whole. But he who is unable to live in society, or who has no need because he is self-sufficient, must be either a beast or a god: he is no part of a state. A social instinct is implanted in all men by nature; whoever founded the first state was the greatest of benefactors. For man, when perfected, is the best of animals, but, when separated from law and justice, he is the worst of all. The reason is that armed injustice is the most dangerous, and man is equipped at birth with weapons, meant to be used by intelligence and virtue, which he may use for the worst ends. So without virtue,[1] man is the most unholy and the most savage of animals, and the most full of lust and gluttony. But justice is the bond of men in states, for the administration of justice, which is the determination of what is just, is the principle of order in political society.

3

Seeing then that the state is made up of households, before speaking of the state we must speak of the management of the household. The elements of household management correspond to the persons who compose the household, and a complete household consists of slaves and freemen.[2] Now we should begin by examining everything in its simplest elements; and these elements of a household are master and slave, husband and wife, father and children. We have therefore to consider what each of these three relations is and ought to be: I mean the relation of master and servant, the marriage relation (the conjunction of man and wife has no name of its own), and thirdly, the procreative relation (this also has no proper name). And there is another element of a household, the so-called art of getting wealth, which, according to some, is identical with household management, according to others, a principal part of it; the nature of this art will also have to be considered by us.

Let us first speak of the master/slave relationship, thinking about the needs of practical life and also seeking to attain some better theory of their relation than exists at present. For some people think that the rule of a master is a science, and that the management of a household, the mastership of slaves, and the political and royal rule are all the same, as I was saying earlier. Others affirm that the rule of a master over slaves is contrary to nature, and that the distinction between slave and freeman exists by law only, and not by nature; and, because it is an interference with nature, it is therefore unjust.

4

Property is a part of the household, and the art of acquiring property is a part of the art of managing the household; for no man can live well, or indeed live at all, unless he be provided with the necessities of life. In all specialized arts, workers must have their own proper instruments for the accomplishment of their work; and so it is in the management of a household. Now instruments are of various sorts; some are living, others lifeless. The rudder is a lifeless instrument for the pilot of a ship, but his look-out man is a living instrument—in every art, a servant is a kind of instrument. Each piece of property is an instrument for maintenance of some sort of life-purpose; one's property as a whole is the aggregate of such instruments. In the arrangement of the family, a slave is a living possession, and the slave is an instrument which takes precedence of all other instruments. For if every instrument could accomplish its own work, obeying or anticipating the will of others, like the statues of Daedalus,[3] or the tripods of Hephaestus,[4] which, says the poet, "of their own accord entered the assembly of the Gods";[5] if, in like manner, the shuttle would weave and the plectrum touch the lyre without a hand to guide them, chief workmen would not need servants, nor masters slaves.

Here, however, another distinction must be drawn; the instruments commonly so called are instruments of production, while a possession is an instrument of action. The shuttle, for example (an instrument of production), is

---

1   *virtue*   This word is often used to translate the Greek word *aretē*, which appears frequently in Aristotle and is very important in his thought. Many commentators note that "virtue" is a somewhat misleading translation for Aristotle's notion, suggesting exclusively *moral* goodness, whereas, for Aristotle, *aretē* is a characteristic that makes anything a good one of its kind; thus the *aretē* of a knife is sharpness, of a racehorse speed. Other translations include "goodness," "merit" and, especially "excellence."

2   *slaves and freeman*   Aristotle speaks of the household slaves as part of the household.

3   *statues of Daedalus*   Daedalus, in Greek mythology, was the craftsman who built wings for his son Icarus. It was also said that he built statues that could walk, talk, see, and so on.

4   *Hephaestus*   Greek god of technology and artisan of the gods.

5   *"of their own accord ... Gods"*   Homer, *Iliad* 18, 376. The ancient Greek tripod was a three-legged altar.

not itself used; but something else is made by it; whereas a garment or a bed (instruments of action) has use, but not for production of something else. Because production and action are different in kind, and both require instruments, the instruments which they employ must likewise differ in kind. But life is action and not production, and therefore the slave is an instrument of action.

We speak of a possession as a *part*. A part is not only a part of something else, but wholly belongs to it; and this is also true of a possession. The master is only the master of the slave; he does not belong to him, whereas the slave is not only the slave of his master, but wholly belongs to him. Hence we see what is the nature and position of a slave; he who is by nature not his own but another's man, is by nature a slave; and he may be said to be another's man who, being a human being, is also a possession. And a possession may be defined as an instrument of action, separable from the possessor.

5

But is there anyone thus intended by nature to be a slave, and for whom such a condition is advantageous and right, or, on the contrary, is all slavery a violation of nature?

There is no difficulty in answering this question, on grounds both of reason and of fact. For that some should rule and others be ruled is a thing not only necessary, but advantageous. From the hour of their birth some are marked out for subjection, others for rule.

There are many kinds both of rulers and subjects; and rule is better when exercised over better subjects—for example, to rule over men is better than to rule over wild beasts; for "a work" (understood as the product of one man's being ruler and another's being ruled) is better which is executed by better workmen. For in all things which form a composite whole and which are made up of parts, whether continuous or discrete, there is this distinction between the ruling and the subject element. Such a duality exists in living creatures, but not in them only; it originates in the constitution of the universe; there is a ruling principle even in things which have no life, as in a musical mode.

But we are wandering from the subject. We will therefore restrict ourselves to the living creature, which, in the first place, consists of soul and body: and of these two, the one is by nature the ruler, and the other the subject. We must look for the intentions of nature in things which re-

tain their nature, and not in things which are corrupted. And therefore we must study the man who is in the most perfect state both of body and soul, for in him we shall see the true relation of the two; although in bad or corrupted natures the body will often appear to rule over the soul, because they are in an evil and unnatural condition. At all events we may firstly observe in living creatures two kinds of rule: similar to that exercised by a master over his slaves, (a despotical rule), the other similar to that exercised by a statesman over his fellow citizens (a constitutional rule). The soul rules the body with a despotical rule, whereas the intellect rules the appetites with a constitutional and royal rule. And it is clear that the rule of the soul over the body, and of the mind and the rational element over the passionate, is natural and expedient (whereas despotical rule when ruler and ruled are equal is always hurtful). The same holds true of animals in relation to men; for tame animals have a better nature than wild ones, and all tame animals are better off when they are ruled by man; for then they are preserved. Again, the male is by nature superior, and the female inferior; and the one rules, and the other is ruled; this principle, of necessity, extends to all mankind.

Where then there a difference between people analogous to that between soul and body, or between men and animals—where it is the business of one sort of person to use his body, and can do nothing better, that lower sort are by nature slaves, and it is better for them, as for all inferiors, that they be under the rule of a master. For a person who can be, and therefore is, another's property—who participates in rationality enough to recognize but not to exercise it—is a slave by nature. The lower animals cannot even recognize rationality; they obey their instincts. And indeed the use made of slaves and of tame animals is not very different; for both minister to the needs of life with their bodies.

Nature would like to distinguish between the bodies of freemen and slaves, making the one strong for servile labor, the other upright—useless for such menial services, but useful for political life in the arts both of war and peace. But the opposite often happens—that some natural slaves have the souls and others have the bodies of freemen. And doubtless if men differed from one another in the mere forms of their bodies as much as the statues of the Gods do from men, everyone would acknowledge that the inferior class should be slaves of the superior. And if this is true of the body, it is even more just that a similar distinction should exist in the soul. But the beauty of the body is seen, whereas the beauty of the soul is not seen. It is clear, then, that some men are

1254b

1255a

by nature free, and others slaves, and that for these latter slavery is both expedient and right.

6

But it may easily be seen that opposite view has something to be said for it. For the words "slavery" and "slave" are used in two senses. There is a slave or slavery *by law* as well as *by nature*. The law of which I speak is convention by which whatever is taken in war is supposed to belong to the victors. But many jurists protest against this supposed right, as they would against an orator who brought forward an unconstitutional measure: they detest the notion that, because one man has the power of doing violence and is superior in brute strength, another should be his slave and subject. Even among philosophers there is a difference of opinion.

The origin of the dispute, and what makes the views invade each other's territory, is as follows: in some sense virtue, when furnished with means, actually has the greatest power of exercising force; and as superior power is only found where there is superior excellence of some kind, power seems to imply virtue. The dispute here is simply one about justice, due to the identification by one party of justice with good will,[1] but by the other party with the rule of the stronger. If these views are thus set out separately, neither has any force when compared with this third view: that the superior *in virtue* ought to rule, or be master.

Others, however, believing that they are simply relying on a principle of justice, assume that slavery in accordance with the custom of war is justified by law, for law and custom are a sort of justice. But they contradict themselves: for what if the cause of the war be unjust? And again, no one would ever say that a person really is a slave who is unworthy to be a slave. Were this the case, men of the highest rank would be slaves and the children of slaves if they or their parents chance to have been taken captive and sold. For this reason, Greeks do not like to call Greeks slaves, but confine the term to barbarians. Yet, in using this language, they really mean the natural slave of whom we spoke at first; for it must be admitted that some are slaves everywhere, others nowhere. The same principle applies to nobility. Greeks regard themselves as noble everywhere, and not only in their own country, but they deem the barbarians noble only when at home, thereby implying that there are two sorts of nobility and freedom, the one absolute, the other relative. In Theodectes's play,[2] Helen says, "Who would presume to call me servant who am on both sides sprung from the stem of the Gods?" What does this mean but that they distinguish freedom and slavery, noble and humble birth, by the two principles of good and evil? They think that as men and animals beget men and animals, so from good men a good man springs. But this is what nature, though she may intend it, cannot always accomplish.

We see then that there is some foundation for this point of view, and that *all* are not either slaves by nature or freemen by nature; but clearly, also, there is in *some* cases a marked distinction between the two classes, rendering it expedient and right for the one to be slaves and the others to be masters: the one practicing obedience, the others exercising the authority and lordship which nature intended them to have. The abuse of this authority is injurious to both; for the interests of part and whole, of body and soul, are the same, and the slave is a part of the master, a living but separated part of his body. Hence, where the relation of master and slave between them is natural they are friends and have a common interest, but where it rests merely on law and force the reverse is true.

7

The previous remarks are quite enough to show that the rule of a master is not a constitutional rule, like that of a statesman, and that all the different kinds of rule are not, as some affirm, the same. For there is one rule exercised over subjects who are by nature free, another over subjects who are by nature slaves. The rule of a household is a monarchy, for every house is under one head: whereas constitutional rule is a government of freemen and equals. The master is so-called not because he has special knowledge, but because he is of a certain character, and the same applies to the slave and the freeman.

Still there may be a body of knowledge appropriate for a master and one for a slave. Slave-knowledge would be such as taught by a man from Syracuse, who made money by instructing slaves in their ordinary duties. And such a knowledge may be extended to include cookery and similar menial arts. For some duties are more necessary, and others

---

1 *good will* Mutual goodwill, which is held to be incompatible with the relation of master and slave.

2 *Theodectes's play* Theodectes was a mid-fourth-century Greek orator and tragic poet. Only fragments of his work quoted by others survive—including this one from his play *Helena*.

of more honorable; as the proverb says, "slave may go before
slave, and master before master." But all such branches of
knowledge are servile. There is likewise a body of knowledge for the master, which teaches how to use slaves; for the
master as such is not concerned with acquiring slaves, but
rather with using them. Yet this knowledge not anything
great or wonderful; for the master need only know how to
give orders that the slave must know how to execute. Hence
those who are in a position which places them above toil
have stewards who attend to their households while they
occupy themselves with philosophy or with politics. But the
art of acquiring slaves, I mean of justly acquiring them, differs both from the art of the master and the art of the slave,
being a species of hunting or war. Enough of the distinction
between master and slave.

8

Let us now inquire into property generally, and into the art
of getting wealth, in accordance with our usual method,[1]
for a slave has been shown to be a part of property. The
first question is whether the art of getting wealth is the
same with the art of managing a household or a part of
it, or instrumental to it; and if instrumental, whether in
the way that the art of making shuttles is instrumental to
the art of weaving, or in the way that the casting of bronze
is instrumental to the art of the statuary, for they are not
instrumental in the same way: but one provides tools and
the other material (by "material" I mean the stuff out of
which something is made; thus wool is the material of the
weaver, bronze of the statuary).

Now it is easy to see that the art of household management is not identical with the art of getting wealth, for
the one uses the material which the other provides: the art
which uses household goods is precisely household management. There is, however, a doubt whether the art of getting
wealth is a part of household management or a distinct
art. Since someone engaged in acquisition has to consider
where wealth and property can be procured; and since there
are many sorts of property and riches, then we should first
ask whether farming and the care and provision of food in
general are parts of the art of wealth-getting art or distinct
arts. Again, there are many sorts of food, and therefore there
are many kinds of lives both animals and men; they must

all have food, and the differences in their food have made
differences in their ways of life. Some animals are gregarious, others are solitary; they live in the way which is best
adapted to sustain them, depending on whether as they are
carnivorous or herbivorous or omnivorous: and their habits
are determined for them by nature to facilitate their obtaining the food of their choice with greater facility. But, as
different species have different tastes, the same things are
not naturally pleasant to all of them; and therefore the lives
of carnivorous or herbivorous animals further differ among
themselves. In the lives of men too there is a great difference. The laziest are shepherds, who lead an idle life, and
get their subsistence without trouble from tame animals.
Their flocks have to wander from place to place in search of
pasture, so they are compelled to follow them, cultivating a
sort of living farm. Others support themselves by hunting;
and there are different kinds of hunters: some, for example,
are brigands, others, who dwell near lakes or marshes or rivers or a sea in which there are fish, are fishermen; and others
live by the pursuit of birds or wild animals. Most humans,
however, obtain a livelihood from cultivating plants.

These different ways of life, then, involving dependence
on one's own labor rather than on exchange and retail trade,
are the shepherd, the farmer, the brigand, the fisherman,
the hunter. Some gain a comfortable maintenance out of
two jobs, making up the deficiencies of one of them with
another: thus the life of a shepherd may be combined with
that of a brigand, the life of a farmer with that of a hunter.
Other modes of life are similarly combined in any way
which the needs of men may require.

Property, in the sense of a bare livelihood, seems to be
given by nature herself to all, both when they are first born,
and when they are grown up. For some animals bring forth,
together with their offspring, enough food to last until the
young are able to supply themselves—for example, those
that bear grubs or eggs; and the live-bearing animals have up
to a certain time a supply of food for their young in themselves, which is called milk. Similarly, we may conclude that
once the young have passed this initial stage, plants exist for
nourishing them, and that the other animals exist for the
sake of man—domestic animals for work and food, wild
animals (if not all of them, at least most) for providing food,
clothing and various tools. Now if nature makes nothing
incomplete, and nothing in vain, the inference must be that
she has made all animals for the sake of man. And so, in one
point of view, the art of war is a natural art of acquisition,
for the art of acquisition includes hunting, an art which we

---

1 *our usual method* That is, examining the whole by consideration
   of its parts.

25 ought to practice against wild beasts, and against men who, though intended by nature to be governed, will not submit; for war of such a kind is naturally just.

There is one form of the art of acquisition, then, which by nature is a part household management, in that the manager must either have or get storable necessities of life, 30 and thus useful for the family or state community. They are the elements of true riches; for the amount of property which is needed for a good life is not unlimited, although Solon[1] in one of his poems says "No bound to riches has been fixed for man." But there is a boundary fixed here, just as there is in the other arts; for the instruments of any art 35 are never unlimited, either in number or size, and riches may be defined as a number of instruments to be used in a household or in a state. And so we see that there is a natural art of acquisition practiced by managers of households and by statesmen, and why this is the case.

9

40 There is another variety of the art of acquisition which is commonly and rightly called an art of wealth-getting, and 1257a has in fact suggested the notion that riches and property have no limit. Being closely connected with the preceding form, it is often identified with it. But though they are not very different, neither are they the same. The form already described is given by nature, the second is gained by experi- 5 ence and skill.

Let us begin our discussion of the question with the following considerations:

There are two uses of everything which we possess: both belong to the thing as such, but not in the same manner. One is the *proper*, and the other the *secondary* use of it. For example, a shoe is used to wear, and is used for exchange; 10 both are uses of the shoe. A person who exchanges a shoe for money or food with someone who wants the shoe does indeed use the shoe as a shoe, but this is not its proper or primary purpose, for a shoe is not made to be an object of barter. The same may be said of all possessions, for the art 15 of exchange extends to all of them.

Exchange arises at first from what is natural, from the circumstance that some have too little, others too much. Hence we may infer that retail trade is not a natural part of the art of getting wealth; had it been so, men would have ceased to exchange when they had enough. In the first com-

munity—the family—this art is obviously of no use, but it 20 begins to be useful when the scope of association increased. For the members of the family originally had all things in common; later, when the family divided into parts, the parts shared in many things, and different parts in differ- ent things, which they had to give in exchange for what they wanted. This kind of barter is still practiced among barbarian tribes who exchange with one another the neces- 25 saries of life and nothing more—giving wine, for example, in exchange for grain, and the like. This sort of barter is not part of the wealth-getting art and is not contrary to nature, but is needed for the satisfaction of men's natural wants. 30

The other or more complex form of exchange grew, as might have been expected, out of the simpler. When the in- habitants of one country became more dependent on those of another, and they imported what they needed and export- ed what they had too much of, money necessarily came into use. For the various necessaries of life are not easily carried about, and hence men agreed to employ in their dealings 35 with each other something which was intrinsically useful and easily applicable to the purposes of life, for example, iron, silver, and the like. The value of this was at first measured simply by size and weight, but in time the metal was stamped to indicate its value, to save the trouble of weighing. 40

Once the use of money had been discovered, the 1257b other art of wealth getting, retail trade, grew out of the barter of necessary articles. This was at first probably a simple matter, but became more complicated as soon as men learned by experience where and how to make the greatest profit. The result is that it is generally thought 5 that wealth-getting is chiefly concerned with accumulating money, and is the art of finding the sources from which it can be obtained. Indeed, many people think that to be rich is only to have a great quantity of money, because the arts of getting wealth and retail trade are concerned with 10 money. Others maintain that money is a mere sham, not something that is natural thing, but merely conventional; because, if the users substitute another commodity for it, it becomes worthless; and because it is not useful as a means to any of the necessities of life; indeed, he who is rich in coin may often lack necessary food. But how could something be wealth if a man could have it in great 15 abundance and yet perish with hunger, like Midas[2] in the

---

1 *Solon* Athenian lawmaker and poet (died 559 BCE).

2 *Midas* In Greek mythology, the king whose wish that everything he touched be turned to gold was granted by Dionysus; disaster resulted when his food turned to gold at his touch.

fable, whose insatiable prayer turned everything that was set before him into gold?

So some people seek a better notion of riches, and of the art of getting wealth—better than the mere acquisition of money—and they are right. For natural riches and the natural art of wealth-getting are a different thing; in their true form they are part of the management of a household; whereas retail trade is the art of producing wealth, not in every way, but by exchange. And it is associated with making money; for money is the unit and measure of exchange.

There is no upper limit to the riches which may spring from this art of wealth getting. As in the art of medicine there is no limit to the pursuit of health, and as in the other arts there is no limit to the pursuit of their various ends, (for they aim at accomplishing their ends to the uttermost, though there is a limit to the means, for the end is always the limit), so, too, there is no upper limit to the spurious riches aimed at by this art of wealth-getting.

But that kind of art of wealth-getting which consists in household management, on the other hand, has a limit; the unlimited acquisition of wealth is not its business. And, therefore, from one point of view, all riches must have a limit; nevertheless, as a matter of fact, we find the opposite to be the case; for all seekers of wealth try to increase their hoard of money without limit. The source of the confusion is the near connection between the two kinds of wealth-getting; in either, the instrument is the same, although the use is different, and so they pass into one another; for each is a use of the same property, but with a difference: accumulation for its own sake is the end in the one case, but there is a further end in the other. Hence some persons are led to believe that getting wealth is the object of household management, and the whole idea of their lives is that they ought either to increase their money without limit, or at any rate not to lose it. The origin of this disposition in men is that they are intent upon living only, and not upon living well; and, as their desires are unlimited they also desire that the means of gratifying them should be without limit. Even those who do aim at a good life seek the means of obtaining bodily pleasures; and, since the enjoyment of these appears to depend on property, they are absorbed with getting wealth: and so there arises the second species of wealth-getting. For, as their enjoyment is in excess, they seek an art which produces the excess of enjoyment; and, if they are not able to supply their pleasures by the art of getting wealth, they try other arts, using in turn every faculty in a manner contrary to nature. The quality of courage,

for example, is not intended to make wealth, but to inspire confidence; neither is this the aim of the general's or of the physician's art; but the one aims at victory and the other at health. Nevertheless, some men turn every quality or art into a means of getting wealth; this they conceive to be the end, and to the promotion of the end they think all things must contribute.

Thus, then, we have considered the unnecessary art of wealth-getting, and why men want it; and also the necessary art of wealth-getting, which we have seen to be different from the other, and to be a natural part of the art of managing a household, concerned with the provision of food. This second kind is not, however, unlimited like the former kind; it has a limit.

10

So now we have found the answer to our original question: Is the art of getting wealth the business of the manager of a household and of the statesman, or is it not their business, but merely presupposed by them? For as the art of statesmanship does not make men, but takes them from nature and uses them, so too nature provides the household with earth or sea or the like as a source of food. This is the point at which the duty of the manager of a household begins: he has to order the things which nature supplies; he may be compared to the weaver who does not make wool, but uses it, and has to know what sort of wool is good and serviceable or bad and unserviceable. Were this otherwise, it would be difficult to see why the art of getting wealth is a part of the management of a household but the art of medicine is not; for surely the members of a household must have health just as they must have life or any other necessity. The answer is that as from one point of view the master of the house and the ruler of the state have to be concerned about health, from another point of view it is not their concern but the physician's; so in one way the art of household management is concerned with wealth, but in another way it is not their concern, but a servant's.

But, strictly speaking, as I have already said, the means of life must be provided beforehand by nature; for the business of nature is to furnish food to whatever is born into the world; this is shown by the fact that newly-born animals are nourished by what remains from their origin. So the art of getting wealth from of plants and animals is always natural.

There are two sorts of wealth-getting, as I have said; one is a part of household management, the other is retail trade:

40 the former necessary and honorable, while the latter, con-
1258b sisting in exchange, is justly censured; for it is unnatural,
as a mode by which men gain from one another. The most
hated sort, and with the greatest reason, is usury, which
makes a gain out of money itself, and not from its natural
object. For money was intended to be used in exchange,
but not to increase by accumulating interest. And originally
5 *tokos*[1] meant "offspring"; interest is, so to speak, the breeding of money, the birth of money from money, because the
offspring resembles the parent. Of all methods of getting
wealth this is the most unnatural.

II

Enough has been said about the theory of wealth-getting;
10 we will now proceed to the practical side. Theoretical discussion may be carried on at length in philosophy, but practice
in particular circumstances is a different matter.

The basic practical modes of acquisition are: first, the
knowledge of livestock—which are most profitable, and
where and how—as, for example, what sort of horses or
sheep or oxen or any other animals are most likely to give
15 a return. A man ought to know which of these pay better
than others, and which pay best in particular places, for
some do better in one place and some in another. Secondly,
farming, which may be either tillage or planting, and the
keeping of bees and of fish, or fowl, or of any animals which
20 may be useful to man. These are the divisions of the true art
of wealth-getting in its pure, original form.

Of the next form, exchange, the first and most important division is commerce (of which there are three
kinds—the provision of a ship, the conveyance of goods,
offering for sale—these again differing as they are safer or
25 more profitable), the second is usury, the third, service for
hire—of this, one kind is employed in the mechanical arts,[2]
the other in unskilled and bodily labor.

There is still a third sort of wealth-getting intermediate
between the second and the first or natural mode; this one is
partly natural, but is also concerned with exchange. It com-
30 prises the industries that make their profit from the earth,
and from things growing from the earth which, although
they bear no fruit, are nevertheless profitable; for example,
the cutting of timber and mining.[3] The art of mining, by

which minerals are obtained, itself has many branches, for
there are various kinds of things dug out of the earth. Of
the several divisions of wealth-getting I speak generally; a
minute consideration of them might be useful in practice, 35
but it would be tiresome to dwell upon them at greater
length now.

Those occupations are most truly arts in which there
is the least element of chance; the worst ones are those in
which the body is most damaged; the most servile in which
there is the greatest use of the body; and the most ignoble
in which there is the least need of excellence.

Works have been written upon these subjects by various 40
persons; for example, by Chares the Parian, and Apollodorus the Lemnian, who have treated of tillage and planting, 1259a
while others have treated of other branches; anyone interested in such matters may refer to their writings. It would
be well also to collect the scattered stories of the ways in
which individuals have succeeded in amassing a fortune; 5
for all this is useful to persons who value the art of getting
wealth. There is the anecdote of Thales the Milesian[4] and
his financial scheme, which involves a principle of universal
application, but is attributed particularly to him because
of his reputation for wisdom. He was reproached for his
poverty, which was taken to show that philosophy was of no 10
use. According to the story, because of his skill in astrology,
he knew when it was still winter that there would be a great
harvest of olives in the coming year; so, having a little money,
he gave deposits for the use of all the olive-presses in Chios
and Miletus, which he hired at a low price because no one
bid against him. When the harvest-time came, and many
presses were suddenly needed all at once, he rented them 15
out at any rate he pleased, and made a quantity of money.
Thus he showed the world that philosophers can easily be
rich if they like, but that their ambition is of another sort.
The story is supposed to illustrate his great wisdom, but, as
I was saying, his scheme for getting wealth is of universal 20
application, and is nothing but the creation of a monopoly.
It is an art often practiced by cities when they are need to
make money; they create a monopoly of provisions.

There was a man of Sicily, who, having money deposited with him, bought up all the iron from the iron mines;
afterwards, when the merchants from their various markets 25

---

1   *tokos*   Greek: interest.
2   *mechanical arts*   Skills involving mechanical assistance, such as
    weaving and pottery-making.
3   *timber and mining*   It may be that Aristotle counts these oc-
    cupations as midway between farming and commerce because

the products of mining and lumbering have to be processed and
exchanged before they are sold.
4   *Thales the Milesian*   Early Greek philosopher (c. 620–c. 546
    BCE). Aristotle, the main source of our information about him,
    identifies Thales as the first natural philosopher/scientist.

came to buy, he was the only seller, and without increasing the usual price very much he gained 200 per cent. When Dionysius[1] heard about this, he told the man that he must leave Syracuse (though he could take his money with him), for he thought that his own interests would be hurt by the money-making scheme this man had discovered. The man made the same discovery as Thales; they both contrived to create a monopoly for themselves. And statesmen as well ought to know these things; for a state often needs money and money-making schemes as much as a household, or even more; thus some politicians devote themselves entirely to finance.

12

As we said earlier, there are three parts to household management: one is the rule of a master over slaves, which has been discussed already, another of a father, and the third of a husband. Husbands and fathers rule over wife and children; both of whom are free people. But the character of the rule differs: over his children, it is a royal rule, but over his wife, it is a constitutional rule.[2] For although there may be exceptions to the order of nature, the male is by nature more suited for command than the female, just as the elder and full-grown is superior to the younger and more immature. But in most constitutional states the citizens take turns being rulers and ruled, for the idea of a constitutional state implies that the natures of the citizens are equal, and do not differ at all. Nevertheless, when one rules and the other is ruled we endeavor to the saying of Amasis about his foot-pan.[3] The relation of the male to the female is of this kind, but there the inequality is permanent. The rule of a father over his children is royal, for he rules by virtue both of love and of the respect due to age, exercising a kind of royal power. And therefore Homer has appropriately called Zeus "father of Gods and men," because he is the king of them all. For a king is the natural superior of his subjects,

---

1 *Dionysius* Dionysius I ruled 405–367 BCE, and his son Dionysius II ruled during two periods thereafter.

2 *royal rule ... constitutional rule* A royal rule is like the absolute power of a monarch over his subjects; a constitutional rule is like that of a statesman over the citizens of a free state.

3 *saying of Amasis ... foot-pan* The story, told by Herodotus, is this: when Amasis became king of Egypt, he was looked down upon because of his humble origins; so he had a golden footpan melted down and made into a statue of a god. When the statue was venerated, he pointed out that this was a parable of his situation: his status as a king deserved respect, whatever his origins.

but he should be of the same stock as they are; and such is the relation of elder and younger, of father and son.

13

So it is clear that household management is concerned more about human beings than with the acquisition of inanimate things, and more about human excellence than about the excellence of property which we call wealth; and more about the excellence pertaining to freemen than that pertaining to slaves.

A question may indeed be raised, whether there is any excellence at all in a slave beyond and higher than merely instrumental and ministerial qualities—whether he can have the virtues of temperance, courage, justice, and the like; or whether slaves possess only bodily and servile qualities. And, whichever way we answer the question, a difficulty arises; for, if they have virtue, how are they different from freemen? On the other hand, since they are men with a share in reason, it seems absurd to say that they have no virtue. A similar question may be raised about women and children, whether they too have virtues: ought a woman to be temperate and brave and just, and is a child to be called temperate, and intemperate, or not? So in general we may ask about the natural ruler, and the natural subject, whether they have the same or different virtues. For if a noble nature is equally required in both, why should one of them always rule, and the other always be ruled? Nor can we say that this is a question of degree, for the difference between ruler and subject is a difference of kind, which the difference of more and less never is. Yet how strange is the supposition that the one ought, and that the other ought not, to have virtue! For if the ruler is intemperate and unjust, how can he rule well? If the subject, how can he obey well? If he be licentious and cowardly, he will certainly not do his duty.

It is evident, therefore, that both of them must have a share of virtue, but varying as natural subjects also vary among themselves. Here the very constitution of the soul has shown us the way; in it one part naturally rules, and the other is subject. Similarly, the virtue of the ruler, we maintain, is different from that of the subject; the ruler's virtue is the virtue of the rational part of the soul, and the subject's of the irrational part. Now, it is obvious that the same principle applies generally, and therefore almost all things rule and are ruled according to nature. But the kind of rule differs; the freeman rules over the slave in a different manner from that in which the male rules over the female, or the man over the child; although the parts of the soul are present in all of them, they are present in different degrees. For the slave has no deliberative faculty at all; the woman has, but it lacks authority, and the child has, but it is immature. So it must necessarily be supposed to be with moral virtue also; all should share in it, but only in such manner and degree as is required by each for the fulfillment of his duty. Hence the ruler ought to have moral virtue in perfection, for his function is essentially that of a master-craftsman, and rationality is such a craftsman. His subjects, on the other hand, require only that quantity of virtue which is proper to each of them. Clearly, then, moral virtue belongs to all of them; but the temperance of a man and of a woman, or the courage and justice of a man and of a woman, are not, as Socrates maintained, the same;[1] the courage of a man is shown in commanding, of a woman in obeying. And this holds of all other virtues, as will be more clearly seen if we look at them in detail, for those who say generally that virtue consists in a good disposition of the soul, or in doing rightly, or the like, only deceive themselves. A far better way to talk than to give definitions like this is to enumerate the virtues, as Gorgias[2] does. All classes must be deemed to have their special attributes; as the poet says of women, "Silence is a woman's glory,"[3] but this is not equally the glory of man. The child is imperfect, and therefore obviously his virtue is not relative to himself alone, but to the perfect man and to his teacher; similarly the virtue of the slave is relative to the ends of his master. Now we determined that a slave is useful for the wants of life, and therefore he will obviously require only so much virtue as will prevent him from failing in his duty through cowardice or lack of self-control.

Someone might ask whether, if what we are saying is true, virtue would not be required also in the artisans, for they often fail in their work through the lack of self control. But is there not a great difference in the two cases? For the slave shares in his master's life; the artisan is less closely connected with him, and only attains excellence in proportion as he becomes a slave. The meaner sort of mechanic[4] has a special and separate slavery; and whereas the slave exists by nature, not so the shoemaker or other artisan.

It is manifest, then, that the master ought to be the source of such excellence in the slave, and not a mere pos-sessor of the art of mastership which trains the slave in his duties. So they are mistaken who forbid us to converse with slaves and say that we should employ command only, for slaves stand even more in need of admonition than children.

So much for this subject. The relations of husband and wife, parent and child, their various virtues, what is good in their relations with one another, and what is evil, and how we may pursue the good and escape the evil, will have to be discussed when we speak of the different forms of government.

Every family is a part of a state, and these relationships are the parts of a family, and the virtue of the part must be considered with reference to the virtue of the whole; thus women and children must be educated with an eye to the constitution[5] of the state, if the virtues of either of them are supposed to make any difference in the virtues of the state. And they must make a difference: for the children grow up to be citizens, and half the free persons in a state are women.

Of these matters, enough has been said; of what remains, let us speak at another time. Regarding, then, our present inquiry as complete, we will make a new beginning, first examining the various theories of the perfect state.

Book 2

I

Our purpose is to consider what form of political community is best of all for those who are most able to realize their ideal of life. We must therefore examine not only constitutions that actually exist in well-governed states, but also any theoretical forms which are held in esteem; this way, what is good and useful may be brought to light. No one should suppose that in looking for good ideas beyond existing constitutions we are eager to show off sophisticated ingenuity at any cost; we only undertake this inquiry because all the constitutions with which we are acquainted are faulty.

We will begin with the natural beginning of the subject. Three alternatives are conceivable: The members of a state must either have (1) all things or (2) nothing in common,

---

1   *Socrates maintained the same*   Plato, *Meno*, 72a–73c.
2   *Gorgias*   Plato, *Meno*, 71e, 72a.
3   *Silence is a woman's glory*   Sophocles, *Ajax*, 293.
4   *mechanic*   Non-agricultural craft worker.

---

5   *constitution*   Aristotle uses this word often to mean the general make-up and organization of a state. He also speaks of a particular *kind* of state as "constitutional" rule (otherwise translated as "polity"). It should be clear in context which sense of the word is meant.

or (3) some things in common and some not. It is clearly impossible that they should have nothing in common, for the state is a community, and its members must at any rate share a common location. As a state has a single locality, so citizens of that state share a location there. But should a well ordered state have all things, as far as may be, in common, or some only and not others? For the citizens might conceivably have wives and children and property in common, as Socrates proposes in the Republic of Plato.[1] Which is better, this proposal or our present condition?

2

There are many difficulties in the system in which women are in common to all. And the purpose which Socrates takes such an institution to serve—that the greater the unity of the state the better—is evidently not established by his arguments. Further, as a means to the end which he ascribes to the state, the scheme, taken literally, is impracticable, and how we are to interpret it is nowhere precisely stated. Is it not obvious that a state may at length attain such a degree of unity as to be no longer a state? The nature of a state is to be a plurality, and in tending to greater unity, from being a state, it becomes a household, and from being a household, an individual; for the household may be said to be more of a unity than the state, and the individual than the household. So that we ought not to attain this greatest unity even if we could, for it would be the destruction of the state.

Again, a state is not made up only of a number of many men, but of different kinds of men; for similar people do not constitute a state. It is not like a military alliance. The aim of an alliance is mutual protection, ant the usefulness of an alliance for this purpose depends entirely upon its quantity, even where there is no difference of kind among its members, just as a large weight tips the balance more than a small. (In like manner, a state differs from a tribe, assuming that the tribe is not organized in scattered villages, but lives an Arcadian sort of life.[2]) But the elements out of which a real unity is to be formed must differ in kind.

Therefore the principle of compensation,[3] as I have already remarked in the *Ethics*, is the salvation of states. Even among freemen and equals this is a principle which must be maintained, for they cannot all rule together, but must change at the end of a year or some other period of time or in some order of succession. The result is that on this plan they all govern; just as if shoemakers and carpenters were to exchange their occupations, and the same persons did not always continue being shoemakers and carpenters. In politics as in these crafts, it might be better that the same persons remained in their positions as long as possible. But this is sometimes not practical because of the natural equality of the citizens; additionally, justice is served when all share in the government (whether governing is a good thing or bad). So we must find an approximation to this: equals should in turn retire from office and thus should be treated equally. Thus one person rules, and others are ruled, in turn, as if they had become different people. In addition, there is a difference between rulers, in the variety of offices held.

Hence it is evident that a state is not by nature a unity in that sense which some persons affirm; and what they call the greatest good of states is in reality their destruction; but surely the good of things must be that which preserves them. And from another point of view, this extreme unification of the state is clearly not good; for a family is more self-suffing than an individual, and a city than a family, and a city only comes into being when the community is large enough to be self-suffing. If then self-sufficiency is to be desired, the lesser degree of unity is more desirable than the greater.

3

But, even supposing that it is best for the community to have the greatest degree of unity, this unity is by no means proved to be achieved by "all men saying 'mine' and 'not mine' at the same instant of time," which, according to Socrates, is the sign of perfect unity in a state.[4] For the word "all" is ambiguous. If the meaning be that every individual says "mine" and "not mine" at the same time, then perhaps the result at which Socrates aims may be in some degree accomplished; each man will call the same person his own

---

1 *Republic of Plato* Books 7 and 8.
2 *Arcadian sort of life* Commentators are unsure what Aristotle intends here. Perhaps the idea is that the Arcadian confederacy was at most a military alliance, not a genuine state.

3 *principle of compensation* The principle that elements in a state must exist in a reciprocal relationship—giving and receiving equivalently. Aristotle refers to his discussion of this in the *Nicomachean Ethics*, 1132b33–1133a5.
4 *unity in a state* Plato, *Republic*, 462 C.

son and the same person his wife, and so of his property and of all that falls to his lot. This, however, is not the way in which people would speak who had their had their wives and children in common; they would all—collectively—call the wives and children "mine," but they would not each—individually, call them that. In like manner their property would be described as belonging to them, not severally but collectively. There is an obvious fallacy in the term "all": like some other words, "both," "odd," "even," it is ambiguous, and even in abstract argument becomes a source of logical puzzles. That all persons call the same thing mine in the sense in which each does so may be a fine thing, but it is impracticable; or if the words are taken in the other sense, such a unity in no way conduces to harmony.

Another objection to the proposal is this: whatever is common to the greatest number has the least care bestowed upon it. Every one thinks chiefly of his own, hardly at all of the common interest; and only when he is himself concerned as an individual. Among the reasons for this is that everybody is more inclined to neglect the duty which he expects another to fulfill; for this reason, in families many attendants are often less useful than a few. Under this proposal, each citizen will have a thousand sons who will not be his sons individually—instead anybody will be equally the son of anybody, and will therefore be neglected by all alike. Further, upon this principle, everyone will use the word "mine" fractionally of one who is prospering or the reverse—the degree of fractional connection being determined by the total number of citizens. The same will be "so and so's son," and "the son of each of the thousand," (or whatever be the number of the citizens); and even about this he will not be positive; for it is impossible to know who fathered a child, or whether, if one came into existence, it has survived.

Which is better—for each to say "mine" in this way, making a man the same relation to two thousand or ten thousand citizens, or to use the word "mine" in the ordinary and more restricted sense? For usually the person one man calls his own son another man calls his own brother or cousin or kinsman—blood relation or connection by marriage either of himself or of some relation of his—and still another calls his clansman or tribesman; and how much better is it to be the real cousin of somebody than to be a son according to Plato's proposal! Nor is there any way of preventing brothers and children and fathers and mothers from sometimes recognizing one another; for children are born like their parents, and they will necessarily be finding

indications of their relationship to one another. Geographers declare such to be the fact; they say that in part of Upper Libya, where the women are common, nevertheless the children who are born are assigned to their respective fathers on the evidence of their resemblance. And some women, like the females of other animals—for example, mares and cows—have a strong tendency to produce offspring resembling their parents, as was the case with the Pharsalian mare called Honest.[1]

4

There are other evils which it would not be easy for constructors of such a community to guard against: assaults and homicides, voluntary as well as involuntary, quarrels and slanders, all which are most unholy acts when committed against fathers and mothers and near relations, but not equally unholy when there is no relationship. Moreover, these evils are much more likely to occur if the relationship is unknown, and, when they have occurred, the customary penance for them (when people know that it is their relatives who were involved) could not be made. Again, how strange it is that Socrates, after having made the children common, should forbid sexual intercourse between lovers, but should permit love and familiarities between father and son or between brother and brother; nothing could be more unseemly than this, since even without these expressions of it, love of this sort is improper. How strange, too, to forbid intercourse for no other reason than the violence of the pleasure, as though the relationship of father and son or of brothers with one another made no difference.[2]

This community of wives and children seems better suited to the farmer than to the guardian,[3] for if the farmers have wives and children in common, they will be bound to one another by weaker ties, as a subject class should be, and they will remain obedient and not rebel. In a word, such a law would have just the opposite result from the one

---

1 *Pharsalian mare called Honest* The mare was called this (or, in other translations, "Honest Wife," or "Just Return" or "Faithful") because she gave back what she received from the stallion. Aristotle mentions this also in *Historia Animalium*, 56a 12.
2 *forbid intercourse ... no difference* Socrates forbids homosexual intercourse but allows other forms of homosexual lovemaking. Aristotle is worried that under Plato's scheme there would be unintentional homosexual relations between relatives.
3 *better suited ... the guardian* Plato's *Republic* proposes for the ideal state three classes: the guardians (that is, the rulers); the soldiers; and the farmers, craftsmen, and traders.

5 a good law should have, and the intention of Socrates in making these regulations about women and children would defeat itself. For we believe that friendship is the greatest good of states, and it preserves them against revolutions; 10 there is nothing Socrates himself praises so highly, after all, as the unity of the state which he and all the world declare to be created by friendship. But the unity which he commends would be like that of the lovers in the Symposium,[1] who, as Aristophanes says, desire to grow together in the excess of their affection, and from being two to become one, in which case one or both would certainly perish. In 15 a state having women and children common, love will be watery; and the father will certainly not say "my son," or the son "my father." As a little sweet wine mingled with a great deal of water is imperceptible in the mixture, so, in this sort of community, the idea of relationship which is 20 based upon these names will be lost; there is no reason why the so-called father should care about the son, or the son about the father, or brothers about one another. Of the two qualities which chiefly inspire regard and affection—that a thing is your own and that it is your only one—neither can exist in such a state as this.

25 Again, the transfer of children as soon as they are born from the rank of farmers or of artisans to that of guardians, and from the rank of guardians into a lower rank,[2] would be very difficult to arrange in Plato's state; those who transfer these children could not but know whom they are transferring, and to whom. And the previously men- 30 tioned evils—assaults, unlawful loves, homicides, and the like—would happen more often amongst those who are transferred to the lower classes, or who have a place assigned to them among the guardians; for they would no longer call the members of the class they have left brothers, and children, and fathers, and mothers, and would not, therefore, be afraid of committing any crimes by reason of close blood 35 relation.

This concludes our treatment of the idea of having wives and children in common.

5

Next let us consider what should be our arrangements about property: should the citizens of the perfect state have

their possessions in common or not? This question may 40 be discussed separately from the proposals about women and children. Even supposing that the women and children 1263a belong to individuals, according to the custom which is at present universal, may there not be an advantage in having and using possessions in common? Three cases are possible: (1) plots of land are be owned separately, but the produce is held for consumption in a common stock; this is the practice of some nations. Or (2) land is owned and cultivated in 5 common, but the produce is divided among individuals for their private use; this is a form of common property which is said to exist among certain barbarian tribes. Or (3) land and the produce are both common property.

When the farmers are not the owners of the land they cultivate, the case will be different and easier to deal with; but when they own the land they cultivate, the question 10 of ownership will give a world of trouble. If they do not share equally in the work and in the benefits, those who labor much and get little will necessarily complain about those who labor little and receive or consume much. There 15 is always a difficulty in men living together and having all human relations in common, but especially in their having common property. People traveling together are an illustration: they generally disagree over everyday matters and quarrel about any trifle which turns up. So with servants: we are most able to take offense at those with whom we most frequently come into contact in daily life. 20

These are only some of the disadvantages which attend the community of property; the present arrangement, if improved as it might be by good customs and laws, would be far better, and would have the advantages of both systems. In one respect property ought to be common,[3] but, as a 25 general rule it should be private; for, when everyone has a distinct interest, men will not complain about one another, and they will make more progress, because everyone will be attending to his own business. But the moral goodness of people will result in sharing the produce; "Friends," as the proverb says, "will have all things common." Even now 30 there are traces of such a principle, showing that it is not impracticable; in well-ordered states, this practice exists already to a certain extent and may be carried further. There, although every man has his own property, he will put some things at the disposal of his friends, and treat other things as common property. The Spartans, for example, use one 35 another's slaves, and horses, and dogs, as if they were their

---

1   *lovers in the Symposium*   Plato, *Symposium*, 191A, 192C.
2   *transfer of children ... lower rank*   In the *Republic*'s ideal state, each class will be populated by persons most suited for it; thus transfers based on different ability will be necessary.

---

3   *one respect ... common*   With regard to certain uses of produce.

own; and when they lack provisions on a journey, they appropriate what they find in the fields throughout the country. It is clearly better that property should be private,
40 but the use of it common; and the special business of the legislator is to create this benevolent disposition in men. Again, how immeasurably greater is the pleasure, when a
1263b man feels a thing to be his own; for surely the love of self is a feeling implanted by nature and not given in vain, although selfishness is rightly censured; this, however, is not the mere love of self, but the love of self in excess, like the miser's love of money; for all, or almost all, men love money and other
5 such objects to some extent. And further, there is the greatest pleasure in doing a kindness or service to friends or guests or companions—but this can be done only when a man has private property. These advantages are lost by excessive unification of the state. Besides, the practice of two virtues is obviously eliminated: first, temperance in sexual relations
10 (for it is an honorable action to abstain from another's wife for the sake of temperance); secondly, generosity in the matter of property. No one, when men have all things in common, will any longer set an example of generosity or do anything generous; for generosity consists in the use which is made of property.
15 Legislation such as proposed by Socrates may have a specious appearance of benevolence; men readily listen to it, and are easily induced to believe that in some miraculous way everybody will become everybody's friend; its attractiveness is increased when one hears of the evils now
20 existing in states—lawsuits about contracts, convictions for perjury, flatteries of rich men and the like—which are said to arise out of the possession of private property. These evils, however, are due to a very different cause—the wickedness of human nature. Indeed, we see that there is much more quarrelling among those who have all things in common,
25 though there are not many of them when compared with the vast numbers who have private property.
Again, we ought to figure in, not just the evils from which the citizens will be saved, but also the advantages which they will lose. The life which they are to lead appears
30 to be quite impracticable. The error of Socrates must be attributed to the false notion of unity from which he starts. There should be unity, both of the family and of the state, but in some respects only. For there is a point at which a state may attain such a degree of unity as to be no longer a state, or at which, without actually ceasing to exist, it will
35 become an inferior state, like harmony passing into unison, or rhythm which has been reduced to a single beat. The

state, as I was saying, is a plurality which should be united and made into a community by education; and it is strange that the author of a system of education which he thinks will make the state virtuous, should expect to improve his citizens by regulations of this sort, and not by philosophy or 40 by customs and laws, like those which prevail at Sparta and Crete respecting common meals, whereby the legislator has made property common.
Let us remember that we should not disregard the ex- 1264a perience of ages. In the multitude of years these things, if they were good, would certainly not have been unknown; for almost everything has been discovered already, although sometimes things are not organized systematically, and in other cases men do not use the knowledge which they have. Great light would be thrown on this subject if we 5 could see such a form of government in the actual process of construction; for the legislator could not form a state at all without distributing and dividing its constituents into associations for common meals, and into clans and tribes. But all Socrates' suggested legislation does is to forbid agriculture to the guardians, a prohibition which the Spartans 10 try to enforce already.
But, indeed, Socrates has not said, and it is not easy to guess, what the general form of his state would be. The citizens who are not guardians are the majority, and nothing has been determined for them: are the farmers, too, to have 15 their property in common? Or is each individual to have his own? And are the wives and children to be individual or common? If, like the guardians, the farmers are to have all things in common, how are they different from the guardians, and what do they gain by submitting to their government? Indeed, what motive would they have for submission at all, unless the governing class adopted the ingenious 20 policy of the Cretans, who give their slaves the same institutions as their own, but forbid them gymnastic exercises and the possession of arms? If, on the other hand, the situation with respect to marriage and property for the farmers is to be the same as in other states, what will be the form of the community? Must it not contain two states in one, each 25 hostile to the other? Socrates makes the guardians into a mere occupying garrison, while the farmers and artisans and the rest are the real citizens. But given this, the lawsuits and quarrels, and all the evils which Socrates agrees exist in other states, would exist equally among them. He says that because they have such a good education, the citizens 30 would not need many laws, for example laws about the city or about the markets; but then he confines his education to

the guardians. Again, he makes the farmers owners of the property on condition that they pay a tribute.[1] But in that case they are likely to be much more unmanageable and conceited than the Helots, or Penestae,[2] or slaves in general. And Socrates has not said whether communal wives and property would be necessary for the lower class as well as the higher class; nor has he answered related questions about the nature of the education, the form of government, or the laws pertaining to the lower class. And it is not easy to answer these questions, but how they are answered would be of great importance if the common life of the guardians is to be maintained.

Again, if Socrates makes the women communal and retains private property, the men will see to the fields, but who will see to the house? And who will do so if the farmers have both their property and their wives in common? Once more: it is absurd to argue, from the analogy of the animals, that men and women should follow the same pursuits, for animals do not have to manage a household.

The government, too, as constituted by Socrates, contains elements of danger; for in his system, there is a permanent ruling class. And if this is often a cause of disturbance among the lower classes, how much more among high-spirited warriors? But evidently he must make the rulers come from a single group, for the gold which the God mingles in the souls of men is not at one time given to one, at another time to another, but always to the same: as he says, "God mingles gold in some, and silver in others, from their very birth; but brass and iron in those who are meant to be artisans and farmers."[3] Again, he deprives the guardians even of happiness, and says that the legislator ought to make the whole state happy. But the whole cannot be happy unless most, or all, or some of its parts enjoy happiness. In this respect happiness is not like the characteristic of evenness in numbers, which may exist only in the whole, but in neither of the parts; not so happiness. And if the guardians

1 *tribute* A portion of their produce, paid to the guardians.
2 *Helots, or Penestae* Helots were serfs in Sparta; Penestae were serfs in Thessaly.
3 *God mingles ... farmers* This passage refers to Plato's "noble lie," in which the inhabitants of the city were told that God had mixed different metals—gold, silver, iron or bronze—into their nature. Those with gold were the rulers and those with silver the guardians, whereas the workers were composed with iron or bronze. The purpose of the lie was to attribute responsibility for the hierarchical social order in the *Republic* to the natural order of things, rather than social arrangements that could otherwise be altered. *Republic* 3, 415a.

are not happy, who is? Surely not the artisans, or the common people. The constitution of which Socrates discourses has all these difficulties, and others just as great.

6

The same, or nearly the same, objections apply to Plato's later work, the *Laws*, and therefore we should briefly examine the constitution there described. In the *Republic*, Socrates has definitely decided only a few matters—such as the communal distribution of women, children, and property, and the constitution of the state. The population is divided into two classes—farmers and warriors; from this latter is taken a third class of counselors and rulers of the state. But Socrates has not determined whether the farmers and artisans are to have a share in the government, and whether they, too, are to carry arms and share in military service. He certainly thinks that the women ought to share in the education of the guardians, and to fight by their side. The remainder of the work is filled up with digressions foreign to the main subject, and with discussions about the education of the guardians.

In the *Laws* there is hardly anything but laws; not much is said about the constitution. He had originally intended his recommendations to be practical, but he gradually turns to consideration of their ideal form. For with the exception of the community of women and property, he supposes everything to be the same as proposed in the *Republic*; there is to be the same education; the citizens of both are to live free from servile occupations, and there are to be common meals in both.

The only difference is that in the *Laws*, the common meals are extended to women, and the warriors number 5000, but in the *Republic* only 1000. The discourses of Socrates are never commonplace; they always exhibit grace and originality and thought; perfection in everything can hardly be expected. We must not overlook the fact that the number of 5000 citizens, just now mentioned, will require a territory as large as Babylon, or some other huge site, if so many persons are to be supported in idleness, together with their women and attendants, who will be a multitude many times as great. In framing an ideal we may assume what we wish, but should avoid impossibilities.

It is said that the legislator ought to have his eye directed to two points—the people and the country. But neighboring countries also must not be forgotten by him, firstly because the state for which he legislates is to have a political and not an isolated life. For a state must have a military force that is useable against its neighbors, and not merely useful at home. Even if the life of action is not admitted to be the best, either for individuals or states, still a city should be formidable to enemies, whether invading or retreating.

There is another point: Should not the amount of property be defined in some different, clearer way? For Socrates says that a man should have as much property as will enable him to live temperately, which is only a way of saying *to live well*; this is too general a conception. Further, a man may live temperately and yet miserably. A better definition would be that a man must have as much property as will enable him to live not only temperately but generously; if the two are separated, generosity will combine with luxury; temperance will be associated with hardship. For generosity and temperance are the only desirable qualities which have to do with the use of property. A man cannot use property with mildness or courage, but he may use it temperately and generously; and therefore the practice of these virtues is inseparable from property.

There is an inconsistency, too, in equalizing the property and not regulating the number of the citizens.[1] The population is to remain unlimited, though he thinks that it will be sufficiently stabilized by a certain number of marriages being unfruitful, however many are born to others, because he finds this to be the case in existing states. But greater care will be required in his state than in existing ones; for in existing states, however many citizens there are, the property is always distributed among them, and therefore no one is needy; but, if the property were not divisible, as specified in the *Laws*, the surplus population, whether few or many, would get nothing. One would have thought that it was even more necessary to limit population than property; and that the limit should be fixed by calculating the chances of mortality in the children, and of sterility in married persons. The neglect of this subject, which in existing states is so common, is a never-failing cause of poverty among the citizens; and poverty is the parent of revolution and crime. Pheidon the Corinthian,[2] who was one of the most ardent legislators, thought that the families and the number of citizens ought to remain the same, although originally all the family allotments may have been of different sizes: but in the Laws the opposite principle is maintained.

What in our opinion is the right arrangement will have to be explained later.

There is another omission in the *Laws*: Socrates does not tell us how the rulers differ from their subjects; he only says that they should be related as the warp and the woof,[3] which are made out of different wools.[4] He allows that a man's whole property may be increased fivefold,[5] but why should not his land also increase to a certain extent? Again, will the good management of a household be promoted by his arrangement of farmhouses? For he assigns to each individual two houses in separate places, and it is difficult to live in two houses.

The whole system of government tends to be neither democracy nor oligarchy, but something in a mean between them, which is usually called a polity; in it, citizenship is restricted to armed soldiers. Now, if he intended to frame a constitution which would suit the greatest number of states, he was very likely right, but not if he meant to say that this constitutional form came nearest to his first or ideal state; for many would prefer the Spartan, or, possibly, some other more aristocratic government. Some, indeed, say that the best constitution is a combination of all existing forms, and they praise the Spartan because it is made up of oligarchy, monarchy, and democracy, the king forming the monarchy, and the council of elders the oligarchy while the democratic element is represented by the ephors;[6] for the ephors are selected from the people. Others, however, declare the ephorate to be a tyranny, and find the element of democracy in the common meals and in the habits of daily life. In the *Laws* it is maintained that the best constitution is made up of democracy and tyranny, which are either not constitutions at all, or are the worst of all. But those thinkers who advocate combination of many forms are nearer the ideal; for the constitution is better which is made up of more numerous elements.

The constitution proposed in the *Laws* has no element of monarchy at all; it is nothing but oligarchy and democracy, leaning rather to oligarchy. This is seen in the mode of appointing magistrates; for although the appointment of them by lot from among those who have been already

---

1 *regulating the number of citizens* Plato did attend to this: in *Laws*, 740b–741a.

2 *Pheidon the Corinthian* Eighth- or seventh-century BCE king of Corinth.

3 *warp and woof* In weaving, the threads that run lengthwise are the warp and the threads that run across are the woof. Metaphorically, it means the essential base or foundation of an organization.

4 *Socrates ... wools* *Laws*, 734e–735a.

5 *increased fivefold* *Laws*, 744d–745a.

6 *ephors* Five elected officials who balanced the power of the kings.

selected combines both elements, the way in which the rich
10 are compelled by law to attend the assembly and vote for
magistrates or discharge other political duties, while the rest
may do as they like, and the endeavor to have the greater
number of the magistrates appointed out of the richer
classes and the highest officers selected from those who have
the greatest incomes, both these are oligarchical features.
The oligarchical principle prevails also in the choice of the
15 council, for all are compelled to choose, but the compulsion
extends only to the choice out of the first class, and of an
equal number out of the second class and out of the third
class, but not in this latter case to all the voters but to those
of the first three classes; and the selection of candidates out
of the fourth class is only compulsory on the first and sec-
20 ond. Then, from the persons so chosen, he says that there
ought to be an equal number of each class selected. Thus a
preponderance will be given to the better sort of people, who
have the larger incomes, because many of the lower classes,
not being compelled will not vote. These considerations,
25 and others which will be adduced when the time comes
for examining similar polities, tend to show that states like
Plato's should not be composed of democracy and monarchy. There is also a danger in electing the magistrates out
of a body who are themselves pre-elected; for, if even a small
number combine, the elections will always go as they desire.
30 Such is the constitution which is described in the *Laws*.

7

Other constitutions, which all come nearer to established
or existing ones than either of Plato's, have been proposed—some by private persons, others by philosophers
and statesmen. No one else has introduced such novelties as
35 the community of women and children, or common meals
for women: other legislators begin with what is necessary.
In the opinion of some, the regulation of property is the
most important matter of all, because that is the issue in
all revolutions. This danger was recognized by Phaleas of
Chalcedon,[1] who was the first to affirm that the citizens of
40 a state ought to have equal possessions. He thought that
1266b in a new colony the equalization might be accomplished
without difficulty, not so easily when a state was already
established; and that then the shortest way of reaching the

desired end would be for the rich to give and not to receive
dowries, and for the poor not to give but to receive them.

In the *Laws*, Plato held that accumulation should be 5
allowed to a certain extent, as I have already observed,
forbidding any citizen to possess more than five times the
amount held by anyone else. But those who make such
laws should remember what they are apt to forget—that
the legislator who fixes the amount of property should also 10
fix the number of children; for, if the children are too many
for the property, the law must be broken. And, besides the
violation of the law, it is a bad thing to turn rich men poor;
for men of ruined fortunes are sure to stir up revolutions.
That the equalization of property exercises an influence on 15
political society was clearly understood even by some of
the old legislators. Laws were made by Solon[2] and others
prohibiting an individual from possessing as much land as
he pleased; and there are other laws in states which forbid
the sale of property: among the Locrians,[3] for example, 20
there is a law that a man is not to sell his property unless he
can prove unmistakably that some misfortune has befallen
him. Again, there have been laws which require keeping
the original lots intact. Such a law existed in the island of
Leucas,[4] and the abrogation of it made the constitution
too democratic, for the rulers no longer had the prescribed
land-holding qualification. Again, where there is equality of
property, the amount may be either too large or too small, 25
and the possessor may be living either in luxury or penury. Clearly, then, the legislator ought not only to aim at
the equalization of properties, but at moderation in their
amount. Further, if he prescribes this moderate amount
equally to all, he will be no nearer the mark; for it is not
the possessions but the desires of mankind which require
to be equalized, and this is impossible, unless a sufficient 30
education is provided by the laws. But Phaleas will probably
reply that this is precisely what he means; and that, in his
opinion, states ought to mandate not only equal property,
but equal education. Still he should tell precisely what sort
of education he means. It would be a bad idea to have one 35
and the same education for all, if that predisposed men to
avarice, or ambition, or both. Moreover, civil troubles arise,

---

1   *Phaleas of Chalcedon* Nothing is known of him except what
Aristotle says in this work.

2   *Solon* (c. 630–c. 530 BCE) Athenian statesman and lawgiver,
known as one of the "Seven Wise Men of Greece." Solon successfully established a constitution for Athens.

3   *Locrians* Locri Epizephyrii was a Greek city in Italy, the first
Greek community to have a written code of laws, the Locrian
code (c. 660 BCE).

4   *Leucas* Greek island in the Ionian Sea.

not only out of the inequality of property, but out of the inequality of honor, though in opposite ways: common
40 people quarrel about the inequality of property, the higher
1267a class about the equality of honor; as the poet says, "The bad and good alike in honor share."[1]

There are crimes motivated by lack of necessities; Phaleas expects to find a cure for these in the equalization of property, which will take away from a man the temptation to be a highwayman because he is hungry or cold. But this
5 is not the sole incentive to crime; men also wish to enjoy themselves and to gratify pressing desires for things beyond the necessities of life. And in addition they may commit crimes because they desire superfluities to provide painless pleasures.

Now what is the cure of these three disorders? Of the
10 first, moderate possessions and occupation; of the second, habits of temperance. As to the third: those who desire pleasures obtained independently of other people will find the satisfaction of their desires nowhere but in philosophy; for all other pleasures we are dependent on others. The fact is that the greatest crimes are caused by excess and not by necessity. Men do not become tyrants in order that they
15 may not suffer cold; so it is a greater honor to kill a tyrant than to kill a thief. Thus we see that the political institutions of Phaleas would work only against petty crimes.

There is another objection to them. They are chiefly designed to promote the internal welfare of the state. But the legislator should consider also its relation to neighboring
20 nations, and to all who are outside of it. The government must be organized with a view to military strength; and he has not said a word about this. Similarly with respect to property: there should be enough not only to supply the internal wants of the state, but also to meet external dangers. The property of the state should not be so large that more
25 powerful neighbors may be tempted by it, while the owners are unable to repel the invaders; nor yet so small that the state is unable to maintain a war even against states of equal power, and of the same character. Phaleas has given no opinions on this; but we should bear in mind that some wealth is an advantage. The best amount is probably set by these
30 considerations: that a more powerful neighbor must have no inducement to go to war with you because of the excess of your wealth, but only if he would have done so anyway, even if you had had less. There is a story that Eubulus,[2]

when Autophradates[3] was going to besiege Atarneus, told him to consider how long the operation would take, and then reckon up the cost which would be incurred in the time. "For," he said, "I am willing for a smaller sum than 35 that to leave Atarneus at once." These words of Eubulus made an impression on Autophradates, and he desisted from the siege.

The equalization of property is one of the things that tend to prevent the citizens from quarrelling. Not that the gain in this direction is very great. For the nobles will be dissatisfied because they think themselves worthy of more 40 than an equal share of honors; and this is often found to be a cause of sedition and revolution. And the avarice of man- 1267b kind is insatiable; at one time two obols[4] was pay enough; but now, when this sum has become customary, men always want more and more without end; for it is of the nature of desire not to be satisfied, and most men live only for the gratification of it. The beginning of reform is not so much 5 to equalize property as to train the nobler sort of natures not to desire more, and to prevent the lower from getting more; that is to say, they must be kept down, but not ill-treated. Besides, the equalization proposed by Phaleas is imperfect; for he only equalizes land, whereas a man may be rich also 10 in slaves, and cattle, and money, and in the abundance of what are called his movables. Now either all these things must be equalized, or some limit must be imposed on them, or they must all be left alone. It would appear that Phaleas is legislating for a small state only, if, as he supposes, all the 15 artisans are to be public slaves and not to form a supplementary part of the body of citizens. But if there is a law that artisans are to be public slaves, it should only apply to those engaged on public works, as at Epidamnus, or at Athens on the plan which Diophantus once introduced.[5]

From these observations any one may judge how far 20 Phaleas was right or wrong in his ideas.

8

Hippodamus,[6] the son of Euryphon, a native of Miletus, the man who invented the art of planning cities, and who

---

1   *The bad ... honor share*   Homer, *Iliad* 9, 319.
2   *Eubulus*   Greek statesman, c. 405–c. 335 BCE.
3   *Autophradates*   Distinguished Persian general who led the fleet in the Aegean Sea against the allies of Alexander the Great.
4   *two obols*   The sum granted to each Athenian citizen to pay for his seat in the theatre.
5   *But if there is a law ... introduced*   Nothing beyond this from Aristotle is known about these schemes.
6   *Hippodamus*   Fifth-century BCE architect, planner of Rhodes.

laid out the Piraeus, was a strange man; his fondness for
distinction led him to eccentricities—affectations, in some
people's view. He would wear flowing hair and expensive
ornaments; but these were worn on a cheap but warm garment both in winter and summer. Besides aspiring to be an
adept in the knowledge of nature, he was the first person
who was not a statesman to make inquiries about the best
form of government.

The city Hippodamus proposed was to be composed of
10,000 citizens divided into three classes: artisans, farmers,
and armed defenders of the state. He also divided the land
into three parts, one sacred, one public, the third private:
the first was set apart to maintain the customary worship of
the Gods, the second was to support the warriors, the third
was the property of the farmers. He also divided laws into
three classes, and no more, for he maintained that there are
three subjects of lawsuits: insult, injury, and homicide. He
likewise instituted a single final court of appeal, to which
all causes seeming to have been improperly decided might
be referred; this court he formed of elders chosen for the
purpose. He was further of opinion that the decisions of the
courts ought not to be given by the use of a voting pebble,[1]
but that every one should have a tablet on which he might
not only write a simple condemnation, or leave the tablet
blank for a simple acquittal, if he partly acquitted and partly
condemned, he was to distinguish accordingly. He objected
to the existing law claiming that obliged a juror to be guilty
of perjury, whichever way he voted. His laws provided for a
reward for anyone who discovered anything for the good of
the state; and he provided that the children of citizens who
died in battle should be maintained at the public expense (as
if such an enactment had never been heard of before—yet
it actually exists in Athens and in other places). He would
have all magistrates elected by the people, that is, by the
three classes already mentioned, and those who were elected
were to watch over the interests of the public, of foreigners,
and of orphans. These are the most striking points in the
constitution of Hippodamus. There is not much else.

The first of these proposals to which objection may be
taken is the threefold division of the citizens. The artisans,
farmers and warriors all have a share in the government. But
the farmers have no arms, and the artisans neither arms nor
land, and therefore they become all but slaves of the warrior class. It is impossible that they share in all the offices;
for generals, police officials, and nearly all the principal
magistrates must be chosen from the class of those who are
armed. Yet, if the two other classes have no share in the government, how can they be loyal citizens? It may be said that
those who have arms must necessarily be masters of both
the other classes, but this is not so easily accomplished unless they are numerous; and if they are superior, why should
the other classes share in the government at all, or have
power to appoint magistrates? Further, what use are farmers
to the state? Artisans are necessary, for these are needed in
every state, and they can live by their craft, as elsewhere; and
the farmers too, if they really provided the warriors with
food, might fairly have a share in the government. But in
the republic of Hippodamus they are supposed to have land
of their own, which they cultivate for their private benefit.
Again, as to this common land out of which the soldiers are
maintained, if they are themselves to be the cultivators of it,
the warrior class will be identical with the farmers, although
the legislator intended to make a distinction between them.
If, again, there are to be other cultivators distinct both from
the farmers, who have land of their own, and from the warriors, they will make a fourth class, which has no place in
the state and no share in anything. Or, if the same persons
are to cultivate their own lands, and those of the public as
well, they will have difficulty in supplying the quantity of
produce which will maintain two households: and why, in
this case, should there be any division, for they might find
food themselves and give to the warriors from the same land
and the same lots? There is surely a great confusion in all
this.

Neither is the law to be commended which says that the
judges might give a qualified judgment, even when the issue
before them is simple and straightforward; for the judge is
thus converted into an arbitrator. Now, in a court of arbitration, when there are several arbitrators, a qualified judgment
is possible, for they confer with one another about the decision; but in courts of law this is impossible; indeed, most
legislators take pains to prevent the judges from conferring
with each other about their decision. Again, will there not
be confusion if the judge thinks that damages should be
given, but not so much as the suitor demands? He asks,
say, for twenty minae, and the judge allows him ten minae
(or in general the suitor asks for more and the judge allows
less), while another judge allows five, another four minae.
In this way they will go on splitting up the damages, and
some will grant the whole and others nothing: how is the
final reckoning to be taken? Again, if the indictment has

---

1   *voting pebble*   Voting was conventionally done in ancient Greece
by casting a pebble into an urn.

been laid in an unqualified form, no one would claim that a juror who votes for a simple acquittal or condemnation perjures himself; and this is just, for the juror who acquits does not decide that the defendant owes nothing, but that he does not owe the twenty minae. A juror would be guilty of perjury who thinks that the defendant ought not to pay twenty minae, and yet condemns him.

The proposal that those who discover anything which is useful to the state be rewarded sounds attractive, but cannot safely be enacted by law, for it may encourage informers, and perhaps even lead to political upheavals. This question involves another. It has been doubted whether it is or is not beneficial to make any change in the laws of a country, even if another law be better. Now, if no change is a gain, we can hardly assent to the proposal of Hippodamus; for, under pretense of doing a public service, a man may introduce measures which are really destructive to the laws or to the constitution.

But, since we have touched upon this subject, perhaps we had better go a little into detail, for, as I was saying, there is a difference of opinion, and it may sometimes seem desirable to make changes. Such changes in the other arts and sciences have certainly been beneficial; medicine, for example, and gymnastic, and every other art and craft have departed from traditional practices. And, if politics is an art, change must be necessary in this as in any other art. That improvement has occurred in the past is shown by the fact that old customs are exceedingly simple and barbarous. For the ancient Greeks went about armed and purchased their brides from each other. The remains of ancient laws still in existence are quite absurd; for example, at Cyme[1] there is a law about murder to the effect that if the accuser produces a certain number of witnesses from among his own kinsmen, the accused shall be held guilty. Again, men in general desire the good, and not merely what is sanctioned by tradition. But the earliest humans, whether they were born of the earth or were the survivors of some cataclysm, may be supposed to have been no better than ordinary or even foolish people among ourselves (such is certainly the tradition concerning the earth-born men); and it would be ridiculous to rest contented with their notions. Even when laws have been written down, they ought not always to remain unaltered. As in other sciences, so in politics, it is impossible that all things should be precisely set down in writing; for enactments must be universal, but actions are concerned with particulars. Hence we infer that sometimes and in certain cases laws may be changed.

But when we look at the matter from another point of view, great caution would seem to be required. For the habit of lightly changing the laws is an evil, and, when the advantage is small, some errors both of lawgivers and rulers had better be left alone; the citizen will not gain so much by making the change as he will lose by the habit of disobedience. The analogy of the arts is false; a change in a law is a very different thing from a change in an art. For the law has no power to command obedience except that of habit, which can only be given by time, so that a readiness to change from old to new laws weakens the power of the law. Even if we admit that the laws are to be changed, are they all to be changed, and in every state? And are they to be changed by anybody who likes, or only by certain persons? These are very important questions; and therefore we had better reserve the discussion of them to a more suitable occasion.

9

When considering the governments of Sparta and Crete, and indeed any government, two questions have to be answered: first, whether any particular law is good or bad, when compared with the perfect state; secondly, whether it is or is not consistent with the idea and character of the constitution of the state as it actually has been established by the lawgiver.

It is generally acknowledged that in a well-ordered state the citizens should have leisure and be free from the necessity of providing their daily wants. But there is a difficulty in seeing how this leisure is to be attained. The Thessalian Penestae[2] have often risen against their masters, and the Helots[3] in like manner against the Spartans, for whose misfortunes they are always lying in wait. Nothing, however, of this kind has as yet happened to the Cretans; the reason probably is that the neighboring states, even when at war with one another, never form an alliance with rebellious serfs, rebellions not being for their interest, since they themselves have a dependent population. Whereas all the neighbors of the Spartans (Argives, Messenians, and Arcadians) were their enemies. In Thessaly, again, the original revolt of the slaves occurred because the Thessalians were still at war with the

---

1   *Cyme*   The city referred to is unknown.

2   *Penestae*   Serfs in Thessaly.
3   *Helots*   Serfs in Sparta.

neighboring Achaeans, Perrhaebians, and Magnesians. Besides, if there were no other difficulty, the treatment or management of slaves is a troublesome affair; for, if not kept in hand, they are insolent, and think that they are as good as their masters, and, if harshly treated, they hate them, and conspire against them. Now it is clear that when these are the results the citizens of a state have not found out the secret of managing their subject population.

Again, the license permitted to the Spartan women defeats the intention of the Spartan constitution, and is harmful to the welfare of the state. For, since each family contains a husband and a wife, the state may be considered as about equally divided into men and women; and, therefore, in those states in which the position of women is badly regulated, half the city may be regarded as having no laws. And this is what has actually happened at Sparta; the legislator wanted to make the whole state hardy and temperate, and he has carried out his intention in the case of the men, but he has neglected the women, who live in every sort of intemperance and luxury. The consequence is that in such a state wealth is too highly valued, especially if a citizen is dominated by his wife, as it is among most warlike races (except the Celts and a few others who openly approve of homosexual attachments). The old mythologer would seem to have been right in uniting Ares and Aphrodite,[1] for all warlike races are prone to the love either of men or of women. This was exemplified among the Spartans in the days of their greatness; many things were managed by their women. But what difference does it make whether women rule, or the rulers are ruled by women? The result is the same. Even in regard to boldness, which is of no use in daily life, and is needed only in war, the influence of the Spartan women has been most harmful. The evil showed itself in the Theban invasion, when, unlike the women in other cities, they were utterly useless and caused more confusion than the enemy.

This license of the Spartan women existed from the earliest times, and was only what might be expected. For, during the wars of the Spartans, first against the Argives, and afterwards against the Arcadians and Messenians, the men were long away from home, and, on the return of peace, they submitted themselves to the legislator's power, already prepared by the discipline of a soldier's life (in which there are many elements of virtue), to receive the legislator's

orders. But, when Lycurgus,[2] as tradition says, wanted to bring the women under his laws, they resisted, and he gave up the attempt. These then are the causes of what then happened, and this defect in the constitution is clearly to be attributed to them. We are not, however, considering what is or is not to be excused, but what is right or wrong, and the disorder of the women, as I have already said, not only gives an air of disharmony to the constitution considered in itself, but tends to foster avarice.

The mention of avarice naturally suggests a criticism of the inequality of property. While some of the Spartan citizens have quite small properties, others have very large ones; hence the land has passed into the hands of a few. And this is due also to faulty laws; for, although the legislator rightly holds up to shame the sale or purchase of an inheritance, he allows anybody who likes to give or bequeath it. Yet both practices lead to the same result. And nearly two-fifths of the whole country is held by women; this is owing to the number of heiresses and to the large dowries which are customary. It would surely have been better to have given no dowries at all, or, if any, but small or moderate ones.

As the law now stands, a man may give in marriage the daughter who stands to inherit his property to any one whom he pleases, and, if he dies but does not specify to whom his daughter is to be given in his will, the privilege of giving her away descends to his male heir. Hence, although the country is able to maintain 1500 cavalry and 30,000 hoplites,[3] the whole number of Spartan citizens fell below 1000. The result proves the faulty nature of their laws respecting property; for the city sank under a single defeat; the lack of men was their ruin. There is a tradition that, in the days of their ancient kings, they were in the habit of giving the rights of citizenship to foreigners, and therefore, in spite of their long wars, no lack of population was experienced by them; indeed, at one time Sparta is said to have numbered not less than 10,000 citizens. Whether this statement is true or not, it would certainly have been better to have maintained their numbers by the equalization of property. Again, the law which relates to the procreation of children is adverse to the correction of this inequality. For the legislator, wanting to have as many Spartans as he could, encouraged the citizens to have large families; and

---

1   *Ares and Aphrodite*   Ares was the god of war; Aphrodite the goddess of sexual love.

2   *Lycurgus*   Possibly legendary seventh-century BCE lawgiver of Sparta.

3   *hoplites*   Heavy infantrymen.

there is a law at Sparta that the father of three sons shall be exempt from military service, and he who has four from all the burdens of the state. Yet it is obvious that, if there were many children, the land being distributed as it is, many of them must necessarily fall into poverty.

The Spartan constitution is defective in another point; I mean the ephorate. This magistracy has authority in the highest matters, but the ephors are chosen from the whole people, and so the office is apt to fall into the hands of very poor men, who, being badly off, are open to bribes. There have been many examples at Sparta of this evil in former times; and quite recently, in the affair in Andros,[1] certain of the ephors who were bribed did their best to ruin the state. And so great and tyrannical is their power, that even the kings have been compelled to court them, so that, in this way as well together with the royal office, the whole constitution has deteriorated, and from being an aristocracy has turned into a democracy. The ephorate certainly does keep the state together; for the people are contented when they have a share in the highest office, and the result, whether due to the legislator or to chance, has been advantageous. For if a constitution is to be permanent, all the parts of the state must desire its continued existence and the maintenance of its arrangements. This is the case at Sparta, where the kings desire its permanence because of the honor that they receive; the nobles because they are represented in the council of elders (for the office of elder is a reward of virtue); and the people, because all are eligible to the ephorate. The election of ephors from the whole populace is perfectly right, but ought not to be carried on in the present fashion, which is too childish. Again, they have the responsibility to decide on important matters, although they are quite ordinary men, and therefore they should not make their decisions merely on their own judgment, but rather according to written rules, and to the laws. Their way of life, too, is not in accordance with the spirit of the constitution—they have too much license; whereas, in the case of the other citizens, the excess of strictness is so intolerable that they run away from the law into the secret indulgence of sensual pleasures.

Again, the council of elders is not free from defects. It may be said that the elders are good men and well trained in manly virtue; and that, therefore, there is an advantage to the state in having them. But that judges of important

causes[2] should hold office for life is a disputable thing, for the mind grows old as well as the body. And when men have been educated in such a manner that even the legislator himself cannot trust them, there is real danger. Many of the elders are well known to have taken bribes and to have been guilty of partiality in public affairs. And therefore they ought not to be free from scrutiny of their conduct; yet at Sparta they are so. But (it may be replied), "All magistracies are accountable to the ephors." Yes, but this prerogative is too great for the ephors, and we maintain that the control should be exercised in some other manner. Further, the mode in which the Spartans elect their elders is childish;[3] and it is improper that the person to be elected should canvass for the office; the worthiest should be appointed, whether he wants the office or not. And here the legislator clearly indicates the same intention which appears in other parts of his constitution: he wants his citizens to be ambitious, and he has reckoned upon this quality in the election of the elders; for only ambitious men would ask to be elected. Yet ambition and avarice, almost more than any other passions, are the motives of crime.

I shall consider later whether kings are an advantage to states; at any rate, they should not be chosen as they are now, but instead with regard to their personal life and conduct. The legislator himself obviously did not suppose that he could produce really good kings; at least he shows a great distrust of their virtue. For this reason the Spartans used to send enemies of kings with them on ambassadorial missions, and the quarrels between the kings were held to be a political safeguard.

Neither did the first introducer of the common meals, called *phiditia*, regulate them well. These ought to have been paid for by public funding, as in Crete; but among the Spartans everyone is expected to contribute, and some of them are too poor to afford the expense; thus the intention of the legislator is frustrated. The common meals were meant to be a popular institution, but the existing manner of regulating them is the reverse of popular. For the very poor can scarcely take part in them; and, according to ancient custom, those who cannot contribute are not allowed to retain their rights of citizenship.

The law about the Spartan admirals has often been censured, and with justice; it is a source of dissension, for the

---

1   *affair in Andros*   Scholars are unsure what events Aristotle refers to here.

2   *judges of important causes*   The council tried cases of homicide.

3   *the mode ... childish*   Those were chosen who received the loudest shouts of approval in the assembly.

40 kings are supreme commanders for life, and this office of admiral is like the setting up of another king.

1271b The charge which Plato brings, in the *Laws*, against the intention of the legislator, is likewise justified: the whole legislative system is directed to fostering one element of virtue only—military excellence, which gives victory in war. So long as the Spartans were at war, therefore, their power was preserved, but when they had attained empire they 5 fell, for they knew nothing of the arts of peace, and had never engaged in any employment higher than war. There is another error, equally great, into which they have fallen. Although they truly think that the goods for which men contend are to be acquired by virtue rather than by vice, they err in supposing that these goods are to be preferred to 10 the virtue which gains them.

In addition: the revenues of the state are ill-managed; there is no money in the treasury, although they are obliged to carry on great wars, and they are unwilling to pay taxes. The greater part of the land being in the hands of the citizens, they do not look closely into one another's contribu-15 tions. The result which the legislator has produced is the reverse of beneficial; for he has made his city poor, and his citizens greedy.

Enough respecting the Spartan constitution, of which these are the principal defects.

10

20 The Cretan constitution closely resembles the Spartan, and in some few points is quite as good; but for the most part less perfect in form. The older constitutions are generally less elaborate than the later, and the Spartan constitution is said to be, and probably is, in a very great measure, a copy 25 of the Cretan. According to tradition, Lycurgus, when he ceased to be the guardian of King Charillus, went abroad and spent most of his time in Crete. For the two countries are closely connected; the Lyctians were a colony of the Spartans, and the colonists, when they came to Crete, adopted the constitution which they found existing among 30 the inhabitants. Even to this day the *perioeci*,[1] or subject population of Crete, are governed by the original laws which Minos is supposed to have enacted. The island seems to be intended by nature for domination in the Greek world, and to be well situated; it extends right across the sea around 35 which nearly all the Greeks are settled; and while one end

---

1 *perioeci* The serfs of the Cretans.

is not far from the Peloponnese, the other almost reaches to the region of Asian Triopium and Rhodes. Hence Minos acquired the empire of the sea, subduing some of the islands and colonizing others; at last he invaded Sicily, where he died near Camicus. 40

The Cretan institutions resemble the Spartan. The helots are the farmers of the one, the *perioeci* of the other, and 1272a both Cretans and Spartans have common meals, which were anciently called by the Spartans not *phiditia* but *andria*; and the Cretans have the same word, the use of which proves that the common meals originally came from Crete. Further, the two constitutions are similar; for the office of the ephors is the same as that of the Cretan *cosmoi*, the only difference 5 being that whereas there are five ephors, there are ten *cosmoi*. The Cretan elders (called the Council) are analogous to the Spartan. And the kingly office once existed in Crete, but was 10 abolished, and the *cosmoi* have now the duty of leading them in war. All classes take part in the assembly, but it can only ratify the decrees of the elders and the cosmoi.

The common meals of Crete are certainly better managed than the Spartan; for in Sparta every one pays so much per head, or, as I have already explained, if he fails, the law 15 forbids him to exercise the rights of citizenship. But in Crete they are of a more popular character. There, all the agriculture produce and livestock raised on the public lands, and all the rent paid by the *perioeci*, is divided; one portion is assigned to public worship of the Gods and to the service of 20 the state, and the other to the common meals, so that men, women, and children are all supported out of a common fund. The legislator has many ingenious ways of securing moderation in eating, which he conceives to be a gain. He encourages the separation of men from women (lest they should have too many children), and homosexual connec-25 tions between men—whether this is a good or bad thing I shall have an opportunity of considering at another time. But there can be no doubt that the Cretan common meals are better ordered than the Spartan.

On the other hand, the *cosmoi* are even a worse in-30 stitution than the ephors, of which they have all the evils without the good. Like the ephors, they have no special qualifications, but in Crete this is not counterbalanced by a corresponding political advantage. In Sparta everyone is eligible, and the body of the people, having a share in the highest office, want the constitution to be permanent. But in Crete the *cosmoi* are drawn from certain families, and not from the whole population, and the elders from those who have been *cosmoi*. 35

The criticism which has been already made about the Spartan elders applies also to the Cretan. Their irresponsibility and life tenure is too great a privilege, and their arbitrary power of acting on their own judgment, and dispensing with 40 written law, is dangerous. It is no proof of the goodness of the institution that the people are not discontented at being excluded from it. For there is no profit to be made out of the office as out of the ephoralty, since, unlike the ephors, 1272b the *cosmoi* live on an island, removed from temptation.

The remedy by which they correct the evil of this institution is an extraordinary one, suited rather to an oligarchy ruled by a small clique than to a constitutional state. For the *cosmoi* are often expelled by a conspiracy of their own colleagues, or of private individuals; and they are allowed 5 also to resign before their term of office has expired. Surely all matters of this kind are better regulated by law than by the will of man, which is a very unsafe rule. Worst of all is the suspension of the office of *cosmoi*, a device to which the nobles often have recourse when they will not submit to justice. This shows that the Cretan government, although 10 possessing some of the characteristics of a constitutional state, is really an oligarchy.

The nobles have a habit, too, of setting up factions— like many little monarchies—among the common people and their own friends, and then to quarrel and fight with one another. What is this but the temporary destruction of 15 the state and dissolution of society? A state is in a dangerous condition when those who are willing are also able to attack her. But, as I have already said, the island of Crete is saved by her situation; distance has the same effect as the Spartan prohibition of foreigners; and the Cretans have 20 no foreign dominions. This is the reason why the *perioeci* are contented in Crete, whereas the helots are perpetually revolting. But when lately foreign invaders found their way into the island, the weakness of the Cretan constitution was revealed. Enough said about the government of Crete.

11

The Carthaginians are also considered to have an excellent form of government, which differs from that of any other 25 state in several respects, though it is in some ways like the Spartan. Indeed, all three states—the Spartan, the Cretan, and the Carthaginian—closely resemble one another, and are very different from any others. Many of the Carthaginian institutions are excellent. The superiority of their consti- 30 tution is proved by the fact that the common people remain loyal to the constitution; the Carthaginians have never had any rebellion worth speaking of, and have never been under the rule of a tyrant.

Among the points in which the Carthaginian constitution resembles the Spartan are the following: The common tables of the clubs correspond to the Spartan phiditia, and their magistracy of the "Hundred and Four" to the eph- 35 ors; but, whereas the ephors are recruited haphazardly, the magistrates of the Carthaginians are elected according to merit—this is an improvement. They have also their kings and their "Gerusia," or council of elders, who correspond to the kings and elders of Sparta. Their kings, unlike the Spartan, are not always drawn from the same family, nor indiscriminately from just any family; but if there is some distinguished family they are selected out of it and not ap- 40 pointed by seniority—this is far better. Such officers have great power, and therefore, if they are persons of little 1273a worth, do a great deal of harm, as they have already done in Sparta.

Most of the defects or deviations from the perfect state, for which the Carthaginian constitution would be censured, apply equally to all the forms of government which we have mentioned. But of the deflections from aristocracy 5 and constitutional government, some incline more to democracy and some to oligarchy. Toward the democratic: the kings and elders, if unanimous, may determine whether they will or will not bring a matter before the people, but when they are not unanimous, the people decide on such matters as well. And whatever the kings and elders bring before the people is not only heard but also determined 10 by them, and any one who likes may oppose it; this is not permitted in Sparta and Crete. Toward the oligarchic: the boards of five magistrates, who have jurisdiction over many important matters, select their own members; they choose the supreme council of one hundred, and hold office longer 15 than other magistrates (for they are virtually rulers both before and after they hold office). There are also aristocratic features, for example, that they are without salary and not elected by lot, and that all suits are tried by the magistrates, 20 and not some by one class of judges or jurors and some by another, as at Sparta. The Carthaginian constitution deviates from aristocracy and inclines to oligarchy, chiefly on a point where popular opinion is on their side. For men in general think that magistrates should be chosen not only for their merit, but for their wealth: a man, they say, who 25 is poor cannot rule well—he does not have leisure. If, then, election of magistrates for their wealth is characteristic of oligarchy, and election for merit of aristocracy, there will be a third form, including the constitution of Carthage: the Carthaginians choose their magistrates, and particularly the highest of them—their kings and generals—with an eye both to merit and to wealth.

But we must acknowledge that, in thus deviating from aristocracy, the legislator has committed an error. Nothing is more absolutely necessary than to ensure that the highest class, not only when in office, but when out of office, should have leisure and not disgrace themselves in any way; and his attention should be directed first to this. Even if wealth must be considered here, in order to secure their leisure, yet it is surely a bad thing that the greatest offices, such as those of kings and generals, should be open to purchase. The law which allows this abuse makes wealth of more account than virtue, and the whole state becomes avaricious. For, whenever the chiefs of the state deem anything honorable, the other citizens are sure to follow their example; and, where virtue does not have priority, their aristocracy cannot be firmly established. Those who have had the expense of purchasing their places will be in the habit of repaying themselves; and it is absurd to suppose that a poor and honest man will be wanting to make gains, but that a lower sort of man who has incurred a great expense will not. Therefore those who should rule are those who are able to rule best. And even if the legislator neglects to protect good rulers from poverty, he should at any rate provide for their leisure when they are in office.

A favorite practice among the Carthaginians is to have one person hold many offices; but this would seem to be a bad principle; one business is better done by one man. The legislator should pay attention to this; you would not appoint the same person to be a flute-player and a shoemaker. Hence, where the state is large, it is more in accordance both with constitutional and with democratic principles that the offices of state should be distributed among a correspondingly large number of people. For, as I said, this arrangement is fairer to all, and any action familiarized by repetition is better and sooner performed. We have a proof in military and naval matters; the duties of command and of obedience in both these services extend to all.

The government of the Carthaginians is oligarchical, but they successfully escape the evils of oligarchy by encouraging the spread of wealth—enriching one section of the population after another by sending them to their colonies. This is their solution for their constitutional problems, and the means by which they give stability to the state. Chance,

then, helps them out; but the legislator should be able to provide against revolution without trusting to accidents. As things are, if any misfortune occurred, and the bulk of the subjects revolted, there would be no way of restoring peace by legal methods.

Such is the character of the Spartan, Cretan, and Carthaginian constitutions, which are justly celebrated.

12

Some people who have put forward views on government have never taken any part in public affairs, but have passed their lives in private positions; about most of them, what was worth telling has been already told. Others have been experienced statesman—lawgivers either in their own or in foreign cities; some of these have only made laws, others have framed whole constitutions; for example, Lycurgus and Solon did both.

I have already spoken of Lycurgus' Spartan constitution. As to Solon, he is thought by some to have been a good legislator, having put an end to the exclusiveness of the oligarchy, emancipated the people, established the ancient Athenian democracy, and harmonized the different elements of the state. According to this view, the council of Areopagus was an oligarchical element, the elected magistracy, aristocratic, and the courts of law, democratic. The truth seems to be that the council and the elected magistracy existed before the time of Solon, and were retained by him, but that he gave all the citizens the right to sit on the court, thus creating the democracy, which is the very reason why he is sometimes blamed. For in giving the supreme power to the law courts, which are elected by lot, he is thought to have destroyed the non-democratic element. When the law courts grew powerful, to flatter the people as one flatters a tyrant, they changed the old constitution into the existing democracy. Ephialtes[1] and Pericles[2] curtailed the power of the Areopagus; Pericles also instituted the payment of the juries, and thus every demagogue in turn increased the

---

1   *Ephialtes*   Actions of this Greek politician which served to diminish the power of the conservative council of the Areopagus c. 460 BCE are now seen as the beginning of Athenian democracy.

2   *Pericles*   Athenian general and orator (c. 495–429 BCE) who, during his rule of Athens (roughly 460–430 BCE) transformed the Delian league into the Athenian empire. He also led the Athenians in the first two years of the Peloponnesian War, and was a patron of the arts (perhaps his most lasting legacy) and advocate of democracy.

power of the democracy until it became what we now see. All this is true; it seems, however, to be the result of circumstances, and not to have been intended by Solon. For the people, having been instrumental in gaining the maritime empire in the Persian War, developed an exaggerated self-esteem, and followed worthless demagogues, whom the better class opposed. Solon, himself, appears to have given the Athenians only the absolutely necessary powers of electing magistrates to offices and calling them to account; without these powers, they would have been in a state of slavery and enmity to the government. He appointed all the magistrates from the notables[1] and the men of wealth, that is to say, from the *pentacosiomedimni*, or from the class called *zeugitae*, or from a third class of so-called knights or cavalry. The fourth class were laborers who had no share in any magistracy.[2]

Other legislators were Zaleucus,[3] who gave laws to the Epizephyrian Locrians, and Charondas,[4] who legislated for his own city of Catana, and for the other Chalcidian cities in Italy and Sicily. Some people attempt to make out that Onomacritus[5] was the first person who had any special skill in legislation, and that he, although a Locrian by birth, was trained in Crete, where he lived in the exercise of his prophetic art; that Thales was his companion, and that Lycurgus and Zaleucus were disciples of Thales, as Charondas was of Zaleucus. But their account is quite inconsistent with chronology.

There was also Philolaus, the Corinthian,[6] who gave laws to Thebes. This Philolaus was one of the family of the Bacchiadae, and a lover of Diocles, the Olympic victor, who left Corinth in horror of the incestuous passion which his mother Halcyone had conceived for him, and retired to Thebes, where the two friends together ended their days.

The inhabitants still point out their tombs, which are in full view of one another, but one is visible from the Corinthian territory, the other not. Tradition says the two friends arranged them thus, Diocles out of horror at his misfortunes, so that the land of Corinth might not be visible from his tomb; Philolaus that it might. This is the reason why they settled at Thebes, and so Philolaus came to legislate for the Thebans. In addition to some other enactments, he gave them laws about the procreation of children, which they call the "Laws of Adoption." These laws were peculiar to him, and were intended to keep the number of family allotments constant.

There is nothing remarkable in the legislation of Charondas, except for the prosecution against false witnesses. He is the first who instituted denunciation for perjury. His laws are more exact and more precisely expressed than even those of our modern legislators.

Peculiar in Phaleas'[7] legislation is the equalization of property; of Plato's, the community of women, children, and property, the common meals of women, and the law about drinking—that the sober shall be masters of the feast; also the idea that soldiers should train to acquire equal skill with each hand, so that one would be as useful as the other.

Draco[8] has left laws, but he adapted them to a constitution which already existed, and there is no peculiarity in them which is worth mentioning, except the severity of the punishments.

Pittacus,[9] too, was only a lawgiver, and not the author of a constitution; he is responsible for an unusual law: that a drunken man who does something wrong should be more heavily punished than if he were sober; he did not consider drunkenness to be an excuse, but considered expediency only: drunken more often than sober people commit acts of violence.

Androdamas of Rhegium[10] gave laws to the Chalcidians of Thrace. Some of them relate to homicide, and to heiresses; but there is nothing remarkable in them.

---

1   *notables*   The usual translation of the Greek word *gnorimoi*; Aristotle contrasts this group of people with the "common people," "the masses," etc.; it refers to those who are eminent or distinguished—not necessarily all or only the rich or the nobility.

2   *He appointed ... magistracy*   The *pentacosiomedimni* were the wealthiest of these four classes, followed by the *zeugitae*, the knights, and the lowest—the laborers.

3   *Zaleucus*   Seventh-century BCE legislator was thought to have constructed the Locrian Code, the first written Greek code of laws.

4   *Charondas*   Lawgiver in Sicily, of uncertain dates: perhaps early fifth century BCE.

5   *Onomacritus*   Attic seer, priest, and poet, c. 530–c. 480 BCE.

6   *Philolaus, the Corinthian*   Philolaus (c. 470–c. 485 BCE) was known primarily as a philosopher.

7   *Phaleas*   Little is known of him other than what Aristotle writes in the *Politics*.

8   *Draco*   Perhaps the first legislator of Athens, seventh century BCE. He is the source of the term "draconian."

9   *Pittacus*   Pittacus of Mytilene (640–568 BCE) was one of the "Seven Sages" of Greece; a general successful against the Athenian forces, he was made ruler of his city.

10   *Androdamas of Rhegium*   Little is known of him other than this mention.

And here let us conclude our inquiry into the various constitutions which either actually exist, or have been devised by theorists.

Book 3

I

To inquire into the essence and attributes of various kinds of governments one must first of all determine "What is a state?" At present this is a disputed question. Some say that the state has done something or other; others, no, not the state, but the oligarchy or the tyrant. And the legislator or statesman is concerned entirely with the state; a constitution or government being an arrangement of the inhabitants of a state. But a state is composite, like any other whole made up of many parts; these are the citizens, who compose it. It is evident, therefore, that we must begin by asking, "Who is a citizen, and what is the meaning of the term?" For here again there may be a difference of opinion. He who is a citizen in a democracy will often not be a citizen in an oligarchy. Leaving out of consideration those who have been made citizens, or who have obtained the name of citizen in any other accidental manner, we may say, first, that what makes someone a citizen is not that he lives in a certain place, for resident aliens and slaves share in the place; nor is he a citizen whose legal rights are limited to suing and being sued; for this may also be true of aliens under the provisions of a treaty, though resident aliens in many places do not possess even such rights completely, for they are obliged to have a patron, so that they participate in citizenship only imperfectly, and we call them citizens only in a qualified sense, as we might apply the term to children who are too young to be on the register, or to old men who have been relieved of state duties. Of these we do not say that they are citizens without qualification, but add in the one case that they are not of age, and in the other, that they are past the age, or something of that sort; the precise expression is immaterial, for our meaning is clear. Similar difficulties to those which I have mentioned may be raised and answered about disenfranchised citizens and about exiles. But the citizen whom we are seeking to define is a citizen in the strictest sense, against whom no such exception can be taken, and his special characteristic is that he shares in the administration of justice, and in the holding of office.

Now offices are of two kinds. Some are discontinuous: either the same persons are not allowed to hold them twice, or else a person can repeat in office only after a fixed interval. Others have no time limit—for example, the office of a juryman or member of the popular assembly. It may, indeed, be argued that these are not magistrates at all, and that their functions give them no share in the government. But surely it is ridiculous to say that those who have supreme power do not govern. Let us not dwell further upon this, which is a purely verbal question; what we want is a common term including juryman assembly member. Let us, for the sake of distinction, call it "indefinite office," and we will assume that those who share in such office are citizens. This is the most comprehensive definition of a citizen, and best suits all those who are generally so called.

But we must not forget that there are certain classes of things based on different sorts of principles—one principle primary, another secondary, another tertiary and so on—and things belonging to a class of this sort have, when regarded with respect to this class membership, nothing, or hardly anything worth mentioning, in common. Now we see that governments differ in kind, and that some of them are prior—superior—and that others are posterior—faulty or perverted. (What we mean by perversion will be explained below.) The citizen then of necessity differs under each form of government; and our definition is best adapted to the citizen of a democracy; but not necessarily to other states. For in some states the people are not acknowledged, nor have they any regular assembly, but only extraordinary ones; and suits are distributed by sections among the magistrates. At Sparta, for instance, the ephors determine suits about contracts (which they determine separately, not as a body), while the council of elders judges homicide, and other cases are decided by other magistrates. A similar principle prevails at Carthage; there certain magistrates decide all cases. We may, indeed, modify our definition of the citizen so as to include these states. In them legislators and judges hold fixed, not indefinite, terms, and the right is reserved to some or all such holders of fixed-term offices of deliberating or judging about some things or about all things. The conception of the citizen now begins to clear up.

He who has the power to take part in the deliberative or judicial administration of any state is said by us to be a citizen of that state; and, speaking generally, a state is a body of citizens large enough to be self-sufficient.

2

But in practice a citizen is defined to be one of whom both the parents are citizens; others insist on going further back; say to two or three or more generations. This is a short and practical definition but there are some who raise the further question: How this third or fourth ancestor came to be a citizen? Gorgias of Leontini,[1] partly because of a sense of this difficulty, partly in irony, said "Mortars are what is made by the mortar-makers, and the citizens of Larissa are those who are made by the magistrates; for it is their trade to make Larissaeans." Yet the question is really simple according to our definition: if they shared in the government, they were citizens. This is a better definition than the other. For the words, "born of a father or mother who is a citizen," cannot possibly apply to the first inhabitants or founders of a state.

There is a greater difficulty in the case of those who have been made citizens after a revolution, as by Cleisthenes at Athens[2] after the expulsion of the tyrants, for he enrolled in tribes many aliens, both foreigners and slaves. The doubt in these cases is, not who is a citizen, but whether he who is a citizen ought to be. But there may be the further question raised whether he who ought not to be a citizen is really one after all, since; for what ought not to be is what is not genuine. Now, there are some who hold office, and yet ought not to hold office, whom we describe as ruling, but ruling unjustly. And the citizen was defined by the fact of his holding some kind of rule or office—this person fits the definition we have given of a citizen: one who holds a judicial or legislative office. It is evident, therefore, that the citizens about whom this doubt has arisen must be called citizens.

3

Whether they ought to be so or not is a question which is bound up with the previous inquiry. For a parallel question is raised respecting the state, whether a certain act is or is not an act of the state; for example, in the transition from an oligarchy or a tyranny to a democracy. In such cases persons refuse to fulfill their contracts or any other obligations, on the ground that the tyrant, and not the state, contracted them; they argue that some constitutions are established by force, and not for the sake of the common good. But this would apply equally to democracies, for they too may be founded on violence, and then the acts of the democracy will be neither more nor less acts of the state in question than those of an oligarchy or of a tyranny. This question leads to another: on what principle shall we ever say that the state is the same, or different? It would be a very superficial view which considered only the place and the inhabitants (for the land and the population may be divided, and some of the inhabitants may live in one place and some in another). This, however, is not a very serious difficulty; we need only remark that the word 'state' is ambiguous.

It is further asked: When are men, living in the same place, to be regarded as a single city-state—what is the limit? Certainly not the wall of the city, for you might surround all Peloponnesus with a wall. Using this doubtful criterion, we might say that Babylon is a city, and likewise every city that has the compass of a nation rather than a city. (Babylon, it is said, had been captured for three days before some part of the inhabitants became aware of the fact.) This difficulty may, however, with advantage be deferred to another occasion; the statesman has to consider the size of the state, and whether it should consist of more than one nation or not.

Again, shall we say that while the racial stock of inhabitants, as well as their place of abode, remain the same, the city is also the same, although the citizens are always dying and being born, as we call rivers and fountains the same, although the water is always flowing away and coming again? Or shall we say that the generations of men, like the rivers, are the same, but that the state changes? For, since the state is a partnership, and is a partnership of citizens in a constitution, when the form of government changes and becomes different, then it may be supposed that the state is no longer the same, just as a tragic chorus differs from a comic chorus, although the members of both may be identical. And in this manner we speak of every union or composition of elements as different when the form of their composition alters; for example, a scale containing the same sounds is said to be different, according to whether the Dorian or the Phrygian mode is employed. And if this is true it is evident that the sameness of the state consists chiefly in the sameness of the constitution, and on this basis it may be called the same or not, whether the inhabitants are the same or entirely different. But it is an entirely different question whether a state ought to fulfill engagements when the form of government changes.

---

1 *Gorgias of Leontini* Greek Sophist and rhetorician (c. 490–383 BCE), subject of Plato's dialogue named after him.

2 *Cleisthenes at Athens* Athenian political leader c. 501 BCE who instituted various democratic constitutional reforms.

4

There is a question closely connected to the preceding: Whether the virtue of a good man and a good citizen is the same or not. But, before entering on this discussion, we certainly must first obtain some general notion of the virtue of the citizen.

20   Like the sailor, the citizen is a member of a community. Now, sailors have different functions, for one of them is a rower, another a pilot, and a third a look-out man, and so on; and while the precise definition of each individual's virtue applies exclusively to him, there is, at the same time, a common definition applicable to them all. For they have all of them a common object, which is safe navigation. Similarly, one citizen differs from another, but the salvation of the community is the common business of them all. This community is the constitution; the virtue of the citizen must therefore be relative to the constitution of which he is a member. If, then, there are many forms of government, it is evident that there is not one single virtue of the good citizen which is perfect virtue. But we say that the good man is he who has one single virtue which is perfect virtue. Hence it is evident that the good citizen need not of necessity possess the virtue which makes a good man.

The same question may also be approached from another direction, by considering the best constitution. If the state cannot be entirely composed of good men, and yet each citizen is expected to do his own business well, and must therefore have virtue, still inasmuch as all the citizens cannot be alike, the virtue of the citizen and of the good man cannot coincide. All must have the virtue of the good citizen—thus, and thus only, can the state be perfect; but they will not have the virtue of a good man, unless we assume that in the good state all the citizens must be good.

Again, the state, composed of unlike elements, may be compared to the living being: as the basic elements of which a living being is composed are soul and body, as the soul is made up of rational principle and appetite, as the family is made up of husband and wife, as property is made up of master and slave, so the state is made up of different and unlike elements. Therefore, the virtue of all the citizens cannot possibly be the same, any more than the excellence of the leader of a chorus is the same as that of the performer who stands by his side. I have said enough to show why the two kinds of virtue cannot be absolutely and always the same.

But will there then be no case in which the virtue of the good citizen and the virtue of the good man coincide?

To this we answer that the good ruler is a good and wise man, and that he who would be a statesman must be a wise man. And some persons say that the education of the ruler should be of a special kind; for are not the children of kings instructed in riding and military exercises? As Euripides[1] says, "No subtle arts for me, but what the state requires," as though there were a special education needed by a ruler. If then the virtue of a good ruler is the same as that of a good man, and we assume further that the subject is a citizen as well as the ruler, the virtue of the good citizen and the virtue of the good man cannot be absolutely the same, although in some cases they may; for the virtue of a ruler differs from that of a citizen. It was the sense of this difference which made Jason[2] say that he felt hungry when he was not a tyrant, meaning that he could not endure to live as merely a private citizen. But, on the other hand, it may be argued that men are praised for knowing both how to rule and how to obey, and he is said to be a citizen of approved virtue who is able to do both. Now if we suppose the virtue of a good man to be that which rules, and the virtue of the citizen to include ruling and obeying, it cannot be said that they are equally worthy of praise. Since, then, it is sometimes thought that the ruler and the ruled must learn different things and not the same, but that the citizen must know and share in them both, the inference is obvious. There is the rule exercised by a master, which is concerned with the menial functions of life; the master need not know how to perform these services (which would be degrading), but rather how to employ others to perform them. And the other sort of knowledge is that involved in doing these menial duties, which vary much in character and are executed by various classes of slaves, such, for example, as handicraftsmen, who, as their name signifies, live by the labor of their hands: under these the mechanic is included. Hence in ancient times, and among some nations, the working classes had no share in the government—a privilege which they only acquired under the most extreme form of democracy. Certainly the good man and the statesman and the good citizen ought not to learn the crafts of inferiors except for their own occasional use; if they habitually practice them, there will cease to be a distinction between master and slave.

1   *Euripides* One of the greatest Ancient Greek tragedians (480–406 BCE). This quote is from his play *Aeolus*, which is (except for fragments quoted by others) now lost.

2   *Jason* Jason of Pherae was a tyrant who ruled Thessaly c. 370 BCE.

This is not the rule of which we are speaking; but there is a rule of another kind, which is exercised over freemen and equals by birth—a constitutional rule,[1] which the ruler must learn by having been ruled himself, as he would learn the duties of a general of cavalry or infantry by being under the orders of one, and by having had the command of a regiment and of a company. It is said that he who has never learned to obey cannot be a good commander. Ruling and obeying are not the same, but the good citizen ought to be capable of both; he should know how to govern like a freeman, and how to obey like a freeman—these are the virtues of a citizen. And, although the temperance and justice of a ruler are distinct from those of a subject, the virtue of a good man will include both; for the virtue of the good man who is free and also a subject, e.g., justice, will not be of a single kind, but will comprise distinct kinds, the one qualifying him to rule, the other to obey, and differing as the temperance and courage of men and women differ. For a man would be thought a coward if he had no more courage than a courageous woman, and a woman would be thought loquacious if she imposed no more restraint on her conversation than the good man; and indeed their part in the management of the household is different, for the duty of the one is to acquire, and of the other to preserve. Practical wisdom only is characteristic of the ruler: it would seem that all other virtues must equally belong to ruler and subject. The virtue of the subject is certainly not wisdom, but only true opinion; he may be compared to the maker of the flute, while his master is like the flute-player or user of the flute.

From these considerations may be gathered the answer to the question, whether, and to what extent, the virtue of the good man is the same as that of the good citizen, or different.

5

There still remains one more question about the citizen: Are only those who have the right to office to be counted as true citizens, or is the mechanic to be included? If they who may not hold office are to be deemed citizens, and thus this man is a citizen, then not every citizen can have this virtue of ruling and obeying. And if none of the lower class are citizens, in which part of the state are they to be placed? For they are not resident aliens, and they are not foreigners. May we not reply that, as far as this objection goes, there is no more absurdity in excluding them than in excluding slaves and freedmen from any of the above-mentioned classes? It must be admitted that we cannot consider all those to be citizens who are necessary to the existence of the state; for example, children are not citizen equally with grown-up men, who are citizens absolutely, but children, not being grown up, are only qualified—"underdeveloped"—citizens. In ancient times, and among some nations the artisan class were slaves or foreigners, and this explains why the majority of them are so now. The best form of state will not admit them to citizenship; but if they are admitted, then our definition of the virtue of a citizen will not apply to every citizen nor to every free man as such, but only to those who are freed from necessary services. The necessary people are either slaves who minister to the wants of individuals, or mechanics and laborers who are the servants of the community. These reflections carried a little further will explain their position—though what has been said already is of itself, when understood, explanation enough.

Since there are many forms of government there must be many varieties of citizen and especially of citizens who are subjects; so that under some governments the mechanic and the laborer will be citizens, but not in others, as, for example, in aristocracy (the so-called rule of the best, where offices are distributed according to virtue and merit); for no man can practice virtue who is living the life of a mechanic or laborer. In oligarchies the qualification for office is high, and therefore no laborer can ever be a citizen; but a mechanic may, for majority of them are rich. At Thebes there was a law that no man could hold office who had not retired from business for ten years. But in many states the law goes to the length of admitting aliens; for in some democracies a man is a citizen though his mother only be a citizen; and a similar principle is applied to illegitimate children; the law is relaxed when there is a dearth of population. But when the number of citizens increases, first the children of a male or a female slave are excluded; then those whose mothers only are citizens; and at last the right of citizenship is confined to those whose fathers and mothers are both citizens.

Hence, as is evident, there are different kinds of citizens; and he is a citizen in the highest sense who shares in the honors of the state. Compare Homer's words, "like some dishonored alien";[2] he who is excluded from the honors of

---

1   *constitutional rule* Sometimes translated as a "political" rule—the sort exercised by a statesman over his fellow-citizens.

2   *like some dishonored alien* Homer, *Iliad* 9, 648; 16, 59.

the state is no better than an alien. But when his exclusion is concealed, then the privileged class is trying to deceive their fellow inhabitants.

As to the question whether the virtue of the good man is the same as that of the good citizen, the considerations already adduced prove that in some states the good man and the good citizen are the same, and in others different. Even when they are the same, it is not every citizen who is a good man, but only the statesman and those who have or may have, alone or in conjunction with others, the direction of public affairs.

6

Having answered these questions, we will next consider whether there is only one form of government or many, and if many, what they are, and how many, and what are the differences between them.

A constitution is the arrangement of offices in a state, especially of the highest offices. The government is everywhere sovereign in the state, and the constitution is in fact the government. For example, in democracies the people are supreme, but in oligarchies, the few; and, therefore, we say that these two forms of government also are different: and so in other cases.

First, let us consider what is the purpose of a state, and how many forms of government for regulating human society there are. We have already said, in the first part of this treatise, when discussing household management and the rule of a master, that man is by nature a political animal. And therefore, men, even when they do not require one another's help, desire to live together; but they are also brought together by their common interests as they individually attain any measure of well-being. This is certainly the chief end, both of individuals and of states. And mankind also come together and maintain the political community for the sake of mere life (in which there is possibly some noble element so long as the evils of existence do not greatly overbalance the good). And we all see that men cling to life even at the cost of enduring great misfortune, seeming to find in life a natural sweetness and happiness.

There is no difficulty in distinguishing the various kinds of authority; they have been often defined already in discussions intended for the general public.[1] The rule of a

master is intended to serve his own interests (though the slave by nature and the master by nature have in reality the same interests), but it incidentally considers the slave, since, if the slave perishes, the rule of the master perishes with him. On the other hand, the government of a wife and children and of a household, which we have called household management, is exercised mainly for the good of the governed or for the common good of both parties, but essentially for the good of the governed, as we see to be the case in medicine, gymnastic, and the arts in general, which are only incidentally concerned with the good of the artists themselves. The trainer or the helmsman considers the good of those committed to his care. But the trainer may sometimes practice gymnastics, and the helmsman is always one of the crew; thus the trainer becomes one of those in training, and the helmsman is also a sailor. Thus, each is one of the persons taken care of, and incidentally participates in the advantage. And so in politics: when the state is constructed on the principle of equality and likeness, the citizens think that they ought to hold office by turns. Formerly, as is natural, each one would take his turn of service; then somebody else would look after his interest, just as he, while in office, had looked after theirs. But nowadays, for the sake of the advantage which is to be gained from the public revenues and from office, men want to be permanently in office. It is almost as if the rulers were sickly, but were kept in health only during their term in office; in that case we may be sure that they would eagerly seek office and want to stay there. The conclusion is evident: that governments which have a regard to the common interest are constituted in accordance with strict principles of justice, and are therefore true forms; but those which regard only the interest of the rulers are all defective and perverted forms, for they are despotic, whereas a state is a community of freemen.

7

Having determined these points, we have next to consider how many forms of government there are, and what they are; and in the first place what are the true forms, for when they are determined the perversions of them will at once be apparent.

The words "constitution" and "government" have the same meaning, and the government, which is the supreme authority in states, must be in the hands of one, or of a few, or of the many. The true forms of government, therefore,

---

1   *discussions intended for the general public* Aristotle refers here (and elsewhere in this work) to writings of his, now lost, that were intended for a wider audience.

30 are those in which the one, or the few, or the many, govern with a view to the common interest; but governments
which rule with a view to the private interest, whether of
the one or of the few, or of the many, are perversions. For
the members of a state, if they are truly citizens, ought to
participate in its advantages.

Of forms of government in which one rules, we call
that which regards the common interests, kingship or
royalty; that in which more than one, but not many, rule,
35 aristocracy;[1] and it is so called, either because the rulers are
the best men, or because they have at heart the best interests of the state and of the citizens. But when the citizens
at large administer the state for the common interest, the
government is called by the generic name—a constitution
or polity. There is a reason to use this generic term. One
40 man or a few may excel in virtue; but as the number increases it becomes more difficult for them to attain perfec-
1279b tion in every kind of virtue, though they may in military
virtues in particular, for this is found in the masses. Hence
in a constitutional government the fighting-men have
the supreme power, and those who possess arms are the
citizens.

Of the above-mentioned forms, the perversions are as
5 follows: of royalty, tyranny; of aristocracy, oligarchy; of constitutional government, democracy. For tyranny is a kind of
monarchy which has in view the interest of the monarch
only; oligarchy has in view the interest of the wealthy; democracy, of the needy—in none of them the common good
10 of all.

8

But there are difficulties about these forms of government,
and it will therefore be necessary to state the nature of each
of them at a little more length. For anyone making a philosophical—not merely a practical—study of the various sci-
15 ences, ought not to overlook or omit anything, but should
set forth the truth in every particular.

Tyranny, as I was saying, is monarchy exercising the
rule of a master over the political society; oligarchy is government by men of property; democracy, the opposite—the
poorer classes, and not the men of property, are the rulers.
20 And here arises the first of our difficulties, and it relates
to the distinction drawn. For democracy is said to be the

government of the many. But what if the many are men of
property and have the power in their hands? In like manner oligarchy is said to be the government of the few; but
what if the poor are fewer than the rich, and have the power
in their hands because they are stronger? In these cases the   25
distinction which we have drawn between these different
forms of government would no longer hold good.

Suppose, then, that we associate wealth with the few
and poverty with the many, and name the governments
accordingly: an oligarchy is said to be that in which the
few and the wealthy are the rulers, and a democracy that in   30
which the many and the poor are the rulers. But there will
still be a difficulty. For, if the only forms of government are
the ones already mentioned, how shall we describe those
other governments also just mentioned by us, in which the
rich are the more numerous and the poor are the fewer, and
both govern in their respective states?

The argument seems to show that, whether in oligarch-   35
ies or in democracies, the size of the governing body—the
greater number, as in a democracy, or the smaller number,
as in an oligarchy—is an accident due to the fact that the
rich generally are few, and the poor numerous. But if so,
there is a misapprehension of the causes of the difference
between them. For the real difference between democracy
and oligarchy is poverty and wealth. Wherever men rule by   40
reason of their wealth, whether they be few or many, that is   1280a
an oligarchy, and where the poor rule, that is a democracy.
But as a matter of fact, the rich are few and the poor many;
for few are well-to-do, whereas freedom is enjoyed by all;   5
and wealth and freedom are the grounds on which the oligarchical and democratic parties, respectively, claim power
in the state.

9

Let us next consider the common definitions of oligarchy
and democracy, and what are the oligarchical and democratic conceptions of justice. For all men cling to justice of
some kind, but their conceptions are imperfect and they do   10
not express the whole idea. For example, justice is thought
by democrats to be equality, and so it is—not equality for
all, however, but only for equals. And inequality is thought
by oligarchs to be justice, and so it is—not for all, again, but
only for unequals. Men judge erroneously when they fail to
consider justice relatively to particular persons. The reason
is that they are passing judgment on themselves, and most   15
people are bad judges in their own case. "Justice" implies a

___
1   *aristocracy*   The Greek *aristos* literally means "best," while *kratein*
    means "to rule," hence *aristokratiā*, "rule of the best."

relation to persons as well as to things, and a just distribution, as I have already said in the *Ethics*,[1] implies the same ratio between the persons receiving as between the things given. The disputing parties here agree about the equality of the things, but dispute about the equality of the persons, chiefly for the reason which I have just given—because they are bad judges in their own affairs; and secondly, because both the parties to the argument are speaking of a limited and partial justice, but imagine themselves to be speaking of absolute justice. The oligarchs consider people unequal in all respects when they are unequal in one respect, for example, wealth; and the democrats, consider people equal in all respects when they are equal in one respect, for example free birth. But they leave out the crucial point. For if men met and associated out of regard to wealth only, their share in the state would be proportioned to their property, and the oligarchical doctrine would then seem to carry the day. It would not be just that he who paid one mina should have the same share of a hundred minae, whether of the principal or of the profits, as he who paid the remaining ninety-nine. But a state exists for the sake of a good life, and not for the sake of life only: if life only were the object, slaves and brute animals might form a state, but they cannot, for they have no share in happiness or in a life of free choice. Nor does a state exist for the sake of alliance and security from injustice, nor yet for the sake of exchange and commercial relations; for then the Etruscans and the Carthaginians, and all who have commercial treaties with one another, would be the citizens of one state. True, they have agreements about imports, and engagements that they will do no wrong to one another, and written articles of alliance. But there are no magistrates common to the contracting parties who will enforce their engagements; different states have each their own magistracies. Nor does one state take care to ensure the moral character of citizens of the other, nor see that those who come under the terms of the treaty do no wrong or wickedness at all, but only that they do no injustice to one another. Whereas, those who care for good government take into consideration virtue and vice in states. This implies that virtue must be the care of a state which is truly so called, and not merely enjoys the name: for without this end the community becomes a mere alliance which differs only in place from alliances of which the members live apart; and law is only a convention, "a guarantor to one another of justice," as the sophist Lycophron[2] says, and has no real power to make the citizens good.

This is obvious; for suppose that distinct places, such as Corinth and Megara, were brought together so that their walls touched, still they would not be one city, not even if the citizens had the right to intermarry, which is one of the rights peculiarly characteristic of states. Again, if men dwelt at a distance from one another, but close enough have associations, and there were laws among them that they should not wrong each other in their exchanges, this would still not make them a single state. Let us suppose that one man is a carpenter, another a farmer, another a shoemaker, and so on, and that there are ten thousand of them all together; nevertheless, if they have nothing in common but exchange, alliance, and the like, this group would not constitute a state. Why is this? Surely not because they are at a distance from one another: for even supposing that such a community were to meet in one place, but that each man had a house of his own, which was in a manner his state, and that they made alliances with one another, but only against evil-doers; still an accurate thinker would not deem this to be a state, if their relations with one another were of the same character after as before their union.

It is clear then that a state is not a mere society, having a common place, established for the prevention of crime and the encouragement of trade. These are conditions without which a state cannot exist; but all of them together do not constitute a state, which is a community of families and aggregations of families in well-being, for the sake of a perfect and self-sufficient life. Such a community can only be established among those who live in the same place and intermarry. Hence arise in cities family connections, brotherhoods, common sacrifices, amusements which draw men together. But these are created by friendship, for the will to live together is friendship. The end of the state is the good life, and these are the means towards it. And the state is the union of families and villages in a perfect and self-sufficing life, by which we mean a happy and honorable life.

Our conclusion, then, is that political society exists for the sake of noble actions, and not of mere companionship. So people who contribute most to such a society have a greater share in it than those who have the same or a greater freedom or nobility of birth but are inferior to them in pol-

---

1   *just distribution ... Ethics*   Nicomachean Ethics, 1131a 14 ff.

2   *Lycophron*   Unknown except for this reference; probably late fifth or early fourth century BCE. The sophist taught that government represents a contractual arrangement among the governed to provide protection and to further self-interested aims.

itical virtue; or than those who exceed them in wealth but are surpassed by them in virtue.

From what has been said it will be clearly seen that all the partisans of different forms of government speak of a part of justice only.

10

There is also a doubt as to what is to be the supreme power in the state: Is it the multitude? Or the wealthy? Or the good? Or the one best man? Or a tyrant? Any of these alternatives seems to involve disagreeable consequences. If the poor, for example, because they are more in number, divide among themselves the property of the rich, is not this unjust? "No, by heaven," someone may reply, "for the supreme authority justly willed it." But if this is not injustice, what is? When taking men as a whole, if the majority divides the property of the minority, is it not evident that they will ruin the state? Yet surely, virtue does not the ruin its possessor, nor is justice destructive of a state; and therefore this law of confiscation clearly cannot be just. If it were, all the acts of a tyrant must of necessity be just; for he only coerces other men by superior power, just as the multitude coerce the rich. But is it just then that the few and the wealthy should be the rulers? And what if they, in like manner, rob and plunder the people—is this just? if so, the other case will likewise be just. But there can be no doubt that all these things are wrong and unjust.

Then ought the good to rule and have supreme power? But in that case everybody else, being excluded from power, will be dishonored. For the offices of a state are posts of honor; and if one set of men always holds them, the rest must be deprived of them. Then should the one best man rule? No, that is still more oligarchical, for the number of those who are dishonored is thereby increased. Someone may say that it is bad in any case for a man, subject as he is to all the accidents of human passion, to have the supreme power, rather than the law. But what if the law itself be democratic or oligarchical, how will that help us out of our difficulties? Not at all; the same consequences will follow.

11

Most of these questions may be reserved for another occasion. Consider further, now, the view that some hold that the multitude ought to be supreme rather than the few best; this is not free from difficulty, yet it seems to contain an element of truth. For a group of many ordinary people meeting together may very likely form a collectivity better than a few good ones, considered individually, just as a feast to which many contribute is better than a dinner provided out of a single purse. For each individual in the group has a share of virtue and prudence, and when they meet together, they become, so to speak, one man with many feet, hands, and senses, and perhaps many good qualities of character and intelligence. In this way, many people taken together are a better judge than a single man of music and poetry; for some understand one part, and some another, and among them they understand the whole. There is a similar combination of qualities in good men, who differ from the others in the way beautiful people are said to differ from those who are not beautiful, and works of art from realities, because in them the scattered elements are combined, although, if taken separately, the eye of one person or some other feature in another person would be more beautiful than in the picture.

Whether this principle can apply to every democracy, and to all bodies of men, is not clear. In some cases it definitely does not apply; for the argument would equally hold about animals; and wherein, it will be asked, do some men differ from animals? But there may be bodies of men about whom our statement is nevertheless true. And if so, the difficulty which has been already raised, and also another which is akin to it—namely, what power should be assigned to the mass of freemen and citizens, who are not rich and have no personal merit—are both solved. There is still a danger in allowing them to share the great offices of state, for their folly will lead them into error, and their dishonesty into crime. But there is a danger also in not letting them share, for a state in which many poor men are excluded from office will necessarily be full of enemies. The only way of escape is to assign to them some deliberative and judicial functions. For this reason Solon and certain other legislators give them the power of electing to offices, and of calling the magistrates to account, but they do not allow them to hold office individually. When they meet together their perceptions are quite good enough, and combined with the better class they are useful to the state (just as impure food when mixed with what is pure sometimes makes the entire mass more wholesome than a small quantity of the pure would be), but each individual, left to himself, judges imperfectly.

On the other hand, the popular form of government involves certain difficulties. In the first place, it might be

40 objected that the only person whose judgment regarding sickness and cure can be trusted is someone—the physician—who could himself heal disease; and so in all professions and arts. As, then, the conduct of a physician ought to be judged by physicians, so ought men in general to be called to account by their peers. But physicians are of three kinds: there is the ordinary practitioner, and there is the specialist, and thirdly the intelligent man who (though not practicing) has studied the art: in all arts there is such a class; and we attribute the power of judging to them quite as much as to practitioners of the art. Secondly, does not the same principle apply to elections? For a right election can only be made by those who have knowledge; those who know geometry, for example, will make a reliable choice of geometrician, and those who know how to navigate, a pilot; and, even if there be some occupations and arts in which private persons share in the ability to choose, they certainly cannot choose better than those who know. So that, according to this argument, neither the election of magistrates, nor the calling of them to account, should be entrusted to the many.

Yet possibly these objections are to a great extent met by our old answer, that if the people are not utterly degraded, although individually they may be worse judges than those who have special knowledge, as a body they are as good or better. Moreover, there are some arts whose products are not judged solely, or best, by the artists themselves, namely those arts whose products are recognized even by those who do not possess the art; for example, the knowledge of the house is not limited to the builder only; the user, or, in other words, the master, of the house will be even a better judge than the builder, just as the pilot will judge better of the quality of a rudder than the carpenter, and the guest will judge better the quality of a feast than will the cook.

This difficulty seems now to be sufficiently answered, but there is another akin to it. It would be strange that inferior persons should have greater authority than good persons in matters of great consequence. Yet the election and oversight of magistrates is the most important matter of all. And these, as I was saying, are functions which in some states are assigned to the people, for the assembly is supreme in all such matters. Yet persons of any age, and having little property, may sit in the assembly and deliberate and judge, although for the great officers of state, such as treasurers and generals, a high qualification is required. But this difficulty may be solved in the same manner as the preceding, and the present practice of democracies may be really defensible. For the power does not reside in the individual members, but rather in the body of the whole, of the court, and the senate, and the assembly. And for this reason the many may claim to have a higher authority than the few; for the people, and the senate, and the courts consist of many persons, and their property collectively is greater than the property of one or of a few individuals holding great offices. But enough of this.

The discussion of the first question shows very clearly that laws, when good, should be supreme; and that magistrates should regulate those matters only on which the laws are unable to speak with precision, owing to the difficulty of general principle applying to particulars. But I have not yet clearly explained what good laws are, so the old difficulty remains. The goodness or badness, justice or injustice, of laws varies of necessity with the constitutions of states. This, however, is clear: that laws must be adapted to constitutions. But if so, true forms of government will of necessity have just laws, and perverted forms of government will have unjust laws.

12

In all sciences and arts the end is some good. The most authoritative of all sciences and arts is political science; its end is the greatest good and the good most to be pursued; and that good is justice, in other words, the common interest. All men think justice to be a sort of equality; and to a certain extent they agree in the philosophical distinctions which have been laid down by us about ethics.[1] For they admit that justice involves things and persons to whom those things are to be assigned, and that equals ought to have equality of assignment.

But there still remains a question: equality or inequality of what? Here is a difficulty which calls for political speculation. For very likely some persons will say that offices of state ought to be unequally distributed according to superiority in any respect, although there is no other difference between one citizen and the rest in other respects; for that those who differ in any one respect have different rights and claims. But, surely, if this is true, the complexion or height of a man, or any other advantage, will be a reason for his obtaining a greater share of political rights. The error here lies upon the surface, and may be illustrated from the other

1   *philosophical distinctions ... ethics*   Aristotle refers here to his conclusions in *Nicomachean Ethics* 5, 3.

arts and sciences. When a number of flute players are equal in their art, there is no reason why those of them who are more nobly born should have better flutes given to them; for they will not play any better on the flute, and the superior instrument should be reserved for him who is the superior
35 artist. If what I am saying is still obscure, it will be made clearer as we proceed. For consider the case of a superior flute-player who was very inferior in birth and beauty. Al-
40 though either of these may be greater assets than the art of flute-playing, and may excel flute-playing in a greater ratio than he excels the others in his art—still he ought to have
1283a the best flutes given to him, unless the advantages of wealth and birth contribute to excellence in flute-playing, which they clearly do not.

There is a further objection to this position: if it were right, then every good characteristic would have to be commensurable with any other. For if a given height may be measured against wealth and against freedom, height in
5 general may be so measured. Thus if A excels in height more than B excels in virtue, even if virtue in general excels height still more, all goods will be commensurable; for if an amount C of one quality is better than an amount D of a second, it is clear that some greater amount of that second quality should be equal to amount C of the first. But since
10 no such comparison can be made, it is evident that there is good reason why in politics a claim to office cannot be grounded on just any sort of inequality. (And the situation is similar in every art.) For if some are slow, and others swift, that is no reason why the one should have little and the others much; it is in gymnastics contests that such excel-
15 lence is rewarded. Whereas the rival claims of candidates for office can only be based on the possession of elements which enter into the composition of a state. And therefore the noble, or free-born, or rich, may with good reason claim office; for holders of offices must be freemen and taxpayers: a state can be no more composed entirely of poor men than entirely of slaves. But if wealth and freedom are necessary
20 elements, justice and valor are equally so; for without the former qualities a state cannot exist at all, without the latter not well.

13

If the mere existence of the state is alone to be considered, then it would seem that all, or some at least, of these claims
25 are just; but, if we take into account a good life, then, as I have already said, education and virtue have superior claims. But because those who are equal in one thing ought not to have an equal share in everything, nor those who are unequal in one thing have an unequal share in everything, it is certain that all forms of government which rest on either of these principles are perversions. All men have a claim in a certain sense, as I have already admitted, but all have not an
30 absolute claim. The rich claim because they have a greater share in the land, and land is the common element of the state; also they are generally more trustworthy in contracts. Freemen claim on the same basis as the nobility; for they are nearly akin. For those of noble birth are citizens in a truer
35 sense than those of lower status, and good birth is always valued in a man's own home and country. Another reason is that those who are sprung from better ancestors are likely to be better men, for high birth implies excellence of one's stock. Virtue, too, may be truly said to have a claim, for justice has been acknowledged by us to be a social virtue, and it implies all others. Again, the many may urge their claim
40 against the few; for, when taken collectively, and compared with the few, they are stronger and richer and better.

But, what if the good, the rich, the noble, and the 1283b other classes who make up a state, are all living together in a single state: will they agree who shall rule? There is no doubt at all in determining who ought to rule in each of the
5 above-mentioned forms of government. For states are characterized by differences in their governing bodies—one of them has a government of the rich, another of the virtuous, and so on. But a difficulty arises when all these elements co-exist. How are we to decide? Suppose the virtuous to
10 be very few in number: may we consider their numbers in relation to their duties, and ask whether there are enough of them to administer the state, or so many as will make up a state? Objections may be urged against all the aspirants to political power. Claims founded on wealth or family might be thought to have no justice; on this foundation, if any
15 one person were richer than all the rest, it is clear that he ought to be ruler of them. In like manner he who is very distinguished by his birth ought to have the superiority over all those whose claim is based on their freeborn status. In
20 an aristocracy, or government of the best, a similar difficulty occurs about virtue; for if one citizen be better than the other members of the government, however good they may be, he too, upon the same principle of just distribution of office, should rule over them. And if the people are to be supreme because they are stronger than the few, then if one man, or more than one, but not a majority, is stronger than
25 the many, they ought to rule, and not the many.

All these considerations appear to show that none of the principles on which men claim to rule and to hold all other men in subjection to them are strictly right. To those who claim to be masters of the government on the ground of their virtue or their wealth, the many might fairly answer that they themselves are often better and richer than the few—not individually, but collectively. And another ingenious objection which is sometimes put forward may be met in a similar manner. Some persons doubt whether the legislator who desires to make laws that are the most just laws ought to legislate with a view to the good of the higher classes or of the many, when the case which we have mentioned occurs.

Now what is just or right is to be interpreted in the sense of "what is equal"; and that which is right in the sense of being equal is to be considered with reference to the advantage of the state, and the common good of the citizens. And a citizen is one who shares in governing and being governed. He differs under different forms of government, but in the best state he is one who is able and willing to be governed and to govern with a view to the life of virtue. If, however, there were some one person, or more than one, although not enough to make up the full complement of a state, whose virtue is so pre-eminent that the virtues or the political capacity of all the rest admit no comparison with his or theirs, he or they can be no longer regarded as part of a state; for justice will not be done to the superior, if he is reckoned only as the equal of those who are so far inferior to him in virtue and in political capacity. Such a person may truly be deemed a god among men. Hence we see that legislation is necessarily concerned only with those who are equal in birth and in capacity; and that for men of pre-eminent virtue there is no law—they are a law in themselves. Anyone would be ridiculous who attempted to make laws for them: they would probably retort what, in the fable of Antisthenes,[1] the lions said to the hares, when in the council of the beasts the hares began haranguing and claiming equality for all.[2] And for this reason democratic states have instituted ostracism;[3] equality is above all things their aim, and therefore they ostracized and banished from the city for a time those who seemed to predominate too much through their wealth, or the number of their friends, or through any other political influence. Mythology tells us that the Argonauts left Heracles behind for a similar reason; the ship Argo would not take him because she feared that he would have been too much for the rest of the crew.[4] So those who denounce tyranny and blame the counsel which Periander[5] gave to Thrasybulus[6] cannot be held altogether just in their censure. The story is that Periander, when the herald was sent to ask counsel of him, said nothing, but only cut off the tallest ears of corn till he had brought the field to a level. The herald did not know the meaning of the action, but came and reported what he had seen to Thrasybulus, who understood that he was to cut off the principal men in the state; and this is a policy not only expedient for tyrants or in practice confined to them, but equally necessary in oligarchies and democracies. Ostracism is a measure of the same kind, which acts by disabling and banishing the most prominent citizens. Great powers do the same to whole cities and nations, as the Athenians did to the Samians, Chians, and Lesbians; no sooner had they obtained a firm grasp of the empire, than they humbled their allies contrary to treaty; and the Persian king has repeatedly crushed the Medes, Babylonians, and other nations, when their spirit has been stirred by the recollection of their former greatness.

The problem is a universal one, and equally concerns all forms of government, correct as well as incorrect forms. Perverted forms with a view to their own interests may adopt this policy, but those which seek the common interest do the same. A similar practice may be observed in the arts and sciences; for the painter will not allow the figure to have a foot which, however beautiful, is not in proportion, nor will the shipbuilder allow the stern or any other part of the vessel to be unduly large, any more than the chorus-master will allow any one who sings louder or better than all the rest to sing in the choir. Monarchs, too, may practice compulsion and still live in harmony with their cities, if their own government is for the interest of the state. Hence where there is an acknowledged superiority the argument in favor of ostracism is based upon a kind of political justice. It would certainly be better that the legislator should from

---

1   *Antisthenes*   (c. 446–366 BCE) companion of Socrates associated with early Cynicism. Only fragments of his works survive.
2   *the lions ... equality for all*   The lions said, "Where are your claws and teeth?"
3   *ostracism*   A practice in Athens from 487–417 BCE that involved banishing a citizen for ten years. Banished citizens retained their citizenship and property. The practice is thought to have been introduced in conjunction with the establishment of Athenian democracy.
4   *Mythology ... crew*   In the story Heracles alone was the equal of Jason, the ship's captain, in prowess at rowing.
5   *Periander*   Ruler of Corinth, around 600 BCE.
6   *Thrasybulus*   Thrasybulus of Miletus, around 600 BCE.

the beginning order his state so as to have no need of such a remedy. But if the need arises, the next best thing is that he should endeavor to correct the evil by this or some similar measure. The principle, however, has not been fairly applied in states; for, instead of looking to the good of their own constitution, they have used ostracism in the spirit of faction. It is true that under perverted forms of government, and from their special point of view, such a measure is just and expedient, but it is also clear that it is not absolutely just. In the perfect state there would be great doubts about the use of it, not when applied to excess in strength, wealth, popularity, or the like, but when used against some one who is pre-eminent in virtue—what is to be done with him? Mankind will not say that such a one is to be expelled and exiled; on the other hand, he ought not to be a subject—that would be as if mankind should claim to rule over Zeus, dividing his offices among them. The only alternative is that all should joyfully obey such a ruler, according to what seems to be the order of nature, and that men like him should be kings for life in their state.

14

The preceding discussion, by a natural transition, leads to the consideration of royalty, which we admit to be one of the correct forms of government. Let us see whether in order to be well governed a state or country should be under the rule of a king or under some other form of government; and whether monarchy, although good for some, may be bad for others.

But first we must determine whether there is one species of royalty or many. It is easy to see that there are many, and that the manner of government is not the same in all of them. Of royalties according to law, (1) the Spartan type is thought to be the best example; but there the royal power is not absolute, with two exceptions: when they take military command during foreign expeditions, and when they supervise religious worship. The kingly office is in truth a kind of independent and perpetual generalship. The king does not have the power of life and death, except in special cases, as for instance, in ancient times, he had it when leading a military campaign, by right of superior force. This custom is described in Homer: Agamemnon is patient when he is attacked in the assembly, but when the army goes out to battle he has the power even of life and death. He says: "When I find a man skulking apart from the battle, nothing shall save him from the dogs and vultures, for in my hands

is death."[1] This, then, is one form of royalty—a generalship for life; some of these are hereditary and others elective.

(2) There is another sort of monarchy common among the barbarians, which nearly resembles tyranny. But this is both legal and hereditary. Barbarians are more servile in character than Greeks, and Asians more than Europeans; so they do not rebel against a despotic government. Such royalties have the nature of tyrannies because the people are by nature slaves; but there is no danger of their being overthrown, for they are hereditary and legal. Thus their guards are such as a king and not such as a tyrant would employ, that is to say, they are composed of citizens, whereas the guards of tyrants are mercenaries. For kings rule according to law over voluntary subjects, but tyrants over involuntary; while kings are guarded by their fellow-citizens, tyrants are guarded against them.

These are two forms of monarchy, and there was a third (3) which existed in ancient Greece, called an *aesymnetia* or dictatorship. This may be broadly defined as an elective tyranny, which, like the barbarian monarchy, is legal, but differs from it in not being hereditary. Sometimes the office was held for life, sometimes for a term of years, or until certain duties had been performed. For example, the Mytilenaeans elected Pittacus leader[2] against the exiles, who were headed by Antimenides and Alcaeus the poet. And Alcaeus himself shows in one of his banquet odes that they chose Pittacus tyrant, for he reproaches his fellow-citizens for "having made the low-born Pittacus tyrant of the spiritless and ill-fated city, with one voice shouting his praises." These forms of government have always had the character of tyrannies, because they possess despotic power; but inasmuch as they are elective and acquiesced in by their subjects, they are kingly.

(4) There is a fourth species of kingly rule—that of the Heroic Age[3]—which was hereditary and legal, and was exercised over willing subjects. For the first chiefs were benefactors of the people in arts or arms; they either gathered them into a community, or procured land for them; and thus they became kings of voluntary subjects, and their power was inherited by their descendants. They took the command in war and presided over the sacrifices, except those which

---

1   *"When I find a man ... death"*   Homer, *Iliad* 2, 391–93.
2   *Mytilenaeans elected Pittacus leader*   Pittacus led the Mytilenaeans from 589 to 579 BCE.
3   *Heroic Age*   The time ending after the Trojan War—that is, around 1300 or 1200 BCE. The Greek account of events during this period is largely mythological.

required a priest. They also decided causes either with or without an oath; and when they swore, the form of the oath was the stretching out of their sceptre. In ancient times their power extended continuously to all things whatsoever, in city and country, as well as in foreign parts; but at a later date they relinquished several of these privileges, and others the people took from them, until in some states nothing was left to them but the sacrifices; and where they retained more of the reality of royal status it consisted only in the right of leadership in foreign wars.

These, then, are the four kinds of royalty. First the monarchy of the Heroic Age; this was exercised over voluntary subjects, but limited to certain functions; the king was a general and a judge, and had the control of religion. The second is that of the barbarians, which is a hereditary despotic government in accordance with law. A third is the power of the so-called *aisynmete* or dictator; this is an elective tyranny. The fourth is the Spartan royal status, which is in fact a generalship, hereditary and perpetual. These four forms differ from one another in the manner which I have described.

(5) There is a fifth form of kingly rule in which one has total sovereignty in every respect, just as each nation or each state has sovereignty over public matters; this form corresponds to the control of a household. For as household management is the kingly rule of a house, so kingly rule is the household management of a city, or of a nation, or of many nations.

15

Of these forms we need only consider two, the Spartan and the absolute royalty (with total sovereignty—the last mentioned); for most of the others lie in a region between them, having less power than the last, and more than the first. Thus the inquiry is reduced to two questions: first, is it advantageous to the state that there should be a perpetual general, and if so, should the office be confined to one family, or open to the citizens in turn? Secondly, is it a good idea to give one man supreme power in all things? The first question falls under the head of laws rather than of constitutions; for perpetual generalship might equally exist under any form of government, so that this matter may be dismissed for the present. The other kind of royalty is a sort of constitution; this we have now to consider, and briefly to run over the difficulties involved in it. We will begin by inquiring whether it is more advantageous to be ruled by the best man or by the best laws.

The advocates of royalty maintain that the laws speak only in general terms, and cannot provide for particular circumstances; and that for any art to abide by written rules is absurd. In Egypt the physician is allowed to alter the rules of treatment after the fourth day; if he does so sooner, it is at his own risk. Similarly, it is clear that a government acting only according to written laws is plainly not the best. Yet surely the ruler cannot dispense with the general principle which exists in law; and this, free from passion, is a better ruler than human judgment, in which passion is innate. Whereas the law is passionless, passion must always sway men's hearts. "Yes," it may be replied, "but then on the other hand an individual will be better at deliberation in some particular cases."

The best man, then, must legislate, and laws must be passed, but these laws will have no authority when they miss the mark, though in all other cases they retain their authority. But when the law cannot determine a point at all, or not well, should the one best man decide, or should all? According to our present practice, assemblies meet, sit in judgment, deliberate, and decide, and their judgments all relate to individual cases. Now any member of the assembly, taken separately, is certainly inferior to the wise man. But the state is made up of many individuals. And as a feast to which all the guests contribute is better than a banquet furnished by a single man, so a multitude is a better judge of many things than any individual.

Again, the many are more incorruptible than the few; they are like a larger quantity of water which is less easily polluted than a smaller quantity. The individual is liable to be overcome by anger or by some other passion, and then his judgment is necessarily perverted; but it is hardly to be supposed that a great number of persons would all get into a passion and go wrong at the same moment. Let us assume that they are the freemen, and that they never act in violation of the law, but fill up the gaps which the law is obliged to leave. Or, if such virtue is scarcely attainable by the multitude, we need only suppose that the majority are good men and good citizens, and ask which will be the more incorruptible, the one good ruler, or the many who are all good? Will not the many? "But," you will say, "there may be factions among them, whereas the one man is not divided against himself." To which we may answer that their character is as good as his. If we call the rule of many men, who are all of them good, aristocracy, and the rule of one man royalty, then aristocracy will be better for states than royalty, whether the government is supported by force or not, provided only that a number of men equal in virtue can be found.

The first governments were kingships, probably because long ago, when cities were small, there were only few men of great virtue. Men were made kings because they were benefactors, and benefits can be bestowed only by good men. But when many persons equal in merit arose, they would no longer endure the pre-eminence of one, and they desired a system they could all share in, and set up a constitution. The ruling class later deteriorated, and enriched themselves out of the public treasury; riches became the path to honor, and so oligarchies naturally grew up. These passed into tyrannies and tyrannies into democracies; for love of gain in the ruling classes was always tending to diminish their number, and so to strengthen the masses, who in the end set upon their masters and established democracies. Since cities have increased in size, no other form of government than democracy appears any longer to be easy to establish.

Even accepting that kingly power is the best thing for states, the question still arises: how about the family of the king? Are his children to succeed him? If they are no better than anybody else, that will be harmful. "But," says the royalist, "the king, though he might hand on his power to his children, would refrain from doing so." That, however, is hardly to be expected, and is too much to ask of human nature. There is also a difficulty about the force which he is to employ; should a king have guards around him for coercing the reluctant? If not, how will he administer his kingdom? Even if he is the lawful sovereign who does nothing arbitrarily or contrary to law, still he must have some force for maintaining the law. In the case of a limited monarchy there is not much difficulty in answering this question: the king must have such force as will be more than a match for one or more individuals, but not so great as that of the people. The ancients observe this principle when they gave guards to those they appointed dictator or tyrant. Thus, when Dionysius asked the Syracusans to allow him guards, somebody advised that they should give him only such a number.

16

1287a At this place in the discussion we turn to an inquiry respecting the king who acts solely according to his own will; he has now to be considered. The so-called limited monarchy, or kingship according to law, as I have already remarked, is not a distinct form of government, for under all governments, as, for example, in a democracy or aristocracy, there may be a general holding office for life, and one person is often made supreme over the administration of a state. A magistracy of this kind exists at Epidamnus, and also at Opus, but in the latter city has a more limited power. Now, absolute monarchy, or the arbitrary rule of a sovereign over all the citizens, in a state which consists of equals, is thought by some to be quite contrary to nature. It is argued that those who are by nature equals must have the same natural right and worth, and that for unequals to have an equal share in the offices of state, or for equals to have an uneven share, is as bad as for people with different body types to have the same food and clothing. So it is thought to be just that among equals everyone be ruled as well as rule, and therefore that all should have their turn. We thus arrive at law; for an order of succession implies law. And the rule of the law, it is argued, is preferable to that of any individual. On the same principle, even if it is better for certain individuals to govern, they should be made only guardians and ministers of the law. For there must be magistrates—this is admitted; but then men say that to give authority to any one man when all are equal is unjust.

There may indeed be cases which the law seems unable to determine, but in such cases can a man? The reply here is that the law trains officers for this express purpose, and appoints them to determine matters which are left undecided by it, to the best of their judgment. Further, it permits them to make any amendment of the existing laws which experience suggests. Therefore he who bids the law rule may be deemed to bid God and reason alone rule, but he who bids man rule adds an element of the beast; for desire is a wild beast, and passion perverts the minds of rulers, even when they are the best of men. The law is reason unaffected by desire.

We are told that a patient should call in a physician; he will not get better if he is doctored out of a book. But the parallel of the arts is clearly not in point; for the physician does nothing contrary to rule from motives of friendship; he only cures a patient and takes a fee; whereas magistrates do many things from spite and partiality. And, indeed, if a man suspected the physician of being in league with his enemies to destroy him for a bribe, he would rather have recourse to the book. But certainly physicians call in other physicians when they are sick, and training-masters call in other training-masters when they are in training, as if they could not judge truly about their own case and might be influenced by their feelings. Hence it is evident that in

seeking for justice men seek for a neutral standard, for this
is what the law is. Customary laws have more weight, and
relate to more important matters, than written laws, and a
man may be a safer ruler than the written law, but not safer
than the customary law.

Another objection is that it is by no means easy for one
man to supervise many things; he will have to appoint a
number of subordinates; and what difference does it make
whether these subordinates were officers from the start, or
were appointed by the ruler because he needed them? If, as
I said before, the good man has a right to rule because he is
better, still two good men are better than one: this is the old
saying, "two going together,"[1] and the prayer of Agamemnon, "Would that I had ten such counselors!"[2] And even
today there are magistrates, for example judges, who have
authority to decide some matters which the law is unable
to determine, since no one doubts that the law would command and decide in the best manner whatever it could.

But some things can, and other things cannot, be comprehended under the law, and this is the origin of the vexed
question whether the best law or the best man should rule.
For matters of detail about which men deliberate cannot be
included in legislation. Nor does any one deny that the decision of such matters must be left to man, but it is argued
that there should be many judges, not just one. For every
ruler who has been trained by the law judges well; and it
would surely seem strange that a single person should see
better with two eyes, or hear better with two ears, or act
better with two hands or feet, than many people with many
of each; indeed, it is already the practice of kings to make
themselves many eyes and ears and hands and feet. For they
make colleagues of those who are their friends and friends
of their government. They must be friends of the monarch
and of his government; if not his friends, they will not do
what he wants; but friendship implies likeness and equality;
and, therefore, if he thinks that his friends ought to rule, he
must think that those equal to him and like him ought to
rule equally with him. These are the principal controversies
relating to monarchy.

17

But might all this be true in some cases and not in others?
For in certain circumstances the rule of a master is just and
advantageous; in other, kingly rule, in still others, constitutional rule. But there is none naturally appropriate to
tyranny, or to any other perverted form of government; for
these come into being contrary to nature. Now, to judge
at least from what has been said, it is manifest that, where
men are alike and equal, it is neither expedient nor just that
one man should be lord of all, if there are laws, or if there
are no laws and he himself takes the place of law. Neither
should a good man be lord over good men, nor a bad man
over bad; not even if he excels in virtue, should he have a
right to rule (except in a particular case at which I have
already hinted, and to which I will shortly return). But first
of all, I must determine what natures are suited for government by a king, and what for an aristocracy, and what for a
constitutional government.

A people who are by nature capable of producing stock
superior in the virtue needed for political rule are fitted for
kingly government. A people whose stock are naturally capable of being ruled as freemen are adapted for aristocracy;
while the people who are suited for constitutional freedom
are those among whom there naturally exists a stock with
military capability, able to rule and to obey in turn, governed by a law which gives office to the well-to-do according to their desert.

But when a whole family or some individual happens to
be so superior in virtue as to surpass all others, then it is just
that they should be the royal family and supreme over all, or
that this one citizen should be king of the whole nation. For,
as I said before, giving them authority is the sort of justice
advocated by the founders of all states, whether aristocratic,
oligarchic, or democratic—for all of them recognize the
claim of excellence, although not the same excellence. For
surely it would not be right to kill, or ostracize, or exile such
a person, or require that he should take his turn in being
governed. The whole is naturally superior to the part, and
he who has this superiority stands in the relation of a whole
to the others' part. But if so, the only alternative is that he
should have the supreme power, and that mankind should
obey him, not in turn, but always.

These are the conclusions at which we arrive respecting
royalty and its various forms, and this is the answer to the
question, whether it is or is not advantageous to states, and
to which, and how.

---

1   *two going together*   Homer, *Iliad* 10, 24.
2   *Would that I had ten such councilors!*   Homer, *Iliad* 2, 372.

18

We maintain that there are three correct forms of government, and that the best must be that which is administered by the best, and in which there is one man, or a whole family, or many persons, excelling all the others together in virtue, and both rulers and subjects are fitted, the one to rule, the others to be ruled, in such a manner as to attain the most desirable life. We showed at the commencement of our inquiry that the virtue of the good man is necessarily the same as the virtue of the citizen of the perfect state. Clearly then in the same manner, and by the same means through which a man becomes truly good, he will frame a state that is to be ruled by an aristocracy or by a king, and the same education and the same habits will be found to make a good man and a man fit to be a statesman or a king.

Having arrived at these conclusions, we must proceed to speak of the perfect state, and describe how it comes into being and is established.

Book 4

1

Every art and science which embraces the whole of any subject, and does not study it in a fragmentary way, necessarily considers all the areas of that subject. For example, the art of gymnastic considers not only the suitableness of different modes of training to different bodies, but what sort is absolutely the best—that is, the sort of training suited to the ideal physique—and also what common form of training is adapted to the great majority of men. And if someone does not seek optimum fitness of body, or the greatest skill in gymnastics possible for him, still the trainer or the teacher of gymnastic should be able to give him skill at the lower level he desires. The same principle equally holds in medicine and shipbuilding, and the making of clothes, and in the arts generally.

Therefore it is obvious that government too is the subject of a single science, which has to consider what government is absolutely the best, and what characteristics it must have, to meet our desires best, if there were no external impediments; and it has also to consider what kind of government is adapted to particular states. For the best is often unattainable, and therefore the true legislator and statesman ought to be acquainted not only with that which is best in the abstract, but also with that which is best relatively to circumstances. We should be able further to say how a state may be constituted under any given conditions; both how it is originally formed and, when formed, how it may be longest preserved, even when it has far from the best constitution, and is not provided with the conditions necessary for the best; and even when it is not the best given its circumstances, but of an inferior type.

He ought, moreover, to know the form of government which is best suited to states in general; for political writers, although they have excellent ideas, are often impractical. We should consider, not only what form of government is best, but also what is possible and what is easily attainable by all. There are some who would have no form of government but the most perfect; but to have this, maximally advantageous external circumstances are required. Others, again, speak of a more attainable form, and, although they reject the constitution under which they are living, they extol some other one, for example the Spartan. Any change of government which has to be introduced should be one which men, will be both willing and able to adopt, starting from their existing constitutions, since there is quite as much trouble in the reformation of an old constitution as in the establishment of a new one, just as to unlearn is as hard as to learn. And therefore, in addition to the qualifications of the statesman already mentioned, he should be able to find remedies for the defects of existing constitutions, as has been said before. This he cannot do unless he knows how many forms of government there are.

It is often supposed that there is only one kind of democracy and one of oligarchy. But this is a mistake; and, in order to avoid such mistakes, we must ascertain what differences there are in the constitutions of states, and in how many ways they are combined. The same political insight will enable a man to know which laws are the best, and which are suited to different constitutions; for the laws are, and ought to be, adapted to the constitution, and not the constitution to the laws. A constitution is the organization of offices in a state, and determines what is to be the governing body, and what is the end of each community. But laws are not to be confused with the principles of the constitution; laws are the rules according to which the magistrates should administer the state, and proceed against offenders. So that we must know the varieties, and the number of varieties, of each form of government, if only with a view to making laws. For the same laws cannot be equally suited to all oligarchies or to all democracies, since there is certainly more than one form both of democracy and of oligarchy.

2

In our original discussion about governments we divided them into three correct forms: kingship, aristocracy, and constitutional government, and three corresponding perversions: tyranny, oligarchy, and democracy. We have already spoken of kingship and of aristocracy, for the study of the ideal state must involve discussion of these two forms, since both involve the idea of a principle of virtue equipped with the external means necessary for its exercise. We have already determined how aristocracy and kingship differ from one another, and when the latter should be established. In what follows we shall describe what is called "polity" or "constitutional government," (which bears the generic name of all constitutions), and the other forms, tyranny, oligarchy, and democracy.

It is obvious which of the three perversions is the worst, and which is the next worse. The one that is the perversion of the first and most nearly divine is necessarily the worst. And just as a royal rule, if not a mere name, must exist by virtue of some great personal superiority in the king, so tyranny, which is the worst of governments, is necessarily the farthest removed from a well-constituted form; oligarchy is little better, for it is a long way from aristocracy, and democracy is the most tolerable of the three.

A writer who preceded me[1] has already made these distinctions, but his point of view is not the same as mine. For he lays down the principle that when all the constitutions are good (the oligarchy and the rest being virtuous), democracy is the worst, but the best when all are bad. Whereas we maintain that they are in any case defective, and that one oligarchy is not to be accounted better than another, but only less bad.

Not to pursue this question further at present, let us begin by determining (1) how many varieties of constitution there are—since there are several forms of democracy and oligarchy; (2) what constitution is the most generally acceptable, that is, second-best after the perfect state; and in addition, what other forms there are which are aristocratic and well-constituted, and at the same time adapted to states in general; (3) what sort of civic body is suited by each of these inferior forms of government—for democracy may meet the needs of some better than oligarchy, and conversely. Next (4) we have to consider how one should proceed who desires to establish one of these various forms, whether of democracy or of oligarchy; and lastly, (5) having briefly discussed these subjects to the best of our power, we will endeavor to ascertain the modes of ruin and preservation both of constitutions generally and of each separately, and to what causes they are to be attributed.

3

The reason why there are many forms of government is that every state contains many elements. In the first place we see that all states are made up of families, and among the many citizens there must be some rich and some poor, and some in a middle condition; the rich are heavily armed, and the poor not. Of the common people, some are farmers, some are traders, and some are artisans. There are also among the notables differences of wealth and property—for example, in the number of horses which they keep, for they cannot afford to keep them unless they are rich. And therefore in old times the cities whose strength lay in their cavalry were oligarchies, and they used cavalry in wars against their neighbors; as was the practice of the Eretrians and Chalcidians, and also of the Magnesians on the river Maeander, and of other peoples in Asia. Besides differences of wealth there are differences of social rank and merit, and there are some other elements which were mentioned by us when, in treating of aristocracy, we enumerated the essentials of a state. Sometimes all of these elements, sometimes many, and sometimes fewer, have a share of control in government. It is evident then that there must be many forms of government, differing in kind, since the parts of which they are composed differ from each other in kind. For a constitution is an organization of offices, which all the citizens distribute among themselves, according to the power of the different classes, for example the rich or the poor, or according to some principle of equality which includes both. There must therefore be as many forms of government as there are modes of arranging the offices, according to the superiorities and differences of the parts of the state.

Just as people speak of two sorts of winds, north and south, and of the rest as only variations of these, there are generally thought to be two principal forms of constitution—democracy and oligarchy. For aristocracy is considered to be a kind of oligarchy, as being the rule of a few, and the so-called constitutional government is considered to be really a democracy, just as among the winds we make the west a variation of the north, and the east of the south wind. Similarly of musical modes there are said to be two kinds,

---

1 *writer who preceded me* Plato in the *Statesman*, 302 ff.

the Dorian and the Phrygian; the other arrangements of the scale are included as varieties of one or other of these two. This is a popular way of thinking about forms of government. But in the both cases—musical modes and governments—a better and more exact way is to distinguish, as I have done, the one or two which are true forms, and to regard the others as perversions, whether of the most perfectly tempered musical mode or of the best form of government. We may compare the severer and more overpowering musical modes to the oligarchical forms, and the more relaxed and gentler ones to the democratic.

4

It must not be assumed, as some are fond of doing, that democracy is simply that form of government in which the greater number are sovereign, for in oligarchies, and indeed in every government, the majority rules; nor again is oligarchy that form of government in which a few are sovereign. Imagine a state with a total population of 1300, of whom 1000 are rich, and do not allow a share of the government to the remaining 300 who are poor, but free, and in an other respects their equals. No one will say that this is a democracy. In like manner, if the poor were few and the masters of the rich who outnumber them, no one would ever call such a government, in which the rich majority have no share of office, an oligarchy. Therefore we should rather say that democracy is the form of government in which the free are rulers, and oligarchy in which the rich rule; it is only an accident that the free are the many and the rich are the few. Otherwise a government in which the offices were given according to height, as is said to be the case in Ethiopia, or according to beauty, would be an oligarchy; for the number of tall or good-looking men is small. And yet oligarchy and democracy are not sufficiently distinguished merely by these two characteristics of wealth and freedom. Both of them contain many other elements, and therefore we must carry our analysis further, and say that the government is not a democracy in which the freemen, being few in number, rule over the many who are not free, as at Apollonia, on the Ionian Gulf, and at Thera (for in each of these states the nobles, who were also the earliest settlers, were held in chief honor, although they were but a few out of many). Neither is it a democracy when the rich have the government because the are the majority, as was the case formerly at Colophon, where the bulk of the inhabitants had substantial property holdings before the Lydian War.

But the form of government is a democracy when the free, who are also poor and the majority, govern, and an oligarchy when the rich and the noble govern, being at the same time a minority.

I have said that there are many forms of government, and have explained to what causes the variety is due. I will now proceed to consider why there are more than those already mentioned, and what they are, and how they arise, starting from the principle already asserted, that every state consists, not of one, but of many parts. If we were going to speak of the different species of animals, we should first of all determine the organs which are indispensable to every animal, as for example some organs of sense, some for receiving and digesting food, such as the mouth and the stomach, and organs of locomotion. Assuming now that there are only so many kinds of organs, but that there may be differences in them—I mean different kinds of mouths, and stomachs, and perceptive and locomotive organs—the possible combinations of these differences will necessarily furnish many varieties of animals. (For animals cannot be the same which have different kinds of mouths or ears.) And when all the combinations are exhausted, there will be as many sorts of animals as there are combinations of the necessary organs. The same, then, is true of the forms of government which have been described; states, as I have repeatedly said, are composed, not of one, but of many elements. One element is the food-producing class, who are called farmers; a second, the class of mechanics who practice the arts without which a city cannot exist; of these arts some are absolutely necessary, others contribute to luxury or to the living of a good life. The third class is that of traders, and by traders I mean those who are engaged in buying and selling, whether in commerce or in retail trade. A fourth class is that of the serfs or laborers. The warriors make up the fifth class, and they are as necessary as any of the others, if the country is not to be the slave of every invader. For how can a state which has any title to the name be of a slavish nature? The state is independent and self-sufficing, but a slave is the reverse of independent.

This subject has been treated ingeniously, but not satisfactorily, in the *Republic*.[1] Socrates says there that a state is made up of four sorts of people who are absolutely necessary; these are a weaver, a farmer, a shoemaker, and a builder; afterwards, finding that they are not enough, he adds a smith, and again a herdsman, to look after the ne-

---

1   *This subject ... Republic* Plato, *Republic* 369d–371e.

cessary animals; then a merchant, and then a retail trader. All these together form the complement of the "first state," as if a state were established merely to supply the necessities of life, rather than for the sake of the good, or stood equally in need of shoemakers and of farmers. But he does not admit a military class into the state until the country has increased in size, and is beginning to encroach on its neighbor's land, whereupon they go to war. Yet even among his four original parts, or whatever be the number of elements whom he associates in the state, there must be some one who will dispense justice and determine what is just. And as the soul may be said to be more truly part of an animal than the body, so the higher parts of states, that is to say, the warrior class, the class engaged in the administration of justice, and that engaged in deliberation, which is the special business of political understanding—these are more essential to the state than the parts which minister to the necessaries of life. Whether their different functions are the functions of different citizens, or of the same—for it may often happen that the same persons are both warriors and farmers—is immaterial to the argument. The higher as well as the lower elements are to be equally considered parts of the state, and if so, the military element at any rate must be included. There are also the wealthy who minister to the state with their property; these form the seventh class. The eighth class is that of magistrates and of officers; for the state cannot exist without rulers. And therefore some must be able to take office and to serve the state, either always or in turn. There only remains the class of those who deliberate and who judge between disputants; we were just now distinguishing them. If the presence of all these elements, and their fair and equitable organization, is necessary to states, then there must also be persons who have the ability of statesmen. Different functions appear to be often combined in the same individual; for example, the warrior may also be a farmer or an artisan; or the counselor a judge. And all claim to possess political ability, and think that they are quite competent to fill most offices. But the same persons cannot be rich and poor at the same time. For this reason the rich and the poor are regarded in an especial sense as parts of a state. Again, because the rich are generally few in number, while the poor are many, they appear to be antagonistic, and as the one or the other prevails they form the government. Hence arises the common opinion that there are two kinds of government—democracy and oligarchy.

I have already explained that there are many forms of constitution, and what causes this variety. Let me now show that there are different forms both of democracy and oligarchy, as will indeed be evident from what has preceded. For various classes are included both in the common people and in the notables. One class of common people are farmers, another artisans; another traders, who are employed in buying and selling; another are the seafaring class, whether engaged in war or in trade, as ferrymen or as fishermen. (In many places any one of these classes forms quite a large population; for example, fishermen at Tarentum and Byzantium, crews of triremes[1] at Athens, merchant seamen at Aegina and Chios, ferrymen at Tenedos.) In addition, there are day-laborers, and those who, owing to their needy circumstances, have no leisure, and those who are not of free birth on both sides; and there may be other classes as well. The notables may be divided according to their wealth, birth, virtue, education, and similar differences.

The first form of democracy is that which is said to be based strictly on equality. In such a democracy the law says that justice demands that the poor and the rich have equal advantage and that neither should be masters. For if liberty and equality, as is thought by some, are chiefly to be found in democracy, they will be best attained when all persons share in the government to the utmost. And since the people are the majority, and the opinion of the majority is decisive, such a government must necessarily be a democracy. This then is one sort of democracy. There is another, in which the magistrates are elected according to a certain property qualification, but a low one; he who has the required amount of property has a share in the government, but he who loses his property loses his rights. Another kind is that in which all the citizens who are of unimpeachable descent share in the government, but still the law is supreme. In another, every citizen can share in office, but the law is supreme as before.

Finally, a fifth form of democracy, in other respects the same, is that in which, not the law, but the multitude, have the supreme power, and may supersede the law by their decrees. This is a state of affairs brought about by the demagogues. For in democracies which are subject to the law the best citizens are predominant, and there are no demagogues; but where the laws are not supreme, there demagogues spring up. For the people collectively become a monarch, and are many in one; and the many have the power in their hands, not as individuals, but collectively.

---

1 *triremes* Greek galley with three banks of oars on each side.

Homer says that "it is not good to have a rule of many,"[1] but whether he means this collective rule, or the rule of many individuals, is uncertain. In any event, in this sort of democracy which has the character of a monarchy uncontrolled by law, the collective rule seeks to exercise monarchical sway, and grows into a despot; the flatterer is held in honor; this sort of democracy is, relative to other democracies, what tyranny is to other forms of monarchy. The spirit of both is the same, and they alike exercise a despotic rule over the better citizens. The decrees of the populace correspond to the edicts of the tyrant; and the demagogue is to the one what the flatterer is to the other. Both have great power; the flatterer with the tyrant, the demagogue with democracies of the kind which we are describing. The demagogues make the decrees of the people override the laws, by referring all things to the popular assembly. And therefore they grow great, because the people are sovereign, and these demagogues hold in their hands the votes of the people, who are too ready to listen to them. Further, those who have any complaint to bring against the magistrates say, "Let the people be judges"; the people are too happy to accept the invitation; and so the authority of every office is undermined. Such a democracy is open to the objection that it is not a constitution at all; for where the laws have no authority, there is no constitution. The law ought to be supreme over all, and the magistracies should judge only about particular cases; and only this should be considered a constitution. So that if democracy be a real form of government, the sort of system in which all things are regulated by decrees is clearly not even a democracy in the true sense of the word, for decrees relate only to particulars—never a general rule.

These then are the different kinds of democracy.

5

Of oligarchies, too, there are different kinds: one where the property qualification for office is such that the poor, although they form the majority, have no share in the government, yet he who acquires enough property may obtain a share. Another sort is when there is a qualification for office, but a high one, and the vacancies in the governing body are filled by appointments made by those who satisfy those requirements. If the choice is made from all qualified persons, a constitution of this kind inclines to an aristocracy;

if out of a privileged class, to an oligarchy. Another sort of oligarchy is when the son succeeds the father. There is a fourth form, likewise hereditary, in which the magistrates are supreme and not the law. Among oligarchies this is what tyranny is among monarchies, and the last-mentioned form of democracy among democracies; and in fact this sort of oligarchy receives the name of a dynasty (or rule of powerful families).

These are the different sorts of oligarchies and democracies. It should, however, be remembered that in many states the constitution which is established by law, although not democratic, may be administered democratically, owing to the education and habits of the people. Conversely in other states the established constitution may incline to democracy, but may be administered in an oligarchical spirit. This most often happens after a revolution: for governments do not change at once; at first the dominant party is content with encroaching only a little upon their opponents. The laws which existed previously continue in force, but the authors of the revolution have the power in their hands.

6

From what has been already said we may safely infer that there are many different kinds of democracies and of oligarchies. For it is evident that either all the classes whom we mentioned must share in the government, or some only and not others. When the class of farmers and of those who possess moderate fortunes have the supreme power, the government is administered according to law. For the citizens being compelled to live by their labor have no leisure; and so they set up the authority of the law, and attend assemblies only when necessary. They all obtain a share in the government when they have acquired the qualification which is fixed by the law—the absolute exclusion of any class would be a step towards oligarchy; hence all who have acquired the property qualification are admitted to a share in government. But leisure cannot be provided for them unless there are revenues to support them. This is one sort of democracy, and these are its causes.

Another kind is based on the distinction which naturally comes next in order: the criterion of birth; in this, everyone who can prove irreproachable descent is eligible, but actually shares in the government only if he can find leisure. Hence in such a democracy the supreme power is vested in the laws, because the state has no means of paying the citizens. A third kind is when all freemen have a

1   it is not good ... many   Homer, Iliad 2, 204.

right to share in the government, but do not actually share
40 for the reason which has been already given; so that in this
form again the law must rule. A fourth kind of democracy
1293a is that which comes latest in the history of states. In our
own day, when cities have far outgrown their original size,
and their revenues have increased, all the citizens have a
place in the government, through the numerical superiority of the masses; and they all, including the poor who
5 receive pay, and therefore have leisure to exercise their
rights, share in the administration. Indeed, when they are
paid, the common people have the most leisure, for they
are not hindered by the care of their property, which often
fetters the rich, who are thereby prevented from taking
part in the assembly or in the courts, and so the state is
10 governed by the poor, who are a majority, and not by the
laws.

These, then, are the many kinds of democracies there
are, and causes from which they arise.

The first form of oligarchies is that in which the majority of the citizens have some property, but not very much;
anyone who obtains the required moderate amount of
15 property has the right of sharing in the government. Because there are a large number of sharers in the government,
it follows that the law must govern, and not individuals.
This sort of oligarchy is quite unlike monarchy. Its citizens
have neither so much property that they are able to live
without attending to business, nor so little that they need
20 state support; so they must seek the rule of law, rather than
claiming to rule themselves.

But if the men of property in the state are fewer than
in the former case, and own more property, there arises a
second form of oligarchy. For the stronger they are, the
more power they claim, and with the aim of increasing their
power they themselves select those of the other classes who
25 are to be admitted to the government. Not strong enough
to rule without the law, they make the law represent their
wishes.

When this power is intensified by a further diminution
of their numbers and increase of their property, there arises
a third and further stage of oligarchy, in which the governing class keep the offices in their own hands, and the law
ordains that the son shall succeed the father in office.

30 When, again, the rulers have great wealth and numerous friends, this sort of family despotism approaches a
monarchy; individuals rule and not the law. This is the
fourth sort of oligarchy, and is analogous to the last sort of
democracy.

7

There are still two forms besides democracy and oligarchy; 35
one of them is universally recognized and included among
the four principal forms of government, which are said to
be (1) monarchy, (2) oligarchy, (3) democracy, and (4) the
so-called aristocracy or government of the best. But there is
also a fifth, which retains the generic name of polity or constitutional government; this is not common, and therefore 40
has not been noticed by writers who attempt to enumerate the different kinds of government; like Plato,[1] in their 1293b
books about the state, they recognize four only.

The term "aristocracy" is rightly applied to the form
of government which is described in the first part of our
treatise; for the only form that can correctly be called aristocracy is one formed of the best men in an absolute sense,
and not merely relatively to some particular standard. In 5
the perfect state the good man is absolutely the same as the
good citizen; whereas in other states the good citizen is only
good relatively to his own form of government. But there
are some states differing from oligarchies and also differing from the so-called polity or constitutional government;
these are termed aristocracies, and in them the magistrates
are certainly chosen, both according to their wealth and ac- 10
cording to their merit. Such a form of government differs
from each of the two just now mentioned, and is termed an
aristocracy. For indeed in states which do not make virtue
the aim of the community, men of merit and reputation
for virtue may be found. And so where a government has
regard to wealth, virtue, and numbers, as at Carthage, that 15
is aristocracy; and also where it has regard only to two out
of the three, as in Sparta, where there is regard to virtue and
numbers; and it is also aristocracy where the two principles
of democracy and virtue temper each other. There are these
two forms of aristocracy in addition to the first and perfect
state, and there is a third form, viz., the constitutions which 20
incline more than the so-called polity towards oligarchy.

8

I have yet to speak of the so-called polity and of tyranny.
I put them in this order, not because a polity or constitutional government is to be regarded as a perversion any
more than the above mentioned aristocracies. The truth is, 25
that they all fall short of the most perfect form of govern-

---

1   *like Plato* See Plato, *Republic* 8, 9.

ment, and so they are reckoned among perversions, and the really perverted forms are perversions of these, as I said in the original discussion. Last of all I will speak of tyranny, which I place last in the series because I am inquiring into the constitutions of states, and this is the very reverse of a constitutional form.

Having explained why I have adopted this order, I will proceed to consider constitutional government; of which the nature will be clearer now that oligarchy and democracy have been defined. For polity or constitutional government may be described generally as a fusion of oligarchy and democracy; but the term is usually applied to those forms of government which incline towards democracy, and the term aristocracy to those which incline towards oligarchy, because birth and education are commonly the accompaniments of wealth. Moreover, the rich already possess those external advantages the lack of which is a temptation to crime, and hence they are called noblemen and gentlemen. And inasmuch as aristocracy seeks to give predominance to the best of the citizens, people say also of oligarchies that they are composed of noblemen and gentlemen.

Now it would seem impossible for a state governed not by the best citizens but by the worst to be well-governed, and equally impossible that the state which is ill-governed should be governed by the best. But we must remember that good laws, if they are not obeyed, do not constitute good government. Hence there are two parts of good government; one is the actual obedience of citizens to the laws, the other part is the goodness of the laws which they obey; they may obey bad laws as well as good. And there may be a further subdivision; they may obey either the best laws which are attainable to them, or the best absolutely.

The distribution of offices according to merit is a special characteristic of aristocracy, for the principle of an aristocracy is virtue, as wealth is the principle of oligarchy and freedom of a democracy. In all of them, of course, there exists the right of the majority, and whatever seems good to the majority of those who share in the government has authority. Now in most states the form called polity exists, for the mixture in them attempts no more than to unite the freedom of the poor and the wealth of the rich, who commonly take the place of the nobility. But as there are three grounds on which men claim an equal share in the government: freedom, wealth, and virtue (for the fourth or good birth is the result of the two last, being only ancient wealth and virtue), it is clear that the mixture of the two elements, that is to say, of the rich and poor, is to be called a polity or constitutional government; and the union of the three is to be called aristocracy or the government of the best, and more than any other form of government, except the correct and ideal, has a right to this name.

Thus far I have shown the existence of forms of states other than monarchy, democracy, and oligarchy, and what they are, and in what aristocracies differ from one another, and polities from aristocracies; that the two latter are quite similar is obvious.

9

Next we have to consider how the so-called polity or constitutional government springs up by the side of oligarchy and democracy, and how it should be organized. Its nature will at once be understood from a comparison of oligarchy and democracy; we must ascertain their different characteristics, and taking a portion from each, put the two together, like the tokens of a contract.[1] Now there are three modes in which fusions of government may be affected. In the first mode we combine the laws made by both governments, say concerning the administration of justice. In oligarchies they impose a fine on the rich if they do not serve as judges, and they give no pay to the poor; but in democracies they give pay to the poor and do not fine the rich. Now the union of these two modes is a common or middle term between them, and is therefore characteristic of a constitutional government, for it is a combination of both. This is one mode of uniting the two elements. Or a mean may be taken between the enactments of the two: thus democracies require no property qualification, or only a small one, from members of the assembly, oligarchies a high one; here neither of these is the common term, but a mean between them. There is a third mode, in which something is borrowed from the oligarchical and something from the democratic principle. For example, the appointment of magistrates by lot is thought to be democratic, and the election of them oligarchical; democratic when there is no property qualification, oligarchical when there is. In the aristocratic or constitutional state, one element will be taken from each: from oligarchy the principle of electing to offices, from democracy the disregard of qualification. Such are the various modes of combination.

---

1   *tokens of a contract*   As a symbol of a contractual arrangement, the Greeks broke a coin, with one half, uniquely fitting to the other, going to each party.

There is a true union of oligarchy and democracy when a state may be called either a democracy or an oligarchy; those who use both names evidently feel that the fusion is complete. There is also this fusion in the mean; for both extremes appear in it. The Spartan constitution, for example, is often described as a democracy, because it has many democratic features. In the first place the youth receive a democratic education: the sons of the poor are brought up with the sons of the rich, who are educated in such a manner as to make it possible for the sons of the poor to be educated by them. A similar equality prevails in the following period of life, and when the citizens are grown to manhood the same rule is observed; there is no distinction between the rich and poor. In like manner they all have the same food at their public tables, and the rich wear only such clothing as any poor man can afford. Again, the people elect to one of the two greatest offices of state, and in the other they share; for they elect the council of elders and share in the ephorate. By others the Spartan constitution is said to be an oligarchy, because it has many oligarchical elements. One of these oligarchic characteristics is that all offices are filled by election and none by lot; another is that only a few persons have the power of inflicting death or banishment; and there are others. In a properly mixed polity there should appear to be both elements and yet neither; also the government should be self-reliant, and not dependent on foreign aid; and its internal support should not come from the good will of a majority—they might be equally well-disposed when there is a bad form of government—but from the general willingness of all classes in the state to maintain the constitution.

So much for the proper manner of organizing constitutional governments and the so-called aristocracies.

10

Still remaining to discuss is the nature of tyranny, so that it has its place in our inquiry (since even tyranny is reckoned by us to be a form of government), although there is not much to be said about it.

Earlier I discussed royalty or kingship according to the most usual meaning of the term, and considered whether it is or is not advantageous to states, and what kind of royalty should be established, and from what source, and how. When speaking of royalty I also spoke of two forms of tyranny, which are both according to law, and therefore easily pass into royalty. First, among barbarians there are elected monarchs who exercise a despotic power; second, despotic rulers, called *aisumnētai* or dictators, were elected in ancient Greece. These monarchies differ from one another in certain ways; but they are both kingly, insofar as the monarch rules according to law over willing subjects, and tyrannical insofar as he is despotic and rules according to his own fancy. There is also a third kind of tyranny, which is the most typical form, and is the opposite of the perfect monarchy. This tyranny exists where an individual rules with arbitrary power, responsible to no one, and governs all alike, whether equals or better, with a view to his own advantage, not to that of his subjects, and therefore against their will. No freeman, if he can escape from it, will endure such a government.

The kinds of tyranny are these, and of this number, for the reasons which I have given.

11

We now have to inquire what is the best constitution for most states, and the best life for most men, without assuming a standard of virtue which is above ordinary persons, nor an education which is exceptionally favored by nature and circumstances, nor an ideal state which is only an aspiration; we shall instead be concerned only with the sort of life in which the majority are able to share, and with the form of government which states in general can attain. The aristocracies, as they are called, of which we were just now speaking, either lie beyond the possibilities of the greater number of states, or they approximate to the so-called constitutional government, and therefore need no separate discussion.

The conclusion we reach regarding all these forms rests upon one principle. If what was said in the *Ethics*[1] is true—that the happy life is the life according to virtue lived without impediment, and that virtue is a mean,[2] then the life which is in a mean, and in a mean attainable by every one, must be the best. And the same principles of virtue and vice are characteristic of states and of constitutions; for the constitution is, in a manner of speaking, the life of the state.

Now in all states there are three elements: one class is very rich, another very poor, and a third in a mean. It

---

1 *If what was said in the Ethics* See Aristotle, *Nicomachean Ethics* 1098a 16; 1153b10; 1177a12.

2 *a mean* For Aristotle's discussion of the mean, see Book 2 of the *Nicomachean Ethics*.

is admitted that moderation and the mean are best, and
therefore it will clearly be best to possess the gifts of fortune
in moderation; for in that condition of life men are most
ready to follow rational principle. But he who greatly excels
in beauty, strength, birth, or wealth, or on the other hand
who is very poor, or very weak, or of very low birth, finds
it difficult to follow rational principle. Those of the first
sort grow arrogant and violent, the others grow into rogues
and petty criminals. And two sorts of offenses correspond to
them, the first committed from arrogance, the second from
petty criminality. But the middle class is least likely to avoid
rule, or to be over-ambitious for it—both of these injure the
state. Those who have too much of the goods of fortune,
strength, wealth, friends, and the like, are neither willing
nor able to submit to authority. The evil begins at home; for
when they are boys, because of the luxury in which they are
brought up, they never learn, even at school, the habit of
obedience. On the other hand, the very poor, who are in the
opposite extreme, are too degraded. So that the first group
cannot obey, and can only rule despotically; the other does
not know how to command and must be ruled like slaves.
Thus arises a city, not of freemen, but of masters and slaves,
the one despising, the other envying; and nothing can be
more fatal to friendship and good fellowship in states than
this: for good fellowship springs from friendship; when
men are enemies, they would rather not even travel in each
other's company. But a state ought to be composed, as far as
possible, of equals and similars; and these are generally the
middle classes. So the state which is composed of middle-
class citizens is necessarily best constituted, with regard to
the elements of which we say the fabric of the state naturally consists. And this is the class of citizens which is most
secure in a state, for they do not, like the poor, desire their
neighbors' goods; nor do others desire theirs, as the poor
desire the goods of the rich; and as they neither plot against
others, nor are themselves plotted against, they pass through
life safely. Wisely then did Phocylides[1] pray "Many things
are best in the mean; I desire to be of a middle condition
in my city."

Clearly, then, the best political community is formed by
citizens of the middle class, and states are likely to be well-
administered when the middle class is large, and stronger if
possible than both the other classes, or at any rate stronger
than either singly; for the addition of the middle class turns
the scale, and prevents either of the extremes from being

dominant. A state has great good fortune, then, when the
citizens have a moderate and sufficient property; for where
some possess much, and the others nothing, there may arise
an extreme democracy, or a pure oligarchy; or a tyranny
may grow out of either extreme—either out of the most
rampant democracy, or out of an oligarchy; but it is not
so likely to arise out of the middle constitutions and those
akin to them. (I will explain the reason for this later, when
I discuss revolution.) The mean condition of states is clearly
best, for no other is free from faction; and where the middle
class is large, there are least likely to be factions and dissensions. For a similar reason large states are less liable to
faction than small ones, because in them the middle class
is large; whereas in small states it is easy to divide all the
citizens into two classes who are either rich or poor, and
to leave nothing in the middle. And democracies are safer
and more permanent than oligarchies, because they have
a middle class which is more numerous and has a greater
share in the government; for when there is no middle class,
and the poor greatly exceed in number, troubles arise, and
the state soon comes to an end. A proof of the superiority
of the middle class is that the best legislators have been of
a middle condition; for example, Solon, as his own verses
testify; and Lycurgus, for he was not a king; and Charondas,
and almost all legislators.

These considerations will help us to understand why
most governments are either democratic or oligarchic.
The reason is that the middle class is seldom numerous;
and when the party of the rich or of the common people
dominates, it oversteps the mean and draws the constitution its own way; thus arises either oligarchy or democracy.
And another reason is that the poor and the rich quarrel
with one another, and whichever side wins, instead of establishing a just or popular government, regards political
supremacy as the prize of victory, and sets up a democracy
or an oligarchy. Further, the two states which had, at one
time or another, supremacy in Greece,[2] were concerned
only with their own interests and their own forms of government, and consequently established democracies or
oligarchies respectively in the states they dominated; they
thought of their own advantage, not that of the public. For
these reasons the middle form of government has rarely, if
ever, existed, and among only a very few states. One man
alone of all who ever ruled in Greece was induced to give

---

1   *Phocylides*   Phocylides of Miletus, sixth-century BCE poet.

2   *two states ... Greece*   Athens and Sparta.

this middle constitution to states.[1] But it has now become a habit among the citizens of states not even to care about equality; all men are seeking domination, or, if conquered, are willing to submit.

It is evident, then, what the best form of government is, and what makes it the best. And, since we say that there are many kinds of democracy and many of oligarchy, it is not difficult to place the other forms second and third in order of excellence, now that we have determined which is the best. For that which is nearest to the best must of necessity be better, and that which is furthest from it worse, if we are judging absolutely and not relatively to given conditions: I say relatively to given conditions, since a particular government may be absolutely preferable, but another form may be better suited for some people.

12

We now consider what kind of government is suitable to what kind of men. I begin by assuming, as a general principle common to all governments, that the portion of the population which desires the permanence of the constitution ought to be stronger than that which desires the reverse.

Now every state is composed of quality and quantity. By quality I mean freedom, wealth, education, and good birth; and by quantity, superiority of numbers. Quality may exist in one of the classes which make up the state, and quantity in the other. For example, the low-born may be more numerous than the well-born, or the poor more numerous than the rich, but fall short in quality more than they exceed in quantity; and therefore quantity must be weighed against quality. Where the number of the poor outweighs the wealth of the rich, there will naturally be a democracy, varying in form with the sort of people who compose it in each case. If, for example, the majority are farmers, the first form of democracy will then arise; if the artisans and laboring class, the last; and so with the intermediate forms. But where the quality of the rich and the notables outweighs their falling-short in quantity, there oligarchy arises, similarly assuming various forms according to the kind of superiority possessed by the oligarchs.

The legislator should always include the middle class in his government. If he makes his laws oligarchic, he should pay attention to the middle class; if he makes them democratic, he should also try, by his laws, to attach this class to the state. The government can be stable only when the middle class exceeds one or both of the others, and by consequence there will be no fear that the rich will unite with the poor against the rulers. For neither of them will ever be willing to serve the other, and if they look for some form of government more suitable to both, they will find none better than this—for the rich and the poor will never consent to rule in turn, because they mistrust one another. The neutral arbitrator—the one in the middle—is always the one trusted. The better the mixture of the political elements, the more lasting will be the constitution. Even those who desire to form aristocratic governments often make the mistakes of giving too much power to the rich and of attempting to overreach the people. There comes a time when out of a false good there arises a true evil, since the encroachments of the rich are more destructive to the constitution than those of the people.

13

There are five techniques by which oligarchies deceive the people: they relate to (1) the assembly; (2) the magistracies; (3) the courts of law; (4) the use of arms; (5) athletic exercises. (1) The assemblies are thrown open to all, but either only the rich are fined for non-attendance, or a much larger fine is inflicted upon them. (2) As regards the magistracies, those who are qualified by property cannot decline office upon oath, but the poor may.[2] (3) Regarding the law courts, the rich, and the rich only, are fined if they do not serve, the poor are let off with impunity, or, as in the laws of Charondas, a larger fine is inflicted on the rich, and a smaller one on the poor. In some states all citizens who have registered themselves are allowed to attend the assembly and to try causes; but if after registration they do not attend either in the assembly or at the courts, heavy fines are imposed upon them. The intention is to get them to avoid registering themselves through fear of the fines, and thereby to prevent them from sitting in the law-courts or in the assembly. Concerning (4) the possession of arms, and (5) athletic exercises, they legislate in a similar spirit. The poor are not obliged to have arms, but the rich are fined for not having them; similarly, no penalty is inflicted on the poor

---

1 *One man ... states* Commentators do not know who Aristotle is referring to here.

2 *decline office ... poor may* An oath swearing that one lacks the financial means to serve in office.

for non-attendance at the gymnasium, and consequently, having nothing to fear, they do not attend, whereas the rich are liable to a fine, and therefore they take care to attend.

35 These are the devices of oligarchical legislators, and in democracies they have counter devices. They pay the poor for attending the assemblies and the law-courts, and they inflict no penalty on the rich for non-attendance. It is obvious that someone who wants to mix the two principles properly should combine the practice of both, and provide 40 that the poor should be paid to attend, and the rich fined if they do not attend, for then all will take part; if there is no 1297b such combination, power will be in the hands of one party only. The government should be confined to those who carry arms. As to the property qualification, no absolute rule can be laid down; but we must determine in each case what is the highest qualification that is sufficient to make 5 the number of those who have the rights of citizens exceed the number of those excluded. Even if they have no share in office, the poor, provided that they are not treated violently or deprived of their property, will keep quiet. But to secure gentle treatment for the poor is not an easy thing, since a 10 ruling class is not always humane. And in time of war the poor are apt to hesitate unless they are fed; when fed, they are willing enough to fight.

In some states the citizenry is constituted not only by those doing military service, but also of those who have served; in Malis, for example, the governing body consisted 15 of the latter, while the magistrates were chosen from those actually in service. And the earliest government which existed among the Greeks, after the overthrow of the kingly power, grew up out of the warrior class; originally, only cavalry soldiers were included—for strength and superiority in war at that time depended on them; indeed, without disci- 20 pline, infantry are useless, and in ancient times there was no military knowledge or tactics, and therefore the strength of armies lay in their cavalry. But when states increased in size and the infantry grew in strength, more had a share in the government; and this is the reason why the states which we call constitutional governments have been hitherto called 25 democracies. Ancient constitutions, as might be expected, were oligarchical and royal. As their population was small they had no significant middle class; the people were weak in numbers and organization, and were therefore more contented to be governed.

I have explained why there is a variety of forms of gov- 30 ernment, and why it is greater than is generally supposed; for democracy, as well as other constitutions, has more than

one form. I have also explained what their differences are, and the causes of the character of each; and also what is the best form of government, generally speaking, and to whom the various forms of government are best suited.

14

We now go on to the next subject. After having provided 35 a proper basis for the discussion, we shall proceed on these topics not only in general but with reference to particular constitutions.

All constitutions have three elements, and a good lawgiver has to consider all three when considering what is suitable for any form of government. When all these elements are well-ordered, the constitution is well-ordered, and as they differ from one another, constitutions dif- 40 fer. There is (1) the deliberative element, concerned with public affairs; secondly (2) the executive element; here 1298a the questions are what public offices there should be, over what they should exercise authority, and how office-holders should be elected; and thirdly (3) the element of judicial power.

The deliberative element has authority in matters of war and peace, in making and dissolving alliances; it passes laws, 5 inflicts capital punishment, exile, and confiscation of property; it elects magistrates and call them to account. These powers may be assigned in different ways: all of them to all the citizens, or to some of them (for example, to one or more magistracies, or different ones to different magistracies), or some of these powers to all citizens, and others of them only to some. It is characteristic of democracy that 10 all things should be decided by all; this is the sort of equality which the people desire. But there are various ways in which all may share in the government; they may deliberate, not all in one body, but by turns, as in the constitution of Telecles the Milesian.[1] There are other constitutions in which the boards of magistrates meet and deliberate, but come into office by turns, and are elected out of the tribes 15 and the very smallest divisions of the state, until every one has obtained office in his turn. The citizens, on the other hand, are assembled only for the purposes of legislation, and to consult about the constitution, and to hear the edicts of the magistrates. In another variety of democracy the citizens form one assembly, but meet only to elect magistrates 20

---

1   *Telecles the Milesian*   Nothing beyond this mention is known of him.

and call them to account, to pass laws, to advise about war and peace. Other matters are referred individually to special magistrates, who are elected by vote or by lot out of all the citizens. Or again, the citizens meet to decide the election of office holders and to call them to account, and to deliberate concerning war or alliances while other matters are administered by the magistrates, who, as far as is possible, are elected by vote. I am speaking of those magistracies in which special knowledge is required. A fourth form of democracy is when all the citizens meet to deliberate about everything, and the magistrates decide nothing, but only make the preliminary inquiries; this is the way the last and worst form of democracy is at present set up. It is a form, I have argued, analogous to dynastic family oligarchy and to tyranny. All these ways of arranging the deliberative element are democratic.

When only some of the citizens, on the other hand, deliberate about all matters, this is the oligarchic arrangement. Like the democratic, this has many forms. When the deliberative class is chosen from among those who have a moderate property qualification, this body is numerous; and they respect and obey the prohibitions of the law without altering it, and anyone who has the required qualification shares in the government. In this case, because of this moderation, the oligarchy inclines towards polity. But when only selected individuals and not the whole people share in the deliberations of the state, then, although, as in the former case, they observe the law, the government is a pure oligarchy. Or, third, when those who have the power of deliberation recruit their own members, and son succeeds father, and they and not the laws are supreme, the government is decidedly oligarchical. And where particular persons have authority in particular matters—for example, when the whole people decide about peace and war and hold officials to account, but the magistrates regulate everything else, and they are elected by vote—there the government is an aristocracy. And if some questions are decided by magistrates elected by vote, and others by magistrates elected by lot (either from among the whole citizenry, or from a selected pool of candidates), or elected partly by vote, partly by lot—these practices are partly characteristic of an aristocratic government, and partly of a pure constitutional government.

These are the various forms of the deliberative body; they correspond to the various forms of government. And the government of each state is administered according to one or other of the principles which have been laid down.

Now it is in the interest of democracy, according to the most prevalent notion of it (I am speaking of that extreme form of democracy in which the people can overrule the laws), to adopt the custom of oligarchies respecting courts of law, with a view to better deliberation. For in oligarchies people called for jury service are compelled to attend under pain of a fine, whereas in democracies the poor are paid to attend. This practice of oligarchies should be adopted by democracies in their public assemblies, for these assemblies will deliberate better if all deliberate together—the people with the notables and the notables with the people. It is also a good plan that those who deliberate should be chosen by vote or by lot in equal numbers, with everyone in the different classes being eligible; and that if the people greatly outnumber those who have political training, pay should not be given to all, but only to as many as would balance the number of the notables, or that the excess number should be eliminated by lot. But in oligarchies either certain persons should be co-opted from the mass, or a class of officers should be appointed such as exist in some states who are termed "preliminary counsellors" or "guardians of the laws"; and the citizens should deal only with matters on which these bodies have previously deliberated. That way the people will have a share in the deliberations of the state, but will not be able to disturb the principles of the constitution. Again, in oligarchies either the people ought to accept the measures of the government, or not pass anything contrary to them; or, if all are allowed to share in counsel, the decision should rest with the magistrates. The opposite of what is done in constitutional governments should be the rule in oligarchies: they should have the power of veto, but should not have power of ultimate assent; any proposals in which they assent should be referred back to the magistrates. In constitutional governments there is the reverse situation: the few have the negative, not the affirmative power; the affirmation of everything rests with the multitude.

These, then, are our conclusions respecting the deliberative, that is, the supreme element in states.

15

Next we will proceed to consider the distribution of offices. This also is a part of politics concerning which many questions arise: How many magisterial offices should there be? Over what should the officers preside, and what should be their term of office? Sometimes they last for six months, sometimes for less; sometimes they are annual, while in other cases offices are held for still longer periods. Shall they be for life or for a long term of years; or, if for a short term only, may the same persons hold additional terms, or once only? Also about the appointment to them—from whom are they to be chosen, by whom, and how? We should first describe the possible varieties of distribution schemes; then we may proceed to determine which are suited to different forms of government.

But what are to be included under the term "offices"? That is a question not quite so easily answered. For a political community requires many officers; and not every one who is chosen by vote or by lot is to be regarded as an office-holder. In the first place there are the priests, who must be distinguished from political officers; masters of choruses and heralds, even ambassadors, are elected by vote. *Political* functions are those that extend either to all the citizens in a single sphere of action (for example, the command of the general who superintends men in the field), or to a section of them only (for example, the inspectorships of women or of youth). Other offices are concerned with economic management, like that of the grain measurers who exist in many states and are elected officers. There are also menial offices which the rich have performed by their slaves. Speaking generally, the term "offices" applies when assigned duties involve deliberating about certain measures and judging and commanding, especially the last; for to command is the special duty of a magistrate. But the question is not of any importance in practice; no one has ever brought into court the meaning of the word, although such problems have a speculative interest.

More important considerations are: what kinds of offices, and how many, are necessary to the existence of a state, or, if not necessary, important for its wellbeing? These matters affect all constitutions, but especially small states; for in large states it is possible, and indeed necessary, that every office should have a special function; where there is a large population, many may hold office. And so it happens there that some offices a man holds a second time only after a long interval, and others he holds once only. Certainly every work is better done which receives the sole, undivided, attention of the worker. But in small states it is necessary to combine many offices in a few hands, since the small number of citizens does not allow that many hold office: for who will there be to succeed them? And yet small states at times require the same offices and laws as large ones; the difference is that large states require the function of such offices all the time, whereas small states merely intermittently.

Thus, in small states, the duties of several offices may be assigned to one person, for these duties will not interfere with each other. When the population is small, offices should be multi-purpose, like the spits for roasting meat which also serve to hold a lamp. We must first ascertain how many magistrates are necessary in every state, and also how many are not exactly necessary, but are nevertheless useful, and then there will be no difficulty in seeing what offices can be combined in one. We should also know over which matters local tribunals are to have jurisdiction, and in which authority should be centralized: for example, should one person keep order in the market and another in somewhere else, or should the same person be responsible everywhere? Again, should offices be divided according to the subjects with which they deal, or according to the persons with whom they deal—I mean to say, should one person see to good order in general, or one look after the boys, another after the women, and so on? Further, under different constitutions, should the magistrates be the same or different? For example, in democracy, oligarchy, aristocracy, monarchy, should there be the same magistrate offices (although they are elected, not out of equal or similar classes of citizen but differently under different constitutions—in aristocracies they are chosen from the educated, in oligarchies from the wealthy, and in democracies from the free) or do these different forms of state require certain different sorts of offices? For in some states it may be convenient that the same office should have a more extensive sphere, in other states a narrower one. Special offices are peculiar to certain forms of government: for example that of preliminary council, which is not a democratic office, although a council is. There must be some body of men whose duty is to prepare measures for the people in order that they not be diverted from their business; when these are few in number, the state inclines to an oligarchy: or rather the preliminary council must always be small in size, and are therefore an oligarchical element. But when both institutions exist in a state, the preliminary council is a check on the council; for the council is a democratic element, but the preliminary council is oligarchic. Even the power of the council disappears when democracy has taken that extreme form in which the people themselves are always meeting and deliberating about everything. This is the case when the members of the assembly receive abundant pay; for they have nothing to do and are always holding assemblies and deciding everything for themselves. A magistracy which controls the boys or the women, or any similar office, is suited to an aristocracy rather than to a democracy; for how can the magistrates prevent the wives of the poor from wandering about out of doors? Neither is it an oligarchical office; for the wives of the oligarchs are too fine to be controlled.

Enough of these matters. I will now inquire into ap-
10 pointments to offices. The varieties depend on three factors, and the combinations of these give all possible modes.
First, who appoints? **Second,** who is eligible? **And third,**
how is the appointment made? Each of these three admits
15 of **a series of** varieties:

- (A) Do all the citizens appoint, or (B) do only some of the citizens appoint?
- (1) Is everyone eligible to be a magistrate? Or (2) are only some eligible, on the basis of a property qualification, or by birth, or merit, or for some special reason. Thus, at Megara only those who had returned from exile and fought together against the democracy were eligible.
- (a) Are they appointed by vote? Or (b) by lot?

20 Further, these several varieties may be coupled—I mean that (C) some officers may be elected by some, others by all; that (3) some offices may be open to everyone, while others have limited eligibility; and that (c) some officers may be selected by vote and others by lot.

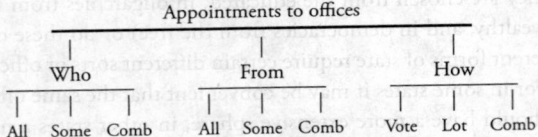

Appointments to offices

	Who				From				How	
All	Some	Comb		All	Some	Comb		Vote	Lot	Comb

Each variety of these terms admits of six modes. Either (A 1 a) all the citizens may appoint from all by vote, or
25 (A 1 b) all citizens may appoint from all by lot; or (A 2 a) all citizens may appoint from some by vote, or (A 2 b) all citizens may appoint some by lot. (If they appoint from all,
30 it may be either by sections, for example, by tribes, wards and phratries,[1] until all citizens have had their turn; or it may be that all citizens are eligible every time.) Or again (A 1 c, A 2 c), appointments may be determined in some cases by vote and in other cases by lot. If some citizens appoint, they may appoint either (B 1 a) from all by vote,
35 or (B 1 b) from all by lot; or (B 2 a) from some by lot, or (B 2 b) from some by lot. Or it may be the case that some offices are determined in one way, while others in another: i.e., (B 1 c) some citizens appoint from all, some by vote,

---

1   *phratries* Social groups whose members were connected by descent. They played a major role in regulating access to citizenship
and inheritance.

others by lot, and (B 2 c) some citizens appoint from some, some by vote, others by lot.[2] Thus arise twelve modes, apart from the two combinations (C, 3).[3]

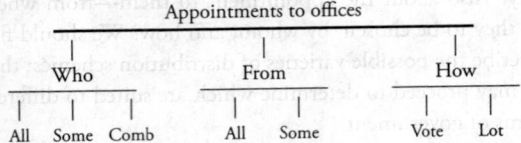

Appointments to offices

	Who			From			How	
All	Some	Comb	All	Some		Vote	Lot

Of these systems, three are democratic: (A 1 a) the system that appoints from all by vote; (A 1 b) the system that 40
appoints all by lot; and (A 1 c) the system that appoints from 1300b
all, with some offices appointed by vote and others by lot. It is characteristic of a polity that not all appoint at once, but rather appoint from all or from some, whether by vote, lot, or both, or appoint to some offices from all and to others from some. ("By both" refers to some office being appointed by lot and others by vote.) And (B 1 C), that some should appoint members selected from all citizens to some offices by vote and to other offices by lot, is also characteristic of a polity, though more oligarchical than the former method. And (A 3 a, b, c, B 3 a, b, c) to appoint from both, to some offices from all, to others from some, is characteristic of a polity with aristocratic tendencies. That (B 2) some should appoint from some is oligarchical—even (B 2 b) that some should appoint from some by lot (and if this does not ac-

---

2   *Thus the modes that arise ... three couplings number twelve* The
following scheme may be useful for reference:
A – all citizens appoint
B – some citizens appoint
C – all citizens appoint some officers; other officers are appointed
only by some
1 – everyone is eligible for office
2 – only some are eligible for office
3 – some offices are open to all; others are only open to some
a – officers are appointed by vote
b – officers are appointed by lot
c – some officers are appointed by vote; others are appointed by lot

3   *Thus arise twelve modes ... two combinations* The twelve modes
are: 1) all appoint from all by vote; 2) all appoint from all by
lot; 3) all appoint from some by vote; 4) all appoint from some
by lot; 5) all appoint from all, in part by vote, in part by lot; 6)
all appoint from some, in part by vote, in part by lot; 7) some
appoint from all by vote; 8) some appoint from all from lot; 9)
some appoint from some by vote; 10) some appoint from some by
lot; 11) some appoint from all in part by election, in part by lot;
12) some appoint from some, in part by election, in part by lot.

The combinations not included are: all appoint for some offices and some appoint for others; and all can be appointed to some offices and some can be appointed for others.

tually occur, it is none the less oligarchical in character), or (B 2 c) that some should appoint from some by both. (B 1 a) that some should appoint from all, and (A 2 a) that all should appoint from some, by vote, is aristocratic.

These are the different modes of constituting magistrates, and these correspond to different forms of government: which are proper to which, or how they ought to be established, will be evident when we determine the nature of their powers. By powers I mean such **powers** as a magistrate exercises over the revenue or in defense of the country; for there are various kinds of power: the power of the general, for example, is not the same as that which regulates contracts in the market.

16

Of the three parts of government, the judicial remains to be considered, and this we shall divide on the same principle. There are three points on which the varieties of law-courts depend: Their membership, the subjects with which they deal, and the manner of their appointment. I mean, (1) are the judges taken from all the population, or from some sections only? (2) how many kinds of law-courts are there? (3) are the judges chosen by vote or by lot?

First, let me determine how many kinds of law-courts there are. There are eight in number: One is the court of audit or scrutiny; a second concerns itself with ordinary offenses against the state; a third is concerned with treason against the constitution; the fourth considers disputes respecting fines, raised by magistrates or by private persons; the fifth decides the more important civil cases; the sixth tries cases of homicide, which are of various kinds: premeditated, involuntary, cases in which the guilt is confessed but the justice is disputed; and in which murderers who have fled from justice are tried after their return; such as the Court of Phreatto is said to be at Athens. (But cases of this sort rarely happen at all even in large states.) The different kinds of homicide may be tried either by the same or by different courts. The seventh is the court for foreigners, with two subdivisions: for the settlement of their disputes with one another; and for the settlement of disputes between them and the citizens. And besides all these there must be an eighth sort: courts for small suits about sums of a drachma up to five drachmas, or a little more; decisions are needed here, but they do not require many judges.

Nothing more need be said of these small suits, nor of the courts for homicide and for foreigners: I would rather speak of political cases, which, when mismanaged, create division and disturbances in constitutions.

Now if all the citizens are eligible to judge in all the different cases which I have distinguished, they may be appointed by vote or by lot, or sometimes by lot and sometimes by vote. Or when all are eligible to serve, but only on a restricted kind of case, the judges who decide them may be appointed, some by vote, and some by lot. These then are the four modes of appointing judges from the whole people, and there will be likewise four modes, if they are elected from a part only; for they may be appointed from some by vote and judge in all causes; or they may be appointed from some by lot and judge in all causes; or they may be chosen in some cases by vote and in some cases by lot, or some courts, even when judging the same causes, may be composed of members some appointed by vote and some by lot. These modes, then, as was said, correspond to those previously mentioned.

Once more, the modes of appointment may be combined; I mean, that some may be chosen out of the whole people, others out of some, some out of both; for example, the same tribunal may be composed of some who were elected out of all, and of others who were elected out of some, either by vote or by lot or by both.

In how many forms law-courts can be established has now been considered. The first form, viz., that in which the judges are taken from all the citizens, and in which all causes are tried, is democratic; the second, which is composed of a few only who try all causes, oligarchic; the third, in which some courts are taken from all classes, and some from certain classes only, is characteristic of aristocracies and "constitutional governments"—that is, polities.

from Book 5

1

We have now nearly completed the tasks earlier proposed. Next in order is consideration of the following topics: the causes of revolution in states, how many, and of what nature they are; what modes of destruction apply to particular states, and out of what, and into what they mostly change; also what are the modes of preservation in states generally, or in a particular state, and by what means each state may be best preserved: these questions remain to be considered.

In the first place we must assume as our starting-point that in the many forms of government which have sprung up there has always been an acknowledgment of justice and proportionate equality, although mankind fail attaining them, as I have already explained. Democracy, for example, arises out of the notion that those who are equal in any respect are equal in all respects; because men are equally free, they claim to be absolutely equal. Oligarchy is based on the notion that those who are unequal in one respect are in all respects unequal; being unequal, that is, in property, they suppose themselves to be unequal absolutely. The democrats think that since they are equal in some respects they ought to have equal shares in everything; while the oligarchs, on the grounds that they are unequal—that some are superior—claim too much. Both of these forms of government have a kind of justice, but, tried by an absolute standard, they are faulty. Both parties stir up revolution whenever their share in the government does not accord with their preconceived ideas. Those who excel in virtue have the best right of all to rebel (for they alone can with reason be deemed absolutely unequal), but they are the least inclined of all men to do so. There is also a superiority which is claimed by men of rank; for they are thought noble because they spring from wealthy and virtuous ancestors.

Here then, so to speak, are opened the sources and springs of revolution; and from here two sorts of changes in governments arise: one affecting the constitution, when men seek to change from an existing form into some other, for example, from democracy into oligarchy, and from oligarchy into democracy, or from either of them into constitutional government or aristocracy, and conversely; the other not affecting the constitution, when, without disturbing the form of government, whether oligarchy, or monarchy, or any other, they try to get the administration into their own hands. Further, there is a question of degree; an oligarchy, for example, may become more or less oligarchic, and a democracy more or less democratic; and in like manner the characteristics of the other forms of government may be more or less strictly maintained. Or the revolution may be directed against a portion of the constitution only, e.g., the establishment or overthrow of a particular office: as at Sparta it is said that Lysander attempted to overthrow the monarchy, and King Pausanias, the ephorate. At Epidamnus, too, the change was partial: a council was appointed to take the place of tribal leaders; but to this day the magistrates are the only members of the ruling class who are compelled to go to the public assembly when an election takes place, and a second oligarchic feature is the office of the single supreme official (the *archōn*).

Everywhere inequality is a cause of revolution, except where unequals are treated justly in proportion to their inequality. A perpetual heredity monarchy, for example, does not involve genuine inequality except when it exists among equals. It is always the desire for equality which rises in rebellion. Now equality is of two kinds, numerical and proportional; by the first I mean sameness or equality in number or size; by the second, equality in proportion to what is deserved—equality *of ratios*. For example, the excess of three over two is numerically equal to the excess of two over one; whereas four exceeds two in the same ratio in which two exceeds one, for two is the same part of four that one is of two, namely, the half. As I was saying before, men agree that justice in the abstract is equality in proportion to desert, but they differ in that some think that if they are equal in any respect they are equal absolutely, others that if they are unequal in any respect they should be unequal in all. For this reason there are two principal forms of government, democracy and oligarchy; for good birth and virtue are rare, but superiority in wealth or in numbers are common. In what state shall we find a hundred persons of good birth and of virtue? But rich people are abundant everywhere. It is not a good thing for a state to be ordered simply and wholly according to either kind of equality. Proof of this is the fact that such forms of government never last. They are originally based on a mistake, and, as they begin badly, they cannot fail to end badly. The inference is that both kinds of equality should be employed; numerical in some cases, and proportionate in others.

Still democracy appears to be safer and less liable to revolution than oligarchy. For in oligarchies there is the double danger of the oligarchs falling out among themselves and also with the people; but in democracies there is only the danger of a quarrel with the oligarchs. No dissension worth mentioning arises among the people themselves. And we may further remark that a government which is composed of the middle class more nearly approximates to democracy than to oligarchy, and is the safest of the imperfect forms of government.

...

8

Next we consider what means there are of preserving constitutions in general, and in particular cases.

In the first place it is evident that if we know the causes which destroy constitutions, we also know the causes which preserve them; for opposites produce opposites, and destruction is the opposite of preservation. In all properly blended governments there is nothing that is more important to maintain than the spirit of obedience to law, more especially in small matters; for transgression creeps in unperceived and at last ruins the state, just as the constant recurrence of small expenses in time eats up a fortune. The expense does not take place at once, and therefore is not observed; the mind is deceived, as in the fallacy which says that if each part is little, then the whole is little. This is true in one way, but not in another, for the whole and the all are not little, although they are made up of littles.

In the first place, then, men should guard against the beginning of change, and in the second place they should not rely on the political devices I have spoken about which are intended to deceive the people, for they are proved by experience to be useless. Further, we note that some states—oligarchies as well as aristocracies—survive, not from any inherent stability in such forms of government, but because the rulers are on good terms both with those without citizens' rights as well as with the enfranchised. They do not mistreat those excluded from the government, but bring their leading members into participation; the ambitious among them are never wronged in a matter of honor, or the common people in a matter of money; and they treat one another and their fellow enfranchised citizens in a spirit of equality.

The equality which the advocates of democracy seek to establish for the multitude is not only just but likewise expedient among equals. Hence, if the governing class are numerous, many democratic institutions are useful—for example, the restriction of the tenure of offices to six months, so that everyone of equal rank may share in them. Indeed, equals or peers, when they are numerous, become a kind of democracy, and therefore demagogues are very likely to arise among them, as I have already remarked. The short tenure of office prevents oligarchies and aristocracies from falling into the hands of families; it is not easy for a person to do any great harm when his tenure of office is short, whereas long possession begets tyranny in oligarchies and democracies. For the aspirants to tyranny are either the principal men of the state, who in democracies are demagogues and in oligarchies members of ruling houses, or those who hold great offices for a long period.

Constitutions are preserved when their destroyers are far away, but sometimes also because they are near, for the fear of those nearby enemies makes the government keep a firm grip on the constitution. Therefore the ruler who has a concern for the constitution should invent terrors, and bring distant dangers near, to keep the citizens on their guard, and, like sentinels in a night watch, never relax their attention. He should also, by help of the laws, endeavor to control the contentions and quarrels of the notables, and to prevent those who have not hitherto taken part in them from catching the spirit of contention. No ordinary man can discern the beginning of evil, but only the true statesman.

Another source of change in oligarchies and constitutional governments is the result of an alternation of the property qualification, as the amount is greater and less. This may come about not only from variation in the qualification itself, but also from the increase of money; so it is a good idea to compare the general valuation of property with that of past years, annually in those cities in which the census is taken annually and in larger cities every third or fifth year. If the whole is many times greater or many times less than when the ratings recognized by the constitution were fixed, there should be power given by law to raise or lower the qualification. Where this is not done a constitutional government passes into an oligarchy, and an oligarchy is narrowed to a rule of families; or in the opposite case constitutional government becomes democracy, and oligarchy either constitutional government or democracy.

It is a principle common to democracy, oligarchy, and every other form of government not to raise anyone too high, compared to his fellow citizens, but to give moderate honor for a long time rather than great honor for a short time. For men are easily spoiled; not every one can bear prosperity. But if this rule is not observed, at any rate the honors which are given all at once should be taken away by degrees rather than all at once. It is important that the laws prohibit any one from having too much power, whether derived from friends or money; if he has, he should be sent clean out of the country.

And since men can become revolutionaries because of circumstances in their private lives, there ought to be a magistracy which will watch out for those whose life is not in harmony with the government, whether oligarchy or democracy or any other. And for a similar reason an increase of prosperity in any part of the state should be carefully watched. The proper remedy for this evil is always to give the management of affairs and offices of state to opposite elements; such opposites are the virtuous and the many, or the rich and the poor. Another way is to combine the poor and the rich in one body, or to increase the middle class: thus an end will be put to the revolutions which arise from inequality.

But above all every state should be so administered and so regulated by law that its magistrates cannot possibly profit from their offices. In oligarchies special precautions should be used against this evil. For the people do not
35 take any great offense at being kept out of the government—indeed they are rather pleased at having leisure for their private business—but what irritates them is to think that their rulers are stealing the public money; then they are doubly annoyed; for they lose both honor and profit. If of-
40 fice brought no profit, then and then only could democracy
1309a and aristocracy be combined; for both notables and ordinary people might have their wishes gratified. All would be able to hold office, which is the aim of democracy, and the notables would be magistrates, which is the aim of aristocracy. And this result may be accomplished when there is no possibility of making money out of the offices; for the poor
5 will not want to have offices when there is nothing to be gained from them—they would rather be attending to their own concerns—and the rich, who do not want money from the public treasury, will be able to take them; and so the poor will keep to their work and grow rich, and the notables will not be governed by the lower class. In order to avoid
10 embezzlement of public funds, the transfer of the revenue should be made at a general assembly of the citizens, and duplicates of the accounts deposited with each clan, ward, and tribe. And honors should be given by law to magistrates who have the reputation of being incorruptible.
15 In democracies the rich should be spared; their property should be left intact; their incomes, which in some states are taken from them imperceptibly, should be protected. It is a good policy also not to allow wealthy citizens, to undertake expensive and useless public services, such as the giving of choruses, torch-races, and the like, even if they are willing.
20 In an oligarchy, on the other hand, great care should be taken of the poor, and lucrative offices should go to them; if any of the wealthy classes insult them, the offender should be punished more severely than if he had wronged one of his own class. Provision should be made that estates pass by inheritance and not by gift, and no person should have
25 more than one inheritance; for in this way properties will be equalized, and more of the poor will rise to affluence. It is also expedient both in a democracy and in an oligarchy to accord to those who have less share in the government (i.e., to the rich in a democracy and to the poor in an oligarchy)
30 equality or preference in all but the principal offices of state (which should be entrusted chiefly or only to members of the governing class).

....

11

Monarchies are preserved, in general, by causes opposite to 1313a those of their destruction;[1] we shall treat each in detail:

Royalty is preserved by the limitation of its powers. 20 The more restricted the functions of kings, the longer their power will last unimpaired; for then they are more moderate and not so despotic in their ways; and they are less envied by their subjects. This is the reason why the kingly office has lasted so long among the Molossians. And for a similar reason it has continued among the Spartans, because there 25 it was always divided between two, and afterwards further limited by Theopompus in various respects, more particularly by the establishment of the ephorate. He diminished the power of the kings, but established on a more lasting basis the kingly office, which was thus made in a certain sense not less, but greater. There is a story that when his wife 30 once asked him whether he was not ashamed to leave to his sons a royal power which was less than he had inherited from his father, "No indeed," he replied, "for the power which I leave to them will be more lasting."

As to tyrannies, they are preserved in two diametrically opposed ways. One of them is the old traditional method in 35 which most tyrants administer their government. Of such arts Periander of Corinth[2] is said to have been the great master, and many similar devices may be gathered from the Persians in the administration of their government. There are firstly the prescriptions I mentioned some distance back for the preservation of tyranny, in so far as this is possible. These are that the tyrant should lop off those who 40 are too high; he must put to death men of spirit; he must not allow common meals, clubs, education, and the like; 1313b he must be upon his guard against anything which is likely to inspire either courage or confidence among his subjects; he must prohibit literary assemblies or other meetings for discussion, and he must take every means to prevent people from knowing one another (for acquaintance produces 5 mutual confidence). Further, he must compel all persons staying in the city to appear in public and hang around at the palace gates; then he will know what they are doing: if they are always kept in a servile position, they will

---

1 *Monarchies ... destruction* Aristotle has spoken of the perils for monarchy in immediately previous sections (omitted here).

2 *Periander of Corinth* Second tyrant of Corinth (seventh century BCE).

learn to be humble. In short, he should practice these and
10 similar Persian and barbaric arts, which all have the same
object. A tyrant should also endeavor to know what each
of his subjects says or does, and should employ spies, like
the "female detectives" at Syracuse, and the eavesdroppers
whom Hieron[1] was in the habit of sending to social gather-
15 ings and public meetings; for the fear of informers prevents
people from speaking their minds, and if they do, they are
more easily discovered. Another art of the tyrant is to sow
quarrels among the citizens; friends should be embroiled
with friends, the people with the notables, and the rich with
one another. Also he should impoverish his subjects; thus
20 they will not be able to afford maintaining a civil guard,
and, having to keep hard at work, they will have no time
for conspiracies. The Pyramids of Egypt afford an example
of this policy; also the offerings of the family of Cypselus,
and the building of the temple of Olympian Zeus by the
family of Peisistratus, and the great monuments at Samos
25 constructed by Polycrates; all these works were alike intended to occupy the people and keep them poor. Another
practice of tyrants is to multiply taxes, after the manner of
Dionysius the Elder[2] at Syracuse, who contrived that within
five years his subjects should bring all their property into
the state's treasury. The tyrant is also fond of making war
in order that his subjects may have something to do and
always need a leader.
30   Whereas the power of a king is preserved by his friends,
the tyrant distrusts his friends, because he knows that all
men want to overthrow him, and his friends, above all, have
the power. The evil practices of the most extreme and worst
form of democracy are all found in tyrannies. For example,
they empower women in their families, in the hope that
35 they will inform against their husbands, and they show indulgence to slaves in order that they may betray their masters; for slaves and women do not conspire against tyrants;
and they are of course friendly to tyrannies and also to democracies, since under them they prosper. For the people too
would like to rule, and therefore they hold the flatterer in
40 honor, as does the tyrant. In democracies the flatterer is the
demagogue; and the tyrant has obsequious associates—flat-
1314a terers of a sort. Hence tyrants are always fond of bad men,
because they love to be flattered, but no man who has the
spirit of a freeman in him will lower himself by flattery; a

---

1 *Hieron* Tyrant of Syracuse, from 478 to c. 467 BCE.
2 *Dionysius the Elder* Tyrant of Syracuse from c. 432 to 367 BCE,
   widely viewed in ancient times as an example of the worst sort of
   despot.

good man may be a friend, but not a flatterer. Moreover,
the bad are useful for bad purposes; "nail knocks out nail," 5
as the proverb says. It is characteristic of a tyrant to dislike
every one who has dignity or independence; he wants to be
alone in his glory, but any one who claims a similar dignity
or asserts his independence encroaches upon his prerogative, and is hated by him as an enemy to his power. Another
mark of a tyrant is that he likes foreigners better than cit- 10
izens, and lives with them and invites them to his table; for
he feels that the citizens are enemies, but that the foreigners
have no rivalry with him.
   Such are the notes of the tyrant and the arts by which
he preserves his power; there is no wickedness too great for
him. All that we have said may be summed up under three
headings, which correspond to the three aims of the tyrant. 15
These are, (1) the humiliation of his subjects; he knows that
a mean-spirited man will not conspire against anybody; (2)
the creation of mistrust among them; for a tyrant is not
overthrown until men begin to have confidence in one another. This is the reason why tyrants are at war with good
people; tyrants think that their power is endangered by 20
good people, not only because the good would not be ruled
despotically but also because they are loyal to one another,
and to other men, and do not inform against one another or
against other men; (3) the tyrant desires that his subjects be
incapable of action, for no one attempts what is impossible,
and they will not attempt to overthrow a tyranny if they are
powerless. Under these three headings the whole policy of 25
a tyrant may be summed up, and to one or other of them
all his ideas may be referred: he sows distrust among his
subjects; he takes away their power; he humbles them.
   This then is one of the two methods by which tyrannies 30
are preserved; and there is another which works in almost
the opposite way. We shall be able better to understand this
next method by recalling the causes of the destruction of
kingdoms discussed earlier: there we saw that one way of
destroying a kingdom is to make the government more
tyrannical; this suggests that the salvation of a tyranny is 35
to make it more like the rule of a king. But the tyrant must
be careful about one matter: he must keep power enough
to rule over his subjects, whether they like him or not, for
if he once gives this up he gives up his tyranny. But though
power must be retained as the foundation, in all else the tyrant should act or appear to act in the character of a king. 40
   In the first place he should pretend to be concerned 1314b
about the public revenues, and not waste money in making presents of a sort which upsets the common people

when they see their hard-earned money snatched from them and lavished on prostitutes and foreigners and artists. He should give an account of what he receives and of what he spends (a practice which has been adopted by some tyrants); for then he will seem to be a steward rather than a tyrant, and as a result he will not have to fear that he will ever lack money while he is the lord of the state. When he is away from home, it is more advantageous for him to leave behind a deficit than a large hoard of property; for then the regents he leaves behind to govern will be less likely to attack his power; and a tyrant, when he is absent from home, has more reason to fear the guardians of his treasure whom he leaves behind than the citizens who accompany him.

In the second place, he should be seen to collect taxes and to require public services only for state purposes and for accumulating a fund for war emergencies; and generally he ought to make himself the guardian and treasurer of them, as if they belonged to the public, not to him.

He should appear dignified, not harsh, and when men meet him they should look upon him with reverence, not fear. Yet it is hard for him to be respected if he inspires no respect, and therefore whatever virtues he may neglect, at least he should maintain the character of a great soldier, and produce the impression that he is one. Neither he nor any of his associates should ever be guilty of the sexual abuse of his young subjects of either sex, and the women of his family should observe a like self-control towards other women; the insolence of women has ruined many tyrannies. In the indulgence of pleasures he should be the opposite of our modern tyrants, who not only begin at dawn and pass whole days in sensuality, but want other men to see them, so that they may admire their happy and blessed lot. In these things a tyrant should if possible be moderate, or at any rate should not parade his vices to the world; for a drunken and drowsy tyrant is soon despised and attacked; but not one who is temperate and wide awake.

His conduct should be the very reverse of nearly everything which has been said before about tyrants. He ought to adorn and improve his city, as though he were not a tyrant, but the guardian of the state. Also he should appear to be particularly earnest in the service of the gods; for if men think that a ruler is religious and has a reverence for the gods, they are less afraid of suffering injustice at his hands, and they are less disposed to conspire against him, because they believe him to have the gods fighting on his side. At the same time his religion must not be thought foolish. And he should honor men of merit, and make them think that they would not be held in more honor by the citizens if they had a free government. He should distribute honors himself, but have punishments inflicted by officers and courts of law. All monarchs take the precaution not to promote just one person to a great position; but if one must be promoted, then two or more should be, so that they can keep watch on one another. If, after all, some one has to hold a high position, he should not be a man of bold spirit; for such dispositions are always most inclined to strike. And if any one is to be deprived of his power, it should be diminished gradually, not taken from him all at once.

The tyrant should abstain from all outrage; in particular from personal violence and from sexual abuse of the young. He should be especially careful of his behavior to men who are lovers of honor; for as the lovers of money are offended when their property is touched, so are the lovers of honor and the virtuous when their honor is affected. Therefore a tyrant ought either not to commit such acts at all; or he should be thought only to employ fatherly correction, and not to trample upon others; and his acquaintance with youth should be supposed to arise from affection, and not from the insolence of power, and in general he should compensate the appearance of dishonor by the increase of honor.

The most dangerous of would-be assassins, and the ones who need to be watched most carefully, are those who are not concerned with surviving, if they succeed. Therefore special precaution should be taken about those men who believe that they, or those they care about, have been insulted; for when men are led by passion to assault others, they have no regard for themselves. As Heraclitus says, "It is difficult to fight against anger; for a man will buy revenge with his soul."

Since states consist of two classes—the poor and the rich—the tyrant should lead both to imagine that they are preserved and prevented from harming one another, and he should attach to his government whichever of the two is stronger; for, having this advantage, he has no need either to emancipate slaves or to disarm the citizens; either party added to the force which he already has, will make him stronger than his assailants.

But enough of these details; what should be the general policy of the tyrant is obvious. He ought to show himself to his subjects in the light, not of a tyrant, but of a steward and a king. He should not appropriate what is theirs, but should be their guardian; he should be moderate, not extravagant in his way of life; he should win the notables by companionship, and the multitude by flattery. For then his rule will of necessity be nobler and happier, because he will rule over better men whose spirits are not crushed, over men to whom he is not an object of hatred, and of whom he is not afraid. His power too will be more lasting. His disposition will be virtuous, or at least half virtuous; and he will not be wicked, but only half wicked.

from Book 7

I

Anyone inquiring about the best form of a state ought first to determine which is the most desirable form of life. While this remains uncertain the best form of the state must also be uncertain; for, in the natural order of things, those who are governed in the best way possible, given their circumstances, are those who may be expected to lead the most desirable life. We ought therefore to ascertain, first of all, what sort of life is generally the most desirable, and then whether that sort of life is best both for the state and for individuals.

Assuming that enough has been already said concerning the best life in discussions in our works intended for the general public, we will now only summarize what is contained in them. Certainly no one will dispute that goods are of three sorts—external goods, goods of the body, and goods of the soul—or deny that the happy man must have all three. For no one would maintain that a man is happy who has in him not a particle of courage or temperance or justice or prudence, who is afraid of every insect which flutters past him, and will commit any crime, however great, in order to gratify his lust of meat or drink, who will sacrifice his dearest friend for the sake of half-a-penny, and is as feeble and false in mind as a child or a madman. These propositions are almost universally acknowledged as soon as they are uttered, but men differ about the degree or relative superiority of this or that good. Some think that a very moderate amount of virtue is enough, but set no limit to their desires of wealth, property, power, reputation, and the like. We reply to this claim by an appeal to facts, which easily prove that mankind do not acquire or preserve virtue by the help of external goods—they acquire and preserve external goods by the help of virtue; and that happiness, whether consisting in pleasure or virtue, or both, is found more often in people who are most highly cultivated in their mind and in their character, and have only a moderate share of external goods, than in people who possess external goods to a useless extent but are deficient in higher qualities.

This is not only matter of experience, but, if reflected upon, will easily appear to be in accordance with reason. External goods have a limit, like any other instrument, and all things useful are of such a nature that where there is too much of them they must either do harm, or at any rate be of no use, to their possessors. But every good of the soul, the greater it is, the more useful—though perhaps "valuable" is a more appropriate word than "useful" here. In general it is obvious that the best state of one thing is better than the best state of a second in a degree corresponding to the superiority of the first thing to the second. So that, if the soul is more noble than our possessions or our bodies, both absolutely and in relation to us, it follows that the best state of the soul is in the same ratio superior to the best state of our possessions or our bodies. Furthermore, the only reason anything else is valuable is for the sake of the soul, and all wise men ought to choose other goods for the sake of the soul, and not the soul for the sake of them.

Let us acknowledge then that the quantity of happiness anyone has is equal to how much he has of virtue and wisdom, and of virtuous and wise action. God is a witness to us of this truth, for he is happy and blessed, not by reason of any external good, but in himself and by reason of his own nature. And the difference between good fortune and happiness lies here; for external goods come of themselves, the result of chance, but no one is just or temperate by or through chance.

In like manner, and by a similar train of argument, it can be shown that the state is happiest that is best and which acts rightly—that is, which does the right actions; neither an individual nor a state can do right actions without virtue and wisdom. Thus the courage, justice, and wisdom of a state have the same form and nature as the qualities because of which we call an individual who possesses them just, wise, or temperate.

I trust that will suffice by way of preface. I could not avoid touching upon these questions, but neither could I go through all the arguments involved here; these are the business of another science.

Let us assume then that the best life, both for individuals and states, is the life of virtue, when virtue has external goods enough for the performance of good actions. We will postpone consideration of any objections for later.

2

A question that remains to be discussed is whether the happiness of the individual is the same as that of the state, or different. Here again there can be no doubt—no one denies that they are the same. For those who hold that the well-being of the individual consists in his wealth, also think that riches make the happiness of the whole state, and those who value the life of a tyrant most highly deem that state the happiest which rules over the greatest number; while they who approve an individual for his virtue say that the more virtuous a state is, the happier it is.

Two questions present themselves at this point for consideration: (1) Which is the more desirable form of life, that of a citizen taking part in the activities of the state, or that of someone who lives as an alien, free from political ties? (2) What is the best form of constitution and the best way of organizing a state, supposing either that political privileges are desirable for all, or for a majority only? Since the good of the state and not of the individual is the proper subject of political thought and speculation, and we are engaged in a political discussion, while the first of these two questions has a secondary interest for us, the second will be the main subject of our inquiry.

Now it is evident that the form of government is best in which every man, whoever he is, can act best and live happily. But even those who agree in thinking that the life of virtue is the most desirable raise the question whether the life of politics and action is more desirable than one which is wholly independent of external goods—I mean than a contemplative life, which by some is maintained to be the only one worthy of a philosopher. For these two lives—the life of the philosopher and the life of the statesman—appear to have been preferred by those who have been most keen in the pursuit of virtue, both in our own and in other ages. Which is the better is a question of no small importance; for the wise man, like the wise state, will necessarily regulate his life according to the best end.

There are some who think that while a despotic rule over others is the greatest injustice, constitutional rule over them, even though not unjust, is a great impediment to the ruler's own individual wellbeing. Others take an opposite view; they maintain that the true life of man is the practical and political, and that every virtue may be practiced as much by statesmen and rulers as by private individuals. But still others think that arbitrary and tyrannical rule alone is consistent with happiness; indeed, in some states the entire aim both of the laws and of the constitution is to give men despotic power over their neighbors. And, therefore, although in most states the laws are somewhat chaotic, still, if they aim at anything, they aim at the maintenance of power: thus in Sparta and Crete the system of education and most of the laws are have been created with a view to war. And in all nations which are able to gratify their ambition military power—for example among the Scythians, Persians, Thracians and Celts, military power is held in highest esteem. In some nations there are laws aiming at encouraging the warlike virtues, as in Carthage, where we are told that men obtain the honor of wearing as many armlets as they have served campaigns. There was once a law in Macedonia that he who had not killed an enemy should wear a halter instead of a belt, and among the Scythians no one who had not slain an enemy was allowed to drink out of the cup which was handed round at a certain feast. Among the Iberians, a warlike nation, the number of enemies whom a man has slain is indicated by the number of obelisks placed around his tomb.

There are numerous similar practices among other nations, some of them established by law and others by custom. Yet to a reflective mind it must appear very strange that the statesman should be always considering how he can dominate and tyrannize over others, with or without their consent. How can that which is not even lawful be the business of the statesman or the legislator? It certainly is unlawful to rule without regard to justice, for there may be might where there is no right. The other arts and sciences offer no parallel: a physician is not expected to persuade or coerce his patients, nor a pilot the passengers in his ship. Yet most men appear to think that the art of despotic government is statesmanship, and what men affirm to be unjust and inexpedient in their own case they are not ashamed of practicing towards others; they demand just rule for themselves, but where other men are concerned they are not interested in it. Such behavior is irrational—unless those under control are born to serve, and their rulers to control, in which case men have a right to command, not indeed all their fellows, but only those who are intended to be subjects, just as we ought not to hunt mankind, whether for food or sacrifice, but only certain animals, those that are wild and edible. It is possible to imagine a state existing happily in isolation from others, and well-governed (for it is quite possible that a city thus isolated might be well-administered and have good laws)—but not be constituted

with any view to war or the conquest of enemies (who, we
assume, do not exist).

Our argument shows that warlike pursuits, although
generally to be deemed honorable, are not the supreme end
of all things, but only means. And the good lawgiver should
inquire how states and races of men and communities may
participate in a good life, and in the degree of happiness
that is possible for them. His enactments will not be always
the same; and where a state has neighbors, he will have to
see what sort of military training would be appropriate, and
what measures would be appropriate regarding each case.
The end at which the best form of government should aim
may be properly made a matter of future consideration.

3

Let us now address those who agree that the life of virtue is
the most desirable, but differ about the manner of practicing it. Some renounce political power, and think that the
life of the freeman is different from the life of the statesman
and the best of all; but others think the life of the statesman
best. The argument of the latter is that he who does nothing
cannot do well, and that virtuous *activity* is identical with
happiness. To both we say: you are partly right and partly
wrong. The first group are right in affirming that the life of
the freeman is better than the life of the despot; for there
is nothing grand or noble in having the use of a slave, in so
far as he is a slave; or in issuing commands about menial
duties. But it is an error to suppose that every sort of rule is
despotic like that of a master over slaves, for there is as great
a difference between the rule over freemen and the rule over
slaves as there is between slavery by nature and freedom by
nature—I have said enough about this at the beginning of
this work. And the second group is correct to place action
above inactivity, for happiness is activity, and the actions of
the just and wise are the realization of much that is noble.

But perhaps someone, accepting these premises, may
still maintain that supreme power is the best of all things,
because those who possess it are able to perform the greatest number of noble actions. It would follow that the man
who possesses power should never surrender any of it to his
neighbor—that instead he ought to take away any power
his neighbor has; and it would also follow that a father
should pay no regard to his son, nor the son to his father,
nor friend to friend; they should not bestow a thought on
one another in comparison with this higher object, for the
best is the most desirable and to do well is the best. There

might be some truth in such a view if we assume that robbers and plunderers attain the chief good. But this can never
be; their hypothesis is false. For the actions of a ruler cannot
be outstandingly honorable unless he is as much superior
to other men as a husband is to a wife, or a father to his
children, or a master to his slaves. And therefore no success,
however great, can ever recover what the man who violates
the law has lost in departing from virtue.

It is honorable and just that equals share equally. But
for equals to receive an unequal share, or for unequals to
receive an equal, is contrary to nature, and nothing which
is contrary to nature is good. If, therefore, there is any one
superior in virtue and in the power of performing the best
actions, we ought to follow and obey that man, but he must
have the capacity for action as well as virtue.

If we are right in our view, and happiness is assumed to
be virtuous activity, the active life will be the best, both for
every city collectively, and for individuals. Not that a life of
action must necessarily involve relations to others, as some
persons think. Nor are only our thoughts to be considered
active when they are directed externally, at objects that have
to be achieved by action. Thoughts and contemplations
which are independent and directed at no external action
can have a stronger claim to be labeled active. The aim is
virtuous activity, and therefore a certain kind of action,
and even in the case of external actions the directing mind
is most truly said to act. Neither is it necessary that states
which are isolated from others and choose to live alone
should be inactive; for activity, as well as other things, may
take place among internal sections; there are many ways in
which the divisions of a state act upon one another. The
same thing is equally true of every individual. If this were
otherwise, God and the universe, who have no external actions over and above their own internal life, would be far
enough from perfection.

It is therefore clear that the same life is best for each
individual, and for states and for mankind collectively.

...

13

Returning to the constitution itself, let us seek to identify
and describe the elements which compose a happy and
well-governed state. There are two things that constitute all
well-being: one of them is the choice of a right end and
aim of action, and the other the discovery of the actions
which are means towards it. Ends and means may not be in

harmony. Sometimes men seek the right end, but in practice fail to attain it; in other cases men are successful in all the means, but their ends are bad; and sometimes they fail in both. Take, for example, the art of medicine; physicians do not always understand the nature of health; sometimes they do not know the means to the desired end. In all arts and sciences both the end and the means should be equally within our control.

Some men have the power to attain the happiness and well-being which all men clearly desire; but this attainment is not granted to others, because of some accident or defect of nature; for a good life requires a supply of external goods, in a less degree when men are in a good state, in a greater degree when they are in a lower state. Others again, who possess the conditions of happiness, go utterly wrong from the first in the pursuit of it. But since our object is to discover the best form of government—the form for the best governing of a state—and since the state is best governed which has the greatest opportunity of obtaining happiness, it is evident that we must clearly ascertain the nature of happiness.

I maintain, and have said in the *Ethics*,[1] if the arguments there are of any value, that happiness is the realization and perfect exercise of virtue, and this not conditional, but absolute. By "conditional" I mean *necessitated externally*, and by "absolute," *good in itself*. Take the case of just actions; just punishments and chastisements do indeed spring from a good principle, but they are good only because we cannot do without them—it would be better if neither individuals nor states needed anything of the sort—but actions which aim at conferring honors and wealth on others are absolutely, intrinsically, good. The conditional action is only the choice of a lesser evil; whereas absolute goods are the foundations and origins of good. A good man may make the best even of poverty and disease, and the other ills of life; but he can only attain happiness under the opposite conditions. (As I have argued elsewhere,[2] the good man is the man for whom, because he is virtuous, the things that are absolutely good are good in practice; it is also plain that his use of these goods must be virtuous and in the absolute sense good.) This makes men suppose that external goods are the cause of happiness, yet we might as well say that a brilliant performance on the lyre was to be attributed to the instrument and not to the skill of the performer.

It follows then from what has been said that some things the legislator must find ready to his hand in a state, others he must provide. And therefore we can only say: May our state be constituted in such a manner as to be blessed with the goods of which fortune disposes (for we acknowledge her power); but nevertheless virtue and goodness in the state are not a matter of chance but the result of knowledge and purpose. A city can be virtuous only when the citizens who have a share in the government are virtuous, and in our state all the citizens share in the government; let us then inquire how a man becomes virtuous. For even if we could suppose the citizen body to be collectively virtuous, without each of them being so individually, yet the latter would be better, for if each is individually good it will follow that the whole is collectively good.

There are three things which make men good and virtuous; these are nature, habit, and rational principle. In the first place, everyone must be born a man and not some other animal; so, too, he must have a certain character, both of body and soul. But there is no use in merely having some qualities by birth, for they are altered by habit, and there are some gifts which are made by nature to be turned by habit to good or bad. Animals lead for the most part a life of nature, although in some less significant ways some are influenced by habit as well. Man uniquely has rationality. So nature, habit, and rational principle must be brought into harmony with one another, for they do not always agree; there are many things men should do against habit and nature, if rational principle persuades them that they ought. We have already determined what natures are likely to be most easily molded by the hands of the legislator. All else is the work of education; we learn some things by habit and some by instruction.

---

1   *I maintain ... Ethics*   See Aristotle, *Nicomachean Ethics* 1098a16; 1176b4.

2   *As I have argued elsewhere*   See Aristotle, *Eudemian Ethics* 1248a26.

POLYBIUS
(c. 200 BCE – c. 120 BCE)

POLYBIUS (PRONOUNCE HIS NAME "PUH-LIB-EE-US"), an ancient Greek historian of Rome, is now ranked among the greatest of the ancient writers of history, behind perhaps only Herodotus and Thucydides. His work is considered important not only for the content of his historical accounts, but also for his innovative methods; he wanted not merely to tell the stories of the past, as other historians had done, but to explain and categorize historical events, look into their causes, and offer political lessons. This approach proved influential on later politicians and social philosophers, especially Cicero, but also Aquinas, Locke, Montesquieu, Machiavelli, and the founding fathers of the United States.

Polybius was born into an aristocratic political family in the Achaean League, a confederation of city states located on the Gulf of Corinth (in present-day Greece). He and a thousand other Achaean noblemen were transported as hostages to Rome, when the Romans became suspicious of the Achaeans' lukewarm support. There he established close contacts with important political figures and became an admirer and supporter of Rome; he traveled widely abroad as a Roman diplomatic and military envoy. His interest in investigating the sources of the Romans' power led him to write a forty-book series narrating the history of Rome from 220 BCE onward. (Only Books 1–5, plus a few excerpts from the rest, survive today.)

"All historians," he wrote, "have insisted that the soundest education and training for political activity is the study of history, and that the surest and indeed the only way to learn how to bear bravely the vicissitudes of fortune is to recall the disasters of others." To this end, he thought, historians should write about military and political matters, instead of amusing their audiences with biography and mythology. His aim was to discover "how and thanks to what kind of constitution the Romans in under fifty-three years have subjected nearly the whole inhabited world to their sole government—a thing unique in history." He argued that it was the institutional set-up of the Roman state, not historical accident or great men, that had been responsible for its success; and that the most important feature of the state was the way in which it balanced three political principles: the monarchical, the aristocratic, and the democratic. Each of these acted as a counterweight to the others, keeping them in check; without this, each if allowed full sway, would degenerate—monarchy into tyranny, aristocracy into oligarchy, and democracy into violent mob rule. Here Polybius anticipated the French thinker Baron de Montesquieu (1689–1755) who advocated a "separation of powers." The American founding fathers appropriated the separation of powers from Polybius and Montesquieu, creating a system of "checks and balances" in which the legislative, judiciary, and executive branches of government check and balance each other. The idea that a government works best for liberty and the social good when limited in this sort of way can be traced back to Polybius.

◆ ◆ ◆ ◆ ◆

The Histories

Fragments of Book 6

1. From the Preface

I am aware that some will wonder why I have deferred until the present occasion my account of the Roman constitution, thus being obliged to interrupt the due course of my narrative. Now, that I have always regarded this account as one of the essential parts of my whole design, I have, I am sure, made evident in numerous passages and chiefly in the prefatory remarks dealing with the fundamental principles of this history, where I said that the best and most valuable result I aim at is that readers of my work may gain a knowledge how it was and by virtue of what peculiar political institutions that in less than in fifty-three years nearly the whole world was overcome and fell under the single dominion[1] of Rome, a thing the like of which had never happened before. Having made up my mind to deal with the matter, I found no occasion more suitable than the present

---

1   *dominion*   Ruling control.

for turning my attention to the constitution and testing the truth of what I am about to say on the subject. For just as those who pronounce in private on the characters of bad or good men, do not, when they really resolve to put their opinion to the test, choose for investigation those periods of their life which they passed in composure and repose, but seasons when they were afflicted by adversity or blessed with success, deeming the sole test of a perfect man to be the power of bearing high-mindedly and bravely the most complete reverses of fortune, so it should be in our judgment of states. Therefore, as I could not see any greater or more violent change in the fortunes of the Romans than this which has happened in our own times,[1] I reserved my account of the constitution for the present occasion....

What chiefly attracts and chiefly benefits students of history is just this—the study of causes and the consequent power of choosing what is best in each case. Now the chief cause of success or the reverse in all matters is the form of a state's constitution; for springing from this, as from a fountain-head,[2] all designs and plans of action not only originate, but reach their consummation.

2. On the Forms of States

In the case of those Greek states which have often risen to greatness and have often experienced a complete change of fortune, it is an easy matter both to describe their past and to pronounce as to their future. For there is no difficulty in reporting the known facts, and it is not hard to foretell the future by inference from the past. But about the Roman state it is neither at all easy to explain the present situation owing to the complicated character of the constitution, nor to foretell the future owing to our ignorance of the peculiar features of public and private life at Rome in the past. Particular attention and study are therefore required if one wishes to attain a clear general view of the distinctive qualities of their constitution.

Most of those whose object it has been to instruct us methodically concerning such matters, distinguish three kinds of constitutions, which they call kingship, aristoc-

racy,[3] and democracy. Now we should, I think, be quite justified in asking them to enlighten us as to whether they represent these three to be the sole varieties or rather to be the best; for in either case my opinion is that they are wrong. For it is evident that we must regard as the best constitution a combination of all these three varieties, since we have had proof of this not only theoretically but by actual experience, Lycurgus[4] having been the first to draw up a constitution— that of Sparta—on this principle. Nor on the other hand can we admit that these are the only three varieties; for we have witnessed monarchical and tyrannical governments, which while they differ very widely from kingship, yet bear a certain resemblance to it, this being the reason why monarchs in general falsely assume and use, as far as they can, the regal title. There have also been several oligarchical[5] constitutions which seem to bear some likeness to aristocratic ones, though the divergence is, generally, as wide as possible. The same holds good about democracies. The truth of what I say is evident from the following considerations. It is by no means every monarchy which we can call straight off a kingship, but only that which is voluntarily accepted by the subjects and where they are governed rather by an appeal to their reason than by fear and force. Nor again can we style every oligarchy an aristocracy, but only that where the government is in the hands of a selected body of the justest and wisest men. Similarly that is no true democracy in which the whole crowd of citizens is free to do whatever they wish or purpose, but when, in a community where it is traditional and customary to reverence the gods, to honor our parents, to respect our elders, and to obey the laws, the will of the greater number prevails, this is to be called a democracy. We should therefore assert that there are six kinds of governments, the three above mentioned which are in everyone's mouth and the three which are naturally allied to them, I mean monarchy, oligarchy, and mob-rule. Now the first of these to come into being is monarchy, its growth being natural and unaided; and next arises kingship derived from monarchy by the aid of art and by the correction of defects. Monarchy first changes into its vicious allied form, tyranny; and next, the abolishment

---

1   *violent change … times*   Polybius is talking about the third Punic war, which ended in 146 BCE with Rome completing its domination of the Western world.

2   *fountain-head*   Literally, the source of a spring; figuratively, the primary source.

3   *aristocracy*   Government by an elite group, often a hereditary nobility.

4   *Lycurgus*   Legendary lawgiver of Sparta, thought to have established the communalistic and militaristic reforms which transformed Spartan society in the first half of the seventh century BCE.

5   *oligarchical*   Involving rule by a small group.

of both gives birth to aristocracy. Aristocracy by its very nature degenerates into oligarchy; and when the commons inflamed by anger take vengeance on this government for its unjust rule, democracy comes into being; and in due course the license and lawlessness of this form of government produces mob-rule to complete the series. The truth of what I have just said will be quite clear to anyone who pays due attention to such beginnings, origins, and changes as are in each case natural. For he alone who has seen how each form naturally arises and develops, will be able to see when, how, and where the growth, perfection, change, and end of each are likely to occur again. And it is to the Roman constitution above all that this method, I think, may be successfully applied, since from the outset its formation and growth have been due to natural causes.

Perhaps this theory of the natural transformations into each other of the different forms of government is more elaborately set forth by Plato and certain other philosophers; but as the arguments are subtle and are stated at great length, they are beyond the reach of all but a few. I therefore will attempt to give a short summary of the theory, as far as I consider it to apply to the actual history of facts and to appeal to the common intelligence of mankind. For if there appear to be certain omissions in my general exposition of it, the detailed discussion which follows will afford the reader ample compensation for any difficulties now left unsolved.

What then are the beginnings I speak of and what is the first origin of political societies? When owing to floods, famines, failure of crops or other such causes there occurs such a destruction of the human race as tradition tells us has more than once happened, and as we must believe will often happen again, all arts and crafts perishing at the same time, then in the course of time, when springing from the survivors as from seeds men have again increased in numbers and just like other animals form herds—it being a matter of course that they too should herd together with those of their kind owing to their natural weakness—it is a necessary consequence that the man who excels in bodily strength and in courage will lead and rule over the rest. We observe and should regard as a most genuine work of nature this very phenomenon in the case of the other animals which act purely by instinct and among whom the strongest are always indisputably the masters—I speak of bulls, boars, cocks, and the like. It is probable then that at the beginning men lived thus, herding together like animals and following the lead of the strongest and bravest, the ruler's strength be-

ing here the sole limit to his power and the name we should give his rule being monarchy.

But when in time feelings of sociability and companionship begin to grow in such gatherings of men, than kingship has struck root; and the notions of goodness, justice, and their opposites begin to arise in men. The manner in which these notions come into being is as follows. Men being all naturally inclined to sexual intercourse, and the consequence of this being the birth of children, whenever one of those who have been reared does not on growing up show gratitude to those who reared him or defend them, but on the contrary takes to speaking ill of them or ill treating them, it is evident that he will displease and offend those who have been familiar with his parents and have witnessed the care and pains they spent on attending to and feeding their children. For seeing that men are distinguished from the other animals by possessing the faculty of reason, it is obviously improbable that such a difference of conduct should escape them, as it escapes the other animals: they will notice the thing and be displeased at what is going on, looking to the future and reflecting that they may all meet with the same treatment. Again when a man who has been helped or succored when in danger by another does not show gratitude to his preserver, but even goes to the length of attempting to do him injury, it is clear that those who become aware of it will naturally be displeased and offended by such conduct, sharing the resentment of their injured neighbor and imagining themselves in the same situation. From all this there arises in everyone a notion of the meaning and theory of duty, which is the beginning and end of justice. Similarly, again, when any man is foremost in defending his fellows from danger, and braves and awaits the onslaught of the most powerful beasts, it is natural that he should receive marks of favor and honor from the people, while the man who acts in the opposite manner will meet with reprobation and dislike. From this again some idea of what is base and what is noble and of what constitutes the difference is likely to arise among the people; and noble conduct will be admired and imitated because it is advantageous, while base conduct will be avoided. Now when the leading and most powerful man among the people always throws the weight of his authority on the side of the notions on such matters which generally prevail, and when in the opinion of his subjects he apportions rewards and penalties according to desert, they yield obedience to him no longer because they fear his force, but rather because their judgment approves him; and they join in maintaining his rule even if he is quite

enfeebled by age, defending him with one consent and bat-
tling against those who conspire to overthrow his rule. Thus
by insensible degrees the monarch becomes a king, ferocity
and force having yielded the supremacy to reason.

Thus is formed naturally among men the first notion of
goodness and justice, and their opposites; this is the beginning and birth of true kingship. For the people maintain the
supreme power not only in the hands of these men themselves, but in those of their descendants, from the conviction that those born from and reared by such men will also
have principles like to theirs. And if they ever are displeased
with the descendants, they now choose their kings and rulers no longer for their bodily strength and brute courage,
but for the excellency of their judgment and reasoning powers, as they have gained experience from actual facts of the
difference between the one class of qualities and the other.
In old times, then, those who had once been chosen to the
royal office continued to hold it until they grew old, fortifying and enclosing fine strongholds with walls and acquiring
lands, in the one case for the sake of the security of their
subjects and in the other to provide them with abundance
of the necessities of life. And while pursuing these aims, they
were exempt from all vituperation or jealousy, as neither in
their dress nor in their food did they make any great distinction, they lived very much like everyone else, not keeping
apart from the people. But when they received the office by
hereditary succession and found their safety now provided
for, and more than sufficient provision of food, they gave
way to their appetites owing to this superabundance, and
came to think that the rulers must be distinguished from
their subjects by a peculiar dress, that there should be a peculiar luxury and variety in the dressing and serving of their
viands,[1] and that they should meet with no denial in the
pursuit of their amours,[2] however lawless. These habits having given rise in the one case to envy and offence and in the
other to an outburst of hatred and passionate resentment,
the kingship changed into a tyranny; the first steps towards
its overthrow were taken by the subjects, and conspiracies
began to be formed. These conspiracies were not the work
of the worst men, but of the noblest, most high-spirited,
and most courageous, because such men are least able to
brook the insolence[3] of princes. The people now having got
leaders, would combined with them against the ruling pow-

ers for the reasons I stated above; kingship and monarchy
would be utterly abolished, and in their place aristocracy
would begin to grow. For the commons,[4] as if bound to pay
at once their debt of gratitude to the abolishers of monarchy,
would make them their leaders and entrust their destinies to
them. At first these chiefs gladly assumed this charge and regarded nothing as of greater importance than the common
interest, administering the private and public affairs of the
people with paternal solicitude.[5] But here again when children inherited this position of authority from their fathers,
having no experience of misfortune and none at all of civil
equality and liberty of speech, and having been brought up
from the cradle amid the evidences of the power and high
position of their fathers, they abandoned themselves some
to greed of gain and unscrupulous money-making, others
to indulgence in wine and the convivial excess which accompanies it, and others again to the violation of women
and the rape of boys; and thus converting the aristocracy
into an oligarchy aroused in the people feelings similar to
those of which I just spoke, and in consequence met with
the same disastrous end as the tyrant. For whenever anyone
who has noticed the jealousy and hatred with which they
are regarded by the citizens, has the courage to speak or
act against the chiefs of the state he has the whole mass of
the people ready to back him. Next, when they have either
killed or banished the oligarchs, they no longer venture to
set a king over them, as they still remember with terror the
injustice they suffered from the former ones, nor can they
entrust the government with confidence to a select few, with
the evidence before them of their recent error in doing so.
Thus the only hope still surviving unimpaired is in themselves, and to this they resort, making the state a democracy
instead of an oligarchy and assuming the responsibility for
the conduct of affairs. Then as long as some of those survive
who experienced the evils of oligarchical dominion, they
are well pleased with the present form of government, and
set a high value on equality and freedom of speech. But
when a new generation arises and the democracy falls into
the hands of the grandchildren of its founders, they have
become so accustomed to freedom and equality that they
no longer value them, and begin to aim at pre-eminence;
and it is chiefly those of ample fortune who fall into this
error. So when they begin to lust for power and cannot at-

---

1   *viands*   Meals.
2   *amours*   Love affairs.
3   *brook the insolence*   Put up with the arrogant disrespect.

4   *commons*   Common people, as distinct from the ruling classes.
5   *paternal solicitude*   Concern and consideration, like that of a
    father.

tain it through themselves or their own good qualities, they ruin their estates,[1] tempting and corrupting the people in every possible way. And hence when by their foolish thirst for reputation they have created among the masses an appetite for gifts and the habit of receiving them, democracy in its turn is abolished and changes into a rule of force and violence. For the people, having grown accustomed to feed at the expense of others and to depend for their livelihood on the property of others, as soon as they find a leader who is enterprising but is excluded from the houses of office by his penury,[2] institute the rule of violence; and now uniting their forces massacre, banish, and plunder, until they degenerate again into perfect savages and find once more a master and monarch.

Such is the cycle of political revolution, the course appointed by nature in which constitutions change, disappear, and finally return to the point from which they started. Anyone who clearly perceives this may indeed in speaking of the future of any state be wrong in his estimate of the time the process will take, but if his judgment is not tainted by animosity or jealousy, he will very seldom be mistaken as to the stage of growth or decline it has reached, and as to the form into which it will change. And especially in the case of the Roman state will this method enable us to arrive at a knowledge of its formation, growth, and greatest perfection, and likewise of the change for the worse which is sure to follow some day. For, as I said, this state, more than any other, has been formed and has grown naturally, and will undergo a natural decline and change to its contrary. The reader will be able to judge of the truth of this from the subsequent parts of this work.

At present I will give a brief account of the legislation of Lycurgus, a matter not alien to my present purpose. Lycurgus had perfectly well understood that all the above changes take place necessarily and naturally, and had taken into consideration that every variety of constitution which is simple and formed on principle is precarious, as it is soon perverted into the corrupt form which is proper to it and naturally follows on it. For just as rust in the case of iron and wood-worms and ship-worms in the case of timber are inbred[3] pests, and these substances, even though they escape all external injury, fall a prey to the evils engendered in them, so each constitution has a vice engendered in it and inseparable from it. In kingship it is despotism, in aristocracy oligarchy, and in democracy the savage rule of violence; and it is impossible, as I said above, that each of these should not in course of time change into this vicious form. Lycurgus, then, foreseeing this, did not make his constitution simple and uniform, but united in it all the good and distinctive features of the best governments, so that none of the principles should grow unduly and be perverted into its allied evil, but that, the force of each being neutralized by that of the others, neither of them should prevail and outbalance another, but that the constitution should remain for long in a state of equilibrium like a well-trimmed boat, kingship being guarded from arrogance by the fear of the commons, who were given a sufficient share in the government, and the commons on the other hand not venturing to treat the kings with contempt from fear of the elders, who being selected from the best citizens would be sure all of them to be always on the side of justice; so that that part of the state which was weakest owing to its subservience to traditional custom, acquired power and weight by the support and influence of the elders. The consequence was that by drawing up his constitution thus he preserved liberty at Sparta for a longer period than is recorded elsewhere.

Lycurgus then, foreseeing, by a process of reasoning, whence and how events naturally happen, constructed his constitution untaught by adversity, but the Romans while they have arrived at the same final result as regards their form of government, have not reached it by any process of reasoning, but by the discipline of many struggles and troubles, and always choosing the best by the light of the experience gained in disaster have thus reached the same result as Lycurgus, that is to say, the best of all existing constitutions.

5. On the Roman Constitution at its Prime

From the crossing of Xerxes to Greece[4] ... and for thirty years after this period, it [Rome] was always one of those polities which was an object of special study, and it was at its best and nearest to perfection at the time of the Hannibalic war,[5] the period at which I interrupted my narrative to deal with it. Therefore now that I have described its growth, I will explain what were the conditions at the time when by

---

1 *estates* Inheritances.
2 *penury* Extreme poverty.
3 *inbred* By their nature.

4 *crossing of Xerxes to Greece* Xerxes was king of Persia from 486 to 465 BCE. He invaded Greece in 480 BCE.
5 *the Hannibalic war* Another name for the second Punic war. Hannibal led the Carthaginians against Rome.

their defeat at Cannae the Romans were brought face to face with disaster.

I am quite aware that to those who have been born and bred under the Roman Republic[1] my account of it will seem somewhat imperfect owing to the omission of certain details. For as they have complete knowledge of it and practical acquaintance with all its parts, having been familiar with these customs and institutions from childhood, they will not be struck by the extent of the information I give but will demand in addition all I have omitted: they will not think that the author has purposely omitted small peculiarities, but owing to ignorance he has been silent regarding the origins of many things and some points of capital importance. Had I mentioned them, they would not have been impressed by my doing so, regarding them as small and trivial points, but as they are omitted they will demand their inclusion as if they were vital matters, through a desire themselves to appear better informed than the author. Now a good critic should not judge authors by what they omit, but by what they relate, and if he finds any falsehood in this, he may conclude that the omissions are due to ignorance; but if all the writer says is true, he should admit that he has been silent about these matters deliberately and not from ignorance.

These remarks are meant for those who find fault with authors in cavilling[2] rather than just spirit....

In so far as any view of matter we form applies to the right occasion, so far expressions of approval or blame are sound. When circumstances change, and when applied to these changed conditions, the most excellent and true reflections of authors seem often not only not acceptable, but utterly offensive....

The three kinds of government that I spoke of above all shared in the control of the Roman state. And such fairness and propriety in all respects was shown in the use of these three elements for drawing up the constitution and in its subsequent administration that it was impossible even for a native to pronounce with certainty whether the whole system was aristocratic, democratic, or monarchical. This was indeed only natural. For if one fixed one's eyes on the power of the consuls, the constitution seemed completely monarchical and royal; if on that of the senate it seemed

again to be aristocratic; and when one looked at the power of the masses, it seemed clearly to be a democracy. The parts of the state falling under the control of each element were and with a few modifications still are as follows.

The consuls, previous to leading out their legions, exercise authority in Rome over all public affairs, since all the other magistrates except the tribunes are under them and bound to obey them, and it is they who introduce embassies to the senate. Besides this it is they who consult the senate on matters of urgency, they who carry out in detail the provisions of its decrees. Again as concerns all affairs of state administered by the people it is their duty to take these under their charge, to summon assemblies, to introduce measures, and to preside over the execution of the popular decrees. As for preparation for war and the general conduct of operations in the field, here their power is almost uncontrolled; for they are empowered to make what demands they choose on the allies, to appoint military tribunes, to levy soldiers and select those who are fittest for service. They also have the right of inflicting, when on active service, punishment on anyone under their command; and they are authorized to spend any sum they decide upon from the public funds, being accompanied by a quaestor[3] who faithfully executes their instructions. So that if one looks at this part of the administration alone, one may reasonably pronounce the constitution to be a pure monarchy or kingship. I may remark that any changes in these matters or in others of which I am about to speak that may be made in present or future times do not in any way affect the truth of the views I here state.

To pass to the senate. In the first place it has the control of the treasury, all revenue and expenditure being regulated by it. For with the exception of payments made to the consuls, the quaestors are not allowed to disburse for any particular object without a decree of the senate. And even the item of expenditure which is far heavier and more important than any other—the outlay every five years by the censors on public works, whether constructions or repairs—is under the control of the senate, which makes a grant to the censors for the purpose. Similarly crimes committed in Italy which require a public investigation, such as treason, conspiracy, poisoning, and assassination, are under the jurisdiction of the senate. Also if any private person or community in Italy is in need of arbitration or indeed

1   *Roman Republic* This began with the overthrow of the monarchy in 510 BCE, and lasted until it was replaced by the Roman Empire (perhaps in 44 BCE when Julius Caesar declared himself dictator, or a little later).

2   *cavilling* Making trivial unjustified objections.

3   *quaestor* Public official in Rome responsible for finance, administration, etc.

claims damages or requires succor or protection, the senate attends to all such matters. It also occupies itself with the dispatch of all embassies sent to countries outside of Italy for the purpose either of settling differences, or of offering friendly advice, or indeed of imposing demands, or of receiving submission, or of declaring war; and in like manner with respect to embassies arriving in Rome it decides what reception and what answer should be given to them. All these matters are in the hands of the senate, nor have the people anything whatever to do with them. So that again to one residing in Rome during the absence of the consuls the constitution appears to be entirely aristocratic; and this is the conviction of many Greek states and many of the kings, as the senate manages all business connected with them.

After this we are naturally inclined to ask what part in the constitution is left for the people, considering that the senate controls all the particular matters I mentioned, and, what is most important, manages all matters of revenue and expenditure, and considering that the consuls again have uncontrolled authority as regards armaments and operations in the field. But nevertheless there is a part and a very important part left for the people. For it is the people which alone has the right to confer honors and inflict punishment, the only bonds by which kingdoms and states and in a word human society in general are held together. For where the distinction between these is overlooked or is observed but ill applied, no affairs can be properly administered. How indeed is this possible when good and evil men are held in equal estimation? It is by the people, then, in many cases the offences punishable by a fine are tried when the accused have held the highest office; and they are the only court which may try on capital charges. As regards the latter they have a practice which is praiseworthy and should be mentioned. Their usage allows those on trial for their lives when found guilty liberty to depart openly, thus inflicting voluntary exile on themselves, if even only one of the tribes that pronounce the verdict has not yet voted. Such exiles enjoy safety in the territories of Naples, Praeneste, Tibur, and other *civitates foederatae*.[1] Again it is the people who bestow office on the deserving, the noblest regard of virtue in a state; the people have the power of approving or rejecting laws, and what is most important of all, they deliberate on the question of war and peace. Further in the case of alliances, terms of peace, and treaties, it is the people who ratify all these or the reverse. Thus here again one might

plausibly say that the people's share in the government is the greatest, and that the constitution is a democratic one.

Having stated how political power is distributed among the different parts of the state, I will now explain how each of the three parts is enabled, if they wish, to counteract or co-operate with the others. The consul, when he leaves with his army invested with the powers I mentioned, appears indeed to have absolute authority in all matters necessary for carrying out his purpose; but in fact he requires the support of the people and the senate, and is not able to bring his operations to a conclusion without them. For it is obvious that the legions require constant supplies, and without the consent of the senate, neither corn,[2] clothing, nor pay can be provided; so that the commander's plans come to nothing, if the senate chooses to be deliberately negligent and obstructive. It also depends on the senate whether or not a general can carry out completely his conceptions and designs, since it has the right of either superseding him when his year's term of office has expired or of retaining him in command. Again it is in its power to celebrate with pomp and to magnify the successes of a general or on the other hand to obscure and belittle them. For the processions they call triumphs, in which the generals bring the actual spectacle of their achievements before the eyes of their fellow-citizens, cannot be properly organized and sometimes even cannot be held at all, unless the senate consents and provides the requisite funds. As for the people it is most indispensable for the consuls to conciliate them, however far away from home they may be; for, as I said, it is the people which ratifies or annuls terms of peace and treaties, and what is most important, on laying down office the consuls are obliged to account for their actions to the people. So that in no respect is it safe for the consuls to neglect keeping in favor with both the senate and the people.

The senate again, which possesses such great power, is obliged in the first place to pay attention to the commons in public affairs and respect the wishes of the people, and it cannot carry out inquiries into the most grave and important offences against the state, punishable with death, and their correction, unless the *senatus consultum*[3] is confirmed by the people. The same is the case in matters which directly affect the senate itself. For if anyone introduces a law meant to deprive the senate of some of its traditional authority, or to abolish the precedence and other distinctions of the

---

1   *civitates foederatae*   Latin: states in the federation.

2   *corn*   Grain.

3   *senatus consultum*   Latin: decree of the Senate.

senators or even to curtail them of their private fortunes, it is the people alone which has the power of passing or rejecting any such measure. And what is most important is that if a single one of the tribunes interposes, the senate is unable to decide finally about any matter, and cannot even meet and hold sittings; and here it is to be observed that the tribunes are always obliged to act as the people decree and to pay every attention to their wishes. Therefore for all these reasons the senate is afraid of the masses and must pay due attention to the popular will.

17. Similarly, again, the people must be submissive to the senate and respect its members both in public and in private. Through the whole of Italy a vast number of contracts, which it would not be easy to enumerate, are given out by the censors for the construction and repair of public buildings, and besides this there are many things which are farmed, such as navigable rivers, harbors, gardens, mines, lands, in fact everything that forms part of the Roman dominion. Now all these matters are undertaken by the people, and one may almost say that everyone is interested in these contracts and the work they involved. For certain people are the actual purchasers from the censors of the contracts, others are the partners of these first, others stand surety[1] for them, others pledge their own fortunes to the state for this purpose. Now in all these matters the senate is supreme. It can grant extension of time; it can relieve the contractor if any accident occurs; and if the work proves to be absolutely impossible to carry out it can liberate him from his contract. There are in fact many ways in which the senate can either benefit or indicate those who manage public property, as all these matters are referred to it. What is even most important is that the judges in most civil trials, whether public or private, are appointed from its members, where the action involves large interests. So that all citizens being at the mercy of the senate, and look-

ing forward with alarm to the uncertainty of litigation,[2] are very shy of obstructing or resisting its decisions. Similarly everyone is reluctant to oppose the projects of the consuls as all are generally and individually under their authority when in the field.

Such being the power that each part has of hampering the others or co-operating with them, their union is adequate to all emergencies, so that it is impossible to find a better political system than this. For whenever the menace of some common danger from abroad compels them to act in concord and support each other, so great does the strength of the state become, that nothing which is requisite can be neglected, as all are zealously competing in devising means of meeting the need of the hour, nor can any decision arrived at fail to be executed promptly, as all are co-operating both in public and in private to the accomplishment of the task which they have set themselves; and consequently this peculiar form of constitution possesses an irresistible power of attaining every object upon which it is resolved. When again they are freed from external menace, and reap the harvest of good fortune and affluence which is the result of their success, and in the enjoyment of this prosperity are corrupted by flattery and idleness and wax insolent and overbearing, as indeed happens often enough, it is then especially that we see the state providing itself a remedy for the evil from which it suffers. For when one part having grown out of proportion to the others aims at supremacy and tends to become too predominant, it is evident that, as for the reasons above given none of the three is absolute, but the purpose of the one can be counterworked and thwarted by the others, none of them will excessively outgrow the others or treat them with contempt. All in fact remains *in statu quo*,[3] on the one hand, because any aggressive impulse is sure to be checked and from the outset each estate[4] stands in dread of being interfered with by the others....

---

2 *litigation* The process of judging a lawsuit.
3 *in statu quo* Latin: in its existing condition; that is, without change.
4 *estate* Political sector.

MARCUS TULLIUS CICERO
(106 BCE – 43 BCE)

CICERO WAS A CENTRAL POLITICAL FIGURE IN ANCIENT Rome in a time of political turmoil, as the Roman Republic, which had lasted almost five centuries, moved toward monarchy. The leading Roman lawyer, he was elected consul, then given unconditional power by the Senate, then forced into exile, then allowed to return, and at last murdered by his political enemies. He was a superb orator and a prolific writer of letters and essays, with a prose style that influenced later writers in all the European languages. But he is best known, and has been most strongly influential, as a political thinker.

Cicero was born of an aristocratic but not wealthy or powerful Roman family. He studied law, rhetoric, and philosophy; succeeding early as a lawyer, he built up a network of powerful friends and soon was elected to a succession of major political offices. In 63 BCE, as consul (the highest Roman office) he exposed a conspiracy involving Cataline and others, who had planned to take over the state by force. Cicero had all of them put to death without trial. In the year 60 he refused to join with the ruling triumvirate (Caesar, Crassus, and Pompey), remaining true to the ideal of constitutional republican governance as put forward by the Senate. He was barred from political activity and forced into exile, where, for a year and a half, he devoted himself to philosophical writing. When allowed to return to Rome, he continued to engage in political wrangling, but his days of great power and influence were over, and he increasingly devoted his energies to speaking and writing. Cicero thought that Caesar's assassination in 44 provided an opportunity to restore the Republic and constitutional government, and spoke and wrote in favor of this idea; but after a power struggle, Mark Antony, Lepidus, and Octavian emerged as rulers, and Antony arranged for Cicero and his other political enemies be killed. His head and hands were cut off and displayed on the speaker's podium in the Forum as a warning to others.

Cicero's thought was influenced by a variety of Greek sources, including the Stoics and traditions descending from Plato and Aristotle. Cicero played an important role in translating Greek philosophy into Latin for a Roman audience, importing the ideas of the Academic skeptics, Stoics and Epicureans. Politically, Cicero was a strong defender of law, constitutionality, and moderation, seeking administrative solutions to problems of public policy and governance. He defended the Roman republic—though in his day it had already disintegrated considerably, and Cicero was thought out of touch by his contemporaries.

In much of his writing, he argued that considerations of morality, which he claimed were a matter of natural law, overrode and took priority over political considerations and positive law, and formed the basis for criticizing and justifying them. His case for the priority of the moral over the political was made in opposition to Plato and Aristotle, who did not strongly distinguish between the two.

Cicero has been enormously influential on future thinkers. He is thought to have been the most widely read ancient political writer during the medieval period, and some have located various strands of Christian social thought in his work. From the Renaissance until the study of Latin in school went into decline halfway through the twentieth century, his elegant Latin prose was a staple of high school study. His work was a strong influence on Enlightenment thought, and on the political thinking of the founding fathers of the United States.

His thoughts on the "just war," expressed in the selection presented here, are perhaps the most important ancestor of subsequent attempts to present conditions under which war may justly be initiated, and under which it may be justly conducted—he is often counted as the father of just-war theory and of the idea that one should try to regulate behavior of those at war through international convention. His ideas would go on to influence Augustine, Aquinas and Christine de Pizan, as well as more recent writers like Michael Walzer.

* * * * *

On Duties (44 BCE)

We have now discussed the first source of duty.[1] Of the three that remain the most wide-reaching one is the reasoning by which the fellowship of men with one another, and the communal life, are held together. There are two parts of this justice, the most illustrious of the virtues, on account of which men are called "good"; and the beneficence connected with it, which may be called either kindness or liberality.

Of justice, the first office[2] is that no man should harm another unless he has been provoked by injustice; the next that one should treat common goods as common and private ones as one's own. Now no property is private by nature, but rather by long occupation (as when men moved into some empty property in the past), or by victory (when they acquired it in war), or by law, by settlement, by agreement, or by lot. The result is that the land of Arpinum is said to belong to the Arpinates, and that of Tusculum to the Tusculani. The distribution of private property is of a similar kind. Consequently, since what becomes each man's own comes from what had in nature been common, each man should hold on to whatever has fallen to him. If anyone else should seek any of it for himself, he will be violating the law of human fellowship.

We are not born for ourselves alone, to use Plato's splendid words,[3] but our country claims for itself one part of our birth, and our friends another. Moreover, as the Stoics[4] believe, everything produced on the earth is created for the use of mankind, and men are born for the sake of men, so

that they may be able to assist one another. Consequently, we ought in this to follow nature as our leader, to contribute to the common stock the things that benefit everyone together, and, by the exchange of dutiful services, by giving and receiving expertise and effort and means, to bind fast the fellowship of men with each other. Moreover, the keeping of faith is fundamental to justice, that is constancy and truth in what is said and agreed. Therefore, though this will perhaps seem difficult to some, let us venture to imitate the Stoics, who hunt assiduously for the derivations of words, and let us trust that keeping faith (*fides*) is so called because what has been said is actually done (*fiat*).

Of injustice there are two types: men may inflict injury; or else, when it is being inflicted upon others, they may fail to deflect it, even though they could. Anyone who makes an unjust attack on another, whether driven by anger or by some other agitation, seems to be laying hands, so to speak, upon a fellow. But also, the man who does not defend someone, or obstruct the injustice when he can, is at fault just as if he had abandoned his parents or his friends or his country.

Those injustices that are purposely inflicted for the sake of harming another often stem from fear; in such cases the one who is thinking of harming someone else is afraid that if he does not do so, he himself will be affected by some disadvantage. In most cases, however, men set about committing injustice in order to secure something that they desire: where this fault is concerned avarice[5] is extremely widespread. Riches are sought both for the things that are necessary to life, and in order to enjoy pleasures. In men of greater spirit, however, the desire for wealth has as its goal influence and the opportunity to gratify others. Marcus Crassus, for example, recently said that no one who wanted to be pre-eminent in the republic would have wealth enough if he could not feed an army on its yield.[6] Magnificent accoutrements and an elegant and plentiful style of life give men further delight. The result of such things is that desire for money has become unlimited. Such expansion of one's personal wealth as harms no one is not, of course, to be disparaged; but committing injustice must always be avoided.

However, men are led most of all to being overwhelmed by forgetfulness of justice when they slip into desiring pos-

---

1   *the first source of duty*   Wisdom, according to Cicero. The second is justice (dealt with in this excerpt) and kindness. The third and fourth are courage and temperance.

2   *office*   Duty assigned to someone.

3   *Plato's splendid words*   "Now it is plain to almost everyone that the pleasantest thing in life is to attend to one's own business, especially when the business one chooses is such as yours; yet you ought also to bear in mind that no one of us exists for himself alone, but one share of our existence belongs to our country, another to our parents, a third to the rest of our friends, while a great part is given over to those needs of the hour with which our life is beset." Plato, *Letters*, 9.357e–9.358a (Jowett trans.).

4   *Stoics*   Ancient Greek school of philosophy; in its later Roman form, referred to by Cicero, they advocated putting aside the passions, concentrating on doing one's duty and calmly accepting one's fate.

5   *avarice*   Greed.

6   *Marcus Crassus ... its yield*   Crassus may have been talking about his own experience. In 71 BCE, when the public treasury was low in funds, he was in charge of fighting the slave revolt led by Spartacus.

itions of command or honor or glory. That is why we find the observation of Ennius to be widely applicable:

> To kingship belongs neither sacred fellowship nor
> faith—

For if there is any area in which is it impossible for many to be outstanding, there will generally be such competition there that it is extremely difficult to maintain a "sacred fellowship." The rash behavior of Gaius Caesar[1] has recently made that clear: he overturned all the laws of gods and men for the sake of the pre-eminence that he had imagined for himself in his mistaken fancy. There is something troubling in this type of case, in that the desire for honor, command, power and glory usually exist in men of the greatest spirit and most brilliant intellectual talent. Therefore one must be all the more careful not to do wrong in this way.

In every case of injustice it matters a great deal whether the injury was committed through some agitation of the spirit, which is generally brief and momentary, or purposefully and with forethought. For those things that happen because of some sudden impulse are less serious than those inflicted after reflection and preparation. But I have now said enough about actually committing injustice.

As for neglecting to defend others and deserting one's duty, there tend to be several causes of this. For some men do not wish to incur enmities, or toil, or expense; others are hindered by indifference, laziness, inactivity or some pursuits or business of their own, to the extent that they allow the people whom they ought to protect to be abandoned. We must therefore watch out in case Plato's words about philosophers prove not to be sufficient. For he said that they are immersed in the investigation of the truth and that, disdaining the very things for which most men vigorously strive and even fight one another to the death, they count them as nothing. Because of that he calls them just. They observe one type of justice, indeed, that they should harm no one else by inflicting injury, but they fall into another; for hindered by their devotion to learning, they abandon those whom they ought to protect. And so, he thinks that they should not even embark upon public life unless they are forced to do so.[2] But that is something done more

fairly when done voluntarily; for something that is done rightly is only just if it is voluntary. There are also some who, whether through devotion to preserving their personal wealth or through some kind of dislike of mankind, claim to be attending to their own business, and appear to do no one any injustice. But though they are free from one type of injustice, they run into another: such men abandon the fellowship of life, because they contribute to it nothing of their devotion, nothing of their effort, nothing of their means.

Since we have set out the two types of injustice, and added the causes of each, and since we established previously what are the things that constitute justice, we shall now be able to judge with ease what is our duty on each occasion—that is, if we do not love ourselves too much. For it is difficult to be concerned about another's affairs. Terence's Chremes, however, thinks "nothing that is human is another's affair";[3] yet in fact we do tend to notice and feel our own good and bad fortune more than that of others, which we see as if a great distance intervenes; accordingly, we do not make the same judgments about them and about ourselves. It is good advice therefore that prevents you from doing anything if you are unsure whether it is fair or unfair. For fairness shines out by itself, and hesitation signifies that one is contemplating injustice.

Occasions often arise when the actions that seem most worthy of a just man, of him whom we call good, undergo a change, and the opposite becomes the case. For example, from time to time it becomes just to set aside such requirements as the returning of a deposit, or the carrying out of a promise, or other things that relate to truth and to keeping faith, and not to observe them. For it is seemly[4] that they should be referred to those fundamentals of justice that I laid down at the beginning: first that one should harm no one; and secondly that one serve the common advantage. Such actions alter with the circumstances, and duty alters likewise, and is not invariable. For it can happen that something that has been promised and agreed, if carried out, would be disadvantageous to the person to whom the promise has been made, or else to him who gave the promise. If Neptune in the myth had not done what he

---

1   *Gaius Caesar* Gaius Julius Caesar, whom we usually call Julius Caesar. They were political enemies, though there was a good deal of mutual respect.

2   *And so ... do so* See Plato's *Republic*, in various places, especially 6, 485b–87a; 7, 520c–21b; 7, 540d–e; 1, 347C; 3, 519C–20d, 539e–40b.

3   *Terence's Chremes ... affair* Chremes is a character in *The Self-Tormentor*, a play by Terence, Roman playwright (d. 159 BCE). This famous quotation, "*Homo sum, humani nihil a me alienum puto,*" is usually translated, "I am human; nothing that is human is alien to me."

4   *seemly* Appropriate and correct.

had promised to Theseus, Theseus would not have been deprived of his son Hippolytus.[1] He made three wishes, as we read, and the third was this: he wished in his anger that Hippolytus should die. When it was granted he fell into the deepest grief. Therefore promises should not be kept if they are disadvantageous to those to whom you have made them. Nor, if they harm you more than they benefit the person whom you have promised, is it contrary to duty to prefer the greater good to the lesser. For example, if you had made an appointment to appear for someone as advocate in the near future, and in the meantime your son had fallen seriously ill, it would not be contrary to your duty not to do as you had said. Rather, the person to whom you had made the promise would be failing in *his* duty if he complained that he had been abandoned. Again, who does not see that if someone is forced to make a promise through fear, or deceived into it by trickery, the promise ought not to stand? One is released from such promises in most cases by the praetor's[2] code of justice, and sometimes by the laws.

Injustices can also arise from a kind of trickery, by an extremely cunning but ill intentioned interpretation of the law. In consequence the saying "the more Justice, the more injustice" has by now become a proverb well worn in conversation. Many wrongs of this type are committed even in public affairs; and example is that of the man who, during a truce of thirty days which had been agreed with the enemy, laid waste the fields by night, on the grounds that the truce had been established for days, but not for nights. We should not approve the action even of our own countryman, if the story is true about Quintus Fabius Labeo (or some other person—for I know of it only from hearsay). He was assigned by the senate to arbitrate about the boundary between the Nolani and the Neapolitani. When he arrived at the place he spoke with each group separately, urging it to do nothing out of covetousness or greed, and to be prepared to retreat rather than to advance. When both of them did that, there was some land left in the middle. Therefore he set a limit to their boundaries exactly where they themselves

had said; but he assigned the land that was left in the middle to the people of Rome. That was not arbitration, that was deception. Cleverness of such a king ought in every case to be avoided.

Moreover, certain duties must be observed even towards those at whose hands you may have received unjust treatment. There is a limit to revenge and to punishment. I am not even sure that it is not enough simply that the man who did the harm should repent of his injustice, so that he himself will do no such thing again, and others will be slower to act unjustly.

Something else that must very much be preserved in public affairs is the justice of warfare. There are two types of conflict: the one proceeds by debate, the other by force. Since the former is the proper concern of a man, but the latter of beasts, one should only resort to the latter if one may not employ the former. Wars, then, ought to be undertaken for this purpose, that we may live in peace, without injustice; and once victory has been secured, those who were not cruel or savage in warfare should be spared. Thus, our forefathers even received the Tusculani, the Aequi, the Volsci, the Sabini, and the Hernici into citizenship. On the other hand they utterly destroyed Carthage and Numantia. I would prefer that they had not destroyed Corinth; but I believe that they had some specific purpose in doing so, in particular in view of its advantageous situation, to prevent the location itself from being some day an incitement to war.[3]

In my opinion, our concern should always be for a peace that will have nothing to do with treachery. If I had been followed in this we would still have some republican government (if perhaps not the very best); whereas now we have none.[4] And while you must have concern for those whom you have conquered by force, you must also take in those who have laid down their arms and seek refuge in the faith of generals, although a battering ram may have crashed against their wall.[5] In this matter, justice was respected so

---

1   *Theseus, Hippolytus* In the mythological story, Phaedra, the young wife of Theseus, king of Athens, was attracted to her stepson, Hippolytus; but Hippolytus turned down Phaedra's advances. In revenge, Phaedra turned her husband against his son, making him insanely jealous, and Theseus used one of his three wishes promised by the sea-god Neptune to ask for the death of his son, but was grief-stricken when he was killed in a chariot-crash as a result.

2   *praetor* High-ranking Roman judge.

3   *Tusculani, Aequi, Volsci, Sabini, Hernici* These were non-Roman Italian peoples, conquered by Rome and later admitted to Roman citizenship in the fourth and third centuries BCE. *Carthage* and *Corinth* were destroyed in 146 BCE, *Numantia* in 133 BCE. Cicero is uncomfortable about the history of Roman imperialistic warfare, but tries here to justify it anyway.

4   *If I had been followed ... none* Cicero had tried to prevent the civil war between Caesar and Pompey and then to end it.

5   *And while you must ... wall* It was traditional Roman battle practice to spare only those who surrendered before the battering ram had touched their walls.

greatly among our countrymen that the very men who had received into their good faith cities or peoples conquered in war would, by the custom of our forefathers, become their patrons.

Indeed, a fair code of warfare has been drawn up, in full accordance with religious scruple, in the fetial laws[1] of the Roman people. From this we can grasp that no war is just unless it is waged after a formal demand for restoration, or unless it has been formally announced and declared beforehand. When Popilius was general in charge of a province, Cato's son was serving as a novice soldier in his army. Popilius then decided to dismiss one of the legions, and included in the dismissal the young Cato, who was serving in that legion. But when, out of love of fighting, he remained in the army, Cato wrote to Popilius saying that if he allowed him to stay in the army he should bind him by a fresh military oath, since he could not in justice fight the enemy when his former oath had become void. Such was their extreme scrupulousness when making war. There actually exists a letter of the Elder Marcus Cato to the younger Marcus, in which he writes that he has heard that his son, who was serving in Macedonia in the war against Perseus, had been discharged by the consul. He warns him therefore to be careful not to enter battle. For, he says, it is not lawful for one who is not a soldier to fight with the enemy.

A further point is that the name given to someone who ought properly to have been called a foe (*perduellis*), is in fact *hostis*. I notice that the grimness of the fact is lessened by the gentleness of the word. For *hostis* meant to our forefathers he whom we now call a stranger. The Twelve Tables show this: for example, "a day appointed for trial with a *hostis*"; and again, "right of ownership cannot be alienated in favor of a *hostis*." What greater courteousness could there be than to call him against whom you are waging war by so tender a name? Long usage, however, has made the name harsher; for the word has abandoned the stranger, and now makes its proper home with him who bears arms against you.

When, then, we are fighting for empire and seeking glory through warfare, those grounds that I mentioned a little above as just grounds for war should be wholly present. But wars in which the goal is the glory of empire are waged less bitterly. For just as in civilian matters we may compete in one way with an enemy, in another with a rival (for the latter contest is for honor and standing, the former

for one's civic life or reputation), similarly the wars against the Celtiberi[2] and the Cimbri[3] were waged with enemies: the question was not who would rule, but who would exist. With the Latins, Sabini, Samnites, Carthaginians, and Pyrrhus,[4] on the other hand, the dispute was over empire. The Carthaginians were breakers of truces, and Hannibal was cruel, but the others were more just.[5] Indeed, Pyrrhus' words about the returning of the captives were splendid:

> My demand is not for gold; nor shall you give me
> a price. Let us each determine our lives by iron,
> not by gold, not by selling, but by fighting war.
> Let us test by our virtue whether Mistress Fortune
> wishes you or me to reign, or what she may bring.
> Hear these words too: if the fortune of war spares
> the virtue of any, take it as certain that I shall
> spare them their liberty. Take them as a gift, and I
> give them with the will of the great gods.

That is certainly the view of a king and one worthy of the race of the Aeacidae.[6]

If any individuals have been constrained by circumstance to promise anything to an enemy, they must keep faith even in that. Indeed, Regulus did so when he was captured by the Carthaginians in the First Punic war and was sent to Rome for the purpose of arranging an exchange of captives, having vowed that he would return. For first of all, upon his arrival he proposed in the senate that the captives should not be returned; and then when his friends and relatives were trying to keep him, he preferred to go

1 *fetial laws* Roman laws relating to war declarations and peace treaties.

2 *wars against the Celtiberi* The three Celtiberian wars, between 181 and 133 BCE, were fought between local tribes and Roman legions in areas now parts of Spain and Portugal. It is not clear that Cicero is justified in considering these threats to Roman existence, rather than disputes over empire.

3 *Cimbri* The Cimbrian War (113–101 BCE), on the other hand, was fought against Germanic tribes that had migrated to Italy and were threatening Rome.

4 *Latins ... Pyrrhus* Various wars for conquest of Italy, fifth to third century BCE.

5 *The Carthaginians ... just* The wars with Carthage were the three Punic Wars (First: 264–241 BCE; Second [against Hannibal, called the "Hannibalic War"] 218–202 BCE; Third 149–146 BCE).

6 *Aeacidae* Quotation from Book 6 of Ennius' epic poem *Annales*. King Pyrrhus of Epirus, who claimed descent from the son of Achilles, grandson of Aeacus, is addressing Roman envoys who offered him a large bribe to surrender Roman prisoners of war; he handed them over without payment.

back to his punishment than to break the faith he had given to an enemy.

In the Second Punic war, after the battle of Cannae, Hannibal sent to Rome ten men, bound by a solemn oath that they would return if they did not succeed in arranging for those whom the Romans had captured to be ransomed. The censors[1] disfranchised[2] all of them for the rest of their lives, on the grounds that they had broken their oath. They treated similarly one of them who incurred blame by fraudulently evading his solemn oath. For after leaving the camp with Hannibal's permission, he returned a little later saying that he had forgotten something or other. He then considered that he had released himself from his oath on leaving the camp; but he had done so only in word and not in fact. For on the question of keeping faith, you just always think of what you meant, not of what you said.

Another very great example of justice towards an enemy was established by our forefathers when a deserter from Pyrrhus promised the senate that he would kill the king by giving him poison. Fabricius and the senate returned him to Pyrrhus. In this way, they did not give approval to killing in a criminal way of even a powerful enemy, and one who was waging war unprovoked. Enough has been said about the duties of war.

Let us remember also that justice must be maintained even towards the lowliest. The lowliest condition and fortune is that of slaves; the instruction we are given to treat them as if they were employees is good advice: that one should require work from them, and grant to them just treatment.[3]

There are two ways in which injustice may be done, either through force or through deceit; and deceit seems to belong to a little fox, force to a lion. Both of them seem most alien to a human being; but deceit deserves a greater hatred. And out of all injustice, nothing deserves punishment more than that of men who, just at the time when they are most betraying trust, act in such a way that they might appear to be good men.

I have now said enough about justice. Next, I must do as I proposed and speak about beneficence and liberality....

---

1   *censors*   Roman magistrates responsible for (among other things) overseeing public morals.

2   *disfranchised*   Deprived of the rights of free citizens.

3   *The lowliest condition ... just treatment*   The Stoics (among them Seneca) sometimes argued for the natural equality of all humans, and for more decent treatment of slaves.

LUCIUS ANNAEUS SENECA
(c. 1 BCE – 65 CE)

Seneca was born in Córdoba, Spain, around the beginning of the Christian era, into a wealthy intellectual family. His father was a famous teacher of rhetoric, which Seneca studied in Rome as a boy, as well as receiving instruction in Stoic philosophy from several masters. Suffering from ill health, he went to Egypt to recover, and when he returned around the year 31, he took up a career in law and politics. In 39 he incurred the displeasure of the Emperor Caligula, and was apparently saved from execution only by his ill health; he was believed to be on the verge of death anyway. In 41 he was charged with adultery with the Emperor Claudius' niece, and he was banished to Corsica, where for eight years he studied science and philosophy and wrote extensively. After an intercession on his behalf by the Emperor's wife, he was allowed to return to Rome in 49. In 50 he married a wealthy woman and made some powerful and influential friends; he was appointed praetor (a high judicial magistrate), and began tutoring the young Nero. After Claudius died in 54, Nero became Emperor while still an adolescent; for several years, Seneca and Nero's other chief advisor actually held the reins of power. In 62, feeling his influence slipping away, Seneca retired. Three years later, having been accused of participation in a conspiracy to oust Nero, he committed suicide.

Stoicism, originally developed in Hellenistic Greece, became the dominant religious/ethical/philosophical system in Ancient Rome. It held that the universe, which can appear chaotic to us, is actually governed by a fundamentally rational principle, defined variously as fate, reason, nature, or God. Everything that happens is part of this meaningful orderly whole, and we can bring calmness and order to our own lives by learning to accept events as necessary, maintaining a tranquil mind despite the difficulties and disasters everyone faces, and doing our duty—in short, by adopting an attitude we still refer to as "stoical."

This doctrine was well-suited to a time of political strife, chaos and uncertainty, and it fit well with the Romans' prizing of *virtus*—manly toughness. The practical Romans adapted the abstract notions of Greek metaphysical and religious stoicism into a more political form. They saw the spread of the Roman empire and its laws throughout the known world as the earthly correlate of the divine plan;

civic virtue was the appropriate way for people to affirm their connection to this rational order, and to do their duties within it. As the Stoics saw it, every place in society has its duties, which we must carry out uncomplainingly and to the best of our abilities; political authority, the agency of the divine order brought to earth, must be respected and obeyed.

Cicero, applying stoicism to politics in an earlier, more optimistic time, had emphasized morality as the test for proper political arrangements, but had still seen politics as the most important practical calling. Seneca, by contrast, reacted to the political deterioration of his day and saw morality not as the guide to politics, but rather as independent from it. The state, he held, was necessary for mitigating our tendencies to harm one another, but what was really important for us was personal, not political—the apolitical pursuit of individual moral perfection. This is not to say that Seneca's views were selfish or individualistic: he emphasized, as few had before him, the moral importance of relieving others' suffering.

Seneca's treatment of slavery is interesting and revealing. He presented his views in explicit contrast to those of Aristotle, who had held that some people were "natural" slaves, without the mental capacity for self-rule. The stoic view, expressed by Seneca, rejected inborn inequality of this sort. All humans, Stoics held, were entitled to full human respect and dignity. Accordingly, Seneca argued, slaves should be treated with respect: they must not be beaten or sexually exploited, and they should be dealt with humanely. On the other hand, Seneca did not see anything particularly wrong with slavery as an institution, and never advocated its abolition. Some critics have argued that the moral blindness in this position is a consequence of the stoic position that individual dignity is the only good, and that one's dignity can survive any mistreatment and misfortune, which is thus rendered insignificant. Anyone—an emperor or a slave—can live with dignity, according to the Stoics.

◆ ◆ ◆ ◆ ◆

Letter on Slaves

Your attitude to your slaves is one of familiarity, as I learn from people who have been in your company. I am pleased; it is what one expects of your good sense and cultivation. "They are slaves"—no, men. "They are slaves"—no, comrades. "They are slaves"—no, humble friends. "They are slaves" —no, fellow slaves, if you remember that Fortune[1] holds equal sway over both.

That is why I laugh at people who think it degrading for a man to dine with his slave. Why, except that conventional exclusiveness has decreed that a master must be surrounded at his dinner by a squad of slaves standing at attention? The master eats more than he can hold; his inordinate greed loads his distended belly, which has unlearned the belly's function, and the digestion of all this food requires more ado than its ingestion. But the unhappy slaves may not move their lips for so much as a word. Any murmur is checked by a rod; not even involuntary sounds—a cough, a sneeze, a choke—are exempted from the lash. If a word breaks the silence the penalty is severe. Hungry and mute, they stand through the whole night.

In consequence, when they cannot speak in the master's presence, they speak *about* him. Yet when slaves spoke not only in the master's presence but *with* him, when their lips were not sewn tight, they were ready to put their necks out for their master, to turn any danger that threatened him upon their own heads; they spoke at dinners, but under torture their lips were sealed. But afterward the arrogance of masters gave currency to the proverb, "So many slaves, so many enemies." We do not acquire them as enemies, we make them such. Other cruel and inhuman treatment I pass over: we abuse them as one does pack animals, not even as one abuses men. When we recline at table[2] one slave wipes up the hawking,[3] another crouches to take up the leavings of the drunks. One carves the costly game, separating the portions by deft sweeps of a practiced hand—unhappy man, to live solely for the purpose of carving fowl neatly, unless the man who teaches the trade for pleasure's sake is

more wretched than the man who learns it for necessity's! Another, who serves the wine, is got up like a woman and must wrestle with his age; he can never escape boyhood but is dragged back to it. His figure may now be a soldier's, but his hairs are rubbed away or plucked out by the roots to make him smooth, and he must divide his sleepless night between his master's drunkenness and his lust; in the bedroom he is a man, in the dining room a boy. Another has the assignment of keeping book[4] on the guests; he stands there, poor fellow, and watches to see whose adulation and whose intemperance of gullet or tongue will get him an invitation for the following day. Add the caterers with their refined *expertise* of the master's palate; they know what flavors will titillate him, what table decorations will please his fancy, what novelty might restore his appetite when he feels nauseous, what his surfeit will scorn, what tidbit he would crave on a particular day. With slaves like these the master cannot bear to dine; he would count it an affront to his dignity to come to table with his own slave. Heaven forbid!

But how many of those slaves are in fact his masters! I have seen Callistus' master a suitor outside Callistus' door and have seen him shut out while others were admitted— the master who tagged him for sale and sent him to market with a job-lot[5] of chattels.[6] But the slave included in this preliminary batch on which the auctioneer tried out his voice paid tit for tat. He crossed Callistus' name from the roster in turn and judged him unfit to enter his house. His master sold Callistus, but how much did Callistus cost his master!

Remember, if you please, that the man you call slave sprang from the same seed, enjoys the same daylight, breathes like you, lives like you, dies like you. You can as easily conceive him a free man as he can conceive you a slave. In the Marian disasters many men of noble birth who had entered military service as the preliminary to a senatorial career were declassed[7] by Fortune and reduced to being shepherds or cottagers;[8] now despise a man for his

---

1   *Fortune*   Fortuna, goddess of chance, is the personification of unpredictable, uncontrollable fate. A central part of the Stoics' attitude toward life is that, because anything can happen, one must rise above whatever wounds Fortuna sends us, and accept life uncomplainingly.

2   *recline at table*   Romans dined lying down—reclining somewhat propped up on couches.

3   *hawking*   Spat-out phlegm.

4   *keeping book*   Keeping track of the behavior of.

5   *job-lot*   Collection of miscellaneous items for sale.

6   *chattels*   Moveable property.

7   *declassed*   Given a lower social status.

8   *shepherds or cottagers*   Up until the end of the second century BCE, the Roman army was composed of soldiers from the landowning classes and volunteers only, and suffered several disastrous defeats. After the consul Marius had no troops to conduct the war in Africa, so he instituted reforms including some policies encouraging the masses to enlist, thus lowering the social status associated with the army, but making it much more effective.

condition when you may find yourself in the same even as you despise it!

I do not wish to take up the large topic of the treatment of slaves, where we show ourselves proud, cruel, and insulting in the highest degree. The essence of my teaching is this: Treat your inferior as you would wish your superior to treat you. Whenever the thought of your wide power over your slave strikes you, be struck, too, by the thought of your master's equally wide power over you. "But I have no master!" you object. All in good time; you may have one. Remember how old Hecuba[1] was when she became a slave, or Croesus, or Darius' mother, or Plato, or Diogenes.[2]

Treat your slave with compassion, even with courtesy; admit him to your conversation, your planning, your society. Here the genteel will protest loudly and unanimously: "Nothing could be more degrading or disgusting!" But these same people I shall catch kissing the hands of other people's slaves. Can't you see how our ancestors stripped the title of master of all invidiousness[3] and the title of slave of all contumely?[4] The master they called "paterfamilias"[5] and the slaves "family"; this usage still obtains in the mimes.[6] They instituted a festival at which masters dined with their slaves—not, of course, the only day they could do so. They allowed slaves to hold office in the household and to act as judges; the household they regarded as a miniature republic.

"What is the upshot? Am I to bring all slaves to my table?" No more than all free men. But if you imagine I would exclude some because their work is dirty, that muleteer,[7] for example, or that cowhand, you are mistaken. I value them not by their jobs but by their character; a man gives himself his own character, accident allots his job. Have some dine with you because they are deserving, some to make them deserving. If their sordid contacts have left a taint, association with respectable people will shake it off. There is no reason to go to the forum or senate house in search of a friend, my dear Lucilius; if you pay careful heed you will find one at home. Without an artisan good material often lies unused; try it and you will find out.

A man is a fool if he looks only at the saddle and bridle and not at the horse itself when he is going to buy one; he is a greater fool if he values a man by his clothing and condition, which only swathes[8] us like clothing. "He is a slave!" But perhaps a free man in spirit. "He is a slave!" Shall that count against him? Show me a man who is not; one is a slave to lust, another to greed, another to ambition, all to fear. I can show you a consular[9] who is slave to a crone, a millionaire who is slave to a housemaid; I can point to young aristocrats indentured to pantomimes. Voluntary slavery is the meanest of all.

Those squeamish types should not deter you, therefore, from camaraderie with your slaves and make you proudly superior. Slaves ought to respect rather than fear you. Here someone will protest that I am now rallying slaves to the cap of liberty and toppling masters from their elevation by saying, "Slaves ought to respect rather than fear a master." "That is what he said: slaves ought to respect him, like his clients or those who pay him formal calls." The protester forgets that what is enough for a god is not too little for a master. If a man is respected he is also loved, and love cannot blend with fear.

Your own attitude is consequently as right as can be, in my judgment; you do not choose to have your slaves fear you, you use words to castigate them. A lash is to admonish dumb beasts. What offends need not wound. It is our daintiness that drives us to distraction, so that anything that does not meet our caprice provokes our wrath. We assume regal lordliness. Kings forget their own strength and others' weakness and fly into a white-hot fury as if they had really been injured, when their exalted position guarantees them complete immunity to any possibility of injury. Nor are they unaware of their immunity; by complaining, they solicit an opening for inflicting harm. They profess they have been injured in order to work injury.

I do not wish to detain you longer; you need no exhortation. Among its other traits good character approves its decisions and abides by them. Wickedness is fickle and changes frequently, not for something better but for something different. Farewell.

---

1   *Hecuba*   Wife of Priam, king of Troy. After the fall of Troy, she was taken captive by the Achaeans and enslaved—presumably at a fairly mature age.
2   *Croesus, Darius' mother, Plato, Diogenes*   All suffered reversal of fortune.
3   *invidiousness*   Disgrace, reproach.
4   *contumely*   Contempt, insult.
5   *paterfamilias*   Latin: father of the family, head of the household.
6   *mimes*   Ancient Greek comedic theatrical performance.
7   *muleteer*   Mule driver.
8   *swathes*   Wraps.
9   *consular*   A chief magistrate of Rome.

PART II

The Medieval Period

ST. AUGUSTINE
(354 – 430)

Who Was St. Augustine?

AURELIUS AUGUSTINUS WAS BORN IN 354 TO A PAGAN Roman father and a Christian mother in Tagaste in Numidia, in what is now Algeria. His mother, St. Monica, was a Berber; that is, a member of an ethnic group that has lived in Northwest Africa for as long as there has been a historical record. Though his family was neither wealthy nor connected, Augustine was very intelligent; at the age of 17 he was able to travel to Carthage, a major city of the ancient world close to the site of what is now Tunis (capital of Tunisia), to advance his studies in rhetoric and oratory, the primary form of "higher education" in his day. His family invested much of their fragile means, and exerted all the influence they could with richer friends, in their efforts to further Augustine's education, hoping that his successful career would lift the family's fortunes. However, he was a turbulent and hedonistic youth—much to the despair of his devout mother, he was by his own account preoccupied with sex and the theatre—and was not a Christian during these years. Instead Augustine was a follower of a relatively new Persian religion called Manichaeism, and also dabbled in magic and astrology.

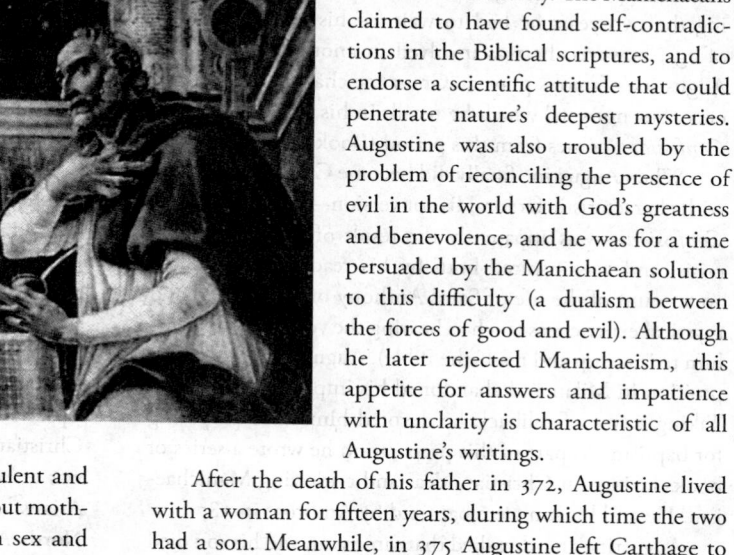

Manichaeism originated in the writings of Mani (210–76) in Babylon and by Augustine's time was firmly established across North Africa. It holds that there is no omnipotent good power—no God, in other words—but instead that there exist two fundamental, opposed, and equally matched powers: light and darkness. Manichaeans associate light with the soul and dark with matter, and hold that the physical universe is a temporary aberration resulting from the invasion of the realm of light by the powers of darkness, while each human person is also a battleground between light (soul) and dark (body). Manichaean theology includes a great variety of figures, including a God of Light and various demons of darkness; it makes a deliberate attempt to encompass other religions and thus treats figures such as Jesus and Buddha as key players in the struggle between light and dark.

Despite what might appear to us bizarre in the Manichaean mythology, Augustine was attracted to Manichaeism by its critical rationalism—its appeal to reason over authority. The Manichaeans claimed to have found self-contradictions in the Biblical scriptures, and to endorse a scientific attitude that could penetrate nature's deepest mysteries. Augustine was also troubled by the problem of reconciling the presence of evil in the world with God's greatness and benevolence, and he was for a time persuaded by the Manichaean solution to this difficulty (a dualism between the forces of good and evil). Although he later rejected Manichaeism, this appetite for answers and impatience with unclarity is characteristic of all Augustine's writings.

After the death of his father in 372, Augustine lived with a woman for fifteen years, during which time the two had a son. Meanwhile, in 375 Augustine left Carthage to return to Tagaste and teach, but two years later the death of a close friend drew him back to Carthage. In 382 he left North Africa for the first time and traveled across the Mediterranean to Rome; Augustine was ambitious to show his mettle with what he thought were the best rhetoricians in the world. He later confessed himself disappointed with the quality of the schools in Rome. However, Manichaean friends introduced him to the Prefect of Rome, a leading pagan rhetorician, who appointed him, at only thirty, professor of rhetoric at the imperial court of Milan—one of the most prestigious academic posts of the Latin world. At that time, Milan was the second largest city in Europe and was soon to become (briefly) the capital of the Western Roman Empire. Its Christian bishop, St. Ambrose, was a highly influential figure with the emperor, Theodosius I. (Christianity had been the religion of most of the Roman emperors since Constantine in 312, and Theodosius was active both in promulgating it as the official state religion and in suppressing paganism.)

It was not until 386 that Augustine converted to Christianity. Before leaving for Italy he had had a disappointing meeting with a leading Manichaean theologian named Faustus, and in Milan he moved away from Manichaeism. But rather than immediately becoming a Catholic, as Ambrose and his mother (who had followed him to Milan, despite Augustine's efforts to leave her behind) urged him to do, he at first enthusiastically adopted pagan Neoplatonism. Meanwhile Monica persuaded Augustine to end his relationship, and arranged a society marriage for him. During the two years he had to wait for his fiancée to come of age, however, he was involved in another relationship. Augustine's famous prayer, "Grant me chastity and continence, but not yet," which he recalls in his autobiographical *Confessions*, comes from this period (Book 8, Chapter 7).

When Augustine finally did become Christian, he did it with characteristic fervor. His conversion—described in *The Confessions*—was apparently the result of a deep personal crisis, and was inspired both by his reading (particularly an account of the life of Saint Anthony of the Desert) and mystical experiences (such as hearing the voice of a child tell him to "take up and read" the Bible). Augustine resigned his position in Milan and abandoned his impending marriage. Taking a vow of celibacy, he devoted himself to preparing for baptism. As part of this preparation he wrote a series of books laying out Christian ideas and criticizing Manichaeism. He and his son were baptized by Ambrose in 387.

Augustine's mother died that same year, and his son died three years later. By 391 Augustine was back in Africa; he founded a Christian retreat—what would later be thought of as a monastery—at Hippo Regius, a major Roman city on the coast between Thagaste and Carthage. He was ordained a priest in 391 and became bishop of Hippo in 395. He remained in this post until his death in 430, leading a monastic life and preaching sermons that gradually became famous all round the Mediterranean.

The years from 395 to 410 were an unusually troubled time, even for that unstable era, and Augustine spent these years preaching and writing against threats to the Catholic church in Africa. The Manicheans presented one such threat, and two heretical Christian splinter groups called the Pelagians and the Donatists presented others. The Donatists were an important sect in Northern Africa, and regarded themselves as the legitimate church. Unlike the Catholics, who held that the emperor was an agent of Christ, the Donatists advocated a strict separation of church and state and regarded the emperor as a personification of the devil. During the persecution of the Christians by the Roman emperor Diocletian (c. 245–c. 312), many Catholic priests and bishops handed Christians over to the Roman authorities, and also handed over sacred texts to be burned. These *traditors* ("people who handed over") returned to power under Constantine (c. 280–337). The Donatists held that *traditors* (even if they had repented) could not administer the sacraments—the Eucharist would remain wafer and wine, rather than being transformed into Christ's body and blood—whereas the Catholics held that the office of the priest, rather than his personal character, was sufficient to enable the Eucharist to be performed, since the sacraments were gifts of Christ. Augustine wrote a number of tracts opposing the Donatists, and eventually he called for their repression by imperial authorities as heretics.

In 410 Rome was sacked by the barbarian general Alaric and his Visigothic armies, and high-born Roman refugees flooded into North Africa. It was becoming clear that these were the last days of the Western Roman Empire.

Between 413 and 427 Augustine wrote what he considered his master work, *City of God*. The writing of this work was begun, at least in part, as a response to the sacking of Rome. The Christian Empire seemed on the verge of collapse, beset on all sides by—and losing ground to—non-Christian or heretical tribes. Alaric, the sacker of Rome, was an adherent of a break-away Christian sect called the Arians.[1] Influential and well-educated pagan refugees in North Africa were arguing that the weakening of Rome was caused by the Christians, who had angered the gods by forbidding sacrifices to them. Augustine, as Bishop of Hippo, felt an obligation to lay out a Catholic Christian worldview that would explain how God could have allowed such disasters to befall the church.

The town of Hippo was attacked and besieged by Vandals—another Germanic tribe that had adopted Arianism—in 430, and Augustine died (of old age—he was now 76) during the 18-month siege. The city fell in 431 and became, for several years, the capital of the Vandal kingdom in North Africa.

---

1   The key difference between the Arians and the mainstream Catholicism of the Nicene Creed was that the Arians believed that Jesus was a separate divine being created by God, rather than an aspect of the Trinity of God the Father, God the Son, and God the Holy Spirit. The word 'Arian' comes from Arius, the sect's founder.

What Was Augustine's Overall Philosophical Project?

Augustine did not construct a complete philosophical system, and his writings were often a response to immediate personal or theological circumstances—as were, for example, his polemics against the Manichaeans or heretical Christian sects—rather than efforts to explore philosophical or theological problems for their own sake. Indeed, Augustine often did not distinguish sharply between philosophy and theology. He accepted doctrinal claims as premises for his arguments, but tested their mutual coherence and drew out their implications through philosophical analysis. One of Augustine's guiding intellectual principles was that mere belief is inferior to *understanding*, and he seems to have held that every mystery can in principle be fully understood by the human intellect (even if only in the afterlife). He believed that the Bible should not be interpreted literally when it conflicts with what we know from reason to be true.

Augustine's theology was influenced by Greek Neoplatonist philosophers, especially Plotinus, and by Roman writers on language and argument, particularly Virgil and Cicero. Academic skepticism also had an important influence on Augustine's thought; his somewhat dismissive attitude toward empirical science and his belief that human knowledge requires divine assistance is a consequence of this influence. He made important and influential contributions to debates on free will, original sin, just war, and the nature of time. Some of his key doctrines include divine predestination, the claim that salvation is impossible outside the Church, and the notion that God exists outside of time in the "eternal present."

Augustine's famous doctrine of predestination is as follows: Because God sees, as it were, all of time at once from his position "outside" of time, he sees all the choices that people have ever made and will ever make, and thus knows who will go to Heaven (the saved) and who is destined for Hell (the reprobates). Thus the lists of the saved and the damned are fixed from the beginning of time. The fall of Adam and Eve introduced the conflict of reason and bodily desires, which dominated human nature unless God granted them the divine grace to overcome their lust. This view lay at the root of Augustine's condemnation of the Pelagians (mentioned above), who taught that salvation depended solely on free human choice. Though Augustine did not deny that a person could freely choose to perform good

works, he held that original sin made salvation impossible without divine grace.

Augustine's ethics were related to the eudemonist ethics of ancient Greece. Like Aristotle, Augustine held that the highest good for human beings is happiness and that the happiest form of life is living in accordance with reason and pursuing a state of wisdom (which, for Augustine, consists in the contemplation of enduring truths about God). From this, Augustine took it that virtue involves acting in accordance with the will of God.

Augustine reacted against the Manichaean belief in the real existence of evil by arguing that everything that exists is good to some degree since it is created by God. Things are evil only to the extent that they lack goodness. In particular, people are not in essence evil, though their actions may be morally evil. (It was Augustine who first formulated the maxim, "love the sinner and hate the sin" [*Opera Omnia*, vol 2. col. 962, letter 211].) The source of evil action, for Augustine, is a turning away from God into prideful self-absorption. By contrast, virtue is a kind of *order* to one's behavior, controlling one's emotions and self-love so that one's actions are in accord with divine eternal law.

The laws of human societies should be framed in accordance with the divine natural law, but Augustine held that laws are given their validity by human political authority. He denied that it was ever justifiable to disobey a properly authorized law, except in very specific cases where the law directly contradicts a command explicitly revealed in Scripture (such as the worship of idols) or commands something that Augustine considered evidently contrary to nature (the example he gives is sodomy). Because Man is a fallen creature, tainted by original sin, Augustine recognizes that the rule of law will generally need to be imposed through coercion. Also, Augustine offers no critique of the social institutions of his day. Private property and slavery, Augustine thought, were consequences of our sinful nature, rather than aspects of the purely natural state for humankind; but he did not argue that the possession of wealth was immoral. Rather, he held—characteristically—that it is *desire* for unnecessary wealth that is sinful.

Augustine's interests differed in some important ways from those of political writers before and after him. He wrote very little on the origin, scope, or proper form of political institutions. What he was primarily concerned about was the operation of *authority*. He viewed it as unnatural—at least outside of the family—for one person to have authority over another, and held that authority was required only because of humankind's sinful nature after the Fall. Thus, Augustine did not see authority as a specifically *political* relationship; indeed, his views on political authority are similar in kind to the views he held on slavery. Furthermore, Augustine broke from his predecessors in the ancient world who thought of politics as crucial to genuine human flourishing. For Augustine, although political authority is of value in producing peace and order (and humbling us and correcting our attachment to worldly things), real human happiness lies in loving God—it comes from membership in the City of God, rather than by being a citizen of any secular state.

In addition to many public letters and sermons, Augustine wrote several larger works including *On Free Choice of the Will* (391), *Confessions* (398), *City of God* (completed 426), and *On Christian Doctrine* (426). In *Retractions* (428), Augustine revisited his works at the end of his life and described what he would have said differently in light of his later thought.

Augustine is considered a saint in the Roman Catholic, Orthodox and Anglican churches, and an important theologian by many Protestant churches.

What Is the Structure of This Reading?

City of God is a long work that falls into two halves: the first ten books criticize various opponents of Catholicism; the final twelve books describe the origin, development and purpose of two "cities"—the city of this world and the City of God.

In engaging with pagan and heretical opponents of the City of God, Augustine knew that his readers would be sophisticated and literate. He attempted to persuade them rationally by showing that their own beliefs entailed the truth of Catholic Christianity; often he would proceed by recasting familiar ideas, such as religious sacrifice, in Christian terms. Augustine does not begin appealing to Christian scripture for authority until the turning point of the work, at the start of Book 10.

In Book 1, Augustine explains the purpose of his work, and argues that the pagan gods did not protect Rome. Book 2, from which there is a selection here, deals with moral evils, and makes the case that God might justifiably be angered by the self-indulgent and decadent lives of the Romans. The rest of the excerpts reprinted here are from Book 19, in which Augustine argues that the supreme good for humankind is peace.

Some Useful Background Information

i) Augustine was highly trained in rhetoric and oratory (the art of persuasion), and his writing style reflects this. He self-consciously—and skillfully—worked on his text to ensure that it would have a similar effect on the reader as a persuasive oration; in this cause he makes extensive use of word-play (in the original Latin) and of stylistic flourishes. Augustine wanted *City of God* to have as much influence as possible—to be read by the educated, and discussed with their friends.

ii) For Augustine, philosophy is centrally "the art of living": one of his key concerns was to understand the nature of true happiness for human beings and how one should live in order to attain that happiness. He did not think of his philosophical or even theological work as at all disconnected from this practical end. For example, he thought that immortality was a key prerequisite for real happiness and he was therefore deeply interested in how that immortality may be secured.

iii) An important part of the background to Augustine's "political philosophy" is his "philosophical psychology." Augustine believed that human beings are motivated by what he calls "loves." There are many kinds of love, but two important categories of love, for Augustine, are what he calls "use" and "enjoyment." To enjoy something is to love it for its own sake; alternatively, something might be loved only as it can be used to secure some other value. True happiness is available only to those who love—"enjoy"—something that is entirely worthy of being loved for its own sake ... that is, in his view, it is available only to those who love God. Perfect justice consists in loving each thing—objects, animals, people, God—according to their real worth. The sin of pride disorders our lives because it causes us to love things more than they are worth.

iv) Augustine's language of the "cities" of man and of God is influenced by his upbringing in late antiquity. The Roman empire began as a city, and the language of "citizenship" in the empire—still of crucial importance to anyone trained for public life in Augustine's day—was formed in line with the ideals of the old Republic. Citizenship—membership in a "city"—in this context has nothing to do with living in the same town or nation, or even at the same time, and everything to do with a common interest that binds a community together across time and place. (There are also various scriptural sources for the idea of a City of God, especially in the psalms.) The city you belong to, then, depends upon the community with which you identify: that of God, or that of man.

A descendant of Manichaean dualism—and also of similar oppositions in Plato or Stoicism—can be seen in Augustine's description of the two opposed cities: the city of man is the dark city ("Babylon") "of men who choose to live by the standards of the flesh," while "Jerusalem" is a city of light occupied by those "who choose to live by the standard of the spirit" (*City of God*, Book 14, Chapter 1).

v) An important feature of Augustine's City of God is that its members—the Saved, destined for Heaven—do not themselves know who they are. No kind of visible observance, including baptism, "church-going," or good works, is sufficient to guarantee citizenship in the City of God. The Christian church on Earth is thus a mixed community, containing both sinners and saved. Similarly, the city of man cannot be simply identified with any secular state or authority; indeed, occupants of the City of God make particularly good citizens of an earthly city, according to Augustine, since they conform to the common good rather than being focused on self-interest.

Augustine's key motivation in opposing the Christian heresies of Pelagianism, Donatism, and so on was the risk that they would draw members of his congregation away from the City of God.

vi) Despite Augustine's (arguably) atavistic Manichaeism, and his much-discussed distress at his own lustfulness and other instinctual urges, Augustine did not denigrate the body. Against the Platonists, he held that God had created us embodied and that this is the natural state for our souls, rather then being a fleshy imprisonment from which we are freed after death.

How Important and Influential Is This Passage?

Augustine is one of the most influential figures in Christian history—the most important thinker of the medieval period, at least until Thomas Aquinas in the thirteenth century—and he thought of *City of God* as the most important, mature, and carefully worked out of his many writings. The passages excerpted here contain some of Augustine's key ideas on justice, community, and the role of political authority.

◆ ◆ ◆ ◆ ◆

City of God (413–427)

1. Preface

The glorious city of God is my theme in this work, which you, my dearest son Marcellinus, suggested, and which is due to you by my promise. I have undertaken its defense against those who prefer their own gods to the Founder of this city—a city surpassingly glorious, whether we view it as it still lives by faith in this fleeting course of time, and sojourns as a stranger in the midst of the ungodly, or as it shall dwell in the fixed stability of its eternal seat, which it now with patience waits for, expecting until "righteousness shall return unto judgment,"[1] and it obtain, by virtue of its excellence, final victory and perfect peace. A great work this, and an arduous; but God is my helper. For I am aware what ability is requisite to persuade the proud how great is the virtue of humility, which raises us, not by a quite human arrogance, but by a divine grace, above all earthly dignities that totter on this shifting scene. For the King and Founder of this city of which we speak, has in Scripture uttered to His people a dictum of the divine law in these words: "God resisteth the proud, but giveth grace unto the humble."[2] But this, which is God's prerogative, the inflated ambition of a proud spirit also affects, and dearly loves that this be numbered among its attributes, to "Show pity to the humbled soul, And crush the sons of pride."[3] And therefore, as the plan of this work we have undertaken requires, and as occasion offers, we must speak also of the earthly city, which, though it be mistress of the nations, is itself ruled by its lust of rule.

1:1. Of the adversaries of the name of Christ, whom the barbarians for Christ's sake spared when they stormed the city

For to this earthly city belong the enemies against whom I have to defend the city of God. Many of them, indeed, being reclaimed from their ungodly error, have become sufficiently creditable citizens of this city; but many are so inflamed with hatred against it, and are so ungrateful to its Redeemer for His signal[4] benefits, as to forget that they

---

1 *righteousness ... unto judgments* Psalms 94.15.
2 *God ... unto the humble* James 4.6 and 1 Peter 5.5.
3 *Show pity ... sons of pride* Virgil, *Æneid*, vi. 854.
4 *signal* Notable.

would now be unable to utter a single word to its prejudice, had they not found in its sacred places, as they fled
from the enemy's steel,[1] that life in which they now boast
themselves. Are not those very Romans, who were spared
by the barbarians through their respect for Christ, become
enemies to the name of Christ? The reliquaries of the martyrs and the churches of the apostles bear witness to this;
for in the sack of the city they were open sanctuary for all
who fled to them, whether Christian or Pagan. To their very
threshold the bloodthirsty enemy raged; there his murderous fury owned a limit. Thither did such of the enemy as
had any pity convey those to whom they had given quarter,
lest any less mercifully disposed might fall upon them. And,
indeed, when even those murderers who everywhere else
showed themselves pitiless came to these spots where that
was forbidden which the license of war permitted in every
other place, their furious rage for slaughter was bridled,
and their eagerness to take prisoners was quenched. Thus
escaped multitudes who now reproach the Christian religion, and impute to Christ the ills that have befallen their
city; but the preservation of their own life—a boon which
they owe to the respect entertained for Christ by the barbarians—they attribute not to our Christ, but to their own
good luck. They ought rather, had they any right perceptions, to attribute the severities and hardships inflicted by
their enemies, to that divine providence which is wont to
reform the depraved manners of men by chastisement, and
which exercises with similar afflictions the righteous and
praiseworthy—either transporting them, when they have
passed through the trial, to a better world, or detaining
them still on earth for ulterior purposes. And they ought
to attribute it to the spirit of these Christian times, that,
contrary to the custom of war, these bloodthirsty barbarians
spared them, and spared them for Christ's sake, whether
this mercy was actually shown in randomly chosen places,
or in those places specially dedicated to Christ's name, and
of which the very largest were selected as sanctuaries, that
full scope might thus be given to the expansive compassion which desired that a large multitude might find shelter
there. Therefore ought they to give God thanks, and with
sincere confession flee for refuge to His name, that so they
may escape the punishment of eternal fire—they who with
lying lips took upon them this name, that they might escape
the punishment of present destruction. For of those whom
you see insolently and shamelessly insulting the servants of

Christ, there are numbers who would not have escaped that
destruction and slaughter had they not pretended that they
themselves were Christ's servants. Yet now, in ungrateful
pride and most impious madness, and at the risk of being
punished in everlasting darkness, they perversely oppose
that name under which they fraudulently protected themselves for the sake of enjoying the light of this brief life.

1:8. Of the advantages and disadvantages which, often indiscriminately accrue to good and wicked men

Will someone say, Why, then, was this divine compassion
extended even to the ungodly and ungrateful? Why, but
because it was the mercy of Him who daily "maketh His
sun to rise on the evil and on the good, and sendeth rain
on the just and on the unjust."[2] For though some of these
men, taking thought of this, repent of their wickedness and
reform, some, as the apostle says, "despising the riches of
His goodness and long-suffering, after their hardness and
impenitent heart, treasure up unto themselves wrath against
the day of wrath and revelation of the righteous judgment
of God, who will render to every man according to his
deeds:"[3] nevertheless does the patience of God still invite the
wicked to repentance, even as the scourge of God educates
the good to patience. And so, too, does the mercy of God
embrace the good that it may cherish them, as the severity
of God arrests the wicked to punish them. To the divine
providence it has seemed good to prepare in the world to
come for the righteous good things, which the unrighteous
shall not enjoy; and for the wicked evil things, by which
the good shall not be tormented. But as for the good things
of this life, and its ills, God has willed that these should
be common to both; that we might not too eagerly covet
the things which wicked men are seen equally to enjoy, nor
shrink with an unseemly fear from the ills which even good
men often suffer.

There is, too, a very great difference in the purpose
served both by those events which we call adverse and those
called prosperous. For the good man is neither uplifted
with the good things of time, nor broken by its ills; but the
wicked man, because he is corrupted by this world's happiness, feels himself punished by its unhappiness. Yet often,
even in the present distribution of temporal things, does

---

1   *steel* Sword.

2   *maketh His sun ... on the unjust* Matthew 5.45.
3   *despising the riches ... his deeds* Romans 2:4.

God plainly evince His own interference. For if every sin were now visited with manifest punishment, nothing would seem to be reserved for the final judgment; on the other hand, if no sin received now a plainly divine punishment, it would be concluded that there is no divine providence at all. And so of the good things of this life: if God did not by a very visible liberality confer these on some of those persons who ask for them, we should say that these good things were not at His disposal; and if He gave them to all who sought them, we should suppose that such were the only rewards of His service; and such a service would make us not godly, but greedy rather, and covetous. Wherefore, though good and bad men suffer alike, we must not suppose that there is no difference between the men themselves, because there is no difference in what they both suffer. For even in the likeness of the sufferings, there remains an unlikeness in the sufferers; and though exposed to the same anguish, virtue and vice are not the same thing. For as the same fire causes gold to glow brightly, and chaff to smoke; and under the same flail the straw is beaten small, while the grain is cleansed; and as the lees are not mixed with the oil, though squeezed out of the vat by the same pressure, so the same violence of affliction proves, purges, clarifies the good, but damns, ruins, exterminates the wicked. And thus it is that in the same affliction the wicked detest God and blaspheme, while the good pray and praise. So material a difference does it make, not what ills are suffered, but what kind of man suffers them. For, stirred up with the same movement, mud exhales a horrible stench, and ointment emits a fragrant odor.

2:21. Cicero's opinion of the Roman republic

But if our adversaries do not care how foully and disgracefully the Roman republic be stained by corrupt practices, so long only as it holds together and continues in being, and if they therefore pooh-pooh the testimony of Sallust[1] to its "utterly wicked and profligate" condition, what will they make of Cicero's[2] statement, that even in his time it had become entirely extinct, and that there remained extant no Roman republic at all? He introduces Scipio[3] (the Scipio who had destroyed Carthage) discussing the republic, at a time when already there were presentiments of its speedy ruin by that corruption which Sallust describes. In fact, at the time when the discussion took place, one of the Gracchi,[4] who, according to Sallust, was the first great instigator of seditions, had already been put to death. His death, indeed, is mentioned in the same book. Now Scipio, in the end of the second book, says: "As, among the different sounds which proceed from lyres, flutes, and the human voice, there must be maintained a certain harmony which a cultivated ear cannot endure to hear disturbed or jarring, but which may be elicited in full and absolute concord by the modulation even of voices very unlike one another; so, where reason is allowed to modulate the diverse elements of the state, there is obtained a perfect concord from the upper, lower, and middle classes as from various sounds; and what musicians call harmony in singing, is concord in matters of state, which is the strictest bond and best security of any republic, and which by no ingenuity can be retained where justice has become extinct." Then, when he had expatiated somewhat more fully, and had more copiously illustrated the benefits of its presence and the ruinous effects of its absence upon a state, Pilus, one of the company present at the discussion, struck in and demanded that the question should be more thoroughly sifted, and that the subject of justice should be freely discussed for the sake of ascertaining what truth there was in the maxim which was then becoming daily more current, that "the republic cannot be governed without injustice." Scipio expressed his willingness to have this maxim discussed and sifted, and gave it as his opinion that it was baseless, and that no progress could be made in discussing the republic unless it was established, not only that this maxim, that "the republic cannot be governed without injustice," was false, but also that the truth is, that it cannot be governed without the most absolute justice. And the discussion of this question, being deferred till the next day, is carried on in the third book with great animation. For Pilus himself undertook to defend the position that the republic cannot be governed without injustice, at the same time being at special pains to clear himself of any real participation in that opinion. He advocated with great keenness the cause of injustice against justice, and endeavored

1 *Sallust* Gaius Sallustius Crispus (86–34 BCE), Roman historian.

2 *Cicero* Marcus Tullius Cicero (106–43 BCE) was a Roman statesman, philosopher, and political theorist.

3 *Scipio* Publius Cornelius Scipio Africanus Major (235–183 BCE), Roman general and statesman, best known for defeating Hannibal of Carthage in the Second Punic War.

4 *Gracchi* The brothers Tiberius Sempronius Gracchus (163–133 BCE) and Gaius Gracchus (154–121 BCE) were Roman politicians. Their efforts to achieve social reform for the benefit of the lower classes led to their assassination by members of the Roman Senate.

by plausible reasons and examples to demonstrate that the former is beneficial, the latter useless, to the republic. Then, at the request of the company, Lælius attempted to defend justice, and strained every nerve to prove that nothing is so hurtful to a state as injustice; and that without justice a republic can neither be governed, nor even continue to exist.

When this question has been handled to the satisfaction of the company, Scipio reverts to the original thread of discourse, and repeats with commendation his own brief definition of a republic, that it is the weal of the people. "The people" he defines as being not every assemblage or mob, but an assemblage associated by a common acknowledgment of law, and by a community of interests. Then he shows the use of definition in debate; and from these definitions of his own he gathers that a republic, or "weal of the people," then exists only when it is well and justly governed, whether by a monarch, or an aristocracy, or by the whole people. But when the monarch is unjust, or, as the Greeks say, a tyrant; or the aristocrats are unjust, and form a faction; or the people themselves are unjust, and become, as Scipio for want of a better name calls them, themselves the tyrant, then the republic is not only blemished (as had been proved the day before), but by legitimate deduction from those definitions, it altogether ceases to be. For it could not be the people's weal when a tyrant factiously lorded it over the state; neither would the people be any longer a people if it were unjust, since it would no longer answer the definition of a people—"an assemblage associated by a common acknowledgment of law, and by a community of interests."

When, therefore, the Roman republic was such as Sallust described it, it was not "utterly wicked and profligate," as he says, but had altogether ceased to exist, if we are to admit the reasoning of that debate maintained on the subject of the republic by its best representatives. Tully[1] himself, too, speaking not in the person of Scipio or anyone else, but uttering his own sentiments, uses the following language in the beginning of the fifth book, after quoting a line from the poet Ennius,[2] in which he said, "Rome's severe morality and her citizens are her safeguard." "This verse," says Cicero, "seems to me to have all the sententious truthfulness of an oracle. For neither would the citizens have managed without the morality of the community, nor would the morality of the common people without out-

standing men have managed either to establish or so long to maintain in vigor so grand a republic with so wide and just an empire. Accordingly, before our day, the hereditary usages formed our foremost men, and they on their part retained the usages and institutions of their fathers. But our age, receiving the republic as a masterpiece of another age which has already begun to grow old, has not merely neglected to restore the colors of the original, but has not even been at the pains to preserve so much as the general outline and most outstanding features. For what survives of that primitive morality which the poet called Rome's safeguard? It is so obsolete and forgotten, that, far from practicing it, one does not even know it. And of the citizens what shall I say? Morality has perished through poverty of great men; a poverty for which we must not only assign a reason, but for the guilt of which we must answer as criminals charged with a capital crime. For it is through our vices, and not by any mishap, that we retain only the name of a republic, and have long since lost the reality."

This is the confession of Cicero, long indeed after the death of Africanus,[3] whom he introduced as an interlocutor in his work De Republica, but still before the coming of Christ. Yet, if the disasters he bewails had been lamented after the Christian religion had been diffused, and had begun to prevail, is there a man of our adversaries who would not have thought that they were to be imputed to the Christians? Why, then, did their gods not take steps then to prevent the decay and extinction of that republic, over the loss of which Cicero, long before Christ had come in the flesh, sings so lugubrious a dirge? Its admirers have need to inquire whether, even in the days of primitive men and morals, true justice flourished in it; or was it not perhaps even then, to use the casual expression of Cicero, rather a colored painting than the living reality? But, if God will, we shall consider this elsewhere. For I mean in its own place to show that—according to the definitions in which Cicero himself, using Scipio as his mouthpiece, briefly propounded what a republic is, and what a people is, and according to many testimonies, both of his own lips and of those who took part in that same debate—Rome never was a republic, because true justice had never a place in it. But accepting the more feasible definitions of a republic, I grant there was a republic of a certain kind, and certainly much better administered by the more ancient Romans than by their modern representatives. But the fact is, true justice has no existence

---

1 *Tully* Cicero.
2 *Ennius* Quintus Ennius (239–169 BCE), sometimes considered the father of Roman poetry.
3 *Africanus* Refers to Scipio.

save in that republic whose founder and ruler is Christ, if at least any choose to call this a republic; and indeed we cannot deny that it is the people's weal. But if perchance this name, which has become familiar in other connections, be considered alien to our common parlance; we may at all events say that in this city is true justice; the city of which Holy Scripture says, "Glorious things are said of thee, O city of God."

19:1. That Varro[1] has made out that two hundred and eighty-eight different sects of philosophy might be formed by the various opinions regarding the supreme good

As I see that I have still to discuss the fit destinies of the two cities, the earthly and the heavenly, must first explain, so far as the limits of this work allow me, the reasonings by which men have attempted to make for themselves a happiness in this unhappy life, in order that it may be evident, not only from divine authority, but also from such reasons as can be adduced to unbelievers, how the empty dreams of the philosophers differ from the hope which God gives to us, and from the substantial fulfillment of it which He will give us as our blessedness. Philosophers have expressed a great variety of diverse opinions regarding the ends of goods and of evils, and this question they have eagerly canvassed, that they might, if possible, discover what makes a man happy. For the end of our good is that for the sake of which other things are to be desired, while it is to be desired for its own sake; and the end of evil is that on account of which other things are to be shunned, while it is avoided on its own account. Thus, by the *end of good*, we at present mean, not that by which good is destroyed, so that it no longer exists, but that by which it is finished, so that it becomes complete; and by the *end of evil* we mean, not that which abolishes it, but that which completes its development. These two ends, therefore, are the supreme good and the supreme evil; and, as I have said, those who have in this vain life professed the study of wisdom have been at great pains to discover these ends, and to obtain the supreme good and avoid the supreme evil in this life. And although they erred in a variety of ways, yet natural insight has prevented them from wandering from the truth so far that they have not placed the supreme good and evil, some in the soul, some in the body, and some in both. From this tripartite distribution

of the sects of philosophy, Marcus Varro, in his book *De Philosophia*,[2] has drawn so large a variety of opinions, that, by a subtle and minute analysis of distinctions, he numbers without difficulty as many as 288 sects—not that these have actually existed, but sects which are possible.

To illustrate briefly what he means, I must begin with his own introductory statement in the above-mentioned book, that there are four things which men desire, as it were by nature without a master, without the help of any instruction, without industry or the art of living which is called virtue, and which is certainly learned: either pleasure, which is an agreeable stirring of the bodily sense; or repose, which excludes every bodily inconvenience; or both these, which Epicurus[3] calls by the one name, pleasure; or the primary objects of nature, which comprehend the things already named and other things, either bodily, such as health, and safety, and integrity of the members, or spiritual, such as the greater and less mental gifts that are found in men. Now these four things—pleasure, repose, the two combined, and the primary objects of nature—exist in us in such sort that we must either desire virtue on their account, or them for the sake of virtue, or both for their own sake; and consequently there arise from this distinction twelve sects, for each is by this consideration tripled. I will illustrate this in one instance, and, having done so, it will not be difficult to understand the others. According, then, as bodily pleasure is subjected, preferred; or united to virtue, there are three sects. It is subjected to virtue when it is chosen as subservient to virtue. Thus it is a duty of virtue to live for one's country, and for its sake to beget children, neither of which can be done without bodily pleasure. For there is pleasure in eating and drinking, pleasure also in sexual intercourse. But when it is preferred to virtue, it is desired for its own sake, and virtue, is chosen only for its sake, and to effect nothing else than the attainment or preservation of bodily pleasure. And this, indeed, is to make life hideous; for where virtue is the slave of pleasure it no longer deserves the name of virtue. Yet even this disgraceful distortion has found some philosophers to patronize[4] and defend it. Then virtue is united to pleasure when neither is desired for the other's sake, but both for their own. And therefore, as pleasure, according as it is subjected, preferred, or united to virtue, makes three sects, so also do repose, pleasure and repose combined, and

---

1 *Varro* Marcus Terentius Varro (116–27 BCE), Roman scholar and writer.

2 *De Philosophia* This book no longer exists today.

3 *Epicurus* (341–270 BCE) Greek philosopher, the founder of Epicureanism.

4 *patronize* Support.

the prime natural blessings, make their three sects each. For as men's opinions vary, and these four things are sometimes subjected, sometimes preferred, and sometimes united to virtue, there are produced twelve sects. But this number again is doubled by the addition of one difference, viz. the social life; for whoever attaches himself to any of these sects does so either for his own sake alone, or for the sake of a companion, for whom he ought to wish what he desires for himself. And thus there will be twelve of those who think some one of these opinions should be held for their own sakes, and other twelve who decide that they ought to follow this or that philosophy not for their own sakes only, but also for the sake of others whose good they desire as their own. These twenty-four sects again are doubled, and become forty-eight by adding a difference taken from the New Academy.[1] For each of these four and twenty sects can hold and defend their opinion as certain, as the Stoics[2] defended the position that the supreme good of man consisted solely in virtue; or they can be held as probable, but not certain, as the New Academics did. There are, therefore, twenty-four who hold their philosophy as certainly true, other twenty-four who hold their opinions as probable, but not certain. Again, as each person who attaches himself to any of these sects may adopt the mode of life either of the Cynics[3] or of the other philosophers, this distinction will double the number, and so make ninety-six sects. Then, lastly, as each of these sects may be adhered to either by men who love a life of ease, as those who have through choice or necessity addicted themselves to study, or by men who love a busy life, as those who, while philosophizing, have been much occupied with state affairs and public business, or by men who choose a mixed life, in imitation of those who have apportioned their time partly to erudite leisure, partly to necessary business: by these differences the number of the sects is tripled, and becomes 288.

---

1   *New Academy*   School of philosophy founded by the skeptical Greek philosopher Arcesilaus (c. 316–c. 241 BCE) as a successor to the original school, the Academy, founded by Plato. (There is confusion about this term: sometimes Arcesilaus's school is called the "Middle Academy" and the successor to his, founded by Carneades [c. 214–129 BCE] the "New Academy.")

2   *Stoics*   Stoicism was the Greek and Roman school of philosophy. Seneca is one of the major representatives of this school and Cicero's work shows its strong influence.

3   *Cynics*   Ancient Greek school of philosophy that was highly critical of many other philosophical systems and conventional social relations. Instead, the Cynics advised reliance on instinct and living according to nature.

I have thus, as briefly and lucidly as I could, given in my own words the opinions which Varro expresses in his book. But how he refutes all the rest of these sects, and chooses one, the Old Academy, instituted by Plato, and continuing to Polemo, the fourth teacher of that school of philosophy which held that their system was certain; and how on this ground he distinguishes it from the New Academy, which began with Polemo's successor Arcesilaus, and held that all things are uncertain; and how he seeks to establish that the Old Academy was as free from error as from doubt—all this, I say, were too long to enter upon in detail, and yet I must not altogether pass it by in silence. Varro then rejects, as a first step, all those differences which have multiplied the number of sects; and the ground on which he does so is that they are not differences about the supreme good. He maintains that in philosophy a sect is created only by its having an opinion of its own different from other schools on the point of the ends-in-chief. For man has no other reason for philosophizing than that he may be happy; but that which makes him happy is itself the supreme good. In other words, the supreme good is the reason of philosophizing; and therefore that cannot be called a sect of philosophy which pursues no way of its own towards the supreme good. Thus, when it is asked whether a wise man will adopt the social life, and desire and be interested in the supreme good of his friend as in his own, or will, on the contrary, do all that he does merely for his own sake, there is no question here about the supreme good, but only about the propriety of associating or not associating a friend in its participation: whether the wise man will do this not for his own sake, but for the sake of his friend in whose good he delights as in his own. So, too, when it is asked whether all things about which philosophy is concerned are to be considered uncertain, as by the New Academy, or certain, as the other philosophers maintain, the question here is not what end should be pursued, but whether or not we are to believe in the substantial existence of that end; or, to put it more plainly, whether he who pursues the supreme good must maintain that it is a true good, or only that it appears to him to be true, though possibly it may be delusive—both pursuing one and the same good. The distinction, too, which is founded on the dress and manners of the Cynics, does not touch the question of the chief good, but only; the question whether he who pursues that good which seems to himself true should live as do the Cynics. There were, in fact, men who, though they pursued different things as the supreme good, some choosing pleasure, others virtue, yet adopted that mode of life which gave the Cynics their name. Thus, whatever it is which distinguishes the Cynics from other philosophers, this has no bearing on the choice and pursuit of that good which constitutes happiness. For if it had any such bearing then the same habits of life would necessitate the pursuit of the same chief good, and diverse habits would necessitate the pursuit of different ends.

19:6. Of the error of human judgments when the truth is hidden

What shall I say of these judgments which men pronounce on men, and which are necessary in communities, whatever outward peace they enjoy? Melancholy and lamentable judgments they are, since the judges are men who cannot discern the consciences of those at their bar, and are therefore frequently compelled to put innocent witnesses to the torture to ascertain the truth regarding the crimes of other men. What shall I say of torture applied to the accused himself? He is tortured to discover whether he is guilty, so that, though innocent, he suffers most undoubted punishment for crime that is still doubtful, not because it is proved that he committed it, but because it is not ascertained that he did not commit it. Thus the ignorance of the judge frequently involves an innocent person in suffering. And what is still more unendurable—a thing, indeed, to be bewailed, and, if that were, possible, watered with fountains of tears—is this, that when the judge puts the accused to the question, that he may not unwittingly put an innocent man to death, the result of this lamentable ignorance is that this very person, whom he tortured that he might not condemn him if innocent, is condemned to death both tortured and innocent. For if he has chosen, in obedience to the philosophical instructions to the wise man, to quit this life rather than endure any longer such tortures, he declares that he has committed the crime which in fact he has not committed. And when he has been condemned and put to death, the judge is still in ignorance whether he has put to death an innocent or a guilty person, though he put the accused to the torture for the very purpose of saving himself from condemning the innocent; and consequently he has both tortured an innocent man to discover his innocence, and has put him to death without discovering it. If such darkness shrouds social life, will a wise judge take his seat on the bench or no? Beyond question he will. For human society, which he thinks it a wickedness to abandon, constrains him and compels him to this duty. And he thinks it no wickedness that innocent witnesses are tortured regarding the crimes of which other men are accused; or that the accused are put to the torture, so that they are often overcome with anguish, and, though innocent, make false confessions regarding themselves, and are punished; or that, though they be not condemned to die, they often die during, or in consequence of, the torture; or that sometimes the accusers, who perhaps have been prompted by a desire to benefit society by bringing criminals to justice, are themselves condemned through the ignorance of the judge, because they are unable to prove the truth of their accusations though they are true, and because the witnesses lie, and the accused endures the torture without being moved to confession. These numerous and important evils he does not consider sins; for the wise judge does these things, not with any intention of doing harm, but because his ignorance compels him, and because human society claims him as a judge. But though we therefore acquit the judge of malice, we must none the less condemn human life as miserable. And if he is compelled to torture and punish the innocent because his office and his ignorance constrain him, is he a happy as well as a guiltless man? Surely it were proof of more profound considerateness and finer feeling were he to recognize the misery of these necessities, and shrink from his own implication in that misery; and had he any piety about him, he would cry to God, "From my necessities deliver Thou me."[1]

19:7. Of the diversity of languages, by which human communication is hindered; and of the misery of wars, even of those called just

After the state or city comes the world, the third circle of human society—the first being the house, and the second the city. And the world, as it is larger, so it is fuller of dangers, as the greater sea is the more dangerous. And here, in the first place, man is separated from man by the difference of languages. For if two men, each ignorant of the other's language, meet, and are not compelled to pass, but, on the contrary, to remain in company, dumb animals, though of different species, would more easily hold intercourse than they, human beings though they be. For their common nature is no help to friendliness when they are prevented by diversity of language from conveying their sentiments to one another; so that a man would more readily hold intercourse with his dog than with a foreigner. But the im-

---

1   *From my necessities deliver thou me*   Psalms 25.27.

perial city has endeavored to impose on subject nations not only her yoke, but her language, as a bond of peace, so that interpreters, far from being scarce, are numberless. This is true; but how many great wars, how much slaughter and bloodshed, have provided this unity! And though these are past, the end of these miseries has not yet come. For though there have never been wanting, nor are yet wanting, hostile nations beyond the empire, against whom wars have been and are waged, yet, supposing there were no such nations, the very extent of the empire itself has produced wars of a more obnoxious description—social and civil wars—and with these the whole race has been agitated, either by the actual conflict or the fear of a renewed outbreak. If I attempted to give an adequate description of these manifold disasters, these stem and lasting necessities, though I am quite unequal to the task, what limit could I set? But, say they, the wise man will wage just wars. As if he would not all the rather lament the necessity of just wars, if he remembers that he is a man; for if they were not just he would not wage them, and would therefore be delivered from all wars. For it is the wrongdoing of the opposing party which compels the wise man to wage just wars; and this wrongdoing, even though it gave rise to no war, would still be matter of grief to man because it is man's wrongdoing. Let every one, then, who thinks with pain on all these great evils, so horrible, so ruthless, acknowledge that this is misery. And if anyone either endures or thinks of them without mental pain, this is a more miserable plight still, for he thinks himself happy because he has lost human feeling.

19:11. Of the happiness of the eternal peace, which constitutes the end or true perfection of the saints

And thus we may say of peace, as we have said of eternal life, that it is the end of our good; and the rather because the Psalmist says of the city of God, the subject of this laborious work, "Praise the Lord; O Jerusalem; praise thy God, O Zion: for He hath strengthened the bars of thy gates; He hath blessed thy children within thee; who hath made thy borders peace."[1] For when the bars of her gates shall be strengthened, none shall go in or come out from her; consequently we ought to understand the peace of her borders as that final peace we are wishing to declare. For even the mystical name of the city itself, that is, Jerusalem,

means, as I have already said, "Vision of Peace." But as the word peace is employed in connection with things in this world in which certainly life eternal has no place, we have preferred to call the end or supreme good of this city life eternal rather than peace. Of this end the apostle says, "But now, being freed from sin, and become servants to God, ye have your fruit unto holiness, and the end life eternal."[2] But, on the other hand, as those who are not familiar with Scripture may suppose that the life of the wicked is eternal life, either because of the immortality of the soul, which some of the philosophers even have recognized, or because of the endless punishment of the wicked, which forms a part of our faith, and which seems impossible unless the wicked live for ever, it may therefore be advisable, in order that every one may readily understand what we mean, to say that the end or supreme good of this city is either peace in eternal life, or eternal life in peace. For peace is a good so great, that even in this earthly and mortal life there is no word we hear with such pleasure, nothing we desire with such zest, or find to be more thoroughly gratifying. So that if we dwell for a little longer on this subject, we shall not, in my opinion, be wearisome to our readers, who will attend both for the sake of understanding what is the end of this city of which we speak, and for the sake of the sweetness of peace which is dear to all.

19:12. That even the fierceness of war and all the disquietude of men make towards this one end of peace, which every nature desires

Whoever gives even moderate attention to human affairs and to our common nature, will recognize that if there is no man who does not to be joyful, neither is there anyone who does not wish to have peace. For even they who make war desire nothing but victory—desire, that is to say, to attain to peace with glory. For what else is victory than the conquest of those who resist us? and when this is done there is peace. It is therefore with the desire for peace that wars are waged, even by those who take pleasure in exercising their warlike nature in command and battle. And hence it is obvious that peace is the end sought for by war. For every man seeks peace by waging war, but no man seeks war by making peace. For even they who intentionally interrupt the peace in which they are living have no hatred of peace, but only wish it changed into a peace that suits them better.

---

1 *Praise the Lord ... thy borders peace* Psalms 147.12-14.

2 *But now ... end life eternal* Romans 6.22.

They do not, therefore, wish to have no peace, but only one more to their mind. And in the case of sedition, when men have separated themselves from the community, they yet do not effect what they wish, unless they maintain some kind of peace with their fellow-conspirators. And therefore even robbers take care to maintain peace with their comrades, that they may with greater effect and greater safety invade the peace of other men. And if an individual happens to be of such unrivalled strength, and to be so jealous of partnership, that he trusts himself with no comrades, but makes his own plots, and commits depredations and murders on his own account, yet he maintains some shadow of peace with such persons as he is unable to kill, and from whom he wishes to conceal his deeds. In his own home, too, he makes it his aim to be at peace with his wife and children, and any other members of his household; for unquestionably their prompt obedience to his every look is a source of pleasure to him. And if this be not rendered, he is angry, he chides and punishes; and even by this storm he secures the calm peace of his own home, as occasion demands. For he sees that peace cannot be maintained unless all the members of the same domestic circle be subject to one head, such as he himself is in his own house. And therefore if a city or nation offered to submit itself to him, to serve him in the same style as he had made his household serve him, he would no longer lurk in a brigand's hiding-places, but lift his head in open day as a king, though the same covetousness and wickedness should remain in him. And thus all men desire to have peace with their own circle whom they wish to govern as suits themselves. For even those whom they make war against they wish to make their own, and impose on them the laws of their own peace.

But let us suppose a man such as poetry and mythology speak of—a man so unsociable and savage as to be called rather a semi-man than a man. Although, then, his kingdom was the solitude of a dreary cave, and he himself was so singularly bad-hearted that he was named Kακός,[1] which is the Greek word for *bad*; though he had no wife to soothe him with endearing talk, no children to play with, no sons to do his bidding, no friend to enliven him with intercourse, not even his father Vulcan (though in one respect he was happier than his father, not having begotten a monster like himself); although he gave to no man, but took as he wished whatever he could, from whomsoever he

could, when he could; yet in that solitary den, the floor of which, as Virgil[2] says, was always reeking with recent slaughter, there was nothing else than peace sought, a peace in which no one should molest him, or disquiet him with any assault or alarm. With his own body he desired to be at peace; and he was satisfied only in proportion as he had this peace. For he ruled his members, and they obeyed him; and for the sake of pacifying his mortal nature, which rebelled when it needed anything, and of allaying the sedition of hunger which threatened to banish the soul from the body, he made forays, slew, and devoured, but used the ferocity and savageness he displayed in these actions only for the preservation of his own life's peace. So that, had he been willing to make with other men the same peace which he made with himself in his own cave, he would neither have been called bad, nor a monster, nor a semi-man. Or if the appearance of his body and his vomiting smoky fires frightened men from having any dealings with him, perhaps his fierce ways arose not from a desire to do mischief, but from the necessity of finding a living. But he may have had no existence, or, at least, he was not such as the poets fancifully describe him, for they had to exalt Hercules, and did so at the expense of Cacus. It is better, then, to believe that such a man or semi-man never existed, and that this, in common with many other fancies of the poets, is mere fiction. For the most savage animals (and he is said to have been almost a wild beast) encompass their own species with a ring of protecting peace. They cohabit, beget, produce, suckle, and bring up their young, though very many of them are not gregarious, but solitary—not like sheep, deer, pigeons, starlings, bees, but such as lions, foxes, eagles, bats. For what tigress does not gently purr over her cubs, and lay aside her ferocity to fondle them? What kite, solitary as he is when circling over his prey, does not seek a mate, build a nest, hatch the eggs, bring up the young birds, and maintain with the mother of his family as peaceful a domestic alliance as he can? How much more powerfully do the laws of man's nature move him to hold fellowship and maintain peace with all men so far as in him lies, since even wicked men wage war to maintain the peace of their own circle, and wish that, if possible, all men belonged to them, that all men and things might serve but one head, and might, either through love or fear, yield themselves to peace with him! It is thus that pride in its perversity apes God. It abhors equality with other men under Him; but, instead of His rule, it seeks to

---

1   *Kακός* Usually referred to by the Latin version of his name, "Cacus."

2   *Virgil* *Æneid*, 8. 195.

impose a rule of its own upon its equals. It abhors, that is to say, the just peace of God, and loves its own unjust peace; but it cannot help loving peace of one kind or other. For there is no vice so clean contrary to nature that it obliterates even the faintest traces of nature.

He, then, who prefers what is right to what is wrong, and what is well-ordered to what is perverted, sees that the peace of unjust men is not worthy to be called peace in comparison with the peace of the just. And yet even what is perverted must of necessity be in harmony with, and in dependence on, and in some part of the order of things, for otherwise it would have no existence at all. Suppose a man hangs with his head downwards, this is certainly a perverted attitude of body and arrangement of its members; for that which nature requires to be above is beneath, and vice versa. This perversity disturbs the peace of the body, and is therefore painful. Nevertheless the spirit is at peace with its body, and labors for its preservation, and hence the suffering; but if it is banished from the body by its pains, then, so long as the bodily framework holds together, there is in the remains a kind of peace among the members, and hence the body remains suspended. And inasmuch as the earthy body tends towards the earth, and rests on the bond by which it is suspended, it tends thus to its natural peace, and the voice of its own weight demands a place for it to rest; and though now lifeless and without feeling, it does not fall from the peace that is natural to its place in creation, whether it already has it, or is tending towards it. For if you apply embalming preparations to prevent the bodily frame from moldering and dissolving, a kind of peace still unites part to part, and keeps the whole body in a suitable place on the earth—in other words, in a place that is at peace with the body. If, on the other hand, the body receive no such care, but be left to the natural course, it is disturbed by exhalations that do not harmonize with one another, and that offend our senses; for it is this which is perceived in putrefaction until it is assimilated to the elements of the world, and particle by particle enters into peace with them. Yet throughout this process the laws of the most high Creator and Governor are strictly observed, for it is by Him the peace of the universe is administered. For although minute animals are produced from the carcass of a larger animal, all these little atoms, by the law of the same Creator, serve the animals they belong to in peace. And although the flesh of dead animals be eaten by others, no matter where it be carried, nor what it be brought into contact with, nor what it be converted and changed into, it still is ruled by the same

laws which pervade all things for the conservation of every mortal race, and which bring things that fit one another into harmony.

19:15. Of the liberty proper to man's nature, and the servitude introduced by sin,—a servitude in which the man whose will is wicked is the slave of his own lust, though he is free so far as regards other men

This is prescribed by the order of nature: it is thus that God has created man. For "let them," He says, "have dominion over the fish of the sea, and over the fowl of the air, and over every creeping thing which creepeth on the earth."[1] He did not intend that His rational creature, who was made in His image, should have dominion over anything but the irrational creation—not man over man, but man over the beasts. And hence the righteous men in primitive times were made shepherds of cattle rather than kings of men, God intending thus to teach us what the relative position of the creatures is, and what the desert of sin; for it is with justice, we believe, that the condition of slavery is the result of sin. And this is why we do not find the word "slave" in any part of Scripture until righteous Noah branded the sin of his son with this name. It is a name, therefore, introduced by sin and not by nature. The origin of the Latin word for slave is supposed to be found in the circumstance that those who by the law of war were liable to be killed were sometimes preserved by their victors, and were hence called servants.[2] And these circumstances could never have arisen save through sin. For even when we wage a just war, our adversaries must be sinning; and every victory, even though gained by wicked men, is a result of the first judgment of God, who humbles the vanquished either for the sake of removing or of punishing their sins. Witness that man of God, Daniel, who, when he was in captivity, confessed to God his own sins and the sins of his people, and declares with pious grief that these were the cause of the captivity.[3] The prime cause, then; of slavery is sin, which brings man under the dominion of his fellow—that which does not happen save by the judgment of God, with whom is no unrighteousness, and who knows how to award fit

---

1   *have dominion ... creepeth on the earth*   Genesis 1.26.
2   *servants* The Latin term *servus*, "a slave," derives from *servare*, "to preserve."
3   *captivity*   See Daniel 9.

punishments to every variety of offence. But our Master in heaven says, "Every one who doeth sin is the servant of sin."[1] And thus there are many wicked masters who have religious men as their slaves, and who are yet themselves in bondage; "for of whom a man is overcome, of the same is he brought in bondage."[2] And beyond question it is a happier thing to be the slave of a man than of a lust; for even this very lust of ruling, to mention no others, lays waste men's hearts with the most ruthless dominion. Moreover, when men are subjected to one another in a peaceful order, the lowly position does as much good to the servant as the proud position does harm to the master. But by nature, as God first created us, no one is the slave either of man or of sin. This servitude is, however, penal, and is appointed by that law which enjoins the preservation of the natural order and forbids its disturbance; for if nothing had been done in violation of that law, there would have been nothing to restrain by penal servitude. And therefore the apostle admonishes slaves to be subject to their masters, and to serve them heartily and with good-will, so that, if they cannot be freed by their masters, they may themselves make their slavery in some sort free, by serving not in crafty fear, but in faithful love, until all unrighteousness pass away, and all principality and every human power be brought to nothing, and God be all in all.

19:16. Of equitable rule

And therefore, although our righteous fathers[3] had slaves, and administered their domestic affairs so as to distinguish between the condition of slaves and the heirship of sons in regard to the blessings of this life, yet in regard to the worship of God, in whom we hope for eternal blessings, they took an equally loving oversight of all the members of their household. And this is so much in accordance with the natural order, that the head of the household was called *paterfamilias*;[4] and this name has been so generally accepted, that even those whose rule is unrighteous are glad to apply it to themselves. But those who are true fathers of their households desire and endeavor that all the members of their household, equally with their own children, should worship and win God, and should come to that heavenly home in which the duty of ruling men is no longer necessary, because the duty of caring for their everlasting happiness has also ceased; but, until they reach that home, masters ought to feel their position of authority a greater burden than servants their service. And if any member of the family interrupts the domestic peace by disobedience, he is corrected either by word or blow, or some kind of just and legitimate punishment, such as society permits, that he may himself be the better for it, and be readjusted to the family harmony from which he had dislocated himself. For as it is not benevolent to give a man help at the expense of some greater benefit he might receive, so it is not innocent to spare a man at the risk of his falling into graver sin. To be innocent, we must not only do harm to no man, but also restrain him from sin or punish his sin, so that either the man himself who is punished may profit by his experience, or others be warned by his example. Since, then, the house ought to be the beginning or element of the city, and every beginning bears reference to some end of its own kind, and every element to the integrity of the whole of which it is an element, it follows plainly enough that domestic peace has a relation to civic peace—in other words, that the well-ordered concord of domestic obedience and domestic rule has a relation to the well-ordered concord of civic obedience and civic rule. And therefore it follows, further, that the father of the family ought to frame his domestic rule in accordance with the law of the city, so that the household may be in harmony with the civic order.

19:21. Whether there ever was a Roman republic answering to the definitions of Scipio in Cicero's dialogue

This, then, is the place where I should fulfill the promise I gave in the second book of this work, and explain, as briefly and clearly as possible, that if we are to accept the definitions laid down by Scipio in Cicero's *De Republica*, there never was a Roman republic; for he briefly defines a republic as the weal[5] of the people. And if this definition be true, there never was a Roman republic, for the people's weal was never attained among the Romans. For the people, according to his definition, is an assemblage associated by a common acknowledgment of right and by a community of interests. And what he means by a common acknowledgment of right he explains at large, showing that a republic

---

1   *Every one ... servant of sin*   John 8.34.

2   *for of whom ... in bondage*   2 Peter 2.19.

3   *righteous fathers*   The patriarchs.

4   *paterfamilias*   Literally, family father.

5   *weal*   Well-being.

cannot be administered without justice. Where, therefore, there is no true justice there can be no right. For that which is done by right is justly done, and what is unjustly done cannot be done by right. For the unjust inventions of men are neither to be considered nor spoken of as rights; for even they themselves say that right is that which flows from the fountain of justice, and deny the definition which is commonly given by those who misconceive the matter, that right is that that which is useful to the stronger party. Thus, where there is not true justice there can be no assemblage of men associated by a common acknowledgment of right, and therefore there can be no people, as defined by Scipio or Cicero; and if no people, then no weal of the people, but only of some promiscuous multitude unworthy of the name of people. Consequently, if the republic is the weal of the people, and there is no people if it be not associated by a common acknowledgment of right, and if there is no right where there is no justice, then most certainly it follows that there is no republic where there is no justice. Further, justice is that virtue which gives everyone his due. Where, then, is the justice of man, when lie deserts the true God and yields himself to impure demons? Is this to give every one his due? Or is he who keeps back a piece of ground from the purchaser, and gives it to a man who has no right to it, unjust, while he who keeps back himself from the God who made him, and serves wicked spirits, is just?

This same book, *De Republica*, advocates the cause of justice against injustice with great force and keenness. The pleading for injustice against justice was first heard, and it was asserted that without injustice a republic could neither increase nor even subsist, for it was laid down as an absolutely unassailable position that it is unjust for some men to rule and some to serve; and yet the imperial city to which the republic belongs cannot rule her provinces without having recourse to this injustice. It was replied in behalf of justice, that this ruling of the provinces is just, because servitude may be advantageous to the provincials, and is so when rightly administered—that is to say, when lawless men are prevented from doing harm. And further, as they became worse and worse so long as they were free, they will improve by subjection. To confirm this reasoning, there is added an, eminent example drawn from nature: for "why," it is asked, "does God rule man, the soul the body; the reason the passions and other vicious parts of the soul?" This example leaves no doubt that, to some, servitude is useful; and, indeed; to serve God is useful to all. And it is when the soul serves God that it exercises a right control over the body; and in the soul itself the reason must be subject to God if it is to govern as it ought the passions and other vices. Hence, when a man does not serve God, what justice can we ascribe to him, since in this case his soul cannot exercise a just control over the body, nor his reason over his vices? And if there is no justice in such an individual, certainly there can be none in a community composed of such persons. Here, therefore, there is not that common acknowledgment of right which makes an assemblage of men a people whose affairs we call a republic. And why need I speak of the advantageousness, the common participation in which, according to the definition, makes a people? For although, if you choose to regard the matter attentively, you will see that there is nothing advantageous to those who live godlessly, as everyone lives who does not serve God but demons, whose wickedness you may measure by their desire to receive the worship of men though they are most impure spirits, yet what I have said of the common acknowledgment of right is enough to demonstrate that, according to the above definition, there can be no people, and therefore no republic, where there is no justice. For if they assert that in their republic the Romans did not serve unclean spirits, but good and holy gods, must we therefore again reply to this evasion, though already we have said enough, and more than enough, to expose it? He must be an uncommonly stupid, or a shamelessly contentious person, who has read through the foregoing books to this point, and can yet question whether the Romans served wicked and impure demons. But, not to speak of their character, it is written in the law of the true God, "He that sacrificeth unto any god save unto the Lord only, he shall be utterly destroyed."[1] He, therefore, who uttered so menacing a commandment decreed that no worship should be given either to good or bad gods.

19:23. Porphyry's[2] account of the responses given by the oracles of the gods concerning Christ

For in his book called *Ek Logion Philosophias*,[3] in which he collects and comments upon the responses which he pre-

---

1   *He that sacrifeth ... utterly destroyed*   Exodus 22.20.
2   *Porphyry's*   Porphyry (c. 233–c. 309) was a Greco-Roman Neoplatonic philosopher and critic of Christianity.
3   *Ek Logion Philosophias*   A work unknown to us—presumably lost.

tends were uttered by the gods concerning divine things, he says—I give his own words as they have been translated from the Greek: "To one who inquired what god he should propitiate in order to recall his wife from Christianity, Apollo replied in the following verses." Then the following words are given as those of Apollo: "You will probably find it easier to write lasting characters on the water, or lightly fly like a bird through the air, than to restore right feeling in your impious wife once she has polluted herself. Let her remain as she pleases in her foolish deception, and sing false laments to her dead God, who was condemned by right-minded judges, and perished ignominiously by a violent death." Then after these verses of Apollo (which we have given in a Latin version that does not preserve the metrical form), he goes on to say: "In these verses Apollo exposed the incurable corruption of the Christians, saying that the Jews; rather than the Christians, recognized God." See how he misrepresents Christ, giving the Jews the preference to the Christians in the recognition of God. This was his explanation of Apollo's verses; in which he says that Christ was put to death by right-minded or just judges—in other words, that He deserved to die. I leave the responsibility of this oracle regarding Christ on the lying interpreter of Apollo, or on this philosopher who believed it or possibly himself invented it; as to its agreement with Porphyry's opinions or with other oracles, we shall in a little have something to say. In this passage, however, he says that the Jews, as the interpreters of God, judged justly in pronouncing Christ to be worthy of the most shameful death. He should have listened, then, to this God of the Jews to whom he bears this testimony, when that God says, "He that sacrificeth to any other god save to the Lord alone shall be utterly destroyed." But let us come to still plainer expressions, and hear how great a God Porphyry thinks the God of the Jews is. Apollo, he says, when asked whether word, *i.e.*, reason, or law is the better thing, replied in the following verses. Then he gives the verses of Apollo, from which I select the following as sufficient: "God, the Generator, and the King prior to all things, before whom heaven and earth, and the sea, and the hidden places of hell tremble, and the deities themselves are afraid, for their law is the Father whom the holy Hebrews honor." In this oracle of his god Apollo, Porphyry avowed that the God of the Hebrews is so great that the deities themselves are afraid before Him. I am surprised, therefore, that when God said, He that sacrificeth to other gods shall be utterly destroyed, Porphyry himself was not afraid lest he should be destroyed for sacrificing to other gods.

This philosopher, however, has also some good to say of Christ, oblivious, as it were, of that contumely of his of which we have just been speaking; or as if his gods spoke evil of Christ only while asleep; and recognized Him to be good, and gave Him His deserved praise, when they awoke. For, as if he were about to proclaim some marvelous thing passing belief, he says, "What we are going to say will certainly take some by surprise. For the gods have declared that Christ was very pious, and has become immortal, and that they cherish his memory: that the Christians, however, are polluted, contaminated, and involved in error. And many other such things," he says, "do the gods say against the Christians." Then he gives specimens of the accusations made, as he says, by the gods against them, and goes on: "But to some who asked Hecate[1] whether Christ were a God, she replied, 'You know the condition of the disembodied immortal soul and that if it has been severed from wisdom it always errs. The soul you refer to is that of a man foremost in piety: they worship it because they mistake the truth.'" To this so-called oracular response he adds the following words of his own: "Of this very pious man, then, Hecate said that the soul, like the souls of other good men, was after death dowered with immortality, and that the Christians through ignorance worship it. And to those who ask why he was condemned to die, the oracle of the goddess replied, 'The body, indeed, is always exposed to torments, but the souls of the pious abide in heaven. And the soul you inquire about has been the fatal cause of error to other souls which were not fated to receive the gifts of the gods, and to have the knowledge of immortal Jove. Such souls are therefore hated by the gods; for they who were fated not to receive the gifts of the gods, and not to know God, were fated to be involved in error by means of him you speak of. He himself, however, was good, and heaven has been opened to him as to other good men. You are not, then, to speak evil of him, but to pity the folly of men: and through him men's danger is imminent.'"

Who is so foolish as not to see that these oracles were either composed by a clever man with a strong animus against the Christians, or were uttered as responses by impure demons with a similar design—that is to say, in order that their praise of Christ may win credence for their vituperation of Christians; and that thus they may, if possible, close the way of eternal salvation, which is identical with Christianity? For they believe that they are by no means

---

1   *Hecate*   Greek goddess of the crossroads.

counterworking their own hurtful craft by promoting belief in Christ, so long as their calumniation of Christians is also accepted; for they thus secure that even the man who thinks well of Christ declines to become a Christian, and is therefore not delivered from their own rule by the Christ he praises. Besides, their praise of Christ is so contrived that whosoever believes in Him as thus represented will not be a true Christian but a Photinian[1] heretic, recognizing only the humanity, and not also the divinity of Christ, and will thus be precluded from salvation and from deliverance out of the meshes of these devilish lies. For our part, we are no better pleased with Hecate's praises of Christ than with Apollo's calumniation of Him. Apollo says that Christ was put to death by right-minded judges, implying that He was unrighteous. Hecate says that He was a most pious man, but no more. The intention of both is the same, to prevent men from becoming Christians, because if this be secured, men shall never be rescued from their power. But it is incumbent on our philosopher, or rather on those who believe in these pretended oracles against the Christians, first of all, if they can, to bring Apollo and Hecate to the same mind regarding Christ, so that either both may condemn or both praise Him. And even if they succeeded in this, we for our part would notwithstanding repudiate the testimony of demons, whether favorable or adverse to Christ. But when our adversaries find a god and goddess of their own at variance about Christ, the one praising, the other vituperating Him, they can certainly give no credence, if they have any judgment, to mere men who blaspheme the Christians.

When Porphyry or Hecate praises Christ, and adds that He gave Himself to the Christians as a fatal gift, that they might be involved in error, he exposes, as he thinks, the causes of this error. But before I cite his words to that purpose, I would ask, *If Christ did thus give Himself to the Christians to involve them in error, did He do so willingly, or against His will? If willingly, how is He righteous? If against His will, how is He blessed?* However, let us hear the causes of this error. "There are," he says, "in a certain place very small earthly spirits, subject to the power of evil demons. The wise men of the Hebrews, among whom was this Jesus, as you have heard from the oracles of Apollo cited above, turned religious persons from these very wicked demons and minor spirits, and taught them rather to worship the

celestial gods, and especially to adore God the Father. This," he said, "the gods enjoin; and we have already shown how they admonish the soul to turn to God, and command it to worship Him. But the ignorant and the ungodly, who are not destined to receive favors from the gods, nor to know the immortal Jupiter, not listening to the gods and their messages, have turned away from all gods, and have not only refused to hate, but have venerated the prohibited demons. Professing to worship God, they refuse to do those things by which alone God is worshipped. For God, indeed, being the Father of all, is in need of nothing; but for us it is good to adore Him by means of justice, chastity, and other virtues, and thus to make life itself a prayer to Him, by inquiring into and imitating His nature. For inquiry," says he, "purifies and imitation deifies us, by moving us nearer to Him." He is right in so far as he proclaims God the Father, and the conduct by which we should worship Him. Of such precepts the prophetic books of the Hebrews are full, when they praise or blame the life of the saints. But in speaking of the Christians he is in error, and calumniates them as much as is desired by the demons whom he takes for gods, as if it were difficult for any man to recollect the disgraceful and shameful actions which used to be done in the theaters and temples to please the gods; and to compare with these things what is heard in our churches, and what is offered to the true God, and from this comparison to conclude where character is edified, and where it is ruined. But who but a diabolical spirit has told or suggested to this man so manifest and vain a lie, as that the Christians reverenced rather than hated the demons, whose worship the Hebrews prohibited? But that God, whom the Hebrew sages worshipped, forbids sacrifice to be offered even to the holy angels of heaven and divine powers, whom we, in this our pilgrimage, venerate and love as our most blessed fellow-citizens. For in the law which God gave to His Hebrew people He utters this menace, as in a voice of thunder: "He that sacrificeth unto any god, save unto the Lord only, he shall be utterly destroyed."[2] And that no one might suppose that this prohibition extends only to the very wicked demons and earthly spirits, whom this philosopher calls very small and inferior—for even these are in the Scripture called gods, not of the Hebrews, but of the nations, as the Septuagint translators have shown in the psalm where it is said, "For all the gods of the nations are demons"[3]—that no one might suppose, I say,

---

1   *Photinian*   Photinius (?–376) was a fourth-century bishop whose teachings were declared heretical, in part because he held that Christ was a mere man; Augustine calls anyone who believes that Christ was a mere man a "Photinian heretic."

2   *He that sacrificeth ... utterly destroyed*   Exodus 22.20.
3   *For all the gods ... demons*   Psalms 96.5.

that sacrifice to these demons was prohibited, but that sacrifice might be offered to all or some of the celestials, it was immediately added, "save unto the Lord alone."[1] The God of the Hebrews, then, to whom this renowned philosopher bears this signal testimony, gave to His Hebrew people a law, composed in the Hebrew language, and not obscure and unknown, but published now in every nation, and in this law it is written, "He that sacrificeth unto any god, save unto the Lord alone, he shall be utterly destroyed." What need is there to seek further proofs in the law or the prophets of this same thing? *Seek*, we need not say, for the passages are neither few nor difficult to find; but what need to collect and apply to my argument the proofs which are thickly sown and obvious, and by which it appears clear as day that sacrifice may be paid to none but the supreme and true God? Here is one brief but decided, even menacing, and certainly true utterance of that God whom the wisest of our adversaries so highly extol. Let this be listened to, feared, fulfilled, that there may be no disobedient soul cut off. "He that sacrifices," He says, not because He needs anything, but because it behooves us to be His possession. Hence the Psalmist in the Hebrew Scriptures sings, "I have said to the Lord, Thou art my God, for Thou needest not my good."[2] For we ourselves, who are His own city, are His most noble and worthy sacrifice, and it is this mystery we celebrate in our sacrifices, which are well known to the faithful, as we have explained in the preceding books. For through the prophets the oracles of God declared that the sacrifices which the Jews offered as a shadow of that which was to be would cease, and that the nations, from the rising to the setting of the sun, would offer one sacrifice. From these oracles, which we now see accomplished, we have made such selections as seemed suitable to our purpose in this work. And therefore, where there is not this righteousness whereby the one supreme God rules the obedient city according to His grace, so that it sacrifices to none but Him, and whereby, in all the citizens of this obedient city, the soul consequently rules the body and reason the vices in the rightful order, so that, as the individual just man, so also the community and people of the just, live by faith, which works by love, that love whereby man loves God as He ought to be loved, and his neighbor as himself—there, I say, there is not an assemblage associated by a common acknowledgment of right, and by a community of interests. But if there is not this, there is not a people, if our definition be true, and therefore there is no republic; for where there is no people there can be no republic.

19:24. The definition which must be given of a people and a republic, in order to vindicate the assumption of these titles by the Romans and by other kingdoms

But if we discard this definition of a people, and, assuming another, say that a people is an assemblage of reasonable beings bound together by a common agreement as to the objects of their love, then, in order to discover the character of any people, we have only to observe what they love. Yet whatever it loves, if only it is an assemblage of reasonable beings and not of beasts, and is bound together by an agreement as to the objects of love, it is reasonably called a people; and it will be a superior people in proportion as it is bound together by higher interests, inferior in proportion as it is bound together by lower. According to this definition of ours, the Roman people is a people, and its weal is without doubt a commonwealth or republic. But what its tastes were in its early and subsequent days, and how it declined into sanguinary seditions and then to social and civil wars, and so burst asunder or rotted off the bond of concord in which the health of a people consists, history shows, and in the preceding books I have related at large. And yet I would not on this account say either that it was not a people, or that its administration was not a republic, so long as there remains an assemblage of reasonable beings bound together by a common agreement as to the objects of love. But what I say of this people and of this republic I must be understood to think and say of the Athenians or any Greek state, of the Egyptians, of the early Assyrian Babylon, and of every other nation, great or small, which had a public government. For, in general, the city of the ungodly, which did not obey the command of God that it should offer no sacrifice save to Him alone, and which, therefore, could not give to the soul its proper command over the body, nor to the reason its just authority over the vices, is void of true justice.

---

1   *save unto the Lord alone* Augustine here warns his readers against a possible misunderstanding of the Latin word for "alone" (*soli*), which might be rendered "the sun."

2   *I have said ... good* Psalms 16.2.

AL-FĀRĀBĪ
(870 – 950)

I N A LETTER TO HIS TRANSLATOR, THE GREAT MEDIEVAL JEW-
ish philosopher Maimonides wrote of al-Fārābī: "Everything that he composed—and particularly his book on the
Principles of Beings—is all finer than fine flour. His arguments enable one to understand and comprehend, for he was
very great in wisdom."[1] The work Maimonides mentioned is
excerpted here, under the title usually given to it nowadays.

Al-Fārābī was one of the earliest and greatest Islamic
philosophers, with enormous influence in the Arab world
and in the West. His importance rests on his having brought
the thought of the great Greek philosophers to the Islamic tradition, and for his original contributions as well. He became
known as the "second Master" in the Arab world (Aristotle
was the first), and was considered by subsequent Muslim
philosophers as the true founder of philosophy in Islam.

Abū Nasr Muhammad al-Fārābī was born around 870
but sources differ about the location of his birth: it may
have been in present day Turkmenistan or Pakistan or Iran.
He studied in Baghdad, living later in Damascus, and
Egypt, and became well versed in a wide range of academic
disciplines and in a great many languages; he worked as a
judge and as a teacher, and died in Damascus in 950.

The work of both Plato and Aristotle were strong influences on al-Fārābī and he wrote a number of commentaries on their works, in addition to over one hundred books
(only some of which survive today) on philosophy, logic,
politics, science, medicine, and music.

The work from which our excerpt is taken was sometimes called *Principles of Beings* because it begins with a very
general metaphysical account of the six principles (the First
Cause, the Second Cause, the Active Intellect, the soul,
form, and matter) which al-Fārābī took to organize all of
existence; but this is preliminary to a much more concrete
and practical account in the second part of that work of the
principles of political life and a description of the types of
polity. (We print only the second part here.)

The Aristotelian influence on al-Fārābī's political
thought is clear: he follows Aristotle in identifying happiness

as the ultimate intrinsic good, and in arguing that politics
is the art of arranging things to allow the attainment of this
good. Both thinkers, while emphasizing the contemplative
life as the prime means to genuine happiness, count human
beings as essentially active and social—as *political* animals.
Al-Fārābī, however, diverges significantly from Aristotle in
adding an Islamic political element, arguing for the necessity of a ruler's reliance on religious truth revealed through
the prophets.

Like Plato in the *Republic*, al-Fārābī presents a vision of
the ideal city led by a wise enlightened ruler. But his originality is revealed in the details of his virtuous city, and of the
kind of ruler and political regime he thinks is necessary for
achieving this ideal. He sets out the ways a political regime
can go wrong, describing several types of "ignorant cities":
the "indispensable city," which places too much importance
on subsistence goods; the "vile city," dominated by greed;
the "base city," whose inhabitants focus on bodily pleasure;
the "timocratic city," where the citizens are preoccupied with
their own vanity; and the "democratic city," a city marked
by the individual liberty and equality of all citizens. The
reading closes with a discussion of "weeds"—people who,
out of ignorance or vice, act contrary to the success of the
virtuous city.

Al-Fārābī had a strong influence on Ibn Sina, Ibn
Rushd, and a great many other Islamic philosophers who
followed him. But his importance is not limited to this
tradition. Moses Maimonides was enormously impressed
by al-Fārābī's work, which had considerable influence on
his own thought. Al-Fārābī's ideas have directly or indirectly
affected the thinking of many western philosophers, including Thomas Aquinas.

◆ ◆ ◆ ◆ ◆

---

1   Quoted by Muhsin Mahdi in his introduction to this selection
from *The Political Regime*, in *Medieval Political Philosophy: A
Sourcebook*, Ralph Lerner and Muhsin Mahdi, eds. (1963).

The Political Regime

Man belongs to the species that cannot accomplish their necessary affairs or achieve their best state, except through the association of many groups of them in a single dwelling-place. Some human societies are large, others are of a medium size, still others are small. The large societies consist of many nations that associate and cooperate with one another; the medium ones consist of a nation; the small are the ones embraced by the city. These three are the perfect societies. Hence the city represents the first degree of perfection. Associations in villages, quarters, streets, and households, on the other hand, are the imperfect associations. Of these the least perfect is the household association, which is a part of the association in the street, the latter being a part of the association in the quarter, and this in turn a part of the political association. Associations in quarters and villages are both for the sake of the city; they differ, however, in that the quarters are parts of the city while the villages only serve it. The political [or civic] society is a part of the nation, and the nation is divided into cities. The absolutely perfect human societies are divided into nations. A nation is differentiated from another by two natural things—natural make-up and natural character—and by something that is composite (it is conventional but has a basis in natural things), which is language—I mean the idiom through which men express themselves. As a result some nations are large and others are small.

The primary natural cause of the differences between nations in these matters consists of a variety of things. One of them is the difference in the parts of the celestial bodies that face them, namely, the first [that is, the outermost] sphere and the sphere of the fixed stars, then the difference in the positions of the inclined spheres from the various parts of the earth and the variation in their proximity and remoteness.[1] From this follows the difference between the parts of the earth that are the nations' dwelling-places; for from the outset, this difference results from the difference in the parts of the first sphere that face them, from the difference in the fixed stars that face them, and from the difference in the positions of the inclined spheres with respect to them. From the difference between the parts of the earth follows the difference in the vapors rising from the earth; since each vapor rises from a certain soil, it is akin to that soil. From the difference in the vapors follows the difference in the air and water, inasmuch as the water of each country is generated from its underground vapors, and the air of each country is mixed with the vapors that work their way up to it from the soil. In the same manner, the difference in the air and water [of each country] follows from the difference [in the parts] of the fixed stars and of the first sphere that face it, and from the difference in the positions of the inclined spheres. From all these differences, in turn, follows the difference in the plants and in the species of irrational animals, as a result of which nations have different diets. From the difference in their diets follows the difference in the materials and crops that go into the composition of the individuals who succeed the ones who die. From this, in turn, follows the difference in the natural make-up and natural character. Moreover, the difference in the parts of the heaven that face them causes further differences in their make-up and character, in a different manner from the one mentioned above. The difference in the air, too, causes differences in make-up and character in a different manner from the one mentioned above. Furthermore, out of the cooperation and combination of these differences there develop different mixtures that contribute to differences in the make-up and character of the nations. It is in this manner and direction that natural things fit together, are connected with each other, and occupy their respective ranks; and this is the extent to which the celestial bodies contribute to their perfection. The remaining perfections are not given by the celestial bodies but by the Active Intellect;[2] and the Active Intellect gives the remaining perfections to no other species but man.

---

1   *the first ... and remoteness*   Al-Fārābi is using a "geocentric" picture of the solar system. According to this view, the earth, which is stationary, is surrounded by invisible concentric crystal spheres on which the astronomical bodies are imbedded. In the original picture, as set out by Aristotle, the closest sphere to the earth was that of the moon, followed by Mercury, the Sun, Mars, Jupiter, Saturn, all the "fixed stars," and, outermost, the "sphere of the prime mover" whose motion propelled all of the inner spheres. Some deficiencies in accounting for astronomical observations were fixed by a more complicated version introduced by Ptolemy (c. 100–c. 170), Greek-origin Roman/Egyptian astronomer, astrologer, and geographer. According to Ptolemy's picture, some objects were on small spheres attached to these larger spheres, and thus moved in complicated "epicycles"—small circles centered on motion around points on a larger circles. Ptolemy's book was translated into Arabic, and had great influence on Al-Fārābi and on medieval Islamic thought—generally both as astronomy and as astrology. It was translated into Latin in the twelfth century, and became the dominant astronomy in Europe until replaced around 1550 by Copernicus' model, which had the moon circling the earth, and all the planets circling the sun.

2   *the Active Intellect*   Cf. Aristotle *De Anima* 3. Al-Fārābi gives an account of the "Active Intellect" in earlier sections of this work,

In giving [these perfections] to man, the Active Intellect follows a course similar to that followed by the celestial bodies. First, it gives him a faculty and a principle with which, of his own accord, he seeks, or is able to seek, the remaining perfections. That principle consists of the primary knowledge and the first intelligibles[1] present in the rational part of the soul; but it gives him this kind of knowledge and those intelligibles only after man (a) first develops the sensitive part of the soul[2] and the appetitive part,[3] which gives rise to the desire and aversion that adhere to the sensitive part. [42] (The instruments of the last two faculties develop from the parts of the body.) They, in turn, give rise to the will. For, at first, the will is nothing but a desire that follows from a sensation; and desire takes place through the appetitive part of the soul, and sensation through the sensitive. (b) Next, there has to develop the imaginative part of the soul and the desire that adheres to it. Hence a second will develops after the first. This will is a desire that follows from [an act of the] imagination. After these two wills develop, it becomes possible for the primary knowledge that emanates from the Active Intellect to the rational part to take place. At this point a third kind of will develops in man—the desire that follows from intellecting—which is specifically called "choice." This choice pertains specifically to man, exclusive of all other animals. By virtue of it, man is able to do either what it commendable or blamable, noble or base; and because of it there is reward and punishment. (The first two wills, on the other hand, can exist in the irrational animals too.) When this will develops in man, with it he is able to seek or not to seek happiness, and to do what is good or evil, noble or base, in so far as this lies in his power.

Happiness is the good without qualification. Everything useful for the achievement of happiness or by which it is attained, is good too, not for its own sake, however, but because it is useful with respect to happiness; and everything that obstructs the way to happiness in any fashion is

unqualified evil. The good that is useful for the achievement of happiness may be something that exists by nature or that comes into being by the will, and the evil that obstructs the way to happiness may be something that exists by nature or that comes into being by the will. That of it which is by nature is given by the celestial bodies, but not because they intend to assist the Active Intellect toward its purpose or to hamper it. For when the celestial bodies give something that contributes to the purpose of the Active Intellect, they do not do so with the intention of assisting the Active Intellect; neither are the natural things that obstruct the way to its purpose intended by the celestial bodies to hamper the Active Intellect. Rather, it is inherent in the substance of the celestial bodies to give all that it is in the nature of matter to receive, without concerning themselves with whether it contributes to, or harms, the purpose of the Active Intellect. Therefore it is possible that the sum total of what is produced by the celestial bodies should comprise at times things that are favorable, and at other times things that are unfavorable, to the purpose of the Active Intellect.

As to voluntary good and evil, which are the noble and the base respectively, they have their origin specifically in man. Now there is only one way in which the voluntary good can come into being. That is because the faculties of the human soul are five: the theoretical-rational, the practical-rational, the appetitive, the imaginative, and the sensitive. Happiness, which only man can know and perceive, is known by the theoretical-rational faculty and by none of the remaining faculties. Man knows it when he makes use of the first principles and the primary knowledge given to him by the Active Intellect. When he knows happiness, desires it by the appetitive faculty, deliberates by the practical rational faculty upon what he ought to do in order to attain it, uses the instruments of the appetitive faculty to do the actions he has discovered by deliberation, and his imaginative and sensitive faculties assist and obey the rational and aid it in arousing man to do the actions with which he attains happiness, then everything that originates from man will be good. It is only in this way that the voluntary good comes into being. As to voluntary evil, it originates in the manner that I shall state. Neither the imaginative nor the appetitive faculty perceives happiness. Not even the rational faculty perceives happiness under all conditions. The rational faculty perceives happiness only when it strives to apprehend it. Now there are many things that man can imagine that they ought to be the aim and end of life, such as the pleasant and the useful, honor, and the like. Whenever man neg-

---

omitted in this selection. In Al-Fārābī's metaphysics (strongly influenced by Aristotle's De Anima), the universe is governed by ten "Intellects." The First is God, the unmoved mover; from this emanates the rest in turn. The Second through Ninth Intellects are the principles of being and action of various planetary bodies; the Tenth (the "Active Intellect") is responsible for the form of earthly matters, including the actualization of the rational potential of man.

1   *intelligibles*   Universal principles capable of being known.
2   *sensitive part of the soul*   That part of the mind capable of sensation.
3   *appetitive part*   That part capable of desire and will.

lects to perfect his theoretical-rational part, fails to perceive happiness and hasten toward it, holds something other than happiness—what is useful, what is pleasant, domination, what is honorable, and the like—as an end toward which he aims in his life, desires it with the appetitive faculty, uses the practical-rational faculty to deliberate in the discovery of what enables him to attain this end, uses the instruments of the appetitive faculty to do the things he has discovered, and is assisted in this by the imaginative and the sensitive faculties, then everything that originates from him is evil. Similarly, when man apprehends and knows happiness but does not make it the aim and the end of his life, has no desire or has only a feeble desire for it, makes something other than happiness the end that he desires in his life, and uses all his faculties to attain that end, then everything that originates from him is evil.

Since what is intended by man's existence is that he attain happiness, which is the ultimate perfection that remains to be given to the possible beings[1] capable of receiving it, it is necessary to state the manner in which man can reach this happiness. Man can reach happiness only when the Active Intellect first gives the first intelligibles, which constitute the primary knowledge. However, not every man is equipped by natural disposition to receive the first intelligibles, because individual human beings are made by nature with unequal powers and different preparations. Some of them are not prepared by nature to receive any of the first intelligibles; others—for instance, the insane—receive them, but not as they really are; and still others receive them as they really are. The last are the ones with sound human natural dispositions; only these, and not the others, are capable of attaining happiness.

• • •

Since what is intended by man's existence is that he attain supreme happiness, he—in order to achieve it—needs to know what happiness is, make it his end, and hold it before his eyes. Then, after that, he needs to know the things he ought to do in order to attain happiness, and then do these actions. In view of what has been said about the differences in the natural dispositions of individual men, not everyone is disposed to know happiness on his own, or the things that he ought to do, but needs a teacher and a guide for this purpose. Some men need little guidance, others need

a great deal of it. In addition, even when a man is guided to these two [that is, happiness and the actions leading to it], he will not, in the absence of an external stimulus and something to arouse him, necessarily do what he has been taught and guided to. This is how most men are. Therefore they need someone to make all this known to them and to arouse them to do it.

Besides, it is not in the power of every man to guide others nor in the power of every man to induce others to do these things. He who does not possess the power to arouse another to do anything whatever, nor to employ him in it, but only has the power always to do what he has been guided to, is never a ruler in anything at all; he is always ruled in everything. He who has the power to guide another to a certain thing, to induce him to do it, and to employ him in it, is in that thing a ruler over the one who cannot do it on his own. And he who cannot discover something on his own, but does it when he is guided to it and instructed in it, and has the power to arouse another to do, and to employ him in, that thing in which he himself has been instructed and to which he has been guided, is a ruler over one man and is ruled by another. Thus the ruler may be a supreme or a subordinate ruler. The subordinate ruler is one who is subject to one man and in turn rules over another. These two types of rule can be in one kind [of art], such as husbandry, trade, or medicine, and can pertain to all kinds of human [arts].

The supreme ruler without qualification is he who does not need anyone to rule him in anything whatever, but has actually acquired the sciences and every kind of knowledge, and has no need of a man to guide him in anything. He is able to comprehend well each one of the particular things that he ought to do. He is able to guide well all others to everything in which he instructs them, to employ all those who do any of the acts for which they are equipped, and to determine, define, and direct these acts toward happiness. This is found only in the one who possesses great and superior natural dispositions, when his soul is in union with the Active Intellect. He can only attain this [union with the Active Intellect] by first acquiring the passive intellect, and then the intellect called the acquired; for, as it is stated in *On the Soul*, union with the Active Intellect results from possessing the acquired intellect.[2] This man is the true prince according to the ancients; he is the one of whom it ought to

1   *possible beings* Distinguished from the "necessary" being that is not caused. The reference here is to the human species.

2   *union with ... acquired intellect* Aristotle *De Anima* 3. 5. 7. The term "acquired intellect" (*nous epiktetos*) does not occur in Aristotle's *De Anima* but in Alexander of Aphrodisias' commentary on that book. Its function is implied by Aristotle, however.

be said that he receives revelation. For man receives revelation only when he attains this rank, that is, when there is no longer an intermediary between him and the Active Intellect; for the passive intellect is like matter and substratum to the acquired intellect, and the latter is like matter and substratum to the Active Intellect. It is then that the power that enables man to understand how to define things and actions and how to direct them toward happiness, emanates from the Active Intellect to the passive intellect. This emanation that proceeds from the Active Intellect to the passive through the mediation of the acquired intellect, is revelation. Now because the Active Intellect emanates from the being of the First Cause,[1] it can for this reason be said that it is the First Cause that brings about revelation to this man through the mediation of the Active Intellect. The rule of this man is the supreme rule; all other human rulerships are inferior to it and are derived from it. Such is his rank.

The men who are governed by the rule of this ruler are the virtuous, good, and happy men. If they form a nation, then that is the virtuous nation; if they are associated in a single dwelling-place, then the dwelling place that brings together all those subject to such a rule is the virtuous city; and if they are not associated together in a single dwelling-place, but live in separate dwelling-places whose inhabitants are governed by rulerships other than this one, then these are virtuous men who are strangers in those dwelling-places. They happen to live separately either because no city happens to exist as yet in which they can be associated, or because they were [associated] in a city, but as a result of certain disasters—such as an enemy attack, pestilence, failure of crops, and so forth—they were forced to separate. If at any one time a group of these princes happens to reside in a single city, in a single nation, or in many nations, then this group is as it were a single prince because they agree in their endeavors, purposes, opinions, and ways of life. If they follow one another in time, their souls will form as it were a single soul, the one who succeeds will be following the way of life of his predecessors, and the living will be following in the way of the ones who have died. Just as it is permissible for each of them to change a Law he had legislated at one time for another if he deems it better to do so, similarly it is permissible for the living who succeeds the one who died to change what the latter had legislated, for the one who

died also would have changed it had he been able to observe the new conditions. But if it does not happen that a man exists with these qualifications, then one will have to adopt the Laws prescribed by the earlier ones, write them down, preserve them, and govern the city by them. The ruler who governs the city according to the written Laws received from the past imams[2] will be the prince of the law (*sunnah*).

As every citizen of the city does what is entrusted to him—either by knowing it on his own or by being guided and induced to it by the ruler—he acquires, by these actions, the good states of the soul, just as by continued practice in good writing a man acquires excellence in the art of writing, which is a state of the soul; and the more he continues practicing, the more firm his excellence in writing becomes, the greater the pleasure he takes in the resulting state, and the stronger the delight of his soul in that state. Similarly, the actions that are determined and directed toward happiness strengthen the part of the soul that is naturally equipped for happiness, and actualize and perfect it—to the extent that the power resulting from the perfection achieved by it enables it to dispense with matter; having been thus freed from matter, it is not destroyed by the destruction of matter, since it is no longer in need of matter in order to exercise its power or to exist—at which time it attains happiness. It is evident that the kinds of happiness attained by the citizens of the city differ in quantity and quality as a result of the difference in the perfections they acquire through political activities. Accordingly, the pleasures they attain vary in excellence. When the soul becomes separated from matter and incorporeal, it is no longer subject to any of the accidents that are attached to bodies as such; therefore it cannot be said of it that it moves or that it rests. Rather one ought then to apply to it the statements appropriate to what is incorporeal. Every one of the things adhering to the human soul and that fits the description of the body as body, ought to be considered as one of the negative attributes of the separate soul. The comprehension and conception of the states of the separate soul are extremely difficult and at variance with common usage, just as it is difficult to conceive the substances that are not bodies or in bodies.

As one group of them passes away, and their bodies are destroyed, their souls have achieved salvation and happiness, and they are succeeded by other men who assume their positions in the city and perform their actions, the souls of the latter will also achieve salvation. As their bodies

---

1   *First Cause*   In Aristotle's *Metaphysics*, the "First Cause" (also known as the Prime Mover) is itself uncaused. Aristotle identifies it with pure intellect—the "thought of thought"—perfect, complete in itself, and immutable.

---

2   *imams*   Islamic scholars/religious leaders.

are destroyed, they join the rank of the former group that had passed away, they will be together with them in the way that incorporeal things are together, and the kindred souls within each group will be in a state of union with one another. The more the kindred separate souls increase in number and unite with one another, the greater the pleasure felt by each soul; and the more they are joined by those who come after them, the greater the pleasure felt by each of the latter through their encounter with the former as well as the pleasure felt by the former through their union with the latter. For each soul will then be intellecting, in addition to itself, many other souls that are of the same kind; and it will be intellecting more souls as the ones that had passed away are joined by the ones succeeding them. Hence the pleasure felt by the very ancient ones will continue to increase indefinitely. Such is the state of every group of them. This, then, is true and supreme happiness, which is the purpose of the Active Intellect.

When the activities of the citizens of a city are not directed toward happiness, they lead them to acquire bad states of the soul—just as when the activities of [the art of] writing are badly performed, they produce bad writing, and similarly, when the activities of any art are badly performed, they produce in the soul bad states, corresponding to the [badly performed] art. As a result their souls become sick. Therefore they take pleasure in the states that they acquire through their activities. Just as because of their corrupt sense [of taste], those with bodily sickness—for example, the ones affected by fever—take pleasure in bitter things and find them sweet, and suffer pain from sweet things, which seem bitter to their palates; similarly, because of their corrupt imagination, those who are sick in their souls take pleasure in the bad states [of the soul]. And just as there are among the sick those who do not feel their malady and those who even think that they are healthy, and such sick men do not at all listen to the advice of a physician; similarly, the sick in their souls who do not feel their sickness and even think that they are virtuous and have sound souls, do not listen at all to the words of a guide, a teacher, or a reformer. The souls of such individuals remain chained to matter and do not reach that perfection by which they can separate from matter, so that when the matter ceases to exist they too will cease to exist.

The ranks of order among the citizens of the city, as regards ruling and serving, vary in excellence according to their natural dispositions and according to the habits of character they have formed. The supreme ruler is the one who orders the various groups and every individual in each group, in the place they merit—that is, gives each a subservient or a ruling rank of order. Therefore, there will be certain ranks of order that are close to his own, others slightly further away, and still others that are far away from it. Such will be the ruling ranks of order: beginning with the highest ruling rank of order, they will descend gradually until they become subservient ranks of order devoid of any element of ruling and below which there is no other rank of order. After having ordered these ranks, if the supreme ruler wishes to issue a command about a certain matter that he wishes to enjoin the citizens of the city or a certain group among them to do, and to arouse them toward it, he intimates this to the ranks closest to him, these will hand it on to their subordinates, and so forth, until it reaches down to those assigned to execute that matter. The parts of the city will thus be linked and fitted together, and ordered by giving precedence to some over the others. Thus the city becomes similar to the natural beings; the ranks of order in it similar to the ranks of order of the beings, which begin with the First and terminate in prime matter[1] and the elements; and the way they are linked and fitted together will be similar to the way the beings are linked and fitted together. The prince of the city will be like the First Cause, which is the cause for the existence of all the other beings. Then the ranks of order of the beings gradually keep descending, each one of them being both ruler and ruled, until they reach down to those possible beings—that is, prime matter and the elements—that possess no ruling element whatever, but are subservient and always exist for the sake of others.

The achievement of happiness takes place only through the disappearance of evils—not only the voluntary but also the natural ones—from the cities and nations, and when these acquire all the goods, both the natural and the voluntary. The function of the city's governor—that is, the prince—is to manage the cities in such a way that all the city's parts become linked and fitted together, and so ordered to enable the citizens to cooperate to eliminate the evils and acquire the goods. He should inquire into everything given by the celestial bodies. Those of them that are in any way helpful and suitable, or in any way useful, in the achievement of happiness, he should maintain and emphasize; those of them that are harmful he should try to turn into useful things; and those of them that cannot be turned

---

1   *prime matter* In Aristotle, this is the material stuff of which everything is made, thought of as stripped of all its form (characteristics).

into useful things he should destroy or reduce in power. In general, he should seek to destroy all the evils and bring into existence all the goods.

Each one of the citizens of the virtuous city is required to know the highest principles of the beings and their ranks of order, happiness, the supreme rulership of the virtuous city, and the ruling ranks of order in it; then, after that, the specified actions that, when performed, lead to the attainment of happiness. These actions are not merely to be known; they should be done and the citizens of the city should be directed to do them.

The principles of the beings, their ranks of order, happiness, and the rulership of the virtuous cities, are either cognized and intellected by man, or he imagines them. To cognize them is to have their essences, as they really are, imprinted in man's soul. To imagine them is to have imprinted in man's soul their images, representations of them, or matters that are imitations of them. This is analogous to what takes place with regard to visible objects, for instance, man. We see him himself, we see a representation of him, we see his image reflected in water and other reflecting substances, and we see the image of a representation of him reflected in water and in other reflecting substances. Our seeing him himself is like the intellect's cognition of the principles of the beings, of happiness, and so forth; while our seeing the reflection of man in water and our seeing a representation of him is like imagination, for our seeing a representation of him or our seeing his reflection in a mirror is seeing that which is an imitation of him. Similarly, when we imagine those things, we are in fact having a cognition of matters that are imitations of them rather than a cognition of them themselves.

Most men, either by nature or by habit, are unable to comprehend and cognize those things; these are the men for whom one ought to represent the manner in which the principles of the beings, their ranks of order, the Active Intellect, and the supreme rulership, exist through things that are imitations of them. Now while the meanings and essences of those things are one and immutable, the matters by which they are imitated are many and varied. Some imitate them more closely, while others do so only remotely—just as is the case with visible objects: for the image of man that is seen reflected in water is closer to the true man than the image of a representation of man that is seen reflected in water. Therefore, it is possible to imitate these things for each group and each nation, using matters that are different in each case. Consequently, there may be a number of virtuous nations and virtuous cities whose religions are

different, even though they all pursue the very same kind of happiness. For religion is but the impressions of these things or the impressions of their images, imprinted in the soul. Because it is difficult for the multitude to comprehend these things themselves as they are, the attempt was made to teach them these things in other ways, which are the ways of imitation. Hence these things are imitated for each group or nation through the matters that are best known to them; and it may very well be that what is best known to the one may not be the best known to the other.

Most men who strive for happiness, follow after an imagined, not a cognized, form of happiness. Similarly, most men accept such principles as are accepted and followed, and are magnified and considered majestic, in the form of images, not of cognitions. Now the ones who follow after happiness as they cognize it and accept the principles as they cognize them, are the wise men. And the ones in whose souls these things are found in the form of images, and who accept them and follow after them as such, are the believers.

The imitations of those things differ in excellence: some of them are better and more perfect imaginative representations, while others are less perfect; some are closer to, others are more removed from, the truth. In some the points of contention are few or unnoticeable, or it is difficult to contend against them, while in others the points of contention are many or easy to detect, or it is easy to contend against them and to refute them. It is also possible that those things be presented to the imagination of men by means of various matters, but that, despite their variety, these matters bear a certain relation to each other: that is, there are certain matters that are the imitations of those things, a second set that are the imitations of these matters, and a third set that are the imitations of the second. Finally, the various matters that are the imitations of those things—that is, of the principles of the beings and of happiness—may be on the same level as imitations. Now if they are of equal excellence as regards imitation, or with respect to having only a few or unnoticeable points of contention, then one can use all or anyone of them indifferently. But if they are not of equal excellence, one should choose the ones that are the most perfect imitations and that either are completely free of points of contention or in which the points of contention are few or unnoticeable; next, those that are closer to the truth; and discard all other imitations.

The virtuous city is the opposite of (*A*) the ignorant city, (*B*) the immoral city, and (*C*) the erring city. (*D*) Then there are the Weeds in the virtuous city. (The position of the Weeds in the cities is like that of the darnel[1] among the wheat, the thorns growing among the crop, or the other grass that is useless or even harmful to the crop or plants.) Finally, there are the men who are bestial by nature. But the bestial by nature are neither political beings nor could they ever form a political association. Instead, some of them are like gregarious beasts and others are like wild beasts, and of the latter some are like ravenous beasts. Therefore some of them live isolated in the wilderness, others live there together in depravity like wild beasts, and still others live near the cities. Some eat only raw meats, others graze on wild vegetation, and still others prey on their victims like wild beasts. These are to be found in the extremities of the inhabited earth, either in the far north or in the far south. They must be treated like animals. Those of them that are gregarious and are in some way useful to the cities, should be spared, enslaved, and employed like beasts of burden. Those of them from whom no use can be derived or who are harmful, should be treated as one treats all other harmful animals. The same applies to those children of the citizens of the cities who turn out to have a bestial nature.

A. The Ignorant Cities

As for the citizens of the ignorant cities, they are political beings. Their cities and their political associations are of many kinds, which comprise (i) indispensable associations, (ii) the association of vile men in the vile cities, (iii) the association of base men in the base cities, (iv) timocratic[2] association in the timocratic city, (v) despotic association in the despotic cities, (vi) free association in the democratic city and the city of the free.

1. The Indispensable City

The indispensable city or the indispensable association is that which leads to cooperation to acquire the bare necessities for the subsistence and the safeguarding of the body. There are many ways to acquire these things, such as hus-

bandry, grazing, hunting, robbery, and so forth. Both hunting and robbery are practiced either by stealth or openly. There are certain indispensable cities that possess all the arts that lead to the acquisition of the bare necessities. In others the bare necessities are obtained through one art only, such as husbandry alone or any other art. The citizens of this city regard the best man to be the one who is most excellent in skill, management, and accomplishment in obtaining the bare necessities through the ways of acquisition that they employ. Their ruler is he who can govern well and is skillful in employing them to acquire the indispensable things, who can govern them well so as to preserve these things for them, or who generously provides them with these things from his own possessions.

2. The Vile City

The vile city or the association of the vile citizens is that whose members (a) cooperate to acquire wealth and prosperity, the excessive possession of indispensable things or their equivalent in coin and in money, and their accumulation beyond the need for them and for no other reason than the love and covetousness of wealth; and (b) avoid spending any of it except on what is necessary for bodily subsistence. This they do either by pursuing all the modes of acquisition or else such modes as are available in that country. They regard the best men to be the wealthiest and the most skillful in the acquisition of wealth. Their ruler is the man who is able to manage them well in what leads them to acquire wealth and always to remain wealthy. Wealth is obtained through all the methods employed to obtain the bare necessities, that is, husbandry, grazing, hunting, and robbery; and also through voluntary transactions like commerce, lease, and so forth.

3. The Base City

The base city or the base association is that in which the citizens cooperate to enjoy sensual pleasures or imaginary pleasures (play and amusement) or both. They enjoy the pleasures of food, drink, and copulation, and strive after what is most pleasant of these, in the pursuit of pleasure alone, rather than what sustains, or is in any way useful to, the body; and they do the same as regards play and amusement. This city is the one regarded by the citizens of the ignorant city as the happy and admirable city; for they can attain the goal of this city only after having acquired the bare necessities and acquired wealth, and only by means of much expenditure. They regard whoever possesses more

---

1   *darnel*   Weedy grass, found in grain fields.
2   *timocratic*   Aristotle and Plato used the Greek word *timokratia*, rendered into English as "timocracy," in two senses: (a) to designate a state which required a certain level of property of political office-holders, and (b) to designate a state in which the pursuit of honor is the dominant political principle motivating rulers. Al-Fārābī's discussion below of the "timocratic state" shows that he had the second primarily in mind, though there is (as in the ancient Greeks) something of an association with the first.

resources for play and the pleasures as the best, the happiest, and the most enviable man.

4. The Timocratic City

The timocratic city or the timocratic association is that in which the citizens cooperate with a view to be honored in speech and deed: that is, to be honored either by the citizens of other cities or by one another. Their honoring of one another consists in the exchange of either equal or unequal honors. The exchange of equal honors takes place through someone bestowing on someone else a certain kind of honor at a certain time so that the latter may at another time return the same kind of honor or another kind of honor that, in their eyes, is of equal worth. The exchange of unequal honors takes place through someone bestowing a certain kind of honor on someone else, with the latter bestowing on the former another kind of honor of greater worth than the first. In every case, moreover, this [exchange of unequal honors] among them takes place on the basis of merit (one of two men merits an honor of a certain worth, while the other merits a greater one), depending on what they consider merit to be. In the eyes of the citizens of the ignorant city, merits are not based on virtue, but (a) on wealth, or (b) on possessing the means of pleasure and play and on obtaining the most of both, or (c) on obtaining most of the necessities of life (when man is served and is well provided with all the necessities he needs), or (d) on man's being useful, that is, doing good to others with respect to these three things. (e) There is one more thing that is well liked by most of the citizens of the ignorant cities, that is, domination. For whoever achieves it is envied by most of them. Therefore this, too, must be regarded as one of the merits in the ignorant cities. For, in their eyes, the highest matter for which a man must be honored is his fame in achieving domination [that is, superiority] in one, two, or many things; not being dominated, because he himself is strong, because his supporters are either numerous or strong, or because of both; and that he be immune to being harmed by others, while able to harm others at will. For, in their eyes, this is a state of felicity for which a man merits honor; hence the better he is in this respect, the more he is honored. Or the man [whom they honor] possesses, in their eyes, distinguished ancestors. But ancestors are distinguished because of the things mentioned above: namely, one's fathers and grandfathers were either wealthy, abundantly favored with pleasure and the means to it, had domination [that is, were superior] in a number of things, were useful to others—

be they a group or the citizens of a city—with respect to these things, or were favored with the instruments of these things, such as nobility, endurance, or the contempt of death, all of which are instruments of domination. Honors of equal worth, on the other hand, are sometimes merited by virtue of an external possession, and sometimes honor itself is the reason for the merit, so that the one who begins and honors someone else merits thereby to be honored by the other, as is the case in market transactions.

Thus, in their eyes, the one who merits more honor rules over the one who merits less of it. This inequality continues on an ascending scale terminating in the one who merits more honors than anyone else in the city. This, therefore, will be the ruler and the prince of the city. By virtue of this office, he ought to be of greater merit than all the rest. Now we have already enumerated what they consider to be the bases of merit. Accordingly, if honor, according to them, is based on distinguished ancestry alone, the ruler ought to have a more distinguished ancestry than the others; and similarly if honor, according to them, is based on wealth alone. Next, men are distinguished and given ranks of order according to their wealth and ancestry; and whoever lacks both wealth and a distinguished ancestry will have no claim to any rulership or honor. Such, then, is the case when merits are based on matters that are good to their possessor alone; and these are the lowest among timocratic rulers. When, on the other hand, the ruler is honored because of his usefulness to the citizens of the city in their pursuits and wishes, it is then because he benefits them with regard to wealth or pleasure; or because he brings others to honor the citizens of the city or to provide them with the other things desired by them; or because he supplies them with these things from his own or he enables them to obtain and preserve them through his good governance. Of such rulers, they consider the best to be the one who provides the citizens of the city with these things without seeking anything for himself except honor: for instance, the one who provides them with wealth or the pleasures without desiring any for himself, but rather seeks only honor (praise, respect, and exaltation in speech and deed), to become famous for it among all nations in his own lifetime and after, and to be remembered for a long time. This is the one who, in their eyes, merits honor. Often, such a man requires money and wealth to spend it on what enables the citizens of the city to fulfill their desires for wealth or pleasure or both, and on what helps them to preserve these things. The more he does in this respect, the greater his wealth must be. His wealth becomes a reserve for the citizens of the city. This is the reason why some of these rulers seek wealth and regard their expenditures as an act of generosity and liberality. They collect this money from the city in the form of taxes, or they conquer another group—other, that is, than the citizens of the city—for its money, which they bring to their treasury. They keep it as a reserve out of which they disburse great expenditures in the city in order to obtain greater honor. The one who covets honor by whatever means, may also claim distinguished ancestry for himself and his offspring after him; and so that his fame survive through his offspring, he designates his immediate offspring or members of his family as his successors. Furthermore, he may appropriate a certain amount of wealth for himself to be honored for it, even though it is of no benefit to others. Also, he honors a certain group so that they may honor him in return. He thus possesses all the things for which men may honor him, reserving for himself alone the things regarded by them as manifesting splendor, embellishment, eminence, and magnificence—such as buildings, costumes, and medals, and, finally, inaccessibility to people. Further, he lays down the laws concerning honors. Once he assumes a certain office and people are accustomed to the fact that he and his family will be their princes, he then orders the people into ranks in such a way as to obtain honor and majesty. To each kind of rank, he assigns (a) a kind of honor and (b) things by virtue of which one merits honor, such as wealth, building, costume, medal, carriage, and so forth, and which contribute to his majesty; and he arranges all this in a definite order. Furthermore, he will show special preference for those men who honor him more or contribute more to the enhancement of his majesty, and he confers honor and distributes favor accordingly. The citizens of his city who covet honor keep honoring him until he acknowledges what they have done and confers honors on them, because of which they will be honored by their inferiors and superiors.

For all these reasons, this city can be likened to the virtuous city, especially when the honors, and men's ranks of order with respect to honors, are conferred because of other, more useful things: for example, wealth, pleasures, or anything else that is desired by whoever seeks after useful things. This city is the best among the ignorant cities; unlike those of the others, its citizens are [more properly] called "ignorant" and so forth. However, when their love of honor becomes excessive, it becomes a city of tyrants, and it is more likely to change into a despotic city.

5. The Despotic City

The despotic city or the despotic association is that in which the members cooperate to achieve domination. This happens when they are all seized by the love of domination, provided that it is in different degrees, and that they seek different kinds of domination and different things for the sake of which to dominate other men; for instance, some like to dominate another man in order to spill his blood, others, to take his property, still others, to possess him so that they may enslave him. People occupy different ranks of order in this city depending on the extent of one's love of domination. Its citizens love to dominate others in order to spill their blood and kill them, to possess them so that they may enslave them, or in order to take their property. In all this, what they love and aim at is to dominate, subdue, and humiliate others, and that the subdued should have no control whatever over himself or any of the things because of which he has been dominated, but should do as the subduer commands and wishes. (Indeed when the lover of domination and subjugation—who is inclined to, or desires, a certain thing obtains it without having to subdue someone else, he does not take it and pays no attention to it.) Some of them choose to dominate through wiliness, others, through open combat alone, and still others, through both wiliness and open combat. Therefore many of those who subjugate others in order to spill their blood, do not kill a man when asleep and do not seize his property until they first wake him up; they prefer to engage him in combat and to be faced with some resistance in order to subdue him and harm him. Since everyone of them loves to dominate the others, each one loves to dominate everyone else, whether a fellow citizen or not. They refrain from dominating one another as regards the spilling of blood or the taking of property, only because they need one another so as to survive, cooperate in dominating others, and defend themselves against outside domination.

Their ruler is he who shows greater strength in governing well with a view to employing them to dominate others; who is the wiliest of them; and who has the soundest judgment about what they ought to do in order to continue to dominate forever and never be dominated by others. Such is their ruler and prince. They are the enemies of all other men.

All their laws and usages are such that, when followed, they enable them better to dominate others. Their rivalries and contentions center on how many times they dominate others or on the extent of their domination, or else on the abundant possession of the equipment and instruments of domination. (The equipment and instruments of domination exist either in man's mind, in his body, or in what is external to his body: in his body, like endurance; external to his body, like arms; and in his mind, like sound judgment regarding that which enables him to dominate others.) At times, such men become rude, cruel, irascible, extravagant, and excessively gluttonous; they consume great quantities of food and drink, overindulge in copulation, and fight each other for all the goods, which they obtain through subjugating and humiliating those who possess them. They think that they should dominate everything and everybody.

(1) Sometimes this is true of the entire city, whose citizens will then choose to dominate those outside the city for no other reason than the citizens' need for association [and hence for a common cause that would promote it]. (2) Sometimes the vanquished and the subjugators live side by side in a single city. The subjugators then either (a) love to subjugate and dominate others to the same degree and hence have the same rank of order in the city, or (b) they occupy various ranks of order, each one of them having a certain kind of domination over their vanquished neighbors, which is lesser or greater than that of the other. In this way, and depending on the power and judgment through which they achieve domination, they occupy their respective places next to a prince who rules them and manages the subjugators' affairs as regards the instruments they use for subjugation. (3) And sometimes there is but a single subjugator, with a group of men as his instruments for subjugating all other men. The group in question does not seek to enable him to dominate and seize something for someone else's sake, but so that he dominate something that would belong to him alone. The single subjugator, in turn, is satisfied with what maintains his life and strength; he gives [the rest] to the others and dominates for the sake of the others, like dogs and falcons do. The rest of the citizens of the city, too, are slaves to that one, serving his every wish; they are submissive and humiliated, possessing nothing whatever of their own. Some of them cultivate the soil, others trade, for him. In all this, he has no other purpose beyond seeing a certain group subjugated and dominated and submissive to him alone, even though he derives no benefit or pleasure from them except that of seeing them humiliated and dominated. This (3), then, is the city whose prince alone is despotic, while the rest of its citizens are not despotic. In the one that preceded it (2), half of the city is despotic. In the first (1), all the citizens are despotic.

The despotic city may thus have such a character that it employs one of these methods in the pursuit of domination alone and the enjoyment of it. But if domination is loved only as a means for the acquisition of bare necessities, prosperity, the enjoyment of pleasures, honors, or all of these together, then this is a despotic city of a different sort; and its citizens belong to the other cities mentioned above. Most people call such cities despotic; but this name applies more properly to the one among them that seeks all of these (three?)[1] things by means of subjugation. There are three sorts of such cities: that is, (3) one of the citizens, (2) half of them, or (1) all of them are despotic. But they [that is, the citizens of these cities], too, do not pursue subjugation and maltreatment for their own sake; rather they pursue, and aim at, something else.

There are, further, other cities that aim at something else and at domination as well. The first of these cities, which aims at domination however and for whatever it may be, may include someone who inflicts harm on others without any benefit to himself, such as to murder for no other reason than the pleasure of subjugation alone; its citizens fight for the sake of base things, as it is told about some of the Arabs. In the second, the citizens love domination for the sake of certain things that they regard as praiseworthy and lofty, not lowly; and when they attain these things without subjugating others, they do not resort to it. The third city does not harm or murder, unless it knows that this enhances one of its noble qualities. Hence when one [of its citizens] gets to the things he wants, without having to dominate and subjugate others—for instance, when the thing exists in abundance, when someone else takes care of seizing it for him, or when someone else gives him the thing voluntarily he will not harm others, remains indifferent to the thing in question, and does not take it from others. Such individuals are also called high-minded and manly. The citizens of the first city confine themselves to such subjugation as is indispensable for the achievement of domination. Sometimes they strive and struggle very hard to possess a certain property or human soul that is denied to them, and they persist until they get it and are able to do with it whatever they please; but at this point they turn away and do not seize it. Such men may also be praised, honored, and respected for

---

1 (three?) This word appears to be an interpolation. It is, however, present in all the manuscripts. Feyzullah punctuates the preceding enumeration in such a manner that it is subdivided into three parts: "bare necessities, prosperity, or the enjoyment of pleasures; honors; or all of these together."

what they do; also, those who seek honor do most of these things so that they may be honored for them. Despotic cities are more often tyrannical than timocratic.

Sometimes the citizens of the [vile or] plutocratic[1] city and the citizens of the [base] city that is dedicated to play and amusement imagine that they are the ones who are lucky, happy, and successful, and that they are more excellent than the citizens of all other cities. These delusions about themselves sometimes lead them to become contemptuous of the citizens of other cities and to suppose that others have no worth, and to love to be honored for whatever caused their happiness. Consequently, they develop traits of arrogance, extravagance, boastfulness, and the love of praise, and suppose that others cannot attain what they themselves have attained, and that the others are therefore too stupid to achieve these two kinds of happiness [which result from wealth, and play and amusement, respectively]. They create for themselves titles with which they embellish their ways of life, such as that they are the talented and the elegant, and that the others are the rude. Therefore they are supposed to be men of pride, magnanimity, and authority. Sometimes they are even called high-minded.

When the lovers of wealth and the lovers of pleasure and play do not happen to possess any of the arts by which wealth is obtained except the power to dominate, and they achieve wealth and play by subjugation and domination, then they become extremely arrogant and join the ranks of tyrants (in contrast, the former group are simply idiots). Similarly, it is possible to find among the lovers of honor some who love it, not for its own sake, but for the sake of wealth. For many of them seek to be honored by others in order to obtain wealth, either from those others or from someone else. They seek to rule, and to be obeyed by, the citizens of the city in order to obtain wealth alone. Many of these seek wealth for the sake of play and pleasure. Thus they seek to rule and to be obeyed in order to obtain wealth to make use of it in play; and they think that the greater and the more complete their authority and the obedience of others to them, the greater their share of these things. Hence they desire to be the sole rulers over the citizens of the city in order to possess majesty, by which to achieve great and incomparable wealth in order to make use of it in obtaining a measure of play and pleasures (food, drink, sex) that no one else can obtain both as regards its quantity and quality.

---

1 *plutocratic*   Ruled by the wealthy.

6. The Democratic City

The democratic city is the one in which each one of the citizens is given free rein and left alone to do whatever he likes. Its citizens are equal and their laws say that no man is in any way at all better than any other man. Its citizens are free to do whatever they like; and no one, be he one of them or an outsider, has any claim to authority unless he works to enhance their freedom. Consequently, they develop many kinds of morals, inclinations, and desires, and they take pleasure in countless things. Its citizens consist of countless similar and dissimilar groups. This city brings together the groups—both the base and the noble—that existed separately in all the other cities; and positions of authority are obtained here by means of anyone of the things we have mentioned. Those from among the multitude of this city, who possess whatever the rulers possess, have the upper hand over those who are called their rulers. Those who rule them do so by the will of the ruled, and the rulers follow the wishes of the ruled. Close investigation of their situation would reveal that, in truth, there is no distinction between ruler and ruled among them. However, they praise and honor those who lead the citizens of the city to freedom and to whatever the citizens like and desire, and who safeguard the citizens' freedom and their varied and different desires against [infringement] by one another and by outside enemies; and who limit their own desires to bare necessities. Such, then, is the one who is honored, regarded as the best, and is obeyed among them. As to any other ruler, he is either (*a*) their equal or (*b*) their inferior. (*a*) He is their equal when it happens that, when he provides them with the good things that they want and desire, they reciprocate with comparable honors and wealth. In this case they do not consider him to be superior to them. (*b*) They are his superiors when they accord him honors and allot him a share of their possessions, without receiving any benefit from him in return. For it is quite possible to find in this city a ruler in this situation: he happens to be magnified in the eyes of the citizens either because they take a fancy to him or because his ancestors ruled them well and they let him rule in gratitude for what his ancestors did. In this case, the multitude would have the upper hand over the rulers.

All the endeavors and purposes of the ignorant cities are present in this city in a most perfect manner; of all of them, this is the most admirable and happy city. On the surface, it looks like an embroidered garment full of colored figures and dyes. Everybody loves it and loves to reside in it, because there is no human wish or desire that this city does not satisfy. The nations emigrate to it and reside there, and it grows beyond measure. People of every race multiply in it, and this by all kinds of copulation and marriages, resulting in children of extremely varied dispositions, with extremely varied education and upbringing. Consequently, this city develops into many cities, distinct yet intertwined, with the parts of each scattered throughout the parts of the others. Strangers cannot be distinguished from the residents. All kinds of wishes and ways of life are to be found in it. Consequently, it is quite possible that, with the passage of time, virtuous men will grow up in it. Thus it may include philosophers, rhetoricians, and poets, dealing with all kinds of things. It is also possible to glean from it certain [men who form] parts of the virtuous city; this is the best thing that takes place in this city. Therefore, this city possesses both good and evil to a greater degree than the rest of the ignorant cities. The bigger, the more civilized, the more populated, the more productive, and the more perfect it is, the more prevalent and the greater are the good and the evil it possesses.

There are as many aims pursued by the ignorant rulerships as there are ignorant cities. Every ignorant rulership aims at having its fill of bare necessities; wealth; delight in the pleasures; honor, reputation, and praise; domination; or freedom. Therefore, such rulerships are actually bought for a price, especially the positions of authority in the democratic city; for here no one has a better claim than anyone else to a position of authority. Therefore, when someone finally holds a position of authority, it is either because the citizens have favored him with it, or else because they have received from him money or something else in return. In their eyes the virtuous ruler is he who has the ability to judge well and to contrive well what enables them to attain their diverse and variegated desires and wishes, safeguards them against their enemies, and takes nothing of their property, but confines himself to the bare necessities of life. As for the truly virtuous man—namely the man who, if he were to rule them, would determine and direct their actions toward happiness—they do not make him a ruler. If by chance he comes to rule them, he will soon find himself either deposed or killed or in an unstable and challenged position. And so are all the other ignorant cities; each one of them only wants the ruler who facilitates the attainment of its wishes and desires, and paves the way for their acquisition and preservation. Therefore, they refuse the rule of virtuous men and resent it. Nevertheless, the construction of virtuous cities and the establishment of the rule of virtuous men are more effective and much easier out of the

indispensable and democratic cities than out of any other ignorant city.

Bare necessity, wealth, the enjoyment of the pleasures and of play, and honors may be attained by subjugation and domination, or they may be attained by other means. Hence the four cities [the indispensable, vile, base, and timocratic] can be subdivided accordingly. Similarly, the rule that aims at these four things, or anyone of them, pursues the achievement of its aim by domination and subjugation, or else pursues it by other means. Those who acquire these things by domination and subjugation, and safeguard what they have acquired by force and compulsion, need to be strong and powerful in body, and to be fierce, rough, rude, and contemptuous of death in moral traits, and not to prefer life to these pursuits; they need skill in the use of arms, and good judgment as regards the means of subjugating others: all this applies to all of them.

But as to the pleasure seekers [that is, the citizens of the base city], they develop, in addition, gluttony and lust for food, drink, and sex. Some of them are dominated by softness and luxury, weakening their irascible faculty to the extent that none or very little of it remains. Others are dominated by anger and its psychical and bodily instruments, and by the appetite and its psychical and bodily instruments, which strengthens and intensifies these two faculties, and facilitates the performance of their functions. Their judgment will be equally devoted to the actions of these two faculties, and their souls equally subservient to them. Of these, the final objective of some are the actions of the appetite. Thus they turn their irascible faculties and actions into instruments by which to achieve the appetitive actions, thus subordinating lofty and higher faculties to the lower; that is, they subordinate their rational faculty to the irascible and appetitive, and further, the irascible faculty to the appetitive. For they devote their judgment to the discovery of what fulfils the irascible and appetitive actions, and devote the actions and instruments of their irascible faculties to what enables them to attain the enjoyment of the pleasures of food, drink, and sex, and all that enables them to seize and safeguard them for themselves, such as you see in the notables of the dwellers of the steppes from among the Arabs and the Turks. For the dwellers of the steppes generally love domination, and have insatiable lust for food, drink, and sex. Consequently, women are of great importance to them, and many of them approve of licentiousness, not considering it as being a degeneration and vileness since their souls are subservient to their appetites. You also see that many of them try to please women in everything they do, in order to gain importance in the eyes of women, considering disgraceful whatever women consider to be disgraceful, fair what women consider to be fair. In everything they do, they follow the desires of their women. In many cases, their women have the upper hand over them and control the affairs of their households. For this reason many of them accustom their women to luxury by shielding them from hard work and keeping them instead in luxury and comfort, while they themselves undertake to do everything that requires toil and labor and the endurance of pain and hardship.

B. The Immoral Cities

Immoral cities are the ones whose citizens once believed in, and cognized, the principles [of beings]; imagined, and believed in, what happiness is; and were guided toward, knew, and believed in, the actions by which to attain happiness. Nevertheless, they did not adhere to any of those actions, but came to desire and will one or another of the aims of the citizens of the ignorant cities—such as honor, domination, and so forth—and directed all their actions and faculties toward them. There are as many kinds of these [immoral] cities as there are ignorant cities, inasmuch as all their actions and morals are identical with those of the ignorant cities. They differ from the citizens of the ignorant cities only in the opinions in which they believe. Not one of the citizens of these cities can attain happiness at all.

C. The Erring Cities

Erring cities are those whose citizens are given imitations of other matters than the ones we mentioned—that is, the principles that are established for, and imitated to, them are other than the ones we mentioned; a kind of happiness that is not true happiness is established for, and represented to, them; and actions and opinions are prescribed for them by none of which true happiness can be attained.

D. The Weeds in Virtuous Cities

The Weeds within the virtuous cities are of many classes. (i) [Members of] one class adhere to the actions conducive to the attainment of happiness; however, they do not do such actions in the pursuit of happiness, but rather of other things that man can attain by means of virtue, such as honor, ruler-

ship, wealth, and so forth. Such individuals are called opportunists (*mutaqannisun*). Some of them have an inclination to one of the ends of the citizens of the ignorant cities and they are prevented by the Laws and the religion of the city from pursuing such ends. Therefore they resort to the expressions of the lawgiver and the statements that embody his precepts, and interpret them as they wish, by which interpretation they make the thing they are after appear good. Such men are called the misinterpreters (*muharrifah*). Others among them do not deliberately misinterpret but, because they do not rightly understand the lawgiver and because of their misconception of his statements, they understand the Laws of the city in a different way than the one intended by the lawgiver. Their actions will therefore not conform to the intention of the supreme ruler. Hence they err without realizing it. These men are the apostates (*mariqah*).

(ii) [Members of] another class do imagine the things we mentioned, yet they are not convinced of what they have imagined of them. Hence they use arguments to falsify them for themselves and for others. In so doing, they are not contending against the virtuous city; rather they are looking for the right path and seeking the truth. He who belongs to this class, should have the level of his imagination raised to things that cannot be falsified by the arguments he has put forward. If he is satisfied with the level to which he has been raised, he should be left alone. But if he is again not satisfied, and discovers here certain places susceptible to contention, then he should be raised to a higher level. This process should continue until he becomes satisfied with one of these levels. And if it happens that he is not satisfied with anyone of these levels of imagination, he should be raised to the level of the truth and be made to comprehend those things as they are, at which point his mind will come to rest.

(iii) [Members of] another class falsify whatever they imagine. Whenever they are raised to a higher level, they falsify it, even when they are conducted to the level of the truth—all this in the pursuit of domination alone, or in the pursuit of ennobling another of the aims of the ignorant cities that is desired by them. They falsify them in every way they can; they do not like to listen to anything that may establish happiness and truth firmly in the soul, or any argument that may ennoble and imprint them in the soul, but meet them with such sham arguments as they think will discredit happiness. Many of them do that with the intention of appearing as having a pretext for turning to one of the aims of the ignorant cities.

(iv) [Members of] another class imagine happiness and the principles [of beings], but their minds are totally lacking in the power to cognize them, or it is beyond the power of their minds to cognize them adequately. Consequently, they falsify the things they imagine and come upon the places of contention in them, and whenever they are raised to a level of imagination that is closer to the truth, they find it to be false. Nor is it possible to raise them to the level of the truth because their minds lack the power to comprehend it. And many of them may find most of what they imagine to be false, not because what they imagine truly contains places of contention, but because they have a defective imagination, and they find these things false because of their defective minds, not because these things contain a place of contention. Many of them—when unable to imagine something sufficiently or discover the real points of contention and in the places where they are to be found, or are unable to comprehend the truth—think that the man who has apprehended the truth and who says that he has apprehended it, is a deliberate liar who is seeking honor or domination, or else think that he is a deluded man. So they try hard to falsify the truth also, and abase the man who has apprehended it. This leads many of them to think that all men are deluded in everything they claim to have apprehended. It leads (1) some of them to a state of perplexity in all things, and (2) others to think that no apprehension whatever is true, and that whenever someone thinks that he has apprehended something that he is lying about it and that he is not sure or certain of what he thinks. These individuals occupy the position of ignorant simpletons in the eyes of reasonable men and in relation to the philosophers. (For this reason it is the duty of the ruler of the virtuous city to look for the Weeds, keep them occupied, and treat each class of them in the particular manner that will cure them: by expelling them from the city, punishing them, jailing them, or forcing them to perform a certain function even though they may not be fond of it.) (3) Others among them think that the truth consists of whatever appears to each individual and what each man thinks it to be at one time or another, and that the truth of everything is what someone thinks it is. (4) Others among them exert themselves to create the illusion that everything that is thought to have been apprehended up to this time is completely false, and that, although a certain truth or reality does exist, it has not as yet been apprehended. (5) Others among them imagine—as if in a dream or as if a thing is seen from a distance—that there is a truth, and it occurs to them that the ones who claim to have ap-

prehended it may have done so, or perhaps that one of them may have apprehended it. They feel that they themselves have missed it, either because they require a long time, and have to toil and exert themselves, in order to apprehend it, when they no longer have sufficient time or the power to toil and persevere; or because they are occupied by certain pleasures and so forth to which they have been accustomed and from which they find it very difficult to free themselves; or because they feel that they cannot apprehend it even if they had access to all the means to it. Consequently, they regret and grieve over what they think others may have attained. Hence, out of jealousy for those who may have apprehended the truth, they think it wise to endeavor, using sham argument, to create the illusion that whoever claims to have apprehended the truth is either deluded or else a liar who is seeking honor, wealth, or some other desirable thing, from the claim he makes. Now many of these perceive their own ignorance and perplexity; they feel sad and suffer pain because of what they perceive to be their condition, they are overcome by anxiety, and it torments them; and they find no way to free themselves of this by means of a science leading them to the truth whose apprehension would give them pleasure. Hence they choose to find rest from all this by turning to the various ends of the ignorant cities, and to find their solace in amusements and games until death comes to relieve them of their burden. Some of these—I mean the ones who seek rest from the torment of ignorance and perplexity—may create the illusion that the [true] ends are those that they themselves choose and desire, that happiness consists of these, and that the rest of men are deluded in what they believe in. They exert themselves to adorn the ends of the ignorant cities and the happiness [that they pursue]. They create the illusion that they have come to prefer some of these ends after a thorough examination of all that the others claim to have apprehended, that they have rejected the latter only after finding out that they are inconclusive, and that their position was arrived at on the basis of personal knowledge—therefore, theirs are the ends, not the ones claimed by the others.

These, then, are the classes of the Weeds growing among the citizens of the city. With such opinions, they constitute neither a city nor a large multitude; rather they are submerged by the citizen body as a whole.

MOSES MAIMONIDES
(1135 – 1204)

MOSES MAIMONIDES IS KNOWN NOW BY A VARIETY OF names. "Maimonides" is the Greek version; "Rabbi Moshe (= Moses) ben Maimon" is the Hebrew; and Jewish scholars often use an acronym of this, "Rambam." However he is named, he is considered the most important medieval Jewish philosopher. His detailed treatment of Jewish law *Mishneh Torah* (c. 1180) was enormously influential; his most important philosophical work, though, was *The Guide for the Perplexed* (c. 1190).

Maimonides was born in Córdoba, in Muslim southern Spain, in 1135. His father, a Jewish scholar, was responsible for much of his early education. After the conquest of Córdoba in 1148 by an intolerant Muslim sect, his family, fleeing forced conversion, escaped to North Africa, where he studied at the university in Fes, Morocco. Continuing to travel, he visited Jerusalem and eventually settled in Egypt, where he lived the last forty years of his life.

Maimonides' philosophical work dealt with, and attempted to reconcile, several great traditions: Jewish law and the commentary on it, Christian and Islamic thought, and the work of Aristotle, whose work had been largely lost to the West after the decline of Rome, but preserved and studied by Arab scholars. Impressed by ancient Greek rationalism, Maimonides aimed at an understanding of religious doctrine in rational terms—terms that were compatible with the discoveries of science.

In the *Guide* he explores issues of how the laws of God are related to secular and religious law, and to the structure of societies. The work is composed of three parts, divided into 178 chapters. In the first part he focuses on questions relating to the nature of God, and in the second on the question of the existence of God. The third part deals with a number of questions, one of which is the nature and role of prophets: since prophets bring God's laws to the people, Maimonides considered it important to be able to tell true from false prophets, and to know what value true prophecy can provide. He argues that divine law is essentially related both to the well-being of our bodies and to the well-being of our souls. The moral virtues that divine law promotes contribute not only to our spiritual well-being, but also to the cohesiveness of society.

Maimonides' idea of the role of politics is very Aristotelian, encompassing the study of the individual human condition and of the good. Like Aristotle, he thinks of humans as essentially social/political animals. The function of a well-ordered state is to facilitate the achievement of our real aim, genuine happiness. Religious and secular law alike, then, function to regulate our lives in accord with the (Aristotelian) "golden mean," to inculcate habits of moral thought and action, to help make us what we can be. The intricacies of traditional Jewish Talmudic law, he argues, can seem arbitrary and useless in this light, and he confesses not to understand the function of some particular requirements; nevertheless, he argues, overall Talmudic law aims at leading us in the direction of divine perfection. Like Aristotle, he stresses the variety of individual personalities, habits, and shortcomings; politics, then, must deal with this diversity, regulating it and producing the most practical arrangement for the best possible social life and the maximum human fulfillment.

In the centuries that followed Maimonides' death, *The Guide for the Perplexed* was read widely by philosophers; it was a strong influence on St. Thomas Aquinas and other Scholastic philosophers as well as on the thought of Leibniz and Spinoza. Though his ideas are today widely studied mostly by Jewish, Christian and Muslim theologians and modern scholars of Judaism, his political and social thought continues to be relevant, especially for those with an interest in contemporary applications of Aristotelian ideas.

◆ ◆ ◆ ◆ ◆

Guide for the Perplexed
(c. 1190)

It has already been fully explained that man is naturally a social being, that by virtue of his nature he seeks to form communities; man is therefore different from other living beings that are not compelled to combine into communities. He is, as you know, the highest form in the creation, and he therefore includes the largest number of constituent elements; this is the reason why the human race contains such a great variety of individuals, that we cannot discover two persons exactly alike in any moral quality, or in external appearance. The cause of this is the variety in man's temperament, and in accidents dependent on his form; for with every physical form there are connected certain special accidents different from those which are connected with the substance.[1] Such a variety among the individuals of a class does not exist in any other class of living beings; for the variety in any other species is limited; only man forms an exception; two persons may be so different from each other in every respect that they appear to belong to two different classes. Whilst one person is so cruel that he kills his youngest child in his anger, another is too delicate and faint-hearted to kill even a fly or worm. The same is the case with most of the accidents. This great variety and the necessity of social life are essential elements in man's nature. But the well-being of society demands that there should be a leader able to regulate the actions of man; he must complete every shortcoming, remove every excess, and prescribe for the conduct of all, so that the natural variety should be counterbalanced by the uniformity of legislation, and the order of society be well established. I therefore maintain that the Law, though not a product of Nature, is nevertheless not entirely foreign to Nature. It being the will of God that

our race should exist and be permanently established, He in His wisdom gave it such properties that men can acquire the capacity of ruling others. Some persons are therefore inspired with theories of legislation, such as prophets and lawgivers; others possess the power of enforcing the dictates of the former, and of compelling people to obey them, and to act accordingly. Such are kings, who accept the code of lawgivers, and [rulers] who pretend to be prophets, and accept, either entirely or partly, the teaching of the prophets. They accept one part while rejecting another part, either because this course appears to them more convenient, or out of ambition, because it might lead people to believe that the rulers themselves had been prophetically inspired with these laws, and did not copy them from others. For when we like a certain perfection, find pleasure in it, and wish to possess it, we sometimes desire to make others believe that we possess that virtue, although we are fully aware that we do not possess it. Thus people, e.g., adorn themselves with the poems of others, and publish them as their own productions. It also occurs in the works of wise men on the various branches of Science, that an ambitious, lazy person sees an opinion expressed by another person, appropriates it, and boasts that he himself originated it.

The same [ambition] occurs also with regard to the faculty of prophecy. There were men who, like Zedekiah, the son of Chenaanah[2] boasted that they received a prophecy, and declared things which have never been prophesied. Others, like Hananiah, son of Azzur,[3] claim the capacity of prophecy, and proclaim things which, no doubt, have been said by God, that is to say, that have been the subject of a divine inspiration, but not to them. They nevertheless say that they are prophets, and adorn themselves with the prophecies of others. All this can easily be ascertained and recognized. I will, however, fully explain this to you, so that no doubt be left to you on this question, and that you may have a test by which you may distinguish between the guidance of human legislation, of the divine law, and of teachings stolen from prophets. As regards those who declare that the laws proclaimed by them are their own ideas, no further test is required; the confession of the defendant makes the evidence of the witness superfluous. I only wish to instruct you about laws which are proclaimed as prophetic. Some of these are truly prophetic, originating in divine inspiration, some are of non-prophetic character, and some, though

---

1   *accidents, form, substance* Accidents are contingent, non-essential properties or attributes. In this sense, being a mammal is (perhaps) an essential (non-accidental) property of a dog—it couldn't be a dog if it weren't an animal—but being brown is an accidental property. A substance (for Aristotle) is the thing itself; its form is its organizational structure—the structure of anything of the same sort. An "accident of form" might therefore be a non-essential variation in the general organization of a type of thing, typical to that type of thing, in contrast to an accident merely pertaining to a substance—a variation in individuals. Having a sheep-herding instinct is an accident relative to dogs in general—it isn't essential for being a dog—but it is a variation typical to the type *dog*.

2   *Zedekiah, the son of Chenaanah* See 1 Kings 22.11, 24.
3   *Hananiah, son of Azzur* See Jeremiah 28.1-5.

prophetic originally, are the result of plagiarism. You will find that the sole object of certain laws, in accordance with the intention of their author, who well considered their effect, is to establish the good order of the state and its affairs, to free it from all mischief and wrong; these laws do not deal with philosophic problems, contain no teaching for the perfecting of our logical faculties, and are not concerned about the existence of sound or unsound opinions. Their sole object is to arrange, under all circumstances, the relations of men to each other, and to secure their well-being, in accordance with the view of the author of these laws. These laws are political, and their author belongs, as has been stated above, to the third class, viz., to those who only distinguish themselves by the perfection of their imaginative faculties. You will also find laws which, in all their rules, aim, as the law just mentioned, at the improvement of the material interests of the people; but, besides, tend to improve the state of the faith of man, to create first correct notions of God, and of angels, and to lead then the people, by instruction and education, to an accurate knowledge of the Universe: this education comes from God; these laws are divine. The question which now remains to be settled is this: Is the person who proclaimed these laws the same perfect man that received them by prophetic inspiration, or a plagiarist, who has stolen these ideas from a true prophet? In order to be enabled to answer this question, we must examine the merits of the person, obtain an accurate account of his actions, and consider his character. The best test is the rejection, abstention, and contempt of bodily pleasures; for this is the first condition of men, and *a fortiori*[1] of prophets; they must especially disregard pleasures of the sense of touch, which, according to Aristotle,[2] is a disgrace to us; and, above all, restrain from the pollution of sensual intercourse. Thus God exposes thereby false prophets to public shame, in order that those who really seek the truth may find it, and not err or go astray; e.g., Zedekiah, son of Maasiah, and Ahab, son of Kolaiah, boasted that they had received a prophecy. They persuaded the people to follow them, by proclaiming utterances of other prophets; but all the time they continued to seek the low pleasures of sensual intercourse, committing even adultery with the wives of their companions and followers. God exposed their falsehood as He has exposed that of other false prophets. The king of Babylon burnt them, as

Jeremiah distinctly states: "And of them shall be taken up a curse by all the captivity of Judah, which are in Babylon, saying, The Lord make thee like Zedekiah, and like Ahab, whom the king of Babylon roasted in the fire. Because they have committed villainy in Israel, and have committed adultery with their neighbors' wives, and have spoken lying words in my name. which I have not commanded them."[3] Note what is meant by these words.

from *Part 3, Chapter 27*

The general object of the Law is twofold: the well-being of the soul, and the well-being of the body. The well-being of the soul is promoted by correct opinions communicated to the people according to their capacity. Some of these opinions are therefore imparted in a plain form, others allegorically; because certain opinions are in their plain form too strong for the capacity of the common people. The well-being of the body is established by a proper management of the relations in which we live one to another. This we can attain in two ways: first by removing all violence from our midst; that is to say, that we do not do every one as he pleases, desires, and is able to do; but everyone of us does that which contributes towards the common welfare. Secondly, by teaching every one of us such good morals as must produce a good social state. Of these two objects, the one, the well-being of the soul, or the communication of correct opinions, comes undoubtedly first in rank, but the other, the well-being of the body, the government of the state, and the establishment of the best possible relations among men, is anterior in nature and time. The latter object is required first; it is also treated [in the Law] most carefully and most minutely, because the well-being of the soul can only be obtained after that of the body has been secured. For it has already been found that man has a double perfection: the first perfection is that of the body, and the second perfection is that of the soul. The first consists in the most healthy condition of his material relations, and this is only possible when man has all his wants supplied, as they arise; if he has his food, and other things needful for his body, e.g., shelter, bath, and the like. But one man alone cannot procure all this; it is impossible for a single man to obtain this comfort; it is only possible in society, since man, as is well known, is by nature social.

The second perfection of man consists in his becoming an actually intelligent being; i.e., he knows about the things

---

1 *a fortiori* Latin: more so, for a stronger reason.

2 *they must ... to Aristotle* Aristotle, *Nicomachean Ethics* (3, 10). Some commentators believe that this is Maimonides' attempt to discredit Mohammed.

3 *And of ... commanded them* Jeremiah 29.22, 23.

in existence all that a person perfectly developed is capable of knowing. This second perfection certainly does not include any action or good conduct, but only knowledge, which is arrived at by speculation, or established by research.

It is clear that the second and superior kind of perfection can only be attained when the first perfection has been acquired; for a person that is suffering from great hunger, thirst, heat, or cold, cannot grasp an idea even if communicated by others, much less can he arrive at it by his own reasoning. But when a person is in possession of the first perfection, then he may possibly acquire the second perfection, which is undoubtedly of a superior kind, and is alone the source of eternal life. The true Law, which as we said is one, and beside which there is no other Law, viz., the Law of our teacher Moses, has for its purpose to give us the twofold perfection. It aims first at the establishment of good mutual relations among men by removing injustice and creating the noblest feelings. In this way the people in every land are enabled to stay and continue in one condition, and every one can acquire his first perfection. Secondly, it seeks to train us in faith, and to impart correct and true opinions when the intellect is sufficiently developed. Compare "And the Lord commanded us to do all these statutes, to fear the Lord our God, for our good always, that he might preserve us alive as it is this day."[1] Here the second perfection is first mentioned because it is of greater importance, being, as we have shown, the ultimate aim of man's existence. This perfection is expressed in the phrase, "for our good always." You know the interpretation of our Sages, "'that it may be well with thee,'[2] namely, in the world that is all good, "and that thou mayest prolong thy days,"[3] i.e., in the world that is all eternal." In the same sense I explain the words, "for our good always," to mean that we may come into the world that is all good and eternal, where we may live permanently; and the words, "that he might preserve us alive as it is this day," I explain as referring to our first and temporal existence, to that of our body, which cannot be in a perfect and good condition except by the co-operation of society, as has been shown by us.

from *Part 3, Chapter 28*

It is necessary to bear in mind that Scripture only teaches the chief points of those true principles which lead to the true perfection of man, and only demands in general terms faith in them. Thus Scripture teaches the Existence, the Unity, the Omniscience, the Omnipotence, the Will, and the Eternity of God. All this is given in the form of final results, but they cannot be understood fully and accurately except after the acquisition of many kinds of knowledge. Scripture further demands belief in certain truths, the belief in which is indispensable in regulating our social relations; such is the belief that God is angry with those who disobey Him, for it leads us to the fear and dread of disobedience [to the will of God]. There are other truths in reference to the whole of the Universe which form the substance of the various and many kinds of speculative sciences, and afford the means of verifying the above-mentioned principles as their final result. But Scripture does not so distinctly prescribe the belief in them as it does in the first case; it is implied in the commandment, "to love the Lord."[4] It may be inferred from the words, "And thou shalt love the Lord thy God with all thy heart, and with all thy soul, and with all thy might,"[5] what stress is laid on this commandment to love God. We have already shown in the Mishneh-torah[6] that this love is only possible when we comprehend the real nature of things, and understand the divine wisdom displayed therein. We have likewise mentioned there what our Sages remark on this subject.

The result of all these preliminary remarks is this: The reason of a commandment, whether positive or negative, is clear, and its usefulness evident, if it directly tends to remove injustice, or to teach good conduct that furthers the well-being of society, or to impart a truth which ought to be believed either on its own merit or as being indispensable for facilitating the removal of injustice or the teaching of good morals. There is no occasion to ask for the object of such commandments; for no one can, e.g., be in doubt as to the reason why we have been commanded to believe that God is one; why we are forbidden to murder, to steal, and to take vengeance, or to retaliate, or why we are commanded to love one another. But there are precepts concerning which people are in doubt, and of divided opinions,

1   *And the Lord ... this day*   Deuteronomy 6.24.
2   *for our ... with thee*   Deuteronomy 22.7.
3   *and that ... thy days*   Deuteronomy 21.7.

4   *to love the Lord*   Deuteronomy 11.13.
5   *And thou ... thy might*   Deuteronomy 6.5
6   *in the Mishneh-torah*   In *Yes. ha-torah* 2.2.

some believing that they are mere commands, and serve no purpose whatever, whilst others believe that they serve a certain purpose, which, however, is unknown to man. Such are those precepts which in their literal meaning do not seem to further any of the three above-named results: to impart some truth, to teach some moral, or to remove injustice. They do not seem to have any influence upon the well-being of the soul by imparting any truth, or upon the well-being of the body by suggesting such ways and rules as are useful in the government of a state, or in the management of a household. Such are the prohibitions of wearing garments containing wool and linen; of sowing divers seeds, or of boiling meat and milk together; the commandment of covering the blood [of slaughtered beasts and birds], the ceremony of breaking the neck of a calf [in case of a person being found slain, and the murderer being unknown]; the law concerning the first-born of an ass, and the like.[1] I am prepared to tell you my explanation of all these commandments, and to assign for them a true reason supported by proof, with the exception of some minor rules, and of a few commandments, as I have mentioned above. I will show that all these and similar laws must have some bearing upon one of the following three things, viz., the regulation of our opinions, or the improvement of our social relations, which implies two things, the removal of injustice, and the teaching of good morals. Consider what we said of the opinions [implied in the laws]; in some cases the law contains a truth which is itself the only object of that law, as e.g., the truth of the Unity, Eternity, and Incorporeality[2] of God; in other cases, that truth is only the means of securing the removal of injustice, or the acquisition of good morals; such is the belief that God is angry with those who oppress their fellow-men, as it is said, "Mine anger will be kindled, and I will slay,"[3] etc.; or the belief that God hears the crying of the oppressed and vexed, to deliver them out of the hands of the oppressor and tyrant, as it is written, "And it shall come to pass, when he will cry unto me, that I will hear, for I am gracious."[4]

Part 3, Chapter 34

It is also important to note that the Law does not take into account exceptional circumstances; it is not based on conditions which rarely occur. Whatever the Law teaches, whether it be of an intellectual, a moral, or a practical character, is founded on that which is the rule and not on that which is the exception; it ignores the injury that might be caused to a single person through a certain maxim or a certain divine precept. For the Law is a divine institution, and [in order to understand its operation] we must consider how in Nature the various forces produce benefits which are general, but in some solitary cases they cause also injury. This is clear from what has been said by ourselves as well as by others. We must consequently not be surprised when we find that the object of the Law does not fully appear in every individual; there must naturally be people who are not perfected by the instruction of the Law, just as there are beings which do not receive from the specific forms in Nature all that they require. For all this comes from one God, is the result of one act; "they are all given from one shepherd."[5] It is impossible to be otherwise; and we have already explained (chap. xv.) that that which is impossible always remains impossible and never changes. From this consideration it also follows that the laws cannot like medicine vary according to the different conditions of persons and times; whilst the cure of a person depends on his particular constitution at the particular time, the divine guidance contained in the Law must be certain and general, although it may be effective in some cases and ineffective in others. If the Law depended on the varying conditions of man, it would be imperfect in its totality, each precept being left indefinite. For this reason it would not be right to make the fundamental principles of the Law dependent on a certain time or a certain place; on the contrary, the statutes and the judgments must be definite, unconditional, and general, in accordance with the divine words: "As for the congregation, one ordinance shall be for you and for the stranger";[6] they are intended, as has been stated before, for all persons and for all times.

After having premised these introductory remarks I will now proceed to the exposition of that which I intended to explain.

---

1 *the prohibitions ... and the like* Deuteronomy 21.11; Leviticus 29.19; Exodus 23.19; Leviticus 17.13; Deuteronomy 21:1 ff.; Exodus 13.13.
2 *Incorporeality* Not having material—bodily—form.
3 *Mine anger ... will slay* Exodus 22.23.
4 *And it ... am gracious* Exodus 22.25.
5 *they are ... one shepherd* Ecclesiastes 12.11.
6 *As for ... the stranger* Numbers 15.15.

ST. THOMAS AQUINAS
(1225 – 1274)

Who Was St. Thomas Aquinas?

SAINT THOMAS WAS BORN IN 1225 IN ROCCASECCA IN southern Italy, the son of the count of Aquino. At the age of five he was sent to be educated at the great Benedictine abbey of Monte Casino, and at 14 he went to university in Naples. His father expected him to join the respectable and wealthy Benedictine order of monks. However, when he was 19, Aquinas instead joined the recently formed Dominican order of celibate, mendicant (begging) friars. These monks had adopted a life of complete poverty and traveled Europe studying, and teaching the gospel. Thomas' father was outraged, and—according to legend—he locked Aquinas in the family castle for a year and offered him bribes, including a beautiful prostitute, to join the Benedictines instead. Aquinas is said to have grabbed a burning brand from the fire and chased away the prostitute; his family eventually allowed him to leave and travel to Paris.

He went on to study Greek and Islamic philosophy, natural science, and theology in Paris and Cologne under Albertus Magnus ("Albert the Great"), a Dominican who was famed for his vast learning. His colleagues in Cologne nicknamed Aquinas "the dumb ox" because of his reserved personality and large size; Albertus is said to have responded that Thomas' bellowing would be heard throughout the world. In 1256 Aquinas was made a regent master—professor—at the University of Paris. He taught in Paris and Naples until, on December 6, 1273, he had a deeply religious experience after which he stopped writing. "All that I have written seems to me like straw compared to what has now been revealed to me," he said. He died four months later.

Aquinas became known to later ages as the Angelic Doctor, and was canonized in 1323. In fact, starting shortly after his death, miraculous powers (such as healing the blind) were attributed to Aquinas' corpse and the Cistercian monks who possessed the body became concerned that members of the Dominican order would steal their treasure: as a safeguard, they "exhumed the corpse of Brother Thomas from its resting place, cut off the head and placed it in a hiding place in a corner of the chapel," so that even if the body were stolen they would still have the skull. His sister was given one of his hands.

Aquinas wrote voluminously—over eight million words of closely reasoned prose, especially amazing considering he was less than 50 when he died. He is said to have committed the entire Bible to memory, and was able to dictate to six or seven secretaries at one time. (His own handwriting was so illegible it has been dubbed the *litera inintelligibilis*.) His two major works, both written in Latin, are *Summa contra Gentiles* and *Summa Theologiae*. The first (written between 1259 and 1264) defends Christianity against a large number of objections, without assuming in advance that Christianity is true—it was reputedly written as a handbook for missionaries seeking to convert Muslims and others to Catholicism. The second (written between 1265 and 1274) attempts to summarize Catholic doctrine in such a way that it is consistent with rational philosophy and the natural science of the day.

What Was Aquinas' Overall Philosophical Project?

Aquinas was the most important philosopher of the middle ages. His great achievement was that he brought together Christian theology with the insights of classical Greek philosophy—especially the work of Aristotle as interpreted by the great Islamic masters, Avicenna and Averroes—and created a formidably systematic and powerful body of thought. Though enormously influential, Aquinas' thought was controversial in his time. Aquinas engaged in polemics with the

"Averroists," late thirteenth-century thinkers who held that Aristotelianism was not compatible with Christianity, and that faith and reason needed to be separated. Subsequent thinkers, including the great Catholic philosophers Dun Scotus (c. 1266–1308) and William of Ockham (c. 1288–c. 1348) (especially the latter) diverged from Aquinas, disagreeing on the extent to which Aristotle's thought, properly understood, conflicted with Christianity. In 1277 the Church authorities in Paris condemned some of Aquinas' doctrines on the grounds that they capitulated to factions attempting to Aristotelianize Christian thought.

Nonetheless, Aquinas was a central figure of the medieval tradition called "scholasticism," which became the standard intellectual worldview for Christian Europe for hundreds of years: in its various forms, it formed the basis of European science and philosophy until the intellectual Renaissance of the sixteenth century, and still underpins much Catholic theology.[1] In 1879 Pope Leo XIII recognized the philosophical system of Aquinas as the official doctrine of the Catholic Church.

The writings of the classical philosophers like Plato and Aristotle were largely lost to Western Europe for centuries after the fall of the Roman empire, though in the sixth century they were available in the original Greek in Italy and elsewhere in the Byzantine empire. Starting in the sixth century CE with Boethius (c. 480–c. 524), these writings, translated into Latin, trickled back into non-Arabic Europe and by the thirteenth century, when Aquinas was writing, most of the texts of Aristotle were again available to Western thinkers. (Aquinas did not read Greek and Plato's only work commonly available in Latin was the *Timaeus*. Much of his knowledge of Plato was second hand, through Boethius and the neo-Platonists.) In particular, in the second half of the twelfth century, Aristotle's writings on physics and metaphysics came to light. This triggered a deep intellectual conflict in Western Europe. Christian theology is ultimately based on *faith* or scriptural revelation, while the conclusions of Plato and Aristotle are supported by *reason*. When theology and philosophy disagree—and in particular, when philosophers provide us with a rationally compelling argument against a theological claim—then which are we to believe? Many conservative Christian theologians at the

time viewed classical philosophy as a pagan threat to Christian dogma, but Aquinas was deeply impressed by the work of Aristotle—he considered him the greatest of all philosophers, often referring to him in his writings as simply "*The Philosopher*"—and set out to reconcile Aristotle's writings with Catholic doctrine. He did this, it is important to note, not because he wanted to remove any threat to Christianity from pagan science, but because he thought a lot of what Aristotle had to say was *demonstrably true*.

Aquinas' reconciliation project had two prongs. First, he tried to show whenever possible that Aristotelian thought did not conflict with Christianity but actually supported it: thus faith could be conjoined with reason—religion could be combined with science—by showing how the human powers of reason allowed us to *better understand* the revealed truths of Catholicism.

Second, Aquinas argued that when Aristotle's conclusions did conflict with revealed truth, his arguments were not rationally compelling ... but that neither were there any rationally compelling arguments on the other side. For example, Aristotle argued that the universe is eternal and uncreated; Christianity holds that the universe was created a finite amount of time ago by God. Aquinas tried to show that *neither* position is provable. In situations like this, Aquinas argued, we discover that reason falls short and some truths can only be known on the basis of faith.

Together, these two kinds of argument were intended to show that there is no conflict between reason and faith ... and in fact that rational argument, properly carried out, can only strengthen faith, either by further supporting points of doctrine and making them comprehensible to the rational mind, or by revealing the limits of reason. Importantly, this only works when we reason rigorously and *well*. The foolish, according to Aquinas, might be led into error by arguments which are only apparently persuasive, and one important solution to this problem is not to suppress reason but to *encourage* trained, critical rational reflection on such arguments. (Of course, this solution, Aquinas realized, was not appropriate for the poor and uneducated; the peasants should instead by urged to rely upon their faith.)

Aquinas distinguished sharply between philosophy and theology. He held that theology begins from faith in God and interprets all things as creatures of God, while philosophy moves in the other direction: it starts with the concrete objects of sense perception—such as animals, rocks and trees—and reasons towards more general conceptions, eventually making its way to God.

---

1   Along with the Scotsman Duns Scotus and the English philosopher William of Ockham, other important scholastic philosophers were Peter Abelard (France, 1079–1142) and Jean Buridan (France, c. 1295–1358).

What Is the Structure of This Reading?

This selection includes, first, some of Aquinas' pronouncements from the start of *Summa contra Gentiles* on the scope and limits of human "natural reason" and the appropriate place of faith in intellectual inquiry. There are then two passages from Book 3 of the same work: the first argues that God is the ultimate governor of the universe and the final end of all purposive action; the second that humankind should arrange society hierarchically in accordance with the natural order of things ordained by God.

The final two excerpts, taken from the First Part of the Second Part of *Summa Theologiae*, give a taste of the medieval "scholastic" method of doing philosophy. Aquinas begins by dividing up his subject matter into a sequence of more precise questions: here, he is dealing with the topic of law, and the two questions included address "The essence of law" and "Human law." Each question is then broken into several parts, and in each part—called an "Article"—Aquinas first considers objections to his position, then lays out his view, and then answers the objections.

Some Useful Background Information

i) Aquinas is perhaps the major historical representative of an important approach to ethics and society called *natural law theory*. Natural law theory was transmitted to Aquinas through the tradition of Roman jurisprudence and the Catholic philosopher Peter Abelard. Originating with the Stoic philosophers (and arguably with Plato), the central idea of natural law theory is that nature—or God—has endowed humankind with an essential nature, and that this human nature entails that we ought to abide by certain rules of conduct. To give a simple example that appears in the writings of Roman jurists, human beings—like other animals—instinctively love their offspring, and social rules and structures must respect and accommodate this fact.

Thus, on this view, law rests on an objective set of principles that exist over and above human law-makers, and is binding on human beings irrespective of their desires or beliefs. This can be contrasted with a view often called *legal positivism* which sees law as having its origin in human conventions.

For Aquinas, the natural law is "nothing else than the rational creature's participation in the eternal law" (ST 1a2ae, Q. 94), where the eternal law is God's plan for the universe. In the case of the material universe, God's eternal law applies deterministically: God intends the universe, and its components, to move towards a particular end, and He directs it to do so through the laws of nature. Unlike mere material objects (or animals), human beings have been granted free will and rational intelligence by God, Aquinas believed, but this does not mean that we are not bound by God's law. On the contrary, like everything else, God has a plan for us and has directed us toward that end. This natural law is made manifest in the nature that God has given us: roughly, when we act in conformity with our real human nature our action is moral and right; when we act against the tendencies of our nature we are behaving wrongly, which is to say, not doing what God intends us to do.

The key issue, then, is how are we directed by our nature to behave. It is important for Aquinas that human nature be considered as a whole, rather than piecemeal in terms of particular instincts or tendencies, and that it must be understood in the light of humanity's place in God's plan. The role of reason is to bring harmony to our conflicting desires and to allow the subordination of the lower instincts—such as hunger or self-preservation—to higher ends when necessary.

Natural law is to be contrasted with—and in Aquinas' view, supplemented by—Divine positive law. Natural law is constituted by God's creative act, and is revealed by reason; divine law is constituted by the arbitrary will of God, and is revealed by supernatural revelation (such as the scriptures).

The selections in this volume contain some snippets of Aquinas' views on natural law, but he wrote very extensively on it, including on the scope and limits of the powers of a sovereign, on international law and the nature of just warfare, and on property rights and fair pricing.

How Important and Influential Is This Passage?

Aquinas is an important representative of classical natural law theory, which was easily the dominant social-political view of the medieval period in Europe and served as a precursor to the modern natural law theory of the seventeenth and eighteenth century. The influence of natural law theory has been on the wane since the early nineteenth century, however. Opponents of natural law theory have generally been skeptical of the notion of a set of timeless normative principles to be found in nature, and legal reformers have argued that law should instead be made to conform with some principle of general welfare, or alternatively that it should be seen as a historically specific expression of the will of the people. Nevertheless, natural law theory is far from moribund—it remains especially important in Catholic thought, but not exclusively there—and its ideas have gained new currency since World War II in connection with the notion of universal natural human rights. Important American legal philosophers Ronald Dworkin and John Finnis see their work as advancing a broadly naturalistic view of law (though with important disagreements with Aquinas), and the agenda of other very influential figures, such as Joseph Raz, has been set in part by opposing and responding to contemporary naturalistic views.

◆ ◆ ◆ ◆ ◆

Summa Contra Gentiles (1258–1264)

Book 1, Chapter 3

That the truths which we confess concerning God fall under two modes or categories

Because not every truth admits of the same mode of manifestation, and "a well-educated man will expect exactness in every class of subject, according as the nature of the thing admits," as is very well remarked by the Philosopher,[1] we must first show what mode of proof is possible for the truth that we have now before us. The truths that we confess concerning God fall under two modes. Some things true of God are beyond all the competence of human reason, as that God is Three and One. Other things there are to which even human reason can attain, as the existence and unity of God, which philosophers have proved to a demonstration under the guidance of the light of natural reason. That there are points of absolute intelligibility in God altogether beyond the compass of human reason, most manifestly appears. For since the leading principle of all knowledge of

any given subject-matter is an understanding of the thing's innermost being, or substance—according to the doctrine of the Philosopher,[2] that the essence is the principle of demonstration—it follows that the mode of our knowledge of the substance must be the mode of knowledge of whatever we know about the substance. Hence if the human understanding comprehends the substance of anything, as of a stone or triangle, none of the points of intelligibility about that thing will exceed the capacity of human reason. But this is not our case with regard to God. The human understanding cannot go so far of its natural power as to grasp His substance, since under the conditions of the present life the knowledge of our understanding commences with sense; and therefore objects beyond sense cannot be grasped by human understanding except so far as knowledge is gathered of them through the senses. But things of sense cannot lead our understanding to read in them the essence of the Divine Substance, inasmuch as they are effects inadequate to the power that caused them. Nevertheless our understanding is thereby led to some knowledge of God, namely, of His existence and of other attributes that must necessarily be attributed to the First Cause. There are, therefore, some points of intelligibility in God, accessible to human reason, and other points that altogether transcend the power of human reason.

The same thing may be understood from consideration of degrees of intelligibility. Of two minds, one of which has a keener insight into truth than the other, the higher mind understands much that the other cannot grasp at all, as is clear in the "plain man" (in rustico), who can in no way grasp the subtle theories of philosophy. Now the intellect of an angel excels that of a man more than the intellect of the ablest philosopher excels that of the plainest of plain men (rudissimi idiotae). The angel has a higher standpoint in creation than man as a basis of his knowledge of God, inasmuch as the substance of the angel, whereby he is led to know God by a process of natural knowledge, is nobler and more excellent than the things of sense, and even than the soul itself, whereby the human mind rises to the knowledge of God. But the Divine Mind exceeds the angelic much more than the angelic the human. For the Divine Mind of its own comprehensiveness covers the whole extent of its substance, and therefore perfectly understands its own essence, and knows all that is knowable about itself; but an

---

1 *remarked by the Philosopher* By "the Philosopher," Thomas always refers to Aristotle (384–322 BCE). The reference here is to his *Nicomachean Ethics*. 1, 3.1094b.

2 *the doctrine of the Philosopher* Aristotle, *Posterior Analytics*, 2, 3. 90b.

angel of his natural knowledge does not know the essence of God, because the angel's own substance, whereby it is led to a knowledge of God, is an effect inadequate to the power of the cause that created it. Hence not all things that God understands in Himself can be grasped by the natural knowledge of an angel; nor is human reason competent to take in all that an angel understands of his own natural ability. As therefore it would be the height of madness in a 'plain man' to declare a philosopher's propositions false, because he could not understand them, so and much more would a man show exceeding folly if he suspected of falsehood a divine revelation given by the ministry of angels, on the mere ground that it was beyond the investigation of reason.

The same thing manifestly appears from the incapacity which we daily experience in the observation of nature. We are ignorant of very many properties of the things of sense; and of the properties that our senses do apprehend, in most cases we cannot perfectly discover the reason. Much more is it beyond the competence of human reason to investigate all the points of intelligibility in that supreme excellent and transcendent substance of God. Consonant with this is the saying of the Philosopher,[1] that "as the eyes of bats are to the light of the sun, so is the intelligence of our soul to the things most manifest by nature." To this truth Holy Scripture also bears testimony. For it is said: "Perchance thou wilt seize upon the traces of God, and fully discover the Almighty."[2] And, "Lo, God is great, and surpassing our knowledge."[3] And, "We know in part."[4] Not everything, therefore, that is said of God, even though it be beyond the power of reason to investigate, is at once to be rejected as false.

Book 1, Chapter 4

That it is an advantage for the truths of God, known by natural reason, to be proposed to men to be believed on faith

If a truth of this nature were left to the sole enquiry of reason, three disadvantages would follow. One is that the knowledge of God would be confined to few. The discov-

ery of truth is the fruit of studious enquiry. From this very many are hindered. Some are hindered by a constitutional unfitness, their natures being ill-disposed to the acquisition of knowledge. They could never arrive by study to the highest grade of human knowledge, which consists in the knowledge of God. Others are hindered by the needs of business and the ties of the management of property. There must be in human society some men devoted to temporal affairs. These could not possibly spend time enough in the learned lessons of speculative enquiry to arrive at the highest point of human enquiry, the knowledge of God. Some again are hindered by sloth. The knowledge of the truths that reason can investigate concerning God presupposes much previous knowledge. Indeed almost the entire study of philosophy is directed to the knowledge of God. Hence, of all parts of philosophy, that part stands over to be learnt last, which consists of metaphysics dealing with points of Divinity. Thus, only with great labor of study is it possible to arrive at the searching out of the aforesaid truth; and this labor few are willing to undergo for sheer love of knowledge. Another disadvantage is that such as did arrive at the knowledge or discovery of the aforesaid truth would take a long time over it, on account of the profundity of such truth, and the many prerequisites to the study, and also because in youth and early manhood, the soul, tossed to and fro on the waves of passion, is not fit for the study of such high truth: only in settled age does the soul become prudent and scientific, as the Philosopher says. Thus, if the only way open to the knowledge of God were the way of reason, the human race would dwell long in thick darkness of ignorance: as the knowledge of God, the best instrument for making men perfect and good, would accrue only to a few, and to those few after a considerable lapse of time.

A third disadvantage is that, owing to the infirmity of our judgment and the perturbing force of imagination, there is some admixture of error in most of the investigations of human reason. This would be a reason to many for continuing to doubt even of the most accurate demonstrations, not perceiving the force of the demonstration, and seeing the divers judgments of divers persons who have the name of being wise men. Besides, in the midst of much demonstrated truth there is sometimes an element of error, not demonstrated but asserted on the strength of some plausible and sophistic reasoning that is taken for a demonstration. And therefore it was necessary for the real truth concerning divine things to be presented to men with fixed certainty

---

1   the saying of the Philosopher Aristotle, *Metaphysics* 2, 1. 993b.
2   *Perchance ... Almighty* Job 11.7.
3   *Lo, God ... knowledge* Job 36.26.
4   *We know in part* 1 Corinthians 13.9.

by way of faith. Wholesome therefore is the arrangement of divine clemency, whereby things even that reason can investigate are commanded to be held on faith, so that all might easily be partakers of the knowledge of God, and that without doubt and error. Hence it is said: "Now ye walk not as the Gentiles walk in the vanity of their own notions, having the understanding darkened";[1] and, "I will make all thy sons taught of the Lord."[2]

Book 1, Chapter 7

That the truth of reason is not contrary to the truth of Christian faith

The natural dictates of reason must certainly be quite true: it is impossible to think of their being otherwise. Nor again is it permissible to believe that the tenets of faith are false, being so evidently confirmed by God. Since therefore falsehood alone is contrary to truth, it is impossible for the truth of faith to be contrary to principles known by natural reason.

2. Whatever is put into the disciple's mind by the teacher is contained in the knowledge of the teacher, unless the teacher is teaching dishonestly, which would be a wicked thing to say of God. But the knowledge of principles naturally known is put into us by God, seeing that God Himself is the author of our nature. Therefore these principles also are contained in the Divine Wisdom. Whatever therefore is contrary to these principles is contrary to Divine Wisdom, and cannot be of God.

3. Contrary reasons fetter our intellect fast, so that it cannot proceed to the knowledge of the truth. If therefore contrary informations were sent us by God, our intellect would be thereby hindered from knowledge of the truth: but such hindrance cannot be of God.

4. What is natural cannot be changed while nature remains. But contrary opinions cannot be in the same mind at the same time: therefore no opinion or belief is sent to man from God contrary to natural knowledge. And therefore the Apostle says: "The word is near in thy heart and in thy mouth, that is, the word of faith which we preach."[3] But because it surpasses reason it is counted by some as contrary to reason, which cannot be. To the same effect is the authority of Augustine:[4] "What truth reveals can nowise be contrary to the holy books either of the Old or of the New Testament." Hence the conclusion is evident, that any arguments alleged against the teachings of faith do not proceed logically from first principles of nature, principles of themselves known, and so do not amount to a demonstration; but are either probable reasons or sophistical; hence room is left for refuting them.

Book 1, Chapter 8

Of the relation of human reason to the first truth of faith

The things of sense, from whence human reason takes its beginning of knowledge, retain in themselves some trace of imitation of God, inasmuch as they are, and are good; yet so imperfect is this trace that it proves wholly insufficient to declare the substance of God Himself. Since every agent acts to the producing of its own likeness, effects in their several ways bear some likeness to their causes: nevertheless the effect does not always attain to the perfect likeness of the agent that produces it. In regard then to knowledge of the truth of faith, which can only be thoroughly known to those who behold the substance of God, human reason stands so conditioned as to be able to argue some true likenesses to it: which likenesses however are not sufficient for any sort of demonstrative or intuitive comprehension of the aforesaid truth. Still it is useful for the human mind to exercise itself in such reasonings, however feeble, provided there be no presumptuous hope of perfect comprehension or demonstration. With this view the authority of Hilary[5] agrees, who says, speaking of such truth: "In this belief start, run, persist; and though I know that you will not reach the goal, still I shall congratulate you as I see you making progress. But intrude not into that sanctuary, and plunge not into the mystery of infinite truth; entertain no presumptuous hope of comprehending the height of intelligence, but understand that it is incomprehensible."

---

1   *Now ye walk ... darkened* Ephesians 4.17, 18.
2   *I will make ... the Lord* Isaiah 54.1, 5.
3   *The word ... we preach* Romans 10.8.

4   *the authority of Augustine* St. Augustine of Hippo (354–430). The reference here is to his *De Genesi ad Litteram*, 2, c. 18.
5   *the authority of Hilary* St. Hilary (or Hilarius) of Poitiers, bishop and theologian (c. 300–67). The quotation is from his *De Trinitate*, 2.10, 2.

Book 3, Chapter 64

That God governs things by His providence

The foregoing conclusions sufficiently show that God is the end of all things. Hence it may be further gathered that by His providence He governs and rules all things. For whatever things are referred to an end, are all subject to His management to whom principally that end belongs, as appears in an army: for all the components of the army and all their works are referred to one last end, the good of the general, which is victory, and therefore it belongs to the general to govern the whole army. In like manner the art which is concerned with the end gives commands and laws to the art which is concerned with the means, as politics to the art of war, the art of war to the management of cavalry, navigation to shipbuilding. Since therefore all things are referred to an end, which is the divine goodness (Chap. 17, 18), God, to whom that goodness principally belongs,—as being His own substance, possessed, understood, and loved,—must have the chief control of all things....

5. Things that are distinct in their natures do not combine into one system, unless they be bound up in one by one directing control (*ab uno ordinante*). But in the universe there are things, having distinct and contrary natures, which nevertheless all combine in one system, some things taking up the activities of other things, some things being aided or even wrought by others. There must then be one ordainer and governor of the universe....

8. Every agent that intends an end cares more for that which is nearer to the last end. But the last end of the divine will is the divine goodness, and the nearest thing to that in creation is the goodness of the order of the entire universe, that being the end to which every particular good of this or that thing is referred, as the less perfect is referred to the more perfect, and every part is for its whole. What therefore God most cares for in creation is the order of the universe: He is therefore its controller....

12. ... Hence Holy Scripture ascribes the course of events to the divine command: "Who giveth command to the sun, and it riseth not, and encloseth the stars as under a seal":[1] "He hath given a command, and it shall not pass away."[2]

---

1   *Who giveth ... a seal*   See Job 9.7.
2   *He hath ... pass away*   See Psalms 148.6.

Book 3, Chapter 81

Of the subordination of men one to another

Since man is endowed with understanding and sense and bodily power, these faculties are arranged in order in him by the disposition of divine providence according to the plan of the order that obtains in the universe, bodily power being put under that of sense and intellect as carrying out their command, and the sentient faculty itself under the faculty of intellect. And similar is the order between man and man. Men pre-eminent in understanding naturally take the command; while men poor in understanding, but of great bodily strength, seem by nature designate for servants, as Aristotle says[3] in his *Politics*, with whom Solomon is of one mind, saying: "The fool shall serve the wise."[4] But as in the works of one man disorder is born of intellect following sense, so in the commonwealth the like disorder ensues where the ruler holds his place, not by pre-eminence of understanding, but by usurpation of bodily strength, or is brought into power by some burst of passion. Nor is Solomon silent upon this disorder: "There is an evil that I have seen under the sun, a fool set in high estate."[5] But even such an anomaly does not carry with it the entire perversion of the natural order: for the dominion of fools is weak, unless strengthened by the counsel of the wise. Hence it is said: "A wise man is strong, and a knowing man stout and valiant: because war is managed by due ordering, and there shall be safety where there are many counsels."[6] And because he who gives counsel rules him who takes it, and becomes in a manner his master, it is said: "A wise servant shall be master over foolish sons."[7]

◆ ◆ ◆ ◆ ◆

---

3   *as Aristotle says*   Aristotle, *Politics*, 1, 5. 1254b.
4   *The fool ... wise*   Proverbs 11.29.
5   *There is ... high estate*   Ecclesiasties 10.5, 6.
6   *A wise ... counsels*   Proverbs 24.5, 6.
7   *A wise ... sons*   Proverbs 17.2.

Summa Theologiae
(1265–1274)

Question 90. The Essence of Law

Article 1. Whether law is something pertaining to reason?

OBJECTION 1. It would seem that law is not something pertaining to reason. For the Apostle says: "I see another law in my members," etc.[1] But nothing pertaining to reason is in the members; since the reason does not make use of a bodily organ. Therefore law is not something pertaining to reason.

OBJECTION 2. Further, in the reason there is nothing else but power, habit, and act. But law is not the power itself of reason. In like manner, neither is it a habit of reason: because the habits of reason are the intellectual virtues of which we have spoken above.[2] Nor again is it an act of reason: because then law would cease, when the act of reason ceases, for instance, while we are asleep. Therefore law is nothing pertaining to reason.

OBJECTION 3. Further, the law moves those who are subject to it to act aright. But it belongs properly to the will to move to act, as is evident from what has been said above.[3] Therefore law pertains, not to the reason, but to the will; according to the words of the Jurist: "Whatsoever pleaseth the sovereign, has force of law."[4]

ON THE CONTRARY, It belongs to the law to command and to forbid. But it belongs to reason to command, as stated above.[5] Therefore law is something pertaining to reason.

I ANSWER THAT, Law is a rule and measure of acts, whereby man is induced to act or is restrained from acting: for "lex" [law] is derived from "ligare" [to bind], because it binds one to act. Now the rule and measure of human acts is the reason, which is the first principle of human acts, as is evident from what has been stated above;[6] since it belongs to the reason to direct to the end, which is the first principle in all matters of action, according to the Philosopher.[7] Now that which is the principle in any genus, is the rule and measure of that genus: for instance, unity in the genus of numbers, and the first movement in the genus of movements. Consequently it follows that law is something pertaining to reason.

REPLY TO OBJECTION 1. Since law is a kind of rule and measure, it may be in something in two ways. First, as in that which measures and rules: and since this is proper to reason, it follows that, in this way, law is in the reason alone. Secondly, as in that which is measured and ruled. In this way, law is in all those things that are inclined to something by reason of some law: so that any inclination arising from a law, may be called a law, not essentially but by participation as it were. And thus the inclination of the members to concupiscence is called "the law of the members."

REPLY TO OBJECTION 2. Just as, in external action, we may consider the work and the work done, for instance the work of building and the house built; so in the acts of reason, we may consider the act itself of reason, i.e., to understand and to reason, and something produced by this act. With regard to the speculative reason, this is first of all the definition; secondly, the proposition; thirdly, the syllogism or argument. And since also the practical reason makes use of a syllogism in respect of the work to be done, as stated above[8] and since as the Philosopher teaches;[9] hence we find in the practical reason something that holds the same position in regard to operations, as, in the speculative intellect, the

---

1   *I see ... members*   Romans 7.23. The full quotation is "But I see another law at work in the members of my body, waging war against the law of my mind and making me a prisoner of the law of sin at work within my members." "Members" here means *organs of the body.*

2   *we have spoken above*   Q. 57. References to this work are standardly designated by the Question number (indicated by "Q.") and sometimes followed by the Article number within that Question.

3   *what has been said above*   Q. 9, 1.

4   *the words of the Jurist*   Thomas always calls the emperor Justinian "the Jurist." Beginning in 527, the emperor ordered work begun on a huge three-part compilation of legal knowledge. The *Digest* is the largest of these three parts, a huge compendium of legal knowledge written by a team of sixteen legal scholars and intended to include every significant feature of Roman law. The reference for this quotation is 1. 4. 1.

5   *as stated above*   Q. 17, 1.

6   *what has been stated above*   Q. 1, 1.

7   *according to the Philosopher*   By "the Philosopher," Thomas always refers to Aristotle (384–322 BCE). The references here are to *Physics* 2, 9. 200a 22 and *Nicomachean Ethics* 7, 8. 1151a 16.

8   *as stated above*   Q.13, 3; Q. 76, 1; Q. 77, 2.

9   *as the Philosopher teaches*   See Aristotle, *Nicomachean Ethics*, 7, 3. 1147a 24.

proposition holds in regard to conclusions. Such like universal propositions of the practical intellect that are directed to actions have the nature of law. And these propositions are sometimes under our actual consideration, while sometimes they are retained in the reason by means of a habit.

REPLY TO OBJECTION 3. Reason has its power of moving from the will, as stated above:[1] for it is due to the fact that one wills the end, that the reason issues its commands as regards things ordained to the end. But in order that the volition of what is commanded may have the nature of law, it needs to be in accord with some rule of reason. And in this sense is to be understood the saying that the will of the sovereign has the force of law; otherwise the sovereign's will would savor of lawlessness rather than of law.

Article 2. Whether the law is always something directed to the common good?

OBJECTION 1. It would seem that the law is not always directed to the common good as to its end. For it belongs to law to command and to forbid. But commands are directed to certain individual goods. Therefore the end of the law is not always the common good.

OBJECTION 2. Further, the law directs man in his actions. But human actions are concerned with particular matters. Therefore the law is directed to some particular good.

OBJECTION 3. Further, Isidore says: "If the law is based on reason, whatever is based on reason will be a law."[2] But reason is the foundation not only of what is ordained to the common good, but also of that which is directed private good. Therefore the law is not only directed to the good of all, but also to the private good of an individual.

ON THE CONTRARY, Isidore says that "laws are enacted for no private profit, but for the common benefit of the citizens."[3]

I ANSWER THAT, As stated above,[4] the law belongs to that which is a principle of human acts, because it is their rule and measure. Now as reason is a principle of human acts, so in reason itself there is something which is the principle in

respect of all the rest: wherefore to this principle chiefly and mainly law must needs be referred. Now the first principle in practical matters, which are the object of the practical reason, is the last end: and the last end of human life is bliss or happiness, as stated above.[5] Consequently the law must needs regard principally the relationship to happiness. Moreover, since every part is ordained to the whole, as imperfect to perfect; and since one man is a part of the perfect community, the law must needs regard properly the relationship to universal happiness. Wherefore the Philosopher, in the above definition of legal matters mentions both happiness and the body politic: for he says[6] that we call those legal matters "just, which are adapted to produce and preserve happiness and its parts for the body politic": since the state is a perfect community, as he says in Politics 1.[7]

Now in every genus, that which belongs to it chiefly is the principle of the others, and the others belong to that genus in subordination to that thing: thus fire, which is chief among hot things, is the cause of heat in mixed bodies, and these are said to be hot in so far as they have a share of fire. Consequently, since the law is chiefly ordained to the common good, any other precept in regard to some individual work, must needs be devoid of the nature of a law, save in so far as it regards the common good. Therefore every law is ordained to the common good.

REPLY TO OBJECTION 1. A command denotes an application of a law to matters regulated by the law. Now the order to the common good, at which the law aims, is applicable to particular ends. And in this way commands are given even concerning particular matters.

REPLY TO OBJECTION 2. Actions are indeed concerned with particular matters: but those particular matters are referable to the common good, not as to a common genus or species, but as to a common final cause, according as the common good is said to be the common end.

REPLY TO OBJECTION 3. Just as nothing stands firm with regard to the speculative reason except that which is traced back to the first indemonstrable principles, so nothing stands firm with regard to the practical reason, unless it be directed to the last end which is the common good: and whatever stands to reason in this sense, has the nature of a law.

---

1   *as stated above*   Q. 17, 1.
2   *Isidore says*   Saint Isidore of Seville (c. 560–636) was Archbishop of Seville and an important medieval scholar. Aquinas refers to his *Etymologiae*, a twenty-volume work, possibly the West's first encyclopedia. (Location of this reference: 2, 10; 5, 3)
3   *Isadore says*   See *Etymolygiae*. 5, 21.
4   *As stated above*   Article 1.

5   *as stated above*   Q. 2, 7; Q. 3, 1; Q. 69, 1.
6   *he says*   See *Nicomachean Ethics* 5, 1. 1129b 17.
7   *he says*   See Aristotle, *Politics*, 1, 1. 1252a 5.

Article 3. Whether the reason of any man is competent to make laws?

OBJECTION 1. It would seem that the reason of any man is competent to make laws. For the Apostle says that "when the Gentiles, who have not the law, do by nature those things that are of the law, ... they are a law to themselves."[1] Now he says this of all in general. Therefore anyone can make a law for himself.

OBJECTION 2. Further, as the Philosopher says, "the intention of the lawgiver is to lead men to virtue."[2] But every man can lead another to virtue. Therefore the reason of any man is competent to make laws.

OBJECTION 3. Further, just as the sovereign of a state governs the state, so every father of a family governs his household. But the sovereign of a state can make laws for the state. Therefore every father of a family can make laws for his household.

ON THE CONTRARY, Isidore says:[3] "A law is an ordinance of the people, whereby something is sanctioned by the Elders together with the Commonalty."

I ANSWER THAT, A law, properly speaking, regards first and foremost the order to the common good. Now to order anything to the common good, belongs either to the whole people, or to someone who is the viceregent[4] of the whole people. And therefore the making of a law belongs either to the whole people or to a public personage who has care of the whole people: since in all other matters the directing of anything to the end concerns him to whom the end belongs.

REPLY TO OBJECTION 1. As stated above,[5] a law is in a person not only as in one that rules, but also by participation as in one that is ruled. In the latter way each one is a law to himself, in so far as he shares the direction that he receives from one who rules him. Hence the same text[6] goes on: "Who shows the work of the law written in their hearts."

REPLY TO OBJECTION 2. A private person cannot lead another to virtue efficaciously: for he can only advise, and if his advice be not taken, it has no coercive power, such as the law should have, in order to prove an efficacious induce-

ment to virtue, as the Philosopher says.[7] But this coercive power is vested in the whole people or in some public personage, to whom it belongs to inflict penalties, as we shall state further on.[8] Wherefore the framing of laws belongs to him alone.

REPLY TO OBJECTION 3. As one man is a part of the household, so a household is a part of the state: and the state is a perfect community, according to *Politics* 1.[9] And therefore, as the good of one man is not the last end, but is ordained to the common good; so too the good of one household is ordained to the good of a single state, which is a perfect community. Consequently he that governs a family, can indeed make certain commands or ordinances, but not such as to have properly the force of law.

Article 4. Whether promulgation is essential to a law?

OBJECTION 1. It would seem that promulgation is not essential to a law. For the natural law above all has the character of law. But the natural law needs no promulgation. Therefore it is not essential to a law that it be promulgated.

OBJECTION 2. Further, it belongs properly to a law to bind one to do or not to do something. But the obligation of fulfilling a law touches not only those in whose presence it is promulgated, but also others. Therefore promulgation is not essential to a law.

OBJECTION 3. Further, the binding force of a law extends even to the future, since "laws are binding in matters of the future," as the jurists say.[10] But promulgation concerns those who are present. Therefore it is not essential to a law.

ON THE CONTRARY, It is laid down in the Decretals,[11] dist. 4, that "laws are established when they are promulgated."

I ANSWER THAT, As stated above (1), a law is imposed on others by way of a rule and measure. Now a rule or measure is imposed by being applied to those who are to be ruled and measured by it. Wherefore, in order that a law obtain the binding force which is proper to a law, it must needs be

---

1   *when ... to themselves*   See Romans 2.14.
2   *the Philosopher says*   See *Nicomachean Ethics* 2, 1. 1103b 3.
3   *Isidore says*   See *Etymologiae* 5, 10.
4   *viceregent*   Official administrative deputy of the regent—the ruler.
5   *As stated above*   Article 1.
6   *the same text*   See Romans 2.15.

7   *the Philosopher says*   See *Nicomachean Ethics* 10, 9. 1180a 20.
8   *as we shall state further on*   Q. 92, 2; Part 2 of Book 2, Q. 64, 3.
9   *Politics 1*   In particular, *Politics* 1, 1. 1252a 5.
10 *the jurists say*   See *Codex Justinianus* 1, 14, 7. The *Codex Justianus* is another part of Justinian's three-part legal compilation; this one collected the legal decrees of the Roman emperors.
11 *It is laid down in the Decretals*   This work is the *Decretum Gratiani*, a collection of Canon law written in the twelfth century by the Italian law scholar Gratian. The reference here is to 1, 4, 3.

applied to the men who have to be ruled by it. Such application is made by its being notified to them by promulgation. Wherefore promulgation is necessary for the law to obtain its force.

Thus from the four preceding articles, the definition of law may be gathered; and it is nothing else than an ordinance of reason for the common good, made by him who has care of the community, and promulgated.

REPLY TO OBJECTION 1. The natural law is promulgated by the very fact that God instilled it into man's mind so as to be known by him naturally.

REPLY TO OBJECTION 2. Those who are not present when a law is promulgated, are bound to observe the law, in so far as it is notified or can be notified to them by others, after it has been promulgated.

REPLY TO OBJECTION 3. The promulgation that takes place now, extends to future time by reason of the durability of written characters, by which means it is continually promulgated. Hence Isidore says[1] that "lex [law] is derived from legere [to read] because it is written."

• • •

Question 94. The Natural Law

Article 1. Whether the natural law is a habit?

OBJECTION 1. It would seem that the natural law is a habit. Because, as the Philosopher says,[2] "there are three things in the soul: power, habit, and passion." But the natural law is not one of the soul's powers: nor is it one of the passions; as we may see by going through them one by one. Therefore the natural law is a habit.

OBJECTION 2. Further, Basil says[3] that the conscience or "synderesis[4] is the law of our mind"; which can only apply to the natural law. But the "synderesis" is a habit, as

was shown in the First Part.[5] Therefore the natural law is a habit.

OBJECTION 3. Further, the natural law abides in man always, as will be shown further on.[6] But man's reason, which the law regards, does not always think about the natural law. Therefore the natural law is not an act, but a habit.

ON THE CONTRARY, Augustine says[7] that "a habit is that whereby something is done when necessary." But such is not the natural law: since it is in infants and in the damned who cannot act by it. Therefore the natural law is not a habit.

I ANSWER THAT, A thing may be called a habit in two ways. First, properly and essentially: and thus the natural law is not a habit. For it has been stated above[8] that the natural law is something appointed by reason, just as a proposition is a work of reason. Now that which a man does is not the same as that whereby he does it: for he makes a becoming speech by the habit of grammar. Since then a habit is that by which we act, a law cannot be a habit properly and essentially.

Secondly, the term habit may be applied to that which we hold by a habit: thus faith may mean that which we hold by faith. And accordingly, since the precepts of the natural law are sometimes considered by reason actually, while sometimes they are in the reason only habitually, in this way the natural law may be called a habit. Thus, in speculative matters, the indemonstrable principles are not the habit itself whereby we hold those principles, but are the principles the habit of which we possess.

REPLY TO OBJECTION 1. The Philosopher proposes[9] there to discover the genus of virtue; and since it is evident that virtue is a principle of action, he mentions only those things which are principles of human acts, viz. powers, habits and passions. But there are other things in the soul besides these three: there are acts; thus "to will" is in the one that wills; again, things known are in the knower; moreover its own natural properties are in the soul, such as immortality and the like.

REPLY TO OBJECTION 2. "Synderesis" is said to be the law of our mind, because it is a habit containing the pre-

1   Isidore says   See Etymologiae 2, 10.
2   as the Philosopher says   See Nicomachean Ethics 2, 5 1105b 20.
3   Basil says   St. Basil the Great (Basil of Caesarea) was a fourth century theologian. The reference here is to his homily "On the Hexaemeron." A secondary source on this work, from the first half of the eighth century, is St. John Damascene, De Fide Orthodoxa (4, 22).
4   synderesis   In Scholastic philosophy, the innate principle in our minds that directs us toward good and away from evil.

5   the First Part   I.e., of this work: 1, Q. 79, 12.
6   further on   See article 6.
7   Augustine says   St. Augustine of Hippo (354–430). The reference here is to his De Bono Coniugali [On the Good of Marriage] 21.
8   it has been stated above   Q. 90, 1.
9   The Philosopher proposes   See Nicomachean Ethics, 2, 5. 1105b 20.

cepts of the natural law, which are the first principles of human actions.

REPLY TO OBJECTION 3. This argument proves that the natural law is held habitually; and this is granted.

To the argument advanced in the contrary sense we reply that sometimes a man is unable to make use of that which is in him habitually, on account of some impediment: thus, on account of sleep, a man is unable to use the habit of science. In like manner, through the deficiency of his age, a child cannot use the habit of understanding of principles, or the natural law, which is in him habitually.

Article 2. Whether the natural law contains several precepts, or only one?

OBJECTION 1. It would seem that the natural law contains, not several precepts, but one only. For law is a kind of precept, as stated above.[1] If therefore there were many precepts of the natural law, it would follow that there are also many natural laws.

OBJECTION 2. Further, the natural law is consequent to human nature. But human nature, as a whole, is one; though, as to its parts, it is manifold. Therefore, either there is but one precept of the law of nature, on account of the unity of nature as a whole; or there are many, by reason of the number of parts of human nature. The result would be that even things relating to the inclination of the concupiscible faculty[2] belong to the natural law.

OBJECTION 3. Further, law is something pertaining to reason, as stated above.[3] Now reason is but one in man. Therefore there is only one precept of the natural law.

ON THE CONTRARY, The precepts of the natural law in man stand in relation to practical matters, as the first principles to matters of demonstration. But there are several first indemonstrable principles. Therefore there are also several precepts of the natural law.

I ANSWER THAT, As stated above,[4] the precepts of the natural law are to the practical reason, what the first principles of demonstrations are to the speculative reason; because both are self-evident principles. Now a thing is said to be self-evident in two ways: first, in itself; secondly, in rela-

tion to us. Any proposition is said to be self-evident in itself, if its predicate is contained in the notion of the subject: although, to one who knows not the definition of the subject, it happens that such a proposition is not self-evident. For instance, this proposition, "Man is a rational being," is, in its very nature, self-evident, since who says "man," says "a rational being": and yet to one who knows not what a man is, this proposition is not self-evident. Hence it is that, as Boethius says,[5] certain axioms or propositions are universally self-evident to all; and such are those propositions whose terms are known to all, as, "every whole is greater than its part," and, "things equal to one and the same are equal to one another." But some propositions are self-evident only to the wise, who understand the meaning of the terms of such propositions: thus to one who understands that an angel is not a body, it is self-evident that an angel is not circumscriptively in a place: but this is not evident to the unlearned, for they cannot grasp it.

Now a certain order is to be found in those things that are apprehended universally. For that which, before aught else, falls under apprehension, is "being," the notion of which is included in all things whatsoever a man apprehends. Wherefore the first indemonstrable principle is that "the same thing cannot be affirmed and denied at the same time," which is based on the notion of "being" and "not-being": and on this principle all others are based, as is stated[6] in *Metaphysics* 4, text. 9. Now as "being" is the first thing that falls under the apprehension simply, so "good" is the first thing that falls under the apprehension of the practical reason, which is directed to action: since every agent acts for an end under the aspect of good. Consequently the first principle of practical reason is one founded on the notion of good, viz. that "good is that which all things seek after." Hence this is the first precept of law, that "good is to be done and pursued, and evil is to be avoided." All other precepts of the natural law are based upon this: so that whatever the practical reason naturally apprehends as man's good (or evil) belongs to the precepts of the natural law as something to be done or avoided.

Since, however, good has the nature of an end, and evil, the nature of a contrary, hence it is that all those things to which man has a natural inclination, are naturally ap-

---

1   *as stated above* Q. 92, 2.
2   *concupiscible faculty* That part of us that has to do with desire—especially sexual desire.
3   *as stated above* Q. 90, 1.
4   *As stated above* Q. 91, 3.

5   *Boethius* Anicius Manlius Severinus Boethius (480–c. 524), Roman statesman and philosopher. His work referred to here is *De Hebdomadibus*.
6   *as it is stated* The correct reference is Aristotle, *Metaphysics*, 3, 3. 1005b 29.

prehended by reason as being good, and consequently as objects of pursuit, and their contraries as evil, and objects of avoidance. Wherefore according to the order of natural inclinations, is the order of the precepts of the natural law. Because in man there is first of all an inclination to good in accordance with the nature which he has in common with all substances: inasmuch as every substance seeks the preservation of its own being, according to its nature: and by reason of this inclination, whatever is a means of preserving human life, and of warding off its obstacles, belongs to the natural law. Secondly, there is in man an inclination to things that pertain to him more specially, according to that nature which he has in common with other animals: and in virtue of this inclination, those things are said to belong to the natural law, "which nature has taught to all animals,"[1] such as sexual intercourse, education of offspring and so forth. Thirdly, there is in man an inclination to good, according to the nature of his reason, which nature is proper to him: thus man has a natural inclination to know the truth about God, and to live in society: and in this respect, whatever pertains to this inclination belongs to the natural law; for instance, to shun ignorance, to avoid offending those among whom one has to live, and other such things regarding the above inclination.

REPLY TO OBJECTION 1. All these precepts of the law of nature have the character of one natural law, inasmuch as they flow from one first precept.

REPLY TO OBJECTION 2. All the inclinations of any parts whatsoever of human nature, e.g., of the concupiscible and irascible parts, in so far as they are ruled by reason, belong to the natural law, and are reduced to one first precept, as stated above: so that the precepts of the natural law are many in themselves, but are based on one common foundation.

REPLY TO OBJECTION 3. Although reason is one in itself, yet it directs all things regarding man; so that whatever can be ruled by reason, is contained under the law of reason.

Article 3. Whether all acts of virtue are prescribed by the natural law?

OBJECTION 1. It would seem that not all acts of virtue are prescribed by the natural law. Because, as stated above[2] it is essential to a law that it be ordained to the common good. But some acts of virtue are ordained to the private good of the individual, as is evident especially in regards to acts of temperance. Therefore not all acts of virtue are the subject of natural law.

OBJECTION 2. Further, every sin is opposed to some virtuous act. If therefore all acts of virtue are prescribed by the natural law, it seems to follow that all sins are against nature: whereas this applies to certain special sins.

OBJECTION 3. Further, those things which are according to nature are common to all. But acts of virtue are not common to all: since a thing is virtuous in one, and vicious in another. Therefore not all acts of virtue are prescribed by the natural law.

ON THE CONTRARY, Damascene says[3] that "virtues are natural." Therefore virtuous acts also are a subject of the natural law.

I ANSWER THAT, We may speak of virtuous acts in two ways: first, under the aspect of virtuous; secondly, as such and such acts considered in their proper species. If then we speak of acts of virtue, considered as virtuous, thus all virtuous acts belong to the natural law. For it has been stated[4] that to the natural law belongs everything to which a man is inclined according to his nature. Now each thing is inclined naturally to an operation that is suitable to it according to its form: thus fire is inclined to give heat. Wherefore, since the rational soul is the proper form of man, there is in every man a natural inclination to act according to reason: and this is to act according to virtue. Consequently, considered thus, all acts of virtue are prescribed by the natural law: since each one's reason naturally dictates to him to act virtuously. But if we speak of virtuous acts, considered in themselves, i.e., in their proper species, thus not all virtuous acts are prescribed by the natural law: for many things are done virtuously, to which nature does not incline at first; but which, through the inquiry of reason, have been found by men to be conducive to well-living.

REPLY TO OBJECTION 1. Temperance is about the natural concupiscences of food, drink and sexual matters, which are indeed ordained to the natural common good, just as other matters of law are ordained to the moral common good.

REPLY TO OBJECTION 2. By human nature we may mean either that which is proper to man—and in this sense all sins, as being against reason, are also against nature, as

---

1   *which nature ... all animals*   See *Digest*, 1, 1, 1.
2   *as stated above*   Q. 90, 2.
3   *Damascene says*   See *De Fide Orthodoxa* 3, 14.
4   *it has been stated*   See article 2, above.

Damascene states:[1] or we may mean that nature which is common to man and other animals; and in this sense, certain special sins are said to be against nature; thus contrary to sexual intercourse, which is natural to all animals, is unisexual lust, which has received the special name of the unnatural crime.

REPLY TO OBJECTION 3. This argument considers acts in themselves. For it is owing to the various conditions of men, that certain acts are virtuous for some, as being proportionate and becoming to them, while they are vicious for others, as being out of proportion to them.

Article 4. Whether the natural law is the same in all men?

OBJECTION 1. It would seem that the natural law is not the same in all. For it is stated[2] in the *Decretals* that "the natural law is that which is contained in the Law and the Gospel." But this is not common to all men; because, as it is written, "all do not obey the gospel."[3] Therefore the natural law is not the same in all men.

OBJECTION 2. Further, "Things which are according to the law are said to be just," as stated in *Ethics* 5.[4] But it is stated[5] in the same book that nothing is so universally just as not to be subject to change in regard to some men. Therefore even the natural law is not the same in all men.

OBJECTION 3. Further, as stated above,[6] to the natural law belongs everything to which a man is inclined according to his nature. Now different men are naturally inclined to different things; some to the desire of pleasures, others to the desire of honors, and other men to other things. Therefore there is not one natural law for all.

ON THE CONTRARY, Isidore says[7] "The natural law is common to all nations."

I ANSWER THAT, As stated above,[8] to the natural law belongs those things to which a man is inclined naturally: and among these it is proper to man to be inclined to act according to reason. Now the process of reason is from the common to the proper, as stated[9] in *Physics* 1. The speculative reason, however, is differently situated in this matter, from the practical reason. For, since the speculative reason is busied chiefly with the necessary things, which cannot be otherwise than they are, its proper conclusions, like the universal principles, contain the truth without fail. The practical reason, on the other hand, is busied with contingent matters, about which human actions are concerned: and consequently, although there is necessity in the general principles, the more we descend to matters of detail, the more frequently we encounter defects. Accordingly then in speculative matters truth is the same in all men, both as to principles and as to conclusions: although the truth is not known to all as regards the conclusions, but only as regards the principles which are called common notions. But in matters of action, truth or practical rectitude is not the same for all, as to matters of detail, but only as to the general principles: and where there is the same rectitude in matters of detail, it is not equally known to all.

It is therefore evident that, as regards the general principles whether of speculative or of practical reason, truth or rectitude is the same for all, and is equally known by all. As to the proper conclusions of the speculative reason, the truth is the same for all, but is not equally known to all: thus it is true for all that the three angles of a triangle are together equal to two right angles, although it is not known to all. But as to the proper conclusions of the practical reason, neither is the truth or rectitude the same for all, nor, where it is the same, is it equally known by all. Thus it is right and true for all to act according to reason: and from this principle it follows as a proper conclusion, that goods entrusted to another should be restored to their owner. Now this is true for the majority of cases: but it may happen in a particular case that it would be injurious, and therefore unreasonable, to restore goods held in trust; for instance, if they are claimed for the purpose of fighting against one's country. And this principle will be found to fail the more, according as we descend further into detail, e.g., if one were to say that goods held in trust should be restored with such and such a guarantee, or in such and such a way; because the greater the number of conditions added, the greater the number of ways in which the principle may fail, so that it be not right to restore or not to restore.

Consequently we must say that the natural law, as to general principles, is the same for all, both as to rectitude

1   *Damascene states*   See *De Fide Orthodoxa* 2, 30.
2   *it is stated*   See *Decretals*, 1, 1, prol.
3   *all do ... gospel*   See Romans 10.16.
4   *as stated*   See *Nicomachean Ethics*, 5, 1. 1129b 12.
5   *it is stated*   See *Nicomachean Ethics*, 5, 7. 1134b 32.
6   *as stated above*   Articles 2 and 3.
7   *Isidore says*   See *Etymologiae*, 5, 4.
8   *As stated above*   Articles 2 and 3.
9   *as stated*   See Aristotle, *Physics*, 1, 1. 184a 16.

and as to knowledge. But as to certain matters of detail, which are conclusions, as it were, of those general principles, it is the same for all in the majority of cases, both as to rectitude and as to knowledge; and yet in some few cases it may fail, both as to rectitude, by reason of certain obstacles (just as natures subject to generation and corruption fail in some few cases on account of some obstacle), and as to knowledge, since in some the reason is perverted by passion, or evil habit, or an evil disposition of nature; thus formerly, theft, although it is expressly contrary to the natural law, was not considered wrong among the Germans, as Julius Caesar relates.[1]

REPLY TO OBJECTION 1. The meaning of the sentence quoted is not that whatever is contained in the Law and the Gospel belongs to the natural law, since they contain many things that are above nature; but that whatever belongs to the natural law is fully contained in them. Wherefore Gratian, after saying that "the natural law is what is contained in the Law and the Gospel," adds at once, by way of example, "by which everyone is commanded to do to others as he would be done by."[2]

REPLY TO OBJECTION 2. The saying of the Philosopher[3] is to be understood of things that are naturally just, not as general principles, but as conclusions drawn from them, having rectitude in the majority of cases, but failing in a few.

REPLY TO OBJECTION 3. As, in man, reason rules and commands the other powers, so all the natural inclinations belonging to the other powers must needs be directed according to reason. Wherefore it is universally right for all men, that all their inclinations should be directed according to reason.

Article 5. Whether the natural law can be changed?

OBJECTION 1. It would seem that the natural law can be changed. Because on Ecclesiastes 17:9, "He gave them instructions, and the law of life," the gloss says:[4] "He wished the law of the letter to be written, in order to correct the law of nature." But that which is corrected is changed. Therefore the natural law can be changed.

OBJECTION 2. Further, the slaying of the innocent, adultery, and theft are against the natural law. But we find these things changed by God: as when God commanded Abraham to slay his innocent son;[5] and when He ordered the Jews to borrow and purloin the vessels of the Egyptians;[6] and when He commanded Hosea to take to himself "a wife of fornications."[7] Therefore the natural law can be changed.

OBJECTION 3. Further, Isidore says[8] that "the possession of all things in common, and universal freedom, are matters of natural law." But these things are seen to be changed by human laws. Therefore it seems that the natural law is subject to change.

ON THE CONTRARY, It is said[9] in the Decretals: "The natural law dates from the creation of the rational creature. It does not vary according to time, but remains unchangeable."

I ANSWER THAT, A change in the natural law may be understood in two ways. First, by way of addition. In this sense nothing hinders the natural law from being changed: since many things for the benefit of human life have been added over and above the natural law, both by the Divine law and by human laws.

Secondly, a change in the natural law may be understood by way of subtraction, so that what previously was according to the natural law, ceases to be so. In this sense, the natural law is altogether unchangeable in its first principles: but in its secondary principles, which, as we have said,[10] are certain detailed proximate conclusions drawn from the first principles, the natural law is not changed so that what it prescribes be not right in most cases. But it may be changed in some particular cases of rare occurrence, through some special causes hindering the observance of such precepts, as stated above.[11]

REPLY TO OBJECTION 1. The written law is said to be given for the correction of the natural law, either because it supplies what was wanting to the natural law; or because

---

1   *Julius Caesar relates*   See Julius Caesar, *Commentarii De Bello Gallico* (*The Gallic Wars*) 6, 23.
2   *the natural ... done by*   Quotation not traced.
3   *the saying of the Philosopher*   See *Nicomachean Ethics*, 5, 1. 1129b 12.
4   *the gloss says*   The "gloss" in this case is a commentary on the scriptures, called *Glossa Ordinaria*, written by the German Walafrid Strabo (died 849); 3, 403E.

5   *God commanded ... innocent son*   See Genesis 22.2.
6   *He ordered ... the Egyptians*   See Exodus 12.35.
7   *He commanded ... of fornications*   See Hosea 1.2.
8   *Isidore says*   See *Etymologicae* 5, 4.
9   *It is said*   See *Decretals*, 1, 5., prol.
10   *as we have said*   Article 4.
11   *as stated above*   Article 4.

the natural law was perverted in the hearts of some men, as to certain matters, so that they esteemed those things good which are naturally evil; which perversion stood in need of correction.

REPLY TO OBJECTION 2. All men alike, both guilty and innocent, die the death of nature: which death of nature is inflicted by the power of God on account of original sin, according to 1 Kings 2.6: "The Lord killeth and maketh alive." Consequently, by the command of God, death can be inflicted on any man, guilty or innocent, without any injustice whatever. In like manner adultery is intercourse with another's wife; who is allotted to him by the law emanating from God. Consequently intercourse with any woman, by the command of God, is neither adultery nor fornication. The same applies to theft, which is the taking of another's property. For whatever is taken by the command of God, to Whom all things belong, is not taken against the will of its owner, whereas it is in this that theft consists. Nor is it only in human things, that whatever is commanded by God is right; but also in natural things, whatever is done by God, is, in some way, natural, as stated in the First Part.[1]

REPLY TO OBJECTION 3. A thing is said to belong to the natural law in two ways. First, because nature inclines thereto: e.g., that one should not do harm to another. Secondly, because nature did not bring in the contrary: thus we might say that for man to be naked is of the natural law, because nature did not give him clothes, but art invented them. In this sense, "the possession of all things in common and universal freedom" are said to be of the natural law, because, to wit, the distinction of possessions and slavery were not brought in by nature, but devised by human reason for the benefit of human life. Accordingly the law of nature was not changed in this respect, except by addition.

Article 6. Whether the law of nature can be abolished from the heart of man?

OBJECTION 1. It would seem that the natural law can be abolished from the heart of man. Because on Romans 2.14, "When the Gentiles who have not the law," etc. a gloss says[2] that "the law of righteousness, which sin had blotted out, is graven on the heart of man when he is restored by grace." But the law of righteousness is the law of nature. Therefore the law of nature can be blotted out.

OBJECTION 2. Further, the law of grace is more efficacious than the law of nature. But the law of grace is blotted out by sin. Much more therefore can the law of nature be blotted out.

OBJECTION 3. Further, that which is established by law is made just. But many things are enacted by men, which are contrary to the law of nature. Therefore the law of nature can be abolished from the heart of man.

ON THE CONTRARY, Augustine says:[3] "Thy law is written in the hearts of men, which iniquity itself effaces not." But the law which is written in men's hearts is the natural law. Therefore the natural law cannot be blotted out.

I ANSWER THAT, As stated above,[4] there belong to the natural law, first, certain most general precepts, that are known to all; and secondly, certain secondary and more detailed precepts, which are, as it were, conclusions following closely from first principles. As to those general principles, the natural law, in the abstract, can nowise be blotted out from men's hearts. But it is blotted out in the case of a particular action, in so far as reason is hindered from applying the general principle to a particular point of practice, on account of concupiscence or some other passion, as stated above.[5] But as to the other, i.e., the secondary precepts, the natural law can be blotted out from the human heart, either by evil persuasions, just as in speculative matters errors occur in respect of necessary conclusions; or by vicious customs and corrupt habits, as among some men, theft, and even unnatural vices, as the Apostle states,[6] were not esteemed sinful.

REPLY TO OBJECTION 1. Sin blots out the law of nature in particular cases, not universally, except perchance in regard to the secondary precepts of the natural law, in the way stated above.

REPLY TO OBJECTION 2. Although grace is more efficacious than nature, yet nature is more essential to man, and therefore more enduring.

REPLY TO OBJECTION 3. This argument is true of the secondary precepts of the natural law, against which some legislators have framed certain enactments which are unjust.

---

1   *as stated in the First Part*   I.e., of this work: 1, Q. 105, 6.
2   *a gloss says*   See *Glossa Ordinaria*, 6, 7E.
3   *Augustine says*   See *Confessions* 2, 4.
4   *As stated above*   Articles 4 and 5.
5   *as stated above*   Q. 77, 2.
6   *as the Apostle states*   Romans 1.24: "Therefore God gave them over in the sinful desires of their hearts to sexual impurity for the degrading of their bodies with one another."

Question 95. Human Law

Article 1. Whether it was useful for laws to be framed by men?

OBJECTION 1. It would seem that it was not useful for laws to be framed by men. Because the purpose of every law is that man be made good thereby, as stated above.[1] But men are more to be induced to be good willingly by means of admonitions, than against their will, by means of laws. Therefore there was no need to frame laws.

OBJECTION 2. Further, as the Philosopher says,[2] "men have recourse to a judge as to animate justice." But animate justice is better than inanimate justice, which contained in laws. Therefore it would have been better for the execution of justice to be entrusted to the decision of judges, than to frame laws in addition.

OBJECTION 3. Further, every law is framed for the direction of human actions, as is evident from what has been stated above.[3] But since human actions are about singulars, which are infinite in number, matter pertaining to the direction of human actions cannot be taken into sufficient consideration except by a wise man, who looks into each one of them. Therefore it would have been better for human acts to be directed by the judgment of wise men, than by the framing of laws. Therefore there was no need of human laws.

ON THE CONTRARY, Isidore says:[4] "Laws were made that in fear thereof human audacity might be held in check, that innocence might be safeguarded in the midst of wickedness, and that the dread of punishment might prevent the wicked from doing harm." But these things are most necessary to mankind. Therefore it was necessary that human laws should be made.

I ANSWER THAT, As stated above,[5] man has a natural aptitude for virtue; but the perfection of virtue must be acquired by man by means of some kind of training. Thus we observe that man is helped by industry in his necessities, for instance, in food and clothing. Certain beginnings of these he has from nature, viz. his reason and his hands; but he has not the full complement, as other animals have, to whom nature has given sufficiency of clothing and food. Now it is difficult to see how man could suffice for himself in the matter of this training: since the perfection of virtue consists chiefly in withdrawing man from undue pleasures, to which above all man is inclined, and especially the young, who are more capable of being trained. Consequently a man needs to receive this training from another, whereby to arrive at the perfection of virtue. And as to those young people who are inclined to acts of virtue, by their good natural disposition, or by custom, or rather by the gift of God, paternal training suffices, which is by admonitions. But since some are found to be depraved, and prone to vice, and not easily amenable to words, it was necessary for such to be restrained from evil by force and fear, in order that, at least, they might desist from evil-doing, and leave others in peace, and that they themselves, by being habituated in this way, might be brought to do willingly what hitherto they did from fear, and thus become virtuous. Now this kind of training, which compels through fear of punishment, is the discipline of laws. Therefore in order that man might have peace and virtue, it was necessary for laws to be framed: for, as the Philosopher says,[6] "as man is the most noble of animals if he be perfect in virtue, so is he the lowest of all, if he be severed from law and righteousness"; because man can use his reason to devise means of satisfying his lusts and evil passions, which other animals are unable to do.

REPLY TO OBJECTION 1. Men who are well disposed are led willingly to virtue by being admonished better than by coercion: but men who are evilly disposed are not led to virtue unless they are compelled.

REPLY TO OBJECTION 2. As the Philosopher says,[7] "it is better that all things be regulated by law, than left to be decided by judges": and this for three reasons. First, because it is easier to find a few wise men competent to frame right laws, than to find the many who would be necessary to judge aright of each single case. Secondly, because those who make laws consider long beforehand what laws to make; whereas judgment on each single case has to be pronounced as soon as it arises: and it is easier for man to see what is right, by taking many instances into consideration, than by considering one solitary fact. Thirdly, because lawgivers judge in the abstract and of future events; whereas those who sit in judgment of things present, towards which

---

1   *as stated above*   Q. 92, 1.
2   *as the Philosopher says*   See *Nicomachean Ethics* 5, 4. 1132a 22.
3   *what has been stated above*   Q. 90, 1 and 2.
4   *Isidore says*   See *Etymologiae* 5, 20.
5   *As stated above*   Q. 63, 1; Q. 94, 3.
6   *as the Philosopher says*   See *Politics* 1, 1. 1253a 31.
7   *As the Philosopher says*   See *Rhetoric* 1, 1. 1354a 31.

they are affected by love, hatred, or some kind of cupidity; wherefore their judgment is perverted.

Since then the animated justice of the judge is not found in every man, and since it can be deflected, therefore it was necessary, whenever possible, for the law to determine how to judge, and for very few matters to be left to the decision of men.

REPLY TO OBJECTION 3. Certain individual facts which cannot be covered by the law "have necessarily to be committed to judges," as the Philosopher says[1] in the same passage: for instance, "concerning something that has happened or not happened," and the like.

Article 2. Whether every human law is derived from the natural law?

OBJECTION 1. It would seem that not every human law is derived from the natural law. For the Philosopher says[2] that "the legal just is that which originally was a matter of indifference." But those things which arise from the natural law are not matters of indifference. Therefore the enactments of human laws are not derived from the natural law.

OBJECTION 2. Further, positive law is contrasted with natural law, as stated by Isidore[3] and the Philosopher.[4] But those things which flow as conclusions from the general principles of the natural law belong to the natural law, as stated above.[5] Therefore that which is established by human law does not belong to the natural law.

OBJECTION 3. Further, the law of nature is the same for all; since the Philosopher says that "the natural just is that which is equally valid everywhere."[6] If therefore human laws were derived from the natural law, it would follow that they too are the same for all: which is clearly false.

OBJECTION 4. Further, it is possible to give a reason for things which are derived from the natural law. But "it is not possible to give the reason for all the legal enactments of the lawgivers," as the jurist says.[7] Therefore not all human laws are derived from the natural law.

ON THE CONTRARY, Tully says:[8] "Things which emanated from nature and were approved by custom, were sanctioned by fear and reverence for the laws."

I ANSWER THAT, As Augustine says[9] "that which is not just seems to be no law at all": wherefore the force of a law depends on the extent of its justice. Now in human affairs a thing is said to be just, from being right, according to the rule of reason. But the first rule of reason is the law of nature, as is clear from what has been stated above.[10] Consequently every human law has just so much of the nature of law, as it is derived from the law of nature. But if in any point it deflects from the law of nature, it is no longer a law but a perversion of law.

But it must be noted that something may be derived from the natural law in two ways: first, as a conclusion from premises, secondly, by way of determination of certain generalities. The first way is like to that by which, in sciences, demonstrated conclusions are drawn from the principles: while the second mode is likened to that whereby, in the arts, general forms are particularized as to details: thus the craftsman needs to determine the general form of a house to some particular shape. Some things are therefore derived from the general principles of the natural law, by way of conclusions; e.g., that "one must not kill" may be derived as a conclusion from the principle that "one should do harm to no man": while some are derived therefrom by way of determination; e.g., the law of nature has it that the evil-doer should be punished; but that he be punished in this or that way, is a determination of the law of nature.

Accordingly both modes of derivation are found in the human law. But those things which are derived in the first way, are contained in human law not as emanating therefrom exclusively, but have some force from the natural law also. But those things which are derived in the second way, have no other force than that of human law.

REPLY TO OBJECTION 1. The Philosopher is speaking of those enactments which are by way of determination or specification of the precepts of the natural law.

REPLY TO OBJECTION 2. This argument avails for those things that are derived from the natural law, by way of conclusions.

---

1 *as the Philosopher says* See *Rhetoric* 1, 1. 1354b 13.
2 *the Philosopher says* See *Nicomachean Ethics* 5, 7. 1134b 20.
3 *as stated by Isidore* See *Etymologiae* 5, 4.
4 *and the Philosopher* See *Nicomachean Ethics* 5, 7. 1134b 18.
5 *as stated above* Q. 94, 4.
6 *the natural ... everywhere* See *Nicomachean Ethics* 5, 7. 1134b 19.
7 *the jurist says* See *Digest* 1, 3, 20.
8 *Tully says* "Tully" is the commonly used nickname for Marcus Tullius Cicero (Roman orator, statesman, philosopher, 106–43 BCE). The reference here is to his *De Inventione* 2, 53.
9 *As Augustine says* See *De Libero Arbitrio* 1, 5.
10 *what has been stated above* Q. 91, 2.

REPLY TO OBJECTION 3. The general principles of the natural law cannot be applied to all men in the same way on account of the great variety of human affairs: and hence arises the diversity of positive laws among various people.

REPLY TO OBJECTION 4. These words of the Jurist are to be understood as referring to decisions of rulers in determining particular points of the natural law: on which determinations the judgment of expert and prudent men is based as on its principles; in so far, to wit, as they see at once what is the best thing to decide.

Hence the Philosopher says[1] that in such matters, "we ought to pay as much attention to the undemonstrated sayings and opinions of persons who surpass us in experience, age and prudence, as to their demonstrations."

Article 3. Whether Isidore's description of the quality of positive law is appropriate?

OBJECTION 1. It would seem that Isidore's description[2] of the quality of positive law is not appropriate, when he says: "Law shall be virtuous, just, possible to nature, according to the custom of the country, suitable to place and time, necessary, useful; clearly expressed, lest by its obscurity it lead to misunderstanding; framed for no private benefit, but for the common good." Because he had previously expressed[3] the quality of law in three conditions, saying that "law is anything founded on reason, provided that it foster religion, be helpful to discipline, and further the common weal." Therefore it was needless to add any further conditions to these.

OBJECTION 2. Further, Justice is included in honesty, as Tully says.[4] Therefore after saying "honest" it was superfluous to add "just."

OBJECTION 3. Further, written law is condivided[5] with custom, according to Isidore.[6] Therefore it should not be stated in the definition of law that it is "according to the custom of the country."

OBJECTION 4. Further, a thing may be necessary in two ways. It may be necessary simply, because it cannot be otherwise: and that which is necessary in this way, is not subject to human judgment, wherefore human law is not concerned with necessity of this kind. Again a thing may be necessary for an end: and this necessity is the same as usefulness. Therefore it is superfluous to say both "necessary" and "useful."

ON THE CONTRARY, stands the authority of Isidore.

I ANSWER THAT, Whenever a thing is for an end, its form must be determined proportionately to that end; as the form of a saw is such as to be suitable for cutting.[7] Again, everything that is ruled and measured must have a form proportionate to its rule and measure. Now both these conditions are verified of human law: since it is both something ordained to an end; and is a rule or measure ruled or measured by a higher measure. And this higher measure is twofold, viz. the Divine law and the natural law, as explained above.[8] Now the end of human law is to be useful to man, as the jurist states.[9] Wherefore Isidore in determining the nature of law, lays down, at first, three conditions; viz. that it "foster religion," inasmuch as it is proportionate to the Divine law; that it be "helpful to discipline," inasmuch as it is proportionate to the nature law; and that it "further the common weal," inasmuch as it is proportionate to the utility of mankind.

All the other conditions mentioned by him are reduced to these three. For it is called virtuous because it fosters religion. And when he goes on to say that it should be "just, possible to nature, according to the customs of the country, adapted to place and time," he implies that it should be helpful to discipline. For human discipline depends first on the order of reason, to which he refers by saying "just": secondly, it depends on the ability of the agent; because discipline should be adapted to each one according to his ability, taking also into account the ability of nature (for the same burdens should be not laid on children as adults); and should be according to human customs; since man cannot live alone in society, paying no heed to others: thirdly, it depends on certain circumstances, in respect of which he says, "adapted to place and time." The remaining words, "necessary, useful," etc. mean that law should further the common weal: so that "necessity" refers to the removal of evils; "usefulness" to the attainment of good; "clearness of expression," to the need of preventing any harm ensuing from the law itself. And since, as stated above,[10] law is or-

---

1   the Philosopher says   See Nicomachean Ethics 6, 11. 1143b 11.

2   Isidore's description   See Etymologiae 5, 21.

3   he had previously expressed   See Etymologiae 5, 3.

4   as Tully says   See De Officiis 1, 7.

5   condivided   Divided in coordination.

6   according to Isidore   See Etymologiae. 2, 10 and 5, 3.

7   Whenever a thing ... suitable for cutting   See Aristotle, Physics 2, 9. 200a 10.

8   as explained above   Article 2; Q. 93, 3.

9   as the jurist states   See Digest, 25, 3.

10   as stated above   Q. 90, 2.

dained to the common good, this is expressed in the last part of the description.

This suffices for the Replies to the Objections.

Article 4. Whether Isidore's division of human laws is appropriate?

OBJECTION 1. It would seem that Isidore wrongly divided human statutes or human law. For under this law he includes the "law of nations," so called, because, as he says,[1] "nearly all nations use it." But as he says,[2] "natural law is that which is common to all nations." Therefore the law of nations is not contained under positive human law, but rather under natural law.

OBJECTION 2. Further, those laws which have the same force, seem to differ not formally but only materially. But "statutes, decrees of the commonalty, senatorial decrees," and the like which he mentions,[3] all have the same force. Therefore they do not differ, except materially. But art takes no notice of such a distinction: since it may go on to infinity. Therefore this division of human laws is not appropriate.

OBJECTION 3. Further, just as, in the state, there are princes, priests and soldiers, so are there other human offices. Therefore it seems that, as this division includes[4] "military law," and "public law," referring to priests and magistrates; so also it should include other laws pertaining to other offices of the state.

OBJECTION 4. Further, those things that are accidental should be passed over. But it is accidental to law that it be framed by this or that man. Therefore it is unreasonable to divide laws according to the names of lawgivers, so that one be called the "Cornelian" law, another[5] the "Falcidian" law, etc.

ON THE CONTRARY, The authority of Isidore[6] suffices.

I ANSWER THAT, A thing can of itself be divided in respect of something contained in the notion of that thing. Thus a soul either rational or irrational is contained in the notion of animal: and therefore animal is divided properly and of itself in respect of its being rational or irrational; but not in the point of its being white or black, which are entirely beside the notion of animal. Now, in the notion of human law, many things are contained, in respect of any of which human law can be divided properly and of itself. For in the first place it belongs to the notion of human law, to be derived from the law of nature, as explained above.[7] In this respect positive law is divided into the "law of nations" and "civil law," according to the two ways in which something may be derived from the law of nature, as stated above.[8] Because, to the law of nations belong those things which are derived from the law of nature, as conclusions from premises, e.g., just buyings and sellings, and the like, without which men cannot live together, which is a point of the law of nature, since man is by nature a social animal, as is proved[9] in *Politics* 1. But those things which are derived from the law of nature by way of particular determination, belong to the civil law, according as each state decides on what is best for itself.

Secondly, it belongs to the notion of human law, to be ordained to the common good of the state. In this respect human law may be divided according to the different kinds of men who work in a special way for the common good: e.g., priests, by praying to God for the people; princes, by governing the people; soldiers, by fighting for the safety of the people. Wherefore certain special kinds of law are adapted to these men.

Thirdly, it belongs to the notion of human law, to be framed by that one who governs the community of the state, as shown above.[10] In this respect, there are various human laws according to the various forms of government. Of these, according to the Philosopher one is "monarchy," i.e., when the state is governed by one; and then we have "Royal Ordinances." Another form is "aristocracy," i.e., government by the best men or men of highest rank; and then we have the "Authoritative legal opinions" [*Responsa Prudentum*] and "Decrees of the Senate" [*Senatus consulta*]. Another form is "oligarchy," i.e., government by a few rich and powerful men; and then we have "Praetorian," also called "Honorary," law. Another form of government is that of the people, which is called "democracy," and there we have "Decrees of the commonalty" [*Plebiscita*]. There is also tyrannical government, which is altogether corrupt, which, therefore, has no corresponding law. Finally, there is a form of government made up of all these, and which is

---

1   *he includes ... he says*   See *Etymologiae* 5, 6.
2   *as he says*   See *Etymologiae* 5, 4.
3   *he mentions*   See *Etymologiae* 5, 9.
4   *this division includes*   See *Etymologiae* 5, 7, 8.
5   *one be called ... another*   See *Etymologiae* 5, 15.
6   *The authority of Isidore*   See Objection 1.

7   *as explained above*   Article 2.
8   *as stated above*   Article 2.
9   *as is proved*   Aristotle, *Politics*, 1, 1. 1253a 2.
10 *as shown above*   Q. 90, 3.

the best:[1] and in this respect we have law sanctioned by the "Lords and Commons," as stated by Isidore.[2]

Fourthly, it belongs to the notion of human law to direct human actions. In this respect, according to the various matters of which the law treats, there are various kinds of laws, which are sometimes named after their authors: thus we have the "Lex Julia"[3] about adultery, the "Lex Cornelia"[4] concerning assassins, and so on, differentiated in this way, not on account of the authors, but on account of the matters to which they refer.

REPLY TO OBJECTION 1. The law of nations is indeed, in some way, natural to man, in so far as he is a reasonable being, because it is derived from the natural law by way of a conclusion that is not very remote from its premises. Wherefore men easily agreed thereto. Nevertheless it is distinct from the natural law, especially it is distinct from the natural law which is common to all animals.

The Replies to the other Objections are evident from what has been said.

---

1   *a form of government ... is the best*   Aristotle, *Politics* 3, 7. 1279a 26.

2   *as stated by Isidore*   See *Etymologiae* 5. 4–9.

3   *Lex Julia*   See *Digest*, 48, 5.

4   *Lex Cornelia*   See *Digest*, 48, 8.

MARSILIUS OF PADUA
(c. 1270 – c. 1342)

IN THE EARLY FOURTEENTH CENTURY, LOUIS IV, EMPEROR of the Holy Roman Empire, was engaged in a power struggle with Pope John XXII. The Pope, claiming that, as God's representative, his approval was necessary for Louis to become emperor, excommunicated him and demanded his removal from power. In response, Louis sought help from Marsilius[1] to provide him with arguments to support his claim to power. The result was *Defensor Pacis*, Marsilius's significant contribution to political scholarship. In this work, Marsilius argued that the power of both political and religious authorities comes from the will of the people; the text is both a defense of democratic principles and an attack on Papal authority.

Little is known about his early life. He was in the military for a time and also studied medicine at the University of Padua. He traveled from Italy to France (where he completed his medical studies), and by 1313 he had become rector of the University of Paris. Marsilius was subsequently made a canon of the Church of Padua by Pope John XXII. He then became an adviser to Louis IV—the position he held when he was commissioned to write *Defensor Pacis*. The work was completed in 1324; within two years it was condemned by the Pope, who had already excommunicated Louis IV. Marsilius continued to be an active supporter of Louis IV, and remained under his protection. Shortly after his death around 1342, Marsilius was described by Pope Clement VI as the most "pestilent heretic" he had ever read.

Like Plato and Al-Fārābi before him, Marsilius explores the nature of a state by first describing how a state should ideally be constructed. (He then argues that intervention in the running of the state by religious authorities, the Pope in particular, is harmful to it.) Throughout *Defensor Pacis* Marsilius advocates the separation of religious and secular authority. He argues that in matters of law and government rulers owe their authority to the people they rule; their objective should thus be to serve the interests of the people. In effect, Marsilius argues for a form of government resembling that of a modern democracy, several centuries before any such system began to take shape.

Defensor Pacis had an enduring influence, providing an intellectual foundation for arguments used in a number of power struggles between religious and secular leaders in the centuries that followed. Thomas Cromwell was responsible for having it translated into English in the sixteenth century; he used it in his position of Principal Secretary of State to help support Henry VIII when England severed its ties with the Pope and established the Church of England. Marsilius's work also had an impact on the thought of the leaders of the Protestant Reformation in the sixteenth century, and in the eighteenth century it greatly influenced Jean-Jacques Rousseau, especially in its emphasis on the central importance of government as the expression of the will of the people.

♦ ♦ ♦ ♦ ♦

The Defender of the Peace
(1324)

Discourse 1, Chapter 10

On differentiating and identifying the significations of this term "law"; and on its most proper signification, which is the one intended by us

1. Now since we have said that election is the more perfect and superior way of instituting the principate,[2] we do well to inquire into its efficient cause,[3] namely, that from which, in its full excellence, it must ensue; for the result of this will

---

1   "Marsilius" is the Latinized version of his name; the Italian version "Marsilio" is also often used. The reference to Padua is conventionally added to distinguish him from Marsilius of Inghen, a fourteenth-century Dutch philosopher.

2   *principate* Jurisdiction of the sovereign. "Instituting the principate" is roughly equivalent to "establishing governments."

3   *efficient cause* One of the four "causes" defined by Aristotle. This one alone corresponds to what we normally call "cause." The ef-

be that the cause both of elected principate, and similarly of the other parts of the polity, becomes apparent. But because the principate must regulate human civil acts (as we demonstrated in chapter 5 of this discourse), and do this according to a standard that is and should be the form of that which exercises it,[1] it is necessary to inquire into this standard: if there is any such thing, what it is, and what is its purpose. For the efficient cause of the standard may turn out to be the same as that of the prince.

2. We suppose, then—as a thing almost self-evident by induction—that this standard, which is called 'statute' or 'custom' or by the common term of 'law,' exists in all perfect communities. Taking this as given, we shall first show what it[2] is. Secondly we shall identify its necessity in terms of its end.[3] Finally we shall determine, through demonstration,[4] by what kind of action, and on the part of what or which agents, it should be instituted. And this will be to inquire into its legislator or active cause; to whom we think that the election of principates also belongs, as we shall show by demonstration in the following chapters. In addition, as a result of these discussions, the matter or subject of the abovementioned standard (which we have called the law) will become apparent. For this is the princely part, to which it belongs[5] to regulate the political or civil acts of men according to law.

3. As we embark on what we have proposed, therefore, it is appropriate to distinguish between the meanings of (or what is signified by) this term 'law,' so that its multiple senses do not lead to frustration. For among its many applications, this term in one of its significations implies a natural inclination of the senses towards some action or passion; and this is the way the Apostle spoke of it in Romans 7, when he said: "But I see another law in my members, warring against the law of my mind."[6] On another understanding, this term 'law' is said of any trained capacity for a work of art,[7] and in general of every form of such a work existing in the mind, from which, as from an exemplar or measure,

the forms of things made by art result. In this sense it says in Ezekiel 43: "Behold, this is the law of the house.... And these are the measures of the altar."[8] In a third way, 'law' is taken as a rule containing admonitions for those human acts that result from an imperative, insofar as they are ordered towards glory or punishment in the world to come. In this sense the Mosaic law[9] was called a law in respect of part of it, and so too the evangelical law[10] is called a law in respect of the whole of it. Hence the Apostle in Hebrews says of these laws: "For the priesthood being changed, there is made of necessity a change also of the law."[11] So too the term 'law' is used of the instruction of the gospel in James 1: "But whoso looketh into the perfect law of liberty, and continueth therein ... this man shall be blessed in his deed."[12] Furthermore on this understanding of law all religious followings are called laws, for example those of Mohammed or the Persians, either wholly or in part; even if of these only the Mosaic and the evangelical, viz. the Christian, contain truth. In this way, too, Aristotle called such followings 'laws' in *Metaphysics* 2, when he said: "Laws show how much force that which is customary has";[13] and in book 7 of the same: "The rest have been introduced as stories to persuade the many to the laws and to what is beneficial."[14] Fourthly, however, and in a more widespread sense, this term 'law' implies a science or doctrine or universal judgment of those things that are just and advantageous in terms of the city, and their opposites.

4. And understood in this sense, law can be considered in two ways: in one way, simply in itself, so that it does no more than give an indication of what is just or unjust, advantageous or harmful; and as such it is called the science or doctrine of right. In a second way it can be considered inasmuch as a command is given in respect of its observation, which coerces by means of penalty or reward meted out in this world; or inasmuch as it is handed down by way of such a command. And considered in this way it is most properly called, and most properly is, law. Moreover Aristotle's definition takes it in this way, when he said in *Ethics* 10, chapter

---

ficient cause is the primary source of change bringing about the effect.

1   *the form of that which exercises it*   The general and ideal pattern for any ruler.

2   *it*   That is, *law*.

3   *end*   That at which it aims, by its very nature.

4   *demonstration*   Proving indubitably by reasoning.

5   *which it belongs*   Whose function it is.

6   *But I see ... my mind*   Romans 7.23.

7   *work of art*   Anything made by human activity, as contrasted with what arises by the processes of nature.

8   *Behold ... to altar*   Ezekiel 43.12-13.

9   *Mosaic law*   Jewish law, as given in the Old Testament. ("Mosaic" is the adjective form of "Moses.")

10   *evangelical law*   Christian—New Testament—law.

11   *For the priesthood ... the law*   Hebrews 7.12.

12   *But whoso ... his deeds*   James 1.25.

13   *Aristotle ... has*   The reference here is to his *Metaphysics* 2, 3. 995a 4.

14   *The rest ... beneficial*   *Metaphysics* 12, 8. 1074b 3.

8: "Law has coercive power, being speech from a certain prudence[1] and understanding."[2] A law, then, is a "speech" (or a pronouncement) "from a certain" (namely, political) "prudence and understanding," i.e., an ordinance concerning the just and the beneficial and their opposites arrived at through political prudence, "having coercive power," i.e., that a command has been given in respect of its observation which an individual is forced to observe, or that it has been enacted by way of such a command.

5. It follows that not every true cognizance of things that are just and beneficial in civil terms is a law, unless a coercive command has been given in respect of its observation, or it has been delivered by way of a command—even though such true cognizance of these matters is necessarily required for a perfect law. On the contrary, sometimes a false cognizance of things that are just and advantageous becomes law, when a command to observe it is given or it is delivered by way of a command. We see this in the lands of some barbarians who cause it to be observed, as a just thing, that a murderer be absolved from civil guilt and penalty if he offers some price in goods for this offence, when however this is simply speaking unjust; and in consequence their laws are not unqualifiedly perfect. For allowing that they have the required form, viz. a coercive command that they be observed, they nonetheless lack the required condition, viz. the requisite true ordinance of what is just.

6. Included in this understanding of law are all those standards of things just and advantageous in civil terms that have been instituted by human authority, such as customs, statutes, plebiscites, decretals[3] and all other things of this kind, namely, which rely (as we have just said) on human authority.

7. Nevertheless we should not be unaware that both the evangelical and the Mosaic law (and perhaps other religious followings too) can be considered and compared in different ways, wholly or in part, in relation to human acts for the status either of this world or of that to come; and that as such they sometimes come—or have come or will come in future under the third signification of law, and sometimes

under the last, as will be made plain in more detail in chapters 8 and 9 of the second discourse. And in some cases this accords with the truth; in others, with a false imagining and a vain promise.

It is clear from what has just been said, therefore, both that there is a standard or law of human civil acts, and what it is.

Discourse 1, Chapter 11

On the necessity of making laws (taken in their most proper signification); and that it is not expedient for any prince, however virtuous or just, to exercise his function without laws

1. Now that we have separated out these understandings of law, we wish to show its necessity in terms of ends, when it is taken in its last and most proper signification. The principal necessity is civil justice and the common advantage, but a secondary necessity is a kind of security for those in the position of prince—especially by hereditary succession—and the long duration of their principate. The first necessity, then, is as follows: since it is necessary to institute within a polity that without which civil judgments cannot be made in a way that is simply speaking correct, and also that through which they are passed in due fashion and saved from defect insofar as this is possible for human acts. Law is a thing of this sort, to the extent that the prince has been limited to passing civil judgments in accordance with it. Therefore it is necessary to institute law within a polity. The first proposition of this demonstration is almost self-evident, and very close to being incapable of demonstration. The certainty of it should and can also be understood from chapter 5 of this discourse, section 7. The second proposition will become clear in the following way: since for a judgment to be completely good there is required, on the part of judges, both a righteous affection[4] and a true cognizance of the matters to be judged, the opposites of which corrupt civil judgments. For a perverted affection on the part of the judge, like hate or love or avarice, corrupts his desire. But these things are kept out of the judgment, and it is saved from them, when the judge or prince has been limited to passing judgments in accordance with the

---

1   *prudence* Aristotle took this to be practical knowledge about matters involving success in our lives—about what is advantageous, useful, expedient, profitable, or fitting for one's self. The contrast is with abstract scientific knowledge.

2   *Law has ... understanding* Aristotle, *Nicomachean Ethics* 10, 9. 1180a 21. An alternative translation of the Greek here would be *discourse emerging from prudence and understanding.*

3   *decretals* Decrees by the Pope on matters of church law.

---

4   *affection* Feeling, emotion, state of mind toward a thing.

laws, because the law lacks all perverted affection. For it has not been made with an eye to friend or foe, help or hurt, but universally with regard to the individual acting well or badly in civil terms. All other things are accidental[1] to the law and outside it, in a way that they are not outside the judge. For persons who are up for judgment can be friendly or hostile to the one who judges, helpful or harmful, giving or promising something; and likewise with all the other attitudes that can give rise to an affection in the judge which corrupts his judgment. For this reason no judgment (so far as possible) should be left to the discretion of the judge, but should rather be defined in law and pronounced in accordance with it.

2. This was the opinion of the divine Aristotle, *Politics* 3, chapter 9, where he asks (following his purpose) whether it is better for a polity to be ruled by the best man without a law, or by the best law,[2] and says: "That has the advantage" i.e., is superior for the purposes of judging "which entirely lacks the element of passion" i.e., the affection that can corrupt a judgment "over that to which it is innate. Now therefore this" viz. passion or affection "is not inherent in the law; but every human soul necessarily has it"—and he said "every," not excepting anyone, however virtuous. Repeating this opinion in his *Rhetoric*, Book 1 chapter 1, he says: "The greatest thing of all" is sought for (namely, that nothing should be left to the discretion of the judge to be judged without a law) "because the judgment of the legislator" i.e., the law "is not partial" i.e., is not passed for the sake of any particular man "but concerns things future and universal. But a prefect and a judge make their judgments concerning things already present and defined, to which love and hate and personal convenience are often annexed, so that they cannot sufficiently discern the truth, but attend in their judgment to what is disagreeable or pleasant to them personally."[3] He says this again in the same book, chapter 2: "For" he says "we do not pass judgment alike[4] when we are unhappy and joyful, when we love or when we hate."[5]

3. Judgment is corrupted further by the ignorance of judges, however good their affection or intention. And this fault or failing is also removed and remedied through the law, for it contains an almost complete definition of what is just and unjust, advantageous or harmful, in respect of any and every human civil act. But this cannot adequately come about through any single man, however resourceful. Because one man alone—and not even, perhaps, all the men of one era—could discover or keep note of all civil actions defined in law. On the contrary, what was said on the subject by the initial discoverers, and even by all the men of the same era who took note of them, amounted to a modest and imperfect thing, which was later supplemented by the contributions of posterity. And familiar experience is enough to see this, in the addition and subtraction and total change to the contrary which has sometimes been made in the laws, depending on different eras and on different times within the same era.

Aristotle too attests to this in *Politics* 2, chapter 3, when he says: "One must not be unaware of this, that it is necessary to recognize much time and many years, in which it may not escape notice, whether these things were well-arranged,"[6] namely, the things that should be laid down as laws. And he says the same in his *Rhetoric*, Book 1 chapter 1: "Then" he says "acts of legislation take place out of things that have been considered for a long time."[7] And this is confirmed by reason, since acts of legislation need prudence (as was plain earlier from the description of law), but prudence needs long experience, and this in turn needs a great deal of time. Hence in *Ethics* 6: "A sign of what has been asserted is also that young men become geometers and trained and knowledgeable about such things, but it does not seem that they become prudent. The reason is, that prudence is of individual things, which are made known by experience; but the young man has none; for it is length of time that yields experience."[8] And accordingly what one man discovers or can know by himself, both in the science of what is just and beneficial in civil terms and in the other sciences, is little or nothing. Going further, what men of one era observe is an imperfect thing in comparison with that which is observed as a result of many eras; and because of this Aristotle, discussing the discovery of truth in each of the arts and disciplines, says in *Metaphysics* 2 chapter 1: "In respect of one" namely, discoverer of any discipline or art "he contributes to it" i.e., discovers about it by himself "little or nothing, but what is jointed together from all of

---

1   *accidental*   Incidental, non-essential.

2   *This was the opinion ... best law*   Aristotle, *Politics* 3, 15. 1286a 17.

3   *but concerns things ... personally*   Aristotle, *Rhetoric* 1, 1. 1354b 4ff.

4   *pass judgment alike*   Render the same judgment.

5   *when we love or when we hate*   Aristotle, *Rhetoric* 1, 2. 1356a 14.

6   *One must ... well-arranged*   *Politics* 2, 5. 1264a 1.

7   *acts of legislation ... long time*   *Rhetoric* 1, 1. 1354b 3.

8   *A sign ... experience*   *Nicomachean Ethics* 6, 9. 1142a 12.

them becomes something sizeable."[1] This passage is clearer, however, in the translation from the Arabic, in which it reads: "And each individual one of them," i.e., of the discoverers of any discipline or art, "grasps either nothing of the truth or a very modest amount. When therefore an assemblage has been made from all those who have grasped something, then the assemblage will be of some quantity"; which is most apparent in the case of astrology.

In this way, by men's mutual aid and by adding together things discovered later and things discovered earlier, all the arts and disciplines have been brought to completion.... Averroes,[2] explaining these words in his *Commentary*, Book 2, says this: "And what he" namely, Aristotle "says in this chapter is plain. For no one by himself can discover the productive and reflective" (i.e., theoretical) "arts in their greater part, because they are not brought to completion except by the aid given by a forerunner to a successor.[3] Aristotle says the same in his *Refutations*, Book 2, last chapter,[4] concerning the discovery of rhetoric and all the other arts (whatever may have been the case with the discovery of logic, which he ascribes in its perfection to himself alone without any discovery or help of a predecessor—in which he was apparently unique). He says this too in *Ethics* 8, chapter 1: "Two men," he says, "coming" i.e., coming together "are more able to act and to understand [than one man alone]."[5] And if two, then it is even more the case with more than two, both together and in succession, that they are better than one alone. And this is what he says on the subject in *Politics* 3, chapter 9: "It will perhaps seem incongruous," he says, "if one person should perceive better, judging with two eyes and two ears and acting with two hands and two feet, than many with many."[6]

Since, therefore, the law is an eye resulting from many eyes, i.e., an understanding forged from the understanding of many, for the purpose of avoiding error with regard to

civil judgments and of judging correctly, it is safer for those judgments to be made in accordance with the law than at the judge's discretion. And for this reason it is necessary that a law should be laid down, if polities are to have the best arrangements with respect to what is just and advantageous for them in civil terms. For it is through the law that civil judgments are saved from ignorance and from the perverted affection of judges; and this was the minor premise of the demonstration we undertook and by which we have tried, from the beginning of this chapter, to identify the necessity of laws.... Laws, therefore, are necessary in order to exclude malice and error from the civil judgments or sentences of judges.

4. Because of this it was Aristotle's advice not to grant any judge or prince the discretion to judge or to command in civil matters without the law, in those things that could be defined in law. Hence in *Ethics* 4 (the treatise on justice), chapter 5, Aristotle said: "For this reason we do not allow the man to be prince, but" in accordance with "reason,"[7] i.e., law; giving the grounds that we introduced earlier, viz. the perverted affection that can occur in the man. Likewise in *Politics* 3, chapter 6, when he said: "But the difficulty stated before makes nothing so plain as that laws, correctly laid down, should have dominion,"[8] i.e., that those in the position of prince should exercise dominion in accordance with them. The same again, in the same book, chapter 9, when he said: "Whoever bids the intellect be prince, seems to bid God and the laws be prince, while he who bids a man" (namely, without a law and at his own discretion) "puts in place a beast";[9] adding the reason a little bit later, when he said: "Because law is intelligence without appetite"[10]—as if to say, the law is intelligence or cognizance without appetite, i.e., without any kind of affection. He reiterates this opinion in his *Rhetoric* as well, Book I chapter I, where he says: "It is therefore most appropriate, that laws correctly laid down should themselves determine everything, whatever arises, and as little as possible be left to judges";[11] giving the reasons for this that were adduced earlier, namely, to keep the malice and ignorance of judges out of civil judgments; which cannot occur in the law as they do in the judge, as

1   *little or nothing ... sizeable*   Metaphysics 2, 1. 993b 2.

2   *Averroes* Ibn Rushd (1126–98), known as Averroes, wrote important commentaries on Aristotle's work. Latin translations of Averroes' oeuvre were largely responsible for the revival of Aristotle in Europe; it is difficult to overestimate his influence on Christian, Muslim and Jewish theology.

3   *arts in their greater part ... successor* Aristotelis opera cum Averrois commentaries, Vol. 8, Book 2, ch. 1, fo. 29r.

4   *last chapter* Aristotle, *On Sophistical Refutations* 34. 183b 34ff.

5   *are more able to act and to understand* Aristotle, *Nicomachean Ethics* 8, 1. 1155a 16.

6   *It will perhaps ... many with many* Aristotle, *Politics* 3, 16. 1287b 26.

7   *"reason"* Aristotle, *Nicomachean Ethics* 5, 6. 1134a 35.

8   *But the difficulty ... dominion* Aristotle, *Politics* 3, 11. 1282b 1.

9   *puts in place a beast* Aristotle, *Politics* 3, 16. 1287a 28.

10   *Because law is intelligence without appetite* Aristotle, *Politics* 3, 16. 1287a 32. *Appetite* here means *strong desire*.

11   *It is therefore most appropriate ... left to judges* Aristotle, *Rhetoric* I, I. 1354a 32.

we showed before. And in amplification of these passages Aristotle says openly in *Politics* 4, chapter 4, that: "where the laws are not prince" (i.e., where those in the position of prince do not exercise their function in accordance with them), "there is no [temperate] polity ... For the law should be prince over all."[1]

5. It remains now to show that all those in the position of prince should exercise their function in accordance with the law, not beyond it, and especially monarchs who exercise this function together with all their posterity, so that their principates may be more secure and long-lasting. (This was given as the secondary necessity of laws at the beginning of this chapter.) We can see that this is so in the first place because to exercise the function of prince according to the laws saves their judgments from defects arising from ignorance and perverted inclination. As a result, being regulated both in themselves and towards the citizens who are their subjects, they suffer fewer acts of sedition (and consequent dissolution of their principate) than they would encounter if they acted badly in accordance with their own discretion. Aristotle says this plainly in *Politics* 5, chapter 5: "For a kingdom," says Aristotle, "is least of all destroyed from without; but many kinds of destruction occur from within itself. It is destroyed in two ways: one, when those who share in the kingship themselves create sedition; two, when they try to govern more tyrannically, demanding to be masters of many and beyond the law. Now it is no longer kingdoms that come into being, but if they come into being, they are rather monarchies and tyrannies."[2]

6. Someone will put forward an objection about the best man, that he has no ignorance or perverted affection. Let us say, though, that this is a very rare occurrence—and even then, not in a way equal to the law. We argued this point earlier on the basis of Aristotle, from reason and the experience of the senses, since it is a fact that every soul has this, i.e., inclination that is sometimes malign. It is easy to believe it from Daniel 13. For it is written there that "two elders came with evil thoughts against Susannah, to put her to death."[3] Now these were old men and priests and judges of the people in that year, who nevertheless bore false witness against her because she had refused to acquiesce in their evil lust. So if elders and old men, of whom one would

scarcely have thought it, were corrupted by carnal lust (and how much more by avarice and all the other vices) what should we think about the rest of men? With certainty, that no one, however virtuous, can lack perverted passion and ignorance in the same way as the law. And therefore it is safer for civil judgments to be regulated by law than committed to the discretion of a judge, however virtuous.

7. Supposing however—even if this is something extremely rare or impossible—that there is some man in the position of prince who is such a hero that neither passion nor ignorance occur in him. What shall we say of his children, who are unlike him and who, because of their unruliness in exercising their function according to their own discretion, commit acts which cause them to lose their principate? Unless perhaps someone will say that their father, the best of men, will not hand the principate on to them? But this should not be given a hearing: firstly because it is not in his power to deprive his sons of this succession, in that the principate is due to his line by succession; and secondly because even if it were in his power to transfer the principate to whomever he wished, he would not deprive his sons of it however bad they were. Hence Aristotle, replying to this objection in *Politics* 3, chapter 9, says: "Moreover this is something difficult to believe" (viz. that a father will deprive his sons of the principate) "and of greater virtue than accords with human nature."[4] For this reason it is more expedient for those who exercise the function of prince to be regulated and limited by law, rather than pass civil judgments at their own discretion; for by following this law they will not do anything wrong or reprehensible, and as a result their principate will be made more secure and long-lasting.

8. And this was the advice of the excellent Aristotle to all those in the position of prince (of which, however, they take little notice) when he said in *Politics* 6, chapter 6: "The fewer the things of which they are masters" (namely, without a law) "the longer, necessarily, that any principate will last; for they" viz. princes "become less despotic, and more equitable in their habits and less the object of ill-will from their subjects."[5] And following up this idea, he adduces the testimony of a certain most prudent king called Theopompus, who gave up some of the power granted to him. We have judged it apt to quote this passage of Aristotle's because of the uniqueness of this prince and his outstand-

---

1   *For the law should be prince over all* Aristotle, *Politics* 4. 1292a 32.

2   *For a kingdom ... monarchies and tyrannies* Aristotle, *Politics* 5, 10. 1312b 38.

3   *two elders ... to death* Daniel 13.28.

4   *Moreover this is something ... human nature* Aristotle, *Politics* 3, 15. 1286b 26.

5   *become less despotic ... subjects* Aristotle, *Politics* 5, 11. 1313a 20.

ing virtue, almost unheard of in anyone else throughout the ages. Aristotle, then, said: "Again, when Theopompus moderated" i.e., lessened his power, which perhaps seemed excessive "and among other things established a principate of ephors;[1] for in taking away from power" namely, his own "he increased his realm in time" i.e., made it more long-lasting "whereby in some way he made it greater, not less. These" i.e., these words "he is reported to have said in response to his wife, who" namely, the wife "had said: Is he nothing" i.e., is he not "ashamed, to hand on to his sons a realm smaller than that which he received from his own father?" (and he gave her in reply the words just referred to:) "that should not be said, for I hand it on more long-lasting." O heroic utterance, issuing from the unheard-of prudence of Theopompus—and how much to be heeded by those who want to wield fullness of power, beyond the law, upon their subjects: for many princes have fallen through failing to take note of it. And indeed we ourselves have seen in these recent times a realm of some significance overturned almost entirely through a failure to take note of Theopompus' utterance, when its prince wanted to impose an unusual and extra-legal tax on his subjects.[2]

It is clear, then, from what we have said, that laws are necessary in polities if they are to be ordered in a way that is simply speaking correct, and if the principate is to last longer.

---

1   *ephors* Magistrates in certain Greek states with power over the king.

2   *when its prince ... his subjects* Marsilius refers to the attempt to institute a severe and unpopular tax by Philip IV ("the Fair") of France in 1314.

CHRISTINE DE PIZAN
(1364 – 1430)

Christine de Pizan was one of the leading intellectual figures in an age in which it was almost unimaginable for a woman to hold such a position. Commonly referred to as "France's first woman of letters," she was a major poet—the author of ten widely known volumes of verse—and was one of the first European women to earn her living by writing. For her essays about women, and their place in society, she has also sometimes been described as the first feminist.

De Pizan was born in Venice, and grew up in the French court, where her father was astrologer to Charles V. She married at fifteen, but her husband died ten years later. Because her husband's estate was contested in lawsuits and her brothers had moved back to Italy, she was in financial trouble; and when in the mid-1390s extended legal battles had resulted in only a small settlement, she turned to writing in an attempt to make a living. Her poems (the earliest of which were expressions of love and grief at the loss of her husband) achieved considerable favor with royalty and nobility, who rewarded her with gifts and commissions to write; such patronage was the usual way in which poets found support, but it was highly unusual for a woman to do so.

Her most famous—and notorious—poetic work, published in 1399, was "L'Epistre au Dieu d'amours" ("Letter to the God of Loves"). This was a reply to "Roman de la rose," ("Romance of the Rose"), a famous poetic work by Guillaume de Lorris. De Pizan's reply argued that the additions Guillaume had made around 1275 to his original poem were misogynistic and bawdy: courtly women, she claimed, would never use the coarse language attributed to them in the poem, and she objected to its demeaning representations of women merely as seducers. The very public literary debate that followed raised the issue of the literary depiction of women in more general terms, and made De Pizan a well-known figure in literary circles.

De Pizan's best-known prose works were written during the first two decades of the fifteenth century. *Le Livre de la cite des dames* (*The Book of the City of Ladies*, c. 1405) imagined a city of historical and contemporary women, telling stories of women from all levels of society, and describing their contributions to society. An excerpt is included below, together with selections from *Livre des fais d'armes et de chevallerie* (*Book of the Deeds of Arms and of Chivalry*, 1410), a scholarly work about the history of warfare, intended to serve as instruction for young noble warriors; and *Livre du corps de policie* (*Book of the Body Politic*, 1406–07).

The *Book of the Deeds of Arms and of Chivalry* was largely inspired by the Roman writer Vegetius' *Epitoma rei militaris* (*Epitome of Military Science*), but served as a text that incorporated much of the theory of warfare known in medieval times. De Pizan examined issues such as the treatment of noncombatants and prisoners, and thereby contributed to the formation of the medieval concept of just war, which had its roots in the work of the Roman jurist Cicero. The *Book of the Body Politic* anticipated Machiavelli's *The Prince* in its depiction of the education of princes. De Pizan also discussed the education of nobles and commoners, using the metaphor of the "body politic" to develop a model of the state as a unified body.

Other books included *Trois vertus ou Tresor de la cité des dames* (*Three Virtues or The Treasure of the City of Ladies*, 1405), intended to teach women strategies with which to combat masculine misogyny; *L'Avision Christine* (*Christine's Vision*, 1405), an allegorical autobiography and defense of her positions; *Fais et bonnes meurs du sage roy Charles V* (*The Deeds and Good Morals of the Wise King Charles V*, 1404), a work about the recently deceased king, written from firsthand knowledge at the request of the Regent.

During the civil war that followed the French defeat by the British at the Battle of Agincourt, Burgundian forces took Paris in 1418, and De Pizan was forced to leave the city; she entered a convent in Poisey, where she spent the rest of her life. *Ditié de Jehanne d'Arc* (*The Song of Joan of Arc*, 1429) was written in response to the jubilation of the French at their military success against the British and in celebration of Joan's part in it. It was the first poem written about Joan, the only major work about her written during her lifetime, and De Pizan's last work.

♦ ♦ ♦ ♦ ♦

City of the Ladies
(c. 1405)

1. Here Begins the Book of the City of the Ladies, in which the First Chapter Tells Why and for What Purpose This Book Was Written

Following the custom and discipline that rules my life, namely the untiring study of the liberal arts, I was sitting one day in my study surrounded by books on many different subjects. My mind a little weary from having studied the science of so many authors, I raised my eyes from my text, and decided to set aside difficult books for a moment to enjoy the work of some poet. In this state of mind I stumbled upon a small work that wasn't mine, but that someone else had been left in storage at my home. I opened it and saw that it was titled *The Lamentations of Mathéole*.[1] I smiled, since though I had never seen it, I had heard that this book had some reputation of saying important things for women!... I therefore thought that I could browse through it as a diversion. But I had hardly begun to read when my good mother called me to the table, it already being time for dinner. Deciding to continue reading the next day, I put it aside.

The next morning, as usual, I returned to my studies, having not forgotten my decision to read Mathéole's book.

I began to read and made some progress. But reading such a book is not very pleasant for those who do not enjoy lies. I found that it did not contribute at all to moral edification or virtue, and I was struck by the indecency of the language and the themes. Nonetheless, I perused it and read the final pages, before turning to more serious, useful studies. But the text of that book, even though it had some authority, disturbed me to the depths of my being. I asked myself what could be the causes and reasons that led so many men, including the educated, to slander women and denounce their conduct, whether with speech or in their treatises and writings. It was not merely one or two men, and certainly not only even this Mathéole, who hardly belongs among the educated, his book being fit only for ridicule; on the contrary, no text is entirely exempt. Philosophers, poets and moralists—and the list is long—all seem to speak with the same voice in concluding that women are wicked and given to vice.

Carefully examining these things in my mind, I reflected on my conduct, having been born a woman; I also thought the many women that I've known, from princesses and great ladies to women of the middle and lower classes, who have confided in me their intimate secrets; all with this evidence in mind, I searched to determine in my soul and conscience whether the testimony of so many illustrious men could be mistaken. But after reflecting hard on these matters, I could neither understand nor admit the truth of their judgment on the nature and conduct of women. I still refrained from accusing them, telling myself that it would be very unlikely that so many illustrious men, so many great scholars with such elevated and deep understanding, who were so clear-sighted in so many things—since it seemed to me that this was the case—could have spoken in such an outrageous manner. Among so many works it was impossible to find a moral text, whoever the author, in which I did not stumble upon some chapter or paragraph condemning women before I had finished reading. This led me to conclude that all of this was true and that my own mind, in its naiveté and ignorance must be unable to recognize the great faults that I also shared with other women. Thus, I accepted the judgments of others rather than what I felt and knew.

I fell so deeply and intensely into dark thoughts that one could have thought I had fallen into a trance. Thoughts welled-up like a fountain. A great number of authors came to mind; I reviewed them one by one and decided at last that God had made a miserable thing in creating woman. It astonished me that such a great artisan would agree to

---

1   *The Lamentations of Mathéolus*   A misogynistic tract written around 1295 by Mathéolus, otherwise known as Mathieu of Boulogne. The book's title is *Liber lamentationum Matheoluli*.

create a work so abominable, since, according to these authors, she was a receptacle containing in her depths every evil and vice. With these reflections, I was inundated with disgust and consternation, despising myself and the female sex altogether as if Nature had given birth to monsters. I lamented thus:

"Oh, God, how can this be? How can I believe, without falling into error, that your infinite wisdom and perfect benevolence could have created something that is not entirely good? Did You not create woman with a purpose? And did You not give her all the inclinations that it pleased You for her to have? Then how could this be possible since you are never in error? Nevertheless, here are so many serious accusations, so many assessments, judgments and condemnations brought against her. I cannot understand such an aberration. And if it is true, Lord, that so many abominations afflict women, as many claim—and, since You Yourself say that the agreement of many witnesses makes faith, it is likely that it is true—alas, my Lord, why did you not make me male so my inclinations would be in your service, so I would not deceive myself in anything and so I would have that great perfection that men are said to have! But since you did not desire this, and since you did not extend your bounty to me, forgive my weakness in your service, Lord, and deign to receive it; since the servant who receives least from his lord is least obliged in his service." I thus poured out my lamentation towards God, saying this and even more. I was sadly afflicted, since in my folly I despaired that God had placed me in a female body.

• • • • •

The Book of the Body Politic (1406–1407)

Chapter 4. Here We Begin to Discuss the Third Estate of the People, and First, Clerics Studying the Branches of Knowledge

In the community of people are found three estates, which means, especially in the city of Paris and other cities, the clergy, the burghers[1] and merchants, and the common people, such as artisans and laborers. Now it is suitable to consider the things to say that are beneficial as examples of good living for each of the distinct estates since they are different. And because the clerical class[2] is high, noble, and worthy of honor amongst the others, I will address it first, that is, the students, whether at the University of Paris or elsewhere.

Oh well advised, oh happy people! I speak to you, the disciples of the study of wisdom, who, by the grace of God and good fortune or nature apply yourselves to seek out the heights of the clear rejoicing star, that is, knowledge, do take diligently from this treasure, drink from this clear and healthy fountain. Fill yourself from this pleasant repast, which can so benefit and elevate you! For what is more worthy for a person than knowledge and the highest learning? Certainly, you who desire it and employ yourself with it, you have chosen the glorious life! For by it, you can understand the choice of virtue and the avoidance of vice as it counsels the one and forbids the other.

Chapter 5. More on the Same Subject

Because it is an important subject and appropriate to know, and because not everyone has the book by Valerius[3] to study at his pleasure the subjects of which he speaks, it pleases me to speak about study. As I said before, the student ought to have great diligence in order to acquire wisdom. Valerius teaches how one ought to have moderate diligence and not be too excessive in this exercise. He says that Scaevola,[4] who was an excellent jurist and expert in common law in Rome and who composed many laws, after his arduous work and study, took recreation in a variety of games. And Valerius explained and approved of it, saying that the nature of things does not allow a person to work continually, but that it is necessary to rest and stay sometimes at leisure.

1 *burghers* Middle-class town-dwellers.
2 *clerical class* The clergy; because virtually all intellectual activity was church-related and church-managed until the fourteenth century, the intellectual class (including students) was included in the clerical class.
3 *Valerius* Valerius Maximus, Roman historian and moralist who wrote (around 20 CE) an important book of historical anecdotes for the use of rhetoricians.
4 *Scaevola* Quintus Mucius Scaevola (?–82 BCE), Roman lawgiver, politician, and chief priest; his major work was an 80-volume treatise on civil law.

Leisure does not mean to do nothing physical, but means any joyful work or sport that will refresh his understanding, because the sensitive qualities of the soul become weak from long attention to study, and they would not be refreshed by complete cessation of all activity. If they give themselves no recreation, those whose work is study become melancholy because the mind is overworked, and if they go to sleep they will suffer from bad dreams. And so the remedy for such labor is to rejoice the spirit in games and play. Just as rich food pleases us more when alternated with plain food, so the work of study is best nourished when one sometimes plays, and so Cato[1] says, "vary your work with diversions." In Book 4 of *Ethics*, Aristotle says "one should exercise the virtue of temperance and moderation in work and play"; to which Seneca,[2] in his book *On Tranquility of Mind*, adds "fertile fields are soon exhausted by continual and uninterrupted cultivation." So continual mental work destroys the strength and leads to frenzy, and so nature gives humans, an inclination to play and relax from time to time. It is for this reason that there are laws establishing certain holidays so that people come together in public to bring joy and a cessation of work. On this, it is said of Socrates, from whom no part of wisdom was hidden, that he was not ashamed when Alcibiades[3] mocked him for playing with little children, because it was an account of this recreation that his understanding was clearer and more lively at study. This is why in his old age he learned to play the harp.

Chapter 6. On the Second Estate of People, That Is, the Burghers and Merchants

I said before that the second rank of people is composed of the burghers and merchants of the cities. Burghers are those who are from old city families and have a surname and an ancient coat of arms. They are the principal dwellers and inhabitants of cities, and they inherit the houses and manors on which they live. Books refer to them as "citizens." Such people ought to be honorable, wise, and of good appearance, dressed in honest clothing without disguise or affectation. They must have true integrity and be people of worth and discretion, and it is the estate of good and beneficial citizens. In some places, they call the more ancient families noble, when they have been people of worthy estate and reputation for a long time. And so, in all places, one ought to praise good burghers and citizens of cities. It is a very good and honorable thing when there is a notable bourgeoisie[4] in a city. It is a great honor to the country and a great treasure to the prince.

These people ought to be concerned with the situation and needs of the cities of which they are a part. They are to ensure that everything concerning commerce and the situation of the population is well governed. For humble people do not commonly have great prudence in words or even in deeds that concern politics and so they should not meddle in the ordinances established by princes. Burghers and the wealthy must take care that the common people are not hurt, so that they have no reason to conspire against the prince or his council. The reason is that these conspiracies and plots by the common people always come back to hurt those that have something to lose. It always was and always will be that the end result is not at all beneficial to them, but evil and detrimental. And so, if there is a case sometime when the common people seem to be aggrieved by some burden, the merchants ought to assemble and from among them choose the wisest and most discreet in action and in speech, and go before the prince or the council, and bring their claims for them in humility and state their case meekly for them, and not allow them to do anything, for that leads to the destruction of cities and of countries.

So, to the extent of their power, they should quiet the complaints of the people because of the evil that could come to all. They must restrain themselves this way, as well as others. And if sometimes the laws of princes and their council seem to them to appear, according to their judgment, to be wrong, they must not interpret this as in bad faith, and there may be danger in foolishly complaining, but they ought to assume that they have good intentions in what they do, although the cause might not be apparent. It is wisdom to learn when to hold one's tongue, said Valerius, citing Socrates, the most noble and praiseworthy philosopher. Once he was in a place where many complained of the laws of princes, and one of them asked him why he alone said nothing when the others spoke. "Because," said he, "I

---

1   *Cato*   Marcus Porcius Cato (234–149 BCE), known as Cato the Censor or Cato the Elder; Roman writer, statesman and orator.
2   *Seneca*   Lucius Annaeus Seneca or Seneca the Younger (c. 4 BCE –65 CE), Roman philosopher, statesman, and dramatist.
3   *Alcibiades*   Athenian politician and commander (450–404 BCE), close associate of Socrates.

4   *bourgeoisie*   Urban, commercial middle class.

have sometimes repented of speaking but never of holding my tongue."

It is a noble thing to keep from speaking, from which evil can come and no benefit and it is a proof of wisdom when someone does it. Likewise, wise Cato said, "the first virtue is to hold one's tongue." For one is close to God who by the teaching of reason knows to keep quiet. And in the fifth book of the last work, Seneca said that "he who would be one of the disciples of Pythagoras[1] must be silent for five years, because it is necessary to know what to say before speaking."

Chapter 8. On Merchants

As we discussed before, the merchant class is very necessary, and without it neither the estate of kings and princes nor even the polities of cities and countries could exist. For by the industry of their labor, all kinds of people are provided for without their having to make everything themselves, because, if they have money, merchants bring from afar all things necessary and proper for human beings to live. For it is a good thing that persons can occupy different offices in the world. For otherwise, one would be so busy with trying to make a living that no one could attend to other aspects of knowledge—thus God and reason have provided well.

And for the good that they do for everyone, this class of people—loyal merchants who in buying and selling, in exchanging things one for another by taking money or by other honest means—are to be loved and commended as necessary, and in many countries are held in high esteem. And there is no important citizen in any city who is not involved with trade, however, they are not considered thereby less noble. So Venice, Genoa, and other places have the most rich and powerful merchants who seek out goods of all kinds, which they distribute all over the world. And thus is the world served all kinds of things, and without doubt, they act honestly. I hold that they have a meritorious office, accepted by God and permitted and approved by the laws.

These people ought to be well advised in their deeds, honest in their labor, truthful in their words, clever in what they do, because they have to know how to buy and resell things at such a price as not to lose money, and ought to be well informed about whether there are enough goods and where they are going short and when to buy and when to sell—otherwise their business will be gone.

They ought to be honest in their work, that is that they ought not, under threat of damnation and awful punishment of the body, treat their goods with any tricks to make them seem better than they are in order to deceive people so that they might be more expensive or more quickly sold, because every trade is punished when there is fraud in one. And those that practice deception ought not to be called merchants but rather deceivers and evil doers. Above all, merchants should be truthful in words and in promises, accustomed to speaking and keeping the truth so that a simple promise by a merchant will be believed as certain as by a contract. And those that keep their promises and are always found honest should prefer to suffer damage rather than fail to keep an agreement, which is a very good and honest custom, and it would please God, if others in France and elsewhere would do the same. Although there may be some that do wrong, I hold that by the mercy of God, there are those who are good, honest, and true. May God keep them rich, honorable and worthy of trust! For it is very good for a country and of great value to a prince and to the common polity when a city has trade and an abundance of merchants. This is why cities on the sea or major rivers are commonly rich and large, because of the goods that are brought by merchants from far away to be delivered there. So these people ought to be of fair and honest life without pomp or arrogance and ought to serve God in courage and reverence and to give alms generously from what God has given them, as one finds among those who give a tenth of their goods to the poor and who found many chapels, places of prayer, and hospitals for the poor. And so there are those of such goodness that if God pleases, they truly deserve merit in heaven and goodness and honor in the world.

Chapter 9. The Third Class of the People

Next comes the third rank of the people who are artisans and agricultural workers, which we call the last part of the body politic and who are like legs and feet, according to Plutarch,[2] and who should be exceptionally well watched over and cared for so that they suffer no hurt, for that which hurts them can dangerously knock the whole body down. It is therefore more necessary to take good care and provide for them, since for the health of the body, they do not cease

---

1   *Pythagoras* Greek philosopher and mathematician (c. 580–c. 500 BCE), discoverer of the theorem that bears his name, and founder of a religious movement.

2   *Plutarch* Greek biographer and author (46–c. 120 CE).

to go "on foot." The varied jobs that the artisans do are necessary for the human body and it cannot do without them, just as a human body cannot go without its feet. It would shamefully and uselessly drag itself in great pain on its hands and body without them, just as, he says, if the republic excluded laborers and artisans, it could not sustain itself. Thus although some think little of the office of the craftsman that the clerics call "artisans," yet it is good, noble, and necessary, as said before. And among all the other good things which exist, so this one should be even more praised because, of all the worldly estates, this one comes closest to science. Artisans put into practice what science teaches, as Aristotle says in his *Metaphysics*, because their works are the result of sciences, such as geometry, which is the science of measurement and proportion without which no craft could exist. To this a writer testifies, saying that the Athenians wanted to make a marvelous altar to Minerva, the goddess of wisdom, and because they wanted a notable and beautiful work above all, they sought advice from the best teachers. They went to the philosopher Plato as the most accomplished master of all the sciences, but he sent them to Euclid[1] instead as the master of the art of measurement, because he created geometry which is read everyday in general studies.

And from this can one see that artisans follow science. For masons, carpenters, and all other workers in whatever crafts work according to the teachings of the sciences. "To be praised is to master a craft," says Valerius, "so that art will follow nature." When a worker properly copies a thing which nature has made, as when a painter who is a great artist makes the portrait of a man so lifelike and so well, that everyone recognizes him, or when he makes a recognizable bird or other beast; so too the sculptor of images makes a likeness, and so on. And so some say that art is the "apess" or the "ape" of nature, because a monkey imitates many of the ways of a man, just as art imitates many of the works of nature.

But nonetheless, they say, art can not imitate everything, so one ought to praise the skillful in art and believe those who have experience in it, for there is no doubt that no one speaks as appropriately of a thing as the one who knows it. And I believe the most skilled artisans of all crafts are more commonly in Paris than elsewhere, which is an important and beautiful thing.

But to speak a little of the fact of their habits: I would to God they pleased God, but in themselves, for it would be pleasing to God if their lives were more sober and less licentious as is appropriate to their estate. For lechery in taverns and the luxuries they use in Paris can lead to many evil and unsuitable things. Aristotle speaks of the voluptuous life that such people and those like them lead, saying that many seem like beasts because they choose lechery before any other pleasures.

And on the false opinion that gluttons have: In the second chapter of Wisdom, Holy Scripture says that they believe "the time of our life is short and full of troubles and in the end we have no rest, and so we use our youth to follow our desires, and we fill ourselves with wine and meat, and in everything leave the traces of our joy." And without doubt, similar foolish and vain words can often be heard not only from simple people but from others believed wise for their position. So the people especially ought to heed preaching and sermons on the Word of God, since for the most part they are not educated in the teachings of Holy Scripture.

Good exhortations and sermons are beneficial for Christians to hear, as Justin recounts in the twentieth book of Trogus Pompeius about the city of Croton.[2] They were pagans and unbelievers, and Pythagoras the philosopher, also a pagan, reformed them through his exhortations on their evil lives. For while the people there were corrupt and inclined to gluttony, vice, and lechery, they were brought to continence and it pure life by the intervention of Pythagoras. This philosopher castigated most the vice of lechery and showed that because of it many cities had gone to ruin. He taught ladies and men the doctrine of honesty and chastity, and to be sober in their food and drink. And so Pythagoras, by his wise admonitions, made the ladies put aside their fancy clothes and the men their gluttonous lives. And for the twenty years that he lived there he continued his instruction. Justin says that in the city of Methaponthus in Puilla, from which Pythagoras came, people had so great a reverence for the house in which he was born that they made it a temple and adored Pythagoras as God because of the good he had done.

Great is the need in many places for such a one, and also for people wanting to put to work that which he taught.

---

1   *Euclid*   Greek mathematician (c. 300 BCE); his work founded the study of geometry.

2   *Good exhortations ... city of Croton*   Gnaeus Pompeius Trogus was a first century BCE Roman historian, whose principal work *Historiae Philippicae* is now lost; what survives is an "Epitome" of that work—an edited paraphrase by Justin (full Latin name Marcus Junianus Justinus), a third century CE Roman historian.

Chapter 10. On Simple Laborers

On the subject of simple laborers of the earth, what should I say of them when so many people despise and oppress them? Of all the estates, they are the most necessary, those who are cultivators of the earth which feed and nourish the human creature, without whom the world would end in little time. And really those who do them so many evils do not take heed of what they do, for anyone who considers himself a rational creature will hold himself obligated to them. It is a sin to be ungrateful for as many services as they give us! And really it is very much the feet which support the body politic, for they support the body of every person with their labor. They do nothing that is unpraiseworthy. God has made their office acceptable, first, because the two heads of the world, from whom all human life is descended, were laborers of the earth. The first head was Adam, the first father, of whom it is written in the second chapter of Genesis, "God took the first man and put him in a paradise of pleasures, to work, cultivate and take care of it."[1] And from this Scripture one can draw two arguments to prove the honesty of labor: The first is that God commanded it and made it first of all crafts. The second, that this craft was created during the state of innocence.

The second head of the world was Noah from whom, after the flood, all humans are descended. It is written in the ninth chapter that Noah was a laborer, and after the flood he put himself to work on the land and planted vineyards. And so our fathers, the ancient patriarchs were all cultivators of the earth and shepherds of beasts (whose stories I will not tell you for the sake of brevity), and in the olden days it was not an ignoble office nor unpraiseworthy.

In his *History of the Romans*, Florus[2] tells us how Diocletian, Emperor of Rome, after many battles and victories, went for the rest of his life to the village called Sallon and his occupation was working on the land. Long after; the rulers of Rome were lacking good government, so Lentulius and Galerius sent to this admirable man to ask that he return to Rome and take over the empire. "Ah," he said, "if you had seen the beautiful cabbages that I planted with my own hands, you would not require me to return to the empire." And this was to say that he had more peace of mind in his state of poverty than in carrying a burden so large and perilous as an empire.

And on this subject, in the third chapter of the fourth book Valerius tells of Actilus, the very worthy Roman who was taken from his work to be emperor. As he worked at his plough in the field, knights came to seek him, and he was made chief and leader of the whole Roman army. And he whose hands had been hardened by labor at the plow, after he had left the leadership of the army, reestablished the republic by his noble courage and with his hands. Said Valerius, "the hand which had governed a team of oxen behind the plow took up governing battle chariots." And after many noble and great victories, he was not ashamed to leave the dignity of emperor and return to the work he had left behind.

Because of these stories, we can understand that the estate of simple laborer or others of low rank should not be denigrated, as others would do. When those of the highest rank choose for their retirement a humble life of simplicity as the best for the soul and the body, then they are surely rich who voluntarily are poor. For they have no fear of being betrayed, poisoned, robbed, or envied, for their wealth is in sufficiency. For no one is rich without it, nor is there any other wealth.

To confirm this, I will tell what Valerius said about sufficiency and about a very rich man who was very poor in having it. There was, Valerius said, a King in Lydia, who was named Gyges. His wealth was reputed to be so great that he went to ask the god Apollo whether there was anyone more happy than he. Apollo answered him that Agamis Soplidius was happier than he was. This Agamis was the poorest in Arcadia and he was very old. He never left his little field and was content with the small yield on which he lived and that which he had. Thus one can see how Apollo understood happiness to be sufficiency and not wealth, because in wealth one cannot have sufficiency, at least, not security, but instead a lot of concerns, and a plenitude of fears and worries. And so, King Gyges, who believed that the god ought to confirm that no one was happier than he, was mistaken in his vain opinion, and learned what pure and firm wealth and happiness were.

Anaxagoras[3] agreed that happiness is to have sufficiency. In the prologue to the *Almagest*, Ptolemy[4] says "he is happy who does not care in whose hands the world is." And that this saying is true is proven by all the sages, the poets, and

---

1 *God took ... care of it* Genesis 2.15.
2 *Florus* First-century Roman historian.
3 *Anaxagoras* Pre-Socratic Greek philosopher (c. 500–428 BCE).
4 *Ptolemy* Claudius Ptolemaeus (90–c. 168), Greek mathematician, geographer, astronomer, and astrologer.

especially, those perfect ones who have chosen a pure and poor life for their greatest surety. For although one can be saved in any estate, nonetheless it is more difficult to pass by flames and not be burned. There is no doubt that the estate of the poor which everyone despises has many good and worthy persons in purity of life.

◆ ◆ ◆ ◆ ◆

The Book of Deeds of Arms and of Chivalry (1410)

Concerning the Prime Causes of Wars and Battles

As it belongs to sovereign princes to undertake and carry on wars and battles, we must now consider the causes by which, according to lawful means, they may be initiated and pursued. In this regard one is well advised, it seems to me, to remember that five grounds are commonly held to be the basis of wars, three of which rest on law and the remaining two on will. The first lawful ground on which wars may be undertaken or pursued is to maintain law and justice; the second is to counteract evildoers who befoul, injure, and oppress the land and the people; and the third is to recover lands, lordships,[1] and other things stolen or usurped for an unjust cause by others who are under the jurisdiction of the prince, the country, or its subjects. As for the two of will, one is to avenge any loss or damage incurred, the other to conquer and take over foreign lands or lordships.

Returning to the first of these points, which concerns justice, it should be remembered that there are three chief causes under which a king or prince is empowered to undertake and carry out wars and battles. The first is to uphold and defend the Church and its patrimony[2] against anyone who would defile it; this is expected of all Christian princes. The second is to act on behalf of a vassal, if he should require it, in cases where the prince must settle a quarrel and is duly obliged to bring about an agreement among various parties,

but then only if the adversary proves to be intractable. And third, the prince, if it pleases him, may justly go to the aid of any other prince, baron, or other ally and friend of his, or to help any country or land, if the need arises and if the quarrel is just. In this point are included widows, orphans, and all who are unjustly trampled under foot by another power.

For this purpose, and likewise for the other two aforementioned purposes, that is, to counteract evildoers and to recover lost property, it is not only permissible for the prince to start a war or to maintain it, indeed he is obliged to do so, through the obligation incurred by his title to lordship and jurisdiction in accordance with his proper duty.

As for the other two points, the one regarding revenge for some damage or loss inflicted by another prince, the other regarding acquisition of foreign lands without title to them—even though conquerors in the past, such as Alexander,[3] the Romans, and others have done so, and have been praised and accorded chivalric titles, as have those who wreaked vengeance upon their enemies, for better or for worse—despite the fact that such actions are commonly undertaken, I do not find in divine law or in any other text, for causes such as these without any other ground, that it is acceptable to start any kind of war or battle upon any Christian land, but rather the contrary.

For according to God's law it is not proper for man either to seize or to usurp anything belonging to another, or even to covet it. Likewise, vengeance is reserved for God alone, and in no way does any man have the right to carry it out.

Thus, to set forth our ideas on this subject more clearly, and to answer any questions that might arise, it is true that it is lawful for any prince to keep for himself the same right that is granted to others. As for what the just prince would do if he considered himself wronged by some other power, should he simply depart, in order to obey divine law, without taking any further actions? In God's name, no, for divine law does not deny justice, but rather mandates that it should be carried out and requires punishment for misdeeds. In order that a prince may go about this matter justly, he will follow this course: he will gather together a great council of wise men in his parliament, or in that of his sovereign if he is a subject, and not only will he assemble

---

1   *lordships* Lands owned by a lord.
2   *patrimony* The Church's patrimony is its estate and endowment—the wealth and property it has accumulated.

3   *Alexander* Alexander the Great (356–323 BCE), king of Macedon, who conquered almost all of the world known to the Greeks.

those of his own realm, but in order that there be no suspicion of favor, he will also call upon some from foreign countries that are known not to take sides, elder statesmen as well as legal advisors and others; he will propose or have proposed the whole matter in full without holding anything back, for God cannot be deceived, everything according to what may be right or wrong, and he will conclude by saying that he wishes to recount everything and hold to the determination of doing right. In short, by these points the affair will be put to order, clearly seen and discussed, and if through such a process it appears that his cause is just, he will summon his adversary to demand of him restitution and amends for his injuries and the wrong done him. Now if it comes about that the adversary in question puts up a defense and tries to contradict what has been said, let him be heard fully without special favor, but also without willfulness or spite. If these things are duly carried out, as the law requires, then the just prince may surely undertake war, which on no account should be called vengeance, but rather the complete carrying out of due justice.

V. Considerations a King or Prince Should Entertain in Initiating War and the Points He Should Keep in Mind While Deliberating the Matter

As it is licit for a prince to engage in wars and battles, pursuing them for the reasons mentioned above, and as these are great and weighty matters that touch the lives, the blood, and the honor and the fortunes of an infinite number of people, it is necessary to look closely into the matter, for without such a look no such thing should be undertaken, nor should it be undertaken lightly by anyone without experience. That one should hesitate to undertake war even on someone weaker there are numerous demonstrations. What great blows the African power dreamed of, or the proud city of Carthage,[1] its capital, and the Spaniards, not to mention the very powerful King Antiochus,[2] lord of a great part of the East, who led so many men into battle that

with their frightful elephants the affair was quickly finished. Then there was also the mighty King Mithradates,[3] who was sovereign of twenty-four powerful countries and even of the whole world, but even these could not and did not subdue the very slight power of the Romans. For this reason, nothing that is in the power of Fortune[4] should be risked lightly, for no one can know which side will be favored.

Therefore, it is necessary for the prince to be wise, or at the very least be disposed to use wise counsel, for as Plato said, fortunate is the country where the wise govern, for otherwise it is cursed, as Holy Scripture also testifies. There is absolutely nothing that so needs to be conducted with good judgment as war and battle, as will be seen later. No mistake made in any other circumstances is less possible to repair than one committed by force of arms and by a battle badly conducted.

What then will the wise prince upon whom it is incumbent do when, for any of the reasons mentioned, he must undertake wars and fight battles? First of all, he will consider how much strength he has or can obtain, how many men are available and how much money. For unless he is well supplied with these two basic elements, it is folly to wage war, for they are necessary to have above all else, especially money. Whoever has I enough and wishes to use it can always find plenty of help from others, even more than he wants; witness the wars of Italy,[5] especially Florence and Venice, that are commonly fought more with their money than with their citizens. For this reason they can scarcely be defeated. So it would be much better for the prince, if he does not consider that he is supported by money from the treasury, or by rich subjects full of goodwill, not to conclude any treaty with his enemies if he feels threatened with invasion, or to undertake to begin a war if he lacks the means to carry it on. For it is quite certain that if he begins it in the hope of extracting more from his subjects than they are able to bear, and without their consent, he will merely increase

1　*city of Carthage*　Carthage, located in present-day Tunisia, in North Africa, engaged in a series of wars (the Sicilian, Pyrrhic, and Punic Wars) against Greece and Rome between 480 and 146 BCE.

2　*King Antiochus*　Antiochus III the Great, ruled the Seleucid Empire between 223 and 187 BCE. The empire stretched from present-day Turkey to India; having increased his area of rule by

several important military victories, Antiochus invaded Europe and was defeated by the Romans.

3　*mighty King Mithradates*　Mithradates VI the Great (132–63 BCE), king of Pontus (in present-day northeastern Turkey) from 120–63 BCE. He waged several successful territorial battles against the Romans, but was eventually defeated by them.

4　*Fortune*　Luck, personified as the Roman goddess Fortuna.

5　*the wars of Italy*　Wars between the Italian city-states (Venice, Florence, Genoa, etc.) were common in the fourteenth and fifteenth centuries. The cities were wealthy, but had inadequate armies; the wars were waged largely by *condottieri*, mercenary soldiers hired from elsewhere.

the number of his enemies. It will profit him little to destroy enemies from the outside in order to acquire them nearby and in his domain. It should be remembered that the prince must not underestimate the power of any enemy, however slight it may appeal to him, for he cannot know what fortune another will have in his favor. It is written of a shepherd named Briacus,[1] that "Fortune was so favorable to him that she sustained him in power with a great number of thieves and pillagers he had assembled to fight Rome, powerful as it was, for a period of more than fourteen years." Much grief he brought to them, and he defeated them several times in battle, nor were they able to destroy him. His life was ended by one of his own men, who killed him.

Therefore, in order that such things may not come about, the prince will assemble in council the four estates[2] of his realm, which should be summoned for such a purpose. That is to say, the elder nobles experienced in arms, who know how to organize and attack; also the law clerks, for in the laws are set forth the cases in which a just war can be undertaken, along with several examples of these; also the burghers, for it is necessary for them to participate in the organization, since they would need to take charge of fortifying towns and cities, and also to persuade the common people to help their lord. Additionally, there should be some representatives of the craftsmen, the more to honor these people. They must be carefully approached so that they will be the more inclined to help the lord financially.

O! how profitable it is for a land, realm, or city to have loyal subjects of great affection, for they lack neither able bodies nor worldly goods. This was evident many times in Rome when the city treasury depended on them for support in wars at the point where there was no other source of revenue. In order to help, the ladies willingly brought their jewels and rich ornaments, lending them to help the city in its dire need. These precious objects were later restored to them, as was only right and reasonable.

In this tradition, to set a good example, the good and wise King Charles, fifth of the name,[3] father of the one who at present reigns, soon after he had been crowned at the age of twenty-five, saw that the English were keeping badly the agreements of the peace treaty he had concluded with them out of necessity and their good fortune, which treaty was so damaging to him. In spite of the agreement that allowed them to keep possession of a great part of the duchy of Guyenne and several other lands and lordships elsewhere in the kingdom of France, this treaty was not good enough for them. Rather, because of their overweening pride they also trampled under foot neighboring territories that did not belong to them. Therefore this king, before he did anything else, peacefully sent envoys to the duke of Lancaster, son of King Edward of England, by whom this outrage was carried out, inquiring if they wished to allow amends to be made for the suffering and damage inflicted since the treaty; whereupon it resulted that although the reply was gracious, the ambassadors themselves were killed. So the aforesaid king, in view of the fact that he had been obliged to agree to a dishonorable treaty, one that even the English did not keep, and for other reasons too long to explain, assembled in his parliament in Paris the aforementioned four estates, and with them wise jurists from Bologna and from other places. To these, in a very wise manner, he made his points against the English, asking their opinion whether he had reason to begin war again, for without just cause, their due consideration of the matter, and the conscience and goodwill of his subjects, he did not wish to undertake it. This council, after long deliberation, concluded that there was due and just cause to begin the war again. So with his own great prudence, all the lost lands were reconquered by the sword, as is well known.

1   *Briacus*   Usually known as Viciathus; leader of a Lusitanian tribe (in present-day Portugal) who led a successful guerilla resistance to Roman expansion mainly between 147 and 139 BCE; he was killed after having been betrayed by his own men.

2   *four estates*   The "estates of the realm" were the main divisions of society from medieval times onward. Traditionally there were three of them: the nobility, the clergy, and the third estate—everyone else. Often, the second estate was divided between the military class and the legal class. This appears to reflect the division De Pizan has in mind.

3   *King Charles*   Charles V The Wise of France (1338–80) ruled 1364 to 1380; during this period of the Hundred Years' War, the French waged successful battles to regain territory previously lost to the English.

PART III
The Early Modern Period

NICCOLÒ MACHIAVELLI
(1469 – 1527)

Who Was Niccolò Machiavelli?

Machiavelli, the author of one of the most controversial texts in Western political thought, was born in 1469 in Florence, an Italian city-state. The capital of Tuscany, Florence was controlled by the great banking house of the Medici; from Machiavelli's birth until his early twenties, his city was ruled by Lorenzo the Magnificent, a prince of the Medici family. An enthusiastic patron of the arts—including Leonardo da Vinci, Botticelli, Donatello, and Michelangelo—Lorenzo made Florence a hub of humanistic Renaissance culture.[1] He died in 1492, and his successor—Piero de' Medici—abandoned the city in the face of an advancing French army in 1494. After a short-lived but disastrous period of quasi-theocratic rule under the charismatic friar Savonarola—a populist religious firebrand who had opposed the humanist rule of the Medici—the newly republican Florence governed itself until 1512, when the Medici family, with the help of the Spanish army and the support of Pope Julius II, recaptured the city.

The second son of a prominent lawyer from an old Florentine family, Machiavelli became a government clerk in 1494 and he very quickly rose to a prominent position. From the death of Savonarola—burned at the stake by the Florentine population in 1498—until the return of the Medici, Machiavelli was Second Chancellor and Secretary to the Ten of War, and he traveled on diplomatic missions to a range of princely and ecclesiastical courts across southern Europe including the king of France, the Emperor Maximilian, and the Papal Court at Rome. During this period Machiavelli visited the military campaign headquarters of the general of the Pope's armies, Cesare Borgia, a figure who has come down through history as being notoriously ruthless and scheming but who Machiavelli is thought to have greatly admired—his exploits are frequently cited approvingly in *The Prince*.[2] Between 1503 and 1506 Machiavelli was in charge of the Florentine militia responsible for the defense of the city. He also organized a military force to attack Pisa, a nearby city that was in revolt against Florentine rule.[3]

After the return of the Medici Machiavelli was removed from office, and in 1513 he was arrested and tortured on suspicion of being involved in a plot to assassinate the Medici brothers, Giuliano and Giovanni. Even on the rack Machiavelli insisted on his innocence, and he was exiled to his family's estates in the Tuscan countryside. It was here, living in semi-seclusion with his wife Marietta and six children, that he wrote the works on which his reputation rests, *The Prince* and *Discourses on Livy*. He also wrote several other pieces, including a ribald play called *Mandragola* ("The Mandrake Root"); *Dell' Arte della Guerra*, a book on military organization; and a history of Florence commissioned by Cardinal—later Pope—Giulio de' Medici.

In 1525 Machiavelli, now in his mid-fifties, was finally allowed to return to public life, this time in the service of the Medici family. He visited Rome to present his *History of Florence* to the Pope, and traveled to Venice—where his play had recently been performed to great acclaim—on a trade mission from Florence. However the spring of 1527

---

1   Lorenzo's collections form the core of the Uffizi museum in Florence. His banking house was also responsible for the creation of the double-entry bookkeeping system for keeping accounts.

2   However, as a Florentine envoy, Machiavelli also strongly criticized Borgia. This has led some commentators to see *The Prince* as a bitter satire on contemporary political life, rather than as a manual in political expedience meant to be taken at face-value. Support for this non-standard interpretation is slim, however.

3   The attack on Pisa was successful, and that city's separatist ambitions were suppressed for a time; however in 1512 Machiavelli's citizen militia lasted just one day when confronted by a professional army come to reclaim the city for the Medici.

saw a terrible upheaval in European politics. To the shock of the continent, the city of Rome was attacked and—after the army ignored a truce agreed with Pope Clement VII—brutally sacked by an army of Germans and Spaniards commanded by the traitorous French Duke of Bourbon (who had turned against the French monarch in favor of Emperor Charles V). In the same month, the Medici were once again expelled from Florence by the rebellious republican citizenry. Machiavelli, however, lived barely long enough to see this new political turmoil: he was already seriously ill, and he died on June 21, 1527.

What Was Machiavelli's Overall Philosophical Project?

One of Machiavelli's central interests was to construct a rule-book for politics: a set of principles that would accurately predict how people will react to various pressures and crises, and thus allow the possessor of this knowledge to exert reliable influence over others—to control their behavior. In *The Prince*, his goal was to explain what a ruler needs to do to hold onto his power. In *Discourses on Livy* he offered an analysis of the early history of Rome in order to discern how the Romans had developed institutions that established a republic and then preserved it for centuries.

What Is the Structure of the Reading?

The Prince consists of a dedication to Lorenzo the Magnificent and then 26 chapters that form five general sections. Chapters 1–11 develop a taxonomy of states; chapters 12–14 deal with military affairs; 15–19 offer prescriptions on the proper character and conduct of a prince; 20–25 give advice on how princes should deal with different situations; and the final chapter is an exhortation to Italy to expel the foreign invaders—from France and the Hapsburg empire—that meddled so much in the affairs of the peninsula.

Discourses on the First Ten Books of Titus Livy is a commentary on Livy's monumental history of Rome, *Ab Urbe Condita* ("From the Founding of the City"). Machiavelli's commentary is divided into three books: Book 1 deals with the internal structure of the republic; Book 2 is on warfare; and Book 3 is a treatise on the qualities desirable in a political leader.

Some Useful Background Information

i) Machiavelli lived during an era when European politics was particularly fractious and brutal. He saw first-hand the machinations that statesmen engaged in to take and hold on to power (including the secular power of the papacy), and the risks that faced them from restless citizenry, from ambitious and vainglorious lieutenants, and even the military ambitions of nearby states. Machiavelli was not a dispassionate observer of these political forces; the ostracism that he underwent after the return of the Medici in 1512 affected him deeply. He had a passionate interest in politics, and loved to consider himself part of the high affairs of great men; he saw his forced exclusion from these circles as a substantial punishment for ending up on the losing side of a power struggle. (Machiavelli spent years making strenuous efforts to win the favor of the Medici—efforts that were just beginning to bear fruit when he died.)

ii) As a youngster, living in one of the great centers of the Italian Renaissance, Machiavelli received a thorough education in the Latin classics. Like many political thinkers of his era, he was deeply impressed by the ideals of the classical Roman republic. In particular, he admired the notion of a society whose institutions fostered virtue in its citizens and encouraged their regular participation in civic life. He was also fully familiar with the classical tradition of rhetoric: the practice of speaking publicly and persuasively in order to convince others of the worthiness of one's own position and the invalidity of that of one's opponents. In the *Discourses* Machiavelli praises rhetorical contention as the basis of civic liberty.

iii) Titus Livius was born in about 59 BCE and died in 17 CE. His history of Rome originally consisted of 142 books, but of these only books 1–10 and 21–45 survived to Machiavelli's day. Although Livy wrote during the reign of the first Roman Emperor, Augustus, he is supposed to have preferred the earlier Roman republic (which lasted from 509 BCE to about 27 BCE); since his books covering the decline of the Republic and the rise of Augustus have been lost, this is not certain.

Some Common Misconceptions

i) Machiavelli's *Prince* is often thought of as a "rule-book" for aspiring (and unprincipled) politicians. However, one of the lessons that Machiavelli was most concerned to impart is that there *are* no hard-and-fast rules in politics; there is no single "virtue" that a politician must display in every circumstance. Instead, every political situation is different and the successful ruler must have the ability to judge what is required on a particular occasion and the flexibility to do what is necessary. Furthermore, although the goal of the shrewd leader is to reduce the role of luck or fate in his affairs—to bring fortune under his control—Machiavelli emphasizes that it is never possible to do this completely. Fortune is a powerful factor in human affairs, and even the greatest leaders are to some extent at its mercy.

ii) Machiavelli is notorious for arguing that "virtuous" princes ought sometimes to act cruelly, violently, or treacherously. However, he does not claim that it is always appropriate to do so—that men who have the power to act as they like therefore have the license to do so. He makes an important distinction between coercive actions that are "well-committed" and those that are "ill-committed." Coercion and deceit, according to Machiavelli, must be part of the prince's toolkit when the end justifies them as means, but they are never ends in themselves.

iii) Machiavelli is sometimes seen as a proponent of opportunistic individualism, a mentor to ambitious men who seek to gain power and influence over their fellows, a sympathizer with tough-minded realists who see that they need to "beat or be beaten" in this dog-eat-dog world. But this is an anachronistic exaggeration. Machiavelli's interest was not individualistic but patriotic—it was the welfare of the *patria*, one's native state, that primarily motivated him. His fervent vision was the restoration of Italy to political health and power.

How Important and Influential Are These Works?

Machiavelli, quite self-consciously, wrote *The Prince* both to form another entry in a particular literary tradition and radically to break from the established pattern of that genre. From Petrarch (1304–74) onwards there had been a humanist habit of writing didactic treatises on the ideal prince, often called "mirror-of-princes" books. These works would typically begin from a discussion of general ethical principles and the role and purpose of the state, and then go on to offer prescriptions for the manner in which a prince should be educated, the qualities required in a good ruler, the relationship that should exist between a prince and his subjects, and so on. Invariably, these handbooks would be full of improving examples taken from the classical world

and bolstered with quotes from Roman historians, poets, and biographers. The central theme was that what it takes to be an effective ruler is *virtue*: princes were praised for their moral goodness, their generosity, their support of culture.

Machiavelli's *The Prince* is patterned on this learned model, which would have been quite familiar to his readers. And, true to this form, he writes extensively about the virtue of princes. However, Machiavelli also boldly asserted that he intended to break from the received wisdom and to take a clear-eyed, non-idealistic look at the way politics *really* operates. As such, when he talks about "virtue," he tends to mean, not moral goodness or Christian piety, but the skill required to keep control of one's kingdom. Machiavelli was aware—indeed, he frequently emphasizes—that this was a radical departure from tradition. It is this then-novel[1] view—that rulers cannot perform their roles effectively if they are bound by the constraints of normal morality; that politics should be governed by a different set of rules than private life—that has since been most associated with Machiavelli.

This view scandalized many and made the author's name synonymous in many quarters with "schemer": the stock character who schemed against and manipulated the other characters in the popular Jacobean tragedies written in the first half of the seventeenth century was called "Machiavelli." Machiavelli's writings were almost immediately placed on the papacy's Index of banned books, where they remained for nearly three centuries. Notwithstanding this, Machiavelli's views became part of the common political education of European rulers for generations after his death, and the doctrine of "reason of state"—that the ruler of a state, unlike a private citizen, may have recourse to force in order to preserve his situation—became an explicit part of political thinking in modern Europe. Along with Thucydides' *Peloponnesian War* and Hobbes' *Leviathan* and *De Cive*, *The Prince* is one of the central statements of political realism, the theory that politics is largely a matter of power, which agents should strive to maximize.

Machiavelli's *Discourses*, though less notorious than *The Prince*, has also been an influential work. It is widely considered the first and most important work on republicanism in the early modern era, and an important influence on the republican movements in England and Scotland in the seventeenth century and America in the eighteenth.

❖ ❖ ❖ ❖ ❖

---

1   Novel, that is, at the level of theory, rather than of practice.

The Prince (written 1513, published 1532)

Dedication

To the Magnificent Lorenzo di Piero de' Medici:[1]

Those who strive to obtain the good graces of a prince[2] are accustomed to come before him with such things as they hold most precious, or in which they see him take most delight; thus one often sees horses, arms, cloth of gold, precious stones, and similar ornaments worthy of their greatness presented to princes.

Desiring therefore to present myself to your Magnificence with some testimony of my devotion towards you, I have looked among my possessions and not found anything which I hold more dear than, or value so much as, the knowledge I hold of the actions of great men, acquired by long experience in contemporary affairs, and a continual study of antiquity; which, having reflected upon it with great and prolonged diligence, I now send this knowledge, condensed into a little volume, to your Magnificence.

And although I may consider this work unworthy of your approval, nevertheless I trust that your humanity will lead you to judge it be acceptable; it is not possible for me to make a better gift than to offer you the opportunity of understanding in the shortest time all that it has taken me many years to learn, through many troubles and dangers. I have not decorated this work with elaborate or magnificent words, nor stuffed it with rhetoric or unnecessary ornamentation, with which so many are accustomed to embellish their works; for I have wished that it receive no honor except by consequence of its truth and the importance of its theme.

Nor do I hold with those who think it presumptuous if a man of low and humble condition dares to discuss and lay down rules for matters of concern to princes. For, just as those who draw landscapes place themselves below in the plain to contemplate the nature of the mountains and of lofty places, and in order to contemplate the plains place themselves upon high mountains, so to understand the nature of the people one must be a prince, and to understand the nature of princes one must be of the people.

Take then, your Magnificence, this little gift in the spirit in which I send it. If you read and consider it diligently, you will discover in it my great desire that you should attain that greatness which fortune and your other attributes promise for you. And if your Magnificence will at some time turn your eyes from the summit of your greatness to these lower regions, you will see how undeservedly I suffer great and continued bad fortune.

[...]

Chapter 5: Concerning the way to govern cities or principalities which lived under their own laws before they were annexed

Whenever states in which people are accustomed to living in freedom under their laws have been acquired as I have described above,[3] there are three courses of action open to those who wish to hold on to them. The first is to ruin them; the next is to reside there in person; the third is to permit the people to live under their own laws, while at the same time exacting from them a tribute,[4] and establishing within the state an oligarchy which will keep it friendly to you. An oligarchical government created by the prince will know that it cannot last without his friendship and interest, and will do its utmost to support him. The ruler who wants to win over a city that is accustomed to freedom will do so more easily by means of its own citizens than in any other way. But establishing an oligarchical government may not be the most reliable approach. Take, for example, the Spartans and the Romans. The Spartans held Athens and Thebes by establishing an oligarchy, but lost both cities. The Romans, in order to hold Capua, Carthage, and Numantia, dismantled them, and did not lose them. They wished to hold Greece as the Spartans had held it, making it free and allowing it to have its laws, and did not succeed. So to hold the region they were compelled to destroy many cities within it, for in truth there is no sure way to retain control of such cities except by ruining them. When a city is accustomed to freedom, he who becomes master of it and does not destroy it runs

---

1   *Lorenzo di Piero de' Medici*   Ruler of Florence (1492–1519); his uncle Pope Leo X made him duke of Urbino. His daughter was Catherine de' Medici, wife of King Henry II of France.

2   *prince*   This word is used here to mean a ruler in general.

3   *as I have described above*   In Chapter 3 (omitted here) Machiavelli discusses the situation of a prince installed in states which are not newly created, but which have been added by their conqueror to an established dominion.

4   *tribute*   Tax.

the risk of being destroyed by it; for the city can always find two rallying points for rebellion: the cause of liberty itself and the cause of maintaining its ancient privileges, which neither time nor new privileges will ever make it forget. Whatever you may do, unless the people are disunited or dispersed, they will never forget the cause of liberty and of those privileges; at every chance they will immediately rally to that cause, as Pisa did after the hundred years she had been held in bondage by the Florentines.

When cities or countries have been accustomed to live under a prince, on the one hand, things are likely to be quite different. If, for example, a prince and his family are exterminated, the people are likely to be uncertain how to react. Being accustomed to obeying a prince but lacking any price to obey, they will not be able to agree on choosing a new prince from amongst themselves, and they will not know how to govern themselves. For this reason they are very slow to take up arms, and a prince can win them over and establish himself much more securely. In republics there is more vitality, greater hatred, and a greater desire for vengeance in such circumstances; republics will never permit the memory of their former liberty to rest; so the safest way is to destroy them or to reside there.

Chapter 6: Concerning new principalities which are acquired through one's own arms and ability

No one should be surprised if, in speaking of entirely new principalities as I shall do, I cite the greatest examples both of prince and of state. Men almost always walk along paths beaten by others and imitate their deeds, although for the most part they are still unable entirely to walk in the path of others or attain to the power of those they imitate. A wise man ought always to follow the paths beaten by great men, and to imitate those who have been supreme, so that if his ability does not equal theirs, at least it will have the tinge of it. Let him act like those prudent archers who, trying to hit the mark which yet appears too far distant, and knowing the limits of the strength of their bow, take aim much higher than the mark, not in order to shoot their arrow to so great a height, but rather, by aiming so high, to hit the mark they wish to reach.

I say, therefore, that in entirely new principalities, where there is a new prince, the likelihood of his remaining in power will depend on whether the new prince displays greater or lesser ability. Now, since a private citizen who becomes a prince must have had either ability or fortune, it is clear that one or other of these two things will mitigate many difficulties to some degree. Nevertheless, he who has relied least on fortune is the best. Further, it facilitates matters when the prince, having no other state to govern, is compelled to reside there in person.

But let us turn to those who have risen to become princes by their own ability and not through fortune. I say that Moses, Cyrus, Romulus, Theseus,[1] and such like are the most excellent examples. Perhaps we should really not include Moses, since he was a mere executor of the will of God, yet he ought to be admired, if only for the grace that made him worthy to speak with God. But Cyrus and others who have acquired or founded kingdoms are all admirable; and if we consider their particular deeds and methods, we will find them to be not inferior to those of Moses, although he had so great a teacher. And if we examine their actions and lives we can see that they owed nothing to fortune except opportunity, which gave them the material to mould into the form which seemed best to them. Without that opportunity their strength of spirit would have been extinguished; but without their strength of spirit the opportunity would have come in vain.

It was therefore necessary for Moses to find the people of Israel in Egypt enslaved and oppressed by the Egyptians, in order that they should be disposed to follow him and be delivered out of bondage. It was necessary that Romulus should not remain in Alba, and that he should be abandoned at birth, in order that he should become King of Rome and founder of the nation. It was necessary that Cyrus should find the Persians discontented with the government of the Medes, and the Medes soft and effeminate as a result of their long peace. Theseus could not have shown his ability had he not found the Athenians dispersed. These opportunities made those men fortunate, and their high ability enabled them to recognize the opportunity through which they could enable their country and make it fortunate.

---

1   *Moses*   The Old Testament religious and military leader of the Jews, who led his people out of slavery in Egypt; *Cyrus*   Cyrus the Great was the sixth-century BCE founder of the Persian Empire; *Romulus*   According to tradition, Romulus, together with his brother Remus, founded Rome in the eighth century BCE and was its first king, conquering and annexing a large territory; *Theseus*   Legendary founder of Athens and hero of Greek mythology.

• Example of Hiero of Syracuse → ability allowed him to keep his kingdom easily

Those, like these men, who through their courage become princes acquire a principality[1] with difficulty, but they keep it with ease. The difficulties they have in acquiring it arise in part from the new rules and methods which they are forced to introduce to establish their government and its security. And it ought to be remembered that there is nothing more difficult to execute, more perilous to conduct, or more uncertain in its success, than taking the lead in the introduction of a new political order. For the innovator has for enemies all those who have done well under the old conditions, and lukewarm defenders in those who may do well under the new. This coolness arises partly from fear of opponents, who have the laws on their side, and partly from the incredulity of men, who do not readily believe in new things until they have had a long experience of them. Thus it happens that whenever those who are hostile have the opportunity to attack, they do it with the zeal of partisans, while the others defend lukewarmly. As a result the prince is endangered along with them.

If we desire to discuss this matter thoroughly, then we must inquire whether these innovators can rely on themselves or have to depend on others. To achieve their goal, do they have to beg for help or can they use force in carrying out their plans? If the first, they always fare badly, and never accomplish anything; but when they can rely on themselves and use force, then they are rarely endangered. Hence it is that all armed prophets have conquered, and the unarmed ones have been destroyed. Besides the reasons mentioned, the nature of the people is variable, and while it is easy to persuade them, it is difficult to keep them convinced. And thus it is necessary to take such measures that, when they believe no longer, they can be made to believe by force.

If Moses, Cyrus, Theseus, and Romulus had been unarmed, they could not have enforced their constitutions for long—as happened in our time to Fra Girolamo Savonarola.[2] Both Savonarola and the new institutions he had created were ruined when the multitude came to believe in him no longer, and he had no means either of keeping steadfast those who believed or of making the unbelievers believe. As we can see, then, such men have great difficulties

and dangers in achieving their goals. But when these are overcome, and those who have envied them their success are exterminated, they will begin to be respected, and they will continue afterwards powerful, secure, honored, and happy.

To these great examples I wish to add one more—that of Hiero of Syracuse.[3] He is a less important figure than those mentioned above, but his case bears some resemblance to theirs, and may serve as an example of circumstances common to many others. This man rose from a private position to be Prince of Syracuse. He owed nothing to Fortune, everything to opportunity; the Syracusans, being oppressed, chose him as their captain. Afterwards they rewarded him by making him their prince. He was of such great ability, even as a private citizen, that according to one source he lacked nothing but a kingdom to be a king.[4] This man abolished the old army, organized a new one, gave up old alliances, made new ones. Since he had his own soldiers and allies, he had strong foundations on which to build any edifice: thus, while he had endured much trouble in acquiring his position, he had little in keeping it.

Chapter 7: Concerning new principalities which are acquired either through the arms of others or by good fortune

Those private citizens who rise to become princes solely as a result of good fortune have little trouble rising, but much trouble remaining on top; they have no difficulty on the way up, since they fly up, but they have many difficulties when they reach the summit. Of this sort are those to whom a principality is given either in exchange for money or else through the favor of him who bestows it. Such things took place in Greece, in the cities of Ionia and of the Hellespont, where princes were installed by Darius[5] to hold the cities both for his security and for his glory. Private citizens who become emperors through the corruption of soldiers are in a similar category. In this sort of situation, everything depends for the rulers on the good will and the fortune of those who have elevated them—two most inconstant and unstable things. They are not likely to have the knowledge required for the position, since, unless they are men of

---

1   *principality*   Position held by a prince.
2   *Fra Girolamo Savonarola*   Italian priest and political leader of Florence (1452–98), known for his agitation for religious reform and his opposition to Renaissance culture (as a burner of books and destroyer of paintings). He drove the Medicis out of Florence and was eventually excommunicated, tortured, and executed for criticizing the Pope.
3   *Hiero of Syracuse*   Hiero II (307–216 BCE) was so successful as an army commander that he was elected king of Syracuse.
4   *he lacked nothing ... to be a king*   Inaccurate quotation from the Roman historian Justin.
5   *Darius*   Last king of Persia who reigned from 336 to 331 BCE.

great worth and ability, it is not reasonable to expect that people who have always lived in private rather than public life should know how to command. Moreover, they cannot be sure of holding their position because they do not have forces which they can keep friendly and faithful to them.

States that rise unexpectedly, then, like all other things in nature which are born and grow rapidly, cannot have foundations stable enough to endure the first storm; unless, as I noted, those who unexpectedly become princes are men of so much ability that they know they have to be prepared both to hold onto that which fortune has thrown into their laps, and afterwards to lay the sort of foundation that others have laid before they became princes.

Let me now cite examples of these two methods of rising to be a prince—through ability or through fortune. These two examples are within our own recollection: Francesco Sforza[1] and Cesare Borgia.[2] Francesco, by proper means and with great ability, rose from his position as a private person to become Duke of Milan. He kept the post, which he had acquired with a thousand anxieties, with little trouble. On the other hand, Cesare Borgia, called by the people Duke Valentino, acquired his state during the ascendancy of his father, and on its decline he lost it, notwithstanding that he had taken every measure and done all that ought to be done by a wise and able man to firmly fix his roots in those states which the arms and fortunes of others had bestowed on him.

For, as I stated above, he who has not first laid his foundations may be able if he possesses great ability to lay them afterwards, but in that case they will be laid with trouble to the architect and danger to the building. The Duke Valentino is one who laid solid foundations for his future power, and I do not consider it superfluous to discuss them, because I do not know what better precepts to give a new prince than the example of Valentino's actions. If his efforts were finally to no avail, that was not his fault, but the extraordinary and extreme malignity of fortune.[3]

Alexander VI,[4] in attempting to advance his son the duke, faced many difficulties. Firstly, he did not see any way in which he could put his son in charge of any state that was not a state of the Church; and if he was willing to try to take a state away from Church control, he knew that the Duke of Milan and the Venetians would not consent, because Faenza and Rimini were already under the protection of the Venetians. Besides this, he saw that the armed forces of Italy, especially those which he might have used, were controlled by those who would fear the greatness of the Pope, namely, the Orsini and the Colonna[5] and their following. It was advantageous to him, therefore, to upset this state of affairs and create turmoil for these powers, so as to safely obtain control of part of their states. This was easy for him to do, because the Venetians wanted for their own reasons to bring back the French into Italy; he would not only not oppose this, but he would render it easier by dissolving the former marriage of King Louis.[6] Therefore the king came into Italy with the assistance of the Venetians and the consent of Alexander. He was no sooner in Milan than the Pope obtained soldiers from him for the Romagna campaign; this was made possible because of the prestige of the king. The duke, having acquired the Romagna and beaten the Colonna, then wished to hold the Romagna and to advance further, but he was hindered by two things. First, a suspicion that his forces were not loyal to him; and second, the will of the King of France. That is to say, he feared that the forces of the Orsini, which he was using, would not stand with him—that they might hinder him from winning more, but also that they might themselves seize what he had won, and that the King might also do the same. He had experienced this with the Orsini when, after taking Faenza and attacking Bologna, he saw them go only reluctantly to battle. And he learned the king's intentions when he himself, after taking the duchy of Urbino, attacked Tuscany, and the king made him desist from that undertaking; hence the duke decided to depend no more upon the troops and fortunes of others.

First he weakened the Orsini and Colonna parties in Rome, by winning over to himself all their adherents who were gentlemen, making them *his* gentlemen, giving them good pay, and, according to their rank, honoring them with office and command in such a way that in a few months all attachment to their factions was destroyed and turned

---

1 *Francesco Sforza* Mercenary for the duke of Milan (1401–66), then duke himself.

2 *Cesare Borgia* Italian military leader (c. 1475–1507), illegitimate son of Pope Alexander VI, and cardinal. He was commander of the papal armies, with a reputation for cruelty, opportunistic ruthlessness, and treachery.

3 *malignity of fortune* As described below, this is his illness after the death of his father.

4 *Alexander VI* Rodrigo Borgia (1431–1503); Pope from 1492 until his death.

5 *the Orsini and the Colonna* Powerful Roman families who played important roles in Italian history. They were hereditary enemies with a rivalry that lasted until the *Pax Romana* of 1511.

6 *King Louis* Louis XII (1462–1515) succeeded Charles VII as king of France in 1498.

entirely to the duke. After this he awaited an opportunity to crush the Orsini, having scattered the adherents of the Colonna. This came to him soon and he used it well; the Orsini, realizing too late that the greatness of the duke and the Church would ruin them, called a meeting at Magione, in the territory of Perugia. From this sprung the rebellion at Urbino and the insurrections in the Romagna, with endless dangers to the duke, all of which he overcame with the help of the French. His authority was restored; and in order not to risk it by trusting either the French or other outside forces, he had turned to strategic deception. He knew very well how to conceal his aims and used as an intermediary Signor Paolo [Orsini]—whom the duke did not fail to secure with all kinds of attention, giving him money, garments, and horses. With Signor Paolo's help, the Orsini were reconciled, so that their stupidity brought them into the duke's power at Sinigaglia. Having exterminated the leaders, and turned their partisans into his friends, the duke had laid sufficiently good foundations for exercising his power; he had control of all the Romagna and of the duchy of Urbino; and he won the support of the people, who had begun to appreciate their prosperity. (And as this last point is worthy of notice, and to be imitated by others, I am not willing to leave it out.)

When the duke occupied the Romagna he found it under the rule of weak masters, who plundered their subjects rather than governed them, and gave them more cause for disunion than for union; so that the country was full of robbery, quarrels, and every kind of violence. Wishing to bring back peace and obedience to authority, the duke considered it necessary to appoint a good governor. He promoted Ramiro d'Orco [de Lorqua], an unscrupulous and cruel man, to whom he gave the fullest power. This man in a short time restored peace and had great success in establishing unity. But afterwards the duke considered that it would not be advisable to confer such excessive authority on him on an ongoing basis, for the duke was sure that Ramiro would become odious. He therefore set up a court of judgment in the country, under a most excellent president, wherein all cities had their advocates. And because the duke knew that the severity of his past behavior had caused some hatred against himself, he desired to clear himself in the minds of the people and win them over to his side. He wanted to show them, indeed, that, if any cruelty had been perpetrated, it had not originated with him, but in the violent nature of Ramiro his minister. Under this pretence he had Ramiro arrested and then and one morning

had him executed and left on the piazza at Cesena, with the block and a bloody knife at his side. The barbarity of this spectacle caused the people to be satisfied and dismayed at the same time.

But let us return to where we left off. The duke now found himself in a powerful position. He had largely secured himself against immediate dangers by having armed himself in his own way, and by having in great measure crushed those forces in his vicinity that could injure him. He had next to consider France, for he knew that the king, who had become aware of his mistake too late, would not support him. And from this time the duke began to seek new alliances and to vacillate with France in the expedition which she was making towards the kingdom of Naples against the Spaniards who were besieging Gaeta. It was the duke's intention to secure himself against them, and he would have quickly accomplished this had Alexander lived.

These were the actions he undertook with a view to the present. As to the future, he had to fear, in the first place, that a new successor to the Church might not be friendly to him and might seek to take from him that which Alexander had given him. So he decided to act in four ways. First, he decided to exterminate the families of those lords whom he had despoiled, so as to take away that opportunity from the Pope. Second, he took it upon himself to win over all the gentlemen of Rome, so as to be able to resist the Pope with their aid, as I have mentioned. Third, he worked at converting the College of Cardinals[1] to his side. Fourth, he endeavored to acquire such a large territory before the Pope died that he could resist the first attack on his own. When Alexander died,[2] he had accomplished three of these four things. He had killed as many of the dispossessed lords as he could lay hands on, and few had escaped; he had won over the Roman gentlemen, and he had the most numerous party in the College of Cardinals. And as to any fresh acquisition, he intended to become master of Tuscany, for he already possessed Perugia and Piombino, and Pisa was under his protection. And since he did not have to pay attention to France any longer (for the French had already been driven out of the kingdom of Naples by the Spaniards, and in this way both were compelled to buy his good will), he pounced on Pisa. After this, Lucca and Siena yielded at once, partly through hatred and partly through fear of the Florentines; and the Florentines would have had no remedy

---

1   *College of Cardinals*   Body that elects the Pope.
2   *Alexander died*   Alexander VI died in 1503.

had he continued to prosper, as he was prospering the year that Alexander died, for he had acquired so much power and reputation that he would have stood by himself, and no longer have depended on the luck and the forces of others, but solely on his own power and ability.

But Alexander died five years after he had first drawn the sword. He left the duke with only the state of Romagna consolidated. The rest was in the air, hanging in the balance between two powerful hostile armies, while the duke himself lay gravely ill. The duke possessed such boldness and ability and knew so well how men are to be won or lost, and had laid down such firm foundations in so short a time, that if he had not had those armies on his back, or if he had been in good health, he would have overcome all difficulties. And it is clear that his foundations were good, for the Romagna awaited him for more than a month. In Rome, although but half alive, he remained secure; though the Baglioni, the Vitelli, and the Orsini came to Rome, they could not accomplish anything against him. Perhaps he could not choose the one he wanted to be Pope, but at least it should have been possible to prevent the one whom he did not want from being elected. If he had been in sound health at the death of Alexander, everything would have been easy for him—but instead he lay deathly ill. On the day that Julius II was elected, he told me that he had thought of everything that might occur at the death of his father, and had provided a remedy for every circumstance, except that he had never anticipated that at the time of his father's death, he would be at the edge of death himself.

When all the actions of the duke are recalled, I do not know how to reproach him. Rather it appears to me, as I have said, that I ought to propose that he be imitated by all those who, through fortune or the troops of others, are raised to government. The duke, having a lofty spirit and far-reaching aims, could not have conducted himself otherwise or achieved greater results; only the shortness of the life of Alexander and his own sickness frustrated his designs. He who considers it necessary to secure himself in his new principality; to win friends; to overcome enemies either by force or fraud; to make himself beloved and feared by the people; to be followed and revered by the soldiers; to exterminate those who have power or reason to hurt him; to change the old order of things for a new one; to be severe and gracious, magnanimous and generous; to destroy a disloyal army and to create a new one; to maintain friendship with kings and princes in such a way that they will help him enthusiastically and will be careful not to offend him; he who desires all

this cannot find a better example to follow than the actions of this man.

The duke can be blamed only for the election of Julius II, in whom he made a bad choice. Although it has been said he was not able to elect the Pope he preferred, he could have prevented any other from being elected Pope; and he ought never to have consented to the election of a cardinal whom he had injured or who had cause to fear him if they became pope. For men injure either from fear or hatred. He had injured, among others, San Pietro ad Vincula, Colonna, San Giorgio, and Ascanio.[1] Any one of the others, on becoming Pope, would have had to fear him, except Rouen[2] and the Spaniards; the latter from their relationship and obligations, the former from his influence (the kingdom of France having relations with him.) Therefore, above all, the duke ought to have created a Spaniard Pope, and, failing him, he ought to have consented to Rouen and not San Pietro ad Vincula. He who believes that new benefits will cause great personages to forget old injuries is deceived. In this case, the duke erred in his choice, and it was the cause of his ultimate ruin.

Chapter 8: Concerning those who have obtained a principality through wickedness

I have spoken of certain methods whereby an ordinary citizen may become a prince—methods that are not entirely matters of fortune or virtue. There are two other methods of which I should say something here (I will also discuss one of them at greater length elsewhere, in discussing republics). The first of these occurs when a private citizen becomes prince through some wicked or nefarious ways, the second when a private citizen becomes prince through the favor of his fellow-citizens. I will illustrate the first of those by two examples—one ancient, the other modern—and not enter further into the subject. I consider these two examples will be enough for those who may be compelled to follow them.

Agathocles,[3] the Sicilian, rose to become King of Syracuse not from the position of an ordinary citizen but from

---

1. *San Pietro ad Vincula* Julius II had been Cardinal of San Pietro ad Vincula; *San Giorgio* Raffaells Riaxis; *Ascanio* Cardinal Ascanio Sforza.
2. *Rouen* Georges d'Amboise.
3. *Agathocles* King of Syracuse (317–289 BCE) and of Sicily (304–289 BCE).

a low and abject position. This man, the son of a potter, led a life of wickedness through a series of changes in his fortunes. But he accompanied his wickedness with so much ability of mind and body that, having devoted himself to the military profession, he rose through its ranks to be Praetor[1] of Syracuse. Once established in that position, he deliberately resolved to make himself prince and to hold on by violence to the position which had been given to him by universal consent, paying no attention to his obligations to others.[2] For this purpose he reached an agreement with Hamilcar,[3] the Carthaginian, who, with his army, was fighting in Sicily. One morning he assembled the people and senate of Syracuse, as if he had to discuss with them matters relating to the Republic, and at a given signal the soldiers killed all the senators and the richest citizens; with them dead, he seized and held the princedom of that city without any opposition from the citizens. And although he was twice defeated by the Carthaginians, and later besieged, not only was he able to defend his city, but leaving part of his men for its defense, he was able to use the rest of his men to attack Africa, and in a short time to free Syracuse. The Carthaginians, in a desperate state, were compelled to come to terms with Agathocles, and, leaving Sicily to him, had to be content with the possession of Africa.[4]

No one who considers the actions and the genius of this man will see anything (or at most a very little) which can be attributed to fortune; Agathocles attained pre-eminence, as is shown above, not by anyone's favor, but step by step in the military profession. He made each step accompanied by a thousand troubles and perils; and afterwards he maintained his position by courageous and dangerous means. Yet it cannot be called virtue to slay fellow-citizens, to deceive friends, to be without faith, without mercy, without religion; such methods may gain empire, but not glory. Still, if the courage of Agathocles in entering into and extricating himself from dangers be considered, together with his greatness of mind in enduring overcoming hardships, it does not seem that he should be esteemed less than the most notable

captain. Nevertheless, his barbarous cruelty, his inhumanity, and his many wicked deeds do not allow him to be celebrated among the most excellent men. What he achieved cannot be attributed either to fortune or to virtue.

In our times, during the rule of Alexander VI, Oliverotto da Fermo, having been left an orphan many years before, was brought up by his maternal uncle, Giovanni Fogliani, and in the early days of his youth was sent to be a soldier under Paolo Vitelli. The idea was that, after being trained under Paolo's discipline, Oliverotto might attain some high position in the military profession. After Paolo died, Oliverotto fought under his brother Vitellozzo, and in a very short time, being endowed with skill and a vigorous body and mind, he became a leader of troops. But since it appeared to him a paltry thing to serve under others, he resolved to seize Fermo, aided by some citizens of Fermo (who evidently preferred the slavery of their country to its liberty), as well as by the Vitelli. So he wrote to Giovanni Fogliani that, having been away from home for many years, he wished to visit him and his city, and to look into the matter of his inheritance. He said that, although he had not labored to acquire anything except honor, yet, in order that the citizens should see he had not spent his time in vain, he desired to come honorably, and so would be accompanied by one hundred horsemen, his friends, and retainers. He begged Giovanni to arrange that he should be received honorably by the citizens of Fermo, which would be not only to his honor, but also to that of Giovanni himself, who had raised him.

Giovanni did not fail in any duty toward his nephew; he had him received honorably by the Fermans, and he lodged him in his own house, where, having passed some days, and having arranged what was necessary for his wicked designs, Oliverotto gave a solemn banquet to which he invited Giovanni Fogliani and the chiefs of Fermo. When the meal and all the entertainment that is usual at such banquets were finished, Oliverotto artfully began certain grave discourses, speaking of the greatness of Pope Alexander and his son Cesare, and of their undertakings. After Giovanni and others replied, he suddenly arose, saying that such matters ought to be discussed in a more private place, and he withdrew to a private room. Giovanni and the rest of the citizens followed him. No sooner were they seated than soldiers emerged from hiding and slaughtered Giovanni and the others. After these murders Oliverotto, mounted on horseback, rode up and down the town and besieged the chief officials in the palace, so that the people were forced to obey him out of fear, and to form a government, of which

---

1   *Praetor*   Chief law officer of the state—second in rank only to Consul.

2   *universal consent ... obligations to others*   He could have become prince by consent of the Senate, but chose not to, because that would have created obligations to them.

3   *Hamilcar*   Statesman (c. 270–228 BCE) and Carthaginian general during the First Punic War.

4   *Africa*   In this case, "Africa" means the region surrounding Carthage in North Africa, on the south shore of the Mediterranean Sea.

he made himself the prince. He killed all those who might be able to harm him, and strengthened himself with new civil and military ordinances, in such a way that, in the year during which he held the principality, not only was he secure in the city of Fermo, but he had become formidable to all his neighbors. To destroy him would have been as difficult in the case of Agathocles if only Oliverotto had not allowed himself to be deceived by Cesare Borgia, who killed him along with the Orsini and Vitelli at Sinigaglia, as was stated above. Thus, one year after he had committed this parricide, he was strangled, together with Vitellozzo, whom he had made his teacher in virtue and wickedness.

Some may wonder how it can happen that Agathocles, and his like, after infinite treacheries and cruelties, are able to live for so long secure in their own country, and are able to defend themselves from external enemies and never be conspired against by their own citizens. After all, many others have never been able to hold the state by means of cruelty even in peaceful times, still less in the uncertain times of war. I believe that this all depends on whether cruelty is badly or properly used. Cruel measures are properly used—if one might speak well of evil—when they are applied a single time, are necessary to one's security, and are not persisted in afterwards unless they can be turned to the advantage of the subjects. Cruel measures badly employed are those which, despite being few at the beginning, multiply with time rather than decrease. Those who practice the first system are able, by aid of God or man, to remedy their condition to some degree, as Agathocles did. It is impossible for those who follow the other system to maintain their position.

We should therefore note that, in seizing a state, the usurper ought to consider carefully which injuries it is necessary for him to inflict, and to do them all at one stroke so as not to have to repeat them daily. By not unduly unsettling men he will be able to reassure them, and win them to himself by offering them benefits. He who does otherwise, either from timidity or evil advice, is always compelled to keep the knife in his hand. He cannot rely on his subjects, and nor can they attach themselves to him, owing to their continued and repeated injuries. As a general rule, then, injuries ought to be inflicted all at one time, so that, being tasted less, they offend less; benefits ought to be given little by little, so that the flavor of them may last longer.

Above all, a prince ought to live among his people in such a way that no unexpected circumstances, whether good or evil, shall make him change; because if the necessity for this comes in troubled times, it will be too late to take harsh measures; and mild ones will not help you, for they will be seen to be forced from you, and no one will owe you any gratitude for them.

Chapter 9: Concerning a civil principality

But now let us consider the second case—where a leading citizen becomes the prince of his country, not by wickedness or any intolerable violence, but by the favor of his fellow citizens. This sort of rule may be called a civil principality; neither genius nor fortune is necessary to achieve this, but rather fortunate astuteness. I believe that such a principality is obtained either by the favor of the people or by the favor of the nobles. These two distinct parties are found in all cities. The people do not wish to be ruled or oppressed by the nobles, but the nobles wish to rule and oppress the people; and from these two opposite desires may arise in cities one of three results: a principality, self-government, or anarchy.

A principality is created either by the people or by the nobles, depending on which of the two groups has the opportunity. The nobles, seeing they cannot withstand the people, begin to support one of themselves, and they try to make him a prince, so that under his shadow they can satisfy their ambitions. The people, finding they cannot resist the nobles, also support one of themselves, and try to make him a prince so as to be defended by his authority. He who obtains sovereignty by the assistance of the nobles maintains himself with more difficulty than he who comes to it by the aid of the people, because the former finds himself with many around him who consider themselves his equals; because of this he can neither rule nor manage them as he likes. But he who reaches sovereignty by popular favor finds himself alone, and has none around him, or few, who are not prepared to obey him.

Moreover, it is impossible to satisfy the nobles by fair dealing, and without causing injury to others, but you can satisfy the people, for their object is more righteous than that of the nobles; the nobles wish to oppress, while the people desire only not to be oppressed. It is to be added also that a prince can never make himself secure against a hostile people, because they are too many, while he can secure himself from the nobles, as they are few in number. The worst that a prince may expect from a hostile people is to be abandoned by them; whereas from hostile nobles he has to fear not only abandonment, but also that they will rise against him. (Nobles, being in these affairs more far-seeing and astute than common people, always come forward in time to save themselves, and to obtain favors from him whom they expect to prevail.) Further, the prince is compelled to live always with the same people, but he can do well without the same nobles, being able to make and unmake them daily, and to give or take away their authority when it pleases him.

To make this point clearer, let me say that the nobles ought to be looked at mainly in two ways: they either commit themselves to your cause entirely, or they do not. Those who so commit themselves, and are not greedy and grasping, ought to be honored and loved; those who do not commit themselves may be dealt with in two ways. First, regarding those who fail to do this through weak-spirited cowardice and a natural lack of courage, you ought to make use of them, especially those who are good advisors; in prosperous times such people will bring you honor, but in adverse times you need not fear them. Second, regarding those who refuse to commit themselves because they are motivated by their own ambitious aims, this shows that they are giving more thought to themselves than to you. A prince ought to guard against this, and to fear them as if they were open enemies, because in adverse times they will always help to ruin him.

One who becomes a prince through the favor of the people ought to keep them friendly, and this he can easily do since they ask only not to be oppressed by him. But one who, in opposition to the people, becomes a prince by the favor of the nobles, ought, above everything, to seek to win the people over to himself; this he may do easily if he takes them under his protection. Because when men receive good from someone from whom they were expecting evil, they are bound more closely to their benefactor; thus the people quickly become more devoted to him than if he had been raised to the principality by their favors. The prince can win their affections in many ways. But as these vary according to the circumstances, one cannot give fixed rules, so I omit them; but, I repeat, it is necessary for a prince to have the people friendly, otherwise he has no security in adverse times.

Nabis,[1] Prince of the Spartans, withstood the attack of all Greece, and of one of Rome's most victorious armies, and defended his country and his government; to overcome this peril it was only necessary for him to secure himself against a few, but this would not have been sufficient if the people had been hostile. And do not let any one cast doubt on this statement with the trite proverb "He who builds on the people, builds on the mud." This is true when a private citizen makes a foundation there, and persuades himself that the people will free him when he is oppressed by his enemies or by the magistrates. In this he would find himself very often deceived, as happened to the Gracchi[2] in Rome and to Giorgio Scali[3] in Florence. But in the case of a prince who can command, and is a man of courage, undismayed in adversity, who does not fail in other qualifications, and who, by his resolution and energy, keeps up the spirit of the people—such a leader will never find himself deceived by them, and it will be shown that he has laid his foundations well.

These principalities are put in danger when they are passing from the civil to the absolute order of government, for such princes either rule personally or through magistrates. In the latter case their government is weaker and more insecure, because it rests entirely on the good will of those citizens who are appointed as magistrates, and who, especially in troubled times, can destroy the government with great ease, either by intrigue or open defiance. The prince cannot exercise absolute authority under tumultuous conditions, because the citizens and subjects, accustomed to receive orders from magistrates, are not inclined to obey him amid these confusions, and in difficult times there will always be a scarcity of men whom he can trust. Such a prince cannot rely upon what he observes in quiet times, when citizens had need of the state, because then everyone agrees with him, everyone makes promises, and when

---

1 *Nabis* Regent, then last king of Sparta (207–192 BCE). He was said to have made himself popular with the people through social reform and a redistribution of wealth, but he was also known for his cruelty.

2 *the Gracchi* Brothers Tiberius Sempronius Gracchus, tribune in 133 BCE, and Gaius Sempronius Gracchus, tribune in 123 and 122 BCE. From a less privileged social class, they attempted to achieve reform (including land redistribution) by limiting the size of large landholdings. Both were killed in political riots—Tiberius in 133 BCE, and Gaius in 121 BCE.

3 *Giorgio Scali* According to Machiavelli, Scali's tyrannical magistracy was ended in 1381 when the populace who had supported him turned against him for his "insolence"; at his execution, Machiavelli says, "he blamed himself for having confided too much in a people who were moved and corrupted by every voice, every act, and every suspicion" (*History of Florence*, Book 3, Section 20).

death is far distant they are all willing to die for him. But in troubled times, when the state has need of its citizens, then he finds but few. And this experiment is very dangerous, inasmuch as it can only be tried once. Therefore a wise prince ought to adopt a course of action that will ensure that his citizens will always need the state and him, in every kind of circumstance. Then he will always find them loyal.

Chapter 10: Concerning the way in which the strength of all principalities ought to be measured

In examining the character of these principalities it is necessary to consider another point: whether a prince has enough power to support himself with his own resources, or whether he needs the assistance of others. Let me make myself quite clear: I count a prince as being able to support himself by his own resources if he can, either by abundance of troops or money, raise a sufficient army to join battle against anyone who comes to attack him. On the other hand, I count a prince as needing others if he cannot face the enemy in the field, but is forced to defend himself by sheltering behind city walls. The first case has been discussed, and I will say more later on. In the second case one can say nothing except to encourage such princes to provision and fortify their towns, and not on any account to defend the countryside. If a prince fortifies his town well, and manages the other concerns of his subjects in the manner I discussed, potential attackers must be very cautious; for men are always adverse to enterprises in which they foresee difficulties, and it cannot seem easy to attack one who has his town well fortified, and is not hated by his people.

The cities of Germany are completely independent; they own only a little country around them; they obey the emperor only when it suits them, and they do not fear the emperor or any other nearby power, because they are fortified in such a way that everyone thinks that it would be tedious and difficult to take them by assault. They have proper moats and walls and sufficient artillery, and they always keep enough food, drink, and fuel for a year in public depots. And beyond this, in order to keep the people quiet without loss to the state, and to support them, they always have the means of providing employment in jobs that are the life and strength of the city. In addition, they hold military exercises in high regard, and have many laws to ensure that they are maintained.

Therefore, a prince who has a strong city, and has not made himself hated, will not be attacked. Or if he is, the attacker will be driven off in disgrace, because things in this world change, and it is almost impossible to sustain a siege for a whole year with an idle army. Someone might object that if people with property outside the city see it burnt, they will not remain patient, and self-interest will make them forget the interests of their prince during a siege. To this I answer that a powerful and courageous prince will overcome all such difficulties by alternately giving hope to his subjects that the evil will not continue for long, and instilling fear of the cruelty of the enemy, all the while protecting himself skillfully from those subjects who seem to him to be too openly critical.

When the enemy has just arrived in such instances, the enemy will naturally at once burn and ruin the country. At that time the people's spirits are still hot and ready for defense; so there is even less reason for the prince to hesitate. After a time, when spirits have cooled, the damage is already done, the ills are incurred, and there is no longer any remedy. The people are then much more ready to unite with their prince, who appears to have obligations to them now that their houses have been burnt and their possessions ruined in his defense. For it is the nature of men to be bound by the benefits they confer as much as by those they receive. Therefore, if everything is well considered, it will not be difficult for a wise prince to keep the minds of his citizens steadfast from first to last, so long as he does not lack provisions and weapons for defense.

Chapter 11: Concerning ecclesiastical principalities

It only remains now to speak of ecclesiastical principalities. All difficulties relating to these occur prior to getting possession. They are acquired either by the prince's ability or by good fortune, and they can be held without either; for they are sustained by the ordinances of religion, which are so all-powerful, and of such a nature that the principalities may be held no matter how their princes behave and live. These princes alone have states and do not defend them, they have subjects and do not rule them. The states, although unguarded, are not taken from them, and the subjects, although not ruled, do not care; they have neither the desire nor the ability to alienate themselves from the state. Such principalities are the only completely secure and successful ones. But being upheld by powers beyond the understanding of the human mind, I shall speak no more of them; because they are exalted and maintained by God, it would be the act of a presumptuous and rash man to discuss them.

How had it come about that the Church has attained such greatness in temporal power, seeing that Alexander and the earlier Italian powers (not only those who have been called powers, but every baron and lord, even the weakest) have placed very little value on temporal power? Yet now a king of France trembles before the power of the church, which has been able to drive him from Italy, and to ruin the Venetians. Although this may be very well known, it doesn't seem superfluous to recall it in some detail.

Before Charles,[1] King of France, invaded Italy, this country was under the dominion of the Pope, the Venetians, the King of Naples, the Duke of Milan, and the Florentines. These potentates had two principal anxieties: one, that no foreigner should enter Italy with his armies; the other, that none of the other Italian potentates should seize more territory. The greatest anxiety concerned the Pope and the Venetians. To restrain the Venetians, the union of all the others was necessary, as it was for the defense of Ferrara. To keep the Pope in check they made use of the barons of Rome, who, being divided into two factions, Orsini and Colonna, were constantly quarrelling. They kept the pontificate weak and powerless by standing with arms in their hands right under the eyes of the Pontiff. And although a courageous pope, such as Sixtus [IV],[2] might sometimes arise, neither fortune nor wisdom could rid him of these annoyances. And the short life of a pope is also a cause of weakness; for in ten years (the average reign of a pope) it is difficult for him to reduce the power of one of the factions. If, for example, one pope should almost destroy the Colonna, a new pope who was hostile to the Orsini would emerge and enable the Colonna to grow powerful again, but would still not have time to suppress them. This was the reason why the temporal powers of the pope were little respected in Italy.

But Alexander VI afterwards showed better than any of the other pontiffs throughout history how a pope with both money and arms could prevail. With Duke Valentino[3] as his

instrument, and because of the invasion of the French, he brought about all those things which I have discussed above when describing the actions of the duke. And although he intended to benefit the duke, not the Church, nevertheless what he did contributed to the greatness of the Church, which, after his death and the ruin of the duke, became heir to the benefits of his labors.

Pope Julius came afterwards and found the Church strong. It possessed all the Romagna, the barons of Rome had been reduced to impotence, and various other factions had been wiped out by Alexander's force. He also found the way open to accumulate money in a manner such as had never been practiced before Alexander's time. Julius pursued these practices, and even improved on them. He intended to gain Bologna, to ruin the Venetians, and to drive the French out of Italy. All of these enterprises prospered for him, and he is even more praiseworthy, inasmuch as he did everything to strengthen the Church rather than any private person. He kept also the Orsini and Colonna factions within the bounds in which he found them. Although they had some intention to disturb things, nevertheless Julius held two things firm: first, the greatness of the church, with which he terrified them; and second, forbidding them to have their own cardinals, since it was these who had caused the disturbances. Whenever these factions have their cardinals they do not remain quiet for long, because cardinals foster factions both within Rome and outside of Rome, and the barons are compelled to support them. Thus the ambitions of church officials give rise to disorder and quarrels among the barons. For these reasons His Holiness Pope Leo[4] found the papacy extremely powerful, and it is to be hoped that, as others made it great in arms, he will make it still greater and more venerated by his goodness and his countless other virtues.

Chapter 12: Of the different types of troops and mercenaries

Having discussed the characteristics of principalities that I proposed to talk about at the beginning, and having considered in some degree the causes of their success or failure,

---

1   *Charles*   King Charles VIII (1470–98), who invaded Naples in 1495.

2   *Sixtus [IV]*   Francesco della Rovere (1414–84), Pope from 1471 until his death.

3   *Duke Valentino*   As Machiavelli mentions above, this is another name for Cesare Borgia.

4   *Pope Leo*   Giovanni de' Medici (1475–1521), Pope Leo X from 1513 until his death. Highly political, he worked to extend the Medici family influence. He is now known for his papal bull against Martin Luther and his failure to check the Protestant Reformation.

and having shown the methods by which many have sought to acquire them and to hold them, it now remains for me to discuss generally the means of offense and defense which each of these principalities can adopt.

We have seen above how necessary it is for a prince to lay foundations well, otherwise he will necessarily come to ruin. The chief foundations of all states, new as well as old or composite, are good laws and good armies; and since there cannot be good laws where there are no good armies, where they are good armies there must be good laws. I shall leave the laws out of the discussion and shall speak of the armies.

I say, therefore, that the armed forces which a prince defends his state are either his own, or they are mercenaries, auxiliaries, or mixed troops. Mercenaries and auxiliaries are useless and dangerous. If one holds his state using these forces, one will stand neither firm nor safe; for they are disunited, ambitious and without discipline, unfaithful, valiant before friends, cowardly before enemies; they have neither the fear of God nor fidelity to men. Ruin is deferred only so long as the attack is; for in peace one is robbed by them, and in war by the enemy. The fact is, they have no other attraction or reason to remain in the field than a trifling wage, which is not sufficient to make them willing to die for you. They are ready enough to be your soldiers while you do not wage war, but if war comes they desert or run from the foe. I have no trouble in proving this, for the ruin of Italy has been caused by nothing else than resting all her hopes for many years on mercenaries. Although they formerly made some display and appeared valiant amongst themselves, yet when the foreigners came they revealed what they were. Thus it was that Charles [VIII], King of France, was easily able to seize Italy with a piece of chalk;[1] and he who said that this was the result of our sins[2] told the truth—but the sins where not the ones they imagined, but were those I have related. And as they were the sins of princes, it is the princes who have also suffered the penalty.

I wish to explain further the problems with this sort of army. The mercenary captains are either capable men or

they are not; if they are, you cannot trust them, because they always aspire to their own greatness, either by oppressing you, who are their master, or oppressing others contrary to your intentions; but if the captain is not skilful, you are ruined in the usual way.

If it is argued that whoever is armed will act in the same way, whether mercenary or not, I reply that when arms have to be resorted to, either by a prince or a republic, then the prince ought to go in person and perform the duty of captain; the republic has to send its citizens, and when one is sent who does not turn out satisfactorily, it must replace him, and when one is worthy, the republic must restrain him so he does not exceed his authority. Experience has shown that only princes and armed republics make great progress, while mercenaries do nothing except damage; and it is more difficult for one of its citizens to take over a republic armed with an army of its own citizens than a republic with a foreign army. Rome and Sparta stood for many ages armed and free. The Swiss are very well armed and quite free.

The Carthaginians provide an example of an ancient use of mercenary armies. They were oppressed by their mercenary soldiers after the first war with the Romans,[3] although the Carthaginians had their own citizens for captains. After the death of Epaminondas, the Thebans made Philip of Macedon[4] captain of their army, and after victory he took away their liberty.

After the death of Duke Filippo,[5] the Milanese hired Francesco Sforza against the Venetians. He, having overcome the enemy at Caravaggio, allied himself with them to crush his own employers, the Milanese. His father, Sforza, who was a soldier for Queen Johanna of Naples, left her unprotected, and as a result she was forced to throw herself into the arms of the King of Aragon, in order to save her kingdom. And if it is objected that the Venetians and Florentines formerly extended their dominions with mercenary armies, without their captains seizing their principalities, I reply that the Florentines in this case have been favored by chance. Among the able leaders, whom they had reason to fear, some failed to conquer, some met with opposition, and

---

1   *with a piece of chalk*   The French had a practice of marking houses in which troops were to be quartered with chalk. Machiavelli is implying here that the French found little Italian resistance to their invasion.

2   *this was the result of our sins*   Quote from Savonarola, who thought that the Italians' problems were punishment for their moral wickedness.

3   *the first war with the Romans*   The First Punic War (264–241 BCE).

4   *Epaminondas ... Philip of Macedon*   Epaminondas (c. 418–362 BCE) was a general and statesman who led Thebes to power and independence. Weakened by his wars, Thebes was taken over in 338 BCE by Philip II of Macedon (382–336 BCE).

5   *Duke Filippo*   Filippo Visconti (1392–1447), duke of Milan.

others have turned their ambitions elsewhere. One who did not conquer was Giovanni Acuto;[1] since he did not conquer his fidelity cannot be proved; but every one will acknowledge that, had he conquered, the Florentines would have been at his mercy. Sforza always had the Bracceschi against him, so they checked each other. Francesco turned his ambition to Lombardy; Braccio[2] against the Church and the kingdom of Naples.

But let us turn to recent events. The Florentines appointed as their captain Paolo Vitelli, a most prudent man, who had risen from the position of private citizen to the greatest renown. If this man had taken Pisa, nobody can deny that it would have been proper for the Florentines to cultivate his friendship, for if he became the soldier of their enemies they had no means of resisting, and if they had engaged him, they would have to obey him. The Venetians, if their achievements are considered, will be seen to have acted safely and gloriously so long as they sent their own men to war, and fought courageously using their armed gentry populace. This was before they began to fight on land. When they began to fight on land they abandoned this virtue and followed the usual practices of waging war in Italy. And in the beginning of the expansion of their territory on the mainland, they did not have much to fear from their captains, because they did not have much territory but had a great reputation. But when they expanded, as under Carmignola, they had a taste of this mistake. On the one hand, they had found him a courageous man (they beat the Duke of Milan under his leadership); but on the other, knowing how he had lost his taste for waging war, they feared they would no longer conquer under him. Yet they could not dismiss him for fear of losing that which they had acquired. In order to secure themselves against him, they were compelled to murder him. Their captains later were Bartolomeo da Bergamo, Roberto da San Severino, the Count of Pitigliano, and the like; under them they had to fear not gain of territory but loss, as happened afterwards at Vailà,[3] where in one battle they lost what they had acquired with so much difficulty over eight hundred years. Because

with soldiers such as these, conquests come slowly, long delayed and inconsequential, but losses tend to be vast and can happen with astonishing speed.

With these examples I have reached Italy,[4] which has been ruled for many years by mercenaries. I wish to discuss them more seriously, in order that, having seen their origin and progress, one may be better prepared to counteract them. You must understand that the empire has recently come to be repudiated in Italy, that the Pope has acquired more temporal power, and that Italy has been divided up into more states. Many of the great cities took up arms against their nobles, who, formerly favored by the emperor, kept them under control. The Church favored these cities so as to gain temporal power; in many others, citizens became princes. From this it came to pass that Italy fell partly into the hands of the Church and of several republics; and, since the priests making up the Church and the citizens making up the republics were both unaccustomed to bearing arms, both began to enlist foreigners.

The first who gave prestige to this sort of soldier was Alberigo da Conio,[5] a native of the Romagna. Trained by him were, among others, Braccio and Sforza, who in their time were the arbiters of Italy. After these came all the other captains who till now have directed Italy's armies; and the end of all their valor has been, that she has been overrun by Charles [VIII], robbed by Louis [XII], ravaged by Ferdinand[6] [II], and insulted by the Swiss. The principle that has guided them has been, first, to discredit the infan-

---

1   *Giovanni Acuto*   This is an Italianized version of the name of John Hawkwood, an English mercenary who fought in Italy beginning in 1360.

2   *Braccio*   Andrea Braccio da Montone (1368–1424), important mercenary leader and later Lord of Perugia, Prince of Capua, and Governor of the Abruzzi.

3   *Vailà*   The Venetians were badly defeated in the battle here (also known as the Battle of Agnadello) by the French in 1509.

4   *With these examples I have reached Italy*   The events mentioned in this section relate to the period of the "Italian Wars," beginning in about 1450 and lasting past the time Machiavelli wrote this work (1513). Italy was divided among rival states, the strongest of which were Venice; Milan (ruled by Ludovico Sforza); Florence, which gained considerably under the rule of Lorenzo the Magnificent; the Papal States, expanding under the political popes of the late fifteenth century; and Naples, ruled by the Aragonese. Continuing battles among the Italians weakened them all, and opened the way, beginning around 1490, for meddling in Italian affairs by the French (under Charles VIII, then Louis XII, then Francis I), the Germans (under Maximilian I, Emperor of the Holy Roman Empire), the Spanish (under Ferdinand of Aragon), and some cantons of Switzerland.

5   *Alberigo da Conio*   Alberigo da Barbiano, count of Cunio (d. 1409); influential in replacing foreign mercenary troops with Italian mercenaries.

6   *Ferdinand*   Ferdinand II (also known as Ferdinand of Aragon, 1452–1516), who unified Spain, gained control of several cities in Italy, and also gained control of large portions of the New World.

try so that they might increase their own prestige. They did this because, subsisting on their pay and without territory, they were unable to support many soldiers themselves, and a few infantry did not give them any authority; so they were led to employ cavalry. With a moderate cavalry force they were well-paid and honored; and it came to pass that in an army of twenty thousand soldiers, there were not to be found even two thousand foot soldiers. They had also used every art to lessen fatigue and danger to themselves and their soldiers, not killing in the fray, but taking prisoners and liberating without ransom. They did not attack towns at night, nor did the garrisons of the towns attack encampments at night; they did not surround a camp either with stockades or trenches, nor did they campaign in the winter. All these things were in line with their military code, and devised by them to avoid, as I have said, both fatigue and dangers; thus they have brought Italy to slavery and contempt.

Chapter 13: Concerning auxiliary, mixed, and citizen soldiers

Auxiliaries are forces that one calls in from a powerful neighbor for aid and defense, and these are as useless as mercenaries. Auxiliaries were used recently by Pope Julius in the Ferrara enterprise. Having seen the failure of his mercenaries, he arranged for armed assistance from Ferdinand, King of Spain. These forces may be useful and good in themselves, but for him who summons them they are always disadvantageous; for losing, one is undone, and winning, one is their captive.

Although ancient histories are full of examples, I want to emphasize the recent case of Pope Julius II, because one cannot fail to see the peril to which he was subjected. Wishing to win Ferrara, he threw himself entirely into the hands of a foreigner. But he had the good fortune that a third development prevented him from suffering the results of his rash choice. After his auxiliaries were routed at Ravenna, the Swiss rose up and drove out the conquerors (against everyone's expectation), and so he did not become prisoner of his enemies, who had fled, nor of his auxiliaries, since he had conquered with other troops than theirs.

The Florentines, being completely unarmed, sent ten thousand Frenchmen to take Pisa, a plan which endangered themselves more than at any of their previous predicaments.

The Emperor of Constantinople,[1] to oppose his neighbors, sent ten thousand Turks into Greece. When the war was finished, the Turks were not willing to leave; this was the beginning of the servitude of Greece to the infidels.

Only those who have no desire to conquer should make use of these armed forces, for they are much more hazardous than mercenaries. With them ruin is assured; they are all united, and they all owe obedience to others. Mercenaries who have conquered, on the other hand, need more time and better opportunities to injure you; they are not united, they are found and paid by you, and the person whom you have made their head is not immediately able to assume enough authority to injure you. In conclusion, cowardice is the most dangerous quality in mercenaries; in auxiliaries, it is courage. The wise prince, therefore, has always avoided these soldiers and turned to his own and has been willing rather to lose using his own forces than to conquer using the forces of others, not deeming a victory real which is gained with foreign troops.

I shall never hesitate to cite Cesare Borgia and his actions. This Duke entered the Romagna with auxiliary troops, taking only French soldiers, and with them he captured Imola and Forli. But afterwards, because these forces did not appear reliable to him, he turned to mercenaries, judging them to be less dangerous, and enlisted the Orsini and Vitelli. But when he found them unreliable, unfaithful, and dangerous, he suppressed them and turned to his own men. The difference between these sorts of forces can easily be seen when one considers the difference there was in the reputation of the duke, on the one hand when he had French troops or when he had the Orsini and Vitelli, and on the other when he relied on his own soldiers, on whose fidelity he could always count. We find that his reputation grew and he was never esteemed more highly than when everyone saw that he was complete master of his own forces.

I did not intend to go beyond Italian and recent examples, but I am unwilling to omit Hiero, the Syracusan, he whom I have named above. This man, as I have said, having been made head of their army by the Syracusans, soon found out that a mercenary army, constituted like our Italian condottieri, was of no use. Since it appeared to him that he could neither keep them nor let them go, he had

---

1   *The Emperor of Constantinople*   John VI Cantacuzenus (c. 1292–1383) was Byzantine emperor (1347–54). In his fight to become emperor, and to keep control later during civil war, he enlisted Turkish aid.

them all cut to pieces. Afterwards he made war with his own troops and not with soldiers belonging to others.

I wish also to call to mind an example from the Old Testament applicable to this subject. David[1] offered himself to Saul to fight Goliath, the Philistine champion. To give David courage, Saul offered him his own weapons; but David rejected them as soon as he had them on his back, saying he could make no use of them, and that he wished to meet the enemy with his own sling and his own knife. In conclusion, the arms of others either fail you, weigh you down, or tie you up.

Charles VII,[2] the father of King Louis XI,[3] having by good fortune and valor liberated France from the English, recognized the necessity of arming himself with his own soldiers, and he established ordinances in his kingdom to procure cavalry and infantry. Afterwards his son, King Louis, abolished the infantry and began to enlist the Swiss. This mistake, followed by others, is now seen to have endangered the kingdom. By raising the reputation of the Swiss, he diminished the value of his own troops. He destroyed the infantry altogether and subordinated his cavalry to others. Being so accustomed to fighting along with the Swiss, the French felt that they could not conquer without them. Hence it arises that the French could not stand against the Swiss, and without the Swiss they did not test their chances against others. The armies of the French have thus become mixed, partly mercenary and partly national. This combined force is much better than mercenaries alone or auxiliaries alone, yet much inferior to one's own forces. And this example proves it: the kingdom of France would be unconquerable if Charles VII's military institutions had been enlarged or maintained.

But men, showing poor judgment when establishing a policy that looks good at first, cannot see the poison that is hidden in it, as I have said above of consumptive fevers. Therefore, if he who rules a principality cannot recognize evils until they are upon him, he is not truly wise; and this insight is given to few. And examination of the first causes of the fall of the Roman Empire will show that it began

when they enlisted the Goths. From that time the vigor of the Roman Empire began to decline, and all the valor which had raised it passed away to others.

I conclude, therefore, that no principality is secure without its own soldiers; on the contrary, it is entirely dependent on good fortune, not having the valor which in adversity would defend it. It has always been the opinion and judgment of wise men that nothing can be so uncertain or unstable as fame or power not founded on one's own strength.[4] One's own forces are those which are composed either of subjects, citizens, or dependants; all others are mercenaries or auxiliaries. And the way to organize one's own forces will be easily found if one reflects on the rules I have suggested, and if one considers how Philip [II], the father of Alexander the Great,[5] and many republics and princes have armed and organized themselves. I have full confidence in their rules.

Chapter 14: That which concerns a prince on the subject of the art of war

A prince ought to have no other aim or thought than war and its organization and discipline. Nor should he study anything else; for this is the sole art that pertains to a ruler, with the power not only to maintain those who are born princes, but also often to enable private citizens to rise to that rank. It has been observed that when princes think more about luxury than of warfare they lose their states. The primary cause of losing power is the neglect of this art; and mastery of it enables the acquisition of a state.

Francesco Sforza, a private citizen, became Duke of Milan because he was armed; and his sons, because they avoided the hardships and troubles of arms, were both reduced from the rank of duke to that of private citizen. Among the many evils which being unarmed brings you is that it makes you contemptible; this is one of those disgraces against which a prince ought to guard himself, as I show later on. There is no comparison between the armed and the unarmed man. It would go against reason that an armed man should willingly obey one who is unarmed, or

---

1   *David*   Ancient king of Israel (c. 1000 BCE?) who extended its territory and influence by a series of military victories. His story is found in several books of the Old Testament, especially 1 Samuel and 2 Samuel.

2   *Charles VII*   King of France (1403–61) from 1422 until his death.

3   *King Louis XI*   King of France (1423–83) from 1461 until his death.

4   *nothing can be … one's own strength*   Machiavelli gives a Latin version: "*Quod nihil sit tam infirmum aut instabile quam fama potentiae non sua vi nixae,*" somewhat misquoting the *Annals* of Tacitus 13, 19.

5   *Alexander the Great*   King of Macedonia (356–323 BCE), Alexander conquered large portions of the Greek world.

that an unarmed man should feel safe among armed servants. Because one is disdainful and the other suspicious, it is not possible for them to work well together. In like fashion a prince who does not understand the art of war, over and above the other misfortunes already mentioned, cannot be respected by his soldiers, and nor can he rely on them. He ought never, therefore, let the subject of war leave his thoughts; he ought to practice it not only in wartime but also in peacetime. This he can do in two ways, the one by action, the other by study.

As regards action, he ought above all things to keep his men well organized and drilled. He ought constantly to be hunting, by which he can accustom his body to hardships and learn something of the nature of localities, how the mountains rise, how the valleys open out, how the plains lie, and understand the nature of rivers and marshes. In all this he should take the greatest care.

This knowledge is useful in two ways. First, he comes to know his country, and is better able to defend it. Second, by means of the knowledge and observation of his own local area, it will be easy for him to understand any other area which he must study later, because the hills, valleys, and plains, and rivers and marshes that are, for instance, in Tuscany, have a certain resemblance to those of other lands, so that with a knowledge of the different aspects of one area he can easily arrive at a knowledge of others. The prince who lacks this skill lacks an essential skill which a captain should possess, for it allows him to surprise his enemy, to select quarters, to lead armies, to organize the battle, and to besiege towns to his advantage.

Among other praises which writers have bestowed on Philopoemen,[1] Prince of the Achaeans, he has been commended because in time of peace he never had anything on his mind except methods of waging war. When he was in the country with friends, he often stopped and reasoned with them: "If the enemy should be upon that hill, and we should find ourselves here with our army, who would have the advantage? How should one best advance to meet the enemy, without breaking formation? If we should wish to retreat, how ought we to set about it? If they should retreat, how ought we to pursue?" And he would set forth to them, as he went, all the contingencies that might arise for an army; he would listen to their opinion and state his, accompanying it with reasons. These continual discussions meant

that there could never arise unexpected circumstances for him to deal with in time of war.

As exercise for the intellect, the prince should read histories, and study there the actions of illustrious men, to see how they have borne themselves in war, and to examine the causes of their victories and defeats, so as to avoid the latter and imitate the former; and above all to do what some illustrious men have done: emulating their predecessors, and remembering their achievements and deeds. It is said that in this way Alexander the Great imitated Achilles, Caesar imitated Alexander, and Scipio[2] imitated Cyrus. Whoever reads Xenophon's[3] life of Cyrus will recognize that the glory of Scipio's life was imitation—that in chastity, affability, humanity, and generosity Scipio conformed to those things written of Cyrus by Xenophon.

A wise prince should follow such methods, and never be idle in peacetime, but rather work to increase his resources then so that they are available to him in adversity—so that if fortune changes it may find him prepared to resist her blows.

Chapter 15: Concerning things for which men, and especially princes, are praised or blamed

It remains now to see what ought to be the rules of conduct for a prince towards his subjects and his allies. As I know that many have written on this point, I expect I shall be considered presumptuous in mentioning the subject again, especially because, in discussing it, I shall depart from the methods of others. But because I intend my writing to be useful for the reader, it appears to me to be more appropriate to pursue real truth rather than imaginary matters. Many have pictured republics and principalities which in fact have never been known or seen, ignoring the great difference between how one ought to live and how one lives in fact. Neglecting to consider what *is* done because one is concentrating on what *ought to be* done is more likely to lead to ruin than to preservation. A man who wishes to

---

1   *Philopoemen*   General of the Achaen league (252–182 BCE), leader of a failed attempt to resist Roman domination of Greece.

2   *Achilles*   Hero of Homer's *Iliad*; *Caesar*   Julius Caesar (102–44 BCE), Roman general, statesman, and historian, who led Roman forces in establishing control over large areas of Europe, was established by the people as dictator for life and then assassinated by republican political enemies; *Scipio*   Scipio Africanus (236–183 BCE), renowned Roman general who defeated Hannibal.

3   *Xenophon*   Soldier and historian (c. 431–355 BCE); the reference here is to his *Anabasis*.

act entirely on the basis of his declarations about morality will soon meet with destruction among those with no such scruples.

Therefore it is necessary that a prince who wishes to hold his own know how to do wrong, and to make use of such knowledge when necessary. Putting aside imaginary matters concerning a prince, and discussing only those that are real, I say that all men when they are spoken of are judged in terms of those qualities which bring them either blame or praise. Such is especially true of princes, because of their high status. Thus it is that one is reputed generous, another miserly (I use a Tuscan term *misero*, because *avaro* in our language means someone who wants to possess by robbery, while *misero* means someone who avoids using what he has). One is reputed generous, one rapacious; one cruel, one compassionate; one faithless, another faithful; one effeminate and cowardly, another bold and brave; one affable, another haughty; one lascivious, another chaste; one sincere, another cunning; one hard, another easy; one grave, another frivolous; one religious, another unbelieving, and the like. And I know that everyone will agree that it would be most praiseworthy in a prince to exhibit all the qualities above that are considered good. But because such qualities can neither be entirely possessed nor completely observed—human conditions do not permit it—it is necessary for him to be prudent enough to know how to avoid scandal because of vices which would result in his losing his state. He should also avoid, if possible, those vices which would not result in this loss. But if this is not possible, he need not overly concern himself with those less serious vices. Moreover, he need not worry about being reproached for those vices without which it would be difficult to save the state; for if everything is considered carefully, it will be found that something which looks like virtue, if followed, would result in ruin; while something else, which looks like vice, when pursued brings him security and prosperity.

Chapter 16: Concerning generosity and miserliness

Let me begin with the first of the above-mentioned qualities; I say that it would be well to be reputed generous. Nevertheless, generosity exercised in a way that does not bring you the reputation for it, injures you; if one exercises it honestly as it should be exercised, it may not become known, and you will not avoid criticism for its opposite.

Therefore, anyone wishing to maintain a reputation for generosity must omit nothing in the way of magnificent display; a prince thus inclined will use up all his property in such acts, and will be compelled in the end, if he wishes to maintain a reputation for generosity, to unduly burden his people, and tax them, and do everything he can to get money. This will soon make him hateful to his subjects, he will become poor, and he will be little valued by anyone. Thus having offended many and rewarded few with his generosity, he will feel the effects of the people's unrest and become imperilled at the first sign of danger. Recognizing this himself, and wishing to draw back from it, he will run into criticism for being miserly.

Since a prince is unable to exercise the virtue of generosity in such a way that it is recognized without damaging his position, he should not be afraid of being considered miserly. That is the wise course to take. For in time he will come to be considered more generous: with good economic management, his revenues will be sufficient; he can defend himself against all attacks, and he will be able to engage in enterprises without burdening his people. Thus he will be able to be generous to the many people from whom he does not take, and miserly towards the few to whom he does not give.

We have not seen great things done in our time except by those who have been considered miserly; the rest have failed. Pope Julius the Second was assisted in reaching the papacy by a reputation for generosity, yet he did not strive afterwards to keep it up. When he made war on the King of France, and when he engaged in many other wars, he did so without imposing any extraordinary tax on his subjects, for he funded his additional expenses out of his long thriftiness. The present King of Spain would not have undertaken or successfully carried out so many enterprises if he were extravagant enough to have a reputation for generosity. Therefore, in order that a prince does not have to rob his subjects, that he can defend himself, that he does not become poor and abject, and that he is not forced to become greedy and grasping, a prince ought to consider the reputation for miserliness unimportant. It is one of those vices which will enable him to govern.

If anyone should say: "Caesar obtained empire by generosity, and many others have reached the highest positions by having been generous, and by being considered so," I answer: "Either you are a prince in fact, or you are on the way to becoming one. In the first case this generosity is dangerous, in the second it is indeed necessary to be considered generous. Caesar was one of those who wished to become pre-eminent in Rome; but if he had not moderated his expenses after taking power, he would have destroyed his government." And if anyone should reply: "Many have been princes, and have done great things with armies, who have been considered very generous," I reply: Either a prince spends his own money, or his subjects', or someone else's. In the first case he ought to be sparing, in the second he ought not to neglect any opportunity for generosity. And to the prince who goes forth with his army, supporting it by pillage, sack, and extortion, dealing with others' belongings, this generosity is necessary, otherwise he would not be followed by his soldiers. And of that which is neither yours nor your subjects' you can be a generous donor, as were Cyrus, Caesar, and Alexander; because it does not take away your reputation if you squander that of others, but adds to it; it is only squandering your own that injures you.

There is nothing that destroys so rapidly as generosity, for as you exercise it you lose the power to do so, and so become either poor or despised, or else, in avoiding poverty, grasping and hated. A prince should guard, above all things, against being despised and hated; and generosity leads you to both. Therefore it is wiser to have a reputation for miserliness, which brings criticism without hatred, than to be compelled, through seeking a reputation for generosity, to incur a name for rapacity and thereby become detested.

Chapter 17: Concerning cruelty and mercy, and whether it is better to be loved than feared

Coming now to the other qualities mentioned above, I say that every prince ought to desire to be considered merciful and not cruel. Nevertheless, he ought to take care not to misuse this mercy. Cesare Borgia was considered cruel, but his cruelty brought order to the Romagna, unified it, and restored it to peace and loyalty. And if this is considered correctly, he will be seen to have been much more merciful than the Florentine people, who, to avoid a reputation for cruelty, permitted Pistoia[1] to be destroyed. So long as a prince keeps his subjects united and loyal, he ought not to mind the criticism of cruelty. If he displays cruelty in a few cases, he will be more merciful than those who, through too much mercy, allow disorder to arise, and murders or robberies follow; these are liable to injure everyone, while executions ordered by a prince offend the individual only.

A new prince, above all, will find it impossible to avoid a reputation for cruelty, because new states are full of dangers. Hence Virgil, through the mouth of Dido, excuses the inhumanity of her reign because it is new, saying "*Res dura, et regni novitas me talia cogunt Moliri, et late fines custode tueri.*"[2]

Nevertheless the prince ought to be slow to believe and to act. Nor should he himself show fear; instead he should proceed in a temperate manner with prudence and humanity, so that too much confidence may not make him incautious and too much distrust render him intolerable.

A question arises here: is it better to be loved than feared, or better to be feared than loved? It may be answered that one should wish to be both. But, because it is difficult to unite them in one person, it is much safer to be feared than to be loved, when one of the two must be dispensed with. This is to be asserted in general of men: they are ungrateful, fickle, false, cowardly, and covetous. As long as you succeed they are yours entirely; they will offer you their blood, property, life and children, as is said above, when the need is far distant; but when it approaches they turn against you. And that prince who, relying entirely on their promises, has neglected other precautions, is ruined; friendships that are obtained by payments, and not by greatness or nobility of mind, may indeed be earned, but they are not secured, and in time of need cannot be relied upon. Men are less hesitant to offend someone who is beloved than someone who is feared, for love is preserved by a link of obligation which, owing to the baseness of men, is broken at every opportunity for their advantage. Fear, on the other hand, preserves you with a dread of punishment which never fails.

A prince ought to inspire fear in such a way that, if he does not win love, he nevertheless avoids hatred, because he can endure being feared easily while he is not hated. This will occur as long as he leaves alone the property of his subjects, and their women. When it is necessary for him to proceed against the life of someone, he must do it with proper justification and manifest cause. But above all things he must keep his hands off the property of others, because men more quickly forget the death of their father than the loss of their patrimony. Besides, pretexts for taking away

---

1   *Pistoia* A city under Florentine rule. Florence forcibly ended a factional conflict there in 1501–02.

2   *Res dura … custode tueri* "Harsh necessity, and the newness of my kingdom, force me to do such things and to guard my frontiers everywhere" (Virgil, *Aeneid* 1, 563–64).

property are never lacking; he who has once begun to live by robbery will always find pretexts for seizing what belongs to others. Reasons for taking lives, on the other hand, are more difficult to find and sooner lapse. But when a prince is with his army, and has a multitude of soldiers under control, then it is quite necessary he not worry about the reputation of cruelty, for without it he would never keep his army united or attentive to its duties.

Among the wonderful deeds of Hannibal[1] is this one. He led an enormous army, composed of many various races of men, to fight in foreign lands, and no dissensions arose either among them or against the prince, either in times of good fortune or bad. This success resulted from nothing else than his inhuman cruelty, which, with his boundless courage, made him revered and terrible in the sight of his soldiers: without that cruelty, his other virtues would not have been sufficient to produce this effect. Short-sighted writers admire his deeds from one perspective and from another condemn the principal cause of them.

That other virtues would not have been sufficient in such a case may be shown too by the case of Scipio, a most excellent man, not just of his own time, but of all times. Nevertheless, his army rebelled against him in Spain; the cause was he was too tolerant, and gave his soldiers more license than is consistent with military discipline. For this he was upbraided in the Senate by Fabius Maximus,[2] and called the corrupter of the Roman soldiery. The Locrians were destroyed by one of Scipio's officers, but he did not avenge this or punish the insolence of the officer. This was the result of his easy nature, so much so that it was said in the Senate by someone wishing to excuse him, that there were many men who knew how not to err better than they knew how to correct the errors of others. Scipio's nature would eventually have destroyed his fame and glory, if he had manifested it during the empire; but since he was under the control of the Senate, this injurious characteristic not only concealed itself, but contributed to his glory.

Returning to the question of being feared or loved, I conclude with this: men love according to their own free will, but fear according to the will of the prince. Therefore a wise prince should base his rule on that which is in his own control and not in the control of others. He must endeavor only to avoid hatred, as I said.

---

1   *Hannibal* Commander of the Carthaginian army (247–183 BCE) during the Second Punic War against Rome.
2   *Fabius Maximus* Roman politician and soldier (c. 275–203 BCE); consul five times, and twice dictator.

Chapter 18: Concerning the way in which princes should keep their word

Everyone knows how praiseworthy it is for a prince to act in good faith—to be honest and keep his word, and to live with integrity and not with deceit. Nevertheless our experience has been that those princes who have done great things have held good faith of little account, and have known how to cunningly manipulate men's minds. In the end they have overcome those who have relied on their word.

You must know there are two ways of fighting—one by the law, the other by force. The first method is appropriate for men, the second for beasts. But because the first is frequently not sufficient, it is often necessary to have recourse to the second. Therefore, it is necessary for a prince to understand how to avail himself of the beast and the man. This has been figuratively taught to princes by ancient writers, who describe how Achilles and many other princes of old were given to the Centaur[3] Chiron to nurse. The centaur brought them up in his discipline; just as they had for a teacher one who was half beast and half man, so it is necessary for a prince to know how to make use of both natures. A prince who has one without the other does not last.

A prince who has to act knowingly as a beast, ought to choose the fox and the lion. The lion cannot defend himself against snares, and the fox cannot defend himself against wolves. Therefore, it is necessary to be a fox to discover the snares and a lion to terrify the wolves. Those who rely simply on the lion lack understanding.

Therefore a wise lord cannot, nor ought he to, keep faith when doing so may be turned against him, and when the reasons that caused him to pledge his good faith exist no longer. If men were entirely good this precept would not hold, but because they are bad, and will not keep faith with you, you too are not bound to observe it with them. There will always be legitimate reasons for a prince to fail to keep his word. Endless modern examples could be given, showing how many treaties and engagements have been made void and of no effect through the faithlessness of princes; he who has known best how to employ the fox has succeeded best.

But it is necessary to know how to disguise this characteristic well, and to be a great pretender and dissembler. Men are so simple-minded, and so subject to present neces-

---

3   *Centaur* In Greek mythology, a half horse, half man.

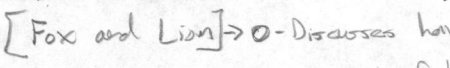

[Fox and Lion] → 0 - Discusses having the balance of gentleman/beast
Knowing when to fight by the law and when to use force

sities, that he who seeks to deceive will always find someone who will allow himself to be deceived. One recent example I cannot pass over in silence. Alexander VI did nothing else but deceive men, and never thought of doing otherwise, and always found victims; there never was a man who had greater power in asserting, or who with greater oaths would affirm a thing, yet would observe it less. Nevertheless his deceits always succeeded according to his wishes, because he well understood this side of humanity.

Therefore, it is not necessary for a prince to have all the good qualities I have enumerated, but it is necessary for him to appear to have them. I shall dare to say this also, that to have them and always to observe them is injurious, while to *appear* to have them is useful. The prince may appear merciful, faithful, humane, religious, upright, and even be so, but he must always keep a mind so disposed that should it become necessary for him not to be so, he will know how to change to the opposite.

You have to understand this: a prince, especially a new one, cannot behave in all those ways for which men are esteemed; in order to maintain the state, he is often forced to act contrary to faith, friendship, humanity, and religion. Therefore it is necessary for him to have a mind ready to turn itself accordingly as the winds and variations of fortune force it. Yet, as I have said above, he should not diverge from the good if he can avoid doing so. It is only if he is compelled to diverge from the good that he must know how to go about it.

For this reason a prince ought to take care that he never let anything slip from his lips that is not full of the above-named five qualities, so that he may appear to anyone who sees and hears him altogether merciful, faithful, humane, upright, and religious. There is nothing more necessary to appear to have than this last quality, since men judge generally more by eye than by hand—anyone can see you, but few can be so close to you that they can touch you. Every one sees what you appear to be, few really know what you are, and those few dare not oppose themselves to the opinion of the many, who have the majesty of the state to defend them. In the actions of all men, and especially of princes, which it is not prudent to challenge, one judges by the result.

For that reason, let a prince have the credit of conquering and holding his state; then his means will always be considered honest, and he will be praised generally, because the vulgar are always taken by what a thing seems to be and by its results; and in the world there are only the vulgar, for the few have no place when the many hold sway.

One prince[1] of the present time, whom it is not well to name, never preaches anything else but peace and good faith, and to both he is most hostile. Either of them, had he kept it, would have deprived him of reputation and kingdom many a time.

Chapter 19: That one should avoid being despised and hated

I have now spoken of the more important characteristics mentioned above, and will discuss the others briefly. The general idea here is that the prince must consider, as I said before, how to avoid what will make him hated or treated with contempt; if he succeeds at this, he will have done his part, and need not fear danger from other vices.

Above all, people would hate him for being greedy and grasping, as I have said—for usurping his subjects' property and women; he must abstain from both. When neither their property nor honor is touched, the majority of men live content, and he has only to contend with the ambition of a few, whom he can easily control in many ways.

What makes him despised is being considered changeable, frivolous, effeminate, mean-spirited, irresolute, from all of which a prince should guard himself as carefully as a sailor avoids reefs. He should try to show greatness, courage, gravity, and fortitude in his actions; and in his private dealings with his subjects let him show that his judgments are irrevocable, and maintain a reputation for himself that would prevent anyone from hoping either to deceive him or to get round him.

That prince is highly esteemed who conveys this impression of himself, and he who is highly esteemed is not easily conspired against; provided it is well known that he is an excellent man and revered by his people, he can be attacked only with difficulty. For this reason a prince ought to have two fears: one internal, regarding his subjects, and the other external, regarding foreign powers. From the latter he is defended by being well armed and having good allies, and if he is well armed he will have good friends. And internal affairs will always remain quiet when things are quiet externally, unless they were already disturbed by conspiracy. And even if there is external trouble, if he has carried out his preparations and has lived as I have said, as long as he does not despair, he will resist every attack, just as I said Nabis the Spartan did.

---

1   *One prince*   Often taken to be Ferdinand of Spain.

But concerning his subjects, when external affairs are disturbed, he has to fear only that they will conspire secretly; and a prince can easily guard himself from this by avoiding being hated and despised, and by keeping the people satisfied with him—this, as I said above at length, must be accomplished. And one of the most efficacious remedies that a prince can have against conspiracies is not to be hated and despised by the people, for conspirators against a prince always expect to please the people by his removal. But when the conspirator can look forward only to offending the people he will not have the courage to take such a course, for the difficulties that confront a conspirator are infinite. As experience shows, there have been many conspiracies, but few successful ones. The reason for this is that if you want to embark on a conspiracy, you cannot act alone; you must have co-conspirators, and you naturally look for them among those you believe to be malcontents. But as soon as you have disclosed your intentions to a malcontent you have given him the means for contenting himself, for he can seek his own advantage by denouncing you. Gain in this way is assured, while participation in the conspiracy is risky and dangerous. So a co-conspirator who keeps faith with you must be a very rare friend of yours, or a thoroughly obstinate enemy of the prince.

Putting matters briefly: on the side of the conspirator, there is nothing but fear, jealousy, and prospect of punishment to terrify him; but on the side of the prince there is the majesty of the principality, the laws, the protection of friends and of the state to defend him; so that, adding to all these things the popular goodwill, it is impossible that anyone should be so rash as to conspire. For whereas in general the conspirator has much to fear before carrying out his plot, in this case he has more to fear afterwards; his plot will make the people his enemy and thus he will have no hope for escape.

Endless examples could be given on this subject, but I will content myself with one, which occurred within the memory of our fathers. Annibale Bentivoglio, who was prince in Bologna (grandfather of the present Annibale), was murdered by the Canneschi, who had conspired against him. Not one of his family survived but Giovanni,[1] who was then a child. Immediately after the assassination the people rose and murdered all the Canneschi. This sprung from the popular goodwill which the house of Bentivoglio

enjoyed in those days in Bologna. Nobody remained there after the death of Annibale who was capable of ruling the state; but the good will of the family was so great that when the Bolognese, who were aware that one of the family, believed to be the son of a blacksmith, lived in Florence, they sent to Florence for him, and installed him as the ruler of the city. He ruled until Giovanni came of age.

For this reason I consider that a prince ought to reckon conspiracies of little account when his people hold him in esteem; but when the people are vehemently hostile and towards him, he should fear everything and everybody. Well-ordered states and wise princes have taken every care not to drive the nobles to desperation, and to keep the people satisfied and contented; this is one of the most important concerns a prince can have.

Among the best ordered and governed kingdoms of our times is France; in it are found many good institutions on which the liberty and security of the king depend. The foremost of these institutions is the parliament. Its authority is of great importance; the founder of the kingdom, knowing the ambition of the nobility and their boldness, thought that a bit in their mouths would be necessary to hold them back. On the other side, knowing the people's hatred of the nobles, founded in fear, he wished to protect them. Yet he was not anxious for this to be the particular concern of the king. Therefore, to protect himself against blame from the nobles for favoring the people, and from the people for favoring the nobles, he set up an arbiter,[2] who could beat down the great and favor the lesser without burdening the king. It is not possible to have a better or a more prudent arrangement, or a greater source of security for the king and kingdom. One can draw another important conclusion from this: princes ought to leave distasteful tasks to others, and keep the pleasant ones for themselves. And further, I consider that a prince ought to cherish the nobles, but not so as to make himself hated by the people.

It may appear, perhaps, to some who have examined the lives and deaths of the Roman emperors that many of them provide examples contrary to my opinion, in that some of them have lived nobly and showed great qualities of soul, but nevertheless have lost their empire or have been killed by subjects who have conspired against them. Wishing, therefore, to answer these objections, I will recall the characters of some of the emperors, and will show that the causes of their ruin were not different from those I have

---

1   *Giovanni*   Giovanni Bentivogli (1438–1508), ruler of Bologna from 1462 to 1506.

2   *arbiter*   That is, the Parliament.

Discusses the last Emperors of Rome

already mentioned; and I will bring forward noteworthy matters for those who study those times.

It seems to me sufficient to take all those emperors who succeeded to the throne from Marcus the philosopher down to Maximinus; they were Marcus and his son Commodus, Pertinax, Julian, Severus and his son Antoninus Caracalla, Macrinus, Heliogabalus, Alexander, and Maximinus.[1]

We should note first that in other principalities only the ambition of the nobles and the insolence of the people have to be contended with, but the Roman emperors had a third difficulty: having to deal with the cruelty and greed of their soldiers, a matter so beset with difficulties that it was the ruin of many. It was difficult to satisfy both the soldiers and the people, because the people loved peace, and for this reason they loved the unambitious prince, while the soldiers loved the warlike prince who was bold, cruel, and rapacious, and were quite willing to see him exercise these characteristics against the people, so that they could get double pay and give vent to their greed and cruelty. So it happened that those emperors who, either by nature and family or by experience, possessed no great reputation, were always overthrown. Most of them, especially those who had come to power recently as new princes, recognizing the difficulty of these two opposing factions, were inclined to appease the soldiers, caring little about injuring the people. This course was necessary, because, as princes cannot help being hated by someone, they ought, first, to avoid being hated by everyone, and when they cannot manage this, they ought to try hard to avoid the hatred of the most power-ful. As a result, those emperors who through inexperience needed special support allied themselves more readily with the soldiers than with the people. Whether this course turned out to be advantageous for them or not depended upon whether the prince knew how to maintain authority over the soldiers.

For these reasons Marcus [Aurelius], Pertinax, and Alexander—all men who lived modest lives, all lovers of justice, enemies of cruelty, humane, and benign—all except

Marcus came to a sad end. Marcus alone lived and died honored, because he had succeeded to the throne by right of birth, and owed nothing either to the soldiers or the people. Afterwards, being respected because of his many virtues, he always kept both groups in their places, and was neither hated nor despised.

But Pertinax was made emperor against the wishes of the soldiers. They had become accustomed to a life free from moral restraint under Commodus, and could not endure the honest life to which Pertinax wished to restrict them. Hating him for this reason, and additionally feeling contempt for his old age, they overthrew him at the very beginning of his administration.

Here it should be noted that hatred is acquired as much by good works as by bad ones. Therefore, as I said before, a prince wishing to keep his state is very often forced to do evil; for when the group you need to support you is corrupt—it may be either the people or the soldiers or the nobles—you have to gratify their corrupt inclinations; to act according to the principles of good works would harm you.

But consider Alexander, a man acknowledged to be of great good. Among the good deeds credited to him is this: that in the fourteen years he held the empire, he put no one to death without trial. Nevertheless, being considered effeminate and a man who allowed himself to be governed by his mother, he was despised, the army conspired against him, and murdered him.

Consider now the characters of the opposite sort of Commodus, Severus, Antoninus Caracalla, and Maximinus. You will find them all cruel and rapacious—men who, to satisfy their soldiers, did not hesitate to commit every kind of iniquity against the people. All except Severus came to a bad end; Severus had so much ability that he reigned suc-cessfully, keeping the soldiers loyal, although he oppressed the people. His valor made him so much admired that the people were astonished and awed and the soldiers respectful and satisfied. And because the actions of this man, as a new prince, were great, I wish to show briefly how well he knew how to play the parts of the fox and the lion—the natures, as I said above, that a prince must imitate.

Learning of the indecisiveness of the Emperor Julian, he persuaded the army in Slavonia, of which he was cap-tain, that it would be right to go to Rome and avenge the death of Pertinax, who had been killed by the praetorian soldiers. Under this pretext, without appearing to aspire to the throne, he moved his army to Rome, and reached Italy

---

1   *Marcus the philosopher*   Marcus Aurelius, emperor from 161 to 180; *Commodus*   Son of Marcus Aurelius, ruled from 180 to 193; *Pertinax*   Ruled next for a short time; *Julian*   Didius Julainus, ruled next for a short time; *Severus and his son Antoninus Caracal-la*   Septimus Severus ruled from 193 to 211, his son Antonius (nicknamed Caracalla) from 211 to 217; *Macrinus*   Ruled next for a little over a year; *Heliogabalus*   Also known as Elagabalus, ruled from 218 to 222; *Alexander*   Severus Alexander ruled from 222 to 235; *Maximinus*   Maximinus Thrax ruled until 238.

before it was known that he had departed. On his arrival at Rome, the Senate, through fear, elected him emperor and killed Julian. After this Severus, who wished to make himself master of the whole empire, faced two problems—one in Asia, where Niger, head of the Asiatic army, had himself proclaimed emperor; the other in the west where Albinus also aspired to the throne. Since he considered it dangerous to declare himself hostile to both, he decided to attack Niger and to deceive Albinus. To the latter he wrote that, having been elected emperor by the Senate, he was willing to share that dignity with him and send him the title of Caesar. Moreover, he said that the Senate had made Albinus his coequal. Albinus accepted these claims as true. But after Severus had conquered and killed Niger, and settled matters in the east, he returned to Rome and complained to the Senate that Albinus did not recognize the benefits that he had received, and had treacherously sought to murder him; so, Severus claimed, he must punish Albinus for this ingratitude. Afterwards he sought him out in France, and took both his government and his life. Anyone who carefully examines the actions of Severus will find him a most savage lion and a most cunning fox; he will be found feared and respected by everyone, and not hated by the army; so nobody should be surprised that he, the new emperor, could hold on to his empire so well, because his great reputation always protected him from that hatred which the people might have conceived against him for his violence.

His son Antoninus was a most eminent man, and had very excellent qualities, which made him admirable in the sight of the people and acceptable to the soldiers. He was a warlike man, inured to fatigue, despising delicate food and other luxuries; this made him loved by the armies. Nevertheless, his ferocity and cruelty were so great, unprecedented even (after countless individual murders, he slaughtered a large number of the people of Rome and all those of Alexandria), that he became hated by the whole world. He also was feared by those he had around him, to such an extent that a centurion murdered him in the midst of his army.

I emphasize that deaths like this, deliberately inflicted by a determined and desperate individual, cannot be avoided by princes, because anyone who does not fear to die can inflict them. But a prince need not fear them greatly because they are very rare; he has only to be careful not to commit any grave injury against those whom he employs or has around him in the service of the state. Antoninus had not taken this care, but had scornfully killed a brother of that centurion, whom he also threatened daily, yet retained

among his bodyguards. This, it turned out, was a rash thing to do, and proved the emperor's ruin.

But we now come to Commodus. It should have been very easy for him to hold on to the rule of the empire, for, being the son of Marcus, he had inherited it, and he had only to follow in the footsteps of his father to please his people and soldiers. But, being by nature cruel and brutal, he turned to pleasing the soldiers and corrupting them, so that he might indulge his greediness at the people's cost. On the other hand, he failed to maintain his dignity, often descending into the arena to compete with gladiators, and doing other vile things unworthy of the imperial majesty. Thus, the soldiers viewed him with contempt, and being hated by one party and despised by the other, he was conspired against and killed.

A discussion of the character of Maximinus remains. He was a very warlike man, and the armies, being disgusted with the softness of Alexander, of whom I have already spoken, killed him and elected Maximinus to the throne. He did not hold it for long, for two things made him hated and despised: first, he was of low birth and had tended sheep on Thrace—this was well known to all, bringing him the contempt of everyone and causing him to lose considerable dignity in everyone's eyes; second, at the beginning of his rule he delayed going to Rome to take possession of the emperor's throne. Further, he had gained a reputation for the utmost ferocity because of his responsibility for many cruelties practiced by his prefects in Rome and elsewhere in the empire, so that the whole world was moved by contempt at his ignoble nature and by hatred caused by fear of his cruelty. First Africa rebelled, then the Senate with all the people of Rome, and all Italy plotted against him—including even his army, which, besieging Aquileia and having difficulty taking it, were disgusted with his cruelties, and fearing him less when they found so many against him, murdered him.

I do not wish to discuss Heliogabalus, Macrinus, or Julian, who, being thoroughly contemptible, were quickly destroyed; but I will conclude this discourse by saying that princes in our times have less difficulty giving extraordinary satisfaction to their soldiers. Although these princes have to give soldiers some indulgence, that is easily done. The reason is that none of these princes have armies that have evolved along with the government and administration of the provinces, as was the case with the armies of the Roman Empire. It was then necessary to give more satisfaction to the soldiers than to the people, but it is now necessary that all princes, except the Turk and the Sultan,[1] satisfy the people more than the soldiers, because the people are more powerful.

From the above I have excepted the Turk. He always keeps around him twelve thousand infantry and fifteen thousand cavalry. The security and strength of the kingdom depend on these forces, and it is necessary that he should keep them loyal, putting aside consideration for the people. The kingdom of the Sultan is similar; it is entirely in the hands of soldiers,[2] and he must also keep them as his friends, without regard to the people. But you must note that the state of the Sultan is unlike all other principalities, in that it is like the Christian pontificate, which cannot be called either a hereditary or a newly formed principality; in both, the sons of the old prince do not rule by inheritance. The new ruler is elected to that position by those who have that authority. And since this is an ancient custom, it cannot be called a new principality, because there are none of those difficulties in it that are met with in new ones. Although the prince is new, the constitution of the state is old, and it is designed so as to receive him as if he were its hereditary lord.

But returning to our topic, I say that everyone who considers it will agree that both hatred and contempt have been fatal to the above-named emperors, and will also recognize how it came to pass that in each of these groups, only some came to a happy end, although some acted in one way, while others acted in a different manner. It would have been useless and dangerous for Pertinax and Alexander, being new princes, to imitate Marcus, who was heir to the principality; likewise, it would have been utterly destructive to Caracalla, Commodus, and Maximinus to have imitated Severus, since they did not have sufficient ability to follow in his footsteps. Therefore a prince, new to the principality, cannot imitate the actions of Marcus; nor, again, should he follow those of Severus. But he ought to take from Severus those methods which are necessary to found his state, and from Marcus those which are proper and glorious to keep a state that may already be stable and firm.

Chapter 21: How a prince should act in order to gain esteem

Nothing makes a prince more esteemed than great undertakings which demonstrate how extraordinary he is. We have in our time Ferdinand of Aragon, the present King of Spain. He can almost be called a new prince, because he has risen, by fame and glory, from being an insignificant king to be the foremost king in Christendom. If you will consider his deeds you will find them all great and some of them extraordinary. In the beginning of his reign he attacked Granada, and this enterprise was the foundation of his dominions. He did this quietly at first and without any fear of opposition, for he kept the barons of Castile occupied with the war so that they did not consider rebellion. They did not perceive that by these means he was acquiring power and authority over them. He was able to sustain his armies with the help of money from the Church and from the people, in that long war he laid the foundation for the military organization which has since distinguished him. Further, he always used religion for the furtherance of his greater schemes; he devoted himself with a pious cruelty to driving the Moors from his kingdom.[3] There could be no more remarkable example of the way he behaved than this. Under the same cloak of religion, he attacked Africa. He then invaded Italy and finally attacked France. His achievements and designs have always been great, and have kept the minds of his people in suspense and wonder, preoccupied with question of how they will turn out. And his actions have followed each other so closely that men have never had time to work steadily against him.

It helps that a prince display outstanding examples of ability in internal affairs, such as those told of Bernabo da Milano.[4] When he had the opportunity, he would find some way to reward or punish anyone in civil life who did some extraordinary good or bad thing; this would be widely discussed. And a prince ought, above all else, to try by every action to gain the reputation of being a great and remarkable man.

A prince is also respected when he is either a true friend or a true enemy—that is, when, he declares himself, with-

---

1   *the Turk and the Sultan*   The ruler of Turkey (that is, of the Ottoman Empire) from 1512 to 1520 was Selim I. "The Sultan" refers to the ruler of Egypt.
2   *in the hands of soldiers*   From 1250 to 1517, Egypt was controlled by the Mamelukes, a powerful military caste.

3   *driving ... his kingdom*   Commentators think Machiavelli was referring to the choice given to Muslims in Granada of baptism or exile from the city.
4   *Bernabo da Milano*   Bernabó Visconti, ruler of the territories of Milan from 1354 to 1385.

out any reservation, to be in favor of one party or against another. This course will always be more advantageous than staying neutral. The reason for this is that when two of your powerful neighbors come to blows, you either have to fear the conqueror or not. In either case it will always be more advantageous for you to declare your allegiance and to make war openly.

In the first case, in which you fear the conqueror, if you have not declared yourself, you will invariably fall a prey to the conqueror, to the pleasure and satisfaction of the conquered party. You will have no excuses or protection or shelter. A conqueror does not want doubtful friends who would not aid him in the time of trial; and a loser will not shelter you; you did not willingly, sword in hand, share his fate.

Antiochus[1] went into Greece, being sent for by the Aetolians to drive out the Romans. He sent envoys to the Achaeans, who were friends of the Romans, exhorting them to remain neutral; on the other side, the Romans urged them to take up arms. This question was discussed in the council of the Achaeans, where the legate of Antiochus urged them to remain neutral. To this the Roman legate answered: "As for what has been said, that it is better and more advantageous for your state not to interfere in our war, nothing can be more erroneous; by not interfering you will be left, without favor or consideration, to be the prize of the conqueror."[2] It will always happen that he who is not your friend will demand your neutrality, while he who is your friend will entreat you to declare yourself with arms. Irresolute princes, to avoid present dangers, generally follow the neutral path, and most of the time come to ruin. But when a prince declares himself gallantly in favor of one side, if the party with whom he allies himself conquers, he is indebted to him, even though the victor may be powerful and may have him at his mercy. A bond of friendship has been established, and men are never so shameless as to show such ingratitude by oppressing an ally. Victories after all are never so complete that the victor must not show some regard, especially to justice. But if he with whom you ally yourself loses, you may be sheltered by him, and while he is able he may aid you, and you become companions in a fortune that may rise again.

In the second case, when you need not fear either of the fighting parties winning, it is even more prudent to be allied, because you assist in the destruction of one prince by another. If he had been wise, he would not have gone to war at all. Since it would have been impossible for him to conquer without your assistance, he will be in your debt.

Here it is to be noted that a prince ought to take care never to make an alliance with one more powerful than himself for the purpose of attacking others, unless necessity compels him to do so. As has been said above, if he conquers, you are under his power, and princes ought to avoid this whenever possible. The Venetians joined with France against the Duke of Milan, and this alliance, which caused their ruin, could have been avoided. But when it cannot be avoided, as happened to the Florentines when the Pope and Spain sent armies to attack Lombardy, then in such a case, for the above reasons, the prince ought to favor one of the parties.

No state should ever believe that it can always choose safe courses of action; rather it should expect that many actions will be risky. It is an everyday fact that in seeking to avoid one danger, one often runs into another. Prudence consists in knowing how to judge the nature of difficulties and risks, and to choose the least damaging path.

A prince ought also to show himself a patron of virtue, and to honor the proficient in every art. At the same time he should encourage his citizens to practice their callings peacefully, in commerce and agriculture, and in every other field, so that no one would be deterred from increasing his wealth for fear that it would be taken away, or from setting up a trade for fear of taxes. The prince ought to reward those who seek honor or enrich their city or state in any way.

Further, he ought to entertain the people with festivals and shows at appropriate times of the year. And, since every city is divided into guilds or groups, he ought to hold such bodies in esteem, and meet with them sometimes, and offer himself as an example of courtesy and generosity—maintaining, nevertheless, the majesty of his rank, which he must never, above all, permit to be doubted.

Chapter 22: Concerning princes' advisors

The choice of ministers is of no little importance to a prince, and they are good or bad depending on his prudence. The first impression one forms of a prince, and of his understanding, comes from observing the men he has around him. When they are capable and faithful he may always be

---

1 *Antiochus* King of Syria (223–187 BCE), frequently involved in battles with Rome.

2 *As for what ... the conqueror* This account is based on that in Livy, *History of Rome*, 35, 49.

considered wise; he has shown that he knows how to recognize the capable and to keep them faithful. But when they are otherwise one cannot form a good opinion of him; for the first error he has made is their selection.

Everyone who knew Antonio da Venafro when he was minister of Pandolfo Petrucci, Prince of Siena, would consider Pandolfo to be a very clever man for having chosen Venafro for his minister. For there are three classes of intellects: one which comprehends by itself; another which appreciates what others comprehend; and a third which comprehends neither by itself nor through the intelligence of others. The first is the most excellent, the second is good, the third is useless. Therefore, it follows necessarily that, if Pandolfo was not in the first rank, he was at least in the second. For a prince may have the judgment to recognize good or bad in other men, even though he himself may not have any original ideas. If he can recognize the good and the bad in his minister, and praise the good and correct the bad. Thus his servant cannot hope to deceive him, and continues to act well.

There is one test which never fails when a prince wishes to form an opinion of his minister. When you see the minister thinking more of his own interests than of yours, and seeking his own happiness and profit, you may know such a man will never make a good minister, and you will never be able to trust him. He who is responsible for a prince's state ought never to think of himself, but always of his prince. He should never pay any attention to matters in which the prince is not concerned.

On the other hand, to keep his minister honest, the prince ought to pay attention to him, honor him, enrich him, share with him honors as well as duties, and thereby place him in his debt. At the same time, let him see that he cannot stand alone, so that many honors not make him desire more, many riches do not make him wish for more, and many duties do not make him fearful of changes. When princes and ministers have this sort of relationship, they can trust each other. But when it is otherwise, the end will always be disastrous for either one or the other.

Chapter 23: How to avoid flatterers

I do not wish to leave out an important issue concerning a danger from which it is difficult to save princes, unless they are very careful and discriminating. The danger comes from flatterers, and courts are full of them. Men are so self-satisfied, and so easily deceived about their own affairs that it is difficult to save them from this plague. If they wish to defend themselves they run the risk of becoming despised, because there is no other way of protecting oneself from flatterers except by letting men understand that you will not be offended if they tell the truth. But when everyone tells you the truth, you lose respect.

Therefore a wise prince ought to take a third course by choosing the wise men in his state, and giving the liberty of speaking the truth to him only to them. Even then, they should be allowed to speak frankly only on those subjects about which he inquires, and about no others. But he ought to question them about everything, and listen to their opinions, and afterwards come to his own conclusions. With these councils and with each of these advisors individually, he ought to conduct himself in such a way that each of them should know that, the more freely he speaks, the more preference he earns. Other than these advisors, the prince should listen to no one; rather, he should pursue what he resolves on doing, and be steadfast in his resolutions. He who does otherwise is either overthrown by flatterers, or so often changes his mind that others lose respect for him.

I wish on this subject to cite a modern example. The present emperor Maximilian's[1] agent, Father Luca, speaking of his majesty, said that the emperor consulted no one, yet never got his own way in anything. This arose because of his following a practice opposite to the above. The emperor is a secretive man—he does not communicate his plans to anyone or receive opinions on them. But as his plans become revealed when he begins to act on them, the men around him at once mount opposition to them, and he, being pliant, is diverted from them. Hence it follows that those things he does one day he undoes the next, and no one ever understands what he wishes or intends to do, and no one can rely on his resolutions.

A prince, therefore, ought always to take counsel, but only when he wishes and not when others wish. He ought rather to discourage everyone from offering him advice unless asked. However, he ought to be a constant inquirer, and afterwards a patient listener concerning the things he has inquired about. Also, if he learns that anyone, for any reason, has not told him the truth, he should let his anger be felt.

---

1   *Maximilian* Maximilian I (1450–1519), Holy Roman Emperor and King of Germany. His involvement in the Italian wars was motivated by his ambition to increase the dominion of the Habsburgs.

⁎Anyone is mistaken who thinks that a prince who impresses people as wise does so through the good advisers that he has around him, rather than through his own ability. This is an axiom which never fails: a prince who is not wise himself will never take good advice, unless by chance he has yielded his affairs entirely to someone else to act on his behalf as a governor—one person who happens to be a very prudent man. In this case the prince may doubtless govern well, but not for long; such a governor would soon take the prince's state away from him.

But if a prince who is not experienced should take counsel from more than one advisor, he will never get the same advice, and will not know how to reconcile the conflicting advice. Each of the counselors will think of his own interests, and the prince will not know how to control his counselors or to see through them. One cannot find counselors who are different from this; men will always prove untrue to you unless they are kept honest by constraint. Therefore it must be inferred that good advice, whatever its origin, must arise from the wisdom of the prince; but the wisdom of the prince does not arise from good advice.

Chapter 24: Why the princes of Italy have lost their states

The suggestions I have made, when observed carefully, will enable a new prince to appear well established, and render him immediately more secure and fixed in the state than if he had possessed it for a long time. For the actions of a new prince are more closely observed than those of a hereditary one, and when these actions demonstrate good ability, they gain the prince more adherents, and bind them to him far tighter than ancient blood. The reason for this is that men are attracted more by the present than by the past, and when they find the present good they enjoy it and seek no further; so they will defend a prince to the utmost so long as he does not neglect his duties. Thus it will be a double glory to him to have established a new principality, and adorned and strengthened it with good laws, a good army, good allies, and good actions; and so it will be a double disgrace to him who, born a prince, shall lose his state through lack of wisdom.

If one considers those rulers who have lost their states in Italy in our times, such as the King of Naples, the Duke of Milan, and others, there will be found the following: First, a common defect with regard to armies, the causes of which have been discussed at length. Second, some of them will be observed either to have faced hostility from the people; or if the people were friendly, from the nobles. In the absence of these defects, states that have enough power to keep an army in the field cannot be lost.

Philip of Macedon, not the father of Alexander the Great,[1] but he who Titus Quintius conquered,[2] had not much territory compared to the Romans and Greece who attacked him. Yet being a warlike man who knew how to attract the people and secure the nobles, he defended against his enemies for many years, and if in the end he lost rule over some of his colonies, nevertheless he retained his kingdom.

⁎ ⁎Those princes who have ruled for many years, but then have been ousted, should not blame bad luck for their loss; it is due instead to their own laziness. In quiet times they never thought there could be a change (it is a common defect in man not to make any provision for storms when the weather is good), and when the bad times came they thought of fleeing and not of defending themselves, and in hope that the people, disgusted with the insolence of the conquerors, would recall them. When other courses of action fail, this one may be good, but it is very bad to have neglected all other means; trusting that someone will later lift you back up should never make you willing to fall. Either you will not be lifted up, or if you are, you will not be secure in your position, because you have relied on this for restoration. Only ⁎⁎ those means which depend solely on yourself and your own abilities are reliable, certain, and durable.

Chapter 25: Of fortune's power in human affairs, and how to deal with her

I know that many men have had, and still have, the opinion that events in this world are controlled by fortune and by God, that men cannot manage them by prudence, and that no one can in any way affect them. Because of this they urge that one not work to change things, saying that everything should be left to chance. This belief has become more widespread in our times because of the great upheavals in human affairs which have taken place—and still are, every day, beyond all human prediction. When I think of this, I am sometimes inclined to agree to some extent. Nevertheless, so as not to deny our free will, I hold the position that

---

1   *the father of Alexander the Great*   Philip II of Macedon (382–336 BCE).

2   *he who Titus Quintius conquered*   Philip V of Macedon (238–179 BCE).

fortune manages only half our actions, and still allows us to direct the other half, (or perhaps a little less).

I compare her to one of those raging rivers, which when in flood overflows the plains, sweeping away trees and buildings, removing the earth from one place and depositing it at another, everyone flees before it, all yield to its violence, without being able to withstand it in any way. Although that is the way it is, it does not follow therefore that men, when the weather becomes calm, cannot not make provisions using embankments and dikes, so that when the waters rise again, they will be channeled off, and their force will not be so unrestrained and dangerous. So it happens with fortune, who shows her power where no measures have been prepared to resist her. She turns her forces to where she knows that embankments and dikes have not been built to restrain her.

If you will consider Italy, which is the seat of these changes, and which has provided their impetus, you will see that it is a country without embankments and dikes—without any defense. If it had been defended by proper measures, as are Germany, Spain, and France, either this invasion would not have caused the great changes it has made, or it would not have come at all. And with this I consider I have said enough about resistance to fortune in general.

But confining myself more to the particular, I say that a prince may live happily today but be ruined tomorrow, without having changed in his disposition or character. This, I believe, arises primarily from causes that have already been discussed at length—namely, that the prince who relies entirely upon fortune is lost when it changes. I believe also that he who directs his actions according to the spirit of the times will be successful, and that he whose actions do not accord with the times will not be successful. We can observe that men attempting to achieve what is everyone's aim—glory and riches—get there by various methods. One achieves that aim with caution, another with haste; one by force, another by skill; one by patience, another by its opposite; and each one succeeds in reaching the goal by a different method. We can also observe two cautious men, one of whom achieves his aims, while another does not; likewise, we can observe two equally successful men with different temperaments—one cautious, the other impetuous. All this arises simply from whether or not their methods conform to the spirit of the times. This follows from what I have said, that two men working differently can bring about the same effect, and of two working similarly, one may attain his object, while the other does not.

Changes in prosperity also result from this. Given a certain sort of convergence of times and affairs, careful and patient management is called for, and one who acts in this way succeeds. But if times and affairs change, he is ruined if he does not change his course of action. Men are seldom sufficiently prudent to be able to accommodate themselves to such a change, both because they cannot deviate from their naturally-arising inclinations, and also because, if they have always prospered by acting in one way, they cannot be persuaded that it is a good idea to change. So the cautious man, when it is time to turn adventurous, does not know how to do it, and so he is ruined; had he changed his conduct with the times, Fortune would not have changed.

Pope Julius II[1] proceeded impetuously in all his affairs, and found the times and circumstances suited so well that line of action that he always met with success. Consider his first enterprise against Bologna, when Giovanni Bentivogli was still alive. The Venetians were unhappy with it, as was the King of Spain, and he was still negotiating with the King of France. Nevertheless he personally entered upon the expedition with his accustomed ferocity and energy, a move which made Spain and the Venetians stand indecisive and passive, the latter from fear, the former from their desire to recover all the kingdom of Naples. On the other hand, Julius drew after him the King of France, because that king, having observed his move and desiring to make the Pope his friend in order to defeat the Venetians, found it impossible to refuse him soldiers without openly offending him. Julius with his impetuous action accomplished what no other pontiff with simple human wisdom could have done; if he had waited in Rome until he could go ahead with everything arranged, as any other pontiff would have done, he would never have succeeded. The King of France would have made a thousand excuses, and the others would have raised a thousand fears.

I will not discuss his other actions alone, as they were all alike, and they all succeeded; his short life did not let him experience the contrary. But if circumstances had arisen which required him to go cautiously, his ruin would have followed, because he would never have deviated from those ways to which nature inclined him.

I conclude that, since fortune changes and men remain obstinate in their ways, men prosper when the two are in

---

1 *Julius II* Pope (1443–1513) from 1503 until 1513. Known as the "Warrior Pope," he effectively increased the power and holdings of the Church.

agreement and languish when they are not. For my part I consider that it is better to be adventurous than cautious, because fortune is a woman, and if you wish to keep her under control it is necessary to beat and mistreat her. It has been observed that she allows herself to be mastered by the adventurous rather than by those who go to work more coldly. She is, therefore, always, like a woman, a lover of young men, because they are less cautious, more violent, and command her more boldly.

Chapter 26: An exhortation to liberate Italy from the barbarians

I have carefully considered the subject of the above discourses, and have been wondering whether the present times are propitious to a new prince, and whether the elements are in place that would give a wise and virtuous one the opportunity to introduce a new order of things which would honor him and benefit the people of this country. It appears to me that so many things concur to favor a new prince that I never knew a time more fit than the present.

If, as I said, it was necessary that the people of Israel should have been captive so as to demonstrate the ability of Moses; that the Persians needed to be oppressed by the Medes so as to discover the greatness of the soul of Cyrus; and that the Athenians should have been dispersed to illustrate the capabilities of Theseus: then at the present time, in order to reveal the ability of an Italian spirit, it was necessary that Italy should be reduced to her present condition, that she should be more enslaved than the Hebrews, more oppressed than the Persians, more scattered than the Athenians; without head, without order, beaten, despoiled, torn, overrun, and suffering every kind of ruin.

Although lately some glimmer of light may have been shown by one man, which made us think he was ordained by God for our redemption,[1] nevertheless it came to pass, in the height of his career, that fortune rejected him; so that Italy, left for dead, waits for the man who shall heal her wounds and put an end to the ravaging and plundering of Lombardy, to the swindling and taxing of the kingdom and of Tuscany, who shall cleanse those sores that have festered for so long. She entreats God to send someone who shall deliver her from barbaric cruelties and insolence. It appears that she is ready and willing to follow a banner if only someone will raise it.

Nor is there anyone in sight in whom she can place more hope than in your illustrious family, with its valor and fortune, favored by God and by the Church of which it is now the chief, and which could lead this redemption. This will not be difficult if you recall the actions and lives of the men I have named.[2] Although they were great and wonderful men, yet they were men, and each one of them had no more opportunity than the present offers, for their enterprises were neither more just nor easier than this, nor was God more their friend than He is yours.

Here there is great justice, because "that war is just which is necessary, and arms are sacred when there is no other hope but in them."[3] Here there is the greatest willingness, and where the willingness is great the difficulties cannot be great if you will only follow those men to whom I have directed your attention. Further than this, we see marvelous manifestations that God is directing you: the sea is divided, a cloud has led the way, the rock has poured forth water, it has rained manna,[4] everything has contributed to your greatness; you must do the rest. God does not want to do everything—that would take away our free will and our share of the glory.

It is not surprising that none of the above-named Italians[5] have been able to accomplish all that is expected from your illustrious family; nor that in so many revolutions in Italy, and in so many campaigns, military vigor has seemed to have been exhausted. This has happened because the old order of things was not good, and none of us has known how to find a new one. And nothing honors a man newly risen to power more than his establishment of new laws and institutions. When they are well founded and dignified, these new arrangements will make him revered and admired. In Italy there is no lack of opportunity to bring about these innovations in every form.

Here in Italy there is great power in the limbs—but not in the heads. Observe duels and hand-to-hand combat: see how superior the Italians are in strength, dexterity, and subtlety. But when it comes to armies they do not compare well. This arises entirely from the insufficiency of the lead-

---

1 *one man ... redemption* Probably Cesare Borgia.

2 *the men I have named* Moses, Cyrus, Theseus.

3 *that war ... in them* This quotation is from Livy, *History of Rome*, 9. 1.

4 *the sea ... rained manna* These events are recounted in Exodus 14.17.

5 *the above-named Italians* It is not perfectly clear to whom Machiavelli refers; it may be Sforza and Borgia (Chapter 7) and perhaps in addition Pope Julius II (Chapter 11).

ers. Those with ability and knowledge are not obeyed, and each one thinks that he is knowledgeable, since there never has been anyone so outstanding in ability or luck that others would yield to him. Hence it is that for so long a time, and during so much of the fighting in the past twenty years, whenever there has been a wholly Italian army, it has always given a poor account of itself. As proof of this, witness Taro, Alessandria, Capua, Genoa, Vaila, Bologna, Mestre.[1]

If, therefore, your illustrious family wishes to follow those remarkable men who have redeemed their country, it is necessary above all, as a true basis for every enterprise, to be provided with your own armed forces, because there can be no more faithful, true, or better soldiers. And although they are good individually, they will be much better when they find themselves commanded by their prince, honored by him, and maintained at his expense. Therefore it is necessary to be prepared with such forces, so that you can defend against foreigners with Italian valor.

Although Swiss and Spanish infantry may be considered very formidable, nevertheless both are defective, and as a result a third power could not only oppose them, but might even overthrow them. For the Spaniards cannot resist cavalry, and the Swiss are afraid of infantry whenever they offer resistance. Because of this, as we have seen and many continue to see, the Spaniards are unable to resist French cavalry, and the Swiss infantry can be decoyed by the Spanish infantry. Although a complete proof cannot be given of the Swiss weakness, there was some evidence of it at the battle of Ravenna,[2] when the Spanish infantry were confronted by German battalions, who follow the same tactics as the Swiss. There the Spaniards, by agility of body and with the aid of their shields, got in under the pikes[3] of the Germans and thus were out of danger and able to attack, while the Germans were helpless. If the cavalry had not raced up, the Spaniards would have slaughtered them all. It is possible, therefore, knowing the defects of both these infantries, to invent a new type, one that will resist cavalry and not be afraid of infantry. This need not be a new form of army; it may be simply a variation on the old. But these are the kind of improvements which confer reputation and power upon a new prince.

The opportunity must not be allowed to pass for Italy to at last behold her liberator. One cannot express the love with which he would be received, in all those provinces which have suffered so much from foreign invasions. Nor can one readily express the thirst for revenge, the stubborn faith, the devotion, and the tears. What door would be closed to him? Who would refuse obedience to him? What envy would hinder him? What Italian would refuse him homage? The current barbarous domination stinks in everyone's nostrils. Let your illustrious family therefore take on this task with the courage and hope with which all just enterprises are undertaken, so that under its banner our native country may be ennobled, and under its auspices may be verified that saying of Petrarch: "Virtu contro al Furore Prendera l'arme, e fia il combatter corto: Che l'antico valore Negli italici cuor non e ancor morto."[4]

◆ ◆ ◆ ◆ ◆

Discourses on the First Ten Books of Titus Livius (1512–17)

Niccolò Machiavelli to Zanobi Buondelmonte and Cosima Rucellai

Greeting

With this I send you a gift which, if it bears no proportion to the extent of the obligations which I owe you, is nevertheless the best that I am able to offer to you; for I have endeavored to embody in it all that long experience and assiduous research have taught me of the affairs of the world. And as neither yourselves nor anyone else can ask more than that of me, you cannot complain that I have not given you more; though you may well complain of my lack

---

1   *Taro ... Mestre*   The French were victorious in Taro (the Battle of Fornovo) in 1495; they sacked Alessandria in 1499 and Capua in 1501; they took Genoa in 1507, defeated the Venetians in Valià (the battle of Agnadello) in 1509, and took Bologna in 1511. In 1513, Mestre, near Venice, was burned by an opposing alliance.

2   *the battle of Ravenna*   A French victory in 1512.

3   *got in under the pikes*   The German and Swiss soldiers held seventeen-foot-long horizontally held pikes; one approached them only by ducking underneath these pikes.

4   *Virtu contro ... ancor morto*   "Virtue against fury shall advance the fight, And in the combat soon shall it put to flight; For the old Roman, valor is not dead, Nor in the Italians' breasts extinguished" (Petrarch, "Italia mia," in Petrarch's letters: *Rerum Vulgarium Fragmenta*, 128 (1344?) 2, 93–96).

of talent when my arguments are poor, and of the fallacies of my judgment on account of the errors into which I have doubtless fallen many times. This being so, however, I know not which of us has the greater right to complain,—I, that you should have forced me to write what I should never have attempted of my own accord, or you, that I should have written without giving you cause to be satisfied.

Accept it, then, as one accepts whatever comes from friends, looking rather to the intention of him who gives, than to the thing offered. And believe me, that I feel a satisfaction in this, that, even if I have often erred in the course of this work, I have assuredly made no mistake in having chosen you above all other friends to whom to dedicate these discourses. In doing this, I give some proof of gratitude, although I may seem to have departed from the ordinary usage of writers, who generally dedicate their works to some prince; and, blinded by ambition or avarice, praise him for all the virtuous qualities he has not, instead of censuring him for his real vices, whilst I, to avoid this fault, do not address myself to such as are princes, but to those who by their infinite good qualities are worthy to be such; not to those who could load me with honors, rank, and wealth, but rather to those who have the desire to do so, but have not the power. For to judge rightly, men should esteem rather those who are, and not those who can be generous; and those who would know how to govern states, rather than those who have the right to govern, but lack the knowledge.

For this reason have historians praised Hiero of Syracuse,[1] a mere private citizen, more than Perseus of Macedon,[2] monarch though he was; for Hiero only lacked a principality to be a prince, whilst the other had nothing of the king except the diadem. Be it good or bad, however, you wanted this work, and such as it is I send it to you; and should you continue in the belief that my opinions are acceptable to you, I shall not fail to continue to examine this history, as I promised you in the beginning of it. Farewell!

---

1   *Hiero of Syracuse*   Hiero II (307–216 BCE) was so successful as an army commander that he was elected king of Syracuse. The remark about lacking only a principality to be a prince is an inaccurate quotation from the Roman historian Justin. Machiavelli also mentions Hiero, and gives this quotation, in *The Prince*.

2   *Perseus of Macedon*   (c. 212–166 BCE) Last king of Macedon, whose antagonistic actions toward Rome led to war in 171 BCE. After his defeat, he was imprisoned in Rome, and Macedon became a Roman possession.

from *First Book*

Introduction

Although the envious nature of men, so prompt to blame and so slow to praise, makes the discovery and introduction of any new principles and systems as dangerous almost as the exploration of unknown seas and continents, yet, animated by that desire which impels me to do what may prove for the common benefit of all, I have resolved to open a new route, which has not yet been followed by anyone, and may prove difficult and troublesome, but may also bring me some reward in the approbation of those who will kindly appreciate my efforts.

And if my poor talents, my little experience of the present and insufficient study of the past, should make the result of my labors defective and of little utility, I shall at least have shown the way to others, who will carry out my views with greater ability, eloquence, and judgment, so that if I do not merit praise, I ought at least not to incur censure.

When we consider the general respect for antiquity, and how often—to say nothing of other examples—a great price *is* paid for some fragments of an antique statue, which we are anxious to possess to ornament our houses with, or to give to artists who strive to imitate them in their own works; and when we see, on the other hand, the wonderful examples which the history of ancient kingdoms and republics presents to us, the prodigies of virtue and of wisdom displayed by the kings, captains, citizens, and legislators who have sacrificed themselves for their country,—when we see these, I say, more admired than imitated, or so much neglected that not the least trace of this ancient virtue remains, we cannot but be at the same time as much surprised as afflicted. The more so as in the differences which arise between citizens, or in the maladies to which they are subjected, we see these same people have recourse to the judgments and the remedies prescribed by the ancients. The civil laws are in fact nothing but decisions given by their jurisconsults,[3] and which, reduced to a system, direct our modern jurists in their decisions. And what is the science of medicine, but the experience of ancient physicians, which their successors have taken for their guide? And yet to found a republic, maintain states, to govern a kingdom, organize an army, conduct a war, dispense justice, and extend empires, you will find neither prince, nor republic, nor

---

3   *jurisconsults*   Persons learned in law.

captain, nor citizen, who has recourse to the examples of antiquity! This neglect, I am persuaded, is due less to the weakness to which the vices of our education have reduced the world, than to the evils caused by the proud indolence which prevails in most of the Christian states, and to the lack of real knowledge of history, the true sense of which is not known, or the spirit of which they do not comprehend. Thus the majority of those who read it take pleasure only in the variety of the events which history relates, without ever thinking of imitating the noble actions, deeming that not only difficult, but impossible; as though heaven, the sun, the elements, and men had changed the order of their motions and power, and were different from what they were in ancient times.

Wishing, therefore, so far as in me lies, to draw mankind from this error, I have thought it proper to write upon those books of Titus Livius[1] that here come to us entire despite the malice of time; touching upon all those matters which, after a comparison between the ancient and modern events, may seem to me necessary to facilitate their proper understanding. In this way those who read my remarks may derive those advantages which should be the aim of all study of history; and although the undertaking is difficult, yet, aided by those who have encouraged me in this attempt, I hope to carry it sufficiently far, so that but little may remain for others to carry it to its destined end.

Chapter 1: Of the Beginning of Cities in General, and Especially that of the City of Rome

Those who read what the beginning of Rome was, and what her lawgivers and her organization, will not be astonished that so much virtue should have maintained itself during so many centuries; and that so great an empire should have sprung from it afterwards. To speak first of her origin, we will premise that all cities are founded either by natives of the country or by strangers.[2] The little security which the natives found in living dispersed; the impossibility for each to resist isolated, either because of the situation or because of their small number, the attacks of any enemy that might present himself; the difficulty of uniting in time for defense

at his approach, and the necessity of abandoning the greater number of their retreats, which quickly became a prize to the assailant,—such were the motives that caused the first inhabitants of a country to build cities for the purpose of escaping these dangers. They resolved, of their own accord, or by the advice of some one who had most authority amongst them, to live together in some place of their selection that might offer them greater conveniences and greater facility of defense. Thus, amongst many others were Athens and Venice; the first was built under the authority of Theseus,[3] who had gathered the dispersed inhabitants; and the second owed its origin to the fact that several tribes had taken refuge on the little islands situated at the head of the Adriatic Sea, to escape from war, and from the Barbarians who after the fall of the Roman Empire had overrun Italy. These refugees of themselves, and without any prince to govern them, began to live under such laws as seemed to them best suited to maintain their new state. In this they succeeded, happily favored by the long peace, for which they were indebted to their situation upon a sea without issue, where the people that ravaged Italy could not harass them, being without any ships. Thus from that small beginning they attained that degree of power in which we see them now.

The second case is when a city is built by strangers; these may be either freemen,[4] or subjects of a republic or of a prince, who, to relieve their states from an excessive population, or to defend a newly acquired territory which they wish to preserve without expense, send colonies there. The Romans founded many cities in this way within their empire. Sometimes cities are built by a prince, not for the purpose of living there, but merely as monuments to his glory; such was Alexandria, built by Alexander the Great.[5] But as all these cities are at their very origin deprived of liberty, they rarely succeed in making great progress, or in being counted amongst the great powers. Such was the origin of Florence; for it was built either by the soldiers of Sylla,[6] or perhaps by the inhabitants of Mount Fiesole, who, trusting to the long peace that prevailed in the reign

---

1 *Titus Livius* (59 BCE?–17 CE?), Roman historian best known for his history of Rome, *Ab Urbe Condita* (often translated as *History of Rome from its Foundation*). He is commonly called Livy in English.

2 *strangers* That is, foreigners.

3 *Theseus* Legendary first king and founder of Athens.

4 *freemen* Not slaves or serfs.

5 *Alexander the Great* (356–323 BCE), king of Macedon. An enormously successful military commander, he conquered most of the Greek world. Having conquered Egypt, he founded Alexandria there in 334 BCE.

6 *Sylla* (More frequently and accurately, *Sulla*.) Publius Cornelius Sulla (c. 138–78 BCE), distinguished Roman general, who was appointed consul in 88, and who defeated his rival Marius in a civil war.

of Octavian,[1] were attracted to the plains along the Arno. Florence, thus built under the Roman Empire, could in the beginning have no growth except what depended on the will of its master.

The founders of cities are independent when they are people who, under the leadership of some prince, or by themselves, have been obliged to fly from pestilence, war, or famine, that was desolating their native country, and are seeking a new home. These either inhabit the cities of the country of which they take possession, as Moses[2] did; or they build new ones, as was done by Aeneas.[3] In such case we are able to appreciate the talents of the founder and the success of his work, which is more or less remarkable according as he, in founding the city, displays more or less wisdom and skill. Both the one and the other are recognized by the selection of the place where he has located the city, and by the nature of the laws which he establishes in it. And as men work either from necessity or from choice, and as it has been observed that virtue has more sway where labor is the result of necessity rather than of choice, it is a matter of consideration whether it might not be better to select for the establishment of a city a sterile region, where the people, compelled by necessity to be industrious, and therefore less given to idleness, would be more united, and less exposed by the poverty of the country to occasions for discord; as was the case with Ragusa,[4] and several other cities that were built upon an ungrateful soil. Such a selection of site would doubtless be more useful and wise if men were content with what they possess, and did not desire to exercise command over others.

Now, as people cannot make themselves secure except by being powerful, it is necessary in the founding of a city to avoid a sterile country. On the contrary, a city should be placed rather in a region where the fertility of the soil affords the means of becoming great, and of acquiring strength to repel all who might attempt to attack it, or oppose the development of its power. As to the idleness which the fertility of a country tends to encourage, the laws should compel men to labor where the sterility of the soil does not do it; as was done by those skilful and sagacious legislators who have inhabited very agreeable and fertile countries, such as are apt to make men idle and unfit for the exercise of valor, These by way of an offset to the pleasures and softness of the climate, imposed upon their soldiers the rigors of a strict discipline and severe exercises, so that they became better warriors than what nature produces in the harshest climates and most sterile countries. Amongst these legislators we may cite the founders of the kingdom of Egypt: despite the charms of the climate, the severity of the institutions there formed excellent men; and if great antiquity had not buried their names in oblivion, we should see that they deserved more praise than Alexander the Great and many others of more recent memory. And whoever has examined the government of the Pachas[5] of Egypt and the discipline of their Mameluke militia before it was destroyed by the Sultan Selim[6] of Turkey, will have seen how much they dreaded idleness, and by what variety of exercises and by what severe laws they prevented in their soldiers that effeminacy which is the natural fruit of the softness of their climate.

I say, then, that for the establishment of a city it is wisest to select the most fertile spot, especially as the laws can prevent the ill effects that would otherwise result from that very fertility.

When Alexander the Great wished to build a city that should serve as a monument to his glory, his architect, Dinocrates, pointed out to him how he could build a city on Mount Athos,[7] which place he said, besides being very strong, could be so arranged as to give the city the appearance of the human form, which would make it a wonder worthy of the greatness of its founder. Alexander having asked him what the inhabitants were to live upon, he replied, "That I have not thought of"; at which Alexander smiled, and, leaving Mount Athos as it was, he built Alexandria, where the inhabitants would be glad to remain on account of the richness of the country and the advantages which the proximity of the Nile and the sea afforded them.

If we accept the opinion that Aeneas was the founder of Rome, then we must count that city as one of those built by

1   *Octavian* Gaius Julius Octavius (usually known as Augustus, 63 BCE–14 CE), first emperor of Rome.
2   *Moses* Machiavelli appears to be talking about the exodus of the Hebrew people from Egypt.
3   *Aeneas* Virgil's *Aenead* tells the mythological story of Aeneas, hero of the Trojan War, who later led a group of Trojans to settle what would become Rome.
4   *Ragusa* City in Sicily (with settlements dating back at least to the second millennium BCE).
5   *Pachas* Civil and military authorities (also spelled *pashas*).
6   *Mameluke militia ... Sultan Selim* The Mamelukes were a military caste that ruled Egypt and other areas during the late medieval period and were defeated by Selim I, Ottoman Sultan of Turkey (c. 1470–1520) in the early 1500s.
7   *Mount Athos* Mountain and peninsula on the Aegean Sea in Macedonia (north-eastern Greece), accessible only by boat.

strangers; but if Romulus[1] is taken as its founder, then must it be classed with those built by the natives of the country. Either way it will be seen that Rome was from the first free and independent; and we shall also see (as we shall show further on) to how many privations the laws of Romulus, of Numa,[2] and of others subjected its inhabitants; so that neither the fertility of the soil, nor the proximity or the sea, nor their many victories, nor the greatness of the Empire, could corrupt them during several centuries, and they maintained there more virtues than have ever been seen in any other republic.

The great things which Rome achieved, and of which Titus Livius has preserved the memory, have been the work either of the government or of private individuals; and as they relate either to the affairs of the interior or of the exterior, I shall begin to discourse of those internal operations of the government which I believe to be most noteworthy, and shall point out their results. This will be the subject of the discourses that will compose this First Book, or rather First Part.

Chapter 2: Of the Different Kinds of Republics, and of what Kind the Roman Republic Was

I will leave aside what might be said of cities which from their very birth have been subject to a foreign power, and will speak only of those whose origin has been independent, and which from the first governed themselves by their own laws, whether as republics or as principalities, and whose constitution and laws have differed as their origin. Some have had at the very beginning, or soon after, a legislator, who, like Lycurgus with the Lacedæmonians,[3] gave them by a single act all the laws they needed. Others have owed theirs to chance and to events, and have received their laws at different times, as Rome did. It is a great good fortune for a republic to have a legislator sufficiently wise to give her

laws so regulated that, without the necessity of correcting them, they afford security to those who live under them. Sparta observed her laws for more than eight hundred years without altering them and without experiencing a single dangerous disturbance. Unhappy, on the contrary, is that republic which, not having at the beginning fallen into the hands of a sagacious and skilful legislator, is herself obliged to reform her laws. More unhappy still is that republic which from the first has diverged from a good constitution. And that republic is furthest from it whose vicious institutions impede her progress, and make her leave the right path that leads to a good end; for those who are in that condition can hardly ever be brought into the right road. Those republics, on the other hand, that started without having even a perfect constitution, but made a fair beginning, and are capable of improvement,—such republics, I say, may perfect themselves by the aid of events. It is very true, however, that such reforms are never effected without danger, for the majority of men never willingly adopt any new law tending to change the constitution of the state, unless the necessity of the change is clearly demonstrated; and as such a necessity cannot make itself felt without being accompanied with danger, the republic may easily be destroyed before having perfected its constitution. That of Florence is a complete proof of this: reorganized after the revolt of Arezzo, in 1502, it was overthrown after the taking of Prato,[4] in 1512.

Having proposed to myself to treat of the kind of government established at Rome, and of the events that led to its perfection, I must at the beginning observe that some of the writers on politics distinguished three kinds of government, viz. the monarchical, the aristocratic, and the democratic and maintain that the legislators of a people must choose from these three the one that seems to them most suitable. Other authors,[5] wiser according to the opinion of many, count six kinds of governments, three of which are very bad, and three good in themselves, but so liable to be corrupted

---

1   *Romulus*   Another legend has it that Rome was founded by the twins Romulus and Remus in 753 BCE. Romulus killed his brother, and became Rome's first ruler, credited with founding many of its institutions.

2   *Numa*   According to legend, Numa Pompilius was the second king of Rome.

3   *Lycurgus ... Lacedæmonians*   Lycurgus was the legendary first leader of Lacedaemon (which we usually refer to by the name of its major city, Sparta). He is credited with having established many of the characteristic features of its laws, government, and culture.

4   *Arezzo ... Prato*   In 1502 Arezzo revolted against Florence and Cesare Borgia seized Urbino. Florence sent Machiavelli and Francesco Soderini as envoys to Borgia, who demanded and was granted a reorganization of government, with Francesco's brother Piero Soderini elected to the high office of Gonfalonier. In 1512, Prato was sacked by the Spaniards, and the Medicis took over Florence, deposed Soderini, and in effect ended the Republic.

5   *some of the writers ... Other authors*   Machiavelli may have been thinking of Polybius as an author who makes the threefold distinction; Polybius, however, is sometimes taken to have agreed with Aristotle, whom Machiavelli certainly and correctly considers a six-fold theorist.

that they become absolutely bad. The three good ones are those which we have just named; the three bad ones result from the degradation of the other three, and each of them resembles its corresponding original, so that the transition from the one to the other is very easy. Thus monarchy becomes tyranny; aristocracy degenerates into oligarchy; and the popular government lapses readily into licentiousness. So that a legislator who gives to a state which he founds, either of these three forms of government, constitutes it but for a brief time; for no precautions can prevent either one of the three that are reputed good, from degenerating into its opposite kind; so great are in these the attractions and resemblances between the good and the evil.

Chance has given birth to these different kinds of governments amongst men; for at the beginning of the world the inhabitants were few in number, and lived for a time dispersed, like beasts. As the human race increased, the necessity for uniting themselves for defense made itself felt; the better to attain this object, they chose the strongest and most courageous from amongst themselves and placed him at their head, promising to obey him. Thence they began to know the good and the honest, and to distinguish them from the bad and vicious; for seeing a man injure his benefactor aroused at once two sentiments in every heart, hatred against the ingrate and love for the benefactor. They blamed the first, and on the contrary honored those the more who showed themselves grateful, for each felt that he in turn might be subject to a like wrong; and to prevent similar evils, they set to work to make laws, and to institute punishments for those who contravened them. Such was the origin of justice. This caused them, when they had afterwards to choose a prince, neither to look to the strongest nor bravest, but to the wisest and most just. But when they began to make sovereignty hereditary and non-elective, the children quickly degenerated from their fathers; and, so far from trying to equal their virtues, they considered that a prince had nothing else to do than to excel all the rest in luxury, indulgence, and every other variety of pleasure. The prince consequently soon drew upon himself the general hatred. An object of hatred, he naturally felt fear; fear in turn dictated to him precautions and wrongs, and thus tyranny quickly developed itself. Such were the beginning and causes of disorders, conspiracies, and plots against the sovereigns, set on foot, not by the feeble and timid, but by those citizens who, surpassing the others in grandeur of soul, in wealth, and in courage, could not submit to the outrages and excesses of their princes.

Under such powerful leaders the masses armed themselves against the tyrant, and, after having rid themselves of him, submitted to these chiefs as their liberators. These, abhorring the very name of prince, constituted themselves a new government; and at first, bearing in mind the past tyranny, they governed in strict accordance with the laws which they had established themselves; preferring public interests to their own, and to administer and protect with greatest care both public and private affairs. The children succeeded their fathers, and ignorant of the changes of fortune, having never experienced its reverses, and indisposed to remain content with this civil equality, they in turn gave themselves up to cupidity, ambition, libertinage, and violence, and soon caused the aristocratic government to degenerate into an oligarchic tyranny, regardless of all civil rights. They soon, however, experienced the same fate as the first tyrant; the people, disgusted with their government placed themselves at the command of whoever was willing to attack them, and this disposition soon produced an avenger, who was sufficiently well seconded to destroy them. The memory of the prince and the wrongs committed by him being still fresh in their minds, and having overthrown the oligarchy, the people were not willing to return to the government of a prince. A popular government was therefore resolved upon, and it was so organized that the authority should not again fall into the hands of a prince or a small number of nobles. And as all governments are at first looked up to with some degree of reverence, the popular state also maintained itself for a time, but which was never of long duration, and lasted generally only about as long as the generation that had established it; for it soon ran into that kind of license which inflicts injury upon public as well as private interests. Each individual only consulted his own passions, and a thousand acts of injustice were daily committed, so that, constrained by necessity, or directed by the counsels of some good man, or for the purpose of escaping from this anarchy, they returned anew to the government of a prince, and from this they generally lapsed again into anarchy, step by step, in the same manner and from the same causes as we have indicated.

Such is the circle which all republics are destined to run through. Seldom, however, do they come back to the original form of government, which results from the fact that their duration is not sufficiently long to be able to undergo these repeated changes and preserve their existence. But it may well happen that a republic lacking strength and good counsel in its difficulties becomes subject after a while to some neighboring state, that is better organized than itself; and if such is not the case, then they will be apt to revolve indefinitely in the circle of revolutions. I say, then, that all kinds of government are defective; those three which we have qualified as good because they are too short-lived, and the three bad ones because of their inherent viciousness. Thus sagacious legislators, knowing the vices of each of these systems of government by themselves, have chosen one that should partake of all of them, judging that to be the most stable and solid. In fact, when there is combined under the same constitution a prince, a nobility, and the power of the people, then these three powers will watch and keep each other reciprocally in check.

Amongst those justly celebrated for having established such a constitution, Lycurgus beyond doubt merits the highest praise. He organized the government of Sparta in such manner that, in giving to the king, the nobles, and the people each their portion of authority and duties, he created a government which maintained itself for over eight hundred years in the most perfect tranquility, and reflected infinite glory upon this legislator. On the other hand, the constitution given by Solon[1] to the Athenians, by which he established only a popular government, was of such short duration that before his death he saw the tyranny of Pisistratus[2] arise. And although forty years afterwards the heirs of the tyrant were expelled, so that Athens recovered her liberties and restored the popular government according to the laws of Solon, yet it did not last over a hundred years; although a number of laws that had been overlooked by Solon were adopted, to maintain the government against the insolence of the nobles and the license of the populace. The fault he had committed in not tempering the power of the people and that of the prince and his nobles, made the duration of the government of Athens very short, as compared with that of Sparta.

But let us come to Rome. Although she had no legislator like Lycurgus, who constituted her government, at her very origin, in a manner to secure her liberty for a length of time, yet the disunion which existed between the Senate and the people produced such extraordinary events, that chance did for her what the laws had failed to do. Thus, if Rome did not attain the first degree of happiness, she at

least had the second. Her first institutions were doubtless defective, but they were not in conflict with the principles that might bring her to perfection. For Romulus and all the other kings gave her many and good laws, well suited even to a free people; but as the object of these princes was to found a monarchy, and not a republic, Rome, upon becoming free, found herself lacking all those institutions that are most essential to liberty, and which her kings had not established. And although these kings lost their empire, for the reasons and in the manner which we have explained, yet those who expelled them appointed immediately two consuls in place of the king; and thus it was found that they had banished the title of king from Rome, but not the regal power. The government, composed of Consuls and a Senate, had but two of the three elements of which we have spoken, the monarchical and the aristocratic; the popular power was wanting. In the course of time, however, the insolence of the nobles, produced by the causes which we shall see further on, induced the people to rise against the others. The nobility, to save a portion of their power, were forced to yield a share of it to the people; but the Senate and the Consuls retained sufficient to maintain their rank in the state. It was then that the Tribunes of the people were created, which strengthened and confirmed the republic, being now composed of the three elements of which we have spoken above. Fortune favored her, so that, although the authority passed successively from the kings and nobles to the people, by the same degrees and for the same reasons that we have spoken of, yet the royal authority was never entirely abolished to bestow it upon the nobles; and these were never entirely deprived of their authority to give it to the people; but a combination was formed of the three powers, which rendered the constitution perfect, and this perfection was attained by the disunion of the Senate and the people, as we shall more fully show in the following two chapters.

Second Book

Introduction

Men ever praise the olden time, and find fault with the present, though often without reason. They are such partisans of the past that they extol not only the times which they know only by the accounts left of them by historians, but, having grown old, they also laud all they remember to have seen in their youth. Their opinion is generally erroneous

---

1   *Solon* Athenian political reformer and lawgiver (638–558 BCE).

2   *Pisistratus* (Preferred spellings: *Peisistratos* or *Peisistratus*; c. 607–528 BCE) was installed as Tyrant in Athens following a popular coup in 561 BCE, and ruled intermittently thereafter.

in that respect, and I think the reasons which cause this illusion are various. The first I believe to be the fact that we never know the whole truth about the past, and very frequently writers conceal such events as would reflect disgrace upon their century, whilst they magnify and amplify those that lend luster to it. The majority of authors obey the fortune of conquerors to that degree that, by way of rendering their victories more glorious, they exaggerate not only the valiant deeds of the victor, but also of the vanquished; so that future generations of the countries of both will have cause to wonder at those men and times, and are obliged to praise and admire them to the utmost. Another reason is that men's hatreds generally spring from fear or envy. Now, these two powerful reasons of hatred do not exist for us with regard to the past, which can no longer inspire either apprehension or envy. But it is very different with the affairs of the present, in which we ourselves are either actors or spectators, and of which we have a complete knowledge, nothing being concealed from us; and knowing the good together with many other things that are displeasing to us, we are forced to conclude that the present is inferior to the past, though in reality it may be much more worthy of glory and fame. I do not speak of matters pertaining to the arts, which shine by their intrinsic merits, which time can neither add to nor diminish; but I speak of such things as pertain to the actions and manners of men, of which we do not possess such manifest evidence.

I repeat, then, that this practice of praising and decrying is very general, though it cannot be said that it is always erroneous; for sometimes our judgment is of necessity correct, human affairs being in a state of perpetual movement, always either ascending or declining. We see, for instance, a city or country with a government well organized by some man of superior ability; for a time it progresses and attains a great prosperity through the talents of its lawgiver. Now, if anyone living at such a period should praise the past more than the time in which he lives, he would certainly be deceiving himself; and this error will be found due to the reasons above indicated. But should he live in that city or country at the period after it shall have passed the zenith of its glory and in the time of its decline, then he would not be wrong in praising the past. Reflecting now upon the course of human affairs, I think that, as a whole, the world remains very much in the same condition, and the good in it always balances the evil; but the good and the evil change from one country to another, as we learn from the history of those ancient kingdoms that differed from each other in manners, whilst the world at large remained the same. The only difference being, that all the virtues that first found a place in Assyria[1] were thence transferred to Media,[2] and afterwards passed to Persia,[3] and from there they came into Italy and to Rome. And if after the fall of the Roman Empire none other sprung up that endured for any length of time, and where the aggregate virtues of the world were kept together, we nevertheless see them scattered amongst many nations, as, for instance, in the kingdom of France, the Turkish empire, or that of the Sultan of Egypt, and nowadays the people of Germany, and before them those famous Saracens,[4] who achieved such great things and conquered so great a part of the world, after having destroyed the Roman Empire of the East. The different peoples of these several countries, then, after the fall of the Roman Empire, have possessed and possess still in great part that virtue which is so much lamented and so sincerely praised. And those who live in those countries and praise the past more than the present may deceive themselves; but whoever is born in Italy and Greece, and has not become either an Ultramontane[5] in Italy or a Turk in Greece, has good reason to find fault with his own and to praise the olden times; for in their past there are many things worthy of the highest admiration, whilst the present has nothing that compensates for all the extreme misery, infamy, and degradation of a period where there is neither observance of religion, law, or military discipline, and which is stained by every species of the lowest brutality; and these vices are the more detestable as they exist amongst those who sit in the tribunals as judges, and hold all power in their hands, and claim to be adored.

But to return to our argument, I say that, if men's judgment is at fault upon the point whether the present age be better than the past, of which latter, owing to its antiquity,

---

1   *Assyria* Ancient empire centered in what is today Iraq; at its height it also included Mesopotamia, Egypt, and parts of Turkey. It lasted, with periods of decline and vassalage, from 2000 BCE until around 600 BCE.

2   *Media* The Medes were an ancient people of Iran; their empire was at its height during the sixth century BCE.

3   *Persia* The Persian Empire was in fact a series of empires centered in Iran, extending from very ancient times until the twentieth century; at one stage (the Achaemenid Persian Empire, 559–330 BCE) it extended west to Egypt, Turkey, and parts of coastal Greece and east to Afghanistan and Pakistan.

4   *Saracens* Western name for the people of the so-called Arab Empire—a succession of caliphates that ruled various significant portions of the Arab world between about 630 and 1170.

5   *Ultramontane* A supporter of the doctrine of papal supremacy.

they cannot have such perfect knowledge as of their own period, the judgment of old men of what they have seen in their youth and in their old age should not be false, inasmuch as they have equally seen both the one and the other. This would be true, if men at the different periods of their lives had the same judgment and the same appetites. But as these vary (though the times do not), things cannot appear the same to men who have other tastes, other delights, and other considerations in age from what they had in youth. For as men when they age lose their strength and energy, whilst their prudence and judgment improve, so the same things that in youth appeared to them supportable and good, will of necessity, when they have grown old, seem to them insupportable and evil; and when they should blame their own judgment they find fault with the times. Moreover, as human desires are insatiable, (because their nature is to have and to do everything whilst fortune limits their possessions and capacity of enjoyment,) this gives rise to a constant discontent in the human mind and a weariness of the things they possess; and it is this which makes them decry the present, praise the past, and desire the future, and all this without any reasonable motive. I know not, then, whether I deserve to be classed with those who deceive themselves, if in these Discourses I shall laud too much the times of ancient Rome and censure those of our own day. And truly, if the virtues that ruled then and the vices that prevail now were not as clear as the sun, I should be more reticent in my expressions, lest I should fall into the very error for which I reproach others. But the matter being so manifest that everybody sees it, I shall boldly and openly say what I think of the former times and of the present, so as to excite in the minds of the young men who may read my writings the desire to avoid the evils of the latter, and to prepare themselves to imitate the virtues of the former, whenever fortune presents them the occasion. For it is the duty of an honest man to teach others that good which the malignity of the times and of fortune has prevented his doing himself; so that amongst the many capable ones whom he has instructed, some one perhaps, more favored by Heaven, may perform it.

Having in the preceding Book treated of the conduct of the Romans in matters relating to their internal affairs, I shall in this Book speak of what the Roman people did in relation to the aggrandizement of their empire.

Chapter 2: What Nations the Romans Had to Contend Against and with What Obstinacy They Defended their Liberty

Nothing required so much effort on the part of the Romans to subdue the nations around them; as well as those of more distant countries, as the love of liberty which these people cherished in those days; and which they defended with so much obstinacy, that nothing but the exceeding valor of the Romans could ever have subjugated them. For we know from many instances to what danger they exposed themselves to preserve or recover their liberty, and what vengeance they practiced upon those who had deprived them of it. The lessons of history teach us also, on the other hand, the injuries people suffer from servitude. And whilst in our own times there is only one country in which we can say that free communities exist,[1] in those ancient times all countries contained numerous cities that enjoyed entire liberty. In the times of which we are now speaking, there were in Italy from the mountains that divide the present Tuscany from Lombardy, down to the extreme point, a number of independent nations, such as the Tuscans,[2] the Romans, the Samnites,[3] and many others, that inhabited the rest of Italy. Nor is there ever any mention of there having been other kings besides those that reigned in Rome, and Porsenna, king of the Tuscans, whose line became extinct in a manner not mentioned in history. But we do see that, at the time when the Romans went to besiege Veii, Tuscany was free, and so prized her liberty and hated the very name of king, that when the Veienti had created a king in their city for its defense, and applied to the Tuscans for help against the Romans, it was resolved, after repeated deliberations, not to grant such assistance to the Veienti so long as they lived under that king; for the Tuscans deemed it not well to engage in the defense of those who had voluntarily subjected themselves to the rule of one man. And it is easy to understand whence that affection for liberty arose in the people, for they had seen that cities never increased in dominion or wealth unless they were free. And certainly it is wonderful to think of the greatness which Athens attained within

---

1   *one country ... free communities exist* Machiavelli probably refers to Germany, though similar free city-states also existed in Switzerland.

2   *Tuscans* Inhabitants of Tuscany, a region including Florence in northern Italy on the Mediterranean coast.

3   *Samnites* Inhabitants of a state centered in Samnium, a region in the Apennine mountains of southern Italy.

the space of a hundred years after having freed herself from the tyranny of Pisistratus; and still more wonderful is it to reflect upon the greatness which Rome achieved after she was rid of her kings. The cause of this is manifest, for it is not individual prosperity, but the general good, that makes cities great; and certainly the general good is regarded nowhere but in republics, because whatever they do is for the common benefit, and should it happen to prove an injury to one or more individuals, those for whose benefit the thing is done are so numerous that they can always carry the measure against the few that are injured by it. But the very reverse happens where there is a prince whose private interests are generally in opposition to those of the city, whilst the measures taken for the benefit of the city are seldom deemed personally advantageous by the prince. This state of things soon leads to a tyranny, the least evil of which is to check the advance of the city in its career of prosperity, so that it grows neither in power nor wealth, but on the contrary rather retrogrades. And if fate should have it that the tyrant is enterprising, and by his courage and valor extends his dominions, it will never be for the benefit of the city, but only for his own; for he will never bestow honors and office upon the good and brave citizens over whom he tyrannizes, so that he may not have occasion to suspect and fear them. Nor will he make the states which he conquers subject or tributary to the city of which he is the despot, because it would not be to his advantage to make that city powerful; but it will always be for his interest to keep the state disunited, so that each place and country shall recognize him only as master; thus he alone, and not his country, profit by his conquests. Those who desire to have this opinion confirmed by many other arguments, need but read Xenophon's treatise *On Tyranny*.[1]

It is no wonder, then, that the ancients hated tyranny and loved freedom, and that the very name of Liberty I should have been held in such esteem by them; as was shown by the Syracusans when Hieronymus, the nephew of Hiero, was killed. When his death became known to his army, which was near Syracuse, it caused at first some disturbances, and they were about committing violence upon his murderers; but when they learnt that the cry of Liberty had been raised in Syracuse, they were delighted, and in, instantly returned

to order. Their fury against the tyrannicides was quelled, and they thought only of how a free government might be established in Syracuse. Nor can we wonder that the people indulge in extraordinary revenge against those who have robbed them of their liberty; of which we could cite many instances, but will quote only one that occurred in Corcyra, a city of Greece, during the Peloponnesian war. Greece was at that time divided into two parties, one of which adhered to the Athenians, and the other to the Spartans, and a similar division of parties existed in most of the Greek cities. It happened that in Corcyra the nobles, being the stronger party, seized upon the liberties of the people; but with the assistance of the Athenians the popular party recovered its power, and, having seized the nobles, they tied their hands behind their backs, and threw them into a prison large enough to hold them all. They thence took eight or ten at a time, under pretence of sending them into exile in different directions; but instead of that they killed them with many cruelties. When the remainder became aware of this, they resolved if possible to escape such an ignominious death; and having armed themselves as well as they could, they resisted those who attempted to enter the prison; but when the people heard this disturbance, they pulled down the roof and upper portion of the prison, and suffocated the nobles within under its ruins. Many such notable and horrible cases occurred in that country, which shows that the people will avenge their lost liberty with more energy than when it is merely threatened.

Reflecting now as to whence it came that in ancient times the people were more devoted to liberty than in the present, I believe that it resulted from this, that men were stronger in those days, which I believe to be attributable to the difference of education, founded upon the difference of their religion and ours. For, as our religion teaches us the truth and the true way of life, it causes us to attach less value to the honors and possessions of this world; whilst the Pagans, esteeming those things as the highest good, were more energetic and ferocious in their actions. We may observe this also in most of their institutions, beginning with the magnificence of their sacrifices as compared with the humility of ours, which are gentle solemnities rather than magnificent ones, and have nothing of energy or ferocity in them, whilst in theirs there was no lack of pomp and show, to which was superadded the ferocious and bloody nature of the sacrifice by the slaughter of many animals, and the familiarity with this terrible sight assimilated the nature of men to their sacrificial ceremonies. Besides this, the Pagan

---

1   *Xenophon's treatise On Tyranny*   Xenophon (c. 431–355 BCE), was a soldier, historian, and pupil of Socrates. *Tyrannicus*, the work Machiavelli refers to, is usually called *Hiero*: it is a dialogue between the tyrant of Syracuse of that name and a poet, in which Hiero appears doubtful about the worth of the life of a tyrant.

religion deified only men who had achieved great glory, such as commanders of armies and chiefs of republics, whilst ours glorifies more the humble and contemplative men than the men of action. Our religion, moreover, places the supreme happiness in humility, lowliness, and a contempt for worldly objects, whilst the other, on the contrary, places the supreme good in grandeur of soul, strength of body, and all such other qualities as render men formidable; and if our religion claims of us fortitude of soul, it is more to enable us to suffer than to achieve great deeds.

These principles seem to me to have made men feeble, and caused them to become an easy prey to evil-minded men, who can control them more securely, seeing that the great body of men, for the sake of gaining Paradise, are more disposed to endure injuries than to avenge them. And although it would seem that the world has become effeminate and Heaven disarmed, yet this arises unquestionably from the baseness of men, who have interpreted our religion according to the promptings of indolence rather than those of virtue. For if we were to reflect that our religion permits us to exalt and defend our country, we should see that according to it we ought also to love and honor our country, and prepare ourselves so as to be capable of defending her. It is this education, then, and this false interpretation of our religion, that is the cause of there not being so many republics nowadays as there were anciently; and that there is no longer the same love of liberty amongst the people now as there was then. I believe, however, that another reason for this will be found in the fact that the Roman Empire, by force of arms, destroyed all the republics and free cities; and although that empire was afterwards itself dissolved, yet these cities could not reunite themselves nor reorganize their civil institutions, except in a very few instances.

Be that, however, as it may, the Romans found everywhere a league of republics, well armed for the most obstinate defense of their liberties, showing that it required the rare ability and extreme valor of the Romans to subjugate men. And to give but one example of this, we will confine ourselves to the case of the Samnites, which really seems marvelous. This people Titus Livius himself admits to have been so powerful and valiant in arms that, until the time of the Consul Papirius Cursor, grandson of the first Papirius, a period of forty years, they were able to resist the Romans, notwithstanding their many defeats, the destruction of their cities, and much slaughter. That country, which was then so thickly inhabited and contained so many cities, is now almost a desert; and yet it was originally so powerful and well governed that it would have been unconquerable by any other than Roman valor. It is easy to discover the cause of this different state of things, for it all comes from this, I that formerly that people enjoyed freedom, and now they live in servitude; for, as I have already said above, only those cities and countries that are free can achieve greatness. Population is greater there because marriages are more free and offer more advantages to the citizen; for people will gladly have children when they know that they can support them, and that they will not be deprived of their patrimony, and where they know that their children not only are born free and not slaves, but, if they possess talents and virtue, can arrive at the highest dignities of the state. In free countries we also see wealth increase more rapidly, both that which results from the culture of the soil and that which is produced by industry and art; for everybody gladly multiplies those things, and seeks to acquire those goods the possession of which he can tranquilly enjoy. Thence men vie with each other to increase both private and public wealth, which consequently increase in an extraordinary manner. But the contrary of all this takes place in countries that are subject to another; and the more rigorous the subjection of the people, the more will they be deprived of all the good to which they had previously been accustomed. And the hardest of all servitudes is to be subject to a republic, and this for these reasons: first, because it is more enduring, and there is no hope of escaping from it; and secondly, because republics aim to enervate and weaken all other states so as to increase their own power. This is not the case with a prince who holds another country in subjection, unless indeed he should be a barbarous devastator of countries and a destroyer of all human civilization, such as the princes of the Orient. But if he be possessed of only ordinary humanity, he will treat all cities that are subject to him equally well, and will leave them in the enjoyment of their arts and industries, and measurably all their ancient institutions. So that if they cannot grow the same as if they were free, they will at least not be ruined whilst in bondage; and by this is understood that bondage into which cities fall that become subject to a stranger, for of that to one of their own citizens we have already spoken above.

Considering now all that has been said, we need not wonder at the power which the Samnites possessed, so long as they were free, nor at the feeble condition to which they afterwards became reduced when they were subjugated. Titus Livius testifies to this in several instances, and mainly in speaking of the war with Hannibal,[1] where he states that the Samnites, pressed by a legion of Romans which was at Nola, sent messengers to Hannibal to implore his assistance. These said in their address that for a hundred years they had combated the Romans with their own soldiers and generals, and had many times sustained the contest against two consular armies and two Consuls at once; but that now they had been reduced so low that they were hardly able to defend themselves against the one small Roman legion that was stationed at Nola.

Chapter 20: Of the Dangers to which Princes and Republic are Exposed that Employ Auxiliary or Mercenary Troops

Were it not that I have in another work of mine[2] treated at length of the uselessness of mercenaries and auxiliaries, and of the advantage of having national troops, I should discuss that subject more fully here; as it is, however, I shall refer to it but briefly, for I do not think that I ought, to pass it over entirely, having found a most striking example of it related by Titus Livius. I understand by auxiliary troops such as a prince or republic sends to your aid, but which are paid, and the commander of which is appointed by the prince or republic. Titus Livius relates the following. The Romans had on different occasions defeated the Samnites with the troops which had been sent from Rome to aid the Capuans;[3] and having relieved these of the war of the Samnites, they returned to Rome, leaving, however, two legions in the country for the protection of the Capuans, who had been deprived of their garrison, so as to save their city from falling again a prey to the Samnites. These legions, plunged in idleness, became so fond of Capua that, forgetful of their own country and of the respect due to the Senate, they conspired to make themselves masters of that country, which they had defended with their valor, deeming the

inhabitants, who were incapable of protecting themselves, unworthy of its possession. When this plot became known to the Romans, they suppressed and punished it, as we shall more fully relate when we come to speak of conspiracies.

I repeat, then, that of all kinds of troops, auxiliaries are the most dangerous; for the prince or republic that calls them to their assistance has no control or authority whatever over them, as that remains entirely with him who sends them; for, as I have said, auxiliary troops that are sent you by any prince are under officers appointed by him, under his banner, and are paid by him, as was the case with the army sent by the Romans to Capua. Such troops, when victorious, generally plunder as well him to whose assistance they were sent as the enemy against whom they have been employed; and this they do either from the perfidy of the prince who sends them, or from their own ambition. And although it was not the intention of the Romans to break the treaty and convention they had made with the Capuans, yet the opportunity and facility of taking the country from the Capuans seemed so great to the soldiers that it suggested the thought and prompted the attempt. We might cite many more examples, but this one suffices, together with that of the people of Rhegium,[4] who lost their city and their lives by a legion which the Romans had sent there to garrison the place. A prince or republic, then, should adopt any other course rather than bring auxiliaries into their state for its defense, especially when their reliance is wholly upon them; for any treaty or convention with the enemy, however hard the conditions, will be less hard to bear than the danger from auxiliaries. And if we read carefully the history of the past, and observe the course of present events, we shall find that for one who derived benefit from auxiliaries there are an endless number who have been disappointed. And in truth no more favorable opportunity could be presented to an ambitious prince or republic for seizing a city or a province, than to be asked to send troops there to assist in its defense. And therefore anyone whose ambition so far misleads him as to call in strangers to aid in its defense, or in an attack upon others, seeks to acquire that which he will not be able to hold, and which after acquiring will be easily taken from him. But the ambition of men is such that, to gratify a present desire, they think not of the evils which will in a short time result from it. Nor will they be

---

1   *war with Hannibal* The Second Punic War (218–201 BCE), during which Hannibal (247–c. 183 BCE) famously led his Carthaginian troops, complete with eighty war elephants, across the Alps to successfully engage the Romans in many battles (eventually, however, losing the war).

2   *another work of mine* Machiavelli refers to *The Prince*.

3   *Capuans* Ancient Capua (not identical with today's town of that name) was located where Santa Maria Capua Vetere stands, in Campania (southern Italy). Capua asked for and received Roman help to free it from its Samnite rulers in 343 BCE; the Capuans proved, however, an unreliable ally of Rome.

4   *Rhegium* City in southern Italy, on the Strait of Messina, site of Reggio di Calabria today. Under Roman rule it was called Rhegium Julium.

influenced by the examples of antiquity, which I have cited upon this and other points; for if they were, they would see that the more liberality they show to their neighbors, and the less desire they manifest to rob them of their territory, the more readily will those neighbors throw themselves into their arms, as we shall see further on from the conduct of the Capuans.

Chapter 29: Fortune Blinds the Minds of Men When She Does Not Wish Them to Oppose Her Designs

If we observe carefully the course of human affairs, we shall often notice accidents and occurrences against which it seems to be the will of Heaven that we should not have provided: And if the events to which I refer occurred at Rome, where there was so much virtue, so much religion, and such order, it is no wonder that similar circumstances occur even much more frequently in a city or province deficient in the above advantages. As the case in point is most remarkable in proving the power of Heaven over human affairs, Titus Livius relates at length in the most effective language, saying that Heaven, wishing to make the Romans feel its power, first caused the Fabii, who had been sent as ambassadors to the Gauls, to commit a grave error; and then, in consequence of this act, it excited the Gauls to make war upon Rome. Afterwards, Heaven ordained that nothing worthy of the Roman people be done to meet this war, having first caused Camillus, the only citizen capable of averting so great an evil, to be exiled to Ardea; and afterwards, the same people who had repeatedly created a Dictator to check the impetuous attacks of the Volscians and other neighboring enemies, failed to do so when the Gauls were marching upon Rome. They also displayed great lack of zeal and diligence in their levies of troops, which were very insufficient; and altogether they were so slow in taking up arms, that they were barely in time to encounter the Gauls upon the river Allia, ten miles from Rome. Here the Tribunes established their camp, without any sign of their customary diligence, without proper examination of the ground, without surrounding the camp with either ditch or stockade, and without any of those precautions which divine or human reason would prompt. And in their order of battle they formed their ranks open and feeble, so that neither the soldiers nor the captains did anything worthy of the Roman discipline; for they fought without bloodshed, and fled even before they were fairly

attacked. The greater part of the army went off to Veii, and the rest retreated to Rome, where they went direct to the Capitol, without entering even their own houses. And the Senate, so far from defending Rome (any more than the others), did not even close its gates; a portion sought safety in flight, and a portion took refuge in the Capitol with the remnant of the army. It is true that in the defense of this citadel they employed some method and prudence; they did not encumber it with useless men; they supplied it with all the provisions possible, so as to be able to support a long siege; and the crowd of useless old men, women, and children fled and dispersed in great part to the neighboring places, and the others remained in Rome, a prey to the Gauls; so that anyone who had read of the deeds done by this people so many years before, and had then witnessed their conduct on that occasion, could not possibly have believed them to be the same people. And Titus Livius, who has given an account of all the above troubles, concludes by saying, "Fortune thus blinds the minds of men when she does not wish them to resist her power."[1]

Nothing could be more true than this conclusion; and therefore men who habitually live in great adversity or prosperity deserve less praise or less blame. For it will generally be found that they have been brought to their ruin or their greatness by some great occasion offered by Heaven, which gives them the opportunity, or deprives them of the power to conduct themselves with courage and wisdom. It certainly is the course of Fortune, when she wishes to effect some great result, to select for her instrument a man of such spirit and ability that he will recognize the opportunity which is afforded him. And thus, in the same way, when she wishes to effect the ruin and destruction of states, she places men at the head who contribute to and hasten such ruin; and if there be anyone powerful enough to resist her, she has him killed or deprives him of all means of doing any good. The instances cited show clearly how Fortune, by way of strengthening Rome and carrying her to that greatness which she attained, deemed it necessary to subject her to defeat (as we shall show in the beginning of the following Book,) but did not wish to ruin her entirely. And therefore *we* see how she caused Camillus to be exiled, but not killed; how she caused the city of Rome to be taken by the Gauls, but not the citadel; and in the same way she caused the Romans to do nothing well for the protection of the city,

---

1   *Fortune thus ... her power*   The quotation is from Livy 5.37. The story about Rome is in Livy, 5.37–38.

whilst their preparations for the defense of the Capitol they omitted nothing. To permit Rome to be taken, Fortune caused the greater part of the troops who were beaten on the Allia to go to Veii, and thus seemingly cut off all means of saving the city; and yet, at the same time whilst doing this, she prepared everything for the recovery of Rome. She caused almost an entire army to go to Veii and Camillus to be exiled to Ardea, so that, under the command of a general with a reputation untarnished by the disgrace of defeat, a sufficient body of troops might be brought together for the recapture of the city.[1]

I might cite some modern examples in confirmation of the views I have advanced, but do not deem it necessary, as that of the Romans suffices. I repeat, then, as an incontrovertible truth, proved by all history, that men may second Fortune, but they cannot oppose her; they may develop her designs, but cannot defeat them. But men should never despair on that account for, not knowing the aims of Fortune, which she pursues by dark and devious ways, men should always be hopeful; and never yield to despair whatever troubles or ill fortune may befall them.

from *Third Book*

Chapter 9: Whoever Desires Constant Success Must Change his Conduct with the Times

I have often reflected that the causes of the success or failure of men depend upon their manner of suiting their conduct to the times. We see one man proceed in his actions with passion and impetuosity; and as in both the one and the other case men are apt to exceed the proper limits, not being able always to observe the just middle course, they are apt to err in both. But he errs least and will be most favored by fortune who suits his proceedings to the times, as I have said above, and always follows the impulses of his nature. Everyone knows how Fabius Maximus[2] conducted the war

against Hannibal with extreme caution and circumspection, and with an utter absence of all impetuosity or Roman audacity. It was his good fortune that this mode of proceeding accorded perfectly with the times and circumstances. For Hannibal arrived in Rome whilst still young and with his fortunes fresh; he had already twice routed the Romans, so that the republic was as it were deprived of her best troops, and greatly discouraged by her reverses. Rome could not therefore have been more favored by fortune, than to have a commander who by his extreme caution and the slowness of his movements kept the enemy at bay. At the same time, Fabius could not have found circumstances more favorable for his character and genius, to which fact he was indebted for his success and glory. And that this mode of proceeding was the result of his character and nature, and not a matter of choice, was shown on the occasion when Scipio[3] wanted to take the same troops to Africa for the purpose of promptly terminating the war. Fabius most earnestly opposed this, like a man incapable of breaking from his accustomed ways and habits; so that, if he had been master, Hannibal would have remained in Italy, because Fabius failed to perceive that the times were changed. But Rome was a republic that produced citizens of various character and dispositions, such as Fabius, who was excellent at the time when it was desirable to protract the war, and Scipio, when it became necessary to terminate it. It is this which assures to republics greater vitality and mere enduring success than monarchies have; for the diversity of the genius of her citizens enables the republic better to accommodate herself to the changes of the times than can be done by a prince. For any man accustomed to a certain mode of proceeding will never change it, as we have said, and consequently when time and circumstances change, so that his ways are no longer in harmony with them, he must of necessity succumb. Piero Soderini, whom we have mentioned several times already, was in all his actions governed by humanity and patience. He and his country prospered so long as the times favored this mode of proceeding; but when afterwards circumstances arose that demanded a course of conduct the opposite to that of patience and humanity, he was unfit for the occasion, and his own and his country's ruin were the consequence. Pope Ju-

---

1   *she caused Camillus ... the city*   Livy, 5.44–54.
2   *Fabius Maximus*   Quintus Fabius Maximus Cunctator (c. 275–203 BCE), commander of the Roman armies facing Hannibal, kept his troops back from engaging the invader; this initially provoked the scorn of the populace, who gave him the epithet "Cunctator" ("Delayer"); eventually his strategy, which conserved the Roman forces and concentrated instead on keeping the enemy short of supplies, proved to be the right one. Livy tells this story in Books 22 and 23.
3   *Scipio*   Scipio Africanus (236–183 BCE), proposed attacking Hannibal in Carthage (Africa); his proposal to the Senate in 205 BCE to do this was opposed by Fabius Maximus; but when Scipio finally did get to attack in Africa, he was successful. See Livy, Book 28.

lius II[1] acted throughout the whole period of his pontificate with the impetuosity and passion natural to his character; and as the times and circumstances well accorded with this; he was successful in all his undertakings. But if the times had changed so that different counsels would have been required, he would unquestionably have been ruined, for he could not have changed his character or mode of action.

That we cannot thus change at will is due to two causes; the one is the impossibility of resisting the natural bent of our characters; and the other is the difficulty of persuading ourselves, after having been accustomed to success by a certain mode of proceeding, that any other can succeed as well. It is this that causes the varying success of a man;

for the times change, but he does not change his mode of proceeding. The ruin of states is caused in like manner, as we have: fully shown above, because they do not modify their institutions to suit the changes of the times. And such changes are more difficult and tardy in republics; for necessarily circumstances will occur that will unsettle the whole state, and when the change of proceeding of one man will not suffice for the occasion.

Having made mention of Fabius Maximus, and the manner in which he held Hannibal at bay, it seems to me opportune in the next chapter to examine the question whether a general who is resolved anyhow to give battle to the enemy can be prevented by the latter from doing so.

---

1   *Pope Julius II* (1443–1513), Pope from 1503 to 1513. Known as the "Warrior Pope," he was strongly engaged in Italian alliances and power struggles.

MARTIN LUTHER
(1483 – 1546)

LUTHER WAS IN MANY WAYS A DEEPLY CONSERVATIVE thinker, but was paradoxically responsible for a revolution—the Reformation—that profoundly changed the religious, political, social, and cultural complexion of Europe.

Luther was born in Saxony, eastern Germany. His parents, of peasant roots but with some recent economic success, had ambitions for him, and sent him to study theology and law. In university he became compulsively anxious about religious matters—especially about his own sinfulness and the possibility of divine redemption—and lost interest in his studies. In 1505 he found himself in a violent thunderstorm, and vowed that if he survived, he would devote himself to the service of God. True to his word, he left university and entered a monastery. There his obsession with his own guilt and with God's anger continued to grow; he felt that his efforts to please God were in vain. At last he found some peace in the idea that God's forgiveness is a free gift given to the faithful through the intercession of Jesus Christ, not something received in recompense for human merit or good deeds. This idea was to form the center of his theological teaching.

At age 23 Luther was ordained a priest. Taking up a position as university teacher of Biblical studies, Luther continued to work out the implications of his insight. One was an ever-increasing disdain for rationalistic scholastic philosophy. Reason, he said later, is the "Devil's whore," useful for earthly matters but worse than useless in the spiritual realm. "Faith," he said, "must trample under foot all reason, sense, and understanding." He was particularly abusive toward the work of Aristotle ("the stinking philosopher") and Aquinas, whose theological opponent William of Ockham, with his anti-rationalism about religious matters, had impressed Luther in his studies.

In 1510, Luther traveled on foot to Rome, where he was shocked by the luxury and worldliness of the priesthood. For Luther, the outrageous practices of the church were epitomized by the sale of indulgences (pardons from temporal punishment for sin). He found this practice offensive not so much as a crass money-making scheme, but rather because religion, he thought, should be concerned with faith only, not reward and punishment for good works or bad.

Revulsion to various Church practices had been growing for a long time, as the Church abused its monopoly on ecclesiastical and temporal power, led by all-powerful popes too often greedy for power and wealth. The Renaissance saw the rise of efforts to transfer Church power to councils, and to revive the humanism of classical culture. But the conciliar and humanist movements were for the most part rejected and suppressed by an adamant Church.

The arrival in Luther's town in 1517 of a papal emissary selling indulgences prompted Luther to write a protest letter to the archbishop, and to nail a copy to the door of the Castle Church in Wittenburg. Within weeks this document, which came to be known as the 95 theses, had been circulated all over Germany, and within a few months, all over Europe. Luther hoped his protest would lead to discussion and reform, but the Church would not budge. Rome examined Luther's document for heresy, and dispatched theologians to argue the case against him. Luther began to write works expressly critical of the Church, requesting that German military force be used in an effort to induce the Church to discuss grievances, and calling for the clergy to revolt openly against Rome. He was excommunicated in 1521, and, because heresy was a civil crime, called before the Diet of Worms, a general assembly of the Holy Roman Empire. There he made his famous statement: "I neither can nor will make any retraction, since it is neither safe nor honorable to act against conscience.... Here I stand. I can do no other. God help me. Amen."

In response to Luther (and to the Church's efforts to suppress him), resistance to the Church grew widely around Europe; in some cases such resistance turned violent. Luther, however, opposed such actions, advocating Christian love and patience, and telling people to trust God, not their own actions, to set things right. He argued that civil authority must be obeyed no matter what: the world is wicked and deserves wicked rulers. In 1525 German peasants rebelled, motivated by political oppression and social injustice, citing Luther's condemnation of the authority of the Church. But Luther urged the princes to suppress the rebellion in the sternest possible way, calling the peasants "mad dogs" and "swine."

His attack on authority was aimed only at the Church (and the Pope in particular). Lutheranism, once established as an official religion in parts of Germany, was arguably as intolerant as the Catholicism it had replaced; Luther championed political absolutism and opposed political freedom. The Reformation led to the Thirty Years War (1618–49), which began as a conflict between Protestants and Catholics and ravaged much of Europe. Luther was also violently anti-Semitic, advocating the confiscation of the property of unconverted Jews. Such views led to a mass expulsion of all Jews from Saxony, Brandenburg, and Silesia. In his treatise *On the Jews and their Lies* (1543) Luther called the Jews a "base, whoring people," covered with the "devil's feces ... which they wallow in like swine." He added that "We are at fault in not slaying them."

Against Luther's temperament and deepest intentions, the rise of Protestantism, with its plethora of non-conforming sects, eventually resulted in civil pluralism and tolerance, anti-authoritarianism, and liberal respect for individual conscience.

◆ ◆ ◆ ◆ ◆

from Temporal Authority: To What Extent It Should Be Obeyed[1] (1523)

First, we must provide a sound basis for the civil law and sword so no one will doubt that it is in the world by God's will and ordinance. The passages which do this are the fol-

lowing: Romans 13, "Let every soul [*seele*] be subject to the governing authority, for there is no authority except from God; the authority which everywhere [*allenthalben*] exists has been ordained by God. He then who resists the governing authority resists the ordinance of God, and he who resists God's ordinance will incur judgment." Again, in I Peter 2 [.13–14], "Be subject to every kind of human ordinance, whether it be to the king as supreme, or to governors, as those who have been sent by him to punish the wicked and to praise the righteous."

The law of this temporal sword has existed from the beginning of the world. For when Cain slew his brother Abel, he was in such great terror of being killed in turn that God even placed a special prohibition on it and suspended the sword for his sake, so that no one was to slay him [Gen. 4.14–15]. He would not have had this fear if he had not seen and heard from Adam that murderers are to be slain. Moreover, after the Flood, God reestablished and confirmed this in unmistakable terms when he said in Genesis 9 [.6], "Whoever sheds the blood of man, by man shall his blood be shed." This cannot be understood as a plague or punishment of God upon murderers, for many murderers who are punished in other ways or pardoned altogether continue to live, and eventually die by means other than the sword. Rather, it is said of the law of the sword, that a murderer is guilty of death and in justice is to be slain by the sword. Now if justice should be hindered or the sword have become negligent so that the murderer dies a natural death, Scripture is not on that account false when it says, "Whoever sheds the blood of man, by man shall his blood be shed." The credit or blame belongs to men if this law instituted by God is not carried out; just as other commandments of God, too, are broken.

Afterward it was also confirmed by the law of Moses, Exodus 21 [.14], "If a man wilfully kills another, you shall take him from my altar, that he may die." And again, in the same chapter, "A life for a life, an eye for an eye, a tooth for a tooth, a foot for a foot, a hand for a hand, a wound for a wound, a stripe for a stripe." In addition, Christ also confirms it when he says to Peter in the garden, "He that

1   *Temporal Authority ... Obeyed* At Worms in 1521 Luther had been commanded by the highest temporal authority, the emperor, to recant his works, and he had refused. Several rulers had burned his works and imprisoned his followers, and Luther himself had been excommunicated and was under the ban of the empire. In the midst of these political consequences of the Reformation, Lu-

ther gave some sermons on temporal authority in October 1522, before Duke John of Saxony and others who urged him to publish his thoughts on the subject. Luther then wrote this relatively non-polemical treatise in order to provide for the Christian a general theory of temporal authority. In it Luther explains the nature of temporal authority, its limitations, and the responsibilities of the Christian subject and the Christian ruler.

takes the sword will perish by the sword" [Matt. 26.52], which is to be interpreted exactly like the Genesis 9 [.6] passage, "Whoever sheds the blood of man," etc. Christ is undoubtedly referring in these words to that very passage which he thereby wishes to cite and to confirm. John the Baptist also teaches the same thing. When the soldiers asked him what they should do, he answered, "Do neither violence nor injustice to anyone, and be content with your wages" [Luke 3.14]. If the sword were not a godly estate, he should have directed them to get out of it, since he was supposed to make the people perfect and instruct them in a proper Christian way. Hence, it is certain and clear enough that it is God's will that the temporal sword and law be used for the punishment of the wicked and the protection of the upright.

Second. There appear to be powerful arguments to the contrary. Christ says in Matthew 5 [.38–41], "You have heard that it was said to them of old: An eye for an eye, a tooth for a tooth. But I say to you, Do not resist evil; but if anyone strikes you on the right cheek, turn to him the other also. And if anyone would sue you and take your coat, let him have your cloak as well. And if anyone forces you to go one mile, go with him two miles," etc. Likewise Paul in Romans 12 [.19], "Beloved, defend not yourselves, but leave it to the wrath of God; for it is written, 'Vengeance is mine; I will repay, says the Lord.'" And in Matthew 5 [.44], "Love your enemies, do good to them that hate you." And again, in 1 Peter 2 [3.9], "Do not return evil for evil, or reviling for reviling," etc. These and similar passages would certainly make it appear as though in the New Testament Christians were to have no temporal sword.

Hence, the sophists also say that Christ has thereby abolished the law of Moses. Of such commandments they make "counsels" for the perfect. They divide Christian teaching and Christians into two classes. One part they call the perfect, and assign to it such counsels. The other they call the imperfect, and assign to it the commandments. This they do out of sheer wantonness and caprice, without any scriptural basis. They fail to see that in the same passage Christ lays such stress on his teaching that he is unwilling to have the least word of it set aside, and condemns to hell those who do not love their enemies. Therefore, we must interpret these passages differently, so that Christ's words may apply to everyone alike, be he perfect or imperfect. For perfection and imperfection do not consist in works, and do not establish any distinct external order among Christians. They exist in the heart, in faith and love, so that those

who believe and love the most are the perfect ones, whether they be outwardly male or female, prince or peasant, monk or layman. For love and faith produce no sects or outward differences.

Third. Here we must divide the children of Adam and all mankind into two classes, the first belonging to the kingdom of God, the second to the kingdom of the world. Those who belong to the kingdom of God are all the true believers who are in Christ and under Christ, for Christ is King and Lord in the kingdom of God, as Psalm 2 [.6] and all of Scripture says. For this reason he came into the world, that he might begin God's kingdom and establish it in the world. Therefore, he says before Pilate, "My kingdom is not of the world, but *every* one who is of the truth hears my voice" [John 18.36–37]. In the gospel he continually refers to the kingdom of God, and says, "Amend your ways, the kingdom of God is at hand" [Matt. 4.17, 10.7]; again, "Seek first the kingdom of God and his righteousness" [Matt. 6.33]. He also calls the gospel a gospel of the kingdom of God; because it teaches, governs, and upholds God's kingdom.

Now observe, these people need no temporal law or sword. If all the world were composed of real Christians, that is, true believers, there would be no need for or benefits from prince, king, lord, sword, or law. They would serve no purpose, since Christians have in their heart the Holy Spirit, who both teaches and makes them to do injustice to no one, to love everyone, and to suffer injustice and even death willingly and cheerfully at the hands of anyone. Where there is nothing but the unadulterated doing of right and bearing of wrong, there is no need for any suit, litigation, court, judge, penalty, law, or sword. For this reason it is impossible that the temporal sword and law should find any work to do among Christians, since they do of their own accord much more than all laws and teachings can demand, just as Paul says in 1 Timothy 1 [.9], "The law is not laid down for the just but for the lawless."

Why is this? It is because the righteous man of his own accord does all and more than the law demands. But the unrighteous do nothing that the law demands; therefore, they need the law to instruct, constrain, and compel them to do good. A good tree needs no instruction or law to bear good fruit; its nature causes it to bear according to its kind without any law or instruction. I would take to be quite a fool any man who would make a book full of laws and statutes for an apple tree telling it how to bear apples and not thorns, when the tree is able by its own nature to do this better than the man with all his books can describe and demand. Just so, by the Spirit and by faith all Christians are so thoroughly disposed and conditioned in their very nature that they do right and keep the law better than one can teach them with all manner of statutes; so far as they themselves are concerned, no statutes or laws are needed.

You ask: Why, then, did God give so many commandments to all mankind, and why does Christ prescribe in the gospel so many things for us to do? Of this I have written at length in the Postils[1] and elsewhere. To put it here as briefly as possible, Paul says that the law has been laid down for the sake of the lawless [I Tim. 1.9], that is, so that those who are not Christians may through the law be restrained outwardly from evil deeds, as we shall hear later. Now since no one is by nature Christian or righteous, but altogether sinful and wicked, God through the law puts them all under restraint so they dare not wilfully implement their wickedness in actual deeds. In addition, Paul ascribes to the law another function in Romans 7 and Galatians 2,[2] that of teaching men to recognize sin in order that it may make them humble unto grace and unto faith in Christ. Christ does the same thing here in Matthew 5 [.39], where he teaches that we should not resist evil; by this he is interpreting the law and teaching what ought to be and must be the state and temper of a true Christian, as we shall hear further later on.

Fourth. All who are not Christians belong to the kingdom of the world and are under the law. There are few true believers, and still fewer who live a Christian life, who do not resist evil and indeed themselves do no evil. For this reason God has provided for them a different government beyond the Christian estate and kingdom of God. He has subjected them to the sword so that, even though they would like to, they are unable to practice their wickedness, and if they do practice it they cannot do so without fear or with success and impunity. In the same way a savage wild beast is bound with chains and ropes so that it cannot bite and tear as it would normally do, even though it would like to; whereas a tame and gentle animal needs no restraint, but is harmless despite the lack of chains and ropes.

If this were not so, men would devour one another, seeing that the whole world is evil and that among thousands there is scarcely a single true Christian. No one could support wife and child, feed himself, and serve God. The

world would be reduced to chaos. For this reason God has ordained two governments: the spiritual, by which the Holy Spirit produces Christians and righteous people under Christ; and the temporal, which restrains the un-Christian and wicked so that—no thanks to them—they are obliged to keep still and to maintain an outward peace. Thus does St. Paul interpret the temporal sword in Romans 13 [.3], when he says it is not a terror to good conduct but to bad. And Peter says it is for the punishment of the wicked [1 Pet. 2.14].

If anyone attempted to rule the world by the gospel and to abolish all temporal law and sword on the plea that all are baptized and Christian, and that, according to the gospel, there shall be among them no law or sword—or need for either—pray tell me, friend, what would he be doing? He would be loosing the ropes and chains of the savage wild beasts and letting them bite and mangle everyone, meanwhile insisting that they were harmless, tame, and gentle creatures; but I would have the proof in my wounds. Just so would the wicked under the name of Christianity abuse evangelical freedom, carry on their rascality, and insist that they were Christians subject neither to law nor sword, as some are already raving and ranting.[3]

To such a one we must say: Certainly it is true that Christians, so far as they themselves are concerned, are subject neither to law nor sword, and have need of neither. But take heed and first fill the world with real Christians before you attempt to rule it in a Christian and evangelical manner. This you will never accomplish; for the world and the masses are and always will be un-Christian, even if they are all baptized and Christian in name. Christians are few and far between (as the saying is). Therefore, it is out of the question that there should be a common Christian government over the whole world, or indeed over a single country or any considerable body of people, for the wicked always outnumber the good. Hence, a man who would venture to govern an entire country or the world with the gospel would be like a shepherd who should put together in one fold wolves, lions, eagles, and sheep, and let them mingle freely with one another, saying, "Help yourselves, and be good and peaceful toward one another. The fold is open, there is plenty of food. You need have no fear of dogs and

---

1   *the Postils*   Collection of sermons expounding the Epistles and Gospels for the Sundays and festivals of the church year.

2   *Galatians 2*   Luther probably was referring to Galatians 3.19, 24.

3   *the wicked ... raving and ranting*   Luther is referring here to the radical religious groups of the time—most prominent among them the Anabaptists (so named for their rejection of infant baptism, on the grounds that only an adult could truly believe in God), who resisted almost all forms of church authority.

clubs." The sheep would doubtless keep the peace and allow themselves to be fed and governed peacefully, but they would not live long, nor would one beast survive another.

For this reason one must carefully distinguish between these two governments. Both must be permitted to remain; the one to produce righteousness, the other to bring about external peace and prevent evil deeds. Neither one is sufficient in the world without the other.

Fifth. But you say: if Christians then do not need the temporal sword or law, why does Paul say to all Christians in Romans 13 [.1], "Let all souls be subject to the governing authority," and St. Peter, "Be subject to every human ordinance" [1 Pet 2.13], etc., as quoted above? Answer: I have just said that Christians, among themselves and by and for themselves, need no law or sword, since it is neither necessary nor useful for them. Since a true Christian lives and labors on earth not for himself alone but for his neighbor, he does by the very nature of his spirit even what he himself has no need of, but is needful and useful to his neighbor. Because the sword is most beneficial and necessary for the whole world in order to preserve peace, punish sin, and restrain the wicked, the Christian submits most willingly to the rule of the sword, pays his taxes, honors those in authority, serves, helps, and does all he can to assist the governing authority, that it may continue to function and be held in honor and fear. Although he has no need of these things for himself—to him they are not essential—nevertheless, he concerns himself about what is serviceable and of benefit to others, as Paul teaches in Ephesians 5 [.21–6.9].

Just as he performs all other works of love which he himself does not need—he does not visit the sick in order that he himself may be made well, or feed others because he himself needs food—so he serves the governing authority not because he needs it but for the sake of others, that they may be protected and that the wicked may not become worse.

[...]

Sixth. You ask whether a Christian too may bear the temporal sword and punish the wicked, since Christ's words, "Do not resist evil," are so clear and definite that the sophists have had to make of them a "counsel." Answer: You have now heard two propositions. One is that the sword can have no place among Christians; therefore, you cannot bear it among Christians or hold it over them, for they do not need it. The question, therefore, must be referred to the other group, the non-Christians, whether you may bear it there in a Christian manner. Here the other proposition applies, that you are under obligation to serve and assist the sword by whatever means you can, with body, goods, honor, and soul. For it is something which you do not need, but which is very beneficial and essential for the whole world and for your neighbor. Therefore, if you see that there is a lack of hangmen, constables, judges, lords, or princes, and you find that you are qualified, you should offer your services and seek the position, that the essential governmental authority may not be despised and become enfeebled or perish. The world cannot and dare not dispense with it.

[...]

To prove our position also by the New Testament, the testimony of John the Baptist in Luke 3 [.14] stands unshaken on this point. There can be no doubt that it was his task to point to Christ, witness for him, and teach about him; that is to say, the teaching of the man who was to lead a truly perfected people to Christ had of necessity to be purely New Testament and evangelical. John confirms the soldiers' calling, saying they should be content with their wages. Now if it had been un-Christian to bear the sword, he ought to have censured them for it and told them to abandon both wages and sword, else he would not have been teaching them Christianity aright. So likewise, when St. Peter in Acts 10 [.34–43] preached Christ to Cornelius, he did not tell him to abandon his profession, which he would have had to do if it had prevented Cornelius from being a Christian. Moreover, before he was baptized the Holy Spirit came upon him [Acts 10.44–48]. St. Luke also praises him as an upright man prior to St. Peter's sermon, and does not criticize him for being a soldier, the centurion of a pagan emperor [Acts 10.1–2]. It is only right that what the Holy Spirit permitted to remain and did not censure in the case of Cornelius, we too should permit and not censure.

[...]

Here you see that Christ is not abrogating the law when he says, "You have heard that it was said to them of old, 'An eye for an eye'; but I say to you: Do not resist evil," etc. [Matt. 5.38–39]. On the contrary, he is expounding the meaning of the law as it is to be understood, as if he were to say, "You Jews think that it is right and proper in the sight of God to recover by law what is yours. You rely on what Moses said, 'An eye for an eye,' etc. But I say to you that Moses set this law over the wicked, who do not belong to God's kingdom, in order that they might not avenge themselves or do worse but be compelled by such outward law to desist from evil, in order that by outward law and rule they might be kept subordinate to the governing authority. You, however, should so conduct yourselves that you neither need nor resort to such law. Although the temporal authority must have such a law by which to judge unbelievers, and although you yourselves may also use it for judging others, still you should not invoke or use it for yourselves and in your own affairs. You have the kingdom of heaven; therefore, you should leave the kingdom of earth to anyone who wants to take it."

There you see that Christ does not interpret his words to mean that he is abrogating the law of Moses or prohibiting temporal authority. He is rather making an exception of his own people. They are not to use the secular authority for themselves but leave it to unbelievers. Yet they may also serve these unbelievers, even with their own law, since they are not Christians and no one can be forced into Christianity. That Christ's words apply only to his own is evident from the fact that later on he says they should love their enemies and be perfect like their heavenly Father [Matt. 5.44, 48]. But he who loves his enemies and is perfect leaves the law alone and does not use it to demand an eye for an eye. Neither does he restrain the non-Christians, however, who do not love their enemies and who do wish to make use of the law; indeed, he lends his help that these laws may hinder the wicked from doing worse.

Thus the word of Christ is now reconciled, I believe, with the passages which establish the sword, and the meaning is this: No Christian shall wield or invoke the sword for himself and his cause. On behalf of another, however, he may and should wield it and invoke it to restrain wickedness and to defend godliness. Even as the Lord says in the same chapter [Matt. 5.34–37]; "A Christian should not swear,[1] but his word should be Yes, yes; No, no." That is, for himself and of his own volition and desire, he should not swear. When it is needful or necessary, however, and salvation or the honor of God demands it, he should swear. Thus, he uses the forbidden oath to serve another, just as he uses the forbidden sword to serve another. Christ and Paul often swore[2] in order to make their teaching and testimony valuable and credible to others, as men do and

have the right to do in covenants and compacts, etc., of which Psalm 63 [.11] says, "They shall be praised who swear by his name."

Here you inquire further, whether constables, hangmen, jurists, lawyers, and others of similar function can also be Christians and in a state of salvation. Answer: If the governing authority and its sword are a divine service, as was proved above, then everything that is essential for the authority's bearing of the sword must also be divine service. There must be those who arrest, prosecute, execute, and destroy the wicked, and who protect, acquit, defend, and save the good. Therefore, when they perform their duties, not with the intention of seeking their own ends but only of helping the law and the governing authority function to coerce the wicked, there is no peril in that; they may use their office like anybody else would use his trade, as a means of livelihood. For, as has been said, love of neighbor is not concerned about its own; it considers not how great or humble, but how profitable and needful the works are for neighbor or community.

You may ask, "Why may I not use the sword for myself and for my own cause, so long as it is my intention not to seek my own advantage but to punish evil?" Answer: Such a miracle is not impossible, but very rare and hazardous. Where the Spirit is so richly present it may well happen. For we read thus of Samson in Judges 15 [.11], that he said, "As they did to me, so have I done to them," even though Proverbs 24 [.29] says to the contrary, "Do not say, I will do to him as he has done to me," and Proverbs 20 [.22] adds, "Do not say, I will repay him his evil." Samson was called of God to harass the Philistines and deliver the children of Israel. Although he used them as an occasion to further his own cause, still he did not do so in order to avenge himself or to seek his own interests, but to serve others and to punish the Philistines [Judg. 14.4]. No one but a true Christian, filled with the Spirit, will follow this example. Where reason too tries to do likewise, it will probably contend that it is not trying to seek its own, but this will be basically untrue, for it cannot be done without grace. Therefore first become like Samson, and then you can also do as Samson did.

Part Two: How Far Temporal Authority Extends

We come now to the main part of this treatise. Having learned that there must be temporal authority on earth, and how it is to be exercised in a Christian and salutary man-

---

1   *swear*   Declare solemnly or forcefully, perhaps by invoking God or heaven.

2   *Christ and Paul often swore*   According to the Bible, Christ frequently emphasized his assertions by saying, "Truly I say unto you," and Paul said, "The God and Father of our Lord Jesus Christ, which is blessed forevermore, knoweth that I lie not" (2 Corinthians 11.31) and "Now the things which I write unto you, behold, before God, I lie not" (Galatians 1.20).

ner, we must now learn how far its arm extends and how widely its hand stretches, lest it extend too far and encroach upon God's kingdom and government. It is essential for us to know this, for where it is given too wide a scope, intolerable and terrible injury follows; on the other hand, injury is also inevitable where it is restricted too narrowly. In the former case, the temporal authority punishes too much; in the latter case, it punishes too little. To err in this direction, however, and punish too little is more tolerable, for it is always better to let a scoundrel live than to put a godly man to death. The world has plenty of scoundrels anyway and must continue to have them, but godly men are scarce.

It is to be noted first that the two classes of Adam's children—the one in God's kingdom under Christ and the other in the kingdom of the world under the governing authority, as was said above—have two kinds of law. For every kingdom must have its own laws and statutes; without law no kingdom or government can survive, as everyday experience amply shows. The temporal government has laws which extend no further than to life and property and external affairs on earth, for God cannot and will not permit anyone but himself to rule over the soul. Therefore, where the temporal authority presumes to prescribe laws for the soul, it encroaches upon God's government and only misleads souls and destroys them. We want to make this so clear that everyone will grasp it, and that our fine gentlemen, the princes and bishops, will see what fools they are when they seek to coerce the people with their laws and commandments into believing this or that.

[...]

Furthermore, every man runs his own risk in believing as he does, and he must see to it himself that he believes rightly. As nobody else can go to heaven or hell for me, so nobody else can believe or disbelieve for me; as nobody else can open or close heaven or hell to me, so nobody else can drive me to belief or unbelief. How he believes or disbelieves is a matter for the conscience of each individual, and since this takes nothing away from the temporal authority the latter should be content to attend to its own affairs and let men believe this or that as they are able and willing, and constrain no one by force. For faith is a free act, to which no one can be forced. Indeed, it is a work of God in the spirit, not something which outward authority should compel or create. Hence arises the common saying, found also in Augustine,[1] "No one can or ought to be forced to believe."

Moreover, the blind, wretched fellows fail to see how utterly hopeless and impossible a thing they are attempting. For no matter how harshly they lay down the law, or how violently they rage, they can do no more than force an outward compliance of the mouth and the hand; the heart they cannot compel, though they work themselves to a frazzle. For the proverb is true: "Thoughts are tax-free." Why do they persist in trying to force people to believe from the heart when they see that it is impossible? In so doing they only compel weak consciences to lie, to disavow, and to utter what is not in their hearts. They thereby load themselves down with dreadful alien sins, for all the lies and false confessions which such weak consciences utter fall back upon him who compels them. Even if their subjects were in error, it would be much easier simply to let them err than to compel them to lie and to utter what is not in their hearts. In addition, it is not right to prevent evil by something even worse.

[...]

If your prince or temporal ruler commands you to side with the pope, to believe thus and so, or to get rid of certain books, you should say, *it* is not fitting that Lucifer[2] should sit at the side of God. Gracious sir, I owe you obedience in body and property; command me within the limits of your authority on earth, and I will obey. But if you command me to believe or to get rid of certain books, I will not obey; for then you are a tyrant and overreach yourself, commanding where you have neither the right nor the authority," etc. Should he seize your property on account of this and punish such disobedience, then blessed are you; thank God that you are worthy to suffer for the sake of the divine word. Let him rage, fool that he is; he will meet his judge. For I tell you, if you fail to withstand him, if you give in to him and let him take away your faith and your books, you have truly denied God.

[...]

You must know that since the beginning of the world a wise prince is a mighty rare bird, and an upright prince even rarer. They are generally the biggest fools or the worst scoundrels on earth; therefore, one must constantly expect the worst from them and look for little good, especially in divine matters which concern the salvation of souls. They are God's executioners and hangmen; his divine wrath uses them to punish the wicked and to maintain outward peace.

---

1 *found also in Augustine* In *Contra litteras Petiliani*, 2.

2 *Lucifer* The rebel angel hurled from heaven, identified with Satan in late medieval and modern Christian thought.

Our God is a great lord and ruler; this is why he must also have such noble, highborn, and rich hangmen and constables. He desires that everyone shall copiously accord them riches, honor, and fear in abundance. It pleases his divine will that we call his hangmen gracious lords, fall at their feet, and be subject to them in all humility, so long as they do not ply their trade too far and try to become shepherds instead of hangmen. If a prince should happen to be wise, upright, or a Christian, that is one of the great miracles, the most precious token of divine grace upon that land. Ordinarily the course of events is in accordance with the passage from Isaiah 8 [.4], "I will make boys their princes, and gaping fools shall rule over them"; and in Hosea 13 [.11], "I will give you a king in my anger, and take him away in my wrath." The world is too wicked, and does not deserve to have many wise and upright princes. Frogs must have their storks.[1]

Again you say, "The temporal power is not forcing men to believe; it is simply seeing to it externally that no one deceives the people by false doctrine; how could heretics otherwise be restrained?" Answer: This the bishops should do; it is a function entrusted to them and not to the princes. Heresy can never be restrained by force. One will have to tackle the problem in some other way, for heresy must be opposed and dealt with otherwise than with the sword. Here God's word must do the fighting. If it does not succeed, certainly the temporal power will not succeed either, even if it were to drench the world in blood. Heresy is a spiritual matter which you cannot hack to pieces with iron, consume with fire, or drown in water. God's word alone avails here, as Paul says in 2 Corinthians 10 [.4–5], "Our weapons are not carnal, but mighty in God to destroy every argument and proud obstacle that exalts itself against the knowledge of God, and to take every thought captive in the service of Christ."

[...]

But you might say, "Since there is to be no temporal sword among Christians, how then are they to be ruled outwardly? There certainly must be authority even among Christians." Answer: Among Christians there shall and can be no authority; rather all are alike subject to one another, as Paul says in Romans 12: "Each shall consider the other

his superior"; and Peter says in 1 Peter 5 [.5], "All of you be subject to one another." This is also what Christ means in Luke 14 [.10], "When you are invited to a wedding, go and sit in the lowest place." Among Christians there is no superior but Christ himself, and him alone. What kind of authority can there be where all are equal and have the same right, power, possession, and honor, and where no one desires to be the other's superior, but each the other's subordinate? Where there are such people, one could not establish authority even if he wanted to, since in the nature of things it is impossible to have superiors where no one is able or willing to be a superior. Where there are no such people, however, there are no real Christians either.

What, then, are the priests and bishops? Answer: Their government is not a matter of authority or power, but a service and an office, for they are neither higher nor better than other Christians. Therefore, they should impose no law or decree on others without their will and consent. Their ruling is rather nothing more than the inculcating of God's word, by which they guide Christians and overcome heresy. As we have said, Christians can be ruled by nothing except God's word, for Christians must be ruled in faith, not with outward works. Faith, however, can come through no word of man, but only through the word of God, as Paul says in Romans 10 [.17], "Faith comes through hearing, and hearing through the word of God." Those who do not believe are not Christians; they do not belong to Christ's kingdom, but to the worldly kingdom where they are constrained and governed by the sword and by outward rule. Christians do every good thing of their own accord and without constraint, and find God's word alone sufficient for them. Of this I have written frequently and at length elsewhere.

Part Three

Now that we know the limits of temporal authority, it is time to inquire also how a prince should use it. We do this for the sake of those very few who would also like very much to be Christian princes and lords, and who desire to enter into the life in heaven.

[...]

First. He must give consideration and attention to his subjects, and really devote himself to it. This he does when he directs his every thought to making himself useful and beneficial to them; when instead of thinking, "The land and people belong to me, I will do what best pleases me," he

---

1 *Frogs must have their storks* I.e., people get the rulers they deserve. This proverbial saying derived from Aesop's fable "The Frogs who Desired a King" in which the frogs are bored and ask Jupiter to send them a king who will really rule over them; Jupiter sends them a stork, who proceeds to devour them.

thinks rather, "I belong to the land and the people, I shall do what is good for them ...

[...]

Second. He must beware of the high and mighty and of his counselors, and so conduct himself toward them that he despises none, but also trusts none enough to leave everything to him.

God cannot tolerate either course.

[...]

Third. He must take care to deal justly with evildoers. Here he must be very wise and prudent, so he can inflict punishment without injury to others. [...] Therefore, he must not follow the advice of those counselors and fire-eaters who would stir and incite him to start a war, saying, "What, must we suffer such insult and injustice?" He is a mighty poor Christian who for the sake of a single castle would put the whole land in jeopardy.

In short, here one must go by the proverb, "He cannot govern who cannot wink at faults." Let this be his rule: Where wrong cannot be punished without greater wrong, there let him waive his rights, however just they may be. He should not have regard to his own injury, but to the wrong others must suffer in consequence of the penalty he imposes. What have the many women and children done to deserve being made widows and orphans in order that you may avenge yourself on a worthless tongue or an evil hand which has injured you?

Here you will ask: "Is a prince then not to go to war, and are his subjects not to follow him into battle? Answer: This is a far-reaching question, but let me answer it very briefly. To act here as a Christian, I say, a prince should not go to war against his overlord—king, emperor, or other liege lord—but let him who takes, take. For the governing authority must not be resisted by force, but only by confession of the truth. If it is influenced by this, well and good; if not, you are excused, you suffer wrong for God's sake. If, however, the antagonist is your equal, your inferior, or of a foreign government, you should first offer him justice and peace, as Moses taught the children of Israel. If he refuses, then—mindful of what is best for you—defend yourself against force by force, as Moses so well describes it in Deuteronomy 20 [.10–12]. But in doing this you must not consider your personal interests and how you may remain lord, but those of your subjects to whom you owe help and protection, that such action may proceed in love. Since your entire land is in peril you must make the venture, so that with God's help all may not be lost. If you

cannot prevent some from becoming widows and orphans as a consequence, you must at least see that not everything goes to ruin until there is nothing left except widows and orphans.

In this matter subjects are in duty bound to follow, and to devote their life and property, for in such a case one must risk his goods and himself for the sake of others. In a war of this sort it is both Christian and an act of love to kill the enemy without hesitation, to plunder and burn and injure him by every method of warfare until he is conquered (except that one must beware of sin, and not violate wives and virgins). And when victory has been achieved, one should offer mercy and peace to those who surrender and humble themselves ...

What if a prince is in the wrong? Are his people bound to follow him then too? Answer: No, for it is no one's duty to do wrong; we must obey God (who desires the right) rather than men [Acts 5.29]. What if the subjects do not know whether their prince is in the right or not? Answer: So long as they do not know, and cannot with all possible diligence find out, they may obey him without peril to their souls. For in such a case one must apply the law of Moses in Exodus 21, where he writes that a murderer who has unknowingly and unintentionally killed a man shall through flight to a city of refuge and by judgment of a court be declared acquitted. Whichever side then suffers defeat, whether it be in the right or in the wrong, must accept it as a punishment from God. Whichever side fights and wins in such ignorance, however, must regard its battle as though someone fell from a roof and killed another, and leave the matter to God. It is all the same to God whether he deprives you of life and property by a just or by an unjust lord. You are His creature and He can do with you as He wills, just so your conscience is clear. Thus in Genesis 20 [.2–7] God himself excuses Abimelech for taking Abraham's wife; not because he had done right, but because he had not known that she was Abraham's wife.

Fourth. Here we come to what should really have been placed first, and of which we spoke above. A prince must act in a Christian way toward his God also; that is, he must subject himself to him in entire confidence and pray for wisdom to rule well, as Solomon did [1 Kings 3.9]. But of faith and trust in God I have written so much that it is not necessary to say more here. Therefore, we will close with this brief summation, that a prince's duty is fourfold: First, toward God there must be true confidence and earnest prayer; second, toward his subjects there must be love and Christian service; third, with respect to his counselors and officials he must maintain an untrammeled reason and unfettered judgment; fourth, with respect to evildoers he must manifest a restrained severity and firmness. Then the prince's job will be done right, both outwardly and inwardly; it will be pleasing to God and to the people. But he will have to expect much envy and sorrow on account of it; the cross will soon rest on the shoulders of such a prince.

Finally, I must add an appendix in answer to those who raise questions about restitution, that is, about the return of goods wrongfully acquired. This is a matter about which the temporal sword is commonly concerned; much has been written about it, and many fantastically severe judgments have been sought in cases of this sort. I will put it all in a few words, however, and at one fell swoop dispose of all such laws and of the harsh judgments based upon them, thus: No surer law can be found in this matter than the law of love. In the first place, when a case of this sort is brought before you in which one is to make restitution to another, if they are both Christians the matter is soon settled; neither will withhold what belongs to the other, and neither will demand that it be returned. If only one of them is a Christian, namely, the one to whom restitution is due, it is again easy to settle, for he does not care whether restitution is ever made to him. The same is true if the one who is supposed to make restitution is a Christian, for he will do so.

But whether one be a Christian or not a Christian, you should decide the question of restitution as follows. If the debtor is poor and unable to make restitution, and the other party is not poor, then you should let the law of love prevail and acquit the debtor; for according to the law of love the other party is in any event obliged to relinquish the debt and, if necessary, to give him something besides. But if the debtor is not poor, then have him restore as much as he can, whether it be all, a half, a third, or a fourth of it, provided that you leave him enough to assure a house, food, and clothing for himself, his wife, and his children. This

much you would owe him in any case, if you could afford it; so much the less ought you to take it away now, since you do not need it and he cannot get along without it.

[...]

A good and just decision must not and cannot be pronounced out of books, but must come from a free mind, as though there were no books. Such a free decision is given, however, by love and by natural law, with which all reason is filled; out of the books come extravagant and untenable judgments. Let me give you an example of this.

This story is told of Duke Charles of Burgundy.[1] A certain nobleman took an enemy prisoner. The prisoner's wife came to ransom her husband. The nobleman promised to give back the husband on condition that she would lie with him. The woman was virtuous, yet wished to set her husband free; so she goes and asks her husband whether she should do this thing in order to set him free. The husband wished to be set free and to save his life, so he gives his wife permission. After the nobleman had lain with the wife, he had the husband beheaded the next day and gave him to her as a corpse. She laid the whole case before Duke Charles. He summoned the nobleman and commanded him to marry the woman. When the wedding day was over he had the nobleman beheaded, gave the woman possession of his property, and restored her to honor. Thus he punished the crime in a princely way.

Observe: No pope, no jurist, no lawbook could have given him such a decision. It sprang from untrammeled reason, above the law in all the books, and is so excellent that everyone must approve of it and find the justice of it written in his own heart. St. Augustine relates a similar story in *The Lord's Sermon on the Mount*.[2] Therefore, we should keep written laws subject to reason, from which they originally welled forth as from the spring of justice. We should not make the spring dependent on its rivulets, or make reason a captive of letters.

---

1   *Duke Charles of Burgundy*   Charles the Bold, Duke of Burgundy from 1467–77.

2   *The Lord's Sermon on the Mount*   St. Augustine wrote a commentary on Jesus' sermon in Matthew 5.1–7.29.

JOHN CALVIN
(1509 – 1564)

WHILE MARTIN LUTHER WAS THE CENTRAL FORCE that began the Protestant Reformation, Calvin, a generation later, established much of its theological, social, and political shape. Calvin was born in France (original name Jean Chauvin or Cauvin, Latinized to Calvinus), son of an attorney of some importance in the town of Noyon. At age 14, he was sent to the University of Paris, where he studied humanities and theology, in preparation for the priesthood, and had some contact with the humanistic and reform movements, with which he was becoming increasingly sympathetic. After receiving a master of arts degree, he moved to Orléans to take a law degree.

By 1534 he had completely broken with his Catholic upbringing, and from then on he devoted himself to the cause of the Reformation. When his mentor announced his support for Martin Luther in 1535, he and Calvin were forced to flee. In 1536 Calvin published the first edition of his major work (revised several times thereafter), *Institutes of the Christian Religion*; this work established him as a leading Protestant thinker.

His travels in 1536 took him through Geneva, a town racked with struggles between the Catholic establishment and the new Protestant forces. Guillaume Farel, a fiery Protestant evangelist, convinced Calvin to stay there to help with their cause; but two years later, the town voted to banish Farel, and Calvin went to Strasbourg, where he became involved with the community's religious affairs, and married. There he published *Commentary on Romans*, the first of many highly influential biblical commentaries.

In 1541, Calvin was persuaded to return to Geneva, which remained his home for the rest of his life. As the Protestants gained dominance in the city, Calvin became influential in government, though he never held public office. He drafted new laws which became the basis of the new constitution for the city, covering secular and sacred matters; and he worked to develop new educational and health institutions, and civil infrastructure.

Protestant rule in Geneva was not more liberal than the Catholic regime it had displaced. It was essentially a theocratic state; Calvin's influence was important in reformation of the government to incorporate the Protestant clergy into the ruling councils of the city, and to impose strict moral and religious codes on the population. In 1553, Calvin was instrumental in the prosecution for heresy of Michael Servetus—a Protestant dissident (considered an ancestor of the Unitarian movement) whose views on various theological matters were condemned by Catholics and Protestants alike. Servetus was condemned and burned at the stake. Calvin approved of his execution, though he claimed afterwards to have suggested that beheading would have been more humane.

By the mid 1550s, Geneva was perhaps the most important Protestant center in Europe; foreign reformers, often expelled from their own countries, flocked there, spreading Calvin's influence when they left. Calvinism was also effectively promulgated across northern Europe by his writings and prodigious correspondence.

Calvin was less of a theological innovator than Luther, whose ideas resemble his in many respects. Like Luther, he emphasized strong reliance on the Christian scriptures, in contrast to the Catholic reliance on the authority of the Pope or on philosophical theology. He rivaled Luther in the strength of his vituperative diatribes against philosophy and its role in scholastic theology. Calvin advised looking to a literal reading of scripture as the source not only for religious belief, but also for the proper structure of temporal government and society. Like Luther again, and unlike the Catholic church and some more moderate Protestant theologies, Calvinism held that salvation for an individual person was pre-ordained by God from the beginning of time, and was not the product of that person's choices or actions. One who is pre-ordained for salvation—a member of the "elect"—can be expected to act well, but right action is not the cause of that person's salvation. And Calvin shared with Luther a strong sense of human evil and corruption: we all deserve destruction, but may achieve salvation as a free gift from God through the intervention of Jesus Christ.

Despite Calvin's contribution to an authoritarian theocracy in Geneva, some twentieth- and twenty-first-century commentators think that Calvinism contributed to the rise of modern civil-libertarian democracy, because of his insistence on the importance of elected officials, rule of law, and on the reliance on conscience in the both church and state.

◆ ◆ ◆ ◆ ◆

from On Civil Government (1534)

Having already stated that man is the subject of two kinds of government, and having sufficiently discussed that which is situated in the soul, or the inner man, and relates to eternal life—we are, in this chapter, to say something of the other kind, which relates to civil justice and the regulation of external conduct. For, though this topic may seem to have no connection with the spiritual doctrine of faith which I have undertaken to discuss, the discussion which follows will show that I have sufficient reason for connecting them together, and, indeed, that necessity obliges me to do so. This is particularly the case since, on the one hand, crazed and barbarous men try madly to subvert the laws established by God, and, on the other hand, the flatterers of princes, extolling their power beyond all just bounds, do not hesitate to set such earthly power against the authority of God himself. Unless both these errors be resisted, the purity of the faith will be destroyed. Besides, it is of no small importance for us to know what benevolent provision God has made for mankind in this instance, so that we may be stimulated by a greater degree of pious zeal to show our gratitude.

In the first place, before we enter into the subject itself, it is necessary for us to return to the distinction which we have already established, lest we fall into an error very common in the world, and injudiciously confound two things, the nature of which is altogether different. For some men, when they hear that the Gospel promises a liberty which acknowledges no king or magistrate[1] among them, but submits to Christ alone, think they cannot take proper ad-

vantage of their liberty so long as they see any power exalted above them. They imagine that nothing will prosper unless the whole world be modeled in a new form, without any governments, or laws, or magistrates, or anything of a similar kind which they consider injurious to their liberty. But he who knows how to distinguish between the body and the soul, between this present transitory life and the future eternal one, will find no difficulty in understanding that the spiritual kingdom of Christ and the civil government are things very different and remote from each other. It is a Jewish folly to seek to include the kingdom of Christ under the elements of this world;[2] let us, on the contrary, (with a view to what the Scripture clearly inculcates, that the benefit which is received from the grace of Christ is spiritual)—let us, I say, remember to confine within its proper limits all this liberty which is promised and offered to us. For why is it that the same apostle who, in one place, exhorts to "stand fast in the liberty that Christ has given us, and be not entangled again with the yoke of bondage,"[3] in another enjoins servants to "care not for" their servile condition,[4] accepting that spiritual liberty may very well co-exist with civil servitude? Likewise, how are we to understand him in the following passages: "There is neither Jew nor Greek, there is neither bond nor free, there is neither male nor female."[5] Again: "There is neither Greek nor Jew, circumcision nor uncircumcision, Barbarian, Scythian, bond nor free: but Christ is all, and in all,"[6] in which he signifies that it is of no importance what our condition is among men or under the laws of what nation we live, since the kingdom of Christ does not consist of these things.

2. Yet this distinction should not lead us to consider the whole system of civil government as a polluted thing which has nothing to do with Christian people. Some fanatics who are pleased with nothing but liberty, or rather licentiousness[7] without any restraint, do indeed boast and argue too loudly that since we are dead with Christ to the

---

1   *magistrate*   Political leader.

2   *a Jewish folly ... this world*   A central tenet of Judaism is an unqualified faith in one god (rather than a trinity or any other dual, tripartite, or multi-partite form); if Jesus is noted at all in Jewish thought, it is as a historical figure, not a divine one. Moreover, Judaism teaches that one should focus on leading a sacred life in this world, rather than hoping for salvation in a future, spiritual existence.

3   *stand fast ... bondage*   Galatians 5.1.

4   *enjoins ... condition*   1 Corinthians 7.21.

5   *There is neither Jew ... female*   Galatians 3.28.

6   *There is neither Greek ... in all*   Colossians 3.11.

7   *licentiousness*   Pursuit of desires unrestricted by moral concerns.

elements of this world, we sit among the inhabitants of heaven, and it is far beneath our dignity to be occupied with those secular and impure cares which relate to things altogether uninteresting to a Christian. Of what use, they ask, are laws without judgments and tribunals? But what have judgments to do with a Christian man? And if it be unlawful to kill, of what use are laws and judgments to us? But as we have just suggested that this kind of government is distinct from that spiritual and internal reign of Christ, so it ought to be known that the two sorts of reign are in no respect at variance with each other. For the spiritual reign, even now upon earth, gives us a preliminary introduction to the heavenly kingdom, and in this mortal and transitory life affords us some foretaste of immortal and incorruptible blessedness. But the civil government is designed, so long as we live in this world, to cherish and support the external worship of God, to preserve the pure doctrine of religion, to defend the constitution of the Church, to regulate our lives in a manner requisite for the society of men, to form our manners to civil justice, to promote our concord with each other, and to establish general peace and tranquility—all of which I confess to be unnecessary if the kingdom of God, as it now exists, extinguishes the present life. But if it is the will of God that while we are aspiring toward our true country, we be pilgrims on the earth, and if such aids are necessary to our pilgrimage, those who try to deny such things to man deprive him of his human nature. They plead that there should be so much perfection in the Church of God that the order it imposes should be enough to take the place of all laws; but they foolishly imagine a perfection which can never be found in any community of men. The insolence of the wicked is so great, and their evil so persistent, that it can scarcely be restrained by all the severity of the laws; what can we expect they would do if they found themselves at liberty to perpetuate crimes with impunity, crimes whose outrages even the arm of government and its laws cannot altogether prevent?

3. But for speaking of the exercise of civil government, there will be another place more suitable. At present we only wish it to be understood that to entertain any thought of eliminating civil government is inhuman barbarism; such government is just as necessary as bread and water, light and air, and far more excellent than those things. For one thing, civil government tends to secure the benefits arising from all these things, so that men may breathe, eat, drink, and be sustained in life. Civil government takes into account all these things as it enables people to live together.

Yet I say this is not its only tendency; it also tries to ensure that idolatry, sacrilege against the name of God, blasphemy against His truth, and other offenses against religion do not openly appear among the people and are not disseminated. It does this so that the public peace may not be disturbed; so that every person may enjoy his property without molestation; so that men may transact their business together without fraud or injustice; and so that integrity and modesty may be cultivated among the people—in short, that there may be a public form of religion among Christians, and that humanity may be maintained among the people. Nor let anyone think it strange that I now assign to human government the responsibility of supporting religion, which I may appear to have placed beyond the jurisdiction of men. I do not allow men to make laws respecting religion and the worship of God now any more than I did before; what I approve of is a civil government that prevents the true religion contained in the law of God from being violated and polluted with impunity by public blasphemies. Setting things out in ordered categories should provide a clearer sense of how we should comprehend the whole system of civil administration. There are three branches of the system: the magistrate, who is the guardian and conservator of the laws; the laws themselves according to which he governs; and the people, who are governed by the laws and obey the magistrate. Let us, therefore, examine, first, the function of a magistrate, asking if it is a legitimate calling approved by God, and inquiring into the nature of the duties of the magistrate, and the extent of his power. Secondly, let us ask by what laws Christian government ought to be regulated. Lastly, let us ask what advantage the people derive from the laws, and what obedience they owe to the magistrate.

[...]

9. Here it is necessary to state in a brief manner the nature of the office of the magistrate, as described in the word of God, and what it consists of. If the Scripture did not teach that the lessons of Scripture apply to civil as well as to religious functions of the magistrate, we might learn of the connection from heathen writers; for not one of them has treated of the office of magistrates, of legislation, and civil government, without beginning with religion and divine worship. They have all admitted that no government can be properly constituted unless its first object be the promotion of piety, and that laws are preposterous if they neglect the claims of God and merely provide for the interests of men. Particularly given that religion holds

pride of place among all the philosophers and that this has always been accepted with universal consent by all nations. Christian princes and magistrates ought to be ashamed of their indolence if they do not make it the object of their most serious care. We have already shown that this duty is particularly commanded of them by God; for it is reasonable that they should employ their utmost efforts in asserting and defending the honor of Him whose viceregents[1] they are, and by whose favor they govern. The principal commendations given in the Scripture to the good kings are for having restored the worship of God when it had been corrupted or abolished, or for having devoted their attention to religion, in order that it might flourish in purity and safety under their reigns. In the other direction, the Bible represents it as one of the evils arising from anarchy, or a want of good government, that when "there was no king in Israel, every man did that which was right in his own eyes."[2] These things show the folly of those who would wish magistrates to neglect all thoughts of God, and to confine themselves entirely to the administration of justice among men, as though God appointed governors in his name to decide secular controversies, and disregarded that which is of far greater importance—the pure worship of Himself according to the rule of law. But a rage for universal innovation, and a desire to escape punishment for wrongdoing leads men of turbulent spirits to wish that all the avengers of violated piety were taken out of circulation. With respect to the civil functions of the magistrate, Jeremiah admonishes kings in the following manner: "Exercise good judgment and be righteous, and deliver the oppressed out of the hand of the oppressor; and do no wrong, do no violence to the stranger, the fatherless, nor the widow, neither shed innocent blood."[3] To the same purpose is the exhortation in the eighty-second psalm: "Defend the poor and fatherless: do justice to the afflicted and needy: deliver the poor and needy from their hardships: take them out of the hand of the wicked."[4] Similarly, Moses "instructed the judges" whom he appointed to supply his place, saying—

Hear the causes between your brethren, and judge righteously between every man and his brother, and the stranger that is with him: you shall not differentiate among persons in judgment; but you

shall hear the small as well as the great; you shall not be afraid of the face of man; for the judgment is God's.[5]

I hardly need to comment on the directions given by him in another place respecting the role of a future king: "He shall not multiply horses to himself; neither shall he greatly multiply to himself silver and gold; his heart shall not be lifted up above his brethren; he shall read in the law all the days of his life";[6] he said also that judges must show no partiality nor take bribes, and similar injunctions abound in the Scriptures. But I will say no more of such things here because, in describing the office of magistrate in this treatise, my intention is not so much to instruct magistrates themselves, as to show to others what magistrates are and for what purpose God has appointed them. We see that they are made the protectors and upholders of the public innocence, modesty, probity, and tranquility, whose sole object it ought to be to promote the peace and security of all. David declares that he will be an example of these virtues when he is raised to the royal throne.

I will set no wicked thing before mine eyes. I will not know a wicked person. I will have nothing to do with anyone who knowingly slanders his neighbor, and the same with anyone who has a high look and a proud heart. My eyes shall be upon the faithful of the land, that they may dwell with me: he that walks in a perfect way, he shall serve me.[7]

Magistrates cannot act rightly unless they defend good men from the injuries of the wicked and aid the oppressed, giving them relief and protection. They must also exercise power for the suppression of crimes, and mete out severe punishment to malefactors whose wickedness disturbs the public peace; Experience fully verifies the observation of Solon:[8] "All states are supported by reward and punishment; and when these two things are removed, all the discipline of human societies is broken and destroyed." For the minds of many lose their regard for equity and justice unless virtue is rewarded and honored; nor can the violence of the wicked be restrained unless crimes are followed by severe punishments. These two related ideas are included in the injunc-

---

1   *viceregents*   Administrative deputies of a ruler.
2   *there was no king ... eyes*   Judges 21.25.
3   *Exercise good judgment ... blood*   Jeremiah 22.3.
4   *Defend the poor ... wicked*   Psalm 82.3–4.
5   *Hear the causes ... judgment is God's*   Deuteronomy 1.16–17.
6   *He shall not ... life*   Deuteronomy 17.16–17.
7   *I will set ... serve me*   Psalm 101.3–6.
8   *Solon*   Athenian lawmaker (c. 638 BCE–558 BCE).

tion of the prophet to kings and other governors to "execute judgment and righteousness."[1] "Righteousness" means the care, patronage, defense, vindication, and liberation of the innocent; "judgment" entails repressing those who are wickedly bold and violent, and punishing the crimes of the impious.

12. The first duty of subjects toward their magistrates is to be respectful of their function, which they know to be a jurisdiction delegated to magistrates from God, and on that account to esteem and reverence magistrates as God's ministers and vicegerents. Some persons show themselves very obedient to their magistrates and have no longing for a world without magistrates, acknowledging that they are necessary to the public good; but nevertheless consider the magistrates themselves as no more than necessary evils. Something more than this is required of us by Peter when he commands us to "honor the king";[2] and by Solomon, when he says, "Fear thou the Lord and the king";[3] for Peter, under the term "honor," comprehends a sincere and candid esteem; and Solomon, by connecting the king with the Lord, attributes to him a kind of sacred and dignified status deserving of veneration. Paul also commends magistrates when he says that we "must needs be subject, not only in order to escape a ruler's wrath, but also for conscience's sake";[4] by which he means that subjects ought to be induced to submit to princes and governors, not merely from a dread of their power, as persons are accustomed to yield to an armed enemy, who they know will immediately take vengeance upon them if they resist; but because obedience which is rendered to prince and magistrates is rendered to God, from whom they have received their authority. I do not suggest that the mask of dignity ought to palliate or excuse folly, ignorance, cruelty, or nefarious behavior and so acquire for vices the praise due to virtues; but I affirm that the office of magistrate is in itself worthy of honor and reverence; whoever our governors are, they ought to be given our esteem and veneration on account of the office which they fill.

[...]

23. Hence follow other duties. With minds disposed to honor and reverence magistrates, subjects express their obedience to them in submitting to their edicts, in paying taxes, in discharging public duties, in bearing burdens which relate to the common defense, and in fulfilling all their other commands. Paul says to the Romans, "Let every soul be subject to the higher powers. Whosoever resisteth the power, resisteth the ordinance of God."[5] He writes to Titus, "Put them in mind to be subject to principalities and powers, to obey magistrates, to be ready to every good work."[6] Peter exhorts, "Submit yourselves to every ordinance of man for the Lord's sake; whether it be to the king, as supreme; or unto governors, as unto them that are sent by him for punishing evildoers, and for praising those that do well."[7] Moreover, in order that subjects may testify that theirs is not a hypocritical but a sincere and cordial submission, Paul teaches that they ought to pray to God for the safety and prosperity of those under whose government they live. "I exhort," he says, "that supplications, prayers, intercessions, and giving of thanks be made for all men; for kings, and for all who are in positions of authority; so that we may lead a quiet and peaceable life in all godliness and honesty."[8]

Here let no man deceive himself. It is impossible to resist the magistrate without at the same time resisting God himself. Though it may seem that one could resist an unarmed magistrate with impunity, yet in such circumstances God is armed to inflict vengeance for the contempt shown to Himself.

Under this category of obedience I also include the moderation which private persons ought to display in relation to public affairs; unless they are called upon to do so, they should not meddle with affairs of state, rashly intrude themselves into the office of magistrates, or undertake anything of a public nature. If there be anything in the public administration which requires to be corrected, let private persons not raise any outburst or take the business into their own hands. Instead, let them refer such matters to the magistrate, who is alone authorized to regulate the concerns of the public. I mean that they ought to attempt nothing without being commanded; for when they have the command of a governor, then they also are invested with public authority. For, as we are accustomed to call the counselors of a prince "his eyes and ears," so it may be appropriate to refer to those he has commissioned to execute his commands as "his hands."

---

1   *execute judgment and righteousness*   Jeremiah 22.3.
2   *honor the king*   1 Peter 2.17.
3   *Fear thou ... king*   Proverbs 24.31.
4   *we must needs be subject ... conscience's sake*   Romans 13.5.
5   *Let every soul ... God*   Romans 13.1–2.
6   *Put them in mind ... good work*   Titus 3.1.
7   *Submit yourselves ... do well*   1 Peter 2.13–14.
8   *that supplications ... honesty*   1 Timothy 2.1–2.

24. We have hitherto described a magistrate who truly answers to his title as one who acts as the father of his country and, as the poet calls him, the pastor of his people, the guardian of peace, the protector of justice, the avenger of innocence; anyone who disapproved of such a government would justly be deemed insane. But it has happened, in almost all ages, that some princes, regardless of everything to which they ought to have directed their attention, give themselves up to their pleasures and pay no heed to any other concern. Some become absorbed in their own interest and allow a price to be put on all laws, privileges, rights, and judgments; others plunder the public purse and afterwards spend the money lavishly in mad prodigality; others commit flagrant outrages, pillaging houses, violating virgins and matrons, and murdering infants. Many persons cannot be persuaded that such "leaders" ought to be acknowledged as princes or magistrates—as leaders whom, as far as possible, they ought to obey. In the case of such outrageous acts—acts incompatible, not only with the office of a magistrate, but with the duty of every man—they discover no appearance of the image of God, which ought to be readily apparent in a magistrate; they perceive no vestige of that minister of God who is "a terror not to good works, but to evil," who is sent "for the punishment of evildoers, and for the praise of them that do well"; they do not recognize in such a governor someone whose dignity and authority the Scripture recommends to us. And certainly human minds have always been naturally disposed to hate and execrate tyrants as much as to love and reverence legitimate kings.

25. But, if we truly pay attention to the word of God, it will lead us to submit to the government, not only of those princes who discharge their duty to us with appropriate integrity and fidelity, but also to the government of those who possess the sovereignty, even though they perform none of the duties of their function. For, though the Lord testifies that the magistrate is an eminently appropriate one to act generously on His behalf to preserve the safety of men, and sets out to magistrates themselves the extent of their duty, yet He at the same time declares that whatever be their characters, they derive their authority to govern only from him. Those who govern for the public good are true specimens and mirrors of his beneficence; and those who rule in an unjust and tyrannical manner are raised up by him to punish the iniquity of the people; both sorts equally possess that sacred majesty with which he has invested legitimate authority. I will not proceed any further till I have

added a few testimonies in proof of this point. It is not difficult to demonstrate that an impious king represents a judgment of God's wrath upon the world, as I have no expectation that anyone will deny it; and in this we say no more of a king than of any other robber who plunders our property, or adulterer who violates our bed, or assassin who attempts to murder us; since the Scripture enumerates all these calamities among the curses inflicted by God. Let us rather insist on the proof of that which the minds of men do not so easily admit—that a man of the worst character, most undeserving of any honor, who holds the sovereign power, really possesses that eminent and divine authority which the Lord has given by his word to the ministers of his justice and judgment; and therefore ought to be regarded by his subjects, as far as pertains to public obedience, with the same reverence and esteem which they would show to the best of kings, if such a one were granted to them.

[...]

31. But whatever opinion be formed of the acts of men, the Lord equally executed his work by them when he broke the bloody scepters[1] of insolent kings and overturned tyrannical governments. Let princes hear and fear. But, in the meanwhile, it is proper for us to use the greatest caution, that we do not despise or violate that authority of magistrates which is entitled to the greatest veneration, which God has established by the most solemn commands, even if it may reside in those who are most unworthy of it, and who pollute it by their iniquity. The correction of tyrannical domination should be a matter for the vengeance of God; we are not, therefore, to conclude that we have a duty to take such vengeance when we have received no other command than to obey and suffer. This observation I always apply to private persons. But if there be, in the present day, any magistrates appointed to protect the people and to moderate the power of kings, such as were, in ancient times, the Ephori,[2] who were a check upon the kings among the Lacedaemonians,[3] or the popular tribunes upon the consuls among the Romans, or the Demarchi[4] upon the senate among the Athenians; or with power such as perhaps is

---

1 *scepters* Staves held by a monarch, symbol of ruling power.
2 *Ephori* Five elected magistrates whose function it was to check the power of kings.
3 *Lacedaemonians* Spartans.
4 *Demarchi* Heads of the local government in ancient Greece. It is not clear that Calvin's understanding of their function was entirely correct.

now possessed by the three estates[1] in every kingdom when they are assembled; I am so far from prohibiting them, in the discharge of their duty, from opposing the violence or cruelty of kings that I affirm that if they shut their eyes to the faults of kings who are oppressing their people, such forbearance involves the most nefarious perfidy[2] because they fraudulently betray the liberty of the people, of which they know that they have been appointed protectors by the ordination of God.

[...]

32. But in the obedience which we have shown to be due to the authority of governors, it is always necessary to make one exception, and that is entitled to our first attention—we must never be led away from obedience to Him to whose will the desires of all kings ought to be subject, to whose decrees all their commands ought to yield, to whose majesty all their scepters ought to submit. And, indeed, how preposterous it would be for us, with a view to satisfy men, to incur the displeasure of Him on whose account we yield obedience to men! The Lord, therefore, is the King of kings; who, when he has opened his sacred mouth, is to be heard alone, above all, for all, and before all. In the next place, we are subject to those men who preside over us, but no otherwise than in Him. If they command anything against Him, it ought not to cause us to pay the least attention, nor, in this case, ought we to pay any regard to all that dignity attached to magistrates, to which no injury is done when it is subjected to the unrivaled and supreme power of God. On this principle Daniel denied that he had committed any crime against the king in disobeying his impious decree;[3] because the king had exceeded the limits of his office, and

had not only done an injury to men, but, by raising his arm against God, had degraded his own authority. On the other hand, the Israelites are condemned for having been too submissive to the impious edict of their king. For when Jeroboam had made his golden calves, in compliance with his will, they deserted the temple of God and turned to new superstitions. Their descendants followed to the decrees of their idolatrous kings with the same ease. The prophet severely condemns them for having "willingly walked after the commandment."[4] Courtly flatterers who excuse themselves and deceive the unwary under the pretext of humility are due no praise; they deny that it is lawful for them to refuse compliance with any command of their kings, as if God had resigned authority over certain mortal men when he made them rulers of mankind, or as if earthly power were diminished by being subordinated to its Creator before whom even the principalities of heaven[5] tremble with awe. I know what great and present danger awaits those who hold constantly to the principle of obedience first and foremost to God, for kings cannot bear to be disregarded without the greatest indignation; and "the wrath of a king," says Solomon, "is as a messenger of death."[6] But since this edict has been proclaimed by that celestial herald, Peter, "We ought to obey God rather than men,"[7]—let us console ourselves with this thought, that we truly perform the obedience which God requires of us when we suffer anything rather than deviate from piety. And so that our hearts may not fail us, Paul stimulates us with another consideration—that Christ has redeemed us at the immense price which our redemption cost him, that we may not be submissive to the corrupt desires of men, much less be slaves to their impiety.[8]

---

1 *three estates* In several areas of sixteenth-century Europe, meetings of legislative or advisory bodies to the monarch representing the three estates, with the first being the clergy, the second the nobility, and the third the commoners.
2 *perfidy* Deliberate treachery.
3 *Daniel denied ... decree* Daniel 6.22.

4 *willingly walked ... commandment* Hosiah 5.11.
5 *principalities of heaven* One of the ranks of angels.
6 *wrath of a king ... death* Proverbs 16.14.
7 *we ought to obey ... men* Acts 5.29.
8 *Paul stimulates ... impiety* 1 Corinthians 7.23.

THOMAS HOBBES
(1588 – 1679)

Who Was Thomas Hobbes?

THOMAS HOBBES WAS BORN, PREMATURELY, IN 1588[1] IN the village of Westport near the small town of Malmesbury, in the southern English county of Wiltshire. Though several relatives had grown wealthy in the family's cloth-making business, Hobbes' father was a poor, ill-educated country clergyman, who frequently ran into trouble with the church authorities for disobedience and volatility. Young Thomas was apparently a studious, unhealthy, rather melancholy boy, who loved music. Because of his black hair he was nicknamed "Crow" by his schoolfellows. Though he grew to be intellectually fearless, he was personally always a rather timid person (and apparently, despite his materialism, had a life-long horror of ghosts).

When Hobbes was 16 his father's long-running feud with a nearby vicar, whom he had publicly slandered as "a knave and an arrant knave and a drunken knave," came to a head when (probably drunk) he encountered his enemy in the churchyard at Malmesbury and set about him with his fists. Any act of violence in a church or churchyard was an excommunicable offence at that time, and laying hands on a clergyman was an even more serious crime, subject to corporal punishment and imprisonment: Hobbes' father was forced to flee. It is not known whether Thomas ever again saw his father, who died "in obscurity beyond London."

By the time of his father's disappearance, however, young Hobbes had already been plucked out of his family situation and sent off to be educated at the university at Oxford (an education paid for by his uncle Francis, a prosperous glover). There, Hobbes attended Magdalen Hall, one of the poorer foundations at Oxford and one which was renowned for its religious Puritanism.[2] He does not seem to have been altogether impressed by the quality of the education he received: later in life he was dismissive of the Aristotelian logic and metaphysics that he was taught there, and claimed that at the time he was more interested in reading about explorations of newly discovered lands, and poring over maps of the world and the stars, than in studying traditional philosophy.

As soon as Hobbes completed his BA in 1608, he was lucky enough to be offered a job as tutor to the eldest son of William Cavendish, a rich and powerful Derbyshire landowner who owned the great stately home at Chatsworth (and who became the first Earl of Devonshire in 1618). Cavendish's son, also called William, was only a few years younger than Hobbes himself, and Hobbes' position quickly became that of a servant, secretary and friend, as well as tutor. In 1614 Hobbes and Cavendish went on a tour of France and Italy, where they both learned Italian and encountered some of the currents of Italian intellectual thought at the time, including the fiercely anti-Papal writings of several Venetian authors.

William Cavendish succeeded his father as the Earl of Devonshire in 1626, but died of disease just two years later. Hobbes, now forty years old, signed on as tutor to the son

---

1   This was the year that the Catholic monarch of Spain, Philip II, dispatched a massive fleet of ships—the Armada—to invade Protestant England. Hobbes later wrote in an autobiographical poem, that "hereupon it was my mother dear / Did bring forth twins at once, both me and fear," and used to joke that this explained his timid nature. (In the event, the Armada was decisively defeated in the English Channel before it could rendezvous with the Spanish invasion force waiting in Flanders.)

2   The Puritans were a group of English Protestants who regarded the Protestant Reformation under Elizabeth I (1558–1603) as incomplete: influenced by Protestant movements from continental Europe, such as Calvinism, they advocated strict religious discipline and simplification of the ceremonies and creeds of the Church of England.

of another rich landowner, Sir Gervase Clifton. During this period he accompanied his charge on another trip to the continent (France and Switzerland), and it was in Geneva that he picked up a copy of Euclid's *Elements* and fell in love with its method of deductive reasoning. A contemporary biographer wrote of the incident:

> Being in a gentleman's library, Euclid's *Elements* lay open, and 'twas the 47th Prop. of Book I. He read the proposition. "By G——," said he (he would now and then swear, by way of emphasis), "this is impossible!" So he read the demonstration of it, which referred him back to such a proposition; which proposition he read. That referred him back to another, which he also read. And so on, until at last he was demonstratively convinced of that truth. This made him in love with geometry.

After his return to England, Hobbes agreed to re-enter the service of the widowed countess of Devonshire as tutor to her thirteen-year-old son, the third earl. The 1630s were important years for Hobbes' intellectual development. His secure, and relatively undemanding, position allowed him time to develop both the main outlines of his political philosophy and also to pursue his interest in science (and especially optics). His connection to a great noble house also gave him contacts with other intellectuals clustered around noble patrons, such as the mathematicians and scientists supported by the earl of Newcastle, and the theologians, lawyers and poets associated with the Viscount Falkland.

In 1634 Hobbes embarked on another European tour with his pupil, and spent more than a year living in Paris where he met French scientists and mathematicians—and especially the influential and well-connected Marin Mersenne—and became finally and fully gripped by the intellectual excitement of the age. "The extreme pleasure I take in study overcomes in me all other appetites," he wrote in a letter at the time. By 1636, when Hobbes had returned to England, he was devoting as much of his energies as possible to philosophical and scientific work: the third earl turned eighteen in 1637, so—although Hobbes remained in his service—he was no longer needed as a tutor and his time was largely his own.

His earliest surviving work is a treatise on the science of optics, in part of which Hobbes attacks Descartes' *Discourse on Method* (published in 1637). Hobbes accused Descartes of inconsistency, of not taking seriously enough his own mechanistic physics. Since perception is caused entirely by physical motions or pressures, then the mind—that which does the perceiving—must also be a physical object, capable of being affected by motion, Hobbes argued.[1] Hobbes, therefore, in his very earliest philosophical writing rejected the dualism of matter and spirit in favor of a purely mechanical view of the world.

Hobbes' philosophical work was pushed in a different direction at the end of the 1630s as political events unfolded in England. As the country moved towards civil war during the final years of the so-called personal rule of King Charles I,[2] there was an intense public debate about the power of the sovereign. Should it be absolute? Should there be any limits at all on the power of the king? It was recognized that the monarch could exceed his normal powers during exceptional circumstances—but the king himself claimed to be the judge of which circumstances were exceptional, and this essentially allowed him to exceed his "normal" powers at any time he chose.

In 1640, after the Scots invaded and occupied northern England, the King recalled Parliament with the intent of having it grant him extra taxes to raise an army. They refused to do so, and what became known as the "Short Parliament" was abruptly dissolved. In the same year Hobbes wrote and circulated an unabashedly pro-royalist work called *The Elements of Law*, which attempted to justify the nature and extent of sovereign power from philosophical first principles. By the end of that year, facing a backlash from anti-royalist parliamentarians as tensions grew, Hobbes called in all his investments and left England for Paris.

Back in Paris, Hobbes was quickly reabsorbed into the intellectual life of the great city, and his reputation was established by the 1642 publication of *De Cive*, a remodeled version of the arguments of *The Elements of Law*. After this, Hobbes returned to the study of scientific philosophy and theology, and he spent several years working on a substantial book on logic, metaphysics and physics, which was eventually published in 1655 as *De Corpore*. However his work was frequently interrupted: once by a serious illness from which he nearly died (in 1647), and repeatedly

---

1 "Since vision is formally and really nothing but motion, it follows that that which sees is also formally and strictly speaking nothing other than that which is moved; for nothing other than a body ... can be moved" (*Tractatus opticus*, p. 207. This translation is by Noel Malcolm).

2 In 1629, after a series of clashes with Parliament, Charles dissolved the legislative body permanently and began an eleven-year period as absolute ruler.

by visitors from England, including royalist exiles from the English Civil War (which had erupted in 1642 and dragged on until 1648). In 1646 Hobbes was even made mathematical tutor to the young Prince Charles, now in exile in Paris. This turned Hobbes' thoughts back to politics, and—secretively and rapidly—Hobbes completed the major work *Leviathan* between the autumn of 1649 and the spring of 1651.

By this time Hobbes was keen to return to England: the war had been won by the Parliamentarians (Charles I was beheaded in 1649, the monarchy and House of Lords abolished, and a Commonwealth, led by Oliver Cromwell, set up) and *Leviathan*—which Hobbes took care to ensure was published in London—was partly intended to ease his passage back home. Hobbes did not abandon, or even substantially modify, the central arguments of his earlier, royalist writings, but in *Leviathan* he emphasizes that his project is to justify *political authority* generally (and not necessarily just that of a monarch), and he discusses extensively the question—which at that time was of vital interest to the former aristocratic supporters of the old king—of when it is legitimate to shift one's allegiance from one ruler to another. Hobbes later said that he had written *Leviathan* on behalf of "those many and faithful servants and subjects of His Majesty," who had fought on the royalist side and lost, and who now were in the position of negotiating with the new Parliamentary rulers for their old lands and titles. "They that had done their utmost endeavor to perform their obligation to the King, had done all that they could be obliged unto; and were consequently at liberty to seek the safety of their lives and livelihood wheresover, and without treachery."

Hobbes probably did not expect his work to cause offence among the court-in-exile of the young Charles II in Paris;[1] he presented a hand-written copy to the king in 1651. But because he denied that kings ruled by a divine right handed down directly from God, Hobbes was perceived as having turned against the monarchy. Furthermore the attack on organized religion, and especially Catholicism, that *Leviathan* contained provoked fury among Charles' courtiers. Hobbes was banned from the court, and shortly afterwards the French clergy attempted to have him arrested; Hobbes quickly fled back to England.

There he settled back into the employ of the earl of Devonshire, and resumed a quiet bachelor life of light secretarial work and intellectual discussion. However, the notoriety of *Leviathan* slowly grew, and—because of its bitter attacks on religion and the universities—Hobbes made enemies of many influential interest groups. When the Royal Society was formed in 1660 Hobbes was pointedly *not* invited to become a member, partly because his fellow exponents of the new "mechanical philosophy" were highly wary of being associated with atheism and reacted by violently attacking Hobbes' supposedly "atheistic" version of the new worldview. Throughout the 1660s and 1670s Hobbes—a.k.a. the "Beast of Malmesbury"—and his works were denounced from pulpits all over England for what was said to be his godlessness and denial of objective moral values. After the Great Fire of London, which destroyed most of the city in 1666 and followed close on the heels of the Great Plague of the previous year, popular feeling against the heretics and atheists whom it was feared were bringing God's wrath down on England reached new heights. *Leviathan* was named in the House of Commons as a book that tended towards atheism, and Hobbes was terrified that he would be charged for heresy—which could, even then, have resulted in his being burned at the stake, though no one had been executed for heresy in England since 1612. King Charles II protected his old tutor, but exacted a price; Hobbes was for the rest of his life no longer allowed to print anything in England on subjects relating to human conduct.

In contrast with the general public vilification which Hobbes faced in his own country, in France and Holland his reputation was soaring and (after the death of the acclaimed scientist Pierre Gassendi in 1655) he was widely regarded by French scientists and men of letters as the greatest living philosopher.

Hobbes, though now well into old age (and suffering severely from Parkinson's disease), continued to write prolifically. His works included several public defenses of *Leviathan* (before the King's ban), several treatises on mathematics, a debate with Robert Boyle about the experimental evidence for vacuums, a short book on six problems in physics, a polemical church history in Latin verse, translations of Homer's *Iliad* and *Odyssey* into English verse, and a history of the English civil war entitled *Behemoth*. When Hobbes died, shortly after suffering a severe stroke in December 1679, he was 91 years old.

---

1   The monarchy was eventually restored, by a vote of Parliament, in 1660.

What Was Hobbes' Overall Philosophical Project?

Hobbes thought of himself as primarily a scientist. He was interested in what we would today think of as science (optics, physics, geometry), but he was also concerned to place the study of human beings—especially psychology, ethics and politics—on what he considered a *scientific* footing. Hobbes was deeply conscious that he was living during a period of intellectual revolution—a time when the old Aristotelian assumptions were being stripped away by the new mechanical and mathematical science which Hobbes enthusiastically endorsed—as well as during an era of political and religious revolution. He wanted to play a significant role in both these movements.

Since Hobbes considered himself a scientist, his view of what *constitutes* science is particularly significant for his thought. Hobbes' scheme of the sciences changes somewhat throughout his writings, but its most stable core looks something like this. The most fundamental science is what Hobbes (like Aristotle) called "first philosophy," and it consists in "universal definitions"—of *body, motion, time, place, cause,* and so on—and their logical consequences. Thus the most basic kind of science, for Hobbes, is more purely rational than it is experimental. After first philosophy comes geometry, which (for Hobbes) was the science of the simple motions of bodies: that is, Hobbes rejected the view that geometry is the study of abstract objects and their relations, insisting instead that it concerns itself with the movements of concrete objects in real space. The next step in the ladder of the sciences is mechanics, which investigates the more complex motions involving whole bodies working together; this is followed by physics, the study of the invisible motions of the parts of bodies (including the effects on the human senses of the motions of external bodies). Then comes moral philosophy, which Hobbes thought of as primarily the investigation of passion and volition, which he considered the internal effects of sensation on the human mind. Finally, civil philosophy—the science of politics—formulates the laws of conduct that will ensure peace and self-preservation for communities of creatures with our particular internal psychological constitution.

A central—and at the time infamous—plank of Hobbes' scientific worldview was his unrelenting *materialism*. According to the new "mechanical" philosophy which had caught Hobbes up in its sweep across the thinkers of Europe, all physical phenomena are ultimately to be explained in terms of the motions and interactions of large numbers of tiny, material bodies. Hobbes enthusiastically accepted this view, and was one of the earliest thinkers to extend it to phenomena which his peers generally did not think of as "physical." In particular, Hobbes declared that *mental* phenomena ought to be just as susceptible to mechanical explanation as anything else in nature. For Hobbes, then, the natural world did not contain both matter and spirit (minds): it was entirely made up of material bodies, and human beings are nothing more than very complex material objects, like sophisticated robots or automata.

Along similar lines, Hobbes was very skeptical of claims to religious knowledge; this was one among several reasons why he devoted so much energy to attacks on the authority of the church. According to Hobbes' theory of language, words have meaning only if they express thoughts, and thoughts are nothing more than the residue in our minds of sensations produced by the action of external objects upon our bodies. Since God is supposed to be an infinite, transcendent being that is beyond our powers to perceive, Hobbes—although it is not at all clear that he was actually an atheist—was led to assert that we can have no meaningful thoughts about God. Furthermore, according to Hobbes' materialism, the notion of an "incorporeal substance" is simply incoherent, and so if God exists at all he must exist as a *material* body (which Hobbes claimed, in fact, to believe).

Like René Descartes, Hobbes saw himself as developing the foundations for a completely new and radical philosophy that was to decisively change the way his contemporaries saw the world. Furthermore, Hobbes did not see moral and political philosophy as a purely intellectual exercise. He firmly believed that the great and tragic upheaval of the English Civil War was directly caused by the promulgation of false and dangerous moral ideas, and could have been avoided by proper appreciation of the moral truth.

In *Leviathan*, then, Hobbes' project was to place social and political philosophy on a *scientific* basis for the first time (a project he thought would be of immense service to humanity). His model for this was the study of geometry: he begins with a sequence of axiomatic definitions—such as "justice," "obligation," "right of nature," and "law of nature"—and then tries to show that his philosophical results are rationally derivable from these basic assumptions. His goal was to derive and prove universal political laws—rather like the laws of physics—from which infallible judgments about particular cases can be made.[1]

What Is the Structure of the Reading?

Leviathan is divided into four parts: "Of Man," which deals primarily with human psychology and the state of nature; "Of Commonwealth," which discusses the formation of political states and the powers of their sovereigns; "Of a Christian Commonwealth," which examines the relationship between secular and religious law; and "Of the Kingdom of Darkness," which is a vitriolic attack on certain kinds of organized religion, especially Roman Catholicism. The excerpts given here come from Part 1 and 2.

First, there is a sequence of chapters that make up much of the second half of Part 1, in which Hobbes describes the unhappy "state of nature" for human beings and argues that several (nineteen, to be precise) moral "laws of nature" or "theorems" arise as "convenient articles of peace upon which men may be drawn to agreement." Included in this discussion, at the end of Chapter 14, is an examination of the way in which natural rights can be transferred or renounced (through contracts, covenants or free gift); there is also (near the beginning of Chapter 15) a lengthy discussion of the nature of justice, *that men perform their covenants made.*

Next are included the first five chapters of "Of Commonwealth," in which Hobbes discusses the way in which political states arise and argues that the sovereigns of those states are entitled to almost absolute power over their subjects. Finally, there are selections on civil laws, things that weaken a commonwealth, and the appropriate role of the sovereign.

Some Useful Background Information

i) The fundamental political problem for Hobbes, and the issue which *Leviathan* primarily sets out to address, was the following: How can any political system unambiguously and indisputably determine the answer to the question *What is the law?* How can one determine universally, uncontroversially acceptable rules of conduct, by which the citizens of a state must lead their public lives? A precondition for achieving this, Hobbes thought, was for there to be only a *single* source of law, and for that source to be *absolute* in the sense that whatever that legislator declared as law *was* law. Any other kind of political system, Hobbes believed, would descend inevitably into factionalism, insecurity, and civil war.

ii) Hobbes was quite self-conscious in rejecting the Aristotelian view of *human nature* that had been passed down to his day. For Aristotle, a human being is a naturally social animal, whose natural situation is as an active member of a political community, and whose highest good is the sort of happiness, or flourishing, for which our biological species is best suited. Furthermore, according to Aristotle, there is a natural hierarchy among human beings, with some people being inherently more noble than others. These inequalities are not *created* by society, on the Aristotelian picture, but ideally should be *mirrored* in the social order.

For Hobbes, by contrast, human beings are *not* naturally social animals, and furthermore there is no single conception of happiness which is tied to the human "essence": instead, according to Hobbes, human happiness is a matter of the continual satisfaction of desires or appetites, and since individual human beings differ in their particular desires so too will what makes people happy. Because people's desires often come into conflict—especially when several people are competing for the same scarce resource, such as land, money, or honor—human beings are naturally *anti*-social. Furthermore, even when civil society has been established, according to Hobbes, most of its citizens will not and should not be active participants in political life, but will simply lead private lives, out of the public sphere, within the constraints of their obedience to the commands of the sovereign. Finally, it was Hobbes' view that human beings in the state of nature are in a state of radical equality, where no one is substantially any better (or worse) than anyone else; similarly, in civil society, although there will be gradations of honor among men, everyone is fundamentally equal under the sovereign.

iii) Like Aristotle, however, Hobbes sees justice, and morality generally, as applying to character traits—what Hobbes calls "manners"—rather than primarily to states of affairs or types of action. For Hobbes, moral virtues are those habits which it is rational for all other people to praise; that is, they are those dispositions which contribute to the preservation, not merely of the individual, but of *everyone* in the community by contributing to peace and stable society.

---

1 On the other hand it is important to note that, unlike physics, politics is a *normative* science: it does not simply describe what people do, but in some sense prescribes what they *ought* to do. In this respect, Hobbes' political science resembles modern economics more than mathematics or experimental science.

Some Common Misconceptions

i) When Hobbes talks about "the state of nature" he is referring *neither* to a particular historical period in human history (such as the age of hunter-gatherers) *nor* to a mere theoretical possibility (a time that never actually occurred). What Hobbes has in mind is any situation, at any time or place, where there is no effective government capable of imposing order on the local population. Thus primitive or prehistoric societies may (or may not) be in the state of nature; but so too may modern societies that are locked in civil war, destroyed by conflict with other countries, or simply experiencing a constitutional crisis. Likewise, the international community of nations (then, as now) is in a state of nature, lacking any over-arching world government capable of determining and enforcing international law. (Hence, as he points out in the text, when Hobbes describes the state of nature as being "a condition of war" he does not mean that it will necessarily involve constant fighting and bloodshed, but rather that no one can feel *secure* against the threat of force.)

ii) Hobbes is not the "immoralist" he is sometimes taken to be: far from arguing *against* the existence of universal moral principles, Hobbes is concerned to *combat* the kind of moral relativism which holds that all laws, including moral laws, are mere matters of arbitrary human convention. Hobbes adopts the assumption of the moral skeptic that the only fundamental, universal moral principle is self-interest, but he then argues that, from the skeptic's *own assumption*, certain "natural" laws of justice follow deductively. In this way, Hobbes tries to show that there can be laws without a lawgiver: moral principles based, not in divine or human command, but in human nature itself. (On the other hand, Hobbes does stress that we are bound by these laws only if we can be sure that others will obey them too—that is, on the whole, only once we have agreed to form a civil society. To that extent at least, the principles of justice remain, for Hobbes, a matter of *convention*.)

iii) A mainspring of Hobbes' political philosophy is the claim that human beings seek their own self-preservation. There is textual evidence that Hobbes saw this desire for self-preservation not merely as a non-rational desire, even one which all human beings naturally share, but as a *primary goal of reason*. That is, one of the dictates *of rationality*, for Hobbes, is that we should take all measures necessary for our self-preservation, and so the ethical laws which Hobbes generates out of this principle are not merely *hypothetical*

commands ("Do this if you care more about your self-preservation than anything else") but are dictates that all rational creatures should recognize as binding on them.

iv) Though Hobbes is, legitimately, often said to be rather pessimistic about human nature, this can be overstated: his view, essentially, is not that *everyone* is fundamentally selfish, but that *enough* people are fundamentally selfish that it would be unwise to construct a civil society on the assumption that people are generally benevolent. According to Hobbes, children are born concerned only with themselves and, though they can learn to care for others, this can be brought about only with proper moral education. Unfortunately, he believed, not very many children are actually brought up in this way, and so most of the citizens of a commonwealth will in fact care primarily for themselves and their families and be not much moved by the interests of strangers.

v) Hobbes did not think that people *in fact* always act to preserve themselves: his claim is not that people always behave in a way which is optimal in avoiding hardship or death for themselves—on the contrary, Hobbes was convinced that people are often rash and vainglorious and prone to irrational quarrels—but that it is always *reasonable* or *rational* for people to seek self-preservation, and furthermore that this fact is so universally recognized by human beings that it is capable of serving as a solid basis for civil society. (Contrary to popular belief, then, Hobbes is not quite what is technically called a "psychological egoist": someone who believes that all people, as a matter of psychological necessity, always act only in their own self-interest.)

vi) Although Hobbes is frequently thought of as a *social contract theorist*, he actually does not see the foundation of the state as involving a contract or covenant between all the members of that society and the sovereign, but instead as a kind of *free gift* by the citizens to their sovereign. That is, people in the state of nature covenant together to freely turn over their right of nature to a sovereign power, in the hope that this sovereign will protect them and allow them to live in greater security. (Importantly, this means that the sovereign cannot *break a covenant* if he or she fails to protect her subjects ... though she does come to be bound by the law of nature prohibiting ingratitude, and so must "endeavor that he which giveth [a gift] have no reasonable cause to repent him of his good will.")

vii) Hobbes thought that his new political science could conclusively demonstrate that all states need a sovereign (an absolute dispenser of law). He did not, however, insist that this sovereign must be a *monarch*; he was quite ready to recognize that a republic, led by an assembly of senators for example, could be an equally effective form of government.

How Important and Influential Is This Work?

Hobbes' *Leviathan* is arguably the most important work of political philosophy in English—even though the work's *conclusions* have been widely rejected from Hobbes' day to this. The project of justifying and delimiting the extent of the state's power over its subjects, without appeal to such supernatural mechanisms as the divine right of kings, is an immensely important one, and Hobbes gave this question its first great answer in modern times. Though his political ideas differed from Hobbes in many important ways, John Locke, writing a couple of decades after Hobbes, nevertheless framed the issues in a similar way: how can human beings live together harmoniously under conditions where religious or traditional justifications of authority are no longer widely persuasive?

◆ ◆ ◆ ◆ ◆

Leviathan (1660)[1]

[1] ## The Introduction

1. Nature (the art[2] whereby God has made and governs the world) is by the art of man, as in many other things, so in this also imitated, that it can make an artificial animal.[3] For seeing life is but a motion of limbs, the beginning whereof is in some principal part within, why may we not say that all *automata* (engines that move themselves by springs and wheels as dos a watch) have an artificial life? For what is the *heart*, but a *spring*; and the *nerves*, but so many *strings*; and the *joints*, but so many *wheels*, giving motion to the whole body, such as was intended by the Artificer? *Art* goes yet further, imitating that rational and most excellent work of nature, *man*. For by art is created that great Leviathan called a Commonwealth, or State[4] (in Latin, *Civitas*), which is but an artificial man, though of greater stature and strength than the natural, for whose protection and defense it was intended; and in which the sovereignty is an artificial *soul*, as giving life and motion to the whole body. The *magistrates* and other *officers* of judicature and execution [are] artificial *joints*. *Reward* and *punishment* (by which fastened to the seat of the sovereignty, every joint and member is moved to perform his duty) are the *nerves* that do the same in the body natural. The *wealth* and *riches* of all the particular members are the *strength*. *Salus populi* (the *people's safety*) [is] its *business*. *Counselors*, by whom all things needful for it to know are suggested unto it, are the *memory*. *Equity* and laws [are] an artificial *reason* and *will*. *Concord* [is] *health*. *Sedition* [is] *sickness*. And *civil war* [is] *death*. Lastly, the *pacts* and *covenants*

---

1   *Leviathan* See Job 41, Psalms 74.15–17, and Isaiah 27.1. In the Bible, Leviathan, sometimes pictured as a whale and sometimes as a crocodile, is a principle of chaos and an enemy of God, whom God defeats. For Hobbes, Leviathan saves people from the state of nature. Elsewhere (28.27), Hobbes quotes the book of Job, which says at 41.34 that Leviathan is "king of all the children of pride." Christian theologians often identified pride as the cause of sin. The word came to mean any sea-monster or other huge creature, and Hobbes is probably using the word figuratively and irreverently, referring to the huge and powerful state.

2   *art* Hobbes uses this word to refer to anything that involves planning and design. A contrast is often made between *art* and *nature*—what happens naturally, not artificially—but Hobbes here rejects that contrast.

3   *an artificial animal* Hobbes is showing that normal beliefs do not pass scrutiny. Nature is actually artificial; machines are alive and humans are machines. Our beliefs must be reconsidered. Since Hobbes is the one to deconstruct these standard distinctions, he is in a good position to construct the correct view, or so he wants the reader to believe.

4   *State* Comparing the state to a living body was common in the seventeenth century: "The head cares for the body, so does the King for his people. As the discourse and direction flows from the head, and the execution thereunto belongs to the rest of the members, everyone according to their office: so it is betwixt a wise King and his people" (James I, "The Trew Law of Free Monarchies," 1598); "As in natural things, the head being cut off, the rest cannot be called a body: no more can in politick things a multitude or commonality, without a head be incorporate" (*Examples for Kings: or Rules for Princes to Govern By*, 1642).

by which the parts of this body politic were at first made, set together, and united, resemble that *fiat*,[1] or the *let us make man*, pronounced by God in the Creation.

[2] 2. To describe the nature of this artificial man, I will consider

First,[2] the *matter* thereof, and the *artificer*, both which is *Man*.

Secondly,[3] *how*, and by what *covenants* it is made; what are the rights and just *power* or authority of a *sovereign*; and what it is that *preserves* and *dissolves* it.

Thirdly,[4] what is a *Christian Commonwealth*.

Lastly,[5] what is the *Kingdom of Darkness*.

3. Concerning the first, there is a saying much usurped[6] of late that *wisdom* is acquired, not by reading of *books*, but of men. Consequently whereunto, those persons, that for the most part can give no other proof of being wise, take great delight to show what they think they have read in men by uncharitable censures of one another behind their backs. But there is another saying, not of late understood, by which they might learn truly to read one another, if they would take the pains; and that is *nosce teipsum*, *read thyself*, which was not meant, as it is now used, to countenance either the barbarous state of men in power towards their inferiors or to encourage men of low degree to a saucy behavior towards their betters. But [it was meant] to teach us that for the similitude of the thoughts and passions of one man to the thoughts and passions of another, whosoever looks into himself and considers what he does when he does *think, opine, reason, hope, fear*, etc., and upon what grounds, he shall thereby read and know what are the thoughts and passions of all other men upon the like occasions. I say the similitude of *passions*, which are the

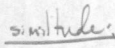

same in all men, *desire, fear, hope*, etc., not the similitude of the *objects* of the passions, which are the things *desired, feared, hoped*, etc.; for these the constitution individual and particular education do so vary, and they are so easy to be kept from our knowledge that the characters of man's heart, blotted and confounded as they are with dissembling, lying, counterfeiting, and erroneous doctrines are legible only to him that searches hearts. And though by men's actions we do discover their design sometimes; yet to do it without comparing them with our own and distinguishing all circumstances by which the case may come to be altered is to decipher without a key and be for the most part deceived by too much trust or by too much diffidence,[7] as he that reads is himself a good or evil man.

4. But let one man read another by his actions never so perfectly, it serves him only with his acquaintance, which are but few. He that is to govern a whole nation must read in himself, not this or that particular man, but mankind, which though it be hard to do, harder than to learn any language or science; yet when I shall have set down my own reading orderly and perspicuously, the pains left another will be only to consider if he also find not the same in himself. For this kind of doctrine admits no other demonstration.

Part 1: Of Man

[...]

Chapter 10: Of Power, Worth, Dignity, Honor, and Worthiness

[41]

1. The power of a man (to take it universally[8]) is his present means to obtain some future apparent good and is either *original* or *instrumental*.

2. *Natural*[9] *power* is the eminence of the faculties of body or mind, as extraordinary strength, form,[10] prudence, arts, eloquence, liberality, nobility. *Instrumental* are those powers which, acquired

---

1   *fiat*   Latin: Let there be. *Fiat lux* means "Let there be light." *Fiat homo* means "Let there be man." These are some of God's words of creation in the Vulgate (or Latin) version of the Bible.
2   *First*   Part 1, Chapters 1–16.
3   *Secondly*   Part 2, Chapters 17–31.
4   *Thirdly*   Part 3, Chapters 32–42.
5   *Lastly*   Part 4, Chapters 44–47.
6   *usurped*   Employed.

7   *diffidence*   Distrust.
8   *universally*   In the most general sense.
9   *Natural*   Original.
10   *form*   Good looks.

by these or by fortune are means and instruments to acquire more, as riches, reputation, friends, and the secret working of God, which men call good luck. For the nature of power is in this point like to fame, increasing as it proceeds, or like the motion of heavy bodies, which, the further they go, make still the more haste.

3. The greatest of human powers is that which is compounded of the powers of most men, united by consent, in one person, natural or civil, that has the use of all their powers depending on his will, such as is the power of a commonwealth; or depending on the wills of each particular, such as is the power of a faction or of divers factions leagued. Therefore to have servants is power; to have friends is power; for they are strengths united.

4. Also, riches joined with liberality[1] is power, because it procures friends and servants; without liberality, not so, because in this case they defend not, but expose men to envy, as a prey.

5. Reputation of power is power, because it draws with it the adherence of those that need protection.

6. So is reputation of love of a man's country called popularity, for the same reason.

7. Also, what quality soever makes a man beloved or feared of[2] many or the reputation of such quality is power, because it is a means to have the assistance and service of many.

8. Good success is power, because it makes reputation of wisdom or good fortune, which makes men either fear him or rely on him.

9. Affability of men already in power is increase of power, because it gains love.

10. Reputation of[3] prudence in the conduct of peace or war is power, because to prudent men we commit the government of ourselves more willingly than to others.

11. Nobility[4] is power, not in all places, but only in those commonwealths where it has privileges; for in such privileges consists their power.

12. Eloquence is power, because it is seeming[5] prudence.

13. Form is power, because being a promise of good, it recommends men to the favor of women and strangers. [42]

14. The sciences are small powers, because not eminent, and therefore not acknowledged in any man; nor are at all, but in a few, and in them, but of a few things. For science is of that nature, as none can understand it to be, but such as in a good measure have attained it.[6]

15. Arts of public use, as fortification, making of engines, and other instruments of war, because they confer to defense and victory, are power; and though the true mother of them be science, namely, the mathematics, yet, because they are brought into the light by the hand of the artificer, they be esteemed (the midwife passing with the vulgar for the mother) as his issue.

16. The *value* or Worth of a man is, as of all other things, his price, that is to say, so much as would be given for the use of his power and therefore is not absolute, but a thing dependent on the need and judgment of another. An able conductor of soldiers is of great price in time of war present or imminent but in peace not so. A learned and uncorrupt judge is much worth in time of peace, but not so much in war. And as in other things, so in men, not the seller, but the buyer determines the price. For let a man, as most men do, rate themselves at the highest value they can; yet their true value is no more than it is esteemed by others.   Worth.

17. The manifestation of the value we set on one another is that which is commonly called honoring and dishonoring. To value a man at a high rate is to *honor* him, at a low rate is to *dishonor* him. But high and low in this case is to be

---

1 *liberality* Generosity.
2 *feared of* Feared by.
3 *Reputation of* Reputation for.
4 *Nobility* Noble rank.

5 *seeming* Giving the appearance of.
6 *The sciences ... attained it* That is: science is only a small power, because nobody has really outstanding scientific knowledge, so nobody is thought of as being very knowledgeable—since only someone who has such knowledge can recognize it in others. Few men have such knowledge, and those that do have it about only a limited range of things.

understood by comparison to the rate that each man sets on himself.

Dignity.

18. The public worth of a man, which is the value set on him by the commonwealth, is that which men commonly call Dignity. And this value of him by the commonwealth is understood by offices of command, judicature, public employment; or by names and titles introduced for distinction of such value.

To honor and dishonor.

19. To pray to[1] another for aid of any kind is *to* Honor [him], because a sign we have an opinion he has power to help; and the more difficult the aid is, the more is the honor.

20. To obey is to honor, because no man obeys them who they think have no power to help or hurt them. And consequently to disobey is to *dishonor.*

21. To give great gifts to a man is to honor him, because it is buying of protection and acknowledging of power. To give little gifts is to dishonor, because it is but alms and signifies an opinion of the need of small helps.

22. To be sedulous in promoting another's good [and] also to flatter is to honor, as a sign we seek his protection or aid. To neglect is to dishonor.

23. To give way or place to another in any commodity is to honor, being a confession of greater power. To arrogate is to dishonor.

[43]

24. To show any sign of love or fear of another is honor, for both to love and to fear is to value. To contemn or less to love or fear than he expects is to dishonor, for it is undervaluing.

25. To praise, magnify, or call happy is to honor, because nothing but goodness, power, and felicity is valued. To revile, mock, or pity is to dishonor.

26. To speak to another with consideration, to appear before him with decency and humility is to honor him, as signs of fear to offend. To speak to him rashly, to do anything before him obscenely, slovenly, impudently is to dishonor.

27. To believe, to trust, to rely on another is to honor him, sign of opinion of his virtue and power. To distrust or not believe is to dishonor.

28. To hearken to a man's counsel or discourse of what kind soever is to honor, as a sign we think him wise or eloquent or witty. To sleep or go forth or talk the while is to dishonor.

29. To do those things to another which he takes for signs of honor or which the law or custom makes so is to honor, because in approving the honor done by others, he acknowledges the power which others acknowledge. To refuse to do them is to dishonor.

30. To agree with in opinion is to honor, as being a sign of approving his judgment and wisdom. To dissent is dishonor and an upbraiding of error, and, if the dissent be in many things, of folly.

31. To imitate is to honor, for it is vehemently to approve. To imitate one's enemy is to dishonor.

32. To honor those another honors is to honor him, as a sign of approbation of his judgment. To honor his enemies is to dishonor him.

33. To employ in counsel or in actions of difficulty is to honor, as a sign of opinion of his wisdom or other power. To deny employment in the same cases to those that seek it is to dishonor.

34. All these ways of honoring are natural, and as well within as without commonwealths. But in commonwealths where he or they that have the supreme authority can make whatsoever they please to stand for signs of honor, there be other honors.

35. A sovereign does honor a subject with whatsoever title or office or employment or action that he himself will have taken for a sign of his will to honor him.

36. The king of Persia honored Mordecai when he appointed [that] he should be conducted through the streets in the king's garment upon one of the king's horses with a crown on his head and a prince before him, proclaiming, *Thus shall it be done to him that the king will honor.*[2] And yet another king of Persia or the same another time to one that demanded for some great service to wear one of the king's robes, gave him leave so to do; but with this addition, that he should wear it as

---

1   *pray to*   Request of.

2   *Thus shall ... honor*   See Esther 1.1–12.

the king's fool,[1] and then it was dishonor. So that of civil honor the fountain[2] is in the person of the commonwealth and depends on the will of the sovereign and is therefore temporary and called [44] *civil honor*, such as are magistracy, offices, titles, and in some places coats and scutcheons painted;[3] and men honor such as have them, as having so many signs of favor in the Commonwealth, which favor is power.

Honorable. 37. *Honorable* is whatsoever possession, action, or quality is an argument[4] and sign of power.

38. And therefore to be honored, loved, or feared of many is honorable, as arguments of pow-Dis- er. To be honored of few or none, *dishonorable*.
honorable. 39. Dominion and victory is honorable because acquired by power; and servitude, for need or fear, is dishonorable.

40. Good fortune (if lasting) honorable, as a sign of the favor of God. Ill fortune and losses, dishonorable. Riches are honorable, for they are power. Poverty, dishonorable. Magnanimity, liberality, hope, courage, [and] confidence are honorable; for they proceed from the conscience[5] of power. Pusillanimity, parsimony, fear, diffidence, are dishonorable.

41. Timely resolution or determination of what a man is to do is honorable, as being the contempt of small difficulties and dangers. And irresolution dishonorable, as a sign of too much valuing of little impediments and little advantages, for when a man has weighed things as long as the time permits and resolves not, the difference of weight is but little; and therefore if he resolve not, he overvalues little things, which is pusillanimity.

42. All actions and speeches that proceed or seem to proceed from much experience, science, discretion, or wit are honorable, for all these are powers. Actions or words that proceed from error, ignorance, or folly, dishonorable.

43. Gravity,[6] as far forth as it seems to proceed from a mind employed on something else, is honorable, because employment is a sign of power. But if it seem to proceed from a purpose to appear grave, it is dishonorable. For the gravity of the former is like the steadiness of a ship laden with merchandise, but of the like the steadiness of a ship ballasted with sand and other trash.

44. To be conspicuous, that is to say, to be known, for wealth, office, great actions, or any eminent good is honorable, as a sign of the power for which he is conspicuous. On the contrary, obscurity is dishonorable.

45. To be descended from conspicuous parents is honorable, because they the more easily attain the aids and friends of their ancestors. On the contrary, to be descended from obscure parentage is dishonorable.

46. Actions proceeding from equity, joined with[7] loss, are honorable, as signs of magnanimity, for magnanimity is a sign of power. On the contrary, craft, shifting, [and] neglect of equity is dishonorable.

47. Covetousness of great riches and ambition of great honors are honorable, as signs of power to obtain them. Covetousness and ambition of little gains or preferments[8] is dishonorable.

48. Nor does it alter the case of honor whether an action (so it be great and difficult and [45] consequently a sign of much power) be just or unjust, for honor consists only in the opinion of power. Therefore, the ancient heathen did not think they dishonored but greatly honored the gods, when they introduced them in their poems committing rapes, thefts, and other great, but unjust or unclean acts, insomuch as nothing is so much celebrated in Jupiter as his adulteries, nor in Mercury as his frauds and thefts, of whose praises in a hymn of Homer the greatest is this, that being born in the morning, he had invented music at noon and before night stolen away the cattle of Apollo from his herdsmen.

---

1 *king's fool* Court jester.
2 *fountain* Source.
3 *scutcheons painted* Shields painted with coats of arms.
4 *argument* Evidence.
5 *conscience* Awareness.
6 *Gravity* Dignified heaviness of manner.
7 *joined with* But in circumstances of.
8 *preferments* Privileges, promotions.

49. Also amongst men, till there were constituted great commonwealths, it was thought no dishonor to be a pirate or a highway thief, but rather a lawful trade, not only amongst the Greeks, but also amongst all other nations, as is manifest by the histories of ancient time. And at this day, in this part of the world, private duels are and always will be honorable, though unlawful, till such time as there shall be honor ordained for them that refuse and ignominy for them that make the challenge. For duels also are many times effects of courage, and the ground of courage is always strength or skill, which are power, though for the most part they be effects of rash speaking and of the fear of dishonor in one or both the combatants, who, engaged by rashness, are driven into the lists to avoid disgrace.

Coats of arms.
50. Scutcheons and coats of arms hereditary, where they have any eminent privileges, are honorable; otherwise not; for their power consists either in such privileges or in riches or some such thing as is equally honored in other men. This kind of honor, commonly called gentry,[1] has been derived from the ancient Germans. For there never was any such thing known where the German customs were unknown. Nor is it now anywhere in use where the Germans have not inhabited. The ancient Greek commanders, when they went to war, had their shields painted with such devices[2] as they pleased, insomuch as an unpainted buckler was a sign of poverty and of a common soldier; but they transmitted not the inheritance of them. The Romans transmitted the marks of their families; but they were the images, not the devices of their ancestors. Amongst the people of Asia, Africa, and America, there is not, nor was ever, any such thing. The Germans only had that custom, from whom it has been derived into England, France, Spain and Italy, when in great numbers they either aided the Romans or made their own conquests in these western parts of the world.

51. For Germany, being anciently, as all other countries in their beginnings, divided amongst an infinite number of little lords or masters of families that continually had wars one with another, those masters or lords, principally to the end they might, when they were covered with arms,[3] be known by their followers and partly for ornament, both painted their armor or their scutcheon or coat with the picture of some beast or other thing and also put some eminent and visible mark upon the crest of their helmets. And this ornament both of the arms and crest descended by inheritance to their children to the eldest pure and to the rest with some note of diversity, such as the old master, that is to say in Dutch, the *Here-alt*, thought fit. But when many such families, joined together, made a greater monarchy, this duty of the herald to distinguish scutcheons was made a private office apart. And the issue of these lords is the great and ancient gentry, which for the most part bear living creatures noted for courage and rapine, or castles, battlements, belts, weapons, bars, palisades, and other notes of war; nothing being then in honor, but virtue military. Afterwards, not only kings but popular commonwealths gave divers manners of scutcheons to such as went forth to the war or returned from it for encouragement or recompense to their service. All which, by an observing reader, may be found in such ancient histories, Greek and Latin, as make mention of the German nation and manners in their times.[4]

[46]

52. Titles of honor, such as are duke, count, marquis, and baron, are honorable, as signifying the value set upon them by the sovereign power of the commonwealth; which titles were in old time titles of office and command derived some from the Romans, some from the Germans and French. Dukes, in Latin, *duces*,[5] being generals in war; counts, *comites*,[6] such as bore the general company out of friendship, and were left to govern and defend places conquered and pacified; marquises, *marchiones*, were counts that governed the marches or bounds of the Empire. Which

Titles of honor.

---

1   *gentry*   High birth or rank.
2   *devices*   Pictures or words.
3   *arms*   Armor.
4   *such ancient histories ... in their times*   See Hobbes' translation of Thucydides, *History of the Peloponnesian War* 1.5–6.
5   *duces*   Leaders.
6   *comites*   Companions.

titles of duke, count, and marquis came into the Empire about the time of Constantine the Great[1] from the customs of the German *militia*. But baron seems to have been a title of the Gauls and signifies a great man, such as were the kings' or princes' men whom they employed in war about their persons and seems to be derived from *vir* [man], to *ber*, and *bar*, that signified the same in the language of the Gauls, that *vir* in Latin, and thence to *bero* and *baro*, so that such men were called *berones*, and after *barones*; and (in Spanish) *varones*. But he that would know more, particularly the original of titles of honor, may find it, as I have done this, in Mr. Selden's most excellent treatise of that subject.[2] In process of time these offices of honor, by occasion of trouble and for reasons of good and peaceable government, were turned into mere titles, serving for the most part to distinguish the precedence, place, and order of subjects in the commonwealth; and men were made dukes, counts, marquises, and barons of places, wherein they had neither possession nor command, and other titles also were devised to the same end.

Worthiness.

53. Worthiness is a thing different from the worth or value of a man and also from his merit or desert, and consists in a particular power or ability for that whereof he is said to be worthy; which particular ability is usually named Fitness or *aptitude*.

Fitness.

[47]

54. For he is worthiest to be a commander, to be a judge, or to have any other charge, that is best fitted with the qualities required to the well discharging of it, and worthiest of riches that has the qualities most requisite for the well using of them, any of which qualities being absent, one may nevertheless be a worthy man and valuable for something else. Again, a man may be worthy of riches, office, and employment that nevertheless can plead no right to have it before another, and therefore cannot be said to merit or deserve it. For merit presupposes a right, and that the thing deserved is due by promise, of which I shall say more hereafter when I shall speak of contracts.

Chapter 11: Of the Difference of Manners

1. By Manners,[3] I mean not here decency of behavior, as how one man should salute another, or how a man should wash his mouth, or pick his teeth before company, and such other points of the *small morals*, but those qualities of mankind that concern their living together in peace and unity. To which end we are to consider that the felicity of this life consists not in the repose of a mind satisfied. For there is no such *finis ultimus* (utmost aim) nor *summum bonum* (greatest good) as is spoken of in the books of the old moral philosophers. Nor can a man any more live whose desires are at an end than he whose senses and imaginations are at a stand.[4] Felicity is a continual progress of the desire from one object to another, the attaining of the former being still but the way to the latter. The cause whereof is that the object of man's desire is not to enjoy once only and for one instant of time, but to assure forever the way of his future desire. And therefore the voluntary actions and inclinations of all men tend not only to the procuring, but also to the assuring of a contented life and differ only in the way, which arises partly from the diversity of passions in divers men and partly from the difference of the knowledge or opinion each one has of the causes which produce the effect desired.

2. So that in the first place, I put for a general inclination of all mankind a perpetual and restless desire of power after power that ceases only

What is here meant by manners.

A restless desire of power in all men.

---

1   *Constantine the Great* Flavius Constantinus (274–337), Roman emperor who made Christianity the state religion. Constantine was praised by John Foxe in his *Book of Martyrs* (English version, 1563) and Hobbes is similarly approving.

2   *Mr. Selden's ... that subject* John Selden, *Titles of Honor* (1614). Selden (1584–1654) was a friend of Hobbes during the early 1650s but they may have met at Great Tew in the 1630s.

3   *Manners* Hobbes does not mean etiquette, but rather ethics.

4   *are at a stand* Have come to a halt. In ancient Greek philosophy, to have a desire was a kind of imperfection, because it meant that one lacked (wanted) the thing desired. For Hobbes, desire is a necessary condition of life.

in death. And the cause of this is not always that a man hopes for a more intensive delight than he has already attained to or that he cannot be content with a moderate power, but because he cannot assure the power and means to live well, which he has present, without the acquisition of more. And from hence it is that kings, whose power is greatest, turn their endeavors to the assuring it at home by laws or abroad by wars; and when that is done, there succeeds a new desire, in some, of fame from new conquest, in others, of ease and sensual pleasure, in others, of admiration or being flattered for excellence in some art or other ability of the mind.

Love of contention from competition.
[48]

3. Competition of riches, honor, command, or other power inclines to contention, enmity, and war, because the way of one competitor to the attaining of his desire is to kill, subdue, supplant, or repel the other. Particularly, competition of praise inclines to a reverence of antiquity. For men contend with the living, not with the dead, to these [dead] ascribing more than due, that they may obscure the glory of the other [living].

Civil obedience from love of ease.
From fear of death or wounds

4. Desire of ease and sensual delight disposes men to obey a common power, because by such desires a man does abandon the protection that might be hoped for from his own industry and labor. Fear of death and wounds disposes to the same and for the same reason. On the contrary, needy men and hardy, not contented with their present condition, as also all men that are ambitious of military command, are inclined to continue the causes of war and to stir up trouble and sedition, for there is no honor military but by war nor any such hope to mend an ill game as by causing a new shuffle.

And from love of arts.

5. Desire of knowledge and arts of peace inclines men to obey a common power, for such desire contains a desire of leisure and consequently protection from some other power than their own.

Love of virtue from love of praise.

6. Desire of praise disposes to laudable actions, such as please them whose judgment they value; for of those men whom we contemn, we contemn also the praises [they give]. Desire of fame after death does the same. And though after death there be no sense of the praise given us on earth, as being joys that are either swallowed up in the unspeakable joys of heaven or extinguished in the extreme torments of hell; yet is not such fame vain,[1] because men have a present delight therein from the foresight of it and of the benefit that may redound thereby to their posterity, which though they now see not, yet they imagine; and anything that is pleasure in the sense the same also is pleasure in the imagination.[2]

Hate from difficulty of requiting great benefits.

7. To have received from one to whom we think ourselves equal greater benefits than there is hope to requite disposes to counterfeit love, but really secret hatred, and puts a man into the estate of a desperate debtor that, in declining the sight of his creditor, tacitly wishes him there where he might never see him more. For benefits oblige; and obligation is thralldom;[3] and unrequitable[4] obligation, perpetual thraldom, which is to one's equal, hateful. But to have received benefits from one whom we acknowledge for superior inclines to love, because the obligation is no new depression;[5] and cheerful acceptation (which men call *gratitude*) is such an honor done to the obliger as is taken generally for retribution.[6] Also to receive benefits, though from an equal or inferior, as long as there is hope of requital, disposes to love; for in the intention of the receiver the obligation is of aid and service mutual, from whence proceeds an emulation of who shall exceed in benefiting, the most noble and profitable contention[7] possible, wherein the victor is pleased with his victory, and the other revenged by confessing it.[8]

And from conscience of deserving to be hated.

8. To have done more hurt to a man than he can or is willing to expiate inclines the doer to

---

1 *is not such fame vain* This fame is not worthless.
2 *Desire of fame ... in the imagination* What a person desires to happen after his death cannot make him happy at that time: the joys of heaven and the pain in hell overwhelm any earthly praise. But these desires for the future can make a person happy in the present.
3 *thralldom* Servitude.
4 *unrequitable* Nondischargeable.
5 *depression* Suppression.
6 *retribution* Repayment.
7 *contention* Competition.
8 *revenged by confessing it* Obtained his revenge by admitting defeat.

[49]

Promptness
to hurt from
fear.

hate the sufferer. For he must expect revenge or forgiveness, both which are hateful.

9. Fear of oppression disposes a man to anticipate or to seek aid by society; for there is no other way by which a man can secure his life and liberty.

And from
distrust of
their own
wit.

10. Men that distrust their own subtlety are in [a time of] tumult and sedition better disposed for victory than they that suppose themselves wise or crafty. For these [the former] love to consult, the other [the latter] (fearing to be circumvented) [love to] to strike first. And in sedition, men being always in the precincts of battle to hold together and use all advantages of force is a better stratagem than any that can proceed from subtlety of wit.

Vain under-
taking from
vain-glory.[1]

11. Vain-glorious men, such as without being conscious to themselves of great sufficiency, delight in supposing themselves gallant men, are inclined only to ostentation, but not to attempt [deeds requiring these virtues], because when danger or difficulty appears, they look for nothing but to have their insufficiency discovered.

12. Vain-glorious men [of a different kind], such as estimate their sufficiency by the flattery of other men or the fortune of some precedent action without assured ground of hope from the true knowledge of themselves, are inclined to rash engaging, and in the approach of danger or difficulty to retire[2] if they can, because not seeing the way of safety they will rather hazard their honor, which may be salved with an excuse than their lives, for which no salve is sufficient.

Ambition
from
opinion of
sufficiency.

13. Men that have a strong opinion of their own wisdom in matter of government are disposed to ambition, because without public employment in counsel or magistracy, the honor of their wisdom is lost. And therefore eloquent speakers are inclined to ambition, for eloquence seems wisdom both to themselves and others.

Irresolution
from too
great valu-
ing of small
matters.

14. Pusillanimity disposes men to irresolution and consequently to lose the occasions and fittest opportunities of action. For after men have been in deliberation till the time of action approach, if

it be not then manifest what is best to be done, it is a sign [that] the difference of motives the one way and the other are not great; therefore not to resolve then is to lose the occasion by weighing of trifles, which is pusillanimity.

15. Frugality (though in poor men a virtue) makes a man unapt to achieve such actions as require the strength of many men at once; for it weakens their endeavor, which is to be nourished and kept in vigor by reward.

Confidence
in others
from ignor-
ance of the
marks of
wisdom and
kindness.

16. Eloquence with flattery disposes men to confide in[3] them that have it, because the former is seeming[4] wisdom, the latter seeming[5] kindness. Add to them military reputation and it disposes men to adhere and subject themselves to those men that have them. The two former, having given them caution against danger from him, the latter gives them caution against danger from others.

And from
ignorance
of natural
causes.

17. Want[6] of science, that is, ignorance of causes, disposes or rather constrains a man to rely on the advice and authority of others. For all men whom the truth concerns, if they rely not on their own, must rely on the opinion of some other whom they think wiser than themselves and see not why he should deceive them.

[50]
And from
want of
under-
standing.

18. Ignorance of the signification of words, which is want of understanding, disposes men to take on trust, not only the truth they know not, but also the errors, and which is more, the nonsense of them they trust; for neither error nor nonsense can without a perfect understanding of words be detected.

19. From the same it proceeds that men give different names to one and the same thing from the difference of their own passions, as they that approve a private opinion call it opinion, but they that mislike[7] it, heresy; and yet heresy signifies no more than private opinion but has only a greater tincture of choler.[8]

1   *vain-glory*   Unwarranted pride or boasting.
2   *retire*   Withdraw.
3   *confide in*   Trust.
4   *the former is seeming*   Eloquence seems to be.
5   *latter seeming*   Flattery seems to be.
6   *Want*   Lack.
7   *mislike*   Dislike.
8   *choler*   Anger.

20. From the same also it proceeds that men cannot distinguish, without study and great understanding, between one action of many men and many actions of one multitude, as for example, between the one action of all the senators of Rome in killing Catiline and the many actions of a number of senators in killing Caesar, and therefore are disposed to take for the action of the people that which is a multitude of actions done by a multitude of men led perhaps by the persuasion of one.[1]

Adherence to custom from ignorance of the nature of right and wrong.

21. Ignorance of the causes and original constitution of right, equity, law, and justice disposes a man to make custom and example the rule of his actions, in such manner as to think that unjust which it has been the custom to punish and that just of the impunity and approbation whereof they can produce an example or (as the lawyers which only use this false measure of justice barbarously call it) a precedent,[2] like little children that have no other rule of good and evil manners but the correction they receive from their parents and masters, save that children are constant to their rule, whereas men are not so, because grown strong and stubborn, they appeal from custom to reason, and from reason to custom, as it serves their turn, receding from custom when their interest requires it and setting themselves against reason as oft as reason is against them; which is the cause that the doctrine of right and wrong is perpetually disputed both by the pen and the sword, whereas the doctrine of lines and figures[3] is not so, because men care not in that subject what be truth, as [it is] a thing that crosses no man's ambition, profit, or lust. For I doubt not but if it had been a thing contrary to any man's right of dominion or to the interest of men that have dominion *that the three angles of a triangle should be equal to two angles of a square*, that doctrine should [would] have been, if not disputed, yet by the burning of all books of geometry suppressed, as far as he whom it concerned was able.

Adherence to private men, from ignorance of the causes of peace.

22. Ignorance of remote causes disposes men to attribute all events to the causes immediate and instrumental; for these are all the causes they perceive. And hence it comes to pass that in all places men that are grieved with payments to the public discharge their anger upon the publicans, that is to say, farmers, collectors, and other officers of the public revenue, and adhere to such as find fault with the public government, and thereby, when they have engaged themselves beyond hope of justification, fall also upon[4] the supreme authority for fear of punishment or shame of receiving pardon.

Credulity from ignorance of nature.

23. Ignorance of natural causes disposes a man to credulity, so as to believe many times impossibilities; for such [a man] knows nothing to the contrary but that they may be true, being unable to detect the impossibility. And credulity, because men love to be hearkened unto[5] in company, disposes them to lying, so that ignorance itself, without malice, is able to make a man both to believe lies and tell them and sometimes also to invent them.

Curiosity to know from care of future time.

24. Anxiety for the future time disposes men to inquire into the causes of things, because the knowledge of them makes men the better able to order the present to their best advantage.

Natural religion from the same.

25. Curiosity or love of the knowledge of causes draws a man from consideration of the effect to seek the cause, and again, the cause of that cause, till of necessity he must come to this thought at last that there is some cause whereof there is no former cause but is eternal; which is it men call God. So that it is impossible to make any profound inquiry into natural causes without being inclined thereby to believe there is one God eternal, though they cannot have any idea of him in their mind answerable to his nature.[6] For as

---

1   *to take ... of one* To mistakenly take what is really a multitude of actions, performed by several people (perhaps with a single leader) to be a single action performed by a collectivity. Hobbes may be alluding to the execution of King Charles I (1649) by the members of the Rump Parliament.

2   *to think ... a precedent* Hobbes is criticizing Edward Coke (1552–1634), who claimed the Common Law was independent of the king.

3   *the doctrine of lines and figures* Geometry.

4   *fall also upon* Attack.

5   *hearkened unto* Listened to.

6   *they cannot ... his nature* Humans can know that God exists, but not what his nature is, because they have no direct or unmediated knowledge of God.

a man that is born blind, hearing men talk of warming themselves by the fire and being brought to warm himself by the same, may easily conceive and assure himself there is somewhat there which men call fire and is the cause of the heat he feels, but cannot imagine what it is like nor have an idea of it in his mind such as they have that see it, so also by the visible things of this world and their admirable order, a man may conceive there is a cause of them, which men call God, and yet not have an idea or image of him in his mind.

26. And they that make little or no inquiry into the natural causes of things, yet from the fear that proceeds from the ignorance itself of what it is that has the power to do them much good or harm are inclined to suppose and feign unto themselves several kinds of powers invisible and to stand in awe[1] of their own imaginations and in time of distress to invoke them, as also in the time of an expected good success, to give them thanks, making the creatures of their own fancy their gods. By which means it has come to pass that from the innumerable variety of fancy,[2] men have created in the world innumerable sorts of gods. And this fear of things invisible is the natural seed of that which every one in himself calls religion, and in them that worship or fear that power otherwise than they do, superstition.

27. And this seed of religion, having been observed by many, some of those that have observed it have been inclined thereby to nourish, dress, and form it into laws, and to add to it of their own invention any opinion of the causes of future events by which they thought they should best be able to govern others and make unto themselves the greatest use of their powers.

[...]

Chapter 13: Of the Natural Condition of Mankind as Concerning Their Felicity and Misery

1. Nature has made men so equal in the faculties of body and mind, as that, though there be found one man sometimes manifestly stronger in body or of quicker mind than another; yet when all is reckoned together, the difference between man and man is not so considerable as that one man can thereupon claim to himself any benefit to which another may not pretend[3] as well as he. For as to the strength of body, the weakest has strength enough to kill the strongest, either by secret machination or by confederacy with others that are in the same danger with himself.

Men by nature equal.

2. And as to the faculties of the mind, setting aside the arts grounded upon words, and especially that skill of proceeding upon general and infallible rules, called science, which very few have and but in few things, as being not a native faculty born with us, nor attained, as prudence, while we look after somewhat else, I find yet a greater equality amongst men than that of strength. For prudence is but experience, which equal time equally bestows on all men in those things they equally apply themselves unto. That which may perhaps make such equality incredible is but a vain conceit of one's own wisdom, which almost all men think they have in a greater degree than the vulgar,[4] that is, than all men but themselves and a few others, whom by fame or for concurring with themselves, they approve. For such is the nature of men that howsoever they may acknowledge many others to be more witty or more eloquent or more learned, they will hardly believe there be many so wise as themselves; for they see their own wit[5] at hand and other men's at a distance. But this proves rather that men are in that point equal, than unequal. For there is not ordinarily a greater sign of the equal distribution of anything than that every man is contented with his share.

[61]

---

1   *awe* This word occurs frequently and importantly in Hobbes. It means *fear, terror, dread*; it does not primarily carry the associations we have with that word of *reverence, respect, wonder*.
2   *fancy* Imagination.

3   *pretend* Claim.
4   *vulgar* Common people.
5   *wit* Wisdom.

[handwritten: 0 — Explanation of the three causes for quarrel: ① competition ② diffidence ③ glory]

From equality proceeds diffidence.

3. From this equality of ability arises equality of hope in the attaining of our ends. And therefore if any two men desire the same thing, which nevertheless they cannot both enjoy, they become enemies; and in the way to their end (which is principally their own conservation,[1] and sometimes their delectation[2] only) endeavor to destroy or subdue one another. And from hence it comes to pass that where an invader has no more to fear than another man's single power, if one plant, sow, build, or possess a convenient seat,[3] others may probably be expected to come prepared with forces united to dispossess and deprive him, not only of the fruit of his labor, but also of his life or liberty. And the invader again is in the like danger of another.

From diffidence war.

4. And from this diffidence[4] of one another, there is no way for any man to secure himself so reasonable as anticipation,[5] that is, by force or wiles, to master the persons of all men he can so long till he see no other power great enough to endanger him; and this is no more than his own conservation requires, and is generally allowed. Also, because there be some that, taking pleasure in contemplating their own power in the acts of conquest, which they pursue farther than their security requires, if others, that otherwise would be glad to be at ease within modest bounds, should not by invasion increase their power, they would not be able, long time, by standing only on their defense, to subsist. And by consequence, such augmentation of dominion over men being necessary to a man's conservation, it ought to be allowed him.

[handwritten margin: Subsist:]

5. Again, men have no pleasure (but on the contrary a great deal of grief) in keeping company where there is no power able to overawe them all. For every man looks that his companion should value him at the same rate he sets upon himself, and upon all signs of contempt or undervaluing naturally endeavors, as far as he dares (which amongst them that have no common power to keep them in quiet is far enough to make them destroy each other), to extort a greater value from his contemners,[6] by damage; and from others, by the example.

6. So that in the nature of man, we find three principal causes of quarrel. First, competition; secondly, diffidence; thirdly, glory.

7. The first makes men invade for gain; the second, for safety; and the third, for reputation. The first use violence to make themselves masters of other men's persons, wives, children, and cattle; the second, to defend them; the third, for trifles, as a word, a smile, a different opinion, and any other sign of undervalue, either direct in their persons or by reflection in their kindred, their friends, their nation, their profession, or their name. [62]

Out of civil states there is always war of every one against every one.

8. Hereby it is manifest that during the time men live without a common power to keep them all in awe, they are in that condition which is called war; and such a war as is of every man against every man. For War consists not in battle only, or the act of fighting, but in a tract[7] of time, wherein the will to contend by battle is sufficiently known; and therefore the notion of *time* is to be considered in the nature of war, as it is in the nature of weather. For as the nature of foul weather lies not in a shower or two of rain, but in an inclination thereto of many days together, so the nature of war consists not in actual fighting, but in the known disposition thereto during all the time there is no assurance to the contrary. All other time is Peace.

The incommodities[8] of such a war.

9. Whatsoever therefore is consequent to[9] a time of war, where every man is enemy to every man, the same consequent to the time wherein men live without other security than what their own strength and their own invention shall furnish them withal. In such condition there is no place for industry, because the fruit thereof is uncertain; and consequently no culture of the earth; no navigation, nor use of the commodities that may be imported by sea; no commodious build-

---

1   *conservation*   Survival.
2   *delectation*   Enjoyment.
3   *convenient seat*   Suitable estate.
4   *diffidence*   Distrust.
5   *anticipation*   Striking first.
6   *contemners*   Scorners.
7   *tract*   Period.
8   *incommodities*   Disadvantages.
9   *is consequent to*   Results from.

ing; no instruments of moving and removing such things as require much force; no knowledge of the face of the earth; no account of time; no arts; no letters; no society; and which is worst of all, continual fear, and danger of violent death; and the life of man, solitary, poor, nasty, brutish, and short.

10. It may seem strange to some man that has not well weighed these things that nature should thus dissociate and render men apt to invade and destroy one another; and he may therefore, not trusting to this inference, made from the passions,[1] desire perhaps to have the same confirmed by experience. Let him therefore consider with himself; when taking a journey, he arms himself and seeks to go well accompanied; when going to sleep, he locks his doors; when even in his house he locks his chests; and this when he knows there be laws and public officers, armed to revenge all injuries shall be done him; what opinion he has of his fellow subjects, when he rides armed; of his fellow citizens, when he locks his doors; and of his children, and servants, when he locks his chests. Does he not there as much accuse mankind by his actions as I do by my words? But neither of us accuse man's nature in it. The desires and other passions of man are in themselves no sin. No more are the actions that proceed from those passions till they know a law that forbids them; which, till laws be made, they cannot know; nor can any law be made till they have agreed upon the person that shall make it.

[63]   11. It may peradventure[2] be thought there was never such a time nor condition of war as this; and I believe it was never generally so, over all the world; but there are many places where they live so now. For the savage people in many places of America, except the government of small families, the concord whereof depends on natural lust, have no government at all, and live at this day in that brutish manner, as I said before. Howsoever, it may be perceived what manner of life there would be, where there were no common

power to fear, by the manner of life which men that have formerly lived under a peaceful government use to degenerate into a civil war.

12. But though there had never been any time wherein particular men were in a condition of war one against another; yet in all times kings and persons of sovereign authority, because of their independency, are in continual jealousies, and in the state and posture of gladiators, having their weapons pointing and their eyes fixed on one another, that is, their forts, garrisons, and guns upon the frontiers of their kingdoms, and continual spies upon their neighbors, which is a posture of war. But because they uphold thereby the industry of their subjects, there does not follow from it that misery which accompanies the liberty of particular men.

13. To this war of every man against every man, this also is consequent; that nothing can be unjust. The notions of right and wrong, justice and injustice, have there no place. Where there is no common power, there is no law; where no law, no injustice. Force and fraud are in war the two cardinal virtues. Justice and injustice are none of the faculties[3] neither of the body nor mind. If they were, they might be in a man that were alone in the world, as well as his senses and passions. They are qualities that relate to men in society, not in solitude. It is consequent also to the same condition that there be no propriety,[4] no dominion, no *mine* and *thine* distinct; but only that to be every man's that he can get, and for so long as he can keep it. And thus much for the ill condition which man by mere nature is actually placed in; though with a possibility to come out of it, consisting partly in the passions, partly in his reason.

In such a war nothing is unjust.

14. The passions that incline men to peace are fear of death, desire of such things as are necessary to commodious living, and a hope by their industry to obtain them. And reason suggests convenient articles of peace upon which men may be drawn to agreement. These articles are they which otherwise are called the laws of nature, whereof I

The passions that incline men to peace.

---

1   *this inference, made from the passions* My derivation of this, from the nature of the passions.
2   *peradventure* Possibly.

3   *faculties* Natural capacities.
4   *propriety* Ownership.

*Explains why property rights don't exist

shall speak more particularly in the two following chapters.

[64] ## Chapter 14: Of the First and Second Natural Laws, and of Contracts

Right of nature what. 1. The right of nature, which writers commonly call *jus naturale*, is the liberty each man has to use his own power as he will himself for the preservation of his own nature; that is to say, of his own life; and consequently, of doing anything which, in his own judgment and reason, he shall conceive to be the aptest means thereunto.

Liberty what. 2. By Liberty is understood, according to the proper signification of the word, the absence of external impediments; which impediments may oft take away part of a man's power to do what he would, but cannot hinder him from using the power left him according as his judgment and reason shall dictate to him.

A law of nature what. 3. A Law of Nature (*lex naturalis*) is a precept or general rule, found out by reason, by which a man is forbidden to do that which is destructive of his life, or takes away the means of preserving the same, and to omit that by which he thinks it may be best preserved. For though they that speak of this subject use to confound[1] *jus* and *lex*, *right* and *law*; yet they ought to be distinguished, because right consists in liberty to do or to forbear; whereas law determines and binds to one of them;[2] so that law and right differ as much as obligation and liberty, which in one and the same matter are inconsistent.

Difference of right and law.

Naturally[3] every man has right to every thing. 4. And because the condition of man (as has been declared in the precedent chapter) is a condition of war of every one against every one, in which case every one is governed by his own reason, and there is nothing he can make use of that may not be a help unto him in preserving his life against his enemies; it follows that in such a condition every man has a right to every thing, even to one another's body. And therefore, as long

as this natural right of every man to every thing endures, there can be no security to any man, how strong or wise soever he be, of living out the time which nature ordinarily allows men to live. And consequently it is a precept, or general rule of reason *that every man ought to endeavor peace, as far as he has hope of obtaining it; and when he cannot obtain it, that he may seek and use all helps and advantages of war.*[4] The first branch of which rule contains the first and fundamental law of nature, which is *to seek peace and follow it*. The second, the sum of the right of nature, which is *by all means we can to defend ourselves*.

The fundamental law of nature, to seek peace.

5. From this fundamental law of nature, by which men are commanded to endeavor peace, is derived this second law: that a man be willing, when others are so too, as far forth as for peace and defense of himself he shall think it necessary, to lay down[5] this right to all things; and be contented with so much liberty against other men as he would allow other men against himself. For as long as every man holds this right of doing anything he likes, so long are all men in the condition of war. But if other men will not lay down their right, as well as he, then there is no reason for anyone to divest himself of his, for that were to expose himself to prey, which no man is bound to, rather than to dispose himself to peace. This is that law of the gospel: Whatsoever you require that others should do to you, that do ye to them.[6] And that law of all men, quod tibi fieri non vis, alteri ne feceris.[7]

The second law of nature. Contract in way of peace. [65]

6. To lay down a man's right to anything is to divest himself of the liberty of hindering another

What it is to lay down a right.

1 *use to confound* Commonly confuse.
2 *determines and binds to one of them* Picks one of them and commands it.
3 *Naturally* In the state of nature.
4 *every man ... of war* The fundamental precept or general rule consists of two parts: the first part is the first or fundamental law of nature; the second part is the right of nature.
5 *lay down* Renounce.
6 *Whatsoever you ... to them* Hobbes is wrong about what is "the law of the gospel." The gospel recommends, "Whatsoever you wish others to do to you, that do ye to them" (Matthew 7.12). At 15.35, Hobbes gives the so-called negative Golden Rule: "*Do not that to another which thou wouldest not have done to thyself.*"
7 *quod tibi ... ne feceris* Latin: what you do not want done to you, do not do to another.

of the benefit of his own right to the same.[1] For he that renounces or passes away his right gives not to any other man a right which he had not before, because there is nothing to which every man had not right by nature, but only stands out of his way that he may enjoy his own original right without hindrance from him, not without hindrance from another. So that the effect which redounds to one man by another man's defect[2] of right is but so much diminution of impediments to the use of his own right original.

Renouncing a right what it is. 7. Right is laid aside either by simply renouncing it or by transferring it to another. By *simply* Renouncing, when he cares not to whom the benefit thereof redoubeth.[3] **Transferring right what.** By Transferring, when he intends the benefit thereof to some certain person or persons. And when a man has in either manner abandoned or granted away his **Obligation.** right, then is he said to be Obliged or Bound, not to hinder those to whom such right is granted, or abandoned, from the benefit of it; and that **Duty.** he *ought*, and it is Duty, not to make void that voluntary act of his own; and that such hindrance **Injustice.** is Injustice and Injury, as being *sine jure*;[4] the right being before renounced or transferred. So that *injury* or *injustice*, in the controversies of the world, is somewhat like to that which in the disputations of scholars is called *absurdity*. For as it is there called an absurdity to contradict what one maintained in the beginning, so in the world it is called injustice and injury voluntarily to undo that which from the beginning he had voluntarily done. The way by which a man either simply renounces or transfers his right is a declaration or signification by some voluntary and sufficient sign or signs that he does so renounce or transfer or has so renounced or transferred the same to him that accepts it. And these signs are either words only, or actions only; or, as it happens most often, both words and actions. And the same are the Bonds, by which men are bound and obliged, bonds that have their strength, not from their own nature (for nothing is more easily broken than a man's word), but from fear of some evil consequence upon the rupture.

8. Whensoever a man transfers his right, or renounces it, it is either in consideration of some right reciprocally transferred to himself, or for some other good he hopes for thereby. For it is a voluntary act; and of the voluntary acts of every man, the object is some *good to himself*. And therefore there be some rights which no man can be understood by any words, or other signs, to have **Not all rights are alienable.** abandoned or transferred. As first a man cannot lay down the right of resisting them that assault him by force to take away his life, because he cannot be understood to aim thereby at any good to himself. The same may be said of wounds, and chains, and imprisonment, both because there is no benefit consequent to such patience,[5] as there is to the patience of suffering another to be wounded or imprisoned, as also because a man cannot tell when he sees men proceed against him by violence whether they intend his death or not. And lastly the motive and end for which this renouncing and transferring of right is introduced is nothing else but the security of a man's person in his life, and in the means of so preserving life as not to be weary of it. And therefore if a man by words, or other signs, seem to despoil [deprive] himself of the end for which those signs were intended, he is not to be understood as if he meant it, or that it was his will, but that he was ignorant of how such words and actions were to be interpreted.

9. The mutual transferring of right is that **Contract what.** which men call Contract.

10. There is difference between transferring of right to the thing, and transferring or tradition,[6] that is, delivery of the thing itself. For the thing may be delivered together with the translation of the right, as in buying and selling with ready money, or exchange of goods or lands; and it may be delivered some time after.

[66]

---

1 *To lay ... the same* That is: when a person renounces his right to something he thus deprives himself of the liberty of blocking someone else from getting the benefit of doing the same thing.
2 *defect* Absence.
3 *redoubeth* Transfers.
4 *sine jure* Latin: without right.
5 *such patience* Putting up with such things.
6 *tradition* Handing over.

11. Again, one of the contractors may deliver the thing contracted for on his part, and leave the other to perform his part at some determinate time after, and in the meantime be trusted; and then the contract on his part is called Pact or Covenant; or both parts may contract now to perform hereafter, in which cases he that is to perform in time to come, being trusted, his performance is called *keeping of promise*, or faith, and the failing of performance, if it be voluntary, *violation of faith*.

Covenant what.

12. When the transferring of right is not mutual, but one of the parties transfers in hope to gain thereby friendship or service from another or from his friends; or in hope to gain the reputation of charity or magnanimity; or to deliver his mind from the pain of compassion; or in hope of reward in heaven; this is not contract, but Gift, Free Gift, Grace; which words signify one and the same thing.

Free gift.

13. Signs of contract are either *express*[1] or *by inference*. Express are words spoken with understanding of what they signify; and such words are either of the time *present* or *past*, as, *I give, I grant, I have given, I have granted, I will that this be yours*; or of the future, as, *I will give, I will grant*, which words of the future are called Promise.

Signs of contract express.

14. Signs by inference are sometimes the consequence of words, sometimes the consequence of silence, sometimes the consequence of actions, sometimes the consequence of forbearing an action, and generally a sign by inference, of any contract, is whatsoever sufficiently argues[2] the will of the contractor.

Signs of contract by inference.
[67]

15. Words alone, if they be of the time to come, and contain a bare promise, are an insufficient sign of a free gift and therefore not obligatory. For if they be of the time to come, as, *tomorrow I will give*, they are a sign I have not given yet, and consequently that my right is not transferred, but remains till I transfer it by some other act. But if the words be of the time present or past, as, *I have given*, or *do give to be delivered tomorrow*, then is my tomorrow's right given away

Free gift passes by words of the present or past.

today; and that by the virtue of the words, though there were no other argument of my will. And there is a great difference in the signification of these words, *volo hoc tuum esse cras*, and *cras dabo*; that is, between *I will that this be thine tomorrow*, and, *I will give it thee tomorrow*, for the word *I will*, in the former manner of speech, signifies an act of the will present; but in the latter, it signifies a promise of an act of the will to come; and therefore the former words, being of the present, transfer a future right; the latter, that be of the future, transfer nothing. But if there be other signs of the will to transfer a right besides words, then, though the gift be free, yet may the right be understood to pass by words of the future, as if a man propound[3] a prize to him that comes first to the end of a race, the gift is free; and though the words be of the future, yet the right passes, for if he would not have his words so be understood, he should not have let them run.

16. In contracts the right passes, not only where the words are of the time present or past, but also where they are of the future, because all contract is mutual translation[4] or change of right; and therefore he that promises only, because he has already received the benefit for which he promises, is to be understood as if he intended the right should pass, for unless he had been content to have his words so understood, the other would not have performed his part first. And for that cause, in buying and selling, and other acts of contract, a promise is equivalent to a covenant, and therefore obligatory.

Signs of contract are words both of the past, present, and future.

17. He that performs first in the case of a contract is said to Merit that which he is to receive by the performance of the other, and he has it as *due*. Also when a prize is propounded to many, which is to be given to him only that wins, or money is thrown amongst many to be enjoyed by them that catch it, though this be a free gift; yet so to win or so to catch is to *merit*, and to have it as Due. For the right is transferred in the propounding of the prize and in throwing down the money, though it be not determined to whom, but by the

Merit what.

---

1   *express* Explicit.
2   *argues* Indicates.

3   *propound* Propose.
4   *translation* Transfer.

event of the contention.[1] But there is between these two sorts of merit this difference, that in contract I merit by virtue of my own power and the contractor's need, but in this case of free gift I am enabled to merit only by the benignity of the giver; in contract I merit at the contractor's hand [68] that he should depart with his right; in this case of gift, I merit not that the giver should part with his right, but that when he has parted with it, it should be mine rather than another's. And this I think to be the meaning of that distinction of the Schools[2] between *meritum congrui*[3] and *meritum condigni*.[4] For God Almighty, having promised paradise to those men, hoodwinked with carnal desires, that can walk through this world according to the precepts and limits prescribed by him, they say he that shall so walk shall merit paradise *ex congruo [from its appropriateness]*. But because no man can demand a right to it by his own righteousness, or any other power in himself, but by the free grace of God only, they say no man can merit paradise *ex condigno [from being deserved]*. This, I say, I think is the meaning of that distinction; but because disputers do not agree upon the signification of their own terms of art[5] longer than it serves their turn,[6] I will not affirm anything of their meaning; only this I say; when a gift is given indefinitely, as a prize to be contended for, he that wins merits, and may claim the prize as due.

Covenants of mutual trust, when invalid.

18. If a covenant be made wherein neither of the parties perform presently, but trust one another, in the condition of mere nature (which is a condition of war of every man against every man) upon any reasonable suspicion, it is void; but if there be a common power set over them both, with right and force sufficient to compel performance, it is not void. For he that performs first has no assurance the other will perform after, because the bonds of words are too weak to bridle men's ambition, avarice, anger, and other passions, without the fear of some coercive power; which in the condition of mere nature, where all men are equal, and judges of the justness of their own fears, cannot possibly be supposed. And therefore he which performs first does but betray himself to his enemy, contrary to the right he can never abandon of defending his life and means of living.

19. But in a civil estate, where there a power set up to constrain those that would otherwise violate their faith, that fear is no more reasonable; and for that cause, he which by the covenant is to perform first is obliged so to do.

20. The cause of fear, which makes such a covenant invalid, must be always something arising after the covenant made, as some new fact or other sign of the will not to perform, else it cannot make the covenant void. For that which could not hinder a man from promising ought not to be admitted as a hindrance of performing.

21. He that transfers any right transfers the means of enjoying it, as far as lies in his power. As he that sells land is understood to transfer the herbage and whatsoever grows upon it; nor can he that sells a mill turn away the stream that drives it. And they that give to a man the right of government in sovereignty are understood to give him the right of levying money to maintain soldiers, and of appointing magistrates for the administration of justice.

Right to the end, contains right to the means.

22. To make covenants with brute beasts is impossible, because not understanding our speech, they understand not, nor accept of any translation of right, nor can translate any right to another; and without mutual acceptation, there is no covenant.

No covenant with beasts.

23. To make covenant with God is impossible but [except] by mediation of such as God speaks to either by revelation supernatural or by his lieutenants that govern under him and in his name; for otherwise we know not whether our covenants be accepted or not. And therefore they that vow anything contrary to any law of nature, vow in vain, as being a thing unjust to pay such vow. And if it be a thing commanded by the law of nature, it is not the vow, but the law that binds them.

Nor with God without special revelation.

---

1   *contention*   Contest.
2   *the Schools*   The Scholastic philosophers—medieval European academics, roughly twelfth to fifteenth century.
3   *meritum congrui*   Latin: what you deserve appropriately (because of having obeyed the rules).
4   *meritum condigni*   Latin: what you deserve because of your own worth.
5   *terms of art*   Technical terms.
6   *serves their turn*   Suits them.

No covenant, but of possible and future.

24. The matter or subject of a covenant is always something that falls under deliberation; for to covenant is an act of the will, that is to say, an act, and the last act, of deliberation, and is therefore always understood to be something to come, and which judged possible for him that covenants to perform.

25. And therefore, to promise that which is known to be impossible is no covenant. But if that prove impossible afterwards, which before was thought possible, the covenant is valid and binds, though not to the thing itself, yet to the value; or, if that also be impossible, to the unfeigned endeavor of performing as much as is possible, for to more no man can be obliged.

Covenants, how made void.

26. Men are freed of their covenants two ways, by performing or by being forgiven. For performance is the natural end of obligation, and forgiveness the restitution of liberty, as being a retransferring of that right in which the obligation consisted.

Covenants extorted by fear are valid.

27. Covenants entered into by fear, in the condition of mere nature, are obligatory. For example, if I covenant to pay a ransom or service for my life to an enemy, I am bound by it. For it is a contract, wherein one receives the benefit of life, the other is to receive money or service for it; and consequently, where no other law (as in the condition of mere nature) forbids the performance, the covenant is valid. Therefore prisoners of war, if trusted with the payment of their ransom, are obliged to pay it; and if a weaker prince make a disadvantageous peace with a stronger, for fear, he is bound to keep it, unless (as has been said before) there arises some new and just cause of fear to renew the war. And even in commonwealths, if I be forced to redeem myself from a thief by promising him money, I am bound to pay it, till the civil law discharge me [of that obligation]. For whatsoever I may lawfully do without obligation, the same I may lawfully covenant to do through fear; and what I lawfully covenant, I cannot lawfully break.

The former covenant to one makes void the later to another.

28. A former[1] covenant makes void a later. For a man that has passed away his right to one man today has it not to pass tomorrow to another; and therefore the later promise passes no right, but is null.

A man's covenant not to defend himself is void. [70]

29. A covenant not to defend myself from force, by force, is always void. For (as I have shown before) no man can transfer or lay down his right to save himself from death, wounds, and imprisonment, the avoiding whereof is the only end of laying down any right; and therefore the promise of not resisting force, in no covenant transfers any right, nor is obliging. For though a man may covenant thus, *unless I do so, or so, kill me*; he cannot covenant thus, *unless I do so, or so, I will not resist you when you come to kill me*. For man by nature chooses the lesser evil, which is danger of death in resisting, rather than the greater, which is certain and present death in not resisting. And this is granted to be true by all men in that they lead criminals to execution and prison with armed men, notwithstanding that such criminals have consented to the law by which they are condemned.

No man obliged to accuse himself.

30. A covenant to accuse oneself, without assurance of pardon, is likewise invalid. For in the condition of nature where every man is judge, there is no place for accusation; and in the civil state the accusation is followed with punishment, which, being force, a man is not obliged not to resist. The same is also true of the accusation of those by whose condemnation a man falls into misery, as of a father, wife, or benefactor. For the testimony of such an accuser, if it be not willingly given, is presumed to be corrupted by nature, and therefore not to be received; and where a man's testimony is not to be credited, he is not bound to give it. Also accusations upon torture are not to be reputed[2] as testimonies. For torture is to be used but as means of conjecture[3] and light in the further examination and search of truth; and what is in that case confessed tends to the ease of him that is tortured, not to the informing of the torturers, and therefore ought not to have the credit of a sufficient testimony, for whether he deliver himself by true or false accusation, he does it by the right of preserving his own life.

1 *former* Earlier.

2 *reputed* Regarded.
3 *conjecture* Hypothesis formation.

The end of an oath.

31. The force of words being (as I have formerly noted) too weak to hold men to the performance of their covenants, there are in man's nature but two imaginable helps to strengthen it. And those are either a fear of the consequence of breaking their word or a glory or pride in appearing not to need to break it. This latter is a generosity too rarely found to be presumed on, especially in the pursuers of wealth, command, or sensual pleasure, which are the greatest part of mankind. The passion to be reckoned upon is fear; whereof there be two very general objects: one, the power of spirits invisible; the other, the power of those men they shall therein offend. Of these two, though the former be the greater power; yet the fear of the latter is commonly the greater fear. The fear of the former is in every man his own religion, which has place in the nature of man before civil society. The latter has not so, at least not place enough to keep men to their promises, because in the condition of mere nature, the inequality of power is not discerned, but by the event of battle. So that before the time of civil society, or in the interruption thereof by war, there is nothing can strengthen a covenant of peace agreed on against the temptations of avarice, ambition, lust, or other strong desire, but the fear of that invisible power which they every one worship as God, and fear as a revenger of their perfidy. All therefore that can be done between two men not subject [71] to civil power is to put one another to swear by the God he fears; which *swearing*, or Oath, is a *form of speech, added to a promise, by which he that promises signifies that unless he perform he renounces the mercy of his God, or calls to him for vengeance on himself.* Such was the heathen form, *Let Jupiter kill me else, as I kill this beast.* So is our form, *I shall do thus, and thus, so help me God.* And this, with the rites and ceremonies which every one uses in his own religion, that the fear of breaking faith might be the greater.

The form of an oath.

No oath, but by God.

32. By this it appears that an oath taken according to any other form or rite than his that swears is in vain and no oath; and that there is no swearing by anything which the swearer thinks not God. For though men have sometimes used to swear by their kings, for fear, or flattery; yet they would have it thereby understood they attributed to them divine honor. And that swearing unnecessarily by God is but profaning of his name; and swearing by other things, as men do in common discourse, is not swearing, but an impious custom, gotten by too much vehemence of talking.

An oath adds nothing to the obligation.

33. It appears also that the oath adds nothing to the obligation. For a covenant, if lawful, binds in the sight of God, without the oath, as much as with it; if unlawful, binds not at all, though it be confirmed with an oath.

Chapter 15: Of Other Laws of Nature

The third law of nature, Justice.

1. From that [second] law of nature by which we are obliged to transfer to another such rights as, being retained, hinder the peace of mankind, there follows a third, which is this; *that men perform their covenants made*; without which, covenants are in vain and but empty words; and the right of all men to all things remaining, we are still in the condition of war.

Justice and injustice what.

2. And in this law of nature consists the fountain and original [source] of Justice. For where no covenant has preceded, there has no right been transferred; and every man has right to everything; and consequently, no action can be unjust. But when a covenant is made, then to break it is *unjust* and the definition of Injustice is no other than *the not performance of covenant.* And whatsoever is not unjust is *just.*[1]

Justice and propriety begin with the constitution of the commonwealth.

3. But because covenants of mutual trust, where there is a fear of not performance on either part (as has been said in the former chapter[2]), are invalid, though the original of justice be the making of covenants; yet injustice actually there can be none till the cause of such fear be taken away;

---

1   *whatsoever is not unjust is just* "Just" and "unjust" are normally contraries, not contradictories. That is: it is not normally understood that everything not one is the other: some things can be neither just nor unjust. However, Hobbes defines "just" in such a way that it becomes the contradictory of "unjust." Taking his definitions strictly, anyone in the state of nature who makes no covenants is just, because he is not unjust.

2   *the former chapter* Chapter 14.

which, while men are in the natural condition of war, cannot be done. Therefore before the names of *just* and *unjust* can have place, there must be some coercive power to compel men equally to the performance of their covenants by the terror of some punishment greater than the benefit they expect by the breach of their covenant, and to make good that propriety[1] which by mutual contract men acquire in recompense of the universal right they abandon; and such power there is none before the erection of a commonwealth. And this is also to be gathered out of the ordinary definition of justice in the Schools, for they say that *justice is the constant* [unwavering] *will of giving to every man his own.* And therefore where there is no *own,* that is, no propriety, there is no injustice; and where there is no coercive power erected, that is, where there is no commonwealth, there is no propriety, all men having right to all things; therefore where there is no commonwealth, there nothing is unjust. So that the nature of justice consists in keeping of valid covenants; but the validity of covenants begins not but with the constitution of a civil power sufficient to compel men to keep them; and then it is also that propriety begins.

Justice not contrary to reason. 4. The fool has said in his heart, there is no such thing as justice;[2] and sometimes also with his tongue, seriously alleging that every man's conservation and contentment being committed to his own care, there could be no reason why every man might not do what he thought conduced thereunto; and therefore also to make or not make, keep or not keep covenants was not against reason when it conduced to one's benefit. He does not therein deny that there be covenants; and that they are sometimes broken, sometimes kept; and that such breach of them may be called injustice, and the observance of them justice; but he questions whether injustice, taking away the fear of God (for the same fool has said in his heart there is no God), not sometimes stand with that reason which dictates to every man his own good; and particularly then, when it conduces to such a

benefit as shall put a man in a condition to neglect not only the dispraise and revilings, but also the power of other men. The kingdom of God is gotten by violence; but what if it could be gotten by unjust violence? Were it against reason so to get it, when it is impossible to receive hurt by it? And if it be not against reason, it is not against justice; or else justice is not to be approved for[3] good. From such reasoning as this, successful wickedness has obtained the name of virtue; and some that in all other things have disallowed the violation of faith, yet have allowed it when it is for the getting of a kingdom. And the heathen that believed that Saturn was deposed by his son Jupiter believed nevertheless the same Jupiter to be the avenger of injustice, somewhat like to a piece of law in Coke's[4] *Commentaries on Littleton,* where he says, if the right heir of the crown be attainted of treason, yet the crown shall descend to him, and *eo instante*[5] the attainder[6] be void; from which instances a man will be very prone to infer that when the heir apparent of a kingdom shall kill him that is in possession, though his father, you may call it injustice or by what other name you will; yet it can never be against reason, seeing all the voluntary actions of men tend to the benefit of themselves; and those actions are most reasonable that conduce most to their ends. This specious reasoning is nevertheless false.

5. For the question is not of promises mutual, where there is no security of performance on either side, as when there is no civil power erected over the parties promising, for such promises are no covenants; but either where one of the parties has performed already or where there is a power to make him perform, there is the question whether it be against reason, that is, against the benefit of

1 *that propriety* Those benefits.
2 *The fool ... as justice* This is a reference to the beginning of Psalm 14 or Psalm 53: "The fool hath said in his heart, There is no God."
3 *approved for* Approved as.
4 *Coke* Edward Coke (1552–1634), in his time England's leading theorist of the common law. This sometimes put him into opposition to King James I and later Charles I. His commentaries on the *Tenures* of Sir Thomas Littleton (c. 1422–81), an English jurist, are among his most famous works. They are in the first part of the *Institutes of the Laws of England* (1629).
5 *eo instante* Latin: at that moment.
6 *attainder* Conviction.

the other to perform or not. And I say it is not against reason. For the manifestation whereof we are to consider, first, that when a man does a thing, which notwithstanding anything can be foreseen and reckoned on[1] tends to his own destruction, howsoever some accident, which he could not expect, arriving may turn it to his benefit; yet such events do not make it reasonably or wisely done. Secondly, that in a condition of war, wherein every man to every man, for want of a common power to keep them all in awe, is an enemy, there is no man can hope by his own strength or wit to defend himself from destruction without the help of confederates, where every one expects the same defense by the confederation that any one else does; and therefore he which declares he thinks it reason to deceive those that help him can in reason expect no other means of safety than what can be had from his own single power. He, therefore, that breaks his covenant and consequently declares that he thinks he may with reason do so, cannot be received into any society that unite themselves for peace and defense but by the error of them that receive him; nor when he is received be retained in it without seeing the danger of their error; which errors a man cannot reasonably reckon upon as the means of his security; and therefore if he be left or cast out of society, he perishes; and if he live in society, it is by the errors of other men, which he could not foresee nor reckon upon, and consequently against the reason of his preservation; and so, as all men that contribute not to his destruction forbear[2] him only out of ignorance of what is good for themselves.

6. As for the instance of gaining the secure and perpetual felicity of heaven by any way, it is frivolous; there being but one way imaginable, and that is not breaking, but keeping of covenant.

7. And for the other instance of attaining sovereignty by rebellion, it is manifest that, though the event follow; yet because it cannot reasonably be expected, but rather the contrary, and because, by gaining it so, others are taught to gain the same in like manner, the attempt thereof is against reason. Justice therefore, that is to say, keeping of covenant, is a rule of reason by which we are forbidden to do anything destructive to our life, and consequently a law of nature.

8. There be some that proceed further and will not have the law of nature to be those rules which conduce to the preservation of man's life on earth, but [only] to the attaining of an eternal felicity after death, to which [felicity] they think the breach of covenant may conduce and consequently be just and reasonable; such are they that think it a work of merit to kill or depose or [74] rebel against the sovereign power constituted over them by their own consent. But because there is no natural knowledge of man's estate after death, much less of the reward that is then to be given to breach of faith, but only a belief grounded upon other men's saying that they know it supernaturally or that they know those that knew them that knew others that knew it supernaturally, breach of faith cannot be called a precept of reason or nature.

9. Others, that allow for a law of nature the keeping of faith, do nevertheless make exception of certain persons, [such] as heretics, and such as use not to[3] perform their covenant to others; and this also is against reason. For if any fault of a man be sufficient to discharge our covenant made, the same ought in reason to have been sufficient to have hindered the making of it.

10. The names of *just* and *unjust*, when they are attributed to men, signify one thing, and, when they are attributed to actions, another. When they are attributed to men, they signify conformity or inconformity of manners to reason. But when they are attributed to action they signify the conformity or inconformity to reason, not of manners, or manner of life, but of particular actions. A just man therefore is he that takes all the care he can that his actions may be all just; and an unjust man is he that neglects it. And such men are more often in our language styled by the names of righteous and unrighteous than

[margin: Covenants not discharged by the vice of the person to whom they are made.]

[margin: Justice of men, & justice of actions what.]

---

1   *notwithstanding ... reckoned on* As far as one can tell in advance.
2   *forbear* Put up with.

3   *use not to* Commonly do not.

just and unjust though the meaning be the same. Therefore a righteous man does not lose that title by one or a few unjust actions that proceed from sudden passion or mistake of things or persons; nor does an unrighteous man lose his character for such actions as he does or forbears to do for fear, because his will is not framed by the justice, but by the apparent benefit of what he is to do. That which gives to human actions the relish[1] of justice is a certain nobleness or gallantness of courage, rarely found, by which a man scorns to be beholding for the contentment of his life to fraud or breach of promise. This justice of the manners[2] is that which is meant where justice is called a virtue; and injustice, a vice.

11. But the justice of actions denominates men, not just, but guiltless; and the injustice of the same (which is also called injury) gives them but the name of guilty.[3]

Justice of manners and justice of actions.

12. Again, the injustice of manners is the disposition or aptitude to do injury, and is injustice before it proceed to act and without supposing any individual person injured. But the injustice of an action (that is to say, injury) supposes an individual person injured; namely him to whom the covenant was made; and therefore many times the injury is received by one man when the damage redounds to another. As when the master commands his servant to give money to a stranger; if it be not done, the injury is done to the master, whom he had before covenanted to obey; but the damage redounds to the stranger, to whom he had no obligation, and therefore could not injure him. And so also in commonwealths private men may remit to one another their debts,[4] but not robberies or other violences, whereby they are endamaged,[5] because the detaining[6] of debt is an injury to themselves; but robbery and violence are injuries to the person of the commonwealth.

[75]

13. Whatsoever is done to a man, conformable to his own will signified to the doer, is not injury to him. For if he that does it has not passed away his original right to do what he please by some antecedent covenant, there is no breach of covenant, and therefore no injury done him. And if he have, then his will to have it done, being signified, is a release of that covenant, and so again there is no injury done him.

Nothing done to a man by his own consent can be injury.

14. Justice of actions is by writers[7] divided into *commutative* and *distributive*; and the former they say consists in proportion arithmetical; the latter in proportion geometrical. Commutative, therefore, they place in the equality of value of the things contracted for; and distributive, in the distribution of equal benefit to men of equal merit. As if it were injustice to sell dearer than we buy, or to give more to a man than he merits. The value of all things contracted for is measured by the appetite[8] of the contractors, and therefore the just value is that which they be contented to give. And merit (besides that which is by covenant, where the performance on one part merits the performance of the other part, and falls under justice commutative, not distributive) is not due by justice, but is rewarded of[9] grace only. And therefore this distinction, in the sense wherein it uses to be expounded, is not right. To speak properly, commutative justice is the justice of a contractor; that is, a performance of covenant in buying and selling, hiring and letting to hire, lending and borrowing, exchanging, bartering, and other acts of contract.

Justice commutative and distributive.

15. And distributive justice [is] the justice of an arbitrator, that is to say, the act of defining what is just. Wherein, being trusted by them that make him arbitrator, if he perform his trust, he is said to distribute to every man his own; and this is indeed just distribution, and may be called, though improperly, distributive justice, but more

---

1   *relish* Savor.
2   *manners* Customary conduct.
3   *But the justice ... of guilty* The fact that an action is just doesn't make the person who did it just—it merely makes him guiltless in this case; and an unjust action (an injury) makes him be called guilty.
4   *remit to one another their debts* Let the debtor off from his debt.
5   *endamaged* Harmed.
6   *detaining* Non-payment.

---

7   *writers* Aristotle, Aquinas, and others.
8   *appetite* Desires.
9   *rewarded of* Rewarded by.

properly equity, which also is a law of nature, as shall be shown in due place.

The fourth law of nature, gratitude.

16. As justice depends on antecedent covenant, so does Gratitude depend on antecedent grace, that is to say, antecedent free gift, and is the fourth law of nature, which may be conceived in this form: *that a man which receives benefit from another of mere grace endeavor that he which gives it have no reasonable cause to repent him of*[1] *[regret] his good will.* For no man gives but with intention of good to himself, because gift is voluntary; and of all voluntary acts, the object is to every man his own good; of which, if men see [that] they shall be frustrated, there will be no beginning of benevolence or trust, nor consequently of mutual help, nor reconciliation of one man to another; and therefore they are to remain still in the condition of *war*, which is contrary to the first and fundamental law of nature which commands men to *seek peace.* The breach of this law is called *ingratitude* and has the same relation to grace that injustice has to obligation by covenant.

[76]

The fifth, mutual accommodation or complaisance.

17. A fifth law of nature is Complaisance; that is to say, *that every man strive to accommodate himself to the rest.* For the understanding whereof we may consider that there is in men's aptness to society a diversity of nature, rising from their diversity of affections, not unlike to that we see in stones brought together for building of an edifice. For as that stone which by the asperity[2] and irregularity of figure takes more room from others than itself fills, and for hardness cannot be easily made plain,[3] and thereby hinders the building, is by the builders cast away as unprofitable and troublesome; so also, a man that by asperity of nature will strive to retain those things which to himself are superfluous and to others necessary, and for the stubbornness of his passions cannot be corrected, is to be left or cast out of society as cumbersome thereunto. For seeing every man, not only by right, but also by necessity of nature, is supposed to endeavor all he can to obtain that which is necessary for his conservation, he that shall oppose himself against it for things superfluous is guilty of the war that thereupon is to follow, and therefore does that which is contrary to the fundamental law of nature, which commands *to seek peace.* The observers of this law may be called Sociable, (the Latins call them *commodi*); the contrary, *stubborn, insociable, forward, intractable.*

The sixth, facility to pardon.

18. A sixth law of nature is this: *that upon caution of the future time,*[4] *a man ought to pardon the offences past of them that, repenting, desire it.* For Pardon is nothing but granting of peace, which though granted to them that persevere in their hostility, be not peace, but fear; yet not granted to them that give caution of the future time is sign of an aversion to peace and therefore contrary to the law of nature.

The seventh, that in revenges men respect on the future good.

19. A seventh is, *that in revenges* (that is, retribution of evil for evil), *men look not at the greatness of the evil past, but the greatness of the good to follow.* Whereby we are forbidden to inflict punishment with any other design than for correction of the offender or direction of others. For this law is consequent to the next before it,[5] that commands pardon upon security of the future time. Besides, revenge without respect to the example and profit to come is a triumph or glorying in the hurt of another, tending to no end (for the end is always somewhat to come[6]); and glorying to no end is vain-glory and contrary to reason; and to hurt without reason tends to the introduction of war, which is against the law of nature, and is commonly styled by the name of *cruelty.*

The eighth, against contumely.[7]

20. And because all signs of hatred or contempt provoke to fight, insomuch as most men choose rather to hazard their life than not to be revenged, we may in the eighth place, for a law of nature, set down this precept; *that no man by deed, word, countenance, or gesture, declare hatred or contempt of another.* The breach of which law is commonly called *contumely.*

---

1   *repent him of* Regret.
2   *asperity* Sharpness.
3   *plain* Smooth.

4   *upon caution of the future time* Being careful with a view to the future.
5   *is consequent to the next before it* Follows from the previous one.
6   *somewhat to come* Something in the future.
7   *contumely* Gratuitous insult.

THE EARLY MODERN PERIOD

The ninth, against pride.

21. The question who is the better man has no place in the condition of mere nature, where (as has been shown before) all men are equal. The inequality that now is has been introduced by the laws civil. I know that Aristotle in the first book of his *Politics*,[1] for a foundation of his doctrine, makes men by nature, some more worthy to command, meaning the wiser sort, such as he thought himself to be for his philosophy; others to serve, meaning those that had strong bodies, but were not philosophers as he, as master and servant were not introduced by consent of men, but by difference of wit;[2] which is not only against reason, but also against experience. For there are very few so foolish that had not rather govern themselves than be governed by others; nor when the wise, in their own conceit, contend by force with them who distrust their own wisdom, do they always, or often, or almost at any time, get the victory.[3] If nature therefore have made men equal, that equality is to be acknowledged; or if nature have made men unequal, yet because men that think themselves equal will not enter into conditions of peace, but upon equal terms, such equality must be admitted. And therefore for the ninth law of nature, I put this, *that every man acknowledge another for his equal by nature*. The breach of this precept is *pride*.

The tenth, against arrogance.

22. On this law depends another, that at the entrance into conditions of peace, no man require to reserve to[4] himself any right which he is not content should be reserved to every one of the rest. As it is necessary for all men that seek peace to lay down certain rights of nature, that is to say, not to have liberty to do all they list,[5] so is it necessary for man's life to retain some, as right to govern their own bodies, enjoy air, water, motion, ways to go from place to place, and all things else without which a man cannot live or not live well. If in this case, at the making of peace, men require

for themselves that which they would not have to be granted to others, they do contrary to the precedent law that commands the acknowledgement of natural equality, and therefore also against the law of nature. The observers of this law are those we call modest, and the breakers arrogant men. The Greeks call the violation of this law pleonexia, that is, a desire of more than their share.

The eleventh, equity.

23. Also, if *a man be trusted to judge between man and man*, it is a precept of the law of nature *that he deal equally between them*. For without that, the controversies of men cannot be determined but by war. He therefore that is partial[6] in judgment does what in him lies to deter men from the use of judges and arbitrators, and consequently (against the fundamental law of nature) is the cause of war.

24. The observance of this law, from the equal distribution to each man of that which in reason belonged to him, is called Equity, and (as I have said before) distributive justice; the violation, *acception of persons, prosopolepsia*.[7]

The twelfth, equal use of things common.

25. And from this follows another law: that such things as cannot be divided be enjoyed in common, if it can be; and if the quantity of the thing permit, without stint;[8] otherwise proportionably to the number of them that have right. For otherwise the distribution is unequal, and contrary to equity.

The thirteenth, of lot. [78]

26. But some things there be that can neither be divided nor enjoyed in common. Then, the law of nature which prescribes equity requires, *that the entire right, or else (making the use alternate) the first possession, be determined by lot*.[9] For equal distribution is of the law of nature; and other means of equal distribution cannot be imagined.

The fourteenth, of primogeniture, and first seizing.

27. Of *lots* there be two sorts, *arbitrary* and *natural*. Arbitrary is that which is agreed on by the competitors; natural is either *primogeniture*[10] (which the Greek calls *klerovomia*, which signifies, *given by lot*) or *first seizure*.

---

1   *the first book of his Politics*   Book 1, 3–7.
2   *wit*   Intellect.
3   *do they ... the victory*   They (those who think themselves wise) don't always, don't often, almost never win.
4   *reserve to*   Keep for.
5   *list*   Desire.
6   *partial*   Biased.
7   *acception of persons, prosopolepsia*   Both mean *favoritism*.
8   *stint*   Restriction.
9   *lot*   Lottery.
10 *primogeniture*   Being first-born.

28. And therefore those things which cannot be enjoyed in common, nor divided, ought to be adjudged to the first possessor; and in some cases to the first born, as acquired by lot.

The fifteenth, of mediators.

29. It is also a law of nature, *that all men that mediate peace be allowed safe conduct.* For the law that commands peace, as the *end*, commands intercession,[1] as the *means*; and to intercession the means is safe conduct.

The sixteenth, of submission to arbitrement.[2]

30. And because, though men be never so willing to observe these laws, there may nevertheless arise questions concerning a man's action; first, whether it were done or not done; secondly, if done, whether against the law or not against the law; the former whereof is called a question *of fact*, the latter a question *of right*; therefore unless the parties to the question covenant mutually to stand to the sentence[3] of another, they are as far from peace as ever. This other, to whose sentence they submit, is called an Arbitrator. And therefore it is of the law of nature *that they that are at controversy submit their right to the judgment of an arbitrator.*

The seventeenth, no man is his own judge.

31. And seeing every man is presumed to do all things in order to his own benefit, no man is a fit arbitrator in his own cause; and if he were never so fit,[4] yet equity allowing to each party equal benefit, if one be admitted to be judge, the other is to be admitted also; and so the controversy, that is, the cause of war, remains, against the law of nature.

The eighteenth, no man is to be judge that has in him a natural cause of partiality.

32. For the same reason no man in any cause ought to be received for arbitrator to whom greater profit or honor or pleasure apparently arises out of the victory of one party than of the other, for he has taken (though an unavoidable bribe, yet) a bribe; and no man can be obliged to trust him. And thus also the controversy and the condition of war remains, contrary to the law of nature.

The nineteenth, of witnesses.

33. And in a controversy of *fact*, the judge being to give no more credit to one than to the other,[5] if there be no other arguments, must give credit to a third; or to a third and fourth; or more, for else the question is undecided, and left to force, contrary to the law of nature.

34. These are the laws of nature, dictating peace, for a means of the conservation of men in multitudes; and which only concern the doctrine of civil society. There be other things tending to the destruction of particular men, as drunkenness, and all other parts of intemperance, which may therefore also be reckoned amongst those things which the law of nature has forbidden, but are not necessary to be mentioned, nor are pertinent enough to this place. [79]

A rule by which the laws of nature may easily be examined.

35. And though this may seem too subtle a deduction of the laws of nature to be taken notice of by all men, whereof the most part are too busy in getting food, and the rest too negligent to understand; yet to leave all men inexcusable, they have been contracted into one easy sum, intelligible even to the meanest capacity; and that is: *Do not that to another which thou wouldest not have done to thyself;* which shows him that he has no more to do in learning the laws of nature but, when weighing the actions of other men with his own they seem too heavy, to put them into the other part of the balance, and his own into their place, that his own passions and self-love may add nothing to the weight; and then there is none of these laws of nature that will not appear unto him very reasonable.

The laws of nature oblige in conscience always, but in effect then only where there is security.

36. The laws of nature oblige *in foro interno,* that is to say, they bind to a desire they should take place; but *in foro externo;*[6] that is, to the putting them in act, not always. For he that should be modest and tractable, and perform all he promises in such time and place where no man else should do so, should but make himself a prey to others, and procure his own certain ruin, contrary to the ground of all laws of nature which tend to nature's

---

1   *intercession* Pleading on behalf of another.
2   *arbitrement* Arbitration.
3   *stand to the sentence* Abide by the judgment.
4   *if he were never so fit* Even if he were fit [to judge his own cause].
5   *being to ... the other* Should not give more credence to one side than to the other.
6   *in foro interno ... in foro externo* Latin: literally, *before the internal court / before the external court.* The usual meaning of these terms is that the "internal court" is the voice of one's conscience, and the "external court" is the judgment of other people or the law court.

preservation. And again, he that having sufficient security that others shall observe the same laws towards him, observes them not himself, seeks not peace, but war, and consequently the destruction of his nature by violence.

37. And whatsoever laws bind *in foro interno* may be broken, not only by a fact[1] contrary to the law, but also by a fact according to it, in case a man think it contrary. For though his action in this case be according to the law; yet his purpose was against the law; which, where the obligation is *in foro interno*, is a breach.

The laws of nature are eternal;

38. The laws of nature are immutable and eternal, for injustice, ingratitude, arrogance, pride, iniquity, acception of persons, and the rest can never be made lawful. For it can never be that war shall preserve life, and peace destroy it.

And yet easy.

39. The same laws, because they oblige only to a desire and endeavor, mean an unfeigned and constant endeavor, are easy to be observed. For in that they require nothing but endeavor, he that endeavors their performance fulfils them; and he that fulfils the law is just.

The science of these laws is the true moral philosophy.

40. And the science of them is the true and only moral philosophy. For moral philosophy is nothing else but the science of what is *good* and *evil* in the conversation [interactions] and society of mankind. *Good* and *evil* are names that signify our appetites and aversions, which in different tempers, customs, and doctrines of men are different; and divers men differ not only in their judgment on the senses of what is pleasant and unpleasant to the taste, smell, hearing, touch, and sight; but also of what is conformable or disagreeable to reason in the actions of common life. Nay, the same man, in divers times, differs from himself; and one time praises, that is, calls *good*, what another time he dispraises, and calls *evil*. From whence arise disputes, controversies, [80] and at last war. And therefore so long a man is in the condition of mere nature (which is a condition of war), as private appetite is the measure of good and evil; and consequently all men agree on this, that peace is good, and therefore also the way or means of peace, which (as I have shown be-

fore) are *justice, gratitude, modesty, equity, mercy,* and the rest of the laws of nature, are good; that is to say, *moral virtues*; and their contrary *vices,* evil. Now the science of virtue and vice is moral philosophy; and therefore the true doctrine of the laws of nature is the true moral philosophy. But the writers of moral philosophy, though they acknowledge the same virtues and vices; yet, not seeing wherein consisted their goodness, nor that they come to be praised as the means of peaceable, sociable, and comfortable living, place them in a mediocrity of[2] passions, as if not the cause, but the degree of daring, made fortitude, or not the cause, but the quantity of a gift, made liberality.

41. These dictates of reason men use to call by the name of laws, but improperly; for they are but conclusions or theorems concerning what conduces to the conservation and defense of themselves; whereas law, properly, is the word of him that by right has command over others. But yet if we consider the same theorems as delivered in the word of God that by right commands all things, then are they properly called *laws.*

Chapter 16: Of Persons, Authors, and Things Personated

A person what.

1. A person is he *whose words or actions are considered, either as his own, or as representing the words or actions of another man,*[3] *or of any other thing to whom they are attributed, whether truly or by fiction.*

Person natural, and artificial.

2. When they are considered as his own, then is he called a *natural person*; and when they are considered as representing the words and actions of another, then is he a *feigned* or *artificial* person.

The word *person,* whence.

3. The word person is Latin, instead whereof the Greeks have *prosopon,* which signifies the *face,* as *persona* in Latin signifies the *disguise* or

---

2   *in a mediocrity of* Among medium-strength.

3   *as representing ... another man* The proviso that an entity can be considered a person when its words and actions represent those of another person is placed here because Hobbes wants to consider the state as a person—and its words and actions represent the people in it.

---

1   *a fact* An action.

[81]

outward appearance of a man, counterfeited on the stage; and sometimes more particularly that part of it which disguises the face, as a mask or vizard;[1] and from the stage has been translated to any represener of speech and action, as well in tribunals as theatres. So that a *person* is the same that an *actor* is, both on the stage and in common conversation; and to *personate* is to *act* or *represent* himself or another; and he that acts another is said to bear his person or act in his name (in which sense Cicero uses it where he says, *Unus sustineo tres personas: mei, adversarii, et judicis;*[2] I bear three persons: my own, my adversary's, and the judge's), and is called in divers occasions, diversely, as a *represener*, or *representative*, a *lieutenant*, a *vicar*, an *attorney*, a *deputy*, a *procurator*, an *actor*, and the like.

Actor, author.

4. Of persons artificial, some have their words and actions *owned*[3] by those whom they represent. And then the person is the *actor*; and he that owns his words and actions is the Author, in which case the actor acts by authority. For that which in speaking of goods and possessions is called an *owner*, and in Latin *dominus* in Greek *kurios*; speaking of actions, is called author. And as the right of possession is called dominion, so the right of doing any action is called Authority

Authority.

and sometimes *warrant*. So that by authority is always understood a right of doing any act; and *done by authority*, done by commission or license from him whose right it is.

Covenants by authority bind the author.

5. From hence it follows that when the actor makes a covenant by authority, he binds thereby the author no less than if he had made it[4] himself, and no less subjects him to all the consequences of the same. And therefore all that has been said formerly (Chapter 14) of the nature of covenants between man and man in their natural capacity is true also when they are made by their actors, representers, or procurators, that have authority from them, so far forth as is in their commission, but no further.

---

1   *vizard* Visor.
2   *Unus sustineo ... et judicis* Cicero, *De oratore* (*On the Orator*, 55 BCE) 2.102.
3   *owned* Identified as their own.
4   *had made it* Said those words.

6. And therefore he that makes a covenant with the actor, or represener, not knowing the authority he hath, does it at his own peril. For no man is obliged by a covenant whereof he is not author, nor consequently by a covenant made against or beside the authority he gave.

But not the actor.

7. When the actor does anything against the law of nature by command of the author, if he be obliged by former covenant to obey him, not he, but the author breaks the law of nature, for though the action be against the law of nature, yet it is not his; but, contrarily, to refuse to do it is against the law of nature that forbids breach of covenant.

The authority is to be shown.

8. And he that makes a covenant with the author by mediation of the actor, not knowing what authority he has, but only takes his word, in case such authority be not made manifest unto him upon demand, is no longer obliged; for the covenant made with the author is not valid without his [the author's] counter-assurance. But if he that so covenants knew beforehand he was to expect no other assurance than the actor's word, then is the covenant valid, because the actor in this case makes himself the author. And therefore, as when the authority is evident, the covenant obliges the author, not the actor, so when the authority is feigned, it obliges the actor only, there being no author but himself.

Things personated, inanimate.

9. There are few things that are incapable of being represented by fiction. Inanimate things, as a church, a hospital, a bridge, may be personated by a rector, master, or overseer. But things inanimate cannot be authors, nor therefore give authority to their actors. Yet the actors may have authority to procure their maintenance, given them by those that are owners or governors of those things. And therefore such things cannot be personated before there be some state of civil government.

[82]

Irrational.

10. Likewise children, fools, and madmen that have no use of reason may be personated by guardians or curators, but can be no authors during that time of any action done by them, longer than (when they shall recover the use of reason) they shall judge the same reasonable. Yet during the folly he that has right of governing them may

give authority to the guardian. But this again has no place but in a state civil, because before such estate there is no dominion of persons.

False gods. 11. An idol or mere figment of the brain may be personated, as were the gods of the heathen, which, by such officers as the state appointed, were personated and held possessions and other goods and rights, which men from time to time dedicated and consecrated unto them. But idols cannot be authors; for an idol is nothing. The authority proceeded from the state; and therefore before introduction of civil government the gods of the heathen could not be personated.

The true God. 12. The true God may be personated.[1] As he was, first, by Moses, who governed the Israelites (that were not his, but God's people), not in his own name (with *hoc dicit Moses* [*thus Moses says*], but in God's name, with (*hoc dicit Dominus* [*thus the Lord says*]). Secondly, by the Son of Man, his own son, our blessed Savior Jesus Christ, that came to reduce[2] the Jews and induce all nations into the kingdom of his Father; not as of himself, but as sent from his Father. And thirdly, by the Holy Ghost or Comforter, speaking and working in the Apostles; which Holy Ghost was a Comforter that came not of himself, but was sent and proceeded from them both on the day of Pentecost.

A multitude of men, how one person. 13. A multitude of men are made *one* person when they are by one man, or one person, represented, so that it be done with the consent of every one of that multitude in particular. For it is the *unity* of the represented, not the *unity* of the represented, that makes the person *one*. And it is the representer that bears the person, and but one person; and *unity* cannot otherwise be understood in multitude.

14. And because the multitude naturally is not *one*, but *many*, they cannot be understood for

one, but in any authors, of everything their representative says or does in their name, every man giving their common representer authority from himself in particular, and owning all the actions the representer does, in case they give him authority without stint; otherwise, when they limit him in what, and [in] how far, he shall represent them, none of them owns more than they gave him commission to act. Every one is author.

15. And if the representative consist of many men, the voice of the greater number must be considered as the voice of them all. For if the lesser number pronounce (for example) in the affirmative, and the greater in the negative, there will be negatives more than enough to destroy the affirmatives; and thereby the excess of negatives, standing uncontradicted, are the only voice the representative hath. An actor may be many men made one by plurality of voices.

16. And a representative of even number, especially when the number is not great, whereby the contradictory voices are oftentimes equal, is therefore oftentimes mute and incapable of action. Yet in some cases contradictory voices, equal in number, may determine a question (as [for example] in condemning or absolving, equality of votes, even in that they condemn not, do absolve) but not on the contrary condemn, in that they absolve not. For when a cause is heard, not to condemn is to absolve; but on the contrary to say that not absolving is condemning is not true. The like it is in deliberation of executing[3] presently or deferring till another time; for when the voices are equal, the not decreeing execution is a decree of dilation.[4] [83]

Representatives, when the number is even, unprofitable.

17. Or if the number be odd, as three or more men or assemblies, whereof every one has, by a negative voice, authority to take away the effect of all the affirmative voices of the rest, this number is no representative; by the diversity of opinions and interests of men, it becomes oftentimes, and in cases of the greatest consequence, a mute person and unapt, as for many things else, so for the government of a multitude, especially in time of war. Negative voice.

18. Of authors there be two sorts. The first simply so called, which I have before defined to

---

1 *The true God may be personated* This passage is Hobbes' attempt to support the idea of the Trinity—the idea that God is three persons in one: God is one person insofar as Moses "personated" God—speaks for God, representing God as the source of his words and deeds; a second person as "personated" by Jesus, and a third as "personated" by the apostles.

2 *reduce* Lead back, restore.

---

3 *executing* Doing something.

4 *dilation* Delaying.

be him that owns the action of another simply. The second is he that owns an action or covenant of another conditionally; that is to say, he undertakes to do it, if the other does it not, at or before a certain time. And these authors conditional are generally called Sureties, in Latin, *fidejussores* and *sponsores*; and particularly for debt, *praedes*; and for appearance before a judge or magistrate, *vades*.

Part 2: Of Commonwealth

[...]

Chapter 17: Of the Causes, Generation, and Definition of a Commonwealth

The end of common-wealth, particularly security.

1. The final cause, end, or design of men (who naturally love liberty, and dominion over others) in the introduction of that restraint upon themselves (in which we see them live in commonwealths) is the foresight [prospect] of their own preservation and of a more contented life thereby, that is to say, of getting themselves out from that miserable condition of war which is necessarily consequent (as has been shown[1]) to the natural passions of men, when there is no visible power to keep them in awe and tie them by fear of punishment to the performance of their covenants and observation of those laws of nature set down in the fourteenth and fifteenth chapters.

Chap 13.

Which is not to be had from the law of nature.

2. For the laws of nature (as *justice, equity, modesty, mercy*, and, in sum, *doing to others as we would be done to*) of themselves, without the terror of some power to cause them to be observed, are contrary to our natural passions that carry us to partiality, pride, revenge, and the like. And covenants without the sword are but words and of no strength to secure a man at all. Therefore, notwithstanding the laws of nature (which every one has then kept, when he has the will to keep them, when he can do it safely), if there be no power erected or not great enough for our security, every man will and may lawfully rely on his own strength and art for caution against all other men. And in all places, where men have lived

by small families, to rob and spoil[2] one another has been a trade, and so far from being reputed against the law of nature, that the greater spoils they gained, the greater was their honor; and men observed no other laws therein but the laws of honor, that is, to abstain from cruelty, leaving to men their lives and instruments of husbandry.[3] And as small families did then, so now do cities and kingdoms, which are but greater families[4] (for their own security), enlarge their dominions, upon all pretences of danger and fear of invasion or assistance that may be given to invaders, endeavor as much as they can to subdue or weaken their neighbors by open force and secret arts, for want of other caution, justly, and are remembered for it in after ages with honor.

Nor from the conjunction of a few men or families. [86]

3. Nor is it the joining together of a small number of men that gives them this security, because in small numbers, small additions on the one side or the other make the advantage of strength so great as is sufficient to carry the victory, and therefore gives encouragement to an invasion. The multitude sufficient to confide in for our security is not determined by any certain number, but by comparison with the enemy we fear; and [it] is then sufficient, when the odds of the enemy is not of so visible and conspicuous moment, to determine the event of war, as to move him to attempt.

Not from a great multitude, unless directed by one judgment.

4. And be there never so great[5] a multitude; yet if their actions be directed according to their particular judgments and particular appetites, they can expect thereby no defense nor protection, neither against a common enemy nor against the injuries of one another. For being distracted in opinions concerning the best use and application of their strength, they do not help but hinder one another; and [they] reduce their strength by

---

1   *as has been shown* See Chapter 13.

2   *rob and spoil* Strip of possessions by force.
3   *husbandry* Farming.
4   *cities and kingdoms ... greater families* Compare 20.15, which seems inconsistent with this passage. One way to make Hobbes' doctrine consistent is to maintain that when a family is big enough to withstand raids from others (and when the members have covenanted to make one or more members the sovereign), then a family is a commonwealth, and not otherwise.
5   *be there never so great* However great.

mutual opposition to nothing, whereby they are easily not only subdued by a very few that agree together, but also, when there is no common enemy, they make war upon each other for their particular interests. For if we could suppose a great multitude of men to consent in the observation of justice and other laws of nature, without a common power to keep them all in awe, we might as well suppose all mankind to do the same; and then there neither would be nor need to be any civil government or commonwealth at all, because there would be peace without subjection.

And that continually. 5. Nor is it enough for the security which men desire should last all the time of their life, that they be governed and directed by one judgment for a limited time, as in one battle or one war. For though they obtain a victory by their unanimous endeavor against a foreign enemy; yet afterwards, when either they have no common enemy, or he that by one part is held for an enemy is by another part held for a friend, they must needs by the difference of their interests dissolve and fall again into a war amongst themselves.

Why certain creatures without reason or speech do nevertheless live in society, without any coercive power. 6. It is true that certain living creatures, as bees and ants, live sociably one with another (which are therefore by Aristotle[1] numbered amongst political creatures), and yet have no other direction than their particular judgments and appetites, nor [do they have] speech, whereby one of them can signify to another what he thinks expedient for the common benefit; and therefore some man may perhaps desire to know why mankind cannot do the same. To which I answer,

7. First, that men are continually in competition for honor and dignity, which these creatures are not; and consequently amongst men there arises on that ground envy and hatred and finally war; but amongst these not so.

8. Secondly, that amongst these creatures the common good differs not from the private; and being by nature inclined to their private, they procure thereby the common benefit. But man, whose joy consists in comparing himself with other men, can relish nothing but what is eminent.[2]

9. Thirdly, that these creatures, having not, as man, the use of reason, do not see, nor think they see, any fault in the administration of their common business; whereas amongst men there are very many that think themselves wiser and abler to govern the public better than the rest; [87] and these strive to reform and innovate, one this way, another that way, and thereby bring it into distraction and civil war.

10. Fourthly, that these creatures, though they have some use of voice in making known to one another their desires and other affections; yet they want that art of words by which some men can represent to others that which is good in the likeness of evil and evil in the likeness of good, and augment or diminish the apparent greatness of good and evil, discontenting men and troubling their peace at their pleasure.

11. Fifthly, irrational creatures cannot distinguish between *injury and damage*;[3] and therefore as long as they be at ease, they are not offended with their fellows; whereas man is then most troublesome when he is most at ease; for then it is that he loves to show his wisdom, and control the actions of them that govern the commonwealth.

12. Lastly, the agreement of these creatures is natural; that of men is by covenant only, which is artificial; and therefore it is no wonder if there be somewhat else required, besides covenant, to make their agreement constant and lasting, which is a common power to keep them in awe and to direct their actions to the common benefit.

The generation of a commonwealth. 13. The only way to erect such a common power as may be able to defend them from the invasion of foreigners and the injuries of one another, and thereby to secure them in such sort as that by their own industry and by the fruits of the earth they may nourish themselves and live contentedly, is to confer all their power and

---

1   *Aristotle* In *History of Animals* 1.1. His assertion about bees and ants (and wasps, cranes, and humans) is usually translated as saying that they are all social animals—creatures "such as have some one common object in view."

2   *eminent* Conspicuous.

3   *injury and damage* The difference is that the former is willfully inflicted.

strength[1] upon one man or upon one assembly of men, that may reduce all their wills by plurality of voices unto one will; which is as much as to say, to appoint one man or assembly of men to bear their person; and every one to own and acknowledge himself to be author of whatsoever he that so bears their person shall act or cause to be acted in those things which concern the common peace and safety; and therein to submit their wills, every one to his will, and their judgments to his judgment.[2] This is more than consent or concord; it is a real unity of them all in one and the same person, made by covenant of every man with every man in such manner as if every man should say to every man, *I authorize and give up my right of governing myself to this man, or to this assembly of men, on this condition: that thou give up thy right to him, and authorize all his actions in like manner.* This done, the multitude so united in one person is called a Commonwealth; in Latin, *Civitas.* This is the generation of that great Leviathan, or rather, to speak more reverently, of that *mortal god* to which we owe, under the *immortal God,* our peace and defense. For by this authority, given him by every particular man in the commonwealth, he has the use of so much power and

[88] strength conferred on him that, by terror thereof, he is enabled to conform[3] the wills of them all to peace at home and mutual aid against their enemies abroad. And in him consists the essence of the commonwealth, which, to define it, is *one*

The definition of a commonwealth. *person, of whose acts a great multitude, by mutual covenants one with another, have made themselves every one the author, to the end he may use the strength and means of them all as he shall think expedient for their peace and common defense.*

14. And he that carries this person is called Sovereign, and said to have *sovereign power*; and every one besides, his Subject.

15. The attaining to this sovereign power is by two ways. One, by natural force, as when a man makes his children to submit themselves and their children to his government, as being able to destroy them if they refuse, or by war subdues his enemies to his will, giving them their lives on that condition. The other is when men agree amongst themselves to submit to some man, or assembly of men, voluntarily, on confidence to be protected by him against all others. This latter may be called a political commonwealth or commonwealth by *institution,* and the former [may be called] a commonwealth by *acquisition.* And first, I shall speak of a commonwealth by institution.

Sovereign, and subject, what.

Chapter 18: Of the Rights of Sovereigns by Institution

1. A *commonwealth* is said to be *instituted* when a *multitude* of men do agree and *covenant, every one with every one,* that to whatsoever *man* or *assembly of men* shall be given by the major part[4] the *right* to *present* the person of them all, that is to say, to be their *representative,* every one, as well he that *voted for it* as he that *voted against it,* shall *authorize* all the actions[5] and judgments of that man, or assembly of men, in the same manner as if they were his own, to the end to live peaceably amongst themselves and be protected against other men.

The act of instituting a commonwealth, what.

2. From this institution of a commonwealth are derived all the *rights* and *faculties*[6] of him or them, on whom the sovereign power is conferred by the consent of the people assembled.[7]

The consequences to such institutions, are:

---

1   *confer ... power and strength* If citizens confer all of their power and strength on the sovereign, it would appear that they would have none left for themselves.

2   *to submit ... his judgment* Each person wills to will what the sovereign wills and to judge as the sovereign judges.

3   *conform* Many editions have "conform," though there is some textual support for "form." "Conform" (shape according to a pattern) appears to make more sense.

4   *the major part* Majority vote.

5   *authorize all the actions* Perhaps an exaggeration. If a subject authorizes all of the sovereign's actions, then he would authorize the sovereign's killing or punishing of him, even though no one can ever lay down his right of self-preservation; though Hobbes sometimes says that a criminal punishes himself because he has authorized all of his sovereign's actions—see 18.3.

6   *faculties* Powers.

7   *on whom ... people assembled* The sovereign is the artificial person who governs his subjects. The sovereign

THOMA HO

1. The subjects cannot change the form of government.

3. First, because they covenant, it is to be understood they are not obliged by former covenant to anything repugnant hereunto. And consequently they that have already instituted a commonwealth, being thereby bound by covenant to own the actions and judgments of one, cannot lawfully make a new covenant amongst themselves to be obedient to any other, in anything whatsoever, without his permission. And therefore, they that are subjects to a monarch cannot without his leave cast off monarchy and return to the confusion of a disunited multitude nor transfer their person from him that bears it to another man or other assembly of men;[1] for

[89] they are bound, every man to every man, to own and be reputed author of all that he that already is their sovereign shall do and judge fit to be done; so that any one man dissenting, all the rest should break their covenant made to that man, which is injustice; and they have also every man given the sovereignty to him that bears their person; and therefore if they depose him, they take from him that which is his own, and so again it is injustice. Besides, if he that attempts to depose his sovereign be killed or punished by him for such attempt, he is author of his own punishment, as being, by the institution, author of all his sovereign shall do; and because it is injustice for a man to do anything for which he may be punished by his own authority, he is also upon that title unjust. And whereas some men have pretended for their disobedience to their sovereign a new covenant, made, not with men but with God, this also is unjust; for there is no covenant with God but by mediation of somebody that represents God's person, which none does but God's lieutenant

who has the sovereignty under God.[2] But this pretence of covenant with God is so evident a lie, even in the pretenders' own consciences, that it is not only an act of an unjust, but also of a vile and unmanly disposition.

4. Secondly, because the right of bearing the person of them all is given to him [whom] they make sovereign by covenant only of one to another and not of him to any of them, there can happen no breach of covenant on the part of the sovereign;[3] and consequently none of his subjects, by any pretence of forfeiture, can be freed from his subjection. That he which is made sovereign makes no covenant with his subjects beforehand is manifest,[4] because either he must make it with the whole multitude, as one party to the covenant, or he must make a several[5] covenant with every man. With the whole, as one party, it is impossible, because as yet they are not one person; and if he make so many several covenants as there be men, those covenants after he has the sovereignty are void, because what act soever can be pretended[6] by any one of them for breach thereof is the act both of himself and of all the rest, because done in the person and by the right of every one of them in particular. Besides, if any one or more of them pretend a breach of the covenant made by the sovereign at his institution, and others or one other of his subjects or himself alone pretend there was no such breach, [then] there is in this case no judge to decide the controversy, [and] it returns therefore to the sword again, and every man recovers the right of protecting himself by his own strength, contrary to the design they had in the institution. It is therefore in vain to grant sovereignty by way of precedent[7] covenant. The opinion that any monarch receives his power by covenant, that is to say, on condition, proceeds

2. Sovereign power cannot be forfeited.

---

is a single human being in a monarchy. In an aristocracy, the sovereign is the group of people who rule. In a democracy, the sovereign is the entire citizenry, considered as a unity, not in the multiplicity of each subject.

1 *nor transfer ... of men* Hobbes is probably criticizing the Scots, who in the National Covenant (1638) made a covenant that appeared to supersede one that Hobbes thought they already had with the king; and criticizing the English who, with the Scots, did the same in the Solemn League and Covenant (1643).

2 *some men ... under God* See previous note.

3 *there can ... the sovereign* The sovereign is not a party of the covenant, as Hobbes says in the next sentence.

4 *That he ... is manifest* King James I wrote, "I deny any such contract to be made [between the king and the people]" ("The Trew Law of Free Monarchies," 1598).

5 *a several* An individual.

6 *pretended* Put forth.

7 *precedent* Pre-existing.

from want of understanding this easy truth: that covenants being but words and breath, have no force to oblige, contain, constrain, or protect any man, but what it has from the public sword, that is, from the untied hands of that man or assembly of men that has the sovereignty, and whose actions [90] are avouched[1] by them all, and performed by the strength of them all in him united. But when an assembly of men is made sovereign, then no man imagines any such covenant to have passed in the institution; for no man is so dull as to say, for example, the people of Rome made a covenant with the Romans to hold the sovereignty on such or such conditions, which not performed, the Romans might lawfully depose the Roman people. That men see not the reason to be alike in a monarchy and in a popular government proceeds from the ambition of some that are kinder to the government of an assembly, whereof they may hope to participate, than of monarchy, which they despair to enjoy.

3. No man can without justice protest against the institution of the sovereign declared by the major part.

5. Thirdly, because the major part[2] has by consenting voices declared a sovereign, he that dissented must now consent with the rest, that is, be contented to avow [accept] all the actions he [the sovereign] shall do, or else justly be destroyed by the rest. For if he voluntarily entered into the congregation of them that were assembled, [then] he sufficiently declared thereby his will and therefore tacitly covenanted to stand to what the major part should ordain; and therefore if he refuse to stand thereto or make protestation against any of their decrees, [then] he does contrary to his covenant and therefore unjustly. And whether he be of the congregation or not and whether his consent be asked or not, he must either submit to their decrees or be left in the condition of war he was in before, wherein he might without injustice be destroyed by any man whatsoever.

4. The sovereign's actions cannot be justly accused by the subject.

6. Fourthly, because every subject is by this institution author of all the actions and judgments of the sovereign instituted, it follows that whatsoever he does can be no injury to any of his subjects nor ought he to be by any of them

accused of injustice. For he that does anything by authority from another does therein no injury to him by whose authority he acts; but by this institution of a commonwealth every particular man is author of all the sovereign does; and consequently he that complains of injury from his sovereign complains of that whereof he himself is author; and therefore [he] ought not to accuse any man but himself; no, nor himself, of injury, because to do injury to oneself is impossible. It is true that they that have sovereign power may commit iniquity, but not injustice or injury[3] in the proper signification.

7. Fifthly, and consequently to that which was said last, no man that has sovereign power can justly be put to death or otherwise in any manner by his subjects punished. For seeing every subject is author of the actions of his sovereign, he punishes another for the actions committed by himself.

5. Whatsoever the sovereign does is unpunishable by the subject.

8. And because the end of this institution is the peace and defense of them all, and whosoever has right to the end has right to the means, it belongs of right to whatsoever man or assembly that has the sovereignty to be judge both of the means of peace and defense and also of the hindrances and disturbances of the same; and to do whatsoever he shall think necessary to be done, both beforehand, for the preserving of peace and security, by prevention of discord at home, and hostility from abroad; and when peace and security are lost, for the recovery of the same. And therefore,

6. The sovereign is judge of what is necessary for the peace and defense of his subjects. [91]

9. Sixthly, it is annexed to the sovereignty to be judge of what opinions and doctrines are averse, and what [opinions and doctrines are] conducing to peace; and consequently on what occasions, how far, and what men are to be trusted withal in speaking to multitudes of people, and who shall examine the doctrines of all books before they be published. For the actions of men

And judge of what doctrines are fit to be taught them.

---

1   *avouched* Taken responsibility for.
2   *major part* Majority.

3   *injustice or injury* Hobbes is playing on the etymology of the Latin word for "right," *jus* (genitive *juris*). Injustice and injury is what is done without *jus* because the wrongdoer has laid down or given up his *jus*. *Iniquity* is merely harm done; the word comes from the Latin "*in + aequus*": not equal.

proceed from their opinions, and in the well governing of opinions consists the well governing of men's actions in order to their peace and concord. And though in matter of doctrine nothing ought to be regarded but the truth; yet this is not repugnant to regulating of the same by peace. For doctrine repugnant to peace can no more be true than peace and concord can be against the law of nature. It is true that in a commonwealth, where by the negligence or unskillfulness of governors and teachers false doctrines are by time generally received, the contrary truths may be generally offensive. Yet the most sudden and rough bustling in of a new truth that can be does never break the peace, but only sometimes awake the war. For those men that are so remissly governed that they dare take up arms to defend or introduce an opinion are still in war; and their condition not peace, but only a cessation of arms for fear of one another; and they live, as it were, in the precincts of battle continually. It belongs therefore to him that has the sovereign power to be judge, or constitute all judges of opinions and doctrines, as a thing necessary to peace, thereby to prevent discord and civil war.

10. Seventhly, is annexed to the sovereignty the whole power of prescribing the rules whereby every man may know what goods he may enjoy and what actions he may do without being molested by any of his fellow subjects; and this is it men call *propriety* [*property*]. For before constitution of sovereign power, as has already been shown, all men had right to all things, which necessarily causes war; and therefore this propriety, being necessary to peace and depending on sovereign power, is the act of that power, in order to the public peace. These rules of propriety (or *meum* and *tuum*[1]) and of *good, evil, lawful,* and *unlawful* in the actions of subjects are the civil laws, that is to say, the laws of each commonwealth in particular; though the name of civil law be now restrained to the ancient civil laws of the city of Rome, which being the head of a great part of the world, her laws at that time were in these parts the civil law.

7. The right of making rules, whereby the subjects may every man know what is so his own, as no other subject can without injustice take it from him.

11. Eighthly, is annexed to the sovereignty the right of judicature, that is to say, of hearing and deciding all controversies which may arise concerning law, either civil or natural, or concerning fact. For without the decision of controversies there is no protection of one subject against the injuries of another, the laws concerning *meum* and *tuum* are in vain, and to every man remains, from the natural and necessary appetite of his own conservation, the right of protecting himself by his private strength, which is the condition of war and contrary to the end for which every commonwealth is instituted.

8. To him also belongs the right of judicature and decision of controversy.

[92]

12. Ninthly, is annexed to the sovereignty the right of making war and peace with other nations and commonwealths, that is to say, of judging when it is for the public good, and how great forces are to be assembled, armed, and paid for that end, and to levy money upon the subjects to defray the expenses thereof. For the power by which the people are to be defended consists in their armies, and the strength of an army in the union of their strength under one command; which command the sovereign instituted, therefore has, because the command of the *militia*, without other institution, makes him that has it sovereign. And therefore, whosoever is made general of an army, he that has the sovereign power is always generalissimo.[2]

9. And of making war, and peace, as he shall think best.

13. Tenthly, is annexed to the sovereignty the choosing of all counselors, ministers, magistrates, and officers, both in peace and war. For seeing the sovereign is charged with the end, which is the common peace and defense, he is understood to have power to use such means as he shall think most fit for his discharge.

10. And of choosing all counselors and ministers, both of peace and war.

14. Eleventhly, to the sovereign is committed the power of rewarding with riches or honor and of punishing with corporal or pecuniary punishment or with ignominy [disgrace], every subject according to the law he has formerly made; or if there be no law made, according as he shall judge most to conduce to the encouraging of men to serve the commonwealth or deterring of them from doing disservice to the same.

11. And of rewarding and punishing, and that (where no former law has

---

1   *meum and tuum*   Latin: mine and yours.

2   *generalissimo*   Commander-in-chief.

determined
the measure
of it)
arbitrary.

12. And of
honor and
order.

15. Lastly, considering what values men are naturally apt to set upon themselves, what respect they look for from others, and how little they value other men, from whence continually arise amongst them emulation,[1] quarrels, factions, and at last war, to the destroying of one another and diminution of their strength against a common enemy, it is necessary that there be laws of honor and a public rate[2] of the worth of such men as have deserved or are able to deserve well of the commonwealth, and that there be force in the hands of some or other to put those laws in execution. But it has already been shown that not only the whole militia or forces of the commonwealth, but also the judicature of all controversies is annexed to the sovereignty. To the sovereign therefore it belongs also to give titles of honor and to appoint what order of place and dignity each man shall hold and what signs of respect in public or private meetings they shall give to one another.

These
rights are
indivisible.

16. These are the rights which make the essence of sovereignty and which are the marks whereby a man may discern in what man or assembly of men the sovereign power is placed and resides. For these are incommunicable[3] and inseparable. The power to coin money, to dispose of the estate and persons of infant heirs, to have preemption in markets,[4] and all other statute prerogatives may be transferred by the sovereign, and yet the power to protect his subjects be retained. But if he transfer the militia, he retains the judicature in vain, for want of execution of the laws; or if he grant away the power of raising money, the militia is in vain; or if he give away the government of doctrines, men will be frighted into rebellion with the fear of spirits. And so if we consider any one of the said rights, we shall presently see that the holding of all the rest will produce no effect in the conservation of peace and justice, the end for which all commonwealths are instituted.

[93]

1   *emulation* Envy.
2   *rate* Price-list.
3   *incommunicable* Cannot be shared.
4   *preemption in markets* The right to buy household provisions in preference to other persons, and at special rates.

And this division [of powers] is it whereof it is said, *A kingdom divided in itself cannot stand*;[5] for unless this division precede, division into opposite armies can never happen. If there had not first been an opinion received of the greatest part of England that these powers were divided between the King and the Lords and the House of Commons, the people had never been divided and fallen into this Civil War, first between those that disagreed in politics and after between the dissenters about the liberty of religion; which have so instructed men in this point of sovereign right that there be few now (in England) that do not see that these rights are inseparable and will be so generally acknowledged at the next return of peace; and so [they will] continue [to see this] till their miseries are forgotten; and [it will be seen] no longer, except the vulgar be better taught than they have hitherto been.[6]

17. And because they are essential and inseparable rights, it follows necessarily that in whatsoever words any of them seem to be granted away, yet if the sovereign power itself be not in direct terms renounced and the name of sovereign no more given by the grantees to him that grants them, [then] the grant is void; for when he has granted all he can, if we grant back the sovereignty, all is restored, as inseparably annexed thereunto.

And can by
no grant
pass away
without
direct
renouncing
of the sovereign power.

18. This great authority being indivisible and inseparably annexed to the sovereignty, there is little ground for the opinion of them that say of sovereign kings, though they be *singulis majores*, of greater power than every one of their subjects; yet they be *universis minores*, of less power than them all together. For if by *all together* they mean not the collective body as one person, then *all together* and *every one* signify the same and the speech is absurd. But if by *all together* they understand them as one person (which person the sovereign bears), then the power of all together is the same with the sovereign's power and so again the speech is absurd, which absurdity they see well enough

The power
and honor
of subjects
vanishes in
the presence
of the power
sovereign.

5   *A kingdom ... cannot stand* Matthew 12.25, Mark 3.24, Luke 11.17.
6   *better taught ... hitherto been* Better teaching would include teaching *Leviathan*, according to Hobbes.

when the sovereignty is in an assembly of the people; but in a monarch they see it not, and yet the power of sovereignty is the same in whomsoever it be placed.

19. And as the power, so also the honor of the sovereign ought to be greater than that of any or all the subjects. For in the sovereignty is the fountain of honor. The dignities of lord, earl, duke, and prince are his creatures.[1] As in the presence of the master the servants are equal and without any honor at all, so are the subjects in the presence of the sovereign. And though they shine some more, some less, when they are out of his sight; yet in his presence they shine no more than the stars in presence of the sun.

20. But a man may here object that the condition of subjects is very miserable, as being obnoxious to[2] the lusts and other irregular passions of him or them that have so unlimited a power in their hands. And commonly they that live under a monarch think it the fault of monarchy; and they that live under the government of democracy or other sovereign assembly attribute all the inconvenience to that form of commonwealth; whereas the power in all forms, if they be perfect enough to protect them, is the same; [and they are] not considering that the estate of man can never be without some incommodity[3] or other, and that the greatest[4] that in any form of government can possibly happen to the people in general is scarce sensible in respect of[5] the miseries and horrible calamities that accompany a civil war or that dissolute condition of masterless men without subjection to laws and a coercive power to tie their hands from rapine[6] and revenge; nor [are they] considering that the greatest pressure of sovereign governors proceeds not from any delight or profit they can expect in the damage or weakening of their subjects (in whose vigor consists their own strength and glory), but in

[94]
Sovereign power not so hurtful as the want of it, and the hurt proceeds for the greatest part from not submitting readily to a less.

the restiveness of themselves that, unwillingly contributing to their own defense, make it necessary for their governors to draw from them what they can in time of peace, [in order] that they may have means on any emergent occasion or sudden need to resist or take advantage on their enemies. For all men are by nature provided of notable multiplying[7] glasses (that is their passions and self-love) through which every little payment appears a great grievance, but are destitute of those prospective glasses[8] (namely moral and civil science) to see afar off the miseries that hang over them and cannot without such payments be avoided.

Chapter 19: Of the Several Kinds of Commonwealth by Institution and of Succession to the Sovereign Power

1. The difference of commonwealths consists in the difference of the sovereign or the person representative of all and every one of the multitude. And because the sovereignty is either in one man or in an assembly of more than one, and into that assembly either every man has right to enter or not every one, but certain men distinguished from the rest; it is manifest there can be but three kinds of commonwealth. For the representative must needs be one man or more; and if more, then it is the assembly of all, or but of a part. When the representative is one man, then is the commonwealth a Monarchy; when an assembly of all that will come together, then it is a Democracy or popular commonwealth; when an assembly of a part only, then it is called an Aristocracy. Other kind of commonwealth there can be none; for either one, or more, or all, must have the sovereign power (which I have shown to be indivisible) entire.

The different forms of commonwealths but three.

2. There be other names of government in the histories and books of policy,[9] as *tyranny* and *oligarchy*; but they are not the names of other forms

---

1   *his creatures*   Created by him.
2   *obnoxious to*   Subject to injury by.
3   *incommodity*   Disadvantage.
4   *greatest*   Worst.
5   *scarce sensible in respect of*   Almost nothing compared to.
6   *rapine*   Robbery.

---

7   *multiplying*   Magnifying.
8   *prospective glasses*   Crystal balls.
9   *books of policy*   "Policy" means political theory. Hobbes is probably thinking here of Aristotle's *Poli-*

[95]

Tyranny and oligarchy, but different names of monarchy, and aristocracy.

of government, but of the same forms misliked.[1] For they that are discontented under *monarchy* call it *tyranny* and they that are displeased with *aristocracy* call it *oligarchy*; so also, they which find themselves grieved under a *democracy* call it *anarchy*, which signifies want of government; and yet I think no man believes that want of government is any new kind of government; nor by the same reason ought they to believe that the government is of one kind when they like it and another when they mislike it or are oppressed by the governors.

3. It is manifest that men who are in absolute liberty may, if they please, give authority to one man to represent them every one, as well as give

Subordinate representatives dangerous.

such authority to any assembly of men whatsoever; and consequently [they] may subject themselves, if they think good, to a monarch as absolutely as to any other representative. Therefore, where there is already erected a sovereign power, there can be no other representative of the same people, but only to certain particular ends by the sovereign limited.[2] For that [that is, to erect a representative in addition to the sovereign power] were to erect two sovereigns and every man to have his person represented by two actors that, by opposing one another, must needs divide that power which (if men will live in peace) is indivisible, and thereby reduce the multitude into the condition of war, contrary to the end for which all sovereignty is instituted.[3] And therefore as it is absurd to think that a sovereign assembly, inviting the people of their dominion to send up their deputies with power to make known their advice or desires, should therefore hold such deputies, rather than themselves, for the absolute representative of the people, so it is absurd also to think the same in

a monarchy. And I know not how this so manifest a truth should of late be so little observed, that in a monarchy he that had the sovereignty from a descent of six hundred years,[4] was alone called sovereign, had the title of Majesty from every one of his subjects, and was unquestionably taken by them for their king, was notwithstanding never considered as their representative, that name without contradiction passing for the title of those men which at his command were sent up by the people to carry their petitions and give him, if he permitted it, their advice.[5] Which may serve as an admonition for those that are the true and absolute representative of a people to instruct men in the nature of that office, and to take heed how they admit of any other general representation upon any occasion whatsoever, if they mean to discharge the trust committed to them.

4. The difference between these three kinds of commonwealth consists not in the difference of power,[6] but in the difference of convenience[7] or aptitude to produce the peace and security of the people, which end they were instituted. And to compare monarchy with the other two, we may observe; first, that whosoever bears the person of the people or is one of that assembly that bears it bears also his own natural person. And though he be careful in his politic person to procure the common interest; yet he is more, or no less, careful to procure the private good of himself, his family, kindred and friends; and for the most part, if the public interest chance to cross the private, he prefers the private, for the passions of men are commonly more potent than their reason. From whence it follows that where the public

Comparison of monarchy, with sovereign assemblies.

[96]

---

1   *misliked* Disliked.

2   *but only ... sovereign limited* Except for certain particular purposes specified by the sovereign.

3   *thereby reduce ... is instituted* Hobbes thinks that genuine separation of powers, as the United States claims for its government, leads to civil war. He was thinking in particular of the English Civil Wars (1642–49), which pitted the king and his followers against a majority of the parliament and their followers.

tics 3.7, and Polybius' *Histories* 6.3–9, among other works.

4   *he that ... six hundred years* The Stuart monarchs traced their lineage back to William I, who conquered England in 1066.

5   *those men ... their advice* Hobbes believed that Parliament had no political power independent of the monarch. He thought it was a purely advisory body, as the French etymology of "parliament" suggests: to talk.

6   *The difference ... of power* All three forms of government are equally sovereign. But Hobbes thinks that monarchy is the most stable form of government; democracy the least.

7   *convenience* Fitness.

and private interest are most closely united, there is the public most advanced. Now in monarchy the private interest is the same with the public. The riches, power, and honor of a monarch arise only from the riches, strength, and reputation of his subjects. For no king can be rich nor glorious nor secure, whose subjects are either poor or contemptible or too weak through want or dissension to maintain a war against their enemies; whereas in a democracy or aristocracy, the public prosperity confers not so much to the private fortune of one that is corrupt or ambitious, as does many times a perfidious advice, a treacherous action, or a civil war.

5. Secondly, that a monarch receives counsel of whom, when, and where he pleases; and consequently may hear the opinion of men versed in the matter about which he deliberates, of what rank or quality soever, and as long before the time of action and with as much secrecy as he will. But when a sovereign assembly has need of counsel, none are admitted but such as have a right thereto from the beginning, which for the most part are of those who have been versed more in the acquisition of wealth than of knowledge and are to give their advice in long discourses which may, and do commonly, excite men to action, but not govern them in it. For the *understanding* is by the flame of the passions never enlightened, but dazzled; nor is there any place or time wherein an assembly can receive counsel with secrecy, because of their own multitude.

6. Thirdly, that the resolutions of a monarch are subject to no other inconstancy than that of human nature; but in assemblies, besides that of nature, there arises an inconstancy from the number. For the absence of a few that would have the resolution, once taken, continue firm (which may happen by security, negligence, or private impediments), or the diligent appearance of a few of the contrary opinion, undoes today all that was concluded yesterday.

7. Fourthly, that a monarch cannot disagree with himself out of envy or interest, but an assembly may, and that to such a height as may produce a civil war.

8. Fifthly, that in monarchy there is this inconvenience:[1] that any subject, by the power of one man, for the enriching of a favorite or flatterer, may be deprived of all he possesses, which I confess is a great and inevitable inconvenience. But the same may as well happen where the sovereign power is in an assembly; for their power is the same, and they are as subject to evil counsel and to be seduced by orators as a monarch by flatterers; and becoming one another's flatterers, serve one another's covetousness and ambition by turns. And whereas the favorites of monarchs are few and they have none else to advance but their own kindred, the favorites of an assembly are many, and the kindred much more numerous than of any monarch. Besides, there is no favorite of a monarch which cannot as well succor his friends as hurt his enemies; but orators, that is to say favorites of sovereign assemblies, though they have great power to hurt, have little to save. For to accuse requires less eloquence (such is man's nature) than to excuse; and condemnation, than absolution, more resembles justice. [97]

9. Sixthly, that it is an inconvenience in monarchy that the sovereignty may descend upon an infant or one that cannot discern between good and evil, and [the inconvenience] consists in this: that the use of his power must be in the hand of another man or of some assembly of men, which are to govern by his right and in his name as curators and protectors of his person and authority. But to say there is inconvenience in putting the use of the sovereign power into the hand of a man or an assembly of men is to say that all government is more inconvenient than confusion and civil war. And therefore all the danger that can be pretended must arise from the contention of those that, for an office of so great honor and profit, may become competitors. To make it appear that this inconvenience proceeds not from that form of government we call monarchy, we are to consider that the precedent monarch has appointed who shall have the tuition[2] of his infant successor, either expressly by testament

---

1   *inconvenience* Unsuitableness.
2   *tuition* Guardianship.

or tacitly by not controlling the custom in that case received; and then such inconvenience, if it happen, is to be attributed not to the monarchy, but to the ambition and injustice of the subjects, which in all kinds of government where the people are not well instructed in their duty and the rights of sovereignty, is the same. Or else the precedent monarch has not at all taken order for such tuition; and then the law of nature has provided this sufficient rule, that the tuition shall be in him that has by nature most interest in the preservation of the authority of the infant, and to whom least benefit can accrue by his death or diminution. For seeing every man by nature seeks his own benefit and promotion, to put an infant into the power of those that can promote themselves by his destruction or damage is not tuition but treachery. So that sufficient provision being taken against all just quarrel about the government under a child, if any contention arise to the disturbance of the public peace, it is not to be attributed to the form of monarchy but to the ambition of subjects and ignorance of their duty. On the other side, there is no great commonwealth, the sovereignty whereof is in a great assembly, which is not, as to consultations of peace and war and making of laws, in the same condition as if the government were in a child. For as a child wants[1] the judgment to dissent from counsel given him and is thereby necessitated to take the advice of them or him to whom he is committed; so an assembly wants the liberty to dissent from the counsel of the major part, be it good or bad. And as a child has need of a tutor or protector to preserve his person and authority, so also in great commonwealths the sovereign assembly, in all great dangers and troubles, have need of *custode libertatis*, that is, of dictators or protectors of their authority, which are as much as temporary [98] monarchs, to whom for a time they may commit the entire exercise of their power; and have (at the end of that time) been oftener deprived thereof than infant kings by their protectors, regents, or any other tutors.

10. Though the kinds of sovereignty be, as I have now shown, but three; that is to say, monarchy, where one man has it; or democracy, where the general assembly of subjects has it; or aristocracy, where it is in an assembly of certain persons nominated or otherwise distinguished from the rest; yet he that shall consider the particular commonwealths that have been and are in the world will not perhaps easily reduce them to three, and may thereby be inclined to think there be other forms arising from these mingled together. As for example elective kingdoms, where kings have the sovereign power put into their hands for a time, or kingdoms wherein the king has a power limited, which governments are nevertheless by most writers called monarchy. Likewise if a popular or aristocratical commonwealth subdue an enemy's country and govern the same by a president, procurator, or other magistrate, this may seem perhaps, at first sight, to be a democratical or aristocratical government. But it is not so. For elective kings are not sovereigns, but ministers of the sovereign; nor limited kings sovereigns, but ministers of them that have the sovereign power; nor are those provinces which are in subjection to a democracy or aristocracy of another commonwealth democratically or aristocratically governed, but monarchically.[2]

11. And first, concerning an elective king whose power is limited to his life, as it is in many places of Christendom at this day, or to certain years or months, as the dictator's power amongst the Romans, if he have right to appoint his successor he is no more elective but hereditary. But if he have no power to elect his successor, then there is some other man or assembly known, which after his decease may elect a new; or else the commonwealth dies and dissolves with him, and re-

---

1   *wants* Lacks.

2   *nor are ... but monarchically* A government may appear to be of one form but really be of another. Some constitutional monarchies, such as the United Kingdom, Canada, and Australia, are in practice not monarchies at all, but representative democracies. When a province, such as first-century Palestine, is ruled by a foreign conqueror, such as Rome, the form of government is monarchy. The people of Rome as sovereign constituted an artificial person and in that capacity governed Palestine.

turns to the condition of war. If it be known who have the power to give the sovereignty after his death, it is known also that the sovereignty was in them before; for none have right to give that which they have not right to possess, and keep to themselves, if they think good. But if there be none that can give the sovereignty after the decease of him that was first elected, then has he power, nay he is obliged by the law of nature, to provide, by establishing his successor, to keep to those that had trusted him with the government from relapsing into the miserable condition of civil war. And consequently he was, when elected, a sovereign absolute.

12. Secondly, that king whose power is limited is not superior to him or them that have the power to limit it; and he that is not superior is not supreme, that is to say, not sovereign. The sovereignty therefore was always in that assembly which had the right to limit him, and by consequence the government [was] not monarchy, but either democracy or aristocracy, as of old [99] time in Sparta, where the kings had a privilege to lead their armies, but the sovereignty was in the Ephori.[1]

13. Thirdly, whereas heretofore the Roman people governed the land of Judea, for example, by a president; yet was not Judea therefore a democracy, because they were not governed by any assembly into which any of them had right to enter, nor by an aristocracy, because they were not governed by any assembly into which any man could enter by their election; but they were governed by one person, which though as to the people of Rome was an assembly of the people, or democracy; yet as to the people of Judea, which had no right at all of participating in the government, was a monarch. For though where the people are governed by an assembly chosen by themselves out of their own number, the government is called a democracy or aristocracy; yet when they are governed by an assembly not of their own choosing, it is a monarchy, not of one

man over another man, but of one people over another people.

14. Of all these forms of government, the matter being mortal, so that not only monarchs but also whole assemblies die, it is necessary for the conservation of the peace of men that as there was order taken for an artificial man, so there be order also taken for an artificial eternity of life, without which men that are governed by an assembly should return into the condition of war in every age, and they that are governed by one man as soon as their governor dies. This artificial eternity is that which men call the right of *succession*. *Of the right of succession.*

15. There is no perfect form of government, where the disposing of the succession is not in the present sovereign. For if it be in any other particular man or private assembly, it is in a person subject, and may be assumed by the sovereign at his pleasure; and consequently the right is in himself. And if it be in no particular man, but left to a new choice, then is the commonwealth dissolved, and the right is in him that can get it, contrary to the intention of them that did institute the commonwealth for their perpetual, and not temporary, security.

16. In a democracy, the whole assembly cannot fail unless the multitude that are to be governed fail. And therefore questions of the right of succession have in that form of government no place at all.

17. In an aristocracy when any of the assembly dies, the election of another into his room belonged to the assembly, as the sovereign, to whom belonged the choosing of all counselors and officers. For that which the representative does as actor, every one of the subjects does as author. And though the sovereign assembly may give power to others to elect new men for supply of their court; yet it is still by their authority that the election is made; and by the same it may, when the public shall require it, be recalled.

18. The greatest difficulty about the right of succession is in monarchy; and the difficulty arises from this, that at first sight it is not manifest who is to appoint the successor nor many times who it is whom he has appointed. For in both these *The present monarch has right to dispose*

---

1   *Ephori* Five senior government officials, elected annually, who advised the king.

of the succession. [100] cases there is required a more exact ratiocination[1] than every man is accustomed to use. As to the question who shall appoint the successor of a monarch that has the sovereign authority, that is to say, who shall determine of the right of inheritance (for elective kings and princes have not the sovereign power in propriety, but in use only), we are to consider that either he that is in possession has right to dispose of the succession or else that right is again in the dissolved multitude. For the death of him that has the sovereign power in propriety leaves the multitude without any sovereign at all, that is, without any representative in whom they should be united and be capable of doing any one action at all. And therefore they are incapable of election of any new monarch, every man having equal right to submit himself to such as he thinks best able to protect him, or, if he can, protect himself by his own sword, which is a return to confusion and to the condition of a war of every man against every man, contrary to the end for which monarchy had its first institution. Therefore it is manifest that by the institution of monarchy the disposing of the successor is always left to the judgment and will of the present possessor.

19. And for the question (which may arise sometimes), *who it is that the monarch in possession has designed to the succession and inheritance of his power*, it is determined by his express words and testament, or by other tacit signs sufficient.

Succession passes by express words. 20. By express words or testament, when it is declared by him in his lifetime, *viva voce*,[2] or by writing, as the first emperors of Rome declared who should be their heirs. For the word *heir* does not of itself imply the children or nearest kindred of a man, but whomsoever a man shall any way declare he would have to succeed him in his estate. If therefore a monarch declare expressly that such a man shall be his heir, either by word or writing, then is that man immediately after the decease of his predecessor invested in the right of being monarch.

Or, by not controlling a custom. 21. But where testament and express words are wanting, other natural signs of the will are to be followed, whereof the one is custom. And therefore where the custom is that the next of kindred absolutely succeeds, there also the next of kindred has right to the succession that, if the will of him that was in possession had been otherwise, he might easily have declared the same in his lifetime. And likewise where the custom is that the next of the male kindred succeeds, there also the right of succession is in the next of the kindred male, for the same reason. And so it is if the custom were to advance the female. For whatsoever custom a man may by a word control and does not, it is a natural sign he would have that custom stand.

Or, by presumption of natural affection. [101] 22. But where neither custom nor testament has preceded, there it is to be understood: first, that a monarch's will is that the government remain monarchical, because he has approved that government in himself. Secondly, that a child of his own, male or female, be preferred before any other, because men are presumed to be more inclined by nature to advance their own children than the children of other men; and of their own, rather a male than a female, because men are naturally fitter than women for actions of labor and danger. Thirdly, where his own issue fails, rather a brother than a stranger, and so still the nearer in blood rather than the more remote, because it is always presumed that the nearer of kin is the nearer in affection and it is evident that a man receives always, by reflection, the most honor from the greatness of his nearest kindred.

To dispose of the succession, though to a king of another nation, not unlawful. 23. But if it be lawful for a monarch to dispose of the succession by words of contract or testament, men may perhaps object a great inconvenience; for he may sell or give his right of governing to a stranger,[3] which, because strangers (that is, men not used to live under the same government, nor speaking the same language) do commonly undervalue one another, may turn to the oppression of his subjects, which is indeed a great inconvenience; but it proceeds not necessarily from the subjection to a stranger's government,

---

1   *ratiocination* Reasoning.
2   *viva voce* Latin: orally.

3   *stranger* Foreigner.

but from the unskillfulness of the governors ignorant of the true rules of politics. And therefore the Romans, when they had subdued many nations, to make their government digestible were wont to take away that grievance as much as they thought necessary by giving sometimes to whole nations, and sometimes to principal men of every nation they conquered, not only the privileges but also the name of Romans, and took many of them into the Senate and offices of charge, even in the Roman city. And this was it our most wise king, King James, aimed at in endeavoring the union of his two realms of England and Scotland.[1] Which, if he could have obtained, had in all likelihood prevented the civil wars which make both those kingdoms, at this present, miserable. It is not therefore any injury to the people for a monarch to dispose of the succession by will, though by the fault of many princes it has been sometimes found inconvenient. Of the lawfulness of it, this also is an argument: that whatsoever inconvenience can arrive by giving a kingdom to a stranger may arrive also by so marrying with strangers, as the right of succession may descend upon them; yet this by all men is accounted lawful.

Chapter 20: Of Dominion Paternal and Despotical

A commonwealth by acquisition.
[102]

1. A commonwealth *by acquisition* is that where the sovereign power is acquired by force; and it is acquired by force when men singly, or many together by plurality of voices, for fear of death or bonds, do authorize all the actions of that man or assembly that has their lives and liberty in his power.

Wherein different from a commonwealth by institution.

2. And this kind of dominion or sovereignty differs from sovereignty by institution only in this, that men who choose their sovereign do it for fear of one another and not of him whom they institute; but in this case, they subject themselves to him they are afraid of. In both cases they do it for fear; which is to be noted by them that hold all such covenants, as proceed from fear of death or violence, void; which, if it were true, no man in any kind of commonwealth could be obliged to obedience. It is true that in a commonwealth once instituted or acquired, promises proceeding from fear of death or violence are no covenants nor obliging when the thing promised is contrary to the laws; but the reason is not because it was made upon fear, but because he that promises has no right in[2] the thing promised. Also, when he may lawfully perform and does not, it is not the invalidity of the covenant that absolves him, but the sentence of the sovereign. Otherwise, whensoever a man lawfully promises, he unlawfully breaks; but when the sovereign, who is the actor, acquits him, then he is acquitted by him that extorted the promise, as by the author of such absolution.

The rights of sovereignty the same in both.

3. But the rights and consequences of sovereignty are the same in both. His power cannot without his consent be transferred to another; he cannot forfeit it; he cannot be accused by any of his subjects of injury; he cannot be punished by them; he is judge of what is necessary for peace and judge of doctrines; he is sole legislator and supreme judge of controversies and of the times and occasions of war and peace; to him it belonged to choose magistrates, counselors, commanders, and all other officers and ministers, and to determine of rewards and punishments, honor and order. The reasons whereof are the same which are alleged in the precedent chapter[3] for the same rights and consequences of sovereignty by institution.

Dominion paternal how attained. Not by generation, but by contract;

4. Dominion is acquired two ways, by generation and by conquest. The right of dominion by generation is that which the parent has over his children and is called Paternal. And is not so derived from the generation, as if therefore the parent had dominion over his child because he begat him, but from the child's consent, either express or by other sufficient arguments declared. For as to the generation, God has ordained to

---

1   *King James ... Scotland*   James I and VI was separately king of Scotland (hence VI) and king of England and Wales (I). His attempt to unite the two realms failed, and union was achieved only in 1707.

2   *right in*   Right to.

3   *the precedent chapter*   This appears to refer to Chapter 18; similarly in Paragraph 14. But these words in Paragraph 9 appear to refer to Chapter 29.

man a helper, and there be always two that are equally parents; the dominion therefore over the child should belong equally to both and he be equally subject to both, which is impossible; for no man can obey two masters. And whereas some[1] have attributed the dominion to the man only, as being of the more excellent sex, they misreckon in it. For there is not always that difference of strength or prudence between the man and the woman as that the right can be determined without war. In commonwealths this controversy is decided by the civil law; and for the most part (but not always) the sentence is in favor of the father, because for the most part commonwealths [103] have been erected by the fathers, not by the mothers of families. But the question lies now in the state of mere nature where there are supposed no laws of matrimony, no laws for the education of children but the law of nature and the natural inclination of the sexes, one to another, and to their children. In this condition of mere nature either the parents between themselves dispose of [settle] the dominion over the child by contract or do not dispose thereof at all. If they dispose thereof, the right passes according to the contract. We find in history that the Amazons[2] contracted with the men of the neighboring countries, to whom they had recourse for issue, that the issue male should be sent back, but the female remain with themselves; so that the dominion of the females was in the mother.

Or education;   5. If there be no contract, the dominion is in the mother. For in the condition of mere nature, where there are no matrimonial laws, it cannot be known who is the father unless it be declared by the mother; and therefore the right of dominion over the child depends on her will, and is consequently hers. Again, seeing the infant is first in the power of the mother, so as she may either nourish or expose[3] it, if she nourish it, it owes its

life to the mother, and is therefore obliged to obey her rather than any other; and by consequence the dominion over it is hers. But if she expose it, and another find and nourish it, dominion is in him that nourishes it. For it ought to obey him by whom it is preserved, because preservation of life being the end for which one man becomes subject to another, every man is supposed to promise obedience to him in whose power it is to save or destroy him.

6. If the mother be the father's subject, the child is in the father's power; and if the father be the mother's subject (as when a sovereign queen marries one of her subjects), the child is subject to the mother, because the father also is her subject.   Or precedent subjection of one of the parents to the other.

7. If a man and a woman, monarchs of two several kingdoms, have a child, and contract concerning who shall have the dominion of him, the right of the dominion passes by the contract. If they contract not, the dominion follows the dominion of the place of his residence. For the sovereign of each country has dominion over all that reside therein.

8. He that has the dominion over the child has dominion also over the children of the child, and over their children's children. For he that has dominion over the person of a man has dominion over all that is his, without which dominion were but a title without the effect.   The right of succession follows the rules of the right of possession.

9. The right of succession to paternal dominion proceeds in the same manner as does the right of succession to monarchy, of which I have already sufficiently spoken in the precedent chapter.

10. Dominion acquired by conquest or victory in war is that which some writers call Despotical from *Despotes*, which signifies a *lord* or *master* and is the dominion of the master over his servant. And this dominion is then acquired to the victor when the vanquished, to avoid the present stroke of death, covenants either in express words or by other sufficient signs of the will that so long as his life and the liberty of his body is allowed him, the victor shall have the use thereof at his pleasure. And after such covenant made, the vanquished is a Servant, and not before; for by the word *servant* (whether it be derived from [the Latin] servire, to serve, or from servare, to save, which I leave to   Despotical dominion how attained. [104]

---

1   *some*   For example, Aristotle and Aquinas.
2   *Amazons*   Ancient nation of warrior women; Hobbes takes accounts of them to be historical, but nowadays these stories are taken to be largely mythological.
3   *expose*   In some cultures, unwanted children were customarily abandoned out in the open, unprotected, where they would die unless rescued by a stranger.

grammarians to dispute)[1] is not meant a captive, which is kept in prison or bonds, till the owner of him that took him or bought him of one that did, shall consider what to do with him; for such men, commonly called slaves, have no obligation at all, but may break their bonds or the prison and kill or carry away captive their master, justly; but one that, being taken, has corporal liberty allowed him, and upon promise not to run away nor to do violence to his master, is trusted by him.

Not by the victory, but by the consent of the vanquished.

11. It is not therefore the victory that gives the right of dominion over the vanquished, but his own covenant. Nor is he obliged because he is conquered, that is to say, beaten and taken or put to flight, but because he comes in and submits to the victor; nor is the victor obliged by an enemy's rendering himself, without promise of life, to spare him for this his yielding to discretion, which obliges not the victor longer than in his own discretion he shall think fit.

12. And that which men do when they demand, as it is now called, *quarter* (which the Greeks called *Zogria, taking alive*) is to evade the present fury of the victor by submission and to compound for their life with ransom or service; and therefore he that has quarter has not his life given, but deferred till further deliberation; for it is not a yielding on condition of life, but to discretion. And then only is his life in security, and his service due, when the victor has trusted him with his corporal liberty. For slaves that work in prisons or fetters do it not of duty, but to avoid the cruelty of their task-masters.

13. The master of the servant is master also of all he has and may exact the use thereof; that is to say, of his goods, of his labor, of his servants, and of his children, as often as he shall think fit. For he holds his life of his master by the covenant of obedience, that is, of owning and authorizing whatsoever the master shall do. And in case the master, if he refuse, kill him or cast him into bonds, or otherwise punish him for his disobedience, he is himself the author of the same and cannot accuse him of injury.

14. In sum, the rights and consequences of both *paternal* and *despotical* dominion are the very same with those of a sovereign by institution, and for the same reasons, which reasons are set down in the precedent chapter. So that for a man that is monarch of divers nations, whereof he has in one the sovereignty by institution of the people assembled, and in another by conquest, that is, by the submission of each particular to avoid death or bonds, to demand of one nation more than of the other, from the title of conquest, as being a conquered nation, is an act of ignorance of the rights of sovereignty. For the sovereign is absolute over both alike or else there is no sovereignty at all, and so every man may lawfully protect himself, if he can, with his own sword, which is the condition of war.

[105]

15. By this it appears that a great family, if it be not part of some commonwealth, is of itself, as to the rights of sovereignty, a little monarchy, whether that family consist of a man and his children, or of a man and his servants, or of a man and his children and servants together,[2] wherein the father or master is the sovereign. But yet a family is not properly a commonwealth unless it be of that power by its own number or by other opportunities,[3] as not to be subdued without the hazard of war. For where a number of men are manifestly too weak to defend themselves united, every one may use his own reason in time of danger to save his own life either by flight or by submission to the enemy, as he shall think best; in the same manner as a very small company of soldiers, surprised by an army, may cast down their arms and demand quarter or run away rather than be put to the sword. And thus much shall suffice concerning what I find by speculation and deduction of sovereign rights, from the nature, need, and designs of men in erecting of commonwealths and putting themselves under monarchs or assemblies entrusted with power enough for their protection.

Difference between a family and a kingdom.

1   *from [the Latin] ... to dispute* The word "servant" derives from *servire*.

2   *whether that ... servants together* The word "family" in Hobbes' time could be used in a broader sense, to include family servants.

3   *a family ... other opportunities* See 17.2, and the footnote regarding families.

The rights
of mon-
archy from
Scripture.
Exodus
20.19.

16. Let us now consider what the Scripture teaches in the same point. To Moses the children of Israel say thus: *Speak thou to us, and we will hear thee; but let not God speak to us, lest we die.* This is absolute obedience to Moses. Concerning the right of kings, God himself, by the mouth of Samuel, says, *This shall be the right of the king you will have to reign over you. He shall take your sons, and set them to drive his chariots and to be his horsemen, and to run before his chariots, and gather in his harvest, and to make his engines of war, and instruments of his chariots; and [he] shall take your daughters to make perfumes, to be his cooks, and bakers. He shall take your fields, your vineyards, and your olive-yards, and give them to his servants. He shall take the tithe of your corn and wine, and give it to the men of his chamber, and to his other servants. He shall take your man-servants, and your maidservants, and the choice of your youth, and employ them in his business. He shall take the tithe of your flocks; and you shall be his servants.* This is

1 Samuel
8.11–17.

absolute power, and summed up in the last words, *you shall be his servants.*[1] Again, when the people heard what power their king was to have; yet they consented thereto, and say thus: *We will be as all other nations, and our king shall judge our causes,*

1 Samuel
8.19–20.

and go before us, to conduct our wars. Here is confirmed the right that sovereigns have, both to the *militia* and to all *judicature*, in which is contained as absolute power as one man can possibly transfer to another. Again, the prayer of King Solomon to God was this: *Give to thy servant understanding, to judge thy people, and to discern between good and*

1 Kings 3.9.

evil. It belonged therefore to the sovereign to be *judge* and to prescribe the rules of *discerning good and evil*, which rules are laws; and therefore in him is the legislative power. Saul sought the life of David; yet when it was in his power to slay Saul, and his servants would have done it, David forbade them, saying, *God forbid I should do such*

1 Samuel
24.9.

an act against my Lord, the anointed of God. For obedience of servants St. Paul says, *Servants obey*

Colossians
3.20.

your masters in all things. and *Children obey your*

parents in all things. There is simple obedience in those that are subject to paternal or despotical dominion. Again, *The scribes and Pharisees sit in Moses' chair, and therefore all that they shall bid you observe, that observe and do.* There again is simple obedience. And St. Paul, *Warn them that they subject themselves to princes, and to those that are in authority, and obey them.* This obedience is also simple. Lastly, our Savior himself acknowledges that men ought to pay such taxes as are by kings imposed where he says, *Give to Caesar that which is Caesar's* and paid such taxes himself. And that the king's word is sufficient to take anything from any subject, when there is need; and that the king is judge of that need; for he himself, as king of the Jews, commanded his Disciples to take the ass and ass's colt to carry him into Jerusalem, saying, *Go into the village over against you, and you shall find a she ass tied, and her colt with her; untie them, and bring them to me. And if any man ask you, what you mean by it, say the Lord has need of them; and they will let them go.* They will not ask whether his necessity be a sufficient title nor whether he be judge of that necessity, but acquiesce in the will of the Lord.

Colossians
3.22.

Matthew
23.2–3.

Titus 3.2.

Matthew
21.2–3.

17. To these places may be added also that of Genesis, *You shall be as gods, knowing good and evil.* And, *Who told thee that thou wast naked? Hast thou eaten of the tree, of which I commanded thee thou shouldest not eat?*[2] For the cognizance or judicature of good and evil, being forbidden by the name of the fruit of the tree of knowledge, as a trial of Adam's obedience, the devil to inflame the ambition of the woman, to whom that fruit already seemed beautiful, told her that by tasting it they should be as gods, knowing good and evil. Whereupon having both eaten, they did indeed take upon them God's office, which is judicature of good and evil, but acquired no new ability to distinguish between them aright.[3] And whereas it is said that having eaten, they saw they were naked, no man has so interpreted that place as if they had been formerly blind and saw not their own skins, the meaning is plain that it was then

Genesis 3.5.

---

1   *you shall be his servants*   It is ironic that Hobbes uses this passage to support absolute sovereignty since the passage clearly is warning the Israelites against establishing a monarchy.

2   *Who told thee ... shouldest not eat?*   Genesis 3.11.
3   *aright*   Correctly.

they first judged their nakedness (wherein it was God's will to create them) to be uncomely, and by being ashamed did tacitly censure God himself. And thereupon God says, *Hast thou eaten*, etc., as if he should say, doest thou that owes me obedience take upon thee to judge of my commandments? Whereby it is clearly, though allegorically, signified that the commands of them that have the right to command are not by their subjects to be censured nor disputed.

Sovereign power ought in all commonwealths to be absolute. [107] 18. So that it appears plainly, to my understanding, both from reason and Scripture, that the sovereign power, whether placed in one man, as in monarchy, or in one assembly of men, as in popular and aristocratical commonwealths, is as great as possibly men can be imagined to make it. And though of so unlimited a power men may fancy many evil consequences; yet the consequences of the want of it, which is perpetual war of every man against his neighbor, are much worse.[1] The condition of man in this life shall never be without inconveniences; but there happens in no commonwealth any great inconvenience but what proceeds from the subjects' disobedience and breach of those covenants from which the commonwealth has its being. And whosoever thinking sovereign power too great will seek to make it less must subject himself to the power that can limit it, that is to say, to a [still] greater [power].

19. The greatest objection is that of the practice[2] when men ask where and when such power has by subjects been acknowledged. But one may ask them again, when or where has there been a kingdom long free from sedition and civil war? In those nations whose commonwealths have been long-lived and not been destroyed but by foreign war the subjects never did dispute of the sovereign power. But howsoever, an argument from the practice of men that have not sifted to the bottom, and with exact reason weighed the causes and nature of commonwealths, and suffer daily those miseries that proceed from the ignorance thereof, is invalid. For though in all places of the world men should lay the foundation of their houses on the sand, it could not thence be inferred that so it ought to be. The skill of making and maintaining commonwealths consists in certain rules, as does arithmetic and geometry, not, as tennis play, on practice only; which rules neither poor men have the leisure, nor men that have had the leisure have hitherto had the curiosity or the method, to find out.

Chapter 21: Of the Liberty of Subjects

Liberty, what. 1. Liberty or Freedom signifies properly the absence of opposition (by opposition I mean external impediments of motion) and may be applied no less to irrational and inanimate creatures than to rational. For whatsoever is so tied or environed, as it cannot move but within a certain space, which space is determined by the opposition of some external body, we say it has not liberty to go further. And so of all living creatures, whilst they are imprisoned or restrained with walls or chains, and of the water, whilst it is kept in by banks or vessels that otherwise would spread itself into a larger space, we use to say they are not at liberty to move in such manner as without those external impediments they would. But when the impediment of motion is in the constitution of the thing itself, we use not to say it wants the liberty, but the power, to move, as when a stone lies still or a man is fastened to his bed by sickness.[3]

[108] **What it is to be free.** 2. And according to this proper and generally received meaning of the word, a Freeman is he that, in those things which by his strength and wit he is able to do, is not hindered to do what he has

---

1 *though of ... much worse* King James I wrote, "For a king cannot be imagined to be so unruly and tyrannous, but the commonwealth will be kept in better order, notwithstanding thereof by him than it can be by his way-taking.... [I]t is better to live in a commonwealth where nothing is lawful, than [a commonwealth] where all things are lawful to all men" ("The Trew Law of Free Monarchies").

2 *the practice* People's actual behavior.

3 *Liberty or Freedom ... by sickness* Liberty or freedom relates to the absence of *external* impediments to motion. Power relates to the *internal* constitution of a thing that makes it able to do things.

a will to. But when the words free and liberty are applied to anything but bodies, they are abused; for that which is not subject to motion is not subject to impediment; and therefore, when it is said, for example, the way[1] is free, no liberty of the way is signified, but of those that walk in it without stop. And when we say a gift is free, there is not meant any liberty of the gift, but of the giver, that was not bound by any law or covenant to give it. So when we speak freely, it is not the liberty of voice or pronunciation, but of the man whom no law has obliged to speak otherwise than he did. Lastly, from the use of the words free will, no liberty can be inferred of the will, desire, or inclination, but the liberty of the man, which consists in this, that he finds no stop in doing what he has the will, desire, or inclination to do.

Fear and liberty consistent. 3. Fear and liberty are consistent, as when a man throws his goods into the sea for *fear* the ship should sink, he does it nevertheless very willingly,[2] and may refuse to do it if he will; it is therefore the action of one that was *free*; so a man sometimes pays his debt only for *fear* of imprisonment, which, because no body hindered him from detaining, was the action of a man at *liberty*. And generally all actions which men do in commonwealths for *fear* of the law are actions which the doers had *liberty* to omit.[3]

Liberty and necessity consistent. 4. *Liberty* and *necessity* are consistent, as in the water that has not only *liberty* but a *necessity* of descending by the channel; so likewise in the actions which men voluntarily do, which, because they proceed from their will, proceed from *liberty*; and yet because every act of man's will and every desire and inclination proceeds from some cause, and that from another cause, in a continual chain (whose first link is in the hand of God, the first of all causes), proceed from *necessity*.[4] So that to him

that could see the connection of those causes, the *necessity* of all men's voluntary actions would appear manifest. And therefore God, that sees and disposes all things, sees also that the *liberty* of man in doing what he will is accompanied with the *necessity* of doing that which God will and no more nor less. For though men may do many things which God does not command nor is therefore author of them;[5] yet they can have no passion nor appetite to anything of which appetite God's will is not the cause. And did not his will assure the *necessity* of man's will, and consequently of all that on man's will depends, the *liberty* of men would be a contradiction and impediment to the omnipotence and *liberty* of God. And this shall suffice, as to the matter in hand, of that natural *liberty*, which only is properly called *liberty*.

Artificial bonds, or covenants. 5. But as men, for the attaining of peace and conservation of themselves thereby, have made an artificial man, which we call a commonwealth, so also have they made artificial chains, called *civil laws*, which they themselves by mutual covenants [109] have fastened at one end to the lips of that man or assembly to whom they have given the sovereign power and at the other to their own ears. These bonds, in their own nature but weak, may nevertheless be made to hold by the danger, though not by the difficulty, of breaking them.

Liberty of subjects consists in liberty from covenants. 6. In relation to these bonds only it is that I am to speak now of the *liberty of subjects*. For seeing there is no commonwealth in the world wherein there be rules enough set down for the regulating of all the actions and words of men (as being a thing impossible); it follows necessarily that in all kinds of actions by the laws pretermitted,[6] men have the liberty of doing what their own reasons shall suggest for the most profitable to themselves. For if we take liberty in the proper

---

1   *way* Path.

2   *when a man ... very willingly* This example is from Aristotle, *Nicomachean Ethics* 3.1.

3   *all actions ... to omit* Hobbes needs freedom to be consistent with fear, because fear motivates people to institute a sovereign.

4   *liberty ... necessity* Liberty concerns absence of external impediments. Necessity concerns what must occur because there is a cause of it.

5   *God, that sees ... author of them* Hobbes agrees with Calvin that God is the cause of sin. Many of Hobbes' contemporaries did not like the fine line he drew when he proposed that God is the cause of everything but not the author of everything, because he does not command people to sin.

6   *pretermitted* Overlooked. Liberty is what is left over after the sovereign has issued all of his laws or commands.

sense, for corporal liberty, that is to say, freedom from chains and prison, it were very absurd for men to clamor as they do for the liberty they so manifestly enjoy. Again, if we take liberty for an exemption from laws, it is no less absurd for men to demand as they do that liberty by which all other men may be masters of their lives. And yet as absurd as it is, this is it they demand, not knowing that the laws are of no power to protect them without a sword in the hands of a man or men to cause those laws to be put in execution. The liberty of a subject lies therefore only in those things which, in regulating their actions, the sovereign has pretermitted, such as is the liberty to buy, and sell, and otherwise contract with one another, to choose their own abode, their own diet, their own trade of life, and institute their children as they themselves think fit, and the like.

Liberty of the subject consistent with the unlimited power of the sovereign. 7. Nevertheless we are not to understand that by such liberty the sovereign power of life and death is either abolished or limited. For it has been already shown that nothing the sovereign representative can do to a subject, on what pretence soever, can properly be called injustice or injury, because every subject is author of every act the sovereign does, so that he never wants right to any thing, otherwise than as he himself is the subject of God and bound thereby to observe the laws of nature. And therefore it may and does often happen in commonwealths that a subject may be put to death by the command of the sovereign power and yet neither do the other wrong, as when Jephthah caused his daughter to be sacrificed;[1] in which, and the like cases, he that so dies had liberty to do the action for which he is nevertheless, without injury, put to death. And the same holds also in a sovereign prince that puts to death an innocent subject. For though the action be against the law of nature, as being contrary to equity, as was the killing of Uriah by David; yet it was not an injury to Uriah, but to God. Not to Uriah, because the right to do what he pleased was given him by Uriah himself; and

yet to God, because David was God's subject and prohibited all iniquity by the law of nature, which distinction David himself, when he repented the fact, evidently confirmed, saying, *To thee only have I sinned.*[2] In the same manner the people of [110] Athens, when they banished the most potent of their commonwealth for ten years, thought they committed no injustice; and yet they never questioned what crime he had done, but what hurt he would do; nay, they commanded the banishment of they knew not whom; and every citizen bringing his oyster shell into the market place, written with the name of him he desired should be banished, without actually accusing him sometimes[3] banished an Aristides,[4] for his reputation of justice, and sometimes a scurrilous jester, as Hyperbolus,[5] to make a jest of it. And yet a man cannot say the sovereign people of Athens wanted right to banish them, or an Athenian the liberty to jest, or to be just.

8. The liberty whereof there is so frequent and honorable mention in the histories and philosophy of the ancient Greeks and Romans and in the writings and discourse of those that from them have received all their learning in the politics is not the liberty of particular men, but the liberty of the commonwealth,[6] which is the same with that which every man then should have if there were no civil laws nor commonwealth at all. And the effects of it also be the same. For as

The liberty which writers praise, is the liberty of sovereigns, not of private men.

---

1 *when Jephthah ... be sacrificed* Jephthah's daughter innocently came to greet him after his military victory; he had made a vow to sacrifice the first to come to him if he won. See Judges 11.29–40.

2 *To thee only have I sinned* Psalm 51:4. The story of David and Uriah is in 2 Samuel 11.

3 *sometimes* At one time.

4 *Aristides* Honored Athenian soldier and statesman (536–468 BCE), known as Aristides "the Just." He was nevertheless banished by ostracism in 482 BCE. This is commonly explained as a consequence of the jealousy of the Athenian populace who voted for his ostracism.

5 *Hyperbolus* (?–411 BCE). Athenian politician. He was variously reported to be universally hated because of the power he wielded (springing from his persuasive rhetoric in the assembly), or, according to one source, because of "the degeneracy of his habits" (Philochorus, *Atthis*, Fragment 30). Hyperbolus was ostracized c. 417 BCE.

6 *The liberty whereof ... of the commonwealth* Hobbes is criticizing the neo-Roman or republican theory of government in 21.8–15.

amongst masterless men there is perpetual war of every man against his neighbor, no inheritance to transmit to the son nor to expect from the father, no propriety of goods or lands, no security, but a full and absolute liberty in every particular man, so in states and commonwealths not dependent on one another every commonwealth (not every man) has an absolute liberty to do what it shall judge (that is to say, what that man or assembly that represents it shall judge) most conducing to their benefit. But withal they live in the condition of a perpetual war and upon the confines of battle, with their frontiers armed and cannons planted against their neighbors round about. The Athenians and Romans were free, that is, free commonwealths; not that any particular men had the liberty to resist their own representative, but that their representative had the liberty to resist, or invade, other people. There is written on the turrets of the city of Luca in great characters at this day the word Libertas; yet no man can thence infer that a particular man has more liberty or immunity from the service of the commonwealth there than in Constantinople. Whether a commonwealth be monarchical or popular, the freedom is still the same.

9. But it is an easy thing for men to be deceived by the specious name of liberty and (for want of judgment to distinguish) mistake that for their private inheritance and birthright which is the right of the public only. And when the same error is confirmed by the authority of men in reputation for their writings on this subject, it is no wonder if it produce sedition and change of government. In these western parts of the world we are made to receive our opinions concerning the institution and rights of commonwealths from Aristotle, Cicero, and other men, Greeks and Romans, that, living under popular states, derived those rights [111] not from the principles of nature, but transcribed them into their books out of the practice of their own commonwealths, which were popular, as the grammarians describe the rules of language out of the practice of the time or the rules of poetry out of the poems of Homer and Virgil. And because the Athenians were taught (to keep them from desire of changing their government) that they

were freemen, and all that lived under monarchy were slaves, therefore Aristotle puts it down in his Politics, In democracy, Liberty is to be supposed; for it is commonly held that no man is Free in any other government.[1] And as Aristotle, so Cicero and other writers have grounded their civil doctrine on the opinions of the Romans, who were taught to hate monarchy, at first by them that, having deposed their sovereign, shared amongst them the sovereignty of Rome, and afterwards by their successors. And by reading of these Greek and Latin authors men from their childhood have gotten a habit, under a false show of liberty, of favoring tumults, and of licentious[2] controlling the actions of their sovereigns, and again of controlling those controllers, with the effusion of so much blood as I think I may truly say there was never anything so dearly bought as these western parts have bought the learning of the Greek and Latin tongues.

10. To come now to the particulars of the true liberty of a subject, that is to say, what are the things which, though commanded by the sovereign, he may nevertheless without injustice refuse to do, we are to consider what rights we pass away when we make a commonwealth or, which is all one, what liberty we deny ourselves by owning all the actions, without exception, of the man or assembly we make our sovereign. For in the act of our *submission* consists both our *obligation* and our *liberty*, which must therefore be inferred by arguments taken from thence; there being no obligation on any man which arises not from some act of his own; for all men equally are by nature free. And because such arguments must either be drawn from the express words, *I authorize all his actions*, or from the intention of him that submits himself to his power (which intention is to be understood by the end for which he so submits), the obligation and liberty of the subject is to be derived either from those words or others equivalent, or else from the end of the

Liberty of subjects, how to be measured.

---

1   *Aristotle ... other government* See Aristotle, *Politics*, 6.2. Aristotle, however, is in this passage reporting a common opinion, one that he does not seem to endorse elsewhere.

2   *licentious* Lawless.

institution of sovereignty; namely, the peace of the subjects within themselves and their defense against a common enemy.[1]

Subjects have liberty to defend their own bodies, even against them that lawfully invade them.

11. First therefore, seeing sovereignty by institution is by covenant of every one to every one, and sovereignty by acquisition by covenants of the vanquished to the victor or child to the parent, it is manifest that every subject has liberty in all those things the right whereof cannot by covenant be transferred. I have shown before, in the fourteenth chapter, that covenants not to defend a man's own body are void. Therefore,

Are not bound to hurt themselves.
[112]

12. If the sovereign command a man (though justly condemned) to kill, wound, or maim himself, or not to resist those that assault him, or to abstain from the use of food, air, medicine, or any other thing without which he cannot live; yet has that man the liberty to disobey.

13. If a man be interrogated by the sovereign or his authority, concerning a crime done by himself, [then] he is not bound (without assurance of pardon) to confess it, because no man, as I have shown in the same chapter, can be obliged by covenant to accuse himself.

14. Again, the consent of a subject to sovereign power is contained in these words, *I authorize, or take upon me, all his actions*, in which there is no restriction at all of his own former natural liberty; for by allowing him to *kill me*, I am not bound to kill myself when he commands me.[2] It is one thing to say, *Kill me, or my fellow, if you please*, another thing to say, *I will kill myself, or my fellow*.[3] It follows, therefore, that

15. No man is bound by the words themselves either to kill himself or any other man; and consequently, that the obligation a man may sometimes have, upon the command of the sovereign, to execute any dangerous or dishonorable office, depends not on the words of our submission, but on the intention, which is to be understood by the end thereof. When therefore our refusal to obey frustrates the end for which the sovereignty was ordained, then there is no liberty to refuse; otherwise, there is.

16. Upon this ground a man that is commanded as a soldier to fight against the enemy, though his sovereign have right enough to punish his refusal with death, may nevertheless in many cases refuse without injustice, as when he substitutes a sufficient soldier in his place; for in this case he deserts not the service of the commonwealth. And there is allowance to be made for natural timorousness, not only to women (of whom no such dangerous duty is expected) but also to men of feminine courage. When armies fight, there is on one side or both a running away; yet when they do it not out of treachery, but fear, they are not esteemed to do it unjustly, but dishonorably. For the same reason to avoid battle is not injustice but cowardice. But he that enrolls himself a soldier, or takes impressed money, takes away the excuse of a timorous nature and is obliged, not only to go to the battle but also not to run from it without his captain's leave. And when the defense of the commonwealth requires at once the help of all that are able to bear arms, every one is obliged, because otherwise the institution of the commonwealth, which they have not the purpose or courage to preserve, was in vain.

Nor to warfare, unless they voluntarily undertake it.

17. To resist the sword of the commonwealth in defense of another man, guilty or innocent, no man has liberty, because such liberty takes away from the sovereign the means of protecting us and is therefore destructive of the very essence of government. But in case a great many men together have already resisted the sovereign power unjustly or committed some capital crime for which every

---

1   *the obligation ... common enemy* Hobbes is emphasizing his theory of authorization in this and the following paragraphs, and suppressing his theory of alienation. He is claiming here that authorization preserves the complete liberty of a subject and that political obligation arises from the subject's intention in entering a civil state.

2   *by allowing ... he commands me* Authorizing the sovereign to kill me does not impose any obligation on me. So if the sovereign tried to "command" me to kill myself, I would be under no obligation to do so.

3   *It is one thing ... my fellow* The sentence "Kill me, or my fellow, if you please" authorizes the addressee to kill me or my fellow. The sentence "I will kill myself, or my fellow" would impose an obligation on me (in virtue of the future tense) if it were possible for a per-

son to lay down his right to self-preservation. But it is not.

one of them expects death, whether have they not the liberty then to join together, and assist, and defend one another? Certainly they have; for [113] they but defend their lives, which the guilty man may as well do as the innocent. There was indeed injustice in the first breach of their duty; their bearing of arms subsequent to it, though it be to maintain what they have done, is no new unjust act. And if it be only to defend their persons, it is not unjust at all. But the offer of pardon takes from them to whom it is offered the plea of self-defense, and makes their perseverance in assisting or defending the rest unlawful.

The greatest liberty of subjects, depends on the silence of the law.   18. As for other liberties, they depend on the silence of the law. In cases where the sovereign has prescribed no rule, there the subject has the liberty to do or forbear, according to his own discretion. And therefore such liberty is in some places more and in some less, and in some times more, in other times less, according as they that have the sovereignty shall think most convenient. As for example, there was a time when in England a man might enter into his own land (and dispossess such as wrongfully possessed it) by force. But in after times that liberty of forcible entry was taken away by a statute made (by the king) in parliament. And in some places of the world men have the liberty of many wives; in other places, such liberty is not allowed.

19. If a subject have a controversy with his sovereign of[1] debt, or of right of possession of lands or goods, or concerning any service required at his hands, or concerning any penalty, corporal or pecuniary, grounded on a precedent law, he has the same liberty to sue for his right as if it were against a subject, and before such judges as are appointed by the sovereign. For seeing the sovereign demands by force of a former law and not by virtue of his power, he declares thereby that he requires no more than shall appear to be due by that law. The suit therefore is not contrary to the will of the sovereign, and consequently the subject has the liberty to demand the hearing of his cause, and sentence according to that law. But if he demand or take anything by pretence of his

power, there lies, in that case, no action of law; for all that is done by him in virtue of his power is done by the authority of every subject, and consequently, he that brings an action against the sovereign brings it against himself.

20. If a monarch or sovereign assembly grant a liberty to all or any of his subjects, which grant standing [and if as a result of this], he is disabled to provide for their safety, [then] the grant is void, unless he directly renounce or transfer the sovereignty to another. For in that he might openly (if it had been his will) and in plain terms have renounced or transferred it and did not, it is to be understood it was not his will, but that the grant proceeded from ignorance of the repugnancy[2] between such a liberty and the sovereign power; and therefore the sovereignty is still retained, and consequently all those powers which are necessary to the exercising thereof, such as are the power of war and peace, of judicature, of appointing officers and counselors, of levying money, and the rest named in the eighteenth chapter.

21. The obligation of subjects to the sovereign is understood to last as long [as] and no longer than the power lasts by which he is able to protect them. For the right men have by nature to protect themselves, when none else can protect them, can by no covenant be relinquished. The sovereignty is the soul of the commonwealth, which, once departed from the body, the members do no more receive their motion from it. The end of obedience is protection, which, wheresoever a man sees it either in his own or in another's sword, nature applies his obedience to it and his endeavor to maintain it. And though sovereignty, in the intention of them that make it, be immortal; yet is it in its own nature not only subject to violent death by foreign war, but also through the ignorance and passions of men, it has in it from the very institution many seeds of a natural mortality, by intestine[3] discord.   *[114] In what cases subjects are absolved of their obedience to their sovereign.*

22. If a subject be taken prisoner in war or his person or his means of life be within the guards of the enemy, and has his life and corporal liberty   *In case of captivity.*

---

1   *of* Regarding.

2   *repugnancy* Conflict.

3   *intestine* Internal.

given him on condition to be subject to the victor, [then] he has liberty to accept the condition; and, having accepted it, is the subject of him that took him, because he had no other way to preserve himself. The case is the same if he be detained on the same terms in a foreign country. But if a man be held in prison or bonds or is not trusted with the liberty of his body, he cannot be understood to be bound by covenant to subjection and therefore may, if he can, make his escape by any means whatsoever.

In case the sovereign cast off the government from himself and his heirs. 23. If a monarch shall relinquish the sovereignty, both for himself and his heirs, his subjects return to the absolute liberty of nature; In case the sovereign cast off nature, because, though nature may declare who are his sons and who are the nearest of his kin; yet it depends on his own will, as has been said in the precedent chapter,[1] who shall be his heir. If therefore he will have no heir, there is no sovereignty, nor subjection. The case is the same if he die without known kindred and without declaration of his heir. For then there can no heir be known, and consequently no subjection be due.

In case of banishment. 24. If the sovereign banish his subject, [then] during the banishment he is not subject. But he that is sent on a message or has leave to travel is still subject, but it is by contract between sovereigns, not by virtue of the covenant of subjection. For whosoever enters into another's dominion is subject to all the laws thereof, unless he have a privilege by the amity[2] of the sovereigns or by special license.

In case the sovereign render himself subject to another. 25. If a monarch subdued by war render himself subject to the victor, his subjects are delivered from their former obligation and become obliged to the victor. But if he be held prisoner or have not the liberty of his own body, he is not understood to have given away the right of sovereignty; and therefore his subjects are obliged to yield obedience to the magistrates formerly placed, governing not in their own name, but in his. For, his right remaining, the question is only of the administration, that is to say, of the magistrates

and officers, which if he have not means to name, [115] he is supposed to[3] approve those which he himself had formerly appointed.

[...]

Chapter 26: Of Civil Laws

Civil law, what. 1. By Civil Laws, I understand the laws that men are therefore bound to observe, because they are members, not of this or that commonwealth in particular, but of a commonwealth. For the knowledge of particular laws belongs to them [137] that profess the study of the laws of their several countries; but the knowledge of civil law in general to any man. The ancient law of Rome was called their *civil law* from the word *civitas*, which signifies a commonwealth; and those countries which, having been under the Roman Empire and governed by that law, retain still such part thereof as they think fit, call that part the civil law to distinguish it from the rest of their own civil laws. But that is not it I intend to speak of here, my design being not to show what is law here and there, but what is law, as Plato, Aristotle, Cicero, and divers others have done, without taking upon them the profession of the study of the law.

2. And first it is manifest that law in general is not counsel, but command, nor a command of any man to any man, but only of him whose command is addressed to one formerly obliged to obey him. And as for civil law, it adds only the name of the person commanding, which is *persona civitatis*, the person of the commonwealth.

3. Which considered, I define civil law in this manner. Civil Law *is to every subject those rules which the commonwealth has commanded him (by word, writing, or other sufficient sign of the will) to make use of, for the distinction of right and wrong, that is to say, of what is contrary and what is not contrary to the rule.*

4. In which definition there is nothing that is not at first sight evident. For every man sees that some laws are addressed to all the subjects in general, some to particular provinces, some to particular vocations, and some to particular men;

---

1   *the precedent chapter*   Apparently 29.20.
2   *amity*   Friendly agreements.

3   *supposed to*   Presumed to.

and are therefore laws to every of those to whom the command is directed, and to none else. As also, that laws are the rules of just and unjust, nothing being reputed unjust that is not contrary to some law. Likewise, that none can make laws but the commonwealth, because our subjection is to the commonwealth only; and that commands are to be signified by sufficient signs, because a man knows not otherwise how to obey them. And therefore, whatsoever can from this definition by necessary consequence be deduced, ought to be acknowledged for truth. Now I deduce from it this that follows.

1. The sovereign is legislator. 5. The legislator in all commonwealths is only the sovereign, be he one man, as in a monarchy, or one assembly of men, as in a democracy or aristocracy. For the legislator is he that makes the law. And the commonwealth only prescribes and commands the observation of those rules which we call law; therefore the commonwealth is the legislator. But the commonwealth is no person, nor has capacity to do anything but by the representative, that is, the sovereign; and therefore the sovereign is the sole legislator.[1] For the same reason, none can abrogate a law made, but the sovereign, because a law is not abrogated but by another law that forbids it to be put in execution.

2. And not subject to civil law.
[138] 6. The sovereign of a commonwealth, be it an assembly or one man, is not subject to the civil laws. For having power to make and repeal laws, he may, when he pleases, free himself from that subjection by repealing those laws that trouble him and making of new, and consequently he was free before. For he is free that can be free when he will; nor is it possible for any person to be bound to himself, because he that can bind can release; and therefore he that is bound to himself only is not bound.

3. Use, a law not by virtue of time, 7. When long use obtains the authority of a law, it is not the length of time that makes the authority, but the will of the sovereign signified by his silence (for silence is sometimes an argument of consent);[2] and it is no longer law, than the sovereign shall be silent therein. And therefore if the sovereign shall have a question of right grounded, not upon his present will, but upon the laws formerly made, the length of time shall bring no prejudice to his right; but the question shall be judged by equity. For many unjust actions and unjust sentences go uncontrolled a longer time than any man can remember. And our lawyers account no customs law but such as are reasonable, and that evil customs are to be abolished; but the judgment of what is reasonable and of what is to be abolished, belonged to him that makes the law, which is the sovereign assembly or monarch. **but of the sovereign's consent.**

8. The law of nature and the civil law contain each other and are of equal extent.[3] For the laws of nature, which consist in equity, justice, gratitude, and other moral virtues on these depending, in the condition of mere nature (as I have said before in the end of the fifteenth Chapter), are not properly laws, but qualities that dispose men to peace and to obedience. When a commonwealth is once settled, then are they actually laws, and not before, as being then the commands of the commonwealth; and therefore also civil laws; for it is the sovereign power that obliges men to obey them. For the differences of private men to declare what is equity, what is justice, and is moral virtue, and to make them binding, there is need of the ordinances of sovereign power; and punishments to be ordained for such as shall break them, which ordinances are therefore part of the civil law. The law of nature therefore is a part of the civil law in all commonwealths of the world. Reciprocally also, the civil law is a part of the dictates of nature. For justice, that is to say, performance of covenant and giving to every man his own is a dictate **4. The law of nature and the civil law contain each other.**

---

1   *therefore the sovereign is the sole legislator*   England had long been a monarchy prior to 1649 and became one again with the Restoration in 1660: Hobbes thought that parliament had no part in England's sovereignty and that the belief that it did had helped to cause the English Civil War.

2   *When long use ... argument of consent*   Hobbes is probably criticizing Edward Coke, the great advocate of Common Law. Hobbes criticized his views at greater length in *A Dialogue Between a Philosopher and a Student of the Common Laws of England.*

3   *The law of nature ... of equal extent*   Hobbes must be speaking metaphorically since the relation "x contains y" is asymmetric: if x contains y, then y cannot contain x. Hobbes certainly thought that civil laws entail the laws of nature. It is harder to see the converse.

of the law of nature. But every subject in a commonwealth has covenanted to obey the civil law; either one with another, as when they assemble to make a common representative, or with the representative itself one by one when, subdued by the sword, they promise obedience that they may receive life; and therefore obedience to the civil law is part also of the law of nature. Civil and natural law are not different kinds, but different parts of law, whereof one part, being written, is called civil, the other unwritten, natural. But the right of nature, that is, the natural liberty of man, may by the civil law be abridged and restrained, nay, the end of making laws is no other but such restraint, without which there cannot possibly be [139] any peace. And law was brought into the world for nothing else but to limit the natural liberty of particular men in such manner as they might not hurt, but assist one another, and join together against a common enemy.

5. Provincial laws are not made by custom, but by the sovereign power.

9. If the sovereign of one commonwealth subdue a people that have lived under other written laws and afterwards govern them by the same laws by which they were governed before; yet those laws are the civil laws of the victor and not of the vanquished commonwealth. For the legislator is he, not by whose authority the laws were first made, but by whose authority they now continue to be laws. And therefore where there be divers provinces within the dominion of a commonwealth and in those provinces diversity of laws, which commonly are called the customs of each several province, we are not to understand that such customs have their force only from length of time, but that they were anciently laws written or otherwise made known for the constitutions and statutes of their sovereigns, and are now laws, not by virtue of the prescription of time, but by the constitutions of their present sovereigns. But if an unwritten law in all the provinces of a dominion shall be generally observed and no iniquity appear in the use thereof, that law can be no other but a law of nature, equally obliging all mankind.

6. Some foolish opinions of lawyers

10. Seeing then all laws, written and unwritten, have their authority and force from the will of the commonwealth, that is to say, from the will of the representative, which in a monarchy is the monarch and in other commonwealths the sovereign assembly, a man may wonder from whence proceed such opinions as are found in the books of lawyers of eminence in several commonwealths, directly or by consequence making the legislative power depend on private men or subordinate judges. As for example, *that the common law has no controller but the parliament*, which is true only where a parliament has the sovereign power and cannot be assembled nor dissolved, but by their own discretion.[1] For if there be a right in any else to dissolve them, there is a right also to control them and consequently to control their controllings. And if there be no such right, then the controller of laws is not *parlamentum*, but *rex in parlamento* [the king in parliament]. And where a parliament is sovereign, if it should assemble never[2] so many or so wise men from the countries subject to them for whatsoever cause; yet there is no man will believe that such an assembly has thereby acquired to themselves a legislative power. *Item* [also it has been claimed], that the two arms of a commonwealth are *force and justice, the first whereof is in the king, the other deposited in the hands of the parliament*.[3] As if a commonwealth could consist where the force were in any hand which justice had not the authority to command and govern.

concerning the making of laws.

11. That law can never be against reason, our lawyers are agreed, and that not the letter (that is, every construction of it), but that which is according to the intention of the legislator is the law. And it is true; but the doubt is of whose reason it is that shall be received for[4] law. It is not meant of any private reason; for then there would be as much contradiction in the laws as there is in the Schools; nor yet, as Sir Edward Coke makes it, an *artificial perfection of reason, gotten by long*

7.

[140]

---

1   *which is true ... their own discretion*   The English parliament when Hobbes was writing was assembled at the command of the monarch, and was also dissolved at his command.

2   *never*   Ever.

3   *the first whereof ... the parliament*   Hobbes is criticizing various actions by parliament in the early 1640s. For example, parliament organized a military force independent of the king.

4   *received for*   Accepted as.

study, observation, and experience, as his was. For it is possible long study may increase and confirm erroneous sentences; and where men build on false grounds, the more they build, the greater is the ruin; and of those that study and observe with equal time and diligence, the reasons and resolutions are and must remain discordant; and therefore it is not that *juris prudential*[1] or wisdom of subordinate judges, but the reason of this our artificial man the commonwealth and his command that makes law; and the commonwealth being in their representative but one person, there cannot easily arise any contradiction in the laws; and when there does [arise contradiction], the same reason is able, by interpretation or alteration, to take it away. In all courts of justice, the sovereign (which is the person of the commonwealth) is he that judges; the subordinate judge ought to have regard to the reason which moved his sovereign to make such law, that his sentence may be according thereunto, which then is his sovereign's sentence; otherwise it is his own, and an unjust one.

12. From this, that the law is a command, and a command consists in declaration or manifestation of the will of him that commands by voice, writing, or some other sufficient argument of the same,[2] we may understand that the command of the commonwealth is law only to those that have means to take notice of it. Over natural fools, children, or madmen there is no law, no more than over brute beasts; nor are they capable of the title of just or unjust, because they had never power to make any covenant or to understand the consequences thereof, and consequently never took upon them to authorize the actions of any sovereign, as they must do that make to themselves a commonwealth. And as those from whom nature or accident has taken away the notice of all laws in general, so also every man, from whom any accident not proceeding from his own default, has taken away the means to take notice of any particular law, is excused if he observe it

not; and to speak properly, that law is no law to him. It is therefore necessary to consider in this place what arguments and signs be sufficient for the knowledge of what is the law, that is to say, what is the will of the sovereign, as well in monarchies as in other forms of government.

13. And first, if it be a law that obliges all the subjects without exception and is not written nor otherwise published in such places as they may take notice thereof, it is a law of nature. For whatever men are to take knowledge of for[3] law, not upon other men's words, but every one from his own reason, must be such as is agreeable to the reason of all men; which no law can be, but the law of nature. The laws of nature therefore need not any publishing nor proclamation, as being contained in this one sentence, approved by all the world, *Do not that to another which thou thinkest unreasonable to be done by another to thyself.*

14. Secondly, if it be a law that obliges only some condition of men or one particular man and be not written nor published by word, then also it is a law of nature and known by the same arguments and signs that distinguish those in such a condition from other subjects. For whatsoever law is not written or some way published by him that makes it law can be known no way but by the reason of him that is to obey it; and is therefore also a law not only civil, but natural. For example, if the sovereign employ a public minister, without written instructions what to do, [then] he is obliged to take for instructions the dictates of reason, as, if he make a judge, the judge is to take notice that his sentence ought to be according to the reason of his sovereign (which being always understood to be equity), he is bound to it by the law of nature; or if an ambassador, he is (in all things not contained in his written instructions), to take for instruction that which reason dictates to be most conducing to his sovereign's interest, and so of all other ministers of the sovereignty, public and private. All which instructions of natural reason may be comprehended under one name of *fidelity*, which is a branch of natural justice.

(margin left): Sir Edw. Coke upon Littleton, Book 2, Chapter 6, Folio 97, b.

8. Law made, if not also made known, is no law.

(margin right): Unwritten laws are all of them laws of nature.

[141]

---

1   *juris prudential* Latin: science of the interpretation of law.
2   *of the same* Similar.

3   *take knowledge of for* Know to be.

15. The law of nature excepted, it belonged to the essence of all other laws to be made known to every man that shall be obliged to obey them, either by word or writing or some other act known to proceed from the sovereign authority. For the will of another cannot be understood but by his own word or act or by conjecture taken from his scope and purpose, which in the person of the commonwealth is to be supposed always consonant to¹ equity and reason. And in ancient time, before letters were in common use, the laws were many times put into verse, [in order] that the rude people, taking pleasure in singing or reciting them, might the more easily retain them in memory. And for the same reason Solomon advises a man to bind the Ten Commandments upon his ten fingers. And for the Law which Moses gave to the people of Israel at the renewing of the Covenant, he bids them to teach it to their children by discoursing of it both at home and upon the way at going to bed and at rising from bed; and to write it upon the posts and doors of their houses and to assemble the people, man, woman, and child, to hear it read.

Proverbs 7.3.

Deuteronomy 11.19.

Deuteronomy 31.12.

Nothing is law where the legislator cannot be known.

16. Nor is it enough the law be written and published, but also that there be manifest signs that it proceeds from the will of the sovereign. For private men, when they have or think they have force enough to secure their unjust designs and convoy them safely to their ambitious ends, may publish for laws what they please, without or against the legislative authority. There is therefore requisite not only a declaration of the law, but also sufficient signs of the author and authority.² The author or legislator is supposed in every commonwealth to be evident, because he is the sovereign, who, having been constituted by the consent of every one, is supposed by every one to be sufficiently known. And though the ignorance and security of men be such, for the most part, as that when the memory of the first constitution of their commonwealth is worn out,³ they do not

[142]

consider by whose power they use to be defended against their enemies and to have their industry protected and to be righted when injury is done them; yet because no man that considers can make question of it, no excuse can be derived from the ignorance of where the sovereignty is placed. And it is a dictate of natural reason and consequently an evident law of nature that no man ought to weaken that power, the protection whereof he has himself demanded or wittingly received against others. Therefore of who is sovereign, no man but by his own fault (whatsoever evil men suggest), can make any doubt. The difficulty consists in the evidence of the authority derived from him, the removing whereof depends on the knowledge of the public registers, public counsels, public ministers, and public seals, by which all laws are sufficiently verified; verified, I say, not authorized; for the verification is but the testimony and record, not the authority of the law, which consists in the command of the sovereign only.

Difference between verifying and authorizing.

17. If therefore a man have a question of injury, depending on the law of nature,⁴ that is to say, on common equity, the sentence of the judge, that by commission has authority to take cognizance of such causes, is a sufficient verification of the law of nature in that individual case. For though the advice of one that professes the study of the law be useful for the avoiding of contention; yet it is but advice; it is the judge must tell men what is law, upon the hearing of the controversy.

The law verified by the subordinate judge.

18. But when the question is of injury or crime upon a written law, every man by recourse to the registers by himself or others may, if he will, be sufficiently informed before he do such injury or commit the crime whether it be an injury or not; nay, he ought to do so; for when a man doubts whether the act he goes about be just or unjust, and may inform himself if he will, the doing is unlawful. In like manner, he that supposes himself injured in a case determined by the written law, which he may by himself or others see and consider; if he complain before he con-

By the public registers.

---

1   *consonant to* Consistent with.
2   *a declaration ... the author and authority* In traditional terms, this is the requirement that a law must be promulgated.
3   *worn out* Faded.

---

4   *depending on the law of nature* The injury in question is claimed to be a violation of a law of nature.

sults with the law, he does unjustly, and bewrays [betrays] a disposition rather to vex other men than to demand his own right.

By letters patent[1] and by public seal.[2] 19. If the question be of obedience to a public officer, to have seen his commission (with the public seal) and heard it read, or to have had the means to be informed of it, if a man would, is a sufficient verification of his authority. For every man is obliged to do his best endeavor to inform himself of all written laws that may concern his own future actions.

The interpretation of the law depends on the sovereign power. 20. The legislator [being] known, and the laws either by writing or by the light of nature sufficiently published, there wants yet another very material circumstance to make them obligatory. For it is not the letter, but the intendment or meaning, that is to say, the authentic interpretation of the law (which is the sense of the legislator), in which the nature of the law consists; and [143] therefore the interpretation of all laws depends on the authority sovereign; and the interpreters can be none but those which the sovereign, to whom only the subject owes obedience, shall appoint. For else, by the craft of an interpreter, the law may be made to bear a sense contrary to that of the sovereign, by which means the interpreter becomes the legislator.

All laws need interpretation. 21. All laws, written and unwritten, have need of interpretation. The unwritten law of nature, though it be easy to such as without partiality and passion make use of their natural reason and therefore leaves the violators thereof without excuse; yet considering there be very few, perhaps none, that in some cases are not blinded by self-love or some other passion, it is now become of all laws the most obscure and has consequently the greatest need of able interpreters. The written laws, if laws, if they be short, are easily misinterpreted, for the divers significations of a word or two; if long, they be more obscure by the divers significations of many words, insomuch as no written law, delivered in few or many words, can be well understood without a perfect understanding of the final causes[3] for which the law was made, the knowledge of which final causes is in the legislator. To him therefore there cannot be any knot in the law insoluble either by finding out the ends to undo it by or else by making what ends he will (as Alexander did with his sword in the Gordian knot)[4] by the legislative power; which no other interpreter can do.

The authentical interpretation of law is not that of writers. 22. The interpretation of the laws of nature in a commonwealth depends not on the books of moral philosophy. The authority of writers without the authority of the commonwealth makes not their opinions law, be they never so true. That which I have written in this treatise concerning the moral virtues and of their necessity for the procuring and maintaining peace, though it be evident truth, is not therefore presently law, but because in all commonwealths in the world it is part of the civil law. For though it be naturally reasonable; yet it is by the sovereign power that it is law; otherwise, it were a great error to call the laws of nature unwritten law, whereof we see so many volumes published and in them so many contradictions of one another and of themselves.

The interpreter of the law is the judge giving sentence *viva voce* in every particular case. 23. The interpretation of the law of nature is the sentence of the judge constituted by the sovereign authority to hear and determine such controversies as depend thereon, and consists in the application of the law to the present case. For in the act of judicature the judge does no more but consider whether the demand of the party be consonant to natural reason and equity; and the sentence he gives is therefore the interpretation of the law of nature; which interpretation is authentic, not because it is his private sentence, but because he gives it by authority of the sovereign, whereby it becomes the sovereign's sentence; which is law for that time to the parties pleading.

1   *letters patent* Open letters from persons in authority for various legal purposes.
2   *by public seal* Authenticated by the official seal of the writer.
3   *final causes* Aims.
4   *Alexander ... Gordian knot* According to legend, whoever untied the Gordian knot would rule Asia. Supposedly, Alexander the Great "untied" the knot by cutting it with his sword. He went on to capture much of Asia. Metaphorically speaking, cutting the Gordian knot means dealing with a difficult problem by a bold shortcut.

[144] The sentence of a judge does not bind him or another judge to give like sentence in like cases ever after.

24. But because there is no judge subordinate nor sovereign, but may err in a judgment of equity, if afterward in another like case he find it more consonant to equity to give a contrary sentence, he is obliged to do it. No man's error becomes his own law nor obliges him to persist in it. Neither, for the same reason, becomes it a law to other judges, though sworn to follow it. For though a wrong sentence given by authority of the sovereign, if he know and allow it, in such laws as are mutable, be a constitution of a new law in cases in which every little circumstance is the same; yet in laws immutable, such as are the laws of nature, they are no laws to the same or other judges in the like cases for ever after. Princes succeed one another; and one judge passes, another cometh; nay, heaven and earth shall pass [away]; but not one tittle[1] of the law of nature shall pass; for it is the eternal law of God. Therefore all the sentences of precedent judges that have ever been cannot all together make a law contrary to natural equity. Nor any examples of former judges can warrant an unreasonable sentence or discharge the present judge of the trouble of studying what is equity (in the case he is to judge) from the principles of his own natural reason. For example sake, it is against the law of nature to punish the innocent; and innocent is he that acquits himself judicially and is acknowledged for innocent by the judge. Put[2] the case now that a man is accused of a capital crime, and seeing the power and malice of some enemy and the frequent corruption and partiality of judges, runs away for fear of the event and afterwards is taken and brought to a legal trial and makes it sufficiently appear he was not guilty of the crime and being thereof acquitted is nevertheless condemned to lose his goods; this is a manifest condemnation of the innocent. I say therefore that there is no place in the world where this can be an interpretation of a law of nature or be made a law by the sentences of precedent judges that had done the same. For he that judged it first judged unjustly; and no injustice can be a pattern of judgment to succeeding judges. A written law may forbid innocent men to fly,[3] and they may be punished for flying; but that flying for fear of injury should be taken for presumption of guilt after a man is already absolved of the crime judicially is contrary to the nature of a presumption, which has no place after judgment given. Yet this is set down by a great lawyer[4] for the common law of England: *If a man*, says he, *that is innocent be accused of felony, and for fear flies for the same; albeit he judicially acquits himself of the felony; yet if it be found that he fled for the felony, he shall, notwithstanding his innocency, forfeit all his goods, chattels, debts, and duties. For as to the forfeiture of them, the law will admit no proof against the presumption in law, grounded upon his flight.* Here you see *an innocent man, judicially acquitted, notwithstanding his innocency* (when no written law forbade him to fly) after his acquittal, *upon a presumption in law*, condemned to lose all the goods he hath. If the law ground upon his flight a presumption of the fact (which was capital), the sentence ought to have been capital: if [145] the presumption were not of the fact, for what then ought he to lose his goods? This therefore is no law of England; nor is the condemnation grounded upon a presumption of law, but upon the presumption of the judges. It is also against law to say that no proof shall be admitted against a presumption of law. For all judges, sovereign and subordinate, if they refuse to hear proof, refuse to do justice; for though the sentence be just; yet the judges that condemn, without hearing the proofs offered, are unjust judges; and their presumption is but prejudice; which no man ought to bring with him to the seat of justice whatsoever precedent judgments or examples he shall pretend to follow. There be other things of this nature, wherein men's judgments have been perverted by trusting to precedents; but this is enough to show that though the sentence of the judge be a law to the party pleading; yet it is no law to any judge that shall succeed him in that office.

---

1   *tittle*   Tiniest bit.
2   *Put*   Consider.
3   *fly*   Flee.
4   *great lawyer*   Sir Edward Coke (1522–1634), whose theories Hobbes often attacked.

25. In like manner, when question is of the meaning of written laws, he is not the interpreter of them that writes a commentary upon them. For commentaries are commonly more subject to cavil[1] than the text, and therefore need other commentaries; and so there will be no end of such interpretation. And therefore unless there be an interpreter authorized by the sovereign, from which the subordinate judges are not to recede, the interpreter can be no other than the ordinary judges, in the same manner as they are in cases of the unwritten law; and their sentences are to be taken by them that plead for laws in that particular case, but not to bind other judges in like cases to give like judgments. For a judge may err in the interpretation even of written laws; but no error of a subordinate judge can change the law, which is the general sentence of the sovereign.

The difference between the letter and the sentence of the law.

26. In written laws men use to make a difference[2] between the letter and the sentence of the law; and when by the letter is meant whatsoever can be gathered from the bare words, it is well distinguished. For the significations of almost all are either in themselves or in the metaphorical use of them ambiguous; and [the words] may be drawn in argument to make many senses; but there is only one sense of the law. But if by the letter be meant the literal sense,[3] then the letter and the sentence or intention of the law is all one. For the literal sense is that which the legislator intended should by the letter of the law be signified. Now the intention of the legislator is always supposed to be equity; for it were a great contumely for a judge to think otherwise of the sovereign. He ought therefore, if the word of the law do not fully authorize a reasonable sentence, to supply it with the law of nature; or if the case be difficult, to respite[4] judgment till he have received more ample authority. For example, a written law ordains that he which is thrust out of his house

by force shall be restored by force. It happens that a man by negligence leaves his house empty and returning is kept out by force, in which case there is no special law ordained. It is evident that this case is contained in the same law; for else there is no remedy for him at all, which is to be supposed against the intention of the legislator. Again, the word of the law commands to judge according to the evidence. A man is accused falsely of a fact which the judge himself saw done by another, and not by him that is accused. In this case neither shall the letter of the law be followed to the condemnation of the innocent, nor shall the judge give sentence against the evidence of the witnesses, because the letter of the law is to the contrary; but [the judge] procure of the sovereign that another be made judge and himself witness. So that the incommodity that follows the bare words of a written law may lead him to the intention of the law, whereby to interpret the same the better; though no incommodity can warrant a sentence against the law. For every judge of right and wrong is not judge of what is commodious or incommodious to the commonwealth. [146]

The abilities required in a judge.

27. The abilities required in a good interpreter of the law, that is to say, in a good judge, are not the same with those of an advocate,[5] namely, the study of the laws. For a judge, as he ought to take notice of the fact from none but the witnesses, so also he ought to take notice of the law from nothing but the statutes and constitutions of the sovereign, alleged in the pleading or declared to him by some that have authority from the sovereign power to declare them; and [the judge] need not take care beforehand what he shall judge; for it shall be given him what he shall say concerning the fact, by witnesses; and what he shall say in point of law, from those that shall in their pleadings show it and by authority interpret it upon the place.[6] The Lords of Parliament in England were judges; and most difficult causes have been heard and determined by them; yet few of them were much versed in the study of the laws, and

---

1   *cavil*   Trivial objections.
2   *use to make a difference*   Customarily distinguish.
3   *the literal sense*   Traditionally, this meant *the sense intended by the author*, not, as it is today, the *dictionary meaning*. The literal sense of the law is the sense intended by the sovereign.
4   *respite*   Postpone.

5   *advocate*   Lawyer.
6   *upon the place*   At that time—that is, not in advance.

fewer had made profession of them; and though they consulted with lawyers that were appointed to be present there for that purpose; yet they alone had the authority of giving sentence. In like manner, in the ordinary trials of right, twelve men of the common people are the judges and give sentence, not only of the fact, but of the right; and pronounce simply for the complainant or for the defendant; that is to say, are judges not only of the fact, but also of the right; and in a question of crime, not only determine whether done or not done, but also whether it be *murder, homicide, felony, assault,* and the like, which are determinations of law; but because they are not supposed to know the law of themselves, there is one that has authority to inform them of it in the particular case they are to judge of. But yet if they judge not according to that he tells them, they are not subject thereby to any penalty, unless it be made appear they did it against their consciences or had been corrupted by reward.

28. The things that make a good judge or good interpreter of the laws are, first, *a right understanding* of that principal law of nature called *equity,* which, depending not on the reading of other men's writings, but on the goodness [147] of a man's own natural reason and meditation, is presumed to be in those most that have had most leisure and had the most inclination to meditate thereon. Secondly, *contempt of unnecessary riches and preferments.* Thirdly, *to be able in judgment to divest himself of all fear, anger, hatred, love, and compassion.* Fourthly, and lastly, *patience to hear, diligent attention in hearing, and memory to retain, digest, and apply what he has heard.*

Divisions of law. 29. The difference and division[1] of the laws has been made in divers manners, according to the different methods of those men that have written of them. For it is a thing that depends not on nature, but on the scope of the writer, and is subservient to every man's proper method. In the *Institutions* of Justinian,[2] we find seven sorts

of civil laws: The *edicts, constitutions,* and *epistles of the prince,* that is, of the emperor, because the whole power of the people was in him. Like these are the proclamations of the kings of England. 1.

30. *The decrees of the whole people of Rome* (comprehending the Senate), when they were put to the question by the *Senate.* These were laws, at first, by the virtue of the sovereign power residing in the people; and such of them as by the emperors were not abrogated remained laws by the authority imperial. For all laws that bind are understood to be laws by his authority that has power to repeal them. Somewhat like to these laws are the Acts of Parliament in England. 2.

31. *The decrees of the common people* (excluding the Senate), when they were put to the question by the *tribune* of the people. For such of them as were not abrogated by the emperors, remained laws by the authority imperial. Like to these were the orders of the House of Commons in England. 3.

32. *Senatus consulta,* the *orders of the Senate,* because when the people of Rome grew so numerous as it was inconvenient to assemble them, it was thought fit by the emperor that men should consult the Senate instead of the people: and these have some resemblance with the Acts of Council. 4.

33. *The edicts of praetors,* and (in some cases) of the *aediles,*[3] such as are the chief justices in the courts of England. 5.

34. *Responsa prudentum,* which were the sentences and opinions of those lawyers to whom the emperor gave authority to interpret the law, and to give answer to such as in matter of law demanded their advice; which answers the judges in giving judgment were obliged by the constitutions of the emperor to observe, and should be like the reports of cases judged, if other judges be by the law of England bound to observe them. For the judges of the common law of England are not properly judges, but *juris consulti,*[4] of whom the judges, who are either the lords or twelve men of the country, are in point of law to ask advice. 6.

---

1   *difference and division* Classification.
2   *Institutions of Justinian* Justinian I (c. 482–565), Eastern Roman Emperor, best known for his writings on Roman law, including a systematic treatise, *Institutiones.*

3   *praetors ... aediles* These were two kinds of magistrates of ancient Rome. The praetors held the higher rank.
4   *juris consulti* Lawyers.

35. Also, *unwritten customs* (which in their own nature are an imitation of law), by the tacit consent of the emperor, in case they be not contrary to the law of nature, are very laws.

[148] 36. Another division of laws is into *natural* and *positive*. Natural are those which have been laws from all eternity, and are called not only natural, but also moral laws, consisting in the moral virtues, as justice, equity, and all habits of the mind that conduce to peace and charity, of which I have already spoken in the fourteenth and fifteenth chapters.

37. *Positive* are those which have not been from eternity, but have been made laws by the will of those that have had the sovereign power over others, and are either written or made known to men by some other argument of the will of their legislator.

Another division of law. 38. Again, of positive laws some are *human*, some *divine*; and of human positive laws, some are *distributive*, some *penal*. *Distributive* are those that determine the rights of the subjects, declaring to every man what it is by which he acquires and holds a propriety in lands or goods, and a right or liberty of action; and these speak to all the subjects. *Penal* are those which declare what penalty shall be inflicted on those that violate the law; and [they] speak to the ministers and officers ordained for execution.[1] For though every one ought to be informed of the punishments ordained beforehand for their transgression, nevertheless the command is not addressed to the delinquent (who cannot be supposed will faithfully punish himself), but to public ministers appointed to see the penalty executed. And these penal laws are for the most part written together with the laws distributive, and are sometimes called judgments. For all laws are general judgments, or sentences of the legislator, as also every particular judgment is a law to him whose case is judged.

Divine positive law how made known to be law. 39. *Divine positive laws* (for natural laws, being eternal and universal, are all divine) are those which, being the commandments of God, not from all eternity, nor universally addressed to all

men, but only to a certain people or to certain persons, are declared for such by those whom God has authorized to declare them. But this authority of man to declare what be these positive laws of God, how can it be known? God may command a man by a supernatural way to deliver laws to other men. But because it is of the essence of law that he who is to be obliged be assured of the authority of him that declares it, which we cannot naturally take notice to be from God, *how can a man without supernatural revelations be assured of the revelation received by the declarer? and how can he be bound to obey them?* For the first question, how a man can be assured of the revelation of another without a revelation particularly to himself, it is evidently impossible; for though a man may be induced to believe such revelation from the miracles they see him do or from seeing the extraordinary sanctity of his life or from seeing the extraordinary wisdom or extraordinary felicity of his actions, all which are marks of God's extraordinary favor; yet they are not assured evidences [positive proof] of special revelation. Miracles are marvelous works; but that which is marvelous to one may not be so to another. Sanctity may be feigned; and the visible felicities of this world are most often the [149] work of God by natural and ordinary causes. And therefore no man can infallibly know by natural reason that another has had a supernatural revelation of God's will but only a belief; every one, as the signs thereof shall appear greater or lesser, a firmer or a weaker belief.[2]

40. But for the second,[3] how he can be bound to obey them, it is not so hard. For if the law declared be not against the law of nature (which is undoubtedly God's law) and he undertake to obey it, he is bound by his own act; bound I say

---

1   *ordained for execution* Appointed to enforce the laws.

2   *know by natural reason ... weaker belief* Hobbes draws a sharp line between belief and knowledge. People can believe or have faith in some person who claims to have had a revelation from God. But this is never knowledge. Hobbes does not commit himself here on the question of whether the person who purportedly has the revelation knows that he had it.

3   *the second* This was the second question posed about halfway through 26.39.

to obey it, but not bound to believe it;[1] for men's belief and interior cogitations are not subject to the commands, but only to the operation of God, ordinary or extraordinary. Faith of[2] supernatural law is not a fulfilling,[3] but only an assenting to the same and not a duty that we exhibit to God, but a gift which God freely gives to whom he pleases, as also unbelief is not a breach of any of his laws, but a rejection of them all, except the laws natural. But this that I say will be made yet clearer by the examples and testimonies concerning this point in Holy Scripture. The covenant God made with Abraham in a supernatural manner was thus, *This is the covenant which thou shalt observe between me* Genesis *and thee and thy seed after thee.* Abraham's seed 17.10. had not this revelation, nor were yet in being; yet they are a party to the covenant and bound to obey what Abraham should declare to them for God's law; which they could not be but in virtue of the obedience they owed to their parents, who (if they be subject to no other earthly power, as here in the case of Abraham) have sovereign power over their children and servants. Again, where God says to Abraham, *In thee shall all nations of the earth be blessed; for I know thou wilt command thy children and thy house after thee to keep the way of the Lord, and to observe righteousness and judgment,* it is manifest the obedience of his family, who had no revelation, depended on their former obligation to obey their sovereign. At Mount Sinai Moses only went up to God; the people were forbidden to approach on pain of death; yet were they bound to obey all that Moses declared to them for God's law. Upon what ground, but on this submission of their own, *Speak thou to us, and we will hear thee; but let not God speak to us, lest we die?*[4] By which two places it sufficiently appears that in a common-

wealth a subject that has no certain and assured revelation particularly to himself concerning the will of God is to obey for such the command of the commonwealth; for if men were at liberty to take for God's commandments their own dreams and fancies or the dreams and fancies of private men, scarce two men would agree upon what is God's commandment; and yet in respect of them every man would despise the commandments of the commonwealth. I conclude, therefore, that in all things not contrary to the moral law (that is to say, to the law of nature), all subjects are bound to obey that for divine law which is declared to be so by the laws of the commonwealth.[5] Which also is evident to any man's reason; for whatsoever is not against the law of nature may be made law in the name of them that have the sovereign power; there is no reason men should be the less [150] obliged by it when it is propounded in the name of God. Besides, there is no place in the world where men are permitted to pretend[6] other commandments of God than are declared for such by the commonwealth. Christian states punish those that revolt from Christian religion; and all other states, those that set up any religion by them forbidden. For in whatsoever is not regulated by the commonwealth, it is equity (which is the law of nature, and therefore an eternal law of God) that every man equally enjoy his liberty.

41. There is also another distinction of laws Another into *fundamental* and *not fundamental*: but I division of could never see in any author what a fundamental laws. law signifies. Nevertheless one may very reasonably distinguish laws in that manner.

42. For a fundamental law in every com- A funda-monwealth is that which, being taken away, the mental law, commonwealth fails and is utterly dissolved, as what? a building whose foundation is destroyed. And therefore a fundamental law is that by which subjects are bound to uphold whatsoever power is given to the sovereign, whether a monarch or a sovereign assembly, without which the common-

---

1   *bound I say to obey it, but not bound to believe it* Hobbes' conventionalist answer—one is required to obey laws about religion commanded by the sovereign, but one is not required to believe them—drove his contemporaries to consternation, and has delighted cynics and some atheists since the eighteenth century.
2   *Faith of* Faith in.
3   *a fulfilling* Obeying it.
4   *Speak thou ... lest we die* Exodus 20.19.

5   *all subjects ... the commonwealth* Hobbes wants to preserve the status quo. Allowing each person to judge what God has revealed is politically destabilizing and hence dangerous.
6   *pretend* Make a claim for.

wealth cannot stand; such as is the power of war and peace, of judicature, of election of officers, and of doing whatsoever he shall think necessary for the public good. Not fundamental is that, the abrogating whereof draws not with it the dissolution of the commonwealth; such as are the laws concerning controversies between subject and subject. Thus much of the division of laws.

Difference between law and right. 43. I find the words *lex civilis* and *jus civile*, that is to say, *law* and *right civil*, promiscuously used for the same thing, even in the most learned authors; which nevertheless ought not to be so. For *right* is liberty, namely that liberty which the civil law leaves us; but *civil law* is an *obligation*, and takes from us the liberty which the law of nature gave us. Nature gave a right to every man to secure himself by his own strength and to invade a suspected neighbor by way of prevention; but the civil law takes away that liberty, in all cases where the protection of the law may be safely stayed for. Insomuch as *lex* and *jus* are as different as *obligation* and *liberty*.

And between a law and a charter. 44. Likewise laws and charters are taken promiscuously for the same thing. Yet charters are donations[1] of the sovereign; and not laws, but exemptions from law. The phrase of a law is *jubeo, injungo*; *I command,* and *enjoin*: the phrase of a charter is *dedi, concessi*; *I have given, I have granted*: but what is given or granted to a man is not forced upon him by a law. A law may be made to bind all the subjects of a commonwealth; a liberty or charter is only to one man or some one part of the people. For to say all the people of a commonwealth have liberty in any case whatsoever is to say that, in such case, there has been no law made; or else, having been made, is now abrogated.

---

1   *donations* Grants.

Chapter 29: Of Those Things that Weaken or Tend to the Dissolution of a Commonwealth

Dissolution of commonwealths proceeds from their imperfect institution.[2] 1. Though nothing can be immortal which mortals make; yet, if men had the use of reason they pretend to, their commonwealths might be secured, at least, from perishing by internal diseases. For by the nature of their institution, they are designed to live as long as mankind or as the laws of nature or as justice itself, which gives them life. Therefore when they come to be dissolved, not by external violence, but intestine disorder, the fault is not in men as they are the matter, but as they are the makers and orderers of them. For men, as they become at last weary of irregular jostling and hewing[3] one another and desire with all their hearts to conform themselves into one firm and lasting edifice, so for want both of the art of making fit laws to square their actions by and also of humility and patience to suffer the rude and cumbersome points of their present greatness to be taken off, they cannot without the help of a very able architect be compiled into any other than a crazy building, such as, hardly lasting out their own time, must assuredly fall upon the heads of their posterity.

2. Amongst the *infirmities* therefore of a commonwealth, I will reckon in the first place those that arise from an imperfect institution and resemble the diseases of a natural body, which proceed from a defectuous[4] procreation.

Want of absolute power. 3. Of which this is one: that a man to obtain a kingdom is sometimes content with less power than to the peace and defense of the commonwealth is necessarily required. From whence it comes to pass that when the exercise of the power laid by is for the public safety to be resumed, it has the resemblance of an unjust act, which disposes great numbers of men, when occasion is presented, to rebel, in the same manner as the bodies of children, gotten by diseased parents, are subject either to untimely death or to purge the ill

---

2   *institution* Construction.
3   *hewing* Striking blows at.
4   *defectuous* Defective.

quality derived from their vicious conception, by breaking out into biles and scabs. And when kings deny themselves some such necessary power, it is not always (though sometimes) out of ignorance of what is necessary to the office they undertake, but many times out of a hope to recover the [168] same again at their pleasure;[1] wherein they reason not well, because such as will hold them to their promises shall be maintained against them by foreign commonwealths, who in order to the good of their own subjects let slip few occasions to weaken the estate of their neighbors. So was Thomas Becket,[2] Archbishop of Canterbury, supported against Henry the Second by the Pope, the subjection of ecclesiastics to the commonwealth having been dispensed with by William the Conqueror at his reception, when he took an oath not to infringe the liberty of the Church. And so were the barons, whose power was by William Rufus,[3] to have their help in transferring the succession from his elder brother to himself, increased to a degree inconsistent with the sovereign power, maintained in their rebellion against King John by the French.

4. Nor does this happen in monarchy only. For whereas the style[4] of the ancient Roman commonwealth was, The Senate and People of Rome, neither Senate nor people pretended to the whole power; which first caused the seditions of Tiberius Gracchus, Caius Gracchus, Lucius Saturninus, and others, and afterwards the wars between the Senate and the people under Marius and Sylla, and again under Pompey and Caesar to the extinction of their democracy and the setting up of monarchy.[5]

5. The people of Athens bound themselves but from one only action, which was that no man on pain of death should propound the renewing of the war for the island of Salamis; and yet thereby, if Solon[6] had not caused to be given out he was mad, and afterwards in gesture and habit of a madman, and in verse, propounded it to the people that flocked about him, they had had an enemy perpetually in readiness, even at the gates of their city; such damage or shifts are all commonwealths forced to that have their power never so little limited.

6. In the second place, I observe the diseases of a commonwealth that proceed from the poison of seditious doctrines, whereof one is that every private man is judge of good and evil actions. This is true in the condition of mere nature, where there are no civil laws, and also under civil government in such cases as are not determined by the law. But otherwise, it is manifest that the measure of good and evil actions is the civil law; and the judge [is] the legislator, who is always representative of the commonwealth. From this false doctrine, men are disposed to debate with themselves and dispute the commands of the commonwealth, and afterwards to obey or disobey them as in their private judgments they shall think fit, whereby the commonwealth is distracted and weakened.

Private judgment of good and evil.

7. Another doctrine repugnant to civil society is that whatsoever a man does against his conscience is sin; and it depends on the presumption of making himself judge of good and evil. For a man's conscience and his judgment is the same thing; and as the judgment, so also the conscience

Erroneous conscience.

---

1   *when kings ... their pleasure*   Hobbes may be thinking of Charles I, who made concessions to Parliament in his "Reply to the Nineteen Propositions," which he probably intended to retract once he had sufficient power to do so.

2   *Thomas Becket*   English martyr (1118–70). King Henry II appointed Becket Archbishop of Canterbury with the expectation that he would support the king's position on the church. Becket did not and when Henry in anger said, "Will none of those who live off my bounty relieve me of this troublesome clerk?" four of Henry's knights murdered Becket in his cathedral.

3   *William Rufus*   King William II (c. 1060–1100) was son of William the Conqueror (c. 1027–87) and fought with Anselm of Canterbury over the issue of lay investiture. William was not well liked. He was shot in the back with an arrow while on a hunting party; no one was prosecuted for the crime.

4   *style*   Inscription used as signature.

5   *Tiberius Gracchus ... of monarchy*   Dates of these seditions [revolts]: Tiberius Gracchus: 132 BCE. Caius Gracchus: 121 BCE. Lucius Saturninus: 100 BCE. Marius and Sulla's civil war of 87 BCE, and Sulla's civil war of 82–81 BCE. Julius Caesar's civil war against Pompey, beginning in 48 BCE.

6   *Solon*   Athenian reformer, statesman, and lawgiver (c. 639–559 BCE). The rich opposed Solon's reforms.

may be erroneous. Therefore, though he that is [169] subject to no civil law sins in all he does against his conscience, because he has no other rule to follow but his own reason; yet it is not so with him that lives in a commonwealth, because the law is the public conscience by which he has already undertaken to be guided. Otherwise in such diversity as there is of private consciences, which are but private opinions, the commonwealth must needs be distracted, and no man dare to obey the sovereign power farther than it shall seem good in his own eyes.

Pretence of inspiration.

8. It has been also commonly taught that faith and sanctity are not to be attained by study and reason, but by supernatural inspiration or infusion. Which granted, I see not why any man should render a reason of his faith, or why every Christian should not be also a prophet; or why any man should take the law of his country rather than his own inspiration for the rule of his action. And thus we fall again into the fault of taking upon us to judge of good and evil, or to make judges of it such private men as pretend to be supernaturally inspired, to the dissolution of all civil government. Faith comes by hearing,[1] and hearing by those accidents which guide us into the presence of them that speak to us; which accidents are all contrived by God Almighty, and yet are not supernatural, but only, for the great number of them that concur to[2] every effect, unobservable. Faith and sanctity are indeed not very frequent; but yet they are not miracles, but brought to pass by education, discipline, correction, and other natural ways by which God works them in his elect, at such time as he thinks fit. And these three opinions, pernicious to peace and government, have in this part of the world proceeded chiefly from tongues and pens of unlearned divines, who, joining the words of Holy Scripture together otherwise is agreeable to reason, do what they can to make men think that sanctity and natural reason cannot stand together.

Subjecting the sovereign power to civil laws.

9. A fourth opinion repugnant to the nature of a commonwealth is this: *that he that has the sovereign power is subject to the civil laws.* It is true that sovereigns are all subject to the laws of nature, because such laws be divine and cannot by any man or commonwealth be abrogated. But to those laws which the sovereign himself, that is, which the commonwealth, makes, he is not subject. For to be subject to laws is to be subject to the commonwealth, that is, to the sovereign representative, that is, to himself which is not subjection, but freedom from the laws. Which error, because it sets the laws above the sovereign, sets also a judge above him, and a power to punish him; which is to make a new sovereign; and again for the same reason a third, to punish the second; and so continually without end, to the confusion[3] and dissolution of the commonwealth.

Attributing of absolute propriety to subjects.

10. A fifth doctrine that tends to the dissolution of a commonwealth is that every private man has an absolute propriety in his goods, such as excludes the right of the sovereign. Every man has indeed a propriety that excludes the right of every other subject; and he has it only from the sovereign power, without the protection whereof every other man should have right to the same. But the right of the sovereign also be excluded, he cannot perform the office they have put him into, which is to defend them both from foreign enemies and from the injuries of one another, and consequently there is no longer a commonwealth.

[170]

11. And if the propriety of subjects exclude not the right of the sovereign representative to their goods, [then] much less to their offices of judicature or execution in which they represent the sovereign himself.

Dividing of the sovereign power.

12. There is a sixth doctrine, plainly and directly against the essence of a commonwealth, and it is this: *that the sovereign power may be divided.* For what is it to divide the power of a commonwealth, but to dissolve it; for powers divided mutually destroy each other. And for these doctrines men are chiefly beholding to some of those that, making profession of the laws, endeavor to make

---

1   *Faith comes by hearing*   A reference to the Epistle to the Romans 10.17: "So then faith cometh by hearing, and hearing by the word of God."

2   *concur to*   Cooperate in producing.

3   *confusion*   Overthrow.

them depend upon their own learning, and not upon the legislative power.

Imitation of neighbor nations.   13. And as false doctrine, so also oftentimes the example of different government in a neighboring nation disposes men to alteration of the form already settled. So the people of the Jews were stirred up to reject God and to call upon the prophet Samuel for a king after the manner of the [other] nations;[1] so also the lesser cities of Greece were continually disturbed with seditions of the aristocratical and democratical factions, one part of almost every commonwealth desiring to imitate the Lacedaemonians,[2] the other, the Athenians. And I doubt not but many men have been contented to see the late troubles in England out of an imitation of the Low Countries,[3] supposing there needed no more to grow rich than to change, as they had done, the form of their government. For the constitution of man's nature is of itself subject to desire novelty; when therefore they are provoked to the same by the neighborhood also of those that have been enriched by it, it is almost impossible to be content with those that solicit them to change, and love the first beginnings, though they be grieved with the continuance of disorder, like hot bloods that, having gotten the itch, tear themselves with their own nails till they can endure the smart no longer.

Imitation of the Greeks and Romans.   14. And as to rebellion in particular against monarchy, one of the most frequent causes of it is the reading of the books of policy and histories of the ancient Greeks and Romans,[4] from which young men and all others that are unprovided of the antidote of solid reason, receiving a strong and delightful impression of the great exploits of war achieved by the conductors of their armies, receive withal a pleasing idea of all they have done besides; and [they] imagine their great prosperity not to have proceeded from the emulation of particular men, but from the virtue of their popular form of government, not considering the frequent seditions and civil wars produced by the imperfection of their policy. From the reading, I say, of such books, men have undertaken to kill their kings, because the Greek and Latin writers in their books and discourses of policy [171] make it lawful and laudable for any man so to do, provided before he do it he call him tyrant. For they say not *regicide*, that is, killing of a king, but *tyrannicide*, that is, killing of a tyrant, is lawful. From the same books they that live under a monarch conceive an opinion that the subjects in a popular commonwealth enjoy liberty, but that in a monarchy they are all slaves. I say, they that live under a monarchy conceive such an opinion, not they that live under a popular government, for they find no such matter. In sum, I cannot imagine how anything can be more prejudicial to a monarchy than the allowing of such books to be publicly read, without present applying such correctives of discreet masters as are fit to take away their venom; which venom I will not doubt to compare to the biting of a mad dog, which is a disease that physicians call *hydrophobia*[5] or *fear of water*. For as he that is so bitten has a continual torment of thirst and yet abhors water; and [he] is in such an estate as if the poison endeavored to convert him into a dog; so when a monarchy is once bitten to the quick by those democratical writers that continually snarl at that estate, it wants nothing more than a strong monarch, which nevertheless out of a certain *tyrannophobia*

---

1   *the people ... the [other] nations* "Then all the elders of Israel gathered themselves together, and came to Samuel unto Ramah, And said unto him, 'Behold, thou art old, and thy sons walk not in thy ways. Now make us a king to judge us, like all the nations.' But the thing displeased Samuel, when they said, 'Give us a king to judge us'; and Samuel prayed unto the Lord. And the Lord said unto Samuel, 'Hearken unto the voice of the people in all that they say unto thee; for they have not rejected thee, but they have rejected me, that I should not reign over them'" (1 Samuel 8.4–7, Authorized Version).

2   *Lacedaemonians* Spartans.

3   *the Low Countries* Roughly, today's Belgium, Netherlands, and Luxembourg.

4   *rebellion in particular ... Greeks and Romans* Hobbes genuinely hated the political views of such thinkers as Aristotle (as represented by his *Politics,* not his *Rhetoric*) and Cicero, who was a republican. Hobbes approved of other ancient Greek and Latin authors, such as Thucydides, whose history of the Peloponnesian war he translated.

5   *hydrophobia* Rabies.

or fear of being strongly governed, when they have him, they abhor.

15. As there have been doctors that hold there be three souls in a man, so there be [doctors] also that think there may be more souls, that is, more sovereigns, than one in a commonwealth; and [they] set up a *supremacy* against [*supreme power over*] the *sovereignty*, *canons* against *laws*, and a *ghostly authority* against the *civil*, working on men's minds with words and distinctions that of themselves signify nothing, but bewray, by their obscurity, that there walks (as some think invisibly) another kingdom, as it were a kingdom of fairies, in the dark. Now seeing it is manifest that the civil power and the power of the commonwealth is the same thing; and that supremacy and the power of making canons and granting faculties, implies a commonwealth; it follows that where one is sovereign, another supreme; where one can make laws and another make canons, there must needs be two commonwealths, of one and the same subjects; which is a kingdom divided in itself and cannot stand. For notwithstanding the insignificant distinction of *temporal* and *ghostly*, they are still two kingdoms,[1] and every subject is subject to two masters.[2] For seeing the *ghostly* power challenges the right to declare what is sin, it challenges by consequence to declare what is law, sin being nothing but the transgression of the law; and again, the civil power challenging to declare what is law, every subject must obey two masters, who both will have their commands be observed as law, which is impossible. Or, if it be but one kingdom, [then] either the civil, which is the power of the commonwealth, must be subordinate to the ghostly, and then there is no sovereignty but the ghostly; or the ghostly must be subordinate to the temporal, and then there is no supremacy but the temporal. When therefore these two powers oppose one another, the com-monwealth cannot but be in great danger of civil [172] war and dissolution. For the civil authority being more visible, and standing in the clearer light of natural reason, cannot choose but draw to it in all times a very considerable part of the people; and the spiritual, though it stand in the darkness of School distinctions and hard words; yet, because the fear of darkness and ghosts is greater than other fears, [the spiritual] cannot want a party sufficient to trouble and sometimes to destroy a commonwealth. And this is a disease which not unfitly may be compared to the epilepsy or falling sickness (which the Jews took to be one kind of possession by spirits) in the body natural. For as in this disease there is an unnatural spirit or wind in the head that obstructs the roots of the nerves and, moving them violently, takes the motion which naturally they should have from the power of the soul in the brain, thereby causes violent and irregular motions, which men call convulsions in the parts, insomuch as he that is seized therewith falls down sometimes into the water and sometimes into the fire, as a man deprived of his senses; so also in the body politic, when the spiritual power moves the members of a commonwealth by the terror of punishments and hope of rewards, which are the nerves of it, otherwise than by the civil power, which is the soul of the commonwealth, they ought to be moved; and [when] by strange and hard words suffocates their understanding, it must needs thereby distract the people and either overwhelm the commonwealth with oppression or cast it into the fire of a civil war.

16. Sometimes also in the merely civil gov- **Mixed** ernment there be more than one soul, as when **government.** the power of levying money, which is the nutritive faculty, has depended on a general assembly;[3] the power of conduct and command, which is the motive faculty, on one man;[4] and the power of making laws, which is the rational faculty, on the accidental consent, not only of those two, but also

---

1   *two kingdoms* Hobbes insisted that every citizen is subject to only one kingdom. This is one reason that he maintained that the kingdom of God did not exist at the present but would exist some time in the indefinite future, with Christ as the sovereign.

2   *two masters* Matthew 5.24: "No man can serve two masters."

3   *the power of levying ... general assembly* The monarch depended on the House of Commons to approve funds.

4   *the power of conduct ... one man* Hobbes is thinking of the monarch of England.

of a third;[1] this endangers the commonwealth, sometimes for want of consent to good laws, but most often for want of such nourishment as is necessary to life and motion. For although few perceive that such government is not government, but division of the commonwealth into three factions, and call it mixed monarchy; yet the truth is that it is not one independent commonwealth, but three independent factions; nor one representative person, but three. In the kingdom of God there may be three persons independent, without breach of unity in God that reigns; but where men reign, that be subject to diversity of opinions, it cannot be so. And therefore if the king bear the person of the people, and the general assembly bear also the person of the people, and another assembly bear the person of a part of the people, they are not one person, nor one sovereign, but three persons and three sovereigns.

17. To what disease in the natural body of man I may exactly compare this irregularity of a commonwealth, I know not. But I have seen a man that had another man growing out of his side, with a head, arms, breast, and stomach of [173] his own; if he had had another man growing out of his other side, the comparison might then have been exact.

Want of money. 18. Hitherto I have named such diseases of a commonwealth as are of the greatest and most present danger. There be other, not so great, which nevertheless are not unfit to be observed. As first, the difficulty of raising money for the necessary uses of the commonwealth, especially in the approach of war.[2] This difficulty arises from the opinion that every subject has of a propriety in his lands and goods exclusive of the sovereign's right to the use of the same. From whence it comes to pass that the sovereign power, which foresees the necessities and dangers of the commonwealth (finding the passage of money to the public treasury obstructed by the tenacity of the people), whereas it ought to extend itself, to encounter and prevent such dangers in their beginnings, contracts itself as long as it can; and when it cannot longer, [the sovereign power] struggles with the people by stratagems of law to obtain little sums, which, not sufficing, he is fain [required] at last violently to open the way for present supply or perish; and, being put often to these extremities, at last reduces the people to their due temper[3] or else the commonwealth must perish.[4] Insomuch as we may compare this distemper[5] very aptly to an ague,[6] wherein, the fleshy parts being congealed or by venomous matter obstructed, the veins which by their natural course empty themselves into the heart, are not (as they ought to be) supplied from the arteries, whereby there succeeds at first a cold contraction and trembling of the limbs, and afterwards a hot and strong endeavor of the heart to force a passage for the blood; and before it can do that, contents itself with the small refreshments of such things as cool for a time, till, if nature be strong enough, it break at last the contumacy[7] of the parts obstructed and dissipates the venom into sweat; or, if nature be too weak, the patient dies.

Monopolies and abuses of publicans. 19. Again, there is sometimes in a commonwealth a disease which resembles the pleurisy; and that is when the treasury of the commonwealth, flowing out of its due course, is gathered together in too much abundance in one or a few private men, by monopolies or by farms of the public revenues; in the same manner as the blood in a pleurisy, getting into the membrane of the breast,

---

1   *the power of making ... a third*   Hobbes is probably thinking of the House of Lords as the third faculty.

2   *the difficulty ... approach of war*   Charles had trouble getting money from Parliament through his entire reign, beginning with his first year of rule, 1625, when, contrary to tradition, Parliament refused to grant him the right to levy tonnage and poundage (customs duties). His imposition of Ship Money in 1634 was legal but extremely unpopular. Charles called his first Parliament since 1629 for the spring of 1640 in order to have funds approved to fight a second Bishops' War. When the members refused to consider levying money until their grievances had been resolved, Charles dissolved Parliament.

3   *due temper*   Proper state.

4   *or else ... must perish*   Although this looks like a prediction or generalization, Hobbes is thinking specifically of the English Civil War.

5   *distemper*   Disorder.

6   *ague*   Fever.

7   *contumacy*   Resistance.

breeds there an inflammation, accompanied with a fever and painful stitches.[1]

Popular men.
20. Also, the popularity of a potent subject, unless the commonwealth have very good caution of his fidelity, is a dangerous disease, because the people, which should receive their motion from the authority of the sovereign, by the flattery and by the reputation of an ambitious man, are drawn away from their obedience to the laws to follow a man of whose virtues and designs they have no knowledge. And this is commonly of more danger in a popular government than in a monarchy, because an army is of so great force and multitude as it may easily be made believe they are the people.

[174] By this means it was that Julius Caesar, who was set up by the people against the Senate, having won to himself the affections of his army, made himself master both of Senate and people. And this proceeding of popular and ambitious men is plain rebellion, and may be resembled to the effects of witchcraft.

Excessive greatness of a town or multitude of corporations.
21. Another infirmity of a commonwealth is the immoderate greatness of a town,[2] when it is able to furnish out of its own circuit the number and expense of a great army, as also the great number of corporations,[3] which are as it were many lesser commonwealths in the bowels of a greater, like worms in the entrails of a natural man. To

Liberty of disputing against sovereign power.
which may be added, the liberty of disputing against absolute power by pretenders to political prudence; which though bred for the most part in the lees [dregs] of the people; yet animated by false doctrines are perpetually meddling with the fundamental laws, to the molestation of the commonwealth, like the little worms which physicians call *ascarides*.[4]

22. We may further add the insatiable appetite or *bulimia* of enlarging dominion, with the incurable *wounds* thereby many times re-ceived from the enemy, and the *wens* [lumps] of ununited conquests, which are many times a burden, and with less danger lost than kept, as also the lethargy of ease, and consumption of riot and vain expense.

Dissolution of the commonwealth.
23. Lastly, when in a war, foreign or intestine, the enemies get a final victory, so as, the forces of the commonwealth keeping the field no longer, there is no further protection of subjects in their loyalty, then is the commonwealth Dissolved, and every man at liberty to protect himself by such courses as his own discretion shall suggest unto him. For the sovereign is the public soul, giving life and motion to the commonwealth, which expiring, the members are governed by it no more than the carcass of a man by his departed, though immortal, soul. For though the right of a sovereign monarch cannot be extinguished by the act of another; yet the obligation of the members may. For he that wants protection may seek it anywhere; and, when he has it, is obliged (without fraudulent pretence of having submitted himself out of fear) to protect his protection as long as he is able. But when the power of an assembly is once suppressed, the right of the same perishes utterly, because the assembly itself is extinct; and consequently, there is no possibility for sovereignty to re-enter.

Chapter 30: Of the Office of the Sovereign Representative

[175]

The procuration of the good of the people.
1. The Office[5] of the sovereign (be it a monarch or an assembly) consists in the end for which he was trusted with the sovereign power, namely the procuration of the safety of the people, to which he is obliged by the law of nature, and to render an account thereof to God, the Author of that law, and to none but him. But by safety here is not meant a bare preservation, but also all other contentments of life, which every man by lawful industry, without danger or hurt to the commonwealth, shall acquire to himself.

By instruction and laws.
2. And this is intended should be done, not by care applied to individuals, further than their

---

1   *stitches*   Stabbing local pains.
2   *town*   Hobbes is thinking of London, which on the one hand, often opposed the king, and on the other, sometimes opposed Parliament. London raised its own army during the Civil War to protect the city against parliamentary troops.
3   *corporations*   Governments of incorporated towns.
4   *ascarides*   Roundworms that infect the intestine.
5   *Office*   Duty attached to position.

protection from injuries when they shall complain, but by a general providence,[1] contained in public instruction, both of doctrine and example; and in the making and executing of good laws to which individual persons may apply their own cases.

Against the duty of a sovereign to relinquish any essential right of sovereignty.

3. And because, if the essential rights of sovereignty (specified before in the eighteenth chapter) be taken away, the commonwealth is thereby dissolved, and every man returns into the condition and calamity of a war with every other man, which is the greatest evil that can happen in this life; it is the office of the sovereign to maintain those rights entire, and consequently against his duty, first, to transfer to another or to lay from himself any of them. For he that deserts the means deserts the ends; and he deserts the means that, being the sovereign, acknowledges himself subject to the civil laws, and renounces the power of supreme judicature; or of making war or peace by his own authority; or of judging of the necessities of the commonwealth; or of levying money and soldiers when and as much as in his own conscience he shall judge necessary; or of making officers and ministers both of war and peace; or of appointing teachers and examining what doctrines are conformable or contrary to the defense, peace, and good of the people. Secondly, it is against his duty to let the people be ignorant or misinformed of the grounds and reasons of those his essential rights, because thereby men are easy to be seduced and drawn to resist him when the commonwealth shall require their use and exercise.

4. And the grounds of these rights have the rather [greater] need to be diligently and truly taught, because they cannot be maintained by any civil law or terror of legal punishment. For a civil law that shall forbid rebellion (and such is [176] all resistance to the essential rights of sovereignty) is not (as a civil law) any obligation but by virtue only of the law of nature that forbids the violation of faith;[2] which natural obligation, if men know not, they cannot know the right of any law the

sovereign makes. And for the punishment, they take it but for an act of hostility; which when they think they have strength enough, they will endeavor, by acts of hostility, to avoid.

5. As I have heard some say that justice is but a word, without substance, and that whatsoever a man can by force or art acquire to himself (not only in the condition of war, but also in a commonwealth) is his own, which I have already shown to be false; so there be also [some] that maintain that there are no grounds nor principles of reason to sustain those essential rights which make sovereignty absolute. For if there were, they would have been found out in some place or other; whereas we see there has not hitherto been any commonwealth where those rights have been acknowledged or challenged. Wherein they argue as ill, as if the savage people of America should deny there were any grounds or principles of reason so to build a house as to last as long as the materials, because they never yet saw any so well built. Time and industry produce every day new knowledge. And as the art of well building is derived from principles of reason, observed by industrious men that had long studied the nature of materials and the divers effects of figure and proportion, long after mankind began, though poorly, to build; so, long time after men have begun to constitute commonwealths, imperfect and apt to relapse into disorder, there may principles of reason be found out by industrious meditation, to make their constitution, excepting by external violence, everlasting. And such are those which I have in this discourse set forth; which, whether they come not into the sight of those that have power to make use of them or be neglected by them or not, concerns my particular interest, at this day, very little. But supposing that these of mine are not such principles of reason; yet I am sure they are principles from authority of Scripture, as I shall make it appear when I shall come to speak of the kingdom of God,[3] administered by Moses, over the Jews, his peculiar people by covenant.

Objection of those that say there are no principles of reason for absolute sovereignty.

---

1 *providence* Provision.
2 *a civil law ... violation of faith* The obligation not to rebel is more basic than any obligation in civil laws. It exists in virtue of the laws of nature, certainly the first,

since rebellion is war, and obviously also the third, that people are to keep their covenants (15.1).
3 *when I ... of God* Chapter 40.

Objection from the incapacity of the vulgar.

6. But they say again that though the principles be right; yet common people are not of capacity enough to be made to understand them. I should be glad that the rich and potent subjects of a kingdom, or those that are accounted the most learned, were no less incapable than they. But all men know that the obstructions to this kind of doctrine proceed not so much from the difficulty of the matter, as from the interest of them that are to learn. Potent men digest hardly anything that sets up a power to bridle their affections; and learned men, anything that discovers their errors, and thereby their authority; whereas the common people's minds, unless they be tainted with dependence on the potent[1] or scribbled over with the opinions of their doctors[2] are like clean paper, fit to receive whatsoever by public authority shall

[177]

be imprinted in them. Shall whole nations be brought to acquiesce in the great mysteries of Christian religion, which are above reason, and millions of men be made believe that the same body may be in innumerable places at one and the same time,[3] which is against reason; and shall not men be able by their teaching and preaching, protected by the law, to make that received which is so consonant to reason that any unprejudiced man needs no more to learn it than to hear it?[4] I conclude therefore that in the instruction of the people in the essential rights which are the natural and fundamental laws of sovereignty, there is no difficulty, whilst a sovereign has his power entire, but what proceeds from his own fault or the fault of those whom he trusts in the administration of the commonwealth; and consequently, it is his duty to cause them so to be instructed; and not only his duty, but his benefit also and security against the danger that may arrive to himself in his natural person from rebellion.

---

1   *potent* Powerful.
2   *doctors* Teachers.
3   *the same ... the same time* Traditional stories of the lives of the saints contain many instances of bilocation and multilocation—appearance in two or more locations at the same time.
4   *shall not men ... to hear it?* Since people have been taught to believe Christian mysteries and even some absurd doctrines, they certainly can be taught to believe the reasonable principles of political obedience.

7. And (to descend to particulars) the people are to be taught, first, that they ought not to be in love with any form of government they see in their neighbor nations, more than with their own, nor, (whatsoever present prosperity they behold in nations that are otherwise governed than they) to desire change. For the prosperity of a people ruled by an aristocratical or democratical assembly comes not from aristocracy nor from democracy, but from the obedience and concord of the subjects; nor do the people flourish in a monarchy because one man has the right to rule them, but because they obey him. Take away in any kind of state the obedience (and consequently the concord of the people) and they shall not only not flourish, but in short time be dissolved. And they that go about by disobedience to do no more than reform the commonwealth shall find they do thereby destroy it, like the foolish daughters of Peleus, in the fable, which desiring to renew the youth of their decrepit father, did by the counsel of Medea cut him in pieces and boil him, together with strange herbs, but made not of him a new man. This desire of change is like the breach of the first of God's commandments; for there God says, *Non habebis Deos alienos*: Thou shalt not have the Gods of other nations; and in another place concerning *kings*, that they are *gods*.[5]

Subjects are to be taught not to affect change of government.

8. Secondly, they are to be taught that they ought not to be led with admiration of the virtue of any of their fellow subjects, how high soever he stand nor how conspicuously soever he shine in the commonwealth; nor [of any admiration of the virtue] of any assembly (except the sovereign assembly), so as to defer to them any obedience or honor appropriate to the sovereign only, whom (in their particular stations) they represent; nor to receive any influence from them, but such as is conveyed by them from the sovereign authority. For that sovereign cannot be imagined to love his people as he ought that is not jealous of them, but suffers [allows] them by the flattery of popular men to be seduced from their loyalty, as they have

Nor adhere[6] (against the sovereign) to popular men.

---

5   *that they are gods* Psalm 82.6: "I have said, Ye are gods; and all of you are children of the most High."
6   *adhere* Become a follower.

often been, not only secretly, but openly, so as to proclaim marriage with them *in facie ecclesiae*[1] by preachers, and by publishing the same in the open streets; which may fitly be compared to the violation of the second of the Ten Commandments.[2]

Nor to dispute the sovereign power. 9. Thirdly, in consequence to this, they ought to be informed how great a fault it is to speak evil of the sovereign representative (whether one man or an assembly of men) or to argue and dispute his power or any way to use his name irreverently, whereby he may be brought into contempt with his people and [with] their obedience (in which the safety of the commonwealth consists) slackened. Which doctrine the third Commandment[3] by resemblance points to.

And to have days set apart to learn their duty. 10. Fourthly, seeing people cannot be taught this, nor, when it is taught, remember it, nor after one generation past so much as know in whom the sovereign power is placed, without setting apart from their ordinary labor some certain times in which they may attend those that are appointed to instruct them; it is necessary that some such times be determined wherein they may assemble together, and (after prayers and praises given to God, the Sovereign of sovereigns), hear those their duties told them, and the positive laws, such as generally concern them all, read and expounded, and be put in mind of the authority that makes them laws. To this end had the Jews every seventh day a Sabbath,[4] in which the law was read and expounded; and in the solemnity whereof they were put in mind that their king was God; that having created the world in six days, he rested on the seventh day; and by their resting on it from their labor, that that God was their

king, which redeemed them from their servile and painful labor in Egypt, and gave them a time, after they had rejoiced in God, to take joy also in themselves, by lawful recreation. So that the first table of the commandments is spent all in setting down the sum of God's absolute power, not only as God, but as King by pact (in peculiar) of the Jews; and [the first table] may therefore give light to those that have sovereign power conferred on them by the consent of men, to see what doctrine they ought to teach their subjects.

And to honor their parents. 11. And because the first instruction of children depends on the care of their parents, it is necessary that they should be obedient to them whilst they are under their tuition; and not only so, but that also afterwards (as gratitude requires) they acknowledge the benefit of their education by external signs of honor. To which end they are to be taught that originally the father of every man was also his sovereign lord, with power over him of life and death; and that the fathers of families, when by instituting a commonwealth they resigned that absolute power; yet it was never intended they should lose the honor due unto them for their education. For to relinquish such right was not necessary to the institution of sovereign power; nor would there be any reason why any man should desire to have children or take the care to nourish and instruct them, if they were afterwards to have no other benefit from them than from other men. And this accords with the fifth Commandment.[5]

[179] And to avoid doing of injury. 12. Again, every sovereign ought to cause justice to be taught, which (consisting in taking from no man what is his) is as much as to say, to cause men to be taught not to deprive their neighbors by violence or fraud of anything which by the sovereign authority is theirs. Of things held in propriety, those that are dearest to a man are his own life and limbs; and in the next degree (in most men) those that concern conjugal affection; and after them riches and means of living. Therefore the people are to be taught to abstain from violence to one another's person by private

---

1 *in facie ecclesiae* Latin: in the appearance [that is, the presence] of the church.

2 *the second of the Ten Commandments* Different traditions number the commandments differently; sometimes "Thou shalt have no other gods before me" is considered to be the Second Commandment, and sometimes "Thou shalt not make thee any graven image."

3 *third Commandment* "Thou shalt not take the name of the Lord thy God in vain."

4 *Sabbath* The implied analogy here is with the fourth Commandment: "Remember the Sabbath and keep it holy."

5 *fifth Commandment* "Honor thy father and thy mother."

revenges, from violation of conjugal honor, and from forcible rapine and fraudulent surreption[1] of one another's goods. For which purpose also it is necessary they be shown the evil consequences of false judgment, by corruption either of judges or witnesses, whereby the distinction of propriety is taken away, and justice becomes of no effect; all which things are intimated in the sixth, seventh, eighth, and ninth commandments.[2]

And to do all this sincerely from the heart. 13. Lastly, they are to be taught that not only the unjust facts [actions], but the designs and intentions to do them (though by accident hindered) are injustice; which consists in the [depravity] of the will, as well as in the irregularity of the act. And this is the intention of the tenth commandment[3] and the sum of the second table;[4] which is reduced all to this one commandment of mutual charity, *Thou shalt love thy neighbor as thy self,* as the sum of the first table is reduced to *the love of God*; whom they had then newly received as their king.

The use of universities. 14. As for the means and conduits by which the people may receive this instruction, we are to search by what means so many opinions contrary to the peace of mankind, upon weak and false principles, have nevertheless been so deeply rooted in them. I mean those which I have in the precedent chapter specified, as that men shall judge of what is lawful and unlawful, not by the law itself, but by their own consciences, that is to say, by their own private judgments; that subjects sin in obeying the commands of the commonwealth, unless they themselves have first judged them to be lawful; that their propriety in their riches is such as to exclude the dominion which the commonwealth has the same; that it is lawful for subjects to kill such as they call tyrants; that

the sovereign power may be divided,[5] and the like; which come to be instilled into the people by this means. They whom necessity or covetousness keeps attent[6] on their trades and labor, and they, on the other side, whom superfluity or sloth carries after their sensual pleasures (which two sorts of men take up the greatest part of mankind), being diverted from the deep meditation which the learning of truth, not only in the matter of natural justice, but also of all other sciences necessarily requires, receive the notions of their duty chiefly from divines in the pulpit, and partly from such of their neighbors or familiar acquaintance as having the faculty of discoursing readily and plausibly seem wiser and better learned in cases of law and conscience than themselves. And the divines and such others as make show of learning [180] derive their knowledge from the universities and from the schools of law or from the books which by men eminent in those schools and universities have been published. It is therefore manifest that the instruction of the people depends wholly on the right teaching of youth in the universities. But are not (may some man say) the universities of England learned enough already to do that? Or is it you [who] will undertake to teach the universities? Hard questions. Yet to the first, I doubt not to answer, that till towards the latter end of Henry the Eighth, the power of the Pope was always upheld against the power of the commonwealth principally by the universities; and that the doctrines by so many preachers against the sovereign power of the king and by so many lawyers and others that had their education there, is a sufficient argument that, though the universities were not authors of those false doctrines, yet they new not how to plant the true. For in such a contradiction of opinions, it is most certain that they have not been sufficiently instructed; and it is no wonder, if they yet retain a relish of that subtle liquor wherewith they were first seasoned against the civil authority. But to the latter ques-

---

1   *surreption* Theft.
2   *sixth, seventh, eighth, and ninth commandments* "Thou shalt not": 6. "kill"; 7. "commit adultery"; 8. "steal"; 9. "bear false witness against thy neighbor."
3   *tenth commandment* "Thou shalt not covet thy neighbor's house, thou shalt not covet thy neighbor's wife, nor his manservant, nor his maidservant, nor his ox, nor his ass, nor any thing that is thy neighbor's."
4   *the second table* Traditionally, commandments 6 through 10.

---

5   *the sovereign power may be divided* Many supporters of Parliament in the 1640s, and some royalists, thought that political authority in England was divided between the monarch and Parliament.
6   *attent* Their attention.

tion, it is not fit nor needful for me to say either aye or no; for any man that sees what I am doing may easily perceive what I think.

15. The safety of the people requires further from him or them that have the sovereign power, that justice be equally administered to all degrees of people, that is, that as well the rich and mighty, as poor and obscure persons, may be righted of[1] the injuries done them, so as the great may have no greater hope of impunity, when they do violence, dishonor or any injury to the meaner sort, than when one of these does the like to one of them; for in this consists equity; to which, as being a precept of the law of nature, a sovereign is as much subject as any of the meanest of his people. All breaches of the law are offences against the commonwealth; but there be some that are also against private persons. Those that concern the commonwealth only may without breach of equity be pardoned; for every man may pardon what is done against himself, according to his own discretion. But an offence against a private man cannot in equity be pardoned without the consent of him that is injured, or reasonable satisfaction.

16. The inequality of subjects proceeds from the acts of sovereign power and therefore has no more place in the presence of the sovereign, that is to say, in a court of justice, than the inequality between kings and their subjects in the presence of the King of kings.[2] The honor of great persons is to be valued for their beneficence and the aids they give to men of inferior rank, or not at all. And the violences, oppressions, and injuries they do are not extenuated, but aggravated, by the greatness of their persons, because they have least need to commit them. The consequences of this partiality towards the great proceed in this man-ner. Impunity makes insolence; insolence, hatred; and hatred, an endeavor to pull down all oppressing and contumelious greatness, though with the ruin of the commonwealth.

17. To equal justice appertains also the equal imposition of taxes; the equality whereof depends not on the equality of riches, but on the equality of the debt that every man owes to the commonwealth for his defense. It is not enough for a man to labor for the maintenance of his life, but also to fight (if need be) for the securing of his labor. They must either do as the Jews did after their return from captivity in re-edifying[3] the Temple, [namely, to] build with one hand and hold the sword in the other, or else they must hire others to fight for them. For the impositions that are laid on the people by the sovereign power are nothing else but the wages due to them that hold the public sword to defend private men in the exercise of several trades and callings. Seeing then the benefit that every one receives thereby is the enjoyment of life, which is equally dear to poor and rich; the debt which a poor man owes them that defend his life is the same which a rich man owes for the defense of his, saving that the rich, who have the service of the poor, may be debtors not only for their own persons, but for many more. Which considered, the equality of imposition consists rather in the equality of that which is consumed than of the riches of the persons that consume the same. For what reason is there that he which labors much and, sparing the fruits of his labor, consumes little should be more charged than he that, living idly, gets little and spends all he gets, seeing the one has no more protection from the commonwealth than the other? But when the impositions are laid upon those things which men consume, every man pays equally for what he uses; nor is the commonwealth defrauded by the luxurious waste of private men.

18. And whereas many men, by accident inevitable, become unable to maintain themselves by their labor, they ought not to be left to the charity of private persons, but to be provided for, as far forth as the necessities of nature require,

[181]

Equal taxes.

Public charity.

---

1   *be righted of*   Given reparation for.

2   *The inequality of subjects ... King of kings*   Hobbes' assertion of the equality of all subjects is surprising, since he had lived off nobility for most of his life. The surprise is moderated somewhat by the fact that the House of Commons abolished the House of Lords on 19 March 1649, the same day that it declared England to be a "Commonwealth and Free State," and two days after abolishing the office of king.

---

3   *re-edifying*   Rebuilding.

by the laws of the commonwealth. For as it is uncharitableness in any man to neglect the impotent; so it is in the sovereign of a commonwealth, to expose them to the hazard of such uncertain charity.

Prevention of idleness.   19. But for such as have strong bodies the case is otherwise; they are to be forced to work; and to avoid the excuse of not finding employment, there ought to be such laws as may encourage all manner of arts, as navigation, agriculture, fishing, and all manner of manufacture that requires labor. The multitude of poor and yet strong people still increasing, they are to be transplanted into countries not sufficiently inhabited; where nevertheless they are not to exterminate those they find there, but constrain them to inhabit closer together, and not range a great deal of ground to snatch what they find, but to court each little plot with art[1] and labor, to give them their sustenance in due season. And when all the world is overcharged with inhabitants, then the last remedy of all is war, which provides for every man, by victory or death.

Good laws, what.   20. To the care of the sovereign belongs the making of good laws. But what is a good law? By a
[182] good law, I mean not a just law; for no law can be unjust. The law is made by the sovereign power; and all that is done by such power is warranted and owned by every one of the people; and that which every man will have so, no man can say is unjust. It is in the laws of a commonwealth, as in the laws of gaming: whatsoever the gamesters all agree on is injustice to none of them. A good law is that which is *needful*, for the *good of the people*, and withal *perspicuous*.

Such as are necessary.   21. For the use of laws (which are but rules authorized) is not to bind the people from all voluntary actions, but to direct and keep them in such a motion as not to hurt themselves by their own impetuous desires, rashness, or indiscretion, as hedges are set, not to stop travelers, but to keep them in the way. And therefore a law that is not needful, having not the true end of a law, is not good. A law may be conceived to be good when it is for the benefit of the sovereign, though it be not necessary for the people, but it is not so. For the good of the sovereign and people cannot be separated. It is a weak sovereign that has weak subjects, and a weak people whose sovereign wants power to rule them at his will. Unnecessary laws are not good laws, but traps for money which, where the right of sovereign power is acknowledged, are superfluous; and where it is not acknowledged, insufficient to defend the people.

Such as are perspicuous.   22. The perspicuity consists not so much in the words of the law itself, as in a declaration of the causes and motives for which it was made. That is it that shows us the meaning of the legislator; and the meaning of the legislator known, the law is more easily understood by few than many words. For all words are subject to ambiguity; and therefore multiplication of words in the body of the law is multiplication of ambiguity; besides it seems to imply (by too much diligence) that whosoever can evade the words is without[2] the compass of the law. And this is a cause of many unnecessary processes.[3] For when I consider how short were the laws of ancient times, and how they grew by degrees still longer, methinks I see a contention between the penners and pleaders of the law; the former seeking to circumscribe the latter and the latter to evade their circumscriptions; and that the pleaders have got the victory. It belongs therefore to the office of a legislator (such as is in all commonwealths the supreme representative, be it one man or an assembly) to make the reason perspicuous why the law was made, and the body of the law itself as short, but in as proper and significant terms, as may be.

Punishments.   23. It belongs also to the office of the sovereign to make a right application of punishments and rewards. And seeing the end of punishing is not revenge and discharge of choler [anger], but correction either of the offender or of others by his example, the severest punishments are to be inflicted for those crimes that are of most danger to the public; such as are those which proceed from malice to the government established; those that spring from contempt of justice; those that

---

1   *art*   Skill.

2   *without*   Outside.

3   *processes*   Legal proceedings.

[183] provoke indignation in the multitude; and those which, unpunished, seem authorized, as when they are committed by sons, servants, or favorites of men in authority; for indignation carries men, not only against the actors and authors of injustice, but against all power that is likely to protect them, as in the case of Tarquin, when for the insolent act of one of his sons he was driven out of Rome and the monarchy itself dissolved.[1] But crimes of infirmity, such as are those which proceed from great provocation, from great fear, great need, or from ignorance whether the fact be a great crime or not, there is place many times for lenity, without prejudice to the commonwealth; and lenity, when there is such place for it, is required by the law of nature. The punishment of the leaders and teachers in a commotion,[2] not the poor seduced people, when they are punished, can profit the commonwealth by their example. To be severe to people is to punish ignorance which may in great part be imputed to the sovereign, whose fault it was they were no better instructed.

Rewards.

24. In like manner it belongs to the office and duty of the sovereign to apply his rewards always so as there may arise from them benefit to the commonwealth; wherein consists their use and end; and is then done when they that have well served the commonwealth are, with as little expense of the common treasury as is possible, so well recompensed as others thereby may be encouraged, both to serve the same as faithfully as they can and to study the arts by which they may be enabled to do it better. To buy with money or preferment from a popular ambitious subject [his agreement] to be quiet and desist from making ill impressions in the minds of the people, has nothing of the nature of reward (which is ordained not for disservice, but for service past); nor a sign of gratitude, but of fear; nor does it tend to the benefit, but to the damage of the public. It is a contention with ambition, like that of Hercules[3] with the monster Hydra, which, having many heads, for every one that was vanquished there grew up three. For in like manner, when the stubbornness of one popular man is overcome with reward, there arise many more by the example, that do the same mischief in hope of like benefit; and as all sorts of manufacture, so also malice increases by being vendible [capable of being sold]. And though sometimes a civil war may be deferred by such ways as that; yet the danger grows still the greater, and the public ruin more assured. It is therefore against the duty of the sovereign, to whom the public safety is committed, to reward those that aspire to greatness by disturbing the peace of their country, and not rather to oppose the beginnings of such men with a little danger, than after a longer time with greater.

25. Another business of the sovereign is   Counselors. to choose good counselors; I mean such whose advice he is to take in the government of the commonwealth. For this word counsel (*consilium, corrupted from considium*[4]) is of a large signification and comprehends all assemblies of men that sit together, not only to deliberate what is to be done hereafter, but also to judge of facts [184] past and of law for the present. I take it here in the first sense only; and in this sense, there is no choice of counsel, neither in a democracy nor aristocracy, because the persons counseling are members of the person counseled. The choice of counselors therefore is proper to[5] monarchy, in which the sovereign that endeavors not to make choice of those that in every kind are the most able, discharges not his office as he ought to do. The most able counselors are they that have least hope of benefit by giving evil counsel and most knowledge of those things that conduce to the peace and defense of the commonwealth. It is a

---

1   *the case of Tarquin ... the monarchy itself dissolved*   The monarchy was abolished (c. 509 BCE) after Tarquin's son (Sextus Tarquinus) raped Lucretia, the wife of his cousin Cullatinus. The entire Tarquin family was exiled.

2   *commotion*   Disturbance.

3   *Hercules*   Latin name for the Greek mythological figure Heracles. Killing the Hydra was one of his fabled ten labors.

4   *consilium, corrupted from considium*   Latin *consilium* means *counsel*; Hobbes is mistaken in thinking that this is derived from Latin *considium*, meaning *a sitting down together*.

5   *is proper to*   Belongs to.

hard matter to know who expects benefit from public troubles; but the signs that guide to a just suspicion is the soothing of the people in their unreasonable or irremediable grievances by men whose estates are not sufficient to discharge their accustomed expenses, and may easily be observed by any one whom it concerns to know it. But to know who has most knowledge of the public affairs is yet harder; and they that know them need them a great deal the less. For to know who knows the rules almost of any art is a great degree of the knowledge of the same art, because no man can be assured of the truth of another's rules but he that is first taught to understand them. But the best signs of knowledge of any art are much conversing in it and constant good effects of it. Good counsel comes not by lot nor by inheritance; and therefore there is no more reason to expect good advice from the rich or noble in matter of state, than in delineating the dimensions of a fortress; unless we shall think there needs no method in the study of the politics (as there does in the study of geometry) but only to be lookers on; which is not so. For the politics is the harder study of the two. Whereas in these parts of Europe it has been taken for a right of certain persons to have place in the highest council of state by inheritance, it derived from the conquests of the ancient Germans; wherein many absolute lords, joining together to conquer other nations, would not enter into the confederacy without such privileges as might be marks of difference in time following between their posterity and the posterity of their subjects; which privileges being inconsistent with the sovereign power, by the favor of the sovereign they may seem to keep; but contending for them as their right, they must needs by degrees let them go and have at last no further honor than adheres naturally to their abilities.

26. And how able soever be the counselors in any affair, the benefit of their counsel is greater when they give every one his advice and the reasons of it apart, than when they do it in an assembly by way of orations, and when they have premeditated, than when they speak on the sudden [extemporaneously], both because they have more time to survey the consequences of action and are less subject to be carried away to contradiction through envy, emulation, or other passions arising from the difference of opinion.

27. The best counsel in those things that concern not other nations, but only the ease and benefit the subjects may enjoy, by laws that look only inward, is to be taken from the general informations and complaints of the people of each province, who are best acquainted with their own wants, and ought therefore, when they demand nothing in derogation of the essential rights of sovereignty, to be diligently taken notice of. For without those essential rights, as I have often before said, the commonwealth cannot at all subsist. [185]

28. A commander of an army in chief, if he be not popular, shall not be beloved, nor feared as he ought to be by his army, and consequently cannot perform that office with good success. He must therefore be industrious, valiant, affable, liberal[1] and fortunate, that he may gain an opinion both of sufficiency and of loving his soldiers. This is popularity and breeds in the soldiers both desire and courage to recommend themselves to his favor; and protects the severity of the general in punishing, when need is, the mutinous or negligent soldiers. But this love of soldiers, if caution be not given of the commander's fidelity, is a dangerous thing to sovereign power, especially when it is in the hands of an assembly not popular. It belongs therefore to the safety of the people, both that they be good conductors and faithful subjects, to whom the sovereign commits his armies. Commanders.

29. But when the sovereign himself is popular, that is, reverenced and beloved of his people, there is no danger at all from the popularity of a subject. For soldiers are never so generally unjust as to side with their captain, though they love him, against their sovereign, when they love not only his person, but also his cause. And therefore those who by violence have at any time suppressed the power of their lawful sovereign before they could settle themselves in his place, have been always put to the trouble of contriving

---

1   *liberal* Generous.

their titles[1] to save the people from the shame of receiving them. To have a known right to sovereign power is so popular a quality as he that has it needs no more for his own part, to turn the hearts of his subjects to him, but that they see him able absolutely to govern his own family: nor, on the part of his enemies, but a disbanding of their armies. For the greatest and most active part of mankind has never hitherto been well contented with the present.

30. Concerning the offices of one sovereign to another, which are comprehended in that law which is commonly called the law of nations, I need not say anything in this place, because the law of nations and the law of nature is the same thing. And every sovereign has the same right in

procuring the safety of his people, that any particular man can have in procuring the safety of his own body. And the same law that dictates to men that have no civil government what they ought to do, and what to avoid in regard of one another, dictates the same to commonwealths, that is, to the consciences of sovereign princes and sovereign assemblies; there being no court of natural justice, but in the conscience only, where not man, but God reigns, whose laws, such of them as oblige all [186] mankind, in respect of God, as he is the author of nature, are *natural*;[2] and in respect of the same God, as he is King of kings, are *laws*. But of the kingdom of God, as King of kings, and as King also of a peculiar people, I shall speak in the rest of this discourse.

---

1   *contriving their titles*   Creating entitlements.

2   *such of them ... are natural*   This is evidence that the laws of nature are genuine laws. If they are not, sovereigns seem to have less motive for obeying the laws of nature.

JOHN LOCKE
(1632 – 1704)

Who Was John Locke?

JOHN LOCKE WAS BORN IN THE SOMERSET COUNTRYSIDE, near the town of Bristol, in 1632. His parents were small landowners—minor gentry—who raised the young Locke according to strict Protestant principles. Thanks to the influence of one of his father's friends Locke was able to gain a place at Westminster School, at the time the best school in England, where he studied Greek, Latin and Hebrew. He went on to Christ Church College, Oxford, and graduated with a B.A. in 1656. Shortly afterwards he was made a senior Student of his college—a kind of teaching position; he would remain at the college until 1684, when the king of England, Charles II, personally (and illegally) demanded his expulsion.

During the 1650s and early 1660s Locke lectured on Greek and rhetoric at Oxford but he was idle and unhappy, and became increasingly bored by the traditional philosophy of his day. He developed an interest in medicine and physical science (in 1675 he tried and failed to gain the degree of Doctor of Medicine), and in 1665 Locke left the confines of the academic world, and began to make his way into the world of politics and science. In the winter of 1665–66 he was ambassador to the German state of Brandenburg, where his first-hand observation of religious toleration between Calvinists, Lutherans, Catholics and Anabaptists made a big impression on him.

A chance encounter in 1666 was the decisive turning-point in Locke's life: he met a nobleman called Lord Ashley, who was then the Chancellor of the Exchequer, and soon went to live at Ashley's London house as his confidant and medical adviser. In 1668, Locke was responsible for a life-saving surgical operation on Ashley, implanting a small silver spigot to drain off fluid from a cyst on his liver; the lord never forgot his gratitude (and wore the small tap in his side for the rest of his life). Under Ashley's patronage, Locke

had both the leisure to spend several years working on his *Essay Concerning Human Understanding*, and a sequence of lucrative and interesting government positions, including one in which he was part of a group drafting the constitution of the new colony of Carolina in the Americas.

Ashley's support was also essential in giving Locke—an introverted and hyper-sensitive soul, who suffered for most of his life from bad asthma and generally poor health—the confidence to do original philosophy. Locke never married, was a life-long celibate, and shied away from drinking parties and a hectic social life, but he enjoyed the attentions of lady admirers and throughout his life he had many loyal friends, and got on especially well with some of his friends' children.

Locke spent the years from 1675 until 1679 traveling in France (where he expected to die of tuberculosis, but survived—Locke spent a large portion of his life confidently expecting an early death), and when he returned to England it was to a very unsettled political situation. The heir to the British throne, Charles II's younger brother James, was a Catholic, and his succession was feared by many politicians, including Ashley—who by this time was now the Earl of Shaftesbury—and his political party, the Whigs. Their greatest worry was that the return of a Catholic monarchy would mean the return of religious oppression to England, as was happening in parts of Europe. Charles, however, stood by his brother and in 1681 Shaftesbury was sent to prison in the Tower of London on a charge of high treason. Shaftesbury was acquitted by a grand jury, but he fled to Holland and died a few months later (spending his last few hours, the story goes, discussing a draft of Locke's *Essay* with his friends). Locke, in danger as a known associate of Shaftesbury's, followed his example in 1683 and secretly moved to the Netherlands, where he had to spend a year underground evading arrest by Dutch government agents acting on King Charles' behalf. While in Holland he re-wrote material for the *Essay*, and molded it towards its final state, and published an abridgement of the book in a French scholarly periodical which immediately attracted international attention.

In 1689, the political tumult in England had subsided enough for Locke to return—James' brief reign (as James II) had ended with the accession of the Protestant William of Orange and his queen Mary—and Locke moved as a permanent house-guest to an estate called Oates about 25 miles from London. He returned to political life (though he refused the post of ambassador to Brandenburg, on the grounds of his ill health), and played a significant role in the loosening of restrictions on publishers and authors.

It was in this year, when Locke was 57, that the results of his 30 years of thinking and writing were suddenly published in a flood. First, published anonymously, came the *Letter on Toleration*, then *Two Treatises on Government*, in which he argued that the authority of monarchs is limited by individuals' rights and the public good and which was influential in the liberal movements of the next century which culminated in the French and American revolutions. Finally, *An Essay Concerning Human Understanding* was published under his own name, to almost instant acclaim: the publication of this book catapulted Locke overnight to what we would now think of as international superstardom.

These three were his most important works, but Locke—by now one of the most famous men in England—continued to write and publish until his death fifteen years later. He wrote, for example, works on the proper control of the currency for the English government; *Some Thoughts Concerning Education* (which, apparently, was historically important in shaping the toilet-training practices of the English educated classes); a work on the proper care and cultivation of fruit trees; and a careful commentary on the *Epistles* of St. Paul. He died quietly, reading in his study, in October 1704.

What Was Locke's Overall Philosophical Project?

Locke is a leading proponent of a school of philosophy usually nowadays called "British empiricism." Some of the central platforms of this doctrine are as follows: First, human beings are born like a blank, white sheet of paper—a *tabula rasa*—without any innate knowledge but with certain natural powers, and we use these powers to adapt ourselves to the social and physical environment into which we are born. Two especially important natural powers are the capacity for conscious sense experience and for feeling pleasure and pain, and it is from the interaction of these capacities with the environment that we acquire all of our ideas, knowledge and habits of mind. All meaningful language must be connected to the ideas that we thus acquire, and the abuse of language to try to talk about things of which we have no idea is a serious source of intellectual errors—errors which can have harmful consequences for social and moral life, as well as the growth of the sciences. British empiricism—whose other main exponents were Hobbes (1588–1679), Berkeley (1685–1753) and Hume (1711–76)—was generally opposed to religious fervor and sectarian strife, and cautious about the human capacity for attaining absolute knowledge about things which go beyond immediate experience.

An Essay Concerning Human Understanding is Locke's attempt to present a systematic and detailed empiricist account of the human mind and human knowledge. It also includes an account of the nature of language, and touches on philosophical issues to do with logic, religion, metaphysics and ethics. Locke was optimistic about the potential and accuracy of his own theory of human understanding—and thus about the potential of human beings to come to know the world. There are some domains in which, according to Locke, our human capacities are sufficient to produce certain knowledge: mathematics, morality, the existence of God, and the existence of things in the world corresponding to our basic sense-perceptions. But he thought that some things human beings just cannot ever come to know with certainty—for example, in the areas of religious doctrine and scientific theory. In these cases the best we can do is to make skilful guesses. God has given us the capacity to effectively get by in the world by making these careful guesses, according to Locke, but he has not given us the capacity ever to know for sure whether our guesses are correct or not. (This is one reason why Locke believed we should be tolerant of other people's religious beliefs.)

A central theme uniting all of Locke's work is his anti-authoritarianism. This manifests itself in his advocacy of reasoning and sense-perception, rather than authority, as the only reliable way to get knowledge, and in his insistence that these faculties be used to determine what political and social institutions would contribute best to human flourishing. His major political works are the *Two Treatises of Government* (with the Second Treatise, included here, being much more important than the First). In this work he argues at length against the divine right of kings, and the idea that people are naturally subject to a monarch; instead, he claims, we are naturally free and equal, possessing natural rights—that is, rights that exist independent of any society's arrangements—to "life, liberty, and property." The restrictions imposed by government are legitimate only when it is rational for us to give up the liberty we would have in the "state of nature" for the sake of the stability and order government may provide; but when a government fails to provide for the public good, it can legitimately be replaced, since it exists only by the agreement of the governed. He considers at length what sorts of arrangements for government might best suit the purposes and constraints he urges. His prescription very closely matches many of the elements of contemporary liberal democracy; Locke played a major part in its invention.

Locke is also important for his views on religious toleration—again propounding what has become a central principle of the modern liberal state. These views are expressed in the selections from his *Letter Concerning Toleration* included here.

He was, in sum, a very early defender of what we have now come to recognize as typically modern values. He advocated abandoning uncritical acceptance of Greek and Roman history, literature and philosophy, and of Christian theology, championing independent thought, secular values, and the power of modern ideas and rationally guided social change.

What Is the Structure of These Readings?

The First Treatise on Government contains an extended attack on the idea of a divinely ordained, hereditary, absolute monarchy, concentrating on the arguments of an influential advocate, Sir Robert Filmer. Locke ridicules Filmer's attempt to prove the divine right of kings on the basis of the claim that God gave sovereignty to Adam, and that this would pass to future kings as Adam's descendants. Commentators have often remarked that Filmer's arguments hardly justify such distinguished and extended philosophical consideration; Locke seems at points a bit apologetic about this, remarking in effect that this was the best presentation he could find of a foolish position.

In the *Second Treatise*, Locke begins with the idea, no doubt derived from Hobbes, that to justify the existence of government we need to think about the state of nature—that is, about what human social arrangements

would be like without government. This state would be anarchy, lacking any written law or enforcement, but, contrary to Hobbes, Locke thought that it would not be lawless: the moral law, provided by God and discoverable by reason ("writ in the hearts of all mankind"), would still bind humans. This law tells us, for example, that all men should be treated as equals—that no one has the right to dominate or enslave another—and that "no one ought to harm another in his life, health, liberty, or possessions." So the state of nature would not necessarily be a Hobbesian state of constant warfare of each against all, and could, at least in principle, be peaceful.

In Chapter 5, Locke attempts to derive the right of property from his considerations about natural moral law. One naturally owns one's own body, and one also legitimately owns unowned things that one "mixes his labor" with; but (the famous "Lockean proviso") only provided one does not take more than he needs, and that he leaves enough, and as good, for others. Locke is sometimes taken in this chapter to have provided an early attempt to justify capitalism.

In Chapter 7 and following chapters, Locke gives what turns out to be, after all, a rather Hobbesian justification for society. In the state of nature, it would be up to each person to discover, interpret, and enforce these natural laws, and doing this is (at best) inconvenient; because people often differ in moral opinion, or are too weak to punish moral infringements, or are simply morally indifferent, this peace would be insecure. Our possessions would be threatened with theft, and our persons with violence. Although obligated by natural law to be peaceful, we would be likely to relapse into Hobbesian general warfare—as we do even in our days, whenever society collapses into anarchy. We would, then, voluntarily be willing to give up some of the freedom we enjoyed in the state of nature in exchange for governmental control of our actions—to transfer the right of enforcement of the law of nature to a civil government, "for the mutual preservation of their lives, liberties and estates, which I call by the general name, property." Interestingly, unlike most political contractarians, he appears to have believed that the state of nature and the contract to form society were both historically real—though so long ago that records have been lost.

But Locke is careful to distance himself from Hobbes' conclusion that the contract justifies dominance by an absolute ruler; a tyrannical sovereign (in extreme cases) puts himself in a state of war with the people—in effect, a breach of the social contract—and (he argues in the last few chapters of the Second Treatise) the people may legitimately revolt.

Chapter 4 of the Treatise has attracted notice because of its peculiarity; here Locke appears to attempt to justify slavery. Commentators have often noted the incongruity of this with Locke's general views about God-given natural rights and equality for all humans.

In 1685, while in exile in Holland, Locke wrote *A Letter Concerning Toleration* to his Dutch friend Philip von Limborch, who had it published (in the original Latin) without Locke's knowledge or permission in 1689, after Locke had returned to England. The letter was quickly translated, and widely republished, to a combination of strong acclaim and bitter criticism. It advocates religious toleration in England—that is, toleration for various Christian denominations. Locke's immediate concern was the use of the power of the state to coerce "nonconformist" Protestants, such as Presbyterians and Quakers, into the Anglican Church, officially established as the Church of England; and with the practice of persecution and denial of full citizenship to non-members of that church; many positions (including university professor and Member of Parliament) were open only to those belonging to the Church of England. (In a section of the *Letter* he went so far as to argue that "neither Pagan nor Mahometan, nor Jew, ought to be excluded from the civil rights of the commonwealth because of his religion." But he drew the line at Roman Catholicism, which cannot be tolerated because "all those who enter into it do thereby *ipso facto* deliver themselves up to the protection and service of another prince." He also supported the exclusion of atheists, on whom "promises, covenants, and oaths, which are the bonds of human society, can have no hold.")

Locke argues in a variety of ways. He claims that religious persecution and exclusion increases civil disorder; that genuine religious faith cannot be coerced; and that there is no certainty that the denomination doing the coercing is really closer to the true faith than its competitors. (As an empiricist, Locke thought that theology—like other branches of theoretical science—could not bring complete certainty. There is no trace of doubt in Locke, however, about the basic truths of religion, such as the existence of God.)

Locke's argument that is most of interest to us, and that holds the most historical significance, is that religion is an interior matter—of only personal concern—while civil authority serves to regulate only "exterior" matters of life,

liberty, and property, and not the care of souls. This radical argument for the separation of church and state ("the Church itself is a thing absolutely separate and distinct from the Commonwealth"), radical and widely unpopular in Locke's day, has become a mainstay of liberal political sensibility, which wants to limit the concerns of the state to matters of public civil concern.

Some Useful Background Information

Locke's 1690 English may be a bit daunting to readers. Sentences are very long, with many subsidiary parts set off in commas. Many words and references need explanation to modern readers; this is provided in a large number of footnotes. Following is a list of a few important terms that Locke uses often, but with special meanings that may be somewhat unfamiliar:

Arbitrary: When Locke speaks of an "arbitrary will" this does not mean just a whim or a random decision without reason. In his day, this meant something that one decides—that depends on someone's choice.

Enjoyment, enjoy: These words in Locke's usage do not imply taking delight in something, but merely making use of it, having benefit of it.

Positive: This can mean explicit; a *positive law*, then, is one that is explicitly written down and passed by a legislative authority; this is contrasted, in Locke's view, with a *natural law*, which is inscribed in no law books, and applies to humans just because of human nature. A *positive agreement* is one explicitly stated and agreed upon; the contrast here is with a tacit (wordless) agreement that is just implied by actions and circumstances. *Positively* can also mean *clearly*.

Prince: Like Machiavelli, Locke uses this term to refer to any ruler. (It does not have the sense more familiar nowadays: *son of the monarch*.)

Some Common Misconceptions

i) Locke did not advocate democracy. His view is that government is legitimate when it has the consent of the governed; but this can occur in a variety of political forms. A monarchy can be legitimate when the monarch has the consent of, expresses the will of, his or her subjects.

ii) Locke is commonly thought to be the father of modern *liberalism*, but that word is very confusing; it has undergone several changes in meaning over the centuries, and must be used with care. Characteristics associated with liberalism in Locke's time and somewhat later, which apply in his case, include an emphasis on intellectual liberty, individual freedom from restraint, individual autonomy, protection of civil liberties and rights, and a generally optimistic view of the innate character of human beings, and of the possibility of social progress. When the word "liberal" is used today (sometimes with an upper-case "L") it often lacks some or all of these implications.

iii) Locke is counted as the first of the British Empiricists (who also include Berkeley and Hume); and according him this title is certainly no mistake. But there are several aspects to his thought that are notably anti-empirical (= "rationalist"). The most notable of these in his ethical/political thought is his treatment of natural rights, which (like other ethical truths) he believes are discovered through the operations of rationality alone, not given by the senses.

How Important and Influential Are These Writings?

Anthony Quinton, the distinguished contemporary philosopher, writes that Locke "must be acknowledged to be the most influential of political thinkers, above even Plato, Aristotle, Hobbes, Rousseau, and Marx.... [His writings] became something like the sacred text of eighteenth-century Whiggism."[1] Locke's idea that government needs the consent of the governed became the official British view, and Locke can be counted as an influence on British voluntary decolonialization after World War II. His argument that it is legitimate to overthrow a government that no longer has the consent of the governed was probably an influence on the French Revolution, through Voltaire, who admired Locke; and it definitely had an enormous effect on the American revolutionists. Thomas Jefferson was a thoroughgoing Lockean, calling him one of "the three greatest men that have ever lived, without any exception."[2] Jefferson's

Declaration of Independence is Lockean in its insistence that government must have the consent of the governed; that rebellion is justified when this consent is missing; in its assertion of the equality of all men; and in its attribution of inalienable natural God-given rights. (Interestingly, the *Declaration* substituted "the pursuit of happiness" for "property" in Locke's "life, liberty, and ... property"; it is sometimes supposed that Jefferson did not want to put the right to own slaves on the same level as the other basic rights.) Locke also had profound influence on the American Constitution—for example, in the tripartite separation of governmental powers. (Locke's division was legislative, executive and federative; Montesquieu modified this into the form that appeared in the Constitution by substituting "judicial" for the third division.) Locke's political liberalism is also apparent in many other of its basic features, including, of course, the separation of church and state argued for in Locke's *Letter*.

The Lockean doctrines of the inborn rights, essential freedom, and natural equality of all humans has been an inspiration for liberals and radicals in all ages. The Utilitarians Bentham and Mill show clear signs of his influence. The socialist Thomas Hodgskin invoked Locke in 1832 in support of his plea for the rights of the oppressed laboring man. Surprisingly, Karl Marx is sometimes also counted among those influenced by Locke: Marx's theories of property and value, both constituted by the addition of labor to what is provided by nature, are in some ways similar to Locke's. However, it is obvious that the two thinkers disagree strongly about most matters. Marxists usually consider Locke as the quintessential apologist for free enterprise capitalism and private property. In general, left-leaning contemporary theorists of many sorts, not just Marxists, tend not to be happy with Locke's libertarianism.

In Locke's own day, the idea of religious toleration was fairly radical, and there were many who disagreed with him on this matter. An Anglican cleric named Jonas Proast, for example, engaged in a public argument against Locke, claiming that when people are too stubborn or stupid or inattentive to be swayed by theological arguments, they must be forced into proper religious faith and practice, for the sake of their salvation; and since the state holds the monopoly on force, it must be the one to do the forcing. Nowadays, the idea of religious toleration has established itself solidly in the mainstream thought of the liberal West, though even here religious zealots and theocrats argue against it; and it is not hard to find other jurisdictions in which religious

---

1   The reference here is to the British Whig Party, the opposition to the Tories. In very general terms, the Whigs represented reformist, parliamentarian, and "liberal" tendencies (see above); they evolved into the Liberal Party (while the Tories, standing for tradition, privilege, and monarchy, evolved into the Conservatives).

2   The other two were Bacon and Newton. Jefferson praised the three for "having laid the foundations of those superstructures which have been raised in the Physical & Moral sciences" (Jefferson's February 15, 1789, letter to John Trumbull, ordering copies of portraits of the three men). Of course, Bacon and Newton were the physical scientists; Locke is the moral scientist.

intolerance is the rule. The tolerance we take for granted is actually unusual from a wider historical and geographical perspective: Locke has had an important hand in creating something extraordinary.

• • • • •

The Second Treatise of Civil Government (1690)

Preface[1]

Reader, you have here the beginning and end of a discourse concerning government; what fate has otherwise disposed of the papers that should have filled up the middle, and were more than all the rest, it is not worth while to tell you.[2] These, which remain, I hope are sufficient to establish the throne of our great restorer, our present King William;[3] to make good his title, in the consent of the people, which being the only one of all lawful governments, he has more fully and clearly, than any prince[4] in Christendom; and to justify to the world the people of England, whose love of their just and natural rights, with their resolution to preserve them, saved the nation when it was on the very brink of slavery and ruin. If these papers have that evidence, I flatter myself is to be found in them, there will be no great miss of those which are lost, and my reader may be satisfied without them: for I imagine, I shall have neither the

time, nor inclination to repeat my pains, and fill up the wanting[5] part of my answer, by tracing Sir Robert again, through all the windings and obscurities, which are to be met with in the several branches of his wonderful[6] system. The king, and body of the nation, have since so thoroughly confuted[7] his hypothesis, that I suppose nobody hereafter will have either the confidence to appear against[8] our common safety, and be again an advocate for slavery; or the weakness to be deceived with contradictions dressed up in a popular style, and well-turned periods:[9] for if anyone will be at the pains, himself, in those parts, which are here untouched, to strip Sir Robert's discourses of the flourish of doubtful expressions, and endeavor to reduce his words to direct, positive,[10] intelligible propositions, and then compare them one with another, he will quickly be satisfied, there was never so much glib nonsense put together in well-sounding English. If he think it not worth while to examine his works all through, let him make an experiment in that part, where he treats of usurpation;[11] and let him try, whether he can, with all his skill, make Sir Robert intelligible, and consistent with himself, or common sense. I should not speak so plainly of a gentleman, long since past answering, had not the pulpit, of late years, publicly owned[12] his doctrine, and made it the current divinity of the times. It is necessary those men, who taking on them to be teachers, have so dangerously misled others, should be openly showed of what authority this their Patriarch is, whom they have so blindly followed, that so they may either retract what upon so ill grounds they have vented, and cannot be maintained; or else justify those principles which they preached up for gospel; though they had no better an author than an English courtier: for I should not have writ against Sir Robert, or taken the pains to show his mistakes, inconsistencies, and want[13] of (what he so much boasts of, and pretends wholly to build on) scrip-

---

1   *Preface*   This is the preface to the whole work consisting of the First and Second Treatises. Only the Second is reprinted below this.

2   *what fate ... tell you*   Some pages that were to go into the Second Treatise were simply lost. They contained an extended attack on the arguments of Sir Robert Filmer, an advocate of the divine right of kings, and of their absolute power to rule. Locke's First Treatise consists largely of an attack on Filmer, and, as you will see, the Second contains a good deal of this also. It is suspected that the lost pages overlapped this attack considerably.

3   *King William*   William of Orange, who took over as king from James II in the Revolution of 1688 (the "Bloodless" or "Glorious" Revolution). William's coming to power is often seen as the beginning of modern English parliamentary government, with limited power for the monarchy.

4   *prince*   Ruler. See the note about this word, which occurs frequently here, in the section called "Some Useful Background Information," in the introduction to Locke.

5   *wanting*   Lacking.

6   *wonderful*   Exciting astonishment.

7   *confuted*   Refuted.

8   *appear against*   Act as witness for the prosecution.

9   *well-turned periods*   Beautifully constructed sentences.

10 *positive*   See the paragraph about this word, which occurs frequently here, in the section called "Some Useful Background Information" on page 494 in the introduction to Locke.

11 *usurpation*   Seizing an office, replacing previous holder, by force.

12 *the pulpit, of late years, publicly owned*   The Church, recently, publicly adopted.

13 *want*   Lack.

ture-proofs, were there not men among us, who, by crying up[1] his books, and espousing his doctrine, save me from the reproach of writing against a dead adversary. They have been so zealous in this point, that, if I have done him any wrong, I cannot hope they should spare me. I wish, where they have done the truth and the public wrong, they would be as ready to redress it, and allow its just weight to this reflection, viz. that there cannot be done a greater mischief[2] to prince and people, than the propagating wrong notions concerning government; that so at last all times might not have reason to complain of the Drum Ecclesiastic.[3] If anyone, concerned really for truth, undertake the confutation of my Hypothesis, I promise him either to recant[4] my mistake, upon fair conviction; or to answer his difficulties. But he must remember two things.

First, That caviling[5] here and there, at some expression, or little incident of my discourse, is not an answer to my book.

Secondly, That I shall not take railing[6] for arguments, nor think either of these worth my notice, though I shall always look on myself as bound to give satisfaction to anyone, who shall appear to be conscientiously scrupulous in the point, and shall show any just grounds for his scruples.

I have nothing more, but to advertise[7] the reader, that Observations stands for *Observations on Hobbs, Milton, &c.* and that a bare quotation of pages always means pages of his *Patriarcha*,[8] Edition 1680.

[...]

Book 2 [*The Second Treatise*]

Chapter 1. Of Political Power

Sec. 1. It having been shown in the foregoing discourse,[9]

1. That Adam had not, either by natural right of fatherhood, or by positive donation from God, any such authority over his children, or dominion[10] over the world, as is pretended:[11]

2. That if he had, his heirs, yet, had no right to it:

3. That if his heirs had, there being no law of nature nor positive law of God that determines which is the right heir in all cases that may arise, the right of succession, and consequently of bearing rule, could not have been certainly determined:

4. That if even that had been determined, yet the knowledge of which is the eldest line of Adam's posterity,[12] being so long since utterly lost, that in the races of mankind and families of the world, there remains not to one above another, the least pretence to be the eldest house,[13] and to have the right of inheritance:

All these premises having, as I think, been clearly made out, it is impossible that the rulers now on earth should make any benefit, or derive any the least shadow of authority from that, which is held to be the fountain[14] of all power, Adam's private dominion and paternal jurisdiction; so that he that will not give just occasion to think that all government in the world is the product only of force and violence, and that men live together by no other rules but that of beasts, where the strongest carries it, and so lay a foundation for perpetual disorder and mischief, tumult, sedition and rebellion, (things that the followers of that hypothesis so loudly cry out against) must of necessity find out another rise[15] of government, another original[16] of political power,

---

1   *crying up* Praising.
2   *mischief* Injury.
3   *Drum Ecclesiastic* Noisy rumblings from the Church.
4   *recant* Withdraw, renounce.
5   *caviling* Making trivial objections.
6   *railing* Scolding.
7   *advertise* Announce to.
8   *Observations on Hobbs, Milton, &c.; Patriarcha* Two works by Filmer.

9   *the foregoing discourse* The *First Treatise of Government*.
10   *dominion* Ruling authority.
11   *pretended* Claimed.
12   *posterity* Descendants.
13   *eldest house* Line of legitimate heirs (through eldest descendants).
14   *fountain* Source.
15   *so that he ... must of necessity find out another rise* This means: So if you don't want to give reason to think that all government is the product of force and violence (etc.), then you must find another account of its origins.
16   *original* Origin, source.

and another way of designing and knowing the persons that have it, than what Sir Robert Filmer has taught us.

Sec. 2. To this purpose, I think it may not be amiss, to set down what I take to be political power; that the power of a magistrate over a subject may be distinguished from that of a father over his children, a master over his servant, a husband over his wife, and a lord over his slave. All which distinct powers happening sometimes together in the same man, if he be considered under these different relations, it may help us to distinguish these powers one from another, and show the difference betwixt a ruler of a commonwealth, a father of a family, and a captain of a galley.

Sec. 3. Political power, then, I take to be a right of making laws with penalties of death, and consequently all less penalties, for the regulating and preserving of property, and of employing the force of the community, in the execution of such laws, and in the defense of the commonwealth from foreign injury; and all this only for the public good.

Chapter 2. Of the State of Nature

Sec. 4. To understand political power right, and derive it from its original,[1] we must consider, what state all men are naturally in, and that is, a state of perfect freedom to order their actions, and dispose of[2] their possessions and persons, as they think fit, within the bounds of the law of nature, without asking leave,[3] or depending upon the will of any other man.

A state also of equality, wherein all the power and jurisdiction is reciprocal,[4] no one having more than another; there being nothing more evident, than that creatures of the same species and rank, promiscuously[5] born to all the same advantages of nature, and the use of the same faculties, should also be equal one among another without subordination or subjection, unless the lord and master of them all[6] should, by any manifest declaration of his will, set one above another, and confer on him, by an evident and clear appointment, an undoubted right to dominion and sovereignty.

Sec. 5. This equality of men by nature, the judicious Hooker[7] looks upon as so evident in itself, and beyond all question, that he makes it the foundation of that obligation to mutual love among men, on which he builds the duties they owe one another, and from whence he derives the great maxims of justice and charity. His words are,

> The like natural inducement has brought men to know that it is no less their duty, to love others than themselves; for seeing those things which are equal, must needs[8] all have one measure;[9] if I cannot but wish to receive good, even as much at every man's hands, as any man can wish unto his own soul, how should I look to have any part of my desire herein satisfied, unless myself be careful to satisfy the like desire, which is undoubtedly in other men, being of one and the same nature? To have any thing offered them repugnant to this desire, must needs in all respects grieve them as much as me; so that if I do harm, I must look to suffer, there being no reason that others should show greater measure of love to me, than they have by me showed unto them: my desire therefore to be loved of my equals in nature as much as possible may be, imposes upon me a natural duty of bearing to them-ward[10] fully the like affection; from which relation of equality between ourselves and them that are as ourselves, what several rules and canons natural reason has drawn, for direction of life, no man is ignorant." *Eccl. Pol. Lib.* 1.

Sec. 6. But though this be a state of liberty, yet it is not a state of license: though man in that state have an uncontrollable liberty to dispose of his person or possessions, yet he has not liberty to destroy himself, or so much as any creature in his possession, but where[11] some nobler use than its bare preservation calls for it. The state of nature has a law of nature to govern it, which obliges everyone: and reason, which is that law, teaches all mankind, who will but consult it, that being all equal and independent, no one ought to

---

1   *original* Proper source.
2   *dispose of* Transfer or get rid of.
3   *leave* Permission.
4   *reciprocal* Existing on both (all) sides.
5   *promiscuously* Indiscriminately.
6   *the lord and master of them all* God.

7   *Hooker* Richard Hooker (1554–1600), influential Anglican theologian. The quote Locke gives is from his *Of the Lawes of Ecclesiastical Politie.*
8   *must needs* Must.
9   *one measure* A single standard.
10   *to them-ward* In their direction.
11   *but where* Except in circumstances in which.

[handwritten margin note at top: We're all created by God, of the same nature, so it is wrong to harm one another → It's only acceptable for self preservation]

harm another in his life, health, liberty, or possessions: for men being all the workmanship of one omnipotent, and infinitely wise maker; all the servants of one sovereign master, sent into the world by his order, and about his business; they are his property, whose workmanship they are, made to last during his, not one another's pleasure:[1] and being furnished with like faculties, sharing all in one community of nature, there cannot be supposed any such subordination among us, that may authorize us to destroy one another, as if we were made for one another's uses, as the inferior ranks of creatures are for ours. Everyone, as he is bound to preserve himself, and not to quit his station willfully, so by the like reason, when his own preservation comes not in competition, ought he, as much as he can, to preserve the rest of mankind, and may not, unless it be to do justice on an offender, take away, or impair the life, or what tends to the preservation of the life, the liberty, health, limb, or goods of another.

Sec. 7. And that[2] all men may be restrained from invading others rights, and from doing hurt to one another, and the law of nature be observed, which wills the peace and preservation of all mankind, the execution of the law of nature is, in that state, put into every man's hands, whereby everyone has a right to punish the transgressors of that law to such a degree, as may hinder its violation: for the law of nature would, as all other laws that concern men in this world be in vain, if there were nobody that in the state of nature had a power to execute that law, and thereby preserve the innocent and restrain offenders. And if anyone in the state of nature may punish another for any evil he has done, everyone may do so: for in that state of perfect equality, where naturally there is no superiority or jurisdiction of one over another, what any may do in prosecution of that law, everyone must needs have a right to do.

Sec. 8. And thus, in the state of nature, one man comes by a power over another; but yet no absolute or arbitrary[3] power, to use a criminal, when he has got him in his hands, according to the passionate heats, or boundless extravagancy of his own will; but only to retribute[4] to him, so far as calm reason and conscience dictate, what

is proportionate to his transgression, which is so much as may serve for reparation[5] and restraint: for these two are the only reasons, why one man may lawfully do harm to another, which is that we call punishment. In transgressing the law of nature, the offender declares himself to live by another rule than that of reason and common equity,[6] which is that measure God has set to the actions of men, for their mutual security; and so he becomes dangerous to mankind, the tie, which is to secure them from injury and violence, being slighted and broken by him. Which being a trespass against the whole species, and the peace and safety of it, provided for by the law of nature, every man upon this score, by the right he has to preserve mankind in general, may restrain, or where it is necessary, destroy things noxious to them, and so may bring such evil on anyone, who has transgressed that law, as may make him repent the doing of it, and thereby deter him, and by his example others, from doing the like mischief. And in the case, and upon this ground, *every man has a right to punish the offender and be executioner of the law of nature.*

Sec. 9. I doubt not but this will seem a very strange doctrine to some men: but before they condemn it, I desire them to resolve[7] me, by what right any prince or state can put to death, or punish an alien, for any crime he commits in their country. It is certain their laws, by virtue of any sanction they receive from the promulgated[8] will of the legislative, reach not a stranger: they speak not to him, nor, if they did, is he bound to hearken to them. The legislative authority, by which they are in force over the subjects of that commonwealth, has no power over him. Those who have the supreme power of making laws in England, France or Holland, are to an Indian, but like the rest of the world, men without authority: and therefore, if by the law of nature every man has not a power to punish offences against it, as he soberly judges the case to require, I see not how the magistrates of any community can punish an alien of another country; since, in reference to him, they can have no more power than what every man naturally may have over another.

Sec. 10. Besides the crime which consists in violating the law, and varying from the right rule of reason, whereby a man so far becomes degenerate, and declares himself to quit the principles of human nature, and to be a noxious

---

1   *during his, not one another's pleasure*   As long as he—not somebody else—wants.

2   *that*   So that.

3   *arbitrary*   See note about this word, which occurs frequently here, in the section called "Some Useful Background Information," in the introduction to Locke.

4   *retribute*   Return in retaliation.

5   *reparation*   Compensation for harm done to one.

6   *equity*   Fairness.

7   *resolve*   Solve (a problem) for.

8   *promulgated*   Officially declared.

[handwritten note at bottom: ● —Explains Right to Retaliation in order to preserve the safety and well-being of mankind against those who break the Natural Law of God]

[handwritten marginal note at top:] — What right does a State have to take action against an alien, aside from he who has received the damage, others may join in in punishing the transgressor

creature, there is commonly injury done to some person or other, and some other man receives damage by his transgression: in which case he who has received any damage, has, besides the right of punishment common to him with other men, a particular right to seek reparation[1] from him that has done it: and any other person, who finds it just, may also join with him that is injured, and assist him in recovering from the offender so much as may make satisfaction for the harm he has suffered.

Sec. 11. From these two distinct rights, the one of punishing the crime for restraint, and preventing the like offence, which right of punishing is in every body; the other of taking reparation, which belongs only to the injured party, comes it to pass that the magistrate, who by being magistrate has the common right of punishing put into his hands, can often, where the public good demands not the execution of the law, remit[2] the punishment of criminal offences by his own authority, but yet cannot remit the satisfaction due to any private man for the damage he has received. That, he who has suffered the damage has a right to demand in his own name, and he alone can remit: the damnified[3] person has this power of appropriating to himself the goods or service of the offender, by right of self-preservation, as every man has a power to punish the crime, to prevent its being committed again, by the right he has of preserving all mankind, and doing all reasonable things he can in order to that end: and thus it is, that every man, in the state of nature, has a power to kill a murderer, both to deter others from doing the like injury, which no reparation can compensate, by the example of the punishment that attends it from every body, and also to secure men from the attempts of a criminal, who having renounced reason, the common rule and measure God has given to mankind, has, by the unjust violence and slaughter he has committed upon one, declared war against all mankind, and therefore may be destroyed as a lion or a tiger, one of those wild savage beasts, with whom men can have no society nor security: and upon this is grounded that great law of nature, "Whoso sheddeth man's blood, by man shall his blood be shed." And Cain was so fully convinced, that everyone had a right to destroy such a criminal, that after the murder of his brother, he cries out, "Every one that findeth me, shall slay me"; so plain was it written in the hearts of all mankind.

Sec. 12. By the same reason may a man in the state of nature punish the lesser breaches of that law. It will perhaps be demanded, with death? I answer, each transgression may be punished to that degree, and with so much severity, as will suffice to make it an ill bargain to the offender, give him cause to repent, and terrify others from doing the like. Every offence, that can be committed in the state of nature, may in the state of nature be also punished equally, and as far forth as it may, in a commonwealth: for though it would be besides my present purpose, to enter here into the particulars of the law of nature, or its measures of punishment; yet, it is certain there is such a law, and that too, as intelligible and plain to a rational creature, and a studier of that law, as the positive laws of commonwealths; nay, possibly plainer; as much as reason is easier to be understood, than the fancies and intricate contrivances of men, following contrary and hidden interests put into words; for so truly are a great part of the municipal laws of countries, which are only so far right, as they are founded on the law of nature, by which they are to be regulated and interpreted.

Sec. 13. To this strange doctrine, viz. That in the state of nature everyone has the executive power of the law of nature, I doubt not but it will be objected, that it is unreasonable for men to be judges in their own cases, that self love will make men partial to themselves and their friends: and on the other side, that ill nature, passion and revenge will carry them too far in punishing others: and hence nothing but confusion and disorder will follow, and that therefore God has certainly appointed government to restrain the partiality and violence of men. I easily grant, that civil government is the proper remedy for the inconveniencies[4] of the state of nature, which must certainly be great, where men may be judges in their own case, since it is easy to be imagined, that he who was so unjust as to do his brother an injury, will scarce be so just as to condemn himself for it: but I shall desire those who make this objection, to remember, that absolute monarchs are but men; and if government is to be the remedy of those evils, which necessarily follow from men's being judges in their own cases, and the state of nature is therefore not to be endured, I desire to know what kind of government that is, and how much better it is than the state of nature, where one man, commanding a multitude, has the liberty to be judge in his own case, and

---

1   *reparation* Repayment.
2   *remit* Give up, forgive, cancel.
3   *damnified* Injured.

[handwritten note, lower center:] Sec. 11 The magistrate has the right of the whole to punish or remit, but cannot prevent the injured party from exacting reparations — By abandonning reason (God's Natural law) he has made an enemy of all mankind and can be subject to punishment by men

4   *inconveniencies* Unsuitable features. This word did not imply, as it does nowadays, trivial unsuitability because of causing discomfort or annoyance, etc.

[handwritten note, lower right:] Men should not be allowed to judge in their own case, but Kings do and command many men

may do to all his subjects whatever he pleases without the least question or control of those who execute his pleasure? and in whatsoever he does, whether led by reason, mistake, or passion, must be submitted to? which men in the state of Nature are not bound to do one to another. And if he that judges, judges amiss in his own or any other case, he is answerable for it to the rest of mankind.

Sec. 14. It is often asked as a mighty objection, "Where are, or ever were there any men in such a state of nature?" To which it may suffice as an answer at present, that since all princes and rulers of independent governments all through the world, are in a state of nature, it is plain the world never was, nor ever will be, without numbers of men in that state. I have named all governors of independent communities, whether they are, or are not, in league with others: for it is not every compact that puts an end to the state of nature between men, but only this one of agreeing together mutually to enter into one community, and make one body politic; other promises, and compacts, men may make one with another, and yet still be in the state of nature. The promises and bargains for truck,[1] &c. between the two men in the desert island, mentioned by Garcilasso de la Vega,[2] in his history of Peru; or between a Swiss and an Indian, in the woods of America, are binding to them, though they are perfectly in a state of nature, in reference to one another: for truth and keeping of faith belongs to men, as men, and not as members of society.

Sec. 15. To those that say, there were never any men in the state of nature, I will not only oppose the authority of the judicious Hooker, *Eccl. Pol. Lib.* 1. sect. 10, where he says,

The laws which have been hitherto mentioned, [i.e., the laws of nature] do bind men absolutely, even as they are men, although they have never any settled fellowship, never any solemn agreement amongst themselves what to do, or not to do: but forasmuch as we are not by ourselves sufficient to furnish ourselves with competent store of things, needful for such a life as our nature doth desire, a life fit for the dignity of man; therefore to supply those defects and imperfections which are in us, as living single and solely by ourselves, we are naturally induced to seek communion and

fellowship with others: this was the cause of men's uniting themselves at first in politic societies.

But I moreover affirm, that all men are naturally in that state, and remain so, till by their own consents they make themselves members of some politic society; and I doubt not in the sequel of this discourse, to make it very clear.

Chapter 3. Of the State of War

Sec. 16. The state of war is a state of enmity[3] and destruction: and therefore declaring by word or action, not a passionate and hasty, but a sedate settled design upon another man's life, puts him in a state of war with him against whom he has declared such an intention, and so has exposed his life to the other's power to be taken away by him, or anyone that joins with him in his defense, and espouses his quarrel; it being reasonable and just, I should have a right to destroy that which threatens me with destruction: for, by the fundamental law of nature, man being to be preserved as much as possible, when all cannot be preserved, the safety of the innocent is to be preferred: and one may destroy a man who makes war upon him, or has discovered an enmity to his being, for the same reason that he may kill a wolf or a lion; because such men are not under the ties of the common law of reason, have no other rule, but that of force and violence, and so may be treated as beasts of prey, those dangerous and noxious creatures, that will be sure to destroy him whenever he falls into their power.

Sec. 17. And hence it is, that he who attempts to get another man into his absolute power, does thereby put himself into a state of war with him; it being to be understood as a declaration of a design upon his life: for I have reason to conclude, that he who would get me into his power without my consent, would use me as he pleased when he had got me there, and destroy me too when he had a fancy to it; for nobody can desire to have me in his absolute power, unless it be to compel me by force to that which is against the right of my freedom, i.e., make me a slave. To be free from such force is the only security of my preservation; and reason bids me look on him, as an enemy to my preservation, who would take away that freedom which is the fence to it; so that he who makes an attempt to enslave me, thereby puts himself into a state of war with me. He that, in the state of nature, would take away the freedom that belongs to

---

1   *truck*   Miscellaneous exchanged goods.
2   *Garcilasso de la Vega*   Peruvian historian (1539–1616).

3   *enmity*   Hostility.

Sec. 17 ✳ { Justification for resisting those who seek to have absolute power over other men → they become enemies

anyone in that state, must necessarily be supposed to have a foundation of all the rest;[1] as he that in the state of society, would take away the freedom belonging to those of that society or commonwealth, must be supposed to design to take away from them every thing else, and so be looked on as in a state of war.

Sec. 18. This makes it lawful for a man to kill a thief, who has not in the least hurt him, nor declared any design upon his life, any farther than, by the use of force, so to get him in his power, as to take away his money, or what he pleases, from him; because using force, where he has no right, to get me into his power, let his pretence be what it will, I have no reason to suppose, that he, who would take away my liberty, would not, when he had me in his power, take away every thing else. And therefore it is lawful for me to treat him as one who has put himself into a state of war with me, i.e., kill him if I can; for to that hazard does he justly expose himself, whoever introduces a state of war, and is aggressor in it.

Sec. 19. And here we have the plain difference between the state of nature and the state of war, which however some men[2] have confounded,[3] are as far distant, as a state of peace, good will, mutual assistance and preservation, and a state of enmity, malice, violence and mutual destruction, are one from another. Men living together according to reason, without a common superior on earth, with authority to judge between them, is properly the state of nature. But force, or a declared design of force, upon the person of another, where there is no common superior on earth to appeal to for relief, is the state of war: and it is the want of such an appeal gives a man the right of war even against an aggressor, though he be in society and a fellow subject. Thus a thief, whom I cannot harm, but by appeal to the law, for having stolen all that I am worth, I may kill, when he sets on me to rob me but of my horse or coat; because the law, which was made for my preservation, where it cannot interpose to secure my life from present force, which, if lost, is capable of no reparation, permits me my own defense, and the right of war, a liberty to kill the aggressor, because the aggressor allows not time to appeal to our common judge, nor the decision of the law, for remedy in a case where the

Distinguishes
between a
State of War
and a
state of
Nature

mischief[4] may be irreparable. Want of a common judge with authority, puts all men in a state of nature: force without right, upon a man's person, makes a state of war, both where there is, and is not, a common judge.

Sec. 20. But when the actual force is over, the state of war ceases between those that are in society, and are equally on both sides subjected to the fair determination of the law; because then there lies open the remedy of appeal for the past injury, and to prevent future harm: but where no such appeal is, as in the state of nature, for want of positive laws, and judges with authority to appeal to, the state of war once begun, continues, with a right to the innocent party to destroy the other whenever he can, until the aggressor offers peace, and desires reconciliation on such terms as may repair any wrongs he has already done, and secure the innocent for the future; nay, where an appeal to the law, and constituted judges, lies open, but the remedy is denied by a manifest perverting of justice, and a barefaced wresting of the laws to protect or indemnify[5] the violence or injuries of some men, or party of men, there it is hard to imagine any thing but a state of war: for wherever violence is used, and injury done, though by hands appointed to administer justice, it is still violence and injury, however colored with the name, pretences, or forms of law, the end whereof being to protect and redress the innocent, by an unbiased application of it, to all who are under it; wherever that is not bona fide done, war is made upon the sufferers, who having no appeal on earth to right them, they are left to the only remedy in such cases, an appeal to heaven.

Sec. 21. To avoid this state of war (wherein there is no appeal but to heaven, and wherein every the least difference is apt to end, where there is no authority to decide between the contenders) is one great reason of men's putting themselves into society, and quitting the state of nature: for where there is an authority, a power on earth, from which relief can be had by appeal, there the continuance of the state of war is excluded, and the controversy is decided by that power. Had there been any such court, any superior jurisdiction on earth, to determine the right between Jephtha and the Ammonites,[6] they had never come to a state of war: but we see

---

1   *have a foundation of all the rest*   Have a basis for (taking away) everything else.

2   *some men*   Locke may be referring to Hobbes here. He is eager to emphasize his difference from Hobbes, who wrote that the state of nature *is* a state of war.

3   *confounded*   Confused.

4   *mischief*   Harm.

5   *indemnify*   Reimburse afterwards for.

6   *Jephtha and the Ammonites*   In the book of Judges, the Israelites, living under the rule of the Ammonites, get Jephtha to lead them in battle for their freedom. Jephtha agrees, on condition that he will be made king if successful. He appeals to God to judge the justice of the Israelites' cause, wins the battle, and frees the Isra-

he was forced to appeal to heaven. The Lord the Judge (says he) be judge this day between the children of Israel and the children of Ammon, Judg. xi. 27. and then prosecuting, and relying on his appeal, he leads out his army to battle: and therefore in such controversies, where the question is put, who shall be judge? It cannot be meant, who shall decide the controversy; everyone knows what Jephtha here tells us, that the Lord the Judge shall judge. Where there is no judge on earth, the appeal lies to God in heaven. That question then cannot mean, who shall judge, whether another has put himself in a state of war with me, and whether I may, as Jephtha did, appeal to heaven in it? of that I myself can only be judge in my own conscience, as I will answer it, at the great day, to the supreme judge of all men.

Chapter 4. Of Slavery

Sec. 22. The natural liberty of man is to be free from any superior power on earth, and not to be under the will or legislative authority of man, but to have only the law of nature for his rule. The liberty of man, in society, is to be under no other legislative power, but that established, by consent, in the commonwealth; nor under the dominion of any will, or restraint of any law, but what that legislative shall enact, according to the trust put in it. Freedom then is not what Sir Robert Filmer tells us, "a liberty for everyone to do what he lists,[1] to live as he pleases, and not to be tied by any laws":[2] but freedom of men under government is, to have a standing rule to live by, common to everyone of that society, and made by the legislative power erected in it; a liberty to follow my own will in all things, where the rule prescribes not; and not to be subject to the inconstant, uncertain, unknown, arbitrary will of another man: as freedom of nature is, to be under no other restraint but the law of nature.

Sec. 23. This freedom from absolute, arbitrary power, is so necessary to, and closely joined with a man's preservation, that he cannot part with it, but by what forfeits his preservation and life together: for a man, not having the power of his own life, cannot, by compact, or his own consent, enslave himself to anyone, nor put himself under the absolute, arbitrary power of another, to take away his

life, when he pleases. Nobody can give more power than he has himself; and he that cannot take away his own life, cannot give another power over it. Indeed, having by his fault forfeited his own life, by some act that deserves death; he, to whom he has forfeited it, may (when he has him in his power) delay to take it, and make use of him to his own service, and he does him no injury by it: for, whenever he finds the hardship of his slavery outweigh the value of his life, it is in his power, by resisting the will of his master, to draw on himself the death he desires.

Sec. 24. This is the perfect condition of slavery, which is nothing else, but the state of war continued, between a lawful conqueror and a captive: for, if once compact enter between them, and make an agreement for a limited power on the one side, and obedience on the other, the state of war and slavery ceases, as long as the compact endures: for, as has been said, no man can, by agreement, pass over to another that which he has not in himself, a power over his own life.

I confess, we find among the Jews, as well as other nations, that men did sell themselves; but, it is plain, this was only to drudgery, not to slavery: for, it is evident, the person sold was not under an absolute, arbitrary, despotical power: for the master could not have power to kill him, at any time, whom, at a certain time, he was obliged to let go free out of his service; and the master of such a servant was so far from having an arbitrary power over his life, that he could not, at pleasure, so much as maim him, but the loss of an eye, or tooth, set him free, Exodus 21.[3]

Chapter 5. Of Property

Sec. 25. Whether we consider natural reason, which tells us, that men, being once born, have a right to their preservation, and consequently to meat and drink, and such other things as nature affords for their subsistence: or revelation, which gives us an account of those grants God made of the world to Adam, and to Noah, and his sons, it is very clear, that God, as king David says, Psalm 115.16.[4] "has given the

---

elites. This story is important to Locke, who discusses it again in Section 109, below.

1   *what he lists*   That which he is inclined to do.

2   *a liberty for ... laws*   From Filmer's *Observations upon Aristotle's Politiques Touching Forms of Government* (1652), p. 55.

3   *Exodus 21*   "And if a man smite the eye of his servant, or the eye of his maid, that it perish; he shall let him go free for his eye's sake. And if he smite out his manservant's tooth, or his maidservant's tooth; he shall let him go free for his tooth's sake" (Exodus 21.26–27).

4   *Psalm 115.16*   "The heaven, even the heavens, are the LORD's: but the earth has he given to the children of men" (Psalm 115, line 16).

\# Gives explicit definition of the Freedom of Men under govt

earth to the children of men"; given it to mankind in common. But this being supposed, it seems to some a very great difficulty, how anyone should ever come to have a property in any thing: I will not content myself to answer, that if it be difficult to make out property, upon a supposition that God gave the world to Adam, and his posterity in common, it is impossible that any man, but one universal monarch, should have any property upon a supposition, that God gave the world to Adam, and his heirs in succession, exclusive of all the rest of his posterity. But I shall endeavor to show, how men might come to have a property in[1] several parts of that which God gave to mankind in common, and that without any express compact of all the commoners.[2]

Sec. 26. God, who has given the world to men in common, has also given them reason to make use of it to the best advantage of life, and convenience. The earth, and all that is therein, is given to men for the support and comfort of their being. And though all the fruits it naturally produces, and beasts it feeds, belong to mankind in common, as they are produced by the spontaneous hand of nature; and nobody has originally a private dominion, exclusive of the rest of mankind, in any of them, as they are thus in their natural state: yet being given for the use of men, there must of necessity be a means to appropriate[3] them some way or other, before they can be of any use, or at all beneficial to any particular man. The fruit, or venison, which nourishes the wild Indian, who knows no enclosure, and is still a tenant in common, must be his, and so his, i.e., a part of him, that another can no longer have any right to it, before it can do him any good for the support of his life.

Sec. 27. Though the earth, and all inferior creatures, be common to all men, yet every man has a property in his own person: this nobody has any right to but himself. The labor of his body, and the work of his hands, we may say, are properly his. Whatsoever then he removes out of the state that nature has provided, and left it in, he has mixed his labor with, and joined to it something that is his own, and thereby makes it his property. It being by him removed from the common state nature has placed it in, it has by this labor something annexed to it, that excludes the common right of other men: for this labor being the unquestionable property of the laborer, no man but he can have a right to

what that is once joined to, at least where there is enough, and as good, left in common for others.

Sec. 28. He that is nourished by the acorns he picked up under an oak, or the apples he gathered from the trees in the wood, has certainly appropriated them to himself. Nobody can deny but the nourishment is his. I ask then, when did they begin to be his? when he digested? or when he eat? or when he boiled? or when he brought them home? or when he picked them up? and it is plain, if the first gathering made them not his, nothing else could. That labor put a distinction between them and common: that added something to them more than nature, the common mother of all, had done; and so they became his private right. And will anyone say, he had no right to those acorns or apples, he thus appropriated, because he had not the consent of all mankind to make them his? Was it a robbery thus to assume to himself what belonged to all in common? If such a consent as that was necessary, man had starved, notwithstanding the plenty God had given him. We see in commons, which remain so by compact, that it is the taking any part of what is common, and removing it out of the state nature leaves it in, which begins the property; without which the common is of no use. And the taking of this or that part, does not depend on the express consent of all the commoners. Thus the grass my horse has bit; the turfs[4] my servant has cut; and the ore I have dug in any place, where I have a right to them in common with others, become my property, without the assignation or consent of anybody. The labor that was mine, removing them out of that common state they were in, has fixed my property in them.

Sec. 29. By making an explicit consent of every commoner, necessary to anyone's appropriating to himself any part of what is given in common, children or servants could not cut the meat, which their father or master had provided for them in common, without assigning to everyone his peculiar part. Though the water running in the fountain be everyone's, yet who can doubt, but that in the pitcher is his only who drew it out? His labor has taken it out of the hands of nature, where it was common, and belonged equally to all her children, and has thereby appropriated it to himself.

Sec. 30. Thus this law of reason makes the deer that Indian's who has killed it; it is allowed to be his goods, who has bestowed his labor upon it, though before it was the common right of everyone. And among those who are

---

1 *have a property in* Own.
2 *commoners* Those who own the land in common.
3 *appropriate* Come to own.
4 *turfs* Peat, used for fuel.

Water Example: WATER in a pitcher, who's is it, merely he who drew of from the fountain?

counted the civilized part of mankind, who have made and multiplied positive laws to determine property, this original law of nature, for the beginning of property, in what was before common, still takes place; and by virtue thereof, what fish anyone catches in the ocean, that great and still remaining common of mankind; or what ambergris[1] anyone takes up here, is by the labor that removes it out of that common state nature left it in, made his property, who takes that pains about it. And even among us, the hare that anyone is hunting, is thought his who pursues her during the chase: for being a beast that is still looked upon as common, and no man's private possession; whoever has employed so much labor about any of that kind, as to find and pursue her, has thereby removed her from the state of nature, wherein she was common, and has begun a property.

Sec. 31. It will perhaps be objected to this, that "if gathering the acorns, or other fruits of the earth, &c. makes a right to them, then anyone may ingross[2] as much as he will." To which I answer, Not so. The same law of nature, that does by this means give us property, does also bound that property too. "God has given us all things richly" 1 Tim. 6.12.[3] is the voice of reason confirmed by inspiration. But how far has he given it us? To enjoy.[4] As much as anyone can make use of to any advantage of life before it spoils, so much he may by his labor fix a property in: whatever is beyond this, is more than his share, and belongs to others. Nothing was made by God for man to spoil or destroy. And thus, considering the plenty of natural provisions there was

---

1   ambergris   A waxy substance, secreted by sperm whales, used in making perfume. It is found on beaches or floating on the ocean.
2   ingross   Collect in large scale.
3   1 Tim. 6.12   It is not clear exactly which line Locke is referring to here. It may be that he meant to cite 1 Timothy 6: [7] For we brought nothing into this world, and it is certain we can carry nothing out.
    [8] And having food and raiment let us be therewith content.
    [9] But they that will be rich fall into temptation and a snare, and into many foolish and hurtful lusts, which drown men in destruction and perdition.
    [10] For the love of money is the root of all evil: which while some coveted after, they have erred from the faith, and pierced themselves through with many sorrows.
    [11] But thou, O man of God, flee these things; and follow after righteousness, godliness, faith, love, patience, meekness.
    [12] Fight the good fight of faith, lay hold on eternal life, whereunto thou art also called, and hast professed a good profession before many witnesses.
4   enjoy   See note about this word, which occurs frequently in Locke, in the section called "Some Useful Background Information," in the introduction to Locke.

a long time in the world, and the few spenders; and to how small a part of that provision the industry of one man could extend itself, and ingross it to the prejudice[5] of others; especially keeping within the bounds, set by reason, of what might serve for his use; there could be then little room for quarrels or contentions about property so established.

Sec. 32. But the chief matter of property being now not the fruits of the earth, and the beasts that subsist on it, but the earth itself; as that which takes in and carries with it all the rest; I think it is plain, that property in that too is acquired as the former. As much land as a man tills, plants, improves, cultivates, and can use the product of, so much is his property. He by his labor does, as it were, enclose it from the common. Nor will it invalidate his right, to say every body else has an equal title to it; and therefore he cannot appropriate, he cannot enclose, without the consent of all his fellow-commoners, all mankind. God, when he gave the world in common to all mankind, commanded man also to labor, and the penury of his condition required it of him. God and his reason commanded him to subdue the earth, i.e., improve it for the benefit of life, and therein lay out something upon it that was his own, his labor. He that in obedience to this command of God, subdued, tilled and sowed any part of it, thereby annexed to it something that was his property, which another had no title to, nor could without injury take from him.

Sec. 33. Nor was this appropriation of any parcel of land, by improving it, any prejudice to any other man, since there was still enough, and as good left; and more than the yet unprovided could use. So that, in effect, there was never the less left for others because of his enclosure for himself: for he that leaves as much as another can make use of, does as good as take nothing at all. Nobody could think himself injured by the drinking of another man, though he took a good draught, who had a whole river of the same water left him to quench his thirst: and the case of land and water, where there is enough of both, is perfectly the same.

Sec. 34. God gave the world to men in common; but since he gave it them for their benefit, and the greatest conveniences of life they were capable to draw from it, it cannot be supposed he meant it should always remain common and uncultivated. He gave it to the use of the industrious and rational, (and labor was to be his title to it;) not to the fancy or covetousness of the quarrelsome and contentious. He that had as good left for his improvement, as was already

---

5   prejudice   Disadvantage or harm.

taken up, needed not complain, ought not to meddle with what was already improved by another's labor: if he did, it is plain he desired the benefit of another's pains, which he had no right to, and not the ground which God had given him in common with others to labor on, and whereof there was as good left, as that already possessed, and more than he knew what to do with, or his industry could reach to.

Sec. 35. It is true, in land that is common in England, or any other country, where there is plenty of people under government, who have money and commerce, no one can enclose or appropriate any part, without the consent of all his fellow-commoners; because this is left common by compact, i.e., by the law of the land, which is not to be violated. And though it be common, in respect of some men, it is not so to all mankind; but is the joint property of this country, or this parish. Besides, the remainder, after such enclosure, would not be as good to the rest of the commoners, as the whole was when they could all make use of the whole; whereas in the beginning and first peopling of the great common of the world, it was quite otherwise. The law man was under, was rather for appropriating. God commanded, and his wants forced him to labor. That was his property which could not be taken from him wherever he had fixed it. And hence subduing or cultivating the earth, and having dominion, we see are joined together. The one gave title to the other. So that God, by commanding to subdue, gave authority so far to appropriate: and the condition of human life, which requires labor and materials to work on, necessarily introduces private possessions.

✻ Sec. 36. ✻ The measure of property nature has well set by the extent of men's labor and the conveniences of life: no man's labor could subdue, or appropriate all; nor could his enjoyment consume more than a small part; so that it was impossible for any man, this way, to entrench[1] upon the right of another, or acquire to himself a property, to the prejudice of his neighbor, who would still have room for as good, and as large a possession (after the other had taken out his) as before it was appropriated. This measure did confine every man's possession to a very moderate proportion, and such as he might appropriate to himself, without injury to anybody, in the first ages of the world, when men were more in danger to be lost, by wandering from their company, in the then vast wilderness of the earth, than to be straitened[2] for want of room to plant in. And the same

measure may be allowed still without prejudice to anybody, as full as the world seems: for supposing a man, or family, in the state they were at first peopling of the world by the children of Adam, or Noah; let him plant in some inland, vacant places of America, we shall find that the possessions he could make himself, upon the measures we have given, would not be very large, nor, even to this day, prejudice the rest of mankind, or give them reason to complain, or think themselves injured by this man's encroachment, though the race of men have now spread themselves to all the corners of the world, and do infinitely exceed the small number was at the beginning. Nay, the extent of ground is of so little value, without labor, that I have heard it affirmed, that in Spain itself a man may be permitted to plough, sow and reap, without being disturbed, upon land he has no other title to, but only his making use of it. But, on the contrary, the inhabitants think themselves beholden to him, who, by his industry on neglected, and consequently waste land, has increased the stock of corn,[3] which they wanted. But be this as it will, which I lay no stress on; this I dare boldly affirm, that the same rule of propriety, (viz.) that every man should have as much as he could make use of, would hold still in the world, without straitening anybody; since there is land enough in the world to suffice double the inhabitants, had not the invention of money, and the tacit agreement of men to put a value on it, introduced (by consent) larger possessions, and a right to them; which, how it has done, I shall by and by show more at large.

Sec. 37. This is certain, that in the beginning, before the desire of having more than man needed had altered the intrinsic value of things, which depends only on their usefulness to the life of man; or had agreed, that a little piece of yellow metal, which would keep without wasting or decay, should be worth a great piece of flesh,[4] or a whole heap of corn; though men had a right to appropriate, by their labor, each one of himself, as much of the things of nature, as he could use: yet this could not be much, nor to the prejudice of others, where the same plenty was still left to those who would use the same industry. To which let me add, that he who appropriates land to himself by his labor, does not lessen, but increase the common stock of mankind: for the provisions serving to the support of human life, produced by one acre of enclosed and cultivated land, are (to speak much within compass) ten times more than those which are

---

1   *entrench* Trespass.
2   *straitened* Restricted.

3   *corn* Grain.
4   *flesh* Meat.

O — You can farm and labor as hard as you please, but if you make things yours and allow them to rot or spoil in your possession, you had no right to take that much

JOHN LOCKE – Second Treatise, Chapter 5   507

yielded by an acre of land of an equal richness lying waste in common. And therefore he that encloses land, and has a greater plenty of the conveniences of life from ten acres, than he could have from an hundred left to nature, may truly be said to give ninety acres to mankind: for his labor now supplies him with provisions out of ten acres, which were but the product of an hundred lying in common. I have here rated the improved land very low, in making its product but as ten to one, when it is much nearer an hundred to one: for I ask, whether in the wild woods and uncultivated waste of America, left to nature, without any improvement, tillage or husbandry, a thousand acres yield the needy and wretched inhabitants as many conveniences of life, as ten acres of equally fertile land do in Devonshire, where they are well cultivated?

Before the appropriation of land, he who gathered as much of the wild fruit, killed, caught, or tamed, as many of the beasts, as he could; he that so employed his pains about any of the spontaneous products of nature, as any way to alter them from the state which nature put them in, by placing any of his labor on them, did thereby acquire a propriety in them: but if they perished, in his possession, without their due use; if the fruits rotted, or the venison putrefied, before he could spend it, he offended against the common law of nature, and was liable to be punished; he invaded his neighbor's share, for he had no right, farther than his use called for any of them, and they might serve to afford him conveniences of life.

Sec. 38. The same measures governed the possession of land too: whatsoever he tilled and reaped, laid up and made use of, before it spoiled, that was his peculiar right; whatsoever he enclosed, and could feed, and make use of, the cattle and product was also his. But if either the grass of his enclosure rotted on the ground, or the fruit of his planting perished without gathering, and laying up, this part of the earth, notwithstanding his enclosure, was still to be looked on as waste, and might be the possession of any other. Thus, at the beginning, Cain might take as much ground as he could till, and make it his own land, and yet leave enough to Abel's sheep to feed on; a few acres would serve for both their possessions. But as families increased, and industry enlarged their stocks, their possessions enlarged with the need of them; but yet it was commonly without any fixed property in the ground they made use of, till they incorporated, settled themselves together, and built cities; and then, by consent, they came in time, to set out the bounds of their distinct territories, and agree on limits between them and their neighbors; and by laws within themselves, settled the properties of those of the same society: for we see, that in that part of the world which was first inhabited, and therefore like to be best peopled, even as low down as Abraham's time, they wandered with their flocks, and their herds, which was their substance, freely up and down; and this Abraham did, in a country where he was a stranger. Whence it is plain, that at least a great part of the land lay in common; that the inhabitants valued it not, nor claimed property in any more than they made use of. But when there was not room enough in the same place, for their herds to feed together, they by consent, as Abraham and Lot did, Gen. xiii. 5. separated and enlarged their pasture, where it best liked them. And for the same reason Esau went from his father, and his brother, and planted in mount Seir, Gen. xxxvi. 6.

Sec. 39. And thus, without supposing any private dominion, and property in Adam, over all the world, exclusive of all other men, which can no way be proved, nor anyone's property be made out from it; but supposing the world given, as it was, to the children of men in common, we see how labor could make men distinct titles to several parcels of it, for their private uses; wherein there could be no doubt of right, no room for quarrel.

Sec. 40. Nor is it so strange, as perhaps before consideration it may appear, that the property of labor should be able to over-balance the community of land: for it is labor indeed that puts the difference of value on every thing; and let anyone consider what the difference is between an acre of land planted with tobacco or sugar, sown with wheat or barley, and an acre of the same land lying in common, without any husbandry upon it,[1] and he will find, that the improvement of labor makes the far greater part of the value. I think it will be but a very modest computation to say, that of the products of the earth useful to the life of man nine tenths are the effects of labor: nay, if we will rightly estimate things as they come to our use, and cast up the several expenses about them, what in them is purely owing to nature, and what to labor, we shall find, that in most of them ninety-nine hundredths are wholly to be put on the account of labor.

Sec. 41. There cannot be a clearer demonstration of any thing, than several nations of the Americans are of this, who are rich in land, and poor in all the comforts of life; whom nature having furnished as liberally as any other people,

---

1   *without any husbandry upon it* Unfarmed.

*It's labor of the ind'l that gives the Naturally acquired base material any Value

with the materials of plenty, i.e., a fruitful soil, apt to produce in abundance, what might serve for food, raiment,[1] and delight; yet for want of improving it by labor, have not one hundredth part of the conveniences we enjoy: and a king of a large and fruitful territory there, feeds, lodges, and is clad worse than a day-laborer in England.

Sec. 42. To make this a little clearer, let us but trace some of the ordinary provisions of life, through their several progresses, before they come to our use, and see how much they receive of their value from human industry. Bread, wine and cloth, are things of daily use, and great plenty; yet notwithstanding, acorns, water and leaves, or skins, must be our bread, drink and clothing, did not labor furnish us with these more useful commodities: for whatever bread is more worth than acorns, wine than water, and cloth or silk, than leaves, skins or moss, that is wholly owing to labor and industry; the one of these being the food and raiment which unassisted nature furnishes us with; the other, provisions which our industry and pains prepare for us, which how much they exceed the other in value, when anyone has computed, he will then see how much labor makes the far greatest part of the value of things we enjoy in this world: and the ground which produces the materials, is scarce to be reckoned in, as any, or at most, but a very small part of it; so little, that even among us, land that is left wholly to nature, that has no improvement of pasturage, tillage, or planting, is called, as indeed it is, waste; and we shall find the benefit of it amount to little more than nothing.

This shows how much numbers of men are to be preferred to largeness of dominions; and that the increase of lands, and the right employing of them, is the great art of government: and that prince, who shall be so wise and godlike, as by established laws of liberty to secure protection and encouragement to the honest industry of mankind, against the oppression of power and narrowness of party, will quickly be too hard for his neighbors: but this by the by.[2] To return to the argument in hand,

Sec. 43. An acre of land, that bears here twenty bushels of wheat, and another in America, which, with the same husbandry, would do the like, are, without doubt, of the same natural intrinsic value: but yet the benefit mankind receives from the one in a year, is worth five pounds and from the other possibly not worth a penny, if all the profit

an Indian received from it were to be valued, and sold here; at least, I may truly say, not one thousandth. It is labor then which puts the greatest part of value upon land, without which it would scarcely be worth any thing: it is to that we owe the greatest part of all its useful products; for all that the straw, bran, bread, of that acre of wheat, is more worth than the product of an acre of as good land, which lies waste, is all the effect of labor: for it is not barely the plough-man's pains, the reaper's and thresher's toil, and the baker's sweat, [that] is to be counted into the bread we eat; the labor of those who broke the oxen, who dug and wrought the iron and stones, who felled and framed the timber employed about the plough, mill, oven, or any other utensils, which are a vast number, requisite to this corn, from its being feed to be sown to its being made bread, must all be charged on the account of labor, and received as an effect of that: nature and the earth furnished only the almost worthless materials, as in themselves. It would be a strange catalogue of things, that industry provided and made use of, about every loaf of bread, before it came to our use, if we could trace them; iron, wood, leather, bark, timber, stone, bricks, coals, lime, cloth, dyeing drugs,[3] pitch, tar, masts, ropes, and all the materials made use of in the ship, that brought any of the commodities made use of by any of the workmen, to any part of the work; all which it would be almost impossible, at least too long, to reckon up.

Sec. 44. From all which it is evident, that though the things of nature are given in common, yet man, by being master of himself, and proprietor of his own person, and the actions or labor of it, had still in himself the great foundation of property; and that, which made up the great part of what he applied to the support or comfort of his being, when invention and arts had improved the conveniences of life, was perfectly his own, and did not belong in common to others.

Sec. 45. Thus labor, in the beginning, gave a right of property, wherever anyone was pleased to employ it upon what was common, which remained a long while the far greater part, and is yet more than mankind makes use of. Men, at first, for the most part, contented themselves with what unassisted nature offered to their necessities: and though afterwards, in some parts of the world, (where the increase of people and stock, with the use of money, had made land scarce, and so of some value) the several communities settled the bounds of their distinct territories,

---

1   *raiment* Clothing.
2   *by the by* After a while. Locke means that he will return to this subject later.

3   *dyeing drugs* Chemicals for dyeing (coloring cloth).

and by laws within themselves regulated the properties of the private men of their society, and so, by compact and agreement, settled the property which labor and industry began; and the leagues that have been made between several states and kingdoms, either expressly or tacitly[1] disowning all claim and right to the land in the others possession, have, by common consent, given up their pretences[2] to their natural common right, which originally they had to those countries, and so have, by positive agreement, settled a property among themselves, in distinct parts and parcels of the earth; yet there are still great tracts of ground to be found, which (the inhabitants thereof not having joined with the rest of mankind, in the consent of the use of their common money) lie waste, and are more than the people who dwell on it do, or can make use of, and so still lie in common; though this can scarce happen among that part of mankind that have consented to the use of money.

Sec. 46. The greatest part[3] of things really useful to the life of man, and such as the necessity of subsisting made the first commoners of the world look after, as it does the Americans now, are generally things of short duration; such as, if they are not consumed by use, will decay and perish of themselves: gold, silver and diamonds, are things that fancy[4] or agreement has put the value on, more than real use, and the necessary support of life. Now of those good things which nature has provided in common, everyone had a right (as has been said) to as much as he could use, and property in all that he could effect with his labor; all that his industry could extend to, to alter from the state nature had put it in, was his. He that gathered a hundred bushels of acorns or apples, had thereby a property in them, they were his goods as soon as gathered. He was only to look, that he used them before they spoiled, else he took more than his share, and robbed others. And indeed it was a foolish thing, as well as dishonest, to hoard up more than he could make use of. If he gave away a part to anybody else, so that it perished not uselessly in his possession, these he also made use of. And if he also bartered away plums, that would have rotted in a week, for nuts that would last good for his eating a whole year, he did no injury; he wasted not the common stock; destroyed no part of the portion of goods that belonged to others, so long as nothing perished

uselessly in his hands. Again, if he would give his nuts for a piece of metal, pleased with its color; or exchange his sheep for shells, or wool for a sparkling pebble or a diamond, and keep those by him all his life he invaded not the right of others, he might heap up as much of these durable things as he pleased; the exceeding of the bounds of his just property not lying in the largeness of his possession, but the perishing of any thing uselessly in it.

Sec. 47. And thus came in the use of money, some lasting thing that men might keep without spoiling, and that by mutual consent men would take in exchange for the truly useful, but perishable supports of life.

Sec. 48. And as different degrees of industry were apt to give men possessions in different proportions, so this invention of money gave them the opportunity to continue and enlarge them:[5] for supposing an island, separate from all possible commerce with the rest of the world, wherein there were but an hundred families, but there were sheep, horses and cows, with other useful animals, wholesome fruits, and land enough for corn for a hundred thousand times as many, but nothing in the island, either because of its commonness, or perishableness, fit to supply the place of money; what reason could anyone have there to enlarge his possessions beyond the use of his family, and a plentiful supply to its consumption, either in what their own industry produced, or they could barter for like perishable, useful commodities, with others? Where there is not some thing, both lasting and scarce, and so valuable to be hoarded up, there men will not be apt to enlarge their possessions of land, were it never so rich, never so free for them to take: for I ask, what would a man value ten thousand, or an hundred thousand acres of excellent land, ready cultivated, and well stocked too with cattle, in the middle of the inland parts of America, where he had no hopes of commerce with other parts of the world, to draw money to him by the sale of the product? It would not be worth the enclosing, and we should see him give up again to the wild common of nature, whatever was more than would supply the conveniences of life to be had there for him and his family.

Sec. 49. Thus in the beginning all the world was America, and more so than that is now; for no such thing as money was anywhere known. Find out something that has the use and value of money among his neighbors, you shall see the same man will begin presently to enlarge his possessions.

---

1   *tacitly*   By understanding or implication, as opposed to open statement.

2   *pretences*   Claims of ownership.

3   *greatest part*   Majority.

4   *fancy*   Impulsive liking or desire.

---

5   *them*   That is, their possessions.

Sec. 50. But since gold and silver, being little useful to the life of man in proportion to food, raiment, and carriage, has its value only from the consent of men, whereof labor yet makes, in great part, the measure, it is plain, that men have agreed to a disproportionate and unequal possession of the earth, they having, by a tacit and voluntary consent, found out, a way how a man may fairly possess more land than he himself can use the product of, by receiving in exchange for the overplus[1] gold and silver, which may be hoarded up without injury to anyone; these metals not spoiling or decaying in the hands of the possessor. This partage[2] of things in an inequality of private possessions, men have made practicable[3] out of the bounds of society, and without compact, only by putting a value on gold and silver, and tacitly agreeing in the use of money: for in governments, the laws regulate the right of property, and the possession of land is determined by positive constitutions.

Sec. 51. And thus, I think, it is very easy to conceive, without any difficulty, how labor could at first begin a title of property in the common things of nature, and how the spending it upon our uses bounded it. So that there could then be no reason of quarrelling about title, nor any doubt about the largeness of possession it gave. Right and conveniency went together; for as a man had a right to all he could employ his labor upon, so he had no temptation to labor for more than he could make use of. This left no room for controversy about the title, nor for encroachment on the right of others; what portion a man carved to himself, was easily seen; and it was useless, as well as dishonest, to carve himself too much, or take more than he needed.

Chapter 6. Of Paternal Power

Sec. 52. It may perhaps be censured as an impertinent[4] criticism, in a discourse of this nature, to find fault with words and names, that have obtained in the world: and yet possibly it may not be amiss to offer new ones, when the old are apt to lead men into mistakes, as this of paternal power probably has done, which seems so to place the power of parents over their children wholly in the father, as if the mother had no share in it; whereas, if we consult reason or revelation, we shall find, she has an equal title.

This may give one reason to ask, whether this might not be more properly called parental power? for whatever obligation nature and the right of generation lays on children, it must certainly bind them equal to both the concurrent causes of it. And accordingly we see the positive law of God every where joins them together, without distinction, when it commands the obedience of children, "Honor thy father and thy mother" (Exod. xx. 12); "Whosoever curseth his father or his mother" (Lev. xx. 9); "Ye shall fear every man his mother and his father" (Lev. xix. 3); "Children, obey your parents," &c. (Eph. vi. 1), is the style of the Old and New Testament.

Sec. 53. Had but this one thing been well considered, without looking any deeper into the matter, it might perhaps have kept men from running into those gross mistakes, they have made, about this power of parents; which, however it might, without any great harshness, bear the name of absolute dominion, and regal authority, when under the title of paternal power it seemed appropriated to the father, would yet have founded but oddly, and in the very name shown the absurdity, if this supposed absolute power over children had been called parental; and thereby have discovered, that it belonged to the mother too: for it will but very ill serve the turn of those men, who contend so much for the absolute power and authority of the fatherhood, as they call it, that the mother should have any share in it; and it would have but ill supported the monarchy they contend for, when by the very name it appeared, that that fundamental authority, from whence they would derive their government of a single person only, was not placed in one, but two persons jointly. But to let this of names pass.

Sec. 54. Though I have said above, (Chapter II) That all men by nature are equal, I cannot be supposed to understand all sorts of equality: age or virtue may give men a just precedency:[5] excellency of parts and merit may place others above the common level: birth may subject some, and alliance or benefits others, to pay an observance to those to whom nature, gratitude, or other respects, may have made it due: and yet all this consists with the equality, which all men are in, in respect of jurisdiction or dominion one over another; which was the equality I there spoke of, as proper to the business in hand, being that equal right, that every man has, to his natural freedom, without being subjected to the will or authority of any other man.

---

1   *overplus* Surplus.
2   *partage* Division.
3   *practicable* Doable.
4   *impertinent* Irrelevant.

---

5   *precedency* Superiority.

Sec. 55. Children, I confess, are not born in this full state of equality, though they are born to it. Their parents have a sort of rule and jurisdiction over them, when they come into the world, and for some time after; but it is but a temporary one. The bonds of this subjection are like the swaddling clothes they are wrapped up in, and supported by, in the weakness of their infancy: age and reason as they grow up, loosen them, till at length they drop quite off, and leave a man at his own free disposal.

Sec. 56. Adam was created a perfect man, his body and mind in full possession of their strength and reason, and so was capable, from the first instant of his being to provide for his own support and preservation, and govern his actions according to the dictates of the law of reason which God had implanted in him. From him the world is peopled with his descendants, who are all born infants, weak and helpless, without knowledge or understanding: but to supply the defects of this imperfect[1] state, till the improvement of growth and age has removed them, Adam and Eve, and after them all parents were, by the law of nature, under an obligation to preserve, nourish, and educate the children they had begotten; not as their own workmanship, but the workmanship of their own Maker, the Almighty, to whom they were to be accountable for them.

Sec. 57. The law, that was to govern Adam, was the same that was to govern all his posterity, the law of reason. But his offspring having another way of entrance into the world, different from him, by a natural birth, that produced them ignorant and without the use of reason, they were not presently under that law; for nobody can be under a law, which is not promulgated to him; and this law being promulgated or made known by reason only, he that is not come to the use of his reason, cannot be said to be under this law; and Adam's children, being not presently as soon as born under this law of reason, were not presently free: for law, in its true notion, is not so much the limitation as the direction of a free and intelligent agent to his proper interest, and prescribes no farther than is for the general good of those under that law: could they be happier without it, the law, as an useless thing, would of itself vanish; and that ill deserves the name of confinement which hedges us in only from bogs and precipices. So that, however it may be mistaken, the end of law is not to abolish or restrain, but to preserve and enlarge freedom: for in all the states of created beings capable of laws, where there is no law, there is no freedom: for liberty is, to be free from restraint and violence from others; which cannot be, where there is no law: but freedom is not, as we are told, a liberty for every man to do what he lists: (for who could be free, when every other man's humor[2] might domineer over him?) but a liberty to dispose, and order as he lists, his person, actions, possessions, and his whole property, within the allowance of those laws under which he is, and therein not to be subject to the arbitrary will of another, but freely follow his own.

Sec. 58. The power, then, that parents have over their children, arises from that duty which is incumbent on them,[3] to take care of their offspring, during the imperfect state of childhood. To inform the mind, and govern the actions of their yet ignorant nonage,[4] till reason shall take its place, and ease them of that trouble, is what the children want, and the parents are bound to: for God having given man an understanding to direct his actions, has allowed him a freedom of will, and liberty of acting, as properly belonging thereunto, within the bounds of that law he is under. But while he is in an estate,[5] wherein he has not understanding of his own to direct his will, he is not to have any will of his own to follow: he that understands for him, must will for him too; he must prescribe to his will, and regulate his actions; but when he comes to the estate that made his father a freeman, the son is a freeman too.

Sec. 59. This holds in all the laws a man is under, whether natural or civil. Is a man under the law of nature? What made him free of[6] that law? what gave him a free disposing of his property, according to his own will, within the compass of that law? I answer, a state of maturity wherein he might be supposed capable to know that law, that so he might keep his actions within the bounds of it. When he has acquired that state, he is presumed to know how far that law is to be his guide, and how far he may make use of his freedom, and so comes to have it; till then, some body else must guide him, who is presumed to know how far the law allows a liberty. If such a state of reason, such an age of discretion made him free, the same shall make his son free too. Is a man under the law of England? What made him free of that law? that is, to have the liberty to dispose of his actions and possessions according to his own will, within

---

1   *imperfect* Incomplete.

2   *humor* Temporary mood or state of mind.
3   *incumbent on them* Their responsibility.
4   *nonage* State of being immature, or under the age required for something.
5   *estate* Condition.
6   *of* Under.

the permission of that law? A capacity of knowing that law; which is supposed by that law, at the age of one and twenty years, and in some cases sooner. If this made the father free, it shall make the son free too. Till then we see the law allows the son to have no will, but he is to be guided by the will of his father or guardian, who is to understand for him. And if the father die, and fail to substitute a deputy in his trust; if he has not provided a tutor, to govern his son, during his minority,[1] during his want of understanding, the law takes care to do it; some other must govern him, and be a will to him, till he has attained to a state of freedom, and his understanding be fit to take the government of his will. But after that, the father and son are equally free as much as tutor and pupil after nonage; equally subjects of the same law together, without any dominion left in the father over the life, liberty, or estate of his son, whether they be only in the state and under the law of nature, or under the positive laws of an established government.

Sec. 60. But if, through defects that may happen out of the ordinary course of nature, anyone comes not to such a degree of reason, wherein he might be supposed capable of knowing the law, and so living within the rules of it, he is never capable of being a free man, he is never let loose to the disposure[2] of his own will (because he knows no bounds to it, has not understanding, its proper guide) but is continued under the tuition and government of others, all the time his own understanding is incapable of that charge. And so lunatics and idiots are never set free from the government of their parents;

> Children, who are not as yet come unto those years whereat they may have; and innocents which are excluded by a natural defect from ever having; thirdly, madmen, which for the present cannot possibly have the use of right reason to guide themselves, have for their guide, the reason that guideth other men which are tutors over them, to seek and procure their good for them

says Hooker (*Ecclesiastical Polity Lib.* 1. sec. 7.). All which seems no more than that duty, which God and nature has laid on man, as well as other creatures, to preserve their offspring, till they can be able to shift for themselves, and

will scarce[3] amount to an instance or proof of parents regal authority.

Sec. 61. Thus we are born free, as we are born rational; not that we have actually the exercise of either: age, that brings one, brings with it the other too. And thus we see how natural freedom and subjection to parents may consist together,[4] and are both founded on the same principle. A child is free by his father's title, by his father's understanding, which is to govern him till he has it of his own. The freedom of a man at years of discretion, and the subjection of a child to his parents, while yet short of that age, are so consistent, and so distinguishable, that the most blinded contenders for monarchy, by right of fatherhood, cannot miss this difference; the most obstinate cannot but allow their consistency: for were their doctrine all true, were the right heir of Adam now known, and by that title settled a monarch in his throne, invested with all the absolute unlimited power Sir Robert Filmer talks of;[5] if he should die as soon as his heir were born, must not the child, notwithstanding he were never so free, never so much sovereign, be in subjection to his mother and nurse, to tutors and governors, till age and education brought him reason and ability to govern himself and others? The necessities of his life, the health of his body, and the information of his mind, would require him to be directed by the will of others, and not his own; and yet will anyone think, that this restraint and subjection were inconsistent with, or spoiled him of that liberty or sovereignty he had a right to, or gave away his empire to those who had the government of his nonage? This government over him only prepared him the better and sooner for it. If anybody should ask me, when my son is of age to be free? I shall answer, just when his monarch is of age to govern. "But at what time," says the judicious Hooker (*Eccl. Pol. Lib.* 1. sect. 6), "a man may be said to have attained so far forth the use of reason, as sufficeth to make him capable of those laws whereby he is then bound to guide his actions: this is a great deal more easy for sense to discern, than for anyone by skill and learning to determine."

---

1   *minority*   Period during which child is younger than the legal age of adulthood.
2   *disposure*   Management.
3   *scarce*   Scarcely.
4   *consist together*   Coexist.
5   *Sir Robert Filmer talks of*   Locke is dwelling on these matters at such length because Filmer's chief argument for the absolute power of the monarch is that the governing of society is based on the same principles as the governing of a family—that God granted Adam and his heirs (i.e., future monarchs) absolute fatherly authority over their people.

Sec. 62. Commonwealths themselves take notice of, and allow, that there is a time when men are to begin to act like free men, and therefore till that time require not oaths of fealty,[1] or allegiance, or other public owning[2] of, or submission to the government of their countries.

Sec. 63. The freedom then of man, and liberty of acting according to his own will, is grounded on his having reason, which is able to instruct him in that law he is to govern himself by, and make him know how far he is left to the freedom of his own will. To turn him loose to an unrestrained liberty, before he has reason to guide him, is not the allowing him the privilege of his nature to be free; but to thrust him out among brutes, and abandon him to a state as wretched, and as much beneath that of a man, as theirs. This is that which puts the authority into the parents' hands to govern the minority of their children. God has made it their business to employ this care on their offspring, and has placed in them suitable inclinations of tenderness and concern to temper this power, to apply it, as his wisdom designed it, to the children's good, as long as they should need to be under it.

Sec. 64. But what reason can hence advance this care of the parents due to their offspring into an absolute arbitrary dominion of the father, whose power reaches no farther, than by such a discipline, as he finds most effectual, to give such strength and health to their bodies, such vigor and rectitude[3] to their minds, as may best fit his children to be most useful to themselves and others; and, if it be necessary to his condition, to make them work, when they are able, for their own subsistence. But in this power the mother too has her share with the father.

Sec. 65. Nay, this power so little belongs to the father by any peculiar right of nature, but only as he is guardian of his children, that when he quits his care of them, he loses his power over them, which goes along with their nourishment and education, to which it is inseparably annexed; and it belongs as much to the foster-father of an exposed child,[4] as to the natural father of another. So little power does the bare act of begetting give a man over his issue; if all his care ends there, and this be all the title he has to the name and authority of a father. And what will become of this paternal power in that part of the world, where one woman has more

than one husband at a time? or in those parts of America, where, when the husband and wife part, which happens frequently, the children are all left to the mother, follow her, and are wholly under her care and provision? If the father die while the children are young, do they not naturally every where owe the same obedience to their mother, during their minority, as to their father were he alive? and will anyone say, that the mother has a legislative power over her children? that she can make standing rules, which shall be of perpetual obligation, by which they ought to regulate all the concerns of their property, and bound their liberty all the course of their lives? or can she enforce the observation of them with capital punishments? for this is the proper power of the magistrate, of which the father has not so much as the shadow. His command over his children is but temporary, and reaches not their life or property: it is but a help to the weakness and imperfection of their non-age, a discipline necessary to their education: and though a father may dispose of his own possessions as he pleases, when his children are out of danger of perishing for want, yet his power extends not to the lives or goods, which either their own industry, or another's bounty has made theirs; nor to their liberty neither, when they are once arrived to the enfranchisement[5] of the years of discretion.[6] The father's empire then ceases, and he can from thence forwards no more dispose of the liberty of his son, than that of any other man: and it must be far from an absolute or perpetual jurisdiction, from which a man may withdraw himself, having license from divine authority to "leave father and mother, and cleave[7] to his wife."

Sec. 66. But though there be a time when a child comes to be as free from subjection to the will and command of his father, as the father himself is free from subjection to the will of anybody else, and they are each under no other restraint, but that which is common to them both, whether it be the law of nature, or municipal law of their country; yet this freedom exempts not a son from that honor which he ought, by the law of God and nature, to pay his parents. God having made the parents instruments in his great design of continuing the race of mankind, and the occasions of life to their children; as he has laid on them an obligation to nourish, preserve, and bring up their offspring; so he has

---

1   *fealty*   Loyalty, faithfulness; oaths of fealty were sworn by medieval vassals to their lords.
2   *owning*   Acknowledgement.
3   *rectitude*   Moral or intellectual correctness.
4   *exposed child*   Child who has been cast out or abandoned.

5   *enfranchisement*   Admission to political rights.
6   *years of discretion*   The time of life at which one is presumed to be capable of prudence and good judgment about one's actions; in English law, beginning at the age of fourteen.
7   *cleave*   Cling.

laid on the children a perpetual obligation of honoring their parents, which containing in it an inward esteem and reverence to be shown by all outward expressions, ties up the child from any thing that may ever injure or affront, disturb or endanger, the happiness or life of those from whom he received his; and engages him in all actions of defense, relief, assistance and comfort of those, by whose means he entered into being, and has been made capable of any enjoyments of life: from this obligation no state, no freedom can absolve children. But this is very far from giving parents a power of command over their children, or an authority to make laws and dispose as they please of their lives or liberties. It is one thing to owe honor, respect, gratitude and assistance; another to require an absolute obedience and submission. The honor due to parents, a monarch in his throne owes his mother; and yet this lessens not his authority, nor subjects him to her government.

Sec. 67. The subjection of a minor places in the father a temporary government, which terminates with the minority of the child: and the honor due from a child, places in the parents a perpetual right to respect, reverence, support and compliance too, more or less, as the father's care, cost, and kindness in his education, has been more or less. This ends not with minority, but holds in all parts and conditions of a man's life. The want[1] of distinguishing these two powers, viz. that which the father has in the right of tuition,[2] during minority, and the right of honor all his life, may perhaps have caused a great part of the mistakes about this matter: for to speak properly of them, the first of these is rather the privilege of children, and duty of parents, than any prerogative[3] of paternal power. The nourishment and education of their children is a charge so incumbent on parents for their children's good, that nothing can absolve them from taking care of it: and though the power of commanding and chastising[4] them go along with it, yet God has woven into the principles of human nature such a tenderness for their offspring, that there is little fear that parents should use their power with too much rigor; the excess is seldom on the severe side, the strong bias of nature drawing the other way. And therefore God almighty when he would express his gentle dealing with the Israelites, he tells them, that though he chastened them, "he chastened them as a man chastens his son" (Deut. viii. 5), i.e., with tenderness and affection, and kept them under no severer discipline than what was absolutely best for them, and had been less kindness to have slackened. This is that power to which children are commanded obedience, that[5] the pains and care of their parents may not be increased, or ill rewarded.

Sec. 68. On the other side, honor and support, all that which gratitude requires to return for the benefits received by and from them, is the indispensable duty of the child, and the proper privilege of the parents. This is intended for the parents advantage, as the other is for the child's; though education, the parents duty, seems to have most power, because the ignorance and infirmities of childhood stand in need of restraint and correction; which is a visible exercise of rule, and a kind of dominion. And that duty which is comprehended in the word "honor," requires less obedience, though the obligation be stronger on grown, than younger children: for who can think the command, "Children obey your parents," requires in a man, that has children of his own, the same submission to his father, as it does in his yet young children to him; and that by this precept he were bound to obey all his father's commands, if, out of a conceit of authority, he should have the indiscretion to treat him still as a boy?

Sec. 69. The first part then of paternal power, or rather duty, which is education, belongs so to the father, that it terminates at a certain season; when the business of education is over, it ceases of itself, and is also alienable[6] before: for a man may put the tuition of his son in other hands; and he that has made his son an apprentice to another, has discharged him, during that time, of a great part of his obedience both to himself and to his mother. But all the duty of honor, the other part, remains never the less entire to them; nothing can cancel that: it is so inseparable from them both, that the father's authority cannot dispossess the mother of this right, nor can any man discharge his son from honoring her that bore him. But both these are very far from a power to make laws, and enforcing them with penalties, that may reach estate, liberty, limbs and life. The power of commanding ends with nonage; and though, after that, honor and respect, support and defense, and whatsoever gratitude can oblige a man to, for the highest benefits he is naturally capable of, be always due from a son to his parents; yet all this puts no scepter[7] into the father's hand,

---

1   *want* Lack.
2   *tuition* Teaching.
3   *prerogative* Privilege restricted to certain people.
4   *chastising* Scolding or punishing.

5   *that* So that.
6   *alienable* Transferable away.
7   *scepter* Ceremonial staff, symbol of royal authority.

no sovereign power of commanding. He has no dominion over his son's property, or actions; nor any right, that his will should prescribe to his son's in all things; however it may become his son in many things, not very inconvenient to him and his family, to pay a deference[1] to it.

Sec. 70. A man may owe honor and respect to an ancient, or wise man; defense to his child or friend; relief and support to the distressed; and gratitude to a benefactor, to such a degree, that all he has, all he can do, cannot sufficiently pay it: but all these give no authority, no right to anyone, of making laws over him from whom they are owing. And it is plain, all this is due not only to the bare title of father; not only because, as has been said, it is owing to the mother too; but because these obligations to parents, and the degrees of what is required of children, may be varied by the different care and kindness, trouble and expense, which is often employed upon one child more than another.

Sec. 71. This shows the reason how it comes to pass, that parents in societies, where they themselves are subjects, retain a power over their children, and have as much right to their subjection, as those who are in the state of nature. Which could not possibly be, if all political power were only paternal, and that in truth they were one and the same thing: for then, all paternal power being in the prince, the subject could naturally have none of it. But these two powers, political and paternal, are so perfectly distinct and separate; are built upon so different foundations, and given to so different ends, that every subject that is a father, has as much a paternal power over his children, as the prince has over his: and every prince, that has parents, owes them as much filial[2] duty and obedience, as the meanest of his subjects do to theirs; and can therefore contain not any part or degree of that kind of dominion, which a prince or magistrate has over his subject.

Sec. 72. Though the obligation on the parents to bring up their children, and the obligation on children to honor their parents, contain all the power on the one hand, and submission on the other, which are proper to this relation, yet there is another power ordinarily in the father, whereby he has a tie on the obedience of his children; which though it be common to him with other men, yet the occasions of showing it, almost constantly happening to fathers in their private families and in instances of it elsewhere being rare, and less taken notice of, it passes in the world for a part of "paternal jurisdiction." And this is the power men generally have to bestow their estates on those who please them best; the possession of the father being the expectation and inheritance of the children, ordinarily in certain proportions, according to the law and custom of each country; yet it is commonly in the father's power to bestow it with a more sparing or liberal hand, according as the behavior of this or that child has comported with[3] his will and humor.

Sec. 73. This is no small tie on the obedience of children: and there being always annexed to the enjoyment of land, a submission to the government of the country, of which that land is a part; it has been commonly supposed, that a father could oblige[4] his posterity to that government, of which he himself was a subject, and that his compact[5] held them; whereas, it being only a necessary condition annexed to the land, and the inheritance of an estate which is under that government, reaches only those who will take it on that condition, and so is no natural tie or engagement, but a voluntary submission: for every man's children being by nature as free as himself, or any of his ancestors ever were, may, while they are in that freedom, choose what society they will join themselves to, what commonwealth they will put themselves under. But if they will enjoy the inheritance of their ancestors, they must take it on the same terms their ancestors had it, and submit to all the conditions annexed to such a possession. By this power indeed fathers oblige their children to obedience to themselves, even when they are past minority, and most commonly too subject them to this or that political power: but neither of these by any peculiar right of fatherhood, but by the reward they have in their hands to enforce and recompense such a compliance; and is no more power than what a French man has over an English man, who by the hopes of an estate he will leave him, will certainly have a strong tie on his obedience: and if, when it is left him, he will enjoy it, he must certainly take it upon the conditions annexed to the possession of land in that country where it lies, whether it be France or England.

Sec. 74. To conclude then, though the father's power of commanding extends no farther than the minority of his children, and to a degree only fit for the discipline and government of that age; and though that honor and respect,

---

3   *has comported with* Was consistent with.
4   *oblige* Connect with bonds of loyalty or obligation.
5   *compact* Agreement. Locke here probably means that the father's tacit social contract with his government might be passed on to his child by inheritance of land.

---

1   *pay a deference* Pay respect.
2   *filial* Of children to parents.

and all that which the Latins called piety, which they indispensably owe to their parents all their lifetime, and in all estates, with all that support and defense is due to them, gives the father no power of governing, i.e., making laws and enacting penalties on his children; though by all this he has no dominion over the property or actions of his son: yet it is obvious to conceive how easy it was, in the first ages of the world, and in places still, where the thinness of people[1] gives families leave to separate into unpossessed quarters,[2] and they have room to remove or plant themselves in yet vacant habitations, for the father of the family to become the prince of[3] it; he had been a ruler from the beginning of the infancy of his children: and since without some government it would be hard for them to live together, it was likeliest it should, by the express or tacit consent of the children when they were grown up, be in the father, where it seemed without any change barely to continue; when indeed nothing more was required to it, than the permitting the father to exercise alone, in his family, that executive power of the law of nature, which every free man naturally has, and by that permission resigning up to him a monarchical power, while they remained in it. But that this was not by any paternal right, but only by the consent of his children, is evident from hence,[4] that nobody doubts, but[5] if a stranger, whom chance or business had brought to his family, had there killed any of his children, or committed any other fact,[6] he might condemn and put him to death, or otherwise have punished him, as well as any of his children; which it was impossible he should do by virtue of any paternal authority over one who was not his child, but by virtue of that executive power of the law of nature, which, as a man, he had a right to: and he alone could punish him in his family, where the respect of his children had laid by the exercise of such a power, to give way to the dignity and authority they were willing should remain in him, above the rest of his family.

Sec. 75. Thus it was easy, and almost natural for children, by a tacit, and scarce avoidable consent, to make way for the father's authority and government. They had been accustomed in their childhood to follow his direction, and to refer their little differences to him, and when they were men, who fitter to rule them? Their little properties, and less covetousness,[7] seldom afforded greater controversies; and when any should arise, where could they have a fitter umpire[8] than he, by whose care they had everyone been sustained and brought up, and who had a tenderness for them all? It is no wonder that they made no distinction betwixt[9] minority and full age; nor looked after one and twenty, or any other age that might make them the free disposers of themselves and fortunes, when they could have no desire to be out of their pupilage:[10] the government they had been under, during it, continued still to be more their protection than restraint; and they could no where find a greater security to their peace, liberties, and fortunes, than in the rule of a father.

Sec. 76. Thus the natural fathers of families, by an insensible change, became the politic[11] monarchs of them too: and as they chanced to live long, and leave able and worthy heirs, for several successions, or otherwise; so they laid the foundations of hereditary, or elective kingdoms, under several constitutions and manners, according as chance, contrivance, or occasions happened to mold them. But if princes have their titles in their fathers' right, and it be a sufficient proof of the natural right of fathers to political authority, because they commonly were those in whose hands we find, de facto,[12] the exercise of government: I say, if this argument be good, it will as strongly prove, that all princes,

---

1   *thinness of people*   Low population density.

2   *unpossessed quarters*   Areas of unowned land.

3   *they have room ... the prince of*   [Locke's note] "It is no improbable opinion therefore, which the arch-philosopher [Aristotle—*Politics* books 3 and 4] was of, that the chief person in every household was always, as it were, a king: so when numbers of households joined themselves in civil societies together, kings were the first kind of governors among them, which is also, as it seemeth, the reason why the name of fathers continued still in them, who, of fathers, were made rulers; as also the ancient custom of governors to do as Melchizedec [Genesis 18.18–20], and being kings, to exercise the office of priests, which fathers did at the first, grew perhaps by the same occasion. Howbeit, this is not the only kind of regiment that has been received in the world. The inconveniencies of one kind have caused sundry others to be devised; so that in a word, all public regiment [rule], of what kind soever, seemeth evidently to have risen from the deliberate advice, consultation and composition between men, judging it convenient and behooveful [advantageous]; there being no impossibility in nature considered by itself, but that man might have lived without any public regiment" (Hooker, *Ecclesiastical Polity Lib.* I. sect. 10).

4   *hence*   The following.

5   *but*   That.

6   *fact*   Evil deed.

7   *covetousness*   Desire to possess others' property.

8   *umpire*   Arbitrator.

9   *betwixt*   Between.

10   *pupilage*   Period of being a young student.

11   *politic*   Political.

12   *de facto*   Latin: in fact (contrasted here with Latin: *de jure* or by law).

nay princes only, ought to be priests, since it is as certain, that in the beginning, the father of the family was priest, as that he was ruler in his own household.

Chapter 7. Of Political or Civil Society

Sec. 77. God having made man such a creature, that in his own judgment, it was not good for him to be alone, put him under strong obligations of necessity, convenience, and inclination to drive him into society, as well as fitted him with understanding and language to continue and enjoy it. The first society was between man and wife, which gave beginning to that between parents and children; to which, in time, that between master and servant came to be added: and though all these might, and commonly did meet together, and make up but one family,[1] wherein the master or mistress of it had some sort of rule proper to a family; each of these, or all together, came short of political society, as we shall see, if we consider the different ends, ties, and bounds of each of these.

Sec. 78. Conjugal[2] society is made by a voluntary compact between man and woman; and though it consist chiefly in such a communion[3] and right in one another's bodies as is necessary to its chief end, procreation; yet it draws with it mutual support and assistance, and a communion of interests too, as necessary not only to unite their care and affection, but also necessary to their common off-spring, who have a right to be nourished, and maintained by them, till they are able to provide for themselves.

Sec. 79. For the end of conjunction,[4] betwixt male and female, being not barely procreation, but the continuation of the species; this conjunction between male and female ought to last, even after procreation, so long as is necessary to the nourishment and support of the young ones, who are to be sustained even after procreation, so long as is necessary to the nourishment and support of the young ones, who are to be sustained by those that got them, till they are able to shift and provide for themselves. This rule, which the infinite wise maker has set to the works of his hands, we find the inferior creatures steadily obey. In those viviparous[5] animals which feed on grass, the conjunction between male and female lasts no longer than the very act of copulation;

because the teat of the dam[6] being sufficient to nourish the young, till it be able to feed on grass, the male only begets,[7] but concerns not himself for the female or young, to whose sustenance he can contribute nothing. But in beasts of prey the conjunction lasts longer: because the dam not being able well to subsist herself, and nourish her numerous off-spring by her own prey alone, a more laborious, as well as more dangerous way of living, than by feeding on grass, the assistance of the male is necessary to the maintenance of their common family, which cannot subsist till they are able to prey for themselves, but by the joint care of male and female. The same is to be observed in all birds, (except some domestic ones, where plenty of food excuses the cock from feeding, and taking care of the young brood) whose young needing food in the nest, the cock and hen continue mates, till the young are able to use their wing, and provide for themselves.

Sec. 80. And herein I think lies the chief, if not the only reason, why the male and female in mankind are tied to a longer conjunction than other creatures, viz. because the female is capable of conceiving, and de facto is commonly with child again, and brings forth too a new birth, long before the former is out of a dependency for support on his parents' help, and able to shift for himself, and has all the assistance is due to him from his parents: whereby the father, who is bound to take care for those he has begot, is under an obligation to continue in conjugal society with the same woman longer than other creatures, whose young being able to subsist of themselves, before the time of procreation returns again, the conjugal bond dissolves of itself, and they are at liberty, till Hymen[8] at his usual anniversary season summons them again to choose new mates. Wherein one cannot but admire the wisdom of the great Creator, who having given to man foresight, and an ability to lay up for the future, as well as to supply the present necessity, has made it necessary, that society of man and wife should be more lasting, than of male and female among other creatures; that so their industry might be encouraged, and their interest better united, to make provision and lay up goods for their common issue, which uncertain mixture, or easy and frequent solutions of conjugal society would mightily disturb.

---

1   *family*   Household.
2   *Conjugal*   Relating to marriage.
3   *communion*   Intimate connection.
4   *conjunction*   Bonding.
5   *viviparous*   Live-bearing (as contrasted with egg-laying).
6   *dam*   Female parent.
7   *begets*   Impregnates the female.
8   *Hymen*   Greek god of marriage.

○ – explains concept of marriage
● – concept of parental responsibility

✱ Comparison of human parents to animal parents w.r.t. offspring

Sec. 81. But though these are ties upon mankind, which make the conjugal bonds more firm and lasting in man, than the other species of animals; yet it would give one reason to enquire, why this compact, where procreation and education are secured, and inheritance taken care for, may not be made determinable,[1] either by consent, or at a certain time, or upon certain conditions, as well as any other voluntary compacts, there being no necessity in the nature of the thing, nor to the ends of it, that it should always be for life; I mean, to such as are under no restraint of any positive law, which ordains all such contracts to be perpetual.

Sec. 82. But the husband and wife, though they have but one common concern, yet having different understandings, will unavoidably sometimes have different wills too; it therefore being necessary that the last determination,[2] i.e., the rule, should be placed somewhere; it naturally falls to the man's share, as the abler and the stronger. But this reaching but to the things of their common interest and property,[3] leaves the wife in the full and free possession of what by contract is her peculiar right,[4] and gives the husband no more power over her life than she has over his; the power of the husband being so far from that of an absolute monarch, that the wife has in many cases a liberty to separate from him, where natural right, or their contract allows it; whether that contract be made by themselves in the state of nature, or by the customs or laws of the country they live in; and the children upon such separation fall to the father or mother's lot, as such contract does determine.

Sec. 83. For all the ends of marriage being to be obtained under politic government, as well as in the state of nature, the civil magistrate does not abridge the right or power of either naturally necessary to those ends, viz. procreation and mutual support and assistance while they are together; but only decides any controversy that may arise between man and wife about them. If it were otherwise, and that absolute sovereignty and power of life and death naturally belonged to the husband, and were necessary to the society between man and wife, there could be no matrimony in any of those countries where the husband is allowed no such absolute authority. But the ends of matrimony requiring no such power in the husband, the condition of conjugal society put it not in him, it being not at all necessary to that state. Conjugal society could subsist and attain its ends without it; nay, community of goods, and the power over them, mutual assistance and maintenance, and other things belonging to conjugal society, might be varied and regulated by that contract which unites man and wife in that society, as far as may consist with procreation and the bringing up of children till they could shift for themselves; nothing being necessary to any society, that is not necessary to the ends for which it is made.

Sec. 84. The society betwixt parents and children, and the distinct rights and powers belonging respectively to them, I have treated of so largely, in the foregoing chapter, that I shall not here need to say any thing of it. And I think it is plain, that it is far different from a politic society.

Sec. 85. Master and servant are names as old as history, but given to those of far different condition; for a freeman makes himself a servant to another, by selling him, for a certain time, the service he undertakes to do, in exchange for wages he is to receive: and though this commonly puts him into the family of his master, and under the ordinary discipline thereof; yet it gives the master but a temporary power over him, and no greater than what is contained in the contract between them. But there is another sort of servants, which by a peculiar name we call slaves, who being captives taken in a just war, are by the right of nature subjected to the absolute dominion and arbitrary power of their masters. These men having, as I say, forfeited their lives, and with it their liberties, and lost their estates; and being in the state of slavery, not capable of any property, cannot in that state be considered as any part of civil society; the chief end whereof is the preservation of property.

Sec. 86. Let us therefore consider a master of a family with all these subordinate relations of wife, children, servants, and slaves, united under the domestic rule of a family; which, whatever resemblance it may have in its order, offices, and number too, with a little commonwealth, yet is very far from it, both in its constitution, power and end: or if it must be thought a monarchy, and the paterfamilias[5] the absolute monarch in it, absolute monarchy will have but a very shattered and short power, when it is plain, by what has been said before, that the master of the family has a very distinct and differently limited power, both as to time and extent, over those several persons that are in it; for excepting

Continued ⇒

---

1 *determinable* Able to be ended.

2 *last determination* The final say in the matter.

3 *But this reaching ... property* But since this extends only to what is their common interest and property.

4 *peculiar right* Private property.

5 *paterfamilias* Literally "father of the family," but with the implication of complete authority.

the slave (and the family is as much a family, and his power as paterfamilias as great, whether there be any slaves in his family or no) he has no legislative power of life and death over any of them, and none too but[1] what a mistress of a family may have as well as he. And he certainly can have no absolute power over the whole family, who has but a very limited one over every individual in it. But how a family, or any other society of men, differ from that which is properly political society, we shall best see, by considering wherein political society itself consists.

Sec. 87. Man being born, as has been proved, with a title to perfect freedom, and an uncontrolled enjoyment of all the rights and privileges of the law of nature, equally with any other man, or number of men in the world, has by nature a power, not only to preserve his property, that is, his life, liberty and estate, against the injuries and attempts of other men; but to judge of, and punish the breaches of that law in others, as he is persuaded the offence deserves, even with death itself, in crimes where the heinousness of the fact,[2] in his opinion, requires it. But because no political society can be, nor subsist, without having in itself the power to preserve the property, and in order thereunto, punish the offences of all those of that society; there, and there only is political society, where everyone of the members has quitted this natural power, resigned[3] it up into the hands of the community in all cases that exclude him not from appealing for protection to the law established by it. And thus all private judgment of every particular member being excluded, the community comes to be umpire, by settled standing rules, indifferent, and the same to all parties; and by men having authority from the community, for the execution of those rules, decides all the differences that may happen between any members of that society concerning any matter of right; and punishes those offences which any member has committed against the society, with such penalties as the law has established: whereby it is easy to discern, who are, and who are not, in political society together. Those who are united into one body, and have a common established law and judicature[4] to appeal to, with authority to decide controversies between them, and punish offenders, are in civil society one with another: but those who have no such common appeal, I mean on earth, are still in the state of nature, each being, where there is no other, judge for himself,

and executioner; which is, as I have before shown it, the perfect state of nature.

Sec. 88. And thus the commonwealth comes by a power to set down what punishment shall belong to the several transgressions which they think worthy of it, committed among the members of that society, (which is the power of making laws) as well as it has the power to punish any injury done unto any of its members, by anyone that is not of it, (which is the power of war and peace;) and all this for the preservation of the property of all the members of that society, as far as is possible. But though every man who has entered into civil society, and is become a member of any commonwealth, has thereby quitted[5] his power to punish offences, against the law of nature, in prosecution[6] of his own private judgment, yet with the judgment of offences, which he has given up to the legislative in all cases, where he can appeal to the magistrate, he has given a right to the commonwealth to employ his force, for the execution of the judgments of the commonwealth, whenever he shall be called to it; which indeed are his own judgments, they being made by himself, or his representative. And herein we have the original of the legislative and executive power of civil society, which is to judge by standing laws, how far offences are to be punished, when committed within the commonwealth; and also to determine, by occasional[7] judgments founded on the present circumstances of the fact, how far injuries from without are to be vindicated;[8] and in both these to employ all the force of all the members, when there shall be need.

Sec. 89. Wherever therefore any number of men are so united into one society, as to quit everyone his executive power of the law of nature, and to resign it to the public, there and there only is a political, or civil society. And this is done, wherever any number of men, in the state of nature, enter into society to make one people, one body politic, under one supreme government; or else when anyone joins himself to, and incorporates with any government already made: for hereby he authorizes the society, or which is all one, the legislative thereof, to make laws for him, as the public good of the society shall require; to the execution whereof, his own assistance (as to his own decrees) is due. And this puts men out of a state of nature into that of a commonwealth, by setting up a judge on earth, with authority

---

1   *none too but*   Nothing but.
2   *heinousness of the fact*   Evil nature of the horrible deed.
3   *resigned*   Relinquished claim to.
4   *judicature*   System for administration of justice.

5   *quitted*   Given up.
6   *prosecution*   Pursuit, as if in court, of legal action.
7   *occasional*   Specific to the occasion.
8   *vindicated*   Punished.

to determine all the controversies, and redress the injuries that may happen to any member of the commonwealth; which judge is the legislative, or magistrates appointed by it. And wherever there are any number of men, however associated, that have no such decisive power to appeal to, there they are still in the state of nature.

Sec. 90. Hence it is evident, that absolute monarchy, which by some men is counted the only government in the world, is indeed inconsistent with civil society, and so can be no form of civil government at all: for the end of civil society, being to avoid, and remedy those inconveniencies of the state of nature, which necessarily follow from every man's being judge in his own case, by setting up a known authority, to which everyone of that society may appeal upon any injury received, or controversy that may arise, and which everyone of the society ought to obey;[1] wherever any persons are, who have not such an authority to appeal to, for the decision of any difference between them, there those persons are still in the state of nature; and so is every absolute prince, in respect of those who are under his dominion.

Sec. 91. For he being supposed to have all, both legislative and executive power in himself alone, there is no judge to be found, no appeal lies open to anyone, who may fairly, and indifferently, and with authority decide, and from whose decision relief and redress may be expected of any injury or inconveniency, that may be suffered from the prince, or by his order: so that such a man, however entitled, "Czar," or "Grand Seignior," or how you please, is as much in the state of nature, with all under his dominion, as he is with the rest of mankind: for wherever any two men are, who have no standing rule, and common judge to appeal to on earth, for the determination of controversies of right betwixt them, there they are still in the state of nature, and under all the inconveniencies of it, with only this woeful difference to the subject, or rather slave of an absolute prince:[2] that whereas,

in the ordinary state of nature, he has a liberty to judge of his right, and according to the best of his power, to maintain it; now, whenever his property is invaded by the will and order of his monarch, he has not only no appeal, as those in society ought to have, but as if he were degraded from the common state of rational creatures, is denied a liberty to judge of, or to defend his right; and so is exposed to all the misery and inconveniencies, that a man can fear from one, who being in the unrestrained state of nature, is yet corrupted with flattery, and armed with power.

Sec. 92. For he that thinks absolute power purifies men's blood, and corrects the baseness of human nature, need read but the history of this, or any other age, to be convinced of the contrary. He that would have been insolent and injurious in the woods of America, would not probably be much better in a throne; where perhaps learning and religion shall be found out to justify all that he shall do to his subjects, and the sword presently silence all those that dare question it: for what the protection of absolute monarchy is, what kind of fathers of their countries it makes princes to be and to what a degree of happiness and security it carries civil society, where this sort of government is grown to perfection, he that will look into the late relation of Ceylon, may easily see.

Sec. 93. In absolute monarchies indeed, as well as other governments of the world, the subjects have an appeal to the law, and judges to decide any controversies, and restrain any violence that may happen betwixt the subjects themselves, one among another. This everyone thinks necessary, and believes he deserves to be thought a declared enemy to society and mankind, who should go about to take it

---

1   *for the end of civil society ... society ought to obey* [Locke's note] "The public power of all society is above every soul contained in the same society; and the principal use of that power is, to give laws unto all that are under it, which laws in such cases we must obey, unless there be reason shown which may necessarily enforce [unavoidably give strength to the idea], that the law of reason, or of God, doth enjoin [impose] the contrary" (Hooker, *Ecclesiastical Polity Lib*. I. sect. 16).

2   *for wherever any two men ... an absolute prince* [Locke's note] "To take away all such mutual grievances, injuries and wrongs," i.e., such as attend men in the state of nature, "there was no way but only by growing into composition and agreement among

themselves, by ordaining some kind of government public, and by yielding themselves subject thereunto, that unto whom they granted authority to rule and govern, by them the peace, tranquility and happy estate of the rest might be procured. Men always knew that where force and injury was offered, they might be defenders of themselves; they knew that however men may seek their own commodity [advantage], yet if this were done with injury unto others, it was not to be suffered, but by all men, and all good means to be withstood. Finally, they knew that no man might in reason take upon him to determine his own right, and according to his own determination proceed in maintenance thereof, in as much as every man is towards himself, and them whom he greatly affects, partial; and therefore that strifes and troubles would be endless, except they gave their common consent, all to be ordered by some, whom they should agree upon, without which consent there would be no reason that one man should take upon him to be lord or judge over another" (Hooker, *Ecclesiastical Polity Lib*. I. sect. 10).

away. But whether this be from a true love of mankind and society, and such a charity as we owe all one to another, there is reason to doubt: for this is no more than what every man, who loves his own power, profit, or greatness, may and naturally must do, keep those animals from hurting, or destroying one another, who labor and drudge only for his pleasure and advantage; and so are taken care of, not out of any love the master has for them, but love of himself, and the profit they bring him: for if it be asked, what security, what fence is there, in such a state, against the violence and oppression of this absolute ruler? the very question can scarce be borne. They are ready to tell you, that it deserves death only to ask after safety. Betwixt and subject, they will grant, there must be measures, laws and judges, for their mutual peace and security: but as for the ruler, he ought to be absolute, and is above all such circumstances; because he has power to do more hurt and wrong, it is right when he does it. To ask how you may be guarded from harm, or injury, on that side where the strongest hand is to do it, is presently the voice of faction and rebellion: as if when men quitting the state of nature entered into society, they agreed that all of them but one, should be under the restraint of laws, but that he should still retain all the liberty of the state of nature, increased with power, and made licentious by impunity.[1] This is to think, that men are so foolish, that they take care to avoid what mischiefs may be done them by polecats, or foxes; but are content, nay, think it safety, to be devoured by lions.

Sec. 94. But whatever flatterers may talk to amuse people's understandings, it hinders not men from feeling; and when they perceive, that any man, in whatever station, is out of the bounds of the civil society which they are of, and that they have no appeal on earth against any harm, they may receive from him, they are apt to think themselves in the state of nature, in respect of him whom they find to be so; and to take care, as soon as they can, to have that safety and security in civil society, for which it was first instituted, and for which only they entered into it. And therefore, though perhaps at first, (as shall be shown more at large hereafter in the following part of this discourse) some one good and excellent man having got a preeminence among the rest, had this deference paid to his goodness and virtue, as to a kind of natural authority, that the chief rule, with arbitration of their differences, by

a tacit consent devolved into his hands, without any other caution, but the assurance they had of his uprightness and wisdom; yet when time, giving authority, and (as some men would persuade us) sacredness of customs, which the negligent, and unforeseeing innocence of the first ages began, had brought in successors of another stamp,[2] the people finding their properties not secure under the government, as then it was,[3] (whereas government has no other end but the preservation of property) could never be safe nor at rest, nor think themselves in civil society, till the legislature was placed in collective bodies of men, call them senate, parliament, or what you please. By which means every single person became subject, equally with other the meanest men, to those laws, which he himself, as part of the legislative, had established; nor could anyone, by his own authority; avoid the force of the law, when once made; nor by any pretence of superiority plead exemption, thereby to license his own, or the miscarriages[4] of any of his dependents.[5] No man in civil society can be exempted from the laws of it: for if any man may do what he thinks fit, and there be no appeal on earth, for redress or security against any harm he shall do; I ask, whether he be not perfectly still in the state of nature, and so can be no part or member of that civil society; unless anyone will say, the state of nature and civil society are one and the same thing, which I have never yet found anyone so great a patron of anarchy as to affirm.

---

1   *made licentious by impunity* Made immoral by freedom from consequences of their actions.

2   *stamp* Type.

3   *the people finding ... under the government, as then it was* [Locke's note] "At the first, when some certain kind of regiment was once appointed, it may be that nothing was then farther thought upon for the manner of governing, but all permitted unto their wisdom and discretion, which were to rule, till by experience they found this for all parts very inconvenient, so as the thing which they had devised for a remedy, did indeed but increase the sore, which it should have cured. They saw, that to live by one man's will, became the cause of all men's misery. This constrained them to come unto laws, wherein all men might see their duty beforehand, and know the penalties of transgressing them" (Hooker, *Ecclesiastical Polity Lib.* I. sect. 10).

4   *miscarriages* Mishandlings.

5   *dependents* [Locke's note] "Civil law being the act of the whole body politic, doth therefore overrule each several part of the same body" (Hooker, *Ibid.*).

Chapter 8. Of the Beginning of Political Societies

Sec. 95. Men being, as has been said, by nature, all free, equal, and independent, no one can be put out of this estate, and subjected to the political power of another, without his own consent. The only way whereby anyone divests himself of his natural liberty, and puts on the bonds of civil society, is by agreeing with other men to join and unite into a community for their comfortable, safe, and peaceable living one among another, in a secure enjoyment of their properties, and a greater security against any, that are not of it. This any number of men may do, because it injures not the freedom of the rest; they are left as they were in the liberty of the state of nature. When any number of men have so consented to make one community or government, they are thereby presently incorporated, and make one body politic, wherein the majority have a right to act and conclude[1] the rest.

Sec. 96. For when any number of men have, by the consent of every individual, made a community, they have thereby made that community one body, with a power to act as one body, which is only by the will and determination of the majority: for that which acts[2] any community, being only the consent of the individuals of it, and it being necessary to that which is one body to move one way; it is necessary the body should move that way whither the greater force carries it, which is the consent of the majority: or else it is impossible it should act or continue one body, one community, which the consent of every individual that united into it, agreed that it should; and so everyone is bound by that consent to be concluded by the majority. And therefore we see, that in assemblies, empowered to act by positive laws, where no number is set by that positive law which empowers them, the act of the majority passes for the act of the whole, and of course determines, as having, by the law of nature and reason, the power of the whole.

Sec. 97. And thus every man, by consenting with others to make one body politic under one government, puts himself under an obligation, to everyone of that society, to submit to the determination of the majority, and to be concluded by it; or else this original compact, whereby he with others incorporates into one society, would signify nothing, and be no compact, if he be left free, and under no other ties than he was in before in the state of nature. For what appearance would there be of any compact? what new engagement if he were no farther tied by any decrees of the society, than he himself thought fit, and did actually consent to? This would be still as great a liberty, as he himself had before his compact, or anyone else in the state of nature has, who may submit himself, and consent to any acts of it if he thinks fit.

Sec. 98. For if the consent of the majority shall not, in reason, be received as the act of the whole, and conclude every individual; nothing but the consent of every individual can make any thing to be the act of the whole: but such a consent is next to impossible ever to be had, if we consider the infirmities of health, and avocations[3] of business, which in a number, though much less than that of a commonwealth, will necessarily keep many away from the public assembly. To which if we add the variety of opinions, and contrariety of interests, which unavoidably happen in all collections of men, the coming into society upon such terms would be only like Cato's coming into the theatre, only to go out again.[4] Such a constitution as this would make the mighty Leviathan[5] of a shorter duration, than the feeblest creatures, and not let it outlast the day it was born in: which cannot be supposed, till we can think, that rational creatures should desire and constitute societies only to be dissolved: for where the majority cannot conclude the rest, there they cannot act as one body, and consequently will be immediately dissolved again.

Sec. 99. Whosoever therefore out of a state of nature unite into a community, must be understood to give up all the power, necessary to the ends for which they unite into society, to the majority of the community, unless they expressly agreed in any number greater than the majority. And this is done by barely agreeing to unite into one

---

3   *avocations* Distractions.
4   *Cato's coming ... go out again* Marcus Porcius Cato (234–149 BCE) was called Cato the Elder, and also Cato the Censor because of his opposition to the introduction into Rome of Greek refinement and luxury and his efforts to enforce a strict moral standard by legislation. Locke's idea here may be that Cato sees the goings-on in the theater and, appalled, walks right back out again.
5   *Leviathan* A large beast or sea-monster in the Bible. The reference here is to Hobbes, who used that term as the title of his famous book and as a name for the huge and formidable state with absolute powers that he advocated as the only effective form of government. Locke was eager to disassociate himself from Hobbes; this is one of the very few more-or-less explicit references to him.

political society, which is all the compact that is, or needs be, between the individuals, that enter into, or make up a commonwealth. And thus that, which begins and actually constitutes any political society, is nothing but the consent of any number of freemen capable of a majority to unite and incorporate into such a society. And this is that, and that only, which did, or could give beginning to any lawful government in the world.

Sec. 100. To this I find two objections made.

First, That there are no instances to be found in story, of a company of men independent, and equal one among another, that met together, and in this way began and set up a government.

Secondly, It is impossible of right, that men should do so, because all men being born under government, they are to submit to that, and are not at liberty to begin a new one.

Sec. 101. To the first there is this to answer, That it is not at all to be wondered, that history gives us but a very little account of men, that lived together in the state of nature. The inconveniencies of that condition, and the love and want of society, no sooner brought any number of them together, but they presently united and incorporated, if they designed to continue together. And if we may not suppose men ever to have been in the state of nature, because we hear not much of them in such a state, we may as well suppose the armies of Salmanasser or Xerxes[1] were never children, because we hear little of them, till they were men, and embodied in armies. Government is every where antecedent to records, and letters seldom come in among a people till a long continuation of civil society has, by other more necessary arts, provided for their safety, ease, and plenty: and then they begin to look after the history of their founders, and search into their original, when they have outlived the memory of it: for it is with common-wealths as with particular persons, they are commonly ignorant of their own births and infancies: and if they know any thing of their original, they are beholden for it, to the accidental records that others have kept of it. And those that we have, of the beginning of any polities in the world, excepting that of the Jews, where God himself immediately interposed, and which favors not at all paternal dominion, are all either

plain instances of such a beginning as I have mentioned, or at least have manifest footsteps of it.

Sec. 102. He must show a strange inclination to deny evident matter of fact, when it agrees not with his hypothesis, who will not allow, that the beginning of Rome and Venice were by the uniting together of several men free and independent one of another, among whom there was no natural superiority or subjection. And if Josephus Acosta's word may be taken, he tells us, that in many parts of America there was no government at all. "There are great and apparent conjectures," says he, "that these men," speaking of those of Peru, "for a long time had neither kings nor commonwealths, but lived in troops, as they do this day in Florida, the Cheriquanas, those of Brazil, and many other nations, which have no certain kings, but as occasion is offered, in peace or war, they choose their captains as they please." I.I. c. 25.[2] If it be said, that every man there was born subject to his father, or the head of his family; that the subjection due from a child to a father took not away his freedom of uniting into what political society he thought fit, has been already proved. But be that as it will, these men, it is evident, were actually free; and whatever superiority some politicians now would place in any of them, they themselves claimed it not, but by consent were all equal, till by the same consent they set rulers over themselves. So that their politic societies all began from a voluntary union, and the mutual agreement of men freely acting in the choice of their governors, and forms of government.

Sec. 103. And I hope those who went away from Sparta with Palantus, mentioned by Justin, I. 3. c. 4.[3] will be allowed to have been freemen independent one of another, and to have set up a government over themselves, by their own consent. Thus I have given several examples, out of history, of people free and in the state of nature, that being met together incorporated and began a commonwealth. And if the want of such instances be an argument to prove that government were not, nor could not be so begun, I

---

1   *Salmanasser*   Shalmaneser V (or IV) (727–722 BCE) was king of Assyria; his fight against the Israelites is referred to in the Bible (2 Kings); *Xerxes*   Xerxes (d. 465 BCE) was king of Persia; he led the second Persian invasion of Greece.

2   *I.I. c. 25*   In *Natural and Moral History of the Indies* by José de Acosta (Spanish, 1540–1600). Acosta's book provided the first detailed description of the geography and culture of Latin America and of Aztec history.

3   *those who went ... Justin, I. 3. c. 4*   Marcus Junianus Justinus, Roman historian of the third century CE. In his major work (now lost) he described the group of young Spartans, who, born out of wedlock and thus denied rights in Sparta, left and, under their leader Phalanthus, conquered Tarentum (modern Taranto) in Southern Italy around 708 BCE and set up a new independent state.

suppose the contenders for paternal empire were better let it alone, than urge it against natural liberty: for if they can give so many instances, out of history, of governments begun upon paternal right, I think (though at best an argument from what has been, to what should of right be, has no great force) one might, without any great danger, yield them the cause. But if I might advise them in the case, they would do well not to search too much into the original of governments, as they have begun de facto, lest they should find, at the foundation of most of them, something very little favorable to the design they promote, and such a power as they contend for.

Sec. 104. But to conclude, reason being plain on our side, that men are naturally free, and the examples of history showing, that the governments of the world, that were begun in peace, had their beginning laid on that foundation, and were made by the consent of the people; there can be little room for doubt, either where the right is, or what has been the opinion, or practice of mankind, about the first erecting of governments.

Sec. 105. I will not deny, that if we look back as far as history will direct us, towards the original of commonwealths, we shall generally find them under the government and administration of one man. And I am also apt to believe, that where a family was numerous enough to subsist by itself, and continued entire together, without mixing with others, as it often happens, where there is much land, and few people, the government commonly began in the father: for the father having, by the law of nature, the same power with every man else to punish, as he thought fit, any offences against that law, might thereby punish his transgressing children, even when they were men, and out of their pupilage; and they were very likely to submit to his punishment, and all join with him against the offender, in their turns, giving him thereby power to execute his sentence against any transgression, and so in effect make him the law-maker, and governor over all that remained in conjunction with his family. He was fittest to be trusted; paternal affection secured their property and interest under his care; and the custom of obeying him, in their childhood, made it easier to submit to him, rather than to any other. If therefore they must have one to rule them, as government is hardly to be avoided among men that live together; who so likely to be the man as he that was their common father; unless negligence, cruelty, or any other defect of mind or body made him unfit for it? But when either the father died, and left his next heir, for want of age, wisdom, courage, or

any other qualities, less fit for rule; or where several families met, and consented to continue together; there, it is not to be doubted, but they used their natural freedom, to set up him, whom they judged the ablest, and most likely, to rule well over them. Conformable hereunto we find the people of America, who (living out of the reach of the conquering swords, and spreading domination of the two great empires of Peru and Mexico) enjoyed their own natural freedom, though, caeteris paribus,[1] they commonly prefer the heir of their deceased king; yet if they find him any way weak, or incapable, they pass him by, and set up the stoutest and bravest man for their ruler.

Sec. 106. Thus, though looking back as far as records give us any account of peopling the world, and the history of nations, we commonly find the government to be in one hand; yet it destroys not that which I affirm, viz. that the beginning of politic society depends upon the consent of the individuals, to join into, and make one society; who, when they are thus incorporated, might set up what form of government they thought fit. But this having given occasion to men to mistake, and think, that by nature government was monarchical, and belonged to the father, it may not be amiss here to consider, why people in the beginning generally pitched upon[2] this form, which though perhaps the father's pre-eminence might, in the first institution of some commonwealths, give a rise to, and place in the beginning, the power in one hand; yet it is plain that the reason, that continued the form of government in a single person, was not any regard, or respect to paternal authority; since all petty monarchies, that is, almost all monarchies, near their original, have been commonly, at least upon occasion, elective.

Sec. 107. First then, in the beginning of things, the father's government of the childhood of those sprung from him, having accustomed them to the rule of one man, and taught them that where it was exercised with care and skill, with affection and love to those under it, it was sufficient to procure and preserve to men all the political happiness they sought for in society. It was no wonder that they should pitch upon, and naturally run into that form of government, which from their infancy they had been all accustomed to: and which, by experience, they had found both easy and safe. To which, if we add, that monarchy being simple, and most obvious to men, whom neither experience

---

1 caeteris paribus Latin: everything else being equal.

2 pitched upon Settled on.

had instructed in forms of government, nor the ambition or insolence of empire had taught to beware of the encroachments[1] of prerogative, or the inconveniencies of absolute power, which monarchy in succession was apt to lay claim to, and bring upon them, it was not at all strange, that they should not much trouble themselves to think of methods of restraining any exorbitances[2] of those to whom they had given the authority over them, and of balancing the power of government, by placing several parts of it in different hands. They had neither felt the oppression of tyrannical dominion, nor did the fashion of the age, nor their possessions, or way of living, (which afforded little matter for covetousness or ambition) give them any reason to apprehend[3] or provide against it; and therefore it is no wonder they put themselves into such a frame of government, as was not only, as I said, most obvious and simple, but also best suited to their present state and condition; which stood more in need of defense against foreign invasions and injuries, than of multiplicity of laws. The equality of a simple poor way of living, confining their desires within the narrow bounds of each man's small property, made few controversies,[4] and so no need of many laws to decide them, or variety of officers to superintend the process, or look after the execution of justice, where there were but few trespasses, and few offenders. Since then those, who like one another so well as to join into society, cannot but be supposed to have some acquaintance and friendship together, and some trust one in another; they could not but have greater apprehensions of others, than of one another: and therefore their first care and thought cannot but be supposed to be, how to secure themselves against foreign force. It was natural for them to put themselves under a frame of government which might best serve to that end, and choose the wisest and bravest man to conduct them in their wars, and lead them out against their enemies, and in this chiefly be their ruler.

Sec. 108. Thus we see, that the kings of the Indians in America, which is still a pattern of the first ages in Asia and Europe, while the inhabitants were too few for the country, and want of people and money gave men no temptation to enlarge their possessions of land, or contest for wider extent of ground, are little more than generals of their armies; and though they command absolutely in war, yet at home and in time of peace they exercise very little dominion, and have

but a very moderate sovereignty, the resolutions of peace and war being ordinarily either in the people, or in a council. Though the war itself, which admits not of plurality of governors, naturally devolves the command into the king's sole authority.

Sec. 109. And thus in Israel itself, the chief business of their judges, and first kings, seems to have been to be captains in war, and leaders of their armies; which (besides what is signified by "going out and in before the people," which was, to march forth to war, and home again in the heads of their forces) appears plainly in the story of Jephtha. The Ammonites making war upon Israel, the Gileadites in fear send to Jephtha, a bastard of their family whom they had cast off, and article with him, if he will assist them against the Ammonites, to make him their ruler; which they do in these words, "And the people made him head and captain over them" (Judges 11.2), which was, as it seems, all one as to be judge. "And he judged Israel" (Judges 7.7), that is, was their captain-general six years. So when Jotham upbraids the Shechemites with the obligation they had to Gideon, who had been their judge and ruler, he tells them, "He fought for you, and adventured his life far, and delivered you out of the hands of Midian" (Judges 9.17). Nothing mentioned of him but what he did as a general: and indeed that is all is found in his history, or in any of the rest of the judges. And Abimelech particularly is called king, though at most he was but their general. And when, being weary of the ill conduct of Samuel's sons, the children of Israel desired a king, "like all the nations to judge them, and to go out before them, and to fight their battles) (1 Samuel 8.20), God granting their desire, says to Samuel, "I will send thee a man, and thou shalt anoint him to be captain over my people Israel, that he may save my people out of the hands of the Philistines" (9.16), as if the only business of a king had been to lead out their armies, and fight in their defense; and accordingly at his inauguration pouring a vial of oil upon him, declares to Saul, that "the Lord had anointed him to be captain over his inheritance" (10.1). And therefore those, who after Saul's being solemnly chosen and saluted king by the tribes at Mispah, were unwilling to have him their king, made no other objection but this, "How shall this man save us?" (5.27), as if they should have said, "This man is unfit to be our king, not having skill and conduct enough in war, to be able to defend us." And when God resolved to transfer the government to David, it is in these words, "But now thy kingdom shall not continue: the Lord has sought him a man after his own heart, and the Lord has commanded

---

1   *encroachments*   Illicit inroads.
2   *exorbitances*   Unreasonable extremes.
3   *apprehend*   Fear.
4   *controversies*   Disputes.

him to be captain over his people" (8.14), as if the whole kingly authority were nothing else but to be their general: and therefore the tribes who had stuck to Saul's family, and opposed David's reign, when they came to Hebron with terms of submission to him, they tell him, among other arguments they had to submit to him as to their king, that he was in effect their king in Saul's time, and therefore they had no reason but to receive him as their king now. "Also," say they, "in time past, when Saul was king over us, thou wast he that leddest out and broughtest in Israel, and the Lord said unto thee, 'Thou shalt feed my people Israel, and thou shalt be a captain over Israel.'"

Sec. 110. Thus, whether a family by degrees grew up into a commonwealth, and the fatherly authority being continued on to the elder son, everyone in his turn growing up under it, tacitly submitted to it, and the easiness and equality of it not offending anyone, everyone acquiesced, till time seemed to have confirmed it, and settled a right of succession by prescription: or whether several families, or the descendants of several families, whom chance, neighborhood, or business brought together, uniting into society, the need of a general, whose conduct might defend them against their enemies in war, and the great confidence the innocence and sincerity of that poor but virtuous age, (such as are almost all those which begin governments, that ever come to last in the world) gave men one of another, made the first beginners of commonwealths generally put the rule into one man's hand, without any other express limitation or restraint, but what the nature of the thing, and the end of government required: which ever of those it was that at first put the rule into the hands of a single person, certain it is nobody was entrusted with it but for the public good and safety, and to those ends, in the infancies of commonwealths, those who had it commonly used it. And unless they had done so, young societies could not have subsisted; without such nursing fathers tender and careful of the public weal, all governments would have sunk under the weakness and infirmities of their infancy, and the prince and the people had soon perished together.

Sec. 111. But though the golden age (before vain ambition, and amor sceleratus habendi,[1] evil concupiscence,[2] had corrupted men's minds into a mistake of true power and honor) had more virtue, and consequently better governors, as well as less vicious subjects, and there was then

no stretching prerogative on the one side, to oppress the people; nor consequently on the other, any dispute about privilege, to lessen or restrain the power of the magistrate, and so no contest betwixt rulers and people about governors or government:[3] yet, when ambition and luxury in future ages would retain and increase the power, without doing the business for which it was given; and aided by flattery, taught princes to have distinct and separate interests from their people, men found it necessary to examine more carefully the original and rights of government; and to find out ways to restrain the exorbitances, and prevent the abuses of that power, which they having entrusted in another's hands only for their own good, they found was made use of to hurt them.

Sec. 112. Thus we may see how probable it is, that people that were naturally free, and by their own consent either submitted to the government of their father, or united together out of different families to make a government, should generally put the rule into one man's hands, and choose to be under the conduct of a single person, without so much as by express conditions limiting or regulating his power, which they thought safe enough in his honesty and prudence; though they never dreamed of monarchy being jure Divino,[4] which we never heard of among mankind, till it was revealed to us by the divinity of this last age; nor ever allowed paternal power to have a right to dominion, or to be the foundation of all government. And thus much may suffice to show, that as far as we have any light from history, we have reason to conclude, that all peaceful beginnings of government have been laid in the consent of the people. I say peaceful, because I shall have occasion in another place to speak of conquest, which some esteem a way of beginning of governments.

The other objection I find urged against the beginning of polities, in the way I have mentioned, is this, viz.

---

1   amor sceleratus habendi   Latin: accursed love of possessing.
2   concupiscence   Lust.
3   nor consequently ... governors or government   [Locke's note] "At first, when some certain kind of regiment was once approved, it may be nothing was then farther thought upon for the manner of governing, but all permitted unto their wisdom and discretion which were to rule, till by experience they found this for all parts very inconvenient, so as the thing which they had devised for a remedy, did indeed but increase the sore which it should have cured. They saw, that to live by one man's will, became the cause of all men's misery. This constrained them to come unto laws wherein all men might see their duty before hand, and know the penalties of transgressing them" (Hooker, Ecclesiastical Polity Lib. 1. sect. 10).
4   jure Divino   Latin: by divine right.

Sec. 113. That all men being born under government, some or other,[1] it is impossible any of them should ever be free, and at liberty to unite together, and begin a new one, or ever be able to erect a lawful government.

If this argument be good; I ask, how came so many lawful monarchies into the world? for if anybody, upon this supposition, can show me any one man in any age of the world free to begin a lawful monarchy, I will be bound to show him ten other free men at liberty, at the same time to unite and begin a new government under a regal, or any other form; it being demonstration, that if anyone, born under the dominion of another, may be so free as to have a right to command others in a new and distinct empire, everyone that is born under the dominion of another may be so free too, and may become a ruler, or subject, of a distinct separate government. And so by this their own principle, either all men, however born, are free, or else there is but one lawful prince, one lawful government in the world. And then they have nothing to do, but barely to show us which that is; which when they have done, I doubt not but all mankind will easily agree to pay obedience to him.

Sec. 114. Though it be a sufficient answer to their objection, to show that it involves them in the same difficulties that it does those they use it against; yet I shall endeavor to discover the weakness of this argument a little farther. "All men," say they, "are born under government, and therefore they cannot be at liberty to begin a new one. Everyone is born a subject to his father, or his prince, and is therefore under the perpetual tie of subjection and allegiance." It is plain mankind never owned nor considered any such natural subjection that they were born in, to one or to the other that tied them, without their own consents, to a subjection to them and their heirs.

Sec. 115. For there are no examples so frequent in history, both sacred and profane,[2] as those of men withdrawing themselves, and their obedience, from the jurisdiction they were born under, and the family or community they were bred up in, and setting up new governments in other places; from whence sprang all that number of petty commonwealths in the beginning of ages, and which always multiplied, as long as there was room enough, till the stronger, or more fortunate, swallowed the weaker; and those great ones again breaking to pieces, dissolved into lesser dominions. All which are so many testimonies against paternal sovereignty, and plainly prove, that it was not the natural right of the father descending to his heirs, that made governments in the beginning, since it was impossible, upon that ground, there should have been so many little kingdoms; all must have been but only one universal monarchy, if men had not been at liberty to separate themselves from their families, and the government, be it what it will, that was set up in it, and go and make distinct commonwealths and other governments, as they thought fit.

Sec. 116. This has been the practice of the world from its first beginning to this day; nor is it now any more hindrance to the freedom of mankind, that they are born under constituted and ancient polities, that have established laws, and set forms of government, than if they were born in the woods, among the unconfined inhabitants, that run loose in them: for those, who would persuade us, that by being born under any government, we are naturally subjects to it, and have no more any title or pretence to the freedom of the state of nature, have no other reason (bating[3] that of paternal power, which we have already answered) to produce for it, but only, because our fathers or progenitors[4] passed away their natural liberty, and thereby bound up themselves and their posterity to a perpetual subjection to the government, which they themselves submitted to. It is true, that whatever engagements or promises anyone has made for himself, he is under the obligation of them, but cannot, by any compact whatsoever, bind his children or posterity: for his son, when a man, being altogether as free as the father, any act of the father can no more give away the liberty of the son, than it can of anybody else: he may indeed annex such conditions to the land, he enjoyed as a subject of any commonwealth, as may oblige his son to be of that community, if he will enjoy those possessions which were his father's; because that estate being his father's property, he may dispose, or settle it, as he pleases.

Sec. 117. And this has generally given the occasion to mistake in this matter; because commonwealths not permitting any part of their dominions to be dismembered, nor to be enjoyed by any but those of their community, the son cannot ordinarily enjoy the possessions of his father, but under the same terms his father did, by becoming a member of the society; whereby he puts himself presently under the government he finds there established, as much as any other subject of that commonwealth. And thus the

---

1   *government, some or other*   Some government or other.
2   *profane*   Secular—not involved with religion.
3   *bating*   Excepting.
4   *progenitors*   Ancestors.

consent of freemen, born under government, which only makes them members of it, being given separately in their turns, as each comes to be of age, and not in a multitude together; people take no notice of it, and thinking it not done at all, or not necessary, conclude they are naturally subjects as they are men.

Sec. 118. But, it is plain, governments themselves understand it otherwise; they claim no power over the son, because of that they had over the father; nor look on children as being their subjects, by their fathers being so. If a subject of England have a child, by an English woman in France, whose subject is he? Not the king of England's; for he must have leave[1] to be admitted to the privileges of it: nor the king of France's; for how then has his father a liberty to bring him away, and breed him as he pleases? and who ever was judged as a traitor or deserter, if he left, or warred against a country, for being barely[2] born in it of parents that were aliens there? It is plain then, by the practice of governments themselves, as well as by the law of right reason, that a child is born a subject of no country or government. He is under his father's tuition and authority, till he comes to age of discretion; and then he is a freeman, at liberty what government he will put himself under, what body politic he will unite himself to: for if an Englishman's son, born in France, be at liberty, and may do so, it is evident there is no tie upon him by his father's being a subject of this kingdom; nor is he bound up by any compact of his ancestors. And why then has not his son, by the same reason, the same liberty, though he be born anywhere else? Since the power that a father has naturally over his children, is the same, where-ever they be born, and the ties of natural obligations, are not bounded by the positive limits of kingdoms and commonwealths.

Sec. 119. Every man being, as has been shown, naturally free, and nothing being able to put him into subjection to any earthly power, but only his own consent; it is to be considered, what shall be understood to be a sufficient declaration of a man's consent, to make him subject to the laws of any government. There is a common distinction of an express and a tacit consent, which will concern our present case. Nobody doubts but an express consent, of any man entering into any society, makes him a perfect member of that society, a subject of that government. The difficulty is, what ought to be looked upon as a tacit

consent, and how far it binds, i.e., how far anyone shall be looked on to have consented, and thereby submitted to any government, where he has made no expressions of it at all. And to this I say, that every man, that has any possessions, or enjoyment, of any part of the dominions of any government, does thereby give his tacit consent, and is as far forth obliged to obedience to the laws of that government, during such enjoyment, as anyone under it; whether this his possession be of land, to him and his heirs forever, or a lodging only for a week; or whether it be barely traveling freely on the highway; and in effect, it reaches as far as the very being of anyone within the territories of that government. ✳ Tacit Consent

Sec. 120. To understand this the better, it is fit to consider, that every man, when he at first incorporates himself into any commonwealth, he, by his uniting himself thereunto, annexed also, and submits to the community, those possessions, which he has, or shall acquire, that do not already belong to any other government: for it would be a direct contradiction, for anyone to enter into society with others for the securing and regulating of property; and yet to suppose his land, whose property is to be regulated by the laws of the society, should be exempt from the jurisdiction of that government, to which he himself, the proprietor of the land, is a subject. By the same act therefore, whereby anyone unites his person, which was before free, to any commonwealth, by the same he unites his possessions, which were before free, to it also; and they become, both of them, person and possession, subject to the government and dominion of that commonwealth, as long as it has a being. Whoever therefore, from thenceforth, by inheritance, purchase, permission, or otherwise, enjoys any part of the land, so annexed to, and under the government of that commonwealth, must take it with the condition it is under; that is, of submitting to the government of the commonwealth, under whose jurisdiction it is, as far forth as any subject of it. ✳ ✳

Sec. 121. But since the government has a direct jurisdiction only over the land, and reaches the possessor of it, (before he has actually incorporated himself in the society) only as he dwells upon, and enjoys that; the obligation anyone is under, by virtue of such enjoyment, to submit to the government, begins and ends with the enjoyment; so that whenever the owner, who has given nothing but such a tacit consent to the government, will, by donation, sale, or otherwise, quit the said possession, he is at liberty to go and incorporate himself into any other commonwealth; or

---

1   *leave* Permission.
2   *barely* Simply.

to agree with others to begin a new one, in vacuis locis,[1] in any part of the world, they can find free and unpossessed: whereas he, that has once, by actual agreement, and any express declaration, given his consent to be of any commonwealth, is perpetually and indispensably obliged to be, and remain unalterably a subject to it, and can never be again in the liberty of the state of nature; unless, by any calamity, the government he was under comes to be dissolved; or else by some public act cuts him off from being any longer a member of it.

Sec. 122. But submitting to the laws of any country, living quietly, and enjoying privileges and protection under them, makes not a man a member of that society: this is only a local protection and homage due to and from all those, who, not being in a state of war, come within the territories belonging to any government, to all parts whereof the force of its laws extends. But this no more makes a man a member of that society, a perpetual subject of that commonwealth, than it would make a man a subject to another, in whose family he found it convenient to abide for some time; though, while he continued in it, he were obliged to comply with the laws, and submit to the government he found there. And thus we see, that foreigners, by living all their lives under another government, and enjoying the privileges and protection of it, though they are bound, even in conscience, to submit to its administration, as far forth as any denison; yet do not thereby come to be subjects or members of that commonwealth. Nothing can make any man so, but his actually entering into it by positive engagement, and express promise and compact. This is that, which I think, concerning the beginning of political societies, and that consent which makes anyone a member of any commonwealth.

Chapter 9. Of the Ends[2] of Political Society and Government

Sec. 123. If man in the state of nature be so free, as has been said; if he be absolute lord of his own person and possessions, equal to the greatest, and subject to nobody, why will he part with his freedom? why will he give up this empire, and subject himself to the dominion and control of any other power? To which it is obvious to answer, that though in the state of nature he has such a right, yet the enjoy-

ment of it is very uncertain, and constantly exposed to the invasion of others: for all being kings as much as he, every man his equal, and the greater part no strict observers of equity and justice, the enjoyment of the property he has in this state is very unsafe, very insecure. This makes him willing to quit a condition, which, however free, is full of fears and continual dangers: and it is not without reason, that he seeks out, and is willing to join in society with others, who are already united, or have a mind to unite, for the mutual preservation of their lives, liberties and estates, which I call by the general name, property.

Sec. 124. The great and chief end, therefore, of men's uniting into commonwealths, and putting themselves under government, is the preservation of their property. To which in the state of nature there are many things wanting.

First, There wants an established, settled, known law, received and allowed by common consent to be the standard of right and wrong, and the common measure to decide all controversies between them: for though the law of nature be plain and intelligible to all rational creatures; yet men being biased by their interest, as well as ignorant for want of study of it, are not apt to allow of it as a law binding to them in the application of it to their particular cases.

Sec. 125. Secondly, In the state of nature there wants a known and indifferent judge, with authority to determine all differences according to the established law: for everyone in that state being both judge and executioner of the law of nature, men being partial to themselves, passion and revenge is very apt to carry them too far, and with too much heat, in their own cases; as well as negligence, and unconcernedness, to make them too remiss in other men's.

Sec. 126. Thirdly, In the state of nature there often wants power to back and support the sentence when right, and to give it due execution, They who by any injustice offended, will seldom fail, where they are able, by force to make good their injustice; such resistance many times makes the punishment dangerous, and frequently destructive, to those who attempt it.

Sec. 127. Thus mankind, notwithstanding all the privileges of the state of nature, being but in an ill condition, while they remain in it, are quickly driven into society. Hence it comes to pass, that we seldom find any number of men live any time together in this state. The inconveniencies that they are therein exposed to, by the irregular and uncertain exercise of the power every man has of punishing the transgressions of others, make them take sanctuary under the established laws of government, and therein seek

---

1   *in vacuis locis*   Latin: in empty places.
2   *ends*   Purposes.

[handwritten margin note: Just holding up in a country does not make one a member of that society]

the preservation of their property. It is this makes them so willingly give up everyone his single power of punishing, to be exercised by such alone, as shall be appointed to it among them; and by such rules as the community, or those authorized by them to that purpose, shall agree on. And in this we have the original right and rise of both the legislative and executive power, as well as of the governments and societies themselves.

Sec. 128. For in the state of nature, to omit the liberty he has of innocent[1] delights, a man has two powers.

The first is to do whatsoever he thinks fit for the preservation of himself, and others within the permission of the law of nature: by which law, common to them all, he and all the rest of mankind are one community, make up one society, distinct from all other creatures. And were it not for the corruption and viciousness of degenerate men, there would be no need of any other; no necessity that men should separate from this great and natural community, and by positive agreements combine into smaller and divided associations.

The other power a man has in the state of nature, is the power to punish the crimes committed against that law. Both these he gives up, when he joins in a private, if I may so call it, or particular politic society, and incorporates into any commonwealth, separate from the rest of mankind.

Sec. 129. The first power, viz. of doing whatsoever he thought for the preservation of himself, and the rest of mankind, he gives up to be regulated by laws made by the society, so far forth as the preservation of himself, and the rest of that society shall require; which laws of the society in many things confine the liberty he had by the law of nature.

Sec. 130. Secondly, The power of punishing he wholly gives up, and engages his natural force, (which he might before employ in the execution of the law of nature, by his own single authority, as he thought fit) to assist the executive power of the society, as the law thereof shall require: for being now in a new state, wherein he is to enjoy many conveniencies, from the labor, assistance, and society of others in the same community, as well as protection from its whole strength; he is to part also with as much of his natural liberty, in providing for himself, as the good, prosperity, and safety of the society shall require; which is not only necessary, but just, since the other members of the society do the like.

Sec. 131. But though men, when they enter into society, give up the equality, liberty, and executive power they had in the state of nature, into the hands of the society, to be so far disposed of by the legislative, as the good of the society shall require; yet it being only with an intention in everyone the better to preserve himself, his liberty and property; (for no rational creature can be supposed to change his condition with an intention to be worse) the power of the society, or legislative constituted by them, can never be supposed to extend farther, than the common good; but is obliged to secure everyone's property, by providing against those three defects above mentioned, that made the state of nature so unsafe and uneasy. And so whoever has the legislative or supreme power of any commonwealth, is bound to govern by established standing laws, promulgated and known to the people, and not by extemporary[2] decrees; by indifferent[3] and upright judges, who are to decide controversies by those laws; and to employ the force of the community at home, only in the execution of such laws, or abroad to prevent or redress foreign injuries, and secure the community from inroads and invasion. And all this to be directed to no other end, but the peace, safety, and public good of the people.

Chapter 10. Of the Forms of a Commonwealth

Sec. 132. The majority having, as has been shown, upon men's first uniting into society, the whole power of the community naturally in them, may employ all that power in making laws for the community from time to time, and executing those laws by officers of their own appointing; and then the form of the government is a perfect democracy: or else may put the power of making laws into the hands of a few select men, and their heirs or successors; and then it is an oligarchy: or else into the hands of one man, and then it is a monarchy: if to him and his heirs, it is an hereditary monarchy: if to him only for life, but upon his death the power only of nominating a successor to return to them; an elective monarchy. And so accordingly of these the community may make compounded and mixed forms of government, as they think good. And if the legislative power be at first given by the majority to one or more persons only for their lives, or any limited time, and then

---

1   *innocent*   Harmless in intention.

2   *extemporary*   Makeshift, without preparation.

3   *indifferent*   Favoring neither side.

the supreme power to revert to them again; when it is so reverted, the community may dispose of it again anew into what hands they please, and so constitute a new form of government: for the form of government depending upon the placing the supreme power, which is the legislative, it being impossible to conceive that an inferior power should prescribe to a superior, or any but the supreme make laws, according as the power of making laws is placed, such is the form of the commonwealth.

Sec. 133. By "commonwealth," I must be understood all along to mean, not a democracy, or any form of government, but any independent community, which the Latins signified by the word *civitas*, to which the word which best answers in our language, is "commonwealth," and most properly expresses such a society of men, which "community" or "city" in English does not; for there may be subordinate communities in a government; and city among us has a quite different notion from commonwealth: and therefore, to avoid ambiguity, I crave leave to use the word commonwealth in that sense, in which I find it used by King James the First;[1] and I take it to be its genuine signification; which if anybody dislike, I consent with him to change it for a better.

Chapter 11. Of the Extent of the Legislative Power

Sec. 134. The great end of men's entering into society, being the enjoyment of their properties in peace and safety, and the great instrument and means of that being the laws established in that society; the first and fundamental positive law of all commonwealths is the establishing of the legislative power; as the first and fundamental natural law, which is to govern even the legislative itself, is the preservation of the society, and (as far as will consist with the public good) of every person in it. This legislative is not only the supreme power of the commonwealth, but sacred and unalterable in the hands where the community have once placed it; nor can any edict of anybody else, in whatever form conceived, or by whatever power backed, have the force and obligation of a law, which has not its sanction from that legislative[2] which the public has chosen and appointed: for without this the

law could not have that, which is absolutely necessary to its being a law,[3] the consent of the society, over whom nobody can have a power to make laws, but by their own consent, and by authority received from them; and therefore all the obedience, which by the most solemn ties anyone can be obliged to pay, ultimately terminates in this supreme power, and is directed by those laws which it enacts: nor can any oaths to any foreign power whatsoever, or any domestic subordinate power, discharge any member of the society from his obedience to the legislative, acting pursuant to their trust; nor oblige him to any obedience contrary to the laws so enacted, or farther than they do allow; it being ridiculous to imagine one can be tied ultimately to obey any power in the society, which is not the supreme.

Sec. 135. Though the legislative, whether placed in one or more, whether it be always in being, or only by intervals, though it be the supreme power in every commonwealth; yet,

First, It is not, nor can possibly be absolutely arbitrary over the lives and fortunes of the people: for it being but the joint power of every member of the society given up to that person, or assembly, which is legislator; it can be no more than those persons had in a state of nature before they entered into society, and gave up to the community: for nobody can transfer to another more power than he has in himself; and nobody has an absolute arbitrary power over himself, or over any other, to destroy his own life, or take away the life or property of another. A man, as has been proved, cannot subject himself to the arbitrary power of another; and having in the state of nature no arbitrary power over the life, liberty, or possession of another, but only so

---

1   *King James the First* James I (1566–1625) ruled England from 1603 to 1625. His writings strongly supported the theory of the divine right of kings.

2   *legislative* Legislator.

3   *for without this the law … necessary to its being a law* [Locke's note] "The lawful power of making laws to command whole politic societies of men, belonging so properly unto the same entire societies, that for any prince or potentate of whatever kind upon earth, to exercise the same of himself, and not by express commission immediately and personally received from God, or else by authority derived at the first from their consent, upon whose persons they impose laws, it is no better than mere tyranny. Laws they are not therefore which public approbation has not made so" (Hooker, *Ecclesiastical Polity Lib.* I. sect. 10). "Of this point therefore we are to note, that men naturally have no full and perfect power to command whole politic multitudes of men, therefore utterly without our consent, we could in such sort be at no man's commandment living. And to be commanded we do consent, when that society, whereof we be a part, hath at any time before consented, without revoking the same after by the like universal agreement. Laws therefore human, of what kind so ever, are available by consent" (*Ibid.*).

much as the law of nature gave him for the preservation of himself, and the rest of mankind; this is all he does, or can give up to the commonwealth, and by it to the legislative power, so that the legislative can have no more than this. Their power, in the utmost bounds of it, is limited to the public good of the society.[1] It is a power, that has no other end but preservation, and therefore can never have a right to destroy, enslave, or designedly to impoverish the subjects. The obligations of the law of nature cease not in society, but only in many cases are drawn closer, and have by human laws known penalties annexed to them, to enforce their observation. Thus the law of nature stands as an eternal rule to all men, legislators as well as others. The rules that they make for other men's actions, must, as well as their own and other men's actions, be conformable to the law of nature, i.e., to the will of God, of which that is a declaration, and the fundamental law of nature being the preservation of mankind, no human sanction can be good, or valid against it.

Sec. 136. Secondly, The legislative, or supreme authority, cannot assume to its self a power to rule by extemporary arbitrary decrees, but is bound to dispense justice, and decide the rights of the subject by promulgated standing laws,[2] and known authorized judges: for the law of nature

being unwritten, and so no where to be found but in the minds of men, they who through passion or interest shall miscite,[3] or misapply it, cannot so easily be convinced of their mistake where there is no established judge: and so it serves not, as it ought, to determine the rights, and fence the properties of those that live under it, especially where everyone is judge, interpreter, and executioner of it too, and that in his own case: and he that has right on his side, having ordinarily but his own single strength, has not force enough to defend himself from injuries, or to punish delinquents. To avoid these inconveniencies, which disorder men's properties in the state of nature, men unite into societies, that they may have the united strength of the whole society to secure and defend their properties, and may have standing rules to bound it, by which everyone may know what is his. To this end it is that men give up all their natural power to the society which they enter into, and the community put the legislative power into such hands as they think fit, with this trust, that they shall be governed by declared laws, or else their peace, quiet, and property will still be at the same uncertainty, as it was in the state of nature.

Sec. 137. Absolute arbitrary power, or governing without settled standing laws, can neither of them consist[4] with the ends of society and government, which men would not quit the freedom of the state of nature for, and tie themselves up under, were it not to preserve their lives, liberties and fortunes, and by stated rules of right and property to secure their peace and quiet. It cannot be supposed that they should intend, had they a power so to do, to give to anyone, or more, an absolute arbitrary power over their persons and estates, and put a force into the magistrate's hand to execute his unlimited will arbitrarily upon them. This were to put themselves into a worse condition than the state of nature, wherein they had a liberty to defend their right against the injuries of others, and were upon equal terms of force to maintain it, whether invaded by a single man, or many in combination. Whereas by supposing they have given up themselves to the absolute arbitrary power and will of a legislator, they have disarmed themselves, and armed him, to make a prey of them when he pleases; he being in a much worse condition, who is exposed to the arbitrary power of one man, who has the command of 100,000, than he that is exposed to the arbitrary power of 100,000 single men; nobody being secure, that his will, who has such a com-

---

1   *Their power ... public good of the society*   [Locke's note] "Two foundations there are which bear up public societies; the one a natural inclination, whereby all men desire sociable life and fellowship; the other an order, expressly or secretly agreed upon, touching the manner of their union in living together: the latter is that which we call the law of a commonweal, the very soul of a politic body, the parts whereof are by law animated, held together, and set on work in such actions as the common good requires. Laws politic, ordained for external order and regiment among men, are never framed as they should be, unless presuming the will of man to be inwardly obstinate, rebellious, and averse from all obedience to the sacred laws of his nature; in a word, unless presuming man to be, in regard of his depraved mind, little better than a wild beast, they do accordingly provide, notwithstanding, so to frame his outward actions, that they be no hindrance unto the common good, for which societies are instituted. Unless they do this, they are not perfect" (Hooker, *Ecclesiastical Polity* Lib. 1. sect. 10).

2   *The legislative ... promulgated standing laws*   [Locke's note] "Human laws are measures in respect of men whose actions they must direct, howbeit such measures they are as have also their higher rules to be measured by, which rules are two, the law of God, and the law of nature; so that laws human must be made according to the general laws of nature, and without contradiction to any positive law of scripture, otherwise they are ill made" (Hooker, *Ecclesiastical Polity* Lib. 3. sect. 9). "To constrain men to any thing inconvenient does seem unreasonable" (Ibid. l. 1. sect. 10).

3   *miscite*   Cite erroneously.
4   *can neither of them consist*   Neither of them are consistent.

mand, is better than that of other men, though his force be 100,000 times stronger. And therefore, whatever form the commonwealth is under, the ruling power ought to govern by declared and received laws, and not by extemporary dictates and undetermined[1] resolutions: for then mankind will be in a far worse condition than in the state of nature, if they shall have armed one, or a few men with the joint power of a multitude, to force them to obey at pleasure the exorbitant and unlimited decrees of their sudden thoughts, or unrestrained, and till that moment unknown wills, without having any measures set down which may guide and justify their actions: for all the power the government has, being only for the good of the society, as it ought not to be arbitrary and at pleasure, so it ought to be exercised by established and promulgated laws; that both the people may know their duty, and be safe and secure within the limits of the law; and the rulers too kept within their bounds, and not be tempted, by the power they have in their hands, to employ it to such purposes, and by such measures, as they would not have known, and own not willingly.

Sec. 138. Thirdly, The supreme power cannot take from any man any part of his property without his own consent: for the preservation of property being the end of government, and that for which men enter into society, it necessarily supposes and requires, that the people should have property, without which they must be supposed to lose that, by entering into society, which was the end for which they entered into it; too gross an absurdity for any man to own.[2] Men therefore in society having property, they have such a right to the goods, which by the law of the community are theirs, that nobody has a right to take their substance or any part of it from them, without their own consent: without this they have no property at all; for I have truly no property in that, which another can by right take from me, when he pleases, against my consent. Hence it is a mistake to think, that the supreme or legislative power of any commonwealth, can do what it will, and dispose of the estates of the subject arbitrarily, or take any part of them at pleasure. This is not much to be feared in governments where the legislative consists, wholly or in part, in assemblies which are variable, whose members, upon the dissolution of the assembly, are subjects under the common laws of their country, equally with the rest. But in governments, where the legislative is in one lasting assembly always in being,

or in one man, as in absolute monarchies, there is danger still, that they will think themselves to have a distinct interest from the rest of the community; and so will be apt to increase their own riches and power, by taking what they think fit from the people: for a man's property is not at all secure, though there be good and equitable laws to set the bounds of it between him and his fellow subjects, if he who commands those subjects have power to take from any private man, what part he pleases of his property, and use and dispose of it as he thinks good.

Sec. 139. But government, into whatsoever hands it is put, being, as I have before shown, entrusted with this condition, and for this end, that men might have and secure their properties; the prince, or senate, however it may have power to make laws, for the regulating of property between the subjects one among another, yet can never have a power to take to themselves the whole, or any part of the subjects property, without their own consent: for this would be in effect to leave them no property at all. And to let us see, that even absolute power, where it is necessary, is not arbitrary by being absolute, but is still limited by that reason, and confined to those ends, which required it in some cases to be absolute, we need look no farther than the common practice of martial[3] discipline: for the preservation of the army, and in it of the whole commonwealth, requires an absolute obedience to the command of every superior officer, and it is justly death to disobey or dispute the most dangerous or unreasonable of them; but yet we see, that neither the sergeant, that could command a soldier to march up to the mouth of a cannon, or stand in a breach,[4] where he is almost sure to perish, can command that soldier to give him one penny of his money; nor the general, that can condemn him to death for deserting his post, or for not obeying the most desperate orders, can yet, with all his absolute power of life and death, dispose of one farthing[5] of that soldier's estate, or seize one jot[6] of his goods; whom yet he can command any thing, and hang for the least disobedience; because such a blind obedience is necessary to that end, for which the commander has his power, viz. the preservation of the rest; but the disposing of his goods has nothing to do with it.

---

1   *undetermined*   Not settled or fixed.
2   *own*   Acknowledge.

3   *martial*   Concerning soldiers.
4   *breach*   Gap in a fortification.
5   *farthing*   Smallest-valued British coin, worth a quarter of a penny—almost nothing.
6   *jot*   Tiny bit.

Sec. 140. It is true, governments cannot be supported without great charge,[1] and it is fit everyone who enjoys his share of the protection, should pay out of his estate his proportion for the maintenance of it. But still it must be with his own consent, i.e., the consent of the majority, giving it either by themselves, or their representatives chosen by them: for if anyone shall claim a power to lay and levy taxes on the people, by his own authority, and without such consent of the people, he thereby invades the fundamental law of property, and subverts the end of government: for what property have I in that, which another may by right take, when he pleases, to himself?

Sec. 141. Fourthly, The legislative cannot transfer the power of making laws to any other hands: for it being but a delegated power from the people, they who have it cannot pass it over to others. The people alone can appoint the form of the commonwealth, which is by constituting the legislative, and appointing in whose hands that shall be. And when the people have said, We will submit to rules, and be governed by laws made by such men, and in such forms, nobody else can say other men shall make laws for them; nor can the people be bound by any laws, but such as are enacted by those whom they have chosen, and authorized to make laws for them. The power of the legislative, being derived from the people by a positive voluntary grant and institution, can be no other than what that positive grant conveyed, which being only to make laws, and not to make legislators, the legislative can have no power to transfer their authority of making laws, and place it in other hands.

Sec. 142. These are the bounds which the trust, that is put in them by the society, and the law of God and nature, have set to the legislative power of every commonwealth, in all forms of government.

First, They are to govern by promulgated established laws, not to be varied in particular cases, but to have one rule for rich and poor, for the favorite at court, and the country man at plow.

Secondly, These laws also ought to be designed for no other end ultimately, but the good of the people.

Thirdly, They must not raise taxes on the property of the people, without the consent of the people, given by themselves, or their deputies. And this properly concerns only such governments where the legislative is always in being, or at least where the people have not reserved any part of the legislative to deputies, to be from time to time chosen by themselves.

Fourthly, The legislative neither must nor can transfer the power of making laws to anybody else, or place it anywhere, but where the people have placed it.

Chapter 12. Of the Legislative, Executive, and Federative Power of the Commonwealth

Sec. 143. The legislative power is that, which has a right to direct how the force of the commonwealth shall be employed for preserving the community and the members of it. But because those laws which are constantly to be executed, and whose force is always to continue, may be made in a little time; therefore there is no need, that the legislative should be always in being, not having always business to do. And because it may be too great a temptation to human frailty, apt to grasp at power, for the same persons, who have the power of making laws, to have also in their hands the power to execute them, whereby they may exempt themselves from obedience to the laws they make, and suit the law, both in its making, and execution, to their own private advantage, and thereby come to have a distinct interest from the rest of the community, contrary to the end of society and government: therefore in well ordered commonwealths, where the good of the whole is so considered, as it ought, the legislative power is put into the hands of divers[2] persons, who duly assembled, have by themselves, or jointly with others, a power to make laws, which when they have done, being separated again, they are themselves subject to the laws they have made; which is a new and near tie upon them, to take care, that they make them for the public good.

Sec. 144. But because the laws, that are at once, and in a short time made, have a constant and lasting force, and need a perpetual execution, or an attendance thereunto; therefore it is necessary there should be a power always in being, which should see to the execution of the laws that are made, and remain in force. And thus the legislative and executive power come often to be separated.

Sec. 145. There is another power in every commonwealth, which one may call natural, because it is that which answers to the power every man naturally had before he entered into society: for though in a commonwealth the members of it are distinct persons still in reference to one another, and as such as governed by the laws of the society;

---

1 *charge* Burden.

2 *divers* Several.

yet in reference to the rest of mankind, they make one body, which is, as every member of it before was, still in the state of nature with the rest of mankind. Hence it is, that the controversies that happen between any man of the society with those that are out of it, are managed by the public; and an injury done to a member of their body, engages the whole in the reparation of it. So that under this consideration, the whole community is one body in the state of nature, in respect of all other states or persons out of its community.

Sec. 146. This therefore contains the power of war and peace, leagues and alliances, and all the transactions, with all persons and communities without the commonwealth, and may be called federative, if anyone pleases. So[1] the thing be understood, I am indifferent as to the name.

Sec. 147. These two powers, executive and federative, though they be really distinct in themselves, yet one comprehending the execution of the municipal laws of the society within itself, upon all that are parts of it; the other the management of the security and interest of the public without,[2] with all those that it may receive benefit or damage from, yet they are always almost united. And though this federative power in the well or ill management of it be of great moment[3] to the commonwealth, yet it is much less capable to be directed by antecedent, standing, positive laws, than the executive; and so must necessarily be left to the prudence and wisdom of those, whose hands it is in, to be managed for the public good: for the laws that concern subjects one among another, being to direct their actions, may well enough precede them. But what is to be done in reference to foreigners, depending much upon their actions, and the variation of designs and interests, must be left in great part to the prudence of those, who have this power committed to them, to be managed by the best of their skill, for the advantage of the commonwealth.

Sec. 148. Though, as I said, the executive and federative power of every community be really distinct in themselves, yet they are hardly to be separated, and placed at the same time, in the hands of distinct persons: for both of them requiring the force of the society for their exercise, it is almost impracticable[4] to place the force of the commonwealth in distinct, and not subordinate hands; or that the executive and federative power should be placed in persons, that

might act separately, whereby the force of the public would be under different commands: which would be apt some time or other to cause disorder and ruin.

Chapter 13. Of the Subordination of the Powers of the Commonwealth

Sec. 149. Though in a constituted commonwealth, standing upon its own basis, and acting according to its own nature, that is, acting for the preservation of the community, there can be but one supreme power, which is the legislative, to which all the rest are and must be subordinate, yet the legislative being only a fiduciary power[5] to act for certain ends, there remains still in the people a supreme power to remove or alter the legislative, when they find the legislative act contrary to the trust reposed in them: for all power given with trust for the attaining an end, being limited by that end, whenever that end is manifestly neglected, or opposed, the trust must necessarily be forfeited, and the power devolve[6] into the hands of those that gave it, who may place it anew where they shall think best for their safety and security. And thus the community perpetually retains a supreme power of saving themselves from the attempts and designs of anybody, even of their legislators, whenever they shall be so foolish, or so wicked, as to lay and carry on designs against the liberties and properties of the subject: for no man or society of men, having a power to deliver up their preservation, or consequently the means of it, to the absolute will and arbitrary dominion of another; whenever anyone shall go about to bring them into such a slavish condition, they will always have a right to preserve, what they have not a power to part with; and to rid themselves of those, who invade this fundamental, sacred, and unalterable law of self-preservation, for which they entered into society. And thus the community may be said in this respect to be always the supreme power, but not as considered under any form of government, because this power of the people can never take place till the government be dissolved.

Sec. 150. In all cases, while the government subsists, the legislative is the supreme power: for what can give laws to another, must needs be superior to him; and since the legislative is no[7] otherwise legislative of the society, but by

1   *So* As long as.
2   *without* Outside.
3   *of great moment* Very important.
4   *impracticable* Impossible.
5   *fiduciary power* The power of a trustee—that is, entrusted to act on behalf of others.
6   *devolve* Transfer.
7   *no* Not.

the right it has to make laws for all the parts, and for every member of the society, prescribing rules to their actions, and giving power of execution, where they are transgressed, the legislative must needs be the supreme, and all other powers, in any members or parts of the society, derived from and subordinate to it.

Sec. 151. In some commonwealths, where the legislative is not always in being, and the executive is vested in a single person, who has also a share in the legislative; there that single person in a very tolerable sense may also be called supreme: not that he has in himself all the supreme power, which is that of lawmaking; but because he has in him the supreme execution, from whom all inferior magistrates derive all their several subordinate powers, or at least the greatest part of them: having also no legislative superior to him, there being no law to be made without his consent, which cannot be expected should ever subject him to the other part of the legislative, he is properly enough in this sense supreme. But yet it is to be observed, that though oaths of allegiance and fealty are taken to him, it is not to him as supreme legislator, but as supreme executor of the law, made by a joint power of him with others; allegiance being nothing but an obedience according to law, which when he violates, he has no right to obedience, nor can claim it otherwise than as the public person vested with the power of the law, and so is to be considered as the image, phantom, or representative of the commonwealth, acted by the will of the society, declared in its laws; and thus he has no will, no power, but that of the law. But when he quits this representation, this public will, and acts by his own private will, he degrades himself, and is but a single private person without power, and without will, that has any right to obedience; the members owing no obedience but to the public will of the society.

Sec. 152. The executive power, placed anywhere but in a person that has also a share in the legislative, is visibly subordinate and accountable to it, and may be at pleasure changed and displaced; so that it is not the supreme executive power, that is exempt from subordination, but the supreme executive power vested in one, who having a share in the legislative, has no distinct superior legislative to be subordinate and accountable to, farther than he himself shall join and consent; so that he is no more subordinate than he himself shall think fit, which one may certainly conclude will be but very little. Of other ministerial and subordinate powers in a commonwealth, we need not speak, they being so multiplied with infinite variety, in the different customs and constitutions of distinct commonwealths, that it is impossible to give a particular account of them all. Only thus much, which is necessary to our present purpose, we may take notice of concerning them, that they have no manner of authority, any of them, beyond what is by positive grant and commission delegated to them, and are all of them accountable to some other power in the commonwealth.

Sec. 153. It is not necessary, no, nor so much as convenient, that the legislative should be always in being; but absolutely necessary that the executive power should, because there is not always need of new laws to be made, but always need of execution of the laws that are made. When the legislative has put the execution of the laws, they make, into other hands, they have a power still to resume[1] it out of those hands, when they find cause, and to punish for any maladministration[2] against the laws. The same holds also in regard of the federative power, that and the executive being both ministerial and subordinate to the legislative, which, as has been shown, in a constituted commonwealth is the supreme. The legislative also in this case being supposed to consist of several persons, (for if it be a single person, it cannot but be always in being, and so will, as supreme, naturally have the supreme executive power, together with the legislative) may assemble, and exercise their legislature, at the times that either their original constitution, or their own adjournment, appoints, or when they please; if neither of these has appointed any time, or there be no other way prescribed to convoke[3] them: for the supreme power being placed in them by the people, it is always in them, and they may exercise it when they please, unless by their original constitution they are limited to certain seasons, or by an act of their supreme power they have adjourned to a certain time; and when that time comes, they have a right to assemble and act again.

Sec. 154. If the legislative, or any part of it, be made up of representatives chosen for that time by the people, which afterwards return into the ordinary state of subjects, and have no share in the legislature but upon a new choice, this power of choosing must also be exercised by the people, either at certain appointed seasons, or else when they are summoned to it; and in this latter case the power of convoking the legislative is ordinarily placed in the executive, and has one of these two limitations in respect of time:

---

1   *resume* Retake.
2   *maladministration* Bad management.
3   *convoke* Call together for a meeting.

that either the original constitution requires their assembling and acting at certain intervals, and then the executive power does nothing but ministerially[1] issue directions for their electing and assembling, according to due forms; or else it is left to his prudence to call them by new elections, when the occasions or exigencies[2] of the public require the amendment of old, or making of new laws, or the redress or prevention of any inconveniencies, that lie on, or threaten the people.

Sec. 155. It may be demanded here, What if the executive power, being possessed of the force of the commonwealth, shall make use of that force to hinder the meeting and acting of the legislative, when the original constitution, or the public exigencies require it? I say, using force upon the people without authority, and contrary to the trust put in him that does so, is a state of war with the people, who have a right to reinstate their legislative in the exercise of their power: for having erected a legislative, with an intent they should exercise the power of making laws, either at certain set times, or when there is need of it, when they are hindered by any force from what is so necessary to the society, and wherein the safety and preservation of the people consists, the people have a right to remove it by force. In all states and conditions, the true remedy of force without authority, is to oppose force to it. The use of force without authority, always puts him that uses it into a state of war, as the aggressor, and renders him liable to be treated accordingly.

Sec. 156. The power of assembling and dismissing the legislative, placed in the executive, gives not the executive a superiority over it, but is a fiduciary trust placed in him, for the safety of the people, in a case where the uncertainty and variableness of human affairs could not bear a steady fixed rule: for it not being possible, that the first framers of the government should, by any foresight, be so much masters of future events, as to be able to prefix so just periods of return and duration to the assemblies of the legislative, in all times to come, that might exactly answer all the exigencies of the commonwealth; the best remedy could be found for this defect, was to trust this to the prudence of one who was always to be present, and whose business it was to watch over the public good. Constant frequent meetings of the legislative, and long continuations of their assemblies, without necessary occasion, could not but be burdensome to the

people, and must necessarily in time produce more dangerous inconveniencies, and yet the quick turn of affairs might be sometimes such as to need their present help: any delay of their convening might endanger the public; and sometimes too their business might be so great, that the limited time of their sitting might be too short for their work, and rob the public of that benefit which could be had only from their mature deliberation. What then could be done in this case to prevent the community from being exposed some time or other to eminent[3] hazard, on one side or the other, by fixed intervals and periods, set to the meeting and acting of the legislative, but to entrust it to the prudence of some, who being present, and acquainted with the state of public affairs, might make use of this prerogative for the public good? and where else could this be so well placed as in his hands, who was entrusted with the execution of the laws for the same end? Thus supposing the regulation of times for the assembling and sitting of the legislative, not settled by the original constitution, it naturally fell into the hands of the executive, not as an arbitrary power depending on his good pleasure, but with this trust always to have it exercised only for the public weal,[4] as the occurrences of times and change of affairs might require. Whether settled periods of their convening, or a liberty left to the prince for convoking the legislative, or perhaps a mixture of both, has the least inconvenience attending it, it is not my business here to inquire, but only to show, that though the executive power may have the prerogative of convoking and dissolving such conventions of the legislative, yet it is not thereby superior to it.

Sec. 157. Things of this world are in so constant a flux,[5] that nothing remains long in the same state. Thus people, riches, trade, power, change their stations, flourishing mighty cities come to ruin, and prove in times neglected desolate corners, while other unfrequented places grow into populous countries, filled with wealth and inhabitants. But things not always changing equally, and private interest often keeping up customs and privileges, when the reasons of them are ceased, it often comes to pass, that in governments, where part of the legislative consists of representatives chosen by the people, that in tract of time this representation becomes very unequal and disproportionate to the reasons it was at first established upon. To what gross

---

1   *ministerially*   In a capacity as minister—administratively.
2   *exigencies*   Urgent needs.
3   *eminent*   Noticeable.
4   *weal*   Well-being.
5   *flux*   State of change.

absurdities the following of custom, when reason has left it, may lead, we may be satisfied, when we see the bare name of a town, of which there remains not so much as the ruins, where scarce so much housing as a sheepcote[1] or more inhabitants than a shepherd is to be found, sends as many representatives to the grand assembly of law-makers, as a whole county numerous in people, and powerful in riches. This strangers stand amazed at, and everyone must confess needs a remedy; though most think it hard to find one, because the constitution of the legislative being the original and supreme act of the society, antecedent to all positive laws in it, and depending wholly on the people, no inferior power can alter it. And therefore the people, when the legislative is once constituted, having, in such a government as we have been speaking of, no power to act as long as the government stands; this inconvenience is thought incapable of a remedy.

Sec. 158. Salus populi suprema lex,[2] is certainly so just and fundamental a rule, that he, who sincerely follows it, cannot dangerously err. If therefore the executive, who has the power of convoking the legislative, observing rather the true proportion, than fashion of representation,[3] regulates, not by old custom, but true reason, the number of members, in all places that have a right to be distinctly represented, which no part of the people however incorporated[4] can pretend[5] to, but in proportion to the assistance which it affords to the public, it cannot be judged to have set up a new legislative, but to have restored the old and true one, and to have rectified the disorders which succession of time had insensibly, as well as inevitably introduced: For it being the interest as well as intention of the people, to have a fair and equal representative; whoever brings it nearest to that, is an undoubted friend to, and establisher of the government, and cannot miss the consent and approbation of the community; prerogative being nothing but a power, in the hands of the prince, to provide for the public good, in such cases, which depending upon unforeseen and uncertain occurrences, certain and unalterable laws could not safely direct; whatsoever shall be done manifestly for the good of the people, and the establishing the government upon its true foundations, is, and always will be, just prerogative, The

power of erecting new corporations,[6] and therewith new representatives, carries with it a supposition, that in time the measures of representation might vary, and those places have a just right to be represented which before had none; and by the same reason, those cease to have a right, and be too inconsiderable for such a privilege, which before had it. It is not a change from the present state, which perhaps corruption or decay has introduced, that makes an inroad upon the government, but the tendency of it to injure or oppress the people, and to set up one part or party, with a distinction from, and an unequal subjection of the rest. Whatsoever cannot but be acknowledged to be of advantage to the society, and people in general, upon just and lasting measures, will always, when done, justify itself; and whenever the people shall choose their representatives upon just and undeniably equal measures, suitable to the original frame of the government, it cannot be doubted to be the will and act of the society, whoever permitted or caused them so to do.

Chapter 14. Of Prerogative

Sec. 159. Where the legislative and executive power are in distinct hands, (as they are in all moderated[7] monarchies, and well-framed governments) there the good of the society requires, that several things should be left to the discretion of him that has the executive power: for the legislators not being able to foresee, and provide by laws, for all that may be useful to the community, the executor of the laws having the power in his hands, has by the common law of nature a right to make use of it for the good of the society, in many cases, where the municipal law has given no direction, till the legislative can conveniently be assembled to provide for it. Many things there are, which the law can by no means provide for; and those must necessarily be left to the discretion of him that has the executive power in his hands, to be ordered by him as the public good and advantage shall require: nay, it is fit that the laws themselves should in some cases give way to the executive power, or rather to this fundamental law of nature and government, viz. That as much as may be,[8] all the members of the society are to be preserved: for since many accidents may happen, wherein a strict and rigid observation of the laws may do harm; (as not

---

1   *sheepcote*   Small building for sheltering sheep.
2   *Salus populi suprema lex*   Latin: the welfare of the people is the supreme law.
3   *fashion of representation*   Appearances.
4   *incorporated*   United into one body.
5   *pretend*   Claim.

6   *corporations*   Bodies of people united to act as collective entities.
7   *moderated*   Not excessive, reasonable.
8   *as much as may be*   To the extent possible.

to pull down an innocent man's house to stop the fire, when the next to it is burning) and a man may come sometimes within the reach of the law, which makes no distinction of persons, by an action that may deserve reward and pardon; it is fit the ruler should have a power, in many cases, to mitigate the severity of the law, and pardon some offenders: for the end of government being the preservation of all, as much as may be, even the guilty are to be spared, where it can prove no prejudice to the innocent.

Sec. 160. This power to act according to discretion, for the public good, without the prescription of the law, and sometimes even against it, is that which is called prerogative: for since in some governments the lawmaking power is not always in being, and is usually too numerous, and so too slow, for the dispatch requisite to execution; and because also it is impossible to foresee, and so by laws to provide for, all accidents and necessities that may concern the public, or to make such laws as will do no harm, if they are executed with an inflexible rigor, on all occasions, and upon all persons that may come in their way; therefore there is a latitude left to the executive power, to do many things of choice which the laws do not prescribe.

Sec. 161. This power, while employed for the benefit of the community, and suitably to the trust and ends of the government, is undoubted prerogative, and never is questioned: for the people are very seldom or never scrupulous or nice[1] in the point; they are far from examining prerogative, while it is in any tolerable degree employed for the use it was meant, that is, for the good of the people, and not manifestly against it: but if there comes to be a question between the executive power and the people, about a thing claimed as a prerogative; the tendency of the exercise of such prerogative to the good or hurt of the people, will easily decide that question.

Sec. 162. It is easy to conceive, that in the infancy of governments, when commonwealths differed little from families in number of people, they differed from them too but little in number of laws: and the governors, being as the fathers of them, watching over them for their good, the government was almost all prerogative. A few established laws served the turn, and the discretion and care of the ruler supplied the rest. But when mistake or flattery prevailed with weak princes to make use of this power for private ends of their own, and not for the public good, the people

were fain[2] by express laws to get prerogative determined in those points wherein they found disadvantage from it: and thus declared limitations of prerogative were by the people found necessary in cases which they and their ancestors had left, in the utmost latitude, to the wisdom of those princes who made no other but a right use of it, that is, for the good of their people.

Sec. 163. And therefore they have a very wrong notion of government, who say, that the people have encroached upon the prerogative, when they have got any part of it to be defined by positive laws: for in so doing they have not pulled from the prince any thing that of right belonged to him, but only declared, that that power which they indefinitely left in his or his ancestors' hands, to be exercised for their good, was not a thing which they intended him when he used it otherwise: for the end of government being the good of the community, whatsoever alterations are made in it, tending to that end, cannot be an encroachment upon anybody, since nobody in government can have a right tending to any other end: and those only are encroachments which prejudice or hinder the public good. Those who say otherwise, speak as if the prince had a distinct and separate interest from the good of the community, and was not made for it; the root and source from which spring almost all those evils and disorders which happen in kingly governments. And indeed, if that be so, the people under his government are not a society of rational creatures, entered into a community for their mutual good; they are not such as have set rulers over themselves, to guard, and promote that good; but are to be looked on as an herd of inferior creatures under the dominion of a master, who keeps them and works them for his own pleasure or profit. If men were so void of reason, and brutish, as to enter into society upon such terms, prerogative might indeed be, what some men would have it, an arbitrary power to do things hurtful to the people.

Sec. 164. But since a rational creature cannot be supposed, when free, to put himself into subjection to another, for his own harm; (though, where he finds a good and wise ruler, he may not perhaps think it either necessary or useful to set precise bounds to his power in all things) prerogative can be nothing but the people's permitting their rulers to do several things, of their own free choice, where the law was silent, and sometimes too against the direct letter of the law, for the public good; and their acquiescing in it when so

1   *nice*   Making subtle discriminations.

2   *fain*   Glad under the circumstances.

done: for as a good prince, who is mindful of the trust put into his hands, and careful of the good of his people, cannot have too much prerogative, that is, power to do good; so a weak and ill prince, who would claim that power which his predecessors exercised without the direction of the law, as a prerogative belonging to him by right of his office, which he may exercise at his pleasure, to make or promote an interest distinct from that of the public, gives the people an occasion to claim their right, and limit that power, which, while it was exercised for their good, they were content should be tacitly allowed.

Sec. 165. And therefore he that will look into the history of England, will find, that prerogative was always largest in the hands of our wisest and best princes; because the people, observing the whole tendency of their actions to be the public good, contested not what was done without law to that end: or, if any human frailty or mistake (for princes are but men, made as others) appeared in some small declinations[1] from that end; yet it was visible, the main of their conduct tended to nothing but the care of the public. The people therefore, finding reason to be satisfied with these princes, whenever they acted without, or contrary to the letter of the law, acquiesced in what they did, and, without the least complaint, let them enlarge their prerogative as they pleased, judging rightly, that they did nothing herein to the prejudice of[2] their laws, since they acted conformable to the foundation and end of all laws, the public good.

Sec. 166. Such godlike princes indeed had some title to arbitrary power by that argument, that would prove absolute monarchy the best government, as that which God himself governs the universe by; because such kings partake of his wisdom and goodness. Upon this is founded that saying, That the reigns of good princes have been always most dangerous to the liberties of their people: for when their successors, managing the government with different thoughts, would draw the actions of those good rulers into precedent, and make them the standard of their prerogative, as if what had been done only for the good of the people was a right in them to do, for the harm of the people, if they so pleased; it has often occasioned contest,[3] and sometimes public disorders, before the people could recover their original right, and get that to be declared not to be prerogative, which truly was never so; since it is impossible that anybody in

the society should ever have a right to do the people harm; though it be very possible, and reasonable, that the people should not go about to set any bounds to the prerogative of those kings, or rulers, who themselves transgressed not the bounds of the public good: for prerogative is nothing but the power of doing public good without a rule.

Sec. 167. The power of calling parliaments in England, as to precise time, place, and duration, is certainly a prerogative of the king, but still with this trust, that it shall be made use of for the good of the nation, as the exigencies of the times, and variety of occasions, shall require: for it being impossible to foresee which should always be the fittest place for them to assemble in, and what the best season; the choice of these was left with the executive power, as might be most subservient to the public good, and best suit the ends of parliaments.

Sec. 168. The old question will be asked in this matter of prerogative, But who shall be judge when this power is made a right use of? I answer: between an executive power in being,[4] with such a prerogative, and a legislative that depends upon his will for their convening, there can be no judge on earth; as there can be none between the legislative and the people, should either the executive, or the legislative, when they have got the power in their hands, design, or go about to enslave or destroy them. The people have no other remedy in this, as in all other cases where they have no judge on earth, but to appeal to heaven: for the rulers, in such attempts, exercising a power the people never put into their hands, (who can never be supposed to consent that anybody should rule over them for their harm) do that which they have not a right to do. And where the body of the people, or any single man, is deprived of their right, or is under the exercise of a power without right, and have no appeal on earth, then they have a liberty to appeal to heaven, whenever they judge the cause of sufficient moment.[5] And therefore, though the people cannot be judge, so as to have, by the constitution of that society, any superior power, to determine and give effective sentence in the case; yet they have, by a law antecedent and paramount to all positive laws of men, reserved that ultimate determination to themselves which belongs to all mankind, where there lies no appeal on earth, viz. to judge, whether they have just cause to make their appeal to heaven. And this judgment they cannot part with, it being out of a man's power so to submit himself to

---

1   *declinations*   Deviations.
2   *to the prejudice of*   Harmful to.
3   *contest*   Struggle for control.

4   *in being*   In existence.
5   *moment*   Importance.

another, as to give him a liberty to destroy him; God and nature never allowing a man so to abandon himself, as to neglect his own preservation: and since he cannot take away his own life, neither can he give another power to take it. Nor let anyone think, this lays a perpetual foundation for disorder; for this operates not, till the inconveniency is so great, that the majority feel it, and are weary of it, and find a necessity to have it amended. But this the executive power, or wise princes, never need come in the danger of: and it is the thing, of all others, they have most need to avoid, as of all others the most perilous.

Chapter 15. Of Paternal, Political, and Despotical Power, considered together

Sec. 169. Though I have had occasion to speak of these separately before, yet the great mistakes of late[1] about government, having, as I suppose, arisen from confounding these distinct powers one with another, it may not, perhaps, be amiss to consider them here together.

Sec. 170. First, then, Paternal or parental power is nothing but that which parents have over their children, to govern them for the children's good, till they come to the use of reason, or a state of knowledge, wherein they may be supposed capable to understand that rule, whether it be the law of nature, or the municipal law of their country, they are to govern themselves by: capable, I say, to know it, as well as several others, who live as freemen under that law. The affection and tenderness which God has planted in the breast of parents towards their children, makes it evident, that this is not intended to be a severe arbitrary government, but only for the help, instruction, and preservation of their offspring. But happen it as it will,[2] there is, as I have proved, no reason why it should be thought to extend to life and death, at any time, over their children, more than over anybody else; neither can there be any pretense[3] why this parental power should keep the child, when grown to a man, in subjection to the will of his parents, any farther than having received life and education from his parents, obliges him to respect, honor, gratitude, assistance and support, all his life, to both father and mother. And thus, it is true, the paternal is a natural government, but not at all extending

itself to the ends and jurisdictions of that which is political. The power of the father does not reach at all to the property of the child, which is only in his own disposing.

Sec. 171. Secondly, Political power is that power, which every man having in the state of nature, has given up into the hands of the society, and therein to the governors, whom the society has set over itself, with this express or tacit trust, that it shall be employed for their good, and the preservation of their property: now this power, which every man has in the state of nature, and which he parts with to the society in all such cases where the society can secure him, is to use such means, for the preserving of his own property, as he thinks good, and nature allows him; and to punish the breach of the law of nature in others, so as (according to the best of his reason) may most conduce[4] to the preservation of himself, and the rest of mankind. So that the end and measure of this power, when in every man's hands in the state of nature, being the preservation of all of his society, that is, all mankind in general, it can have no other end or measure, when in the hands of the magistrate, but to preserve the members of that society in their lives, liberties, and possessions; and so cannot be an absolute, arbitrary power over their lives and fortunes, which are as much as possible to be preserved; but a power to make laws, and annex such penalties to them, as may tend to the preservation of the whole, by cutting off those parts, and those only, which are so corrupt, that they threaten the sound and healthy, without which no severity is lawful. And this power has its original only from compact and agreement, and the mutual consent of those who make up the community.

Sec. 172. Thirdly, Despotical power is an absolute, arbitrary power one man has over another, to take away his life, whenever he pleases. This is a power, which neither nature gives, for it has made no such distinction betwixt one man and another; nor compact can convey: for man not having such an arbitrary power over his own life, cannot give another man such a power over it; but it is the effect only of forfeiture,[5] which the aggressor makes of his own life, when he puts himself into the state of war with another: for having quitted reason, which God has given to be the rule between man and man, and the common bond whereby human kind is united into one fellowship and society; and having renounced the way of peace which that teaches, and made use of the force of war, to compass his unjust ends

---

1 *of late* Recently.
2 *happen it as it will* That is, however individual families manage this.
3 *pretense* Unwarranted claim.

4 *conduce* Contribute.
5 *forfeiture* Giving up.

upon another, where he has no right; and so revolting from his own kind to that of beasts, by making force, which is theirs, to be his rule of right, he renders himself liable to be destroyed by the injured person, and the rest of mankind, that will join with him in the execution of justice, as any other wild beast, or noxious brute, with whom mankind can have neither society nor security.[1] And thus captives, taken in a just and lawful war, and such only, are subject to a despotical power, which, as it arises not from compact, so neither is it capable of any, but is the state of war continued: for what compact can be made with a man that is not master of his own life? what condition can he perform? and if he be once allowed to be master of his own life, the despotical, arbitrary power of his master ceases. He that is master of himself, and his own life, has a right too to the means of preserving it; so that as soon as compact enters, slavery ceases, and he so far quits his absolute power, and puts an end to the state of war, who enters into conditions with his captive.

Sec. 173. Nature gives the first of these, viz. paternal power to parents for the benefit of their children during their minority, to supply their want of ability, and understanding how to manage their property. (By property I must be understood here, as in other places, to mean that property which men have in their persons as well as goods.) Voluntary agreement gives the second, viz. political power to governors for the benefit of their subjects, to secure them in the possession and use of their properties. And forfeiture gives the third despotical power to lords for their own benefit, over those who are stripped of all property.

Sec. 174. He, that shall consider the distinct rise and extent, and the different ends of these several powers, will plainly see, that paternal power comes as far short of that of the magistrate, as despotical exceeds it; and that absolute dominion, however placed, is so far from being one kind of civil society, that it is as inconsistent with it, as slavery is with property. Paternal power is only where minority makes the child incapable to manage his property; political, where men have property in their own disposal; and despotical, over such as have no property at all.

Chapter 16. Of Conquest

Sec. 175. Though governments can originally have no other rise than that before mentioned, nor polities be founded on any thing but the consent of the people; yet such have been the disorders ambition has filled the world with, that in the noise of war, which makes so great a part of the history of mankind, this consent is little taken notice of: and therefore many have mistaken the force of arms for the consent of the people, and reckon conquest as one of the originals of government. But conquest is as far from setting up any government, as demolishing an house is from building a new one in the place. Indeed, it often makes way for a new frame of a commonwealth, by destroying the former; but, without the consent of the people, can never erect a new one.

Sec. 176. That the aggressor, who puts himself into the state of war with another, and unjustly invades another man's right, can, by such an unjust war, never come to have a right over the conquered, will be easily agreed by all men, who will not think, that robbers and pirates have a right of empire over whomsoever they have force enough to master; or that men are bound by promises, which unlawful force extorts from them. Should a robber break into my house, and with a dagger at my throat make me seal deeds to convey my estate to him, would this give him any title? Just such a title, by his sword, has an unjust conqueror, who forces me into submission. The injury and the crime is equal, whether committed by the wearer of a crown, or some petty villain. The title of the offender, and the number of his followers, make no difference in the offence, unless it be to aggravate it. The only difference is, great robbers punish little ones, to keep them in their obedience; but the great ones are rewarded with laurels[2] and triumphs,[3] because they are too big for the weak hands of justice in this world, and have the power in their own possession, which should punish offenders. What is my remedy against a robber, that so broke into my house? Appeal to the law for justice. But perhaps justice is denied, or I am crippled and cannot stir, robbed and have not the means to do it. If God has taken away all means of seeking remedy, there is nothing left but patience.[4] But my son, when able, may seek the relief of the law, which I am denied: he or his son may renew his appeal, till he recover his right. But the conquered, or their

---

1   *and so revolting ... society nor security*   [note in originally published edition] Another copy corrected by Mr. Locke, has it thus, "Noxious brute that is destructive to their being."

2   *laurels*   Wreath of leaves, ancient symbol of victory.

3   *triumphs*   Ancient Roman victory parade.

4   *patience*   Calm endurance.

children, have no court, no arbitrator on earth to appeal to. Then they may appeal, as Jephtha did, to heaven, and repeat their appeal till they have recovered the native right of their ancestors, which was, to have such a legislative over them, as the majority should approve, and freely acquiesce in. If it be objected, This would cause endless trouble; I answer, no more than justice does, where she lies open to all that appeal to her. He that troubles his neighbor without a cause, is punished for it by the justice of the court he appeals to: and he that appeals to heaven must be sure he has right on his side; and a right too that is worth the trouble and cost of the appeal, as he will answer at a tribunal that cannot be deceived, and will be sure to retribute to everyone according to the mischiefs he has created to his fellow subjects; that is, any part of mankind: from whence it is plain, that he that conquers in an unjust war can thereby have no title to the subjection and obedience of the conquered.

Sec. 177. But supposing victory favors the right side, let us consider a conqueror in a lawful war, and see what power he gets, and over whom.

First, It is plain he gets no power by his conquest over those that conquered with him. They that fought on his side cannot suffer by the conquest, but must at least be as much freemen as they were before. And most commonly they serve upon terms,[1] and on condition to share with their leader, and enjoy a part of the spoil, and other advantages that attend the conquering sword; or at least have a part of the subdued country bestowed upon them. And the conquering people are not, I hope, to be slaves by conquest, and wear their laurels only to show they are sacrifices to their leaders triumph. They that found absolute monarchy upon the title of the sword, make their heroes, who are the founders of such monarchies, arrant Draw-can-sirs,[2] and forget they had any officers and soldiers that fought on their side in the battles they won, or assisted them in the subduing, or shared in possessing, the countries they mastered. We are told by some, that the English monarchy is founded in the Norman conquest, and that our princes have thereby a title to absolute dominion: which if it were true, (as by the history it appears otherwise) and that William had a right to make war on this island; yet his dominion by conquest could reach no farther than to the Saxons and Britons, that were then inhabitants of this country. The Normans that

came with him, and helped to conquer, and all descended from them, are freemen, and no subjects by conquest; let that give what dominion it will. And if I, or anybody else, shall claim freedom, as derived from them, it will be very hard to prove the contrary: and it is plain, the law, that has made no distinction between the one and the other, intends not there should be any difference in their freedom or privileges.

Sec. 178. But supposing, which seldom happens, that the conquerors and conquered never incorporate into one people, under the same laws and freedom; let us see next what power a lawful conqueror has over the subdued: and that I say is purely despotical. He has an absolute power over the lives of those who by an unjust war have forfeited them; but not over the lives or fortunes of those who engaged not in the war, nor over the possessions even of those who were actually engaged in it.

Sec. 179. Secondly, I say then the conqueror gets no power but only over those who have actually assisted, concurred, or consented to that unjust force that is used against him: for the people having given to their governors no power to do an unjust thing, such as is to make an unjust war, (for they never had such a power in themselves) they ought not to be charged as guilty of the violence and injustice that is committed in an unjust war, any farther than they actually abet it;[3] no more than they are to be thought guilty of any violence or oppression their governors should use upon the people themselves, or any part of their fellow subjects, they having empowered them no more to the one than to the other. Conquerors, it is true, seldom trouble themselves to make the distinction, but they willingly permit the confusion of war to sweep all together: but yet this alters not the right; for the conquerors power over the lives of the conquered, being only because they have used force to do, or maintain an injustice, he can have that power only over those who have concurred in that force; all the rest are innocent; and he has no more title over the people of that country, who have done him no injury, and so have made no forfeiture of their lives, than he has over any other, who, without any injuries or provocations, have lived upon fair terms with him.

Sec. 180. Thirdly, The power a conqueror gets over those he overcomes in a just war, is perfectly despotical: he has an absolute power over the lives of those, who, by putting themselves in a state of war, have forfeited them; but

---

1   *upon terms*   By agreement.
2   *Draw-can-sirs*   Drawcansir is a blustering braggart and bully in a 1672 play by George Villiers called *The Rehearsal*.

3   *abet it*   Help them do it.

he has not thereby a right and title to their possessions. This I doubt not, but at first sight will seem a strange doctrine, it being so quite contrary to the practice of the world; there being nothing more familiar in speaking of the dominion of countries, than to say such an one conquered it; as if conquest, without any more ado, conveyed a right of possession. But when we consider, that the practice of the strong and powerful, however universal it may be, is seldom the rule of right, however it be one part of the subjection of the conquered, not to argue against the conditions cut out to them by the conquering sword.

Sec. 181. Though in all war there be usually a complication of force and damage, and the aggressor seldom fails to harm the estate, when he uses force against the persons of those he makes war upon; yet it is the use of force only that puts a man into the state of war: for whether by force he begins the injury, or else having quietly, and by fraud, done the injury, he refuses to make reparation, and by force maintains it, (which is the same thing, as at first to have done it by force) it is the unjust use of force that makes the war: for he that breaks open my house, and violently turns me out of doors; or having peaceably got in, by force keeps me out, does in effect the same thing; supposing we are in such a state, that we have no common judge on earth, whom I may appeal to, and to whom we are both obliged to submit: for of such I am now speaking. It is the unjust use of force then, that puts a man into the state of war with another; and thereby he that is guilty of it makes a forfeiture of his life: for quitting reason, which is the rule given between man and man, and using force, the way of beasts, he becomes liable to be destroyed by him he uses force against, as any savage ravenous beast, that is dangerous to his being.

Sec. 182. But because the miscarriages[1] of the father are no faults of the children, and they may be rational and peaceable, notwithstanding the brutishness and injustice of the father; the father, by his miscarriages and violence, can forfeit but his own life, but involves not his children in his guilt or destruction. His goods, which nature, that wills the preservation of all mankind as much as is possible, has made to belong to the children to keep them from perishing, do still continue to belong to his children: for supposing them not to have joined in the war, either through infancy, absence, or choice, they have done nothing to forfeit them: nor has the conqueror any right to take them away, by the bare title of having subdued him that by force attempted his destruction; though perhaps he may have some right to them, to repair the damages he has sustained by the war, and the defense of his own right; which how far it reaches to the possessions of the conquered, we shall see by and by. So that he that by conquest has a right over a man's person to destroy him if he pleases, has not thereby a right over his estate to possess and enjoy it: for it is the brutal force the aggressor has used, that gives his adversary a right to take away his life, and destroy him if he pleases, as a noxious creature; but it is damage sustained that alone gives him title to another man's goods: for though I may kill a thief that sets on me in the highway, yet I may not (which seems less) take away his money, and let him go: this would be robbery on my side. His force, and the state of war he put himself in, made him forfeit his life, but gave me no title to his goods. The right then of conquest extends only to the lives of those who joined in the war, not to their estates, but only in order to make reparation for the damages received, and the charges of the war, and that too with reservation of the right of the innocent wife and children.

Sec. 183. Let the conqueror have as much justice on his side, as could be supposed, he has no right to seize more than the vanquished could forfeit: his life is at the victor's mercy; and his service and goods he may appropriate, to make himself reparation; but he cannot take the goods of his wife and children; they too had a title to the goods he enjoyed, and their shares in the estate he possessed: for example, I in the state of nature (and all commonwealths are in the state of nature one with another) have injured another man, and refusing to give satisfaction, it comes to a state of war, wherein my defending by force what I had gotten unjustly, makes me the aggressor. I am conquered: my life, it is true, as forfeit, is at mercy, but not my wife's and children's. They made not the war, nor assisted in it. I could not forfeit their lives; they were not mine to forfeit. My wife had a share in my estate; that neither could I forfeit. And my children also, being born of me, had a right to be maintained out of my labor or substance.[2] Here then is the case: the conqueror has a title[3] to reparation for damages received, and the children have a title to their father's estate for their subsistence: for as to the wife's share, whether her own labor, or compact, gave her a title to it, it is plain, her husband could not forfeit what was hers. What must be

---

1   *miscarriages* Mismanagements.

2   *substance* Possessions.
3   *title* Right to possess.

done in the case? I answer; the fundamental law of nature being, that all, as much as may be, should be preserved, it follows, that if there be not enough fully to satisfy both, viz, for the conqueror's losses, and children's maintenance, he that has, and to spare, must remit something of his full satisfaction, and give way to the pressing and preferable title of those who are in danger to perish without it.

Sec. 184. But supposing the charge and damages of the war are to be made up to the conqueror, to the utmost farthing; and that the children of the vanquished, spoiled of all their father's goods, are to be left to starve and perish; yet the satisfying of what shall, on this score, be due to the conqueror, will scarce give him a title to any country he shall conquer: for the damages of war can scarce amount to the value of any considerable tract of land, in any part of the world, where all the land is possessed, and none lies waste. And if I have not taken away the conqueror's land, which, being vanquished, it is impossible I should; scarce any other spoil I have done him[1] can amount to the value of mine, supposing it equally cultivated, and of an extent any way coming near what I had overrun of his. The destruction of a year's product or two (for it seldom reaches four or five) is the utmost spoil that usually can be done: for as to money, and such riches and treasure taken away, these are none of nature's goods, they have but a fantastical[2] imaginary value: nature has put no such upon them: they are of no more account by her standard, than the wampompeke[3] of the Americans to an European prince, or the silver money of Europe would have been formerly to an American. And five years product is not worth the perpetual inheritance of land, where all is possessed, and none remains waste, to be taken up by him that is deceased: which will be easily granted, if one do but take away the imaginary value of money, the disproportion being more than between five and five hundred; though, at the same time, half a year's product is more worth than the inheritance, where there being more land than the inhabitants possess and make use of, anyone has liberty to make use of the waste: but there conquerors take little care to possess themselves of the lands of the vanquished, No damage therefore, that men in the state of nature (as all princes and governments are in reference to one another) suffer from one another, can give a conqueror power to dispossess the posterity of the vanquished, and

turn them out of that inheritance, which ought to be the possession of them and their descendants to all generations. The conqueror indeed will be apt to think himself master: and it is the very condition of the subdued not to be able to dispute their right. But if that be all, it gives no other title than what bare force gives to the stronger over the weaker: and, by this reason, he that is strongest will have a right to whatever he pleases to seize on.

Sec. 185. Over those then that joined with him in the war, and over those of the subdued country that opposed him not, and the posterity even of those that did, the conqueror, even in a just war, has, by his conquest, no right of dominion: they are free from any subjection to him, and if their former government be dissolved, they are at liberty to begin and erect another to themselves.

Sec. 186. The conqueror, it is true, usually, by the force he has over them, compels them, with a sword at their breasts, to stoop to his conditions, and submit to such a government as he pleases to afford them; but the enquiry is, what right he has to do so? If it be said, they submit by their own consent, then this allows their own consent to be necessary to give the conqueror a title to rule over them. It remains only to be considered, whether promises extorted by force, without right, can be thought consent, and how far they bind. To which I shall say, they bind not at all; because whatsoever another gets from me by force, I still retain the right of, and he is obliged presently to restore. He that forces my horse from me, ought presently to restore him, and I have still a right to retake him. By the same reason, he that forced a promise from me, ought presently[4] to restore it, i.e., quit me of the obligation of it; or I may resume it myself, i.e., choose whether I will perform it: for the law of nature laying an obligation on me only by the rules she[5] prescribes, cannot oblige me by the violation of her rules: such is the extorting any thing from me by force. Nor does it at all alter the case to say, I gave my promise, no more than it excuses the force, and passes the right, when I put my hand in my pocket, and deliver my purse myself to a thief, who demands it with a pistol at my breast.

Sec. 187. From all which it follows, that the government of a conqueror, imposed by force on the subdued, against whom he had no right of war, or who joined not in the war against him, where he had right, has no obligation upon them.

---

1   *spoil I have done him*   Property of his I have destroyed or taken.
2   *fantastical*   In fantasy—unreal.
3   *wampompeke*   "Wampum"—money of the North American aboriginal peoples.

4   *presently*   Soon.
5   *she*   Nature.

Sec. 188. But let us suppose, that all the men of that community, being all members of the same body politic, may be taken to have joined in that unjust war wherein they are subdued, and so their lives are at the mercy of the conqueror.

Sec. 189. I say, this concerns not their children who are in their minority: for since a father has not, in himself, a power over the life or liberty of his child, no act of his can possibly forfeit it. So that the children, whatever may have happened to the fathers, are freemen, and the absolute power of the conqueror reaches no farther than the persons of the men that were subdued by him, and dies with them: and should he govern them as slaves, subjected to his absolute arbitrary power, he has no such right of dominion over their children. He can have no power over them but by their own consent, whatever he may drive them to say or do; and he has no lawful authority, while force, and not choice, compels them to submission.

Sec. 190. Every man is born with a double right: first, a right of freedom to his person, which no other man has a power over, but the free disposal of it lies in himself. Secondly, a right, before any other man, to inherit with his brethren his father's goods.

Sec. 191. By the first of these, a man is naturally free from subjection to any government, though he be born in a place under its jurisdiction; but if he disclaim the lawful government of the country he was born in, he must also quit the right that belonged to him by the laws of it, and the possessions there descending to him from his ancestors, if it were a government made by their consent.

Sec. 192. By the second, the inhabitants of any country, who are descended, and derive a title to their estates from those who are subdued, and had a government forced upon them against their free consents, retain a right to the possession of their ancestors, though they consent not freely to the government, whose hard conditions were by force imposed on the possessors of that country: for the first conqueror never having had a title to the land of that country, the people who are the descendants of, or claim under those who were forced to submit to the yoke of a government by constraint, have always a right to shake it off, and free themselves from the usurpation or tyranny which the sword has brought in upon them, till their rulers put them under such a frame of government as they willingly and of choice consent to. Who doubts but the Grecian Christians, descendants of the ancient possessors of that country, may justly cast off the Turkish yoke, which they have so long groaned under, whenever they have an opportunity to do it? For no government can have a right to obedience from a people who have not freely consented to it; which they can never be supposed to do, till either they are put in a full state of liberty to choose their government and governors, or at least till they have such standing laws, to which they have by themselves or their representatives given their free consent, and also till they are allowed their due property, which is so to be proprietors of what they have, that nobody can take away any part of it without their own consent, without which, men under any government are not in the state of freemen, but are direct slaves under the force of war.

Sec. 193. But granting that the conqueror in a just war has a right to the estates, as well as power over the persons, of the conquered; which, it is plain, he has not:[1] nothing of absolute power will follow from hence, in the continuance of the government; because the descendants of these being all freemen, if he grants them estates and possessions to inhabit his country, (without which it would be worth nothing) whatsoever he grants them, they have, so far as it is granted, property in. The nature whereof is, that without a man's own consent it cannot be taken from him,

Sec. 194. Their persons are free by a native[2] right, and their properties, be they more or less, are their own, and at their own dispose,[3] and not at his; or else it is no property. Supposing the conqueror gives to one man a thousand acres, to him and his heirs forever; to another he lets[4] a thousand acres for his life, under the rent of 50 pounds or 500 pounds per annum has not the one of these a right to his thousand acres forever, and the other, during his life, paying the said rent? and has not the tenant for life a property in all that he gets over and above his rent, by his labor and industry during the said term, supposing it be double the rent? Can anyone say, the king, or conqueror, after his grant, may by his power of conqueror take away all, or part of the land from the heirs of one, or from the other during his life, he paying the rent? or can he take away from either the goods or money they have got upon the said land, at his pleasure? If he can, then all free and voluntary contracts cease, and are void in the world; there needs nothing to dissolve them at any time, but power enough: and all the grants and prom-

---

1   *But granting ... he has not*   Locke means here: Even supposing that the conquerer ... has a right ... —which he plainly does not.
2   *native*   Inborn, natural.
3   *at their own dispose*   To be dealt with by their own choice.
4   *lets*   Rents.

ises of men in power are but mockery and collusion:[1] for can there be any thing more ridiculous than to say, I give you and yours this forever, and that in the surest and most solemn way of conveyance can be devised; and yet it is to be understood, that I have right, if I please, to take it away from you again tomorrow?

Sec. 195. I will not dispute now whether princes are exempt from the laws of their country; but this I am sure, they owe subjection to the laws of God and nature. Nobody, no power, can exempt them from the obligations of that eternal law. Those are so great, and so strong, in the case of promises, that omnipotency[2] itself can be tied by them. Grants, promises, and oaths, are bonds that hold the Almighty: whatever some flatterers say to princes of the world, who all together, with all their people joined to them, are, in comparison of the great God, but as a drop of the bucket, or a dust on the balance, inconsiderable, nothing!

Sec. 196. The short of the case in conquest is this: the conqueror, if he have a just cause, has a despotical right over the persons of all, that actually aided, and concurred in the war against him, and a right to make up his damage and cost out of their labor and estates, so he injure not the right of any other. Over the rest of the people, if there were any that consented not to the war, and over the children of the captives themselves, or the possessions of either, he has no power; and so can have, by virtue of conquest, no lawful title himself to dominion over them, or derive it to his posterity; but is an aggressor, if he attempts upon their properties, and thereby puts himself in a state of war against them, and has no better a right of principality, he, nor any of his successors, than Hingar, or Hubba, the Danes, had here in England;[3] or Spartacus,[4] had he conquered Italy, would have had; which is to have their yoke cast off, as soon as God shall give those under their subjection courage and opportunity to do it. Thus, notwithstanding whatever title the kings of Assyria had over Judah, by the sword, God assisted Hezekiah to throw off the dominion of that conquering empire. "And the lord was with Hezekiah, and he prospered; wherefore he went forth, and he rebelled against the king of Assyria, and served him not" (2 Kings xviii. 7). Whence it is plain, that shaking off a power, which force, and not right, has set over anyone, though it has the name of rebellion, yet is no offence before God, but is that which he allows and countenances, though even promises and covenants, when obtained by force, have intervened: for it is very probable, to anyone that reads the story of Ahaz and Hezekiah attentively, that the Assyrians subdued Ahaz, and deposed him, and made Hezekiah king in his father's lifetime; and that Hezekiah by agreement had done him homage, and paid him tribute all this time.

Chapter 17. Of Usurpation

Sec. 197. As conquest may be called a foreign usurpation, so usurpation is a kind of domestic conquest, with this difference, that an usurper can never have right on his side, it being no usurpation, but where one is got into the possession of what another has right to.[5] This, so far as it is usurpation, is a change only of persons, but not of the forms and rules of the government: for if the usurper extend his power beyond what of right belonged to the lawful princes, or governors of the commonwealth, it is tyranny added to usurpation.

Sec. 198. In all lawful governments, the designation of the persons, who are to bear rule, is as natural and necessary a part as the form of the government itself, and is that which had its establishment originally from the people; the anarchy being much alike, to have no form of government at all, or to agree that it shall be monarchical, but to appoint no way to design the person that shall have the power, and be the monarch. Hence all commonwealths, with the form of government established, have rules also of appointing those who are to have any share in the public authority, and settled methods of conveying the right to them. Whoever gets into the exercise of any part of the power, by other ways than what the laws of the community have prescribed, has no right to be obeyed, though the form of the commonwealth be still preserved; since he is not the person the laws have appointed, and consequently not the person the people have consented to. Nor can such an usurper, or any deriving from him, ever have a title, till the people are both at liberty to consent, and have actually consented to allow, and confirm in him the power he has till then usurped.

---

1   *collusion*   Secret fraudulent agreement.

2   *omnipotency*   The state of being all-powerful, infinitely powerful.

3   *Hingar, or Hubba ... in England*   Hingar and Hubba, known now as Hengist and Horsa, were two Jutish brothers (from Jutland, an island of Denmark) who, according to tradition, led the invasion of Britain in the fifth century CE and founded the kingdom of Kent.

4   *Spartacus*   Gladiator-slave who led a slave rebellion against Rome, defeated in 71 BCE.

5   *it being no usurpation ... another has right to*   Locke means: It is not usurpation when one has the right to what one gets.

Chapter 18. Of Tyranny

Sec. 199. As usurpation is the exercise of power, which another has a right to; so tyranny is the exercise of power beyond right, which nobody can have a right to. And this is making use of the power anyone has in his hands, not for the good of those who are under it, but for his own private separate advantage. When the governor, however entitled, makes not the law, but his will, the rule; and his commands and actions are not directed to the preservation of the properties of his people, but the satisfaction of his own ambition, revenge, covetousness, or any other irregular passion.

Sec. 200. If one can doubt this to be truth, or reason, because it comes from the obscure hand of a subject, I hope the authority of a king will make it pass with him. King James the First, in his speech to the parliament, 1603, tells them thus,

> I will ever prefer the weal of the public, and of the whole commonwealth, in making of good laws and constitutions, to any particular and private ends of mine; thinking ever the wealth and weal of the commonwealth to be my greatest weal and worldly felicity; a point wherein a lawful king doth directly differ from a tyrant: for I do acknowledge, that the special and greatest point of difference that is betwixt a rightful king and an usurping tyrant, is this, that whereas the proud and ambitious tyrant doth think his kingdom and people are only ordained for satisfaction of his desires and unreasonable appetites, the righteous and just king doth by the contrary acknowledge himself to be ordained for the procuring of the wealth and property of his people.

And again, in his speech to the parliament, 1609, he had these words:

> The king binds himself by a double oath, to the observation of the fundamental laws of his kingdom; tacitly, as by being a king, and so bound to protect as well the people, as the laws of his kingdom; and expressly, by his oath at his coronation, so as every just king, in a settled kingdom, is bound to observe that paction[1] made to his people, by his laws, in framing his government agreeable thereunto, according to that paction which God made with Noah after the deluge "Hereafter, seed-time and harvest, and cold and heat, and summer and winter, and day and night, shall not cease while the earth remaineth." And therefore a king governing in a settled kingdom, leaves to be a king, and degenerates into a tyrant, as soon as he leaves off to rule according to his laws.

And a little after:

> Therefore all kings that are not tyrants, or perjured, will be glad to bound themselves within the limits of their laws; and they that persuade them the contrary, are vipers, and pests both against them and the commonwealth. Thus that learned king, who well understood the notion of things, makes the difference between a king and a tyrant to consist only in this, that one makes the laws the bounds of his power, and the good of the public, the end of his government; the other makes all give way to his own will and appetite.

Sec. 201. It is a mistake, to think this fault is proper only to monarchies; other forms of government are liable to it, as well as that: for wherever the power, that is put in any hands for the government of the people, and the preservation of their properties, is applied to other ends, and made use of to impoverish, harass, or subdue them to the arbitrary and irregular commands of those that have it; there it presently becomes tyranny, whether those that thus use it are one or many. Thus we read of the thirty tyrants[2] at Athens, as well as one at Syracuse;[3] and the intolerable dominion of the Decemviri[4] at Rome was nothing better.

---

1   *paction* Agreement.

2   *thirty tyrants* Ruling group installed after Athens's defeat in the Peloponnesian War in 404 BCE. They disregarded their assignment (to draft a new constitution), abused their power, and killed off their opponents, confiscating their possessions.

3   *one at Syracuse* Opinions differ about which ruler of Syracuse (in Sicily) Locke meant here. Perhaps Dionysius I, also known as Dionysius the Elder (430–367 BCE), perhaps Agathocles (361?–289 BCE); both were known for their cruelty.

4   *Decemviri* Latin: ten men. There were various ten-man groups in ancient Rome, but Locke here refers to the group of magistrates (lawgivers) appointed with strong powers in 451 BCE; they became increasingly violent and tyrannical, refusing to leave at the end of their term, but they were forced out by an uprising afterwards.

Sec. 202. Wherever law ends, tyranny begins, if the law be transgressed to another's harm; and whosoever in authority exceeds the power given him by the law, and makes use of the force he has under his command, to compass that upon the subject, which the law allows not,[1] ceases in that to be a magistrate; and, acting without authority, may be opposed, as any other man, who by force invades the right of another. This is acknowledged in subordinate magistrates. He that has authority to seize my person in the street, may be opposed as a thief and a robber, if he endeavors to break into my house to execute a writ,[2] notwithstanding that I know he has such a warrant, and such a legal authority, as will empower him to arrest me abroad.[3] And why this should not hold in the highest, as well as in the most inferior magistrate, I would gladly be informed. Is it reasonable, that the eldest brother, because he has the greatest part of his father's estate, should thereby have a right to take away any of his younger brothers' portions? or that a rich man, who possessed a whole country, should from thence have a right to seize, when he pleased, the cottage and garden of his poor neighbor? The being rightfully possessed of great power and riches, exceedingly beyond the greatest part of the sons of Adam, is so far from being an excuse, much less a reason, for rapine[4] and oppression, which the endamaging[5] another without authority is, that it is a great aggravation of it:[6] for the exceeding the bounds of authority is no more a right in a great, than in a petty officer; no more justifiable in a king than a constable; but is so much the worse in him, in that he has more trust put in him, has already a much greater share than the rest of his brethren, and is supposed, from the advantages of his education, employment, and counselors, to be more knowing in the measures of right and wrong.

Sec. 203. May the commands then of a prince be opposed? may he be resisted as often as anyone shall find himself aggrieved, and but imagine he has not right done him? This will unhinge and overturn all polities, and, instead of government and order, leave nothing but anarchy and confusion.

Sec. 204. To this I answer, that force is to be opposed to nothing, but to unjust and unlawful force; whoever makes any opposition in any other case, draws on himself a just condemnation both from God and man; and so no such danger or confusion will follow, as is often suggested: for,

Sec. 205. First, As, in some countries, the person of the prince by the law[7] is sacred; and so, whatever he commands or does, his person is still free from all question or violence, not liable to force, or any judicial censure or condemnation. But yet opposition may be made to the illegal acts of any inferior officer, or other commissioned by him; unless he will, by actually putting himself into a state of war with his people, dissolve the government, and leave them to that defense which belongs to everyone in the state of nature: for of such things who can tell what the end will be? and a neighbor kingdom has shown the world an odd example. In all other cases the sacredness of the person exempts him from all inconveniencies, whereby he is secure, while the government stands, from all violence and harm whatsoever; than which there cannot be a wiser constitution: for the harm he can do in his own person not being likely to happen often, nor to extend itself far; nor being able by his single strength to subvert the laws, nor oppress the body of the people, should any prince have so much weakness, and ill nature as to be willing to do it, the inconveniency of some particular mischiefs, that may happen sometimes, when a heady prince comes to the throne, are well recompensed by the peace of the public, and security of the government, in the person of the chief magistrate, thus set out of the reach of danger: it being safer for the body, that some few private men should be sometimes in danger to suffer, than that the head of the republic should be easily, and upon slight occasions, exposed.

Sec. 206. Secondly, But this privilege, belonging only to the king's person, hinders not, but they may be questioned, opposed, and resisted, who use unjust force, though they pretend a commission from him, which the law authorizes not;[8] as is plain in the case of him that has the king's writ to arrest a man, which is a full commission from the king; and yet he that has it cannot break open a man's house to

---

1   *compass ... law allows not*   Do to the subject that which the law does not allow.

2   *execute a writ*   Carry out the provisions of a legal order.

3   *abroad*   Outside (my house).

4   *rapine*   Illicit seizing of another's property.

5   *endamaging*   Bringing damage to.

6   *The being rightfully possessed ... aggravation of it*   Locke means here: Being the owner of great power and riches ... far from being an excuse for robbery and oppression (for this is what doing damage to someone without authority amounts to) makes it much worse.

7   *by the law*   As a matter of law.

8   *But this privilege ... authorizes not*   Locke means here: This privilege for the king's person does not extend to those who use unjust force, claiming to be commissioned by the king; they may be questioned, opposed, and resisted.

do it, nor execute this command of the king upon certain days, nor in certain places, though this commission have no such exception in it; but they are the limitations of the law, which if anyone transgress, the king's commission excuses him not: for the king's authority being given him only by the law, he cannot empower anyone to act against the law, or justify him, by his commission, in so doing; the commission, or command of any magistrate, where he has no authority, being as void and insignificant, as that of any private man; the difference between the one and the other, being that the magistrate has some authority so far, and to such ends, and the private man has none at all: for it is not the commission, but the authority, that gives the right of acting; and against the laws there can be no authority. But, notwithstanding such resistance, the king's person and authority are still both secured, and so no danger to governor or government,

Sec. 207. Thirdly, Supposing a government wherein the person of the chief magistrate is not thus sacred; yet this doctrine of the lawfulness of resisting all unlawful exercises of his power, will not upon every slight occasion endanger him, or embroil the government: for where the injured party may be relieved, and his damages repaired by appeal to the law, there can be no pretence for force, which is only to be used where a man is intercepted from appealing to the law: for nothing is to be accounted[1] hostile force, but where[2] it leaves not the remedy of such an appeal; and it is such force alone, that puts him that uses it into a state of war, and makes it lawful to resist him. A man with a sword in his hand demands my purse in the highway, when perhaps I have not twelve pence in my pocket: this man I may lawfully kill. To another I deliver 100 pounds to hold only while I alight, which he refuses to restore me, when I am got up again, but draws his sword to defend the possession of it by force, if I endeavor to retake it. The mischief this man does me is a hundred, or possibly a thousand times more than the other perhaps intended me (whom I killed before he really did me any); and yet I might lawfully kill the one, and cannot so much as hurt the other lawfully. The reason whereof is plain; because the one using force, which threatened my life, I could not have time to appeal to the law to secure it: and when it was gone, it was too late to appeal. The law could not restore life to my dead carcass: the loss was irreparable; which to prevent, the law of nature

gave me a right to destroy him, who had put himself into a state of war with me, and threatened my destruction. But in the other case, my life not being in danger, I may have the benefit of appealing to the law, and have reparation for my 100 pounds that way.

Sec. 208. Fourthly, But if the unlawful acts done by the magistrate be maintained (by the power he has got), and the remedy which is due by law, be by the same power obstructed; yet the right of resisting, even in such manifest acts of tyranny, will not suddenly, or on slight occasions, disturb the government: for if it reach no farther than some private men's cases, though they have a right to defend themselves, and to recover by force what by unlawful force is taken from them; yet the right to do so will not easily engage them in a contest, wherein they are sure to perish; it being as impossible for one, or a few oppressed men to disturb the government, where the body of the people do not think themselves concerned in it, as for a raving madman, or heady malcontent to overturn a well settled state; the people being as little apt to follow the one, as the other.

Sec. 209. But if either these illegal acts have extended to the majority of the people; or if the mischief and oppression has lighted only on some few, but in such cases, as the precedent, and consequences seem to threaten all; and they are persuaded in their consciences, that their laws, and with them their estates, liberties, and lives are in danger, and perhaps their religion too; how they will be hindered from resisting illegal force, used against them, I cannot tell. This is an inconvenience, I confess, that attends all governments whatsoever, when the governors have brought it to this pass, to be generally suspected of their people; the most dangerous state which they can possibly put themselves in. Wherein they are the less to be pitied, because it is so easy to be avoided; it being as impossible for a governor, if he really means the good of his people, and the preservation of them, and their laws together, not to make them see and feel it, as it is for the father of a family, not to let his children see he loves, and takes care of them.

Sec. 210. But if all the world shall observe pretences of one kind, and actions of another; arts used to elude the law, and the trust of prerogative (which is an arbitrary power in some things left in the prince's hand to do good, not harm to the people) employed contrary to the end for which it was given: if the people shall find the ministers and subordinate magistrates chosen suitable to such ends, and favored, or laid

---

1 *accounted* Counted as.
2 *but where* Except if.

by, proportionably as[1] they promote or oppose them: if they see several experiments[2] made of arbitrary power, and that religion underhand[3] favored, (though publicly proclaimed against) which is readiest to introduce it; and the operators[4] in it supported, as much as may be; and when that cannot be done, yet approved still, and liked the better: if a long train of actions show the councils all tending that way; how can a man any more hinder himself from being persuaded in his own mind, which way things are going; or from casting about how to save himself, than he could from believing the captain of the ship he was in, was carrying him, and the rest of the company, to Algiers,[5] when he found him always steering that course, though cross winds, leaks in his ship, and want of men and provisions did often force him to turn his course another way for some time, which he steadily returned to again, as soon as the wind, weather, and other circumstances would let him?

Chapter 19. Of the Dissolution of Government

Sec. 211. He that will with any clearness speak of the dissolution of government, ought in the first place to distinguish between the dissolution of the society and the dissolution of the government. That which makes the community, and brings men out of the loose state of nature, into one politic society, is the agreement which everyone has with the rest to incorporate, and act as one body, and so be one distinct commonwealth. The usual, and almost only way whereby this union is dissolved, is the inroad of foreign force making a conquest upon them: for in that case, (not being able to maintain and support themselves, as one entire and independent body) the union belonging to that body which consisted therein, must necessarily cease, and so everyone return to the state he was in before, with a liberty to shift for himself, and provide for his own safety, as he thinks fit, in some other society. Whenever the society is dissolved, it is certain the government of that society cannot remain. Thus conquerors' swords often cut up governments by[6] the roots, and mangle societies to pieces, separating the subdued or

scattered multitude from the protection of, and dependence on, that society which ought to have preserved them from violence. The world is too well instructed in, and too forward[7] to allow of, this way of dissolving of governments, to need any more to be said of it; and there wants not much argument to prove, that where the society is dissolved, the government cannot remain; that being as impossible, as for the frame of an house to subsist when the materials of it are scattered and dissipated by a whirlwind, or jumbled into a confused heap by an earthquake.

Sec. 212. Besides this overturning from without,[8] governments are dissolved from within,

First, When the legislative is altered. Civil society being a state of peace, among those who are of it, from whom the state of war is excluded by the umpirage,[9] which they have provided in their legislative, for the ending all differences that may arise among any of them, it is in their legislative, that the members of a commonwealth are united, and combined together into one coherent living body. This is the soul that gives form, life, and unity, to the commonwealth: from hence the several members have their mutual influence, sympathy, and connection: and therefore, when the legislative is broken, or dissolved, dissolution and death follows: for the essence and union of the society consisting in having one will, the legislative, when once established by the majority, has the declaring, and as it were keeping of that will. The constitution of the legislative is the first and fundamental act of society, whereby provision is made for the continuation of their union, under the direction of persons, and bonds of laws, made by persons authorized thereunto, by the consent and appointment of the people, without which no one man, or number of men, among them, can have authority of making laws that shall be binding to the rest. When any one, or more, shall take upon them to make laws, whom the people have not appointed so to do, they make laws without authority, which the people are not therefore bound to obey; by which means they come again to be out of subjection, and may constitute to themselves a new legislative, as they think best, being in full liberty to resist the force of those, who without authority would impose any thing upon them. Everyone is at the disposure of his own will,[10] when those who had, by the delegation of the society, the declaring of the public will, are

---

1   *laid by, proportionably as* Dismissed, depending on whether they promote or oppose them.
2   *experiments* Tryouts.
3   *underhand* Secretly.
4   *operators* Officials (of the religion).
5   *Algiers* A particularly nasty—pirate-ridden—place in Locke's day.
6   *cut up governments by* Cut off governments at.

7   *forward* Ready.
8   *without* Outside.
9   *umpirage* Arbitration.
10   *at the disposure of his own will* Free to do what he wants.

excluded from it, and others usurp the place, who have no such authority or delegation.

Sec. 213. This being usually brought about by such in the commonwealth who misuse the power they have; it is hard to consider it aright, and know at whose door to lay it,[1] without knowing the form of government in which it happens. Let us suppose then the legislative placed in the concurrence[2] of three distinct persons.

1. A single hereditary person, having the constant, supreme, executive power, and with it the power of convoking and dissolving the other two within certain periods of time.

2. An assembly of hereditary nobility.

3. An assembly of representatives chosen, pro tempore,[3] by the people. Such a form of government supposed,[4] it is evident,

Sec. 214. First, That when such a single person, or prince, sets up his own arbitrary will in place of the laws, which are the will of the society, declared by the legislative, then the legislative is changed: for that being in effect the legislative, whose rules and laws are put in execution, and required to be obeyed; when other laws are set up, and other rules pretended, and enforced, than what the legislative, constituted by the society, have enacted, it is plain that the legislative is changed.[5] Whoever introduces new laws, not being thereunto authorized by the fundamental appointment of the society, or subverts the old, disowns and overturns the power by which they were made, and so sets up a new legislative.

Sec. 215. Secondly, When the prince hinders the legislative from assembling in its due time, or from acting freely, pursuant to those ends for which it was constituted, the legislative is altered: for it is not a certain number of men, no, nor their meeting, unless they have also freedom of debating, and leisure of perfecting, what is for the good of the society, wherein the legislative consists: when these are taken away or altered, so as to deprive the society of the due exercise of their power, the legislative is truly altered; for it

is not names that constitute governments, but the use and exercise of those powers that were intended to accompany them; so that he, who takes away the freedom, or hinders the acting of the legislative in its due seasons, in effect takes away the legislative, and puts an end to the government.

Sec. 216. Thirdly, When, by the arbitrary power of the prince, the electors,[6] or ways of election, are altered, without the consent, and contrary to the common interest of the people, there also the legislative is altered: for, if others than those whom the society has authorized thereunto, do choose, or in another way than what the society has prescribed, those chosen are not the legislative appointed by the people.

Sec. 217. Fourthly, The delivery also of the people into the subjection of a foreign power, either by the prince, or by the legislative, is certainly a change of the legislative, and so a dissolution of the government: for the end why people entered into society being to be preserved one entire, free, independent society, to be governed by its own laws; this is lost, whenever they are given up into the power of another.

Sec. 218. Why, in such a constitution as this, the dissolution of the government in these cases is to be imputed to[7] the prince, is evident; because he, having the force, treasure[8] and offices of the state to employ, and often persuading himself, or being flattered by others, that as supreme magistrate he is incapable of control; he alone is in a condition to make great advances toward such changes, under pretence of lawful authority, and has it in his hands to terrify or suppress opposers, as factious,[9] seditious, and enemies to the government: whereas no other part of the legislative, or people, is capable by themselves to attempt any alteration of the legislative, without open and visible rebellion, apt enough to be taken notice of, which, when it prevails, produces effects very little different from foreign conquest. Besides, the prince in such a form of government, having the power of dissolving the other parts of the legislative, and thereby rendering them private persons, they can never in opposition to him, or without his concurrence, alter the legislative by a law, his consent being necessary to give any of their decrees that sanction. But yet so far as the other parts of the legislative any way contribute to any attempt upon[10] the government, and do either promote, or not, what

---

1   *at whose door to lay it*   Whom to blame it on.
2   *concurrence*   Cooperation.
3   *pro tempore*   Latin: for a limited period.
4   *supposed*   Presupposes.
5   *for that being in effect ... legislative is changed*   This means: What constitutes a legislature is applying rules and laws, and requiring them to be obeyed; so when laws are set up and rules announced and enforced other than those enacted by the legislature set up by the society, clearly the legislature has changed.

6   *electors*   People who are to vote.
7   *imputed to*   Blamed on.
8   *treasure*   Treasury.
9   *factious*   Promoting internal dissension.
10 *attempt upon*   Assault on.

lies in them,[1] hinder such designs, they are guilty, and partake in this, which is certainly the greatest crime men can be guilty of one towards another.

Sec. 219. There is one way more whereby such a government may be dissolved, and that is: When he who has the supreme executive power, neglects and abandons that charge, so that the laws already made can no longer be put in execution. This is demonstratively[2] to reduce all to anarchy, and so effectually to dissolve the government: for laws not being made for themselves, but to be, by their execution, the bonds of the society, to keep every part of the body politic in its due place and function; when that totally ceases, the government visibly ceases, and the people become a confused multitude, without order or connection. Where there is no longer the administration of justice, for the securing of men's rights, nor any remaining power within the community to direct the force, or provide for the necessities of the public, there certainly is no government left. Where the laws cannot be executed, it is all one as if there were no laws; and a government without laws is, I suppose, a mystery in politics, unconceivable to human capacity, and inconsistent with human society.

Sec. 220. In these and the like cases, when the government is dissolved, the people are at liberty to provide for themselves, by erecting a new legislative, differing from the other, by the change of persons, or form, or both, as they shall find it most for their safety and good: for the society can never, by the fault of another, lose the native and original right it has to preserve itself, which can only be done by a settled legislative, and a fair and impartial execution of the laws made by it. But the state of mankind is not so miserable that they are not capable of using this remedy, till it be too late to look for any. To tell people they may provide for themselves, by erecting a new legislative, when by oppression, artifice, or being delivered over to a foreign power, their old one is gone, is only to tell them, they may expect relief when it is too late, and the evil is past cure. This is in effect no more than to bid them first be slaves, and then to take care of their liberty; and when their chains are on, tell them, they may act like freemen. This, if barely so, is rather mockery than relief; and men can never be secure from tyranny, if there be no means to escape it till they are perfectly under it: and therefore it is, that they have not only a right to get out of it, but to prevent it.

Sec. 221. There is therefore, secondly, another way whereby governments are dissolved, and that is, when the legislative, or the prince, either of them, act contrary to their trust. First, The legislative acts against the trust reposed in them, when they endeavor to invade the property of the subject, and to make themselves, or any part of the community, masters, or arbitrary disposers of the lives, liberties, or fortunes of the people.

Sec. 222. The reason why men enter into society, is the preservation of their property; and the end why they choose and authorize a legislative, is, that there may be laws made, and rules set, as guards and fences to the properties of all the members of the society, to limit the power, and moderate the dominion, of every part and member of the society: for since it can never be supposed to be the will of the society, that the legislative should have a power to destroy that which everyone designs to secure, by entering into society, and for which the people submitted themselves to legislators of their own making; whenever the legislators endeavor to take away, and destroy the property of the people, or to reduce them to slavery under arbitrary power, they put themselves into a state of war with the people, who are thereupon absolved from any farther obedience, and are left to the common refuge, which God has provided for all men, against force and violence. Whenever therefore the legislative shall transgress this fundamental rule of society; and either by ambition, fear, folly or corruption, endeavor to grasp themselves, or put into the hands of any other, an absolute power over the lives, liberties, and estates of the people; by this breach of trust they forfeit the power the people had put into their hands for quite contrary ends, and it devolves to the people, who. have a right to resume their original liberty, and, by the establishment of a new legislative, (such as they shall think fit) provide for their own safety and security, which is the end for which they are in society. What I have said here, concerning the legislative in general, holds true also concerning the supreme executor, who having a double trust put in him, both to have a part in the legislative, and the supreme execution of the law, acts against both, when he goes about to set up his own arbitrary will as the law of the society. He acts also contrary to his trust, when he either employs the force, treasure, and offices of the society, to corrupt the representatives, and gain them to his purposes; or openly preengages[3] the electors, and prescribes to their choice, such, whom he has, by solicita-

---

1 *what lies in them* When they could have done so.
2 *demonstratively* Manifestly.

3 *preengages* Courts.

tions, threats, promises, or otherwise, won to his designs; and employs them to bring in such,[1] who have promised beforehand what to vote, and what to enact. Thus to regulate candidates and electors, and new-model[2] the ways of election, what is it but to cut up the government by the roots, and poison the very fountain of public security? for the people having reserved to themselves the choice of their representatives, as the fence to their properties, could do it for no other end, but that they might always be freely chosen, and so chosen, freely act, and advise, as the necessity of the commonwealth, and the public good should, upon examination, and mature debate, be judged to require. This, those who give their votes before they hear the debate, and have weighed the reasons on all sides, are not capable of doing. To prepare such an assembly as this, and endeavor to set up the declared abettors of his own will, for the true representatives of the people, and the law-makers of the society, is certainly as great a breach of trust, and as perfect a declaration of a design to subvert the government, as is possible to be met with. To which, if one shall add rewards and punishments visibly employed to the same end, and all the arts of perverted law made use of, to take off and destroy all that stand in the way of such a design, and will not comply and consent to betray the liberties of their country, it will be past doubt what is doing. What power they ought to have in the society, who thus employ it contrary to the trust went along with it in its first institution, is easy to determine; and one cannot but see, that he, who has once attempted any such thing as this, cannot any longer be trusted.

Sec. 223. To this perhaps it will be said,[3] that the people being ignorant, and always discontented, to lay the foundation of government in the unsteady opinion and uncertain humor of the people, is to expose it to certain ruin; and no government will be able long to subsist, if the people may set up a new legislative, whenever they take offence at the old one. To this I answer, Quite the contrary. People are not so easily got out of their old forms, as some are apt to suggest. They are hardly to be prevailed with to amend the acknowledged faults in the frame they have been accustomed to. And if there be any original defects, or adventitious[4] ones introduced by time, or corruption; it is not an easy thing to get them changed, even when all the world sees there is an opportunity for it. This slowness and aversion in the people

to quit their old constitutions, has, in the many revolutions which have been seen in this kingdom, in this and former ages, still kept us to, or, after some interval of fruitless attempts, still brought us back again to our old legislative of king, lords and commons: and whatever provocations have made the crown be taken from some of our princes' heads, they never carried the people so far as to place it in another line.[5]

Sec. 224. But it will be said, this hypothesis lays[6] a ferment for frequent rebellion. To which I answer,

First, No more than any other hypothesis: for when the people are made miserable, and find themselves exposed to the ill usage of arbitrary power, cry up their governors, as much as you will, for sons of Jupiter;[7] let them be sacred and divine, descended, or authorized from heaven; give them out for whom or what you please, the same will happen. The people generally ill treated, and contrary to right, will be ready upon any occasion to ease themselves of a burden that sits heavy upon them. They will wish, and seek for the opportunity, which in the change, weakness and accidents of human affairs, seldom delays long to offer itself. He must have lived but a little while in the world, who has not seen examples of this in his time; and he must have read very little, who cannot produce examples of it in all sorts of governments in the world.

Sec. 225. Secondly, I answer, such revolutions happen not upon every little mismanagement in public affairs. Great mistakes in the ruling part, many wrong and inconvenient laws, and all the slips of human frailty, will be born by the people without mutiny or murmur. But if a long train of abuses, prevarications[8] and artifices, all tending the same way, make the design visible to the people, and they cannot but feel what they lie under, and see whither they are going; it is not to be wondered, that they should then rouse themselves, and endeavor to put the rule into such hands which may secure to them the ends for which government was at first erected; and without which, ancient names, and specious forms,[9] are so far from being better, that they are much worse, than the state of nature, or pure anarchy; the inconveniencies being all as great and as near, but the remedy farther off and more difficult.

---

1   *bring in such*   Elect those.
2   *new-model*   Reshape.
3   *it will be said*   It will be objected.
4   *adventitious*   Added from outside.
5   *line*   Line of descent.
6   *lays*   Creates.
7   *Jupiter*   Patron deity of the ancient Roman state; god of laws and social order.
8   *prevarications*   Avoidances of telling the truth.
9   *specious forms*   Deceptively attractive rituals.

Sec. 226. Thirdly, I answer, that this doctrine of a power in the people of providing for their safety anew, by a new legislative, when their legislators have acted contrary to their trust, by invading their property, is the best fence against rebellion, and the probablest[1] means to hinder it: for rebellion being an opposition, not to persons, but authority, which is founded only in the constitutions and laws of the government; those, whoever they be, who by force break through, and by force justify their violation of them, are truly and properly rebels: for when men, by entering into society and civil-government, have excluded force, and introduced laws for the preservation of property, peace, and unity among themselves, those who set up force again in opposition to the laws, do rebellare,[2] that is, bring back again the state of war, and are properly rebels: which they who are in power, (by the pretence they have to authority, the temptation of force they have in their hands, and the flattery of those about them) being likeliest to do; the most proper way to prevent the evil, is to show them the danger and injustice of it, who are under the greatest temptation to run into it.

Sec. 227. In both the aforementioned cases, when either the legislative is changed, or the legislators act contrary to the end for which they were constituted; those who are guilty are guilty of rebellion: for if anyone by force takes away the established legislative of any society, and the laws by them made, pursuant to their trust, he thereby takes away the umpirage, which everyone had consented to, for a peaceable decision of all their controversies, and a bar to the state of war among them. They, who remove, or change the legislative, take away this decisive power, which nobody can have, but by the appointment and consent of the people; and so destroying the authority which the people did, and nobody else can set up, and introducing a power which the people has not authorized, they actually introduce a state of war, which is that of force without authority: and thus, by removing the legislative established by the society, (in whose decisions the people acquiesced and united, as to that of their own will) they untie the knot, and expose the people a-new to the state of war, And if those, who by force take away the legislative, are rebels, the legislators themselves, as has been shown, can be no less esteemed so; when they,

who were set up for the protection, and preservation of the people, their liberties and properties, shall by force invade and endeavor to take them away; and so they putting themselves into a state of war with those who made them the protectors and guardians of their peace, are properly, and with the greatest aggravation, rebellantes,[3] rebels.

Sec. 228. But if they, who say it lays a foundation for rebellion, mean that it may occasion civil wars, or intestine broils,[4] to tell the people they are absolved from[5] obedience when illegal attempts are made upon their liberties or properties, and may oppose the unlawful violence of those who were their magistrates, when they invade their properties contrary to the trust put in them; and that therefore this doctrine is not to be allowed, being so destructive to the peace of the world: they may as well say, upon the same ground, that honest men may not oppose robbers or pirates, because this may occasion disorder or bloodshed. If any mischief come in such cases, it is not to be charged upon him who defends his own right, but on him that invades his neighbors. If the innocent honest man must quietly quit all he has, for peace sake, to him who will lay violent hands upon it, I desire it may be considered, what a kind of peace there will be in the world, which consists only in violence and rapine; and which is to be maintained only for the benefit of robbers and oppressors. Who would not think it an admirable peace betwixt the mighty and the mean, when the lamb, without resistance, yielded his throat to be torn by the imperious wolf? Polyphemus's den[6] gives us a perfect pattern of such a peace, and such a government, wherein Ulysses and his companions had nothing to do, but quietly to suffer themselves to be devoured. And no doubt Ulysses, who was a prudent man, preached up passive obedience, and exhorted them to a quiet submission, by representing to them of what concernment peace was to mankind; and by showing the inconveniencies might happen, if they should offer to resist Polyphemus, who had now the power over them.

Sec. 229. The end of government is the good of mankind; and which is best for mankind, that the people should be always exposed to the boundless will of tyranny, or that

---

1 *probablest* Most likely.
2 *rebellare* Latin: rebel. This word derives from *bellare*, to make war; so adding the initial *re* (= again) suggests making war again. That may be why Locke uses the Latin word: for him, to rebel and destroy the government is to re-institute a state of war.

3 *rebellantes* Latin: rebels; but see previous note.
4 *intestine broils* Internal unrest.
5 *absolved from* Relieved of the obligation of.
6 *Polyphemus's den* In Homer's *Odyssey*, Polyphemus is a ferocious and horrible one-eyed giant (a Cyclops) who traps Ulysses and his men in his cave and begins eating them. Ulysses hatches an ingenious scheme to blind Polyphemus and escape.

the rulers should be sometimes liable to be opposed, when they grow exorbitant in the use of their power, and employ it for the destruction, and not the preservation of the properties of their people?

Sec. 230. Nor[1] let anyone say, that mischief can arise from hence, as often as it shall please a busy head, or turbulent spirit, to desire the alteration of the government. It is true, such men may stir, whenever they please; but it will be only to their own just ruin and perdition: for till the mischief be grown general, and the ill designs of the rulers become visible, or their attempts sensible to the greater part,[2] the people, who are more disposed to suffer than right themselves by resistance, are not apt to stir. The examples of particular injustice, or oppression of here and there an unfortunate man, moves them not. But if they universally have a persuasion, grounded upon manifest evidence, that designs are carrying on[3] against their liberties, and the general course and tendency of things cannot but give them strong suspicions of the evil intention of their governors, who is to be blamed for it? Who can help it, if they, who might avoid it, bring themselves into this suspicion? Are the people to be blamed, if they have the sense of rational creatures, and can think of things no otherwise than as they find and feel them? And is it not rather their fault, who put things into such a posture, that they would not have them thought to be as they are? I grant, that the pride, ambition, and turbulency of private men have sometimes caused great disorders in commonwealths, and factions have been fatal to states and kingdoms. But whether the mischief has oftener begun in the people's wantonness,[4] and a desire to cast off the lawful authority of their rulers, or in the rulers insolence, and endeavors to get and exercise an arbitrary power over their people; whether oppression, or disobedience, gave the first rise to the disorder, I leave it to impartial history to determine. This I am sure, whoever, either ruler or subject, by force goes about to invade the rights of either prince or people, and lays the foundation for overturning the constitution and frame of any just government, is highly guilty of the greatest crime, I think, a man is capable of, being to answer for all those mischiefs of blood, rapine, and desolation, which the breaking to pieces of governments bring on a country. And he who does it, is justly to be esteemed the common enemy and pest of mankind, and is to be treated accordingly.

Sec. 231. That subjects or foreigners, attempting[5] by force on the properties of any people, may be resisted with force, is agreed on all hands. But that magistrates, doing the same thing, may be resisted, has of late been denied: as if those who had the greatest privileges and advantages by the law, had thereby a power to break those laws, by which alone they were set in a better place than their brethren: whereas their offence is thereby the greater, both as being ungrateful for the greater share they have by the law, and breaking also that trust, which is put into their hands by their brethren.

Sec. 232. Whosoever uses force without right, as everyone does in society, who does it without law, puts himself into a state of war with those against whom he so uses it; and in that state all former ties are cancelled, all other rights cease, and everyone has a right to defend himself, and to resist the aggressor. This is so evident, that Barclay[6] himself, that great assertor of the power and sacredness of kings, is forced to confess, that it is lawful for the people, in some cases, to resist their king; and that too in a chapter, wherein he pretends to show, that the divine law shuts up[7] the people from all manner of rebellion. Whereby it is evident, even by his own doctrine, that, since they may in some cases resist, all resisting of princes is not rebellion.

His words are these:[8]

> Quod siquis dicat, Ergone populus tyrannicae crudelitati et furori jugulum semper praebebit? Ergone multitudo civitates suas fame, ferro, et flamma vastari, seque, conjuges, et liberos fortunae ludibrio et tyranni libidini exponi, inque omnia vitae pericula omnesque miserias et molestias a rege deduci patientur? Num illis quod omni animantium generi est a natura tributum, denegari debet, ut sc. vim vi repellant, seseque ab injuria tueantur? Huic breviter responsum sit, populo universo negari defensionem, quae juris naturalis est, neque ultionem quae praeter naturam est adversus regem concedi debere. Quapropter si

---

1   *Nor*   Do not.
2   *greater part*   The majority (of people).
3   *designs are carrying on*   Plots are being carried out.
4   *wantonness*   Unruliness, irresponsibility.
5   *attempting*   Attacking.
6   *Barclay*   William Barclay (c. 1546–1608), obscure Scottish jurist and political theorist.
7   *shuts up*   Blocks.
8   *His words are these*   See below for Locke's English translation. (This is one of a series of Latin quotations that Locke translates.)

rex non in singulares tantum personas aliquot privatum odium exerceat, sed corpus etiam reipublicae, cujus ipse, caput est—i.e., totum populum, vel insignem aliquam ejus partem immani et intoleranda saevitia seu tyrannide divexet; populo, quidem hoc casu resistendi ac tuendi se ab injuria potestas competit, sed tuendi se tantum, non enim in principem invadendi: et restituendae injuriae illatae, non recedendi a debita reverentia propter acceptum injuriam. Praesentem denique impetum propulsandi non vim praeteritam ulciscendi jus habet. Horum enim alterum a natura est, ut vitani scilicet corpusque tueamur. Alterum vero contra naturam, ut inferior de superiori supplicium sumat. Quod itaque populus malum, antequam factum sit, impedire potest, ne fiat, id postquam factum est, in regem authorem sceleris vindicare non potest, populus igitur hoc amplius quam privatus quispiam habet: Quod huic, vel ipsis adversariis judicibus, excepto Buchanano, nullum nisi in patientia remedium superest. Cum ille si intolerabilis tyrannis est (modicum enim ferre omnino debet) resistere cum reverentia possit.—Barclay, *Contra Monarchomachos*, iii. 8.

In English thus:

Sec. 233. But if anyone should ask, Must the people then always lay themselves open to the cruelty and rage of tyranny? Must they see their cities pillaged, and laid in ashes, their wives and children exposed to the tyrant's lust and fury, and themselves and families reduced by their king to ruin, and all the miseries of want and oppression, and yet sit still? Must men alone be debarred the common privilege of opposing force with force, which nature allows so freely to all other creatures for their preservation from injury? I answer: Self-defense is a part of the law of nature; nor can it be denied the community, even against the king himself: but to revenge themselves upon him, must by no means be allowed them; it being not agreeable to[1] that law. Wherefore if the king shall show an hatred, not only to some particular persons, but sets himself against the body of the commonwealth, whereof he is the head, and shall,

with intolerable ill usage, cruelly tyrannize over the whole, or a considerable part of the people, in this case the people have a right to resist and defend themselves from injury: but it must be with this caution, that they only defend themselves, but do not attack their prince: they may repair the damages received, but must not for any provocation exceed the bounds of due reverence and respect. They may repulse the present attempt, but must not revenge past violences: for it is natural for us to defend life and limb, but that an inferior should punish a superior, is against nature. The mischief which is designed them, the people may prevent before it be done; but when it is done, they must not revenge it on the king, though author of the villainy. This therefore is the privilege of the people in general, above what any private person has; that particular men are allowed by our adversaries themselves (Buchanan[2] only excepted) to have no other remedy but patience; but the body of the people may with respect resist intolerable tyranny; for when it is but moderate, they ought to endure it.

Sec. 234. Thus far that great advocate of monarchical power allows of resistance.

Sec. 235. It is true, he has annexed two limitations to it, to no purpose:

First, He says, it must be with reverence.

Secondly, It must be without retribution, or punishment; and the reason he gives is, because an inferior cannot punish a superior.

First, How to resist force without striking again, or how to strike with reverence, will need some skill to make intelligible. He that shall oppose an assault only with a shield to receive the blows, or in any more respectful posture, without a sword in his hand, to abate the confidence and force of the assailant, will quickly be at an end of his resistance, and will find such a defense serve only to draw on himself the worse usage. This is as ridiculous a way of resisting, as Juvenal thought it of fighting; ubi tu pulsas, ego vapulo tantum.[3]

---

1   *agreeable to*   In conformity with.

2   *Buchanan*   George Buchanan (1506–82), Scottish poet and political writer who argued that the monarch's power came from the people, not from divine right.

3   *ubi tu ... tantum*   Latin: when you do all the thrashing and I get all the blows. This and the following quotation are from Juvenal, Roman satirist (60?–140? CE). In his *Third Satire*, this quote appears at line 289, and the following at lines 299-301.

And the success of the combat will be unavoidably the same he there describes it:

> Libertas pauperis haec est:
> Pulsatus rogat, & pugnis concisus, adorat,
> Ut liceat paucis cum dentibus inde reverti.[1]

This will always be the event of such an imaginary resistance, where men may not strike again. He therefore who may resist, must be allowed to strike. And then let our author, or anybody else, join a knock on the head, or a cut on the face, with as much reverence and respect as he thinks fit. He that can reconcile blows and reverence, may, for aught I know, desire for his pains, a civil, respectful cudgeling wherever he can meet with it.

Secondly, As to his second, An inferior cannot punish a superior; that is true, generally speaking, while he is his superior. But to resist force with force, being the state of war that levels the parties, cancels all former relation of reverence, respect, and superiority: and then the odds that remains, is, that he, who opposes the unjust aggressor, has this superiority over him, that he has a right, when he prevails, to punish the offender, both for the breach of the peace, and all the evils that followed upon it. Barclay therefore, in another place, more coherently to himself,[2] denies it to be lawful to resist a king in any case. But he there assigns two cases, whereby a king may un-king himself. His words are,

> Quid ergo, nulline casus incidere possunt quibus populo sese erigere atque in regem impotentius dominantem arma capere et invadere jure suo suaque authoritate liceat? Nulli certe quamdiu rex manet. Semper enim ex divinis id obstat, Regem honorificato, et qui potestati resistit, Dei ordinationi resistit; non alias igitur in eum populo potestas est quam si id committat propter quod ipso jure rex esse desinat. Tunc enim se ipse principatu exuit atque in privatis constituit liber; hoc modo populus et superior efficitur, reverso ad eum scilicet jure illo quod ante regem inauguratum in interregno habuit. At sunt paucorum generum commissa ejusmodi quae hunc effectum pariunt. At ego cum plurima animo perlustrem,

duo tantum invenio, duos, inquam, casus quibus rex ipso facto ex rege non regem se facit et omni honore et dignitate regali atque in subditos potestate destituit; quorum etiam meminit Winzerus. Horum unus est, si regnum disperdat, quemadmodum de Nerone fertur, quod is nempe senatum populumque Romanum atque adeo urbem ipsam ferro flammaque vastare, ac novas sibi sedes quaerere decrevisset. Et de Caligula, quod palam denunciarit se neque civem neque principem senatui amplius fore, inque animo habuerit, interempto utriusque ordinis electissimo, quoque Alexandriam commigrare, ac ut populum uno ictu interimeret, unam ei cervicem optavit. Talia cum rex aliquis meditatur et molitur serio, omnem regnandi curam et animum ilico abjicit, ac proinde imperium in subditos amittit, ut dominus servi pro derelicto habiti, dominium.

Sec. 236. Alter casus est, si rex in alicujus clientelam se contulit, ac regnum quod liberum a majoribus et populo traditum accepit, alienae ditioni mancipavit. Nam tunc quamvis forte non ea mente id agit populo plane ut incommodet; tamen quia quod praecipuum est regiae dignitatis amisit, ut summus scilicet in regno secundum Deum sit, et solo Deo inferior, atque populum etiam totum ignorantem vel invitum, cujus libertatem sartam et tectam conservare debuit, in alterius gentis ditionem et potestatem dedidit; hac velut quadam rengi abalienatione effecit, ut nec quod ipse in regno imperium habuit retineat, nec in eum cui collatum voluit, juris quicquam transferat, atque ita eo facto liberum jam et suae potestatis populum relinquit, cujus rei exemplum unum annales Scotici suppeditant.—Barclay, Contra Monarchomachos, I. iii., c. 16.

Which in English runs thus:

Sec. 237. What then, can there no case happen wherein the people may of right, and by their own authority, help themselves, take arms, and set upon their king, imperiously domineering over them? None at all, while he remains a king. "Honor the king," and "He that resists the power, resists the ordinance of God," are divine oracles[3]

---

1   *Libertas pauperis ... inde reverti* Latin: such is the liberty of the poor man: having been pounded and cuffed into a jelly, he begs and prays to be allowed to return home with a few teeth in his head.

2   *coherently to himself* Consistently.

---

3   *oracles* Wise sayings.

that will never permit it, The people therefore can never come by a power over him, unless he does something that makes him cease to be a king: for then he divests himself of his crown and dignity, and returns to the state of a private man, and the people become free and superior, the power which they had in the interregnum,[1] before they crowned him king, devolving[2] to them again. But there are but few miscarriages which bring the matter to this state. After considering it well on all sides, I can find but two. Two cases there are, I say, whereby a king, ipso facto,[3] becomes no king, and loses all power and regal authority over his people; which are also taken notice of by Winzerus.[4]

The first is, If he endeavor to overturn the government, that is, if he have a purpose and design to ruin the kingdom and commonwealth, as it is recorded of Nero,[5] that he resolved to cut off the senate and people of Rome, lay the city waste with fire and sword, and then remove to some other place. And of Caligula,[6] that he openly declared, that he would be no longer a head to the people or senate, and that he had it in his thoughts to cut off the worthiest men of both ranks, and then retire to Alexandria: and he wished that the people had but one neck, that he might dispatch them all at a blow, Such designs as these, when any king harbors in his thoughts, and seriously promotes, he immediately gives up all care and thought of the commonwealth; and consequently forfeits the power of governing his subjects, as a master does the dominion over his slaves whom he has abandoned.

Sec. 238. The other case is, When a king makes himself the dependent of another, and subjects his kingdom which his ancestors left

him, and the people put free into his hands, to the dominion of another: for however perhaps it may not be his intention to prejudice the people; yet because he has hereby lost the principal part of regal dignity, viz. to be next and immediately under God, supreme in his kingdom; and also because he betrayed or forced his people, whose liberty he ought to have carefully preserved, into the power and dominion of a foreign nation. By this, as it were, alienation[7] of his kingdom, he himself loses the power he had in it before, without transferring any the least right to those on whom he would have bestowed it; and so by this act sets the people free, and leaves them at their own disposal. One example of this is to be found in the *Scotch Annals*.

Sec. 239. In these cases Barclay, the great champion of absolute monarchy, is forced to allow, that a king may be resisted, and ceases to be a king. That is, in short, not to multiply cases, in whatsoever he has no authority, there he is no king, and may be resisted: for wherever the authority ceases, the king ceases too, and becomes like other men who have no authority. And these two cases he instances in, differ little from those above mentioned, to be destructive to governments, only that he has omitted the principle from which his doctrine flows: and that is, the breach of trust, in not preserving the form of government agreed on, and in not intending the end of government itself, which is the public good and preservation of property. When a king has dethroned himself, and put himself in a state of war with his people, what shall hinder them from prosecuting him who is no king, as they would any other man, who has put himself into a state of war with them, Barclay, and those of his opinion, would do well to tell us. This farther I desire may be taken notice of out of Barclay, that he says, "The mischief that is designed them, the people may prevent before it be done," whereby he allows resistance when tyranny is but in design. "Such designs as these," says he, "when any king harbors in his thoughts and seriously promotes, he immediately gives up all care and thought of the commonwealth," so that, according to him, the neglect of the public good is to be taken as an evidence of such design, or at least for a sufficient cause of resistance. And the reason of all, he gives in these words: "Because he betrayed or forced his people, whose liberty he ought carefully to have preserved." What

---

1   *interregnum*   Latin: time between one reign and the next.
2   *devolving*   Transferring.
3   *ipso facto*   Latin: as a result of that fact in particular.
4   *Winzerus*   Ninian Winzet (c. 1518–92), Scottish Benedictine Abbot, author of pamphlets replying to Barclay, defending the power of the (constitutional) monarch.
5   *Nero*   Nero Claudius Caesar (37–68), emperor of Rome, with a very bad reputation: thought to have murdered his mother, wife, and mistress, to have set fire to Rome, etc.
6   *Caligula*   Gaius Julius Caesar Germanicus (12–41), Roman emperor with a reputation for madness and misrule.

---

7   *alienation*   Transfer away.

he adds, "into the power and dominion of a foreign nation," signifies nothing, the fault and forfeiture[1] lying in the loss of their liberty, which he ought to have preserved, and not in any distinction of the persons to whose dominion they were subjected. The people's right is equally invaded, and their liberty lost, whether they are made slaves to any of their own, or a foreign nation; and in this lies the injury, and against this only have they the right of defense. And there are instances to be found in all countries, which show, that it is not the change of nations in the persons of their governors, but the change of government, that gives the offence. Bilson,[2] a bishop of our church, and a great stickler for the power and prerogative of princes, does, if I mistake not, in his treatise of Christian subjection, acknowledge, that princes may forfeit their power, and their title to the obedience of their subjects; and if there needed authority in a case where reason is so plain, I could send my reader to Bracton, Fortescue, and the author of the Mirrour,[3] and others, writers that cannot be suspected to be ignorant of our government, or enemies to it. But I thought Hooker alone might be enough to satisfy those men, who relying on him for their ecclesiastical polity,[4] are by a strange fate carried to deny those principles upon which he builds it. Whether they are herein made the tools of more cunning workmen, to pull down their own fabric, they were best look.[5] This I am sure, their civil policy is so new, so dangerous, and so destructive to both rulers and people, that as former ages never could bear the broaching[6] of it; so it may be hoped, those to come, redeemed[7] from the impositions

of these Egyptian under-task-masters,[8] will abhor the memory of such servile flatterers, who, while it seemed to serve their turn, resolved[9] all government into absolute tyranny, and would have all men born to, what their mean souls fitted them for, slavery.

Sec. 240. Here, it is like,[10] the common question will be made,[11] "Who shall be judge, whether the prince or legislative act contrary to their trust?" This, perhaps, ill-affected and factious men may spread among the people, when the prince only makes use of his due prerogative. To this I reply, The people shall be judge; for who shall be judge whether his trustee or deputy acts well, and according to the trust reposed in him, but he who deputes him, and must, by having deputed him, have still a power to discard him, when he fails in his trust? If this be reasonable in particular cases of private men, why should it be otherwise in that of the greatest moment,[12] where the welfare of millions is concerned, and also where the evil, if not prevented, is greater, and the redress very difficult, dear, and dangerous?

Sec. 241. But farther, this question, ("Who shall be judge?") cannot mean, that there is no judge at all: for where there is no judicature on earth, to decide controversies among men, God in heaven is judge. He alone, it is true, is judge of the right. But every man is judge for himself, as in all other cases, so in this, whether another has put himself into a state of war with him, and whether he should appeal to the Supreme Judge, as Jeptha did.

Sec. 242. If a controversy arise betwixt a prince and some of the people, in a matter where the law is silent, or doubtful, and the thing be of great consequence, I should think the proper umpire, in such a case, should be the body of the people: for in cases where the prince has a trust reposed in him, and is dispensed from the common ordinary rules of the law; there, if any men find themselves aggrieved,[13] and think the prince acts contrary to, or beyond that trust, who so proper to judge as the body of the people, (who, at first, lodged that trust in him) how far they meant it should extend? But if the prince, or whoever they be in the administration, decline that way of determination, the appeal then

---

1 *forfeiture* That which had to be given up as a penalty.

2 *Bilson* Thomas Bilson (c. 1546–1616), author of *The True Difference Between Christian Subjection and Unnatural Rebellion* (1586), which argued that, despite the fact that subjects must submit to royal authority in general, in certain cases revolt against this authority is justified.

3 *Bracton* Henry de Bracton (d. 1268), English lawyer, argued in *De legibus et consuietudinibus Angliae* (1569) that the king is supreme ruler in his realm, but subject to law; *Fortescue* Sir John Fortescue (1394–1476) wrote several books defending the idea that laws required consent of both king and people; *author of the Mirrour* The editor and principal contributor to *The Mirror for Magistrates* (1559) was William Baldwin; it is a collection of poems about the downfall of historical rulers, intended to warn against abuse of power.

4 *ecclesiastical polity* Principles of governance of the church.

5 *they were best look* They had better watch out.

6 *broaching* Bringing up a difficult matter.

7 *redeemed* Set free.

8 *Egyptian under-task-masters* Locke metaphorically refers to the slave-drivers under whom the Israelites labored while in captivity in Egypt.

9 *resolved* Transformed.

10 *like* Likely.

11 *made* Asked.

12 *moment* Importance.

13 *aggrieved* Injured, harmed.

lies nowhere but to heaven; force between either persons, who have no known superior on earth, or which permits no appeal to a judge on earth, being properly a state of war, wherein the appeal lies only to heaven; and in that state the injured party must judge for himself, when he will think fit to make use of that appeal, and put himself upon it.

Sec. 243. To conclude, The power that every individual gave the society, when he entered into it, can never revert to the individuals again, as long as the society lasts, but will always remain in the community; because without this there can be no community, no commonwealth, which is contrary to the original agreement: so also when the society has placed the legislative in any assembly of men, to continue in them and their successors, with direction and authority for providing such successors, the legislative can never revert to the people while that government lasts; because having provided a legislative with power to continue forever, they have given up their political power to the legislative, and cannot resume it. But if they have set limits to the duration of their legislative, and made this supreme power in any person, or assembly, only temporary; or else, when by the miscarriages of those in authority, it is forfeited; upon the forfeiture, or at the determination of the time set, it reverts to the society, and the people have a right to act as supreme, and continue the legislative in themselves; or erect a new form, or under the old form place it in new hands, as they think good.

◆ ◆ ◆ ◆ ◆

A Letter Concerning Toleration (1689)

Honored Sir,

Since you are pleased to inquire what are my thoughts about the mutual toleration of Christians in their different professions of[1] religion, I must needs[2] answer you freely that I esteem that toleration to be the chief characteristic mark of the true Church. For whatsoever some people boast of the antiquity of places and names, or of the pomp of their outward worship; others, of the reformation of their discipline; all, of the orthodoxy of their faith—for everyone

is orthodox to himself—these things, and all others of this nature, are much rather marks of men striving for power and empire over one another than of the Church of Christ. Let anyone have never so true a claim to all these things,[3] yet if he be destitute of charity, meekness, and good-will in general towards all mankind, even to those that are not Christians, he is certainly yet short of being a true Christian himself. "The kings of the Gentiles exercise leadership over them," said our Saviour to his disciples, "but ye shall not be so."[4] The business of true religion is quite another thing. It is not instituted in order to the erecting of an external pomp, nor to the obtaining of ecclesiastical dominion,[5] nor to the exercising of compulsive[6] force, but to the regulating of men's lives, according to the rules of virtue and piety.... If the Gospel and the apostles may be credited, no man can be a Christian without charity and without that faith which works, not by force, but by love. Now, I appeal to the consciences of those that persecute, torment, destroy, and kill other men upon pretence of religion, whether they do it out of friendship and kindness towards them or no? And I shall then indeed, and not until then, believe they do so, when I shall see those fiery zealots correcting, in the same manner, their friends and familiar acquaintance for the manifest[7] sins they commit against the precepts of the Gospel; when I shall see them persecute with fire and sword the members of their own communion[8] that are tainted with enormous vices and without amendment are in danger of eternal perdition;[9] and when I shall see them thus express their love and desire of the salvation of their souls by the infliction of torments and exercise of all manner of cruelties. ...

The toleration of those that differ from others in matters of religion is so agreeable to[10] the Gospel of Jesus Christ, and to the genuine reason of mankind, that it seems monstrous for men to be so blind as not to perceive the necessity and advantage of it in so clear a light. I will not here tax[11] the pride and ambition of some, the passion and uncharitable zeal of others. These are faults from which human affairs can perhaps scarce[12] ever be perfectly freed; but yet such as

---

1   *professions of* Declarations of belief in.
2   *must needs* Must.

3   *Let anyone ... all these things* Despite the truth of these claims.
4   *The kings ... not be so* Luke 22.25.
5   *ecclesiastical dominion* Rule by the church.
6   *compulsive* Powerful.
7   *manifest* Obvious.
8   *communion* Religious group.
9   *perdition* Damnation.
10   *agreeable to* In harmony with.
11   *tax* Determine the extent of.
12   *scarce* Scarcely.

nobody will bear the plain imputation of, without covering them with some specious color;[1] and so pretend to[2] commendation, whilst they are carried away by their own irregular passions. But, however, that some may not color their spirit of persecution and unchristian cruelty with a pretence of care of the public weal[3] and observation of the laws; and that others, under pretence of religion, may not seek impunity[4] for their libertinism and licentiousness;[5] in a word, that none may impose either upon himself or others, by the pretences of loyalty and obedience to the prince, or of tenderness and sincerity in the worship of God; I esteem it above all things necessary to distinguish exactly the business of civil government from that of religion and to settle the just bounds that lie between the one and the other.[6] If this be not done, there can be no end put to the controversies that will be always arising between those that have, or at least pretend to have, on the one side, a concernment[7] for the interest of men's souls, and, on the other side, a care of the commonwealth.

The commonwealth seems to me to be a society of men constituted only for the procuring, preserving, and advancing their own civil interests.

Civil interests I call life, liberty, health, and indolency[8] of body; and the possession of outward things, such as money, lands, houses, furniture, and the like.

It is the duty of the civil magistrate, by the impartial execution of equal laws, to secure unto all the people in general and to every one of his subjects in particular the just possession of these things belonging to this life. If anyone presume to violate the laws of public justice and equity, established for the preservation of those things, his presump-

tion[9] is to be checked by the fear of punishment, consisting of the deprivation or diminution of those civil interests, or goods, which otherwise he might and ought to enjoy.[10] But seeing[11] no man does willingly suffer[12] himself to be punished by the deprivation of any part of his goods, and much less of his liberty or life, therefore, is the magistrate armed with the force and strength of all his subjects, in order to the punishment of those[13] that violate any other man's rights.

Now that the whole jurisdiction of the magistrate reaches only to these civil concernments, and that all civil power, right and dominion, is bounded and confined to the only care of promoting these things; and that it neither can nor ought in any manner to be extended to the salvation of souls, these following considerations seem unto me abundantly to demonstrate.

First, because the care of souls is not committed to the civil magistrate, any more than to other men. It is not committed unto him, I say, by God; because it appears not that God has ever given any such authority to one man over another as to compel anyone to his religion. Nor can any such power be vested in[14] the magistrate by the consent of the people, because no man can so far abandon the care of his own salvation as blindly to leave to the choice of any other, whether prince or subject, to prescribe to him what faith or worship he shall embrace. For no man can, if he would, conform his faith to the dictates of another. All the life and power of true religion consist in the inward and full persuasion of the mind; and faith is not faith without believing. Whatever profession we make, to whatever outward worship we conform, if we are not fully satisfied in our own mind that the one is true and the other well pleasing unto God, such profession and such practice, far from being any furtherance, are indeed great obstacles to our salvation. For in this manner, instead of expiating[15] other sins by the exercise of religion, I say, in offering thus unto God Almighty such a worship as we esteem to be displeasing unto Him, we add unto the number of our other sins those also of hypocrisy and contempt of His Divine Majesty.

---

1   *covering them with some specious color* Making them appear something they are not.
2   *pretend to* Make a dubious claim for.
3   *weal* Welfare.
4   *impunity* Freedom from punishment.
5   *libertinism and licentiousness* Living without moral restraint, especially in sexual matters.
6   *I esteem it ... the other* The beginning of this sentence means: To prevent some people from disguising their spirit of persecution and unchristian charity by pretending to be religious, and to prevent others from avoiding blame for their immoral pleasure-seeking under cover of religion—in short, so that nobody should enforce their will on others, by insincere claims of loyalty and obedience to the prince or of claiming kindness and sympathy in the worship of God—I judge that it is necessary above all....
7   *concernment* Concern.
8   *indolency* Freedom from pain; rest, ease.
9   *presumption* Arrogance.
10 *enjoy* See note about this word, which occurs frequently here, in the section called "Some Useful Background Information," in the introduction to Locke.
11 *seeing* Since.
12 *suffer* Allow.
13 *to the punishment of those* To punish those.
14 *be vested in* Be granted to.
15 *expiating* Atoning for.

In the second place, the care of souls cannot belong to the civil magistrate, because his power consists only in outward force; but true and saving religion consists in the inward persuasion of the mind, without which nothing can be acceptable to God. And such is the nature of the understanding, that it cannot be compelled to the belief of anything by outward force. Confiscation of estate, imprisonment, torments, nothing of that nature can have any such efficacy as to make men change the inward judgment that they have framed of things.

It may indeed be alleged that the magistrate may make use of arguments, and, thereby; draw the heterodox[1] into the way of truth, and procure their salvation. I grant it; but this is common to him with other men. In teaching, instructing, and redressing the erroneous by reason, he may certainly do what becomes[2] any good man to do. Magistracy[3] does not oblige him to put off either humanity or Christianity; but it is one thing to persuade, another to command; one thing to press with arguments, another with penalties. This civil power alone has a right to do; to the other, goodwill is authority enough. Every man has commission[4] to admonish, exhort, convince another of error, and, by reasoning, to draw him into truth; but to give laws, receive obedience, and compel with the sword, belongs to none but the magistrate. And, upon this ground, I affirm that the magistrate's power extends not to the establishing of any articles of faith, or forms of worship, by the force of his laws. For laws are of no force at all without penalties, and penalties in this case are absolutely impertinent,[5] because they are not proper to convince the mind. Neither the profession of any articles of faith, nor the conformity to any outward form of worship (as has been already said), can be available to the salvation of souls, unless the truth of the one and the acceptableness of the other unto God be thoroughly believed by those that so profess and practice. But penalties are no way capable to produce such belief. It is only light and evidence that can work a change in men's opinions; which light can in no manner proceed from corporal[6] sufferings, or any other outward penalties.

In the third place, the care of the salvation of men's souls cannot belong to the magistrate; because, though[7] the rigor of laws and the force of penalties were capable to convince and change men's minds, yet would not that help at all to the salvation of their souls. For there being but one truth, one way to heaven, what hope is there that more men would be led into it if they had no rule but the religion of the court and were put under the necessity to quit the light of their own reason, and oppose the dictates of their own consciences, and blindly to resign themselves up to the will of their governors and to the religion which either ignorance, ambition, or superstition had chanced to establish in the countries where they were born? In the variety and contradiction of opinions in religion, wherein the princes of the world are as much divided as in their secular interests, the narrow way would be much straitened;[8] one country alone would be in the right, and all the rest of the world put under an obligation of following their princes in the ways that lead to destruction; and that which heightens the absurdity, and very ill suits the notion of a Deity, men would owe their eternal happiness or misery to the places of their nativity.[9]

These considerations, to omit many others that might have been urged to the same purpose, seem unto me sufficient to conclude that all the power of civil government relates only to men's civil interests, is confined to the care of the things of this world, and hath nothing to do with the world to come.[10]

Let us now consider what a church is. A church, then, I take to be a voluntary society of men, joining themselves together of their own accord in order to the public worshipping of God in such manner as they judge acceptable to Him, and effectual to the salvation of their souls.

I say it is a free and voluntary society. Nobody is born a member of any church; otherwise the religion of parents would descend unto children by the same right of inheritance as their temporal[11] estates, and everyone would hold

---

1   *the heterodox*   Those disagreeing with standardly established views.
2   *becomes*   Is appropriate for.
3   *Magistracy*   Position in the executive of the government.
4   *commission*   Authority.
5   *impertinent*   Irrelevant.
6   *corporal*   Bodily.

7   *though*   Even if.
8   *much straitened*   Made much more narrow. The reference here is to Matthew 7.13–14: "Enter ye in by the narrow gate: for wide is the gate, and broad is the way, that leads to destruction, and many are they that enter in thereby. For narrow is the gate, and straitened the way, that leads unto life, and few are they that find it."
9   *nativity*   Birth.
10   *the world to come*   The afterlife.
11   *temporal*   Of this world—material as opposed to spiritual.

his faith by the same tenure[1] he does his lands, than which nothing can be imagined more absurd. Thus, therefore, that matter stands. No man by nature is bound unto any particular church or sect, but everyone joins himself voluntarily to that society in which he believes he has found that profession and worship which is truly acceptable to God. The hope of salvation, as it was the only cause of his entrance into that communion, so it can be the only reason of his stay there. For if afterwards he discover anything either erroneous in the doctrine or incongruous[2] in the worship of that society to which he has joined himself, why should it not be as free for him to go out as it was to enter? No member of a religious society can be tied with any other bonds but what proceed from the certain expectation of eternal life. A church, then, is a society of members voluntarily uniting to that end.

It follows now that we consider what is the power of this church and unto what laws it is subject.

Forasmuch as no society, however free, or upon whatsoever slight occasion instituted, whether of philosophers for learning, of merchants for commerce, or of men of leisure for mutual conversation and discourse, no church or company, I say, can in the least subsist and hold together, but will presently dissolve and break in pieces, unless it be regulated by some laws, and the members all consent to observe some order.[3] Place and time of meeting must be agreed on; rules for admitting and excluding members must be established; distinction of officers, and putting things into a regular course, and suchlike, cannot be omitted. But since the joining together of several members into this church-society, as has already been demonstrated, is absolutely free and spontaneous, it necessarily follows that the right of making its laws can belong to none but the society itself; or, at least (which is the same thing), to those whom the society by common consent has authorized thereunto.

Some, perhaps, may object that no such society can be said to be a true church unless it have in it a bishop or presbyter,[4] with ruling authority derived from the very apostles, and continued down to the present times by an uninterrupted succession.

To these I answer: In the first place, let them show me the edict by which Christ has imposed that law upon His Church. And let not any man think me impertinent, if in a thing of this consequence I require that the terms of that edict be very express and positive;[5] for the promise He has made us, that "wheresoever two or three are gathered together in His name, He will be in the midst of them,"[6] seems to imply the contrary. Whether such an assembly want anything necessary to a true church, pray do you consider.[7] Certain I am that nothing can be there wanting unto[8] the salvation of souls, which is sufficient to our purpose.

Next, pray observe how great have always been the divisions amongst even those who lay so much stress upon the Divine institution and continued succession of a certain order of rulers in the Church. Now, their very dissension unavoidably puts us upon a necessity of deliberating and, consequently, allows a liberty of choosing that which upon consideration we prefer.

And, in the last place, I consent that these men have a ruler in their church, established by such a long series of succession as they judge necessary, provided I may have liberty at the same time to join myself to that society in which I am persuaded those things are to be found which are necessary to the salvation of my soul. In this manner ecclesiastical liberty will be preserved on all sides, and no man will have a legislator imposed upon him but whom himself has chosen. ...

The end of a religious society (as has already been said) is the public worship of God and, by means thereof, the acquisition of eternal life. All discipline ought, therefore, to tend to that end, and all ecclesiastical laws to be thereunto confined. Nothing ought nor can be transacted in this society relating to the possession of civil and worldly goods. No force is here to be made use of upon any occasion whatsoever. For force belongs wholly to the civil magistrate, and the possession of all outward goods is subject to his jurisdiction. ...

---

1 *tenure* Property right.

2 *incongruous* Unsuitable.

3 *I say ... order* This sentence means: "Since no society—whether of philosophers ... merchants ... or men of leisure ... —however free it is, and no matter how trivial the reason for its organization—no church or company can last and hold together, but instead will break up, if it is not regulated...."

4 *presbyter* Church official.

5 *express and positive* Stated clearly, directly, unambiguously.

6 *wheresoever ... midst of them* Matthew 18.20.

7 *Whether such an assembly ... consider* This sentence means: "Please consider whether such a group lacks anything necessary for a true church."

8 *wanting unto* Lacking for.

Another more secret evil, but more dangerous to the commonwealth, is when men arrogate to themselves, and to those of their own sect, some peculiar prerogative covered over with a specious show of deceitful words, but in effect opposite to the civil right of the community. For example: we cannot find any sect that teaches, expressly and openly, that men are not obliged to keep their promise; that princes may be dethroned by those that differ from them in religion; or that the dominion of all things belongs only to themselves. For these things, proposed thus nakedly and plainly, would soon draw on them the eye and hand of the magistrate and awaken all the care of the commonwealth to a watchfulness against the spreading of so dangerous an evil. But, nevertheless, we find those that say the same things in other words. What else do they mean who teach that faith is not to be kept with heretics? Their meaning, forsooth, is that the privilege of breaking faith belongs unto themselves; for they declare all that are not of their communion to be heretics, or at least may declare them so whensoever they think fit. What can be the meaning of their asserting that kings excommunicated forfeit their crowns and kingdoms? It is evident that they thereby arrogate[1] unto themselves the power of deposing kings, because they challenge the power of excommunication, as the peculiar right of their hierarchy. That dominion is founded in grace is also an assertion by which those that maintain it do plainly lay claim to the possession of all things. For they are not so wanting to themselves as not to believe, or at least as not to profess themselves to be the truly pious and faithful. These, therefore, and the like, who attribute unto the faithful, religious, and orthodox, that is, in plain terms, unto themselves, any peculiar privilege or power above other mortals, in civil concernments; or who upon pretence of religion do challenge any manner of authority over such as are not associated with them in their ecclesiastical communion, I say these have no right to be tolerated by the magistrate; as neither those that will not own and teach the duty of tolerating all men in matters of mere religion. For what do all these and the like doctrines signify, but that they may and are ready upon any occasion to seize the Government and possess themselves of the estates and fortunes of their fellow subjects; and that they only ask leave to be tolerated by the magistrate so long until they find themselves strong enough to effect it?

Again: That Church can have no right to be tolerated by the magistrate which is constituted upon such a bottom that all those who enter into it do thereby *ipso facto*[2] deliver themselves up to the protection and service of another prince. For by this means the magistrate would give way to the settling of a foreign jurisdiction in his own country and suffer his own people to be listed, as it were, for soldiers against his own Government. Nor does the frivolous and fallacious distinction between the Court and the Church afford any remedy to this inconvenience; especially when both the one and the other are equally subject to the absolute authority of the same person, who has not only power to persuade the members of his Church to whatsoever he lists, either as purely religious, or in order thereunto, but can also enjoin it them on pain of eternal fire. It is ridiculous for any one to profess himself to be a Mahometan[3] only in his religion, but in everything else a faithful subject to a Christian magistrate, whilst at the same time he acknowledges himself bound to yield blind obedience to the Mufti[4] of Constantinople, who himself is entirely obedient to the Ottoman Emperor and frames the feigned oracles of that religion according to his pleasure. But this Mahometan living amongst Christians would yet more apparently renounce their government if he acknowledged the same person to be head of his Church who is the supreme magistrate in the state.

Lastly, those are not at all to be tolerated who deny the being of a God. Promises, covenants, and oaths, which are the bonds of human society, can have no hold upon an atheist. The taking away of God, though but even in thought, dissolves all; besides also, those that by their atheism undermine and destroy all religion, can have no pretence of religion whereupon to challenge the privilege of a toleration. As for other practical opinions, though not absolutely free from all error, if they do not tend to establish domination over others, or civil impunity to the Church in which they are taught, there can be no reason why they should not be tolerated.

---

1   *arrogate*   Assign illegitimately.

2   *ipso facto*   Latin: by that very fact.
3   *Mahometan*   Muslim.
4   *Mufti*   Islamic scholar who interprets Islamic law (sharia).

MARY ASTELL
(1666 – 1731)

MARY ASTELL IS NOW BEST KNOWN FOR HER FAMOUS rhetorical question in the 1706 Preface to *Some Reflections upon Marriage*: "If all men are born free, how is it that all women are born slaves?" These well-chosen words have earned her a place not only in the feminist canon, but also the Republican one, as a theorist of "freedom from domination." Prior to her recent resurrection she was best known as the author of *A Serious Proposal*, which advocates a Platonist academy for women, a project which would have attracted the support of Queen Anne, to whom it was dedicated, were it not that the ridicule to which it was subjected made it too politically risky. As a promoter of women's causes, and particularly women's education, Astell has frequently been depicted in literature: she is said to have been the model for the protagonist of Samuel Richardson's landmark novel *Clarissa*; and, as late as 1847, Lilia, of Alfred, Lord Tennyson's *The Princess*, dreams of a women's college cut off from male society, over whose gates the inscription would read, "Let no man enter on pain of death." A truncated version of the famous inscription that adorned the doors of Plato's Academy, "Let No Man Enter Here Unless He Study Mathematics," this slogan was to be famously lampooned in Gilbert and Sullivan's *Princess Ida*, also based on Astell's *Proposal*.

It is noteworthy that Astell, who has been deemed "England's First Feminist," has only recently been readmitted to the canon of philosophers and political commentators, in which she held a prominent place in the eighteenth and nineteenth centuries. The twentieth-century reception of Astell's works focuses on her proto-feminist critique of the condition of women. Her proto-feminism sits uneasily with her Anglican High Church and Tory views, however, and modern commentary on her work has rarely done justice to the full range of her thought, or treated in sufficient detail her substantive arguments.

Debate over the reception of Locke's anonymously published *Two Treatises of Government* (1690), for instance, has never given Astell her due. Her argument, in the first edition of *Some Reflections upon Marriage* (1700), that the very men who press for liberty in the public sphere are the first to exempt themselves from constraints on the exercise of their power at home, is an important anticipation of the argument mounted against the social contract theory

of "Great L—k in his *Two Discourses of Government*" by Charles Leslie in 1703. It is an argument that Astell develops in high style in her famous 1706 Preface to *Some Reflections upon Marriage*. Not only does her critique pre-date that of Leslie (having been introduced in *Some Reflections upon Marriage* as early as 1700, and also made implicitly in *A Serious Proposal, Part 2*); it is also more trenchant than his. Nor is this the only instance of Leslie receiving undue credit for ideas that originated with Astell. In *A Fair Way with the Dissenters and their Patrons* (1704), she bitterly protested against Leslie getting credit for her earlier pamphlet of that year, *Moderation truly Stated* (evidence enough, were any needed, that women in her era who were obliged to publish anonymously could often be plagiarized at will).

Astell's *Proposal* made her famous, and eventually ran to five editions. But for every George Wheler, who gave unqualified acknowledgement to Astell's influence in *A Protestant Monastery* of 1698, there were ten who stole her ideas without acknowledgement and then satirized her to cover their tracks. Gilbert Burnet (1643–1715), Bishop of Salisbury, while arguing that Astell's project was too monastic, himself proposed that, for women, "something like Monasteries without Vows ... would be a glorious design." Daniel Defoe (1661?–1731), although expressing admiration for Astell's proposal, argued against it on account of women's incorrigible levity, and then put forward his own proposal for an "Academy for Women" (1697) which differed in no significant aspects from hers. Richard Steele (1672–1729), Irish essayist, dramatist and politician, lampooned Astell in *The Tatler* as the founder of an "order of Platonick Ladies ... who ... gave out, that their Virginity was to be their State of Life during their Mortal condition, and therefore resolv'd to join their Fortunes and erect a Nunnery." Even the stage did not spare her. Susanna Centlivre (c. 1667–1723) in her play, *The Basset Table* (1706), has Valeria, "that little She-Philosopher" (doubtless modeled on Astell) "founding a College for the Study of Philosophy where none but Women should be admitted."

Astell has outlasted her critics and is now increasingly recognized as the author of perhaps the first systematic critique of Locke. Her *Some Reflections upon Marriage* (1700) presents a highly original critique of patriarchalism and contractarianism in the thought of Locke (and Hobbes).

To Locke's claim that the monarch does not have absolute sovereignty and that men have the right to rebel against tyranny, she places the analogy of the *husband's sovereignty*. Ironically, she argues *for* absolute sovereignty, both of the state and in the family. But, at the same time, she argues that women should not marry. This argument anticipates feminist critiques of the distinction between the public and private spheres, while her recommendation that women form a separate sphere and that they not marry anticipates radical feminism.

◆ ◆ ◆ ◆ ◆

Some Reflections upon Marriage (1700)

from *Preface*

These *Reflections* being made in the country, where the book that occasioned them came but late to hand,[1] the *Reader* is desired to excuse their unseasonableness[2] as well as other faults; and to believe that they have no other design than to correct some abuses, which are not the less because power and prescription[3] seem to authorize them. If any is so needlessly curious as to enquire from what hand they come,[4] they may please to know, that it is not good manners to ask, since the title-page does not tell them: we are all of us sufficiently vain, and without doubt the celebrated name of *Author*, which most are so fond of, had not been avoided but for very good reasons: To name but one; *who will care to pull upon themselves a hornet's nest?* 'Tis a very great fault to regard rather who it is that speaks, than what is spoken; and either to submit to authority, when we should only yield to reason; or if reason press too hard, to think to ward it off by personal objections and reflections. Bold truths may pass while the speaker is *incognito*,[5] but are not endured when he is known; few minds being strong enough to bear what

contradicts their principles and practices without recriminating[6] when they can. And though to tell the truth be the most friendly office,[7] yet whosoever is so hardy as to venture at it, shall be counted an enemy for so doing.

Thus far the old Advertisement, when the Reflections first appeared, A.D. 1700.

But the Reflector[8] who hopes Reflector is not bad English, now governor is happily of the feminine gender,[9] had as good or better have said nothing; for people by being forbid, are only excited to a more curious enquiry. A certain ingenious gentleman (as she is informed) had the good-nature to own these Reflections, so far as to affirm that he had the original ms.[10] in his closet, a proof she is not able to produce; and so to make himself responsible for all their faults, for which she returns him all due acknowledgment. However, the generality being of opinion, that a man would have had more prudence and manners than to have published such unseasonable truths, or to have betrayed the *arcana imperii*[11] of his sex, she humbly confesses, that the contrivance[12] and execution of this design, which is unfortunately accused of being so destructive to the government, of the men I mean, is entirely her own. She neither advised with friends, nor turned over ancient or modern authors, nor prudently submitted to the correction of such as are, or such as think they are good judges, but with an English spirit and genius, set out upon the forlorn hope,[13] meaning no hurt to any body, nor designing any thing but the public good, and to retrieve, if possible, the native liberty, the rights and privileges of the subject.[14]

Far be it from her to stir up sedition of any sort, none can abhor it more; and she heartily wishes that our masters would pay their civil and ecclesiastical governors the same submission, which they themselves exact from their domestic subjects. Nor can she imagine how she any way undermines the masculine empire, or blows the trumpet of rebellion to the moiety[15] of mankind. Is it by exhorting women, not to expect to have their own will in any thing,

---

1   *the book ... late to hand*   This is one of a number of references in this excerpt to writers and books that Astell has left unidentified. An impressive job of locating their sources has been done by Patricia Springborg, editor of the definitive collection of Astell's work, *Political Writings*, 1996.
2   *unseasonableness*   Unsuitability, inappropriateness.
3   *prescription*   Long-standing custom, regarded as authoritative.
4   *from what hand they come*   Who wrote them.
5   *incognito*   With disguised identity.

6   *recriminating*   Accusing the accuser.
7   *friendly office*   Helpful, kindly service.
8   *Reflector*   Astell means herself.
9   *governor ... feminine gender*   Because the ruler of England was then female.
10   *ms.*   Manuscript.
11   *arcana imperii*   Latin: state secrets.
12   *contrivance*   Plotting.
13   *forlorn hope*   A dangerous or hopeless venture.
14   *subject*   Citizen in a monarchy.
15   *the moiety*   Half.

but to be entirely submissive, when once they have made choice of a lord and master, though he happen not to be so wise, so kind, or even so just a governor as was expected? She did not indeed advise them to think his folly wisdom, nor his brutality that love and worship he promised in his matrimonial oath, for this required a flight of wit and sense much above her poor ability, and proper only to masculine understandings. However she did not in any manner prompt them to resist, or to abdicate[1] the perjured spouse, though, the laws of God and the land make special provision for it, in a case wherein, as is to be feared, few men can truly plead not guilty.

'Tis true, through want of learning, and of that superior genius which men as men lay claim to, she was ignorant of the natural inferiority of our sex, which our masters lay down as a self-evident and fundamental truth. She saw nothing in the reason of things, to make this either a principle or a conclusion, but much to the contrary; it being sedition at least, if not treason to assert it in this reign.[2] For if by the natural superiority of their sex, they mean that *every* man is by nature superior to *every* woman, which is the obvious meaning, and that which must be stuck to if they would speak sense, it would be a sin in *any* woman to have dominion over *any* man, and the greatest queen ought not to command but to obey her footman, because no municipal laws can supersede or change the law of nature; so that if the dominion of the men be such, the *Salique Law*[3] as unjust as English men have ever thought it, ought to take place over all the Earth, and the most glorious reigns in the English, Danish, Castilian, and other annals,[4] were wicked violations of the law of nature!

If they mean that *some* men are superior to *some* women this is no great discovery; had they turned the tables they might have seen that *some* women are superior to *some* men. Or had they been pleased to remember their Oaths of Allegiance and Supremacy,[5] they might have known that *one*

woman is superior to *all* the men in these nations, or else they have sworn to very little purpose. And it must not be supposed, that their reason and religion would suffer them to take oaths, contrary to the law of nature and reason of things.

By all which it appears, that our Reflector's ignorance is very pitiable, it may be her misfortune but not her crime, especially since she is willing to be better informed, and hopes she shall never be so obstinate as to shut her eyes against the light of truth, which is not to be charged with novelty, how late soever we may be blessed with the discovery. Nor can error, be it as ancient as it may, ever plead prescription against truth. And since the only way to remove all doubts, to answer all objections, and to give the mind entire satisfaction, is not by *affirming*, but by *proving*, so that every one may see with their own eyes, and judge according to the best of their *own* understandings, she hopes it is no presumption to insist on this natural right of judging for her self, and the rather, because by quitting it, we give up all the means of rational conviction. Allow us then as many glasses as you please to help our sight, and as many good arguments as you can afford to convince our understandings: But don't exact of us we beseech you, to affirm that we see such things as are only the discovery of men who have quicker senses; or that we understand and know what we have by hear-say only; for to be so excessively complaisant is neither to see nor to understand.

That the custom of the world has put women, generally speaking, into a state of subjection, is not denied; but the right can no more be proved from the fact, than the predominancy of vice can justify it. A certain great man has endeavored to prove by reasons not contemptible, that in the original state of things the woman was the superior, and that her subjection to the man is an effect of the Fall,[6] and the punishment of her sin. And that ingenious theorist Mr. Whiston asserts, that before the Fall there was a greater equality between the two sexes. However this be 'tis certainly no arrogance in a woman to conclude, that she was made for the service of God, and that this is her end. Because God made all things for Himself, and a rational mind is too noble a being to be made for the sake and service of any creature. The service she at any time becomes obliged to pay to a man, is only a business by the bye.[7] Just as it may be any man's business and duty to keep hogs; he was not made for this, but if he hires himself out to such an employment,

---

1   *abdicate*   Cut (themselves) off from.

2   *in this reign*   Here (or now).

3   *Salique Law*   The Salic Law was a wide-ranging code of laws originating in sixth-century France and important in various ways thereafter; its most famous and influential provision, to which Astell refers here, was the prohibiting of a female occupying the throne.

4   *annals*   Histories. Elizabeth I of England, Margaret I of Denmark, and Isabella I of Castile were all acknowledged to have been among the most important monarchs in their respective nations' histories.

5   *Oaths of Allegiance and Supremacy*   Oaths sworn to the Queen.

---

6   *Fall*   The original sin committed by Adam and Eve in the Christian tradition.

7   *business by the bye*   Matter of secondary importance.

he ought conscientiously to perform it. Nor can anything be concluded to the contrary from St. Paul's argument, 1 Corinthians 11. For he argues only for decency and order, according to the present custom and state of things. Taking his words strictly and literally, they prove too much, in that praying and prophesying in the Church are allowed the women, provided they do it with their head covered, as well as the men; and no inequality can be inferred from hence, neither from the gradation the Apostle there uses, that "the head of every man is Christ, and that the head of the woman is the man, and the head of Christ is God,"[1] It being evident from the Form of baptism, that there is no natural inferiority among the Divine Persons, but that they are in all things coequal. The Apostle indeed adds, that "the man is the glory of God, and the woman the glory of the man,"[2] etc. But what does he infer from hence? he says not a word of inequality, or natural inferiority, but concludes, that a woman ought to cover her head, and a man ought not to cover his, and that "even nature itself teaches" us, that "if a man have long hair it is a shame unto him."[3]

Whatever the Apostle's argument proves in this place nothing can be plainer, than that there is much more said against the present fashion of men's wearing long hair, than for that supremacy they lay claim to. For by all that appears in the text, it is not so much a law of nature, that women should obey men, as that men should not wear long hair. Now how can a Christian nation allow fashions contrary to the law of nature, forbidden by an Apostle and declared by him to be a shame to man? Or if custom may make an alteration in one case it may in another, but what then becomes of the nature and reason of things? Besides, the conclusion the Apostle draws from his argument concerning women, viz.[4] that they "should have power on their heads because of the angels"[5] is so very obscure a text, that that ingenious paraphrast who pleads so much for the natural subjection of women, ingenuously confesses, that he does not understand it. Probably it refers to some custom among the Corinthians, which being well known to them the Apostle only hints at it, but which we are ignorant of, and therefore apt to mistake him. 'Tis like that the false Apostle whom St. Paul writes against had led *captive* some of their

rich and powerful but silly women[6] who having as mean an opinion of the reason God had given them, as any deceiver could desire, did not like the noble minded Bereans, search the Scriptures whether those things were so,[7] but lazily took up with having men's persons in admiration, and followed their leaders blindfold, the certain rout to destruction. And it is also probable that the same cunning seducer, employed these women to carry on his own designs and putting them upon what he might not think fit to appear in himself, made them guilty of indecent behavior in the church of Corinth. And therefore St. Paul thought it necessary to reprove them so severely in order to humble them, but this being done, he takes care in the conclusion to set the matter on a right foot, placing the two sexes on a level, to keep men as much as might be, from taking those advantages which people who have strength in their hands, are apt to assume over those who can't contend with them. For, says he, nevertheless, or notwithstanding the former argument, the man is not without the woman, nor the woman without the man, but all things of God.[8] The relation between the two sexes is mutual, and the dependence reciprocal, both of them depending entirely upon God, and upon Him only; which one would think is no great argument of the natural inferiority of either sex.

Our Reflector is of opinion that disputes of this kind, extending to human nature in general, and not peculiar to those to whom the Word of God has been revealed, ought to be decided by natural reason only. And that the Holy Scriptures should not be interested[9] in the present controversy, in which it determines nothing, any more than it does between the Copernican and Ptolomean systems. The design of those holy Books being to make us excellent moralists and perfect Christians, not great philosophers. And being writ for the vulgar as well as for the learned, they are accommodated to the common way of speech and the usage of the world; in which we have but a short probation,[10] so that it matters not much what part we act, whether of governing or obeying, provided we perform it well with respect to the world to come.

One does not wonder indeed, that when an adversary is driven to a nonplus[11] and reason declares against him, he

---

1 *the head ... God* 1 Corinthians 11.3.
2 *the man ... the man* 1 Corinthians 11.7.
3 *even nature ... shame unto him* 1 Corinthians 11.14.
4 *viz.* Namely.
5 *should have power ... angels* 1 Corinthians 11.10.

6 *false Apostle ... silly women* See 2 Timothy 3.6.
7 *as mean an opinion ... things were so* See Acts 17.11.
8 *the man is not ... things of God* 1 Corinthians 11.11–12.
9 *interested* Involved.
10 *probation* Trial period.
11 *nonplus* State of confusion.

flies to authority, especially to divine, which is infallible, and therefore ought not to be disputed. But Scripture is not always on their side who make parade[1] of it, and through their skill in languages and the tricks of the Schools,[2] wrest it from its genuine sense to their own inventions. And supposing, not granting, that it were apparently to the woman's disadvantage, no fair and generous adversary but would be ashamed to urge this advantage. Because women without their own fault, are kept in ignorance of the original, wanting languages and other helps to criticize on the sacred text, of which they know no more, than men are pleased to impart in their translations. In short, they show their desire to maintain their hypotheses, but by no means their reverence to the sacred oracles who engage them in such disputes. And therefore the blame be theirs, who have unnecessarily introduced them in the present subject, and who by saying that the *Reflections* were not agreeable to Scripture, oblige the Reflector to show that those who affirm it must either mistake her meaning, or the sense of Holy Scripture, or both, if they think what they say, and do not find fault merely because they resolve to do so. For had she ever writ any thing contrary to those sacred truths, she would be the first in pronouncing its condemnation.

But what says the Holy Scripture? It speaks of women as in a state of subjection, and so it does of the Jews and Christians when under the dominion of the Chaldeans[3] and Romans, requiring of the one as well as of the other a quiet submission to them under whose power they lived. But will anyone say that these had a natural superiority and right to dominion? that they had a superior understanding, or any pre-eminence, except what their greater strength acquired? Or that the other were subjected to their adversaries for any other reason but the punishment of their sins, and in order to their reformation? Or for the exercise of their virtue, and because the order of the world and the good of society required it?

If mankind had never sinned, reason would always have been obeyed, there would have been no struggle for dominion, and brutal power would not have prevailed. But in the lapsed state of mankind,[4] and now that men will not be guided by their reason but by their appetites, and do not what they *ought* but what they *can*, the reason, or that which stands for it, the will and pleasure of the governor is to be the reason of those who will not be guided by their own, and must take place for order's sake, although it should not be conformable to right reason. Nor can there be any society great or little, from empires down to private families, without a last resort, to determine the affairs of that society by an irresistible sentence.[5] Now unless this supremacy be fixed somewhere, there will be a perpetual contention about it, such is the love of dominion, and let the reason of things be what it may, those who have least force, or cunning to supply it, will have the disadvantage. So that since women are acknowledged to have least bodily strength, their being commanded to obey is in pure kindness to them and for their quiet and security, as well as for the exercise of their virtue. But does it follow that domestic governors have more sense than their subjects, any more than that other governors have? We do not find that any man thinks the worse of his own understanding because another has superior power; or concludes himself less capable of a post of honor and authority, because he is not preferred[6] to it. How much time would lie on men's hands, how empty would the places of concourse[7] be, and how silent most companies[8] did men forbear to censure their governors, that is in effect to think themselves wiser. Indeed government would be much more desirable than it is, did it invest the possessor with a superior understanding as well as power. And if mere power gives a right to rule, there can be no such thing as usurpation; but a highway-man so long as he has strength to force, has also a right to require our obedience.

Again, if absolute sovereignty be not necessary in a state, how comes it to be so in a family? or if in a family why not in a state; since no reason can be alleged for the one that will not hold more strongly for the other? If the authority of the husband so far as it extends, is sacred and inalienable, why not of the prince? The domestic sovereign is without dispute elected, and the stipulations and contract are mutual, is it not then partial in men to the last degree, to contend for, and practice that arbitrary dominion in their families, which they abhor and exclaim against in the state? For if arbitrary power is evil in itself, and an improper

---

1   *parade*   A display.
2   *Schools*   The medieval universities, where, according to a common view, scholarship was "scholastic"—dogmatic, church-dominated, pedantic, conservative.
3   *Chaldeans*   The ancient Babylonians, who, in the Old Testament, held the Jews in captivity.
4   *lapsed state of mankind*   State of sin, resulting from Adam and Eve's original one.

---

5   *Nor can there ... irresistible sentence*   I.e., every group can be governed by somebody's decision.
6   *preferred*   Promoted to it.
7   *concourse*   Public gathering.
8   *companies*   Gatherings of people.

method of governing rational and free agents it ought not to be practiced any where; nor is it less, but rather more mischievous in families than in kingdoms, by how much 100,000 tyrants are worse than one. What though a husband can't deprive a wife of life without being responsible to the law, he may however do what is much more grievous to a generous mind, render life miserable, for which she has no redress, scarce pity which is afforded to every other complainant. It being thought a wife's duty to suffer everything without complaint. If all men are born free, how is it that all women are born slaves, as they must be if being subjected to the inconstant, uncertain, unknown, arbitrary will of men, be the perfect condition of slavery, and if the essence of freedom consists, as our masters say it does, in having a standing rule to live by? And why is slavery so much condemned and strove against in one case, and so highly applauded and held so necessary and so sacred in another?

'Tis true that God told Eve after the Fall that her husband should rule over her:[1] And so it is that he told Esau by the mouth of Isaac his father, that he should serve his younger brother, and should in time, and when he was strong enough to do it, break the yoke from off his neck.[2] Now why one text should be a command any more than the other, and not both of them be predictions only; or why the former should prove Adam's natural right to rule, and much less every man's, any more than the latter is a proof of Jacob's right to rule, and of Esau's to rebel, one is yet to learn? The text in both cases foretelling what would be; but, in neither of them determining what ought to be.

But the Scripture commands wives to submit themselves to their own husbands. True; for which St. Paul gives a mystical reason (Eph 5.22, etc.) and St. Peter a prudential and charitable one (1 St. Pet. 3.) but neither of them derive that subjection from the law of nature. Nay St. Paul, as if he foresaw and meant to prevent this plea, giving directions for their conduct to women in general, 1 Tim. 2, when he comes to speak of subjection, he changes his phrase from women, which denotes the whole sex, to woman, which in the New Testament is appropriated to a wife.

As for his not suffering[3] women to speak in the church, no sober person that I know of pretends to it.[4] That learned paraphrast indeed, who lays so much stress on the natural

subjection, provided this prerogative[5] be secured, is willing to give up the other.[6] For he endeavors to prove that inspired women as well as men used to speak in the church, and that St. Paul does not forbid it, but only takes care that the women should signify their subjection by wearing a veil. But the Apostle is his own best expositor,[7] let us therefore compare his precepts with his practice, for he was all of a piece, and did not contradict himself. Now by this comparison we find, that though he forbids women to teach in the church, and this for several prudential reasons, like those he introduces with an *I give my opinion, and now speak I not the Lord*, and not because of any law of nature, or positive[8] divine precept, for that the words *they are commanded* (1 Cor.14.34.) are not in the original, appears from the italic character,[9] yet he did not found this prohibition on any supposed want of understanding in woman, or of ability to teach; neither does he confine them at all times to learn in silence. For the eloquent Apollos who was himself a teacher, was instructed by Priscilla as well as by her husband Aquila, and was improved by them both in the Christian faith.[10] Nor does St. Paul blame her for this, or suppose that she usurped authority over that great man, so far from this, that as she is always honorably mentioned in Holy Scripture, so our Apostle in his salutations, Rom. 16 places her in the front, even before her husband, giving to her as well as to him, the noble title of his helper in Christ Jesus, and of one to whom all the churches of the Gentiles had great obligations.[11]

But it will be said perhaps, that in 1 Tim. 2.13, etc. St. Paul argues for the woman's subjection from the reason of things. To this I answer, that it must be confessed that this (according to the vulgar interpretation) is a very obscure place, and I should be glad to see a natural, and not a forced interpretation given of it by those who take it literally. Whereas if it be taken allegorically, with respect to the mystical union between Christ and his Church, to

---

1 *her husband ... rule over her* Genesis 3.16.
2 *break the yoke ... neck* Genesis 27.40.
3 *suffering* Allowing.
4 *pretends to it* Makes that claim.
5 *prerogative* Privilege.
6 *That learned paraphrast ... give up the other* Astell means that the "paraphrast" is willing to give up the claim that women not be allowed to speak in the church, provided that their "natural subjection" is allowed.
7 *expositor* Commentator on what is meant.
8 *positive* Explicit.
9 *italic character* It was customary to insert passages into translations of the Bible, printed in italics, which were not translations of the original, but were rather added by translators to make clear what they took the sense of the original to be.
10 *For the eloquent Apollos ... Christian faith* Acts 18.24–26.
11 *Rom. 16 ... obligations* Romans 16.3–4.

which St. Paul frequently accommodates the matrimonial relation, the difficulties vanish. For the earthly Adam's being formed before Eve, seems as little to prove her natural subjection to him, as the living creatures, fishes, birds and beasts being formed before them both, proves that mankind must be subject to these animals. Nor can the Apostle mean that Eve only sinned; or that she only was deceived, for if Adam sinned willfully and knowingly, he became the greater transgressor. But it is very true that the second Adam, the man Christ Jesus, was first formed, and then his spouse the Church. He was not in any respect deceived, nor does she pretend to infallibility. And from this second Adam, promised to Eve in the day of our first parent's transgression, and from Him only, do all their race, men as well as women, derive their hopes of salvation. Nor is it promised to either sex on any other terms besides perseverance in faith, charity, holiness and sobriety.

If the learned will not admit of this interpretation I know not how to contend with them. For sense is a portion that God Himself has been pleased to distribute to both sexes with an impartial hand, but learning is what men have engrossed to themselves, and one can't but admire their great improvements! For after doubting whether there was such a thing as truth, and after many hundred years disputes about it, in the last century an extraordinary genius arose, (whom yet some are pleased to call a visionary) enquired after it, and laid down the best method of finding it. Not to the general liking of the men of letters, perhaps, because it was wrote in a vulgar language, and was so natural and easy as to debase truth to common understandings, showing too plainly that learning and true knowledge are two very different things. "For it often happens," (says that author), "that women and children acknowledge the falsehood of those prejudices we contend with, because they do not dare to judge without examination, and they bring all the attention they are capable of to what they read. Whereas on the contrary, the learned continue wedded to their own opinions, because they will not take the trouble of examining what is contrary to their received doctrines."

Sciences indeed have been invented and taught long ago, and, as men grew better advised, new modeled. So that it is become a considerable piece of learning to give an account of the rise and progress of the sciences, and of the various opinions of men concerning them. But certainty and demonstration are much pretended to in this present age, and being obtained in many things, 'tis hoped men will never dispute them away in that which is of greatest

importance, the way of salvation. And because there is not any thing more certain than what is delivered in the oracles of God, we come now to consider what they offer in favor of our sex.

Let it be premised,[1] (according to the reasoning of a very ingenious person in a like case) that one text for us, is more to be regarded than many against us. Because that one being different from what custom has established, ought to be taken with philosophical strictness; whereas the many being expressed according to the vulgar mode of speech, ought to have no greater stress laid on them, than that evident condescension[2] will bear. One place then were sufficient, but we have many instances wherein Holy Scripture considers women very differently from what they appear in the common prejudices of mankind....

[Here Astell provides lengthy analyses of several biblical presentations of women and argues that one need not interpret the Bible as advocating the subordination of women.]

The world will hardly allow a woman to say any thing well, unless as she borrows it from men, or is assisted by them: But God Himself allows that the Daughters of Zelophehad spake right, and passes their request into a law.[3] Considering how much the tyranny shall I say, or the superior force of men, keeps women from acting in the world, or doing any thing considerable, and remembering withal the conciseness of the sacred story, no small part of it is bestowed in transmitting the history of women famous in their generations: Two of the Canonical Books[4] bearing the names of those great women whose virtues and actions are there recorded. Ruth being called from among the Gentiles to be an ancestor of the Messiah, and Esther being raised up by God to be the great instrument of the deliverance and prosperity of the Jewish Church.

The character of Isaac, though one of the most blameless men taken notice of in the Old Testament, must give place to Rebecca's, whose affections are more reasonably placed than his, her favorite son being the same who was God's favorite. Nor was the blessing bestowed according to

---

1   *premised*   Assumed for the purposes of argument.
2   *condescension*   Descent to something unworthy.
3   *But God Himself ... law*   Numbers 27.2.
4   *Canonical Books*   Those books of the Bible officially considered to give a true account of divine revelation of history. Some bibles, including the King James version of 1611, include the *apocrypha* (Greek: hidden), non-canonical texts whose authenticity is questioned.

his but to her desire; so that if you will not allow, that her command to Jacob superseded Isaac's to Esau, his desire to give the blessing to this son, being evidently an effect of his partiality:[1] you must at least grant that she paid greater deference to the Divine Revelation, and for this reason at least, had a right to oppose her husband's design; which it seems Isaac was sensible of when upon his disappointment he "trembled so exceedingly."[2] And so much notice is taken even of Rebecca's nurse that we have an account where she died and where she was buried.[3]

God is pleased to record it among His favors to the ungrateful Jews, that He sent before them His servants Moses, Aaron, and Miriam; who was also a prophetess, and instructed the women how to bear their part with Moses in his triumphal hymn. Is she to be blamed for her ambition? and is not the High Priest Aaron also [to blame], who has his share in the reproof as well as in the crime? Nor could she have moved[4] sedition if she had not been a considerable person, which appears also by the respect the people paid her, in deferring their journey till she was ready.[5]

Where shall we find a nobler piece of poetry than Deborah's Song? or a better and greater ruler than that re-nowned woman whose government so much excelled that of the former judges? And though she had a husband, she herself judged Israel and consequently was his sovereign, of whom we know no more than the name.[6] Which instance, as I humbly suppose, overthrows the pretence of natural inferiority. For it is not the bare relation of a fact, by which none ought to be concluded, unless it is conformable to a rule, and to the reason of things: But Deborah's govern-ment was conferred on her by God Himself. Consequently the sovereignty of a woman is not contrary to the law of nature; for the law of nature is the law of God, who cannot contradict Himself; and yet it was God who inspired and approved that great woman, raising her up to judge and to deliver His people Israel.

Not to insist on the courage of that valiant woman who delivered Thebez by slaying the assailant;[7] nor upon the preference which God thought fit to give to Sampson's mother, in sending the angel to her, and not to her hus-band, whose vulgar fear she so prudently answered, as plainly shows her superior understanding:[8] to pass over Abigail's wise conduct, whereby she preserved her family and deserved David's acknowledgments, for restraining him from doing a rash and unjustifiable action; the holy penman giving her the character of a woman of good understanding, whilst her husband has that of a churlish[9] and foolish per-son, and a son of Belial:[10] to say nothing of the wise *woman* (as the text calls her) of Tekoah;[11] or of her of Abel who has the same epithet,[12] and who by her prudence delivered the city and appeased a dangerous rebellion:[13] Nor of the Queen of Sheba whose journey to hear the wisdom of Solomon, shows her own good judgment and great share in that excel-lent endowment![14] Solomon does not think himself too wise to be instructed by his mother, nor too great to record her lessons, which if he had followed he might have spared the trouble of repentance, and been delivered from a great deal of that vanity he so deeply regrets.[15]

What reason can be assigned why the mothers of the kings of Judah are so frequently noted in those very short accounts that are given of their reigns, but not the great respect paid them, or perhaps their influence on the govern-ment, and share in the administrations. This is not improb-able, since the wicked Athaliah had power to carry on her intrigues so far as to get possession of the throne, and to keep it for some years.[16] Neither was there any necessity for Asa's removing his mother (or grandmother) from being queen, if this were merely titular, and did not carry power and author-ity along with it![17] And we find what influence Jezabel had in Israel, indeed to her husband's and her own destruction.[18]

It was a widow-woman whom God made choice of to sustain his Prophet Elijah at Zarephah![19] And the history of the Shunamite is a noble instance of the account that is made of women in Holy Scripture. For whether it was not the custom in Shunem for the husband to dictate, or

---

1   *partiality* Preference.
2   *Isaac ... trembled so exceedingly* Genesis 25, 26, 27.
3   *Rebecca's nurse ... buried* Genesis 24.59 and 35.8.
4   *moved* Promoted.
5   *Nor could she ... she was ready* Numbers 12.
6   *she herself ... name* Judges 4 and 5.
7   *valiant woman ... assailant* Judges 9.53.
8   *preference which God ... understanding* Judges 13.
9   *churlish* Crass, unkind, grumpy.
10 *Abigail's wise conduct ... son of Belial* 1 Samuel 25.
11 *wise* woman ... *Tekoah* 2 Samuel 14.
12 *epithet* Descriptive term attached to one's name.
13 *her of Abel ... rebellion* 2 Samuel 20.16–22.
14 *Queen of Sheba ... endowment* 1 Kings 10.
15 *Solomon does not ... regrets* 1 Kings 2.
16 *wicked Athaliah ... years* 2 Kings 8.25–11.16.
17 *Asa's removing ... along with it* 1 Kings 15.13.
18 *what influence Jezabel ... destruction* 1 Kings 16.31–33; 18.4; 19.2; 21.
19 *widow-woman ... Zarephah* 1 Kings 17.9.

whether hers was conscious of her superior virtue, or whatever was the reason, we find it is she who governs, dwelling with great honor and satisfaction among her own people. Which happiness she understood so well, and was so far from a troublesome ambition, that she desires no recommendation to the king or Captain of the Host when the prophet offered it, being already greater than they could make her. The text calls her a great woman, whilst her husband is hardly taken notice of, and this no otherwise than as performing the office of a bailiff.[1] It is *her* piety and hospitality that are recorded, *she* invites the prophet to *her house*; who converses with and is entertained by *her*. She gives her husband no account of *her* affairs any further than to tell him *her* designs that he may see them executed. And when he desires to know the reason of her conduct, all the answer she affords is, "well," or as the margin has it from the Hebrew, "peace."[2] Nor can this be thought assuming, since it is no more than what the prophet encourages, for all his addresses are to *her*, he takes no notice of her husband. His benefits are conferred on *her*, 'tis *she* and *her household* whom he warns of a famine, and 'tis *she* who appeals to the king for the restitution of *her house and land*.[3] I would not infer from hence that women generally speaking, ought to govern in their families when they have a husband, but I think this instance and example is a sufficient proof, that if by custom or contract, or the laws of the country, or birth-right (as in the case of sovereign princesses) they have the supreme authority, it is no usurpation, nor do they act contrary to Holy Scripture, nor consequently to the law of nature. For they are no where that I know of forbidden to claim their just right: the Apostle 'tis true would not have them usurp authority where custom and the law of the strongest had brought them into subjection, as it has in these parts of the world. Though in remoter regions, if travelers rightly inform us, the succession to the Crown is entailed on the female line.

God Himself who is no respecter of persons, with whom there is neither bond nor free, male nor female, but they are all one in Christ Jesus, did not deny women that divine gift the spirit of prophecy, neither under the Jewish nor Christian dispensation. We have named two great prophetesses already, Min'am and Deborah, and besides other instances, Huldah the prophetess was such an oracle that the good king Josiah, that great pattern of virtue, sends even the High Priest himself to consult her, and to receive directions from her in the most arduous affairs.[4] "It shall come to pass," saith the Lord, "that I will pour out my spirit upon all flesh, and your sons and your daughters shall prophesy,"[5] which was accordingly fulfilled by the mission of the Holy Ghost on the day of Pentecost, as St. Peter tells us. And besides others, there is mention of four daughters of Philip, virgins who did prophesy.[6] For as in the Old, so in the New Testament, women make a considerable figure; the Holy Virgin receiving the greatest honor that human nature is capable of, when the Son of God vouchsafed to be her Son and to derive his humanity from her only. And if it is a greater blessing to hear the Word of God and keep it, who are more considerable for their assiduity[7] in this than the female disciples of our Lord? Mary being exemplary and receiving a noble encomium[8] from Him, for her choice of the better part.

It would be thought tedious to enumerate all the excellent women mentioned in the New Testament, whose humble penitence and ardent love, as Magdalen's; their lively faith and holy importunity, as the Syrophenician's;[9] extraordinary piety and uprightness, as Elizabeth's;[10] hospitality, charity and diligence, as Martha's,[11] Tabitha's;[12] etc. (see St. Luc. 8)[13] frequent and assiduous devotions and austerities, as Anna's;[14] constancy and courage, perseverance and ardent zeal, as that of the holy women who attended our Lord to His Cross, when His disciples generally forsook, and the most courageous had denied Him; are recorded for our example. Their love was stronger than death, it followed our Savior into the grave. And as a reward, both the angel and even the Lord Himself appears first to them, and sends them to preach the great article of the resurrection to the very apostles, who being as yet under the power of the prejudices of their sex, esteemed the holy women's words as idle tales and believed them not.[15]

---

1   *bailiff*   Minor legal official.
2   *the Shunamite ... peace*   2 Kings 4.
3   *she and her household ... land*   2 Kings 8.1–6.
4   *Huldah ... affairs*   2 Kings 22.14.
5   *It shall come ... prophesy*   Joel 2.28.
6   *four daughters ... prophesy*   Acts 21.9.
7   *assiduity*   Great care and attention.
8   *encomium*   Statement of high praise.
9   *Syrophenician*   Mark 7.25–30.
10   *Elizabeth*   Luke 1.5–80.
11   *Martha*   Luke 10.38–42.
12   *Tabitha*   Acts 9.36–42.
13   *(see St. Luc. 8)*   Astell's reference is incorrect. The correct citation has been inserted in the next note.
14   *Anna*   Luke 2.36–38.
15   *apostles ... believed them not*   Luke 24.11.

Some men will have it, that the reason of our Lord's appearing first to the women, was their being least able to keep a secret; a witty and masculine remark and wonderfully reverent! But not to dispute whether those women were blabs[1] or no, there are many instances in Holy Scripture of women who did not betray the confidence reposed in them. Thus Rahab though formerly an ill woman, being converted by the report of those miracles, which though the Israelites saw, yet they believed not in God, nor put their trust in his word, she acknowledges the God of Heaven, and as a reward of her faithful service in concealing Joshua's spies, is with her family exempted from the ruin of her country, and also has the honor of being named in the Messiah's genealogy.[2] Michal to save David's life exposes herself to the fury of a jealous and tyrannical prince.[3] A girl was trusted by David's grave councilors to convey him intelligence in his son's rebellion; and when a lad had found it out and blabbed it to Absalom, the king's friends confiding in the prudence and fidelity of a woman were secured by her.[4] When our Lord escaped from the Jews, he trusted Himself in the hands of Martha and Mary.[5] So does St. Peter with another Mary when the angel delivered him from Herod, the damsel Rhoda too was acquainted with the secret.[6] More might be said, but one would think here is enough to show, that whatever other great and wise reasons men may have for despising women, and keeping them in ignorance and slavery, it can't be from their having learnt to do so in Holy Scripture. The Bible is for, and not against us, and cannot, without great violence done to it, be urged to our prejudice.

However, there are strong and prevalent reasons which demonstrate the superiority and pre-eminence of the men. For in the first place, boys have much time and pains, care and cost bestowed on their education; girls have little or none. The former are early initiated in the sciences, are made acquainted with ancient and modern discoveries, they study books and men, have all imaginable encouragement; not only fame (a dry reward nowadays), but also title, authority, power, and riches themselves which purchase all things, are the reward of their improvement. The latter are restrained, frowned upon, and beat, not for but from the Muses;[7] laughter and ridicule that never-failing scarecrow is set up to drive them from the Tree of Knowledge. But if in spite of all difficulties nature prevails, and they can't be kept so ignorant as their masters would have them, they are stared upon as monsters, censured, envied, and every way discouraged, or at the best they have the fate the proverb assigns them, virtue is praised and starved. And therefore since the coarsest materials need the most curing,[8] as every workman can inform you, and the worst ground the most elaborate culture, it undeniably follows, that men's understandings are superior to women's, for after many years study and experience they become wise and learned, and women are not born so!

Again, men are possessed of all places of power, trust and profit, they make laws and exercise the magistracy, not only the sharpest sword, but even all the swords and blunderbusses[9] are theirs, which by the strongest logic in the world, gives them the best title to every thing they please to claim as their prerogative; who shall contend with them? Immemorial prescription is on their side in these parts of the world, ancient tradition and modern usage! Our fathers have all along both taught and practiced superiority over the weaker sex, and consequently women are by nature inferior to men, as was to be demonstrated. An argument which must be acknowledged unanswerable, for as well as I love my sex, I will not pretend a reply to such demonstration!

Only let me beg to be informed, to whom we poor fatherless maids, and widows who have lost their masters, owe subjection? It can't be to all men in general, unless all men were agreed to give the same commands; do we then fall as strays to the first who finds us? By the maxims of some men, and the conduct of some women one would think so. But whoever he be that thus happens to become our master, if he allows us to be reasonable creatures, and does not merely compliment us with that title, since no man denies our readiness to use our tongues, it would tend, I should think, to our master's advantage, and therefore he may please to be advised to teach us to improve our reason. But if reason is only allowed us by way of raillery, and the secret maxim is that we have none, or little more than

---

1 *blabs* Persons without sufficient control over what they say.
2 *Rahab ... genealogy* Joshua 2 and 6.22–5.
3 *Michal ... prince* 2 Samuel 3.
4 *A girl ... secured by her* 2 Samuel 17.17–20.
5 *When our Lord ... Mary* Luke 10.38 and 39.
6 *St. Peter ... secret* Acts 12.12–14.
7 *not for but from the Muses* The Muses were Greek goddesses personifying inspiration in the arts; Astell means here that women are chastised not for the sake of encouraging artistic achievement, but for discouraging it.
8 *curing* Technique for preservation, for example of tobacco or leather.
9 *blunderbusses* Seventeenth-century guns.

brutes, 'tis the best way to confine us with chain and block to the chimney-corner,[1] which probably might save the estates of some families and the honor of others.

I do not propose this to prevent a rebellion, for women are not so well united as to form an insurrection. They are for the most part wise enough to love their chains, and to discern how very becomingly they set. They think as humbly of themselves as their masters can wish, with respect to the other sex, but in regard to their own, they have a spice of masculine ambition, every one would lead, and none will follow. Both sexes being too apt to envy, and too backward in emulating, and take more delight in detracting from their neighbor's virtue than in improving their own. And therefore as to those women who find themselves born for slavery and are so sensible of their own meanness[2] as to conclude it impossible to attain to any thing excellent, since they are, or ought to be best acquainted with their own strength and genius, she's a fool who would attempt their deliverance or improvement. No, let them enjoy the great honor and felicity of their tame, submissive and depending temper! Let the men applaud, and let them glory in, this wonderful humility! Let them receive the flatteries and grimaces of the other sex, live unenvied by their own, and be as much beloved as one such woman can afford to love another! Let them enjoy the glory of treading in the footsteps of their predecessors, and of having the prudence to avoid that audacious attempt of soaring beyond their sphere! Let them housewife or play, dress and be pretty entertaining company! Or which is better, relieve the poor to ease their own compassions, read pious books, say their prayers and go to church, because they have been taught and used to do so, without being able to give a better reason for their faith and practice! Let them not by any means aspire at being women of understanding, because no man can endure a woman of superior sense, or would treat a reasonable woman civilly, but that he thinks he stands on higher ground, and that she is so wise as to make exceptions in his favor, and to take her measures by his directions; they may pretend to sense indeed, since mere pretences only render one the more ridiculous! Let them in short be what is called very women, for this is most acceptable to all sorts of men; or let them aim at the title of *good devout* women, since some men can bear with this; but let them not judge of the sex by their own

scantling.[3] for the great Author of nature and Fountain of all perfection, never designed that the mean[4] and imperfect, but that the most complete and excellent of His creatures in every kind, should be the standard to the rest.

To conclude, if that Great Queen who has subdued the proud, and made the pretended invincible more than once fly before her; who has rescued an empire, reduced a kingdom, conquered provinces in as little time almost as one can travel them, and seems to have chained victory to her standard; who disposes of crowns, gives laws and liberty to Europe, and is the chief instrument in the hand of the Almighty to pull down and to set up the great men of the Earth; who conquers everywhere for others, and no where for her self but in the hearts of the conquered, who are of the number of those who reap the benefit of her triumphs; whilst she only reaps for her self the laurels of disinterested glory, and the royal pleasure of doing heroically; if this glory of her own sex and envy of the other, will not think we need, or does not hold us worthy of, the protection of her ever victorious arms, and men have not the gratitude for her sake at least, to do justice to her sex, who has been such a universal benefactress to theirs: Adieu to the liberties not of this or that nation or region only, but of the moiety of mankind! To all the great things that women might perform, inspired by her example, encouraged by her smiles, and supported by her power! To their discovery of new worlds for the exercise of her goodness, new sciences to publish her fame, and reducing nature itself to a subjection to her empire! To their destroying those worst of tyrants impiety and immorality, which dare to stalk about even in her own dominions, and to devour souls almost within view of her throne, leaving a stench behind them scarce to be corrected even by the incense of her devotions! To the women's tracing a new path to honor, in which none shall walk but such as scorn to cringe in order to rise, and who are proof both against giving and receiving flattery! In a word, to those halcyon,[5] or if you will millennium days,[6] in which the wolf and the lamb shall feed together, and a tyrannous domination which nature never meant, shall no longer render useless if not hurtful, the industry and understandings of half mankind!

---

1   *chimney-corner* Seat at the side of a fireplace, traditionally regarded as the place for the old, the infirm, and the idle.

2   *meanness* Insignificance, lowness of rank.

3   *scantling* Measuring-stick.

4   *mean* Low-born, insignificant.

5   *halcyon* Tranquil.

6   *millennium days* The thousand-year period of peace traditionally expected to follow the second coming of Christ; figuratively, any hoped-for future period of happiness.

MONTESQUIEU
(1689 – 1755)

CHARLES-LOUIS DE SECONDAT, BARON DE MONTES-quieu, was one of the foremost figures of the eighteenth-century Enlightenment. His condemnations of the Inquisition and the Spanish conquest of the Americas, and his pleas for a more humane penal code and an end to slavery stamped him as a part of the larger intellectual movement (led by such figures as Voltaire in France, Kant in Germany, and Hume in Scotland) that aimed to rethink the workings of human society using rational principles. Most of all, Montesquieu is remembered as the champion of new forms of constitutional government, based on the principle of a separation of powers into executive, legislative, and judicial branches.

Unlike many other French intellectuals, Montesquieu chose to spend his life in the provinces rather than in Paris. In his inherited capacity as a member of the local judicial body, the *parlement* of Bordeaux, he witnessed the use of torture in the judicial system; this is probably one of the reasons why he soon resigned his post. Another reason was that he wished to devote his attention to the scientific activities of the Academy of Bordeaux.

Although not a scientist, Montesquieu attempted to apply the methods of scientific reasoning to the study of society and politics. In a small book that he published in 1734, he disputed Machiavelli's contention that the Roman republic had declined into monarchy by accident or misfortune, and he took issue with Bishop Bossuet, who in the seventeenth century had argued that Providence had stepped in to punish Rome for its reign of bloodshed. Neither Fortune nor Providence provided the answer, argued Montesquieu in his *Considerations on the Grandeur of the Romans and the Cause of Their Decline*. Instead, he looked to human causes and effects, arguing that a classical republic had to remain small to survive. If it expanded indefinitely, as the Roman republic had tried to do, its civic life would necessarily give way to a different kind of society and government. In Montesquieu's analysis, a scientific approach to causality swept aside both the pagan goddess *Fortuna* and the Christian deity, *Providence*.

Montesquieu had no desire, however, to sweep aside moral concerns. Already in his earliest work, the highly entertaining *Persian Letters* (1721), he put forward a case against injustice, arguing that tyranny is as self-destructive as it is morally repugnant. The book is a collection of fictionalized letters written by Persian travelers in France. Many of the letters display the often amusing sort of mistakes tourists make in their efforts to understand foreign cultural practices. Yet the novel has a serious message: despotism is a miserable form of government from which no one benefits, not even the despot. As he travels through Europe the Persian prince Usbek comes, over the years, to appreciate the presence of a degree of freedom there—a freedom that is contrasted with the "Oriental despotism" of his own country. He refuses, however, to understand that he is a despot in his relationship with his wives, and at the end of the story learns that Roxanne, the one woman he has loved, has decided to commit suicide rather than submit to his despotic ways.

Montesquieu was well aware that Western societies had their own form of despotism to worry about, the kind that had changed Spain from a great power into a backward country. In *The Spirit of the Laws* (1748), Montesquieu's most influential book, he argued that France should learn from Spain what to avoid, and learn from England that to which she might aspire. On the English side of the Channel the clergy no longer sat as a separate order in Parliament, and the aristocracy was no longer a feudal nobility. Also in contrast to France, the King of England did not claim to rule by divine right. For Montesquieu England, more than any other country, exemplified a desirable form of constitutional government. It is from the English experience that he derived his model of the separation of powers, which he based on his perception of the British constitutional system, divided between the king, Parliament and the courts of laws. Montesquieu argued that political power should be divided between an executive, in charge of enforcing the law; a legislature, which writes the law; and a judiciary, which implements and interprets it. This arrangement, Montesquieu argued, was most likely to preserve liberty and prevent oppression.

Montesquieu sometimes spoke of the "spirit of the age"; when he applied that expression to the modern world, he insisted that its spirit was that of commerce. Holland and England were commercial, progressive countries and, not by coincidence, countries in which the citizenry enjoyed a high degree of freedom. Long before Adam Smith, Montesquieu held that through commerce ordinary persons demonstrate their capacity to act for themselves. Economic retardation and political unfreedom are linked, as seen in Portugal and Spain; commerce and constitutional government also go hand in hand, as witnessed by England and Holland.

Internationally, Montesquieu upheld the view that if European nations wished to assert their power, they should do so through trade rather than conquest. A new day of imperialism was at hand, he feared; the rising Leviathans of the Western world could not be stopped, so he did his best to explain why, even from the standpoint of narrow self-interest, the European countries would be better served by a policy of international commerce than by one of war.

Montesquieu achieved considerable fame in his day. Some intellectuals of his era challenged his view that Asian countries were doomed by climate and other "physical causes" to endure oppressive regimes in perpetuity, but his constitutional scheme became highly influential at the time of the founding of the United States, when his writings were frequently quoted; the Americans followed Montesquieu in the New World by substituting the President for the Monarch and a Senate for a House of Lords.

◆ ◆ ◆ ◆ ◆

The Spirit of the Laws (1748)

[...]

from *Part 2, Book 11*

Chapter 5: On the Purpose of Various States

Although all states have the same purpose in general, which is to maintain themselves, yet each state has a purpose that is peculiar to it. Expansion was the purpose of Rome; war, that of Lacedaemonia;[1] religion, that of the Jewish laws; commerce, that of Marseilles;[2] public tranquility, that of the laws of China;[3] navigation, that of the laws of the Rhodians;[4] natural liberty was the purpose of the police of the savages; in general, the delights of the prince are the purpose of the despotic states; his glory and that of his state, that of monarchies; the independence of each individual is the purpose of the laws of Poland;[5] and what results from this is the oppression of all.

There is also one nation in the world whose constitution has political liberty for its direct purpose. We are going to examine the principles on which this nation founds political liberty. If these principles are good, liberty will appear there as in a mirror.

Not much trouble need be taken to discover political liberty in the constitution. If it can be seen where it is, if it has been found, why seek it?

Chapter 6: On the Constitution of England

In each state there are three sorts of powers: legislative power, executive power over the things depending on the right of nations, and executive power over the things depending on civil right.

By the first, the prince or the magistrate makes laws for a time or for always and corrects or abrogates those that have

---

1   *Lacedaemonia*   More commonly known as Sparta.
2   *Marseilles*   This historically important port did not become part of France until 1481.
3   *public tranquility, that of the laws of China*   [Montesquieu's note] The natural purpose of a state having no enemies on the outside or believing them checked by barriers.
4   *Rhodians*   Ancient inhabitants of the Greek island of Rhodes.
5   *the laws of Poland*   [Montesquieu's note] Drawback of the *liberum veto*. [Until 1764, this provision of Polish law meant that any member of the legislature could by his vote alone defeat a bill, end the current session, and nullify all legislation passed during it.]

been made. By the second, he makes peace or war, sends or receives embassies, establishes security, and prevents invasions. By the third, he punishes crimes or judges disputes between individuals. The last will be called the power of judging, and the former simply the executive power of the state.

Political liberty in a citizen is that tranquility of spirit which comes from the opinion each one has of his security, and in order for him to have this liberty the government must be such that one citizen cannot fear another citizen.

When legislative power is united with executive power in a single person or in a single body of the magistracy, there is no liberty, because one can fear that the same monarch or senate that makes tyrannical laws will execute them tyrannically.

Nor is there liberty if the power of judging is not separate from legislative power and from executive power. If it were joined to legislative power, the power over the life and liberty of the citizens would be arbitrary, for the judge would be the legislator. If it were joined to executive power, the judge could have the force of an oppressor.

All would be lost if the same man or the same body of principal men, either of nobles, or of the people, exercised these three powers: that of making the laws, that of executing public resolutions, and that of judging the crimes or the disputes of individuals.

In most kingdoms in Europe, the government is moderate because the prince, who has the first two powers, leaves the exercise of the third to his subjects. Among the Turks, where the three powers are united in the person of the sultan, an atrocious despotism reigns.

In the Italian republics, where the three powers are united, there is less liberty than in our monarchies. Thus, in order to maintain itself, the government needs means as violent as in the government of the Turks; witness the state inquisitors[1] and the lion's maw into which an informer can, at any moment, throw his note of accusation.

Observe the possible situation of a citizen in these republics. The body of the magistracy, as executor of the laws, retains all the power it has given itself as a legislator. It can plunder the state by using its general wills; and, as it also has the power of judging, it can destroy each citizen by using its particular wills.

There, all power is one; and, although there is none of the external pomp that reveals a despotic prince, it is felt at every moment.

Thus princes who have wanted to make themselves despotic have always begun by uniting in their person all the magistracies, and many kings of Europe have begun by uniting all the great posts of their state.

I do believe that the pure hereditary aristocracy of the Italian republics is not precisely like the despotism of Asia. The multitude of magistrates sometimes softens the magistracy; not all the nobles always concur in the same designs; there various tribunals are formed that temper one another. Thus, in Venice, the *Great Council* has legislation, the *Pregadi*, execution; *Quarantia*, the power of judging. But the ill is that these different tribunals are formed of magistrates taken from the same body; this makes them nearly a single power.

The power of judging should not be given to a permanent senate but should be exercised by persons drawn from the body of the people[2] at certain times of the year in the manner prescribed by law to form a tribunal which lasts only as long as necessity requires.

In this fashion the power of judging, so terrible[3] among men, being attached neither to a certain state nor to a certain profession, becomes, so to speak, invisible and null. Judges are not continually in view; one fears the magistracy, not the magistrates.

In important accusations, the criminal in cooperation with the law must choose the judges, or at least he must be able to challenge so many of them that those who remain are considered to be of his choice.

The two other powers may be given instead to magistrates or to permanent bodies because they are exercised upon no individual, the one being only the general will of the state, and the other, the execution of that general will.

But though tribunals should not be fixed, judgments should be fixed to such a degree that they are never anything but a precise text of the law. If judgments were the individual opinion of a judge, one would live in this society without knowing precisely what engagements one has contracted.

Further, the judges must be of the same condition[4] as the accused, or his peers, so that he does not suppose that he has fallen into the hands of people inclined to do him violence.

---

1 *state inquisitors* [Montesquieu's note] In Venice.

2 *exercised by persons drawn from the body of the people* [Montesquieu's note] As in Athens.
3 *terrible* Montesquieu means *capable of inspiring such terror.*
4 *the same condition* The same social rank.

If the legislative power leaves to the executive power the right to imprison citizens who can post bail for their conduct, there is no longer any liberty, unless the citizens are arrested in order to respond without delay to an accusation of a crime the law has rendered capital; in this case they are really free because they are subject only to the power of the law.

But if the legislative power believed itself endangered by some secret conspiracy against the state or by some correspondence with its enemies on the outside, it could, for a brief and limited time, permit the executive power to arrest suspected citizens who would lose their liberty for a time only so that it would be preserved forever.

And this is the only means consistent with reason of replacing the tyrannical magistracy of the *ephors*[1] and the *state inquisitors* of Venice, who are also despotic.

As, in a free state, every man, considered to have a free soul, should be governed by himself, the people as a body should have legislative power; but, as this is impossible in large states and is subject to many drawbacks in small ones, the people must have their representatives do all that they themselves cannot do.

One knows the needs of one's own town better than those of other towns, and one judges the ability of one's neighbors better than that of one's other compatriots. Therefore, members of the legislative body must not be drawn from the body of the nation at large; it is proper for the inhabitants of each principal town to choose a representative from it.

The great advantage of representatives is that they are able to discuss public business. The people are not at all appropriate for such discussions; this forms one of the great drawbacks of democracy.

It is not necessary that the representatives, who have been generally instructed by those who have chosen them, be instructed about each matter of business in particular, as is the practice in the Diets of Germany. It is true that, in their way, the word of the deputies would better express the voice of the nation; but it would produce infinite delays and make each deputy the master of all the others, and on the most pressing occasions the whole force of the nation could be checked by a caprice.

Mr. Sidney[2] says properly that when the deputies represent a body of people, as in Holland, they should be accountable to those who have commissioned them; it is another thing when they are deputed by boroughs, as in England.

In choosing a representative, all citizens in the various districts should have the right to vote except those whose estate is so humble that they are deemed to have no will of their own.

A great vice in most ancient republics was that the people had the right to make resolutions for action, resolutions which required some execution, which altogether exceeds the people's capacity. The people should not enter the government except to choose their representatives; this is quite within their reach. For if there are few people who know the precise degree of a man's ability, yet every one is able to know, in general, if the one he chooses sees more clearly than most of the others.

Nor should the representative body be chosen in order to make some resolution for action, a thing it would not do well, but in order to make laws or in order to see if those they have made have been well executed; these are things it can do very well and that only it can do well.

In a state there are always some people who are distinguished by birth, wealth, or honors; but if they were mixed among the people and if they had only one voice like the others, the common liberty would be their enslavement and they would have no interest in defending it, because most of the resolutions would be against them. Therefore, the part they have in legislation should be in proportion to the other advantages they have in the state, which will happen if they form a body that has the right to check the enterprises of the people, as the people have the right to check theirs.

Thus, legislative power will be entrusted both to the body of the nobles and to the body that will be chosen to represent the people, each of which will have assemblies and deliberations apart and have separate views and interests.

Among the three powers of which we have spoken, that of judging is in some fashion, null.[3] There remain only two; and, as they need a power whose regulations temper them,

---

1   *ephors*   Officials elected in ancient Sparta to balance the power of the two kings. They were sometimes considered to have excessive dictatorial power.

2   *Mr. Sidney*   Algernon Sidney (1622–83), an English Whig politician and author of *Discourses Concerning Government* (1698), chap. 3, sect. 38.

3   *that of judging is in some fashion, null*   Montesquieu means that the judiciary has negligible power compared to the other branches.

that part of the legislative body composed of the nobles is quite appropriate for producing this effect.

The nobility should be hereditary. In the first place, it is so by its nature; and, besides, it must have a great interest in preserving its prerogatives, odious in themselves, and which, in a free state, must always be endangered.

But, as a hereditary power could be induced to follow its particular interests and forget those of the people, in the things about which one has a sovereign interest in corrupting, for instance, in the laws about levying silver coin, it must take part in legislation only through its faculty of vetoing and not through its faculty of enacting.

I call the right to order by oneself, or to correct what has been ordered by another, the *faculty of enacting*. I call the right to render null a resolution taken by another the *faculty of vetoing*, which was the power of the tribunes of Rome. And, although the one who has the faculty of vetoing can also have the right to approve, this approval is no more than a declaration that one does not make use of one's faculty of vetoing, and it derives from that faculty.

The executive power should be in the hands of a monarch, because the part of the government that almost always needs immediate action is better administered by one than by many, whereas what depends on legislative power is often better ordered by many than by one.

If there were no monarch and the executive power were entrusted to a certain number of persons drawn from the legislative body, there would no longer be liberty, because the two powers would be united, the same persons sometimes belonging and always able to belong to both.

If the legislative body were not convened for a considerable time, there would no longer be liberty. For one of two things would happen: either there would no longer be any legislative resolution and the state would fall into anarchy; or these resolutions would be made by the executive power, and it would become absolute.

It would be useless for the legislative body to be convened without interruption. That would inconvenience the representatives and besides would overburden the executive power, which would not think of executing, but of defending its prerogatives and its right to execute.

In addition, if the legislative body were continuously convened, it could happen that one would do nothing but replace the deputies who had died with new deputies; and in this case, if the legislative body were once corrupted, the ill would be without remedy. When various legislative bodies follow each other, the people, holding a poor opinion of the current legislative body, put their hopes, reasonably enough, in the one that will follow; but if the legislative body were always the same, the people, seeing it corrupted, would expect nothing further from its laws; they would become furious or would sink into indolence.

The legislative body should not convene itself. For a body is considered to have a will only when it is convened; and if it were not convened unanimously, one could not identify which part was truly the legislative body, the part that was convened or the one that was not. For if it had the right to prorogue[1] itself, it could happen that it would never prorogue itself; this would be dangerous in the event that it wanted to threaten executive power. Besides, there are some times more suitable than others for convening the legislative body; therefore, it must be the executive power that regulates, in relation to the circumstances it knows, the time of the holding and duration of these assemblies.

If the executive power does not have the right to check the enterprises of the legislative body, the latter will be despotic, for it will wipe out all the other powers, since it will be able to give to itself all the power it can imagine.

But the legislative power must not have the reciprocal faculty of checking the executive power. For, as execution has the limits of its own nature, it is useless to restrict it; besides, executive power is always exercised on immediate things. And the power of the tribunes in Rome was faulty in that it checked not only legislation but even execution; this caused great ills.

But if, in a free state, legislative power should not have the right to check executive power, it has the right and should have the faculty to examine the manner in which the laws it has made have been executed; and this is the advantage of this government over that of Crete and Lacedaemonia, where the *kosmoi*[2] and the *ephors* were not held accountable for their administration.

But, whether or not this examination is made, the legislative body should not have the power to judge the person, and consequently the conduct, of the one who executes. His person should be sacred because, as he is necessary to the state so that the legislative body does not become tyrannical, if he were accused or judged there would no longer be liberty.

---

1 *prorogue* Discontinue its sittings without formally ending the legislative session.
2 *kosmoi* Officials in ancient Crete (corresponding closely to the ephors in Sparta).

In this case, the state would not be a monarchy but an unfree republic. But, as he who executes cannot execute badly without having as ministers wicked counselors who hate the law although the laws favor them as men, these counselors can be sought out and punished. And this is the advantage of this government over that of Cnidus,[1] where the people could never get satisfaction for the injustices that had been done to them, as the law did not permit calling the *amymones*[2] to judgment even after their administration.[3]

Although in general the power of judging should not be joined to any part of the legislative power, this is subject to three exceptions founded on the particular interests of the one who is to be judged.

Important men are always exposed to envy; and if they were judged by the people, they could be endangered and would not enjoy the privilege of the last citizen of a free state, of being judged by his peers. Therefore, nobles must not be called before the ordinary tribunals of the nation but before that part of the legislative body composed of nobles.

It could happen that the law, which is simultaneously clairvoyant[4] and blind, might be too rigorous in certain cases. But the judges of the nation are, as we have said, only the mouth that pronounces the words of the law, inanimate beings who can moderate neither its force nor its rigor. Therefore, the part of the legislative body, which we have just said is a necessary tribunal on another occasion, is also one on this occasion; it is for its supreme authority to moderate the law in favor of the law itself by pronouncing less rigorously than the law.

It could also happen that a citizen, in matters of public business, might violate the rights of the people and commit crimes that the established magistrates could not or would not want to punish. But, in general, the legislative power cannot judge, and even less so in this particular case, where it represents the interested party, the people. Therefore, it can be only the accuser. But, before whom will it make its accusation? Will it bow before the tribunals of law, which are lower than it and are, moreover, composed of those who, being also of the people, would be swept along by the authority of such a great accuser? No: in order to preserve the dignity of the people and the security of the individual, that part of the legislature drawn from the people must make its accusation before the part of the legislature drawn from the nobles, which has neither the same interests nor the same passions.

This last is the advantage of this government over most of the ancient republics, where there was the abuse that the people were judge and accuser at the same time.

Executive power, as we have said, should take part in legislation by its faculty of vetoing; otherwise it will soon be stripped of its prerogatives. But if legislative power takes part in execution,[5] executive power will equally be lost.

If the monarch took part in legislation by the faculty of enacting, there would no longer be liberty. But as in spite of this, he must take part in legislation in order to defend himself, he must take part in it by the faculty of vetoing.

The cause of the change in government in Rome was that the senate, which had one part of the executive power, and the magistrates, who had the other, did not have the faculty of vetoing, as the people had.

Here, therefore, is the fundamental constitution of the government of which we are speaking. As its legislative body is composed of two parts, the one will be chained to the other by their reciprocal faculty of vetoing. The two will be bound by the executive power, which will itself be bound by the legislative power.

The form of these three powers should be rest or inaction. But as they are constrained to move by the necessary motion of things, they will be forced to move in concert.

As executive power belongs to the legislative only through its faculty of vetoing, it cannot enter into the discussion of public business. It is not even necessary for it to propose, because, as it can always disapprove of resolutions, it can reject decisions on propositions it would have wanted left unmade.

In some ancient republics, where the people as a body discussed the public business, it was natural for the executive power to propose and discuss with them; otherwise, there would have been a strange confusion in the resolutions.

If the executive power enacts on the raising of public funds without the consent of the legislature, there will no longer be liberty, because the executive power will become the legislator on the most important point of legislation.

---

1   *Cnidus*   Ancient colony of Sparta.
2   *amymones*   [Montesquieu's note] These were magistrates elected annually by the people. See Stephanus of Byzantium. [Sixth-century author of a geographical dictionary entitled *Ethnica*.]
3   *even after their administration*   [Montesquieu's note] One could accuse the Roman magistrates after their magistracy. In Dionysius Halicarnassus, Book 9 see the affair of the tribune Genutius. [The work is *Antiquitates Romanae* by Dionysius of Halicarnassus.]
4   *clairvoyant*   Having the ability to see things beyond the reach of normal human senses.

---

5   *execution*   Carrying out (the law).

If the legislative power enacts, not from year to year, but forever, on the raising of public funds, it runs the risk of losing its liberty, because the executive power will no longer depend upon it; and when one holds such a right forever, it is unimportant whether that right comes from oneself or from another. The same is true if the legislative power enacts, not from year to year, but forever, about the land and sea forces, which it should entrust to the executive power.

So that the one who executes is not able to oppress, the armies entrusted to him must be of the people and have the same spirit as the people, as they were in Rome until the time of Marius.[1] This can be so in only two ways: either those employed in the army must have enough goods to be answerable for their conduct to the other citizens and be enrolled for a year only, as was practiced in Rome; or, if the troops must be a permanent body, whose soldiers come from the meanest parts of the nation, legislative power must be able to disband them as soon as the legislature so desires; the soldiers must live with the citizens, and there must not be a separate camp, a barracks, or a fortified place.

Once the army is established, it should be directly dependent on the executive power, not on the legislative body; and this is in the nature of the thing, as its concern is more with action than with deliberation.

Men's manner of thinking is to make more of courage than of timidity; more of activity than of prudence; more of force than of counsel. The army will always scorn a senate and respect its officers. It will not make much of the orders sent from a body composed of people it believes timid and, therefore, unworthy to command it. Thus, whenever the army depends solely on the legislative body, the government will become military. And if the contrary has ever occurred, it is the effect of some extraordinary circumstances; it is because the army there is always separate, because it is composed of several bodies each of which depends upon its particular province, because the capitals are in excellent locations whose situation alone defends them and which have no troops.

Holland is even more secure than Venice; it could flood rebellious troops; it could leave them to die of hunger; since the troops are not in towns that could give them sustenance, their sustenance is precarious.

For if, in the case of an army governed by the legislative body, particular circumstances keep the government from becoming military, one will encounter other drawbacks; one of these two things must happen, either the army must destroy the government, or the government must weaken the army.

And this weakening will have a fatal cause: it will arise from the very weakness of the government.

If one wants to read the admirable work by Tacitus, *On the Mores of the Germans*, one will see that the English have taken their idea of political government from the Germans.[2] This fine system was found in the forests.

Since all human things have an end, the state of which we are speaking will lose its liberty; it will perish. Rome, Lacedaemonia, and Carthage have surely perished. This state will perish when legislative power is more corrupt than executive power.

It is not for me to examine whether at present the English enjoy this liberty or not. It suffices for me to say that it is established by their laws, and I seek no further.

I do not claim hereby to disparage other governments, or to say that this extreme political liberty should humble those who have only a moderate one. How could I say that, I who believe that the excess even of reason is not always desirable and that men almost always accommodate themselves better to middles than to extremities?

Harrington, in his Oceana,[3] has also examined the furthest point of liberty to which the constitution of a state can be carried. But of him it can be said that he sought this liberty only after misunderstanding it, and that he built Chalcedon with the coast of Byzantium before his eyes.[4]

---

1   *Marius*   Gaius Marius (157–86 BCE), Roman general and politician. He broke with the tradition of having an army composed of land-holders, offering work as soldiers to the poor and landless.

2   *the English have taken their idea of political government from the Germans*   [Montesquieu's note] On lesser matters the princes consult, on greater ones, everybody does; yet even when a decision is in the power of the people, it is thoroughly considered by the princes. [This quotation is from Tacitus, *Germania*, chap. 11.]

3   *Harrington, in his Oceana*   James Harrington, *Commonwealth of Oceana*, a work of utopian fiction published in 1656.

4   *he built Chalcedon with the coast of Byzantium before his eyes*   Chalcedon was an ancient town just across the Bosporus from Byzantium (both are now part of Istanbul). The Chalcedonian founders picked a far less advantageous and defensible site for their town, within sight of the superior location where Byzantium was founded seventeen years later.

DAVID HUME
(1711 – 1776)

DAVID HUME HAS BEEN CALLED THE MOST IMPORTANT philosopher ever to have written in English. He was born to a strict Calvinist family in Edinburgh, Scotland's capital, in 1711, and spent his youth there and in Ninewells, his family's small land-holding near the border with England. He was a precociously intelligent and well-read child, and by the age of 16 he had begun composing his first philosophical masterwork, *A Treatise of Human Nature*, on which he was to work, more or less continually, for the next ten years. Hume spent the years between 1723 and 1726 (i.e., between the ages of 12 and 15) studying a wide range of subjects at the University of Edinburgh. Like many students of that era, however, he did not take a degree. His father and grandfather had both been lawyers, and his family expected him also to go into law, but, Hume later wrote, he found the law "nauseous" and discovered in himself "an unsurmountable aversion to every thing but the pursuits of philosophy and general learning." Hume continued to read and write and, as a result of his feverish intellectual activity—motivated by his belief that he had made a major philosophical discovery—he suffered a nervous breakdown in 1734. He was forced to put philosophy aside for several months. He then left Britain for France. There, in the following three years, living frugally in the countryside in Anjou (and using up all his savings), he completed most of his book.

Hume's *A Treatise of Human Nature* was published anonymously when he was 27. Hume later wrote, it "fell *dead-born from the press*, without reaching such distinction as even to excite a murmur among the zealots." Hume's career as an intellectual and man of letters seemed to have ended before it had begun. He returned to Scotland to live with his mother, and began to recast the material of the *Treatise* into two new books, which have become philosophical classics in their own right: *An Enquiry Concerning Human Understanding* (1748), and *An Enquiry Concerning the Principles of Morals* (1751). These books were more suc-cessful than the *Treatise*, but they too were slow to become influential during Hume's own lifetime.

Needing money, Hume got his first real job at the age of 34; he spent a well-paid year as tutor to a mad nobleman (the Marquess of Annandale). In 1746 Hume accepted a position as secretary to General St. Clair, and for two years was part of a secret diplomatic and military embassy to the courts of Vienna and Turin. During this period Hume was twice refused academic appointments at Scot-tish universities—first Edinburgh, then Glasgow—because of his reputation as a religious skeptic. Shortly afterwards, between 1755 and 1757, unsuccessful attempts were made in Edinburgh to have Hume excommunicated from the Church of Scotland.

In 1763 Hume was made secretary of the English embassy at Paris, where he found himself very much in fashion and seems to have enjoyed the experience. There he fell in love with, but failed to win the hand of, the Comtesse de Boufflers, the mistress of a prominent French noble. (Some unkindly suggest this might have been partly because at the time, when Hume was in his fifties, he had come to resemble "a fat well-fed Bernardine monk.") In 1767, back in Scotland and now a fairly wealthy man, Hume was ap-pointed an Under-Secretary of State, a senior position in the British civil service. By the time Hume died, in 1776, he had become respected as one of Europe's leading men of letters and a principal architect of the Enlightenment.

Hume can be called the first "post-skeptical" modern philosopher. He was wholly convinced (by, among others, the writings of his predecessors Descartes, Locke and Berkeley) that no knowledge which goes beyond the mere data of our own minds has anything like secure and reli-able foundations: that is, he believed, we have no certain knowledge of the inner workings of the physical world and its laws, or of God, or of absolute moral "truth," or even of our own "real selves." All we have secure knowledge of is our own mental states and their relations: our sensory impressions, our ideas, our emotions, and so on. Nevertheless, Hume's philosophical project was a positive one: he wanted to develop a new, constructive science of human nature that would provide a defensible foundation for all the sciences, including ethics, physics and politics. Where Hume's predecessors tried in vain to argue against philosophical skepticism, Hume argued that a certain kind of skepticism was actually true and tried to go beyond it, to say something positive about how we are to get on with our lives (including our lives as scientists and philosophers). Much of Hume's philosophical writing, therefore, begins by showing the unstoppable power of skepticism in some domain—such as skepticism about causation or objective ethical truths—and then goes on to show how we can still talk sensibly about causation or ethics after all.

Hume's *Dialogues Concerning Natural Religion* (1779) was published only after his death, due to the controversial nature of its religious skepticism. In this work, written in the 1750s, Hume raises powerful doubts about whether we could ever have good reasons for believing in God—all religion, if Hume is right, may be no more than "mere superstition." Why then is religious belief so common? In *The Natural History of Religion*, published in 1757, Hume argues that the causes of religious belief are independent of rationality but are instead based on human fear of the unpredictable and uncontrollable influences in our lives—such as the forces of nature—which we try to propitiate through worship. Furthermore, Hume suggests, religious belief is more harmful than it is beneficial. Even apart from the suffering and strife which they have historically caused, religions invent spurious sins such as suicide, which (Hume argued) are not really harmful, and create "frivolous merits" which are not grounded in any genuine good (such as attending certain ceremonies and abstaining from particular foods).

In Book 3 of the *Treatise* and in his *Enquiry Concerning the Principles of Morals* Hume develops a secular alternative to religion-based morality; the theory of moral life which he develops there is based entirely upon an analysis of human nature and human needs, and is completely independent of religion. Hume's moral theory is a development of the "moral sense" tradition, exemplified by the writings of the Earl of Shaftesbury (1671–1713), Joseph Butler (1692–1752) and, especially, Francis Hutcheson (1694–1747). What these views have in common is the thesis that humans have a faculty of moral *perception*, analogous to sensory perception; that we experience feelings of approval or disapproval when we observe certain external actions or events; and that it is these feelings, rather than a priori deliverances of reason, that form the basis of morality. Earlier writers often tended to see moral sensations as giving insight into a relatively objective realm of moral fact. Hume shifted the debate by treating moral sensations as informing us not about the external world but about *human nature*—the structure of these sensations is to be explained by facts about our sympathies for those who are affected.

Hume's moral theory includes the following components. First, there are moral agents, whose actions are motivated by their character traits, which may be either virtuous or vicious, and may be either natural (instinctive) or artificial (acquired through social conditioning). Then there is the effect of such actions on others, who may experience either agreeable or disagreeable feelings as a result. Finally, there are moral spectators, who pronounce judgment on the agent's character traits—their virtues and vices—based on the observer's sympathetic experience of the feelings of those affected by the agent's action.[1]

Book 3 of the *Treatise* has three parts. Part 1 famously attacks two influential ideas about morality: the first is that moral distinctions are derived from reason; the second that moral judgments are judgments about empirical facts. It is in the context of the second critique that Hume formulated his famous doctrine that "ought" cannot be derived from "is"—that claims about how the world ought to be never follow trivially from claims about how the world actually is. Part 2, three sections of which are reprinted here, deals with justice. Hume argues that justice is an "artificial virtue," and describes how it emerges with the development of society and how it comes to be surrounded by a scaffolding of social rules and institutions. It is here that Hume sets out his famous "conditions of justice." Justice is needed under conditions in which there is moderate scarcity and imperfect benevolence. If there were sufficient goods so that everyone could acquire everything they wanted, justice would be unnecessary. Similarly, a world in which everyone was perfectly benevolent would have no need of coercive laws and institutions to determine the division of goods. Thus, people create justice as an artificial virtue because it is useful, contributing (for the most part) to the welfare of all. In Part 3 Hume discusses the natural virtues, and explains further the difference between the natural and the artificial virtues.

---

1   Of course, on occasion, one and the same person may be the agent of an action, affected by it, and an observer of their own behavior.

Like several other authors in this volume, Hume sets himself the problem of explaining how social institutions arise and are justified. But unlike many of his early modern predecessors Hume rejects any kind of contractualist account of the origin of government. Like social contract theorists—but unlike thinkers from the Aristotelian or Thomistic traditions—Hume insists that social institutions, and the accompanying virtues, are human creations: they are *artificial* virtues. But unlike the social contract theorists, Hume denies that any mere act of collective will is sufficient to create meaningful social practices. So he faces the special problem of developing what one might call a "naturalistic" account of the origin and development of society, rooted in an empirical account of human psychological motivation.

Importantly, Hume distinguished between a contract—the kind of contract adduced by social contract theorists—and a convention. A convention, for Hume, does not require any explicitly stated promise. Rather, conventions arise when two or more people have a shared interest in a coordinated course of action, and where there is a mutually understood intention by each party to act in accordance with this course of action, so long as everybody else does as well. Much of Hume's account of justice rests on his notion of a convention.

Hume is often considered one of the founding figures of conservative thought; he repeatedly emphasizes the importance of the rule of law, moderation, stability, and pragmatism in his essays. At the same time, Hume defended the liberty of the press and moderate democracy; his legacy extends far beyond conservative thought. James Madison read Hume carefully and the *Federalist* essay No. 10 on factions is greatly influenced by Hume's essay "Of Parties in General." Hume's claim that justice is an artificial virtue has had a major influence on constructivist approaches to ethics and political philosophy (for example, the work of Rawls). Despite his rejection of the social contract, Hume plays a role in the social contract tradition. Rawls uses Hume's account of the conditions of justice in *Theory of Justice*.

It would be misleading, however, to think of Hume's influence only as a matter of influence on specific figures. His political writings and his secular approach to morality and politics are part of the philosophical vocabulary and have been absorbed—directly or indirectly—by most social and political philosophers.

◆ ◆ ◆ ◆ ◆

A Treatise of Human Nature (1739–1740)

Part 2: *Of Justice and Injustice*

Section 1: Justice, Whether a Natural or Artificial Virtue?

I have already hinted, that our sense of every kind of virtue is not natural; but that there are some virtues, that produce pleasure and approbation by means of an artifice or contrivance,[1] which arises from the circumstances and necessity of mankind. Of this kind I assert justice to be; and shall endeavor to defend this opinion by a short, and, I hope, convincing argument, before I examine the nature of the artifice, from which the sense of that virtue is derived.

It is evident, that when we praise any actions, we regard only the motives that produced them, and consider the actions as signs or indications of certain principles in the mind and temper. The external performance has no merit. We must look within to find the moral quality. This we cannot do directly; and therefore fix our attention on actions, as on external signs. But these actions are still considered as signs; and the ultimate object of our praise and approbation is the motive, that produced them.

After the same manner, when we require any action, or blame a person for not performing it, we always suppose, that one in that situation should be influenced by the proper motive of that action, and we esteem it vicious in him to be regardless of it.[2] If we find, upon enquiry, that the virtuous motive was still powerful over his breast, though checked in its operation by some circumstances unknown to us, we retract our blame, and have the same esteem for him, as if he had actually performed the action, which we require of him.

It appears, therefore, that all virtuous actions derive their merit only from virtuous motives, and are considered merely as signs of those motives. From this principle I conclude, that the first virtuous motive, which bestows a merit

---

1   *natural ... artifice or contrivance* Hume holds that the "natural" virtues are those characteristic dispositions to act because of an inborn, instinctive associated "agreeable" feeling—of pleasure or approval. The "artificial" ones involve actions whose associations with "agreeable" feelings are learned—which we are trained by society to feel.

2   *regardless of it* Motivated without regard to the proper motive—motivated otherwise.

on any action, can never be a regard to the virtue of that action, but must be some other natural motive or principle. To suppose, that the mere regard to the virtue of the action, may be the first motive, which produced the action, and rendered it virtuous, is to reason in a circle. Before we can have such a regard, the action must be really virtuous; and this virtue must be derived from some virtuous motive: And consequently the virtuous motive must be different from the regard to the virtue of the action. A virtuous motive is requisite to render an action virtuous. An action must be virtuous, before we can have a regard to its virtue. Some virtuous motive, therefore, must be antecedent to[1] that regard.

Nor is this merely a metaphysical subtlety; but enters into all our reasonings in common life, though perhaps we may not be able to place it in such distinct philosophical terms. We blame a father for neglecting his child. Why? because it shows a want of natural affection, which is the duty of every parent. Were not natural affection a duty, the care of children could not be a duty; and it were impossible we could have the duty in our eye in the attention we give to our offspring. In this case, therefore, all men suppose a motive to the action distinct from a sense of duty.

Here is a man, that does many benevolent actions; relieves the distressed, comforts the afflicted, and extends his bounty even to the greatest strangers. No character can be more amiable and virtuous. We regard these actions as proofs of the greatest humanity. This humanity bestows a merit on the actions. A regard to this merit is, therefore, a secondary consideration, and derived from the antecedent principle of humanity, which is meritorious and laudable.

In short, it may be established as an undoubted maxim, that no action can be virtuous, or morally good, unless there be in human nature some motive to produce it, distinct from the sense of its morality.

But may not the sense of morality or duty produce an action, without any other motive? I answer, It may: But this is no objection to the present doctrine. When any virtuous motive or principle is common in human nature, a person, who feels his heart devoid of that motive, may hate himself upon that account, and may perform the action without the motive, from a certain sense of duty, in order to acquire by practice, that virtuous principle, or at least, to disguise to himself, as much as possible, his want of it. A man that really feels no gratitude in his temper, is still pleased to perform grateful actions, and thinks he has, by that means,

fulfilled his duty. Actions are at first only considered as signs of motives: But it is usual, in this case, as in all others, to fix our attention on the signs, and neglect, in some measure, the thing signified. But though, on some occasions, a person may perform an action merely out of regard to its moral obligation, yet still this supposes in human nature some distinct principles, which are capable of producing the action, and whose moral beauty renders the action meritorious.

Now to apply all this to the present case; I suppose a person to have lent me a sum of money, on condition that it be restored in a few days; and also suppose, that after the expiration of the term agreed on, he demands the sum: I ask, What reason or motive have I to restore the money? It will, perhaps, be said, that my regard to justice, and abhorrence of villainy and knavery, are sufficient reasons for me, if I have the least grain of honesty, or sense of duty and obligation. And this answer, no doubt, is just and satisfactory to man in his civilized state, and when trained up according to a certain discipline and education. But in his rude[2] and more natural condition, if you are pleased to call such a condition natural, this answer would be rejected as perfectly unintelligible and sophistical. For one in that situation would immediately ask you, Wherein consists this honesty and justice, which you find in restoring a loan, and abstaining from the property of others? It does not surely lie in the external action. It must, therefore, be placed in the motive, from which the external action is derived. This motive can never be a regard to the honesty of the action. For it is a plain fallacy to say, that a virtuous motive is requisite to render an action honest, and at the same time that a regard to the honesty is the motive of the action. We can never have a regard to the virtue of an action, unless the action be antecedently virtuous. No action can be virtuous, but so far as it proceeds from a virtuous motive. A virtuous motive, therefore, must precede the regard to the virtue; and it is impossible, that the virtuous motive and the regard to the virtue can be the same.

It is requisite, then, to find some motive to acts of justice and honesty, distinct from our regard to the honesty; and in this lies the great difficulty. For should we say, that a concern for our private interest or reputation is the legitimate motive to all honest actions; it would follow, that wherever that concern ceases, honesty can no longer have place. But it is certain, that self-love, when it acts at its liberty, instead of engaging us to honest actions, is the source of all injustice and violence; nor can a man ever correct those

---

1 *antecedent to* Logically prior to—independent of.

2 *rude* Untrained by society.

vices, without correcting and restraining the natural movements of that appetite.

But should it be affirmed, that the reason or motive of such actions is the regard to public interest, to which nothing is more contrary than examples of injustice and dishonesty; should this be said, I would propose the three following considerations, as worthy of our attention. First, public interest is not naturally attached to the observation of the rules of justice; but is only connected with it, after an artificial convention for the establishment of these rules, as shall be shown more at large[1] hereafter. Secondly, if we suppose, that the loan was secret, and that it is necessary for the interest of the person, that the money be restored in the same manner (as when the lender would conceal his riches) in that case the example ceases, and the public is no longer interested in the actions of the borrower; though I suppose there is no moralist, who will affirm, that the duty and obligation ceases. Thirdly, experience sufficiently proves, that men, in the ordinary conduct of life, look not so far as the public interest, when they pay their creditors, perform their promises, and abstain from theft, and robbery, and injustice of every kind. That is a motive too remote and too sublime to affect the generality of mankind, and operate with any force in actions so contrary to private interest as are frequently those of justice and common honesty.

In general, it may be affirmed, that there is no such passion in human minds, as the love of mankind, merely as such, independent of personal qualities, of services, or of relation to oneself. It is true, there is no human, and indeed no sensible, creature, whose happiness or misery does not, in some measure, affect us, when brought near to us, and represented in lively colors: But this proceeds merely from sympathy,[2] and is no proof of such an universal affection to mankind, since this concern extends itself beyond our own species. An affection betwixt the sexes is a passion evidently implanted in human nature; and this passion not only appears in its peculiar symptoms, but also in inflaming every other principle of affection, and raising a stronger love from beauty, wit, kindness, than what would otherwise flow from them. Were there an universal love among all human creatures, it would appear after the same manner. Any degree of a good quality would cause a stronger affection than the same degree of a bad quality would cause hatred; contrary

to what we find by experience. Men's tempers are different, and some have a propensity to the tender, and others to the rougher, affections: But in the main, we may affirm, that man in general, or human nature, is nothing but the object both of love and hatred, and requires some other cause, which by a double relation of impressions and ideas, may excite these passions. In vain would we endeavor to elude this hypothesis. There are no phenomena that point out any such kind affection to men, independent of their merit, and every other circumstance. We love company in general; but it is as we love any other amusement. An Englishman in Italy is a friend: A European in China; and perhaps a man would be beloved as such, were we to meet him in the moon. But this proceeds only from the relation to ourselves; which in these cases gathers force by being confined to a few persons.

If public benevolence, therefore, or a regard to the interests of mankind, cannot be the original motive to justice, much less can private benevolence, or a regard to the interests of the party concerned, be this motive. For what if he be my enemy, and has given me just cause to hate him? What if he be a vicious man, and deserves the hatred of all mankind? What if he be a miser, and can make no use of what I would deprive him of? What if he be a profligate debauchee, and would rather receive harm than benefit from large possessions? What if I be in necessity, and have urgent motives to acquire something to my family? In all these cases, the original motive to justice would fail; and consequently the justice itself, and along with it all property, right, and obligation.

A rich man lies under a moral obligation to communicate to those in necessity a share of his superfluities. Were private benevolence the original motive to justice, a man would not be obliged to leave others in the possession of more than he is obliged to give them. At least the difference would be very inconsiderable. Men generally fix their affections more on what they are possessed of, than on what they never enjoyed: For this reason, it would be greater cruelty to dispossess a man of any thing, than not to give it him. But who will assert, that this is the only foundation of justice?

Besides, we must consider, that the chief reason, why men attach themselves so much to their possessions is, that they consider them as their property, and as secured to them inviolably by the laws of society. But this is a secondary consideration, and dependent on the preceding notions of justice and property.

A man's property is supposed to be fenced against every mortal, in every possible case. But private benevolence is,

---

1   *more at large* At greater length.

2   *sympathy* Hume uses this word in a broad sense, meaning the broad capacity to share in another's feelings—not just to feel unhappy at another's pain.

and ought to be, weaker in some persons, than in others: And in many, or indeed in most persons, must absolutely fail. Private benevolence, therefore, is not the original motive of justice.

From all this it follows, that we have no real or universal motive for observing the laws of equity, but the very equity and merit of that observance; and as no action can be equitable or meritorious, where it cannot arise from some separate motive, there is here an evident sophistry and reasoning in a circle. Unless, therefore, we will allow, that nature has established a sophistry, and rendered it necessary and unavoidable, we must allow, that the sense of justice and injustice is not derived from nature, but arises artificially, though necessarily from education, and human conventions.

I shall add, as a corollary to this reasoning, that since no action can be laudable or blamable, without some motives or impelling passions, distinct from the sense of morals, these distinct passions must have a great influence on that sense. It is according to their general force in human nature, that we blame or praise. In judging of the beauty of animal bodies, we always carry in our eye the economy[1] of a certain species; and where the limbs and features observe that proportion, which is common to the species, we pronounce them handsome and beautiful. In like manner we always consider the natural and usual force of the passions, when we determine concerning vice and virtue; and if the passions depart very much from the common measures on either side, they are always disapproved as vicious. A man naturally loves his children better than his nephews, his nephews better than his cousins, his cousins better than strangers, where every thing else is equal. Hence arise our common measures of duty, in preferring the one to the other. Our sense of duty always follows the common and natural course of our passions.

To avoid giving offence, I must here observe, that when I deny justice to be a natural virtue, I make use of the word, natural, only as opposed to artificial. In another sense of the word; as no principle of the human mind is more natural than a sense of virtue; so no virtue is more natural than justice. Mankind is an inventive species; and where an invention is obvious and absolutely necessary, it may as properly be said to be natural as any thing that proceeds immediately from original principles, without the intervention of thought or reflection. Though the rules of

justice be artificial, they are not arbitrary. Nor is the expression improper to call them Laws of Nature; if by natural we understand what is common to any species, or even if we confine it to mean what is inseparable from the species.

Section 2: Of the Origin of Justice and Property

We now proceed to examine two questions, viz. concerning the manner, in which the rules of justice are established by the artifice of men; and concerning the reasons, which determine us to attribute to the observance or neglect of these rules a moral beauty and deformity. These questions will appear afterwards to be distinct. We shall begin with the former.

Of all the animals, with which this globe is peopled, there is none towards whom nature seems, at first sight, to have exercised more cruelty than towards man, in the numberless wants and necessities, with which she has loaded him, and in the slender means, which she affords to the relieving these necessities. In other creatures these two particulars generally compensate each other. If we consider the lion as a voracious and carnivorous animal, we shall easily discover him to be very necessitous;[2] but if we turn our eye to his make and temper, his agility, his courage, his arms, and his force, we shall find, that his advantages hold proportion with his wants. The sheep and ox are deprived of all these advantages; but their appetites are moderate, and their food is of easy purchase. In man alone, this unnatural conjunction of infirmity, and of necessity, may be observed in its greatest perfection. Not only the food, which is required for his sustenance, flies his search and approach, or at least requires his labor to be produced, but he must be possessed of clothes and lodging, to defend him against the injuries of the weather; though to consider him only in himself, he is provided neither with arms, nor force, nor other natural abilities, which are in any degree answerable to so many necessities.

It is by society alone he is able to supply his defects, and raise himself up to an equality with his fellow-creatures, and even acquire a superiority above them. By society all his infirmities are compensated; and though in that situation his wants multiply every moment upon him, yet his abilities are still more augmented, and leave him in every respect more satisfied and happy, than it is possible for him, in his savage and solitary condition, ever to become. When

1 *economy* Structure, arrangement, proportion of parts; organization and apportionment of functions.

2 *necessitous* Needy (as if in poverty).

every individual person labors apart, and only for himself, his force is too small to execute any considerable work; his labor being employed in supplying all his different necessities, he never attains a perfection in any particular art; and as his force and success are not at all times equal, the least failure in either of these particulars must be attended with inevitable ruin and misery. Society provides a remedy for these three inconveniences.[1] By the conjunction of forces, our power is augmented: By the partition of employments, our ability increases: And by mutual succor we are less exposed to fortune and accidents. it is by this additional force, ability, and security, that society becomes advantageous.

But in order to form society, it is requisite not only that it be advantageous, but also that men be sensible of these advantages; and it is impossible, in their wild uncultivated state, that by study and reflection alone, they should ever be able to attain this knowledge. Most fortunately, therefore, there is conjoined to those necessities, whose remedies are remote and obscure, another necessity, which having a present and more obvious remedy, may justly be regarded as the first and original principle of human society. This necessity is no other than that natural appetite betwixt the sexes, which unites them together, and preserves their union, till a new tie takes place in their concern for their common offspring. This new concern becomes also a principle of union betwixt the parents and offspring, and forms a more numerous society; where the parents govern by the advantage of their superior strength and wisdom, and at the same time are restrained in the exercise of their authority by that natural affection, which they bear their children. In a little time, custom and habit operating on the tender minds of the children, makes them sensible of the advantages, which they may reap from society, as well as fashions them by degrees for it, by rubbing off those rough corners and untoward affections, which prevent their coalition.

For it must be confessed, that however the circumstances of human nature may render a union necessary, and however those passions of lust and natural affection may seem to render it unavoidable; yet there are other particulars in our natural temper, and in our outward circumstances, which are very incommodious, and are even contrary to the requisite conjunction. Among the former, we may justly esteem our selfishness to be the most considerable. I am sensible, that, generally speaking, the representations of this quality have been carried much too far; and that the descriptions, which

certain philosophers delight so much to form of mankind in this particular, are as wide of nature as any accounts of monsters, which we meet with in fables and romances. So far from thinking, that men have no affection for any thing beyond themselves, I am of opinion, that though it be rare to meet with one, who loves any single person better than himself; yet it is as rare to meet with one, in whom all the kind affections, taken together, do not over-balance all the selfish. Consult common experience: Do you not see, that though the whole expense of the family be generally under the direction of the master of it, yet there are few that do not bestow the largest part of their fortunes on the pleasures of their wives, and the education of their children, reserving the smallest portion for their own proper use and entertainment. This is what we may observe concerning such as have those endearing ties; and may presume, that the case would be the same with others, were they placed in a like situation.

But though this generosity must be acknowledged to the honor of human nature, we may at the same time remark, that so noble an affection, instead of fitting men for large societies, is almost as contrary to them, as the most narrow selfishness. For while each person loves himself better than any other single person, and in his love to others bears the greatest affection to his relations and acquaintance, this must necessarily produce an opposition of passions, and a consequent opposition of actions; which cannot but be dangerous to the new-established union.

It is however worth while to remark, that this contrariety of passions would be attended with but small danger, did it not concur with a peculiarity in our outward circumstances, which affords it an opportunity of exerting itself. There are three different species of goods, which we are possessed of; the internal satisfaction of our minds, the external advantages of our body, and the enjoyment of such possessions as we have acquired by our industry and good fortune. We are perfectly secure in the enjoyment of the first. The second may be ravished[2] from us, but can be of no advantage to him who deprives us of them. The last only are both exposed to the violence of others, and may be transferred without suffering any loss or alteration; while at the same time, there is not a sufficient quantity of them to supply every one's desires and necessities. As the improvement, therefore, of these goods is the chief advantage of society, so the instability of their possession, along with their scarcity, is the chief impediment.

---

1 *inconveniences* Harms.

2 *ravished* Removed by force.

In vain should we expect to find, in uncultivated nature, a remedy to this inconvenience; or hope for any inartificial principle of the human mind, which might control those partial affections, and make us overcome the temptations arising from our circumstances. The idea of justice can never serve to this purpose, or be taken for a natural principle, capable of inspiring men with an equitable conduct towards each other. That virtue, as it is now understood, would never have been dreamed of among rude and savage men. For the notion of injury or injustice implies an immorality or vice committed against some other person: And as every immorality is derived from some defect or unsoundness of the passions, and as this defect must be judged of, in a great measure, from the ordinary course of nature in the constitution of the mind; it will be easy to know, whether we be guilty of any immorality, with regard to others, by considering the natural, and usual force of those several affections, which are directed towards them. Now it appears, that in the original frame of our mind, our strongest attention is confined to ourselves; our next is extended to our relations and acquaintance; and it is only the weakest which reaches to strangers and indifferent persons. This partiality, then, and unequal affection, must not only have an influence on our behavior and conduct in society, but even on our ideas of vice and virtue; so as to make us regard any remarkable transgression of such a degree of partiality, either by too great an enlargement, or contraction of the affections, as vicious and immoral. This we may observe in our common judgments concerning actions, where we blame a person, who either centers all his affections in his family, or is so regardless of them, as, in any opposition of interest, to give the preference to a stranger, or mere chance acquaintance. From all which it follows, that our natural uncultivated ideas of morality, instead of providing a remedy for the partiality of our affections, do rather conform themselves to that partiality, and give it an additional force and influence.

The remedy, then, is not derived from nature, but from artifice; or more properly speaking, nature provides a remedy in the judgment and understanding, for what is irregular and incommodious in the affections. For when men, from their early education in society, have become sensible of the infinite advantages that result from it, and have besides acquired a new affection to[1] company and conversation; and when they have observed, that the principal disturbance in society arises from those goods, which we call external, and from their looseness and easy transition from one person to another; they must seek for a remedy, by putting these goods, as far as possible, on the same footing with the fixed and constant advantages of the mind and body. This can be done after no other manner, than by a convention entered into by all the members of the society to bestow stability on the possession of those external goods, and leave every one in the peaceable enjoyment of what he may acquire by his fortune and industry. By this means, every one knows what he may safely possess; and the passions are restrained in their partial and contradictory motions. Nor is such a restraint contrary to these passions; for if so, it could never be entered into, nor maintained; but it is only contrary to their heedless and impetuous movement. Instead of departing from our own interest, or from that of our nearest friends, by abstaining from the possessions of others, we cannot better consult both these interests, than by such a convention; because it is by that means we maintain society, which is so necessary to their well-being and subsistence, as well as to our own.

This convention is not of the nature of a promise: For even promises themselves, as we shall see afterwards, arise from human conventions. It is only a general sense of common interest; which sense all the members of the society express to one another, and which induces them to regulate their conduct by certain rules. I observe, that it will be for my interest to leave another in the possession of his goods, provided he will act in the same manner with regard to me. He is sensible of a like interest in the regulation of his conduct. When this common sense of interest is mutually expressed, and is known to both, it produces a suitable resolution and behavior. And this may properly enough be called a convention or agreement betwixt us, though without the interposition of a promise; since the actions of each of us have a reference to those of the other, and are performed upon the supposition, that something is to be performed on the other part. Two men, who pull the oars of a boat, do it by an agreement or convention, though they have never given promises to each other. Nor is the rule concerning the stability of possession the less derived from human conventions, that it arises gradually, and acquires force by a slow progression, and by our repeated experience of the inconveniences of transgressing it. On the contrary, this experience assures us still more, that the sense of interest has become common to all our fellows, and gives us a confidence of the future regularity of their conduct: And it is only on the expectation of this, that our moderation

---

1   *affection to* Fondness for.

and abstinence are founded. In like manner are languages gradually established by human conventions without any promise. In like manner do gold and silver become the common measures of exchange, and are esteemed sufficient payment for what is of a hundred times their value.

After this convention, concerning abstinence from the possessions of others, is entered into, and every one has acquired a stability in his possessions, there immediately arise the ideas of justice and injustice; as also those of property, right, and obligation. The latter are altogether unintelligible without first understanding the former. Our property is nothing but those goods, whose constant possession is established by the laws of society; that is, by the laws of justice. Those, therefore, who make use of the words property, or right, or obligation, before they have explained the origin of justice, or even make use of them in that explication, are guilty of a very gross fallacy, and can never reason upon any solid foundation. A man's property is some object related to him. This relation is not natural, but moral, and founded on justice. It is very preposterous, therefore, to imagine, that we can have any idea of property, without fully comprehending the nature of justice, and showing its origin in the artifice and contrivance of man. The origin of justice explains that of property. The same artifice gives rise to both. As our first and most natural sentiment of morals is founded on the nature of our passions, and gives the preference to ourselves and friends, above strangers; it is impossible there can be naturally any such thing as a fixed right or property, while the opposite passions of men impel them in contrary directions, and are not restrained by any convention or agreement.

No one can doubt, that the convention for the distinction of property, and for the stability of possession, is of all circumstances the most necessary to the establishment of human society, and that after the agreement for the fixing and observing of this rule, there remains little or nothing to be done towards settling a perfect harmony and concord. All the other passions, besides this of interest, are either easily restrained, or are not of such pernicious consequence, when indulged. Vanity is rather to be esteemed a social passion, and a bond of union among men. Pity and love are to be considered in the same light. And as to envy and revenge, though pernicious, they operate only by intervals, and are directed against particular persons, whom we consider as our superiors or enemies. This avidity alone, of acquiring goods and possessions for ourselves and our nearest friends, is insatiable, perpetual, universal, and directly destructive of society. There scarce is any one, who is not actuated by it; and there is no one, who has not reason to fear from it, when it acts without any restraint, and gives way to its first and most natural movements. So that upon the whole, we are to esteem the difficulties in the establishment of society, to be greater or less, according to those we encounter in regulating and restraining this passion.

It is certain, that no affection of the human mind has both a sufficient force, and a proper direction to counterbalance the love of gain, and render men fit members of society, by making them abstain from the possessions of others. Benevolence to strangers is too weak for this purpose; and as to the other passions, they rather inflame this avidity, when we observe, that the larger our possessions are, the more ability we have of gratifying all our appetites. There is no passion, therefore, capable of controlling the interested affection, but the very affection itself, by an alteration of its direction. Now this alteration must necessarily take place upon the least reflection; since it is evident, that the passion is much better satisfied by its restraint, than by its liberty, and that in preserving society, we make much greater advances in the acquiring possessions, than in the solitary and forlorn condition, which must follow upon violence and a universal license. The question, therefore, concerning the wickedness or goodness of human nature, enters not in the least into that other question concerning the origin of society; nor is there any thing to be considered but the degrees of men's sagacity or folly. For whether the passion of self-interest be esteemed vicious or virtuous, it is all a case; since itself alone restrains it: So that if it be virtuous, men become social by their virtue; if vicious, their vice has the same effect.

Now as it is by establishing the rule for the stability of possession, that this passion restrains itself; if that rule be very abstruse, and of difficult invention; society must be esteemed, in a manner, accidental, and the effect of many ages. But if it be found, that nothing can be more simple and obvious than that rule; that every parent, in order to preserve peace among his children, must establish it; and that these first rudiments of justice must every day be improved, as the society enlarges: If all this appear evident, as it certainly must, we may conclude, that it is utterly impossible for men to remain any considerable time in that savage condition, which precedes society; but that his very first state and situation may justly be esteemed social. This, however, hinders not, but that philosophers may, if they please, extend their reasoning to the supposed state of nature;

provided they allow it to be a mere philosophical fiction, which never had, and never could have any reality. Human nature being composed of two principal parts, which are requisite in all its actions, the affections and understanding; it is certain, that the blind motions of the former, without the direction of the latter, incapacitate men for society: And it may be allowed us to consider separately the effects, that result from the separate operations of these two component parts of the mind. The same liberty may be permitted to moral, which is allowed to natural philosophers; and it is very usual with the latter to consider any motion as compounded and consisting of two parts separate from each other, though at the same time they acknowledge it to be in itself uncompounded and inseparable.

This state of nature, therefore, is to be regarded as a mere fiction, not unlike that of the golden age, which poets have invented; only with this difference, that the former is described as full of war, violence and injustice; whereas the latter is painted out to us, as the most charming and most peaceable condition, that can possibly be imagined. The seasons, in that first age of nature, were so temperate, if we may believe the poets, that there was no necessity for men to provide themselves with clothes and houses as a security against the violence of heat and cold. The rivers flowed with wine and milk: The oaks yielded honey; and nature spontaneously produced her greatest delicacies. Nor were these the chief advantages of that happy age. The storms and tempests were not alone removed from nature; but those more furious tempests were unknown to human breasts, which now cause such uproar, and engender such confusion. Avarice, ambition, cruelty, selfishness, were never heard of: Cordial affection, compassion, sympathy, were the only movements, with which the human mind was yet acquainted. Even the distinction of mine and thine was banished from that happy race of mortals, and carried with them the very notions of property and obligation, justice and injustice.

This, no doubt, is to be regarded as an idle fiction; but yet deserves our attention, because nothing can more evidently show the origin of those virtues, which are the subjects of our present enquiry. I have already observed, that justice takes its rise from human conventions; and that these are intended as a remedy to some inconveniences, which proceed from the concurrence of certain qualities of the human mind with the situation of external objects. The qualities of the mind are selfishness and limited generosity: And the situation of external objects is their easy change, joined to their scarcity in comparison of the wants and

desires of men. But however philosophers may have been bewildered in those speculations, poets have been guided more infallibly, by a certain taste or common instinct, which in most kinds of reasoning goes farther than any of that art and philosophy, with which we have been yet acquainted. They easily perceived, if every man had a tender regard for another, or if nature supplied abundantly all our wants and desires, that the jealousy of interest, which justice supposes, could no longer have place; nor would there be any occasion for those distinctions and limits of property and possession, which at present are in use among mankind. Increase to a sufficient degree the benevolence of men, or the bounty of nature, and you render justice useless, by supplying its place with much nobler virtues, and more valuable blessings. The selfishness of men is animated by the few possessions we have, in proportion to our wants; and it is to restrain this selfishness, that men have been obliged to separate themselves from the community, and to distinguish betwixt their own goods and those of others.

Nor need we have recourse to the fictions of poets to learn this; but beside the reason of the thing, may discover the same truth by common experience and observation. It is easy to remark, that a cordial affection renders all things common among friends; and that married people in particular mutually lose their property, and are unacquainted with the mine and thine, which are so necessary, and yet cause such disturbance in human society. The same effect arises from any alteration in the circumstances of mankind; as when there is such a plenty of any thing as satisfies all the desires of men: In which case the distinction of property is entirely lost, and every thing remains in common. This we may observe with regard to air and water, though the most valuable of all external objects; and may easily conclude, that if men were supplied with every thing in the same abundance, or if every one had the same affection and tender regard for every one as for himself; justice and injustice would be equally unknown among mankind.

Here then is a proposition, which, I think, may be regarded as certain, that it is only from the selfishness and confined generosity of men, along with the scanty provision nature has made for his wants, that justice derives its origin. If we look backward we shall find, that this proposition bestows an additional force on some of those observations, which we have already made on this subject.

First, we may conclude from it, that a regard to public interest, or a strong extensive benevolence, is not our first and original motive for the observation of the rules of justice; since it is allowed, that if men were endowed with such a benevolence, these rules would never have been dreamt of.

Secondly, we may conclude from the same principle, that the sense of justice is not founded on reason, or on the discovery of certain connections and relations of ideas, which are eternal, immutable, and universally obligatory. For since it is confessed, that such an alteration as that above-mentioned, in the temper and circumstances of mankind, would entirely alter our duties and obligations, it is necessary upon the common system, that the sense of virtue is derived from reason, to show the change which this must produce in the relations and ideas. But it is evident, that the only cause, why the extensive generosity of man, and the perfect abundance of every thing, would destroy the very idea of justice, is because they render it useless; and that, on the other hand, his confined benevolence, and his necessitous condition, give rise to that virtue, only by making it requisite to the public interest, and to that of every individual. It was therefore a concern for our own, and the public interest, which made us establish the laws of justice; and nothing can be more certain, than that it is not any relation of ideas, which gives us this concern, but our impressions and sentiments, without which every thing in nature is perfectly indifferent to us, and can never in the least affect us. The sense of justice, therefore, is not founded on our ideas, but on our impressions.[1]

Thirdly, we may farther confirm the foregoing proposition, that those impressions, which give rise to this sense of justice, are not natural to the mind of man, but arise from artifice and human conventions. For since any considerable alteration of temper and circumstances destroys equally justice and injustice; and since such an alteration has an effect only by changing our own and the public interest; it

follows, that the first establishment of the rules of justice depends on these different interests. But if men pursued the public interest naturally, and with a hearty affection, they would never have dreamed of restraining each other by these rules; and if they pursued their own interest, without any precaution, they would run headlong into every kind of injustice and violence. These rules, therefore, are artificial, and seek their end in an oblique and indirect manner; nor is the interest, which gives rise to them, of a kind that could be pursued by the natural and inartificial passions of men.

To make this more evident, consider, that though the rules of justice are established merely by interest, their connection with interest is somewhat singular, and is different from what may be observed on other occasions. A single act of justice is frequently contrary to public interest; and were it to stand alone, without being followed by other acts, may, in itself, be very prejudicial to society. When a man of merit, of a beneficent disposition, restores a great fortune to a miser, or a seditious bigot, he has acted justly and laudably, but the public is a real sufferer. Nor is every single act of justice, considered apart, more conducive to private interest, than to public; and it is easily conceived how a man may impoverish himself by a signal instance of integrity, and have reason to wish, that with regard to that single act, the laws of justice were for a moment suspended in the universe. But however single acts of justice may be contrary, either to public or private interest, it is certain, that the whole plan or scheme is highly conducive, or indeed absolutely requisite, both to the support of society, and the well-being of every individual. It is impossible to separate the good from the ill. Property must be stable, and must be fixed by general rules. Though in one instance the public be a sufferer, this momentary ill is amply compensated by the steady prosecution of the rule, and by the peace and order, which it establishes in society. And even every individual person must find himself a gainer, on balancing the account; since, without justice, society must immediately dissolve, and every one must fall into that savage and solitary condition, which is infinitely worse than the worst situation that can possibly be supposed in society. When therefore men have had experience enough to observe, that whatever may be the consequence of any single act of justice, performed by a single person, yet the whole system of actions, concurred in by the whole society, is infinitely advantageous to the whole, and to every part; it is not long before justice and property take place. Every member of society is sensible of this interest: Every one expresses this sense to his

---

1   *ideas ... impressions* In Hume's theory of knowledge, impressions are the inner sensations we have when perceiving external objects. Ideas are the generalized copies of these impressions that we store mentally. Knowledge about particular things arises from perception and only from perception; but once we have stored ideas, we can have knowledge without (further) perception by recognizing the relations of ideas. Thus, for example, we know that snow is white by having an impression of whiteness when we look at snow; but we know that all bachelors are unmarried by examining the stored ideas corresponding to the words "bachelor" and "unmarried," and recognizing that the second idea is included within the first. Hume's point here is that knowledge about justice is not of this second sort; it is not discoverable that some action is just by mere operation of the mind (comparing ideas). Instead, that knowledge comes from the accompanying internal feelings we have when perceiving (or imagining) some event.

fellows, along with the resolution he has taken of squaring his actions by it, on condition that others will do the same. No more is requisite to induce any one of them to perform an act of justice, who has the first opportunity. This becomes an example to others. And thus justice establishes itself by a kind of convention or agreement; that is, by a sense of interest, supposed to be common to all, and where every single act is performed in expectation that others are to perform the like. Without such a convention, no one would ever have dreamed, that there was such a virtue as justice, or have been induced to conform his actions to it. Taking any single act, my justice may be pernicious in every respect; and it is only upon the supposition, that others are to imitate my example, that I can be induced to embrace that virtue; since nothing but this combination can render justice advantageous, or afford me any motives to conform my self to its rules.

We come now to the second question we proposed, viz. Why we annex the idea of virtue to justice, and of vice to injustice. This question will not detain us long after the principles, which we have already established. All we can say of it at present will be dispatched in a few words: And for farther satisfaction, the reader must wait till we come to the third part of this book. The natural obligation to justice, viz. interest, has been fully explained; but as to the moral obligation, or the sentiment of right and wrong, it will first be requisite to examine the natural virtues, before we can give a full and satisfactory account of it.

After men have found by experience, that their selfishness and confined generosity, acting at their liberty, totally incapacitate them for society; and at the same time have observed, that society is necessary to the satisfaction of those very passions, they are naturally induced to lay themselves under the restraint of such rules, as may render their commerce[1] more safe and commodious.[2] To the imposition then, and observance of these rules, both in general, and in every particular instance, they are at first induced only by a regard to interest; and this motive, on the first formation of society, is sufficiently strong and forcible. But when society has become numerous, and has increased to a tribe or nation, this interest is more remote; nor do men so readily perceive, that disorder and confusion follow upon every breach of these rules, as in a more narrow and contracted society.

But though in our own actions we may frequently lose sight of that interest, which we have in maintaining order, and may follow a lesser and more present interest, we never fail to observe the prejudice we receive, either mediately or immediately,[3] from the injustice of others; as not being in that case either blinded by passion, or biased by any contrary temptation. Nay when the injustice is so distant from us, as no way to affect our interest, it still displeases us; because we consider it as prejudicial to human society, and pernicious to every one that approaches the person guilty of it. We partake of their uneasiness by sympathy; and as every thing, which gives uneasiness in human actions, upon the general survey, is called Vice, and whatever produces satisfaction, in the same manner, is denominated Virtue; this is the reason why the sense of moral good and evil follows upon justice and injustice. And though this sense, in the present case, be derived only from contemplating the actions of others, yet we fail not to extend it even to our own actions. The general rule reaches beyond those instances, from which it arose; while at the same time we naturally sympathize with others in the sentiments they entertain of us. Thus self-interest is the original motive to the establishment of justice: but a sympathy with public interest is the source of the moral approbation, which attends that virtue.

Though this progress of the sentiments be natural, and even necessary, it is certain, that it is here forwarded by the artifice of politicians, who, in order to govern men more easily, and preserve peace in human society, have endeavored to produce an esteem for justice, and an abhorrence of injustice. This, no doubt, must have its effect; but nothing can be more evident, than that the matter has been carried too far by certain writers on morals, who seem to have employed their utmost efforts to extirpate all sense of virtue from among mankind. Any artifice of politicians may assist nature in the producing of those sentiments, which she suggests to us, and may even on some occasions, produce alone an approbation or esteem for any particular action; but it is impossible it should be the sole cause of the distinction we make betwixt vice and virtue. For if nature did not aid us in this particular, it would be in vain for politicians to talk of honorable or dishonorable, praiseworthy or blamable. These words would be perfectly unintelligible, and would no more have any idea annexed to them, than if they were of a tongue perfectly unknown to us. The utmost politicians

---

1   *commerce*   Dealings by people with one another, in various life-matters—not just buying and selling.

2   *commodious*   Advantageous, convenient, serviceable.

3   *mediately or immediately*   Indirectly (mediated by other events) or directly.

can perform, is, to extend the natural sentiments beyond their original bounds; but still nature must furnish the materials, and give us some notion of moral distinctions.

As public praise and blame increase our esteem for justice; so private education and instruction contribute to the same effect. For as parents easily observe, that a man is the more useful, both to himself and others, the greater degree of probity and honor he is endowed with; and that those principles have greater force, when custom and education assist interest and reflection: For these reasons they are induced to inculcate on their children, from their earliest infancy, the principles of probity, and teach them to regard the observance of those rules, by which society is maintained, as worthy and honorable, and their violation as base and infamous. By this means the sentiments of honor may take root in their tender minds, and acquire such firmness and solidity, that they may fall little short of those principles, which are the most essential to our natures, and the most deeply radicated[1] in our internal constitution.

What farther contributes to increase their solidity, is the interest of our reputation, after the opinion, that a merit or demerit attends justice or injustice, is once firmly established among mankind. There is nothing, which touches us more nearly than our reputation, and nothing on which our reputation more depends than our conduct, with relation to the property of others. For this reason, every one, who has any regard to his character, or who intends to live on good terms with mankind, must fix an inviolable law to himself, never, by any temptation, to be induced to violate those principles, which are essential to a man of probity and honor.

I shall make only one observation before I leave this subject, viz. that though I assert, that in the state of nature, or that imaginary state, which preceded society, there be neither justice nor injustice, yet I assert not, that it was allowable, in such a state, to violate the property of others. I only maintain, that there was no such thing as property; and consequently could be no such thing as justice or injustice. I shall have occasion to make a similar reflection with regard to promises, when I come to treat of them; and I hope this reflection, when duly weighed, will suffice to remove all odium from the foregoing opinions, with regard to justice and injustice.

Section 7: Of the Origin of Government

Nothing is more certain, than that men are, in a great measure, governed by interest, and that even when they extend their concern beyond themselves, it is not to any great distance; nor is it usual for them, in common life, to look farther than their nearest friends and acquaintance. it is no less certain, that it is impossible for men to consult their interest in so effectual a manner, as by an universal and inflexible observance of the rules of justice, by which alone they can preserve society, and keep themselves from falling into that wretched and savage condition, which is commonly represented as the state of nature. And as this interest, which all men have in the upholding of society, and the observation of the rules of justice, is great, so is it palpable and evident, even to the most rude and uncultivated of human race; and it is almost impossible for any one, who has had experience of society, to be mistaken in this particular. Since, therefore, men are so sincerely attached to their interest, and their interest is so much concerned in the observance of justice, and this interest is so certain and avowed; it may be asked, how any disorder can ever arise in society, and what principle there is in human nature so powerful as to overcome so strong a passion, or so violent as to obscure so clear a knowledge?

It has been observed, in treating of the passions, that men are mightily governed by the imagination, and proportion their affections more to the light, under which any object appears to them, than to its real and intrinsic value. What strikes upon them with a strong and lively idea commonly prevails above what lies in a more obscure light; and it must be a great superiority of value, that is able to compensate this advantage. Now as every thing, that is contiguous to us, either in space or time, strikes upon us with such an idea, it has a proportional effect on the will and passions, and commonly operates with more force than any object, that lies in a more distant and obscure light. Though we may be fully convinced, that the latter object excels the former, we are not able to regulate our actions by this judgment; but yield to the solicitations of our passions, which always plead in favor of whatever is near and contiguous.

This is the reason why men so often act in contradiction to their known interest; and in particular why they prefer any trivial advantage, that is present, to the maintenance of order in society, which so much depends on the observance of justice. The consequences of every breach of equity seem to lie very remote, and are not able to counterbalance

---

1 *radicated* Rooted.

any immediate advantage, that may be reaped from it. They are, however, never the less real for being remote; and as all men are, in some degree, subject to the same weakness, it necessarily happens, that the violations of equity must become very frequent in society, and the commerce of men, by that means, be rendered very dangerous and uncertain. You have the same propension,[1] that I have, in favor of what is contiguous above what is remote. You are, therefore, naturally carried to commit acts of injustice as well as me. Your example both pushes me forward in this way by imitation, and also affords me a new reason for any breach of equity, by showing me, that I should be the cully of[2] my integrity, if I alone should impose on myself a severe restraint amidst the licentiousness of others.

This quality, therefore, of human nature, not only is very dangerous to society, but also seems, on a cursory view, to be incapable of any remedy. The remedy can only come from the consent of men; and if men be incapable of themselves to prefer remote to contiguous, they will never consent to any thing, which would oblige them to such a choice, and contradict, in so sensible a manner, their natural principles and propensities. Whoever chooses the means, chooses also the end; and if it be impossible for us to prefer what is remote, it is equally impossible for us to submit to any necessity, which would oblige us to such a method of acting.

But here it is observable, that this infirmity of human nature becomes a remedy to itself, and that we provide against our negligence about remote objects, merely because we are naturally inclined to that negligence. When we consider any objects at a distance, all their minute distinctions vanish, and we always give the preference to whatever is in itself preferable, without considering its situation and circumstances. This gives rise to what in an improper sense we call reason, which is a principle, that is often contradictory to those propensities that display themselves upon the approach of the object. In reflecting on any action, which I am to perform a twelve-month hence, I always resolve to prefer the greater good, whether at that time it will be more contiguous or remote; nor does any difference in that particular make a difference in my present intentions and resolutions. My distance from the final determination makes all those minute differences vanish, nor am I affected by any thing, but the general and more discernible qualities of good and evil. But on my nearer approach, those circumstances, which I at first over-looked, begin to appear, and have an influence on my conduct and affections. A new inclination to the present good springs up, and makes it difficult for me to adhere inflexibly to my first purpose and resolution. This natural infirmity I may very much regret, and I may endeavor, by all possible means, to free my self from it. I may have recourse to study and reflection within myself; to the advice of friends; to frequent meditation, and repeated resolution: And having experienced how ineffectual all these are, I may embrace with pleasure any other expedient, by which I may impose a restraint upon myself, and guard against this weakness.

The only difficulty, therefore, is to find out this expedient, by which men cure their natural weakness, and lay themselves under the necessity of observing the laws of justice and equity, notwithstanding their violent propension to prefer contiguous to remote. It is evident such a remedy can never be effectual without correcting this propensity; and as it is impossible to change or correct any thing material in our nature, the utmost we can do is to change our circumstances and situation, and render the observance of the laws of justice our nearest interest, and their violation our most remote. But this being impracticable with respect to all mankind, it can only take place with respect to a few, whom we thus immediately interest in the execution of justice. These are the persons, whom we call civil magistrates, kings and their ministers, our governors and rulers, who being indifferent persons to the greatest part of the state,[3] have no interest, or but a remote one, in any act of injustice; and being satisfied with their present condition, and with their part in society, have an immediate interest in every execution of justice, which is so necessary to the upholding of society. Here then is the origin of civil government and society. Men are not able radically to cure, either in themselves or others, that narrowness of soul, which makes them prefer the present to the remote. They cannot change their natures. All they can do is to change their situation, and render the observance of justice the immediate interest of some particular persons, and its violation their more remote. These persons, then, are not only induced to observe those rules in their own conduct, but also to constrain others to a like regularity, and enforce the dictates of equity

---

1   *propension*   Inclination.
2   *the cully of*   Duped by, taken in or cheated as a result of.

3   *indifferent persons to the greatest part of the state*   On the whole, unbiased, not predisposed to further the interests of one particular group over another.

through the whole society. And if it be necessary, they may also interest others more immediately in the execution of justice, and create a number of officers, civil and military, to assist them in their government.

But this execution of justice, though the principal, is not the only advantage of government. As violent passion hinders men from seeing distinctly the interest they have in an equitable behavior towards others; so it hinders them from seeing that equity itself, and gives them a remarkable partiality in their own favors. This inconvenience is corrected in the same manner as that above-mentioned. The same persons, who execute the laws of justice, will also decide all controversies concerning them; and being indifferent to the greatest part of the society, will decide them more equitably than every one would in his own case.

By means of these two advantages, in the execution and decision of justice, men acquire a security against each other's weakness and passion, as well as against their own, and under the shelter of their governors, begin to taste at ease the sweets of society and mutual assistance. But government extends farther its beneficial influence; and not contented to protect men in those conventions they make for their mutual interest, it often obliges them to make such conventions, and forces them to seek their own advantage, by a concurrence in some common end or purpose. There is no quality in human nature, which causes more fatal errors in our conduct, than that which leads us to prefer whatever is present to the distant and remote, and makes us desire objects more according to their situation than their intrinsic value. Two neighbors may agree to drain a meadow, which they possess in common; because it is easy for them to know each other's mind; and each must perceive, that the immediate consequence of his failing in his part, is the abandoning the whole project. But it is very difficult, and indeed impossible, that a thousand persons should agree in any such action; it being difficult for them to concert so complicated a design, and still more difficult for them to execute it; while each seeks a pretext to free himself of the trouble and expense, and would lay the whole burden on others. Political society easily remedies both these inconveniences. Magistrates find an immediate interest in the interest of any considerable part of their subjects. They need consult no body but themselves to form any scheme for the promoting of that interest. And as the failure of any one piece in the execution is connected, though not immediately, with the failure of the whole, they prevent that failure, because they find no interest in it, either im-

mediate or remote. Thus bridges are built; harbors opened; ramparts raised; canals formed; fleets equipped; and armies disciplined; every where, by the care of government, which, though composed of men subject to all human infirmities, becomes, by one of the finest and most subtle inventions imaginable, a composition, which is, in some measure, exempted from all these infirmities.

◆ ◆ ◆ ◆ ◆

An Enquiry Concerning the Principles of Morals (1751)

Appendix 3: Some Farther Considerations with Regard to Justice

The intention of this Appendix is to give some more particular explication of the origin and nature of Justice, and to mark some differences between it and the other virtues.

The social virtues of humanity and benevolence exert their influence immediately by a direct tendency or instinct, which chiefly keeps in view the simple object, moving the affections, and comprehends not any scheme or system, nor the consequences resulting from the concurrence, imitation, or example of others. A parent flies to the relief of his child; transported by that natural sympathy which actuates him, and which affords no leisure to reflect on the sentiments or conduct of the rest of mankind in like circumstances. A generous man cheerfully embraces an opportunity of serving his friend; because he then feels himself under the dominion of the beneficent affections, nor is he concerned whether any other person in the universe were ever before actuated by such noble motives, or will ever afterwards prove their influence. In all these cases the social passions have in view a single individual object, and pursue the safety or happiness alone of the person loved and esteemed. With this they are satisfied: in this they acquiesce. And as the good, resulting from their benign influence, is in itself complete and entire, it also excites the moral sentiment of approbation, without any reflection on farther consequences, and without any more enlarged views of the concurrence or imitation of the other members of society. On the contrary, were the generous friend or disinterested patriot to stand alone in the practice of beneficence, this would rather enhance his value in our eyes, and join the praise of rarity and novelty to his other more exalted merits.

The case is not the same with the social virtues of justice and fidelity. They are highly useful, or indeed absolutely necessary to the well-being of mankind: but the benefit resulting from them is not the consequence of every individual single act; but arises from the whole scheme or system concurred in by the whole, or the greater part of the society. General peace and order are the attendants of justice or a general abstinence from the possessions of others; but a particular regard to the particular right of one individual citizen may frequently, considered in itself, be productive of pernicious consequences. The result of the individual acts is here, in many instances, directly opposite to that of the whole system of actions; and the former may be extremely hurtful, while the latter is, to the highest degree, advantageous. Riches, inherited from a parent, are, in a bad man's hand, the instrument of mischief. The right of succession[1] may, in one instance, be hurtful. Its benefit arises only from the observance of the general rule; and it is sufficient, if compensation be thereby made for all the ills and inconveniences which flow from particular characters and situations.

Cyrus, young and inexperienced, considered only the individual case before him, and reflected on a limited fitness and convenience, when he assigned the long coat to the tall boy, and the short coat to the other of smaller size. His governor instructed him better, while he pointed out more enlarged views and consequences, and informed his pupil of the general, inflexible rules, necessary to support general peace and order in society.[2]

The happiness and prosperity of mankind, arising from the social virtue of benevolence and its subdivisions, may be compared to a wall, built by many hands, which still rises by each stone that is heaped upon it, and receives increase proportional to the diligence and care of each workman. The same happiness, raised by the social virtue of justice and its subdivisions, may be compared to the building of a vault,[3] where each individual stone would, of itself, fall to the ground; nor is the whole fabric supported but by the mutual assistance and combination of its corresponding parts.

All the laws of nature, which regulate property, as well as all civil laws, are general, and regard alone some essential circumstances of the case, without taking into consideration the characters, situations, and connections of the person concerned, or any particular consequences which may result from the determination of these laws in any particular case which offers. They deprive, without scruple, a beneficent man of all his possessions, if acquired by mistake, without a good title; in order to bestow them on a selfish miser, who has already heaped up immense stores of superfluous riches. Public utility requires that property should be regulated by general inflexible rules; and though such rules are adopted as best serve the same end of public utility, it is impossible for them to prevent all particular hardships, or make beneficial consequences result from every individual case. It is sufficient, if the whole plan or scheme be necessary to the support of civil society, and if the balance of good, in the main, do thereby preponderate much above that of evil. Even the general laws of the universe, though planned by infinite wisdom, cannot exclude all evil or inconvenience in every particular operation.

It has been asserted by some, that justice arises from Human Conventions, and proceeds from the voluntary choice, consent, or combination of mankind. If by *convention* be here meant a *promise* (which is the most usual sense of the word) nothing can be more absurd than this position. The observance of promises is itself one of the most considerable parts of justice, and we are not surely bound to keep our word because we have given our word to keep it. But if by convention be meant a sense of common interest, which sense each man feels in his own breast, which he remarks in his fellows, and which carries him, in concurrence with others, into a general plan or system of actions, which tends to public utility; it must be owned, that, in this sense, justice arises from human conventions. For if it be allowed (what is, indeed, evident) that the particular consequences of a particular act of justice may be hurtful to the public as well as to individuals; it follows that every man, in embracing that virtue, must have an eye to the whole plan or system, and must expect the concurrence of his fellows in the same conduct and behavior. Did all his views terminate in the consequences of each act of his own, his benevolence and humanity, as well as his self-love, might often prescribe to him measures of conduct very different from those which are agreeable to the strict rules of right and justice.

---

1   *right of succession* Principle determining inheritance of an estate, an office, a title, etc.; the primary use of this term, which Hume may have had in mind here, is with reference to the rules determining who takes over at the death of a monarch.

2   *Cyrus ... in society* This story, found in Xenophon's *Memorabilia*, concerns the young prince who would become Cyrus the Great, ruler of Persia (sixth century BCE). A big boy has taken a coat that fitted him from the small boy by force, and given him his smaller one; Cyrus, asked by his teacher to judge this case, decides that the situation is just because both coats fit; but his teacher corrects him, telling him that all that is relevant here is enforcing the law against violent appropriation of someone else's property.

3   *vault* Arched roof or ceiling.

Thus, two men pull the oars of a boat by common convention for common interest, without any promise or contract; thus gold and silver are made the measures of exchange; thus speech and words and language are fixed by human convention and agreement. Whatever is advantageous to two or more persons, if all perform their part; but what loses all advantage if only one perform, can arise from no other principle There would otherwise be no motive for any one of them to enter into that scheme of conduct.[1]

The word *natural* is commonly taken in so many senses and is of so loose a signification, that it seems vain to dispute whether justice be natural or not. If self-love, if benevolence be natural to man; if reason and forethought be also natural; then may the same epithet be applied to justice, order, fidelity, property, society. Men's inclination, their necessities, lead them to combine; their understanding and experience tell them that this combination is impossible where each governs himself by no rule, and pays no regard to the possessions of others: and from these passions and reflections conjoined, as soon as we observe like passions and reflections in others, the sentiment of justice, throughout all ages, has infallibly and certainly had place to some degree or other in every individual of the human species. In so sagacious an animal, what necessarily arises from the exertion of his intellectual faculties may justly be esteemed natural.[2]

Among all civilized nations it has been the constant endeavor to remove everything arbitrary and partial from the decision of property, and to fix the sentence of judges by such general views and considerations as may be equal to every member of society. For besides, that nothing could be more dangerous than to accustom the bench, even in the smallest instance, to regard private friendship or enmity; it is certain, that men, where they imagine that there was no other reason for the preference of their adversary but personal favor, are apt to entertain the strongest ill-will against the magistrates and judges. When natural reason, therefore, points out no fixed view of public utility by which a controversy of property can be decided, positive laws[3] are often framed to supply its place, and direct the procedure of all courts of judicature. Where these too fail, as often happens, precedents are called for; and a former decision, though given itself without any sufficient reason, justly becomes a sufficient reason for a new decision. If direct laws and precedents be wanting, imperfect and indirect ones are brought in aid; and the controverted[4] case is ranged under them by analogical reasonings and comparisons, and similitudes, and correspondencies, which are often more fanciful than real. In general, it may safely be affirmed that jurisprudence is, in this respect, different from all the sciences; and that in many of its nicer[5] questions, there cannot properly be said to be truth or falsehood on either side. If one pleader bring the case under any former law or precedent, by a refined

---

1   *Whatever is ... conduct* [Hume's note] This theory concerning the origin of property, and consequently of justice, is, in the main, the same with that hinted at and adopted by Grotius, "Hence a notion may be formed of the reason why men departed from the primeval state of holding all things in common, attaching the ideas of property, first to moveable and next to immoveable things. When the inhabitants of the earth began to acquire a taste for more delicate fare than the spontaneous productions of the ground, and to look for more commodious habitations than caves, or the hollow of trees, and to long for more elegant clothing than the skins of wild beasts, industry became necessary to supply those wants, and each individual began to apply his attention to some particular art. The distance of the places too, into which men were dispersed, prevented them from carrying the fruits of the earth to a common stock, and in the next place, the want of just principle and equitable kindness would destroy that equality which ought to subsist both in the labor of producing and consuming the necessaries of life. At the same time, we learn how things passed from being held in common to a state of property. It was not by the act of the mind alone that this change took place. For men in that case could never know, what others intended to appropriate to their own use, so as to exclude the claim of every other pretender to the same; and many too might desire to possess the same thing. Property therefore must have been established either by express agreement, as by division, or by tacit consent, as by occupancy (Hugo Grotius, *The Rights of War and Peace including the Law of Nature and of Nations*) [625; trans. A.C. Campbell, 1901]. [Grotius (1583–1645), also known as Huig de Groot, was an important Dutch philosopher, jurist, and natural law theorist. This work was influential in establishing the idea of international law.]

2   *esteemed natural* [Hume's note] Natural may be opposed, either to what is UNUSUAL, MIRACULOUS or ARTIFICIAL. In the two former senses, justice and property are undoubtedly natural. But as they suppose reason, forethought, design, and a social union and confederacy among men, perhaps that epithet cannot strictly, in the last sense, be applied to them. Had men lived without society, property had never been known, and neither justice nor injustice had ever existed. But society among human creatures had been impossible without reason and forethought. Inferior animals, that unite, are guided by instinct, which supplies the place for reason. But all these disputes are merely verbal.

3   *positive laws* Laws of social origin, explicitly enacted by government or laid down by custom; the contrast here is usually with *natural* laws: rules discovered or created by natural reason.

4   *controverted* Disputed.

5   *nicer* More subtle, involving close consideration and minute distinctions; not obvious.

analogy or comparison; the opposite pleader is not at a loss to find an opposite analogy or comparison: and the preference given by the judge is often founded more on taste and imagination than on any solid argument. Public utility is the general object of all courts of judicature; and this utility too requires a stable rule in all controversies: but where several rules, nearly equal and indifferent,[1] present themselves, it is a very slight turn of thought which fixes the decision in favor of either party.[2]

1   *indifferent*   Equally apt.
2   *either party*   [Hume's note] That there be a separation or distinction of possessions, and that this separation be steady and constant; this is absolutely required by the interests of society, and hence the origin of justice and property. What possessions are assigned to particular persons; this is, generally speaking, pretty indifferent; and is often determined by very frivolous views and considerations. We shall mention a few particulars.

Were a society formed among several independent members, the most obvious rule, which could be agreed on, would be to annex property to *present* possession, and leave every one a right to what he at present enjoys. The relation of possession, which takes place between the person and the object, naturally draws on the relation of property.

For a like reason, occupation or first possession becomes the foundation of property.

Where a man bestows labor and industry upon any object, which before belonged to no body; as in cutting down and shaping a tree, in cultivating a field, &c., the alterations, which he produces, causes a relation between him and the object, and naturally engages us to annex it to him by the new relation of property. This cause here concurs with the public utility, which consists in the encouragement given to industry and labor.

Perhaps too, private humanity towards the possessor concurs, in this instance, with the other motives, and engages us to leave with him what he has acquired by his sweat and labor; and what he has flattered himself in the constant enjoyment of. For though private humanity can, by no means, be the origin of justice; since the latter virtue so often contradicts the former; yet when the rule of separate and constant possession is once formed by the indispensable necessities of society, private humanity, and an aversion to the doing a hardship to another, may, in a particular instance, give rise to a particular rule of property.

I am much inclined to think, that the right succession or inheritance much depends on those connections of the imagination, and that the relation to a former proprietor begetting a relation to the object, is the cause why the property is transferred to a man after the death of his kinsman. It is true; industry is more encouraged by the transference of possession to children or near relations: but this consideration will only have place in a cultivated society: whereas the right of succession is regarded even among the greatest Barbarians.

Acquisition of property by accession can be explained no way but by having recourse to the relations and connections of the

We may just observe, before we conclude this subject, that after the laws of justice are fixed by views of general utility, the injury, the hardship, the harm, which result to any individual from a violation of them, enter very much into consideration, and are a great source of that universal blame which attends every wrong or iniquity. By the laws of society, this coat, this horse is mine, and *ought* to remain perpetually in my possession: I reckon on the secure enjoyment of it: by depriving me of it, you disappoint my expectations, and doubly displease me, and offend every bystander. It is a public wrong, so far as the rules of equity are violated: it is a private harm, so far as an individual is injured. And though the second consideration could have no place, were not the former previously established: for otherwise the distinction of *mine* and *thine* would be unknown in society:

imaginations. [*Accession* refers to an assortment of legal conventions for ownership of property. For example, one can come to own new property: by growth out of, or construction from, old property (as one owns the apples produced by one's apple tree, or as one owns the wine one makes out of one's grapes); more complicated cases arise when one person constructs something out of someone else's raw materials, and ownership of the product is contested.]

The property of rivers, by the laws of most nations, and by the natural turn of our thoughts, is attributed to the proprietors of their banks, excepting such vast rivers as the Rhine or the Danube, which seem too large to follow as an accession to the property of the neighboring fields. Yet even these rivers are considered as the property of that nation, through whose dominions they run; the idea of a nation being of a suitable bulk to correspond with them, and bear them such a relation in the fancy.

The accessions, which are made to land, bordering upon rivers, follow the land, say the civilians, provided it be made by what they call alluvion, that is, insensibly and imperceptibly; which are circumstances, that assist the imagination in the conjunction. [*Alluvion* is the formation of new land by the slow and imperceptible action of flowing water; in law, provided this action has been slow and imperceptible, this added land is considered to be the property of the owner of the land to which it is annexed.]

Where there is any considerable portion torn at once from one bank and added to another, it becomes not his property, whose land it falls on, till it unite with the land, and till the trees and plants have spread their roots into both. Before that, the thought does not sufficiently join them.

In short, we must ever distinguish between the necessity of a separation and constancy in men's possession, and the rules, which assign particular objects to particular persons. The first necessity is obvious, strong, and invincible: the latter may depend on a public utility more light and frivolous, on the sentiment of private humanity and aversion to private hardship, on positive laws, on precedents, analogies, and very fine connections and turns of the imagination.

yet there is no question but the regard to general good is much enforced by the respect to particular. What injures the community, without hurting any individual, is often more lightly thought of. But where the greatest public wrong is also conjoined with a considerable private one, no wonder the highest disapprobation attends so iniquitous a behavior.

◆ ◆ ◆ ◆ ◆

Of the Original Contract (1748)

As no party, in the present age, can well support itself without a philosophical or speculative system of principles annexed to its political or practical one, we accordingly find, that each of the factions into which this nation is divided has reared up a fabric of the former kind, in order to protect and cover that scheme of actions which it pursues. The people being commonly very rude builders, especially in this speculative way, and more especially still when actuated by party-zeal, it is natural to imagine that their workmanship must be a little unshapely, and discover evident marks of that violence and hurry in which it was raised. The one party, by tracing up government to the Deity, endeavored to render it so sacred and inviolate, that it must be little less than sacrilege, however, tyrannical it may become, to touch or invade it in the smallest article. The other party,[1] by founding government altogether on the consent of the people, suppose that there is a kind of *original contract*, by which the subjects have tacitly reserved the power of resisting their sovereign, whenever they find themselves aggrieved by that authority, with which they have, for certain purposes, voluntarily entrusted him. These are the speculative principles of the two parties, and these, too, are the practical consequences deduced from them.

I shall venture to affirm, *That both these systems of speculative principles are just; though not in the sense intended by the parties*: and, *That both the schemes of practical consequences are prudent; though not in the extremes to which each party, in opposition to the other, has commonly endeavored to carry them.*

That the Deity is the ultimate author of all government, will never be denied by any, who admit a general providence,

and allow, that all events in the universe are conducted by an uniform plan, and directed to wise purposes. As it is impossible for the human race to subsist, at least in any comfortable or secure state, without the protection of government, this institution must certainly have been intended by that beneficent Being, who means the good of all his creatures: and as it has universally, in fact, taken place, in all countries, and all ages, we may conclude, with still greater certainty, that it was intended by that omniscient Being who can never be deceived by any event or operation. But since he gave rise to it, not by any particular or miraculous interposition, but by his concealed and universal efficacy, a sovereign cannot, properly speaking, be called his vicegerent in any other sense than every power or force, being derived from him, may be said to act by his commission. Whatever actually happens is comprehended in the general plan or intention of Providence; nor has the greatest and most lawful prince any more reason, upon that account, to plead a peculiar sacredness or inviolable authority, than an inferior magistrate, or even an usurper, or even a robber and a pirate. The same Divine Superintendent, who, for wise purposes, invested a Titus or a Trajan with authority, did also, for purposes no doubt equally wise, though unknown, bestow power on a Borgia or an Angria.[2] The same causes, which gave rise to the sovereign power in every state, established likewise every petty jurisdiction in it, and every limited authority. A constable, therefore, no less than a king, acts by a divine commission, and possesses an indefeasible right.

When we consider how nearly equal all men are in their bodily force, and even in their mental powers and faculties, till cultivated by education, we must necessarily allow, that nothing but their own consent could, at first, associate them together, and subject them to any authority. The people, if we trace government to its first origin in the woods and deserts, are the source of all power and jurisdiction, and voluntarily, for the sake of peace and order, abandoned their native liberty, and received laws from their equal and companion. The conditions upon which they were willing

---

1 *one party ... The other party* The Tories and the Whigs, respectively.

2 *Titus ... Angria* Titus Flavius Vespasianus (39–81 CE) and Marcus Ulpius Traianus (c. 53–117 CE) were both emperors of Rome. Cesare Borgia (1476–1507) was an Italian cardinal, military leader, and ruler of part of northern Italy. His methods were a model for Machiavelli's prince. Tulagee Angria was the leader of a pirate family ruling the coast of India between Goa and Bombay; he was defeated by a British force in 1755. Hume contrasts the vicious cruelty of Borgia and the pirate with the reputation for humanity and enlightened rule of the two Roman emperors.

to submit, were either expressed, or were so clear and obvious, that it might well be esteemed superfluous to express them. If this, then, be meant by the *original contract*, it cannot be denied, that all government is, at first, founded on a contract, and that the most ancient rude combinations of mankind were formed chiefly by that principle. In vain are we asked in what records this charter of our liberties is registered. It was not written on parchment, nor yet on leaves or barks of trees. It preceded the use of writing, and all the other civilized arts of life. But we trace it plainly in the nature of man, and in the equality, or something approaching equality, which we find in all the individuals of that species. The force, which now prevails, and which is founded on fleets and armies, is plainly political, and derived from authority, the effect of established government. A man's natural force consists only in the vigor of his limbs, and the firmness of his courage; which could never subject multitudes to the command of one. Nothing but their own consent, and their sense of the advantages resulting from peace and order, could have had that influence.

Yet even this consent was long very imperfect, and could not be the basis of a regular administration. The chieftain, who had probably acquired his influence during the continuance of war, ruled more by persuasion than command; and till he could employ force to reduce the refractory and disobedient, the society could scarcely be said to have attained a state of civil government. No compact or agreement, it is evident, was expressly formed for general submission; an idea far beyond the comprehension of savages: each exertion of authority in the chieftain must have been particular, and called forth by the present exigencies of the case: the sensible utility, resulting from his interposition, made these exertions become daily more frequent; and their frequency gradually produced a habitual, and, if you please to call it so, a voluntary, and therefore precarious, acquiescence in the people.

But philosophers, who have embraced a party (if that be not a contradiction in terms), are not contented with these concessions. They assert,[1] not only that government in its earliest infancy arose from consent, or rather the voluntary acquiescence of the people; but also that, even at present, when it has attained its full maturity, it rests on no other foundation. They affirm, that all men are still born equal, and owe allegiance to no prince or government, unless bound by the obligation and sanction of a *promise*. And as no man, without some equivalent, would forego the advantages of his native liberty, and subject himself to the will of another, this promise is always understood to be conditional, and imposes on him no obligation, unless he meet with justice and protection from his sovereign. These advantages the sovereign promises him in return; and if he fail in the execution, he has broken, on his part, the articles of engagement, and has thereby freed his subject from all obligations to allegiance. Such, according to these philosophers, is the foundation of authority in every government, and such the right of resistance possessed by every subject.

But would these reasoners look abroad into the world, they would meet with nothing that, in the least, corresponds to their ideas, or can warrant so refined and philosophical a system. On the contrary, we find every where princes who claim their subjects as their property, and assert their independent right of sovereignty, from conquest or succession. We find also everywhere subjects who acknowledge this right in their prince, and suppose themselves born under obligations of obedience to a certain sovereign, as much as under the ties of reverence and duty to certain parents. These connections are always conceived to be equally independent of our consent, in Persia and China; in France and Spain; and even in Holland and England, wherever the doctrines abovementioned have not been carefully inculcated. Obedience or subjection becomes so familiar, that most men never make any inquiry about its origin or cause, more than about the principle of gravity, resistance, or the most universal laws of nature. Or if curiosity ever move them; as soon as they learn that they themselves and their ancestors have, for several ages, or from time immemorial, been subject to such a form of government or such a family, they immediately acquiesce, and acknowledge their obligation to allegiance. Were you to preach, in most parts of the world, that political connections are founded altogether on voluntary consent or a mutual promise, the magistrate would soon imprison you as seditious for loosening the ties of obedience; if your friends did not before shut you up as delirious, for advancing such absurdities. It is strange that an act of the mind, which every individual is supposed to have formed, and after he came to the use of reason too, otherwise it could have no authority; that this act, I say, should be so much unknown to all of them, that over the face of the whole earth, there scarcely remain any traces or memory of it.

---

1   *They assert*   Hume has in mind here the "contractarian" philosophers, especially John Locke, who claimed that an original contract or (at least implied) consent of the governed, was the basis of legitimacy of government. Hume's account of their position is loosely adapted from that given in Locke's *Second Treatise*.

But the contract, on which government is founded, is said to be the *original contract*; and consequently may be supposed too old to fall under the knowledge of the present generation. If the agreement, by which savage men first associated and conjoined their force, be here meant, this is acknowledged to be real; but being so ancient, and being obliterated by a thousand changes of government and princes, it cannot now be supposed to retain any authority. If we would say any thing to the purpose, we must assert that every particular government which is lawful, and which imposes any duty of allegiance on the subject, was, at first, founded on consent and a voluntary compact. But, besides that this supposes the consent of the fathers to bind the children, even to the most remote generations (which republican writers will never allow), besides this, I say, it is not justified by history or experience in any age or country of the world.

Almost all the governments which exist at present, or of which there remains any record in story, have been founded originally, either on usurpation or conquest, or both, without any presence of a fair consent or voluntary subjection of the people. When an artful and bold man is placed at the head of an army or faction, it is often easy for him, by employing, sometimes violence, sometimes false presences, to establish his dominion over a people a hundred times more numerous than his partisans. He allows no such open communication, that his enemies can know, with certainty, their number or force. He gives them no leisure to assemble together in a body to oppose him. Even all those who are the instruments of his usurpation may wish his fall; but their ignorance of each other's intention keeps them in awe, and is the sole cause of his security. By such arts as these many governments have been established; and this is all the *original contract* which they have to boast of.

The face of the earth is continually changing, by the increase of small kingdoms into great empires, by the dissolution of great empires into smaller kingdoms, by the planting of colonies, by the migration of tribes. Is there any thing discoverable in all these events but force and violence? Where is the mutual agreement or voluntary association so much talked of?

Even the smoothest way by which a nation may receive a foreign master, by marriage or a will, is not extremely honorable for the people; but supposes them to be disposed of, like a dowry or a legacy, according to the pleasure or interest of their rulers.

But where no force interposes, and election takes place; what is this election so highly vaunted? It is either the combination of a few great men, who decide for the whole, and will allow of no opposition; or it is the fury of a multitude, that follow a seditious ringleader, who is not known, perhaps, to a dozen among them, and who owes his advancement merely to his own impudence, or to the momentary caprice of his fellows.

Are these disorderly elections, which are rare too, of such mighty authority as to be the only lawful foundation of all government and allegiance?

In reality, there is not a more terrible event than a total dissolution of government, which gives liberty to the multitude, and makes the determination or choice of a new establishment depend upon a number, which nearly approaches to that of the body of the people: for it never comes entirely to the whole body of them. Every wise man then wishes to see, at the head of a powerful and obedient army, a general who may speedily seize the prize, and give to the people a master which they are so unfit to choose for themselves. So little correspondent is fact and reality to those philosophical notions.

Let not the establishment at the Revolution[1] deceive us, or make us so much in love with a philosophical origin to government, as to imagine all others monstrous and irregular. Even that event was far from corresponding to these refined ideas. It was only the succession, and that only in the regal part of the government, which was then changed: and it was only the majority of seven hundred, who determined that change for near ten millions. I doubt not, indeed, but the bulk of those ten millions acquiesced willingly in the determination: but was the matter left, in the least, to their choice? Was it not justly supposed to be, from that moment, decided, and every man punished, who refused to submit to the new sovereign? How otherwise could the matter have ever been brought to any issue or conclusion?

The republic of Athens was, I believe, the most extensive democracy that we read of in history: yet if we make the requisite allowances for the women, the slaves, and the strangers, we shall find, that that establishment was not at first made, nor any law ever voted, by a tenth part of those

---

1 *the establishment at the Revolution* The transfer of the British crown to William and Mary, and the establishment of rules for succession thereafter, in "the Glorious Revolution" of 1688–89. This was approved by parliamentary conventions, and Hume's reference to the "majority of seven hundred" apparently refers to those voting for this.

who were bound to pay obedience to it; not to mention the islands and foreign dominions, which the Athenians claimed as theirs by right of conquest. And as it is well known that popular assemblies in that city were always full of license and disorder, not withstanding the institutions and laws by which they were checked; how much more disorderly must they prove, where they form not the established constitution, but meet tumultuously on the dissolution of the ancient government, in order to give rise to a new one? How chimerical must it be to talk of a choice in such circumstances?

The Achæans enjoyed the freest and most perfect democracy of all antiquity; yet they employed force to oblige some cities to enter into their league, as we learn from Polybius.[1]

Harry the IVth and Harry the VIIth of England,[2] had really no title to the throne but a parliamentary election; yet they never would acknowledge it, lest they should thereby weaken their authority. Strange, if the only real foundation of all authority be consent and promise?

It is in vain to say, that all governments are, or should be, at first, founded on popular consent, as much as the necessity of human affairs will admit. This favors entirely my pretension. I maintain, that human affairs will never admit of this consent, seldom of the appearance of it; but that conquest or usurpation, that is, in plain terms, force, by dissolving the ancient governments, is the origin of almost all the new ones which were ever established in the world. And that in the few cases where consent may seem to have taken place, it was commonly so irregular, so confined, or so much intermixed either with fraud or violence, that it cannot have any great authority.

My intention here is not to exclude the consent of the people from being one just foundation of government where it has place. It is surely the best and most sacred of any. I only pretend, that it has very seldom had place in any degree, and never almost in its full extent; and that, therefore, some other foundation of government must also be admitted.

Were all men possessed of so inflexible a regard to justice, that, of themselves, they would totally abstain from the properties of others; they had for ever remained in a state of absolute liberty, without subjection to any magistrate or political society: but this is a state of perfection, of which human nature is justly deemed incapable. Again, were all men possessed of so perfect an understanding as always to know their own interests, no form of government had ever been submitted to but what was established on consent, and was fully canvassed by every member of the society: but this state of perfection is likewise much superior to human nature. Reason, history, and experience show us, that all political societies have had an origin much less accurate and regular; and were one to choose a period of time when the people's consent was the least regarded in public transactions, it would be precisely on the establishment of a new government. In a settled constitution their inclinations are often consulted; but during the fury of revolutions, conquests, and public convulsions, military force or political craft usually decides the controversy.

When a new government is established, by whatever means, the people are commonly dissatisfied with it, and pay obedience more from fear and necessity, than from any idea of allegiance or of moral obligation. The prince is watchful and jealous, and must carefully guard against every beginning or appearance of insurrection. Time, by degrees, removes all these difficulties, and accustoms the nation to regard, as their lawful or native princes, that family which at first they considered as usurpers or foreign conquerors. In order to found this opinion, they have no recourse to any notion of voluntary consent or promise, which, they know, never was, in this case, either expected or demanded. The original establishment was formed by violence, and submitted to from necessity. The subsequent administration is also supported by power, and acquiesced in by the people, not as a matter of choice, but of obligation. They imagine not that their consent gives their prince a title: but they willingly consent, because they think, that, from long possession, he has acquired a title, independent of their choice or inclination.

Should it be said, that, by living under the dominion of a prince which one might leave, every individual has given a *tacit* consent to his authority, and promised him obedience; it may be answered, that such an implied consent can only have place where a man imagines that the matter depends on his choice. But where he thinks (as all mankind do who are born under established governments) that, by his birth, he owes allegiance to a certain prince or certain form of government; it would be absurd to infer a consent or choice, which he expressly, in this case, renounces and disclaims.

---

1   *as we learn from Polybius*   Book 2, Chapter 38 of *The Rise of the Roman Empire*.

2   *Harry the IVth and Harry the VIIth of England*   Henry IV reigned from 1399 to 1413; Henry VII from 1485 to 1509. Neither acceded to the throne by the regular process of succession. (The name *Harry* is a familiar form of *Henry*.)

Can we seriously say, that a poor peasant or artisan has a free choice to leave his country, when he knows no foreign language or manners, and lives, from day to day, by the small wages which he acquires? We may as well assert that a man, by remaining in a vessel, freely consents to the dominion of the master; though he was carried on board while asleep, and must leap into the ocean and perish, the moment he leaves her.

What if the prince forbid his subjects to quit his dominions; as in Tiberius's time, it was regarded as a crime in a Roman knight that he had attempted to fly to the Parthians, in order to escape the tyranny of that emperor?[1] Or as the ancient Muscovites prohibited all traveling under pain of death? And did a prince observe, that many of his subjects were seized with the frenzy of migrating to foreign countries, he would, doubtless, with great reason and justice, restrain them, in order to prevent the depopulation of his own kingdom. Would he forfeit the allegiance of all his subjects by so wise and reasonable a law? Yet the freedom of their choice is surely, in that case, ravished from them.

A company of men, who should leave their native country, in order to people some uninhabited region, might dream of recovering their native freedom; but they would soon find, that their prince still laid claim to them, and called them his subjects, even in their new settlement. And in this he would but act conformably to the common ideas of mankind.

The truest *tacit* consent of this kind that is ever observed, is when a foreigner settles in any country, and is beforehand acquainted with the prince, and government, and laws, to which he must submit: yet is his allegiance, though more voluntary, much less expected or depended on, than that of a natural born subject. On the contrary, his native prince still asserts a claim to him. And if he punish not the renegade, where he seizes him in war with his new prince's commission; this clemency is not founded on the municipal law, which in all countries condemns the prisoner; but on the consent of princes, who have agreed to this indulgence, in order to prevent reprisals.

Did one generation of men go off the stage at once, and another succeed, as is the case with silkworms and butterflies, the new race, if they had sense enough to choose their government, which surely is never the case with men, might voluntarily, and by general consent, establish their own form of civil polity, without any regard to the laws or precedents which prevailed among their ancestors. But as human society is in perpetual flux, one man every hour going out of the world, another coming into it, it is necessary, in order to preserve stability in government, that the new brood should conform themselves to the established constitution, and nearly follow the path which their fathers, treading in the footsteps of theirs, had marked out to them. Some innovations must necessarily have place in every human institution; and it is happy where the enlightened genius of the age give these a direction to the side of reason, liberty, and justice: but violent innovations no individual is entitled to make: they are even dangerous to be attempted by the legislature: more ill than good is ever to be expected from them: and if history affords examples to the contrary, they are not to be drawn into precedent, and are only to be regarded as proofs, that the science of politics affords few rules, which will not admit of some exception, and which may not sometimes be controlled by fortune and accident. The violent innovations in the reign of Henry VIII[2] proceeded from an imperious monarch, seconded by the appearance of legislative authority: those in the reign of Charles I were derived from faction and fanaticism; and both of them have proved happy in the issue. But even the former were long the source of many disorders, and still more dangers; and if the measures of allegiance were to be taken from the latter, a total anarchy must have place in human society, and a final period at once be put to every government.

Suppose that an usurper, after having banished his lawful prince and royal family, should establish his dominion for ten or a dozen years in any country, and should preserve so exact a discipline in his troops, and so regular a disposition in his garrisons that no insurrection had ever been raised, or even murmur heard against his administration: can it be asserted that the people, who in their hearts abhor his treason, have tacitly consented to his authority, and

---

1   *as in ... of that emperor* [Hume's note] "Rubrius Fabatus was put under surveillance, on a suspicion that, in despair of the fortunes of Rome, he meant to throw himself on the mercy of the Parthians. He was, at any rate, found near the Straits of the Sicily, and, when dragged back by a centurion, he assigned no adequate reason for his long journey. Still, he lived on in safety, thanks to forgetfulness rather than to mercy" (Tacitus, *Annals*, Book 6, Chapter 14).

2   *violent innovations in the reign of Henry VIII* Henry reigned from 1509 until his death in 1547. His "violent innovations" included breaking with the Roman Catholic Church, destroying the powerful monasteries, and installing himself as the spiritual leader of the Church of England.

promised him allegiance, merely because, from necessity, they live under his dominion? Suppose again their native prince restored, by means of an army, which he levies in foreign countries: they receive him with joy and exultation, and show plainly with what reluctance they had submitted to any other yoke. I may now ask, upon what foundation the prince's title stands? Not on popular consent surely: for though the people willingly acquiesce in his authority, they never imagine that their consent made him sovereign. They consent; because they apprehend him to be already by birth, their lawful sovereign. And as to that tacit consent, which may now be inferred from their living under his dominion, this is no more than what they formerly gave to the tyrant and usurper.

When we assert, that all lawful government arises from the consent of the people, we certainly do them a great deal more honor than they deserve, or even expect and desire from us. After the Roman dominions became too unwieldy for the republic to govern them, the people over the whole known world were extremely grateful to Augustus for that authority which, by violence, he had established over them; and they showed an equal disposition to submit to the successor whom he left them by his last will and testament. It was afterwards their misfortune, that there never was, in one family, any long regular succession; but that their line of princes was continually broken, either by private assassinations or public rebellions. The *prætorian* bands, on the failure of every family, set up one emperor; the legions in the East a second; those in Germany, perhaps a third; and the sword alone could decide the controversy. The condition of the people in that mighty monarchy was to be lamented, not because the choice of the emperor was never left to them, for that was impracticable, but because they never fell under any succession of masters who might regularly follow each other. As to the violence, and wars, and bloodshed, occasioned by every new settlement, these were not blamable because they were inevitable.

The house of Lancaster ruled in this island about sixty years; yet the partisans of the white rose[1] seemed daily to multiply in England. The present establishment has taken place during a still longer period. Have all views of right in another family been utterly extinguished, even though scarce any man now alive had arrived at the years of dis-

cretion when it was expelled, or could have consented to its dominion, or have promised it allegiance?—a sufficient indication, surely, of the general sentiment of mankind on this head. For we blame not the partisans of the abdicated family merely on account of the long time during which they have preserved their imaginary loyalty. We blame them for adhering to a family which we affirm has been justly expelled, and which, from the moment the new settlement took place, had forfeited all title to authority.

But would we have a more regular, at least a more philosophical, refutation of this principle of an original contract, or popular consent, perhaps the following observations may suffice.

All *moral* duties may be divided into two kinds. The *first* are those to which men are impelled by a natural instinct or immediate propensity which operates on them, independent of all ideas of obligation, and of all views either to public or private utility. Of this nature are love of children, gratitude to benefactors, pity to the unfortunate. When we reflect on the advantage which results to society from such humane instincts, we pay them the just tribute of moral approbation and esteem: but the person actuated by them feels their power and influence antecedent to any such reflection.

The *second* kind of moral duties are such as are not supported by any original instinct of nature, but are performed entirely from a sense of obligation, when we consider the necessities of human society, and the impossibility of supporting it, if these duties were neglected. It is thus *justice*, or a regard to the property of others, *fidelity*, or the observance of promises, become obligatory, and acquire an authority over mankind. For as it is evident that every man loves himself better than any other person, he is naturally impelled to extend his acquisitions as much as possible; and nothing can restrain him in this propensity but reflection and experience, by which he learns the pernicious effects of that license, and the total dissolution of society which must ensue from it. His original inclination, therefore, or instinct, is here checked and restrained by a subsequent judgment or observation.

The case is precisely the same with the political or civil duty of *allegiance* as with the natural duties[2] of justice and

---

1   *The house of Lancaster ... partisans of the white rose*   The kings of the house of Lancaster were Henry IV, Henry V, and Henry VI; together they ruled from 1399 to 1461. Their emblem was the red rose; the white was that of their rivals, the house of York.

2   *the natural duties*   Hume's terminology here is somewhat puzzling, given his position as explained both here and at greater length in the *Treatise* and in Appendix 3 of his *Enquiry Concerning the Principles of Morals*, that keeping promises and acting justly are "artificial," as opposed to "natural" virtues.

fidelity. Our primary instincts lead us either to indulge ourselves in unlimited freedom, or to seek dominion over others; and it is reflection only which engages us to sacrifice such strong passions to the interests of peace and public order. A small degree of experience and observation suffices to teach us, that society cannot possibly be maintained without the authority of magistrates, and that this authority must soon fall into contempt where exact obedience is not paid to it. The observation of these general and obvious interests is the source of all allegiance, and of that moral obligation which we attribute to it.

What necessity, therefore, is there to found the duty of *allegiance* or obedience to magistrates on that of *fidelity* or a regard to promises, and to suppose, that it is the consent of each individual which subjects him to government, when it appears that both allegiance and fidelity stand precisely on the same foundation, and are both submitted to by mankind, on account of the apparent interests and necessities of human society? We are bound to obey our sovereign, it is said, because we have given a tacit promise to that purpose. But why are we bound to observe our promise? It must here be asserted, that the commerce and intercourse[1] of mankind, which are of such mighty advantage, can have no security where men pay no regard to their engagements. In like manner, may it be said that men could not live at all in society, at least in a civilized society, without laws, and magistrates, and judges, to prevent the encroachments of the strong upon the weak, of the violent upon the just and equitable. The obligation to allegiance being of like force and authority with the obligation to fidelity, we gain nothing by resolving the one into the other. The general interests or necessities of society are sufficient to establish both.

If the reason be asked of that obedience, which we are bound to pay to government, I readily answer, *Because society could not otherwise subsist*; and this answer is clear and intelligible to all mankind. Your answer is, *Because we should keep our word*. But besides, that no body, till trained in a philosophical system, can either comprehend or relish this answer; besides this, I say, you find yourself embarrassed when it is asked, *Why we are bound to keep our word?* Nor can you give any answer but what would, immediately, without any circuit, have accounted for our obligation to allegiance.

But *to whom is allegiance due? And who is our lawful sovereign?* This question is often the most difficult of any,

and liable to infinite discussions. When people are so happy that they can answer, *Our present sovereign, who inherits, in a direct line, from ancestors that have governed us for many ages*, this answer admits of no reply, even though historians, in tracing up to the remotest antiquity the origin of that royal family, may find, as commonly happens, that its first authority was derived from usurpation and violence. It is confessed that private justice, or the abstinence from the properties of others, is a most cardinal virtue. Yet reason tells us that there is no property in durable objects, such as lands or houses, when carefully examined in passing from hand to hand, but must, in some period, have been founded on fraud and injustice. The necessities of human society, neither in private nor public life, will allow of such an accurate inquiry; and there is no virtue or moral duty but what may, with facility, be refined away, if we indulge a false philosophy in sifting and scrutinizing it, by every captious rule of logic, in every light or position in which it may be placed.

The questions with regard to private property have filled infinite volumes of law and philosophy, if in both we add the commentators to the original text; and in the end, we may safely pronounce, that many of the rules there established are uncertain, ambiguous, and arbitrary. The like opinion may be formed with regard to the succession and rights of princes, and forms of government. Several cases no doubt occur, especially in the infancy of any constitution, which admit of no determination from the laws of justice and equity; and our historian Rapin pretends, that the controversy between Edward the Third and Philip de Valois was of this nature, and could be decided only by an appeal to heaven, that is, by war and violence.[2]

Who shall tell me, whether Germanicus or Drusus ought to have succeeded to Tiberius,[3] had he died while they were both alive, without naming any of them for his

2   *Rapin pretends ... war and violence* Paul de Rapin-Thoyras (1661–1725), in *Histoire d'Angleterre* (1723–27). Charles IV of France died in 1328; if his then pregnant wife gave birth to a son, he would succeed to the throne; but an assembly was formed to appoint a successor if she gave birth to a daughter. The assembly rejected the claim of Edward III of England, Charles' nephew and nearest male relative, and appointed Charles' cousin Philip of Valois, who became king (as Philip VI) when a daughter was born.

3   *Germanicus ... Tiberius* Tiberius, future emperor of Rome, adopted his nephew Germanicus in 13 BCE, as his son and successor, though he already had a son Drusus. Tiberius became emperor in 14 CE and ruled till his death in 37. But Germinicus died

1   *intercourse* Mutual exchange (of any sort).

successor? Ought the right of adoption to be received as equivalent to that of blood, in a nation where it had the same effect in private families, and had already, in two instances, taken place in the public? Ought Germanicus to be esteemed the elder son, because he was born before Drusus; or the younger, because he was adopted after the birth of his brother? Ought the right of the elder to be regarded in a nation, where he had no advantage in the succession of private families? Ought the Roman empire at that time to be deemed hereditary, because of two examples; or ought it, even so early, to be regarded as belonging to the stronger, or to the present possessor, as being founded on so recent an usurpation?

Commodus mounted the throne after a pretty long succession of excellent emperors, who had acquired their title, not by birth, or public election, but by the fictitious rite of adoption. That bloody debauchee being murdered by a conspiracy, suddenly formed between his wench and her gallant, who happened at that time to be *Prætorian Præfect*; these immediately deliberated about choosing a master to human kind, to speak in the style of those ages; and they cast their eyes on Pertinax. Before the tyrant's death was known, the *Præfect* went secretly to that senator, who, on the appearance of the soldiers, imagined that his execution had been ordered by Commodus. He was immediately saluted emperor by the officer and his attendants, cheerfully proclaimed by the populace, unwillingly submitted to by the guards, formally recognized by the senate, and passively received by the provinces and armies of the empire.

The discontent of the *Prætorian* bands broke out in a sudden sedition, which occasioned the murder of that excellent prince; and the world being now without a master, and without government, the guards thought proper to set the empire formally to sale. Julian, the purchaser, was proclaimed by the soldiers, recognized by the senate, and submitted to by the people; and must also have been submitted to by the provinces, had not the envy of the legions begotten opposition and resistance. Pescennius Niger in Syria elected himself emperor, gained the tumultuary consent of his army, and was attended with the secret good-will of the senate and people of Rome. Albinus in Britain found an equal right to set up his claim; but Severus, who governed Pannonia, prevailed in the end above both of them. That able politician and warrior, finding his own birth and dignity too much inferior to the imperial crown, professed, at first, an intention only of revenging the death of Pertinax. He marched as general into Italy, defeated Julian, and, without our being able to fix any precise commencement even of the soldiers' consent, he was from necessity acknowledged emperor by the senate and people, and fully established in his violent authority, by subduing Niger and Albinus.[1]

"*Inter hæc Gordianus Cæsar*" (says Capitolinus, speaking of another period) "*sublatus a militibus.* [Imperator] *est appellatus, quia non erat alius in præsenti.*"[2] It is to be remarked, that Gordian was a boy of fourteen years of age.

Frequent instances of a like nature occur in the history of the emperors; in that of Alexander's successors; and of many other countries: nor can any thing be more unhappy than a despotic government of this kind; where the succession is disjointed and irregular, and must be determined, on every vacancy, by force or election. In a free government, the matter is often unavoidable, and is also much less dangerous. The interests of liberty may there frequently lead the people, in their own defense, to alter the succession of the crown. And the constitution, being compounded of parts, may still maintain a sufficient stability, by resting on the aristocratical or democratical members, though the monarchical be altered, from time to time, in order to accommodate it to the former.

In an absolute government, when there is no legal prince who has a title to the throne, it may safely be determined to belong to the first occupant. Instances of this kind are but too frequent, especially in the eastern monarchies. When any race of princes expires, the will or destination of the last sovereign will be regarded as a title. Thus the edict of Louis the XIVth, who called the bastard princes to the succession in case of the failure of all the legitimate princes,

---

1   *He marched ... Albinus*   [Hume's note] Herodian, Book 2 [Hume refers to Herodian's *History of the Empire From the Time of Marcus Aurelius*, written in 238 CE or afterward. Commodus was emperor of Rome 180–92 CE. Pertinax ruled for only three months after his death. The following power struggles mentioned took place during the next four years.]

2   *Inter hæc ... in præsenti*   [Hume's note] "In the meantime, Gordianus Caesar was lifted up by the soldiers and named ["Augustus" in the original, meaning *emperor*] because there was nobody else at the moment." [Hume is quoting from Julius Capitolinus, *Maximus et Balbinus*, sec. 14, in *Scriptores Historiae Augustae*. Gordian II was killed after serving as emperor for all of three weeks in 238 CE.]

---

in 19, leaving Drusus as heir, and Drusus died in 23; so neither became emperor.

would, in such an event, have some authority.[1] Thus the will of Charles the Second disposed of the whole Spanish monarchy. The cession of the ancient proprietor, especially when joined to conquest, is likewise deemed a good title. The general obligation, which binds us to government, is the interest and necessities of society; and this obligation is very strong. The determination of it to this or that particular prince, or form of government, is frequently more uncertain and dubious. Present possession has considerable authority in these cases, and greater than in private property; because of the disorders which attend all revolutions and changes of government.

We shall only observe, before we conclude, that though an appeal to general opinion may justly, in the speculative sciences of metaphysics, natural philosophy, or astronomy, be deemed unfair and inconclusive, yet in all questions with regard to morals, as well as criticism, there is really no other standard, by which any controversy can ever be decided. And nothing is a clearer proof, that a theory of this kind is erroneous, than to find, that it leads to paradoxes repugnant to the common sentiments of mankind, and to the practice and opinion of all nations and all ages. The doctrine, which founds all lawful government on an *original contract*, or consent of the people, is plainly of this kind; nor has the most noted of its partisans, in prosecution of it, scrupled to affirm, *that absolute monarchy is inconsistent with civil society, and so can be no form of civil government at all;*[2] *and that the supreme power in a state cannot take from any man, by taxes and impositions, any part of his property, without his own consent or that of his representatives.*[3] What authority any moral reasoning can have, which leads into opinions so wide of the general practice of mankind, in every place but this single kingdom, it is easy to determine.

The only passage I meet with in antiquity, where the obligation of obedience to government is ascribed to a promise, is in Plato's *Crito*; where Socrates refuses to escape from prison, because he had tacitly promised to obey the laws. Thus he builds a *Tory* consequence of passive obedience on a *Whig*[4] foundation of the original contract.

New discoveries are not to be expected in these matters. If scarce any man, till very lately, ever imagined that government was founded on compact, it is certain that it cannot, in general, have any such foundation.

The crime of rebellion among the ancients was commonly expressed by the terms νεοτεριζειν, νουας ρες μολιρι *novas res moliri*.[5]

1   *Thus the edict ... some authority* [Hume's note] It is remarkable, that in the remonstrance of the Duke of Bourbon and the legitimate princes, against this destination of Louis the XIVth, the doctrine of the *original contract* is insisted on even in that absolute government. The French nation, say they, choosing Hugh Capet and his posterity to rule over them and their posterity, where the former line fails, there is a tacit right reserved to choose a new royal family; and this right is invaded by calling the bastard princes to the throne, without the consent of the nation. But the Comte de Boulainvilliers, who wrote in defense of the bastard princes, ridicules this notion of an original contract, especially when applied to Hugh Capet; who mounted the throne, says he, by the same arts which have ever been employed by all conquerors and usurpers. He got his title, indeed, recognized by the states after he had put himself in possession: but is this a choice or contract? The Comte de Boulainvilliers, we may observe, was a noted republican; but being a man of learning, and very conversant in history, he knew that the people were almost never consulted in these revolutions and new establishments, and that time alone bestowed right and authority on what was commonly at first founded on force and violence. See *État de la France*, vol. 3. [Hume refers to Henri de Boulainvilliers' book of 1727.]

2   *The doctrine ... at all* [Hume's note] See Locke on Government, chapter 7, §90. [Hume paraphrases Locke.]

3   *that the supreme ... representatives* [Hume's note] Ibid., chapter 9, §138, 139, 140.

4   *Tory ... Whig* In Hume's time, the Tories believed that kings were owed allegiance because they were ordained to rule by God; and the Whigs argued that monarchs' rule was contingent upon consent of the governed (or, at least, of the important citizens). Unquestioned "passive obedience" is thus more closely associated with the former.

5   *terms ... novas res moliri* The Greek and Latin terms both mean to make changes, especially political ones.

JEAN-JACQUES ROUSSEAU
(1712 – 1778)

Who Was Jean-Jacques Rousseau?

JEAN-JACQUES ROUSSEAU WAS THE SON OF A WATCHMAKER from the independent Calvinist republic of Geneva (today part of Switzerland). As a young man Rousseau's first love was music, and he composed several quite successful operas. But in his late thirties he, almost accidentally, began a new career as an essayist, and by the time of his death in 1778 he was one of the most famous intellectuals in Europe and a leading figure of the French Enlightenment. His ideas also influenced the growth of both socialism and nationalism, and his fictional and autobiographical works were an important influence on Romanticism.

Rousseau was born in 1712, and his mother died from complications from his birth. Jean-Jacques was raised by his sentimental, apparently rather irresponsible, father until he was ten. (His older brother, his only sibling, ran away from home when Jean-Jacques was still young.) In 1722 his father was involved in an illegal duel with a French captain and had to flee Geneva, leaving his son in the care of his uncle. His uncle, in turn, placed young Jean-Jacques with the pastor of a nearby village, M. Lambercier, where he was regularly beaten by the pastor's sister but also, he later wrote, came to develop an abiding love of the countryside. In 1725 Rousseau returned to Geneva and was apprenticed to an engraver, Abel Ducommun, who features in Rousseau's autobiographical *Confessions* as a violent and ignorant master.

Throughout his childhood, then, Rousseau had virtually no formal education. However his father did teach him to read, and Rousseau later recalled reading classical literature (such as Plutarch's *Lives*) with his father in a public garden as the most tranquil part of growing up.

In 1728, aged fifteen, Rousseau abruptly decided to leave Geneva and seek his fortune in the wider world. A Catholic priest sent him to see Françoise-Louise de la Tour, Baronne de Warens, who had been given money by the House of Savoy to attempt to secure converts to Catholicism as a buffer against the influence of Protestant Geneva. In order to win her patronage and secure an education for himself Rousseau converted to Catholicism (which forced him to give up his Genevan citizenship) and Madame de Warens sent him to study in Turin, where Rousseau supported himself through a series of odd jobs.[1] A year later Rousseau returned to Madame de Warrens in Annecy and lived with her for the following eight years. After a few years they became lovers, although de Warrens was thirteen years older than Rousseau (and he continued to call her "maman"). Rousseau spent this period reading, educating himself, and developing a passion for music.

In 1738 de Warrens broke off their romantic relationship, and in 1740 Rousseau moved to Lyons to serve as a private tutor. This did not last long—Rousseau did not take to the work—and soon he moved again, this time to Paris, where he presented a paper on musical notation to the Academy of Sciences and embarked on his career as a composer. In 1743 he went to Venice as secretary to the French Ambassador, but Rousseau quarreled with his master (who was lazy, and neglected to pay him) and returned to Paris. The experience remained with him, however; he was impressed by Venice's republican form of government yet struck by the corrupting effects of luxury and special-interest politics. At this time he also began his lifelong relationship with a semi-literate linen-maid named Thérèse Levasseur. (They eventually married in 1768; they had several children together, all of whom—to Rousseau's belated shame—were abandoned as infants to a Parisian orphanage, where they most likely soon died.)

---

1   Rousseau reports in his *Confessions* one incident from this time that, he said, haunted him the rest of his life: he stole a ribbon and put the blame on an innocent serving girl.

Rousseau's literary career finally began in 1749 when he noticed an essay competition in the newspaper on the question: have advances in the sciences and arts improved morals? Although he was on his way to visit his friend Denis Diderot, imprisoned near Paris for what seemed to the authorities to be his relativistic anti-religious writings (he was later to edit the famous French rationalist *Encyclopédie*), Rousseau was so overwhelmed with ideas about this topic, he tells us, that he had to stop his journey and write an essay for the competition. His main argument in that essay—*Discourse on the Sciences and Arts* (1750)—was that, far from being improved, human morals had been corrupted and weakened by advances in the sciences and culture. The essay won the prize, and set the tone for the rest of Rousseau's life's work.

Rousseau followed up his essay with another on similar questions, *Discourse on the Origin of Inequality* (1755)[1] and retired to the countryside, away from Parisian society, in order to think and write. (A cottage in the valley of Montmorency was bought for him by writer Louise d'Épinay, with whom Rousseau had an affair.) These were his most productive years, during which he wrote on educational theory (*Émile*, 1762), political philosophy (*On Political Economy*, 1755; *On the Social Contract*, 1762), and a novel (*Julie, ou la Nouvelle Héloïse*, 1761). *La Nouvelle Héloïse* was one of the best-selling novels of its time—indeed, one of the best-selling of the eighteenth century—and was an important influence on the aesthetic movement called Romanticism. Rousseau also returned to the Protestant faith and reclaimed his Genevan citizenship (only to renounce it again in 1764).

During these years, Rousseau gradually became estranged from most of his old friends and supporters, including Diderot and the *Encyclopédistes*, and Madame d'Épinay, though he was able to secure the new patronage of such wealthy and powerful figures as the Duc de Luxembourg and Frederick the Great of Prussia.

In his writings of the late 1750s and early 1760s, Rousseau made a number of radical proposals. Perhaps the most striking, given the extraordinary neglect he had displayed towards his own children, were those concerning childhood education. Rousseau called on society to show far greater respect—even reverence—for children and the state of childhood. Such views brought him unwelcome and unfriendly attention from the French church and state, who considered them anti-religious. In 1762—after *The Social Contract* and *Émile* were condemned and publicly burned by the Archbishop and *Parlement* of Paris—he was forced to flee to Switzerland, only to find his writings condemned in Geneva also.

Rousseau spent much of the following fourteen years suffering from depression and even paranoia. During this period he wrote his autobiographical *Confessions*, a work saturated with apology and self-justification.[2] He abandoned Geneva for the nearby Prussian principality of Neuchâtel, and then—after being drummed out of there by clergy-led peasant protests against him—spent a year in Britain as a guest of philosopher David Hume, who offered him sanctuary, but left after becoming convinced (wrongly) that Hume was planning to publicly humiliate him.[3] In 1767, Rousseau returned to France incognito, more or less a broken man and he lived in seclusion in Grenoble, under the assumed name Renou, cared for by Levasseur. In addition to his various self-justificatory writings of this period, Rousseau also developed an interest in, and wrote about, botany.

The final years of Rousseau's life were somewhat less anguished. Though he continued to be banned from publishing or speaking publicly on anything controversial, his reputation was gradually resuscitated and in 1770 he was able to return to Paris as a literary celebrity. In 1776 he was knocked down by a dog while out walking (he was now in his mid-sixties). Oddly, this accident seems to have had the unexpected effect of clearing away his mental distress, and during his final two years he wrote *Reveries of the Solitary Walker*, a calmer, clearer reflection on his life and experiences.

After his sudden death, while studying plants, he was buried at Erménonville, north of Paris (where he was staying at the time of his death). But in 1794, at the feverish height of the French Revolution, his ashes were transported, in a dramatic torchlit procession, into the heart of Paris and laid in the Panthéon—a mausoleum reserved for France's greatest intellectual heroes—across from the remains of Voltaire.

---

1 Like the first discourse, this essay was written as an entry for the Academy of Dijon's essay contest. Rousseau considered it the better work but, this time, the Academy's judges were irritated by its length and boldness and did not even finish reading it.

2 To complete his misery Rousseau also suffered for most of his adult life from constriction of the urethra, which caused him great pain.

3 An exchange of letters, in which Rousseau accused his erstwhile host of treachery, was published in France to widespread titillation.

What Was Rousseau's Overall Philosophical Project?

Rousseau's modern reputation rests on his work on ethics, social-political thought, and education. One of his key themes is the liberty of the individual with respect to the state; one of the remarks most frequently quoted from his writings is the opening line from *The Social Contract*: "Man is born free; and everywhere he is in chains" (*L'homme est né libre, et partout il est dans les fers*). A second theme of Rousseau's philosophical works is the principle of the innate goodness of human beings in their natural state. A third abiding preoccupation for Rousseau is the distorting effect of social prestige. The search for individual distinction, according to Rousseau, leads people to pursue vain and useless activities, and to belittle and keep down those around them, instead of working for the common good. This theme is explored especially in Rousseau's *Discourse on the Origin and Foundations of Inequality Among Men* (1755). In his work on education, especially *Émile* (1762), he tried to describe a manner of educating children—or at least boys—that would encourage them to cooperate with other men from a position of mutual respect, and would eliminate the desire to dominate others. *Émile*, therefore, is more than "just" a treatise on education; it is also an essay in social criticism.

These themes come together in Rousseau's most famous work, *On the Social Contract* (1762), in which he describes a just society in which every member has equal political authority, regardless of birth or wealth (though not, probably, of gender), and laws are effected by the general will of the people. Such a society, however, requires a new kind of citizen: a radical reformulation of human nature ... or rather a kind of return to the original, undistorted human nature. Immoral societies create immoral citizens who are acculturated into conniving with and perpetuating their inequalities. The only way to break this vicious cycle, in Rousseau's view, would be to create a new kind of citizen—brought up from an early age in a new way, in relative isolation from the prevailing society. These "new men" would then re-make society.

What Is the Structure of the Reading?

Discourse on the Origin and Foundations of Inequality Among Men is preceded by a long and adulatory dedication to the state of Geneva, and then sets out to describe the history of humankind as it develops from the state of nature towards civil society. Part One describes the state of nature; Part Two deals with the establishment of society. As the story progresses, Rousseau seeks to show how moral/political inequality first develops, and then how it intensifies.

On the Social Contract is divided into four books. The first book considers the question of how humankind passes from a state of nature to society, and the conditions of the "social compact" that this transition requires. Book 2 deals with legislation (by the sovereign), while Book 3 addresses government: its proper form, and its scope and limits. The final book goes into more detail about the business of government.

Some Useful Background Information

i) Rousseau saw himself as an inheritor of the ancient tradition of political theory, from Aristotle and Plato, adopting the wide range of its interconnected concerns (including psychology, civic religion, education, the role of art in society, and so on). Ancient social models, such as Sparta, Rome and Athens, were often his touchstones.

ii) While it is perhaps not quite right to think of Rousseau as a systematizer, nevertheless his various writings are deeply connected with one another and explore a unified set of themes. "I have written on diverse subjects but always on the same principles, always the same morals, the same beliefs, the same maxims, and, if you will, the same opinions," Rousseau wrote in 1763. (This was written in defense of *Émile*.)

iii) A useful starting point for understanding Rousseau's *Social Contract* is this: for Rousseau, a social structure is legitimate only if it exists according to the active will of all the people who make it up. That is, the proper basis of society is not force, or even passive consent, but the on-going will of the people.

From this, much of what is distinctive about Rousseau's political philosophy tends to follow: for example, that a basic principle of society is the equality of all citizens; that humans in a legitimate society are fully free; that individual wills are complementary and mutually dependent, not competing and separate (otherwise society would not be possible); that good societies are not accidental, distorting artifacts but rather a natural outgrowth of human development; that the sovereign is a corporate entity made up of all the individuals in society (rather than any individual or smaller group); that the powers of the sovereign are unlimited and infallible with respect to, but only to, the general interest; and so on.

iv) Rousseau made two important distinctions which we need to be sensitive to in reading his work. The first is between self-love (*amour de soi*) and self-interest (*amour-propre*); for Rousseau these are quite different. Self-love is a basic, natural feeling of, roughly, well-being, self-sufficiency, and contentment. Self-interest, by contrast, is a feeling that arises only in social settings when we compare ourselves to others; it is this feeling that gives rise to envy and competition.

The second distinction is that between goodness (*bonté*) and virtue (*vertu*). According to Rousseau, human beings are innately good, and if raised properly are all capable of becoming good people. Humans in the state of nature are good, but only unconsciously so; society adds moral awareness, and may tend to produce either good or bad human beings depending on how well it is constituted. Virtue is a social quality, and consists, roughly, in the effort we exert to overcome bad influences, both internal and external.

v) Another helpful distinction for understanding Rousseau is between the state, the sovereign, and the government. His view, roughly, is that the state (*état*) is composed of all the inhabitants of the society; the sovereign (*souverain*) is the common will of all the people acting together, and is the ultimate source of all political authority; the government (*gouvernement*) is the body—the subset of the population—responsible for executing the wishes of the sovereign. Notice that on this view members of the government, even a monarch, are fundamentally equal with all other members of the state, no matter their social status: all citizens participate equally in sovereignty.

Some Common Misconceptions

i) Despite his well-known praise of the "noble savage" (*bon sauvage*), Rousseau was not a primitivist—he did not prefer a pre-social state for humanity over any possible society. He certainly thought that existing societies tended to corrupt and distort human nature, and he argued that humanity was in some sense "naturally good," rather than savage and violent. However, in *The Social Contract* Rousseau envisaged a social condition that he considered vastly preferable to any version of the state of nature.

ii) Rousseau held that government is accountable to the will of the people, but he denied that any government can *represent* that sovereign will. The individual will is, for Rousseau, inalienable, and so cannot be given away to a representative, even willingly.

iii) For Rousseau, law-making is something that can be done only by the sovereign; that is to say, by the general will of the people as a whole. According to Rousseau's way of thinking, therefore, the *government* does not and cannot make laws; it can only issue decrees that *apply* the laws to particular sub-sets of the population. From this it follows that laws proper apply equally to all citizens; they are, in the words of G.D.H. Cole something like "the fundamental declarations of principle on which the entire social order rests." Most of what we would call "laws," however, are what Rousseau would think of as decrees, applications of the law to particular groups and circumstances.

How Important and Influential Are These Works?

Rousseau wrote *The Social Contract* in 1762, criticizing as unjust societies based on inequality and the centralization of political authority. Less that thirty years later, in 1789, the *ancien régime* was overthrown by the French Revolution. Rousseau's name was frequently invoked by the authors of the revolution,[1] but it is unclear to what extent his writings actively influenced those events. What is clear, though, is that Rousseau was one of the key figures crystallizing a set of ideas that swept through Europe and America in the second half of the eighteenth century. Important as his influence may have been on the French Revolutionaries, it also extended into many other areas.

In *The Cambridge Companion to Rousseau*, Rousseau scholar Patrick Riley has called him:

> the greatest of all critics of inequality, the purest social contract theorist of the eighteenth century (and simultaneously the deepest critic of contractarianism after Hume), the greatest writer on civic education after Plato, the most perceptive understander of mastery and slavery after Aristotle and before Hegel, the finest critic of Hobbes, the most important predecessor of Kant, the most accomplished didactic novelist between Richardson and Tolstoy, the greatest confessor since Augustine,

---

1   The revolutionary slogan, later the motto of the French Republic, "liberté, égalité, fraternité," can be seen as almost a summary of Rousseau's main concerns: liberty and equality arising from, and sustaining, fraternity.

the author of paradoxes ("the general will is always right" but "not enlightened") that continue to fascinate and infuriate.

Two of the connections mentioned by Riley are particularly worth emphasizing. Rousseau was perhaps the last great social contract theorist, and his reactions against and reformulation of previous social contract theories, particularly that of Hobbes, changed the nature of subsequent political theory.

Second, Rousseau can be seen as a key influence on Kant's moral and political theory. In particular, Rousseau's notion of the general will and its laws, and his doctrine that true liberty and morality are to be found in acting in accordance with the general will, strongly anticipate Kant.

◆ ◆ ◆ ◆ ◆

Discourse on the Origin and Foundations of Inequality Among Men (1755)

"Not in depraved things but in those well oriented according to nature, are we to consider what is natural."

—Aristotle, *Politics*, 1

To The Republic of Geneva

Magnificent, Most Honored and Sovereign Lords:

Convinced that only a virtuous man may bestow on his homeland those honors which it can acknowledge, I have labored for thirty years to earn the right to offer you public homage. And since this happy occasion supplements to some extent what my efforts have been unable to accomplish, I believed I might be allowed here to give heed to the zeal that urges me on, instead of the right that ought to have given me authorization. Having had the good fortune to be born among you, how could I meditate on the equality which nature has established among men and upon the inequality they have instituted without thinking of the profound wisdom with which both, felicitously combined in this state, cooperate in the manner that most closely

approximates the natural law and that is most favorable to society, to the maintenance of public order and to the happiness of private individuals? In searching for the best maxims that good sense could dictate concerning the constitution of a government, I have been so struck on seeing them all in operation in your own, that even if I had not been born within your walls, I would have believed myself incapable of dispensing with offering this picture of human society to that people which, of all peoples, seems to me to be in possession of the greatest advantages, and to have best prevented its abuses.[1]

If I had had to choose my birthplace, I would have chosen a society of a size limited by the extent of human faculties, that is to say, limited by the possibility of being well governed, and where, with each being sufficient to his task, no one would have been forced to relegate to others the functions with which he was charged; a state where, with all private individuals being known to one another, neither the obscure maneuvers of vice nor the modesty of virtue could be hidden from the notice and the judgment of the public, and where that pleasant habit of seeing and knowing one another turned love of homeland into love of the citizens rather than into love of the land.

I would have wanted to be born in a country where the sovereign and the people could have but one and the same interest, so that all the movements of the machine always tended only to the common happiness. Since this could not have taken place unless the people and the sovereign were one and the same person, it follows that I would have wished to be born under a democratic government, wisely tempered.

I would have wanted to live and die free, that is to say, subject to the laws in such wise that neither I nor anyone else could shake off their honorable yoke: that pleasant and salutary yoke, which the most arrogant heads bear with all the greater docility, since they are made to bear no other.

I would therefore have wanted it to be impossible for anyone in the state to say that he was above the law and for anyone outside to demand that the state was obliged to give him recognition. For whatever the constitution of a government may be, if a single man is found who is not subject to the law, all the others are necessarily at his discre-

---

1   *that people … its abuses*   Rousseau's picture of Geneva's political situation in his day is exaggeratedly rosy; his remarks here are of interest not as accurate history, but rather as a picture of what a society should be like.

tion.[1] And if there is a national leader and a foreign leader as well, whatever the division of authority they may make, it is impossible for both of them to be strictly obeyed and for the state to be well governed.

I would not have wanted to dwell in a newly constituted republic, however good its laws may be, out of fear that, with the government perhaps constituted otherwise than would be required for the moment and being unsuited to the new citizens or the citizens to the new government, the state would be subject to being overthrown and destroyed almost from its inception. For liberty is like those solid and tasty foods or those full-bodied wines which are appropriate for nourishing and strengthening robust constitutions that are used to them, but which overpower, ruin and intoxicate the weak and delicate who are not suited for them. Once peoples are accustomed to masters, they are no longer in a position to get along without them. If they try to shake off the yoke, they put all the more distance between themselves and liberty, because, in mistaking for liberty an unbridled license which is its opposite, their revolutions nearly always deliver them over to seducers who simply make their chains heavier. The Roman people itself—that model of all free peoples—was in no position to govern itself when it

emerged from the oppression of the Tarquins.[2] Debased by slavery and the ignominious labors the Tarquins had imposed on it, at first it was but a stupid rabble that needed to be managed and governed with the greatest wisdom, so that, as it gradually became accustomed to breathe the salutary air of liberty, these souls, enervated or rather brutalized under tyranny, acquired by degrees that severity of mores and that high-spirited courage which eventually made them, of all the peoples, most worthy of respect. I would therefore have sought for my homeland a happy and tranquil republic, whose antiquity was somehow lost in the dark recesses of time, which had experienced only such attacks as served to manifest and strengthen in its inhabitants courage and love of homeland, and where the citizens, long accustomed to a wise independence, were not only free but worthy of being so.

I would have wanted to choose for myself a homeland diverted by a fortunate impotence from the fierce love of conquest, and protected by an even more fortunate position from the fear of becoming itself the conquest of another state; a free city, situated among several peoples none of whom had any interest in invading it, while each had an interest in preventing the others from invading it themselves; in a word, a republic that did not tempt the ambition of its neighbors and that could reasonably count on their assistance in time of need. It follows that in so fortunate a position, it would have had nothing to fear except from itself; and that, if its citizens were trained in the use of arms, it would have been more to maintain in them that martial fervor and that high-spirited courage that suit liberty so well and whet the appetite for it, than out of the necessity to provide for their defense.

I would have searched for a country where the right of legislation was common to all citizens, for who can know better than they the conditions under which it suits them to live together in a single society? But I would not have approved of plebiscites like those of the Romans where the state's leaders and those most interested in its preservation were excluded from the deliberations on which its safety often depended, and where, by an absurd inconsistency, the magistrates were deprived of the rights enjoyed by ordinary citizens.

On the contrary, I would have desired that, in order to stop the self-centered and ill-conceived projects and the

---

1   *For whatever ... at his discretion* [Annotations within Rousseau's notes on the part of the editors are placed within square brackets.]

[Rousseau's note] Herodotus relates [*Histories,* 3.83; these events took place during the second half of the fifth century BCE] that after the murder of the false Smerdis, the seven liberators of Persia being assembled to deliberate on the form of government they would give the state, Otanes was fervently in support of a republic: an opinion all the more extraordinary in the mouth of a satrap, since, over and above the claim he could have to the empire, a grandee fears more than death a type of government that forces him to respect men. Otanes, as may readily be believed, was not listened to; and seeing that things were progressing toward the election of a monarch, he, who wanted neither to obey nor command, voluntarily yielded to the other rivals his right to the crown, asking as his sole compensation that he and his descendants be free and independent. This was granted him. If Herodotus did not inform us of the restriction that was placed on this privilege, it would be necessary to suppose it, otherwise Otanes, not acknowledging any sort of law and not being accountable to anyone, would have been all powerful in the state and more powerful than the king himself. But there was hardly any likelihood that a man capable of contenting himself, in similar circumstances, with such a privilege, was capable of abusing it. In fact, there is no evidence that this right ever caused the least trouble in the kingdom, either from wise Otanes or from any of his descendants.

2   *Tarquins* A dynasty of seven kings of Etruscan origin who ruled Rome until the last one, Tarquin the Proud, was overthrown in 509 BCE, and his government replaced by the Republic.

dangerous innovations that finally ruined Athens, no one would have the power to propose new laws according to his fancy; that this right belonged exclusively to the magistrates; that even they used it with such caution that the populace, for its part, was so hesitant about giving its consent to these laws, and that their promulgation could only be done with such solemnity that before the constitution was overturned one had time to be convinced that it is above all the great antiquity of the laws that makes them holy and venerable; that the populace soon holds in contempt those laws that it sees change daily; and that in becoming accustomed to neglect old usages on the pretext of making improvements, great evils are often introduced in order to correct the lesser ones.

Above all, I would have fled, as necessarily ill-governed, a republic where the people, believing it could get along without its magistrates or permit them but a precarious authority, would imprudently have held on to the administration of civil affairs and the execution of its own laws. Such must have been the rude constitution of the first governments immediately emerging from the state of nature, and such too was one of the vices which ruined the republic of Athens.

But I would have chosen that republic where private individuals, being content to give sanction to the laws and to decide as a body and upon the recommendation of their leaders the most important public affairs, would establish respected tribunals, distinguish with care their various departments, annually elect the most capable and most upright of their fellow citizens to administer justice and to govern the state; and where, with the virtue of the magistrates thus bearing witness to the wisdom of the people, they would mutually honor one another. Thus if some fatal misunderstandings were ever to disturb public concord, even those periods of blindness and errors were marked by indications of moderation, reciprocal esteem, and a common respect for the laws: presages and guarantees of a sincere and perpetual reconciliation.

Such, magnificent, most honored, and sovereign lords, are the advantages that I would have sought in the homeland that I would have chosen for myself. And if in addition providence had joined to it a charming location, a temperate climate, a fertile country and the most delightful appearance there is under the heavens, to complete my happiness I would have desired only to enjoy all these goods in the bosom of that happy homeland, living peacefully in sweet society with my fellow citizens, and practicing toward them (following their own example), humanity, friendship,

and all the virtues; and leaving behind me the honorable memory of a good man and a decent and virtuous patriot.

If, less happy or too late grown wise, I had seen myself reduced to end an infirm and languishing career in other climates, pointlessly regretting the repose and peace of which an imprudent youth deprived me, I would at least have nourished in my soul those same sentiments I could not have used in my native country; and penetrated by a tender and disinterested affection for my distant fellow citizens, I would have addressed them from the bottom of my heart more or less along the following lines:

My dear fellow citizens, or rather my brothers, since the bonds of blood as well as the laws unite almost all of us, it gives me pleasure to be incapable of thinking of you without at the same time thinking of all the good things you enjoy, and of which perhaps none of you appreciates the value more deeply than I who have lost them. The more I reflect upon your political and civil situation, the less I am capable of imagining that the nature of human affairs could admit of a better one. In all other governments, when it is a question of assuring the greatest good of the state, everything is always limited to imaginary projects, and at most to simple possibilities. As for you, your happiness is complete; it remains merely to enjoy it. And to become perfectly happy you are in need of nothing more than to know how to be satisfied with being so. Your sovereignty, acquired or recovered at the point of a sword, and preserved for two centuries by dint of valor and wisdom, is at last fully and universally recognized. Honorable treaties fix your boundaries, secure your rights and strengthen your repose. Your constitution is excellent, since it is dictated by the most sublime reason and is guaranteed by friendly powers deserving of respect. Your state is tranquil; you have neither wars nor conquerors to fear. You have no other masters but the wise laws you have made, administered by upright magistrates of your own choosing. You are neither rich enough to enervate yourself with softness and to lose in vain delights the taste for true happiness and solid virtues, nor poor enough to need more foreign assistance than your industry procures for you. And this precious liberty, which in large nations is maintained only by exorbitant taxes, costs you almost nothing to pursue.

For the happiness of its citizens and the examples of the peoples, may a republic so wisely and so happily constituted last forever! This is the only wish left for you to make, and the only precaution left for you to take. From here on, it is for you alone, not to bring about your own happiness, your ancestors having saved you the trouble, but to render it lasting by the wisdom of using it well. It is upon your perpetual union, your obedience to the laws, your respect for their ministers that your preservation depends. If there remains among you the slightest germ of bitterness or distrust, hasten to destroy it as a ruinous leaven that sooner or later results in your misfortunes and the ruin of the state. I beg you all to look deep inside your hearts and to heed the secret voice of your conscience. Is there anyone among you who knows of a body that is more upright, more enlightened, more worthy of respect than that of your magistracy? Do not all its members give you the example of moderation, of simplicity of mores, of respect for the laws, and of the most sincere reconciliation? Then freely give such wise chiefs that salutary confidence that reason owes to virtue. Bear in mind that they are of your choice, that they justify it, and that the honors due to those whom you have established in dignity necessarily reflect back upon yourselves. None of you is so unenlightened as to be ignorant of the fact that where the vigor of laws and the authority of their defenders cease, there can be neither security nor freedom for anyone. What then is the point at issue among you except to do wholeheartedly and with just confidence what you should always be obliged to do by a true self-interest, by duty and for the sake of reason? May a sinful and ruinous indifference to the maintenance of the constitution never make you neglect in time of need the wise teachings of the most enlightened and most zealous among you. But may equity, moderation, and the most respectful firmness continue to regulate all your activities and display in you, to the entire universe, the example of a proud and modest people, as jealous of its glory as of its liberty. Above all, beware (and this will be my last counsel) of ever listening to sinister interpretations and venomous speeches, whose secret motives are often more dangerous than the actions that are their object. An entire household awakens and takes warning at the first cries of a good and faithful watchdog who never barks except at the approach of burglars. But people hate the nuisance caused by those noisy animals that continually disturb the public repose and whose continual and ill-timed warnings are not heeded even at the moment when they are necessary.

And you, magnificent and most honored, you upright and worthy magistrates of a free people, permit me to offer you in particular my compliments and my respects. If there is a rank in the world suited to conferring honor on those who hold it, it is without doubt the one that is given by talents and virtue, that of which you have made yourselves worthy, and to which your fellow citizens have raised you. Their own merit adds still a new luster to yours. And I that find you, who were chosen by men capable of governing others in order that they themselves may be governed, are as much above other magistrates as a free people; and above all that the one which you have the honor of leading, is, by its enlightenment and reason, above the populace of the other states.

May I be permitted to cite an example of which better records ought to remain, and which will always be near to my heart. I never call to mind without the sweetest emotion the memory of the virtuous citizen to whom I owe my being, and who often spoke to me in my childhood of the respect that was owed you. I still see him living from the work of his hands, and nourishing his soul on the most sublime truths. I see Tacitus, Plutarch and Grotius mingled with the instruments of his craft before him. I see at his side a beloved son receiving with too little profit the tender instruction of the best of fathers. But if the aberrations of foolish youth made me forget such wise lessons for a time, I have the happiness to sense at last that whatever the inclination one may have toward vice, it is difficult for an education in which the heart is involved to remain forever lost.

Such, magnificent and most honored lords, are the citizens and even the simple inhabitants born in the state you govern. Such are those educated and sensible men concerning whom, under the name of workers and people, such base and false ideas are entertained in other nations. My father, I gladly acknowledge, was in no way distinguished among his fellow citizens; he was only what they all are; and such as he was, there was no country where his company would not have been sought after, cultivated, and profitably too, by the most upright men. It does not behoove me, nor, thank heaven, is it necessary to speak to you of the regard which men of that stamp can expect from you: your equals by education as well as by the rights of nature and of birth; your inferiors by their will and by the preference they owe your merit, which they have granted to it, and for which you in turn owe them some sort of gratitude. It is with intense satisfaction that I learn how much, in your dealings with them, you temper with gentleness and cooperativeness the gravity suited to the ministers of the law; how much you repay them in esteem and attention for the obedience and respect they owe you; conduct full of justice and wisdom, suited to putting at a greater and greater distance the memory of unhappy events which must be forgotten so as never to see them again; conduct all the more judicious because this equitable and generous people makes a pleasure out of its duty, because it naturally loves to honor you, and because those who are most zealous in upholding their rights are the ones who are most inclined to respect yours.

It should not be surprising that the leaders of a civil society love its glory and happiness; but, unfortunately for the tranquility of men, that those who consider themselves as the magistrates, or rather as the masters, of a more holy and more sublime homeland manifest some love for the earthly homeland which nourishes them. How sweet it is for me to be able to make such a rare exception in our favor, and to place in the rank of our best citizens those zealous trustees of the sacred dogmas authorized by the laws, those venerable pastors of souls, whose lively and sweet eloquence the better instills the maxims of the Gospel into people's hearts as they themselves always begin by practicing them. Everyone knows the success with which the great art of preaching is cultivated in Geneva. But since people are too accustomed to seeing things said in one way and done in another, few of them know the extent to which the spirit of Christianity, the saintliness of mores, severity to oneself and gentleness to others reign in the body of our ministers. Perhaps it behooves only the city of Geneva to provide the edifying example of such a perfect union between a society of theologians and of men of letters. It is in large part upon their wisdom and their acknowledged moderation and upon their zeal for the prosperity of the state that I base my hopes for its eternal tranquility. And I note, with a pleasure mixed with amazement and respect, how much they abhor the atrocious maxims of those sacred and barbarous men of whom history provides more than one example, and who, in order to uphold the alleged rights of God—that is to say, their own interests—were all the less sparing of human blood because they hoped their own would always be respected.

Could I forget that precious half of the republic which produces the happiness of the other and whose gentleness and wisdom maintain peace and good mores? Amiable and virtuous women citizens, it will always be the fate of your sex to govern ours. Happy it is when your chaste power, exercised only within the conjugal union, makes itself felt only for the glory of the state and the public happiness! Thus it was that in Sparta women were in command, and thus it is that you deserve to be in command in Geneva. What barbarous man could resist the voice of honor and reason in the mouth of an affectionate wife? And who would not despise vain luxury on seeing your simple and modest attire, which, from the luster it derives from you, seems the most favorable to beauty? It is for you to maintain always, by your amiable and innocent dominion and by your insinuating wit, the love of laws in the state and concord among the citizens; to reunite, by happy marriages, divided families; and above all, to correct, by the persuasive sweetness of your lessons and by the modest graces of your conversation, those extravagances which our young people come to acquire in other countries, whence, instead of the many useful things they could profit from, they bring back, with a childish manner and ridiculous airs adopted among fallen women, nothing more than an admiration for who knows what pretended grandeurs, frivolous compensations for servitude, which will never be worth as much as august liberty. Therefore always be what you are, the chaste guardians of mores and the gentle bonds of peace; and continue to assert on every occasion the rights of the heart and of nature for the benefit of duty and virtue.

I flatter myself that events will not prove me wrong in basing upon such guarantees hope for the general happiness of the citizens and for the glory of the republic. I admit that with all these advantages it will not shine with that brilliance which dazzles most eyes; and the childish and fatal taste for this is the deadliest enemy of happiness and liberty. Let a dissolute youth go elsewhere in search of easy pleasures and lengthy repentances. Let the alleged men of taste admire someplace else the grandeur of palaces, the beauty of carriages, the sumptuous furnishings, the pomp of spectacles, and all the refinements of softness and luxury. In Geneva we will find only men; but such a sight has a value of its own, and those who seek it are well worth the admirers of the rest.

May you all, magnificent, most honored and sovereign lords, deign to receive with the same goodness the respectful testimonies of the interest I take in your common prosperity. If I were unfortunate enough to be guilty of some indiscreet rapture in this lively effusion of my heart, I beg you to pardon it as the tender affection of a true patriot, and to the ardent and legitimate zeal of a man who envisages no greater happiness for himself than that of seeing all of you happy.

With the most profound respect, I am, magnificent, most honored and sovereign lords, your most humble and most obedient servant and fellow citizen.

Jean-Jacques Rousseau
Chambéry
12 June 1754

Preface

Of all the branches of human knowledge, the most useful and the least advanced seems to me to be that of man;[1] and I dare say that the inscription on the temple at Delphi[2] alone contained a precept more important and more difficult than all the huge tomes of the moralists. Thus I regard the subject of this discourse as one of the most interesting questions that philosophy is capable of proposing, and unhappily for us, one of the thorniest that philosophers can attempt to resolve. For how can the source of the inequality among men be known unless one begins by knowing men themselves? And how will man be successful in seeing himself as nature formed him, through all the changes that the succession of time and things must have produced in his original constitution, and in separating what he derives from his own wherewithal from what circumstances and his progress have added to or changed in his primitive state? Like the statue of Glaucus,[3] which time, sea and storms had disfigured to such an extent that it looked less like a god than a wild beast, the human soul, altered in the midst

of society by a thousand constantly recurring causes, by the acquisition of a multitude of bits of knowledge and of errors, by changes that took place in the constitution of bodies, by the constant impact of the passions,[4] has, as it were, changed its appearance to the point of being nearly unrecognizable. And instead of a being active always by certain and invariable principles, instead of that heavenly and majestic simplicity whose mark its author had left on it, one no longer finds anything but the grotesque contrast of passion which thinks it reasons and an understanding in a state of delirium.

What is even more cruel is that, since all the progress of the human species continually moves away from its primitive state, the more we accumulate new knowledge, the more we deprive ourselves of the means of acquiring the most important knowledge of all. Thus, in a sense, it is by dint of studying man that we have rendered ourselves incapable of knowing him.

It is easy to see that it is in these successive changes of the human constitution that we must seek the first origin of the differences that distinguish men, who, by common consensus, are naturally as equal among themselves as were the animals of each species before various physical causes had introduced into certain species the varieties we now observe among some of them. In effect, it is inconceivable that these first changes, by whatever means they took place, should have altered all at once and in the same manner all the individuals of the species. But while some improved or declined and acquired various good or bad qualities which were not inherent in their nature, the others remained longer in their original state. And such was the first source of inequality among men, which it is easier to demonstrate thus in general than to assign with precision its true causes.

Let my readers not imagine, then, that I dare flatter myself with having seen what appears to me so difficult to see. I have begun some lines of reasoning; I have hazarded some guesses, less in the hope of resolving the question than with the intention of clarifying it and of reducing it to its true state. Others will easily be able to go farther on this same route, though it will not be easy for anyone to reach the end of it. For it is no light undertaking to separate what is original from what is artificial in the present nature of man, and to have a proper understanding of a state which no longer exists, which perhaps never existed, which probably never will exist, and yet about which it is necessary to have

---

1   *Of all the branches of human knowledge ... of man*   [Rousseau's note] From the start I rely with confidence on one of those authorities that are respectable for philosophers, because they come from a solid and sublime reason, which they alone know how to find and perceive:

Whatever interest we may have in knowing ourselves, I do not know whether we do not have a better knowledge of everything that is not us. Provided by nature with organs uniquely destined for our preservation, we use them merely to receive impressions of external things; we seek merely to extend ourselves outward and to exist outside ourselves. Too much taken with multiplying the functions of our senses and with increasing the external range of our being, we rarely make use of that internal sense which reduces us to our true dimensions, and which separates us from all that is not us. Nevertheless, this is the sense we must use if we wish to know ourselves. It is the only one by which we can judge ourselves. But how can this sense be activated and given its full range? How can our soul, in which it resides, be rid of all the illusions of our mind? We have lost the habit of using it; it has remained unexercised in the midst of the tumult of our bodily sensations; it has been dried out by the fire of our passions; the heart, the mind, the senses, everything has worked against it. *Hist. Nat.*, Vol. 4: *de la Nat. de l'homme*, p. 151. [Georges Buffon (1707–88), "The Natural History of Man" in *Natural History*]

2   *the inscription on the temple at Delphi*   "Know thyself."

3   *statue of Glaucus*   The reference is to Plato's *Republic*, Book 10, 611. Rousseau is here talking about the problem of discovering the true primitive state of man; Plato used this image in connection with the immortality of the soul, a totally unrelated matter.

4   *passions*   Feelings, emotions.

accurate notions in order to judge properly our own present state. He who would attempt to determine precisely which precautions to take in order to make solid observations on this subject would need even more philosophy than is generally supposed; and a good solution of the following problem would not seem to me unworthy of the Aristotles and Plinys[1] of our century: *What experiments would be necessary to achieve knowledge of natural man? And what are the means of carrying out these experiments in the midst of society?* Far from undertaking to resolve this problem, I believe I have meditated sufficiently on the subject to dare respond in advance that the greatest philosophers will not be too good to direct these experiments, nor the most powerful sovereigns to carry them out. It is hardly reasonable to expect such a combination, especially with the perseverance or rather the succession of understanding and good will needed on both sides in order to achieve success.

These investigations, so difficult to carry out and so little thought about until now, are nevertheless the only means we have left of removing a multitude of difficulties that conceal from us the knowledge of the real foundations of human society. It is this ignorance of the nature of man which throws so much uncertainty and obscurity on the true definition of natural right. For the idea of right, says M. Burlamaqui,[2] and even more that of natural right, are manifestly ideas relative to the nature of man. Therefore, he continues, the principles of this science must be deduced from this very nature of man from man's constitution and state.

It is not without surprise and a sense of outrage that one observes the paucity of agreement that prevails among the various authors who have treated it. Among the most serious writers one can hardly find two who are of the same opinion on this point. The Roman jurists—not to mention the ancient philosophers who seem to have done their best to contradict each other on the most fundamental principles—subject man and all other animals indifferently to the same natural law, because they take this expression to refer to the law that nature imposes on itself rather than the law she prescribes, or rather because of the particular sense in which those jurists understood the word "law," which on this occasion they seem to have taken only for the expression of the general relations established by nature among all animate beings for their common preservation. The moderns, in acknowledging under the word "law" merely a rule prescribed to a moral being, that is to say, intelligent, free and considered in his relations with other beings, consequently limit the competence of the natural law to the only animal endowed with reason, that is, to man. But with each one defining this law in his own fashion, they all establish it on such metaphysical principles that even among us there are very few people in a position to grasp these principles, far from being able to find them by themselves. So that all the definitions of these wise men, otherwise in perpetual contradiction with one another, agree on this alone, that it is impossible to understand the law of nature and consequently to obey it without being a great reasoner and a profound metaphysician, which means precisely that for the establishment of society, men must have used enlightenment which develops only with great difficulty and by a very small number of people within the society itself.

Knowing nature so little and agreeing so poorly on the meaning of the word "law," it would be quite difficult to come to some common understanding regarding a good definition of natural law. Thus all those definitions that are found in books have, over and above a lack of uniformity, the added fault of being drawn from several branches of knowledge which men do not naturally have, and from advantages the idea of which they cannot conceive until after having left the state of nature. Writers begin by seeking the rules on which, for the common utility, it would be appropriate for men to agree among themselves; and then they give the name *natural law* to the collection of these rules, with no other proof than the good which presumably would result from their universal observance. Surely this is a very convenient way to compose definitions and to explain the nature of things by virtually arbitrary views of what is seemly.

But as long as we are ignorant of natural man, it is futile for us to attempt to determine the law he has received or which is best suited to his constitution. All that we can see very clearly regarding this law is that, for it to be law, not only must the will of him who is obliged by it be capable of knowing submission to it, but also, for it to be natural, it must speak directly by the voice of nature.

Leaving aside therefore all the scientific books which teach us only to see men as they have made themselves, and meditating on the first and most simple operations of the human soul, I believe I perceive in it two principles that are

---

1   *Plinys* Pliny the Elder (Gaius Plinius Secundus, 23–79 CE), ancient Roman author, philosopher, and military commander, author of *Naturalis Historia* (*Natural History*, an encyclopedia).

2   *M. Burlamaqui* Jean Jacques Burlamaqui, *Principes du Droit Naturel*, 1,1,2. (*Principles of Natural Law*)

prior to reason, of which one makes us ardently interested in our well-being and our self-preservation, and the other inspires in us a natural repugnance to seeing any sentient[1] being, especially our fellow man, perish or suffer. It is from the conjunction and combination that our mind is in a position to make regarding these two principles, without the need for introducing that of sociability, that all the rules of natural right appear to me to flow; rules which reason is later forced to reestablish on other foundations, when, by its successive developments, it has succeeded in smothering nature.

In this way one is not obliged to make a man a philosopher before making him a man. His duties toward others are not uniquely dictated to him by the belated lessons of wisdom; and as long as he does not resist the inner impulse of compassion, he will never harm another man or even another sentient being, except in the legitimate instance where, if his preservation were involved, he is obliged to give preference to himself. By this means, an end can also be made to the ancient disputes regarding the participation of animals in the natural law. For it is clear that, lacking intelligence and liberty, they cannot recognize this law; but since they share to some extent in our nature by virtue of the sentient quality with which they are endowed, one will judge that they should also participate in natural right, and that man is subject to some sort of duties toward them. It seems, in effect, that if I am obliged not to do any harm to my fellow man, it is less because he is a rational being than because he is a sentient being: a quality that, since it is common to both animals and men, should at least give the former the right not to be needlessly mistreated by the latter.

This same study of original man, of his true needs and the fundamental principles of his duties, is also the only good means that can be used to remove those multitudes of difficulties which present themselves regarding the origin of moral inequality, the true foundations of the body politic, the reciprocal rights of its members, and a thousand other similar questions that are as important as they are poorly explained.

In considering human society from a tranquil and disinterested point of view it seems at first to manifest merely the violence of powerful men and the oppression of the weak. The mind revolts against the harshness of the former; one is inclined to deplore the blindness of the latter. And since nothing is less stable among men than those external relationships which chance brings about more often than wisdom, and which are called weakness or power, wealth or poverty, human establishments appear at first glance to be based on piles of shifting sand. It is only in examining them closely, only after having cleared away the dust and sand that surround the edifice, that one perceives the unshakeable base on which it is raised and one learns to respect its foundations. Now without a serious study of man, of his natural faculties and their successive developments, one will never succeed in making these distinctions and in separating, in the present constitution of things, what the divine will has done from what human art has pretended to do. The political and moral investigations occasioned by the important question I am examining are therefore useful in every way; and the hypothetical history of governments is an instructive lesson for man in every respect. In considering what we would have become, left to ourselves, we ought to learn to bless him whose beneficent hand, in correcting our institutions and giving them an unshakeable foundation, has prevented the disorders that must otherwise result from them, and has brought about our happiness from the means that seemed likely to add to our misery.

> *Learn whom God has ordered you to be, and in what part of human affairs you have been placed.*[2]

Notice on the Notes

I have added some notes to this work, following my indolent custom of working in fits and starts. Occasionally these notes wander so far from the subject that they are not good to read with the text. I therefore have consigned them to the end of the Discourse, in which I have tried my best to follow the straightest path. Those who have the courage to begin again will be able to amuse themselves the second time as they beat the bushes and try to run through the notes. There will be little harm done if others do not read them at all.

Question proposed by the Academy of Dijon: What is the Origin of Inequality Among Men, and is it Authorized by the Natural Law?

---

1 *sentient* Capable of sensation, feeling; conscious.

2 *Learn whom ... been placed* Persius, *Satires* 3.17–72.

Discourse on the Origin and Foundations of Inequality among Men

It is of man that I have to speak, and the question I am examining indicates to me that I am going to be speaking to men, for such questions are not proposed by those who are afraid to honor the truth. I will therefore confidently defend the cause of humanity before the wise men who invite me to do so, and I will not be displeased with myself if I make myself worthy of my subject and my judges.

I conceive of two kinds of inequality in the human species: one which I call natural or physical, because it is established by nature and consists in the difference of age, health, bodily strength, and qualities of mind or soul. The other may be called moral or political inequality, because it depends on a kind of convention[1] and is established, or at least authorized, by the consent of men. This latter type of inequality consists in the different privileges enjoyed by some at the expense of others, such as being richer, more honored, more powerful than they, or even causing themselves to be obeyed by them.

There is no point in asking what the source of natural inequality is, because the answer would be found enunciated in the simple definition of the word. There is still less of a point in asking whether there would not be some essential connection between the two inequalities, for that would amount to asking whether those who command are necessarily better than those who obey, and whether strength of body or mind, wisdom or virtue are always found in the same individuals in proportion to power or wealth. Perhaps this is a good question for slaves to discuss within earshot of their masters, but it is not suitable for reasonable and free men who seek the truth.

Precisely what, then, is the subject of this discourse? To mark, in the progress of things, the moment when, right taking the place of violence, nature was subjected to the law. To explain the sequence of wonders by which the strong could resolve to serve the weak, and the people to buy imaginary repose at the price of real felicity.

The philosophers who have examined the foundations of society have all felt the necessity of returning to the state of nature, but none of them has reached it. Some have not hesitated to ascribe to man in that state the notion of just and unjust, without bothering to show that he had to have that notion, or even that it was useful to him. Others have spoken of the natural right that everyone has to preserve what belongs to him, without explaining what they mean by "belonging." Others started out by giving authority to the stronger over the weaker, and immediately brought about government, without giving any thought to the time that had to pass before the meaning of the words "authority" and "government" could exist among men. Finally, all of them, speaking continually of need, avarice, oppression, desires, and pride, have transferred to the state of nature the ideas they acquired in society. They spoke about savage man, and it was civil man they depicted. It did not even occur to most of our philosophers to doubt that the state of nature had existed, even though it is evident from reading the Holy Scriptures that the first man, having received enlightenment and precepts immediately from God, was not himself in that state; and if we give the writings of Moses the credence that every Christian owes them, we must deny that, even before the flood, men were ever in the pure state of nature, unless they had fallen back into it because of some extraordinary event: a paradox that is quite awkward to defend and utterly impossible to prove.

Let us therefore begin by putting aside all the facts, for they have no bearing on the question. The investigations that may be undertaken concerning this subject should not be taken for historical truths, but only for hypothetical and conditional reasonings, better suited to shedding light on the nature of things than on pointing out their true origin, like those our physicists make everyday with regard to the formation of the world. Religion commands us to believe that since God himself drew men out of the state of nature, they are unequal because he wanted them to be so; but it does not forbid us to form conjectures, drawn solely from the nature of man and the beings that surround him, concerning what the human race could have become, if it had been left to itself. That is what I am asked, and what I propose to examine in this discourse. Since my subject concerns man in general, I will attempt to speak in terms that suit all nations, or rather, forgetting times and places in order to think only of the men to whom I am speaking, I will imagine I am in the Lyceum[2] in Athens, reciting the lessons of my masters, having men like Plato and Xenocrates[3] for my judges, and the human race for my audience.

---

1   *convention*   Custom.

2   *Lyceum*   Famous school in Athens founded by Aristotle in 335 BCE.

3   *Plato and Xenocrates*   Plato (427–347 BCE), the famous ancient Greek philosopher; Xenocrates of Chalcedon (396–314 BCE) was

O man, whatever country you may be from, whatever your opinions may be, listen: here is your history, as I have thought to read it, not in the books of your fellowmen, who are liars, but in nature, who never lies. Everything that comes from nature will be true; there will be nothing false except what I have unintentionally added. The times about which I am going to speak are quite remote: how much you have changed from what you were! It is, as it were, the life of your species that I am about to describe to you according to the qualities you have received, which your education and your habits have been able to corrupt but have been unable to destroy. There is, I feel, an age at which an individual man would want to stop. You will seek the age at which you would want your species to have stopped. Dissatisfied with your present state for reasons that portend even greater grounds for dissatisfaction for your unhappy posterity, perhaps you would like to be able to go backwards in time. This feeling should be a hymn in praise of your first ancestors, the criticism of your contemporaries, and the dread of those who have the unhappiness of living after you.

Part One

However important it may be, in order to render sound judgments regarding the natural state of man, to consider him from his origin and to examine him, so to speak, in the first embryo of the species, I will not follow his nature through its successive developments. I will not stop to investigate in the animal kingdom what he might have been at the beginning so as eventually to become what he is. I will not examine whether, as Aristotle thinks,[1] man's elongated nails were not at first hooked claws, whether man was not furry like a bear, and whether, if man walked on all fours,[2] his gaze, directed toward the ground and limited to a hor-

izon of a few steps—did not provide an indication of both the character and the limits of his ideas. On this subject I could form only vague and almost imaginary conjectures. Comparative anatomy has as yet made too little progress; the observations of naturalists are as yet too uncertain for one to be able to establish the basis of solid reasoning on such foundations. Thus, without having recourse to the supernatural knowledge we have on this point, and without taking note of the changes that must have occurred in the internal as well as the external conformation of man, as he applied his limbs to new purposes and nourished himself on new foods, I will suppose him to have been formed from all time as I see him today: walking on two feet, using his hands as we use ours, directing his gaze over all of nature, and measuring with his eyes the vast expanse of the heavens.

When I strip that being, thus constituted, of all the supernatural gifts he could have received and of all the artificial faculties he could have acquired only through long progress; when I consider him, in a word, as he must have left the hands of nature, I see an animal less strong than some, less agile than others, but all in all, the most advantageously organized of all. I see him satisfying his hunger under an oak tree, quenching his thirst at the first stream, finding his bed at the foot of the same tree that supplied his meal; and thus all his needs are satisfied.

When the earth is left to its natural fertility[3] and covered with immense forests that were never mutilated by the axe, it offers storehouses and shelters at every step to animals of every species. Men, dispersed among the animals, observe and imitate their industry, and thereby raise themselves to the level of animal instinct, with the advantage that, whereas each species has only its own instincts, man, who may perhaps have none that belongs to him, appropriates all of them to himself, feeds himself equally well on most of the various foods[4] which the other animals divide among

---

a student of Plato who became head of the school Plato founded, the Academy, in 339 BCE.

1   *as Aristotle thinks*   Aristotle certainly did not believe in anything like the evolutionary view Rousseau has, though he did speak of the analogy between claws and human nails. See his *Parts of Animals* 4.10.687b and his *History of Animals* 1.1.486b, 2.8.502b, and 3.9.517a.

2   *if man walked on all fours*   [Rousseau's note] The changes that a long-established habit of walking on two feet could have brought about in the conformation of man, the relations that are still observed between his arms and the forelegs of quadrupeds, and the induction drawn from their manner of walking, could have given rise to doubts about the manner that must have been the most natural to us. All children begin by walking on all fours, and need

our example and our lessons to learn to stand upright.... [A long note on bipeds and quadrupeds, which is omitted here, follows.]

3   *When the earth ... natural fertility*   Rousseau here appends a long note on the natural fertility of the earth.

4   *feeds himself ... various foods*   [Rousseau's note] Among the quadrupeds, the two most universal distinguishing traits of voracious species are derived, on the one hand, from the shape of the teeth, and, on the other, from the conformation of the intestines. Animals that live solely on vegetation have all flat teeth, like the horse, ox, sheep and hare, but voracious animals have pointed teeth, like the cat, dog, wolf and fox. And as for the intestines, the frugivorous [fruit-eating] ones have some, such as the colon, which are not found in voracious animals. It appears therefore that man, hav-

themselves, and consequently finds his sustenance more easily than any of the rest can.

Accustomed from childhood to inclement weather and the rigors of the seasons, acclimated to fatigue, and forced, naked and without arms, to defend their lives and their prey against other ferocious beasts, or to escape them by taking flight, men develop a robust and nearly unalterable temperament. Children enter the world with the excellent constitution of their parents and strengthen it with the same exercises that produced it, thus acquiring all the vigor that the human race is capable of having. Nature treats them precisely the way the law of Sparta treated the children of its citizens: it renders strong and robust those who are well constituted and makes all the rest perish, thereby differing from our present-day societies, where the state, by making children burdensome to their parents, kills them indiscriminately before their birth.

Since the savage man's body is the only instrument he knows, he employs it for a variety of purposes that, for lack of practice, ours are incapable of serving. And our industry deprives us of the force and agility that necessity obliges him to acquire. If he had had an axe, would his wrists break such strong branches? If he had had a sling, would he throw a stone with so much force? If he had had a ladder, would he climb a tree so nimbly? If he had had a horse, would he run so fast? Give a civilized man time to gather all his machines around him, and undoubtedly he will easily overcome a savage man. But if you want to see an even more unequal fight, pit them against each other naked and disarmed, and you will soon realize the advantage of constantly having all of one's forces at one's disposal, of always being ready for any event, and of always carrying one's entire self, as it were, with one.[1]

Hobbes maintains that man is naturally intrepid and seeks only to attack and to fight.[2] On the other hand, an illustrious philosopher thinks,[3] and Cumberland[4] and Pufendorf[5] also affirm, that nothing is as timid as man in the state of nature, and that he is always trembling and ready to take flight at the slightest sound he hears or at the slightest movement he perceives. That may be the case with regard to objects with which he is not acquainted. And I do not doubt that he is frightened by all the new sights that present themselves to him every time he can neither discern the physical good and evil he may expect from them nor compare his forces with the dangers he must run: rare circumstances in the state of nature, where everything takes place in such a uniform manner and where the face of the earth is not subject to those sudden and continual changes caused by the passions and inconstancy of peoples living together. But since a savage man lives dispersed among the animals and, finding himself early on in a position to measure himself against them, he soon makes the comparison; and, aware that he surpasses them in skillfulness more than they surpass him in strength, he learns not to fear them any more. Pit a bear or a wolf against a savage who is robust, agile, and courageous, as they all are, armed with stones and a hefty cudgel, and you will see that the danger will be at least equal on both sides, and that after several such experiences, ferocious beasts, which do not like to attack one another, will be quite reluctant to attack a man, having found

---

ing teeth and intestines like frugivorous animals, should naturally be placed in that class. And not only do anatomical observations confirm this opinion, but the monuments of antiquity are also very favorable to it. "Dicaearchus" [(c. 350–c. 285 BCE) Greek philosopher and scholar], says St. Jerome, "relates in his books on Greek antiquities that under the reign of Saturn, when the earth was still fertile by itself, no man ate flesh, but that all lived on fruits and vegetables that grew naturally" (*Adversus Jovinianum* [395 CE], Book 2). This opinion can also be supported by the reports of several modern travelers.... [Rousseau provides several examples.]

1 *But if you want ... with me* [Rousseau's note] All the kinds of knowledge that demand reflection, all those acquired only by the concatenation of ideas and perfected only successively, appear to be utterly beyond the grasp of savage man, owing to the lack of communication with his fellow-men, that is to say, owing to the

lack of the instrument which is used for that communication, and to the lack of the needs that make it necessary. His understanding and his industry are limited to jumping, running, fighting, throwing a stone, climbing a tree. But if he knows only those things, in return he knows them much better than we, who do not have the same need for them as he. And since they depend exclusively on bodily exercise and are not capable of any communication or progress from one individual to another, the first man could have been just as adept at them as his last descendants. [Rousseau concludes his note with several paragraphs of examples.]

2 *Hobbes maintains ... to fight.* Thomas Hobbes (1588–1679), English philosopher and central figure in the social contract tradition. Hobbes famously held that the life of man in the state of nature is "solitary, poor, nasty, brutish, and short" (*Leviathan*, Chapter 13).

3 *an illustrious philosopher thinks* See Montesquieu (1689–1755), *The Spirit of the Laws*, 1.2.

4 *Cumberland* Richard Cumberland (1631–1718), English philosopher. *De Legibus Naturae*, translated into English as *A Treatise of the Laws of Nature*, or *On Natural Laws*, 2.29.

5 *Pufendorf* Samuel Pufendorf (1632–94), German jurist. *De Jure Naturae et Gentium*, translated into English as *Of the Law of Nature and of Nations*, 2.1.8, 2.2.2.

him to be as ferocious as themselves. With regard to animals that actually have more strength than man has skillfulness, he is in the same position as other weaker species, which nevertheless subsist. Man has the advantage that, since he is no less adept than they at running and at finding almost certain refuge in trees, he always has the alternative of accepting or leaving the encounter and the choice of taking flight or entering into combat. Moreover, it appears that no animal naturally attacks man, except in the case of self-defense or extreme hunger, or shows evidence of those violent antipathies toward him that seem to indicate that one species is destined by nature to serve as food for another.

<No doubt these are the reasons why negroes and savages bother themselves so little about the ferocious beasts they may encounter in the woods. In this respect, the Caribs of Venezuela, among others, live in the most profound security and without the slightest inconvenience. Although they are practically naked, says Francisco Coreal,[1] they boldly expose themselves in the forest, armed only with bow and arrow, but no one has ever heard of one of them being devoured by animals.>[2]

There are other, more formidable enemies, against which man does not have the same means of self-defense: natural infirmities, childhood, old age, and illnesses of all kinds—sad signs of our weakness, of which the first two are common to all animals, with the last belonging principally to man living in society. On the subject of childhood, I even observe that a mother, by carrying her child everywhere with her, can feed it much more easily than females of several animal species, which are forced to be continually coming and going, with great fatigue, to seek their food and to suckle or feed their young. It is true that if a woman were to perish, the child runs a considerable risk of perishing with her. But this danger is common to a hundred other species, whose young are for quite some time incapable of going off to seek their nourishment for themselves. And although childhood is longer among us, our lifespan is also longer; thus things are more or less equal in this respect,[3] although

there are other rules, not relevant to my subject, which are concerned with the duration of infancy and the number of young.[4] Among the elderly, who are less active and perspire little, the need for food diminishes with the faculty of providing for it. And since savage life shields them from gout and rheumatism, and since old age is, of all ills, the one that human assistance can least alleviate, they eventually die without anyone being aware that they are ceasing to exist, and almost without being aware of it themselves.

With regard to illnesses, I will not repeat the vain and false pronouncements made against medicine by the majority of people in good health. Rather, I will ask whether there is any solid observation on the basis of which one can conclude that the average lifespan is shorter in those countries where the art of medicine is most neglected than in those

---

grow, can live six or seven times as long, that is to say, ninety or a hundred years. The horse, whose growth period is four years, can live six or seven times as long, that is to say, twenty-five or thirty years. The examples that could be contrary to this rule are so rare, that they should not even be regarded as an exception from which conclusions can be drawn. And just as large horses achieve their growth in less time than slender horses, they also have a shorter lifespan and are old from the age of fifteen."

4   *number of young*   [Rousseau's note] I believe I see another difference between carnivorous and frugivorous animals still more general than the one I have remarked upon [in Note 5], since this one extends to birds. This difference consists in the number of young, which never exceeds two in each litter for the species that lives exclusively on plant life, and which ordinarily exceeds this number for voracious animals. It is easy to know nature's plan in this regard by the number of teats, which is only two in each female of the first species, like the mare, the cow, the goat, the doe, the ewe, etc., and which is always six or eight in the other females, such as the dog, the cat, the wolf, the tigress, etc. The hen, the goose, the duck, which are all voracious birds (as are the eagle, the sparrow hawk, the screech owl), also lay and hatch a large number of eggs, which never happens to the pigeon, the turtle-dove, or to birds that eat nothing but grain, which lay and hatch scarcely more than two eggs at a time. The reason that can be given for this difference is that the animals that live exclusively on grass and plants, remaining nearly the entire day grazing and being forced to spend considerable time feeding themselves, could not be up to the task of nursing several young; whereas the voracious animals, taking their meal almost in an instant, can more easily and more often return to their young and to their hunting, and can compensate for the loss of so large a quantity of milk. There would be many particular observations and reflections to make on all this, but this is not the place to make them, and it is enough for me to have shown in this part the most general system of nature, a system which furnishes a new reason to remove man from the class of carnivorous animals and to place him among the frugivorous species.

---

1   *Francisco Coreal*   (1648–1708), Spanish travel writer who visited North and South America and wrote a narrative about his travels, *Viaje a las Indias Occidentales* (Voyage to the Occidental Indies).

2   <*No doubt ... by animals*> This and further passages in the text enclosed inside the symbols < > were added by Rousseau to the 1782 edition.

3   *equal in this respect*   [Rousseau's note] "The lifespan of horses," says M. de Buffon ["Natural History of the Horse," *Natural History*] "is, as in all other species of animals, proportionate to the length of their growth period. Man, who takes fourteen years to

where it is cultivated most assiduously. And how could that be the case, if we give ourselves more ills than medicine can furnish us remedies? The extreme inequality in our lifestyle: excessive idleness among some, excessive labor among others; the ease with which we arouse and satisfy our appetites and our sensuality; the overly refined foods of the wealthy, which nourish them with irritating juices and overwhelm them with indigestion; the bad food of the poor, who most of the time do not have even that, and who, for want of food, are inclined to stuff their stomachs greedily whenever possible; staying up until all hours, excesses of all kinds, immoderate outbursts of every passion, bouts of fatigue and mental exhaustion; countless sorrows and afflictions which are felt in all levels of society and which perpetually gnaw away at souls: these are the fatal proofs that most of our ills are of our own making, and that we could have avoided nearly all of them by preserving the simple, regular and solitary lifestyle prescribed to us by nature. If nature has destined us to be healthy, I almost dare to affirm that the state of reflection is a state contrary to nature and that the man who meditates is a depraved animal. When one thinks about the stout constitutions of the savages, at least of those whom we have not ruined with our strong liquors; when one becomes aware of the fact that they know almost no illnesses but wounds and old age, one is strongly inclined to believe that someone could easily write the history of human maladies by following the history of civil societies. This at least was the opinion of Plato,[1] who believed that, from certain remedies used or approved by Podalirius and Machaon at the siege of Troy, various illnesses which these remedies should exacerbate were as yet unknown among men. <And Celsus[2] reports that diet, so necessary today, was only an invention of Hippocrates.>[3]

With so few sources of ills, man in the state of nature hardly has any need therefore of remedies, much less of physicians. The human race is in no worse condition than all the others in this respect; and it is easy to learn from hunters whether in their chases they find many sick animals. They find quite a few that have received serious wounds that healed quite nicely, that have had bones or even limbs broken and reset with no other surgeon than time, no other regimen than their everyday life, and that are no less per-

fectly cured for not having been tormented with incisions, poisoned with drugs, or exhausted with fasting. Finally, however correctly administered medicine may be among us, it is still certain that although a sick savage, abandoned to himself, has nothing to hope for except from nature, on the other hand, he has nothing to fear except his illness. This frequently makes his situation preferable to ours.

Therefore we must take care not to confuse savage man with the men we have before our eyes. Nature treats all animals left to their own devices with a predilection that seems to show how jealous she is of that right. The horse, the cat, the bull, even the ass, are usually taller, and all of them have a more robust constitution, more vigor, more strength, and more courage in the forests than in our homes. They lose half of these advantages in becoming domesticated; it might be said that all our efforts at feeding them and treating them well only end in their degeneration. It is the same for man himself. In becoming habituated to the ways of society and a slave, he becomes weak, fearful, and servile; his soft and effeminate lifestyle completes the enervation of both his strength and his courage. Let us add that the difference between the savage man and the domesticated man should be still greater than that between the savage animal and the domesticated animal; for while animal and man have been treated equally by nature, man gives more comforts to himself than to the animals he tames, and all of these comforts are so many specific causes that make him degenerate more noticeably.

It is therefore no great misfortune for those first men, nor, above all, such a great obstacle to their preservation, that they are naked, that they have no dwelling, and that they lack all those useful things we take to be so necessary. If they do not have furry skin, they have no need for it in warm countries, and in cold countries they soon learn to help themselves to the skins of animals they have vanquished. If they have but two feet to run with, they have two arms to provide for their defense and for their needs. Perhaps their children learn to walk late and with difficulty, but mothers carry them easily: an advantage that is lacking in other species, where the mother, on being pursued, finds herself forced to abandon her young or to conform her pace to theirs. <It is possible there are some exceptions to this. For example, the animal from the province of Nicaragua which resembles a fox and which has feet like a man's hands, and, according to Coreal, has a pouch under its belly in which the mother places her young when she is forced to take flight. No doubt this is the same animal that is called *tlaquatzin*

---

1   *the opinion of Plato*   See the *Republic*, 405 ff.
2   *Celsus*   Second-century Greek philosopher best known for his writing in opposition to Christianity.
3   *Hippocrates*   (460–370 BCE) Greek physician, often called the father of medicine.

in Mexico; the female of the species Laët describes as having a similar pouch for the same purpose.>[1] Finally, unless we suppose those singular and fortuitous combinations of circumstances of which I will speak later, and which might very well have never taken place, at any rate it is clear that the first man who made clothing or a dwelling for himself was giving himself things that were hardly necessary, since he had done without them until then and since it is not clear why, as a grown man, he could not endure the kind of life he had endured ever since he was a child.

Alone, idle, and always near danger, savage man must like to sleep and be a light sleeper like animals which do little thinking and, as it were, sleep the entire time they are not thinking. Since his self-preservation was practically his sole concern, his best trained faculties ought to be those that have attack and defense as their principal object, either to subjugate his prey or to prevent his becoming the prey of another animal. On the other hand, the organs that are perfected only by softness and sensuality must remain in a state of crudeness that excludes any kind of refinement in him. And with his senses being divided in this respect, he will have extremely crude senses of touch and taste; those of sight, hearing and smell will have the greatest subtlety. Such is the state of animals in general, and, according to the reports of travelers, such also is that of the majority of savage peoples. Thus we should not be surprised that the Hottentots of the Cape of Good Hope can sight ships with the naked eye as far out at sea as the Dutch can with telescopes; or that the savages of America were as capable of trailing Spaniards by smell as the best dogs could have done; or that all these barbarous nations endure their nakedness with no discomfort, whet their appetites with hot peppers, and drink European liquors like water.

So far I have considered only physical man. Let us now try to look at him from a metaphysical and moral point of view.

In any animal I see nothing but an ingenious machine to which nature has given senses in order for it to renew its strength and to protect itself, to a certain point, from all that tends to destroy or disturb it. I am aware of precisely the same things in the human machine, with the difference that nature alone does everything in the operations of an animal, whereas man contributes, as a free agent, to his own operations. The former chooses or rejects by instinct and the later by an act of freedom. Hence an animal cannot deviate from the rule that is prescribed to it, even when it would be advantageous to do so, while man deviates from it, often to his own detriment. Thus a pigeon would die of hunger near a bowl filled with choice meats, and so would a cat perched atop a pile of fruit or grain, even though both could nourish themselves quite well with the food they disdain, if they were of a mind to try some. And thus dissolute men abandon themselves to excesses which cause them fever and death, because the mind perverts the senses and because the will still speaks when nature is silent.

Every animal has ideas, since it has senses; up to a certain point it even combines its ideas, and in this regard man differs from an animal only in degree. Some philosophers[2] have even suggested that there is a greater difference between two given men than between a given man and an animal. Therefore it is not so much understanding which causes the specific distinction of man from all other animals as it is his being a free agent. Nature commands every animal, and beasts obey. Man feels the same impetus, but he knows he is free to go along or to resist; and it is above all in the awareness of this freedom that the spirituality of his soul is made manifest. For physics explains in some way the mechanism of the senses and the formation of ideas; but in the power of willing, or rather of choosing, and in the feeling of this power, we find only purely spiritual acts, about which the laws of mechanics explain nothing.

But if the difficulties surrounding all these questions should leave some room for dispute on this difference between man and animal, there is another very specific quality which distinguishes them and about which there can be no argument: the faculty of self-perfection, a faculty which, with the aid of circumstances, successively develops all the others, and resides among us as much in the species as in the individual. On the other hand, an animal, at the end of a few months, is what it will be all its life; and its species, at the end of a thousand years, is what it was in the first of those thousand years. Why is man alone subject to becoming an imbecile? Is it not that he thereby returns to his primitive state, and that, while the animal which has acquired nothing and which also has nothing to lose, always retains its instinct, man, in losing through old age or other

---

1   the animal ... same purpose   The *tlaquatzin* is a large squirrel, but it appears that the pouched animal in question is an opossum. Joannes de Laët (1581–1649) was a Flemish geographer and director of the Dutch West India Company, author of *History of the New World*.

2   *Some philosophers*   Rousseau may be referring to Montaigne's "Of the Inequality Among Us" (*Essays*, 1, 42).

accidents all that his *perfectibility* has enabled him to acquire, thus falls even lower than the animal itself? It would be sad for us to be forced to agree that this distinctive and almost unlimited faculty is the source of all man's misfortunes; that this is what, by dint of time, draws him out of that original condition in which he would pass tranquil and innocent days; that this is what, through centuries of giving rise to his enlightenment and his errors, his vices and his virtues, eventually makes him a tyrant over himself and nature.[1] It would be dreadful to be obliged to praise as a beneficent being the one who first suggested to the inhabitant on the banks of the Orinoco the use of boards which he binds to his children's temples, and which assure them of at least part of their imbecility and their original happiness.

Savage man, left by nature to instinct alone, or rather compensated for the instinct he is perhaps lacking by faculties capable of first replacing them and then of raising him to the level of instinct, will therefore begin with purely animal functions.[2] Perceiving and feeling will be his first state, which he will have in common with all animals. Willing and not willing, desiring, and fearing will be the first and nearly the only operations of his soul until new circumstances bring about new developments in it.

Whatever the moralists may say about it, human understanding owes much to the passions, which, by common consensus, also owe a great deal to it. It is by their activity that our reason is perfected. We seek to know only because we desire to find enjoyment; and it is impossible to conceive why someone who had neither desires nor fears would go to the bother of reasoning. The passions in turn take their origin from our needs, and their progress from our knowledge. For one can desire or fear things only by virtue of the ideas one can have of them, or from the simple impulse of nature; and savage man, deprived of every sort of enlightenment, feels only the passion of this latter sort. His desires do not go beyond his physical needs.[3] The only goods he knows in the universe are nourishment, a woman and rest; the only evils he fears are pain and hunger. I say pain and not death because an animal will never know what it is to die; and knowledge of death and its terrors is one of the first acquisitions that man has made in withdrawing from the animal condition.

Were it necessary, it would be easy for me to support this view with facts and to demonstrate that, among all the nations of the world, the progress of the mind has been precisely proportioned to the needs received by peoples from nature or to those needs to which circumstances have subjected them, and consequently to the passions which inclined them to provide for those needs. I would show the arts coming into being in Egypt and spreading with the flooding of the Nile. I would follow their progress among the Greeks, where they were seen to germinate, grow and rise to the heavens among the sands and rocks of Attica,[4] though never being able to take root on the fertile banks of the Eurotas.[5] I would point out that in general the peoples of the north are more industrious than those of the south, because they cannot get along as well without being so, as if nature thereby wanted to equalize things by giving to their minds the fertility it refuses their soil.

But without having recourse to the uncertain testimony of history, does anyone fail to see that everything seems to remove savage man from the temptation and the means of ceasing to be savage? His imagination depicts nothing to him; his heart asks nothing of him. His modest needs are so easily found at hand, and he is so far from the degree of knowledge necessary to make him desire to acquire greater knowledge, that he can have neither foresight nor curiosity. The spectacle of nature becomes a matter of indifference to him by dint of its becoming familiar to him. It is always the same order, always the same succession of changes. He does not have a mind for marveling at the greatest wonders; and we must not seek in him the philosophy that a man needs in order to know how to observe once what he has seen everyday. His soul, agitated by nothing, is given over to the single feeling of his own present existence, without any idea of the future, however, near it may be, and his projects, as limited as his views, hardly extend to the end of the day.

---

1   *his vices and his virtues ... nature*   The long note Rousseau appends here has been included as Appendix 1 below.

2   *animal functions*   The long note that Rousseau appends here on human variety has been included as Appendix 2 below.

3   *His desires ... physical needs*   [Rousseau's note] That appears utterly evident to me and I am unable to conceive whence our philosophers can derive all the passions they ascribe to natural man. With the single exception of the physically necessary which nature itself demands, all our other needs are such merely out of habit (previous to which they were not needs), or by our own desires; and we do not desire what we are not in a position to know. Whence it follows that since savage man desires only the things he knows and knows only those things whose possession is in his power or easily acquired, nothing should be so tranquil as his soul and nothing so limited as his mind.

4   *the sands and rocks of Attica*   The location of Athens.

5   *the fertile banks of the Eurotas*   The location of Sparta.

Such is, even today, the extent of the Carib's[1] foresight. In the morning he sells his bed of cotton and in the evening he returns in tears to buy it back, for want of having foreseen that he would need it that night.

The more one meditates on this subject, the more the distance from pure sensations to the simplest knowledge increases before our eyes; and it is impossible to conceive how a man could have crossed such a wide gap by his forces alone, without the aid of communication and without the provocation of necessity. How many centuries have perhaps gone by before men were in a position to see any fire other than that from the heavens? How many different risks did they have to run before they learned the most common uses of that element? How many times did they let it go out before they had acquired the art of reproducing it? And how many times perhaps did each of these secrets die with the one who had discovered it? What will we say about agriculture, an art that requires so much labor and foresight, that depends on so many other arts, that quite obviously is practicable only in a society which is at least in its beginning stages, and that serves us not so much to derive from the earth food it would readily provide without agriculture, as to force from it those preferences that are most to our taste? But let us suppose that men multiplied to the point where the natural productions were no longer sufficient to nourish them: a supposition which, it may be said in passing, would show a great advantage for the human species in that way of life. Let us suppose that, without forges or workshops, farm implements had fallen from the heavens into the hands of the savages; that these men had conquered the mortal hatred they all have for continuous work; that they had learned to foresee their needs far enough in advance; that they had guessed how the soil is to be cultivated, grains sown, and trees planted; that they had discovered the arts of grinding wheat and fermenting grapes: all things they would need to have been taught by the gods, for it is inconceivable how they could have picked these things up on their own. Yet, after all this, what man would be so foolish as to tire himself out cultivating a field that will be plundered by the first comer, be it man or beast, who takes a fancy to the crop? And how could each man resolve to spend his life in hard labor, when, the more necessary to him the fruits of his labor may be, the surer he is of not realizing them? In a

word, how could this situation lead men to cultivate the soil as long as it is not divided among them, that is to say, as long as the state of nature is not wiped out?

Were we to want to suppose a savage man as skilled in the art of thinking as our philosophers make him out to be; were we, following their example, to make him a full-fledged philosopher, discovering by himself the most sublime truths, and, by chains of terribly abstract reasoning, forming for himself maxims of justice and reason drawn from the love of order in general or from the known will of his creator; in a word, were we to suppose there was as much intelligence and enlightenment in his mind as he needs, and is in fact found to have been possessed of dullness and stupidity, what use would the species have for all that metaphysics, which could not be communicated and which would perish with the individual who would have invented it? What progress could the human race make, scattered in the woods among the animals? And to what extent could men mutually perfect and enlighten one another, when, with neither a fixed dwelling nor any need for one another, they would hardly encounter one another twice in their lives, without knowing or talking to one another.

Let us consider how many ideas we owe to the use of speech; how much grammar trains and facilitates the operations of the mind. And let us think of the inconceivable difficulties and the infinite amount of time that the first invention of languages must have cost. Let us join their reflections to the preceding ones, and we will be in a position to judge how many thousands of centuries would have been necessary to develop successively in the human mind the operations of which it was capable.

May I be permitted to consider for a moment the obstacles to the origin of languages. I could be content here to cite or repeat the investigations that the Abbé de Condillac[2] has made on this matter, all of which completely confirm my view, and may perhaps have given me the idea in the first place. But since the way in which this philosopher resolves the difficulties he himself raises concerning the origin of conventional signs shows that he assumed what I question (namely, a kind of society already established among the inventors of language), I believe that, in referring to his reflections, I must add to them my own, in order to present the same difficulties from a standpoint that is pertinent to

---

1 *Carib's* The Caribs are the native people of the Lesser Antilles, the island chain running from east of Puerto Rico down to and along the north coast of South America.

2 *Abbé de Condillac* Étienne Bonnot de Condillac (1715–80), French philosopher. Rousseau may be referring to his *Essay on the Origin of Human Knowledge* (1746), 2.1.

my subject. The first that presents itself is to imagine how languages could have become necessary; for since men had no communication among themselves nor any need for it, I fail to see either the necessity of this invention or its possibility, if it were not indispensable. I might well say, as do many others, that languages were born in the domestic intercourse[1] among fathers, mothers, and children. But aside from the fact that this would not resolve the difficulties, it would make the mistake of those who, reasoning about the state of nature, intrude into it ideas taken from society. They always see the family gathered in one and the same dwelling, with its members maintaining among themselves a union as intimate and permanent as exists among us, where so many common interests unite them. But the fact of the matter is that in that primitive state, since nobody had houses or huts or property of any kind, each one bedded down in some random spot and often for only one night. Males and females came together fortuitously as a result of chance encounters, occasion, and desire, without there being any great need for words to express what they had to say to one another. They left one another with the same nonchalance.[2] The mother at first nursed her children for her own need; then, with habit having endeared them to her, she later nourished them for their own need. Once they had the strength to look for their food, they did not hesitate to leave the mother herself. And since there was practically no other way of finding one another than not to lose sight of one another, they were soon at the point of not even recognizing one another. It should also be noted that, since the child had all his needs to explain and consequently more things to say to the mother than the mother to the child, it is the child who must make the greatest effort toward inventing a language, and that the language he uses should in large part be of his own making, which multiplies languages as many times as there are individuals to speak them. This tendency was abetted by a nomadic and vagabond life, which does not give any idiom time to gain a foothold. For claiming that the mother teaches her child the words he ought to use in asking her for this or that is a good way of showing how already formed languages are taught, but it does not tell us how languages are formed.

Let us suppose this first difficulty has been overcome. Let us disregard for a moment the immense space that there

must have been between the pure state of nature and the need for languages. And, on the supposition that they are necessary,[3] let us inquire how they might have begun to be established. Here we come to a new difficulty, worse still than the preceding one. For if men needed speech in order to learn to think, they had a still greater need for knowing how to think in order to discover the art of speaking. And even if it were understood how vocal sounds had been taken for the conventional expressions of our ideas, it would still remain for us to determine what could have been the conventional expressions for ideas that, not having a sensible object, could not be indicated either by gesture or by voice. Thus we are scarcely able to form tenable conjectures regarding the birth of this art of communicating thoughts and establishing intercourse between minds, a sublime art which is already quite far from its origin, but which the philosopher still sees at so prodigious a distance from its perfection that there is no man so foolhardy as to claim that it will ever achieve it, even if the sequences of change that time necessarily brings were suspended in its favor, even if prejudices were to be barred from the academies or be silent before them, and even if they were able to occupy themselves with that thorny problem for whole centuries without interruption.

Man's first language, the most universal, the most energetic and the only language he needed before it was necessary to persuade men assembled together, is the cry of nature. Since this cry was elicited only by a kind of instinct in pressing circumstances, to beg for help in great dangers,

---

1   *intercourse* Dealings or communications of any sort between individuals.

2   *They left ... same nonchalance* The long note Rousseau appends here on Locke's views has been included as Appendix 3 below.

3   *on the supposition ... necessary* [Rousseau's note] I will hold back from embarking on the philosophical reflections that there would be to engage in concerning the advantages and disadvantages of this institution of languages. It is not for me to be permitted to attack vulgar errors; and educated people respect their prejudices too much to abide patiently my alleged paradoxes. Let us therefore allow men to speak, to whom it has not been made a crime to risk sometimes taking the part of reason against the opinion of the multitude. *Nor would anything disappear from the happiness of the human race, if, when the disaster and confusion of so many languages has been cast out, mortals should cultivate one art, and if it should be allowed to explain anything by means of signs, movements and gestures. But now it has been so established that the condition of animals commonly believed to be brutes is considerably better than ours in this respect, inasmuch as they articulate their feelings and their thoughts without an interpreter more readily and perhaps more felicitously than any mortals can, especially if they use a foreign language.* Is. Vossius *de Poëmat. Cant. et Viribus Rythmi,* p. 66. [Rousseau gives the Latin text. Isaac Vossius, *De Poematum Cantu et Viribus Rythmi* (1673).]

or for relief of violent ills, it was not used very much in the ordinary course of life, where more moderate feelings prevail. When the ideas of men begin to spread and multiply, and closer communication was established among them, they sought more numerous signs and a more extensive language. They multiplied vocal inflections and combined them with gestures, which, by their nature, are more expressive, and whose meaning is less dependent on a prior determination. They therefore signified visible and mobile objects by means of gestures, and audible ones by imitative sounds. But since a gesture indicates hardly anything more than present or easily described objects and visible actions; since its use is not universal, because darkness or the interposition of a body renders it useless; and since it requires rather than stimulates attention, men finally thought of replacing them with vocal articulations, which, while not having the same relationship to certain ideas, were better suited to represent all ideas as conventional signs. Such a substitution could only be made by a common consent and in a way rather difficult to practice for men whose crude organs had as yet no exercise, and still more difficult to conceive in itself, since that unanimous agreement had to have had a motive, and speech appears to have been necessary in order to establish the use of speech.

We must infer that the first words men used had a much broader meaning in their mind than do those used in languages that are already formed; and that, being ignorant of the division of discourse into its constitutive parts, at first they gave each word the meaning of a whole sentence. When they began to distinguish subject from attribute and verb from noun, which was no mean effort of genius, substantives were at first only so many proper nouns; the <present> infinitive was the only verb tense; and the notion of adjectives must have developed only with considerable difficulty, since every adjective is an abstract word, and abstractions are difficult and not particularly natural operations.

At first each object was given a particular name, without regard to genus and species which those first founders were not in a position to distinguish; and all individual things presented themselves to their minds in isolation, as they are in the spectacle of nature. If one oak tree was called A, another was called B. <For the first idea one draws from two things is that they are not the same; and it often requires quite some time to observe what they have in common.> Thus the more limited the knowledge, the more extensive becomes the dictionary. The difficulty inherent in all this nomenclature could not easily be alleviated, for in order to group beings under various common and generic denominations, it was necessary to know their properties and their differences. Observations and definitions were necessary, that is to say, natural history and metaphysics, and far more than men of those times could have had.

Moreover, general ideas can be introduced into the mind only with the aid of words, and the understanding grasps them only through sentences. That is one reason why animals cannot form such ideas or even acquire the perfectibility that depends on them. When a monkey moves unhesitatingly from one nut to another, does anyone think the monkey has the general idea of that type of fruit and that he compares its archetype with these two individuals? Undoubtedly not; but the sight of one of these nuts recalls to his memory the sensations he received of the other; and his eyes, modified in a certain way, announce to his sense of taste the modification it is about to receive. Every general idea is purely intellectual. The least involvement of the imagination thereupon makes the idea particular. Try to draw for yourself the image of a tree in general; you will never succeed in doing it. In spite of yourself, it must be seen as small or large, barren or leafy, light or dark; and if you were in a position to see in it nothing but what you see in every tree, this image would no longer resemble a tree. Purely abstract beings are perceived in the same way, or are conceived only through discourse. The definition of a triangle alone gives you the true idea of it. As soon as you behold one in your mind, it is a particular triangle and not some other one, and you cannot avoid making its lines to be perceptible or its plane to have color. It is therefore necessary to utter sentences, and thus to speak, in order to have general ideas. For as soon as the imagination stops, the mind proceeds no further without the aid of discourse. If, then, the first inventors of language could give names only to ideas they already had, it follows that the first substantives could not have been anything but proper nouns.

But when, by means I am unable to conceive, our new grammarians began to extend their ideas and to generalize their words, the ignorance of the inventors must have subjected this method to very strict limitations. And just as they had at first unduly multiplied the names of individual things, owing to their failure to know the genera and species, they later made too few species and genera, owing to their failure to have considered beings in all their differences. Pushing these divisions far enough would have required more experience and enlightenment than they could have had, and more investigations and work than they were willing to put into it. Now if even today new species are discovered every-day that until now had escaped all our observations, just imagine how many species must have escaped the attention of men who judged things only on first appearance! As for primary classes and the most general notions, it is super-fluous to add that they too must have escaped them. How, for example, would they have imagined or understood the words "matter," "mind," "substance," "mode," "figure," and "movement," when our philosophers, who for so long have been making use of them, have a great deal of difficulty understanding them themselves; and when, since the ideas attached to these words are purely metaphysical, they found no model of them in nature?

I stop with these first steps, and I implore my judges to suspend their reading here to consider, concerning the invention of physical substantives alone, that is to say, concerning the easiest part of the language to discover, how far language still had to go in order to express all the thoughts of men, assume a durable form, be capable of being spoken in public, and influence society. I im-plore them to reflect upon how much time and know-ledge were needed to discover numbers,[1] abstract words,

---

1   *discover numbers* [Rousseau's note] In showing how ideas of discrete quantity and its relationships are necessary in the hum-blest of the arts, Plato [*Republic*, 7.522] mocks with good reason the authors of his time who alleged that Palamedes had invented numbers at the siege of Troy, as if, says this philosopher, Agamem-non could have been ignorant until then of how many legs he had. In fact, one senses the impossibility that society and the arts should have arrived at the point where they already were at the time of the siege of Troy, unless men had the use of numbers and arithmetic. But the necessity for knowing numbers, before acquir-ing other types of knowledge, does not make their invention easier to imagine. Once the names of the numbers are known, it is easy to explain their meaning and to elicit the ideas which these names represent; but in order to invent them, it was necessary, prior to conceiving of these same ideas, to be, as it were, on familiar terms with philosophical meditations, to be trained to consider beings by their essence alone and independently of all other per-ception—a very difficult, very metaphysical, hardly natural abstraction, and yet one without which these ideas could never have been transported from one species or genus to another, nor could numbers have become universal. A savage could consider separately his right leg and his left leg, or look at them together under the indivisible idea of a pair without ever thinking that he had two of them; for the representative idea that portrays for us an object is one thing, and the numerical idea which determines it is another. Even less was he able to count to five. And although, by placing his hands one on top of the other, he could have noticed that the fingers corresponded exactly, he was far from thinking of their numerical equality. He did not know the sum of his fingers

aorists,[2] and all the tenses of verbs, particles, syntax, the connecting of sentences, reasoning, and the forming of all the logic of discourse. As for myself, being shocked by the unending difficulties and convinced of the almost de-monstrable impossibility that languages could have arisen and been established by merely human means, I leave to anyone who would undertake it the discussion of the fol-lowing difficult problem: which was the more necessary: an already formed society for the invention of languages, or an already invented language for the establishment of society?

Whatever these origins may be, it is clear, from the little care taken by nature to bring men together through mutual needs and to facilitate their use of speech, how little she pre-pared them for becoming habituated to the ways of society, and how little she contributed to all that men have done to establish the bonds of society. In fact, it is impossible to imagine why, in that primitive state, one man would have a greater need for another man than a monkey or a wolf has for another of its respective species; or, assuming this need, what motive could induce the other man to satisfy it; or even, in this latter instance, how could they be in mutual agreement regarding the conditions. I know that we are re-peatedly told that nothing would have been so miserable as man in that state; and if it is true, as I believe I have proved, that it is only after many centuries that men could have had the desire and the opportunity to leave that state, that would be a charge to bring against nature, not against him whom nature has thus constituted. But if we understand the word *miserable* properly, it is a word which is without meaning or which signifies merely a painful privation and suffering of the body or the soul. Now I would very much like someone to explain to me what kind of misery can there be for a free being whose heart is at peace and whose body is in good health? I ask which of the two, civil or natural life, is more likely to become insufferable to those who live it? We see about us practically no people who do not complain about their existence; many even deprive themselves of it to the extent they are able, and the combination of divine and human laws is hardly enough to stop this disorder. I

---

any more than that of his hairs. And if, after having made him understand what numbers are, someone had said to him that he had as many fingers as toes, he perhaps would have been quite surprised, in comparing them, to find that this was true.

2   *aorists* Verbs of a form that does not imply continuance or completion: a specialized form in Classical Greek and other languages.

ask if anyone has ever heard tell of a savage who was living in liberty ever dreaming of complaining about his life and of killing himself. Let the judgment therefore be made with less pride on which side real misery lies. On the other hand, nothing would have been so miserable as savage man, dazzled by enlightenment, tormented by passions, and reasoning about a state different from his own. It was by a very wise providence that the latent faculties he possessed should develop only as the occasion to exercise them presents itself, so that they would be neither superfluous nor troublesome to him beforehand, nor underdeveloped and useless in time of need. In instinct alone, man had everything he needed in order to live in the state of nature; in a cultivated reason, he has only what he needs to live in society.

At first it would seem that men in that state, having among themselves no type of moral relations or acknowledged duties, could be neither good nor evil, and had neither vices nor virtues, unless, if we take these words in a physical sense, we call those qualities that can harm an individual's preservation "vices" in him, and those that can contribute to it "virtues." In that case it would be necessary to call the one who least resists the simple impulses of nature the most virtuous. But without departing from the standard meaning of these words, it is appropriate to suspend the judgment we could make regarding such a situation and to be on our guard against our prejudices, until we have examined with scale in hand whether there are more virtues than vices among civilized men; or whether their virtues are more advantageous than their vices are lethal; or whether the progress of their knowledge is sufficient compensation for ills they inflict on one another as they learn of the good they ought to do; or whether, all things considered, they would not be in a happier set of circumstances if they had neither evil to fear nor good to hope for from anyone, rather than subjecting themselves to a universal dependence and obliging themselves to receive everything from those who do not oblige themselves to give them anything.

Above all, let us not conclude with Hobbes that because man has no idea of goodness he is naturally evil; that he is vicious because he does not know virtue; that he always refuses to perform services for his fellow men he does not believe he owes them; or that, by virtue of the right, which he reasonably attributes to himself, to those things he needs, he foolishly imagines himself to be the sole proprietor of the entire universe. Hobbes has very clearly seen the defect of all modern definitions of natural right, but the consequences he draws from his own definition show that he takes it in a

sense that is no less false. Were he to have reasoned on the basis of the principles he establishes, this author should have said that since the state of nature is the state in which the concern for our self-preservation is the least prejudicial to that of others, that state was consequently the most appropriate for peace and the best suited for the human race. He says precisely the opposite, because he had wrongly injected into the savage man's concern for self-preservation the need to satisfy a multitude of passions which are the product of society and which have made laws necessary. The evil man, he says, is a robust child. It remains to be seen whether savage man is a robust child. Were we to grant him this, what would we conclude from it? That if this man were as dependent on others when he is robust as he is when he is weak, there is no type of excess to which he would not tend: he would beat his mother if she were too slow in offering him her breast; he would strangle one of his younger brothers, should he find him annoying he would bite someone's leg, should he be assaulted or aggravated by him. But being robust and being dependent are two contradictory suppositions in the state of nature. Man is weak when he is dependent, and he is emancipated from that dependence before he is robust. Hobbes did not see that the same cause preventing savages from using their reason, as our jurists claim, is what prevents them at the same time from abusing their faculties, as he himself maintains. Hence we could say that savages are not evil precisely because they do not know what it is to be good; for it is neither the development of enlightenment nor the restraint imposed by the law, but the calm of the passions and the ignorance of vice which prevents them from doing evil. *So much more profitable to these is the ignorance of vice than the knowledge of virtue is to those.*[1] Moreover, there is another principle that Hobbes failed to notice, and which, having been given to man in order to mitigate, in certain circumstances, the ferocity of his egocentrism or the desire for self-preservation before this egocentrism of his came into being,[2] tempers the ardor he has for his own well-being by an innate repugnance to seeing his fellow

---

1   *So much ... to those* Justin, *Histories*, 2.2. Rousseau quotes the original Latin.

2   *egocentrism ... came into being* [Rousseau's note] We must not confuse egocentrism with love of oneself, two passions very different by virtue of both their nature and their effects. Love of oneself is a natural sentiment which moves every animal to be vigilant in its own preservation and which, directed in man by reason and modified by pity, produces humanity and virtue. Egocentrism is merely a sentiment that is relative, artificial and born in society, which moves each individual to value himself more than anyone

men suffer. I do not believe I have any contradiction to fear in granting the only natural virtue that the most excessive detractor of human virtues[1] was forced to recognize. I am referring to pity, a disposition that is fitting for beings that are as weak and as subject to ills as we are; a virtue all the more universal and all the more useful to man in that it precedes in him any kind of reflection, and so natural that even animals sometimes show noticeable signs of it. Without speaking of the tenderness of mothers for their young and of the perils they have to brave in order to protect them, one daily observes the repugnance that horses have for trampling a living body with their hooves. An animal does not go undisturbed past a dead animal of its own species. There are even some animals that give them a kind of sepulcher; and the mournful lowing of cattle entering a slaughterhouse voices the impression they receive of the horrible spectacle that strikes them. One notes with pleasure the author of *The Fable of the Bees*, having been forced to acknowledge man as a compassionate and sensitive being, departing from his cold and subtle style in the example he gives, to offer us the pathetic image of an imprisoned man who sees outside his cell a ferocious animal tearing a child from its mother's breast, mashing its frail limbs with its murderous teeth, and ripping with its claws the child's quivering entrails. What

horrible agitation must be felt by this witness of an event in which he has no personal interest! What anguish must he suffer at this sight, being unable to be of any help to the fainting mother or to the dying child?

Such is the pure movement of nature prior to all reflection. Such is the force of natural pity, which the most depraved mores still have difficulty destroying, since everyday one sees in our theaters someone affected and weeping at the ills of some unfortunate person, and who, were he in the tyrant's place, would intensify the torments of his enemy still more; <like the bloodthirsty Sulla,[2] so sensitive to ills he had not caused, or like Alexander of Pherae,[3] who did not dare attend the performance of any tragedy, for fear of being seen weeping with Andromache and Priam,[4] and yet who listened impassively to the cries of so many citizens who were killed every day on his orders. *Nature, in giving men tears, bears witness that she gave the human race the softest hearts.*>[5] Mandeville has a clear awareness that, with all their mores, men would never have been anything but monsters, if nature had not given them pity to aid their reason; but he has not seen that from this quality alone flow all the social virtues that he wants to deny in men. In fact, what are generosity, mercy, and humanity, if not pity applied to the weak, to the guilty, or to the human species in general. Benevolence and even friendship are, properly understood, the products of a constant pity fixed on a particular object; for is desiring that someone not suffer anything but desiring that he be happy? Were it true that commiseration were merely a sentiment that puts us in the position of the one who suffers, a sentiment that is obscure and powerful in savage man, developed but weak in man dwelling in civil society, what importance would this idea have to the truth of what I say, except to give it more force? In fact, commiseration will be all the more energetic as the witnessing animal identifies itself more intimately with the suffering animal. Now it is evident that this identification must have been infinitely closer in the state of nature than in the state of reasoning. Reason is what engenders egocentrism, and

---

else, which inspires in men all the evils they cause one another, and which is the true source of honor.

With this well understood, I say that in our primitive state, in the veritable state of nature, egocentrism does not exist; for since each particular man regards himself as the only spectator who observes him, as the only being in the universe that takes an interest in him, as the only judge of his own merit, it is impossible that a sentiment which has its source in comparisons that he is not in a position to make could germinate in his soul. For the same reason, this man could not have either hatred or desire for revenge, passions which can arise only from the belief that offense has been received. And since what constitutes the offense is scorn or the intention to harm and not the harm, men who know neither how to appraise nor to compare themselves can do considerable violence to one another when it returns them some advantage for doing it, without ever offending one another. In a word, on seeing his fellow-men hardly otherwise than he would see animals of another species, each man can carry away the prey of the weaker or yield his own to the stronger, viewing these lootings as merely natural events, without the least stirring of insolence or resentment, and without any other passion but the sadness or the joy of a good or bad venture.

1   *the most excessive detractor of human virtues*   Rousseau is referring to Bernard Mandeville (1670–1733), Dutch-English philosopher and economist, author of the work mentioned just below, *Fable of the Bees: or, Private Vices, Public Benefits* (1714).

2   *Sulla*   Lucius Cornelius Sulla Felix (c. 138–78 BCE), Roman general and dictator; he was praised by Machiavelli for his ruthlessness in killing his enemies once in power.

3   *Alexander of Pherae*   Tyrannical ruler of Pherae in Thessaly, 369–358 BCE.

4   *Andromache and Priam*   Greek mythological figures. Andromache was the wife of the Trojan hero Hector; Priam was king of Troy. Both are represented in Greek drama and poetry as suffering piteous fates.

5   *Nature, in ... softest hearts*   Juvenal, *Satires* 15, 131–33.

reflection strengthens it. Reason is what turns man in upon himself. Reason is what separates him from all that troubles him and afflicts him. Philosophy is what isolates him and what moves him to say in secret, at the sight of a suffering man, "Perish if you will; I am safe and sound." No longer can anything but danger to the entire society trouble the tranquil slumber of the philosopher and yank him from his bed. His fellow man can be killed with impunity underneath his window. He has merely to place his hands over his ears and argue with himself a little in order to prevent nature, which rebels within him, from identifying him with the man being assassinated. Savage man does not have this admirable talent, and for lack of wisdom and reason he is always seen thoughtlessly giving in to the first sentiment of humanity. When there is a riot or a street brawl, the populace gathers together; the prudent man withdraws from the scene. It is the rabble, the women of the marketplace, who separate the combatants and prevent decent people from killing one another.

It is therefore quite certain that pity is a natural sentiment, which, by moderating in each individual the activity of the love of oneself, contributes to the mutual preservation of the entire species. Pity is what carries us without reflection to the aid of those we see suffering. Pity is what, in the state of nature, takes the place of laws, mores, and virtue, with the advantage that no one is tempted to disobey its sweet voice. Pity is what will prevent every robust savage from robbing a weak child or an infirm old man of his hard-earned subsistence, if he himself expects to be able to find his own someplace else. Instead of the sublime maxim of reasoned justice, *Do unto others as you would have them do unto you*, pity inspires all men with another maxim of natural goodness, much less perfect but perhaps more useful than the preceding one: *Do what is good for you with as little harm as possible to others*. In a word, it is in this natural sentiment, rather than in subtle arguments that one must search for the cause of the repugnance at doing evil that every man would experience, even independently of the maxims of education. Although it might be appropriate for Socrates and minds of his stature to acquire virtue through reason, the human race would long ago have ceased to exist, if its preservation had depended solely on the reasonings of its members.

With passions so minimally active and such a salutary restraint, being more wild than evil, and more attentive to protecting themselves from the harm they could receive than tempted to do harm to others, men were not subject to very dangerous conflicts. Since they had no sort of intercourse among themselves; since, as a consequence, they knew neither vanity, nor deference, nor esteem, nor contempt; since they had not the slightest notion of mine and thine, nor any true idea of justice; since they regarded the acts of violence that could befall them as an easily redressed evil and not as an offense that must be punished; and since they did not even dream of vengeance except perhaps as a knee-jerk response right then and there, like the dog that bites the stone that is thrown at him, their disputes would rarely have had bloody consequences, if their subject had been no more sensitive than food. But I see a more dangerous matter that remains for me to discuss.

Among the passions that agitate the heart of man, there is an ardent, impetuous one that renders one sex necessary to the other; a terrible passion which braves all dangers, overcomes all obstacles, and which, in its fury, seems fitted to destroy the human race it is destined to preserve. What would become of men, victimized by this unrestrained and brutal rage, without modesty and self-control, fighting everyday over the object of their passion at the price of their blood?

There must first be agreement that the more violent the passions are, the more necessary the laws are to contain them. But over and above the fact that the disorders and the crimes these passions cause daily in our midst show quite well the insufficiency of the laws in this regard, it would still be good to examine whether these disorders did not come into being with the laws themselves; for then, even if they were capable of repressing them, the least one should expect of them would be that they call a halt to an evil that would not exist without them.

Let us begin by distinguishing between the moral and the physical aspects of the sentiment of love. The physical aspect is that general desire which inclines one sex to unite with another. The moral aspect is what determines this desire and fixes it exclusively on one single object, or which at least gives it a greater degree of energy for this preferred object. Now it is easy to see that the moral aspect of love is an artificial sentiment born of social custom, and extolled by women with so much skill and care in order to establish their hegemony and make dominant the sex that ought to obey. Since this feeling is founded on certain notions of merit or beauty that a savage is not in a position to have, and on comparisons he is incapable of making, it must be almost non-existent for him. For since his mind could not form abstract ideas of regularity and proportion, his heart is not susceptible to sentiments of admiration and love, which, even without its being observed come into being from the application of these ideas. He pays exclusive attention to the temperament he has received from nature, and not the taste <aversion> he has been unable to acquire; any woman suits his purpose.

Limited merely to the physical aspect of love, and fortunate enough to be ignorant of those preferences which stir up the feeling and increase the difficulties in satisfying it, men must feel the ardors of their temperament less frequently and less vividly, and consequently have fewer and less cruel conflicts among themselves. Imagination, which wreaks so much havoc among us, does not speak to savage hearts; each man peacefully awaits the impetus of nature, gives himself over to it without choice, and with more pleasure than frenzy; and once the need is satisfied, all desire is snuffed out.

Hence it is incontestable that love itself, like all other passions, had acquired only in society that impetuous ardor which so often makes it lethal to men. And it is all the more ridiculous to represent savages as continually slaughtering each other in order to satisfy their brutality, since this opinion is directly contrary to experience; and since the Caribs, of all existing peoples, are the people that until now has wandered least from the state of nature, they are the people least subject to jealousy, even though they live in a hot climate which always seems to occasion greater activity in these passions.

As to any inferences that could be drawn, in the case of several species of animals, from the clashes between males that bloody our poultry yards throughout the year, and which make our forests resound in the spring with their cries as they quarrel over a female, it is necessary to begin by excluding all species in which nature has manifestly established, in the relative power of the sexes, relations other than those that exist among us. Hence cockfights do not form the basis for an inference regarding the human species. In species where the proportion is more closely observed, these fights can have for their cause only the scarcity of females in relation to the number of males, or the exclusive intervals during which the female continually rejects the advances of the male, which adds up to the cause just cited. For if each female receives the male for only two months a year, in this respect it is as if the number of females were reduced by five-sixths. Now neither of these two cases is applicable to the human species where the number of females generally surpasses the number of males, and where human females,

unlike those of other species, have never been observed to have periods of heat and exclusion, even among savages. Moreover, among several of these animal species, where the entire species goes into heat simultaneously, there comes a terrible moment of common ardor, tumult, disorder and combat: a moment that does not happen in the human species where love is never periodic. Therefore one cannot conclude from the combats of certain animals for the possession of females that the same thing would happen to man in the state of nature. And even if one could draw that conclusion, given that these conflicts do not destroy the other species, one should conclude that they would not be any more lethal for ours. And it is quite apparent that they would wreak less havoc in the state of nature than in society, especially in countries where mores still count for something and where the jealousy of lovers and the vengeance of husbands every day give rise to duels, murders and still worse things; where the duty of eternal fidelity serves merely to create adulterers, and where even the laws of continence and honor necessarily spread debauchery and multiply the number of abortions.

Let us conclude that, wandering in the forests, without industry, without speech, without dwelling, without war, without relationships, with no need for his fellow men, and correspondingly with no desire to do them harm, perhaps never even recognizing any of them individually, savage man, subject to few passions and self-sufficient, had only the sentiments and enlightenment appropriate to that state; he felt only his true needs, took notice of only what he believed he had an interest in seeing, and that his intelligence made no more progress than his vanity. If by chance he made some discovery, he was all the less able to communicate it to others because he did not even know his own children. Art perished with its inventor. There was neither education nor progress; generations were multiplied to no purpose. Since each one always began from the same point, centuries went by with all the crudeness of the first ages; the species was already old, and man remained ever a child.

If I have gone on at such length about the supposition of that primitive condition, it is because, having ancient errors and inveterate prejudices to destroy, I felt I should dig down to the root and show, in the depiction of the true state of nature how far even natural inequality is from having as much reality and influence in that state as our writers claim.

In fact, it is easy to see that, among the differences that distinguish men, several of them pass for natural ones which are exclusively the work of habit and of the various sorts of life that men adopt in society. Thus a robust or delicate temperament, and the strength or weakness that depend on it, frequently derive more from the harsh or effeminate way in which one has been raised than from the primitive constitution of bodies. The same holds for mental powers; and not only does education make a difference between cultivated minds and those that are not, it also augments the difference among the former in proportion to their culture; for were a giant and a dwarf walking on the same road, each step they both take would give a fresh advantage to the giant. Now if one compares the prodigious diversity of educations and lifestyles in the different orders of the civil state with the simplicity and uniformity of animal and savage life, where all nourish themselves from the same foods live in the same manner, and do exactly the same things, it will be understood how much less the difference between one man and another must be in the state of nature than in that of society, and how much natural inequality must increase in the human species through inequality occasioned by social institutions.

But even if nature were to affect, in the distribution of her gifts, as many preferences as is claimed, what advantage would the most favored men derive from them, to the detriment of others, in a state of things that allowed practically no sort of relationships among them? Where there is no love, what use is beauty? What use is wit for people who do not speak, and ruse to those who have no dealing with others? I always hear it repeated that the stronger will oppress the weaker. But let me have an explanation of the meaning of the word "oppression." Some will dominate with violence; others will groan, enslaved to all their caprices. That is precisely what I observe among us; but I do not see how this could be said of savage men, to whom it would be difficult even to explain what servitude and domination are. A man could well lay hold of the fruit another has gathered, the game he has killed, the cave that served as his shelter. But how will he ever succeed in making himself be obeyed? And what can be the chains of dependence among men who possess nothing? If someone chases me from one tree, I am free to go to another; if someone torments me in one place, who will prevent me from going elsewhere? Is there a man with strength sufficiently superior to mine and who is, moreover, sufficiently depraved, sufficiently lazy and sufficiently ferocious to force me to provide for his subsistence while he remains idle? He must resolve not to take his eyes off me for a single instant, to keep me carefully tied down while he sleeps, for fear that I may escape or that I would kill him. In other words, he is obliged to expose himself voluntarily to a much greater hardship than the one he wants to avoid and gives me. After all that, were his vigilance to relax for an instant, were an unforeseen noise to make him turn his head, I take twenty steps into the forest; my chains are broken, and he never sees me again for the rest of his life.

Without needlessly prolonging these details, anyone should see that, since the bonds of servitude are formed merely from the mutual dependence of men and the reciprocal needs that unite them, it is impossible to enslave a man without having first put him in the position of being incapable of doing without another. This being a situation that did not exist in the state of nature, it leaves each person free of the yoke, and renders pointless the law of the strongest.

After having proved that inequality is hardly observable in the state of nature, and that its influence there is almost nonexistent, it remains for me to show its origin and progress in the successive developments of the human mind. After having shown that *perfectibility*, social virtues, and the other faculties that natural man had received in a state of potentiality could never develop by themselves, that to achieve this development they required the chance coming together of several unconnected causes that might never have come into being and without which he would have remained eternally in his primitive constitution, it remains for me to consider and to bring together the various chance happenings that were able to perfect human reason while deteriorating the species, make a being evil while rendering it habituated to the ways of society, and, from so distant a beginning, finally bring man and the world to the point where we see them now.

I admit that, since the events I have to describe could have taken place in several ways, I cannot make a determination among them except on the basis of conjecture. But over and above the fact that these conjectures become reasons when they are the most probable ones that a person can draw from the nature of things and the sole means that a person can have of discovering the truth, the consequences I wish to deduce from mine will not thereby be conjectural, since, on the basis of the principles I have just established, no other system is conceivable that would not furnish me with the same results, and from which I could not draw the same conclusions.

This will excuse me from expanding my reflections on the way in which the lapse of time compensates for the slight probability of events; concerning the surprising power that quite negligible causes may have when they act without interruption; concerning the impossibility, on the one hand, of a person's destroying certain hypotheses, even though, on the other hand, one is not in a position to accord them the level of factual certitude; concerning a situation in which two facts given as real are to be connected by a series of intermediate facts that are unknown or regarded as such, it belongs to history, when it exists, to provide the facts that connect them; it belongs to philosophy, when history is unavailable, to determine similar facts that can connect them; finally, concerning how, with respect to events, similarity reduces the facts to a much smaller number of different classes than one might imagine. It is enough for me to offer these objects to the consideration of my judges; it is enough for me to have seen to it that ordinary readers would have no need to consider them.

Part Two

The first person who, having enclosed a plot of land, took it into his head to say *this is mine* and found people simple enough to believe him, was the true founder of civil society. What crimes, wars, murders, what miseries and horrors would the human race have been spared, had someone pulled up the stakes or filled in the ditch and cried out to his fellow men: "Do not listen to this impostor. You are lost if you forget that the fruits of the earth belong to all and the earth to no one!" But it is quite likely that by then things had already reached the point where they could no longer continue as they were. For this idea of property, depending on many prior ideas which could only have arisen successively, was not formed all at once in the human mind. It was necessary to make great progress, to acquire much industry and enlightenment, and to transmit and augment them from one age to another, before arriving at this final stage in the state of nature. Let us therefore take things farther back and try to piece together under a single viewpoint that slow succession of events and advances in knowledge in their most natural order.

Man's first sentiment was that of his own existence; his first concern was that of his preservation. The products of the earth provided him with all the help he needed; instinct led him to make use of them. With hunger and other appetites making him experience by turns various ways of existing, there was one appetite that invited him to perpetuate his species; and this blind inclination, devoid of any sentiment of the heart, produced a purely animal act. Once this need had been satisfied, the two sexes no longer took cognizance of one another, and even the child no longer meant anything to the mother once it could do without her.

Such was the condition of man in his nascent stage; such was the life of an animal limited at first to pure sensations, and scarcely profiting from the gifts nature offered him, far from dreaming of extracting anything from her. But difficulties soon presented themselves to him; it was necessary to learn to overcome them. The height of trees, which kept him from reaching their fruits, the competition of animals that sought to feed themselves on these same fruits, the ferocity of those animals that wanted to take his own life: everything obliged him to apply himself to bodily exercises. It was necessary to become agile, fleet-footed and vigorous in combat. Natural arms, which are tree branches and stones, were soon found ready at hand. He learned to surmount nature's obstacles, combat other animals when necessary, fight for his subsistence even with men, or compensate for what he had to yield to those stronger than himself.

In proportion as the human race spread, difficulties multiplied with the men. Differences in soils, climates and seasons could force them to inculcate these differences in their lifestyles. Barren years, long and hard winters, hot summers that consume everything required new resourcefulness from them. Along the seashore and the riverbanks they invented the fishing line and hook, and became fishermen and fish-eaters. In the forests they made bows and arrows, and became hunters and warriors. In cold countries they covered themselves with the skins of animals they had killed. Lightning, a volcano, or some fortuitous chance happening acquainted them with fire: a new resource against the rigors of winter. They learned to preserve this element, then to reproduce it, and finally to use it to prepare meats that previously they devoured raw.

This repeated appropriation of various beings to himself, and of some beings to others, must naturally have engendered in man's mind the perceptions of certain relations. These relationships which we express by the words "large," "small," "strong," "weak," "fast," "slow," "timorous," "bold," and other similar ideas, compared when needed and almost without thinking about it, finally produced in him a kind of reflection, or rather a mechanical prudence which pointed out to him the precautions that were most necessary for his safety.

The new enlightenment which resulted from this development increased his superiority over the other animals by making him aware of it. He trained himself to set traps for them; he tricked them in a thousand different ways. And although several surpassed him in fighting strength or in swiftness in running, of those that could serve him or hurt him, he became in time the master of the former and the scourge of the latter. Thus the first glance he directed upon himself produced within him the first stirring of pride; thus, as yet hardly knowing how to distinguish the ranks, and contemplating himself in the first rank by virtue of his species, he prepared himself from afar to lay claim to it in virtue of his individuality.

Although his fellowmen were not for him what they are for us, and although he had hardly anything more to do with them than with other animals, they were not forgotten in his observations. The conformities that time could make him perceive among them, his female, and himself, made him judge those he did not perceive. And seeing that they all acted as he would have done under similar circumstances, he concluded that their way of thinking and feeling was in complete conformity with his own. And this important truth, well established in his mind, made him follow, by a presentiment as sure as dialectic and more prompt, the best rules of conduct that it was appropriate to observe toward them for his advantage and safety.

Taught by experience that love of well-being is the sole motive of human actions, he found himself in a position to distinguish the rare occasions when common interest should make him count on the assistance of his fellowmen, and those even rarer occasions when competition ought to make him distrust them. In the first case, he united with them in a herd, or at most in some sort of free association, that obligated no one and that lasted only as long as the passing need that had formed it. In the second case, everyone sought to obtain his own advantage, either by overt force, if he believed he could, or by cleverness and cunning, if he felt himself to be the weaker.

This is how men could imperceptibly acquire some crude idea of mutual commitments and of the advantages to be had in fulfilling them, but only insofar as present and perceptible interests could require it, since foresight meant nothing to them, and far from concerning themselves about a distant future, they did not even give a thought to the next day. Were it a matter of catching a deer, everyone was quite aware that he must faithfully keep to his post in order to achieve this purpose; but if a hare happened to pass within reach of one of them, no doubt he would have pursued it without giving it a second thought, and that, having obtained his prey, he cared very little about causing his companions to miss theirs.

It is easy to understand that such intercourse did not require a language much more refined than that of crows or monkeys, which flock together in practically the same way. Inarticulate cries, many gestures, and some imitative noises must for a long time have made up the universal language. By joining to this in each country a few articulate and conventional sounds, whose institution, as I have already said, is not too easy to explain, there were individual languages, but crude and imperfect ones, quite similar to those still spoken by various savage nations today. Constrained by the passing of time, the abundance of things I have to say, and the practically imperceptible progress of the beginnings, I am flying like an arrow over the multitudes of centuries. For the slower events were in succeeding one another, the quicker they can be described.

These first advances enabled man to make more rapid ones. The more the mind was enlightened, the more industry was perfected. Soon they ceased to fall asleep under the first tree or to retreat into caves, and found various types of hatchets made of hard, sharp stones, which served to cut wood, dig up the soil, and make huts from branches they later found it useful to cover with clay and mud. This was the period of a first revolution which formed the establishment of the distinction among families and which introduced a kind of property, whence perhaps there already arose many quarrels and fights. However, since the strongest were probably the first to make themselves lodgings they felt capable of defending, presumably the weak found it quicker and safer to imitate them than to try to dislodge them; and as for those who already had huts, each of them must have rarely sought to appropriate that of his neighbor, less because it did not belong to him than because it was of no use to him, and because he could not seize it without exposing himself to a fierce battle with the family that occupied it.

The first developments of the heart were the effect of a new situation that united the husbands and wives, fathers and children in one common habitation. The habit of living together gave rise to the sweetest sentiments known to men: conjugal love and paternal love. Each family became a little society all the better united because mutual attachment and liberty were its only bonds; and it was then that the first difference was established in the lifestyle of the two sexes, which until then had had only one. Women became more sedentary and grew accustomed to watch over the hut and the children, while the man went to seek their common subsistence. With their slightly softer life the two sexes also began to lose something of their ferocity and vigor. But while each one separately became less suited to combat savage beasts, on the other hand it was easier to assemble in order jointly to resist them.

In this new state, with a simple and solitary life, very limited needs, and the tools they had invented to provide for them, since men enjoyed a great deal of leisure time, they used it to procure for themselves many types of conveniences unknown to their fathers; and that was the first yoke they imposed on themselves without realizing it, and the first source of evils they prepared for their descendants. For in addition to their continuing thus to soften body and mind (those conveniences having through habit lost almost all their pleasure, and being at the same time degenerated into true needs), being deprived of them became much more cruel than possessing them was sweet; and they were unhappy about losing them without being happy about possessing them.

At this point we can see a little better how the use of speech was established or imperceptibly perfected itself in the bosom of each family; and one can further conjecture how various particular causes could have extended the language and accelerated its progress by making it more necessary. Great floods or earthquakes surrounded the inhabited areas with water or precipices. Upheavals of the globe detached parts of the mainland and broke them up into islands. Clearly among men thus brought together and forced to live together, a common idiom must have been formed sooner than among those who wandered freely about the forests of the mainland. Thus it is quite possible that after their first attempts at navigation, the islanders brought the use of speech to us; and it is at least quite probable that society and languages came into being on islands and were perfected there before they were known on the mainland.

Everything begins to take on a new appearance. Having previously wandered about the forests and having assumed a more fixed situation, men slowly came together and united into different bands, eventually forming in each country a particular nation, united by mores and characteristic features, not by regulations and laws, but by the same kind of life and foods and by the common influence of the climate. Eventually a permanent proximity cannot fail to engender some intercourse among different families. Young people of different sexes live in neighboring huts; the passing intercourse demanded by nature soon leads to another, through frequent contact with one another, no less sweet and more permanent. People become accustomed to consider different objects and to make comparisons. Imperceptibly they acquire the ideas of merit and beauty which produce feelings of preference. By dint of seeing one another, they can no longer get along without seeing one another again. A sweet and tender feeling insinuates itself into the soul and at the least opposition becomes an impetuous fury. Jealousy awakens with love; discord triumphs, and the sweetest passion receives sacrifices of human blood.

In proportion as ideas and sentiments succeed one another and as the mind and heart are trained, the human race continues to be tamed, relationships spread and bonds are tightened. People grew accustomed to gather in front of their huts or around a large tree; song and dance, true children of love and leisure, became the amusement or rather the occupation of idle men and women who had flocked together. Each one began to look at the others and to want to be looked at himself, and public esteem had a value. The one who sang or danced the best, the handsomest, the strongest, the most adroit or the most eloquent became the most highly regarded. And this was the first step toward inequality and, at the same time, toward vice. From these first preferences were born vanity and contempt on the one hand, and shame and envy on the other. And the fermentation caused by these new leavens eventually produced compounds fatal to happiness and innocence.

As soon as men had begun mutually to value one another, and the idea of esteem was formed in their minds, each one claimed to have a right to it, and it was no longer possible for anyone to be lacking it with impunity. From this came the first duties of civility, even among savages; and from this every voluntary wrong became an outrage, because along with the harm that resulted from the injury, the offended party saw in it contempt for his person, which often was more insufferable than the harm itself. Hence each man punished the contempt shown him in a manner proportionate to the esteem in which he held himself; acts of revenge became terrible, and men became bloodthirsty and cruel. This is precisely the stage reached by most of the savage people known to us; and it is for want of having made adequate distinctions among their ideas or of having noticed how far these peoples already were from the original state of nature that many have hastened to conclude that man is naturally cruel, and that he needs civilization in order to soften him. On the contrary, nothing is so gentle as man in his primitive state, when, placed by nature at an equal distance from the stupidity of brutes and the fatal enlightenment of civil man, and limited equally by instinct and reason to protecting himself from the harm that threatens him, he is restrained by natural pity from needlessly harming anyone himself, even if he has been harmed. For according to the axiom of the wise Locke, *where there is no property, there is no injury.*[1]

But it must be noted that society in its beginning stages and the relations already established among men required in them qualities different from those they derived from their primitive constitution; that, with morality beginning to be introduced into human actions, and everyone, prior to the existence of laws, being sole judge and avenger of the offenses he had received, the goodness appropriate to the pure state of nature was no longer what was appropriate to an emerging society; that it was necessary for punishments to become more severe in proportion as the occasions for giving offense became more frequent; and that it was for the fear of vengeance to take the place of the deterrent character of laws. Hence although men had become less forbearing, and although natural pity had already undergone some alteration, this period of the development of human faculties, maintaining a middle position between the indolence of our primitive state and the petulant activity of our egocentrism, must have been the happiest and most durable epoch. The more one reflects on it, the more one finds that this state was the least subject to upheavals and the best for man,[2] and that he must have left it only by virtue of some fatal chance happening that, for the common good, ought never have happened. The example of savages, almost all of whom have been found in this state, seems to confirm that the human race had been made to remain in it always; that this state is the veritable youth of the world; and that all the subsequent progress has been in appearance so many steps toward the perfection of the individual, and in fact toward the decay of the species.

As long as men were content with the rustic huts, as long as they were limited to making their clothing out of skins sewn together with thorns or fish bones, adorning themselves with feathers and shells, painting their bodies with various colors, perfecting or embellishing their bows and arrows, using sharp-edged stones to make some fishing canoes or some crude musical instruments; in a word, as long as they applied themselves exclusively to tasks that a single individual could do and to the arts that did not require the cooperation of several hands, they lived as free, healthy, good and happy as they could in accordance with their nature; and they continued to enjoy among themselves the sweet rewards of independent intercourse. But as soon as one man needed the help of another, as soon as one man realized that it was useful for a single individual to have provisions for two, equality disappeared, property came into existence, labor became necessary. Vast forests were transformed into smiling fields which had to be watered with men's sweat, and in which slavery and misery were soon seen to germinate and grow with the crops.

Metallurgy and agriculture were the two arts whose invention produced great revolution. For the poet, it is gold and silver; but for the philosopher, it is iron and wheat that have civilized men and ruined the human race. Thus they were both unknown to the savages of America, who for that reason have always remained savages. Other peoples even appear to have remained barbarous, as long as they practiced one of those arts without the other. And perhaps one of the best reasons why Europe has been, if not sooner, at least more constantly and better governed than the other parts of the world, is that it is at the same time the most abundant in iron and the most fertile in wheat.

It is very difficult to guess how men came to know and use iron, for it is incredible that by themselves they thought of drawing the ore from the mine and performing the necessary preparations on it for smelting it before they knew what would result. From another point of view, it is even less plausible to attribute this discovery to some accidental fire, because mines are set up exclusively in arid places devoid of trees and plants, so that one would say that nature had taken precautions to conceal this deadly secret from us. Thus there remains only the extraordinary circumstance of some volcano that, in casting forth molten metal, would have given observers the idea of imitating this operation of nature. Even still we must suppose them to have had a great deal of courage and foresight to undertake such a difficult task and to have envisaged so far in advance the advantages

---

1   *where there ... no injury*   John Locke, *Essay Concerning Human Understanding*, 4, 3 §18. We print a translation of Rousseau's French translation of Locke; Locke's actual words were "Where there is no property there is no injustice."

2   *best for man*   The long note Rousseau appends here, on humans living in an intermediate stage between the "primitive state" and "the fatal enlightenment of civil man," has been included as Appendix 4 below.

they could derive from it. This is hardly suitable for minds already better trained than theirs must have been.

As for agriculture, its principle was known long before its practice was established, and it is hardly possible that men, constantly preoccupied with deriving their subsistence from trees and plants, did not rather quickly get the idea of the methods used by nature to grow plant life. But their industry probably did not turn in that direction until very late either because trees, which, along with hunting and fishing, provided their nourishment, had no need of their care; or for want of knowing how to use wheat; or for want of tools with which to cultivate it; or for want of foresight regarding future needs; or, finally, for want of the means of preventing others from appropriating the fruits of their labors. Having become more industrious, it is believable that, with sharp stones and pointed sticks, they began by cultivating some vegetables or roots around their huts long before they knew how to prepare wheat and had the tools necessary for large-scale cultivation. Moreover, to devote oneself to that occupation and to sow the lands, one must be resolved to lose something at first in order to gain a great deal later: a precaution quite far removed from the mind of the savage man, who, as I have said, finds it quite difficult to give thought in the morning to what he will need at night.

The invention of the other arts was therefore necessary to force the human race to apply itself to that of agriculture. Once men were needed in order to smelt and forge the iron, other men were needed in order to feed them. The more the number of workers increased, the fewer hands there were to obtain food for the common subsistence, without there being fewer mouths to consume it; and since some needed foodstuffs in exchange for their iron, the others finally found the secret of using iron to multiply foodstuffs. From this there arose farming and agriculture, on the one hand, and the art of working metals and multiplying their uses, on the other.

From the cultivation of land, there necessarily followed the division of land; and from property once recognized, the first rules of justice. For in order to render everyone what is his, it is necessary that everyone can have something. Moreover, as men began to look toward the future and as they saw that they all had goods to lose, there was not one of them who did not have to fear reprisals against himself for wrongs he might do to another. This origin is all the more natural as it is impossible to conceive of the idea of property arising from anything but manual labor,

for it is not clear what man can add, beyond his own labor, in order to appropriate things he has not made. It is labor alone that, in giving the cultivator a right to the product of the soil he has tilled, consequently gives him a right, at least until the harvest, and thus from year to year. With this possession continuing uninterrupted, it is easily transformed into property. When the ancients, says Grotius,[1] gave Ceres the epithet of legislatrix, gave the name Thesmophories[2] to a festival celebrated in her honor, they thereby made it apparent that the division of lands has produced a new kind of right: namely, the right of property, different from that which results from the natural law.

Things in this state could have remained equal, if talents had been equal, and if the use of iron and the consumption of foodstuffs had always been in precise balance. But this proportion, which was not maintained by anything, was soon broken. The strongest did the most work; the most adroit turned theirs to better advantage: the most ingenious found ways to shorten their labor. The farmer had a greater need for iron, or the blacksmith had a greater need for wheat; and in laboring equally, the one earned a great deal while the other barely had enough to live. Thus it is that natural inequality imperceptibly manifests itself together with inequality occasioned by the socialization process. Thus it is that the differences among men, developed by those of circumstances, make themselves more noticeable, more permanent in their effects, and begin to influence the fate of private individuals in the same proportion.

With things having reached this point, it is easy to imagine the rest. I will not stop to describe the successive invention of the arts, the progress of languages, the testing and use of talents, the inequality of fortunes, the use or abuse of wealth, nor all the details that follow these and that everyone can easily supply. I will limit myself exclusively to taking a look at the human race placed in this new order of things.

---

1   *Grotius*   Hugo Grotius (1583–1645), Dutch philosopher, jurist, playwright, and poet. The reference is to *On the Laws of War and Peace*, 2.2.2.

2   *gave Ceres the epithet of legislatrix, gave the name Thesmophories* Ceres was the Roman name for the goddess of agriculture, called Demeter by the Greeks. "Legislatrix" is the feminine version of the Latin word "legislator." The Thesmophoria was a secret women-only ritual/festival in Athens connected with marriage customs. It is associated with Demeter/Ceres, whom the Greeks gave the title Thesmophoros, meaning in Greek: "giver of customs" or even "legislator."

Thus we find here all our faculties developed, memory and imagination in play, egocentrism looking out for its interests, reason rendered active, and the mind having nearly reached the limit of the perfection of which it is capable. We find here all the natural qualities put into action, the rank and fate of each man established not only on the basis of the quantity of goods and the power to serve or harm, but also on the basis of mind, beauty, strength or skill, on the basis of merit or talents. And since these qualities were the only ones that could attract consideration, he was soon forced to have them or affect them. It was necessary, for his advantage, to show himself to be something other than what he in fact was. Being something and appearing to be something became two completely different things; and from this distinction there arose grand ostentation, deceptive cunning, and all the vices that follow in their wake. On the other hand, although man had previously been free and independent, we find him, so to speak, subject, by virtue of a multitude of fresh needs, to all of nature and particularly to his fellowmen, whose slave in a sense he becomes even in becoming their master; rich, he needs their services; poor, he needs their help; and being midway between wealth and poverty does not put him in a position to get along without them. It is therefore necessary for him to seek incessantly to interest them in his fate and to make them find their own profit, in fact or in appearance, in working for his. This makes him two-faced and crooked with some, imperious and harsh with others, and puts him in the position of having to abuse everyone he needs when he cannot make them fear them and does not find it in his interests to be of useful service to them. Finally, consuming ambition, the zeal for raising the relative level of his fortune, less out of real need than in order to put himself above others, inspires in all men a wicked tendency to harm one another, a secret jealousy all the more dangerous because, in order to strike its blow in greater safety, it often wears the mask of benevolence; in short, competition and rivalry on the one hand, opposition of interest<s> on the other, and always the hidden desire to profit at the expense of someone else. All these ills are the first effect of property and the inseparable offshoot of incipient inequality.

Before representative signs of wealth had been invented, it could hardly have consisted of anything but lands and livestock, the only real goods men can possess. Now when inheritances had grown in number and size to the point of covering the entire landscape and of all bordering on one another, some could no longer be enlarged except at the expense of others; and the supernumeraries, whom weakness or indolence had prevented from acquiring an inheritance in their turn, became poor without having lost anything, because while everything changed around them, they alone had not changed at all. Thus they were forced to receive or steal their subsistence from the hands of the rich. And from that there began to arise, according to the diverse characters of the rich and the poor, domination and servitude, or violence and thefts. For their part, the wealthy had no sooner known the pleasure of domination, than before long they disdained all others, and using their old slaves to subdue new ones, they thought of nothing but the subjugation and enslavement of their neighbors, like those ravenous wolves which, on having once tasted human flesh, reject all other food and desire to devour only men.

Thus, when both the most powerful or the most miserable made of their strength or their needs a sort of right to another's goods, equivalent, according to them, to the right of property, the destruction of equality was followed by the most frightful disorder. Thus the usurpations of the rich, the acts of brigandage by the poor, the unbridled passions of all, stifling natural pity and the still weak voice of justice, made men greedy, ambitious and wicked. There arose between the right of the strongest and the right of the first occupant a perpetual conflict that ended only in fights and murders.[1] Emerging society gave way to the most horrible state of war; since the human race, vilified and desolated, was no longer able to retrace its steps or give up the unfortunate acquisitions it had made, and since it labored only toward its shame by abusing the faculties that honor it, it brought itself to the brink of its ruin. *Horrified by the newness of the ill, both the poor man and the rich man hope to*

[1]   *fights and murders*   [Rousseau's note] One could raise against me the objection that, in such a disorder, men, instead of willfully murdering one another, would have dispersed, had there been no limits to their dispersion. But first, these limits would at least have been those of the world. And if one thinks about the excessive population that results from the state of nature, one will judge that the earth in that state would not have taken long to be covered with men thus forced to keep together. Besides, they would have dispersed, had the evil been rapid, and had it been an overnight change. But they were born under the yoke; they were in the habit of carrying it when they felt its weight, and they were content to wait for the opportunity to shake it off. Finally, since they were already accustomed to a thousand conveniences which forced them to keep together, dispersion was no longer so easy as in the first ages, when, since no one had need for anyone but himself, everyone made his decision without waiting for someone else's consent.

flee from wealth, hating what they once had prayed for.[1] It is not possible that men should not have eventually reflected upon so miserable a situation and upon the calamities that overwhelm them. The rich in particular must have soon felt how disadvantageous to them it was to have a perpetual war in which they alone paid all the costs, and in which the risk of losing one's life was common to all and the risk of losing one's goods was personal. Moreover, regardless of the light in which they tried to place their usurpations, they knew full well that they were established on nothing but a precarious and abusive right, and that having been acquired merely by force, force might take them away from them without their having any reason to complain. Even those enriched exclusively by industry could hardly base their property on better claims. They could very well say: "I am the one who built that wall; I have earned this land with my labor." In response to them it could be said: "Who gave you the boundary lines? By what right do you claim to exact payment at our expense for labor we did not impose upon you? Are you unaware that a multitude of your brothers perish or suffer from need of what you have in excess, and that you needed explicit and unanimous consent from the human race for you to help yourself to anything from the common subsistence that went beyond your own?" Bereft of valid reasons to justify himself and sufficient forces to defend himself; easily crushing a private individual, but himself crushed by troops of bandits; alone against all and unable on account of mutual jealousies to unite with his equals against enemies united by the common hope of plunder, the rich, pressed by necessity, finally conceived the most thought-out project that ever entered the human mind. It was to use in his favor the very strength of those who attacked him, to turn his adversaries into his defenders, to instill in them other maxims, and to give them other institutions which were as favorable to him as natural right was unfavorable to him.

With this end in mind, after having shown his neighbors the horror of a situation which armed them all against each other and made their possessions as burdensome as their needs, and in which no one could find safety in either poverty or wealth, he easily invented specious reasons to lead them to his goal. "Let us unite," he says to them, "in order to protect the weak from oppression, restrain the ambitious, and assure everyone of possessing what belongs to him. Let us institute rules of justice and peace to which all will be obliged to conform, which will make special exceptions for no one, and which will in some way compensate for the caprices of fortune by subjecting the strong and the weak to mutual obligations. In short, instead of turning our forces against ourselves, let us gather them into one supreme power that governs us according to wise laws, that protects and defends all the members of the association, repulses common enemies, and maintains us in an eternal concord."

Considerably less than the equivalent of this discourse was needed to convince crude, easily seduced men who also had too many disputes to settle among themselves to be able to get along without arbiters, and too much greed and ambition to be able to get along without masters for long. They all ran to chain themselves, in the belief that they secured their liberty, for although they had enough sense to realize the advantages of a political establishment, they did not have enough experience to foresee its dangers. Those most capable of anticipating the abuses were precisely those who counted on profiting from them; and even the wise saw the need to be resolved to sacrifice one part of their liberty to preserve the other, just as a wounded man has his arm amputated to save the rest of his body.

Such was, or should have been, the origin of society and laws, which gave new fetters to the weak and new forces to the rich,[2] irretrievably destroyed natural liberty, established forever the law of property and of inequality, changed adroit usurpation into an irrevocable right, and for the profit of a few ambitious men henceforth subjected the entire human race to labor, servitude and misery. It is readily apparent how the establishment of a single society rendered indispensable that of all the others, and how, to stand head to head against the united forces, it was necessary to unite in turn. Societies, multiplying or spreading rapidly, soon covered the entire surface of the earth; and it was no longer possible to find a single corner in the universe where someone could free himself from the yoke and withdraw his head from the often ill-guided sword which everyone

---

1   *Horrified by ... prayed for*   This quotation (given by Rousseau in Latin) is from Ovid, *Metamorphoses* 11. The context is the story of Midas, who is horrified by the results after his wish was granted that everything he touched would turn to gold.

2   *new forces to the rich*   [Rousseau's note] Marshal de V*** related that, on one of his campaigns, when the excessive knavery of a provisions supplier had made the army suffer and complain, he gave him a severe dressing down and threatened to have him hanged. "This threat has no effect on me," the knave boldly replied to him, "and I am quite pleased to tell you that nobody hangs a man with a hundred thousand crowns at his disposal." I do not know how it happened, the Marshal added naïvely, but in fact he was not hanged, even though he deserved to be a hundred times over.

saw perpetually hanging over his own head. With civil right thus having become the common rule of citizens, the law of nature no longer was operative except between the various societies, when, under the name of the law of nations, it was tempered by some tacit conventions in order to make intercourse possible and to serve as a substitute for natural compassion which, losing between one society and another nearly all the force it had between one man and another, no longer resides anywhere but in a few great cosmopolitan souls, who overcome the imaginary barriers that separate peoples, and who, following the example of the sovereign being who has created them, embrace the entire human race in their benevolence.

Remaining thus among themselves in the state of nature, the bodies politic soon experienced the inconveniences that had forced private individuals to leave it; and that state became even more deadly among these great bodies than that state had among the private individuals of whom they were composed. Whence came the national wars, battles, murders, and reprisals that make nature tremble and offend reason, and all those horrible prejudices that rank the honor of shedding human blood among the virtues. The most decent people learned to consider it one of their duties to kill their fellow men. Finally, men were seen massacring one another by the thousands without knowing why. More murders were committed in a single day of combat and more horrors in the capture of a single city than were committed in the state of nature during entire centuries over the entire face of the earth. Such are the first effects one glimpses of the division of mankind into different societies. Let us return to the founding of these societies.

I know that many have ascribed other origins to political societies, such as conquests by the most powerful, or the union of the weak; and the choice among these causes is indifferent to what I want to establish. Nevertheless, the one I have just described seems to me the most natural, for the following reasons. 1. In the first case, the right of conquest, since it is not a right, could not have founded any other, because the conqueror and conquered peoples always remain in a state of war with one another, unless the nation, returned to full liberty, were to choose voluntarily its conqueror as its leader. Until then, whatever the capitulations that may have been made, since they have been founded on violence alone and are consequently null by this very fact, on this hypothesis there can be neither true society nor body politic, nor any other law than that of the strongest. 2. These words *strong* and *weak* are equivocal in the second

case, because in the interval between the establishment of the right of property or of the first occupant and that of political governments, the meaning of these terms is better rendered by the words *poor* and *rich,* because, before the laws, man did not in fact have any other means of placing his equals in subjection except by attacking their goods or by giving them part of his. 3. Since the poor had nothing to lose but their liberty, it would have been utter folly for them to have voluntarily surrendered the only good remaining to them, gaining nothing in return. On the contrary, since the rich men were, so to speak, sensitive in all parts of their goods, it was much easier to do them harm, and consequently they had to take greater precautions to protect themselves. And finally it is reasonable to believe that a thing was invented by those to whom it is useful rather than by those to whom it is harmful.

Incipient government did not have a constant and regular form. The lack of philosophy and experience permitted only present inconveniences to be perceived, and there was thought of remedying the others only as they presented themselves. Despite all the labors of the wisest legislators, the political state always remained imperfect, because it was practically the work of chance and, because it had been badly begun, time, in discovering faults and suggesting remedies, could never repair the vices of the constitution. People were continually patching it up, whereas they should have begun by clearing the air and putting aside all the old materials, as Lycurgus[1] did in Sparta, in order to raise a good edifice later on. At first, society consisted merely of some general conventions that all private individuals promised to observe, and concerning which the community became the guarantor for each of them. Experience had to demonstrate how weak such a constitution was, and how easy it was for lawbreakers to escape conviction or punishment for faults of which the public alone was to be witness and judge. The law had to be evaded in a thousand ways; inconveniences and disorders had to multiply continually in order to make them finally give some thought to confiding to private individuals the dangerous trust of public authority, and to make them entrust to magistrates the care of enforcing the observance of the deliberations of the people. For to say that the leaders were chosen before the confederation was brought about and that the ministers of the laws existed

---

1   *Lycurgus*   Legendary seventh-century BCE lawgiver of Sparta, said to have been primarily responsible for a good deal of the social organization of that state.

before the laws themselves is a supposition that does not allow of serious debate.

It would be no more reasonable to believe that initially the peoples threw themselves unconditionally and for all time into the arms of an absolute master, and that the first means of providing for the common security dreamed up by proud and unruly men was to rush headlong into slavery. In fact, why did they give themselves over to superiors, if not to defend themselves against oppression and to protect their goods, their liberties and their lives, which are, as it were, the constitutive elements of their being? Now, since, in relations between men, the worst that can happen to someone is for him to see himself at the discretion of someone else, would it not have been contrary to good sense to begin by surrendering into the hands of a leader the only things for whose preservation they needed his help? What equivalent could he have offered them for the concession of so fine a right? And if he had dared to demand it on the pretext of defending them, would he not have immediately received the reply given in the fable: "what more will the enemy do to us?" It is therefore incontestable, and it is a fundamental maxim of all political right, that peoples have given themselves leaders in order to defend their liberty and not to enslave themselves. *If we have a prince*, Pliny said to Trajan,[1] *it is so that he may preserve us from having a master.*

<Our> political theorists produce the same sophisms about the love of liberty that <our> philosophers have made about the state of nature. By the things they see they render judgments about very different things they have not seen; and they attribute to men a natural inclination to servitude owing to the patience with which those who are before their eyes endure their servitude, without giving a thought to the fact that it is the same for liberty as it is for innocence and virtue: their value is felt only as long as one has them oneself, and the taste for them is lost as soon as one has lost them. "I know the delights of your country," said Brasidas to a satrap who compared the life of Sparta to that of Persepolis,[2] "but you cannot know the pleasures of mine."

As an unbroken steed bristles his mane, paws the ground with his hoof, and struggles violently at the mere approach of the bit, while a trained horse patiently endures the whip and the spur, barbarous man does not bow his head for the yoke that civilized man wears without a murmur, and he prefers the most stormy liberty to tranquil subjection. Thus it is not by the degradation of enslaved peoples that man's natural dispositions for or against servitude are to be judged, but by the wonders that all free peoples have accomplished to safeguard themselves from oppression. I know that enslaved peoples do nothing but boast of the peace and tranquility they enjoy in their chains and that *they give the name 'peace' to the most miserable slavery.*[3] But when I see free peoples sacrificing pleasures, tranquility, wealth, power, and life itself for the preservation of this sole good which is regarded so disdainfully by those who have lost it; when I see animals born free and abhorring captivity break their heads against the bars of their prison; when I see multitudes of utterly naked savages scorn European pleasures and brave hunger, fire, sword and death, simply to preserve their independence, I sense that it is inappropriate for slaves to reason about liberty.

As for paternal authority, from which several have derived absolute government and all society, it is enough, without having recourse to the contrary proofs of Locke and Sidney,[4] to note that nothing in the world is farther from the ferocious spirit of despotism than the gentleness of that authority which looks more to the advantage of the one who obeys than to the utility of the one who commands; that by the law of nature, the father is master of the child as long as his help is necessary for him; that beyond this point they become equals, and the son, completely independent of the father, then owes him merely respect and not obedience; for gratitude is clearly a duty that must be rendered, but not a right that can be demanded. Instead of saying that civil society derives from paternal power, on the contrary it must be said that it is from civil society that this power draws its principal force. An individual was not recognized as the father of several children until the children remained gathered about him. The goods of the father, of which he is truly the master, are the goods that keep his children in a state of dependence toward him, and he can cause their receiving a share in his estate to be consequent upon the extent to which they will have well merited it from him by

---

1   *Pliny ... Trajan* Pliny the Younger, *Panegyricus* 55.7. Trajan (53–117) was one of the so-called Good Emperors of Rome.

2   *Brasidas* Spartan officer during the Peloponnesian War. A satrap is a minor official in the ancient Persian empire. Persepolis was a city of ancient Persia.

3   *they give ... miserable slavery* Quotation (given by Rousseau in Latin) ascribed by Tacitus, *Histories* 4.17, to Gaius Julius Civilis who was, during the first century CE, attempting to urge the Gauls to revolt against the rule of Rome.

4   *the contrary proofs of Locke and Sidney* John Locke, *First Treatise* 2, 6, 7, 9, and *Second Treatise*, 6. Algernon Sidney, *Discourses Concerning Government*, 1, 2, and 3.

continuous deference to his wishes. Now, far from having some similar favor to expect from their despot (since they belong to him as personal possessions—they and all they possess—or at least he claims this to be the case), subjects are reduced to receiving as a favor what he leaves them of their goods. He does what is just when he despoils them; he does them a favor when he allows them to live.

In continuing thus to examine facts from the viewpoint of right, no more solidity than truth would be found in the belief that the establishment of tyranny was voluntary; and it would be difficult to show the validity of a contract that would obligate only one of the parties, where all the commitments would be placed on one side with none on the other, and that it would turn exclusively to the disadvantage of the one making the commitments. This odious system is quite far removed from being, even today, that of wise and good monarchs, and especially of the kings of France, as may be seen in various places in their edicts, and particularly in the following passage of a famous writing[1] published in 1667 in the name of and by order of Louis XIV: *Let it not be said therefore that the sovereign is not subject to the laws of his state, for the contrary statement is a truth of the law of nations, which flattery has on occasion attacked, but which good princes have always defended as a tutelary divinity of their states. How much more legitimate is it to say, with the wise Plato, that the perfect felicity of a kingdom is that a prince be obeyed by his subjects, that the prince obey the law, and that the law be right and always directed to the public good.* I will not stop to investigate whether, with liberty being the most noble of man's faculties, he degrades his nature, places himself on the level of animals enslaved by instinct, offends even his maker, when he unreservedly renounces the most precious of all his gifts, and allows himself to commit all the crimes he forbids us to commit, in order to please a ferocious or crazed master; nor whether this sublime workman should be more irritated at seeing his finest work destroyed rather than at seeing it dishonored. <I will disregard, if you will, the authority of Barbeyrac, who flatly declares, following Locke,[2] that no one can sell his liberty to the point of submitting himself to an arbitrary power that treats him

according to its fancy. *For,* he adds, *this would be selling his own life, of which he is not the master.*> I will merely ask by what right those who have not been afraid of debasing themselves to this degree have been able to subject their posterity to the same ignominy and to renounce for it goods that do not depend on their liberality, and without which life itself is burdensome to all who are worthy of it.

Pufendorf says[3] that just as one transfers his goods to another by conventions and contracts, one can also divest himself of his liberty in favor of someone. That, it seems to me, is very bad reasoning; for, in the first place, the goods I give away become something utterly foreign to me, and it is a matter of indifference to me whether or not these goods are abused; but it is important to me that my liberty is not abused, and I cannot expose myself to becoming the instrument of crime without making myself guilty of the evil I will be forced to commit. Moreover, since the right of property is merely the result of convention and human institution, every man can dispose of what he possesses as he sees fit. But it is not the same for the essential gifts of nature such as life and liberty, which everyone is allowed to enjoy, and of which it is at least doubtful that one has the right to divest himself. In giving up the one he degrades his being; in giving up the other he annihilates that being insofar as he can. And because no temporal goods can compensate for the one or the other, it would offend at the same time both nature and reason to renounce them, regardless of the price. But even if one could give away his liberty as he does his goods, the difference would be very great for the children who enjoy the father's goods only by virtue of a transmission of his right; whereas, since liberty is a gift they receive from nature in virtue of being men, their parents had no right to divest them of it. Thus, just as violence had to be done to nature in order to establish slavery, nature had to be changed in order to perpetuate this right. And the jurists, who have gravely pronounced that the child of a slave woman is born a slave, have decided, in other words, that a man is not born a man.

Thus it appears certain to me not only that governments did not begin with arbitrary power, which is but their corruption and extreme limit, and which finally brings them back simply to the law of the strongest, for which they were initially to have been the remedy; but also that even if they

---

1   *passage of a famous writing*   "Traité des Droits de la Reine très Chrétienne sur divers États de la Monarchie d'Espagne" (French: Treaty of the Rights of the very Christian Queen on Different States of the Spanish Monarchy). In this work the king attempted to justify his ambitions to annex some possessions of Spain.

2   *Barbeyrac ... following Locke*   Jean Barbeyrac (1674–1744), French jurist. The work referred to here is his translation of Pufen-

dorf, *Le Droit de la Nature et des Gens*, 7.8. 6, n2. Rousseau here attacks Barbeyrac, but not Locke; Locke's *Second Treatise*, 4 §23.

3   *Pufendorf says*   See *De Jure Naturae et Gentium*, 7.3 §1, 7.6. §5.

had begun thus, this power, being illegitimate by its nature, could not have served as a foundation for the rights of society, nor, as a consequence, for the inequality occasioned by social institutions.

Without entering at present into the investigations that are yet to be made into the nature of the fundamental compact of all government, I restrict myself, in following common opinion, to considering here the establishment of the body politic as a true contract between the populace and the leaders it chooses for itself: a contract by which the two parties obligate themselves to observe the laws that are stipulated in it and that form the bonds of their union. Since, with respect to social relations, the populace has united all its wills into a single one, all the articles on which this will is explicated become so many fundamental laws obligating all the members of the state without exception, and one of these regulates the choice and power of the magistrates charged with watching over the execution of the others. This power extends to everything that can maintain the constitution, without going so far as to change it. To it are joined honors that make the laws and their ministers worthy of respect, and, for the ministers personally, prerogatives that compensate them for the troublesome labors that a good administration requires. The magistrate, for his part, obligates himself to use the power entrusted to him only in accordance with the intention of the constituents, to maintain each one in the peaceful enjoyment of what belongs to him, and to prefer on every occasion the public utility to his own interest.

Before experience had shown or knowledge of the human heart had made men foresee the inevitable abuses of such a constitution, it must have seemed all the better because those who were charged with watching over its preservation were themselves the ones who had the greatest interest in it. For since the magistracy and its rights were established exclusively on fundamental laws, were they to be destroyed, the magistracy would immediately cease to be legitimate; the people would no longer be bound to obey them. And since it was not the magistrate but the law that had constituted the essence of the state, everyone would rightfully return to his natural liberty.

The slightest attentive reflection on this point would confirm this by new reasons, and by the nature of the contract it would be seen that it could not be irrevocable. For were there no superior power that could guarantee the fidelity of the contracting parties or force them to fulfill their reciprocal commitments, the parties would remain sole

judges in their own case, and each of them would always have the right to renounce the contract as soon as he should find that the other party violated the conditions of the contract, or as soon as the conditions should cease to suit him. It is on this principle that it appears the right to abdicate can be founded. Now to consider, as we are doing, only what is of human institution, if the magistrate, who has all the power in his hands and who appropriates to himself all the advantages of the contract, nevertheless had the right to renounce the authority, a fortiori the populace, which pays for all the faults of the leaders, should have the right to renounce their dependence. But the horrible dissensions, the infinite disorders that this dangerous power would necessarily bring in its wake, demonstrate more than anything else how much need human governments had for a basis more solid than reason alone, and how necessary it was for public tranquility that the divine will intervened to give to sovereign authority a sacred and inviolable character which took from the subjects the fatal right to dispose of it. If religion had brought about this good for men, it would be enough to oblige them to cherish and adopt it, even with its abuses, since it spares even more blood than fanaticism causes to be shed. But let us follow the thread of our hypothesis.

The various forms of government take their origin from the greater or lesser differences that were found among private individuals at the moment of institution. If a man were eminent in power, virtue, wealth or prestige, he alone was elected magistrate, and the state became monarchical. If several men, more or less equal among themselves, stood out over all the others, they were elected jointly, and there was an aristocracy. Those whose fortune or talents were less disproportionate, and who least departed from the state of nature, kept the supreme administration and formed a democracy. Time made evident which of these forms was the most advantageous to men. Some remained in subjection only to the laws; the others soon obeyed masters. Citizens wanted to keep their liberty; the subjects thought only of taking it away from their neighbors, since they could not endure others enjoying a good they themselves no longer enjoyed. In a word, on the one hand were riches and conquests, and on the other were happiness and virtue.

In these various forms of government all the magistratures were at first elective; and when wealth did not prevail, preference was given to merit, which gives a natural ascendancy, and to age, which gives experience in conducting business and cool-headedness in deliberation. The elders of the Hebrews, the gerontes of Sparta, the senate of Rome, and even the etymology of our word seigneur[1] show how much age was respected in former times. The more elections fell upon men of advanced age, the more frequent elections became, and the more their difficulties were made to be felt. Intrigues were introduced; factions were formed; parties became embittered; civil wars flared up. Finally, the blood of citizens was sacrificed to the alleged happiness of the state, and people were on the verge of falling back into the anarchy of earlier times. The ambition of the leaders profited from these circumstances to perpetuate their offices within their families. The people, already accustomed to dependence, tranquility and the conveniences of life, and already incapable of breaking their chains, consented to let their servitude increase in order to secure their tranquility. Thus it was that the leaders, having become hereditary, grew accustomed to regard their magistratures as family property, to regard themselves as the proprietors of the state (of which at first they were but the officers), to call their fellow citizens their slaves, to count them like cattle in the number of things that belonged to them, and to call themselves equals of the gods and kings of kings.

If we follow the progress of inequality in these various revolutions, we will find that the first stage was the establishment of the law and of the right of property, the second stage was the institution of the magistracy, and the third and final stage was the transformation of legitimate power into arbitrary power. Thus the class of rich and poor was authorized by the first epoch, that of the strong and the weak by the second, and that of master and slave by the third: the ultimate degree of inequality and the limit to which all the others finally lead, until new revolutions completely dissolve the government or bring it nearer to its legitimate institution.

To grasp the necessity of this progress, we must consider less the motives for the establishment of the body politic than the form it takes in its execution and the disadvantages that follow in its wake. For the vices that make social institutions necessary are the same ones that make their abuses inevitable. And with the sole exception of Sparta, where the law kept watch chiefly over the education of children, and where Lycurgus established mores that nearly dispensed with having to add laws to them, since laws are generally

less strong than passions and restrain men without changing them, it would be easy to prove that any government that always moved forward in conformity with the purpose for which it was founded without being corrupted or altered, would have been needlessly instituted, and that a country where no one eluded the laws and abused the magistrature would need neither magistracy nor laws.

Political distinctions necessarily lend themselves to civil distinctions. The growing inequality between the people and its leaders soon makes itself felt among private individuals, and is modified by them in a thousand ways according to passions, talents and events. The magistrate cannot usurp illegitimate power without producing protégés for himself to whom he is forced to yield some part of it. Moreover, citizens allow themselves to be oppressed only insofar as they are driven by blind ambition; and looking more below than above them, domination becomes more dear to them than independence, and they consent to wear chains in order to be able to give them in turn to others. It is very difficult to reduce to obedience someone who does not seek to command; and the most adroit politician would never succeed in subjecting men who wanted merely to be free. But inequality spreads easily among ambitious and cowardly souls always ready to run the risks of fortune and, almost indifferently, to dominate or serve, according to whether it becomes favorable or unfavorable to them. Thus it is that there must have come a time when the eyes of people were beguiled to such an extent that its leaders merely had to say to the humblest men, "Be great, you and all your progeny," and he immediately appeared great to everyone as well as in his own eyes, and his descendants were elevated even more in proportion as they were at some remove from him. The more remote and uncertain the cause, the more the effect increased; the more loafers one could count in a family, the more illustrious it became.

If this were the place to go into detail, I would easily explain how <even without government involvement> the inequality of prestige and authority becomes inevitable among private individuals,[2] as soon as they are united in one

---

1   *gerontes of Sparta ... word seigneur* "Gerontes" and "senate," names of ruling bodies in Sparta and Rome, both derive directly from roots meaning "older," as does the French word "*seigneur*," meaning "lord," which derives from the Latin "*senior*," which has the same meaning it does in English.

2   *inequality of prestige ... private individual* [Rousseau's note] Distributive justice would still be opposed to this rigorous equality of the state of nature, if it were workable in civil society. And since all the members of the state owe it services proportionate to their talents and forces, the citizens for their part should be distinguished and favored in proportion to their services. It is in this sense that one must understand a passage of Isocrates, in which he praises the first Athenians for having known well how to distinguish

single society and are forced to make comparisons among themselves and to take into account the differences they discover in the continual use they have to make of one another. These differences are of several sorts, but in general, since wealth, nobility or rank, power and personal merit are the principal distinctions by which someone is measured in society, I would prove that the agreement or conflict of these various forces is the surest indication of a well- or ill-constituted state. I would make it apparent that among these four types of inequality, since personal qualities are the origin of all the others, wealth is the last to which they are ultimately reduced, because it readily serves to buy all the rest, since it is the most immediately useful to well-being and the easiest to communicate. This observation enables one to judge rather precisely the extent to which each people is removed from its primitive institution, and of the progress it has made toward the final stage of corruption. I would note how much that universal desire for reputation, honors, and preferences, which devours us all, trains and compares our talents and strengths; how much it excites and multiplies the passions; and, by making all men competitors, rivals, or rather enemies, how many setbacks, successes and catastrophes of every sort it causes every day, by making so many contenders run the same course. I would show that

it is to this ardor for making oneself the topic of conversation, to this furor to distinguish oneself which nearly always keeps us outside ourselves, that we owe what is best and worst among men, our virtues and vices, our sciences and our errors, our conquerors and our philosophers, that is to say, a multitude of bad things against a small number of good ones. Finally, I would prove that if one sees a handful of powerful and rich men at the height of greatness and fortune while the mob grovels in obscurity and misery, it is because the former prize the things they enjoy only to the extent that the others are deprived of them; and because, without changing their position, they would cease to be happy, if the people ceased to be miserable.

But these details alone would be the subject of a large work in which one would weigh the advantages and the disadvantages of every government relative to the rights of the state of nature, and where one would examine all the different faces under which inequality has appeared until now and may appear in <future> ages, according to the nature of these governments and the upheavals that time will necessarily bring in its wake. We would see the multitude oppressed from within as a consequence of the very precautions it had taken against what menaced it from without. We would see oppression continually increase, without the oppressed ever being able to know where it would end or what legitimate means would be left for them to stop it. We would see the rights of citizens and national liberties gradually die out, and the protests of the weak treated like seditious murmurs. We would see politics restrict the honor of defending the common cause to a mercenary portion of the people. We would see arising from this the necessity for taxes, the discouraged farmer leaving his field, even during peacetime, and leaving his plow in order to gird himself with a sword. We would see the rise of fatal and bizarre rules in the code of honor. We would see the defenders of the homeland sooner or later become its enemies, constantly holding a dagger over their fellow citizens, and there would come a time when we would hear them say to the oppressor of their country: "*If you order me to plunge my sword into my brother's breast or my father's throat, and into my pregnant wife's entrails, I will do so, even though my right hand is unwilling.*"[1]

From the extreme inequality of conditions and fortunes, from the diversity of passions and talents, from use-

---

which of the two sorts of equality was the more advantageous, one of which consists in portioning out indifferently to all citizens the same advantages, and the other in distributing them according to each one's merit. These able politicians, adds the orator, in banishing that unjust equality that makes no differentiation between wicked and good men, adhered inviolably to that equality which rewards and punishes each according to one's merit. But first, no society has ever existed, regardless of the degree of corruption they could have achieved, in which no differentiation between wicked and good men was made. And in the matter of mores, where the law cannot set a sufficiently precise measurement to serve as a rule for the magistrate, the law very wisely prohibits him from the judgment of persons, leaving him merely the judgment of actions, in order not to leave the fate or the rank of citizens to his discretion. Only mores as pure as those of the ancient Romans could withstand censors; such tribunals would soon have overturned everything among us. It is for public esteem to differentiate between wicked and good men. The magistrate is judge only of strict law [*droit*]; but the populace is the true judge of mores—an upright and even enlightened judge on this point, occasionally deceived but never corrupted. The ranks of citizens ought therefore to be regulated not on the basis of their personal merit, which would be to leave to the magistrate the means of making an almost arbitrary application of the law, but upon the real services which they render to the state and which lend themselves to a more precise reckoning.

---

1 *If you ... is unwilling* Lucan, *Pharsalia* 1. Rousseau quotes the (slightly modified) original Latin.

less arts, from pernicious arts, from frivolous sciences there would come a pack of prejudices equally contrary to reason, happiness and virtue. One would see the leaders fomenting whatever can weaken men united together by disuniting them; whatever can give society an air of apparent concord while sowing the seeds of real division; whatever can inspire defiance and hatred in the various classes through the opposition of their rights and interests, and can as a consequence strengthen the power that contains them all.

It is from the bosom of this disorder and these upheavals that despotism, by gradually raising its hideous head and devouring everything it had seen to be good and healthy in every part of the state, would eventually succeed in trampling underfoot the laws and the people, and in establishing itself on the ruins of the republic. The times that would precede this last transformation would be times of troubles and calamities; but in the end everything would be swallowed up by the monster, and the peoples would no longer have leader or laws, but only tyrants. Also, from that moment on, there would no longer be any question of mores and virtue, for wherever despotism, *in which decency affords no hope*,[1] reigns, it tolerates no other master. As soon as it speaks, there is neither probity nor duty to consult, and the blindest obedience is the only virtue remaining for slaves.

Here is the final stage of inequality, and the extreme point that closes the circle and touches the point from which we started. Here all private individuals become equals again, because they are nothing. And since subjects no longer have any law other than the master's will, nor the master any rule other than his passions, the notions of good and the principles of justice again vanish. Here everything is returned solely to the law of the strongest, and consequently to a new state of nature different from the one with which we began, in that the one was the state of nature in its purity, and this last one is the fruit of an excess of corruption. Moreover, there is so little difference between these two states, and the governmental contract is so utterly dissolved by despotism, that the despot is master only as long as he is the strongest; and as soon as he can be ousted, he has no cause to protest against violence. The uprising that ends in the strangulation or the dethronement of a sultan is as lawful an act as those by which he disposed of the lives and goods of his subjects the day before. Force alone maintained him; force alone brings him down. Thus everything happens in accordance with the natural order, and whatever the outcome of these brief and frequent upheavals may be, no one can complain about someone else's injustice, but only of his own imprudence or his misfortune.

In discovering and following thus the forgotten and lost routes that must have led man from the natural state to the civil state; in reestablishing, with the intermediate positions I have just taken note of, those that time constraints on me have made me suppress or that the imagination has not suggested to me, no attentive reader can fail to be struck by the immense space that separates these two states. It is in this slow succession of things that he will see the solution to an infinity of moral and political problems which the philosophers are unable to resolve. He will realize that, since the human race of one age is not the human race of another age, the reason why Diogenes did not find his man[2] is because he searched among his contemporaries for a man who no longer existed. Cato,[3] he will say, perished with Rome and liberty because he was out of place in his age; and this greatest of men merely astonished the world, which five hundred years earlier he would have governed. In short, he will explain how the soul and human passions are imperceptibly altered and, as it were, change their nature; why, in the long run, our needs and our pleasures change their objects; why, with original man gradually disappearing, society no longer offers to the eyes of the wise man anything but an assemblage of artificial men and factitious passions which are the work of all these new relations and have no true foundation in nature. What reflection teaches us on this subject is perfectly confirmed by observation: savage man and civilized man differ so greatly in the depths of their hearts and in their inclinations, that what constitutes the supreme happiness of the one would reduce the other to despair. Savage man breathes only tranquility and liberty; he wants simply to live and rest easy; and not even the unperturbed tranquility of the Stoic[4] approaches his profound indifference for any other objects. On the other hand, the citizen is always active and in a sweat, always agitated, and

---

1   *in which decency affords no hope*   Tacitus, *Annals* 5.3. Rousseau quotes the (slightly modified) original Latin.

2   *Diogenes did not find his man*   Diogenes (c. 412–323 BCE) was an ancient Greek philosopher who expressed contempt for human institutions and foibles. He was supposed to have walked around the streets of Athens searching for an honest man, but finding none.

3   *Cato*   Marcus Porcius Cato (234–149 BCE), Roman statesman.

4   *unperturbed tranquility of the Stoic*   Stoicism was a philosophical school developed in Ancient Greece, advocating the use of reason to free one from emotional trouble and to produce inner calm.

unceasingly tormenting himself in order to seek still more laborious occupations. He works until he dies; he even runs to his death in order to be in a position to live, or renounces life in order to acquire immortality. He pays court to the great whom he hates and to the rich whom he scorns. He stops at nothing to obtain the honor of serving them. He proudly crows about his own baseness and their protection; and proud of his slavery, he speaks with disdain about those who do not have the honor of taking part in it. What a spectacle for the Carib are the difficult and envied labors of the European minister! How many cruel deaths would that indolent savage not prefer to the horror of such a life, which often is not mollified even by the pleasure of doing good. But in order to see the purpose of so many cares, the words *power* and *reputation* would have to have a meaning in his mind; he would have to learn that there is a type of men who place some value on the regard the rest of the world has for them, and who know how to be happy and content with themselves on the testimony of others rather than on their own. Such, in fact, is the true cause of all these differences; the savage lives in himself; the man accustomed to the ways of society is always outside himself and knows how to live only in the opinion of others. And it is, as it were, from their judgment alone that he draws the sentiment of his own existence. It is not pertinent to my subject to show how, from such a disposition, so much indifference for good and evil arises, along with such fine discourse on morality; how, with everything reduced to appearances, everything becomes factitious and bogus: honor, friendship, virtue, and often even our vices, about which we eventually find the secret of boasting; how, in a word, always asking others what we are and never daring to question ourselves on this matter, in the midst of so much philosophy, humanity, politeness, and sublime maxims, we have merely a deceitful and frivolous exterior: honor without virtue, reason without wisdom, and pleasure without happiness. It is enough for me to have proved that this is not the original state of man, and that this is only the spirit of society, and the inequality that society engenders, which thus change and alter all our natural inclinations.

I have tried to set forth the origin and progress of inequality, the establishment and abuse of political societies, to the extent that these things can be deduced from the nature of man by the light of reason alone, and independently of the sacred dogmas that give to sovereign authority the sanction of divine right. It follows from this presentation that, since inequality is practically non-existent in the state

of nature, it derives its force and growth from the development of our faculties and the progress of the human mind, and eventually becomes stable and legitimate through the establishment of property and laws. Moreover, it follows that moral inequality, authorized by positive right alone, is contrary to natural right whenever it is not combined in the same proportion with physical inequality: a distinction that is sufficient to determine what one should think in this regard about the sort of inequality that reigns among all civilized people, for it is obviously contrary to the law of nature, however it may be defined, for a child to command an old man, for an imbecile to lead a wise man, and for a handful of people to gorge themselves on superfluities while the starving multitude lacks necessities.

Appendix 1: Note [On Good and Evil in Human Life]

A famous author, on calculating the goods and evils of human life and comparing the two sums, has found that the latter greatly exceeded the former, and that, all things considered, life was a pretty poor present for man. I am not surprised by his conclusion; he has drawn all of his arguments from the constitution of civil man. Had he gone back as far as natural man, the judgment can be made that he would have found very different results, that he would have realized that man has scarcely any evils other than those he has given himself, and that nature would have been justified. It is not without trouble that we have managed to make ourselves so unhappy. When, on the one hand, one considers the immense labors of men, so many sciences searched into, so many arts invented, and so many forces employed, abysses filled up, mountains razed, rocks broken, rivers made navigable, lands cleared, lakes dug, marshes drained, enormous buildings raised upon the earth, the sea covered with ships and sailors; and when, on the other hand, one searches with a little meditation for the true advantages that have resulted from all this for the happiness of the human species, one cannot help being struck by the astonishing disproportion that obtains between these things, and to deplore man's blindness, which, to feed his foolish pride and who knows what vain sense of self-importance, makes him run ardently after all the miseries to which he is susceptible, and which beneficent nature has taken pains to keep from him.

Men are wicked; a sad and continual experience dispenses us from having to prove it. Nevertheless, man is naturally good; I believe I have demonstrated it. What therefore can have depraved him to this degree, if not the changes that have befallen his constitution, the progress he has made, and the sorts of knowledge he has acquired? Let human society be admired as much as one wants; it will be no less true for it that it necessarily brings men to hate one another to the extent that their interests are at cross-purposes with one another, to render mutually to one another apparent services and in fact do every evil imaginable to one another. What is one to think of an interaction where the reason of each private individual dictates to him maxims directly contrary to those that public reason preaches to the body of society, and where each finds his profit in the misfortune of another? Perhaps there is not a wealthy man whose death is not secretly hoped for by greedy heirs and often by his own children; not a ship at sea whose wreck would not be good news to some merchant; not a firm that a debtor of bad faith would not wish to see burn with all the papers it contains; not a people that does not rejoice at the disasters of its neighbors. Thus it is that we find our advantage in the setbacks of our fellow-men, and that one person's loss almost always brings about another's prosperity. But what is even more dangerous is that public calamities are anticipated and hoped for by a multitude of private individuals. Some want diseases, others death, others war, others famine. I have seen ghastly men weep with the sadness at the likely prospects of a fertile year. And the great and deadly fire of London, which cost the life or the goods of so many unfortunate people, made the fortunes of perhaps more than ten thousand people. I know that Montaigne ["The Profit of One Man is the Damage of Another," *Essays*, 1.22] blames the Athenian Demades for having had a worker punished, who, by selling coffins at a high price, made a great deal from the death of the citizens. But since the reason Montaigne proposes is that everyone would have to be punished, it is evident that it confirms my own. Let us therefore penetrate, through our frivolous demonstration of good will, to what happens at the bottom of our hearts; and let us reflect on what the state of things must be where all men are forced to caress and destroy one another, and where they are born enemies by duty and crooks by interest. If someone answers me by claiming that society is constituted in such a manner that each man gains by serving others, I will reply that this would be very well and good, provided he did not gain still more by harming them. There is no profit, however legitimate, that is not surpassed by one that can be made il-

legitimately, and wrong done to a neighbor is always more lucrative than services. It is therefore no longer a question of anything but finding the means of being assured of impunity. And this is what the powerful spend all their forces on, and the weak all their ruses.

Savage man, when he has eaten, is at peace with all nature, and the friend of all his fellow-men. Is it sometimes a question of his disputing over his meal? He never comes to blows without having first compared the difficulty of winning with that of finding his sustenance elsewhere. And since pride is not involved in the fight, it is ended by a few swings of the fist. The victor eats; the vanquished is on his way to seek his fortune, and everything is pacified. But for man in society, these are quite different affairs. It is first of all a question of providing for the necessary and then for the superfluous; next come delights, and then immense riches, and then subjects, and then slaves. He has not a moment's respite. What is most singular is that the less natural and pressing the needs, the more the passions increase and, what is worse, the power to satisfy them; so that after long periods of prosperity, after having swallowed up many treasures and ruined many men, my hero will end by butchering everything until he is the sole master of the universe. Such in brief is the moral portrait, if not of human life, then at least of the secret pretensions of the heart of every civilized man.

Compare, without prejudices, the state of civil man with that of savage man and seek, if you can, how many new doors to suffering and death (other than his wickedness, his needs and his miseries) the former has opened. If you consider the emotional turmoil that consumes us, the violent passions that exhaust and desolate us, the excessive labors with which the poor are overburdened, the still more dangerous softness to which the rich abandon themselves, and which cause the former to die of their needs and the latter of their excesses; if you call to mind the monstrous combinations of foods, their pernicious seasonings, the corrupted foodstuffs, tainted drugs, the knavery of those who sell them, the errors of those who administer them, the poison of the vessels in which they are prepared; if you pay attention to the epidemic diseases engendered by the bad air among the multitudes of men gathered together, to the illnesses occasioned by the effeminacy of our lifestyle, by the coming and going from the inside of our houses to the open air, the use of garments put on or taken off with too little precaution, and all the cares that our excessive sensuality has turned into necessary habits, the neglect or privation of which then costs us our life or our health; if you take into account fires and earthquakes, which, in consuming or turning upside down whole cities, cause their inhabitants to die by the thousands; in a word, if you unite the dangers that all these causes continually gather over our heads, you will realize how dearly nature makes us pay for the scorn we have shown for its lessons.

I will not repeat here what I have said elsewhere [in *L'etat de guerre*, translated as *The State of War*] about war, but I wish that informed men would, for once, want or dare to give the public the detail of the horrors that are committed in armies by provisions and hospital suppliers. One would see that their not too secret maneuvers, on account of which the most brilliant armies dissolve into less than nothing, cause more soldiers to perish than are cut down by enemy swords. Moreover, no less surprising is the calculation of the number of men swallowed up by the sea every year, either by hunger, or scurvy, or pirates, or fire, or shipwrecks. It is clear that we must also put to the account of established property, and consequently to that of society, the assassinations, the poisonings, the highway robberies, and even the punishments of these crimes, punishments necessary to prevent greater ills, but which, costing the lives of two or more for the murder of one man, do not fail really to double the loss to the human species. How many are the shameful ways to prevent the birth of men or to fool nature: either by those brutal and depraved tastes which insult its most charming work, tastes that neither savages nor animals ever knew, and that have arisen in civilized countries only as the result of a corrupt imagination; or by those secret abortions, worthy fruits of debauchery and vicious honor; or by the exposure or the murder of a multitude of infants, victims of the misery of their parents or of the barbarous shame of their mothers; or, finally by the mutilation of those unfortunates, part of whose existence and all of whose posterity are sacrificed to vain songs, or what is worse still, to the brutal jealousy of a few men: a mutilation which, in this last case, doubly outrages nature, both by the treatment received by those who suffer it and by the use to which they are destined.

<But are there not a thousand more frequent and even more dangerous cases where paternal rights overtly offend humanity? How many talents are buried and inclinations are forced by the imprudent constraint of fathers! How many men would have distinguished themselves in a suitable station who die unhappy and dishonored in another station for which they have no taste! How many happy but

unequal marriages have been broken or disturbed, and how many chaste wives dishonored by this order of conditions always in contradiction with that of nature! How many other bizarre unions formed by interests and disavowed by love and by reason! How many even honest and virtuous couples cause themselves torment because they were ill-matched! How many young and unhappy victims of their parent's greed plunge into vice or pass their sorrowful days in tears, and moan in indissoluble chains which the heart rejects and which gold alone has formed! Happy sometimes are those whose courage and even virtue tear them from life before a barbarous violence forces them into crime or despair. Forgive me, father and mother forever deplorable. I regrettably worsen your sorrows; but may they serve as an eternal and terrible example to whoever dares, in the name of nature, to violate the most sacred of its rights!

If I have spoken only of those ill-formed relationships that are the result of our civil order, is one to think that those where love and sympathy have presided are themselves exempt from drawbacks?>

What would happen if I were to undertake to show the human species attacked in its very source, and even in the most holy of all bonds, where one no longer dares to listen to nature until after having consulted fortune, and where, with civil disorder confounding virtues and vices, continence becomes a criminal precaution, and the refusal to give life to one's fellow-man an act of humanity? But without tearing away the veil that covers so many horrors, let us content ourselves with pointing out the evil, for which others must supply the remedy.

Let us add to all this that quantity of unwholesome trades which shorten lives or destroy one's health, such as work in mines, various jobs involving the processing of metals, minerals, and especially lead, copper, mercury, cobalt, arsenic, realgar; those other perilous trades which everyday cost the lives of a number of workers, some of them roofers, others carpenters, others masons, others working in quarries; let us bring all of these objects together, I say, and we will be able to see in the establishment and the perfection of societies the reasons for the diminution of the species, observed by more than one philosopher.

Luxury, impossible to prevent among men who are greedy for their own conveniences and for the esteem of others, soon completes the evil that societies have begun; and on the pretext of keeping the poor alive (which it was not necessary to do), luxury impoverishes everyone else, and sooner or later depopulates the state.

Luxury is a remedy far worse than the evil it means to cure; or rather it is itself the worst of all evils in any state, however large or small it may be, and which, in order to feed the hordes of lackeys and wretches it has produced, crushes and ruins the laborer and the citizen—like those scorching south winds that, by covering grass and greenery with devouring insects, take sustenance away from useful animals, and bring scarcity and death to all the places where they make themselves felt.

From society and the luxury it engenders, arise the liberal and mechanical arts, commerce, letters, and all those useless things that make industry flourish, enriching and ruining states. The reason for this decay is quite simple. It is easy to see that agriculture, by its nature, must be the least lucrative of all the arts, because, with its product being of the most indispensable use to all men, its price must be proportionate to the abilities of the poorest. From the same principle can be drawn this rule: that, in general, the arts are lucrative in inverse proportion to their usefulness, and that the most necessary must finally become the most neglected. From this it is clear what must be thought of the true advantages of industry and of the real effect that results from its progress.

Such are the discernible causes of all the miseries into which opulence finally brings down the most admired nations. To the degree that industry and the arts expand and flourish, the scorned farmer, burdened with taxes necessary to maintain luxury and condemned to spend his life between toil and hunger, abandons his fields to go to the cities in search of the bread he ought to be carrying there. The more the capital cities strike the stupid eyes of the people as wonderful, the more it will be necessary to groan at the sight of countrysides abandoned, fields fallow, and main roads jammed with unhappy citizens who have become beggars or thieves, destined to end their misery one day on the rack or on a dung-heap. Thus it is that the state, enriching itself on the one hand, weakens and depopulates itself on the other; and that the most powerful monarchies, after much labor to become opulent and deserted, end by becoming the prey of poor nations which succumb to the deadly temptation to invade them, and which enrich and enfeeble themselves in their turn, until they are themselves invaded and destroyed by others.

Let someone deign to explain to us for once what could have produced those hordes of barbarians which for so many centuries have overrun Europe, Asia and Africa. Was it to the industry of their arts, the wisdom of their laws, the excellence of their civil order that they owed that prodigious population? Would our learned ones be so kind as to tell us why, far from multiplying to that degree, those ferocious and brutal men, without enlightenment, without restraint, without education, did not all kill one another at every moment to argue with one another over their food or game? Let them explain to us how these wretches even had the gall to look right in the eye such capable people as we were, with such fine military discipline, such fine codes, and such wise laws, and why, finally, after society was perfected in the countries of the north, and so many pains were taken there to teach men their mutual duties and the art of living together agreeably and peaceably, nothing more is seen to come from them like those multitudes of men it produced formerly. I am very much afraid that someone might finally get it into his head to reply to me that all these great things, namely the arts, sciences, and laws, have been very wisely invented by men as a salutary plague to prevent the excessive multiplication of the species, out of fear that this world, which is destined for us, might finally become too small for its inhabitants.

What then! Must we destroy societies, annihilate thine and mine, and return to live in the forests with bears?—a conclusion in the style of my adversaries, which I prefer to anticipate, rather than leave to them the shame of drawing it. Oh you, to whom the heavenly voice has not made itself heard, and who recognize for your species no other destination except to end this brief life in peace; you who can leave in the midst of the cities your deadly acquisitions, your troubled minds, your corrupt hearts and your unbridled desires. Since it depends on you, retake your ancient and first innocence; go into the woods to lose sight and memory of the crimes of your contemporaries, and have no fear of cheapening your species in renouncing its enlightenment in order to renounce its vices. As for men like me, whose passions have forever destroyed their original simplicity, who can no longer feed on grass and acorn<s>, nor get by without laws and chiefs; those who were honored in their first father with supernatural lessons [that is, who are descended (they believe) from a divinely inspired prophet]; those who will see, in the intention of giving human actions from the beginning a morality they would not have acquired for a long time, the reason for a precept indifferent in itself and inexplicable in any other system; those, in a word, who are convinced that the divine voice called the entire human race to the enlightenment and the happiness of the celestial intelligences; all those latter ones will attempt, through the exercise of virtues they oblige themselves to practice while learning to know them, to merit the eternal reward that they ought to expect for them. They will respect the sacred bonds of the societies of which they are members; they will love their fellow-men and will serve them with all their power; they will scrupulously obey the laws and the men who are their authors and their ministers; they will honor above all the good and wise princes who will know how to prevent, cure or palliate that pack of abuses and evils always ready to overpower us; they will animate the zeal of these worthy chiefs by showing them without fear or flattery the greatness of their task and the rigor of their duty. But they will despise no less for it a constitution that can be maintained only with the help of so many respectable people, who are desired more often than they are obtained, and from which, despite all their care, always arise more real calamities than apparent advantages.

Appendix 2: Note [On Human Variety]

Among the men we know, whether by ourselves, or from historians, or from travelers, some are black, others white, others red. Some wear their hair long; others have merely curly wool. Some are almost entirely covered with hair; others do not even have a beard. There have been and perhaps there still are nations of men of gigantic size; and apart from the fable of the Pygmies (which may well be merely an exaggeration), we know that the Laplanders and above all the Greenlanders are considerably below the average size of man. It is even maintained that there are entire peoples who have tails like quadrupeds. And without putting blind faith in the accounts of Herodotus and Ctesias, we can at least draw from them the very likely opinion that had one been able to make good observations in those ancient times when various peoples followed lifestyles differing more greatly among themselves than do those of today, one would have also noted in the shape and posture of the body, much more striking varieties. All these facts, for which it is easy to furnish incontestable proofs, are capable of surprising only those who are accustomed to look solely at the objects that surround them and who are ignorant of the powerful effects of the diversity of climates, air, foods, lifestyle, habits in general, and especially the astonishing force of the same causes when they act continually for long successions of generations. Today, when commerce, voyages and conquests reunite various peoples further, and their lifestyles are constantly approximating one another through frequent communication, it is evident that certain national differences have diminished; and, for example, everyone can take note of the fact that today's Frenchmen are no longer those large, colorless and blond-haired bodies described by Latin historians, although time, together with the mixture of the Franks and the Normans, themselves colorless and blond-haired, should have reestablished what commerce with the Romans could have removed from the influence of the climate in the natural constitution and complexion of the inhabitants. All of these observations on the varieties that a thousand causes can produce and have in fact produced in the human species cause me to wonder whether the various animals similar to men, taken without much scrutiny by travelers for beasts, either because of some differences they noticed in their outward structure or simply because these animals did not speak, would not in fact be veritable savage men, whose race, dispersed in the woods during olden times, had not had an occasion to develop any of its virtual faculties, had not acquired any degree of perfection, and was still found in the primitive state of nature. Let us give an example of what I mean.

"There are found in the kingdom of the Congo," says the translator of the *Histoire des Voyages*, "many of those large animals called *orangutans* in the East Indies, which occupy a middle ground between the human species and the baboons. Battel relates that in the forests of Mayomba, in the kingdom of Loango, one sees two kinds of monsters, the larger of which are called *pongos* and the others *enjocos*. The former bear an exact resemblance to man, except they are much larger and very tall. With a human face, they have very deep-set eyes. Their hands, cheeks and ears are without hair, except for their eyebrows, which are very long. Although the rest of their body is quite hairy, the hair is not very thick; the color of the hair is brown. Finally, the only part that distinguishes them from men is their leg, which has no calf. They walk upright, grasping the hair of their neck with their hand. Their retreat is in the woods. They sleep in the trees, and there they make a kind of roof which offers them shelter from the rain. Their foods are fruits or wild nuts; they never eat flesh. The custom of the Negroes who cross the forests is to light fires during the night. They note that in the morning, at their departure, the pongos take their place around the fire, and do not withdraw until it is out; because, for all their cleverness, they do not have enough sense to lay wood on the fire to keep it going.

"They occasionally walk in groups and kill the Negroes who cross the forests. They even fall upon elephants who come to graze in the places they inhabit, and they irritate the elephants so much with punches or with whacks of a stick that they force them howling to take flight. Pongos are never taken alive, because they are so strong that ten men would not be enough to stop them. But the Negroes take a good many young ones after having killed the mother, to whose body the young stick very closely. When one of these animals dies, the others cover its body with a pile of branches or leaves. Purchass adds that, in the conversations he has had with Battel, he had learned from him also that a pongo abducted a little Negro who passed an entire month in the society of these animals, for they do not harm men they take by surprise, at least when these men do not pay any attention to them, as the little Negro had observed. Battel had not described the second species of monster.

"Dapper confirms that the kingdom of the Congo is filled with those animals which in the Indies bear the name orangutans, that is to say, inhabitants of the woods, and which the Africans call *quojas-morros*. This beast, he says, is so similar to man, that it has occurred to some travelers that it could have issued from a woman and a monkey: a myth which even the Negroes reject. One of these animals was transported from the Congo to Holland and presented to the Prince of Orange, Frederick Henry. It was the height of a three-year old child, moderately stocky, but square and well-proportioned, very agile and lively; its legs fleshy and robust; the entire front of the body naked, but the rear covered with black hairs. At first sight, its face resembled that of a man, but it had a flat and turned up nose; its ears were also those of the human species; its breast (for it was a female), was plump, its navel sunken, its shoulders very well joined, its hands divided into fingers and thumbs, its calves and heels fat and fleshy. It often walked upright on its legs; it was capable of lifting and carrying heavy burdens. When it wanted to drink, it took the cover of the pot in one hand, and held the base with the other; afterward it graciously wiped its lips. It lay down to sleep with its head on a cushion, covering itself with such skill that it would have been taken for a man in bed. The Negroes tell strange stories about this animal. They assert not only that it takes women and girls by force, but that it dares to attack armed men. In a word, there is great likelihood that it is the satyr of the ancients. Perhaps Merolla is speaking only of these animals whom he relates that Negroes sometimes lay hold of savage men and women in their hunts."

These species of anthropomorphic animals are again discussed in the third volume of the same *Histoire des Voyages* under the name of *beggos* and *mandrills*. But sticking to the preceding accounts, we find in the description of these alleged monsters striking points of conformity with the human species and lesser differences than those that would be assigned between one man and another. From these pages it is not clear what the reasons are that the authors have for refusing to give the animals in question the name "savage men"; but it is easy to conjecture that it is on account of their stupidity and also because they did not speak—feeble reasons for those who know that although the organ of speech is natural to man, nevertheless speech itself is not natural to him, and who knows to what point his perfectibility can have elevated civil man above his original state. The small number of lines these descriptions contain can cause us to judge how badly these animals have been observed and with what prejudices they have been viewed. For example, they are categorized as monsters, and yet there is agreement that they reproduce. In one place, Battel says that the pongos kill the Negroes who cross the forests; in another place, Purchass adds that they do not do any harm, even when they surprise them, at least when the Negroes do not fix their gaze upon them. The pongos gather around fires lit by the Negroes upon the Negroes' withdrawal, and withdraw in their turn when the fire is out. There is the fact. Here now is the commentary of the observer: *because, for all their cleverness, they do not have enough sense to lay wood on the fire to keep it going*. I would like to hazard a guess how Battel, or Purchass, his compiler, could have known that the withdrawal of the pongos was an effect of their stupidity rather than their will. In a climate such as Loango, fire is not something particularly necessary for the animals; and if the Negroes light a fire, it is less against the cold than to frighten ferocious beasts. It is therefore a very simple matter that, after having been for some time delighted with the flame or being well warmed, the pongos grow tired of always remaining in the same place and go off to graze, which requires more time than if they ate flesh. Moreover, we know that most animals, man not excluded, are naturally lazy, and that they refuse all sorts of cares which are not absolutely necessary. Finally, it seems very strange that pongos, whose adroitness and strength are praised, the pongos who know how to bury their dead and to make themselves roofs out of branches, should not know how to push fagots into the fire. I recall having seen a monkey perform the same maneuver that people deny the pongos can do. It is true that since my ideas were not oriented in this direction, I myself committed the mistake for which I reproach our travelers; I neglected to examine whether the intention of the monkey was actually to sustain the fire or simply, as I believe is the case, to imitate the actions of a man. Whatever the case may be, it is well demonstrated that the monkey is not a variety of man: not only because he is deprived of the faculty of speech, but above all because it is certain that his species does not have the faculty of perfecting itself, which is the specific characteristic of the human species: experiments that do not seem to have been made on the pongos and the orangutan with sufficient care to enable one to draw the same conclusion in their case. However, there would be a means by which, if the orangutan or others were of the human species, even the least sophisticated observers could assure themselves of it by means of demonstration [Rousseau means: the attempt to cross-breed humans and apes]. But beyond the fact that a single generation would not be sufficient for this experiment, it should pass as unworkable, since it would be necessary that what is merely a supposition be demonstrated to be true, before the test that should establish the fact could be innocently tried.

Precipitous judgments, which are not the fruit of an enlightened reason, are prone to be excessive. Without any fanfare, our travelers made into beasts, under the names *pongos, mandrills, orangutans*, the same beings that the ancients, under the names *satyrs, fauns, sylvans*, made into divinities. Perhaps, after more precise investigations it will be found that they are <neither beasts nor gods but> men. Meanwhile, it would seem to me that there is as much reason to defer on this point to Merolla, an educated monk, an eyewitness, and one who, with all his naïveté, did not fail to be a man of wit, as to the merchant Battel, Dapper, Purchass, and the other compilers.

What judgment do we think such observers would have made regarding the child found in 1694, of whom I have spoken before, who gave no indication of reason, walked on his feet and hands, had no language, and made sounds that bore no resemblance whatever to those of a man? It took a long time, continues the same philosopher who provided me with this fact [Condillac, *Essai*], before he could utter a few words, and then he did it in a barbarous manner. Once he could speak, he was questioned about his first state, but he did not recall it any more than we recall what happened to us in the cradle. If, unhappily for him, this child had fallen into the hands of our travelers, there can be no doubt that after having observed his silence and stupidity, they

would have resolved to send him back to the woods or lock him up in a menagerie; after which they would have spoken eruditely about him in their fine accounts as a very curious beast who looked rather like a man.

For the three or four hundred years since the inhabitants of Europe inundated the other parts of the world and continually published new collections of travels and stories, I am convinced that we know no other men but the Europeans alone. Moreover, it would appear, from the ridiculous prejudices that have not been extinguished even among men of letters, that everybody does hardly anything under the pompous name of "the study of man" except study the men of his country. Individuals may well come and go; it seems that philosophy travels nowhere; moreover, the philosophy of one people is little suited to another. The reason for this is manifest, at least for distant countries. There are hardly more than four sorts of men who make long voyages: sailors, merchants, soldiers, and missionaries. Now we can hardly expect the first three classes to provide good observers; and as for those in the fourth, occupied by the sublime vocation that calls them, even if they were not subject to the prejudices of social position as are all the rest, we must believe that they would not voluntarily commit themselves to investigations that would appear to be sheer curiosity, and which would sidetrack them from the more important works to which they are destined. Besides, to preach the Gospel in a useful manner, zeal alone is needed, and God gives the rest. But to study men, talents are needed which God is not required to give anyone, and which are not always the portion of saints. One does not open a book of voyages where one does not find descriptions of characters and mores. But one is utterly astonished to see that these people who have described so many things have said merely what everyone already knew, that, at the end of the world, they knew how to understand only what it was for them to notice without leaving their street; and that those true qualities which characterize nations and strike eyes made to see have almost always escaped theirs. Whence this fine moral slogan, so bandied about by the philosophizing rabble: that men are everywhere the same; that, since everywhere they have the same passions and the same vices, it is rather pointless to seek to characterize different peoples—which is about as well reasoned as it would be for someone to say that Peter and James cannot be distinguished from one another, because they both have a nose, a mouth and eyes.

Will we never see those happy days reborn when the people did not dabble in philosophizing, but when a Plato, a Thales, a Pythagoras, taken with an ardent desire to know, undertook the greatest voyages merely to inform themselves, and went far away to shake off the yoke of national prejudices, in order to learn to know men by their similarities and their differences, and to acquire those sorts of universal knowledge that are exclusively those of a single century or country, but which, since they are of all times and all places, are, as it were, the common science of the wise?

We admire the splendor of some curious men who, at great expense, made or caused to be made voyages to the Orient with learned men and painters, in order to sketch hovels and to decipher or copy inscriptions. But I have trouble conceiving how, in a century where people take pride in fine sorts of knowledge, there are not to be found two closely united men—rich, one in money, the other in genius, both loving glory and aspiring for immortality—one of whom sacrifices twenty thousand crowns of his goods and the other ten years of his life for a famous voyage around the world, in order to study, not always rocks and plants, but, for once, men and mores, and who, after so many centuries used to measure and examine the house, would finally be of a mind to want to know its inhabitants.

The academicians who have traveled through the northern parts of Europe and the southern parts of America had for their object to visit them more as geometers than as philosophers. Nevertheless, since they were both simultaneously, we cannot regard as utterly unknown the regions that have been seen and described by La Condamine and Maupertuis. The jeweler Chardin, who has traveled like Plato, has left nothing to be said about Persia. China appeared to have been well observed by the Jesuits. Kempfer gives a passable idea of what little he has seen in Japan. Except for these reports, we know nothing about the peoples of the East Indies, who have been visited exclusively by Europeans interested more in filling their purses than their heads. All of Africa and its numerous inhabitants, as unique in character as in color, are yet to be examined. The entire earth is covered with nations of which we know only the names, and we dabble in judging the human race! Let us suppose a Montesquieu, a Buffon, a Diderot, a Duclos, a d'Alembert, a Condillac, or men of that ilk traveling in order to inform their compatriots, observing and describing as they know how to do, Turkey, Egypt, Barbary, the empire of Morocco, Guinea, the land of the Bantus, the interior of Africa and its eastern coastlines, the Malabars, Mogul, the banks of the Ganges, the kingdoms of Siam, Peru, and Ava, China, Tartary, and especially Japan; then in the other hemisphere, Mexico, Peru, Chile, the straits of Magellan, not to forget the Patagonias true or false, Tucuman, Paraguay (if possible), Brazil; finally the Caribbean Islands, Florida, and all the savage countries—the most important voyage of all and the one that should be embarked upon with the greatest care. Let us suppose that these new Hercules, back from these memorable treks, then wrote at leisure the natural, moral, and political history of what they would have seen; we ourselves would see a new world sally forth from their pen, and we would thus learn to know our own. I say that when such observers will affirm of an animal that it is a man and of another that it is a beast, we will have to believe them. But it would be terribly simpleminded to defer in this to unsophisticated travelers, concerning whom we will sometimes be tempted to put the same question that they dabble at resolving concerning other animals.

Appendix 3: Note [On the Views of John Locke]

I find in Locke's *Civil Government* an objection which seems to me too specious for me to be permitted to hide it. "Since the purpose of the society between male and female," says this philosopher, "is not merely to procreate, but to continue the species, this society should last, even after procreation, at least as long as it is necessary for the nurture and support of the procreated, that is to say, until they are capable of seeing to their needs on their own. This rule, which the infinite wisdom of the creator has established upon the works of his hands, we see creatures inferior to man observing constantly and strictly. In those animals which live on grass, the society between male and female lasts no longer than each act of copulation, because, the teats of the mother being sufficient to feed the young until they are able to feed on grass, the male is content to beget and no longer mingles with the female or the young, to whose sustenance he has nothing to contribute. But as far as beasts of prey are concerned, the society lasts longer, because, with the mother being unable to see to her own sustenance and at the same time feed her young by means of her prey alone (which is a more laborious and more dangerous way of taking in nourishment than by feeding on grass), the assistance of the male is utterly necessary for the maintenance of their common family (if one may use that term), which is able to subsist to the point where it can go hunt for prey only through the efforts of the male and the female. We note the same thing in all the birds (with the exception of some domestic birds which are found in places where the continual abundance of nourishment exempts the male from the effort of feeding the young). It is clear that when the young in their nest need food, the male and female bring it to them until the young there are capable of flying and seeing to their own sustenance.

"And, in my opinion, herein lies the principal, if not the only reason why the male and the female in mankind are bound to a longer period of society than is undertaken by other creatures: namely, that the female is capable of conceiving and is ordinarily pregnant again and has a new child long before the previous child is in a position to do without the help of its parents and can take care of itself. Thus, since the father is bound to take care of those he has produced, and to take that care for a long time, he is also under an obligation to continue in conjugal society with the same woman by whom he has had them, and to remain in that society much longer than other creatures, whose young being capable of subsisting by themselves before the time comes for a new procreation, the bond of the male and female breaks of its own accord, and they are both at complete liberty, until such time as that season, which usually solicits the animals to join with one another, obliges them to choose new mates. And here we cannot help admiring the wisdom of the creator, who, having given to man the qualities needed to provide for the future as well as for the present, has willed and has brought it about that the society of man should last longer than that of the male and female among other creatures, so that thereby the industry of man and woman might be stimulated more, and that their interests might be better united, with a view to making provisions for their children and to leaving them their goods—nothing being more to the detriment of the children than an uncertain and vague conjunction, or an easy and frequent dissolution of the conjugal society." [Locke, Second Treatise, 7. Here is presented not Locke's original text, but a retranslation into English of Rousseau's French version.]

The same love of truth which has made me to set forth sincerely this objection, moves me to accompany it with some remarks, if not to resolve it, at least to clarify it.

1. I will observe first that moral proofs do not have great force in matters of physics, and that they serve more to explain existing facts than to establish the real existence of those facts. Now such is the type of proof that M. Locke employs in the passage I have just quoted; for although it may be advantageous to the human species for the union

between man and woman to be permanent, it does not follow that it has been thus established by nature; otherwise it would be necessary to say that it also instituted civil society, the arts, commerce, and all that is asserted to be useful to men.

2. I do not know where M. Locke has found that among animals of prey, the society of the male and female lasts longer than does the society of those that live on grass, and that the former assists the latter to feed the young; for it is not manifest that the dog, the cat, the bear, or the wolf recognize their female better than the horse, the ram, the bull, the stag, or all the other quadruped animals do theirs. On the contrary, it seems that if the assistance of the male were necessary to the female to preserve her young, it would be particularly in the species that live only on grass, because a long period of time is needed by the mother to graze, and during that entire interval she is forced to neglect her brood, whereas the prey of a female bear or wolf is devoured in an instant, and, without suffering hunger, she has more time to nurse her young. This line of reasoning is confirmed by an observation upon the relative number of teats and young which distinguishes carnivorous from frugivorous species, and of which I have spoken in Note 8. If this observation is accurate and general, since a woman has only two teats and rarely has more than one child at a time, this is one more strong reason for doubting that the human species is naturally carnivorous. Thus it seems that, in order to draw Locke's conclusion, it would be necessary to reverse completely his reasoning. There is no more solidity in the same distinction when it is applied to birds. For who could be persuaded that the union of the male and the female is more durable among vultures and crows than among turtle-doves? We have two species of domestic birds, the duck and the pigeon, which furnish us with examples directly contrary to the system of this author. The pigeon, which lives solely on grain, remains united to its female, and they feed their young in common. The duck, whose voraciousness is known, recognizes neither his female nor his young, and provides no help in their sustenance. And among hens, a species hardly less carnivorous, we do not observe that the rooster bothers himself in the least with the brood. And if in the other species the male shares with the female the care of feeding the young, it is because birds, which at first are unable to fly and which the mother cannot nurse, are much less in a position to get along without the help of the father than are quadrupeds, for which the mother's teat is sufficient, at least for a time.

3. There is much uncertainty about the principal fact that serves as a basis for all of M. Locke's reasoning; for in order to know whether, as he asserts, in the pure state of nature the female ordinarily is pregnant again and has a new child long before the preceding one could see to its needs for itself, it would be necessary to perform experiments that M. Locke surely did not perform and that no one is in a position to perform. The continual cohabitation of husband and wife is so near an occasion for being exposed to a new pregnancy that it is very difficult to believe that the chance encounter or the mere impulsion of temperament produced such frequent effects in the pure state of nature as in that of conjugal society: a slowness that would contribute perhaps toward making the children more robust, and that, moreover, might be compensated by the power to conceive, prolonged to a greater age in the women who would have abused it less in their youth. As to children, there are several reasons for believing that their forces and their organs develop much later among us than they did in the primitive state of which I am speaking. The original weakness which they derive from the constitution of the parents, the cares taken to envelop and constrain all of their members, the softness in which they are raised, perhaps the use of milk other than that of their mother, everything contradicts and slows down in them the initial progress of nature. The heed they are forced to pay to a thousand things on which their attention is continually fixed, while no exercise is given to their bodily forces, can also bring about considerable deflection from their growth. Thus, if, instead of first overworking and exhausting their minds in a thousand ways, their bodies were allowed to be exercised by the continual movements that nature seems to demand of them, it is to be believed that they would be in a much better position to walk and to provide for their needs by themselves.

4. Finally, M. Locke at most proves that there could well be in a man a motive for remaining attached to a woman when she has a child but in no way does he prove that the man must have been attached to her before the childbirth and during the nine months of pregnancy. If a given woman is indifferent to the man during those nine months, if she even becomes unknown to him, why will he help her after childbirth? Why will he help her to raise a child that he does not know belongs to him alone, and whose birth he has neither decided upon nor foreseen? Evidently M. Locke presumes what is in question, for it is not a matter of knowing why the man will remain attached to the woman after childbirth, but why he will be attached to her after concep-

tion. Once his appetite is satisfied, the man has no further need for a given woman, nor the woman for a given man. The man does not have the least care or perhaps the least idea of the consequences of his action. The one goes off in one direction, the other in another, and there is no likelihood that at the end of nine months they have the memory of having known one another. For this type of memory, by which one individual gives preference to another for the act of generation, requires, as I prove in the text, more progress or corruption in human understanding than may be supposed in man in the state of animality we are dealing with here. Another woman can therefore satisfy the new desires of the man as congenially as the one he has already known, and another man in the same manner satisfy the woman, supposing she is impelled by the same appetite during the time of pregnancy, about which one can reasonably be in doubt. And if in the state of nature the woman no longer feels the passion of love after the conception of the child, the obstacle to her society with the man thus becomes much greater still, since she then has no further need either for the man who has made her pregnant or for anyone else. There is not, therefore, in the man any reason to seek the same woman, or in the woman any reason to seek the same man. Thus Locke's reasoning falls in ruin, and all the dialectic of this philosopher has not shielded him from the mistake committed by Hobbes and others. They had to explain a fact of the state of nature, that is to say, of a state where men lived in isolation and where a given man did not have any motive for living in proximity to another given man, nor perhaps did a given group of men have a motive for living in proximity to another given group of men, which is much worse. And they gave no thought to transporting themselves beyond the centuries of society, that is to say, of those times when men always have a reason for living in proximity to one another, and when a given man often has a reason for living in proximity to a given man or woman.

Appendix 4: Note [On Humans Living in an Intermediate Stage]

It is something extremely remarkable that, for the many years that the Europeans torment themselves in order to acclimate the savages of various countries to their lifestyle, they have not yet been able to win over a single one of them, not even by means of Christianity; for our missionaries sometimes turn them into Christians, but never into civilized men. Nothing can overcome the invincible repugnance they have against appropriating our mores and living in our way. If these poor savages are as unhappy as is alleged, by what inconceivable depravity of judgment do they constantly refuse to civilize themselves in imitation of us, or to learn to live happily among us; whereas one reads in a thousand places that the French and other Europeans have voluntarily taken refuge among those nations, and have spent their entire lives there, no longer able to leave so strange a lifestyle; and whereas we even see level-headed missionaries regret with tenderness the calm and innocent days they have spent among those much scorned peoples? If one replies that they do not have enough enlightenment to make a sound judgment about their state and ours, I will reply that the reckoning of happiness is less an affair of reason than of sentiment. Moreover, this reply can be turned against us with still greater force; for there is a greater distance between our ideas and the frame of mind one needed to be in in order to conceive the taste which the savages find in their lifestyle, than between the ideas of savages and those that can make them conceive our lifestyle. In fact, after a few observations it is easy for them to see that all our labors are directed toward but two objects: namely, the conveniences of life for oneself and esteem among others. But what are the means by which we are to imagine the sort of pleasure a savage takes in spending his life alone amidst the woods, or fishing, or blowing into a sorry-looking flute, without ever knowing how to derive a single tone from it and without bothering himself to learn?

Savages have frequently been brought to Paris, London and other cities; people have been eager to display our luxury, our wealth, and all our most useful and curious arts. None of this has ever excited in them anything but a stupid admiration, without the least stirring of covetousness. I recall, among others, the story of a chief of some North Americans who was brought to the court of England about thirty years ago. A thousand things were made to pass before his eye in an attempt to give him some present that could please him, but nothing was found about which he seemed to care. Our weapons seemed heavy and cumbersome to him, our shoes hurt his feet, our clothes restricted him; he rejected everything. Finally, it was noticed that, having taken a wool blanket, he seemed to take some pleasure in wrapping it around his shoulders. You will agree at least, someone immediately said to him, on the usefulness of this furnishing? Yes, he replies, this seems to me to be nearly as good as an animal skin. However, he would not have said that, had he worn them both in the rain.

Perhaps someone will say to me that it is habit which, in attaching everyone to his lifestyle, prevents savages from realizing what is good in ours. And at that rate, it must at least appear quite extraordinary that habit has more force in maintaining the savages in the taste for their misery than the Europeans in the enjoyment of their felicity. But to give to this last objection a reply to which there is not a word to make in reply, without adducing all the young savages that people have tried in vain to civilize, without speaking of the Greenlanders and the inhabitants of Iceland, whom people have tried to raise and feed in Denmark, and all of whom sadness and despair caused to perish, whether from languor or in the sea when they attempted to regain their homeland by swimming back to it, I will be content to cite a single, well-documented example, which I give to the admirers of European civilization to examine.

"All the efforts of the Dutch missionaries at the Cape of Good Hope have never been able to convert a single Hottentot. Van der Stel, Governor of the Cape, having taken one from infancy, had raised him in the principles of the Christian religion and in the practice of the customs of Europe. He was richly clothed; he was taught several languages and his progress corresponded very closely to the care that was taken for his education. Having great hopes for his wit, the Governor sent him to the Indies with a commissioner general who employed him usefully in the affairs of the company. He returned to the Cape after the death of the commissioner. A few days after his return, on a visit he made to some of his Hottentot relatives, he made the decision to strip himself of his European dress in order to clothe himself with a sheepskin. He returned to the fort in this new outfit, carrying a bundle containing his old clothes, and, on presenting them to the Governor, he made the following speech to him: *Please, sir, be so kind as to pay heed to the fact that I forever renounce this clothing. I also renounce the Christian religion for the rest of my life. My resolution is to live and die in the religion, ways and customs of my ancestors. The only favor I ask of you is that you let me keep the necklace and cutlass I am wearing. I will keep them for love of you.* Thereupon, without waiting for Van der Stel's reply, he escaped by taking flight and was never seen again at the Cape." *Histoire des Voyages [History of Voyages]*, Volume 5.

◆ ◆ ◆ ◆ ◆

On the Social Contract or Principles of Political Right (1762)

—foederis aequas
Dicamus leges

—Aeneid, XI[1]

Foreword

This little treatise is part of a longer work I undertook some time ago without taking stock of my abilities, and have long since abandoned. Of the various selections that could have been drawn from what had been completed, this is the most considerable, and, it appears to me, the one least unworthy of being offered to the public. The rest no longer exists.

Book I

I want to inquire whether there can be some legitimate and sure rule of administration in the civil order, taking men as they are and laws as they might be. I will always try in this inquiry to bring together what right permits with what interest prescribes, so that justice and utility do not find themselves at odds with one another.

I begin without demonstrating the importance of my subject. It will be asked if I am a prince or a legislator that I should be writing about politics. I answer that I am neither, and that is why I write about politics. Were I a prince or a legislator, I would not waste my time saying what ought to be done. I would do it or keep quiet.

Born a citizen of a free state and a member of the sovereign,[2] the right to vote is enough to impose upon me the duty to instruct myself in public affairs, however little influence my voice may have in them. Happy am I, for every time I meditate on governments, I always find new reasons in my inquiries for loving that of my country.

Chapter 1: Subject of the First Book

Man is born free, and everywhere he is in chains. He who believes himself the master of others does not escape being more of a slave than they. How did this change take place? I have no idea. What can render it legitimate? I believe I can answer this question.

Were I to consider only force and the effect that flows from it, I would say that so long as a people is constrained to obey and does obey, it does well. As soon as it can shake off the yoke and does shake it off, it does even better. For by recovering its liberty by means of the same right that stole it, either the populace is justified in getting it back or else those who took it away were not justified in their actions. But the social order is a sacred right which serves as a foundation for all other rights. Nevertheless, this right does not come from nature. It is therefore founded upon convention. Before coming to that, I ought to substantiate what I just claimed.

Chapter 2: Of the First Societies

The most ancient of all societies and the only natural one, is that of the family. Even so children remain bound to their father only so long as they need him to take care of them. As soon as the need ceases, the natural bond is dissolved. Once the children are freed from the obedience they owed the father and their father is freed from the care he owed his children, all return equally to independence. If they continue to remain united, this no longer takes place naturally but voluntarily, and the family maintains itself only by means of convention.

This common liberty is one consequence of the nature of man. Its first law is to see to his maintenance; its first concerns are those he owes himself; and, as soon as he reaches the age of reason, since he alone is the judge of the proper means of taking care of himself, he thereby becomes his own master.

The family therefore is, so to speak, the prototype of political societies; the leader is the image of the father, the populace is the image of the children, and, since all are born equal and free, none give up their liberty except for their utility. The entire difference consists in the fact that in the family the love of the father for his children repays him for the care he takes for them, while in the state, where the leader does not have love for his peoples, the pleasure of commanding takes the place of this feeling.

---

1   *foederis aequas / Dicamus leges*   Latin: "In an equitable federation, we will make the laws." Virgil, *Aeneid*, 11.321.

2   *the sovereign*   See the last paragraph of Book I, Chapter 6, and the following chapter, below, for an explanation of what Rousseau means by this.

Grotius[1] denies that all human power is established for the benefit of the governed, citing slavery as an example. His usual method of reasoning is always to present fact as a proof of right.[2] A more logical method could be used, but not one more favorable to tyrants.

According to Grotius, it is therefore doubtful whether the human race belongs to a hundred men, or whether these hundred men belong to the human race. And throughout his book he appears to lean toward the former view. This is Hobbes'[3] position as well. On this telling, the human race is divided into herds of cattle, each one having its own leader who guards it in order to devour it.

Just as a herdsman possesses a nature superior to that of his herd, the herdsmen of men who are the leaders, also have a nature superior to that of their peoples. According to Philo, Caligula[4] reasoned thus, concluding quite properly from this analogy that kings were gods, or that the peoples were beasts.

Caligula's reasoning coincides with that of Hobbes and Grotius. Aristotle,[5] before all the others, had also said that men are by no means equal by nature, but that some were born for slavery and others for domination.

Aristotle was right, but he took the effect for the cause. Every man born in slavery is born for slavery; nothing is more certain. In their chains slaves lose everything, even the desire to escape. They love their servitude the way the companions of Ulysses loved their degradation.[6] If there are slaves by nature, it is because there have been slaves against nature. Force has produced the first slaves; their cowardice has perpetuated them.

I have said nothing about King Adam or Emperor Noah, father of three great monarchs who partitioned the universe, as did the children of Saturn,[7] whom some have believed they recognize in them. I hope I will be appreciated for this moderation, for since I am a direct descendent of these princes, and perhaps of the eldest branch, how am I to know whether, after the verification of titles, I might not find myself the legitimate king of the human race? Be that as it may, we cannot deny that Adam was the sovereign of the world, just as Robinson Crusoe was sovereign of his island,[8] so long as he was its sole inhabitant. And the advantage this empire had was that the monarch, securely on his throne, had no rebellions, wars or conspirators to fear.

Chapter 3: On the Right of the Strongest

The strongest is never strong enough to be master all the time, unless he transforms force into right and obedience into duty. Hence the right of the strongest, a right that seems like something intended ironically and is actually established as a basic principle. But will no one explain this word to me? Force is a physical power; I fail to see what morality can result from its effects. To give in to force is an act of necessity, not of will. At most, it is an act of prudence. In what sense could it be a duty?

Let us suppose for a moment that there is such a thing as this alleged right. I maintain that all that results from it is an inexplicable mish-mash. For once force produces the right, the effect changes places with the cause. Every force that is superior to the first succeeds to its right. As soon as one can disobey with impunity, one can do so legitimately; and since the strongest is always right, the only thing to do is to make oneself the strongest. For what kind of right is it that perishes when the force on which it is based ceases? If one must obey because of force, one need not do so out of duty; and if one is no longer forced to obey one is no

---

1   *Grotius*   Hugo Grotius (1583–1645), Dutch jurist and writer. Rousseau here refers to *The Law of War and Peace*, Book 1.

2   *proof of right*   [Rousseau's note] "Learned research on public right is often nothing more than the history of ancient abuses, and taking a lot of trouble to study them too closely gets one nowhere." *Treatise on the Interests of France Along With Her Neighbors*, by the Marquis [Pierre de Voyer] d'Argenson [1626–1710]. This is just what Grotius has done.

3   *Hobbes*   Thomas Hobbes (1588–1679), English philosopher.

4   *Philo, Caligula*   Philo (20 BCE–50 CE), Greek-Jewish philosopher, was sent as an envoy to the Court of the Roman Emperor Gaius Caligula by the Alexandrian (Egyptian) Jews in 40 CE. Philo wrote about the emperor in his *Embassy to Gaius*.

5   *Aristotle*   (384–322 BCE) The reference here is *Politics*, 1.2 in which Aristotle argues that some people are "natural" slaves.

6   *companions of Ulysses ... degradation*   [Rousseau's note] See a short treatise of Plutarch entitled "That Animals Reason." [Plutarch (Mestrius Plutarchus c. 46–127 CE), was a Greek historian and essayist. The story of Ulysses' companions on his voyage is in Homer's *Odyssey*.]

7   *the children of Saturn*   In Greek mythology, Saturn destroyed his children who, it had been foretold, would overthrow him, but one child, Jupiter (Zeus), escaped to become king of the Gods.

8   *Robinson Crusoe ... island*   In the famous 1719 novel bearing his name by Daniel Defoe (1660?–1731), Robinson Crusoe is a survivor of a shipwreck cast ashore on an island. He was not the sole inhabitant on his island—there were other castaways and some natives.

longer obliged. Clearly then, this word "right" adds nothing to force. It is utterly meaningless here.

Obey the powers that be. If that means giving in to force, the precept is sound, but superfluous. I reply it will never be violated. All power comes from God—I admit it—but so does every disease. Does this mean that calling in a physician is prohibited? If a brigand takes me by surprise at the edge of a wooded area, is it not only the case that I must surrender my purse, but even that I am in good conscience bound to surrender it, if I were able to withhold it? After all, the pistol he holds is also a power.

Let us then agree that force does not bring about right, and that one is obliged to obey only legitimate powers. Thus my original question keeps returning.

Chapter 4: On Slavery

Since no man has a natural authority over his fellow man, and since force does not give rise to any right, conventions therefore remain the basis of all legitimate authority among men.

If, says Grotius, a private individual can alienate his liberty and turn himself into the slave of a master,[1] why could not an entire people alienate its liberty and turn itself into the subject of a king? There are many equivocal words here which need explanation, but let us confine ourselves to the word *alienate*. To alienate is to give or to sell. A man who makes himself the slave of someone else does not give himself; he sells himself, at least for his subsistence. But why does a people sell itself? Far from furnishing his subjects with their subsistence, a king derives his own from them alone, and, according to Rabelais,[2] a king does not live cheaply. Do subjects then give their persons on the condition that their estate will also be taken? I fail to see what remains for them to preserve.

It will be said that the despot assures his subjects of civil tranquility. Very well. But what do they gain, if the wars his ambition drags them into, if his insatiable greed, if the oppressive demands caused by his ministers occasion more grief for his subjects than their own dissensions would have done? What do they gain, if this very tranquility is one of their miseries? A tranquil life is also had in dungeons; is

that enough to make them desirable? The Greeks who were locked up in the Cyclops'[3] cave lived a tranquil existence as they awaited their turn to be devoured.

To say that a man gives himself gratuitously is to say something absurd and inconceivable. Such an act is illegitimate and null, if only for the fact that he who commits it does not have his wits about him. To say the same thing of an entire populace is to suppose a populace composed of madmen. Madness does not bring about right.

Even if each person can alienate himself, he cannot alienate his children. They are born men and free. Their liberty belongs to them; they alone have the right to dispose of it. Before they have reached the age of reason, their father can, in their name, stipulate conditions for their maintenance and for their well-being. But he cannot give them irrevocably and unconditionally, for such a gift is contrary to the ends of nature and goes beyond the rights of paternity. For an arbitrary government to be legitimate, it would therefore be necessary in each generation for the people to be master of its acceptance or rejection. But in that event this government would no longer be arbitrary.

Renouncing one's liberty is renouncing one's dignity as a man, the rights of humanity and even its duties. There is no possible compensation for anyone who renounces everything. Such a renunciation is incompatible with the nature of man. Removing all morality from his actions is tantamount to taking away all liberty from his will. Finally, it is a vain and contradictory convention to stipulate absolute authority on one side and a limitless obedience on the other. Is it not clear that no commitments are made to a person from whom one has the right to demand everything? And does this condition alone not bring with it, without equivalent or exchange, the nullity of the act? For what right would my slave have against me, given that all he has belongs to me, and that, since his right is my right, my having a right against myself makes no sense?

Grotius and others derive from war another origin for the alleged right of slavery.[4] Since, according to them, the victor has the right to kill the vanquished, these latter can repurchase their lives at the price of their liberty—a convention all the more legitimate, since it turns a profit for both of them.

---

1   *Grotius ... master* See Hugo Grotius, *The Law of War and Peace*, Book 1.

2   *Rabelais* François Rabelais (c. 1494–1553), French satirical writer.

3   *Cyclops* Race of mythical giants with one central eye. In Homer's *Odyssey*, Odysseus and his men are held captive in the cave of one of the Cyclops, who begins eating them one by one.

4   *Grotius ... slavery* See Hugo Grotius, *The Law of War and Peace*, Book 3, Chapter 7.

But clearly this alleged right to kill the vanquished does not in any way derive from the state of war. Men are not naturally enemies, for the simple reason that men living in their original state of independence do not have sufficiently constant relationships among themselves to bring about either a state of peace or a state of war. It is the relationship between things and not that between men that brings about war. And since this state of war cannot come into existence from simple personal relations, but only from real [proprietary] relations,[1] a private war between one man and another can exist neither in the state of nature, where there is no constant property, nor in the social state, where everything is under the authority of the laws.

Fights between private individuals, duels, encounters are not acts which produce a state. And with regard to private wars, authorized by the ordinances of King Louis IX of France[2] and suspended by the Peace of God,[3] they are abuses of feudal government, an absurd system if there ever was one, contrary to the principles of natural right and to all sound polity.

War is not therefore a relationship between one man and another, but a relationship between one state and another. In war private individuals are enemies only incidentally: not as men or even as citizens, but as soldiers; not as members of the homeland but as its defenders. <The Romans, who had a better understanding of and a greater respect for the right of war than any other nation, carried their scruples so far in this regard that a citizen was not allowed to serve as a volunteer unless he had expressly committed himself against the enemy and against a specifically named enemy. When a legion in which Cato the Younger first served had been reorganized, Cato the Elder[4] wrote Popilius that if he wanted his grandson to continue to serve under him, he would have to make him swear the military oath afresh, since, with the first one having been annulled, he could no longer take up arms against the enemy. And this very same Cato wrote his son to take care to avoid going into battle without swearing this military oath afresh. I know the siege of Clusium[5]

and other specific cases can be raised as counter-examples to this, but for my part I cite laws and customs. The Romans were the ones who transgressed their laws least often, and are the only ones to have had such noble laws.>[6] Finally, each state can have as enemies only other states and not men, since there can be no real relationship between things of disparate natures.

This principle is even in conformity with the established maxims of all times and with the constant practice of all civilized peoples. Declarations of war are warnings not so much to powers as to their subjects. The foreigner (be he king, private individual, or a people) who robs, kills or detains subjects of another prince without declaring war on the prince, is not an enemy but a brigand. Even in the midst of war a just prince rightly appropriates to himself everything in an enemy country belonging to the public, but respects the person and goods of private individuals. He respects the rights upon which his own rights are founded. Since the purpose of war is the destruction of the enemy state, one has the right to kill the defenders of that state so long as they bear arms. But as soon as they lay down their arms and surrender, they cease to be enemies or instruments of the enemy. They return to being simply men; and one no longer has a right to their lives. Sometimes a state can be killed without a single one of its members being killed. For war does not grant a right that is unnecessary to its purpose. These principles are not those of Grotius. They are not based on the authority of poets. Rather they are derived from the nature of things; they are based on reason.

As to the right of conquest, the only basis it has is the law of the strongest. If war does not give the victor the right to massacre the vanquished peoples, this right (which he does not have) cannot be the basis for the right to enslave them. One has the right to kill the enemy only when one cannot enslave him. The right to enslave him does not therefore derive the right to kill him. Hence it is an iniquitous exchange to make him buy his life, to which no one has any right, at the price of his liberty. In establishing the right of life and death on the right of slavery, and the right of slavery on the right of life and death, is it not clear that one falls into a vicious circle?

Even if we were to suppose that there were this terrible right to kill everyone, I maintain that neither a person enslaved during wartime nor a conquered people bears any

---

1   *real [proprietary] relations*   Relations having to do with exclusive ownership of property.

2   *King Louis IX of France*   This king (1215–70), known as Saint Louis, led two failed crusades to the Holy Land.

3   *the Peace of God*   Supposedly perpetual truce arranged by the medieval church to end hostilities between warring lords.

4   *Cato the Elder*   Marcus Porcius Cato (234–149 BCE) Roman statesman.

5   *siege of Clusium*   Clusium, a Roman city in northern Italy, was besieged by the Gauls in the early fourth century BCE.

6   *<The Romans ... noble laws>*   Material within the symbols < > was added by Rousseau to the 1782 edition.

obligation whatever toward its master, except to obey him for as long as it is forced to do so. In taking the equivalent of his life, the victor has done him no favor. Instead of killing him unprofitably he kills him usefully. Hence, far from the victor having acquired any authority over him beyond force, the state of war subsists between them just as before. Their relationship itself is the effect of war, and the usage of the right to war does not suppose any peace treaty. They have made a convention. Fine. But this convention, far from destroying the state of war, presupposes its continuation.

Thus, from every point of view, the right of slavery is null, not simply because it is illegitimate, but because it is absurd and meaningless. These words, *slavery* and *right*, are contradictory. They are mutually exclusive. Whether it is the statement of one man to another man, or one man to a people, the following sort of talk will always be equally nonsensical. *I make a convention with you which is wholly at your expense and wholly to my advantage; and, for as long as it pleases me, I will observe it and so will you.*

Chapter 5: That It Is Always Necessary to Return to a First Convention

Even if I were to grant all that I have thus far refuted, the supporters of despotism would not be any better off. There will always be a great difference between subduing a multitude and ruling a society. If scattered men, however many they may be, were successively enslaved by a single individual, I see nothing there but a master and slaves; I do not see a people and its leader. It is, if you will, an aggregation, but not an association. There is neither a public good nor a body politic there. Even if that man had enslaved half the world, he is always just a private individual. His interest, separated from that of others, is never anything but a private interest. If this same man is about to die, after his passing his empire remains scattered and disunited, just as an oak tree dissolves and falls into a pile of ashes after fire has consumed it.

"A people," says Grotius, "can give itself to a king."[1] According to Grotius, therefore, a people is a people before it gives itself to a king. This gift itself is a civil act; it presupposes a public deliberation. Thus, before examining the act whereby a people chooses a king, it would be well to examine the act whereby a people is a people. For since this act is necessarily prior to the other, it is the true foundation of society.

In fact, if there were no prior convention, then, unless the vote were unanimous, what would become of the minority's obligation to submit to the majority's choice, and where do one hundred who want a master get the right to vote for ten who do not? The law of majority rule is itself an established convention, and presupposes unanimity on at least one occasion.

Chapter 6: On the Social Compact

I suppose that men have reached the point where obstacles that are harmful to their maintenance in the state of nature gain the upper hand by their resistance to the forces that each individual can bring to bear to maintain himself in that state. Such being the case, that original state cannot subsist any longer, and the human race would perish if it did not alter its mode of existence.

For since men cannot engender new forces, but merely unite and direct existing ones, they have no other means of maintaining themselves but to form by aggregation a sum of forces that could gain the upper hand over the resistance, so that their forces are directed by means of a single moving power and made to act in concert.

This sum of forces cannot come into being without the cooperation of many. But since each man's force and liberty are the primary instruments of his maintenance, how is he going to engage them without hurting himself and without neglecting the care that he owes himself? This difficulty, seen in terms of my subject, can be stated in the following terms:

"Find a form of association which defends and protects with all common forces the person and goods of each associate, and by means of which each one, while uniting with all, nevertheless obeys only himself and remains as free as before?" This is the fundamental problem for which the social contract provides the solution.

The clauses of this contract are so determined by the nature of the act that the least modification renders them vain and ineffectual, that, although perhaps they have never been formally promulgated, they are everywhere the same, everywhere tacitly accepted and acknowledged. Once the social compact is violated, each person then regains his first rights and resumes his natural liberty, while losing the conventional liberty for which he renounced it.

---

1   *A people ... a king* See Grotius, *The Law of War and Peace*, Book 1, Chapter 3.

These clauses, properly understood, are all reducible to a single one, namely the total alienation of each associate, together with all of his rights, to the entire community. For first of all, since each person gives himself whole and entire, the condition is equal for everyone; and since the condition is equal for everyone, no one has an interest in making it burdensome for the others.

Moreover, since the alienation is made without reservation, the union is as perfect as possible, and no associate has anything further to demand. For if some rights remained with private individuals, in the absence of any common superior who could decide between them and the public, each person would eventually claim to be his own judge in all things, since he is on some point his own judge. The state of nature would subsist and the association would necessarily become tyrannical or hollow.

Finally, in giving himself to all, each person gives himself to no one. And since there is no associate over whom he does not acquire the same right that he would grant others over himself, he gains the equivalent of everything he loses, along with a greater amount of force to preserve what he has.

If, therefore, one eliminates from the social compact whatever is not essential to it, one will find that it is reducible to the following terms. *Each of us places his person and all his power in common under the supreme direction of the general will; and as one we receive each member as an indivisible part of the whole.*

At once, in place of the individual person of each contracting party, this act of association produces a moral and collective body composed of as many members as there are voices in the assembly, which receives from this same act its unity, its common *self,* its life and its will. This public person, formed thus by union of all the others formerly took the name *city*,[1] and at present takes the name *republic* or

body politic, which is called *state* by its members when it is passive, *sovereign* when it is active, *power* when compared to others like itself. As to the associates, they collectively take the name *people*; individually they are called *citizens*, insofar as participants in the sovereign authority, and *subjects*, insofar as they are subjected to the laws of the state. But these terms are often confused and mistaken for one another. It is enough to know how to distinguish them when they are used with absolute precision.

Chapter 7: On the Sovereign

This formula shows that the act of association includes a reciprocal commitment between the public and private individuals, and that each individual, contracting, as it were, with himself, finds himself under a twofold commitment: namely as a member of the sovereign to private individuals, and as a member of the state toward the sovereign. But the maxim of civil law that no one is held to commitments made to himself cannot be applied here, for there is a considerable difference between being obligated to oneself, or to a whole of which one is a part.

It must be further noted that the public deliberation that can obligate all the subjects to the sovereign, owing to the two different relationships in which each of them is viewed, cannot, for the opposite reason, obligate the sovereign to itself, and that consequently it is contrary to the nature of the body politic that the sovereign impose upon itself a law it could not break. Since the sovereign can be considered under but one single relationship, it is then in the position of a private individual contracting with himself. Whence it is apparent that there neither is nor can be any type of fundamental law that is obligatory for the people as a body, not even the social contract. This does not mean that the whole body cannot perfectly well commit itself to another body with respect to things that do not infringe on this contract. For in regard to the foreigner, it becomes a simple being, an individual.

---

1   *city* [Rousseau's note] The true meaning of this word is almost entirely lost on modern men. Most of them mistake a town for a city and a townsman for a citizen. They do not know that houses make a town but citizens make a city. Once this mistake cost the Carthaginians dearly. I have not found in my reading that the title of *citizen* has ever been given to the subjects of a prince, not even in ancient times to the Macedonians or in our own time to the English, although they are closer to liberty than all the others. Only the French adopt this name *citizen* with complete familiarity, since they have no true idea of its meaning, as can be seen from their dictionaries. If this were not the case, they would become guilty of treason for using it. For them, this name expresses a virtue and not a right. When Bodin [Jean Bodin (1530–96) *Les*

six livres de la République, 1,6] wanted to speak about our citizens and townsmen, he committed a terrible blunder when he mistook the one group for the other. M. *[Jean d'Alembert (1717–83), "Geneva" in Encyclopédie 7] was not in error, and in his article entitled *Geneva* he has carefully distinguished the four orders of men (even five, counting ordinary foreigners) who are in our towns, and of whom only two make up the republic. No other French author I am aware of has grasped the true meaning of the word *citizen*.

However, since the body politic or the sovereign derives its being exclusively from the sanctity of the contract, it can never obligate itself, not even to another power, to do anything that derogates from the original act, such as alienating some portion of itself or submitting to another sovereign. Violation of the act whereby it exists would be self-annihilation, and whatever is nothing produces nothing.

As soon as this multitude is thus united in a body, one cannot harm one of the members without attacking the whole body. It is even less likely that the body can be harmed without the members feeling it. Thus duty and interest equally obligate the two parties to come to one another's aid, and the same men should seek to combine in this two-fold relationship all the advantages that result from it.

For since the sovereign is formed entirely from the private individuals who make it up, it neither has nor could have an interest contrary to theirs. Hence, the sovereign power has no need to offer a guarantee to its subjects, since it is impossible for a body to want to harm all of its members, and, as we will see later, it cannot harm any one of them in particular. The sovereign, by the mere fact that it exists, is always all that it should be.

But the same thing cannot be said of the subjects in relation to the sovereign, for which, despite their common interest, their commitments would be without substance if it did not find ways of being assured of their fidelity.

In fact, each individual can, as a man, have a private will contrary to or different from the general will that he has as a citizen. His private interest can speak to him in an entirely different manner than the common interest. His absolute and naturally independent existence can cause him to envisage what he owes the common cause as a gratuitous contribution, the loss of which will be less harmful to others than its payment is burdensome to him. And in viewing the moral person which constitutes the state as a being of reason because it is not a man, he would enjoy the rights of a citizen without wanting to fulfill the duties of a subject, an injustice whose growth would bring about the ruin of the body politic.

Thus, in order for the social compact to avoid being an empty formula, it tacitly entails the commitment—which alone can give force to the others—that whoever refuses to obey the general will will be forced to do so by the entire body. This means merely that he will be forced to be free. For this is the sort of condition that, by giving each citizen to the homeland, guarantees him against all personal dependence—a condition that produces the skill and the performance of the political machine, and which alone bestows legitimacy upon civil commitments. Without it such commitments would be absurd, tyrannical and subject to the worst abuses.

Chapter 8: On the Civil State

This passage from the state of nature to the civil state produces quite a remarkable change in man, for it substitutes justice for instinct in his behavior and gives his actions a moral quality they previously lacked. Only then, when the voice of duty replaces physical impulse and right replaces appetite, does man, who had hitherto taken only himself into account, find himself forced to act upon other principles and to consult his reason before listening to his inclinations. Although in this state he deprives himself of several of the advantages belonging to him in the state of nature, he regains such great ones. His faculties are exercised and developed, his ideas are broadened, his feelings are ennobled, his entire soul is elevated to such a height that, if the abuse of this new condition did not often lower his status to beneath the level he left, he ought constantly to bless the happy moment that pulled him away from it forever and which transformed him from a stupid, limited animal into an intelligent being and a man.

Let us summarize this entire balance sheet so that the credits and debits are easily compared. What man loses through the social contract is his natural liberty and an unlimited right to everything that tempts him and that he can acquire. What he gains is civil liberty and the proprietary ownership of all he possesses. So as not to be in error in these compensations, it is necessary to draw a careful distinction between natural liberty (which is limited solely by the force of the individual involved) and civil liberty (which is limited by the general will), and between possession (which is merely the effect of the force or the right of the first occupant) and proprietary ownership (which is based solely on a positive title).

To the preceding acquisitions could be added the acquisition in the civil state of moral liberty, which alone makes man truly the master of himself. For to be driven by appetite alone is slavery, and obedience to the law one has prescribed for oneself is liberty. But I have already said too much on this subject, and the philosophical meaning of the word *liberty* is not my subject here.

Chapter 9: On the Real [i.e., Proprietary] Domain

Each member of the community gives himself to it at the instant of its constitution, just as he actually is, himself and all his forces, including all the goods in his possession. This is not to say that by this act possession changes its nature as it changes hands and becomes property in the hands of the sovereign. Rather, since the forces of the city are incomparably greater than those of a private individual, public possession is by that very fact stronger and more irrevocable, without being more legitimate, at least to strangers. For with regard to its members, the state is master of all their goods in virtue of the social contract, which serves in the state as the basis of all rights. But with regard to other powers, the state is master only in virtue of the right of the first occupant, which it derives from private individuals.

The right of first occupant, though more real than the right of the strongest, does not become a true right until after the establishment of the right of property. Every man by nature has a right to everything he needs; however, the positive act whereby he becomes a proprietor of some goods excludes him from all the rest. Once his lot has been determined, he should limit himself thereto, no longer having any right against the community. This is the reason why the right of the first occupant, so weak in the state of nature, is able to command the respect of every man living in the civil state. In this right, one respects not so much what belongs to others as what does not belong to oneself.

In general, the following rules must obtain in order to authorize the right of the first occupant on any land. First, this land may not already be occupied by anyone. Second, no one may occupy more than the amount needed to subsist. Third, one is to take possession of it not by an empty ceremony, but by working and cultivating it—the only sign of property that ought, in the absence of legal titles, to be respected by others.

In fact, by according to need and work the right of the first occupant, is it not extended as far as it can go? Is it possible to avoid setting limits to this right? Will setting one's foot on a piece of common land be sufficient to claim it at once as one's own? Will having the force for a moment to drive off other men be sufficient to deny them the right ever to return? How can a man or a people seize a vast amount of territory and deprive the entire human race of it except by a punishable usurpation, since this seizure deprives all other men of the shelter and sustenance that nature gives them in common? When Núñez Balboa[1] stood on the shoreline and took possession of the South Sea and all of South America in the name of crown of Castille, was this enough to dispossess all the inhabitants and to exclude all the princes of the world? On that basis, those ceremonies would be multiplied quite in vain. All the Catholic King had to do was to take possession of the universe all at once from his private room, excepting afterwards from his empire only what already belonged to other princes.

One can imagine how the combined and contiguous lands of private individuals became public territory; and how the right of sovereignty, extending from subjects to the land they occupied, becomes at once real and personal. This places its owners in a greater dependence, turning their very own forces into guarantees of their loyalty. This advantage does not seem to have been fully appreciated by the ancient monarchs, who, calling themselves merely King of the Persians, the Scythians, and the Macedonians, appeared to regard themselves merely as the leaders of men rather than the masters of the country. Today's monarchs more shrewdly call themselves King of France, Spain, England, and so on. In holding the land thus, they are quite sure of holding the inhabitants.

What is remarkable about this alienation is that, in accepting the goods of private individuals, the community is far from despoiling them; rather, in so doing, it merely assures them of legitimate possession, changing usurpation into a true right, and enjoyment into proprietary ownership. In that case, since owners are considered trustees of the public good, and since their rights are respected by all members of the state and maintained with all its force against foreigners, through an advantageous surrender to the public and still more so to themselves, they have, so to speak, acquired all they have given. This paradox is easily explained by the distinction between the rights of the sovereign and those of the proprietor to the same store, as will be seen later.

It can also happen, as men begin to unite before possessing anything and later appropriate a piece of land sufficient for everyone, that they enjoy it in common or divide it among themselves either in equal shares or according to

---

1   *Núñez Balboa* Vasco Núñez de Balboa (1475–1519), Spanish explorer. In 1513, he crossed Panama, and became the first European to see the eastern Pacific Ocean, claiming all lands that bordered on that ocean for Spain, in the name of the "Catholic King" Ferdinand II.

proportions laid down by the sovereign. In whatever way this acquisition is accomplished, each private individual's right to his very own store is always subordinate to the community's right to all, without which there could be neither solidity in the social fabric nor real force in the exercise of sovereignty.

I will end this chapter and this book with a remark that should serve as a basis for every social system. It is that instead of destroying natural equality, the fundamental compact, on the contrary, substitutes a moral and legitimate equality to whatever physical inequality nature may have been able to impose upon men, and that, however, unequal in force or intelligence they may be, men all become equal by convention and by right.[1]

Book 2

Chapter 1: That Sovereignty Is Inalienable

The first and most important consequence of the principles established above is that only the general will can direct the forces of the state according to the purpose for which it was instituted, which is the common good. For if the opposition of private interests made necessary the establishment of societies, it is the accord of these same interests that made it possible. It is what these different interests have in common that forms the social bond, and, were there no point of agreement among all these interests, no society could exist. For it is utterly on the basis of this common interest that society ought to be governed.

I therefore maintain that since sovereignty is merely the exercise of the general will, it can never be alienated, and that the sovereign, which is only a collective being, cannot be represented by anything but itself. Power can perfectly well be transmitted, but not the will.

In fact, while it is not impossible for a private will to be in accord on some point with the general will, it is impossible at least for this accord to be durable and constant. For by its nature the private will tends toward having preferences, and the general will tends toward equality. It is even

more impossible for there to be a guarantee of this accord even if it ought always to exist. This is not the result of art but of chance. The sovereign may well say, "Right now I want what a certain man wants or at least what he says he wants." But it cannot say, "What this man will want tomorrow I too will want," since it is absurd for the will to tie its hands for the future and since it does not depend upon any will's consenting to anything contrary to the good of the being that wills. If, therefore, the populace promises simply to obey, it dissolves itself by this act, it loses its standing as a people. The very moment there is a master, there no longer is a sovereign, and thenceforward the body politic is destroyed.

This is not to say that the commands of the leaders could not pass for manifestations of the general will, so long as the sovereign, who is free to oppose them, does not do so. In such a case, the consent of the people ought to be presumed on the basis of universal silence. This will be explained at greater length.

Chapter 2: That Sovereignty Is Indivisible

Sovereignty is indivisible for the same reason that it is inalienable. For either the will is general,[2] or it is not. It is the will of either the people as a whole or of only a part. In the first case, this declared will is an act of sovereignty and constitutes law. In the second case, it is merely a private will, or an act of magistracy. At most it is a decree.

However, our political theorists, unable to divide sovereignty in its principle, divide it in its object. They divide it into force and will, into legislative and executive power, into rights of imposing taxes, of justice and of war, into internal administration and power to negotiate with foreigners. Occasionally they confuse all these parts and sometimes they separate them. They turn the sovereign into a fantastic being made of interconnected pieces. It is as if they built a man out of several bodies, one of which had eyes, another had arms, another feet, and nothing more. Japanese sleight-of-hand artists are said to dismember a child before the eyes of spectators, then, throwing all the parts in the air one after the other, they make the child fall back down alive and all in one piece. These conjuring acts of our political theorists are more or less like these

---

1   *men all become equal ... by right*   [Rousseau's note] Under bad governments this equality is only apparent and illusory. It serves merely to maintain the poor man in his misery and the rich man in his usurpation. In actuality, laws are always useful to those who have possessions and harmful to those who have nothing. Whence it follows that the social state is advantageous to men only insofar as they all have something and none of them has too much.

2   *will is general*   [Rousseau's note] For a will to be general, it need not always be unanimous; however, it is necessary for all the votes to be counted. Any formal exclusion is a breach of generality.

performances. After having taken apart the social body by means of a sleight-of-hand worthy of a carnival, they put the pieces back together who knows how.

This error comes from not having formed precise notions of sovereign authority, and from having taken for parts of that authority what were merely emanations from it. Thus, for example, the acts of declaring war and making peace have been viewed as acts of sovereignty, which they are not, since each of these acts is not a law but merely an application of the law, a particular act determining the legal circumstances, as will be clearly seen when the idea attached to the word *law* comes to be defined.

In reviewing the other divisions in the same way, one would find that one is mistaken every time one believes one sees sovereignty divided, and that the rights one takes to be the parts of this sovereignty are all subordinated to it and always presuppose supreme wills which these rights merely put into effect.

It would be impossible to say how much this lack of precision has obscured the decisions of authors who have written about political right when they wanted to judge the respective rights of kings and peoples on the basis of the principles they had established. Anyone can see, in Chapters 3 and 4 of Book 1 of Grotius, how this learned man and his translator, Barbeyrac, become entangled and caught up in their sophisms, for fear of either saying too much or too little according to their perspectives, and of offending the interests they needed to reconcile. Grotius, taking refuge in France, unhappy with his homeland and desirous of paying court to Louis XIII (to whom his book is dedicated), spares no pain to rob the people of all their rights and to invest kings with them by every possible artifice. This would also have been the wish of Barbeyrac, who dedicated his translation to King George I of England. But unfortunately the expulsion of James II (which he calls an abdication) forced him to be evasive and on his guard and to beat around the bush, in order to avoid making William out to be a usurper. If these two writers had adopted the true principles, all their difficulties would have been alleviated and they would always have been consistent. However, sad to say, they would have told the truth and paid court only to the people. For truth does not lead to fortune, and the populace grants neither ambassadorships, university chairs nor pensions.

Chapter 3: Whether the General Will Can Err

It follows from what has preceded that the general will is always right and always tends toward the public utility. However, it does not follow that the deliberations of the people always have the same rectitude. We always want what is good for us, but we do not always see what it is. The populace is never corrupted, but it is often tricked, and only then does it appear to want what is bad.

There is often a great deal of difference between the will of all and the general will. The latter considers only the general interest, whereas the former considers private interest and is merely the sum of private wills. But remove from these same wills the pluses and minuses that cancel each other out,[1] and what remains as the sum of the differences is the general will.

If, when a sufficiently informed populace deliberates, the citizens were to have no communication among themselves, the general will would always result from the large number of small differences, and the deliberation would always be good. But when intrigues and partial associations come into being at the expense of the large association, the will of each of these associations becomes general in relation to its members and particular in relation to the state. It can be said, then, that there are no longer as many voters as there are men, but merely as many as there are associations. The differences become less numerous and yield a result that is less general. Finally, when one of these associations is so large that it dominates all the others, the result is no longer a sum of minor differences, but a single difference. Then there is no longer a general will, and the opinion that dominates is merely a private opinion.

For the general will to be well articulated, it is therefore important that there should be no partial society in the state and that each citizen make up his own mind.[2] Such was

---

1   *But remove ... cancel each other out* [Rousseau's note] *Each interest*, says the Marquis d'Argenson, *has different principles. The accord of two private interests is formed in opposition to that of a third.* He could have added that the accord of all the interests is found in the opposition to that of each. If there were no different interests, the common interest, which would never encounter any obstacle, would scarcely be felt. Everything would proceed on its own and politics would cease being an art.

2   *each citizen ... own mind* [Rousseau's note; he quotes Machiavelli in Italian] "It is true," says Machiavelli, "that some divisions are harmful to the republic while others are helpful to it. Those that are accompanied by sects and partisan factions are harmful. Since, therefore, a ruler of a republic cannot prevent enmities from aris-

the unique and sublime institution of the great Lycurgus.[1] If there are partial societies, their number must be multiplied and inequality among them prevented, as was done by Solon, Numa and Servius.[2] These precautions are the only effective way of bringing it about that the general will is always enlightened and that the populace is not tricked.

Chapter 4: On the Limits of Sovereign Power

If the state or the city is merely a moral person whose life consists in the union of its members, and if the most important of its concerns is that of its own conservation, it ought to have a universal compulsory force to move and arrange each part in the manner best suited to the whole. Just as nature gives each man an absolute power over all his members, the social compact gives the body politic an absolute power over all its members, and it is the same power which, as I have said, is directed by the general will and bears the name sovereignty.

But over and above the public person, we need to consider the private persons who make it up and whose life and liberty are naturally independent of it. It is, therefore, a question of making a rigorous distinction between the respective rights of the citizens and the sovereign,[3] and between the duties the former have to fulfill as subjects and the natural right they should enjoy as men.

We grant that each person alienates, by the social compact, only that portion of his power, his goods, and liberty whose use is of consequence to the community; but we must also grant that only the sovereign is the judge of what is of consequence.

A citizen should render to the state all the services he can as soon as the sovereign demands them. However, for its part, the sovereign cannot impose on the subjects any

fetters that are of no use to the community. It cannot even will to do so, for under the law of reason nothing takes place without a cause, any more than under the law of nature.

The commitments that bind us to the body politic are obligatory only because they are mutual, and their nature is such that in fulfilling them one cannot work for someone else without also working for oneself. Why is the general will always right, and why do all constantly want the happiness of each of them, if not because everyone applies the word *each* to himself and thinks of himself as he votes for all? This proves that the quality of right and the notion of justice it produces are derived from the preference each person gives himself, and thus from the nature of man; that the general will, to be really such, must be general in its object as well as in its essence; that it must derive from all in order to be applied to all; and that it loses its natural rectitude when it tends toward any individual, determinate object. For then, judging what is foreign to us, we have no true principle of equity to guide us.

In effect, once it is a question of a state of affairs or a particular right concerning a point that has not been regulated by a prior, general convention, the issue becomes contentious. It is a suit in which the interested private individuals are one of the parties and the public the other, but in which I fail to see either what law should be followed or what judge should render the decision. In these circumstances it would be ridiculous to want to defer to an express decision of the general will, which can only be the conclusion reached by one of its parts, and which, for the other party, therefore, is merely an alien, particular will, inclined on this occasion to injustice and subject to error. Thus, just as a private will cannot represent the general will, the general will, for its part, alters its nature when it has a particular object; and as general, it is unable to render a decision on either a man or a state of affairs. When, for example, the populace of Athens appointed or dismissed its leaders, decreed that honors be bestowed on one or inflicted penalties on another, and by a multitude of particular decrees, indiscriminately exercised all the acts of government, the people in this case no longer had a general will in the strict sense. It no longer functioned as sovereign but as magistrate. This will appear contrary to commonly held opinions, but I must be given time to present my own.

It should be seen from this that what makes the will general is not so much the number of votes as the common interest that unites them, for in this institution each person necessarily submits himself to the conditions he imposes

---

ing within it, he at least ought to prevent them from becoming sects," *The History of Florence*, Book 7.

1   *Lycurgus* Legendary lawgiver of ancient Sparta, supposed to have established, in the first half of the seventh century BCE, the important features of Spartan society.

2   *Solon, Numa and Servius* Solon (c. 638–558 BCE) was an Athenian statesman; Numa Pompilius (d. 673 BCE) the second king of ancient Rome; Servius Tullius, the sixth legendary king of ancient Rome, said to have reigned 578–535 BCE. All three instituted significant transformations of their states.

3   *rigorous distinction ... sovereign* [Rousseau's note] Attentive readers, please do not rush to accuse me of contradiction here. I have been unable to avoid it in my choice of words, given the poverty of the language. But wait.

on others, an admirable accord between interest and justice which bestows on common deliberations a quality of equity that disappears when any particular matter is discussed, for lack of a common interest uniting and identifying the role of the judge with that of the party.

From whatever viewpoint one approaches this principle, one always arrives at the same conclusion, namely that the social compact establishes among the citizens an equality of such a kind that they all commit themselves under the same conditions and should all enjoy the same rights. Thus by the very nature of the compact, every act of sovereignty (that is, every authentic act of the general will) obligates or favors all citizens equally, so that the sovereign knows only the nation as a body and does not draw distinctions between any of those members that make it up. Strictly speaking, then, what is an act of sovereignty? It is not a convention between a superior and an inferior, but a convention of the body with each of its members. This convention is legitimate, because it has the social contract as a basis; equitable, because it is common to all; useful, because it can have only the general good for its object; and solid, because it has the public force and the supreme power as a guarantee. So long as the subjects are subordinated only to such convention, they obey no one but their own will alone. And asking how far the respective rights of the sovereign and the citizens extend is asking how far the latter can commit themselves to one another, each to all and all to each.

We can see from this that the sovereign power, absolute, wholly sacred and inviolable as it is, does not and cannot exceed the limits of general conventions, and that every man can completely dispose of such goods and freedom as has been left to him by these conventions. This results in the fact that the sovereign never has the right to lay more charges on one subject than on another, because in that case the matter becomes particular, no longer within the range of the sovereign's competence.

Once these distinctions are granted, it is so false that there is, in the social contract, any genuine renunciation on the part of private individuals that their situation, as a result of this contract, is really preferable to what it was beforehand; and, instead of an alienation, they have merely made an advantageous exchange of an uncertain and precarious mode of existence for another that is better and surer. Natural independence is exchanged for liberty; the power to harm others is exchanged for their own security; and their force, which others could overcome, for a right which the social union renders invincible. Their life itself, which they

have devoted to the state, is continually protected by it; and when they risk their lives for its defense, what are they then doing but returning to the state what they have received from it? What are they doing, that they did not do more frequently and with greater danger in the state of nature, when they would inevitably have to fight battles, defending at the peril of their lives the means of their preservation? It is true that everyone has to fight, if necessary, for the homeland; but it also is the case that no one ever has to fight on his own behalf. Do we not still gain by running, for something that brings about our security, a portion of the risks we would have to run for ourselves once our security is taken away?

Chapter 5: On the Right of Life or Death

The question arises how private individuals who have no right to dispose of their own lives can transfer to the sovereign this very same right which they do not have. This question seems difficult to resolve only because it is poorly stated. Every man has the right to risk his own life in order to preserve it. Has it ever been said that a person who jumps out a window to escape a fire is guilty of committing suicide? Has this crime ever been imputed to someone who perishes in a storm, unaware of its danger when he embarked?

The social treaty has as its purpose the conservation of the contracting parties. Whoever wills the end also wills the means, and these means are inseparable from some risks, even from some losses. Whoever wishes to preserve his life at the expense of others should also give it up for them when necessary. For the citizen is no longer judge of the peril to which the law wishes he be exposed, and when the prince has said to him, "it is expedient for the state that you should die," he should die. Because it is under this condition alone that he has lived in security up to then, and because his life is not only a kindness of nature, but a conditional gift of the state.

The death penalty inflicted on criminals can be viewed from more or less the same point of view. It is in order to avoid being the victim of an assassin that a person consents to die, were he to become one. According to this treaty, far from disposing of his own life, one thinks only of guaranteeing it. And it cannot be presumed that any of the contracting parties is then planning to get himself hanged.

Moreover, every malefactor who attacks the social right becomes through his transgressions a rebel and a traitor to the homeland; in violating its laws, he ceases to be a member, and he even wages war with it. In that case the preservation of the state is incompatible with his own. Thus one of the two must perish; and when the guilty party is put to death, it is less as a citizen than as an enemy. The legal proceeding and the judgment are the proofs and the declaration that he has broken the social treaty, and consequently that he is no longer a member of the state. For since he has acknowledged himself to be such, at least by his living there, he ought to be removed from it by exile as a violator of the compact, or by death as a public enemy. For such an enemy is not a moral person, but a man, and in this situation the right of war is to kill the vanquished.

But it will be said that the condemnation of a criminal is a particular act. Fine. So this condemnation is not a function of the sovereign. It is a right the sovereign can confer without itself being able to exercise it. All of my opinions are consistent, but I cannot present them all at once.

In addition, frequency of physical punishment is always a sign of weakness or of torpor in the government. There is no wicked man who could not be made good for something. One has the right to put to death, even as an example, only someone who cannot be preserved without danger.

With regard to the right of pardon, or of exempting a guilty party from the penalty decreed by the law and pronounced by the judge, this belongs only to one who is above the judge and the law, that is, to the sovereign. Still its right in this regard is not clearly defined, and the cases in which it is used are quite rare. In a well governed state, there are few punishments, not because many pardons are granted, but because there are few criminals. When a state is in decline, the sheer number of crimes insures impunity. Under the Roman Republic,[1] neither the senate nor the consuls ever tried to grant pardons. The people itself did not do so, even though it sometimes revoked its own judgment. Frequent pardons indicate that transgressions will eventually have no need of them, and everyone sees where that leads. But I feel that my heart murmurs and holds back my pen. Let us leave these questions to be discussed by a just man who has not done wrong and who himself never needed pardon.

Chapter 6: On Law

Through the social compact we have given existence and life to the body politic. It is now a matter of giving it movement and will through legislation. For the primitive act whereby

this body is formed and united still makes no determination regarding what it should do to preserve itself.

Whatever is good and in conformity with order is such by the nature of things and independently of human conventions. All justice comes from God; he alone is its source. But if we knew how to receive it from so exalted a source, we would have no need for government or laws. Undoubtedly there is a universal justice emanating from reason alone; but this justice, to be admitted among us, ought to be reciprocal. Considering things from a human standpoint, the lack of a natural sanction causes the laws of justice to be without teeth among men. They do nothing but good to the wicked and evil to the just, when the latter observes them in his dealings with everyone while no one observes them in their dealings with him. There must therefore be conventions and laws to unite rights and duties and to refer justice back to its object. In the state of nature where everything is commonly held, I owe nothing to those to whom I have promised nothing. I recognize as belonging to someone else only what is not useful to me. It is not this way in the civil state where all rights are fixed by law.

But what then is a law? So long as we continue to be satisfied with attaching only metaphysical ideas to this word, we will continue to reason without coming to any understanding. And when they have declared what a law of nature is, they will not thereby have a better grasp of what a law of the state is.

I have already stated that there is no general will concerning a particular object. In effect, this particular object is either within or outside of the state. If it is outside of the state, a will that is foreign to it is not general in relation to it. And if this object is within the state, that object is part of it; in that case, a relationship is formed between the whole and its parts which makes two separate beings, one of which is the part, and the other is the whole less that same part. But the whole less a part is not the whole, and so long as this relationship obtains, there is no longer a whole, but rather two unequal parts. Whence it follows that the will of the one is not more general in relation to the other.

But when the entire populace enacts a statute concerning the entire populace, it considers only itself, and if in that case a relationship is formed, it is between the entire object seen from one perspective and the entire object seen from another, without any division of the whole. Then the subject matter about which a statute is enacted is general like the will that enacts it. It is this act that I call a law.

---

1   *Roman Republic* The republic lasted from the sixth to the first century BCE.

When I say that the object of the laws is always general, I have in mind that the law considers subjects as a body and actions in the abstract, never a man as an individual or a particular action. Thus the law can perfectly well enact a statute to the effect that there be privileges, but it cannot bestow them by name on anyone. The law can create several classes of citizens, and even stipulate the qualifications that determine membership in these classes, but it cannot name specific persons to be admitted to them. It can establish a royal government and a hereditary line of succession, but it cannot elect a king or name a royal family. In a word, any function that relates to an individual does not belong to the legislative power. On this view, it is immediately obvious that it is no longer necessary to ask who is to make the laws, since they are the acts of the general will; nor whether the prince is above the laws, since he is a member of the state; nor whether the law can be unjust, since no one is unjust to himself; nor how one is both free and subject to the laws, since they are merely the record of our own wills.

Moreover, it is apparent that since the law combines the universality of the will and that of the object, what a man, whoever he may be, decrees on his own authority is not a law. What even the sovereign decrees concerning a particular object is no closer to being a law; rather, it is a decree. Nor is it an act of sovereignty but of magistracy.

I therefore call every state ruled by laws a republic, regardless of the form its administration may take. For only then does the public interest govern, and only then is the "public thing" [in Latin: *res publica*] something real. Every legitimate government is republican.[1] I will explain later on what government is.

Strictly speaking, laws are merely the conditions of civil association. The populace that is subjected to the laws ought to be their author. The regulating of the conditions of a society belongs to no one but those who are in association with one another. But how will they regulate these conditions? Will it be by a common accord, by a sudden inspiration? Does the body politic have an organ for making known its will? Who will give it the necessary foresight to formulate acts and to promulgate them in advance, or how will it announce them in time of need? How will a blind multitude, which often does not know what it wants (since it rarely knows what is good for it), carry out on its own an enterprise as great and as difficult as a system of legislation? By itself the populace always wants the good, but by itself it does not always see it. The general will is always right, but the judgment that guides it is not always enlightened. It must be made to see objects as they are, and sometimes as they ought to appear to it. The good path it seeks must be pointed out to it. It must be made safe from the seduction of private wills. It must be given a sense of time and place. It must weigh present, tangible advantages against the danger of distant, hidden evils. Private individuals see the good they reject. The public wills the good that it does not see. Everyone is equally in need of guides. The former must be obligated to conform their wills to their reason; the latter must learn to know what it wants. Then public enlightenment results in the union of the understanding and the will in the social body; hence the full cooperation of the parts, and finally the greatest force of the whole. Whence there arises the necessity of having a legislator.

Chapter 7: On the Legislator

Discovering the rules of society best suited to nations would require a superior intelligence that beheld all the passions of men without feeling any of them; who had no affinity with our nature, yet knew it through and through; whose happiness was independent of us, yet who nevertheless was willing to concern itself with ours; finally, who, in the passage of time, procures for himself a distant glory, being able to labor in one age and find enjoyment in another.[2] Gods would be needed to give men laws.

The same reasoning used by Caligula regarding matters of fact was used by Plato regarding right in defining the civil or royal man he looks for in his dialogue *The Statesman*. But if it is true that a great prince is a rare man, what about a great legislator? The former merely has to follow the model the latter should propose to him. The latter is the engineer who invents the machine; the former is merely the workman who constructs it and makes it run. "At the birth of societies," says Montesquieu, "it is

---

1   *republican* [Rousseau's note] By this word I do not have in mind merely an aristocracy or a democracy, but in general every government guided by the general will, which is the law. To be legitimate, the government need not be made indistinguishable from the sovereign, but it must be its minister. Then the monarchy itself is a republic. This will become clear in the next Book.

2   *finally, who ... enjoyment in another* [Rousseau's note] A people never becomes famous except when its legislation begins to decline. It is not known for how many centuries the institution established by Lycurgus caused the happiness of the Spartans before the rest of Greece took note of it.

the leaders of republics who bring about the institution, and thereafter it is the institution that forms the leaders of the republic."[1]

He who dares to undertake the establishment of a people should feel that he is, so to speak, in a position to change human nature, to transform each individual (who by himself is a perfect and solitary whole), into a part of a larger whole from which this individual receives, in a sense, his life and his being; to alter man's constitution in order to strengthen it; to substitute a partial and moral existence for the physical and independent existence we have all received from nature. In a word, he must deny man his own forces in order to give him forces that are alien to him and that he cannot make use of without the help of others. The more these natural forces are dead and obliterated, and the greater and more durable are the acquired forces, the more too is the institution solid and perfect. Thus if each citizen is nothing and can do nothing except in concert with all the others, and if the force acquired by the whole is equal or superior to the sum of the natural forces of all the individuals, one can say that the legislation has achieved the highest possible point of perfection.

The legislator is in every respect an extraordinary man in the state. If he ought to be so by his genius, he is no less so by his office, which is neither magistracy nor sovereignty. This office, which constitutes the republic, does not enter into its constitution. It is a particular and superior function having nothing in common with the dominion over men. For if he who has command over men must not have command over laws, he who has command over the laws must no longer have any authority over men. Otherwise, his laws, ministers of his passions, would often only serve to perpetuate his injustices, and he could never avoid private opinions altering the sanctity of his work.

When Lycurgus gave laws to his homeland, he began by abdicating the throne. It was the custom of most Greek cities to entrust the establishment of their laws to foreigners. The modern republics of Italy often imitated this custom. The republic of Geneva did the same and things worked out well.[2] In its finest age Rome saw the revival within its midst

of all the crimes of tyranny and saw itself on the verge of perishing as a result of having united the legislative authority and the sovereign power in the same hands.

Nevertheless, the decimvirs[3] themselves never claimed the right to have any law passed on their authority alone. *Nothing we propose*, they would tell the people, *can become law without your consent. Romans, be yourselves the authors of the laws that should bring about your happiness.*

He who frames the laws, therefore, does not or should not have any legislative right. And the populace itself cannot, even if it wanted to, deprive itself of this incommunicable right, because, according to the fundamental compact, only the general will obligates private individuals, and there can never be any assurance that a private will is in conformity with the general will until it has been submitted to the free vote of the people. I have already said this, but it is not a waste of time to repeat it.

Thus we find together in the work of legislation two things that seem incompatible: an undertaking that transcends human force, and, to execute it, an authority that is nil.

Another difficulty deserves attention. The wise men who want to speak to the common masses in the former's own language rather than in the common vernacular cannot be understood by the masses. For there are a thousand kinds of ideas that are impossible to translate in the language of the populace. Overly general perspectives and overly distant objects are equally beyond its grasp. Each individual, in having no appreciation for any other plan of government but the one that relates to his own private interest, finds it difficult to realize the advantages he ought to draw from the continual privations that good laws impose. For an emerging people to be capable of appreciating the sound maxims of politics and to follow the fundamental rules of statecraft, the effect would have to become the cause. The social spirit which ought to be the work of that institution, would have to preside over the institution itself. And men would be, prior to the advent of laws, what they ought to

---

1   *At the birth ... the republic*   Charles-Louis de Secondat, Baron de Montesquieu (1689–1755), *Grandeur et décadence des Romains*, Chapter 1.

2   *republic of Geneva ... worked out well*   [Rousseau's note] Those who view [John] [Calvin (1509–64), French Protestant theologian and legal reformer] simply as a theologian fail to grasp the extent of his genius. The codification of our wise edicts, in which

he had a large role, does him as much honor as his *Institutes* [*of the Christian Religion*, 1536]. Whatever revolution time may bring out in our cult, so long as the love of homeland and of liberty is not extinguished among us, the memory of this great man will never cease to be held sacred.

3   *decimvirs*   Often spelled *decemvirs* (from *decemviri*, Latin: *ten men*). Judicial/executive commissions in ancient Rome; the most famous of these established the Laws of the Twelve Tables, the basic Roman legal code, in the fifth century BCE.

become by means of laws. Since, therefore, the legislator is incapable of using either force or reasoning, he must of necessity have recourse to an authority of a different order, which can compel without violence and persuade without convincing.

This is what has always forced the fathers of nations to have recourse to the intervention of heaven and to credit the gods with their own wisdom, so that the peoples, subjected to the laws of the state as to those of nature and recognizing the same power in the formation of man and of the city, might obey with liberty and bear with docility the yoke of public felicity.

It is this sublime reason, which transcends the grasp of ordinary men, whose decisions the legislator puts in the mouth of the immortals in order to compel by divine authority those whom human prudence could not move.[1] But not everybody is capable of making the gods speak or of being believed when he proclaims himself their interpreter. The great soul of the legislator is the true miracle that should prove his mission. Any man can engrave stone tablets, buy an oracle, or feign secret intercourse with some divinity, or train a bird to talk in his ear, or find other crude methods of imposing his beliefs on the people. He who knows no more than this may perchance assemble a troupe of lunatics, but he will never found an empire and his extravagant work will soon die with him. Pointless sleights-of-hand form a fleeting connection; only wisdom can make it lasting. The Judaic Law, which still exists, and that of the child of Ishmael,[2] which has ruled half the world for ten centuries, still proclaim today the great men who enunciated them. And while pride-ridden philosophy or the blind spirit of factionalism sees in them nothing but lucky impostors, the true political theoretician admires in their institutions that great and powerful genius which presides over establishments that endure.

We should not, with Warburton,[3] conclude from this that politics and religion have a common object among us, but that in the beginning stages of nations the one serves as an instrument of the other.

Chapter 8: On the People

Just as an architect, before putting up a large building, surveys and tests the ground to see if it can bear the weight, the wise teacher does not begin by laying down laws that are good in themselves. Rather he first examines whether the people for whom they are destined are fitted to bear them. For this reason, Plato refused to give laws to the Arcadians and to the Cyrenians, knowing that these two peoples were rich and could not abide equality. For this reason, one finds good laws and evil men in Crete, because Minos[4] had disciplined nothing but a vice-ridden people.

A thousand nations have achieved brilliant earthly success that could never have abided good laws; and even those that could have would have been able to have done so for a very short period of their entire existence. Peoples,[5] like men, are docile only in their youth. As they grow older they become incorrigible. Once customs are established and prejudices have become deeply rooted, it is a dangerous and vain undertaking to want to reform them. The people cannot abide having even their evils touched in order to eliminate them, just like those stupid and cowardly patients who quiver at the sight of a physician.

This is not to say that, just as certain maladies unhinge men's minds and remove from them the memory of the past, one does not likewise sometimes find in the period during which states have existed violent epochs when revolutions do to peoples what certain crises do to individuals, when the horror of the past takes the place of forgetfulness, and when the state, set afire by civil wars, is reborn, as it were, from its ashes and takes on again the vigor of youth as it escapes death's embrace. Such was Sparta at the time of Lycurgus; such was Rome after the Tarquins;[6] and such in our time have been Holland and Switzerland after the expulsion of the tyrants.

---

1   *It is this sublime reason ... could not more*   [Rousseau's note; he quotes Machiavelli in Italian.] And in truth, says Machiavelli, there has never been among a people a single legislator who, in proposing extraordinary laws, did not have recourse to God, for otherwise they would not be accepted, since there are many benefits known to a prudent man that do not have in themselves evident reasons enabling him to persuade others. *Discourses on Titus Livy*, Book 1, Ch. 11.

2   *that of the child of Ishmael*   Reference to Islam; in this tradition, Ishmael is considered the ancestor of the Arabic peoples, and of the prophet Mohammed.

3   *Warburton*   William Warburton (1698–1779), Anglican bishop and religious writer.

4   *Minos*   Mythological king of Crete.

5   *Peoples*   In the 1782 edition, this sentence was revised to read: "Most people, like men...."

6   *the Tarquins*   Tarquin I (616–579 BCE); Tarquin II ("Tarquin the Proud"—535–510 BCE).

But these events are rare. They are exceptions whose cause is always to be found in the particular constitution of the states in question. They cannot take place even twice to the same people, for it can make itself free so long as it is merely barbarous; but it can no longer do so when civil strength is exhausted. At that point troubles can destroy it with revolutions being unable to reestablish it. And as soon as its chains are broken, it falls apart and exists no longer. Henceforward a master is needed, not a liberator. Free peoples, remember this axiom: Liberty can be acquired, but it can never be recovered.

For nations, as for men, there is a time of maturity that must be awaited before subjecting them to the laws.[1] But the maturity of a people is not always easily recognized; and if it is foreseen, the work is ruined. One people lends itself to discipline at its inception; another, not even after ten centuries. The Russians will never be truly civilized, since they have been civilized too early. Peter[2] had a genius for imitation. He did not have true genius, the kind that creates and makes everything out of nothing. Some of the things he did were good; most of them were out of place. He saw that his people was barbarous; he did not see that it was not ready for civilization. He wanted to civilize it when all it needed was toughening. First he wanted to make Germans and Englishmen, when he should have made Russians. He prevented his subjects from ever becoming what they could have been by persuading them that they were something they are not. This is exactly how a French tutor trains his pupil to shine for a short time in his childhood, and afterwards never to amount to a thing. The Russian Empire would like to subjugate Europe and will itself be subjugated. The Tartars, its subjects or its neighbors, will become its masters and ours. This revolution appears inevitable to me. All the kings of Europe are working in concert to hasten its occurrence.

Chapter 9: The People (continued)

Just as nature has set limits to the status of a well-formed man, beyond which there are but giants or dwarfs, so too, with regard to the best constitution of a state, there are limits to the size it can have, so as not to be too large to be capable of being well governed, nor too small to be capable of preserving itself on its own. In every body politic there is a *maximum* force that it cannot exceed, and which has often fallen short by increasing in size. The more the social bond extends the looser it becomes, and in general a small state is proportionately stronger than a large one.

A thousand reasons prove this maxim. First, administration becomes more difficult over great distances, just as a weight becomes heavier at the end of a longer lever. It also becomes more onerous as the number of administrative levels multiplies, because first each city has its own administration which the populace pays for; each district has its own, again paid for by the people; next each province has one and then the great governments, the satrapies and vice royalties, requiring a greater cost the higher you go, and always at the expense of the unfortunate people. Finally, there is the supreme administration which weights down on everyone. All these surcharges continually exhaust the subjects. Far from being better governed by these different orders, they are worse governed than if there were but one administration over them. Meanwhile, hardly any resources remain for meeting emergencies; and when recourse must be made to them, the state is always on the verge of its ruin.

This is not all. Not only does the government have less vigor and quickness in enforcing the observance of the laws, preventing nuisances, correcting abuses and foreseeing the seditious undertakings that can occur in distant places, but also the populace has less affection for its leaders when it never sees them, for the homeland, which, to its eyes, is like the world, and for its fellow citizens, the majority of whom are foreigners to it. The same laws cannot be suitable to so many diverse provinces which have different customs, live in contrasting climates, and which are incapable of enduring the same form of government. Different laws create only trouble and confusion among the peoples who live under the same rulers and are in continuous communication. They intermingle and intermarry, and, being under the sway of other customs, never know whether their patrimony is actually their own. Talents are hidden; virtues are unknown; vices are unpunished in this multitude of men who are unknown to one another which the seat of supreme administration brings together in one place. The leaders, overwhelmed with work, see nothing for themselves; clerks govern the state. Finally, the measures that need to be taken to maintain the general authority, which so many distant officials want to avoid or harass, absorb all the public at-

---

1 *For nations ... the laws* In the 1782 edition, this sentence was revised to read: "Youth is not childhood. For nations, as for men, maturity must be awaited...."

2 *Peter* Peter I ("Peter the Great"—1672–1725), ruler of Russia 1682–1725, known for his sweeping reforms aimed at modernizing Russia.

tention. Nothing more remains for the people's happiness, and there barely remains enough for its defense in time of need. And thus a body which is too big for its constitution collapses and perishes, crushed by its own weight.

On the other hand, the state ought to provide itself with a firm foundation to give it solidity, to resist the shocks it is bound to experience, as well as the efforts it will have to make to sustain itself. For all the peoples have a kind of centrifugal force, by which they continually act one against the other and tend to expand at the expense of their neighbors, like Descartes' vortices.[1] Thus the weak risk being soon swallowed up; scarcely any people can preserve itself except by putting itself in a kind of equilibrium with all, which nearly equalizes the pressure on all sides.

It is clear from this that there are reasons for expanding and reasons for contracting, and it is not the least of the political theorist's talents to find, between these and other reasons, the proportion most advantageous to the preservation of the state. In general, it can be said that the former reasons, being merely external and relative, should be subordinated to the latter reasons, which are internal and absolute. A strong, healthy constitution is the first thing one needs to look for, and one should count more on the vigor born of a good government than on the resources furnished by a large territory.

Moreover, there have been states so constituted that the necessity for conquests entered into their very constitution, and that, to maintain themselves, they were forced to expand endlessly. Perhaps they congratulated themselves greatly on account of this happy necessity, which nevertheless showed them, together with the limit of their size, the inevitable moment of their fall.

Chapter 10: The People (continued)

A body politic can be measured in two ways: namely, by the size of its territory and by the number of its people. And between these measurements there is a relationship suitable for giving the state its true greatness. Men are what make up the state and land is what feeds men. This relationship therefore consists in there being enough land for the maintenance of its inhabitants and as many inhabitants as the land can feed. It is in this proportion that the *maximum* force of a given population size is found. For if there is too much land, its defense is onerous, its cultivation inadequate, and its yield surplus. This is the proximate cause of defensive wars. If there is not enough land, the state finds itself at the discretion of its neighbors for what it needs as a supplement. This is the proximate cause of offensive wars. Any people whose position provides it an alternative merely between commerce and war is inherently weak. It depends on its neighbors; it depends on events. It never has anything but an uncertain and brief existence. Either it conquers and changes the situation, or it is conquered and obliterated. It can keep itself free only by means of smallness or greatness.

No one can provide in mathematical terms a fixed relationship between the size of land and the population size which are sufficient for one another, as much because of the differences in the characteristics of the terrain, its degrees of fertility, the nature of its crops, the influence of its climates, as because of the differences to be noted in the temperaments of the men who inhabit them, some of whom consume little in a fertile country, while others consume a great deal on a barren soil. Again, attention must be given to the greater or lesser fertility of women, to what the country can offer that is more or less favorable to the population, to the number of people that the legislator can hope to bring together through his institutions. Thus, the legislator should not base his judgment on what he sees but on what he foresees. And he should dwell less upon the present state of the population as upon the state it should naturally attain. Finally, there are a thousand situations where the idiosyncrasies of a place require or permit the assimilation of more land than appears necessary. Thus, there is considerable expansion in mountainous country, where the natural crops—namely, woods and pastures—demand less work; where experience shows that women are more fertile than on the plains; and where a large amount of sloping soil provides only a very small amount of flat land, the only thing that can be counted on for vegetation. On the other hand, people can draw closer to one another at the seashore, even on rocks and nearly barren sand, because fishing can make up to a great degree for the lack of land crops, since men should be more closely gathered together in order to repulse pirates, and since in addition it is easier to unburden the country of surplus inhabitants by means of colonies.

To these conditions for instituting a people must be added one that cannot be a substitute for any other, but without which all the rest are useless: the enjoyment of the

---

1   *Descartes' vortices*   René Descartes (1596–1650), French philosopher, constructed a theory of celestial phenomena, initially very influential, according to which the universe was composed of material particles in interlocking circling bands.

fullness of peace. For the time when a state is organized, like the time when a battalion is formed, is the instant when the body is the least capable of resisting and easiest to destroy. There would be better resistance at a time of absolute disorder than at a moment of fermentation, when each man is occupied with his own position rather than with the danger. Were a war, famine, or sedition to arise in this time of crisis the state inevitably is overthrown.

This is not to say that many governments are not established during such storms; but in these instances it is these governments themselves that destroy the state. Usurpers always bring about or choose these times of trouble to use public terror to pass destructive laws that the people never adopt when they have their composure. The choice of the moment of a government's institution is one of the surest signs by which the work of a legislator can be distinguished from that of a tyrant.

What people, therefore, is suited for legislation? One that, finding itself bound by some union of origin, interest or convention, has not yet felt the true yoke of laws. One that has no custom or superstitions that are deeply rooted. One that does not fear being overpowered by sudden invasion. One that can, without entering into the squabbles of its neighbors, resist each of them single-handed or use the help of one to repel another. One where each member can be known to all, and where there is no need to impose a greater burden on a man than a man can bear. One that can get along without peoples and without which every other people can get along.[1] One that is neither rich nor poor and can be sufficient unto itself; finally, one that brings together the stability of an ancient people and the docility of a new people. What makes the work of legislation trying is not so much what must be established or what must be destroyed. And what makes success so rare is the impossibility of finding the simplicity of nature together with the needs of society. All these conditions, it is true, are hard to

find in combination. Hence few well constituted states are to be seen.

In Europe there is still one country capable of receiving legislation. It is the island of Corsica. The valor and constancy with which this brave people has regained and defended its liberty would well merit having some wise man teaching them how to preserve it. I have a feeling that some day that little island will astonish Europe.

Chapter 11: On the Various Systems of Legislation

If one enquires into precisely wherein the greatest good of all consists, which should be the purpose of every system of legislation, one will find that it boils down to the two principal objects, *liberty* and *equality*. Liberty, because all particular dependence is that much force taken from the body of the state; equality, because liberty cannot subsist without it.

I have already said what civil liberty is. Regarding equality, we need not mean by this word that degrees of power and wealth are to be absolutely the same, but rather that, with regard to power, it should transcend all violence and never be exercised except by virtue of rank and laws; and, with regard to wealth, no citizen should be so rich as to be capable of buying another citizen, and none so poor that he is forced to sell himself. This presupposes moderation in goods and credit on the part of the great, and moderation in avarice and covetousness[2] on the part of the lowly.

This equality is said to be a speculative fiction that cannot exist in practice. But if abuse is inevitable, does it follow that it should not at least be regulated? It is precisely because the force of things tends always to destroy equality that the force of legislation should always tend to maintain it.

But these general objects of every good institution should be modified in each country in accordance with the relationships that arise as much from the local situation as from the temperament of the inhabitants. And it is on the basis of these relationships that each people must be as-

---

1 *get along without peoples ... people can get along* [Rousseau's note] If there were two neighboring peoples, one being unable to get along without the other, it would be a very tough situation for the former and very dangerous for the latter. In such a case, every wise nation will work very quickly to free the other of its dependency. The republic of Thlascala, enclosed within the Mexican empire, preferred to do without salt, rather than buy it from the Mexicans or even take it from them for nothing. The wise Thlascalans saw the trap hidden beneath this generosity. They kept themselves free, and this small state, enclosed within this great empire, was finally the instrument of its ruin.

2 *avarice and covetousness* [Rousseau's note] Do you therefore want to give constancy to the State? Bring the extremes as close together as possible. Tolerate neither rich men nor beggars. These two estates, which are naturally inseparable, are equally fatal to the common good. From the one come the fomenters of tyranny, and from the other the tyrants. It is always between them that public liberty becomes a matter of commerce. The one buys it and the other sells it.

signed a particular institutional system that is the best, not perhaps in itself, but for the state for which it is destined. For example, is the soil barren and unproductive, or the country too confining for its inhabitants? Turn to industry and crafts, whose products you will exchange for the foodstuffs you lack. On the other hand, do you live in rich plains and fertile slopes? Do you lack inhabitants on a good terrain? Put all your effort into agriculture, which increases the number of men, and chase out the crafts that seem only to achieve the depopulation of the country by grouping in a few sectors what few inhabitants there are.[1] Do you occupy long, convenient coastlines? Cover the sea with vessels; cultivate commerce and navigation. You will have a brilliant and brief existence. Does the sea wash against nothing on your coasts but virtually inaccessible rocks? Remain barbarous and fish-eating. You will live in greater tranquility, better perhaps and certainly happily. In a word, aside from the maxims common to all, each people has within itself some cause that organizes them in a particular way and renders its legislation proper for it alone. Thus it was that long ago the Hebrews and recently the Arabs have had religion as their main object; the Athenians had letters; Carthage and Tyre, commerce; Rhodes, seafaring; Sparta, war; and Rome, virtue. The author of *The Spirit of the Laws*[2] has shown with a large array of examples the art by which the legislator directs the institution toward each of its objects.

What makes the constitution of a state truly solid and lasting is that proprieties are observed with such fidelity that the natural relations and the laws are always in agreement on the same points, and that the latter serve only to assure, accompany and rectify them. But if the legislator is mistaken about his object and takes a principle different from the one arising from the nature of things (whether the one tends toward servitude and the other toward liberty; the one toward riches, the other toward increased population; the one toward peace, the other toward conquests), the laws will weaken imperceptibly, the constitution will be altered, and the state will not cease being agitated until it is destroyed or changed, and invincible nature has regained her empire.

---

1   *Put all your effort ... inhabitants there are*   [Rousseau's note] Any branch of foreign trade, says the Marquis d'Argenson, creates hardly anything more than a false utility for a kingdom in general. It can enrich some private individuals, even some towns, but the nation as a whole gains nothing and the populace is none the better for it.

2   *The author of The Spirit of the Laws*   Montesquieu, in *Grandeur et décadence des Romains*, Chapter 1.

Chapter 12: Classification of the Laws

To set the whole in order or to give the commonwealth the best possible form, there are various relations to consider. First, the action of the entire body acting upon itself, that is, the relationship of the whole to the whole, or of the sovereign to the state, and this relationship, as we will see later, is composed of relationships of intermediate terms.

The laws regulating this relationship bear the name political laws, and are also called fundamental laws, not without reason if these laws are wise. For there is only one way of organizing in each state. The people who have found it should stand by it. But if the established order is evil, why should one accept as fundamental, laws that prevent it from being good? Besides, a people is in any case always in a position to change its laws, even the best laws. For if it wishes to do itself harm, who has the right to prevent it from doing so?

The second relation is that of the members to each other or to the entire body. And this relationship should be as small as possible in regard to the former and as large as possible in regard to the latter, so that each citizen would be perfectly independent of all the others and excessively dependent upon the city. This always takes place by the same means, for only the force of the state brings about the liberty of its members. It is from this second relationship that civil laws arise.

We may consider a third sort of relation between man and law, namely that of disobedience and penalty. And this gives rise to the establishment of criminal laws, which basically are not so much a particular kind of law as the sanction for all the others.

To these three sorts of law is added a fourth, the most important of all. It is not engraved on marble or bronze, but in the hearts of citizens. It is the true constitution of the state. Every day it takes on new forces. When other laws grow old and die away, it revives and replaces them, preserves a people in the spirit of its institution and imperceptibly substitutes the force of habit for that of authority. I am speaking of mores, customs, and especially of opinion, a part of the law unknown to our political theorists but one on which depends the success of all the others; a part with which the great legislator secretly occupies himself, though he seems to confine himself to the particular regulations that are merely the arching of the vault, whereas mores, slower to arise, form in the end its immovable keystone.

Among these various classes, only political laws, which constitute the form of government, are relevant to my subject.

Book 3

Before speaking of the various forms of government, let us try to determine the precise meaning of this word, which has not as yet been explained very well.

Chapter 1: On Government in General

I am warning the reader that this chapter should be read carefully and that I do not know the art of being clear to those who do not want to be attentive.

Every free action has two causes that come together to produce it. The one is moral, namely the will that determines the act; the other is physical, namely the power that executes it. When I walk toward an object, I must first want to go there. Second, my feet must take me there. A paralyzed man who wants to walk or an agile man who does not want to walk will both remain where they are. The body politic has the same moving causes. The same distinction can be made between force and the will; the one under the name *legislative power* and the other under the name *executive power*. Nothing is done and ought to be done without their concurrence.

We have seen that legislative power belongs to the people and can belong to it alone. On the contrary, it is easy to see, by the principles established above, that executive power cannot belong to the people at large in its role as legislator or sovereign, since this power consists solely of particular acts that are not within the province of the law, nor consequently of the sovereign, none of whose acts can avoid being laws.

Therefore the public force must have an agent of its own that unifies it and gets it working in accordance with the directions of the general will, that serves as a means of communication between the state and the sovereign, and that accomplishes in the public person just about what the union of soul and body accomplishes in man. This is the reason for having government in the state, something often badly confused with the sovereign, of which it is merely the minister.

What then is the government? An intermediate body established between the subjects and the sovereign for their mutual communication, and charged with the execution of the laws and the preservation of liberty, both civil and political.

The members of this body are called magistrates or *kings*, that is to say, *governors*, and the entire body bears the name *prince*.[1] Therefore those who claim that the act by which a people submits itself to leaders is not a contract are quite correct. It is absolutely nothing but a commission, an employment in which the leaders, as simple officials of the sovereign, exercise in its own name the power with which it has entrusted them. The sovereign can limit, modify, or appropriate this power as it pleases, since the alienation of such a right is incompatible with the nature of the social body and contrary to the purpose of the association.

Therefore, I call *government* or supreme administration the legitimate exercise of executive power; I call prince or magistrate the man or the body charged with that administration.

In government one finds the intermediate forces whose relationships make up that of the whole to the whole or of the sovereign to the state. This last relationship can be represented as one between the extremes of a continuous proportion, whose proportional mean is the government. The government receives from the sovereign the orders it gives the people, and, for the state to be in good equilibrium, there must, all things considered, be an equality between the output or the power of the government, taken by itself, and the output or power of the citizens, who are sovereigns on the one hand and subjects on the other.

Moreover, none of these three terms could be altered without the simultaneous destruction of the proportion. If the sovereign wishes to govern, or if the magistrate wishes to give laws, or if the subjects refuse to obey, disorder replaces rule, force and will no longer act in concert, and thus the state dissolves and falls into despotism or anarchy. Finally, since there is only one proportional mean between each relationship, there is only one good government possible for a state. But since a thousand events can change the relationships of a people, not only can different governments be good for different peoples, but also for the same people at different times.

In trying to provide an idea of the various relationships that can obtain between these two extremes, I will take as an example the number of people, since it is a more easily expressed relationship.

---

1   *prince* [Rousseau's note] Thus in Venice the College [of government] is given the name *Most Serene Prince* even when the Doge is not present.

Suppose the state is composed of ten thousand citizens. The sovereign can only be considered collectively and as a body. But each private individual in his position as a subject is regarded as an individual. Thus the sovereign is to the subject as ten thousand is to one. In other words, each member of the state has as his share only one ten-thousandth of the sovereign authority, even though he is totally in subjection to it. If the populace is made up of a hundred thousand men, the condition of the subjects does not change, and each bears equally the entire dominion of the laws, while his vote, reduced to one hundred-thousandth, has ten times less influence in the drafting of them. In that case, since the subject always remains one, the ratio of the sovereign to the subject increases in proportion to the number of citizens. Whence it follows that the larger the state becomes, the less liberty there is.

When I say that the ratio increases, I mean that it places a distance between itself and equality. Thus the greater the ratio is in the sense employed by geometricians, the less relationship there is in the everyday sense of the word. In the former sense, the ratio, seen in terms of quantity, is measured by the quotient; in the latter sense, ratio, seen in terms of identity, is reckoned by similarity.

Now the less relationship there is between private wills and the general will, that is, between mores and the laws, the more repressive force ought to increase. Therefore, in order to be good, the government must be relatively stronger in proportion as the populace is more numerous.

On the other hand, as the growth of the state gives the trustees of the public authority more temptations and the means of abusing their power, the more the force the government must have in order to contain the people, the more the force the sovereign must have in order to contain the government. I am speaking here not of an absolute force but of the relative force of the various parts of the state.

It follows from this twofold relationship that the continuous proportion between the sovereign, the prince and the people, is in no way an arbitrary idea, but a necessary consequence of the nature of the body politic. It also follows that since one of the extremes, namely the people as subject, is fixed and represented by unity, whenever the doubled ratio increases or decreases, the simple ratio increases or decreases in like fashion, and that as a consequence the middle term is changed. This makes it clear that there is no unique and absolute constitution of government, but that there can be as many governments of differing natures as there are states of differing sizes.

If, in ridiculing this system, someone were to say that in order to find this proportional mean and to form the body of the government, it is necessary merely, in my opinion, to derive the square root of the number of people, I would reply that here I am taking this number only as an example; that the relationships I am speaking of are not measured solely by the number of men, but in general by the quantity of action, which is the combination of a multitude of causes; and that, in addition, if to express myself in fewer words I borrow for the moment the terminology of geometry, I nevertheless am not unaware of the fact that geometrical precision has no place in moral quantities.

The government is on a small scale what the body politic which contains it is on a large scale. It is a moral person endowed with certain faculties, active like the sovereign and passive like the state, and capable of being broken down into other similar relationships whence there arises as a consequence a new proportion and yet again another within this one according to the order of tribunals, until an indivisible middle term is reached; that is, a single leader or supreme magistrate, who can be represented in the midst of this progression as the unity between the series of fractions and that of whole numbers.

Without involving ourselves in this multiplication of terms, let us content ourselves with considering the government as a new body in the state, distinct from the people and sovereign, and intermediate between them.

The essential difference between these two bodies is that the state exists by itself, while the government exists only through the sovereign. Thus the dominant will of the prince is not and should not be anything other than the general will or the law. His force is merely the public force concentrated in him. As soon as he wants to derive from himself some absolute and independent act, the bond that links everything together begins to come loose. If it should finally happen that the prince had a private will more active than that of the sovereign, and that he had made use of some of the public force that is available to him in order to obey this private will, so that there would be, so to speak, two sovereigns—one de jure and the other de facto,[1] at that moment the social union would vanish and the body politic would be dissolved.

---

1   *de jure ... de facto*   "De jure" is Latin for *as a matter of law*—what the law prescribes. "De facto," translated from the Latin, means *as a matter of fact*—what happens in practice, which may be quite different.

However, for the body of the government to have an existence, a real life that distinguishes it from the body of the state, and for all its members to be able to act in concert and to fulfill the purpose for which it is instituted, there must be a particular *self*, a sensibility common to all its members, a force or will of its own that tends toward its preservation. This particular existence presupposes assemblies, councils, a power to deliberate and decide, rights, titles and privileges that belong exclusively to the prince and that render the condition of the magistrate more honorable in proportion as it is more onerous. The difficulties lie in the manner in which this subordinate whole is so organized within the whole, that it in no way alters the general constitution by strengthening its own, that it always distinguishes its particular force, which is intended for its own preservation, from the public force intended for the preservation of the state, and that, in a word, it is always ready to sacrifice the government to the people and not the people to the government.

In addition, although the artificial body of the government is the work of another artificial body and has, in a sense, only a borrowed and subordinate life, this does not prevent it from being capable of acting with more or less vigor or speed, or from enjoying, so to speak, more or less robust health. Finally, without departing directly from the purpose of its institution, it can deviate more or less from it, according to the manner in which it is constituted.

From all these differences arise the diverse relationships that the government should have with the body of the state, according to the accidental and particular relationships by which the state itself is modified. For often the government that is best in itself will become the most vicious, if its relationships are not altered according to the defects of the body politic to which it belongs.

Chapter 2: On the Principle that Constitutes the Various Forms of Government

In order to lay out the general cause of these differences, a distinction must be made here between the prince and the government, as I had done before between the state and the sovereign.

The body of the magistrates can be made up of a larger or smaller number of members. We have said that the ratio of the sovereign to the subjects was greater in proportion as the populace was more numerous, and by a manifest analogy we can say the same thing about the government in relation to the magistrates.

Since the total force of the government is always that of the state, it does not vary. Whence it follows that the more of this force it uses on its own members, the less that is left to it for acting on the whole populace.

Therefore, the more numerous the magistrates, the weaker the government. Since this maxim is fundamental, let us attempt to explain it more clearly.

We can distinguish in the person of the magistrate three essentially different wills. First, the individual's own will, which tends only to its own advantage. Second, the common will of the magistrates which is uniquely related to the advantage of the prince. This latter can be called the corporate will, and is general in relation to the government, and particular in relation to the state, of which the government forms a part. Third, the will of the people or the sovereign will, which is general both in relation to the state considered as the whole and in relation to the government considered as a part of the whole.

In a perfect act of legislation, the private or individual will should be nonexistent; the corporate will proper to the government should be very subordinate; and consequently the general or sovereign will should always be dominant and the unique rule of all the others.

According to the natural order, on the contrary, these various wills become more active in proportion as they are the more concentrated. Thus the general will is always the weakest, the corporate will has second place, and the private will is first of all, so that in the government each member is first himself, then a magistrate, and then a citizen—a gradation directly opposite to the one required by the social order.

Granting this, let us suppose the entire government is in the hands of one single man. In that case the private will and the corporate will are perfectly united, and consequently the latter is at the highest degree of intensity it can reach. But since the use of force is dependent upon the degree of will, and since the absolute force of the government does not vary one bit, it follows that the most active of governments is that of one single man.

On the other hand, let us suppose we are uniting the government to the legislative authority. Let us make the sovereign the prince and all the citizens that many magistrates. Then the corporate will, confused with the general will, will have no more activity than the latter, and will leave the private will all its force. Thus the government, always with the same absolute force, will have its *minimum* relative force or activity.

These relationships are incontestable, and there are still other considerations that serve to confirm them. We see, for example, that each magistrate is more active in his body than each citizen is in his, and consequently that the private will has much more influence on the acts of the government than on those of the sovereign. For each magistrate is nearly always charged with the responsibility for some function of government, whereas each citizen, taken by himself, exercises no function of sovereignty. Moreover, the more the state is extended, the more its real force increases, although it does not increase not in proportion to its size. But if the state remains the same, the magistrates may well be multiplied without the government acquiring any greater real force, since this force is that of the state, whose size is always equal. Thus the relative force or activity of the government diminishes without its absolute or real force being able to increase.

It is also certain that the execution of public business becomes slower in proportion as more people are charged with the responsibility for it; that in attaching too much importance to prudence, too little importance is attached to fortune, opportunities are missed, and the fruits of deliberation are often lost by dint of deliberation.

I have just proved that the government becomes slack in proportion as the magistrates are multiplied; and I have previously proved that the more numerous the people, the greater should be the increase of repressive force. Whence it follows that the ratio of the magistrate to the government should be the inverse of the ratio of the subjects to the sovereign; that is to say, the more the state increases in size, the more the government should shrink, so that the number of leaders decreases in proportion to the increase in the number of people.

I should add that I am speaking here only about the relative force of the government and not about its rectitude. For, on the contrary, the more numerous the magistrates, the more closely the corporate will approaches the general will, whereas under a single magistrate, the same corporate will is, as I have said, merely a particular will. Thus what can be gained on the one hand is lost on the other, and the art of the legislator is to know how to determine the point at which the government's will and force, always in a reciprocal proportion, are combined in the relationship that is most advantageous to the state.

Chapter 3: Classification of Governments

We have seen in the previous chapter why the various kinds or forms of government are distinguished by the number of members that compose them. It remains to be seen in this chapter how this classification is made.

In the first place, the sovereign can entrust the government to the entire people or to the majority of the people, so that there are more citizens who are magistrates than who are ordinary private citizens. This form of government is given the name *democracy*.

Or else it can restrict the government to the hands of a small number, so that there are more ordinary citizens than magistrates; and this form is called *aristocracy*.

Finally, it can concentrate the entire government in the hands of a single magistrate from whom all the others derive their power. This third form is the most common and is called *monarchy* or royal government.

It should be noted that all these forms, or at least the first two, can be had in greater or lesser degrees, and even have a rather wide range. For democracy can include the entire populace or be restricted to half. Aristocracy, for its part, can be indeterminately restricted from half the people down to the smallest number. Even royalty can be had in varying levels of distribution. Sparta always had two kings, as required by its constitution; and the Roman Empire is known to have had up to eight emperors at a time, without it being possible to say that the empire was divided. Thus there is a point at which each form of government is indistinguishable from the next, and it is apparent that, under just three names, government can take on as many diverse forms as the state has citizens.

Moreover, since this same government can, in certain respects, be subdivided into other parts, one administered in one way, another in another, there can result from the combination of these three forms a multitude of mixed forms, each of which can be multiplied by all the simple forms.

There has always been a great deal of argument over the best form of government, without considering that each one of them is best in certain cases and the worst in others.

If the number of supreme magistrates in the different states ought to be in inverse ratio to that of the citizens, it follows that in general democratic government is suited to small states, aristocratic government to states of intermediate size, and monarchical government to large ones. This rule is derived immediately from the principle; but how is one to count the multitude of circumstances that can furnish exceptions?

Chapter 4: On Democracy

He who makes the law knows better than anyone else how it should be executed and interpreted. It seems therefore to be impossible to have a better constitution than one in which the executive power is united to the legislative power. But this is precisely what renders such a government inadequate in certain respects, since things that should be distinguished are not, and the prince and sovereign, being merely the same person, form, as it were, only a government without a government.

It is not good for the one who makes the laws to execute them, nor for the body of the people to turn its attention away from general perspectives in order to give it particular objects. Nothing is more dangerous than the influence of private interests on public affairs; and the abuse of the laws by the government is a lesser evil than the corruption of the legislator, which is the inevitable outcome of particular perspectives. In such a situation, since the state is being substantially altered, all reform becomes impossible. A people that would never misuse the government would never misuse independence. A people that would always govern well would not need to be governed.

Taking the term in the strict sense, a true democracy has never existed and never will. It is contrary to the natural order that the majority govern and the minority is governed. It is unimaginable that the people would remain constantly assembled to handle public affairs; and it is readily apparent that it could not establish commissions for this purpose without changing the form of administration.

In fact, I believe I can lay down as a principle that when the functions of the government are shared among several tribunals, those with the fewest members sooner or later acquire the greatest authority, if only because of the facility in expediting public business which brings this about naturally.

Besides, how many things that are difficult to unite are presupposed by this government? First, a very small state where it is easy for the people to gather together and where each citizen can easily know all the others. Second, a great simplicity of mores, which prevents the multitude of public business and thorny discussions. Next, a high degree of equality in ranks and fortunes, without which equality in rights and authority cannot subsist for long. Finally, little

or no luxury, for luxury either is the effect of wealth or it makes wealth necessary. It simultaneously corrupts both the rich and the poor, the one by possession, the other by covetousness. It sells the homeland to softness and vanity. It takes all its citizens from the state in order to make them slaves to one another, and all of them to opinion.

This is why a famous author[1] has made virtue the principle of the republic. For all these conditions could not subsist without virtue. But owing to his failure to have made the necessary distinctions, this great genius often lacked precision and sometimes clarity. And he did not realize that since the sovereign authority is everywhere the same, the same principle should have a place in every well constituted state, though in a greater or lesser degree, it is true, according to the form of government.

Let us add that no government is so subject to civil wars and internal agitations as a democratic or popular one, since there is none that tends so forcefully and continuously to change its form, or that demands greater vigilance and courage to be maintained in its own form. Above all, it is under this constitution that the citizen ought to arm himself with force and constancy, and to say each day of his life from the bottom of his heart what a virtuous Palatine[2] said in the Diet of Poland: *Better to have liberty fraught with danger than servitude in peace.*

Were there a people of gods, it would govern itself democratically. So perfect a government is not suited to men.

Chapter 5: On Aristocracy

We have here two very distinct moral persons, namely the government and the sovereign, and consequently two general wills, one in relation to all the citizens, the other only for the members of the administration. Thus, although the government can regulate its internal administration as it chooses, it can never speak to the people except in the name of the sovereign, that is to say, in the name of the populace itself. This is something not to be forgotten.

The first societies governed themselves aristocratically. The leaders of families deliberated among themselves about

---

1   *a famous author* Montesquieu, *The Spirit of the Laws*, Book 3, Chapter 3.
2   *a virtuous Palatine* [Rousseau's note] The Palatine of Posen, father of the King of Poland, Duke of Lorraine. [The Diet was the ruling council of Poland. Rousseau quotes in Latin the maxim which follows.]

public affairs. Young people deferred without difficulty. to the authority of experience. This is the origin of the words *priests, ancients, senate* and *elders.* The savages of North America still govern themselves that way to this day, and are very well governed.

But to the extent that inequality occasioned by social institutions came to prevail over natural inequality, wealth or power[1] was preferred to age, and aristocracy became elective. Finally, the transmission of the father's power, together with his goods, to his children created patrician families; the government was made hereditary, and we know of senators who were only twenty years old.

There are therefore three sorts of aristocracy: natural, elective and hereditary. The first is suited only to simple people; the third is the worst of any government. The second is the best; it is aristocracy properly so-called.

In addition to the advantage of the distinction between the two powers, aristocracy has that of the choice of its members. For in popular government all the citizens are born magistrates; however, this type of government limits them to a small number, and they become magistrates only through election,[2] a means by which probity, enlightenment, experience, and all the other reasons for public preference and esteem are so many new guarantees of being well governed.

Furthermore, assemblies are more conveniently held, public business better discussed and carried out with more orderliness and diligence, the reputation of the state is better sustained abroad by venerable senators than by a multitude that is unknown or despised.

In a word, it is the best and most natural order for the wisest to govern the multitude, when it is certain that they will govern for its profit and not for their own. There is no need for multiplying devices uselessly or for doing with twenty thousand men what one hundred hand-picked men can do even better. But it must be noted here that the corporate interest begins to direct the public force in less strict a conformity with the rule of the general will, and that

another inevitable tendency removes from the laws a part of the executive power.

With regard to the circumstances that are specifically suitable, a state must not be so small, nor its people so simple and upright that the execution of the laws follows immediately from the public will, as is the case in a good democracy. Nor must a nation be so large that the leaders, scattered about in order to govern it, can each play the sovereign in his own department, and begin by making themselves independent in order finally to become the masters.

But if aristocracy requires somewhat fewer virtues than popular government, it also demands others that are proper to it, such as moderation among the wealthy and contentment among the poor. For it appears that rigorous equality would be out of place here. It was not observed even in Sparta.

Moreover, if this form of government carries with it a certain inequality of fortune, this is simply in order that in general the administration of public business may be entrusted to those who are best able to give all their time to it, but not, as Aristotle claims,[3] in order that the rich may always be given preference. On the contrary, it is important that an opposite choice should occasionally teach the people that more important reasons for preference are to be found in a man's merit than in his wealth.

Chapter 6: On Monarchy

So far, we have considered the prince as a moral and collective person, united by the force of laws, and as the trustee of the executive power in the state. We have now to consider this power when it is joined together in the hands of a natural person, of a real man, who alone has the right to dispose of it in accordance with the laws. Such a person is called a monarch or a king.

In utter contrast with the other forms of administration where a collective entity represents an individual, in this form of administration an individual represents a collective entity; so that the moral unity constituting the prince is at the same time a physical unity, in which all the faculties which are combined by the law in the other forms

---

1   *power* [Rousseau's note] It is clear that among the ancients the word *optimates* does not mean the best, but the most powerful.

2   *only through election* [Rousseau's note] It is of great importance that laws should regulate the form of the election of magistrates, for if it is left to the will of the prince, it is impossible to avoid falling into a hereditary aristocracy, as has taken place in the Republics of *Venice* and *Berne.* Thus the former has long been a state in dissolution, while the latter maintains itself through the extreme wisdom of its senate. It is a very honorable and very dangerous exception.

3   *as Aristotle claims* As several commentators have pointed out, this is not in fact Aristotle's position either in *Politics* or in *Nicomachean Ethics.* His claim is something quite different: that aristocracy (rule of the best) is to be preferred to oligarchy (rule by the few, who tended also to be rich).

of administration with such difficulty are found naturally combined.

Thus the will of the people, the will of the prince, the public force of the state, and the particular force of the government, all respond to the same moving agent; all the springs of the machine are in the same hand; everything moves toward the same end; there are no opposing movements which are at cross purposes with one another; and no constitution is imaginable in which a lesser effort produces a more considerable action. Archimedes sitting serenely on the shore and effortlessly launching a huge vessel[1] is what comes to mind when I think of a capable monarch governing his vast states from his private study, and making everything move while appearing himself to be immovable.

But if there is no government that has more vigor, there is none where the private will has greater sway and more easily dominates the others. Everything moves toward the same end, it is true; but this end is not that of public felicity, and the very force of the administration unceasingly operates to the detriment of the state.

Kings want to be absolute, and from a distance one cries out to them that the best way to be so is to make themselves loved by their peoples. This maxim is very noble and even very true in certain respects. Unfortunately it will always be an object of derision in courts. The power that comes from the peoples' love is undoubtedly the greatest, but it is precarious and conditional. Princes will never be satisfied with it. The best kings want to be able to be wicked if it pleases them, without ceasing to be the masters. A political sermonizer might well say to them that since the people's force is their force, their greatest interest is that the people should be flourishing, numerous and formidable. They know perfectly well that this is not true. Their personal interest is first of all that the people should be weak and miserable and incapable of ever resisting them. I admit that, assuming the subjects were always in perfect submission, the interest of the prince would then be for the people to be powerful, so that this power, being his own, would render him formidable in the eyes of his neighbors. But since this interest is merely secondary and subordinate, and since the two suppositions are incompatible, it is natural that the princes should always give preference to the maxim that is the most immediately useful to them. This is the point that Samuel made so forcefully to the Hebrews,[2] and that Machiavelli has made apparent. Under the pretext of teaching kings, he has taught important lessons to the peoples. Machiavelli's *The Prince* is the book of republicans. <Machiavelli was a decent man and a good citizen. But since he was attached to the house of Medici, he was forced during the oppression of his homeland to disguise his love of liberty. The very choice of his execrable hero makes clear enough his hidden intention. And the contrast between the maxims of his book *The Prince* and those of his *Discourses on Titus Livy* and of his *History of Florence* shows that this profound political theorist has until now had only superficial or corrupt readers. The court of Rome has sternly prohibited his book. I can well believe it; it is the court he most clearly depicts.>

We have found, through general relationships, that the monarchy is suited only to large states, and we find this again in examining the monarchy itself. The more numerous the public administration, the more the ratio of the prince to subject diminishes and approaches equality, so that this ratio increases in proportion as the government is restricted, and is at its *maximum* when the government is in the hands of a single man. Then there is too great a distance between the prince and the people, and the state lacks cohesiveness. In order to bring about this cohesiveness, there must therefore be intermediate orders; there must be princes, grandees, and a nobility to fill them. Now none of this is suited to a small state, which is ruined by all these social levels.

But if it is difficult for a large state to be well governed, it is much harder still for it to be well governed by just one man, and everyone knows what happens when the king appoints substitutes.

An essential and inevitable defect, which will always place the monarchical form of government below the republican form, is that in the latter form the public voice hardly ever raises to the highest positions men who are not enlightened and capable and who would not fill their positions with honor. On the other hand, those who attain these positions in monarchies are most often petty bunglers, petty swindlers, petty intriguers, whose petty talents, which cause them to attain high positions at court, serve only to display their incompetence to the public as soon as they reach these positions. The populace is much less often in

---

1   *Archimedes ... launching a huge vessel* Archimedes (287–212 BCE), Greek mathematician, physicist, and inventor. He is reputed to have said, "Give me a place to stand and I will move the world," and to have demonstrated by using levers and pulleys how to launch single-handedly one of the largest ships made up to that time, with the crew aboard.

2   *Samuel made so forcefully to the Hebrews* See 1 Samuel 8.11–18.

error in its choice than the prince, and a man of real merit in the ministry is almost as rare as a fool at the head of a republican government. Thus, when by some happy chance one of these men who are born to govern takes the helm of public business in a monarchy that has nearly been sunk by this crowd of fine managers, there is utter amazement at the resources he finds, and his arrival marks an era in the history of the country.

For a monarchical state to be capable of being well governed, its size or extent must be proportionate to the faculties of the one who governs. It is easier to conquer than to rule. With a long enough lever it is possible for a single finger to make the world shake; but holding it in place requires the shoulders of Hercules.[1] However small a state may be, the prince is nearly always too small for it. When, on the contrary, it happens that the state is too small for its leader, which is quite rare, it is still poorly governed, since the leader, always pursuing his grand schemes, forgets the interests of the peoples, making them no less wretched through the abuse of talents he has too much of than does a leader who is limited for want of what he lacks. A kingdom must, so to speak, expand or contract with each reign, depending on the ability of the prince. On the other hand, since the talents of a senate have a greater degree of stability, the state can have permanent boundaries without the administration working any less well.

The most obvious disadvantage of the government of just one man is the lack of that continuous line of succession which forms an unbroken bond of unity in the other two forms of government. When one king dies, another is needed. Elections leave dangerous intervals and are stormy. And unless the citizens have a disinterestedness and integrity that seldom accompanies this form of government, intrigue and corruption enter the picture. It is difficult for one to whom the state has sold itself not to sell it in turn, and reimburse himself at the expense of the weak for the money extorted from him by the powerful. Sooner or later everything becomes venal under such an administration, and in these circumstances, the peace enjoyed under kings is worse than the disorders of the interregna.

What has been done to prevent these ills? In certain families, crowns have been made hereditary, and an order of succession has been established which prevents all

dispute when kings die. That is to say, by substituting the disadvantage of regencies for that of elections, an apparent tranquility has been preferred to a wise administration, the risk of having children, monsters, or imbeciles for leaders has been preferred to having to argue over the choice of good kings. No consideration has been given to the fact that in being thus exposed to the risk of the alternative, nearly all the odds are against them. There was a lot of sense in what Dionysius the Younger[2] said in reply to his father, who, while reproaching his son for some shameful action, said "Have I given you such an example?" "Ah," replied the son, "but your father was not king."

When a man has been elevated to command others, everything conspires to deprive him of justice and reason. A great deal of effort is made, it is said, to teach young princes the art of ruling. It does not appear that this education does them any good. It would be better to begin by teaching them the art of obeying. The greatest kings whom history celebrates were not brought up to reign. It is a science one is never less in possession of than after one has learned too much, and that one acquires it better in obeying than in commanding. *For the most useful as well as the shortest method of finding out what is good and what is bad is to consider what you would have wished or not wished to have happened under another prince.*[3]

One result of this lack of coherence is the instability of the royal form of government, which, now regulated by one plan now by another according to the character of the ruling prince or of those who rule for him, cannot have a fixed object for very long or a consistent policy. This variation always causes the state to drift from maxim to maxim, from project to project, and does not take place in the other forms of government, where the prince is always the same. It is also apparent that in general, if there is more cunning in a royal court, there is more wisdom in a senate; and that republics proceed toward their objectives by means of policies that are more consistent and better followed. On the other hand, each revolution in the ministry produces a revolution in the state, since the maxim common to all ministers and nearly all kings is to do the reverse of their predecessor in everything.

From this same incoherence we derive the solution to a sophism that is very familiar to royalist political theorists.

---

1   *shoulders of Hercules* Figuratively, enormous strength. In Greek mythology, Atlas held the heavens on his shoulders, but to get Atlas to aid him, Hercules relieved him of this weight for awhile.

2   *Dionysius the Younger* (397–343 BCE) Ruler of Syracuse, who succeeded his father in 367.

3   *For the most useful ... another prince* [Rousseau's note; he quotes the Latin.] Tacitus, *Histories,* 1.16.

Not only is civil government compared to domestic government and the prince to the father of the family (an error already refuted), but this magistrate is also liberally given all the virtues he might need, and it is always presupposed that the prince is what he ought to be. With the help of this presupposition, the royal form of government is obviously preferable to any other, since it is unquestionably the strongest; and it lacks only a corporate will that is more in conformity with the general will in order to be the best as well.

But if according to Plato,[1] a king by nature is such a rare person, how many times will nature and fortune converge to crown him; and if a royal education necessarily corrupts those who receive it, what is to be hoped from a series of men who have been brought up to reign? Surely then it is deliberate self-deception to confuse the royal form of government with that of a good king. To see what this form of government is in itself, we need to consider it under princes who are incompetent or wicked, for either they come to the throne wicked or incompetent, or else the throne makes them so.

These difficulties have not escaped the attention of our authors, but they have not been troubled by them. The remedy, they say, is to obey without a murmur. God in his anger gives us bad kings, and they must be endured as punishments from heaven. No doubt this sort of talk is edifying, however I do not know but that it belongs more in a pulpit than in a book on political theory. What is to be said of a physician who promises miracles, and whose art consists entirely of exhorting his sick patient to practice patience? It is quite obvious that we must put up with a bad government when that is what we have. The question would be how to find a good one.

Chapter 7: On Mixed Government

Strictly speaking, there is no such thing as a simple form of government. A single leader must have subordinate magistrates; a popular government must have a leader. Thus in the distribution of the executive power there is always a gradation from the greater to the lesser number, with the difference that sometimes the greater number depends on the few, and sometimes the few depend on the greater number.

At times the distribution is equal, either when the constitutive parts are in a state of mutual dependence, as in the government of England; or when the authority of each part is independent but imperfect, as in Poland. This latter form is bad, since there is no unity in the government and the state lacks a bond of unity.

Which one is better, a simple or a mixed form of government? A question much debated among political theorists, to which the same reply must be given that I gave above regarding every form of government.

In itself the simple form of government is the best, precisely because it is simple. But when the executive power is not sufficiently dependent upon the legislative power, that is to say, when there is more of a ratio between the prince and the sovereign than between the people and the prince, this defect in the proportion must be remedied by dividing the government; for then all of its parts have no less authority over the subjects, and their division makes all of them together less forceful against the sovereign.

The same disadvantage can also be prevented through the establishment of intermediate magistrates, who, by being utterly separate from the government, serve merely to balance the two powers and to maintain their respective rights. In that case, the government is not mixed; it is tempered.

The opposite difficulty can be remedied by similar means. And when the government is too slack, tribunals can be set up to give it a concentrated focus. This is done in all democracies. In the first case the government is divided in order to weaken it, and in the second to strengthen it. For the *maximum* of force and weakness are found equally in the simple forms of government, while the mixed forms of government provide an intermediate amount of strength.

Chapter 8: That Not All Forms of Government Are Suited to All Countries

Since liberty is not a fruit of every climate, it is not within the reach of all peoples. The more one meditates on this principle established by Montesquieu,[2] the more one is aware of its truth. The more one contests it, the more occasions there are for establishing it by means of new proofs.

In all the governments in the world, the public person consumes, but produces nothing. Whence therefore does it get the substance it consumes? It is from the labor of its members. It is the surplus of private individuals that produ-

---

1   *according to Plato*   [Rousseau's note] *The Statesman.*

2   *Montesquieu*   The position attributed to him is expressed in several places in *Spirit of the Laws*; see, for example, Book 17.

ces what is needed by the public. Whence it follows that the civil state can subsist only so long as men's labor produces more than they need.

Now this surplus is not the same in every country in the world. In many countries it is considerable; in others it is moderate; in others it is nil; in still others it is negative.

This ratio depends on the fertility of the climate, the sort of labor the land requires, the nature of its products, the force of its inhabitants, the greater or lesser consumption they need, and many other similar ratios of which it is composed.

On the other hand, not all governments are of the same nature. They are more or less voracious; and the differences are founded on this added principle that the greater the distance the public contributions are from their source, the more onerous they are. It is not on the basis of the amount of the taxes that this burden is to be measured, but on the basis of the path they have to travel in order to return to the hands from which they came. When this circulation is prompt and well established, it is unimportant whether one pays little or a great deal. The populace is always rich and the finances are always in good shape. On the contrary, however little the populace gives, when this small amount does not return, it is soon wiped out by continual giving. The state is never rich and the populace is always destitute.

It follows from this that the greater the distance between the people and the government, the more onerous the taxes become. Thus in a democracy the populace is the least burdened; in an aristocracy it is more so; in a monarchy it bears the heaviest weight. Monarchy, therefore, is suited only to wealthy nations; aristocracy to states of moderate wealth and size; democracy to states that are small and poor.

In fact, the more one reflects on it, the more one finds in it the difference between free and monarchical states. In the former, everything is used for the common utility. In the latter, the public and private forces are reciprocal, the one being augmented by the weakening of the other. Finally, instead of governing subjects in order to make them happy, despotism makes them miserable in order to govern them.

Thus in each climate there are natural causes on the basis of which one can assign the form of government that the force of the climate requires, and can even say what kind of inhabitants it should have. Barren and unproductive lands, where the product is not worth the labor, ought to remain uncultivated and deserted, or peopled only by savages. Places where men's labor yields only what is necessary ought to be inhabited by barbarous peoples; in places such as these all polity would be impossible. Places where the surplus of products over labor is moderate are suited to free peoples. Those where an abundant and fertile soil produces a great deal in return for a small amount of labor require a monarchical form of government, in order that the subject's excess of surplus may be consumed by the prince's luxurious living. For it is better for this excess to be absorbed by the government than dissipated by private individuals. I realize that there are exceptions; but these exceptions themselves prove the rule, in that sooner or later they produce revolutions that restore things to the order of nature.

General laws should always be distinguished from the particular causes that can modify their effect. Even if the entire south were covered with republics and the entire north with despotic states, it would still be no less true that the effect of climate makes despotism suited to hot countries, barbarism to cold countries, and good polity to intermediate regions. I also realize that, while granting the principle, disputes may arise over its application. It could be said that there are cold countries that are very fertile and southern ones that are quite barren. But this poses a difficulty only for those who have not examined the thing in all its relationships. As I have said, it is necessary to take into account those of labor, force, consumption, and so on.

Let us suppose that there are two parcels of land of equal size, one of which yields five units and the other yields ten. If the inhabitants of the first parcel consume four units and the inhabitants of the second consume nine, the excess of the first will be one-fifth and that of the other will be one-tenth. Since the ratio of these two excesses is therefore the inverse of that of the products, the parcel of land that produces only five units will yield a surplus that is double that of the parcel of land that produces ten.

But it is not a question of a double product, and I do not believe that anyone dares, as a general rule, to place the fertility of a cold country even on an equal footing with that of hot countries. Nevertheless, let us assume that this equality does obtain. Let us, if you will, reckon England to be the equal of Sicily, and Poland the equal of Egypt. Further south we have Africa and the Indies; further north we have nothing at all. To achieve this equality of product, what difference must there be in agricultural techniques? In Sicily one needs merely to scratch the soil; in England what efforts it demands to work it! Now where more hands are needed to obtain the same product, the surplus ought necessarily to be less.

Consider too that the same number of men consumes much less in hot countries. The climate demands that a person keep sober in order to be in good health. Europeans wanting to live there just as they do at home would all die of dysentery and indigestion. *We are*, says Chardin,[1] *carnivorous beasts, wolves, in comparison with the Asians. Some attribute the sobriety of the Persians to the fact that their land is less cultivated. On the contrary, I believe that this country is less abundant in commodities because the inhabitants need less. If their frugality*, he continues, *were an effect of the country's scarcity, only the poor would eat little; however, it is generally the case that everyone does so. And more or less would be eaten in each province according to the fertility of the country; however, the same sobriety is found throughout the kingdom. They take great pride in their lifestyle, saying that one has only to look at their complexions to recognize how far it excels that of the Christians. In fact, the complexion of the Persians is clear. They have fair skin, fine and polished, whereas the complexion of their Armenian subjects, who live in the European style, is coarse and blotchy, and their bodies are fat and heavy.*

The closer you come to the equator, the less people live on. They rarely eat meat; rice, maize, couscous, millet and cassava are their usual diet. In the Indies there are millions of men whose sustenance costs less than a penny a day. In Europe itself we see noticeable differences in appetite between the peoples of the north and the south. A Spaniard will live for eight days on a German's dinner. In countries where men are the most voracious, luxury too turns toward things edible. In England, luxury is shown in a table loaded with meats; in Italy you are regaled on sugar and flowers.

Luxury in clothing also offers similar differences. In the climate where the seasonal changes are sudden and violent, people have better and simpler clothing. In climates where people clothe themselves merely for ornamental purposes, flashiness is more sought after than utility. The clothes themselves are a luxury there. In Naples you see men strolling everyday along the Posillippo[2] decked out in gold-embroidered coats and bare legged. It is the same with buildings; magnificence is the sole consideration when there is nothing to fear from the weather. In Paris or London, people want to be housed warmly and comfortably. In Madrid, there are superb salons, but no windows that close, and people sleep in rat holes.

In hot countries foodstuffs are considerably more substantial and succulent. This is a third difference which cannot help but influence the second. Why do people eat so many vegetables in Italy? Because there they are good, nourishing, and have an excellent flavor. In France, where they are fed nothing but water, they are not nourishing at all, and are nearly counted for nothing at table. Be that as it may, they occupy no less land and cost at least as much effort to cultivate. It is a known fact that the wheats of Barbary,[3] in other respects inferior to those of France, yield far more flour, and that those of France, for their part, yield more wheats than those of the north. It can be inferred from this that a similar gradation in the same direction is generally observed from the equator to the pole. Now is it not a distinct disadvantage to have a smaller quantity of food in an equal amount of produce?

To all these different considerations, I can add one which depends on and strengthens them. It is that hot countries have less of a need for inhabitants than do cold countries, and yet could feed more of them. This produces a double surplus, always to the advantage of despotism. The greater the area occupied by the same number of inhabitants, the more difficult it becomes to revolt, since concerted action cannot be taken promptly and secretly; and it is always easy for the government to discover plots and cut off communications. But the closer together a numerous people is drawn, the less the government can usurp from the sovereign. The leaders deliberate as safely in their rooms as the prince does in his council; and the crowd assembles as quickly in public squares as do troops in their quarters. In this regard, the advantage of a tyrannical government, therefore, is that of acting over great distances. With the help of the points of support it establishes, its force increases with distance like that of levers.[4] On the other hand, the strength of the people acts only when concentrated; it evaporates and is lost as it spreads, like the effect of gunpowder scattered on the ground, which catches fire only one grain at a time.

---

1 *Chardin* Jean (or Sir John) Chardin (1643–1713), French travel writer on Persia and the Near East. The quotation here is from his *Voyages en Perse* (Voyages in Persia), 3.76.

2 *Posillippo* Scenic shore road in Naples.

3 *Barbary* The coastal regions of Morocco, Algeria, Tunisia, and Libya.

4 *its force ... levers* [Rousseau's note] This does not contradict what I said earlier in Book 2, Chapter 9, regarding the disadvantages of large states, for there it was a question of the authority of the government over its members, and here it is a question of its force against the subjects. Its scattered members serve it as points of support for acting from a distance upon the people, but it has no support for acting directly on these members themselves. Thus in the one case the length of the lever causes its weakness, and in the other case its force.

The least populated countries are thus the best suited for tyranny. Ferocious animals reign only in deserts.

Chapter 9: On the Signs of a Good Government

When the question arises which one is absolutely the best government, an insoluble question is being raised because it is indeterminate. Or, if you wish, it has as many good answers as there are possible combinations in the absolute and relative positions of peoples.

But if it is asked by what sign it is possible to know that a given people is well or poorly governed, this is another matter, and the question of fact could be resolved.

However, nothing is answered, since each wants to answer it in his own way. The subjects praise public tranquility; the citizens praise the liberty of private individuals. The former prefers the security of possessions; the latter that of persons. The former has it that the best government is the one that is most severe; the latter maintains that the best government is the one that is mildest. This one wants crimes to be punished, and that one wants them prevented. The former think it a good thing to be feared by their neighbors; the latter prefer to be ignored by them. The one is content so long as money circulates; the other demands that the people have bread. Even if agreement were had on these and similar points, would we be any closer to an answer? Since moral quantities do not allow of precise measurement, even if there were agreement regarding the sign, how could there be agreement regarding the evaluation.

For my part, I am always astonished that such a simple sign is overlooked or that people are of such bad faith as not to agree on it. What is the goal of the political association? It is the preservation and prosperity of its members. And what is the surest sign that they are preserved and prospering? It is their number and their population. Therefore do not go looking elsewhere for this much disputed sign. All other things being equal, the government under which, without external means, without naturalizations, without colonies, the citizens become populous and multiply the most, is infallibly the best government. That government under which a populace diminishes and dies out is the worst. Calculators, it is now up to you. Count, measure, compare.[1]

---

1   *Count, measure, compare* [Rousseau's note] We should judge on this same principle the centuries that merit preference with respect to the prosperity of the human race. Those in which let-

Chapter 10: On the Abuse of Government and Its Tendency to Degenerate

Just as the private will acts constantly against the general will, so the government makes a continual effort against sovereignty. The more this effort increases, the more the constitution is altered. And since there is here no other corporate will which, by resisting the will of the prince, would create an equilibrium with it, sooner or later the prince must finally oppress the sovereign and break the social treaty. That is the inherent and inevitable vice which, from the birth of the body politic, tends unceasingly to destroy it, just as old age and death destroy the human body.

There are two general ways in which a government degenerates, namely, when it shrinks, or when the state dissolves.

---

ters and arts are known to have nourished have been admired too much, without penetrating the secret object of their cultivation, and without considering its devastating effect, *and this was called humanity by the inexperienced, when it was a part of servitude.* [Rousseau here and in the passage below quotes Tacitus, *Agricola*, 31, in Latin.] Will we never see in the maxims of books the crude interest that causes the authors to speak? No. Whatever they may say, when a country is depopulated, it is not true, despite its brilliance, that all goes well; and the fact that a poet has an income of one hundred thousand livres is not sufficient to make his century the best of all. The apparent calm and tranquility of the leader ought to be less of an object of consideration than the well-being of whole nations and especially of the most populous states. A hailstorm may devastate a few cantons, but it rarely causes famine. Riots and civil wars may greatly disturb the leaders, but they are not the true misfortunes of the people, who may even have a reprieve while people argue over who will tyrannize them. It is their permanent condition that causes real periods of prosperity or calamity. It is when everything remains crushed under the yoke that everything decays. It is then that the leaders destroy them at will, *where they bring about solitude they call it peace.* When the quarrels of the great disturbed the kingdom of France, and the Coadjutor of Paris [assistant to a bishop] brought with him to the Parliament a knife in his pocket, this did not keep the French people from living happily and in great numbers in a free and decent ease. Long ago, Greece flourished in the midst of the cruelest wars. Blood flowed in waves, and the whole country was covered with men. It seemed, says Machiavelli [*History of Florence*, Introduction], that in the midst of murders, proscriptions, and civil wars, our republic became more powerful; the virtue of its citizens, their mores, and their independence did more to reinforce it than all its dissensions did to weaken it. A little agitation gives strength to souls, and what truly brings about prosperity for the species is not so much peace as liberty.

The government shrinks when it passes from a large to a small number, that is to say, from democracy to aristocracy, and from aristocracy to royalty. That is its natural inclination.[1] If it were to go backward from a small number to a large number, it could be said to slacken, but this reverse progression is impossible.

1 *That is its natural inclination* [Rousseau's note] The slow formation and the progress of the Republic of Venice in its lagoons offers a notable example of this succession. And it is rather astonishing that after more than twelve hundred years the Venetians seem to be no further than the second stage, which began with *Serrar di Consiglio* in 1198. As for the ancient dukes, for whom the Venetians are reproached, whatever the *squitinio della libertà veneta* [Anonymous 1612 pamphlet attacking the republic of Venice and advocating the sovereignty of the Emperor over it] may say about them, it has been proved that they were not their sovereigns.
  The Roman Republic does not fail to be brought forward as an objection against me, which, it will be said, followed a completely opposite course, passing from monarchy to aristocracy to democracy. I am quite far from thinking of it in this way.
  The first establishment of Romulus was a mixed government that promptly degenerated into despotism. For some particular reasons, the state perished before its time, just as one sees a newborn die before reaching manhood. The expulsion of the Tarquins was the true epoch of the birth of the republic. But it did not at first take on a constant form, because in failing to abolish the patriciate, only half the work was completed. For in this way, since hereditary aristocracy, which is the worst of all forms of legitimate administration, remained in conflict with democracy, a form of government that was always uncertain and adrift, it was not determined, as Machiavelli has proved [Rousseau may be referring to *Discourses on Titus Livy*, 1, 2–4], until the establishment of the tribunes. It was only then that there was a true government and a veritable democracy. In fact, the populace then was not merely sovereign but also magistrate and judge. The senate was merely a subordinate tribunal whose purpose was to temper and concentrate the government; and the consuls themselves, though they were patricians, magistrates, and absolute generals in war, in Rome were merely presidents of the people.
  From that point on, the government was also seen to follow its natural inclination and to tend strongly toward aristocracy. With the patriciate having abolished itself, as it were, the aristocracy was no longer in the body of patricians, as it was in Venice and Genoa, but in the body of the senate which was composed of patricians and plebeians, and even in the body of the tribunes when they began to usurp an active power. For words do not affect things, and when the populace has leaders who govern for it, it is always an aristocracy, regardless of the name these leaders bear.
  The abuse of aristocracy gave birth to civil wars and the triumvirate. Sulla [ruled 82–80 BCE], Julius Caesar [ruled 49–44 BCE], and Augustus [ruled 27 BCE–14 CE] became in fact veritable monarchs, and finally, under the despotism of Tiberius [ruled 14–37 CE], the state was dissolved. Roman history therefore does not invalidate my principle; it confirms it.

In fact, the government never changes its form except when its exhausted energy leaves it too enfeebled to be capable of preserving what belongs to it. Now if it were to become still more slack while it expanded, its force would become entirely nil; it would be still less likely to subsist. It must therefore wind up and tighten its force in proportion as it gives way; otherwise the state it sustains would fall into ruin.

The dissolution of the state can come about in two ways.

First, when the prince no longer administers the state in accordance with the laws and usurps the sovereign power. In that case a remarkable change takes place, namely that it is not the government but the state that shrinks. I mean that the state as a whole is dissolved, and another is formed inside it, composed exclusively of the members of the government, and which is no longer anything for the rest of the populace but its master and tyrant. So that the instant that the government usurps sovereignty, the social compact is broken, and all ordinary citizens, on recovering by right their natural liberty, are forced but not obliged to obey.

The same thing happens also when the members of the government separately usurp the power they should only exercise as a body. This is no less an infraction of the laws, and produces even greater disorder. Under these circumstances, there are, so to speak, as many princes as magistrates, and the state, no less divided than the government, perishes or changes its form.

When the state dissolves, the abuse of government, whatever it is, takes the common name *anarchy*. To distinguish, democracy degenerates into *ochlocracy*,[2] aristocracy into *oligarchy*. I would add that royalty degenerates into *tyranny*, however this latter term is equivocal and requires an explanation.

In the ordinary sense a tyrant is a king who governs with violence and without regard for justice and the laws. In the strict sense, a tyrant is a private individual who arrogates to himself royal authority without having any right to it. This is how the Greeks understood the word tyrant. They gave the name indifferently to good and bad princes whose authority was not legitimate.[3] Thus *tyrant* and *usurper* are two perfectly synonymous words.

2 *ochlocracy* Government by the lowest: mob rule.
3 *They gave ... not legitimate* [Rousseau's note; he gives the quote in Latin.] For all are considered and are called tyrants who use perpetual power in a city accustomed to liberty. Cornelius Nepos, *Life of Miltiades*. It is true that Aristotle, *Nicomachean Ethics*, Book

To give different names to different things, I call the usurper of royal authority a *tyrant*, and the usurper of sovereign power a *despot*. The tyrant is someone who intrudes himself, contrary to the laws, in order to govern according to the laws. The despot is someone who places himself above the laws themselves. Thus the tyrant cannot be a despot, but the despot is always a tyrant.

Chapter 11: On the Death of the Body Politic

Such is the natural and inevitable tendency of the best constituted governments. If Sparta and Rome perished, what state can hope to last forever? If we wish to form a durable establishment, let us then not dream of making it eternal. To succeed, one must not attempt the impossible or flatter oneself with giving to the work of men a solidity that things human do not allow.

The body politic, like the human body, begins to die from the very moment of its birth, and carries within itself the causes of its destruction. But both can have a constitution that is more or less robust and suited to preserve them for a longer or shorter time. The constitution of man is the work of nature; the constitution of the state is the work of art. It is not within men's power to prolong their lives; it is within their power to prolong the life of the state as far as possible, by giving it the best constitution it can have. The best constituted state will come to an end, but later than another, if no unforeseen accident brings about its premature fall.

The principle of political life is in the sovereign authority. Legislative power is the heart of the state; the executive power is the brain, which gives movement to all the parts. The brain can fall into paralysis and yet the individual may still live. A man may remain an imbecile and live. But once the heart has ceased its functions, the animal is dead.

It is not through laws that the state subsists; it is through legislative power. Yesterday's law does not obligate today, but tacit consent is presumed from silence, and the sovereign is taken to be giving incessant confirmation to the laws it does not abrogate while having the power to do

so. Whatever it has once declared it wants, it always wants, unless it revokes its declaration.

Why then is so much respect paid to ancient laws? For just this very reason. We must believe that nothing but the excellence of the ancient wills that could have preserved them for so long. If the sovereign had not constantly recognized them to be salutary, it would have revoked them a thousand times. This is why, far from growing weak, the laws continually acquire new force in every well constituted state. The prejudice in favor of antiquity each day renders them more venerable. On the other hand, wherever the laws weaken as they grow old, this proves that there is no longer a legislative power, and that the state is no longer alive.

Chapter 12: How the Sovereign Authority Is Maintained

The sovereign, having no other force than legislative power, acts only through the laws. And since the laws are only authentic acts of the general will, the sovereign can act only when the populace is assembled. With the populace assembled, it will be said: what a chimera![1] It is a chimera today, but two thousand years ago it was not. Have men changed their nature?

The boundaries of what is possible in moral matters are less narrow than we think. It is our weaknesses, our vices and our prejudices that shrink them. Base souls do not believe in great men; vile slaves smile with an air of mockery at the word liberty.

Let us consider what can be done in the light of what has been done. I will not speak of the ancient republics of Greece; however, the Roman Republic was, to my mind, a great state, and the town of Rome was a great town. The last census in Rome gave four thousand citizens bearing arms, and the last census count of the empire gave four million citizens, not counting subjects, foreigners, women, children, and slaves.

What difficulty might not be imagined in frequently calling assemblies of the immense populace of that capital and its environs. Nevertheless, few weeks passed by without the Roman people being assembled, and even several times in one week. It exercised not only the rights of sovereignty but also a part of those of the government. It took care of certain matters of public business; it tried certain cases; and

---

18, Chapter 10, distinguishes between a tyrant and a king, in that the former governs for his own utility and the latter governs only for the utility of his subjects. But besides the fact that generally all the Greek authors used the word *tyrant* in another sense, as appears most clearly in Xenophon's *Hiero*, it would follow from Aristotle's distinction that there has not yet been a single king since the beginning of the world.

---

1   *chimera*   Imaginary creature.

this entire populace was in the public meeting place hardly less often as magistrate than as citizen.

In looking back to the earliest history of nations, one would find that most of the ancient governments, even the monarchical ones such as those of the Macedonians and the Franks, had similar councils. Be that as it may, this lone contestable fact answers every difficulty: arguing from the actual to the possible seems like good logic to me.

Chapter 13: Continuation

It is not enough for an assembled people to have once determined the constitution of the state by sanctioning a body of laws. It is not enough for it to have established a perpetual government or to have provided once and for all for the election of magistrates. In addition to the extraordinary assemblies that unforeseen situations can necessitate, there must be some fixed, periodic assemblies that nothing can abolish or prorogue, so that on a specified day the populace is rightfully convened by law, without the need for any other formal convocation.

But apart from these assemblies which are lawful by their date alone, any assembly of the people that has not been convened by the magistrates appointed for that task and in accordance with the prescribed forms should be regarded as illegitimate, and all that takes place there should be regarded as null, since the order itself to assemble ought to emanate from the law.

As to the question of the greater or lesser frequency of legitimate assemblies, this depends on so many considerations that no precise rules can be given about it. All that can be said is that in general the more force a government has, the more frequently the sovereign ought to show itself.

I will be told that this may be fine for a single town, but what is to be done when the state includes several? Will the sovereign authority be divided, or will it be concentrated in a single town with all the rest made subject to it?

I answer that neither should be done. In the first place, the sovereign authority is simple and one; it cannot be divided without being destroyed. In the second place, a town cannot legitimately be in subjection to another town, any more than a nation can be in subjection to another nation, since the essence of the body politic consists in the harmony of obedience and liberty; and the words *subject* and *sovereign* are identical correlatives, whose meaning is combined in the single word "citizen."

I answer further that it is always an evil to unite several towns in a single city, and that anyone wanting to bring about this union should not expect to avoid its natural disadvantages. The abuses of large states should not be raised as an objection against someone who wants only small ones. But how are small states to be given enough force to resist the large ones, just as the Greek cities long ago resisted a great king, and more recently Holland and Switzerland have resisted the house of Austria?

Nevertheless, if the state cannot be reduced to appropriate boundaries, one expedient still remains: not to allow a fixed capital, to make the seat of government move from one town to another, and to assemble the estates of the country in each of them in their turn.

Populate the territory uniformly, extend the same rights everywhere, spread abundance and life all over. In this way the state will become simultaneously as strong and as well governed as possible. Recall that town walls are made from the mere debris of rural houses. With each palace I see being erected in the capital, I believe I see an entire countryside turned into hovels.

Chapter 14: Continuation

Once the populace is legitimately assembled as a sovereign body, all jurisdiction of the government ceases; the executive power is suspended, and the person of the humblest citizen is as sacred and inviolable as that of the first magistrate, for where those who are represented are found, there is no longer any representative. Most of the tumults that arose in the comitia in Rome were due to ignorance or neglect of this rule. On such occasions the consuls were merely the presidents of the people; the tribunes, ordinary speakers;[1] the senate, nothing at all.

These intervals of suspension, during which the prince recognizes or ought to recognize an actual superior, have always been disturbing to him. And these assemblies of the people, which are the aegis of the body politic and the curb on the government, have at all times been the horror of leaders. Thus they never spare efforts, objections, difficulties, or promises to keep the citizens from having them. When the citizens were greedy, cowardly, and pusillanimous, more enamored of repose than with liberty, they do not hold out

---

1   *the tribunes, ordinary speakers* [Rousseau's note] In nearly the same sense as is given this word in English Parliament. The similarity between these activities would have put the consuls and the tribunes in conflict, even if all jurisdiction had been suspended.

very long against the redoubled efforts of the government. Thus it is that, as the resisting force constantly grows, the sovereign authority finally vanishes, and the majority of the cities fall and perish prematurely.

But between the sovereign authority and arbitrary government, there sometimes is introduced an intermediate power about which we must speak.

Chapter 15: On Deputies or Representatives

Once public service ceases to be the chief business of the citizens, and they prefer to serve with their wallet rather than with their person, the state is already near its ruin. Is it necessary to march off to battle? They pay mercenary troops and stay at home. Is it necessary to go to the council? They name deputies and stay at home. By dint of laziness and money, they finally have soldiers to enslave the country and representatives to sell it.

The hustle and bustle of commerce and the arts, the avid interest in profits, softness and the love of amenities: these are what change personal services into money. A person gives up part of his profit in order to increase it at leisure. Give money and soon you will be in chains. The word *finance* is a slave's word. It is unknown in the city. In a truly free state the citizens do everything with their own hands and nothing with money. Far from paying to be exempted from their duties, they would pay to fulfill them themselves. Far be it from me to be sharing commonly held ideas. I believe that forced labor is less opposed to liberty than are taxes.

The better a state is constituted, the more public business takes precedence over private business in the minds of the citizens. There even is far less private business, since, with the sum of common happiness providing a more considerable portion of each individual's happiness, less remains for him to look for through private efforts. In a well run city everyone flies to the assemblies; under a bad government no one wants to take a step to get to them, since no one takes an interest in what happens there, for it is predictable that the general will will not predominate, and that in the end domestic concerns absorb everything. Good laws lead to making better laws; bad laws bring about worse ones. Once someone says *what do I care?* about the affairs of state, the state should be considered lost.

The cooling off of patriotism, the activity of private interest, the largeness of states, conquests, the abuse of government: these have suggested the route of using deputies or representatives of the people in the nation's assemblies. It

is what in certain countries is called the third estate.[1] Thus the private interest of two orders is given first and second place; the public interest is given merely third place.

Sovereignty cannot be represented for the same reason that it cannot be alienated. It consists essentially in the general will, and the will does not allow of being represented. It is either itself or something else; there is nothing in between. The deputies of the people, therefore, neither are nor can be its representatives; they are merely its agents. They cannot conclude anything definitively. Any law that the populace has not ratified in person is null; it is not a law at all. The English people believes itself to be free. It is greatly mistaken; it is free only during the election of the members of Parliament. Once they are elected, the populace is enslaved; it is nothing. The use the English people makes of that freedom in the brief moments of its liberty certainly warrants their losing it.

The idea of representatives is modern. It comes to us from feudal government, that iniquitous and absurd government in which the human race is degraded and the name of man is in dishonor. In the ancient republics and even in monarchies, the people never had representatives. The word itself was unknown. It is quite remarkable that in Rome where the tribunes were so sacred, no one even imagined that they could usurp the functions of the people, and that in the midst of such a great multitude, they never tried to pass a single plebiscite on their own authority. However, we can size up the difficulties that were sometimes caused by the crowd by what took place in the time of the Gracchi, when part of the citizenry voted from the rooftops.[2]

Where right and liberty are everything, inconveniences are nothing. In the care of this wise people, everything was handled correctly. It allowed its lictors to do what its tribunes[3] would not have dared to do. It had no fear that its lictors would want to represent it.

---

1   *third estate* In France (and elsewhere) separate governing councils represented each of the three "estates" (social groups): the first estate was the clergy; the second, the nobility, and the third, everyone else.
2   *the time of the Gracchi ... rooftops* The three Gracchus brothers were statesmen during a time of social unrest in Rome, in the second century BCE; two of the three were killed in the struggle for reform. During his 123 BCE election, citizens found no room in the assembly to voice their support for Gaius Gracchus, and climbed on the roofs of neighboring buildings to shout it.
3   *lictors ... tribunes* The tribunes were powerful Roman magistrates representing the lower classes. Lictors were civil-servants serving a magistrate as bodyguards and police.

However, to explain how the tribunes sometimes represented it, it is enough to conceive how the government represents the sovereign. Since the law is merely the declaration of the general will, it is clear that the people cannot be represented in the legislative power. But it can and should be represented in the executive power, which is merely force applied to the law. This demonstrates that, on close examination, very few nations would be found to have laws. Be that as it may, it is certain that, since they have no share in the executive power, the tribunes could never represent the Roman people by the rights of their office, but only by usurping those of the senate.

Among the Greeks, whatever the populace had to do, it did by itself. It was constantly assembled at the public square. It inhabited a mild climate; it was not greedy; its slaves did the work; its chief item of business was its liberty. No longer having the same advantages, how are the same rights to be preserved? Your harsher climates cause you to have more needs;[1] six months out of the year the public square is uninhabitable; your muted tongues cannot make themselves understood in the open air; you pay more attention to your profits than to your liberty; and you are less fearful of slavery than you are of misery.

What! Can liberty be maintained only with the support of servitude? Perhaps. The two extremes meet. Everything that is not in nature has its drawbacks, and civil society more so than all the rest. There are some unfortunate circumstances where one's liberty can be preserved only at the expense of someone else's, and where the citizen can be perfectly free only if the slave is completely enslaved. Such was the situation in Sparta. As for you, modern peoples, you do not have slaves, but you yourselves are slaves. You pay for their liberty with your own. It is in vain that you crow about that preference. I find more cowardice in it than humanity.

I do not mean by all this that having slaves is necessary, nor that the right of slavery is legitimate, for I have proved the contrary. I am merely stating the reasons why modern peoples who believe themselves free have representatives, and why ancient peoples did not have them. Be that as it may, the moment a people gives itself representatives, it is no longer free; it no longer exists.

All things considered, I do not see that it is possible henceforth for the sovereign to preserve among us the exercise of its rights, unless the city is very small. But if it is very small, will it be subjugated? No. I will show later[2] how the external power of a great people can be combined with the ease of administration and the good order of a small state.

Chapter 16: That the Institution of Government Is Not a Contract

Once the legislative power has been well established, it is a matter of establishing the executive power in the same way. For this latter, which functions only by means of particular acts, not being of the essence of the former, is naturally separate from it. Were it possible for the sovereign, considered as such, to have the executive power, right and fact would be so completely confounded that we would no longer know what is law and what is not. And the body politic, thus denatured, would soon fall prey to the violence against which it was instituted.

Since the citizens are all equal by the social contract, what everyone should do can be prescribed by everyone. On the other hand, no one has the right to demand that someone else do what he does not do for himself. Now it is precisely this right, indispensable for making the body politic live and move, that the sovereign gives the prince in instituting the government.

Several people have claimed that this act of establishment was a contract between the populace and the leaders it gives itself, a contract by which are stipulated between the two parties the conditions under which the one obliges itself to command and the other to obey. It will be granted, I am sure, that this is a strange way of entering into a social contract! But let us see if this opinion is tenable.

First, the supreme authority cannot be modified any more than it can be alienated; to limit it is to destroy it. It is absurd and contradictory for the sovereign to acquire a superior. To obligate oneself to obey a master is to return to full liberty.

Moreover, it is evident that this contract between the people and some or other persons would be a particular act. Whence it follows that this contract could be neither a law

---

1 *Your harsher climates ... more needs* [Rousseau's note] To adopt in cold countries the luxury and softness of the orientals is to desire to be given their chains; it is submitting to these with even greater necessity than they did.

2 *I will show later* [Rousseau's note] This is what I intended to do in the rest of this work, when in treating external relations I would have come to confederations. An entirely new subject, and its principles have yet to be established.

nor an act of sovereignty, and that consequently it would be illegitimate.

It is also clear that the contracting parties would, in relation to one another, be under only the law of nature and without any guarantee of their reciprocal commitments, which is contrary in every way to the civil state. Since the one who has force at his disposal is always in control of its employment, it would come to the same thing if we were to give the name contract to the act of a man who would say to another, "I am giving you all my goods, on the condition that you give me back whatever you wish."

There is only one contract in the state, that of the association, and that alone excludes any other. It is impossible to imagine any public contract that was not a violation of the first contract.

Chapter 17: On the Institution of the Government

What should be the terms under which we should conceive the act by which the government is instituted? I will begin by saying that this act is complex or composed of two others, namely the establishment of the law and the execution of the law.

By the first, the sovereign decrees that there will be a governing body established under some or other form. And it is clear that this act is a law.

By the second, the people names the leaders who will be placed in charge of the established government. And since this nomination is a particular act, it is not a second law, but merely a consequence of the first and a function of the government.

The problem is to understand how there can be an act of government before a government exists, and how the people, which is only sovereign or subject, can in certain circumstances become prince or magistrate.

Moreover, it is here that we discover one of those remarkable properties of the body politic, by which it reconciles seemingly contradictory operations. For this takes place by a sudden conversion of sovereignty into democracy, so that, without any noticeable change, and solely by a new relation of all to all, the citizens, having become magistrates, pass from general to particular acts, and from the law to its execution.

This change of relation is not a speculative subtlety without exemplification in practice. It takes place everyday in the English Parliament, where the lower chamber on cer-

tain occasions turns itself into a committee of the whole in order to discuss better the business of the sovereign court, thus becoming the simple commission of the sovereign court (the latter being what it was the moment before), so that it later reports to itself, as the House of Commons, the result of what it has just settled in the committee of the whole, and deliberates all over again under one title about what it had already settled under another.

The peculiar advantage to democratic government is that it can be established in actual fact by a simple act of the general will. After this, the provisional government remains in power, if this is the form adopted, or establishes in the name of the sovereign the government prescribed by the law; and thus everything is in accordance with the rule. It is not possible to institute the government in any other legitimate way without renouncing the principles established above.

Chapter 18: The Means of Preventing Usurpations of the Government

From these clarifications, it follows, in confirmation of Chapter 16, that the act that institutes the government is not a contract but a law; that the trustees of the executive power are not the masters of the populace but its officers; that it can establish and remove them when it pleases; that for them there is no question of contracting, but of obeying; and that in taking on the functions the state imposes on them, they merely fulfill their duty as citizens, without in any way having the right to dispute over the conditions.

Thus, when it happens that the populace institutes a hereditary government, whether it is monarchical within a single family or aristocratic within a class of citizens, this is not a commitment it is entering. It is a provisional form that it gives the administration, until the populace is pleased to order it otherwise.

It is true that these changes are always dangerous, and that the established government should never be touched except when it becomes incompatible with the public good. But this circumspection is a maxim of politics and not a rule of law and the state is no more bound to leave civil authority to its leaders than it is to leave military authority to its generals.

Again, it is true that in such cases it is impossible to be too careful about observing all the formalities required in order to distinguish a regular and legitimate act from a seditious tumult, and the will of an entire people from the clamor of a faction. And it is here above all that one must not grant anything to odious cases except what cannot be refused according to the full rigor of the law. And it is also from this obligation that the prince derives a great advantage in preserving his power in spite of the people, without anyone being able to say that he has usurped it. For in appearing to use only his rights, it is quite easy for him to extend them, and under the pretext of public peace, to prevent assemblies destined to reestablish good order. Thus he avails himself of a silence he keeps from being broken, or of irregularities he causes to be committed, to assume that the opinion of those who are silenced by fear is supportive of him, and to punish those who dare to speak. This is how the decemvirs, having been first elected for one year and then continued for another year, tried to retain their power in perpetuity by no longer permitting the comitia[1] to assemble. And it is by this simple means that all the governments of the world, once armed with the public force, sooner or later usurp the public authority.

The periodic assemblies I have spoken of earlier are suited to the prevention or postponement of this misfortune, especially when they have no need for a formal convocation. For then the prince could not prevent them without openly declaring himself a violator of the laws and an enemy of the state.

The opening of these assemblies, which have as their sole object the preservation of the social treaty, should always take place through two propositions which can never be suppressed, and which are voted on separately:

The first: *Does it please the sovereign to preserve the present form of government?*

The second: *Does it please the people to leave its administration to those who are now in charge of it?*

I am presupposing here what I believe I have demonstrated, namely that in the state there is no fundamental law that cannot be revoked, not even the social compact. For if all the citizens were to assemble in order to break this compact by common agreement, no one could doubt that it was legitimately broken. Grotius even thinks[2] that each person can renounce the state of which he is a member and recover his natural liberty and his goods by leaving the country.[3]

But it would be absurd that all the citizens together could not do what each of them can do separately.

Book 4

Chapter 1: That the General Will Is Indestructible

So long as several men together consider themselves to be a single body, they have but a single will, which is concerned with their common preservation and the general well-being. Then all the energies of the state are vigorous and simple; its maxims are clear and luminous; there are no entangled, contradictory interests; the common good is clearly apparent everywhere, demanding only good sense in order to be perceived. Peace, union, equality are enemies of political subtleties. Upright and simple men are difficult to deceive on account of their simplicity. Traps and clever pretexts do not fool them. They are not even clever enough to be duped. When, among the happiest people in the world, bands of peasants are seen regulating their affairs of state under an oak tree,[4] and always acting wisely, can one help scorning the refinements of other nations, which make themselves illustrious and miserable with so much art and mystery?

A state thus governed needs very few laws; and in proportion as it becomes necessary to promulgate new ones, this necessity is universally understood. The first to propose them merely says what everybody has already felt; and there is no question of either intrigues or eloquence to secure the passage into law of what each has already resolved to do, once he is sure the others will do likewise.

What misleads argumentative types is the fact that, since they take into account only the states that were badly constituted from the beginning, they are struck by the impossibility of maintaining such an administration. They laugh when they imagine all the foolishness a clever knave or a sly orator could get the people of Paris or London to believe. They do not know that Cromwell would have been sentenced to hard labor by the people of Berne, and the Duc de Beaufort imprisoned by the Genevans.

But when the social bond begins to relax and the state to grow weak, when private interests begin to make themselves

---

1   *comitia*   Powerful assemblies in the Roman Republic.
2   *Grotius even thinks*   See Hugo Grotius, *The Law of War and Peace*, Book 2, Chapter 5.
3   *leaving the country*   [Rousseau's note] On the understanding that one does not leave in order to evade one's duty and to be exempt from serving the homeland the moment it needs us. In such cir-

cumstances, taking flight would be criminal and punishable; it would no longer be withdrawal, but desertion.
4   *oak tree*   Traditionally a sacred tree, under which important things happen.

felt and small societies begin to influence the large one, the common interest changes and finds opponents. Unanimity no longer reigns in the votes; the general will is no longer the will of all. Contradictions and debates arise, and the best advice does not pass without disputes.

Finally, when the state, on the verge of ruin, subsists only in an illusory and vain form, when the social bond of unity is broken in all hearts, when the meanest interest brazenly appropriates the sacred name of the public good, then the general will becomes mute. Everyone, guided by secret motives, no more express their opinions as citizens than if the state had never existed; and iniquitous decrees having as their sole purpose the private interest are falsely passed under the name of laws.

Does it follow from this that the general will is annihilated or corrupted? No, it is always constant, unalterable and pure; but it is subordinate to other wills that prevail over it. Each man, in detaching his interest from the common interest, clearly sees that he cannot totally separate himself from it; but his share of the public misfortune seems insignificant to him compared to the exclusive good he intends to make his own. Apart from this private good, he wants the general good in his own interest, just as strongly as anyone else. Even in selling his vote for money he does not extinguish the general will in himself; he evades it. The error he commits is that of changing the thrust of the question and answering a different question from the one he was asked. Thus, instead of saying through his vote *it is advantageous to the state*, he says *it is advantageous to this man or that party that this or that view should pass*. Thus the law of the public order in the assemblies is not so much to maintain the general will, as to bring it about that it is always questioned and that it always answers.

I could present here a number of reflections about the simple right to vote in every act of sovereignty, a right that nothing can take away from the citizens; and on the right to state an opinion, to offer proposals, to divide, to discuss, which the government always takes great care to allow only to its members. But this important subject would require a separate treatise, and I cannot say everything in this one.

Chapter 2: On Voting

It is clear from the preceding chapter that the manner in which general business is taken care of can provide a rather accurate indication of the present state of mores and of the health of the body politic. The more harmony reigns in the assemblies, that is to say, the closer opinions come to unanimity, the more dominant too is the general will. But long debates, dissensions, and tumult betoken the ascendance of private interests and the decline of the state.

This seems less evident when two or more orders enter into its constitution, as had been done in Rome by the patricians and the plebeians, whose quarrels often disturbed the comitia, even in the best of times in the Republic. But this exception is more apparent than real. For then, by the vice inherent in the body politic, there are, as it were, two states in one. What is not true of the two together is true of each of them separately. And indeed even in the most tumultuous times, the plebiscites of the people, when the senate did not interfere with them, always passed quietly and by a large majority of votes. Since the citizens have but one interest, the people had but one will.

At the other extreme of the circle, unanimity returns. It is when the citizens, having fallen into servitude, no longer have either liberty or will. Then fear and flattery turn voting into acclamations. People no longer deliberate; either they adore or they curse. Such was the vile manner in which the senate expressed its opinions under the emperors; sometimes it did so with ridiculous precautions. Tacitus[1] observes that under Otho, the senators, while heaping curses upon Vitellius, contrived at the same time to make a frightening noise, so that, if by chance he became master, he would be unable to know what each of them had said.

From these various considerations there arise the maxims by which the manner of counting votes and comparing opinions should be regulated, depending on whether the general will is more or less easy to know and the state more or less in decline.

There is but one law that by its nature requires unanimous consent. This is the social compact. For civil association is the most voluntary act in the world. Since every man is born free and master of himself, no one can, under any pretext whatever, place another under subjection without his consent. To decide that the son of a slave is born a slave is to decide that he was not a man.

If, therefore, at the time of the social compact, there are opponents to it, their opposition does not invalidate the contract; it merely prevents them from being included in it. They are foreigners among citizens. Once the state is insti-

---

1   *Tacitus History*, 1.85. Marcus Salvius Otho (32–69 CE) was emperor of Rome for a mere three months before his death. His rival Aulus Vitellius Germanicus (15–69 CE) succeeded him, and ruled for eight months.

tuted, residency implies consent. To inhabit the territory is to submit to sovereignty.[1]

Aside from this primitive contract, the vote of the majority always obligates all the others. This is a consequence of the contract itself. But it is asked how a man can be both free and forced to conform to wills that are not his own. How can the opponents be both free and be placed in subjection to laws to which they have not consented?

I answer that the question is not put properly. The citizen consents to all the laws, even to those that pass in spite of his opposition, and even to those that punish him when he dares to violate any of them. The constant will of all the members of the state is the general will; through it they are citizens and free.[2] When a law is proposed in the people's assembly, what is asked of them is not precisely whether they approve or reject, but whether or not it conforms to the general will that is theirs. Each man, in giving his vote, states his opinion on this matter, and the declaration of the general will is drawn from the counting of votes. When, therefore, the opinion contrary to mine prevails, this proves merely that I was in error, and that what I took to be the general will was not so. If my private opinion had prevailed, I would have done something other than what I had wanted. In that case I would not have been free.

This presupposes, it is true, that all the characteristics of the general will are still in the majority. When they cease to be free, there is no longer any liberty regardless of the side one takes.

In showing earlier how private wills were substituted for the general will in public deliberations, I have given an adequate indication of the possible ways of preventing this abuse. I will discuss this again at a later time. With respect to the proportional number of votes needed to declare this will, I have also given the principles on the basis of which it can be determined. The differences of a single vote breaks a

tie vote; a single opponent destroys a unanimous vote. But between a unanimous and a tie vote there are several unequal divisions, at any of which this proportionate number can be fixed in accordance with the condition and needs of the body politic.

Two general maxims can serve to regulate these ratios. One, that the more important and serious the deliberations are, the closer the prevailing opinion should be to unanimity. The other, that the more the matter at hand calls for alacrity, the smaller the prescribed difference in the division of opinion should be. In decisions that must be reached immediately, a majority of a single vote should suffice. The first of these maxims seems more suited to the laws, and the second to public business. Be that as it may, it is the combination of the two that establishes the ratios that best help the majority to render its decision.

Chapter 3: On Elections

With regard to the elections of the prince and the magistrates, which are, as I have said, complex acts, there are two ways to proceed, namely by choice or by lots. Both of these have been used in various republics, and at present we still see a very complicated mixture of the two in the election of the Doge of Venice.[3]

Voting by lot, says Montesquieu,[4] *is of the essence of democracy.* I agree, but why is this the case? *Drawing lots*, he continues, *is a way of electing that harms no one; it leaves each citizen a reasonable hope of serving the homeland.* These are not reasons.

If we keep in mind that the election of leaders is a function of government and not of the sovereignty, we will see why the method of drawing lots is more in the nature of democracy, where the administration is better in proportion as its acts are less numerous.

In every true democracy the magistrature is not an advantage but a heavy responsibility that cannot justly be imposed on one private individual rather than another. The law alone can impose this responsibility on the one to

---

1   *To inhabit ... sovereignty* [Rousseau's note] This should always be understood in connection with a free state, for otherwise the family, goods, the lack of shelter, necessity, or violence can keep an inhabitant in a country in spite of himself; and then his sojourn alone no longer presupposes his consent to the contract or to the violation of the contract.

2   *The constant will ... free* [Rousseau's note] In Genoa, the word *libertas* [Latin: liberty] can be read on the front of prisons and on the chains of galley-slaves. This application of the motto is fine and just. Indeed it is only malefactors of all social classes who prevent the citizen from being free. In a country where all such people were in the galleys, the most perfect liberty would be enjoyed.

3   *a very complicated mixture ... Doge of Venice* The Doge was the elected leader of the Republic of Venice. The complicated procedure, designed to minimize the influence of the powerful Venetian families, involved a succession of several councils: a subset of each council, chosen by lot, elected the succeeding council, and the final one at last elected the Doge.

4   *says Montesquieu* See Montesquieu, *The Spirit of the Laws*, Book 2, Chapter 2.

whom it falls by lot. For in that case, with the condition being equal for all and the choice not depending on any human will, there is no particular application that alters the universality of the law.

In any aristocracy, the prince chooses the prince; the government is preserved by itself, and it is there that voting is appropriate.

The example of the election of the Doge of Venice, far from destroying this distinction, confirms it. This mixed form suits a mixed government. For it is an error to regard the government of Venice as a true aristocracy. For although the populace there has no part in the government, the nobility is itself the people. A multitude of poor Barnabites[1] never came near any magistrature, have nothing to show for their nobility but the vain title of excellency and the right to be present at the grand council. Since this grand council is as numerous as our general council in Geneva, its illustrious members have no more privileges than our single citizens. It is certain that, aside from the extreme disparity between the two republics, the bourgeoisie of Geneva exactly corresponds to the Venetian patriciate. Our natives and inhabitants correspond to the townsmen and people of Venice. Our peasants correspond to the subjects on the mainland. Finally, whatever way one considers this Republic, apart from its size, its government is no more aristocratic than ours. The whole difference lies in the fact that, since we do not have leaders who serve for life, we do not have the same need to draw lots.

Elections by lot would have few disadvantages in a true democracy where, all things being equal both in mores and talents as well as in maxims and fortunes, the choice would become almost indifferent. But I have already said there is no such thing as a true democracy.

When choice and lots are mixed, the former should fill the position requiring special talents, such as military posts. The latter is suited to those positions, such as the responsibilities of judicature, where good sense, justice, and integrity are enough, because in a well constituted state these qualities are common to all the citizens.

Neither the drawing of lots nor voting have any place in a monarchical government. Since the monarch is by right the only prince and sole magistrate, the choice of his lieutenants belongs to him alone. When the Abbé de St. Pierre[2]

proposed multiplying the Councils of the King of France and electing the members by ballot, he did not realize that he was proposing to change the form of government.

It remains for me to speak of the manner in which the votes are cast and gathered in the people's assembly. But perhaps in this regard the history of the Roman system of administration will explain more clearly all the maxims I could establish. It is not beneath the dignity of a judicious reader to consider in some detail how public and private business was conducted in a council made of two hundred thousand men.

Chapter 4: On the Roman Comitia

We have no especially reliable records of the earliest period of Rome's history. It even appears quite likely that most of the things reported about it are fables.[3] And in general the most instructive part of the annals of peoples, which is the history of their founding, is the part we most lack. Experience teaches us every day the causes that lead to the revolutions of empires. But since peoples are no longer being formed, we have almost nothing but conjecture to explain how they were formed.

The customs we find established attest at the very least to the fact that these customs had an origin. Of the traditions that go back to these origins, those that are supported by the greatest authorities and that are confirmed by the strongest reasons should pass for the most certain. These are the maxims I have tried to follow in attempting to find out how the freest and most powerful people on earth exercised its supreme power.

After the founding of Rome, the new-born Republic, that is, the army of the founder, composed of Albans, Sabines,[4] and foreigners, was divided into three classes, which took the name *tribus* [tribes] by nature of this division. Each of these tribes was divided into ten curiae, and each curia into decuriae, at the head of which were placed leaders called *curiones* and *decuriones*.

Moreover, from each tribe was drawn a body of one hundred horsemen or knights, called a *century*. It is clear

---

1   *Barnabites*   Poor members of the nobility living in St. Barnabas, a quarter of Venice.

2   *Abbé de St. Pierre*   Charles Irénée Castel, Abbé de Saint Pierre (1658–1743), French philosopher. The reference is to *Project for*

Perpetual Peace (1713).

3   *It even appears ... fables*   [Rousseau's note] The name *Rome*, which presumably comes from *Romulus*, is Greek, and means *force*. The name *Numa* is also Greek, and means *law*. What is the likelihood that the first two kings of that town would have borne in advance names so clearly related to what they did?

4   *Albans, Sabines*   Italic tribes in pre-Roman Italy.

from this that these divisions, being hardly necessary in a market-town, originally were exclusively military. But it appears that an instinct for greatness led the small town of Rome to provide itself in advance with a system of administration suited to the capital of the world.

One disadvantage soon resulted from this initial division. With the tribes of the Albans[1] and the Sabines[2] always remaining constant, while that of the foreigners[3] grew continually, thanks to their perpetual influx, this latter group soon outnumbered the other two. The remedy that Servius found for this dangerous abuse was to change the division and, in place of the division based on race, which he abolished, to substitute another division drawn from the areas of the town occupied by each tribe. In place of the three tribes, he made four. Each of them occupied one of the hills of Rome and bore its name. Thus, in remedying the inequality of the moment, he also prevented it from happening in the future. And in order that this division might not be merely one of localities but of men, he prohibited the inhabitants of one quarter from moving into another, which prevented the races from mingling with one another.

He also doubled the three ancient centuries of horsemen and he added to them twelve others, but always under the old names, a simple and judicious means by which he achieved the differentiation of the body of knights from that of the people, without causing the latter to murmur.

To the four urban tribes, Servius added fifteen others called rural tribes, because they were formed from the inhabitants of the countryside, divided into the same number of cantons. Subsequently, the same number of new ones were brought into being, and the Roman people finally found itself divided into thirty-five tribes, a number at which they remained fixed until the end of the Republic.

There resulted from this distinction between the tribes of the city and those of the countryside an effect worth noting, because there is no other example of it, and because Rome owed it both the preservation of its mores and the growth of its empire. One might have thought that the urban tribes soon would have arrogated to themselves power and honors, and wasted no time in vilifying the rural tribes. What took place was quite the opposite. The early Romans'

taste for country life is well known. They inherited this taste from the wise founder who united liberty with rural and military labors, and, so to speak, relegated to the town arts, crafts, intrigue, fortune and slavery.

Thus, since all the illustrious men in Rome lived in the country and tilled the soil, people became accustomed to look only there for the mainstays of the Republic. Since this condition was that of the worthiest patricians, it was honored by everyone. The simple and laborious life of the townsmen was preferred to the lazy and idle life of the bourgeois of Rome. And someone who would have been merely a miserable proletarian in the town, became a respected citizen as a field worker. It was not without reason, said Varro,[4] that our great-souled ancestors established in the village the nursery of those robust and valiant men who defended them in time of war and nourished them in time of peace. Pliny[5] says positively that the tribes of the fields were honored on account of the men who made them up; on the other hand, cowards whom men wished to vilify were transferred in disgrace to the tribes of the town. When the Sabine Appius Claudius came to settle in Rome, he was decked with honors and inscribed in a rural tribe that later took the name of his family. Finally, freedmen[6] all entered the urban tribes, never the rural ones. And during the entire period of the Republic, there was not a single example of any of these freedmen reaching any magistrature, even if he had become a citizen.

This maxim was excellent, but it was pushed so far that it finally resulted in a change and certainly an abuse in the administration.

First, the censors,[7] after having long arrogated to themselves the right to transfer citizens arbitrarily from one tribe to another, permitted most of them to have themselves inscribed in whatever tribe they pleased. Certainly this permission served no useful purpose and deprived the censorship of one of its greatest resources. Moreover, with the great and the powerful having themselves inscribed in the tribes of the countryside, and the freedmen who had become citizens remaining with the populace in the tribes of the town, the tribes in general no longer had either place

---

1 *Albans* [Rousseau's note] Ramnenses. [This and the next two notes name the respective classes of Roman society, divided according to tribal origin, for various governmental, military, and religious institutional purposes.]

2 *Sabines* [Rousseau's note] Tatienses.

3 *foreigners* [Rousseau's note] Luceres.

4 *Varro* Marcus Terentius Varro, *De Re Rustica* (*On Agriculture*, 37 BCE).

5 *Pliny* Pliny the Elder, *Naturalis Historia* (*Natural History*, c. 77 CE).

6 *freedmen* Former slaves.

7 *censors* Roman magistrates with responsibilities for the census and for supervision of public morality and government finances.

or territory. On the contrary, they all found themselves so intermixed that the number of each could no longer be identified except by the registers, so that in this way the idea of the word *tribe* passed from being proprietary to personal, or rather, it became almost a chimera.

In addition, it happened that since the tribes of the town were nearer at hand, they were often the strongest in the comitia, and sold the state to those who deigned to buy the votes of the mob that made them up.

Regarding the curiae, since the founder had created ten curiae in each tribe, the entire Roman people, which was then contained within the town walls, was composed of thirty curiae, each of which had its temples, its gods, its officials, its priests and its feasts called *compitalia*, similar to the *paganalia* later held by the rural tribes.

When Servius established this new division, since this number thirty could not be divided equally among his four tribes, and since he did not want to alter it, the curiae became another division of the inhabitants of Rome, independent of the tribes. But there was no question of the curiae either in the rural tribes or among the people that make them up, for since the tribes had become a purely civil establishment and another system of administration had been introduced for the raising of troops, the military divisions of Romulus[1] were found to be superfluous. Thus, even though every citizen was inscribed in a tribe, there were quite a few who were not inscribed in a curia.

Servius established still a third division which bore no relationship to the two preceding ones and which became, in its effects, the most important of all. He divided the entire Roman people into six classes, which he distinguished neither by place nor by person, but by wealth. Thus the first classes were filled by the rich, the last by the poor, and the middle ones by those who enjoyed a moderate fortune. These six classes were subdivided into one hundred ninety-three other bodies called centuries, and these bodies were divided in such wise that the first class alone contained more than half of them, and the last contained only one. Thus it was that the class with the smallest number of men was the one with the greatest number of centuries, and that the entire last class counted only as a subdivision, even though it alone contained more than half the inhabitants of Rome.

In order that the people might have less of a grasp of the consequences of this last form, Servius feigned giving it

a military air. He placed in the second class two centuries of armorers, and two instruments of war in the fourth. In each class, with the exception of the last, he made a distinction between the young and old, that is to say, between those who were obliged to carry arms and those whose age exempted them by law. This distinction, more than that of wealth, produced the necessity for frequently retaking the census or counting. Finally, he wished the assembly to be held in the Campus Martius, and that all those who were of age to serve should come there with their arms.

The reason he did not follow this same division of young and old in the last division is that the populace of which it was composed was not accorded the honor of bearing arms for the homeland. It was necessary to possess a hearth in order to obtain the right to defend it. And of the innumerable troops of beggars who today grace the armies of kings, there is perhaps no one who would not have been disdainfully chased from a Roman cohort, when the soldiers were the defenders of liberty.

There still is a distinction in the last class between the *proletarians* and those that are called *capite censi*.[2] The former, not completely reduced to nothing, at least gave citizens to the state, sometimes even soldiers in times of pressing need. As for those who possessed nothing at all and could be reckoned only by counting heads, they were reckoned to be absolutely worthless, and Marius[3] was the first who deigned to enroll them.

Without deciding here whether this third method of reckoning was good or bad in itself, I believe I can affirm that it could be made practicable only by the simple mores of the early Romans, their disinterestedness, their taste for agriculture, their dislike for commerce and for the passion for profits. Where is the modern people among whom their devouring greed, their unsettled spirit, their intrigue, their continual displacements, their perpetual revolutions of fortunes could allow such an establishment to last twenty years without overturning the entire state? It must also be duly noted that the mores and the censorship, which were stronger than this institution, corrected its defects in Rome, and that a rich man found himself relegated to the class of the poor for having made too much of a show of his wealth.

1　*Romulus*　(c. 771–c. 717 BCE) Traditionally counted (with his brother Remus) as the founder of Rome; its first king.

2　*capite censi*　(Latin) Literally, *those counted by head*; as opposed to all the other classes, who were classified on the basis of property distinctions.

3　*Marius*　Gaius Marius (157–86 BCE), Roman general and politician, known for his institution of reforms of the army.

From all this, it is easy to grasp why mention is almost never made of more than five classes, even though there actually were six. The sixth, since it furnished neither soldiers for the army nor voters for the Campus Martius[1] and was of virtually no use in the Republic, was hardly ever counted for anything.

Such were the various divisions of the Roman people. Let us now look at the effect these divisions had on the assemblies. When legitimately convened, these assemblies were called *comitia*. Ordinarily they were held in the Roman forum or in the Campus Martius, and were distinguished as comitia curiata, comitia centuriata, and comitia tributa, according to which of the three forms was the basis on which they were organized. The comitia curiata were based on the institution of Romulus, the comitia centuriata on that of Servius, and the comitia tributa on that of the tribunes of the people. No law received sanction, no magistrate was elected save in the comitia. And since there was no citizen who was not inscribed in a curia, in a century, or in a tribe, it followed that no citizen was excluded from the right of suffrage, and that the Roman people was truly sovereign both de jure and de facto.

For the comitia to be legitimately assembled and for what took place to have the force of law, three conditions had to be met: first, the body or the magistrate who called these assemblies had to be invested with the necessary authority to do so; second, the assembly had to be held on one of the days permitted by law; third, the auguries had to be favorable.

The reason for the first regulation needs no explanation. The second is an administrative matter. Thus the comitia were not allowed to be held on holidays and market days, when people from the country, coming to Rome on business, did not have time to spend the day in the public forum. By means of the third rule, the senate held in check a proud and restless people, and appropriately tempered the ardor of seditious tribunes. But these latter found more than one way of getting around this constraint.

The laws and the election of leaders were not the only matters submitted to the judgment of the comitia. Since the Roman people had usurped the most important functions of government, it can be said that the fate of Europe was decided in its assemblies. This variety of objects gave rise to the various forms these assemblies took on according to the matters on which they had to pronounce.

In order to judge these various forms, it is enough to compare them. In instituting the curiae, Romulus had intended to contain the senate by means of the people and the people by means of the senate, while he dominated both equally. He therefore gave the people, by means of this form, all the authority of number to balance that of power and wealth which he left to the patricians. But in conformity with the spirit of the monarchy, he nevertheless left a greater advantage to the patricians through their clients' influence on the majority of the votes. This admirable institution of patrons and clients was a masterpiece of politics and humanity, without which the patriciate, so contrary to the spirit of the Republic, could not have subsisted. Only Rome had the honor of giving the world this fine example, which never led to any abuse, and which, for all that, has never been followed.

Since this same form of curiae had subsisted under the kings until Servius, and since the reign of the last Tarquin was not considered legitimate, royal laws were generally known by the name *leges curiatae*.[2]

Under the Republic, the curiae, always limited to the four urban tribes and including no more than the populace of Rome, was unable to suit either the senate, which was at the head of the patricians, or the tribunes, who, plebeians though they were, were at the head of the citizens who were in comfortable circumstances. The curiae therefore fell into discredit and their degradation was such that their thirty assembled lictors together did what the comitia curiata should have done.

The division by centuries was so favorable to the aristocracy, that at first difficult it is to see how the senate did not always prevail in the comitia which bears this name, and by which the consuls, the censors, and other curule magistrates were elected. In fact, of the one hundred ninety-three centuries that formed the six classes of the entire Roman people, the first class contained ninety-eight, and, since the voting was counted by centuries only, this first class alone prevailed in the number of votes over all the rest. When all its centuries were in agreement, they did not even continue to gather the votes. Decisions made by the smallest number passed for a decision of the multitude; and it can be said

---

1 *Campus Martius* [Rousseau's note] I say *Campus Martius* because it was here that the *comitia centuriata* gathered. In the two other forms of assembly, the people gathered in the *forum* or elsewhere, and then the *capite censi* had as much influence and authority as the first citizens.

2 *leges curiatae* Latin: laws passed by the *Comitia Curiata*, one of the three Roman assemblies.

that in the comitia centuriata business was regulated more by the majority of money than by one of votes.

But this extreme authority was tempered in two ways. First, since ordinarily the tribunes, and always a large number of plebeians, were in the class of the rich, they balanced the credit of the patricians in this first class.

The second way consisted in the following. Instead of at the outset making the centuries vote according to their order, which would have meant always beginning with the first, one century was chosen by lot, and that one[1] alone proceeded to the election. After this, all the centuries were called on another day according to their rank, repeated the same election and usually confirmed it. Thus the authority of example was removed from rank in order to give it to lot, in accordance with the principle of democracy.

There resulted from this custom still another advantage; namely that the citizens from the country had time between the two elections to inform themselves of the merit of the provisionally named candidate, so as to give their votes only on condition of their having knowledge of the issue. But on the pretext of speeding things up, this custom was finally abolished and the two elections were held on the same day.

Strictly speaking, the comitia tributa were the council of the Roman people. They were convened only by the tribunes. The tribunes were elected and passed their plebiscites there. Not only did the senate hold no rank in them, it did not even have the right to be present. And since the senators were forced to obey the laws upon which they could not vote, they were less free in this regard than the humblest citizens. This injustice was altogether ill-conceived, and was by itself enough to invalidate the decrees of a body to which all its members were not admitted. If all the patricians had been present at these comitia in virtue of the right they had as citizens, having then become simple private individuals, they would not have had a great deal of influence on a form of voting that was tallied by counting heads, and where the humblest proletarian had as much clout as the prince of the senate.

Thus it can be seen that besides the order that resulted from these various distributions for gathering the votes of so great a people, these distributions were not reducible to forms indifferent in themselves, but each one had effects relative to the viewpoints that caused it to be preferred.

Without going further into greater detail here, it is a consequence of the preceding clarifications that the comitia tributa were the most favorable to the popular government, and the comitia centuriata more favorable to the aristocracy. Regarding the comitia curiata, in which the populace of Rome alone formed the majority, since these were good only for favoring tyranny and evil designs, they fell of their own weight into disrepute, and even the seditious abstained from using a means that gave too much exposure to their projects. It is certain that all the majesty of the Roman people is found only in the curia centuriata, which alone were complete, for the comitia curiata excluded the rural tribes, and the comitia tributa the senate and the patricians.

As to the manner of counting the votes, among the early Romans it was as simple as their mores, though not so simple as in Sparta. Each gave his vote in a loud voice, and a clerk marked it down accordingly. The majority vote in each tribe determined the tribe's vote; the majority vote of the tribes determined the people's vote; and the same went for the curia and the centuries. This custom was good so long as honesty reigned among the citizens and each was ashamed to give his vote publicly in favor of an unjust proposal or an unworthy subject. But when the people became corrupt and votes were bought, it was fitting that they should give their votes in secret in order to restrain the buyers through distrust and to provide scoundrels the means of not being traitors.

I know that Cicero[2] condemns this change and attributes the ruin of the Republic partly to it. But although I am aware of the weight that Cicero's authority should have here, I cannot agree with him. On the contrary, I think that, by having made not enough of these changes, the fall of the state was accelerated. Just as the regimen of healthy people is not suitable for the sick, one should not want to govern a corrupt people by means of the same laws that are suited to a good people. Nothing proves this maxim better than the long life of the Republic of Venice, whose shadow still exists, solely because its laws are suited only to wicked men.

Tablets were therefore distributed to the citizens by mean of which each man could vote without anyone knowing what his opinion was. New formalities were also established for collecting the tablets, counting the votes, comparing the numbers, and so on. None of this prevented

---

1   *that one* [Rousseau's note] This century, having been chosen thus by lot, was called *prae rogativa*, on account of the fact that it was the first to be asked for its vote, and it is from this that the word *prerogative* is derived.

2   *Cicero* Marcus Tullius Cicero (106–43 BCE) was a Roman statesman, lawyer and philosopher. The reference is to his *Laws*, 3.

the integrity of the officials in charge of these functions[1] from often being under suspicion. Finally, to prevent intrigue and vote trafficking, edicts were passed whose sheer multiplicity is proof of their uselessness.

Toward the end of the period of the Republic, it was often necessary to have recourse to extraordinary expedients in order to make up for the inadequacy of the law. Sometimes miracles were alleged. But this means, which could deceive the populace, did not deceive those who governed it. Sometimes an assembly was unexpectedly convened before the candidates had time to carry out their intrigues. Sometimes an entire session was spent on talk, when it was clear that the populace was won over and ready to take the wrong side on an issue. But finally ambition eluded everything; and what is unbelievable is that in the midst of so much abuse, this immense people, by virtue of its ancient regulations, did not cease to choose magistrates, pass laws, judge cases, or expedite private and public business, almost as easily as the senate itself could have done.

Chapter 5: On the Tribunate

When it is not possible to establish an exact proportion between the constitutive parts of the state, or when indestructible causes continually alter the relationships between them, a special magistrature is then established that does not make up a larger body along with them. This magistrature restores each term to its true relationship to the others, and which creates a link or a middle term either between the prince and the people or between the prince and the sovereign, or on both sides at once, if necessary.

This body, which I will call the *tribunate*, is the preserver of the laws and the legislative power. It serves sometimes to protect the sovereign against the government, as the tribunes of the people did in Rome; sometimes to sustain the government against the people, as the Council of Ten now does in Venice; and sometimes to maintain equilibrium between the two, as the ephors did in Sparta.

The tribunate is not a constitutive part of the city and it should have no share in either the legislative or the executive power. But this is precisely what makes its own power the greater. For although it is unable to do anything, it can prevent everything. It is more sacred and more revered as a defender of the laws than the prince who executes them

and the sovereign who gives them. This was very clearly apparent in Rome when the proud patricians, who always scorned the entire populace, were forced to bow before a humble official of the people, who had neither auspices nor jurisdiction.

A well tempered tribunate is the firmest support of a good constitution. But if it has the slightest bit too much force, it undermines everything. As to weakness, there is none in its nature; and provided it is something, it is never less than it ought to be.

It degenerates into tyranny when it usurps the executive power, of which it is merely the moderator, and when it wants to dispense the laws it ought only protect. The enormous power of the ephors, which was without danger so long as Sparta preserved its mores, hastened corruption once it had begun. The blood of Agis,[2] who was slaughtered by these tyrants, was avenged by his successor. The crime and the punishment of the ephors equally hastened the fall of the republic; and after Cleomenes[3] Sparta was no longer anything. Rome also perished in the same way, and the excessive power of the tribunes, which they had gradually usurped, finally served, with the help of the laws that were made to protect liberty, as a safeguard for the emperors who destroyed it. As for the Council of Ten in Venice, it is a tribunal of blood, equally horrible to the patricians and the people, and which, far from proudly protecting the laws, no longer serves any purpose, after their degradation, beyond that of delivering blows in the dark which no one dares notice.

Just like the government, the tribunate weakened as a result of the multiplication of its members. When the tribunes of the Roman people, who at first were two in number, then five, wanted to double this number, the senate let them do so, certain that one part would hold the others in check; and this did not fail to happen.

The best way to prevent usurpations by so formidable a body, one that no government has yet made use of, would be not to make this body permanent, but to regulate the intervals during which it would be suppressed. These intervals, which ought not be so long as to allow abuses time to grow in strength, can be fixed by law in such a way that it is easy to shorten them, as needed, by means of extraordinary commissions.

---

1   *officials in charge of these functions*   [Rousseau's note] Custodes, diribitores, rogatores suffragiorum.

2   *Agis*   King of Sparta who attempted to reform Sparta's economic and political structure. His rule began in 245 BCE; he was overthrown and killed in prison 241 BCE.

3   *Cleomenes*   King of Sparta c. 520–c. 490 BCE.

This way seems to me to have no disadvantage, for since, as I have said, the tribunate is not part of the constitution, it can be set aside without doing the constitution any harm, because a newly established magistrate begins not with the power his predecessor had, but with the power the law gives him.

Chapter 6: On Dictatorship

The inflexibility of the laws, which prevents them from adapting to circumstances, can in certain instances make them harmful and render them the instrument of the state's downfall in time of crisis. The order and the slowness of formal procedures require a space of time which circumstances sometimes do not permit. A thousand circumstances can present themselves which the legislator has not foreseen, and it is a very necessary bit of foresight to realize that not everything can be foreseen.

It is therefore necessary to avoid the desire to strengthen political institutions to the point of removing the power to suspend their effect. Sparta itself allowed its laws to lie dormant.

But only the greatest dangers can counterbalance the danger of altering the public order, and the sacred power of the laws should never be suspended except when it is a question of the safety of the homeland. In these rare and obvious cases, public safety can be provided for by a special act which confers the responsibility for it on someone who is most worthy. This commission can be carried out in two ways, according to the type of danger.

If increasing the activity of government is enough to remedy the situation, it is concentrated in one or two members. Thus it is not the authority of the laws that is altered, but merely the form of their administration. But if the peril is such that the apparatus of the laws is an obstacle to their being protected, then a supreme leader is named who silences all the laws and briefly suspends the sovereign authority. In such a case, the general will is not in doubt, and it is evident that the first intention of the people is that the state should not perish. In this manner, the suspension of legislative authority does not abolish it. The magistrate who silences it cannot make it speak; he dominates it without being able to represent it. He can do anything but make laws.

The first way was used by the Roman senate when, by a sacred formula, it entrusted the consuls with the responsibility for providing for the safety of the Republic. The second took place when one of the two consuls named a

dictator,[1] a custom for which Alba[2] had provided Rome the precedent.

In the beginning days of the Republic, there was frequent recourse to dictatorship, since the state did not yet have a sufficiently stable basis to be capable of sustaining itself by the force of its constitution. Since the mores at that time made many of the precautions superfluous that would have been necessary in other times, there was no fear either that a dictator would abuse his authority or that he would try to hold on to it beyond his term of office. On the contrary, it seemed that such a great power was a burden to the one in whom it was vested, so quickly did he hasten to rid himself of it, as if a position that took the place of the laws would have been too troublesome and dangerous!

Thus it is not so much the danger of its being abused as it is that of its being degraded which makes one criticize the injudicious use of this supreme magistrature in the early days of the Republic. For while it was being wasted on elections, dedications and purely formal proceedings, there was reason to fear that it would become less formidable in time of need, and that people would become accustomed to regard as empty a title that was used exclusively in empty ceremonies.

Toward the end of the Republic, the Romans, having become more circumspect, were as unreasonably sparing in their use of the dictatorship as they had formerly been lavish. It was easy to see that their fear was ill-founded; that the weakness of the capital then protected it against the magistrates who were in its midst; that a dictator could, under certain circumstances, defend the public liberty without ever being able to make an attack on it; and that Rome's chains would not be forged in Rome itself, but in its armies. The weak resistance that Marius offered Sulla[3] and Pompey[4] offered Caesar clearly demonstrated what could be expected of internal authority in the face of external force.

---

1   *two consuls ... dictator*   [Rousseau's note] This nomination was made at night and in secret, as if it were shameful to place a man beyond the laws.

2   *Alba*   Legendary fifth king of Alba Longa, a city in pre-Roman Italy.

3   *Sulla*   Lucius Cornelius Sulla Felix (c. 138–78 BCE), Roman general and dictator, rival of, and victor over, Marius.

4   *Pompey*   Cnaeus Pompeius Magnus (106–48 BCE), former political ally, then rival, of Julius Caesar; defeated in the Civil War against Caesar, then assassinated in exile.

This error caused them to make huge mistakes; for example, failing to name a dictator in the Catalinian affair.[1] For since this was a question merely of the interior of the town and, at most, of some province in Italy, with the unlimited authority that the laws give the dictator, he would have easily quelled the conspiracy, which was stifled only by a coming together of favor chance happenings, which human prudence has no right to expect.

Instead of that, the senate was content to entrust all its power to the consuls. Whence it happened that, in order to act effectively, Cicero was forced to exceed this power on a crucial point. And although the first transports of joy indicated approval of his conduct, eventually Cicero was justly called to account for the blood of citizens shed against the laws, a reproach that could not have been delivered against a dictator. But the eloquence of the consul carried the day. And since even he, Roman though he was, preferred his own glory to his homeland, he sought not so much the most legitimate and safest way of saving the state as he did the way that would get him all the honor for settling this affair.[2] Thus he was justly honored as the liberator of Rome and justly punished as a law-breaker. However brilliant his recall may have been, it undoubtedly was a pardon.

For the rest, whatever the manner in which this important commission was conferred, it is important to limit a dictatorship's duration to a very short period of time which cannot be prolonged. In the crises that call for its being established, the state is soon either destroyed or saved; and once the pressing need has passed, the dictatorship becomes tyrannical or needless. In Rome, where the dictators had terms of six months only, most of them abdicated before their terms had expired. If the term had been longer, perhaps they would have been tempted to prolong it further, as did the decemvirs with a one year term. The dictator only had time enough to see to the need that got him elected. He did not have time to dream up other projects.

Chapter 7: On the Censorship[3]

Just as the declaration of the general will takes place through the law, the declaration of the public judgment takes place through the censorship. Public opinion is the sort of law whose censor is the minister, and which he only applies to particular cases, after the example of the prince.

Thus the censorial tribunal, far from being the arbiter of the people's opinion, is merely its spokesman; and as soon as it deviates from this opinion, its decisions are vain and futile.

It is useless to distinguish the mores of a nation from the objects of its esteem, for all these things derive from the same principle and are necessarily intermixed. Among all the peoples of the world, it is not nature but opinion which decides the choice of their pleasures. Reform men's opinions, and their mores will soon become purified all by themselves. Men always love what is good or what they find to be so; but it is in this judgment that they make mistakes. Hence this is the judgment whose regulation is the point at issue. Whoever judges mores judges honor; and whoever judges honor derives his law from opinion.

The opinions of a people arise from its constitution. Although the law does not regulate mores, legislation is what gives rise to them. When legislation weakens, mores degenerate; but then the judgment of the censors will not do what the force of the laws has not done.

It follows from this that the censorship can be useful for preserving mores, but never for reestablishing them. Establish censors while the laws are vigorous. Once they have lost their vigor, everything is hopeless. Nothing legitimate has any force once the laws no longer have force.

The censorship maintains mores by preventing opinions from becoming corrupt, by preserving their rectitude through wise applications, and sometimes even by making a determination on them when they are still uncertain. The use of seconds in duels,[4] which had been carried to the point of being a craze in the kingdom of France, was abolished by the following few words of the king's edict: *as for those who are cowardly enough to call upon seconds.* This judgment anticipated that of the public and suddenly made a determination. But when the same edicts tried to declare

---

1   *the Catalinian affair* Lucius Sergius Catilina (108–62 BCE), Roman politician who was at the center of the Catiline conspiracy (famously opposed by Cicero), which tried to overthrow the Roman Republic in 63–62 BCE.
2   *all the honor ... affair* [Rousseau's note] He could not have been sure of this, had he proposed a dictator, since he did not dare name himself, and he could not be sure that his colleague would name him.

3   *Censorship* Rousseau means the function performed by the Roman censor; this included legal enforcement of public morality, so it covered what we would call (legal) censorship and more.
4   *seconds in duels* Assistants to the dueling parties, sometimes finishing the fight when a dueler was unable to continue.

that it was also an act of cowardice to fight duels (which of course is quite true, but contrary to common opinion), the public mocked this decision; it concerned a matter about which its mind was already made up.

I have said elsewhere[1] that since public opinion is not subject to constraint, there should be no vestige of it in the tribunal established to represent it. It is impossible to show too much admiration for the skill with which this device, entirely lost among us moderns, was put into effect among the Romans and even better among the Lacedemonians.[2]

When a man of bad mores put forward a good proposal in the council of Sparta, the ephors ignored it and had the same proposal put forward by a virtuous citizen. What honor for the one, what shame for the other; and without having given praise or blame to either of the two! Certain drunkards of Samos—<they are from another island[3] which the delicacy of our language prohibits me from naming at this time>—defiled the tribunals of the ephors. The next day, a public edict gave the Samians permission to be filthy. A true punishment would have been less severe than impunity such as this. When Sparta made a pronouncement on what was or was not decent, Greece did not appeal its judgments.

Chapter 8: On Civil Religion

At first men had no other kings but the gods, and no other government than a theocratic one. They reasoned like Caligula, and then they reasoned correctly. A lengthy alteration of feelings and ideas is necessary before men can be resolved to accept a fellow man as a master, in the hope that things will turn out well for having done so.

By the mere fact that a god was placed at the head of every political society, it followed that there were as many gods as there were peoples. Two peoples who were alien to one another and nearly always enemies, could not recognize the same master for very long. Two armies in combat with one another could not obey the same leader. Thus national divisions led to polytheism, and this in turn led to theological and civil intolerance which are by nature the same, as will be stated later.

The fanciful notion of the Greeks that they had rediscovered their gods among the beliefs of barbarian peoples arose from another notion they had of regarding themselves as the natural sovereigns of these peoples. But in our day it is a ridiculous bit of erudition which equates the gods of different nations: as if Moloch, Saturn, and Chronos[4] could have been the same god; as if the Phoenicians' Baal, the Greeks' Zeus, and the Romans' Jupiter could have been the same; as if there could be anything in common among chimerical beings having different names!

But if it is asked how in pagan cultures, where each state has its own cult and its own gods, there are no wars of religion, I answer that it was for this very reason that each state, having its own cult as well as its own government, did not distinguish its gods from its laws. Political war was theological as well. The departments of the gods were, so to speak, fixed by national boundaries. The gods of one people had no rights over other peoples. The gods of the pagans were not jealous gods. They divided dominion over the world among themselves. Moses himself and the Hebrew people sometimes countenanced this idea in speaking of the god of Israel. It is true they regarded as nothing the gods of the Canaanites, a proscribed people destined for destruction, and whose land they were to occupy. But note how they spoke of the divinities of neighboring peoples whom they were forbidden to attack! *Is not the possession of what belongs to your god Chamos*, said Jephthah to the Ammonites, *lawfully yours? By the same right we possess the lands our victorious god has acquired for himself.*[5] It appears to me that here was a clear recognition of the parity between the rights of Chamos and those of the god of Israel.

But when the Jews, while in subjection to the kings of Babylon and later to the kings of Syria, wanted to re-

---

1   *I have said elsewhere* [Rousseau's note] I merely call attention in this chapter to what I have treated at greater length in my *Letter to D'Alembert*.

2   *Lacedemonians* Spartans.

3   *another island* It was in fact Chios.

4   *Moloch, Saturn, and Chronos* Moloch was a god of the ancient Phoenicians; Saturn of the Romans; and Chronos of the Greeks. In some contexts, various pairs of the six gods mentioned here were identified with each other—for example, it is often said that the god called Zeus by the Greeks was called Jupiter by the Romans.

5   *Is not the possession ... acquired for himself* [Rousseau's note] Nonne ea quae possidet Chamos deus tuus, tibi jure debentur? [Judges 11.24] Such is the text of the Vulgate. Father de Carrières has translated it: Do you not believe that you have the right to possess what belongs to your god Chamos? I do not know the force of the Hebrew text; but I see that in the Vulgate Jephthah positively acknowledges the right of the god Chamos, and that the French translator weakened this recognition by adding an "according to you" which is not in the Latin.

main steadfast in not giving recognition to any other god but their own, their refusal, seen as rebellion against the victor, brought them the persecutions we read of in their history, and of which there is no other precedent prior to Christianity.[1]

Since, therefore, each religion was uniquely tied to the laws of the state which prescribed it, there was no other way of converting a people except by enslaving it, nor any other missionaries than conquerors. And with the obligation to change cult being the law of the vanquished, it was necessary to begin by conquering before talking about it. Far from men fighting for the gods, it was, as it was in Homer, the gods who fought for men; each asked his own god for victory and paid for it with new altars. Before taking an area, the Romans summoned that area's gods to leave it. And when they allowed the Tarentines[2] to keep their angry gods, it was because at that point they considered these gods to be in subjection to their own and forced to do them homage. They left the vanquished their gods, just as they left them their laws. A wreath to the Capitoline Jupiter was often the only tribute they imposed.

Finally, the Romans having spread this cult and their gods, along with their empire, and having themselves often adopted the gods of the vanquished by granting the right of the city to both alike, the peoples of this vast empire gradually found themselves to have multitudes of gods and cults, which were nearly the same everywhere. And that is how paganism finally became a single, identical religion in the known world.

Such were the circumstances under which Jesus came to establish a spiritual kingdom on earth. In separating the theological system from the political system, this made the state to cease being united and caused internal divisions that never ceased to agitate Christian peoples. But since this new idea of an otherworldly kingdom had never entered the heads of the pagans, they always regarded the Christians as true rebels who, underneath their hypocritical submission, were only waiting for the moment when they would become independent and the masters, and adroitly usurp

the authority they pretended in their weakness to respect. This is the reason for the persecutions.

What the pagans feared happened. Then everything changed its appearance. The humble Christians changed their language, and soon this so-called otherworldly kingdom became, under a visible leader, the most violent despotism in this world.

However, since there has always been a prince and civil laws, this double power has given rise to a perpetual jurisdictional conflict that has made all good polity impossible in Christian states, and no one has ever been able to know whether it is the priest or the master whom one is obliged to obey.

Nevertheless, several peoples, even in Europe or nearby have wanted to preserve or reestablish the ancient system, but without success. The spirit of Christianity has won everything. The sacred cult has always remained or again become independent of the sovereign and without any necessary link to the state. Mohammed had very sound opinions. He tied his political system together very well, and so long as the form of his government subsisted under his successors, the caliphs, this government was utterly unified, and for that reason it was good. But as the Arabs became prosperous, lettered, polished, soft and cowardly, they were subjugated by barbarians. Then the division between the two powers began again. Although it is less apparent among the Mohammedans than among the Christians, it is there all the same, especially in the sect of Ali;[3] and there are states, such as Persia,[4] where it never ceases to be felt.

Among us, the kings of England have established themselves as heads of the Church, and the czars have done the same. But with this title, they became less its masters than its ministers. They have acquired not so much the right to change it as the power to maintain it. They are not its legislators; they are merely its princes. Wherever the clergy constitutes a body,[5] it is master and legislator in its own realm.

---

1   *no other precedent ... Christianity* [Rousseau's note] It is quite clear that the Phocian War [355–346 BCE ended in the conquest of Phocis by Philip II of Macedon], called the Holy War, was not a war of religion at all. It had for its object to punish sacrileges, and not to make unbelievers submit.

2   *Tarentines* Tarentum (Taranto), was a southern Italian city, sometimes quarreling with Rome, and conquered by the Romans in 272 BCE.

3   *sect of Ali* Ali was Mohammed's son-in-law; his followers formed one of the major divisions within Islam, the Shiites.

4   *Persia* Today's Iran.

5   *clergy constitutes a body* [Rousseau's note] It should be carefully noted that it is not so much the formal assemblies, such as those of France, which bind the clergy together into a body, as it is the communion of the churches. Communion and excommunication are the social compact of the clergy, one with which it will always be the master of the peoples and the kings. All the priests who communicate together are citizens, even if they should be from the opposite ends of the world. This invention is a political mas-

Thus there are two powers, two sovereigns, in England and in Russia, just as there are everywhere else.

Of all the Christian writers, the philosopher Hobbes[1] is the only one who clearly saw the evil and the remedy, who dared to propose the reunification of the two heads of the eagle and the complete restoration of political unity, without which no state or government will ever be well constituted. But he should have seen that the dominating spirit of Christianity was incompatible with his system, and that the interest of the priest would always be stronger than that of the state. It is not so much what is horrible and false in his political theory as what is just and true that has caused it to be hated.[2]

I believe that if the facts of history were developed from this point of view, it would be easy to refute the opposing sentiments of Bayle[3] and Warburton,[4] the one holding that no religion is useful to the body politic, while the other maintains, to the contrary, that Christianity is its firmest support. We could prove to the first that no state has ever been founded without religion serving as its base, and to the second that Christian law is at bottom more injurious than it is useful for the strong constitution of the state. To succeed in making myself understood, I need only give a bit more precision to the excessively vague ideas about religion that are pertinent to my subject.

When considered in relation to society, which is either general or particular, religion can also be divided into two kinds, namely the religion of the man and that of the citizen. The first—without temples, altars or rites, and limited to the purely internal cult of the supreme God and to the eternal duties of morality—is the pure and simple religion of the Gospel, the true theism, and what can be called natural divine law [droit]. The other, inscribed in a single country, gives it its gods, its own titulary patrons. It has its dogmas, its rites, its exterior cult prescribed by laws. Outside the nation that practices it, everything is infidel, alien and barbarous to it. It extends the duties and rights of man only as far as its altars. Such were all the religions of the early peoples, to which the name of civil or positive divine law [droit] can be given.

There is a third sort of religion which is more bizarre. In giving men two sets of legislation, two leaders, and two homelands, it subjects them to contradictory duties and prevents them from being simultaneously devout men and citizens. Such is the religion of the Lamas and of the Japanese, and such is Roman Christianity. It can be called the religion of the priest. It leads to a kind of mixed and unsociable law [droit] which has no name.

Considered from a political standpoint, these three types of religion all have their faults. The third is so bad that it is a waste of time to amuse oneself by proving it. Whatever breaks up social unity is worthless. All institutions that place man in contradiction with himself are of no value.

The second is good in that it unites the divine cult with love of the laws, and that, in making the homeland the object of its citizens' admiration, it teaches them that all service to the state is service to its tutelary god. It is a kind of theocracy in which there ought to be no pontiff other than the prince and no priests other than the magistrates. To die for one's country is then to become a martyr; to violate its laws is to be impious. To subject a guilty man to public execration is to deliver him to the wrath of the gods: sacer estod.[5]

On the other hand, it is bad in that, being based on error and lies, it deceives men, makes them credulous and superstitious, and drowns the true cult of the divinity in an empty ceremony. It is also bad when, on becoming exclusive and tyrannical, it makes a people bloodthirsty and intolerant, so that men breathe only murder and massacre, and believe they are performing a holy action in killing anyone who does not accept its gods. This places such a people in a natural state of war with all others, which is quite harmful to its own security.

Thus there remains the religion of man or Christianity (not that of today, but that of the Gospel, which is completely different). Through this holy, sublime, true religion,

terpiece. There is nothing like this among the pagan priests; thus they never made up a body of clergy.

1 Hobbes His De Cive (1642) contains the first important argument for the supremacy of secular over church authority in the state.

2 It is not so much ... caused it to be hated [Rousseau's note] Notice, among other things, in Grotius' letter to his brother, dated April 11, 1643, what this learned man approves of and what he criticizes in his book De Cive. It is true that, prone to being indulgent, he appears to forgive the author for his good points for the sake of his bad ones. But not everyone is so merciful.

3 Bayle Pierre Bayle (1647–1706), French Protestant philosopher and essayist, who spent most of his life in exile in Holland. See his Pensées sur la comété.

4 Warburton See his The Divine Legation of Moses Demonstrated on the Principles of a Religious Deist (1737–41).

5 sacer estod Latin: let him be damned. This formula was uttered when someone was to be cut off from contact with society and left to the judgment of the gods.

men, in being the children of the same God, all acknowledge one another as brothers, and the society that unites them is not dissolved even at death.

But since this religion has no particular relation to the body politic, it leaves laws with only the force the laws derive from themselves, without adding any other force to them. And thus one of the great bonds of a particular society remains ineffectual. Moreover, far from attaching the hearts of the citizens to the state, it detaches them from it as from all the other earthly things. I know of nothing more contrary to the social spirit.

We are told that a people of true Christians would form the most perfect society imaginable. I see but one major difficulty in this assumption, namely that a society of true Christians would no longer be a society of men.

I even say that this supposed society would not, for all its perfection, be the strongest or the most durable. By dint of being perfect, it would lack a bond of union; its destructive vice would be in its very perfection.

Each man would fulfill his duty; the people would be subject to the laws; the leaders would be just and moderate, the magistrates would be upright and incorruptible; soldiers would scorn death; there would be neither vanity nor luxury. All of this is very fine, but let us look further.

Christianity is a completely spiritual religion, concerned exclusively with things heavenly. The homeland of the Christian is not of this world. He does his duty, it is true, but he does it with a profound indifference toward the success or failure of his efforts. So long as he has nothing to reproach himself for, it matters little to him whether anything is going well or poorly down here. If the state is flourishing, he hardly dares to enjoy the public felicity, for fear of becoming puffed up with his country's glory. If the state is in decline, he blesses the hand of God that weighs heavily on his people.

For the society to be peaceful and for harmony to be maintained, every citizen without exception would have to be an equally good Christian. But if, unhappily, there is a single ambitious man, a single hypocrite, a Cataline, for example, or a Cromwell, he would quite undoubtedly gain the upper hand on his pious compatriots. Christian charity does not readily allow one to think ill of his neighbors. Once he has discovered by some ruse the art of deceiving them and of laying hold of a part of the public authority, behold a man established in dignity! God wills that he be respected. Soon, behold a power! God wills that he be obeyed. Does the trustee of his power abuse it? He is the rod with which God punishes his children. It would be against one's conscience to expel the usurper. It would be necessary to disturb the public tranquility, use violence and shed blood. All this accords ill with the meekness of a Christian. And after all, what difference does it make whether one is a free man or a serf in this vale of tears? The essential thing is getting to heaven, and resignation is but another means to that end.

What if a foreign war breaks out? The citizens march without reservation into combat; none among them dreams of deserting. They do their duty, but without passion for victory; they know how to die better than how to be victorious. What difference does it make whether they are the victors or the vanquished? Does not providence know better than they what they need? Just imagine the advantage a fierce, impetuous and passionate enemy could draw from their stoicism! Set them face to face with those generous peoples who were devoured by an ardent love of glory and homeland. Suppose your Christian republic is face to face with Sparta or Rome. The pious Christians will be beaten, crushed and destroyed before they realize where they are, or else they will owe their safety only to the scorn their enemies will conceive for them. To my way of thinking, the oath taken by Fabius'[1] soldiers was a fine one. They did not swear to die or to win; they swore to return victorious. And they kept their promise. Christians would never have taken such an oath; they would have believed they were tempting God.

But I am deceiving myself in talking about a Christian republic; these terms are mutually exclusive. Christianity preaches only servitude and dependence. Its spirit is too favorable to tyranny for tyranny not to take advantage of it at all times. True Christians are made to be slaves. They know it and are hardly moved by this. This brief life has too little value in their eyes.

Christian troops, we are told, are excellent. I deny this. Is someone going to show me some? For my part, I do not know of any Christian troops. Someone will mention the crusades. Without disputing the valor of the crusaders, I will point out that quite far from being Christians, they were soldiers of the priest; they were citizens of the church; they were fighting for its spiritual country which the church, God knows how, had made temporal. Properly understood, this is a throwback to paganism. Since the Gospel does not

---

1   *Fabius*   Quintus Fabius Maximus Verrucosus (c. 275–203 BCE), Roman soldier in the Punic Wars, and politician.

establish a national religion, no holy war is possible among Christians.

Under the pagan emperors, Christian soldiers were brave. All the Christian authors affirm this, and I believe it. This was a competition for honor against the pagan troops. Once the emperors were Christians, this competition ceased. And when the cross expelled the eagle, all Roman valor disappeared.

But leaving aside political considerations, let us return to right and determine the principles that govern this important point. The right which the social compact gives the sovereign over the subjects does not, as I have said, go beyond the limits of public utility.[1] The subjects, therefore, do not have to account to the sovereign for their opinions, except to the extent that these opinions are of importance to the community. For it is of great importance to the state that each citizen have a religion that causes him to love his duties. But the dogmas of that religion are of no interest either to the state or its members, except to the extent that these dogmas relate to morality and to the duties which the one who professes them is bound to fulfill toward others. Each man can have in addition such opinions as he pleases, without it being any of the sovereign's business to know what they are. For since the other world is outside the province of the sovereign, whatever the fate of subjects in the life to come, it is none of its business, so long as they are good citizens in this life.

There is, therefore, a purely civil profession of faith, the articles of which it belongs to the sovereign to establish, not exactly as dogmas of religion, but as sentiments of sociability, without which it is impossible to be a good citizen or a faithful subject.[2] While not having the ability to obligate anyone to believe them, the sovereign can banish from the state anyone who does not believe them. It can banish him not for being impious but for being unsociable, for being incapable of sincerely loving the laws and justice, and of sacrificing his life, if necessary, for his duty. If, after having publicly acknowledged these same dogmas, a person acts as if he does not believe them, he should be put to death; he has committed the greatest of crimes: he has lied before the laws.

The dogmas of the civil religion ought to be simple, few in number, precisely worded, without explanations or commentaries. The existence of a powerful, intelligent, beneficent divinity that foresees and provides; the life to come; the happiness of the just; the punishment of the wicked; the sanctity of the social contract and of the laws. These are the positive dogmas. As for the negative dogmas, I am limiting them to just one, namely intolerance. It is part of the cults we have excluded.

Those who distinguish between civil and theological intolerance are mistaken, in my opinion. Those two types of intolerance are inseparable. It is impossible to live in peace with those one believes to be damned. To love them would be to hate God who punishes them. It is absolutely necessary either to reclaim them or torment them. Whenever theological intolerance is allowed, it is impossible for it not to have some civil effect;[3] and once it does, the sovereign no

---

1 *The right ... limits of public utility* [Rousseau's note] *In the Republic*, says the Marquis d'Argenson, *each man is perfectly free with respect to what does not harm others.* [Commentators have been unable to find this quotation in the surviving publications of d'Argenson.] This is the invariable boundary. It cannot be expressed more precisely. I have been unable to deny myself the pleasure of occasionally citing this manuscript, even though it is unknown to the public, in order to pay homage to the memory of a famous and noteworthy man, who, even as a minister [French Minister of Foreign Affairs], retained the heart of a citizen, along with just and sound opinions on the government of his country.

2 *purely civil profession ... faithful subject* [Rousseau's note] By pleading for Cataline, Caesar tried to establish the dogma of the mortality of the soul. To refute him, Cato and Cicero did not waste time philosophizing. They contented themselves with showing that Caesar spoke like a bad citizen and advanced a doctrine that was injurious to the state. In fact, this was what the Roman senate had to judge, and not a question of theology.

3 *civil effect* [Rousseau's note] Marriage, for example, being a civil contract, has civil effects without which it is impossible for a society even to subsist. Suppose then that a clergy reaches the point where it ascribes to itself alone the right to permit this act (a right that must necessarily be usurped in every intolerant religion). In that case, is it not clear that in establishing the authority of the church in this matter, it will render ineffectual that of the prince, who will have no more subjects than those whom the clergy wishes to give him? Is it not also clear that the clergy—if master of whether to marry or not to marry people according to whether or not they accept this or that doctrine, according to whether they accept or reject this or that formula, according to whether they are more or less devout—in behaving prudently and holding firm, will alone dispose of inheritance, offices, the citizens, the state itself, which could not subsist, if composed solely of bastards? But, it will be said, abuses will be appealed; summonses and decrees will be issued; temporal holdings will be seized. What a pity! If it has a little—I will not say courage—but good sense, the clergy will serenely allow the appeals, the summonses, the decrees and the seizures, and it will end up master. It is not, it seems to me, a big sacrifice to abandon a part when one is sure of securing the whole.

longer is sovereign, not even over temporal affairs. Thenceforward, priests are the true masters; kings are simply their officers.

Now that there no longer is and never again can be an exclusive national religion, tolerance should be shown to all those that tolerate others, so long as their dogmas contain nothing contrary to the duties of a citizen. But whoever dares to say *outside the church there is no salvation* ought to be expelled from the state, unless the state is the church and the prince is the pontiff. Such a dogma is good only in a theocratic government; in all other forms of government it is ruinous. The reason why Henry IV is said to have embraced the Roman religion should make every

decent man, and above all any prince who knows how to reason, leave it.

Chapter 9: Conclusion

After laying down the true principles of political right and attempting to establish the state on this basis, it remains to support the state by means of its external relations, which would include the laws of nations, commerce, the right of war and conquest, public law, leagues, negotiations, treaties, and so on. But all that forms a new subject which is too vast for my nearsightedness. I should always set my sights on things that are nearer at hand to me.

ADAM SMITH
(1723 – 1790)

WHEN ADAM SMITH PUBLISHED HIS MOST FAMOUS book, *An Inquiry into the Nature and Causes of the Wealth of Nations* (1776), he was already well-known for his contributions to moral philosophy, most particularly *A Theory of Moral Sentiments* (1759). Smith was well versed in many different fields and had lectured and written on logic, rhetoric, and jurisprudence. But it is in the field of economics that he has left his most indelible mark. He is arguably the most important writer in the history of economics and, to the extent that economic thought has come to occupy a central place in political philosophy, a figure of real importance in the latter as well. The influence of *The Wealth of Nations* can hardly be overestimated.

Smith was born in 1723 in Kirkcaldy, Fife, Scotland and raised by his mother, as his father had died before he was born. In 1737, when he was fourteen, Smith began his advanced studies at the University of Glasgow. There he studied under Francis Hutcheson, one of the first prominent philosophers to advance the idea that morality was based on natural human sentiments. In 1740 Smith went to Balliol College, Oxford to continue his studies. Two years later he embarked on a series of lectures in Edinburgh, mostly dealing with literature and rhetoric, but some also touching on philosophy and economics.

Shortly thereafter, he met David Hume for the first time. Hume, who would become the most influential British philosopher of the eighteenth century, was also a Scotsman and also significantly influenced by Francis Hutcheson's work. The two developed a close personal and professional friendship which would continue throughout their lives.

In 1751 Smith returned to the University of Glasgow as professor of logic. A year later he was appointed chair of moral philosophy. In 1759 Smith published *A Theory of Moral Sentiments*, which was based on his Edinburgh lectures and his teaching in Glasgow. The book attempts to explain the nature of our moral practices through an examination of human psychology. Smith would employ a similar approach to the subject of economics when he began writing *The Wealth of Nations*.

In 1763 Smith left his University post to become the private tutor for the Duke of Buccleuch. In his new vocation, Smith traveled to France and came into contact with many of the great figures of the Enlightenment, including Voltaire and Rousseau. He also met Benjamin Franklin, who was influenced by Smith's arguments for limitations on government power and who brought those ideas to the attention of others as an independent United States of America was being formed. Smith also met members of the French physiocrat school, whose views on the importance of agricultural labor and whose rejection of mercantilism had a significant impact on Smith's economic thinking. After two years abroad, Smith returned to Scotland and began writing *The Wealth of Nations*. The book was published ten years later, in 1776.

While Smith was certainly not the first writer to discuss economics, his treatment of the subject was an important step in its development as a distinct area of study. He had argued that sympathy provided the chief human psychological underpinning of morality; he argued that prudential self-interest provided the chief psychological underpinning for economic relationships. If markets were left free of political interference, he argued, the collective result of each person pursuing his own good would be the promotion of the collective good. It was, he said, as though an "invisible hand" were directing our activities to optimize the outcome for all. This force would naturally help to ensure that supply and demand, when unmanipulated, would adjust as needed to reach a natural balance. His arguments supporting free markets within nations and free trade among them have influenced politicians and economists to the present day.

Smith also saw labor rather than raw materials or land as central to economic relationships. He pointed out that how a workforce was organized could have a dramatic impact on productivity, most prominently in his analysis of the division of labor. Smith pointed out that a pin factory, with each employee performing a specific task, could produce thousands more pins than individuals performing each step. Such ideas were not only influential in capitalist thought; Karl Marx would incorporate them into his analysis, placing economic relationships at the core of all political and social history and regarding the power of the laborer as fundamental to change. Smith also discussed the relationship between population and consumption, a topic central to the later thinking of Thomas Malthus.

Two years after publishing *The Wealth of Nations* Smith accepted an appointment as a customs commissioner, a post he held until his death. But he did not give up his scholarly pursuits; he worked on revisions to *The Wealth of Nations* and *A Theory of Moral Sentiments* as well as on new writings during his final years. In 1783 Smith helped to found The Royal Society of Edinburgh, Scotland's national academy of sciences and letters.

Smith's mother died in 1784. He had been devoted to her throughout his life and lived with her for much of it. Her death marked the beginning of the decline of his health; he died in 1790 at the age of 67.

◆ ◆ ◆ ◆ ◆

The Wealth of Nations (1776)

from *Book 1. Of the Causes of Improvement in the Productive Powers of Labor, and of the Order According to Which Its Produce is Naturally Distributed Among the Different Ranks of the People*

Chapter 1: Of the Division of Labor

The greatest improvement in the productive powers of labor, and the greater part of the skill, dexterity, and judgment with which it is anywhere directed, or applied, seem to have been the effects of the division of labor.

The effects of the division of labor, in the general business of society, will be more easily understood by considering in what manner it operates in some particular manufactures. It is commonly supposed to be carried furthest in some very trifling ones; not perhaps that it really is carried further in them than in others of more importance: but in those trifling manufactures which are destined to supply the small wants of but a small number of people, the whole number of workmen must necessarily be small; and those employed in every different branch of the work can often be collected into the same workhouse, and placed at once under the view of the spectator. In those great manufactures, on the contrary, which are destined to supply the great wants of the great body of the people, every different branch of the work employs so great a number of workmen that it is impossible to collect them all into the same workhouse. We can seldom see more, at one time, than those employed in one single branch. Though in such manufactures, therefore, the work may really be divided into a much greater number of parts than in those of a more trifling nature, the division is not near so obvious, and has accordingly been much less observed.

To take an example, therefore, from a very trifling manufacture; but one in which the division of labor has been very often taken notice of, the trade of the pin-maker; a workman not educated to this business (which the division of labor has rendered a distinct trade), nor acquainted with the use of the machinery employed in it (to the invention of which the same division of labor has probably given occasion), could scarce, perhaps, with his utmost industry, make one pin in a day, and certainly could not make twenty. But in the way in which this business is now carried on, not only the whole work is a peculiar trade, but it is divided into a number of branches, of which the greater part are likewise peculiar[1] trades. One man draws out the wire, another straights it, a third cuts it, a fourth points it, a fifth grinds it at the top for receiving, the head; to make the head requires two or three distinct operations; to put it on is a peculiar business, to whiten the pins is another; it is even a trade by itself to put them into the paper; and the important business of making a pin is, in this manner, divided into about eighteen distinct operations, which, in some manufactories, are all performed by distinct hands, though in others the same man will sometimes perform two or three of them. I have seen a small manufactory of this kind where ten men only were employed, and where some of them consequently performed two or three distinct operations. But though they were very poor, and therefore but indifferently accom-

---

1 *peculiar* Individual, particular.

modated[1] with the necessary machinery, they could, when they exerted themselves, make among them about twelve pounds of pins in a day. There are in a pound upwards of four thousand pins of a middling size. Those ten persons, therefore, could make among them upwards of forty-eight thousand pins in a day. Each person, therefore, making a tenth part of forty-eight thousand pins, might be considered as making four thousand eight hundred pins in a day. But if they had all wrought separately and independently, and without any of them having been educated to this peculiar business, they certainly could not each of them have made twenty, perhaps not one pin in a day; that is, certainly, not the two hundred and fortieth, perhaps not the four thousand eight hundredth part of what they are at present capable of performing, in consequence of a proper division and combination of their different operations.

[...]

It is the great multiplication of the productions of all the different arts, in consequence of the division of labor, which occasions, in a well-governed society, that universal opulence which extends itself to the lowest ranks of the people. Every workman has a great quantity of his own work to dispose of beyond what he himself has occasion for; and every other workman being exactly in the same situation, he is enabled to exchange a great quantity of his own goods for a great quantity, or, what comes to the same thing, for the price of a great quantity of theirs. He supplies them abundantly with what they have occasion for, and they accommodate him as amply with what he has occasion for, and a general plenty diffuses itself through all the different ranks of the society.

Observe the accommodation of the most common artificer or day-laborer in a civilized and thriving country, and you will perceive that the number of people of whose industry a part, though but a small part, has been employed in procuring him this accommodation, exceeds all computation. The woolen coat, for example, which covers the day-laborer, as coarse and rough as it may appear, is the produce of the joint labor of a great multitude of workmen. The shepherd, the sorter of the wool, the wool-comber or carder, the dyer, the scribbler, the spinner, the weaver, the fuller, the dresser,[2] with many others, must all join their different arts in order to complete even this homely production. How many merchants and carriers, besides, must have been employed in transporting the materials from some of those workmen to others who often live in a very distant part of the country! How much commerce and navigation in particular, how many ship-builders, sailors, sail-makers, rope-makers, must have been employed in order to bring together the different drugs made use of by the dyer, which often come from the remotest corners of the world! What a variety of labor, too, is necessary in order to produce the tools of the meanest of those workmen! To say nothing of such complicated machines as the ship of the sailor, the mill of the fuller, or even the loom of the weaver, let us consider only what a variety of labor is requisite in order to form that very simple machine, the shears with which the shepherd clips the wool. The miner, the builder of the furnace for smelting the ore, the seller of the timber, the burner of the charcoal to be made use of in the smelting-house, the brickmaker, the brick-layer, the workmen who attend the furnace, the mill-wright, the forger, the smith, must all of them join their different arts in order to produce them. Were we to examine, in the same manner, all the different parts of his dress and household furniture, the coarse linen shirt which he wears next his skin, the shoes which cover his feet, the bed which he lies on, and all the different parts which compose it, the kitchen-grate at which he prepares his victuals,[3] the coals which he makes use of for that purpose, dug from the bowels of the earth, and brought to him perhaps by a long sea and a long land carriage, all the other utensils of his kitchen, all the furniture of his table, the knives and forks, the earthen or pewter plates upon which he serves up and divides his victuals, the different hands employed in preparing his bread and his beer, the glass window which lets in the heat and the light, and keeps out the wind and the rain, with all the knowledge and art requisite for preparing that beautiful and happy invention, without which these northern parts of the world could scarce have afforded a very comfortable habitation, together with the tools of all the different workmen employed in producing those different conveniences; if we examine, I say, all these things, and consider what a variety of labor is employed about each of them, we shall be sensible that, without the assistance and co-operation of many thousands, the very meanest person in a civilized country could not be provided, even according to what we very falsely imagine the easy and

---

1 *indifferently accommodated* Not well provided.

2 *the scribbler* Runs wool through a machine, which cards or teases it coarsely; *the fuller* Treads or beats cloth to clean and thicken it; *the dresser* Finishes fabrics, to give them a nap (smooth surface, or gloss).

3 *victuals* Food.

simple manner in which he is commonly accommodated. Compared, indeed, with the more extravagant luxury of the great, his accommodation must no doubt appear extremely simple and easy; and yet it may be true, perhaps, that the accommodation of a European prince does not always so much exceed that of an industrious and frugal peasant as the accommodation of the latter exceeds that of many an African king, the absolute master of the lives and liberties of ten thousand naked savages.

Chapter 2: Of the Principle Which Gives Occasion to the Division of Labor

This division of labor, from which so many advantages are derived, is not originally the effect of any human wisdom, which foresees and intends that general opulence to which it gives occasion. It is the necessary, though very slow and gradual consequence of a certain propensity in human nature which has in view no such extensive utility; the propensity to truck,[1] barter, and exchange one thing for another.

Whether this propensity be one of those original principles in human nature of which no further account can be given; or whether, as seems more probable, it be the necessary consequence of the faculties of reason and speech, it belongs not to our present subject to inquire. It is common to all men, and to be found in no other race of animals, which seem to know neither this nor any other species of contracts. Two greyhounds, in running down the same hare, have sometimes the appearance of acting in some sort of concert.[2] Each turns her towards his companion, or endeavors to intercept her when his companion turns her towards himself. This, however, is not the effect of any contract, but of the accidental concurrence of their passions in the same object at that particular time. Nobody ever saw a dog make a fair and deliberate exchange of one bone for another with another dog. Nobody ever saw one animal by its gestures and natural cries signify to another, this is mine, that yours; I am willing to give this for that. When an animal wants to obtain something either of a man or of another animal, it has no other means of persuasion but to gain the favor of those whose service it requires. A puppy fawns upon its dam,[3] and a spaniel endeavors by a thousand attractions to engage the attention of its master who is at dinner, when it wants to be fed by him. Man sometimes uses the same arts with his brethren, and when he has no other means of engaging them to act according to his inclinations, endeavors by every servile and fawning attention to obtain their good will. He has not time, however, to do this upon every occasion. In civilized society he stands at all times in need of the cooperation and assistance of great multitudes, while his whole life is scarce[4] sufficient to gain the friendship of a few persons. In almost every other race of animals each individual, when it is grown up to maturity, is entirely independent, and in its natural state has occasion for the assistance of no other living creature. But man has almost constant occasion for the help of his brethren, and it is in vain for him to expect it from their benevolence only. He will be more likely to prevail if he can interest their self-love in his favor, and show them that it is for their own advantage to do for him what he requires of them. Whoever offers to another a bargain of any kind, proposes to do this. Give me that which I want, and you shall have this which you want, is the meaning of every such offer; and it is in this manner that we obtain from one another the far greater part of those good offices[5] which we stand in need of. It is not from the benevolence of the butcher, the brewer, or the baker that we expect our dinner, but from their regard to their own interest. We address ourselves, not to their humanity but to their self-love, and never talk to them of our own necessities but of their advantages. Nobody but a beggar chooses to depend chiefly upon the benevolence of his fellow-citizens. Even a beggar does not depend upon it entirely. The charity of well-disposed people, indeed, supplies him with the whole fund of his subsistence. But though this principle ultimately provides him with all the necessaries of life which he has occasion for,[6] it neither does nor can provide him with them as he has occasion for them. The greater part of his occasional[7] wants are supplied in the same manner as those of other people, by treaty, by barter, and by purchase. With the money which one man gives him he purchases food. The old clothes which another bestows upon him he exchanges for other old clothes which suit him better, or for lodging, or for food, or for money, with which he can buy either food, clothes, or lodging, as he has occasion.

As it is by treaty, by barter, and by purchase that we obtain from one another the greater part of those mutual

1   *truck*   Trade.
2   *concert*   Cooperation or harmony.
3   *dam*   Mother.

4   *scarce*   Scarcely.
5   *good offices*   Beneficial acts.
6   *occasion for*   Need of.
7   *occasional*   Arising out of particular occasions.

good offices which we stand in need of, so it is this same trucking disposition which originally gives occasion to the division of labor. In a tribe of hunters or shepherds a particular person makes bows and arrows, for example, with more readiness and dexterity than any other. He frequently exchanges them for cattle or for venison with his companions; and he finds at last that he can in this manner get more cattle and venison than if he himself went to the field to catch them. From a regard to his own interest, therefore, the making of bows and arrows grows to be his chief business, and he becomes a sort of armorer. Another excels in making the frames and covers of their little huts or movable houses. He is accustomed to be of use in this way to his neighbors, who reward him in the same manner with cattle and with venison, till at last he finds it his interest to dedicate himself entirely to this employment, and to become a sort of house-carpenter. In the same manner a third becomes a smith or a brazier,[1] a fourth a tanner or dresser of hides or skins, the principal part of the clothing of savages. And thus the certainty of being able to exchange all that surplus part of the produce of his own labor, which is over and above his own consumption, for such parts of the produce of other men's labor as he may have occasion for, encourages every man to apply himself to a particular occupation, and to cultivate and bring to perfection whatever talent or genius he may possess for that particular species of business.

The difference of natural talents in different men is, in reality, much less than we are aware of; and the very different genius which appears to distinguish men of different professions, when grown up to maturity, is not upon many occasions so much the cause as the effect of the division of labor. The difference between the most dissimilar characters, between a philosopher and a common street porter, for example, seems to arise not so much from nature as from habit, custom, and education. When they came into the world, and for the first six or eight years of their existence, they were perhaps very much alike, and neither their parents nor playfellows could perceive any remarkable difference. About that age, or soon after, they come to be employed in very different occupations. The difference of talents comes then to be taken notice of, and widens by degrees, till at last the vanity of the philosopher is willing to acknowledge scarce any resemblance. But without the disposition to truck, barter, and exchange, every man must

have procured to himself every necessary and conveniency[2] of life which he wanted. All must have had the same duties to perform, and the same work to do, and there could have been no such difference of employment as could alone give occasion to any great difference of talents.

As it is this disposition which forms that difference of talents, so remarkable among men of different professions, so it is this same disposition which renders that difference useful. Many tribes of animals acknowledged to be all of the same species derive from nature a much more remarkable distinction of genius,[3] than what, antecedent to custom and education, appears to take place among men. By nature a philosopher is not in genius and disposition half so different from a street porter, as a mastiff is from a greyhound, or a greyhound from a spaniel, or this last from a shepherd's dog. Those different tribes of animals, however, though all of the same species, are of scarce any use to one another. The strength of the mastiff is not, in the least, supported either by the swiftness of the greyhound, or by the sagacity of the spaniel, or by the docility of the shepherd's dog. The effects of those different geniuses and talents, for want of the power or disposition to barter and exchange, cannot be brought into a common stock, and do not in the least contribute to the better accommodation and conveniency of the species. Each animal is still obliged to support and defend itself, separately and independently, and derives no sort of advantage from that variety of talents with which nature has distinguished its fellows. Among men, on the contrary, the most dissimilar geniuses are of use to one another; the different produces of their respective talents, by the general disposition to truck, barter, and exchange, being brought, as it were, into a common stock, where every man may purchase whatever part of the produce of other men's talents he has occasion for.

Chapter 3: That the Division of Labor Is Limited by the Extent of the Market

As it is the power of exchanging that gives occasion to the division of labor, so the extent of this division must always be limited by the extent of that power, or, in other words, by the extent of the market. When the market is very small, no person can have any encouragement to dedicate himself entirely to one employment, for want of the power to

---

1   *brazier*   One who works in brass.

2   *necessary and conveniency*   Necessity and convenience.
3   *genius*   Specific skill.

exchange all that surplus part of the produce of his own labor, which is over and above his own consumption, for such parts of the produce of other men's labor as he has occasion for.

[...]

Chapter 10, Part 2: Inequalities by the Policy of Europe

Such are the inequalities in the whole of advantages and disadvantages of the different employments of labor and stock, which the defect of any of the three requisites above mentioned must occasion,[1] even where there is the most perfect liberty. But the policy of Europe, by not leaving things at perfect liberty, occasions other inequalities of much greater importance.

It does this chiefly in the three following ways. First, by restraining the competition in some employments to a smaller number than would otherwise be disposed to enter into them; secondly, by increasing it in others beyond what it naturally would be; and, thirdly, by obstructing the free circulation of labor and stock, both from employment to employment and from place to place.

First, the policy of Europe occasions a very important inequality in the whole of the advantages and disadvantages of the different employments of labor and stock, by restraining the competition in some employments to a smaller number than might otherwise be disposed to enter into them.[...]

The property which every man has in his own labor, as it is the original foundation of all other property, so it is the most sacred and inviolable. The patrimony of a poor man lies in the strength and dexterity of his hands; and to hinder him from employing this strength and dexterity of his hands; and to hinder him from employing this strength and dexterity in what manner he thinks proper without injury to his neighbor is a plain violation of this most sacred property. It is a manifest encroachment upon the just liberty both of the workman and of those who might be disposed to employ him. As it hinders the one from working at what he thinks proper, so it hinders the others from employing whom they think proper. To judge whether he is fit to be employed may surely be trusted to the discretion of the employers whose interest it so much concerns. The affected[2] anxiety of the law-giver lest they should employ an improper person is evidently as impertinent[3] as it is oppressive.[...]

People of the same trade seldom meet together, even for merriment and diversion, but the conversation ends in a conspiracy against the public, or in some contrivance to raise prices. It is impossible indeed to prevent such meetings, by any law which either could be executed, or would be consistent with liberty and justice. But though the law cannot hinder people of the same trade from sometimes assembling together, it ought to do nothing to facilitate such assemblies, much less to render them necessary.

[...]

Secondly, the policy of Europe, by increasing the competition in some employments beyond what it naturally would be, occasions another inequality of an opposite kind in the whole of the advantages and disadvantages of the different employments of labor and stock.

It has been considered as of so much importance that a proper number of young people should be educated for certain professions, that sometimes the public and sometimes the piety of private founders have established many pensions, scholarships, exhibitions, bursaries, etc., for this purpose, which draw many more people into those trades than could otherwise pretend to follow them.

[...]

Thirdly, the policy of Europe, by obstructing the free circulation of labor and stock both from employment to employment, and from place to place, occasions in some cases a very inconvenient inequality in the whole of the advantages and disadvantages of their different employments.

The Statute of Apprenticeship[4] obstructs the free circulation of labor from one employment to another, even in the same place. The exclusive privileges of corporations obstruct it from one place to another, even in the same employment.

It frequently happens that while high wages are given to the workmen in one manufacture, those in another are obliged to content themselves with bare subsistence. The

---

1 *three requisites ... occasion* In the preceding section, Smith wrote that there are three circumstances, in addition to perfect freedom, which are necessary for people to have "equality in the whole of their advantages or disadvantages.... First, the employments must be well known and long established in the neighborhood; secondly, they must be in their ordinary, or what may be called their natural state; and, thirdly, they must be the sole or principal employments of those who occupy them."

2 *affected* Artificial, designed to make an impression.

3 *impertinent* Irrelevant.

4 *The Statute of Apprenticeship* English law specifying seven years as the required term of an apprenticeship.

one is in an advancing state, and has, therefore, a continual demand for new bands: the other is in a declining state, and the superabundance of hands is continually increasing. Those two manufactures may sometimes be in the same town, and sometimes in the same neighborhood, without being able to lend the least assistance to one another. The Statute of Apprenticeship may oppose it in the one case, and both that and an exclusive corporation in the other. In many different manufactures, however, the operations are so much alike, that the workmen could easily change trades with one another, if those absurd laws did not hinder them. The arts of weaving plain linen and plain silk, for example, are almost entirely the same. That of weaving plain woolen is somewhat different; but the difference is so insignificant that either a linen or a silk weaver might become a tolerable work in a very few days. If any of those three capital manufactures, therefore, were decaying, the workmen might find a resource in one of the other two which was in a more prosperous condition; and their wages would neither rise too high in the thriving, nor sink too low in the decaying manufacture. The linen manufacture indeed is, in England, by a particular statute, open to everybody; but as it is not much cultivated through the greater part of the country, it can afford no general resource to the workmen of other decaying manufactures, who, wherever the Statute of Apprenticeship takes place, have no other choice but either to come upon the parish,[1] or to work as common laborers, for which, by their habits, they are much worse qualified than for any sort of manufacture that bears any resemblance to their own. They generally, therefore, choose to come upon the parish.

[...]

from *Book 4*

Chapter 2: Of Restraints upon the Importation from Foreign Countries of Such Goods as Can Be Produced At Home

[...]

Every individual is continually exerting himself to find out the most advantageous employment for whatever capital he can command. It is his own advantage, indeed, and not that of the society, which he has in view. But the study of his own advantage naturally, or rather necessarily, leads him to prefer that employment which is most advantageous to the society.

First, every individual endeavors to employ his capital as near home as he can, and consequently as much as he can in the support of domestic industry; provided always that he can thereby obtain the ordinary, or not a great deal less than the ordinary profits of stock.

[...]

Secondly, every individual who employs his capital in the support of domestic industry, necessarily endeavors so to direct that industry that its produce may be of the greatest possible value.

The produce of industry is what it adds to the subject or materials upon which it is employed. In proportion as the value of this produce is great or small, so will likewise be the profits of the employer. But it is only for the sake of profit that any man employs a capital in the support of industry; and he will always, therefore, endeavor to employ it in the support of that industry of which the produce is likely to be of the greatest value, or to exchange for the greatest quantity either of money or of other goods.

But the annual revenue of every society is always precisely equal to the exchangeable value[2] of the whole annual produce of its industry, or rather is precisely the same thing with that exchangeable value. As every individual, therefore, endeavors as much as he can both to employ his capital in the support of domestic industry, and so to direct that industry that its produce may be of the greatest value; every individual necessarily labors to render the annual revenue of the society as great as he can. He generally, indeed, neither intends to promote the public interest, nor knows how much he is promoting it. By preferring the support of domestic to that of foreign industry, he intends only his own security; and by directing that industry in such a manner as its produce may be of the greatest value, he intends only his own gain, and he is in this, as in many other cases, led by an invisible hand[3] to promote an end which was no part of his

---

1   *come upon the parish*   To live in poverty, relying on public support. In England prior to the nineteenth century, relief for those in dire poverty was provided (if at all) through local parishes, not by the national government.

2   *exchangeable value*   What people are willing to exchange for it.

3   *invisible hand*   This famous term, often associated with arguments for unrestrained capitalism, was originated by Smith. The term is used only three times in his writing. It occurs once in a book on astronomy, as a metaphor for the divine agency sometimes thought to be behind unusual natural events—"acts of God." The other two uses of the term, once here and once in *The Theory of Moral Sentiments*, refer to unseen, unconscious forces of economic

intention. Nor is it always the worse for the society that it was no part of it. By pursuing his own interest he frequently promotes that of the society more effectually than when he really intends to promote it. I have never known much good done by those who affected to trade for the public good. It is an affectation, indeed, not very common among merchants, and very few words need be employed in dissuading them from it.

Chapter 9: Of the Agricultural Systems

[...]

It is thus that every system which endeavors, either by extraordinary encouragements to draw towards a particular species of industry a greater share of the capital of the society than what would naturally go to it, or, by extraordinary restraints, force from a particular species of industry some share of the capital which would otherwise be employed in it, is in reality subversive of the great purpose which it means to promote. It retards, instead of accelerating, the progress of the society towards real wealth and greatness; and diminishes, instead of increasing, the real value of the annual produce of its land and labor.

All systems either of preference or of restraint, therefore, being thus completely taken away, the obvious and simple system of natural liberty establishes itself of its own accord. Every man, as long as he does not violate the laws of justice, is left perfectly free to pursue his own interest his own way, and to bring both his industry and capital into competition with those of any other man, or order of men. The sovereign is completely discharged from a duty, in the attempting to perform which he must always be exposed

to innumerable delusions, and for the proper performance of which no human wisdom or knowledge could ever be sufficient; the duty of superintending the industry of private people, and of directing it towards the employments most suitable to the interest of the society. According to the system of natural liberty, the sovereign has only three duties to attend to; three duties of great importance, indeed, but plain and intelligible to common understandings: first, the duty of protecting the society from violence and invasion of other independent societies; secondly, the duty of protecting, as far as possible, every member of the society from the injustice or oppression of every other member of it, or the duty of establishing an exact administration of justice; and, thirdly, the duty of erecting and maintaining certain public works and certain public institutions which it can never be for the interest of any individual, or small number of individuals, to erect and maintain; because the profit could never repay the expense to any individual or small number of individuals, though it may frequently do much more than repay it to a great society.

The proper performance of those several duties of the sovereign necessarily supposes a certain expense; and this expense again necessarily requires a certain revenue to support it. In the following book, therefore, I shall endeavor to explain, first, what are the necessary expenses of the sovereign or commonwealth; and which of those expenses ought to be defrayed by the general contribution of the whole society; and which of them by that of some particular part only, or of some particular members of the society; secondly, what are the different methods in which the whole society may be made to contribute towards defraying the expenses incumbent on the whole society, and what are the principal advantages and inconveniences of each of those methods; and thirdly, what are the reasons and causes which have induced almost all modern governments to mortgage some part of this revenue, or to contract debts, and what have been the effects of those debts upon the real wealth, the annual produce of the land and labor of the society.

---

law which Smith, suggests, produce public good as a by-product of private, self-interested action. In Part 4,1,10 of *The Theory of Moral Sentiments*, he writes: "The produce of the soil maintains at all times nearly that number of inhabitants which it is capable of maintaining. The rich only select from the heap what is most precious and agreeable. They consume little more than the poor, and in spite of their natural selfishness and rapacity, though they mean only their own conveniency, though the sole end which they propose from the labors of all the thousands whom they employ, be the gratification of their own vain and insatiable desires, they divide with the poor the produce of all their improvements. They are led by an invisible hand to make nearly the same distribution of the necessaries of life, which would have been made, had the earth been divided into equal portions among all its inhabitants, and thus without intending it, without knowing it, advance the interest of the society, and afford means to the multiplication of the species."

IMMANUEL KANT
(1724 – 1804)

Who Was Immanuel Kant?

IMMANUEL KANT—CONSIDERED BY MANY THE MOST IM-portant philosopher of the past 300 years—was born in 1724 on the coast of the Baltic Sea, in a regionally import-ant harbor city in East Prussia[1] called Königsberg. Kant spent his whole life living in this town, and never ventured outside its region. His family were devout members of an evangelical Protestant sect (rather like the Quakers or early Methodists) called the Piet-ists, and Pietism's strong emphasis on the inner life, emotional religiosity, and distrust of religious dogma had a deep effect on Kant's character. Kant's father was a craftsman (making har-nesses and saddles for horses) and his family was fairly poor; Kant's mother, whom he loved deeply, died when he was thirteen.

Kant's life is notorious for its outward uneventfulness. He was educated at a strict Lutheran school in Königsberg, and after graduating from the University of Königsberg in 1746 (where he supported himself by some tutoring and also by his skill at billiards and card games) he served as a private tutor to various families in the area until he was ap-pointed as a lecturer at the university in 1755. However his position—that of *Privatdozent*—carried no salary, and Kant was expected to support himself by the income from his lecturing; financial need caused Kant to lecture for thirty or more hours a week, on a huge range of subjects (including mathematics, physics, geography, anthropology, ethics, and law). During this period Kant published several scientific works and his reputation as a scholar grew; he turned down opportunities for professorships in other towns (Erlangen and Jena). Finally, at the age of 46, Kant became professor of logic and metaphysics at the University of Königsberg, a position he held until his retirement twenty-six years later in 1796. After a tragic period of sen-ility he died in 1804, and was buried with pomp and circumstance in the "professors' vault" at the Königsberg cathedral.[2]

Kant's days were structured by a rigorous and unvarying routine—in-deed, it is often said (perhaps with exaggeration) that the housewives of Königsberg were able to set their clocks by the regularity of his after-noon walk. He never married (though twice he nearly did) and lived by all accounts a quite austere and outwardly unemotional life. He was something of a hypochondriac, hated noise, and disliked all music except for military marches. Nevertheless, anecdotes by those who knew him give the impression of a warm, impressive, rather noble human being, capable of great kindness and dignity and sparkling conversation. He did not shun society, and in fact his regular daily routine included an extended lunchtime gathering at which he and his guests—drawn from the cosmopolitan stratum of Königsberg society—would discuss politics, science, phil-osophy, and poetry.

Kant's philosophical life is often divided into three phases: his "pre-Critical" period, his "silent" period, and his "Critical" period. His pre-Critical period began in 1747 when he published his first work (*Thoughts on the True Esti-mation of Living Forces*) and ended in 1770 when he wrote his Inaugural Dissertation—*Concerning the Form and Prin-ciples of the Sensible and Intelligible World*—and became a professor. Between 1770 and 1780, Kant published almost

---

1   Prussia is a historical region which included what is today north-ern Germany, Poland, and the western fringes of Russia. It became a kingdom in 1701, and then a dominant part of the newly uni-fied Germany in 1871. Greatly reduced after World War I, the state of Prussia was formally abolished after World War II, and Königsberg—renamed Kaliningrad during the Soviet era, after one of Stalin's henchmen—now sits on the western rump of Rus-sia (between Poland and Lithuania).

2   His body no longer remains there: in 1950 his sarcophagus was broken open by unknown vandals; Kant's corpse was stolen and never recovered.

nothing. In 1781, however, at the age of 57, Kant made his first major contribution to philosophy with his monumental *Critique of Pure Reason* (written, Kant said, over the course of a few months "as if in flight"). He spent the next twenty years in unrelenting intellectual labor, trying to develop and answer the new problems laid out in this masterwork. First, in order to clarify and simplify the system of the *Critique* for the educated public, Kant published the much shorter *Prolegomena to Any Future Metaphysics* in 1783. In 1785 came Kant's *Groundwork for the Metaphysics of Morals*, his first important work on moral theory. During this period he published a number of moral, social, and political works, including the essay "What is Enlightenment?" (1784), where he provides a seminal definition of the age of enlightenment in which "Enlightenment (*Aufklärung*) is the human being's emergence from his self-incurred immaturity." In 1788 he published what is now known as his "second Critique": the *Critique of Practical Reason*. His third and final Critique, the *Critique of Judgement*, was published in 1790.

Other celebrated moral and political essays followed, including "On the Common Saying: 'That may be right in theory but does not work in practice'" (1795) and "To Perpetual Peace: A Philosophical Sketch" (1795) (included here), which contains the central statement of his cosmopolitanism, as well as the notorious essay, "On the Supposed Right to Lie from Philanthropy" (1797), in which Kant argues that one should never lie, even to prevent a murderer from reaching his victim. Also in 1797 he published his long awaited *The Metaphysics of Morals*, which contains the *Doctrine of Right* and the *Doctrine of Virtue*, laying out his legal and political theory, followed by his last major work, *Anthropology from a Pragmatic Point of View* (1798).

By the time he died, Kant had already become known as a great philosopher. Over his grave was inscribed a quote from one of his books (the *Critique of Practical Reason*), which sums up the impulse for his philosophy: "Two things fill the mind with ever new and increasing admiration and reverence, the more often and more steadily one reflects on them: the starry heavens above me and the moral law within me."

What Was Kant's Overall Philosophical Project?

Kant's critical philosophy is a turning point in the history of philosophy and he revolutionized virtually every area of philosophy, especially metaphysics, epistemology, ethics and aesthetics. Though some scholars dispute the aptness of

this distinction, seventeenth- and eighteenth-century philosophers are often grouped into two camps, the rationalists and the empiricists.[1] The rationalists (chiefly Descartes, Spinoza and Leibniz) held that knowledge could be obtained a priori through the use of reason; the empiricists (represented by Locke, Berkeley and Hume) claimed that knowledge could only be gained through experience.

Kant bridged these two approaches. Rather than siding with either of the rationalists or the empiricists, Kant instead asked, "How is knowledge possible?" and introduced "transcendental" arguments which concern "all knowledge which is occupied not so much with objects as with the mode of our knowledge of objects insofar as this mode of knowledge is to be possible *a priori*" (Immanuel Kant, *Critique of Pure Reason*, Introduction, 7). In order to answer the question of how knowledge is possible, he made two separate distinctions: between "a priori" judgments (independent from and prior to experience) and "a posteriori" judgments (after experience), and between "analytic" and "synthetic" judgments. What earlier philosophers had termed truths of reason were categorized by Kant as instances of "analytic a priori" knowledge, while empirical truths of fact were classed by Kant as "synthetic a posteriori" knowledge. To this classification Kant adds *synthetic a priori judgments*, judgments that we know *a priori* and therefore do not learn from experience, but that nevertheless go beyond merely "analytic" claims about our own concepts.[2] Synthetic a priori knowledge is possible insofar as it is knowledge of the *conditions of our experience of the world*—they are prior to any *possible* experience.

Kant, famously, described this insight as constituting a kind of "Copernican revolution" in philosophy: just as Copernicus set cosmology on a totally new path by suggesting (in 1543) that the Earth orbits the Sun and not the other way around, so Kant suggested that rather than assuming that "all our knowledge must conform to objects," instead we might "suppose that objects must conform to

---

1   Like any crude classification, the rationalist/empiricist divide does not do justice to the individual thinkers, who, not surprisingly, rely *both* on reason independent of experience, and on experience. For example, the empiricists typically accepted the seemingly trivial "relations of ideas" as being knowable independent of experience. Ironically, Descartes and Leibniz were both great scientists (relying on empirical observation), a distinction that Locke, Berkeley and Hume did not hold.

2   There are no analytic *a posteriori* judgments: if a judgment is analytic, there is no need for experience to determine whether or not it is true.

our knowledge." Rather than merely passively representing objects in the world independent of mental contribution, Kant held that the mind actively *constitutes* its objects with the categories of time, space and causation as conditions of experience.

On this view, limits are placed on metaphysical knowledge. By establishing the limits of experience, Kant denies that there are theoretically adequate arguments for the existence of God, the soul, freedom or the nature of the world, but argues we can nonetheless use philosophical arguments concerning such matters as "regulative" notions for our inquiry.

In such a context, the limits on reason give rise to a series of "antinomies," paired propositions, a thesis and antithesis, both of which seem in each case to be provable by reason but which are contradictory. Particularly relevant for Kant's ethics (and political thought) is the third antinomy between freedom and determinism. Kant worried about the conflict between free will and natural causality (i.e., causality according to the laws of nature). He was impressed by the scientific advances of his age, particularly those stemming from the work of Isaac Newton, in which scientific laws had come to include the principle of universal causal determination—the principle that nothing happens (including choosing to do X rather than rather than Y) without a cause. At the same time, on Kant's view, we cannot disprove the claim that we are free. In order to resolve this antinomy, Kant argues that we must give each side its due by limiting the domain over which the claims hold.

Thus, Kant argues that we are entitled to assume that we are free—and indeed (as we will see) bases his moral and political thought on an assumption of freedom. Morality rests on the conviction that agents can freely will their actions.[1] Simply by posing the question "what ought I to do" to ourselves we presuppose that we are free. In the *Groundwork*, Kant seeks the foundational principle of morality, providing a precise formulation implicit in our common-sense ideas about morality. To this purpose, Kant begins the *Groundwork* with the assertion that the only thing that is good in itself is a good will. Though many characteristics or objects are typically considered to be good, they can be applied towards dubious ends. For example, courage and intelligence are often considered to be good, but a brilliant, courageous bank robber might well do more harm than a dull, cowardly one. Kant also rejects happiness as the good. Indeed, a good will is necessary to deserve happiness. Furthermore, whether we achieve our ends (including happiness) is beyond our control, so our moral judgments typically evaluate people's *intentions*, not their actions.

The good will, for Kant, is manifested in actions that are performed for the sake of duty. These actions are autonomous (self-determined), in that the agent, as a free being, is the author of the law which she obeys. This is opposed to heteronomous actions—ones determined by factors outside of the agent, including her desires and emotions. (Actions determined by factors in the phenomenal world are part of the causal chain and therefore cannot be free for Kant.)

In order to understand what Kant means by "autonomy,"[2] it is necessary to discuss imperatives. Kant distinguishes hypothetical and categorical imperatives. Hypothetical imperatives exemplify instrumental or means/ends reasoning. They have the form of "if you want x, then do y." Hypothetical imperatives are not unconditionally binding, since agents can always reject or modify their ends—they are commands for an agent only if she has the relevant goal. A categorical imperative, on the other hand, commands unconditionally, no matter what goals the agent has. Kant argues that there is a single categorical imperative, which is a synthetic a priori principle (that is, one known independently of experience). Morality is only possible if there is a categorical imperative, and much of the *Groundwork* tries to show that this is the case, as well as set out the form of the categorical imperative.

Kant offers a number of "formulations" of the categorical imperative.[3] The first formulation is usually called the "Formula of Universal Law" and commands that you "Act only on that maxim whereby you can at the same time will that it become a universal law." Thus, when we act, we must

---

1   We typically do not hold people morally responsible for actions they did not choose or intend.

2   "Autonomy" comes from the Greek words for self—*autos*—and law—*nomos*—and hence means something like "following one's own laws."

3   There is controversy around how many formulations of the categorical imperative Kant provides in the *Groundwork*. He follows this version with "Act as if the maxim of your action were to become by your will a universal law of nature," which is arguably distinct. If this is correct, there are four formulations. The Formula of Universal Law and the Formula of Humanity as an End in Itself are the most important, though the Formula of the Kingdom of Ends is perhaps the most relevant to his political philosophy. Kant claimed that all of the formulations of the categorical imperative are equivalent, though there is considerable disagreement about whether this is true and even about what this claim might mean.

test our maxim (the principle of action) to see if it can be universalized. If there is a contradiction when it is universalized (that is, if it can't be willed as universal law), our action is not permitted. Kant gives the example of giving a false promise and argues that any attempt to universalize the maxim "Everyone may make a deceitful promise when he finds himself in a difficulty from which he cannot otherwise extricate himself" would destroy the practice of promising altogether, thus demonstrating the impermissibility of false promising.

Many moral and political philosophers find that Kant's "Formula of Humanity as an End in Itself" offers better guidance. This commands: "*So act as to treat humanity, whether in your own person or in that of any other, in every case at the same time as an end, never as a means only.*" Under this formula, every rational agent must take into account that not only does she set her ends, but that other autonomous agents do the same. When interacting with other rational and autonomous agents, it is necessary to respect their ends and obtain their *consent*. To do otherwise is to treat them as a *mere means*, ignoring their rationality and their freedom. Thus, false promising is ruled out since we cannot possibly consent to someone deceiving us. The Formula of Humanity as an End in Itself also establishes positive duties—to promote humanity as an end in itself—including positive duties to others (such as performing charitable acts) and positive duties to one's self (such as developing one's talents).

This brings us to the third formulation, which is of particular relevance to Kant's political philosophy, the formula of the Kingdom of Ends: "Act according to the maxims of a member of a merely possible kingdom of ends legislating in it universally." In this formula, all free and rational agents harmonize their ends by legislating a set of universal laws.

Though Kant's political philosophy is clearly related to his moral thought, it is not simply an extension of his moral views. Perhaps most importantly, Kant holds that the state neither can nor should attempt to regulate the moral behavior of its members. In the *Groundwork*, Kant stresses that actions can be performed *in accordance* with duty, but not necessarily *from* duty, depending on whether the agent is motivated by the moral law or mere inclination. The avaricious shopkeeper who does not cheat her clients because she knows that it will hurt her business in the long run does not act morally, though her actions may be indistinguishable to the observer from those of the honest shopkeeper motivated by the moral law. In *The Metaphysics of Morals* Kant divides duties into duties of right and duties of virtue. Only duties

of right are subject to law and external coercion, since "no external lawgiving can bring about someone's setting an end for himself" (*Metaphysics of Morals*, 6.239). In other words, the state may compel people to behave in certain ways (i.e., regulate their external behavior), but it cannot coerce them to endorse particular ends.

Kant is a central figure in the liberal tradition due to his emphasis on rights, his use of contract theory, and his division between justice and virtue. As well, he strongly resisted paternalism, arguing that so long as action is rightful, the state should respect and protect the agent's freedom (e.g., see *Perpetual Peace*, 8.290–91). He does not think the state should attempt to set citizens' ends, or compel virtuous behavior. His doctrine of right is grounded in a principle related to the categorical imperative: "Freedom (independence from being constrained by another's choice) insofar as it can coexist with the freedom of every other in accordance with a universal law, is the only original right belonging to every man by virtue of his humanity" (*Metaphysics of Morals*, 6.237). Thus, "any action is right if it can coexist with everyone's freedom in accordance with a universal law" (*Metaphysics of Morals*, 6.230–31). Similarly, Kant argues that a republican constitution (i.e., a system of government that protects liberty, and upholds the rule of law) is the only form of government compatible with the rights of human beings.

Despite the centrality of freedom in his political thought, Kant's specific views seem surprisingly authoritarian to the modern reader. Kant asserts that each partner in marriage has the right to force the other to remain in the marriage ("if one of the partners in a marriage has left or given itself into someone else's possession, their partner is justified, always and without question, in bringing its partner back under its control, just as it is justified in retrieving a thing" (*Metaphyiscs of Morals*, 6.278).[1] Similarly, he advocates a harsh retributive form of justice, based on *ius talionis* (the legal principle that argues on the basis of like for like, as in "eye for an eye, tooth for a tooth"). In a notorious passage, Kant writes:

> Even if a civil society were to be dissolved by the consent of all of its members ... the last murderer remaining in prison would first have to be executed, so that each has done to him what his deeds deserve and blood guilt does not cling to

---

1 Kant also says women and those who labor for others should not be allowed to vote.

the people for having insisted upon this punishment; for otherwise the people can be regarded as collaborators in this public violation of justice. (*Metaphysics of Morals*, 6.333)

Furthermore, Kant explicitly denies (unlike John Locke) any right to rebel against the state—in fact, Kant claims that such a right would be "self-contradictory" (*Metaphysics of Morals*, 6.371). Civil disobedience is also condemned.

However, Kant does stress the importance of *public reason* (a notion adopted by one of Kant's most important political heirs, John Rawls):

The public use of one's reason must always be free, and it alone can bring about enlightenment among human beings; the private use of one's reason may, however, often be very narrowly restricted without this particularly hindering the progress of enlightenment. ("What is Enlightenment?" 8.37)

By public reason, Kant refers to the work of scholars presented before the public; he advocates academic freedom, as long as it does not amount to rebellion. But the private reason of the civil servant can be restricted, as civil servants are expected to behave passively and follow orders. While Kant does suggest that our duty to obey the state extends only to those cases in which its edicts do not conflict with "inner morality" (*Metaphysics of Morals*, 6.371), this is not a call for rebellion, but an assertion of a duty to accept execution rather than act immorally.

Kant's authoritarianism is directly related to his conception of the state, which he develops from his highly original version of the social contract. For Kant the social contract is not based on actual or even hypothetical consent.

[The original contract] is instead *only an idea* of reason, which, however, has its undoubtable practical reality, namely to bind every legislator to give his laws in such a way that they *could* have arisen from the united will of a whole people and to regard each subject, insofar as he wants to be a citizen, as if he has joined in voting for such a will. ("To Perpetual Peace," 8.297)

Unlike the social contracts of Hobbes, Locke, and Rousseau, all of whom influenced him, Kant does not base his social contract on the individual consent of the members of society. In fact, agents in the state of nature can compel others to enter civil society against their will. In an important passage from *The Metaphysics of Morals*, Kant writes:

[H]owever well disposed and law-abiding human beings might be, it still lies a priori in the rational idea of such a condition (one that is not rightful) that before a public lawful condition is established individual human beings, peoples and states can never be secure against violence from one another, since each has its own right to do *what seems right and good to it* and not to be dependent upon another's opinion about this. So, unless it wants to renounce any concepts of right, the first thing it has to resolve upon is the principle that it must leave the state of nature, in which each follows its own judgment, unite itself with all others (with which it cannot avoid interacting), subject itself to a public lawful external coercion, and so enter into a condition in which what is to be recognized as belonging to it is determined *by law* ... (*Metaphysics of Morals*, 6.312)

It is a mistake to identify Kant's vision of the state of nature with Hobbes'. Kant believes that people in the state of nature can be sociable. But this does not rule out the fact that conflict will occur. Importantly, for Kant, it is not experience that teaches us that people living side by side can be violent.[1] Rather, in the state of nature, "each has its own right to do *what seems right and good to it* and not to be dependent upon another's opinion about this" (*Metaphysics of Morals*, 6.312). This does not refer to a clash of selfish interests (though the human tendency to favor the "dear self" over the commands of morality is no doubt a problem for Kant). Instead, each individual has her own interpretation of what is right.[2] In many ways, this is even more problematic than a mere clash of selfish desires. Selfish desires can give way to bargaining or compromise, whereas a dispute over principles can be resolved only by entering a

---

1 For Kant, if people were widely dispersed around the world and did not encounter each other, there would be no need for civil society since nobody would threaten anybody else's freedom or compete for the same resources. Instead—one can surmise—there would simply be "cosmopolitan right," a right to hospitality entailing non-aggression.

2 This can be seen today when people disagree over the interpretation of rights. For example, does a right to free speech guarantee the right to publicly denigrate minorities? Does a woman's right to control her body give her the right to an abortion? Reasonable people disagree.

law-governed civil society with the authority to adjudicate these principles. On Kant's constructivist theory of rights, rights do not exist (they are merely "provisional") until enacted by a government. Since justice is only possible in civil society and justice is an end that we should have, we have a *duty* to bring ourselves into civil status (and force others nearby to join us).

An example may help to illustrate Kant's point. As is the case in Locke, Hume, and Rousseau, one of Kant's major concerns in political philosophy is property. A property right, for Kant, is the right to exclude others. A property right, however, is not something that we can observe (it is not empirical), but, rather, an instance of *intelligible possession*. (The fact that something belongs to me doesn't depend on my physical control of an object, but rather on the public recognition that the object is mine.) Thus, when I claim that an object is mine, I am imposing an obligation on everyone else to refrain from appropriating it. But this claim implies a universal claim that everyone should respect everyone else's property right, since a unilateral will cannot serve as a coercive law for everyone. Without this universal agreement there is no obligation to respect anyone's property. Thus, what is needed is a collective agreement that places everyone in a civil condition of law. According to Kant, the very *possibility* of having a property right requires a civil condition under which property claims can be enforced and mediated.

Kant also investigated the rights of nations, most notably in "To Perpetual Peace" (and in *The Metaphysics of Morals*, 6.352–54). He divides justice or right into "civil right" (concerned with domestic relations); "international right" (dealing with rights governing the interaction of states, such as those dealing with treaties or war); and "cosmopolitan right," which he limits to universal hospitality, the right for aliens not be treated as enemies in foreign states, and the right for merchants to conduct trade.

The school of political realism, following Hobbes, views the international sphere as a state of nature, ungoverned by law or morality. In the state of nature, the only right is the right to self-preservation, and there are no duties. Kant disputes this: just as he sees an obligation of individuals in the state of nature to form a civil society, so he argues that nations must also try to escape their lawless state and form a federation of free states. This federation of states should not be confused with a world government. Instead, its goal is to end war forever, with the narrow function of guaranteeing each state's security and freedom (similar to the function of the League of Nations after World War I and the current United Nations Security Council).

What Is the Structure of These Readings?

In the First Section of the *Groundwork*, Kant attempts to derive the principles of morality from common sense notions of morality. He analyzes the concepts of the good will and of duty and sets out the Formulation of the Universal Law. The Second Section develops common sense notions into a proper "metaphysics of morals," embedded in a general theory of practical reason. Kant discusses the difference between hypothetical and categorical imperatives, and explains why categorical imperatives are binding. He also sets out the Formulation of the End in Itself and the Formulation of the Kingdom of Ends in this section. The Third Section (which is not reprinted here) argues that the human will is not subject to the laws of nature—in other words, that we are free—and that if we understand ourselves as rational, we must also consider ourselves free. Thus, to be rational is to be governed by the moral law.

"To Perpetual Peace" begins with a series of preliminary articles concerning peace among nations. Kant follows these with three definitive articles: 1) The civil constitution of every nation should be republican; 2) The right of nations shall be based on a federation of free states; and 3) Cosmopolitan right shall be limited to conditions of universal hospitality. To these articles, he adds two supplements, the first of which presents a teleological theory of history suggesting that *nature* is moving toward perpetual peace, and the second of which provides arguments as to why philosophers should be consulted by nations armed for war. A long appendix discusses the relationship between morality and politics in relation to perpetual peace.

Some Common Misconceptions

i) It is sometimes thought that Kant claims that we only act morally when we do something we don't want to do. (In the *Groundwork*, Kant discusses a philanthropist with a sympathetic soul that leads him to help others out of inclination. He claims that this philanthropist deserves praise, but not esteem, and that only if this person were to fall into despair and act solely because of duty would the action have genuine moral worth.) But Kant does not say that the mere presence of an inclination detracts from an action's moral worth; he says rather that the primary motive must be duty. Kant is constantly aware of the tendency for the "dear self" to lead people to immoral actions and, for this reason, stresses the importance of acting from duty. Kant also doubts that we can ever entirely divine true motives—even our own true motives.

ii) Kant does not claim that the good will is the *only thing* which is good, that everything which is good is merely a *means* to the achievement of a good will, or even that a good will is *all* we require for a completely good life. It is perfectly consistent with Kant's views to point out that, say, health or pleasure are valuable for their own sake. Kant's claim is that the good will is the *highest* good, and that it is the *precondition* of all the other goods (i.e., nothing else is good unless it is combined with a good will). By contrast, a good will is unconditionally good: it has its goodness in all possible circumstances, independent of its relation to anything else.

iii) It is an error to consider Kant's moral philosophy as authoritarian. For Kant, moral duty is not imposed from the outside. Rather, the moral law is self-legislated and comes from the agent. Genuine freedom is only possible through rational action guided by the moral law.

iv) When reading Kant's political philosophy, it is necessary to keep in mind the ways in which he distinguishes between moral and political questions. Political philosophy concerns positive law—laws that are actually implemented in civil society and that govern the actions of citizens. In fact, Kant claims in the First Supplement of "To Perpetual Peace" that "the problem of organizing a nation is solvable even for a people comprised of devils (if only they possess understanding)." Needless to say, though these devils may outwardly conform to the rules of morality, they are in no way moral.

How Influential Are These Readings?

Kant's *Groundwork for the Metaphysics of Morals* is one of the central works of philosophy. The philosopher H.J. Paton called it "one of the small books which are truly great: it has exercised on human thought an influence almost ludicrously disproportionate to its size.... Its main topic—the supreme principle of morality—is of the utmost importance to all who are not indifferent to the struggle of good against evil." Many of the most important twentieth- and twenty-first-century moral and political theorists, including John Rawls, Jürgen Habermas, Christine Korsgaard, Onora O'Neill, and Thomas Nagel, descend from Kant.

"To Perpetual Peace" has been accorded a good deal of attention in the late twentieth and early twenty-first centuries as philosophers have grappled with the need for an international political theory that addresses the reality of an increasingly globalized world. It is central to John Rawls' *Law of Peoples*, and it has become a touchstone for philosophers attempting to formulate cosmopolitan theories of justice.

◆ ◆ ◆ ◆ ◆

Groundwork for the Metaphysics of Morals (1785)

Preface

Ancient Greek philosophy was divided into three sciences:[1] physics, ethics, and logic. This division is perfectly suitable to the nature of the thing; and the only improvement that can be made in it is to add the principle on which it is based, so that we may both satisfy ourselves of its completeness, and also be able to determine correctly the necessary subdivisions.

All rational cognition is either *material* or *formal*: the former considers some object, the latter is concerned only with the form of the understanding and of reason itself, and with the universal laws of thought in general without distinction of its objects. Formal philosophy is called logic. Material philosophy, however, which has to do with determinate[2] objects and the laws to which they are subject, is again twofold; for these laws are either laws of **nature** or of **freedom**. The science of the former is **physics**, that of the latter, **ethics**; they are also called natural philosophy[3] and moral philosophy respectively.

[...]

As my concern here is with moral philosophy, I limit the question suggested to this: whether it is not of the utmost necessity to construct a pure moral philosophy, perfectly cleared of everything which is only empirical and which belongs to anthropology? For that such a philosophy must be possible is evident from the common idea of duty and of the moral laws. Everyone must admit that if a law is to

---

1   *sciences* Branches of knowledge.
2   *determinate* Definite and particular.
3   *natural philosophy* "Natural philosophy" corresponds to what is today called "natural science."

have moral force, that is, to be the basis of an obligation, it must carry with it absolute necessity; that, for example, the precept, "You ought not to lie," is not valid for human beings alone, as if other rational beings had no need to observe it; and so with all the other moral laws properly so called; that therefore, the basis of obligation must not be sought in the nature of the human being, or in the circumstances in the world in which he is placed, but *a priori*[1] simply in the concepts of pure reason;[2] and although any other precept which is founded on principles of mere experience may be in certain respects universal, yet in as far as it rests even in the least degree on an empirical basis, perhaps only as to a motive, such a precept, while it may be a practical rule, can never be called a moral law.

Thus not only are moral laws with their principles essentially distinguished from every other kind of practical cognition in which there is anything empirical, but all moral philosophy rests wholly on its pure part. When applied to human beings, it does not borrow the least thing from acquaintance with them (anthropology), but gives laws *a priori* to them as rational beings. No doubt these laws require a judgment sharpened by experience, in order, on the one hand, to distinguish in what cases they are applicable, and, on the other, to procure for them access to the will of the human being, and effectual influence on conduct; since the human being is acted on by so many inclinations[3] that, though capable of the idea of a practical pure reason, he is not so easily capable of making it effective *in concreto*[4] in his life. A metaphysics of morals is therefore indispensably necessary, not merely because of a motive of speculation, in order to investigate the sources of the practical principles which are to be found *a priori* in our reason, but also because morals themselves are liable to all sorts of corruption as long as we are without that guide and supreme canon by which to estimate them correctly. For in order that an action should be morally good, it is not enough that it *conform* to the moral law, but it must also be done *for the sake* of the

law, otherwise that conformity is only very contingent[5] and uncertain; since a principle which is not moral, although it may now and then produce actions conformable to the law, will also often produce actions which contradict it. Now it is only in a pure philosophy that we can look for the moral law in its purity and genuineness (and, in a practical matter, this is of the utmost consequence): we must, therefore, begin with pure philosophy (metaphysics), and without it there cannot be any moral philosophy at all. That which mingles these pure principles with the empirical does not deserve the name of philosophy (for what distinguishes philosophy from common rational knowledge is that it treats in separate sciences what the latter only comprehends confusedly); much less does it deserve that of moral philosophy, since by this confusion it even spoils the purity of morals themselves and counteracts its own end.

[...]

First Section: Transition from the Common Rational Moral Cognition to the Philosophical Moral Cognition

Nothing can possibly be conceived in the world, or even out of it, which can be called good without qualification, except a *good will*. Intelligence, wit, judgment, and the other *talents* of the mind, however they may be named, or courage, resolution, perseverance, as qualities of *temperament*, are undoubtedly good and desirable in many respects; but these gifts of nature may also become extremely bad and mischievous if the will which is to make use of them, and which, therefore, constitutes what is called *character*, is not good. It is the same with the *gifts of fortune*. Power, riches, honor, even health, and the general well-being and contentment with one's condition which is called *happiness*, inspire pride, and often presumption, if there is not a good will to correct the influence of these on the mind, and with this also to rectify the whole principle of acting, and adapt it to its end. The sight of a being who is not adorned with a single feature of a pure and good will, enjoying unbroken prosperity, can never give pleasure to an impartial spectator. Thus a good will appears to constitute the indispensable condition even of being worthy of happiness.

---

1 *a priori*   Latin: from what comes first. The *a priori* is independent of any empirical (sense-based) investigation.

2 *pure reason*   That is, reason untainted by any empirical concepts or beliefs.

3 *inclinations*   Desires, emotions or feelings that motivate people to act in a heteronomous (unfree) way. Kant holds that the moral law, not inclination, motivates autonomous (free) actions, and he contrasts inclination with reason.

4 *in concreto*   In actual practice, with regard to particular real "concrete" examples; in contrast to "*in abstracto*"—in the abstract.

5 *contingent*   Conditional, dependent on the specific ends of the agent, which may change, or other unpredictable factors.

There are even some qualities which are of service to this good will itself, and may facilitate its action, yet which have no inner unconditional value, but always presuppose a good will, and this qualifies the esteem that we justly have for them, and does not permit us to regard them as absolutely good. Moderation in the affections and passions, self-control, and calm deliberation are not only good in many respects, but even seem to constitute part of the *inner* worth of the person; but they are far from deserving to be called good without qualification, although they have been so unconditionally praised by the ancients. For without the principles of a good will, they may become extremely evil; and the coldness of a villain not only makes him far more dangerous, but also directly makes him more abominable in our eyes than he would have been without it.

A good will is good not because of what it accomplishes or effects, not by its aptness for the attainment of some proposed end, but simply by virtue of the volition—that is, it is good in itself, and considered by itself is to be esteemed much higher than all that can be brought about by it in favor of any inclination, or even the sum total of all inclinations. Even if it should happen that, owing to a step-motherly nature, this will should wholly lack power to accomplish its purpose, if with its greatest efforts it should yet achieve nothing, and there should remain only the good will (not, to be sure, a mere wish, but the summoning of all means in our power), then, like a jewel, it would still shine by its own light, as a thing which has its whole value in itself. Its usefulness or fruitlessness can neither add to nor take away anything from this value. It would be, as it were, only the setting to enable us to handle it more conveniently in common commerce, or to attract to it the attention of those who are not yet connoisseurs, but not to recommend it to true connoisseurs, or to determine its value.

There is, however, something so strange in this idea of the absolute value of a mere will, in which no account is taken of its utility, that notwithstanding the thorough assent of even common reason to the idea, yet a suspicion must arise that it may perhaps really be the product of mere high-flown fancy, and that we may have misunderstood the purpose of nature in assigning reason as the governor of our will. Therefore we will examine this idea from this point of view.

In the natural constitution of an organized being, that is, a being adapted suitably to the purposes of life, we assume it as a fundamental principle that no organ for any purpose will be found but what is also the fittest and best adapted for that purpose. Now in a being which has reason and a will, if the proper object of nature were its *preservation*, its *welfare*, in a word, its *happiness*, then nature would have hit upon a very bad arrangement in selecting the reason of the creature to carry out this purpose. For all the actions which the creature has to perform with a view to this purpose, and the whole rule of its conduct, would be far more surely prescribed to it by instinct, and that end would have been attained thereby much more certainly than it ever can be by reason. Should reason have been imparted to this favored creature over and above, it must only have served it to contemplate the happy constitution of its nature, to admire it, to congratulate itself on it, and to feel thankful for it to the beneficent cause, but not that it should subject its desires to that weak and delusive guidance, and meddle incompetently with the purpose of nature. In a word, nature would have taken care that reason should not break forth into *practical use*, nor have the presumption, with its weak insight, to think out for itself the plan of happiness and of the means of attaining it. Nature would not only have taken on herself the choice of the ends but also of the means, and with wise foresight would have entrusted both to instinct.

And, in fact, we find that the more a cultivated reason applies itself with deliberate purpose to the enjoyment of life and happiness, so much more does one fall short of true satisfaction. And from this circumstance there arises in many, if they are candid enough to confess it, a certain degree of *misology*, that is, hatred of reason, especially in the case of those who are most experienced in the use of it, because after calculating all the advantages they derive—I do not say from the invention of all the arts of common luxury, but even from the sciences (which seem to them to be after all only a luxury of the understanding)—they find that they have, in fact, only brought more trouble on their shoulders rather than gained in happiness; and they end by envying rather than despising the more common run of human beings who keep closer to the guidance of mere instinct, and do not allow their reason much influence on their conduct. And this we must admit, that the judgment of those who would very much lower the lofty eulogies of the advantages which reason gives us in regard to the happiness and satisfaction of life, or who would even reduce them below zero, is by no means morose or ungrateful to the goodness with which the world is governed, but that there lies at the root of these judgments the idea that our existence has a different and far worthier end, to which, and not to happiness, is reason's proper vocation, and which must, therefore, be regarded as the supreme condition to which private ends of human beings must, for the most part, defer.

For as reason is not competent to guide the will with certainty in regard to its objects and the satisfaction of all our needs (which it to some extent even multiplies), this being an end to which an implanted instinct would have led with much greater certainty; and since, nevertheless, reason is imparted to us as a practical faculty, that is, as one which is to have influence on the *will*, therefore admitting that nature generally in the distribution of her capacities has adapted the means to the end, its true vocation must be to produce a *will*, not merely good as a *means* to something else, but *good in itself*, for which reason was absolutely necessary. This will then, though not indeed the sole and complete good, must be the supreme good and the condition of every other, even of the desire of happiness. Under these circumstances, there is nothing inconsistent with the wisdom of nature in the fact that the cultivation of reason, which is requisite for the first and unconditioned purpose, does in many ways interfere, at least in this life, with the attainment of the second, which is always conditional—namely, happiness. Indeed, it may even reduce it to nothing, without nature thereby failing of her purpose. For reason recognizes the establishment of a good will as its highest practical vocation, and in attaining this purpose is capable only of a satisfaction of its own proper kind, namely, that from the attainment of an end, which in turn is determined by reason only, notwithstanding that this may involve many a disappointment to the ends of inclination.

We have then to develop the concept of a will which deserves to be highly esteemed for itself, and is good without a view to anything further, a concept which exists already in the sound natural understanding, requiring rather to be clarified than to be taught, and which in estimating the value of our actions always takes the first place and constitutes the condition of all the rest. In order to do this, we will take the concept of duty, which includes that of a good will, although implying certain subjective limitations and hindrances. These, however, far from concealing it or rendering it unrecognizable, rather bring it out by contrast and make it shine forth so much the brighter.

I omit here all actions which are already recognized as contrary to duty, although they may be useful for this or that purpose, for with these the question whether they are done *from duty* cannot arise at all, since they even conflict with it. I also set aside those actions which really conform to duty, but to which men have *no* immediate *inclination*,

performing them because they are impelled thereto by some other inclination. For in this case we can readily distinguish whether the action which agrees with duty is done *from duty* or from a selfish purpose. It is much harder to make this distinction when the action accords with duty, and the subject has besides an *immediate* inclination to it. For example, it is always a matter of duty that a dealer should not overcharge an inexperienced purchaser; and wherever there is much commerce the prudent tradesman does not overcharge, but keeps a fixed price for everyone, so that a child buys from him as well as any other. People are thus *honestly* served; but this is not enough to make us believe that the tradesman has so acted from duty and from principles of honesty; his own advantage required it; it is unwarranted in this case to suppose that he might besides have an immediate inclination in favor of the buyers, so that, as it were, from love he should give no advantage to one over another. Accordingly the action was done neither from duty nor from immediate inclination, but merely with a selfish purpose.

On the other hand, it is a duty to preserve one's life; and, in addition, everyone has also an immediate inclination to do so. But on this account the often anxious care which most people take for it has no intrinsic worth, and their maxim[1] has no moral content. They preserve their life *in conformity with duty*, no doubt, but not *from duty*. On the other hand, if adversity and hopeless sorrow have completely taken away the relish for life, if the unfortunate one, strong in mind, indignant to his fate rather than desponding or dejected, wishes for death, and yet preserves his life without loving it—not from inclination or fear, but from duty—then his maxim has moral content.

To be beneficent when one can is a duty; and besides this, there are many minds so sympathetically constituted that, without any other motive of vanity or self-interest, they find a pleasure in spreading joy around them, and can take delight in the satisfaction of others so far as it is their own work. But I maintain that in such a case an action of this kind, however proper, however amiable it may be, has nevertheless no true moral worth, but is on a level with other inclinations, for example, the inclination to honor, which if it is happily directed to that which is in fact of public utility and accordant with duty, and consequently honorable, deserves praise and encouragement, but not esteem. For the maxim lacks the moral content, namely, that such actions be done *from duty*, not from inclination. Put the case that

---

1   *their maxim*   Principle of volition.

the mind of that philanthropist was clouded by sorrow of his own, extinguishing all sympathy with the lot of others, and that while he still has the power to benefit others in distress, he is not touched by their trouble because he is absorbed with his own; and now suppose that he tears himself out of this dead insensibility and performs the action without any inclination to it, but simply from duty, then for the first time his action has its genuine moral worth. Further still, if nature has put little sympathy in the heart of this or that man, if he, supposed to be an upright man, is by temperament cold and indifferent to the sufferings of others, perhaps because in respect of his own he is provided with the special gifts of patience and fortitude, and supposes, or even requires, that others should have the same—and such a man would certainly not be the meanest product of nature—but if nature had not specially framed him for a philanthropist, would he not still find in himself a source from which to give himself a far higher worth than that of a good-natured temperament could be? Unquestionably. It is just in this that the moral worth of the character is brought out which is incomparably the highest of all, namely, that he is beneficent, not from inclination, but from duty.

To secure one's own happiness is a duty, at least indirectly; for discontent with one's condition, under a pressure of many anxieties and amidst unsatisfied needs, might easily become a great *temptation to transgression of duty*. But here again, without looking to duty, all men have already the strongest and most intimate inclination to happiness, because it is just in this idea that all inclinations are combined in one total. But the precept of happiness is often of such a sort that it greatly interferes with some inclinations, and yet a human being cannot form any definite and certain conception of the sum of satisfaction of all of them which is called happiness. It is not then to be wondered at that a single inclination, definite both as to what it promises and as to the time within which it can be gratified, is often able to overcome such a fluctuating idea, and that a gouty patient,[1] for instance, can choose to enjoy what he likes, and to suffer what he may, since, according to his calculation, on this occasion at least, he has not sacrificed the enjoyment of the present moment to a possibly mistaken expectation of a happiness which is supposed to be found in health. But even in this case, if the general inclination to happiness did not influence his will, and supposing that in his particular case health was not a necessary element in this calculation, there yet remains in this, as in all other cases, this law—namely, that he should promote his happiness not from inclination but from duty, and by this would his conduct first acquire true moral worth.

It is in this manner, undoubtedly, that we are to understand those passages of Scripture also in which we are commanded to love our neighbor, even our enemy. For love, as an inclination, cannot be commanded, but beneficence for duty's sake may, even though we are not impelled to it by any inclination—indeed, are even repelled by a natural and unconquerable aversion. This is *practical* love, and not *pathological*[2]—a love which is seated in the will, and not in the propensities of feeling—in principles of action and not of tender sympathy; and it is this love alone which can be commanded.

The second proposition is: That an action done from duty derives its moral worth, *not from the purpose* which is to be attained by it, but from the maxim by which it is determined, and therefore does not depend on the realization of the object of the action, but merely on the *principle of volition* by which the action has taken place, without regard to any object of desire. It is clear from what precedes that the purposes which we may have in view in our action, or their effects regarded as ends and incentives of the will, cannot give to actions any unconditional or moral worth. In what, then, can their worth lie if it is not to consist in the will in reference to its expected effect? It cannot lie anywhere but in the *principle of the will* without regard to the ends which can be attained by the action. For the will stands between its *a priori* principle, which is formal, and its *a posteriori* incentive, which is material, as between two roads, and as it must be determined by something, it follows that it must be determined by the formal principle of volition when an action is done from duty, in which case every material principle has been withdrawn from it.

The third proposition, which is a consequence of the two preceding, I would express thus: *Duty is the necessity of acting from respect for the law.*[3] I may have *inclination* for an object as the effect of my proposed action, but *never respect* for it, just because it is an effect and not an activity of will. Similarly, I cannot have respect for inclination, whether my own or another's; I can at most, if my own, approve

---

1   *a gouty patient*   Gout, an illness involving painful swelling of the joints, can be triggered by alcohol or certain foods.

2   *pathological*   Dependent on sensibility or feeling, rather than reason.

3   *law*   Kant means the moral law—not governmental law.

it; if another's, sometimes even love it, that is, look on it as favorable to my own interest. It is only what is connected with my will as a principle, by no means as an effect—what does not serve my inclination, but outweighs it, or at least in case of choice excludes it from its calculation—in other words, simply the law of itself, which can be an object of respect, and hence a command. Now an action done from duty must wholly exclude the influence of inclination, and with it every object of the will, so that nothing remains which can determine the will except objectively the *law*, and subjectively *pure respect* for this practical law, and consequently the maxim that I should follow this law even to the thwarting of all my inclinations.

Thus the moral worth of an action does not lie in the effect expected from it, nor in any principle of action which needs to borrow its motive from this expected effect. For all these effects— agreeableness of one's condition, and even the promotion of the happiness of others—could have been also brought about by other causes, so that for this there would have been no need of the will of a rational being; whereas it is in this alone that the supreme and unconditional good can be found. The pre-eminent good which we call moral can therefore consist in nothing else than *the representation[1] of the law* in itself, *which certainly is only possible in a rational being*, insofar as this representation, and not the expected effect, determines the will. This is a good which is already present in the person who acts accordingly, and we need not wait for it to appear first in the result.

But what sort of law can that be, the conception of which must determine the will, even without paying any regard to the effect experienced from it, in order that this will may be called good absolutely and without qualification? As I have deprived the will of every impulse which could arise for it from obedience to any particular law, there remains nothing but the universal conformity of its actions to law in general, which alone is to serve the will as a principle, that is, I am never to act otherwise than so *that I could also will that my maxim should become a universal law*. Here, now, it is the simple lawfulness in general, without assuming any particular law applicable to certain actions, that serves the will as its principle, and must so serve it if duty is not to be a vain delusion and a chimerical notion. The common reason of human beings in its practical judgments perfectly coincides with this, and always has in view the principle here suggested.

Let the question be, for example: May I when in distress make a promise with the intention not to keep it? I readily distinguish here between the two significations which the question may have: whether it is prudent or whether it is right to make such a false promise. The former may undoubtedly often be the case. I see clearly indeed that it is not enough to extricate myself from a present difficulty by means of this subterfuge, but it must be well considered whether there may not hereafter spring from this lie much greater inconvenience than that from which I now seek to free myself, and as, with all my supposed *cunning*, the consequences cannot be so easily foreseen but that credit once lost may be much more injurious to me than any mischief which I seek to avoid at present, it should be considered whether it would not be *more prudent* to act herein according to a universal maxim, and to make it a habit to promise nothing except with the intention of keeping it. But it is soon clear to me that such a maxim will still only be based on the fear of consequences. Now it is a wholly different thing to be truthful from duty than to be so from apprehension of injurious consequences. In the first case, the very notion of the action already implies a law for me; in the second case, I must first look about elsewhere to see what results may be combined with it which would affect myself. For to deviate from the principle of duty is beyond all doubt evil; but to be unfaithful to my maxim of prudence may often be very advantageous to me, although to abide by it is certainly safer. The shortest way, however, and an unerring one, to discover the answer to this question whether a lying promise is consistent with duty, is to ask myself: Would I be content that my maxim (to extricate myself from difficulty by a false promise) should hold as a universal law, for myself as well as for others? And would I be able to say to myself, "Everyone may make a deceitful promise when he finds himself in a difficulty from which he cannot otherwise extricate himself"? Then I presently become aware that, while I can will the lie, I can by no means will that lying become a universal law. For with such a law there would be no promises at all, since it would be in vain to profess my intention in regard to my future actions to those who would not believe this profession, or if they over-hastily did so, would pay me back in my own coin. Hence my maxim, as soon as it should be made a universal law, would necessarily destroy itself.

I do not, therefore, need any far-reaching penetration to discern what I have to do in order that my volition may be morally good. Inexperienced in the course of the world, incapable of being prepared for all its contingencies, I only

---

1   *representation*   Mental representation.

ask myself: Can you also will that your maxim should be a universal law? If not, then it must be rejected, and that not because of a disadvantage accruing from it to myself or even to others, but because it cannot enter as a principle into a possible universal legislation, and reason extorts from me immediate respect for such legislation. I do not indeed as yet *discern* on what this respect is based (this the philosopher may inquire), but at least I understand this—that it is an estimation of the worth which far outweighs all worth of what is recommended by inclination, and that the necessity of acting from *pure* respect for the practical law is what constitutes duty, to which every other motive must give place because it is the condition of a will that is good *in itself*, and the worth of such a will is above everything.

Thus, then, without quitting the moral cognition of common human reason, we have arrived at its principle. And although, no doubt, common human reason does not conceive it in such an abstract and universal form, yet it really always has it before its eyes and uses it as the standard of judgment. Here it would be easy to show how, with this compass in hand, common human reason is well able to distinguish, in every case that occurs, what is good, what evil, conformable to duty or inconsistent with it, if, without in the least teaching it anything new, we only, like Socrates, direct its attention to the principle it itself employs; and that, therefore, we do not need science and philosophy to know what we should do to be honest and good, yes, even to be wise and virtuous. Indeed we might well have conjectured beforehand that the acquaintance with what every human being is obligated to do, and therefore also to know, would be within the reach of every human being, even the commonest. Here we cannot withhold admiration when we see how great an advantage practical judgment has over the theoretical in the common human understanding. In the latter, if common reason ventures to depart from the laws of experience and from the perceptions of the senses, it falls into mere inconceivabilities and self-contradictions, at least into a chaos of uncertainty, obscurity, and instability. But in the practical sphere it is just when the common understanding excludes all sensible incentives from practical laws that its power of judgment begins to show itself to advantage. It then becomes even subtle, whether it be that it quibbles with its own conscience or with other claims regarding what is to be called right, or whether it desires for its own instruction to determine honestly the worth of its actions; and, in the latter case, it may even have as good a hope of hitting the mark as any philosopher whatever can promise himself. Indeed it is almost more sure of doing so, because the philosopher cannot have any other principle, while he may easily perplex his judgment by a multitude of considerations foreign to the matter, and so turn aside from the right way. Would it not therefore be wiser in moral concerns to acquiesce in the judgment of common reason, or at most only to call in philosophy for the purpose of rendering the system of morals more complete and intelligible, and its rules more convenient for use (especially disputation), but not so as to draw off the common understanding from its happy simplicity, or bring it by means of philosophy into a new path of inquiry and instruction? Innocence is indeed a glorious thing; but, on the other hand, it is very sad that it cannot well maintain itself, and is easily seduced. On this account even wisdom—which otherwise consists more in conduct than in knowledge—still has need of science, not in order to learn from it, but to secure for its precepts admission and permanence. Against all the commands of duty which reason represents to the human being as so deserving of respect, he feels in himself a powerful counterweight in his needs and inclinations, the entire satisfaction of which he sums up under the name of happiness. Now reason issues commands unyieldingly, without promising anything to the inclinations, and, as it were, with disregard and contempt for these claims, which are so impetuous and at the same time so plausible, and which will not allow themselves to be suppressed by any command.

Hence there arises a *natural dialectic*,[1] that is, a disposition to argue against these strict laws of duty and to question their validity, or at least their purity and strictness; and if possible, to make them more compatible with our wishes and inclinations, that is to say, to corrupt them at their very source and entirely destroy their worth—a thing which even common practical reason cannot ultimately approve.

Thus is the *common human reason* compelled to go out of its sphere and to take a step into the field of *practical philosophy*, not to satisfy any speculative need (which never occurs to it as long as it is content to be mere sound reason), but rather on practical grounds, in order to attain in it information and clear instruction respecting the source of its principle, and the correct determination of it in opposition to the maxims which are based on wants and inclinations, so that it may escape from the perplexity of opposite claims, and not run the risk of losing all genuine moral principles

---

1   *dialectic*   Tension or debate between two conflicting or contradictory ideas or approaches.

through the equivocation[1] into which it easily falls. Thus, when practical reason cultivates itself, there insensibly arises in it a dialectic which forces it to seek aid in philosophy, just as happens to it in its theoretical use; and in this case, therefore, as well as in the other, it will find rest nowhere but in a thorough critical examination of our reason.

Second Section: Transition from Popular Moral Philosophy to the Metaphysics of Morals

[...]

Everything in nature works according to laws. Rational beings alone have the capacity to act *in accordance with the representation* of laws—that is, according to principles, that is, have a *will*. Since the deduction of actions from principles requires *reason*, the will is nothing but practical reason. If reason infallibly determines the will, then the actions of such a being which are recognized as objectively necessary are subjectively necessary also, that is, the will is a capacity to choose *that only* which reason independent of inclination recognizes as practically necessary, that is, as good. But if reason of itself does not sufficiently determine the will, if the latter is subject also to subjective conditions (particular incentives) which do not always coincide with the objective conditions, in a word, if the will does not *in itself* completely accord with reason (which is actually the case with human beings), then the actions which objectively are recognized as necessary are subjectively contingent, and the determination of such a will according to objective laws is *necessitation*, that is to say, the relation of the objective laws to a will that is not thoroughly good is conceived as the determination of the will of a rational being by principles of reason, but which the will from its nature does not necessarily follow.

The conception of an objective principle, in so far as it is obligatory for a will, is called a command (of reason), and the formula of the command is called an imperative.

All imperatives are expressed through an *ought*, and thereby indicate the relation of an objective law of reason to a will which from its subjective constitution is not necessarily determined by it (a necessitation). They say that something would be good to do or to forbear, but they say it to a will which does not always do a thing because it is represented to be good to do it. That is *practically good*, however, which determines the will by means of the representations of reason, and consequently not from subjective causes, but objectively, that is, on principles which are valid for every rational being as such. It is distinguished from the agreeable as that which influences the will only by means of feeling from merely subjective causes, valid only for the senses of this or that one, and not as a principle of reason which holds for everyone.

A perfectly good will would therefore be equally subject to objective laws (viz. laws of good), but could not be conceived as *necessitated* thereby to act lawfully, because of itself from its subjective constitution it can only be determined by the conception of good. Therefore no imperatives hold for the Divine will, or in general for a *holy* will; *ought* is here out of place because the volition is already of itself necessarily in unison with the law. Therefore imperatives are only formulae to express the relation of objective laws of all volition to the subjective imperfection of the will of this or that rational being, for example, a human will.

Now all imperatives command either *hypothetically* or *categorically*. The former represent the practical necessity of a possible action as means to something else that is willed (or at least which one might possibly will). The categorical imperative would be that which represented an action as necessary of itself without reference to another end, that is, as objectively necessary.

Since every practical law represents a possible action as good, and on this account, for a subject who is practically determinable by reason, as necessary, all imperatives are formulae determining an action which is necessary according to the principle of a will good in some respects. If now the action is good only as a means *to something else*, then the imperative is *hypothetical*; if it is conceived as good *in itself* and consequently as being necessarily the principle of a will which of itself conforms to reason, then it is *categorical*.

[...]

Finally, there is an imperative which commands a certain conduct immediately, without having as its condition any other purpose to be attained by it. This imperative is categorical. It concerns not the matter of the action, or its intended result, but its form and the principle of which it is itself a result; and what is essentially good in it consists in the mental disposition, let the consequence be what it may. This imperative may be called that of morality.

[...]

If then there is a supreme practical principle or, with respect to the human will, a categorical imperative, it must

---

1   *equivocation* In this case, the ambiguity about "ought"—which may be read morally or prudentially.

be one which, being drawn from the conception of that which is necessarily an end for everyone because it is *an end in itself*, constitutes an *objective* principle of will, and can therefore serve as a universal practical law. The foundation of this principle is: *rational nature exists as an end in itself*. The human being necessarily conceives of his own existence as being so; so far then this is a *subjective* principle of human actions. But every other rational being regards its existence similarly, just on the same rational principle that holds for me; so that it is at the same time an objective principle from which as a supreme practical law all laws of the will must be capable of being deduced. Accordingly the practical imperative will be as follows: *So act as to treat humanity, whether in your own person or in that of any other, in every case at the same time as an end, never as a means only.* We will now inquire whether this can be practically carried out.

To abide by the previous examples: *First*, under the head of necessary duty to oneself: Someone who contemplates suicide should ask himself whether his action can be consistent with the idea of humanity *as an end in itself*. If he destroys himself in order to escape from painful circumstances, he uses a person merely as a *means* to maintain a tolerable condition up to the end of life. But a human being is not a thing, that is to say, something which can be used merely as a means, but must in all his actions be always considered as an end in itself. I cannot, therefore, dispose in any way of a human being in my own person by mutilating, damaging, or killing him. (It belongs to morals proper to define this principle more precisely, so as to avoid all misunderstanding, for example, as to the amputation of the limbs in order to preserve myself; as to exposing my life to danger with a view to preserve it, etc. This question is therefore omitted here.)

Second, as regards necessary duties, or those of strict obligation, towards others: He who is thinking of making a lying promise to others will see at once that he would be using another human being *merely as a means*, without the latter at the same time containing in himself the end. For he whom I propose by such a promise to use for my own purposes cannot possibly assent to my mode of acting toward him, and therefore cannot himself contain the end of this action.[1] This violation of the principle of human-

ity in other human beings is more obvious if we take in examples of attacks on the freedom and property of others. For then it is clear that he who transgresses the rights of human beings intends to use the person of others merely as means, without considering that as rational beings they ought always to be esteemed also as ends, that is, as beings who must be capable of containing in themselves the end of the very same action.

Third, as regards contingent (meritorious) duties to oneself: It is not enough that the action does not violate humanity in our own person as an end in itself, it must also *harmonize with* it. Now there are in humanity capacities of greater perfection which belong to the end that nature has in view with regard to humanity in ourselves as the subject; to neglect these might perhaps be consistent with the *maintenance* of humanity as an end in itself, but not with the *advancement* of this end.

Fourth, as regards meritorious duties toward others: The natural end which all human beings have is their own happiness. Now humanity might indeed subsist although no one should contribute anything to the happiness of others, provided he did not intentionally withdraw anything from it; but after all, this would only harmonize negatively, not positively, with *humanity as an end in itself*, if everyone does not also endeavor, as far as he can, to forward the ends of others. For the ends of any subject which is an end in itself ought as far as possible to be *my* ends also, if that conception is to have its *full* effect in me.

◆ ◆ ◆ ◆ ◆

To Perpetual Peace: A Philosophical Sketch (1795)

"To Perpetual Peace"

Whether this satirical inscription on a certain Dutch shopkeeper's sign, on which a graveyard was painted, holds for *men* in general, or especially for heads of state who can never get enough of war, or perhaps only for philosophers who dream that sweet dream, is not for us to decide. However, the author of this essay does set out one condition: The practical politician tends to look down with great smugness on the political theorist, regarding him as an academic

---

1 *cannot himself contain the end of this action* In other words, the aim of my action (to deceive him with a lying promise) is not *his* aim.

whose empty ideas cannot endanger the nation since the nation must proceed on principles [derived from] experience; consequently, the theorist is allowed to fire his entire volley, without the *worldly-wise* statesman becoming the least bit concerned. Now if he is to be consistent—and this is the condition I set out—the practical politician must not claim, in the event of a dispute with a theorist, to detect some danger to the nation in those views that the political theorist expresses openly and without ulterior motive. By this *clausula salvatoria*,[1] the author of this essay will regard himself to be expressly protected in the best way possible from all malicious interpretation.

First Section: Which Contains the Preliminary Articles for Perpetual Peace Among Nations (1795)

1. No treaty of peace that tacitly reserves issues for a future war shall be held valid

For if this were the case, it would be a mere truce, a suspension of hostilities, not *peace*, which means the end of all hostilities, so much so that even to modify it by "perpetual" smacks of pleonasm. A peace treaty nullifies all existing causes for war, even if they are unknown to the contracting parties, and even if they are assiduously ferreted out from archival documents. When one or both parties to a peace treaty, being too exhausted to continue the war, has a mental reservation (*reservatio mentalis*) concerning some presently unmentioned pretension that will be revived at the first opportune moment, since ill will between the warring parties still remains, that reservation is a bit of mere Jesuitical casuistry.[2] If we judge such actions in their true character, they are beneath the dignity of a ruler, just as a willingness to indulge in reasoning of this sort is beneath his minister's dignity.

If, however, enlightened concepts of political prudence lead us to believe that the true honor of a nation lies in its continual increase of power by whatever means necessary, this judgment will appear academic and pedantic.

2. No independent nation, be it large or small, may be acquired by another nation by inheritance, exchange, purchase, or gift

A nation is not (like the ground on which it is located) a possession (*partrimonium*). It is a society of men whom no other than the nation itself can command or dispose of. Since, like a tree, each nation has its own roots, to incorporate it into another nation as a graft, denies its existence as a moral person, turns it into a thing, and thus contradicts the concept of the original contract, without which a people has no rights.[3] Everyone is aware of the danger that this purported right of acquisition by the marriage of nations to one another—a custom unknown in other parts of the world—has brought to Europe, even in the most recent times. It is a new form of industry, in which influence is increased without expending energy, and territorial possessions are extended merely by establishing family alliances. The hiring out of one nation's troops[4] to another for use against an enemy not common to both of them falls under this principle, for by this practice subjects are used and wasted as mere objects to be manipulated at will.

3. Standing armies (*miles perpetuus*) shall be gradually abolished

For they constantly threaten other nations with war by giving the appearance that they are prepared for it, which goads nations into competing with one another in the number of men under arms, and this practice knows no bounds. And since the costs related to maintaining peace will in this way finally become greater than those of a short war, standing armies are the cause of wars of aggression that are intended to end burdensome expenditures. Moreover, paying men to kill or be killed appears to use them as mere machines and tools in the hand of another (the nation), which is inconsistent with the rights of humanity. The voluntary, periodic

---

1 *clausula salvatoria* Latin: disclaimer.
2 *Jesuitical casuistry* Casuistry is a form of case-based ethical reasoning. It is often used in a pejorative sense to refer to an extremely subtle contorted reasoning intended to mislead or deceive. It was a frequent slur in Protestant nations in Kant's time to allege such reasoning to be typical of the Catholic order of Jesuits.

3 *Since, like a tree ... no rights* [Kant's note] A hereditary monarch is not a nation that can be inherited by another nation; only the right to rule it can be inherited by another physical person. Consequently, the nation acquires a ruler, but the ruler as such (i.e., as one who already has another kingdom) does not acquire the nation.

4 *hiring out of one nation's troops* Kant was thinking in particular here of the recent hiring of a large number of "Hessian" troops (many from the German region of Hesse) by the British to fight on their side during the American Revolution.

military training of citizens so that they can secure their homeland against external aggression is an entirely different matter. The same could be said about the hoarding of treasure (for of the three sorts of power, the *power of an army*, the *power of alliance*, and the *power of money*, the third is the most reliable instrument of war). Thus, except for the difficulty in discovering the amount of wealth another nation possesses, the hoarding of treasure could be regarded as preparation for war that necessitates aggression.

4. No national debt shall be contracted in connection with the foreign affairs of the nation

Seeking either internal or external help for the national economy (e.g., for improvement of roads, new settlements, storage of food against years of bad harvest, and so on) is above suspicion. However, as an instrument in the struggle among powers, the credit system—the ingenious invention of a commercial people[1] during this century—of endlessly growing debts that remain safe against immediate demand (since the demand for payment is not made by all creditors at the same time) is a dangerous financial power. It is a war chest exceeding the treasure of all nations taken together, and it can be exhausted only by an inevitable default in taxes (although it can also be forestalled indefinitely by the economic stimulus that derives from credit's influence on industry and commerce). This ease in making war, combined with the inclination of those in power to do so—an inclination that seems innate in human nature—is a great obstacle to perpetual peace. Thus, forbidding foreign debt must be a preliminary article for perpetual peace, for eventual yet unavoidable national bankruptcy must entangle many innocent nations, and that would clearly injure them. Consequently, other nations are justified in allying themselves against such a nation and its pretensions.

5. No nation shall forcibly interfere with the constitution and government of another

For what can justify its doing so? Perhaps some offense that one nation's subjects give to those of another? Instead, this should serve as a warning by providing an example of the great evil that a people falls into through its lawlessness.

Generally, the bad example that one free person furnishes for another (as a *scandalum acceptum*[2]) does not injure the latter. But it would be different if, as a result of internal discord, a nation were divided in two and each part, regarding itself as a separate nation, lay claim to the whole; for (since they are in a condition of anarchy) the aid of a foreign nation to one of the parties could not be regarded as interference by the other in its constitution. So long, however, as this internal conflict remains undecided, a foreign power's interference would violate the rights of an independent people struggling with its internal ills. Doing this would be an obvious offense and would render the autonomy of every nation insecure.

6. No nation at war with another shall permit such acts of war as shall make mutual trust impossible during some future time of peace: Such acts include the use of Assassins (*percussores*), Poisoners (*venefici*), breach of surrender, instigation of treason (*perduello*) in the opposing nation, etc.

These are dishonorable stratagems. Some level of trust in the enemy's way of thinking must be preserved even in the midst of war, for otherwise no peace can ever be concluded and the hostilities would become a war of extermination (*bellum internecinum*). Yet war is but a sad necessity in the sate of nature (where no tribunal empowered to make judgments supported by the power of law exists), one that maintains the rights of a nation by mere might, where neither party can be declared an unjust enemy (since this already presupposes a judgment of right) and the outcome of the conflict (as if it were a so-called "judgment of God") determines the side on which justice lies. A war of punishment (*bellum punitivum*) between nations is inconceivable (for there is no relation of superior and inferior between them). From this it follows that a war of extermination—where the destruction of both parties along with all rights is the result—would permit perpetual peace to occur only in the vast graveyard of humanity as a whole. Thus, such a war, including all means used to wage it, must be absolutely pro-

---

1   *a commercial people*   Kant means the British.

2   *scandalum acceptum*   Latin: scandal received. In Catholic theology, this is a sin that one is led to by another's actions, not because they really incite sin, but rather because they are seen that way due to the viewer's own ignorance, weakness, or malice.

hibited. But that the means named above inexorably lead to such war becomes clear from the following: Once they come into use, these intrinsically despicable, infernal acts cannot long be confined to war alone. This applies to the use of spies (*uti exploratoribus*), where only the dishonorableness *of others* (which can never be entirely eliminated) is exploited; but such activities will also carry over to peacetime and will thus undermine it.

Although the laws set out above are objectively, i.e., from the perspective of the intention of those in power, merely *prohibitive laws* (*leges prohibitivae*), some of them are of that *strict* kind—that is, of that class of laws that holds regardless of the circumstances (*leges strictae*)—that demands *immediate* implementation (viz., Nos. 1, 5, and 6). However, others (viz., Nos. 2, 3, 4), while not exceptions to the rule of law, do permit, depending on circumstances, some subjective leeway in their *implementation* (*leges latae*) as long as one does not lose sight of their end. This permission, e.g., of the *restoration* of freedom to certain nations in accord with No. 2, cannot be put off until doomsday (or as Augustus was wont to promise, *ad calendas graecas*[1]), that is, we cannot fail to implement them. Delay is permitted only to prevent such premature implementation as might injure the intention of the article. For in the case of the second article, the prohibition concerns only the *mode of acquisition*, which is henceforth forbidden, but not the *state of ownership*, which, though not supported by the necessary title of right, was at the time (of the putative acquisition) accepted as lawful by public opinion in all nations.[2]

---

1   *ad calendas graecas*   Latin: at the Greek Calends. The Calends was the first day of the month in the Roman calendar. The Greeks did not have this term, so the expression in effect means *never*. The reference is to Suetonius' *Lives of the Caesars*: Augustus, chapter 87, section 1.

2   *prohibition concerns ... in all nations*   [Kant's note] It has previously been doubted, not unjustifiably, whether in addition to *commands* (*leges praeceptivae*) and *prohibitions* (*leges prohibitivae*) pure reason could provide *permissive laws* (*leges permissivae*). For in general laws contain a foundation of objective practical necessity, while permission only provides a foundation for certain acts that depend on practical contingencies. Thus a *permissive* law would necessitate an action that one cannot be compelled to perform, which, if the object of law has the same sense in both cases, would entail a contradiction. But the permissive law here under consideration only prohibits certain modes of acquiring a right in the future (e.g., through inheritance), while the exception from this prohibition, i.e., the permission, applies to a present state of pos-

Second Section: Which Contains the Definitive Articles for Perpetual Peace Among Nations

The state of peace among men living in close proximity is not the natural state (*status naturalis*); instead, the natural state is a one of war, which does not just consist in open hostilities, but also in the constant and enduring threat of them. The state of peace must therefore be *established*, for the suspension of hostilities does not provide the security of peace, and unless this security is pledged by one neighbor to another (which can happen only in a state of *lawfulness*), the latter, from whom such security has been requested, can treat the former as an enemy.[3]

---

session. In the transition from the state of nature to that of civil society, then, this possession, while unjust in itself, may nonetheless be regarded as *honest* (*possessio putativa*) and can continue to endure by virtue of a permissive law derived from natural right. However, as soon as any putative possession comes to be regarded as prohibited in the state of nature, every similar form of acquisition is subsequently prohibited in civil society, and this putative right to continuing possession would not hold if such a supposed acquisition had occurred in the civil state. In that case it would, as an offense against natural law, have to cease existing as soon as its illegality were discovered.

My desire here has been simply to draw the attention of proponents of natural right to the concept of a *lex permissiva*, a concept that reason in its systematically analytic use sets out and that is often used in civil (statutory) law, though with this difference, namely, that the prohibitive part of law stands on its own, while the permissive part is not (as it should be) included in the law as a limiting condition, but is regarded instead as among the exceptions to it. This means that this or that will be forbidden, *as is the case with* Nos. 1, 2, and 3, and so on indefinitely, for permissions arise only circumstantially, not according to a principle, that is, they arise only in considering specific situations. Otherwise the conditions would have to be stated in the *formulation of the prohibitive laws* and would in that way have to become laws of permission. It is therefore regrettable that the incisive, but unsolved Prize question posed by the wise and acute Count von Windischgrätz, a question that directly concerns this issue, has been forgotten so quickly. [Joseph Niklaus, Imperial Count of Windischgraetz (1744–1802) offered a prize for a method for writing contracts that would have only one possible interpretation, thus eliminating disputes.] For the possibility of a formula (such as exists in mathematics) is the only true criterion of all subsequent legislation, and without it the so-called *ius certum* will forever remain a pious wish. In its absence, we shall merely have *general* laws (which are valid in general), but no universal ones (which are universally valid), and it is the latter that the concept of a law requires.

3   *The state of peace ... as an enemy*   [Kant's note] It is commonly assumed that one ought not take hostile action against another

First definitive article for a perpetual peace: The civil constitution of every nation should be republican

The sole established constitution that follows from the idea of an original contract, the one on which all of a nation's rightful legislation must be based, is republican. For, first, it accords with the principles of the *freedom* of the members of a society (as men), second, it accords with the principles of the *dependence* of everyone on a single, common [source of] legislation (as subjects), and third, it accords with the law of equality of them all (as citizens).[1] Thus, so far as [the

matter of] right is concerned, republicanism is the original foundation of all forms of civil constitution. Thus, the only question remaining is this, does it also provide the only foundation for perpetual peace?

Now in addition to the purity of its origin, a purity whose source is the pure concept[2] of right, the republican constitution also provides for this desirable result, namely, perpetual peace, and the reason for this is as follows: If (as must inevitably be the case, given this form of constitution) the consent of the citizenry is required in order to deter-

---

unless one has already been actively *injured* by that person and that is entirely correct if both parties live in a state [governed by] *civil law*. For by entering into civil society, each person gives every other (by virtue of the sovereignty that has power over them both) the requisite security. However, a man (or a people) who is merely in a state of nature denies me this security and injures me merely by being in this state. For although he does not actively (*facto*) injure me, he does so by virtue of the lawlessness of his state (*statu iniusto*), by which he constantly threatens me, and I can require him either to enter with me into a state of civil law or to remove himself from my surroundings. Thus, the postulate on which all the following articles rest is: "All men who can mutually influence one another must accept some civil constitution."

Every just constitution, as far as the persons who accept it are concerned, will be one of the three following:

   1. one conforming to the civil rights of men in a nation (*ius civitatis*);

   2. one conforming to the *rights of nations* in relations to one another;

   3. one conforming to the *rights of world citizenship*, so far as men and nations stand in mutually influential relations as citizens of a universal nation of men (*ius cosmopoliticum*). These are not arbitrary divisions, but ones that are necessary in relationship to the idea of perpetual peace. Because if even only one of these [nations] had only physical influence on another, they would be in a state of nature, and consequently they would be bound together in a state of war. Our intention here is to free them from this.

1 *For, first, it accords ... (as citizens)* [Kant's note] *Rightful* (consequently external) *freedom* cannot be defined in the way it usually is, as the privilege to do whatever one will as long as one does no injustice. For what does privilege mean? The possibility of action as long as one does no wrong. Thus, the clarification would read: Freedom is the possibility of action as long as one does no wrong. One does no wrong (one may thus do what one wills), if only one does no wrong. This is a mere empty tautology. Instead, external (*rightful*) *freedom* is to be clarified as follows: It is the privilege not to obey any external laws except those to which I have been able to give my consent. In just the same way, external (*rightful*) *equal-*

ity in a nation is that relation among citizens whereby no citizen can be bound by a law, unless all are subject to it simultaneously and in the very same way. (The principle of *rightful* dependence requires no clarification, for it is already contained in the concept of a political constitution in general.) The validity of these innate rights that necessarily and inalienably belong to humanity is confirmed and raised to an even higher level by virtue of the principle that man has rightful relations to higher beings (if he believes in them), since by these very same principles he represents himself as a citizen in the supersensuous world. Now so far as my freedom is concerned, I have no obligation even to divine laws knowable only by reason, except only insofar as I am able to consent to them. (For it is through the law of freedom that I am first able rationally to create a concept of the divine will.) But as regards the principle of equality, even the highest worldly being that I can think of (say a great Aeon [the Greek personification of eternal time])—but excepting God—has no reason (assuming I perform my duty in my position, as that Aeon performs his duty in his) to expect it to be my duty only to obey, leaving the right of command to him. This principle of *equality* does not (as does that of freedom) pertain to one's relation to God because God is the sole being excepted from the concept of duty.

Concerning all citizens' right of equality as subjects, one can resolve the issue of whether a hereditary nobility is permissible by asking whether some rank making one citizen superior to another granted by the nation is antecedent to *merit*, or whether merit must precede rank. Now clearly, when rank is tied to birth it is completely uncertain whether merit (skill and integrity in one's office) will accompany it. Consequently, this hereditary arrangement is no different from conferring command on some favorite person who is wholly lacking in merit. This is something that the general will of a people would never agree to in an original contract (which is the principle that underlies all rights). For a nobleman is not, by virtue of that fact alone, a *noble* man. Concerning the *nobility of office* (as one can designate the rank of a higher magistrate, which one must earn by virtue of merit), here rank does not belong to the person, but to the position he holds, and this does not violate [the principle of] equality, because when that person resigns his office he gives up his rank at the same time and again becomes one of the people.

2 *pure concept* This is, for Kant, an understanding of something based solely on reasoning—unmixed with information from the senses (empirical information).

mine whether or not there will be war, it is natural that they consider all its calamities before committing themselves to so risky a game. (Among these are doing the fighting themselves, paying the costs of war from their own resources, having to repair at great sacrifice the war's devastation, and, finally, the ultimate evil that would make peace itself better, never being able—because of new and constant wars—to expunge the burden of debt.) By contrast, under a non-republican constitution, where subjects are not citizens, the easiest thing in the world to do is to declare war. Here the ruler is not a fellow citizen, but the nation's owner, and war does not affect his table, his hunt, his places of pleasure, his court festivals, and so on. Thus, he can decide to go to war for the most meaningless of reasons, as if it were a kind of pleasure party, and he can blithely leave its justification (which decency requires) to his diplomatic corps, who are always prepared for such exercises.

The following comments are necessary to prevent confusing (as so often happens) the republican form of constitution with the democratic one: The forms of a nation (*civitas*) can be analyzed either on the basis of the persons who possess the highest political authority or on the basis of the way the people are *governed* by their ruler, whoever he may be. The first is called the form of sovereignty (*forma imperii*), of which only three kinds are possible, specifically, where either *one*, or *several* in association, or *all* those together who make up civil society possess the sovereign power (autocracy, aristocracy, and democracy, the power of a monarch, the power of a nobility, the power of a people). The second is the form of government (*forma regiminis*) and concerns the way in which a nation, based on its constitution (the act of the general will whereby a group becomes a people), exercises its authority. In this regard, government is either *republican* or *despotic. Republicanism* is that political principle whereby executive power (the government) is separated from legislative power. In a despotism the ruler independently executes laws that it has itself made; here rulers have taken hold of the public will and treated it as their own private will. Among the three forms of government, *democracy*, in the proper sense of the term, is necessarily a *despotism*, because it sets up an executive power in which all citizens make decisions about and, if need be, against one (who therefore does not agree); consequently, all, who are not quite all, decide, so that the general will contradicts both itself and freedom.

Every form of government that is not *representative* is properly speaking *without form*, because one and the same

person can no more be at one and the same time the legislator and executor of his will (than the universal proposition can serve as the major premise in a syllogism and at the same time be the subsumption of the particular under it in the minor premise[1]). And although the other two forms of political constitution are defective inasmuch as they always leave room for a democratic form of government, it is nonetheless possible that they assume a form of government that accords with the *spirit* of a representative system: As Friederick II[2] at least *said*, "I am merely the nation's highest servant."[3] The democratic system makes this impossible, for everyone wants to rule. One can therefore say, the smaller the number of persons who exercise the power of the nation (the number of rulers), the more they represent and the closer the political constitution approximates the possibility of republicanism, and thus, the constitution can hope through gradual reforms finally to become republican. For this reason, attaining this state that embodies a completely just constitution is more difficult in an aristocracy than in a monarchy, and, except by violent revolution, there is no possibility of attaining it in a democracy.

Nonetheless, the people are incomparably more concerned with the form of government[4] than with the form of

---

1   *than the universal proposition ... minor premise* This is an impossibility in certain kinds of argument-form; its details are not relevant here.

2   *Friederick II* Friederick the Great (1712–86), King of Prussia.

3   *I am merely ... highest servant* From Friederick II's book *Anti-Macchiavel* (1740). [Kant's note] People have often criticized the lofty titles that are normally bestowed on a ruler ("the divinely anointed" and "the representative and executor of the divine will on earth") as gross and extravagant flatteries; but it seems to me that this is without basis. Far from stirring arrogance in the ruler of a country, they should instead humble his soul, providing he possesses reason (which one must assume) and has reflected on the fact that he has undertaken an office that is too great for a single man, the holiest one that God has established on earth, the protector of the *rights of mankind*, and he must always be careful not to tread upon this apple of God's eye.

4   *the people ... form of government* [Kant's note] In his important sounding but hollow and empty language, Mallet du Pan boasts of having after many years of experience finally come to be convinced of Pope's well known saying, "For forms of government let fools contest;/Whate'er is best administered is best." If that means that the best administered government is the best administered, then he has, in Swift's expression, "cracked a nut and been rewarded with only a worm." But if it means that it is the best form of government, i.e., political constitution, then it is fundamentally false, for good governments prove nothing about form of government. Who has ruled better than a Titus and a Marcus Aurelius, and yet one was succeeded by a Domitian and

the constitution (although a great deal depends on the degree to which the latter is suited to the goals of the former). But if the form of government is to cohere with the concept of right, it must include the representative system, which is possible only in a republican form of government and without which (no matter what the constitution may be) government is despotic and brutish. None of the ancient so-called republics were aware of this, and consequently they inevitably degenerated into despotism; still, this is more bearable under a single person's rulership than other forms of government are.

Second definitive article for a perpetual peace: The right of nations shall be based on a federation of free states

As nations, peoples can be regarded as single individuals who injure one another through their close proximity while living in the state of nature (i.e., independently of external laws). For the sake of its own security, each nation can and should demand that the others enter into a contract resembling the civil one and guaranteeing the rights of each. This would be a federation of *nations*, but it must not be a nation consisting of nations. The latter would be contradictory, for in every nation there exists the relation of *ruler* (legislator) to *subject* (those who obey, the people); however, many nations in a single nation would constitute only a single nation, which contradicts our assumption (since we are here weighing the rights of *nations* in relation to one another, rather than fusing them into a single nation).

Just as we view with deep disdain the attachment of savages to their lawless freedom—preferring to scuffle without end rather than to place themselves under lawful restraints that they themselves constitute, consequently preferring a mad freedom to a rational one—and consider it barbarous, rude, and brutishly degrading of humanity, so also should we think that civilized peoples (each one united into a nation) would hasten as quickly as possible to escape so similar a state of abandonment. Instead, however, each *nation* sees its majesty (for it is absurd to speak of the majesty of a people) to consist in not being subject to any external legal constraint, and the glory of its ruler consists in being able, without endangering himself, to command many thousands to sacrifice themselves for a matter that does not concern them.[1] The primary difference between European and American savages is this, while many latter tribes have been completely eaten by their enemies, the former know how to make better use of those they have conquered than to consume them: They increase the number of their subjects and thus also the quantity of instruments they have to wage even more extensive wars.

Given the depravity of human nature which is revealed and can be glimpsed in the free relations among nations (though deeply concealed by governmental restraints in law governed civil-society), one must wonder why the word *right* has not been completely discarded from the politics of war as pedantic, or why no nation has openly ventured to declare that it should be. For while, Hugo Grotius, Pufendorf, Vattel,[2] and others whose philosophically and diplomatically formulated codes do not and cannot have the slightest legal force (since nations do not stand under any common external constraints), are always piously cited in justification of a war of aggression (and who therefore provide only cold comfort), no example can be given of a nation having foregone its intention [of going to war] based on the arguments provided by such important men. The homage that every nation pays (at least in words) to the concept of right proves, nonetheless, that there is in man a still greater, though presently dormant, moral aptitude to master the evil principle in himself (a principle he cannot deny) and to hope that

---

the other by Commodus, which could not have happened under a good political constitution, since their unfitness for the post was known early enough and the power of the ruler was sufficient to have excluded them from it. [The writers referred to in this note are Jacques Mallet du Pan (1749–1800), Swiss Royalist writer, in his *Über die französische Revolution* (1794); Alexander Pope (1688–1744), English poet, in his *Essay on Man*, 3; and Jonathan Swift (1667–1745), Irish satirist—the quotation is a paraphrase from *Tale of a Tub*, 1. The Roman Emperors are Titus Flavius Vespasianus (39–81), ruled 79–81; Marcus Aurelius Antoninus (121–80), ruled 161–80; Titus Flavius Domitianus (51–96), ruled 81–96; and Lucius Aurelius Commodus (161–92), ruled 180–92. The first two have a reputation as benevolent rulers, the second two as cruel ones.]

---

1   *glory of its ruler ... not concern them*   [Kant's note] Thus a Bulgarian prince gave this answer to a Greek emperor who kindly offered to settle a conflict between them by duel: "A smith who has tongs will not use his hands to take the glowing iron from the fire."

2   *Hugo Grotius, Pufendorf, Vattel*   Hugo Grotius (1583–1645), Dutch philosopher, jurist, and literary writer, author of *On the Law of War and Peace* (1625); Baron Samuel von Pufendorf (1632–94), German philosopher, jurist, economist, historian and statesman, author of *The Law of Nature and of Nations* (1672); Emmerich de Vattel (1714–67), Swiss philosopher, jurist, and diplomat, best known for *The Law of Nations* (1758). All three made important contributions to international law.

others will also overcome it. For otherwise the word *right* would never leave the mouths of those nations that want to make war on one another, unless it were mockingly, as when that Gallic prince declared, "Nature has given the strong the prerogative of making the weak obey them."

Nations can press for their rights only by waging war and never in a trial before an independent tribunal, but war and its favorable consequence, victory, cannot determine the right. And although a *treaty of peace* can put an end to some particular war, it cannot end the state of war (the tendency always to find a new pretext for war). (And this situation cannot straightforwardly be declared unjust, since in this circumstance each nation is judge of its own case.) Nor can one say of nations as regards their rights what one can say concerning the natural rights of men in a state of lawlessness, to wit, that "they should abandon this state." (For as nations they already have an internal, legal constitution and therefore have outgrown the compulsion to subject themselves to another legal constitution that is subject to someone else's concept of right.) Nonetheless, from the throne of its moral legislative power, reason absolutely condemns war as a means of determining the right and makes seeking the state of peace a matter of unmitigated duty. But without a contract among nations peace can be neither inaugurated nor guaranteed. A league of a special sort must therefore be established, one that we can call a *league of peace* (*foedus pacificum*), which will be distinguished from a *treaty of peace* (*pactum pacis*) because the latter seeks merely to stop one war, while the former seeks to end *all* wars forever. This league does not seek any power of the sort possessed by nations, but only the maintenance and security of each nation's own freedom, as well as that of the other nations leagued with it, without their having thereby to subject themselves to civil laws and their constraints (as men in the state of nature must do). It can be shown that this *idea of federalism* should eventually include all nations and thus lead to perpetual peace. For if good fortune should so dispose matters that a powerful and enlightened people should form a republic (which by its nature must be inclined to seek perpetual peace), it will provide a focal point for a federation association among other nations that will join it in order to guarantee a state of peace among nations that is in accord with the idea of the right of nations, and through several associations of this sort such a federation can extend further and further.

That a people might say, "There should be no war among us, for we want to form ourselves into a nation,

i.e., place ourselves under a supreme legislative, executive, and judicial power to resolve our conflicts peacefully," is understandable. But when a nation says, "There should be no war between me and other nations, though I recognize no supreme legislative power to guarantee me my rights and him his," then if there does not exist a surrogate of the union in a civil society, which is a free federation, it is impossible to understand what the basis for so entrusting my rights is. Such a federation is necessarily tied rationally to the concept of the right of nations, at least if this latter notion has any meaning.

The concept of the right of nations as a right to go to war is meaningless (for it would then be the right to determine the right not by independent, universally valid laws that restrict the freedom of everyone, but by one-sided maxims backed by force). Consequently, the concept of the right of nations must be understood as follows: that it serves justly those men who are disposed to seek one another's destruction and thus find perpetual peace in the grave that covers all the horrors of violence and its perpetrators. Reason can provide related nations with no other means for emerging from the state of lawlessness, which consists solely of war, than that they give up their savage (lawless) freedom, just as individual persons do, and, by accommodating themselves to the constraints of common law, establish a *nation of peoples* (*civitas gentium*), that (continuingly growing) will finally include all the people of the earth. But they do not will to do this because it does not conform to their idea of the right of nations, and consequently they discard in *hypothesis* what is true in *thesis*. So (if everything is not to be lost) in place of the positive idea of *a world republic* they put only the *negative* surrogate of an enduring, ever expanding *federation* that prevents war and curbs the tendency of that hostile inclination to defy the law, though there will always be constant danger of their breaking loose (*Furor impius intus ... fremit horridus ore cruento.* Virgil).[1,2]

---

1   *Fuor impius ... ore cruento* Latin: "Within impious rage ... roars with blood-stained mouth." Virgil, *Aeneid* 1, 294–96. The full passage reads, "The gates of war, grim with iron and close-fitting bars, shall be closed: within, impious Rage, sitting on savage arms, his hands bound behind with a hundred brazen knots shall roar in the ghastliness of blood-stained lips" (H.R. Fairclough translation).

2   [Kant's note] It would not be inappropriate at the end of a war concluded by peace for a people to set aside, after a festival of thanksgiving, a day of atonement so that in the name of the nation they might ask heaven to forgive them for the great sin that the human race continues to be guilty of by failing to establish a lawful contract in relation to other peoples, preferring instead,

Third definitive article for a perpetual peace: Cosmopolitan right shall be limited to conditions of universal hospitality

As in the preceding articles, our concern here is not with philanthropy but with *right*, and in this context *hospitality* (hospitableness) means the right of an alien not to be treated as an enemy upon his arrival in another's country. If it can be done without destroying him, he can be turned away; but, as long as he behaves peaceably he cannot be treated as an enemy. He may request the *right* to be a *permanent visitor* (which would require a special, charitable agreement to make him a fellow inhabitant for a certain period), but the *right to visit*, to associate, belongs to all men by virtue of their common ownership of the earth's surface; for since the earth is a globe, they cannot scatter themselves infinitely, but must, finally, tolerate living in close proximity, because originally no one had a greater right to any region of the earth than anyone else. Uninhabitable parts of this surface—the sea and deserts—separate these communities, and yet ships and camels (the *ships* of the desert) make it possible to approach one another across these unowned regions, and the right to the *earth's surface* that belongs in common to the totality of men makes commerce possible. The inhospitableness that coastal dwellers (e.g., on the Barbary Coast[1]) show by robbing ships in neighboring seas and by making slaves of stranded seafarers, or of desert dwellers (the Arabic Bedouins), who regard their proximity to nomadic peoples as giving them a right to plunder, is contrary to natural right, even though the latter extends the right to hospitality, i.e., the privilege of aliens to enter, only so far as makes attempts at commerce with native inhabitants possible. In this way distant parts of the world can establish with one another peaceable relations that will eventually become matters of public law, and the human race can gradually be brought closer and closer to a cosmopolitan constitution.

Compare this with the inhospitable conduct of civilized nations in our part of the world, especially commercial ones: The injustice that they display towards foreign lands and peoples (which is the same as *conquering* them), is terrifying. When discovered, America, the lands occupied by the blacks, the Spice Islands, the Cape, etc., were regarded as lands belonging to no one because their inhabitants were counted for nothing. Foreign soldiers were imported into East India under the pretext of merely establishing economic relations, and with them came subjection of the natives, incitement of various nations to widespread wars among themselves, famine, rebellion, treachery, and the entire litany of evils that can afflict the human race.

China[2] and Japan (*Nippon*), which have had experience with such guests, have therefore wisely restricted contact

---

through pride in their independence, to employ the barbarous means of war (by use of which they cannot secure what they seek, namely, the rights of each particular nation). The festivals of thanksgiving for victories during war, the hymns that are sung (in good Israelitic fashion) to the *Lord of Lords*, could not stand in greater contrast with the ideas of a Father of men, for besides displaying an indifference to the way in which peoples seek their mutual right (which is sad enough), they actually express joy at having destroyed numerous humans and their happiness.

1 *Barbary Coast* Part of the coast of North Africa.

2 *China* [Kant's note] [For the reasons why] we should call this great kingdom by the name it gives itself (namely, China, not Sina, or anything similar), one has only to consult [Antonio Agostino] Georgi's *Alpha[betum] Tibet[anum ...]*. According to the observation of Professor [Johann Eberhard] Fischer of Petersburg [1697–1771, *Quaestiones Petropolitanae*, 1770], there is actually no determinate name that it uses in reference to itself. The most common one is the word *Kin*, namely, gold (which the Tibetans call *Ser*), and therefore the emperor is called the king of *Gold* (i.e., of the most magnificent country in the world). In the kingdom itself, this word is probably pronounced *Chen*, but is pronounced *Kin* by the Italian missionaries (who cannot make the guttural sound). From this one can see that the Romans' so-called "Land of Seres" was China, and silk was brought from there to Europe across *Greater-Tibet* (probably through *Lesser Tibet*, Bukhara, Persia and so on). This leads to many speculations concerning the antiquity of this amazing nation in comparison with that of Hindustan, as well as regarding its connections with Tibet and also with Japan. But the name Sina or Tshina, which neighbors of this land give it, leads nowhere. Perhaps this also allows us to clarify the very ancient but never properly understood commerce of Europe with Tibet from what *Hysichius* [Hesychius of Alexandra, Greek grammarian c. fifth century CE, author of a dictionary] has recorded about the hierophants' cry "Κονε Ομπαξ" (*Konx Ompax*) in the Eleusinian mysteries. [Hierophants were the chief priests at the Eleusinian mysteries, initiation ceremonies of an ancient Greek religious cult.] (See [Abbé Jean Jacques Barthélemy,] *Travels of the Young Anacharsis [in Greece ...*, 1788] Part V.) For according to Georgi's *Alph. Tibet.*, the word "*Concoia*" means God, which has a striking resemblance to Knox. *Pah-cio* (*ibid.*), which the Greeks might well have pronounced *pax*, means the *promulgator legis*, the divinity that pervades all of nature (also called *Cencresi*). However, *Om*, which [Mathurin Veyssière de] La Croze translated *benedictus, blessed*, can be related to divinity, but probably means nothing other than the *beatified*. Now Fr. Franz [Franciscus] Horatius often asked the Tibetan Lamas what they understood God (*Concoia*) to be and always received this answer, "It is the gathering of all the Saints" (i.e., the gathering of all blessed ones who, according to the Lama's doctrine of rebirth, have finally returned, after many migrations through all sorts of bodies, to the

with them. China only permits contact with a single European people, the Dutch, whom they nonetheless exclude as if they were prisoners from associating with the natives. The worst (or, considered from the perspective of a moral judge, the best) consequence of all this is that such violence profits these trading companies not at all and that all of them are at the point of near collapse. The Sugar Islands,[1] the seat of the cruelest and most ingenious slavery, yield no true profit, but serve only the indirect and not very profitable purpose of training sailors for ships of war, which in turn aids the pursuit of wars in Europe. And this is the action of powers who, while imbibing injustice like water, make much of their piety and who in matters of orthodoxy want to be regarded as the elect.

Because a (narrower or wider) community widely prevails among the Earth's peoples, a transgression of rights in *one* place in the world is felt *everywhere*; consequently, the idea of cosmopolitan right is not fantastic and exaggerated, but rather an amendment to the unwritten code of national and international rights, necessary to the public rights of men in general. Only such amendment allows us to flatter ourselves with the thought that we are making continual progress towards perpetual peace.

First Supplement on the Guarantee of Perpetual Peace

Perpetual peace is *insured* (guaranteed) by nothing less than that great artist nature (*natura daedala rerum*)[2] whose mechanical process makes her purposiveness visibly manifest, permitting harmony to emerge among men through

their discord, even against their wills. If we regard this design as a compulsion resulting from one of her causes whose laws of operation are unknown to us, we call it *fate*, while, if we reflect on nature's purposiveness in the flow of world events, and regard it to be the underlying wisdom of a higher cause that directs the human race toward its objective goal and predetermines the world's course, we call it *providence*.[3] We cannot actually have *cognitive* knowledge

---

1   *Sugar Islands* Caribbean islands (including Barbados, Antigua, and Montserrat), settled first in the 1620s by slave-holding European sugar-planters.

2   *natura daedala rerum* Latin: "Nature the contriver of [all] things"—Lucretius, *De Rerum Naturae*, 5.

3   *providence* [Kant's note] There is manifest in the mechanism of nature to which man (as a sensory being) belongs a form that is fundamental to its existence, a form that we cannot conceive except insofar as it underlies the purpose of a predetermining creator of the world. We call this predetermination (divine) *providence* in general; so far as it is established at the *beginning* of the world, we call it *grounding providence* (*providentia conditrix; semel iussit, semper parent* ["Providence is a founder; as soon as she commands, they obey without fail"], Augustine); where this purposiveness in nature's course is maintained through universal laws, we call it *ruling providence* (*providentia gubernatrix*); where it leads to specific ends that men cannot foresee but can only infer from its results, we call it *guiding providence* (*providentia directrix*); finally, where we regard particular events as divine ends, we no longer speak of providence but of *dispensation* (*directio extraordinaria*). However, it is a foolish presumption for men to want to be able to recognize these latter for what they are (for in fact they are miracles, even though the events are not described in that way). No matter how pious and humble such language may be, it is absurd and altogether self-conceited to make an inference from some single event to some special principle as its efficient cause (so that this event is [regarded as] an end and not merely the natural and mechanical consequence of some other end completely unknown to us). In the same way, applying the distinction between *universal* and *special* providence (considered *materially*) to *objects* in the world is unjustifiable and self-contradictory (as when, for example, one claims that nature is concerned to preserve the species, but leaves individuals to chance); for the point of saying that providence applies universally is that no single thing is taken into consideration. Presumably, one intends by this to distinguish between the ways in which providence (considered *formally*) carries out its intentions, that is, in ordinary [fashion] (e.g., the annual death and revival of nature in accordance with the change of seasons) or in *extraordinary* fashion (e.g., the transport of wood by ocean currents to icebound coasts, where it cannot grow, so as to provide for the needs of their natives, who could not live without it). Here, while we can readily explain the physical and mechanical causes of these appearances to ourselves (e.g., by the fact that the banks of rivers in temperate lands are heavily wooded so that trees fall into them and are carried off by the Gulf Stream), we must nonetheless not overlook teleological causes, which indicate the care of a wisdom that governs nature. Only the scholastic concept of a divine *participation* in or concurrence (*concursus*) with every effect experienced in the world of sense must be given up. *First*, that scholastic view attempts to conjoin dissimilar kinds of things (*gryphes iungere equis* ["To mate griffins with horses"—Virgil,

---

divinity, or *Burchane*, i.e., souls metamorphosed into being that is worthy of worship). Thus that mysterious term *Konx Ompax* might well refer to that *holy* (Konx), *blessed* (Om) and *wise* (Pax) supreme Being who pervades the world (nature personified), and its use in the Greek *Mystery religions* may have signified a monotheism to the Epopts [initiates into the Eleusinian mysteries] that contrasted with the polytheism of the people, though Fr. Horatius (among others) detected an *atheism* in it. But just how that mysterious term made its way from Tibet to Greece may apparently be explained in the foregoing way, as well as Europe's early commerce with China (which may have begun earlier than with Hindustan) through Tibet.

of these intricate designs in nature, nor can we *infer* their actual existence from it, but (as with all relations between the forms of things and purposes in general) we can and must *attribute* them to objects only in thought so as to conceive of their possibility on an analogy with mankind's productive activities. The relationship of objects to and their conformity with the purposes that reason itself sets out for us (the end of morality) can be represented from a *theoretical* point of view as a transcendent idea, but from the practical point of view (where, e.g., it is employed in relation to our concept of duty regarding *perpetual peace*), it is represented as a dogmatic idea and it is here that its reality is properly established. When, as in the context of this essay, our concern is entirely theoretical (and not religious) it is most appropriate to the limits of human reason to use the term *nature* (for in reflecting on the relations of effects to their causes, human reason must remain within the bounds of possible experience); the term *nature* is less *pretentious* than a term connoting that there is a *providence* of which we can have cognitive knowledge, and on which we take flight as on Icarus's wings[1] in order more closely to approach the secrets of some unfathomable intention.

Before we define this guarantee [of perpetual peace] more closely, we must examine the state in which nature has placed her actors on her vast stage, a state that ultimately and necessarily secures their peace—then we shall see how she guarantees the latter.

Nature's provisional arrangement consists of the following: 1. She has taken care that men can live in all regions of the world. 2. Through *war* she has driven them everywhere, even into the most inhospitable regions in order to populate them. 3. Also through war she has constrained them to establish more or less legal relationships. It is truly wonderful that moss grows even in the cold wastes by the Arctic Ocean and that *reindeer* can dig it from beneath the snow so that they can become food or transportation for the Ostiak or Samoyed; or that the salt deserts are inhabited by the *camel*, which appears to have been created for traveling over them, so that the deserts do not go unused. But purpose is even more clearly evident when one realizes that not only do furbearing animals exist on the shores of the Arctic Ocean, but also seals, walruses, and whales, whose flesh provides food and whose blubber provides warmth for the inhabitants. However, what most arouses our wonder is nature's care to bring (in what way we do not really know) driftwood to these barren regions, for without this material the natives could have neither their canoes and spears nor their huts to dwell in. In these regions they are sufficiently occupied with their war against animals that they live in peace among themselves. But it was probably nothing but war that *drove* them there. Among all the animals, the *horse* was the first that man learned to tame and to domesticate in the process of populating the earth and the first *instrument of war* (for the elephant belongs to a later period, to the luxury of already established nations). The art of cultivating certain kinds of grasses, called *grains*, whose original characteristics are no longer known, as well as the propagation and refinement of various *fruits* by transplanting and grafting (in Europe perhaps only two species, the crab apple and the wild pear), could arise only under conditions provided by already established nations, where property was secure; and it could occur only after men had already undergone the transition from the lawless freedom of hunting,[2] fishing,

---

Eclogues 8.27. slightly altered]) and it is self-contradictory to let that which is itself the wholly sufficient cause of all changes in the world supplement its own predetermining providence in the course of the world (implying that providence must originally have therefore been lacking). It is, for example, self-contradictory to say that *after* God, the physician assisted in curing the illness. For *causa solitaria non iuvat* ["a single cause does not suffice"] God creates the physician and all his medicines, and if we want to go back to the highest, but theoretically inconceivable, original cause we must ascribe the action entirely to Him. Of course, if we explain this event as following from the chain of causes in the world and in accordance with the natural order, one can ascribe healing to the physician alone. *Second*, with that scholastic way of thinking we give up all determinant principles for making judgments about an effect. But from a *morally-practical* perspective (which is wholly directed to the supersensuous [beyond perception by the senses])—e.g., in the belief that if only our interactions are pure, God will compensate for our own injustices by means that are inconceivable to us and that we should not, therefore, give up our striving to do good—the concept of a divine *concursus* is entirely appropriate and even necessary. But it is self-evident that one must not attempt to *explain* a good action (as an event in the world) in this way, for that is a vain and consequently absurd attempt at theoretical knowledge of the supersensuous.

1   *Icarus's wings*   In Greek mythology, Icarus fell into the sea after flying too close to the sun, which melted the wax wings his father Daedalus had made for him.

2   *freedom of hunting*   [Kant's note] Of all forms of life, the *life of the hunter* is without doubt most contrary to a civilized constitution, for, having to live separately, families soon become estranged and, dispersed as they become in immense forest, also soon become enemies, for each requires a great deal of room in order to provide for its nourishment and clothing. The Noachic prohibition

and herding to the life of *agriculture*. *Salt* and *iron* were discovered next, and these were probably the first articles of trade sought far and wide by different peoples. In this way they entered into *peaceful relations* with one another, and from this common understanding, community of interest and peaceful relations arose with the most distant peoples.

In taking care that men *could* live everywhere on earth, nature has also despotically chosen that they *should* live everywhere, even against their inclinations, and without presupposing that this should rest on a concept of duty that binds men as a moral law; instead, she has chosen war as the means whereby this purpose is to be fulfilled. Specifically, we see peoples whose unity of language reveals the unity of their origins, for instance, the *Samoyeds* of the Arctic Ocean, on the one hand, and a people with a similar language living two hundred miles distant, in the Altai Mountains, on the other; between them lives another people, of Mongolian origin, who are adept at horsemanship and, consequently, war and who drove the two parts of the other race into inhospitable arctic regions, where they would certainly not have gone of their own inclination.[1] Similarly, in the northern-most regions of Europe, Gothic and Sarmitic peoples, who pushed their way in, separated the *Finns*, called *Lapps*, by an equal distance from the linguistically related *Hungarians*. And what else but war—which nature uses as a means to populate the entire earth—could have driven the Eskimos (who are perhaps very ancient European adventurers, and totally distinct as a race from all Americans) to the north, and the Pescherais to the south of America, to Tierra del Fuego. Nonetheless, war itself requires no particular

motivation, but appears to be ingrained in human nature and is even valued as something noble; indeed, the desire for glory inspires men to it, even independently of selfish motives. Consequently, *courage in war* (among American Indians as well as during Europe's chivalric period) is judged to be of immediate and great worth not only *during war* (as is reasonable), but also in order that *war might be*, and often war is begun only as a means to display courage. As a result, an intrinsic worth is bestowed on war, even to the extent that philosophers, unmindful of that Greek saying, "War is a bad bet because it produces more evil people than it eliminates," have praised it as having a certain ennobling influence on mankind. So much for what nature does to further *her own ends* in respect to the human race as a class of animal.

Our concern now is the most important question regarding the objective of perpetual peace: How does nature further this purpose that man's own reason sets out as a duty for him, i.e., how does she foster his *moral objective*, and how has it been guaranteed that what man ought to do through the laws of freedom, but does not, he shall, notwithstanding his freedom, do through nature's constraint? This question arises with respect to all three aspects of public right, *civil, international,* and *cosmopolitan right*. When I say of nature that she *wills* that this or that happen, that does not mean that she sets it out as a duty that we do it (because only practical reason, which is free of constraint, can do that); rather, she does it herself whether or not we will it (*fata volentem ducunt, nolentem trahunt*[2]).

1. Even if a people were not constrained by internal discord to submit to public laws, war would make them do it, for according to the natural arrangement explained above, every people finds itself neighbor to another people that threatens it, and it must form itself into a *nation* so as to be able to prepare itself to meet this threat with *military might*. Now the republican constitution is the only one wholly compatible with the rights of men, but it is also the most difficult to establish and still harder to maintain, so much so that many contend[3] that a republic must be a nation of *angels*, for men's self-seeking inclinations make them incapable of adhering to so sublime a form of government. But now nature comes to the aid of that revered but practically

---

against blood (Genesis 9.4–5) (is repeated often, and Jewish Christians imposed it on pagans newly converted to Christianity as a condition of their acceptance, though for different reasons, Acts 15.20, 21.25) appears originally to have been nothing other than a command against the *hunting life*, since the latter often required eating raw flesh, and when the later is forbidden, the other must also be.

1 *their own inclination* [Kant's note] One could ask, if nature has chosen that these icy coasts should not remain uninhabited and if (as we can expect) nature no longer provides them with driftwood, what will become of their inhabitants? For one must believe that as culture progresses, the natives in the temperate zone might make better use of the wood that grows on the banks of their rivers if they did not allow it to fall into rivers and float away into the sea, I answer: Those who dwell along the Ob, the Yenisei, the Lena, etc., will provide it through trade, exchanging it for products from the animal kingdom, in which the sea along the Arctic coasts abounds—but only if she (nature) first compels them to peace.

2 *fata volentem ducunt, nolentem trahunt* Latin: the fates lead the willing, drag the unwilling. Slightly misquoted from Seneca, *Epistle* 107.11.

3 *many contend* Kant may have Rousseau in mind here (*Social Contract* 3.4).

impotent general will, which is grounded in reason. Indeed, this aid comes directly from those self-seeking inclinations, and it is merely by organizing the nation well (which is certainly within man's capacities) that they are able to direct their power against one another, and one inclination is able to check or cancel the destructive tendencies of the others. The result for reason is the same as if neither sets of opposing inclinations existed, and so man, even though he is not morally good, is forced to be a good citizen. As hard as it may sound, the problem of organizing a nation is solvable even for a people comprised of devils (if only they possess understanding). The problem can be stated in this way: "So order and organize a group of rational beings who require universal laws for their preservation—though each is secretly inclined to exempt himself from such laws—that, while their private attitudes conflict, these nonetheless so cancel one another that these beings behave publicly just as if they had no evil attitudes." This kind of problem must be *solvable*. For it does not require the moral improvement of man; it requires only that we know how to apply the mechanism of nature to men so as to organize the conflict of hostile attitudes present in a people in such a way that they must compel one another to submit to coercive laws and thus to enter into a state of peace, where laws have power. One can see that although the inner core of morality is certainly not its cause, presently existing but still very imperfectly organized nations have in their foreign relations already approached what the idea of right prescribes (so that a good national constitution cannot be expected to arise from morality, but, rather, quite the opposite, a people's good moral condition is to be expected only under a good constitution). Consequently, the mechanism of nature, in which self-seeking inclinations naturally counteract one another in their external relations, can be used by reason as a means to prepare the way for its own end, the rule of right, as well as to promote and secure the nation's internal and external peace. This means that nature irresistibly *wills* that right should finally triumph. What one neglects to do will ultimately occur of its own accord, though with a great deal of inconvenience. "If one bends the reed too much, it breaks; and whoever wills too much, wills nothing."[1]

2. The idea of international right presupposes the existence of many *separate*, independent, adjoining nations; and although such a situation is in itself a state of war (assuming that a federative union among them does not prevent the outbreak of hostilities), yet this situation is rationally preferable to their being overrun by a superior power that melds them into a universal monarchy. For laws invariably lose their impact with the expansion of their domain of governance, and after it has uprooted the soul of good a soulless despotism finally degenerates into anarchy. Nonetheless, the desire of every nation (or its ruler) is to establish an enduring peace, hoping, if possible, to dominate the entire world. But nature *wills* otherwise. She uses two means to prevent peoples from intermingling and to separate them, differences in *language* and *religion*,[2] which do indeed dispose men to mutual hatred and to pretexts for war. But the growth of culture and men's gradual progress toward greater agreement regarding their principles lead to mutual understanding and peace. Unlike that peace that despotism (in the graveyard of freedom) brings about by vitiating all powers, this one is produced and secured by an equilibrium of the liveliest competing powers.

3. Just as nature wisely separates peoples that the will of every nation, based on principles of international right, would gladly unite through cunning or force, so also by virtue of their mutual interest does nature unite peoples against violence and war, for the concept of cosmopolitan right does not protect them from it. The *spirit of trade* cannot coexist with war, and sooner or later this spirit dominates every people. For among all those powers (or means) that belong to a nation, financial power may be the most reliable in forcing nations to pursue the noble cause of peace (though not from moral motives); and wherever in the world war threatens to break out, they will try to head it off through mediation, just as if they were permanently leagued for this purpose. By the very nature of things, large alliances for [purposes of waging] war are very rare and are even more rarely successful. In this fashion nature guarantees perpetual peace by virtue of the mechanism of man's inclinations themselves; to be sure, it does not do so with a

---

1 *If one bends ... wills nothing* A commentator attributes this quotation to Kant's disciple Friedrich Bouterwek (1766–1828).

2 *differences in language and religion* [Kant's note] *Differences in religion*: an odd expression! Just as if one spoke of different *moralities*. No doubt there can be different kinds of historical *faiths*, though these do not pertain to religion, but only to the history of the means used to promote it, and these are the province of learned investigation; the same holds of different religious *books* (*Zendavesta*, the *Vedas*, *Koran*, and so on). But there is only a single *religion*, valid for all men in all times. Those [faiths and books] can thus be nothing more than the accidental vehicles of religion and can only thereby be different in different times and places.

certainty sufficient to *prophesy* it from a theoretical point of view, but we can do so from a practical one, which makes it our duty to work toward bringing about this goal (which is not a chimerical one).

Second Supplement: Secret Article for Perpetual Peace

Objectively, i.e., in the terms of its content, a secret article in proceedings concerning public right is a contradiction; but subjectively, i.e., judged from the perspective of the kind of person who dictates it, an article can certainly contain a secret [provision], for a person may find it beneath his dignity to declare openly that he is its author.

The sole article of this kind is contained in this sentence: *The maxims of philosophers concerning the conditions under which public peace is possible shall be consulted by nations armed for war.*

While it seems humiliating for the legislative authority of a nation, to whom we must naturally ascribe the greatest wisdom, to seek instruction from *subjects* (the philosophers) concerning the principles on which it should act toward other nations, yet it is very advisable to do so. Thus, the nation will *silently* (that is secretly) *seek their advice,* which is to say, it will *allow* them *to speak* freely and publicly about the universal maxims concerning the conduct of war and the search for peace (for they do it of their own accord already, if only one does not forbid it). And an arrangement concerning this issue among nations does not require a special agreement, since it is already present as an obligation in universal (morally legislative) human reason. This does not, however, mean that the nation must give the principles of the philosophers precedence over the decisions of the jurist (the representatives of national power), but only that they be *heard*. The jurist, who has adopted as his symbol not only the *scales* of right but also the *sword* of justice, normally uses the latter not merely to keep the alien influences away from the former, but when one side of the scales will not sink, to throw the sword into it (*vae victis*[1]). Every jurist who is not at the same time a philosopher (even in morality), is severely tempted by this practice; but his only function is to apply existing laws and to investigate whether they require improvement, even though, because his function is invested with power (as are the other two), he regards it as the higher one, when, in

fact, it is the lower. The philosophical faculty occupies a very low position in the face of the combined power of the other two.[2] Thus it is said, for example, that philosophy is the *handmaid* of theology (and this is said of the two others as well). But one does not rightly know "whether this handmaid carries the torch before her gracious lady or bears her train behind her."

That kings should be philosophers, or philosophers kings is neither to be expected nor to be desired, for the possession of power inevitably corrupts reason's free judgment. However, that kings or sovereign peoples (who rule themselves by laws of equality) should not allow the class of philosophers to disappear or to be silent, but should permit them to speak publicly is indispensable to the enlightenment of their affairs. And because this class is by nature incapable of sedition and of forming cliques, it cannot be suspected of being the formulator of *propaganda.*

Appendix

1: On the Disagreement between Morals and Politics in Relation to Perpetual Peace

Taken objectively, morality is in itself practical, for it is the totality of unconditionally binding laws according to which we *ought* to act, and once one has acknowledged the authority of its concept of duty, it would be utterly absurd to continue wanting to say that one *cannot* do his duty. For if that were so, then this concept would disappear from morality (*ultra posse nemo obligatur*[3]); consequently, there can be no conflict between politics as an applied doctrine of right and morals as a theoretical doctrine of right (thus no conflict between practice and theory). [If such a conflict were to occur], one would have to understand morality as a universal *doctrine of prudence,* i.e., a theory of maxims by which to choose the most efficient means of furthering one's own interests, which is to deny that morality exists at all.

Politics says, *"Be ye wise as serpents,"* to which *morality adds (as a limiting condition), "and innocent as doves."*[4] Where both of these maxims cannot coexist in a command, there

---

1   *vae victis*   Latin: "woe to the vanquished."

2   *The philosophical faculty ... the other two*   Kant here is thinking about the rivalry among the divisions of philosophy, theology, law, and medicine in the German universities of his day.

3   *ultra posse nemo obligatur*   Latin: no one is obliged to do what is beyond his ability.

4   *Be ye wise as serpents ... and innocent as doves*   Matthew 19.16.

one finds an actual conflict between politics and morality; but if the two are completely united the concept of opposition is absurd, and the question as to how the conflict is to be resolved cannot even be posed as a problem. However, the proposition, *"Honesty is the best policy,"* is beyond all refutation, and is the indispensable condition of all policy. The divinity who protects the boundaries of morality does not yield to Jupiter (the protector of power), for the latter is still subject to fate. That is, reason is not yet sufficiently enlightened that it can survey the series of predetermining causes and predict with certainty what the happy or unhappy consequences that follow in accord with nature's mechanism from men's activities will be (though one can hope that they come out as one wishes). But with respect to everything we have to do in order to remain on the path of duty (according to rules of wisdom), reason does provide us with enlightenment sufficient to pursue our ultimate goals.

Now even if the practical man (for whom morality is mere theory) admits that we can do what we ought to do, he bases his disconsolate rejection of our fond hope on the following consideration: He asserts that, human nature being what it is, we can predict that man will never want to do what is required to achieve the goal of perpetual peace. Certainly, the will of all *individual* men (the *distributive* unity of the wills of *all*) to live under a lawful constitution that accords with principles of freedom is not sufficient to attain this goal; only the will of *all together* (the *collective* unity of combined wills) is. The solution to so difficult a task requires that civil society become a whole. Implementing this state of right (in practice) can begin only with *force*, and this coercion will subsequently provide a basis for public right, because an additional unifying cause must be superimposed on the differences among each person's particular desires in order to transform them into a common will—and this is something no single person can do. Furthermore, in actual experience we can certainly anticipate great deviations from that (theoretical) idea of right (for we can hardly expect the legislator to have such moral sensibilities that having united the wild mass into a people, he will then allow them to create a legal constitution through their general will).

For this reason it is said that he who once has power in hand will not have laws prescribed to him by the people. And once a nation is no longer subject to external laws it will not allow itself to be subjected to the judgment of other nations regarding the way in which it should seek to uphold its rights against them. Even a continent that feels itself to be superior to another, regardless of whether or not the lat-

ter stands in the way of the former, will not fail to exercise the means of increasing its power, plundering and conquering. Thus, all theoretical plans for civil, international, and cosmopolitan rights dissolve into empty, impractical ideals; by contrast, a practice that is based on empirical principles of human nature and that does not regard it demeaning to formulate its maxims in accord with the way of the world can alone hope to find a secure foundation for its structure of political prudence.

To be sure, if neither freedom nor the moral law that is based on it exist, and if everything that happens or can happen is mere mechanism of nature, then politics (as the art of using that mechanism to govern men) would be the whole of practical wisdom, and the concept of right would be contentless thought. But if we find it absolutely necessary to couple politics with the concept of right, and even to make the latter a limiting condition of politics, the compatibility of the two must be conceded. I can actually think of a *moral politician*, i.e., one who so interprets the principles of political prudence that they can be coherent with morality, but I cannot think of a *political moralist*, i.e., one who forges a morality to suit the statesman's advantage.

The moral politician will make it a principle that once a fault that could not have been anticipated is found in a nation's constitution or in its relations with other nations, it becomes a duty, particularly for the rulers of nations, to consider how it can be corrected as soon as possible and in such a way as to conform with natural right, which stands in our eyes as a model presented by an idea of reason; and this ought to be done even at the cost of self-sacrifice. Since it is contrary to all political prudence consistent with morality to sever a bond of political or cosmopolitan union before a better constitution is prepared to put in its place, it would also be truly absurd that such a fault be immediately and violently repaired. However, it can be required of those in power that they at least take to heart the maxim that such changes are necessary so as continuously to approach the goal (of the constitution most in accord with the laws of right). A nation may already possess republican rule, even if under its present constitution it has a despotic *ruling power*, until gradually the people are capable of being influenced by the mere idea of the law's authority (just as if it possessed physical power) and thus is found able to be its own legislator (which [ability] is originally based on [natural] right). If—through a violent *revolution* caused by a bad constitution—a constitution conforming to law were introduced by illegal means, it must not be permissible to lead the people back to the old one, even though everyone who violently or covertly participated in the revolution would rightly have been subject to the punishment due rebels. But as to the external relations among nations, it cannot be expected that a nation will give up its constitution, even if despotic (which is the stronger in relation to foreign enemies), so long as it risks the danger of being overrun by other nations; consequently, it is permissible to delay the intention to implement improvements until a better opportunity arises.[1]

It may be that despotic moralists (those who fail in practice) violate rules of political prudence in many ways (by adopting or proposing premature measures); still, experience will gradually bring them to give up their opposition to nature and to follow a better course. By contrast with this, the moralizing politician attempts, on the pretext that human nature is not *capable* of attaining the good as prescribed in the idea of reason, to extenuate political principles that are contrary to right, and thus these principles make progress *impossible* and perpetuate the violation of right.

Instead of employing the practical science that these politically prudent men make so much of they use devious *practices* to influence the current ruling power (so as to insure their own private advantage), even at the expense of the people and, where possible, the entire world, acting just like lawyers (for whom law is a *trade*, not a matter of *legislation*) when they go into politics. For since it is not their business to be overly concerned with legislation, but rather to carry out momentary commands under the law of the land, they must always regard every existing legal constitution as best—and when it is amended in higher places, they regard these amendments as for the best, too; in that way, everything follows in its proper mechanical order. But, granted that this deftness at being all things to all men gives the politically prudent the illusion of being able to judge

a *national constitution* in general against concepts of right (consequently, a *priori*,[2] not empirically); and granted that they make a great to do of knowing *men* (which is certainly to be expected, since they deal with so many of them), though without knowing *man* and what can be made of him (for which a high standpoint of anthropological observation is required); nonetheless, if, as reason prescribes, they attempt to use these concepts in civil and international law, they cannot make the transition except in a spirit of charlatanism. For they will continue to follow their customary procedure (of mechanically applying despotically imposed laws of coercion) in an area where the concepts of reason only permit lawful compulsion that accords with principles of freedom, and it is under such principles alone that a rightful and enduring constitution is possible. The supposed practical man believes he can ignore the idea of right and solve this problem empirically, the solution being based on his experience of the national constitutions that have heretofore been most lasting, though oftentimes contrary to right. The maxims that he uses to this end (though he does not make them public) consist, roughly speaking, of the following sophistries.

1. *Fac et excusa*.[3] Seize every favorable opportunity for arbitrary usurpation (of a right of a nation either over its own people or over another neighboring people); the justification can be presented far more easily and elegantly *after the fact*, and the violence more easily glossed over (especially in the first case, where the supreme internal power is also the legislative authority, which one must obey without argument), than if one first thinks out convincing reasons and waits for objections to them. This audacity itself gives a certain appearance of an inner conviction that the act is right, and after the fact the god of success, *Bonus Eventus*,[4] is the best advocate.

2. *Si fecisti, nega*.[5] Whatever crime you have committed—e.g., that you have reduced your people to despair and hence brought them to rebellion—deny that the guilt is *yours*; instead, maintain that it is the obstinacy of the subjects, or, if you have conquered a neighboring people, that the guilt belongs to human nature, for if one does not

---

1 consequently, it is permissible ... opportunity arises [Kant's note] These are permissive laws of reason: To allow a condition of public right afflicted with injustice to continue until everything is either of itself or through peaceful means ripe for a complete transformation, for any *legal* constitution, even if it conforms with right only to a small degree, is better than none, and the latter fate (anarchy) would result from *premature* reform. Political wisdom, therefore, will make it a duty, given the present state of things, to evaluate reforms against the ideal of public right. Revolutions brought about by nature itself will not find excuses for still greater oppression, but will use revolution as nature's call to create a lawful constitution based on principles of freedom, for only this fundamental reform is enduring.

2 a *priori* Prior to—independently of—sense [empirical] observation.

3 *Fac et excusa* Latin: act first, justify later.

4 *Bonus Eventus* Latin: good outcome. Bonus Eventus was the Roman god of good luck and fortune.

5 *Si fecisti, nega* Latin: if you did it, deny it.

forestall others by using force, one can surely count on their anticipating it and becoming one's conqueror.

3. *Divide et impera.*[1] That is, if there are certain privileged persons among your people who have merely chosen you to be their leader (*primus inter pares*[2]), destroy their unity and separate them from the people; and if, in turn, the people have delusions of greater freedom, everyone will depend on your unchecked will. Or if you are concerned with foreign nations, then sowing discord among them is a relatively certain method of subjecting them one after another to your will, all the while appearing to defend the weaker.

Certainly no one will be taken in by these political maxims, for all of them are widely known; nor are men ashamed of them, as if their injustice were altogether too apparent. For great powers never heed the judgment of the masses, feeling shame only in the face of others like them; and as regards the foregoing principles, not their becoming public knowledge, but only their *failure* can make those powers feel ashamed (for among themselves they agree on the morality of the maxims). And in this way their *political* honor, on which they can always count, is retained, namely, by the expansion of their power by whatever means they choose.[3]

---

1   *Divide et impera*   Latin: divide and rule.
2   *primus inter pares*   Latin: first among equals.
3   *means they choose*   [Kant's note] Although we might doubt the existence of a certain inherent wickedness in *men* who live together within a nation, and instead might plausibly point to the lack of a sufficiently advanced culture (barbarism) as the cause of the unlawful aspects of their way of thinking, this wickedness is still completely and incontrovertibly apparent in foreign relations among *nations*. Within each nation this wickedness is concealed by the coercive power of civil law, for the citizens' inclination toward violence against one another is counteracted by a greater power, namely, that of the government. Not only does this provide a veneer of morality (*causae non causae* [perhaps: "An apparent reason is not a real reason"]), but by placing these inclinations toward outbreaks of lawlessness behind bars, it also actually makes it easier to develop the moral capacity for direct and immediate respect for the law. Everyone believes of himself that he would truly venerate and abide by the concept of right, if only he could expect the same from everyone else, which it is government's part to insure; and by this means a large step towards morality is taken (although it is still not a moral step)—a large step towards willing the concept of duty for its own sake, without regard for any reciprocity. But since all persons have a good opinion of themselves but presuppose evil intentions in everyone else, they mutually have this opinion of one another, that they are all in point of *fact*, of little worth (though how this might be remains inexplicable, since it cannot be blamed on the *nature* of man as a free being). Since, however, respect for the concept of right, which no man

From all these twistings and turnings of an immoral doctrine of prudence regarding how men are to be brought out of the warlike state of nature into the state of peace, we receive at least this much illumination: Men can no more escape the concept of right in their private relations than in their public ones; nor can they properly risk basing their politics on the handiwork of prudence alone, and, consequently, they cannot altogether refuse obedience to the concept of public right (which is particularly important in the case of international right). Instead, they give this concept all due honor, even if they also invent a hundred excuses and evasions to avoid observing it in practice, attributing to cunning force the authority that is the original source and bond of right. In order to end this sophistry (if not the injustice that it glosses over) and to force the false representatives of those in earthly power to confess that rather than right it is might that they advocate—a fact that is clear from the tone they adopt, as if they were entitled to give orders—it will do well to expose the fraud to which they subject themselves and others and to reveal the highest principle from which perpetual peace as an end proceeds. We will show that all the evil that stands in the way of perpetual peace derives from the fact that the political moralist begins where the moral politician rightly stops; and, since the former subordinates his principles to his ends (i.e., puts the cart before the horse), he defeats his own purpose of effecting an agreement between politics and morals.

In order to bring practical philosophy into harmony with itself, it is first necessary to resolve this question: In problems of practical reason, must we begin from *material principles*, the end (as object of the will), or from its *formal* one, i.e., the one (which rests only on freedom in external relations) that is expressed thus: "Act so that you can will that your maxim ought to become a universal law (no matter what the end may be)"?

Without doubt the latter principle must take precedence, because as a principle of right it has unconditioned necessity, whereas the former is necessary only if one assumes the existence of those empirical conditions through which the proposed end can be realized. And if this end (e.g., perpetual peace) were also a duty, it must itself be derived from the formal principle of external action. Now the first principle, that of the *political moralists* (concerning

---

is capable of denying, provides the most solemn sanction for the theory that man has the ability to act according to it, everyone sees that for one's own part one must act in accord with it, no matter how others may act.

the problem of civil, international and cosmopolitan right), proposes a mere *technical task* (*problema technicum*); by contrast, the second is the principle of the *moral politician*, for whom it is a *moral task* (*problema morale*), and its method of pursuing perpetual peace—which one now desires not merely as a physical good, but also as a condition that arises from acknowledging one's duty—is completely distinct.

Solving the first problem, namely, the problem that political prudence proposes, requires considerable natural knowledge so that one can use nature's mechanism to attain the desired end; yet it is uncertain how this mechanism will function as far as its consequences for perpetual peace are concerned; and this is so in all three areas of public right. Whether the people's obedience and prosperity will be better preserved over a long period of time by harshness or by appeals to vanity, by granting supreme power to a single ruler or to several united ones, or, perhaps, merely by a devoted aristocracy or by the power of the people is uncertain. History furnishes examples of the opposite effects being produced by all forms of government (with the singular exception of true republicanism, which alone can appeal to the sensibility of a moral politician). Still more uncertainty arises in the area of *international right*—a form of right purportedly based on statutes worked out by ministers—for in fact it is a term without content, and it rests on contracts whose very act of conclusion contains the secret reservation for their violation. By contrast, the solution to the second problem, the problem of *political wisdom*, impresses itself on us, as it were, for it obviously puts all artificiality to shame, and leads directly to the end. Yet prudence cautions us not to employ power in direct pursuit of it, but rather to approach it indirectly through those conditions presented by favorable circumstances.

Thus, it may be said: "Seek first the kingdom of pure practical reason and its *righteousness*, and your end (the blessing of perpetual peace) will come to you of itself." For this characteristic is inherent in morals—especially as regards its fundamental principle of public right (consequently, in relation to a politics that is *a priori* knowable)—that the less it makes conduct depend on the proposed end, be it a physical or moral advantage, the more conduct will in general harmonize with morality. And this is because such conduct derives directly from the general will that is given *a priori* (in a single people or in the relations of different peoples to one another), which alone determines what is right among men. If only it is acted on in a consistent way, this unity of the will of all can, along with the mechanism of nature, be

the cause of the desired result and can make the concept of right effective. So, for example, it is a fundamental principle of moral politics that in uniting itself into a nation a people ought to subscribe to freedom and equality as the sole constituents of its concept of right, and this is not a principle of prudence, but is founded on duty. By contrast, political moralists do not even deserve a hearing, no matter how much they argue that the natural mechanism of a group of people who enter into society invalidates that fundamental principle and vitiates its intention, or seek to substantiate their contentions by use of ancient and modern examples of badly organized constitutions (e.g., of democracies without systems of representation). This is especially so since such a damaging theory may bring about the evil that it prophesies, for in it man is thrown into the same class as other living machines, which need only to become conscious that they are not free in order to become in their own eyes the most wretched of all the earth's creatures.

The true, albeit somewhat boastful proverb, *Fiat iustia, pereat mundus*[1]—"Let justice reign, even if all the rogues in the world should perish"—is a sound principle of right that cuts across the sinuous paths of deceit and power. But it must not be misunderstood nor, perhaps, taken as permission simply to press with the utmost vigor for one's own right (for that would conflict with moral duty); instead, those in power should understand it to pose an obligation not to deny or diminish anyone's rights through either dislike or sympathy. Above all, this requires that the nation have an internal constitution founded on principles of right and that it also unite itself (analogously to a universal nation) with other neighboring and distant nations so they can settle their differences legally. This proposition means only that adherence to political maxims must not be based on the benefit or happiness that each nation anticipates from so doing—thus, not on the end that each nation makes an object (of its desire) and its supreme (though empirical) principle of political wisdom; instead, adherence must derive from the pure concept of the duty of right (from the *ought*, whose principle is given *a priori* through pure reason), let the physical consequences be what they may. The world will certainly not cease to exist if there are fewer bad men. The intrinsic characteristic of moral evil is that its aims (especially in relation to other like-minded persons) are self-contradictory and self-destructive, and it

---

1   *Fiat iustia, pereat mundus* Latin: let there be justice, even if the world perishes.

thus makes way for the (moral) principle of goodness, even if progress in doing so is slow.

Objectively (i.e., in theory) there is utterly no conflict between morality and politics. But subjectively (in the self-seeking inclinations of men, which, because they are not based on maxims of reason, must not be called the [sphere of] practice) this conflict will always remain, as well it should; for it serves as the whetstone of virtue, whose true courage (according to the principle, "*tu ne cede malis, sed contra audentior ito*"[1]) in the present case consists not so much in resolutely standing up to the evils and sacrifices that must be taken on; rather, it consists in detecting, squarely facing, and conquering the deceit of the evil principle in ourselves, which is the more dangerously devious and treacherous because it excuses all our transgressions with an appeal to human nature's frailty.

In fact, the political moralist can say that the ruler and the people, or the people and the people, do not treat *one another* wrong if, through violence and fraud they war against one another, although they do in general act wrong when they deny respect to the concept of right, on which alone peace can be perpetually based. When one person violates the rights of another who is just as lawlessly disposed towards him, then whatever *happens* to them as they destroy themselves is entirely right; enough of their race will always survive so that this game will not cease, even into the remotest age, and they can serve as a warning to later generations. In this manner, the course of world events justifies providence. For the moral principle in man never dies out, and with the continuous progress of culture, reason, which is able pragmatically to apply the ideas of right in accordance with the moral principle, grows through its persistence in doing so, and guilt for transgressions grows concomitantly. (Given that the human race never can and never will be in a better condition) it seems impossible to be able to use a theodicy[2] to provide any justification whatsoever for creation, namely, that such a race of generally corrupt beings should have been put on earth. We will be unavoidably driven to such skeptical conclusions, if we do not assume that pure principles of right have objective reality, i.e., that they permit themselves to be applied and

that peoples in nations and even nations in their relations with one another must for their parts behave in conformity with them, no matter how objectionable empirical politics may find them. Thus, true politics cannot progress without paying homage to morality; and although politics by itself is a difficult art, its union with morality is not art at all, for this union cuts through the [Gordian] knot[3] that politics cannot solve when politics and morality come into conflict. The rights of men must be held sacred, however great the cost of sacrifice may be to those in power. Here one cannot go halfway, cooking up hybrid, pragmatically-conditioned rights (which are somewhere between the right and the expedient); instead, all politics must bend its knee before morality, and by so doing it can hope to reach, though but gradually, the stage where it will shine in light perpetual.

2: On the Agreement between Politics and Morality under the Transcendental Concept[4] of Public Right

If, in thinking about public right as jurists customarily do, I abstract from its *matter* (i.e., the different empirically given relations among men in a nation or among nations), the *form of publicity*, whose possibility every claim of right intrinsically contains, still remains, and unless every such claim has this form there can be no justice (that can be regarded as *publicly knowable*), thus no right either, since the right can be conferred only through justice. Every claim of right must have this capacity for publicity, and since one can easily judge whether or not it is present in a particular case, i.e., whether or not publicity is compatible with the agent's principles, it provides us with a readily applicable criterion that is found *a priori* in reason; for the purported claim's (*praetensio iuris*) falseness (contrariness to right) is immediately recognized by an experiment of pure reason.

Having abstracted in this way from everything empirical contained in the concept of national and international right (such as the wickedness in human nature that makes coercion necessary), one can call the following proposition the *transcendental formula* of public right:

---

1   *tu ne cede malis, sed contra audentior ito*   Latin: you should not yield to evils, but should go against them more strongly. Virgil, *Aeneid* 6.95.

2   *theodicy*   Branch of religious thought which attempts to reconcile the idea of a perfectly good and all-powerful God with the apparent existence of evil in the world.

3   *[Gordian] knot*   An oracle prophesied that whoever untied the knot at Gordium, capital of Phrygia, would become king of Asia. Alexander the Great, failing to untie it, sliced it in half with his sword, providing the "Alexandrian solution" in 333 BCE.

4   *Transcendental Concept*   Type of concepts given not by experience, but rather that provide the necessary conditions for experience.

All actions that affect the rights of other men are wrong if their maxim is not consistent with publicity.

This principle is to be considered not only *ethical* (as belonging to the doctrine of virtue), but also *juridical* (as pertaining to the rights of men). If my maxim cannot be *openly divulged* without at the same time defeating my own intention, i.e., must be kept *secret* for it to succeed, or if I cannot *publicly acknowledge* it without thereby inevitably arousing everyone's opposition to my plan, then this necessary and universal, and thus *a priori* foreseeable, opposition of all to me could not have come from anything other than the injustice with which it threatens everyone. Further, it is merely *negative*, i.e., it serves only as a means for recognizing what is *not right* in regard to others. Like any axiom, it is seen in the following examples of public right.

1. In regard to *civil right* (*ius civitas*), namely, rights internal to a nation, the following question arises, one that many believe is difficult to answer, but that the transcendental principle of publicity solves with utter ease: "May a people rightfully use rebellion to overthrow the oppressive power of a so-called tyrant (*nontitulo, sed exercitio talis*[1])?" The rights of the people are injured, and no injustice comes to him (the tyrant) who is deposed, of that there is no doubt. Nonetheless, it remains wrong in the highest degree for the subjects to pursue their rights in this way, and they can in no way complain of injustice if they are defeated in this conflict and must subsequently suffer the harshest punishment for it.

A great many arguments can be offered on both sides when one attempts to settle this issue by a dogmatic deduction of the foundations of right. Only the transcendental principle of the publicity of public right will spare us this long-windedness. According to this principle, before establishing the social contract, the people have to ask whether it dare make known the maxim of its intention to revolt in some circumstances. One can readily see, first, that if one were to make revolt a condition of the establishment of a nation's constitution that force might then in certain circumstances be used against the ruler and, second, that the people must in such an instance claim some rightful power over the ruler. In that case, he would not be the ruler; or if as a condition of establishing the nation, both the people and the ruler were given power, there would be no possibility whatsoever of doing what it was the people's intention to do. The wrongness of revolt revealed by the fact that the maxim through which one *publicly declares it* renders one's own intention impossible. One must therefore necessarily keep it secret. This secrecy, however, is not necessary on the part of the nation's ruler. He can say quite openly that he will punish with death the ringleader of every rebellion, even if they believe that he has been the first to transgress the fundamental law. For if he knows that he possesses *irresistibly* supreme power (which must be assumed in every civil constitution, since he who lacks sufficient might to protect each of his people against every other, also does not have the right to give orders), he does not have to worry that his own intention will be defeated if his maxim becomes known. It is perfectly consistent with this view that if the people's revolt succeeds, the ruler, returning to the status of a subject, cannot begin a new revolt to return himself to power, nor should he have to fear being called to account for his previous administration of the nation.

2. *Concerning international right*: There can be talk of international right only on the assumption that a state of law-governedness exists (i.e., that external condition under which a right can actually be accorded man). For as a public right, its concept already contains the public recognition of a general will that determines the rights of everyone, and this *status iuridicus*[2] must proceed from some contract that cannot be founded on coercive laws (like those from which the nation springs), but can at best be an *enduring free* association, like the federation of different nations mentioned above. For in the state of nature, in the absence of a state of law-governedness, only private right can exist. Here another conflict between politics and morality (considering the latter as a doctrine of right) arises, to which, however, the criterion of the publicity of maxims finds easy application, though only if the contract binds the nations for the sole purpose of maintaining peace among themselves and between them and other nations, and not with the intention of conquest. This introduces the following instances of antinomy[3] between politics and morality, along with their solution.

(a) "If one of these nations has promised something to another, be it aid, cession of certain territories, or subsidies, and so on, it may be asked whether, in those cases where the nation's well-being is at stake, it can be released from its

---

1   *nontitulo, sed exercitio talis* Latin: not in title, but acting that way.

2   *status iuridicus* Latin: legal status.

3   *antinomy* Conflict between two apparently valid ideas.

promise by maintaining that it must be considered to have two roles: first, that of a sovereign, who is answerable to no one in the nation; and, on the other hand, merely that of the highest *political official*, who must give an account of his actions to the nation. From this we draw the following conclusion, that what the nation had bound itself to by virtue of its first role, it frees itself from in its second." But if a nation (or its ruler) were to allow its maxim to be known, then all others would quite naturally either flee from it or would unite with others in order to oppose its arrogance. This proves that, given all its cunning, politics would in this way (through openness) defeat its end; consequently, that maxim is wrong.

(b) "If a neighboring power grows so formidably great (*potentia tremenda*) as to cause anxiety, can one assume that it will want to oppress others because it *can*; and does this give the lesser powers a right to (unified) attack on it, even without previous injury?" A nation that *let it be known* that it affirmed this maxim would suffer evil even more certainly and quickly. For the greater power would beat the lesser ones to the punch, and, as far as concerns the union of the latter, that would only be a feeble reed against one who knew how to employ the maxim *divide et impera*.

(c) "If a smaller nation is so located that it divides some territory that a larger one regards as necessary to its preservation, is not the latter justified in subjugating the smaller one and incorporating it into itself?" One can easily see that the larger must not allow it to become known that it has adopted such a maxim; for either the smaller nations would unite very early, or other powers would fight over the prey, and, consequently, openness would render the maxim ineffectual, a sign that it is wrong, and, indeed, perhaps to a very high degree. For a small object of wrong [action] does not prevent the wrong done to it from being very great.

3. Here I silently pass over the issue of *cosmopolitan right*, for, given its analogy with international right, its maxims are easy to adduce and validate.

In the principle of the incompatibility between the maxims of international right and publicity one has a good indication of the *incommensurability* of politics and morality (as a doctrine of right). But one now needs also to become aware of the conditions under which the maxims of politics agree with the right of peoples. For it cannot be conversely concluded that whatever maxims are compatible with publicity are also for that reason right, for he who has decisively supreme power, has no need to keep his maxims secret. The condition underlying the possibility of international right

in general is that there first exist a *state of right*. For without this there is no public right, and all right other than this (in the state of nature) that one can think of is merely private right. Now we have seen above that a federative state of nations whose only purpose is to prevent war is the only state of *right* compatible with their *freedom*. Thus, it is possible to make politics commensurable with morality only in a federative union (which is therefore necessary and given *a priori* in conformity with the principles of right); and the foundation of right underlying all political prudence is the establishment of this union to the greatest possible extent, for without this as an end all the sophistry of political prudence is contrary to wisdom, hence mere veiled wrong. The *casuistry* of this pseudopolitics is unsurpassed by the best of the Jesuit scholars, including as it does the *reservatio mentalis*,[1] i.e., formulating public contracts in such terms (e.g., the distinction between a *status quo* of *fact* and of *right*) that, whatever the occasion, one can interpret them in one's own favor; including, further, the *probabilismus*,[2] i.e., attributing evil intentions to others, or making the likelihood of their possible superior power into a justification of the right to undercut other, peaceful nations; and, finally, the *peccatum philosophicum*[3] (*peccatillum, baggatelle*[4]), i.e., maintaining it to be an easily dismissible triviality to devour a *small* nation when some purportedly very much *greater* benefit to the world is a result.[5]

Politics' duplicitous relation to morality by first using one of its branches and then the other in pursuit of its purposes is fed by this casuistry. Both the love of man and the respect for the rights of man are our duty; the former is only *conditional, while the latter is an unconditional*, absolutely imperative duty, a duty that one must be completely certain of not having transgressed, if one is to be able to enjoy the sweet sense of having done right. Politics readily

---

1 *reservatio mentalis* Latin: tacit reservation.
2 *probabilismus* Latin: probabilism (the position that one is free to choose when things are not certain).
3 *peccatum philosophicum* Latin: the philosophical sin.
4 *peccatillum, baggatelle* Latin: little sin, trifle.
5 *maintaining it ... world is a result* [Kant's note] Documentation for such maxims can be found in Counselor [Christian] Garve's treatise "*Über die Verbindung der Moral mit der Politik*" [*On the Unity of Morality and Politics*], 1788. This worthy scholar admits at the outset that he is unable to give an adequate answer to this question. But to approve of this union while granting that one cannot fully meet the objections that can be brought against it seems to be more forebearing than is advisable toward those who will most tend to misuse it.

agrees with morality in the first sense (as ethics) for both surrender men's rights to their rulers. But with regard to morality in the second sense (as doctrine of right), before which it must bend the knee, politics finds it advisable not to enter into any relation whatsoever and, unfortunately, denies all reality to morality and reduces all duties to mere benevolence. This ruse of a secretive politics could be easily defeated were philosophy to give publicity to the maxims of politics, if politicians would only allow philosophers to give publicity to their own.

With this in mind, I propose another transcendental and affirmative principle of right, whose formula is:

> All maxims that *require* publicity (in order not to fail of their end) agree with both politics and morality.

For if they can achieve their end only through publicity, they must also conform to the universal public end (happiness), and it is the singular task of politics to establish this (to make the public satisfied with its state). But if this

end can be attained only by publicity, i.e., by removing all mistrust of the maxims through which it is to be achieved, these maxims must harmonize with public right, for in this latter alone is the unity of all ends possible. I must postpone the further development and explanation of this principle for another occasion. But that it is a transcendental formula can be seen from the absence of all empirical conditions (of the doctrine of happiness), as material of the law, and from the reference it makes to the mere form of universal lawfulness.

If it is a duty to make the state of public right actual, though only through an unending process of approximation to it, and if at the same time there is a well founded hope that we can do it, then *perpetual peace*, which will follow the hitherto falsely so-called treaties of peace (but which are really only suspension of war), is no empty idea, but a task that, gradually completed, steadily approaches its goal (since the times during which equal progress occurs will, we hope, become ever shorter).

THOMAS JEFFERSON
(1743 – 1826)

JEFFERSON WAS BORN IN SHADWELL, VIRGINIA, ON APRIL 13, 1743. He was the third of ten children born to plantation owners. At the age of fourteen, Jefferson inherited 5000 acres of land when his father died of a sudden illness at the age of forty-nine. From age sixteen to eighteen Jefferson attended the College of William and Mary, where he studied philosophy and mathematics. By the time he ended his studies there, he also had mastered French, Greek, and Latin. He then studied law, and was admitted to the bar in Virginia at the age of twenty-four. He worked in Virginia as a lawyer and in several positions in local and state governments from 1767 to 1774. Jefferson gained a wider reputation in 1774 when he published "A Summary View of the Rights of British America." In it he argued that loyalty to the King was voluntary and that the colonies had the right to become independent of his rule.

By the middle of 1775 the American colonies were at war with England. On June 11, 1776, members of the Second Continental Congress chose Jefferson to write *The Declaration of Independence*. With only minor alterations, it was adopted on July 4, 1776. During the revolutionary war Jefferson served as a legislator in Virginia before becoming Governor of that state. After the war, Jefferson became Minister to France, Secretary of State, Vice President, and finally President of the United States (1801–09). After leaving office Jefferson continued to be active in public life, most notably founding the University of Virginia in 1819. Thomas Jefferson died at the age of 83 on July 4, 1826, the fiftieth anniversary of *The Declaration of Independence*.

Inspired in part by the writings of philosophers such as John Locke and Jean-Jacques Rousseau, *The Declaration of Independence* comprises a straightforward statement of political ideals, accompanied by a series of complaints against King George III. Composed in simple prose, it was criticized by some of Jefferson's contemporaries as insufficiently eloquent for such an important document. In a letter written shortly before his death, Jefferson defended its style: "Neither aiming at originality of principle or sentiment, nor yet copied from any particular and previous writing, it was intended to be an expression of the American mind ... in terms so plain and firm as to command their assent."

Jefferson expressed democratic ideals through this document in a concise form that has continued to resonate both within the United States and outside it; the *Declaration*'s formulation of principles of political and human rights has been an inspiration and a model for many nations around the world as they too threw off the reins of former colonial masters.

◆ ◆ ◆ ◆ ◆

The Declaration of Independence [as amended and adopted in Congress], July 4, 1776

The unanimous declaration of the thirteen United States of America

When, in the course of human events, it becomes necessary for one people to dissolve the political bands which have connected them with another, and to assume, among the powers of the earth, the separate and equal station[1] to which the laws of nature and of nature's God entitle them, a decent respect to the opinions of mankind requires that they should declare the causes which impel them to the separation.

---

1   *station* Standing, position, status.

763

We hold these truths to be self-evident: That all men are created equal; that they are endowed by their creator with certain unalienable rights; that among these are life, liberty, and the pursuit of happiness; that, to secure these rights, governments are instituted among men, deriving their just powers from the consent of the governed; that whenever any form of government becomes destructive of these ends, it is the right of the people to alter or to abolish it, and to institute new government, laying its foundation on such principles, and organizing its power in such form, as to them shall seem most likely to effect their safety and happiness. Prudence, indeed, will dictate that governments long established should not be changed for light and transient causes; and accordingly all experience hath shown that mankind are more disposed to suffer, while evils are sufferable, than to right themselves by abolishing the forms to which they are accustomed. But when a long train of abuses and usurpations,[1] pursuing invariably the same object, evinces a design to reduce them under absolute despotism, it is their right, it is their duty, to throw off such government, and to provide new guards for their future security. Such has been the patient sufferance[2] of these colonies; and such is now the necessity which constrains them to alter their former systems of government. The history of the present King of Great Britain is a history of repeated injuries and usurpations, all having in direct object the establishment of an absolute tyranny over these states. To prove this, let facts be submitted to a candid world.

He has refused his assent to laws, the most wholesome and necessary for the public good.

He has forbidden his governors to pass laws of immediate and pressing importance, unless suspended in their operation till his assent should be obtained; and, when so suspended, he has utterly neglected to attend to them.

He has refused to pass other laws for the accommodation of large districts; of people, unless those people would relinquish the right of representation in the legislature, a right inestimable to them, and formidable to tyrants only.

He has called together legislative bodies at places unusual, uncomfortable, and distant from the depository of their public records, for the sole purpose of fatiguing them into compliance with his measures.

He has dissolved representative houses repeatedly, for opposing, with manly firmness, his invasions on the rights of the people.

He has refused for a long time, after such dissolutions, to cause others to be elected; whereby the legislative powers, incapable of annihilation, have returned to the people at large for their exercise; the state remaining, in the mean time, exposed to all the dangers of invasions from without and convulsions within.

He has endeavored to prevent the population of these states; for that purpose obstructing the laws for naturalization of foreigners; refusing to pass others to encourage their migration hither, and raising the conditions of new appropriations of lands.

He has obstructed the administration of justice, by refusing his assent to laws for establishing judiciary powers.

He has made judges dependent on his will alone, for the tenure of their offices,[3] and the amount and payment of their salaries.

He has erected a multitude of new offices, and sent hither swarms of officers to harass our people and eat out their substance.

He has kept among us, in times of peace, standing armies, without the consent of our legislatures.

He has affect to render the military independent of, and superior to, the civil power.

He has combined with others to subject us to a jurisdiction foreign to our constitution, and unacknowledged by our laws, giving his assent to their acts of pretended legislation:

For quartering large bodies of armed troops among us;

For protecting them, by a mock trial, from punishment for any murders which they should commit on the inhabitants of these states;

For cutting off our trade with all parts of the world;

For imposing taxes on us without our consent;

For depriving us, in many cases, of the benefits of trial by jury;

For transporting us beyond seas, to be tried for pretended offenses;

---

1   *usurpations* Seizures without right.
2   *sufferance* Endurance.

3   *tenure of their offices* Getting and keeping of their positions.

For abolishing the free system of English laws in a neighboring province,[1] establishing therein an arbitrary government, and enlarging its boundaries, so as to render it at once an example and fit instrument for introducing the same absolute rule into these colonies;

For taking away our charters, abolishing our most valuable laws, and altering fundamentally the forms of our governments;

For suspending our own legislatures, and declaring themselves invested with power to legislate for us in all cases whatsoever.

He has abdicated government[2] here, by declaring us out of his protection and waging war against us.

He has plundered our seas, ravaged our coasts, burned our towns, and destroyed the lives of our people.

He is at this time transporting large armies of foreign mercenaries to complete the works of death, desolation, and tyranny already begun with circumstances of cruelty and perfidy[3] scarcely paralleled in the most barbarous ages, and totally unworthy the head of a civilized nation.

He has constrained our fellow-citizens, taken captive on the high seas, to bear arms against their country, to become the executioners of their friends and brethren, or to fall themselves by their hands.

He has excited domestic insurrection among us, and has endeavored to bring on the inhabitants of our frontiers the merciless Indian savages, whose known rule of warfare is an undistinguished destruction of all ages, sexes, and conditions.

In every stage of these oppressions we have petitioned for redress in the most humble terms; our repeated petitions have been answered only by repeated injury. A prince, whose character is thus marked by every act which may define a tyrant, is unfit to be the ruler of a free people.

Nor have we been wanting in our attentions to our British brethren. We have warned them, from time to time, of attempts by their legislature to extend an unwarrantable[4] jurisdiction over us. We have reminded them of the circumstances of our emigration and settlement here. We have appealed to their native justice and magnanimity; and we

have conjured[5] them, by the ties of our common kindred, to disavow these usurpations, which would inevitably interrupt our connections and correspondence.[6] They, too, have been deaf to the voice of justice and of consanguinity. We must, therefore, acquiesce in the necessity which denounces[7] our separation, and hold them, as we hold the rest of mankind, enemies in war, in peace friends.

We, therefore, the representatives of the United States of America, in General Congress assembled, appealing to the Supreme Judge of the world for the rectitude of our intentions, do, in the name and by the authority of the good people of these colonies, solemnly publish and declare, that these United Colonies are, and of right ought to be, FREE AND INDEPENDENT STATES, that they are absolved from[8] all allegiance to the British crown, and that all political connection between them and the state of Great Britain is, and ought to be, totally dissolved; and that, as free and independent states, they have full power to levy war, conclude peace, contract alliances, establish commerce, and do all other acts and things which independent states may of right do. And for the support of this declaration, with a firm reliance on the protection of Divine Providence, we mutually pledge to each other our lives, our fortunes, and our sacred honor.

---

1 *neighboring province* Canada.
2 *abdicated government* Neglected to govern.
3 *perfidy* Treachery, deceit.
4 *unwarrantable* Unjustifiable.
5 *conjured* Begged.
6 *correspondence* Relations.
7 *denounces* Formally announces.
8 *absolved from* Relieved of obligation regarding.

ALEXANDER HAMILTON
(1755 – 1804)
and
JAMES MADISON
(1751 – 1836)

BETWEEN OCTOBER 27, 1787 AND MAY 28, 1788 A SERies of eighty-five essays, collectively known as *The Federalist Papers* was published. They were originally published under the pen name "Publius" in honor of Roman consul Publius Valerius Publicola (d. 503 BCE), whose surname means "friend of the people." They were actually written by three men—Alexander Hamilton, James Madison, and John Jay. Each man made significant contributions to the United States in its infancy: Hamilton was the first Secretary of the Treasury, Madison the fourth President of the United States, and Jay the first Chief Justice of the Supreme Court. It is particularly as a result of their status as "founding fathers" of the United States that the views they advanced in *The Federalist Papers* continue to be extremely important in contemporary American constitutional scholarship.

Alexander Hamilton was born and raised in the West Indies. He was an illegitimate child whose father abandoned him and whose mother was jailed for adultery before her early death (when Hamilton was thirteen). Hamilton became a success in business before moving to New York at age seventeen to attend school. He quickly became sympathetic to colonial grievances against Britain, eventually coming to work for George Washington in 1777. Hamilton was a military leader during the revolutionary war and became a legislator in various capacities afterward. He wrote 51 of the 85 articles that comprise *The Federalist Papers* (including articles number 10 and 51), a series of articles presenting arguments in support of ratifying the proposed constitution. From 1789 to 1795 Hamilton served as Secretary of the Treasury, and in the last decade of his life he continued

James Madison

to be an influential political figure. He died as a result of a gunshot wound he received in a duel with Vice President Aaron Burr.

James Madison spent his childhood on the successful plantation his father owned in Virginia. He was educated at Princeton University and then entered public life, where he worked closely with Thomas Jefferson. Madison led the campaign to ratify the Constitution in Virginia. He wrote 29 of *The Federalist Papers* (including article number 78), to support that cause.[1] After the Constitution was adopted, Madison, as a member of Congress, proposed ten amendments that have come to be known collectively as the American Bill of Rights. In 1809, Madison was elected President; he served in that role for eight years. Following his Presidency, Madison devoted his time to running his plantation and working for the University of Virginia. He died the day before what would have been his eighty-fifth birthday.

The battle over ratification of the Constitution of the United States was a war of words that was fought both in elected assemblies and in the newspapers of the day. In 1787 prominent politicians using the pen names "Cato" and "Brutus" began writing columns in opposition to ratification. Hamilton, Madison, and Jay responded by writing and publishing articles in support. They argued for the importance of a federal union (as opposed to a confederation or a collection of independent states) to the economic and political development of the newly independent colonies.

---

1   The author of the remaining five *Federalist Papers*, none of which is included here, was John Jay.

They also argued that the specific provisions of the proposed constitution best served those ends. They warned against the oppressive powers of sectarianism and advocated a strong constitutional union to protect all individuals. They further argued that "checks and balances" of one arm of government by others would provide the best protection against the abuses of power. Additionally, they set out the principles according to which the role of the judiciary had been defined by the constitution.

The Federalist Papers are acknowledged as vitally important aids in interpreting the provisions of the American constitution; they continue to be cited as important touchstones by the Supreme Court of the United States in rendering decisions, and by leading politicians and political writers in discussing current political issues. The "founders' intent" behind the various articles of the constitution continues to be regarded by many as fundamental to issues over their implementation today, and *The Federalist Papers* offer an important window into the thoughts of those who created and originally enacted these articles.

◆ ◆ ◆ ◆ ◆

The Federalist No. 9

Alexander Hamilton

from *The Independent Journal*, November 21, 1787. This essay appeared on the same day in *The Daily Advertiser* and on November 23 in *The New York Packet*.

To the People of the State of New York.

A Firm Union will be of the utmost moment[1] to the peace and liberty of the States as a barrier against domestic faction and insurrection. It is impossible to read the history of the petty Republics of Greece and Italy, without feeling sensations of horror and disgust at the distractions with which they were continually agitated, and at the rapid succession of revolutions, by which they were kept in a state of perpetual vibration, between the extremes of tyranny and anarchy. If they exhibit occasional calms, these only serve as short-lived contrasts to the furious storms that are to succeed. If now and then intervals of felicity[2] open themselves to view, we behold them with a mixture of regret arising from the reflection that the pleasing scenes before us are soon to be overwhelmed by the tempestuous waves of sedition[3] and party-rage. If momentary rays of glory break forth from the gloom, while they dazzle us with a transient and fleeting brilliancy, they at the same time admonish us to lament that the vices of government should pervert the direction and tarnish the luster of those bright talents and exalted endowments, for which the favored soils, that produced them, have been so justly celebrated.

From the disorders that disfigure the annals of those republics, the advocates of despotism have drawn arguments, not only against the forms of republican government, but against the very principles of civil liberty. They have decried all free government, as inconsistent with the order of society, and have indulged themselves in malicious exultation over its friends and partisans.[4] Happily for mankind, stupendous fabrics reared on the basis of liberty, which have flourished for ages, have in a few glorious instances refuted their gloomy sophisms.[5] And, I trust, America will be the broad and solid foundation of other edifices not less magnificent, which will be equally permanent monuments of their errors.

But it is not to be denied that the portraits, they have sketched of republican government, were too just[6] copies of the originals from which they were taken. If it had been found impracticable, to have devised models of a more perfect structure, the enlightened friends to liberty would have been obliged to abandon the cause of that species of government as indefensible. The science of politics, however, like most other sciences has received great improvement. The efficacy of various principles is now well understood, which were either not known at all, or imperfectly known to the ancients. The regular distribution of power into distinct departments—the introduction of legislative balances and checks—the institution of courts composed of judges, holding their offices during good behavior—the representation of the people in the legislature by deputies of their own election—these are either wholly new discoveries or have made their principal progress towards perfection in modern times. They are means, and powerful means, by which the

---

1   *moment*   Importance.

2   *felicity*   Happiness.

3   *sedition*   Rebellion against the government.

4   *partisans*   Strong supporters.

5   *sophisms*   Flawed reasoning.

6   *just*   Correct.

excellencies of republican government may be retained and its imperfections lessened or avoided; To this catalogue of circumstances, that tend to the amelioration[1] of popular systems of civil government, I shall venture, however novel it may appear to some, to add one more on a principle, which has been made the foundation of an objection to the New Constitution, I mean the ENLARGEMENT of the ORBIT within which such systems are to revolve either in respect to the dimensions of a single State, or to the consolidation of several smaller States into one great confederacy. The latter is that which immediately concerns the object under consideration. It will however be of use to examine the principle in its application to a single State which shall be attended to in another place.[2]

The utility of a confederacy, as well to suppress faction and to guard the internal tranquility of States, as to increase their external force and security, is in reality not a new idea. It has been practiced upon in different countries and ages, and has received the sanction of the most applauded writers, on the subjects of politics. The opponents of the PLAN proposed have with great assiduity[3] cited and circulated the observations of Montesquieu on the necessity of a contracted territory for a republican government. But they seem not to have been apprised[4] of the sentiments of that great man expressed in another part of his work, nor to have adverted[5] to the consequences of the principle to which they subscribe, with such ready acquiescence.[6]

When Montesquieu recommends a small extent for republics, the standards he had in view were of dimensions, far short of the limits of almost every one of these States. Neither Virginia, Massachusetts, Pennsylvania, New-York, North-Carolina, nor Georgia, can by any means be compared with the models, from which he reasoned and to which the terms of his description apply. If we therefore take his ideas on this point, as the criterion of[7] truth, we shall be driven to the alternative, either of taking refuge at once in the arms of monarchy, or of splitting ourselves into an infinity of little jealous, clashing, tumultuous commonwealths, the wretched nurseries of unceasing discord and the miserable objects of universal pity or contempt. Some of

the writers, who have come forward on the other side of the question, seem to have been aware of the dilemma; and have even been bold enough to hint at the division of the larger States, as a desirable thing. Such an infatuated[8] policy, such a desperate expedient, might, by the multiplication of petty offices, answer the views of men, who possess not qualifications to extend their influence beyond the narrow circles of personal intrigue, but it could never promote the greatness or happiness of the people of America.

Referring the examination of the principle itself to another place,[9] as has been already mentioned, it will be sufficient to remark here, that in the sense of the author who has been most emphatically quoted upon the occasion, it would only dictate a reduction of the SIZE of the more considerable MEMBERS of the Union; but would not militate against their being all comprehended in one Confederate Government. And this is the true question, in the discussion of which we are at present interested.

So far are the suggestions of Montesquieu from standing in opposition to a general Union of the States, that he explicitly treats of a CONFEDERATE REPUBLIC as the expedient for extending the sphere of popular government and reconciling the advantages of monarchy with those of republicanism.

"It is very probable (says he[10]) that mankind would have been obliged, at length, to live constantly under the government of a SINGLE PERSON, had they not contrived a kind of constitution, that has all the internal advantages of a republican, together with the external force of a monarchial government. I mean a CONFEDERATE REPUBLIC.

"This form of Government is a Convention, by which several smaller *States* agree to become members of a larger *one*, which they intend to form. It is a kind of assemblage of societies, that constitute a new one, capable of increasing by means of new associations, till they arrive to such a degree of power as to be able to provide for the security of the united body.

"A republic of this kind, able to withstand an external force, may support itself without any internal corruption. The form of this society prevents all manner of inconveniencies.

"If a single member should attempt to usurp the supreme authority, he could not be supposed to have an equal

---

1 *amelioration* Betterment.
2 *in another place* See Essays 10 and 14.
3 *assiduity* Care.
4 *apprised* Informed.
5 *adverted* Referred.
6 *acquiescence* Agreement.
7 *criterion of* Standard for.

8 *infatuated* Irrational, foolish.
9 *to another place* See Essays 10 and 14.
10 *says he* [Publius' note] *Spirit of Laws*, Vol. 1, Book 9. Chapter 1.

authority and credit, in all the confederate states. Were he to have too great influence over one, this would alarm the rest. Were he to subdue a part, that which would still remain free might oppose him with forces, independent of those which he had usurped, and overpower him before he could be settled in his usurpation.

"Should a popular insurrection happen, in one of the confederate States, the others are able to quell it. Should abuses creep into one part, they are reformed by those that remain sound. The State may be destroyed on one side, and not on the other; the confederacy may be dissolved, and the confederates preserve their sovereignty.

"As this government is composed of small republics it enjoys the internal happiness of each, and with respect to its external situation it is possessed, by means of the association of all the advantages of large monarchies."

I have thought it proper to quote at length these interesting passages, because they contain a luminous abridgement[1] of the principal arguments in favor of the Union, and must effectually remove the false impressions, which a misapplication of other parts of the work was calculated to produce. They have at the same time an intimate connection with the more immediate design of this Paper; which is to illustrate the tendency of the Union to repress domestic faction and insurrection.

A distinction, more subtle than accurate has been raised between a *confederacy* and a *consolidation* of the States. The essential characteristic of the first is said to be, the restriction of its authority to the members in their collective capacities, without reaching to the individuals of whom they are composed. It is contended that the national council ought to have no concern with any object of internal administration. An exact equality of suffrage[2] between the members has also been insisted upon as a leading feature of a Confederate Government. These positions are in the main arbitrary; they are supported neither by principle nor precedent. It has indeed happened that governments of this kind have generally operated in the manner, which the distinction, taken notice of, supposes to be inherent in their nature—but there have been in most of them extensive exceptions to the practice, which serve to prove as far as example will go, that there is no absolute rule on the subject. And it will be clearly shown, in the course of this investigation, that as far as the

principle contended[3] for has prevailed, it has been the cause of incurable disorder and imbecility in the government.

The definition of a *Confederate Republic* seems simply to be, an "assemblage of societies" or an association of two or more States into one State. The extent, modifications and objects of the Federal authority are mere matters of discretion.[4] So long as the separate organization of the members be not abolished, so long as it exists by a constitutional necessity for local purposes, though it should be in perfect subordination[5] to the general authority of the Union, it would still be, in fact and in theory, an association of States, or a confederacy. The proposed Constitution, so far from implying an abolition of the State Governments, makes them constituent parts of the national sovereignty by allowing them a direct representation in the Senate, and leaves in their possession certain exclusive and very important portions of sovereign power. This fully corresponds, in every rational import of the terms, with the idea of a Federal Government.

In the Lycian confederacy,[6] which consisted of twenty three CITIES or republics, the largest were entitled to *three* votes in the COMMON COUNCIL, those of the middle class to *two* and the smallest to *one*. The COMMON COUNCIL had the appointment of all the judges and magistrates of the respective CITIES. This was certainly the most delicate species of interference in their internal administration; for if there be any thing, that seems exclusively appropriated to the local jurisdictions, it is the appointment of their own officers. Yet Montesquieu, speaking of this association, says "Were I to give a model of an excellent confederate republic, it would be that of Lycia." Thus we perceive that the distinctions insisted upon were not within the contemplation of this enlightened civilian, and we shall be led to conclude that they are the novel refinements of an erroneous theory.

PUBLIUS.

◆ ◆ ◆ ◆ ◆

---

1   *abridgement* Summary.
2   *suffrage* Right to vote.
3   *contended* Argued.
4   *discretion* Free decision—that is, decision as is seen fit.
5   *in perfect subordination* Completely subject to.
6   *Lycian confederacy* The Lycian League, a federation of several states in what is now Turkey, founded around 150 BCE and lasting several centuries, was the world's first federal republic; it was of great interest to Enlightenment and especially early American political theorists.

The Federalist No. 10

James Madison
November 22, 1787

from *The Daily Advertiser*, November 22, 1787. This essay appeared in *The New-York Packet* on November 23 and in *The Independent Journal* on November 24.

To the People of the State of New York.

Among the numerous advantages promised by a well constructed Union, none deserves to be more accurately developed than its tendency to break and control the violence of faction.[1] The friend of popular governments, never finds himself so much alarmed for their character and fate, as when he contemplates their propensity to this dangerous vice. He will not fail therefore to set a due value on any plan which, without violating the principles to which he is attached, provides a proper cure for it. The instability, injustice and confusion introduced into the public councils, have in truth been the mortal diseases under which popular governments have every where perished; as they continue to be the favorite and fruitful topics from which the adversaries to liberty derive their most specious[2] declamations.[3] The valuable improvements made by the American Constitutions on the popular models, both ancient and modern, cannot certainly be *too* much admired; but it would be an unwarrantable partiality,[4] to contend that they have as effectually obviated[5] the danger on this side as was wished and expected. Complaints are every where heard from our most considerate and virtuous citizens, equally the friends of public and private faith, and of public and personal liberty; that our governments are *too* unstable; that the public good is disregarded in the conflicts of rival parties; and that measures are too often decided, not according to the rules of justice, and the rights of the minor party;[6] but by the superior force of an interested[7] and over-bearing majority. However anxiously we may wish that these complaints had no foundation, the evidence of known facts will not permit us to deny that they are in some degree true. It will be found indeed, on a candid review of our situation, that some of the distresses under which we labor, have been erroneously charged on the operation of our governments; but it will be found, at the same time, that other causes will not alone account for many of our heaviest misfortunes; and particularly, for that prevailing and increasing distrust of public engagements, and alarm for private rights, which are echoed from one end of the continent to the other. These must be chiefly, if not wholly, effects of the unsteadiness and injustice, with which a factious spirit has tainted our public administrations.

By a faction I understand a number of citizens, whether amounting to a majority or minority of the whole, who are united and actuated[8] by some common impulse of passion, or of interest, adverse to the rights of other citizens, or to the permanent and aggregate interests of the community. There are two methods of curing the mischiefs[9] of faction: the one, by removing its causes; the other, by controlling its effects. There are again two methods of removing the causes of faction: the one by destroying the liberty which is essential to its existence; the other, by giving to every citizen the same opinions, the same passions, and the same interests. It could never be more truly said than of the first remedy, that it is worse than the disease. Liberty is to faction, what air is to fire, an aliment[10] without which it instantly expires. But it could not be a less folly to abolish liberty, which is essential to political life, because it nourishes faction, than it would be to wish the annihilation of air, which is essential to animal life, because it imparts to fire its destructive agency. The second expedient is as impracticable, as the first would be unwise. As long as the reason of man continues fallible, and he is at liberty to exercise it, different opinions will be formed. As long as the connection subsists between his reason and his self-love, his opinions and his passions will have a reciprocal[11] influence on each other; and the former will be objects to which the latter will attach themselves. The diversity in the faculties of men from which the rights of property originate, is not less an insuperable[12] obstacle to a uniformity of interests. The protection of these faculties is the first object of Government. From the protection of different and unequal faculties of acquiring property, the

---

1   *faction*   Conflict within.
2   *specious*   Attractive, but false.
3   *declamations*   Public rhetoric.
4   *unwarrantable partiality*   Unjustifiable bias.
5   *obviated*   Anticipated and avoided.
6   *minor party*   Minority group.
7   *interested*   Having a concern for their own advantage or disadvantage.
8   *actuated*   Moved to action.
9   *mischiefs*   Harms.
10 *aliment*   Something that sustains.
11 *reciprocal*   Produced by each side.
12 *insuperable*   Impossible to overcome.

possession of different degrees and kinds of property immediately results: and from the influence of these on the sentiments[1] and views of the respective proprietors,[2] ensues a division of the society into different interests and parties. The latent causes of faction are thus sown in the nature of man; and we see them every where brought into different degrees of activity, according to the different circumstances of civil society. A zeal for different opinions concerning religion, concerning Government and many other points, as well of speculation as of[3] practice; an attachment to different leaders ambitiously contending for pre-eminence and power; or to persons of other descriptions whose fortunes have been interesting to the human passions, have in turn divided mankind into parties, inflamed them with mutual animosity, and rendered them much more disposed to vex and oppress each other, than to co-operate for their common good. So strong is this propensity of mankind to fall into mutual animosities, that where no substantial occasion presents itself, the most frivolous and fanciful distinctions have been sufficient to kindle their unfriendly passions, and excite their most violent conflicts. But the most common and durable source of factions, has been the various and unequal distribution of property. Those who hold, and those who are without property, have ever formed distinct interests in society. Those who are creditors, and those who are debtors, fall under a like discrimination. A landed interest, a manufacturing interest, a mercantile interest, a monied interest, with many lesser interests, grow up of necessity in civilized nations, and divide them into different classes, actuated by different sentiments and views. The regulation of these various and interfering interests forms the principal task of modern Legislation, and involves the spirit of party and faction in the necessary and ordinary operations of Government.

No man is allowed to be a judge in his own cause; because his interest would certainly bias his judgment, and, not improbably, corrupt his integrity. With equal, nay with greater reason, a body of men, are unfit to be both judges and parties, at the same time; yet, what are many of the most important acts of legislation, but so many judicial determinations, not indeed concerning the rights of single persons, but concerning the rights of large bodies of citizens; and what are the different classes of legislators, but

advocates and parties to the causes which they determine? Is a law proposed concerning private debts? It is a question to which the creditors are parties on one side, and the debtors on the other. Justice ought to hold the balance between them. Yet the parties are and must be themselves the judges; and the most numerous party, or, in other words, the most powerful faction must be expected to prevail. Shall domestic manufactures be encouraged, and in what degree, by restrictions on foreign manufactures? are questions which would be differently decided by the landed and the manufacturing classes; and probably by neither, with a sole regard to justice and the public good. The apportionment of taxes on the various descriptions of property, is an act which seems to require the most exact impartiality; yet, there is perhaps no legislative act in which greater opportunity and temptation are given to a predominant party, to trample on the rules of justice. Every shilling[4] with which they over-burden the inferior number, is a shilling saved to their own pockets.

It is in vain to say, that enlightened statesmen will be able to adjust these clashing interests, and render them all subservient to the public good. Enlightened statesmen will not always be at the helm: Nor, in many cases, can such an adjustment be made at all, without taking into view indirect and remote considerations, which will rarely prevail over the immediate interest which one party may find in disregarding the rights of another, or the good of the whole. The inference to which we are brought, is, that the *causes* of faction cannot be removed; and that relief is only to be sought in the means of controlling its *effects*.

If a faction consists of less than a majority, relief is supplied by the republican principle, which enables the majority to defeat its sinister[5] views by regular vote: It may clog the administration, it may convulse[6] the society; but it will be unable to execute and mask its violence under the forms of the Constitution. When a majority is included in a faction, the form of popular government on the other hand enables it to sacrifice to its ruling passion or interest, both the public good and the rights of other citizens. To secure the public good, and private rights, against the danger of such a faction, and at the same time to preserve the spirit and the form of popular government, is then the great object to which our enquiries are directed: Let me add

1   *sentiments* Feelings, opinions.
2   *proprietors* Owners.
3   *as well of ... as of* Involving both ... and.

4   *Every shilling* A shilling is a now-defunct currency denomination; "every shilling" means "every cent."
5   *sinister* Unfavorable, threatening.
6   *convulse* Cause extreme disruption in.

that it is the great desideratum,[1] by which alone this form of government can be rescued from the opprobrium[2] under which it has so long labored, and be recommended to the esteem and adoption of mankind.

By what means is this object attainable? Evidently by one of two only. Either the existence of the same passion or interest in a majority at the same time, must be prevented; or the majority, having such co-existent passion or interest, must be rendered, by their number and local situation, unable to concert[3] and carry into effect schemes of oppression. If the impulse and the opportunity be suffered[4] to coincide, we well know that neither moral nor religious motives can be relied on as an adequate control. They are not found to be such on the injustice and violence of individuals, and lose their efficacy in proportion to the number combined together; that is, in proportion as their efficacy becomes needful.

From this view of the subject, it may be concluded, that a pure Democracy, by which I mean, a Society, consisting of a small number of citizens, who assemble and administer the Government in person, can admit of no cure for the mischiefs of faction. A common passion or interest will, in almost every case, be felt by a majority of the whole; a communication and concert results from the form of Government itself; and there is nothing to check the inducements to sacrifice the weaker party, or an obnoxious individual. Hence it is, that such Democracies have ever been spectacles of turbulence and contention; have ever been found incompatible with personal security, or the rights of property; and have in general been as short in their lives, as they have been violent in their deaths. Theoretic politicians, who have patronized[5] this species of Government, have erroneously supposed, that by reducing mankind to a perfect equality in their political rights, they would, at the same time, be perfectly equalized and assimilated in their possessions, their opinions, and their passions.

A Republic, by which I mean a Government in which the scheme of representation takes place, opens a different prospect, and promises the cure for which we are seeking. Let us examine the points in which it varies from pure Democracy, and we shall comprehend both the nature of the cure, and the efficacy which it must derive from the Union.

The two great points of difference between a Democracy and a Republic are, first, the delegation of the Government, in the latter, to a small number of citizens elected by the rest: secondly, the greater number of citizens, and greater sphere of country, over which the latter may be extended.

The effect of the first difference is, on the one hand to refine and enlarge the public views, by passing them through the medium of a chosen body of citizens, whose wisdom may best discern the true interest of their country, and whose patriotism and love of justice, will be least likely to sacrifice it to temporary or partial[6] considerations. Under such a regulation, it may well happen that the public voice pronounced by the representatives of the people, will be more consonant to[7] the public good, than if pronounced by the people themselves convened for the purpose. On the other hand, the effect may be inverted. Men of factious tempers, of local prejudices, or of sinister designs, may by intrigue, by corruption or by other means, first obtain the suffrages,[8] and then betray the interests of the people. The question resulting is, whether small or extensive Republics are most favorable to the election of proper guardians of the public weal:[9] and it is clearly decided in favor of the latter by two obvious considerations.

In the first place it is to be remarked that however small the Republic may be, the Representatives must be raised to a certain number, in order to guard against the cabals[10] of a few; and that however large it may be, they must be limited to a certain number, in order to guard against the confusion of a multitude. Hence the number of Representatives in the two cases, not being in proportion to that of the Constituents, and being proportionally greatest in the small Republic, it follows, that if the proportion of fit characters, be not less, in the large than in the small Republic, the former will present a greater option, and consequently a greater probability of a fit choice.

In the next place, as each Representative will be chosen by a greater number of citizens in the large than in the small Republic, it will be more difficult for unworthy candidates to practice with success the vicious arts, by which elections are too often carried; and the suffrages of the people being more free, will be more likely to center on men who pos-

---

1 *desideratum* That which is desired.
2 *opprobrium* Shame, disgrace.
3 *concert* Settle by discussion and mutual consent.
4 *suffered* Allowed.
5 *patronized* Supported.

6 *partial* Biased.
7 *consonant to* In harmony with.
8 *suffrages* Votes.
9 *weal* Well-being.
10 *cabals* Secret plots.

sess the most attractive merit, and the most diffusive[1] and established characters.

It must be confessed, that in this, as in most other cases, there is a mean, on both sides of which inconveniencies[2] will be found to lie. By enlarging too much the number of electors, you render the representative too little acquainted with all their local circumstances and lesser interests; as by reducing it too much, you render him unduly attached to these, and too little fit to comprehend and pursue great and national objects. The Federal Constitution forms a happy combination in this respect; the great and aggregate interests being referred to the national, the local and particular, to the state legislatures.

The other point of difference is, the greater number of citizens and extent of territory which may be brought within the compass of Republican, than of Democratic Government; and it is this circumstance principally which renders factious combinations less to be dreaded in the former, than in the latter. The smaller the society, the fewer probably will be the distinct parties and interests composing it; the fewer the distinct parties and interests, the more frequently will a majority be found of the same party; and the smaller the number of individuals composing a majority, and the smaller the compass within which they are placed, the more easily will they concert and execute their plans of oppression. Extend the sphere, and you take in a greater variety of parties and interests; you make it less probable that a majority of the whole will have a common motive to invade the rights of other citizens; or if such a common motive exists, it will be more difficult for all who feel it to discover their own strength, and to act in unison with each other. Besides other impediments, it may be remarked, that where there is a consciousness of unjust or dishonorable purposes, communication is always checked by distrust, in proportion to the number whose concurrence is necessary.

Hence it clearly appears, that the same advantage, which a Republic has over a Democracy, in controlling the effects of faction, is enjoyed by a large over a small Republic—is enjoyed by the Union over the States composing it. Does this advantage consist in the substitution of Representatives, whose enlightened views and virtuous sentiments render them superior to local prejudices, and to schemes of injustice? It will not be denied, that the Representation of the Union will be most likely to possess these requisite

endowments. Does it consist in the greater security afforded by a greater variety of parties, against the event of anyone party being able to outnumber and oppress the rest? In an equal degree does the increased variety of parties, comprised within the Union, increase this security. Does it, in fine,[3] consist in the greater obstacles opposed to the concert and accomplishment of the secret wishes of an unjust and interested majority? Here, again, the extent of the Union gives it the most palpable advantage.

The influence of factious leaders may kindle a flame within their particular States, but will be unable to spread a general conflagration[4] through the other States: a religious sect, may degenerate into a political faction in a part of the Confederacy; but the variety of sects dispersed over the entire face of it, must secure the national Councils against any danger from that source: a rage for paper money, for an abolition of debts, for an equal division of property, or for any other improper or wicked project, will be less apt to pervade the whole body of the Union, than a particular member of it; in the same proportion as such a malady is more likely to taint a particular county or district, than an entire State.

In the extent and proper structure of the Union, therefore, we behold a Republican remedy for the diseases most incident to Republican Government. And according to the degree of pleasure and pride, we feel in being Republicans, ought to be our zeal in cherishing the spirit, and supporting the character of Federalists.

PUBLIUS.

◆ ◆ ◆ ◆ ◆

The Federalist No. 51

James Madison
February 6, 1788

from *The Independent Journal*, February 6, 1788. This essay appeared on February 8 in *The New-York Packet* and on February 11 in *The Daily Advertiser*. Standard numbering (from the McLean edition of all the essays) gives it the number 51, but it was numbered 50 in the newspapers.

---

1 *diffusive* Bountiful, generous.
2 *inconveniencies* Difficulties.

3 *in fine* In conclusion.
4 *conflagration* Large destructive fire.

To the People of the State of New York.

To what expedient[1] then shall we finally resort for maintaining in practice the necessary partition of power among the several departments, as laid down in the *constitution*? The only answer that can be given is, that as all these exterior provisions are found to be inadequate, the defect must be supplied, by so contriving the interior structure of the government, as that its several constituent parts may, by their mutual relations, be the means of keeping each other in their proper places. Without presuming to undertake a full development of this important idea, I will hazard a few general observations, which may perhaps place it in a clearer light, and enable us to form a more correct judgment of the principles and structure of the government planned by the convention.

In order to lay a due foundation for that separate and distinct exercise of the different powers of government, which to a certain extent, is admitted on all hands to be essential to the preservation of liberty, it is evident that each department should have a will of its own; and consequently should be so constituted, that the members of each should have as little agency as possible in the appointment of the members of the others. Were this principle rigorously adhered to, it would require that all the appointments for the supreme executive, legislative, and judiciary magistracies, should be drawn from the same fountain of authority, the people, through channels, having no communication whatever with one another. Perhaps such a plan of constructing the several departments would be less difficult in practice than it may in contemplation appear. Some difficulties however, and some additional expense, would attend the execution of it. Some deviations therefore from the principle must be admitted. In the constitution of the judiciary department in particular, it might be inexpedient to insist rigorously on the principle; first, because peculiar qualifications being essential in the members, the primary consideration ought to be to select that mode of choice, which best secures these qualifications; secondly, because the permanent tenure[2] by which the appointments are held in that department, must soon destroy all sense of dependence on the authority conferring them.

It is equally evident that the members of each department should be as little dependent as possible on those of the others, for the emoluments annexed to their offices.[3] Were the executive magistrate, or the judges, not independent of the legislature in this particular, their independence in every other would be merely nominal.[4]

But the great security against a gradual concentration of the several powers in the same department, consists in giving to those who administer each department, the necessary constitutional means, and personal motives, to resist encroachments of the others. The provision for defense must in this, as in all other cases, be made commensurate[5] to the danger of attack. Ambition must be made to counteract ambition. The interest of the man must be connected with the constitutional rights of the place. It may be a reflection on human nature, that such devices should be necessary to control the abuses of government. But what is government itself but the greatest of all reflections on human nature? If men were angels, no government would be necessary. If angels were to govern men, neither external nor internal controls on government would be necessary. In framing a government which is to be administered by men over men, the great difficulty lies in this: You must first enable the government to control the governed; and in the next place, oblige it to control itself. A dependence on the people is no doubt the primary control on the government; but experience has taught mankind the necessity of auxiliary precautions.

This policy of supplying by opposite and rival interests, the defect of better motives, might be traced through the whole system of human affairs, private as well as public. We see it particularly displayed in all the subordinate distributions of power; where the constant aim is to divide and arrange the several offices in such a manner as that each may be a check on the other; that the private interest of every individual, may be a sentinel[6] over the public rights. These inventions of prudence cannot be less requisite in the distribution of the supreme powers of the state.

But it is not possible to give to each department an equal power of self defense. In republican government the legislative authority, necessarily, predominates. The remedy for this inconveniency is, to divide the legislature into different branches; and to render them by different modes of election, and different principles of action, as little con-

---

nected with each other, as the nature of their common functions, and their common dependence on the society, will admit. It may even be necessary to guard against dangerous encroachments by still further precautions. As the weight of the legislative authority requires that it should be thus divided, the weakness of the executive may require, on the other hand, that it should be fortified. An absolute negative,[1] on the legislature, appears at first view to be the natural defense with which the executive magistrate should be armed. But perhaps it would be neither altogether safe, nor alone sufficient. On ordinary occasions, it might not be exerted with the requisite firmness; and on extraordinary occasions, it might be perfidiously[2] abused. May not this defect of an absolute negative be supplied, by some qualified connection between this weaker department, and the weaker branch of the stronger department, by which the latter may be led to support the constitutional rights of the former, without being too much detached from the rights of its own department?

If the principles on which these observations are founded be just, as I persuade myself they are, and they be applied as a criterion, to the several state constitutions, and to the federal constitution, it will be found, that if the latter does not perfectly correspond with them, the former are infinitely less able to bear such a test.

There are moreover two considerations particularly applicable to the federal system of America, which place that system in a very interesting point of view.

First. In a single republic, all the power surrendered by the people, is submitted to the administration of a single government; and usurpations[3] are guarded against by a division of the government into distinct and separate departments. In the compound republic of America, the power surrendered by the people, is first divided between two distinct governments, and then the portion allotted to each, subdivided among distinct and separate departments. Hence a double security arises to the rights of the people. The different governments will control each other; at the same time that each will be controlled by itself.

Second. It is of great importance in a republic, not only to guard the society against the oppression of its rulers; but to guard one part of the society against the injustice of the other part. Different interests necessarily exist in different classes of citizens. If a majority be united by a common interest, the rights of the minority will be insecure. There are but two methods of providing against this evil: The one by creating a will in the community independent of the majority, that is, of the society itself; the other by comprehending[4] in the society so many separate descriptions of citizens, as will render an unjust combination of a majority of the whole, very improbable, if not impracticable.[5] The first method prevails in all governments possessing an hereditary or self appointed authority. This at best is but a precarious[6] security; because a power independent of the society may as well espouse[7] the unjust views of the major, as the rightful interests, of the minor party, and may possibly be turned against both parties. The second method will be exemplified in the federal republic of the United States. Whilst all authority in it will be derived from and dependent on the society, the society itself will be broken into so many parts, interests and classes of citizens, that the rights of individuals or of the minority, will be in little danger from interested combinations of the majority. In a free government, the security for civil rights must be the same as for religious rights. It consists in the one case in the multiplicity of interests, and in the other, in the multiplicity of sects. The degree of security in both cases will depend on the number of interests and sects; and this may be presumed to depend on the extent of country and number of people comprehended under the same government. This view of the subject must particularly recommend a proper federal system to all the sincere and considerate friends of republican government: Since it shows that in exact proportion as the territory of the union may be formed into more circumscribed[8] confederacies or states, oppressive combinations of a majority will be facilitated, the best security under the republican form, for the rights of every class of citizens, will be diminished; and consequently, the stability and independence of some member of the government, the only other security, must be proportionally increased. Justice is the end of government. It is the end of civil society. It ever has been, and ever will be pursued, until it be obtained, or until liberty be lost in the pursuit. In a society under the forms of which the stronger faction can readily unite and oppress the weaker, anarchy may as truly be said to reign,

---

1 *negative* Right of veto.
2 *perfidiously* Treacherously.
3 *usurpations* Wrongful seizures.

4 *comprehending* Including.
5 *impracticable* Impossible.
6 *precarious* Uncertain, unstable.
7 *espouse* Take as its own.
8 *circumscribed* Restricted in area.

as in a state of nature where the weaker individual is not secured against the violence of the stronger: And as in the latter state even the stronger individuals are prompted by the uncertainty of their condition, to submit to a government which may protect the weak as well as themselves: So in the former state, will the more powerful factions or parties be gradually induced by a like motive, to wish for a government which will protect all parties, the weaker as well as the more powerful. It can be little doubted, that if the state of Rhode Island[1] was separated from the confederacy, and left to itself, the insecurity of rights under the popular form of government within such narrow limits, would be displayed by such reiterated[2] oppressions of factious majorities, that some power altogether independent of the people would soon be called for by the voice of the very factions whose misrule had proved the necessity of it. In the extended republic of the United States, and among the great variety of interests, parties and sects which it embraces, a coalition of a majority of the whole society could seldom take place on any other principles than those of justice and the general good; and there being thus less danger to a minor from the will of the major party, there must be less pretext[3] also, to provide for the security of the former, by introducing into the government a will not dependent on the latter; or in other words, a will independent of the society itself. It is no less certain than it is important, notwithstanding the contrary opinions which have been entertained, that the larger the society, provided it lie within a practicable sphere, the more duly capable it will be of self government. And happily for the *republican cause*, the practicable sphere may be carried to a very great extent, by a judicious modification and mixture of the *federal principle*.

PUBLIUS.

◆ ◆ ◆ ◆ ◆

---

1   *Rhode Island*   Still the state with the smallest area.
2   *reiterated*   Repeated.
3   *pretext*   Excuse.

The Federalist No. 78

Alexander Hamilton
May 28, 1788

from J. and A. McLean, *The Federalist*, II, 290-99, where this essay was first published on May 28, 1788. and numbered 78. It appeared on June 14 in *The Independent Journal* where it was numbered 77; it was begun on June 17 and concluded on June 20 in *The New-York Packet* where it was numbered 78.

We proceed now to an examination of the judiciary department of the proposed government.

In unfolding the defects of the existing confederation, the utility and necessity of a federal judicature have been clearly pointed out.[4] It is the less necessary to recapitulate[5] the considerations there urged; as the propriety of the institution in the abstract is not disputed: The only questions which have been raised being relative to the manner of constituting it, and to its extent. To these points therefore our observations shall be confined.

The manner of constituting it seems to embrace these several objects—First: The mode of appointing the judges. Second: The tenure by which they are to hold their places. Third: The partition of the judiciary authority between different courts, and their relations to each other.

First. As to the mode of appointing the judges: This is the same with that of appointing the officers of the union in general, and has been so fully discussed in the two last numbers, that nothing can be said here which would not be useless repetition.

Second. As to the tenure by which the judges are to hold their places: This chiefly concerns their duration in office; the provisions for their support; and the precautions for their responsibility.

According to the plan of the convention, all the judges who may be appointed by the United States are to hold their offices *during good behavior*, which is conformable to the most approved of the state constitutions; and among the rest, to that of this state. Its propriety having been drawn into question by the adversaries of that plan, is no light symptom of the rage for objection which disorders their imaginations and judgments. The standard of good behavior for the

---

4   *have been clearly pointed out* See Essay 22.
5   *recapitulate* Restate.

continuance in office of the judicial magistracy is certainly one of the most valuable of the modern improvements in the practice of government. In a monarchy it is an excellent barrier to the despotism of the prince: In a republic it is a no less excellent barrier to the encroachments and oppressions of the representative body. And it is the best expedient which can be devised in any government, to secure a steady, upright and impartial administration of the laws.

Whoever attentively considers the different departments of power must perceive, that in a government in which they are separated from each other, the judiciary, from the nature of its functions, will always be the least dangerous to the political rights of the constitution; because it will be least in a capacity to annoy[1] or injure them. The executive not only dispenses the honors, but holds the sword of the community. The legislature not only commands the purse, but prescribes the rules by which the duties and rights of every citizen are to be regulated. The judiciary on the contrary has no influence over either the sword or the purse, no direction either of the strength or of the wealth of the society, and can take no active resolution whatever. It may truly be said to have neither Force nor Will, but merely judgment; and must ultimately depend upon the aid of the executive arm even for the efficacy of its judgments.

This simple view of the matter suggests several important consequences. It proves incontestably that the judiciary is beyond comparison the weakest of the three departments of power;[2] that it can never attack with success either of the other two; and that all possible care is requisite to enable it to defend itself against their attacks. It equally proves, that though individual oppression may now and then proceed from the courts of justice, the general liberty of the people can never be endangered from that quarter: I mean, so long as the judiciary remains truly distinct from both the legislative and executive. For I agree that "there is no liberty, if the power of judging be not separated from the legislative and executive powers."[3] And it proves, in the last place, that as liberty can have nothing to fear from the judiciary alone, but would have every thing to fear from its union with either of the other departments; that as all the effects of such an union must ensue from a dependence of the former

on the latter, notwithstanding a nominal and apparent separation; that as from the natural feebleness of the judiciary, it is in continual jeopardy of being overpowered, awed or influenced by its coordinate branches; and that as nothing can contribute so much to its firmness and independence, as permanency in office, this quality may therefore be justly regarded as an indispensable ingredient in its constitution; and in a great measure as the citadel of the public justice and the public security.

The complete independence of the courts of justice is peculiarly essential in a limited constitution. By a limited constitution I understand one which contains certain specified exceptions to the legislative authority; such for instance as that it shall pass no bills of attainder,[4] no *ex post facto laws*,[5] and the like. Limitations of this kind can be preserved in practice no other way than through the medium of the courts of justice; whose duty it must be to declare all acts contrary to the manifest tenor[6] of the constitution void. Without this, all the reservations of particular rights or privileges would amount to nothing.

Some perplexity respecting the right of the courts to pronounce legislative acts void, because contrary to the constitution, has arisen from an imagination that the doctrine would imply a superiority of the judiciary to the legislative power. It is urged that the authority which can declare the acts of another void, must necessarily be superior to the one whose acts may be declared void. As this doctrine is of great importance in all the American constitutions, a brief discussion of the grounds on which it rests cannot be unacceptable.

There is no position which depends on clearer principles, than that every act of a delegated authority, contrary to the tenor of the commission under which it is exercised, is void. No legislative act therefore contrary to the constitution can be valid. To deny this would be to affirm that the deputy is greater than his principal; that the servant is above his master; that the representatives of the people are superior to the people themselves; that men acting by

---

1   *annoy* Interfere with.

2   *three departments of power* [Publius' footnote] The celebrated Montesquieu speaking of them says, "of the three powers above mentioned, the *judiciary* is next to nothing." *Spirit of Laws*, volume 1.

3   *there is no liberty ... executive powers* [Publius' footnote] Ibid.

4   *bills of attainder* Acts of the legislature declaring someone (or some group) guilty of a crime, and sentencing to punishment, without trial. Regarded as an abuse of governmental power, the power to enact these laws was abolished in the United Kingdom in 1870 (they had been only rarely used before that).

5   *ex post facto laws* Laws changing the legal status of acts retroactively, that is, after they have been committed. Another practice regarded as an abuse.

6   *manifest tenor* Clear general nature.

virtue of powers may do not only what their powers do not authorize, but what they forbid.

If it be said that the legislative body are themselves the constitutional judges of their own powers, and that the construction they put upon them is conclusive upon the other departments, it may be answered, that this cannot be the natural presumption, where it is not to be collected from any particular provisions in the constitution. It is not otherwise to be supposed that the constitution could intend to enable the representatives of the people to sub-stitute their *will* to that of their constituents. It is far more rational to suppose that the courts were designed to be an intermediate body between the people and the legislature, in order, among other things, to keep the latter within the limits assigned to their authority. The interpretation of the laws is the proper and peculiar province of the courts. A constitution is in fact, and must be, regarded by the judges as a fundamental law. It therefore belongs to them to ascer-tain its meaning as well as the meaning of any particular act proceeding from the legislative body. If there should happen to be an irreconcilable variance between the two, that which has the superior obligation and validity ought of course to be preferred; or in other words, the constitution ought to be preferred to the statute, the intention of the people to the intention of their agents.

Nor does this conclusion by any means suppose a su-periority of the judicial to the legislative power. It only sup-poses that the power of the people is superior to both; and that where the will of the legislature declared in its statutes, stands in opposition to that of the people declared in the constitution, the judges ought to be governed by the latter, rather than the former. They ought to regulate their deci-sions by the fundamental laws, rather than by those which are not fundamental.

This exercise of judicial discretion in determining be-tween two contradictory laws, is exemplified in a familiar instance. It not uncommonly happens, that there are two statutes existing at one time, clashing in whole or in part with each other, and neither of them containing any repeal-ing[1] clause or expression. In such a case, it is the province of the courts to liquidate and fix their meaning and operation: So far as they can by any fair construction be reconciled to each other; reason and law conspire to dictate that this should be done. Where this is impracticable, it becomes a matter of necessity to give effect to one, in exclusion of the other. The rule which has obtained in the courts for determining their relative validity is that the last in order of time shall be preferred to the first. But this is mere rule of construction, not derived from any positive[2] law, but from the nature and reason of the thing. It is a rule not enjoined[3] upon the courts by legislative provision, but adopted by themselves, as consonant to truth and propriety, for the direction of their conduct as interpreters of the law. They thought it reasonable, that between the interfering acts of an *equal* authority, that which was the last indication of its will, should have the preference.

But in regard to the interfering acts of a superior and subordinate authority, of an original and derivative power, the nature and reason of the thing indicate the converse of that rule as proper to be followed. They teach us that the prior act of a superior ought to be preferred to the subse-quent act of an inferior and subordinate authority; and that, accordingly, whenever a particular statute contravenes the constitution, it will be the duty of the judicial tribunals to adhere to the latter, and disregard the former.

It can be of no weight to say, that the courts on the pre-tense of a repugnancy,[4] may substitute their own pleasure to the constitutional intentions of the legislature. This might as well happen in the case of two contradictory statutes; or it might as well happen in every adjudication upon any single statute. The courts must declare the sense of the law; and if they should be disposed to exercise WILL instead of JUDGMENT, the consequence would equally be the sub-stitution of their pleasure to that of the legislative body. The observation, if it proved any thing, would prove that there ought to be no judges distinct from that body,

If then the courts of justice are to be considered as the bulwarks[5] of a limited constitution against legislative encroachments, this consideration will afford a strong argu-ment for the permanent tenure[6] of judicial offices, since nothing will contribute so much as this to that independent spirit in the judges, which must be essential to the faithful performance of so arduous a duty.

This independence of the judges is equally requisite to guard the constitution and the rights of individuals from the effects of those ill humors[7] which the arts of design-

---

1   *repealing*   Retracting, annulling.

2   *positive*   Explicit.

3   *enjoined*   Imposed.

4   *repugnancy*   Strong feeling of disgust.

5   *bulwarks*   Defensive walls.

6   *tenure*   Term of appointment to a job.

7   *ill humors*   Fits of irritation or surliness.

ing[1] men, or the influence of particular conjunctures,[2] sometimes disseminate among the people themselves, and which, though they speedily give place to better information and more deliberate reflection, have a tendency in the mean time to occasion dangerous innovations in the government, and serious oppressions of the minor party in the community. Though I trust the friends of the proposed constitution will never concur with its enemies[3] in questioning that fundamental principle of republican government, which admits the right of the people to alter or abolish the established constitution whenever they find it inconsistent with their happiness; yet it is not to be inferred from this principle, that the representatives of the people, whenever a momentary inclination happens to lay hold of a majority of their constituents incompatible with the provisions in the existing constitution, would on that account be justifiable in a violation of those provisions; or that the courts would be under a greater obligation to connive[4] at infractions in this shape, than when they had proceeded wholly from the cabals of the representative body. Until the people have by some solemn and authoritative act annulled or changed the established form, it is binding upon themselves collectively, as well as individually; and no presumption, or even knowledge of their sentiments, can warrant their representatives in a departure from it, prior to such an act. But it is easy to see that it would require an uncommon portion of fortitude in the judges to do their duty as faithful guardians of the constitution, where legislative invasions of it had been instigated by the major voice of the community.

But it is not with a view to infractions of the constitution only that the independence of the judges may be an essential safeguard against the effects of occasional ill humors in the society. These sometimes extend no farther than to the injury of the private rights of particular classes of citizens, by unjust and partial laws. Here also the firmness of the judicial magistracy is of vast importance in mitigating[5] the severity, and confining the operation of such laws. It not only serves to moderate the immediate mischiefs of those which may have been passed, but it operates as a check upon the legislative body in passing them; who, perceiving that obstacles to the success of an iniquitous[6] intention are to be expected from the scruples of the courts, are in a manner compelled by the very motives of the injustice they meditate, to qualify their attempts. This is a circumstance calculated to have more influence upon the character of our governments, than but few may be aware of. The benefits of the integrity and moderation of the judiciary have already been felt in more states than one; and though they may have displeased those whose sinister expectations they may have disappointed, they must have commanded the esteem and applause of all the virtuous and disinterested.[7] Considerate men of every description ought to prize whatever will tend to beget or fortify that temper in the courts; as no man can be sure that he may not be tomorrow the victim of a spirit of injustice, by which he may be a gainer today. And every man must now feel that the inevitable tendency of such a spirit is to sap the foundations of public and private confidence, and to introduce in its stead, universal distrust and distress.

That inflexible and uniform adherence to the rights of the constitution and of individuals, which we perceive to be indispensable in the courts of justice, can certainly not be expected from judges who hold their offices by a temporary commission. Periodical appointments, however regulated, or by whomsoever made, would in some way or other be fatal to their necessary independence. If the power of making them was committed either to the executive or legislature, there would be danger of an improper complaisance to[8] the branch which possessed it; if to both, there would be an unwillingness to hazard the displeasure of either; if to the people, or to persons chosen by them for the special purpose, there would be too great a disposition to consult popularity, to justify a reliance that nothing would be consulted but the constitution and the laws.

There is yet a further and a weighty reason for the permanency of the judicial offices; which is deducible from the nature of the qualifications they require. It has been fre-

---

1   *designing* Scheming.
2   *conjunctures* Combinations of events and circumstances.
3   *Though I trust ... enemies* [Publius' footnote] Vide [see] Protest of the minority of the convention of Pennsylvania, Martin's speech, etc. [The "Protest" was against Pennsylvania's ratification of the Constitution, signed by twenty-one members of that state's Constitutional Convention, and printed in *The Pennsylvania Packet and Daily Advertiser*, December 18, 1787. "Martin's speech" may be one opposing the proposed Constitution by Luther Martin, member of the Constitutional Convention, before the Maryland House of Delegates on January 27, 1788.]
4   *connive* Give unspoken consent (to something wrong).

5   *mitigating* Reducing (severity).
6   *iniquitous* Unjust or unfair.
7   *disinterested* Impartial.
8   *complaisance to* Seeking to please.

quently remarked with great propriety,[1] that a voluminous code of laws is one of the inconveniences necessarily connected with the advantages of a free government. To avoid an arbitrary discretion in the courts, it is indispensable that they should be bound down by strict rules and precedents, which serve to define and point out their duty in every particular case that comes before them; and it will readily be conceived from the variety of controversies which grow out of the folly and wickedness of mankind, that the records of those precedents must unavoidably swell to a very considerable bulk, and must demand long and laborious study to acquire a competent knowledge of them. Hence it is that there can be but few men in the society, who will have sufficient skill in the laws to qualify them for the stations of judges. And making the proper deductions for the ordinary depravity of human nature, the number must be still smaller of those who unite the requisite integrity with the requisite knowledge. These considerations apprise us, that the government can have no great option between fit characters; and that a temporary duration in office, which

would naturally discourage such characters from quitting a lucrative line of practice to accept a seat on the bench, would have a tendency to throw the administration of justice into hands less able, and less well qualified to conduct it with utility and dignity. In the present circumstances of this country, and in those in which it is likely to be for a long time to come, the disadvantages on this score would be greater than they may at first sight appear; but it must be confessed that they are far inferior to those which present themselves under the other aspects of the subject.

Upon the whole there can be no room to doubt that the convention acted wisely in copying from the models of those constitutions which have established *good behavior* as the tenure of their judicial offices in point of duration; and that so far from being blamable on this account, their plan would have been inexcusably defective if it had wanted this important feature of good government. The experience of Great Britain affords an illustrious comment on the excellence of the institution.

PUBLIUS.

---

1   *with great propriety*   Properly.

OLYMPE DE GOUGES
(1748 – 1793)

Olympe de Gouges was a playwright, pamphleteer, and feminist revolutionary. Born and christened Marie Gouze in the southwest of France into a *petit bourgeois* family, her first language was Occitan (Provençal). She received little formal education and, in 1865, she married a French officer, Louis Aubrey, with whom she had a son. After the death of her husband three years later, she left for Paris, declaring marriage to be *le tombeau de la confiance et de l'amour*—the death of trust and love.

In Paris, she improved her French and began her literary career. Her play *Zamore et Mirza, ou l'heureux naufrage* ("Zamora and Mirza, or the Happy Shipwreck") was performed by the Comédie-Française on June 30, 1785 and later published as *L'Esclavage des nègres* ("Black Slavery") in 1792. This work, along with *Réflexions sur les hommes nègres* (1788) ("Reflections on Black Men") and *Le Marché des Noirs* (1790) ("The March of the Blacks") established her as an early anti-slavery advocate.

During this time, she published political posters and manifestos calling for the equality of the sexes, including the right to vote and the rights of divorce and sexual freedom; the full recognition of illegitimate children; solidarity with the poor, including the creation of national workshops for the unemployed and shelters for beggars; people's juries for criminal trials; and the abolition of the death penalty. When the French Revolution began in 1789, she initially greeted it with enthusiasm. This enthusiasm waned when she found the revolutionaries reluctant to extend the rights they had successfully fought for to women. In 1791 the French Constituent National Assembly published "*Déclaration des droits de l'homme et du citoyen*" ("Declaration of the Rights of Man and of the Citizen") as the preamble to the constitutional law that Louis XVI was to sign. Only a few days later, Gouges distributed her most famous work, "*Déclaration des droits de la femme et de la citoyenne*" ("Declaration of the Rights of Woman and of the Female Citizen,") a slightly but crucially amended work in which women were accorded equal and full political rights.

Her opposition to what she saw as the injustices of the revolution grew, and she associated with the Griondistes, a political group which had strongly advocated the Revolution, but who afterwards, repelled by post-revolutionary terror and anarchy, urged moderation. In 1792, her opposition to the execution of King Louis XVI brought her a good deal of criticism. In 1793, she published *Les trois urnes, ou le salut de la Patrie, par un voyageur aérien* ("The Three Urns, or the Health of the Country, By An Aerial Voyager"); here she argued that the French should be given a choice among three modes of government: a federal republic, a more monolithic republic, or a constitutional monarchy. This led to her arrest and trial. Charged with monarchist anti-Republican sympaties and counter-revolutionary agitation, she was condemned to death. Though she had the opportunity to escape, she chose instead to contest the decision, publishing two pamphlets *Olympe de Gouges au Tribunal révolutionnaire* ("Olympe de Gouges before the Revolutionary Court") and *Une patriote persécutée* ("A Persecuted Patriot"). On November 3, 1793, she was executed on the guillotine.

◆ ◆ ◆ ◆ ◆

Declaration of the Rights of Woman and the Female Citizen (1791)

[*The main part of Gouge's* Declaration *is a rewriting of the French National Assembly's* Declaration of the Rights of Man and the Citizen. *Both consist of a "Preamble" and twenty-seven articles. The translation of Gouge's rewrite is in the left column below; to the right, for the purpose of comparison, is the translation of the* Declaration of the Rights of Man and the Citizen. *Gouge's* Declaration *is preceded by her introductory passage and followed by her "Postamble."*]

Man, are you capable of being just? It is a woman who asks you this question; at least you will not deny her this right. Tell me! Who has given you the sovereign authority to oppress my sex? Your strength? Your talents? Observe the creator in his wisdom; survey nature in all her grandeur, with which you seem to want to be in harmony; and give me, if you dare, an example of such tyrannical empire. Go back to the animals, consider the elements, study the plants, then glance over all the modifications of organized matter, and yield to the evidence when I offer you the means. Seek, probe, and distinguish, if you can, the sexes in the administration of nature. Everywhere you will find them mingled, everywhere they cooperate in harmony in this immortal masterpiece.

♦ ♦ ♦ ♦ ♦

Preamble

The mothers, daughters, and sisters, representatives of the nation, demand to be constituted a national assembly. Believing that ignorance, disregard of or contempt for the rights of women are the only causes of public calamities and of governmental corruption, they have resolved to set forth, in a solemn declaration, the natural, inalienable and sacred rights of woman; in order that this declaration, being constantly before all members of society, shall remind them continually of their rights and duties; in order that the acts based on women's power and those based on the power of men, may be constantly compared with the goal of all political institutions, may thus be more respected; and so that the demands of female citizens, based henceforth on simple and indisputable principles, may always uphold the constitution and good morals, and may contribute to the happiness of all.

Therefore, the sex that is superior in beauty as well as in courage of maternal suffering, recognizes and proclaims, in the presence, and under the auspices, of the Supreme Being, the following rights of woman and citizen.

1. Women are born free and remain equal in rights to man. Social distinctions may be based only on considerations of the general good.

2. The aim of every political association is the preservation of the natural and irrevocable rights of women and men. These rights are liberty, property, security, and especially resistance to oppression.

Man alone has made his exceptional circumstance a principle. He—bizarre, blind, bloated by science, degenerate, grossly ignorant in this century of enlightenment and wisdom, wishes to exercise despotic command of a sex in full possession of its intellectual faculties; he claims to rejoice in the Revolution and claims his own rights to equality, but then says say nothing more about it.

Preamble

The representatives of the French people, organized in National Assembly, believing that ignorance, disregard of, or contempt for the rights of man are the only causes of public calamities and of the governmental corruption, have resolved to set forth, in a solemn declaration, the natural, inalienable, and sacred rights of man, in order that this declaration, being constantly before all members of the society, shall remind them continually of their rights and duties; in order that the acts of the legislative power, as well as those of the executive power, may be constantly compared with the goal of all political institutions and may thus be more respected, and in order that the demands of citizens, based henceforth on simple and indisputable principles, may always uphold the constitution and contribute to the happiness of all.

Therefore the National Assembly recognizes and proclaims, in the presence, and under the auspices, of the Supreme Being, the following rights of man and of the citizen:

1. Men are born and remain free and equal in rights. Social distinctions may be based only on considerations of the general good.

2. The aim of every political association is the preservation of the natural and irrevocable rights of man. These rights are liberty, property, security, and resistance to oppression.

3. The principle of all sovereignty resides essentially in the Nation, which is nothing other than the union of women and man; no group nor individual may exercise any authority that is not expressly derived from it.

4. Liberty and justice consist of rendering to persons those things that belong to them; thus, the exercise of woman's natural rights is limited only by the perpetual tyranny with which man opposes her; these limits must be changed according to the laws of nature and reason.

5. The laws of nature and of reason prohibit all acts harmful to society; whatever is not prohibited by these wise and divine laws may not be interfered with, and no one may be forced to do anything not required by law.

6. The law should be the expression of the general will: all female and male citizens must participate in its making, personally or through their representatives. It must be the same for all; all female and male citizens, being equal in the eyes of the law, should be equally eligible for all high offices, public positions, and occupations, according to their abilities and with no distinction other than those of their virtues and talents.

7. No woman is immune; she can be accused, arrested, or detained in the cases determined by law. Women, like men, must obey these rigorous laws.

8. Only punishments strictly and obviously necessary may be established by law. No one may be punished except under a law established and promulgated before the offense occurred, and which is legally applicable to women.

9. If any woman is declared guilty, then the law must be rigorously enforced.

10. People shall not be punished for their opinions. Women have the right to mount the scaffold; they should equally have the right to speak in public, provided that this expression of their views does not disrupt the public order established by law.

3. The principle of all sovereignty resides essentially in the nation. No group nor individual may exercise any authority that is not expressly derived from it.

4. Liberty consists in the freedom to do anything that harms no one else; hence the exercise of man's natural rights has no limits except those that assure other members of society the enjoyment of the same rights. These limits can only be determined by law.

5. Law can prohibit only those actions that are harmful to society. Whatever is not prohibited by law may not be interfered with, and no one may be forced to do anything not required by law.

6. Law is the expression of the general will. Every citizen must participate in its making, personally, or through his representative. It must be the same for all, whether it protects or punishes. All citizens, being equal in the eyes of the law, should be equally eligible for all high offices, public positions, and occupations, according to their abilities, and without distinction other than those of their virtues and talents.

7. No person shall be accused, arrested, or detained except in the cases, and according to the procedures, determined by law. Those who solicit, expedite, carry out, or cause to be carried out, any arbitrary order, shall be punished. But any citizen summoned or apprehended in accord with the law shall submit without delay, as resistance constitutes an offense.

8. Only punishments strictly and obviously necessary may be established by law. No one may be punished except under a law established and promulgated before the offense occurred, and which is legally applied.

9. As all persons are held innocent until they have been declared guilty; if arrest is deemed necessary, any force beyond the minimum essential for security shall be strictly prevented by law.

10. People shall not be punished for their opinions, even their religious views, provided that the expression of their views does not disrupt the public order established by law.

11. Free communication of thought and opinion is one of the most precious rights of woman, since this liberty assures the recognition of the paternity of children by their fathers. Every female citizen can therefore freely say: "I am the mother of a child that belongs to you," without being subject to the barbaric prejudice forcing her to conceal the truth; but she must also be responsible for abuse of this freedom, as determined by law.

12. Guarantee of the rights of woman and female citizens requires the existence of army and police. Such guarantee is therefore to be established for the good of everyone, not for the personal benefit of those who are entrusted to perform this service.

13. For the maintenance of public forces and administrative expenses, taxation of women and men shall be equal; women share in all forced labor and all painful tasks, therefore they should have the same share in the distribution of positions, tasks, assignments, honors, and jobs.

14. Female and male citizens have the right to determine the necessity for a public tax, either by themselves or through their representatives. This can apply to female citizens only if they are given an equal share not only of wealth, but also of the public administration and the determination of the amount, the method of assessment, and the duration of taxes.

15. The collectivity of women, their contributions joined with those of men, have the right make public officials give an account of their administration.

16. Any society in which the guarantee of rights is not assured, or the separation of powers not determined, has no constitution at all. The constitution is invalid if the majority of individuals who make up the nation have not participated in its creation.

17. Property belongs to both sexes, whether united or separate, and is for each an inviolable and sacred right; since it is a true inheritance of nature, no one may be deprived of it except in cases of legally determined public necessity, and then only on condition that the owner shall have been previously and equitably compensated.

11. The free communication of ideas and opinions is one of the most precious rights of man. Every citizen may therefore freely speak, write, and publish, but he must also shall be responsible for abuse of this freedom as determined by law.

12. The security of the rights of man and of the citizen requires the existence of army and police. These forces are, therefore, to be established for the good of everyone and not for the personal benefit of those who are entrusted to perform this service.

13. For the maintenance of public forces and administrative expenses, a common tax is essential. This should be equitably shared by all citizens in proportion to their means.

14. All citizens have a right to determine the necessity for a public tax, either personally or through their representatives; to grant this freely; to watch over how it is used; and to determine the amount, the method of assessment, and the duration of taxes.

15. Society has the right to make public officials give an account of their administration.

16. A society in which the guarantee of rights is not assured, or the separation of powers not determined, has no constitution at all.

17. Since property is an inviolable and sacred right, no one may be deprived of it except in cases of legally determined public necessity, and then only on condition that the owner shall have been previously and equitably compensated.

Postamble

Women, wake up! The alarm bell of reason is sounding throughout the Universe; discover your rights. The powerful empire of nature is no longer surrounded by prejudices, fanaticism, superstition, and lies. The torch of truth has dispelled all the clouds of stupidity and usurpation. When he was enslaved, man gathered his strength and multiplied his forces; he needed to draw upon your strength to break his own chains. Having become free, he has become unjust toward his companion. Oh Women! Women! When will you cease to be blind? What advantages have you gained in the Revolution?[1] A more marked scorn, a more pronounced disdain. During centuries of corruption, you reigned only over the weakness of men. Your empire is destroyed; what then remains for you? The proof of man's injustice. To claim of your inheritance founded on the wise decrees of nature—what have you to fear from such a splendid enterprise? The good word of the governor at the marriage of Cana?[2] Do you not fear that our French legislators, correcting this morality, attached for so long to the realm of politics but no longer fashionable, will again say to you, "Women, what do we have in common with you?" You must answer, "Everything!" If, in their weakness, they persist in drawing this conclusion contradicting their principles, you must courageously use the force of reason against their vain pretensions of superiority. Unite yourselves under the banner of philosophy; deploy all the energy of your character, and soon you will see these prideful ones not longer groveling with servile adoration at your feet, but proud to share with you the treasures of the Supreme Being. Whatever the obstacles that are put in your way, it is in your power to overturn them; you have only to want to do it. Let us turn now to the frightful picture of what you have been in society; and since there is currently a question of national education, let us see if our wise legislators will think wisely about the education of women.

Women have done more evil than good. They have had their share in coercion and deceit. When forcibly abused, they have reacted with deceptive scheming; they have had recourse to all the resources of their charms, and the most irreproachable have not resisted them. They have used poison and the sword; they have called up crime and virtue alike. For centuries, the French government in particular has depended on the night-time administration of women; officials kept no secrets from their indiscretion: embassy, military command, the ministry, presidency of a court, the papacy, the college of cardinals—one might say everything profane and sacred subject to the foolishness of man has been subordinated to the greed and ambition of the female sex, which was formerly respected yet contemptible and, since the revolution, is still respectable and yet contemptible....

---

1   *Revolution* Gouges refers to the French Revolution, which began in 1789 and was still underway when she wrote in 1791.

2   *The good word ... Cana* The reference here is to John 2. The wine ran out at this wedding, and Jesus performed his first miracle, turning water into wine. Then: "When the ruler of the feast had tasted the water that had been made into wine, and knew not where it had come from (but the servants which drew the water knew), the governor of the feast called the bridegroom and said unto him, 'Every man at the beginning of a feast sets out good wine; and when men have drunk well of that, the host starts to serve the lower-quality wine: but you have kept the good wine until now'" (John 2, 9–10). This story is sometimes taken by Christians to confirm the sanctity of marriage.

MARY WOLLSTONECRAFT
(1759 – 1797)

Who Was Mary Wollstonecraft?

As one of the first to formulate an extended set of arguments that gave questions of gender a central place in social and political matters, Mary Wollstonecraft, an eighteenth-century British writer, has secured a lasting place of prominence in Western political philosophy.

Wollstonecraft was born in 1759 into a well-off London family. Her father, however, was a drunken, violent, spendthrift who squandered the family's modest fortune during Mary's childhood years (including money that Mary was to have inherited from another relative at 21). The family moved frequently as her father tried, and repeatedly failed, to make a go of farming in Epping, Whalebone (East London), Essex, Yorkshire, and Wales. They finally moved back to London when Mary was 18.

During these years Mary came to adopt a protective role toward her mother and two younger sisters. She sometimes slept outside the door of her mother's bedroom as a teenager in order to protect her from her father's alcohol-fueled rages. Later she nursed her sister, Eliza, after the difficult birth of Eliza's daughter. Eliza was probably suffering from postpartum depression, and Mary also suspected that her husband abused her; Mary convinced her sister to leave her husband, and helped her to do so. Unfortunately, Eliza was forced to leave behind her baby, who died within the year; this left Eliza disgraced in society, unable to remarry, and she spent the rest of her life struggling against poverty.

Wollstonecraft was also a passionate friend. A key friendship in her early life was with Fanny Blood, with whom she dreamed of setting up a female utopia. Together with Wollstonecraft's sisters they set up a school in Newington Green, London (a center for non-conformist religious communities). Before long, however, Blood became engaged and left the school. Blood's husband, Hugh Skeys, took her to Europe to try to improve her delicate health, but when she became pregnant she fell seriously ill. Wollstonecraft visited her in Lisbon to try and nurse her to health, but Blood died of complications from premature childbirth in 1785. This was a severe emotional blow for Wollstonecraft, and part of the inspiration for her first novel *Mary, a Fiction* (1788).

On Wollstonecraft's return to England[1] she closed the school—which had declined in her absence—and took a position as governess to the daughters of Lord Viscount Kingsborough in Ireland. She stayed with the Kingsboroughs for a year, and then made a decision which, for that time, was almost unprecedented: she decided to attempt to support herself as an author. Some of the reasons for doing so are set out in her first work, *Thoughts on the Education of Daughters* (1787), subtitled "The Unfortunate Situation of Females, Fashionably Educated, and Left Without a Fortune," in which she expresses her frustration at the very limited opportunities available for "respectable" women who nevertheless needed to work.

Wollstonecraft moved to London where, encouraged and assisted by the radical liberal publisher and bookseller Joseph Johnson, she settled down to make her living by writing. She learned French and German so that she could work as a translator of Continental texts, and wrote reviews, some of which were published in Johnson's liberal *Analytical Review*. She also published two books. *A Vindication of the Rights of Man* (1790) was a response to Edmund Burke's conservative critique of the French Revolution in *Reflections on the Revolution in France*. Its even more famous and influential partner was *A Vindication of the Rights of Woman* (1792).

Wollstonecraft soon began to move in radical intellectual circles, and became acquainted with Thomas Paine,

---

1   One anecdote from this period is illustrative of Wollstonecraft's character: on the voyage home from Portugal, she brow-beat the captain of the ship into rescuing a wrecked French vessel that he wanted to pass by.

Joseph Priestley, Samuel Coleridge, William Blake, William Wordsworth and William Godwin. During this period she became enraptured with the painter Henry Fuseli and pursued a relationship with him even though he was already married. In typically forthright fashion, Wollstonecraft proposed that she come to live with Fuseli and his wife in order to carry on a platonic relationship with the artist; Fuseli's wife was appalled and he broke off his relationship with her.

Humiliated, Wollstonecraft left for Paris late in 1792 in order to escape London and to witness first-hand the revolutionary events in France. She arrived alone in a country in turmoil, only a few weeks before the execution of the deposed king, Louis XVI. Wollstonecraft plunged into the excitement, and quickly fell passionately in love with an American adventurer named Gilbert Imlay (formerly an officer in the American Revolutionary War, he was acting as a diplomatic representative of the US while simultaneously lining his pockets by running the British blockade of French ports). Although Imlay had no interest in marrying her—and Wollstonecraft herself had strong reservations about marriage—she became pregnant with her first daughter, Fanny. After Britain declared war on France in 1793 Imlay registered Wollstonecraft as his wife in order to protect her from being arrested as a British citizen; however he did not marry her, and after leaving her at Le Havre, where she was to give birth, he never returned. Through all this Wollstonecraft continued her writing, publishing *An Historical and Moral View of the French Revolution* in 1794. The violent excesses she had witnessed caused her to temper her radical zeal somewhat, but she remained committed to democratic and egalitarian principles.

Wollstonecraft finally returned to London in 1795 and sought out Imlay, who had left France for England sometime earlier. Imlay, who had begun an affair with a young actress, rejected her,[1] but when she attempted to commit suicide with an overdose of tincture of opium he saved her life. In a last desperate attempt to win back his affections Wollstonecraft undertook to travel to Scandinavia—taking only her maid and young daughter—to attempt to track down a ship's captain who had absconded with a small fortune in Imlay's money intended to buy Swedish goods

to import to France. But when she got back to England it became clear to her that Imlay would never return her love for him. Once again, she attempted suicide—by jumping into the Thames—and once again she was saved, this time by a passing stranger.

Gradually Wollstonecraft's depression began to lift and—throwing off any financial support from Imlay—she returned to the literary life she had previously pursued in London. Cautiously, she entered once more into a love affair, this time with the journalist, novelist and utilitarian philosopher, William Godwin. The relationship was a happy and mutually reciprocated one, and when Wollstonecraft became pregnant they decided to marry. This forced Wollstonecraft to reveal publicly that her "marriage" to Imlay had been a fake one, and once again she became the subject of social scandal. Godwin, too, was attacked, this time by some of his radical friends, because he had argued in his *Enquiry Concerning Political Justice* (1793) that marriage should be abolished as a social institution.

Wollstonecraft and Godwin were wed in March 1797; so that they could retain their independence, they moved into adjoining houses in London. Wollstonecraft was full of plans for the future, and embarked on a new novel, to be called *Maria; or, The Wrongs of Woman*. In August, Wollstonecraft gave birth to her second daughter, Mary; but although at first the delivery seemed to go well, Wollstonecraft developed septicemia and died several days later. She was 38.

Godwin was grief-stricken. In 1798 he published his *Memoirs of the Author of a Vindication of the Rights of Woman* which, though deeply felt and sincere, caused yet more scandal for revealing in print the history of his dead wife's love affairs, illegitimate child, and suicide attempts. Their daughter, Mary Godwin, went on to elope with the Romantic poet Percy Bysshe Shelley, and to write *Frankenstein* (1818), as well as a number of other novels.

What Was Wollstonecraft's Overall Philosophical Project?

Wollstonecraft is best known for her argument, presented in *A Vindication of the Rights of Woman*, that women and men are inherently equal—equally rational, equally intelligent, equally moral—and that any appearances of intellectual or moral inequality are an artifact of differing education and social upbringing. She proposed a new social order, which would better serve the natural capacities of human beings,

---

1 Virginia Woolf's diagnosis of Imlay's feelings about Wollstonecraft is delightful (though possibly too charitable to him): "Tickling minnows he had hooked a dolphin, and the creature rushed him through the waters till he was dizzy and only wanted to escape" (from "Four Figures").

in which men and women are both treated as rational, autonomous beings. She argued that social changes of this sort would produce citizens—especially female citizens—that were better able to serve social justice, which would in turn produce a better, more robust, and more healthy society, which would then raise even more virtuous citizens, and so on in an upward spiral of social progress. Thus, equality for women would benefit all members of society, male as well as female.

A key concern for Wollstonecraft was the importance of personal independence. For her, self-government was a key aspect of individual human development. In particular, moral virtue essentially involves acting autonomously on the basis of moral principles. These principles, according to Wollstonecraft, do not arise merely out of sympathy for others or other moral passions, or in accordance with merely social strictures, but are grasped by rational reflection on the attributes of God and on God's design as manifested through human nature.

The importance of stressing rational thought in the education of females was another significant theme for Wollstonecraft, beginning with one of her earliest works, the children's book *Original Stories from Real Life* (1788), which encourages a balance between reason and emotion. In *A Vindication of the Rights of Woman*, though she does not denigrate passion, Wollstonecraft urges women not to be "blown about by every momentary gust of feeling" but to temper feeling with rational reflection.

What Is the Structure of the Reading?

A Vindication of the Rights of Woman is divided into thirteen chapters; Wollstonecraft wrote these chapters hurriedly, as a response to current events, and intended them to be only Volume 1 of the work. However she died before she was able to complete Volume 2, which she envisaged as a more deliberate discussion of the issues raised in the first volume. A large portion of chapters 1 to 6 are reprinted here, plus long excerpts from chapters 9 and 12. These are preceded by an introduction and by Wollstonecraft's dedication to Talleyrand—whose report on education to the French National Assembly, in which he recommended that women be educated only in domestic science, spurred her into writing.

Wollstonecraft begins by discussing the relation between human nature and the good society, and then describes the harmful social effects of "artificial manners and virtues." She applies this discussion to the social asymmetries between women and men; she criticizes various arguments purporting to show that women are naturally inferior to men, while arguing that it is distorting social forces that make them appear so. Chapter 4 discusses the "state of degradation" to which these social forces, particularly early education, have reduced womankind.

In Chapter 5 Wollstonecraft debates four writers who had belittled the status of women; we reprint here her discussion of the first, Rousseau. Chapter 6 deals with the importance of early education, while Chapter 9 emphasizes the harm caused to both women and society by "the unnatural distinctions established in society." The twelfth chapter is on public education, and Wollstonecraft argues in particular for co-educational day schools. A concluding section from Chapter 13 is also included here.

Some Useful Background Information

i) Wollstonecraft was primarily a political reformer, rather than a philosopher. She saw herself as applying quasi-scientific reasoning—generalizations from her own experience and that of others—to the practical, social problems of the day. She had little interest in formulating an overarching, comprehensive conceptual framework for her ideas.

ii) Wollstonecraft divided human attributes into natural and non-natural characteristics. Society plays a major role in guiding the development of individuals, and thus may either be beneficial in fostering natural characteristics or harmful in distorting human nature. A rationally constructed society, then, can be a powerful force for progress.

Artificial distinctions between the sexes are, for Wollstonecraft, a key example of social corruption of human nature, giving rise to social injustice and personal immorality, and preventing individuals from developing their full natural potential.

iii) Among the currents in eighteenth-century thought that influenced Wollstonecraft was the notion of sensibility—a term then widely used to refer to a heightened sensitivity or responsiveness towards aspects of one's environment, especially beauty, moral truth, or emotional tone. Sensibility was often considered a sign of fragility—those sensible to their environment in these ways might easily be overcome by their heightened experiences. But it was also considered by many to be a virtue, and those possessing it to display a kind of perceptiveness lacking in those less sensitive.

Some Common Misconceptions

i) Wollstonecraft would not have called herself a feminist—the word did not come into currency until the end of the nineteenth century—and it is unclear to what extent she can be treated as a thinker putting forward an early version of modern feminism. Certainly, she needs to be seen in the context of her own time as well as through the lens of modern feminism. Wollstonecraft did not argue for equal political or economic rights for men and women, and she did not argue that women should be allowed the vote. Although she generally thought of men and women as being, innately, mental and moral equals, she acknowledged that men were typically stronger than women, and believed them also to be physically braver than women.

ii) Wollstonecraft is often identified with the liberal tradition in feminism, particularly because of her debt to John Locke's thought on education and her emphasis on the rational, self-determining individual as the key unit of society. But she also placed heavy emphasis on the familial and civic duties of women, as well as their rights, and was sensitive to the need for bringing change to, as it were, indirectly oppressive social structures such as *male* education.

iii) In most of her writings, Wollstonecraft also differs from modern writers on the same topics in that she focuses on the plight of middle-class (Western) women, and shows no signs of an awareness that women may share similar interests, in virtue of their gender, no matter what their income-level or ethnicity. However, her final, uncompleted novel *Maria* contains some hints that Wollstonecraft had begun to take more seriously the similarities between the oppression of middle-class and of poor women.

iv) The notion that men and women should be treated as equally rational and educated along similar lines may seem banal today in modern Western democracies, but in Wollstonecraft's day it emphatically was not. Wollstonecraft was responding to popular conduct-books, such as James Fordyce's *Sermons for Young Women* (1760) and John Gregory's *A Father's Legacy to His Daughters* (1774), and to educational philosophers such as Rousseau, who notoriously wrote in book 5 of *Emile* (1762) that "all the education of women must be relative to men. To please them, to be useful to them, to make oneself loved and honored by them, to raise them when they are young, to care for them when they are grown ... these are the duties of women at all times and what one ought to teach them from their childhood."

How Important and Influential Is This Work?

Mary Wollstonecraft's reputation—never very secure during her own lifetime—was heavily affected by her husband's memoir of her "scandalous" and emotionally turbulent life. For many decades, she was, more than anything else, a figure of derision and pity (see, e.g., Richard Polwhele's 1798 poem "The Unsex'd Females"). In the late nineteenth century figures within the nascent feminist movement rediscovered the power of her ideas—and, for some, the inspirational example of her own unconventional life story. (For example, Virginia Woolf praised Wollstonecraft for her "experiments in living.") By the 1970s Wollstonecraft was recognized as a trail blazer for modern feminism. A further re-evaluation of Wollstonecraft occurred in the 1990s, with more focus on her ideas and the source of those ideas in the intellectual currents of the eighteenth century. Today, *A Vindication of the Rights of Woman* is considered a classic in the history of Western thought, and an important bridge between Enlightenment and Romantic ideas.

◆ ◆ ◆ ◆ ◆

A Vindication of the Rights of Woman: with Strictures on Political and Moral Subjects (1792)

To M. Talleyrand-Pélleyrand-Périgord, Late Bishop of Autun[1]

Sir,

Having read with great pleasure a pamphlet which you have lately published,[2] I dedicate this volume to you; to induce you to reconsider the subject, and maturely weigh what I have advanced respecting the rights of woman and national education: and I call with the firm tone of humanity; for my arguments, Sir, are dictated by a disinterested spirit—I plead for my sex—not for myself. Independence I have long considered as the grand blessing of life, the basis of every virtue—and independence I will ever secure by contracting my wants, though I were to live on a barren heath.

It is then an affection for the whole human race that makes my pen dart rapidly along to support what I believe to be the cause of virtue: and the same motive leads me earnestly to wish to see woman placed in a station in which she would advance, instead of retarding, the progress of those glorious principles that give a substance to morality. My opinion, indeed, respecting the rights and duties of woman, seems to flow so naturally from these simple principles, that I think it scarcely possible, but that some of the enlarged minds who formed your admirable constitution, will coincide with me.

---

1   *M. Talleyrand-Pélleyrand-Périgord, Late Bishop of Autun*   Charles-Maurice de Talleyrand-Périgord (1754–1838) was made Bishop of Autun in 1788. As minister of finance in the French revolutionary government, he initiated the confiscation of church property that so exercised Burke in *Reflections on the Revolution in France*. He resigned his bishopric in January 1791 and was excommunicated that April.

2   *pamphlet which you have lately published*   The pamphlet referred to was entitled *Rapport sur l'instruction publique, fait au nom du Comité de Constitution à l'Assemblée Nationale, les 10, 11, et 19 Septembre 1791, par M. de Talleyrand-Périgord, Ancien Évêque d'Autun.* (*Report on public instruction, written in the name of the Constitutional Committee of the National Assembly, September, 10, 11 and 19, by Mr. de Talleyrand-Périgord, Late Bishop of Autun.*) Talleyrand prepared the report with the help of such distinguished thinkers as Condorcet and Laplace.

In France there is undoubtedly a more general diffusion of knowledge than in any part of the European world, and I attribute it, in a great measure, to the social intercourse which has long subsisted between the sexes. It is true, I utter my sentiments with freedom, that in France the very essence of sensuality has been extracted to regale the voluptuary, and a kind of sentimental lust has prevailed, which, together with the system of duplicity that the whole tenour of their political and civil government taught, have given a sinister sort of sagacity to the French character, properly termed finesse; from which naturally flow a polish of manners that injures the substance, by hunting sincerity out of society.—And, modesty, the fairest garb of virtue! has been more grossly insulted in France than even in England, till their women have treated as *prudish* that attention to decency, which brutes instinctively observe.

Manners and morals are so nearly allied that they have often been confounded; but, though the former should only be the natural reflection of the latter, yet, when various causes have produced factitious and corrupt manners, which are very early caught, morality becomes an empty name. The personal reserve, and sacred respect for cleanliness and delicacy in domestic life, which French women almost despise, are the graceful pillars of modesty; but, far from despising them, if the pure flame of patriotism have reached their bosoms, they should labor to improve the morals of their fellow-citizens, by teaching men, not only to respect modesty in women, but to acquire it themselves, as the only way to merit their esteem.

Contending for the rights of woman, my main argument is built on this simple principle, that if she be not prepared by education to become the companion of man, she will stop the progress of knowledge and virtue; for truth must be common to all, or it will be inefficacious with respect to its influence on general practice. And how can woman be expected to co-operate unless she know why she ought to be virtuous? unless freedom strengthen her reason till she comprehend her duty, and see in what manner it is connected with her real good? If children are to be educated to understand the true principle of patriotism, their mother must be a patriot; and the love of mankind, from which an orderly train of virtues spring, can only be produced by considering the moral and civil interest of mankind; but the education and situation of woman, at present, shuts her out from such investigations.

In this work I have produced many arguments, which to me were conclusive, to prove that the prevailing notion respecting a sexual[1] character was subversive of morality, and I have contended, that to render the human body and mind more perfect, chastity must more universally prevail, and that chastity will never be respected in the male world till the person of a woman is not, as it were, idolized, when little virtue or sense embellish it with the grand traces of mental beauty, or the interesting simplicity of affection.

Consider, Sir, dispassionately, these observations—for a glimpse of this truth seemed to open before you when you observed, "that to see one half of the human race excluded by the other from all participation of government, was a political phaenomenon that, according to abstract principles, it was impossible to explain."[2] If so, on what does your constitution rest? If the abstract rights of man will bear discussion and explanation, those of woman, by a parity of reasoning, will not shrink from the same test: though a different opinion prevails in this country, built on the very arguments which you use to justify the oppression of woman—prescription.

Consider, I address you as a legislator, whether, when men contend for their freedom, and to be allowed to judge for themselves respecting their own happiness, it be not inconsistent and unjust to subjugate women, even though you firmly believe that you are acting in the manner best calculated to promote their happiness? Who made man the exclusive judge, if woman partake with him the gift of reason?

In this style, argue tyrants of every denomination, from the weak king to the weak father of a family; they are all eager to crush reason; yet always assert that they usurp its throne only to be useful. Do you not act a similar part, when you *force* all women, by denying them civil and political rights, to remain immured in their families groping in the dark? for surely, Sir, you will not assert, that a duty can be binding which is not founded on reason? If indeed this be their destination, arguments may be drawn from reason: and thus augustly supported, the more understanding women acquire, the more they will be attached to their duty—comprehending it—for unless they comprehend it, unless their morals be fixed on the same immutable principle as those of man, no authority can make them discharge

it in a virtuous manner. They may be convenient slaves, but slavery will have its constant effect, degrading the master and the abject dependent.

But, if women are to be excluded, without having a voice, from a participation of the natural rights of mankind, prove first, to ward off the charge of injustice and inconsistency, that they want reason—else this flaw in your new constitution will ever show that man must, in some shape, act like a tyrant, and tyranny, in whatever part of society it rears its brazen front, will ever undermine morality.

I have repeatedly asserted, and produced what appeared to me irrefragable[3] arguments drawn from matters of fact, to prove my assertion, that women cannot, by force, be confined to domestic concerns; for they will, however ignorant, intermeddle with more weighty affairs, neglecting private duties only to disturb, by cunning tricks, the orderly plans of reason which rise above their comprehension.

Besides, whilst they are only made to acquire personal accomplishments, men will seek for pleasure in variety, and faithless husbands will make faithless wives; such ignorant beings, indeed, will be very excusable when, not taught to respect public good, nor allowed any civil rights, they attempt to do themselves justice by retaliation.

The box of mischief thus opened in society, what is to preserve private virtue, the only security of public freedom and universal happiness?

Let there be then no coercion *established* in society, and the common law of gravity prevailing, the sexes will fall into their proper places. And, now that more equitable laws are forming your citizens, marriage may become more sacred: your young men may choose wives from motives of affection, and your maidens allow love to root out vanity.

The father of a family will not then weaken his constitution and debase his sentiments, by visiting the harlot, nor forget, in obeying the call of appetite, the purpose for which it was implanted. And, the mother will not neglect her children to practice the arts of coquetry, when sense and modesty secure her the friendship of her husband.

But, till men become attentive to the duty of a father, it is vain to expect women to spend that time in their nursery which they, "wise in their generation,"[4] choose to spend at their glass; for this exertion of cunning is only an instinct of nature to enable them to obtain indirectly a little of that power of which they are unjustly denied a share: for, if

---

1 *sexual* Wollstonecraft almost always uses this word to mean "gender-specific."

2 *that to see one half ... impossible to explain* Talleyrand, *Rapport* 118 (Appendix B.1.2). The French constitution of 1791 recognized only men over 25 as citizens; French women did not get the vote until 1944.

3 *irrefragable* Irrefutable.

4 *wise in their generation* Luke 16.8.

women are not permitted to enjoy legitimate rights, they will render both men and themselves vicious, to obtain illicit privileges.

I wish, Sir, to set some investigations of this kind afloat in France; and should they lead to a confirmation of my principles, when your constitution is revised the Rights of Woman may be respected, if it be fully proved that reason calls for this respect, and loudly demands justice for one half of the human race.

I am, Sir,
Yours respectfully,
M.W.

Advertisement

When I began to write this work, I divided it into three parts, supposing that one volume would contain a full discussion of the arguments which seemed to me to rise naturally from a few simple principles; but fresh illustrations occurring as I advanced, I now present only the first part to the public.

Many subjects, however, which I have cursorily alluded to, call for particular investigation, especially the laws relative to women, and the consideration of their peculiar duties. These will furnish ample matter for a second volume, which in due time will be published, to elucidate some of the sentiments, and complete many of the sketches begun in the first.[1]

Introduction

After considering the historic page, and viewing the living world with anxious solicitude, the most melancholy emotions of sorrowful indignation have depressed my spirits, and I have sighed when obliged to confess, that either nature has made a great difference between man and man, or that the civilization which has hitherto taken place in the world has been very partial. I have turned over various books written on the subject of education, and patiently observed the conduct of parents and the management of schools; but what has been the result?—a profound conviction that the neglected education of my fellow-creatures is

the grand source of the misery I deplore; and that women, in particular, are rendered weak and wretched by a variety of concurring causes, originating from one hasty conclusion. The conduct and manners of women, in fact, evidently prove that their minds are not in a healthy state; for, like the flowers which are planted in too rich a soil, strength and usefulness are sacrificed to beauty; and the flaunting leaves, after having pleased a fastidious eye, fade, disregarded on the stalk, long before the season when they ought to have arrived at maturity.—One cause of this barren blooming I attribute to a false system of education, gathered from the books written on this subject by men who, considering females rather as women than human creatures, have been more anxious to make them alluring mistresses than affectionate wives and rational mothers; and the understanding of the sex has been so bubbled by this specious homage, that the civilized women of the present century, with a few exceptions, are only anxious to inspire love, when they ought to cherish a nobler ambition, and by their abilities and virtues exact respect.

In a treatise, therefore, on female rights and manners, the works which have been particularly written for their improvement must not be overlooked; especially when it is asserted, in direct terms, that the minds of women are enfeebled by false refinement; that the books of instruction, written by men of genius, have had the same tendency as more frivolous productions; and that, in the true style of Mahometanism,[2] they are treated as a kind of subordinate beings, and not as a part of the human species, when improveable reason is allowed to be the dignified distinction which raises men above the brute creation, and puts a natural scepter in a feeble hand.

Yet, because I am a woman, I would not lead my readers to suppose that I mean violently to agitate the contested question respecting the equality or inferiority of the sex; but as the subject lies in my way, and I cannot pass it over without subjecting the main tendency of my reasoning to misconstruction, I shall stop a moment to deliver, in a few words, my opinion.—In the government of the physical world it is observable that the female in point of strength is, in general, inferior to the male. This is the law of nature; and it does not appear to be suspended or abrogated in favor of woman. A degree of physical superiority cannot, therefore, be denied—and it is a noble prerogative! But not content with this natural pre-eminence, men endeavor

---

1   *sketches begun in the first*   The second volume was never written; most scholars assume its place was taken by Wollstonecraft's unfinished novel *Maria; or, The Wrongs of Woman* (1798), which devotes considerable attention to "the laws relative to women."

2   *Mahometanism*   Islam.

to sink us still lower, merely to render us alluring objects for a moment; and women, intoxicated by the adoration which men, under the influence of their senses, pay them, do not seek to obtain a durable interest in their hearts, or to become the friends of the fellow creatures who find amusement in their society.

I am aware of an obvious inference—from every quarter have I heard exclamations against masculine women; but where are they to be found? If by this appellation men mean to inveigh against their ardor in hunting, shooting, and gaming, I shall most cordially join in the cry; but if it be against the imitation of manly virtues, or, more properly speaking, the attainment of those talents and virtues, the exercise of which ennobles the human character, and which raise females in the scale of animal being, when they are comprehensively termed mankind;—all those who view them with a philosophic eye must, I should think, wish with me, that they may every day grow more and more masculine.

This discussion naturally divides the subject. I shall first consider women in the grand light of human creatures, who, in common with men, are placed on this earth to unfold their faculties; and afterwards I shall more particularly point out their peculiar designation.

I wish also to steer clear of an error which many respectable writers have fallen into; for the instruction which has hitherto been addressed to women, has rather been applicable to *ladies*, if the little indirect advice, that is scattered through Sandford and Merton,[1] be excepted; but, addressing my sex in a firmer tone, I pay particular attention to those in the middle class, because they appear to be in the most natural state. Perhaps the seeds of false-refinement, immorality, and vanity, have ever been shed by the great. Weak, artificial beings, raised above the common wants and affections of their race, in a premature unnatural manner, undermine the very foundation of virtue, and spread corruption through the whole mass of society! As a class of mankind they have the strongest claim to pity; the education of the rich tends to render them vain and helpless, and the unfolding mind is not strengthened by the practice of those duties which dignify the human character.—They only live to amuse themselves, and by the same law which

in nature invariably produces certain effects, they soon only afford barren amusement.

But as I purpose taking a separate view of the different ranks of society, and of the moral character of women, in each, this hint is, for the present, sufficient; and I have only alluded to the subject, because it appears to me to be the very essence of an introduction to give a cursory account of the contents of the work it introduces.

My own sex, I hope, will excuse me, if I treat them like rational creatures, instead of flattering their *fascinating* graces, and viewing them as if they were in a state of perpetual childhood, unable to stand alone. I earnestly wish to point out in what true dignity and human happiness consists—I wish to persuade women to endeavor to acquire strength, both of mind and body, and to convince them that the soft phrases, susceptibility of heart, delicacy of sentiment, and refinement of taste, are almost synonymous with epithets of weakness, and that those beings who are only the objects of pity and that kind of love, which has been termed its sister, will soon become objects of contempt.

Dismissing then those pretty feminine phrases, which the men condescendingly use to soften our slavish dependence, and despising that weak elegancy of mind, exquisite sensibility, and sweet docility of manners, supposed to be the sexual characteristics of the weaker vessel, I wish to show that elegance is inferior to virtue, that the first object of laudable ambition is to obtain a character as a human being, regardless of the distinction of sex; and that secondary views should be brought to this simple touchstone.

This is a rough sketch of my plan; and should I express my conviction with the energetic emotions that I feel whenever I think of the subject, the dictates of experience and reflection will be felt by some of my readers. Animated by this important object, I shall disdain to cull my phrases or polish my style;—I aim at being useful, and sincerity will render me unaffected; for, wishing rather to persuade by the force of my arguments, than dazzle by the elegance of my language, I shall not waste my time in rounding periods, or in fabricating the turgid bombast of artificial feelings, which, coming from the head, never reach the heart.—I shall be employed about things, not words!—and, anxious to render my sex more respectable members of society, I shall try to avoid that flowery diction which has slided from essays into novels, and from novels into familiar letters and conversation.

These pretty superlatives, dropping glibly from the tongue, vitiate the taste, and create a kind of sickly delicacy

---

1   *Sandford and Merton* Thomas Day (1748–89), *The History of Sandford and Merton*, 3 vols. (1783–89), a moral tale written for nineteenth-century children. Wollstonecraft reviewed the third volume for the *Analytical Review* (*Works* 7: 174–76).

that turns away from simple unadorned truth; and a deluge of false sentiments and overstretched feelings, stifling the natural emotions of the heart, render the domestic pleasures insipid, that ought to sweeten the exercise of those severe duties, which educate a rational and immortal being for a nobler field of action.

The education of women has, of late, been more attended to than formerly; yet they are still reckoned a frivolous sex, and ridiculed or pitied by the writers who endeavor by satire or instruction to improve them. It is acknowledged that they spend many of the first years of their lives in acquiring a smattering of accomplishments; meanwhile strength of body and mind are sacrificed to libertine notions of beauty, to the desire of establishing themselves,—the only way women can rise in the world,—by marriage. And this desire making mere animals of them, when they marry they act as such children may be expected to act—they dress; they paint, and nickname God's creatures.—Surely these weak beings are only fit for a seraglio!—Can they be expected to govern a family with judgment, or take care of the poor babes whom they bring into the world?

If then it can be fairly deduced from the present conduct of the sex, from the prevalent fondness for pleasure which takes place of ambition and those nobler passions that open and enlarge the soul; that the instruction which women have hitherto received has only tended, with the constitution of civil society, to render them insignificant objects of desire—mere propagators of fools!—if it can be proved that in aiming to accomplish them, without cultivating their understandings, they are taken out of their sphere of duties, and made ridiculous and useless when the short-lived bloom of beauty is over,[1] I presume that *rational* men will excuse me for endeavoring to persuade them to become more masculine and respectable.

Indeed the word masculine is only a bugbear: there is little reason to fear that women will acquire too much courage or fortitude; for their apparent inferiority with respect to bodily strength, must render them, in some degree, dependent on men in the various relations of life; but why should it be increased by prejudices that give a sex to virtue, and confound simple truths with sensual reveries?

---

1   *when the short-lived bloom of beauty is over* [Wollstonecraft's note] A lively writer, I cannot recollect his name, asks what business women turned of forty have to do in the world? [Wollstonecraft may be thinking of a remark made by Lord Merton, a character in Frances Burney (1752–1840), *Evelina; or, The History of a Young Lady's Entrance into the World* (1778), Vol. 3, letter 1.]

Women are, in fact, so much degraded by mistaken notions of female excellence, that I do not mean to add a paradox when I assert, that this artificial weakness produces a propensity to tyrannize, and gives birth to cunning, the natural opponent of strength, which leads them to play off those contemptible infantine airs that undermine esteem even whilst they excite desire. Let men become more chaste and modest, and if women do not grow wiser in the same ratio, it will be clear that they have weaker understandings. It seems scarcely necessary to say, that I now speak of the sex in general. Many individuals have more sense than their male relatives; and, as nothing preponderates where there is a constant struggle for an equilibrium, without it has naturally more gravity, some women govern their husbands without degrading themselves, because intellect will always govern.

Part 1

from Chapter 1: The Rights and Involved Duties of Mankind Considered

In the present state of society it appears necessary to go back to first principles in search of the most simple truths, and to dispute with some prevailing prejudice every inch of ground. To clear my way, I must be allowed to ask some plain questions, and the answers will probably appear as unequivocal as the axioms on which reasoning is built; though, when entangled with various motives of action, they are formally contradicted, either by the words or conduct of men.

In what does man's pre-eminence over the brute creation consist? The answer is as clear as that a half is less than the whole; in Reason.

What acquirement exalts one being above another? Virtue; we spontaneously reply.

For what purpose were the passions implanted? That man by struggling with them might attain a degree of knowledge denied to the brutes; whispers Experience.

Consequently the perfection of our nature and capability of happiness, must be estimated by the degree of reason, virtue, and knowledge, that distinguish the individual, and direct the laws which bind society: and that from the exercise of reason, knowledge and virtue naturally flow, is equally undeniable, if mankind be viewed collectively.

The rights and duties of man thus simplified, it seems almost impertinent to attempt to illustrate truths that appear so incontrovertible; yet such deeply rooted prejudices have clouded reason, and such spurious qualities have assumed the name of virtues, that it is necessary to pursue the course of reason as it has been perplexed and involved in error, by various adventitious circumstances, comparing the simple axiom with casual deviations.

Men, in general, seem to employ their reason to justify prejudices, which they have imbibed, they can scarcely trace how, rather than to root them out. The mind must be strong that resolutely forms its own principles; for a kind of intellectual cowardice prevails which makes many men shrink from the task, or only do it by halves. Yet the imperfect conclusions thus drawn, are frequently very plausible, because they are built on partial experience, on just, though narrow, views.

Going back to first principles, vice skulks, with all its native deformity, from close investigation; but a set of shallow reasoners are always exclaiming that these arguments prove too much, and that a measure rotten at the core may be expedient. Thus expediency is continually contrasted with simple principles, till truth is lost in a mist of words, virtue, in forms, and knowledge rendered a sounding nothing, by the specious prejudices that assume its name.

That the society is formed in the wisest manner, whose constitution is founded on the nature of man, strikes, in the abstract, every thinking being so forcibly, that it looks like presumption to endeavor to bring forward proofs; though proof must be brought, or the strong hold of prescription will never be forced by reason; yet to urge prescription as an argument to justify the depriving men (or women) of their natural rights, is one of the absurd sophisms which daily insult common sense.

The civilization of the bulk of the people of Europe is very partial; nay, it may be made a question, whether they have acquired any virtues in exchange for innocence, equivalent to the misery produced by the vices that have been plastered over unsightly ignorance, and the freedom which has been bartered for splendid slavery. The desire of dazzling by riches, the most certain pre-eminence that man can obtain, the pleasure of commanding flattering sycophants, and many other complicated low calculations of doting self-love, have all contributed to overwhelm the mass of mankind, and make liberty a convenient handle for mock patriotism. For whilst rank and titles are held of the utmost importance, before which Genius "must hide its diminished head,"[1] it is, with a few exceptions, very unfortunate for a nation when a man of abilities, without rank or property, pushes himself forward to notice.—Alas! what unheard of misery have thousands suffered to purchase a cardinal's hat for an intriguing obscure adventurer, who longed to be ranked with princes, or lord it over them by seizing the triple crown![2]

Such, indeed, has been the wretchedness that has flowed from hereditary honors, riches, and monarchy, that men of lively sensibility have almost uttered blasphemy in order to justify the dispensations of providence. Man has been held out as independent of his power who made him, or as a lawless planet darting from its orbit to steal the celestial fire of reason; and the vengeance of heaven, lurking in the subtle flame, like Pandora's pent up mischiefs, sufficiently punished his temerity, by introducing evil into the world.[3]

Impressed by this view of the misery and disorder which pervaded society, and fatigued with jostling against artificial fools, Rousseau became enamored of solitude, and, being at the same time an optimist, he labors with uncommon eloquence to prove that man was naturally a solitary animal.[4] Misled by his respect for the goodness of God, who certainly—for what man of sense and feeling can doubt it!—gave life only to communicate happiness, he considers evil as positive, and the work of man; not aware that he was exalting one attribute at the expense of another, equally necessary to divine perfection.

Reared on a false hypothesis his arguments in favor of a state of nature are plausible, but unsound. I say unsound; for to assert that a state of nature is preferable to civilization, in all its possible perfection, is, in other words, to arraign supreme wisdom; and the paradoxical exclamation, that God has made all things right, and that error has been introduced by the creature, whom he formed,[5] knowing what he formed, is as unphilosophical as impious.

---

1   *must hide its diminished head* Milton, *Paradise Lost* 4.35.

2   *triple crown* The papal tiara.

3   *Pandora's pent up mischiefs ... evil into the world* In the Greek myth, Prometheus stole fire from heaven for the benefit of humanity. Zeus punished the theft by sending Pandora, the first woman, whose curiosity led her to open the "box of mischief," thus introducing evil into human life.

4   *solitary animal* Rousseau expresses his love of solitude in *Confessions* (1781–88) Books 8 and 9. Wollstonecraft reviewed the second part, which includes these books (*Works* 7: 228–34). Rousseau sets out his theory that humans are naturally solitary in *Discourse on the Origin and Foundations of Inequality among Men* (1755).

5   *and the paradoxical exclamation ... whom he formed* This is a paraphrase of the first sentence of Book 1 of Rousseau, *Emile*, 37.

When that wise Being who created us and placed us here, saw the fair idea, he willed, by allowing it to be so, that the passions should unfold our reason, because he could see that present evil would produce future good. Could the helpless creature whom he called from nothing break loose from his providence, and boldly learn to know good by practicing evil, without his permission? No.—How could that energetic advocate for immortality argue so inconsistently?[1] Had mankind remained for ever in the brutal state of nature, which even his magic pen cannot paint as a state in which a single virtue took root, it would have been clear, though not to the sensitive unreflecting wanderer, that man was born to run the circle of life and death, and adorn God's garden for some purpose which could not easily be reconciled with his attributes.

But if, to crown the whole, there were to be rational creatures produced, allowed to rise in excellence by the exercise of powers implanted for that purpose; if benignity itself thought fit to call into existence a creature above the brutes,[2] who could think and improve himself, why should that inestimable gift, for a gift it was, if man was so created as to have a capacity to rise above the state in which sensation produced brutal ease, be called, in direct terms, a curse? A curse it might be reckoned, if the whole of our existence were bounded by our continuance in this world; for why should the gracious fountain of life[3] give us passions, and the power of reflecting, only to imbitter our days and inspire us with mistaken notions of dignity? Why should he lead us from love of ourselves to the sublime emotions which the discovery of his wisdom and goodness excites, if these feelings were not set in motion to improve our nature, of which they make a part,[4] and render us capable of enjoying a more godlike portion of happiness? Firmly persuaded that no evil exists in the world that God did not design to take place, I build my belief on the perfection of God.

Rousseau exerts himself to prove that all *was* right originally: a crowd of authors that all *is* now right: and I, that all will *be* right.

But, true to his first position, next to a state of nature, Rousseau celebrates barbarism, and apostrophizing the shade of Fabricius,[5] he forgets that, in conquering the world, the Romans never dreamed of establishing their own liberty on a firm basis, or of extending the reign of virtue. Eager to support his system, he stigmatizes, as vicious, every effort of genius; and, uttering the apotheosis of savage virtues, he exalts those to demi-gods, who were scarcely human—the brutal Spartans, who, in defiance of justice and gratitude, sacrificed, in cold blood, the slaves who had shown themselves heroes to rescue their oppressors.[6]

Disgusted with artificial manners and virtues, the citizen of Geneva,[7] instead of properly sifting the subject, threw away the wheat with the chaff,[8] without waiting to inquire whether the evils which his ardent soul turned from indignantly, were the consequence of civilization or the vestiges of barbarism. He saw vice trampling on virtue, and the semblance of goodness taking place of the reality; he saw talents bent by power to sinister purposes, and never thought of tracing the gigantic mischief up to arbitrary power, up to the hereditary distinctions that clash with the mental superiority that naturally raises a man above his fellows. He did not perceive that regal power, in a few genera-

1 *How could that energetic advocate ... so inconsistently* See "Profession of Faith of the Savoyard Vicar," in Rousseau, *Emile*.

2 *above the brutes* [Wollstonecraft's note] Contrary to the opinion of anatomists, who argue by analogy from the formation of the teeth, stomach, and intestines, Rousseau will not allow a man to be a carnivorous animal. And, carried away from nature by a love of system, he disputes whether man be a gregarious animal, though the long and helpless state of infancy seems to point him out as particularly impelled to pair, the first step towards herding.

3 *gracious fountain of life* See Psalms 36.9 and Proverbs 14.27.

4 *make a part* [Wollstonecraft's note] What would you say to a mechanic whom you had desired to make a watch to point out the hour of the day, if, to show his ingenuity, he added wheels to make it a repeater, etc. that perplexed the simple mechanism; should he urge, to excuse himself—had you not touched a certain spring, you would have known nothing of the matter, and that he should have amused himself by making *an experiment* with-

out doing you any harm: would you not retort fairly upon him, by insisting that if he had not added those needless wheels and springs, the accident could not have happened? [A "repeater" was a watch that could strike the hour. The watch-maker analogy was a commonplace of eighteenth-century natural religion.]

5 *Fabricius* Rousseau addresses the shade of Gaius Fabricius (third century BCE), the virtuous Roman, who urged his countrymen to conquer the world, in *Discourse on the Sciences and Arts* (1750).

6 *brutal Spartans ... rescue their oppressors* During the Peloponnesian War, the Spartans invited their slaves to pick out those who had most distinguished themselves in fighting against the Athenians; two thousand were chosen. Instead of giving them their freedom, as they had promised, the Spartans murdered them, on the grounds that they were the most high-spirited and likely to rebel (Thucydides, *The Peloponnesian War* 4.14.81). For Rousseau's praise, see *Discourse on the Sciences and Arts* 43.

7 *citizen of Geneva* This is how Rousseau identifies himself on the title pages of both *Discourses*.

8 *wheat with the chaff* See Matthew 3.12.

tions, introduces idiotism into the noble stem, and holds out baits to render thousands idle and vicious.

[...]

Society, therefore, as it becomes more enlightened, should be very careful not to establish bodies of men who must necessarily be made foolish or vicious by the very constitution of their profession.

In the infancy of society, when men were just emerging out of barbarism, chiefs and priests, touching the most powerful springs of savage conduct, hope and fear, must have had unbounded sway. An aristocracy, of course, is naturally the first form of government. But, clashing interests soon losing their equipoise, a monarchy and hierarchy break out of the confusion of ambitious struggles, and the foundation of both is secured by feudal tenures. This appears to be the origin of monarchical and priestly power, and the dawn of civilization. But such combustible materials cannot long be pent up; and, getting vent in foreign wars and intestine insurrections, the people acquire some power in the tumult, which obliges their rulers to gloss over their oppression with a show of right. Thus, as wars, agriculture, commerce, and literature, expand the mind, despots are compelled, to make covert corruption hold fast the power which was formerly snatched by open force.[1] And this baneful lurking gangrene is most quickly spread by luxury and superstition, the sure dregs of ambition. The indolent puppet of a court first becomes a luxurious monster, or fastidious sensualist, and then makes the contagion which his unnatural state spread, the instrument of tyranny.

It is the pestiferous[2] purple which renders the progress of civilization a curse, and warps the understanding, till men of sensibility doubt whether the expansion of intellect produces a greater portion of happiness or misery. But the nature of the poison points out the antidote; and had Rousseau mounted one step higher in his investigation, or could his eye have pierced through the foggy atmosphere, which he almost disdained to breathe, his active mind would have darted forward to contemplate the perfection of man in the establishment of true civilization, instead of taking his ferocious flight back to the night of sensual ignorance.

---

1   *Thus, as wars ... snatched by open force*   [Wollstonecraft's note] Men of abilities scatter seeds that grow up and have a great influence on the forming opinion; and when once the public opinion preponderates, through the exertion of reason, the overthrow of arbitrary power is not very distant.

2   *pestiferous*   Pernicious; bringing disease.

from Chapter 2: The Prevailing Opinion of a Sexual Character Discussed

To account for, and excuse the tyranny of man, many ingenious arguments have been brought forward to prove, that the two sexes, in the acquirement of virtue, ought to aim at attaining a very different character: or, to speak explicitly, women are not allowed to have sufficient strength of mind to acquire what really deserves the name of virtue. Yet it should seem, allowing them to have souls, that there is but one way appointed by Providence to lead *mankind* to either virtue or happiness.

If then women are not a swarm of ephemeron triflers, why should they be kept in ignorance under the specious name of innocence? Men complain, and with reason, of the follies and caprices of our sex, when they do not keenly satirize our headstrong passions and groveling vices.—Behold, I should answer, the natural effect of ignorance! The mind will ever be unstable that has only prejudices to rest on, and the current will run with destructive fury when there are no barriers to break its force. Women are told from their infancy, and taught by the example of their mothers, that a little knowledge of human weakness, justly termed cunning, softness of temper, *outward* obedience, and a scrupulous attention to a puerile kind of propriety, will obtain for them the protection of man; and should they be beautiful, every thing else is needless, for, at least, twenty years of their lives.

Thus Milton describes our first frail mother; though when he tells us that women are formed for softness and sweet attractive grace,[3] I cannot comprehend his meaning, unless, in the true Mahometan strain, he meant to deprive us of souls, and insinuate that we were beings only designed by sweet attractive grace, and docile blind obedience, to gratify the senses of man when he can no longer soar on the wing of contemplation.

How grossly do they insult us who thus advise us only to render ourselves gentle, domestic brutes! For instance, the winning softness so warmly, and frequently, recommended, that governs by obeying. What childish expressions, and how insignificant is the being—can it be an immortal one? who will condescend to govern by such sinister methods! "Certainly," says Lord Bacon, "man is of kin to the beasts by his body; and if he be not of kin to God by his spirit, he

---

3   *Thus Milton describes ... sweet attractive grace*   Milton, *Paradise Lost* 4.297–98.

is a base and ignoble creature!"[1] Men, indeed, appear to me to act in a very unphilosophical manner when they try to secure the good conduct of women by attempting to keep them always in a state of childhood. Rousseau was more consistent when he wished to stop the progress of reason in both sexes, for if men eat of the tree of knowledge, women will come in for a taste;[2] but, from the imperfect cultivation which their understandings now receive, they only attain a knowledge of evil.

Children, I grant, should be innocent; but when the epithet is applied to men, or women, it is but a civil term for weakness. For if it be allowed that women were destined by Providence to acquire human virtues, and by the exercise of their understandings, that stability of character which is the firmest ground to rest our future hopes upon, they must be permitted to turn to the fountain of light, and not forced to shape their course by the twinkling of a mere satellite. Milton, I grant, was of a very different opinion; for he only bends to the indefeasible right of beauty, though it would be difficult to render two passages which I now mean to contrast, consistent. But into similar inconsistencies are great men often led by their senses.

> To whom thus Eve with *perfect beauty* adorn'd.
> My Author and Disposer, what thou bidst
> *Unargued* I obey; so God ordains;
> God is *thy law, thou mine*: to know no more
> Is Woman's *happiest* knowledge and her *praise*.[3]

These are exactly the arguments that I have used to children; but I have added, your reason is now gaining strength, and, till it arrives at some degree of maturity, you must look up to me for advice—then you ought to *think*, and only rely on God.

Yet in the following lines Milton seems to coincide with me; when he makes Adam thus expostulate with his Maker.

> Hast thou not made me here thy substitute,
> And these inferior far beneath me set?
> Among *unequals* what society
> Can sort, what harmony or true delight?

> Which must be mutual, in proportion due
> Giv'n and receiv'd; but in *disparity*
> The one intense, the other still remiss
> Cannot well suit with either, but soon prove
> Tedious alike: of *fellowship* I speak
> Such as I seek, fit to participate
> All rational delight—[4]

In treating, therefore, of the manners of women, let us, disregarding sensual arguments, trace what we should endeavor to make them in order to co-operate, if the expression be not too bold, with the supreme Being.

By individual education, I mean, for the sense of the word is not precisely defined, such an attention to a child as will slowly sharpen the senses, form the temper, regulate the passions as they begin to ferment, and set the understanding to work before the body arrives at maturity; so that the man may only have to proceed, not to begin, the important task of learning to think and reason.

To prevent any misconstruction, I must add, that I do not believe that a private education can work the wonders which some sanguine writers have attributed to it. Men and women must be educated, in a great degree, by the opinions and manners of the society they live in. In every age there has been a stream of popular opinion that has carried all before it, and given a family character, as it were, to the century. It may then fairly be inferred, that, till society be differently constituted, much cannot be expected from education. It is, however, sufficient for my present purpose to assert, that, whatever effect circumstances have on the abilities, every being may become virtuous by the exercise of its own reason; for if but one being was created with vicious inclinations, that is positively bad, what can save us from atheism? or if we worship a God, is not that God a devil?

Consequently, the most perfect education, in my opinion, is such an exercise of the understanding as is best calculated to strengthen the body and form the heart. Or, in other words, to enable the individual to attain such habits of virtue as will render it independent. In fact, it is a farce to call any being virtuous whose virtues do not result from the exercise of its own reason. This was Rousseau's opinion respecting men:[5] I extend it to women, and confidently assert that they have been drawn out of their sphere by false refinement, and not by an endeavor to acquire mas-

---

1   *man is of kin ... base and ignoble creature*   Francis Bacon (1561–1626), *Essays or Counsels Civil and Moral* (1625), Essay 16, "Of Atheism."

2   *if men eat ... for a taste*   See Genesis 2–3.

3   *To whom thus ... her praise*   Milton, *Paradise Lost* 4.634–38; Wollstonecraft's italics.

4   *Hast thou not ... All rational delight*   Milton, *Paradise Lost* 8.381–91; Wollstonecraft's italics.

5   *Rousseau's opinion respecting men*   See Rousseau, *Emile*.

culine qualities. Still the regal homage which they receive is so intoxicating, that till the manners of the times are changed, and formed on more reasonable principles, it may be impossible to convince them that the illegitimate power, which they obtain, by degrading themselves, is a curse, and that they must return to nature and equality, if they wish to secure the placid satisfaction that unsophisticated affections impart. But for this epoch we must wait—wait, perhaps, till kings and nobles, enlightened by reason, and, preferring the real dignity of man to childish state, throw off their gaudy hereditary trappings: and if then women do not resign the arbitrary power of beauty—they will prove that they have *less* mind than man.

I may be accused of arrogance; still I must declare what I firmly believe, that all the writers who have written on the subject of female education and manners from Rousseau to Dr. Gregory,[1] have contributed to render women more artificial, weak characters, than they would otherwise have been; and, consequently, more useless members of society. I might have expressed this conviction in a lower key; but I am afraid it would have been the whine of affectation, and not the faithful expression of my feelings, of the clear result, which experience and reflection have led me to draw. When I come to that division of the subject, I shall advert to the passages that I more particularly disapprove of, in the works of the authors I have just alluded to; but it is first necessary to observe, that my objection extends to the whole purport of those books, which tend, in my opinion, to degrade one half of the human species, and render women pleasing at the expense of every solid virtue.

Though, to reason on Rousseau's ground, if man did attain a degree of perfection of mind when his body arrived at maturity, it might be proper, in order to make a man and his wife *one*, that she should rely entirely on his understanding; and the graceful ivy, clasping the oak that supported it, would form a whole in which strength and beauty would be equally conspicuous. But, alas! husbands, as well as their helpmates, are often only overgrown children; nay, thanks to early debauchery, scarcely men in their outward form—and if the blind lead the blind, one need not come from heaven to tell us the consequence.[2]

Many are the causes that, in the present corrupt state of society, contribute to enslave women by cramping their understandings and sharpening their senses. One, perhaps, that silently does more mischief than all the rest, is their disregard of order.

To do every thing in an orderly manner, is a most important precept, which women, who, generally speaking, receive only a disorderly kind of education, seldom attend to with that degree of exactness that men, who from their infancy are broken into method, observe. This negligent kind of guess-work, for what other epithet can be used to point out the random exertions of a sort of instinctive common sense, never brought to the test of reason? prevents their generalizing matters of fact—so they do to-day, what they did yesterday, merely because they did it yesterday.

This contempt of the understanding in early life has more baneful consequences than is commonly supposed; for the little knowledge which women of strong minds attain, is, from various circumstances, of a more desultory kind than the knowledge of men, and it is acquired more by sheer observations on real life, than from comparing what has been individually observed with the results of experience generalized by speculation. Led by their dependent situation and domestic employments more into society, what they learn is rather by snatches; and as learning is with them, in general, only a secondary thing, they do not pursue any one branch with that persevering ardor necessary to give vigor to the faculties, and clearness to the judgment. In the present state of society, a little learning[3] is required to support the character of a gentleman; and boys are obliged to submit to a few years of discipline. But in the education of women, the cultivation of the understanding is always subordinate to the acquirement of some corporeal accomplishment; even while enervated by confinement and false notions of modesty, the body is prevented from attaining that grace and beauty which relaxed half-formed limbs never exhibit. Besides, in youth their faculties are not brought forward by emulation; and having no serious scientific study, if they have natural sagacity it is turned too soon on life and manners. They dwell on effects, and modifications, without tracing them back to causes; and complicated rules to adjust behavior are a weak substitute for simple principles.

As a proof that education gives this appearance of weakness to females, we may instance the example of military men, who are, like them, sent into the world before their

---

1   *Rousseau to Dr. Gregory*   Rousseau, *Emile*, Book 5; John Gregory (1724–73), *A Father's Legacy to his Daughters* (1774). Wollstonecraft included substantial excerpts from Gregory in *The Female Reader* (1789).

2   *if the blind ... the consequence*   Matthew 15.14. The speaker is Jesus, who has "come from heaven."

3   *a little learning*   See Pope, *An Essay on Criticism* (1711) 215.

minds have been stored with knowledge or fortified by principles. The consequences are similar; soldiers acquire a little superficial knowledge, snatched from the muddy current of conversation, and, from continually mixing with society, they gain, what is termed a knowledge of the world; and this acquaintance with manners and customs has frequently been confounded with a knowledge of the human heart. But can the crude fruit of casual observation, never brought to the test of judgment, formed by comparing speculation and experience, deserve such a distinction? Soldiers, as well as women, practice the minor virtues with punctilious politeness. Where is then the sexual difference, when the education has been the same? All the difference that I can discern, arises from the superior advantage of liberty, which enables the former to see more of life.

[…]

I now principally allude to Rousseau, for his character of Sophia is, undoubtedly, a captivating one, though it appears to me grossly unnatural;[1] however it is not the superstructure, but the foundation of her character, the principles on which her education was built, that I mean to attack; nay, warmly as I admire the genius of that able writer, whose opinions I shall often have occasion to cite, indignation always takes place of admiration, and the rigid frown of insulted virtue effaces the smile of complacency, which his eloquent periods are wont to raise, when I read his voluptuous reveries. Is this the man, who, in his ardor for virtue, would banish all the soft arts of peace, and almost carry us back to Spartan discipline? Is this the man who delights to paint the useful struggles of passion, the triumphs of good dispositions, and the heroic flights which carry the glowing soul out of itself?—How are these mighty sentiments lowered when he describes the pretty foot and enticing airs of his little favorite! But, for the present, I wave the subject, and, instead of severely reprehending the transient effusions of overweening sensibility, I shall only observe, that whoever has cast a benevolent eye on society, must often have been gratified by the sight of humble mutual love, not dignified by sentiment, or strengthened by a union in intellectual pursuits. The domestic trifles of the day have afforded matters for cheerful converse, and innocent caresses have softened toils which did not require great exercise of mind or stretch of thought: yet, has not the sight of this moderate felicity excited more tenderness than respect? An

emotion similar to what we feel when children are playing, or animals sporting,[2] whilst the contemplation of the noble struggles of suffering merit has raised admiration, and carried our thoughts to that world where sensation will give place to reason.

Women are, therefore, to be considered either as moral beings, or so weak that they must be entirely subjected to the superior faculties of men.

Let us examine this question. Rousseau declares that a woman should never, for a moment, feel herself independent, that she should be governed by fear to exercise her *natural* cunning, and made a coquetish slave in order to render her a more alluring object of desire, a *sweeter* companion to man, whenever he chooses to relax himself. He carries the arguments, which he pretends to draw from the indications of nature, still further, and insinuates that truth and fortitude, the corner stones of all human virtue, should be cultivated with certain restrictions, because, with respect to the female character, obedience is the grand lesson which ought to be impressed with unrelenting rigor.

What nonsense! when will a great man arise with sufficient strength of mind to puff away the fumes which pride and sensuality have thus spread over the subject! If women are by nature inferior to men, their virtues must be the same in quality, if not in degree, or virtue is a relative idea; consequently, their conduct should be founded on the same principles, and have the same aim.[3]

Connected with man as daughters, wives, and mothers, their moral character may be estimated by their manner of fulfilling those simple duties; but the end, the grand end of their exertions should be to unfold their own faculties and acquire the dignity of conscious virtue. They may try to render their road pleasant; but ought never to forget, in common with man, that life yields not the felicity which can satisfy an immortal soul. I do not mean to insinuate, that either sex should be so lost in abstract reflections or

---

1 *character of Sophia … unnatural* Rousseau, *Emile*, Book 5.

2 *animals sporting* [Wollstonecraft's note] Similar feelings has Milton's pleasing picture of paradisiacal happiness ever raised in my mind; yet, instead of envying the lovely pair, I have, with conscious dignity, or Satanic pride, turned to hell for sublimer objects. In the same style, when viewing some noble monument of human art, I have traced the emanation of the Deity in the order I admired, till, descending from that giddy height, I have caught myself contemplating the grandest of all human sights;—for fancy quickly placed, in some solitary recess, an outcast of fortune, rising superior to passion and discontent.

3 *their conduct … same aim* Rousseau argues in *Emile* that men's and women's virtues are essentially different.

distant views, as to forget the affections and duties that lie before them, and are, in truth, the means appointed to produce the fruit of life; on the contrary, I would warmly recommend them, even while I assert, that they afford most satisfaction when they are considered in their true, sober light.

Probably the prevailing opinion, that woman was created for man, may have taken its rise from Moses's poetical story;[1] yet, as very few, it is presumed, who have bestowed any serious thought on the subject, ever supposed that Eve was, literally speaking, one of Adam's ribs, the deduction must be allowed to fall to the ground; or, only be so far admitted as it proves that man, from the remotest antiquity, found it convenient to exert his strength to subjugate his companion, and his invention to show that she ought to have her neck bent under the yoke, because the whole creation was only created for his convenience or pleasure.

Let it not be concluded that I wish to invert the order of things; I have already granted, that, from the constitution of their bodies, men seem to be designed by Providence to attain a greater degree of virtue. I speak collectively of the whole sex; but I see not the shadow of a reason to conclude that their virtues should differ in respect to their nature. In fact, how can they, if virtue has only one eternal standard? I must therefore, if I reason consequentially, as strenuously maintain that they have the same simple direction, as that there is a God.

It follows then that cunning should not be opposed to wisdom, little cares to great exertions, or insipid softness, varnished over with the name of gentleness, to that fortitude which grand views alone can inspire.

I shall be told that woman would then lose many of her peculiar graces, and the opinion of a well known poet might be quoted to refute my unqualified assertion. For Pope has said, in the name of the whole male sex,

Yet ne'er so sure our passion to create,
As when she touch'd the brink of all we hate.[2]

In what light this sally places men and women, I shall leave to the judicious to determine; meanwhile I shall content myself with observing, that I cannot discover why, unless they are mortal, females should always be degraded by being made subservient to love or lust.

To speak disrespectfully of love is, I know, high treason against sentiment and fine feelings; but I wish to speak the simple language of truth, and rather to address the head than the heart. To endeavor to reason love out of the world, would be to out-Quixote Cervantes,[3] and equally offend against common sense; but an endeavor to restrain this tumultuous passion, and to prove that it should not be allowed to dethrone superior powers, or to usurp the scepter which the understanding should ever coolly wield, appears less wild.

Youth is the season for love in both sexes; but in those days of thoughtless enjoyment provision should be made for the more important years of life, when reflection takes place of sensation. But Rousseau, and most of the male writers who have followed his steps, have warmly inculcated that the whole tendency of female education ought to be directed to one point: to render them pleasing.

Let me reason with the supporters of this opinion who have any knowledge of human nature, do they imagine that marriage can eradicate the habitude of life? The woman who has only been taught to please will soon find that her charms are oblique sunbeams, and that they cannot have much effect on her husband's heart when they are seen every day, when the summer is passed and gone. Will she then have sufficient native energy to look into herself for comfort, and cultivate her dormant faculties? or, is it not more rational to expect that she will try to please other men; and, in the emotions raised by the expectation of new conquests, endeavor to forget the mortification her love or pride has received? When the husband ceases to be a lover—and the time will inevitably come, her desire of pleasing will then grow languid, or become a spring of bitterness; and love, perhaps, the most evanescent of all passions, gives place to jealousy or vanity.

I now speak of women who are restrained by principle or prejudice; such women, though they would shrink from an intrigue with real abhorrence, yet, nevertheless, wish to be convinced by the homage of gallantry that they are cruelly neglected by their husbands; or, days and weeks are spent in dreaming of the happiness enjoyed by congenial souls till their health is undermined and their spirits broken

1 *Moses's poetical story* Genesis 2.18–25. Moses was believed to be the author of Genesis.
2 *Yet ne'er ... all we hate* Pope, "Of the Characters of Women," 51–52.
3 *out-Quixote Cervantes* An allusion to the impossibly idealistic hero of Miguel de Cervantes Saavedra (1547–1615), *Don Quixote* (1604–14). Burke compared Price to Don Quixote (*Reflections*; *Writings* 8.58); in turn, radical writers and cartoonists applied the comparison to Burke, because of his lament for the age of chivalry (*Writings* 8.17).

by discontent. How then can the great art of pleasing be such a necessary study? it is only useful to a mistress; the chaste wife, and serious mother, should only consider her power to please as the polish of her virtues, and the affection of her husband as one of the comforts that render her task less difficult and her life happier.—But, whether she be loved or neglected, her first wish should be to make herself respectable, and not to rely for all her happiness on a being subject to like infirmities with herself.

[...]

Women ought to endeavor to purify their heart;[1] but can they do so when their uncultivated understandings make them entirely dependent on their senses for employment and amusement, when no noble pursuit sets them above the little vanities of the day, or enables them to curb the wild emotions that agitate a reed over which every passing breeze has power? To gain the affections of a virtuous man is affectation necessary? Nature has given woman a weaker frame than man; but, to ensure her husband's affections, must a wife, who by the exercise of her mind and body whilst she was discharging the duties of a daughter, wife, and mother, has allowed her constitution to retain its natural strength, and her nerves a healthy tone, is she, I say, to condescend to use art and feign a sickly delicacy in order to secure her husband's affection? Weakness may excite tenderness, and gratify the arrogant pride of man; but the lordly caresses of a protector will not gratify a noble mind that pants for, and deserves to be respected. Fondness is a poor substitute for friendship!

In a seraglio,[2] I grant, that all these arts are necessary; the epicure[3] must have his palate tickled, or he will sink into apathy; but have women so little ambition as to be satisfied with such a condition? Can they supinely dream life away in the lap of pleasure, or the languor of weariness, rather than assert their claim to pursue reasonable pleasures and render themselves conspicuous by practicing the virtues which dignify mankind? Surely she has not an immortal soul who can loiter life away merely employed to adorn her

person, that she may amuse the languid hours, and soften the cares of a fellow-creature who is willing to be enlivened by her smiles and tricks, when the serious business of life is over.

Besides, the woman who strengthens her body and exercises her mind will, by managing her family and practicing various virtues, become the friend, and not the humble dependent of her husband; and if she, by possessing such substantial qualities, merit his regard, she will not find it necessary to conceal her affection, nor to pretend to an unnatural coldness of constitution to excite her husband's passions. In fact, if we revert to history, we shall find that the women who have distinguished themselves have neither been the most beautiful nor the most gentle of their sex.

[...]

A mistaken education, a narrow, uncultivated mind, and many sexual prejudices, tend to make women more constant than men; but, for the present, I shall not touch on this branch of the subject. I will go still further, and advance, without dreaming of a paradox, that an unhappy marriage is often very advantageous to a family, and that the neglected wife is, in general, the best mother. And this would almost always be the consequence if the female mind were more enlarged: for, it seems to be the common dispensation of Providence, that what we gain in present enjoyment should be deducted from the treasure of life, experience; and that when we are gathering the flowers of the day and reveling in pleasure, the solid fruit of toil and wisdom should not be caught at the same time. The way lies before us, we must turn to the right or left; and he who will pass life away in bounding from one pleasure to another, must not complain if he acquire neither wisdom nor respectability of character.

Supposing, for a moment, that the soul is not immortal, and that man was only created for the present scene,—I think we should have reason to complain that love, infantine fondness, ever grew insipid and palled upon the sense. Let us eat, drink, and love, for tomorrow we die,[4] would be, in fact, the language of reason, the morality of life; and who but a fool would part with a reality for a fleeting shadow? But, if awed by observing the improbable powers of the mind, we disdain to confine our wishes or thoughts to such a comparatively mean field of action; that only ap-

---

1   *Women ought ... purify their heart*   Matthew 5.8.

2   *seraglio*   Part of the Sultan's palace where the harem is situated.

3   *epicure*   Person devoted to sensual pleasure, after the Greek philosopher Epicurus (341–270 BCE), who taught that the highest good is pleasure. The term is used pejoratively, in a sense that misrepresents the thought of Epicurus and his followers, who identified pleasure with "tranquil pleasures" such as peace of mind and freedom from fear.

4   *Let us eat ... for tomorrow we die*   Isaiah 22.13; 1 Corinthians 15.32.

pears grand and important, as it is connected with a boundless prospect and sublime hopes, what necessity is there for falsehood in conduct, and why must the sacred majesty of truth be violated to detain a deceitful good that saps the very foundation of virtue? Why must the female mind be tainted by coquetish arts to gratify the sensualist, and prevent love from subsiding into friendship, or compassionate tenderness, when there are not qualities on which friendship can be built? Let the honest heart show itself, and *reason* teach passion to submit to necessity; or, let the dignified pursuit of virtue and knowledge raise the mind above those emotions which rather embitter than sweeten the cup of life, when they are not restrained within due bounds.

[...]

Gentleness of manners, forbearance and long-suffering, are such amiable Godlike qualities,[1] that in sublime poetic strains the Deity has been invested with them; and, perhaps, no representation of his goodness so strongly fastens on the human affections as those that represent him abundant in mercy and willing to pardon.[2] Gentleness, considered in this point of view, bears on its front all the characteristics of grandeur, combined with the winning graces of condescension; but what a different aspect it assumes when it is the submissive demeanor of dependence, the support of weakness that loves, because it wants protection; and is forbearing, because it must silently endure injuries; smiling under the lash at which it dare not snarl. Abject as this picture appears, it is the portrait of an accomplished woman, according to the received opinion of female excellence, separated by specious reasoners from human excellence. Or, they[3] kindly restore the rib, and make one moral being of a man and woman; not forgetting to give her all the "submissive charms."[4]

How women are to exist in that state where there is to be neither marrying nor giving in marriage,[5] we are not told. For though moralists have agreed that the tenor of life seems to prove that *man* is prepared by various circumstances for a future state, they constantly concur in advising *woman* only to provide for the present. Gentleness, docility, and a spaniel-like affection are, on this ground, consistently recommended as the cardinal virtues of the sex; and, disregarding the arbitrary economy of nature, one writer has declared that it is masculine for a woman to be melancholy.[6] She was created to be the toy of man, his rattle, and it must jingle in his ears whenever, dismissing reason, he chooses to be amused.

To recommend gentleness, indeed, on a broad basis is strictly philosophical. A frail being should labor to be gentle. But when forbearance confounds right and wrong, it ceases to be a virtue; and, however convenient it may be found in a companion—that companion will ever be considered as an inferior, and only inspire a vapid tenderness, which easily degenerates into contempt. Still, if advice could really make a being gentle, whose natural disposition admitted not of such a fine polish, something towards the advancement of order would be attained; but if, as might quickly be demonstrated, only affectation be produced by this indiscriminate counsel, which throws a stumbling-block in the way of gradual improvement, and true melioration of temper, the sex is not much benefited by sacrificing solid virtues to the attainment of superficial graces, though for a few years they may procure the individuals regal sway.

As a philosopher, I read with indignation the plausible epithets which men use to soften their insults; and, as a moralist, I ask what is meant by such heterogeneous associations, as fair defects, amiable weaknesses,[7] &c.? If there be but one criterion of morals, but one archetype for man, women appear to be suspended by destiny, according to the vulgar tale of Mahomet's coffin;[8] they have neither the unerring instinct of brutes, nor are allowed to fix the eye of reason on a perfect model. They were made to be loved, and must not aim at respect, lest they should be hunted out of society as masculine.

But to view the subject in another point of view. Do passive indolent women make the best wives? Confining

1. *Gentleness of manners ... Godlike qualities* Galatians 5.22, Ephesians 4.2.
2. *those that represent ... willing to pardon* Isaiah 55.7.
3. *they* Wollstonecraft refers to Rousseau, *Emile* and to Emmanuel Swedenborg (1688–1772), Swedish philosopher, scientist and Christian mystic, who wrote *On Marriages in Heaven; and On the Nature of Heavenly Conjugal Love* (1768; trans. 1789), which Wollstonecraft reviewed (*Works* 7: 94–95).
4. *submissive charms* Milton, *Paradise Lost* 4.498.
5. *there is to be neither marrying nor giving in marriage* Matthew 22.30; Mark 12.25; Luke 20.35.
6. *one writer ... melancholy* The source is unidentified.
7. *I read with indignation ... amiable weaknesses* Milton, *Paradise Lost* 10.891; Pope, "Of the Characters of Women" 44 (misquoted).
8. *Mahomet's coffin* According to the legend, Mohammed's coffin was suspended in midair by magnets. See Milton, *Eikonoklastes* (1649); Samuel Butler (1613–80), *Hudibras* (1663–78) 2.3.442, 3.2.605; Matthew Prior (1664–1721), *Alma; or, The Progress of the Mind* (1718) 2.198–99.

our discussion to the present moment of existence, let us see how such weak creatures perform their part? Do the women who, by the attainment of a few superficial accomplishments, have strengthened the prevailing prejudice, merely contribute to the happiness of their husbands? Do they display their charms merely to amuse them? And have women, who have early imbibed notions of passive obedience, sufficient character to manage a family or educate children? So far from it, that, after surveying the history of woman, I cannot help, agreeing with the severest satirist, considering the sex as the weakest as well as the most oppressed half of the species. What does history disclose but marks of inferiority, and how few women have emancipated themselves from the galling yoke of sovereign man?—So few, that the exceptions remind me of an ingenious conjecture respecting Newton: that he was probably a being of a superior order, accidentally caged in a human body.[1] Following the same train of thinking, I have been led to imagine that the few extraordinary women who have rushed in eccentrical directions out of the orbit prescribed to their sex, were *male* spirits, confined by mistake in female frames. But if it be not philosophical to think of sex when the soul is mentioned, the inferiority must depend on the organs; or the heavenly fire, which is to ferment the clay, is not given in equal portions.

But avoiding, as I have hitherto done, any direct comparison of the two sexes collectively, or frankly acknowledging the inferiority of woman, according to the present appearance of things, I shall only insist that men have increased that inferiority till women are almost sunk below the standard of rational creatures. Let their faculties have room to unfold, and their virtues to gain strength, and then determine where the whole sex must stand in the intellectual scale. Yet let it be remembered, that for a small number of distinguished women I do not ask a place.

It is difficult for us purblind[2] mortals to say to what height human discoveries and improvements may arrive when the gloom of despotism subsides, which makes us stumble at every step; but, when morality shall be settled on a more solid basis, then, without being gifted with a prophetic spirit, I will venture to predict that woman will be either the friend or slave of man. We shall not, as at present, doubt whether she is a moral agent, or the link which unites man with brutes. But, should it then appear, that like the brutes they were principally created for the use of man, he will let them patiently bite the bridle, and not mock them with empty praise; or, should their rationality be proved, he will not impede their improvement merely to gratify his sensual appetites. He will not, with all the graces of rhetoric, advise them to submit implicitly their understanding to the guidance of man. He will not, when he treats of the education of women, assert that they ought never to have the free use of reason, nor would he recommend cunning and dissimulation to beings who are acquiring, in like manner as himself, the virtues of humanity.

Surely there can be but one rule of right, if morality has an eternal foundation, and whoever sacrifices virtue, strictly so called, to present convenience, or whose *duty* it is to act in such a manner, lives only for the passing day, and cannot be an accountable creature.

The poet then should have dropped his sneer when he says,

> If weak women go astray,
> The stars are more in fault than they.[3]

For that they are bound by the adamantine chain of destiny is most certain, if it be proved that they are never to exercise their own reason, never to be independent, never to rise above opinion, or to feel the dignity of a rational will that only bows to God, and often forgets that the universe contains any being but itself and the model of perfection to which its ardent gaze is turned, to adore attributes that, softened into virtues, may be imitated in kind, though the degree overwhelms the enraptured mind.

If, I say, for I would not impress by declamation when Reason offers her sober light, if they be really capable of acting like rational creatures, let them not be treated like slaves; or, like the brutes who are dependent on the reason of man, when they associate with him; but cultivate their minds, give them the salutary, sublime curb of principle, and let them attain conscious dignity by feeling themselves only dependent on God. Teach them, in common with man, to submit to necessity, instead of giving, to render them more pleasing, a sex to morals.

---

1   *conjecture respecting Newton ... caged in a human body*   See James Thomson (1700–48), *A Poem Sacred to the Memory of Sir Isaac Newton* (1727); Pope, *An Essay on Man* (1733–34) 2.31–34; "Epitaph. Intended for Sir Isaac Newton, In Westminster-Abbey" (1730).

2   *purblind*   Totally blind.

3   *If weak women ... fault than they*   Prior, "Hans Carvel" (1700), 11–12.

Further, should experience prove that they cannot attain the same degree of strength of mind, perseverance, and fortitude, let their virtues be the same in kind, though they may vainly struggle for the same degree; and the superiority of man will be equally clear, if not clearer; and truth, as it is a simple principle, which admits of no modification, would be common to both. Nay, the order of society as it is at present regulated would not be inverted, for woman would then only have the rank that reason assigned her, and arts could not be practiced to bring the balance even, much less to turn it.

These may be termed Utopian dreams.—Thanks to that Being who impressed them on my soul, and gave me sufficient strength of mind to dare to exert my own reason, till, becoming dependent only on him for the support of my virtue, I view, with indignation, the mistaken notions that enslave my sex.

I love man as my fellow; but his scepter, real, or usurped, extends not to me, unless the reason of an individual demands my homage; and even then the submission is to reason, and not to man. In fact, the conduct of an accountable being must be regulated by the operations of its own reason; or on what foundation rests the throne of God?

It appears to me necessary to dwell on these obvious truths, because females have been insulated, as it were; and, while they have been stripped of the virtues that should clothe humanity, they have been decked with artificial graces that enable them to exercise a short-lived tyranny. Love, in their bosoms, taking place of every nobler passion, their sole ambition is to be fair, to raise emotion instead of inspiring respect; and this ignoble desire, like the servility in absolute monarchies, destroys all strength of character. Liberty is the mother of virtue, and if women be, by their very constitution, slaves, and not allowed to breathe the sharp invigorating air of freedom, they must ever languish like exotics, and be reckoned beautiful flaws in nature.

As to the argument respecting the subjection in which the sex has ever been held, it retorts on man. The many have always been enthralled by the few; and monsters, who scarcely have shown any discernment of human excellence, have tyrannized over thousands of their fellow-creatures. Why have men of superior endowments submitted to such degradation? For, is it not universally acknowledged that kings, viewed collectively, have ever been inferior, in abilities and virtue, to the same number of men taken from the common mass of mankind—yet, have they not, and are they not still treated with a degree of reverence that is an insult to reason? China is not the only country where a living man has been made a God. *Men* have submitted to superior strength to enjoy with impunity the pleasure of the moment—*women* have only done the same, and therefore till it is proved that the courtier, who servilely resigns the birthright of a man, is not a moral agent, it cannot be demonstrated that woman is essentially inferior to man because she has always been subjugated.

Brutal force has hitherto governed the world, and that the science of politics is in its infancy, is evident from philosophers scrupling to give the knowledge most useful to man that determinate distinction.

I shall not pursue this argument any further than to establish an obvious inference, that as sound politics diffuse liberty, mankind, including woman, will become more wise and virtuous.

from Chapter 3: The Same Subject Continued

Bodily strength from being the distinction of heroes is now sunk into such unmerited contempt that men, as well as women, seem to think it unnecessary: the latter, as it takes from their feminine graces, and from that lovely weakness the source of their undue power; and the former, because it appears inimical to the character of a gentleman.

That they have both by departing from one extreme run into another, may easily be proved; but first it may be proper to observe, that a vulgar error has obtained a degree of credit, which has given force to a false conclusion, in which an effect has been mistaken for a cause.

People of genius have, very frequently, impaired their constitutions by study or careless inattention to their health, and the violence of their passions bearing a proportion to the vigor of their intellects, the sword's destroying the scabbard has become almost proverbial,[1] and superficial observers have inferred from thence, that men of genius have commonly weak, or, to use a more fashionable phrase, delicate constitutions. Yet the contrary, I believe, will appear to be the fact; for, on diligent inquiry, I find that strength of mind has, in most cases, been accompanied by superior strength of body,—natural soundness of constitution,—not that robust tone of nerves and vigor of muscles, which arise from bodily labor, when the mind is quiescent, or only directs the hands.

---

1 *the sword's destroying ... almost proverbial* Rousseau, *Confessions,* Book 5.

Dr. Priestley has remarked, in the preface to his biographical chart,[1] that the majority of great men have lived beyond forty-five. And, considering the thoughtless manner in which they have lavished their strength, when investigating a favorite science they have wasted the lamp of life, forgetful of the midnight hour; or, when, lost in poetic dreams, fancy has peopled the scene, and the soul has been disturbed, till it shook the constitution, by the passions that meditation had raised; whose objects, the baseless fabric of a vision,[2] faded before the exhausted eye, they must have had iron frames. Shakespeare never grasped the airy dagger with a nerveless hand,[3] nor did Milton tremble when he led Satan far from the confines of his dreary prison.[4]—These were not the ravings of imbecility, the sickly effusions of distempered brains; but the exuberance of fancy, that "in a fine phrenzy" wandering,[5] was not continually reminded of its material shackles.

I am aware that this argument would carry me further than it may be supposed I wish to go; but I follow truth, and, still adhering to my first position, I will allow that bodily strength seems to give man a natural superiority over woman; and this is the only solid basis on which the superiority of the sex can be built. But I still insist, that not only the virtue, but the *knowledge* of the two sexes should be the same in nature, if not in degree, and that women, considered not only as moral, but rational creatures, ought to endeavor to acquire human virtues (or perfections) by the *same* means as men, instead of being educated like a fanciful kind of *half* being—one of Rousseau's wild chimeras.[6]

But, if strength of body be, with some show of reason, the boast of men, why are women so infatuated as to be proud of a defect? Rousseau has furnished them with a plausible excuse, which could only have occurred to a man, whose imagination had been allowed to run wild, and refine on the impressions made by exquisite senses;—that they might, forsooth, have a pretext for yielding to a natural appetite without violating a romantic species of modesty, which gratifies the pride and libertinism of man.

Women, deluded by these sentiments, sometimes boast of their weakness, cunningly obtaining power by playing on the *weakness* of men; and they may well glory in their illicit

---

1   *Dr. Priestly ... biographical chart*   Joseph Priestley (1733–1804) was a British natural philosopher who co-discovered oxygen (with Antoine Lavoisier), as well as a theologian, political theorist, and educator. Wollstonecraft refers to his *A Description of a Chart of Biography* (1765).

2   *baseless fabric of vision*   Shakespeare, *The Tempest* 4.1.151.

3   *airy dagger with a nerveless hand*   Shakespeare, *Macbeth* 2.1.33–49.

4   *led Satan ... dreary prison*   Milton, *Paradise Lost* 2.629–1055.

5   *"in a fine phrenzy" wandering*   Shakespeare, *A Midsummer Night's Dream* 5.1.12.

6   *Rousseau's wild chimeras*   [Wollstonecraft's note] "Researches into abstract and speculative truths, the principles and axioms of sciences, in short, every thing which tends to generalize our ideas, is not the proper province of women; their studies should be relative to points of practice; it belongs to them to apply those principles which men have discovered; and it is their part to make observations, which direct men to the establishment of general principles. All the ideas of women, which have not the immediate tendency to points of duty, should be directed to the study of men, and to

the attainment of those agreeable accomplishments which have taste for their object; for as to works of genius, they are beyond their capacity; neither have they sufficient precision or power of attention to succeed in sciences which require accuracy: and as to physical knowledge, it belongs to those only who are most active, most inquisitive; who comprehend the greatest variety of objects: in short, it belongs to those who have the strongest powers, and who exercise them most, to judge of the relations between sensible beings and the laws of nature. A woman who is naturally weak, and does not carry her ideas to any great extent, knows how to judge and make a proper estimate of those movements which she sets to work, in order to aid her weakness; and these movements are the passions of men. The mechanism she employs is much more powerful than ours; for all her levers move the human heart. She must have the skill to incline us to do every thing which her sex will not enable her to do herself, and which is necessary or agreeable to her; therefore she ought to study the mind of man thoroughly, not the mind of man in general, abstractedly, but the dispositions of those men to whom she is subject, either by the laws of her country or by the force of opinion. She should learn to penetrate into their real sentiments from their conversation, their actions, their looks, and gestures. She should also have the art, by her own conversation, actions, looks, and gestures, to communicate those sentiments which are agreeable to them, without seeming to intend it. Men will argue more philosophically about the human heart; but women will read the heart of man better than they. It belongs to women, if I may be allowed the expression, to form an experimental morality, and to reduce the study of man to a system. Women have most wit, men have most genius; women observe, men reason: from the concurrence of both we derive the clearest light and the most perfect knowledge, which the human mind is, of itself, capable of attaining. In one word, from hence we acquire the most intimate acquaintance, both with ourselves and others, of which our nature is capable; and it is thus that art has a constant tendency to perfect those endowments which nature has bestowed.—The world is the book of women." Rousseau's *Emilius*. I hope my readers still remember the comparison, which I have brought forward, between women and officers. [Rousseau, *Emile* 386–87; Wollstonecraft quotes from *Emilius and Sophia; or, A New System of Education*, trans. William Kenrick (1763).]

sway, for, like Turkish bashaws,[1] they have more real power than their masters: but virtue is sacrificed to temporary gratifications, and the respectability of life to the triumph of an hour.

Women, as well as despots, have now, perhaps, more power than they would have if the world, divided and sub-divided into kingdoms and families, were governed by laws deduced from the exercise of reason; but in obtaining it, to carry on the comparison, their character is degraded, and licentiousness spread through the whole aggregate of society. The many become pedestal to the few. I, therefore, will venture to assert, that till women are more rationally educated, the progress of human virtue and improvement in knowledge must receive continual checks. And if it be granted that woman was not created merely to gratify the appetite of man, or to be the upper servant, who provides his meals and takes care of his linen, it must follow, that the first care of those mothers or fathers, who really attend to the education of females, should be, if not to strengthen the body, at least, not to destroy the constitution by mistaken notions of beauty and female excellence; nor should girls ever be allowed to imbibe the pernicious notion that a defect can, by any chemical process of reasoning, become an excellence.

[...]

But should it be proved that woman is naturally weaker than man, whence does it follow that it is natural for her to labor to become still weaker than nature intended her to be? Arguments of this cast are an insult to common sense, and savor of passion. The *divine right* of husbands, like the divine right of kings, may, it is to be hoped, in this enlightened age, be contested without danger, and, though conviction may not silence many boisterous disputants, yet, when any prevailing prejudice is attacked, the wise will consider, and leave the narrow-minded to rail with thoughtless vehemence at innovation.

The mother, who wishes to give true dignity of character to her daughter, must, regardless of the sneers of ignorance, proceed on a plan diametrically opposite to that which Rousseau has recommended with all the deluding charms of eloquence and philosophical sophistry: for his eloquence renders absurdities plausible, and his dogmatic conclusions puzzle, without convincing, those who have not ability to refute them.

Throughout the whole animal kingdom every young creature requires almost continual exercise, and the infancy of children, comformable to this intimation, should be passed in harmless gambols, that exercise the feet and hands, without requiring very minute direction from the head, or the constant attention of a nurse. In fact, the care necessary for self-preservation is the first natural exercise of the understanding, as little inventions to amuse the present moment unfold the imagination. But these wise designs of nature are counteracted by mistaken fondness or blind zeal. The child is not left a moment to its own direction, particularly a girl, and thus rendered dependent—dependence is called natural.

To preserve personal beauty, woman's glory! the limbs and faculties are cramped with worse than Chinese bands,[2] and the sedentary life which they are condemned to live, whilst boys frolic in the open air, weakens the muscles and relaxes the nerves.—As for Rousseau's remarks, which have since been echoed by several writers, that they have naturally, that is from their birth, independent of education, a fondness for dolls, dressing, and talking—they are so puerile as not to merit a serious refutation. That a girl, condemned to sit for hours together listening to the idle chat of weak nurses, or to attend at her mother's toilet, will endeavor to join the conversation, is, indeed, very natural; and that she will imitate her mother or aunts, and amuse herself by adorning her lifeless doll, as they do in dressing her, poor innocent babe! is undoubtedly a most natural consequence. For men of the greatest abilities have seldom had sufficient strength to rise above the surrounding atmosphere; and, if the page of genius have always been blurred by the prejudices of the age, some allowance should be made for a sex, who, like kings, always see things through a false medium.

Pursuing these reflections, the fondness for dress, conspicuous in women, may be easily accounted for, without supposing it the result of a desire to please the sex on which they are dependent. The absurdity, in short, of supposing that a girl is naturally a coquette, and that a desire connected with the impulse of nature to propagate the species, should appear even before an improper education has, by heating the imagination, called it forth prematurely, is so unphilosophical, that such a sagacious observer as Rousseau would not have adopted it, if he had not been accustomed

---

1   *bashaws* High-ranking officers of the Ottoman Empire, also referred to as "pashas."

2   *Chinese bands* An allusion to the practice of foot-binding. See John Locke (1632–1704), *Some Thoughts Concerning Education* (1693).

to make reason give way to his desire of singularity, and truth to a favorite paradox.

Yet thus to give a sex to mind was not very consistent with the principles of a man who argued so warmly, and so well, for the immortality of the soul.—But what a weak barrier is truth when it stands in the way of a hypothesis! Rousseau respected—almost adored virtue—and yet he allowed himself to love with sensual fondness. His imagination constantly prepared inflammable fuel for his inflammable senses; but, in order to reconcile his respect for self-denial, fortitude, and those heroic virtues, which a mind like his could not coolly admire, he labors to invert the law of nature, and broaches a doctrine pregnant with mischief and derogatory to the character of supreme wisdom.

[...]

I have, probably, had an opportunity of observing more girls in their infancy than J.J. Rousseau—I can recollect my own feelings, and I have looked steadily around me; yet, so far from coinciding with him in opinion respecting the first dawn of the female character, I will venture to affirm, that a girl, whose spirits have not been damped by inactivity, or innocence tainted by false shame, will always be a romp, and the doll will never excite attention unless confinement allows her no alternative.[1] Girls and boys, in short, would play harmlessly together, if the distinction of sex was not inculcated long before nature makes any difference.—I will go further, and affirm, as an indisputable fact, that most of the women, in the circle of my observation, who have acted like rational creatures, or shown any vigor of intellect, have accidentally been allowed to run wild—as some of the elegant formers of the fair sex would insinuate.

The baneful consequences which flow from inattention to health during infancy, and youth, extend further than is supposed—dependence of body naturally produces dependence of mind; and how can she be a good wife or mother, the greater part of whose time is employed to guard against or endure sickness? Nor can it be expected that a woman will resolutely endeavor to strengthen her constitution and abstain from enervating indulgencies, if artificial notions of beauty, and false descriptions of sensibility, have been early entangled with her motives of action. Most men are sometimes obliged to bear with bodily inconveniencies, and to endure, occasionally, the inclemency of the elements; but

genteel women are, literally speaking, slaves to their bodies, and glory in their subjection.

[...]

Women are everywhere in this deplorable state; for, in order to preserve their innocence, as ignorance is courteously termed, truth is hidden from them, and they are made to assume an artificial character before their faculties have acquired any strength. Taught from their infancy that beauty is woman's scepter, the mind shapes itself to the body, and, roaming round its gilt cage, only seeks to adorn its prison. Men have various employments and pursuits which engage their attention, and give a character to the opening mind; but women, confined to one, and having their thoughts constantly directed to the most insignificant part of themselves, seldom extend their views beyond the triumph of the hour. But were their understanding once emancipated from the slavery to which the pride and sensuality of man and their short-sighted desire, like that of dominion in tyrants, of present sway, has subjected them, we should probably read of their weaknesses with surprise. I must be allowed to pursue the argument a little farther.

Perhaps, if the existence of an evil being were allowed, who, in the allegorical language of scripture, went about seeking whom he should devour,[2] he could not more effectually degrade the human character than by giving a man absolute power.

[...]

It is time to effect a revolution in female manners—time to restore to them their lost dignity—and make them, as a part of the human species, labor by reforming themselves to reform the world. It is time to separate unchangeable morals from local manners.—If men be demi-gods—why let us serve them! And if the dignity of the female soul be as disputable as that of animals—if their reason does not afford sufficient light to direct their conduct whilst unerring instinct is denied—they are surely of all creatures the most miserable! and, bent beneath the iron hand of destiny, must submit to be a *fair defect* in creation. But to justify the ways of Providence respecting them,[3] by pointing out some irrefragable reason for thus making such a large portion of

---

1   *whose spirits ... no alternative*   In fact, Rousseau approves of exercise (within limits) for girls.

2   *went about seeking ... devour*   1 Peter 5.8.

3   *justify the ways of Providence respecting them*   Milton, *Paradise Lost* 10.891–92, 1.25–26.

mankind accountable and not accountable, would puzzle the subtilest casuist.

The only solid foundation for morality appears to be the character of the supreme Being; the harmony of which arises from a balance of attributes;—and, to speak with reverence, one attribute seems to imply the *necessity* of another. He must be just, because he is wise, he must be good, because he is omnipotent. For to exalt one attribute at the expence of another equally noble and necessary, bears the stamp of the warped reason of man—the homage of passion. Man, accustomed to bow down to power in his savage state, can seldom divest himself of this barbarous prejudice, even when civilization determines how much superior mental is to bodily strength; and his reason is clouded by these crude opinions, even when he thinks of the Deity.—His omnipotence is made to swallow up, or preside over his other attributes, and those mortals are supposed to limit his power irreverently, who think that it must be regulated by his wisdom.

[…]

Let fancy now present a woman with a tolerable understanding, for I do not wish to leave the line of mediocrity, whose constitution, strengthened by exercise, has allowed her body to acquire its full vigor; her mind, at the same time, gradually expanding itself to comprehend the moral duties of life, and in what human virtue and dignity consist.

Formed thus by the discharge of the relative duties of her station, she marries from affection, without losing sight of prudence, and looking beyond matrimonial felicity, she secures her husband's respect before it is necessary to exert mean arts to please him and feed a dying flame, which nature doomed to expire when the object became familiar, when friendship and forbearance take place of a more ardent affection.—This is the natural death of love, and domestic peace is not destroyed by struggles to prevent its extinction. I also suppose the husband to be virtuous; or she is still more in want of independent principles.

Fate, however, breaks this tie.—She is left a widow, perhaps, without a sufficient provision; but she is not desolate! The pang of nature is felt; but after time has softened sorrow into melancholy resignation, her heart turns to her children with redoubled fondness, and anxious to provide for them, affection gives a sacred heroic cast to her maternal duties. She thinks that not only the eye sees her virtuous efforts from whom all her comfort now must flow, and whose approbation is life; but her imagination, a little abstracted

and exalted by grief, dwells on the fond hope that the eyes which her trembling hand closed, may still see how she subdues every wayward passion to fulfill the double duty of being the father as well as the mother of her children. Raised to heroism by misfortunes, she represses the first faint dawning of a natural inclination, before it ripens into love, and in the bloom of life forgets her sex—forgets the pleasure of an awakening passion, which might again have been inspired and returned. She no longer thinks of pleasing, and conscious dignity prevents her from priding herself on account of the praise which her conduct demands. Her children have her love, and her brightest hopes are beyond the grave, where her imagination often strays.

I think I see her surrounded by her children, reaping the reward of her care. The intelligent eye meets hers, whilst health and innocence smile on their chubby cheeks, and as they grow up the cares of life are lessened by their grateful attention. She lives to see the virtues which she endeavored to plant on principles, fixed into habits, to see her children attain a strength of character sufficient to enable them to endure adversity without forgetting their mother's example.

The task of life thus fulfilled, she calmly waits for the sleep of death, and rising from the grave, may say—Behold, thou gavest me a talent—and here are five talents.[1]

I wish to sum up what I have said in a few words, for I here throw down my gauntlet, and deny the existence of sexual virtues, not excepting modesty. For man and woman, truth, if I understand the meaning of the word, must be the same; yet the fanciful female character, so prettily drawn by poets and novelists, demanding the sacrifice of truth and sincerity, virtue becomes a relative idea, having no other foundation than utility, and of that utility men pretend arbitrarily to judge, shaping it to their own convenience.

Women, I allow, may have different duties to fulfill; but they are *human* duties, and the principles that should regulate the discharge of them, I sturdily maintain, must be the same.

To become respectable, the exercise of their understanding is necessary, there is no other foundation for independence of character; I mean explicitly to say that they must only bow to the authority of reason, instead of being the *modest* slaves of opinion.

---

1 *Behold, thou gavest me a talent—and here are five talents* Matthew 25.14–30; Luke 19.12–26.

In the superior ranks of life how seldom do we meet with a man of superior abilities, or even common acquirements? The reason appears to me clear, the state they are born in was an unnatural one. The human character has ever been formed by the employments the individual, or class, pursues; and if the faculties are not sharpened by necessity, they must remain obtuse. The argument may fairly be extended to women; for, seldom occupied by serious business, the pursuit of pleasure gives that insignificancy to their character which renders the society of the *great* so insipid. The same want of firmness, produced by a similar cause, forces them both to fly from themselves to noisy pleasures, and artificial passions, till vanity takes place of every social affection, and the characteristics of humanity can scarcely be discerned. Such are the blessings of civil governments, as they are at present organized, that wealth and female softness equally tend to debase mankind, and are produced by the same cause; but allowing women to be rational creatures, they should be incited to acquire virtues which they may call their own, for how can a rational being be ennobled by any thing that is not obtained by its *own* exertions?

from Chapter 4: Observations on the State of Degradation to Which Woman Is Reduced by Various Causes

That woman is naturally weak, or degraded by a concurrence of circumstances, is, I think, clear. But this position I shall simply contrast with a conclusion, which I have frequently heard fall from sensible men in favor of an aristocracy: that the mass of mankind cannot be any thing, or the obsequious slaves, who patiently allow themselves to be driven forward, would feel their own consequence, and spurn their chains. Men, they further observe, submit every where to oppression, when they have only to lift up their heads to throw off the yoke; yet, instead of asserting their birthright, they quietly lick the dust, and say, let us eat and drink, for tomorrow we die.[1] Women, I argue from analogy, are degraded by the same propensity to enjoy the present moment; and, at last, despise the freedom which they have not sufficient virtue to struggle to attain. But I must be more explicit.

With respect to the culture of the heart, it is unanimously allowed that sex is out of the question; but the line of subordination in the mental powers is never to be passed over.[2] Only "absolute in loveliness,"[3] the portion of rationality granted to woman, is, indeed, very scanty; for, denying her genius and judgment, it is scarcely possible to divine what remains to characterize intellect.

The stamen[4] of immortality, if I may be allowed the phrase, is the perfectibility of human reason; for, were man created perfect, or did a flood of knowledge break in upon him, when he arrived at maturity, that precluded error, I should doubt whether his existence would be continued after the dissolution of the body. But, in the present state of things, every difficulty in morals that escapes from human discussion, and equally baffles the investigation of profound thinking, and the lightning glance of genius, is an argument on which I build my belief of the immortality of the soul. Reason is, consequentially, the simple power of improvement; or, more properly speaking, of discerning truth. Every individual is in this respect a world in itself. More or less may be conspicuous in one being than another; but the nature of reason must be the same in all, if it be an emanation of divinity, the tie that connects the creature with the Creator; for, can that soul be stamped with the heavenly image, that is not perfected by the exercise of its own reason?[5] Yet outwardly ornamented with elaborate care, and so adorned to delight man, "that with honor he may love,"[6] the soul of woman is not allowed to have this distinction, and man, ever placed between her and reason,

1   *let us eat and drink, for tomorrow we die*   Isaiah 22.13; 1 Corinthians 15.32.

2   *but the line of subordination ... passed over*   [Wollstonecraft's note] Into what inconsistencies do men fall when they argue without the compass of principles. Women, weak women, are compared with angels; yet, a superior order of beings should be supposed to possess more intellect than man; or, in what does their superiority consist? In the same strain, to drop the sneer, they are allowed to possess more goodness of heart, piety, and benevolence.—I doubt the fact, though it be courteously brought forward, unless ignorance be allowed to be the mother of devotion; for I am firmly persuaded that, on an average, the proportion between virtue and knowledge, is more upon a par than is commonly granted.

3   *absolute in loveliness*   Milton, *Paradise Lost* 8.547.

4   *stamen*   Part of the flower bearing pollen for reproduction.

5   *for, can that soul ... its own reason*   [Wollstonecraft's note] "The brutes," says Lord Monboddo, "remain in the state in which nature has placed them, except in so far as their natural instinct is improved by the culture *we* bestow upon them." [James Burnett, Lord Monboddo (1714–99), *Of the Origin and Progress of Language* (1773–92); Wollstonecraft's italics.]

6   *that with honor he may love*   Milton, *Paradise Lost* 8.577.

she is always represented as only created to see through a gross medium, and to take things on trust. But dismissing these fanciful theories, and considering woman as a whole, let it be what it will, instead of a part of man, the inquiry is whether she have reason or not. If she have, which, for a moment, I will take for granted, she was not created merely to be the solace of man, and the sexual should not destroy the human character.

Into this error men have, probably, been led by viewing education in a false light; not considering it as the first step to form a being advancing gradually towards perfection;[1] but only as a preparation for life. On this sensual error, for I must call it so, has the false system of female manners been reared, which robs the whole sex of its dignity, and classes the brown and fair with the smiling flowers that only adorn the land. This has ever been the language of men, and the fear of departing from a supposed sexual character, has made even women of superiour sense adopt the same sentiments. Thus understanding, strictly speaking, has been denied to woman; and instinct, sublimated into wit and cunning, for the purposes of life, has been substituted in its stead.

The power of generalizing ideas, of drawing comprehensive conclusions from individual observations, is the only acquirement, for an immortal being, that really deserves the name of knowledge. Merely to observe, without endeavoring to account for any thing, may (in a very incomplete manner) serve as the common sense of life; but where is the store laid up that is to clothe the soul when it leaves the body?

This power has not only been denied to women; but writers have insisted that it is inconsistent, with a few exceptions, with their sexual character. Let men prove this, and I shall grant that woman only exists for man. I must, however, previously remark, that the power of generalizing ideas, to any great extent, is not very common amongst men or women. But this exercise is the true cultivation of the understanding; and every thing conspires to render the cultivation of the understanding more difficult in the female than the male world.

[...]

Ignorance is a frail base for virtue! Yet, that it is the condition for which woman was organized, has been insisted upon by the writers who have most vehemently argued in favor of the superiority of man; a superiority not in degree, but essence; though, to soften the argument, they have labored to prove, with chivalrous generosity, that the sexes ought not to be compared; man was made to reason, woman to feel: and that together, flesh and spirit, they make the most perfect whole, by blending happily reason and sensibility into one character.

[...]

I come round to my old argument; if woman be allowed to have an immortal soul, she must have, as the employment of life, an understanding to improve. And when, to render the present state more complete, though every thing proves it to be but a fraction of a mighty sum, she is incited by present gratification to forget her grand destination, nature is counteracted, or she was born only to procreate and rot. Or, granting brutes, of every description, a soul, though not a reasonable one, the exercise of instinct and sensibility may be the step, which they are to take, in this life, towards the attainment of reason in the next; so that through all eternity they will lag behind man, who, why we cannot tell, had the power given him of attaining reason in his first mode of existence.

[...]

In tracing the causes that, in my opinion, have degraded woman, I have confined my observations to such as universally act upon the morals and manners of the whole sex, and to me it appears clear that they all spring from want of understanding. Whether this arise from a physical or accidental weakness of faculties, time alone can determine; for I shall not lay any great stress on the example of a few women[2] who, from having received a masculine education,

---

1   *perfection* [Wollstonecraft's note] This word is not strictly just, but I cannot find a better.

2   *a few women* [Wollstonecraft's note] Sappho, Eloisa, Mrs. Macaulay, the Empress of Russia, Madame d'Eon, etc. These, and many more, may be reckoned exceptions; and, are not all heroes, as well as heroines, exceptions to general rules? I wish to see women neither heroines nor brutes; but reasonable creatures. [Sappho (c. 600 BCE) was a distinguished poet. Héloïse (c. 1101–64), secretly married to the philosopher Peter Abelard (1079–1142), was herself a scholar; their love letters inspired Pope's "Eloisa to Abelard" (1717) and Rousseau's *Julie; ou, La Nouvelle Héloïse*. Catharine Macaulay Graham (1731–91) was the author of an eight-volume *History of England* (1763–83) and other works including *Observations on the Reflections of the Right Honourable Edmund Burke on the Revolution in France* (1790) and *Letters on Education* (1790). Catherine II of Russia (1729–96) displayed her "courage and resolution" by deposing and murdering her husband; but she also introduced vaccination for smallpox and promoted religious

have acquired courage and resolution; I only contend that the men who have been placed in similar situations, have acquired a similar character—I speak of bodies of men, and that men of genius and talents have started out of a class, in which women have never yet been placed.

from Chapter 5: Animadversions[1] on Some of the Writers Who Have Rendered Women Objects of Pity, Bordering on Contempt

The opinions speciously supported, in some modern publications on the female character and education, which have given the tone to most of the observations made, in a more cursory manner, on the sex, remain now to be examined.

Section 1

I shall begin with Rousseau, and give a sketch of his character of woman, in his own words, interspersing comments and reflections. My comments, it is true, will all spring from a few simple principles, and might have been deduced from what I have already said; but the artificial structure has been raised with so much ingenuity, that it seems necessary to attack it in a more circumstantial manner, and make the application myself.

Sophia, says Rousseau, should be as perfect a woman as Emilius is a man, and render her so, it is necessary to examine the character which nature has given to the sex.

He then proceeds to prove that woman ought to be weak and passive, because she has less bodily strength than man; and hence infers, that she was formed to please and to be subject to him; and that it is her duty to render herself *agreeable* to her master—this being the grand end of her existence. Still, however, to give a little mock dignity to lust, he insists that man should not exert his strength, but depend on the will of the woman, when he seeks for pleasure with her.

"Hence we deduce a third consequence from the different constitutions of the sexes; which is, that the strongest should be master in appearance, and be dependent in fact on the weakest; and that not from any frivolous practice of gallantry or vanity of protectorship, but from an invariable law of nature, which, furnishing woman with a greater facility to excite desires than she has given man to satisfy them, makes the latter dependent on the good pleasure of the former, and compels him to endeavor to please in his turn, *in order to obtain her consent that he should be strongest.*[2] On these occasions, the most delightful circumstance a man finds in his victory is, to doubt whether it was the woman's weakness that yielded to his superior strength, or whether her inclinations spoke in his favor: the females are also generally artful enough to leave this matter in doubt. The understanding of women answers in this respect perfectly to their constitution: so far from being ashamed of their weakness, they glory in it; their tender muscles make no resistance; they affect to be incapable of lifting the smallest burthens, and would blush to be thought robust and strong. To what purpose is all this? Not merely for the sake of appearing delicate, but through an artful precaution: it is thus they provide an excuse beforehand, and a right to be feeble when they think it expedient."[3]

I have quoted this passage, lest my readers should suspect that I warped the author's reasoning to support my own arguments. I have already asserted that in educating women these fundamental principles lead to a system of cunning and lasciviousness.

Supposing woman to have been formed only to please, and be subject to man, the conclusion is just, she ought to sacrifice every other consideration to render herself agreeable to him: and let this brutal desire of self-preservation be the grand spring of all her actions, when it is proved to be the iron bed of fate, to fit which her character should be stretched or contracted, regardless of all moral or physical distinctions.[4] But, if, as I think, may be demonstrated, the purposes, of even this life, viewing the whole, be subverted by practical rules built upon this ignoble base, I may be allowed to doubt whether woman were created for man: and, though the cry of irreligion, or even atheism, be raised against me, I will simply declare, that were an angel from

---

toleration and the education of women. Charles de Beaumont, Chevalier d'Eon (1728–1810), a distinguished French diplomat, dressed as a woman for much of his life, and (in consequence of litigation over wagers about his sex) had been legally declared one in 1777. Rousseau repeatedly accuses feminists of basing their arguments on exceptions.

1 *Animadversions* Strong criticisms.

2 *compels him to endeavor ... he should be strongest* [Wollstonecraft's note] What nonsense!

3 *Hence we deduce ... it expedient* Rousseau, *Emile*; Wollstonecraft's italics.

4 *iron bed of fate ... physical distinctions* An allusion to the bed of Procrustes, which he made to fit all his guests: if they were too short, he stretched them on the rack; if they were too tall, he cut off their extremities.

heaven to tell me that Moses's beautiful, poetical cosmogony, and the account of the fall of man, were literally true, I could not believe what my reason told me was derogatory to the character of the Supreme Being: and, having no fear of the devil before mine eyes, I venture to call this a suggestion of reason, instead of resting my weakness on the broad shoulders of the first seducer of my frail sex.

"It being once demonstrated," continues Rousseau, "that man and woman are not, nor ought to be, constituted alike in temperament and character, it follows of course that they should not be educated in the same manner. In pursuing the directions of nature, they ought indeed to act in concert, but they should not be engaged in the same employments: the end of their pursuits should be the same, but the means they should take to accomplish them, and of consequence their tastes and inclinations, should be different."[1]

[...]

"Here then we see a primary propensity firmly established, which you need only to pursue and regulate. The little creature will doubtless be very desirous to know how to dress up her doll, to make its sleeve-knots, its flounces, its head-dress, &c. she is obliged to have so much recourse to the people about her, for their assistance in these articles, that it would be much more agreeable to her to owe them all to her own industry. Hence we have a good reason for the first lessons that are usually taught these young females: in which we do not appear to be setting them a task, but obliging them, by instructing them in what is immediately useful to themselves. And, in fact, almost all of them learn with reluctance to read and write; but very readily apply themselves to the use of their needles. They imagine themselves already grown up, and think with pleasure that such qualifications will enable them to decorate themselves."[2]

This is certainly only an education of the body; but Rousseau is not the only man who has indirectly said that merely the person of a *young* woman, without any mind, unless animal spirits come under that description, is very pleasing. To render it weak, and what some may call beautiful, the understanding is neglected, and girls forced to sit still, play with dolls and listen to foolish conversations;—the effect of habit is insisted upon as an undoubted indication of nature. I know it was Rousseau's opinion that the first years of youth should be employed to form the body, though in educating Emilius he deviates from this plan; yet, the difference between strengthening the body, on which strength of mind in a great measure depends, and only giving it an easy motion, is very wide.

Rousseau's observations, it is proper to remark, were made in a country where the art of pleasing was refined only to extract the grossness of vice. He did not go back to nature, or his ruling appetite disturbed the operations of reason, else he would not have drawn these crude inferences.

In France boys and girls, particularly the latter, are only educated to please, to manage their persons, and regulate their exterior behavior; and their minds are corrupted, at a very early age, by the worldly and pious cautions they receive to guard them against immodesty. I speak of past times. The very confessions which mere children were obliged to make, and the questions asked by the holy men, I assert these facts on good authority, were sufficient to impress a sexual character; and the education of society was a school of coquetry and art. At the age of ten or eleven; nay, often much sooner, girls began to coquet, and talked, unreproved,[3] of establishing themselves in the world by marriage.

In short, they were treated like women, almost from their very birth, and compliments were listened to instead of instruction. These, weakening the mind, Nature was supposed to have acted like a step-mother, when she formed this after-thought of creation.

[...]

Men have superiour strength of body; but were it not for mistaken notions of beauty, women would acquire sufficient to enable them to earn their own subsistence, the true definition of independence; and to bear those bodily inconveniencies and exertions that are requisite to strengthen the mind.

Let us then, by being allowed to take the same exercise as boys, not only during infancy, but youth, arrive at perfection of body, that we may know how far the natural superiority of man extends. For what reason or virtue can be expected from a creature when the seed-time of life is neglected? None—did not the winds of heaven casually scatter many useful seeds in the fallow ground.

"Beauty cannot be acquired by dress, and coquetry is an art not so early and speedily attained. While girls are yet

---

1   *It being once demonstrated ... should be different*   Rousseau, *Emile.*
2   *Here then we see ... decorate themselves*   Rousseau, *Emile.*
3   *unreproved*   Not rebuked.

young, however, they are in a capacity to study agreeable gesture, a pleasing modulation of voice, an easy carriage and behavior; as well as to take the advantage of gracefully adapting their looks and attitudes to time, place, and occasion. Their application, therefore, should not be solely confined to the arts of industry and the needle, when they come to display other talents, whose utility is already apparent."[1]

"For my part, I would have a young Englishwoman cultivate her agreeable talents, in order to please her future husband, with as much care and assiduity as a young Circassian cultivates her's, to fit her for the Haram of an Eastern bashaw."[2]

To render women completely insignificant, he adds— "The tongues of women are very voluble; they speak earlier, more readily, and more agreeably, than the men; they are accused also of speaking much more: but so it ought to be, and I should be very ready to convert this reproach into a compliment; their lips and eyes have the same activity, and for the same reason. A man speaks of what he knows, a woman of what pleases her; the one requires knowledge, the other taste; the principal object of a man's discourse should be what is useful, that of a woman's what is agreeable. There ought to be nothing in common between their different conversation but truth."

"We ought not, therefore, to restrain the prattle of girls, in the same manner as we should that of boys, with that severe question; *To what purpose are you talking?* but by another, which is no less difficult to answer, *How will your discourse be received?* In infancy, while they are as yet incapable to discern good from evil, they ought to observe it, as a law, never to say any thing disagreeable to those whom they are speaking to: what will render the practice of this rule also the more difficult, is, that it must ever be subordinate to the former, of never speaking falsely or telling an untruth."[3] To govern the tongue in this manner must require great address indeed; and it is too much practiced both by men and women.—Out of the abundance of the heart how few speak![4] So few, that I, who love simplicity, would gladly give up politeness for a quarter of the virtue that has been sacrificed to an equivocal quality which at best should only be the polish of virtue.

But, to complete the sketch. "It is easy to be conceived, that if male children be not in a capacity to form any true notions of religion, those ideas must be greatly above the conception of the females.

[...]

"As authority ought to regulate the religion of the women, it is not so needful to explain to them the reasons for their belief, as to lay down precisely the tenets they are to believe: for the creed, which presents only obscure ideas to the mind, is the source of fanaticism; and that which presents absurdities, leads to infidelity."[5]

Absolute, uncontroverted authority, it seems, must subsist somewhere: but is not this a direct and exclusive appropriation of reason? The *rights* of humanity have been thus confined to the male line from Adam downwards. Rousseau would carry his male aristocracy still further, for he insinuates, that he should not blame those, who contend for leaving woman in a state of the most profound ignorance, if it were not necessary in order to preserve her chastity and justify the man's choice, in the eyes of the world, to give her a little knowledge of men, and the customs produced by human passions; else she might propagate at home without being rendered less voluptuous and innocent by the exercise of her understanding: excepting, indeed, during the first year of marriage, when she might employ it to dress like Sophia. "Her dress is extremely modest in appearance, and yet very coquettish in fact: she does not make a display of her charms, she conceals them; but in concealing them, she knows how to affect your imagination. Every one who sees her will say, There is a modest and discreet girl; but while you are near her, your eyes and affections wander all over her person, so that you cannot withdraw them; and you would conclude, that every part of her dress, simple as it seems, was only put in its proper order to be taken to pieces by the imagination."[6] Is this modesty? Is this a preparation for immortality? Again.—What opinion are we to form of a system of education, when the author says of his heroine, "that with her,

1 *Beauty cannot be acquired ... apparent* Rousseau, *Emile.*
2 *For my part ... Eastern bashaw* Rousseau, *Emile*, 374. Circassia, on the northeastern coast of the Black Sea, was proverbial for the beauty of its women.
3 *We ought not, therefore, to restrain ... an untruth* Rousseau, *Emile.*
4 *Out of the abundance of the heart how few speak* See Matthew 12.34. Wollstonecraft inverts the meaning of the original.
5 *As authority ought ... leads to infidelity* Rousseau, *Emile.*
6 *Her dress is extremely modest ... taken to pieces by the imagination* Rousseau, *Emile*, 394.

doing things well, is but a *secondary* concern; her principal concern is to do them *neatly*."[1]

Secondary, in fact, are all her virtues and qualities, for, respecting religion, he makes her parents thus address her, accustomed to submission—"Your husband will instruct you in *good time*."[2]

After thus cramping a woman's mind, if, in order to keep it fair, he have not made it quite a blank, he advises her to reflect, that a reflecting man may not yawn in her company, when he is tired of caressing her.—What has she to reflect about who must obey? and would it not be a refinement on cruelty only to open her mind to make the darkness and misery of her fate *visible*?[3] Yet, these are his sensible remarks; how consistent with what I have already been obliged to quote, to give a fair view of the subject, the reader may determine.

[...]

Why was Rousseau's life divided between ecstasy and misery? Can any other answer be given than this, that the effervescence of his imagination produced both; but, had his fancy been allowed to cool, it is possible that he might have acquired more strength of mind. Still, if the purpose of life be to educate the intellectual part of man, all with respect to him was right; yet, had not death led to a nobler scene of action, it is probable that he would have enjoyed more equal happiness on earth, and have felt the calm sensations of the man of nature instead of being prepared for another stage of existence by nourishing the passions which agitate the civilized man.

But peace to his manes! I war not with his ashes, but his opinions. I war only with the sensibility that led him to degrade woman by making her the slave of love.

> ———Curs'd vassalage,
> First idoliz'd till love's hot fire be o'er,
> Then slaves to those who courted us before.
> *Dryden.*[4]

---

1   *that with her ... neatly* Rousseau, *Emile*, 395; Wollstonecraft's italics.
2   *Your husband ... in good time* Rousseau, *Emile*, 397; Wollstonecraft's italics.
3   *her fate visible* Milton, *Paradise Lost* 1.63.
4   *Curs'd vassalage ... courted us before* John Dryden (1631–1700), *The State of Innocence and Fall of Man* (1677) 5.1.58–60. The speaker is Eve.

The pernicious tendency of those books, in which the writers insidiously degrade the sex whilst they are prostrate before their personal charms, cannot be too often or too severely exposed.

Let us, my dear contemporaries, arise above such narrow prejudices! If wisdom be desirable on its own account, if virtue, to deserve the name, must be founded on knowledge; let us endeavor to strengthen our minds by reflection, till our heads become a balance for our hearts; let us not confine all our thoughts to the petty occurrences of the day, or our knowledge to an acquaintance with our lovers' or husbands' hearts; but let the practice of every duty be subordinate to the grand one of improving our minds, and preparing our affections for a more exalted state!

[...]

from Chapter 6: The Effect Which an Early Association of Ideas Has Upon the Character

Educated in the enervating style recommended by the writers on whom I have been animadverting; and not having a chance, from their subordinate state in society, to recover their lost ground, is it surprising that women every where appear a defect in nature? Is it surprising, when we consider what a determinate effect an early association of ideas has on the character, that they neglect their understandings, and turn all their attention to their persons?

The great advantages which naturally result from storing the mind with knowledge, are obvious from the following considerations. The association of our ideas is either habitual or instantaneous; and the latter mode seems rather to depend on the original temperature of the mind than on the will. When the ideas, and matters of fact, are once taken in, they lie by for use, till some fortuitous circumstance makes the information dart into the mind with illustrative force, that has been received at very different periods of our lives. Like the lightning's flash are many recollections; one idea assimilating and explaining another, with astonishing rapidity. I do not now allude to that quick perception of truth, which is so intuitive that it baffles research, and makes us at a loss to determine whether it is reminiscence or ratiocination, lost sight of in its celerity,[5] that with her, doing things well, is but a *secondary* concern; her principal concern is to do them *neatly* that opens the dark cloud.

---

5   *celerity* Swiftness.

Over those instantaneous associations we have little power; for when the mind is once enlarged by excursive flights, or profound reflection, the raw materials will, in some degree, arrange themselves. The understanding, it is true, may keep us from going out of drawing[1] when we group our thoughts, or transcribe from the imagination the warm sketches of fancy; but the animal spirits, the individual character, give the coloring. Over this subtle electric fluid,[2] how little power do we possess, and over it how little power can reason obtain! These fine intractable spirits appear to be the essence of genius, and beaming in its eagle eye, produce in the most eminent degree the happy energy of associating thoughts that surprise, delight, and instruct. These are the glowing minds that concentrate pictures for their fellow-creatures; forcing them to view with interest the objects reflected from the impassioned imagination, which they passed over in nature.

I must be allowed to explain myself. The generality of people cannot see or feel poetically, they want fancy, and therefore fly from solitude in search of sensible objects; but when an author lends them his eyes they can see as he saw, and be amused by images they could not select, though lying before them.

Education thus only supplies the man of genius with knowledge to give variety and contrast to his associations; but there is an habitual association of ideas, that grows "with our growth,"[3] which has a great effect on the moral character of mankind; and by which a turn is given to the mind that commonly remains throughout life. So ductile[4] is the understanding, and yet so stubborn, that the associations which depend on adventitious circumstances, during the period that the body takes to arrive at maturity, can seldom be disentangled by reason. One idea calls up an-

other, its old associate, and memory, faithful to the first impressions, particularly when the intellectual powers are not employed to cool our sensations, retraces them with mechanical exactness.

This habitual slavery, to first impressions, has a more baneful effect on the female than the male character, because business and other dry employments of the understanding, tend to deaden the feelings and break associations that do violence to reason. But females, who are made women of when they are mere children, and brought back to childhood when they ought to leave the go-cart for ever, have not sufficient strength of mind to efface the superinductions[5] of art that have smothered nature.

[…]

from Chapter 9: Of the Pernicious Effects Which Arise from the Unnatural Distinctions Established in Society

From the respect paid to property flow, as from a poisoned fountain, most of the evils and vices which render this world such a dreary scene to the contemplative mind. For it is in the most polished society that noisome reptiles and venomous serpents lurk under the rank herbage; and there is voluptuousness pampered by the still sultry air, which relaxes every good disposition before it ripens into virtue.

One class presses on another; for all are aiming to procure respect on account of their property: and property, once gained, will procure the respect due only to talents and virtue. Men neglect the duties incumbent on man, yet are treated like demi-gods; religion is also separated from morality by a ceremonial veil, yet men wonder that the world is almost, literally speaking, a den of sharpers or oppressors.

There is a homely proverb, which speaks a shrewd truth, that whoever the devil finds idle he will employ.[6] And what but habitual idleness can hereditary wealth and titles produce? For man is so constituted that he can only attain a proper use of his faculties by exercising them, and will not exercise them unless necessity, of some kind, first set the wheels in motion. Virtue likewise can only be acquired by the discharge of relative duties; but the im-

---

1   *may keep us from going out of drawing*   I.e., out of perspective.
2   *subtle electric fluid*   [Wollstonecraft's note] I have sometimes, when inclined to laugh at materialists, asked whether, as the most powerful effects in nature are apparently produced by fluids, the magnetic, etc. the passions might not be fine volatile fluids that embraced humanity, keeping the more refractory elementary parts together—or whether they were simply a liquid fire that pervaded the more sluggish materials, giving them life and heat? [Scientists believed that electricity and magnetism were "subtle"—that is, very thin—fluids. In the life sciences, vitalists believed that life itself was such a fluid, which is the materialist position Wollstonecraft is mocking here.]
3   *with our growth*   Pope, *An Essay on Man* 2.136.
4   *ductile*   Capable of changing form without breaking, often used to describe metals which can be hammered thin to make wire.

5   *superinductions*   Added features.
6   *whoever the devil ... he will employ*   See Isaac Watts (1674–1748), *Divine Songs* (1720), "Song 20" 11–12.

portance of these sacred duties will scarcely be felt by the being who is cajoled out of his humanity by the flattery of sycophants. There must be more equality established in society, or morality will never gain ground, and this virtuous equality will not rest firmly even when founded on a rock,[1] if one half of mankind be chained to its bottom by fate, for they will be continually undermining it through ignorance or pride.

It is vain to expect virtue from women till they are, in some degree, independent of men; nay, it is vain to expect that strength of natural affection, which would make them good wives and mothers. Whilst they are absolutely dependent on their husbands they will be cunning, mean, and selfish, and the men who can be gratified by the fawning fondness of spaniel-like affection, have not much delicacy, for love is not to be bought, in any sense of the words, its silken wings are instantly shriveled up when any thing beside a return in kind is sought. Yet whilst wealth enervates men; and women live, as it were, by their personal charms, how can we expect them to discharge those ennobling duties which equally require exertion and self-denial. Hereditary property sophisticates the mind, and the unfortunate victims to it, if I may so express myself, swathed from their birth, seldom exert the locomotive faculty of body or mind; and, thus viewing every thing through one medium, and that a false one, they are unable to discern in what true merit and happiness consist. False, indeed, must be the light when the drapery of situation hides the man, and makes him stalk in masquerade, dragging from one scene of dissipation to another the nerveless limbs that hang with stupid listlessness, and rolling round the vacant eye which plainly tells us that there is no mind at home.

I mean, therefore, to infer that the society is not properly organized which does not compel men and women to discharge their respective duties, by making it the only way to acquire that countenance from their fellow-creatures, which every human being wishes some way to attain. The respect, consequently, which is paid to wealth and mere personal charms, is a true north-east blast, that blights the tender blossoms of affection and virtue. Nature has wisely attached affections to duties, to sweeten toil, and to give that vigor to the exertions of reason which only the heart can give. But, the affection which is put on merely because it is the appropriated insignia of a certain character, when its duties are not fulfilled, is one of the empty compliments which vice and folly are obliged to pay to virtue and the real nature of things.

To illustrate my opinion, I need only observe, that when a woman is admired for her beauty, and suffers herself to be so far intoxicated by the admiration she receives, as to neglect to discharge the indispensable duty of a mother, she sins against herself by neglecting to cultivate an affection that would equally tend to make her useful and happy. True happiness, I mean all the contentment, and virtuous satisfaction, that can be snatched in this imperfect state, must arise from well regulated affections; and an affection includes a duty. Men are not aware of the misery they cause, and the vicious weakness they cherish, by only inciting women to render themselves pleasing; they do not consider that they thus make natural and artificial duties clash, by sacrificing the comfort and respectability of a woman's life to voluptuous notions of beauty, when in nature they all harmonize.

Cold would be the heart of a husband, were he not rendered unnatural by early debauchery, who did not feel more delight at seeing his child suckled by its mother, than the most artful wanton tricks could ever raise; yet this natural way of cementing the matrimonial tie, and twisting esteem with fonder recollections, wealth leads women to spurn. To preserve their beauty, and wear the flowery crown of the day, which gives them a kind of right to reign for a short time over the sex, they neglect to stamp impressions on their husbands' hearts, that would be remembered with more tenderness when the snow on the head began to chill the bosom, than even their virgin charms. The maternal solicitude of a reasonable affectionate woman is very interesting, and the chastened dignity with which a mother returns the caresses that she and her child receive from a father who has been fulfilling the serious duties of his station, is not only a respectable, but a beautiful sight. So singular, indeed, are my feelings, and I have endeavored not to catch factitious ones, that after having been fatigued with the sight of insipid grandeur and the slavish ceremonies that with cumberous[2] pomp supplied the place of domestic affections, I have turned to some other scene to relieve my eye by resting it on the refreshing green every where scattered by nature. I have then viewed with pleasure a woman nursing her children, and discharging the duties of her station with, perhaps, merely a servant maid to take off her hands the servile part of the household business. I have seen her

---

1 *founded on a rock* Matthew 7.24–25.

2 *cumberous* Cumbersome.

prepare herself and children, with only the luxury of cleanliness, to receive her husband, who returning weary home in the evening found smiling babes and a clean hearth. My heart has loitered in the midst of the group, and has even throbbed with sympathetic emotion, when the scraping of the well known foot has raised a pleasing tumult.

Whilst my benevolence has been gratified by contemplating this artless picture, I have thought that a couple of this description, equally necessary and independent of each other, because each fulfilled the respective duties of their station, possessed all that life could give.—Raised sufficiently above abject poverty not to be obliged to weigh the consequence of every farthing they spend, and having sufficient to prevent their attending to a frigid system of economy, which narrows both heart and mind. I declare, so vulgar are my conceptions, that I know not what is wanted to render this the happiest as well as the most respectable situation in the world, but a taste for literature, to throw a little variety and interest into social converse, and some superfluous money to give to the needy and to buy books. For it is not pleasant when the heart is opened by compassion and the head active in arranging plans of usefulness, to have a prim urchin continually twitching back the elbow to prevent the hand from drawing out an almost empty purse, whispering at the same time some prudential maxim about the priority of justice.

Destructive, however, as riches and inherited honors are to the human character, women are more debased and cramped, if possible, by them, than men, because men may still, in some degree, unfold their faculties by becoming soldiers and statesmen.

[...]

The preposterous distinctions of rank, which render civilization a curse, by dividing the world between voluptuous tyrants, and cunning envious dependents, corrupt, almost equally, every class of people, because respectability is not attached to the discharge of the relative duties of life, but to the station, and when the duties are not fulfilled the affections cannot gain sufficient strength to fortify the virtue of which they are the natural reward. Still there are some loopholes out of which a man may creep, and dare to think and act for himself; but for a woman it is an Herculean task, because she has difficulties peculiar to her sex to overcome, which require almost super-human powers.

A truly benevolent legislator always endeavors to make it the interest of each individual to be virtuous; and thus private virtue becoming the cement of public happiness,[1] an orderly whole is consolidated by the tendency of all the parts towards a common centre. But, the private or public virtue of woman is very problematical; for Rousseau, and a numerous list of male writers, insist that she should all her life be subjected to a severe restraint, that of propriety. Why subject her to propriety—blind propriety, if she be capable of acting from a nobler spring, if she be an heir of immortality? Is sugar always to be produced by vital blood?[2] Is one half of the human species, like the poor African slaves, to be subject to prejudices that brutalize them, when principles would be a surer guard, only to sweeten the cup of man? Is not this indirectly to deny woman reason? for a gift is a mockery, if it be unfit for use.

Women are, in common with men, rendered weak and luxurious by the relaxing pleasures which wealth procures; but added to this they are made slaves to their persons, and must render them alluring that man may lend them his reason to guide their tottering steps aright. Or should they be ambitious, they must govern their tyrants by sinister tricks, for without rights there cannot be any incumbent duties. The laws respecting woman, which I mean to discuss in a future part, make an absurd unit of a man and his wife; and then, by the easy transition of only considering him as responsible, she is reduced to a mere cypher.[3]

The being who discharges the duties of its station is independent; and, speaking of women at large, their first duty is to themselves as rational creatures, and the next, in point of importance, as citizens, is that, which includes so many, of a mother. The rank in life which dispenses with their fulfilling this duty, necessarily degrades them by making them mere dolls. Or, should they turn to something more important than merely fitting drapery upon a smooth

---

1   *A truly benevolent legislator ... public happiness* Allusion to Mandeville, *The Fable of the Bees; or, Private Vices, Public Benefits* (1705). In this satirical work, the philosopher and political economist Bernard de Mandeville (1670–1733) argued against the belief that it is possible to educate for virtue. He describes a community of bees who thrive until they decide to abandon private ambition for public honesty and virtue, much to their demise. In other words, Mandeville claimed that progress is largely due to private vices.

2   *Is sugar ... vital blood* A boycott of slave-produced sugar was one of the most successful aspects of the abolition campaign (and one in which women could play an active part): by 1792, between three and four hundred thousand consumers were taking part.

3   *she is reduced to a mere cipher* See William Blackstone (1723–80), *Commentaries on the Laws of England* (1765–69) 430; 1.15.

block, their minds are only occupied by some soft platonic attachment; or, the actual management of an intrigue may keep their thoughts in motion; for when they neglect domestic duties, they have it not in their power to take the field and march and counter-march like soldiers, or wrangle in the senate to keep their faculties from rusting.

I know that, as a proof of the inferiority of the sex, Rousseau has exultingly exclaimed, How can they leave the nursery for the camp![1]—And the camp has by some moralists been termed the school of the most heroic virtues; though, I think, it would puzzle a keen casuist to prove the reasonableness of the greater number of wars that have dubbed heroes. I do not mean to consider this question critically; because, having frequently viewed these freaks of ambition as the first natural mode of civilization, when the ground must be torn up, and the woods cleared by fire and sword, I do not choose to call them pests; but surely the present system of war has little connection with virtue of any denomination, being rather the school of *finesse* and effeminacy, than of fortitude.

Yet, if defensive war, the only justifiable war, in the present advanced state of society, where virtue can show its face and ripen amidst the rigors which purify the air on the mountain's top, were alone to be adopted as just and glorious, the true heroism of antiquity might again animate female bosoms.—But fair and softly, gentle reader, male or female, do not alarm thyself, for though I have compared the character of a modern soldier with that of a civilized woman, I am not going to advise them to turn their distaff into a musket, though I sincerely wish to see the bayonet converted into a pruning-hook.[2] I only recreated an imagination, fatigued by contemplating the vices and follies which all proceed from a feculent stream of wealth that has muddied the pure rills of natural affection, by supposing that society will some time or other be so constituted, that man must necessarily fulfill the duties of a citizen, or be despised, and that while he was employed in any of the departments of civil life, his wife, also an active citizen, should be equally intent to manage her family, educate her children, and assist her neighbors.

But, to render her really virtuous and useful, she must not, if she discharge her civil duties, want, individually, the protection of civil laws; she must not be dependent on her husband's bounty for her subsistence during his life, or support after his death—for how can a being be generous who has nothing of its own? or, virtuous, who is not free? The wife, in the present state of things, who is faithful to her husband, and neither suckles nor educates her children, scarcely deserves the name of a wife, and has no right to that of a citizen. But take away natural rights, and duties become null.

Women then must be considered as only the wanton solace of men, when they become so weak in mind and body, that they cannot exert themselves, unless to pursue some frothy pleasure, or to invent some frivolous fashion. What can be a more melancholy sight to a thinking mind, than to look into the numerous carriages that drive helter-skelter about this metropolis in a morning full of pale-faced creatures who are flying from themselves. I have often wished, with Dr. Johnson,[3] to place some of them in a little shop with half a dozen children looking up to their languid countenances for support. I am much mistaken, if some latent vigor would not soon give health and spirit to their eyes, and some lines drawn by the exercise of reason on the blank cheeks, which before were only undulated by dimples, might restore lost dignity to the character, or rather enable it to attain the true dignity of its nature. Virtue is not to be acquired even by speculation, much less by the negative supineness that wealth naturally generates.

Besides, when poverty is more disgraceful than even vice, is not morality cut to the quick? Still to avoid misconstruction, though I consider that women in the common walks of life are called to fulfill the duties of wives and mothers, by religion and reason, I cannot help lamenting that women of a superiour cast have not a road open by which they can pursue more extensive plans of usefulness and independence. I may excite laughter, by dropping an hint, which I mean to pursue, some future time, for I really think that women ought to have representatives, instead of being arbitrarily governed without having any direct share allowed them in the deliberations of government.[4]

But, as the whole system of representation is now, in this country, only a convenient handle for despotism, they need not complain, for they are as well represented as a numerous class of hard working mechanics, who pay

---

1   *How can they leave ... for the camp*   Rousseau, *Emile*.

2   *bayonet converted into a pruning-hook*   See Isaiah 2.4: "They shall beat their swords into plowshares, and their spears into pruning-hooks."

3   *Dr. Johnson*   Johnson, *The Rambler* 85 (8 January 1751), "The Mischiefs of Total Idleness."

4   *without having ... deliberations of government*   British women were granted the vote with some property restrictions in 1918, and without restriction in 1928.

for the support of royalty when they can scarcely stop their children's mouths with bread. How are they represented whose very sweat supports the splendid stud of an heir apparent, or varnishes the chariot of some female favorite who looks down on shame? Taxes on the very necessaries of life, enable an endless tribe of idle princes and princesses to pass with stupid pomp before a gaping crowd, who almost worship the very parade which costs them so dear. This is mere gothic grandeur, something like the barbarous useless parade of having sentinels on horseback at Whitehall,[1] which I could never view without a mixture of contempt and indignation.

How strangely must the mind be sophisticated when this sort of state impresses it! But, till these monuments of folly are leveled by virtue, similar follies will leaven the whole mass. For the same character, in some degree, will prevail in the aggregate of society: and the refinements of luxury, or the vicious repinings[2] of envious poverty, will equally banish virtue from society, considered as the characteristic of that society, or only allow it to appear as one of the stripes of the harlequin coat, worn by the civilized man.

In the superiour ranks of life, every duty is done by deputies, as if duties could ever be waved, and the vain pleasures which consequent idleness forces the rich to pursue, appear so enticing to the next rank, that the numerous scramblers for wealth sacrifice every thing to tread on their heels. The most sacred trusts are then considered as sinecures, because they were procured by interest, and only sought to enable a man to keep *good company*. Women, in particular, all want to be ladies. Which is simply to have nothing to do, but listlessly to go they scarcely care where, for they cannot tell what.

But what have women to do in society? I may be asked, but to loiter with easy grace; surely you would not condemn them all to suckle fools and chronicle small beer![3] No. Women might certainly study the art of healing, and be physicians as well as nurses. And midwifery, decency seems to allot to them, though I am afraid the word midwife, in our dictionaries, will soon give place to *accoucheur*, and one proof of the former delicacy of the sex be effaced from the language.

They might, also, study politics, and settle their benevolence on the broadest basis; for the reading of history will scarcely be more useful than the perusal of romances, if read as mere biography; if the character of the times, the political improvements, arts, &c. be not observed. In short, if it be not considered as the history of man; and not of particular men, who filled a niche in the temple of fame, and dropped into the black rolling stream of time, that silently sweeps all before it, into the shapeless void called—eternity.—For shape, can it be called, "that shape hath none?"[4]

Business of various kinds, they might likewise pursue, if they were educated in a more orderly manner, which might save many from common and legal prostitution. Women would not then marry for a support, as men accept of places under government, and neglect the implied duties; nor would an attempt to earn their own subsistence, a most laudable one! sink them almost to the level of those poor abandoned creatures who live by prostitution. For are not milliners and mantua[5]-makers reckoned the next class? The few employments open to women, so far from being liberal, are menial; and when a superior education enables them to take charge of the education of children as governesses, they are not treated like the tutors of sons, though even clerical tutors are not always treated in a manner calculated to render them respectable in the eyes of their pupils, to say nothing of the private comfort of the individual. But as women educated like gentlewomen, are never designed for the humiliating situation which necessity sometimes forces them to fill; these situations are considered in the light of a degradation; and they know little of the human heart, who need to be told, that nothing so painfully sharpens sensibility as such a fall in life.

Some of these women might be restrained from marrying by a proper spirit or delicacy, and others may not have had it in their power to escape in this pitiful way from servitude; is not that government then very defective, and very unmindful of the happiness of one half of is members, that does not provide for honest, independent women, by encouraging them to fill respectable stations? But in order to render their private virtue a public benefit,[6] they must have a civil existence in the State, married or single; else we shall continually see some worthy woman, whose sensibility

---

1   *Whitehall* Whitehall is the location of the most important offices of the British government. The horse guards are still there.

2   *repinings* Complaints.

3   *suckle fools and chronicle small beer* Shakespeare, *Othello* 2.1.159.

4   *that shape hath none* Milton, *Paradise Lost* 3.11–12, 2.667.

5   *mantua* Loose gown worn by women.

6   *private virtue a public benefit* Another allusion to Mandeville, *The Fable of the Bees; or, Private Vices, Public Benefits*.

has been rendered painfully acute by undeserved contempt, droop like "the lily broken down by a plow-share."[1]

It is a melancholy truth; yet such is the blessed effect of civilization! the most respectable women are the most oppressed;[2] and, unless they have understandings far superiour to the common run of understandings, taking in both sexes, they must, from being treated like contemptible beings, become contemptible. How many women thus waste life away the prey of discontent, who might have practiced as physicians, regulated a farm, managed a shop, and stood erect, supported by their own industry,[3] instead of hanging their heads surcharged with the dew of sensibility, that consumes the beauty to which it at first gave lustre;[4] nay, I doubt whether pity and love are so near akin as poets feign, for I have seldom seen much compassion excited by the helplessness of females, unless they were fair; then, perhaps, pity was the soft handmaid of love, or the harbinger of lust.

How much more respectable is the woman who earns her own bread by fulfilling any duty, than the most accomplished beauty!—beauty did I say?—so sensible am I of the beauty of moral loveliness, or the harmonious propriety that attunes the passions of a well-regulated mind, that I blush at making the comparison; yet I sigh to think how few women aim at attaining this respectability by withdrawing from the giddy whirl of pleasure, or the indolent calm that stupifies the good sort of women it sucks in.

Proud of their weakness, however, they must always be protected, guarded from care, and all the rough toils that dignify the mind.—If this be the fiat of fate, if they will make themselves insignificant and contemptible, sweetly to waste "life away," let them not expect to be valued when their beauty fades, for it is the fate of the fairest flowers to be admired and pulled to pieces by the careless hand that plucked them. In how many ways do I wish, from the purest benevolence, to impress this truth on my sex; yet I fear that they will not listen to a truth that dear bought

experience has brought home to many an agitated bosom, nor willingly resign the privileges of rank and sex for the privileges of humanity, to which those have no claim who do not discharge its duties.

Those writers are particularly useful, in my opinion, who make man feel for man, independent of the station he fills, or the drapery of factitious sentiments. I then would fain convince reasonable men of the importance of some of my remarks; and prevail on them to weigh dispassionately the whole tenor of my observations.—I appeal to their understandings; and, as a fellow-creature, claim, in the name of my sex, some interest in their hearts. I entreat them to assist to emancipate their companion, to make her a *help meet* for them!

Would men but generously snap our chains, and be content with rational fellowship instead of slavish obedience, they would find us more observant daughters, more affectionate sisters, more faithful wives, more reasonable mothers—in a word, better citizens. We should then love them with true affection, because we should learn to respect ourselves; and the peace of mind of a worthy man would not be interrupted by the idle vanity of his wife, nor the babes sent to nestle in a strange bosom, having never found a home in their mother's.

[...]

Chapter 12: On National Education

The good effects resulting from attention to private education will ever be very confined, and the parent who really puts his own hand to the plow, will always, in some degree, be disappointed, till education becomes a grand national concern. A man cannot retire into a desert with his child, and if he did, he could not bring himself back to childhood, and become the proper friend and play-fellow of an infant or youth. And when children are confined to the society of men and women, they very soon acquire that kind of premature manhood which stops the growth of every vigorous power of mind or body. In order to open their faculties they should be excited to think for themselves; and this can only be done by mixing a number of children together, and making them jointly pursue the same objects.

A child very soon contracts a benumbing indolence of mind, which he has seldom sufficient vigor to shake off, when he only asks a question instead of seeking for information, and then relies implicitly on the answer he receives.

---

1   *the lily ... plow-share* Fénelon, *The Adventures of Telemachus*, trans. Isaac Littlebury (1699) 1.152; see Robert Burns (1759–96), "To a Mountain-Daisy, On Turning One Down, with the Plough, in April—1786" 49–54.

2   *the most respectable women ... most oppressed* Ironic echo of the opening sentences of Jonathan Swift's "A Modest Proposal" (1729).

3   *How many women ... their own industry* See Thomas Gray, "Elegy Written in a Country Church-Yard" (1768) 53–60.

4   *consumes the beauty ... first gave lustre* See Shakespeare, Sonnet 73, line 12.

With his equals in age this could never be the case, and the subjects of inquiry, though they might be influenced, would not be entirely under the direction of men, who frequently damp, if not destroy abilities, by bringing them forward too hastily: and too hastily they will infallibly be brought forward, if the child could be confined to the society of a man, however sagacious that man may be.

Besides, in youth the seeds of every affection should be sown, and the respectful regard, which is felt for a parent, is very different from the social affections that are to constitute the happiness of life as it advances. Of these, equality is the basis, and an intercourse of sentiments unclogged by that observant seriousness which prevents disputation, though it may not enforce submission. Let a child have ever such an affection for his parent, he will always languish to play and chat with children; and the very respect he entertains, for filial esteem always has a dash of fear mixed with it, will, if it do not teach him cunning, at least prevent him from pouring out the little secrets which first open the heart to friendship and confidence, gradually leading to more expansive benevolence. Added to this, he will never acquire that frank ingenuousness of behavior, which young people can only attain by being frequently in society, where they dare to speak what they think; neither afraid of being reproved for their presumption, nor laughed at for their folly.

Forcibly impressed by the reflections which the sight of schools, as they are at present conducted, naturally suggested, I have formerly delivered my opinion rather warmly in favor of a private education; but further experience has led me to view the subject in a different light. I still, however, think schools, as they are now regulated, the hot-beds of vice and folly, and the knowledge of human nature, supposed to be attained there, merely cunning selfishness.

At school, boys become gluttons and slovens,[1] and, instead of cultivating domestic affections, very early rush into the libertinism which destroys the constitution before it is formed; hardening the heart as it weakens the understanding.

I should, in fact, be averse to boarding-schools, if it were for no other reason than the unsettled state of mind which the expectation of the vacations produce. On these the children's thoughts are fixed with eager anticipating hopes, for, at least, to speak with moderation, half of the time, and when they arrive they are spent in total dissipation and beastly indulgence.

But, on the contrary, when they are brought up at home, though they may pursue a plan of study in a more orderly manner than can be adopted, when near a fourth part of the year is actually spent in idleness, and as much more in regret and anticipation; yet they there acquire too high an opinion of their own importance, from being allowed to tyrannize over servants, and from the anxiety expressed by most mothers, on the score of manners, who, eager to teach the accomplishments of a gentleman, stifle, in their birth, the virtues of a man. Thus brought into company when they ought to be seriously employed, and treated like men when they are still boys, they become vain and effeminate.

The only way to avoid two extremes equally injurious to morality, would be to contrive some way of combining a public and private education. Thus to make men citizens, two natural steps might be taken, which seem directly to lead to the desired point; for the domestic affections, that first open the heart to the various modifications of humanity would be cultivated, whilst the children were nevertheless allowed to spend great part of their time, on terms of equality, with other children.

I still recollect, with pleasure, the country day school; where a boy trudged in the morning, wet or dry, carrying his books, and his dinner, if it were at a considerable distance; a servant did not then lead master by the hand, for, when he had once put on coat and breeches, he was allowed to shift for himself, and return alone in the evening to recount the feats of the day close at the parental knee. His father's house was his home, and was ever after fondly remembered; nay, I appeal to some superior men who were educated in this manner, whether the recollection of some shady lane where they conned their lesson; or, of some stile, where they sat making a kite, or mending a bat, has not endeared their country to them?

But, what boy ever recollected with pleasure the years he spent in close confinement, at an academy near London? unless indeed he should by chance remember the poor scare-crow of an usher whom he tormented; or, the tart-man, from whom he caught a cake, to devour it with the cattish appetite of selfishness. At boarding schools of every description, the relaxation of the junior boys is mischief; and of the senior, vice. Besides, in great schools what can be more prejudicial to the moral character, than the system of tyranny and abject slavery which is established amongst the boys, to say nothing of the slavery to forms, which

---

1   *slovens* People who are careless regarding their personal appearance.

makes religion worse than a farce? For what good can be expected from the youth who receives the sacrament of the Lord's supper, to avoid forfeiting half-a-guinea, which he probably afterwards spends in some sensual manner? Half the employment of the youths is to elude the necessity of attending public worship; and well they may, for such a constant repetition of the same thing must be a very irksome restraint on their natural vivacity. As these ceremonies have the most fatal effect on their morals, and as a ritual performed by the lips, when the heart and mind are far away, is not now stored up by our church as a bank to draw on for the fees of the poor souls in purgatory, why should they not be abolished?

[...]

In order then to inspire a love of home and domestic pleasures, children ought to be educated at home, for riotous holidays only make them fond of home for their own sakes. Yet, the vacations, which do not foster domestic affections, continually disturb the course of study, and render any plan of improvement abortive which includes temperance; still, were they abolished, children would be entirely separated from their parents, and I question whether they would become better citizens by sacrificing the preparatory affections, by destroying the force of relationships that render the marriage state as necessary as respectable. But, if a private education produce self-importance, or insulates a man in his family, the evil is only shifted, not remedied.

This train of reasoning brings me back to a subject, on which I mean to dwell, the necessity of establishing proper day-schools.

But these should be national establishments, for whilst school-masters are dependent on the caprice of parents, little exertion can be expected from them, more than is necessary to please ignorant people. Indeed, the necessity of a master's giving the parents some sample of the boy's abilities, which during the vacation, is shown to every visitor, is productive of more mischief than would at first be supposed. For they are seldom done entirely, to speak with moderation, by the child itself; thus the master countenances falsehoods, or winds the poor machine up to some extraordinary exertion, that injures the wheels, and stops the progress of gradual improvement. The memory is loaded with unintelligible words, to make a show of, without the understanding's acquiring any distinct ideas: but only that education deserves emphatically to be termed cultivation of mind, which teaches young people how to begin to think. The imagina-

tion should not be allowed to debauch the understanding before it gained strength, or vanity will become the forerunner of vice: for every way of exhibiting the acquirements of a child is injurious to its moral character.

How much time is lost in teaching them to recite what they do not understand! whilst, seated on benches, all in their best array, the mammas listen with astonishment to the parrot-like prattle, uttered in solemn cadences, with all the pomp of ignorance and folly. Such exhibitions only serve to strike the spreading fibers of vanity through the whole mind; for they neither teach children to speak fluently, nor behave gracefully. So far from it, that these frivolous pursuits might comprehensively be termed the study of affectation: for we now rarely see a simple, bashful boy, though few people of taste were ever disgusted by that awkward sheepishness so natural to the age, which schools and an early introduction into society, have changed into impudence and apish grimace.

Yet, how can these things be remedied whilst school-masters depend entirely on parents for a subsistence; and when so many rival schools hang out their lures to catch the attention of vain fathers and mothers, whose parental affection only leads them to wish, that their children should outshine those of their neighbors?

Without great good luck, a sensible, conscientious man, would starve before he could raise a school, if he disdained to bubble weak parents, by practicing the secret tricks of the craft.

In the best regulated schools, however, where swarms are not crammed together many bad habits must be acquired; but, at common schools, the body, heart, and understanding, are equally stunted, for parents are often only in quest of the cheapest school, and the master could not live, if he did not take a much greater number than he could manage himself; nor will the scanty pittance, allowed for each child, permit him to hire ushers sufficient to assist in the discharge of the mechanical part of the business. Besides, whatever appearance the house and garden may make, the children do not enjoy the comforts of either, for they are continually reminded, by irksome restrictions, that they are not at home, and the state-rooms, garden, &c. must be kept in order for the recreation of the parents; who, of a Sunday, visit the school, and are impressed by the very parade that renders the situation of their children uncomfortable.

With what disgust have I heard sensible women, for girls are more restrained and cowed than boys, speak of the wearisome confinement which they endured at school. Not allowed, perhaps, to step out of one broad walk in a superb garden, and obliged to pace with steady deportment stupidly backwards and forwards, holding up their heads, and turning out their toes, with shoulders braced back, instead of bounding, as nature directs to complete her own design, in the various attitudes so conducive to health. The pure animal spirits, which make both mind and body shoot out, and unfold the tender blossoms of hope are turned sour, and vented in vain wishes, or pert repinings, that contract the faculties and spoil the temper; else they mount to the brain and sharpening the understanding before it gains proportionable strength, produce that pitiful cunning which disgracefully characterizes the female mind—and I fear will ever characterize it whilst women remain the slaves of power!

The little respect which the male world pay to chastity is, I am persuaded, the grand source of many of the physical and moral evils that torment mankind, as well as of the vices and follies that degrade and destroy women; yet at school, boys infallibly lose that decent bashfulness, which might have ripened into modesty at home.

And what nasty indecent tricks do they not also learn from each other, when a number of them pig together in the same bedchamber, not to speak of the vices, which render the body weak, whilst they effectually prevent the acquisition of delicacy of mind. The little attention paid to the cultivation of modesty, amongst men, produces great depravity in all the relationships of society; for, not only love—love that ought to purify the heart, and first call forth all the youthful powers, to prepare the man to discharge the benevolent duties of life, is sacrificed to premature lust; but, all the social affections are deadened by the selfish gratifications, which very early pollute the mind, and dry up the generous juices of the heart. In what an unnatural manner is innocence often violated; and what serious consequences ensue to render private vices a public pest. Besides, a habit of personal order, which has more effect on the moral character, than is, in general, supposed, can only be acquired at home, where that respectable reserve is kept up which checks the familiarity, that sinking in beastliness, undermines the affection it insults.

I have already animadverted on the bad habits which females acquire when they are shut up together; and I think that the observation may fairly be extended to the other sex, till the natural inference is drawn which I have had in view throughout—that to improve both sexes they ought, not only in private families, but in public schools, to be educated together. If marriage be the cement of society, mankind should all be educated after the same model, or the intercourse of the sexes will never deserve the name of fellowship, nor will women ever fulfill the peculiar duties of their sex, till they become enlightened citizens, till they become free, by being enabled to earn their own subsistence, independent of men; in the same manner, I mean, to prevent misconstruction, as one man is independent of another. Nay, marriage will never be held sacred till women by being brought up with men, are prepared to be their companions, rather than their mistresses; for the mean doublings of cunning will ever render them contemptible, whilst oppression renders them timid. So convinced am I of this truth, that I will venture to predict, that virtue will never prevail in society till the virtues of both sexes are founded on reason; and, till the affection common to both are allowed to gain their due strength by the discharge of mutual duties.

Were boys and girls permitted to pursue the same studies together, those graceful decencies might early be inculcated which produce modesty, without those sexual distinctions that taint the mind. Lessons of politeness, and that formulary of decorum, which treads on the heels of falsehood, would be rendered useless by habitual propriety of behavior. Not, indeed put on for visitors like the courtly robe of politeness, but the sober effect of cleanliness of mind. Would not this simple elegance of sincerity be a chaste homage paid to domestic affections, far surpassing the meretricious compliments that shine with false lustre in the heartless intercourse of fashionable life? But, till more understanding preponderate in society, there will ever be a want of heart and taste, and the harlot's *rouge* will supply the place of that celestial suffusion which only virtuous affections can give to the face. Gallantry, and what is called love, may subsist without simplicity of character; but the main pillars of friendship, are respect and confidence—esteem is never founded on it cannot tell what!

A taste for the fine arts requires great cultivation; but not more than a taste for the virtuous affections: and both suppose that enlargement of mind which opens so many sources of mental pleasure. Why do people hurry to noisy scenes and crowded circles? I should answer, because they want activity of mind, because they have not cherished the virtues of the heart. They only, therefore, see and feel in the gross, and continually pine after variety, finding every thing that is simple, insipid.

This argument may be carried further than philosophers are aware of, for if nature destined woman, in particular, for the discharge of domestic duties, she made her susceptible of the attached affections in a great degree. Now women are notoriously fond of pleasure; and naturally must be so, according to my definition, because they cannot enter into the minutiae of domestic taste; lacking judgment the foundation of all taste. For the understanding, in spite of sensual cavillers, reserves to itself the privilege of conveying pure joy to the heart.

With what a languid yawn have I seen an admirable poem thrown down, that a man of true taste returns to, again and again with rapture; and, whilst melody has almost suspended respiration, a lady has asked me where I bought my gown. I have seen also an eye glanced coldly over a most exquisite picture, rest, sparkling with pleasure, on a caricature rudely sketched; and whilst some terrific feature in nature has spread a sublime stillness through my soul, I have been desired to observe the pretty tricks of a lap-dog, that my perverse fate forced me to travel with. Is it surprising, that such a tasteless being should rather caress this dog than her children? Or, that she should prefer the rant of flattery to the simple accents of sincerity?

To illustrate this remark I must be allowed to observe, that men of the first genius, and most cultivated minds, have appeared to have the highest relish for the simple beauties of nature; and they must have forcibly felt, what they have so well described, the charm, which natural affections, and unsophisticated feelings spread round the human character. It is this power of looking into the heart, and responsively vibrating with each emotion, that enables the poet to personify each passion, and the painter to sketch with a pencil of fire.

True taste is ever the work of the understanding employed in observing natural effects; and till women have more understanding, it is vain to expect them to possess domestic taste. Their lively senses will ever be at work to harden their hearts, and the emotions struck out of them will continue to be vivid and transitory, unless a proper education stores their minds with knowledge.

It is the want of domestic taste, and not the acquirement of knowledge, that takes women out of their families, and tears the smiling babe from the breast that ought to afford it nourishment. Women have been allowed to remain in ignorance, and slavish dependence, many, very many years, and still we hear of nothing but their fondness of pleasure and sway, their preference of rakes and soldiers, their childish attachment to toys, and the vanity that makes them value accomplishments more than virtues.

History brings forward a fearful catalogue of the crimes which their cunning has produced, when the weak slaves have had sufficient address to over-reach their masters. In France, and in how many other countries have men been the luxurious despots, and women the crafty ministers? Does this prove that ignorance and dependence domesticate them? Is not their folly the by-word of the libertines, who relax in their society; and do not men of sense continually lament, that an immoderate fondness for dress and dissipation carries the mother of a family for ever from home? Their hearts have not been debauched by knowledge, nor their minds led astray by scientific pursuits; yet, they do not fulfill the peculiar duties, which as women they are called upon by nature to fulfill. On the contrary, the state of warfare which subsists between the sexes, makes them employ those wiles, that frustrate the more open designs of force.

When, therefore, I call women slaves, I mean in a political and civil sense; for, indirectly they obtain too much power, and are debased by their exertions to obtain illicit sway.

Let an enlightened nation then try what effect reason would have to bring them back to nature, and their duty; and allowing them to share the advantages of education and government with man, see whether they will become better, as they grow wiser and become free. They cannot be injured by the experiment; for it is not in the power of man to render them more insignificant than they are at present.

To render this practicable, day schools for particular ages should be established by government, in which boys and girls might be educated together. The school for the younger children, from five to nine years of age, ought to be absolutely free and open to all classes. A sufficient number of masters should also be chosen by a select committee, in each parish, to whom any complaint of negligence, &c. might be made, if signed by six of the children's parents.

Ushers would then be unnecessary; for, I believe, experience will ever prove, that this kind of subordinate authority is particularly injurious to the morals of youth. What, indeed, can tend to deprave the character more than outward submission and inward contempt? Yet, how can boys be expected to treat an usher with respect when the master seems to consider him in the light of a servant, and almost to countenance the ridicule which becomes the chief amusement of the boys during the play hours?

But nothing of this kind could occur in an elementary day-school, where boys and girls, the rich and poor, should meet together. And to prevent any of the distinctions of vanity, they should be dressed alike, and all obliged to submit to the same discipline, or leave the school. The school-room ought to be surrounded by a large piece of ground, in which the children might be usefully exercised, for at this age they should not be confined to any sedentary employment for more than an hour at a time. But these relaxations might all be rendered a part of elementary education, for many things improve and amuse the senses, when introduced as a kind of show, to the principles of which dryly laid down, children would turn a deaf ear. For instance, botany, mechanics, and astronomy. Reading, writing, arithmetic, natural history, and some simple experiments in natural philosophy, might fill up the day; but these pursuits should never encroach on gymnastic plays in the open air. The elements of religion, history, the history of man, and politics, might also be taught by conversations, in the Socratic form.

After the age of nine, girls and boys, intended for domestic employments, or mechanical trades, ought to be removed to other schools, and receive instruction, in some measure appropriated to the destination of each individual, the two sexes being still together in the morning; but in the afternoon, the girls should attend a school, where plain work, mantua-making, millinery,[1] &c. would be their employment.

The young people of superior abilities, or fortune, might now be taught, in another school, the dead and living languages, the elements of science, and continue the study of history and politics, on a more extensive scale, which would not exclude polite literature.

Girls and boys still together? I hear some readers ask: yes. And I should not fear any other consequence, than that some early attachment might take place; which, whilst it had the best effect on the moral character of the young people, might not perfectly agree with the views of the parents, for it will be a long time, I fear, before the world is so enlightened, that parents, only anxious to render their children virtuous, will let them choose companions for life themselves.

Besides, this would be a sure way to promote early marriages, and from early marriages the most salutary physical and moral effects naturally flow. What a different character does a married citizen assume from the selfish coxcomb, who lives but for himself, and who is often afraid to marry lest he should not be able to live in a certain style. Great emergencies excepted, which would rarely occur in a society of which equality was the basis, a man could only be prepared to discharge the duties of public life, by the habitual practice of those inferior ones which form the man.

In this plan of education, the constitution of boys would not be ruined by the early debaucheries, which now make men so selfish, nor girls rendered weak and vain, by indolence and frivolous pursuits. But, I presuppose, that such a degree of equality should be established between the sexes as would shut out gallantry and coquetry, yet allow friendship and love to temper the heart for the discharge of higher duties.

These would be schools of morality—and the happiness of man, allowed to flow from the pure springs of duty and affection, what advances might not the human mind make? Society can only be happy and free in proportion as it is virtuous; but the present distinctions, established in society, corrode all private, and blast all public virtue.

[...]

Chapter 13: Some Instances of the Folly Which the Ignorance of Women Generates; with Concluding Reflections on the Moral Improvement that a Revolution in Female Manners Might Naturally Be Expected to Produce

[...]

Asserting the rights which women in common with men ought to contend for, I have not attempted to extenuate their faults; but to prove them to be the natural consequence of their education and station in society. If so, it is reasonable to suppose that they will change their character, and correct their vices and follies, when they are allowed to be free in a physical, moral, and civil sense.

Let woman share the rights and she will emulate the virtues of man; for she must grow more perfect when emancipated, or justify the authority that chains such a weak being to her duty.—If the latter, it will be expedient to open a fresh trade with Russia for whips; a present which a father should always make to his son-in-law on his wedding day, that a husband may keep his whole family in order by the

---

1   *millinery*   Hat-making.

same means; and without any violation of justice reign, wielding this scepter, sole master of his house, because he is the only being in it who has reason:—the divine, indefeasible earthly sovereignty breathed into man by the Master of the universe. Allowing this position, women have not any inherent rights to claim, and by the same rule, their duties vanish, for rights and duties are inseparable.

Be just then, O ye men of understanding! and mark not more severely what women do amiss, than the vicious tricks of the horse or the ass for whom ye provide provender—and allow her the privileges of ignorance, to whom ye deny the rights of reason, or ye will be worse than Egyptian task-masters, expecting virtue where nature has not given understanding!

EDMUND BURKE
(1729 – 1797)

EDMUND BURKE WAS A MEMBER OF THE ENGLISH PAR-
liament and a renowned orator as well as a prolific and
distinguished writer. His most famous work was an attack
on the French Revolution, published in 1790 very soon
after the Revolution had begun, and predicting with some
accuracy the revolutionary excesses still
to come. *Reflections on the Revolution in
France* was widely read and hugely influential—provoking both enthusiastic
support and impassioned opposition.
"Read it," urged the half-mad and
reactionary King George III, "It will
do you good—do you good! Every
gentleman should read it."[1] On the
other side, Thomas Paine, the hero of
the American revolutionary movement,
declared at the beginning of *The Rights
of Man* (a work largely devoted to refuting Burke), "Among the incivilities by
which nations or individuals provoke
and irritate each other, Mr. Burke's
pamphlet on the French Revolution is
an extraordinary instance ... Everything
which rancour, prejudice, ignorance or
knowledge could suggest, is poured forth in the copious
fury of near four hundred pages."[2]

Burke's *Reflections* earned him the reputation of a defender of aristocracy and monarchy, of status and hierarchy,
of tradition and custom, of religion and the established
social order—in short, of political conservatism (in one important form). And he is still considered a founding figure
of the conservative movement.

Burke was born in Dublin, Ireland, in 1729. His father
was a successful Protestant attorney, and his mother a
Catholic; he was brought up a Catholic. After finishing his
education at Trinity College in Dublin, he went to England
intending to start a career in the law, but instead turned

to writing, on, among other things, aesthetics and social
philosophy. In 1765 he took a job with the leader of the
Whig party, and shortly thereafter took a seat in Parliament,
elected member for Bristol, England's second most important city at the time.

Over the next twenty-five years,
he was a prolific producer of political
pamphlets and speeches. His well-
known speech to the electors of Bristol
defended representative democracy, the
system in which elected members are
not expected always to represent exactly
the views of the majority of their constituents; as "trustees" they should in
Burke's view vote reflecting their own
conscience and their understanding of
the long-term public good, rather than
as mere "delegates"—mouthpieces for
the views of those who elected them.

The most important political and
literary event of Burke's life was the
1790 publication of his strongly critical
work on the French Revolution. Paine
and other commentators on this work
expressed surprise that Burke's views had undergone such
a drastic reversal: Burke had previously been a strong advocate of the "progressive" views of the Whig party, supporting limitations on the power of the monarch, attacking the
corrupt and harmful policies of the East India Company
in the Indian colonies, condemning the persecution of the
Catholics in Ireland, and criticizing the unjust treatment
of the colonists in pre-revolutionary America. "The temper
and character which prevail in our [American] Colonies,"
he had written, "are, I am afraid, unalterable by any human art. We cannot, I fear, falsify the pedigree of this fierce
people, and persuade them that they are not sprung from
a nation in whose veins the blood of freedom circulates....
An Englishman is the unfittest person on earth to argue
another Englishman into slavery."[3]

---

1   Quoted by William Ebenstein, "Burke" in *Great Political Thinkers:
    Plato to the Present*, Fourth Edition (Hinsdale, IL: Dryden Press,
    1969), 475.

2   In "Part The First: Being An Answer To Mr. Burke's Attack On
    The French Revolution" (1791).

3   Burke's 1775 speech "*On Conciliation with the Colonies.*"

But Burke saw the French Revolution as being different in character from the American one. In 1790 the French Revolution had not yet reached its worst excesses, but even then he saw it as a descent into chaos, a rupture of the social contract, threatening Europe with atheism, destruction, anarchy, and terror. And in 1790 Burke argued on behalf of small, gradual reforms, suggesting that these would serve to disarm revolutionary social critics and preserve the basic traditions and institutions of society. "I love a manly, moral, regulated liberty as well as any gentleman" he said in *Reflections*, but "the circumstances are what render every civil and political scheme beneficial or noxious to mankind." And in the circumstances of revolutionary France, Burke argued, the ideal of liberty, as put into practice by the revolutionaries, was noxious, producing tyranny and chaos.

The attempt to radically reconstruct society, Burke argued, must inevitably have terrible results; the only way to avoid disaster is to preserve historical inequalities and hierarchies. So the French Revolution, which aimed at the destruction of the traditional, was horrifying to him. He preferred property, tradition, and community to the French ideals of *liberté*, *egalité*, and *fraternité*.

These views put Burke in the company of Enlightenment figures such as David Hume, and in opposition to those who (in a tradition stemming largely from John Locke) believed that an intellectual understanding of the functions and mechanisms of society, and of the God-given rights of individuals, could result in a rational social reconstruction, and in freedom from the disfunctions of tradition. But Burke distrusted reason as a basis for choosing among social institutions. Some commentators see a source of this distrust in his Christian pessimism: the fallen state of humans makes them forever prone to suffering and disaster, and the traditional social framework has at least worked to mitigate (to the limited extent this was possible) the human propensity for violence and chaos.[1] The best we can do then is to try to hold on to what has worked in the past; even if it has not worked well, it is likely to be superior to anything human reason could design as a replacement.

Burke thought of society not as the sum of individuals, but rather as a kind of living organism, operating rather sluggishly by its own slow laws of adaptive development. Its well-established customs and institutions are a system of obligations and privileges that have stood the test of time, and must not be overthrown by abstract theoretical idealism. Our common-sense "prejudices"—automatic unreflective beliefs and values, without conscious justification—are more reliable, he thought, than the pronouncements of theory. His background in practical politics is reflected by his advocacy of a pragmatic political approach which works slowly and experimentally, and of political thought anchored within the context of practice.

Burke took it that people are made what they are by the historically evolved society they live in. And he thought that this state of affairs constituted an implied justification for his traditionalism—his opposition to radical change, and his conservative attachment to the status quo. Interestingly, the idea of the social construction of individuals is a basic tenet of contemporary communitarianism, which may owe more to Burke than is generally acknowledged. Communitarianism nowadays is often associated with left-wing views, but its similarities with Burke's position—both reject Enlightenment individualism and rationalism—are instructive to contemplate.

Though Burke is best known for the strong stance he took in response to the American and French revolutions, he put forward important arguments in a wide variety of contexts. His 1788 attack on the alleged tendency of the colonial administrator Warren Hastings to be too accommodating of local laws and customs (referred to by Burke as a "geographical morality"), for example, has considerable relevance to today's debates about moral relativism.

◆ ◆ ◆ ◆ ◆

---

1   For this view see Maurice Cranston, "Burke, Edmund" in *The Encyclopedia of Philosophy*, ed. by Paul Edwards (New York: Macmillan Publishing Company, November 1973), v. 1, 430.

from Reflections on the Revolution in France (1790)

It may not be unnecessary to inform the reader that the following reflections had their origin in a correspondence between the author and a very young gentleman at Paris, who did him the honor of desiring his opinion upon the important transactions which then, and ever since, have so much occupied the attention of all men....

Dear Sir

You are pleased to call again, and with some earnestness, for my thoughts on the late proceedings in France....

I flatter myself that I love a manly, moral, regulated liberty as well as any gentleman...; and perhaps I have given as good proofs of my attachment to that cause in the whole course of my public conduct.[1]... But I cannot stand forward and give praise or blame to anything which relates to human actions, and human concerns, on a simple view of the object, as it stands stripped of every relation, in all the nakedness and solitude of metaphysical abstraction. Circumstances (which with some gentlemen pass for nothing) give in reality to every political principle its distinguishing color and discriminating effect. The circumstances are what render every civil and political scheme beneficial or noxious[2] to mankind. Abstractedly speaking, government, as well as liberty, is good; yet could I, in common sense, ten years ago, have felicitated[3] France on her enjoyment of a government (for she then had a government) without inquiry what the nature of that government was, or how it was administered? Can I now congratulate the same nation upon its freedom? Is it because liberty in the abstract may be classed amongst the blessings of mankind, that I am seriously to felicitate a madman, who has escaped from the protecting restraint and wholesome darkness of his cell, on his restoration to the enjoyment of light and liberty? Am I to congratulate a highwayman and murderer who has broke prison upon the recovery of his natural rights?...

When I see the spirit of liberty in action, I see a strong principle at work; and this, for a while, is all I can pos-

sibly know of it. The wild gas, the fixed air, is plainly broke loose; but we ought to suspend our judgment until the first effervescence is a little subsided, till the liquor is cleared, and until we see something deeper than the agitation of a troubled and frothy surface. I must be tolerably sure, before I venture publicly to congratulate men upon a blessing, that they have really received one. Flattery corrupts both the receiver and the giver, and adulation is not of more service to the people than to kings. I should, therefore, suspend my congratulations on the new liberty of France until I was informed how it had been combined with government, with public force, with the discipline and obedience of armies, with the collection of an effective and well-distributed revenue, with morality and religion, with the solidity of property, with peace and order, with civil and social manners. All these (in their way) are good things, too, and without them liberty is not a benefit whilst it lasts, and is not likely to continue long. The effect of liberty to individuals is that they may do what they please; we ought to see what it will please them to do, before we risk congratulations which may be soon turned into complaints. Prudence would dictate this in the case of separate, insulated, private men, but liberty, when men act in bodies, is power. Considerate people, before they declare themselves, will observe the use which is made of power....

... [Doctor Richard Price, a non-conforming minister of eminence][4] tells the Revolution Society in this political sermon that his Majesty "is almost the only lawful king in the world because the only one who owes his crown to the choice of his people."... This doctrine, as applied to the prince now on the British throne, either is nonsense and therefore neither true nor false, or it affirms a most unfounded, dangerous, illegal, and unconstitutional position. According to this spiritual doctor of politics, if his Majesty does not owe his crown to the choice of his people, he is no lawful king. Now nothing can be more untrue than that the crown of this kingdom is so held by his Majesty....

... At some time or other, to be sure, all the beginners of dynasties were chosen by those who called them to govern. There is ground enough for the opinion that all the kingdoms of Europe were, at a remote period, elective, with more or fewer limitations in the objects of choice. But whatever kings might have been here or elsewhere a thousand years

---

1   *in the whole ... conduct*   Burke had been a strong public advocate for the right of the American colonies to declare independence from Britain, and a strong public critic of what he saw as a tendency towards tyranny by the British in India.

2   *noxious*   Harmful.

3   *felicitated*   Congratulated.

4   *Doctor ... eminence*   Price (1723–91), a political philosopher, was also a dissenting clergyman.

ago, or in whatever manner the ruling dynasties of England or France may have begun, the king of Great Britain is, at this day, king by a fixed rule of succession according to the laws of his country; and whilst the legal conditions of the compact of sovereignty are performed by him[1] (as they are performed), he holds his crown in contempt of the choice of the Revolution Society,[2] who have not a single vote for a king amongst them, either individually or collectively....

Whatever may be the success of evasion in explaining away the gross error of fact, which supposes that his Majesty (though he holds it in concurrence with the wishes) owes his crown to the choice of his people, yet nothing can evade their full explicit declaration concerning the principle of a right in the people to choose; ... the political divine proceeds dogmatically to assert[3] that, by the principles of the Revolution, the people of England have acquired three fundamental rights, ... namely, that we have acquired a right:

(1) to choose our own governors.
(2) to cashier[4] them for misconduct.
(3) to frame a government for ourselves.

This new and hitherto unheard-of bill of rights, though made in the name of the whole people, belongs to those gentlemen and their faction only. The body of the people of England have no share in it. They utterly disclaim it. They will resist the practical assertion of it with their lives and fortunes. They are bound to do so by the laws of their country made at the time of that very Revolution which is appealed to in favor of the fictitious rights claimed by the Society which abuses its name.

... It is now sixteen or seventeen years since I saw the queen of France, then the dauphiness,[5] at Versailles, and surely never lighted on this orb, which she hardly seemed to touch, a more delightful vision. I saw her just above the horizon, decorating and cheering the elevated sphere she just began to move in—glittering like the morning star, full of life and splendor and joy. Oh! what a revolution! and what a heart must I have to contemplate without emotion that elevation and that fall! Little did I dream when she added titles of veneration to those of enthusiastic, distant, respectful love, that she should ever be obliged to carry the sharp antidote against disgrace concealed in that bosom; little did I dream that I should have lived to see such disasters fallen upon her in a nation of gallant men, in a nation of men of honor and of cavaliers. I thought ten thousand swords must have leaped from their scabbards to avenge even a look that threatened her with insult. But the age of chivalry is gone. That of sophisters,[6] economists, and calculators has succeeded; and the glory of Europe is extinguished forever. Never, never more shall we behold that generous loyalty to rank and sex, that proud submission, that dignified obedience, that subordination of the heart which kept alive, even in servitude itself, the spirit of an exalted freedom. The unbought grace of life, the cheap defense of nations, the nurse of manly sentiment and heroic enterprise, is gone! It is gone, that sensibility of principle, that chastity of honor which felt a stain like a wound, which inspired courage whilst it mitigated ferocity, which ennobled whatever it touched, and under which vice itself lost half its evil by losing all its grossness.

This mixed system of opinion and sentiment had its origin in the ancient chivalry; and the principle, though varied in its appearance by the varying state of human affairs, subsisted and influenced through a long succession of generations even to the time we live in. If it should ever be totally extinguished, the loss I fear will be great. It is this which has given its character to modern Europe. It is this which has distinguished it under all its forms of government, and distinguished it to its advantage, from the states of Asia and possibly from those states which flourished in the most brilliant periods of the antique world. It was this which, without confounding ranks, had produced a noble equality and handed it down through all the gradations of social life. It was this opinion which mitigated kings into companions and raised private men to be fellows with kings. Without force or opposition, it subdued the fierceness of pride and power, it obliged sovereigns to submit to the soft collar of social esteem, compelled stern authority to submit to elegance, and gave a domination, vanquisher of laws, to be subdued by manners.

But now all is to be changed. All the pleasing illusions which made power gentle and obedience liberal, which harmonized the different shades of life, and which, by a bland

---

1   *whilst the legal ... by him*   While he acts according to the legal agreements regarding the sovereign.

2   *Revolution Society*   A British organization offering a forum for views in favor of the French Revolution.

3   *the political divine ... to assert*   [Burke's note] *Discourse on the Love of our Country*, by Dr. Price.

4   *cashier*   Dismiss.

5   *dauphiness*   Marie Antoinette, then wife of the dauphin (i.e., the crown prince, heir to the throne of France).

6   *sophisters*   Those skilled at misleading by devious argument.

assimilation, incorporated into politics the sentiments which beautify and soften private society, are to be dissolved by this new conquering empire of light and reason. All the decent drapery of life is to be rudely torn off. All the super-added ideas, furnished from the wardrobe of a moral imagination, which the heart owns and the understanding ratifies as necessary to cover the defects of our naked, shivering nature, and to raise it to dignity in our own estimation, are to be exploded as a ridiculous, absurd, and antiquated fashion.

On this scheme of things, a king is but a man, a queen is but a woman; a woman is but an animal, and an animal not of the highest order. All homage paid to the sex in general as such, and without distinct views, is to be regarded as romance and folly. Regicide,[1] and parricide,[2] and sacrilege are but fictions of superstition, corrupting jurisprudence by destroying its simplicity. The murder of a king, or a queen, or a bishop, or a father are only common homicide; and if the people are by any chance or in any way gainers by it, a sort of homicide much the most pardonable, and into which we ought not to make too severe a scrutiny.

On the scheme of this barbarous philosophy, which is the offspring of cold hearts and muddy understandings, and which is as void of solid wisdom as it is destitute of all taste and elegance, laws are to be supported only by their own terrors and by the concern which each individual may find in them from his own private speculations or can spare to them from his own private interests. In the groves of their academy, at the end of every vista, you see nothing but the gallows. Nothing is left which engages the affections on the part of the commonwealth.... To make us love our country, our country ought to be lovely.

But power, of some kind or other, will survive the shock in which manners and opinions perish; and it will find other and worse means for its support.... When the old feudal and chivalrous spirit of fealty,[3] which, by freeing kings from fear, freed both kings and subjects from the precautions of tyranny, shall be extinct in the minds of men, plots and assassinations will be anticipated by preventive murder and preventive confiscation.... Kings will be tyrants from policy when subjects are rebels from principle.

When ancient opinions and rules of life are taken away, the loss cannot possibly be estimated. From that moment we have no compass to govern us; nor can we know distinctly to what port we steer. Europe, undoubtedly, taken in a mass, was in a flourishing condition the day on which your revolution was completed. How much of that prosperous state was owing to the spirit of our old manners and opinions is not easy to say; but as such causes cannot be indifferent in their operation, we must presume that on the whole their operation was beneficial.

We are but too apt to consider things in the state in which we find them, without sufficiently adverting[4] to the causes by which they have been produced and possibly may be upheld. Nothing is more certain than that our manners, our civilization, and all the good things which are connected with manners and with civilization have, in this European world of ours, depended for ages upon two principles and were, indeed, the result of both combined: I mean the spirit of a gentleman and the spirit of religion....

When the people have emptied themselves of all the lust of selfish will, which without religion it is utterly impossible they ever should, when they are conscious that they exercise, and exercise perhaps in a higher link of the order of delegation, the power, which to be legitimate must be according to that eternal, immutable law in which will and reason are the same, they will be more careful how they place power in base and incapable hands. In their nomination to office, they will not appoint to the exercise of authority as to a pitiful job, but as to a holy function, not according to their sordid, selfish interest, nor to their wanton caprice,[5] nor to their arbitrary will, but they will confer that power (which any man may well tremble to give or to receive) on those only in whom they may discern that predominant proportion of active virtue and wisdom, taken together and fitted to the charge, such as in the great and inevitable mixed mass of human imperfections and infirmities is to be found....

To avoid, therefore, the evils of inconstancy and versatility,[6] ten thousand times worse than those of obstinacy and the blindest prejudice, we have consecrated[7] the state, that no man should approach to look into its defects or corruptions but with due caution, that he should never dream of beginning its reformation by its subversion, that he should approach to the faults of the state as to the wounds of a father, with pious awe and trembling solicitude. By this

---

1   *Regicide*   Murder of a king.

2   *parricide*   Murder of one's father.

3   *fealty*   Loyalty, allegiance, sometimes by oath.

4   *adverting*   Referring.

5   *wanton caprice*   Random sudden impulsive decision.

6   *inconstancy, versatility*   Liability for frequent, rapid, or unpredictable change.

7   *consecrated*   Sanctified, made worthy of veneration.

wise prejudice we are taught to look with horror on those children of their country who are prompt rashly to hack that aged parent in pieces and put him into the kettle of magicians, in hopes that by their poisonous weeds and wild incantations they may regenerate the paternal constitution and renovate their father's life.

Society is indeed a contract. Subordinate contracts for objects of mere occasional interest may be dissolved at pleasure—but the state ought not to be considered as nothing better than a partnership agreement in a trade of pepper and coffee, calico, or tobacco, or some other such low concern, to be taken up for a little temporary interest, and to be dissolved by the fancy of the parties. It is to be looked on with other reverence, because it is not a partnership in things subservient only to the gross animal existence of a temporary and perishable nature. It is a partnership in all science; a partnership in all art;[1] a partnership in every virtue and in all perfection. As the ends of such a partnership cannot be obtained in many generations, it becomes a partnership not only between those who are living, but between those who are living, those who are dead, and those who are to be born. Each contract of each particular state is but a clause in the great primeval[2] contract of eternal society, linking the lower with the higher natures, connecting the visible and invisible world, according to a fixed compact sanctioned by the inviolable oath which holds all physical and all moral natures, each in their appointed place. This law is not subject to the will of those who by an obligation above them, and infinitely superior, are bound to submit their will to that law....

But am I so unreasonable as to see nothing at all that deserves commendation in the indefatigable[3] labors of this Assembly?[4] I do not deny that, among an infinite number of acts of violence and folly, some good may have been done. They who destroy everything certainly will remove some grievance. They who make everything new have a chance that they may establish something beneficial. To give them credit for what they have done in virtue of the authority they have usurped, or which can excuse them in the crimes

by which that authority has been acquired, it must appear that the same things could not have been accomplished without producing such a revolution. Most assuredly they might, because almost every one of the regulations made by them which is not very equivocal was either in the cession of the king, voluntarily made at the meeting of the states, or in the concurrent instructions to the orders. Some usages have been abolished on just grounds, but they were such that if they had stood as they were to all eternity, they would little detract from the happiness and prosperity of any state. The improvements of the National Assembly are superficial, their errors fundamental.

Whatever they are, I wish my countrymen rather to recommend to our neighbors the example of the British constitution[5] than to take models from them for the improvement of our own. In the former, they have got an invaluable treasure. They are not, I think, without some causes of apprehension and complaint, but these they do not owe to their constitution but to their own conduct. I think our happy situation owing to our constitution, but owing to the whole of it, and not to any part singly, owing in a great measure to what we have left standing in our several reviews and reformations as well as to what we have altered or super-added. Our people will find employment enough for a truly patriotic, free, and independent spirit in guarding what they possess from violation. I would not exclude alteration neither, but even when I changed, it should be to preserve.

[...]

I have told you candidly my sentiments. I think they are not likely to alter yours. I do not know that they ought. You are young; you cannot guide but must follow the fortune of your country. But hereafter they may be of some use to you, in some future form which your commonwealth may take. In the present it can hardly remain; but before its final settlement it may be obliged to pass, as one of our poets

---

1 *art* Creation by human action, rather than by nature.
2 *primeval* Ancient or original.
3 *indefatigable* Tireless.
4 *Assembly* The National Assembly, a legislature established by the French Revolution in June 1789 to give France a constitution. On 9 July 1789 it reconstituted itself as the National Constituent Assembly, which abolished feudalism and established the *Declaration of the Rights of Man*.
5 *the British constitution* The English constitution is not one single document, like the US Constitution, for example. Rather, it is composed of a series of documents which include Magna Carta, issued in 1215, and the 1688 Declaration of Rights. The structure of the government and the rights of the subjects of Great Britain were and are contingent upon a shared cultural understanding shaped by these documents and English common law. This explains why Burke refers to the English constitution with a lower-case "c"; there is not a specific document that bears the title of Constitution.

says, "through great varieties of untried being," and in all its transmigrations to be purified by fire and blood.

I have little to recommend my opinions but long observation and much impartiality. They come from one who has been no tool of power, no flatterer of greatness; and who in his last acts does not wish to belie the tenor[1] of his life. They come from one almost the whole of whose public exertion has been a struggle for the liberty of others; from one in whose breast no anger, durable or vehement, has ever been kindled but by what he considered as tyranny....

◆ ◆ ◆ ◆ ◆

from On "Geographical Morality"

from Speech on the Impeachment of Warren Hastings[2] (15–19 February, 1788)

My Lords, we contend that Mr. Hastings, as a British governor, ought to govern on British principles.... We call for that spirit of equity, that spirit of justice, that spirit of safety, that spirit of protection, that spirit of lenity,[3] which ought to characterize every British subject in power; and on these, and these principles only, he will be tried.

But he has told your lordships, in his defense, that actions in Asia do not bear the same moral qualities which the same actions would bear in Europe.... And having stated at large what he means by saying that the same actions have not the same qualities in Asia and in Europe, ... [he and others] have formed a plan of geographical morality, by which the duties of men in public and in private situations are not to be governed by their relations to the great governor of the universe, or by their relations to men, but by climates, degrees of longitude and latitude, parallels not of life but of latitudes; as if, when you have crossed the equinoctial, all the virtues die, as they say some insects die when they

cross the line; as if there were a kind of baptism, like that practiced by seamen, by which they unbaptize themselves of all that they learned in Europe, and commence a new order and system of things.

This geographical morality we do protest against.... We think it necessary, in justification of ourselves, to declare that the laws of morality are the same everywhere, and that there is no action which would pass for an act of extortion, of peculation,[4] of bribery, and of oppression in England, that is not an act of extortion, of peculation, of bribery, and oppression in Europe, Asia, Africa, and all the world over....

Mr. Hastings comes before your lordships not as a British governor answering to a British tribunal, but as a subahdar....[5] He says, "I had an arbitrary power to exercise; I exercised it. Slaves I found the people; slaves they are. They are so by their constitution; and if they are, I did not make it for them. I was unfortunately bound to exercise this arbitrary power, and accordingly I did exercise it. It was disagreeable to me, but I did exercise it, and no other power can be exercised in that country."

[...]

Think of an English governor tried before you as a British subject, and yet declaring that he governed upon the principles of arbitrary power! This plea is, that he did govern there upon arbitrary and despotic, and, as he supposes, Oriental principles.

---

1 *belie the tenor* Disguise the nature.
2 *Warren Hastings* Hastings had been appointed Governor of Bengal in 1772, and Governor General of Bengal (with authority over Madras and Bombay) the following year, with the passage of the East India Company Act. He resigned in 1785 and impeachment proceedings against him began in 1786. Hastings was finally acquitted of all charges in 1794.
3 *lenity* Mildness, mercy.

4 *peculation* Appropriation of public funds.
5 *subahdar* Governor of an Indian province.

PART IV

The Nineteenth Century

BENJAMIN CONSTANT
(1767 – 1830)

Henri Benjamin Constant de Rebecque (often called simply Benjamin Constant[1]) was a Swiss-French man-of-many-trades: a successful novelist, a publisher, a politician, and a political writer. Sometimes overshadowed by the fame of his contemporary, the French political commentator Tocqueville, Constant nevertheless had considerable influence on the political future of France and on political thought in general. He was a champion of personal freedom; Sir Isaiah Berlin, the eminent twentieth-century philosopher, called him "the most eloquent of all defenders of freedom and privacy," and credited him with the invention of the idea of "negative liberty"—the protection of individual choices and preferences (*Two Concepts of Liberty*, 1968).

Constant's ancestors were Huguenots, French Protestants forced into exile in Switzerland. He studied briefly at the University of Oxford, but more substantially at the universities in Erlangen, Germany, and Edinburgh. This last university was the center of Scottish Enlightenment thought—Adam Smith was there at the time—and those intellectual currents certainly influenced Constant's future views. In France he obtained the position of chamberlain to a duke, a position that must have been rather uncomfortable to someone with Constant's republican leanings; he sided with the revolutionaries, and left this job in 1794. Divorcing his wife (a court-connected woman 27 years his senior) he began a relationship with Germaine de Staël, the well-known novelist; during the relationship with her, he married twice more. It is thought to have been her influence that crystallized his political thinking and turned him towards a career as political commentator.

In 1799, Constant became a tribune under Napoleon, but a couple of years later, as a leader of the opposition to the Bonapartist regime, he was removed from this position and shortly thereafter followed Madame de Staël into exile in Switzerland and Germany. While away he published many political pamphlets, his major work on religion, and *Adolphe*, a well received semi-autobiographical work (based largely on his relationship with de Staël), now sometimes counted as the first psychological novel. After an exile of twelve years, Constant returned to France, where he continued his phampleteering, and served as an active member of the chamber of deputies. He was appointed president of the council of state in 1830, but died the same year.

Among political theorists, Constant is best known for his distinction between the "liberties of the ancients" and "the liberties of the moderns." The liberties of the ancients are democratic liberties, modeled on the participatory democracy of the classical city-states and revived by Jean-Jacques Rousseau. They are "positive liberties," permitting citizens to influence the path of their community through collective deliberation and voting. However, these liberties were only possible in small communities where decision-makers enjoyed significant leisure (made possible by slave labor); they could no longer be effectively exercised in large, anonymous communities. Moreover, as Constant wrote, the liberties of the ancients were compatible with "the complete subjection of the individual to the authority of the community."

While the ancients (or, more precisely, the minority in Greek and Roman society comprising males who had been accorded citizen status) had considerably more control over public affairs, they enjoyed fewer opportunities for individual choice. In Constant's view, the liberties of the moderns were more appropriate to larger societies dominated by commerce, where individuals had little time to participate in public life. These liberties restrained the state, guaranteeing freedom from interference, and included the rule of law. Though Constant eloquently defended modern liberty, he also appreciated the merits of ancient liberty and attempted

---

1   But beware of ambiguity: two other historical figures are also sometimes called Benjamin Constant: Benjamin Constant Botelho de Magalhães, Brazillian politician and soldier (1836–91), and the well-known French painter Jean Joseph Benjamin Constant (1805–1902).

to combine these in a form of representative government. Along these lines, Constant made important contributions towards the theory and practice of constitutional monarchy with legal restraints to protect liberty.

◆ ◆ ◆ ◆ ◆

The Liberty of Ancients Compared with that of Moderns (1816)

Gentlemen,

I wish to submit for your attention a few distinctions, still rather new, between two kinds of liberty: these differences have thus far remained unnoticed, or at least insufficiently remarked. The first is the liberty the exercise of which was so dear to the ancient peoples; the second the one the enjoyment of which is especially precious to the modern nations. If I am right, this investigation will prove interesting from two different angles.

Firstly, the confusion of these two kinds of liberty has been amongst us, in the all too famous days of our revolution, the cause of many an evil. France was exhausted by useless experiments, the authors of which, irritated by their poor success, sought to force her to enjoy the good she did not want, and denied her the good which she did want. Secondly, called as we are by our happy revolution (I call it happy, despite its excesses, because I concentrate my attention on its results) to enjoy the benefits of representative government, it is curious and interesting to discover why this form of government, the only one in the shelter of which we could find some freedom and peace today, was totally unknown to the free nations of antiquity.

I know that there are writers who have claimed to distinguish traces of it among some ancient peoples, in the Lacedaemonian republic[1] for example, or amongst our ancestors the Gauls;[2] but they are mistaken.

The Lacedaemonian government was a monastic aristocracy, and in no way a representative government. The power of the kings was limited, but it was limited by the ephors,[3] and not by men invested with a mission similar to that which election confers today on the defenders of our liberties. The ephors, no doubt, though originally created by the kings, were elected by the people. But there were only five of them. Their authority was as much religious as political; they even shared in the administration of government, that is, in the executive power. Thus their prerogative, like that of almost all popular magistrates in the ancient republics, far from being simply a barrier against tyranny became sometimes itself an insufferable tyranny.

The regime of the Gauls, which quite resembled the one that a certain party would like to restore to us, was at the same time theocratic and warlike. The priests enjoyed unlimited power. The military class or nobility had markedly insolent and oppressive privileges; the people had no rights and no safeguards.

In Rome the tribunes had, up to a point, a representative mission. They were the organs of those plebeians whom the oligarchy—which is the same in all ages—had submitted, in overthrowing the kings, to so harsh a slavery. The people, however, exercised a large part of the political rights directly. They met to vote on the laws and to judge the patricians[4] against whom charges had been leveled: thus there were, in Rome, only feeble traces of a representative system.

This system is a discovery of the moderns, and you will see, Gentlemen, that the condition of the human race in antiquity did not allow for the introduction or establishment of an institution of this nature. The ancient peoples could neither feel the need for it, nor appreciate its advantages. Their social organization led them to desire an entirely different freedom from the one which this system grants to us. Tonight's lecture will be devoted to demonstrating this truth to you.

First ask yourselves, Gentlemen, what an Englishman, a Frenchman, and a citizen of the United States of America understand today by the word "liberty." For each of them it is the right to be subjected only to the laws, and to be neither arrested, detained, put to death or maltreated in any way by the arbitrary will of one or more individuals. It is the right of everyone to express their opinion, choose a profession and practice it, to dispose of property, and even to abuse it; to come and go without permission, and without having to account for their motives or undertakings. It is

---

1   *Lacedaemonian republic* City-state in Ancient Greece, more often known by the name of its city, Sparta.
2   *the Gauls* Celtic people widespread in France and neighboring regions of Europe during ancient Roman times.

3   *ephors* Five elected magistrates exercising a supervisory power over the kings of Sparta.
4   *patricians* The nobility, upper classes.

everyone's right to associate with other individuals, either to discuss their interests, or to profess the religion which they and their associates prefer, or even simply to occupy their days or hours in a way which is most compatible with their inclinations or whims. Finally it is everyone's right to exercise some influence on the administration of the government, either by electing all or particular officials, or through representations, petitions, demands to which the authorities are more or less compelled to pay heed. Now compare this liberty with that of the ancients.

The latter consisted in exercising collectively, but directly, several parts of the complete sovereignty; in deliberating, in the public square, over war and peace; in forming alliances with foreign governments; in voting laws, in pronouncing judgments; in examining the accounts, the acts, the stewardship of the magistrates; in calling them to appear in front of the assembled people, in accusing, condemning or absolving them. But if this was what the ancients called liberty, they admitted as compatible with this collective freedom the complete subjection of the individual to the authority of the community. You find among them almost none of the enjoyments which we have just seen form part of the liberty of the moderns. All private actions were submitted to a severe surveillance. No importance was given to individual independence, neither in relation to opinions, nor to labor, nor, above all, to religion. The right to choose one's own religious affiliation, a right which we regard as one of the most precious, would have seemed to the ancients a crime and a sacrilege. In the domains which seem to us the most useful, the authority of the social body interposed itself and obstructed the will of individuals. Among the Spartans, Therpandrus could not add a string to his lyre without causing offense to the ephors. In the most domestic of relations the public authority again intervened. The young Lacedaemonian could not visit his new bride freely. In Rome, the censors[1] cast a searching eye over family life. The laws regulated customs, and as customs touch on everything, there was hardly anything that the laws did not regulate.

Thus among the ancients the individual, almost always sovereign in public affairs, was a slave in all his private relations. As a citizen, he decided on peace and war; as a private individual, he was constrained, watched and repressed in all his movements; as a member of the collective body, he

interrogated, dismissed, condemned, beggared,[2] exiled, or sentenced to death his magistrates and superiors; as a subject of the collective body he could himself be deprived of his status, stripped of his privileges, banished, put to death, by the discretionary will of the whole to which he belonged. Among the moderns, on the contrary, the individual, independent in his private life, is, even in the freest of states, sovereign only in appearance. His sovereignty is restricted and almost always suspended. If, at fixed and rare intervals, in which he is again surrounded by precautions and obstacles, he exercises this sovereignty, it is always only to renounce it.

I must at this point, Gentlemen, pause for a moment to anticipate an objection which may be addressed to me. There was in antiquity a republic where the enslavement of individual existence to the collective body was not as complete as I have described it. This republic was the most famous of all: you will guess that I am speaking of Athens. I shall return to it later, and in subscribing to the truth of this fact, I shall also indicate its cause. We shall see why, of all the ancient states, Athens was the one which most resembles the modern ones. Everywhere else social jurisdiction was unlimited. The ancients, as Condorcet[3] says, had no notion of individual rights. Men were, so to speak, merely machines, whose gears and cog-wheels were regulated by the law. The same subjection characterized the golden centuries of the Roman republic; the individual was in some way lost in the nation, the citizen in the city. We shall now trace this essential difference between the ancients and ourselves back to its source.

All ancient republics were restricted to a narrow territory. The most populous, the most powerful, the most substantial among them, was not equal in extension to the smallest of modern states. As an inevitable consequence of their narrow territory, the spirit of these republics was bellicose; each people incessantly attacked their neighbors or was attacked by them. Thus driven by necessity against one another, they fought or threatened each other constantly. Those who had no ambition to be conquerors, could still not lay down their weapons, lest they should themselves be conquered. All had to buy their security, their independence, their whole existence at the price of war. This was the constant interest, the almost habitual occupation of the free

1   *censors*   Two officials in ancient Rome responsible for taking the public census and supervising public behavior and morals.

2   *beggared*   Made into a beggar, impoverished.
3   *Condorcet*   Marie Jean Antoine Nicolas Caritat, marquis de Condorcet (1743–94), French philosopher, advocate of freedom and equality.

states of antiquity. Finally, by an equally necessary result of this way of being, all these states had slaves. The mechanical professions and even, among some nations, the industrial ones, were committed to people in chains.

The modern world offers us a completely opposing view. The smallest states of our day are incomparably larger than Sparta or than Rome was over five centuries. Even the division of Europe into several states is, thanks to the progress of enlightenment, more apparent than real. While each people, in the past, formed an isolated family, the born enemy of other families, a mass of human beings now exists, that under different names and under different forms of social organization are essentially homogeneous in their nature. This mass is strong enough to have nothing to fear from barbarian hordes. It is sufficiently civilized to find war a burden. Its uniform tendency is towards peace.

This difference leads to another one. War precedes commerce. War and commerce are only two different means of achieving the same end, that of getting what one wants. Commerce is simply a tribute paid to the strength of the possessor by the aspirant to possession. It is an attempt to conquer, by mutual agreement, what one can no longer hope to obtain through violence. A man who was always the stronger would never conceive the idea of commerce. It is experience, by proving to him that war, that is the use of his strength against the strength of others, exposes him to a variety of obstacles and defeats, that leads him to resort to commerce, that is to a milder and surer means of engaging the interest of others to agree to what suits his own. War is all impulse, commerce, calculation. Hence it follows that an age must come in which commerce replaces war. We have reached this age.

I do not mean that amongst the ancients there were no trading peoples. But these peoples were to some degree an exception to the general rule. The limits of this lecture do not allow me to illustrate all the obstacles which then opposed the progress of commerce; you know them as well as I do; I shall only mention one of them.

Their ignorance of the compass meant that the sailors of antiquity always had to keep close to the coast. To pass through the pillars of Hercules, that is, the straits of Gibraltar,[1] was considered the most daring of enterprises.

The Phoenicians and the Carthaginians, the most able of navigators, did not risk it until very late, and their example for long remained without imitators. In Athens, of which we shall talk soon, the interest on maritime enterprises was around 60%, while current interest was only 12%: that was how dangerous the idea of distant navigation seemed.

Moreover, if I could permit myself a digression which would unfortunately prove too long, I would show you, Gentlemen, through the details of the customs, habits, way of trading with others of the trading peoples of antiquity, that their commerce was itself impregnated by the spirit of the age, by the atmosphere of war and hostility which surrounded it. Commerce then was a lucky accident, today it is the normal state of things, the only aim, the universal tendency, the true life of nations. They want repose, and with repose comfort, and as a source of comfort, industry. Every day war becomes a more ineffective means of satisfying their wishes. Its hazards no longer offer to individuals benefits that match the results of peaceful work and regular exchanges.

Among the ancients, a successful war increased both private and public wealth in slaves, tributes and lands shared out. For the moderns, even a successful war costs infallibly more than it is worth. Finally, thanks to commerce, to religion, to the moral and intellectual progress of the human race, there are no longer slaves among the European nations. Free men must exercise all professions, provide for all the needs of society.

It is easy to see, Gentlemen, the inevitable outcome of these differences. Firstly, the size of a country causes a corresponding decrease of the political importance allotted to each individual. The most obscure republican[2] of Sparta or Rome had power. The same is not true of the simple citizen of Britain or of the United States. His personal influence is an imperceptible part of the social will which impresses on the government its direction.

Secondly, the abolition of slavery has deprived the free population of all the leisure which resulted from the fact that slaves took care of most of the work. Without the slave population of Athens, 20,000 Athenians could never have spent every day at the public square in discussions.

Thirdly, commerce does not, like war, leave in men's lives intervals of inactivity. The constant exercise of political rights, the daily discussion of the affairs of the state, disagreements, confabulations, the whole entourage and movement

---

1   *straits of Gibraltar*   Straits separating the Mediterranean Sea from the Atlantic Ocean. In Greek mythology, Hercules, instead of crossing the mountain that was once the titan Atlas, split it in half, connecting the Mediterranean to the Atlantic (hence the pillars of Hercules).

2   *republican*   Citizen of the republic.

of factions, necessary agitations, the compulsory filling, if I may use the term, of the life of the peoples of antiquity, who, without this resource would have languished under the weight of painful inaction, would only cause trouble and fatigue to modern nations, where each individual, occupied with his speculations, his enterprises, the pleasures he obtains or hopes for, does not wish to be distracted from them other than momentarily, and as little as possible.

Finally, commerce inspires in men a vivid love of individual independence. Commerce supplies their needs, satisfies their desires, without the intervention of the authorities. This intervention is almost always—and I do not know why I say almost—this intervention is indeed always a trouble and an embarrassment. Every time collective power wishes to meddle with private speculations, it harasses the speculators. Every time governments pretend to do our own business, they do it more incompetently and expensively than we would.

I said, Gentlemen, that I would return to Athens, whose example might be opposed to some of my assertions, but which will in fact confirm all of them.

Athens, as I have already pointed out, was of all the Greek republics the most closely engaged in trade, thus it allowed to its citizens an infinitely greater individual liberty than Sparta or Rome. If I could enter into historical details, I would show you that, among the Athenians, commerce had removed several of the differences which distinguished the ancient from the modern peoples. The spirit of the Athenian merchants was similar to that of the merchants of our days. Xenophon[1] tells us that during the Peloponnesian war,[2] they moved their capitals from the continent of Attica to place them on the islands of the archipelago. Commerce had created among them the circulation of money. In Isocrates[3] there are signs that bills of exchange[4] were used. Observe how their customs resemble our own. In their relations with women, you will see, again I cite Xenophon, husbands, satisfied when peace and a decorous friendship reigned in their households, make allowances for the wife who is too vulnerable before the tyranny of nature, close their eyes to the irresistible power of passions, forgive the

first weakness and forget the second.[5] In their relations with strangers, we shall see them extending the rights of citizenship to whoever would, by moving among them with his family, establish some trade or industry. Finally, we shall be struck by their excessive love of individual independence. In Sparta, says a philosopher, the citizens quicken their step when they are called by a magistrate; but an Athenian would be desperate if he were thought to be dependent on a magistrate.

However, as several of the other circumstances which determined the character of ancient nations existed in Athens as well; as there was a slave population and the territory was very restricted; we find there too the traces of the liberty proper to the ancients. The people made the laws, examined the behavior of the magistrates, called Pericles[6] to account for his conduct, sentenced to death the generals who had commanded the battle of the Arginusae.[7] Similarly ostracism, that legal arbitrariness, extolled by all the legislators of the age; ostracism, which appears to us, and rightly so, a revolting iniquity, proves that the individual was much more subservient to the supremacy of the social body in Athens, than he is in any of the free states of Europe today.

It follows from what I have just indicated that we can no longer enjoy the liberty of the ancients, which consisted in an active and constant participation in collective power. Our freedom must consist of peaceful enjoyment and private independence. The share which in antiquity everyone held in national sovereignty was by no means an abstract presumption as it is in our own day. The will of each individual had real influence: the exercise of this will was a vivid and repeated pleasure. Consequently the ancients were ready to make many a sacrifice to preserve their political rights and their share in the administration of the state. Everybody, feeling with pride all that his suffrage was worth, found in this awareness of his personal importance a great compensation.

This compensation no longer exists for us today. Lost in the multitude, the individual can almost never perceive

---

1 *Xenophon* Greek historian, c. 400 BCE.
2 *Peloponnesian war* War between Athens and Sparta, lasting from 431 BCE until 404 BCE, chronicled by Xenophon and Thucydides.
3 *Isocrates* Greek rhetorician, c. 400 BCE.
4 *bill of exchange* Written order directing that a specified sum of money be paid to a specified person.

5 *forgive the first ... forget the second* Presumably Constant is talking obliquely about a wife being sexually unfaithful to her husband.
6 *Pericles* Influential statesman during the "Golden Age" in Athens, c. 400 BCE.
7 *battle of the Arginusae* Battle of the Peloponnesian war that took place in 406 BCE, in which Athens defeated Sparta. Afterwards, however, bad weather prevented rescue of a large number of Athenian sailors, and for this six commanders (including Pericles' son) were punished with death.

the influence he exercises. Never does his will impress itself upon the whole; nothing confirms in his eyes his own cooperation. The exercise of political rights, therefore, offers us but a part of the pleasures that the ancients found in it, while at the same time the progress of civilization, the commercial tendency of the age, the communication amongst peoples, have infinitely multiplied and varied the means of personal happiness.

It follows that we must be far more attached than the ancients to our individual independence. For the ancients when they sacrificed that independence to their political rights, sacrificed less to obtain more; while in making the same sacrifice, we would give more to obtain less.

The aim of the ancients was the sharing of social power among the citizens of the same fatherland: this is what they called liberty. The aim of the moderns is the enjoyment of security in private pleasures; and they call liberty the guarantees accorded by institutions to these pleasures.

I said at the beginning that, through their failure to perceive these differences, otherwise well-intentioned men caused infinite evils during our long and stormy revolution. God forbid that I should reproach them too harshly. Their error itself was excusable. One could not read the beautiful pages of antiquity, one could not recall the actions of its great men, without feeling an indefinable and special emotion, which nothing modern can possibly arouse. The old elements of a nature, one could almost say, earlier than our own, seem to awaken in us in the face of these memories. It is difficult not to regret the time when the faculties of man developed along an already trodden path, but in so wide a career, so strong in their own powers, with such a feeling of energy and dignity. Once we abandon ourselves to this regret, it is impossible not to wish to imitate what we regret. This impression was very deep, especially when we lived under vicious governments, which, without being strong, were repressive in their effects; absurd in their principles; wretched in action; governments which had as their strength arbitrary power; for their purpose the belittling of mankind; and which some individuals still dare to praise to us today, as if we could ever forget that we have been the witnesses and the victims of their obstinacy, of their impotence and of their overthrow. The aim of our reformers was noble and generous. Who among us did not feel his heart beat with hope at the outset of the course which they seemed to open up? And shame, even today, on whoever does not feel the need to declare that acknowledging a few errors committed by our first guides does not mean blighting their memory or

disowning the opinions which the friends of mankind have professed throughout the ages.

But those men had derived several of their theories from the works of two philosophers who had themselves failed to recognize the changes brought by two thousand years in the dispositions of mankind. I shall perhaps at some point examine the system of the most illustrious of these philosophers, of Jean-Jacques Rousseau,[1] and I shall show that, by transposing into our modern age an extent of social power, of collective sovereignty, which belonged to other centuries, this sublime genius, animated by the purest love of liberty, has nevertheless furnished deadly pretexts for more than one kind of tyranny. No doubt, in pointing out what I regard as a misunderstanding which it is important to uncover, I shall be careful in my refutation, and respectful in my criticism. I shall certainly refrain from joining myself to the detractors of a great man. When chance has it that I find myself apparently in agreement with them on some one particular point, I suspect myself; and to console myself for appearing for a moment in agreement with them on a single partial question, I need to disown and denounce with all my energies these pretended allies.

Nevertheless, the interests of truth must prevail over considerations which make the glory of a prodigious talent and the authority of an immense reputation so powerful. Moreover, as we shall see, it is not to Rousseau that we must chiefly attribute the error against which I am going to argue; this is to be imputed much more to one of his successors, less eloquent but no less austere and a hundred times more exaggerated. The latter, the Abbé de Mably,[2] can be regarded as the representative of the system which, according to the maxims of ancient liberty, demands that the citizens should be entirely subjected in order for the nation to be sovereign, and that the individual should be enslaved for the people to be free.

The Abbé de Mably, like Rousseau and many others, had mistaken, just as the ancients did, the authority of the social body for liberty; and to him any means seemed good if it extended his area of authority over that recalcitrant part of human existence whose independence he deplored. The

---

1 *Jean-Jacques Rousseau* French philosopher (1712–78) who importantly influenced the thought of the Enlightenment and Romanticism, as well as French revolutionary ideology.

2 *Abbé de Mably* French historian, philosopher, legal thinker, and politician (1709–85); variously taken to be a utopian communist, a source of republican thought, or an enemy of the Enlightenment, religious toleration, and civil liberties.

regret he expresses everywhere in his works is that the law can only cover actions. He would have liked it to cover the most fleeting thoughts and impressions; to pursue man relentlessly, leaving him no refuge in which he might escape from its power. No sooner did he learn, among no matter what people, of some oppressive measure, than he thought he had made a discovery and proposed it as a model. He detested individual liberty like a personal enemy; and whenever in history he came across a nation totally deprived of it, even if it had no political liberty, he could not help admiring it. He went into ecstasies over the Egyptians, because, as he said, among them everything was prescribed by the law, down to relaxations and needs: everything was subjected to the empire of the legislator. Every moment of the day was filled by some duty; love itself was the object of this respected intervention, and it was the law that in turn opened and closed the curtains of the nuptial bed.

Sparta, which combined republican forms with the same enslavement of individuals, aroused in the spirit of that philosopher an even more vivid enthusiasm. That vast monastic barracks to him seemed the ideal of a perfect republic. He had a profound contempt for Athens, and would gladly have said of this nation, the first of Greece, what an academician and great nobleman said of the French Academy: What an appalling despotism! Everyone does what he likes there. I must add that this great nobleman was talking of the Academy as it was thirty years ago.

Montesquieu,[1] who had a less excitable and therefore more observant mind, did not fall into quite the same errors. He was struck by the differences which I have related; but he did not discover their true cause. The Greek politicians who lived under the popular government did not recognize, he argues, any other power but virtue. Politicians of today talk only of manufactures, of commerce, of finances, of wealth and even of luxury. He attributes this difference to the republic and the monarchy. It ought instead to be attributed to the opposed spirit of ancient and modern times. Citizens of republics, subjects of monarchies, all want pleasures, and indeed no-one, in the present condition of societies can help wanting them. The people most attached to their liberty in our own days, before the emancipation of France, was also the most attached to all the pleasures of life; and it valued its liberty especially because it saw in this the guarantee of the pleasures which it cherished. In the past, where there was

liberty, people could bear hardship. Now, wherever there is hardship, despotism is necessary for people to resign themselves to it. It would be easier today to make Spartans of an enslaved people than to turn free men into Spartans.

The men who were brought by events to the head of our revolution were, by a necessary consequence of the education they had received, steeped in ancient views which are no longer valid, which the philosophers whom I mentioned above had made fashionable. The metaphysics of Rousseau, in the midst of which flashed the occasional sublime thought and passages of stirring eloquence; the austerity of Mably, his intolerance, his hatred of all human passions, his eagerness to enslave them all, his exaggerated principles on the competence of the law, the difference between what he recommended and what had ever previously existed, his declamations against wealth and even against property; all these things were bound to charm men heated by their recent victory, and who, having won power over the law, were only too keen to extend this power to all things. It was a source of invaluable support that two disinterested writers anathematizing human despotism, should have drawn up the text of the law in axioms. They wished to exercise public power as they had learnt from their guides it had once been exercised in the free states. They believed that everything should give way before collective will, and that all restrictions on individual rights would be amply compensated by participation in social power.

We all know, Gentlemen, what has come of it. Free institutions, resting upon the knowledge of the spirit of the age, could have survived. The restored edifice of the ancients collapsed, notwithstanding many efforts and many heroic acts which call for our admiration. The fact is that social power injured individual independence in every possible war, without destroying the need for it. The nation did not find that an ideal share in an abstract sovereignty was worth the sacrifices required from her. She was vainly assured, on Rousseau's authority, that the laws of liberty are a thousand times more austere than the yoke of tyrants. She had no desire for those austere laws, and believed sometimes that the yoke of tyrants would be preferable to them. Experience has come to undeceive her. She has seen that the arbitrary power of men was even worse than the worst of laws. But laws too must have their limits.

If I have succeeded, Gentlemen, in making you share the persuasion which in my opinion these facts must produce, you will acknowledge with me the truth of the following principles.

---

1   *Montesquieu* French Enlightenment political thinker (1689–1755), known best for his theory of separation of powers.

Individual independence is the first need of the moderns: consequently one must never require from them any sacrifices to establish political liberty.

It follows that none of the numerous and too highly praised institutions which in the ancient republics hindered individual liberty is any longer admissible in the modern times.

You may, in the first place, think, Gentlemen, that it is superfluous to establish this truth. Several governments of our days do not seem in the least inclined to imitate the republics of antiquity. However, little as they may like republican institutions, there are certain republican usages for which they feel a certain affection. It is disturbing that they should be precisely those which allow them to banish, to exile, or to despoil. I remember that in 1802, they slipped into the law on special tribunals an article which introduced into France Greek ostracism;[1] and God knows how many eloquent speakers, in order to have this article approved, talked to us about the freedom of Athens and all the sacrifices that individuals must make to preserve this freedom! Similarly, in much more recent times, when fearful authorities attempted, with a timid hand, to rig the elections, a journal which can hardly be suspected of republicanism proposed to revive Roman censorship to eliminate all dangerous candidates.

I do not think therefore that I am engaging in a useless discussion if, to support my assertion, I say a few words about these two much vaunted institutions.

Ostracism in Athens rested upon the assumption that society had complete authority over its members. On this assumption it could be justified; and in a small state, where the influence of a single individual, strong in his credit, his clients, his glory, often balanced the power of the mass, ostracism may appear useful. But amongst us individuals have rights which society must respect, and individual interests are, as I have already observed, so lost in a multitude of equal or superior influences, that any oppression motivated by the need to diminish this influence is useless and consequently unjust. No-one has the right to exile a citizen, if he is not condemned by a regular tribunal, according to a formal law which attaches the penalty of exile to the action of which he is guilty. No-one has the right to tear the citizen from his country, the owner away from his possessions, the merchant away from his trade, the husband from his wife, the father from his children, the writer from his studious meditations, the old man from his accustomed way of life.

All political exile is a political abuse. All exile pronounced by an assembly for alleged reasons of public safety is a crime which the assembly itself commits against public safety, which resides only in respect for the laws, in the observance of forms, and in the maintenance of safeguards.

Roman censorship implied, like ostracism, a discretionary power. In a republic where all the citizens, kept by poverty to an extremely simple moral code, lived in the same town, exercised no profession which might distract their attention from the affairs of the state, and thus constantly found themselves the spectators and judges of the usage of public power, censorship could on the one hand have greater influence: while on the other, the arbitrary power of the censors was restrained by a kind of moral surveillance exercised over them. But as soon as the size of the republic, the complexity of social relations and the refinements of civilization deprived this institution of what at the same time served as its basis and its limit, censorship degenerated even in Rome. It was not censorship which had created good morals; it was the simplicity of those morals which constituted the power and efficacy of censorship.

In France, an institution as arbitrary as censorship would be at once ineffective and intolerable. In the present conditions of society, morals are formed by subtle, fluctuating, elusive nuances, which would be distorted in a thousand ways if one attempted to define them more precisely. Public opinion alone can reach them; public opinion alone can judge them, because it is of the same nature. It would rebel against any positive authority which wanted to give it greater precision. If the government of a modern people wanted, like the censors in Rome, to censure a citizen arbitrarily, the entire nation would protest against this arrest by refusing to ratify the decisions of the authority.

What I have just said of the revival of censorship in modern times applies also to many other aspects of social organization, in relation to which antiquity is cited even more frequently and with greater emphasis. As for example, education; what do we not hear of the need to allow the government to take possession of new generations to shape them to its pleasure, and how many erudite quotations are employed to support this theory! The Persians, the Egyptians, Gaul, Greece and Italy are one after another set before us. Yet, Gentlemen, we are neither Persians subjected to a

---

1   *ostracism*   Practice in Ancient Greece of temporarily banishing, by popular vote, someone thought to be a threat to the state, or a political troublemaker.

despot, nor Egyptians subjugated by priests, nor Gauls who can be sacrificed by their druids, nor, finally, Greeks or Romans, whose share in social authority consoled them for their private enslavement. We are modern men, who wish each to enjoy our own rights, each to develop our own faculties as we like best, without harming anyone; to watch over the development of these faculties in the children whom nature entrusts to our affection, the more enlightened as it is more vivid; and needing the authorities only to give us the general means of instruction which they can supply, as travelers accept from them the main roads without being told by them which route to take.

Religion is also exposed to these memories of bygone ages. Some brave defenders of the unity of doctrine cite the laws of the ancients against foreign gods, and sustain the rights of the Catholic church by the example of the Athenians, who killed Socrates for having undermined polytheism,[1] and that of Augustus, who wanted the people to remain faithful to the cult of their fathers; with the result, shortly afterwards, that the first Christians were delivered to the lions. Let us mistrust, Gentlemen, this admiration for certain ancient memories. Since we live in modern times, I want a liberty suited to modern times; and since we live under monarchies, I humbly beg these monarchies not to borrow from the ancient republics the means to oppress us.

Individual liberty, I repeat, is the true modern liberty. Political liberty is its guarantee, consequently political liberty is indispensable. But to ask the peoples of our day to sacrifice, like those of the past, the whole of their individual liberty to political liberty, is the surest means of detaching them from the former and, once this result has been achieved, it would be only too easy to deprive them of the latter.

As you see, Gentlemen, my observations do not in the least tend to diminish the value of political liberty. I do not draw from the evidence I have put before your eyes the same conclusions that some others have. From the fact that the ancients were free, and that we cannot any longer be free like them, they conclude that we are destined to be slaves. They would like to reconstitute the new social state with a small number of elements which, they say, are alone appro-

priate to the situation of the world today. These elements are prejudices to frighten men, egoism to corrupt them, frivolity to stupefy them, gross pleasures to degrade them, despotism to lead them; and, indispensably, constructive knowledge and exact sciences to serve despotism the more adroitly. It would be odd indeed if this were the outcome of forty centuries during which mankind has acquired greater moral and physical means: I cannot believe it. I derive from the differences which distinguish us from antiquity totally different conclusions. It is not security which we must weaken; it is enjoyment which we must extend. It is not political liberty which I wish to renounce; it is civil liberty which I claim, along with other forms of political liberty. Governments, no more than they did before, have the right to arrogate to themselves an illegitimate power.

But the governments which emanate from a legitimate source have even less right than before to exercise an arbitrary supremacy over individuals. We still possess today the rights we have always had, those eternal rights to assent to the laws, to deliberate on our interests, to be an integral part of the social body of which we are members. But governments have new duties; the progress of civilization, the changes brought by the centuries require from the authorities greater respect for customs, for affections, for the independence of individuals. They must handle all these issues with a lighter and more prudent hand.

This reserve on the part of authority, which is one of its strictest duties, equally represents its well-conceived interest; since, if the liberty that suits the moderns is different from that which suited the ancients, the despotism which was possible amongst the ancients is no longer possible amongst the moderns. Because we are often less concerned with political liberty than they could be, and in ordinary circumstances less passionate about it, it may follow that we neglect, sometimes too much and always wrongly, the guarantees which this assures us. But at the same time, as we are much more preoccupied with individual liberty than the ancients, we shall defend it, if it is attacked, with much more skill and persistence; and we have means to defend it which the ancients did not.

Commerce makes the action of arbitrary power over our existence more oppressive than in the past, because, as our speculations are more varied, arbitrary power must multiply itself to reach them. But commerce also makes the action of arbitrary power easier to elude, because it changes the nature of property, which becomes, in virtue of this change, almost impossible to seize.

1   *who killed Socrates … polytheism* A jury of 500 Athenian citizens condemned Socrates to death for corrupting the youth and worshipping false gods (a reference to his personal spirit or "daimon"). Plato chronicles the trial and its aftermath in his dialogues the *Apology*, *Crito*, and *Phaedo*, as well as in the *Euthyphro*.

Commerce confers a new quality on property, circulation. Without circulation, property is merely a usufruct;[1] political authority can always affect usufruct, because it can prevent its enjoyment; but circulation creates an invisible and invincible obstacle to the actions of social power.

The effects of commerce extend even further: not only does it emancipate individuals, but, by creating credit, it places authority itself in a position of dependence. Money, says a French writer, "is the most dangerous weapon of despotism; yet it is at the same time its most powerful restraint; credit is subject to opinion; force is useless; money hides itself or flees; all the operations of the state are suspended." Credit did not have the same influence amongst the ancients; their governments were stronger than individuals, while in our time individuals are stronger than the political powers. Wealth is a power which is more readily available in all circumstances, more readily applicable to all interests, and consequently more real and better obeyed. Power threatens; wealth rewards: one eludes power by deceiving it; to obtain the favors of wealth one must serve it: the latter is therefore bound to win.

As a result, individual existence is less absorbed in political existence. Individuals carry their treasures far away; they take with them all the enjoyments of private life. Commerce has brought nations closer, it has given them customs and habits which are almost identical; the heads of states may be enemies: the peoples are compatriots. Let power therefore resign itself: we must have liberty and we shall have it. But since the liberty we need is different from that of the ancients, it needs a different organization from the one which would suit ancient liberty. In the latter, the more time and energy man dedicated to the exercise of his political rights, the freer he thought himself; on the other hand, in the kind of liberty of which we are capable, the more the exercise of political rights leaves us the time for our private interests, the more precious will liberty be to us.

Hence, Sirs, the need for the representative system. The representative system is nothing but an organization by means of which a nation charges a few individuals to do what it cannot or does not wish to do herself. Poor men look after their own business; rich men hire stewards. This is the history of ancient and modern nations. The representative system is a proxy given to a certain number of men by the mass of the people who wish their interests to be defended and who nevertheless do not have the time to defend them themselves. But, unless they are idiots, rich men who employ stewards keep a close watch on whether these stewards are doing their duty, lest they should prove negligent, corruptible, or incapable; and, in order to judge the management of these proxies, the landowners, if they are prudent, keep themselves well-informed about affairs, the management of which they entrust to them. Similarly, the people who, in order to enjoy the liberty which suits them, resort to the representative system, must exercise an active and constant surveillance over their representatives, and reserve for themselves, at times which should not be separated by too lengthy intervals, the right to discard them if they betray their trust, and to revoke the powers which they might have abused.

For from the fact that modern liberty differs from ancient liberty, it follows that it is also threatened by a different sort of danger. The danger of ancient liberty was that men, exclusively concerned with securing their share of social power, might attach too little value to individual rights and enjoyments.

The danger of modern liberty is that, absorbed in the enjoyment of our private independence, and in the pursuit of our particular interests, we should surrender our right to share in political power too easily. The holders of authority are only too anxious to encourage us to do so. They are so ready to spare us all sort of troubles, except those of obeying and paying! They will say to us: what, in the end, is the aim of your efforts, the motive of your labors, the object of all your hopes? Is it not happiness? Well, leave this happiness to us and we shall give it to you. No, Sirs, we must not leave it to them. No matter how touching such a tender commitment may be, let us ask the authorities to keep within their limits. Let them confine themselves to being just. We shall assume the responsibility of being happy for ourselves.

Could we be made happy by diversions, if these diversions were without guarantees? And where should we find guarantees, without political liberty? To renounce it, Gentlemen, would be a folly like that of a man who, because he only lives on the first floor, does not care if the house itself is built on sand.

Moreover, Gentlemen, is it so evident that happiness, of whatever kind, is the only aim of mankind? If it were so, our course would be narrow indeed, and our destination far from elevated. There is not one single one of us who, if he wished to abase himself, restrain his moral faculties, lower his desires, abjure activity, glory, deep and generous emotions, could not demean himself and be happy. No,

---

1 usufruct Legal right to use another's property.

Sirs, I bear witness to the better part of our nature, that noble disquiet which pursues and torments us, that desire to broaden our knowledge and develop our faculties. It is not to happiness alone, it is to self-development that our destiny calls us; and political liberty is the most powerful, the most effective means of self-development that heaven has given us.

Political liberty, by submitting to all the citizens, without exception, the care and assessment of their most sacred interests, enlarges their spirit, ennobles their thoughts, and establishes among them a kind of intellectual equality which forms the glory and power of a people.

Thus, see how a nation grows with the first institution which restores to her the regular exercise of political liberty. See our countrymen of all classes, of all professions, emerge from the sphere of their usual labors and private industry, find themselves suddenly at the level of important functions which the constitutions confers upon them, choose with discernment, resist with energy—, brave threats, nobly withstand seduction. See a pure, deep and sincere patriotism triumph in our towns, revive even our smallest villages, permeate our workshops, enliven our countryside, penetrate the just and honest spirits of the useful farmer and the industrious tradesman with a sense of our rights and the need for safeguards; they, learned in the history of the evils they have suffered, and no less enlightened as to the remedies which these evils demand, take in with a glance the whole of France and, bestowing a national gratitude, repay with their suffrage, after thirty years, the fidelity to principles embodied in the most illustrious of the defenders of liberty.

Therefore, Sirs, far from renouncing either of the two sorts of freedom which I have described to you, it is necessary, as I have shown, to learn to combine the two together. Institutions, says the famous author of the history of the republics in the Middle Ages, must accomplish the destiny of the human race; they can best achieve their aim if they elevate the largest possible number of citizens to the highest moral position.

The work of the legislator is not complete when he has simply brought peace to the people. Even when the people are satisfied, there is much left to do. Institutions must achieve the moral education of the citizens. By respecting their individual rights, securing their independence, refraining from troubling their work, they must nevertheless consecrate their influence over public affairs, call them to contribute by their votes to the exercise of power, grant them a right of control and supervision by expressing their opinions; and, by forming them through practice for these elevated functions, give them both the desire and the right to discharge these.

GEORG WILHELM FRIEDRICH HEGEL
(1770 – 1831)

GEORG WILHELM FRIEDRICH HEGEL WAS BORN IN Stuttgart, Germany in 1770. Celebrated in his time, he won professorships in Heidelberg (1816) and Berlin (1818). He is remembered for his dialectical method, his philosophy of history, and his distinctive place in the German Idealist tradition. In political philosophy, he is known as a critic of contract theory. Responding to the perceived emptiness of Kant's ethics and to Romanticism's individualistic attack on convention, Hegel argued that freedom requires assuming customary roles and duties. There is debate over the implications of his views, some reading him as a proto-totalitarian, others as a liberal.

Hegel's dialectic is a system of logic—in his view, the correct philosophical method. It systematically resolves oppositions. Each concept, on his view, generates its own opposite. Reason transcends the resulting contradictions, combining them in a third concept. For instance, the opposing concepts "being" and "nothing" are transcended in "becoming." (The dialectic is sometimes explained with the terms "thesis, antithesis, synthesis," but this simplifying terminology is not Hegel's.) Hegel uses the dialectic to explain historical change and the natural world. For example, he explains sexual reproduction as combining and transcending the two sexes, which are oppositionally incomplete on their own.

Idealism licenses Hegel to interpret the world dialectically. Hegelian Idealism holds that the world is the continuous development of Spirit or Mind (*Geist*). The world is thus essentially mental and so operates in accordance with reason, that is, dialectically. On the traditional interpretation, his theory is pantheistic: the universe is Spirit thinking itself. Some recent interpreters have argued that Hegel is not committed to a metaphysical thesis of divine immanence; Spirit can be understood as the collective spirit of each historical age, as opposed to an independent, conscious entity. Thus Allen Wood describes Hegel's view as "histori-cized naturalism," in which human nature and, derivatively, ethical standards are essentially social or historical.

On either reading, Hegel's Idealism implies that the world is rationally intelligible. His Preface to *Philosophy of Right* explains that the task of philosophy is to reconcile us to the world by uncovering its inner rationality—"the rose in the cross of the present" (22). Philosophy cannot prescribe how things ought to be. Instead, it can only examine forms of life which have already completely developed their inner rationality: "the owl of Minerva begins its flight only with the onset of dusk" (23). At first glance, Hegel's axiom that "What is rational is actual; and what is actual is rational" (20) appears conservative. But Hegel carefully distinguishes what *exists* from what is *actual* (what has successfully developed its nature) and so leaves conceptual room for reform (§270).

Another distinctive Hegelian view is that self-consciousness depends on recognizing others and being recognized in turn. His famous exposition of this, the parable of lordship and bondage in *Phenomenology of Spirit*, imagines two individuals in mutual confrontation, each recognizing his own personhood as he recognizes the other recognizing him. This prompts a "trial by death" in a mutual attempt to secure recognition. The risk of life involved demonstrates each man's transcendence of mere existence. Eventually, one combatant yields and becomes a slave; the other becomes master. Paradoxically, the slave now finds self-recognition through his work, while the master becomes dependent on the slave. For Hegel, this generates the central political problem of how everyone can secure stable equal recognition.

Hegel's main political work, *Elements of the Philosophy of Right*, begins by examining the will. In the modern world the individual is inherently free: "the will is *free*, so that freedom constitutes its substance and destiny" (§4). Right (*Recht*, also translated *law* or *justice*) is a rational order in which human freedom develops in a dialectical progression of the will. The will is inherently indeterminate: it can abstract itself from "every limitation, every content" (§4). Indeterminacy is not freedom: if we do not will anything particular, we are not persons at all. Freedom requires limiting the will through commitment to some self-definition, yet simultaneously being able to recognize this role as one's own. How can an inherently indeterminate being recognize itself in limitation? Hegel's dialectical solution is that the content of the will must be "universal," expressing the collective social spirit.

Hegel writes that freedom is usually understood as an absence of restraint, allowing the pursuit of desires. But this is not true freedom, because the will is determined randomly by indiscriminate urges such as hunger and thirst. Hegelian "absolute freedom" is achieved by taming the will through a "purification of the drives" which integrates desires into a system ordered by customary roles and duties.

In apparent paradox, Hegel insists that duty is freedom: "The individual ... finds his *liberation* in duty" (§149). In absolute freedom, the individual identifies with his social role. He sees it as self-expressive, not limiting: it is "not something *alien* to the subject," but "*its own essence*" (§147). Internalizing the role, he desires to do that which is also his duty. Further, the system of Right organizes the desires of everyone harmoniously, overcoming the conflict between individual and community. The roles of "ethical life" (*Sittlichkeit*), or customary morality, remove the individual from isolation by connecting him to a larger whole, express his historically shaped nature, and secure mutual recognition. Ethical life is the highest stage of Right.

The system of Right exists in three stages simultaneously. The first, abstract right, concerns property, contract, and punishment. Considered in this stage, the person has rights over property (including the body). Abstract right secures equal mutual recognition between citizens as rights-bearers—property owners or contractors: "The commandment of right is ...: *be a person and respect others as persons*" (§36). In Hegel's retributive account, punishment recognizes the criminal "as a rational being" who chose his crime (§100). Abstract right focuses only on that which is external to the individual, and so is an incomplete development of freedom.

So the next stage of right is morality, which focuses on the individual's interiority or subjectivity. Morality, understood as Kant's Categorical Imperative, is not sufficiently defined to guide action. Rousseau's understanding of conscience as independent of society is likewise inadequate. For Hegel,

duty and judgment, like the self, exist in a social context, in relation to others. Absolute freedom is realized only at the stage of ethical life—social institutions and shared customs. Its three levels are family, civil society, and the state.

The spirit of the family is non-contractual and non-individualistic. Here individuals understand themselves as members of a larger unit, a role which is self-defining, not limiting. In Hegel's system, women are confined to the family, the unreflective or un-self-conscious stage of ethical life. However, the family is crucial to the whole: its non-contractual bonds reappear as the principle of the state after dissolution in individualistic civil society.

What Hegel calls "civil society," which he distinguishes from the political, includes the economic sphere, the administration of justice, the police, and corporations (trade or professional associations). Here men interact as self-interested independent individuals. However, in trade their needs are organized into "a system of all-round interdependence" (§183) and in the corporations, foreshadowing citizenship and recalling the family, they belong as members in a united larger whole.

Freedom is only fully realized (and only by men) in the state. Hegel rejects social contract theory because it represents membership in the state as self-interested and contingent. For Hegel, it necessarily involves belonging in a union in which the opposition between individual and society is overcome in a relationship of trust, and men see themselves represented in the legislature and the monarch.

Hegel died in 1831. His philosophy has exerted tremendous, and diverse, influence. Shortly after his death his followers divided into Left and Right Hegelians. Karl Marx "turned Hegel on his head" by reinterpreting the dialectic as a material, not spiritual, progression. Simone de Beauvoir endorsed Hegel's dialectical view of gender but argued that it is contingent, not necessary. Hegel's influence extends as well to existentialism and to contemporary communitarian critiques of liberal individualism.

◆ ◆ ◆ ◆ ◆

The Phenomenology of Spirit (1807)

A. Independence and Dependence of Self-Consciousness: Lordship and Bondage

178. Self-consciousness exists in and for itself[1] when, and by the fact that, it so exists for another; that is, it exists only in being acknowledged. The Notion[2] of this its unity in its duplication embraces many and varied meanings. Its moments, then, must on the one hand be held strictly apart, and on the other hand must in this differentiation at the same time also be taken and known as not distinct, or in their opposite significance. The twofold significance of the distinct moments has in the nature of self-consciousness to be infinite,[3] or directly the opposite of the determinateness in which it is posited. The detailed exposition of the Notion of this spiritual unity in its duplication will present us with the process of Recognition.

179. Self-consciousness is faced by another self-consciousness; it has come *out of itself*. This has a twofold significance: first, it has lost itself, for it finds itself as an *other* being; secondly, in doing so it has superseded[4] the other, for it does not see the other as an essential being, but in the other sees its own self.

180. It must supersede this otherness of itself. This is the supersession of the first ambiguity, and is therefore itself a second ambiguity. First, it must proceed to supersede the *other* independent being in order thereby to become certain of *itself* as the essential being; secondly, in so doing it proceeds to supersede its own self, for this other is itself.

181. This ambiguous supersession of its ambiguous otherness is equally an ambiguous return *into itself*. For first, through the supersession, it receives back its own self, because, by superseding its otherness, it again becomes equal to itself; but secondly, the other self-consciousness equally gives it back again to itself, for it saw itself in the other, but supersedes this being of itself in the other and thus lets the other again go free.

182. Now, this movement of self-consciousness in relation to another self-consciousness has in this way been represented as the action of *one* self-consciousness, but this action of the one has itself the double significance of being both its own action and the action of the other as well. For the other is equally independent and self-contained, and there is nothing in it of which it is not itself the origin. The first does not have the object before it merely as it exists primarily for desire, but as something that has an independent existence of its own, which, therefore, it cannot utilize for its own purposes, if that object does not of its own accord do what the first does to it. Thus the movement is simply the double movement[5] of the two self-consciousnesses. Each sees the *other* do the same as it does; each does itself what it demands of the other, and therefore also does what it does only in so far as the other does the same. Action by one side only would be useless because what is to happen can only be brought about by both.

183. Thus the action has a double significance not only because it is directed against itself as well as against the other, but also because it is indivisibly the action of one as well as of the other.

184. In this movement we see repeated the process which presented itself as the play of Forces, but repeated now in consciousness. What in that process was *for us*,[6] is true here of the extremes[7] themselves. The middle term[8] is self-consciousness which splits into the extremes; and each extreme is this exchanging of its own determinateness and an absolute transition into the opposite. Although, as consciousness, it does indeed come *out of itself*, yet, though out of itself, it is at the same time kept back within itself,

---

1   *in and for itself*   Implicitly and on its own account; rather like the English expression "in and of itself."

2   *Notion*   The German term, *Begriff* is also translated as "concept." Note that all nouns are capitalized in German; capitals in the present text are introduced by the translator.

3   *infinite*   Hegel gives this term a distinctive sense: able to transcend any limitations and incorporate them into itself.

4   *superseded*   Translating the German *Aufhebung*, which can mean *cancel, retain* and *go beyond*. Hegel frequently intends all three senses. See §188 below.

5   *double movement*   Reciprocal interaction is an important motif in Hegel's thought.

6   *for us*   Hegel here identifies what we as philosophical observers notice, in contrast to what the self-consciousness being talked about is aware of.

7   *extremes*   This term can also refer to the subject and predicate of the conclusion in a syllogism.

8   *middle term*   The reference is to the "middle term" of a syllogism in Aristotelian logic which occurs in both premises. For example, in the syllogism

All *men* are mortal
Socrates is a *man*

Therefore, Socrates is mortal
"man" is the middle term.

is *for itself*, and the self outside it, is for *it*.[1] It is aware that it at once is, and is not, another consciousness, and equally that this other is *for itself* only when it supersedes itself as being for itself, and is for itself only in the being-for-self[2] of the other. Each is for the other the middle term, through which each mediates itself with itself and unites with itself; and each is for itself, and for the other, an immediate being on its own account, which at the same time is such only through this mediation. They *recognize* themselves as *mutually recognizing* one another.

185. We have now to see how the process of this pure Notion of recognition, of the duplicating of self-consciousness in its oneness, appears to self-consciousness. At first, it will exhibit the side of the inequality of the two, or the splitting-up of the middle term into the extremes which, as extremes, are opposed to one another, one being only *recognized*, the other only *recognizing*.

186. Self-consciousness is, to begin with, simple being-for-self, self-equal through the exclusion from itself of everything else. For it, its essence and absolute object is "I"; and in this immediacy, or in this [mere] being, of its being-for-self, it is an *individual*. What is "other" for it is an unessential, negatively characterized[3] object. But the "other" is also a self-consciousness; one individual is confronted by another individual. Appearing thus immediately on the scene, they are for one another like ordinary objects, *independent* shapes, individuals submerged in the being [or immediacy] of *Life*—for the object in its immediacy is here determined as Life. They are, *for each other*,[4] shapes of consciousness which have not yet accomplished the movement of absolute abstraction,[5] of rooting-out all immediate being, and of being merely the purely negative being of self-identical consciousness; in other words, they have not as yet exposed themselves to each other in the form of pure being-for-self, or as self-consciousnesses. Each is indeed certain of its own self, but not of the other, and therefore its own self-certainty still has no truth.[6] For it would have truth only if its own being-for-self had confronted it as an independent object,

or, what is the same thing, if the object had presented itself as this pure self-certainty. But according to the Notion of recognition this is possible only when each is for the other what the other is for it,[7] only when each in its own self through its own action, and again through the action of the other, achieves this pure abstraction of being-for-self.

187. The presentation of itself, however, as the pure abstraction of self-consciousness consists in showing itself as the pure negation of its objective mode,[8] or in showing that it is not attached to any specific *existence*, not to the individuality common to existence as such, that it is not attached to life. This presentation is a twofold action: action on the part of the other, and action on its own part. In so far as it is the action of the *other*, each seeks the death of the other. But in doing so, the second kind of action, action on its own part, is also involved; for the former involves the staking of its own life. Thus the relation of the two self-conscious individuals is such that they prove themselves and each other through a life-and-death struggle. They must engage in this struggle, for they must raise their certainty of being *for themselves* to truth, both in the case of the other and in their own case. And it is only through staking one's life that freedom is won; only thus is it proved that for self-consciousness, its essential being is not [just] being, not the *immediate* form in which it appears, not its submergence in the expanse of life, but rather that there is nothing present in it which could not be regarded as a vanishing moment, that it is only pure *being-for-self*. The individual who has not risked his life may well be recognized as a *person*, but he has not attained to the truth of this recognition as an independent self-consciousness. Similarly, just as each stakes his own life, so each must seek the other's death, for it values the other no more than itself; its essential being is present to it in the form of an "other," it is outside of itself and must rid itself of its self-externality. The other is an immediate consciousness entangled in a variety of relationships, and it must regard its otherness as a pure being-for-self or as an absolute negation.[9]

188. This trial by death, however, does away with the truth which was supposed to issue from it, and so, too, with

---

1   *for itself . . . for it*   Two quite different expressions. The first means "on its own account"; the second, "what consciousness is aware of."

2   *being-for-self*   Something that is on its own account.

3   *negatively characterized*   Defined by what it is *not*.

4   *for each other*   Each is aware of the other only in this way.

5   *absolute abstraction*   Distinguishing in a thoroughgoing way from all non-essential details of our existence.

6   *self-certainty . . . truth*   Throughout the *Phenomenology* the goal is to overcome any discrepancy between what a consciousness holds for certain and what is true. "Self-certainty" is found when we

are confident that we know who and what we are. We may later discover we have been mistaken, so our certainty is not true.

7   *each is . . . for it*   Other persons are to be aware of us in the same way that we are aware of them.

8   *pure negation . . . mode*   Reflection in which we radically distinguish the self from the body (or object) in which it lives.

9   *as an absolute negation*   As being in no way related to anything else, entirely on one's own.

the certainty of self generally. For just as life is the *natural* setting of consciousness, independence without absolute negativity,[1] so death is the *natural* negation of consciousness, negation without independence,[2] which thus remains without the required significance of recognition. Death certainly shows that each staked his life and held it of no account, both in himself and in the other; but that is not for those who survived this struggle. They put an end to their consciousness in its alien setting of natural existence, that is to say, they put an end to themselves, and are done away with as *extremes* wanting to be *for themselves*, or to have an existence of their own. But with this there vanishes from their interplay the essential moment of splitting into extremes with opposite characteristics; and the middle term collapses into a lifeless unity which is split into lifeless, merely immediate, unopposed extremes; and the two do not reciprocally give and receive one another back from each other consciously, but leave each other free only indifferently, like things. Their act is an abstract negation, not the negation coming from consciousness, which supersedes in such a way as to preserve and maintain what is superseded, and consequently survives its own supersession.[3]

189. In this experience, self-consciousness learns that life is as essential to it as pure self-consciousness. In immediate self-consciousness the simple "I" is absolute mediation, and has as its essential moment lasting independence. The dissolution of that simple unity is the result of the first experience; through this there is posited a pure self-consciousness, and a consciousness which is not purely for itself but for another, i.e., is a merely *immediate* consciousness, or consciousness in the form of *thinghood*. Both moments are essential. Since to begin with they are unequal and opposed, and their reflection into a unity has not yet been achieved, they exist as two opposed shapes of consciousness; one is the independent consciousness whose essential nature is to be for itself, the other is the dependent consciousness whose essential nature is simply to live or to be for another. The former is lord, the other is bondsman.

190. The lord is the consciousness that exists *for itself*, but no longer merely the Notion of such a consciousness. Rather, it is a consciousness existing *for itself* which is mediated with itself through another consciousness, i.e., through a consciousness whose nature it is to be bound up with an existence that is independent, or thinghood in general.[4] The lord puts himself into relation with both of these moments, to a *thing* as such, the object of desire, and to the consciousness for which thinghood is the essential characteristic. And since he is (a) *qua* the Notion of self-consciousness an immediate relation of *being-for-self*, but (b) is now at the same time mediation, or a being-for-self which is for itself only through another, he is related (a) immediately to both, and (b) mediately to each through the other. The lord relates himself mediately to the bondsman through a being [a thing] that is independent, for it is just this which holds the bondsman in bondage; it is his chain from which he could not break free in the struggle, thus proving himself to be dependent, to possess his independence in thinghood.[5] But the lord is the power over this thing, for he proved in the struggle that it is something merely negative;[6] since he is the power over this thing and this again is the power over the other [the bondsman], it follows that he holds the other in subjection. Equally, the lord relates himself mediately to the thing through the bondsman; the bondsman, *qua* self-consciousness in general, also relates himself negatively to the thing, and takes away its independence; but at the same time the thing is independent *vis-à-vis* the bondsman, whose negating of it, therefore, cannot go the length of being altogether done with it to the point of annihilation;[7] in other words, he only *works* on it. For the lord, on the other hand, the *immediate* relation becomes through this mediation the sheer negation of the thing, or the enjoyment of it. What desire[8] failed to achieve, he succeeds in doing, viz. to have done with the thing altogether, and to achieve

---

1   *independence ... negativity* A separate existence in which we do not consciously separate ourselves from others around us.

2   *negation without independence* I.e., through death we become what we were not, but we thereby cease to have a separate existence.

3   *abstract ... supersession* Hegel here contrasts a kind of negating which totally abandons any implicit relationship from the kind of negating which presupposes and requires its opposite.

4   *through ... in general* The bondsman or slave simply becomes one thing among many, both in the eyes of the lord and in his or her own eyes.

5   *it is ... thinghood* The bondsman's life is essentially tied up with the other things that the lord owns.

6   *that it is something merely negative* I.e., that things (including the bondsman) make no contribution to the lord's sense of himself.

7   *whose negating ... annihilation* I.e., the bondsman can overcome the independence of the things around him, but he cannot simply absorb them into the satisfaction of his own desires.

8   *desire* Earlier in the *Phenomenology* self-consciousness on its own fails to achieve the truth of its self-certainty as desiring, because satisfaction always leads to the dissatisfaction of renewed desire.

satisfaction in the enjoyment of it. Desire failed to do this because of the thing's independence; but the lord, who has interposed the bondsman between it and himself, takes to himself only the dependent aspect of the thing and has the pure enjoyment of it. The aspect of its independence he leaves to the bondsman, who works on it.

191. In both of these moments the lord achieves his recognition through another consciousness; for in them, that other consciousness is expressly something unessential, both by its working on the thing, and by its dependence on a specific existence. In neither case can it be lord over the being of the thing and achieve absolute negation of it. Here, therefore, is present this moment of recognition, viz. that the other consciousness sets aside its own being-for-self, and in so doing itself does what the first does to it. Similarly, the other moment too is present, that this action of the second is the first's own action; for what the bondsman does is really the action of the lord. The latter's essential nature is to exist only for himself; he is the sheer negative power for whom the thing is nothing. Thus he is the pure, essential action in this relationship, while the action of the bondsman is impure and unessential. But for recognition proper the moment is lacking, that what the lord does to the other he also does to himself, and what the bondsman does to himself he should also do to the other. The outcome is a recognition that is one-sided and unequal.

192. In this recognition the unessential consciousness is for the lord the object, which constitutes the *truth* of his certainty of himself. But it is clear that this object does not correspond to its Notion, but rather that the object in which the lord has achieved his lordship has in reality turned out to be something quite different from an independent consciousness. What now really confronts him is not an independent consciousness, but a dependent one. He is, therefore, not certain of *being-for-self* as the truth of himself.[1] On the contrary, his truth is in reality the unessential consciousness and its unessential action.

193. The *truth* of the independent consciousness is accordingly the servile consciousness of the bondsman. This, it is true, appears at first *outside* of itself and not as the truth of self-consciousness. But just as lordship showed that its essential nature is the reverse of what it wants to be, so too servitude in its consummation will really turn into the op-

posite of what it immediately is; as a consciousness forced back into itself, it will withdraw into itself and be transformed into a truly independent consciousness.

194. We have seen what servitude is only in relation to lordship. But it is a self-consciousness, and we have now to consider what as such it is in and for itself. To begin with, servitude has the lord for its essential reality; hence the *truth* for it is the independent consciousness that is *for itself*. However, servitude is not yet aware that this truth is implicit in it. But it does in fact contain within itself this truth of pure negativity and being-for-self, for it has experienced this its own essential nature. For this consciousness has been fearful, not of this or that particular thing or just at odd moments, but its whole being has been seized with dread; for it has experienced the fear of death, the absolute Lord. In that experience it has been quite unmanned, has trembled in every fiber of its being, and everything solid and stable has been shaken to its foundations. But this pure universal movement, the absolute melting-away of everything stable, is the simple, essential nature of self-consciousness, absolute negativity, *pure being-for-self*, which consequently is *implicit* in this consciousness. This moment of pure being-for-self is also *explicit* for the bondsman, for in the lord it exists for him as his *object*. Furthermore, his consciousness is not this dissolution of everything stable merely in principle; in his service he actually brings this about. Through his service he rids himself of his attachment to natural existence in every single detail; and gets rid of it by working on it.[2]

195. However, the feeling of absolute power both in general, and in the particular form of service, is only implicitly this dissolution, and although the fear of the lord is indeed the beginning of wisdom,[3] consciousness is not therein aware that it is a being-for-self. Through work, however, the bondsman becomes conscious of what he truly is. In the moment which corresponds to desire in the lord's consciousness, it did seem that the aspect of unessential relation to the thing fell to the lot of the bondsman, since in that relation the thing retained its independence. Desire has reserved to itself the pure negating of the object and thereby

---

1 *He is ... himself* Since the bondsman only does what the lord commands, the lord does not receive any independent confirmation of his own sense of self, and so he loses his original sense of self-certainty.

2 *But this pure ... working on it* When confronted with the immediate threat of death, the bondsman learns that nothing else is really of any importance other than his own self-conscious life. At first he attributes that independence to the lord. But he puts his insight into practice by working on things that are of really no interest to him.

3 *fear of the lord ... wisdom* See Psalm 111.10: "The fear of the Lord is the beginning of wisdom."

its unalloyed feeling of self. But that is the reason why this satisfaction is itself only a fleeting one, for it lacks the side of objectivity and permanence.[1] Work, on the other hand, is desire held in check, fleetingness staved off; in other words, work forms and shapes the thing. The negative relation to the object becomes its *form* and something *permanent*, because it is precisely for the worker that the object has independence. This *negative* middle term or the formative *activity* is at the same time the individuality or pure being-for-self of consciousness which now, in the work outside of it, acquires an element of permanence. It is in this way, therefore, that consciousness, *qua* worker, comes to see in the independent being [of the object] its *own* independence.[2]

196. But the formative activity has not only this positive significance that in it the pure being-for-self of the servile consciousness acquires an existence; it also has, in contrast with its first moment, the negative significance of *fear*. For, in fashioning the thing, the bondsman's own negativity, his being-for-self, becomes an object for him only through his setting at nought the existing *shape* confronting him. But this objective *negative* moment[3] is none other than the alien being before which it has trembled. Now, however, he destroys this alien negative moment, posits *himself* as a negative in the permanent order of things, and thereby becomes *for himself*, someone existing on his own account. In the lord, the being-for-self is an "other" for the bondsman, or is only *for* him[4] [i.e., is not his own]; in fear, the being-for-self is present in the bondsman himself; in fashioning the thing, he becomes aware that being-for-self belongs to *him*, that he himself exists essentially and actually in his own right. The shape does not become something other than himself through being made external to him; for it is precisely this shape that is his pure being-for-self, which in this externality is seen by him to be the truth.[5] Through this rediscovery of himself by himself, the bondsman realizes that it is precisely

in his work wherein he seemed to have only an alienated existence that he acquires a mind of his own. For this reflection, the two moments of fear and service as such, as also that of formative activity, are necessary, both being at the same time in a universal mode. Without the discipline of service and obedience, fear remains at the formal stage, and does not extend to the known real world of existence. Without the formative activity, fear remains inward and mute, and consciousness does not become explicitly *for itself*. If consciousness fashions the thing without that initial absolute fear, it is only an empty self-centered attitude; for its form or negativity is not negativity *per se*, and therefore its formative activity cannot give it a consciousness of itself as essential being. If it has not experienced absolute fear but only some lesser dread, the negative being has remained for it something external, its substance has not been infected by it through and through. Since the entire contents of its natural consciousness have not been jeopardized, determinate being still *in principle* attaches to it; having a 'mind of one's own' is self-will, a freedom which is still enmeshed in servitude.[6] Just as little as the pure form can become essential being for it, just as little is that form, regarded as extended to the particular, a universal formative activity, an absolute Notion; rather it is a skill which is master over some things, but not over the universal power and the whole of objective being.

◆ ◆ ◆ ◆ ◆

---

1   *But that … permanence*   The lord can enjoy the delightful thing produced by the bondsman, but once that enjoyment is over, he is back wanting more exciting pleasures.

2   *This negative … independence*   The fear of death revealed the bondsman's self was essentially the pure dynamic of living. Through work, that dynamic gives form and shape to the object worked upon. After the work is completed, the bondsman can look at it and see an objective embodiment of his own activity.

3   *objective negative moment*   I.e., a moment in which the thing being worked on is independent and other than himself.

4   *only for him*   Only something he is aware of as present.

5   *it is precisely … is seen by him to be the truth*   I.e., he becomes certain of who he really is.

6   *If it has not experienced … servitude*   Without the experience of total terror when faced with death, there is no discovery that the independent form of the object created is the bondsman's own being. The object would then remain simply one external entity among many, and any self-assertion would be an unjustified claim to uniqueness.

Philosophy of Right (1821)

from *Preface*

The immediate occasion for me to publish this outline is the need to provide my audience with an introduction to the lectures on the *Philosophy of Right* which I deliver in the course of my official duties.[1] This textbook is a more extensive, and in particular a more systematic, exposition of the same basic concepts which, in relation to this part of philosophy, are already contained in a previous work designed to accompany my lectures, namely my *Encyclopaedia of the Philosophical Sciences* (Heidelberg, 1817).[2]

The fact that this outline was due to appear in print and thus to come before a wider public gave me the opportunity to amplify in it some of those *Remarks*[3] whose primary purpose was to comment briefly on ideas [*Vorstellungen*][4] akin to or divergent from my own, on further consequences of my argument, and on other such matters as would be properly elucidated in the lectures themselves.

I have amplified them here so as to clarify on occasion the more abstract contents of the text and to take fuller account of related ideas [*Vorstellungen*] which are current at the present time. As a result, some of these Remarks have become more extensive than the aim and style of a compendium would normally lead one to expect. A genuine compendium, however, has as its subject-matter what is considered to be the entire compass of a science;[5] and what distinguishes it—apart, perhaps, from a minor addition here or there—is above all the way in which it arranges and orders the essential elements [*Momente*][6] of a content which has long been familiar and accepted, just as the form in which it is presented has its rules and conventions which have long been agreed. But a philosophical outline is not expected to conform to this pattern, if only because it is imagined that what philosophy puts forward is as ephemeral a product as Penelope's weaving, which is begun afresh every day.[7]

It is certainly true that the primary difference between the present outline and an ordinary compendium is the method which constitutes its guiding principle. But I am here presupposing that the philosophical manner of progressing from one topic to another and of conducting a scientific proof—this entire speculative mode of cognition[8]—is essentially different from other modes of cognition. The realization that such a difference is a necessary one is the only thing which can save philosophy from the shameful decline into which it has fallen in our times. It has indeed been recognized that the forms and rules of the older logic—of definition, classification, and inference—which include the rules of the understanding's cog-

---

1 *publish ... duties* In German universities, professors frequently start from a condensed paragraph which they will dictate (if it is not already published in a handbook), and then comment on. The *Philosophy of Right* is just such a handbook. After Hegel's death, his students collected student notes from these lectures, and edited them into a series of "Additions" that are connected to the various paragraphs. In this text the additions come from notes taken by H.G. Hotho in 1822–23 (H) and K.G. von Griesheim in 1824–25 (G).

2 *Encyclopaedia ... 1817* The *Philosophy of Right* is an expansion of the section on "Objective Spirit" contained in the third part of the *Encyclopaedia of the Philosophical Sciences*, called the *Philosophy of Spirit* or *Philosophy of Mind*. The *Encyclopaedia* is also a compendium of condensed paragraphs designed to be used in Hegel's lectures. The 1817 edition was revised twice in Hegel's lifetime, in 1827 and 1830.

3 *Remarks* Hegel's "Remarks" are to be distinguished from the "Additions" in that they are elaborations of the basic paragraphs written by Hegel himself. In the following text, they are indented. Under every numbered paragraph, then, we can have three distinct components: the paragraph itself, a Remark expanding on this (written by Hegel), and an Addition containing material from students' notes.

4 *ideas* Hegel draws a sharp distinction between "ideas" or "representations" (German *Vorstellungen*) which are the common thoughts people have, and the more carefully defined "concepts" or "notions" which are the result of disciplined reflection. They are not to be confused with Ideas with a capital I.

5 *science* By "science" Hegel means a disciplined body of knowledge that follows systematically from point to point.

6 *essential elements [Momente]* Hegel's use of the German term *Momente* for the components of an analysis suggests that they are not static and permanent, but transient stages in a continuous development.

7 *Penelope's ... day* The reference is to the wife of Odysseus in Homer's epic, who would unravel overnight the cloth she had woven during the day. Her husband's overlong absence had generated a number of suitors for her hand, and she had promised to choose one of them once her weaving was finished.

8 *speculative mode of cognition* In the first part of the *Encyclopaedia* and in a separate treatise, both called *Science of Logic*, Hegel endeavored to show how thought leads necessarily from concept to concept following a method of continual elaboration. Once thought turns to the real world of nature and politics it can use the same method to show how the interconnections among natural and social phenomena can be grasped in a comprehensive way.

nition [*Verstandeserkenntnis*], are inadequate for speculative science. Or rather, their inadequacy has not so much been recognized as merely felt, and then the rules in question have been cast aside, as if they were simply fetters, to make way for the arbitrary pronouncements of the heart, of fantasy, and of contingent intuition; and since, in spite of this, reflection and relations of thought inevitably also come into play, the despised method of commonplace deduction and ratiocination is unconsciously adopted.[1]—Since I have fully developed the nature of speculative knowledge in my *Science of Logic*,[2] I have only occasionally added an explanatory comment on procedure and method in the present outline. Given that the subject-matter is concrete and inherently of so varied a nature, I have of course omitted to demonstrate and bring out the logical progression in each and every detail. But on the one hand, it might have been considered superfluous to do so in view of the fact that I have presupposed a familiarity with scientific method; and on the other, it will readily be noticed that the work as a whole, like the construction [*Ausbildung*] of its parts, is based on the logical spirit. It is also chiefly from this point of view that I would wish this treatise to be understood and judged. For what it deals with is *science*, and in science, the content is essentially inseparable from the *form*.[3]

It is true that we may hear it said by those who seem to adopt the most thorough approach that form is a purely external quality, indifferent to the matter [*Sache*] itself, which is alone of consequence; furthermore, the task of the writer, especially the philosophical writer, may be said to consist in the discovery of *truths*, the statement of *truths*, and the dissemination of *truths* and correct concepts. But if we consider how this task is actually performed, we see on the one hand how the same old brew is reheated again and again and served up to all and sundry—a task that may not be without its merits in educating and arousing the emotions, though it might sooner be regarded as the superfluous product of over-zealous activity—"for they have Moses and the prophets; let them hear them."[4] Above all, we have ample opportunity to wonder at the tone and pretentiousness that can be detected in such writers, as if all that the world had hitherto lacked was these zealous disseminators of truths, and as if their reheated brew contained new and unheard-of truths which ought, as they always claim, to be taken particularly to heart, above all "at the present time." But on the other hand, we can see how whatever truths of this kind are handed out by one party are displaced and swept away by truths of precisely the same kind dispensed by other parties. And if, amidst this jumble of truths, there is something that is neither old nor new but enduring, how can it be extracted from these formlessly fluctuating reflections—how can it be distinguished and verified other than by *scientific* means?

The *truth* concerning *right*,[5] *ethics, and the state* is at any rate *as old* as its *exposition and promulgation* in *public laws and in public morality and religion*. What more does this truth require, inasmuch as the thinking mind [*Geist*][6] is not content to possess it in this proximate manner? What it needs is to be *comprehended* as well, so that the content which is already rational in itself may also gain a rational form[7] and thereby appear justified to free thinking. For such thinking does not stop at what is *given,* whether the latter is supported by the external positive authority of the state or of mutual agreement among human beings, or by the authority of inner feeling and the heart and by the testimony of the spirit which immediately concurs with this, but starts out from itself and thereby demands to know itself as united in its innermost being with the truth.

The simple reaction [*Verhalten*] of ingenuous emotion is to adhere with trusting conviction to the publicly recognized truth and to base one's conduct and fixed position in life on this firm foundation. But this simple reaction may

---

1 *felt ... adopted* Hegel is here referring to the Romantic thinkers of his day who rejected the tyranny of thought and advocated greater reliance on the immediate intuitions of the heart.

2 *Science of Logic* Originally published in 1812–16, with a second edition of the first part in 1831. A condensed version for his lectures is included in his *Encyclopaedia*.

3 *content ... form* For Hegel, the form of the discussion must follow from the nature of the concepts being discussed. It is not a template that is simply applied from outside to satisfy some other interests.

4 *for they have Moses ... hear them* See Luke 16.29.

5 *right* The human interest in justice and fairness, both in public institutions and personal morality.

6 *mind [Geist]* The German term names self-conscious life, and Hegel uses it to cover all stages of life, from that of the incipient human individual to that of the most complex organizations of international relations, and even to interactions between humans and the divine. It is thus frequently translated "spirit." Since Hegel is here talking about "thinking spirit," *mind* is an appropriate alternative.

7 *content ... form* Hegel's conviction is that the world of nature and human society operates according to rational principles. This is why we can use our minds to understand how it works. He wants to bring this inherent rationality out through the structure of his argument.

well encounter the supposed difficulty of how to distinguish and discover, among the *infinite variety of opinions*, what is universally acknowledged and valid in them; and this perplexity may easily be taken for a just and genuine concern with the matter [*Sache*] itself. But in fact, those who pride themselves on this perplexity are in the position of not being able to see the wood for the trees and the only perplexity and difficulty that is present is the one they have themselves created; indeed, this perplexity and difficulty, is rather a proof that they want something other than what is universally acknowledged and valid, something other than the substance of the right and the ethical. For if they were genuinely concerned with the latter and not with the *vanity* and *particularity* of opinions and being, they would adhere to the substantial right, namely to the commandments of ethics and of the state, and regulate their lives accordingly.—A further difficulty arises, however, from the fact that human beings *think* and look for their freedom and the basis of ethics in [the realm of] thought. But however exalted, however divine this right may be, it is nevertheless transformed into wrong if the only criterion of thought, and the only way in which thought can know itself to be free is the extent to which it *diverges from what is universally acknowledged and valid* and manages to invent something *particular* for itself.[1]

The notion [*Vorstellung*][2] that freedom of thought, and of spirit in general, can be demonstrated only by divergence from, and even hostility towards, what is publicly acknowledged might seem to be most firmly rooted nowadays in *relation* [*Beziehung*] *to the state*; for this very reason, it might seem to be the essential task of a philosophy of the state to invent and propound *yet another theory*, and specifically, a new and particular theory. If we examine this notion [*Vorstellung*] and the activity that is associated with it, we might well imagine that no state or constitution had ever previously existed or were in existence today, but that we had *now* (and this "now" is of indefinite duration) to start right from the beginning, and that the ethical world had been waiting only for such intellectual constructions, discoveries, and proofs as are *now* available. As far as *nature* is concerned, it is readily admitted that philosophy must recognize it *as it is*, that the philosopher's stone lies hidden

somewhere, but *within nature itself*, that nature is *rational within itself*, and that it is this *actual* reason present within it which knowledge must investigate and grasp conceptually—not the shapes and contingencies which are visible on the surface, but, nature's eternal harmony, conceived, however, as the law and essence *immanent* within it. The ethical world, on the other hand, the state, or, reason as it actualizes itself in the element of self-consciousness, is not supposed to be happy in the knowledge that it is reason itself which has in fact gained power and authority [*Gewalt*] within this element, and which asserts itself there and remains inherent within it.

Addition (H). There are two kinds of laws, laws of nature and laws of right: the laws of nature are simply there and are valid as they stand: they suffer no diminution, although they may be infringed in individual cases. To know what the law of nature is, we must familiarize ourselves with nature, for these laws are correct and it is only our notions [*Vorstellungen*] concerning them which may be false. The measure of these laws is external to us, and our cognition adds nothing to them and does not advance them: it is only our cognition of them which can expand. Knowledge [*Kenntnis*] of right is in one respect similar to this and in another respect different. We get to know the laws of right in just the same way, simply as they are; the citizen knows them more or less in this way, and the positive jurist[3] also stops short at what is given. But the difference is that, with the laws of right, the spirit of reflection comes into play and their very diversity draws attention to the fact that they are not absolute. The laws of right are something *laid down*, something *derived from* human beings. It necessarily follows that our inner voice may either come into collision with them or concur with them. The human being does not stop short at the existent [*dem Daseienden*], but claims to have within himself the measure of what is right; he may be subjected to the necessity and power of external authority, but never in the same way as to natural necessity, for his inner self always tells him how things ought to be, and he finds within himself the confirmation or repudiation of what is accepted as valid. In nature, the highest truth is that a law *exists at all*; in laws of right, however, the thing [*Sache*] is not valid because it exists; on the contrary, everyone demands that it should match his own criterion. Thus a conflict may

---

1   *it is ... for itself*   Hegel here challenges the belief that independent thought always requires originality.

2   *notion [Vorstellung]*   The translator here uses "notion" (rather than "idea" or "representation") for the more casual thoughts of ordinary reflection.

3   *positive jurist*   Jurist who works only with the laws actually recognized by the courts.

arise between what is and what ought to be, between the right which has being in and for itself,[1] which remains unaltered, and the arbitrary determination of what is supposed to be accepted as right. A disjunction and conflict of this kind is found only in the sphere [*Boden*] of the spirit, and since the prerogative of the spirit thus seems to lead to discord and unhappiness, we often turn away from the arbitrariness of life to the contemplation of nature and are inclined to take the latter as a model. But these very discrepancies [*Gegensätze*] between that right which has being in and for itself and what arbitrariness proclaims as right make it imperative for us to learn to recognize precisely what right is. In right, the human being must encounter his own reason; he must therefore consider the rationality of right; and this is the business of our science, in contrast with positive jurisprudence, which is often concerned only with contradictions. Besides, the present-day world has a more urgent need of such an investigation, for in olden times there was still respect and veneration for the existing [*bestehenden*] law, whereas the culture [*Bildung*] of the present age has taken a new direction, and thought has adopted a leading role in the formation of values. Theories are put forward in opposition to what already exists [*dem Daseienden*], theories which seek to appear correct and necessary in and for themselves. From now on, there is a more special need to recognize and comprehend the thoughts of right. Since thought has set itself up as the essential form, we must attempt to grasp right, too, in terms of thought. If thought is to take precedence over right, this would seem to throw open the door to contingent opinions; but genuine thought is not an opinion about something [*die Sache*], but the concept of the thing [*Sache*] itself. The concept of the thing does not come to us by nature. Everyone has fingers and can take a brush and paint, but that does not make him a painter. It is precisely the same with thinking. The thought of right is not, for example, what everybody knows at first hand; on the contrary, correct thinking is knowing [*das Kennen*] and recognizing the thing, and our cognition should therefore be scientific.

The spiritual universe[2] is supposed rather to be at the mercy of contingency and arbitrariness, to be *god-forsaken*, so that, according to this atheism of the ethical world, *truth* lies *outside* it, and at the same time, since reason is never-

theless *also* supposed to be present in it, truth is nothing but a problem. But, we are told, this very circumstance justifies, indeed obliges, every thinker to take his own initiative; though not *in search of* the philosopher's stone, for this search is made superfluous by the philosophizing of our times and everyone, whatever his condition, can be assured that he has this stone in his grasp. Now it does admittedly happen that those who live within the actuality of the state and are able to satisfy their knowledge and volition within it—and there are many of them, more in fact than think or know it, for *basically* this includes *everyone*—or at least those who *consciously* find satisfaction within the state, laugh at such initiatives and assurances and regard them as an empty game, now more amusing, now more serious, now pleasing, now dangerous. This restless activity of vain reflection, along with the reception and response it encounters, might be regarded as a separate issue [*Sache*], developing independently in its own distinct way, were it not that *philosophy* in general has incurred all kinds of contempt and discredit as a result of such behavior. The worst kind of contempt it has met with is, as already mentioned, that everyone, whatever his condition, is convinced that he knows all about philosophy in general and can pass judgment upon it. No other art or science is treated with this ultimate degree of contempt, namely the assumption that one can take possession of it outright.

[...]

It should therefore be considered a stroke of *good fortune* for science—although in fact, as I have already mentioned it is a *necessary consequence* of the *thing* [*Sache*] itself—that this philosophizing, which could well have continued to spin itself into its own web of *scholastic wisdom*, has come into closer contact with actuality, in which the principles of rights and duties are a serious matter, and which lives in the light of its consciousness of these principles, and that a *public* split has consequently resulted between the two. It is *this very relation of philosophy to actuality* which is the subject of misunderstandings, and I accordingly come back to my earlier observation that, since philosophy is *exploration of the rational*, it is for that very reason the *comprehension of the present and the actual*, not the setting up of a *world beyond* which exists God knows where—or rather, of which we can very well say that we know where it exists, namely in the errors of a one-sided and empty ratiocination. In the course of the following treatise, I have remarked that even Plato's *Republic*, a proverbial example of an *empty ideal*, is

---

1   *in and for itself*   What is implicit and on its own account; "in and of itself."

2   *spiritual universe*   World of spirit or mind [*Geist*].

essentially the embodiment of nothing other than the nature of Greek ethics; and Plato, aware that the ethics of his time were being penetrated by a deeper principle which, within this context could appear immediately only as an as yet unsatisfied longing and hence only as a destructive force, was obliged, in order to counteract it, to seek the help of that very longing itself. But the help he required had to come from above, and he could seek it at first only in a particular *external* form of Greek ethics. By this means, he imagined he could overcome the destructive force, and he thereby inflicted the gravest damage on the deeper drive behind it, namely free infinite personality. But he proved his greatness of spirit by the fact that the very principle on which the distinctive character of his Idea[1] turns is the pivot on which the impending world revolution turned.

What is rational is actual;
and what is actual is rational.[2]

This conviction is shared by every ingenuous consciousness as well as by philosophy, and the latter takes it as its point of departure in considering both the *spiritual* and the *natural* universe. If reflection, feeling, or whatever form the subjective consciousness may assume regards the *present* as *vain* and looks beyond it in a spirit of superior knowledge, it finds itself in a vain position; and since it has actuality only in the present, it is itself mere vanity. Conversely, if the *Idea* is seen as "only an idea," a representation [*Vorstellung*] in the realm of opinion, philosophy affords the opposite insight that nothing is actual except the Idea. For what matters is to recognize in the semblance of the temporal and transient the substance which is immanent and the eternal which is present. For since the rational, which is synonymous with the Idea, becomes actual by entering into external existence [*Existenz*], it emerges in an infinite wealth of forms, appearances, and shapes and surrounds its core with a brightly colored covering in which consciousness at first resides, but which only the concept can penetrate in order to find the inner pulse, and detect its continued beat

even within the external shapes.[3] But the infinitely varied circumstances which take shape within this externality as the essence manifests itself within it, this infinite material and its organization, are not the subject-matter of philosophy. To deal with them would be to interfere in things [*Dinge*] with which philosophy has no concern, and it can save itself the trouble of giving good advice on the subject. Plato could well have refrained from recommending nurses never to stand still with children but to keep rocking them in their arms;[4] and Fichte likewise need not have perfected his *passport regulations* to the point of "constructing," as the expression ran, the requirement that the passports of suspect persons should carry not only their personal description but also their painted likeness.[5] In deliberations of this kind, no trace of philosophy remains, and it can the more readily abstain from such ultra-wisdom because it is precisely in relation to this infinite multitude of subjects that it should appear at its most liberal. In this way, philosophical science will also show itself furthest removed from the hatred which the vanity of superior wisdom displays towards a multitude of circumstances and institutions—a hatred in which pettiness takes the greatest of pleasure, because this is the only way in which it can attain self-esteem [*Selbstgefühl*].

This treatise, therefore, in so far as it deals with political science, shall be nothing other than an attempt *to comprehend and portray the state as an inherently rational entity.* As a philosophical composition, it must distance itself as far as possible from the obligation to construct a *state as it ought to be*; such instruction as it may contain cannot be aimed at instructing the state on how it ought to be, but rather at showing how the state, as the ethical universe, should be recognized.

Ἰδού ἡ Ρόδος, ιδού και το πήδημα
Hic Rhodus, *hic* saltus.[6]

To comprehend *what is* is the task of philosophy, for *what is* is reason. As far as the individual is concerned, each

---

1 *Idea* For Hegel, "Idea" with a capital "I" is where concept and the inherent rationality of the actual world come together and match each other. This term when capitalized should be distinguished from our more causal ideas, representations, or notions [*Vorstellung*].

2 *What is ... rational* I.e., the universe is ultimately grounded in reason, so that everything that is actual has its own rationale. This statement is defended in *The Encyclopaedia Logic* §6.

3 *but which only ... shapes* I.e., it requires the discipline of conceiving with concepts rather than the causal association of ideas and representations to get at the rationality of the universe.

4 *Plato ... arms* See Plato, *Laws* vii, 789ᵉ.

5 *Fichte ... likeness* See Fichte, *Science of Rights* §21.

6 Ἰδού ... *saltus* Literally (in Greek, then Latin): Here is Rhodes, jump here. More loosely translated: Pretend this is Rhodes; let's see you jump. It comes from a proverb from one of Aesop's fables in which an athlete boasts that he completed a great jump in Rhodes; the suggestion is that one should be able to do here what one boasts one can do elsewhere.

individual is in any case a *child of his time*; thus philosophy, too, is *its own time comprehended in thoughts*. It is just as foolish to imagine that any philosophy can transcend its contemporary world as that an individual can overleap his own time or leap over Rhodes. If his theory does indeed transcend his own time, if it builds itself a world *as it ought to be*, then it certainly has an existence, but only within his opinions—a pliant medium in which the imagination can construct anything it pleases.

With little alteration, the saying just quoted would read:

Here is the rose, dance *here*.[1]

What lies between reason as self-conscious spirit and reason as present actuality, what separates the former from the latter and prevents it from finding satisfaction in it, is the fetter of some abstraction or other which has not been liberated into [the form of] the concept.[2] To recognize reason as the rose in the cross of the present[3] and thereby to delight in the present—this rational insight is the *reconciliation* with actuality which philosophy grants to those who have received the inner call *to comprehend*, to preserve their subjective freedom in the realm of the substantial, and at the same time to stand with their subjective freedom not in a particular and contingent situation, but in what has being in and for itself.

This is also what constitutes the more concrete sense of what was described above in more abstract terms as the *unity of form and content*. For *form* in its most concrete significance is reason as conceptual cognition, and *content* is reason as the substantial essence of both ethical and natural actuality; the conscious identity of the two is the philosophical Idea.—It is a great obstinacy, the kind of obstinacy which does honor to human beings, that they are unwilling to acknowledge in their attitudes [*Gesinnung*] anything which has not been justified by thought—and this obstinacy is the characteristic property of the modern age, as well as being the distinctive principle of Protestantism. What Luther inaugurated as faith in feeling and in the testimony of the spirit is the same thing that the spirit, at a more mature stage of its development, endeavors to grasp

in the *concept* so as to free itself in the present and thus find itself therein. It has become a famous saying that "a half-philosophy leads away from God"—and it is the same half-measure which defines cognition as an *approximation* to the truth—"whereas true philosophy leads to God";[4] the same applies to philosophy and the state. Reason is not content with an approximation which, as something "neither cold nor hot," it "spews out of its mouth";[5] and it is as little content with that cold despair which confesses that, in this temporal world, things are bad or at best indifferent, but that nothing better can be expected here, so that for this reason alone we should live at peace with actuality. The peace which cognition establishes with the actual world has more warmth in it than this.

A further word on the subject of *issuing instructions* on how the world ought to be: philosophy, at any rate, always comes too late to perform this function. As the *thought* of the world, it appears only at a time when actuality has gone through its formative process and attained its completed state. This lesson of the concept is necessarily also apparent from history, namely that it is only when actuality has reached maturity that the ideal appears opposite the real and reconstructs this real world, which it has grasped in its substance, in the shape of an intellectual *realm*. When philosophy paints its grey in grey, a shape of life has grown old, and it cannot be rejuvenated, but only recognized, by the grey in grey of philosophy; the owl of Minerva[6] begins its flight only with the onset of dusk.

But it is time to conclude this foreword; as a foreword, its function was in any case merely to make external and subjective comments on the point of view of the work to which it is prefaced. If a content is to be discussed philosophically, it will bear only scientific and objective treatment; in the same way, the author will regard any criticism expressed in a form other than that of scientific discussion of the matter [*Sache*] itself merely as a subjective postscript and random assertion, and will treat it with indifference.

Berlin, 25 June 1820

---

1   *Here ... here*   Hegel is playing on words. In Greek the word for Rhodes could also be "rose," whereas in Latin, the word for jump (*saltum*) is related to "dance" (*salta*).

2   *concept*   Disciplined thought.

3   *reason ... present*   A reference to the seal of Martin Luther, which has a black cross superimposed on a red heart on a white rose.

4   *It has become ... God*   See Francis Bacon's essay, "Of Atheism": "A little philosophy inclineth man's mind to atheism; but depth in philosophy bringeth men's minds about to religion."

5   *neither cold ... mouth*   See Revelations 3.15–16.

6   *owl of Minerva*   Minerva (or the Greek Athena) is the goddess of wisdom.

from *Introduction*

§1. The subject-matter of the philosophical science of right is the Idea of right—the concept of right and its actualization.[1]

Philosophy has to do with Ideas and therefore not with what are commonly described as *mere concepts*. On the contrary, it shows that the latter are one-sided and lacking in truth, and that it is the *concept* alone (not what is so often called by that name, but which is merely an abstract determination of the understanding) which has *actuality*, and in such a way that it gives actuality to itself. Everything other than this actuality which is posited by the concept itself is transitory *existence* [*Dasein*], external contingency, opinion, appearance without essence, untruth, deception, etc. The *shape* which the concept assumes in its actualization, and which is essential for cognition of the *concept* itself, is different from its *form* of being purely as concept, and is the other essential moment of the Idea.

Addition (H). The concept and its existence [*Existenz*] are two aspects [of the same thing], separate and united, like soul and body. The body is the same life as the soul, and yet the two can be said to lie outside one another. A soul without a body would not be a living thing, and vice versa. Thus the existence [*Dasein*] of the concept is its body, just as the latter obeys the soul which produced it.[2] The buds have the tree within them and contain its entire strength, although they are not yet the tree itself. The tree corresponds entirely to the simple image of the bud. If the body does not correspond to the soul, it is a wretched thing indeed. The unity of existence [*Dasein*] and the concept, of body and soul, is the Idea. It is not just a harmony, but a complete interpenetration. Nothing lives which is not in some way Idea. The Idea of right is freedom, and in order to be truly apprehended, it must be recognizable in its concept and in the concept's existence [*Dasein*].

§2. The science of right is *a part of philosophy*. It has therefore to develop the *Idea*, which is the reason within an object [*Gegenstand*] out of the concept; or what comes to the same thing, it must observe the proper immanent development of the thing [*Sache*] itself. As a part [of philosophy], it has a determinate *starting point*, which is the *result* and truth of what *preceded* it, and what preceded it is the so-called *proof* of that result. Hence the concept of right, so far as its *coming into being* is concerned, falls outside the science of right; its deduction is presupposed here and is to be taken as *given*.[3]

Addition (G). Philosophy forms a circle. It has an initial or immediate point—for it must begin somewhere—a point which is not demonstrated and is not a result. But the starting point of philosophy is immediately relative, for it must appear at another end-point as a result. Philosophy is a sequence which is not suspended in mid-air; it does not begin immediately, but is rounded off within itself.

According to the formal, non-philosophical method of the sciences, the first thing which is sought and required, at least for the sake of external scientific form, is the *definition*. The positive science of right cannot be much concerned with this, however, since its chief aim is to state *what* is right and legal [*Rechtens*], i.e., what the particular legal determinations are. This is the reason for the warning: "omnis definitio in iure civili periculosa."[4] And in fact, the more incoherent and internally contradictory the determinations of a [system of] right are, the less possible it will be to make definitions within it; for definitions should contain universal determinations, but in the present context, these would immediately make the contradictory element—in this case, what is unjust [*das Unrechtliche*]—visible in all its nakedness. Thus, in Roman law [*das römische Recht*], for example, no definition of a *human being* would be possible, for the slave could not be subsumed under it; indeed, the status [*Stand*] of the slave does violence to that concept. The definitions of "property" and "proprietor" would seem equally hazardous in many situations.—But the deduction of the definition may perhaps be reached by means of etymology, or chiefly by abstraction from particular cases, so that it is ultimately based on the feelings and ideas [*Vorstellung*] of human beings. The correctness of the definition is then made to depend on its agreement with prevailing ideas [*Vorstellungen*]. This method leaves out of account

---

1   *Idea of right ... actualization* As Hegel has mentioned in the Preface, an Idea involves the full (conceptual) comprehension of the rational essence of things as they actually are. In the *Philosophy of Right* Hegel is focusing on questions of fairness and justice as they are embodied in individual, social, and political relations.

2   *like soul and ... produced it* In Hegel's *Logic* life, and particularly the living individual, is the basic form of the Idea, because concept (soul) and actuality (body) are there fully integrated.

3   *its deduction ... given* This can be found in the *Philosophy of Mind* or *Spirit*, §§485–487, the third part of the *Encyclopaedia of the Philosophical Sciences*.

4   *omnis definitio ... periculosa* Latin: in civil law all definitions are hazardous.

what is alone essential to science—with regard to content, the *necessity of the thing* [*Sache*] in and for itself (in this case, of right), and with regard to form, the nature of the concept. In philosophical cognition, on the other hand, the chief concern is the *necessity* of a concept, and the route by which it has become a *result* [is] its proof and deduction. Thus, given that its *content* is necessary *for itself*, the second step is to look around for what corresponds to it in our ideas [*Vorstellungen*] and language. But this concept as it is for itself in its *truth* may not only be different from our *representation* [*Vorstellung*] of it: the two must also differ in their form and shape. If, however, the representation is not also false in its content, the concept may well be shown to be contained in it and present in essence within it; that is, the representation may be raised to the form of the concept. But it is so far from being the measure and criterion of the concept which is necessary and true for itself that it must rather derive its truth from the concept, and recognize and correct itself with the help of the latter.—But if, on the other hand, the former manner of cognition with its formal definitions, inferences, proofs, and the like has now virtually disappeared, the other mode which has replaced it is a bad substitute: that is, Ideas in general, and hence also the Idea of right and its further determinations, are taken up and asserted in immediate fashion as *facts of consciousness*, and our natural or intensified feelings, our *own heart* and *enthusiasm*, are made the source of right. If this is the most convenient method of all, it is also the least philosophical—not to mention here other aspects of this view, which has immediate relevance [*Beziehung*] to action and not just to cognition. Whereas the first—admittedly formal—method does at least require the *form* of the concept in its definitions and the *form* of *necessary* cognition in its proofs, the mode of immediate consciousness and feeling makes the subjectivity, contingency, and arbitrariness of knowledge into its principle.—A familiarity with the nature of scientific procedure in philosophy, as expounded in philosophical logic, is here presupposed.

§3. Right is in general *positive*[1] (a) through its *form* of having validity within a [particular] state; and this legal authority is the principle which underlies knowledge [*Kenntnis*] of right, i.e., *the positive science of right*. (b) In terms of *content*, this right acquires a positive element (α) through the particular *national character* of a people, its stage of *historical* develop-

ment, and the whole context of relations governed by *natural necessity*;[2] (β) through the necessity whereby a system of legal right must contain the *application* of the universal concept to the particular and *externally* given characteristics of objects [*Gegenstände*] and instances—an application which is no longer [a matter of] speculative thought and the development of the concept, but [of] subsumption by the understanding;[3] (γ) through the *final* determinations required for *making decisions* in actuality.[4]

[...]

§4. The basis [*Boden*] of right is the *realm of spirit* in general and its precise location and point of departure is the *will*; the will is *free*, so that freedom constitutes its substance and destiny [*Bestimmung*] and the system of right is the realm of actualized freedom, the world of spirit produced from within itself as a second nature.

Addition (H,G). The freedom of the will can best be explained by reference to physical nature. For freedom is just as much a basic determination of the will as weight is a basic determination of bodies. If matter is described as heavy, one might think that this predicate is merely contingent; but this is not so, for nothing in matter is weightless: on the contrary, matter is weight itself. Heaviness constitutes the body and is the body. It is just the same with freedom and the will, for that which is free is the will. Will without freedom is an empty word, just as freedom is actual only as will or as subject. But as for the connection between the will and thought, the following remarks are necessary. Spirit is thought in general, and the human being is distinguished from the animal by thought. But it must not be imagined [*sich vorstellen*] that a human being thinks on the one hand and wills on the other, and that he has thought in one pocket and volition in the other, for this would be an empty representation [*Vontellung*]. The distinction between thought and will is simply that between theoretical and practical attitudes. But they are not two separate faculties; on the contrary, the will is a particular way of thinking—thinking translating itself into existence [*Dasein*], thinking

---

1 *positive* Positive law is law that is actually in force in a state.

2 *through the particular ... necessity* I.e., each state will develop distinctive laws to reflect its particular culture and history.

3 *through the necessity ... understanding* I.e., law becomes modified as it comes to be applied to situations that do not quite fit its original mold.

4 *through ... actuality* I.e., law is not simply a matter of theory but also of practice. Officials and judges have to decide how the general rules are to be applied.

as the drive to give itself existence. This distinction between thought and will can be expressed as follows. When I think of an object [Gegenstand], I make it into a thought and deprive it of its sensuous quality; I make it into something which is essentially and immediately mine. For it is only when I think that I am with myself [bei mir], and it is only by comprehending it that I can penetrate an object; it then no longer stands opposed to me, and I have deprived it of that quality of its own which it had for itself in opposition to me. Just as Adam says to Eve: "You are flesh of my flesh and bone of my bone,"[1] so does spirit say: "This is spirit of my spirit, and its alien character has disappeared." Every representation [Vorstellung] is a generalization, and this is inherent in thought. To generalize something means to think it. "I" is thought and likewise the universal. When I say "I," I leave out of account every particularity such as my character, temperament, knowledge [Kenntnisse], and age. "I" is totally empty; it is merely a point—simple, yet active in this simplicity. The colorful canvas of the world is before me; I stand opposed to it and in this [theoretical] attitude I overcome [aufhebe][2] its opposition and make its content my own. "I" is at home in the world when it knows it, and even more so when it has comprehended it. So much for the theoretical attitude. The practical attitude, on the other hand, begins with thought, with the "I" itself, and seems at first to be opposed [to the world] because it immediately sets up a separation. In so far as I am practical or active, i.e., in so far as I act, I determine myself, and to determine myself means precisely to posit a difference. But these differences which I posit are nevertheless also mine, the determinations apply to me, and the ends to which I am impelled belong to me. Now even if I let go of these determinations and differences, i.e., if I posit them in the so-called external world, they still remain mine: they are what I have done or made, and they bear the imprint of my mind [Geist]. This, then, is the distinction between theoretical and practical attitudes; the relationship between them must now be described. The theoretical is essentially contained within the practical; the idea [Vorstellung] that the two are separate must be rejected, for one cannot have a will without intelligence. On the contrary, the will contains the theoretical within itself. The will determines itself, and this

determination is primarily of an inward nature, for what I will I represent to myself as my object [Gegenstand]. The animal acts by instinct, it is impelled by something inward and is therefore also practical; but it has no will, because it does not represent to itself what it desires. It is equally impossible to adopt a theoretical attitude or to think without a will, for in thinking we are necessarily active. The content of what is thought certainly takes on the form of being; but this being is something mediated, something posited by our activity. These distinct attitudes are therefore inseparable: they are one and the same thing, and both moments can be found in every activity, of thinking and willing alike.

[...]

§5. The will contains (α) the element of pure indeterminacy[3] or of the "I"'s pure reflection into itself, in which every limitation, every content, whether present immediately through nature, through needs, desires, and drives, or given and determined in some other way, is dissolved; this is the limitless infinity of absolute abstraction or universality, the pure thinking of oneself.

Those who regard thinking as a particular and distinct faculty, divorced from the will as an equally distinct faculty, and who in addition even consider that thinking is prejudicial to the will—especially the good will—show from the very outset that they are totally ignorant of the nature of the will (a remark which we shall often have occasion to make on this same subject).—Only one aspect of the will is defined here—namely this absolute possibility of abstracting from every determination in which I find myself or which I have posited in myself, the flight from every content as a limitation. If the will determines itself in this way, or if representational thought [die Vorstellung] considers this aspect in itself [für sich] as freedom and holds fast to it, this is negative freedom or the freedom of the understanding.—This is the freedom of the void, which is raised to the status of an actual shape and passion. If it remains purely theoretical, it becomes in the religious realm the Hindu fanaticism of pure contemplation; but if it turns to actuality it becomes in the realm of both politics and religion the fanaticism of destruction, demolishing the whole existing social order, eliminating all individuals regarded as suspect by a given order, and annihilating any organization which attempts to

---

1 *You are ... bone* See Genesis 2.23: "This at last is bone of my bones and flesh of my flesh."

2 *overcome* This is the same German term as "supersession" in the selection "Lordship and Bondage" above. The translator sometimes also uses the term "cancel."

3 *pure indeterminacy* I.e., the will starts from the thought that all options are open, that nothing about the future is yet fully determined.

rise up anew.[1] Only in destroying something does this negative will have a feeling of its own existence [*Dasein*]. It may well believe that it wills some positive condition, for instance the condition of universal equality or of universal religious life, but it does not in fact will the positive actuality of this condition, for this at once gives rise to some kind of order, a particularization both of institutions and of individuals; but it is precisely through the annihilation of particularity and of objective determination that the self-consciousness of this negative freedom arises. Thus, whatever such freedom believes [*meint*] that it wills can in itself [*für sich*] be no more than an abstract representation [*Vorstellung*], and its actualization can only be the fury of destruction.

Addition (H,G). It is inherent in this element of the will that I am able to free myself from everything, to renounce all ends, and to abstract from everything. The human being alone is able to abandon all things, even his own life: he can commit suicide. The animal cannot do this; it always remains only negative,[2] in a determination which is alien to it and to which it merely grows accustomed. The human being is pure thinking of himself, and only in thinking is he this power to give himself universality, that is, to extinguish all particularity, all determinacy. This negative freedom, or freedom of the understanding is one-sided, but this one-sidedness always contains within itself an essential determination and should therefore not be dismissed; but the defect of the understanding is that it treats a one sided determination as unique and elevates it to supreme status. This form of freedom occurs frequently in history. The Hindus, for example, place the highest value on mere persistence in the knowledge of one's simple identity with oneself, on remaining within this empty space of one's inwardness like colorless light in pure intuition, and on renouncing every activity of life, every end, and every representation [*Vorstellung*]. In this way, the human being becomes *Brahman*. There is no longer any distinction between the finite human being and Brahman; instead, every difference [*Differenz*] has disappeared in this universality. This form [of freedom] appears more concretely in the active fanaticism of both political and religious life. An example of this was the Reign of Terror in the French Revolution, during which all differences of talents and authority were supposed to be cancelled

out [*aufgehoben*]. This was a time of trembling and quaking and of intolerance towards everything particular. For fanaticism wills only what is abstract, not what is articulated, so that whenever differences emerge, it finds them incompatible with its own indeterminacy and cancels them [*hebt sie auf*]. This is why the people during the French Revolution, destroyed once more the institutions they had themselves created, because all institutions are incompatible with the abstract self-consciousness of equality.

§6. (β) In the same way, "I" is the transition from undifferentiated indeterminacy to *differentiation, determination,* and the *positing* of a determinacy as a content and object.—This content may further be given by nature, or generated by the concept of spirit. Through this positing of itself as something *determinate*, "I" steps into existence [*Dasein*] in general—the absolute moment of the *finitude* or *particularization* of the "I."[3]

This second moment of *determination* is just as much *negativity* and cancellation [*Aufheben*] as the first—for it is the cancellation of the first abstract negativity.—Just as the particular is in general contained within the universal, so in consequence is this second moment already contained within the first and is merely a *positing* of what the first already is *in itself*. The first moment—that is, the first as it is for itself—is not true infinity or the *concrete* universality of the concept, but only something *determinate* and one-sided. For since it is abstraction from all determinacy, it is itself not *without* determinacy; and the fact that it is abstract and one-sided constitutes its determinacy, deficiency, and finitude. [...]

Addition (H,G). This second moment appears as the opposing one. It is to be apprehended in its universal mode: it belongs to freedom, but does not constitute the whole of freedom. The "I" here emerges from undifferentiated indeterminacy to become differentiated, to posit something determinate as its content and object [*Gegenstand*]. I do not merely will—I will *something*. A will which, as described in the previous paragraph, wills only the abstract universal, wills *nothing* and is therefore not a will at all. The particular [thing] which the will wills is a limitation, for the will, in order to be a will, must in some way limit itself. The fact that the will wills *something* is the limit or negation.

1 *the fanaticism of destruction ... anew* The reference is to the Reign of Terror during the French Revolution.

2 *The animal ... negative* The animal simply reacts to what is given or alien; it cannot free itself from this "other" to establish its own positive identity.

3 *In the same way ... "I"* I.e., into the initial indeterminacy created by thought and understanding the will introduces a definite decision, which can either pick out one thing already present in the world or try to create something proposed by thought or spirit.

Thus particularization is what as a rule is called finitude. Reflective thought usually regards the first moment, namely the indeterminate, as the absolute and higher moment, and conversely regards the limited as a mere negation of this indeterminacy. But this indeterminacy is itself merely a negation with regard to the determinate, to finitude: "I" is this solitude and absolute negation. The indeterminate will is to this extent just as one-sided as that which exists in mere determinacy.

§7. (γ) The will is the unity of both these moments—*particularity* reflected *into itself* and thereby restored to *universality*. It is *individuality* [*Einzelheit*], the *self-determination* of the "I," in that it posits itself as the negative of itself, that is, as *determinate* and *limited*, and at the same time remains with itself [*bei sich*], that is, in its *identity with itself* and universality; and in this determination, it joins together with itself alone.—"I" determines itself in so far as it is the self-reference of negativity. As this *reference to itself*, it is likewise indifferent to this determinacy; it knows the latter as its own and as *ideal*, as a mere *possibility* by which it is not restricted but in which it finds itself merely because it posits itself in it.—This is the *freedom* of the will, which constitutes the concept or substantiality of the will, its gravity, just as gravity constitutes the substantiality of a body.[1]

Every self-consciousness knows itself as universal, as the possibility of abstracting from everything determinate, and as particular, with a determinate object [*Gegenstand*], content, and end. But these two moments are only abstractions; what is concrete and true (and everything true is concrete) is the universality which has the particular as its opposite, but this particular, through its reflection into itself, has been reconciled [*ausgeglichen*] with the universal. This unity is *individuality*, but not in its immediacy as a single unit—as in our common idea [*Vorstellung*] of individuality—but rather in accordance with the concept of individuality ...; in other words, this individuality is in fact none other than the concept itself.[2] The first two mo-

ments—that the will can abstract from everything and that it is *also* determined (by itself or by something else)—are easy to accept and grasp, because they are, in themselves [*für sich*], moments of the understanding and devoid of truth. But it is the third moment, the true and speculative[3] (and everything true, in so far as it is comprehended, can be thought of only speculatively), which the understanding refuses to enter into, because the concept is precisely what the understanding always describes as incomprehensible. The task of proving and explaining in more detail this innermost insight of speculation—that is, infinity as self-referring negativity,[4] this ultimate source of all activity, life, and consciousness—belongs to *logic* as purely speculative philosophy.—The only thing which remains to be noted here is that, when we say that *the will is* universal and that *the will* determines itself, we speak as if the will were already assumed to be a *subject* or *substratum*. But the will is not complete and universal until it is determined, and until this determination is superseded and idealized; it does not become will until it is this self-mediating activity and this return into itself.

Addition (H). What is properly called the will contains both the preceding moments. "I" as such is primarily pure activity, the universal which is with itself [*bei sich*]; but this universal determines itself, and to that extent is no longer with itself but posits itself as an other and ceases to be the universal. Then the third moment is that "I" is with itself in its limitation, in this other; as it determines itself, it nevertheless still remains with itself and does not cease to hold fast to the universal. This, then, is the concrete concept of freedom, whereas the two previous moments have been found to be thoroughly abstract and one-sided. But we already possess this freedom in the form of feeling [*Empfindung*], for example in friendship and love. Here, we are not one-sidedly within ourselves, but willingly limit ourselves with reference to an other, even while knowing ourselves in this limitation as ourselves. In this determinacy, the human being, should not feel determined; on the contrary, he attains his self-awareness only by regarding the other

---

1   *This is the freedom of the will ... body* I.e., the will involves both the abstract indeterminacy of indecision and the particular choice. The choice remains something that emerges within our more general, abstract, ability to think. So each of the first two moments presupposes and requires the other.

2   *Every self-consciousness ... itself* In his *Logic* Hegel identifies three moments: abstract universality, a particular determination of that universality, and individuality or singularity. The individual is an integrated union of the two previous moments, a kind of totality. So it becomes a new, more concrete, universality. Hegel here refers

the reader to what would become §§163–65 in the 3rd edition of *The Encyclopaedia Logic*.

3   *speculative* Apprehending the unity that binds opposed determinations together. See *The Encyclopaedia Logic* §82.

4   *infinity as self-referring negativity* Infinity as the ability to transcend any limits, particularly those that are reciprocal opposites and so refer back and forth to each other, and incorporate them into a single self-contained totality.

as other. Thus, freedom lies neither in indeterminacy nor in determinacy, but is both at once. The will which limits itself exclusively to a *this* is the will of the stubborn person who considers himself unfree unless he has *this* will. But the will is not tied to something limited; on the contrary, it must proceed further, for the nature of the will is not this one-sidedness and restriction. Freedom is to will something determinate, yet to be with oneself [*bei sich*] in this determinacy and to return once more to the universal.

[...]

§29. *Right* is any existence [*Dasein*] in general which is the existence of free will. Right is therefore in general freedom, as Idea.[1]

In the Kantian definition [*Bestimmung*] of right (see the introduction to Kant's *Theory of Right* [*Metaphysische Anfangsgründe der Rechtslehre*, 1797]), which is also more widely accepted, the essential element [*Moment*] is "the *limitation* of my freedom or *arbitrary will* in such a way that it may coexist with the arbitrary will of everyone else in accordance with a universal law." On the one hand, this definition contains only a *negative* determination—that of limitation; and on the other hand, the positive [element]—the universal law or so-called "law of reason," the consonance of the arbitrary will of one individual with that of the other—amounts simply to the familiar [principle of] formal identity and the law of contradiction. The definition of right in question embodies the view, especially prevalent since Rousseau, according to which the substantial basis and primary factor is supposed to be not the will as rational will which has being in and for itself or the spirit as *true* spirit, but will and spirit as the *particular* individual, as the will of the single person [*des Einzelnen*] in his distinctive arbitrariness. Once this principle is accepted, the rational can of course appear only as a limitation on the freedom in question, and not as an immanent rationality, but only as an external and formal universal. This view is devoid of any speculative thought and is refuted by the philosophical concept, and has at the same time produced phenomena [*Erscheinungen*] in people's minds and in the actual world whose terrifying nature is matched only by the shallowness of the thoughts on which they are based.

[...]

from *Subdivisions*

§33. In accordance with the stages in the development of the Idea of the will which is free in and for itself, the will is

A. *immediate*; its concept is therefore abstract, as that of *personality*, and its *existence* [*Dasein*] is an immediate external thing [*Sache*];—the sphere of *abstract* or *formal right*;[2]

B. reflected from its external existence *into itself*, determined as *subjective individuality* [*Einzelheit*] in opposition to the *universal*—the universal partly as something internal, the *good*, and partly as something external, an *existent world*, with these two aspects of the Idea mediated only *through each other*; the Idea in its division or *particular* existence [*Existenz*], *the right of the subjective will* in relation to the right of the world and to the *right* of the Idea—which, however, *has being* only *in itself*;—*the sphere of morality*;[3]

C. the *unity* and *truth* of these two abstract moments—the thought Idea of the good realized in the internally *reflected will* and in the *external world*;—so that freedom, as the *substance*, exists no less as *actuality* and *necessity* than as *subjective* will;—the *Idea* in its universal existence [*Existenz*] in and for itself; [the sphere of] *ethical life*.[4]

But the ethical substance is likewise

(a) *natural* spirit;—the *family*,
(b) in its *division* and *appearance*;—*civil society*,
(c) the *state* as freedom, which is equally universal and objective in the free self-sufficiency of the particular will; this

---

1   *freedom, as Idea*   Freedom as involving not only the will to be free, but also what it has actually brought about—the union of what we conceive and what is actually the case.

2   *immediate ... right*   Hegel starts by considering individual acts of will isolated or abstracted from any responsibility to the general social context. These involve the appropriation of property and actions that result from such claims to ownership, such as contracts and fraud.

3   *reflected from ... morality*   Reflection on the bare formalism of property law leads to the realization that one cannot avoid relying on the subjective moral intentions of the individuals involved. The discussion of morality thus introduces a tension between these intentions and the objective world where actions take place. In this sphere, then, the Idea—which is to be the union of subjective conceiving and objective actuality—becomes internally divided into opposing moments.

4   *the unity ... ethical life*   Subjective intentions and objective structures become integrated in the concrete settings of social life: family, the economic order, and government. In these spheres our moral purposes are structured and defined by the roles we play in society, and society itself is constituted and structured by the individuals who conscientiously perform their duties. This integration of the subjective and the objective realms is where freedom comes to be fully actualized.

actual and organic spirit (α) of a people (β) actualizes and reveals itself through the relationship between the particular national spirits (γ) and in world history as the universal world spirit whose *right* is *supreme*.[1]

[...]The subdivisions may ... be regarded as a *historical* preview of the parts [of the book], for the various stages must generate themselves from the nature of the content itself as moments in the development of the Idea. Philosophical subdivisions are certainly not an external classification—i.e., an outward classification of a given material based on one or more extraneous principles of organization—but the immanent differentiation of the concept itself.—*Morality* and *ethics*, which are usually regarded as roughly synonymous, are taken here in essentially distinct senses. [...]

Addition (H). When we speak here of right, we mean not merely civil right, which is what is usually understood by this term, but also morality, ethics, and world history. These likewise belong here, because the concept brings thoughts together in their true relationship. If it is not to remain abstract, the free will must first give itself an existence [*Dasein*], and the primary sensuous constituents of this existence are things [*Sachen*], i.e., external objects [*Dinge*]. This first mode of freedom is the one which we should know as *property*, the sphere of formal and abstract right; property in its mediated shape as *contract*, and right in its infringement as *crime* and *punishment*, are no less a part of this sphere. The freedom which we have here is what we call the person, that is, the subject which is free, and indeed free for itself, and which gives itself an existence [*Dasein*] in the realm of things [*Sachen*]. But this mere immediacy of existence is not in keeping with freedom, and the negation[2] of this determination is the sphere of *morality*. I am

then free no longer merely in this immediate thing [*Sache*], but also in a superseded immediacy[3]—that is, I am free in myself, in the subjective realm. In this sphere, everything depends on my insight, my intention, and the end I pursue, because externality is now regarded as indifferent. But the good, which is here the universal end should not simply remain with me; on the contrary, it should be realized. For the subjective will demands that what is internal to it—that is, its end—should attain an external existence [*Dasein*], and hence that the good should be accomplished in external existence [*Existenz*]. Morality and the earlier moment of formal right are both abstractions whose truth is attained only in *ethical life*. Thus, ethical life is the unity of the will in its concept and the will of the individual [*des Einzelnen*], that is, of the subject. Its initial existence [*Dasein*] is again something natural, in the form of love and feeling [*Empfindung*]—the *family*; here, the individual [*das Individuum*] has overcome [*aufgehoben*] his personal aloofness and finds himself and his consciousness within a whole. But at the next stage, we witness the disappearance of ethical life in its proper sense and of substantial unity: the family becomes fragmented and its members behave towards each other as self-sufficient individuals, for they are held together only by the bond of mutual need. This stage of *civil society* has often been equated with the state. But the *state* emerges only at the third stage, that of ethical life and spirit, at which the momentous unification of self-sufficient individuality with universal substantiality takes place. The right of the state is therefore superior to the other stages: it is freedom in its most concrete shape, which is subordinate only to the supreme absolute truth of the world spirit.

from *Part One: Abstract Right*

[...]

§35. The *universality* of this will which is free for itself is formal universality, i.e., the will's self-conscious (but otherwise contentless) and *simple* reference to itself in its individuality [*Einzelheit*]; to this extent, the subject is a *person*. It is inherent in *personality* that, as *this* person, I am completely determined in all respects (in my inner arbitrary will, drive, and desire, as well as in relation to my immediate external existence [*Dasein*]), and that I am finite, yet totally pure

---

1 *But the ethical ... supreme* The third stage of ethical life can itself be divided into three consecutive stages: in the family, personal commitments to each other create a tightly knit bond; in civil or economic society, individuals in their diversity interact to produce a social order structured by conventions and the division of labor; in the state, governing structures take account of the economic institutions of civil society but the whole is also held together by personal bonds of patriotism—diversity and common purpose are integrated into a single complex structure. Even the state is not the final stage, for there is also the realm of international relations and (finally) the comprehensive overview provided by human history, in which various states and cultures emerge and disappear.

2 *negation* Other or opposite.

3 *superseded immediacy* The simple facts of property and ownership are canceled but also preserved within a more reflective and mediated perspective—that of subjective intention or morality.

self-reference, and thus know myself in my finitude as *infinite, universal*, and *free*.

> Personality begins only at that point where the subject has not merely a consciousness of itself in general as concrete and in some way determined, but a consciousness of itself as a completely abstract "I," in which all concrete limitation and validity are negated and invalidated. In the personality, therefore, there is knowledge of the self as an object [Gegenstand], but as an object raised by thought to simple infinity[1] and hence purely identical with itself. In so far as they have not yet arrived at this pure thought and knowledge of themselves, individuals and peoples do not yet have a personality. The spirit which has being in and for itself[2] differs in this respect from spirit in its appearance, for in the same determination in which the latter is only self-consciousness—consciousness of itself, but only in accordance with the natural will and its as yet external oppositions [...][3]—the former has itself, as abstract and free "I," as its object and end and is consequently a person.

Addition (H). The will which has being for itself, or the abstract will, is the person. The highest achievement of a human being is to be a person; yet in spite of this, the simple abstraction "person" has something contemptuous about it, even as an expression. The person is essentially different from the subject, for the subject is only the possibility of personality, since any living thing whatever is a subject. A person is therefore a subject which is aware of this subjectivity, for as a person, I am completely for myself: the person is the individuality of freedom in pure being-for-itself.[4] As *this* person, I know myself as free in myself, and I can abstract from everything, since nothing confronts me but pure personality. And yet as *this* person I am something wholly determinate: I am of such an age, of such a height, in this room and whatever other particular things [Partikularitäten] I happen to be. Personality is thus

at the same time the sublime and the wholly ordinary; it contains this unity of the infinite and the utterly finite, of the determinate boundary and the completely unbounded. The supreme achievement of the person is to support this contradiction, which nothing in the natural realm contains or could endure.

§36. 1. Personality contains in general the capacity for right[5] and constitutes the concept and the (itself abstract) basis of abstract and hence *formal* right. The commandment of right is therefore: *be a person and respect others as persons*.

§37. 2. The *particularity* of the will is indeed a moment within the entire consciousness of the will [...], but it is not yet contained in the abstract personality as such. Thus, although it is present—as desire, need, drives, contingent preference, etc.—it is still different from personality, from the determination of freedom.—In formal right, therefore, it is not a question of particular interests, of my advantage or welfare, and just as little of the particular ground by which my will is determined, i.e., of my insight and intention.[6]

Addition (H). Since particularity, in the person, is not yet present as freedom, everything which depends on particularity is here a *matter of indifference*. If someone is interested only in his formal right, this may be pure stubbornness, such as is often encountered in emotionally limited people [einem beschränkten Herzen und Gemüte]; for uncultured people insist most strongly on their rights, whereas those of nobler mind seek to discover what other aspects there are to the matter [Sache] in question. Thus abstract right is initially a mere possibility, and in that respect is formal in character as compared with the whole extent of the relationship. Consequently, a determination of right gives me a warrant, but it is not absolutely necessary that I should pursue my rights, because this is only one aspect of the whole relationship. For possibility is being, which also has the significance of not being.

§38. With reference to *concrete* action and to moral and ethical relations, abstract right is only a *possibility* as com-

---

1   *infinity*   Self-contained dynamic that regards any limitations as moments of its own life.

2   *being in and for itself*   Something that is implicit, yet also exists on its own account.

3   *self-consciousness ... oppositions*   See "Lordship and Bondage" above.

4   *being-for-itself*   Self-contained being.

5   *Personality ... right*   Law presupposes that all those governed by the law be persons—independent and in charge of their own affairs.

6   *The particularity ... intention*   Someone's particular interests and wishes are not part of what is included in "person" as understood in a legal sense. Therefore they cannot be considered part of one's rights.

pared with the rest of their content, and the determination of right is therefore only a *permission or warrant*. For the same reason [*Grund*] of its abstractness, the necessity of this right is limited to the negative—*not to violate* personality and what ensues from personality. Hence there are only *prohibitions of right*, and the positive form of commandments of right is, in its ultimate content, based on prohibition.

§39. 3. The resolving and *immediate* individuality [*Einzelheit*] of the person relates itself to a nature which it encounters before it. Hence the personality of the will stands in opposition to nature as *subjective*. But since personality within itself is infinite and universal, the limitation of being merely subjective is in contradiction with it and is *null and void*. Personality is that which acts to overcome [*aufzuheben*] this limitation and to give itself reality—or, what amounts to the same thing, to posit that existence [*Dasein*] as its own.[1]

§40. Right is primarily that immediate existence [*Dasein*] which freedom, gives itself in an immediate way,

(a) as *possession,* which is *property*; freedom is here the freedom of the abstract will *in general*, or, by the same token, the freedom *of an individual* person who relates only to himself.

(b) A person, in distinguishing himself from himself, relates himself to *another person*, and indeed it is only as owners of property that the two have existence [*Dasein*] for each other. Their identity *in themselves* acquires existence [*Existenz*] through the transference of the property of the one to the other by common will and with due respect of the rights of both—that is, by *contract*.

(c) The will which, as in (a), is differentiated within itself in its self-reference rather than distinguished from another person as in (b), is, as a *particular* will, different from and opposed to itself as the will *which has being in and for itself.* This constitutes *wrong* and *crime*.[2]

The division of right into the right of *persons and things* [*Sachen*] and the right of *actions* [*Aktionen*], like the many other divisions of this kind, aims primarily to impose an external order upon the mass of disorganized material before us. The chief characteristic of this division is the confused way in which it jumbles together rights which presuppose substantial relations, such as family and state, with those which refer only to abstract personality. ... Here, it is clear at least that *personality* alone confers a right to *things*, and consequently that personal right is in essence a *right of things*— "thing" [*Sache*] being understood in its general sense as everything external to my freedom, including even my body and my life. This right of things is the right of *personality* as such. [...]

[...]

Section 2: Contract

§72. That [kind of] property of which the *aspect* of existence [*Dasein*] or *externality* is no longer merely a thing [*Sache*] but contains the moment of a will (and hence the will of another person) comes into being through *contract*.[3] This is the process in which the following contradiction is represented and mediated: I *am* and *remain* an owner of property, having being for myself and excluding the will of another; only in so far as, in identifying my will with that of another, I *cease* to be an owner of property.

§73. It is not only *possible* for me to dispose of an item of property as an external thing [*Sache*] [...]—I am also *compelled* by the concept to dispose of it as property in order that *my* will, as *existent,* may become objective [*gegenständlich*] to me.[4] But according to this moment, my will, as externalized, is at the same time *another* will. Hence this moment, in which this necessity of the concept is real, is *the unity* of different wills, which therefore relinquish their difference and distinctiveness. Yet it is also implicit (at this stage) in this identity of different wills that each of them is and remains a will distinctive for itself and *not identical* with the other.

---

1   *Personality ... own* The pure concept of being a person is not enough; one has to put it into practice to show what it really is.
2   *The will ... crime* While as a person one wills that property rights in general be respected, one may also will to violate rights to accomplish one's own particular interests. This is where crime comes in.
3   *That [kind of] property ... contract* My ownership of property needs to be recognized by others. This recognition acquires a public existence when I am able to transfer ownership to another, while assuming ownership of something belonging to her. This happens when contracts are signed and executed.
4   *in order ... me* When I dispose of property I demonstrate to myself that my will is not inextricably bound up with my possessions, but has power over them.

§74. This relationship is therefore the mediation of an identical will within the absolute distinction between owners of property who have being for themselves.[1] It contains the implication that each party, in accordance with his own and the other party's will, *ceases* to be an owner of property, *remains* one, and *becomes* one. This is the mediation of the will to give up a property (an individual property) and the will to accept such a property (and hence the property of someone else). The context of this mediation is one of identity, in that the one volition comes to a decision only in so far as the other volition is present.

§75. Since the two contracting parties relate to each other as *immediate* self sufficient persons, it follows that (α) the contract is the product of the *arbitrary will*; (β) the identical will which comes into existence [*Dasein*] through the contract is only *a will posited by the contracting parties*, hence only a *common* will, not a will which is universal in and for itself;[2] (γ) the object [*Gegenstand*] of the contract is an *individual external* thing [*Sache*], for only things of this kind are subject to the purely arbitrary will of the contracting parties to alienate them [...].

Marriage cannot therefore be subsumed under the concept of contract; this subsumption—which can only be described as disgraceful—is proposed in Kant's Metaphysical Elements of the Theory of Right [*Metaphysische Anfangsgründe der Rechtslehre*].—The nature of the *state* has just as little to do with the relationship of contract, whether it is assumed that the state is a contract of all with all, or a contract of all with the sovereign and the government.[3]—The intrusion of this relationship, and of relationships concerning private property in general, into political relationships has created the greatest confusion in constitutional law

[*Staatsrecht*] and in actuality. Just as in earlier times political rights and duties were regarded as, and declared to be, the immediate private property of particular individuals in opposition to the right of the sovereign and the state, so also in more recent times have the rights of the sovereign and the state been regarded as objects of contract and based on a contract, as the result merely of a *common* will and proceeding from the arbitrary will of those who have combined to form a state.—However different these two points of view may be, in one respect, they do have this in common: they have transferred the determinations of private property to a sphere of a totally different and higher nature. (See below, "Ethical Life" and "The State.")

Addition (H). In recent times, it has become very popular to regard the state as a contract of all with all. Everyone, we are told, makes a contract with the sovereign, and he in turn with the subjects. This view is the result of superficial thinking, which envisages only a *single* unity of different wills. But in a contract, there are two identical wills, both of which are persons and wish to remain owners of property; the contract accordingly, originates in the arbitrary will of the person—an origin which marriage also has in common with contract. But in the case of the state, this is different from the outset, for the arbitrary will of individuals [*Individuen*] is not in a position to break away from the state, because the individual is already by nature a citizen of it. It is the rational destiny [*Bestimmung*] of human beings to live within a state, and even if no state is yet present, reason requires that one be established. The state itself must give permission for individuals [*Einzelne*] to enter or leave it, so that this does not depend on the arbitrary will of the individuals concerned; consequently the state is not based on contract, which presupposes an arbitrary will. It is false to say that the arbitrary will of everyone is capable of founding a state: on the contrary, it is absolutely necessary for each individual to live within the state. The great advance made by the state in modern times is that it remains an end in and for itself, and that each individual may no longer base his relationship [*Beziehung*] to it on his own private stipulation, as was the case in the Middle Ages.

[...]

---

1   *the mediation ... themselves* In a contract each party must be independent and act freely; but at the same time the act is a single act where the two wills are willing the same thing.

2   *only a common will ... itself* Hegel draws a distinction between an agreement between two contracting agents, and the will of a corporate body or state, which is a will encompassing the purposes of the social organism as a whole and is thus universal both implicitly and on its own account.

3   *The nature ... government* Hegel is referring to social contract theories, such as those of Hobbes, Locke, Rousseau, Kant, and Fichte.

from *Part Three: Ethical Life*

§145. The fact that the ethical sphere[1] is the *system* of these determinations of the Idea[2] constitutes its *rationality*. In this way, the ethical sphere is freedom, or the will which has being in and for itself as objectivity, as a circle of necessity whose moments are the *ethical powers* which govern the lives of individuals. In these individuals—who are accidental to them—these powers have their representation [*Vorstellung*], phenomenal shape [*erscheinende Gestalt*], and actuality.

Addition (H). Since the determinations of ethics constitute the concept of freedom, they are the substantiality or universal essence of individuals, who are related to them merely as accidents.[3] Whether the individual exists or not is a matter of indifference to objective ethical life, which alone has permanence and is the power by which the lives of individuals are governed. Ethical life has therefore been represented to nations as eternal justice, or as gods who have being in and for themselves, and in relation to whom the vain pursuits of individuals are merely a play of the waves. [...]

§147. On the other hand, [the ethical substance and its laws and powers] are not something *alien* to the subject. On the contrary, the subject bears *spiritual witness* to them as to *its own essence*, in which it has its *self-awareness* [*Selbstgefühl*] and lives as in its element which is not distinct from itself—a relationship which is immediate and closer to identity than even [a relationship of] *faith* or *trust*.

Faith and trust arise with the emergence of reflection, and they presuppose representations and distinctions [*Vorstellung und Unterschied*]. For example, to believe in pagan religion and to be a pagan are two different things. That relationship—or rather, that relationless identity—in which the ethical is the actual living principle [*Lebendigkeit*] of self-consciousness, may indeed turn into a relationship of faith and conviction or a relationship mediated by *further reflection*, into insight grounded on reasons, which may also begin with certain particular ends, interests, and considerations, with hope or fear, or with historical presuppositions. But *adequate cognition* of this identity belongs to conceptual thought [*dem denkenden Begriffe*].

§148. All these substantial determinations are *duties* which are binding on the will of the individual; for the individual, as subjective and inherently undetermined—or determined in a particular way—is distinct from them and *consequently stands in a relationship to them* as to his own substantial being.

The ethical *theory of duties* [*Pflichtenlehre*]—i.e., in its *objective* sense, not as supposedly comprehended in the empty principle of moral subjectivity, which in fact determines nothing [...]—therefore consists in that systematic development of the circle of ethical necessity which follows here in *Part Three* of the work. The difference between its presentation here and the form of a *theory of duties* lies solely in the fact that the following account merely shows that ethical determinations are necessary relations, and does not proceed to add in every case "this determination is therefore a duty for human beings."—A theory of duties, unless it forms part of philosophical science, will take its material from existing relations and show its connection with one's own ideas [*Vorstellungen*] and with commonly encountered principles and thoughts, ends, drives, feelings [*Empfindungen*], etc.; and as reasons in favor of each duty, it may also adduce the further consequences which this duty may have with reference to other ethical relations and to welfare and opinion. But an immanent and consistent theory of duties can be nothing other than the development of *those relations* which are necessitated by the Idea of freedom, and are therefore *actual* in their entirety, within the state.

§149. A binding duty can appear as a *limitation* only in relation to indeterminate subjectivity or abstract freedom, and

---

1   *ethical sphere*   This includes not only the state, but also the family, economic institutions such as corporations, and legal institutions such as civil courts.

2   *the system ... Idea*   In the previous § Hegel has referred to the customs and laws of society which make up the structure of a variety of institutions and has given each of them a determinate character. They can only function as the willed intentions of many individuals, yet they have an objective life of their own. They thus integrate subjectivity and objectivity, and the result can be called an Idea.

3   *individuals ... accidents*   Social structures carry on while individual people come and go.

to the drives of the natural will or of the moral will which arbitrarily determines its own indeterminate good. The individual, however, finds his *liberation* in duty. On the one hand, he is liberated from his dependence on mere natural drives, and from the burden he labors under as a particular subject in his moral reflections on obligation and desire; and on the other hand, he is liberated from that indeterminate subjectivity which does not attain existence [*Dasein*] or the objective determinacy of action, but remains *within itself* and has no actuality. In duty, the individual liberates himself so as to attain substantial freedom.

Addition (H). Duty places limits only on the arbitrary will of subjectivity and clashes only with that abstract good to which subjectivity clings. When people say that they want to be free, this means primarily only that they want to be free in an abstract sense, and every determination and division [*Gliederung*] within the state is regarded as a limitation of that freedom. To this extent, duty is not a limitation of freedom, but only of freedom in the abstract, that is, of unfreedom: it is the attainment of essential being, the acquisition of affirmative freedom.

[...]

§151. But if it is simply *identical* with the actuality of individuals, the ethical [*das Sittliche*], as their general mode of behavior, appears as *custom* [*Sitte*]; and the *habit* of the ethical appears as a *second nature* which takes the place of the original and purely natural will and is the all-pervading soul, significance, and actuality of individual existence [*Dasein*]. It is *spirit* living and present as a world, and only thus does the substance of spirit begin to exist as spirit.

Addition (H,G). Just as nature has its laws, and as animals, trees, and the sun obey their law, so is custom the law appropriate to the spirit of freedom. Custom is what [abstract] right and morality have not yet reached, namely spirit. For in right, particularity is not yet that of the concept, but only of the natural will. Similarly, from the point of view of morality, self-consciousness is not yet spiritual consciousness. At this stage, it is merely a question of the value of the subject in itself—that is, the subject which determines itself in accordance with good as opposed to evil still has the form of arbitrary will. Here, on the other hand, at the level of ethics, the will is present as the will of spirit and has a substantial content which is in conformity with itself. Education [*Pädagogik*] is the art of making human beings ethical: it considers them as natural beings and shows them how they can be reborn, and how their

original nature can be transformed into a second, spiritual nature so that this spirituality becomes *habitual* to them. In habit, the opposition between the natural and the subjective will disappears, and the resistance of the subject is broken; to this extent, habit is part of ethics, just as it is part of philosophical thought, since the latter requires that the mind [*der Geist*] should be trained to resist arbitrary fancies and that these should be destroyed and overcome to clear the way for rational thought. Human beings even die as a result of habit—that is, if they have become totally habituated to life and mentally [*geistig*] and physically blunted, and the opposition between subjective consciousness and mental activity has disappeared. For they are active only in so far as they have not yet attained something and wish to assert themselves and show what they can do in pursuit of it. Once this is accomplished, their activity and vitality disappear, and the loss of interest which ensues is mental or physical death.

[...]

Section 3: The State

§257. The state is the actuality of the ethical Idea—the ethical spirit as substantial will, *manifest* and clear to itself, which thinks and knows itself and implements what it knows in so far as it knows it. It has its immediate existence [*Existenz*] in *custom* and its mediate existence in the *self-consciousness* of the individual [*des Einzelnen*], in the individual's knowledge and activity, just as self-consciousness, by virtue of its disposition, has its *substantial freedom* in the state as its essence, its end, and the product of its activity.

[...]

§258. The state is the actuality of the substantial *will*, an actuality which it possesses in the particular *self-consciousness* when this has been raised to its universality;[1] as such, it is the *rational*[2] *in and for itself. This substantial unity is an absolute and unmoved end in itself, and in it, freedom enters into*

---

1 *the particular ... universality* As citizens individuals implicitly accept the actions of the state as their own actions, whether they approve of them or not; so their will is no longer concerned simply with their particular interests, but with the well-being of the whole social order.

2 *rational* Reason, for Hegel, involves the move from a starting point over to its opposite and back again; then grasping the double transition as a single complex totality. The state embodies this because individual wills interact to create a structure of social and

its highest right, just as this ultimate end possesses the highest right in relation to individuals [die Einzelnen], whose highest duty is to be members of the state.

If the state is confused with civil society and its determination is equated with the security and protection of property and personal freedom, *the interest of individuals [der Einzelnen] as such* becomes the ultimate end for which they are united; it also follows from this that membership of the state is an optional matter.—But the relationship of the state to the individual [*Individuum*] is of quite a different kind. Since the state is objective spirit,[1] it is only through being a member of the state that the individual [*Individuum*] himself has objectivity, truth, and ethical life. *Union* as such is itself the true content and end, and the destiny [*Bestimmung*] of individuals [*Individuen*] is to lead a universal life; their further particular satisfaction, activity, and mode of conduct have this substantial and universally valid basis as their point of departure and result.—Considered in the abstract, rationality consists in general in the unity and interpenetration of universality and individuality [*Einzelheit*]. Here, in a concrete sense and in terms of its content, it consists in the unity of objective freedom (i.e., of the universal substantial will[2]) and subjective freedom (as the freedom of individual [*individuellen*] knowledge and of the will in its pursuit of particular ends). And in terms of its form, it therefore consists in self-determining action in accordance with laws and principles based on *thought* and hence *universal*.—This Idea[3] is the being of spirit as necessary and eternal in and for itself.—As far as the Idea of the state itself is concerned, it makes no difference what is

or was the *historical* origin of the state in general (or rather of any particular state with its rights and determinations)—whether it first arose out of patriarchal conditions, out of fear or trust, out of corporations etc., or how the basis of its rights has been understood and fixed in the consciousness as divine and positive right or contract, habit, etc. In relation to scientific cognition, which is our sole concern here, these are questions of appearance, and consequently a matter [*Sache*] for history. In so far as the authority of any actual state concerns itself with the question of reasons, these will be derived from the forms of right which are valid within that state.—The philosophical approach deals only with the internal aspect of all this, with the *concept as thought* [*mit dem gedachten Begriffe*]. As far as the search for this concept is concerned, it was the achievement of Rousseau[4] to put forward the *will* as the principle of the state, a principle which has *thought* not only as its form (as with the social instinct, for example, or divine authority) but also as its content, and which is in fact *thinking* itself. But Rousseau considered the will only in the determinate form of the *individual* [*einzelnen*] will (as Fichte[5] subsequently also did) and regarded the universal will not as the will's rationality in and for itself, but only as the *common element* arising out of this individual [*einzelnen*] will *as a conscious will*. The union of individuals [*der Einzelnen*] within the state thus becomes a *contract*,[6] which is accordingly based on their arbitrary will and opinions, and on their express consent given at their own discretion; and the further consequences which follow from this, and which relate merely to the understanding, destroy the divine [element] which has being in and for itself and its absolute authority and majesty. Consequently, when these abstractions were invested with power, they afforded the tremendous spectacle, for the first time we know of in human history, of the overthrow of all existing and given conditions

economic relations; and the resulting structure becomes a single complex entity that has a life of its own.

1　*objective spirit*　Spirit is self-conscious life; objective spirit is Hegel's name for the public social reality that is formed when self-conscious individuals act and interact.

2　*universal substantial will*　The willed actions of the state are in essence the actions of the whole social body, and thus are universal; they also remain and continue to be valid through all the accidental changes that might happen to the individuals that make it up, and thus are substantial.

3　*Idea*　Integrating subjective rationality with a rational, public, and objective reality.

4　*Rousseau*　Jean-Jacques Rousseau (1712–78), author of *The Social Contract* (1762) (included in this volume).

5　*Fichte*　Johann Gottlieb Fichte (1762–1814), German idealist philosopher and author of *Science of Rights* (1796), which Hegel refers to here.

6　*contract*　See above §§72–75.

within an actual major state[1] and the revision of its constitution from first principles and purely in terms of *thought*; the *intention* behind this was to give it what was *supposed* to be a purely *rational* basis. On the other hand, since these were only abstractions divorced from the Idea, they turned the attempt into the most terrible and drastic event.—In opposition to the principle of the individual will, we should remember the fundamental concept according to which the objective will is rational in itself, i.e., in its *concept*, whether or not it is recognized by individuals [*Einzelnen*] and willed by them at their discretion—and that its opposite, knowledge and volition, the subjectivity of freedom (which is the *sole* content of the principle of the individual will) embodies only *one* (consequently one-sided) moment of the *Idea of the rational* will, which is rational solely because it has being both *in itself* and *for itself*.—Also at variance with the thought that the state may be apprehended by cognition as something rational for itself is [the practice of] taking the *externality* of appearance and the contingencies of want, need of protection, strength, wealth, etc. not as moments of historical development, but as the *substance* of the state. Here, the principle of cognition is once again that of separate individuality [*die Einzelheit der Individuen*], but not so much the *thought* of this individuality as the converse of this, namely empirical individuality with all its contingent qualities of strength and weakness, wealth and poverty, etc. [...]

Addition (G) The state in and for itself is the ethical whole, the actualization of freedom, and it is the absolute end of reason that freedom should be actual. The state is the spirit which is present in the world and which *consciously* realizes itself therein, whereas in nature it actualizes itself only as the other of itself, as dormant spirit. Only when it is present in consciousness, knowing itself as an existent object [*Gegenstand*], is it the state. Any discussion of freedom must begin not with individuality [*Einzelheit*] or the individual self-consciousness, but only with the essence of self-consciousness; for whether human beings know it or not, this essence realizes itself as a self-sufficient power of which single individuals [*die einzelnen Individuen*] are only

moments. The state consists in the march of God[2] in the world, and its basis is the power of reason actualizing itself as will. In considering the Idea of the state, we must not have any particular states or particular institutions in mind; instead, we should consider the Idea, this actual God, in its own right [*für sich*]. Any state, even if we pronounce it bad in the light of our own principles, and even if we discover this or that defect in it, invariably has the essential moments of its existence [*Existenz*] within itself (provided it is one of the more advanced states of our time). But since it is easier to discover deficiencies than to comprehend the affirmative, one may easily fall into the mistake of overlooking the inner organism of the state in favor of individual [*einzelne*] aspects. The state is not a work of art; it exists in the world, and hence in the sphere of arbitrariness, contingency, and error, and bad behavior may disfigure it in many respects. But the ugliest man, the criminal, the invalid, or the cripple is still a living human being; the affirmative aspect—life—survives [*besteht*] in spite of such deficiencies, and it is with this affirmative aspect that we are here concerned.

§259. The Idea of the state (a) has *immediate* actuality and is the individual state as a self-related organism—the *constitution* or constitutional law [*inneres Staatsrecht*];
(b) passes over into the *relationship* of the individual state to other states—international law [*äußeres Staatsrecht*];
(c) is the universal Idea as a *genus* [*Gattung*][3] and as an absolute power in relation to individual states—the spirit which gives itself its actuality in the process of *world history*.

Addition (G). The state as actual is essentially an individual state, and beyond that a particular state. Individuality should be distinguished from particularity; it is a moment within the very Idea of the state, whereas particularity belongs to history. States as such are independent of one another, and their relationship can consequently only be an external one, so that there must be a third factor above them to link them together. This third factor is in fact the spirit which gives itself actuality in world history and is the absolute judge of states. Admittedly, several states may form a league and sit

1   *the overthrow ... state* The French Revolution.

2   *God* For Hegel, "God" names the ultimate rationality that governs the universe. The state, as the form rationality takes in human society (for all of its inadequacies), is thus the form God assumes in human history.

3   *universal Idea ... genus* The panorama of world history integrates into one totality all the interactions of particular states over the ages, and is thus the genus under which they all serve as species.

in judgment, as it were, on other states, or they may enter into alliances (like the Holy Alliance,[1] for example), but these are always purely relative and limited, like [the ideal of] perpetual peace. The one and only absolute judge which always asserts its authority over the particular is the spirit which has being in and for itself, and which reveals itself as the universal and as the active genus in world history.

A. CONSTITUTIONAL LAW

[...]

§268. The political *disposition*, i.e., *patriotism* in general, is certainty based on *truth*[2] (*whereas merely subjective certainty does not originate in truth*, but is only opinion) and a volition which has become *habitual*. As such, it is merely a consequence of the institutions within the state, a consequence in which rationality is *actually* present, just as rationality receives its practical application through action in conformity with the state's institutions.—This disposition is in general one of *trust* (which may pass over into more or less educated insight), or the consciousness that my substantial and particular interest is preserved and contained in the interest and end of an other (in this case, the state), and in the latter's relation to me as an individual [*als Einzelnem*]. As a result, this other immediately ceases to be another for me, and in my consciousness of this, I am free.[3]

> Patriotism is frequently understood to mean only a willingness to perform *extraordinary* sacrifices and actions. But in essence, it is that disposition which, in the normal conditions and circumstances of life, habitually knows that the community is the substantial basis and end. It is this same consciousness, tried and tested in all circumstances of ordinary life, which underlies the willingness to make extraordinary efforts. But

just as human beings often prefer to be guided by magnanimity instead of by right, so also do they readily convince themselves that they possess this extraordinary patriotism in order to exempt themselves from the genuine disposition, or to excuse their lack of it.—Furthermore, if we take this disposition to be something which can originate independently [*für sich*] and arise out of subjective representations [*Vorstellungen*) and thoughts, we are confusing it with opinion; for in this interpretation, it is deprived of its true ground, i.e., objective reality.[4]

Addition (H). Uneducated people delight in argument [*Räsonieren*) and fault-finding, for it is easy to find fault, but difficult to recognize the good and its inner necessity. Education in its early stages always begins with fault-finding, but when it is complete, it sees the positive element in everything. In religion, it is equally easy to say that this or that is superstition, but it is infinitely more difficult to comprehend the truth which it contains. Thus people's apparent political disposition should be distinguished from what they genuinely will; for inwardly, they in fact will the thing [*Sache*], but they fasten on to details and delight in the vanity of claiming superior insight. They trust that the state will continue to exist [*bestehen*] and that particular interests can be fulfilled within it alone; but habit blinds us to the basis of our entire existence [*Existenz*]. It does not occur to someone who walks the streets in safety at night that this might be otherwise, for this habit of [living in] safety has become second nature, and we scarcely stop to think that it is solely the effect of particular institutions. Representational thought often imagines that the state is held together by force; but what holds it together is simply the basic sense of order which everyone possesses.

---

1. *Holy Alliance* Alliance among Austria, Russia, and Prussia after the fall of Napoleon.
2. *The political ... truth* The personal commitment of patriotism is based on the real relations of custom and culture that integrate a community into a state. Since these relations contribute to the character and development of citizens, they constitute the underlying truth of their spiritual life.
3. *ceases to be another ... free* Once I recognize the role the whole social structure plays in constituting my makeup, I no longer regard the state in which I live as something alien to me. By accepting my position and status within this complex, my actions become genuinely free: determined solely by my own volition.
4. *Furthermore ... reality* Since genuine patriotism is our sense of belonging to our community, it is not something we arbitrarily assume or discard. When we think that we can decide to be patriotic or not, we are simply giving way to our subjective feelings, and articulating arbitrary opinions.

JEREMY BENTHAM
(1748 – 1832)

ONE OF THE MOST ENDURINGLY INFLUENTIAL THEORIES in both moral philosophy and economics is utilitarianism. The basis of the theory, put most simply, is that actions should be judged based on their consequences and that the actions that result in the greatest amount of pleasure or happiness are best, while those that result in the greatest amount of harm or pain are worst. Utilitarian (or more broadly, consequentialist) thinking is one of the dominant approaches in current philosophical discussions of morality. It also continues to be fundamental to discussions of policies related to economic distribution. Jeremy Bentham is generally regarded as the first modern Western philosopher to give utilitarian ideas a central place in his thought. He discusses the "principle of utility" at length in both of his best known works, *A Fragment on Government* (1776) and *An Introduction to the Principles of Morals and Legislation* (1789).

Bentham was born in 1748 in London, England. His father was a wealthy, well-educated, politically ambitious lawyer who wanted to ensure that Jeremy, his eldest son, was well prepared for economic and political success in life. Bentham began to read Latin at age three and attended the prestigious Westminster School before being sent to Oxford at age twelve. He received a Bachelor's degree at age fifteen. As his father and grandfather had done, he then studied law, passing the bar in 1769 at age twenty-one. Despite his father's hopes that he would then begin a successful legal career, Bentham decided that he wanted to devote his career to further academic study aimed at finding ways to reform public institutions.

In 1768 Bentham read Joseph Priestley's just-published *The First Principles of Government*. Priestley's ideas—and in particular, his use of the phrase "the greatest happiness for the greatest number"—greatly influenced Bentham in his first formulations of utilitarian ideas in *A Fragment on Government*. He argued, for example, that an assessment of the quality of a legal system should be based on how it contributes to the overall happiness of the members of society.

Bentham's first interest was reform of the penal system. He argued that rehabilitation, not punishment, should be the central feature of the system. Bentham's first book, *A Fragment on Government* critiqued the writings of William Blackstone, the most prominent English legal scholar at the time.

By 1780 Bentham had finished writing *An Introduction to the Principles of Morals and Legislation* (though the book was not actually published until 1789). In this work he elaborates and extends his utilitarian arguments to cover all areas of moral philosophy, proposing a "felicific calculus" for evaluating pleasures and pains in terms of intensity, duration, certainty, propinquity, fecundity (or how likely it is to be followed by sensations of the same kind), purity and extent (i.e., the number of people affected). Since Bentham saw human motivation as rooted in seeking pleasures and avoiding pains, the best political and legal systems would help citizens to achieve those goals.

During the last half of Bentham's life he was an extremely active writer, but much of his output was never published in his lifetime. He left voluminous manuscripts, some of which were not published until more than a century after his death. His later writings include a more comprehensive version of his *A Fragment on Government* and work on such varied topics as the relationship between the state and religious institutions, political equality for women, slavery, animal rights, opposition to corporal punishment, and support for tolerance of homosexuality (in the essay "Offences Against One's Self," included here); on many of these subjects Bentham's views were far ahead of his time.

Bentham also endeavored to put many of his ideas into practice. He became actively engaged with politicians in England to try to exert influence on legislation. He visited Russia in the 1780s to persuade Catherine the Great to implement his ideas for legal reform. And his efforts to influence the new government of France after the revolution earned him the title of honorary citizen. His *Panopticon Writings* (1787) provided a design for a prison that allowed the jailers to observe all the inmates at any time, all the while preventing them from knowing they were being watched. Bentham extended this idea to hospitals, schools and other institutions, suggesting that it would increase efficiency and discipline, fostering reform. French philosopher Michel Foucault famously discussed Bentham's design in *Discipline and Punish* (1975) as a means of control and normalization.

Bentham also influenced a great many important scholars of his time. He and Adam Smith engaged in lively public and private correspondence, most notably on interest rates. Bentham's ideas were also central to the education of the son of his secretary, James Mill; John Stuart Mill's *On Liberty* and *Utilitarianism* became texts central to utilitarian philosophy.

In 1828 University College London was founded, in large part as a result of Bentham's advocacy of an expansion of educational opportunities. Upon his death in 1832, Bentham's will stipulated that his body was to be preserved and placed on display at the college. His "auto-icon," as it is called, can still be found there to this day. The College has also honored Bentham's legacy in more traditional ways. Since 1968 they have been working on a project to publish all of Bentham's writings in a single collection. To date twenty-five of the seventy projected volumes have been published.

◆ ◆ ◆ ◆ ◆

An Introduction to the Principles of Morals and Legislation (1780, published 1789)

Chapter 1: Of the Principle of Utility

I. Nature has placed mankind under the governance of two sovereign masters, *pain* and *pleasure*. It is for them alone to point out what we ought to do, as well as to determine what we shall do. On the one hand the standard of right and wrong, on the other the chain of causes and effects, are fastened to their throne. They govern us in all we do, in all we say, in all we think: every effort we can make to throw off our subjection, will serve but to demonstrate and confirm it. In words a man may pretend to abjure their empire: but in reality he will remain subject to it all the while. The *principle of utility*[1] recognizes this subjection, and assumes it for the foundation of that system, the object of which is to rear the fabric of felicity by the hands of reason and of law. Systems which attempt to question it, deal in sounds instead of sense, in caprice instead of reason, in darkness instead of light.

But enough of metaphor and declamation: it is not by such means that moral science is to be improved.

---

1   *principle of utility* [Bentham's note] To this denomination has of late been added, or substituted, the *greatest happiness* or *greatest felicity* principle: this for shortness, instead of saying at length that principle which states the greatest happiness of all those whose interest is in question, as being the right and proper, and only right and proper and universally desirable, end of human action: of human action in every situation, and in particular in that of a functionary [i.e., *official*] or set of functionaries exercising the powers of Government. The word *utility* does not so clearly point to the ideas of *pleasure* and *pain* as the words *happiness* and *felicity* do: nor does it lead us to the consideration of the *number*, of the interests affected; to the *number*, as being the circumstance, which contributes, in the largest proportion, to the formation of the standard here in question; the *standard of right and wrong*, by which alone the propriety of human conduct, in every situation, can with propriety be tried [i.e., *determined*]. This want [i.e., *lack*] of a sufficiently manifest connection between the ideas of *happiness* and *pleasure* on the one hand, and the idea of *utility* on the other, I have every now and then found operating, and with but too much efficiency, as a bar to the acceptance, that might otherwise have been given, to this principle.

II. The principle of utility is the foundation of the present work: it will be proper therefore at the outset to give an explicit and determinate account of what is meant by it. By the principle[1] of utility is meant that principle which approves or disapproves of every action whatsoever, according to the tendency it appears to have to augment or diminish the happiness of the party whose interest is in question: or, what is the same thing in other words, to promote or to oppose that happiness. I say of every action whatsoever, and therefore not only of every action of a private individual, but of every measure of government.

III. By utility is meant that property in any object, whereby it tends to produce benefit, advantage, pleasure, good, or happiness, (all this in the present case comes to the same thing) or (what comes again to the same thing) to prevent the happening of mischief, pain, evil, or unhappiness to the party whose interest is considered: if that party be the community in general, then the happiness of the community: if a particular individual, then the happiness of that individual.

IV. The interest of the community is one of the most general expressions that can occur in the phraseology of morals: no wonder that the meaning of it is often lost. When it has a meaning, it is this. The community is a fictitious *body*, composed of the individual persons who are considered as constituting as it were its *members*. The interest of the community then is, what?—the sum of the interests of the several members who compose it.

V. It is in vain to talk of the interest of the community, without understanding what is the interest of the individual. A thing is said to promote the interest, or to be *for the* interest, of an individual, when it tends to add to the sum total of his pleasures: or, what comes to the same thing, to diminish the sum total of his pains.

VI. An action then may be said to be conformable to the principle of utility, or, for shortness sake, to utility, (meaning with respect to the community at large) when the tendency it has to augment the happiness of the community is greater than any it has to diminish it.

VII. A measure of government (which is but a particular kind of action, performed by a particular person or persons) may be said to be conformable to or dictated by the principle of utility, when in like manner the tendency which it has to augment the happiness of the community is greater than any which it has to diminish it.

VIII. When an action, or in particular a measure of government, is supposed by a man to be conformable to the principle of utility, it may be convenient, for the purposes of discourse, to imagine a kind of law or dictate, called a law or dictate[2] of utility: and to speak of the action in question, as being conformable to such law or dictate.

IX. A man may be said to be a partisan of the principle of utility, when the approbation or disapprobation he annexes to any action, or to any measure, is determined by and proportioned to the tendency which he conceives it to have to augment or to diminish the happiness of the community: or in other words, to its conformity or unconformity to the laws or dictates of utility.

X. Of an action that is conformable to the principle of utility one may always say either that it is one that ought to be done, or at least that it is not one that ought not to be done. One may say also, that it is right it should be done; at least that it is not wrong it should be done: that it is a right action; at least that it is not a wrong action. When thus interpreted, the words *ought*, and *right* and *wrong* and others of that stamp, have a meaning: when otherwise, they have none.

XI. Has the rectitude of this principle been ever formally contested? It should seem that it had, by those who have not known what they have been meaning. Is it susceptible of

---

1   *principle* [Bentham's note] The word *principle* is derived from the Latin *principium*: which seems to be compounded of the two words *primus*, first, or chief, and *cipium* a termination which seems to be derived from *capio*, to take, as in *mancipium, municipium*; to which are analogous, *auceps, forceps*, and others. It is a term of very vague and very extensive signification: it is applied to any thing which is conceived to serve as a foundation or beginning to any series of operations: in some cases, of physical operations; but of mental operations in the present case.

    The principle here in question may be taken for an act of the mind; a sentiment; a sentiment of approbation; a sentiment which, when applied to an action, approves of its utility, as that quality of it by which the measure of approbation or disapprobation bestowed upon it ought to be governed.

2   *dictate* Command, guiding principle.

any direct proof? it should seem not: for that which is used to prove everything else, cannot itself be proved: a chain of proofs must have their commencement somewhere. To give such proof is as impossible as it is needless.

XII. Not that there is or ever has been that human creature at breathing, however stupid or perverse, who has not on many, perhaps on most occasions of his life, deferred to it. By the natural constitution of the human frame, on most occasions of their lives men in general embrace this principle, without thinking of it: if not for the ordering of their own actions, yet for the trying of their own actions, as well as of those of other men. There have been, at the same time, not many perhaps, even of the most intelligent, who have been disposed to embrace it purely and without reserve. There are even few who have not taken some occasion or other to quarrel with it, either on account of their not understanding always how to apply it, or on account of some prejudice or other which they were afraid to examine into, or could not bear to part with. For such is the stuff that man is made of: in principle and in practice, in a right track and in a wrong one, the rarest of all human qualities is consistency.

XIII. When a man attempts to combat the principle of utility, it is with reasons drawn, without his being aware of it, from that very principle itself. His arguments, if they prove any thing, prove not that the principle is *wrong*, but that, according to the applications he supposes to be made of it, it is *misapplied*. Is it possible for a man to move the earth? Yes; but he must first find out another earth to stand upon.

XIV. To disprove the propriety of it by arguments is impossible; but, from the causes that have been mentioned, or from some confused or partial view of it, a man may happen to be disposed not to relish it. Where this is the case, if he thinks the settling of his opinions on such a subject worth the trouble, let him take the following steps, and at length, perhaps, he may come to reconcile himself to it.

1. Let him settle with himself, whether he would wish to discard this principle altogether; if so, let him consider what it is that all his reasonings (in matters of politics especially) can amount to?

2. If he would, let him settle with himself, whether he would judge and act without any principle, or whether there is any other he would judge an act by?

3. If there be, let him examine and satisfy himself whether the principle he thinks he has found is really any separate intelligible principle; or whether it be not a mere principle in words, a kind of phrase, which at bottom expresses neither more nor less than the mere averment[1] of his own unfounded sentiments;[2] that is, what in another person he might be apt to call caprice?

4. If he is inclined to think that his own approbation or disapprobation, annexed to the idea of an act, without any regard to its consequences, is a sufficient foundation for him to judge and act upon, let him ask himself whether his sentiment is to be a standard of right and wrong, with respect to every other man, or whether every man's sentiment has the same privilege of being a standard to itself?

5. In the first case, let him ask himself whether his principle is not despotical, and hostile to all the rest of human race?

6. In the second case, whether it is not anarchial, and whether at this rate there are not as many different standards of right and wrong as there are men? and whether even to the same man, the same thing, which is right today, may not (without the least change in its nature) be wrong tomorrow? and whether the same thing is not right and wrong in the same place at the same time? and in either case, whether all argument is not at an end? and whether, when two men have said, "I like this," and "I don't like it," they can (upon such a principle) have any thing more to say?

7. If he should have said to himself, No: for that the sentiment which he proposes as a standard must be grounded on reflection, let him say on what particulars the reflection is to turn? if on particulars having relation to the utility of the act, then let him say whether this is not deserting his own principle, and borrowing assistance from that very one in opposition to which he sets it up: or if not on those particulars, on what other particulars?

8. If he should be for compounding the matter, and adopting his own principle in part, and the principle of utility in part, let him say how far he will adopt it?

9. When he has settled with himself where he will stop, then let him ask himself how he justifies to himself the adopting it so far? and why he will not adopt it any farther?

10. Admitting any other principle than the principle of utility to be a right principle, a principle that it is right

---

1 *averment* Declaration.
2 *sentiments* Feelings of approval or disapproval.

for a man to pursue; admitting (what is not true) that the word *right* can have a meaning without reference to utility, let him say whether there is any such thing as a *motive* that a man can have to pursue the dictates of it: if there is, let him say what that motive is, and how it is to be distinguished from those which enforce the dictates of utility: if not, then lastly let him say what it is this other principle can be good for?

Chapter 4: *Value of a Lot of Pleasure or Pain, How to Be Measured*

I. Pleasures then, and the avoidance of pains, are the *ends* that the legislator has in view; it behooves him therefore to understand their *value*. Pleasures and pains are the *instruments* he has to work with: it behooves him therefore to understand their force, which is again, in other words, their value.

II. To a person considered by *himself*, the value of a pleasure or pain considered *by itself*, will be greater or less, according to the four following *circumstances*:[1]

1. Its *intensity*.
2. Its *duration*.
3. Its *certainty* or *uncertainty*.
4. Its *propinquity*[2] or *remoteness*.

III. These are the circumstances which are to be considered in estimating a pleasure or a pain considered each of them by itself. But when the value of any pleasure or pain is considered for the purpose of estimating the tendency of any *act*

by which it is produced, there are two other circumstances to be taken into the account; these are,

5. Its *fecundity*, or the chance it has of being followed by sensations of the *same* kind: that is, pleasures, if it be a pleasure: pains, if it be a pain.
6. Its *purity*, or the chance it has of not being followed by sensations of the *opposite* kind: that is, pains, if it be a pleasure: pleasures, if it be a pain.

These two last, however, are in strictness scarcely to be deemed properties of the pleasure or the pain itself; they are not, therefore, in strictness to be taken into the account of the value of that pleasure or that pain. They are in strictness to be deemed properties only of the act, or other event, by which such pleasure or pain has been produced; and accordingly are only to be taken into the account of the tendency of such act or such event.

IV. To a *number* of persons, with reference to each of whom to the value of a pleasure or a pain is considered, it will be greater or less, according to seven circumstances: to wit, the six preceding ones; viz.

1. Its *intensity*.
2. Its *duration*.
3. Its *certainty* or *uncertainty*.
4. Its *propinquity* or *remoteness*.
5. Its *fecundity*.
6. Its *purity*.

   And one other; to wit:

7. Its *extent*; that is, the number of persons to whom it *extends*; or (in other words) who are affected by it.

V. To take an exact account then of the general tendency of any act, by which the interests of a community are affected, proceed as follows. Begin with any one person of those whose interests seem most immediately to be affected by it: and take an account,

1. Of the value of each distinguishable *pleasure* which appears to be produced by it in the *first* instance.
2. Of the value of each *pain* which appears to be produced by it in the *first* instance.

---

1   *four following circumstances*   [Bentham's note] These circumstances have since been denominated *elements* or *dimensions* of *value* in a pleasure or a pain.

   Not long after the publication of the first edition, the following memoriter [*connected with memorizing*] verses were framed, in the view of lodging more effectually, in the memory, these points, on which the whole fabric of morals and legislation may be seen to rest.

   Intense, long, certain, speedy, fruitful, pure—
   Such marks in *pleasures* and in *pains* endure.
   Such pleasures seek if *private* be thy end:
   If it be *public*, wide let them *extend*
   Such *pains* avoid, whichever be thy view:
   If pains *must* come, let them *extend* to few.

2   *propinquity*   Closeness.

3. Of the value of each pleasure which appears to be produced by it *after* the first. This constitutes the *fecundity* of the first *pleasure* and the *impurity* of the first *pain*.

4. Of the value of each *pain* which appears to be produced by it after the first. This constitutes the *fecundity* of the first *pain*, and the *impurity* of the first pleasure.

5. Sum up all the values of all the *pleasures* on the one side, and those of all the pains on the other. The balance, if it be on the side of pleasure, will give the *good* tendency of the act upon the whole, with respect to the interests of that *individual* person; if on the side of pain, the *bad* tendency of it upon the whole.

6. Take an account of the *number* of persons whose interests appear to be concerned; and repeat the above process with respect to each. *Sum up* the numbers expressive of the degrees of *good* tendency, which the act has, with respect to each individual, in regard to whom the tendency of it is *good* upon the whole: do this again with respect to each individual, in regard to whom the tendency of it is *good* upon the whole: do this again with respect to each individual, in regard to whom the tendency of it is *bad* upon the whole. Take the *balance* which if on the side of *pleasure*, will give the general *good tendency* of the act, with respect to the total number or community of individuals concerned; if on the side of pain, the general *evil tendency*, with respect to the same community.

VI. It is not to be expected that this process should be strictly pursued previously to every moral judgment, or to every legislative or judicial operation. It may, however, be always kept in view: and as near as the process actually pursued on these occasions approaches to it, so near will such process approach to the character of an exact one.

VII. The same process is alike applicable to pleasure and pain, in whatever shape they appear: and by whatever denomination they are distinguished: to pleasure, whether it be called *good* (which is properly the cause or instrument of pleasure) or *profit* (which is distant pleasure, or the cause or instrument of distant pleasure,) or *convenience*, or *advantage, benefit, emolument*,[1] *happiness*, and so forth: to pain, whether it be called *evil*, (which corresponds to *good*) or *mischief*, or *inconvenience*, or *disadvantage*, or *loss*, or *unhappiness*, and so forth.

---

1 *emolument* Payment (for work done).

VIII. Nor is this a novel and unwarranted, any more than it is a useless theory. In all this there is nothing but what the practice of mankind, wheresoever they have a clear view of their own interest, is perfectly conformable to. An article of property, an estate in land, for instance, is valuable, on what account? On account of the pleasures of all kinds which it enables a man to produce, and what comes to the same thing the pains of all kinds which it enables him to avert. But the value of such an article of property is universally understood to rise or fall according to the length or shortness of the time which a man has in it: the certainty or uncertainty of its coming into possession: and the nearness or remoteness of the time at which, if at all, it is to come into possession. As to the *intensity* of the pleasures which a man may derive from it, this is never thought of, because it depends upon the use which each particular person may come to make of it; which cannot be estimated till the particular pleasures he may come to derive from it, or the particular pains he may come to exclude by means of it, are brought to view. For the same reason, neither does he think of the *fecundity* or *purity* of those pleasures.

Thus much for pleasure and pain, happiness and unhappiness, in *general*. We come now to consider the several particular kinds of pain and pleasure.

Chapter 13: Cases Unmeet for Punishment

§1. General View of Cases Unmeet for Punishment

I. The general object which all laws have, or ought to have, in common, is to augment the total happiness of the community; and therefore, in the first place, to exclude, as far as may be, every thing that tends to subtract from that happiness: in other words, to exclude mischief.

II. But all punishment is mischief: all punishment in itself is evil. Upon the principle of utility, if it ought at all to be admitted, it ought only to be admitted in as far as it promises to exclude some greater evil.[2]

---

2 *greater evil* [Bentham's note] The immediate principal end of punishment is to control action. This action is either that of the offender, or of others: that of the offender it controls by its influence, either on his will, in which case it is said to operate in the way of *reformation*; or on his physical power, in which case it

III. It is plain, therefore, that in the following cases punishment ought not to be inflicted.

1. Where it is *groundless:* where there is no mischief for it to prevent; the act not being mischievous upon the whole.

2. Where it must be *inefficacious*: where it cannot act so as to prevent the mischief.

3. Where it is *unprofitable*, or too *expensive*: where the mischief it would produce would be greater than what it prevented.

4. Where it is *needless*: where the mischief may be prevented, or cease of itself, without it: that is, at a cheaper rate.

§2. Cases In Which Punishment Is Groundless

These are,

V. 1. Where there has never been any mischief: where no mischief has been produced to anybody by the act in question. Of this number are those in which the act was such as might, on a some occasions, be mischievous or disagreeable, but the person whose interest it concerns gave his *consent* to the performance of it. This consent, provided it be free, and fairly obtained, is the best proof that can be produced, that, to the person who gives it, no mischief, at least no immediate mischief, upon the whole, is done. For no man

---

is said to operate by *disablement*: that of others it can influence otherwise than by its influence over their wills, in which case it is said to operate in the way of *example*. A kind of collateral end, which it has a natural tendency to answer, is that of affording a pleasure or satisfaction to the party injured, where there is one, and, in general, to parties whose ill-will whether on a self-regarding account, or on the account of sympathy or antipathy, has been excited by the offense. This purpose, as far as it can be answered *gratis*, is a beneficial one. But no punishment ought to be allotted merely to this purpose, because (setting aside its effects in the way of control) no such pleasure is ever produced by punishment as can be equivalent to the pain. The punishment, however, which is allotted to the other purpose, ought, as far as it can be done without expense, to be accommodated to this. Satisfaction thus administered to a party injured, in the shape of a dissocial pleasure, may be styled a vindictive satisfaction or compensation: as a compensation, administered in the shape of self-regarding profit, or stock of pleasure, may be styled a lucrative one. Example is the most important end of all, in proportion as the *number* of the persons under temptation to offend is to *one*.

---

can be so good a judge as the man himself, what it is gives him pleasure or displeasure.

V. 2. Where the mischief was *outweighed*: although a mischief was produced by that act, yet the same act was necessary to the production of a benefit which was of greater value than the mischief. This may be the case with anything that is done in the way of precaution against instant calamity, as also with anything that is done in the exercise of the several sorts of powers necessary to be established in every community, to wit, domestic, judicial, military, and supreme.

VI. 3. Where there is a certainty of an adequate compensation: and that in all cases where the offense can be committed. This supposes two things: 1. That the offence is such as admits of an adequate compensation. 2. That such a compensation is sure to be forthcoming. Of these suppositions, the latter will be found to be a merely ideal one: a supposition that cannot, in the universality here given to it, be verified by fact. It cannot, therefore, in practice, be numbered amongst the grounds of absolute impunity. It may, however, be admitted as a ground for an abatement of that punishment, which other considerations, standing by themselves, would seem to dictate.[1]

§3. Cases In Which Punishment Must Be Inefficacious

These are,

VII. 1. Where the penal provision is *not established* until after the act is done. Such are the cases, 1. Of an *ex-post-facto* law; where the legislator himself appoints not a punishment till after the act is done. 2. Of a sentence beyond the law; where the judge, of his own authority, appoints a punishment which the legislator had not appointed.

---

1 *seem to dictate* [Bentham's note] This, for example, seems to have been one ground, at least, of the favor shown by perhaps all systems of laws, to such offenders as stand upon a footing of responsibility: shown, not directly indeed to the persons themselves; but to such offenses as none but responsible persons are likely to have the opportunity of engaging in. In particular, this seems to be the reason why embezzlement, in certain cases, has not commonly been punished upon the footing of theft: nor mercantile frauds upon that of common sharping.

VIII. 2. Where the penal provision, though established, is *not conveyed* to the notice of the person on whom it seems intended that it should operate. Such is the case where the law has omitted to employ any of the expedients which are necessary, to make sure that every person whatsoever, who is within the reach of the law, be apprised of all the cases whatsoever, in which (being in the station of life he is in) he can be subjected to the penalties of the law.

IX. 3. Where the penal provision, though it were conveyed to a man's notice, *could produce no effect* on him, with respect to the preventing him from engaging in any act of the *sort* in question. Such is the case, 1. In extreme *infancy*; where a man has not yet attained that state or disposition of mind in which the prospect of evils so distant as those which are held forth by the law, has the effect of influencing his conduct. 2. In *insanity*; where the person, if he has attained to that disposition, has since been deprived of it through the influence of some permanent though unseen cause. 3. In *intoxication*; where he has been a deprived of it by the transient influence of a visible cause: such as the use of wine, or opium, or other drugs, that act in this manner on the nervous system: which condition is indeed neither more nor less than a temporary insanity produced by an assignable cause.

X. 4. Where the penal provision (although, being conveyed to the party's notice, it might very well prevent his engaging in acts of the sort in question, provided he knew that it related to those acts) could not have this effect, with regard to the *individual* act he is about to engage in: to wit, because he knows not that it is of the number of those to which the penal provision relates. This may happen, 1. In the case of *unintentionality*; where he intends not to engage, and thereby knows not that he is about to engage, in the *act* in which eventually he is about to engage. 2. In the case of *unconsciousness*; where, although he may know that he is about to engage in the *act* itself, yet, from not knowing all the material *circumstances* attending it, he knows not of the *tendency* it has to produce that mischief, in contemplation of which it has been made penal in most instances. 3. In the case of *missupposal*;[1] where, although he may know of the tendency the act has to produce that degree of mischief, he supposes it, though mistakenly, to be attended with some circumstance, or set of circumstances, which, if it had been

attended with, it would either not have been productive of that mischief, or have been productive of such a greater degree of good, as has determined the legislator in such a case not to make it penal.

XI. 5. Where, though the penal clause might exercise a full and prevailing influence, were it to act alone, yet by the *predominant* influence of some opposite cause upon the will, it must necessarily be ineffectual; because the evil which he sets himself about to undergo, in the case of his *not* engaging in the act, is so great, that the evil denounced by the penal clause, in case of his engaging in it, cannot appear greater. This may happen, 1. In the case of *physical danger*; where the evil is such as appears likely to be brought about by the unassisted powers of *nature*. 2. In the case of a *threatened mischief*; where it is such as appears likely to be brought about through the intentional and conscious agency of *man*.[2]

XII. 6. Where (though the penal clause may exert a full and prevailing influence over the *will* of the party) yet his *physical faculties* (owing to the predominant influence of some physical cause) are not in a condition to follow the determination of the will: insomuch that the act is absolutely *involuntary*. Such is the case of physical *compulsion* or *restraint*, by whatever means brought about; where the man's hand, for instance, is pushed against some object which his will disposes him *not* to touch; or tied down from touching some object which his will disposes him to touch.

§4. Cases Where Punishment Is Unprofitable

These are,

XIII. 1. Where, on the one hand, the nature of the offense, on the other hand, that of the punishment, are, *in the ordin-*

---

1 *missupposal* Mistaken assumption.

2 *conscious agency of man* [Bentham's note] The influences of the *moral* and *religious* sanctions, or, in other words, of the motives of *love of reputation* and *religion*, are other causes, the force of which may, upon particular occasions, come to be greater than that of any punishment which the legislator is *able*, or at least which he will *think proper*, to apply. These, therefore, it will be proper for him to have his eye upon. But the force of these influences is variable and different in different times and places: the force of the foregoing influences is constant and the same, at all times and every where. These, therefore, it can never be proper to look upon as safe grounds for establishing absolute impunity: owing (as in the above-mentioned cases of infancy and intoxication) to the impracticability of ascertaining the matter of fact.

ary state of things, such, that when compared together, the evil of the latter will turn out to be greater than that of the former.

XIV. Now the evil of the punishment divides itself into four branches, by which so many different sets of persons are affected. 1. The evil of *coercion* or *restraint*: or the pain which it gives a man not to be able to do the act, whatever it be, which by the apprehension of the punishment he is deterred from doing. This is felt by those by whom the law is *observed*. 2. The evil of *apprehension*: or the pain which a man, who has exposed himself to punishment, feels at the thoughts of undergoing it. This is felt by those by whom the law has been *broken*, and who feel themselves in *danger* of its being executed upon them. 3. The evil of *sufferance*: or the pain which a man feels, in virtue of the punishment itself, from the time when he begins to undergo it. This is felt by those by whom the law is broken, and upon whom it comes actually to be executed. 4. The pain of sympathy, and the other *derivative* evils resulting to the persons who are in *connection* with the several classes of original sufferers just mentioned. Now of these four lots of evil, the first will be greater or less, according to the nature of the act from which the party is restrained: the second and third according to the nature of the punishment which stands annexed to that offence.

XV. On the other hand, as to the evil of the offense, this will also, of course, be greater or less, according to the nature of each offense. The proportion between the one evil and the other will therefore be different in the case of each particular offence. The cases, therefore, where punishment is unprofitable on this ground, can by no other means be discovered, than by an examination of each particular offense; which is what will be the business of the body of the work.

XVI. 2. Where, although in the *ordinary state* of things, the evil resulting from the punishment is not greater than the benefit which is likely to result from the force with which it operates, during the same space of time, towards the excluding the evil of the offenses, yet it may have been rendered so by the influence of some *occasional circumstances*. In the number of these circumstances may be, 1. The multitude of delinquents at a particular juncture;[1] being such as would increase, beyond the ordinary measure, the *quantum*[2] of the second and third lots, and thereby also of a part of the fourth lot,[3] in the evil of the punishment. 2. The extraordinary value of the services of some one delinquent; in the case where the effect of the punishment would be to deprive the community of the benefit of those services. 3. The displeasure of the *people*; that is, of an indefinite number of the members of the *same* community, in cases where (owing to of the influence of some occasional incident) they happen to conceive, that the offense or the offender ought not to be punished at all, or at least ought not to be punished in the way in question. 4. The displeasure of *foreign powers*; that is, of the governing body, or a considerable number of the members of some *foreign* community or communities, with which the community in question is connected.

§5. Cases Where Punishment Is Needless

These are,

XVII. 1. Where the purpose of putting an end to the practice may be attained as effectually at a cheaper rate: by instruction, is for instance, as well as by terror: by informing the understanding, as well as by exercising an immediate influence on the will. This seems to be the case with respect to all those offenses which consist in the disseminating pernicious principles in matters of *duty*; of whatever kind the duty be; whether political, or moral, or religious. And this, whether such principles be disseminated *under*, or even *without*; a sincere persuasion of their being beneficial. I say, even *without*: for though in such a case it is not instruction that can prevent the writer from endeavoring to inculcate his principles, yet it may the readers from adopting them: without which, his endeavoring to inculcate them will do no harm. In such a case, the sovereign will commonly have little need to take an active part: if it be the interest of *one* individual to inculcate principles that are pernicious, it will as surely be the interest of *other* individuals to expose them. But if the sovereign must needs take a part in the controversy, the pen is the proper weapon to combat error with, not the sword.

◆ ◆ ◆ ◆ ◆

---

1   *multitude of delinquents at a particular juncture*   Large number of wrong-doers at a particular occasion.

2   *quantum*   Quantity.

3   *second and third lots … fourth lot*   The "lots" here are the quantities of pain resulting in cases 2, 3, and 4 mentioned in section XIV above.

Offences Against One's Self: Paederasty, Part 1 (1785)

To what class of offences shall we refer these irregularities of the venereal[1] appetite which are styled unnatural? Whence hidden from the public eye there could be no color[2] for placing them anywhere else: could they find a place anywhere it would be here. I have been tormenting myself for years to find if possible a sufficient ground for treating them with the severity with which they are treated at this time of day by all European nations: but upon the principle of utility I can find none.

Offences of Impurity—Their Varieties

The abominations that come under this head have this property in common, in this respect, that they consist in procuring certain sensations by means of an improper object. The impropriety then may consist either in making use of an object

1. Of the proper species but at an improper time: for instance, after death.
2. Of an object of the proper species and sex, and at a proper time, but in an improper part.
3. Of an object of the proper species but the wrong sex. This is distinguished from the rest by the name of pederasty.
4. Of a wrong species.
5. In procuring this sensation by one's self without the help of any other sensitive object.

Pederasty Makes the Greatest Figure

The third being that which makes the most figure in the world it will be proper to give that the principal share of our attention. In settling the nature and tendency of this offence we shall for the most part have settled the nature and tendency of all the other offences that come under this disgusting catalogue.

Whether They Produce Any Primary Mischief

1. As to any primary mischief, it is evident that it produces no pain in anyone. On the contrary it produces pleasure, and that a pleasure which, by their perverted taste, is by this supposition preferred to that pleasure which is in general reputed the greatest. The partners are both willing. If either of them be unwilling, the act is not that which we have here in view: it is an offence totally different in its nature of effects: it is a personal injury; it is a kind of rape.

As a Secondary Mischief Whether They Produce Any Alarm in the Community

2. As to any secondary mischief, it produces not any pain of apprehension. For what is there in it for anybody to be afraid of? By the supposition, those only are the objects of it who choose to be so, who find a pleasure, for so it seems they do, in being so.

Whether Any Danger

3. As to any danger exclusive of pain, the danger, if any, must consist in the tendency of the example. But what is the tendency of this example? To dispose others to engage in the same practices: but this practice for anything that has yet appeared produces not pain of any kind to anyone.

Reasons That Have Commonly Been Assigned

Hitherto we have found no reason for punishing it at all: much less for punishing it with the degree of severity with which it has been commonly punished. Let us see what force there is in the reasons that have been commonly assigned for punishing it.

The whole tribe of writers on English law, who none of them knows any more what they mean by the word "peace" than they do by many other of the expressions that are most familiar to them, reckon this among offences against the peace. It is accordingly treated in all respects as an offence against the peace. They likewise reckon forgery, coining,[3] and all sorts of frauds among offences against the peace. According to the same writers it is doubted whether

---

1 *venereal* Sexual.
2 *color* Seeming reason.

3 *coining* Manufacturing (false) coins.

adultery be not a breach of the peace. It is certain however that whenever a gallant[1] accepts an invitation of another man's wife he does it with force and arms. This needs no comment.

Whether Against the Security of the Individual

Sir W. Blackstone[2] is more particular. According to him it is not only an offence against the peace, but it is of that division of offences against the peace which are offences against security. According to the same writer, if a man is guilty of this kind of filthiness, for instance, with a cow, as some men have been known to be, it is an offence against somebody's security. He does not say whose security, for the law makes no distinction in its ordinances, so neither does this lawyer or any other English lawyer in his comments make any distinction between this kind of filthiness when committed with the consent of the patient[3] and the same kind of filthiness when committed against his consent and by violence. It is just as if a man were to make no distinction between concubinage[4] and rape.

Whether It Debilitates—Montesquieu

The reason that Montesquieu[5] gives for reprobating[6] it is the weakness which he seems to suppose it to have a tendency to bring upon those who practice it. (*Spirit of Laws*, Book 12, Chapter 6) "Il faudroit le proscrire quand il ne feroit que donner à un sexe les faiblesses de l'autre et preparer à une vieillesse infame par une jeunesse honteuse." / "It ought to be proscribed were it only for its giving to the one sex the weaknesses of the other and paving the way by a scandalous youth for an infamous old age.") This, if it be true in fact, is a reason of a very different complexion from any of the preceding and it is on the ground of this reason as being the most plausible one that I have ranked the offence under its present head. As far as it is true in fact, the act ought to be regarded in the first place as coming within the list of offences against one's self, of offences of imprudence: in the next place, as an offence against the state, an offence the tendency of which is to diminish the public force.

If however it tends to weaken a man it is not any single act that can in any sensible degree have that effect. It can only be the habit: the act thus will become obnoxious as evidencing the existence, in probability, of the habit. This enervating tendency, be it what it may, if it is to be taken as a ground for treating the practice in question with a degree of severity which is not bestowed upon the regular way of gratifying the venereal appetite, must be greater in the former case than in the latter. Is it so? If the affirmative can be shown it must be either by arguments *a priori*[7] drawn from considerations of the nature of the human frame[8] or from experience. Are there any such arguments from physiology? I have never heard of any: I can think of none.

What Says History?

What says historical experience? The result of this can be measured only upon a large scale or upon a very general survey. Among the modern nations it is comparatively but rare. In modern Rome it is perhaps not very uncommon; in Paris probably not quite so common; in London still less frequent; in Edinburgh or Amsterdam you scarce hear of it two or three times in a century. In Athens and in ancient Rome in the most flourishing periods of the history of those capitals, regular intercourse between the sexes was scarcely much more common. It was upon the same footing throughout Greece: everybody practiced it; nobody was ashamed of it. They might be ashamed of what they looked upon as an excess in it, or they might be ashamed of it as a weakness, as a propensity that had a tendency to distract men from more worthy and important occupations, just as a man with us might be ashamed of excess or weakness in his love for women. In itself one may be sure they were not ashamed of it. Agesilaus,[9] upon somebody's taking notice of the care he took to avoid taking any familiarities with a youth who

---

1 *gallant* Ladies' man.

2 *Sir W. Blackstone* William Blackstone (1723–80), English author of *Commentaries on the Laws of England* (1765–69), a very important work on the history and nature of English common law.

3 *patient* One to whom something is done.

4 *concubinage* The living together of a man and woman not legally married.

5 *Montesquieu* French Enlightenment social and political thinker (1689–1755). His rarely used full name was Charles-Louis de Secondat, Baron de La Brède et de Montesquieu.

6 *reprobating* Condemning.

7 *a priori* Latin: *from beforehand*—that is, before, independent of, direct observation.

8 *frame* Body.

9 *Agesilaus* Agesilaus (440–360 BCE) was King of Sparta for 41 years beginning in 401 BCE.

passed for being handsome acknowledges it, indeed, but upon what ground? Not on account of the turpitude but the danger. Xenophon[1] in his retreat of the ten thousand gives an anecdote of himself in which he mentions himself as particularly addicted to this practice without seeming to entertain the least suspicion that any apology was necessary. In his account of Socrates's conversation he introduces that philosopher censuring or rather making merry with a young man for his attachment to the same practice. But in what light does he consider it? As a weakness unbecoming to a philosopher, not as a turpitude or a crime unbecoming to a man. It is not because an object of the one sex more than one of the other is improper game: but on account of the time that must be spent and the humiliation submitted to in the pursuit.

What is remarkable is that there is scarce a striking character in antiquity, nor one that in other respects men are in use to cite as virtuous, of whom it does not appear by one circumstance or another, that he was infected with this inconceivable propensity. It makes a conspicuous figure in the very opening of Thucydides's[2] history, and by an odd accident it was to the spirit of two young men kindled and supported by this passion that Athens according to that historian stood indebted on a trying occasion for the recovery of its liberty. The firmness and spirit of the Theban band—the band of lovers as it was called—is famous in history; and the principle by which the union among the members of it was commonly supposed to be cemented is well known. Many moderns, and among others Mr. Voltaire,[3] dispute the fact, but that intelligent philosopher sufficiently intimates the ground[4] of his incredulity—if he does not believe it, it is because he likes not to believe it. What the ancients called love in such a case was what we call Platonic, that is, was not love but friendship. But the Greeks knew the difference between love and friendship as well as we—they had distinct terms to signify them by: it seems reasonable therefore to suppose that when they say love they mean love, and that when they say friendship only they mean friendship only. And with regard to Xenophon and his master, Socrates, and his fellow-scholar Plato, it seems more reasonable to believe them to have been addicted to this taste when they or any

of them tell us so in express terms than to trust to the interpretations, however ingenious and however well-intended, of any men who write at this time of day, when they tell us it was no such thing. Not to insist upon Agesilaus and Xenophon, it appears by one circumstance or another that Themistocles, Aristides, Epaminondus, Alcibiades, Alexander[5] and perhaps the greatest number of the heroes of Greece were infected with this taste. Not that the historians are at the pains of informing us so expressly, for it was not extraordinary enough to make it worth their while, but it comes out collaterally in the course of the transactions they have occasion to relate.

[…]

Whether It Enervates the Patient More than the Agent

Montesquieu however seems to make a distinction—he seems to suppose these enervating effects to be exerted principally upon the person who is the patient in such a business. This distinction does not seem very satisfactory in any point of view. Is there any reason for supposing it to be a fixed one? Between persons of the same age actuated by the same incomprehensible desires would not the parts they took in the business be convertible? Would not the patient be the agent in his turn? If it were not so, the person on whom he supposes these effects to be the greatest is precisely the person with regard to whom it is most difficult to conceive whence those consequences should result. In the one case there is exhaustion which when carried to excess may be followed by debility: in the other case there is no such thing.

Whether It Hurts Population?

A notion more obvious, but perhaps not much better founded than the former is that of its being prejudicial to population. Mr. Voltaire appears inclined in one part of his works to give some countenance to this opinion. He speaks of it as a vice which would be destructive to the human race if it were general. "How did it come about that a vice which

---

1 *Xenophon*   Greek historian (c. 427–355 BCE).

2 *Thucydides*   Greek historian (c. 460 BCE–c. 400 BCE), author of the *History of the Peloponnesian War*.

3 *Voltaire*   Pen-name of François-Marie Arouet (1694–1778), French Enlightenment writer and philosopher.

4 *intimates the ground*   Hints at the basis.

5 *Themistocles … Alexander*   All ancient Greek figures of great achievement: Themistocles and Aristides were statesmen, Epaminondus a general, Alcibiades both a statesman and a general, and Alexander ("the Great") king of Macedon and military conqueror.

would destroy mankind if it were general, that an infamous outrage against nature...?"[1]

A little further on, speaking of Sextus Empiricus[2] who would have us believe that this practice was "recommended" in Persia by the laws, he insists that the effect of such a law would be to annihilate the human race if it were literally observed. "No," says he, "it is not in human nature to make a law that contradicts and outrages nature, a law that would annihilate mankind if it were observed to the letter." This consequence however is far enough from being a necessary one. For a law of the purport he represents to be observed, it is sufficient that this unprolific kind of venery[3] be practiced; it is not necessary that it should be practiced to the exclusion of that which is prolific.[4] Now that there should ever be wanting such a measure of the regular and ordinary inclination of desire for the proper object as is necessary for keeping up the numbers of mankind upon their present footing is a notion that stands warranted by nothing that I can find in history. To consider the matter *a priori*, if we consult Mr. Hume[5] and Dr. Smith,[6] we shall find that it is not the strength of the inclination of the one sex for the other that is the measure of the numbers of mankind, but the quantity of subsistence which they can find or raise upon a given spot. With regard to the mere object of population, if we consider the time of gestation in the female sex we shall find that much less than a hundredth part of the activity a man is capable of exerting in this way is sufficient to produce all the effect that can be produced by ever so much more. Population therefore cannot suffer till the inclination of the male sex for the female be considerably less than a hundredth part as strong as for their own. Is there the least probability that should ever be the case? I must confess I see not anything that should lead us to suppose it. Before this can happen the nature of the human composition must receive a total change and that propensity which is com-

monly regarded as the only one of the two that is. Natural must have become altogether an unnatural one.

I have already observed that I can find nothing in history to countenance the notion I am examining. On the contrary the country in which the prevalence of this practice is most conspicuous happens to have been remarkable for its populousness. The bent of popular prejudice has been to exaggerate this populousness: but after all deductions made, still it will appear to have been remarkable. It was such as, notwithstanding the drain of continual wars in a country parceled out into paltry states as to be all of it frontier, gave occasion to the continued necessity of emigration.

This reason however well grounded soever it were in itself could not with any degree of consistency be urged in a country where celibacy was permitted, much less where it was encouraged. The proposition which (as will be shewn more fully by and by) is not at all true with respect to pederasty, I mean that were it to prevail universally it would put an end to the human race, is most evidently and strictly true with regard to celibacy. If then merely out of regard to population it were right that pederasts should be burnt alive monks ought to be roasted alive by a slow fire. If a pederast, according to the monkish canonist Bermondus,[7] destroys the whole human race, Bermondus destroyed it I don't know how many thousand times over. The crime of Bermondus[8] is I don't know how many times worse than pederasty.

◆ ◆ ◆ ◆ ◆

1 *How did it come ... against nature* Voltaire, *Questions on the Encyclopedia*, "Socratic Love" (1764).
2 *Sextus Empiricus* Ancient Greek philosopher who flourished towards the end of second century CE (his biographical details are largely unknown). He is known for his association with the school of skeptical philosophy.
3 *venery* Pursuit of sexual pleasure.
4 *prolific* Productive of offspring.
5 *Mr. Hume* David Hume (1711–76), Scottish philosopher, economist, and historian.
6 *Dr. Smith* Adam Smith (1723–90), Scottish political economist.
7 *Bermondus* Little is known of this figure in the Roman Catholic Church other than his denunciation of pederasty at the Fifth Council of the Lateran (1512–17).
8 *crime of Bermondus* I.e., celibacy.

Panopticon; or the Inspection-House (1787)[1]

Letter 1: Idea of the Inspection Principle

Crecheff in White Russia, 1787.

Dear ****,

I observed t'other day in one of your English papers, an advertisement relative to a House of Correction therein spoken of, as intended for ******. It occurred to me, that the plan of a building, lately contrived by my brother, for purposes in some respects similar, and which, under the name of the *Inspection House*, or the *Elaboratory*, he is about erecting here, might afford some hints for the above establishment.[2] I have accordingly obtained some drawings

---

1   *Panopticon*   The full title reads as follows: Panopticon; or the Inspection-House: containing the idea of a new principle of construction applicable to any sort of establishment, in which persons of any description are to be kept under inspection; and in particular to penitentiary-houses, prisons, houses of industry, work-houses, poor-houses, lazarettos, manufactories, hospitals, mad-houses, and schools: with a plan of management adapted to the principle: in a series of letters written in the year 1787, from Crecheff in White Russia. To a friend in England by Jeremy Bentham, of Lincoln's Inn, Esquire.

2   *It occurred to me ... establishment*   [Bentham's note] The sudden breaking out of the war between the Turks and Russians, in consequence of an unexpected attack made by the former on the latter concurred with some other incidents in putting a stop to the design. The person here spoken of, at that time Lieutenant-Colonel Commandant of a battalion in the Empress's service, having obtained a regiment and other honors for his services in the course of the war, is now stationed with his regiment in a distant part of the country.

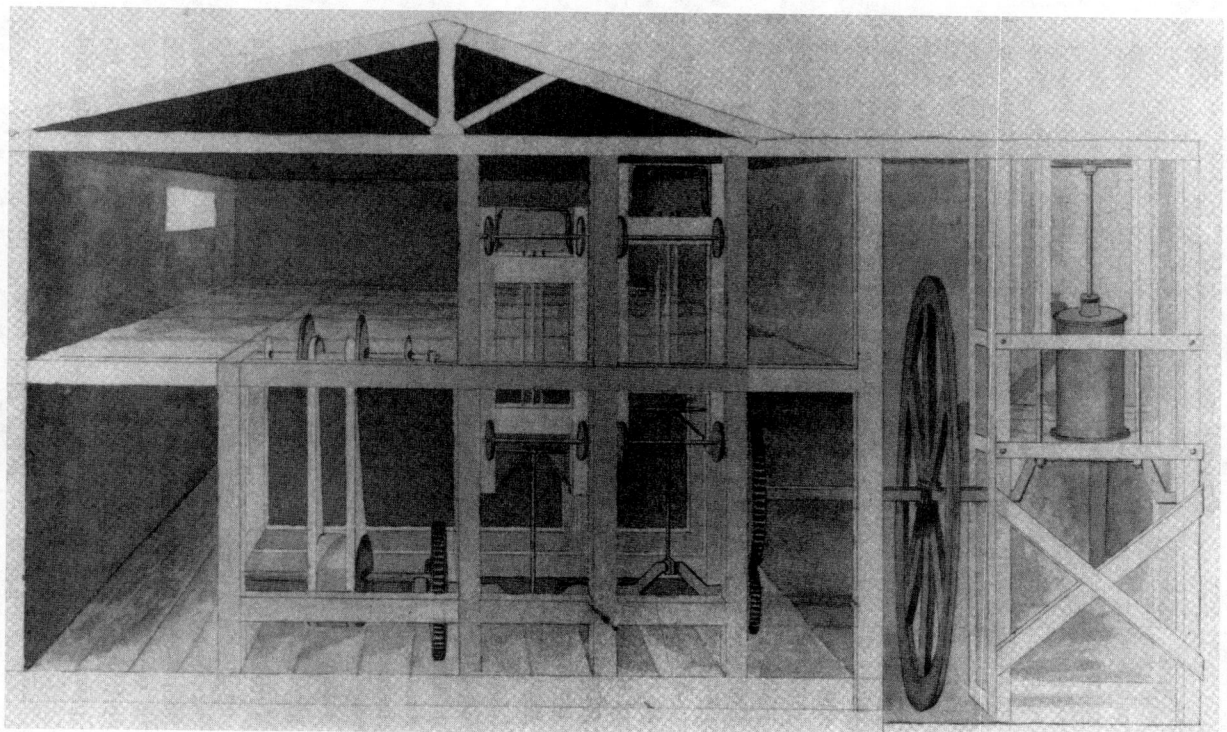

Illustration 1 of Bentham's panopticon.

relative to it, which I here enclose. Indeed I look upon it as capable of applications of the most extensive nature; and that for reasons which you will soon perceive.

To say all in one word, it will be found applicable, I think, without exception, to all establishments whatsoever, in which, within a space not too large to be covered or commanded by buildings, a number of persons are meant to be kept under inspection. No matter how different, or even opposite the purpose: whether it be that of *punishing the incorrigible, guarding the insane, reforming the vicious, confining the suspected, employing the idle, maintaining the helpless, curing the sick, instructing the willing* in any branch of industry, or *training the rising race* in the path of *education*: in a word, whether it be applied to the purposes of *perpetual prisons* in the room of death, or *prisons for confinement* before trial, or *penitentiary-houses, or houses of correction, or work-houses, or manufactories, or mad-houses, or hospitals, or schools.*

It is obvious that, in all these instances, the more constantly the persons to be inspected are under the eyes of the persons who should inspect them, the more perfectly will the purpose X of the establishment have been attained.

Ideal perfection, if that were the object, would require that each person should actually be in that predicament, during every instant of time. This being impossible, the next thing to be wished for is, that, at every instant, seeing reason to believe as much, and not being able to satisfy himself to the contrary, he should *conceive* himself to be so. This point, you will immediately see, is most completely secured by my brother's plan; and, I think, it will appear equally manifest, that it cannot be compassed by any other, or to speak more properly, that if it be compassed by any other, it can only be in proportion as such other may approach to this.

To cut the matter as short as possible, I will consider it at once in its application to such purposes as, being most complicated, will serve to exemplify the greatest force and variety of precautionary contrivance. Such are those which have suggested the idea of *penitentiary-houses*: in which the objects of *safe custody, confinement, solitude, forced labor,* and *instruction*, were all of them to be kept in view. If all these objects can be accomplished together, of course with at least equal certainty and facility may any lesser number of them.

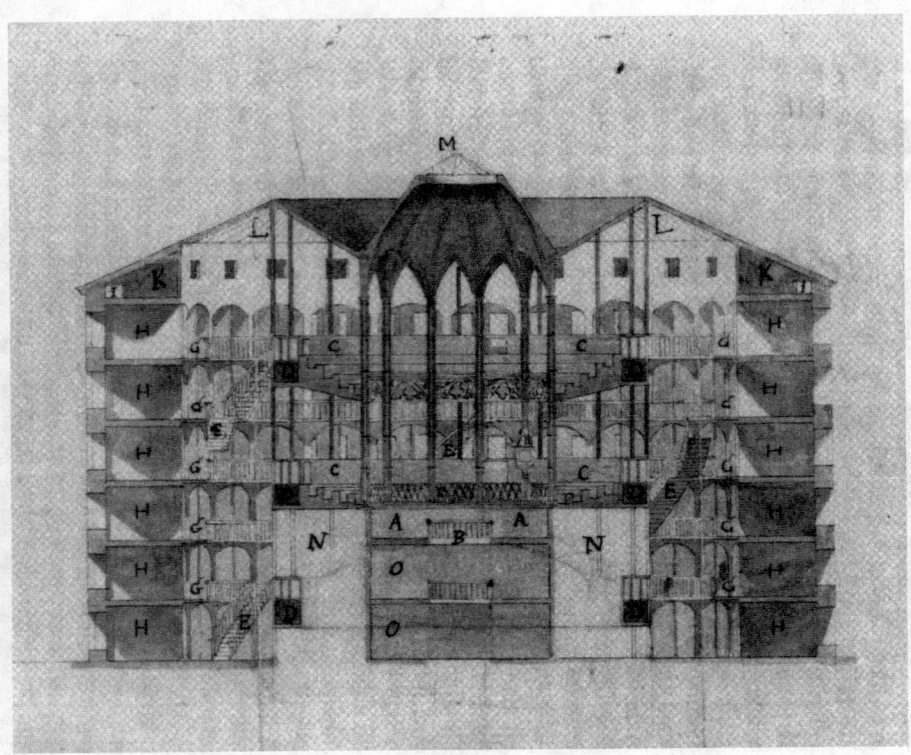

Illustration 2 of Bentham's panopticon.

Letter 2: Plan for a Penitentiary Inspection-House

Before you look at the plan, take in words the general idea of it.

The building is circular.

The apartments of the prisoners occupy the circumference. You may call them, if you please, the *cells*.

These *cells* are divided from one another, and the prisoners by that means secluded from all communication with each other, by *partitions* in the form of *radii* issuing from the circumference towards the centre, and extending as many feet as shall be thought necessary to form the largest dimension of the cell.

The apartment of the inspector occupies the centre; you may call it if you please the *inspector's lodge*.

It will be convenient in most, if not in all cases, to have a vacant space or *area* all round, between such centre and such circumference. You may call it if you please the *intermediate* or *annular* area.

About the width of a cell may be sufficient for a *passage* from the outside of the building to the lodge.

Each cell has in the outward circumference, a *window*, large enough, not only to light the cell, but, through the cell, to afford light enough to the correspondent part of the lodge.

The inner circumference of the cell is formed by an iron *grating*, so light as not to screen any part of the cell from the inspector's view.

Of this grating, a part sufficiently large opens, in form of a *door*, to admit the prisoner at his first entrance; and to give admission at any time to the inspector or any of his attendants.

To cut off from each prisoner the view of every other, the partitions are carried on a few feet beyond the grating into the intermediate area: such projecting parts I call the *protracted partitions*.

It is conceived, that the light, coming in in this manner through the cells, and so across the intermediate area, will be sufficient for the inspector's lodge. But, for this purpose, both the windows in the cells, and those corresponding to them in the lodge, should be as large as the strength of the building, and what shall be deemed a necessary attention to economy, will permit.

To the windows of the lodge there are *blinds*, as high up as the eyes of the prisoners in their cells can, by any means they can employ, be made to reach.

To prevent *thorough light*, whereby, notwithstanding the blinds, the prisoners would see from the cells whether or not any person was in the lodge, that apartment is divided into quarters, by *partitions* formed by two diameters to the circle, crossing each other at right angles. For these partitions the thinnest materials might serve; and they might be made removable at pleasure; their height, sufficient to prevent the prisoners seeing over them from the cells. Doors to these partitions, if left open at any time, might produce the thorough light. To prevent this, divide each partition into two, at any part required, setting down the one-half at such distance from the other as shall be equal to the aperture of a door.

These windows of the inspector's lodge open into the intermediate area, in the form of *doors*, in as many places as shall be deemed necessary to admit of his communicating readily with any of the cells.

Small *lamps*, in the outside of each window of the lodge, backed by a reflector, to throw the light into the corresponding cells, would extend to the night the security of the day.

To save the troublesome exertion of voice that might otherwise be necessary, and to prevent one prisoner from knowing that the inspector was occupied by another prisoner at a distance, a small *tin tube* might reach from each cell to the inspector's lodge, passing across the area, and so in at the side of the correspondent window of the lodge. By means of this implement, the slightest whisper of the one might be heard by the other, especially if he had proper notice to apply his ear to the tube.

With regard to *instruction*, in cases where it cannot be duly given without the instructor's being close to the work, or without setting his hand to it by way of example before the learner's face, the instructor must indeed here as elsewhere, shift his station as often as there is occasion to visit different workmen; unless he calls the workmen to him, which in some of the instances to which this sort of building is applicable, such as that of imprisoned felons, could not so well be. But in all cases where directions, given verbally and at a distance, are sufficient, these tubes will be found of use. They will save, on the one hand, the exertion of voice it would require, on the part of the instructor, to communicate instruction to the workmen without quitting his central station in the lodge; and, on the other, the confusion which would ensue if different instructors or persons in the lodge were calling to the cells at the same time. And, in the case of hospitals, the quiet that may be insured by this little contrivance, trifling as it may seem at first sight, affords an additional advantage.

A *bell*, appropriated exclusively to the purposes of *alarm*, hangs in a *belfry* with which the building is crowned, communicating by a rope with the inspector's lodge.

The most economical, and perhaps the most convenient, way of *warming* the cells and area, would be by flues[1] surrounding it, upon the principle of those in hot-houses. A total want of every means of producing artificial heat might, in such weather as we sometimes have in England, be fatal to the lives of the prisoners; at any rate, it would often times be altogether incompatible with their working at any sedentary employment. The flues, however, and the fire-places belonging to them, instead of being on the outside, as in hot-houses, should be in the inside. By this means, there would be less waste of heat, and the current of air that would rush in on all sides through the cells, to supply the draught made by the fires, would answer so far the purpose of ventilation. But of this more under the head of Hospitals.[2]

Letter 5: Essential Points of the Plan

It may be of use, that among all the particulars you have seen, it should be clearly understood what circumstances are, and what are not, essential to the plan. The essence of it consists, then, in the *centrality* of the inspector's situation, combined with the well-known and most effectual contrivances for *seeing without being seen*. As to the *general form* of the building, the most commodious for most purposes seems to be the circular: but this is not an absolutely

1 *flues* Pipes to carry heat.
2 *of this more ... Hospitals* [Bentham's note] There is one subject, which, though not of the most dignified kind, nor of the most pleasant kind to expatiate upon, is of too great importance to health and safe custody to be passed over unconsidered: I mean the provision to be made for carrying off the result of necessary evacuations. A common necessary might be dangerous to security, and would be altogether incompatible with the plan of solitude. To have the filth carried off by the attendants, would be altogether as incompatible with cleanliness, since without such a degree of regularity as it would be difficult, if not ridiculous, to attempt to enforce in case of health, and altogether impossible in case of sickness, the air of each cell, and by that means the lodge itself would be liable to be kept in a state of constant contamination, in the intervals betwixt one visit and another. This being the case, I can see no other eligible means, than that of having in each cell a fixed provision made for this purpose in the construction of the building.

essential circumstance. Of all figures, however, this, you will observe, is the only one that affords a perfect view, and the same view, of an indefinite number of apartments of the same dimensions: that affords a spot from which, without any change of situation, a man may survey, in the same perfection, the whole number, and without so much as a change of posture, the half of the whole number, at the same time: that, within a boundary of a given extent, contains the greatest quantity of room:—that places the centre at the least distance from the light:—that gives the cells most width, at the part where, on account of the light, most light may, for the purposes of work, be wanted:—and that reduces to the greatest possible shortness the path taken by the inspector, in passing from each part of the field of inspection to every other.

You will please to observe, that though perhaps it is the most important point, that the persons to be inspected should always feel themselves as if under inspection, at least as standing a great chance of being so, yet it is not by any means the *only* one. If it were, the same advantage might be given to buildings of almost any form. What is also of importance is, that for the greatest proportion of time possible, each man should actually *be* under inspection. This is material in *all* cases, that the inspector may have the satisfaction of knowing, that the discipline actually has the effect which it is designed to have: and it is more particularly material in such cases where the inspector, besides seeing that they conform to such standing rules as are prescribed, has more or less frequent occasion to give them such transient and incidental directions as will require to be given and enforced, at the commencement at least of every course of industry. And I think, it needs not much argument to prove, that the business of inspection, like every other, will be performed to a greater degree of perfection, the less trouble the performance of it requires.

Not only so, but the greater chance there is, of a given person's being at a given time actually under inspection, the more strong will be the persuasion—the more *intense*, if I may say so, the *feeling*, he has of his being so. How little turn soever the greater number of persons so circumstanced may be supposed to have for calculation, some rough sort of calculation can scarcely, under such circumstances, avoid forcing itself upon the rudest mind. Experiment, venturing first upon slight trangressions, and so on, in proportion to success, upon more and more considerable ones, will not fail to teach him the difference between a loose inspection and a strict one.

It is for these reasons, that I cannot help looking upon every form as less and less eligible, in proportion as it deviates from the *circular*.

A very material point is, that room be allotted to the lodge, sufficient to adapt it to the purpose of a complete and constant habitation for the principal inspector or head-keeper, and his family. The more numerous also the family, the better; since, by this means, there will in fact be as many inspectors, as the family consists of persons, though only one be paid for it. Neither the orders of the inspector himself, nor any interest which they may feel, or not feel, in the regular performance of his duty, would be requisite to find them motives adequate to the purpose. Secluded oftentimes, by their situation, from every other object, they will naturally, and in a manner unavoidably, give their eyes a direction conformable to that purpose, in every momentary interval of their ordinary occupations. It will supply in their instance the place of that great and constant fund of entertainment to the sedentary and vacant in towns—the looking out of the window. The scene, though a confined, would be a very various, and therefore, perhaps, not altogether an unamusing one.

Letter 6: Advantages of the Plan

I flatter myself there can now be little doubt of the plan's possessing the fundamental advantages I have been attributing to it: I mean, the *apparent omnipresence*[1] of the inspector (if divines will allow me the expression,) combined with the extreme facility of his *real presence*.

A collateral advantage it possesses, and on the score of frugality a very material one, is that which respects the *number* of the inspectors requisite. If this plan required more than another, the additional number would form an objection, which, were the difference to a certain degree considerable, might rise so high as to be conclusive: so far from it, that a greater multitude than ever were yet lodged in one house might be inspected by a single person; for the trouble of inspection is diminished in no less proportion than the strictness of inspection is increased.

Another very important advantage, whatever purposes the plan may be applied to, particularly where it is applied to the severest and most coercive purposes, is, that the *under*

keepers or inspectors, the servants and subordinates of every kind, will be under the same irresistible control with respect to the *head* keeper or inspector, as the prisoners or other persons to be governed are with respect to *them*. On the common plans, what means, what possibility, has the prisoner of appealing to the humanity of the principal for redress against the neglect or oppression of subordinates in that rigid sphere, but the *few* opportunities which, in a crowded prison, the most conscientious keeper *can* afford—but the none at all which many a keeper *thinks* fit to give them? How different would their lot be upon this plan!

In no instance could his subordinates either perform or depart from their duty, but he must know the time and degree and manner of their doing so. It presents an answer, and that a satisfactory one, to one of the most puzzling of political questions—*quis custodiet ipsos custodes?*[2] And, as the fulfilling of his, as well as their, duty would be rendered so much easier, than it can ever have been hitherto, so might, and so should any departure from it be punished with the more inflexible severity. It is this circumstance that renders the influence of this plan not less beneficial to what is called *liberty*, than to necessary coercion; not less powerful as a control upon subordinate power, than as a curb to delinquency; as a shield to innocence, than as a scourge to guilt.

Another advantage, still operating to the same ends, is the great load of trouble and disgust which it takes off the shoulders of those occasional inspectors of a higher order, such as *judges* and other *magistrates*, who, called down to this irksome task from the superior ranks of life, cannot but feel a proportionable repugnance to the discharge of it. Think how it is with them upon the present plans, and how it still must be upon the best plans that have been hitherto devised! The cells or apartments, however constructed, must, if there be nine hundred of them (as there were to have been upon the penitentiary-house plan,) be opened to the visitors, one by one. To do their business to any purpose, they must approach near to, and come almost in contact with each inhabitant; whose situation being watched over according to no other than the loose methods of inspection at present practicable, will on that account require the more minute and troublesome investigation on the part of these occasional superintendents. By this new plan, the disgust is entirely removed, and the trouble of going into such a

---

1 *omnipresence* Presence everywhere (a characteristic usually associated only with God—thus the joking remark about "divines" following).

2 *quis custodiet ipsos custodes?* Latin: who will guard the guardians?

room as the lodge, is no more than the trouble of going into any other.

Were *Newgate* upon this plan, all Newgate might be inspected by a quarter of an hour's visit to Mr. Akerman.[1]

Among the other causes of that reluctance, none at present so forcible, none so unhappily well grounded, none which affords so natural an excuse, nor so strong a reason against accepting of any excuse, as the danger of *infection*—a circumstance which carries death, in one of its most tremendous forms, from the seat of guilt to the seat of justice, involving in one common catastrophe the violator and the upholder of the laws. But in a spot so constructed, and under a course of discipline so insured, how should infection ever arise? or how should it continue? Against every danger of this kind, what private house of the poor, one might almost say, or even of the most opulent, can be equally secure?

Nor is the disagreeableness of the task of superintendence diminished by this plan, in a much greater degree than the efficacy of it is increased. On all others, be the superintendent's visit ever so unexpected, and his motions ever so quick, time there must always be for preparations blinding the real state of things. Out of nine hundred cells, he can visit but one at a time, and, in the meanwhile, the worst of the others may be arranged, and the inhabitants threatened, and tutored how to receive him. On this plan, no sooner is the superintendent announced, than the whole scene opens instantaneously to his view.

In mentioning inspectors and superintendents who are such by office, I must not overlook that system of inspection, which, however little heeded, will not be the less useful and efficacious: I mean, the part which individuals may be disposed to take in the business, without intending, perhaps, or even without thinking of, any other effects of their visits, than the gratification of their own particular curiosity. What the inspector's or keeper's family are with respect to him, that, and more, will these spontaneous visitors be to the superintendent,—assistants, deputies, in so far as he is faithful, witnesses and judges should he ever be unfaithful, to his trust. So as they are but there, what the motives were that drew them thither is perfectly immaterial; whether the relieving of their anxieties by the affecting prospect of their respective friends and relatives thus detained in durance,[2] or merely the satisfying that general curiosity, which an establishment, on various accounts so interesting to human feelings, may naturally be expected to excite.

You see, I take for granted as a matter of course, that under the necessary regulations for preventing interruption and disturbance, the doors of these establishments will be, as, without very special reasons to the contrary, the doors of all public establishments ought to be, thrown wide open to the body of the curious at large—the great *open committee* of the tribunal of the world. And who ever objects to such publicity, where it is practicable, but those whose motives for objection afford the strongest reasons for it?

---

1   *Mr. Ackerman*   Richard Ackerman, keeper in Bentham's time of Newgate Prison in London.

2   *durance* Imprisonment.

JOHN STUART MILL
(1806 – 1873)

Who Was John Stuart Mill?

JOHN STUART MILL, THE MOST IMPORTANT BRITISH PHIL-osopher of the nineteenth century, was born in London in 1806, the eldest son of Scottish utilitarian philosopher and political radical James Mill. His father brought up John to prove his theory that all variations in adult abilities were the result of childhood experiences and education. In an effort to make him a genius, he isolated him from other human company, and home-schooled him, beginning his training in Greek at age three. By age eight, when he began study of arith-metic and logic, he had studied large chunks of Greek literature in the ori-ginal. At twelve, he took on philoso-phy, and political economy at thirteen; when he was fourteen he was sent to France for a year to become fluent in the language and to study chemistry and mathematics. He never had toys or children's books, never learned to play, and had no friends of his own age before he was fourteen. An early draft of his autobiography says "I believe there is less personal affection in England than in any other coun-try of which I know."

At the age of twenty Mill suffered a nervous breakdown and was plunged into suicidal despair. The trigger—accord-ing to his autobiography—was his sudden realization that living the life his father had trained him for could not make him happy. He later claimed that his sanity was saved by his discovery of Romantic poetry, particularly Wordsworth, and his philosophical views were to emphasize the proper development of the emotional and sentimental side of one's character, as well as one's intellect.

In 1830, at 24, Mill began a deeply passionate (but non-sexual) love affair with Harriet Hardy Taylor—a rela-tionship that was emotionally and intellectually central to the rest of his life. (See the introduction for Harriet Taylor Mill for more on this.)

Mill never held an academic position, but spent 35 years working as an administrator for the British East India Company in London. This left him plenty of time for his writing, and he was also very active in public life. In 1823 he was arrested for distributing birth-control pamphlets, and in 1825 he helped to found the London Debating Society. He was a frequent contributor to the *Westminster Review*, a radical magazine founded by his father; and began and edited the influential *London Review* (renamed *London and Westminster Re-view*). Between 1865 and 1868 Mill was the Liberal Member of Parliament for Westminster, and in 1866 he secured a law guaranteeing freedom of speech in London's Hyde Park, where Speakers' Corner survives today as a place where "soapbox orators" can say whatever they like with legal impunity. In 1867 he tried, but failed, to amend the second Reform Bill to introduce proportional representation and the vote for women. In 1866—by now something of a grand old man of English society—he was made Rector of the University of St. Andrew's in Scotland. In 1872 he became godfather to the new-born Bertrand Russell.

Mill died suddenly, from a fever, in 1873 at Aix-en-Provence, France. From about 1860 until 1870 he had been at the peak of his powers and influence. The moral philosopher Henry Sidgwick wrote in 1873 that "from about 1860–1865 or thereabouts he ruled England in the region of thought as very few men ever did. I do not expect to see anything like it again," and a few decades later the former Prime Minister James Arthur Balfour noted that the authority of Mill's thought in English universities had been "comparable to that wielded ... by Hegel in Germany and in the middle ages by Aristotle." By World War I, however, Mill's reputation as a philosopher had suffered a precipitous decline, and he remained in ill-favor in the English-speaking philosophical world until the early 1970s, when new scholarship and changing philosophical fashions made possible a gradual increase in the appreciation of Mill as a major philosophical figure, as the finest flowering of nineteenth-century British philosophy, and as a precursor for the "naturalist" philosophers of the second-half of the twentieth century.

What Was Mill's Overall Philosophical Project?

Mill is philosophically important perhaps less for the *originality* of his thought than for its brilliant *synthesis* of several major strands in nineteenth-century (and especially British) thought into a single, compelling, well-developed picture. The main ingredients for his worldview were empiricism, associationism, utilitarianism, and elements of German Romanticism: together, these elements became what John Skorupski has called Mill's "liberal naturalism."

The bedrock of Mill's philosophy was empiricism: he believed that all human knowledge comes ultimately from sense-experience, and his most substantial intellectual project was the attempt to construct a system of empirical knowledge that could underpin not just science but also moral and social affairs. One of his main interests was in showing that empiricism need not lead to skepticism, such as that espoused by the eighteenth-century Scottish philosopher David Hume. Mill's main discussion of the foundation of knowledge and the principles of inference is the massive *System of Logic*, published in six volumes in 1843. In this work he discussed both deductive inference (including mathematics, which Mill argued was—like all human knowledge—reducible to a set of generalizations of relations among sense-experience) and inductive inference in the natural sciences. He also tried to show how these methods could be applied in politics and the social sciences: social phenomena, he argued, are just as much the result of causal laws as are natural events, and thus the social sciences—though they will never permit us perfectly to predict human behavior—are capable of putting social policy on an objective footing which goes beyond the mere "intuitions" of conservative common sense.

His prescriptions for scientific practice—today called "Mill's methods"—were highly influential in the development of the philosophy of science in the twentieth century, and his work is still the foundation of modern methodologies for discovering causal laws. The key engine of science, for Mill, is simply *enumerative induction*: generalization from experience. That is, crudely put, once we have observed a sequence of events which all obey some regularity—ravens which are black, say, or moving magnetic fields being accompanied by an electrical current—we are justified in inferring that all future events of that type will follow the same law.

Mill's work also foreshadowed what is today called "naturalized epistemology." He proposed that the phenomena of the human mind (including rationality) be treated as the upshot of the operation of psychological laws operating upon the data of experience. This psychological theory is called "associationism"—since it thinks of ideas as arising from the psychological *associations* between sensations—and was particularly defended by Mill in his *Examination of Sir William Hamilton's Philosophy* (1865).

In his own time, Mill was for many years most widely known for his *Principles of Political Economy* (1848), which tried to show that the science of economics—criticized in his day by Mill's friend, the writer Thomas Carlyle, as a "dismal science" that could only predict disaster and starvation—could be reformulated as a progressive force for social progress. Mill pointed out that there is a mismatch between what economics measures and what human beings really value, and this led him to argue for such theses as that economic growth should be limited for the sake of the environment, that populations should be controlled in order to allow an adequate standard of living for everyone, and that the economically ideal form of society would be a system of worker-owned cooperatives.

Mill's main ethical position is *utilitarianism*, which he sets out in his book with that title, selections of which are reprinted here. As he wrote in his autobiography, once he had read Jeremy Bentham's work on utilitarianism (at the age of 15), "it gave unity to my conceptions of things. I now had opinions; a creed, a doctrine, a philosophy; in one among all the best senses of the word, a religion; the inculcation and diffusion of which could be made the principal outward purpose of a life." Mill was also concerned to apply this moral theory to wider questions of social policy. Of all social institutions—including both formal institutions such as laws and churches, and informal ones like social norms—Mill wants to ask: does this institution contribute to human welfare, and does it do so better than any of the alternatives? If the answer was No, Mill argued, then that institution should (gradually and non-violently) be changed for the better.

Mill's *On Liberty* (1859)—which, during his lifetime, was probably his most notorious writing—is a classic defense of the freedom of thought and discussion, arguing that the

"the only purpose for which power can be rightfully exercised over any member of a civilized community, against his will, is to prevent harm to others. His own good, either physical or moral, is not a sufficient warrant." This essay, reprinted here, was sparked partly by Mill's growing fear of the middle-class conformism (which he saw in America and detected increasing signs of in Britain) that he thought dangerously stifled originality and the critical consideration of ideas. Central to these concerns is Mill's view of human nature as "progressive," and of the importance of individuality and autonomy. These themes, with their emphasis on the power and importance of the human spirit, were part of what he took from the Romantic movement on the continent of Europe.

One of Mill's last works, *The Subjection of Women* (1869), is a classic statement of liberal feminism. Mill argues that women should have just as much freedom as men, and attacks the conservative view that women and men have different "natures" which suit them for different spheres of life by arguing that no one could possibly know this—since all knowledge comes only from experience—unless women were first allowed to throw off their oppression and, over several generations, to *try* and do all the things that men were allowed to do.

What Is the Structure of These Readings?

Utilitarianism was written not as a scholarly treatise but as a sequence of articles, published in a monthly magazine, intended for the general educated reader: consequently, although *Utilitarianism* is philosophically weighty and—just below the surface—often quite difficult, its overall structure is pretty straightforward. Mill begins in Chapter 1 (not included in our selection) by making some general remarks, attacking moral intuitionism (the view that we can know ethical truths through immediate intellectual awareness or "intuition") and suggesting, among other things, that the principle of utilitarianism has always had a major tacit influence on moral beliefs. In Chapter 2 he defines utilitarianism, attempts to head off several common objections of the doctrine, and raises and responds to about ten possible objections to the theory (such as that utilitarianism is a godless morality worthy only of pigs, or alternatively that it sets an impracticably high standard which can never be attained by mere mortal human beings). In the third chapter Mill considers the question of moral motivation, and discusses how people might come to feel themselves

morally bound by the principles of utilitarianism: he argues that utilitarianism is grounded in the natural social feelings of humanity. In chapter 4 (not included here) Mill sets out to give a positive "proof" (insofar as that is possible) for the claim that utilitarianism is the correct moral theory: he argues, first, that one's own happiness is desirable to oneself; second that it follows that happiness is simply desirable in itself, no matter whose it is; and third that *only* happiness is intrinsically desirable. The final chapter of *Utilitarianism*, most of which is reprinted here, discusses the relationship between utilitarianism and justice.

On Liberty (1859) begins with a clarification of its subject matter: Mill tells us that he will be dealing with "civil or social liberty," rather than with "liberty of the will" [free will]. It might seem that democratic government automatically produces civil liberty, but Mill is concerned with the danger that democracy will open the way for "tyranny of the majority." His cure for this is his central principle of liberty: that the only actions that should be subject to civil control are those that harm others—not those that might harm only the agent himself. He goes on to add that this principle does not prevent attempting to persuade others; and lists some minor exceptions to his rule. The justification of this principle, he argues, is utilitarian.

Chapter 2 is primarily concerned with freedom of speech. The general idea here is that this will promote truth, by allowing free competition between diverse opinions, and by encouraging the habits of open-minded consideration of alternatives and rational defense of one's own position.

Chapter 3 treats freedom of action. Mill argues here that this will enhance happiness and human progress through the encouragement of experimentation and individuality.

Chapter 4 considers when social control is justified. Mill argues that it is when the aim is to prevent individuals from harming the interests of others that are considered rights, and to make sure individuals share the task of defending society and other individuals from harm. Otherwise, society should not interfere; and Mill argues carefully, and at length, that society is not justified in interfering when only the individual's own welfare is at stake.

Chapter 5 considers various applications of Mill's position.

Mill had been working for years with his wife Harriet Taylor on a book about the place of women in society when she died in 1858. He continued working on the book with her daughter Helen, finishing it a couple of years later. *The Subjection of Women* was published in 1869, under his name alone; nevertheless, he wrote "Whoever, either now or here-after, may think of me and my work I have done, must never forget that it is the product not of one intellect and conscience but of three, the least considerable of whom, and above all the least original, is the one whose name is attached to it."

The book is divided into four chapters. The first one introduces his position: that the "legal subordination of one sex to the other is wrong in itself, and now one of the chief hindrances to human improvement; and that it ought to be replaced by a principle of perfect equality, admitting no power or privilege on the one side, nor disability on the other." The fact that women have traditionally been subordinate to men gives no reason to think that this is a good social arrangement. In the second chapter he considers the marriage laws of nineteenth-century England, and argues for equality in the family. The third chapter considers employment, and argues for the equal competence of women in many jobs from which they have been traditionally, sometimes legally, excluded. In the last chapter, Mill considers what good—in utilitarian terms, what gains in human happiness for all—might result from the emancipation of women.

Representative Government was published in 1861. As in the case of all of his political works, his defense of that form of government is on utilitarian grounds: he argues that (in the ideal case, anyway) it is better than any alternative at encouraging individuality (always a primary concern for Mill). It does this by getting people actively involved in the political process, by exercising their intelligence and their socially directed moral concerns. He goes on to discuss his chief worry about representative democracy: that it can exercise tyranny of the majority, oppressing groups such as the blacks in America, the Catholics in Northern Ireland and the Protestants in Southern Ireland, the poor in all countries. He proposes various ways to ensure that they are adequately represented, endorsing for example the idea of proportional representation, and giving voting rights to women and the poor. Excerpts reprinted here apply utilitarian considerations to particular political issues: the secret ballot and nationalism.

Some Useful Background Information

i) Mill frames much of *Utilitarianism* in terms of a debate between two basic positions on the nature of morality: the "intuitive" school versus the "inductive" school. The intuitionists, whom Mill attacks, believed that ethical facts—though as real and as objectively true as any other—are *non-empirical*: that is, moral truths cannot be detected or confirmed through the activities of the five senses, but instead are known through a special faculty of "moral intuition." This philosophical position was represented in Mill's time by, among others, Sir William Hamilton (1788–1856) and William Whewell (1794–1866), and Mill's frequent criticism of the notion of "transcendental" moral facts is directed at intuitionists such as these. Mill considered intuitionism to be not only false but also a serious obstacle to social and moral progress: he thought the claim that (educated) human beings can "just tell" which moral principles are true, without needing or being able to cite *evidence* for these beliefs, tended merely to act as a disguise for prejudice and social conservatism. Mill's own moral methodology, by contrast, was what he called "inductive": he believed that *all* human knowledge, including ethical knowledge, comes ultimately from sense experience, and thus that moral judgments must be explained and defended by showing their connections to actual human experience.

ii) The notion of *happiness* is a very important part of Mill's moral philosophy, so it is useful to be clear about exactly what his theory of happiness was. Because of Mill's empiricist and associationist philosophical upbringing, the view of happiness it was most natural for him to adopt was a kind of *hedonism*. That is—in keeping with his emphasis on sense experience as the key to understanding knowledge and the mind—he thinks of happiness as a kind of *pleasurable mental state* (*hēdonē* is the classical Greek word for "pleasure"). For Mill, a happy life is, roughly, one filled with as many pleasurable sensations as possible, and as few painful ones.

Mill followed his philosophical predecessors in thinking that pleasurable experiences can be classified according to their duration and their intensity: thus rational people seeking their own happiness will aim to arrange their lives so that, over time, they will have more longer-lasting pleasures than short-lived ones, and more intense pleasures than dilute ones. For example, the initial painfulness of learning the violin, and the cost of missing a few TV sitcoms to practice, might be more than off-set by the intense and long-lasting pleasure of playing it well.[1] Furthermore, un-

---

[1] Mill's mentor Jeremy Bentham even proposed what he called a "felicific calculus": a mathematical system for measuring the total net quantity of pleasure that can be expected from a given course of action. Roughly, one calculates the balance of pleasure

like some of his philosophical forebears, Mill additionally distinguished between different *qualities* of pleasure: for Mill (unlike, say, Bentham), pleasure is not just one type of mental sensation but comes in "higher" and "lower" varieties. For example, according to Mill, the pleasant feeling that accompanies advanced intellectual or creative activity is a more valuable kind of pleasure—even if it were no more intense or long-lasting—than that which comes from physical satisfactions like eating and sex.

iii) One of Mill's philosophical presuppositions which is significant for his moral and social philosophy is *individualism*. That is, Mill assumed that individual persons are the basic unit of political analysis—that social structures are nothing more than constructions out of these individuals and are nothing over and above particular people and the relations between them. It follows from this that the analysis of social phenomena must be approached through a study of the actions and intentions of individuals, and similarly that social change is only possible through a large number of changes to individual people. What mattered to Mill was not "the general happiness" in some abstract sense, but the happiness of large numbers of individual human beings, and social institutions are to be seen as merely *instruments* for benefiting all these people. Furthermore, for Mill (influenced, as he was, by European Romanticism), there is a special kind of *value* in individuality: the particular uniqueness of each person is a thing to be treasured in itself.

iv) Some of the argumentation in *The Subjection of Women* may seem overly long or unnecessary for today's reader insisting on, and defending what often now seems to be obvious. It's important, though, to bear in mind that in Mill's day his claims were considered extremely radical, and he believed, with reason, that they all needed thorough justification.

Some Common Misconceptions

i) For Mill, mere *exemption* from pain is not itself a good—he holds that pleasure is the only good, and pain the only bad, and the overall goodness of states of affairs consists in the *balance* of pleasure over pain. The absence of pain is thus merely morally neutral, unless it is accompanied by the positive presence of pleasure.

ii) Mill is not arguing that people already *do* act in order to produce the greatest happiness of the greatest number: he is arguing that we *should*. He is not merely describing an already prevalent moral psychology, but arguing for a certain set of moral attitudes that he thinks we ought to cultivate in ourselves and in society in general.

iii) Utilitarianism is a theory of actions and not motives: it does not require that people *intend* to maximize utility, just that their behavior in fact does so. Mill insists that the criterion for what makes an action right is that it maximize utility; it does not follow from this that all our actions must have the conscious goal of maximizing utility. In fact, there is a good case to be made that a community where everyone is *trying* to maximize utility all the time would actually be self-defeating: it would be a much less happy society than it would be if people acted from other motivations. If this is right it would follow that, according to utilitarianism itself, it would be immoral to be always consciously trying to maximize utility. This is not a paradox or a problem for the theory however: it simply shows that there is a difference between the criterion of right action, and the best advice one can give moral agents for actually meeting that criterion.

Actions, however, do include within themselves two parts, according to Mill: an *intention* (which is different from a motive—it is not *why* the action is done but *what* the action is intended to achieve), and the action's *effects*. Mill sometimes appeals to differences of intention to differentiate between kinds of actions, but strictly speaking only the *effects* or consequences of an action can be morally relevant to the utilitarian.

iv) One common complaint against utilitarianism is that it makes *every* action, no matter how trivial, a moral issue: pretty much everything we do (e.g., getting a haircut) will have *some* effect on someone's pleasure and pain, and so it appears that we have a moral duty to ensure that we *always* act in such a way as to maximize the general happiness—and this, to say the least, would seem to put a bit of a strain on everyday life. However, even if this in fact is an implication of Mill's utilitarian theory, he himself did not intend to commit us to such an onerous regime. Here is a quote from another of Mill's works (*Auguste Comte and Positivism*): "It is not good that persons should be bound, by other people's opinion, to do everything that they would deserve praise for doing. There is a standard of altruism to

---

and pain that would accompany a particular outcome of your action (taking into account their intensity and duration), and then multiplies this number by the probability of that outcome actually occurring. This yields what Bentham called the "expected utility" of an action; the rational agent—according to Bentham—acts in a way which has the greatest expected utility.

which all should be required to come up, and a degree beyond which it is not obligatory, but meritorious."

v) Despite the way *Utilitarianism* can strike us today, in the aftermath of the grand and often massively destructive social engineering projects of the twentieth century, Mill was actually a bitter foe of what might be called "social constructivism." He emphatically did *not* see society as merely a machine built to help human beings to live together, a machine which can be broken into bits and reconstructed if it is not working optimally, and one where the rational, technical vision of collective planners should override individual initiative in the public good. On the contrary, Mill was very much an *individualist* and a humanist: he saw society as built from the actions of separate individual human beings and held that it is a kind of historical "consensus" which has created traditions and cultural practices which are continually but gradually evolving over time. Mill's vision for the reform of society, then, was not the imposition of central planning, but instead the gradual construction of a set of cultural norms—and especially, a progressive educational system—which will create human beings with the best possible moral character.

vi) Despite the obvious radical (for his day) feminism of *The Subjection of Women*, it is interesting that Mill is not entirely free of what some would count as sexist views about the place of women in the family and in society. He held, for example, that it can be assumed in general that a woman choosing to be married is voluntarily undertaking the management of the household and the raising of children as her first priority; and that it is in general undesirable for this reason that they work outside the home. And while he urged that women be accepted in roles traditionally assigned to men, he did not also suggest that men assume traditionally female roles.

How Influential Are These Writings?

John Stuart Mill did not *invent* utilitarianism (and never pretended to have done so): indeed, he was brought up by people who already considered themselves utilitarians. Mill's importance to utilitarianism is that he gave it what is arguably its single greatest and most influential formulation, in the essay *Utilitarianism*. It is this work which, ever since it was written, has been the starting point for both defenders and foes of utilitarianism. Furthermore, utilitarianism is itself a very important and influential moral theory: indeed, along with Marxism, it was arguably the

most prevalent moral theory among philosophers, economists, political scientists and other social theorists for much of the twentieth century (eclipsing the moral "intuitionism" which Mill saw as his theory's main competitor in 1861). Utilitarianism's influence has waned in some circles, having been subject to several very damaging philosophical attacks: but it is still uncontroversially one of the main three or four moral theories available today and continues to dominate economics.

Mill's book on the status of women, published in 1869, was strongly influential on radical thought, though of course it generated a great deal of opposition. The women's movement relied on the book for philosophical justification, and it has always been counted as a classic of liberal feminism.

On Liberty remains one of the central works of liberalism and its defense of freedom of thought and speech, and of individuality continues to inspire political theorists. Though Mill's form of liberalism has suffered repeated attacks and changes of fashion, few would deny its influence and importance.

◆ ◆ ◆ ◆

On Liberty (1859)

from *Chapter 1: Introductory*

[...]

The object of this Essay is to assert one very simple principle, as entitled to govern absolutely the dealings of society with the individual in the way of compulsion and control, whether the means used be physical force in the form of legal penalties, or the moral coercion of public opinion. That principle is, that the sole end for which mankind are warranted, individually or collectively in interfering with the liberty of action of any of their number, is self-protection. That the only purpose for which power can be rightfully exercised over any member of a civilized community, against his will, is to prevent harm to others. His own good, either physical or moral, is not a sufficient warrant. He cannot rightfully be compelled to do or forbear because it will be better for him to do so, because it will make him happier, because, in the opinions of others, to do so would be wise, or even right. These are good reasons for remonstrating with him, or reasoning with him, or persuading him, or entreating him, but not for compelling him, or visiting him with any evil, in case he do otherwise. To justify that, the conduct from which it is desired to deter him must be calculated to produce evil to some one else. The only part of the conduct of any one, for which he is amenable to society, is that which concerns others. In the part which merely concerns himself, his independence is, of right, absolute. Over himself, over his own body and mind, the individual is sovereign.

It is, perhaps, hardly necessary to say that this doctrine is meant to apply only to human beings in the maturity of their faculties. We are not speaking of children, or of young persons below the age which the law may fix as that of manhood or womanhood. Those who are still in a state to require being taken care of by others, must be protected against their own actions as well as against external injury. For the same reason, we may leave out of consideration those backward states of society in which the race itself may be considered as in its nonage.[1] The early difficulties in the way of spontaneous progress are so great, that there is seldom any choice of means for overcoming them; and a ruler full of the spirit of improvement is warranted in the use of any expedients that will attain an end, perhaps otherwise unattainable. Despotism is a legitimate mode of government in dealing with barbarians, provided the end be their improvement, and the means justified by actually effecting that end. Liberty, as a principle, has no application to any state of things anterior to the time when mankind have become capable of being improved by free and equal discussion. Until then, there is nothing for them but implicit obedience to an Akbar or a Charlemagne,[2] if they are so fortunate as to find one. But as soon as mankind have attained the capacity of being guided to their own improvement by conviction or persuasion (a period long since reached in all nations with whom we need here concern ourselves), compulsion, either in the direct form or in that of pains and penalties for non-compliance, is no longer admissible as a means to their own good, and justifiable only for the security of others.

It is proper to state that I forego any advantage which could be derived to my argument from the idea of abstract right as a thing independent of utility. I regard utility as the ultimate appeal on all ethical questions; but it must be utility in the largest sense, grounded on the permanent interests of man as a progressive being. Those interests, I contend, authorize the subjection of individual spontaneity to external control, only in respect to those actions of each, which concern the interest of other people. If any one does an act hurtful to others, there is a prima facie[3] case for punishing him, by law, or, where legal penalties are not safely applicable, by general disapprobation. There are also many positive acts for the benefit of others, which he may rightfully be compelled to perform; such as, to give evidence in a court of justice; to bear his fair share in the common defense, or in any other joint work necessary to the interest of the society of which he enjoys the protection; and to perform certain acts of individual beneficence, such as saving a fellow-creature's life, or interposing to protect the defenseless against ill-usage, things which whenever it is obviously a man's duty to do, he may rightfully be made responsible to society for not doing. A person may cause evil to others not only by his actions but by his inaction, and in neither case he is justly accountable to them for the injury. The latter case, it is true, requires a much more cautious exercise of compulsion than the former. To make any one answerable for doing evil to others, is the rule; to make him answerable for not preventing evil, is, comparatively speaking, the exception. Yet there are many cases clear enough and grave enough to justify that exception. In all things which regard the external relations of the individual, he is de jure[4] amenable to those whose interests are concerned, and if need be, to society as their protector. There are often good reasons for not holding him to the responsibility; but these reasons must arise from the special expediencies of the case: either because it is a kind of case in which he is on the whole likely to act better, when left to his own discretion, than when controlled in any way in which society have it in their power to control him; or because the attempt to exercise control would produce other evils, greater than those which it would prevent. When such reasons as these preclude the enforcement of responsibility, the conscience of the agent himself should step into the vacant judgment-seat, and protect those interests of others which have no external protection; judging himself all the more rigidly, because the case does not admit of his being made accountable to the judgment of his fellow-creatures.

---

1 *in its nonage* Below the age of responsibility.
2 *Akbar ... Charlemagne* Great, widely respected, historically important, but autocratic rulers—Akbar of Northern India at the end of the sixteenth century, Charlemagne of much of Europe, late eighth, early ninth centuries.

3 *prima facie* [Latin: on its face] At first sight.
4 *de jure* By law.

But there is a sphere of action in which society, as distinguished from the individual, has, if any, only an indirect interest; comprehending all that portion of a person's life and conduct which affects only himself, or, if it also affects others, only with their free, voluntary, and undeceived consent and participation. When I say only himself, I mean directly, and in the first instance: for whatever affects himself, may affect others through himself; and the objection which may be grounded on this contingency, will receive consideration in the sequel. This, then, is the appropriate region of human liberty. It comprises, first, the inward domain of consciousness; demanding liberty of conscience, in the most comprehensive sense; liberty of thought and feeling; absolute freedom of opinion and sentiment on all subjects, practical or speculative, scientific, moral, or theological. The liberty of expressing and publishing opinions may seem to fall under a different principle, since it belongs to that part of the conduct of an individual which concerns other people; but, being almost of as much importance as the liberty of thought itself, and resting in great part on the same reasons, is practically inseparable from it. Secondly, the principle requires liberty of tastes and pursuits; of framing the plan of our life to suit our own character; of doing as we like, subject to such consequences as may follow; without impediment from our fellow-creatures, so long as what we do does not harm them even though they should think our conduct foolish, perverse, or wrong. Thirdly, from this liberty of each individual, follows the liberty, within the same limits, of combination among individuals; freedom to unite, for any purpose not involving harm to others: the persons combining being supposed to be of full age, and not forced or deceived.

No society in which these liberties are not, on the whole, respected, is free, whatever may be its form of government; and none is completely free in which they do not exist absolute and unqualified. The only freedom which deserves the name, is that of pursuing our own good in our own way, so long as we do not attempt to deprive others of theirs, or impede their efforts to obtain it. Each is the proper guardian of his own health, whether bodily, or mental or spiritual. Mankind are greater gainers by suffering each other to live as seems good to themselves, than by compelling each to live as seems good to the rest.

[...]

It will be convenient for the argument, if, instead of at once entering upon the general thesis, we confine ourselves

in the first instance to a single branch of it, on which the principle here stated is, if not fully, yet to a certain point, recognized by the current opinions. This one branch is the Liberty of Thought: from which it is impossible to separate the cognate[1] liberty of speaking and of writing. Although these liberties, to some considerable amount, form part of the political morality of all countries which profess religious toleration and free institutions, the grounds, both philosophical and practical, on which they rest, are perhaps not so familiar to the general mind, nor so thoroughly appreciated by many even of the leaders of opinion, as might have been expected. Those grounds, when rightly understood, are of much wider application than to only one division of the subject, and a thorough consideration of this part of the question will be found the best introduction to the remainder. Those to whom nothing which I am about to say will be new, may therefore, I hope, excuse me, if on a subject which for now three centuries has been so often discussed, I venture on one discussion more.

from *Chapter 2: Of the Liberty of Thought and Discussion*

The time, it is to be hoped, is gone by when any defense would be necessary of the "liberty of the press" as one of the securities against corrupt or tyrannical government. No argument, we may suppose, can now be needed, against permitting a legislature or an executive, not identified in interest with the people, to prescribe opinions to them, and determine what doctrines or what arguments they shall be allowed to hear. This aspect of the question, besides, has been so often and so triumphantly enforced by preceding writers, that it needs not be specially insisted on in this place. Though the law of England, on the subject of the press, is as servile to this day as it was in the time of the Tudors, there is little danger of its being actually put in force against political discussion, except during some temporary panic, when fear of insurrection drives ministers and judges from their propriety;[2] and, speaking generally, it is

---

1 *cognate* Related.
2 *gloss word(s)* [Mill's footnote] These words had scarcely been written, when, as if to give them an emphatic contradiction, occurred the Government Press Prosecutions of 1858. That ill-judged interference with the liberty of public discussion has not, however, induced me to alter a single word in the text, nor has it at all weakened my conviction that, moments of panic excepted, the era of pains and penalties for political discussion has, in our

not, in constitutional countries, to be apprehended that the government, whether completely responsible to the people or not, will often attempt to control the expression of opinion, except when in doing so it makes itself the organ of the general intolerance of the public. Let us suppose, therefore, that the government is entirely at one with the people, and never thinks of exerting any power of coercion unless in agreement with what it conceives to be their voice. But I deny the right of the people to exercise such coercion, either by themselves or by their government. The power itself is illegitimate. The best government has no more title to it than the worst. It is as noxious, or more noxious, when exerted in accordance with public opinion, than when in opposition to it. If all mankind minus one, were of one opinion, and only one person were of the contrary opinion, mankind would be no more justified in silencing that one person, than he, if he had the power, would be justified in silencing mankind. Were an opinion a personal possession of no value except to the owner; if to be obstructed in the enjoyment of it were simply a private injury, it would make some difference whether the injury was inflicted only on a few persons or on many. But the peculiar evil of silencing the expression of an opinion is, that it is robbing the human race; posterity as well as the existing generation; those who dissent from the opinion, still more than those who hold it.

own country, passed away. For, in the first place, the prosecutions were not persisted in; and in the second, they were never, properly speaking, political prosecutions. The offence charged was not that of criticizing institutions, or the acts or persons of rulers, but of circulating what was deemed an immoral doctrine, the lawfulness of Tyrannicide [assassination of a tyrant].

If the arguments of the present chapter are of any validity, there ought to exist the fullest liberty of professing and discussing, as a matter of ethical conviction, any doctrine, however immoral it may be considered. It would, therefore, be irrelevant and out of place to examine here, whether the doctrine of Tyrannicide deserves that title. I shall content myself with saying, that the subject has been at all times one of the open questions of morals, that the act of a private citizen in striking down a criminal, who, by raising himself above the law, has placed himself beyond the reach of legal punishment or control, has been accounted by whole nations, and by some of the best and wisest of men, not a crime, but an act of exalted virtue and that, right or wrong, it is not of the nature of assassination but of civil war. As such, I hold that the instigation to it, in a specific case, may be a proper subject of punishment, but only if an overt act has followed, and at least a probable connection can be established between the act and the instigation. Even then it is not a foreign government, but the very government assailed, which alone, in the exercise of self-defense, can legitimately punish attacks directed against its own existence.

If the opinion is right, they are deprived of the opportunity of exchanging error for truth: if wrong, they lose, what is almost as great a benefit, the clearer perception and livelier impression of truth, produced by its collision with error.

It is necessary to consider separately these two hypotheses, each of which has a distinct branch of the argument corresponding to it. We can never be sure that the opinion we are endeavoring to stifle is a false opinion; and if we were sure, stifling it would be an evil still.

First: the opinion which it is attempted to suppress by authority may possibly be true. Those who desire to suppress it, of course deny its truth; but they are not infallible. They have no authority to decide the question for all mankind, and exclude every other person from the means of judging. To refuse a hearing to an opinion, because they are sure that it is false, is to assume that their certainty is the same thing as absolute certainty. All silencing of discussion is an assumption of infallibility. Its condemnation may be allowed to rest on this common argument, not the worse for being common.

Unfortunately for the good sense of mankind, the fact of their fallibility is far from carrying the weight in their practical judgment, which is always allowed to it in theory; for while every one well knows himself to be fallible, few think it necessary to take any precautions against their own fallibility, or admit the supposition that any opinion of which they feel very certain, may be one of the examples of the error to which they acknowledge themselves to be liable. Absolute princes, or others who are accustomed to unlimited deference, usually feel this complete confidence in their own opinions on nearly all subjects. People more happily situated, who sometimes hear their opinions disputed, and are not wholly unused to be set right when they are wrong, place the same unbounded reliance only on such of their opinions as are shared by all who surround them, or to whom they habitually defer: for in proportion to a man's want of confidence in his own solitary judgment, does he usually repose, with implicit trust, on the infallibility of "the world" in general. And the world, to each individual, means the part of it with which he comes in contact; his party, his sect, his church, his class of society: the man may be called, by comparison, almost liberal and large-minded to whom it means anything so comprehensive as his own country or his own age. Nor is his faith in this collective authority at all shaken by his being aware that other ages, countries, sects, churches, classes, and parties have thought, and even now think, the exact reverse.

He devolves upon[1] his own world the responsibility of being in the right against the dissentient[2] worlds of other people; and it never troubles him that mere accident has decided which of these numerous worlds is the object of his reliance, and that the same causes which make him a Churchman[3] in London, would have made him a Buddhist or a Confucian in Pekin.[4] Yet it is as evident in itself as any amount of argument can make it, that ages are no more infallible than individuals; every age having held many opinions which subsequent ages have deemed not only false but absurd; and it is as certain that many opinions, now general, will be rejected by future ages, as it is that many, once general, are rejected by the present.

The objection likely to be made to this argument, would probably take some such form as the following. There is no greater assumption of infallibility in forbidding the propagation of error, than in any other thing which is done by public authority on its own judgment and responsibility. Judgment is given to men that they may use it. Because it may be used erroneously, are men to be told that they ought not to use it at all? To prohibit what they think pernicious, is not claiming exemption from error, but fulfilling the duty incumbent on them, although fallible, of acting on their conscientious conviction. If we were never to act on our opinions, because those opinions may be wrong, we should leave all our interests uncared for, and all our duties unperformed. An objection which applies to all conduct can be no valid objection to any conduct in particular.

It is the duty of governments, and of individuals, to form the truest opinions they can; to form them carefully, and never impose them upon others unless they are quite sure of being right. But when they are sure (such reasoners may say), it is not conscientiousness but cowardice to shrink from acting on their opinions, and allow doctrines which they honestly think dangerous to the welfare of mankind, either in this life or in another, to be scattered abroad without restraint, because other people, in less enlightened times, have persecuted opinions now believed to be true. Let us take care, it may be said, not to make the same mistake: but governments and nations have made mistakes in other things, which are not denied to be fit subjects for the exercise of authority: they have laid on bad taxes, made unjust wars. Ought we therefore to lay on no taxes, and, under whatever provocation, make no wars? Men, and governments, must act to the best of their ability. There is no such thing as absolute certainty, but there is assurance sufficient for the purposes of human life. We may, and must, assume our opinion to be true for the guidance of our own conduct: and it is assuming no more when we forbid bad men to pervert society by the propagation of opinions which we regard as false and pernicious.

I answer, that it is assuming very much more. There is the greatest difference between presuming an opinion to be true, because, with every opportunity for contesting it, it has not been refuted, and assuming its truth for the purpose of not permitting its refutation. Complete liberty of contradicting and disproving our opinion, is the very condition which justifies us in assuming its truth for purposes of action; and on no other terms can a being with human faculties have any rational assurance of being right.

When we consider either the history of opinion, or the ordinary conduct of human life, to what is it to be ascribed that the one and the other are no worse than they are? Not certainly to the inherent force of the human understanding; for, on any matter not self-evident, there are ninety-nine persons totally incapable of judging of it, for one who is capable; and the capacity of the hundredth person is only comparative; for the majority of the eminent men of every past generation held many opinions now known to be erroneous, and did or approved numerous things which no one will now justify. Why is it, then, that there is on the whole a preponderance[5] among mankind of rational opinions and rational conduct? If there really is this preponderance—which there must be, unless human affairs are, and have always been, in an almost desperate state—it is owing to a quality of the human mind, the source of everything respectable in man, either as an intellectual or as a moral being, namely, that his errors are corrigible.[6] He is capable of rectifying his mistakes by discussion and experience. Not by experience alone. There must be discussion, to show how experience is to be interpreted. Wrong opinions and practices gradually yield to fact and argument: but facts and arguments, to produce any effect on the mind, must be brought before it. Very few facts are able to tell their own story, without comments to bring out their meaning. The whole strength and value, then, of human judgment, depending on the one property, that it can be set right

---

1   *devolves upon*   Gives to.
2   *dissentient*   Disagreeing.
3   *Churchman*   Member of the Church of England.
4   *Pekin*   Beijing.

5   *preponderance*   Majority.
6   *corrigible*   Capable of being corrected.

when it is wrong, reliance can be placed on it only when the means of setting it right are kept constantly at hand. In the case of any person whose judgment is really deserving of confidence, how has it become so? Because he has kept his mind open to criticism of his opinions and conduct. Because it has been his practice to listen to all that could be said against him; to profit by as much of it as was just, and expound to himself, and upon occasion to others, the fallacy of what was fallacious. Because he has felt, that the only way in which a human being can make some approach to knowing the whole of a subject, is by hearing what can be said about it by persons of every variety of opinion, and studying all modes in which it can be looked at by every character of mind. No wise man ever acquired his wisdom in any mode but this; nor is it in the nature of human intellect to become wise in any other manner. The steady habit of correcting and completing his own opinion by collating[1] it with those of others, so far from causing doubt and hesitation in carrying it into practice, is the only stable foundation for a just reliance on it: for, being cognizant of all that can, at least obviously, be said against him, and having taken up his position against all gainsayers[2] knowing that he has sought for objections and difficulties, instead of avoiding them, and has shut out no light which can be thrown upon the subject from any quarter—he has a right to think his judgment better than that of any person, or any multitude, who have not gone through a similar process.

[…]

In the present age—which has been described as "destitute of faith, but terrified at skepticism,"—in which people feel sure, not so much that their opinions are true, as that they should not know what to do without them—the claims of an opinion to be protected from public attack are rested not so much on its truth, as on its importance to society. There are, it is alleged, certain beliefs, so useful, not to say indispensable to well-being, that it is as much the duty of governments to uphold those beliefs, as to protect any other of the interests of society. In a case of such necessity, and so directly in the line of their duty, something less than infallibility may, it is maintained, warrant, and even bind, governments, to act on their own opinion, confirmed by the general opinion of mankind. It is also often argued, and still oftener thought, that none but bad men would desire

to weaken these salutary beliefs; and there can be nothing wrong, it is thought, in restraining bad men, and prohibiting what only such men would wish to practice. This mode of thinking makes the justification of restraints on discussion not a question of the truth of doctrines, but of their usefulness; and flatters itself by that means to escape the responsibility of claiming to be an infallible judge of opinions. But those who thus satisfy themselves, do not perceive that the assumption of infallibility is merely shifted from one point to another. The usefulness of an opinion is itself matter of opinion: as disputable, as open to discussion and requiring discussion as much, as the opinion itself. There is the same need of an infallible judge of opinions to decide an opinion to be noxious, as to decide it to be false, unless the opinion condemned has full opportunity of defending itself. And it will not do to say that the heretic may be allowed to maintain the utility or harmlessness of his opinion, though forbidden to maintain its truth. The truth of an opinion is part of its utility. If we would know whether or not it is desirable that a proposition should be believed, is it possible to exclude the consideration of whether or not it is true? In the opinion, not of bad men, but of the best men, no belief which is contrary to truth can be really useful: and can you prevent such men from urging that plea, when they are charged with culpability for denying some doctrine which they are told is useful, but which they believe to be false? Those who are on the side of received opinions, never fail to take all possible advantage of this plea; you do not find them handling the question of utility as if it could be completely abstracted from that of truth: on the contrary, it is, above all, because their doctrine is "the truth," that the knowledge or the belief of it is held to be so indispensable. There can be no fair discussion of the question of usefulness, when an argument so vital may be employed on one side, but not on the other. And in point of fact, when law or public feeling do not permit the truth of an opinion to be disputed, they are just as little tolerant of a denial of its usefulness. The utmost they allow is an extenuation of its absolute necessity or of the positive guilt of rejecting it.

In order more fully to illustrate the mischief of denying a hearing to opinions because we, in our own judgment, have condemned them, it will be desirable to fix down the discussion to a concrete case; and I choose, by preference, the cases which are least favorable to me—in which the argument against freedom of opinion, both on the score of truth and on that of utility, is considered the strongest. Let the opinions impugned be the belief in a God and in a future

---

1   *collating* Comparing.
2   *gainsayers* Those who contradict (him).

state, or any of the commonly received doctrines of morality. To fight the battle on such ground, gives a great advantage to an unfair antagonist; since he will be sure to say (and many who have no desire to be unfair will say it internally), Are these the doctrines which you do not deem sufficiently certain to be taken under the protection of law? Is the belief in a God one of the opinions, to feel sure of which, you hold to be assuming infallibility? But I must be permitted to observe, that it is not the feeling sure of a doctrine (be it what it may) which I call an assumption of infallibility. It is the undertaking to decide that question for others, without allowing them to hear what can be said on the contrary side. And I denounce and reprobate[1] this pretension not the less, if put forth on the side of my most solemn convictions. However positive any one's persuasion may be, not only of the falsity, but of the pernicious consequences—not only of the pernicious consequences, but (to adopt expressions which I altogether condemn) the immorality and impiety of an opinion; yet if, in pursuance of that private judgment, though backed by the public judgment of his country or his contemporaries, he prevents the opinion from being heard in its defense, he assumes infallibility. And so far from the assumption being less objectionable or less dangerous because the opinion is called immoral or impious, this is the case of all others in which it is most fatal. These are exactly the occasions on which the men of one generation commit those dreadful mistakes which excite the astonishment and horror of posterity. It is among such that we find the instances memorable in history, when the arm of the law has been employed to root out the best men and the noblest doctrines; with deplorable success as to the men, though some of the doctrines have survived to be (as if in mockery) invoked, in defense of similar conduct towards those who dissent from them, or from their received interpretation.

Mankind can hardly be too often reminded, that there was once a man named Socrates, between whom and the legal authorities and public opinion of his time, there took place a memorable collision. Born in an age and country abounding in individual greatness, this man has been handed down to us by those who best knew both him and the age, as the most virtuous man in it; while we know him as the head and prototype of all subsequent teachers of virtue, the source equally of the lofty inspiration of Plato and the judicious utilitarianism of Aristotle, "i maestri di color che sanno,"[2]

the two headsprings of ethical as of all other philosophy. This acknowledged master of all the eminent thinkers who have since lived—whose fame, still growing after more than two thousand years, all but outweighs the whole remainder of the names which make his native city illustrious—was put to death by his countrymen, after a judicial conviction, for impiety and immorality. Impiety, in denying the gods recognized by the State; indeed his accuser asserted (see the "Apologia"[3]) that he believed in no gods at all. Immorality, in being, by his doctrines and instructions, a "corrupter of youth." Of these charges the tribunal, there is every ground for believing, honestly found him guilty, and condemned the man who probably of all then born had deserved best of mankind, to be put to death as a criminal.

[...]

Let us now pass to the second division of the argument, and dismissing the Supposition that any of the received opinions may be false, let us assume them to be true, and examine into the worth of the manner in which they are likely to be held, when their truth is not freely and openly canvassed. However unwillingly a person who has a strong opinion may admit the possibility that his opinion may be false, he ought to be moved by the consideration that however true it may be, if it is not fully, frequently, and fearlessly discussed, it will be held as a dead dogma, not a living truth.

There is a class of persons (happily not quite so numerous as formerly) who think it enough if a person assents undoubtingly to what they think true, though he has no knowledge whatever of the grounds of the opinion, and could not make a tenable defense of it against the most superficial objections. Such persons, if they can once get their creed taught from authority, naturally think that no good, and some harm, comes of its being allowed to be questioned. Where their influence prevails, they make it nearly impossible for the received opinion to be rejected wisely and considerately, though it may still be rejected rashly and ignorantly; for to shut out discussion entirely is seldom possible, and when it once gets in, beliefs not grounded on conviction are apt to give way before the slightest semblance of an argument. Waiving, however, this possibility—assum-

---

1   *reprobate* Condemn.
2   *i maestri di color che sanno* Italian: "The teachers of those who know." Quotation from Dante's *Inferno* IV, slightly adapted:

Dante's "il maestro di color che sanno" refers to one teacher only (Aristotle).
3   "*Apologia*" Plato's dialogue the *Apology* puts forward Socrates' defense against these charges. (The word "apology" is used here in an archaic sense, meaning a formal defense of one's views or actions, not an expression of regret for one's mistakes.)

ing that the true opinion abides in the mind, but abides as a prejudice, a belief independent of, and proof against, argument—this is not the way in which truth ought to be held by a rational being. This is not knowing the truth. Truth, thus held, is but one superstition the more, accidentally clinging to the words which enunciate a truth.

If the intellect and judgment of mankind ought to be cultivated, a thing which Protestants at least do not deny, on what can these faculties be more appropriately exercised by any one, than on the things which concern him so much that it is considered necessary for him to hold opinions on them? If the cultivation of the understanding consists in one thing more than in another, it is surely in learning the grounds of one's own opinions. Whatever people believe, on subjects on which it is of the first importance to believe rightly, they ought to be able to defend against at least the common objections. But, some one may say, "Let them be taught the grounds of their opinions. It does not follow that opinions must be merely parroted because they are never heard controverted.[1] Persons who learn geometry do not simply commit the theorems to memory, but understand and learn likewise the demonstrations;[2] and it would be absurd to say that they remain ignorant of the grounds of geometrical truths, because they never hear any one deny, and attempt to disprove them." Undoubtedly: and such teaching suffices on a subject like mathematics, where there is nothing at all to be said on the wrong side of the question. The peculiarity of the evidence of mathematical truths is, that all the argument is on one side. There are no objections, and no answers to objections. But on every subject on which difference of opinion is possible, the truth depends on a balance to be struck between two sets of conflicting reasons. Even in natural philosophy,[3] there is always some other explanation possible of the same facts; some geocentric theory instead of heliocentric,[4] some phlogiston instead of oxygen;[5] and it has to be shown why that other theory cannot be the true one: and until this is shown and until we know how it is shown, we do not understand the grounds of our opinion. But when we turn to subjects infinitely more complicated, to morals, religion, politics, social relations, and the business of life, three-fourths of the arguments for every disputed opinion consist in dispelling the appearances which favor some opinion different from it. The greatest orator, save one, of antiquity, has left it on record that he always studied his adversary's case with as great, if not with still greater, intensity than even his own. What Cicero practiced as the means of forensic[6] success, requires to be imitated by all who study any subject in order to arrive at the truth. He who knows only his own side of the case, knows little of that. His reasons may be good, and no one may have been able to refute them. But if he is equally unable to refute the reasons on the opposite side; if he does not so much as know what they are, he has no ground for preferring either opinion. The rational position for him would be suspension of judgment, and unless he contents himself with that, he is either led by authority, or adopts, like the generality of the world, the side to which he feels most inclination. Nor is it enough that he should hear the arguments of adversaries from his own teachers, presented as they state them, and accompanied by what they offer as refutations. This is not the way to do justice to the arguments, or bring them into real contact with his own mind. He must be able to hear them from persons who actually believe them; who defend them in earnest, and do their very utmost for them. He must know them in their most plausible and persuasive form; he must feel the whole force of the difficulty which the true view of the subject has to encounter and dispose of, else he will never really possess himself of the portion of truth which meets and removes that difficulty. Ninety-nine in a hundred of what are called educated men are in this condition, even of those who can argue fluently for their opinions. Their conclusion may be true, but it might be false for anything they know: they have never thrown themselves into the mental position of those who think differently from them, and considered what such persons may have to say; and consequently they do not, in any proper sense of the word, know the doctrine which they themselves profess. They do not know those parts of it which explain and justify the remainder; the considerations which show that a fact which seemingly conflicts with another is reconcilable with it, or that, of two apparently

---

1   *controverted*   Disputed by reasoning.

2   *theorems ... demonstrations*   The theorems of geometry are its accepted truths that can be proven by demonstrations.

3   *natural philosophy*   Natural science.

4   *geocentric ... heliocentric*   The first is the theory in astronomy which places the earth at the center of the system including sun, moon, planets, and stars; the second has planets revolving around the sun as the center.

5   *phlogiston ... oxygen*   The first is a hypothetical substance—the essence of fire—supposed to be given off when something burned. Modern theory sees burning instead not as giving off anything, but rather as combining fuel with oxygen.

6   *forensic*   Debating.

strong reasons, one and not the other ought to be preferred. All that part of the truth which turns the scale, and decides the judgment of a completely informed mind, they are strangers to; nor is it ever really known, but to those who have attended equally and impartially to both sides, and endeavored to see the reasons of both in the strongest light. So essential is this discipline to a real understanding of moral and human subjects, that if opponents of all important truths do not exist, it is indispensable to imagine them and supply them with the strongest arguments which the most skilful devil's advocate[1] can conjure up.

To abate the force of these considerations, an enemy of free discussion may be supposed to say, that there is no necessity for mankind in general to know and understand all that can be said against or for their opinions by philosophers and theologians. That it is not needful for common men to be able to expose all the misstatements or fallacies of an ingenious opponent. That it is enough if there is always somebody capable of answering them, so that nothing likely to mislead uninstructed persons remains unrefuted. That simple minds, having been taught the obvious grounds of the truths inculcated on them, may trust to authority for the rest, and being aware that they have neither knowledge nor talent to resolve every difficulty which can be raised, may repose in the assurance that all those which have been raised have been or can be answered, by those who are specially trained to the task.

Conceding to this view of the subject the utmost that can be claimed for it by those most easily satisfied with the amount of understanding of truth which ought to accompany the belief of it; even so, the argument for free discussion is no way weakened. For even this doctrine acknowledges that mankind ought to have a rational assurance that all objections have been satisfactorily answered; and how are they to be answered if that which requires to be answered is not spoken? or how can the answer be known to be satisfactory, if the objectors have no opportunity of showing that it is unsatisfactory? If not the public, at least the philosophers and theologians who are to resolve the difficulties, must make themselves familiar with those difficulties in their most puzzling form; and this cannot be accomplished unless they are freely stated, and placed in the most advantageous light which they admit of. The Catholic Church has its own way of dealing with this embarrassing problem. It makes a broad separation between those who can be permitted to receive its doctrines on conviction, and those who must accept them on trust. Neither, indeed, are allowed any choice as to what they will accept; but the clergy, such at least as can be fully confided in, may admissibly and meritoriously make themselves acquainted with the arguments of opponents, in order to answer them, and may, therefore, read heretical books; the laity, not unless by special permission, hard to be obtained. This discipline recognizes a knowledge of the enemy's case as beneficial to the teachers, but finds means, consistent with this, of denying it to the rest of the world: thus giving to the elite more mental culture, though not more mental freedom, than it allows to the mass. By this device it succeeds in obtaining the kind of mental superiority which its purposes require; for though culture without freedom never made a large and liberal mind, it can make a clever *nisi prius*[2] advocate of a cause. But in countries professing Protestantism, this resource is denied; since Protestants hold, at least in theory, that the responsibility for the choice of a religion must be borne by each for himself, and cannot be thrown off upon teachers. Besides, in the present state of the world, it is practically impossible that writings which are read by the instructed can be kept from the uninstructed. If the teachers of mankind are to be cognizant of all that they ought to know, everything must be free to be written and published without restraint.

If, however, the mischievous operation of the absence of free discussion, when the received opinions are true, were confined to leaving men ignorant of the grounds of those opinions, it might be thought that this, if an intellectual, is no moral evil, and does not affect the worth of the opinions, regarded in their influence on the character. The fact, however, is, that not only the grounds of the opinion are forgotten in the absence of discussion, but too often the meaning of the opinion itself. The words which convey it, cease to suggest ideas, or suggest only a small portion of those they were originally employed to communicate. Instead of a vivid conception and a living belief, there remain

1　*devil's advocate* One who takes a position for the sake of argument, not necessarily believed. (Originally this term was applied to the person involved in hearings considering conferring sainthood in the Church whose job it was to present a case, as strong as possible, against the candidate, with the object of making sure that a positive decision was without defect.)

2　*nisi prius* [Latin: unless before] Refers literally to certain local court proceedings in England: trials were to take place centrally, at Westminster, *unless beforehand* they were tried locally. Figuratively Mill here is calling the Catholic intellectual elite the "*nisi prius*" experts—the court where issues get settled first.

only a few phrases retained by rote; or, if any part, the shell and husk only of the meaning is retained, the finer essence being lost. The great chapter in human history which this fact occupies and fills, cannot be too earnestly studied and meditated on.

It is illustrated in the experience of almost all ethical doctrines and religious creeds. They are all full of meaning and vitality to those who originate them, and to the direct disciples of the originators. Their meaning continues to be felt in undiminished strength, and is perhaps brought out into even fuller consciousness, so long as the struggle lasts to give the doctrine or creed an ascendancy over other creeds. At last it either prevails, and becomes the general opinion, or its progress stops; it keeps possession of the ground it has gained, but ceases to spread further. When either of these results has become apparent, controversy on the subject flags, and gradually dies away. The doctrine has taken its place, if not as a received opinion, as one of the admitted sects or divisions of opinion: those who hold it have generally inherited, not adopted it; and conversion from one of these doctrines to another, being now an exceptional fact, occupies little place in the thoughts of their professors.[1] Instead of being, as at first, constantly on the alert either to defend themselves against the world, or to bring the world over to them, they have subsided into acquiescence, and neither listen, when they can help it, to arguments against their creed, nor trouble dissentients[2] (if there be such) with arguments in its favor. From this time may usually be dated the decline in the living power of the doctrine. We often hear the teachers of all creeds lamenting the difficulty of keeping up in the minds of believers a lively apprehension of the truth which they nominally recognize, so that it may penetrate the feelings, and acquire a real mastery over the conduct. No such difficulty is complained of while the creed is still fighting for its existence: even the weaker combatants then know and feel what they are fighting for, and the difference between it and other doctrines; and in that period of every creed's existence, not a few persons may be found, who have realized its fundamental principles in all the forms of thought, have weighed and considered them in all their important bearings, and have experienced the full effect on the character, which belief in that creed ought to produce in a mind thoroughly imbued with it. But when it has come to be an hereditary creed, and to be received passively, not act-

ively—when the mind is no longer compelled, in the same degree as at first, to exercise its vital powers on the questions which its belief presents to it, there is a progressive tendency to forget all of the belief except the formularies,[3] or to give it a dull and torpid assent, as if accepting it on trust dispensed with the necessity of realizing it in consciousness, or testing it by personal experience; until it almost ceases to connect itself at all with the inner life of the human being. Then are seen the cases, so frequent in this age of the world as almost to form the majority, in which the creed remains as it were outside the mind, encrusting and petrifying it against all other influences addressed to the higher parts of our nature; manifesting its power by not suffering any fresh and living conviction to get in, but itself doing nothing for the mind or heart, except standing sentinel over them to keep them vacant.

[…]

But what! (it may be asked) Is the absence of unanimity an indispensable condition of true knowledge? Is it necessary that some part of mankind should persist in error, to enable any to realize the truth? Does a belief cease to be real and vital as soon as it is generally received—and is a proposition never thoroughly understood and felt unless some doubt of it remains? As soon as mankind have unanimously accepted a truth, does the truth perish within them? The highest aim and best result of improved intelligence, it has hitherto been thought, is to unite mankind more and more in the acknowledgment of all important truths: and does the intelligence only last as long as it has not achieved its object? Do the fruits of conquest perish by the very completeness of the victory?

I affirm no such thing. As mankind improve, the number of doctrines which are no longer disputed or doubted will be constantly on the increase: and the well-being of mankind may almost be measured by the number and gravity of the truths which have reached the point of being uncontested. The cessation, on one question after another, of serious controversy, is one of the necessary incidents of the consolidation of opinion; a consolidation as salutary in the case of true opinions, as it is dangerous and noxious when the opinions are erroneous. But though this gradual narrowing of the bounds of diversity of opinion is necessary in both senses of the term, being at once inevitable and indispensable, we are not therefore obliged to conclude

1   *professors*   Those who profess the doctrine—i.e., claim belief in it.
2   *dissentients*   Those who express disagreement.

3   *formularies*   Fixed formulas.

that all its consequences must be beneficial. The loss of so important an aid to the intelligent and living apprehension of a truth, as is afforded by the necessity of explaining it to, or defending it against, opponents, though not sufficient to outweigh, is no trifling drawback from, the benefit of its universal recognition. Where this advantage can no longer be had, I confess I should like to see the teachers of mankind endeavoring to provide a substitute for it; some contrivance for making the difficulties of the question as present to the learner's consciousness, as if they were pressed upon him by a dissentient champion, eager for his conversion.

But instead of seeking contrivances for this purpose, they have lost those they formerly had. The Socratic dialectics,[1] so magnificently exemplified in the dialogues of Plato, were a contrivance of this description. They were essentially a negative discussion of the great questions of philosophy and life, directed with consummate skill to the purpose of convincing any one who had merely adopted the commonplaces of received opinion, that he did not understand the subject—that he as yet attached no definite meaning to the doctrines he professed; in order that, becoming aware of his ignorance, he might be put in the way to attain a stable belief, resting on a clear apprehension both of the meaning of doctrines and of their evidence. The school disputations of the Middle Ages had a somewhat similar object. They were intended to make sure that the pupil understood his own opinion, and (by necessary correlation) the opinion opposed to it, and could enforce the grounds of the one and confute[2] those of the other. These last-mentioned contests had indeed the incurable defect, that the premises appealed to were taken from authority, not from reason; and, as a discipline to the mind, they were in every respect inferior to the powerful dialectics which formed the intellects of the "*Socratici viri*":[3] but the modern mind owes far more to both than it is generally willing to admit, and the present modes of education contain nothing which in the smallest degree supplies the place either of the one or of the other. A person who derives all his instruction from teachers or books, even if he escape the besetting temptation of contenting himself with cram,[4] is under no compulsion to hear both sides; accordingly it is far from a frequent accomplishment, even among thinkers, to know both sides; and the weakest part

of what everybody says in defense of his opinion, is what he intends as a reply to antagonists. It is the fashion of the present time to disparage negative logic—that which points out weaknesses in theory or errors in practice, without establishing positive truths. Such negative criticism would indeed be poor enough as an ultimate result; but as a means to attaining any positive knowledge or conviction worthy the name, it cannot be valued too highly; and until people are again systematically trained to it, there will be few great thinkers, and a low general average of intellect, in any but the mathematical and physical departments of speculation. On any other subject no one's opinions deserve the name of knowledge, except so far as he has either had forced upon him by others, or gone through of himself, the same mental process which would have been required of him in carrying on an active controversy with opponents. That, therefore, which when absent, it is so indispensable, but so difficult, to create, how worse than absurd is it to forego, when spontaneously offering itself! If there are any persons who contest a received opinion, or who will do so if law or opinion will let them, let us thank them for it, open our minds to listen to them, and rejoice that there is some one to do for us what we otherwise ought, if we have any regard for either the certainty or the vitality of our convictions, to do with much greater labor for ourselves.

It still remains to speak of one of the principal causes which make diversity of opinion advantageous, and will continue to do so until mankind shall have entered a stage of intellectual advancement which at present seems at an incalculable distance. We have hitherto considered only two possibilities: that the received opinion may be false, and some other opinion, consequently, true; or that, the received opinion being true, a conflict with the opposite error is essential to a clear apprehension and deep feeling of its truth. But there is a commoner case than either of these; when the conflicting doctrines, instead of being one true and the other false, share the truth between them; and the nonconforming opinion is needed to supply the remainder of the truth, of which the received doctrine embodies only a part. Popular opinions, on subjects not palpable to sense, are often true, but seldom or never the whole truth. They are a part of the truth; sometimes a greater, sometimes a smaller part, but exaggerated, distorted, and disjoined from the truths by which they ought to be accompanied and limited. Heretical opinions, on the other hand, are generally some of these suppressed and neglected truths, bursting the bonds which kept them down, and either seeking reconciliation

---

1   *dialectics* Debates.

2   *confute* Prove wrong.

3   *Socratici viri* Latin: "Socrates' men." Followers of Socrates.

4   *cram* The temporary storage of large amounts of information for a particular purpose—for example, an examination.

with the truth contained in the common opinion, or fronting[1] it as enemies, and setting themselves up, with similar exclusiveness, as the whole truth. The latter case is hitherto the most frequent, as, in the human mind, one-sidedness has always been the rule, and many-sidedness the exception. Hence, even in revolutions of opinion, one part of the truth usually sets while another rises. Even progress, which ought to superadd,[2] for the most part only substitutes one partial and incomplete truth for another; improvement consisting chiefly in this, that the new fragment of truth is more wanted, more adapted to the needs of the time, than that which it displaces. Such being the partial character of prevailing opinions, even when resting on a true foundation; every opinion which embodies somewhat of the portion of truth which the common opinion omits, ought to be considered precious, with whatever amount of error and confusion that truth may be blended. No sober judge of human affairs will feel bound to be indignant because those who force on our notice truths which we should otherwise have overlooked, overlook some of those which we see. Rather, he will think that so long as popular truth is one-sided, it is more desirable than otherwise that unpopular truth should have one-sided asserters too; such being usually the most energetic, and the most likely to compel reluctant attention to the fragment of wisdom which they proclaim as if it were the whole.

Thus, in the eighteenth century, when nearly all the instructed, and all those of the uninstructed who were led by them, were lost in admiration of what is called civilization, and of the marvels of modern science, literature, and philosophy, and while greatly overrating the amount of unlikeness between the men of modern and those of ancient times, indulged the belief that the whole of the difference was in their own favor; with what a salutary shock did the paradoxes of Rousseau[3] explode like bombshells in the midst, dislocating the compact mass of one-sided opinion, and forcing its elements to recombine in a better form and with additional ingredients. Not that the current opinions were on the whole farther from the truth than Rousseau's were; on the contrary, they were nearer to it; they contained more of positive truth, and very much less of error. Nevertheless there lay in Rousseau's doctrine, and has floated down the stream of opinion along with it, a considerable amount of exactly those truths which the popular opinion wanted; and these are the deposit which was left behind when the flood subsided. The superior worth of simplicity of life, the enervating and demoralizing effect of the trammels[4] and hypocrisies of artificial society, are ideas which have never been entirely absent from cultivated minds since Rousseau wrote; and they will in time produce their due effect, though at present needing to be asserted as much as ever, and to be asserted by deeds, for words, on this subject, have nearly exhausted their power.

In politics, again, it is almost a commonplace, that a party of order or stability, and a party of progress or reform, are both necessary elements of a healthy state of political life; until the one or the other shall have so enlarged its mental grasp as to be a party equally of order and of progress, knowing and distinguishing what is fit to be preserved from what ought to be swept away. Each of these modes of thinking derives its utility from the deficiencies of the other; but it is in a great measure the opposition of the other that keeps each within the limits of reason and sanity. Unless opinions favorable to democracy and to aristocracy, to property and to equality, to co-operation and to competition, to luxury and to abstinence, to sociality and individuality, to liberty and discipline, and all the other standing antagonisms of practical life, are expressed with equal freedom, and enforced and defended with equal talent and energy, there is no chance of both elements obtaining their due; one scale is sure to go up, and the other down. Truth, in the great practical concerns of life, is so much a question of the reconciling and combining of opposites, that very few have minds sufficiently capacious[5] and impartial to make the adjustment with an approach to correctness, and it has to be made by the rough process of a struggle between combatants fighting under hostile banners. On any of the great open questions just enumerated, if either of the two opinions has a better claim than the other, not merely to be tolerated, but to be encouraged and countenanced, it is the one which happens at the particular time and place to be in a minority. That is the opinion which, for the time being, represents the neglected interests, the side of human well-being which is in danger of obtaining less than its share. I am aware that there is not, in this country, any intolerance

1 *fronting* Facing.

2 *superadd* Put in a further addition.

3 *the paradoxes of Rousseau* Jean-Jacques Rousseau (1712–78), Swiss-French philosopher of the Enlightenment, was fond of expressing himself in the form of unresolved "paradoxes," the best known of which is "Man was born free, and is everywhere in chains."

4 *trammels* Confinements, hindrances.

5 *capacious* Able to hold a great deal.

of differences of opinion on most of these topics. They are adduced to show, by admitted and multiplied examples, the universality of the fact, that only through diversity of opinion is there, in the existing state of human intellect, a chance of fair play to all sides of the truth. When there are persons to be found, who form an exception to the apparent unanimity of the world on any subject, even if the world is in the right, it is always probable that dissentients have something worth hearing to say for themselves, and that truth would lose something by their silence.

[...]

We have now recognized the necessity to the mental well-being of mankind (on which all their other well-being depends) of freedom of opinion, and freedom of the expression of opinion, on four distinct grounds; which we will now briefly recapitulate.

First, if any opinion is compelled to silence, that opinion may, for aught[1] we can certainly know, be true. To deny this is to assume our own infallibility.

Secondly, though the silenced opinion be an error, it may, and very commonly does, contain a portion of truth; and since the general or prevailing opinion on any object is rarely or never the whole truth, it is only by the collision of adverse opinions that the remainder of the truth has any chance of being supplied.

Thirdly, even if the received opinion be not only true, but the whole truth; unless it is suffered to be, and actually is, vigorously and earnestly contested, it will, by most of those who receive it, be held in the manner of a prejudice, with little comprehension or feeling of its rational grounds. And not only this, but, fourthly, the meaning of the doctrine itself will be in danger of being lost, or enfeebled, and deprived of its vital effect on the character and conduct: the dogma becoming a mere formal profession, inefficacious for good, but cumbering[2] the ground, and preventing the growth of any real and heartfelt conviction, from reason or personal experience.

Before quitting the subject of freedom of opinion, it is fit to take notice of those who say, that the free expression of all opinions should be permitted, on condition that the manner be temperate, and do not pass the bounds of fair discussion. Much might be said on the impossibility of fixing where these supposed bounds are to be placed; for if the

test be offence to those whose opinion is attacked, I think experience testifies that this offence is given whenever the attack is telling and powerful, and that every opponent who pushes them hard, and whom they find it difficult to answer, appears to them, if he shows any strong feeling on the subject, an intemperate opponent. But this, though an important consideration in a practical point of view, merges in a more fundamental objection. Undoubtedly the manner of asserting an opinion, even though it be a true one, may be very objectionable, and may justly incur severe censure. But the principal offences of the kind are such as it is mostly impossible, unless by accidental self-betrayal, to bring home to conviction. The gravest of them is, to argue sophistically,[3] to suppress facts or arguments, to misstate the elements of the case, or misrepresent the opposite opinion. But all this, even to the most aggravated degree, is so continually done in perfect good faith, by persons who are not considered, and in many other respects may not deserve to be considered, ignorant or incompetent, that it is rarely possible on adequate grounds conscientiously to stamp the misrepresentation as morally culpable; and still less could law presume to interfere with this kind of controversial misconduct. With regard to what is commonly meant by intemperate discussion, namely, invective, sarcasm, personality, and the like, the denunciation of these weapons would deserve more sympathy if it were ever proposed to interdict them equally to both sides; but it is only desired to restrain the employment of them against the prevailing opinion: against the unprevailing they may not only be used without general disapproval, but will be likely to obtain for him who uses them the praise of honest zeal and righteous indignation. Yet whatever mischief arises from their use, is greatest when they are employed against the comparatively defenseless; and whatever unfair advantage can be derived by any opinion from this mode of asserting it, accrues[4] almost exclusively to received opinions. The worst offence of this kind which can be committed by a polemic, is to stigmatize those who hold the contrary opinion as bad and immoral men. To calumny[5] of this sort, those who hold any unpopular opinion are peculiarly exposed, because they are in general few and uninfluential, and nobody but themselves feels much interest in seeing justice done them; but this weapon is, from the nature of the case, denied to those who attack a prevailing

1 *aught* Anything.
2 *cumbering* Obstructively occupying.
3 *sophistically* With clever-sounding but flawed reasoning.
4 *accrues* Comes.
5 *calumny* Malicious falsehoods.

opinion: they can neither use it with safety to themselves, nor if they could, would it do anything but recoil on their own cause. In general, opinions contrary to those commonly received can only obtain a hearing by studied moderation of language, and the most cautious avoidance of unnecessary offence, from which they hardly ever deviate even in a slight degree without losing ground: while unmeasured vituperation[1] employed on the side of the prevailing opinion, really does deter people from professing contrary opinions, and from listening to those who profess them. For the interest, therefore, of truth and justice, it is far more important to restrain this employment of vituperative language than the other; and, for example, if it were necessary to choose, there would be much more need to discourage offensive attacks on infidelity, than on religion. It is, however, obvious that law and authority have no business with restraining either, while opinion ought, in every instance, to determine its verdict by the circumstances of the individual case; condemning every one, on whichever side of the argument he places himself, in whose mode of advocacy either want of candor, or malignity, bigotry or intolerance of feeling manifest themselves, but not inferring these vices from the side which a person takes, though it be the contrary side of the question to our own; and giving merited honor to every one, whatever opinion he may hold, who has calmness to see and honesty to state what his opponents and their opinions really are, exaggerating nothing to their discredit, keeping nothing back which tells, or can be supposed to tell, in their favor. This is the real morality of public discussion; and if often violated, I am happy to think that there are many controversialists[2] who to a great extent observe it, and a still greater number who conscientiously strive towards it.

from *Chapter 3: On Individuality, as One of the Elements of Well-being*

Such being the reasons which make it imperative that human beings should be free to form opinions, and to express their opinions without reserve; and such the baneful consequences to the intellectual, and through that to the moral nature of man, unless this liberty is either conceded, or asserted in spite of prohibition; let us next examine whether the same reasons do not require that men should be free to act upon their opinions—to carry these out in

their lives, without hindrance, either physical or moral, from their fellow-men, so long as it is at their own risk and peril. This last proviso[3] is of course indispensable. No one pretends that actions should be as free as opinions. On the contrary, even opinions lose their immunity, when the circumstances in which they are expressed are such as to constitute their expression a positive instigation to some mischievous act. An opinion that corn-dealers[4] are starvers of the poor, or that private property is robbery, ought to be unmolested when simply circulated through the press, but may justly incur punishment when delivered orally to an excited mob assembled before the house of a corn-dealer, or when handed about among the same mob in the form of a placard.[5] Acts of whatever kind, which, without justifiable cause, do harm to others, may be, and in the more important cases absolutely require to be, controlled by the unfavorable sentiments, and, when needful, by the active interference of mankind. The liberty of the individual must be thus far limited; he must not make himself a nuisance[6] to other people. But if he refrains from molesting others in what concerns them, and merely acts according to his own inclination and judgment in things which concern himself, the same reasons which show that opinion should be free, prove also that he should be allowed, without molestation, to carry his opinions into practice at his own cost. That mankind are not infallible; that their truths, for the most part, are only half-truths; that unity of opinion, unless resulting from the fullest and freest comparison of opposite opinions, is not desirable, and diversity not an evil, but a good, until mankind are much more capable than at present of recognizing all sides of the truth, are principles applicable to men's modes of action, not less than to their opinions. As it is useful that while mankind are imperfect there should be different opinions, so is it that there should be different experiments of living; that free scope should be given to varieties of character, short of injury to others; and that the worth of different modes of life should be proved practically, when any one thinks fit to try them. It is desirable, in short, that in things which do not primarily concern others, individuality should assert itself. Where, not the person's own character, but the traditions of customs of other people are the rule of conduct, there is wanting one of the prin-

---

1   *vituperation*   Outbursts of abuse.
2   *controversialists*   Disputants.

3   *proviso*   Condition.
4   *corn-dealers*   Buyers and sellers of grain.
5   *placard*   Single-sheet document.
6   *nuisance*   One who causes harm.

cipal ingredients of human happiness, and quite the chief ingredient of individual and social progress.

In maintaining this principle, the greatest difficulty to be encountered does not lie in the appreciation of means towards an acknowledged end, but in the indifference of persons in general to the end itself. If it were felt that the free development of individuality is one of the leading essentials of well-being; that it is not only a coordinate[1] element with all that is designated by the terms civilization, instruction, education, culture, but is itself a necessary part and condition of all those things; there would be no danger that liberty should be undervalued, and the adjustment of the boundaries between it and social control would present no extraordinary difficulty. But the evil is, that individual spontaneity is hardly recognized by the common modes of thinking as having any intrinsic worth, or deserving any regard on its own account. The majority, being satisfied with the ways of mankind as they now are (for it is they who make them what they are), cannot comprehend why those ways should not be good enough for everybody; and what is more, spontaneity forms no part of the ideal of the majority of moral and social reformers, but is rather looked on with jealousy, as a troublesome and perhaps rebellious obstruction to the general acceptance of what these reformers, in their own judgment, think would be best for mankind. Few persons, out of Germany, even comprehend the meaning of the doctrine which Wilhelm von Humboldt,[2] so eminent both as a savant and as a politician, made the text of a treatise—that "the end of man, or that which is prescribed by the eternal or immutable dictates of reason, and not suggested by vague and transient desires, is the highest and most harmonious development of his powers to a complete and consistent whole;" that, therefore, the object "towards which every human being must ceaselessly direct his efforts, and on which especially those who design to influence their fellow-men must ever keep their eyes, is the individuality of power and development;" that for this there are two requisites, "freedom, and a variety of situations;" and that from the union of these arise "individual vigor and manifold diversity," which combine themselves in "originality."[3]

Little, however, as people are accustomed to a doctrine like that of Von Humboldt, and surprising as it may be to them to find so high a value attached to individuality, the question, one must nevertheless think, can only be one of degree. No one's idea of excellence in conduct is that people should do absolutely nothing but copy one another. No one would assert that people ought not to put into their mode of life, and into the conduct of their concerns, any impress[4] whatever of their own judgment, or of their own individual character. On the other hand, it would be absurd to pretend that people ought to live as if nothing whatever had been known in the world before they came into it; as if experience had as yet done nothing towards showing that one mode of existence, or of conduct, is preferable to another. Nobody denies that people should be so taught and trained in youth, as to know and benefit by the ascertained results of human experience. But it is the privilege and proper condition of a human being, arrived at the maturity of his faculties, to use and interpret experience in his own way. It is for him to find out what part of recorded experience is properly applicable to his own circumstances and character. The traditions and customs of other people are, to a certain extent, evidence of what their experience has taught them; presumptive[5] evidence, and as such, have a claim to this deference: but, in the first place, their experience may be too narrow; or they may not have interpreted it rightly. Secondly, their interpretation of experience may be correct but unsuitable to him. Customs are made for customary circumstances, and customary characters: and his circumstances or his character may be uncustomary. Thirdly, though the customs be both good as customs, and suitable to him, yet to conform to custom, merely as custom, does not educate or develop in him any of the qualities which are the distinctive endowment of a human being. The human faculties of perception, judgment, discriminative feeling, mental activity, and even moral preference, are exercised only in making a choice. He who does anything because it is the custom, makes no choice. He gains no practice either in discerning or in desiring what is best. The mental and moral, like the muscular powers, are improved only by being used. The faculties are called into no exercise by doing a thing merely because others do it, no more than by believing a thing only because others believe it. If the grounds of an opinion are

1 *coordinate* Equal.
2 *Wilhelm von Humboldt* German diplomat and Enlightenment philosopher (1767–1835); his writings anticipated Mill's defense of liberty.
3 *that "the end of man" ... "originality"* [Mill's footnote] *The Sphere and Duties of Government*, from the German of Baron Wilhelm

von Humboldt.
4 *impress* Characteristic mark.
5 *presumptive* Reasonably regarded as.

not conclusive to the person's own reason, his reason cannot be strengthened, but is likely to be weakened by his adopting it: and if the inducements to an act are not such as are consentaneous[1] to his own feelings and character (where affection, or the rights of others are not concerned), it is so much done towards rendering his feelings and character inert and torpid, instead of active and energetic.

He who lets the world, or his own portion of it, choose his plan of life for him, has no need of any other faculty than the ape-like one of imitation. He who chooses his plan for himself, employs all his faculties. He must use observation to see, reasoning and judgment to foresee, activity to gather materials for decision, discrimination to decide, and when he has decided, firmness and self-control to hold to his deliberate decision. And these qualities he requires and exercises exactly in proportion as the part of his conduct which he determines according to his own judgment and feelings is a large one. It is possible that he might be guided in some good path, and kept out of harm's way, without any of these things. But what will be his comparative worth as a human being? It really is of importance, not only what men do, but also what manner of men they are that do it. Among the works of man, which human life is rightly employed in perfecting and beautifying, the first in importance surely is man himself. Supposing it were possible to get houses built, corn grown, battles fought, causes tried, and even churches erected and prayers said, by machinery—by automatons in human form—it would be a considerable loss to exchange for these automatons even the men and women who at present inhabit the more civilized parts of the world, and who assuredly are but starved specimens of what nature can and will produce. Human nature is not a machine to be built after a model, and set to do exactly the work prescribed for it, but a tree, which requires to grow and develop itself on all sides, according to the tendency of the inward forces which make it a living thing.

It will probably be conceded that it is desirable people should exercise their understandings, and that an intelligent following of custom, or even occasionally an intelligent deviation from custom, is better than a blind and simply mechanical adhesion to it. To a certain extent it is admitted, that our understanding should be our own: but there is not the same willingness to admit that our desires and impulses should be our own likewise; or that to possess impulses of our own, and of any strength, is anything but a peril and

a snare. Yet desires and impulses are as much a part of a perfect human being, as beliefs and restraints: and strong impulses are only perilous when not properly balanced; when one set of aims and inclinations is developed into strength, while others, which ought to coexist with them, remain weak and inactive. It is not because men's desires are strong that they act ill; it is because their consciences are weak. There is no natural connection between strong impulses and a weak conscience. The natural connection is the other way. To say that one person's desires and feelings are stronger and more various than those of another, is merely to say that he has more of the raw material of human nature, and is therefore capable, perhaps of more evil, but certainly of more good. Strong impulses are but another name for energy. Energy may be turned to bad uses; but more good may always be made of an energetic nature, than of an indolent and impassive one. Those who have most natural feeling, are always those whose cultivated feelings may be made the strongest. The same strong susceptibilities which make the personal impulses vivid and powerful, are also the source from whence are generated the most passionate love of virtue, and the sternest self-control. It is through the cultivation of these, that society both does its duty and protects its interests: not by rejecting the stuff of which heroes are made, because it knows not how to make them. A person whose desires and impulses are his own—are the expression of his own nature, as it has been developed and modified by his own culture—is said to have a character. One whose desires and impulses are not his own, has no character, no more than a steam-engine has a character. If, in addition to being his own, his impulses are strong, and are under the government of a strong will, he has an energetic character. Whoever thinks that individuality of desires and impulses should not be encouraged to unfold itself, must maintain that society has no need of strong natures—is not the better for containing many persons who have much character—and that a high general average of energy is not desirable.

In some early states of society, these forces might be, and were, too much ahead of the power which society then possessed of disciplining and controlling them. There has been a time when the element of spontaneity and individuality was in excess, and the social principle had a hard struggle with it. The difficulty then was, to induce men of strong bodies or minds to pay obedience to any rules which required them to control their impulses. To overcome this difficulty, law and discipline, like the Popes struggling against the Emperors, asserted a power over the whole man, claiming to control

---

1 *consentaneous* In agreement with.

all his life in order to control his character—which society had not found any other sufficient means of binding. But society has now fairly got the better of individuality; and the danger which threatens human nature is not the excess, but the deficiency, of personal impulses and preferences. Things are vastly changed, since the passions of those who were strong by station or by personal endowment were in a state of habitual rebellion against laws and ordinances, and required to be rigorously chained up to enable the persons within their reach to enjoy any particle of security. In our times, from the highest class of society down to the lowest every one lives as under the eye of a hostile and dreaded censorship. Not only in what concerns others, but in what concerns only themselves, the individual, or the family, do not ask themselves—what do I prefer? or, what would suit my character and disposition? or, what would allow the best and highest in me to have fair play, and enable it to grow and thrive? They ask themselves, what is suitable to my position? what is usually done by persons of my station and pecuniary circumstances? or (worse still) what is usually done by persons of a station and circumstances superior to mine? I do not mean that they choose what is customary, in preference to what suits their own inclination. It does not occur to them to have any inclination, except for what is customary. Thus the mind itself is bowed to the yoke: even in what people do for pleasure, conformity is the first thing thought of; they like in crowds; they exercise choice only among things commonly done: peculiarity of taste, eccentricity of conduct, are shunned equally with crimes: until by dint of not following their own nature, they have no nature to follow: their human capacities are withered and starved: they become incapable of any strong wishes or native pleasures, and are generally without either opinions or feelings of home growth, or properly their own. Now is this, or is it not, the desirable condition of human nature?

[...]

from *Chapter 4: Of the Limits of the Authority of Society Over the Individual*

What, then, is the rightful limit to the sovereignty of the individual over himself? Where does the authority of society begin? How much of human life should be assigned to individuality, and how much to society?

Each will receive its proper share, if each has that which more particularly concerns it. To individuality should be-

long the part of life in which it is chiefly the individual that is interested; to society, the part which chiefly interests society.

Though society is not founded on a contract, and though no good purpose is answered by inventing a contract in order to deduce social obligations from it, every one who receives the protection of society owes a return for the benefit, and the fact of living in society renders it indispensable that each should be bound to observe a certain line of conduct towards the rest. This conduct consists, first, in not injuring the interests of one another; or rather certain interests, which, either by express legal provision or by tacit understanding, ought to be considered as rights; and secondly, in each person's bearing his share (to be fixed on some equitable principle) of the labors and sacrifices incurred for defending the society or its members from injury and molestation. These conditions society is justified in enforcing, at all costs to those who endeavor to withhold fulfillment. Nor is this all that society may do. The acts of an individual may be hurtful to others, or wanting in due consideration for their welfare, without going the length of violating any of their constituted rights. The offender may then be justly punished by opinion, though not by law. As soon as any part of a person's conduct affects prejudicially the interests of others, society has jurisdiction over it, and the question whether the general welfare will or will not be promoted by interfering with it, becomes open to discussion. But there is no room for entertaining any such question when a person's conduct affects the interests of no persons besides himself, or needs not affect them unless they like (all the persons concerned being of full age, and the ordinary amount of understanding). In all such cases there should be perfect freedom, legal and social, to do the action and stand the consequences.

It would be a great misunderstanding of this doctrine, to suppose that it is one of selfish indifference, which pretends that human beings have no business with each other's conduct in life, and that they should not concern themselves about the well-doing or well-being of one another, unless their own interest is involved. Instead of any diminution, there is need of a great increase of disinterested[1] exertion to promote the good of others. But disinterested benevolence can find other instruments to persuade people to their good, than whips and scourges, either of the literal or the metaphorical sort. I am the last person to undervalue the self-re-

---

1   *disinterested*   Free from bias or self-interest.

garding virtues; they are only second in importance, if even second, to the social. It is equally the business of education to cultivate both. But even education works by conviction and persuasion as well as by compulsion, and it is by the former only that, when the period of education is past, the self-regarding virtues should be inculcated. Human beings owe to each other help to distinguish the better from the worse, and encouragement to choose the former and avoid the latter. They should be forever stimulating each other to increased exercise of their higher faculties, and increased direction of their feelings and aims towards wise instead of foolish, elevating instead of degrading, objects and contemplations. But neither one person, nor any number of persons, is warranted in saying to another human creature of ripe years, that he shall not do with his life for his own benefit what he chooses to do with it. He is the person most interested in his own well-being, the interest which any other person, except in cases of strong personal attachment, can have in it, is trifling, compared with that which he himself has; the interest which society has in him individually (except as to his conduct to others) is fractional, and altogether indirect: while, with respect to his own feelings and circumstances, the most ordinary man or woman has means of knowledge immeasurably surpassing those that can be possessed by any one else. The interference of society to overrule his judgment and purposes in what only regards himself, must be grounded on general presumptions; which may be altogether wrong, and even if right, are as likely as not to be misapplied to individual cases, by persons no better acquainted with the circumstances of such cases than those are who look at them merely from without. In this department, therefore, of human affairs, Individuality has its proper field of action. In the conduct of human beings towards one another, it is necessary that general rules should for the most part be observed, in order that people may know what they have to expect; but in each person's own concerns, his individual spontaneity is entitled to free exercise. Considerations to aid his judgment, exhortations to strengthen his will, may be offered to him, even obtruded[1] on him, by others; but he, himself, is the final judge. All errors which he is likely to commit against advice and warning, are far outweighed by the evil of allowing others to constrain him to what they deem his good.

I do not mean that the feelings with which a person is regarded by others, ought not to be in any way affected by his self-regarding qualities or deficiencies. This is neither

possible nor desirable. If he is eminent in any of the qualities which conduce to his own good, he is, so far, a proper object of admiration. He is so much the nearer to the ideal perfection of human nature. If he is grossly deficient in those qualities, a sentiment the opposite of admiration will follow. There is a degree of folly, and a degree of what may be called (though the phrase is not unobjectionable) lowness or depravation of taste, which, though it cannot justify doing harm to the person who manifests it, renders him necessarily and properly a subject of distaste, or, in extreme cases, even of contempt: a person could not have the opposite qualities in due strength without entertaining these feelings. Though doing no wrong to any one, a person may so act as to compel us to judge him, and feel to him, as a fool, or as a being of an inferior order: and since this judgment and feeling are a fact which he would prefer to avoid, it is doing him a service to warn him of it beforehand, as of any other disagreeable consequence to which he exposes himself. It would be well, indeed, if this good office were much more freely rendered than the common notions of politeness at present permit, and if one person could honestly point out to another that he thinks him in fault, without being considered unmannerly or presuming. We have a right, also, in various ways, to act upon our unfavorable opinion of any one, not to the oppression of his individuality, but in the exercise of ours. We are not bound, for example, to seek his society; we have a right to avoid it (though not to parade the avoidance), for we have a right to choose the society most acceptable to us. We have a right, and it may be our duty, to caution others against him, if we think his example or conversation likely to have a pernicious effect on those with whom he associates. We may give others a preference over him in optional good offices, except those which tend to his improvement. In these various modes a person may suffer very severe penalties at the hands of others, for faults which directly concern only himself; but he suffers these penalties only in so far as they are the natural, and, as it were, the spontaneous consequences of the faults themselves, not because they are purposely inflicted on him for the sake of punishment. A person who shows rashness, obstinacy, self-conceit—who cannot live within moderate means—who cannot restrain himself from hurtful indulgences—who pursues animal pleasures at the expense of those of feeling and intellect—must expect to be lowered in the opinion of others, and to have a less share of their favorable sentiments, but of this he has no right to complain, unless he has merited their

---

1 *obtruded* Imposed.

favor by special excellence in his social relations, and has thus established a title to their good offices, which is not affected by his demerits towards himself.

What I contend for is, that the inconveniences which are strictly inseparable from the unfavorable judgment of others, are the only ones to which a person should ever be subjected for that portion of his conduct and character which concerns his own good, but which does not affect the interests of others in their relations with him. Acts injurious to others require a totally different treatment. Encroachment on their rights; infliction on them of any loss or damage not justified by his own rights; falsehood or duplicity in dealing with them; unfair or ungenerous use of advantages over them; even selfish abstinence from defending them against injury—these are fit objects of moral reprobation, and, in grave cases, of moral retribution and punishment. And not only these acts, but the dispositions which lead to them, are properly immoral, and fit subjects of disapprobation which may rise to abhorrence. Cruelty of disposition; malice and ill-nature; that most anti-social and odious of all passions, envy; dissimulation and insincerity, irascibility on insufficient cause, and resentment disproportioned to the provocation; the love of domineering over others; the desire to engross[1] more than one's share of advantages (the *pleonexia*[2] of the Greeks); the pride which derives gratification from the abasement of others; the egotism which thinks self and its concerns more important than everything else, and decides all doubtful questions in his own favor;—these are moral vices, and constitute a bad and odious moral character: unlike the self-regarding faults previously mentioned, which are not properly immoralities, and to whatever pitch[3] they may be carried, do not constitute wickedness. They may be proofs of any amount of folly, or want of personal dignity and self-respect; but they are only a subject of moral reprobation when they involve a breach of duty to others, for whose sake the individual is bound to have care for himself. What are called duties to ourselves are not socially obligatory, unless circumstances render them at the same time duties to others. The term duty to oneself, when it means anything more than prudence, means self-respect or self-development; and for none of these is any one accountable to his fellow-creatures, because for none of them is it for the good of mankind that he be held accountable to them.

The distinction between the loss of consideration which a person may rightly incur by defect of prudence or of personal dignity, and the reprobation which is due to him for an offence against the rights of others, is not a merely nominal distinction.[4] It makes a vast difference both in our feelings and in our conduct towards him, whether he displeases us in things in which we think we have a right to control him, or in things in which we know that we have not. If he displeases us, we may express our distaste, and we may stand aloof from a person as well as from a thing that displeases us; but we shall not therefore feel called on to make his life uncomfortable. We shall reflect that he already bears, or will bear, the whole penalty of his error; if he spoils his life by mismanagement, we shall not, for that reason, desire to spoil it still further: instead of wishing to punish him, we shall rather endeavor to alleviate his punishment, by showing him how he may avoid or cure the evils his conduct tends to bring upon him. He may be to us an object of pity, perhaps of dislike, but not of anger or resentment; we shall not treat him like an enemy of society: the worst we shall think ourselves justified in doing is leaving him to himself, If we do not interfere benevolently by showing interest or concern for him. It is far otherwise if he has infringed the rules necessary for the protection of his fellow-creatures, individually or collectively. The evil consequences of his acts do not then fall on himself, but on others; and society, as the protector of all its members, must retaliate on him; must inflict pain on him for the express purpose of punishment, and must take care that it be sufficiently severe. In the one case, he is an offender at our bar,[5] and we are called on not only to sit in judgment on him, but, in one shape or another, to execute our own sentence: in the other case, it is not our part to inflict any suffering on him, except what may incidentally follow from our using the same liberty in the regulation of our own affairs, which we allow to him in his.

The distinction here pointed out between the part of a person's life which concerns only himself, and that which concerns others, many persons will refuse to admit. How (it may be asked) can any part of the conduct of a member of society be a matter of indifference to the other members? No person is an entirely isolated being; it is impossible for a person to do anything seriously or permanently hurtful to himself, without mischief reaching at least to his near

---

1   *engross*   Collect up all of, or in excess of.
2   *pleonexia*   Greek: greed.
3   *pitch*   Degree.

4   *nominal distinction*   A matter of words only, not a difference in reality.
5   *bar*   Law court.

connections, and often far beyond them. If he injures his property, he does harm to those who directly or indirectly derived support from it, and usually diminishes, by a greater or less amount, the general resources of the community. If he deteriorates his bodily or mental faculties, he not only brings evil upon all who depended on him for any portion of their happiness, but disqualifies himself for rendering the services which he owes to his fellow-creatures generally; perhaps becomes a burden on their affection or benevolence; and if such conduct were very frequent, hardly any offence that is committed would detract more from the general sum of good. Finally, if by his vices or follies a person does no direct harm to others, he is nevertheless (it may be said) injurious by his example; and ought to be compelled to control himself, for the sake of those whom the sight or knowledge of his conduct might corrupt or mislead.

And even (it will be added) if the consequences of misconduct could be confined to the vicious or thoughtless individual, ought society to abandon to their own guidance those who are manifestly unfit for it? If protection against themselves is confessedly due to children and persons under age, is not society equally bound to afford it to persons of mature years who are equally incapable of self-government? If gambling, or drunkenness, or incontinence, or idleness, or uncleanliness,[1] are as injurious to happiness, and as great a hindrance to improvement, as many or most of the acts prohibited by law, why (it may be asked) should not law, so far as is consistent with practicability and social convenience, endeavor to repress these also? And as a supplement to the unavoidable imperfections of law, ought not opinion at least to organize a powerful police against these vices, and visit rigidly with social penalties those who are known to practice them? There is no question here (it may be said) about restricting individuality, or impeding the trial of new and original experiments in living. The only things it is sought to prevent are things which have been tried and condemned from the beginning of the world until now; things which experience has shown not to be useful or suitable to any person's individuality. There must be some length of time and amount of experience, after which a moral or prudential truth may be regarded as established, and it is merely desired to prevent generation after generation from falling over the same precipice which has been fatal to their predecessors.

I fully admit that the mischief which a person does to himself, may seriously affect, both through their sympathies and their interests, those nearly connected with him, and in a minor degree, society at large. When, by conduct of this sort, a person is led to violate a distinct and assignable obligation to any other person or persons, the case is taken out of the self-regarding class, and becomes amenable to moral disapprobation in the proper sense of the term. If, for example, a man, through intemperance or extravagance, becomes unable to pay his debts, or, having undertaken the moral responsibility of a family, becomes from the same cause incapable of supporting or educating them, he is deservedly reprobated, and might be justly punished; but it is for the breach of duty to his family or creditors, not for the extravagance. If the resources which ought to have been devoted to them, had been diverted from them for the most prudent investment, the moral culpability would have been the same. George Barnwell murdered his uncle to get money for his mistress, but if he had done it to set himself up in business, he would equally have been hanged. Again, in the frequent case of a man who causes grief to his family by addiction to bad habits, he deserves reproach for his unkindness or ingratitude; but so he may for cultivating habits not in themselves vicious, if they are painful to those with whom he passes his life, or who from personal ties are dependent on him for their comfort. Whoever fails in the consideration generally due to the interests and feelings of others, not being compelled by some more imperative duty, or justified by allowable self-preference, is a subject of moral disapprobation for that failure, but not for the cause of it, nor for the errors, merely personal to himself, which may have remotely led to it. In like manner, when a person disables himself, by conduct purely self-regarding, from the performance of some definite duty incumbent on him to the public, he is guilty of a social offence. No person ought to be punished simply for being drunk; but a soldier or a policeman should be punished for being drunk on duty. Whenever, in short, there is a definite damage, or a definite risk of damage, either to an individual or to the public, the case is taken out of the province of liberty, and placed in that of morality or law.

But with regard to the merely contingent[2] or, as it may be called, constructive[3] injury which a person causes to society, by conduct which neither violates any specific duty to the public, nor occasions perceptible hurt to any assignable individual except himself; the inconvenience is one which

---

1   *uncleanliness* Mill may mean moral impurity.

2   *contingent* Dependent on variable external events.

3   *constructive* Resulting from interpretation or inference—indirect or incidental.

society can afford to bear, for the sake of the greater good of human freedom. If grown persons are to be punished for not taking proper care of themselves, I would rather it were for their own sake, than under pretence of preventing them from impairing their capacity of rendering to society benefits which society does not pretend it has a right to exact. But I cannot consent to argue the point as if society had no means of bringing its weaker members up to its ordinary standard of rational conduct, except waiting till they do something irrational, and then punishing them, legally or morally, for it. Society has had absolute power over them during all the early portion of their existence: it has had the whole period of childhood and nonage in which to try whether it could make them capable of rational conduct in life. The existing generation is master both of the training and the entire circumstances of the generation to come; it cannot indeed make them perfectly wise and good, because it is itself so lamentably deficient in goodness and wisdom; and its best efforts are not always, in individual cases, its most successful ones; but it is perfectly well able to make the rising generation, as a whole, as good as, and a little better than, itself. If society lets any considerable number of its members grow up mere children, incapable of being acted on by rational consideration of distant motives,[1] society has itself to blame for the consequences. Armed not only with all the powers of education, but with the ascendancy which the authority of a received opinion always exercises over the minds who are least fitted to judge for themselves; and aided by the natural penalties which cannot be prevented from falling on those who incur the distaste or the contempt of those who know them; let not society pretend that it needs, besides all this, the power to issue commands and enforce obedience in the personal concerns of individuals, in which, on all principles of justice and policy, the decision ought to rest with those who are to abide the consequences. Nor is there anything which tends more to discredit and frustrate the better means of influencing conduct, than a resort to the worse. If there be among those whom it is attempted to coerce into prudence or temperance, any of the material of which vigorous and independent characters are made, they will infallibly rebel against the yoke. No such person will ever feel that others have a right to control him in his concerns, such as they have to prevent him from injuring them in theirs; and it easily comes to be considered a mark of spirit and courage to fly in the face of such usurped authority, and do with ostentation the exact opposite of what it enjoins; as in the fashion of grossness which succeeded, in the time of Charles II, to the fanatical moral intolerance of the Puritans. With respect to what is said of the necessity of protecting society from the bad example set to others by the vicious or the self-indulgent; it is true that bad example may have a pernicious effect, especially the example of doing wrong to others with impunity to the wrong-doer. But we are now speaking of conduct which, while it does no wrong to others, is supposed to do great harm to the agent himself: and I do not see how those who believe this, can think otherwise than that the example, on the whole, must be more salutary than hurtful, since, if it displays the misconduct, it displays also the painful or degrading consequences which, if the conduct is justly censured, must be supposed to be in all or most cases attendant on it.

But the strongest of all the arguments against the interference of the public with purely personal conduct, is that when it does interfere, the odds are that it interferes wrongly, and in the wrong place. On questions of social morality, of duty to others, the opinion of the public, that is, of an overruling majority, though often wrong, is likely to be still oftener right; because on such questions they are only required to judge of their own interests; of the manner in which some mode of conduct, if allowed to be practiced, would affect themselves. But the opinion of a similar majority, imposed as a law on the minority, on questions of self-regarding conduct, is quite as likely to be wrong as right; for in these cases public opinion means, at the best, some people's opinion of what is good or bad for other people; while very often it does not even mean that; the public, with the most perfect indifference, passing over the pleasure or convenience of those whose conduct they censure, and considering only their own preference. There are many who consider as an injury to themselves any conduct which they have a distaste for, and resent it as an outrage to their feelings; as a religious bigot, when charged with disregarding the religious feelings of others, has been known to retort that they disregard his feelings, by persisting in their abominable worship or creed. But there is no parity between the feeling of a person for his own opinion, and the feeling of another who is offended at his holding it; no more than between the desire of a thief to take a purse, and the desire of the right owner to keep it. And a person's taste is as much his own peculiar concern as his opinion or

---

1 *rational consideration of distant motives* That is, motivated by considerations about the future. Mill is contrasting this with being motivated only by what is immediate.

his purse. It is easy for any one to imagine an ideal public, which leaves the freedom and choice of individuals in all uncertain matters undisturbed, and only requires them to abstain from modes of conduct which universal experience has condemned. But where has there been seen a public which set any such limit to its censorship? or when does the public trouble itself about universal experience. In its interferences with personal conduct it is seldom thinking of anything but the enormity of acting or feeling differently from itself; and this standard of judgment, thinly disguised, is held up to mankind as the dictate of religion and philosophy, by nine tenths of all moralists and speculative writers. These teach that things are right because they are right; because we feel them to be so. They tell us to search in our own minds and hearts for laws of conduct binding on ourselves and on all others. What can the poor public do but apply these instructions, and make their own personal feelings of good and evil, if they are tolerably unanimous in them, obligatory on all the world?

The evil here pointed out is not one which exists only in theory; and it may perhaps be expected that I should specify the instances in which the public of this age and country improperly invests its own preferences with the character of moral laws. I am not writing an essay on the aberrations of existing moral feeling. That is too weighty a subject to be discussed parenthetically, and by way of illustration. Yet examples are necessary, to show that the principle I maintain is of serious and practical moment, and that I am not endeavoring to erect a barrier against imaginary evils. And it is not difficult to show, by abundant instances, that to extend the bounds of what may be called moral police, until it encroaches on the most unquestionably legitimate liberty of the individual, is one of the most universal of all human propensities.

As a first instance, consider the antipathies which men cherish on no better grounds than that persons whose religious opinions are different from theirs, do not practice their religious observances, especially their religious abstinences. To cite a rather trivial example, nothing in the creed or practice of Christians does more to envenom the hatred of Mahomedans[1] against them, than the fact of their eating pork. There are few acts which Christians and Europeans regard with more unaffected disgust, than Mussulmans[2] regard this particular mode of satisfying hunger. It is, in

the first place, an offence against their religion; but this circumstance by no means explains either the degree or the kind of their repugnance; for wine also is forbidden by their religion, and to partake of it is by all Mussulmans accounted wrong, but not disgusting. Their aversion to the flesh of the "unclean beast" is, on the contrary, of that peculiar character, resembling an instinctive antipathy, which the idea of uncleanness, when once it thoroughly sinks into the feelings, seems always to excite even in those whose personal habits are anything but scrupulously cleanly and of which the sentiment of religious impurity, so intense in the Hindoos,[3] is a remarkable example. Suppose now that in a people, of whom the majority were Mussulmans, that majority should insist upon not permitting pork to be eaten within the limits of the country. This would be nothing new in Mahomedan countries.[4] Would it be a legitimate exercise of the moral authority of public opinion? and if not, why not? The practice is really revolting to such a public. They also sincerely think that it is forbidden and abhorred by the Deity. Neither could the prohibition be censured as religious persecution. It might be religious in its origin, but it would not be persecution for religion, since nobody's religion makes it a duty to eat pork. The only tenable ground of condemnation would be, that with the personal tastes and self-regarding concerns of individuals the public has no business to interfere.

To come somewhat nearer home: the majority of Spaniards consider it a gross impiety, offensive in the highest degree to the Supreme Being, to worship him in any other manner than the Roman Catholic; and no other public worship is lawful on Spanish soil. The people of all Southern Europe look upon a married clergy as not only irreligious, but unchaste, indecent, gross, disgusting. What do Protestants think of these perfectly sincere feelings, and of

---

1 *Mahomedans* Muslims.
2 *Mussulmans* Muslims.

3 *Hindoos* Hindus.
4 *Mahomedan countries* [Mill's footnote] The case of the Bombay Parsees is a curious instance in point. When this industrious and enterprising tribe, the descendants of the Persian fire-worshippers, flying from their native country before the Caliphs, arrived in Western India, they were admitted to toleration by the Hindoo sovereigns, on condition of not eating beef. When those regions afterwards fell under the dominion of Mahomedan conquerors, the Parsees obtained from them a continuance of indulgence, on condition of refraining from pork. What was at first obedience to authority became a second nature, and the Parsees to this day abstain both from beef and pork. Though not required by their religion, the double abstinence has had time to grow into a custom of their tribe; and custom, in the East, is a religion.

the attempt to enforce them against non-Catholics? Yet, if mankind are justified in interfering with each other's liberty in things which do not concern the interests of others, on what principle is it possible consistently to exclude these cases? or who can blame people for desiring to suppress what they regard as a scandal in the sight of God and man?

No stronger case can be shown for prohibiting anything which is regarded as a personal immorality, than is made out for suppressing these practices in the eyes of those who regard them as impieties; and unless we are willing to adopt the logic of persecutors, and to say that we may persecute others because we are right, and that they must not persecute us because they are wrong, we must beware of admitting a principle of which we should resent as a gross injustice the application to ourselves.

The preceding instances may be objected to, although unreasonably, as drawn from contingencies impossible among us: opinion, in this country, not being likely to enforce abstinence from meats, or to interfere with people for worshipping, and for either marrying or not marrying, according to their creed or inclination. The next example, however, shall be taken from an interference with liberty which we have by no means passed all danger of. Wherever the Puritans have been sufficiently powerful, as in New England, and in Great Britain at the time of the Commonwealth,[1] they have endeavored, with considerable success, to put down all public, and nearly all private, amusements: especially music, dancing, public games, or other assemblages for purposes of diversion, and the theatre. There are still in this country large bodies of persons by whose notions of morality and religion these recreations are condemned; and those persons belonging chiefly to the middle class, who are the ascendant power in the present social and political condition of the kingdom, it is by no means impossible that persons of these sentiments may at some time or other command a majority in Parliament. How will the remaining portion of the community like to have the amusements that shall be permitted to them regulated by the religious and moral sentiments of the stricter Calvinists and Methodists? Would they not, with considerable peremptoriness,[2] desire these intrusively pious members of society to mind their own business? This is precisely what should be said to every government and every public, who have the pretension that

no person shall enjoy any pleasure which they think wrong. But if the principle of the pretension be admitted, no one can reasonably object to its being acted on in the sense of the majority, or other preponderating power in the country; and all persons must be ready to conform to the idea of a Christian commonwealth, as understood by the early settlers in New England, if a religious profession similar to theirs should ever succeed in regaining its lost ground, as religions supposed to be declining have so often been known to do.

To imagine another contingency, perhaps more likely to be realized than the one last mentioned. There is confessedly a strong tendency in the modern world towards a democratic constitution of society, accompanied or not by popular political institutions. It is affirmed that in the country where this tendency is most completely realized—where both society and the government are most democratic—the United States—the feeling of the majority, to whom any appearance of a more showy or costly style of living than they can hope to rival is disagreeable, operates as a tolerably effectual sumptuary law,[3] and that in many parts of the Union it is really difficult for a person possessing a very large income, to find any mode of spending it, which will not incur popular disapprobation. Though such statements as these are doubtless much exaggerated as a representation of existing facts, the state of things they describe is not only a conceivable and possible, but a probable result of democratic feeling, combined with the notion that the public has a right to a veto on the manner in which individuals shall spend their incomes. We have only further to suppose a considerable diffusion of Socialist opinions, and it may become infamous in the eyes of the majority to possess more property than some very small amount, or any income not earned by manual labor. Opinions similar in principle to these, already prevail widely among the artisan class, and weigh oppressively on those who are amenable to the opinion chiefly of that class, namely, its own members. It is known that the bad workmen who form the majority of the operatives in many branches of industry, are decidedly of opinion that bad workmen ought to receive the same wages as good, and that no one ought to be allowed, through piecework or otherwise, to earn by superior skill or industry more than others can without it. And they employ a moral police, which occasionally becomes a physical one,

---

1   *Commonwealth* Period between 1649–60 in which the monarchy had been overthrown and the Puritan Oliver Cromwell ruled as "Lord Protector."

2   *peremptoriness* Determination so strong as to admit no denial.

3   *sumptuary law* A law which attempts to prohibit display of wealth, especially showy clothing.

to deter skilful workmen from receiving, and employers from giving, a larger remuneration for a more useful service. If the public have any jurisdiction over private concerns, I cannot see that these people are in fault, or that any individual's particular public can be blamed for asserting the same authority over his individual conduct, which the general public asserts over people in general.

[...]

from *Chapter 5: Applications*

[...]

It was pointed out in an early part of this Essay, that the liberty of the individual, in things wherein the individual is alone concerned, implies a corresponding liberty in any number of individuals to regulate by mutual agreement such things as regard them jointly, and regard no persons but themselves. This question presents no difficulty, so long as the will of all the persons implicated remains unaltered; but since that will may change, it is often necessary, even in things in which they alone are concerned, that they should enter into engagements with one another; and when they do, it is fit, as a general rule, that those engagements should be kept. Yet in the laws probably, of every country, this general rule has some exceptions. Not only persons are not held to engagements which violate the rights of third parties, but it is sometimes considered a sufficient reason for releasing them from an engagement, that it is injurious to themselves. In this and most other civilized countries, for example, an engagement by which a person should sell himself, or allow himself to be sold, as a slave, would be null and void; neither enforced by law nor by opinion. The ground for thus limiting his power of voluntarily disposing of his own lot in life, is apparent, and is very clearly seen in this extreme case. The reason for not interfering, unless for the sake of others, with a person's voluntary acts, is consideration for his liberty. His voluntary choice is evidence that what he so chooses is desirable, or at the least endurable, to him, and his good is on the whole best provided for by allowing him to take his own means of pursuing it. But by selling himself for a slave, he abdicates his liberty; he foregoes any future use of it, beyond that single act. He therefore defeats, in his own case, the very purpose which is the justification of allowing him to dispose of himself. He is no longer free; but is thenceforth in a position which has no longer the presumption in its favor, that would be afforded by his voluntarily remaining

in it. The principle of freedom cannot require that he should be free not to be free. It is not freedom, to be allowed to alienate his freedom. These reasons, the force of which is so conspicuous in this peculiar case, are evidently of far wider application; yet a limit is everywhere set to them by the necessities of life, which continually require, not indeed that we should resign our freedom, but that we should consent to this and the other limitation of it. The principle, however, which demands uncontrolled freedom of action in all that concerns only the agents themselves, requires that those who have become bound to one another, in things which concern no third party, should be able to release one another from the engagement: and even without such voluntary release, there are perhaps no contracts or engagements, except those that relate to money or money's worth, of which one can venture to say that there ought to be no liberty whatever of retraction[1]....

[...]

I have reserved for the last place a large class of questions respecting the limits of government interference, which, though closely connected with the subject of this Essay, do not, in strictness, belong to it. These are cases in which the reasons against interference do not turn upon the principle of liberty: the question is not about restraining the actions of individuals, but about helping them: it is asked whether the government should do, or cause to be done, something for their benefit, instead of leaving it to be done by themselves, individually, or in voluntary combination.

The objections to government interference, when it is not such as to involve infringement of liberty, may be of three kinds.

The first is, when the thing to be done is likely to be better done by individuals than by the government. Speaking generally, there is no one so fit to conduct any business, or to determine how or by whom it shall be conducted, as those who are personally interested in it. This principle condemns the interferences, once so common, of the legislature, or the officers of government, with the ordinary processes of industry. But this part of the subject has been sufficiently enlarged upon by political economists, and is not particularly related to the principles of this Essay.

The second objection is more nearly allied to our subject. In many cases, though individuals may not do the particular thing so well, on the average, as the officers of

---

1   *retractation* Retraction.

government, it is nevertheless desirable that it should be done by them, rather than by the government, as a means to their own mental education—a mode of strengthening their active faculties, exercising their judgment, and giving them a familiar knowledge of the subjects with which they are thus left to deal. This is a principal, though not the sole, recommendation of jury trial (in cases not political); of free and popular local and municipal institutions; of the conduct of industrial and philanthropic enterprises by voluntary associations. These are not questions of liberty, and are connected with that subject only by remote tendencies; but they are questions of development. It belongs to a different occasion from the present to dwell on these things as parts of national education; as being, in truth, the peculiar training of a citizen, the practical part of the political education of a free people, taking them out of the narrow circle of personal and family selfishness, and accustoming them to the comprehension of joint interests, the management of joint concerns—habituating them to act from public or semi-public motives, and guide their conduct by aims which unite instead of isolating them from one another. Without these habits and powers, a free constitution can neither be worked nor preserved, as is exemplified by the too-often transitory nature of political freedom in countries where it does not rest upon a sufficient basis of local liberties. The management of purely local business by the localities, and of the great enterprises of industry by the union of those who voluntarily supply the pecuniary means, is further recommended by all the advantages which have been set forth in this Essay as belonging to individuality of development, and diversity of modes of action. Government operations tend to be everywhere alike. With individuals and voluntary associations, on the contrary, there are varied experiments, and endless diversity of experience. What the State can usefully do, is to make itself a central depository, and active circulator and diffuser, of the experience resulting from many trials. Its business is to enable each experimentalist to benefit by the experiments of others, instead of tolerating no experiments but its own.

The third, and most cogent reason for restricting the interference of government, is the great evil of adding unnecessarily to its power. Every function superadded to those already exercised by the government, causes its influence over hopes and fears to be more widely diffused, and converts, more and more, the active and ambitious part of the public into hangers-on of the government, or of some party which aims at becoming the government. If the roads, the railways, the banks, the insurance offices, the great joint-stock companies, the universities, and the public charities, were all of them branches of the government; if, in addition, the municipal corporations and local boards, with all that now devolves on them, became departments of the central administration; if the employees of all these different enterprises were appointed and paid by the government, and looked to the government for every rise in life; not all the freedom of the press and popular constitution of the legislature would make this or any other country free otherwise than in name. And the evil would be greater, the more efficiently and scientifically the administrative machinery was constructed—the more skilful the arrangements for obtaining the best qualified hands and heads with which to work it. In England it has of late been proposed that all the members of the civil service of government should be selected by competitive examination, to obtain for those employments the most intelligent and instructed persons procurable; and much has been said and written for and against this proposal. One of the arguments most insisted on by its opponents is that the occupation of a permanent official servant of the State does not hold out sufficient prospects of emolument[1] and importance to attract the highest talents, which will always be able to find a more inviting career in the professions, or in the service of companies and other public bodies. One would not have been surprised if this argument had been used by the friends of the proposition, as an answer to its principal difficulty. Coming from the opponents it is strange enough. What is urged as an objection is the safety-valve of the proposed system. If indeed all the high talent of the country could be drawn into the service of the government, a proposal tending to bring about that result might well inspire uneasiness. If every part of the business of society which required organized concert, or large and comprehensive views, were in the hands of the government, and if government offices were universally filled by the ablest men, all the enlarged culture and practiced intelligence in the country, except the purely speculative, would be concentrated in a numerous bureaucracy, to whom alone the rest of the community would look for all things: the multitude for direction and dictation in all they had to do; the able and aspiring for personal advancement. To be admitted into the ranks of this bureaucracy, and when admitted, to rise therein, would be the sole objects of ambition. Under this regime, not only is the outside public

1   *emolument* Payment.

ill-qualified, for want of practical experience, to criticize or check the mode of operation of the bureaucracy, but even if the accidents of despotic or the natural working of popular institutions occasionally raise to the summit a ruler or rulers of reforming inclinations, no reform can be effected which is contrary to the interest of the bureaucracy ...

[...]

It is not, also, to be forgotten, that the absorption of all the principal ability of the country into the governing body is fatal, sooner or later, to the mental activity and progressiveness of the body itself. Banded together as they are—working a system which, like all systems, necessarily proceeds in a great measure by fixed rules—the official body are under the constant temptation of sinking into indolent routine, or, if they now and then desert that mill-horse round,[1] of rushing into some half-examined crudity which has struck the fancy of some leading member of the corps: and the sole check to these closely allied, though seemingly opposite, tendencies, the only stimulus which can keep the ability of the body itself up to a high standard, is liability to the watchful criticism of equal ability outside the body. It is indispensable, therefore, that the means should exist, independently of the government, of forming such ability, and furnishing it with the opportunities and experience necessary for a correct judgment of great practical affairs. If we would possess permanently a skilful and efficient body of functionaries—above all, a body able to originate and willing to adopt improvements; if we would not have our bureaucracy degenerate into a pedantocracy,[2] this body must not engross all the occupations which form and cultivate the faculties required for the government of mankind.

... A government cannot have too much of the kind of activity which does not impede, but aids and stimulates, individual exertion and development. The mischief begins when, instead of calling forth the activity and powers of individuals and bodies, it substitutes its own activity for theirs; when, instead of informing, advising, and upon occasion denouncing, it makes them work in fetters or bids them stand aside and does their work instead of them. The worth of a State, in the long run, is the worth of the individ-

uals composing it; and a State which postpones the interests of their mental expansion and elevation, to a little more of administrative skill or that semblance of it which practice gives, in the details of business; a State, which dwarfs its men, in order that they may be more docile instruments in its hands even for beneficial purposes, will find that with small men no great thing can really be accomplished; and that the perfection of machinery to which it has sacrificed everything, will in the end avail it nothing, for want of the vital power which, in order that the machine might work more smoothly, it has preferred to banish.

◆ ◆ ◆ ◆ ◆

Considerations on Representative Government (1861)

Chapter 10: Of the Mode of Voting

The Question of greatest moment in regard to modes of voting is that of secrecy or publicity; and to this we will at once address ourselves.

It would be a great mistake to make the discussion turn on sentimentalities about skulking or cowardice. Secrecy is justifiable in many cases, imperative in some, and it is not cowardice to seek protection against evils which are honestly avoidable. Nor can it be reasonably maintained that no cases are conceivable in which secret voting is preferable to public. But I must contend that these cases, in affairs of a political character, are the exception, not the rule.

The present is one of the many instances in which, as I have already had occasion to remark, the spirit of an institution, the impression it makes on the mind of the citizen, is one of the most important parts of its operation. The spirit of vote by ballot—the interpretation likely to be put on it in the mind of an elector—is that the suffrage is given to him for himself; for his particular use and benefit, and not as a trust for the public.[3] For if it is indeed a trust, if the public are entitled to his vote, are not they entitled to know his vote? This false and pernicious impression may well be made on the generality,[4] since it has been made on most of

---

1   *mill-horse round* Routine repetitive work. (Horses working in mills turned horizontal wheels by walking round in the same circle over and over.)

2   *pedantocracy* A pedant is someone too concerned with rules and details. Mill invented this term to apply to a bureaucracy consisting of such people.

3   *trust for the public* Position of public obligation.

4   *on the generality* In general.

those who of late years have been conspicuous advocates of the ballot.

The doctrine was not so understood by its earlier promoters; but the effect of a doctrine on the mind is best shown, not in those who form it, but in those who are formed by it. Mr. Bright[1] and his school of democrats think themselves greatly concerned in maintaining that the franchise is what they term a right, not a trust.

Now this one idea, taking root in the general mind, does a moral mischief outweighing all the good that the ballot could do, at the highest possible estimate of it. In whatever way we define or understand the idea of a right, no person can have a right (except in the purely legal sense) to power over others: every such power, which he is allowed to possess, is morally, in the fullest force of the term, a trust. But the exercise of any political function, either as an elector or as a representative, is power over others.

Those who say that the suffrage is not a trust but a right will scarcely accept the conclusions to which their doctrine leads. If it is a right, if it belongs to the voter for his own sake, on what ground can we blame him for selling it, or using it to recommend himself to any one whom it is his interest to please? A person is not expected to consult exclusively the public benefit in the use he makes of his house, or his three per cent stock, or anything else to which he really has a right. The suffrage is indeed due to him, among other reasons, as a means to his own protection, but only against treatment from which he is equally bound, so far as depends on his vote, to protect every one of his fellow-citizens. His vote is not a thing in which he has an option; it has no more to do with his personal wishes than the verdict of a juryman. It is strictly a matter of duty; he is bound to give it according to his best and most conscientious opinion of the public good. Whoever has any other idea of it is unfit to have the suffrage; its effect on him is to pervert, not to elevate his mind. Instead of opening his heart to an exalted patriotism and the obligation of public duty, it awakens and nourishes in him the disposition to use a public function for his own interest, pleasure, or caprice; the same feelings and purposes, on a humbler scale, which actuate a despot and oppressor. Now an ordinary citizen in any public position, or on whom there devolves any social function, is certain to

think and feel, respecting the obligations it imposes on him, exactly what society appears to think and feel in conferring it. What seems to be expected from him by society forms a standard which he may fall below, but which he will seldom rise above. And the interpretation which he is almost sure to put upon secret voting is that he is not bound to give his vote with any reference to those who are not allowed to know how he gives it; but may bestow it simply as he feels inclined.

This is the decisive reason why the argument does not hold, from the use of the ballot in clubs and private societies, to its adoption in parliamentary elections. A member of a club is really, what the elector falsely believes himself to be, under no obligation to consider the wishes or interests of any one else. He declares nothing by his vote but that he is or is not willing to associate, in a manner more or less close, with a particular person. This is a matter on which, by universal admission, his own pleasure or inclination is entitled to decide: and that he should be able so to decide it without risking a quarrel is best for everybody, the rejected person included. An additional reason rendering the ballot unobjectionable in these cases is that it does not necessarily or naturally lead to lying. The persons concerned are of the same class or rank, and it would be considered improper in one of them to press another with questions as to how he had voted. It is far otherwise in parliamentary elections, and is likely to remain so, as long as the social relations exist which produce the demand for the ballot; as long as one person is sufficiently the superior of another to think himself entitled to dictate his vote. And while this is the case, silence or an evasive answer is certain to be construed as proof that the vote given has not been that which was desired.

In any political election, even by universal suffrage (and still more obviously in the case of a restricted suffrage), the voter is under an absolute moral obligation to consider the interest of the public, not his private advantage, and give his vote, to the best of his judgment, exactly as he would be bound to do if he were the sole voter, and the election depended upon him alone. This being admitted, it is at least a prima facie[2] consequence that the duty of voting, like any other public duty, should be performed under the eye and criticism of the public; every one of whom has not only an interest in its performance, but a good title to consider himself wronged if it is performed otherwise than honestly and carefully.

---

1   *Mr. Bright*   John Bright (1811–89) was a radical British politician who supported the secret ballot, arguing that newly enfranchised tenants would face the threat of eviction were they to vote against the wishes of their landlord. The secret ballot was finally adopted by Britain in 1872.

2   *prima facie*   [Latin: on its face.] At first sight.

Undoubtedly neither this nor any other maxim of political morality is absolutely inviolable; it may be overruled by still more cogent considerations. But its weight is such that the cases which admit of a departure from it must be of a strikingly exceptional character.

It may, unquestionably, be the fact that if we attempt, by publicity,[1] to make the voter responsible to the public for his vote, he will practically be made responsible for it to some powerful individual, whose interest is more opposed to the general interest of the community than that of the voter himself would be if, by the shield of secrecy, he were released from responsibility altogether.

When this is the condition, in a high degree, of a large proportion of the voters, the ballot may be the smaller evil. When the voters are slaves, anything may be tolerated which enables them to throw off the yoke. The strongest case for the ballot is when the mischievous power of the Few over the Many is increasing. In the decline of the Roman republic the reasons for the ballot were irresistible. The oligarchy was yearly becoming richer and more tyrannical, the people poorer and more dependent, and it was necessary to erect stronger and stronger barriers against such abuse of the franchise as rendered it but an instrument the more in the hands of unprincipled persons of consequence.[2] As little can it be doubted that the ballot, so far as it existed, had a beneficial operation in the Athenian constitution. Even in the least unstable of the Grecian commonwealths freedom might be for the time destroyed by a single unfairly obtained popular vote; and though the Athenian voter was not sufficiently dependent to be habitually coerced, he might have been bribed, or intimidated by the lawless outrages of some knot of individuals, such as were not uncommon even at Athens among the youth of rank and fortune. The ballot was in these cases a valuable instrument of order, and conduced to the Eunomia[3] by which Athens was distinguished among the ancient commonwealths.

But in the more advanced states of modern Europe, and especially in this country, the power of coercing voters has declined and is declining; and bad voting is now less to be apprehended from the influences to which the voter is subject at the hands of others than from the sinister interests and discreditable feelings which belong to himself, either individually or as a member of a class. To secure him

against the first, at the cost of removing all restraint from the last, would be to exchange a smaller and a diminishing evil for a greater and increasing one. [...]

Chapter 16: Of Nationality, as Connected with Representative Government

A portion of mankind may be said to constitute a Nationality if they are united among themselves by common sympathies which do not exist between them and any others—which make them co-operate with each other more willingly than with other people, desire to be under the same government, and desire that it should be government by themselves or a portion of themselves exclusively. This feeling of nationality may have been generated by various causes. Sometimes it is the effect of identity of race and descent. Community of language, and community of religion, greatly contribute to it. Geographical limits are one of its causes. But the strongest of all is identity of political antecedents; the possession of a national history, and consequent community of recollections; collective pride and humiliation, pleasure and regret, connected with the same incidents in the past. None of these circumstances, however, are either indispensable, or necessarily sufficient by themselves. Switzerland has a strong sentiment of nationality, though the cantons[4] are of different races, different languages, and different religions. Sicily has, throughout history, felt itself quite distinct in nationality from Naples, notwithstanding identity of religion, almost identity of language, and a considerable amount of common historical antecedents. The Flemish[5] and the Walloon[6] provinces of Belgium, notwithstanding diversity of race and language, have a much greater feeling of common nationality than the former have with Holland, or the latter with France. Yet in general the national feeling is proportionally weakened by the failure of any of the causes which contribute to it. Identity of language, literature, and, to some extent, of race and recollections, have maintained the feeling of nationality in considerable strength among the different portions of the German name, though they have at no time been really united under the same government;

---

1 *publicity* Making (voting) public.
2 *of consequence* Important in rank or social position.
3 *Eunomia* Ancient Greek goddess of good order and legislation (and thus the personification of a well-ordered community).

4 *cantons* States into which Switzerland is divided.
5 *Flemish* Of the Dutch-speaking people inhabiting the north of Belgium.
6 *Walloon* Of the French-speaking people inhabiting the south of Belgium.

but the feeling has never reached to making the separate states desire to get rid of their autonomy. Among Italians an identity far from complete, of language and literature, combined with a geographical position which separates them by a distinct line from other countries, and, perhaps more than everything else, the possession of a common name, which makes them all glory in the past achievements in arts, arms, politics, religious primacy, science, and literature, of any who share the same designation, give rise to an amount of national feeling in the population which, though still imperfect, has been sufficient to produce the great events now passing before us,[1] notwithstanding a great mixture of races, and although they have never, in either ancient or modern history, been under the same government, except while that government extended or was extending itself over the greater part of the known world.[2]

Where the sentiment of nationality exists in any force, there is a prima facie case for uniting all the members of the nationality under the same government, and a government to themselves apart. This is merely saying that the question of government ought to be decided by the governed. One hardly knows what any division of the human race should be free to do if not to determine with which of the various collective bodies of human beings they choose to associate themselves.

But, when a people are ripe for free institutions, there is a still more vital consideration. Free institutions are next to impossible in a country made up of different nationalities. Among a people without fellow-feeling, especially if they read and speak different languages, the united public opinion, necessary to the working of representative government, cannot exist. The influences which form opinions and decide political acts are different in the different sections of the country. An altogether different set of leaders have the confidence of one part of the country and of another. The same books, newspapers, pamphlets, speeches, do not reach them. One section does not know what opinions, or what instigations, are circulating in another. The same incidents, the same acts, the same system of government, affect them in different ways; and each fears more injury to itself from the other nationalities than from the common arbiter, the state. Their mutual antipathies are generally much stronger than jealousy of the government. That any one of them feels

aggrieved by the policy of the common ruler is sufficient to determine another to support that policy. Even if all are aggrieved, none feel that they can rely on the others for fidelity in a joint resistance; the strength of none is sufficient to resist alone, and each may reasonably think that it consults its own advantage most by bidding for the favor of the government against the rest. Above all, the grand and only effectual security in the last resort against the despotism of the government is in that case wanting: the sympathy of the army with the people. The military are the part of every community in whom, from the nature of the case, the distinction between their fellow-countrymen and foreigners is the deepest and strongest. To the rest of the people foreigners are merely strangers; to the soldier, they are men against whom he may be called, at a week's notice, to fight for life or death. The difference to him is that between friends and foes—we may almost say between fellow-men and another kind of animals: for as respects the enemy, the only law is that of force, and the only mitigation the same as in the case of other animals—that of simple humanity. Soldiers to whose feelings half or three-fourths of the subjects of the same government are foreigners will have no more scruple in mowing them down, and no more desire to ask the reason why, than they would have in doing the same thing against declared enemies. An army composed of various nationalities has no other patriotism than devotion to the flag. Such armies have been the executioners of liberty through the whole duration of modern history. The sole bond which holds them together is their officers and the government which they serve; and their only idea, if they have any, of public duty is obedience to orders. A government thus supported, by keeping its Hungarian regiments in Italy and its Italian in Hungary, can long continue to rule in both places with the iron rod of foreign conquerors.

If it be said that so broadly marked a distinction between what is due to a fellow-countryman and what is due merely to a human creature is more worthy of savages than of civilized beings, and ought, with the utmost energy, to be contended against, no one holds that opinion more strongly than myself. But this object, one of the worthiest to which human endeavor can be directed, can never, in the present state of civilization, be promoted by keeping different nationalities of anything like equivalent strength under the same government. In a barbarous state of society the case is sometimes different. The government may then be interested in softening the antipathies of the races that peace may be preserved and the country more easily governed. But when

---

1   *great events now passing before us* The Italian struggle for unification.

2   *except while ... known world* That is, in ancient Roman times.

there are either free institutions or a desire for them, in any of the peoples artificially tied together, the interest of the government lies in an exactly opposite direction. It is then interested in keeping up and envenoming their antipathies that they may be prevented from coalescing, and it may be enabled to use some of them as tools for the enslavement of others. The Austrian Court has now for a whole generation made these tactics its principal means of government; with what fatal success, at the time of the Vienna insurrection and the Hungarian contest,[1] the world knows too well. Happily there are now signs that improvement is too far advanced to permit this policy to be any longer successful.

For the preceding reasons, it is in general a necessary condition of free institutions that the boundaries of governments should coincide in the main with those of nationalities. But several considerations are liable to conflict in practice with this general principle. In the first place, its application is often precluded by geographical hindrances. There are parts even of Europe in which different nationalities are so locally intermingled that it is not practicable for them to be under separate governments. The population of Hungary is composed of Magyars, Slovaks, Croats, Serbs, Roumans,[2] and in some districts Germans, so mixed up as to be incapable of local separation; and there is no course open to them but to make a virtue of necessity, and reconcile themselves to living together under equal rights and laws. Their community of servitude, which dates only from the destruction of Hungarian independence in 1849, seems to be ripening and disposing them for such an equal union. The German colony of East Prussia is cut off from Germany by part of the ancient Poland, and being too weak to maintain separate independence, must, if geographical continuity is to be maintained, be either under a non-German government, or the intervening Polish territory must be under a German one. Another considerable region in which the dominant element of the population is German, the provinces of Courland, Esthonia, and Livonia,[3] is condemned by its local situation to form part of a Slavonian state. In Eastern Germany itself there is a large Slavonic population: Bohemia is principally Slavonic, Silesia and other districts partially so. The most united country in Europe, France, is far from being homogeneous: independently of the fragments of foreign nationalities at its remote extremities, it consists, as language and history prove, of two portions, one occupied almost exclusively by a Gallo-Roman population, while in the other the Frankish, Burgundian, and other Teutonic races form a considerable ingredient.

When proper allowance has been made for geographical exigencies, another more purely moral and social consideration offers itself. Experience proves that it is possible for one nationality to merge and be absorbed in another: and when it was originally an inferior and more backward portion of the human race the absorption is greatly to its advantage. Nobody can suppose that it is not more beneficial to a Breton, or a Basque of French Navarre, to be brought into the current of the ideas and feelings of a highly civilized and cultivated people—to be a member of the French nationality, admitted on equal terms to all the privileges of French citizenship, sharing the advantages of French protection, and the dignity and prestige of French power—than to sulk on his own rocks, the half-savage relic of past times, revolving in his own little mental orbit, without participation or interest in the general movement of the world. The same remark applies to the Welshman or the Scottish Highlander as members of the British nation.

Whatever really tends to the admixture of nationalities, and the blending of their attributes and peculiarities in a common union, is a benefit to the human race. Not by extinguishing types, of which, in these cases, sufficient examples are sure to remain, but by softening their extreme forms, and filling up the intervals between them. The united people, like a crossed breed of animals (but in a still greater degree, because the influences in operation are moral as well as physical), inherits the special aptitudes and excellences of all its progenitors, protected by the admixture from being exaggerated into the neighboring vices. But to render this admixture possible, there must be peculiar conditions. The combinations of circumstances which occur, and which effect the result, are various.

The nationalities brought together under the same government may be about equal in numbers and strength, or they may be very unequal. If unequal, the least numerous of the two may either be the superior in civilization, or the inferior. Supposing it to be superior, it may either, through that superiority, be able to acquire ascendancy over the other, or it may be overcome by brute strength and reduced to subjection. This last is a sheer mischief to the human race, and one which civilized humanity with one accord

---

1   *Vienna insurrection and Hungarian contest*   The Vienna insurrection and the Hungarian revolt, 1848, were both nationalist uprisings against the Hapsburg rule.

2   *Roumans*   Romanians.

3   *Courland, Esthonia, and Livonia*   Now parts of Latvia, Lithuania, and Estonia.

should rise in arms to prevent. The absorption of Greece by Macedonia was one of the greatest misfortunes which ever happened to the world: that of any of the principal countries of Europe by Russia would be a similar one.

If the smaller nationality, supposed to be the more advanced in improvement, is able to overcome the greater, as the Macedonians, reinforced by the Greeks, did Asia, and the English India, there is often a gain to civilization: but the conquerors and the conquered cannot in this case live together under the same free institutions. The absorption of the conquerors in the less advanced people would be an evil: these, must be governed as subjects, and the state of things is either a benefit or a misfortune, according as the subjugated people have or have not reached the state in which it is an injury not to be under a free government, and according as the conquerors do or do not use their superiority in a manner calculated to fit the conquered for a higher stage of improvement. This topic will be particularly treated of in a subsequent chapter.

When the nationality which succeeds in overpowering the other is both the most numerous and the most improved; and especially if the subdued nationality is small, and has no hope of reasserting its independence; then, if it is governed with any tolerable justice, and if the members of the more powerful nationality are not made odious by being invested with exclusive privileges, the smaller nationality is gradually reconciled to its position, and becomes amalgamated with the larger. No Bas-Breton, nor even any Alsatian, has the smallest wish at the present day to be separated from France. If all Irishmen have not yet arrived at the same disposition towards England, it is partly because they are sufficiently numerous to be capable of constituting a respectable nationality by themselves; but principally because, until of late years, they had been so atrociously governed, that all their best feelings combined with their bad ones in rousing bitter resentment against the Saxon rule. This disgrace to England, and calamity to the whole empire, has, it may be truly said, completely ceased for nearly a generation. No Irishman is now less free than an Anglo-Saxon, nor has a less share of every benefit either to his country or to his individual fortunes than if he were sprung from any other portion of the British dominions. The only remaining real grievance of Ireland, that of the State Church, is one which half, or nearly half, the people of the larger island have in common with them. There is now next to nothing, except the memory of the past, and the difference in the predominant religion, to keep apart two races, perhaps the most fitted of any two in the world to be the completing counterpart of one another. The consciousness of being at last treated not only with equal justice but with equal consideration is making such rapid way in the Irish nation as to be wearing off all feelings that could make them insensible to the benefits which the less numerous and less wealthy people must necessarily derive from being fellow-citizens instead of foreigners to those who are not only their nearest neighbors, but the wealthiest, and one of the freest, as well as most civilized and powerful, nations of the earth.

The cases in which the greatest practical obstacles exist to the blending of nationalities are when the nationalities which have been bound together are nearly equal in numbers and in the other elements of power. In such cases, each, confiding in its strength, and feeling itself capable of maintaining an equal struggle with any of the others, is unwilling to be merged in it: each cultivates with party obstinacy its distinctive peculiarities; obsolete customs, and even declining languages, are revived to deepen the separation; each deems itself tyrannized over if any authority is exercised within itself by functionaries[1] of a rival race; and whatever is given to one of the conflicting nationalities is considered to be taken from all the rest. When nations, thus divided, are under a despotic government which is a stranger to all of them, or which, though sprung from one, yet feeling greater interest in its own power than in any sympathies of nationality, assigns no privilege to either nation, and chooses its instruments indifferently from all; in the course of a few generations, identity of situation often produces harmony of feeling, and the different races come to feel towards each other as fellow-countrymen; particularly if they are dispersed over the same tract of country. But if the era of aspiration to free government arrives before this fusion has been effected, the opportunity has gone by for effecting it. From that time, if the unreconciled nationalities are geographically separate, and especially if their local position is such that there is no natural fitness or convenience in their being under the same government (as in the case of an Italian province under a French or German yoke), there is not only an obvious propriety, but, if either freedom or concord is cared for, a necessity, for breaking the connection altogether. There may be cases in which the provinces, after separation, might usefully remain united by a federal tie: but it generally happens that if they are willing to forego complete independence, and become members of a federa-

---

1   *functionaries* Officials.

tion, each of them has other neighbors with whom it would prefer to connect itself, having more sympathies in common, if not also greater community of interest.

♦ ♦ ♦ ♦ ♦

Utilitarianism (1863)

from *Chapter 2: What Utilitarianism Is*

[...]

The creed which accepts as the foundation of morals, Utility, or the Greatest Happiness Principle, holds that actions are right in proportion as they tend to promote happiness, wrong as they tend to produce the reverse of happiness. By happiness is intended pleasure, and the absence of pain; by unhappiness, pain, and the privation of pleasure. To give a clear view of the moral standard set up by the theory, much more requires to be said; in particular, what things it includes in the ideas of pain and pleasure; and to what extent this is left an open question. But these supplementary explanations do not affect the theory of life on which this theory of morality is grounded—namely, that pleasure, and freedom from pain, are the only things desirable as ends; and that all desirable things (which are as numerous in the utilitarian as in any other scheme) are desirable either for the pleasure inherent in themselves, or as means to the promotion of pleasure and the prevention of pain.

Now, such a theory of life excites in many minds, and among them in some of the most estimable in feeling and purpose, inveterate dislike. To suppose that life has (as they express it) no higher end than pleasure—no better and nobler object of desire and pursuit—they designate as utterly mean and groveling; as a doctrine worthy only of swine, to whom the followers of Epicurus[1] were, at a very early period, contemptuously likened; and modern holders of the doctrine are occasionally made the subject of equally polite comparisons by its German, French, and English assailants.

When thus attacked, the Epicureans have always answered, that it is not they, but their accusers, who represent human nature in a degrading light; since the accusation supposes human beings to be capable of no pleasures except those of which swine are capable. If this supposition were true, the charge could not be gainsaid,[2] but would then be no longer an imputation; for if the sources of pleasure were precisely the same to human beings and to swine, the rule of life which is good enough for the one would be good enough for the other. The comparison of the Epicurean life to that of beasts is felt as degrading, precisely because a beast's pleasures do not satisfy a human being's conceptions of happiness. Human beings have faculties more elevated than the animal appetites, and when once made conscious of them, do not regard anything as happiness which does not include their gratification. I do not, indeed, consider the Epicureans to have been by any means faultless in drawing out their scheme of consequences from the utilitarian principle. To do this in any sufficient manner, many Stoic,[3] as well as Christian elements require to be included. But there is no known Epicurean theory of life which does not assign to the pleasures of the intellect, of the feelings and imagination, and of the moral sentiments, a much higher value as pleasures than to those of mere sensation. It must be admitted, however, that utilitarian writers in general have placed the superiority of mental over bodily pleasures chiefly in the greater permanency, safety, uncostliness, etc., of the former—that is, in their circumstantial advantages rather than in their intrinsic nature. And on all these points utilitarians have fully proved their case; but they might have taken the other, and, as it may be called, higher ground, with entire consistency. It is quite compatible with the principle of utility to recognize the fact, that some kinds of pleasure are more desirable and more valuable than others. It would be absurd that while, in estimating all other things, quality is considered as well as quantity, the estimation of pleasures should be supposed to depend on quantity alone.

If I am asked, what I mean by difference of quality in pleasures, or what makes one pleasure more valuable than another, merely as a pleasure, except its being greater in amount, there is but one possible answer. Of two pleasures, if there be one to which all or almost all who have experience

---

1   *Epicurus*   Greek philosopher (341 BCE–270 BCE), founder of the school named after him, Epicureanism; he held that pleasure and pain-avoidance were the whole basis of morality, the only thing worth seeking. Epicureans did not, however, advocate rampant pleasure-seeking (as has sometimes been thought); their ideal was rather absence of pain—tranquility of mind.

2   *gainsaid*   Contradicted.
3   *Stoic*   Stoicism, an ancient Greek (and later Roman) school, held as ideals self-control, concentration on what was important, strength of character, mastery of emotions, and adherence to duty; the aim (as with Epicureanism) was tranquility.

of both give a decided preference, irrespective of any feeling of moral obligation to prefer it, that is the more desirable pleasure. If one of the two is, by those who are competently acquainted with both, placed so far above the other that they prefer it, even though knowing it to be attended with a greater amount of discontent, and would not resign it for any quantity of the other pleasure which their nature is capable of, we are justified in ascribing to the preferred enjoyment a superiority in quality, so far outweighing quantity as to render it, in comparison, of small account.

Now it is an unquestionable fact that those who are equally acquainted with, and equally capable of appreciating and enjoying, both, do give a most marked preference to the manner of existence which employs their higher faculties. Few human creatures would consent to be changed into any of the lower animals, for a promise of the fullest allowance of a beast's pleasures; no intelligent human being would consent to be a fool, no instructed person would be an ignoramus, no person of feeling and conscience would be selfish and base, even though they should be persuaded that the fool, the dunce, or the rascal is better satisfied with his lot than they are with theirs. They would not resign what they possess more than he for the most complete satisfaction of all the desires which they have in common with him. If they ever fancy they would, it is only in cases of unhappiness so extreme, that to escape from it they would exchange their lot for almost any other, however undesirable in their own eyes. A being of higher faculties requires more to make him happy, is capable probably of more acute suffering, and certainly accessible to it at more points, than one of an inferior type; but in spite of these liabilities, he can never really wish to sink into what he feels to be a lower grade of existence. We may give what explanation we please of this unwillingness; we may attribute it to pride, a name which is given indiscriminately to some of the most and to some of the least estimable feelings of which mankind are capable: we may refer it to the love of liberty and personal independence, an appeal to which was with the Stoics one of the most effective means for the inculcation of it; to the love of power, or to the love of excitement, both of which do really enter into and contribute to it: but its most appropriate appellation is a sense of dignity, which all human beings possess in one form or other, and in some, though by no means in exact, proportion to their higher faculties, and which is so essential a part of the happiness of those in whom it is strong, that nothing which conflicts with it could be, otherwise than momentarily, an object of desire

to them. Whoever supposes that this preference takes place at a sacrifice of happiness—that the superior being, in anything like equal circumstances, is not happier than the inferior—confounds the two very different ideas, of happiness, and content. It is indisputable that the being whose capacities of enjoyment are low, has the greatest chance of having them fully satisfied; and a highly endowed being will always feel that any happiness which he can look for, as the world is constituted, is imperfect. But he can learn to bear its imperfections, if they are at all bearable; and they will not make him envy the being who is indeed unconscious of the imperfections, but only because he feels not at all the good which those imperfections qualify. It is better to be a human being dissatisfied than a pig satisfied; better to be Socrates dissatisfied than a fool satisfied. And if the fool, or the pig, are a different opinion, it is because they only know their own side of the question. The other party to the comparison knows both sides.

It may be objected, that many who are capable of the higher pleasures, occasionally, under the influence of temptation, postpone them to the lower. But this is quite compatible with a full appreciation of the intrinsic superiority of the higher. Men often, from infirmity of character, make their election for the nearer good, though they know it to be the less valuable; and this no less when the choice is between two bodily pleasures, than when it is between bodily and mental. They pursue sensual indulgences to the injury of health, though perfectly aware that health is the greater good. It may be further objected, that many who begin with youthful enthusiasm for everything noble, as they advance in years sink into indolence and selfishness. But I do not believe that those who undergo this very common change, voluntarily choose the lower description of pleasures in preference to the higher. I believe that before they devote themselves exclusively to the one, they have already become incapable of the other. Capacity for the nobler feelings is in most natures a very tender plant, easily killed, not only by hostile influences, but by mere want of sustenance; and in the majority of young persons it speedily dies away if the occupations to which their position in life has devoted them, and the society into which it has thrown them, are not favorable to keeping that higher capacity in exercise. Men lose their high aspirations as they lose their intellectual tastes, because they have not time or opportunity for indulging them; and they addict themselves to inferior pleasures, not because they deliberately prefer them, but because they are either the only ones to which they have access, or the only ones which they are any longer capable of enjoying. It may be questioned whether any one who has remained equally susceptible to both classes of pleasures, ever knowingly and calmly preferred the lower; though many, in all ages, have broken down in an ineffectual attempt to combine both.

From this verdict of the only competent judges, I apprehend there can be no appeal. On a question which is the best worth having of two pleasures, or which of two modes of existence is the most grateful to the feelings, apart from its moral attributes and from its consequences, the judgment of those who are qualified by knowledge of both, or, if they differ, that of the majority among them, must be admitted as final. And there needs be the less hesitation to accept this judgment respecting the quality of pleasures, since there is no other tribunal to be referred to even on the question of quantity. What means are there of determining which is the acutest of two pains, or the intensest of two pleasurable sensations, except the general suffrage of those who are familiar with both? Neither pains nor pleasures are homogeneous, and pain is always heterogeneous with pleasure. What is there to decide whether a particular pleasure is worth purchasing at the cost of a particular pain, except the feelings and judgment of the experienced? When, therefore, those feelings and judgment declare the pleasures derived from the higher faculties to be preferable in kind, apart from the question of intensity, to those of which the animal nature, disjoined from the higher faculties, is susceptible, they are entitled on this subject to the same regard.

I have dwelt on this point, as being a necessary part of a perfectly just conception of Utility or Happiness, considered as the directive rule of human conduct. But it is by no means an indispensable condition to the acceptance of the utilitarian standard; for that standard is not the agent's own greatest happiness, but the greatest amount of happiness altogether; and if it may possibly be doubted whether a noble character is always the happier for its nobleness, there can be no doubt that it makes other people happier, and that the world in general is immensely a gainer by it. Utilitarianism, therefore, could only attain its end by the general cultivation of nobleness of character, even if each individual were only benefited by the nobleness of others, and his own, so far as happiness is concerned, were a sheer deduction from the benefit. But the bare enunciation of such an absurdity as this last, renders refutation superfluous.

According to the Greatest Happiness Principle, as above explained, the ultimate end, with reference to and for the sake of which all other things are desirable (whether we are considering our own good or that of other people), is an existence exempt as far as possible from pain, and as rich as possible in enjoyments, both in point of quantity and quality; the test of quality, and the rule for measuring it against quantity, being the preference felt by those who in their opportunities of experience, to which must be added their habits of self-consciousness and self-observation, are best furnished with the means of comparison. This, being, according to the utilitarian opinion, the end of human action, is necessarily also the standard of morality; which may accordingly be defined, the rules and precepts for human conduct, by the observance of which an existence such as has been described might be, to the greatest extent possible, secured to all mankind; and not to them only, but, so far as the nature of things admits, to the whole sentient creation.

[...]

Though it is only in a very imperfect state of the world's arrangements that any one can best serve the happiness of others by the absolute sacrifice of his own, yet so long as the world is in that imperfect state, I fully acknowledge that the readiness to make such a sacrifice is the highest virtue which can be found in man. I will add, that in this condition the world, paradoxical as the assertion may be, the conscious ability to do without happiness gives the best prospect of realizing, such happiness as is attainable. For nothing except that consciousness can raise a person above the chances of life, by making him feel that, let fate and fortune do their worst, they have not power to subdue him: which, once felt, frees him from excess of anxiety concerning the evils of life, and enables him, like many a Stoic in the worst times of the Roman Empire, to cultivate in tranquility the sources of satisfaction accessible to him, without concerning himself about the uncertainty of their duration, any more than about their inevitable end.

Meanwhile, let utilitarians never cease to claim the morality of self devotion as a possession which belongs by as good a right to them, as either to the Stoic or to the Transcendentalist.[1] The utilitarian morality does recognize in human beings the power of sacrificing their own greatest good for the good of others. It only refuses to admit that the sacrifice is itself a good. A sacrifice which does not increase,

---

1   *Transcendentalist*   Mill refers here to Kant and his philosophical school, which located the source of moral obligation outside of the empirical world.

or tend to increase, the sum total of happiness, it considers as wasted. The only self-renunciation which it applauds, is devotion to the happiness, or to some of the means of happiness, of others; either of mankind collectively, or of individuals within the limits imposed by the collective interests of mankind.

I must again repeat, what the assailants of utilitarianism seldom have the justice to acknowledge, that the happiness which forms the utilitarian standard of what is right in conduct, is not the agent's own happiness, but that of all concerned. As between his own happiness and that of others, utilitarianism requires him to be as strictly impartial as a disinterested and benevolent spectator.

Chapter 3: Of the Ultimate Sanction of the Principle of Utility

The Question is often asked, and properly so, in regard to any supposed moral standard—What is its sanction? what are the motives to obey it? or more specifically, what is the source of its obligation? whence does it derive its binding force? It is a necessary part of moral philosophy to provide the answer to this question; which, though frequently assuming the shape of an objection to the utilitarian morality, as if it had some special applicability to that above others, really arises in regard to all standards. It arises, in fact, whenever a person is called on to adopt a standard, or refer morality to any basis on which he has not been accustomed to rest it. For the customary morality, that which education and opinion have consecrated, is the only one which presents itself to the mind with the feeling of being in itself obligatory; and when a person is asked to believe that this morality derives its obligation from some general principle round which custom has not thrown the same halo, the assertion is to him a paradox; the supposed corollaries seem to have a more binding force than the original theorem; the superstructure seems to stand better without, than with, what is represented as its foundation. He says to himself, I feel that I am bound not to rob or murder, betray or deceive; but why am I bound to promote the general happiness? If my own happiness lies in something else, why may I not give that the preference?

If the view adopted by the utilitarian philosophy of the nature of the moral sense be correct, this difficulty will always present itself, until the influences which form moral character have taken the same hold of the principle which

they have taken of some of the consequences—until, by the improvement of education, the feeling of unity with our fellow-creatures shall be (what it cannot be denied that Christ intended it to be) as deeply rooted in our character, and to our own consciousness as completely a part of our nature, as the horror of crime is in an ordinarily well brought up young person. In the meantime, however, the difficulty has no peculiar application to the doctrine of utility, but is inherent in every attempt to analyze morality and reduce it to principles; which, unless the principle is already in men's minds invested with as much sacredness as any of its applications, always seems to divest them of a part of their sanctity.

The principle of utility either has, or there is no reason why it might not have, all the sanctions which belong to any other system of morals. Those sanctions are either external or internal. Of the external sanctions it is not necessary to speak at any length. They are, the hope of favor and the fear of displeasure, from our fellow creatures or from the Ruler of the Universe, along with whatever we may have of sympathy or affection for them, or of love and awe of Him, inclining us to do his will independently of selfish consequences. There is evidently no reason why all these motives for observance should not attach themselves to the utilitarian morality, as completely and as powerfully as to any other. Indeed, those of them which refer to our fellow creatures are sure to do so, in proportion to the amount of general intelligence; for whether there be any other ground of moral obligation than the general happiness or not, men do desire happiness; and however imperfect may be their own practice, they desire and commend all conduct in others towards themselves, by which they think their happiness is promoted. With regard to the religious motive, if men believe, as most profess to do, in the goodness of God, those who think that conduciveness to the general happiness is the essence, or even only the criterion of good, must necessarily believe that it is also that which God approves. The whole force therefore of external reward and punishment, whether physical or moral, and whether proceeding from God or from our fellow men, together with all that the capacities of human nature admit of disinterested[1] devotion to either, become available to enforce the utilitarian morality, in proportion as that morality is recognized; and the more powerfully, the more the appliances[2] of education and general cultivation are bent to the purpose.

---

1   *disinterested*   Without bias or self-interest.
2   *appliances*   Apparatuses.

So far as to external sanctions. The internal sanction of duty, whatever our standard of duty may be, is one and the same—a feeling in our own mind; a pain, more or less intense, attendant on violation of duty, which in properly cultivated moral natures rises, in the more serious cases, into shrinking from it as an impossibility. This feeling, when disinterested, and connecting itself with the pure idea of duty, and not with some particular form of it, or with any of the merely accessory circumstances, is the essence of Conscience; though in that complex phenomenon as it actually exists, the simple fact is in general all encrusted over with collateral associations, derived from sympathy, from love, and still more from fear; from all the forms of religious feeling; from the recollections of childhood and of all our past life; from self-esteem, desire of the esteem of others, and occasionally even self-abasement. This extreme complication is, I apprehend, the origin of the sort of mystical character which, by a tendency of the human mind of which there are many other examples, is apt to be attributed to the idea of moral obligation, and which leads people to believe that the idea cannot possibly attach itself to any other objects than those which, by a supposed mysterious law, are found in our present experience to excite it. Its binding force, however, consists in the existence of a mass of feeling which must be broken through in order to do what violates our standard of right, and which, if we do nevertheless violate that standard, will probably have to be encountered afterwards in the form of remorse. Whatever theory we have of the nature or origin of conscience, this is what essentially constitutes it.

The ultimate sanction, therefore, of all morality (external motives apart) being a subjective feeling in our own minds, I see nothing embarrassing to those whose standard is utility, in the question, what is the sanction of that particular standard? We may answer, the same as of all other moral standards—the conscientious feelings of mankind. Undoubtedly this sanction has no binding efficacy on those who do not possess the feelings it appeals to; but neither will these persons be more obedient to any other moral principle than to the utilitarian one. On them morality of any kind has no hold but through the external sanctions. Meanwhile the feelings exist, a fact in human nature, the reality of which, and the great power with which they are capable of acting on those in whom they have been duly cultivated, are proved by experience. No reason has ever been shown why they may not be cultivated to as great intensity in connection with the utilitarian, as with any other rule of morals.

[...]

Chapter 5: On the Connection between Justice and Utility

In all ages of speculation, one of the strongest obstacles to the reception of the doctrine that Utility or Happiness is the criterion of right and wrong, has been drawn from the idea of justice. The powerful sentiment, and apparently clear perception, which that word recalls with a rapidity and certainty resembling an instinct, have seemed to the majority of thinkers to point to an inherent quality in things; to show that the just must have an existence in Nature as something absolute, generically distinct from every variety of the Expedient,[1] and, in idea, opposed to it, though (as is commonly acknowledged) never, in the long run, disjoined from it in fact.

In the case of this, as of our other moral sentiments, there is no necessary connection between the question of its origin, and that of its binding force. That a feeling is bestowed on us by Nature, does not necessarily legitimate all its promptings. The feeling of justice might be a peculiar instinct, and might yet require, like our other instincts, to be controlled and enlightened by a higher reason. If we have intellectual instincts, leading us to judge in a particular way, as well as animal instincts that prompt us to act in a particular way, there is no necessity that the former should be more infallible in their sphere than the latter in theirs: it may as well happen that wrong judgments are occasionally suggested by those, as wrong actions by these. But though it is one thing to believe that we have natural feelings of justice, and another to acknowledge them as an ultimate criterion of conduct, these two opinions are very closely connected in point of fact. Mankind are always predisposed to believe that any subjective feeling, not otherwise accounted for, is a revelation of some objective reality. Our present object is to determine whether the reality, to which the feeling of justice corresponds, is one which needs any such special revelation; whether the justice or injustice of an action is a thing intrinsically peculiar, and distinct from all its other qualities, or only a combination of certain of those qualities, presented under a peculiar aspect. For the purpose of this inquiry it is practically important to consider whether the feeling itself, of justice and injustice, is *sui generis*[2] like our

---

1   *Expedient* An action is "expedient" in Mill's terms when it produces utility—when, that is, it will result in the greatest happiness for the greatest number of people.
2   *sui generis* Latin: of its own kind.

sensations of color and taste, or a derivative feeling, formed by a combination of others. And this it is the more essential to examine, as people are in general willing enough to allow, that objectively the dictates of justice coincide with a part of the field of General Expediency; but inasmuch as the subjective mental feeling of justice is different from that which commonly attaches to simple expediency, and, except in the extreme cases of the latter, is far more imperative in its demands, people find it difficult to see, in justice, only a particular kind or branch of general utility, and think that its superior binding force requires a totally different origin.

To throw light upon this question, it is necessary to attempt to ascertain what is the distinguishing character of justice, or of injustice: what is the quality, or whether there is any quality, attributed in common to all modes of conduct designated as unjust (for justice, like many other moral attributes, is best defined by its opposite), and distinguishing them from such modes of conduct as are disapproved, but without having that particular epithet of disapprobation[1] applied to them. If in everything which men are accustomed to characterize as just or unjust, some one common attribute or collection of attributes is always present, we may judge whether this particular attribute or combination of attributes would be capable of gathering round it a sentiment of that peculiar character and intensity by virtue of the general laws of our emotional constitution, or whether the sentiment is inexplicable, and requires to be regarded as a special provision of Nature. If we find the former to be the case, we shall, in resolving this question, have resolved also the main problem: if the latter, we shall have to seek for some other mode of investigating it.

To find the common attributes of a variety of objects, it is necessary to begin by surveying the objects themselves in the concrete. Let us therefore advert successively[2] to the various modes of action, and arrangements of human affairs, which are classed, by universal or widely spread opinion, as Just or as Unjust. The things well known to excite the sentiments associated with those names are of a very multifarious character. I shall pass them rapidly in review, without studying any particular arrangement.

In the first place, it is mostly considered unjust to deprive any one of his personal liberty, his property, or any other thing which belongs to him by law. Here, therefore, is one instance of the application of the terms just and un-

just in a perfectly definite sense, namely, that it is just to respect, unjust to violate, the legal rights of any one. But this judgment admits of several exceptions, arising from the other forms in which the notions of justice and injustice present themselves. For example, the person who suffers the deprivation may (as the phrase is) have forfeited the rights which he is so deprived of: a case to which we shall return presently. But also,

Secondly; the legal rights of which he is deprived, may be rights which ought not to have belonged to him; in other words, the law which confers on him these rights, may be a bad law. When it is so, or when (which is the same thing for our purpose) it is supposed to be so, opinions will differ as to the justice or injustice of infringing it. Some maintain that no law, however bad, ought to be disobeyed by an individual citizen; that his opposition to it, if shown at all, should only be shown in endeavoring to get it altered by competent authority. This opinion (which condemns many of the most illustrious benefactors of mankind, and would often protect pernicious institutions against the only weapons which, in the state of things existing at the time, have any chance of succeeding against them) is defended, by those who hold it, on grounds of expediency; principally on that of the importance, to the common interest of mankind, of maintaining inviolate the sentiment of submission to law. Other persons, again, hold the directly contrary opinion, that any law, judged to be bad, may blamelessly be disobeyed, even though it be not judged to be unjust, but only inexpedient; while others would confine the license of disobedience to the case of unjust laws: but again, some say, that all laws which are inexpedient are unjust; since every law imposes some restriction on the natural liberty of mankind, which restriction is an injustice, unless legitimated by tending to their good. Among these diversities of opinion, it seems to be universally admitted that there may be unjust laws, and that law, consequently, is not the ultimate criterion of justice, but may give to one person a benefit, or impose on another an evil, which justice condemns. When, however, a law is thought to be unjust, it seems always to be regarded as being so in the same way in which a breach of law is unjust, namely, by infringing somebody's right; which, as it cannot in this case be a legal right, receives a different appellation, and is called a moral right. We may say, therefore, that a second case of injustice consists in taking or withholding from any person that to which he has a moral right.

Thirdly, it is universally considered just that each person should obtain that (whether good or evil) which he de-

---

1   *epithet of disapprobation*   Insulting term of disapproval.
2   *advert successively*   Refer, one-by-one, in turn.

serves; and unjust that he should obtain a good, or be made to undergo an evil, which he does not deserve. This is, perhaps, the clearest and most emphatic form in which the idea of justice is conceived by the general mind. As it involves the notion of desert, the question arises, what constitutes desert? Speaking in a general way, a person is understood to deserve good if he does right, evil if he does wrong; and in a more particular sense, to deserve good from those to whom he does or has done good, and evil from those to whom he does or has done evil. The precept of returning good for evil has never been regarded as a case of the fulfillment of justice, but as one in which the claims of justice are waived, in obedience to other considerations.

Fourthly, it is confessedly unjust to break faith with any one: to violate an engagement, either express or implied, or disappoint expectations raised by our conduct, at least if we have raised those expectations knowingly and voluntarily. Like the other obligations of justice already spoken of, this one is not regarded as absolute, but as capable of being overruled by a stronger obligation of justice on the other side; or by such conduct on the part of the person concerned as is deemed to absolve us from our obligation to him, and to constitute a forfeiture of the benefit which he has been led to expect.

Fifthly, it is, by universal admission, inconsistent with justice to be partial; to show favor or preference to one person over another, in matters to which favor and preference do not properly apply. Impartiality, however, does not seem to be regarded as a duty in itself, but rather as instrumental to some other duty; for it is admitted that favor and preference are not always censurable, and indeed the cases in which they are condemned are rather the exception than the rule. A person would be more likely to be blamed than applauded for giving his family or friends no superiority in good offices[1] over strangers, when he could do so without violating any other duty; and no one thinks it unjust to seek one person in preference to another as a friend, connection, or companion. Impartiality where rights are concerned is of course obligatory, but this is involved in the more general obligation of giving to every one his right. A tribunal, for example, must be impartial, because it is bound to award, without regard to any other consideration, a disputed object to the one of two parties who has the right to it. There are other cases in which impartiality means, being solely influenced by desert; as with those who, in the cap-

acity of judges, preceptors, or parents, administer reward and punishment as such. There are cases, again, in which it means, being solely influenced by consideration for the public interest; as in making a selection among candidates for a government employment. Impartiality, in short, as an obligation of justice, may be said to mean, being exclusively influenced by the considerations which it is supposed ought to influence the particular case in hand; and resisting the solicitation of any motives which prompt to conduct different from what those considerations would dictate.

Nearly allied to the idea of impartiality is that of equality; which often enters as a component part both into the conception of justice and into the practice of it, and, in the eyes of many persons, constitutes its essence. But in this, still more than in any other case, the notion of justice varies in different persons, and always conforms in its variations to their notion of utility. Each person maintains that equality is the dictate of justice, except where he thinks that expediency requires inequality. The justice of giving equal protection to the rights of all, is maintained by those who support the most outrageous inequality in the rights themselves. Even in slave countries it is theoretically admitted that the rights of the slave, such as they are, ought to be as sacred as those of the master; and that a tribunal which fails to enforce them with equal strictness is wanting in justice; while, at the same time, institutions which leave to the slave scarcely any rights to enforce, are not deemed unjust, because they are not deemed inexpedient. Those who think that utility requires distinctions of rank, do not consider it unjust that riches and social privileges should be unequally dispensed; but those who think this inequality inexpedient, think it unjust also. Whoever thinks that government is necessary, sees no injustice in as much inequality as is constituted by giving to the magistrate powers not granted to other people. Even among those who hold leveling[2] doctrines, there are as many questions of justice as there are differences of opinion about expediency. Some Communists consider it unjust that the produce of the labor of the community should be shared on any other principle than that of exact equality; others think it just that those should receive most whose wants are greatest; while others hold that those who work harder, or who produce more, or whose services are more valuable to the community, may justly claim a larger quota in the division of the produce. And the sense of natural justice may be plausibly appealed to on behalf of every one of these opinions.

---

1 *good offices* Services, kindnesses, attentions.

2 *leveling* Producing equality.

Among so many diverse applications of the term justice, which yet is not regarded as ambiguous, it is a matter of some difficulty to seize the mental link which holds them together, and on which the moral sentiment adhering to the term essentially depends....

[...]

... We do not call anything wrong, unless we mean to imply that a person ought to be punished in some way or other for doing it; if not by law, by the opinion of his fellow-creatures; if not by opinion, by the reproaches of his own conscience. This seems the real turning point of the distinction between morality and simple expediency. It is a part of the notion of Duty in every one of its forms, that a person may rightfully be compelled to fulfill it. Duty is a thing which may be exacted from a person, as one exacts a debt. Unless we think that it may be exacted from him, we do not call it his duty. Reasons of prudence, or the interest of other people, may militate against actually exacting it; but the person himself, it is clearly understood, would not be entitled to complain. There are other things, on the contrary, which we wish that people should do, which we like or admire them for doing, perhaps dislike or despise them for not doing, but yet admit that they are not bound to do; it is not a case of moral obligation; we do not blame them, that is, we do not think that they are proper objects of punishment. How we come by these ideas of deserving and not deserving punishment, will appear, perhaps, in the sequel;[1] but I think there is no doubt that this distinction lies at the bottom of the notions of right and wrong; that we call any conduct wrong, or employ, instead, some other term of dislike or disparagement, according as we think that the person ought, or ought not, to be punished for it; and we say, it would be right, to do so and so, or merely that it would be desirable or laudable, according as we would wish to see the person whom it concerns, compelled, or only persuaded and exhorted, to act in that manner.

This, therefore, being the characteristic difference which marks off, not justice, but morality in general, from the remaining provinces of Expediency and Worthiness; the character is still to be sought which distinguishes justice from other branches of morality. Now it is known that ethical writers divide moral duties into two classes, denoted by the ill-chosen expressions, duties of perfect and of imperfect obligation; the latter being those in which, though the act is obligatory, the particular occasions of performing it are left to our choice, as in the case of charity or beneficence, which we are indeed bound to practice, but not towards any definite person, nor at any prescribed time. In the more precise language of philosophic jurists, duties of perfect obligation are those duties in virtue of which a correlative right resides in some person or persons; duties of imperfect obligation are those moral obligations which do not give birth to any right. I think it will be found that this distinction exactly coincides with that which exists between justice and the other obligations of morality. In our survey of the various popular acceptations of justice, the term appeared generally to involve the idea of a personal right—a claim on the part of one or more individuals, like that which the law gives when it confers a proprietary or other legal right. Whether the injustice consists in depriving a person of a possession, or in breaking faith with him, or in treating him worse than he deserves, or worse than other people who have no greater claims, in each case the supposition implies two things—a wrong done, and some assignable person who is wronged. Injustice may also be done by treating a person better than others; but the wrong in this case is to his competitors, who are also assignable persons. It seems to me that this feature in the case—a right in some person, correlative to the moral obligation—constitutes the specific difference between justice, and generosity or beneficence. Justice implies something which it is not only right to do, and wrong not to do, but which some individual person can claim from us as his moral right. No one has a moral right to our generosity or beneficence, because we are not morally bound to practice those virtues towards any given individual. And it will be found with respect to this, as to every correct definition, that the instances which seem to conflict with it are those which most confirm it. For if a moralist attempts, as some have done, to make out that mankind generally, though not any given individual, have a right to all the good we can do them, he at once, by that thesis, includes generosity and beneficence within the category of justice. He is obliged to say, that our utmost exertions are due to our fellow creatures, thus assimilating them to a debt; or that nothing less can be a sufficient return for what society does for us, thus classing the case as one of gratitude; both of which are acknowledged cases of justice. Wherever there is right, the case is one of justice, and not of the virtue of beneficence: and whoever does not place the distinction between justice and morality in general, where we have now placed it, will be found to make no distinction between them at all, but to merge all morality in justice.

---

1 *the sequel* What follows (in this work).

Having thus endeavored to determine the distinctive elements which enter into the composition of the idea of justice, we are ready to enter on the inquiry, whether the feeling, which accompanies the idea, is attached to it by a special dispensation of nature, or whether it could have grown up, by any known laws, out of the idea itself; and in particular, whether it can have originated in considerations of general expediency.

I conceive that the sentiment itself does not arise from anything which would commonly, or correctly, be termed an idea of expediency; but that though the sentiment does not, whatever is moral in it does.

We have seen that the two essential ingredients in the sentiment of justice are, the desire to punish a person who has done harm, and the knowledge or belief that there is some definite individual or individuals to whom harm has been done.

Now it appears to me, that the desire to punish a person who has done harm to some individual is a spontaneous outgrowth from two sentiments, both in the highest degree natural, and which either are or resemble instincts; the impulse of self-defense, and the feeling of sympathy.

It is natural to resent, and to repel or retaliate, any harm done or attempted against ourselves, or against those with whom we sympathize. The origin of this sentiment it is not necessary here to discuss. Whether it be an instinct or a result of intelligence, it is, we know, common to all animal nature; for every animal tries to hurt those who have hurt, or who it thinks are about to hurt, itself or its young. Human beings, on this point, only differ from other animals in two particulars. First, in being capable of sympathizing, not solely with their offspring, or, like some of the more noble animals, with some superior animal who is kind to them, but with all human, and even with all sentient, beings. Secondly, in having a more developed intelligence, which gives a wider range to the whole of their sentiments, whether self-regarding or sympathetic. By virtue of his superior intelligence, even apart from his superior range of sympathy, a human being is capable of apprehending a community of interest between himself and the human society of which he forms a part, such that any conduct which threatens the security of the society generally, is threatening to his own, and calls forth his instinct (if instinct it be) of self-defense. The same superiority of intelligence joined to the power of sympathizing with human beings generally, enables him to attach himself to the collective idea of his tribe, his country, or mankind, in such a manner that any act hurtful to them, raises his instinct of sympathy, and urges him to resistance.

The sentiment of justice, in that one of its elements which consists of the desire to punish, is thus, I conceive, the natural feeling of retaliation or vengeance, rendered by intellect and sympathy applicable to those injuries, that is, to those hurts, which wound us through, or in common with, society at large. This sentiment, in itself, has nothing moral in it; what is moral is, the exclusive subordination of it to the social sympathies, so as to wait on and obey their call. For the natural feeling would make us resent indiscriminately whatever any one does that is disagreeable to us; but when moralized by the social feeling, it only acts in the directions conformable to the general good: just persons resenting a hurt to society, though not otherwise a hurt to themselves, and not resenting a hurt to themselves, however painful, unless it be of the kind which society has a common interest with them in the repression of.

It is no objection against this doctrine to say, that when we feel our sentiment of justice outraged, we are not thinking of society at large, or of any collective interest, but only of the individual case. It is common enough certainly, though the reverse of commendable, to feel resentment merely because we have suffered pain; but a person whose resentment is really a moral feeling, that is, who considers whether an act is blamable before he allows himself to resent it—such a person, though he may not say expressly to himself that he is standing up for the interest of society, certainly does feel that he is asserting a rule which is for the benefit of others as well as for his own. If he is not feeling this—if he is regarding the act solely as it affects him individually—he is not consciously just; he is not concerning himself about the justice of his actions. This is admitted even by anti-utilitarian moralists. When Kant (as before remarked) propounds as the fundamental principle of morals, "So act, that thy rule of conduct might be adopted as a law by all rational beings," he virtually acknowledges that the interest of mankind collectively, or at least of mankind indiscriminately, must be in the mind of the agent when conscientiously deciding on the morality of the act. Otherwise he uses words without a meaning: for, that a rule even of utter selfishness could not possibly be adopted by all rational beings—that there is any insuperable obstacle in the nature of things to its adoption—cannot be even plausibly maintained. To give any meaning to Kant's principle, the sense put upon it must be, that we ought to shape our conduct by a rule which all rational beings might adopt with benefit to their collective interest.

To recapitulate: the idea of justice supposes two things; a rule of conduct, and a sentiment which sanctions the rule. The first must be supposed common to all mankind, and intended for their good. The other (the sentiment) is a desire that punishment may be suffered by those who infringe the rule. There is involved, in addition, the conception of some definite person who suffers by the infringement; whose rights (to use the expression appropriated to the case) are violated by it. And the sentiment of justice appears to me to be, the animal desire to repel or retaliate a hurt or damage to oneself, or to those with whom one sympathizes, widened so as to include all persons, by the human capacity of enlarged sympathy, and the human conception of intelligent self-interest. From the latter elements, the feeling derives its morality; from the former, its peculiar impressiveness, and energy of self-assertion.

I have, throughout, treated the idea of a right residing in the injured person, and violated by the injury, not as a separate element in the composition of the idea and sentiment, but as one of the forms in which the other two elements clothe themselves. These elements are, a hurt to some assignable person or persons on the one hand, and a demand for punishment on the other. An examination of our own minds, I think, will show, that these two things include all that we mean when we speak of violation of a right. When we call anything a person's right, we mean that he has a valid claim on society to protect him in the possession of it, either by the force of law, or by that of education and opinion. If he has what we consider a sufficient claim, on whatever account, to have something guaranteed to him by society, we say that he has a right to it. If we desire to prove that anything does not belong to him by right, we think this done as soon as it is admitted that society ought not to take measures for securing it to him, but should leave him to chance, or to his own exertions. Thus, a person is said to have a right to what he can earn in fair professional competition; because society ought not to allow any other person to hinder him from endeavoring to earn in that manner as much as he can. But he has not a right to three hundred a-year, though he may happen to be earning it; because society is not called on to provide that he shall earn that sum. On the contrary, if he owns ten thousand pounds three per cent stock, he has a right to three hundred a-year; because society has come under an obligation to provide him with an income of that amount.

To have a right, then, is, I conceive, to have something which society ought to defend me in the possession of. If the objector goes on to ask, why it ought? I can give him no other reason than general utility.

[. . .]

It appears from what has been said, that justice is a name for certain moral requirements, which, regarded collectively, stand higher in the scale of social utility, and are therefore of more paramount obligation, than any others; though particular cases may occur in which some other social duty is so important, as to overrule any one of the general maxims of justice. Thus, to save a life, it may not only be allowable, but a duty, to steal, or take by force, the necessary food or medicine, or to kidnap, and compel to officiate, the only qualified medical practitioner. In such cases, as we do not call anything justice which is not a virtue, we usually say, not that justice must give way to some other moral principle, but that what is just in ordinary cases is, by reason of that other principle, not just in the particular case. By this useful accommodation of language, the character of indefeasibility[1] attributed to justice is kept up, and we are saved from the necessity of maintaining that there can be laudable injustice.

The considerations which have now been adduced resolve, I conceive, the only real difficulty in the utilitarian theory of morals. It has always been evident that all cases of justice are also cases of expediency: the difference is in the peculiar sentiment which attaches to the former, as contradistinguished from the latter. If this characteristic sentiment has been sufficiently accounted for; if there is no necessity to assume for it any peculiarity of origin; if it is simply the natural feeling of resentment, moralized by being made coextensive with the demands of social good; and if this feeling not only does but ought to exist in all the classes of cases to which the idea of justice corresponds; that idea no longer presents itself as a stumbling-block to the utilitarian ethics. Justice remains the appropriate name for certain social utilities which are vastly more important, and therefore more absolute and imperative, than any others are as a class (though not more so than others may be in particular cases); and which, therefore, ought to be, as well as naturally are, guarded by a sentiment not only different in degree, but also in kind; distinguished from the milder feeling which attaches to the mere idea of promoting human pleasure or convenience, at once by the

---

1 *indefeasibility* Impossibility of annulment, of making inapplicable.

more definite nature of its commands, and by the sterner character of its sanctions.

◆ ◆ ◆ ◆ ◆

from The Subjection of Women (1869)

The object of this Essay is to explain as clearly as I am able grounds of an opinion which I have held from the very earliest period when I had formed any opinions at all on social political matters, and which, instead of being weakened or modified, has been constantly growing stronger by the progress of reflection and the experience of life. That the principle which regulates the existing social relations between the two sexes—the legal subordination of one sex to the other—is wrong itself, and now one of the chief hindrances to human improvement; and that it ought to be replaced by a principle of perfect equality, admitting no power or privilege on the one side, nor disability on the other.

The very words necessary to express the task I have undertaken, show how arduous it is. But it would be a mistake to suppose that the difficulty of the case must lie in the insufficiency or obscurity of the grounds of reason on which my conviction rests. The difficulty is that which exists in all cases in which there is a mass of feeling to be contended against. So long as opinion is strongly rooted in the feelings, it gains rather than loses instability by having a preponderating[1] weight of argument against it. For if it were accepted as a result of argument, the refutation of the argument might shake the solidity of the conviction; but when it rests solely on feeling, the worse it fares in argumentative contest, the more persuaded adherents are that their feeling must have some deeper ground, which the arguments do not reach; and while the feeling remains, it is always throwing up fresh entrenchments of argument to repair any breach made in the old. And there are so many causes tending to make the feelings connected with this subject the most intense and most deeply-rooted of those which gather round and protect old institutions and custom, that we need not wonder to find them as yet less undermined and loosened than any of the rest by the progress the great modern spiritual and social transition; nor suppose that the barbarisms to which

men cling longest must be less barbarisms than those which they earlier shake off.

In every respect the burthen[2] is hard on those who attack an almost universal opinion. They must be very fortunate well as unusually capable if they obtain a hearing at all. They have more difficulty in obtaining a trial, than any other litigants have in getting a verdict. If they do extort a hearing, they are subjected to a set of logical requirements totally different from those exacted from other people. In all other cases, burthen of proof is supposed to lie with the affirmative. If a person is charged with a murder, it rests with those who accuse him to give proof of his guilt, not with himself to prove his innocence. If there is a difference of opinion about the reality of an alleged historical event, in which the feelings of men general are not much interested, as the Siege of Troy[3] example, those who maintain that the event took place expected to produce their proofs, before those who take the other side can be required to say anything; and at no time these required to do more than show that the evidence produced by the others is of no value. Again, in practical matters, the burthen of proof is supposed to be with those who are against liberty; who contend for any restriction or prohibition either any limitation of the general freedom of human action or any disqualification or disparity of privilege affecting one person or kind of persons, as compared with others. The *a priori* presumption[4] is in favor of freedom and impartiality. It is held that there should be no restraint not required by the general good, and that the law should be no respecter of persons[5] but should treat all alike, save where dissimilarity of treatment is required by positive reasons, either of justice or of policy. But of none of these rules of evidence will the benefit be allowed to those who maintain the opinion I profess. It is useless [for] me to say that those who maintain the doctrine that men have a right to command and women are under an obligation [to] obey, or that men are fit for government and women unfit, on the affirmative side of the question, and that they are bound to show positive evidence for the asser-

---

1   *preponderating* Outweighing.

2   *burthen* Burden.

3   *Siege of Troy* Homer's *Iliad* tells the story of the last year of a ten-year siege of the city of Troy by the Achaeans during the Trojan War. The Greeks supposed this to be a historical event, but many later historians doubted it.

4   *a priori presumption* *a priori* is literally translated from the Latin as *from before-hand.* Mill refers to what is assumed before serious investigation begins.

5   *should be no respecter of persons* Should show no special concern for one person over another.

tions, or submit to their rejection. It is equally unavailing for me to say that those who deny to women any freedom or privilege rightly allow to men, having the double presumption against them that they are opposing freedom and recommending partiality, must held to the strictest proof of their case, and unless their success be such as to exclude all doubt, the judgment ought to against them. These would be thought good pleas in any common case; but they will not be thought so in this instance. Before I could hope to make any impression, I should be expected not only to answer all that has ever been said by those who take the other side of the question, but to imagine that could be said by them—to find them in reasons, as I answer all I find: and besides refuting all arguments for the affirmative, I shall be called upon for invincible positive arguments to prove a negative. And even if I could do all and leave the opposite party with a host of unanswered arguments against them, and not a single unrefuted one on side, I should be thought to have done little; for a cause supported on the one hand by universal usage, and on the other by so great a preponderance of popular sentiment, is supposed to have a presumption in its favor, superior to any conviction which an appeal to reason has power to produce in any intellects but those of a high class.

I do not mention these difficulties to complain of them; first, because it would be useless; they are inseparable from having to contend through people's understandings against the hostility their feelings and practical tendencies: and truly the understandings of the majority of mankind would need to be much better cultivated than has ever yet been the case, before they be asked to place such reliance in their own power of estimating arguments, as to give up practical principles in which have been born and bred, and which are the basis of much existing order of the world, at the first argumentative attack which they are not capable of logically resisting. I do not therefore quarrel with them for having too little faith in argument, but for having too much faith in custom and the general feeling. It is one of the characteristic prejudices of the reaction of the nineteenth century against the eighteenth, to accord to the unreasoning elements in human nature the infallibility which the eighteenth century is supposed to have ascribed to the reasoning elements. For the apotheosis[1] of Reason we have substituted that of Instinct; and we call a thing instinct which we find in ourselves and for which we cannot trace any rational foundation. This idolatry, infinitely more degrading than

the other, and the most pernicious of the false worships of the present day, of all of which it is now the main support, will probably hold its ground until it gives way before a sound psychology laying bare the real root of much that is bowed down to as the intention of Nature and ordinance of God. As regards the present question, I am willing to accept the unfavorable conditions which the prejudice assigns to me. I consent that established custom, and the general feelings, should be deemed conclusive against me, unless that custom and feeling from age to age can be shown to have owed their existence to other causes than their soundness, and to have derived their power from the worse rather than the better parts of human nature. I am willing that judgment should go against me, unless I can show that my judge has been tampered with. The concession is not so great as it might appear; for to prove this, is by far the easiest portion of my task.

The generality of a practice is in some cases a strong presumption that it is, or at all events once was, conducive to laudable ends. This is the case, when the practice was first adopted, or afterwards kept up, as a means to such ends, and was grounded on experience of the mode in which they could be most effectually attained. If the authority of men over women, when first established, had been the result of a conscientious comparison between different modes of constituting the government of society; if, after trying various other modes of social organization—the government of women over men, equality between the two, and such mixed and divided modes of government as might be invented—it had been decided, on the testimony of experience, that the mode in which women are wholly under the rule of men, having no share at all in public concerns, and each in private being under the legal obligation of obedience to the man with whom she has associated her destiny, was the arrangement most conducive to the happiness and well-being of both; its general adoption might then be fairly thought to be some evidence that, at the time when it was adopted, it was the best: though even then the considerations which recommended it may, like so many other primeval social facts of the greatest importance, have subsequently, in the course of ages, ceased to exist. But the state of the case is in every respect the reverse of this. In the first place, the opinion in favor of the present system, which entirely subordinates the weaker sex to the stronger, rests upon theory only; for there never has been trial made of any other: so that experience, in the sense in which it is vulgarly opposed to theory, cannot be pretended to have pronounced

---

1   *apotheosis* Transformation into a god.

any verdict. And in the second place, the adoption of this system of inequality never was the result of deliberation, or forethought, or any social ideas, or any notion whatever of what conduced to the benefit of humanity or the good order of society. It arose simply from the fact that from the very earliest twilight of human society, every woman (owing to the value attached to her by men, combined with her inferiority in muscular strength) was found in a state of bondage to some man. Laws and systems of polity always begin by recognizing the relations they find already existing between individuals. They convert what was a mere physical fact into a legal right, give it the sanction of society, and principally aim at the substitution of public and organized means of asserting and protecting these rights, instead of the irregular and lawless conflict of physical strength. Those who had already been compelled to obedience became in this manner legally bound to it. Slavery, from being a mere affair of force between the master and the slave, became regularized and a matter of compact[1] among the masters, who, binding themselves to one another for common protection, guaranteed by their collective strength the private possessions of each, including his slaves. In early times, the great majority of the male sex were slaves, as well as the whole of the female. And many ages elapsed, some of them ages of high cultivation, before any thinker was bold enough to question the rightfulness, and the absolute social necessity, either of the one slavery or of the other. By degrees such thinkers did arise; and (the general progress of society assisting) the slavery of the male sex has, in all the countries of Christian Europe at least (though, in one of them, only within the last few years[2]) been at length abolished, and that of the female sex has been gradually changed into a milder form of dependence. But this dependence, as it exists at present, is not an original institution, taking a fresh start from considerations of justice and social expediency—it is the primitive state of slavery lasting on, through successive mitigations and modifications occasioned by the same causes which have softened the general manners, and brought all human relations more under the control of justice and the influence of humanity. It has not lost the taint of its brutal origin. No presumption in its favor, therefore, can be drawn from the fact of its existence. The only such

presumption which it could be supposed to have, must be grounded on its having lasted till now, when so many other things which came down from the same odious source have been done away with. And this, indeed, is what makes it strange to ordinary ears, to hear it asserted that the inequality of rights between men and women has no other source than the law of the strongest.

That this statement should have the effect of a paradox, is in some respects creditable to the progress of civilization, and the improvement of the moral sentiments of mankind. We now live—that is to say, one or two of the most advanced nations of the world now live—in a state in which the law of the strongest seems to be entirely abandoned as the regulating principle of the world's affairs: nobody professes it, and, as regards most of the relations between human beings, nobody is permitted to practice it. When anyone succeeds in doing so, it is under cover of some pretext which gives him the semblance of having some general social interest on his side. This being the ostensible state of things, people flatter themselves that the rule of mere force is ended; that the law of the strongest cannot be the reason of existence of anything which has remained in full operation down to the present time. However any of our present institutions may have begun, it can only, they think, have been preserved to this period of advanced civilization by a well-grounded feeling of its adaptation to human nature, and conduciveness to the general good. They do not understand the great vitality and durability of institutions which place right on the side of might; how intensely they are clung to; how the good as well as the bad propensities and sentiments of those who have power in their hands, become identified with retaining it; how slowly these bad institutions give way, one at a time, the weakest first. Beginning with those which are least interwoven with the daily habits of life; and how very rarely those who have obtained legal power because they first had physical, have ever lost their hold of it until the physical power had passed over to the other side. Such shifting of the physical force not having taken place in the case of women; this fact, combined with all the peculiar and characteristic features of the particular case, made it certain from the first that this branch of the system of right founded on might, though softened in its most atrocious features at an earlier period than several of the others, would be the very last to disappear. It was inevitable that this one case of a social relation grounded on force, would survive through generations of institutions grounded on equal justice, an almost solitary exception to the general character of their laws and

---

1   *compact* Agreement.
2   *last few years* Mill may be referring to the Netherlands, which abolished slavery at home and in its colonies in 1863. Mill wrote this six years later. (Slavery was abolished throughout the British Empire in 1833.)

customs; but which, so long as it does not proclaim its own origin, and as discussion has not brought out its true character, is not felt to jar with modern civilization, any more than domestic slavery among the Greeks jarred with their notion of themselves as a free people.

The truth is, that people of the present and the last two or three generations have lost all practical sense of the primitive condition of humanity; and only the few who have studied history accurately, or have much frequented the parts of the world occupied by the living representatives of ages long past, are able to form any mental picture of what society then was. People are not aware how entirely, in former ages, the law of superior strength was the rule of life; how publicly and openly it was avowed, I do not say cynically or shamelessly—for these words imply a feeling that there was something in it to be ashamed of, and no such notion could find a place in the faculties of any person in those ages, except a philosopher or a saint. History gives a cruel experience of human nature, in showing how exactly the regard due to the life, possessions, and entire earthly happiness of any class of persons, was measured by what they had the power of enforcing; how all who made any resistance to authorities that had arms in their hands, however dreadful might be the provocation, had not only the law of force but all other laws, and all the notions of social obligation against them; and in the eyes of those whom they resisted, were not only guilty of crime, but of the worst of all crimes, deserving the most cruel chastisement which human beings could inflict. The first small vestige of a feeling of obligation in a superior to acknowledge any right in inferiors, began when he had been induced, for convenience, to make some promise to them. Though these promises, even when sanctioned by the most solemn oaths, were for many ages revoked or violated on the most trifling provocation or temptation, it is probably that this, except by persons of still worse than the average morality, was seldom done without some twinges of conscience. The ancient republics, being mostly grounded from the first upon some kind of mutual compact, or at any rate formed by an union of persons not very unequal in strength, afforded, in consequence, the first instance of a portion of human relations fenced round, and placed under the dominion of another law than that of force. And though the original law of force remained in full operation between them and their slaves, and also (except so far as limited by express compact) between a commonwealth and its subjects, or other independent commonwealths; the banishment of that primitive law even from so narrow a field, commenced the regeneration of human nature, by giving birth to sentiments of which experience soon demonstrated the immense value even for material interests, and which thence forward only required to be enlarged, not created. Though slaves were no part of the commonwealth, it was in the free states that slaves were first felt to have rights as human beings. The Stoics[1] were, I believe, the first (except so far as the Jewish law constitutes an exception) who taught as a part of morality that men were bound by moral obligations to their slaves. No one, after Christianity became ascendant, could ever again have been a stranger to this belief, in theory; nor, after the rise of the Catholic Church, was it ever without persons to stand up for it. Yet to enforce it was the most arduous task which Christianity ever had to perform. For more than thousand years the Church kept up the contest, with hardly any perceptible success. It was not for want of power over men's minds. Its power was prodigious. It could make kings and nobles resign their most valued possessions to enrich the Church. It could make thousands in the prime of life and the height of worldly advantages, shut themselves up in convents to work out their salvation by poverty, fasting, and prayer. It could send hundreds of thousands across land and sea, Europe and Asia, to give their lives for the deliverance of the Holy Sepulcher.[2] It could make kings relinquish wives who were the object of their passionate attachment, because the Church declared that they were within the seventh (by our calculation the fourteenth) degree of relationship.[3] All this it did; but it could not make men fight less with one another, nor tyrannize less cruelly over the serfs, and when they were able, over burgesses.[4] It could not make them renounce either of the applications of force; force militant, or force triumphant. This they could never be induced to do until they were themselves in their turn compelled by superior force. Only by the growing power of kings was an end put to fighting except between kings, or competitors for kingship; only by the growth of a wealthy and warlike bourgeoisie[5] in the fortified towns, and of a plebeian[6] in-

---

1   *Stoics*   Ancient Greek and Roman school of philosophy, founded by Zeno.
2   *Sepulcher*   Burial vault. Taking back possession of Christ's sepulcher, supposedly in Jerusalem, was one of the objectives of the Crusades.
3   *degree of relationship*   A measure of how closely two people were related.
4   *burgesses*   Citizens of an English borough.
5   *bourgeoisie*   Middle class.
6   *plebeian*   Lower class.

fantry which proved more powerful in the field than the undisciplined chivalry,[1] was the insolent tyranny of the nobles over the bourgeoisie and peasantry brought within some bounds. It was persisted in not only until, but long after, the oppressed had obtained a power enabling them often to take conspicuous vengeance; and on the Continent much of it continued to the time of the French Revolution, though in England the earlier and better organization of the democratic classes put an end to it sooner, by establishing equal laws and free national institutions.

If people are mostly so little aware how completely, during the greater part of the duration of our species, the law of force was the avowed rule of general conduct, any other being only a special and exceptional consequence of peculiar ties—and from how very recent a date it is that the affairs of society in general have been even pretended to be regulated according to any moral law; as little do people remember or consider, how institutions and customs which never had any ground but the law of force, last on into ages and states of general opinion which never would have permitted their first establishment. Less than forty years ago, Englishmen might still by law hold human beings in bondage as saleable property: within the present century they might kidnap them and carry them off, and work them literally to death. This absolutely extreme case of the law of force, condemned by those who can tolerate almost every other form of arbitrary power, and which, of all others presents features the most revolting to the feelings of all who look at it from an impartial position, was the law of civilized and Christian England within the memory of persons now living: and in one half of Anglo-Saxon America three or four years ago, not only did slavery exist, but the slave-trade, and the breeding of slaves expressly for it, was a general practice between slave states. Yet not only was there a greater strength of sentiment against it, but, in England at least, a less amount either of feeling or of interest in favor of it, than of any other of the customary abuses of force: for its motive was the love of gain, unmixed and undisguised; and those who profited by it were a very small numerical fraction of the country, while the natural feeling of all who were not personally interested in it, was unmitigated abhorrence. So extreme an instance makes it almost superfluous to refer to any other: but consider the long duration of absolute monarchy. In England at present it is the almost universal conviction that military despotism is a case of the law of force,

having no other origin or justification. Yet in all the great nations of Europe except England it either still exists, or has only just ceased to exist, and has even now a strong party favorable to it in all ranks of the people, especially among persons of station and consequence. Such is the power of an established system, even when far from universal; when not only in almost every period of history there have been great and well-known examples of the contrary system, but these have almost invariably been afforded by the most illustrious and most prosperous communities. In this case, too, the possessor of the undue power, the person directly interested in it, is only one person, while those who are subject to it and suffer from it are literally all the rest. The yoke is naturally and necessarily humiliating to all persons, except the one who is on the throne, together with, at most, the one who expects to succeed to it. How different are these cases from that of the power of men over women! I am not now prejudging the question of its justifiableness. I am showing how vastly more permanent it could not but be, even if not justifiable, than these other dominations which have nevertheless lasted down to our own time. Whatever gratification of pride there is in the possession of power, and whatever personal interest in its exercise, is in this case not confined to a limited class, but common to the whole male sex. Instead of being, to most of its supporters) a thing desirable chiefly in the abstract, or, like the political ends usually contended for by factions, of little private importance to any but the leaders; it comes home to the person and hearth of every male head of a family, and of everyone who looks forward to being so. The clodhopper[2] exercises, or is to exercise, his share of the power equally with the highest nobleman. And the case is that in which the desire of power is the strongest: for everyone who desires power, desires it most over those who are nearest to him, with whom his life is passed, with whom he has most concerns in common and in whom any independence of his authority is oftenest likely to interfere with his individual preferences. If, in the other cases specified, powers manifestly grounded only on force, and having so much less to support them, are so slowly and with so much difficulty got rid of, much more must it be so with this, even if it rests on no better foundation than those. We must consider, too, that the possessors of the power have facilities in this case, greater than in any other, to prevent any uprising against it. Every one of the subjects lives under the very eye, and almost, it may be said, in the hands, of

1   *chivalry*   Medieval knights.

2   *clodhopper*   Unsophisticated coarse person.

one of the masters in closer intimacy with him than with any of her fellow-subjects; with no means of combining against him, no power of even locally over mastering him, and, on the other hand, with the strongest motives for seeking his favor and avoiding to give him offence. In struggles for political emancipation, everybody knows how often its champions are bought off by bribes, or daunted by terrors. In the case of women, each individual of the subject-class is in a chronic state of bribery and intimidation combined. In setting up the standard of resistance, a large number of the leaders, and still more of the followers, must make an almost complete sacrifice of the pleasures or the alleviations of their own individual lot. If ever any system of privilege and enforced subjection had its yoke tightly riveted on the necks of those who are kept down by it, this has. I have not yet shown that it is a wrong system: but everyone who is capable of thinking on the subject must see that even if it is, it was certain to outlast all other forms of unjust authority. And when some of the grossest of the other forms still exist in many civilized countries, and have only recently been got rid of in others, it would be strange if that which is so much the deepest rooted had yet been perceptibly shaken anywhere. There is more reason to wonder that the protests and testimonies against it should have been so numerous and so weighty as they are.

Some will object, that a comparison cannot fairly be made between the government of the male sex and the forms of unjust power which I have adduced in illustration of it, since these are arbitrary, and the effect of mere usurpation, while it on the contrary is natural. But was there ever any domination which did not appear natural to those who possessed it? There was a time when the division of mankind into two classes, a small one of masters and a numerous one of slaves, appeared, even to the most cultivated minds, to be natural, and the only natural, condition of the human race. No less an intellect, and one which contributed no less to the progress of human thought, than Aristotle, held this opinion without doubt or misgiving; and rested it on the same premises on which the same assertion in regard to the dominion of men over women is usually based, namely that there are different natures among mankind, free natures, and slave natures; that the Greeks were of a free nature, the barbarian races of Thracians and Asiatics of a slave nature. But why need I go back to Aristotle? Did not the slave-owners of the Southern United States maintain the same doctrine, with all the fanaticism with which men cling to the theories that justify their passions and legitimate their

personal interests? Did they not call heaven and earth to witness that the dominion of the white man over the black is natural, that the black race is by nature incapable of freedom, and marked out for slavery? some even going so far as to say that the freedom of manual laborers is an unnatural order of things anywhere. Again, the theorists of absolute monarchy have always affirmed it to be the only natural form of government; issuing from the patriarchal, which was the primitive and spontaneous form of society, framed on the model of the paternal, which is anterior to society itself, and, as they contend, the most natural authority of all. Nay, for that matter, the law of force itself, to those who could not plead any other has always seemed the most natural of all grounds for the exercise of authority. Conquering races hold it to be Nature's own dictate that the conquered should obey the conquerors, or as they euphoniously paraphrase it, that the feebler and more unwarlike races should submit to the braver and manlier. The smallest acquaintance with human life in the middle ages, shows how supremely natural the dominion of the feudal nobility over men of low condition appeared to the nobility themselves, and how unnatural the conception seemed, of a person of the inferior class claiming equality with them, or exercising authority over them. It hardly seemed less so to the class held in subjection. The emancipated serfs and burgesses, even in their most vigorous struggles, never made any pretension to a share of authority; they only demanded more or less of limitation to the power of tyrannizing over them. So true is it that unnatural generally means only uncustomary, and that everything which is usual appears natural. The subjection of women to men being a universal custom, any departure from it quite naturally appears unnatural. But how entirely, even in this case, the feeling is dependent on custom, appears by ample experience. Nothing so much astonishes the people of distant parts of the world, when they first learn anything about England, as to be told that it is under a queen; the thing seems to them so unnatural as to be almost incredible. To Englishmen this does not seem in the least degree unnatural, because they are used to it; but they do feel it unnatural that women should be soldiers or Members of Parliament. In the feudal ages, on the contrary, war and politics were not thought unnatural to women, because not unusual; it seemed natural that women of the privileged classes should be of manly character, inferior in nothing but bodily strength to their husbands and fathers. The independence of women seemed rather less unnatural to the Greeks than to other ancients, on account of the fabulous Amazons[1] (whom they believed to be historical), and the partial example afforded by the Spartan women; who, though no less subordinate by law than in other Greek states, were more free in fact, and being trained to bodily exercises in the same manner with men, gave ample proof that they were not naturally disqualified for them. There can be little doubt that Spartan experience suggested to Plato, among many other of his doctrines, that of the social and political equality of the two sexes.

But, it will be said, the rule of men over women differs from all these others in not being a rule of force: it is accepted voluntarily; women make no complaint, and are consenting parties to it. In the first place, a great number of women do not accept it. Ever since there have been women able to make their sentiments known by their writings (the only mode of publicity[2] which society permits to them), an increasing number of them have recorded protests against their present social condition: and recently many thousands of them, headed by the most eminent women known to the public, have petitioned Parliament for their admission to the Parliamentary Suffrage.[3] The claim of women to be educated as solidly, and in the same branches of knowledge, as men, is urged with growing intensity, and with a great prospect of success; while the demand for their admission into professions and occupations hitherto closed against them, becomes every year more urgent. Though there are not in this country, as there are in the United States, periodical conventions and an organized party to agitate for the Rights of Women, there is a numerous and active society organized and managed by women, for the more limited object of obtaining the political franchise. Nor is it only in our own country and in America that women are beginning to protest, more or less collectively, against the disabilities under which they labor. France, and Italy, and Switzerland, and Russia now afford examples of the same thing. How many more women there are who silently cherish similar aspirations, no one can possibly know; but there are abundant tokens how many would cherish them, were they not so strenuously taught to repress them as contrary to the proprieties of their sex. It must be remembered, also, that no

enslaved class ever asked for complete liberty at once. When Simon de Montfort[4] called the deputies of the commons to sit for the first time in Parliament, did any of them dream of demanding that an assembly, elected by their constituents) should make and destroy ministries, and dictate to the king in affairs of State? No such thought entered into the imagination of the most ambitious of them. The nobility had already these pretensions;[5] the commons[6] pretended to nothing but to be exempt from arbitrary taxation, and from the gross individual oppression of the king's officers. It is a political law of nature that those who are under any power of ancient origin, never begin by complaining of the power itself, but only of its oppressive exercise. There is never any want of women who complain of ill-usage by their husbands. There would be infinitely more, if complaint were not the greatest of all provocatives[7] to a repetition and increase of the ill-usage. It is this which frustrates all attempts to maintain the power but protect the woman against its abuses. In no other case (except that of a child) is the person who has been proved judicially to have suffered an injury, replaced under the physical power of the culprit who inflicted it. Accordingly wives, even in the most extreme and protracted cases of bodily ill-usage, hardly ever dare avail themselves of the laws made for their protection: and if, in a moment of irrepressible indignation, or by the interference of neighbors, they are induced to do so, their whole effort afterwards is to disclose as little as they can, and to beg off their tyrant from his merited chastisement.

All causes, social and natural, combine to make it unlikely that women should be collectively rebellious to the power of men. They are so far in a position different from all other subject classes, that their masters require something more from them than actual service. Men do not want solely the obedience of women, they want their sentiments. All men, except the most brutish, desire to have, in the woman most nearly connected with them, not a forced slave but a willing one, not a slave merely, but a favorite. They have therefore put everything in practice to enslave their minds. The masters of all other slaves rely, for maintaining obedience, on fear; either fear of themselves, or religious fears. The masters

---

1   *Amazons* In Greek mythology, a nation of female warriors.

2   *publicity* Public communication of their views.

3   *for their admission to the Parliamentary Suffrage* For the right to vote for members of Parliament. Mill was an early, strong (and unsuccessful) advocate of extending voting rights to women. Women achieved some voting rights in Britain in 1918, but did not achieve full voting equality until 1928.

4   *Simon de Montfort* de Montfort (1208–65) led the barons' opposition to King Henry III of England; after the rebellion of 1263–64, de Montfort organized the first directly elected parliament since those of ancient Athens.

5   *these pretensions* Claims to this.

6   *commons* Common people.

7   *provocatives* Things that provoke.

of women wanted more than simple obedience, and they turned the whole force of education to effect their purpose. All women are brought up from the very earliest years in the belief that their ideal of character is the very opposite to that of men; not self-will, and government by self-control, but submission, and yielding to the control of other. All the moralities tell them that it is the duty of women, and all the current sentimentalities that it is their nature, to live for others; to make complete abnegation of themselves, and to have no life but in their affections. And by their affections are meant the only ones they are allowed to have—those to the men with whom they are connected, or to the children who constitute an additional and indefeasible[1] tie between them and a man. When we put together three things—first, the natural attraction between opposite sexes; secondly, the wife's entire dependence on the husband, every privilege or pleasure she has being either his gift, or depending entirely on his will; and lastly, that the principal object of human pursuit, consideration, and all objects of social ambition, can in general be sought or obtained by her only through him, it would be a miracle if the object of being attractive to men had not become the polar star[2] of feminine education and formation of character. And, this great means of influence over the minds of women having been acquired, an instinct of selfishness made men avail themselves of it to the utmost as a means of holding women in subjection, by representing to them meekness, submissiveness, and resignation of all individual will into the hands of a man, as an essential part of sexual attractiveness. Can it be doubted that any of the other yokes which mankind have succeeded in breaking, would have subsisted till now if the same means had existed, and had been so sedulously[3] used, to bow down their minds to it? If it had been made the object of the life of every young plebeian to find personal favor in the eyes of some patrician, of every young serf with some seigneur;[4] if domestication with him, and a share of his personal affections, had been held out as the prize which they all should look out for, the most gifted and aspiring being able to reckon on the most desirable prizes; and if, when this prize had been obtained, they had been shut out by a wall of brass from all interests not centering in him, all feelings and desires but those which he shared or inculcated; would not serfs and seigneurs, plebeians and patri-

cians, have been as broadly distinguished at this day as men and women are? and would not all but a thinker here and there, have believed the distinction to be a fundamental and unalterable fact in human nature?

The preceding considerations are amply sufficient to show that custom, however universal it may be, affords in this case no presumption, and ought not to create any prejudice, in favor of the arrangements which place women in social and political subjection to men. But I may go farther, and maintain that the course of history, and the tendencies of progressive human society, afford not only no presumption in favor of this system of inequality of rights, but a strong one against it; and that, so far as the whole course of human improvement up to the time, the whole stream of modern tendencies, warrants any inference on the subject, it is, that this relic of the past is discordant with the future, and must necessarily disappear.

For, what is the peculiar character of the modern world—the difference which chiefly distinguishes modern institutions, modern social ideas, modern life itself, from those of times long past? It is, that human beings are no longer born to their place in life, and chained down by an inexorable bond to the place they are born to, but are free to employ their faculties, and such favorable chances as offer, to achieve the lot which may appear to them most desirable. Human society of old was constituted on a very different principle. All were born to a fixed social position, and were mostly kept in it by law, or interdicted[5] from any means by which they could emerge from it. As some men are born white and others black, so some were born slaves and others freemen and citizens; some were born patricians, others plebeians; some were born feudal nobles, others commoners and *roturiers.*[6] A slave or serf could never make himself free, nor, except by the will of his master, become so. In most European countries it was not till towards the close of the middle ages, and as a consequence of the growth of regal power, that commoners could be ennobled. Even among nobles, the eldest son was born the exclusive heir to the paternal possessions, and a long time elapsed before it was fully established that the father could disinherit him. Among the industrious classes, only those who were born members of a guild,[7] or were admitted into it by its members, could lawfully practice their calling within its lo-

---

1 *indefeasible* Impossible to annul.
2 *polar star* Guiding principle.
3 *sedulously* Painstakingly, zealously, persistently.
4 *seigneur* Medieval lord.

5 *interdicted* Prohibited by authority.
6 *roturiers* French: commoners.
7 *guild* Medieval association for regulation and protection of a town's craftsmen. Each guild held a monopoly on that craft.

cal limits; and nobody could practice any calling deemed important, in any but the legal manner—by processes authoritatively prescribed. Manufacturers have stood in the pillory[1] for presuming to carry on their business by new and improved methods. In modern Europe, and most in those parts of it which have participated most largely in all other modern improvements, diametrically opposite doctrines now prevail. Law and government do not undertake to prescribe by whom any social or industrial operation shall or shall not be conducted, or what modes of conducting them shall be lawful. These things are left to the unfettered choice of individuals. Even the laws which required that workmen should serve an apprenticeship, have in this country been repealed: there being ample assurance that in all cases in which an apprenticeship is necessary, its necessity will suffice to enforce it. The old theory was, that the least possible should be left to the choice of the individual agent; that all he had to do should, as far as practicable, be laid down for him by superior wisdom. Left to himself he was sure to go wrong. The modern conviction, the fruit of a thousand years of experience, is, that things in which the individual is the person directly interested, never go right but as they are left to his own discretion; and that any regulation of them by authority, except to protect the rights of others, is sure to be mischievous. This conclusion slowly arrived at, and not adopted until almost every possible application of the contrary theory had been made with disastrous result, now (in the industrial department) prevails universally in the most advanced countries, almost universally in all that have pretensions to any sort of advancement. It is not that all processes are supposed to be equally good, or all persons to be equally qualified for everything; but that freedom of individual choice is now known to be the only thing which procures the adoption of the best processes, and throws each operation into the hands of those who are best qualified for it. Nobody thinks it necessary to make a law that only a strong-armed man shall be a blacksmith. Freedom and competition suffice to make blacksmiths strong-armed men, because the weak armed can earn more by engaging in occupations for which they are more fit. In consonance with this doctrine, it is felt to be an overstepping of the proper bounds of authority to fix beforehand, on some general presumption, that certain persons are not fit to do certain things. It is now thoroughly known and admitted

that if some such presumptions exist, no such presumption is infallible. Even if it be well grounded in a majority of cases, which it is very likely not to be, there will be a minority of exceptional cases in which it does not hold: and in those it is both an injustice to the individuals, and a detriment to society, to place barriers in the way of their using their faculties for their own benefit and for that of others. In the cases, on the other hand, in which the unfitness is real, the ordinary motives of human conduct will on the whole suffice to prevent the incompetent person from making, or from persisting in, the attempt.

If this general principle of social and economical science is not true; if individuals, with such help as they can derive from the opinion of those who know them, are not better judges than the law and the government, of their own capacities and vocation; the world cannot too soon abandon this principle, and return to the old system of regulations and disabilities. But if the principle is true, we ought to act as if we believed it, and not to ordain that to be born a girl instead of a boy, any more than to be born black instead of white, or a commoner instead of a nobleman, shall decide the person's position through all life—shall interdict people from all the more elevated social positions, and from all, except a few, respectable occupations. Even were we to admit the utmost that is ever pretended to the superior fitness of men for all the functions now reserve to them, the same argument applies which forbids a legal qualification for Members of Parliament. If only once in a dozen years the conditions of eligibility exclude a fit person, there is a real loss, while the exclusion of thousands of unfit persons is no gain; for if the constitution of the electoral body disposes them to choose unfit persons, there are always plenty of such persons to choose from. In all things of any difficulty and importance, those who can do them well are fewer than the need, even with the most unrestricted latitude of choice: and any limitation of the field of selection deprives society of some chances of being served by the competent, without ever saving it from the incompetent.

At present, in the more improved countries, the disabilities of women are the only case, save one, in which laws and institutions take persons at their birth, and ordain that they shall never in all their lives be allowed to compete for certain things. The one exception is that of royalty. Persons still are born to the throne; no one, not of the reigning family, can occupy it, and no one even of that family can, by any means but the course of hereditary succession, attain it. All other dignities and social advantages are open to the

---

1   *pillory*   Device for public punishment: one's head and arms were locked in a wooden frame.

whole male sex: many indeed are only attainable by wealth, but wealth may be striven for by anyone, and is actually obtained by many men of the very humblest origin. The difficulties, to the majority, are indeed insuperable without the aid of fortunate accidents; but no male human being is under any legal ban: neither law nor opinion superadd[1] artificial obstacles to the natural ones. Royalty, as I have said, is excepted: but in this case everyone feels it to be an exception—an anomaly in the modern world, in marked opposition to its customs and principles, and to be justified only by extraordinary special expediencies, which, though individuals and nations differ in estimating their weight, unquestionably do in fact exist. But in this exceptional case, in which a high social function is, for important reasons, bestowed on birth instead of being put up to competition, all free nations contrive to adhere in substance to the principle from which they nominally derogate;[2] for they circumscribe this high function by conditions avowedly intended to prevent the person to whom it ostensibly belongs from really performing it; while the person by whom it is performed, the responsible minister, does obtain the post by a competition from which no full-grown citizen of the male sex is legally excluded. The disabilities, therefore, to which women are subject from the mere fact of their birth, are the solitary examples of the kind in modern legislation. In no instance except this, which comprehends[3] half the human race, are the higher social functions closed against anyone by a fatality[4] of birth which no exertions, and no change of circumstances, can overcome; for even religious disabilities (besides that in England and in Europe they have practically almost ceased to exist) do not close any career to the disqualified person in case of conversion.

The social subordination of women thus stands out an isolated fact in modern social institutions; a solitary breach of what has become their fundamental law; a single relic of an old world of thought and practice exploded in everything else, but retained in the one thing of most universal interest; as if a gigantic dolmen,[5] or a vast temple of Jupiter Olym-

pus, occupied the site of St. Paul's[6] and received daily worship, while the surrounding Christian churches were only resorted to on fasts and festivals. This entire discrepancy between one social fact and all those which accompany it, and the radical opposition between its nature and the progressive movement which is the boast of the modern world, and which has successively swept away everything else of an analogous character, surely affords, to a conscientious observer of human tendencies, serious matter for reflection. It raises a *prima facie*[7] presumption on the unfavorable side, far outweighing any which custom and usage could in such circumstances create on the favorable; and should at least suffice to make this, like the choice between republicanism[8] and royalty, a balanced question.

The least that can be demanded is, that the question should not be considered as prejudged by existing fact and existing opinion, but open to discussion on its merits, as a question of justice and expediency: the decision on this, as on any of the other social arrangements of mankind, depending on what an enlightened estimate of tendencies and consequences may show to be most advantageous to humanity in general, without distinction of sex. And the discussion must be a real discussion, descending to foundations, and not resting satisfied with vague and general assertions. It will not do, for instance to assert in general terms, that the experience of mankind has pronounced in favor of the existing system. Experience cannot possibly have decided between two courses, so long as there has only been experience of one. If it be said that the doctrine of the equality of the sexes rests only on theory, it must be remembered that the contrary doctrine also has only theory to rest upon. All that is proved in its favor by direct experience, is that mankind have been able to exist under it, and to attain the degree of improvement and prosperity which we now see; but whether that prosperity has been attained sooner, or is now greater, than it would have been under the other system, experience does not say, on the other hand, experience does say, that every step in improvement has been so invariably accompanied by a step made in raising the social position of women, that historians and philosophers have been led to adopt their elevation or debasement as on the whole the surest test and most correct measure of the civil-

---

1   *superadd*   Add on top of.
2   *to adhere in substance to the principle from which they nominally derogate*   To obey in fact the principle which they deviate from in words only.
3   *comprehends*   Includes.
4   *fatality*   Predetermination by fate.
5   *dolmen*   Prehistoric primitive stone structure, of a type found around the English countryside, thought to have been used as a tomb.

6   *St. Paul's*   Landmark London Anglican Cathedral.
7   *prima facie*   [Latin: on its face.] At first sight.
8   *republicanism*   Belief that government should be in the form of a republic—that is, by elected representatives, rather than by a monarch.

ization of a people or an age. Through all the progressive period of human history, the condition of women has been approaching nearer to equality with men. This does not of itself prove that the assimilation must go on to complete equality; but it assuredly affords some presumption that such is the case.

Neither does it avail anything to say that the nature of the two sexes adapts them to their present functions and position, and renders these appropriate to them. Standing on the ground of common sense and the constitution of the human mind, I deny that anyone knows, or can know, the nature of the two sexes, as long as they have only been seen in their present relation to one another. If men had ever been found in society without women, or women without men, or if there had been a society of men and women in which the women were not under the control of the men, something might have been positively known about the mental and moral differences which may be inherent in the nature of each. What is now called the nature of women is an eminently artificial thing—the result of forced repression in some directions, unnatural stimulation in others. It may be asserted without scruple, that no other class of dependents have had their character so entirely distorted from its natural proportions by their relation with their masters; for, if conquered and slave races have been, in some respects, more forcibly repressed, whatever in them has not been crushed down by an iron heel has generally been let alone, and if left with any liberty of development, it has developed itself according to its own laws; but in the case of women, a hot-house and stove cultivation[1] has always been carried on of some of the capabilities of their nature, for the benefit and pleasure of their masters. Then, because certain products of the general vital force sprout luxuriantly and reach a great development in this heated atmosphere and under this active nurture and watering, while other shoots from the same root, which are left outside in the wintry air, with ice purposely heaped all round them, have a stunted growth, and some are burnt off with fire and disappear; men, with that inability to recognize their own work which distinguishes the unanalytic mind, indolently believe that the tree grows of itself in the way they have made it grow, and that it would die if one half of it were not kept in a vapor bath and the other half in the snow.

Of all difficulties which impede the progress of thought, and the formation of well-grounded opinions on life and social arrangements, the greatest is now the unspeakable ignorance and inattention of mankind in respect to the influences which form human character. Whatever any portion of the human species now are, or seem to be, such, it is supposed, they have a natural tendency to be: even when the most elementary knowledge of the circumstances in which they have been placed, clearly points out the causes that made them what they are. Because a cottier[2] deeply in arrears to his landlord is not industrious, there are people who think that the Irish are naturally idle. Because constitutions can be overthrown when the authorities appointed to execute them turn their arms against them, there are people who think the French incapable of free government. Because the Greeks cheated the Turks, and the Turks only plundered the Greeks, there are persons who think that the Turks are naturally more sincere: and because women, as is often said, care nothing about politics except their personalities, it is supposed that the general good is naturally less interesting to women than to men. History, which is now so much better understood than formerly, teaches another lesson: if only by showing the extraordinary susceptibility of human nature to external influences, and the extreme variableness of those of its manifestations which are supposed to be most universal and uniform. But in history, as in traveling, men usually see only what they already had in their own minds; and few learn much from history, who do not bring much with them to its study.

Hence, in regard to that most difficult question, what are the natural differences between the two sexes—a subject on which it is impossible in the present state of society to obtain complete and correct knowledge—while almost everybody dogmatizes[3] upon it, almost all neglect and make light of the only means by which any partial insight can be obtained into it. This is, an analytic study of the most important department of psychology, the laws of the influence of circumstances on character. For, however great and apparently ineradicable the moral and intellectual differences between men and women might be, the evidence of there being natural differences could only be negative. Those only could be inferred to be natural which could not possibly

---

1 *hot-house and stove cultivation* Artificial—likened to the raising of plants in a heated greenhouse.

2 *cottier* In Ireland, a peasant working a small parcel of rented land.

3 *dogmatizes* Expresses strongly held views without reference to evidence or argument.

be artificial—the residuum,[1] after deducting every characteristic of either sex which can admit of being explained from education or external circumstances. The profoundest knowledge of the laws of the formation of character is indispensable to entitle anyone to affirm even that there is any difference, much more what the difference is, between the two sexes considered as moral and rational beings; and since no one, as yet, has that knowledge (for there is hardly any subject which, in proportion to its importance, has been so little studied), no one is thus far entitled to any positive opinion on the subject. Conjectures are all that can at present be made; conjectures more or less probable, according as more or less authorized by such knowledge as we yet have of the laws of psychology, as applied to the formation of character.

Even the preliminary knowledge, what the differences between the sexes now are, apart from all question as to how they are made what they are, is still in the crudest and most incomplete state. Medical practitioners and physiologists have ascertained, to some extent, the differences in bodily constitution; and this is an important element to the psychologist: but hardly any medical practitioner is a psychologist. Respecting the mental characteristics of women; their observations are of no more worth than those of common men. It is a subject on which nothing final can be known, so long as those who alone can really know it, women themselves, have given but little testimony, and that little, mostly suborned. It is easy to know stupid women. Stupidity is much the same all the world over. A stupid person's notions and feelings may confidently be inferred from those which prevail in the circle by which the person is surrounded. Not so with those whose opinions and feelings are an emanation from their own nature and faculties. It is only a man here and there who has any tolerable knowledge of the character even of the women of his own family. I do not mean, of their capabilities; these nobody knows, not even themselves, because most of them have never been called out. I mean their actually existing thoughts and feelings. Many a man thinks he perfectly understands women, because he has had amatory relations with several, perhaps with many of them. If he is a good observer, and his experience extends to quality as well as quantity, he may have learnt something of one narrow department of their nature—an important department, no doubt. But of all the rest of it, few persons are generally more ignorant,

because there are few from whom it is so carefully hidden. The most favorable case which a man can generally have for studying the character of a woman, is that of his own wife: for the opportunities are greater, and the cases of complete sympathy not so unspeakably rare. And in fact, this is the source from which any knowledge worth having on the subject has, I believe, generally come. But most men have not had the opportunity of studying in this way more than a single case: accordingly one can, to an almost laughable degree, infer what a man's wife is like, from his opinions about women in general. To make even this one case yield any result, the woman must be worth knowing, and the man not only a competent judge, but of a character so sympathetic in itself, and so well adapted to hers, that he can either read her mind by sympathetic intuition, or has nothing in himself which makes her shy of disclosing it, Hardly anything, I believe, can be more rare than this conjunction. It often happens that there is the most complete unity of feeling and community of interests as to all external things, yet the one has as little admission into the internal life of the other as if they were common acquaintance. Even with true affection, authority on the one side and subordination on the other prevent perfect confidence. Though nothing may be intentionally withheld, much is not shown. In the analogous relation of parent and child, the corresponding phenomenon must have been in the observation of everyone. As between father and son, how many are the cases in which the father, in spite of real affection on both sides, obviously to all the world does not know, nor suspect, parts of the son's character familiar to his companions and equals. The truth is, that the position of looking up to another is extremely unpropitious to[2] complete sincerity and openness with him. The fear of losing ground in his opinion or in his feelings is so strong, that even in an upright character, there is an unconscious tendency to show only the best side, or the side which, though not the best, is that which he most likes to see: and it may be confidently said that thorough knowledge of one another hardly ever exists, but between persons who, besides being intimates, are equals. How much more true, then, must all this be, when the one is not only under the authority of the other, but has it inculcated on her as a duty to reckon everything else subordinate to his comfort and pleasure, and to let him neither see nor feel anything coming from her, except what is agreeable to him. All these difficulties stand in the way of a man's obtaining

---

1   *residuum* What is left over.

2   *unpropitious to* Unfavorable for.

any thorough knowledge even of the one woman whom alone, in general, he has sufficient opportunity of studying. When we further consider that to understand one woman is not necessarily to understand any other woman; that even if he could study many women of one rank, or of one country, he would not thereby understand women of other ranks or countries; and even if he did, they are still only the women of a single period of history; we may safely assert that the knowledge which men can acquire of women, even as they have been and are, without reference to what they might be, is wretchedly imperfect and superficial, and always will be so, until women themselves have told all that they have to tell.

And this time has not come; nor will it come otherwise than gradually. It is but of yesterday that women have either been qualified by literary accomplishments or permitted by society, to tell anything to the general public. As yet very few of them dare tell anything, which men, on whom their literary success depends, are unwilling to hear. Let us remember in what manner, up to a very recent time, the expression, even by a male author, of uncustomary opinions, or what are deemed eccentric feelings, usually was, and in some degree still is, received; and we may form some faint conception under what impediments a woman, who is brought up to think custom and opinion her sovereign rule, attempts to express in books anything drawn from the depths of her own nature. The greatest woman who has left writings behind her sufficient to give her an eminent rank in the literature of her country, thought it necessary to prefix as a motto to her boldest work, *Un homme peut braver l'opinion; une femme doit s'y soumettre*.[1] The greater part of what women write about women is mere sycophancy[2] to men. In the case of unmarried women, much of it seems only intended to increase their chance of a husband. Many, both married and unmarried, overstep the mark, and inculcate a servility beyond what is desired or relished by any man, except the very vulgarest. But this is not so often the case as, even at a quite late period, it still was. Literary women are becoming more free-spoken, and more willing to express their real sentiments. Unfortunately, in this country especially, they are themselves such artificial products, that their sentiments are compounded of a small element of individual observation and consciousness, and a very large one of acquired associations. This will be less and less the case, but it will remain true to a great extent, as long as social institutions do not admit the same free development of originality in women which is possible to men. When that time comes, and not before, we shall see, and not merely hear, as much as it is necessary to know of the nature of women, and the adaptation of other things to it.

I have dwelt so much on the difficulties which at present obstruct any real knowledge by men of the true nature of women, because in this as in so many other things *opinio copiae inter maximas causas inopiae est*;[3] and there is little chance of reasonable thinking on the matter while people flatter themselves that they perfectly understand a subject of which most men know absolutely nothing, and of which it is at present impossible that any man, or all men taken together, should have knowledge which can qualify them to lay down the law to women as to what is, or is not, their vocation. Happily, no such knowledge is necessary for any practical purpose connected with the position of women is relation to society and life. For, according to all the principles involved in modern society, the question rests with women themselves—to be decided by their own experience, and by the use of their own faculties. There are no means of finding what either one person or many can do, but by trying—and no means by which anyone else can discover for them what it is for their happiness to do or leave undone.

One thing we may be certain of—that what is contrary to women's nature to do, they never will be made to do by simply giving their nature free play. The anxiety of mankind to interfere in behalf of nature, for fear lest nature should not succeed in effecting its purpose, is an altogether unnecessary solicitude. What women by nature cannot do, it is quite superfluous to forbid them from doing. What they can do, but not so well as the men who are their competitors, competition suffices to exclude them from; since nobody asks for protective duties and bounties in favor of women; it is only asked that the present bounties and protective duties in favor of men should be recalled. If women have a greater natural inclination for some things than for others, there is no need of laws or social inculcation to make the majority of them do the former in preference to the latter. Whatever women's services are most wanted for, the free play of competition will hold out the strongest inducements to them to undertake. And, as the words imply, they

---

1　*Un home peut braver ... une femme doit s'y soumettre* French: A man can defy opinion; a woman must submit to it. Motto on the title page of Germaine de Staël's 1802 novel *Delphine*.

2　*sycophancy* Insincere flattery designed to elicit advantage.

3　*opinio copiae inter maximas causas inopiae est* Latin: Popular opinion is deficient on many matters. –Francis Bacon.

are most wanted for the things for which they are most fit; by the apportionment of which to them, the collective faculties of the two sexes can be applied on the whole with the greatest sum of valuable result.

The general opinion of men is supposed to be, that the natural vocation of a woman is that of a wife and mother. I say, is supposed to be, because, judging from acts—from the whole of the present constitution of society—one might infer that their opinion was the direct contrary. They might be supposed to think that the alleged natural vocation of women was of all things the most repugnant to their nature; insomuch that if they are free to do anything else—if any other means of living or occupation of their time and faculties, is open, which has any chance of appearing desirable to them—there will not be enough of them who will be willing to accept the condition said to be natural to them. If this is the real opinion of men in general, it would be well that it should be spoken out. I should like to hear somebody openly enunciating the doctrine (it is already implied in much that is written on the subject)—It is necessary to society that women should marry and produce children. They will not do so unless they are compelled. Therefore it is necessary to compel them. The merits of the case would then be clearly defined. It would be exactly that of the slaveholders of South Carolina and Louisiana. It is necessary that cotton and sugar should be grown. White men cannot produce them. Negroes will not, for any wages which we choose to give. Ergo[1] they must be compelled. An illustration still closer to the point is that of impressment.[2] Sailors must absolutely be had to defend the country. It often happens that they will not voluntarily enlist. Therefore there must be the power of forcing them. How often has this logic been used! and, but for one flaw in it, without doubt it would have been successful up to this day. But it is open to the retort—First pay the sailors the honest value of their labor. When you have made it as well worth their while to serve you, as to work for other employers, you will have no more difficulty than others have in obtaining their services. To this there is no logical answer except I will not: and as people are now not only ashamed, but are not desirous, to rob the laborer of his hire, impressment is no longer advocated. Those who attempt to force women into marriage by closing all other doors against them, lay them-

selves open to a similar retort. If they mean what they say, their opinion must evidently be, that men do not render the married condition so desirable to women, as to induce them to accept it for its own recommendations. It is not a sign of one's thinking the boon one offers very attractive, when one allows only Hobson's choice,[3] that or none. And here, I believe, is the clue to the feelings of those men, who have a real antipathy to the equal freedom of women. I believe they are afraid, not lest women should be unwilling to marry, for I do not think that anyone in reality has that apprehension; but lest they should insist that marriage should be on equal conditions; lest all women of spirit and capacity should prefer doing almost anything else, not in their own eyes degrading, rather than marry, when marrying is giving themselves a master, and a master too of all their earthly possessions. And truly, if this consequence were necessarily incident to[4] marriage, I think that the apprehension would be very well founded. I agree in thinking it probable that few women, capable of anything else, would, unless under an irresistible entrainment, rendering them for the time insensible to anything but itself, choose such a lot, when any other means were open to them of filling a conventionally honorable place in life: and if men are determined that the law of marriage shall be a law of despotism, they are quite right, in point of mere policy, in leaving to women only Hobson's choice. But, in that case, all that has been done in the modern world to relax the chain on the minds of women, has been a mistake. They never should have been allowed to receive a literary education. Women who read, much more women who write, are, in the existing constitution of things, a contradiction and a disturbing element: and it was wrong to bring women up with any acquirements[5] but those of an odalisque,[6] or of a domestic servant.

---

1   *Ergo* Latin: therefore (the mark of a conclusion of an argument).

2   *impressment* The practice of forcibly inducting men into military service.

3   *Hobson's choice* The choice of taking something offered or nothing.

4   *incident to* An accompaniment of.

5   *acquirements* Learned skills.

6   *odalisque* Enslaved woman in a harem.

HARRIET (HARDY) TAYLOR MILL
(1807 – 1858)

HARRIET TAYLOR MILL WAS AN EARLY FEMINIST AND radical philosopher, an advocate of women's rights to vote and to education, a socialist defender of the working class and an eloquent spokeswoman for individual expression, liberty, and the toleration of dissenting opinions. She criticized marriage as an institution designed for the gratification of men and bemoaned the loss to humanity caused by preventing women from acquiring the education and experience necessary to flourish as independent individuals.

Taylor Mill was raised in a Unitarian household, and was largely self-educated. At age eighteen she married John Taylor, a wealthy pharmaceutical merchant, eleven years her senior. They initially had a happy marriage, but later she became frustrated by his lack of interest in intellectual and artistic matters, and, having met John Stuart Mill, began to spend a good deal of time with him. When apart (her tuberculosis forced her to spend months in the warm south of France) they maintained a voluminous correspondence, exchanging personal thoughts, discussing intellectual matters and passing drafts of writings back and forth. Those who knew about this relationship were scandalized, especially after the Taylors agreed to a separation in 1833. She struggled for years to find a satisfactory way out of her problems: divorce was almost impossible; she hated subjecting her husband to scandal; she treasured her children and was terrified of losing the right to see and raise them. When John Taylor was dying of cancer, she returned to him; after remaining in mourning for a respectable two years, she married Mill. They lived together mostly in seclusion, possibly to try to keep to a minimum any lingering taint of scandal, but probably also because they enjoyed each others' company so much, and were so busy with their joint work. In 1858 her tuberculosis flared up, and they traveled again to southern Europe; she died in Avignon in the south of France. Till his death, Mill spent part of each year in Avignon, where he daily visited his wife's grave.

Exactly how much authorship of a number of works should be attributed to Taylor Mill remains unclear. Both Taylor Mill and Mill were clearly aware that, at that time, many readers would discount writing listing a woman's name as author (and, indeed, joint authorship where a woman was involved). In his *Autobiography*, John Stuart Mill wrote:

> The whole mode of thinking of which [*On Liberty*] was the expression, was emphatically hers. But I also was so thoroughly imbued with it that the same thoughts naturally occurred to us both. When two persons have their thoughts and speculations completely in common; when all subjects of intellectual or moral interest are discussed between them in daily life, and probed to much greater depths than are usually or conveniently sounded in writings intended for general readers; when they set out from the same principles, and arrive at their conclusions by processes pursued jointly, it is of little consequence in respect to the question of originality, which of them holds the pen; the one who contributes least to the composition may contribute most to the thought; the writings which result are the joint product of both, and it must often be impossible to disentangle their respective parts, and affirm that this belongs to one and that to the other. (Vol 1, 251)

Though Mill's own assessment of the extent of their collaborating has been questioned, there is little other firm evidence to fall back on to resolve the issues of their respective contributions and authorship. She first collaborated with Mill on his *Principles of Political Economy* (1848) and he credited her with prompting him to write the chapter "On the Probable Futurity of the Laboring Classes." As mentioned above, her ideas played an important role in the production of *On Liberty* (1859). Finally, correspondence between the two suggests that she first drafted some of the paragraphs on marriage from *The Subjection of Women* (1869).

The Enfranchisement of Women (1851), from which we include a selection here, is the major philosophical work for which there is the most convincing case for Taylor Mill's sole authorship. Originally published in the *Westminster Review*, it defends women's suffrage and advocates the elimination of restrictions on women's political participation and occupation. Taylor Mill sets out feminist claims that some have argued are more radical than those put forward in *Subjection of Women*: "We deny the right of any portion of the species to decide for another portion, or any individual for another individual, what is and what is not their 'proper sphere.'" As an explanation for the current state of things, she adds, "When ... we ask why the existence of one-half the species should be merely ancillary to that of the other—why each woman should be a mere appendage to a man, allowed to have no interest of her own, that there may be nothing to compete in her mind with his interests and his pleasure; the only reason which can be given is, that men like it."

◆ ◆ ◆ ◆ ◆

The Enfranchisement of Women (1851)

Most of our readers will probably learn from these pages for the first time, that there has arisen in the United States, and in the most civilized and enlightened portion of them, an organized agitation on a new question—new, not to thinkers, nor to anyone by whom the principles of free and popular government are felt as well as acknowledged, but new, and even unheard-of, as a subject for public meetings and practical political action. This question is, the enfranchisement[1] of women; their admission, in law and in fact, to equality in all rights, political, civil, and social, with the male citizens of the community.

It will add to the surprise with which many will receive this intelligence, that the agitation which has commenced is not a pleading by male writers and orators for women, those who are professedly to be benefited remaining either

indifferent or ostensibly hostile. It is a political movement, practical in its objects, carried on in a form which denotes an intention to persevere. And it is a movement not merely *for* women, but *by* them. Its first public manifestation appears to have been a Convention of Women, held in the State of Ohio, in the spring of 1850. Of this meeting we have seen no report. On the 23rd and 24th of October last, a succession of public meetings was held at Worcester in Massachusetts under the name of a "Women's Rights Convention," of which the president was a woman, and nearly all the chief speakers women; numerously reinforced, however, by men, among whom were some of the most distinguished leaders in the kindred cause of negro emancipation. A general and four special committees were nominated, for the purpose of carrying on the undertaking until the next annual meeting.

According to the report in the *New York Tribune*, above a thousand persons were present throughout, and "if a larger place could have been had, many thousands more would have attended." The place was described as "crowded from the beginning with attentive and interested listeners." In regard to the quality of the speaking, the proceedings bear an advantageous comparison with those of any popular movement with which we are acquainted, either in this country or in America. Very rarely in the oratory of public meetings is the part of the verbiage and declamation so small, that of calm good sense and reason so considerable. The result of the Convention was in every respect encouraging to those by whom it was summoned: and it is probably destined to inaugurate one of the most important of the movements towards political and social reform, which are the best characteristics of the present age.

That the promoters of this new agitation take their stand on principles, and do not fear to declare these in their widest extent, without time-serving or compromise, will be seen from the resolutions adopted by the Convention, part of which we transcribe.

Resolved—That every human being, of full age, and resident for a proper length of time on the soil of the nation, who is required to obey the law, is entitled to a voice in its enactment; that every such person, whose property or labor is taxed for the support of the government, is entitled to a direct share in such government; therefore,

Resolved—That women are entitled to the right of suffrage, and to be considered eligible to office, ... and that every party which claims to represent the humanity, the civilization, and the progress of the age, is bound to inscribe

---

1 *enfranchisement* (Narrowly) getting the right to vote; (more broadly) being admitted to membership, or political privileges, in a state.

on its banner equality before the law, without distinction of sex or color.

Resolved—That civil and political rights acknowledge no sex, and therefore the word "male" should be struck from every State Constitution.

Resolved—That, since the prospect of honorable and useful employment in after-life[1] is the best stimulus to the use of educational advantages, and since the best education is that we give ourselves, in the struggles, employments, and discipline of life; therefore it is impossible that women should make full use of the instruction already accorded to them, or that their career should do justice to their faculties, until the avenues to the various civil and professional employments are thrown open to them.

Resolved—That every effort to educate women, without according to them their rights, and arousing their conscience by the weight of their responsibilities, is futile, and a waste of labor.

Resolved—That the laws of property, as affecting married persons, demand a thorough revisal, so that all rights be equal control over the property gained by their mutual toil and sacrifices, and be heir to her husband precisely to that extent that he is heir to her, and entitled at her death to dispose by will of the same share of the joint property as he is.

The following is a brief summary of the principal demands.

1. *Education* in primary and high schools, universities, medical, legal, and theological institutions.
2. *Partnership* in the labors and gains, risks and remunerations, of productive industry.
3. A *coequal share* in the formation and administration of laws—municipal, state and national—through legislative assemblies, courts, and executive offices.

It would be difficult to put so much true, just, and reasonable meaning into a style so little calculated to recommend it as that of some of the resolutions. But whatever objection may be made to some of the expressions, none, in our opinion, can be made to the demands themselves. As a question of justice, the case seems to us too clear for dispute. As one of expediency, the more thoroughly it is examined the stronger it will appear.

The women have as good as claim as men have, in point of personal right, to the suffrage, or to a place in the jury-box, it would be difficult for anyone to deny. It cannot certainly be denied by the United States of America, as a people or as a community. Their democratic institutions rest avowedly on the inherent right of every one to a voice in the government. Their Declaration of Independence, framed by the men who are still great constitutional authorities—that document which has been from the first, and is now, the acknowledged basis of their polity, commences with this express statement:

> We hold these truths to be self-evident: that all men are created equal; that they are endowed by their Creator with certain inalienable rights; that among these are life, liberty, and the pursuit of happiness; that to secure these rights, governments are instituted among men, deriving their just powers from the consent of the governed.

We do not imagine that any American democrat will evade the force of these expressions by the dishonest or ignorant subterfuge, that "men," in this memorable document, does not stand for human beings, but for one sex only; that "life, liberty, and the pursuit of happiness" are "inalienable rights" of only one moiety of the human species; and that "the governed," whose consent is affirmed to be the only source of just power, are meant for that half of mankind only, who, in relation to the other, have hitherto assumed the character of governors. The contradiction between principle and practice cannot be explained away. A like dereliction of the fundamental maxims of their political creed has been committed by the Americans in the flagrant instance of the negroes; of this they are learning to recognize the turpitude. After a struggle which, by many of its incidents, deserves the name of heroic, the abolitionists[2] are now so strong in numbers and in influence that they hold the balance of parties in the United States. It was fitting that the men whose names will remain associated with the extirpation, for the democratic soil of America, of the aristocracy of color, should be among the originators, for America and for the rest of the world, of the first collective protest against the aristocracy of sex; a distinction as accidental as that of color, and fully as irrelevant to all questions of government.

Not only to the democracy of America, the claim of women to civil and political equality makes an irresistible appeal, but also to those Radicals and Chartists[3] in the

---

1 *after-life* Life following education.

2 *abolitionists* Advocates of the abolition of slavery.
3 *Chartists* Supporters of a working-class movement in England between 1838 and 1848 for political and social reform. The first of the six points of the "People's Charter" listing their demands was

British islands, and democrats on the continent, who claim what is called universal suffrage as an inherent right, unjustly and oppressively withheld from them. For with what truth or rationality could the suffrage be termed universal, while half the human species remained excluded from it? To declare that a voice in the government is the right of all, and demand it only for a part—the part, namely, to which the claimant himself belongs—is to renounce even the appearance of principle. The Chartist who denies the suffrage to women, is a Chartist only because he is not a lord: he is one of those levelers[1] who would level only down to themselves.

Even those who do not look upon a voice in the government as a matter of personal right, nor profess principles which require that it should be extended to all, have usually traditional maxims of political justice with which it is impossible to reconcile the exclusion of all women from the common rights of citizenship. It is an axiom of English freedom that taxation and representation should be co-extensive. Even under the laws which give the wife's property to the husband, there are many unmarried women who pay taxes. It is one of the fundamental doctrines of the British Constitution, that all persons should be tried by their peers: yet women, whenever tried, are by male judges and a male jury. To foreigners the law accords the privilege of claiming that half the jury should be composed of themselves; not so to women. Apart from maxims of detail, which represent local and national rather than universal ideas; it is an acknowledged dictate of justice to make no degrading distinctions without necessity. In all things the presumption ought to be on the side of equality. A reason must be given why anything should be permitted to one person and interdicted to another. But when that which is interdicted includes nearly everything which those to whom it is permitted most prize, and to be deprived of which they feel to be most insulting; when not only political liberty but personal freedom of action is the prerogative of a caste; when even in the exercise of industry, almost all employments which task the higher faculties in an important field, which lead to distinction, riches, or even pecuniary independence, are fenced around as the exclusive domain of the predominant section, scarcely any doors being left open to the dependent class, except such as all who can enter elsewhere disdainfully pass by; the

miserable expediencies which are advanced as excuses for so grossly partial a dispensation, would not be sufficient, even if they were real, to render it other than a flagrant justice. While, far from being expedient, we are firmly convinced that the division of mankind into two castes, one born to rule over the other, is in this case, as in all cases, an unqualified mischief; a source of perversion and demoralization, both to the favored class and to those at whose expense they are favored; producing none of the good which it is the custom to ascribe to it, and forming a bar, almost insuperable while it lasts, to any really vital improvement, either in the character or in the social condition of the human race.

These propositions it is now our purpose to maintain. But before entering on them, we would endeavor to dispel the preliminary objections which, in the minds of persons to whom the subject is new, are apt to prevent a real and conscientious examination of it. The chief of these obstacles is that most formidable one, custom. Women never have had equal rights with men. The claim in their behalf, of the common rights of mankind, is looked upon as barred by universal practice. This strongest of prejudices, the prejudice against what is new and unknown, has, indeed, in an age of changes like the present, lost much of its force; if it had not, there would be little hope of prevailing against it. Over three-fourths of the habitable world, even at this day, the answer, "it has always been so," closes all discussion. But it is the boast of modern Europeans, and of their American kindred, that they know and do many things which their forefathers neither knew nor did; and it is perhaps the most unquestionable point of superiority in the present above former ages, that habit is not now the tyrant it formerly was over opinions and modes of action, and that the worship of custom is a declining idolatry. An uncustomary thought, on a subject which touches the greater interests of life, still startles when first presented; but if it can be kept before the mind until the impression of strangeness wears off, it obtains a hearing, and as rational a consideration as the intellect of the hearer is accustomed to bestow on any other subject.

In the present case, the prejudice of custom is doubtless on the unjust side. Great thinkers, indeed, at different times, from Plato to Condorcet,[2] besides some of the most eminent names of the present age, have made emphatic protest in favor of the equality of women. And there have been voluntary societies, religious or secular, of which the Society

---

"a vote for every man twenty-one years of age, of sound mind, and not undergoing punishment for crime."

1   levelers   Believers in social equality.

2   Condorcet   Marie Jean Antoine Nicolas Caritat, marquis de Condorcet (1743–94).

of Friends[1] is the most known, by whom that principle was recognized. But there has been no political community or nation in which, by laws and usage, women have not been in a state of political and civil inferiority. In the ancient world the same fact was alleged, with equal truth, in behalf of slavery. It might have been alleged in favor of the mitigated form of slavery, serfdom, all through the middle ages. It was urged against freedom of industry, freedom of conscience, freedom of the press; none of these liberties were thought compatible with a well-ordered state, until they had proved their possibility by actually existing as facts. That an institution or a practice is customary is no presumption of its goodness, when any other sufficient cause can be assigned for its existence. There is no difficulty in understanding why the subjection of women has been a custom. No other explanation is needed than physical force.

That those who were physically weaker should have been made legally inferior, is quite conformable to the mode in which the world has been governed. Until very lately, the rule of physical strength was the general law of human affairs. Throughout history, the nations, races, classes, which found themselves the strongest, either in muscles, in riches, or in military discipline, have conquered and held in subjection the rest. If, even in the most improved nations, the law of the sword is at last discountenanced[2] as unworthy, it is only since the calumniated[3] eighteenth century. Wars of conquest have only ceased since democratic revolutions began. The world is very young, and has but just begun to cast off injustice. It is only now getting rid of monarchial despotism. It is only now getting rid of hereditary feudal nobility. It is only now getting rid of disabilities on the ground of religion. It is only beginning to treat any men as citizens, except the rich and a favored portion of the middle class. Can we wonder that it has not yet done as much for women? As society was constituted until the last few generations, inequality was its very basis; association grounded on equal rights scarcely existed; to be equals was to be enemies; two persons could hardly cooperate in anything, or meet in any amicable relation, without the law's appointing that one of them should be superior of the other. Mankind have outgrown this state, and all things now tend to substitute, as the general principle of human relations, a just equality, instead of the dominion of the strongest. But of all relations, that between men and women being the nearest and most intimate, and connected with the greatest number of strong emotions, was sure to be the last to throw off the old rule and receive the new: for in proportion to the strength of a feeling, is the tenacity with which it clings to the forms and circumstances with which it has even accidentally become associated.

When a prejudice, which has any hold on the feelings, finds itself reduced to the unpleasant necessity of assigning reasons, it thinks it had done enough when it has reasserted the very point in dispute, in phrases which appeal to the pre-existing feeling. Thus, many persons think they have sufficiently justified the restrictions on women's field of action, when they have said that the pursuits from which women are excluded are *unfeminine*, and that the *proper sphere* of women is not politics or publicity, but private and domestic life.

We deny the right of any portion of the species to decide for another portion, or any individual for another individual, what is and what is not their "proper sphere." The proper sphere for all human beings is the largest and highest which they are able to attain to. What this is, cannot be ascertained, without complete liberty of choice. The speakers at the Convention in America have therefore done wisely and right, in refusing to entertain the question of the peculiar aptitudes either of women or of men, or the limits within this or that occupation may be supposed to be more adapted to the one or to the other. They justly maintain, that these questions can only be more adapted to the one or to the other. They justly maintain, that these questions can only be satisfactorily answered by perfect freedom. Let every occupation be open to all, without favor or discouragement to any, and employments will fall into the hands of those men or women who are found by experience to be most capable of worthily exercising them. There need be no fear that women will take out of the hands of men any occupation which men perform better than they. Each individual will prove his or her capacities, in the only way in which capacities can be proved—by trial; and the world will have the benefit of the best faculties of all its inhabitants. But to interfere beforehand by an arbitrary limit, and declare that whatever be the genius, talent, energy, or force of mind of an individual of a certain sex or class, those faculties shall not be exerted, or shall be exerted only in some few of the many modes in which others are permitted to use theirs, is not only an injustice to the individual, and a detriment to society, which loses what it can ill spare, but is also the most effectual mode of providing that, in the sex or class so fet-

---

1   *Society of Friends*   The official name for the religious group more informally known as Quakers.
2   *discountenanced*   Disapproved of, discouraged.
3   *calumniated*   Falsely accused.

tered, the qualities which are not permitted to be exercised shall not exist.

Individuals now-a-days are seldom called upon to fight hand to hand, even with peaceful weapons; personal enmities and rivalries count for little in worldly transactions; the general pressure of circumstances, not the adverse will of individuals, is the obstacle men now have to make head against. That pressure, when excessive, breaks the spirit, and cramps and sours the feelings, but not less of women than of men, since they suffer certainly not less from its evils. There are still quarrels and dislikes, but the sources of them are changed. The feudal chief once found his bitterest enemy in his powerful neighbor, the minister or courtier in his rival for place: but opposition of interest in active life, as a cause of personal animosity, is out of date; the enmities of the present day arise not from great things but small, from what people say of one another, more than from what they do; and if there are hatred, malice, and all uncharitableness, they are to be found among women fully as much as among men. In the present state of civilization, the notion of guarding women from hardening influences of the world, could only be realized by secluding them from society altogether. The common duties of common life, as at present constituted, are incompatible with any other softness in women than weakness. Surely weak minds in weak bodies must ere long cease to be even supposed to be either attractive or amiable.

But, in truth, none of these arguments and considerations touch the foundations of the subject. The real question is, whether it is right and expedient that one-half of the human race should pass through life in a state of forced subordination to the other half. If the best state of human society is that of being divided into two parts, one consisting of persons with a will and a substantive existence, the other of humble companions to these persons, attached, each of them to one, for the purpose of bringing up *his* children, and making *his* home pleasant to him; if this is the place assigned to women, it is but kindness to educate them for this; to make them believe that the greatest good fortune which can befall them, is to be chosen by some man for this purpose; and that every other career which the world deems happy or honorable, is closed to them by the law, not social institutions, but of nature and destiny.

When, however, we ask why the existence of one-half the species should be merely ancillary to that of the other—why each woman should be a mere appendage to a man, allowed to have no interest of her own, that there may be nothing to compete in her mind with his interests and his pleasure; the only reason which can be given is, that men like it. It is agreeable to them that men should live for their own sake, women for the sake of men: and the qualities and conduct in subjects which are agreeable to rulers, they succeed for a long time in making the subjects themselves consider as their appropriate virtues. Helvetius[1] has met with much obloquy for asserting, that persons usually mean by virtues the qualities which are useful or convenient to themselves. How truly this is said of mankind in general, and how wonderfully the ideas of virtue set afloat by the powerful, are caught and imbibed by those under the dominion, is exemplified by the manner in which the world were once persuaded that the supreme virtue of subjects was loyalty to kings, and are still persuaded that the paramount virtue of womanhood is loyalty to men. Under a nominal[2] recognition of a moral code common to both, in practice self-will and self-assertion form the type of what are designated as manly virtues, while abnegation of self, patience, resignation, and submission to power, unless when resistance is commanded by other interests than their own, have been stamped by general consent as pre-eminently the duties and graces required of women. The meaning being merely, that power makes itself the center of moral obligation, and that a man likes to have his own will, but does not like that his domestic companion should have a will different from his.

In the beginning, and among tribes which are still in a primitive condition, women were and are the slaves of men for purposes of toil. All the hard bodily labor devolves on them. The Australian savage is idle, while women painfully dig up the roots on which he lives. An American Indian, when he has killed a deer, leaves it, and sends a woman to carry it home. In a state somewhat more advanced, as in Asia, women were and are the slaves of men for purposes of sensuality. In Europe there early succeeded a third and milder dominion, secured not by blows, nor by locks and bars, but by sedulous inculcation on the mind; feelings also of kindness, and ideas of duty, such as a superior owes to inferiors under his protection, became more and more involved in the relation of companionship, even between unequals. The lives of the two persons were apart. The wife was part of the furniture of home—of the resting-place to which the man returned from business or pleasure.

---

1   *Helvetius*   Claude Adrien Helvetius (1715–71), a French philosopher and poet well known for his utilitarian views.
2   *nominal*   In name, but not in fact.

Thus the position is corrupting equally to both; in the one it produces the vices of power, in the other those of artifice. Women, in their present physical and moral state, having stronger impulses, would naturally be franker and more direct than men; yet all the old saws and traditions represent them as artful and dissembling. Why? Because their only way to their objects is by indirect paths. In all countries where women have strong wishes and active minds, this consequence is inevitable; and if it is less conspicuous in England than in some other places, it is because Englishwomen, saving occasional exceptions, have ceased to have either strong wishes or active minds.

We are not now speaking of cases in which there is anything deserving the name of strong affection on both sides. That, where it exists, is too powerful a principle not to modify greatly the bad influences of the situation; it seldom, however, destroys them entirely. Much oftener the bad influences are too strong for the affection, and destroy it. The highest order of durable and happy attachments would be a hundred times more frequent than they are, if the affection which the two sexes sought from one another were that genuine friendship, which only exists between equals in privileges as in faculties.

With respect to the influence personally exercised by women over men, it, no doubt, renders them less harsh and brutal; in ruder times, it was often the only softening influence to which they were accessible. But the assertion, that the wife's influence renders the man less selfish, contains, as things now are, fully as much error as truth. Selfishness towards the wife herself, and towards those in whom she is interested, the children, though favored by her dependence, the wife's influence, no doubt, tends to counteract. But the general effect on him of her character, so long as her interests are concentrated in the family, tends but to substitute for individual selfishness a family selfishness, wearing an amiable guise, and putting on the mask of duty. How rarely is the wife's influence on the side of public virtue; how rarely does it do otherwise that discourage any effort of principle by which the private interests or worldly vanities of the family can be expected to suffer. Public spirit, sense of duty towards the public good, is of all virtues, as women are now educated and situated, the most rarely to be found among them; they have seldom even, what in men is often a partial substitute for public spirit, a sense of personal honor connected with any public duty. Many a man, whom no money or personal flattery would have bought, has bartered his political opinions against a title or invitations for his wife; and a still greater number are made mere hunters after the puerile vanities of society, because their wives value them. As for opinions; in Catholic countries, the wife's influence is another name for that of the priest; he gives her, in hopes and emotions connected with a future life, a consolation for the sufferings and disappointments which are her ordinary lot in this. Elsewhere, her weight is thrown into the scale either of the most commonplace, or of the most outwardly prosperous opinions: either those by which censure will be escaped, or by which worldly advancement is likeliest to be procured. In England, the wife's influence is usually on the illiberal[1] and anti-popular side: this is generally the gaining side for personal interest and vanity; and what to her is the democracy of liberalism in which she has no part—which leaves her the Pariah it found her? The man himself, when he marries, usually declines into Conservatism; begins to sympathize with the holders of power, more than with its victims, and thinks it his part to be on the side of authority. As to mental progress, except those vulgar attainments by which vanity or ambition are promoted, there is generally an end to it in a man who marries a woman mentally his inferior; unless, indeed, he is unhappy in marriage, or becomes indifferent. From a man of twenty-five or thirty, after he is married, an experienced observer seldom expects any further progress in mind or feelings. It is rare that the progress already made is maintained. Any spark of the *mens divinior*[2] which might otherwise have spread and become a flame, seldom survives for any length of time unextinguished. For a mind which learns to be satisfied with what it already is—which does not incessantly look forward to a degree of improvement not yet reached—becomes relaxed, self-indulgent, and loses the spring and the tension which maintain it even at the point already attained. And there is no fact in human nature to which experience bears more invariable testimony than to this—that all social or sympathetic influences which do not raise up, pull down; if they do not tend to stimulate and exalt the mind, they tend to vulgarize it.

For the interest, therefore, not only of women but of men, and of human improvement in which the modern world often boasts of having effected, and for which credit is sometimes given to civilization, and sometimes to Christianity, cannot stop where it is. If it were either necessary or just that one portion of mankind should remain mentally and spiritually only half developed, the development of the

1 *illiberal* Narrow-minded, ungenerous.
2 *mens divinior* Latin: more divinely inspired mind.

other portion ought to have been made, as far as possible, independent of their influence. Instead of this, they have become the most intimate, and it may now be said, the only intimate associates of those to whom yet they are sedulously kept inferior; and have been raised just high enough to drag the others down to themselves.

We have left behind a host of vulgar objections either as not worthy of an answer, or as answered by the general course of our remarks. A few words, however, must be said on one plea, which in England is made much use of for giving an unselfish air to the upholding of selfish privileges, and which, with unobserving, unreflecting people, passes for much more than it is worth. Women, it is said, do not desire—do not seek, what is called their emancipation. On the contrary, they generally disown such claims when made in their behalf, and fall with *acharnement*[1] upon anyone of themselves who identifies herself with their common cause.

Supposing the fact to be true in the fullest extent ever asserted, if it proves that European women ought to remain as they are, it proves exactly the same with respect to Asiatic women; for they too, instead of murmuring at their seclusion, and at the restraint imposed upon them, pride themselves on it, and are astonished at the effrontery of women who receive visits from male acquaintances, and are seen in the streets unveiled. Habits of submission make men as well as women servile-minded. The vast population of Asia do not desire or value, probably would not accept, political liberty, nor the savage of the forest, civilization; which does not prove that either of those things is undesirable for them, or that they will not, at some future time, enjoy it. Custom hardens human beings to any kind of degradation, by deadening the part of their nature which would resist it. And the case of women is, in this respect, even a peculiar one, for no other inferior caste that we have heard of have been taught to regard degradation as their honor. The argument, however, implies a secret consciousness that the alleged preference of women for their dependent state is merely apparent; and arises from their being allowed no choice; for if the preference be natural, there can be no necessity for enforcing it by law. To make laws compelling people to follow their inclination, had not hitherto been thought necessary by any legislator. The plea that women do not desire any change, is the same that has been urged, times out of mind, against the proposal of abolishing any social evil—"there is no complaint"; which is generally not true, and when true, only so because there is not that hope of success, without which complaint seldom makes itself audible to unwilling ears. How does the objector know that women do not desire equality and freedom? He never knew a woman who did not, or would not, desire it for herself individually. It would be very simple to suppose, that if they do desire it they will say so. Their position is like that of the tenants or laborers who vote against their own political interest to please their landlords or employers; with the unique addition, that submission is inculcated on them from childhood, as the peculiar attention and grace of their character. They are taught to think, that to repel actively even an admitted injustice done to themselves, is somewhat unfeminine, and had better be left to some male friend or protector.

The professions of women in this matter remind us of the State offenders of old, who, on the point of execution, used to protest their love and devotion to the sovereign by whose unjust mandate they suffered. *Griselda*[2] herself might be matched from the speeches put by Shakespeare into the mouths of male victims of kingly caprice and tyranny: the Duke of Buckingham, for example, in *Henry the Eighth*, and even Wolsey.[3] The literary class of women, especially in England, are ostentatious in disclaiming the desire for equality or citizenship, and proclaiming their complete satisfaction with the place which society assigns to them; exercising in this, as in many other respects, a most noxious influence over the feelings and opinions of men, who unsuspectingly accept the servilities of toadyism as concessions to the force of truth, not considering that it is the personal interest of these women to profess whatever opinions they expect will be agreeable to men. It is not among men of talent, sprung from the people, and patronized and flattered by the aristocracy, that we look for the leaders of a democratic movement. Successful literary women are just as unlikely to prefer the cause of women to their own social consideration.

---

1   *acharnement* French: fierceness, fury, determination.

2   *Griselda* Character in *The Decameron* (1353) by Boccaccio (1313–75). She reacts to spousal abuse with what is presented as heroic patience and obedience.

3   *Duke of Buckingham ... Wolsey* In Shakespeare's play, the Duke, a victim of Cardinal Wolsey's scheming, is unjustly on trial for treason but nevertheless reacts "sweetly," showing "a most noble patience." Wolsey later, fallen into misfortune, understands his own wrongdoing, and becomes, through suffering, serene and humble.

SOJOURNER TRUTH
(1797 – 1883)

SOJOURNER TRUTH IS AN ICON BOTH FOR FEMINISTS AND for African-Americans. Born into slavery in a Dutch settlement in New York State, her original name was Isabella Baumfree. She was sold several times, and compelled by one of her masters to marry another slave with whom she had five children (several were sold and taken away from her). Around the time New York State law freed its slaves (1827) she ran away from her master with her youngest child, and became a housekeeper; the family she was working for helped her sue successfully for the return of a child of hers who had been taken to Alabama. Having experienced a religious conversion, she moved to a commune of believers in the imminent arrival of Judgment Day; their leader, calling himself Prophet Matthias, exploited his followers financially and sexually, and was eventually tried for murder (but not convicted). In 1843, after the commune had fallen apart, Isabella felt prompted by the Holy Spirit to change her name to Sojourner Truth and to become a traveling preacher. ("Sojourner" means a traveler staying for only a short time.) She became a popular speaker both for the abolitionist movement, and a few years later, for the women's suffrage movement. Her most famous speech was delivered at a convention on women's rights in Akron, Ohio in 1851. A white abolitionist, Frances Gage, published a version of that speech a few years later, in which (she reports) Truth was confronted by a hostile audience, and said, "That man over there says that women need to be helped into carriages, and lifted over ditches, and to have the best place everywhere. Nobody helps me to any best place. *And ain't I a woman?*" Her fame increased after a laudatory article by Harriet Beecher Stowe was published in the *Atlantic Monthly Magazine* in 1863. ("I do not recollect ever to have been conversant with any one who had more of that silent and subtle power which we call personal presence than this woman.") During the Civil War, Truth raised contributions for black regiments and met Abraham Lincoln in the White House. After the war, she continued speaking, mostly on religion, equal rights for African-Americans, and temperance. She died in 1883.

Truth is important less for what she said, than for how she said it and for what she was taken to represent. According to contemporary sources, she was an enormously strong and forceful presence and a moving orator—an important role model of strong African-American womanhood who rallied the forces for feminism, for the abolition of slavery, for equal rights for blacks. Contemporary academics have become especially interested in the use of her words and persona for various political purposes—and Truth herself was clearly an early participant in this process of myth-making and symbol-construction. Written reports of her life and speeches have been highly selective and variable, filtered through political agendas—including those of Truth herself, in her dictated autobiography, and those of the people who wrote about her and gave accounts of her speeches. (Truth herself was illiterate, so all written material is second-hand.) These accounts tell us as much about how different ages conceptualized race and gender politics, as they do about Truth herself, who remains in many respects elusive. Even her most famous speech is surrounded by question marks; several accounts survive, each different in various ways. The most famous one by Gage was almost certainly highly shaped by the author's desire to connect the abolitionist cause with the issue of women's rights. Scholars agree now that the quote "Ain't I a woman?" was probably Gage's invention, as was the southern black dialect (Truth was raised in New York, and her first language was Dutch).

963

Speech Delivered at the Akron, Ohio Convention on Women's Rights, 1851

As Reported by the Anti-Slavery Bugle, 21 June 1851

One of the most unique and interesting speeches of the Convention was made by Sojourner Truth, an emancipated slave. It is impossible to transfer it to paper, or convey any adequate idea of the effect it produced upon the audience. Those only can appreciate it who saw her powerful form, her whole-souled, earnest gestures, and listened to her strong and truthful tones. She came forward to the platform and addressing the President said with great simplicity:

May I say a few words? Receiving an affirmative answer, she proceeded; I want to say a few words about this matter. I am a woman's rights. I have as much muscle as any man, and can do as much work as any man. I have plowed and reaped and husked and chopped and mowed, and can any man do more than that? I have heard much about the sexes being equal; I can carry as much as any man, and can eat as much too, if I can get it. I am as strong as any man that is now. As for intellect, all I can say is, if woman have a pint and man a quart—why cant she have her little pint full? You need not be afraid to give us our rights for fear we will take too much,—for we cant take more than our pint'll hold. The poor men seem to be all in confusion, and dont know what to do. Why children, if you have woman's rights give it to her and you will feel better. You will have your own rights, and they wont be so much trouble. I cant read, but I can hear. I have heard the bible and have learned that Eve caused man to sin. Well if woman upset the world, do give her a chance to set it right side up again. The Lady has spoken about Jesus, how he never spurned woman from him, and she was right. When Lazarus died, Mary and Martha came to him with faith and love and besought him to raise their brother. And Jesus wept—and Lazarus came forth. And how came Jesus into the world? Through God who created him and woman who bore him. Man, where is your part? But the women are coming up blessed be God and a few of the men are coming up with them. But man is in a tight place, the poor slave is on him, woman is coming on him, and he is surely between a hawk and a buzzard.

As Reported by F.D. Gage for the National Anti-Slavery Standard, 2 May 1863

"Well, chillen, what dar's so much racket dar must be som'ting out o'kilter. I tink dat 'twixt de niggers of de South and de women at de Norf, all a-talking 'bout rights, de white men will be in a fix pretty soon. But what's all this here talking 'bout? Dat man ober dar say dat woman needs to be helped into carriages, and lifted ober ditches, and to have de best place eberywhar. Nobody eber helps me into carriages, or ober mud-puddles, or gives me any best place,"; and, raising herself to her full height, and her voice to a pitch like rolling thunder, she asked, "And ar'n't I a woman? Look at me. Look at my arm," and she bared her right arm to the shoulder, showing its tremendous muscular power. "I have plowed and planted and gathered into barns, and no man could head me—and ar'n't I a woman? I could work as much and eat as much as a man (when I could get it) and bear de lash as well-and ar'n't I a woman? I have borne thirteen chillen, and seen 'em mos' all sold off to slavery, and when I cried out with a mother's grief, none but Jesus heard—and ar'n't' I a woman? Den dey talks 'bout dis ting in de head. What dis dey call it" "Intellect," whispered some one near. "Dat's it, honey. What's dat got to do with woman's rights or niggers' rights? If my cup won't hold but a pint, and youm holds a quart, wouldn't ye be mean not to let me have my little half-measure full?" and she pointed her significant finger and sent a keen glance at the minister who had made the argument. The cheering was long and loud. "Den dat little man in black dar, he say woman can't have as much rights as man, 'cause Christ wa'n't a woman. *Whar did your Christ come from?*"

Rolling thunder could not have stilled that crowd as did those deep, wonderful tones, as she stood there with outstretched arms and eye of fire. Raising her voice still louder, she repeated,

"Whar did your Christ come from? From God and a woman. Man had not'ing to do with him." Oh, what a rebuke she gave the little man. Turning again to another objector, she took up the defense of Mother Eve. I cannot follow her through it all. It was pointed and witty and solemn, eliciting at almost every sentence deafening applause, and she ended by asserting: "that if de fust woman God ever made was strong enought to turn de world upside down all her one lone, all dese togeder," and she glanced her eye over us, "ought to be able to turn it back, and git it right side up again, and now dey is asking to, de men better let 'em." (long and continued cheering). "Bleeged[1] to ye for hearin' on me, and now ole Sojourner ha'n't got nothing more to say."

- - - - -

---

1 *Bleeged* Obliged.

ALEXIS DE TOCQUEVILLE
(1805 – 1859)

IN 1830, FRENCH POLITICAL THEORIST ALEXIS DE TOCQUEville came to see the US as a concrete representation of democratic ideals. After a research trip there, he wrote the first part of *Democracy in America*, a classic work of political sociology that was to become the chief tool for the world's understanding of that new country. Tocqueville predicted what few other Europeans saw at the time: that the US was not just an infantile wild and uncultured offshoot of Europe, but that it was destined to be a world leader—a power to be reckoned with and also an example to be emulated of a successful democracy.

Tocqueville was born into a family active in politics, and decided early on to seek a career in public life. Having studied law, he took the position of assistant public magistrate, but when Louis-Philippe came to the French throne in 1830, Tocqueville's previous association with the ousted king put him in an uneasy political position, and he and a friend sought permission to go to America to study prison reform. Tocqueville by then had already sensed that America would provide him with a model for the future of democratic France, and he extended his research in America far beyond an examination of the penal situation: he observed and read widely, and interviewed many eminent Americans. On his return, he wrote the book that was widely hailed as a masterwork.

Tocqueville's admiration for democracy always had a touch of ambivalence (later, as Minister of Foreign Affairs in the Second Republic, he would curtail freedom of association and freedom of the press). His aristocratic sensibilities tended toward a certain distrust of the "mob mentality" that had long been associated in certain minds with the notion of majority rule; he feared too that it might lead to lawlessness and curtailment of individual rights. For him, the central problem for democracy was whether it could be compatible, in the long run, with equality and liberty. He saw dangers in the centralization of a monolithic and powerful government, and in the possibility of rule by the majority becoming the tyranny of the majority. He argued in the first part of *Democracy in America* that the characteristically American practice of forming local political associations was an effective way of dealing with both issues. Participation through associations would teach

people to work together for common causes, blunting rampant individualism and countering excessive state power. This account of associations has continued to inspire democratic theorists, especially those advocating "participative" or "deliberative" democracy, calling for a more robust role for ordinary citizens in public affairs.

The second part of *Democracy in America* appeared four years after the first, and its tone was rather different. Tocqueville had become depressed by the curtailment of liberties and the political apathy in France, and he was less optimistic about the possibility of genuine libertarian democracy. Elected to the Chamber of Deputies in 1837, he never achieved the political effectiveness he had hoped for. In 1851 he was ousted from his office by the new regime of Louis-Napoleon. He began *The Old Regime and the Revolution*, an iconoclastic book on the French Revolution arguing that the French Revolution, instead of breaking with the Old Regime, continued the process of government centralization in France.

◆ ◆ ◆ ◆ ◆

Democracy in America (1835)

Chapter 5: On the Use that Americans Make of Public Associations in Civil Life

I do not propose to speak of the political associations which men use to defend themselves against the despotic influence of a majority or the aggressions of royal power. I have already treated that subject. As each citizen becomes individually weaker and consequently less able to preserve his freedom single-handedly, if he did not learn to join with his fellow-citizens to defend his freedom, it is clear that increase of equality would inevitably bring with it increase of tyranny.

I refer here only to those associations which are formed in civil life, not to political bodies. The political associations which exist in the United States are only one of the country's many kinds of association. Americans of all ages, all conditions, and all dispositions, constantly form associations. They have not only commercial and manufacturing companies, in which all take part, but also associations of a thousand other kinds—religious, moral, serious, trivial, extensive, or restricted, enormous or tiny. Americans form associations for entertainment, to found educational institutions, to build inns, to construct churches, to distribute books, to send missionaries to the other side of the earth. In this manner they found hospitals, prisons, and schools. If they propose to advance some doctrine, or to foster some feeling with the help of a great example, they form a society. Wherever there is a new undertaking, in the place of the government in France or of a man of high rank in England, in the United States you will be sure to find an association. I encountered several kinds of associations in America which, I confess, I had no idea existed; and I have often admired the extreme skill of the inhabitants in proposing a common aim for the efforts of a great many men, and in getting them to pursue it voluntarily. I have since traveled in England, from where the Americans have taken some of their laws and many of their customs, and it seemed to me that the principle of association was by no means used so constantly or so skillfully in that country. The English often do great deeds single-handedly, whereas the Americans form associations for the smallest tasks. It is evident that the English consider association as a powerful means for action, while the Americans seem to regard it as the only means for acting.

Thus the most democratic country on the face of the earth is the one where people have carried the art of pursuing their common desires together to the highest perfection, and have applied this new science to the greatest number of purposes. Is this merely accident, or is there actually a connection between the principles of association and equality? Aristocratic communities[1] always contain, among a multitude of individuals who by themselves are powerless, a small number of powerful and wealthy citizens, each of whom can achieve great undertakings single-handedly. In aristocratic societies men do not need to join together in order to act, because they are strongly held together. Every wealthy and powerful citizen is, in effect, the head of a permanent and compulsory association composed of all those who are dependent upon him, or whom he makes subservient to his

aims. In democratic nations, on the contrary, all the citizens are independent and weak; they can do hardly anything by themselves, and they cannot force their fellow citizens to assist them. They all are helpless, therefore, unless they voluntarily learn to help each other. If men living in democratic countries had no right or no inclination to associate for political purposes, their independence would be in great jeopardy; still, they could preserve their wealth and their enlightenment for some time to come. On the other hand, if they never acquired the habit of forming associations in ordinary life, civilization itself would be endangered. A people whose individuals lost the power of achieving great things single-handedly, but did not acquire the means of producing them together, would soon relapse into barbarism.

Unfortunately, the social conditions which make associations so necessary in democratic nations, make achieving them more difficult than elsewhere. When several members of an aristocracy agree to combine, they can do it easily. Each of them brings great strength to the partnership, so the number of its members can be very small; and consequently they may easily become acquainted, understand each other, and establish fixed regulations. The same opportunities do not occur in democratic nations, where associations must always be very large to have any power.

I am aware that many of my countrymen are not in the least embarrassed by this difficulty. They contend that the weaker and more incompetent the citizens become, the more the nation requires an able and active government, so that society as a whole may accomplish what individuals no longer can. Though they believe this solves the whole problem, I think they are mistaken. A government might take the place of some of the largest American companies—several U.S. states have already attempted this—but what political power could ever carry out the vast number of smaller undertakings the American citizens perform every day by means of associations? It is easy to see that the time is coming when man will be less and less able to produce the most common necessities of life by himself. The task of the governing power and its efforts will therefore perpetually increase. The more it takes the place of associations, the more individuals will require its assistance, forgetting the idea of combining together. These are causes and effects which unceasingly bring about each other. Will the administration of the country ultimately assume the management of every industry that no single citizen is capable of? And if it eventually happens that land is split into an infinite number of lots, due to the extreme subdivision of property, so that it

---

1   *Aristocratic communities*   An "aristocracy," in the sense Tocqueville speaks of it, is a society in which government or leadership more broadly is in the hands of a ruling class, either hereditary or composed of those judged best qualified to lead.

can only be cultivated by groups of farmers, will it be necessary that the head of the government leave the helm of state to become a farm-worker? The morals and the intelligence of a democratic people would be as much endangered as its business and manufactures, if the government ever wholly took over the place of private companies.

Feelings and opinions are renewed, the heart is enlarged, and the human mind is developed by no other means than by people's reciprocal influence upon each other. I have shown that these influences are almost nonexistent in democratic countries; they must therefore be artificially created, and this can only be accomplished through associations.

When the members of an aristocratic community adopt a new opinion, or develop a new feeling, they display it on the great stage in which they are players; opinions or feelings so conspicuous to the eyes of the crowd are easily introduced into the minds or hearts of all around. In democratic countries the governing power alone is naturally in a condition to act in this manner; but it is easy to see that its action is always inadequate, and often dangerous. A government alone can no more sustain and renew the circulation of opinions and feelings among a large population, than it can control all of industry's activities. The minute a government attempts to go beyond its political sphere and embark on this new path, it becomes insupportably tyrannical, if only unintentionally. For a government can dictate only strict rules; the opinions which it favors are rigidly enforced; and it is never easy to discriminate between its advice and its commands. Worse still is the case where the government really believes itself interested in preventing the circulation of ideas. It will then stand motionless, oppressed by the weight of voluntary inaction. Governments therefore should not be the only active powers: associations ought to stand in place of those powerful private individuals that the equality of conditions has eliminated.

As soon as several of the inhabitants of the United States have taken up an opinion or a feeling which they wish to bring to the world's attention, they search for similarly minded people; and as soon as they have found each other, they combine. From that moment on they are no longer isolated individuals, but a power to be reckoned with, whose actions serve as an example, and whose language is listened to. The first time I heard in the United States that 100,000 men had publicly vowed to abstain from alcohol, it appeared to me more like a joke than a serious pledge; and I did not immediately see why these temperate citizens could not content themselves with drinking water by their own firesides. At last I understood that 100,000 Americans, alarmed by the progress of drunkenness around them, had made up their minds to support temperance. They acted in just the same way as a man of high rank who dresses very plainly in order to inspire a contempt of luxury in ordinary citizens. It is probable that if these 100,000 men had lived in France, each of them would have individually petitioned the government to watch the taverns all over the kingdom.

Nothing, in my opinion, deserves our attention more than the intellectual and moral associations of America. The political and industrial associations of that country are obvious and vivid to us; but the other associations elude our observation, or if we discover them, we understand them imperfectly, because we have hardly ever seen anything of the kind. However it must be acknowledged that they are as necessary to the American people as political and industrial associations, and perhaps more so. In democratic countries the science of association is the fundamental science; the progress of the other sciences depends upon the progress it has made. Among the laws which rule human societies there is one which seems to be more precise and clear than all others: if men are to become or remain civilized, the art of associating together must grow in proportion to the growth of equality.

Chapter 6: Of the Relation between Associations and Newspapers

When men are no longer united by firm and lasting ties, it is impossible to obtain widespread cooperation, unless you can persuade each man that it is in his self-interest to work with others voluntarily. This can be habitually and conveniently achieved only through a newspaper; nothing but a newspaper can communicate the same thought to a thousand minds at the same moment. A newspaper is an adviser you do not need to seek out, but who comes uninvited, and every day talks briefly of public affairs without distracting you from your private pursuits.

Newspapers therefore become more necessary as men become more equal, and as individualism becomes more to be feared. To suppose that they serve only to protect freedom would be to diminish their importance: they maintain civilization. I shall not deny that in democratic countries newspapers frequently lead the citizens to engage in rash undertakings; but if there were no newspapers there would be no common activity. The evil which they produce is therefore much less than that which they cure.

The effect of a newspaper is not only to suggest the same purpose to a great number of people, but also to provide means for jointly executing the plans which they may have individually conceived. The leading citizens who inhabit an aristocratic country discern each other from afar; and if they wish to unite their forces, they move towards each other, drawing a multitude of others after them. It frequently happens, by contrast, in democratic countries, that a great number of men who would like to combine cannot do so, because they are very insignificant and lost in the crowd—they cannot see, and do not know where to find, one another. A newspaper then takes up the idea or the feeling which had occurred to each of them simultaneously, but singly. All are then immediately guided towards this light; and these wandering minds, which had long sought each other in darkness, at last meet and unite.

The newspaper brought them together, and the newspaper is then necessary to keep them united. For an association among a democratic people to have any power, it must be a large body. Its members are therefore scattered over a wide area, and each of them is bound to his home by low income or the demands of work. They must therefore find the means for communicating every day without seeing each other, and for taking steps in common without having met. Thus hardly any democratic association can do without newspapers. There is consequently a necessary connection between public associations and newspapers: newspapers make associations, and associations make newspapers. And if it is correct that that the number of associations will grow as the conditions of men become more equal, it is as certain that the number of newspapers increases along with the number of associations. Thus it is that in America we find at the same time the greatest number of associations and of newspapers.

Consideration of this connection between the number of newspapers and of associations leads us to discover a further connection between the state of the periodical press and the form of the administration in a country. It shows that the number of newspapers must increase as the country's administration becomes decentralized. For among democratic nations the exercise of local powers cannot be entrusted to the leading members of the community as in aristocracies. Those powers must either be abolished, or placed in the hands of very large numbers of men, who then in fact constitute an association permanently established by law for the purpose of administering the affairs of an area; and they require a newspaper, to bring to them every day, in the midst of their own petty concerns, some news of current affairs. The greater the number of local powers, the greater the number of men required by law to exercise them; and the greater this need is felt, the more profusely newspapers appear.

The extraordinary subdivision of administrative power has much more to do with the enormous number of American newspapers than the great political freedom of the country and the absolute liberty of the press. If all the inhabitants of the Union had the vote—but a vote which only extended to electing legislators in Congress—they would require only a few newspapers, because they would have to act together on only a few very important but very rare occasions. But within the scope of the great association of the nation, lesser associations for local administration have been established by law in every country, every city, and indeed in every village. The laws of the country thus compel all Americans to cooperate every day with some of their fellow citizens for a common purpose, and they all require a newspaper to inform them what all the others are doing.

In my opinion a democratic people[1] without any national representative assemblies, but with a great number of small local powers, would have, in the end, more newspapers than another people governed by a centralized administration and an elective legislation. The best explanation of the enormous circulation of the daily press in the United States seems to me to be that Americans enjoy utmost national freedom combined with local freedom of every kind. There is a prevailing opinion in France and England that the circulation of newspapers would be strongly increased by removing the taxes imposed on the press. This exaggerates the effects of such a reform. Newspapers increase in numbers, not according to their cheapness, but in proportion to the frequency the desire is felt for intercommunication and combination.

Similarly, I would attribute the increasing influence of the daily press to more general causes than those commonly offered. A newspaper can survive only by publishing sentiments or principles common to a large number of men. A newspaper therefore always represents an association which is composed of its habitual readers. This association may be

---

1   *democratic people*   [Tocqueville's note] I say a *democratic* people. When the administration of an aristocratic people is not centralized, the lack of newspapers is not strongly felt, because local powers are then in the hands of a very small number of men, who either act apart, or who know each other and can easily meet and come to an understanding.

more or less defined, more or less restricted, more or less numerous; but the fact that the newspaper remains in publication is proof that at least the germ of such an association exists in the minds of its readers.

This leads me to a last reflection, with which I shall conclude this chapter. The more equal men's conditions become, and the weaker individual men are, the more easily mass opinion influences them and the more difficult is it for them to hold an opinion rejected by the multitude. A newspaper represents an association; it may be said to address each of its readers in the name of all the others, and to exert its influence over them in proportion to their individual weakness. The power of the press must therefore increase as social conditions become more equal.

Chapter 7: The Relationship between Civil and Political Associations

There is only one country on the face of the earth where citizens enjoy unlimited freedom of association for political purposes. This country is the only one in the world where the continual exercise of the right of association has been introduced into civil life, and where all the advantages which civilization can confer are procured by means of this exercise. In all the countries where political associations are prohibited, civil associations are rare. It is hardly probable that this an accident; rather, we should infer that there is a natural, and perhaps a necessary, connection between these two kinds of associations. Certain men happen to have a common interest in some concern—perhaps it involves the management of a commercial undertaking or the negotiation of an industrial contract; they meet, they combine, and thus by degrees they become familiar with the principle of association. The greater the multiplicity of small affairs, the more do men acquire facility in undertaking great projects together, even without knowing it. Civil association, therefore, facilitates political association: but, on the other hand, political association singularly strengthens and improves associations for civil purposes. Men might imagine that they can provide for their own needs in civil life, but not in politics. So when people know anything about public life, the idea of association and the wish to associate occur constantly. Whatever natural reluctance may restrain men from acting together, they will always be ready to combine for political interests. Thus political life makes the love and practice of association more general; it imparts a desire of union, and teaches the means of uniting to men who would have always lived apart.

Politics gives birth not only to a large number of associations, but to larger associations as well. In civil life it seldom happens that any one interest draws a very large number of men to act together; much skill is required to bring such an interest into existence: but in politics opportunities present themselves every day. Now it is solely in great associations that the general value of the principle of association is displayed. Citizens who are individually powerless do not very clearly anticipate the strength they can acquire by uniting together; they must be shown in order to understand. Hence it is often easier to gather a crowd for a public purpose than a few persons; while a thousand citizens do not see what interest they have in joining forces, ten thousand will be perfectly aware of it. In politics people combine for great undertakings; and the use they make of the principle of association in important affairs teaches them, in practical terms, that it is their interest to help each other in less important ones. A political association draws a number of individuals out of their own circle at the same time: however different they may be in age, mind, and fortune, it brings them nearer, and into contact. Once having met, they can always meet again.

Men can undertake few civil partnerships without risking a portion of their possessions; this is the case with all manufacturing and trading companies. If men are not familiar with the art of association and its principal rules, they are afraid when they first cooperate in this manner, since it may cost them a good deal. Therefore they therefore would prefer to deprive themselves of a powerful instrument of success, rather than to run its risks. They are, however, less reluctant to join political associations, which appear to them to safe, because their money is not at risk. But they cannot belong to these associations for any length of time without finding out how order is maintained among a large number of men, and how they are made to advance, harmoniously and methodically, to the same object. Thus they learn to surrender their own will to the group and to make their own efforts subordinate to the common impulse—things that are no less necessary to know in civil than in political associations. Political associations may therefore be considered as large free schools, where all the members of the community go to learn the general theory of association.

But even if political association did not directly contribute to the progress of civil association, to destroy the former would be to impair the latter. When citizens can meet in public only for certain purposes, they regard such meetings as an unusual undertaking and they rarely think about it. When they are allowed to meet freely for all purposes, they ultimately look upon public association as the universal or the sole means for accomplishing their various purposes. Every new desire instantly revives the idea. The art of association then becomes, as I have said before, the fundamental science, studied and applied by all.

When some types of associations are prohibited and others allowed, it is difficult to distinguish the former from the latter. In this state of doubt men abstain from them altogether and a sort of public opinion tends to cause any association whatsoever to be regarded as a bold and almost an illicit enterprise.[1]

It is therefore a delusion to suppose that the spirit of association, when it is repressed at one point, will nevertheless display the same vigor at all others; and that if men are allowed to carry out certain undertakings in common, that is quite enough to motivate them. When the members of a community are allowed and accustomed to associate for all purposes, they will associate as readily for less as for more important ones; but if they are only allowed to associate for small affairs, they will be neither inclined nor able to do so. It does no good to leave them entirely free to engage in matters of trade: they will hardly care to exercise the rights you have granted to them; and, after having exhausted your strength in useless efforts to suppress prohibited associa-

tions, you will be surprised that you cannot persuade men to form the associations you encourage.

I do not say that there can be no civil associations in a country where political association is prohibited; for men can never live in society without embarking in some common undertakings: but I maintain that in such a country civil associations will always be few in number, poorly planned, unskillfully managed, that they will never engage in great projects, or that they will fail in executing them.

This naturally leads me to think that freedom of association in political matters is not so dangerous to public peace as is supposed; and that possibly, after having threatened society for some time, it may strengthen the state in the end. In democratic countries political associations are, so to speak, the only powerful persons who aspire to rule the state. Accordingly, the governments of our time look upon associations of this kind just as sovereigns in the Middle Ages regarded the great vassals of the Crown: they entertain a sort of instinctive hatred of them, and they fight them on all occasions. They bear, on the contrary, a natural good will to civil associations, because they readily discover that, instead of directing the minds of the community to public affairs, these institutions serve to distract them from such reflections; and that, by engaging them more and more in projects that require public peace, they avert revolutions. But these governments do not pay attention to the fact that political associations tend amazingly to multiply and to facilitate civil associations, and that in avoiding a dangerous evil they deprive themselves of an effective remedy.

When you see Americans freely and constantly forming associations for the purpose of promoting some political principle, or of getting someone elected or removed from power, you have some difficulty understanding that men who are so independent do not constantly abuse their freedom. If, on the other hand, you survey the infinite number of trading companies which are in operation in the United States, and see that Americans are everywhere always involved in the execution of important and difficult plans that the slightest revolution would throw into confusion, you will readily comprehend why they are not at all tempted to disrupt the State, nor to destroy the public peace by which they all profit.

Is it enough to observe these things separately, or should we not discover the hidden link which connects them? In their political associations, the Americans of all conditions, minds, and ages, daily acquire a general taste for association, and grow accustomed to its use. There they

1   *In this state ... illicit enterprise* [Tocqueville's note] This is especially true when the executive government has a discretionary power of allowing or prohibiting associations. When certain associations are simply prohibited by law, and the courts have to punish infringements of that law, the evil is far less considerable. Then every citizen knows beforehand pretty much what to expect. He judges himself before he is judged by the law, and abstains from prohibited associations, and joins those which are legally permitted. All free nations have always admitted that the right of association might be limited by these restrictions. But if the legislature should give a man the power to determine beforehand which associations are dangerous and which are useful, and should authorize him to nip all associations in the bud or allow them to be formed, then, because nobody would be able to predict in what cases associations might be established and in what cases they might not, the spirit of association would be entirely paralyzed. The former of these arrangements—in which laws govern associations—would only attack certain associations; the latter arrangement—with power given to one person—would inflict injury on society itself. I can conceive that a regular government may have recourse to the former, but I do not concede that any government has the right to enact the latter.

meet together in large numbers, they converse, they listen to each other, and they are mutually stimulated to all sorts of undertakings. Afterwards, they transfer the ideas they have thus acquired to civil life, and put them to a thousand uses. Thus it is by the enjoyment of a dangerous freedom that the Americans learn the art of rendering the dangers of freedom less formidable.

If we select a certain moment in the existence of a nation, it is easy to prove that political associations disrupt the state and paralyze industry. But take the whole life of a people, and it may perhaps be easy to demonstrate that freedom of association in political matters is favorable to the prosperity and even to the peace of the community.

I said earlier that the unrestrained liberty of political association cannot be entirely assimilated to the liberty of the press. The one is at the same time less necessary and more dangerous than the other. A nation may confine it within certain limits without ceasing to be its own master; and it may sometimes be obliged to do so in order to maintain its own authority. And further on I added that it cannot be denied that the unrestrained liberty of association for political purposes is the last degree of liberty which a people can tolerate. If it does not throw them into anarchy, it perpetually brings them, as it were, to the verge of it. Thus I do not think that a nation is always at liberty to give its citizens an absolute right of association for political purposes; and I doubt that it is wise to set no limits on freedom of association in any country or in any age. Consider a nation that could not maintain peace in the community, produce respect for law, or establish a lasting government, if it did not confine the right of association within narrow limits. These goods are doubtless of great value, and I can imagine that, to acquire or to preserve them, the nation may impose upon itself severe temporary restrictions. Nevertheless, it should know at what price these goods are purchased. I can understand that it may be advisable to cut off a man's arm in order to save his life; but it would be ridiculous to assert that he will be as nimble as he was before he lost it.

Chapter 8: How Americans Combat Individualism with the Principle of Self-Interest Rightly Understood

When a few rich and powerful individuals led the world, they loved to imagine man's duties in lofty terms. They were fond of professing that it is praiseworthy to forget one's self, and that good should be done without hope of reward, as it is by God himself. Such were the standard opinions of that age of morality. I doubt whether men were more virtuous in aristocratic ages than in others; but they were constantly talking of the beauties of virtue, and its utility was studied only in secret. But since the imagination now takes less lofty flights and every man's thoughts are now centered on himself, moralists are alarmed by this ideal of self-sacrifice, and they no longer attempt to present it to the human mind. They therefore content themselves with inquiring whether the personal advantage of each member of the community does not consist in working for the good of all; and when they have hit upon some point on which private interest and public interest meet and converge, they are eager to point it out. Observations of this kind are gradually multiplied: what was only a single remark becomes a general principle; and it is held as a truth that man serves himself in serving his fellow-creatures, and that his private interest is to do good.

I have already shown, in several parts of this work, how the inhabitants of the United States almost always manage to combine their own advantage with that of their fellow citizens: my present purpose is to point out the general rule which enables them to do this. In the United States hardly anybody talks of the beauty of virtue; but they maintain that virtue is useful, and prove it every day. The American moralists do not claim that men ought to sacrifice themselves for their fellow-creatures because it is noble to make such sacrifices; but they boldly claim that such sacrifices are as necessary to him who imposes them on himself, as to him for whose sake they are made. They have found out that in their country and their age man is driven back to himself by an irresistible force; and losing all hope of stopping that force, they turn all their thoughts to following it. They therefore do not deny that every man may follow his own interest; but they endeavor to prove that it is the interest of every man to be virtuous. I shall not examine here their justifications, which would divert me from my subject: suffice it to say that they have convinced their fellow countrymen.

Montaigne said long ago: "Were I not to follow the straight road for its straightness, I should follow it for having found by experience that in the end it is commonly the happiest and most useful track." The doctrine of interest rightly understood is not new, then. But among Americans of our time it finds universal acceptance: it has become popular there; you may notice it at the root of all their actions, you will notice it in everything they say. It is as often to be encountered on the lips of a poor man as a rich one. In Europe the principle of interest is much cruder than it is in America, but at the same time it is less common, and especially it is less publicized. Among us, men still constantly pretend great self-denial which they no longer feel. The Americans, on the contrary, are fond of explaining almost all the actions of their lives by the principle of interest rightly understood; they complacently show how an enlightened regard for themselves constantly prompts them to assist each other, and inclines them willingly to sacrifice a portion of their time and property to the welfare of the state. In this respect I think they frequently fail to do themselves justice; for in the United States, as well as elsewhere, people are sometimes seen to give way to those disinterested and spontaneous impulses which are natural to man; but the Americans seldom admit that they yield to emotions of this kind; they are more anxious to do honor to their philosophy than to themselves.

I might here pause, without attempting to pass judgment on what I have described. The extreme difficulty of the subject would be my excuse, but I shall not avail myself of it; and I would prefer that my readers, clearly perceiving my purpose, should disagree with me than that I should leave them in suspense.

The principle of interest rightly understood is not a lofty one, but it is clear and sure. It does not aim at a great goal, but it attains the goals it has without excessive effort. Since it lies within everyone's capacities, everyone can learn and remember it without difficulty. By its admirable conformity to human weaknesses, it easily obtains great prominence; and this prominence is not precarious, since the principle balances one personal interest with another, and uses the very same instrument that excites the passions to direct them. The principle of interest, rightly understood, produces no great acts of self-sacrifice, but it suggests daily small acts of self-denial. By itself it is not sufficient to make a man virtuous, but it disciplines a number of citizens in habits of consistency, temperance, moderation, foresight, self-command; and, if it does not lead men straight to virtue by the will, it gradually draws them in that direction by their habits. If the principle of interest rightly understood were to sway the whole moral world, extraordinary virtues would doubtless be rarer; but I think that gross depravity would then also be less common. The principle of interest rightly understood perhaps prevents some men from rising far above the general level; but a great number of other men,

who were falling far below it, are caught and restrained by it. Observe a few individuals, they are lowered by it; survey mankind, it is raised. I am not afraid to say that the principle of interest, rightly understood, appears to me the best suited of all philosophical theories to the wants of men of our time, and that I regard it as their chief remaining security against themselves. The minds of the moralists of our age should therefore turn towards it; even should they judge it to be incomplete, it must nevertheless be adopted as necessary.

I do not think that, on the whole, there is more egotism among us than in America; the only difference is that there it is enlightened—here it is not. Americans will sacrifice a portion of their private interests to preserve the rest; we try to preserve everything, and often we lose it all. Everybody I see about me seems bent on teaching their contemporaries, by principle and example, that what is useful is never wrong. Will nobody attempt to make them understand how what is right may be useful? No power on earth can prevent the increasing equality of conditions from prompting the human mind to seek out what is useful, or from leading every member of the community to be self-interested. It must therefore be expected that personal interest will become, more than ever, the principal, if not the sole, origin of men's actions; but it remains to be seen how each man will understand his personal interest. If the members of a community, as they become more equal, become more ignorant and coarse, it is difficult to predict what stupid lengths their egotism may lead them to; and no one can predict to what disgrace and wretchedness they would plunge themselves for fear that they should have to sacrifice something of their own well-being to the prosperity of their fellow-creatures. I do not think that the system of interest, as it is professed in America, is, in all its parts, self-evident; but it contains a great number of truths that are so evident that anyone who is educated must see them. Educate them, then; for the age of implicit self-sacrifice and instinctive virtues is already behind us, and the time is fast approaching when freedom, public peace, and social order itself will not be able to exist without education.

HENRY DAVID THOREAU
(1817 – 1862)

DURING A TWO YEAR PERIOD FROM 1845 TO 1847, Henry David Thoreau conducted a famous experiment at Walden Pond near Concord, Massachusetts; he lived in near isolation and as self-sufficiently as possible. This experience led to his two most famous publications, *Civil Disobedience* (1849) and *Walden* (1854). In the earlier work he argued for the legitimacy and, in some cases, the necessity of individual citizens resisting the demands of government. In the later work he presented a wide range of social, political, and economic thoughts in the course of describing his life in the woods. While he published several dozen other pieces of writing, Thoreau's reputation in political philosophy and literature rests primarily on these two works; they are still widely read and studied and continue to be important influences on contemporary social and political thought.

Thoreau was born on July 12, 1817 in Concord and would live his entire life in or near that small town. His education at Concord Academy and later at Harvard in nearby Cambridge exposed him to Immanuel Kant, which helped to shape the newly developing American transcendentalism of Thoreau and his mentor, Ralph Waldo Emerson. American transcendentalism is notoriously difficult to define, but arose largely as a reaction to Lockean empiricism—roughly, the view that all knowledge comes from sense experience. The transcendentalists thought that the mind could apprehend spiritual truths without having to derive such truths from information received through the senses. They rejected the authority of past institutions, stressing individualism in faith and social affairs. Though in full flower only from the mid 1830s to late 1840s, American transcendentalism has had a continuing influence on American politics, philosophy (especially through the American pragmatists William James and John Dewey), and literature.

After graduating from Harvard, Thoreau opened a school with his brother John in 1838. But this effort was cut short by the death of John from tetanus resulting from a minor cut. Thoreau then worked for Ralph Waldo Emerson and later for his brother William Emerson, primarily as a tutor for their children. During this time Thoreau began to write and publish both essays and poetry in Emerson's publication, *The Dial*. But by 1845 Thoreau decided he wanted to try something different. He built his own home on property owned by Emerson, surviving on what he could produce for himself.

In 1846 Thoreau was arrested for his refusal to pay the poll tax; he was unwilling to pay taxes to a government that condoned the institute of slavery and that was engaging in what he saw as an unjust war against Mexico. He only spent one night in jail and was released when, against his wishes, his aunt paid his taxes for him. The event inspired him to write *Civil Disobedience* (originally entitled *Resistance to Civil Government*). In that work, Thoreau expressed his general skepticism about the legitimacy of any form of government, and more specifically his concern that citizens too often substitute the judgment of their leaders for their own. He defended action in support of justice, even if that action went against the laws of the land.

After his release from jail, Thoreau returned to his home by Walden Pond, where he lived until 1847. A further seven years elapsed before he published his book about his time there. *Walden* was part autobiography, part novel, and part philosophical treatise. Throughout, he emphasizes the values of simplicity, self-reliance, and personal responsibility, and extols the value of nature itself. The book remains highly regarded and widely studied both as a literary work and as a philosophical one.

In the years following the publication of *Walden*, Thoreau continued to write and travel throughout New England. But he suffered increasingly from the tuberculosis he had contracted in 1835, and from 1859 on he lived largely as an invalid. Henry David Thoreau died on May 6, 1862 at the age of forty-four.

Civil Disobedience continues to be seen by both modern anarchists and libertarians as a work of vital importance. His argument for the legitimacy of resistance to government when it violates principles of justice has been a factor in many social revolutions in the years since Thoreau's death. Gandhi's civil disobedience in the cause of Indian independence and Martin Luther King, Jr.'s activism in support of civil rights for all Americans both have strong roots in Thoreau's thoughts and writings. His ideas have also been credited with influencing such diverse groups as the British labor movement and the counterculture of the 1960s and 1970s.

◆ ◆ ◆ ◆ ◆

from Civil Disobedience (1849)

I heartily accept the motto, "That government is best which governs least"; and I should like to see it acted up to more rapidly and systematically. Carried out, it finally amounts to this, which also I believe—"That government is best which governs not at all"; and when men are prepared for it, that will be the kind of government which they will have. Government is at best but an expedient; but most governments are usually, and all governments are sometimes, inexpedient. The objections which have been brought against a standing[1] army, and they are many and weighty, and deserve to prevail, may also at last be brought against a standing government. The standing army is only an arm of the standing government. The government itself, which is only the mode which the people have chosen to execute their will, is equally liable to be abused and perverted before the people can act through it. Witness the present Mexican war,[2] the work of comparatively a few individuals using the standing government as their tool; for in the outset, the people would not have consented to this measure.

This American government—what is it but a tradition, though a recent one, endeavoring to transmit itself unimpaired to posterity, but each instant losing some of its integrity? It has not the vitality and force of a single living man; for a single man can bend it to his will. It is a sort of wooden gun[3] to the people themselves. But it is not the less necessary for this; for the people must have some complicated machinery or other, and hear its din, to satisfy that idea of government which they have. Governments show thus how successfully men can be imposed upon, even impose on themselves, for their own advantage. It is excellent, we must all allow. Yet this government never of itself furthered any enterprise, but by the alacrity[4] with which it got out of its way. *It* does not keep the country free. *It* does not settle the West. *It* does not educate. The character inherent in the American people has done all that has been accomplished; and it would have done somewhat more, if the government had not sometimes got in its way. For government is an expedient, by which men would fain succeed in letting one another alone; and, as has been said, when it is most expedient, the governed are most let alone by it. Trade and commerce, if they were not made of India rubber, would never manage to bounce over obstacles which legislators are continually putting in their way; and if one were to judge these men wholly by the effects of their actions and not partly by their intentions, they would deserve to be classed and punished with those mischievous persons who put obstructions on the railroads.

But, to speak practically and as a citizen, unlike those who call themselves no-government men, I ask for, not at once no government, but *at once* a better government. Let every man make known what kind of government would command his respect, and that will be one step toward obtaining it.

After all, the practical reason why, when the power is once in the hands of the people, a majority are permitted, and for a long period continue, to rule is not because they are most likely to be in the right, nor because this seems fairest to the minority, but because they are physically the strongest. But a government in which the majority rule in all cases can not be based on justice, even as far as men understand it. Can there not be a government in which the majorities do not virtually decide right and wrong, but conscience?—in which majorities decide only those questions to which the

---

1   *standing* Permanently established (as opposed to temporary, for the duration of service for a particular purpose).

2   *Mexican war* Mexican-American war, a seventeen-month long war between the United States and Mexico, beginning in 1846 and ending with Mexico being forced to recognize Texas as part of the US. It also ceded California and New Mexico to the US in 1848 under the Treaty of Guadalupe Hidalgo for $15,000,000. Critics of the war have argued that it was deliberately provoked by the US to serve its territorial ambitions.

---

3   *wooden gun* Something weak and ineffective.

4   *but by the alacrity* Except by the speedy readiness.

rule of expediency is applicable? Must the citizen ever for a moment, or in the least degree, resign his conscience to the legislator? Why has every man a conscience then? I think that we should be men first, and subjects afterward. It is not desirable to cultivate a respect for the law, so much as for the right. The only obligation which I have a right to assume is to do at any time what I think right. It is truly enough said that a corporation[1] has no conscience; but a corporation of conscientious men is a corporation with a conscience. Law never made men a whit more just; and, by means of their respect for it, even the well-disposed are daily made the agents on injustice. A common and natural result of an undue respect for the law is, that you may see a file of soldiers, colonel, captain, corporal, privates, powder-monkeys,[2] and all, marching in admirable order over hill and dale to the wars, against their wills, aye, against their common sense and consciences, which makes it very steep marching indeed, and produces a palpitation of the heart. They have no doubt that it is a damnable business in which they are concerned; they are all peaceably inclined. Now, what are they? Men at all? or small movable forts and magazines,[3] at the service of some unscrupulous man in power? Visit the Navy Yard, and behold a marine, such a man as an American government can make, or such as it can make a man with its black arts—a mere shadow and reminiscence of humanity, a man laid out alive and standing, and already, as one may say, buried under arms with funeral accompaniment, though it may be,

> Not a drum was heard, not a funeral note,
> As his corpse to the rampart we hurried;
> Not a soldier discharged his farewell shot
> O'er the grave where out hero was buried."[4]

The mass of men serve the state thus, not as men mainly, but as machines, with their bodies. They are the standing army, and the militia, jailers, constables, *posse comitatus*,[5] etc. In most cases there is no free exercise whatever of the judgment or of the moral sense; but they put themselves on a level with wood and earth and stones; and wooden men

can perhaps be manufactured that will serve the purpose as well. Such command no more respect than men of straw or a lump of dirt. They have the same sort of worth only as horses and dogs. Yet such as these even are commonly esteemed good citizens. Others—as most legislators, politicians, lawyers, ministers, and office-holders—serve the state chiefly with their heads; and, as the rarely make any moral distinctions, they are as likely to serve the devil, without intending it, as God. A very few—as heroes, patriots, martyrs, reformers in the great sense, and men—serve the state with their consciences also, and so necessarily resist it for the most part; and they are commonly treated as enemies by it. A wise man will only be useful as a man, and will not submit to be "clay," and "stop a hole to keep the wind away," but leave that office to his dust at least:

> I am too high born to be propertied,
> To be a second at control,
> Or useful serving-man and instrument
> To any sovereign state throughout the world.[6]

He who gives himself entirely to his fellow men appears to them useless and selfish; but he who gives himself partially to them is pronounced a benefactor and philanthropist.

How does it become a man to behave toward the American government today? I answer, that he cannot without disgrace be associated with it. I cannot for an instant recognize that political organization as my government which is the *slave*'s government also.

All men recognize the right of revolution; that is, the right to refuse allegiance to, and to resist, the government, when its tyranny or its inefficiency are great and unendurable. But almost all say that such is not the case now. But such was the case, they think, in the Revolution of '75.[7] If one were to tell me that this was a bad government because it taxed certain foreign commodities brought to its ports, it is most probable that I should not make an ado about it, for I can do without them. All machines have their friction; and possibly this does enough good to counter-balance the evil. At any rate, it is a great evil to make a stir about it. But when the friction comes to have its machine, and oppression and robbery are organized, I say, let us not have such a machine any longer. In other words, when a sixth of the population of a nation which has undertaken to be the

---

1   *corporation*   Group acting as a single individual.
2   *powder-monkeys*   Soldiers whose job it is to carry explosives.
3   *magazines*   Storehouses for military supplies.
4   *Not a drum ... was buried*   From "The Burial of Sir John Moore after Corunna" by Charles Wolfe (1791–1823).
5   *posse comitatus*   Latin: *power of the county*: temporary police force, recruited from the general population, known for short (in Western films) as a *posse*.

6   *I am too ... the world*   Shakespeare, *The Life and Death of King John*, 5.2.79–82. (Shakespeare wrote "secondary," where Thoreau has "a second.")
7   *Revolution of '75*   American War of Independence, 1775–83.

refuge of liberty are slaves, and a whole country is unjustly overrun and conquered by a foreign army, and subjected to military law, I think that it is not too soon for honest men to rebel and revolutionize. What makes this duty the more urgent is that fact that the country so overrun is not our own, but ours is the invading army.

Paley, a common authority with many on moral questions, in his chapter on the "Duty of Submission to Civil Government,"[1] resolves all civil obligation into expediency; and he proceeds to say that "so long as the interest of the whole society requires it, that is, so long as the established government cannot be resisted or changed without public inconveniency, it is the will of God, that the established government be obeyed, and no longer. This principle being admitted, the justice of every particular case of resistance is reduced to a computation of the quantity of the danger and grievance on the one side, and of the probability and expense of redressing it on the other." Of this, he says, every man shall judge for himself. But Paley appears never to have contemplated those cases to which the rule of expediency[2] does not apply, in which a people, as well and an individual, must do justice, cost what it may. If I have unjustly wrested a plank from a drowning man, I must restore it to him though I drown myself. This, according to Paley, would be inconvenient. But he that would save his life, in such a case, shall lose it. This people must cease to hold slaves, and to make war on Mexico, though it cost them their existence as a people.

In their practice, nations agree with Paley; but does anyone think that Massachusetts does exactly what is right at the present crisis?

> A drab of state, a cloth-o'-silver slut,
> To have her train borne up, and her soul trail in the dirt.[3]

Practically speaking, the opponents to a reform in Massachusetts are not a hundred thousand politicians at the South, but a hundred thousand merchants and farmers here, who are more interested in commerce and agriculture than they are in humanity, and are not prepared to do justice to the slave and to Mexico, *cost what it may.* I quarrel not with far-off foes, but with those who, neat at home, co-operate with, and do the bidding of, those far away, and without whom the latter would be harmless. We are accustomed to say, that the mass of men are unprepared; but improvement is slow, because the few are not as materially wiser or better than the many. It is not so important that many should be good as you, as that there be some absolute goodness somewhere; for that will leaven the whole lump.[4] There are thousands who are in opinion opposed to slavery and to the war, who yet in effect do nothing to put an end to them; who, esteeming themselves children of Washington and Franklin, sit down with their hands in their pockets, and say that they know not what to do, and do nothing; who even postpone the question of freedom to the question of free trade, and quietly read the prices-current[5] along with the latest advices from Mexico, after dinner, and, it may be, fall asleep over them both. What is the price-current of an honest man and patriot today? They hesitate, and they regret, and sometimes they petition; but they do nothing in earnest and with effect. They will wait, well disposed, for other to remedy the evil, that they may no longer have it to regret. At most, they give up only a cheap vote, and a feeble countenance and Godspeed,[6] to the right, as it goes by them. There are nine hundred and ninety-nine patrons of virtue to one virtuous man. But it is easier to deal with the real possessor of a thing than with the temporary guardian of it.

All voting is a sort of gaming, like checkers or backgammon, with a slight moral tinge to it, a playing with right and wrong, with moral questions; and betting naturally accompanies it. The character of the voters is not staked. I cast my vote, perchance, as I think right; but I am not vitally concerned that that right should prevail. I am willing to leave it to the majority. Its obligation, therefore, never exceeds that of expediency. Even voting for the right is doing nothing for it. It is only expressing to men feebly your

---

1   *"Duty of Submission to Civil Government"* William Paley, *The Principles of Moral and Political Philosophy* (1785), Book 6, Section 3: "The Duty of Submission to Civil Government Explained." In the original, Paley adds, after the word "God," the parenthetical remark, "(which *will* universally determine our duty)."

2   *expediency* Based on practical (as opposed to moral) considerations.

3   *A drab ... dirt* Cyril Tourneur, *The Revenger's Tragaedie* (1607), Act V. Thoreau gives a modernized version of the original:
> A drab of State, a cloath, a siluery slut!
> To haue her traine borne up, and her soule traile
> I' th' durt—Great!—

4   *leaven the whole lump* Literally, alter the whole lump (of dough) by the action of yeast; figuratively, in this case: transform the whole matter.

5   *prices-current* List of current prices of commodities.

6   *Godspeed* Wish for a pleasant journey.

desire that it should prevail. A wise man will not leave the right to the mercy of chance, nor wish it to prevail through the power of the majority. There is but little virtue in the action of masses of men. When the majority shall at length vote for the abolition of slavery, it will be because they are indifferent to slavery, or because there is but little slavery left to be abolished by their vote. They will then be the only slaves. Only his vote can hasten the abolition of slavery who asserts his own freedom by his vote.

I hear of a convention to be held at Baltimore, or elsewhere, for the selection of a candidate for the Presidency, made up chiefly of editors, and men who are politicians by profession; but I think, what is it to any independent, intelligent, and respectable man what decision they may come to? Shall we not have the advantage of this wisdom and honesty, nevertheless? Can we not count upon some independent votes? Are there not many individuals in the country who do not attend conventions? But no: I find that the respectable man, so called, has immediately drifted from his position, and despairs of his country, when his country has more reasons to despair of him. He forthwith adopts one of the candidates thus selected as the only available one, thus proving that he is himself available for any purposes of the demagogue. His vote is of no more worth than that of any unprincipled foreigner or hireling[1] native, who may have been bought. O for a man who is a man, and my neighbor says, has a bone is his back which you cannot pass your hand through! Our statistics are at fault: the population has been returned too large. How many men are there to a square thousand miles in the country? Hardly one. Does not America offer any inducement for men to settle here? The American has dwindled into an Odd Fellow[2]—one who may be known by the development of his organ of gregariousness, and a manifest lack of intellect and cheerful self-reliance; whose first and chief concern, on coming into the world, is to see that the almshouses[3] are in good repair; and, before yet he has lawfully donned the virile garb,[4] to collect a fund to the support of the widows and orphans that may be; who, in short, ventures to live

only by the aid of the Mutual Insurance company, which has promised to bury him decently.

It is not a man's duty, as a matter of course, to devote himself to the eradication of any, even to most enormous, wrong; he may still properly have other concerns to engage him; but it is his duty, at least, to wash his hands of it, and, if he gives it no thought longer, not to give it practically his support. If I devote myself to other pursuits and contemplations, I must first see, at least, that I do not pursue them sitting upon another man's shoulders. I must get off him first, that he may pursue his contemplations too. See what gross inconsistency is tolerated. I have heard some of my townsmen say, "I should like to have them order me out to help put down an insurrection of the slaves, or to march to Mexico—see if I would go"; and yet these very men have each, directly by their allegiance, and so indirectly, at least, by their money, furnished a substitute.[5] The soldier is applauded who refuses to serve in an unjust war by those who do not refuse to sustain the unjust government which makes the war; is applauded by those whose own act and authority he disregards and sets at naught; as if the state were penitent to that degree that it hired one to scourge[6] it while it sinned, but not to that degree that it left off sinning for a moment. Thus, under the name of Order and Civil Government, we are all made at last to pay homage to and support our own meanness. After the first blush of sin comes its indifference; and from immoral it becomes, as it were, unmoral, and not quite unnecessary to that life which we have made.

The broadest and most prevalent error requires the most disinterested[7] virtue to sustain it. The slight reproach to which the virtue of patriotism is commonly liable, the noble are most likely to incur. Those who, while they disapprove of the character and measures of a government, yield to it their allegiance and support are undoubtedly its most conscientious supporters, and so frequently the most serious obstacles to reform. Some are petitioning the State to dissolve the Union, to disregard the requisitions of the President. Why do they not dissolve it themselves—the union between themselves and the State—and refuse to pay their quota into its treasury? Do not they stand in same relation to the State that the State does to the Union? And have not the same reasons prevented the State from resist-

---

1   *hireling*   Person working only for money.
2   *Odd Fellow*   Member of a secret society with initiatory rites and mystic signs of recognition, organized for social and benevolent purposes.
3   *almshouses*   Publicly funded institutions for housing those in poverty.
4   *before yet he has lawfully donned the virile garb*   That is, before he has become a full adult.

5   *substitute*   At this time it was possible to pay someone to take one's place in the military.
6   *scourge*   Whip (for the purpose of obtaining absolution from sin).
7   *disinterested*   Unbiased, unmoved by self-interest.

ing the Union which have prevented them from resisting the State?

How can a man be satisfied to entertain and opinion merely, and enjoy it? Is there any enjoyment in it, if his opinion is that he is aggrieved? If you are cheated out of a single dollar by your neighbor, you do not rest satisfied with knowing you are cheated, or with saying that you are cheated, or even with petitioning him to pay you your due; but you take effectual steps at once to obtain the full amount, and see to it that you are never cheated again. Action from principle, the perception and the performance of right, changes things and relations; it is essentially revolutionary, and does not consist wholly with anything which was. It not only divided States and churches, it divides families; aye, it divides the individual, separating the diabolical in him from the divine.

Unjust laws exist: shall we be content to obey them, or shall we endeavor to amend them, and obey them until we have succeeded, or shall we transgress them at once? Men, generally, under such a government as this, think that they ought to wait until they have persuaded the majority to alter them. They think that, if they should resist, the remedy would be worse than the evil. But it is the fault of the government itself that the remedy is worse than the evil. It makes it worse. Why is it not more apt to anticipate and provide for reform? Why does it not cherish its wise minority? Why does it cry and resist before it is hurt? Why does it not encourage its citizens to put out its faults, and do better than it would have them? Why does it always crucify Christ and excommunicate Copernicus and Luther, and pronounce Washington and Franklin rebels?

One would think, that a deliberate and practical denial of its authority was the only offense never contemplated by its government; else, why has it not assigned its definite, its suitable and proportionate, penalty? If a man who has no property refuses but once to earn nine shillings for the State, he is put in prison for a period unlimited by any law that I know, and determined only by the discretion of those who put him there; but if he should steal ninety times nine shillings from the State, he is soon permitted to go at large again.

If the injustice is part of the necessary friction of the machine of government, let it go, let it go: perchance it will wear smooth—certainly the machine will wear out. If the injustice has a spring, or a pulley, or a rope, or a crank, exclusively for itself, then perhaps you may consider whether the remedy will not be worse than the evil; but if it is of such a nature that it requires you to be the agent of injustice to another, then I say, break the law. Let your life be a counter-friction to stop the machine. What I have to do is to see, at any rate, that I do not lend myself to the wrong which I condemn.

As for adopting the ways of the State has provided for remedying the evil, I know not of such ways. They take too much time, and a man's life will be gone. I have other affairs to attend to. I came into this world, not chiefly to make this a good place to live in, but to live in it, be it good or bad. A man has not everything to do, but something; and because he cannot do everything, it is not necessary that he should be petitioning the Governor or the Legislature any more than it is theirs to petition me; and if they should not hear my petition, what should I do then? But in this case the State has provided no way: its very Constitution is the evil. This may seem to be harsh and stubborn and unconciliatory; but it is to treat with the utmost kindness and consideration the only spirit that can appreciate or deserves it. So is all change for the better, like birth and death, which convulse the body.

I do not hesitate to say, that those who call themselves Abolitionists should at once effectually withdraw their support, both in person and property, from the government of Massachusetts, and not wait till they constitute a majority of one, before they suffer the right to prevail through them. I think that it is enough if they have God on their side, without waiting for that other one. Moreover, any man more right than his neighbors constitutes a majority of one already.

I meet this American government, or its representative, the State government, directly, and face to face, once a year—no more—in the person of its tax-gatherer; this is the only mode in which a man situated as I am necessarily meets it; and it then says distinctly, recognize me; and the simplest, the most effectual, and, in the present posture of affairs, the indispensable mode of treating with it on this head, of expressing your little satisfaction with and love for it, is to deny it then. My civil neighbor, the tax-gatherer, is the very man I have to deal with—for it is, after all, with men and not with parchment that I quarrel—and he has voluntarily chosen to be an agent of the government. How shall he ever know well that he is and does as an officer of the government, or as a man, until he is obliged to consider whether he will treat me, his neighbor, for whom he has respect, as a neighbor and well-disposed man, or as a maniac and disturber of the peace, and see if he can get over this obstruction to his neighborliness without a ruder and more impetuous thought or speech corresponding with his action. I know this well, that if one thousand, if one hundred, if ten men whom I could name—if ten honest men only—aye, if *one* honest man, in this State of Massachusetts, ceasing to hold slaves, were actually to withdraw from this co-partnership, and be locked up in the county jail therfor, it would be the abolition of slavery in America. For it matters not how small the beginning may seem to be: what is once well done is done forever. But we love better to talk about it: that we say is our mission. Reform keeps many scores of newspapers in its service, but not one man. If my esteemed neighbor, the State's ambassador, who will devote his days to the settlement of the question of human rights in the Council Chamber, instead of being threatened with the prisons of Carolina, were to sit down the prisoner of Massachusetts, that State which is so anxious to foist the sin of slavery upon her sister—though at present she can discover only an act of inhospitality to be the ground of a quarrel with her—the Legislature would not wholly waive the subject of the following winter.

Under a government which imprisons unjustly, the true place for a just man is also a prison. The proper place today, the only place which Massachusetts has provided for her freer and less despondent spirits, is in her prisons, to be put out and locked out of the State by her own act, as they have already put themselves out by their principles. It is there that the fugitive slave, and the Mexican prisoner on parole, and the Indian come to plead the wrongs of his race should find them; on that separate but more free and honorable ground, where the State places those who are not with her, but against her—the only house in a slave State in which a free man can abide with honor. If any think that their influence would be lost there, and their voices no longer afflict the ear of the State, that they would not be as an enemy within its walls, they do not know by how much truth is stronger than error, nor how much more eloquently and effectively he can combat injustice who has experienced a little in his own person. Cast your whole vote, not a strip of paper merely, but your whole influence. A minority is powerless while it conforms to the majority; it is not even a minority then; but it is irresistible when it clogs by its whole weight. If the alternative is to keep all just men in prison, or give up war and slavery, the State will not hesitate which to choose. If a thousand men were not to pay their tax bills this year, that would not be a violent and bloody measure, as it would be to pay them, and enable the State to commit violence and shed innocent blood. This is, in fact, the definition of a peaceable revolution, if any such is possible. If the tax-gatherer, or any other public officer, asks me, as one has done, "But what shall I do?" my answer is, "If you really wish to do anything, resign your office." When the subject has refused allegiance, and the officer has resigned from office, then the revolution is accomplished. But even suppose blood shed when the conscience is wounded? Through this wound a man's real manhood and immortality flow out, and he bleeds to an everlasting death. I see this blood flowing now.

[...]

The authority of government, even such as I am willing to submit to—for I will cheerfully obey those who know and can do better than I, and in many things even those who neither know nor can do so well—is still an impure one: to be strictly just, it must have the sanction and consent of the governed. It can have no pure right over my person and property but what I concede to it. The progress from an absolute to a limited monarchy, from a limited monarchy to a democracy, is a progress toward a true respect for the individual. Even the Chinese philosopher[1] was wise enough to regard the individual as the basis of the empire. Is a democracy, such as we know it, the last improvement possible in government? Is it not possible to take a step further towards recognizing and organizing the rights of man? There will never be a really free and enlightened State until the State comes to recognize the individual as a higher and independent power, from which all its own power and authority are derived, and treats him accordingly. I please myself with imagining a State at last which can afford to be just to all men, and to treat the individual with respect as a neighbor; which even would not think it inconsistent with its own repose if a few were to live aloof from it, not meddling with it, nor embraced by it, who fulfilled all the duties of neighbors and fellow men. A State which bore this kind of fruit, and suffered it to drop off as fast as it ripened, would prepare the way for a still more perfect and glorious State, which I have also imagined, but not yet anywhere seen.

---

1   *Chinese philosopher*   Confucius (551–479 BCE).

KARL MARX
(1818 – 1883) and
FRIEDRICH ENGELS
(1820 – 1895)

Who Were Karl Marx and Friedrich Engels?

KARL HEINRICH MARX WAS BORN IN 1818 IN THE TOWN of Trier in the Rhineland, a region of Prussia that lies next to the French border and is today part of Germany. Both his parents were Jewish, descended from a long line of rabbis and Jewish intellectuals; they were among the first generation of German Jews to enjoy equal legal status with Christians and to be granted free choice of residence and profession. The Rhineland had been under French rule during the Napoleonic period, from 1792 until 1815, and Marx's father Heinrich had also benefited from the relatively enlightened French regime: he had used these opportunities to forge a successful career as a respected lawyer. However, after the restoration of Prussian power in Trier in 1815, Marx's father had felt obliged to convert himself and his family to Lutheranism in order to protect his career, and so Marx was not brought up as a Jew.

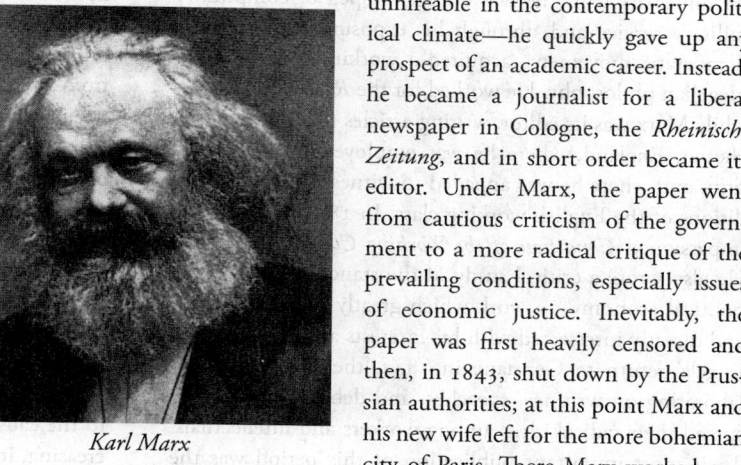

Karl Marx

Marx's father wanted him to become a lawyer, but Marx was a rowdy, rebellious child and, as a young man, chose instead to spend his time studying philosophy and history, dueling, and writing romantic verses to his childhood sweetheart, the daughter of his neighbor, Jenny von Westphalen (whom he eventually married in 1843). From 1835 to 1841 Marx studied at the universities of Bonn (where he spent a year studying law) and Berlin, where he was exposed to, and heavily influenced by, the idealist philosophy of G.W.F. Hegel. Marx's early writings show a preoccupation with the notion of human self-realization through the struggle for freedom, and a view of the nature of reality as turbulently changing—both themes which find resonance in Hegel. However, like many contemporary "Young Hegelians,"

Marx found the Hegelian system, as it was then taught in the Prussian universities, to be politically and religiously much too conservative.

In 1841 Marx successfully submitted a doctoral dissertation (on Greek philosophy) to the university of Jena, but—because his political radicalism made him effectively unhireable in the contemporary political climate—he quickly gave up any prospect of an academic career. Instead, he became a journalist for a liberal newspaper in Cologne, the *Rheinische Zeitung*, and in short order became its editor. Under Marx, the paper went from cautious criticism of the government to a more radical critique of the prevailing conditions, especially issues of economic justice. Inevitably, the paper was first heavily censored and then, in 1843, shut down by the Prussian authorities; at this point Marx and his new wife left for the more bohemian city of Paris. There Marx worked as a journalist for another radical publication, the *Deutsch-Französische Jahrbücher* [*German-French Annals*], and realizing that he knew little about the economic issues which he saw to be politically so significant, threw himself into the study of political economy. Even before these studies began, however, Marx was already—like many of his compatriots—politically left-wing in a way which could loosely be called "communist": he was convinced of the need for the "cooperative" rather than individual control of economic resources, and was ferociously concerned about the need to alleviate the living conditions of the swelling numbers of urban poor.

In 1845 pressure from the Prussian government caused Marx to be expelled from France, and he and his family moved to Brussels. There he developed a close friendship, begun in France, with Friedrich Engels, the man who was to be Marx's most important intellectual collaborator, supporter, and friend (indeed, the only lasting friend that Marx ever had). Engels was born in 1820 in Barmen, near Düsseldorf. His family were wealthy mill owners in the rapidly industrializing Ruhr valley in northwest Germany, and although Engels had hoped for a career in literature his father insisted that he leave school at seventeen in order to work for the family firm. He worked first in a local factory, then in an export office in the port city of Bremen, and finally as an accountant for the English branch of the firm Ermen and Engels. Thus, from the time he was a young man, Engels saw first-hand the profound social changes brought about by the introduction of new methods of production in the textile industry. Although he never formally attended university, he did sit in on some lectures at Berlin university while he was doing his spell of compulsory military service and, through his exposure to the radical democratic movement, acquired a working knowledge of Hegelian philosophy. He worked for the *Rheinische Zeitung* while Marx was its editor, writing articles for it from Manchester, England, where he was employed by the family firm, and where he was appalled to witness the living conditions of the English working class. In 1844 he wrote the impassioned *Condition of the Working Classes in England.* He also wrote a critical study of the standard positions in political economy—a work which greatly impressed Marx and directly intersected with his interests at the time. After Engels' return to Germany in 1844, the two began collaborating on writings, speeches, and debates intended to spread their radical ideas among workers and intellectuals. Their most important publication of this period was the *Communist Manifesto.*

1848, the year of the publication of the *Communist Manifesto*, was a year of revolution in Europe: most of the countries of Europe (the notable exceptions being Britain, Belgium, and Russia) underwent a spasm of social upheaval in which old, aristocratic regimes fell and were replaced (briefly) by bold, new republican governments. Marx and Engels, in their different ways, attempted to play a role in this revolutionary process: Marx, now expelled from Belgium for his activism, returned to Cologne and started up a new radical broadsheet, the *Neue Reinische Zeitung*, whose goal was to inspire and educate the revolutionary leaders (along the lines of the *Communist Manifesto*); Engels was an officer in a short-lived military uprising in the German region of Baden. Within a matter of months, however, the upheaval was over and (everywhere in Europe except France), the new democratic, republican regimes began

to collapse and the old order reasserted itself. Marx and his associates were tried in a Cologne court for charges of inciting revolt and, although Marx successfully defended himself against the indictment, he was nevertheless exiled from Prussian territory in 1849. As a result, Marx and Engels emigrated permanently to England: Marx, to live and write in London, and Engels to work for his family firm in Manchester.

Conditions were extremely hard for the Marx family, especially for the first decade or so of their lives in London. Marx was unwilling to take work that would interfere with his writing, and when he did seek stable employment he was unable to get it. (At one point he applied for a job as a railway clerk, but was unsuccessful because of the—now notorious—illegibility of his handwriting.) He and his family—his wife, her servant, and six children—subsisted on financial gifts from family and friends and the income from Marx's occasional freelance journalism (mostly as a European correspondent for the *New York Tribune*, for which he was paid £1 per article). Their main financial benefactor was Engels, who sent them grants and allowances taken from his own income and the money from his investments: nevertheless, the Marx household lived in relative poverty for many years, enduring poor housing and bad food. Three of Marx's children died young, in part because of these hard conditions, and his own health suffered a collapse from which it never fully recovered.[1]

Meanwhile, Marx was single-mindedly devoting his life to the cause of ending what he saw as the serious, and increasing, inequalities and exploitation inherent in capitalist society. His role in doing this, he thought, was to formulate a theoretical framework that would reveal the true state of things to the masses of workers and that, by doing so, would both incite and guide the impending revolutionary replacement of capitalism by communism. He saw himself mainly as an "ideas man" and as a publicist for the communist movement, rather than as an organizer or leader (and indeed, during his lifetime, his personal political influence was always quite small). He spent ten hours a day, most days, in the Reading Room of the British Museum, conducting research and writing; after returning home, he would often continue to write late into the night. His main work during these years was a massive, wide-ranging, detailed analysis of capitalist society and what Marx saw as the

---

1   Despite these hardships, Marx's marriage was apparently a very happy one, and he was a devoted husband and father.

tensions intrinsic to it, which was eventually published in three substantial volumes as *Das Kapital* or *Capital*.[1]

Engels, meanwhile, ran his family's cotton mills in Lancashire and became a respected figure in Manchester society. He rode two days a week with the aristocratic Cheshire Hunt (which, he unconvincingly claimed, was valuable training for a future leader of the armies of the revolution). But at heart Engels was unquestionably a devoted revolutionary, sincerely committed to the cause of communism, and he did his best to support Marx's work. He lived with an Irish factory girl called Mary Burns, and when she died he took in, and eventually married, her sister Lizzie.

In 1864 the International Working Men's Association was formed, otherwise known as the First International. This was a watershed in the history of the working class movement, and for the next eight years the organization was highly influential in European left-wing politics. Marx was one of its main leaders, and was heavily engaged with its internal politics. By the 1870s he had become the leading theoretician for the radical movement in Europe, especially in Germany, and had become notorious across the continent as the "Red Doctor Marx."

Marx died, of chronic respiratory disease, in London in 1883. (Despite Engels' best efforts: he took him on a tour of France, Switzerland, and Algiers in the hope that the change of climate might help his condition.) He is buried next to his wife in Highgate Cemetery. After 1870 Engels—who retired at fifty, an independently wealthy man—had devoted all of his time to helping Marx with his research, and after Marx's death he continued the writing of *Capital* from Marx's notes, completing it in 1894, a year before his own death.

In a speech given at Marx's graveside, Engels attested that Marx was above all else a revolutionary. His real mission in life was to contribute, in one way or another, to the overthrow of capitalist society and of the state institutions which it had brought into being, to contribute to the liberation of the modern proletariat, which *he* was the first to make conscious of its own position and needs, and the conditions of its emancipation. Fighting was his element. And he fought with a passion, a tenacity and a success such as few could rival.

What Was Marx's Overall Philosophical Project?

Marx's work integrates German philosophy, French socialism and British (or Scottish) political economy. Though Marx is commonly thought of as primarily a political economist, following in the tradition of Adam Smith (1723–90) and David Ricardo (1772–1823), he was trained as a political philosopher and is deeply indebted to German philosophy—most centrally Hegel and his followers, the Young Hegelians. When Marx was a student, Hegel's idealism dominated the German intellectual scene. According to Hegelian Idealism, the world is the continuous evolution of Spirit or Mind (*Geist*), which develops through a dialectical process. In the Hegelian dialectic, concepts generate their opposite, with reason transcending this apparent contradiction, forming a third concept. For example, the opposing concepts "being" and "nothing" are transcended in "becoming." The traditional interpretation of Hegel (dominant in Marx's time) is that Hegel is a pantheist, with the universe being Spirit thinking itself. Hegel's followers quickly split into two factions: the right-wing Hegelians, who attempted to synthesize his philosophy with orthodox Christianity, and the left-wing Hegelians, who attempted to provide a materialist alternative to Hegel's idealism. Besides Marx these included Arnold Ruge (1802–80), Ludwig Feuerbach (1804–72), Bruno Bauer (1809–82), and Marx's lifelong collaborator and benefactor, Friedrich Engels (1820–95).

Many of Marx's earlier works are preoccupied with Hegel's *Philosophy of Right*, most prominently his *Contribution to a Critique of Hegel's Philosophy of Right* (1843), the source of his remark that religion is the "opiate of the people." Here Marx claimed that religion is a response to alienation from work and community, creating a false community to substitute for a world of social and economic inequality. Contrary to Hegel's idealism, Marx held that the evolution of history is driven by relations of production which develop over time.[2] It is worthwhile quoting Marx's succinct rejection of idealism in *A Contribution to the Critique of Political Economy* (1859):

---

1 Marx's mother is said to have commented that it was a shame that her boy merely wrote about capital and never acquired any.

2 Though "historical materialism" (Engels' term) or "dialectical materialism" (the term introduced by Russian revolutionary and Marxist Georgi Plekhanov (1856–1918)) hold a central place in Marxist thought, Marx himself wrote relatively little about history. Much of what he wrote can be found in *The German Ideology* (discussed below) and the 1859 preface to *A Contribution to the Critique of Political Economy*.

In the social production of their existence, men inevitably enter into definite relations, which are independent of their will, namely relations of production appropriate to a given stage in the development of their material forces of production. The totality of these relations of production constitutes the economic structure of society, the real foundation, on which arises a legal and political superstructure and to which correspond definite forms of social consciousness. The mode of production of material life conditions the general process of social, political and intellectual life. It is not the consciousness of men that determines their existence, but their social existence that determines their consciousness.

Besides Hegel himself, Marx was particularly taken by, though critical of, Feuerbach's materialism and atheism, which attempted to analyze philosophy and religion as human products. This anthropological perspective (drawing on Kant's last major work, *Anthropology from a Pragmatic Point of View* [1798; revised edition 1800]) would influence Marx throughout his career. With the Young Hegelians, Marx became critical of Hegelianism and of philosophy in general as socially inefficacious. The task, as he would say in the *Theses on Feuerbach* is not merely to interpret the world, but to change it.[1]

Marx began to be influenced by a variety of non-Hegelian intellectual currents, including the ideas of the French utopian socialists Charles Fourier (1772–1837) and Henri de Saint-Simon (1760–1825). The utopian socialists advocated the reorganization of society into socialist communes. From historian and politician Louis Jean Joseph Charles Blanc (1811–92), Marx took the principle, "From each according to his abilities, to each according to his needs." The anarchist Pierre-Joseph Proudhon (1809–65) attracted Marx's attention with *What is Property?* where we find the declaration that "property is theft." Their subsequent correspondence and collaboration ended with Marx's criticism of Proudhon's work, *The Poverty of Philosophy* (1847). Marx would later direct scathing criticisms at the utopian socialists, rejecting the call for justice as a form of ideology arising from and reinforcing the current economic relations of production. Instead, he came to advocate a value-neutral

"scientific socialism." Still, the influence of utopian socialism on his work remains considerable.

The political economists, particularly Smith and Ricardo, provided the third major influence on Marx. He appropriated Smith's discussion of the division of labor and technological progress, along with Ricardo's labor theory of value—the view that the value of a commodity derives from the amount of labor it took to produce it. The details of Marx's economic project do not concern us here (and are no longer widely accepted, at least in the form he presented them); what remains important is that Marx brought a historical dimension to political economy. While Smith and Ricardo tended to view economic behavior as a constant, Marx saw it as dynamic, subject to fundamental change. And of the three, it was Marx who did the most to define capitalism as a social system in which labor-power itself becomes a commodity—where a class of workers, the proletariat, bereft of property, had only their labor-power to sell.

This provides much of the background to Marx's political philosophy. In 1852 he summarized his three most important political ideas as being the following:

(1) Social classes are not permanent features of society, but instead are phases in the historical development of the relations of economic production.

(2) The struggle between these classes will necessarily lead to the "dictatorship of the proletariat," in which the working people will forcibly take over political power from the property-owners.

(3) The dictatorship of the proletariat is not an end in itself, but a transition period on the way to a classless communist society devoted to the free development and flourishing of individuals.

Marx's analysis of capitalism points to how social class divisions were produced and perpetuated by a particular type of economic system. A society is capitalist, according to Marx, if the production of goods is dominated by the use of wage-labor: that is, by the use of labor power sold, as their only way to make a living, by people who have no significant control over means of production (the proletariat), and bought by other people who do have control over means of production such as raw materials, capital, and machinery (the bourgeoisie). The bourgeoisie make their money mostly by combining the labor power they have bought with the means of production they own, and

---

1   A detailed discussion of Marx's criticisms of Feuerbach and Brauer can be found below in the sections on the *Theses on Feuerbach* and *the Jewish Question*.

selling the commodities thus produced. Marx held that the relationship between these two classes, bourgeoisie and proletariat, was intrinsically and inescapably *antagonistic*, and he attempted to explain all the main institutional features of capitalist society in terms of this relation. Since, in Marx's view, the main institutions of a capitalist society have the function of preserving the interests of the bourgeoisie, and since these interests are opposed to those of the proletarians, capitalist society is therefore a kind of class rule, or oppression, of the majority by the minority.

Furthermore, for Marx, social structures such as capitalism which are based on the oppression of one class by another give rise to what he called *ideologies*. An ideology is a (socially influential) system of beliefs or assumptions that reflects a false perception of reality—a perception of reality that is distorted by the social forces involved in class oppression. Central examples, for Marx, were systems of religious belief and the capitalist doctrine of the "free market." The dominance of a ruling class, whose members usually make up only a tiny minority of society, cannot be preserved through physical coercion alone: it can only survive as long as most people believe (falsely) that the social status quo is in their own interests, or that there is no realistic alternative to the current system.

One of the best-known components of Marx's philosophical system is his *historical materialism*: "[t]he mode of production of material life conditions the social, political, and intellectual life-process in general." This is the view that the foundation or "base" of society is its economic structure, which is defined by historical facts about the means of production (for example, facts about the level of agricultural sophistication, industrial technology, trade and transportation networks, and so on). As productive forces change, economic adjustments—changes to the relations of production—give rise to revolutions in society's "superstructure": the political, legal, moral, religious and philosophical components of culture. In other words, political and social changes do not cause economic change, but the other way around: political and social systems are determined by their economic basis.

Marx's second main political-philosophical idea, in his 1852 summary, was the view that capitalism contains internal tensions which, in time, will inevitably produce the revolutionary overthrow of the bourgeoisie by the workers and usher in a "dictatorship of the proletariat." This view is, in part, the heritage of Marx's early influence by, and reaction to, the philosophical system of Hegel. For Hegel,

history is a "dialectical" movement in which a thesis—a principle or idea—is challenged by its antithesis, and from this conflict there emerges a synthesis of the two, a new principle. In time this new principle meets *its* antithesis, and so on (until the ideal, final synthesis is achieved). Thus Hegel was an *idealist*, in the sense that for him the engine of world change was the clash of *Ideas*. In Engels' words, Marx turned this Hegelian system on its head: instead of conflicts between ideas (in the shape of political structures) driving change, Marx held that the world contains its own internal conflicts and that political ideas actually spring up *from* this conflict rather than causing it. And these built-in conflicts, the mainspring of historical change, are *economic* in nature: they are generated by people's attempts to satisfy their material needs—for food, clothing, shelter and so on—and their subsequent pursuit of personal wealth, within the context of their society's particular level of economic development. (Thus, Marx's system is often called *dialectical materialism*, though Marx himself never used this label.)

A notion central to Marx's diagnosis of the economic conflicts driving capitalism towards revolution is that of *alienation* (or *estrangement*),[1] which in turn arises from two other fundamental ideas in Marx's system: his theory of human nature, and his "labor theory of value." According to Marx, human beings are essentially *active* and *creative* beings: human flourishing consists in the continual transformation of one's inherent creative power into objective products, the constant *realization* of one's "subjectivity." Thus, productive activity—that is, work—is an essential component of human well-being: Marx's concern for the poor was never merely concern for their basic "material needs," such as food and housing, but was part of his view of human flourishing as being a matter of "free self-activity," of true self-expression in a social context.

The institution of private property, in Marx's view, stifles the flourishing of the human spirit. Since private property represents the products of labor as if they were mere *things*, it alienates labor—and thus, human nature—from itself. Workers in a modern economy typically do not experience the economic goods they spend their lives producing as expressions of *themselves*, but merely as things to be sold.

---

1   Marx used two German words for what commentators have generally taken to be the same concept: *Entäußerung* and *Entfremdung*. Some translations—including the one included here—render these by two English words, "alienation" and "estrangement," respectively. Others use the word "alienation" to translate both.

Furthermore, capitalism intensifies this process of alienation by treating *labor itself* as a commodity, to be bought and sold: not only is the product of your creative activity alienated from you, but that very activity, work itself, is alienated—it is no longer *yours*, once you have sold it to an employer.

Marx did not invent the concept of alienation. It has a long history, dating back perhaps to early Christianity, but a more immediate source for Marx was German Romanticism, a philosophical, literary, and generally cultural movement that flourished from perhaps 1790 till 1850. Romantics tended to look back with nostalgia to pre-industrial times, when, they thought, our lives were more natural, more whole—when we were more in touch with our real selves. Modern alienation for them is separation—from nature and from human nature. Hegel, sometimes considered a German Romantic himself, was a more immediate influence on Marx's concept. For Hegel, alienation involves the view of the external world as outside—foreign to us—as objective and mind independent. We recover from this alienation when we see all truth as "our" truth—when we see it as a facet of mind and its self-consciousness, of the "Spirit" which creates the world and its history, and which is in fact embodied in nature and in our society.

While accepting certain aspects of the Romantic and Hegelian views, Marx insisted on some important changes. He agreed that contemporary industrial society was particularly alienating, but gave a "materialistic"—economic—account of this, as a consequence of the condition of wage laborers under capitalism. Their lives are unfulfilling—alienated— because they are deprived of the ownership of the products of their labor—and thus the pride of production—deprived of any sense of communal action, powerless over their lives, in the grip of an autonomous external inhuman "market" which enslaves them and separates them from one-another, from their human nature, and thus from themselves. Marxist alienation, in sum, has four aspects: the worker is alienated from his product; from his act of production; from nature; and from his "species-being"—that is, his human nature. Marx rejected Hegel's acceptance of contemporary society and religion as a possible embodiment of unalienated wholeness, and Hegel's philosophical recipe for ending alienation. Religion was essentially alienating, Marx argued, transferring what should be seen as human power to an external God; society could be unalienating only when its economic structure restored power and ownership to the workers to whom these belonged.

On Marx's analysis, the capitalist sale of goods for profit is inherently exploitative. According to the labor theory of value, which Marx took over from British economists Adam Smith (1723–90) and David Ricardo (1772–1823) and developed into his own economic theory, the fair value of anything in a free market is determined by the amount of labor that is required to produce it. This has two major implications. First it means, according to Marx, that *capital* adds no value to goods over and above the labor taken to produce them, and thus the capitalist, after recompensing his workers for the value of the labor they have expended in his factories, simply appropriates the "surplus value" which is generated as profits. Although not economically "unfair," in Marx's view, this is nevertheless a form of exploitation. Second, when the labor theory of value is applied to a free market for *labor itself*, it has the implication that the working classes will necessarily (and not "unjustly," by the lights of capitalism) be forced into permanent poverty. This is because the labor-value of labor itself is simply the amount necessary to keep the worker healthy and ready to work each day—that is the minimum amount of food and shelter necessary to sustain the worker. This therefore, no more and no less, is the labor wage in a free capitalist market, and this produces a huge class of workers with no security, no prospects, no savings, no interest in preserving the current social conditions . . . in short, "nothing to lose but their chains."

Interestingly, Marx had relatively little to say about the nature of a future communist society. It is clear, however, that he saw it as a society in which the tensions inherent in capitalism have annihilated themselves and produced an economic system that—because there is no private property or capital—does not generate alienation and exploitation. Instead, it allows for genuine human flourishing as active, creative individuals, self-determined and self-sufficient within a community of other self-determined human beings.

What Is the Structure of the Readings?

I. *On the Jewish Question.* This essay, written in 1843, is among the earliest of Marx's works. The essay is to a large extent an attack on the views of Bruno Bauer (1809–82), philosopher, historian, and theologian. Bauer, a leader of the Young Hegelian movement, had argued against Jewish emancipation, on the basis that religion in general—Jewish or Christian—was the problem, and that *human* emancipation, flowing from a political regime which granted rights and liberties—was the answer. Marx was not opposed to human emancipation, and was no friend of religion. His argument with Bauer here is that state protection of rights and freedoms is the wrong approach: that these presuppose a liberal capitalist state, which is the problem, not the solution. Freedom in the liberal state protects us in our efforts to seek our self-interest, free from the interference of others; but what is needed is a radically different social situation in which we find our real freedom in our participation in the human community, not in protected isolation. When we insist on rights, then, we in effect reinforce the capitalist individualistic state, and postpone real emancipation.

An uncomfortable aspect of Marx's writing here (and periodically elsewhere, as in his *Thesis on Feuerbach*) is the degree to which he partakes of the anti-Semitism that was endemic in the European culture of the time. He clearly shares in the prejudice that attributed to Jews an inherent tendency towards "money-grubbing"; the acceptance of anti-Semitic stereotypes of this sort no doubt facilitated the conflation of those supposed Jewish tendencies with capitalist ones. In fact, Jews in England, Germany, and most of the rest of Europe were prevented (usually by legal restrictions as well as through social strictures) from entering most respectable professions, but were nevertheless disparaged for pursuing the few occupations (such as money-lending) that were open to them.

II. *Essays from Economic and Philosophic Manuscripts of 1844.* In 1844, while living in Paris, Marx completed rough drafts of several essays he intended to form part of a book; but his work on this project went no further. More than eighty years later, an incomplete translation into Russian of the four surviving essays was published under the title *Economic and Philosophic Manuscripts of 1844*; a more complete German translation appeared soon afterwards, and now this collection is a well-known standard part of the Marx bibliography; sometimes it is referred to as the Paris Manuscripts of 1844.

A few years after having written these manuscripts, Marx's thought had undergone several important changes, and he had rejected many of the views and standpoints demonstrated here. But these manuscripts remain important reading, for a couple of reasons. First, they are of historical interest in showing Marx's thought at an early stage: still very Hegelian in content, form, vocabulary, and mode of expression; still quite abstract and philosophical, still somewhat humanist and individualist; still akin to the

ethical socialists he would firmly denounce later. Second, many prefer Marx's emphasis in these earlier works on human self-fulfillment, cooperation, sociability, even love, to his later views on issues such as the dictatorship of the proletariat which have been seen as precursors of the orthodox communist ideology promulgated by Lenin and Stalin under the totalitarian Soviet system.

III. *The German Ideology*, written in 1845–46, is the first substantial work of Marx[1] showing him rejecting his earlier liberal, humanistic, individualistic socialism. Much of this work is a scathing attack on thinkers representing, in one way or another, something like his own earlier views: Marx later stated that he wrote it "to settle accounts with our erstwhile [earlier] philosophical conscience" ("Preface," *A Contribution to the Critique of Political Economy*). Marx's witty sarcasm directed against Bruno Bauer, Max Stirner, and others makes for lively reading; but because there is little attention given to these people nowadays, and because Marx's invective goes on at enormous length, these parts of the book are nowadays mostly ignored. What is instead of great interest is the opening section of the book, called "Feuerbach: Opposition of the Materialistic and Idealistic Outlook." This title is not very accurate, because although this section clearly is directed against Feuerbach's views, these are hardly mentioned; instead what we have here is mostly a positive restatement, this time without all the contorted Hegelian philosophical rhetoric, of the theory of history Marx presented in his 1844 manuscripts.

Ludwig Feuerbach (1804–72) was often seen as a bridge between Hegel and Marx. Originally a Hegelian, he argued that Hegel's views suffered from internal inconsistency, and proposed a naturalistic materialism to take the place of Hegel's idealism. His views on religion were the best known—and the most scandalous—part of his philosophy: he was accused by some of atheism, of taking a merely anthropological view of religion, of treating it as a merely symbolic expression of human yearnings. Marx, of course, could agree with much of the spirit of this critique. But, as always, he directs his bitterest polemics against those who are largely on his side. Marx's main objection to Feuerbach, and to the rest of the Young Hegelians—indeed perhaps to German philosophy in general—is that it takes ideas as

---

1   The manuscript of this work, and its published form (which did not appear until 1932) list Marx and Engels as co-authors, but most scholars are inclined to attribute almost all the writing to Marx.

basic causes, responding to human phenomena in general, and to human problems in particular, as if a mode of consciousness was the cause. He insists instead that consciousness does not cause our social existence, but the reverse: our social existence determines our consciousness.

IV. Marx wrote the *Theses on Feuerbach* in 1845 as he and Engels were beginning work on *The German Ideology*. After Marx's death, Engels found it in one of Marx's notebooks, and published it over forty years after it was written, describing it as "the brilliant gem of the new world outlook." It is often seen as a note summarizing the main points he would make in *The German Ideology*, and it does a good job of compressing many of the major Marxist themes into an accessible format. Thesis XI, "The philosophers have only *interpreted* the world in different ways; the point is to *change* it," has become one of the most frequently quoted Marxian utterances, and it perfectly expresses his most central, decidedly un-Hegelian idea.

V. The *Communist Manifesto* was written to be a statement of the ideals and aims of the Communist League. The Communist League was an umbrella organization linking the main centers of communist activity in London, Paris, Brussels, and Cologne; it was formed in June 1847, largely at the instigation of Marx and Engels, and was descended from a shadowy "secret society" formed in Paris called the League of the Just. Most of its (few) members were German émigrés, and included several tailors, a few students, a typesetter, a cobbler, a watchmaker, a painter of miniatures, a disgraced Prussian officer, and Marx's aristocratic brother-in-law. A Congress of the League was held in London in November of 1847. To quote the eminent British historian A.J.P. Taylor:

> Marx attended in person. He listened impatiently while the worthy tailors lamented the wickedness of capitalism and preached universal brotherhood. He rose and denounced brotherhood in the name of class war. The tailors were entranced. Where they relied on sentiment, a learned man explained to them how society worked and placed the key to the future in their hands. They invited Marx to write a declaration of principles for them. He agreed.

Engels wrote a first draft—a question and answer brief on the main principles of communism—which was then completely rewritten by Marx in the space of fewer than six weeks. Marx was less than thirty years old at the time.

The *Manifesto* has four sections. The first part is a history of society from the Middle Ages to the present day, presenting it as a succession of class struggles, and predicting the imminent victory of the proletariat over the present ruling class, the bourgeoisie. Part II describes the position of the communists with respect to the proletarian class, and then goes on to reject a sequence of bourgeois objections to communism. This is followed by a brief characterization of the nature of the forthcoming communist revolution. The third part, not included here, contains an extended criticism of other forms of socialism—reactionary, bourgeois and utopian—and the final section provides a short description of communist tactics towards other opposition parties and culminates with a call for proletarian unity.

VI. "Critique of the Gotha Program" was written in 1875, eight years before Marx's death. The "Gotha Program" was named after the German town of Gotha where a congress of a social-democratic party with which Marx was associated was to be held. The Program was a compromise proposal aimed at uniting the party by including a non-Marxist faction that had been led by the German political economist Ferdinand Lassalle (1825–64). The Lassalle faction argued for reform, rather than revolution; and Marx condemned them for their willingness to limit demands on behalf of workers in exchange for concessions from the government, and in broader terms, for what he took to be their acceptance of the basic structure of, and philosophical assumptions behind, capitalist society. The "Critique" offers Marx's criticisms of the proposal, in a letter written to the leaders of his faction of the Party. (Despite his efforts, the proposal was presented and accepted, and the party united.)

Because he is writing to others thoroughly familiar with the issues, his notes here are comparatively brief and sketchy; he does not bother to explain things very carefully, and it is sometimes difficult for the reader to form a clear idea of exactly what the Gotha Program proposes, or what Marx's objections are. Often he mocks his opponents' ideas, without clearly explaining where he thinks they are mistaken. But overall, the main themes should become clear: Marx discusses (sometimes only indirectly) several subjects central to his idea of communism, and important in its later development, including the dictatorship of the proletariat, the period of transition from capitalism to communism, the anticipated development of communist society, the production and distribution of the social goods, proletarian internationalism, and the party of the working class. Of special interest is his deconstructive critique of the less radical socialist faction's idea of "fair" distribution of the products of labor. His positive proposal for economic justice is sketched lightly, though he does introduce here what was to become the famous communist slogan: "From each according to his ability, to each according to his needs." Throughout this document, however, we may find expressions of Marx's view that an economically just state would not be created out of abstract philosophical ideas, but would rather be the consequence of the implementation of the basic material aims of the communist revolution.

Some Useful Background Information

i) For Marx, no external force or random accident is required to topple capitalism: he believed that the overthrow of capitalism by socialism was inevitable, and that it would come about because of the very internal nature of capitalism itself. An accurate grasp of the forces which sustain almost all social systems throughout history, Marx thought, will show that they must inevitably, as a result of internal processes, decline and be replaced by a radically different social system. However *inevitably* does not mean *spontaneously*: the actual overthrow of existing society must be performed by a band of determined revolutionaries who join the already existing, day-to-day class struggles and introduce revolutionary ideas to combat the ruling ideology, emphasize the need for unity among the oppressed, and, when the time is ripe, boldly lead the revolution. The key is to follow the course of history *knowingly* by controlling the circumstances which generate it.

ii) There are a few terms that appear frequently in Marx's writings that it is worth defining here:

"Species-being": our essence as a species, as biological creatures; our human nature, what makes us distinctively human. An important theme (especially in the early writing) is alienation from our species-being. The two components of our species-being are consciousness of ourselves as human, part of the human collectivity; and our characteristically human free creative activity.

"Alienation" (or "estrangement") is distancing from, opposition to, being out of touch with something, making something foreign, seeing it as something apart from one's self. Thus the alienation of labor happens when labor becomes foreign—separated from—the laborer. To be

alienated from our species being is to be distanced from our fundamental nature. Capitalism, Marx argued, necessarily alienates in both these ways.

"Civil Society" is a term used by Marx in two distinct ways. Sometimes he merely means any sort of structured society. But more often he means society structured in a particular sort of way: with autonomous economic activity, unrestricted by governmental or religious authority. This society, arising as feudalism broke down, facilitated the accumulation of property and economic power in a few hands, and made it necessary for workers to sell their labor.

"Reactionary" is the term Marx and other socialists often use to refer to their right-wing conservative opposition. The contrast is with left-wing radicals and socialists: "progressives." Reactionaries are so-called because they are seen as opposing social change: they merely *react* against it.

"Bourgeois, bourgeoisie, proletariat." In Marx's writings, a bourgeois is a capitalist, someone who owns the means of production and hires others to perform the labor. "Bourgeois" can also be a plural noun: "the bourgeois were …" and an adjective: "bourgeois society" (meaning capitalist society). The social class containing the bourgeois is called "the bourgeoisie." (These French words are pronounced, roughly, "Boor-zhwa" and "Boor-zhwazee.") The working class in capitalist society is called the "proletariat."

Some Common Misconceptions

i) Although Marx believed that all the main institutions of society function to preserve the interests of the ruling class, he was not a conspiracy theorist: he did not believe, for example, that leading political figures receive covert orders from the business community. Instead, he held that institutional mechanisms press the actions of successful political figures into reflecting the long-term interests of the bourgeoisie (including the need for social and economic stability and the suppression of revolution). One especially important mechanism for this, according to Marx, is the national debt: governments depend on capitalists to renew huge but routine loans, and these financiers could throw national finances into chaos if their interests are too directly threatened. Another major influence is the pace of investment: if capitalists are displeased, the rate of investment slows and this has serious repercussions for employment rates and income levels. A third major factor is the bourgeois ownership of the media (in Marx's time, the mass-circulation newspapers), and their consequent ability to manipulate and mould public opinion.

ii) Marx's philosophy, as it is found in his writings, may be distinguished from the ideological system that we often call "Marxism" today. His thought has been built on and interpreted by many other writers, starting with Engels; and including several prominent Russian thinkers such as Georgy Plekhanov (1856–1918) and Vladimir Ilich Lenin (1870–1924) who formulated an "orthodox," systematic Soviet version of Marxism; as well as the so-called Western Marxists such as Georg Lukács (1885–1971), Theodor Adorno (1903–69), and Louis Althusser (1918–90). Nor is Marxism quite the same thing as communism. The "communist" notion of the abolition of private property dates back at least to the early Christians, and was proposed during the French Revolution by a few fringe groups whom even the revolutionaries considered beyond the pale. And of course, the modern association of Communism with the political and economic structures of China and the Soviet Union is a development which occurred after Marx's death (and it is highly unlikely that Marx himself would have unconditionally approved of those regimes).

How Important and Influential Are These Writings?

The *Communist Manifesto* is the most successful political pamphlet of all time, inspiring the thought of Vladimir Lenin, Leon Trotsky and Mao Zedong and leading to the Russian and Chinese revolutions. While the relationship between Marx's thought and communism under Stalin and Mao's brutal dictatorships is controversial, for a substantial period of the twentieth century, roughly a third of the human race was ruled by governments that claimed allegiance to the ideas expressed by Marx. Practically, Marx's thought remains the chief inspiration for many of the modern forms of social radicalism; intellectually, according to the *Blackwell Encyclopedia of Political Thought*, "[o]ver the whole range of the social sciences, Marx has proved probably the most influential figure of the twentieth century." Marx's central ideas—"historical materialism," the labor theory of value, the notion of class struggle—have had an inestimable influence on the development of contemporary economics, history, and sociology.

In social and political philosophy, Marx remains a towering, though sometimes unacknowledged and frequently controversial, figure. No major social or political thinker has been untouched by Marx's work. The great sociologist Max Weber reacted against and learned from Marx's oeuvre. The members of the Frankfurt school—most prominently Max Horkheimer, Theodor Adorno, Herbert Marcuse, and their intellectual heir, Jurgen Habermas—rejected economic determinism and other aspects of Marx's philosophy, but developed from it highly original critiques of ideology and capitalism. And analytic Marxists such as G.A. Cohen, John Roemer, and John Elster have applied the tools of analytic philosophy and contemporary economics to transform Marx's ideas about history, ideology, economics, and social justice.

Marx is also reflected in twentieth-century communitarianism, especially in its skepticism of the language of rights and individualism. Liberal philosophy has both reacted against and learned from Marxism, and Marx's influence (both positive and negative) can be seen in the work of philosophers as diverse as Isaiah Berlin, Robert Nozick, and John Rawls. Though liberals take issue with many of Marx's claims, the rise of liberal egalitarianism as a major philosophical standpoint can be plausibly traced in large part to his work.

◆ ◆ ◆ ◆ ◆

On Bruno Bauer's *On the Jewish Question* (1843)[1]

The German Jews seek emancipation. What kind of emancipation do they want? Civic, political emancipation. Bruno Bauer replies to them: In Germany no one is pol-

[1] *Bruno Bauer* (1809–82), German philosopher, historian, and theologian, taught the teen-aged Marx in 1836, and introduced him to Hegelianism. Originally a right-wing Hegelian, Bauer turned left during the 1840s, and published *On the Jewish Question (Die Judenfrage)* in 1843. In it, Bauer criticized both the conservative Prussian state for its restrictions on Jews, and also the Jews for maintaining their traditions and separateness. The Jewish religion, he claimed, was inferior to Christianity in terms of compatibility with full citizenship. As long as Jews maintained their beliefs they could expect persecution and exclusion, which was, then, for all intents and purposes, their own fault. Bauer managed to alienate both the conservative state (which revoked his teaching license) and the radical left. This article by Marx discussing Bauer's work first appeared in *Deutsch-Französische Jahrbücher*, October 1843. The first part focuses on Bauer's *On the Jewish Question*, the second on Bauer's *The Capacity of Present-day Jews and Christians to Become Free.*

itically emancipated. We ourselves are not free. How then could we liberate you? You Jews are egoists if you demand for yourselves, as Jews, a special emancipation. You should work, as Germans, for the political emancipation of Germany, and as men, for the emancipation of mankind. You should feel the particular kind of oppression and shame which you suffer, not as an exception to the rule but rather as a confirmation of the rule.

Or do the Jews want to be placed on a footing of equality with the *Christian subjects?* If they recognize the *Christian state* as legally established they also recognize the regime of general enslavement. Why should their particular yoke be irksome when they accept the general yoke? Why should the German be interested in the liberation of the Jew, if the Jew is not interested in the liberation of the German?

The *Christian* state recognizes nothing but *privileges.* The Jew himself, in this state, has the privilege of being a Jew. As a Jew he possesses rights which the Christians do not have. Why does he want rights which he does not have but which the Christians enjoy?

In demanding his emancipation from the Christian state he asks the Christian state to abandon its *religious* prejudice. But does he, the Jew, give up *his* religious prejudice? Has he then the right to insist that someone else should forswear his religion?

The *Christian* state, *by its very nature,* is incapable of emancipating the Jew. But, adds Bauer, the Jew, by his very nature, cannot be emancipated. As long as the state remains Christian, and as long as the Jew remains a Jew, they are equally incapable, the one of conferring emancipation, the other of receiving it.

With respect to the Jews the Christian state can only adopt the attitude of a Christian state. That is, it can permit the Jew, as a matter of privilege, to isolate himself from its other subjects; but it must then allow the pressures of all the other spheres of society to bear upon the Jew, and all the more heavily since he is in *religious* opposition to the dominant religion. But the Jew likewise can only adopt a Jewish attitude, i.e., that of a foreigner, towards the state, since he opposes his illusory nationality to actual nationality, his illusory law to actual law. He considers it his right to separate himself from the rest of humanity; as a matter of principle he takes no part in the historical movement and looks to a future which has nothing in common with the future of mankind as a whole. He regards himself as a member of the Jewish people, and the Jewish people as the chosen people.

On what grounds, then, do you Jews demand emancipation? On account of your religion? But it is the mortal enemy of the state religion. As citizens? But there are no citizens in Germany. As men? But you are not men any more than are those to whom you appeal.

Bauer, after criticizing earlier approaches and solutions, formulates the question of Jewish emancipation in a new way. What, he asks, is the nature of the Jew who is to be emancipated, and the *nature* of the Christian state which is to emancipate him? He replies by a critique of the Jewish religion, analyses the religious opposition between Judaism and Christianity, explains the essence of the Christian state; and does all this with dash, clarity, wit and profundity, in a style which is as precise as it is pithy and vigorous.

How then does Bauer resolve the Jewish question? What is the result? To formulate a question is to resolve it. The critical study of the Jewish question is the answer to the Jewish question. Here it is in brief: we have to emancipate ourselves before we can emancipate others.

The most stubborn form of the opposition between Jew and Christian is the *religious* opposition. How is an opposition resolved? By making it impossible. And how is *religious* opposition made impossible? By abolishing *religion.* As soon as Jew and Christian come to see in their respective religions nothing more than *stages in the development of the human mind*—snake skins which have been cast off by *history*, and *man* as the snake who clothed himself in them—they will no longer find themselves in religious opposition, but in a purely critical, *scientific* and human relationship. *Science* will then constitute their unity. But scientific oppositions are resolved by science itself.

The *German* Jew, in particular, suffers from the general lack of political freedom and the pronounced Christianity of the state. But in Bauer's sense the Jewish question has a general significance, independent of the specifically German conditions. It is the question of the relations between religion and the state, of the *contradiction between religious prejudice and political emancipation.* Emancipation from religion is posited as a condition, both for the Jew who wants political emancipation, and for the state which should emancipate him and itself be emancipated.

Very well, it may be said (and the Jew himself says it) but the Jew should not be emancipated because he is a Jew, because he has such an excellent and universal moral creed; the *Jew* should take second place to the citizen, and he will be a *citizen* although he is and desires to remain a Jew. In other words, he is and remains a *Jew*, even though he is a *citizen* and as such lives in a universal human condition; his restricted Jewish nature always finally triumphs over his human and political obligations. The bias persists even though it is overcome by general principles. But if it persists, it would be truer to say that it overcomes all the rest. It is only in a sophistical[1] and superficial sense that the Jew could remain a Jew in political life. Consequently, if he wanted to remain a Jew, this would mean that the superficial became the essential and thus triumphed. In other words, his life *in the state* would be only a semblance, or a momentary exception to the essential and normal. (Bauer, "Die Fahigkeit der heutigen Juden und Christen frei zu warden")[2]

Let us see also how Bauer establishes the role of the state.

France [he says] has provided us recently,[3] in connection with the Jewish question (and for that matter all other *political* questions), with the spectacle of a life which is free but which revokes its freedom by law and so declares it to be merely an appearance; and which, on the other hand, denies its free laws by its acts.

In France, universal liberty is not yet established by law, nor is the *Jewish question as yet resolved*, because legal liberty, i.e., the equality of all citizens, is restricted in actual life, which is still dominated and fragmented by religious privileges, and because the lack of liberty in actual life influences law in its turn and obliges it to sanction the division of citizens who are by nature free into oppressors and oppressed. (Bauer, *Die Judenfrage*)[4]

When, therefore, would the Jewish question be resolved in France?

The Jew would really have ceased to be Jewish, for example, if he did not allow his religious code to prevent his fulfillment of his duties towards the state and his fellow citizens; if he attended and took part in the public business of the Chamber of Deputies on the Sabbath. It would be necessary, further, to abolish *all religious privilege* including the monopoly of a privileged church. If, thereafter, some or many or *even the overwhelming majority felt obliged to fulfill their religious duties*, such practices should be left to them as an absolutely private matter."

There is no longer any religion when there is no longer a privileged religion. Take away from religion its power to excommunicate and it will no longer exist.

Mr. Martin du Nord has seen, in the suggestion to omit any mention of Sunday in the law, a proposal to declare that Christianity has ceased to exist. With equal right (and the right is well founded) the declaration that the law of the Sabbath is no longer binding upon the Jew would amount to proclaiming the end of Judaism.

Thus Bauer demands, on the one hand, that the Jew should renounce Judaism, and in general that man should renounce religion, in order to be emancipated as a citizen. On the other hand, he considers, and this follows logically, that the political abolition of religion is the abolition of all religion. The state which presupposes religion is not yet a true or actual state. "Clearly, the religious idea gives some assurances to the state. But to what state? *To what kind of state?*"

At this point we see that the Jewish question is considered only from one aspect.

It was by no means sufficient to ask: who should emancipate? who should be emancipated? The critic should ask a third question: *what kind of emancipation* is involved? What are the essential conditions of the emancipation which is demanded? The criticism of *political emancipation* itself was only the final criticism of the Jewish question and its genuine resolution into the "*general question of the age.*"

Bauer, since he does not formulate the problem at this level, falls into contradictions. He establishes conditions which are not based upon the nature of *political* emancipation. He raises questions which are irrelevant to his problem, and he resolves problems which leave his question

1   *sophistical* Based on flawed reasoning.
2   *"Die Fahigkeit ... zu warden"* "The Capacity of Present-Day Jews and Christians to Become Free," emphases added by Marx.
3   *France ... recently* [Marx's footnote] Chamber of Deputies. Debate of 26th December, 1840.
4   *Bauer, Die Judenfrage* The original German title of *On the Jewish Question*. Unless otherwise noted, Marx's quotations from Bauer are all from this work.

unanswered. When Bauer says of the opponents of Jewish emancipation that "Their error was simply to assume that the Christian state was the only true one, and not to subject it to the same criticism as Judaism," we see his own error in the fact that he subjects *only* the "Christian state," and not the "state as such" to criticism, that he does not examine *the relation between political emancipation and human emancipation*, and that he, therefore, poses conditions which are only explicable by his lack of critical sense in confusing political emancipation and universal human emancipation. Bauer asks the Jews: Have you, from your standpoint, the right to demand *political emancipation?* We ask the converse question: from the standpoint of *political* emancipation can the Jew be required to abolish Judaism, or man be asked to abolish religion?

The Jewish question presents itself differently according to the state in which the Jew resides. In Germany, where there is no political state, no state as such, the Jewish question is purely *theological*. The Jew finds himself in *religious* opposition to the state, which proclaims Christianity as its foundation. This state is a theologian *ex professo*.[1] Criticism here is criticism of theology; a double-edged criticism, of Christian and of Jewish theology. And so we move always in the domain of theology, however *critically* we may move therein.

In France, which is a *constitutional* state, the Jewish question is a question of constitutionalism, of the incompleteness *of political emancipation*. Since the *semblance* of a state religion is maintained here, if only in the insignificant and self-contradictory formula of a *religion of the majority*, the relation of the Jews to the state also retains a semblance of religious, theological opposition.

It is only in the free states of North America, or at least in some of them, that the Jewish question loses its *theological* significance and becomes a truly *secular* question. Only where the state exists in its completely developed form can the relation of the Jew, and of the religious man in general, to the political state appear in a pure form, with its own characteristics. The criticism of this relation ceases to be theological criticism when the state ceases to maintain a *theological* attitude towards religion, that is, when it adopts the attitude of a state, i.e., a *political* attitude. Criticism then becomes *criticism of the political state*. And at this point, where the question ceases to be *theological*, Bauer's criticism ceases to be critical.

There is not, in the United States, either a state religion or a religion declared to be that of a majority, or a predominance of one religion over another. The state remains aloof from all religions. (Gustave de Beaumont, *Marie ou l'esclavage aux Etats-Unis*)[2]

There are even some states in North America in which "the constitution does not impose any religious belief or practice as a condition of political rights." And yet, "no one in the United States believes that a man without religion can be an honest man." And North America is pre-eminently the country of religiosity, as Beaumont, (op. cit) Tocqueville (A. de Tocqueville, *De la democratie en Amerique*) and the Englishman, Hamilton, (Thomas Hamilton, *Men and Manners in North America*, 1833, 2 vols.) assure us in unison. However, the states of North America only serve as an example. The question is: what is the relation between *complete* political emancipation and religion? If we find in the country which has attained full political emancipation, that religion not only continues to *exist* but is *fresh* and *vigorous*, this is proof that the existence of religion is not at all opposed to the perfection of the state. But since the existence of religion is the existence of a defect, the source of this defect must be sought in the *nature* of the state itself. Religion no longer appears as the basis, but as, the *manifestation* of secular narrowness. That is why we explain the religious constraints upon the free citizens by the secular constraints upon them. We do not claim that they must transcend their religious narrowness in order to get rid of their secular limitations. We do not turn secular questions into theological questions; we turn theological questions into secular ones. History has for long enough been resolved into superstition; but we now resolve superstition into history. The question of the *relation between political emancipation and religion* becomes for us a question of the *relation between political emancipation and human emancipation*. We criticize the religious failings of the political state by criticizing the political state in its *secular* form, disregarding its religious failings. We express in human terms the contradiction between the state and a *particular religion*, for example *Judaism*, by showing the contradiction between the state and particular *secular elements*, between the state and *religion* in *general* and between the state and its general *presuppositions*.

1   *ex professo* Latin: avowedly, expressly.

2   *Marie ou l'esclavage aux Etats-Unis* French: Mary, or Slavery in the United States.

The *political* emancipation of the Jew or the Christian—of the *religious* man in general—is the *emancipation of* the state from Judaism, Christianity, and *religion* in general. The *state* emancipates itself from religion in its own particular way, in the mode which corresponds to its nature, by emancipating itself from the *state religion*; that is to say, by giving recognition to no religion and affirming itself purely and simply as a state. To be *politically* emancipated from religion is not to be finally and completely emancipated from religion, because political emancipation is not the final and absolute form of *human* emancipation.

The limits of political emancipation appear at once in the fact that the *state* can liberate itself from a constraint without man himself being *really* liberated; that a state may be a *free state* without man himself being a *free man*. Bauer himself tacitly admits this when he makes political emancipation depend upon the following condition—

> It would be necessary, moreover, to abolish all religious privileges, including the monopoly of a privileged church: If some people, or even the *immense majority, still felt obliged to fulfill their religious duties*, this practice should be left to them as a *completely private matter*.

Thus the state may have emancipated itself from religion, even though the *immense majority* of people continue to be religious. And the immense majority do not cease to be religious by virtue of being religious *in private*.

The attitude of the state, especially the *free state*, towards religion is only the attitude towards religion of the individuals who compose the state. It follows that man frees himself from a constraint in a *political* way, through the state, when he transcends his limitations, in contradiction with himself, and in an *abstract, narrow* and partial way. Furthermore, by emancipating himself *politically*, man emancipates himself in a *devious way*, through an intermediary, however *necessary* this intermediary may be. Finally, even when he proclaims himself an atheist through the intermediary of the state, that is, when he declares the state to be an atheist, he is still engrossed in religion, because he only recognizes himself as an atheist in a roundabout way, through an intermediary. Religion is simply the recognition of man in a roundabout fashion; that is, through an intermediary. The state is the intermediary between man and human liberty. Just as Christ is the intermediary to whom man attributes all his own divinity and all his religious *bonds*, so the state is the intermediary to which man confides all his non-divinity and all his *human freedom*.

The *political* elevation of man above religion shares the weaknesses and merits of all such political measures. For example, the state as a state abolishes *private property* (i.e., man decrees by *political* means the *abolition* of private-property) when it abolishes the *property qualification* for electors and representatives, as has been done in many of the North American States. Hamilton interprets this phenomenon quite correctly from the political standpoint: *The masses have gained a victory over property owners and financial wealth.*

Is not private property ideally abolished when the non-owner-comes to legislate for the owner of property? The *property qualification* is the last *political* form in which private property is recognized.

But the political suppression of private property not only does not abolish private property; it actually presupposes its existence. The state abolishes, after its fashion, the distinctions established by *birth, social rank, education, occupation*, when it decrees that birth, social rank, education, occupation are *non-political* distinctions; when it proclaims, without regard to these distinctions, that every member of society is an *equal* partner in popular sovereignty, and treats all the elements which compose the real life of the nation from the standpoint of the state. But the state, none the less, allows private property, education, occupation, to *act* after *their* own fashion, namely as private property, education, occupation, and to manifest their *particular* nature. Far from abolishing these *effective* differences, it only exists so far as they are presupposed; it is conscious of being a *political state* and it manifests its *universality* only in opposition to these elements. Hegel, therefore, defines the relation of the political state to religion quite correctly when he says:

> In order for the state to come in to existence as the *self-knowing* ethical actuality of spirit, it is essential that it should be distinct from the forms of authority and of faith. But this distinction emerges only in so far as divisions occur within the ecclesiastical sphere itself. It is only in this way that the state, above the *particular* churches; has attained to the universality of thought—its formal principle—and is bringing this universality into existence. (Hegel, *Philosophy of Right*, §270)

To be sure! Only in this manner, *above* the *particular* elements, can the state constitute itself as universality.

The perfected political state is, by its nature, the *species-life*[1] of Man as opposed to his material life. All the presuppositions of this egoistic life continue to exist in *civil society outside* the political sphere, as qualities of civil society. Where the political state has attained to its full development, man leads, not only in thought, in consciousness, but in *reality*, in *life*, a double existence—celestial and terrestrial. He lives in the *political community* where he regards himself as a *communal being*, and in *civil society*, where he acts simply as a private individual, treats other men as means, degrades himself to the role of a mere means, and becomes the plaything of alien powers. The political state, in relation to civil society, is just as spiritual as is heaven in relation to earth. It stands in the same opposition to civil society, and overcomes it in the same manner as religion overcomes the narrowness of the profane world; i.e., it has always to acknowledge it again, re-establish it, and allow itself to be dominated by it. Man in his *most intimate* reality, in civil society, is a profane[2] being. Here, where he appears both to himself and to others as a real individual he is an *illusory* phenomenon. In the state, on the contrary, where he is regarded as a species-being, man, is the imaginary member of an imaginary sovereignty, divested of his real individual life, and infused with an unreal universality.

The conflict in which the individual, as the professor[3] of a *particular* religion, finds himself involved with his own quality of citizenship and with other men as members of the community, may be resolved into the *secular* schism between the *political* state and *civil society*. For man as a *bourgeois*, "*life* in the state" is "only an appearance or a fleeting exception to the normal and essential." It is true that the *bourgeois*, like the Jew, participates in political life only in a sophistical way, just as the *citoyen*[4] is a Jew or a *bourgeois* only in a sophistical way. But this sophistry is not personal. It is the *sophistry of the political state* itself. The difference between the religious man and the citizen is the same as that between the shopkeeper and the citizens, between the day-laborer and the citizen, between the landed proprietor and the citizen, between the *living individual* and the *citizen*. The contradiction in which the religious man finds himself with the political man, is the same contradiction in which the *bourgeois* finds himself with the citizen, and the member of civil society with his *political lion's skin*.[5]

This secular opposition, to which the Jewish question reduces itself—the relation between the political state and its presuppositions, whether the latter are material elements such as private property, etc., or spiritual elements such as culture or religion, the conflict between the *general interest*, and *private interest*, the schism between the *political* state and *civil society*—*these* profane contradictions, Bauer leaves intact, while he directs his polemic against their *religious* expression.

> It is precisely this basis—that is, the needs which assure the existence of *civil society* and *guarantee its necessity*—which exposes its existence to continual danger, maintains an element of uncertainty in civil society, produces this continually changing compound of wealth and poverty, of prosperity and distress, and above all generates change.

Compare the whole section entitled "Civil society," which follows closely the distinctive features of Hegel's philosophy of right. Civil society, in its opposition to this political state, is recognized as necessary because the political state is recognized as necessary.

Political emancipation certainly represents a great progress. It is not, indeed, the final form of human emancipation, but it is the final form of human emancipation *within* the framework of the prevailing social order. It goes without saying that we are speaking here of real, practical emancipation.

---

1   *species-life*   The term "species-life" (*Gattungsleben*) and "species-being" (*Gattungswesen*) are derived from the German materialist philosopher Ludwig Feuerbach (1804–72). In the first chapter of *Das Wesen des Christentums* [*The Essence of Christianity*], Feuerbach discusses the nature of humans and argues that we are to be distinguished from animals not by "consciousness" as such but by a particular kind of consciousness. Humans are not only conscious of themselves as individuals; they are also conscious of themselves as members of the human species and so they apprehend a "human essence" which is the same in all humans. According to Feuerbach this ability to conceive of "species" is the fundamental element in the human power of reasoning: "Science is the consciousness of species." Marx, while not departing from this meaning of the terms, employs them in other contexts; and he insists more strongly than Feuerbach that since this "species-consciousness" defines the nature of the human, humans are only living and acting authentically (i.e., in accordance with their nature) when they live and act deliberately as a "species-being," that is, as a *social* being.

2   *profane*   Not a matter of religion.

3   *professor*   One who claims belief.

4   *citoyen*   French: *citizen*—that is, the individual with political rights.

5   *with his political lion's skin*   Disguised as a frighteningly powerful individual.

Man emancipates himself *politically* from religion by expelling it from the sphere of public law to that of private law. Religion is no longer the spirit of the state, in which man behaves, albeit in a specific and limited way and in a particular sphere, as a species-being, in community with other men. It has become the spirit of *civil society*, of the sphere of egoism and of the *bellum omnium contra omnes*.[1] It is no longer the essence of *community*, but the essence of *differentiation*. It has become what it was at the *beginning*, an expression of the fact that man is *separated* from the *community*, from himself and from other men. It is now only the abstract avowal of an individual folly, a private whim or caprice. The infinite fragmentation of religion in North America, for example, already gives it the *external* form of a strictly private affair. It has been relegated among the numerous private interests and exiled from the life of the community as such. But one should have no illusions about the scope of political emancipation. The division of man into the *public person* and the *private person*, the *displacement* of religion from the state to civil society—all this is not a stage in political emancipation but its consummation. Thus political emancipation does not abolish, and does not even strive to abolish, man's *real* religiosity.

The *decomposition* of man into Jew and citizen, Protestant and citizen, religious man and citizen, is not a deception practised *against* the political system nor yet an evasion of political emancipation. It is *political emancipation itself*, the *political* mode of emancipation from religion. Certainly, in periods when the political state as such comes violently to birth in civil society, and when men strive to liberate themselves through political emancipation, the state can, and must, proceed to *abolish and destroy religion*; but only in the same way as it proceeds to abolish private property, by declaring a maximum, by confiscation, or by progressive taxation,[2] or in the same way as it proceeds to abolish life, by the *guillotine*. At those times when the state is most aware of itself, political life seeks to stifle its own prerequisites—civil society and its elements—and to establish itself as the genuine and harmonious species-life of man. But it can only achieve this end by setting itself in *violent* contradiction with its own conditions of existence, by declaring a *permanent* revolution. Thus the political drama ends necessarily with the restoration of religion, of private property,

of all the elements of civil society, just as war ends with the conclusion of peace.

In fact, the perfected Christian state is not the so-called *Christian* state which acknowledges Christianity as its basis, as the state religion, and thus adopts an exclusive attitude towards other religions; it is, rather, the *atheistic* state, the democratic state, the state which relegates religion among the other elements of civil society. The state which is still theological, which still professes officially the Christian creed, and which has not yet dared to declare itself a *state*, has not yet succeeded in expressing in a human and *secular* form, in its political *reality*, the human basis of which Christianity is the transcendental expression. The so-called Christian state is simply a *non-state*; since it is not Christianity as a religion, but only the *human core* of the Christian religion which can realize itself in truly human creations.

The so-called Christian state is the Christian negation of the state, but not at all the political realization of Christianity. The state which professes Christianity as a religion does not yet profess it in a political form, because it still has a religious attitude towards religion. In other words, such a state is not the *genuine realization* of the human basis of religion, because it still accepts the *unreal, imaginary* form of this human core. The so-called Christian state is an *imperfect* state, for which the Christian religion serves as the *supplement* and *sanctification* of its imperfection. Thus religion becomes necessarily one of its *means*; and so it is the *hypocritical* state. There is a great difference between saying: (i) that the *perfect* state, owing to a deficiency in the general *nature* of the state, counts religion as one of its *prerequisites*, or (ii) that the *imperfect* state, owing to a deficiency in its *particular existence* as an imperfect state, declares that religion is its *basis*. In the latter, religion becomes *imperfect politics*. In the former, the imperfection even of perfected *politics* is revealed in religion. The so-called Christian state needs the Christian religion in order to complete itself *as a state*. The democratic state, the real state, does not need religion for its political consummation. On the contrary, it can dispense with religion, because in this case the human core of religion is realized in a profane manner. The so-called Christian state, on the other hand, has a political attitude towards religion, and a religious attitude towards politics. It reduces political institutions and religion to mere appearances.

In order to make this contradiction clearer we shall examine Bauer's model of the Christian state, a model which is derived from his study of the German-Christian state.

---

1 *bellum omnium contra omnes* Latin: *war of each against all.* This is Hobbes' phrase in *Leviathan*, describing the "State of Nature."

2 *progressive taxation* System of taxation under which higher incomes are taxed at progressively higher rates.

Quite recently, [says Bauer] in order to demonstrate the *impossibility* or the *non-existence* of a Christian state, those passages in the Bible have been frequently quoted with which the state *does not conform* and *cannot conform unless* it *wishes* to *dissolve itself entirely.*

But the question is not so easily settled. What do these Biblical passages demand? Supernatural renunciation, submission to the authority of revelation, turning away from the state, the abolition of profane conditions. But the Christian state proclaims and accomplishes all these things. It has assimilated the *spirit of the Bible*, and if it does not reproduce it exactly in the terms which the Bible uses, that is simply because it expresses this spirit in political forms, in forms which are borrowed from the political system of this world but which, in the religious rebirth which they are obliged to undergo, are reduced to simple appearances. Man turns away from the state and by this means realizes and completes the political institutions.

Bauer continues by showing that the members of a Christian state no longer constitute a nation with a will of its own. The nation has its true existence in the leader to whom it is subjected, but this leader is, by his origin and nature, alien to it since he has been imposed by God without the people having any part in the matter. The laws of such a nation are not its own work, but are direct revelations. The supreme leader, in his relations with the real nation, the masses, requires privileged intermediaries; and the nation itself disintegrates into a multitude of distinct spheres which are formed and determined by chance, are differentiated from each other by their interests and their specific passions and prejudices, and acquire as a privilege the permission to isolate themselves from each other, etc.

But Bauer himself says: "Politics, if it is to be nothing more than religion, should not be politics; any more than the scouring of pans, if it is treated as a religious matter, should be regarded as ordinary housekeeping." But in the German-Christian state religion is an "economic matter" just as "economic matters" are religion. In the German-Christian state the power of religion is the religion of power.

The separation of the "spirit of the Bible" from the "letter of the Bible" is an *irreligious* act. The state which expresses the Bible in the letter of politics, or in any letter other than that of the Holy Ghost, commits sacrilege, if not

in the eyes of men at least in the eyes of its own religion. The state which acknowledges the Bible as its charter and Christianity as its supreme rule must be assessed according to the words of the Bible; for even the language of the Bible is sacred. Such a state, as well as the *human rubbish* upon which it is based, finds itself involved in a painful contradiction, which is insoluble from the standpoint of religious consciousness, when it is referred to those words of the Bible "with which it does not conform and *cannot conform unless it wishes to dissolve itself entirely.*" And why does it not wish to dissolve itself entirely? The state itself cannot answer either itself or others. In its own consciousness the official Christian state is an "ought" whose realization is impossible. It cannot affirm the *reality* of its own existence without lying to itself, and so it remains always in its own eyes an object of doubt, an uncertain and problematic object. Criticism is, therefore, entirely within its rights in forcing the state, which supports itself upon the Bible, into a total disorder of thought in which it no longer knows whether it is *illusion* or *reality*; and in which the infamy of its *profane* ends (for which religion serves as a cloak) enter into an insoluble conflict with the probity of its *religious* consciousness (for which religion appears as the goal of the world). Such a state can only escape its inner torment by becoming the *myrmidon*[1] of the Catholic Church. In the face of this Church, which asserts that secular power is entirely subordinate to its commands, the state is powerless; powerless the secular power which claims to be the rule of the religious spirit.

What prevails in the so-called Christian state is not man but alienation. The only man who counts—the *King*—is specifically differentiated from other men and is still a religious being associated directly with heaven and with God. The relations which exist here are relations still based upon *faith*. The religious spirit is still not really secularized.

But the religious spirit cannot be *really* secularized. For what is it but the *non-secular* form of a stage in the development of the human spirit? The religious spirit can only be realized if the stage of development of the human spirit which it expresses in religious form, manifests and constitutes itself in its *non-secular* form. This is what happens in the *democratic* state. The basis of this state is not Christianity but the *human basis* of Christianity. Religion remains the ideal, non-secular consciousness of its members, because it

---

1   *myrmidon* Faithful follower; one who obeys orders unquestioningly.

is the ideal form of the *stage of human development* which has been attained.

The members of the political state are religious because of the dualism between individual life and species-life, between the life of civil society and political life. They are religious in the sense that man treats political life, which is remote from his own individual existence, as if it were his true life; and in the sense that religion is here the spirit of civil society and expresses the separation and withdrawal of man from man. Political democracy is Christian in the sense that man, not merely one man but every man, is there considered a sovereign being, a supreme being; but it is uneducated, unsocial man, man just as he is in his fortuitous existence, man as he has been corrupted, lost to himself, alienated, subjected to the rule of inhuman conditions and elements, by the whole organization of our society—in short man who is not yet a *real* species-being. Creations of fantasy, dreams, the postulates of Christianity, the sovereignty of man—but of man as an alien being distinguished from the real man—all these become, in democracy, the tangible and present reality, secular maxims.

In the perfected democracy, the religious and theological consciousness appears to itself all the more religious and theological in that it is apparently without any political significance or terrestrial aims, is an affair of the heart withdrawn from the world, an expression of the limitations of reason, a product of arbitrariness and fantasy, a veritable life in the beyond. Christianity here attains the *practical* expression of its universal religious significance, because the most varied views are brought together in the form of Christianity, and still more because Christianity does not ask that anyone should profess Christianity, but simply that he should have some kind of religion. The religious consciousness runs riot in a wealth of contradictions and diversity.

We have shown, therefore, that political emancipation from religion leaves religion in existence, although this is no longer a privileged religion. The contradiction in which the adherent of a particular religion finds himself in relation to his citizenship is only *one aspect* of the universal *secular contradiction between the political state and* civil society. The consummation of the Christian state is a state which acknowledges itself simply as a state and ignores the religion of its members. The emancipation of the state from religion is not the emancipation of the real man from religion.

We do not say to the Jews, therefore, as does Bauer: you cannot be emancipated politically without emancipating yourselves completely from Judaism. We say rather:

it is because you can be emancipated politically, without renouncing Judaism complete and absolutely, that *political emancipation* itself is not *human* emancipation. If you want to be politically emancipated, without emancipating yourselves humanly, the inadequacy and the contradiction is not entirely in yourselves but in the *nature* and the *category* of political emancipation. If you are preoccupied with this category you share the general prejudice. Just as the state *evangelizes*[1] when, although it is a state, it adopts a Christian attitude towards the Jews, the Jew *acts politically* when, though a Jew, he demands civil rights.

But if a man, though a Jew, can be emancipated politically and acquire civil rights, can he claim and acquire what are called the *rights of man?* Bauer *denies* it.

> The question is whether the Jew as such, that is, the Jew who himself avows that he is constrained by his true nature to live eternally separate from men, is able to acquire and to concede to others the *universal rights of man*.
>
> The idea of the rights of man was only discovered in the Christian world, in the last century. It is not an innate idea; on the contrary, it is acquired in a struggle against the historical traditions in which man has been educated up to the present time. The rights of man are not, therefore, a gift of nature, nor a legacy from past history, but the reward of a struggle against the accident of birth and against the privileges which history has hitherto transmitted from generation to generation. They are the results of culture, and only he can possess them who has merited and earned them.
>
> But can the Jew really take possession of them? As long as he remains Jewish the limited nature which makes him a Jew must prevail over the human nature which should associate him, as a man, with other men; and it will isolate him from everyone who is not a Jew. He declares, by this separation, that the particular nature which makes him Jewish is his true and supreme nature, before which human nature has to efface itself.
>
> Similarly, the Christian as such cannot grant the rights of man.

---

1   *evangelizes*   Seeks to win religious converts.

According to Bauer man has to sacrifice the "*privilege of faith*" in order to acquire the general rights of man. Let us consider for a moment the so-called rights of man; let us examine them in their most authentic form, that which they have among those who have *discovered* them, the North Americans and the French! These rights of man are, in part, *political rights*, which can only be exercised if one is a member of a community. Their content is *participation* in the *community* life, in the *political* life the community, the life of the state. They fall in the category of *political liberty*, of *civil rights*, which as we have seen do not at all presuppose the consistent and positive abolition of religion; nor consequently, of Judaism. It remains to consider the other part, namely the *rights of man* as distinct from the *rights of the citizen*.

Among them is to be found the freedom of conscience, the right to practice a chosen religion. The *privilege of faith* is expressly recognized, either as a *right of man* or as a consequence of a right of man, namely liberty. *Declaration of the Rights of Man and of the Citizen*, 1791, Article 10: "No one is to be disturbed on account of his opinions, even religious opinions." There is guaranteed, as one of the rights of man, "the liberty of every man to practice the *religion* to which he adheres."

The *Declaration of the Rights of Man, etc.* 1793, enumerates among the rights of man (Article 7): "The liberty of religious observance." Moreover, it is even stated, with respect to the right to express ideas and opinions, to hold meetings, to practice a religion, that: "The necessity of enunciating these *rights* presupposes either the existence or the recent memory of despotism." Compare the Constitution of 1795, Section 12, Article 354.

Constitution of Pennsylvania, Article 9, S 3: "All men have received from nature the imprescriptible[1] *right* to worship the Almighty according to the dictates of their conscience, and no one can be legally compelled to follow, establish or support against his will any religion or religious ministry. No human authority can, in any circumstances intervene in a matter of conscience or control the forces of the soul."

Constitution of New Hampshire, Articles 5 and 6: "Among these natural rights some are by nature inalienable[2] since nothing can replace them. The rights of conscience—are among them."

The incompatibility between religion and the rights of man is so little manifest in the concept of the rights of man that the *right to be religious*, in one's own fashion, and to practice one's own particular religion, is expressly included among the rights of man. The privilege of faith is a *universal right of man.*

A distinction is made between the rights of man and the rights of the citizen. Who is this *man* distinct from the *citizen*? No one but the *member of civil society.* Why is the member of civil society called "man," simply man, and why are his rights called the "rights of man"? How is this fact to be explained? By the relation between the political state and civil society, and by the nature of political emancipation.

Let us notice first of all that the so-called *rights of man*, as distinct from the *rights of the citizen*, are simply the *rights of a member of civil society*, that is, of egoistic man, of man separated from other men and from the community. The most radical constitution, that of 1793, says: "These rights, etc. (the natural and imprescriptible rights) are: *equality, liberty, security, property*" (*Declaration of the Rights of Man and of the Citizen*, Article 2).

What Constitutes Liberty?

Article 6 (*Declaration of the Rights of Man and of the Citizen*). "Liberty is the power which man has to do everything which does not harm the rights of others."

Liberty is, therefore, the right to do everything which does not harm others. The limits within which each individual can act without harming others are determined by law, just as the boundary between two fields is marked by a stake. It is a question of the liberty of man regarded as an isolated monad, withdrawn into himself. Why, according to Bauer, is the Jew not fitted to acquire the rights of man? "As long as he remains Jewish the limited nature which makes him a Jew must prevail over the human nature which should associate him, as a man, with other men; and it will isolate him from everyone who is not a Jew." But liberty as a right of man is not founded upon the relations between man and man, but rather upon the separation of man from man. It is the right of such separation. The right of the *circumscribed* individual, withdrawn into himself.

The practical application of the right of liberty is the right of private property. What constitutes the right of private property?

---

1 *imprescriptible* Cannot be legally taken away.
2 *inalienable* Not able to be taken away.

Article 16 (*Constitution of 1793*). "The right of *property* is that which belongs to every citizen of enjoying and disposing *as he will* of his goods and revenues, of the fruits of his work and industry."

The right of property is, therefore, the right to enjoy one's fortune and to dispose of it as one will; without regard for other men and independently of society. It is the right of self-interest. This individual liberty, and its application, form the basis of civil society. It leads every man to see in other men, not the *realization*, but rather the *limitation* of his own liberty. It declares above all the right "to enjoy and to dispose *as one will*, one's goods and revenues, the fruits of one's work and industry."

There remain the other rights of man, equality and security.

The term "equality" has here no political significance. It is only the equal right to liberty as defined above; namely that every man is equally regarded as a self-sufficient monad.[1] The Constitution of 1795 defines the concept of liberty in this sense.

Article 5 (*Constitution* of 1795). "Equality consists in the fact that the law is the same for all, whether it protects or punishes."

And Security?

Article 8 (*Constitution of 1793*). "Security consists in the protection afforded by society to each of its members for the preservation of his person, his rights, and his property."

Security is the supreme social concept of civil society; the concept of the police. The whole society exists only in order to guarantee for each of its members the preservation of his person, his rights, and his property. It is in this sense that Hegel calls civil society "the state of need and of reason."

The concept of security is not enough to raise civil society above its egoism. Security is, rather, the *assurance* of its egoism.

None of the supposed rights of man, therefore, go beyond the egoistic man, man as he is, as a member of civil society; that is an individual separated from the community, withdrawn into himself, wholly preoccupied with his private interest and acting in accordance with his private

caprice. Man is far from being considered, in the rights of man, as species-being; on the contrary, species-life itself—society—appears as a system which is external to the individual an as a limitation of his original independence. The only bond between men is natural necessity, need and private interest, the preservation of their property and their egoistic persons.

It is difficult enough to understand that a nation which has just begun to liberate itself, to tear down all the barriers between different sections of the people and to establish a political community, should solemnly proclaim (*Declaration of 1791*) the rights of the egoistic man, separated from the community, and should renew this proclamation at a moment when only the most heroic devotion can save the nation (and is, therefore, urgently called for), and when the sacrifice of all the interests of civil society is in question and egoism should be punished as a crime. (*Declaration of the Rights of Man, etc.* 1793). The matter becomes still more incomprehensible when we observe that the political liberators reduce citizenship, the *political community*, to a *mere means* for preserving these so-called rights of man; and consequently, that the citizen is declared to be the servant of egoistic "man," that the sphere in which man functions as a partial being, and finally that it is man a bourgeois and not man as a citizen who is considered the *true* and *authentic* man.

"The end of every *political association is* the *preservation* of the natural and imprescriptible rights of man (*Declaration of the Rights of Man,* 1791) "Government is instituted in order to guarantee man's enjoyment of his natural and imprescriptible rights." (*Declaration, etc.* 1793) Thus, even in the period of its youthful enthusiasm, which is raised to fever pitch by the force of circumstances, political life declares itself to be only a *means,* whose end is the life of civil society. It is true that its revolutionary practice is in flagrant contradiction with its theory. While, for instance, security is declared to be one of the rights of man, the violation of the privacy of correspondence is openly considered. While the "unlimited freedom of the press" (*Constitution* of 1793), as a corollary of the right of individual liberty, is guaranteed, the freedom of the press is completely destroyed, since "the freedom of the press should not be permitted when it endangers public liberty" (Buchez et Roux, "Robespierre jeune," *Histoire parlementaire de la Révolution française*, volume 28).[2] This amounts to saying: the right to

---

1   *monad* Self-sufficient independent basic entity—not subject to further analysis.

2   *Buchez et Roux ... la Révolution française* French: Buchez and Roux, "Young Robespierre" in the *Parlimentary History of the*

liberty ceases to be a right as soon as it comes into conflict with *political* life, whereas in theory political life is no more than the guarantee of the rights of man—the rights of the individual man—and should, therefore, be suspended as soon as it comes into contradiction with its *end*, these rights of man. But practice is only the exception, while theory is the rule. Even if one decided to regard revolutionary practice as the correct expression of this relation, the problem would remain as to why it is that in the minds of political liberators the relation is inverted, so that the end appears as the means and the means as the end? This optical illusion of their consciousness would always remain a problem, though a psychological and theoretical one.

But the problem is easily solved.

Political emancipation is at the same time the *dissolution* of old society, upon which the sovereign power, the alienated political life of the people, rests. Political revolution is a revolution of civil society. What was the nature of the old society? It can be characterized in one word: feudalism. The old civil society had a *directly political* character; that is, the elements of civil life such as property, the family, and types of occupation had been raised, in the form of lordship, caste[1] and guilds,[2] to elements of political life. They determined, in this form, the relation of the individual to the *state as a whole*; that is, his *political* situation, or in other words, his separation and exclusion from the other elements of society. For this organization of national life did not constitute property and labor as social elements; it rather succeeded in *separating* them from the body of the state, and made them *distinct* societies within society. Nevertheless, at least in the feudal sense, the vital functions and conditions of civil society remained political. They excluded the individual from the body of the state, and transformed the *particular* relation which existed between his corporation and the state into a general relation between the individual and social life, just as they transformed his specific civil activity and situation into a general activity and situation. As a result of this organization, the state as a whole and its consciousness, will and activity—the general political power—also necessarily appeared as the *private* of a ruler and his servants, separated from the people.

The political revolution which overthrew this power of the ruler, which made state affairs the affairs of the people,

and the political state a matter of *general* concern, i.e., a real state, necessarily shattered everything—estates, corporations, guilds, privileges—which expressed the separation of the people from community life. The political revolution therefore *abolished* the *political character of civil society.* It dissolved civil society into its basic elements, on the one hand *individuals*, and on the other hand the *material and cultural elements* which formed the life experience and the civil situation of these individuals. It set free the political spirit which had, so to speak, been dissolved, fragmented and lost in the various culs-de-sac[3] of feudal society; it reassembled these scattered fragments, liberated the political spirit from its connexion with civil life and made of it the community sphere, the *general* concern of the people, in principle independent of these particular elements of civil life. A *specific* activity and situation in life no longer had any but an individual significance. They no longer constituted the general relation between the individual and the state as a whole. Public affairs as such became the general affair of each individual, and political functions became general functions.

But the consummation of the idealism of the state was at the same time the consummation of the materialism of civil society. The bonds which had restrained the egoistic spirit of civil society were removed along with the political yoke. Political emancipation was at the same time an emancipation of civil society from politics and from even the *semblance* of a general content.

Feudal society was dissolved into its basic element, *man*; but into *egoistic* man who was its real foundation.

Man in this aspect, the member of civil society, is now the foundation and presupposition of the *political* state. He is recognized as such in the rights of man.

But the liberty of egoistic man, and the recognition of this liberty, is rather the recognition of the *frenzied* movement of the cultural and material elements which form the content of his life.

Thus man was not liberated from religion; he received religious liberty. He was not liberated from property; he received the liberty to own property. He was not liberated from the egoism of business; he received the liberty to engage in business.

The *formation* of the *political state*, and the dissolution of civil society into independent *individuals* whose relations are regulated by *law*, as the relations between men in the

French Revolution, volume 28.

1 *caste* Hereditary social class within a rigid societal system.
2 *guilds* Medieval European organizations of craftspeople, with strong political power.

3 *culs-de-sac* Dead-ends.

corporations and guilds regulated by *privilege*, are accomplished by one *and the same act.* Man as a member of civil society—*non-political* man—necessarily appears as natural man. The rights of man appear as natural rights because *conscious* activity is concentrated upon political *action.* *Egoistic* man is the *passive, given* result of the dissolution of society, an object of *direct apprehension* and consequently a *natural* object. The *political revolution* dissolves civil society into its elements without *revolutionizing* these elements themselves or subjecting them to criticism. This revolution regards civil society, the sphere of human needs, labor, private interests and civil law, as the *basis of its* own *existence,* as a self-subsistent *precondition*, and thus as its *natural basis.* Finally, man as a member of civil society is identified with *authentic man*, man as distinct from citizen, because he is man in his sensuous, individual and *immediate* existence, whereas *political* man is only abstract, artificial man, man as an *allegorical, moral* person. Thus man as he really is, is seen only in the form of *egoistic* man, and man in his true nature only in the form of the *abstract citizen.*

The abstract notion of political man is well formulated by Rousseau:

Whoever dares undertake to establish a people's institutions must feel himself capable of *changing*, as it were, *human nature* itself, of *transforming* each individual who, in isolation, is a complete but solitary whole, into a *part* of something greater than himself, from which in a sense, he derives his life and his being; [of changing man's nature in order to strengthen it;] of substituting a limited and moral existence for the physical and independent life [with which all of us are endowed by nature]. His task, in short, is to take from *a man his own powers*, and to give him in exchange alien powers which he can only employ with the help of other men. (J.J. Rousseau, *The Social Contract*, Book 2, Chapter 7, "The Legislator.")

Every emancipation is a *restoration* of the human world and of human relationships to *man himself.*

Political emancipation is a reduction of man, on the one hand to a member of civil society, an *independent* and *egoistic* individual, and on the other hand, to a *citizen*, to a moral person.

Human emancipation will only be complete when the real, individual man has absorbed into himself the abstract citizen; when as an individual man, in his everyday life, in his work, and in his relationships, he has become a *species-being*; when he has recognized and organized his own powers (*forces propres*) as social powers so that he no longer separates this *social* power from himself as *political* power.

◆ ◆ ◆ ◆ ◆

On Bruno Bauer's *The Capacity for the Present-day Jews and Christians to Become Free*

It is in this form that Bauer studies the relation between the *Jewish and Christian religions*, and also their relation with modem criticism. This latter relation is their relation with "the capacity to become free."

He reaches this conclusion: "The Christian has only to raise himself one degree, to rise above his religion, in order to abolish religion in general," and thus to become free; but "the Jew, on the contrary, has to break not only with his Jewish nature, but also with the process towards the consummation of his religion, a process which has remained alien to him."[1]

Thus Bauer here transforms the question of Jewish emancipation into a purely religious question. The theological doubt about whether the Jew or the Christian has the better chance of attaining salvation is reproduced here in the more enlightened form: which of the two is more *capable of emancipation*? It is indeed no longer asked: which makes free—Judaism or Christianity? On the contrary, it is now asked: which makes free—the negation of Judaism or the negation of Christianity?

"If they wish to become free the Jews should not embrace Christianity as such, but Christianity in dissolution, religion in dissolution; that is to say, the Enlightenment, criticism, and its outcome, a free humanity."

It is still a matter, therefore, of the Jews professing some kind of faith; no longer Christianity as such, but Christianity in dissolution.

1　*The Christian ... to him* Unless otherwise noted, Marx's quotations from Bauer in this section are all from *The Capacity for Present-day Jews and Christians to Become Free.*

Bauer asks the Jews to break with the essence of the Christian religion, but this demand does not follow, as he himself admits, from the development of the Jewish nature.

From the moment when Bauer, at the end of his *The Jewish Question [Judenfrage]*, saw in Judaism only a crude religious criticism of Christianity, and, therefore, attributed to it only a religious significance, it was to be expected that he would transform the emancipation of the Jews into a philosophico-theological act.

Bauer regards the *ideal* and abstract essence of the Jew—his *religion*—as the *whole* of his nature. He, therefore, concludes rightly that "The Jew contributes nothing to mankind when he disregards his own limited law," when he renounces all his Judaism.

The relation between Jews and Christians thus becomes the following: the only interest which the emancipation of the Jew presents for the Christian is a general human and *theoretical* interest.

Judaism is a phenomenon which offends the religious eye of the Christian. As soon as the Christian ceases to be religious the phenomenon ceases to offend it. The emancipation of the Jew is not in itself, therefore, a task which falls to the Christian to perform.

The Jew, on the other hand, if he wants to emancipate himself has to undertake, besides his own work, the work of the Christian—the "criticism of the gospels," of the "life of Jesus," etc.[1]

"It is for them to arrange matters; they will decide their own destiny. But history does not allow itself to be mocked."

We will attempt to escape from the theological formulation of the question. For us the question concerning the capacity of the Jew for emancipation is transformed into another question: what specific *social* element is it necessary to overcome in order to abolish Judaism? For the capacity of the present day Jew to emancipate himself expresses the relation of Judaism to the emancipation of the contemporary world. The relation results necessarily from the particular situation—of Judaism in the present enslaved world.

Let us consider the real Jew: not the *Sabbath Jew*,[2] whom Bauer considers, but the *everyday Jew*.

Let us not seek the secret of the Jew in his religion, but let us seek the secret of the religion in the real Jew.

What is the profane basis of Judaism? *Practical* need, *self-interest*. What is the worldly cult of the Jew? *Huckstering*.[3] What is his worldly god? *Money*.[4]

Very well: then in emancipating itself from *huckstering* and *money*, and thus from real and practical Judaism, our age would emancipate itself.

An organization of society which would abolish the preconditions and thus the very possibility of huckstering, would make the Jew impossible. His religious consciousness would evaporate like some insipid vapor in the real, life-giving air of society. On the other hand, when the Jew recognizes his *practical* nature as invalid and endeavors to abolish it, he begins to deviate from his former path of development, works for general *human emancipation* and turns against the *supreme practical* expression of human self-estrangement.

We discern in Judaism, therefore a universal *antisocial* element of the *present time* whose historical development, zealously aided in its harmful aspects by the Jews, has now attained its culminating point, a point at which it must necessarily begin to disintegrate.

In the final analysis, the *emancipation of* the Jews is the emancipation of mankind from *Judaism*.

The Jew has already emancipated himself in a Jewish fashion. "The Jew, who is merely tolerated in Vienna for example, determines the fate of the whole Empire by his financial power. The Jew, who may be entirely without rights in the smallest German state, decides the destiny of Europe. While the corporations and guilds exclude the Jew, or at least look on him with disfavor, the audacity of industry mocks the obstinacy of medieval institutions." (Bauer, *The Jewish Question*)

This is not an isolated instance. The Jew has emancipated himself in a Jewish manner, not only by acquiring the power of money, but also because *money* has become, through him and also apart from him, a world power, while the practical Jewish spirit has become the practical spirit of

1 Marx alludes here to two books: Bruno Bauer's, *Kritik der evangelischen Geschichte der Synoptiker (Critique of the Gospel History of the Synoptics* [i.e., Matthew, Mark, and Luke]) (1841–42), and David Friedrich Strauss, *Das Leben Jesu* (1835–36). An English translation of Strauss' book by Marian Evans (George Eliot) was published in 1846 under the title *Life of Jesus Critically Examined*.

2 *Sabbath Jew* Largely secular Jew, who engages in some religious practices on the Sabbath, but who is just like everyone else every other day.

3 *Huckstering* Aggressive retailing.

4 *What is his worldly god? Money* See the introduction for a discussion of Marx's evident acceptance of anti-Semitic stereotypes.

the Christian nations. The Jews have emancipated themselves in so far as the Christians have become Jews.

Thus, for example, Captain Hamilton reports that the devout and politically free inhabitant of New England is a kind of Laocoon[1] who makes not the least effort to escape from the serpents which are crushing him. Mammon[2] is his idol which he adores not only with his lips but with the whole force of his body and mind. In his view the world is no more than a Stock Exchange, and he is convinced that he has no other destiny here below than to become richer than his neighbor. Trade has seized upon all his thoughts, and he has no other recreation than to exchange objects. When he travels he carries, so to speak, his goods and his counter on his back and talks only of interest and profit. If he loses sight of his own business for an instant it is only in order to pry into the business of his competitors (Hamilton).

In North America, indeed, the effective domination of the Christian world by Judaism has come to be manifested in a common and unambiguous form; the *preaching of the Gospel* itself, Christian preaching, has become an article of commerce, and the bankrupt trader in the church behaves like the prosperous clergyman in business. "This man whom you see at the head of a respectable congregation began as a trader; his business having failed he has become a minister. This other began as a priest, but as soon as he had accumulated some money he abandoned the priesthood for trade. In the eyes of many people the religious ministry is a veritable industrial career" (Beaumont).

According to Bauer, it is "a hypocritical situation when, in theory, the Jew is deprived of political rights, while in practice he wields tremendous power and exercises on a wholesale scale the political influence which is denied him in minor matters" (Bauer, *The Jewish Question*).

The contradiction which exists between the effective political power of the Jew and his political rights, is the contradiction between politics and the power of money in general. Politics is in principle superior to the power of money, but in practice it has become its bondsman.[3]

Judaism has maintained itself *alongside* Christianity, not only because it constituted the religious criticism of Christianity and embodied the doubt concerning the religious origins of Christianity, but equally because the practical Jewish spirit—Judaism or commerce[4]—has perpetuated itself in Christian society and has even attained its highest development there. The Jew, who occupies a distinctive place in civil society, only manifests in a distinctive way the Judaism of civil society.

Judaism has been preserved, not in spite of history, but by history.

It is from its own entrails that civil society ceaselessly engenders the Jew.

What was, in itself, the basis of the Jewish religion? Practical need, egoism.

The monotheism of the Jews is, therefore, in reality, a polytheism of the numerous needs of man, a polytheism which makes even the lavatory an object of divine regulation. *Practical need, egoism*, is the principle of *civil society*, and is revealed as such in its pure form as soon as civil society has fully engendered the political state. *The god of practical need and self-interest is money.*

Money is the jealous god of Israel, beside which no other god may exist. Money is the universal and self-sufficient *value* of all things. It has, therefore, deprived the whole world, both the human world and nature, of their own proper value. Money is the alienated essence of man's work and existence; this essence dominates him and he worships it.

The god of the Jews has been secularized and has become the god of this world. The bill of exchange is the real god of the Jew. His god is only an illusory bill of exchange.

The mode of perceiving nature, under the rule of private property and money, is a real contempt for, and a practical degradation of nature, which does indeed exist in the Jewish religion but only as a creature of the imagination.

It is in this sense that Thomas Munzer declares it intolerable "that every creature should be transformed into property—the fishes in the water, the birds of the air, the plants of the earth: the creature too should become free."

That which is contained in an abstract form in the Jewish religion—contempt for theory, for art, for history, and for man as an end in himself—is the *real, conscious* stand-

---

1   *Laocoon* In Greek mythology, a Trojan priest who warned his people about the Trojan Horse—that they should beware of Greeks bearing gifts—and was punished when a god who favored the Greeks sent sea serpents who curled around him and his twin sons, killing them.

2   *Mammon* False god in the Old Testament, representing riches and greed.

3   *bondsman* Slave.

4   *Judaism or commerce* The German word *Judentum* had, in the language of the time, the secondary meaning of "commerce"; in this and other passages Marx exploits the two senses of the word.

point and the virtue of the man of money. Even the species-relation itself, the relation between man and woman, becomes an object of commerce. Woman is bartered away.

The *chimerical* nationality of the Jew is the nationality of the trader, and above all of the financier.

The law, without basis or reason, of the Jew, is only the religious caricature of morality and right in general, without basis or reason; the purely *formal* rites with which the world of self-interest encircles itself.

Here again the supreme condition of man is his *legal* status, his relationship to laws, which are valid for him, not because they are the laws of his own will and nature, but because they are dominant and any infraction of them will be *avenged*.

Jewish Jesuitism, the same practical Jesuitism which Bauer discovers in the Talmud,[1] is the relationship of the world of self-interest to the laws which govern this world, laws which the world devotes its principal arts to circumventing.

Indeed, the operation of this world within its framework of laws is impossible without the continual supersession[2] of law.

Judaism could not develop further as a *religion*, in a theoretical form, because the world view of practical need is, by its very nature, circumscribed, and the delineation of its characteristics soon completed.

The religion of practical need could not, by its very nature, find its consummation in theory, but only in *practice*, just because practice is its truth.

Judaism could not create a new world. It could only bring the new creations and conditions of the world within its own sphere of activity, because practical need, the spirit of which is self-interest, is always passive, cannot expand at will, but *finds* itself extended as a result of the continued development of society.

Judaism attains its apogee[3] with the perfection of civil society; but civil society only reaches perfection in the *Christian* world. Only under the sway of Christianity, which *objectifies all* national, natural, moral and theoretical relationships, could civil society separate itself completely from the life of the state, sever all the species-bonds of man, establish egoism and selfish need in their place, and dissolve the human world into a world of atomistic,[4] antagonistic individuals.

Christianity issued from Judaism. It has now been reabsorbed into Judaism.

From the beginning, the Christian was the theorizing Jew; consequently, the Jew is the practical Christian. And the practical Christian has become a Jew again.

It was only in appearance that Christianity overcame real Judaism. It was too *refined,* too spiritual to eliminate the crudeness of practical need except by raising it into the ethereal realm.

Christianity is the sublime thought of Judaism; Judaism is the vulgar practical application of Christianity. But this practical application could only become universal when Christianity as perfected religion had accomplished, in a *theoretical* fashion, the alienation of man from himself and from nature.

It was only then that Judaism could attain universal domination and could turn alienated man and alienated nature into *alienable,* saleable objects, in thrall to egoistic need and huckstering.

Objectification is the practice of alienation. Just as man, so long as he is engrossed in religion, can only objectify his essence by an *alien* and fantastic being; so under the sway of egoistic need, he can only affirm himself and produce objects in practice by subordinating his products and his own activity to the domination of an alien entity, and by attributing to them the significance of an alien entity, namely money.

In its perfected practice the spiritual egoism of Christianity necessarily becomes the material egoism of the Jew, celestial need is transmuted[5] into terrestrial need, subjectivism into self-interest. The tenacity of the Jew is to be explained, not by his religion, but rather by the human basis of his religion—practical need and egoism.

It is because the essence of the Jew was universally realized and secularized in civil society, that civil society could not convince the Jew of the *unreality* of his *religious* essence, which is precisely the ideal representation of practical need. It is not only, therefore, in the Pentateuch[6] and the Talmud, but also in contemporary society, that we find the essence of the present-day Jew; not as an abstract essence, but as one

---

1 *Talmud* Collection of ancient Rabbinic writings, the basis of religious authority for Orthodox Jews.
2 *supersession* Setting aside.
3 *apogee* High point.

4 *atomistic* Considered as basic, independent building-blocks of larger structures, not themselves to be analyzed.
5 *transmuted* Changed from one basic sort to another.
6 *Pentateuch* First five books of the Hebrew scriptures.

which is supremely empirical, not only as a limitation of the Jew, but as the Jewish narrowness of society.

As soon as society succeeds in abolishing the *empirical* essence of Judaism—huckstering and its conditions—the Jew becomes *impossible*, because his consciousness no longer has an object. The subjective basis of Judaism—practical need—assumes a human form, and the conflict between the individual, sensuous existence of man and his species-existence, is abolished.

The *social* emancipation of the Jew is the *emancipation of society from Judaism.*

◆ ◆ ◆ ◆ ◆

Economic and Philosophical Manuscripts (1844)

Estranged[1] Labor

We have proceeded from the premises of political economy.[2] We have accepted its language and its laws. We presupposed private property, the separation of labor, capital and land, and of wages, profit of capital and rent of land—likewise division of labor, competition, the concept of exchange-value, etc. On the basis of political economy itself, in its own words, we have shown that the worker sinks to the level of a commodity and becomes indeed the most wretched of commodities; that the wretchedness of the worker is in proportion to the power and magnitude of his production;[3] that the necessary result of competition is the accumulation of capital in a few hands, and thus the restoration of monopoly in a more terrible form; that finally the distinction between capitalist and land-rentier,[4] like that between the tiller of the soil and the factory-worker,

disappears and that the whole of society must fall apart into the two classes—the *property-owners* and the propertyless *workers.*

Political economy proceeds from the fact of private property, but it does not explain it to us. It expresses in general, abstract formulae the *material* process through which private property actually passes, and these formulae it then takes for *laws.* It does not *comprehend* these laws—i.e., it does not demonstrate how they arise from the very nature of private property. Political economy does not disclose the source of the division between labor and capital, and between capital and land. When, for example, it defines the relationship of wages to profit, it takes the interest of the capitalists to be the ultimate cause; i.e., it takes for granted what it is supposed to evolve. Similarly, competition comes in everywhere. It is explained from external circumstances. As to how far these external and apparently fortuitous circumstances are but the expression of a necessary course of development, political economy teaches us nothing. We have seen how, to it, exchange itself appears to be a fortuitous fact. The only wheels which political economy sets in motion are *avarice* and the *war amongst the avaricious—competition.*

Precisely because political economy does not grasp the connections within the movement, it was possible to counterpose,[5] for instance, the doctrine of competition to the doctrine of monopoly, the doctrine of craft-liberty to the doctrine of the corporation, the doctrine of the division of landed property to the doctrine of the big estate—for competition, craft-liberty and the division of landed property were explained and comprehended only as fortuitous, premeditated and violent consequences of monopoly, the corporation, and feudal property, not as their necessary, inevitable and natural consequences.

Now, therefore, we have to grasp the essential connection between private property, avarice, and the separation of labor, capital and landed property; between exchange and competition, value and the devaluation of men, monopoly and competition, etc.; the connection between this whole estrangement and the *money*-system.

Do not let us go back to a fictitious primordial condition as the political economist does, when he tries to explain. Such a primordial condition explains nothing. He merely pushes the question away into a grey nebulous distance. He assumes in the form of fact, of an event, what

---

1 *Estranged* This important term (German: *entfremdete*) is also often translated as "alienated."

2 *political economy* By this term, Marx refers to classical macroeconomics—the work of Adam Smith, David Ricardo, David Hume, and Thomas Malthus, investigating the laws of large-scale production and exchange. He means that his thought *starts* from this outlook—but he goes on to criticize it.

3 *that the wretchedness . . . production* I.e., the less power the worker has, the more he has to work, and the more miserable he is.

4 *land-rentier* In pre-industrial society, a land-owner who did not labor himself, but lived off the rent charged to farmers on his property.

5 *counterpose* Oppose—set in opposition to each other.

he is supposed to deduce—namely, the necessary relationship between two things—between, for example, division of labor and exchange. Theology in the same way explains the origin of evil by the fall of man: that is, it assumes as a fact, in historical form, what has to be explained.

We proceed from an *actual*[1] economic fact.

The worker becomes all the poorer the more wealth he produces, the more his production increases in power and range. The worker becomes an ever cheaper commodity the more commodities he creates. With the increasing value of the world of things proceeds in direct proportion the devaluation of the world of men.[2] Labor produces not only commodities; it produces itself and the worker as a commodity—and does so in the proportion in which it produces[3] commodities generally.[4]

This fact expresses merely that the object which labor produces—labor's product—confronts it as *something alien*, as a *power independent* of the producer. The product of labor is labor which has been congealed in an object, which has become material: it is the *objectification* of labor.[5] Labor's realization[6] is its objectification. In the conditions dealt with by political economy this realization of labor appears as *loss of reality* for the workers; objectification as *loss of the object* and *object-bondage*;[7] appropriation as *estrangement*, as *alienation*.

So much does labor's realization appear as loss of reality that the worker loses reality to the point of starving to death. So much does objectification appear as loss of the object that the worker is robbed of the objects most necessary not only for his life but for his work. Indeed, labor itself becomes an object which he can get hold of only with the greatest effort and with the most irregular interruptions. So much does the appropriation of the object appear as estrangement that the more objects the worker produces the fewer can he possess and the more he falls under the dominion of his product, capital.

All these consequences are contained in the definition that the worker is related to the *product of his labor* as to an *alien* object. For on this premise it is clear that the more the worker spends himself, the more powerful the alien objective world becomes which he creates over-against himself, the poorer he himself—his inner world—becomes, the less belongs to him as his own. It is the same in religion. The more man puts into God, the less he retains in himself. The worker puts his life into the object; but now his life no longer belongs to him but to the object. Hence, the greater this activity, the greater is the worker's lack of objects. Whatever the product of his labor is, he is not. Therefore the greater this product, the less is he himself. The *alienation* of the worker in his product means not only that his labor becomes an object, an *external* existence, but that it exists *outside him*, independently, as something alien to him, and that it becomes a power of its own confronting him; it means that the life which he has conferred on the object confronts him as something hostile and alien.

Let us now look more closely at the *objectification*, at the production of the worker; and therein at the *estrangement*, the *loss* of the object, his product.

The worker can create nothing without *nature*, without the *sensuous*[8] external world. It is the material on which his labor is manifested, in which it is active, from which and by means of which it produces.

But just as nature provides labor with the *means of life*, in the sense that labor cannot *live* without objects on which to operate, on the other hand, it also provides the *means of life* in the more restricted sense—i.e., the means for the physical subsistence of the *worker* himself.

Thus the more the worker by his labor *appropriates* the external world, sensuous nature, the more he deprives himself of *means of life* in the double respect: first, that the sensuous external world more and more ceases to be an object belonging to his labor—to be his labor's *means of life*; and secondly, that it more and more ceases to be *means of life* in the immediate sense, means for the physical subsistence of the worker.

Thus in this double respect the worker becomes a slave of his object, first, in that he receives an *object of labor*, i.e., in that he receives *work*; and secondly, in that he receives

---

1   *actual*   The word in the original (German: *gegenwärtigen*) is sometimes translated *contemporary*.

2   *With the increasing . . . world of men*   I.e., the increase in value of the world of things is in direct relation to the decrease in value of the human world.

3   *in the proportion in which it produces*   I.e., in proportion to the production of.

4   *commodities generally*   I.e., labor is bought and sold just as other objects are.

5   *The product . . . labor*   Labor becomes an object—a thing—rather than what people *do*.

6   *realization*   This translates the German word *Verwirklichung*, *making-real*. This contrasts with the *making-unreal* (German: *Entwirklichung*) of the workers, referred to in the following sentence.

7   *object-bondage*   Slavery to the object.

8   *sensuous*   Appearing to our senses.

means of subsistence. Therefore, it enables him to exist, first, as a *worker*; and, second, as a *physical subject.* The extremity of this bondage is that it is only as a *worker* that he continues to maintain himself as a *physical subject,* and that it is only as a *physical subject* that he is a *worker.*

(The laws of political economy express the estrangement of the worker in his object thus: the more the worker produces, the less he has to consume; the more values he creates, the more valueless, the more unworthy he becomes; the better formed his product, the more deformed becomes the worker; the more civilized his object, the more barbarous becomes the worker; the mightier labor becomes, the more powerless becomes the worker; the more ingenious labor becomes, the duller becomes the worker and the more he becomes nature's bondsman.)

Political economy conceals the estrangement inherent in the nature of labor by not considering the direct relationship between the worker (labor) *and production.* It is true that labor produces for the rich wonderful things—but for the worker it produces privation. It produces palaces—but for the worker, hovels. It produces beauty—but for the worker, deformity. It replaces labor by machines—but some of the workers it throws back to a barbarous type of labor, and the other workers it turns into machines. It produces intelligence—but for the worker idiocy, cretinism.

The direct relationship of labor to its produce is the relationship of the worker to the objects of his production. The relationship of the man of means[1] to the objects of production and to production itself is only a *consequence* of this first relationship—and confirms it. We shall consider this other aspect later.

When we ask, then, what is the essential relationship of labor we are asking about the relationship of the *worker* to production.

Till now we have been considering the estrangement, the alienation of the worker only in one of its aspects, i.e., the worker's *relationship to the products of his labor.* But the estrangement is manifested not only in the result but in the *act of production* within the *producing activity* itself. How would the worker come to face the product of his activity as a stranger, were it not that in the very act of production he was estranging himself from himself? The product is after all but the summary of the activity of production. If then the product of labor is alienation, production itself must be active alienation, the alienation of activity, the activity

of alienation. In the estrangement of the object of labor is merely summarized the estrangement, the alienation, in the activity of labor itself.

What, then, constitutes the alienation of labor?

First, the fact that labor is *external* to the worker, i.e., it does not belong to his essential being; that in his work, therefore, he does not affirm himself but denies himself, does not feel content but unhappy, does not develop freely his physical and mental energy but mortifies[2] his body and ruins his mind. The worker therefore only feels himself outside his work, and in his work feels outside himself. He is at home when he is not working, and when he is working he is not at home. His labor is therefore not voluntary, but coerced; it is *forced labor.* It is therefore not the satisfaction of a need; it is merely a *means* to satisfy needs external to it. Its alien character emerges clearly in the fact that as soon as no physical or other compulsion exists, labor is shunned like the plague. External labor, labor in which man alienates himself, is a labor of self-sacrifice, of mortification. Lastly, the external character of labor for the worker appears in the fact that it is not his own, but someone else's, that it does not belong to him, that in it he belongs, not to himself, but to another. Just as in religion the spontaneous activity of the human imagination, of the human brain and the human heart, operates independently of the individual—that is, operates on him as an alien, divine or diabolical activity—in the same way the worker's activity is not his spontaneous activity. It belongs to another; it is the loss of his self.

As a result, therefore, man (the worker) no longer feels himself to be freely active in any but his animal functions—eating, drinking, procreating, or at most in his dwelling and in dressing-up, etc.; and in his human functions he no longer feels himself to be anything but an animal. What is animal becomes human and what is human becomes animal.

Certainly eating, drinking, procreating, etc., are also genuinely human functions. But in the abstraction which separates them from the sphere of all other human activity and turns them into sole and ultimate ends, they are animal.

We have considered the act of estranging practical human activity, labor, in two of its aspects. (1) The relation of the worker to the *product of labor* as an alien object exercising power over him. This relation is at the same time the relation to the sensuous external world, to the objects of

---

1   *man of means* Property-owner.

2   *mortifies* Imposes hardship on.

nature as an alien world antagonistically opposed to him. (2) The relation of labor to the *act* of *production* within the *labor* process. This relation is the relation of the worker to his own activity as an alien activity not belonging to him; it is activity as suffering, strength as weakness, begetting as emasculating, the worker's own physical and mental energy, his personal life or what is life other than activity—as an activity which is turned against him, neither depends on nor belongs to him. Here we have *self-estrangement*, as we had previously the estrangement of the *thing*.

We have yet a third aspect of *estranged labor* to deduce from the two already considered.

Man is a species being, not only because in practice and in theory he adopts the species as his object (his own as well as those of other things), but—and this is only another way of expressing it—but also because he treats himself as the actual, living species; because he treats himself as a *universal* and therefore a free being.[1]

The life of the species, both in man and in animals, consists physically in the fact that man (like the animal) lives on inorganic nature; and the more universal man is compared with an animal, the more universal is the sphere of inorganic nature on which he lives. Just as plants, animals, stones, the air, light, etc., constitute a part of human consciousness in the realm of theory, partly as objects of natural science, partly as objects of art—his spiritual inorganic nature, spiritual nourishment which he must first prepare to make it palatable and digestible—so too in the realm of practice they constitute a part of human life and human activity. Physically man lives only on these products of nature, whether they appear in the form of food, heating, clothes, a dwelling, or whatever it may be. The universality of man is in practice manifested precisely in the universality which makes all nature his *inorganic* body—both inasmuch as nature is (1) his direct means of life, and (2) the material, the object, and the instrument of his life-activity. Nature is man's *inorganic body-nature*, that is, in so far as it is not

itself the human body. Man *lives* on nature—means that nature is his *body*, with which he must remain in continuous intercourse[2] if he is not to die. That man's physical and spiritual life is linked to nature means simply that nature is linked to itself, for man is a part of nature.

In estranging from man (1) nature, and (2) himself, his own active functions, his life-activity, estranged labor estranges the *species* from man. It turns for him the *life of the species* into a means of individual life. First it estranges the life of the species and individual life, and secondly it makes individual life in its abstract form the purpose of the life of the species, likewise in its abstract and estranged form.

For in the first place labor, *life-activity, productive life* itself, appears to man merely as a *means* of satisfying a need—the need to maintain the physical existence. Yet the productive life is the life of the species. It is life-engendering life. The whole character of a species—its species character—is contained in the character of its life-activity; and free, conscious activity is man's species character. Life itself appears only as *a means* to *life*.

The animal is immediately identical with its life-activity. It does not distinguish itself from it. It is *its life-activity.* Man makes his life-activity itself the object of his will and of his consciousness. He has conscious life-activity. It is not a determination with which he directly merges. Conscious life-activity directly distinguishes man from animal life-activity. It is just because of this that he is a species being. Or it is only because he is a species being that he is a Conscious Being, i.e., that his own life is an object for him. Only because of that is his activity free activity. Estranged labor reverses this relationship, so that it is just because man is a conscious being that he makes his life-activity, his *essential being*, a mere means to his *existence*.

In creating an *objective world* by his practical activity, in *working-up*[3] inorganic nature, man proves himself a conscious species being, i.e., as a being that treats the species as its own essential being, or that treats itself as a species being. Admittedly animals also produce. They build themselves nests, dwellings, like the bees, beavers, ants, etc. But an animal only produces what it immediately needs for itself or its young. It produces one-sidedly, whilst man produces universally. It produces only under the dominion of immediate physical need, while man produces even when

---

1   *he treats ... free being* I.e., humans (alone) can be conscious of their universal nature as a "species-being"—that is, of their general nature as a species—their general human nature; and this consciousness produces freedom. (Other animals, conscious only of their own particular needs, do not have this freedom.) Most male writers from the classical era through the nineteenth century use "man" either to refer exclusively to adult males or in a way that is nominally gender-inclusive but in practice presumes the male to be the norm and the female unworthy of notice. See, however, Marx and Engels' discussion of gender issues in *The Communist Manifesto*.

2   *intercourse* Mutual dealings, social activity. Marx's German term "*Verkehr*," often translated in this way, refers particularly to economic activity.

3   *working-up* Manipulating.

he is free from physical need and only truly produces in freedom therefrom.[1] An animal produces only itself, while man reproduces the whole of nature. An animal's product belongs immediately to its physical body, while man freely confronts his product. An animal forms things in accordance with the standard and the need of the species to which it belongs, whilst man knows how to produce in accordance with the standard of every species, and knows how to apply everywhere the inherent standard to the object. Man therefore also forms things in accordance with the laws of beauty.

It is just in the working-up of the objective world, therefore, that man first really proves himself to be a *species being*. This production is his active species life. Through and because of this production, nature appears as *his* work and his reality. The object of labor is, therefore, the *objectification*[2] of man's species life: for he duplicates himself not only, as in consciousness, intellectually, but also actively, in reality, and therefore he contemplates himself in a world that he has created. In tearing away from man the object of his production, therefore, estranged labor tears from him his *species life*, his real species objectivity, and transforms his advantage over animals into the disadvantage that his inorganic body, nature, is taken from him.

Similarly, in degrading spontaneous activity, free activity, to a means, estranged labor makes man's species life a means to his physical existence.

The consciousness which man has of his species is thus transformed by estrangement in such a way that the species life becomes for him a means.

Estranged labor turns thus:

(3) *Man's species being*, both nature and his spiritual species property, into a being *alien* to him, into a *means* to his *individual existence*. It estranges man's own body from him, as it does external nature and his spiritual essence, his *human* being.

(4) An immediate consequence of the fact that man is estranged from the product of his labor, from his life-activity, from his species being is the *estrangement of man* from *man*. If a man is confronted by himself, he is confronted by the *other* man. What applies to a man's relation to his work, to the product of his labor and to himself, also holds of a man's relation to the other man, and to the other man's labor and object of labor.

In fact, the proposition that man's species nature is estranged from him means that one man is estranged from the other, as each of them is from man's essential nature.

The estrangement of man, and in fact every relationship in which man stands to himself, is first realized and expressed in the relationship in which a man stands to other men.

Hence within the relationship of estranged labor each man views the other in accordance with the standard and the position in which he finds himself as a worker.

We took our departure from a fact of political economy—the estrangement of the worker and his production. We have formulated the concept of this fact—*estranged, alienated* labor. We have analyzed this concept—hence analyzing merely a fact of political economy.

Let us now see, further, how in real life the concept of estranged, alienated labor must express and present itself.

If the product of labor is alien to me, if it confronts me as an alien power, to whom, then, does it belong?

If my own activity does not belong to me, if it is an alien, a coerced activity, to whom, then, *does* it belong?

To a being *other* than me.

Who is this being?

The *gods?* To be sure, in the earliest times the principal production (for example, the building of temples, etc., in Egypt, India and Mexico) appears to be in the service of the gods, and the product belongs to the gods. However, the gods on their own were never the lords of labor. No more was[3] *nature*. And what a contradiction it would be if, the more man subjugated nature by his labor and the more the miracles of the gods were rendered superfluous by the miracles of industry, the more man were to renounce the joy of production and the enjoyment of the produce in favor of these powers.

The *alien* being, to whom labor and the produce of labor belongs, in whose service labor is done and for whose benefit the produce of labor is provided, can only be *man* himself.

If the product of labor does not belong to the worker, if it confronts him as an alien power, this can only be because it belongs to some *other man than the worker*. If the worker's activity is a torment to him, to another it must be *delight* and his life's joy. Not the gods, not nature, but only man himself can be this alien power over man.

---

1   *only truly produces in freedom therefrom*   Truly produces only when free from this (physical need).

2   *objectification*   Presentation in an external object.

3   *No more was*   Neither was.

We must bear in mind the above-stated proposition that man's relation to himself only becomes *objective* and *real* for him through his relation to the other man. Thus, if the product of his labor, his labor *objectified*, is for him an *alien*, hostile, powerful object independent of him, then his position towards it is such that someone else is master of this object, someone who is alien, hostile, powerful, and independent of him. If his own activity is to him an unfree activity, then he is treating it as activity performed in the service, under the dominion, the coercion and the yoke of another man.

Every self-estrangement of man from himself and from nature appears in the relation in which he places himself and nature to men other than and differentiated from himself.[1] For this reason religious self-estrangement necessarily appears in the relationship of the layman to the priest, or again to a mediator, etc., since we are here dealing with the intellectual world. In the real practical world self-estrangement can only become manifest through the real practical relationship to other men. The medium through which estrangement takes place is itself *practical*. Thus through estranged labor man not only engenders his relationship to the object and to the act of production as to powers that are alien and hostile to him; he also engenders the relationship in which other men stand to his production and to his product, and the relationship in which he stands to these other men. Just as he begets his own production as the loss of his reality, as his punishment; just as he begets his own product as a loss, as a product not belonging to him; so he begets the dominion of the one who does not produce over production and over the product.[2] Just as he estranges from himself his own activity, so he confers to the stranger activity which is not his own.

Till now we have only considered this relationship from the standpoint of the worker and later we shall be considering it also from the standpoint of the non-worker.

Through *estranged, alienated labor*, then, the worker produces the relationship to this labor of a man alien to labor and standing outside it.[3] The relationship of the worker to labor engenders the relation to it of the capitalist, or whatever one chooses to call the master of labor. *Private property* is thus the product, the result, the necessary consequence, of *alienated labor*, of the external relation of the worker to nature and to himself.

Private property thus results by analysis from the concept of *alienated labor*—i.e., of *alienated man*, of estranged labor, of estranged life, of *estranged* man.

True, it is as a result of the *movement of private property* that we have obtained the concept of *alienated labor (of alienated life)* from political economy. But on analysis of this concept it becomes clear that though private property appears to be the source, the cause of alienated labor, it is really its consequence, just as the gods *in the beginning* are not the cause but the effect of man's intellectual confusion. Later this relationship becomes reciprocal.

Only at the very culmination of the development of private property does this, its secret, re-emerge, namely, that on the one hand it is the *product* of alienated labor, and that secondly it is the *means* by which labor alienates itself, the *realization of this alienation*.

This exposition immediately sheds light on various hitherto unsolved conflicts.

(1) Political economy starts from labor as the real soul of production; yet to labor it gives nothing, and to private property everything. From this contradiction Proudhon[4] has concluded in favor of labor and against private property. We understand, however, that this apparent contradiction is the contradiction of *estranged labor* with itself, and that political economy has merely formulated the laws of estranged labor.

We also understand, therefore, that *wages* and *private property* are identical: where the product, the object of labor pays for labor itself, the wage is but a necessary consequence of labor's estrangement, for after all in the wage of labor, labor does not appear as an end in itself but as the servant of the wage. We shall develop this point later, and meanwhile will only deduce some conclusions.

A *forcing-up*[5] of wages (disregarding all other difficulties, including the fact that it would only be by force, too, that the higher wages, being an anomaly, could be maintained) would therefore be nothing but *better payment for the slave*,

---

1   *Every ... from himself*   I.e., every self-estrangement of man, from himself and from nature, appears in the relation which he postulates between other men and himself and nature.

2   *so he begets ... over the product*   In the same way he creates the domination of the non-producer over production and its product.

3   *produces the relationship ... standing outside it*   I.e., creates the relation of another man to this labor—a man who does not work,

and is outside the work process.

4   *Proudhon*   Pierre-Joseph Proudhon (1809–65), French political philosopher, one of the first anarchist theoreticians, famous for his slogan, "Property is theft!"

5   *forcing-up*   Enforced increase.

and would not conquer either for the worker or for labor their human status and dignity.

Indeed, even the *equality of wages* demanded by Proudhon only transforms the relationship of the present-day worker to his labor into the relationship of all men to labor. Society is then conceived as an abstract capitalist.

Wages are a direct consequence of estranged labor, and estranged labor is the direct cause of private property. The downfall of the one aspect must therefore mean the downfall of the other.

(2) From the relationship of estranged labor to private property it further follows that the emancipation of society from private property, etc., from servitude, is expressed in the *political* form of the *emancipation of the workers*; not that *their* emancipation alone was at stake but because the emancipation of the workers contains universal human emancipation—and it contains this, because the whole of human servitude is involved in the relation of the worker to production, and every relation of servitude is but a modification and consequence of this relation.

Just as we have found the concept of *private property* from the concept of *estranged, alienated labor* by *analysis*, in the same way every *category* of political economy can be evolved with the help of these two factors; and we shall find again in each category, e.g., trade, competition, capital, money, only a *definite* and *developed expression* of the first foundations.

Before considering this configuration, however, let us try to solve two problems.

(1) To define the general *nature of private property*, as it has arisen as a result of estranged labor, in its relation to *truly human, social property*.

(2) We have accepted the *estrangement of labor*, its *alienation*, as a fact, and we have analyzed this fact. How, we now ask, does *man* come to *alienate*, to estrange, *his labor*? How is this estrangement rooted in the nature of human development? We have already gone a long way to the solution of this problem by *transforming* the question as to the *origin of private property* into the question as to the relation of *alienated labor* to the course of humanity's development. For when one speaks of *private property*, one thinks of being concerned with something external to man. When one speaks of labor, one is directly concerned with man himself. This new formulation of the question already contains its solution.

As to (1): *The general nature of private property and its relation to truly human property.*

Alienated labor has resolved itself for us into two elements which mutually condition one another, or which are but different expressions of one and the same relationship. *Appropriation* appears as *estrangement*, as *alienation*; and *alienation* appears as *appropriation, estrangement* as true *enfranchisement.*[1]

We have considered the one side—*alienated* labor in relation to the *worker* himself, i.e., the *relation of alienated labor to itself*. The *property-relation of the non-worker to the worker and to labor* we have found as the product, the necessary outcome of this relation of alienated labor. *Private property*, as the material, summary expression of alienated labor, embraces both relations—the *relation of the worker to work, to the product of his labor and to the non-worker*, and the relation of the *non-worker to the worker and to the product of his labor*.

Having seen that in relation to the worker who *appropriates* nature by means of his labor, this appropriation *appears* as estrangement, his own spontaneous activity as activity for another and as activity of another, vitality as a sacrifice of life, production of the object as loss of the object to an alien power, to an *alien* person—we shall now consider the relation to the worker, to labor and its object of this person who is *alien* to labor and the worker.

First it has to be noticed, that everything which appears in the worker as an *activity of alienation, of estrangement*, appears in the non-worker as a *state of alienation, of estrangement*.

Secondly, that the worker's *real, practical attitude* in production and to the product (as a state of mind) appears in the non-worker confronting him as a *theoretical* attitude.

Thirdly, the non-worker does everything against the worker which the worker does against himself; but he does not do against himself what he does against the worker.

Let us look more closely at these three relations.[2]

Private Property and Communism

The antithesis of *propertylessness* and *property* so long as it is not comprehended as the antithesis of *labor* and *capital*, still remains an antithesis of indifference, not grasped in its

---

1 *Appropriation ... enfranchisement* I.e., appropriation (taking possession of something) and alienation (or estrangement) are two aspects of the same thing; and the estranged state constitutes enfranchisement—full acceptance into the community.

2 The manuscript breaks off unfinished at this point.

[handwritten note at top: uses Marx as an example to explain his concept of Universal P.P. vs. P.P.]

active connection, its *internal* relation—an antithesis not yet grasped as a *contradiction*. It can find expression in this *first* form even without the advanced development of private property (as in ancient Rome, Turkey, etc.). It does not yet *appear* as having been established by private property itself. But labor, the subjective essence of private property as exclusion of property, and capital, objective labor as exclusion of labor, constitute *private property* as its developed state of contradiction—hence a dynamic relationship moving inexorably to its resolution.

Re. the same page. The transcendence of self-estrangement[1] follows the same course as self-estrangement. *Private property* is first considered only in its objective aspect—but nevertheless with labor as its essence. Its form of existence is therefore *capital*, which is to be annulled[2] "as such" (Proudhon). Or a *particular form* of labor—labor leveled down, parceled, and therefore unfree—is conceived as the source of private property's *perniciousness* and of its existence in estrangement from men; for instance, *Fourier*,[3] who, like the physiocrats,[4] also conceived *agricultural labor* to be at least the *exemplary* type, whilst *Saint-Simon*[5] declares in contrast that *industrial labor* as such is the essence, and now also aspires to[6] the *exclusive* rule of the industrialists and the improvement of the workers' condition. Finally, *communism is the positive* expression of annulled private property—at first as *universal* private property. By embracing this relation as a *whole*, communism is:

(1) In its first form only a *generalization* and *consummation* of this relationship. It shows itself as such in a twofold form: on the one hand, the dominion of *material* property bulks so large that it wants to destroy *everything* which is not capable of being possessed by all as *private property*. It wants to abstract *by force* from talent, etc. For it the sole purpose of life and existence is direct, physical *possession*. The category of *laborer* is not done away with, but extended to all men. The relationship of private property persists as the relationship of the community to the world of things. Finally,

this movement of counterposing[7] universal private property to private property finds expression in the bestial form of counterposing to *marriage* (certainly a *form of exclusive private property*) the *community of women*, in which a woman becomes a piece of *communal* and *common* property. It may be said that this idea of the *community of women* gives away the *secret* of this as yet completely crude and thoughtless communism. Just as the woman passes from marriage to general prostitution,[8] so the entire world of wealth (that is, of man's objective substance[9]) passes from the relationship of exclusive marriage with the owner of private property to a state of universal prostitution with the community. In negating the *personality* of man in every sphere; this type of communism is really nothing but the logical expression of private property, which is this negation. General *envy* constituting itself as a power is the disguise in which *avarice* reestablishes itself and satisfies itself, only in *another* way. The thoughts of every piece of private property—inherent in each piece as such—are *at least* turned against all *wealthier* private property in the form of envy and the urge to reduce to a common level,[10] so that this envy and urge even constitute the essence of competition. The crude communism is only the consummation of this envy and of this leveling down to a *preconceived* minimum. It has a *definite, limited* standard. How little this annulment of private property is really an appropriation is in fact proved by the abstract negation of the entire world of culture and civilization, the regression to the *unnatural* simplicity of the *poor and undemanding* man who has not only failed to go beyond private property, but has not yet even attained to it.

The community[11] is only a community of *labor*, and an equality of *wages* paid out by the communal capital—the *community* as the universal capitalist. Both sides of the relationship are raised to an *imagined*[12] universality—labor as a state in which every person is put, and *capital* as the acknowledged universality and power of the community.

---

1   *transcendence of self-estrangement*   Overcoming of self-alienation.
2   *annulled*   Abolished.
3   *Fourier*   François Marie Charles Fourier (1772–1837), French utopian socialist and early theorist of alienation.
4   *physiocrats*   French economists, influential during the second half of the eighteenth century, who idealized agriculture and rural life.
5   *Saint-Simon*   Claude Henri de Rouvroy, comte de Saint-Simon (1760–1825), the founder of French socialism.
6   *aspires to*   Demands.
7   *counterposing*   Contrasting.
8   *Just as the woman ... prostitution*   [Marx's note] Prostitution is only a *specific* expression of the *general* prostitution of the *laborer*, and since it is a relationship in which falls not the prostitute alone, but also the one who prostitutes—and the latter's abomination is still greater—the capitalist, etc., also comes under this head.
9   *substance*   Essence.
10   *The thoughts ... common level*   I.e., each thought about a piece of private property ... is turned against all wealthier property....
11   *The community*   According to this "first form" of communism, that is.
12   *imagined*   False.

In the approach to *woman* as the spoil and handmaid of communal lust is expressed the infinite degradation in which man exists for himself, for the secret of this approach has its *unambiguous*, decisive, *plain* and undisguised expression in the relation of *man* to *woman* and in the manner in which the *direct* and *natural* procreative relationship is conceived. The direct, natural, and necessary relation of person to person is the *relation* of *man* to *woman*. In this *natural* relationship of the sexes man's relation to nature is immediately his relation to man, just as his relation to man is immediately his relation to nature—his own *natural* function. In this relationship, therefore, is *sensuously manifested*, reduced to an observable *fact*, the extent to which the human essence has become nature to man, or to which nature has to him become the human essence of man. From this relationship one can therefore judge man's whole level of development. It follows from the character of this relationship how much *man as a species being*, as *man*, has come to be himself and to comprehend himself; the relation of man to woman is *the most natural* relation of human being to human being. It therefore reveals the extent to which man's *natural* behavior has become *human*, or the extent to which the *human* essence in him has become a *natural* essence—the extent to which his *human nature* has come to be *nature to him*. In this relationship is revealed, too, the extent to which man's *need* has become a *human* need; the extent to which, therefore, the *other* person as a person has become for him a need—the extent to which he in his individual existence is at the same time a social being. The first positive annulment of private property—crude communism—is thus merely one *form* in which the vileness of private property, which wants to set itself up as the *positive community, comes to the surface*.

(2) Communism[1] (a) of a political nature still—democratic or despotic; (b) with the annulment of the state, yet still incomplete, and being still affected by private property (i.e., by the estrangement of man). In both forms communism already knows itself to be re-integration or return of man to himself, the transcendence[2] of human self-estrangement; but since it has not yet grasped the positive essence of private property, and just as little the *human* nature of need, it remains captive to it and infected by it. It has, indeed, grasped its concept, but not its essence.

(3) *Communism*[3] as the *positive* transcendence of *private property*, or *human self-estrangement*, and therefore as the real *appropriation of the human* essence by and for man; communism therefore as the complete return of man to himself as a *social* (i.e., human) being—a return become conscious, and accomplished within the entire wealth of previous development. This communism, as fully-developed naturalism, equals humanism, and as fully-developed humanism equals naturalism; it is the *genuine* resolution of the conflict between man and nature and between man and man—the true resolution of the strife between existence and essence, between objectification and self-confirmation, between freedom and necessity, between the individual and the species. Communism is the riddle of history solved, and it knows itself to be this solution.

The entire movement of history is, therefore, both its *actual* act of genesis (the birth act of its empirical existence) and also for its thinking consciousness, the *comprehended* and *known* process of its *coming-to-be*. That other, still immature communism, meanwhile, seeks an *historical* proof for itself—a proof in the realm of the existent—amongst disconnected historical phenomena opposed to private property, tearing single phases from the historical process and focusing attention on them as proofs of its historical pedigree (a horse ridden hard especially by Cabet, Villegardelle,[4] etc.). By so doing it simply makes clear that by far the greater part of this process contradicts its claims, and that, if it has once been, precisely its being in the *past* refutes its pretension to being *essential*.

That the entire revolutionary movement necessarily finds both its empirical and its theoretical basis in the movement of *private property*—in that of the economy, to be precise—is easy to see.

This *material*, immediately *sensuous* private property is the material sensuous expression of *estranged human* life. Its movement—production and consumption—is the *sensuous* revelation of the movement of all production hitherto—i.e., the realization or the reality of man. Religion, family, state, law, morality, science, art, etc., are only *particular* modes of production, and fall under its general law. The positive transcendence of *private property* as the appropriation

---

1 *Communism* Here Marx talks about a second form of communism.
2 *transcendence* Passing beyond.

3 *Communism* And here the third stage.
4 *Cabet, Villegardelle* Etienne Cabet (1788–1856) and François Villegardelle (1810–56), French utopian socialists. Cabet developed a theory of communism influenced by Robert Owen. Several "Icarian" communities (so called after Cabet's *Voyage en Icarie* [1840]) were founded in the United States.

of human life is, therefore, the positive transcendence of all estrangement—that is to say, the return of man from religion, family, state, etc., to his *human*, i.e., *social* mode of existence. Religious estrangement as such occurs only in the realm of *consciousness*, of man's inner life, but economic estrangement is that of *real life*; its transcendence therefore embraces both aspects. It is evident that the *initial* stage of the movement amongst the various peoples depends on whether the true and for them *authentic* life of the people manifests itself more in consciousness or in the external world—is more ideal or real. Communism begins from the outset (*Owen*[1]) with atheism; but atheism is at first far from being *communism*; indeed, it is still mostly an abstraction.

The philanthropy of atheism is therefore at first only *philosophical*, abstract, philanthropy, and that of communism is at once *real* and directly bent on *action*.

We have seen how on the premise of positively annulled private property man produces man—himself and the other man; how the object, being the direct embodiment of his individuality, is simultaneously his own existence for the other man, the existence of the other man, and that existence for him. Likewise, however, both the material of labor and man as the subject, are the point of departure as well as the result of the movement (and precisely in this fact, that they must constitute the *point of departure*, lies the historical *necessity* of private property). Thus the *social* character is the general character of the whole movement: *just as* society itself produces *man as man*, so is society *produced* by him. Activity and consumption, both in their content and in their *mode of existence*, are *social*: *social* activity and *social* consumption; the *human* essence of nature first exists only for *social* man; for only here does nature exist for him as a *bond* with man—as his existence for the other and the other's existence for him—as the life-element of the human world; only here does nature exist as the *foundation* of his own *human* existence. Only here has what is to him his *natural* existence become his *human* existence, and nature become man for him. Thus *society* is the consummated oneness in substance of man and nature—the true resurrection of nature—the naturalism of man and the humanism of nature both brought to fulfillment.

Social activity and social consumption exist by no means *only* in the form of some *directly* communal activity and *directly* communal consumption, although *communal* activity and *communal* consumption—i.e., activity and consumption which are manifested and directly confirmed in *real association* with other men—will occur wherever such a *direct* expression of sociality[2] stems from the true character of the activity's content and is adequate to the nature of consumption.

But again when I am active *scientifically*, etc.,—when I am engaged in activity which I can seldom perform in direct community with others—then I am *social*, because I am active as a *man*. Not only is the material of my activity given to me as a social product (as is even the language in which the thinker is active): my own existence *is* social activity, and therefore that which I make of myself, I make of myself for society and with the consciousness of myself as a social being.

My *general* consciousness is only the *theoretical* shape of that of which the *living* shape is the *real* community, the social fabric, although at the present day *general* consciousness is an abstraction from real life and as such antagonistically confronts it. Consequently, too, the *activity* of my general consciousness, as an activity, is my *theoretical* existence as a social being.

What is to be avoided above all is the re-establishing of "Society" as an abstraction *vis-à-vis*[3] the individual. The individual *is the social being*. His life, even if it may not appear in the direct form of a *communal* life carried out together with others—is therefore an expression and confirmation of *social life*. Man's individual and species life are not *different*, however much—and this is inevitable—the mode of existence of the individual is a more *particular*, or more *general* mode of the life of the species, or the life of the species is a more *particular* or more *general* individual life.

In his *consciousness of species* man confirms his real *social* life and simply repeats his real existence in thought, just as conversely the being of the species confirms itself in species-consciousness and is for *itself* in its generality as a thinking being.

Man, much as he may therefore be a *particular* individual (and it is precisely his particularity which makes him an individual, and a real *individual* social being), is just as much the *totality*—the ideal totality—the subjective existence of thought and experienced society present for itself; just as he exists also in the real world as the awareness and

---

1   *Owen*   Robert Owen (1771–1851), Welsh industrialist and social reformer. He formed a model industrial community at New Lanark, Scotland, and pioneered cooperative societies.

2   *sociality*   Sociability.

3   *vis-à-vis*   With respect to.

the real enjoyment of social existence, and as a totality of human life-activity.

Thinking and being are thus no doubt *distinct*, but at the same time they are in *unity* with each other.

Death seems to be a harsh victory of the species over the *definite* individual and to contradict their unity. But the determinate individual is only a *determinate species being*, and as such mortal.

(4) Just as *private property* is only the sensuous expression of the fact that man becomes *objective* for himself and at the same time becomes to himself a strange and inhuman object; just as it expresses the fact that the assertion of his life is the alienation of his life, that his realization is his loss of reality, is an *alien* reality: conversely, the positive transcendence of private property—i.e., the *sensuous* appropriation for and by man of the human essence and of human life, of objective man, of human *achievements*—is not to be conceived merely in the sense of *direct*, one-sided *gratification*—merely in the sense of *possessing*, of *having*. Man appropriates his total essence in a total manner, that is to say, as a whole man. Each of his *human* relations to the world—seeing, hearing, smelling, tasting, feeling, thinking, being aware, sensing, wanting, acting, loving—in short, all the organs of his individual being, like those organs which are directly social in their form, are in their *objective* orientation or in their *orientation* to *the object*, the appropriation of that object, the appropriation of the *human* world; their orientation to the object is the *manifestation of the human world*;[1] it is human *efficaciousness* and human *suffering*, for suffering, apprehended humanly, is an enjoyment of self in man.

Private property has made us so stupid and one-sided that an object is only *ours* when we have it—when it exists for us as capital, or when it is directly possessed, eaten, drunk, worn, inhabited, etc.,—in short, when it is *used* by us. Although private property itself again conceives all these direct realizations of possession as *means of life*, and the life which they serve as means is the life of private property—labor and conversion into capital.

In place of *all* these physical and mental senses there has therefore come the sheer estrangement of *all* these senses—the sense of *having*. The human being had to be reduced to this absolute poverty in order that he might yield his inner wealth to the outer world. (On the category of "*having*," see Hess in the *Twenty-One Sheets*.)[2]

The transcendence of private property is therefore the complete *emancipation* of all human senses and attributes; but it is this emancipation precisely because these senses and attributes have become, subjectively and objectively, *human*. The eye has become a *human* eye, just as its *object* has become a social, *human* object—an object emanating from man for man. The *senses* have therefore become directly in their practice *theoreticians*. They relate themselves to the *thing* for the sake of the thing, but the thing itself is an *objective human* relation to itself and to man,[3] and vice versa. Need or enjoyment have consequently lost their *egotistical* nature, and nature has lost its mere *utility* by use becoming *human* use.

In the same way, the senses and enjoyments of other men have become my own appropriation. Besides these direct organs, therefore, *social* organs develop in the *form* of society; thus, for instance, activity in direct association with others, etc., has become an organ for *expressing* my own *life*, and a mode of appropriating *human life*.

It is obvious that the *human* eye gratifies itself in a way different from the crude, non-human eye; the human *ear* different from the crude ear, etc.

To recapitulate; man is not lost in his object only when the object becomes for him a *human* object or objective man. This is possible only when the object becomes for him a *social* object, he himself for himself a social being, just as society becomes a being for him in this object.

On the one hand, therefore, it is only when the objective world becomes everywhere for man in society the world of man's essential powers—human reality, and for that reason the reality of his own essential powers—that all *objects* become for him the *objectification of himself*, become objects which confirm and realize his individuality, become *his* objects: that is, *man himself* becomes the object. The manner in which they become *his* depends on the *nature of the objects* and on the nature of the *essential power* corresponding *to it*; for it is precisely the *determinateness* of this relationship which shapes the particular, *real* mode of affirmation. To

---

1 *manifestation of the human world* [Marx's note] For this reason it is just as highly priced as the *determinations* of human *essence* and *activities*.

2 *Hess … Twenty-One Sheets* Moses Hess (1812–75), a German writer, was a pioneer of socialist thought, and a precursor of Zionist thinkers; Marx here refers to his *Philosophische und Sozialistische Aufsätze*.

3 *They relate … to man* [Marx's note] In practice I can relate myself to a thing humanly only if the thing relates itself to the human being humanly.

the *eye* an object comes to be other than it is to the *ear*, and the object of the eye is another object than the object of the *ear*. The peculiarity of each essential power is precisely its *peculiar essence*, and therefore also the peculiar mode of its objectification, of its *objectively actual* living *being*. Thus man is affirmed in the objective world not only in the act of thinking, but with *all* his senses.

On the other hand, looking at this in its subjective aspect: just as music alone awakens in man the sense of music, and just as the most beautiful music has no sense for the unmusical ear—is no object for it, because my object can only be the confirmation of one of my essential powers and can therefore only be so for me as my essential power is present for itself as a subjective capacity, because the sense of an object for me goes only so far as my senses go (has only sense for a sense corresponding to that object)—for this reason the *senses* of the social man are *other* senses than those of the non-social man. Only through the objectively unfolded richness of man's essential being is the richness of subjective *human* sensibility (a musical ear, an eye for beauty of form—in short, *senses* capable of human gratifications, senses confirming themselves as essential powers of man) either cultivated or brought into being. For not only the five senses but also the so-called mental senses—the practical senses (will, love, etc,)—in a word, *human* sense—the humanness of the senses—comes to be by virtue of its object, by virtue of *human* nature. The *forming* of the five senses is a labor of the entire history of the world down to the present.

The *sense* caught up in crude practical need has only a *restricted* sense. For the starving man, it is not the human form of food that exists, but only its abstract being as food; it could just as well be there in its crudest form, and it would be impossible to say wherein this feeding-activity differs from that of *animals*. The care-burdened man in need has no sense for the finest play; the dealer in minerals sees only the mercantile value but not the beauty and the unique nature of the mineral: he has no mineralogical sense. Thus, the objectification of the human essence both in its theoretical and practical aspects is required to make man's *sense human*, as well as to create the *human sense* corresponding to the entire wealth of human and natural substance.

Just as resulting from the movement of *private property*, of its wealth as well as its poverty—or of its material and spiritual wealth and poverty—the budding society finds to hand all the material for this *development*: so *established* society produces man in this entire richness of his be-ing—produces the *rich* man *profoundly endowed with all the senses*—as its enduring reality.

It will be seen how subjectivism and objectivism, spiritualism and materialism, activity and suffering, only lose their antithetical character, and thus their existence, as such antitheses in the social condition; it will be seen how the resolution of the *theoretical* antitheses is *only* possible in *a practical* way, by virtue of the practical energy of men. Their resolution is therefore by no means merely a problem of knowledge, but a *real* problem of life, which *philosophy* could not solve precisely because it conceived this problem as *merely* a theoretical one.

It will be seen how the history of *industry* and the established *objective* existence of industry are the *open* book of *man's essential powers*, the exposure to the senses of human *psychology*. Hitherto this was not conceived in its inseparable connection with man's *essential being*, but only in an external relation of utility, because, moving in the realm of estrangement, people could only think man's general mode of being—religion or history in its abstract-general character as politics, art, literature, etc.,—to be the reality of man's essential powers and *man's species-activity*. We have before us the *objectified essential powers* of man in the form of *sensuous, alien, useful objects*, in the form of estrangement, displayed in *ordinary material industry* (which can be conceived as a part of that general movement, just as that movement can be conceived as a particular part of industry, since all human activity hitherto has been labor—that is, industry-activity estranged from itself).

A *psychology* for which this, the part of history most contemporary and accessible to sense, remains a closed book, cannot become a genuine, comprehensive and *real* science. What indeed are we to think of a science which *airily abstracts from*[1] this large part of human labor and which fails to feel its own incompleteness, while such a wealth of human endeavor unfolded before it means nothing more to it than, perhaps, what can be expressed in one word—"need," "*vulgar need*"?

The *natural sciences* have developed an enormous activity and have accumulated a constantly growing mass of material. Philosophy, however, has remained just as alien to them as they remain to philosophy. Their momentary unity was only a *chimerical*[2] illusion. The will was there, but the means were lacking. Even historiography[3] pays regard

---

1   *airily abstracts from*   Casually disregards.
2   *chimerical*   Imaginary.
3   *historiography*   The study of the writing of history.

to natural science only occasionally, as a factor of enlightenment and utility arising from individual great discoveries. But natural science has invaded and transformed human life all the more *practically* through the medium of industry; and has prepared human emancipation, however directly and much it had to consummate dehumanization. *Industry* is the *actual*, historical relation of nature, and therefore of natural science, to man. If, therefore, industry is conceived as the *exoteric* revelation of man's *essential powers*, we also gain an understanding of the *human* essence of nature or the *natural* essence of man. In consequence, natural science will lose its abstractly material[1]—or rather, its idealistic tendency, and will become the basis of *human* science, as it has already become the basis of actual human life, albeit in an estranged form. *One basis* for life and another basis for *science* is *a priori* a lie. The nature which comes to be in human history—the genesis of human society—is man's *real* nature; hence nature as it comes to be through industry, even though in an *estranged* form, is true *anthropological* nature.

Sense-perception (see Feuerbach) must be the basis of all science. Only when it proceeds from sense-perception in the twofold form both of *sensuous* consciousness and of *sensuous* need—that is, only when science proceeds from nature—is it *true* science. All history is the preparation for "*man*" to become the object of *sensuous* consciousness, and for the needs of "man as man" to become [natural, sensuous] needs. History itself is a *real* part of *natural history*—of nature's coming to be man. Natural science will in time subsume under itself the science of man, just as the science of man will subsume under itself natural science: there will be *one* science.

Man is the immediate object of natural science: for immediate, *sensuous nature* for man is, immediately, human sensuousness (the expressions are identical)—presented immediately in the form of the *other* man sensuously present for him. For his own sensuousness first exists as human sensuousness for himself through the *other* man. But *nature* is the immediate object of the *science of man*: the first object of man—man—is nature, sensuousness; and the particular human sensuous essential powers can only find their self-knowledge in the science of the natural world in general, since they can find their objective realization in *natural* objects only. The element of thought itself—the element of thought's living expression—*language*—is of a sensuous nature. The *social* reality of nature, and *human* natural science, or the *natural science about man*, are identical terms.

It will be seen how in place of the *wealth* and *poverty* of political economy come the *rich human being* and rich *human* need. The *rich* human being is simultaneously the human being *in need of* a totality of human life-activities—the man in whom his own realization exists as an inner necessity, as *need*. Not only *wealth*, but likewise the *poverty* of man—given socialism—receives in equal measure a *human* and therefore social significance. Poverty is the passive bond which causes the human being to experience the need of the greatest wealth—the *other* human being. The dominion of the objective being in me, the sensuous outburst of my essential activity, is *emotion*, which thus becomes here the *activity* of my being.

(5) A *being* only considers himself independent when he stands on his own feet; and he only stands on his own feet when he owes his *existence* to himself. A man who lives by the grace of another regards himself as a dependent being. But I live completely by the grace of another if I owe him not only the sustenance of my life, but if he has, moreover, *created* my *life*—if he is the *source* of my life; and if it is not of my own creation, my life has necessarily a source of this kind outside it. The *Creation* is therefore an idea very difficult to dislodge from popular consciousness. The self-mediated being of nature and of man is *incomprehensible* to it, because it contradicts everything *palpable* in practical life.

The creation of the *earth* has received a mighty blow from geogeny—i.e., from the science which presents the formation of the earth, the coming-to-be of the earth, as a process, as self-generation. *Generatio aequivoca*[2] is the only practical refutation of the theory of creation.

Now it is certainly easy to say to the single individual what Aristotle has already said: You have been begotten by your father and your mother; therefore in you the mating of two human beings—a species-act of human beings—has produced the human being. You see, therefore, that even physically, man owes his existence to man. Therefore you must not only keep sight of the one aspect—the *infinite* progression which leads you further to enquire: "Who begot my father? Who his grandfather?" etc. You must also hold on to the *circular movement* sensuously percep-

---

1   *material* Materialist.

2   *Generatio aequivoca* Latin: spontaneous generation—the pre-scientific idea that non-living material can produce living organisms—for example, that mud produces frogs.

tible in that progression, by which *man* repeats himself in procreation, thus always remaining the subject. You will reply, however: I grant you this circular movement; now grant me the progression which drives me even further until I ask: Who begot the first man, and nature as a whole? I can only answer you: Your question is itself a product of abstraction. Ask yourself how you arrived at that question. Ask yourself whether your question is not posed from a standpoint to which I cannot reply, because it is a perverse one. Ask yourself whether that progression as such exists for a reasonable mind. When you ask about the creation of nature and man, you are abstracting, in so doing, from man and nature. You postulate them as *non-existent*, and yet you want me to prove them to you as *existing*. Now I say to you: Give up your abstraction and you will also give up your question. Or if you want to hold on to your abstraction, then be consistent, and if you think of man and nature as *non-existent*, then think of yourself as non-existent, for you too are surely nature and man. Don't think, don't ask me, for as soon as you think and ask, your *abstraction* from the existence of nature and man has no meaning. Or are you such an egoist that you postulate everything as nothing, and yet want yourself to be?

You can reply: I do not want to postulate the nothing-ness of nature. I ask you about *its genesis*, just as I ask the anatomist about the formation of bones, etc.

But since for the socialist man the *entire so-called history of the world* is nothing but the begetting of man through human labor, nothing but the coming-to-be of nature for man, he has the visible, irrefutable proof of his *birth* through himself, of his *process* of *coming-to-be*. Since the *real existence* of man and nature has become practical, sensuous and perceptible—since man has become for man as the be-ing of nature, and nature for man as the being of man—the question about an *alien* being, about a being above nature and man—a question which implies the admission of the inessentiality of nature and of man—has become impos-sible in practice. *Atheism*, as the denial of this inessentiality, has no longer any meaning, for atheism is a *negation of God*, and postulates the *existence of man* through this negation; but socialism as socialism no longer stands in any need of such a mediation. It proceeds from the *practically and theor-etically sensuous consciousness* of man and of nature as the *essence*. Socialism is man's *positive self-consciousness* no longer mediated through the annulment of religion, just as *real life* is man's positive reality, no longer mediated through the annulment of private property, through *communism*. Com-munism is the position as the negation of the negation, and is hence the *actual* phase necessary for the next stage of his-torical development in the process of human emancipation and recovery. *Communism* is the necessary pattern and the dynamic principle of the immediate future, but commun-ism as such is not the goal of human development—the structure of human society.

◆ ◆ ◆ ◆ ◆

The German Ideology (1845)

A. Ideology in General, German Ideology in Particular

German criticism has, right up to its latest efforts, never quitted the realm of philosophy. Far from examining its general philosophic premises, the whole body of its inquir-ies has actually sprung from the soil of a definite philosoph-ical system, that of Hegel. Not only in their answers but in their very questions there was a mystification. This depend-ence on Hegel is the reason why not one of these modern critics has even attempted a comprehensive criticism of the Hegelian system, however much each professes to have advanced beyond Hegel. Their polemics against Hegel and against one another are confined to this—each extracts one side of the Hegelian system and turns this against the whole system as well as against the sides extracted by the others. To begin with they extracted pure unfalsified Hegelian categor-ies such as "substance" and "self-consciousness," later they desecrated these categories with more secular names such as "species," "the Unique," "Man," etc.

The entire body of German philosophical criticism from Strauss[1] to Stirner[2] is confined to criticism of religious conceptions. [The following passage is crossed out in the manuscript:] claiming to be the absolute redeemer of the world from all evil. Religion was continually regarded and treated as the arch-enemy, as the ultimate cause of all rela-tions repugnant to these philosophers. The critics started

---

1 *Strauss* David Friedrich Strauss (1808–74), German Hegelian theologian who created a scandal with his historical account of Jesus, calling into question his divinity.

2 *Stirner* Max Stirner (pen name of Johann Kaspar Schmidt, 1806–56), German philosopher, important in the development of nihilism, existentialism, and individualistic anarchism.

from real religion and actual theology. What religious consciousness and a religious conception really meant was determined variously as they went along. Their advance consisted in subsuming the allegedly dominant metaphysical, political, juridical, moral and other conceptions under the class of religious or theological conceptions; and similarly in pronouncing political, juridical, moral consciousness as religious or theological, and the political, juridical, moral man—"man" in the last resort—as religious. The dominance of religion was taken for granted. Gradually every dominant relationship was pronounced a religious relationship and transformed into a cult, a cult of law, a cult of the State, etc. On all sides it was only a question of dogmas and belief in dogmas. The world was sanctified to an ever-increasing extent till at last our venerable Saint Max[1] was able to canonize it en bloc and thus dispose of it once for all.

The Old Hegelians had comprehended everything as soon as it was reduced to an Hegelian logical category. The Young Hegelians criticized everything by attributing to it religious conceptions or by pronouncing it a theological matter. The Young Hegelians are in agreement with the Old Hegelians in their belief in the rule of religion, of concepts, of a universal principle in the existing world. Only, the one party[2] attacks this dominion as usurpation while the other[3] extols it as legitimate.

Since the Young Hegelians consider conceptions, thoughts, ideas, in fact all the products of consciousness, to which they attribute an independent existence, as the real chains of men (just as the Old Hegelians declared them the true bonds of human society) it is evident that the Young Hegelians have to fight only against these illusions of consciousness. Since, according to their fantasy, the relationships of men, all their doings, their chains and their limitations are products of their consciousness, the Young Hegelians logically put to men the moral postulate of exchanging their present consciousness for human, critical or egoistic[4] consciousness, and thus of removing their limitations. This demand to change consciousness amounts to a

demand to interpret reality in another way, i.e., to recognize it by means of another interpretation. The Young-Hegelian ideologists, in spite of their allegedly "world-shattering" statements, are the staunchest conservatives. The most recent of them have found the correct expression for their activity when they declare they are only fighting against "phrases." They forget, however, that to these phrases they themselves are only opposing other phrases, and that they are in no way combating the real existing world when they are merely combating the phrases of this world. The only results which this philosophic criticism could achieve were a few (and at that thoroughly one-sided) elucidations of Christianity from the point of view of religious history; all the rest of their assertions are only further embellishments of their claim to have furnished, in these unimportant elucidations, discoveries of universal importance.

It has not occurred to any one of these philosophers to inquire into the connection of German philosophy with German reality, the relation of their criticism to their own material surroundings.

The premises from which we begin are not arbitrary ones, not dogmas, but real premises from which abstraction can only be made in the imagination. They are the real individuals, their activity and the material conditions under which they live, both those which they find already existing and those produced by their activity. These premises can thus be verified in a purely empirical way.

The first premise of all human history is, of course, the existence of living human individuals. Thus the first fact to be established is the physical organization of these individuals and their consequent relation to the rest of nature. Of course, we cannot here go either into the actual physical nature of man, or into the natural conditions in which man finds himself—geological, hydrographical,[5] climatic and so on. The writing of history must always set out from these natural bases and their modification in the course of history through the action of men.

Men can be distinguished from animals by consciousness, by religion or anything else you like. They themselves begin to distinguish themselves from animals as soon as they begin to produce their means of subsistence, a step which is conditioned by their physical organization. By producing their means of subsistence men are indirectly producing their actual material life.

---

1 *Saint Max* Stirner (see above note). Marx gives him this nickname indicating that Stirner interprets material relationships as spiritual. "Saint Bruno" below refers with the same implication to Bruno Bauer.

2 *the one party* I.e., the Young or left-wing Hegelians.

3 *the other* I.e., the Old or right-wing Hegelians.

4 *human … egoistic* These words refer to catch-phrases associated with the work of Feuerbach ("human"), Bauer ("critical") and Stirner ("egoistic").

5 *hydrographical* Having to do with the scientific study of bodies of water.

O - Different forms of Divided Labour; tribal, slavery
↳ First Form

The way in which men produce their means of subsistence depends first of all on the nature of the actual means of subsistence they find in existence and have to reproduce. This mode of production must not be considered simply as being the production of the physical existence of the individuals. Rather it is a definite form of activity of these individuals, a definite form of expressing their life, a definite mode of life on their part. As individuals express their life, so they are. What they are, therefore, coincides with their production, both with what they produce and with how they produce. The nature of individuals thus depends on the material conditions determining their production.

This production only makes its appearance with the increase of population. In its turn this presupposes the intercourse[1] of individuals with one another. The form of this intercourse is again determined by production.

The relations of different nations among themselves depend upon the extent to which each has developed its productive forces, the division of labor and internal intercourse. This statement is generally recognized. But not only the relation of one nation to others, but also the whole internal structure of the nation itself depends on the stage of development reached by its production and its internal and external intercourse. How far the productive forces of a nation are developed is shown most manifestly by the degree to which the division of labor has been carried. Each new productive force, insofar as it is not merely a quantitative extension of productive forces already known (for instance the bringing into cultivation of fresh land), causes a further development of the division of labor.

The division of labor inside a nation leads at first to the separation of industrial and commercial from agricultural labor, and hence to the separation of town and country and to the conflict of their interests. Its further development leads to the separation of commercial from industrial labor. At the same time through the division of labor inside these various branches there develop various divisions among the individuals cooperating in definite kinds of labor. The relative position of these individual groups is determined by the methods employed in agriculture, industry and commerce (patriarchalism, slavery, estates,[2] classes). These same condi-tions are to be seen (given a more developed intercourse) in the relations of different nations to one another.

The various stages of development in the division of labor are just so many different forms of ownership, i.e., the existing stage in the division of labor determines also the relations of individuals to one another with reference to the material, instrument, and product of labor.

The first form of ownership is tribal ownership. It corresponds to the undeveloped stage of production, at which a people lives by hunting and fishing, by the rearing of beasts or, in the highest stage, agriculture. In the latter case it presupposes a great mass of uncultivated stretches of land. The division of labor is at this stage still very elementary and is confined to a further extension of the natural division of labor existing in the family. The social structure is, therefore, limited to an extension of the family; patriarchal family chieftains, below them the members of the tribe, finally slaves. The slavery latent in the family only develops gradually with the increase of population, the growth of wants, and with the extension of external relations, both of war and of barter.

The second form is the ancient communal and State ownership which proceeds especially from the union of several tribes into a city by agreement or by conquest, and which is still accompanied by slavery. Beside communal ownership we already find movable, and later also immovable, private property[3] developing, but as an abnormal form subordinate to communal ownership. The citizens hold power over their laboring slaves only in their community, and on this account alone, therefore, they are bound to the form of communal ownership. It is the communal private property which compels the active citizens to remain in this spontaneously derived form of association over against their slaves. For this reason the whole structure of society based on this communal ownership, and with it the power of the people, decays in the same measure as, in particular, immovable private property evolves. The division of labor is already more developed. We already find the antagonism of town and country; later the antagonism between those states which represent town interests and those which represent country interests, and inside the towns themselves the antagonism between industry and maritime commerce. The

---

1   *intercourse* Mutual dealings, social activity (particularly, in this case, activity having to do with economic relations).

2   *estates* Historical divisions of European society into sectors of political power, traditionally the clergy, the nobility, and the middle class.

3   *movable ... immovable* The former is property which can be given a monetary value, and transformed into money; the latter is property which cannot, such as land and buildings.

O - Second Form

class relation between citizens and slaves is now completely developed.

With the development of private property, we find here for the first time the same conditions which we shall find again, only on a more extensive scale, with modern private property. On the one hand, the concentration of private property, which began very early in Rome (as the Licinian agrarian law[1] proves) and proceeded very rapidly from the time of the civil wars and especially under the Emperors; on the other hand, coupled with this, the transformation of the plebeian small peasantry into a proletariat,[2] which, however, owing to its intermediate position between propertied citizens and slaves, never achieved an independent development.

The third form of ownership is feudal or estate property. If antiquity started out from the town and its little territory, the Middle Ages started out from the country. This different starting-point was determined by the sparseness of the population at that time, which was scattered over a large area and which received no large increase from the conquerors. In contrast to Greece and Rome, feudal development at the outset, therefore, extends over a much wider territory, prepared by the Roman conquests and the spread of agriculture at first associated with it. The last centuries of the declining Roman Empire and its conquest by the barbarians destroyed a number of productive forces; agriculture had declined, industry had decayed for want of a market, trade had died out or been violently suspended, the rural and urban population had decreased. From these conditions and the mode of organization of the conquest determined by them, feudal property developed under the influence of the Germanic military constitution. Like tribal and communal ownership, it is based again on a community; but the directly producing class standing over against it is not, as in the case of the ancient community, the slaves, but the enserfed[3] small peasantry. As soon as feudalism is fully developed, there also arises antagonism to the towns.

The hierarchical structure of land ownership, and the armed bodies of retainers[4] associated with it, gave the nobility power over the serfs. This feudal organization was, just as much as the ancient communal ownership, an association against a subjected[5] producing class; but the form of association and the relation to the direct producers were different because of the different conditions of production.

This feudal system of land ownership had its counterpart in the towns in the shape of corporative property, the feudal organization of trades. Here property consisted chiefly in the labor of each individual person. The necessity for association against the organized robber-nobility, the need for communal covered markets in an age when the industrialist was at the same time a merchant, the growing competition of the escaped serfs swarming into the rising towns, the feudal structure of the whole country: these combined to bring about the guilds. The gradually accumulated small capital of individual craftsmen and their stable numbers, as against the growing population, evolved the relation of journeyman and apprentice,[6] which brought into being in the towns a hierarchy similar to that in the country.

Thus the chief form of property during the feudal epoch consisted on the one hand of landed property with serf labor chained to it, and on the other of the labor of the individual with small capital commanding the labor of journeymen. The organization of both was determined by the restricted conditions of production—the small-scale and primitive cultivation of the land, and the craft type of industry. There was little division of labor in the heyday of feudalism. Each country bore in itself the antithesis of town and country; the division into estates was certainly strongly marked; but apart from the differentiation of princes, nobility, clergy and peasants in the country, and masters, journeymen, apprentices and soon also the rabble of casual laborers in the towns, no division of importance took place. In agriculture it was rendered difficult by the strip-system,[7] beside which

1   *Licinian agrarian law*   Roman law passed in 367 BCE, limiting the amount of public land that a single citizen could hold.
2   *plebeian small peasantry ... proletariat*   "Plebeians" were the ordinary people (as opposed to the nobility) in ancient Rome; the "small peasantry" was the class of people who farmed small parcels of land, with the produce being intended largely for their own use, not for trade. The "proletariat" is the working class—people who do not own any means of production, and who therefore must sell their labor to earn a living.
3   *enserfed*   In the position of serfhood. Serfs received the use of land from a lord in exchange for rent or labor. Serfs inherited their position of obligation to a lord from their parents and were bought and sold with the land.
4   *retainers*   Paid servants.
5   *subjected*   Subject to the rule of another.
6   *journeyman and apprentice*   An apprentice was bound legally to work for a skilled craftsman for a certain time, in exchange for training. A journeyman was one who had completed his apprenticeship, and was a qualified workman, but who was still employed by another.
7   *strip-system*   System according to which land is divided into small strips, several of which were allotted to the peasant for working. Crops were rotated among the strips.

the cottage industry[1] of the peasants themselves emerged. In industry there was no division of labor at all in the individual trades themselves, and very little between them. The separation of industry and commerce was found already in existence in older towns; in the newer it only developed later, when the towns entered into mutual relations.

The grouping of larger territories into feudal kingdoms was a necessity for the landed nobility as for the towns. The organization of the ruling class, the nobility, had, therefore, everywhere a monarch at its head.

The fact is, therefore, that definite individuals who are productively active in a definite way enter into these definite social and political relations. Empirical observation must in each separate instance bring out empirically, and without any mystification and speculation, the connection of the social and political structure with production. The social structure and the State are continually evolving out of the life-process of definite individuals, but of individuals, not as they may appear in their own or other people's imagination, but as they really are; i.e., as they operate, produce materially, and hence as they work under definite material limits, presuppositions and conditions independent of their will.

The production of ideas, of conceptions, of consciousness, is at first directly interwoven with the material activity and the material intercourse of men, the language of real life. Conceiving, thinking, the mental intercourse of men, appear at this stage as the direct efflux[2] of their material behavior. The same applies to mental production as expressed in the language of politics, laws, morality, religion, metaphysics, etc., of a people. Men are the producers of their conceptions, ideas, etc.—real, active men, as they are conditioned by a definite development of their productive forces and of the intercourse corresponding to these, up to its furthest forms. Consciousness can never be anything else than conscious existence, and the existence of men is their actual life-process. If in all ideology men and their circumstances appear upside-down as in a camera obscura,[3] this phenomenon arises just as much from their historical life-process as the inversion of objects on the retina does from their physical life-process.

In direct contrast to German philosophy which descends from heaven to earth, here we ascend from earth to heaven. That is to say, we do not set out from what men say, imagine, conceive, nor from men as narrated, thought of, imagined, conceived, in order to arrive at men in the flesh. We set out from real, active men, and on the basis of their real life-process we demonstrate the development of the ideological reflexes and echoes of this life-process. The phantoms formed in the human brain are also, necessarily, sublimates[4] of their material life-process, which is empirically verifiable and bound to material premises. Morality, religion, metaphysics, all the rest of ideology and their corresponding forms of consciousness, thus no longer retain the semblance of independence. They have no history, no development; but men, developing their material production and their material intercourse, alter, along with this their real existence, their thinking and the products of their thinking. Life is not determined by consciousness, but consciousness by life. In the first method of approach the starting-point is consciousness taken as the living individual; in the second method, which conforms to real life, it is the real living individuals themselves, and consciousness is considered solely as their consciousness.

This method of approach is not devoid of premises. It starts out from the real premises and does not abandon them for a moment. Its premises are men, not in any fantastic isolation and rigidity, but in their actual, empirically perceptible process of development under definite conditions. As soon as this active life-process is described, history ceases to be a collection of dead facts as it is with the empiricists[5] (themselves still abstract), or an imagined activity of imagined subjects, as with the idealists.

Where speculation ends—in real life—there real, positive science begins: the representation of the practical activity, of the practical process of development of men. Empty talk about consciousness ceases, and real knowledge has to take its place. When reality is depicted, philosophy as an independent branch of knowledge loses its medium of existence. At the best its place can only be taken by a summing-up of the most general results, abstractions which arise from the observation of the historical development of

---

1 *cottage industry* System according to which individual craftsworkers work at home, sometimes getting their supplies and selling their products to a central larger industry.

2 *efflux* Outflow.

3 *camera obscura* Darkened chamber with a hole or lens in one side, designed to throw an (upside-down) image of whatever is outside on the opposite wall; painters traced images from the camera obscura as an aid in representation.

4 *sublimates* Results of a change from one state to another.

5 *empiricists* Philosophers who take all knowledge to be derived from direct sense experience.

men. Viewed apart from real history, these abstractions have in themselves no value whatsoever. They can only serve to facilitate the arrangement of historical material, to indicate the sequence of its separate strata. But they by no means afford a recipe or schema, as does philosophy, for neatly trimming the epochs of history. On the contrary, our difficulties begin only when we set about the observation and the arrangement—the real depiction—of our historical material, whether of a past epoch or of the present. The removal of these difficulties is governed by premises which it is quite impossible to state here, but which only the study of the actual life-process and the activity of the individuals of each epoch will make evident. We shall select here some of these abstractions, which we use in contradistinction to the ideologists, and shall illustrate them by historical examples.

1. History

Since we are dealing with the Germans, who are devoid of premises,[1] we must begin by stating the first premise of all human existence and, therefore, of all history, the premise, namely, that men must be in a position to live in order to be able to "make history." But life involves before everything else eating and drinking, a habitation, clothing and many other things. The first historical act is thus the production of the means to satisfy these needs, the production of material life itself. And indeed this is an historical act, a fundamental condition of all history, which today, as thousands of years ago, must daily and hourly be fulfilled merely in order to sustain human life. Even when the sensuous world is reduced to a minimum, to a stick as with Saint Bruno, it presupposes the action of producing the stick. Therefore in any interpretation of history one has first of all to observe this fundamental fact in all its significance and all its implications and to accord it its due importance. It is well known that the Germans have never done this, and they have never, therefore, had an earthly basis for history and consequently never a historian. The French and the English, even if they have conceived the relation of this fact with so-called history only in an extremely one-sided fashion, particularly as long as they remained in the toils of political ideology, have nevertheless made the first attempts to give the writing of history a materialistic basis by being the first to write histories of civil society, of commerce and industry.

The second point is that the satisfaction of the first need (the action of satisfying, and the instrument of satisfaction which has been acquired) leads to new needs; and this production of new needs is the first historical act. Here we recognize immediately the spiritual ancestry of the great historical wisdom of the Germans who, when they run out of positive material and when they can serve up neither theological nor political nor literary rubbish, assert that this is not history at all, but the "prehistoric era." They do not, however, enlighten us as to how we proceed from this nonsensical "prehistory" to history proper; although, on the other hand, in their historical speculation they seize upon this "prehistory" with especial eagerness because they imagine themselves safe there from interference on the part of "crude facts," and, at the same time, because there they can give full rein to their speculative impulse and set up and knock down hypotheses by the thousand.

The third circumstance which, from the very outset, enters into historical development, is that men, who daily remake their own life, begin to make other men, to propagate their kind: the relation between man and woman, parents and children, the family. The family, which to begin with is the only social relationship, becomes later, when increased needs create new social relations and the increased population new needs, a subordinate one (except in Germany), and must then be treated and analyzed according to the existing empirical data, not according to "the concept of the family," as is the custom in Germany. These three aspects of social activity are not of course to be taken as three different stages, but just as three aspects or, to make it clear to the Germans, three "moments,"[2] which have existed simultaneously since the dawn of history and the first men, and which still assert themselves in history today.

The production of life, both of one's own in labor and of fresh life in procreation, now appears as a double relationship: on the one hand as a natural, on the other as a social relationship. By social we understand the cooperation of several individuals, no matter under what conditions, in what manner and to what end. It follows from this that a certain mode of production, or industrial stage, is always combined with a certain mode of cooperation, or social stage, and this mode of cooperation is itself a "productive force." Further, that the multitude of productive forces accessible to men determines the nature of society, hence,

---

1   *are devoid of premises*   Do not start off by assuming anything.

2   *moments*   This philosophical term here means *aspects*, but can also refer to *stages*.

that the "history of humanity" must always be studied and treated in relation to the history of industry and exchange. But it is also clear how in Germany it is impossible to write this sort of history, because the Germans lack not only the necessary power of comprehension and the material but also the "evidence of their senses," for across the Rhine you cannot have any experience of these things since history has stopped happening. Thus it is quite obvious from the start that there exists a materialistic connection of men with one another, which is determined by their needs and their mode of production, and which is as old as men themselves. This connection is ever taking on new forms, and thus presents a "history" independently of the existence of any political or religious nonsense which in addition may hold men together.

Only now, after having considered four moments, four aspects of the primary historical relationships, do we find that man also possesses "consciousness," but, even so, not inherent,[1] not "pure" consciousness. From the start the "spirit" is afflicted with the curse of being "burdened" with matter, which here makes its appearance in the form of agitated layers of air, sounds, in short, of language. Language is as old as consciousness, language is practical consciousness that exists also for other men, and for that reason alone it really exists for me personally as well; language, like consciousness, only arises from the need, the necessity, of intercourse with other men. Where there exists a relationship, it exists for me: the animal does not enter into "relations" with anything, it does not enter into any relation at all. For the animal, its relation to others does not exist as a relation. Consciousness is, therefore, from the very beginning a social product, and remains so as long as men exist at all. Consciousness is at first, of course, merely consciousness concerning the immediate sensuous environment and consciousness of the limited connection with other persons and things outside the individual who is growing self-conscious. At the same time it is consciousness of nature, which first appears to men as a completely alien, all-powerful and unassailable force, with which men's relations are purely animal and by which they are overawed like beasts; it is thus a purely animal consciousness of nature (natural religion) just because nature is as yet hardly modified historically.

We see here immediately: this natural religion or this particular relation of men to nature is determined by the form of society and vice versa. Here, as everywhere, the identity of nature and man appears in such a way that the restricted relation of men to nature determines their restricted relation to one another, and their restricted relation to one another determines men's restricted relation to nature. On the other hand, man's consciousness of the necessity of associating with the individuals around him is the beginning of the consciousness that he is living in society at all. This beginning is as animal as social life itself at this stage. It is mere herd-consciousness, and at this point man is only distinguished from sheep by the fact that with him consciousness takes the place of instinct or that his instinct is a conscious one. This sheep-like or tribal consciousness receives its further development and extension through increased productivity, the increase of needs, and, what is fundamental to both of these, the increase of population. With these there develops the division of labor, which was originally nothing but the division of labor in the sexual act, then that division of labor which develops spontaneously or "naturally" by virtue of natural predisposition (e.g., physical strength), needs, accidents, etc., etc. Division of labor only becomes truly such from the moment when a division of material and mental labor appears. (The first form of ideologists, priests, is concurrent.) From this moment onwards consciousness can really flatter itself that it is something other than consciousness of existing practice, that it really represents something without representing something real; from now on consciousness is in a position to emancipate itself from the world and to proceed to the formation of "pure" theory, theology, philosophy, ethics, etc. But even if this theory, theology, philosophy, ethics, etc., comes into contradiction with the existing relations, this can only occur because existing social relations have come into contradiction with existing forces of production; this, moreover, can also occur in a particular national sphere of relations through the appearance of the contradiction, not within the national orbit, but between this national consciousness and the practice of other nations, i.e., between the national and the general consciousness of a nation (as we see it now in Germany).

Moreover, it is quite immaterial what consciousness starts to do on its own: out of all such muck we get only the one inference that these three moments, the forces of production, the state of society, and consciousness, can and must come into contradiction with one another, because the division of labor implies the possibility, nay the fact that intellectual and material activity—enjoyment and

---

1   *inherent* Belonging to humans by their very nature.

labor, production and consumption—devolve on[1] different individuals, and that the only possibility of their not coming into contradiction lies in the negation in its turn of the division of labor. It is self-evident, moreover, that "specters," "bonds," "the higher being," "concept," "scruple," are merely the idealistic, spiritual expression, the conception apparently of the isolated individual, the image of very empirical fetters and limitations, within which the mode of production of life and the form of intercourse coupled with it move.

With the division of labor, in which all these contradictions are implicit, and which in its turn is based on the natural division of labor in the family and the separation of society into individual families opposed to one another, is given simultaneously the distribution, and indeed the unequal distribution, both quantitative and qualitative, of labor and its products, hence property: the nucleus, the first form, of which lies in the family, where wife and children are the slaves of the husband. This latent slavery in the family, though still very crude, is the first property, but even at this early stage it corresponds perfectly to the definition of modern economists who call it the power of disposing of the labor-power of others. Division of labor and private property are, moreover, identical expressions: in the one the same thing is affirmed with reference to activity as is affirmed in the other with reference to the product of the activity.

Further, the division of labor implies the contradiction between the interest of the separate individual or the individual family and the communal interest of all individuals who have intercourse with one another. And indeed, this communal interest does not exist merely in the imagination, as the "general interest," but first of all in reality, as the mutual interdependence of the individuals among whom the labor is divided. And finally, the division of labor offers us the first example of how, as long as man remains in natural society, that is, as long as a cleavage exists between the particular and the common interest, as long, therefore, as activity is not voluntarily, but naturally, divided, man's own deed becomes an alien power opposed to him, which enslaves him instead of being controlled by him. For as soon as the distribution of labor comes into being, each man has a particular, exclusive sphere of activity, which is forced upon him and from which he cannot escape. He is a hunter, a fisherman, a herdsman, or a critical critic, and

must remain so if he does not want to lose his means of livelihood; while in communist society, where nobody has one exclusive sphere of activity but each can become accomplished in any branch he wishes, society regulates the general production and thus makes it possible for me to do one thing today and another tomorrow, to hunt in the morning, fish in the afternoon, rear cattle in the evening, criticize after dinner, just as I have a mind, without ever becoming hunter, fisherman, herdsman or critic. This fixation of social activity, this consolidation of what we ourselves produce into an objective power above us, growing out of our control, thwarting our expectations, bringing to naught our calculations, is one of the chief factors in historical development up till now.

[And out of this very contradiction between the interest of the individual and that of the community the latter takes an independent form as the State, divorced from the real interests of individual and community, and at the same time as an illusory communal life, always based, however, on the real ties existing in every family and tribal conglomeration—such as flesh and blood, language, division of labor on a larger scale, and other interests—and especially, as we shall enlarge upon later, on the classes, already determined by the division of labor, which in every such mass of men separate out, and of which one dominates all the others. It follows from this that all struggles within the State, the struggle between democracy, aristocracy, and monarchy, the struggle for the franchise,[2] etc., are merely the illusory forms in which the real struggles of the different classes are fought out among one another (of this the German theoreticians have not the faintest inkling, although they have received a sufficient introduction to the subject in the *Deutsch-Französische Jahrbücher*[3] and *Die heilige Familie*[4]). Further, it follows that every class which is struggling for mastery, even when its domination, as is the case with the proletariat, postulates the abolition of the old form of society in its entirety and of domination itself, must first conquer for itself political power in order to represent its interest in turn as the general interest, which in the first mo-

1   *devolve on* Become the responsibility of.

2   *franchise* Right conferred by the state—in particular the right to vote.

3   *Deutsch-Französische Jahrbücher* German: *The German-French Annals* by Marx, 1844. Marx particularly refers here to his articles, "On the Jewish Question" (above) and "A Contribution to the Critique of the Hegelian Philosophy of Law."

4   *Die heilige Familie* German: *The Holy Family* by Marx and Engels, 1845.

ment it is forced to do. Just because individuals seek only their particular interest, which for them does not coincide with their communal interest (in fact the general is the illusory form of communal life), the latter will be imposed on them as an interest "alien" to them, and "independent" of them as in its turn a particular, peculiar "general" interest; or they themselves must remain within this discord, as in democracy. On the other hand, too, the practical struggle of these particular interests, which constantly really run counter to the communal and illusory communal interests, makes practical intervention and control necessary through the illusory "general" interest in the form of the State. The social power, i.e., the multiplied productive force, which arises through the cooperation of different individuals as it is determined by the division of labor, appears to these individuals, since their cooperation is not voluntary but has come about naturally, not as their own united power, but as an alien force existing outside them, of the origin and goal of which they are ignorant, which they thus cannot control, which on the contrary passes through a peculiar series of phases and stages independent of the will and the action of man, nay even being the prime governor of these.][1]

This "alienation" (to use a term which will be comprehensible to the philosophers) can, of course, only be abolished given two practical premises. For it to become an "intolerable" power, i.e., a power against which men make a revolution, it must necessarily have rendered the great mass of humanity "propertyless," and produced, at the same time, the contradiction of an existing world of wealth and culture, both of which conditions presuppose a great increase in productive power, a high degree of its development. And, on the other hand, this development of productive forces (which itself implies the actual empirical existence of men in their world-historical, instead of local, being) is an absolutely necessary practical premise because without it want is merely made general, and with destitution the struggle for necessities and all the old filthy business would necessarily be reproduced; and furthermore, because only with this universal development of productive forces is a universal intercourse between men established, which produces in all nations simultaneously the phenomenon of the "propertyless" mass (universal competition), makes each nation dependent on the revolutions of the others, and finally has put world-historical, empirically universal individuals in place

of local ones. Without this, (1) communism could only exist as a local event; (2) the forces of intercourse themselves could not have developed as universal, hence intolerable powers: they would have remained home-bred conditions surrounded by superstition; and (3) each extension of intercourse would abolish local communism. Empirically, communism is only possible as the act of the dominant peoples "all at once" and simultaneously, which presupposes the universal development of productive forces and the world intercourse bound up with communism. How otherwise could for instance property have had a history at all, have taken on different forms, and landed property, for example, according to the different premises given, have proceeded in France from parcellation to centralization in the hands of a few, in England from centralization in the hands of a few to parcellation, as is actually the case today?[2] Or how does it happen that trade, which after all is nothing more than the exchange of products of various individuals and countries, rules the whole world through the relation of supply and demand—a relation which, as an English economist[3] says, hovers over the earth like the fate of the ancients, and with invisible hand allots fortune and misfortune to men, sets up empires and overthrows empires, causes nations to rise and to disappear—while with the abolition of the basis of private property, with the communistic regulation of production (and, implicit in this, the destruction of the alien relation between men and what they themselves produce), the power of the relation of supply and demand is dissolved into nothing, and men get exchange, production, the mode of their mutual relation, under their own control again?

Communism is for us not a state of affairs which is to be established, an ideal to which reality will have to adjust itself. We call communism the real movement which abolishes the present state of things. The conditions of this movement result from the premises now in existence. Moreover, the mass of propertyless workers—the utterly precarious position of labor—power on a mass scale cut off from capital or from even a limited satisfaction and, there-

---

1   *And out of this very contradiction ... governor of these* This paragraph appears as a marginal note in the manuscript.

2   *in France ... today* Some have suggested that Marx may have carelessly interchanged "France" and "England" here; elsewhere Marx tells the story of how land in *England* passed out of the hands of many into the hands of the few (*Capital*, 2, 27–29).

3   The phrase "invisible hand" originates with the Scottish economist and philosopher Adam Smith (1723–90). He used this as a metaphorical way of referring to economic forces in capitalism. Each individual pursuing his or her private interest in the market would produce social benefits for the benefit of rich and poor alike.

fore, no longer merely temporarily deprived of work itself as a secure source of life—presupposes the world market through competition. The proletariat can thus only exist world-historically, just as communism, its activity, can only have a "world-historical" existence. World-historical existence of individuals means existence of individuals which is directly linked up with world history.

The form of intercourse determined by the existing productive forces at all previous historical stages, and in its turn determining these, is civil society. The latter, as is clear from what we have said above, has as its premises and basis the simple family and the multiple, the so-called tribe, the more precise determinants of this society are enumerated in our remarks above. Already here we see how this civil society is the true source and theatre of all history, and how absurd is the conception of history held hitherto, which neglects the real relationships and confines itself to high-sounding dramas of princes and states.

Civil society embraces the whole material intercourse of individuals within a definite stage of the development of productive forces. It embraces the whole commercial and industrial life of a given stage and, insofar, transcends the State and the nation, though, on the other hand again, it must assert itself in its foreign relations as nationality, and inwardly must organize itself as State. The word "civil society" emerged in the eighteenth century, when property relationships had already extricated themselves from the ancient and medieval communal society. Civil society as such only develops with the bourgeoisie; the social organization evolving directly out of production and commerce, which in all ages forms the basis of the State and of the rest of the idealistic superstructure, has, however, always been designated by the same name.

[...]

The ideas of the ruling class are in every epoch the ruling ideas, i.e., the class which is the ruling material force of society, is at the same time its ruling intellectual force. The class which has the means of material production at its disposal, has control at the same time over the means of mental production, so that thereby, generally speaking, the ideas of those who lack the means of mental production are subject to it. The ruling ideas are nothing more than the ideal expression of the dominant material relationships, the dominant material relationships grasped as ideas; hence of the relationships which make the one class the ruling one, therefore, the ideas of its dominance. The individuals

composing the ruling class possess among other things consciousness, and therefore think. Insofar, therefore, as they rule as a class and determine the extent and compass of an epoch, it is self-evident that they do this in its whole range, hence among other things rule also as thinkers, as producers of ideas, and regulate the production and distribution of the ideas of their age: thus their ideas are the ruling ideas of the epoch. For instance, in an age and in a country where royal power, aristocracy, and bourgeoisie are contending for mastery and where, therefore, mastery is shared, the doctrine of the separation of powers proves to be the dominant idea and is expressed as an "eternal law."

The division of labor, which we already saw above as one of the chief forces of history up till now, manifests itself also in the ruling class as the division of mental and material labor, so that inside this class one part appears as the thinkers of the class (its active, conceptive ideologists, who make the perfecting of the illusion of the class about itself their chief source of livelihood), while the others' attitude to these ideas and illusions is more passive and receptive, because they are in reality the active members of this class and have less time to make up illusions and ideas about themselves. Within this class this cleavage can even develop into a certain opposition and hostility between the two parts, which, however, in the case of a practical collision, in which the class itself is endangered, automatically comes to nothing, in which case there also vanishes the semblance[1] that the ruling ideas were not the ideas of the ruling class and had a power distinct from the power of this class. The existence of revolutionary ideas in a particular period presupposes the existence of a revolutionary class; about the premises for the latter sufficient has already been said above.

If now in considering the course of history we detach the ideas of the ruling class from the ruling class itself and attribute to them an independent existence, if we confine ourselves to saying that these or those ideas were dominant at a given time, without bothering ourselves about the conditions of production and the producers of these ideas, if we thus ignore the individuals and world conditions which are the source of the ideas, we can say, for instance, that during the time that the aristocracy was dominant, the concepts honor, loyalty, etc. were dominant, during the dominance of the bourgeoisie the concepts freedom, equality, etc. The ruling class itself on the whole imagines this to be so. This conception of history, which is common to all historians,

---

1   *semblance* Outward appearance.

particularly since the eighteenth century, will necessarily come up against the phenomenon that increasingly abstract ideas hold sway, i.e., ideas which increasingly take on the form of universality. For each new class which puts itself in the place of one ruling before it, is compelled, merely in order to carry through its aim, to represent its interest as the common interest of all the members of society, that is, expressed in ideal form: it has to give its ideas the form of universality, and represent them as the only rational, universally valid ones. The class making a revolution appears from the very start, if only because it is opposed to a *class*, not as a class but as the representative of the whole of society; it appears as the whole mass of society confronting the one ruling class. It can do this because, to start with, its interest really is more connected with the common interest of all other non-ruling classes, because under the pressure of hitherto existing conditions its interest has not yet been able to develop as the particular interest of a particular class. Its victory, therefore, benefits also many individuals of the other classes which are not winning a dominant position, but only insofar as it now puts these individuals in a position to raise themselves into the ruling class. When the French bourgeoisie overthrew the power of the aristocracy, it thereby made it possible for many proletarians to raise themselves above the proletariat, but only insofar as they become bourgeois. Every new class, therefore, achieves its hegemony[1] only on a broader basis than that of the class ruling previously, whereas the opposition of the non-ruling class against the new ruling class later develops all the more sharply and profoundly. Both these things determine the fact that the struggle to be waged against this new ruling class, in its turn, aims at a more decided and radical negation of the previous conditions of society than could all previous classes which sought to rule.

This whole semblance, that the rule of a certain class is only the rule of certain ideas, comes to a natural end, of course, as soon as class rule in general ceases to be the form in which society is organized, that is to say, as soon as it is no longer necessary to represent a particular interest as general or the "general interest" as ruling.

◆ ◆ ◆ ◆ ◆

---

1 *hegemony* Authority and control in society by one group over the others.

Theses On Feuerbach (1845)[2]

1

The chief defect of all hitherto existing materialism—that of Feuerbach included—is that the thing, reality, sensuousness, is conceived only in the form of the object or of contemplation, but not as sensuous human activity, practice, not subjectively. Hence, in contradistinction to materialism, the active side was developed abstractly by idealism—which, of course, does not know real, sensuous activity as such. Feuerbach wants sensuous objects, really distinct from the thought objects, but he does not conceive human activity itself as objective activity. Hence, in *The Essence of Christianity*, he regards the theoretical attitude as the only genuinely human attitude, while practice is conceived and fixed only in its dirty-judaical[3] manifestation. Hence he does not grasp the significance of "revolutionary," of "practical-critical," activity.

2

The question whether objective truth can be attributed to human thinking is not a question of theory but is a practical question. Man must prove the truth—i.e., the reality and power, the this-sidedness of his thinking in practice. The dispute over the reality or non-reality of thinking that is isolated from practice is a purely *scholastic* question.

---

2 *Feuerbach* Ludwig Feuerbach (1804–72), German philosopher and proponent of materialism. Marx initially shared many of Feuerbach's ideas, but in the 1840s increasingly differentiated his own form of materialist philosophy from that of Feuerbach.

3 *dirty-judaical* Another translation has been "dirty-Jewish." A common manifestation of anti-Semitism was (and is) the association of Jews with allegedly less attractive aspects of "money-grubbing" capitalism such as money lending; in Germany, Britain, and most other European societies Jews were prevented from entering most respectable professions, but were nevertheless disparaged for pursuing those few occupations (such as money-lending) that were open to them. Commentators differ on the question of whether the comment here expresses anti-Semitism on Marx's part, or is meant to imply that Feuerbach was anti-Semitic. (Though Marx's parents came from a Jewish background, he was raised in part as a Lutheran, and some other passages in his works indicate that he shared to some degree in the anti-Semitism that was prevalent at the time.)

3

The materialist doctrine concerning the changing of circumstances and upbringing forgets that circumstances are changed by men and that it is essential to educate the educator himself. This doctrine must, therefore, divide society into two parts, one of which is superior to society.

The coincidence of the changing of circumstances and of human activity or self-changing can be conceived and rationally understood only as revolutionary practice.

4

Feuerbach starts out from the fact of religious self-alienation, of the duplication of the world into a religious world and a secular one. His work consists in resolving the religious world into its secular basis. But that the secular basis detaches itself from itself and establishes itself as an independent realm in the clouds can only be explained by the cleavages and self-contradictions within this secular basis. The latter must, therefore, in itself be both understood in its contradiction and revolutionized in practice. Thus, for instance, after the earthly family is discovered to be the secret of the holy family, the former must then itself be destroyed in theory and in practice.

5

Feuerbach, not satisfied with abstract thinking, wants contemplation; but he does not conceive sensuousness as practical, human-sensuous activity.

6

Feuerbach resolves the religious essence into the human essence. But the human essence is no abstraction inherent in each single individual. In its reality it is the ensemble of the social relations.

Feuerbach, who does not enter upon a criticism of this real essence, is consequently compelled:

(1) To abstract from the historical process and to fix the religious sentiment as something by itself and to presuppose an abstract—*isolated*—human individual.

(2) Essence, therefore, can be comprehended only as "genus," as an internal, dumb generality which naturally unites the many individuals.

7

Feuerbach, consequently, does not see that the "religious sentiment" is itself a social product, and that the abstract individual whom he analyses belongs to a particular form of society.

8

All social life is essentially practical. All mysteries which lead theory to mysticism find their rational solution in human practice and in the comprehension of this practice.

9

The highest point reached by contemplative materialism, that is, materialism which does not comprehend sensuousness as practical activity, is contemplation of single individuals and of civil society.

10

The standpoint of the old materialism is civil society; the standpoint of the new is human society, or social humanity.

11

The philosophers have only interpreted the world, in various ways; the point is to change it.

◆ ◆ ◆ ◆ ◆

The Communist Manifesto (1848)

A specter is stalking Europe—the specter of Communism. All the Powers of Old Europe have bound themselves in a crusade against this specter: the Pope[1] and the Czar,[2] Metternich[3] and Guizot,[4] French Radicals[5] and German police.

Where is the opposition party that has not been denounced as Communistic by its opponents in power? Where the opposition party that has not hurled back the branding reproach of Communism against the more progressive members of the opposition as well as against its reactionary adversaries?

Two things stem from this fact:

    1. Communism is already acknowledged by all European Powers to be a Power.

    2. It is high time that the Communists openly set forth before the whole world their perspective, their aims, their tendencies, and meet this fairy tale about the Specter of Communism with a Manifesto of the Party itself.

To this end, Communists of the most diverse nationalities have assembled in London, and devised the following Manifesto, that is to be published in the English, French, German, Italian, Flemish and Danish languages.[6]

1. Bourgeois and Proletarians

    The history of all society hitherto is the history of class struggles.[7]

Freeman and slave, patrician and plebeian, lord and serf, guild-master and journeyman, in short, oppressor and oppressed, situated in constant opposition to one another, carried on an uninterrupted, now hidden, now open, conflict, a fight that each time ended in a revolutionary transformation of the entire society or in the common ruin of the contending classes.

In the earlier epochs of history, we find almost everywhere a comprehensive articulation[8] of society into various orders, a manifold gradation of social ranks. In ancient Rome we have patricians, knights, plebeians, slaves; in the Middle Ages, feudal lords, vassals, guild-masters, journeymen, apprentices, serfs;[9] and in almost all of these classes further specific gradations.

The modern bourgeois society that has sprouted from the ruins of feudal society has not done away with class antagonisms. It has but established new classes, new conditions of oppression, new forms of struggle in place of the old ones.

---

1   *the Pope*   Pius IX.

2   *the Czar*   Nicholas I.

3   *Metternich*   Klemens Wenzel von Metternich (1773–1859), prince responsible for shoring up what Marx called the "mouldering edifice" of the Austro-Hungarian empire.

4   *Guizot*   François Guizot (1787–1874), conservative French Foreign Minister 1840–48.

5   *French Radicals*   Not the revolutionary sort but bourgeois moderates, both anti-monarchist and anti-populist.

6   However only one translation—into Swedish—was published in 1848–49, and widespread translation and reprinting of the *Manifesto* did not begin until after 1870.

7   *class struggles*   [Engels' note, added to the 1888 edition] That is, all *written* history. In 1847, the pre-history of society, the social organization existing previous to recorded history, was all but unknown. Since then, [August von] Haxthausen discovered common ownership of land in Russia, [Georg Ludwig von] Maurer proved it to be the social foundation from which all Teutonic races started in history, and by and by village communities were found to be, or to have been the primitive form of society everywhere from India to Ireland. The inner organization of this primitive Communistic society was laid bare, in its typical form, by [Lewis Henry] Morgan's crowning discovery of the true nature of the *gens* and its relation to the *tribe*. With the dissolution of these primaeval communities society begins to be differentiated into separate and finally antagonistic classes. I have attempted to retrace this dissolution in *Der Ursprung der Familie, des Privateigenthums und des Staats* [*The Origins of the Family, Private Property and the State*], second edition, Stuttgart, 1886.

8   *articulation*   Distinguished into distinct units that are nonetheless joined together.

9   *ancient Rome ... serfs*   In ancient Rome, patricians were hereditary nobility; knights were an upper class defined by their high level of property ownership; plebeians the common people. In medieval feudal Europe, serfs were low-class farmers, bound to the lord's land (with which they could be sold), and forced to work for him; vassals were those held under bonds of obedience to a lord, in exchange for land and protection, and could be nobles, subservient to a king. Guilds were associations of independent craftsmen, formed both for their protection and to regularize their procedures. A guild-master was a skilled and qualified craftsman ("master craftsman") within a guild; apprentices were trainees, attached by contract for a specified period to a skilled craftsman; journeymen were qualified tradesmen who were not yet allowed (by the guild) to work independently, and so worked as day-laborers, receiving wages from employers.

However, our epoch, the epoch of the bourgeoisie distinguishes itself by the fact it has simplified the class antagonisms. Society as a whole is more and more splitting up into two great hostile camps, into two great classes directly confronting each other: Bourgeoisie and Proletariat.

From the serfs of the Middle Ages sprang the chartered burghers[1] of the earliest towns. From this bourgeoisification the first elements of the bourgeoisie were developed.

The discovery of America, the rounding of the Cape,[2] opened up a new terrain for the rising bourgeoisie. The East-Indian and Chinese markets, the colonization of America, trade with the colonies, the increase in the means of exchange and in commodities generally, gave to commerce, to navigation, to industry, an impulse never before known, and thereby, to the revolutionary element in the tottering feudal society, a rapid development.

The hitherto existing feudal or guild system of industry could no longer cope with the growing needs of the new markets. The manufacturing system took its place. The guild-masters were pushed to one side by the manufacturing[3] middle class; the division of labor between the different corporate guilds vanished before the division of labor within the selfsame workshop.

But the markets kept constantly growing, the demand constantly rising. Even manufacture no longer coped. Thereupon, steam and machinery revolutionized industrial production. The place of manufacture was taken by modern big industry, the place of the industrial middle class by industrial millionaires, the leaders of whole industrial armies, the modern bourgeois.

Big industry has established the world market, for which the discovery of America prepared the way. This market has given an inestimable development to commerce, to navigation, to communication by land. This development has, in its turn, reacted on the extension of industry; and in proportion as industry, commerce, navigation, railways extended, in the same proportion the bourgeoisie extended, increased its capital, and pushed into the background all of the classes handed down from the Middle Ages.

We see, therefore, how the modern bourgeoisie is itself the product of a long course of development, of a series of revolutions in the modes of production and of exchange.

Each of these steps in the development of the bourgeoisie was accompanied by a corresponding political advance of that class. An oppressed cohort[4] under the sway of the feudal nobility, armed and self-governing associations in the commune;[5] here independent urban republic, there taxable third estate[6] of the monarchy, afterwards, in the period of manufacture proper, serving either the semi-feudal or the absolute monarchy as a counterpoise[7] against the nobility, and as cornerstone of the great monarchies in general. The bourgeoisie has at last, since the establishment of big industry and of the world market, acquired for itself, in the modern representative State,[8] exclusive political sway. The executive of the modern State is but a committee for managing the common affairs of the whole bourgeoisie.

The bourgeoisie has played an intensely revolutionary part in history.

The bourgeoisie, wherever it has got the upper hand, has put an end to all feudal, patriarchal,[9] idyllic relations. It has remorselessly torn asunder the motley feudal ties that bound people to their natural superiors, and has left remaining no other nexus between two people than naked self-interest, than callous "cash payment." It has drowned the heavenly ecstasies of religious fervor, of chivalrous enthusiasm, of philistine sentimentalism, in the ice-cold water of egotistical calculation. It has dispersed personal worth into exchange value, and in place of the numberless chartered, fully earned freedoms has set up a single, unconscionable freedom—Free Trade. In a word, in place of exploitation, veiled by religious and political illusions, it has substituted public, shameless, direct, blatant exploitation.

The bourgeoisie has stripped of its halo every occupation hitherto honored and looked up to with reverent awe.

---

1   *chartered burghers*   A *burgher* was a middle-class citizen of a town; a *chartered burgher* was a citizen of a town by virtue of being a full member of a legally chartered trade association or guild.

2   *Cape*   Cape of Good Hope, at the southern tip of Africa.

3   *manufacturing*   This word is used here in its original sense of making by hand.

4   *cohort*   Group of people.

5   *commune*   In medieval Europe, alliances of members of a town for mutual defense. (There is no suggestion of "communism" in the word used this way.)

6   *third estate*   In pre-Revolutionary France society was considered divided into three "estates": the First Estate was the clergy; the Second was the nobility; and the Third was everyone else—though sometimes this term is used the way Marx does, excluding the peasantry, including just the middle class.

7   *counterpoise*   Counterweight.

8   *modern representative State*   One whose institutions are based on the political representation of *individuals*, in contrast to earlier states where social corporations (such as towns or guilds) or estates (such as the nobility or the clergy) were politically represented.

9   *patriarchal*   Relating to historical societies in which the important organizational unit is the (very) extended family, or clan.

It has converted the physician, the lawyer, the priest, the poet, the researcher, into its paid wage-laborers.

The bourgeoisie has torn away from the connectedness of the family its consoling veil, and has reduced it to a merely monetary relation.

The bourgeoisie has disclosed how the brutal display of vigor in the Middle Ages, which reactionaries so much admire, found its fitting complement in the most slothful indolence. It has been the first to show what human effort can achieve. It has worked wonders of a different order than Egyptian pyramids, Roman aqueducts, and Gothic cathedrals; it has conducted expeditions of a different order than all diasporas[1] of peoples and crusades.

The bourgeoisie cannot exist without constantly revolutionizing the instruments of production, thereby the relations of production, and hence social relations in their entirety. Retaining the old mode of production in unaltered form, was, by contrast, the first condition of existence for all earlier industrial classes. Constant, radical transformation of production, uninterrupted disturbance of all social conditions, everlasting insecurity and mobility distinguish the bourgeois epoch from all earlier ones. All relations fixed, corroded fast, with their retinue of ancient and venerable thinking and opinion, are dispersed, all new-formed ones become antiquated before they can ossify. Everything set and stolid turns to vapor, all that is holy is profaned, and people are at last compelled to confront soberly their situation in life, their relations to others.

The need for a constantly expanding market for its products chases the bourgeoisie over the whole surface of the globe. It must nestle everywhere, settle everywhere, establish connections everywhere.

The bourgeoisie has through its exploitation of the world market given a cosmopolitan character to production and consumption of all countries. To the great chagrin of reactionaries, it has removed from under the feet of industry the national ground. All venerable national industries have been destroyed or are daily being destroyed. They are dislodged by new industries, whose introduction becomes a life-and-death question for all civilized nations, by industries that no longer work up native raw material, but raw material drawn from the remotest zones; industries whose products are consumed not only at home but in every part of the world. In place of the old wants, satisfied by the productions of the country, emerge new wants requiring for their satisfaction the products of the most remote lands and climes. In place of the old local and national seclusion and self-sufficiency, there emerges multifaceted intercourse,[2] a comprehensive interdependence of nations. And as in material, so also in intellectual production the intellectual products of individual nations become common property. National one-sidedness and narrow-mindedness become more and more impossible, and from the numerous national and local literatures a world literature forms itself.

The bourgeoisie, by the rapid improvement of all instruments of production, by the immensely facilitated means of communication, draws all nations, even the most barbarian, into civilization. The cheap prices of its commodities are the heavy artillery with which it batters down all Chinese walls, with which it forces the barbarians' most entrenched hatred of foreigners to capitulate.[3] It compels all nations, if they are not to be overwhelmed, to adopt the bourgeois mode of production; it compels them to introduce what it calls civilization into their midst, i.e., to become bourgeois themselves. In a word, it creates a world after its own image.

The bourgeoisie has subjected the country to the rule of the towns. It has created enormous cities, has greatly increased the urban population as compared with the rural, and has thus rescued a considerable part of the population from the idiotism of rural life. Just as it has made the country dependent on the town, so it has made barbarian and semi-barbarian countries dependent on the civilized ones, nations of peasants on nations of bourgeois, the East on the West.

The bourgeoisie keeps more and more doing away with the scattered state of the population, of the means of production, and of property. It has agglomerated[4] the population, centralized means of production, and concentrated property in a few hands. The necessary consequence of this was political centralization. Independent or but loosely connected provinces with separate interests, laws, governments and systems of taxation, were pressed together into one nation, one government, one code of laws, one national class-interest, one tariff-zone.[5]

---

1   *diasporas* Dispersions from their home location.

2   *intercourse* Mutual dealings, social activity. In Marx, this refers particularly to economic relations.

3   *The cheap prices ... capitulate* This is a reference to the first Opium War in China (1839–43); the Chinese capitulated and were forced to cede Hong Kong to the British and to open five of their ports to foreign trade.

4   *agglomerated* Gathered together into a mass.

5   *tariff-zone* Zone in which taxes on imports are the same.

The bourgeoisie, during its rule of scarce one hundred years, has created more massive and more colossal productive forces than have all preceding generations together. Subjection of Nature's forces to man, machinery, application of chemistry to industry and agriculture, steam-navigation, railways, electric telegraphs, clearing of whole continents for cultivation, making river-traffic possible, whole populations conjured out of the ground—what earlier century had even a presentiment that such productive forces slumbered in the lap of social labor?

We have seen then, that the means of production and of exchange, on whose foundation the bourgeoisie built itself up, were generated in feudal society. At a certain stage in the development of these means of production and of exchange, the conditions under which feudal society produced and exchanged, the feudal organization of agriculture and manufacturing industry, in a word, the feudal relations of property became no longer compatible with the already developed productive forces; they transformed themselves into so many fetters. They had to be burst asunder; they were burst asunder.

Into their place stepped free competition, accompanied by the social and political constitution adapted to it, and by the economical and political sway of the bourgeois class.

A similar movement is going on before our very eyes. Modern bourgeois society with its relations of production, of exchange and of property, a society that has conjured up such gigantic means of production and of exchange, is like the sorcerer who is no longer able to control the powers of the nether world whom he has summoned by his spells. For many a decade past the history of industry and commerce is but the history of the revolt of modern productive forces against the modern conditions of production, against the property relations that are the conditions of existence of the bourgeoisie and of its rule. It is enough to mention the commercial crises that by their political return put on trial, ever more threateningly, the existence of the entire bourgeois society. In these commercial crises a great part not only of the products produced but also of the previously created productive forces, are regularly destroyed.[1] In these

crises there breaks out a social epidemic that in all earlier epochs would have seemed an absurdity—the epidemic of over-production. Society suddenly finds itself returned to a state of passing barbarism; it appears as if a famine, a universal war of devastation had cut off the supply of every means of subsistence; industry and commerce seem to be destroyed. And why? Because there is too much civilization, too much means of subsistence, too much industry, too much commerce. The productive forces at our disposal no longer tend to further the development of the relations of bourgeois civilization; on the contrary, they have become too powerful for these relations by which they are encumbered, and so soon as they overcome these encumbrances, they bring into disorder the whole of bourgeois society, then endanger the existence of bourgeois property. The relations of bourgeois society have become too narrow to comprise the wealth created by them. And how does the bourgeoisie get over these crises? On the one hand by the enforced destruction of a mass of productive forces; on the other by the conquest of new markets, and by the more thorough exploitation of the old ones. And by what means? By preparing the way for more general and more destructive crises, and by diminishing the means whereby crises are prevented.

The weapons with which the bourgeoisie felled feudalism to the ground are now turned against the bourgeoisie itself.

But not only has the bourgeoisie forged the weapons that bring death to itself; it has also called into existence the people who are to wield those weapons—the modern workers, the proletarians.

To the same degree as the bourgeoisie, i.e., capital, is developed, so is the proletariat, the modern working class, developed—a class of laborers, who live only so long as they find work, and who find work only so long as their labor increases capital. These workers who must sell themselves piecemeal are a commodity, like every other article of commerce, and are consequently exposed equally to all the vicissitudes of competition, all the fluctuations of the market.

---

1   *commerical crises ... destroyed* Such crises occurred regularly in advanced capitalist economies from 1825 until 1939. Periodically, as more and more companies joined a particular industry, firms found themselves facing a glut of their products on the market. This over-supply depressed the price of each good below expected profit levels, and so companies suddenly began to cut back their production: each time, these cutbacks started a vicious chain reaction, as their suppliers were also forced to make cutbacks, which increased the unemployment rate, which reduced consumer spending and so increased over-supply, which depressed prices still further, and so on. At the height of the Great Depression of the 1930s, the worst such crisis, unemployment reached 25 per cent in the United States. Marx provided a sophisticated analysis of such crises in *Capital*.

Owing to the expanded use of machinery and to division of labor, the work of the proletarians has lost all individual character, and, consequently, all charm for the worker. He becomes a mere appendage of the machine, and it is only the most simple, most monotonous, and most easily acquired dexterity that is required of them. The cost of production of workers is restricted, almost entirely, to the means of subsistence that they require to maintain themselves and reproduce their stock.[1] But the price of a commodity, and therefore also of labor, is equal to its cost of production. In proportion, therefore, as the repulsiveness of the work increases, the wage decreases. Nay more, in proportion as the use of machinery and division of labor increases, in the same proportion the burden of toil also increases, whether by extension of the working hours, by increase of the work exacted in a given time, by increased speed of the machinery, etc.

Modern industry has converted the little workshop of the patriarchal master into the great factory of the industrial capitalist. Masses of workers, pressed together in the factory, are organized like soldiers. As ordinary soldiers in the industrial army they are placed under the command of a comprehensive hierarchy of sub-officers and officers. Not only are they slaves of the bourgeois class, and of the bourgeois state; they are daily and hourly enslaved by the machine, by the overseer, and, above all, by the individual bourgeois manufacturer himself. The more openly this despotism proclaims gain to be its ultimate goal, the more petty, hateful and the more embittering it is.

The less the skill and exertion of strength implied in manual labor, in other words, the more modern industry becomes developed, the more is the labor of men superseded by that of women. Differences of age and sex have no longer any social validity for the working class. They are only instruments of labor, more or less costly to use, according to their age and sex.

No sooner is the exploitation of the laborer by the manufacturer, so far, at an end, and he receives his wages in cash, than he is set upon by the other portions of the bourgeoisie, the landlord, the shopkeeper, the pawnbroker, etc.

The lower strata of the middle class—the small tradespeople, shopkeepers, and retired tradesmen, the handicraftsmen and peasants—all these cohorts sink into the proletariat, partly because their meager capital does not suffice for the scale on which big industry is carried on, and is swamped in the competition with the bigger capitalists, partly because their skill is rendered worthless by new methods of production. Thus the proletariat is recruited from all classes of the population.

The proletariat goes through various stages of development. With its birth begins its struggle with the bourgeoisie.

At first the contest is carried on by individual laborers, then by the workpeople of a factory, then by the operatives of one trade, in one locality, against the individual bourgeois who directly exploits them. They direct their attacks not only against the bourgeois conditions of production, but they direct them against the instruments of production themselves; they destroy imported wares that compete with their labor, they smash machinery, they set factories ablaze, they seek to restore by force the vanished status of the worker in the Middle Ages.

At this stage the workers form a mass scattered over the whole country and fragmented by competition. Uniting to form more compact bodies is not yet the consequence of their own active union, but the uniting of the bourgeoisie, which, in order to attain its own political ends, is compelled to set the whole proletariat in motion, and is yet for a time able to do so. At this stage, then, the proletarians do not fight their enemies, but the enemies of their enemies, the remnants of absolute monarchy, the landowners, the non-industrial bourgeois, the petty bourgeoisie.[2] In this fashion, the whole historical movement is concentrated in the hands of the bourgeoisie; every victory so obtained is a victory for the bourgeoisie.

But with the development of industry the proletariat not only increases in number; it becomes concentrated into greater masses, its strength grows, and it feels its strength more. The interests and conditions of life within the ranks of the proletariat are more and more alike, in proportion as machinery obliterates distinctions of labor, and nearly everywhere reduces wages to the same low level. The growing competition among the bourgeois, and the resulting commercial crises, make the wages of the workers ever more fluctuating. The unceasing improvement of machinery, ever more rapidly developing, makes their situation in life more and more precarious; the collisions between individual

---

1 *stock* "Family," "race," "line of descent."

2 *petty bourgeoisie* Lower middle-class, including independent shopkeepers and small farmers; they control means of production (as do the bourgeoisie), but unlike the bourgeoisie they operate the means of production that they control. (In relying on their own labor they resemble the proletariat.)

workers and individual bourgeois take more and more the character of collisions between two classes. Thereupon the workers begin to form combinations against the bourgeois; they club together in order to keep up wages. They enter into long-term associations in order to make provision beforehand for these occasional revolts. Here and there the struggle breaks out into riots.

From time to time the workers are victorious, but only for a time. The real fruit of their struggles lies, not in the immediate result, but in the ever more inclusive union of the workers. It is assisted by the enhanced means of communication that are created by big industry and that place the workers of different localities in contact with one another. It was just this contact that was needed to centralize the numerous local struggles, all of the same character, into one national struggle between classes. But every class struggle is a political struggle. And that union, to attain which the burghers[1] of the Middle Ages with their miserable highways required centuries, the modern proletarians by means of railways achieve in a few years.

This organization of the proletarians into a class, and consequently into a political party, is at every instant unsettled again by the competition between the workers themselves. But it always rises up again, stronger, firmer, mightier. It compels legislative recognition of particular interests of the workers by making use of the divisions within the bourgeoisie itself. And so the Ten Hours Bill in England.[2]

Overall, collisions within the old society further, in many ways, the course of development of the proletariat. The bourgeoisie is embroiled in an ongoing struggle: at first with the aristocracy; later on with those portions of the bourgeoisie itself whose interests have been set at odds with the progress of industry; at all times, with the bourgeoisie of all foreign countries. In all these struggles it sees itself required to appeal to the proletariat, to ask for its help, and thus to propel it into the political arena. The bourgeoisie itself, therefore, supplies the proletariat with its own elements of education, that is to say, with weapons usable against itself.

Moreover, as we saw, entire sections of the ruling classes are by the advance of industry precipitated into the proletariat or are at least threatened in their conditions of existence. These also supply the proletariat with a significant amount of educational elements.

Finally, in times when the class struggle nears decision, the process of dissolution inside the ruling class, within the whole of old society, assumes such a violent, glaring character, that a small section of the ruling class cuts itself adrift to join the revolutionary class, the class that holds the future in its hands. Just as, therefore, at an earlier period, a section of the nobility went over to the bourgeoisie, so now a portion of the bourgeoisie goes over to the proletariat, and in particular a portion of the bourgeois ideologists, who have raised themselves to a theoretical understanding of the historical in its entirety.

Of all the classes that stand face to face with the bourgeoisie today, the proletariat alone is a really revolutionary class. The other classes decay and go under in the presence of big industry; the proletariat is its very own product.

The middling levels—the small manufacturer, the small trader, the artisan, the peasant—all these fight against the bourgeoisie to save from extinction their existence as fractions of the middle class. They are therefore not revolutionary, but conservative. Nay more, they are reactionary, for they try to roll back the wheel of history. Should they be revolutionary, they are so in view of their impending transfer into the proletariat; they thus defend not their present but their future interests, they abandon their own standpoint in order to set themselves on proletarian ground.

The lumpenproletariat,[3] that passive putrifying of the lowest layers of old society, may here and there be swept into the movement by a proletarian revolution; its lot in life, however, disposes it more readily to be bought for the cause of reactionary intrigue.[4]

---

1   *burghers*   The middle-class: merchants, etc.

2   *Ten Hours Bill in England*   This law—part of the 1847 Factory Act—limited the daily working hours of women and children to 58 hours a week. It was highly controversial, and succeeded in being passed by Parliament only because of the willingness of conservative "Old England" landowners to oppose the interests of the ever-more-powerful industrialists and mill owners.

3   *lumpenproletariat*   German: "proletariat in rags." Permanent underclass, composed of criminals, the homeless, the permanently unemployed. "This scum of the depraved elements of all classes ... decayed roués, vagabonds, discharged soldiers, discharged jailbirds, escaped galley slaves, swindlers, mountebanks [itinerants selling fake cures and patent medicines], lazzaroni [homeless of Naples], pickpockets, tricksters, gamblers, brothel keepers, tinkers, beggars, the dangerous class, the social scum, that passively rotting mass thrown off by the lowest layers of the old society" (Marx, *The Eighteenth Brumaire of Louis Bonaparte*).

4   *intrigue*   Secret underhanded schemes. For Marx and Engels, the hopeless and displaced state of the lumpenproletariat makes them susceptible to becoming bribed agents of the state.

The conditions of existence of old society are already nullified in the conditions of existence of the proletariat. The proletarian is without property; his relation to wife and children has nothing else in common with bourgeois family relations; modern industrial labor, modern subjection to capital, the same in England as in France, in America as in Germany, has stripped him of every trace of national character. Law, morality, religion, are to him so many bourgeois prejudices, behind which lurk many bourgeois interests.

All the preceding classes that got the upper hand, ought to secure their already acquired status by subjecting society at large to their conditions of appropriation. The proletarians cannot take command of the productive forces of society, except by abolishing their own previous mode of appropriation, and thereby also every other previous mode of appropriation. The proletarians have nothing of their own to protect; their mission is to destroy all hitherto existing protection and insurance for private holdings.

All previous historical movements were movements of minorities, or in the interest of minorities. The proletarian movement is the independent movement of the immense majority in the interest of the immense majority. The proletariat, the lowest stratum of our present society, cannot raise itself up, cannot stand up straight, without exploding the whole stratified superstructure of official society.

Though not in substance, yet in form, the struggle of the proletariat with the bourgeoisie is at first a national one. The proletariat of each country must naturally first of all settle matters with its own bourgeoisie.

In depicting the most general phases of the development of the proletariat, we traced the more or less concealed civil war within existing society, up to the point where that war breaks out into open revolution, and where the forceful overthrow of the bourgeoisie lays the foundation for the sway of the proletariat.

Hitherto, every form of society has been based, as we have already seen, on the antagonism of oppressing and oppressed classes. But in order to oppress a class, certain conditions must be assured to it under which it can, at least, continue its slavish existence. The serf, in the period of serfdom, raised himself to membership in the commune, just as the petty bourgeois, under the yoke of feudal absolutism, managed to develop into a bourgeois. The modern worker, on the contrary, instead of rising with the progress of industry, sinks deeper and deeper below the conditions of existence of his own class. He becomes a pauper, and pauperism develops more rapidly than population and wealth.

And here it becomes evident that the bourgeoisie is unfit any longer to be the ruling class in society, and to impose its conditions of existence upon society as directive law. It is unfit to rule because it is incompetent to assure an existence to its slave within his slavery, because it cannot help letting them sink into such a state that it has to feed him instead of being fed by him. Society can no longer live under it; i.e., its existence is no longer compatible with society.

The most essential condition for the existence and for the sway of the bourgeois class is the accumulation of riches in private hands, the formation and augmentation of capital. The condition for capital is wage-labor. Wage-labor rests exclusively on competition between the laborers. The advance of industry, whose unwilling and unstoppable instrument is the bourgeoisie, replaces the isolation of the workers due to competition by their revolutionary combination due to association. The development of big industry, therefore, cuts from under its feet the very foundation on which the bourgeoisie produces and appropriates products. It produces, above all, its own grave-diggers. Its fall and the victory of the proletariat are alike inevitable.

2. Proletarians and Communists

In what relation do the Communists stand to the proletarians in general?

The Communists do not constitute a party distinct from other workers parties.

They have no interests separate from those of the proletariat as a whole.

They do not lay out any principles peculiar to themselves, through which they wish to mould the proletarian movement.

The Communists are distinguished from the other working-class parties by this only, that, in the various national struggles common to the proletarians, they point out and bring to prominence the shared interests of the entire proletariat, independent of nationality; and that, on the other hand, in the various stages of development which the struggle of the working class against the bourgeoisie passes through, they always represent the interests of the movement as a whole.

The Communists, therefore, are in effect, the most resolute section of the workers parties of every country, always pressing further; on the other hand, they have over the great mass of the proletariat the theorizing edge in understanding the conditions, heading, and the general results of the proletarian movement.

The immediate aim of the Communists is the same as that of all the other proletarian parties: formation of the proletariat into a class, overthrow of the bourgeois rule, conquest of political power by the proletariat.

The theoretical conclusions of the Communists are in no way based on ideas or principles that have been invented, discovered by this or that global improver.

They are simply general versions of actual relations in an existing class struggle, in a historical movement going on before our eyes. The abolition of existing property relations is not an indicator exclusive to Communism.

All property relations have been subject to continual historical change, a persistent historical alteration.

The French Revolution, for example, abolished feudal property in favor of bourgeois property.

What distinguishes Communism is not the abolition of property generally, but the abolition of bourgeois property.

But modern bourgeois private property is the final and most complete expression of the production and appropriation of products based on class antagonisms, on the exploitation of some by others.

In this sense, the Communists can sum up their theory in this one motto: abolition of private property.

We Communists have been reproached for wishing to abolish the right to acquire personal property by working for it oneself, which property is alleged to be the foundation of all personal freedom, activity and independence.

Hard-won, self-acquired, self-earned property! Do you mean the property of the petty bourgeois and the small peasant, a form of property that preceded bourgeois property? We have no need to abolish it; the development of industry has abolished it and abolishes it every day.

Or do you speak of modern bourgeois private property?

But does wage-labor, the work of the proletarian, produce any property for him? Not a bit. It produces capital, i.e., the property which exploits wage-labor, which cannot increase except when it begets fresh wage-labor. Property, in its current form, derives from the antagonism of capital and wage-labor. Let us examine both sides of this antagonism.

To be a capitalist is to have not only a purely personal, but a social status in production. Capital is a collective product, and only by the united action of many members, nay, in the last resort, only by the united action of all members of society, can it be set in motion.

Therefore, capital is not a personal but a social power.

When, therefore, capital is converted into common property, into the property of all members of society, personal property is not transformed into social property. Only the social character of the property is changed. It loses its class character.

We come now to wage-labor.

The average price of wage-labor is the minimum wage, i.e., the amount of the means of subsistence necessary to keep the worker functioning as a worker. What, therefore, the wage-laborer appropriates by means of his labor, suffices merely to prolong and reproduce his bare existence. We are by no means inclined to abolish this personal appropriation of the products of labor for the reproduction of human life, an appropriation that leaves no surplus wherewith to command the labor of others. We want to do away only with the miserable character of this appropriation, through which the laborer lives merely to increase capital and lives only in so far as the interest of the ruling class requires it.

In bourgeois society, living labor is simply a means to increase accumulated labor. In communist society, accumulated labor is simply a means to expand, to enrich, to promote the workers' way of life.

In bourgeois society, therefore, the past dominates the present; in communist society, the present dominates the past. In bourgeois society capital is independent and individualized, while the living individual is dependent and depersonalized.

And the elimination of these conditions is called by the bourgeois the death of individuality and freedom! And rightly so. It is undoubtedly a matter of making bourgeois individuality, independence, and freedom disappear.

By freedom, under the present bourgeois conditions of production, is understood free trade, free buying and selling.

But if dealing disappears, the free dealing disappears as well. The talk about free dealing, like the rest of our bourgeoisie's bold hyping of freedom, is generally meaningful only in contrast with restricted dealing, with the fettered traders of the Middle Ages, but not when opposed to the communistic elimination of dealing, of the bourgeois conditions of production, and of the bourgeoisie itself.

You are horrified by our intending to do away with private property. But in your existing society, private property is no longer an option for nine-tenths of the population; it exists precisely because for nine-tenths it does not exist. You charge us, therefore, with intending to do away with a form of property whose necessary precondition is that the immense majority of society should have no property at all.

In a word, you charge us with intending to put an end to your property. Precisely so; that is just what we intend.

From the moment when labor can no longer be converted into capital, money, or ground rent, in short into a social power that may be monopolized, i.e., from the moment when individual property can no longer be transformed into bourgeois property, into capital, from that moment, you claim, individuality is suspended.

You therefore confess that by the individual you mean none other than the bourgeois, the bourgeois owner of property. And this person must certainly be eliminated.

Communism deprives no one of the power to appropriate the products of society; it deprives one only of the power to subjugate others' labor by means of such appropriation.

It has been objected that with the abolition of private property all effort will cease and universal laziness take over.

According to this, bourgeois society ought long ago to have succumbed to idleness; for those of its number who work in it acquire nothing, and those who do not make acquisitions. This objection expresses in sum the tautology that there can no longer be any wage-labor when there is no longer any capital.

All objections urged against the communistic mode of producing and appropriating material products, have similarly been urged against the communistic modes of producing and appropriating intellectual products. Just as for the bourgeois the disappearance of class property is the disappearance of production itself, so the disappearance of class culture is to him identical with the disappearance of culture more generally.

The culture whose loss he laments, is, for the enormous majority, training to be machines.

But don't wrangle with us by judging our intended abolition of bourgeois property against your bourgeois notions of freedom, culture, law, etc. Your very ideas are born of the conditions of bourgeois production and property, just as your law is but the will of your class made into regulation for all, a will, whose content is determined by the material conditions of existence of your class.

The selfish notion you use to transform into eternal laws of nature and of reason the social forms springing from your current relations of production and property—historical relations that come and go in the course of production—this misconception you share with every ruling class

that has preceded you. What you understand about ancient property, what you understand about feudal property, you are yet unwilling to grasp about bourgeois.

Abolition of the family! Even the most radical flare up at this infamous proposal of the Communists.

On what foundation is today's family, the bourgeois family, based? On capital, on private gain. Fully developed, it exists only among the bourgeoisie; but it finds its complement in the lack of family imposed on proletarians and in public prostitution.

The bourgeois family will vanish as a matter of course when this its complement vanishes, and both will vanish with the vanishing of capital.

Do you charge us with wanting to stop the exploitation of children by their parents? To this crime we plead guilty.

But, you say, we destroy the most revered relations when we replace home education by social.

And is not your education also social—determined by the social conditions under which you educate, by the intervention, direct or indirect, of society, by means of schools, etc.? The Communists have not invented the intervention of society in education; they do but alter its character, seizing education from the influence of a ruling class.

The bourgeois discourse of the family and education, about the revered bond between parent and child, becomes all the more disgusting, the more, by the action of big industry, all family ties among the proletarians are torn asunder and the children transformed into simple articles of commerce and instruments of labor.

But you Communists would introduce community of women, screams the whole bourgeoisie at us in chorus.

The bourgeois sees in his wife a mere instrument of production. He hears that the instruments of production are to be exploited in common, and, naturally, can come to no other conclusion than that the lot of being common to all will likewise fall to women.

He has not a clue that it is exactly a matter of erasing the status of women as mere instruments of production.

At any rate, nothing is more ridiculous than the ultra-righteous indignation shown by our bourgeois at the alleged community of women ratified by the Communists. The Communists have no need to introduce community of women; it has existed almost always.

Our bourgeois, not content with having the wives and daughters of their proletarians at their disposal, not to mention official prostitution, take considerable pleasure in seducing each others' wives.

Bourgeois marriage is in reality a communality system of wives. At most, the Communists can be reproached with desiring to replace a hypocritically concealed community of women with an openly approved one. Besides, it is self-evident that the abolition of the present relations of production must entail the passing of the community of women deriving from them, i.e., of official and unofficial prostitution.

The Communists are further reproached with desiring to abolish countries and nationality.

The workers have no fatherland. One cannot take from them what they have not got. In that the proletariat must first acquire political supremacy, must elevate itself to be the national class, must constitute itself the nation, it is itself yet national, though by no means in the bourgeois sense.

National differences and antagonisms between peoples are daily vanishing more and more with the development of the bourgeoisie, with freedom of trade, the world market, uniformity in industrial production and in the corresponding conditions of existence.

The supremacy of the proletariat will cause them to vanish still more. United action of the leading civilized countries at least, is one of the first conditions for the emancipation of the proletariat.

In proportion as the exploitation of one individual by another is prohibited, the exploitation of one nation by another will also be put an end to.

In proportion as the exploitation of one individual by another is prohibited, the exploitation of one nation by another will also cease.

The charges against communism made from religious, philosophical, and generally ideological standpoints do not deserve a detailed response.

Does it require deep insight to comprehend that people's ideas, views and conceptions—in a word, their consciousness—changes with their conditions of existence, their social relations and their life in society?

What does the history of ideas indicate other than that intellectual production changes along with material production? The ruling ideas of any age are always the ideas of the ruling class.

People speak of ideas that revolutionize an entire society; in this they do but express the fact that within the old society the elements of a new one have been developed, that the dissolution of the old ideas proceeds at the same pace as the dissolution of the old conditions of existence.

When the ancient world was in its last throes, the ancient religions were overcome by Christianity. When Christian ideas succumbed in the eighteenth century to Enlightenment ideas, feudal society engaged in its mortal struggle with the then revolutionary bourgeoisie. The ideas of freedom of conscience and religion conveyed merely the domination by free competition of the realm of conscience.

"But," it will be said, "religious, moral, philosophical, juridical ideas, etc. have indeed been modified in the course of historical development. Religion, morality, philosophy, politics, law, constantly survived this exchange."

"There are, besides, eternal truths, such as Freedom, Justice, etc., that are common to all states of society. Communism, however, abolishes eternal truths; it abolishes all religion and all morality instead of remodeling them afresh; it therefore contradicts all historical experience hitherto."

What does this accusation reduce itself to? The history of all society to date has taken the path of class antagonisms, antagonisms that assumed different forms in different epochs.

But whatever form they may have taken, the exploitation of one part of society by the other is a fact common to all preceding centuries. No wonder, then, that the social consciousness of all centuries, notwithstanding all the multiplicity and variety it displays, moves in certain common forms, forms of consciousness, which cannot completely vanish except with the total disappearance of class antagonisms.

The Communist revolution is the most radical rupture with traditional property relations; no wonder that in the course of its development there occurs the most radical rupture with traditional ideas.

But let us have done with the bourgeoisie's objections to communism.

We have already seen above that the first step in the worker-revolution is the raising of the proletariat to the ruling class, prevailing in democracy.

The proletariat will use its political supremacy to wrest all capital gradually from the bourgeoisie, to centralize all instruments of production in the hands of the State, i.e., of the proletariat organized as the ruling class; and to increase the body of productive forces as rapidly as possible.

Of course, in the beginning this cannot be achieved except by means of despotic inroads on the right of property, and on the relations of bourgeois production; by means of measures, therefore, which appear economically insufficient and untenable, but which, in the course of implementation outstrip themselves and are unavoidable as a means of transforming the whole mode of production.

These measures will of course be different in different countries.

Nevertheless, in the most advanced countries the following will be pretty generally applicable.

1. Expropriation of landed property and application of ground rent of land to state expenditures.
2. A heavy progressive tax.
3. Abolition of right of inheritance.
4. Confiscation of the property of all emigrants and rebels.
5. Centralization of credit in the hands of the state through a national bank with state capital and an exclusive monopoly.
6. Centralization of all modes of transportation in the hands of the state.
7. Expansion of national factories and instruments of production owned by the state; reclamation and improvement of estates according to a common plan.
8. Equal liability of all to labor. Establishment of industrial armies, especially for agriculture.
9. Combination of agriculture and industry, to effect the gradual undoing of the opposition between town and country.
10. Free public education for all children. Doing away with children's factory labor in its present form. Combination of education with material production, etc., etc.

When, in the course of development, class distinctions have disappeared, and all production is concentrated in the hands of associated individuals, public power loses its political character. Political power in the proper sense is the organized power of one class for the subjugation of another. When the proletariat during its struggle with the bourgeoisie is compelled to organize itself as a class, by means of a revolution makes itself the ruling class, and as the ruling class forcibly removes the old conditions of production, then, along with these conditions, it eradicates the conditions for the existence of class conflict and of classes generally, and thereby its own supremacy as a class.

In place of the old bourgeois society, with its classes and class antagonisms, there emerges an association, in which the free development of each is the condition for the free development of all.

3. *Socialist and Communist Literature*

1. Reactionary Socialism

A. FEUDAL SOCIALISM. Owing to their historical position, the aristocracies of France and England were called upon to write pamphlets against modern bourgeois society. In the July revolution of 1830 in France, and in the English reform movement, they once again succumbed to the hateful upstart. Thenceforth, a serious political contest was out of the question. A literary battle alone remained possible. But even in the realm of literature the old discourse of the restoration period had become impossible. In order to arouse sympathy, the aristocracy were obliged to lose sight apparently of their own interests, and to formulate their list of grievances against the bourgeoisie in the interest of the exploited working class alone. Thus they prepared for restitution by singing lampoons about their new master, and permitting themselves to whisper in his ear more or less ominous prophecies.

In this way arose feudal Socialism: half lamentation, half squib;[1] half echo of the past, half menace of the future; at times, by its bitter, witty and incisive criticism striking the bourgeoisie to the heart; always comic in effect through total inability to grasp the operation of modern history.

They brandished the proletarian alms-bag like a banner, in order to rally the people behind them. But every popular following saw on their hindquarters the old feudal coats of arms and broke ranks midst loud and irreverent laughter.[2]

A section of the French Legitimists[3] and Young England[4] exhibited this spectacle best.

In pointing out that their mode of exploitation was cast otherwise than that of the bourgeoisie, the feudalists simply forgot that they exploited under circumstances and conditions wholly different and now outmoded. In demonstrating that under their rule the modern proletariat never existed, they simply forget that the modern bourgeoisie was the necessary offspring of their social structure.

---

1 *squib* Lampoon.
2 *hindquarters ... laughter* Marx borrows this image from Heinrich Heine's satirical poem, *A Winter's Tale* (1844).
3 *French Legitimists* Royalists, agitating for restoration of the hereditary monarchy, in post-Revolutionary France.
4 *Young England* Conservative political movement in Victorian England, in favor of an absolute monarchy and a strong established church.

At any rate, they conceal the reactionary character of their criticism so little that their chief grievance against the bourgeoisie amounts to this, that under their regime a class is emerging which will explode the whole of the old social order.

What they reproach the bourgeoisie more for is producing not so much a proletariat as a revolutionary one.

In political practice, therefore, they join in all coercive measures against the working class; and in ordinary life, despite their inflated rhetoric, they stoop to pick up the golden apples and to barter truth, love, and honor for traffic in wool, sugar beets, and schnapps.

As the parson has ever gone hand in hand with the feudalist, so has clerical socialism with feudal socialism.

Nothing is easier than to give Christian asceticism a socialist coating. Has not Christianity come out strongly against private property, against marriage, against the State? Has it not preached in the place of these, charity and mendicancy, celibacy and mortification of the flesh, monastic life and the Church? Religious socialism is but the holy water with which the priest consecrates the aristocrat's ire.

B. PETTY-BOURGEOIS SOCIALISM. The feudal aristocracy was not the only class brought down by the bourgeoisie, or whose conditions of existence wasted away and perished in modern bourgeois society. The medieval burgesses and small peasantry were the precursors of the modern bourgeoisie. In countries which are little developed, industrially and commercially, these classes still vegetate beside the rising bourgeoisie.

In countries where modern civilization has developed, a new petty bourgeoisie has been formed which floats between proletariat and bourgeoisie while renewing itself constantly as a supplementary part of bourgeois society. The individual members of this class, however, are constantly hurled down into the proletariat by the action of competition; assuredly as modern industry develops, they even see the moment approaching when they completely disappear as an independent section of modern society, to be replaced in commerce, manufacturing, and agriculture by overseers and shopmen.

In countries like France, where the peasant class constitutes far more than half of the population, it was natural that writers who sided with the proletariat against the bourgeoisie should use, in their criticism of the bourgeois regime, the standard of the small peasant and petty bourgeois, and took up the cause of the working class from the standpoint of the petty bourgeoisie. Thus arose petty-bourgeois socialism. Sismondi[1] is the chief among its authors, in France as well as England.

This school of Socialism dissected with great acuteness the contradictions in modern relations of production. It laid bare the hypocritical alibis of economists. It proved, incontrovertibly, the disastrous effects of machinery and division of labor; the concentration of capital and landed property; overproduction, crises, the unavoidable ruination of the petty bourgeois and peasants, the misery of the proletariat, anarchy in production, the crying inequalities in the distribution of wealth, the industrial war of extermination between nations, the dissolution of old moral bonds, of old family connections, of old nationalities.

In its positive import, however, this socialism aspires either to restoring the old means of production and of exchange, and with them the old property relations, and the old society, or to forcibly reconfining modern means of production and of exchange within the framework of the old property relations which they exploded, had to explode. In either case, it is at the same time reactionary and utopian.[2]

Its last words are: corporate guilds for manufacture; patriarchal relations in agriculture.

In its fuller expression, this commitment ended with a hangover for the uncourageous.

C. GERMAN OR TRUE SOCIALISM. The Socialist and Communist literature of France, which originated under the pressure of a bourgeoisie in power, and that was the expression of the struggle against this power, was introduced into Germany at a time when the bourgeoisie had just begun its struggle against feudal absolutism.

German philosophers, semi-philosophers, and *beaux esprits*[3] seized eagerly on this literature, only forgetting that when these writings emigrated from France French social conditions did not emigrate along with them. In the German context, this French literature lost all immediate practical significance and assumed a purely literary aspect. It was sure to look like idle speculation about the True Society, about the realization of Human Nature. Thus, for the German philosophers of the eighteenth century, the demands of the first French Revolution were nothing more than the

---

1 *Sismondi* Léonard Simonde de Sismondi (1773–1842), Swiss-born historian and economist; he criticized capitalism, but was too politically moderate for Marx.

2 *utopian* With an impractical vision of ideal society.

3 *beaux esprits* French: beautiful spirits. Witty cultured people.

demands of Practical Reason[1] in general, the disclosure of the will of the revolutionary French bourgeoisie representing in their eyes the laws of pure Will, of Will as it was bound to be, of true human Will.

The work of the German *literati*[2] consisted solely in bringing the new French ideas into harmony with their ancient philosophical conscience, or rather, in annexing the French ideas from their own philosophic point of view.

This annexation took place in the same way in which a foreign language is appropriated, in and as translation.

We are familiar with how the monks wrote silly lives of Catholic saints over the manuscripts on which the classical works of ancient heathendom had been transcribed. The German littérateurs[3] reversed this process with the profane French literature. They wrote their philosophical nonsense underneath the French original. For instance, underneath the French criticism of money relations they wrote "Alienation of Humanity," and underneath the French criticism of the bourgeois State they wrote "Abolition of the Category of the General," and so forth.

This insertion of their philosophical language underneath the French contributions they dubbed "Philosophy of Action," "True Socialism," "German Science of Socialism," "Philosophical Foundation of Socialism," and so on.

The French-socialist, communist literature was thus in effect emasculated. And since it ceased in German hands to express the struggle of one class against the other, the German felt conscious of overcoming French one-sidedness, of representing not true needs but the needs of Truth; not the interests of the proletariat but the interests of Human Nature, of Humanity in general who belong to no class in the real world but only in the misty firmament of philosophical fantasy.

This German Socialism, which took its awkward school work so seriously and solemnly, and pitched its value like a costermonger,[4] meanwhile gradually lost its pedantic innocence.

The struggle of the German, and especially the Prussian bourgeoisie against the feudalists and absolute monarchy—in sum, the liberal movement—became more earnest.

True Socialism was thus offered the longed-for opportunity to confront the political movement with the Social-

ist demands: the traditional anathemas against liberalism, against representative government, bourgeois competition, bourgeois freedom of the press, bourgeois legislation, bourgeois liberty and equality, and of preaching to the masses that they had nothing to gain and everything to lose from this bourgeois movement. German Socialism conveniently forgot that the French criticism, whose silly echo it was, presupposed the existence of modern bourgeois society with its corresponding material conditions of existence and political constitution adapted thereto, the very goals in dispute for the first time within the German struggle.

To the German absolute governments, with their claque of priests, teachers, cabbage-boors and bureaucrats, it served as a welcome scarecrow against the increasingly threatening bourgeoisie.

It represented a sweet completion after the bitter floggings and shootings to which these same governments treated German working-class uprisings.

While this True Socialism thus served the governments as a weapon for fighting the German bourgeoisie, it also represented directly a reactionary interest, the interest of middle-class German Philistines. In Germany the petty-bourgeois class, a relic of the sixteenth century, and since then constantly cropping up here again under various forms, is the real social basis of the existing state of things.

Its preservation is the preservation of the German status quo. From the industrial and political supremacy of the bourgeoisie it anticipates certain destruction: on the one hand, in the wake of capital concentration; on the other, from the rise of a revolutionary proletariat. True Socialism appeared to kill two birds with one stone. It spread like an epidemic.

The robe of speculative[5] cobwebs, embroidered with the rhetorical flowers of *beaux esprits*, drenched with the dew of erotic sentiment—this overwrought robe in which the German socialists wrapped some of their emaciated eternal truths, merely increased the sale of their wares to this public.

For its part, German socialism recognized more and more its vocation as the stilted stand-in for this middle-class Philistine.

It proclaimed the German nation to be the typical nation, and the German petty Philistine to be the typical man. To each of his deficiencies it gave a hidden, higher,

---

1   *Practical Reason* A reference, perhaps, to Immanuel Kant's *Critique of Practical Reason* (1788) and other works of moral philosophy.

2   *literati* Intellectuals.

3   *littérateurs* French: literary hack.

4   *costermonger* Street-vender of fruits and vegetables.

5   *speculative* Hegel used this term to describe his style of philosophy.

socialistic spin so as to signify its opposite. It extracted the extreme conclusion from directly countering the brutally destructive tendency of communism while proclaiming its own ability to rise impartially above all class struggles. With very few exceptions, all the so-called socialist and communist publications that now circulate in Germany belong to the domain of this foul, enervating literature.

2. Conservative, or Bourgeois, Socialism

A part of the bourgeoisie wishes to redress social grievances in order to secure the continued existence of bourgeois society.

To this cohort belong economists, philanthropists, humanitarians, improvers of the condition of the working class, organizers of charity, preventers of cruelty to animals, temperance societies, hole-and-corner[1] reformers of every imaginable kind.

This form of Socialism has, moreover, been worked out into complete systems. We cite Proudhon's *Philosophie de la Misère*[2] as an example.

The socialistic bourgeois want the conditions of existence without the struggles and dangers necessarily resulting therefrom. They want the existing state of society minus its revolutionizing and disintegrating elements. They want the bourgeoisie without the proletariat. Bourgeois socialism conceives the world of its ascendancy to be naturally the best world; and bourgeois Socialism contrives from this consoling conception a semi- or complete system. When it calls on the proletariat to implement such a system in order to enter the New Jerusalem, it is basically asking only that the proletariat remain within existing society while rejecting its odious ideas about it.

A second, less systematic and more practical form of socialism sought to make the working class recoil from every revolutionary movement by showing that neither this nor that political change but only a change in the material conditions of existence, in economical relations, could be of advantage to them. By change in the material conditions of existence, however, this socialism by no means understands the eradication of the bourgeois relations of production,

which is achievable only by way of revolution, but rather administrative improvements that advance on the basis of these relations of production, that therefore change not at all the relation between capital and wage-labor, but in the best case for the bourgeoisie lessen the cost of its rule and simplify the ways in which it is administered.

Bourgeois socialism finds fit expression only when it becomes a mere figure of speech.

Free trade!—in the interests of the working class. Protective duties!—in the interests of the working class. Prison cells now!—in the interests of the working class. This is the last, the only earnestly intended word of bourgeois Socialism.

Its socialism resides precisely in the proposition that the bourgeois are bourgeois—in the interests of the working class.

3. Critical-Utopian Socialism and Communism

We do not here refer to that literature which, in every great modern revolution, has always given voice to the demands of the proletariat (writings of Babœuf and others).[3]

The first direct attempts of the proletariat, in a time of general excitement, when feudal society was being overthrown, necessarily foundered because of the undeveloped state of the proletariat itself, as well as the absence of the material conditions for its emancipation, conditions unproducible in advance of the bourgeois era. The revolutionary literature that accompanied these first movements of the proletariat is unavoidably reactionary in content. It teaches a general asceticism and rude leveling.

The Socialist and Communist systems proper, the systems of Saint-Simon,[4] Fourier,[5] Owen[6] and others, emerge in the early undeveloped period of the struggle between proletariat and bourgeoisie we described above.

The creators of these systems admittedly see the class antagonisms, as well as the action of the fragmenting ele-

---

1 *hole-and-corner* Out-of-the-way, secretive.

2 *Proudhon's Philosophie de la Misère* Pierre Joseph Proudhon (1809–65) published in 1846 *Système des Contradictions Economiques ou Philosophie de la Misère* [*The System of Economic Conditions; or the Philosophy of Poverty*]. Marx replied in 1847 with *Misère de la Philosophie* [*The Poverty of Philosophy*].

3 *Babœuf* François Noël ["Gracchus"] Babœuf (1760–97); Marx approved of his defense of the ideals of the French Revolution.

4 *Saint-Simon* Count Claude Saint-Simon (1760–1825), influential nineteenth-century socialist writer.

5 *Fourier* Charles Fourier (1772–1837) was a French writer on social reform, socialist association, and model communities (phalansteries).

6 *Owen* Robert Owen (1771–1858) was a leading British advocate and organizer of co-operatives and model industrial villages.

ments in the dominant society itself. But they witness no historical self-determination on the part of the proletariat, no political movement particular to it.

Since the development of class antagonism proceeds in step with the development of industry, they do not as yet encounter the material conditions for the emancipation of the proletariat, and therefore seek after a social science, after new social laws, in order to bring about these conditions.

Social action has to yield to their personal inventive action; historical conditions of emancipation to those born of fantasy; and the gradual class-formation of the proletariat to a privately contrived shaping of society. Future world-history resolves itself for them into propaganda for, and practical implementation of, their social plans.

In their planning they are conscious of capturing mainly the interests of the working class as the class that suffers most. Only from this perspective of being the most suffering class does the proletariat exist for them.

The undeveloped state of the class struggle, as well as their own situation in life, brings them to believe themselves far superior to the class antagonism referred to above. They want to improve the life situation of every member of society, even those best off. Hence, they habitually appeal to the whole of society without distinction; nay, preferably to the ruling class. Assuredly, to see their system is to understand it as the best possible plan of the best possible society.

They consequently reject all political, and especially all revolutionary, action; they wish to attain their objective by peaceful means, and endeavor, by minor experiments that fail as a matter of course, by the force of example to clear the path for the new social gospel.

Such fantasizing about the society of the future, at a time when the proletariat is still in a very undeveloped state and can but fancifully conceive of its own position, corresponds to its earliest, fully prescient impulses towards a general reconstruction of society.

But these socialist and communist publications contain critical elements too. They attack all the foundations of existing society. Hence they have furnished most valuable materials for the enlightenment of the workers. Their positive proposals for the society of the future—for example, the abolition of the distinction between town and country, of the family, of private accumulation, of wage labor, the proclamation of social harmony, the conversion of the state into a mere superintendence of production—all these proposals

of theirs signify solely the disappearance of class antagonism which is only just forming and which they register only in its earliest, inchoate[1] forms. These proposals, therefore, retain a purely utopian significance.

The meaning of critical utopian socialism and communism bears an inverse relation to historical development. In proportion as the class struggle unfolds and takes definite shape, this imaginary elevation above it, these fantastic attacks upon it, lose all practical value, all theoretical justification. Therefore, although the originators of these systems were in many respects revolutionary, their disciples form reactionary sects all the time. They hold fast to the old views of their masters as opposed to the further historical development of the proletariat. They therefore endeavor consistently to deaden the class struggle and to resolve conflicts. They still dream of experimental realization of their social utopias, of founding separate phalansteries, of establishing home colonies,[2] of setting up a little Icaria[3]–duodecimo editions[4] of the New Jerusalem;[5] and to construct all these castles in the air, they are compelled to appeal to the hearts and money-bags of the bourgeois. By degrees they sink into the category of the aforementioned reactionary or conservative socialists, differing from them only by more systematic pedantry, by fanatical superstitious belief in the miraculous effects of their social science.

They therefore violently oppose all political action on the part of the workers, such action as could result only from blind unbelief in the new Gospel.

The Owenites in England and the Fourierists in France opposed the Chartists[6] and the *Réformistes*[7] respectively.

---

1   *inchoate*   Just beginning, as yet imperfectly developed.

2   *home colonies*   Cooperative communities established by Robert Owen in the early nineteenth century.

3   *Icaria*   A fictitious ideal society, subject of a book by Étienne Cabet (1788–1856), French philosopher and utopian socialist; the "Icarian communities" he established in the US eventually failed.

4   *duodecimo editions*   Literally, books with a very small page size; figuratively, miniature versions.

5   *New Jerusalem*   A literal or figurative ideal city.

6   *Chartists*   Chartism was a popular reformist movement that lasted from 1837 to 1848: among its demands (outlined in a "People's Charter" of 1837) were universal male suffrage, equal electoral districts, abolition of the property qualification for running for Parliament, and annual parliaments.

7   *Réformistes*   A political party grouped around the Paris newspaper, *La Réforme*, which included radical opponents of the July monarchy, republican democrats and petty-bourgeois socialists.

Position of the Communists in Relation to the Various Existing Opposition Parties

From Section 2 the relation of the Communists to the already constituted workers parties is plain, and accordingly their relation to the Chartists in England and the Agrarian Reformers in North America.[1]

They battle for the attainment of the immediate aims and interests of the working class; but in the current movement they at the same time represent the future of the movement. In France the Communists ally themselves with the Social-Democrats, against the conservative and radical bourgeoisie, without relinquishing the right to critique the phrases and illusions born of the revolutionary tradition.

In Switzerland they support the Radicals, without losing sight of the fact that this party consists of antagonistic elements, partly of democratic socialists in the French sense, partly of radical bourgeois.

Among Poles the Communists support the party that insists on an agrarian revolution as essential to national emancipation, the same party that brought about the Kraków insurrection[2] in 1846.

In Germany, as soon as the bourgeoisie acts in a revolutionary fashion the Communist party battles along with them against the absolute monarchy, feudal land tenure, and the petty bourgeoisie.

But they do not for an instant cease to nourish among the workers the clearest possible awareness of the hostile antagonism of bourgeoisie and proletariat, so that the German workers can instantly appropriate and adapt the social and political features which the bourgeoisie must introduce along with its dominance as so many weapons against the bourgeoisie, so that after the overthrow of the reactionary classes in Germany the struggle against the bourgeoisie itself can at once commence.

It is to Germany that the Communists are most attentive because Germany stands on the eve of a bourgeois revolution, and, because it is undertaking this radical change amid the more advanced conditions of European civilization generally and with a much more developed proletariat than England's in the seventeenth and France's in the eighteenth century, Germany's bourgeois revolution will thus be only the immediate forerunner of a proletarian revolution.

In a word, the Communists everywhere support every revolutionary movement against the existing social and political order of things.

In all these movements they foreground the property question as the fundamental question for the movement, no matter its degree of development.

Finally, the communists labor everywhere for the solidarity and agreement of the democratic parties of all countries.

The Communists disdain to conceal their views and aims. They openly declare that their objectives can be attained only by the forcible overthrow of all existing social orders. Let the ruling classes tremble at a communist revolution. In it proletarians have nothing to lose but their chains.

Proletarians of all lands unite![3]

♦ ♦ ♦ ♦ ♦

Critique of the Gotha Program[4] (1875)

I

1. "Labor is the source of wealth and all culture, and since useful labor is possible only in society and through society, the proceeds of labor belong undiminished with equal right to all members of society."

---

1   *Agrarian Reformers ... America*   The National Reform Association was founded in the US in 1844 to campaign for the free settlement of the landless on public lands, a moratorium on the seizure of family farms for non-payment of debt, and the establishment of a 160 acre ceiling on land ownership to ensure that there would be enough small-holdings to go round.

2   *Kraków insurrection*   A nationalist, republican uprising in southern Poland against the Russians, Prussians, and Austrians who had jointly occupied it since the collapse of Napoleon's empire in 1815: the rebellion was crushed, and Kraków was incorporated into the Austrian empire.

3   *Proletarians of all lands unite!*   In German, *Proletarier aller Länder, vereinigt euch!* This famous conclusion has also been translated into English as "Workers of the world, unite! You have nothing to lose but your chains."

4   *Gotha Program*   Common program for political change agreed on by the two branches of the German socialist movement at meetings held in the town of Gotha in central German in May

First part of the paragraph: "Labor is the source of all wealth and all culture."

Labor is not the source of all wealth. Nature is just as much the source of use values[1] (and it is surely of such that material wealth consists!) as labor, which itself is only the manifestation of a force of nature, human labor power. The above phrase is to be found in all children's primers and is correct insofar as it is implied that labor is performed with the appurtenant subjects and instruments.[2] But a socialist program cannot allow such bourgeois phrases to pass over in silence the conditions that alone give them meaning. And insofar as man from the beginning behaves toward nature, the primary source of all instruments and subjects of labor, as an owner, treats her as belonging to him, his labor becomes the source of use values, therefore also of wealth. The bourgeois have very good grounds for falsely ascribing supernatural creative power to labor; since precisely from the fact that labor depends on nature it follows that the man who possesses no other property than his labor power must, in all conditions of society and culture, be the slave of other men who have made themselves the owners of the material conditions of labor. He can only work with their permission, hence live only with their permission.

Let us now leave the sentence as it stands, or rather limps. What could one have expected in conclusion? Obviously this:

"Since labor is the source of all wealth, no one in society can appropriate wealth except as the product of labor. Therefore, if he himself does not work, he lives by the labor of others and also acquires his culture at the expense of the labor of others."

Instead of this, by means of the verbal rivet "and since," a proposition is added in order to draw a conclusion from this and not from the first one.

Second part of the paragraph: "Useful labor is possible only in society and through society."

According to the first proposition, labor was the source of all wealth and all culture; therefore no society is possible without labor. Now we learn, conversely, that no "useful" labor is possible without society.

One could just as well have said that only in society can useless and even socially harmful labor become a branch of gainful occupation, that only in society can one live by being idle, etc., etc.—in short, one could just as well have copied the whole of Rousseau.

And what is "useful" labor? Surely only labor which produces the intended useful result. A savage—and man was a savage after he had ceased to be an ape—who kills an animal with a stone, who collects fruit, etc., performs "useful" labor.

Thirdly, the conclusion: "Useful labor is possible only in society and through society, the proceeds of labor belong undiminished with equal right to all members of society."

A fine conclusion! If useful labor is possible only in society and through society, the proceeds of labor belong to society—and only so much therefrom accrues to the individual worker as is not required to maintain the "condition" of labor, society.

In fact, this proposition has at all times been made use of by the champions of the state of society prevailing at any given time. First comes the claims of the government and everything that sticks to it, since it is the social organ for the maintenance of the social order; then comes the claims of the various kinds of private property, for the various kinds of private property are the foundations of society, etc. One sees that such hollow phrases are the foundations of society, etc. One sees that such hollow phrases can be twisted and turned as desired.

The first and second parts of the paragraph have some intelligible connection only in the following wording:

"Labor becomes the source of wealth and culture only as social labor," or, what is the same thing, "in and through society."

This proposition is incontestably correct, for although isolated labor (its material conditions presupposed) can create use value, it can create neither wealth nor culture.

But equally incontestable is this other proposition:

"In proportion as labor develops socially, and becomes thereby a source of wealth and culture, poverty and destitution develop among the workers, and wealth and culture among the nonworkers."

1875. In Marx's view the more radical socialists (led by his protégé Wilhelm Liebknecht) had ceded too much in the agreement to the moderate socialist faction (led by Ferdinand Lassalle).

1 *use values* The "use value" of something is a measure of how much the consumer gets from its use. This is contrasted with the "exchange value" of something—how much of something else it can bring in return when exchanged on the market. These are distinct: often, one is far out of line with the other.

2 *appurtenant subjects and instruments* Accessory people and tools.

This is the law of all history hitherto. What, therefore, had to be done here, instead of setting down general phrases about "labor" and "society," was to prove concretely how in present capitalist society the material, etc., conditions have at last been created which enable and compel the workers to lift this social curse.

In fact, however, the whole paragraph, bungled in style and content, is only there in order to inscribe the Lassallean catchword of the "undiminished proceeds of labor" as a slogan at the top of the party banner. I shall return later to the "proceeds of labor," "equal right," etc., since the same thing recurs in a somewhat different form further on.

> 2. "In present-day society, the instruments of labor are the monopoly of the capitalist class; the resulting dependence of the working class is the cause of misery and servitude in all forms."

This sentence, borrowed from the Rules of the International,[1] is incorrect in this "improved" edition.

In present-day society, the instruments of labor are the monopoly of the landowners (the monopoly of property in land is even the basis of the monopoly of capital) and the capitalists. In the passage in question, the Rules of the International do not mention either one or the other class of monopolists. They speak of the "monopolizer of the means of labor, that is, the sources of life." The addition, "sources of life," makes it sufficiently clear that land is included in the instruments of labor.

The correction was introduced because Lassalle, for reasons now generally known, attacked only the capitalist class and not the landowners. In England, the capitalist class is usually not even the owner of the land on which his factory stands.

> 3. "The emancipation of labor demands the promotion of the instruments of labor to the common property of society and the co-operative regulation of the total labor, with a fair distribution of the proceeds of labor.

"Promotion of the instruments of labor to the common property" ought obviously to read their "conversion into the common property"; but this is only passing.

What are the "proceeds of labor"? The product of labor, or its value? And in the latter case, is it the total value of the product, or only that part of the value which labor has newly added to the value of the means of production consumed?

"Proceeds of labor" is a loose notion which Lassalle has put in the place of definite economic conceptions.

What is "a fair distribution"?

Do not the bourgeois assert that the present-day distribution is "fair"? And is it not, in fact, the only "fair" distribution on the basis of the present-day mode of production? Are economic relations regulated by legal conceptions, or do not, on the contrary, legal relations arise out of economic ones? Have not also the socialist sectarians the most varied notions about "fair" distribution?

To understand what is implied in this connection by the phrase "fair distribution," we must take the first paragraph and this one together. The latter presupposes a society wherein the instruments of labor are common property and the total labor is co-operatively regulated, and from the first paragraph we learn that "the proceeds of labor belong undiminished with equal right to all members of society."

"To all members of society"? To those who do not work as well? What remains then of the "undiminished" proceeds of labor? Only to those members of society who work? What remains then of the "equal right" of all members of society?

But "all members of society" and "equal right" are obviously mere phrases. The kernel consists in this, that in this communist society every worker must receive the "undiminished" Lassallean "proceeds of labor."

Let us take, first of all, the words "proceeds of labor" in the sense of the product of labor; then the co-operative proceeds of labor are the total social product.

From this must now be deducted: First, cover for replacement of the means of production used up. Second, additional portion for expansion of production. Third, reserve or insurance funds to provide against accidents, dislocations caused by natural calamities, etc.

These deductions from the "undiminished" proceeds of labor are an economic necessity, and their magnitude is to be determined according to available means and forces, and partly by computation of probabilities, but they are in no way calculable by equity.[2]

---

1   *Rules of the International*   "Rules of the International Workingmen's Association," London, 1864. This association, known as the IWA or the First International, aimed to unite all left-wing socialist and trade-union associations.

---

2   *equity*   Considerations of fairness.

There remains the other part of the total product, intended to serve as means of consumption.

Before this is divided among the individuals, there has to be deducted again, from it: First, the general costs of administration not belonging to production. This part will, from the outset, be very considerably restricted in comparison with present-day society, and it diminishes in proportion as the new society develops. Second, that which is intended for the common satisfaction of needs, such as schools, health services, etc. From the outset, this part grows considerably in comparison with present-day society, and it grows in proportion as the new society develops. Third, funds for those unable to work, etc., in short, for what is included under so-called official poor relief today.

Only now do we come to the "distribution" which the program, under Lassallean influence, alone has in view in its narrow fashion—namely, to that part of the means of consumption which is divided among the individual producers of the co-operative society.

The "undiminished" proceeds of labor have already unnoticeably become converted into the "diminished" proceeds, although what the producer is deprived of in his capacity as a private individual benefits him directly or indirectly in his capacity as a member of society.

Just as the phrase of the "undiminished" proceeds of labor has disappeared, so now does the phrase of the "proceeds of labor" disappear altogether.

Within the co-operative society based on common ownership of the means of production, the producers do not exchange their products; just as little does the labor employed on the products appear here as the value of these products, as a material quality possessed by them, since now, in contrast to capitalist society, individual labor no longer exists in an indirect fashion but directly as a component part of total labor. The phrase "proceeds of labor," objectionable also today on account of its ambiguity, thus loses all meaning.

What we have to deal with here is a communist society, not as it has developed on its own foundations, but, on the contrary, just as it emerges from capitalist society; which is thus in every respect, economically, morally, and intellectually, still stamped with the birthmarks of the old society from whose womb it emerges. Accordingly, the individual producer receives back from society—after the deductions have been made—exactly what he gives to it. What he has given to it is his individual quantum of labor. For example, the social working day consists of the sum of the individual hours of work; the individual labor time of the individual producer is the part of the social working day contributed by him, his share in it. He receives a certificate from society that he has furnished such-and-such an amount of labor (after deducting his labor for the common funds); and with this certificate, he draws from the social stock of means of consumption as much as the same amount of labor cost. The same amount of labor which he has given to society in one form, he receives back in another.

Here, obviously, the same principle prevails as that which regulates the exchange of commodities, as far as this is exchange of equal values. Content and form are changed, because under the altered circumstances no one can give anything except his labor, and because, on the other hand, nothing can pass to the ownership of individuals, except individual means of consumption. But as far as the distribution of the latter among the individual producers is concerned, the same principle prevails as in the exchange of commodity equivalents: a given amount of labor in one form is exchanged for an equal amount of labor in another form.

Hence, equal right here is still in principle—bourgeois right, although principle and practice are no longer at loggerheads, while the exchange of equivalents in commodity exchange exists only on the average and not in the individual case.

In spite of this advance, this equal right is still constantly stigmatized by a bourgeois limitation. The right of the producers is proportional to the labor they supply; the equality consists in the fact that measurement is made with an equal standard, labor.

But one man is superior to another physically, or mentally, and supplies more labor in the same time, or can labor for a longer time; and labor, to serve as a measure, must be defined by its duration or intensity, otherwise it ceases to be a standard of measurement. This equal right is an unequal right for unequal labor. It recognizes no class differences, because everyone is only a worker like everyone else; but it tacitly recognizes unequal individual endowment, and thus productive capacity, as a natural privilege. It is, therefore, a right of inequality, in its content, like every right. Right, by its very nature, can consist only in the application of an equal standard; but unequal individuals (and they would not be different individuals if they were not unequal) are measurable only by an equal standard insofar as they are brought under an equal point of view, are taken from one definite side only—for instance, in the present case, are regarded only as workers and nothing more is seen in them, everything else being ignored. Further, one worker is married, another is not; one has more children than another, and so on and so forth. Thus, with an equal performance of labor, and hence an equal in the social consumption fund, one will in fact receive more than another, one will be richer than another, and so on. To avoid all these defects, right, instead of being equal, would have to be unequal.

But these defects are inevitable in the first phase of communist society as it is when it has just emerged after prolonged birth pangs from capitalist society. Right can never be higher than the economic structure of society and its cultural development conditioned thereby.

In a higher phase of communist society, after the enslaving subordination of the individual to the division of labor, and therewith also the antithesis between mental and physical labor, has vanished; after labor has become not only a means of life but life's prime want; after the productive forces have also increased with the all-around development of the individual, and all the springs of co-operative wealth flow more abundantly—only then can the narrow horizon of bourgeois right be crossed in its entirety and society inscribe on its banners: From each according to his ability, to each according to his needs!

I have dealt more at length with the "undiminished" proceeds of labor, on the one hand, and with "equal right" and "fair distribution," on the other, in order to show what a crime it is to attempt, on the one hand, to force on our Party again, as dogmas, ideas which in a certain period had some meaning but have now become obsolete verbal rubbish, while again perverting, on the other, the realistic outlook, which it cost so much effort to instill into the Party but which has now taken root in it, by means of ideological nonsense about right and other trash so common among the democrats and French socialists.

Quite apart from the analysis so far given, it was in general a mistake to make a fuss about so-called distribution and put the principal stress on it.

Any distribution whatever of the means of consumption is only a consequence of the distribution of the conditions of production themselves. The latter distribution, however, is a feature of the mode of production itself. The capitalist mode of production, for example, rests on the fact that the material conditions of production are in the hands of nonworkers in the form of property in capital and land, while the masses are only owners of the personal condition of production, of labor power. If the elements of produc-

tion are so distributed, then the present-day distribution of the means of consumption results automatically. If the material conditions of production are the co-operative property of the workers themselves, then there likewise results a distribution of the means of consumption different from the present one. Vulgar socialism (and from it in turn a section of the democrats) has taken over from the bourgeois economists the consideration and treatment of distribution as independent of the mode of production and hence the presentation of socialism as turning principally on distribution. After the real relation has long been made clear, why retrogress[1] again?

> 4. "The emancipation of labor must be the work of the working class, relative to which all other classes are only one reactionary mass."

The first strophe[2] is taken from the introductory words of the Rules of the International, but "improved." There it is said: "The emancipation of the working class must be the act of the workers themselves"; here, on the contrary, the "working class" has to emancipate—what? "Labor." Let him understand who can.

In compensation, the antistrophe,[3] on the other hand, is a Lassallean quotation of the first water:[4] "relative to which" (the working class) "all other classes are only one reactionary mass."

In the *Communist Manifesto* it is said:

"Of all the classes that stand face-to-face with the bourgeoisie today, the proletariat alone is a really revolutionary class. The other classes decay and finally disappear in the face of modern industry; the proletariat is its special and essential product."

The bourgeoisie is here conceived as a revolutionary class—as the bearer of large-scale industry—relative to the feudal lords and the lower middle class, who desire to maintain all social positions that are the creation of obsolete modes of production. Thus, they do not form together with the bourgeoisie "only one reactionary mass."

On the other hand, the proletariat is revolutionary relative to the bourgeoisie because, having itself grown up on the basis of large-scale industry, it strives to strip off from production the capitalist character that the bourgeoisie

---

1   *retrogress*   Go backwards.
2   *strophe*   Part of the traditional song and dance of the chorus in ancient Greek drama.
3   *antistrophe*   Part following the strophe.
4   *of the first water*   Of the highest quality.

seeks to perpetuate. But the Manifesto adds that the "lower middle class" is becoming revolutionary "in view of [its] impending transfer to the proletariat."

From this point of view, therefore, it is again nonsense to say that it, together with the bourgeoisie, and with the feudal lords into the bargain, "form only one reactionary mass" relative to the working class.

Has one proclaimed to the artisan, small manufacturers, etc., and peasants during the last elections: Relative to us, you, together with the bourgeoisie and feudal lords, form one reactionary mass?

Lassalle knew the Communist Manifesto by heart, as his faithful followers know the gospels written by him. If, therefore, he has falsified it so grossly, this has occurred only to put a good color on his alliance with absolutist and feudal opponents against the bourgeoisie.

In the above paragraph, moreover, his oracular saying is dragged in by main force without any connection with the botched quotation from the Rules of the International. Thus, it is simply an impertinence, and indeed not at all displeasing to Herr Bismarck,[1] one of those cheap pieces of insolence in which the Marat of Berlin[2] deals.

5. "The working class strives for its emancipation first of all within the framework of the present-day national states, conscious that the necessary result of its efforts, which are common to the workers of all civilized countries, will be the international brotherhood of peoples."

Lassalle, in opposition to the *Communist Manifesto* and to all earlier socialism, conceived the workers' movement from the narrowest national standpoint. He is being followed in this—and that after the work of the International!

It is altogether self-evident that, to be able to fight at all, the working class must organize itself at home as a class and that its own country is the immediate arena of its struggle—insofar as its class struggle is national, not in substance, but, as the *Communist Manifesto* says, "in form."

But the "framework of the present-day national state," for instance, the German Empire, is itself, in its turn, economically "within the framework" of the world market, politically "within the framework" of the system of states. Every businessman knows that German trade is at the same time foreign trade, and the greatness of Herr Bismarck consists, to be sure, precisely in his pursuing a kind of international policy.

And to what does the German Workers' party reduce its internationalism? To the consciousness that the result of its efforts will be "the international brotherhood of peoples"— a phrase borrowed from the bourgeois League of Peace and Freedom,[3] which is intended to pass as equivalent to the international brotherhood of working classes in the joint struggle against the ruling classes and their governments. Not a word, therefore, about the international functions of the German working class! And it is thus that it is to challenge its own bourgeoisie—which is already linked up in brotherhood against it with the bourgeois of all other countries—and Herr Bismarck's international policy of conspiracy.

In fact, the internationalism of the program stands even infinitely below that of the Free Trade party.[4] The latter also asserts that the result of its efforts will be "the international brotherhood of peoples." But it also does something to make trade international and by no means contents itself with the consciousness that all people are carrying on trade at home.

The international activity of the working classes does not in any way depend on the existence of the International Working Men's Association. This was only the first attempt to create a central organ for the activity; an attempt which was a lasting success on account of the impulse which it gave but which was no longer realizable in its historical form after the fall of the Paris Commune.[5]

Bismarck's *Norddeutsche*[6] was absolutely right when it announced, to the satisfaction of its master, that the Ger-

1 *Herr Bismarck* Otto von Bismarck (1815–98), Chancellor of the German Empire.
2 *the Marat of Berlin* By this phrase, Marx refers to Wilhelm Hasselmann, editor of the *Neuer Social-Democrat*, a journal associated with the General German Workers' Association (*Allgemeiner Deutscher Arbeiterverein*, ADAV), a non-revolutionary reformist socialist group founded by Lassalle. Jean-Paul Marat (1743–93), an activist in the French Revolution, was a ferocious radical who played an instrumental role in the Reign of Terror.
3 *League of Peace and Freedom* Pacifist organization founded in Switzerland in 1867. It urged formation of a United States of Europe as a way to prevent wars.
4 *Free Trade party* A German movement advocating free trade as a way of increasing economic productivity, and thus of helping the poor.
5 *Paris Commune* Socialist government that ruled Paris for two months in 1871.
6 *Norddeutsche* Berlin newspaper (*Norddeutsche Allgemeine Zeitung*), the official organ of Bismarck's government at the time.

man Workers' party had sworn off internationalism in the new program.

II

"Starting from these basic principles, the German workers' party strives by all legal means for the free state—and—socialist society: that abolition of the wage system together with the iron law of wages—and—exploitation in every form; the elimination of all social and political inequality."

I shall return to the "free" state later.

So, in future, the German Workers' party has got to believe in Lassalle's "iron law of wages"! That this may not be lost, the nonsense is perpetrated of speaking of the "abolition of the wage system" (it should read: system of wage labor), "together with the iron law of wages." If I abolish wage labor, then naturally I abolish its laws also, whether they are of "iron" or sponge. But Lassalle's attack on wage labor turns almost solely on this so-called law. In order, therefore, to prove that Lassalle's sect has conquered, the "wage system" must be abolished "together with the iron law of wages" and not without it.

It is well known that nothing of the "iron law of wages" is Lassalle's except the word "iron" borrowed from Göethe's "great, eternal iron laws."[1] The word "iron" is a label by which the true believers recognize one another. But if I take the law with Lassalle's stamp on it, and consequently in his sense, then I must also take it with his substantiation[2] for it. And what is that? As Lange[3] already showed, shortly after Lassalle's death, it is the Malthusian theory of population[4] (preached by Lange himself). But if this theory is correct, then again I cannot abolish the law even if I abolish wage labor a hundred times over, because the law then governs not only the system of wage labor but every social system.

Basing themselves directly on this, the economists have been proving for 50 years and more that socialism cannot abolish poverty, which has its basis in nature, but can only make it general, distribute it simultaneously over the whole surface of society!

But all this is not the main thing. Quite apart from the false Lassallean formulation of the law, the truly outrageous retrogression[5] consists in the following:

Since Lassalle's death, there has asserted itself in our party the scientific understanding that wages are not what they appear to be—namely, the value, or price, of labor—but only a masked form for the value, or price, of labor power. Thereby, the whole bourgeois conception of wages hitherto, as well as all the criticism hitherto directed against this conception, was thrown overboard once and for all. It was made clear that the wage worker has permission to work for his own subsistence—that is, to live, only insofar as he works for a certain time gratis[6] for the capitalist (and hence also for the latter's co-consumers of surplus value[7]); that the whole capitalist system of production turns on the increase of this gratis labor by extending the working day, or by developing the productivity—that is, increasing the intensity or labor power, etc.; that, consequently, the system of wage labor is a system of slavery, and indeed of a slavery which becomes more severe in proportion as the social productive forces of labor develop, whether the worker receives better or worse payment. And after this understanding has gained more and more ground in our party, some return to Lassalle's dogma although they must have known that Lassalle did not know what wages were, but, following in the wake of the bourgeois economists, took the appearance for the essence of the matter.

It is as if, among slaves who have at last got behind the secret of slavery and broken out in rebellion, a slave still in thrall to[8] obsolete notions were to inscribe on the program of the rebellion: Slavery must be abolished because the feed-

---

1   *Göethe's great, eternal iron laws*   Principles set out by German poet, novelist, scientist and statesman Johann Wolfgang von Göethe in "Das Göttlich" ("The Divine").

2   *substantiation*   Evidence.

3   *Lange*   Friedrich Albert Lange (1828–75) German philosopher and journalist, active in the German labor movement and in the development of social democratic thought.

4   *the Malthusian theory of population*   English economist Thomas Malthus (1766–1834) argued that population would increase at a geometric rate but the food supply at an arithmetic rate; this would lead to poverty and starvation which could be counteracted only by disease, famine, war, or moral restraint.

5   *retrogression*   Backward movement.

6   *gratis*   For free.

7   *surplus value*   Marx's term for the value of unpaid work for extra hours of labor appropriated by the capitalist. Marx held that, in the capitalist system, a worker's labor would be worth the subsistence wage. He explained profit by noting that while the capitalist would pay workers the subsistence wage, they would work hours beyond what is needed to earn this wage. The capitalist would then pass along the "true value" of the products to consumers, making a profit at the expense of the workers.

8   *in thrall to*   Dominated by.

ing of slaves in the system of slavery cannot exceed a certain low maximum!

Does not the mere fact that the representatives of our party were capable of perpetrating such a monstrous attack on the understanding that has spread among the mass of our party prove, by itself, with what criminal levity and with what lack of conscience they set to work in drawing up this compromise program!

Instead of the indefinite concluding phrase of the paragraph, "the elimination of all social and political inequality," it ought to have been said that with the abolition of class distinctions all social and political inequality arising from them would disappear of itself.

III

> "The German workers' party, in order to *pave the way to the solution of the social question,* demands the establishment of producers' co-operative societies *with state aid under the democratic control of the toiling people.* The producers' co-operative societies *are* to *be called into being* for industry and agriculture on such a scale *that the socialist organization of the total labor will arise from them.*"

After the Lassallean "iron law of wages,"[1] the physic of the prophet.[2] The way to it is "paved" in worthy fashion. In place of the existing class struggle appears a newspaper scribbler's phrase: "the social *question,*" to the "*solution*" of which one "paves the way." Instead of arising from the revolutionary process of transformation of society, the "socialist organization of the total labor" "arises" from: the "state aid" that the state gives to the producers' co-operative societies and which the *state,* not the worker, "*calls into being.*" It is worthy of Lassalle's imagination that with state loans one can build a new society just as well as a new railway!

From the remnants of a sense of shame, "state aid" has been put—under the democratic control of the "toiling people."

In the first place, the majority of the "toiling people" in Germany consists of peasants, and not of proletarians.

Secondly, "democratic" means in German "*volksherrschaftlich.*"[3] But what does "control by the rule of the people of the toiling people"[4] mean? And particularly in the case of a toiling people which, through these demands that it puts to the state, expresses its full consciousness that it neither rules nor is ripe for ruling!

It would be superfluous to deal here with the criticism of the recipe prescribed by Buchez in the reign of Louis Philippe in *opposition* to the French Socialists and accepted by the reactionary workers of the *Atelier.*[5] The chief offence does not lie in having inscribed this specific nostrum[6] in the program, but in taking, in general, a retrograde step from the standpoint of a class movement to that of a sectarian[7] movement.

That the workers desire to establish the conditions for co-operative production on a social scale, and first of all on a national scale in their own country, only means that they are working to revolutionize the present conditions of production, and it has nothing in common with the foundation of co-operative societies with state aid. But as far as the present co-operative societies are concerned, they are of value *only* in so far as they are the independent creations of the workers and not protégés either of the government or of the bourgeois.

IV

I come now to the democratic section.

A. "The Free Basis of the State"

First of all, according to II, the German workers' party strives for "the free state."

Free state—what is this?

It is by no means the aim of the workers, who have got rid of the narrow mentality of humble subjects, to set

---

1   *iron law of wages* This "law" of economics, named but not invented by Lassalle, says that wages tend to revert to subsistence levels, just sufficient for workers to live.

2   *physic of the prophet* A physic is a supposedly cure-all potion; Marx refers to Lassalle as the "Prophet" and to his proposal for cooperative societies as a cure-all.

3   *volksherrschaftlich* Literally, "by the rule of the people."

4   *control by the rule ... toiling people* Marx is making fun of the redundancy in the passage which mentions both "democratic" and "rule of the people."

5   *recipe ... the Atelier* Buchez was a Christian Socialist who became President of the Constituent Assembly in France after Louis-Philippe was ousted by the Revolution of 1848. *Atelier* was a journal which represented his views.

6   *nostrum* Ineffective remedy.

7   *sectarian* Narrow, pertaining to a small "sect" as opposed to a mass movement.

the state free. In the German Empire the "state" is almost as "free" as in Russia. Freedom consists in converting the state from an organ superimposed upon society into one completely subordinate to it, and today, too, the forms of state are more free or less free to the extent that they restrict the "freedom of the state."

The German workers' party—at least if it adopts the program—shows that its socialist ideas are not even skin-deep; in that, instead of treating existing society (and this holds good for any future one) as the *basis* of the existing state (or of the future state in the case of future society), it treats the state rather as independent entity that possesses its own *intellectual, ethical and libertarian bases.*

And what of the riotous misuse which the program makes of the words "*present-day state,*" "*present-day society,*" and of the still more riotous misconception it creates in regard to the state to which it addresses its demands?

"Present-day society" is capitalist society, which exists in all civilized countries, more or less free from medieval admixture, more or less modified by the special historical development of each country, more or less developed. On the other hand, the "present-day state" changes with a country's frontier. It is different in the Prusso-German Empire from what it is in Switzerland, it is different in England from what it is in the United States. The "present-day state" is, therefore, a fiction.

Nevertheless, the different states of the different civilized countries, in spite of their manifold diversity of form, all have this in common, that they are based on modern bourgeois society, only one more or less capitalistically developed. They have, therefore, also certain essential features in common. In this sense it is possible to speak of the "present-day state," in contrast with the future, in which its present root, bourgeois society, will have died off.

The question then arises: what transformation will the state undergo in communist society? In other words, what social functions will remain in existence there that are analogous to present functions of the state? This question can only be answered scientifically, and one does not get a flea-hop nearer to the problem by a thousand-fold combination of the word 'people' with the word 'state.'

Between capitalist and communist society lies the period of the revolutionary transformation of the one into the other. There corresponds to this also a political transition period in which the state can be nothing but *the revolutionary dictatorship of the proletariat.*

Now the program does not deal with this nor with the future state of communist society.

Its political demands contain nothing beyond the old democratic litany familiar to all: universal suffrage,[1] direct legislation, popular rights, a people's militia, etc. They are a mere echo of the bourgeois People's Party,[2] of the League of Peace and Freedom. They are all demands which, in so far as they are not exaggerated in fantastic presentation, have already been *realized.* Only the state to which they belong does not lie within the borders of the German Empire, but in Switzerland, the United States, etc. This sort of "state of the future" is a present-day state, although existing outside the "framework" of the German Empire.

But one thing has been forgotten. Since the German workers' party expressly declares that it acts within "the present-day national state," hence within *its own* state, the Prusso-German Empire—its demands would indeed otherwise be largely meaningless, since one only demands what one has not got—it should not have forgotten the chief thing, namely, that all those pretty little gewgaws rest on the recognition of the so-called sovereignty of the people and hence are appropriate only in a *democratic republic.*

Since one has not the courage—and wisely so, for the circumstances demand caution—to demand the democratic republic, as the French workers' programs under Louis Philippe and under Louis Napoleon did, one should not have resorted, either, to the subterfuge, neither "honest" nor decent, of demanding things which have meaning only in a democratic republic from a state which is nothing but a police-guarded military despotism, embellished with parliamentary forms, alloyed with a feudal admixture, already influenced by the bourgeoisie and bureaucratically carpentered, and then to assure this state into the bargain that one imagines one will be able to force such things upon it "by legal means."

Even vulgar democracy, which sees the millennium[3] in the democratic republic and has no suspicion that it is precisely in this last form of state of bourgeois society that the class struggle has to be fought out to a conclusion—even it

---

1   *universal suffrage* Voting rights for all adult individuals in a society.
2   *People's Party* Established in Germany in 1865, this party unsuccessfully opposed the unification of Germany as a centralized democratic republic under Prussian domination, advocating instead a German federation including Prussia and Austria.
3   *millennium* Hoped-for utopian age.

towers mountains above this kind of democratism which keeps within the limits of what is permitted by the police and not permitted by logic.

That, in fact, by the word "state" is meant the government machine, or the state in so far as it forms a special organism separated from society through division of labor, is shown by the words "the German worker's party demands *as the economic basis of the state*: a single progressive income tax," etc. Taxes are the economic basis of the government machinery and of nothing else. In the state of the future, existing in Switzerland, this demand has been pretty well fulfilled. Income tax presupposes various sources of income of the various social classes, and hence capitalist society. It is, therefore, nothing remarkable that the Liverpool financial reformers, bourgeois headed by Gladstone's brother, are putting forward the same demand as the program.

B. "The German Workers' Party Demands as the Intellectual and Ethical Basis of the State:

1. 'UNIVERSAL AND EQUAL ELEMENTARY EDUCATION BY THE STATE. UNIVERSAL COMPULSORY SCHOOL ATTENDANCE. FREE INSTRUCTION.'"

Equal elementary education? What idea lies behind these words? Is it believed that in present-day society (and it is only with this one has to deal) education can be *equal* for all classes? Or is it demanded that the upper classes also shall be compulsorily reduced to the modicum of education—the elementary school—that alone is compatible with the economic conditions not only of the wageworkers but of the peasants as well?

"Universal compulsory school attendance. Free instruction." The former exists even in Germany, the second in Switzerland and in the United States in the case of elementary schools. If in some states of the latter country higher educational institutions are also "free" that only means in fact defraying the cost of the education of the upper classes from the general tax receipts. Incidentally, the same holds good for "free administration of justice" demanded under A, 5. The administration of criminal justice is to be had free everywhere; that of civil justice is concerned almost exclusively with conflicts over property and hence affects almost exclusively the possessing classes. Are they to carry on their litigation at the expense of the national coffers?

The paragraph on the schools should at least have demanded technical schools (theoretical and practical) in combination with the elementary school.

"*Elementary education by the state*" is altogether objectionable. Defining by a general law the expenditures on the elementary schools, the qualifications of the teaching staff, the branches of instruction, etc., and, as is done in the United States, supervising the fulfillment of these legal specifications by state inspectors, is a very different thing from appointing the state as the educator of the people! Government and Church should rather be equally excluded from any influence on the school. Particularly, indeed, in the Prusso-German Empire (and one should not take refuge in the rotten subterfuge that one is speaking of a "state of the future"; we have seen how matters stand in this respect) the state has need, on the contrary, of a very stern education by the people.

But the whole program, for all its democratic clang, is tainted through and through by the Lassallean sect's servile belief in the state, or, what is no better, by a democratic belief in miracles, or rather it is a compromise between these two kinds of belief in miracles, both equally remote from socialism.

"*Freedom of science*" says a paragraph of the Prussian Constitution. Why, then, here?

"*Freedom of conscience!*" If one desired at this time of the *Kulturkampf*[1] to remind liberalism of its old catchwords, it surely could have been done only in the following form: Everyone should be able to attend to his religious as well as his bodily needs without the police sticking their noses in. But the workers' party ought at any rate in this connection to have expressed its awareness of the fact that bourgeois "freedom of conscience" is nothing but the toleration of all possible kinds of *religious freedom of conscience*, and that for its part it endeavors rather to liberate the conscience from the witchery of religion. But one chooses not to transgress the "bourgeois" level.

I have now come to the end, for the appendix that now follows in the program does not constitute a characteristic component part of it. Hence I can be very brief here.

---

1 *Kulturkampf* German: battle of civilizations. Here the reference is to Bismarck's struggle in the 1870s against the German Catholic Party, a Party of the "Center," by means of police persecution of Catholicism.

"The German Workers' Party Demands as the Intellectual and Ethical Basis of the State:

2. 'Normal Working Day'"

In no other country has the workers' party limited itself to such an indefinite demand, but has always fixed the length of the working day that it considers normal under the given circumstances.

"The German Workers' Party Demands as the Intellectual and Ethical Basis of the State:

3. 'Restriction of Female Labor and Prohibition of Child Labor'"

The standardization of the working day must include the restriction of female labor, in so far as it relates to the duration, intermissions, etc., of the working day; otherwise it could only mean the exclusion of female labor from branches of industry that are especially unhealthy for the female body or are objectionable morally for the female sex. If that is what was meant, it should have been said so.

"*Prohibition of child labor.*" Here it was absolutely essential to state the age limit.

A *general prohibition* of child labor is incompatible with the existence of large-scale industry and hence an empty, pious wish. Its realization—if it were possible—would be reactionary, since, with a strict regulation of the working time according to the different age groups and other safety measures for the protection of children, an early combination of productive labor with education is one of the most potent means for the transformation of present-day society.

"The German Workers' Party Demands as the Intellectual and Ethical Basis of the State:

4. 'State Supervision of Factory, Workshop and Domestic Industry'"

In consideration of the Prusso-German state it should definitely have been demanded that the inspectors are to be removable only by a court of law; that any worker can have them prosecuted for neglect of duty; that they must belong to the medical profession.

"The German Workers' Party Demands as the Intellectual and Ethical Basis of the State:

5. 'Regulation of Prison Labor'"

A petty demand in a general workers' program. In any case, it should have been clearly stated that there is no intention from fear of competition to allow ordinary criminals to be treated like beasts, and especially that there is no desire to deprive them of their sole means of betterment, productive labor. This was surely the least one might have expected from Socialists.

"The German Workers' Party Demands as the Intellectual and Ethical Basis of the State:

6. 'An Effective Liability Law'"

It should have been stated what is meant by an "effective" liability law.

Be it noted, incidentally, that in speaking of the normal working day the part of factory legislation that deals with health regulations and safety measures, etc., has been overlooked. The liability law only comes into operation when these regulations are infringed.

In short, this appendix also is distinguished by slovenly editing.

Dixi et salvavi animam meam.[1]

---

1   *Dixi et salvavi animam meam*   Latin: I have spoken and saved my soul.

FRIEDRICH NIETZSCHE
(1844 – 1900)

In the end, what is there for it? There is no other means to bring philosophy again into honor: one must first hang all moralists.

—Friedrich Nietzsche

Who Was Friedrich Nietzsche?

FRIEDRICH WILHELM NIETZSCHE WAS ONE OF THE MOST original, important and—belatedly—influential voices of the nineteenth century, and is among the greatest of the German-speaking philosophers since Kant. He was born in 1844, on the birthday of King Friedrich Wilhelm IV of Prussia (after whom he was named), in the village of Röcken near Leipzig in the region of Saxony. His father and both grandfathers were Lutheran ministers. Nietzsche's father, Carl Ludwig, died of a head injury before he was five and Nietzsche's younger brother died the next year, and so he and his sister Elisabeth were brought up by his mother, Franziska, and two aunts. As a young boy he struggled with his schoolwork, but persevered, rising at 5 am to begin his school day and then studying extra hours in the evening to keep up with his Greek. He spent much of his free time playing the piano—Nietzsche was a skilled pianist—and, beginning before the age of ten and continuing throughout his life, he composed many pieces of music and wrote a great deal of poetry.

In 1858 Nietzsche was admitted to Schulpforta, one of Germany's oldest and most prestigious private boarding schools. The fourteen-year-old Nietzsche found the transition to the school's rigorous, almost monastic, regime hard, but again he persevered and played an energetic role in the school's intellectual, musical and cultural life. By 1861, however, he was beginning to be plagued by headaches, fevers, eye strain and weakness—the first real signs of the ill health from which he was to suffer for the rest of his life. In 1864 Nietzsche graduated from Pforta: although his grades were patchy he had already shown signs of great intellectual promise, especially in the study of languages.

After a brief stint as a theology student at the University of Bonn, Nietzsche enrolled at the university in Leipzig and began work in classical philology—the study of the linguistic, interpretative and historical aspects of Greek and Roman literature. At this time he discovered the work of Arthur Schopenhauer (1788–1860), a pessimistic German philosopher who saw the world as an irrational, godless place of ceaseless striving and suffering. He also met and became friends with the composer Richard Wagner (1813–83), a creative genius who revolutionized opera with his concept of a "music drama" fusing music, poetry, drama, and legend (the most famous expression of which is his *Ring* cycle). Both of these men were to be great influences on Nietzsche's philosophical thought.

Before he had completed his studies Nietzsche was invited to take up a post as professor of classical philology at the University of Basel in Switzerland, at the unprecedentedly young age of 24; and Leipzig University hastily gave him a doctorate without even bothering with the formality of an examination. Nietzsche began his new job at Basel in 1869, after renouncing his Prussian citizenship, and in 1870 was immediately promoted to the rank of full professor. In that same year the French parliament declared war on Prussia. Nietzsche volunteered for military service but, because of Switzerland's neutrality, he was allowed only to serve as a medical orderly. He was on the front lines for approximately a week before falling ill himself—of diphtheria—and he spent most of the rest of the short Franco-Prussian war (Paris surrendered in January 1871) recuperating, and continuing his academic work.

His first book, *The Birth of Tragedy out of the Spirit of Music*, appeared in 1872 and was expected to secure his reputation as a brilliant young scholar: instead, it caused a small tempest of academic controversy—a battle which

Nietzsche was deemed by his professional contemporaries to have lost. Rather than publishing a traditional work of classical scholarship, Nietzsche had instead presented a rhapsodic, free-flowing essay which attempted to apply Schopenhauer's philosophical ideas to an interpretation of the origins of Greek tragedy, and which argued that the spirit of Greek tragedy was once again reborn in the music-dramas of Richard Wagner. Nietzsche hoped that this work would establish his reputation as a philosopher (and allow him to transfer to the philosophy department at Basel), but it no more resembled a traditional work of philosophy than it did one of philology. Nietzsche's reputation as a professional scholar was from this point on irreparably damaged.

For several years after the publication of *The Birth of Tragedy*, Nietzsche was generally shunned by students but he continued to teach philosophy at Basel until 1879. In that year he was forced to resign due to ill health: by this time he could often hardly see to read and write, and was beset with headaches and other pains. He was given a pension of two-thirds his salary. It was not quite enough for Nietzsche to live on comfortably, but now he was free to devote all his time to his real love—the writing of philosophy.

Disliking the increasingly nationalist climate of Bismarck's "Second Reich," Nietzsche spent most of the next decade, from 1880 until 1889, in self-imposed exile, wandering around Europe (France, Italy, Switzerland) staying with various friends. In 1882, in Rome, Nietzsche met the bewitching Lou von Andreas-Salomé and fell madly in love with her. Within two months he asked her to marry him; she refused. A month later in Lucerne he proposed again, and was again rejected. Nevertheless, Nietzsche, Salomé, and their mutual friend Paul Rée became for a time firm companions, traveling together and calling themselves the *Dreieinigkeit* or "trinity" of free spirits. The capricious Salomé, however, was not warmly received by Nietzsche's possessive mother and sister—eventually his mother refused to have Lou in the house. This caused such family bickering that Nietzsche, upset and depressed, broke off his relations with Rée and Salomé and also ceased his correspondence with his mother and sister for a few months. On his (rather bumpy) reconciliation with his sister Elisabeth, she began a campaign to turn Nietzsche decisively against Rée and Salomé, and was quite quickly successful in making the split between Nietzsche and his former friends irrevocable.

Despite this and various other emotional upsets, Nietzsche produced several substantial philosophical books during the first few years of his "wandering" decade: *Hu-*

man, All Too Human: A Book for Free Spirits (1878–80), *Daybreak: Thoughts on the Prejudices of Morality* (1881), *The Gay Science* (1882), and *Thus Spake Zarathustra* (1883–85). They sold so few copies, however, that by the time he came to write *Beyond Good and Evil* (1886) he was having great difficulty finding publishers and was rapidly running out of money. The late 1880s were lonely, worried years for Nietzsche: his health was very bad, he had little money, he had destroyed his relationships with most of his friends (including Wagner and his circle), and his philosophical work was falling on deaf ears.

In 1887 Nietzsche published *On the Genealogy of Morals*, and in 1888, at long last, he began to see the first signs of public recognition he craved; the new book reached a much broader readership. Nietzsche, never a modest man, soon began to show signs of full-blown megalomania, referring to himself in letters as, for example, "the first spirit of the age" and "a genius of the Truth." In this final year of his sanity he managed to write no fewer than five new books: *The Case of Wagner*, *Twilight of the Idols* (or *How to Philosophize with a Hammer*), *The Anti-Christ*, *Ecce Homo*, and *Nietzsche Contra Wagner*. By January of 1889, however, his communications were so bizarre—they are the so-called *Wahnbriefe*, or "mad letters"—that his remaining friends became concerned and called in the director of the Psychiatric Clinic in Basel, Dr. Ludwig Wille.

Nietzsche, by now completely insane, was tracked down in Turin and (with the help of a local dentist named Dr. Bettmann) was brought back to Basel and then quickly transferred to a psychiatric clinic in the central German city of Jena. He was only 44. The doctors quickly agreed that the prospects for Nietzsche's recovery were slim, even after his condition improved somewhat with confinement and treatment. They reported that "he speaks more coherently and ... the episodes with screaming are more seldom. Different delirious notions appear continually, and auditory hallucinations still occur.... He recognizes his environment only partially, e.g., he calls the chief orderly Prince Bismarck etc. He does not know exactly where he is."

In 1890, Nietzsche was released into the care of his mother and his mental health declined even further into a kind of permanent apathy and, gradually, paralysis.

Meanwhile, his sister Elisabeth seized control of Nietzsche's literary remains.[1] She created a Nietzsche Archive in

---

1   She and her racist husband Bernhard Förster (whom Nietzsche detested) had been living in Paraguay, South America, where

Naumburg, near Leipzig, in 1894 and quickly turned out a biography of her brother in which she presented herself as his major influence and closest friend. She even hired a tutor, Rudolf Steiner, to teach her about her brother's philosophy, but after a few months Steiner resigned in disgust, declaring that it was impossible to teach her anything about philosophy. After much legal wrangling, editions of many of Nietzsche's previously unpublished works were released, several of his books were translated into English and other languages, and (partly because of his sister's energetic, if self-serving, proselytizing) Nietzsche's intellectual influence began to increase. It is now widely agreed, however, that Elisabeth's editing practices caused great harm to Nietzsche's reputation for many years after his death; many of his thoughts were twisted to fit her virulent German nationalism and Christianity—and her virulent anti-Semitism.

Nietzsche finally died in the German city of Weimar—where Elisabeth had relocated the Nietzsche Archive, along with her helpless brother—on August 25, 1900.[1] For some time before his death, his sister—who was still enthusiastically encouraging the formation of a "Nietzsche cult"—had taken to dressing the half-paralyzed Nietzsche in ridiculous "holy" outfits and propping him up on the balcony of his home for the adoring groups below to witness, an indignity which Nietzsche would have loathed.

What Was Nietzsche's Overall Philosophical Project?

Nietzsche's unusual philosophical approach makes him one of the most difficult philosophers to interpret. His arguments are rarely straightforward and require considerable diligence on the part of the reader. With some exceptions (the *Untimely Mediations* and *Genealogy of Morals*, included here, come to mind), he prefers to write in short sections (which may extend to a few pages) or aphorisms. One of the few great stylists among philosophers, Nietzsche employs many literary devices, including metaphor, hyperbole, and irony (not to mention invective and sarcasm), designed to provoke the reader. He expects his readers to struggle act-

---

Förster was attempting to establish the pure Aryan colony of "New Germany." However Förster committed suicide in 1889 and, after unsuccessfully trying for a few months to hold the colony together, Elisabeth returned to Germany.

1   Although there is still controversy about this issue, most commentators agree that he probably suffered from and succumbed to syphilis.

ively with the problems he raises and to that end he often refuses to set out his claims in a straightforward manner. In a passage from the *Gay Science*, he writes, "It is not by any means necessarily an objection to a book when anyone finds it impossible to understand: perhaps that was part of the author's intention—he did not want to be understood by just 'anybody.' All the nobler spirits and tastes select their audience when they wish to communicate; and choosing that, one at the same time erects barriers against 'the others'" (*Gay Science* 381). Needless to say, this doesn't make for easy reading!

Beyond this, Nietzsche often presents various perspectives on the same issue, raising further interpretative problems, especially when different passages either explicitly or implicitly contradict each other. This isn't simply a result of his views evolving over time (though they did) or his reliance on multiple discourses, including philology, law, medicine, economics, and biology. In an oft-quoted passage from his early unpublished work, "On Truth and Lies in a Non-moral Sense" (1873), Nietzsche claimed that "truth" is only "a mobile army of metaphors, metonyms, and anthropomorphisms." Nietzsche savagely critiques how philosophers have been led by words to make claims about reality; he is acutely aware of how language shapes our concepts, potentially leading us astray. Nietzsche doesn't hold a crude relativism where every view has equal warrant—if he did, it would be hard to see how he could hold any substantial views. He believed instead that various of these perspectives have merit and need to be evaluated in terms of their human value. In the *Genealogy of Morals* he asserts, "There is *only* a perspective seeing, *only* a perspective 'knowing'; and the *more* affects we allow to speak about one thing, the *more* eyes, different eyes, we can use to observe one thing, the more complete will our 'concept' of this thing, our 'objectivity,' be" (Third Essay, Section 12). As a result, scholars often diverge widely on fundamental issues. Any attempt to present a non-controversial summary of Nietzsche's philosophy is bound to fail.

A further obstacle for anyone writing about his social and political philosophy is that, while Nietzsche is widely recognized as an important moral philosopher, it is not clear that he has a well-developed social or political philosophy. In *Ecce Homo*, he claims, "It is only beginning with me that the earth knows *great politics*" (*Ecce Homo*, "Why I Am a Destiny," 1). However, in the same book he suggests, "I am perhaps more German than present-day Germans, mere citizens of the German *Reich*, could possibly be—I, the last *anti-political* German" ("Why I am So Wise," 3). Though he has many remarks expressing political views, these are rarely developed and, at times, are naïve or odious. Nietzsche clearly did not believe that every human being has equal moral worth and denigrates liberalism, egalitarianism and democracy. This has sometimes been taken to imply a coherent political stance.[1] At the same time, Nietzsche never presents a developed *theory* of the state, justice, political legitimacy, liberty, toleration, international affairs, gender relations, or other major political topic.

Some philosophers have seized on Nietzsche's discussion of the Hindu Laws of Manu in the *Antichrist* (section 57), which appear to support a hierarchical caste based society. While this resonates in some ways with Nietzsche's claim that there are different types of people—masters and slaves (more on this below)—other remarks explicitly criticize such laws (*Twilight of the Idols*, "The 'Improvers' of Mankind," 3). Indeed, when taken in context, the passage in the *Antichrist* should be read as a rhetorical contrast to Christianity, *not* as an endorsement of Manu.[2]

One might seize on the "anti-political" remark mentioned above in setting out Nietzsche's political philosophy. For example, in *Thus Spake Zarathustra*, Nietzsche adds, "Only where the state ends, there begins the human being who is not superfluous" (*Zarathustra* I:11). There are other passages where Nietzsche considers the state antithetical to culture and creativity. This suggests that Nietszche is a sort of anarchist (as he was considered to be by Emma Goldman). But elsewhere Nietzsche identifies anarchists and Christians as "both decadents, both incapable of having any effect other than disintegrating, poisoning, withering, bloodsucking ..." (*The Antichrist* 58).

Why, then, include Nietzsche in an anthology of social and political philosophy? First, he provides one of the most original and subtle analyses of morality, as he pursues his ambition of providing a re-evaluation of morals. Though he has some predecessors, notably the character of Callicles in Plato's *Gorgias* (and, to a lesser extent, Thrasymachus in Book I of the *Republic*), Nietzsche presents a critique of morality that is far more detailed and wide-ranging.[3] Nietzsche's re-

examination of the moral tradition is radical and powerful, casting doubt on the transparency and desirability of much of the moral and political tradition. Second, Nietzsche has had a major influence on political ideas, beginning with his unfortunate appropriation by Nazi philosopher Alfred Baeumler. It is generally agreed that Nietzsche's philosophy is antithetical to the Nazis, but the stigma—at least in popular conception—has remained. More positively, he also influenced Max Weber, particularly in Weber's writings on power. In the twentieth century, Nietzsche inspired French post-structuralist Michel Foucault, who developed his genealogical method, focusing on the nature and importance of power. Nietzsche has also exerted a surprising amount of influence on left-wing and liberal thought.

What, exactly, then, is Nietzsche's project? Broadly speaking, Nietzsche undertakes an examination of our moral prejudices and their biological and historical origins. Nietzsche denies that people are equal, a fundamental claim in most modern moral theories; instead, he suggests that there are natural differences between types of people, with some "higher" than the rest, and these natural facts lead to different types of morality. Nietzsche contrasts master morality and slave morality, arguing that master morality is historically prior. Master morality is the morality of the "nobles" or "aristocrats"—not in the sense of social position, but in terms of natural superiority—and involves a contrast between "good" and "bad." According to Nietzsche, "Moral designations were everywhere first applied to human beings and only later, derivatively, to actions" (*Beyond Good and Evil* 260). For master morality, then, "good" is identified with noble; it is what the masters endorse: "The noble type of man experiences *itself* as determining values; ... it is *value-creating*" (*Beyond Good and Evil* 260). "Bad," in master morality, is quite different from "evil"—it simply means not-noble or "contemptible."

The nobles are only a small part of society and, understandably, cause resentment. This leads to an inversion of values, and to "the vengefulness of the impotent" (*Genealogy of Morals* 1, 10), who react against noble morality. Everything noble—selfishness, inequality, self-reverence, the affirmation of suffering—is transformed and labeled

---

1   Most notoriously, the Nazis appropriated a distorted version of Nietzsche, in part influenced by his sister's anti-Semitic distortions.

2   This reflects the danger of reading Nietzsche literally and out of context.

3   The claim of Callicles' paralleled in Nietzsche is that the inferior use morality to enslave those who are naturally better. (*Gorgias*

491e–492a) In other words, morality is in the rational self-interest of the weak and is used to bind the stronger to their will. In *The Genealogy of Morals*, he refers to "slave" morality as "prudence of the lowest order" (Book 1: 13) Nietzsche rejects Callicles' other, less interesting view, that we should let our appetites grow unchecked (*Gorgias* 419e).

"evil." In their place, "those qualities are brought out and flooded with light which serve to ease existence for those who suffer: here pity, the complaisant and obliging hand, the warm heart, patience, industry, humility, and friendliness are honored—for here these are the most useful qualities and almost the only means of enduring the pressure of existence. Slave morality is essentially a morality of utility" (*Beyond Good and Evil* 260).

The problem with the ascendancy of slave morality is that it can only be accomplished at the expense of the excellent. Nietzsche accused slave morality of being "life-denying," suggesting that it follows Christianity in denying this world and encouraging people to set their sights on the afterlife. It denies growth, sexuality, and the body, and demands the repression of the instincts and self-mortification, what Nietzsche called the "ascetic ideal." Slave morality is a morality of the majority or of the lowest common denominator. As mentioned above, Nietzsche held that there is a natural hierarchy among human beings; he valued the flourishing of higher men. Slave morality actively suppresses exceptional people, the "free spirits" who disdain democracy, equality and social convention, and are "*delivered* from the crowd, the multitude, the majority, where [they are] allowed to forget the rule of 'humanity,' being the exception to it."[1]

Who are these free spirits? In different places, Nietzsche condemns Jesus, St. Paul, Socrates, Rousseau, and Mill (among many others), while praising Napoleon, Caesar, Goethe, Beethoven, and Nietzsche himself as free spirits. He even classifies "the man of prey," Cesare Borgia (who also appears in Machiavelli's *The Prince*), as a free spirit; it would be difficult to set out a list of characteristics shared by all these "free spirits." It might be suggested that instead of toiling for "objectivity" and consensus, "free spirits" will revel in their subjectivity and strive for the *extraordinary*. They are in touch with their own instinctual life—their "will to power"—and rise beyond, or "overcome," traditional morality and religion.[2] According to Nietzsche, these traditional ethical systems are merely historical creations which serve the self-interested purposes of their creators and artificially constrain the horizons of human possibility.

Another way of identifying these "free spirits" is through Nietzsche's famous thesis of "eternal recurrence": the idea that time is cyclical, repeating itself in an endless loop over and over again. It is not fully clear whether Nietzsche actually *believed* this cosmological claim, but he did use it as a way of expressing what he thought of as a more positive attitude to life than the moral or Christian one. Instead of the value of one's life being judged *at its end*, Nietzsche suggests that we should see our lives as being subject to eternal recurrence, and thus that we should strive to make *each moment* of our life one that we would want to repeat over and over again for eternity.

What Is the Structure of These Readings?

Beyond Good and Evil and the *Genealogy of Morals* are both later—post-*Zarathustra*—works. *Beyond Good and Evil* is divided into eight sections and a poem:

On the Prejudices of Philosophers
The Free Spirit
What Is Religious
Epigrams and Interludes
Natural History of Morals
We Scholars
Our Virtues
People and Fatherlands
What is Noble
From High Mountains: *Aftersong*

Beyond Good and Evil is a vast book. It attacks philosophical practice from Plato onwards, and deals with many of the major philosophical conundrums, such as free will, knowledge and consciousness. It also sets out a "life-affirming" philosophy in *The Free Spirit*. For our purposes, the sections *Natural History of Morals* and *What is Noble* are particularly important. *Natural History of Morals* contains scathing criticisms of Plato, Christianity, utilitarianism, Kant, and democracy as degenerate and life-denying. Nietzsche also begins to develop the notion of herd morality, particularly in section 260 of *What is Noble*. Here he elaborates on the contrast between master morality and slave morality (a subject broached in section 45 of *Human, All-Too-Human*, and further developed in *The Genealogy of Morals*).

---

1   One of Nietzsche's most celebrated notions is the "overman" or "superman" (*Übermensch*), but its role is not as prominent as one might expect. It appears mostly in *Thus Spoke Zarathustra* and is later replaced by the notion of "higher men."

2   One of Nietzsche's most famous aphorisms occurs in *The Gay Science*, where he proclaims that "God is dead" (Book 3, Section 125). In *Beyond Good and Evil* he calls Christianity "an ongoing suicide of reason."

Nietzsche called the *Genealogy* a sequel to *Beyond Good and Evil*. He develops many of its themes in three essays, "'Good and Evil,' 'Good and Bad'"; "'Guilt' 'Bad Conscience' and the Like"; and "What is the Meaning of Ascetic Ideals?" The first essay includes his most detailed development of a contrast between master and slave morality. The second essay contains a profound—and disturbing—discussion of punishment, contractual relations, promising, and guilt. For social and political philosophers, this is of central importance. Nietzsche challenges the standard connection between punishment and free will—the idea that people should only be punished if they have intended their actions. He claims that this is a recent view and that "throughout the greater part of human history punishment was *not* imposed *because* one held the wrongdoer responsible for his deed, thus *not* on the presupposition that only the guilty one should be punished" (*Genealogy of Morals*, Second Essay, Section 4). Rather, he sees the idea as having its origin in the "contractual relationship between *creditor* and *debtor*, which is as old as the idea of 'legal subjects' and in turn points back to the fundamental forms of buying, selling, barter, trade and traffic" (*Genealogy of Morals*, Second Essay, Section 4). (Nietzsche ties guilt to debts, noting the German connection between Schuld [guilt] and Schulden [debts]). Nietzsche goes on to argue ingeniously that "justice," "fairness," "good will," and "objectivity," all developed as moral and political concepts out of the relationship between buyer and seller.

The third essay, "What is the Meaning of Ascetic Ideals?" contains some of Nietzsche's most penetrating analyses of asceticism and life-denying morality.

The Will to Power is composed of Nietzsche's uncollected notebooks, composed between 1883 and 1888, which his sister brought together under that title. Scholars disagree about the place of these notes in Nietzsche's oeuvre, but it is here that Nietzsche sets forth his diagnosis of nihilism, and most fully develops the will to power.

Some Useful Background Information

One of the central concepts in Nietzsche's philosophy is that of the will to power. According to Nietzsche, the will to power is the basic disposition of all life, including human life: it is the principle which provides the ultimate force for everything that happens in the natural (or at least the biological) world. Thus, every organic phenomenon—plant growth, predation, or even the establishment of a religion—can be understood, according to Nietzsche, as being brought about by an underlying set of power relationships, where each term of the relation is exerting a "force of will" that strives, with varying success, to expand towards and transform the other terms. "Slave morality," for example, can be analyzed in terms of the will to power of the oppressed and their vindictive inversion of values.

i) Though Nietzsche makes it clear in his writings that he admires master morality more than slave morality, there is nevertheless controversy over whether Nietzsche actually *endorsed* master morality. In an oft-cited passage from the *Antichrist* 57, Nietzsche asserts: "When the exceptional human being treats the mediocre more tenderly than himself and his peers, this is not mere politeness of the heart—it is simply his duty." The free spirits certainly have more in common with master than slave morality, but might nevertheless supersede *both* types and give expression to a third form of "morality" altogether.

ii) Nietzsche's "master" and "slave" moralities are ideal types. As he writes, "in all higher and more mixed cultures there also appear attempts at mediation between these two moralities, and yet more often the interpenetration and mutual misunderstanding of both, and at times they occur directly alongside each other—even in the same human being, within a single soul" (*Beyond Good and Evil* 260).

iii) Though Nietzsche called himself an "immoralist," and attacks morality—particularly "slave" morality, which he thought dominated his era—he is not encouraging people to *behave immorally*. In one of his earlier works, *The Dawn* (1881), he firmly asserts that:

> it goes without saying that I do not deny, presupposing I am no fool, that many actions called immoral ought to be avoided and resisted, or that many called moral ought to be done and encouraged—but *for different reasons than formerly*.

iv) Although Nietzsche certainly did equate the rise of Judeo-Christianity with the ascendance of "slave morality"—the issues of anti-Semitism and his supposed sympathy for what became the ideological themes of the Nazi party, largely arose out of misunderstandings and deliberate distortions of his work after his death. Numerous passages in Nietzsche's works explicitly condemn anti-Semitism. To be sure, in his earlier writings from the time of his association with the rabid anti-Semite Richard Wagner, there are passages in which he expresses anti-Semitic views. But he later repudiated these views; indeed, when he was writing

Beyond Good and Evil, he split with his previous publisher Ernst Schmeitzner, in part because Nietzsche objected to Schmeitzner's close association with the anti-Semitic movement in Germany.

• • • • •

Beyond Good and Evil

from *Part Five: A Natural History of Morals*

186. Moral feeling in Europe is now just as refined, old, multi-faceted, sensitive, and sophisticated as the "Science of Morality" associated with it is still young, amateurish, awkward, and fumbling: an attractive contrast which now and then even becomes visibly incorporated in the person of a moralist. Even the phrase "Science of Morals" is, so far as what it designates is concerned, much too arrogant and contrary to good taste, which tends always to prefer more modest terms. We should in all seriousness admit to ourselves what we have needed to do for a long time and still need to do, the only thing that is justified at this point, that is, to assemble materials, organize conceptually, and set in order an immense realm of delicate feelings of value and differences in values, which live, grow, reproduce, and die off—and, perhaps, to attempt to clarify the recurring and more frequent forms of these living crystallizations, as a preparation for a theory of types of morality. Naturally, so far we have not been so modest.

As soon as philosophers busied themselves with morality as a science, they collectively have demanded from themselves, with a formal seriousness which makes one laugh, something very much higher, more ambitious, more solemn. They have been looking for the rational basis of morality, and every philosopher so far has believed that he has provided such a rational grounding for morality. But morality itself has been considered something "given." How distant from their stodgy pride lay that apparently unspectacular task, left in the dust and mould, of a description, although for that task the subtlest hands and senses could hardly be subtle enough!

The very fact that the moral philosophers had only a crude knowledge of the moral facts, in an arbitrary selection or an accidental abbreviation, something like the morality of their surroundings, their class, their church, the spirit of their age, their climate and region of the world—the very

fact that they were poorly educated and not even very curious with respect to peoples, ages, and past events—meant that they never confronted at all the essential problems of morality, all of which come to the surface only with a comparison of several moralities.

In all the "science of morality" up to this point what is still lacking, odd as it may sound, is the problem of morality itself. What's missing is the suspicion that here there may be something problematic. What the philosophers have called a "rational grounding of morality" and demanded from themselves was, seen in the right light, only a scholarly version of good faith in the ruling morality, some new way of expressing it, and thus itself an element in the middle of a determined morality, even indeed, in the final analysis, a form of denial that this morality could be grasped as a problem—and, at any rate, the opposite of a test, analysis, questioning, or vivisection of this particular belief.

Listen, for example, to how even Schopenhauer[1] presents his own task with such an almost admirable innocence, and make your own conclusions about the scientific nature of a "science" whose ultimate masters still talk like children and old women: "The principle," he says (in *The Fundamental Problem of Morality*), "the basic assumption whose meaning all ethicists are essentially in agreement about— *neminem laede, immo omnes, quantum potes, juve*[2]—that is really the principle which all teachers of morality struggle to ground in reason ... the essential foundation of ethics, which people have been seeking for thousands of years as the philosopher's stone."

The difficulty of rationally grounding the principle quoted above may, of course, be great—as we know, it's not something Schopenhauer was successful in doing—and whoever has once thoroughly understood just how tastelessly false and sentimental this principle is in a world whose essence is the will to power may permit himself to recall that Schopenhauer, although a pessimist, really played the flute.... Every day, after his meal: just read his biographers on this point. And here's an incidental question: a pessimist, a man who denies god and the world, who stops in front

---

1 *Schopenhauer* Arthur Schopenhauer, German philosopher (1788–1860) whose ethics stressed the importance of overcoming egoism, of alleviating suffering, and of compassion. Much of Nietzsche's mature philosophical work was written in response to Schopenhauer's work, and in particular to his pessimism, which Nietzsche strives to overcome.

2 *neminen ... juve* Latin: hurt no one; rather, help all as much as you can.

of morality, who says yes to morality and blows his flute, the *laede-neminem*[1] morality—How's that? Is that really—a pessimist?

187. Even apart from the value of such claims as "There is in us a categorical imperative," we can still always ask: What does such a claim express about the person making it? There are moralities which are intended to justify their creators before other people; other moralities are meant to calm him down and make him satisfied with himself; with others he wants to nail himself to the cross and humiliate himself; with others he wants to practice revenge; with others to hide himself; with others to be transfigured and set himself above, high up and far away. This morality serves its originator so that he forgets; that morality so that he or something about him is forgotten; some moralists may want to exercise their power and creative mood on humanity, some on others. Perhaps even Kant[2] wants us to understand with his morality: "What is respectable about me is that I can obey—and things should be no different for you than they are for me"—in short, moralities are also only sign languages of the feelings.

188. Every morality is—in contrast to *laisser aller*[3]—a part of tyranny against "nature," also against "reason": that is, however, not yet an objection to it. To object, we would have to decree, once again, on the basis of some morality or other, that all forms of tyranny and irrationality are not permitted. The essential and invaluable part of every morality is that it is a lengthy compulsion: to understand Stoicism[4] or Port Royal[5] or Puritanism[6] people should remember the compulsion under which every language so far has achieved strength and freedom—the metrical compulsion, the tyranny of rhyme and rhythm.

In every people how much trouble poets and orators have made for themselves—including some contemporary prose writers in whose ears a relentless conscience dwells—"for the sake of some foolishness," as utilitarian fools say, who think that makes them clever,—"out of obsequiousness to arbitrary laws," as the anarchists say, who think that makes them "free," even free spirited. The strange fact, however, is that everything there is or has been on earth to do with freedom, refinement, boldness, dance, and masterly certainty, whether it is in thinking itself, or in governing, or in speaking and persuading, in arts just as much as in morals, developed only thanks to the "tyranny of such arbitrary laws," and in all seriousness, the probability is not insignificant that this is "nature" and "natural"—and not that laisser aller!

Every artist knows how far from the feeling of letting himself go his "most natural" condition is, the free ordering, setting, disposing, shaping in the moment of "inspiration"—and how strictly and subtly he obeys at that very moment the thousand-fold laws which make fun of all conceptual formulations precisely because of their hardness and decisiveness (even the firmest idea, on the other hand, contains something fluctuating, multiple, ambiguous—).

The essential thing "in heaven and on earth," so it appears, is, to make the point again, that there is obedience for a long time in one direction: in the process there always comes and always has come eventually something for whose sake living on earth is worthwhile, for example, virtue, art, music, dance, reason, spirituality—something or other transfiguring, subtle, amazing, and divine.

The long captivity of the spirit, the mistrustful compulsion in our ability to communicate our thoughts, the discipline which the thinker imposed on himself to think within the guiding principles of a church or court or with Aristotelian assumptions, the long spiritual will to interpret everything which happens according to a Christian scheme and to discover and justify the Christian god once again in every coincidence—all this powerful, arbitrary, hard, dreadful, anti-rational activity has turned out to be the means by which the European spirit cultivated its strength, its reckless curiosity, and its subtle flexibility. Admittedly in the process a great deal of irreplaceable force and spirit must have also been overwhelmed, crushed, and ruined (for here as everywhere "nature" reveals herself as she is, in her

1   *laede neminem* Latin: hurt no one.
2   *Kant* Immanuel Kant, German philosopher (1724–1804) whose moral theory is grounded on the principle that we should freely act on our duty to obey the categorical imperative (universal moral law) within us.
3   *laisser aller* French: letting go.
4   *Stoicism* School of philosophy originating in the Hellenistic period (around 301 BCE) that advocated detachment from the emotions, and observation of the natural law.
5   *Port Royal* French Jansenist Catholic school of philosophy (after Cornelius Jansen [1585–1638]) that emphasized original sin, the necessity of divine grace, and predestination.
6   *Puritanism* Strand of Protestant Christianity which emphasized moral purity, private study of the Bible, and God's authority over human affairs.

totally extravagant and indifferent magnificence, which is an outrage, but something noble).

The fact that for thousands of years European thinkers thought in order to prove something—nowadays, by contrast, we distrust any thinker who "wants to prove something"—and the fact that for them what was going to emerge as the result of their strictest thinking was always already clearly established, something like the Asiatic astrologers earlier or like the harmless Christian moralistic interpretation of the most intimate personal experience "for the honor of God" or "for the salvation of the soul" still present today—this tyranny, this arbitrariness, this strict and grandiose stupidity, has trained the spirit. Apparently slavery is, in the cruder and more refined sense, the indispensable means for disciplining and cultivating the spirit.

We can examine every morality in this way: "nature" in it is what teaches hatred of the *laisser aller*, of that all-too-great freedom, and plants the need for limited horizons, for work close at hand—it teaches the narrowing of perspective and also, in a certain sense, stupidity as a condition of living and growth. "You should obey someone or other and for a long time: otherwise you perish and lose final respect for yourself"—this seems to me to be the moral imperative of nature, which, of course, is neither "categorical," as old Kant wanted the imperative to be (thus the "otherwise"), nor directed at the individual (what does nature care about individuals!), but rather at peoples, races, ages, classes, but above all at the whole animal "man," at human beings.

189. The industrious races complain a great deal about having to tolerate idleness: it was a masterpiece of the English instinct to make Sunday so holy and so tedious that the Englishman, without being aware of the fact, became eager again for weekdays and workdays—a form of cleverly invented and shrewdly introduced fasting. Things like it are frequently seen also in the ancient world (even if, as is reasonable among southern people, not exactly connected to work). There must be fasts of several kinds, and everywhere where powerful impulses and habits rule, the lawgivers had to take care to set aside empty days in which such an impulse is placed in chains and learns once again to go hungry.

Seen from a higher viewpoint, the periods when entire races and ages get afflicted with some moral fanaticism or other look like such imposed times of compulsion and fasting, during which an impulse learns to cower down and abase itself, but also to cleanse itself and become sharper. Individual philosophical sects (for example the Stoa in the midst of Hellenistic culture and its lecherous air heavy with aphrodisiac scents) can also be given this sort of interpretation. And with this is also given a hint for an explanation of that paradox why it was precisely in Europe's Christian period and, in general, first under the pressure of Christian value judgments that the sex drive sublimated itself into love (amour-passion).

190. There is something in Plato's morality which does not really belong to Plato, but is found in his philosophy, one might say, only in spite of Plato, namely, the Socratism for which Plato was essentially too noble. "No one will do harm to himself; thus, everything bad happens unwillingly. For the bad man inflicts damage on himself: he would not do that, if he knew that bad is bad. Thus, the bad man is bad only from error. If we take his error away from him, we necessarily make him—'good.'"

This sort of conclusion stinks of the rabble, which sees in bad actions only the wretched consequences and, in fact, makes the judgment "It is stupid to act badly," while "good" it assumes without further thought is identical to "useful and agreeable." So far as every utilitarianism of morality is concerned, we may guess from the start it had the same origin and follow our noses: we will seldom go wrong. Plato did everything to interpret something subtle and noble in the principle of his teacher, above all, himself.

Plato is the most daring of all interpreters who took all of Socrates only like a popular tune and folk song from the alleys, in order to vary it into something infinite and impossible, that is, into all his own masks and multiplicities. To speak in jest—and one based on Homer: What is the Platonic Socrates if not *prosthe Platon opithen te Platon messe te Chimera*?[1]

191. The old theological problem of "believing" and "knowing"—or, to put the matter more clearly—of instinct and reason—as well as the question whether in assessing the value of things instinct deserves more authority than rationality, which wants to assess and act according to reasons, according to a "Why?"—according to expediency and utility—it is always still that old moral problem, as it first appeared in the person of Socrates, which had already divided our minds long before Christianity.

---

1   *prosthe Platon … Chimera* Latin: Plato in front, Plato behind, and in the middle the Chimera.

Socrates, in fact, set himself, with a taste for his talent—which was that of a superior dialectical thinker—at first on the side of reason, and, in truth, what did he do his whole life long but laugh at the awkward inability of his noble Athenians, who were men of instinct, like all noble men, and who could never provide enough information about the reasons for their actions? Finally, however, in stillness and secret he also laughed at himself. With his more subtle conscience and self-enquiry he found in himself the same difficulty and inability. But, he said to himself, does that mean releasing oneself from instincts! We must give the instincts and reason the proper help. We must follow the instincts but convince reason to assist with good reasons. This was the real falsehood of that great ironist, so full of secrets. He brought his conscience to the point where it was satisfied with a kind of trick played on itself.

Socrates basically had seen through the irrational in moral judgments. Plato, who was more innocent in such things and without the mischievousness of a common man, wanted to use all his power—the greatest power which a philosopher up to that time had had at his command—to prove that reason and instinct inherently move to a single goal, to the good, to "God," and since Plato all the theologians and philosophers have been on the same road—that is, in things concerning morality up to now, instinct, or as the Christians call it "faith," or as I call it, "the herd," has triumphed. We must grant that Descartes is an exception, the father of rationalism (and thus the grandfather of the revolution), a man who conferred sole authority on reason. But reason is only a tool, and Descartes was superficial.

192. Anyone who has followed the history of a particular science finds in its development a textbook case for understanding the oldest and commonest event in all "knowing and perceiving." There, as here, the rash hypotheses, the fabrications, the good, stupid will to "believe," the lack of suspicion and of patience develop first of all—our senses learn late and never learn well enough to be subtle, true, and cautious organs of perception. With any given stimulus, our eyes find it more comfortable to produce once more an image which has already been produced frequently than to capture something different and new in an impression. To do the latter requires more power, more "morality." To listen to something new is embarrassing and hard on our ears; we hear strange music badly. When we hear some different language, we spontaneously try to reshape the sounds we hear into words which sound more familiar and native to us:

that's how, for example, in earlier times, when the German heard the word *arcubalista* he changed it into *Armbrust*.[1]

Something new finds our senses hostile and reluctant, and in general, even with the "simplest" perceptual processes, the emotions like fear, love, hate, including the passive feeling of idleness, are in control. Just as a reader nowadays hardly reads all the individual words (or even syllables) on a page—he's much more likely to take about five words out of twenty and "guess" on the basis of these five words the presumed sense they contain—so we hardly look at a tree precisely and completely, considering the leaves, branches, color, and shape; we find it so very much easier to imagine an approximation of the tree.

Even in the midst of the most peculiar experiences we still act in the same way: we make up the greatest part of experiences for ourselves and are hardly ever compelled not to look upon any event as an "inventor." What this adds up to is that basically from time immemorial we have been accustomed to lie. Or to express the matter more virtuously and hypocritically, in short, more pleasantly: we are much more the artist than we realize.

In a lively conversation I often see the face of the person with whom I am speaking so clearly and subtly determined according to the idea which he expresses or which I think I have brought out in him that this degree of clarity far exceeds the power of my ability to see—the delicacy of the play of muscles and of the expression in his eyes must also be something I have added out of my own head. The person probably had a totally different expression or none at all.

193. *Quidquid luce fuit, tenebris agit*[2] but the other way around as well. What we experience in a dream, provided we experience it frequently, finally is as much a part of the collective household of our souls as anything "truly" experienced. Thanks to this, we are richer or poorer, have one more need or one less, and finally in the bright light of day and even in the brightest moments of our waking spirit we are ordered around a little by the habits of our dreams.

Suppose that an individual in his dreams has often flown and, finally, as soon as he dreams, becomes aware of the power and art of flying as his privilege and also as his own enviable happiness, such a man who believes he is capable of realizing every kind of curving or angled flight

1 *arcubalista ... Armbrust* Both words, in Latin and German, mean "crossbow."
2 *Quidquid ... agit* Latin: What goes on in the light, acts in the darkness.

with the easiest impulse, who knows the feeling of a certain godlike carelessness, an "upward" without tension and compulsion, a "downward" without condescension and without humiliation—without difficulty—how should a man with such dream experiences and dream habits not also finally discover in his waking day that the word "happiness" has a different color and definition. How could he not want a different happiness? "A swing upward," as described by poets, for him must be, in comparison with that "flying," too earthbound, too muscular, too forceful, even too "heavy."

194. The difference between men does not manifest itself only in the difference between the tables of the goods they possess but also in the fact that they consider different goods worthy of striving for and that they are at odds among themselves about what is more or less valuable, about the rank ordering of the commonly acknowledged goods—the difference becomes even clearer in what counts for them as something really worth having and possessing.

So far as women are concerned, for example, a more modest man considers having at his disposal her body and sexual gratification as a satisfactory and sufficient sign of having, of possession. Another man, with his more suspicious and more discriminating thirst for possessions sees the "question mark," the fact that such a possession is only apparent, and wants a more refined test, above all, to know whether the woman not only gives herself to him but also for his sake gives up what she has or would like to have. Only that counts for him as "possessing." A third man, however, is at this point not yet finished with his suspicion and desire to possess. He asks himself if the woman, when she gives up everything for him, is doing this for something like a phantom of himself: he wants to be well known first, fundamentally, even profoundly, in order to be able to be loved. He dares to allow himself to be revealed. Only then does he feel that the loved one is fully in his possession, when she is no longer deceived about him, when she loves him just as much for his devilry and hidden insatiability as for his kindness, patience, and spirituality.

One man wants to possess a people: and all the higher arts of Cagliostro and Cataline he thinks appropriate for this purpose. Another, with a more refined thirst for possession, tells himself "One should not deceive where one wants to possess." He is irritable and impatient at the idea that a mask of him rules the hearts of his people: "Hence I must let myself be known and, first of all, learn about myself."

Among helpful and charitable men one finds almost regularly that crude hypocrisy which first prepares the person who should be helped, as if, for example, he "earns" help, wants precisely their help, and would show himself deeply thankful, devoted, and obsequious to them for all their help. With these fantasies they dispose of the needy as if they were property, as if they were charitable and helpful people out of a demand for property. One finds them jealous if one crosses them or anticipates them in their helping.

With their child, parents involuntarily act something like these helpers: they call it "an upbringing." No mother doubts at the bottom of her heart that with a child she has given birth to a possession; no father denies himself the right to be allowed to subjugate the child to his ideas and value judgments. In fact, in earlier times it seemed proper to the father to dispose of the life and death of newborns at his own discretion (as among the ancient Germans). And like the father, even today the teacher, the state, the priest, and the prince still see in each new man a harmless opportunity for a new possession. And from that follows. . . .

195. The Jews—a people "born for slavery," as Tacitus and the entire ancient world said, "the chosen people among peoples," as they themselves said and believed—the Jews achieved the amazing feat of inverting values, thanks to which life on earth for two millennia has possessed a new and dangerous appeal. Their prophets fused "rich," "godless," "evil," "violent," and "sensuous" into a unity and for the first time coined the word "world" as a word connoting shame. In this inversion of value (to which belongs the use of the word for "poor" as a synonym for "holy" and "friend") lies the significance of the Jewish people: with them the slave condition in morality begins.

196. We can conclude that there are countless dark bodies in the region of our sun—bodies we will never see. Between us, that's a parable, and a psychologist of morality reads the entire writing in the stars only as a language of parable and sign language which allows a great deal to remain silent.

197. We fundamentally misunderstand predatory animals and predatory men, for example, Cesare Borgia, and we misunderstand "Nature," so long as we still look for a "pathology" at the bottom of these healthiest of all tropical monsters and growths or even for some "Hell" born in them, as almost all moralists so far have done. It seems that among moralists there is a hatred for the primaeval forest and the

tropics? And the "tropical man" must at all accounts be discredited, whether as a sickness and degeneration of human beings or as his own hell and self-torture? But why? For the benefit of the "moderate zones"? For the benefit of the moderate human beings? The "moral human beings"? The mediocre? This for the chapter "morality as timidity."—

198. All these moralities that direct themselves at the individual person, for the sake of his "happiness," as people say—what are they except proposals about conduct in relation to the degree of danger in which the individual person lives with himself, recipes against his passions, his good and bad inclinations, to the extent that they may have a will to power and want to play the master; small and great clever sayings and affectations, afflicted with the musty enclosed smell of ancient household remedies or old women's advice, all baroque and unreasonable in form—because they direct themselves at "everything," because they generalize where we should not generalize—, all speaking absolutely, taking themselves absolutely, all spiced with more than one grain of salt, and much more bearable, sometimes even seductive, only when they learn to smell over-seasoned and dangerous, above all "about the other world."

By any intellectual standard, all that is worth little and still a far cry from "science," to say nothing of "wisdom," but, to say it again and to say it three times: prudence, prudence, prudence, mixed in with stupidity, stupidity, stupidity—whether it is now that indifference and coldness of a metaphorical statute against the hot-headed foolishness of the emotions, which the Stoics recommended and applied as a cure; or even that no-more-laughing and no-more-crying of Spinoza, his excessively naïve support for the destruction of the emotions through their analysis and vivisection; or that repression of the emotions to a harmless mean, according to which they should be satisfied, the Aristotelianism of morality; even morality as the enjoyment of emotions in a deliberate dilution and spiritualization through artistic symbolism, something like music or the love of god and of man for god's sake—for in religion the passions have civil rights once more, provided that—; and finally even that accommodating and wanton dedication to the emotions, as Hafis and Goethe taught, that daring permission to let go of the reins, that physical-spiritual *licentia morum*[1] in the exceptional examples of wise old owls and drunkards,

for whom it "has little danger any more." This also for the chapter "morality as timidity."

199. Given that at all times, so long as there have been human beings, there have also been herds of human beings (racial groups, communities, tribes, peoples, states, churches) and always a great many followers in relation to the small number of those issuing orders, and taking into consideration also that so far nothing has been better and longer practiced and cultivated among human beings than obedience, we can reasonably assume that typically now the need for obedience is inborn in each individual, as a sort of formal conscience which states "You should do something or other without conditions, and leave aside something else without conditions," in short, "Thou shalt."

This need seeks to satisfy itself and to fill its form with some content. Depending on its strength, impatience, and tension, it seizes on something, without being very particular, like a coarse appetite, and accepts what someone or other issuing commands shouts in people's ears—parents, teachers, laws, class bias, public opinion. The curiously limited intelligence of human development—the way it hesitates, takes so long, often regresses, and turns around on itself—is based on the fact that the herd instinct of obedience is passed on best and at the expense of the art of commanding.

If we imagine this instinct for once striding right to its ultimate excess, then there would finally be a total lack of commanders and independent people, or they would suffer inside from a bad conscience and find it necessary to prepare a deception for themselves in order to be able to command, as if they, too, were only obeying orders. This condition is what, in fact, exists nowadays in Europe: I call it the moral hypocrisy of those in command. They don't know how to protect themselves from their bad conscience except by behaving as if they were carrying out older or higher orders (from ancestors, the constitution, rights, law, or even God), or they even borrow maxims of the herd and from the herd way of thinking, for example, as "the first servant of their people" or as "tools of the common good."

On the other hand, the herd man in Europe today makes himself appear as if he is the single kind of human being allowed, and he glorifies those characteristics of his thanks to which he is tame, good natured, and useful to the herd as the really human virtues, as well as public spiritedness, wishing everyone well, consideration, diligence, moderation, modesty, forbearance, and compassion. For those

---

1   *licentia morum* Latin: freedom in behavior.

cases, however, where people believe they cannot do without a leader and bellwether,[1] they make attempt after attempt to replace the commander by adding together collections of clever herd people. All the representative constitutional assemblies, for example, have this origin.

But for all that, what a blissful relief, what a release from a pressure which is growing unbearable is the appearance of an absolute commander for these European herd animals. The effect which the appearance of Napoleon made was the most recent major evidence for that:—the history of the effect of Napoleon is almost the history of the higher happiness which this entire century derived from its most valuable men and moments.

200. The man from an age of dissolution, which mixes the races all together, such a man has an inheritance of a multiple ancestry in his body, that is, conflicting and frequently not merely conflicting drives and standards of value which war among themselves and rarely give each other rest—such a man of late culture and disturbed lights will typically be a weaker man. His most basic demand is that the war which constitutes him should finally end. Happiness seems to him, in accordance with a calming medicine and way of thinking (for example, Epicurean[2] or Christian), principally the happiness of resting, of having no interruptions, of smugness, of the final unity, as the "Sabbath of Sabbaths," to use the words of the saintly rhetorician Augustine,[3] who was himself such a man.

But if the opposition and war in such a nature work like one more charm or thrill in life and bring, in addition to its powerful and irreconcilable drives, also the real mastery and refinement in waging war with itself, and thus transmit and cultivate self-ruling and outwitting of the self, then arise those delightfully amazing and unimaginable people, those enigmatic men predestined for victory and temptation, whose most beautiful expressions are Alcibiades[4] and Caesar (in their company I'd like to place the first European, according to my taste, the Hohenstaufer Frederick II),[5] and among artists perhaps Leonardo da Vinci. They appear

precisely in the same ages when that weaker type, with its demands for quiet, steps into the foreground—both types belong with one another and arise from the same causes.

201. As long as the utility which rules in moral value judgments is merely the utility of the herd, as long as our gaze is directed only at the preservation of the community and what is precisely and conclusively immoral is sought in what appears dangerous to the survival of the community, there can be no "morality of loving one's neighbor." Assuming there existed in society already a constant small habit of consideration, compassion, fairness, kindness, and mutual assistance, assuming that in this condition of society all these drives were already active which later were described with honorable names as "virtues" and which finally were almost synonymous with the idea "morality": at that time they are not at all yet in the realm of moral value judgments—they are still outside morality. For example, a compassionate action in the best Roman period was called neither good nor evil, neither moral nor immoral. And even if it was praised, this praise brought with it at best still a kind of reluctant disdain, as soon as it was compared with any other action which served the demands of the totality, of the *res publica*.[6]

Ultimately the "love of one's neighbor"[7] is always something of minor importance, partly conventional, arbitrary, and apparent in relation to the fear of one's neighbor. After the structure of society in its entirety is established and appears secure against external dangers, it is this fear of one's neighbors which creates once again new perspectives of moral value judgments. Certain strong and dangerous instincts, like a love of enterprise, daring, desire for revenge, shiftiness, rapacity, desire for mastery, which up to this point were not only honored in a sense useful to the community, under different names, of course, from those chosen here, but also had to be really inculcated and cultivated (because people constantly needed them for the dangers to the totality, against the enemy of that totality)—these are now experienced as doubly dangerous when there is a lack of diversionary channels for them—and they are gradually abandoned, branded as immoral and slanderous.

Now the opposing impulses and inclinations acquire moral honor. The herd instinct draws its conclusions, step

---

1   *bellwether*   Sheep that lead the flock.
2   *Epicurean*   Associated with the school of philosophy founded by Epicurus (341–270 BCE), which identified good and bad with pleasure and pain.
3   *Augustine*   Augustine of Hippo (354–430), one of the founding figures in the history of Christianity.
4   *Alcibiades*   Athenian statesman and general (c. 450–404 BCE).
5   *Hohenstaufer Frederick II*   Medieval German emperor, 1215–50.

6   *res publica*   Latin: state or republic.
7   *love … neighbor*   "Thou shalt love thy neighbor as thyself," Matthew 19.19.

by step. How much or how little something is dangerous to the community, dangerous to equality, in an opinion, in a condition and emotion, in a will, in a talent, that is now the moral perspective. Here also fear is once again the mother of morality. When the highest and strongest drives break out passionately and impel the individual far above and beyond the average and low level of the herd's conscience, the feeling of commonality in the community is destroyed; its belief in itself, its spine, as it were, breaks: as a result people brand these very drives the most and slander them. The high independent spirituality, the will to stand alone, even powerful reasoning are experienced as a danger. Everything which lifts the individual up over the herd and creates fear of one's neighbor from now on is called evil. The proper, modest, conforming faith in equality and mediocrity in desire take on the name of morality and honor.

Finally, under very peaceful conditions, there is an increasing lack of opportunity and need to educate the feelings in strength and hardness. Now every strength, even justice, begins to disrupt the conscience. A high and hard nobility and self-responsibility are almost an insult and awaken mistrust; "the lamb" and even more "the sheep" acquire respect.

There is a point of decay and decadence in the history of society when it itself takes sides on behalf of the person who harms it, the criminal, and does so, in fact, seriously and honestly. Punishment: that seems to society somehow or other unreasonable. What's certain is that the idea of "punishment" and "We should punish" causes it distress, arouses fear. "Is it not enough to make him un-dangerous? Why still punish? To punish is itself dreadful!" With this question the morality of the herd, the morality of timidity, draws its last consequence. Assuming people could do away with the danger, the basis of the fear, then people would have done away with this morality: it would be no longer necessary; it would no longer consider itself necessary.

Whoever tests the conscience of the contemporary European will always have to pull out from the thousand moral folds and hiding places the same imperative, the imperative of the timidity of the herd: "Our wish is that at some point or other there is nothing more to fear!" At some point or other—nowadays the will and the way there everywhere in Europe are called "progress."

202. Let us state right away one more time what we have already said a hundred times, for today's ears don't listen willingly to such truths—to our truths. We already know well enough how insulting it sounds when an individual reckons human beings in general plain and simply (without metaphor) among the animals, but one thing will make people consider us almost guilty, the fact that we, so far as men of "modern ideas" are concerned, constantly use the terms "herd," "herd instincts," and the like. What help is there? We cannot do anything else: for precisely here lies our new insight.

We have found that in all major moral judgments Europe, together with those countries where Europe's influence dominates, has become unanimous. People in Europe apparently know what Socrates thought he didn't know[1] and what that famous old snake[2] once promised to teach: today people "know" what good and evil are. Now, it must ring hard and badly on their ears when we keep claiming all the time that what here thinks it knows, what here glorifies itself with its praise and censure and calls itself good, is the instinct of the herd animal man, which has come to break through, to overpower, and to dominate other instincts— and continues increasingly to do so, in accordance with the growing physiological assimilation and homogeneity, whose symptom it is.

Morality today in Europe is the morality of the herd animal—thus only, as we understand the matter, one kind of human morality, alongside which, before which, and after which there are many other possible moralities, above all higher ones, or there should be. Against such a "possibility," in opposition to such a "should be," however, this morality turns itself with all its force: it says stubbornly and relentlessly, "I am morality itself, and nothing outside me is moral"—in fact, with the help of a religion which was willed by and which catered to the most sublime desires of the herd animal, it has reached the point where we find even in the political and social arrangements an always visible expression of this morality: the democratic movement has come into the inheritance of the Christian movement.

But the fact is that its tempo is still much too slow and drowsy for the impatient, the sick, and those addicted to the above-mentioned instincts—evidence for that comes from the wailing, which grows constantly more violent, and the increasingly open snarling fangs of the anarchist hounds

---

1   *Socrates ... know* Plato reports in his dialogue *The Apology* that the Oracle at Delphi pronounced Socrates (c. 470–399 BCE) the wisest man in Greece because he alone knew that he did not possess knowledge.

2   *famous ... snake* Serpent who convinced Eve to eat the fruit from the tree of the knowledge of good and evil. Genesis 3.1–6.

who now swarm through the alleys of European culture, apparently in contrast to the peacefully industrious democrats and ideologues of the revolution, even more to the foolish pseudo-philosophers and those ecstatic about brotherhood, who call themselves socialists and want a "free society."

But in reality these anarchists are at one with all of them in their fundamental and instinctive hostility to every other form of society than the autonomous herd (all the way to the rejection of the very idea of "master" and "servant"—*ni dieu ni maître*[1] is the way one socialist formula goes—); at one in their strong resistance to all special claims, all special rights and privileges (that means, in the last analysis, every right, for when all people are equal, then no one needs "rights" any more); at one in their mistrust of a justice which punishes (as if it were a violation of the weaker people, a wrong against the necessary consequences of all earlier society—); and equally at one in the religion of compassion, of sympathy, wherever there is feeling, living, and suffering (right down to the animals, right up to "God":—the excessive outpouring of "sympathy with God" belongs to a democratic age—); at one collectively in their cries for and impatience in their pity, in their deadly hatred for suffering generally, in their almost feminine inability to stand there as spectators, to let suffering happen; at one in their involuntary gloom and softness, under whose spell Europe seems threatened by a new Buddhism; at one in their faith in the morality of mutual compassion, as if that was morality in and of itself, as the height, the attained height of humanity, the sole hope of the future, the means of consolation for the present, the great absolution from the guilt of earlier times; all together at one in their belief in the community as their savior, thus in the herd, in themselves …

203. Those of us who have a different belief, who do not consider the democratic movement merely a degenerate form of political organization but a degenerate form of humanity, that is, as something that diminishes humanity, makes it mediocre and of lesser worth, where must we reach out to with our hopes?

There's no choice: we must reach for new philosophers, for spirits strong and original enough to provide the stimuli for an opposing way of estimating value and to re-evaluate and invert "eternal values," for those sent out as forerunners, for men of the future who at the present time take up the compulsion and the knot which forces the will of the millennia into new paths. To teach man the future of humanity as his will, as dependent on a man's will, and to prepare for great exploits and comprehensive attempts at discipline and cultivation, so as to put an end to that horrifying domination of nonsense and contingency which up to now has been called "history"—the nonsense of the "greatest number" is only its latest form. For that some new type of philosophers and commanders will at some point be necessary, at the sight of which all hidden, fearsome, and benevolent spirits on earth may well look pale and dwarfish. The image of such a leader is what hovers before our eyes: may I say that out loud, you free spirits?

The conditions which we must partly create and partly exploit for the origin of these leaders, the presumed ways and trials thanks to which a soul might grow to such height and power to feel the compulsion for these tasks, a revaluation of value under whose new pressure and hammer a conscience would be hardened, a heart transformed to bronze, so that it might endure the weight of such responsibility and, on the other hand, the necessity for such leaders, the terrifying danger that they might not appear or could fail and turn degenerate—those are our real worries, the things that make us gloomy. Do you know that, you free spirits? Those are the heavy, distant thoughts and thunderstorms which pass over the heaven of our lives.

There are few pains as severe as having once seen, guessed, and felt how an extraordinary man goes astray and degenerates: someone who has the rare eye for the overall danger that "man" himself is degenerating, someone who, like us, has recognized the monstrous accident which has played its game up to this point with respect to the future of humanity—a game in which there is no hand and not even a "finger of god" playing along!—someone who guesses the fate which lies hidden in the idiotic innocence and the blissful trust in "modern ideas," and even more in the entire Christian-European morality, such a man suffers from an anxiety which cannot be compared with any other—with one look, in fact, he grasps everything that still might be cultivated in man, given a favorable combination and increase of powers and tasks; he knows with all the knowledge of his conscience how the greatest possibilities for man are still inexhaustible and how often the type man has already stood up to mysterious decisions and new paths: he knows even better, from his own painful memory, what wretched things have so far usually broken apart a being of the highest rank, shattered him, sunk him, and made him pathetic.

---

1 *ni dieu ni maître*   French: neither god nor master.

The overall degeneration of man, down to what nowadays shows up as the socialist fool and flat head, as their "man of the future," as their ideal!—this degeneration and diminution of man to a perfect herd animal (or, as I put it, to a man of "free society"), this beastialization of man into a dwarf animal of equal rights and claims is possible—no doubt of that! Anyone who has once thought this possibility through to the end understands one more horror than the remaining men—and perhaps a new task, as well!...

from *Part Nine: What is Noble?*

257. Every enhancement in the type "man" up to this point has been the work of an aristocratic society—and that's how it will always be, over and over again—a society which believes in a long scale of rank ordering and differences in worth between man and man and which, in some sense or other, requires slavery. Without the pathos of distance, the sort which grows out of the deeply rooted difference between the classes, out of the constant gazing outward and downward of the ruling caste on the subjects and work implements, and out of its equally sustained practice of obedience and command, holding down and holding at a distance, that other more mysterious pathos would have no chance of growing at all, that longing for an ever-widening of new distances inside the soul itself, the development of ever higher, rarer, more distant, more expansive, more comprehensive states, in short, that very enhancement in the type "man," the constant "self-conquest of man," to cite a moral formula in a supra-moral sense.

Of course, where the history of the origins of aristocratic society is concerned (and thus the precondition for that raising of the type "man"), we should not surrender to humanitarian illusions: truth is hard. So without further consideration, let's state how up to this point every higher culture on earth has started! Men with a still natural nature, barbarians in every dreadful sense of the word, predatory men still in possession of an unbroken power of the will and a desire for power, threw themselves on weaker, more civilized, more peaceful, perhaps trading or cattle-raising races, or on old, worn cultures, in which at that very moment the final forces of life were flaring up in a brilliant fireworks display of spirit and corruption. At the start the noble caste has always been the barbarian caste: its superiority has lain not primarily in physical might but in spiritual power—it has been a matter of more complete human beings (which at every level also means "more complete beasts").

258. Corruption as the expression of the fact that within the instincts anarchy is threatening and that the foundation of the affects, what we call "life," has been shaken: according to the living structure in which it appears, corruption is something fundamentally different. When, for example, an aristocracy, like France's at the start of the Revolution, throws away its privileges with a sublime disgust and sacrifices itself to a dissipation of its moral feelings, this is corruption. Essentially it was only the final act in that centuries-long corruption, thanks to which step-by-step it gave up its ruling authority and reduced itself to a function of the monarchy (finally even to the monarch's finery and display pieces).

But the essential thing in a good and healthy aristocracy is that it feels itself not as a function (whether of a monarchy or of a community) but as their significance and highest justification, that it therefore with good conscience accepts the sacrifice of an enormous number of men, who for its sake must be oppressed and reduced to incomplete men, slaves, and instruments of work. Its fundamental belief must, in fact, be that the society should exist, not for the sake of the society, but only as a base and framework on which an exceptional kind of nature can raise itself to its higher function and, in general, to a higher form of being, comparable to those heliotropic climbing plants on Java—people call them *Sipo Matador*[1]—*whose branches clutch an oak tree so much and for so long until finally, high over the tree but supported by it, they can unfold their crowns in the open light and make a display of their happiness.*

259. Mutually refraining from wounding each other, from violence, and from exploitation, and setting one's will on the same level as others—these can in a certain crude sense become good habits among individuals, if conditions exist for that (namely, a real similarity in the quality of their power and their estimates of value, as well as their belonging together within a single body). However, as soon as people wanted to take this principle further and, where possible, establish it as the basic principle of society, it immediately revealed itself for what it is, as the willed denial of life, as the principle of disintegration and decay.

Here we must think through to the basics and push away all sentimental weakness: living itself is essentially appropriation from and wounding and overpowering stran-

---

1   *Sipo Matador* Murdering Creeper.

gers and weaker men, oppression, hardness, imposing one's own forms, annexing, and at the very least, in its mildest actions, exploitation. But why should we always use these precise words, which have from ancient times carried the stamp of a slanderous purpose? Even that body in which, as previously mentioned, the individuals deal with each other as equals—and that happens in every healthy aristocracy—must itself, if it is a living body and not dying out, do to other bodies all those things which the individuals in it refrain from doing to each other: it will have to be the living will to power, it will grow, grab things around it, pull to itself, and want to acquire predominance—not because of some morality or immorality, but because it is alive and because living is precisely the will to power.

But in no point is the common consciousness of the European more reluctant to be instructed than here. Nowadays people everywhere, even those in scientific disguises, are raving about the coming conditions of society from which "the exploitative character" is to have disappeared. To my ears that sounds as if people had promised to invent a life which abstained from all organic functions. The "exploitation" is not part of a depraved or incomplete and primitive society: it belongs in the essential nature of what is living, as a basic organic function. It is a consequence of the real will to power, which is precisely the will to live. Granted that this is something new as a theory, but it is, in reality, the fundamental fact of all history: we should at least be honest with ourselves to this extent!

260. As the result of a stroll though the many more sophisticated and cruder moral systems which up to this point have ruled or still rule on earth, I found certain characteristics routinely return with each other, bound up together, until finally two basic types revealed themselves to me and a fundamental difference sprang up. There is master morality and slave morality. To this I immediately add that in all higher and mixed cultures attempts at a mediation between both moralities make an appearance as well as, even more often, a confusion and mutual misunderstanding between the two, in fact, sometimes their harsh juxtaposition, even in the same man, within a single soul.

Distinctions in moral value have arisen either among a ruling group, which was happily conscious of its difference with respect to the ruled, or among the ruled, the slaves and dependent people of every degree. In the first case, when it's the masters who establish the idea of the good, it's the elevated and proud conditions of the soul which emotionally register as the distinguishing and defining order of rank. The noble man separates his own nature from that of people in whom the opposite of such exalted and proud states expresses itself. He despises them.

We should notice at once that in this first kind of morality the opposites "good" and "bad" mean no more than "noble" and "despicable." The opposition between "good" and "evil" has another origin. The despised one is the coward, the anxious, the small, the man who thinks about narrow utility—also the suspicious man with his inhibited look, the self-abasing man, the species of human dogs who allow themselves to be mistreated, the begging flatterer, above all, the liar. It is a basic belief of all aristocrats that the common folk are liars. "We tellers of the truth"—that's what the nobility called themselves in ancient Greece. It's evident that distinctions of moral worth everywhere were first applied to men and later were established for actions; hence, it is a serious mistake when historians of morality take as a starting point a question like "Why was the compassionate action praised?"

The noble kind of man experiences himself as a person who determines value and does not need to have other people's approval. He makes the judgment "What is harmful to me is harmful in itself." He understands himself as something which in general first confers honor on things, as someone who creates values. Whatever he recognizes in himself he honors. Such a morality is self-glorification. In the foreground stands the feeling of fullness and power, which wants to overflow, the happiness of high tension, the consciousness of riches which wants to give and deliver; the noble man also helps the unfortunate, but not, or hardly ever, from pity, more in response to an impulse which the excess of power produces.

The noble man honors the powerful man in himself and also the man who has power over himself, who understands how to speak and how to keep silent, who takes delight in dealing with himself severely and toughly and respects, above all, severity and toughness. "Wotan[1] set a hard heart in my breast," it says in an old Scandinavian saga: that's how poetry emerged, with justice, from the soul of a proud Viking. A man of this sort is even proud of the fact that he has not been made for compassion. That's why the hero of the saga adds a warning, "In a man whose heart is not hard when he is still young the heart will never become hard." Noble and brave men who think this way are furthest re-

---

1   *Wotan*   Chief of the Norse gods, also known as Odin.

moved from that morality which sees the badge of morality in pity or actions for others or *désintéressement*;[1] the belief in oneself, pride in oneself, a fundamental hostility and irony against "selflessness" clearly belong to noble morality, just as much as an easy contempt and caution before feelings of compassion and a "warm heart."

Powerful men are the ones who understand how to honor—that is their art, their realm of invention. The profound reverence for age and for tradition—all justice stands on this double reverence—the belief and the prejudice favoring ancestors and working against newcomers are typical in the morality of the powerful, and when, by contrast, the men of "modern ideas" believe almost instinctively in "progress" and the "future" and an ever-increasing lack of respect for age, then in that attitude the ignoble origin of these "ideas" reveals itself well enough.

However, a morality of the rulers is most alien and embarrassing to the present taste because of the severity of its basic principle that man has duties only with respect to those like him, that man should act towards those beings of lower rank, towards everything strange, at his own discretion, "as his heart dictates," and, in any case, "beyond good and evil." Here pity and things like that may belong. The capacity for and obligation to a long gratitude and a long revenge—both only within the circle of those like oneself—the sophistication in paying back again, the refined idea in friendship, a certain necessity to have enemies (as, so to speak, drainage ditches for the feelings of envy, quarrelsomeness, and high spirits—basically in order to be capable of being a good friend): all those are typical characteristics of a noble morality, which, as indicated, is not the morality of "modern ideas" and which is thus nowadays difficult to sympathize with, as well as difficult to dig up and expose.

Things are different with the second type of moral system, slave morality. Suppose the oppressed, depressed, suffering, and unfree people, those ignorant of themselves and tired out, suppose they moralize: what will be the common feature of their moral estimates of value? Probably a pessimistic suspicion directed at the entire human situation will express itself, perhaps a condemnation of man, along with his situation. The gaze of a slave is not well disposed towards the virtues of the powerful; he possesses skepticism and mistrust; he has a subtlety of mistrust against everything "good" and what is honored in it; he would like to persuade himself that even happiness is not genuine there.

By contrast, those characteristics will be pulled forward and flooded with light which serve to mitigate existence for those who suffer: here respect is given to pity, to the obliging hand ready to help, to the warm heart, to patience, diligence, humility, and friendliness, for these are the most useful characteristics and almost the only means to endure the pressure of existence. Slave morality is essentially a morality of utility. Here is the focus for the origin of that famous opposition of "good" and "evil": power and danger are felt within evil itself, a certain terror, subtlety, and strength, which does not permit contempt to spring up. According to slave morality, the "evil" man thus inspires fear; according to master morality, it is precisely the "good" man who inspires and will inspire fear, while the "bad" man will be felt as despicable.

This opposition reaches its peak when, in accordance with the consequences of slave morality, finally a trace of disregard is also attached to the "good" of this morality—it may be light and benevolent—because within the way of thinking of the slave the good man must definitely be an harmless man: he is good natured, easy to deceive, perhaps a bit stupid, a *bonhomme*.[2] Wherever slave morality gains predominance the language reveals a tendency to bring the words "good" and "stupid" into closer proximity. A final basic difference: the longing for freedom, the instinct for happiness and the refinements of the feeling for freedom belong just as necessarily to slave morality and morals as art and enthusiasm in reverence and devotion are the regular symptoms of an aristocratic way of thinking and valuing. From this we can without further ado understand why love as passion—which is our European specialty—must clearly have a noble origin: as is well known, its invention belongs to the Provencal knightly poets, those splendidly inventive men of the "*gay saber*"[3] to whom Europe owes so much—almost its very self.

◆ ◆ ◆ ◆ ◆

---

1 *désintéressement* French: selflessness.

2 *a bonhomme* French: a good human being.
3 *gai saber* Provençal: Gay science.

On the Genealogy of Morals

from *First Essay: Good and Evil, Good and Bad*

1

These English psychologists whom we have to thank for the only attempts up to this point to produce a history of the origins of morality—in themselves they serve up to us no small riddle. In the way of a lively riddle, they even offer, I confess, something substantially more than their books—they are interesting in themselves! These English psychologists—what do they really want? We find them, willingly or unwillingly, always at the same work, that is, hauling the *partie honteuse*[1] of our inner world into the foreground, in order to look right there for the truly effective and operative force which has determined our development, the very place where man's intellectual pride least wishes to find it (for example, in the *vis inertiae*[2] of habit or in forgetfulness or in a blind, contingent, mechanical joining of ideas or in something else purely passive, automatic, reflex, molecular, and completely stupid)—what is it that really drives these psychologists always in this particular direction?

Is it a secret, malicious, common instinct (perhaps one which is self-deceiving) for belittling humanity? Or something like a pessimistic suspicion, the mistrust of idealists who've become disappointed, gloomy, venomous, and green. Or a small underground hostility and rancor towards Christianity (and Plato), which perhaps has never once managed to cross the threshold of consciousness? Or even a lecherous taste for what is odd or painfully paradoxical, for what in existence is questionable and ridiculous? Or finally a bit of all of these—a little vulgarity, a little gloominess, a little hostility to Christianity, a little thrill, and a need for pepper?...

But people tell me that these men are simply old, cold, boring frogs, who creep and hop around people as if they were in their own proper element, that is, in a swamp. I resist that idea when I hear it. What's more, I don't believe it. And if one is permitted to hope where one cannot know, then I hope from my heart that the situation with these men could be reversed, that these investigators peering at the soul through their microscopes could be thoroughly brave, generous, and proud animals, who know how to control their hearts and their pain and who have educated themselves to sacrifice everything desirable for the sake of the truth, for the sake of every truth, even the simple, the bitter, the hateful, the repellent, the unchristian, the unmoral truth.... For there are such truths.—

2

So all respect to the good spirits that may govern in these historians of morality! But it's certainly a pity that they lack the historical spirit itself, that they've been left in the lurch by all the good spirits of history! Collectively they all think essentially unhistorically, in what is now the traditional manner of philosophers. Of that there is no doubt. The incompetence of their genealogies of morals reveals itself at the very beginning, where the issue is to determine the origin of the idea and of the judgment "good."

"People," so they proclaim, "originally praised unegoistic actions and called them good from the perspective of those for whom they were done, that is, those for whom such actions were useful. Later people forgot how this praise began, and because unegoistic actions had, according to custom, always been praised as good, people then simply felt them as good, as if they were something inherently good."

We see right away that this initial derivation already contains all the typical characteristics of the idiosyncrasies of English psychologists—we have "usefulness," "forgetting," "habit," and finally "error," all as the foundation for an evaluation in which the higher man up to this time has taken pride, as if it were a sort of privilege of men generally. This pride should be humbled, this evaluation of worth emptied of value. Has that been achieved?

Now, first of all, it's obvious to me that from this theory the origin of the idea "good" has been sought for and established in the wrong place: the judgment "good" did not move here from those to whom "goodness" was shown! It is much more that case that the "good people" themselves, that is, the noble, powerful, higher-ranking, and higher-thinking people felt and set themselves and their actions up as good, that is to say, of the first rank, in contrast to everything low, low-minded, common, and vulgar. From this pathos of distance they first arrogated to themselves the right to create values, to stamp out the names for values. What did they care about usefulness!

---

1   *partie honteuse*   French: shameful part.
2   *vis inertiae*   Latin: force of inertia.

In relation to such a hot pouring out of the highest rank-ordering, rank-setting judgments of value, the point of view which considers utility is as foreign and inappropriate as possible. Here the feeling has reached the opposite of that low level of warmth which is a condition for that calculating shrewdness, that calculation by utility—and not just for a moment, not for an exceptional hour, but permanently. The pathos of nobility and distance, as mentioned, the lasting and domineering feeling, something total and complete, of a higher ruling nature in relation to a lower nature, to a "beneath"—that is the origin of the opposition between "good" and "bad." (The right of the master to give names extends so far that we could permit ourselves to grasp the origin of language itself as an expression of the power of the rulers: they say "that is such and such," seal every object and event with a sound and, in the process, as it were, take possession of it.)

Given this origin, the word "good" was not in any way necessarily tied up with "unegoistic" actions, as it is in the superstitions of those genealogists of morality. Rather, that occurs for the first time with the collapse of aristocratic value judgments, when this entire contrast between "egoistic" and "unegoistic" pressed itself ever more strongly into human awareness—it is, to use my own words, the instinct of the herd which, through this contrast, finally gets its word (and its words). And even so, it took a long time until this instinct in the masses became master, with the result that moral evaluation got thoroughly hung up and bogged down on this opposition (as is the case, for example, in modern Europe: today the prejudice that takes "moralistic," "unegoistic," and "désintéressé"[1] as equally valuable ideas already governs, with the force of a "fixed idea" and a disease of the brain).

3

Secondly, however, and quite separate from the fact that this hypothesis about the origin of the value judgment "good" is historically untenable, it suffers from an inherent psychological contradiction. The utility of the unegoistic action is supposed to be the origin of the praise it receives, and this origin has allegedly been forgotten: but how is this forgetting even possible? Could the usefulness of such actions at some time or other perhaps just have stopped? The case is the opposite: this utility has rather been an everyday

experience throughout the ages, and thus something that has always been constantly re-emphasized. Hence, instead of disappearing out of consciousness, instead of becoming something forgettable, it must have pressed itself into the consciousness with ever-increasing clarity.

How much more sensible is the contrasting theory (which is not therefore closer to the truth), for example, the one which is advocated by Herbert Spencer:[2] he proposes that the idea "good" is essentially the same as the idea "useful" or "functional," so that in judgments about "good" and "bad" human beings sum up and endorse the experiences they have not forgotten and cannot forget concerning the useful-functional and the harmful-useless. According to this theory, good is something which has always proved useful, so that it may assert its validity as "valuable in the highest degree" or as "valuable in itself." This path to an explanation is, as mentioned, also false, but at least the account itself is sensible and psychologically tenable.

4

I was given a hint of the right direction by this question: What, from an etymological perspective, do the meanings of "Good" as manifested in different languages really mean? There I found that all of them lead back to the same transformation of ideas, that everywhere "noble" or "aristocratic" in a social sense is the fundamental idea out of which "good" in the sense of "spiritually noble," "aristocratic," "spiritually high-minded," "spiritually privileged" necessarily develop—a process which always runs in parallel with that other one which finally transforms "common," "vulgar," and "low" into the concept "bad." The most eloquent example of the latter is the German word "schlect"[3] itself—which is identical with the word "schlicht"[4]—compare "schlectweg"[5] and "schlechterdings."[6] Originally these words designated the plain, common man, but without any suspicious side glance, simply in contrast to the nobility. Around the time of the Thirty Years War[7] approximately—hence late enough—this sense changed into the one used now.

1 désinteressé French: selfless.
2 Herbert Spencer English philosopher (1820–1903) famous for endeavoring to apply Darwin's theory of evolution to many fields, including ethics.
3 schlect German: bad.
4 schlicht German: plain.
5 schlectweg German: quite simply.
6 schlechterdings German: simply.
7 Thirty Years War War between Protestant and Catholic nations

As far as the genealogy of morals is concerned, this point strikes me as a fundamental insight—that it was first discovered so late we can ascribe to the repressive influence which democratic prejudice in the modern world exercises over all questions of origin. And this occurs in what appears to be the most objective realm of natural science and physiology, a point which I can only hint at here. But the sort of mischief this prejudice can cause, once it has become unleashed as hatred, particularly where morality and history are concerned, is revealed in the well-known case of Buckle:[1] the plebeian nature of the modern spirit, which originated in England, broke out once again on its home turf, as violently as a muddy volcano and with the same salty, overloud, and common eloquence with which all previous volcanoes have spoken.

6

From this rule that the concept of political superiority always resolves itself into the concept of spiritual priority, it is not really an exception (although there is room for exceptions), when the highest caste is also the priest caste and consequently for its total range of meanings prefers a scale of values which recalls its priestly function. So, for example, for the first time the words "pure" and "impure" appear as marks of one's social position and later a "good" and a "bad" develop which no longer refer to social position.

Incidentally, people should be warned not to take these ideas of "pure" and "impure" from the outset too seriously, too broadly, or even symbolically. All the ideas of ancient humanity are initially to be understood to a degree we can hardly imagine, much more as coarse, crude, superficial, narrow, blunt and, in particular, unsymbolic. The "pure man" is from the start simply a man who washes himself, who forbids himself certain foods which produce diseases of the skin, who doesn't sleep with the dirty women of the lower people, who has a horror of blood—no more, not much more!

On the other hand, from the very nature of an essentially priestly aristocracy it is clear enough how even here early on the opposition between different evaluations could become dangerously internalized and sharpened. And in fact they finally ripped open fissures between man and man, over which even an Achilles of the free spirit could not cross without shivering. From the very beginning there is something unhealthy about such priestly aristocracies and about the customary attitudes which govern in them, which turn away from action, sometimes brooding, sometimes exploding with emotion, as a result of which in the priests of almost all ages there have appeared almost unavoidably debilitating intestinal illness and neurasthenia.[2]

But what they themselves came up with as a remedy for this pathological disease—surely we can assert that it has finally shown itself, through its effects, as even a hundred times more dangerous than the illness for which it was meant to provide relief. Human beings are still sick from the after-effects of this priestly naïveté in healing! Let's think, for example, of certain forms of diet (avoiding meat), of fasting, of celibacy, of the flight "into the desert" (Weir Mitchell's isolation,[3] but naturally without the fattening up cure and overeating which follow it—a treatment which constitutes the most effective treatment for all hysteria induced by the ideals of asceticism): consider also the whole metaphysic of the priests—so hostile to the senses, making men so lazy and sophisticated—or the way they hypnotize themselves in the manner of fakirs and Brahmins—Brahmanism employed as a glass head and a fixed idea. Consider finally the only too understandable and common dissatisfaction with its radical cure, with nothingness (or God—the desire for a *unio mystica*[4] with God is the desire of the Buddhist for nothingness, nirvana—nothing more!).

Among the priests, everything mentioned above becomes more dangerous—not only the remedies and arts of healing, but also pride, vengeance, mental acuity, excess, love, thirst for power, virtue, illness—although it's fair enough to add that on the foundation of this basically dangerous form of human existence, the priest, for the first time the human being became, in general, an interesting animal, that here the human soul first attained depth in a higher sense and became evil—and, indeed, these are the two fundamental reasons for humanity's superiority, up to now, over other animals.

---

between 1618 and 1648, involving most of the major European powers of the time.
1 *Buckle* Henry Thomas Buckle, English historian (1821–62), author of *History of Civilization* (1857).
2 *neurasthenia* Psychic disorder characterized by chronic fatigue, weakness, aches and pains.
3 *Weir Mitchell's isolation* Cure developed by American doctor Silas Weir Mitchell (1829–1914) for nervous disorders; it involved weeks or even months of enforced rest in bed.
4 *unio mystica* Latin: mystical union.

7

You will have already guessed how easily the priestly way of evaluating could split from the knightly-aristocratic and then continue to develop into its opposite. Such a development receives a special stimulus every time the priest caste and the warrior caste confront each other jealously and are not willing to agree about the winner. The knightly-aristocratic judgments of value have as their basic assumption a powerful physicality, a blooming, rich, even overflowing health, together with those things which are required to maintain these qualities—war, adventure, hunting, dancing, war games, and in general everything which involves strong, free, happy action. The priestly-noble method of evaluating has, as we saw, other preconditions: these make it difficult enough for them when it comes to war!

As is well known, priests are the most evil of enemies—but why? Because they are the most powerless. From their powerlessness, their hate grows into something immense and terrifying, to the most spiritual and most poisonous manifestations. Those who have been the greatest haters in world history and the most spiritually rich haters have always been the priests—in comparison with the spirit of priestly revenge all the remaining spirits are, in general, hardly worth considering. Human history would be a really stupid affair without that spirit which entered it from the powerless.

Let us quickly consider the greatest example. Everything on earth which has been done against "the nobility," "the powerful," "the masters," "the possessors of power" is not worth mentioning in comparison with what the Jews have done against them—the Jews, that priestly people who knew how to get final satisfaction from their enemies and conquerors through a radical transformation of their values, that is, through an act of the most spiritual revenge. This was appropriate only to a priestly people with the most deeply rooted priestly desire for revenge.

In opposition to the aristocratic value equations (good = noble = powerful = beautiful = fortunate = loved by god), the Jews, with a consistency inspiring fear, dared to reverse it and to hang on to that with the teeth of the most profound hatred (the hatred of the powerless), that is, to "only those who suffer are good; the poor, the powerless, the low are the only good people; the suffering, those in need, the sick, the ugly are also the only pious people; only they are blessed by God; for them alone there is salvation. By contrast, you privileged and powerful people, you are for all

eternity the evil, the cruel, the lecherous, the insatiable, the godless—you will also be the unblessed, the cursed, and the damned for all eternity!"... We know who inherited this Judaic transformation of values ...

In connection with that huge and immeasurably disastrous initiative which the Jews launched with this most fundamental of all declarations of war, I recall the sentence I wrote at another time (in *Beyond Good and Evil*, section 195)—namely, that with the Jews the slave condition in morality begins: that condition which has a two-thousand-year-old history behind it and which we nowadays no longer notice because it has triumphed.

10

The slave revolt in morality begins when the resentment itself becomes creative and gives birth to values: the resentment of those beings who are prevented from a genuinely active reaction and who compensate for that with a merely imaginary vengeance. While all noble morality grows out of a triumphant self-affirmation, slave morality from the start says "No" to what is "outside," "other," "a non-self". And this "No" is its creative act. This transformation of the glance which confers value—this necessary projection towards what is outer instead of back onto itself—that is inherent in resentment. In order to arise, slave morality always requires first an opposing world, a world outside itself. Psychologically speaking, it needs external stimuli in order to act at all. Its action is basically reaction.

The reverse is the case with the noble method of valuing: it acts and grows spontaneously. It seeks its opposite only to affirm itself even more thankfully, with even more rejoicing. Its negative concept of "low," "common," "bad" is only a pale contrasting image after the fact in relation to its positive basic concept, thoroughly intoxicated with life and passion, "We are noble, good, beautiful, and happy!" When the noble way of evaluating makes a mistake and abuses reality, that happens with reference to the sphere which it does not know well enough, indeed, the sphere it has strongly resisted learning the truth about: under certain circumstances it misjudges the sphere it despises—the sphere of the common man, the low people.

On the other hand, we should consider that even assuming that the feeling of contempt, of looking down, or of looking superior falsifies the image of the person despised, such distortion will fall short by a long way of the distortion with which the repressed hatred and vengeance of the powerless man mistakenly assault his opponent—naturally, in effigy. In fact, in contempt there is too much negligence, too much dismissiveness, too much looking away and impatience, all mixed together, even too much feeling of joy, for it to be capable of converting its object into a truly distorted monster.

We should not fail to hear the almost benevolent nuances which for a Greek noble, for example, lay in all the words with which he set himself above the lower people—how a constant form of pity, consideration, and forbearance is mixed in there, sweetening the words, to the point where almost all words which refer to the common man finally remain as expressions for "unhappy," "worthy of pity" (compare *deilos*,[1] *deilaios*,[2] *poneros*,[3] *mochtheros*[4]—the last two basically designating the common man as a slave worker and beast of burden). On the other hand, for the Greek ear the words "bad," "low," "unhappy" have never stopped echoing a single note, one tone color, in which "unhappy" predominates. That is the inheritance of the old, noble, aristocratic way of evaluating, which does not betray its principles even in contempt.

(Philologists might recall the sense in which *oizuros*,[5] *anolbos*,[6] *tlemon*,[7] *dustychein*,[8] *xymfora*[9] were used). The "well born" felt that they were "the happy ones"; they did not have to construct their happiness artificially first by looking at their enemies, or in some circumstance to talk themselves into it, to lie to themselves (the way all men of resentment habitually do). Similarly they knew, as complete men, overloaded with power and thus necessarily active, they must not separate action from happiness. They considered being active necessarily associated with happiness (that's where the phrase *eu prattein*[10] derives its origin)—all this is very much the opposite of "happiness" at the level of the powerless, the oppressed, those festering with poisonous and hostile feelings, among whom happiness comes out essentially as a narcotic, an anesthetic, quiet, peace, "Sabbath", relaxing the soul, stretching one's limbs, in short, as something passive.

1 *deilos* Greek: cowardly.
2 *deilaios* Greek: lowly, mean.
3 *poneros* Greek: oppressed by toil, wretched.
4 *mochtheros* Greek: suffering, wretched.
5 *oizuros* Greek: miserable.
6 *anolbos* Greek: unblessed.
7 *tlemon* Greek: wretched.
8 *dustychein* Greek: unfortunate.
9 *xymfora* Greek: misfortune.
10 *eu prattein* Greek: do well, succeed.

While the noble man lives for himself with trust and candour (*gennaios*, meaning "of noble birth" stresses the nuance "upright" and also probably "naïve"); the man of resentment is neither upright nor naïve, nor honest and direct with himself. His soul squints. His spirit loves hiding places, secret paths, and back doors. Everything furtive attracts him as his world, his security, his refreshment. He understands about remaining silent, not forgetting, waiting, temporarily diminishing himself, humiliating himself. A race of such men of resentment will necessarily end up cleverer than any noble race. It will value cleverness to a very different extent, that is, as a condition of existence of the utmost importance; whereas, cleverness among noble men easily acquires a delicate aftertaste of luxury and sophistication about it. Here it is not nearly so important as the complete certainly of the ruling unconscious instincts or even a certain lack of cleverness, something like brave recklessness, whether in the face of danger or of an enemy, or wildly enthusiastic, sudden fits of anger, love, reverence, thankfulness, and vengefulness, by which in all ages noble souls have recognized each other.

The resentment of the noble man himself, if it comes over him, consumes and exhausts itself in an immediate reaction and therefore does not poison. On the other hand, in countless cases it just does not appear at all; whereas, in the case of all weak and powerless people it is unavoidable. The noble man cannot take his enemies, his misfortunes, even his bad deeds seriously for very long—that is the mark of strong, complete natures, in whom there is a surplus of plastic, creative, healing power, as well as the power to forget (a good example for that from the modern world is Mirabeau,[11] who had no memory of the insults and maliciousness people directed at him, and who therefore could not forgive, because he just forgot). Such a man with a single shrug throws off himself all those worms which eat into other men. Only here is possible (provided that it is at all possible on earth) the real "love for one's enemy." How much respect a noble man already has for his enemies! And such a respect is already a bridge to love … In fact, he demands his enemy for himself, as his mark of honor. Indeed, he has no enemy other than one who has nothing to despise and a great deal to respect! By contrast, imagine for yourself "the enemy" as a man of resentment conceives him—and right here we have his action, his creation: he has concep-

11 *Mirabeau* Honoré Gabriel Riqueti, comte de Mirabeau (1749–91), French writer and statesman during the French Revolution.

tualized "the evil enemy," "the evil one," as a fundamental idea—and from that he now thinks his way to an opposite image and counterpart, a "good man"—himself!

11

We see exactly the opposite with the noble man, who conceives the fundamental idea "good" in advance and spontaneously by himself and from there first creates a picture of "bad" for himself. This "bad" originating from the noble man and that "evil" arising out of the stew pot of insatiable hatred—of these the first is a later creation, an afterthought, a complementary color; whereas, the second is the original, the beginning, the essential act of conception in slave morality.

Although the two words "bad" and "evil" both seem opposite to the same idea of "good," how different they are. But it is not the same idea of the "good"; it is much rather a question of who the "evil man" really is, in the sense of the morality of resentment. The strict answer to that is as follows: precisely the "good man" of the other morality, the noble man himself, the powerful, the ruling man, only colored over, reinterpreted, and seen only through the poisonous eyes of resentment.

Here there is one thing we will be the last to deny: the man who knows these "good men" only as enemies, knows them as nothing but evil enemies, and the same men who are so strongly bound by custom, honor, habit, thankfulness, even more by mutual suspicion and jealousy *inter pares*[1] and who, by contrast, demonstrate in relation to each other such resourceful consideration, self-control, refinement, loyalty, pride, and friendship—these men, once outside where the strange world, the foreign, begins, are not much better than beasts of prey turned loose. There they enjoy freedom from all social constraints. In the wilderness they make up for the tension which a long fenced-in confinement within the peace of the community brings about. They go back to the innocent consciousness of a wild beast of prey, as joyful monsters, who perhaps walk away from a dreadful sequence of murder, arson, rape, and torture with exhilaration and spiritual equilibrium, as if they had merely pulled off a student prank, convinced that the poets now have something more to sing about and praise for a long time to come.

At the bottom of all these noble races we cannot fail to recognize the beast of prey, the blond beast splendidly roaming around in its lust for loot and victory. This hidden basis from time to time needs to be discharged: the animal must come out again, must go back into the wilderness,— Roman, Arab, German, Japanese nobility, Homeric heroes, Scandinavian Vikings—in this need they are all alike.

It was the noble races which left behind the concept of the "barbarian" in all their tracks, wherever they went. A consciousness of and a pride in this fact reveals itself even in their highest culture (for example, when Pericles[2] says to his Athenians, in that famous Funeral Speech, "our audacity has broken a way through to every land and sea, putting up permanent memorials to itself for good and ill."[3])—this "audacity" of the noble races, mad, absurd, sudden in the way it expresses itself, its unpredictability, even the improbability of its undertakings—Pericles emphatically praises the *raythumia*[4] of the Athenians—its indifference to and contempt for safety, body, life, comfort, its fearsome cheerfulness and the depth of its joy in all destruction, in all the physical pleasures of victory and cruelty—everything summed up for those who suffer from such audacity in the image of the "barbarian," the "evil enemy," something like the "Goth" or the "Vandal."

The deep, icy mistrust which the German evokes, as soon as he comes to power—even today—is still an after-effect of that unforgettable terror with which for centuries Europe confronted the rage of the blond German beast (although there is hardly any idea linking the old Germanic tribes and we Germans, let alone any blood relationship).

Once before I have remarked on Hesiod's dilemma when he thought up his sequence of cultural periods and sought to express them as Gold, Silver, and Iron. But he didn't know what to do with the contradiction presented to him by the marvelous but, at the same time, horrifying and violent world of Homer, other than to make two cultural ages out of one and then place one after the other—first the age of Heroes and Demi-gods from Troy and Thebes, just as that world remained as a memorial for the noble races who had their own ancestors in it, and then the Iron Age, as that same world appeared to the descendants of the downtrodden, exploited, ill treated, those carried off and sold—a metallic age, as mentioned: hard, cold, cruel, empty of feeling and scruples, with everything crushed and covered over in blood.

---

1   *inter pares*   Latin: among equals.

2   *Pericles*   Greek statesman, orator and general (c. 495–429 BCE).

3   *our audacity … for good and ill*   From Thucydides, *Peloponnesian War*, 2.41.

4   *raythumia*   Greek: mental balance, freedom from anxiety.

Assuming as true what in any event is taken as "the truth" nowadays, that it is precisely the purpose of all culture to breed a tame and civilized animal, a domestic pet, out of the beast of prey "man," then we would undoubtedly have to consider the essential instruments of culture all those instinctive reactions and resentments by means of which the noble races with all their ideals were finally disgraced and overpowered—but that would not be to claim that the bearers of these instincts also in themselves represented culture. It would much rather be the case that the opposite is not only probable—no! nowadays it is visibly apparent. These people carrying instincts for oppression and a lust for revenge, the descendants of all European and non-European slavery, and all pre-Aryan populations in particular, represent the regression of mankind! These "instruments of culture" are a disgrace to humanity, more a reason to be suspicious of or a counterargument against "culture" in general!

We may well be right when we hang onto our fear of the blond beast at the base of all noble races and keep up our guard. But who would not find it a hundred times better to fear if he could at the same time be allowed to admire, rather than not fear and no longer be able to rid himself of the disgusting sight of the failures, the stunted, the emaciated, the poisoned? Is not that our fate? Today what is it that constitutes our aversion to "man"? For we suffer from man—there's no doubt of that. It's not a matter of fear. Rather it's the fact that we have nothing more to fear from men, that the maggot "man" is in the foreground swarming around, that the "tame man," the hopelessly mediocre and unpleasant man, has already learned to feel that he is the goal, the pinnacle, the meaning of history, "the higher man,"—yes indeed, he even has a certain right to feel that about himself, insofar as he feels separate from the excess of failed, sick, tired, spent people, who are nowadays beginning to make Europe stink, and feels at least somewhat successful, at least still capable of life, at least able to say "Yes" to life . . .

from *Second Essay: Guilt, Bad Conscience and Related Matters*

I

To breed an animal that is entitled to make promises— surely that is the essence of the paradoxical task nature has set itself where human beings are concerned? Isn't that the real problem of human beings? The fact that this problem has largely been resolved must seem all the more astonishing to a person who knows how to appreciate fully the power which works against this promise-making, namely forgetfulness. Forgetfulness is not merely a *vis interiae*, as superficial people think. Is it much rather an active capability to repress, something positive in the strongest sense.

We can ascribe to forgetfulness the fact what while we are digesting what we alone live through and experience and absorb (we might call the process mental ingestion *[Einverseelung]*), we are conscious of what is going on as little as we are with the thousand-fold process which our bodily nourishment goes through (so-called physical ingestion *[Einverleibung]*). The doors and windows of consciousness are shut from time to time, so that it stays undisturbed by the noise and struggle with which the underworld of our functional organs keeps working for and against one another—a small quiet place, a little *tabula rasa*[1] of the consciousness, so that there will again be room for something new, above all, for the nobler functions and officials, for ruling, thinking ahead, determining what to do (for our organism is arranged as an oligarchy)—that is, as I said, the use of active forgetfulness, like some porter at the door, a maintainer of psychic order, quiet, and etiquette. From that we can see at once how, if forgetfulness were not present, there could be no happiness, no cheerfulness, no hoping, no pride, no present. The man in whom this repression apparatus is harmed and not working properly we can compare to a dyspeptic (and not just compare)—he is "finished" with nothing.

Now this necessarily forgetful animal in which forgetfulness is present as a force, as a form of strong health, has had an opposing capability bred into it, a memory, with the help of which, in certain cases, its forgetfulness will cease to function—that is, for those cases where promises are to be made. This is in no way a merely passive inability ever to be rid of an impression once it has been etched into the mind, nor is it merely indigestion over a word one has pledged at a particular time and which one can no longer be over and done with. No, it's an active wish not to be free of the matter, a continuing desire for what one willed at a particular time, a real memory of one's will, so that between the original "I will" or "I will do" and the actual discharge of the will, its real action, without thinking about it, a world

---

1   *tabula rasa* Latin: blank slate.

of strange new things, circumstances, even acts of the will can intervene, without breaking this long chain of the will.

But consider what that presupposes! In order to organize the future in this manner, human beings must have first learned to separate necessary events from chance events, to think in terms of cause and effect, to see distant events as if they were present, to anticipate them, to set goals and the means to reach them safely, to develop a capability for figures and calculations in general—and for that to occur, a human being must necessarily have first become something one could predict, something bound by regular rules, even in the way he imagined himself to himself, so that finally he is able to act like someone who makes promises—he can make himself into a pledge for the future!

2

Precisely that development is the long history of the origin of responsibility. The task of breeding an animal with a right to make promises contains within it, as we have already grasped, as a condition and prerequisite, the earlier task of first making a human being necessarily uniform to some extent, one among many others like him, regular and consequently predictable. The immense task involved in this, what I have called the "morality of custom" (cf. *Daybreak*, Sections 9, 14, 16), the essential work of a man on his own self in the longest-lasting age of the human race, his entire pre-historical work, derives its meaning, its grand justification, from the following point, no matter how much hardship, tyranny, monotony and idiocy it also manifested: with the help of the morality of custom and the social strait jacket, the human being was rendered truly predictable.

Now, let's position ourselves, by contrast, at the end of this immense process, in the place where the tree finally yields its fruit, where society and the morality of custom finally bring to light the end for which they were simply the means. We find—as the ripest fruit on that tree—the sovereign individual, something which resembles only itself, which has broken loose again from the morality of custom—the autonomous individual beyond morality (for "autonomous" and "moral" are mutually exclusive terms)—in short, the human being who possesses his own independent and enduring will, who is entitled to make promises—and in him a proud consciousness, quivering in every muscle, of what has finally been achieved and given living embodiment in him: a real consciousness of power and freedom, a feeling of completion for human beings generally.

This man who has become free, who really has the right to make promises, this master of free will, this sovereign—how can he not realize the superiority he enjoys over everyone who does not have the right to make a promise and make pledges on his own behalf, knowing how much trust, how much fear, and how much respect he creates (he is worthy of all three) and how, with this mastery over himself, he has necessarily been given in addition mastery over his circumstances, over nature, and over all creatures with a shorter and less reliable will?

The "free" man, the owner of an enduring unbreakable will, by possessing this, also acquires his own standard of value: he looks out from himself at others and confers respect or withholds it. And just as it will be necessary for him to honor those like him, the strong and dependable (who are entitled to make promises), in other words, everyone who makes promises like a sovereign, seriously, rarely, and slowly, who is sparing with his trust, who honors another when he does trust, who gives his word as something reliable, because he knows he is strong enough to remain upright when opposed by misfortune, even when "opposed by fate," so it will be necessary for him to keep his foot ready to kick the scrawny unreliable men, who make promises without being entitled to, and to hold his cane ready to punish the liar who breaks his word in the very moment it comes out of his mouth.

The proud knowledge of the extraordinary privilege of responsibility, the consciousness of this rare freedom, this power over oneself and destiny, have become internalized into the deepest parts of him and grown instinctual, have now become a dominating instinct. What will he call it, this dominating instinct, given that he finds he needs a word for it? There's no doubt about this question: the sovereign man calls this instinct his conscience.

3

His conscience?... To begin with, we can conjecture that the idea of "conscience," which we are encountering here in its highest, almost perplexing form, already has a long history and developmental process behind it. To be entitled to pledge one's word, to do it with pride, and also to say "Yes" to oneself—that right is a ripe fruit, as I have mentioned, but it is also a late fruit. For what a long stretch of time this fruit must have hung tart and sour on the tree! And for an even longer time it was impossible to see any such fruit. It would appear that no one would have been entitled to make promises, even if everything about the tree was getting ready for it and was growing in that very direction.

"How does one create a memory for the human animal? How does one stamp something like that into his partly dull, partly flickering, momentary understanding, this living embodiment of forgetfulness, so that it stays there?" This ancient problem, as you can imagine, was not resolved right away with tender answers and methods. There is perhaps nothing more fearful and more terrible in the entire pre-history of human beings than the technique for developing his memory. "We burn something in so that it remains in the memory. Only something which never ceases to cause pain stays in the memory"—that is a leading principle of the most ancient (and unfortunately the most recent) psychology on earth.

We might even say that everywhere on earth nowadays where there is still solemnity, seriousness, mystery, and gloomy colors in the lives of men and people, something of that terror is still at work, the fear with which in earlier times on earth people made promises, pledged their word, or praised something. The past, the longest, deepest, most severe past, breathes on us and surfaces in us when we become "solemn." When the human being considered it necessary to make a memory for himself, it never happened without blood, martyrs, and sacrifices—the most terrible sacrifices and pledges (among them the sacrifice of the first born), the most repulsive self-mutilations (for example castration), the cruellest forms of ritual in all the religious cults (and all religions are at bottom systems of cruelty)—all that originates in that instinct which discovered that pain was the most powerful means of helping to develop the memory.

In a certain sense all asceticism belongs here: a couple of ideas need to be made indissoluble, omnipresent, unforgettable, "fixed," in order to hypnotize the entire nervous and intellectual system through these "fixed ideas"—and the ascetic procedures and forms of life are the means whereby these ideas are freed from jostling around with all the other ideas, in order to make them "unforgettable." The worse the human being's "memory" was, the more terrible his customs have always appeared. The harshness of the laws of punishment provide a special standard for measuring how much trouble people went to in order to triumph over forgetfulness and to maintain a present awareness of a few primitive demands of social living together for this slave of momentary feelings and desires.

We Germans certainly do not think of ourselves as a particularly cruel and hard-hearted people, even less as par-

ticularly careless people who live only in the present. But have a look at our old penal code in order to understand how much trouble it took on this earth to breed a "People of Thinkers" (by that I mean the peoples of Europe, among whom today we still find a maximum of trust, seriousness, tastelessness, and practicality, and who, with these characteristics, have a right to breed all sorts of European mandarins). These Germans have used terrible means to make themselves a memory in order to attain mastery over their vulgar and brutally crude basic instincts. Think of the old German punishments, for example, stoning (the legend even lets the mill stone fall on the head of the guilty person), breaking on the wheel (the unique invention and specialty of the German genius in the area of punishment!), impaling on a stake, ripping people apart or stamping them to death with horses ("quartering"), boiling the criminal in oil or wine (still done in the fourteenth and fifteenth centuries), the well-loved practice of flaying ("cutting flesh off in strips"), carving flesh out of the chest, along with, of course, covering the offender with honey and leaving him to the flies in the burning sun.

With the help of such images and procedures people finally retained five or six "I will not's" in their memory, and so far as these precepts were concerned they gave their word in order to live with the advantages of society—and that was that! With the assistance of this sort of memory people finally came to "reason"! Ah, reason, seriousness, mastery over emotions, the whole gloomy business called reflection, all these privileges and ceremonies of human beings—how expensive they were! How much blood and horror is the basis for all "good things"!...

4

But then how did that other "gloomy business," the consciousness of guilt, the whole "bad conscience" come into the world? With this we turn back to our genealogists of morality. I'll say it once more—or perhaps I haven't said it at all yet—they are useless. With their own purely "modern" experience extending only through five periods, with no knowledge of or any desire to know the past, and even less historical insight, a "second perspective"—something so necessary at this point—they nonetheless pursue the history of morality. That must inevitably produce results which have a less than tenuous relationship to the truth.

Have these genealogists of morality up to this point allowed themselves to dream, even remotely, that, for instance, the major moral principle "guilt" *[Schuld]* derives its origin from the very materialistic idea "debt" *[Schulden]* or that punishment developed entirely as repayment, without reference to any assumption about the freedom or lack of freedom of the will—and did so to the point where it first required a high degree of human development so that the animal "man" began to make those much more primitive distinctions between "intentional," "negligent," "accidental," "responsible," and their opposites and bring them to bear when meting out punishment? That unavoidable idea, nowadays so trite and apparently natural, which has really had to serve as the explanation how the feeling of justice in general came into existence on earth—"The criminal deserves punishment because he could have acted otherwise"—this idea, in fact, is an extremely late achievement, indeed, a sophisticated form of human judgment and decision making.

Anyone who moves this idea back to the very beginnings is sticking his coarse fingers inappropriately into the psychology of primitive humanity. For the most extensive period of human history, punishment was certainly not meted out because people held the instigator of evil responsible for his actions, nor was it assumed that only the guilty party should be punished. It was much more the case, as it still is now when parents punish their children, of anger over some harm which people have suffered, anger vented on the perpetrator. But this anger was restrained and modified through the idea that every injury had some equivalent and that compensation for it could, in fact, be paid out, even if that was through the pain of the perpetrator.

Where did this primitive, deeply rooted, and perhaps by now ineradicable idea derive its power, the idea of an equivalence between punishment and pain? I have already given away the answer: in the contractual relationship between creditor and debtor, which is as ancient as the idea of "someone subject to law" and which, in itself, refers back to the basic forms of buying, selling, bartering, trading, and exchanging goods.

5

It's true that recalling this contractual relationship arouses, as we might expect from what I have observed above, all sorts of suspicion of and opposition to primitive humanity, which established or allowed it. It's precisely at this point that people make promises. Here the pertinent issue is that the person who makes a promise has to have a memory created for him, so that precisely at this point, we can surmise, there exists a site where we find harshness, cruelty, and pain. In order to inspire trust in his promise to pay back, in order to give his promise a guarantee of its seriousness and sanctity, in order to impress on his own conscience the idea of paying back as a duty, an obligation, the debtor, by virtue of the contract, pledges to the creditor, in the event that he does not pay, something that he still "owns," something over which he still exercises power, for example, his body or his wife or his freedom or even his life (or, under certain religious conditions, even his blessedness, the salvation of his soul, or finally his peace in the grave, as was the case in Egypt, where the dead body of the debtor even in the tomb found no peace from the creditor—and it's certain that with the Egyptians such peace was particularly important). That means that the creditor could inflict all kinds of ignominy and torture on the body of the debtor—for instance, slicing off the body as much as seemed appropriate for the size of the debt. And this point of view early on and everywhere gave rise to precise, sometimes horrific estimates going into finer and finer details, legally established estimates about individual limbs and body parts. I consider it already a step forward, as evidence of a freer conception of the law, something which calculates more grandly, a more Roman idea of justice, when Rome's Twelve Tables of Laws decreed it was all the same, no matter how much or how little the creditor cut off in such cases: *"si plus minusve secuerunt, ne fraude esto."*[1]

Let us clarify the logic of this whole method of compensation—it is weird enough. The equivalency is given in this way: instead of an advantage making up directly for the harm (hence, instead of compensation in gold, land, possessions of some sort or another), the creditor is given a kind of pleasure as repayment and compensation—the pleasure of being allowed to discharge his power on a powerless person without having to think about it, the delight in *"de fair le mal pour le plaisir de le faire,"*[2] the enjoyment of violation. This enjoyment is more highly prized the lower and baser the debtor stands in the social order, and it can easily seem to the creditor a delicious mouthful, even a foretaste of a higher rank. By means of the "punishment" of the debtor, the creditor participates in a right belonging to the masters. Finally he himself for once comes to the lofty feeling of

---

1   *si plus … fraude esto*   Latin: let it not be thought a crime if they cut off more or less.

2   *de fair le mal pour le plaisir de le faire*   French: doing wrong for the pleasure of doing it.

despising a being as someone "below him," as someone he is entitled to mistreat—or at least, in the event that the real force of punishment, of inflicting punishment, has already been transferred to the "authorities," the feeling of seeing the debtor despised and mistreated. The compensation thus consist of a permission for and right to cruelty.

6

In this area, that is, in the laws of obligation, the world of the moral concepts "guilt," "conscience," and "sanctity of obligations" originated. Its beginnings, just like the beginnings of everything great on earth, were watered thoroughly and for a long time with blood. And can we not add that this world deep down has never again been completely free of a certain smell of blood and torture—(not even with old Kant whose categorical imperative[1] stinks of cruelty . . .)? In addition, here the weird knot linking the ideas of "guilt and suffering," which perhaps has become impossible to undo, was first knit together.

Let me pose the question once more: to what extent can suffering be a compensation for "debts"? To the extent that making someone suffer provides the highest degree of pleasure, to the extent that the person hurt by the debt, in exchange for the injury and for the distress caused by the injury, got an extraordinary offsetting pleasure—making someone suffer—a real celebration, something that, as I've said, was valued all the more, the greater the difference between him and the rank and social position of the creditor. I have been speculating here, for it's difficult to see such subterranean things from the surface, quite apart from the fact that it's an embarrassing subject.

Anyone who crudely throws into the middle of all this the idea of "revenge" has merely buried and dimmed his insights rather than illuminated them (revenge itself takes us back to the very same problem "How can making someone suffer give us a feeling of satisfaction?"). It seems to me that the delicacy and even more the hypocrisy of tame house pets (I mean modern man, I mean us) resist a really powerful understanding of just how much cruelty contributes to the great celebratory joy of primitive humanity, as an ingredient mixed into almost all their enjoyments and, from another perspective, how naïve and innocent their need for cruelty appears, how they basically accept "disinterested malice" (or to use Spinoza's words, the *sympathia malevolens*[2] as a normal human characteristic, and hence as something to which their conscience says a heartfelt Yes!

A more deeply penetrating eye might still notice, even today, enough of this most ancient and most basic celebratory human joy. In *Beyond Good and Evil*, section 229 (even earlier in *Daybreak*, sections 18, 77, 113), I pointed a cautious finger at the constantly growing spiritualization and "deification" of cruelty, which runs through the entire history of higher culture (and, in a significant sense, even constitutes that culture). In any case, it's not so long ago that people wouldn't think of an aristocratic wedding and folk festival in a grandest style without executions, tortures, or something like an *auto-da-fé*,[3] and similarly no noble household lacked creatures on whom people could vent their malice and cruel taunts without a second thought (remember Don Quixote at the court of the duchess.[4] Today we read all of *Don Quixote* with a bitter taste on the tongue—it's almost an ordeal. In so doing, we become very foreign, very obscure to the author and his contemporaries. They read it with a fully clear conscience as the most cheerful of books. They almost died laughing at it).

Watching suffering is good for people, making someone suffer is even better—that is a harsh principle, but an old, powerful, and human, all-too-human major principle, which, by the way, even the apes might agree with. For people say that, in thinking up bizarre cruelties, the apes already anticipate a great many human actions and, as it were, "act them out." Without cruelty there is no celebration: that's what the oldest and longest era of human history teaches us—and with punishment, too, there is so much celebration!—

8

To resume the path of our enquiry, the feeling of guilt, of personal obligation has, as we saw, its origin in the oldest and most primitive personal relationship there is and has been—in the relationship between seller and buyer, creditor and debtor. Here for the first time one person encountered

---

1   *categorical imperative* In its first formulation, from Kant's *Groundwork of the Metaphysics of Morals* (1785): "Act only according to that maxim whereby you can at the same time will that it should become a universal law."

2   *sympathia malevolens* Latin: malevolent sympathy.

3   *auto-da-fé* Portuguese: act of faith.

4   *Don Quixote . . . the duchess* See Miguel de Cervantes (1547–1616), *Don Quixote*, Volume 2, Chapters 30 to 57.

another person and measured himself against him. We have not yet found a civilization at such a low level that something of this relationship is not already perceptible. To set prices, measure values, think up equivalencies, to exchange things—that preoccupied man's very first thinking to such a degree that in a certain sense it's what thinking is.

The very oldest form of astuteness was bred here—here, too, we can assume are the first beginnings of human pride, his feeling of pre-eminence in relation to other animals. Perhaps our word "man" [Mensch] (manas) continues to express directly something of this feeling of the self: the human being describes himself as a being which assesses values, which values and measures, as the "inherently calculating animal." Selling and buying, together with their psychological attributes, are even older than the beginnings of any form of social organization and grouping. It is much rather the case that out of the most rudimentary form of personal legal rights the budding feeling of exchange, contract, guilt, law, duty, and compensation were first transferred to the crudest and earliest social structures (in their relationships with similar social structures), along with the habit of comparing power with power, of measuring, of calculating. The eye was now at any rate adjusted to this perspective, and with that awkward consistency characteristic of the thinking in ancient human beings, hard to get started but then inexorably moving forward in the same direction, people soon reached the great generalization "Everything has its price, everything can be paid off"—the oldest and most naïve moral principle of justice, the beginning of all "good nature," all "fairness," all "good will," all "objectivity" on earth. Justice at this first stage is good will among those approximately equal in power to come to terms with each other, to "understand" each other again by compensation—and in relation to those less powerful, to compel them to arrive at some settlement among themselves.

9

Still measuring by the standard of pre-history (a pre-history which, by the way, is present at all times or is capable of returning), the community also stands in relation to its members in that important basic relationship of the creditor to his debtors. People live in a community. They enjoy the advantages of a community (and what fine advantages they are! Nowadays we sometimes underestimate them)—they live protected, cared for, in peace and trust, without worries concerning certain injuries and enmities from which

the man outside the community, the "man without peace," is excluded—a German understands what "misery" [Elend] or êlend[1] originally meant—and how people pledged themselves to and entered into obligations with the community bearing in mind precisely these injuries and enmities.

What will happen with an exception to this case? The community, the defrauded creditor, will see that it gets paid as well as it can—on that people can rely. The issue here is least of all the immediate damage which the offender has caused. Setting this to one side, the lawbreaker [Verbrecher] is above all a "breaker" [Brecher]—a breaker of contracts and a breaker of his word against the totality, with respect to all the good features and advantages of the communal life in which, up to that point, he has had a share. The lawbreaker is a debtor who does not merely not pay back the benefits and advances given to him, but who even attacks his creditor. So from this point on not only does he lose, as is reasonable, all these good things and benefits, but he is also more pertinently reminded what these good things are all about.

The anger of the injured creditor, the community, gives him back the wild condition, as free as a bird, from which he was earlier protected. It pushes him away from it, and now every form of hostility can vent itself on him. At this stage of cultural behavior "punishment" is simply the copy, the mimus, of the normal conduct towards the hated, disarmed enemy who has been thrown down, who has forfeited not only all legal rights and protection but also all mercy—hence it is a case of the rights of war and the victory celebration of vae victis[2] in all its ruthlessness and cruelty, which accounts for the fact that war itself (including the warlike cult of sacrifice) has given us all the ways in which punishment has appeared in history.

10

As it acquires more power, a community considers the crimes of a single individual less serious, because they no longer make him dangerous and unsettling for the existence of the community as much as they did before. The wrong doer is no longer "left without peace" and thrown out, and the common anger can no longer vent itself on him without restraint to the same extent it did before. It is rather the case that the wrong doer from now on is carefully protected

---

1 êlend   German: other country.
2 vae victis   Latin: woe to the conquered.

by the community against this anger, particularly from that of the injured person, and is taken into protective custody. The compromise with the anger of those most immediately affected by the wrong doing, and thus the effort to localize the case and to avert a wider or even a general participation and unrest, the attempts to find equivalents and to settle the whole business (the *compositio*), above all the desire, appearing with ever-increasing clarity, to consider every crime as, in some sense or other, capable of being paid off, and thus, at least to some extent, to separate the criminal and his crime from each other—those are the characteristics stamped more and more clearly on the further development of criminal law.

If the power and the self-confidence of a community keeps growing, the criminal law grows constantly milder. Every weakening and profound jeopardizing of the community brings the harsher forms of criminal law to light once more. The "creditor" always became proportionally more human as he became richer. Finally the amount of his wealth itself establishes how much damage he can sustain without suffering from it. It would not be impossible to imagine a society with a consciousness of its own power which allowed itself the most privileged luxury which it can have—letting its criminals go free without punishment. "Why should I really bother about my parasites," it could then say. "May they live and prosper—for that I am still sufficiently strong!"… Justice, which started by stating "Everything is capable of being paid for, everything must be paid off" ends at that point, by covering its eyes and letting the person incapable of payment go free—it ends, as every good thing on earth ends, by doing away with itself. This self-negation of justice—we know what a beautiful name it calls itself—mercy. It goes without saying that mercy remains the privilege of the most powerful man, or even better, his beyond the law.

11

Now a critical word about a recently published attempt to find the origin of justice in quite a different place—that is, in resentment. But first let me speak a word in the ear of the psychologists, provided that they have any desire to study resentment itself up close for once: this plant grows most beautifully nowadays among anarchists and anti-Semites—in addition, it blooms, as it always has, in hidden places, like the violet, although it has a different fragrance. And since like always has to emerge from like, it is not surprising

to see attempts coming forward again from just such circles, as they have already done many times before, to sanctify revenge under the name of justice, as if justice were basically simply a further development of a feeling of being injured, and to bring belated respect to emotional reactions generally, all of them, using the idea of revenge.

With this last point I personally take the least offence. It even seems to me a service, so far as the entire biological problem is concerned (in connection with which the worth of these emotions has been underestimated up to now). The only thing I'm calling attention to is the fact that it is the very idea of resentment itself out of which this new emphasis on scientific fairness grows (which favors hate, envy, resentment, suspicion, rancor, and revenge). This "scientific fairness," that is, ceases immediately and gives way to tones of mortal enmity and prejudice as soon as it deals with another group of emotions which, it strikes me, have a much higher biological worth than those reactive ones and which therefore have earned the right to be scientifically assessed and given a high value—namely, the truly active emotions, like desire for mastery, acquisitiveness, and so on (E. Dühring,[1] *The Value of Life: A Course in Philosophy*, the whole book really). So much against this tendency in general.

But in connection with Dühring's single principle that we must seek the homeland of justice in the land of the reactive feeling, we must, for love of the truth, rudely turn this around by setting out a different principle: the last territory to be conquered by the spirit of justice is the land of the reactive emotions! If it is truly the case that the just man remains just even towards someone who has injured him (and not just cold, moderate, strange, indifferent: being just is always a positive attitude), if under the sudden attack of personal injury, ridicule, and suspicion, the gaze of the lofty, clear, deep, and benevolent objectivity of the just and judging eye does not grow dark, well, that's a piece of perfection and the highest mastery on earth, even something that it would be wise for people not to expect. In any event they should not believe in it too easily.

It's certainly true that, on average, even among the most just people even a small dose of hostility, malice, and insinuation is enough to make them see red and chase fairness out of their eyes. The active, aggressive, over-reaching hu-

---

1 *E. Dühring* Eugen Karl Dühring (1833–1921) was a German philosopher and economist, and a socialist who criticized Marxism. He is chiefly remembered as the subject of Engels' polemic *Anti-Dühring: Herr Eugen Dühring's Revolution in Science*.

man being is always placed a hundred steps closer to justice than the reactive person. For him it is not even necessary in the slightest to estimate an object falsely and with bias, the way the reactive man does and must do. Thus, as a matter of fact, at all times the aggressive human being—the stronger, braver, more noble man—has always had on his side a better conscience as well as a more independent eye. And by contrast, we can already guess who generally has the invention of "bad conscience" on his conscience—the man of resentment!

Finally, let's look around in history: up to now in what area has the whole implementation of law in general as well as the essential need for law been at home? Could it be in the area of the reactive human beings? That is entirely wrong. It is much more the case that it's been at home with the active, strong, spontaneous, and aggressive men. Historically considered, the law on earth—let me say this to the annoyance of the above-mentioned agitator (who himself once made the confession "The doctrine of revenge runs through all my work and efforts as the red thread of justice")—represents that very struggle against the reactive feelings, the war with them on the part of active and aggressive powers, which have partly used up their strength to put a halt to or restrain reactive pathos and to compel some settlement with it.

Everywhere where justice is practiced, where justice is upheld, we see a power stronger in relation to a weaker power standing beneath it (whether with groups or individuals), seeking ways to bring an end among the latter to the senseless rage of resentment, partly by dragging the object of resentment out of the hands of revenge, partly by setting in the place of revenge a battle against the enemies of peace and order, partly by coming up with compensation, proposing it, under certain circumstances making it compulsory, sometimes establishing certain equivalents for injuries as a norm, which from now on resentment is channeled into once and for all.

The most decisive factor, however, which the highest power carries out and sets in place against the superior power of the feelings of hostility and animosity—something that power always does as soon as it is somehow strong enough to do it—is to set up laws, the imperative explanation of those things which, in its own eyes, are considered allowed and legal and things which are considered forbidden and illegal. In the process, after the establishment of the law, the authorities treat attacks and arbitrary acts of individuals or entire groups as an outrage against the law, as rebellion against the highest power itself, and they steer the feelings of those beneath them away from the immediate damage caused by such outrages and thus, in the long run, achieve the reverse of what all revenge desires, which sees only the viewpoint of the injured party and considers only that valid. From now on, the eye becomes trained to evaluate actions always impersonally, even the eye of the harmed party itself (although this would be the very last thing to occur, as I have remarked earlier).

Consequently, only with the setting up of the law is there a "just" and "unjust" (and not, as Dühring will have it, from the time of the injurious action). To talk of just and unjust in themselves has no sense whatsoever—it's obvious that in themselves harming, oppressing, exploiting, destroying cannot be "unjust," inasmuch as life essentially works that way, that is, in its basic functions it harms, oppresses, exploits, and destroys—and cannot be conceived at all without these characteristics. We must acknowledge something even more alarming—the fact that from the highest biological standpoint, conditions of law must always be exceptional conditions, partial restrictions on the basic will to live, which is set on power—they are subordinate to the total purpose of this will as its individual means, that is, as means to create a larger unit of power. A legal system conceived of as sovereign and universal, not as a means in the struggle of power complexes, but as a means against all struggles in general, something along the lines of Dühring's communist cliché in which each will must be considered as equal to every will, that would be a principle hostile to life, a destroyer and dissolver of human beings, an assassination attempt on the future of human beings, a sign of exhaustion, a secret path to nothingness.

12

Here one more word concerning the origin and purpose of punishment—two problems which are separate or should be separate. Unfortunately people normally throw them together into one. How do the previous genealogists of morality deal with this issue? Naively—the way they always work. They find some "purpose" or other for punishment, for example, revenge or deterrence, then in a simple way set this purpose at the beginning as the *causa fiendi*[1] of punishment and then that's it—they're finished. The "purpose in law," however, is the very last idea we should use in the history of the emergence of law. It is much rather the case

---

1 *causa fiendi* Latin: cause of origin.

that for all forms of history there is no more important principle than the one which we reach with such difficulty but which we also really should reach, namely that what causes a particular thing to arise and the final utility of that thing, its actual use and arrangement in a system of purposes, are separate *toto coelo*,[1] that something existing, which has somehow come to its present state, will again and again be interpreted by the higher powers over it from a new perspective, appropriated in a new way, reorganized for and redirected to new uses, that all events in the organic world involve overpowering, acquiring mastery and that, in turn, all overpowering and acquiring mastery involve a re-interpretation, a readjustment, in which the "sense" and "purpose" up to then must necessarily be obscured or entirely erased.

No matter how well we have understood the usefulness of some physiological organ or other (or a legal institution, a social custom, a political practice, some style in art or in religious cults), we have not, in that process, grasped anything about its origin—no matter how uncomfortable and unpleasant this may sound in elderly ears. From time immemorial people have believed that in demonstrable purposes, the usefulness of a thing, a form, or an institution, they could understand the reasons it came into existence— the eye as something made to see, the hand as something made to grasp. So people also imagined punishment as invented to punish. But all purposes, all uses, are only signs that a will to power has become master over something with less power and has stamped on it its own meaning of some function, and the entire history of a "thing," an organ, a practice can by this process be seen as a continuing chain of signs of constantly new interpretations and adjustments, whose causes need not be connected to each other—they rather follow and take over from each other under merely contingent circumstances.

Consequently, the "development" of a thing, a practice, or an organ has nothing to do with its progress towards a single goal, even less is it the logical and shortest progress reached with the least expenditure of power and resources, but rather the sequence of more or less profound, more or less mutually independent processes of overpowering which take place on that thing, together with the resistance which arises against that overpowering each time, the transformations of form which have been attempted for the purpose of defense and reaction, as well as the results of successful

countermeasures. Form is fluid—the "meaning," however, is even more so ... Even within each individual organism things are no different: with every essential growth in the totality, the "meaning" of an individual organ also shifts— in certain circumstances its partial destruction, a reduction of its numbers (for example, through the destruction of intermediate structures) can be a sign of growing power and perfection.

Let me say this: the partial loss of utility, decline, and degeneration, the loss of meaning, and purposelessness, in short, death, also belong to the conditions of a real progress, which always appears in the form of a will and a way to greater power constantly establishing itself at the expense of a huge number of smaller powers. The size of a "step forward" can even be estimated by a measure of everything that had to be sacrificed to it. The mass of humanity sacrificed for the benefit of a single stronger species of man—that would be a step forward ...

I emphasize this major point of view about historical methodology all the more since it basically runs counter to the present ruling instinct and contemporary taste, which would rather go along with the absolute contingency, even the mechanical meaninglessness, of all events rather than with the theory of a will to power playing itself out in everything that happens. The democratic idiosyncrasy of being hostile to everything which rules and wants to rule, the modern ruler-hatred *[Misarchismus]* (to make up a bad word for a bad thing), has gradually transformed itself and dressed itself up in intellectual activity, the most intellectual activity, to such an extent that nowadays step by step it infiltrates the strictest, apparently most objective scientific research, and is allowed to infiltrate it. Indeed, it seems to me already to have attained mastery over all of physiology and the understanding of life, to their detriment, as is obvious, because it has conjured away from them their fundamental concept—that of real activity.

By contrast, under the pressure of this idiosyncrasy we push "adaptation" into the foreground, that is, a second-order activity, a mere re-activity—in fact, people have defined life itself as an always purposeful inner adaptation to external circumstances (Herbert Spencer). But that simply misjudges the essence of life, its will to power. That overlooks the first priority of the spontaneous, aggressive, overreaching, re-interpreting, re-directing, and shaping powers, after whose effects the "adaptation" first follows. Thus, the governing role of the highest functions in an organism, ones in which the will for living appear active and creative, are

---

1   *toto coelo*   Latin: by all the heavens, i.e., absolutely.

denied. People should remember the criticism Huxley[1] directed at Spencer for his "administrative nihilism." But the
issue here concerns much more than "administration" …

13

Returning to the business at hand, that is, to punishment,
we have to differentiate between two aspects of it: first its
relative duration, the way it is carried out, the action, the
"drama," a certain strict sequence of procedures and, on
the other hand, its fluidity, the meaning, the purpose, the
expectation linked to the implementation of such procedures. In this matter, we can here assume, without further
comment, *per analogium*,[2] in accordance with the major
viewpoints about the historical method we have just established, that the procedure itself will be somewhat older
and earlier than its use as a punishment, that the latter was
only injected and interpreted into the procedure (which
had been present for a long time but was a tradition with a
different meaning), in short, that it was not what our naïve
genealogists of morality and law up to now assumed, who
collectively imagined that the procedure was invented for
the purpose of punishment, just as people earlier thought
that the hand was invented for the purpose of grasping.

Now, so far as that other element in punishment is
concerned, the fluid element, its "meaning," in a very
late cultural state (for example in contemporary Europe)
the idea of "punishment" actually presents not simply one
meaning but a whole synthesis of "meanings." The history
of punishment up to now, in general, the history of its use
for different purposes, finally crystallizes into a sort of unity,
which is difficult to untangle, difficult to analyze, and, it
must be stressed, totally incapable of definition. (Today
it is impossible to say clearly why we really have punishment—all ideas in which an entire process is semiotically
summarized elude definition—only something which has
no history is capable of being defined).

At an earlier stage, by contrast, that synthesis of "meanings" appears much easier to untangle, as well as easier to
adjust. We can still see how in every individual case the
elements in the synthesis alter their valence and rearrange
themselves to such an extent that soon this or that ele-

ment steps forward and dominates at the expense of the
rest—indeed, under certain circumstances one element
(say, the purpose of deterrence) appears to rise above all
the other elements. In order to give at least an idea of how
uncertain, how belated, how accidental "the meaning" of
punishment is and how one and the same procedure can
be used, interpreted, or adjusted for fundamentally different purposes, let me offer here an example which presented
itself to me on the basis of relatively little random material:
punishment as a way of rendering someone harmless, as a
prevention from further harm; punishment as compensation for the damage to the person injured, in some form
or other (also in the form of emotional compensation);
punishment as isolation of some upset to an even balance in
order to avert a wider outbreak of the disturbance; punishment as way of bringing fear to those who determine and
carry out punishment; punishment as a sort of compensation for the advantages which the law breaker has enjoyed
up until that time (for example, when he is made useful as
a slave working the mines); punishment as a cutting out
of a degenerate element (in some circumstances an entire
branch, as in Chinese law, and thus a means to keep the
race pure or to sustain a social type); punishment as festival,
that is, as the violation and humiliation of some enemy one
has finally thrown down; punishment as a way of making
a conscience, whether for the man who suffers the punishment—so-called "reform"—or whether for those who
witness the punishment being carried out; punishment as
the payment of an honorarium, set as a condition by those
in power, which protects the wrong doer from the excesses
of revenge; punishment as a compromise with the natural
condition of revenge, insofar as the latter is still upheld and
assumed as a privilege by powerful families; punishment as
a declaration of war and a war measure against an enemy to
peace, law, order, and authority, which people fight with the
very measures war makes available, as something dangerous
to the community, like a contract breaker with respect to its
conditions, like a rebel, traitor, and breaker of the peace.

14

Of course, this list is not complete. Obviously punishment
is overloaded with all sorts of useful purposes—all the more
reason why people infer from it an alleged utility, which in
the popular consciousness at least is considered the most
essential one. Faith in punishment, which nowadays for
several reasons is getting very shaky, always finds its most

---

1   *Huxley* Thomas Henry Huxley (1825–95), English biologist
    and writer, sometimes referred to as "Darwin's bulldog" for his
    spirited defense of Darwinism.
2   *per analogium* Latin: by analogy.

powerful support in precisely this: Punishment is supposed to be valuable in waking a feeling of guilt in the guilty party. In punishment people are looking for the actual instrument for that psychic reaction called "bad conscience" and "pangs of conscience." In doing this, people still apply reality and psychology incorrectly to present issues—and how much more incorrectly to the greater part of man's history, his prehistory!

Real pangs of conscience are something extremely rare, especially among criminals and prisoners. Prisons and penitentiaries are not breeding grounds in which this species of gnawing worm particularly likes to thrive—on that point all conscientious observers agree, in many cases delivering such a judgment with sufficient unwillingness, going against their own desires. In general, punishment makes people hard and cold. It concentrates. It sharpens the feeling of estrangement and strengthens powers of resistance. If it comes about that punishment shatters a man's energy and brings on a wretched prostration and self-abasement, such a consequence is surely even less pleasant than the ordinary results of punishment—characteristically a dry and gloomy seriousness.

However, if we consider the millennia before the history of humanity, without a second thought we can conclude that the very development of a feeling of guilt was most powerfully hindered by punishment, at least with respect to the victims onto whom this force of punishment was vented. For let us not underestimate just how much the criminal is prevented by the sight of judicial and executive processes from sensing the nature of his action as something inherently reprehensible, for he sees exactly the same kind of actions undertaken in the service of justice, applauded and practiced in good conscience, like espionage, lying, bribery, entrapment, the whole tricky and sly art of the police and prosecution, as it develops in the various kinds of punishment—the robbery, oppression, abuse, imprisonment, torture, murder (all done as a matter of principle, without any emotional involvement as an excuse). All these actions are in no way rejected or condemned in themselves by his judges, but only in particular respects when used for certain purposes.

"Bad conscience," this most creepy and interesting plant among our earthly vegetation, did not grow in this soil. In fact, for the longest period in the past no notion of dealing with a "guilty party" penetrated the consciousness of judges or even those doing the punishing.. They were dealing with someone who had caused harm, with an irresponsible piece of fate. And even the man on whom punishment later fell, once again like a piece of fate, experienced in that no "inner pain," other than what came from the sudden arrival of something unpredictable, a terrible natural event, a falling, crushing boulder against which there is no way to fight.

15

At one point Spinoza became aware of this point in an incriminating way (something which irritates his interpreters, like Kino Fischer,[1] who really go to great lengths to misunderstand him on this issue), when one afternoon, he came up against some memory or other (who knows what?) and pondered the question about what, as far as he was concerned, was left of the celebrated *morsus conscientiae*[2]—for he had expelled good and evil into the human imagination and had irascibly defended the honor of his "free" God against those blasphemers who claimed that in everything God worked *sub ratione boni*[3] ("but that means that God would be subordinate to Fate, a claim which, if true, would be the greatest of all contradictions"). For Spinoza the world had gone back again into that state of innocence in which it existed before the fabrication of the idea of a bad conscience. So what, then, had happened to the *morsus conscientiae*?

"The opposite of *gaudium*,"[4] Spinoza finally told himself "is sorrow, accompanied by the image of something over and done with which happened contrary to all expectation."[5] Just like Spinoza, those instigating evil who incurred punishment have for thousands of years felt in connection with their crime "Something has unexpectedly gone awry here," not "I should not have done that." They submitted to their punishment as people submit to a sickness or some bad luck or death, with that brave fatalism free of revolt which, for example, even today gives the Russians an advantage over us westerners in coping with life. If back then there was some criticism of the act, such criticism came from prudence: without question we must seek the essential effect of punishment above all in an increase of prudence, in a extension of memory, in a will to go to work from now on more carefully, mistrustfully, and secretly, with the

---

1   *Kino Fischer*   Professor at Heidelberg (1824–1907) and author of a ten-volume history of modern philosophy.

2   *morsus conscientiae*   Latin: the bite of conscience.

3   *sub ratione boni*   Latin: with good reason.

4   *gaudium*   Latin: joy.

5   *The opposite ... to all expectation*   Spinoza, *Ethics* 3, Proposition 18, Schol. 1, 2.

awareness that we are in many things definitely too weak, in a kind of improved ability to judge ourselves.

In general, what can be achieved through punishment, in human beings and animals, is an increase in fear, a honing of prudence, control over desires. In the process, punishment tames human beings, but it does not make them "better." People might be more justified in asserting the opposite (Popular wisdom says "Injury makes people prudent," but to the extent that it makes them prudent, it also makes them bad. Fortunately, often enough it makes people stupid.)

16

At this point, I can no longer avoid setting out, in an initial, provisional statement, my own hypothesis about the origin of "bad conscience." It is not easy to get people to attend to it, and it requires them to consider it at length, to guard it, and to sleep on it. I consider bad conscience the profound illness which human beings had to come down with, under the pressure of the most fundamental of all the changes which they experienced—that change when they finally found themselves locked within the confines of society and peace. Just like the things water animals must have gone though when they were forced either to become land animals or to die off, so events must have played themselves out with this half-beast so happily adapted to the wilderness, war, wandering around, adventure—suddenly all its instincts were devalued and "disengaged."

From this point on, these animals were to go on foot and "carry themselves"; whereas previously they had been supported by the water. A terrible heaviness weighed them down. In performing the simplest things they felt ungainly. In dealing with this new unknown world, they no longer had their old leader, the ruling unconscious drives which guided them safely. These unfortunate creatures were reduced to thinking, inferring, calculating, bringing together cause and effect, reduced to their "consciousness," their most impoverished and error-prone organ! I believe that on earth there has never been such a feeling of misery, such a leaden discomfort—while at the same time those old instincts had not all at once stopped imposing their demands! Only it was difficult and seldom possible to do their bidding. For the most part, they had to find new and, as it were, underground satisfactions for them.

All instincts which are not discharged to the outside are turned back inside. This is what I call the internal-

ization of man. From this first grows in man what people later call his "soul." The entire inner world, originally as thin as if stretched between two layers of skin, expanded and extended itself, acquired depth, width, and height, to the extent that the discharge of human instinct out into the world was obstructed. Those frightening fortifications with which the organization of the state protected itself against the old instincts for freedom—punishment belongs above all to these fortifications—made all those instincts of the wild, free, roaming man turn backwards, against man himself. Enmity, cruelty, joy in pursuit, in attack, in change, in destruction—all those turned themselves against the possessors of such instincts. That is the origin of "bad conscience."

The man who lacked external enemies and opposition and was forced into an oppressive narrowness and regularity of custom, impatiently tore himself apart, persecuted himself, gnawed away at himself, grew upset, and did himself damage—this animal which scraped itself raw against the bars of its cage, which people want to "tame," this impoverished creature, consumed with longing for the wild, had to create in itself an adventure, a torture chamber, an uncertain and dangerous wilderness, this fool, this yearning and puzzled prisoner, was the inventor of "bad conscience." With him was introduced the greatest and weirdest illness, from which human beings up to the present time have not recovered, the suffering of man from his humanness, from himself, a consequence of the forcible separation from his animal past, a leap and, so to speak, a fall into new situations and living conditions, a declaration of war against the old instincts, on which, up to that point, his power, joy, and ability to inspire fear had been based.

Let us at once add that, on the other hand, the fact that there was now an animal soul turned against itself, taking sides against itself, provided this earth with something so new, profound, unheard of, enigmatic, contradictory, and portentous, that the picture of the earth was fundamentally changed. In fact, it required divine spectators to approve the dramatic performance which then began and whose conclusion is not yet in sight, a spectacle too fine, too wonderful, too paradoxical, to be allowed to play itself out senselessly and unobserved on some ridiculous star or other. Since then man has been included among the most unexpected and most thrillingly lucky rolls of the dice in the game played by Heraclitus' "great child," whether he's called Zeus or chance. In himself he arouses a certain interest, tension, hope, almost a certainty, as if something is announcing itself in him, is preparing itself, as if the human being were not the goal but only the way, an episode, a great promise …

17

Inherent in this hypothesis about the origin of bad conscience is, firstly, the assumption that this change was not gradual or voluntary and did not manifest an organic growth into new conditions, but was a break, a leap, something forced, an irrefutable disaster, against which there was no struggle nor any resentment. Secondly, it assumes that the adaptation of a populace which had hitherto been unchecked and shapeless into a fixed form was initiated by an act of violence and was carried to its conclusion by nothing but sheer acts of violence, that consequently the very oldest "State" emerged as a terrible tyranny, as an oppressive and inconsiderate machinery, and continued working until such a raw materials of people and half-animals finally were not only thoroughly kneaded and submissive but also given a shape.

I used the word "State"—it is self-evident who is meant by that term—some pack of blond predatory animals, a race of conquerors and masters, which, organized for war and with the power to organize, without thinking about it, sets its terrifying paws on a subordinate population which may perhaps be vast in numbers but is still without any shape, is still wandering about. That's surely the way the "State" begins on earth. I believe that that fantasy has been done away with which sees the beginning of the state in some "contract." The man who can command, who is naturally a "master," who comes forward with violence in his actions and gestures—what has a man like that to do with making contracts! We cannot negotiate with such beings. They come like fate, without cause, reason, consideration, or pretext. They are present as lightning is present, too fearsome, too sudden, too convincing, too "different" even to become hated. Their work is the instinctive creation of forms, the imposition of forms. They are the most involuntary and unconscious artists in existence. Where they appear something new is soon present, a living power structure, something in which the parts and functions are demarcated and coordinated, in which there is, in general, no place for anything which does not first derive its "meaning" from its relationship to the totality.

These men, these born organizers, have no idea what guilt, responsibility, and consideration are. In them that fearsome egotism of the artist is in charge, which stares

out like bronze and knows how to justify itself for all time in the "work," just like a mother with her child. They are not the ones in whom "bad conscience" grew—that point is obvious from the outset. But this hateful plant would not have grown without them. It would have failed if an immense amount of freedom had not been driven from the world under the pressure of their hammer blows, their artistic violence—or at least driven from sight and, as it were, had become latent. This powerful instinct for freedom, once made latent (we already understand how), this instinct driven back, repressed, imprisoned inside, and finally able to discharge and direct itself only against itself—that and that alone is what bad conscience is in its beginnings.

18

We need to be careful not to entertain a low opinion of this entire phenomenon simply because it is from the start hateful and painful. Basically it is the same active force which is at work on a grander scale in those artists of power and organization and which builds states. Here it is inner, smaller, more mean spirited, directing itself backwards, into "the labyrinth of the breast,"[1] to use Goethe's words, and it creates bad conscience and builds negative ideals, that very instinct for freedom (to use my own language, the will to power). But the material on which the shaping and violating nature of this force directs itself here is man himself, all his old animal self, and not, as in that greater and more striking phenomenon, on another man or on other men.

This furtive violation of the self, this artistic cruelty, this pleasure in giving a shape to oneself as if to a tough, resisting, suffering material, to burn into it a will, a critique, a contradiction, a contempt, a denial—this weird and horribly pleasurable work of a soul willingly divided against itself, which makes itself suffer for the pleasure of creating suffering, all this active "bad conscience," as the essential womb of ideal and imaginative events, finally brought to light—we have already guessed—also an abundance of strange new beauty and affirmation, perhaps for the first time the idea of the beautiful…. For what would be "beautiful," if its opposite had not yet come to an awareness of itself, if ugliness had not already said to itself, "I am ugly" …

At least, after this hint one paradox will be less puzzling—how contradictory ideas, like selflessness, self-denial,

---

1 *labyrinth … breast* From Goethe's poem *An den Mond* (To the Moon) (1789).

and self-sacrifice, can connote an ideal, something beautiful. And beyond that, one thing we do know—I have no doubt about it—namely, the nature of the pleasure which the selfless, self-denying, self-sacrificing person experiences from the beginning: this pleasure belongs to cruelty.

So much for the moment on the origin of the "unegoistic" as something of moral worth and on the demarcation of the soil out of which this value has grown: only bad conscience, only the will to abuse the self, provides the condition for the value of the unegoistic.

19

Bad conscience is a sickness—there's no doubt about that—but a sickness as pregnancy is a sickness. Let's look for the conditions in which this illness has arrived at its most terrible and most sublime peak. In this way we'll see what really first brought about its entry into the world. But that requires a lot of endurance—and we must first go back again to an earlier point. The relationship in civil law between the debtor and the creditor, which I have reviewed extensively already, has been reinterpreted once again in an extremely remarkable and dubious historical manner into a relationship which we modern men are perhaps least capable of understanding, namely, into the relationship between those people presently alive and their ancestors.

Within the original tribal cooperatives—we're talking about primeval times—the living generation always acknowledged a legal obligation to the previous generations, and especially to the earliest one which had founded the tribe (and this was in no way merely a sentimental obligation—the latter is something we could reasonably claim was absent for the longest period of the human race). Here the reigning conviction was that the tribe exists only because of the sacrifices and achievements of its ancestors, and that people had to pay them back with sacrifices and achievements. In this people recognize a debt which keeps steadily growing because these ancestors in their continuing existence as powerful spirits do not stop giving the tribe new advantages and lending them their power. Do they do this gratuitously? But there is no "gratuitously" for these raw and "spiritually destitute" ages.

What can people give back to them? Sacrifices (at first as nourishment understood very crudely), festivals, chapels, signs of honor, and, above all, obedience—for all customs, as work of one's ancestors, are also their statutes and commands. Do people ever give them enough? This suspicion

remains and grows. From time to time it forcefully requires wholesale redemption, something huge as a payment back to the "creditor" (the notorious sacrifice of the first born, for example, blood, human blood in any case).

Fear of ancestors and their power, the awareness of one's debt to them, according to this kind of logic, necessarily increases directly in proportion to the increase in the power of the tribe itself, as the tribe finds itself constantly more victorious, more independent, more honored, and more feared. It's not the other way around! Every step towards the decline of the tribe, all conditions of misery, all indications of degeneration, of approaching dissolution, much rather lead to a constant diminution of the fear of the spirit of its founder and give a constantly smaller image of his wisdom, providence, and present power.

If we think this crude logic through to its conclusion, then the ancestors of the most powerful tribes must, because of the fantasy of increasing fear, finally have grown into something immense and have been pushed into the darkness of a divine mystery, something beyond the powers of imagination, so that finally the ancestor is necessarily transfigured into a god. Here perhaps lies even the origin of the gods, thus an origin out of fear!... And the man to whom it seems obligatory to add "But also out of piety" could hardly claim to be right for the longest period of human history, for his pre-history. Of course, he would be all the more correct for the middle period in which the noble tribes developed, those who in fact paid back their founders, their ancestors (heroes, gods), with interest, all the characteristics which in the meantime had become manifest in themselves, the noble qualities. Later we will have another look at the process by which the gods were ennobled and exalted (which is naturally not at all the same thing as their becoming "holy"). But now, for the moment, let's follow the path of this whole development of the consciousness of guilt to its conclusion.

20

As history teaches us, the consciousness of being in debt to the gods did not in any way come to an end after the downfall of communities organized on the basis of blood relationships. Just as humanity inherited the ideas of "good and bad" from the nobility of the tribe (together with its fundamental psychological tendency to set up orders of rank), in the same way people also inherited, as well as the divinities of the tribe and of the extended family, the pressure of as yet unpaid debts and the desire to be relieved of them. (The transition is made with those numerous slave and indentured populations which adapted themselves to the divine cults of their masters, whether through compulsion or through obsequiousness and mimicry; from them this inheritance overflowed in all directions). The feeling of being indebted to the gods did not stop growing for several thousands of years—always, in fact, in direct proportion to the extent to which the idea of god and the feeling for god grew and were carried to the heights.

(The entire history of ethnic fighting, victory, reconciliation, mergers—everything which comes before the final rank ordering of all the elements of a people in that great racial synthesis—is mirrored in the tangled genealogies of its gods, in the sagas of their fights, victories, and reconciliations. The progress towards universal kingdoms is at the same time always also the progress toward universal divinities. In addition, despotism, with its overthrow of the independent nobles always builds the way to some variety of monotheism).

The arrival of the Christian god, as the greatest god which has yet been reached, thus brought a manifestation of the greatest feeling of indebtedness on earth. Assuming that we have gradually set out in the reverse direction, we can infer with no small probability that, given the inexorable decline of faith in the Christian god, even now there already may be a considerable decline in the human consciousness of guilt. Indeed, we cannot dismiss the idea that the complete and final victory of atheism could release humanity from this entire feeling of being indebted to its origins, its *causa prima*.[1] Atheism and a kind of second innocence belong together.

21

So much for a brief and rough preface concerning the connection between the ideas "guilt" and "obligation" with religious assumptions. Up to this point I have deliberately set aside the actual moralizing of these ideas (the repression of them into the conscience, or more precisely, the complex interaction between a bad conscience and the idea of god). At the end of the previous section I even talked as if there was no such thing as this moralizing and thus as if now these ideas had necessarily come to an end after the collapse of their presuppositions, the faith in our "creditor," in God.

But to a terrifying extent the facts indicate something different. The moralizing of the ideas of debt and duty, with their repression into bad conscience, actually gave rise to the attempt to reverse the direction of the development I have just described, or at least to bring its motion to a halt. Now, in a fit of pessimism, the prospect of a final installment must once and for all be denied. Now, our gaze is to bounce and ricochet back despairingly off an iron impossibility, now those ideas of "debt" and "duty" are supposed to turn back. But against whom?

There can be no doubt: first of all against the "debtor," in whom from this point on bad conscience, firmly set in him, eating into him and spreading out like a polyp, grows wide and deep, until finally, with the impossibility of discharging the debt, people conceive of the idea of the impossibility of removing the penance, the idea that the debt cannot be paid off ("eternal punishment"). Finally however, those ideas of "debt" and "duty" turn back even against the "creditor." People should, in this matter, now think about the causa prima of humanity, about the beginning of the human race, about their ancestor who from now on is loaded down with a curse ("Adam," "original sin," "no freedom of the will,") or about nature from whose womb human beings arose and into whom from now on the principle of evil is inserted ("the demonizing of nature") or about existence in general, which remains something without value in itself (nihilistic turning away from existence, longing for nothingness, or a desire for its "opposite," in an alternate state of being, Buddhism and things like that)—until all of a sudden we confront the paradoxical and horrifying expedient with which a martyred humanity found temporary relief, that stroke of genius of Christianity—God's sacrifice of himself for the guilt of human beings, God paying himself back with himself, God as the only one who can redeem man from what for human beings has become impossible to redeem—the creditor sacrifices himself for the debtor, out of love (can people believe that?), out of love for his debtor!...

---

1 *causa prima* Latin: first cause.

Sources/Permission Acknowledgments

The list below includes source information and copyright acknowledgments for all texts in the anthology that are in copyright, and all texts in translation, whether in copyright or in the public domain. Texts originally written in English and in the public domain are generally not included in the list below; unless otherwise noted the annotations to all such texts appearing in this anthology may be presumed to have been prepared for the anthology, and to be copyright © Broadview Press.

◆ ◆ ◆ ◆ ◆

AL-FĀRĀBĪ

♦ "The Political Regime," from *Medieval Political Philosophy: A Sourcebook*. Translated by Fauzi M. Najjar. Edited by Ralph Lerner and Muhsin Mahdi. New York: The Free Press of Glencoe/Collier-Macmillan Ltd., 1963. pp. 31–57. Reprinted by permission of Ralph Lerner.

AQUINAS, St. Thomas

♦ Excerpts from *The "Summa Theologica" of St. Thomas Aquinas*. Second and revised edition. Literally translated by Fathers of the English Dominican Province. London: Burns, Oates and Washbourne, 1920.

♦ Excerpts from "Book I," from *The "Summa Contra Gentiles" of Saint Thomas Aquinas*. Translated by Joseph Rickaby. London: Burns and Oates, 1905.

ARISTOTLE

♦ "Book I," "Book II," "Book III: 6–9," "Book V," "Book VIII" and "Book X: 6–9," from *Nicomachean Ethics, Second Edition*. Indianapolis, IN: Hackett Publishing Company, 1999. Translated by Terence Irwin. Copyright © 2000 by Hackett Publishing Company, Inc. Reprinted by permission of Hackett Publishing Company, Inc. All rights reserved.

♦ Excerpts from *Politics*. Based on the translation by Benjamin Jowett. Revised by Robert M. Martin. Copyright © 2007 Broadview Press.

AUGUSTINE, Saint, Bishop of Hippo

♦ "Book I: Preface, Chapters 1 and 8," "Book II: Chapter 21" and "Book XIX: Chapters 1, 6, 7, 11, 12, 15, 16, 21, 23 and 24," from *The City of God*. Translated by Marcus Dods, D.D. New York: Random House, 1950. Reprinted by permission of Random House, Inc.

CALVIN, John

♦ Excerpts from *On Civil Government*. Loosely based on the John Allen translation, substantially revised by Broadview Press. Copyright © 2007 Broadview Press.

CICERO, Marcus Tullius

♦ Excerpt from *On Duties*. Loosely based on the Walter Miller translation, substantially revised by Robert M. Martin. Copyright © 2007 Broadview Press.

CONSTANT, Benjamin

♦ "The Liberty of the Ancients Compared with that of the Moderns," from *Constant: Political Writings*. Translated by Biancamaria Fontana. New York: Cambridge University Press, 1988. Copyright © 1988 Cambridge University Press. Reprinted by permission of Cambridge University Press.

de GOUGES, Olympe

♦ "Declaration of the Rights of Women and the Citizen," from *Women, the Family, and Freedom, Volume I*. Edited by Susan Groag Bell and Karen M. Offen. Stanford, CA: Stanford University Press, 1983. Copyright © 1983 by the Board of Trustees of the Leland Stanford Jr. University. All rights reserved. Reprinted by permission of Stanford University Press. <http://www.sup.org>.

de PIZAN, Christine

♦ Excerpts from "Chapters 4, 5, 6, 8, 9 and 10," from *The Book of the Body Politic*. Translated and edited by Kate Langdon Forhan. New York: Cambridge University Press, 1994. Copyright © 1994 Cambridge University Press. Reprinted by permission of Cambridge University Press.

♦ Excerpts from "Parts III, IV and V," from *The Books of Deeds of Arms and of Chivalry*. Translated by Sumner Willard. University Park, PA: Pennsylvania State University Press, 1999. Copyright © 1999 by The Pennsylvania State University Press. Reprinted by permission of The Pennsylvania State University Press.

♦ Excerpt from *City of the Ladies*. Translated by Alex Sager. Copyright © 2007 Broadview Press.

de TOCQUEVILLE, Alexis

♦ "Chapters 5, 6, 7 and 8," from *Democracy in America*. Based on the Henry Reeve translation, substantially revised by Robert M. Martin and Alex Sager. Copyright © 2007 Broadview Press.

HEGEL, Georg Wilhelm Friedrich

♦ Excerpts from "Preface," "Introduction," "Subdivisions," "Part One: Abstract Right" and "Part Three: Ethical Life," from *Hegel: Elements of the Philosophy of Right*. New York: Cambridge University Press, 1991. Copyright © 1991 Cambridge University Press. Reprinted by permission of Cambridge University Press.

HOBBES, Thomas

♦ Excerpts from *Leviathan*. Edited and annotated by A.P. Martinich. Peterborough, ON: Broadview Press, 2002. Copyright © 2002 by A.P. Martinich. Reprinted by permission of A.P. Martinich and Broadview Press.

KANT, Immanuel

♦ Excerpts from *Groundwork for Metaphysics of Morals*. Loosely based on the Thomas Abbott translation, substantially revised by Lara Denis. Peterborough, ON: Broadview Press, 2005. Copyright © 2005. Reprinted by permission of Broadview Press.

♦ Excerpts from *To Perpetual Peace*. Translated by Ted Humphrey. Indianapolis, IN: Hackett Publishing Company, 2003. Copyright © 2003 by Hackett Publishing Company, Inc. Reprinted by permission of Hackett Publishing Company, Inc. All rights reserved.

LUTHER, Martin

- Excerpts from "Temporal Authority: To What Extent it Should be Obeyed," from *Luther: Selected Political Writings*. Translated by J.J. Schindel. Revised by Walther I. Brandt. Philadelphia: Fortress Press, 1974.

MACHIAVELLI, Niccolò

- Excerpts from *The Prince*. Loosely based on the W.K. Marriott translation, substantially revised by Don LePan, Robert M. Martin and Alex Sager. Copyright © 2007 Broadview Press.
- Excerpts from *The Prince and The Discourses*. Translated by Eric R.P. Vincent. Revised by Christian E. Detmold. New York: The Modern Library, Random House, 1940. Reprinted by permission of Random House, Inc.

MAIMONIDES, Moses

- "Part II: Chapter 40 and Part III: Chapters 27, 28 and 34, from *The Political Regime*," from *Medieval Political Philosophy: A Sourcebook*. Translated by Ralph Lerner and Muhsin Mahdi. New York: The Free Press of Glencoe/Collier-Macmillan Ltd., 1963. pp. 212–15 and 221–25. Reprinted by permission of Ralph Lerner.

MARSILIUS OF PADUA

- Excerpts from *The Defender of the Peace: Marsilius of Padua*. Translated and edited by Annabel Brett. New York: Cambridge University Press, 2005. Copyright © 2005 by Cambridge University Press. Reprinted by permission of Cambridge University Press.

MARX, Karl, and Friedrich Engels

- Excerpts from *The Communist Manifesto*. Translated and edited by L.M. Findlay. Peterborough, ON: Broadview Press, 2004. Copyright © 2004. Reprinted by permission of Broadview Press.

MONTESQUIEU, Charles de Secondat

- Excerpts from *Montesquieu: Spirit of the Laws*. Translated and edited by Anne M. Cohler, Basia C. Miller and Harold S. Stone. New York: Cambridge University Press, 1989. Copyright © 1989 Cambridge University Press. Reprinted by permission of Cambridge University Press.

NIETZSCHE, Friedrich

- Excerpts from *Beyond Good and Evil* and *On the Genealogy of Morals*. Translated by Ian Johnston. Copyright © 2003 Ian Johnston. Reprinted by permission of Ian Johnston.

PLATO

- "The Apology," "Crito" and "Phaedo—Death Scene," from *The Trial and Death of Socrates*. Translated by G.M.A. Grube. Indianapolis, IN: Hackett Publishing Company, 2000. Copyright © 2000 by Hackett Publishing Company, Inc. Reprinted by permission of Hackett Publishing Company, Inc. All rights reserved.
- "Book I," "Book II," "Book III: Selection of Rulers," "Book IV: The Guardians of Happiness/Wealth and Poverty, Virtues in the State, Three Parts of the Soul, and The Virtues in the Individual," "Book V: Men and Women, The Philosopher as King," "Book VII: The Allegory of the Cave," "Book VIII" and "Book IX: The Tyrant," from *The Republic*. Translated by G.M.A. Grube. Indianapolis, IN: Hackett Publishing Company, 1974. Copyright © 1974 by Hackett Publishing Company, Inc. Reprinted by permission of Hackett Publishing Company, Inc. All rights reserved.
- "Book I," from *Laws*. Translated by Janet Sisson. Copyright © 2007 Broadview Press.

POLYBIUS

- Excerpts from "Book VI," from *Polybius: The Histories: Volume III*. Translated by W.R. Patton. Cambridge, MA: Harvard University Press, 1923. Loeb Classical Library® Volume 138, pp. 269–311. Reprinted by permission of Harvard University Press and the Trustees of Loeb Classical Library. The Loeb Classical Library® is a registered trademark of the President and Fellows of Harvard College.

ROUSSEAU, Jean-Jacques

- Excerpts from *The Basic Political Writings*. Translated by Donald A. Cress. Indianapolis, IN: Hackett Publishing Company, 1987. Copyright © 1987 Hackett Publishing Company. Reprinted by permission of Hackett Publishing Company, Inc. All rights reserved.

SENECA, Lucius Annaeus

- "Letters on Slaves," from *The Stoic Philosophy of Seneca: Essays and Letters of Seneca*. Translated by Moses Hadas. New York: Random House, 1958. Copyright © 1958 by Moses Hadas. Reprinted by permission of Doubleday, a division of Random House, Inc.

THUCYDIDES

- Excerpts from *Melian Dialogue* and *Pericles' Funeral Oration*. Based on the translation by Richard Crowley. Revised by Robert M. Martin. Copyright © 2007 Broadview Press.

◆ ◆ ◆ ◆ ◆

The publisher has endeavoured to contact the rights holders of all copyrighted works and translations published in this text and would appreciate receiving any information regarding errors or omissions so that we may correct them in future reprints and editions of the work.

Index of Authors and Titles